3 v.s.t 15⁰⁰

THE
READER'S
ADVISER

THE READER'S ADVISER

A LAYMAN'S GUIDE TO LITERATURE

12TH EDITION

Volume 3: The best in the reference literature of the world

Edited by Jack A. Clarke

R. R. BOWKER COMPANY
NEW YORK & LONDON, 1977

Published by R. R. Bowker Co.
1180 Avenue of the Americas, New York, New York 10036
Copyright © 1977 by Xerox Corporation
All rights reserved
International Standard Book Number 0-8352-0853-2
International Standard Serial Number 0094-5943
Library of Congress Card Number 57-13277
Printed and bound in the United States of America

Contents

v

FEB 17 1977

Preface

THE ORDER OF the chapters in this volume, as in the previous edition of *"The Reader's Adviser,"* is planned so that the background or reference books necessary to the general reader and to the bookman come before the main subject divisions—preceded only by the chapter on General Biography, which continues the last chapter of Volume 1 on Literary Biography. The arrangement of the entries in each chapter has a logical sequence. Reference Books, Histories and Studies, and suggested Reading Lists of books which can throw light on the general subject of each chapter are given in the opening pages, arranged alphabetically by author or editor. The authors who have main entries are arranged (in general) chronologically. Their volumes of collected and selected works come first, followed by the in-print titles belonging in that specific chapter in the order of their publication. Last in the listing of titles (except in the Biography chapter where these are the main books treated) come the autobiographical works including letters. If an autobiographer also writes on history, these additional titles are mentioned in the biographical and critical note or a new main entry appears in another chapter and a cross-reference to that chapter is given. In the book entries, if known, the date of the first publication is given, the publisher, the edition or series if named, and the price. If the edition now available is not issued by the original publisher, the date of the first publication follows the title. Most often the original publisher and original publication date are given first, followed by the reprints. Where there are many editions of a single title the publishers' names are arranged alphabetically.

In the preparation of this edition every title from the previous volume was reviewed and either updated or replaced. While the main emphasis continues to be on recently published material, many standard works available once again in reprint form have been added. Exigencies of time and space have required that many still useful titles had to be replaced by newer books and in some cases by older reprints. We have also listed many new works that reflect the accelerating pace of social developments in the United States. These titles include women's studies, Black studies, revisionist works on the American Indians, and the general reexamination of our revolutionary heritage. As in previous editions, the value judgments are based on a wide variety of reviews, select lists, literary prizes and awards. The annual lists of books for academic libraries in *Choice* and the *Library Journal* lists of books in science, technology and business have been particularly helpful. Portions of this volume have been completed at widely different times, which accounts for the discrepancy in many prices and in some editions of classic works.

The editor of a volume covering this many subjects must rely heavily on the professional expertise and good will of many individuals. Several persons merit special thanks for suggesting select lists of titles in their subject field: For Latin American history, Professor Jack Ray Thomas, Bowling Green State University, and Ellen Brouw, University of Kansas; for African history, Dr. Joseph Lauer, University of Wisconsin; for diplomatic history, Dr. Richard Werding, Lawrence

University; for Canadian history, Kathryn F. Dean, University of Manitoba; for Catholic theology, Sister Jerome Heyman, Edgewood College of the Sacred Heart; for Protestant theology and Bibles, Father Robert Smith; for women's studies, Joan Durrance; for a list of works on films and filmmaking, Rose Caruso, University of Wisconsin College Library; for journalism and mass communications, Barbara Schmiechen, University of Wisconsin Journalism Library; for assistance in revising the folklore titles, Professor Gertrude Herman, University of Wisconsin Library School; and for assistance in revising the science chapter, Professor Richard Walker, University of Wisconsin Library School, Nancy Crossfield, University of Wisconsin Earth Sciences Library, and Philip Sullivan, Madison Public Library. My wife Anna Clarke acted as an editorial and research associate in the revision of this volume.

J. A. Clarke

Madison, Wis. 1977

Abbreviations

abr.	abridged	ltd. ed.	limited edition
annot.	annotated	MLA	Modern Language Association
Am.	American		
app.	appendix	Mod.	Modern
arr.	arranged	mor.	morocco
bibliog.	bibliography	ms., mss.	manuscript(s)
bd.	bound	NYPL	New York Public Library *Branch Library Book News*, etc.
bdg.	binding		
Bks.	Books		
Booklist	*Booklist and Subscription Books Bulletin*	*N.Y. Times*	*New York Times*
		orig.	original
c.	circa	o.p.	out of print
Chil.	Children's	pap.	paper
Class.	Classics	*PBIP*	*Paperbound Books in Print*
coll.	collected		
coll. ed.	collected edition	Perenn.	Perennial
comp.	compiled, compiler	Pock.	Pocket
d.	died	pref.	preface
Devot.	Devotional	pseud.	pseudonym
dist.	distributed	pt.	part
ed.	edited, editor, edition	ptg.	printing
Eng.	English	*PW*	*Publishers Weekly*
enl.	enlarged	*q.v.*	*quod vide* (which see)
Enrich.	Enrichment	repr.	reprint
fl.	flourished	rev. ed.	revised edition
fwd.	foreword	Riv.	Riverside
gen. eds.	general editors	sel.	selected
Gt.	Great	Ser.	Series
ill.	illustrated, illustrations	*SR*	*Saturday Review*
		Stand.	Standard
imit. lea.	imitation leather	*TLS*, London	*Times Literary Supplement*
(in prep.)	in preparation		
introd.	introduction	trans.	translated, translator, translation
lea.	leather		
lg.-type ed.	large-type edition	Univ.	University, Universal
lib. ed.	library edition	Vol., Vols.	Volume(s)
Lib.	Library, Liberal	*(WLB)*	*Wilson Library Bulletin*
Lit.	Literature		
LJ	*Library Journal*		

Chapter 1

Reference Books—General

For the organization of this Chapter, see table of contents. Purely literary reference materials have been excluded and will be found in Chapter 3, Reference Books—Literature, *Reader's Adviser*, Volume I. We have duplicated a good many entries from that Chapter which apply to the subjects treated in this third volume, in order to make the latter as self-contained as practicable. Reference books relating to particular chapters should be sought in the early sections of the chapter concerned (again, consult the table of contents), though a few of the very basic ones in special fields have been included here. Reference books of particular interest to librarians, catalogs such as the National Union Catalog, foreign bibliographies and other similar materials will be found in Chapter 2, Bibliography, *Reader's Adviser*, Volume I.

Two interesting recent developments related to this general field are the Xerox Publishing Division's DATRIX II program which is a computerized information retrieval system that can compile a list of dissertations on any subject. Its data base includes more than 430,000 dissertations written at over 300 degree-granting institutions in North America. The New York Times Information Bank is an "on-line computerized service" that contains nearly a million abstracts from 60 publications. It "searches out facts and ideas with amazing speed" drastically reducing the search time for current information.

GENERAL BIBLIOGRAPHIC AND REFERENCE TOOLS

See also Reader's Adviser, *Vol. 1, Chapter 2, Bibliography, and Chapter 3, Reference Books—Literature.*

AMERICAN BOOK PUBLISHING RECORD. 12 issues a year. *Bowker* annual subscription $19.00. Annual Cumulatives 14 vols.: 1960–64 4 vols. set $105.00 1965–69 5 vols. set $129.50 1970 1971 1972 each annual vol. $36.50 1973 $38.50 1974 $39.50 1975 $42.50. Cumulation of the Weekly Record listings from *Publishers' Weekly* of over 37,000 books a year, as catalogued by the Library of Congress; arranged by subject under Dewey numbers.

AMERICAN PERIODICAL INDEX TO 1850. Comp. by Nelson F. Adkins *Readex Microprint* $575.00

"Index to 352 periodicals published in the U.S. from beginning to 1850. Originally compiled by the W.P.A. Microprint edition has 650,000 entries, arranged by author, title, and subject. Covers material prior to that covered by Poole's index [*see below*] plus a great deal of additional material not in Poole's"—(Publisher's catalog).

ANGLO-AMERICAN GENERAL ENCYCLOPEDIAS, 1703–1967: A Historical Bibliography. Comp. by S. Padraig Walsh *Bowker* 1968 $12.00

"This is the only comprehensive historical bibliography of English-language encyclopedias. Alphabetically arranged, it evaluates the worth and historical importance of over 400 British and American general encyclopedias from the early 18th century to the present"—(Publisher's catalog).

AYER DIRECTORY OF PUBLICATIONS. *Ayer Press* annually $49.00. Authoritative directory of print media published in the United States; Puerto Rico; Virgin Islands; the Dominion of Canada; Bahamas; Bermuda; The Republics of Panama and the Philippines. Arranged geographically with classified lists.

BIBLIOGRAPHIC INDEX. 1938– . *Wilson* Permanent vols. in print: Vol. 1 1937–1942 $54.00 Vol. 2 1943–1946 $30.00 Vol. 3 1947–1950 $30.00 Vol. 4 1951–1955 $26.00. Succeeding volumes sold on a service basis to libraries. Vol. 5 1956–1959 Vol. 6 1960–

1962 Vol. 7 1963–1965 Vol. 8 1966–1968 Vol. 9 1969 Vol. 10 1970 Vol. 11 1971 Vol. 12 1972 Vol. 13 1973

"Indexes by subject current bibliographies, including those published separately as books and pamphlets, and those appearing as parts of books, pamphlets, and articles, both in English and foreign languages. In addition, approximately 1,900 periodicals are regularly examined for bibliographical material and bibliographical lists containing 40 or more bibliographical citations are indexed. References to new editions and supplements are included"—(Publisher's catalog).

BIOGRAPHY INDEX. 1946– . *Wilson* Vol. 1 Jan. 1946–July 1949 Vol. 2 Aug. 1949–Aug. 1952 Vol. 3 Sept. 1952–Aug. 1955 Vol. 4 Sept. 1955–Aug. 1958 Vol. 5 Sept. 1958– Aug. 1961 Vol. 6 Sept. 1961–Aug. 1964 Vol. 7 Sept. 1964–Aug. 1967 Vol. 8 Sept. 1967–Aug. 1970 Vol. 9 Sept. 1970–Aug. 1973 each $58.00. Issued quarterly (in November, February, May and August), with annual and permanent three-year cumulations; annual subscription $29.00.

"Covers biographical material appearing in approximately 1,900 periodicals indexed in other Wilson indexes; current books of individual and collective biography in the English language; obituaries, including those of national interest published in the *New York Times*; and incidental biographical material in otherwise non-biographical books. Bibliographies and portraits and other illustrations are noted when they appear in connection with indexed material. Biography Index consists of a main or "name" alphabet and an index by professions and occupations"—(Publisher's catalog).

THE BOOKMAN'S GLOSSARY. *Bowker* 5th ed. 1975 $10.50

"This edition has been revised by subject specialists, the format has been enlarged, and the number of terms defined has been increased"—(*LJ*).

BOOK REVIEW DIGEST. *Wilson* annually, service basis

"Since 1905 this digest of quotations from book reviews has been issued annually. About 6,000 books a year are listed by author, with price, publisher, year of publication, descriptive note, citations for all reviews, International Standard Book Numbers when available, and excerpts from as many reviews as are necessary to reflect the balance of critical opinion. Published monthly (except February and July) with permanent bound annual cumulations. Every fifth year the annual volume contains a cumulated subject and title index of the previous five years. Reprints of annual volumes, from 1905 through 1959, are available at prices ranging from $9.00 to $26.00; annuals for 1960–1973 are sold on the service basis"—(Publisher's catalog).

BOOK REVIEW INDEX. *Gale Research Co.* Annual clothbound cumulations for 1965 1966 1967 1968 1970 1971 1972 1973 1974 and 1975 each $68.00. Annual subscription for six bimonthly issues published in February, April, June, August, October, December $68.00

BOOKS FOR COLLEGE LIBRARIANS. *American Lib. Assn.* 6 vols. 2d ed. 1975 set $52.00

"Nearly 40,000 titles . . . have been selected and evaluated by subject specialists"—(Publisher's catalog).

BOOKS FOR PUBLIC LIBRARIES: Nonfiction for Small Collections. Comp. by an American Library Association committee. *Bowker* 2nd ed. 1975 $13.95. Lists about 5,000 non-fiction titles by Dewey classification with an author and title index.

BOOKS IN PRINT. *Bowker* 4 vols. 1975 set $75.00; Supplement annually in Spring $37.50

Over 425,000 books in print in the U.S., arranged alphabetically by author and title. Each entry includes: author, editor, title, price, publisher, date, number of vols., series, grade level, whether illustrated, LC card number and ISBN. A publishers' directory with name and address of every known U.S. publisher is also included. The Supplement provides data on new, forthcoming, backlist and o.p. titles. Indexed by author and title. Forthcoming and new books are also indexed by subject.

BOWKER ANNUAL OF LIBRARY AND BOOK TRADE INFORMATION. Ed. by Madeline Miele, Roberta Moore, and Sarah Prakken; consulting ed. Frank L. Schick *Bowker* 21st ed. 1976 $23.50

BRITISH BOOKS IN PRINT. *Whitaker*, London (dist. by Bowker) Annual 1974 2 vols. set $46.50

"All British books in print at the end of April each year. This is the continuation of 'The Reference Catalogue of Current Literature' first published in 1874 and subsequently at four- or five-year intervals."

CANADIAN BOOKS IN PRINT: Catalogue des Livres Canadiens en Librairie. Ed. by Harald Bohne and Martha Pluskauskas *Canadian Books in Print Committee* (dist. by Univ. of Toronto Press and Conseil Superieur du Livre) 1975 ed. $25.00. Arranged by author, publisher and title indexes with English and French-Canadian listings interfiled.

CANADIAN ESSAY AND LITERATURE INDEX, 1973. Ed. by Andrew Armitage and Nancy Tudor *Univ. of Toronto Press* 1975 $27.50

CELI "has five sections: essays, book reviews, poems, plays, and short stories"—*(LJ)*.

CATALOG OF REPRINTS IN SERIES. Ed. by Robert Merritt Orton *Scarecrow* 21st ed. 1972 $27.50

"Anyone working with series would save countless hours and countless steps by having this book within reach. It will surely become one of our most-used tools"—*(Journal of Cataloging & Classification)*.

Choice. American Lib. Assn., Assn. of College and Research Libraries annual subscription $35.00, single copies $3.50. A monthly publication with a combined July-August issue designed to assist college and university libraries in their selection of books. Cumulative index issued in February.

"A current book selection guide for librarians and faculties of undergraduate colleges, universities, junior colleges. . . . Concise, often comparative evaluations of 500–700 new publications each month are written by undergraduate faculty or librarian subject specialists"—(Publisher's catalog).

Cleary, Florence Damon. DISCOVERING BOOKS AND LIBRARIES: A Handbook for the Upper Elementary and Junior High School Grades. *Wilson* 1966 pap. $2.50

CONSUMER SOURCEBOOK. Ed. by Paul Wasserman and Jean Morgan *Gale Research Co.* 1974 $35.00

"A comprehensive guide to services, printed and otherwise, available to the American consumer, . . . it is a one-stop source of supply for the consumer's needs. Consumer Sourcebook gives specific names for corporate consumer complaint executives. Another unique feature of Consumer Sourcebook is its geographical listing of newspaper, radio, and television ombudsmen (and women) who answer questions and investigate dissatisfactions in their own local areas"—(Publisher's catalog).

THE CUMULATIVE BOOK INDEX. *Wilson* 1957–73, sold on service basis; 1928–56 write publisher for additional information

The CBI began publication in 1898 as the "U.S. Book Catalog." Since 1928, the last single-volume cumulation under this title, it has been an author, title and subject index to current books in the English language published in all countries. Monthly supplements are cumulated frequently during the year with bound semiannual and larger cumulations.

CUMULATIVE PAPERBACK INDEX, 1939–1959. Ed. by Robert Reginald and M. R. Burgess *Gale Research Co.* 1973 $24.00

"The time saved on an exhaustive and perhaps futile search of *Publishers Weekly, Paperbound Books in Print* (1955–), and *The National Union Catalog* makes this volume well worth its price . . . highly recommended for public and academic libraries"—*(RQ)*.

David, Nina. REFERENCE GUIDE FOR CONSUMERS. *Bowker* 1975 $14.95

". . . an annotated bibliography of consumer media in print, including film. . . . this is an excellent entry in a.crowded field"—*(LJ)*.

DIRECTORY OF SPECIAL LIBRARIES AND INFORMATION CENTERS. Ed. by Margaret L. Young and others. *Gale Research Co.* 1974 Vol. 1 Special Libraries and Information Centers in the United States and Canada $55.00 Vol. 2 Geographic-Personnel Index 3rd ed. $35.00 Vol. 3 New Special Libraries, Four Periodic Supplements to the Base Volume $57.50

Downs, Robert B., and Elizabeth C. Downs. HOW TO DO LIBRARY RESEARCH. *Univ. of Illinois Press* 1974 $7.95

EDUCATION INDEX. *Wilson* Vols. 1–23 1929–1973 service basis. Published monthly from September to June with permanent bound annual cumulations.

EL-HI TEXTBOOKS IN PRINT. (Orig. "Textbooks in Print") *Bowker* annually in spring 7th
    ed. 1976 $25.00

"Lists 20,000 textbooks and related teaching materials under 20 main subject headings, with
some 140 sub-categories. Entry information includes: author, title, grade level, series affiliation,
publication date, binding, ISBN, price, and publisher.... A directory of the 374 publishers
represented is also provided for added ordering convenience"—(Publisher's catalog).

ENCYCLOPEDIA OF LIBRARY AND INFORMATION SCIENCE. Ed. by Allen Kent and others
    Marcel Dekker for subscribers to complete set each vol. $45.00 for nonsubscribers each
    vol. $55.00

A projected 18-volume work "concerned with the present practices and backgrounds of the fields
of librarianship and documentation"—(Publisher's note).

ENCYCLOPEDIA OF PHILOSOPHY. Ed. by Paul Edwards *Macmillan* (Free Press) 4 vols. 1973 set
    $99.50

ENCYCLOPEDIA OF THE SOCIAL SCIENCES. Ed. by E. R. Seligman *Macmillan* 8 vols. each
    $40.00 set $195.00. (*See also* International Encyclopedia of the Social Sciences, *below*.)

Enoch Pratt Free Library, Baltimore. REFERENCE BOOKS: A Brief Guide for Students and
    Other Users of the Library. Comp. by Mary Neill Barton and Marion V. Bell *Enoch
    Pratt* 7th ed. 1970 $1.75 10 or more each $1.35

EUROPEAN BIBLIOGRAPHY. Ed. by Hjalmar Pehrsson and Hanna Wulf; comp. by the
    European Cultural Center, Geneva. *A. W. Sythoff*, Leyden, Netherlands (dist. by
    Bowker) 1965 $13.50. Includes 1,300 books of a historical and philosophical nature
    on European art and culture as a unity. Each entry is given in English, French and
    German.

FORTHCOMING BOOKS. *Bowker* bimonthly, annual subscription $24.00 with "Subject Guide
    to Forthcoming Books" $32.00 single copies each $6.00. Each issue includes books to
    be published during the next five months, plus a continuing, cumulative index to
    books published since the latest (annual) edition of "Books in Print." 5–7,000 titles per
    issue. Separate author and title index.

Hutchins, Margaret. INTRODUCTION TO REFERENCE WORK. *American Lib. Assn.* 1944 $6.00.
    A textbook for library schools dealing with the principles and methods of reference
    work in general.

INDUSTRIAL RESEARCH LABORATORIES OF THE UNITED STATES. Ed. by the Jaques Cattell
    Press *Bowker* 1975 $49.75

The 14th edition of this directory gives full details on 6,661 research facilities in the United
States with emphasis on research and development activities in the physical, biological, and social
and behavioral sciences. Companies are arranged alphabetically; subject, geographical and
personnel indexes.

INTERNATIONAL ENCYCLOPEDIA OF THE SOCIAL SCIENCES. Ed. by D. E. Sills. *Macmillan* 17
    vols. 1968 each $55.00 set $495.00. The successor to "Encyclopedia of the Social
    Sciences" listed above.

IRREGULAR SERIALS AND ANNUALS: An International Directory. *Bowker* 4th ed. 1976
    $45.00

"Current data on 25,000 serials, annuals, continuations, conference proceedings, and other
publications issued irregularly or less frequently than twice a year is provided in this updated,
expanded bibliography. Designed as a companion to *Ulrich's International Periodicals Directory*, it is
world-wide in scope. Entries are arranged alphabetically by title under 249 subject headings, and
include: frequency of issue, publisher, Dewey Decimal number, language(s) of text, year first
published, price, and editor. International Standard Serial Numbers (ISSN) are included and for
the first time, a special index of international publications—those of the U.N., European communities and international organizations—simplifies the location of materials that are world-wide in
scope. It also provides a title index of all publications contained within, complete with ISSN and
Country Codes, and a Cessations section with listings for 800 serials which have ceased publication
since the 2nd edition"—(Publisher's catalog).

THE JULIAN STREET LIBRARY: A Preliminary List of Titles. Comp. by Warren Kuhn *Bowker* 1966 $16.95. A list of 8,555 titles selected over a 5-year period for the Julian Street Undergraduate Library at Princeton University.

LIBRARY JOURNAL. *Bowker* issued twice a month, except monthly in July and August annual subscription $19.00 single copies $1.35 Spring, Summer, and Fall Announcement issues each $3.25. Its reviewing service by professional librarians offers objective appraisals of more than 7,000 titles annually.

THE LIBRARY JOURNAL BOOK REVIEW. *Bowker* 7 vols. to date Vol. 1 (1967 reviews) 1968 ed. by Margaret Cooley Vol. 2 (1968 reviews) 1969 ed. by Margaret Cooley Vol. 3 (1969 reviews) 1970 ed. by Judith Serebnick Vol. 4 (1970 reviews) 1971 ed. by Judith Serebnick Vol. 5 (1971 reviews) 1972 ed. by Judith Serebnick Vol. 6 (1972 reviews) 1973 ed. by Janet Fletcher Vol. 7 (1973 reviews) 1974 ed. by Janet Fletcher each $21.00

"Cumulative bound volumes of adult reviews which appeared in *LJ* during the year, arranged by subject with author and title indexes. Over 5,000 reviews in more than 20 categories are included in each volume"—(Publisher's catalog).

Merrill, John C., and others. THE FOREIGN PRESS: A Survey of the World's Journalism. Revised edition of "A Handbook of the Foreign Press" (1959). *Louisiana State Univ. Press* 1970 pap. $7.95

Murphey, Robert W. HOW AND WHERE TO LOOK IT UP: A Guide to Standard Sources of Information. *McGraw-Hill* 1958 $16.50

THE NEGRO IN AMERICA: A Bibliography. Ed. by Elizabeth W. Miller and Mary Fisher *Harvard Univ. Press* 1970 $12.50 pap. $4.95

NEW SERIAL TITLES 1950–1970. Ed. by Emery Koltay *Bowker* 4 vols. 1973 $220.00

"This 21-year cumulation contains basic bibliographic data for 220,000 serials issued throughout the world between the years 1950 and 1970 which are held by 800 U.S. and Canadian libraries reporting to the Library of Congress. It combines and supersedes *New Serial Titles* volumes 1950–1960, 1961–1965, 1966–1969, and quarterly issues for 1970. It includes 200,000 new library holdings and 13,000 data revisions never before published"—(Publisher's catalog).

THE NEW YORK TIMES BOOK REVIEW 1896–1973. *Arno* 130 vols. including 5 vol. index $6,410.00

THE NEW YORK TIMES INDEX. *New York Times.* Issued semimonthly with annual cumulation, semimonthly subscription $125.00 annual cumulation $125.00 combination $225.00 per year. A complete *Times Index* file is available from the *N.Y. Times* Library Services back to the establishment of the paper in 1851.

NINETEENTH-CENTURY READERS' GUIDE TO PERIODICAL LITERATURE: 1890–1899. *Wilson* 2 vols. set $35.00. Author-subject index to 51 American and English periodicals; includes some periodicals up to 1922.

NOBEL LECTURES. *American Elsevier* Chemistry Vol. 1 1901–1921 (1967) $30.80 Vol. 2 1922–1941 (1966) $30.80 Vol. 3 1942–1962 (1964) $30.80 Vol. 4 1963–1970 (1973) $42.30. Literature 1901–1967 ed. by Horst Frenz (1969) $15.40. Peace Vol. 1 1901–1925 $30.80 Vol. 2 1926–1950 $30.80 Vol. 3 1951–1970 $30.80. Physics Vol. 1 1901–1921 (1967) $30.80 Vol. 2 1922–1941 (1965) $30.80 Vol. 3 1942–1962 (1964) $30.80 Vol. 4 1963–1970 (1973) $42.30. Physiology-Medicine Vol. 1 1901–1921 (1967) $30.80 Vol. 2 1922–1941 (1965) $30.80 Vol. 3 1942–1962 (1964) $30.80 Vol. 4 1963–1970 (1973) $42.30

Since 1901, more than 330 men and women have won Nobel Prizes for outstanding achievement in the five categories of award: physics, chemistry, physiology or medicine, literature and peace. Their lectures and personal statements on the occasion of their receipt of the awards provide a treasury of the scientific and cultural advances of our time. In 1963 *American Elsevier Publishing Company* began the publication of the complete versions never before available in English or in a systematic, ready-reference manner. Every ten years cumulative volumes in each of the five subject categories will be published.

The work of translation is handled by teams who combine foreign language ability with knowledge of the specific field of science. In addition to the illustrated acceptance speeches of the winners these volumes contain biographies of the winners and the introductory lectures—a speech for each winner by a member of the awards committee, summing up the winner's accomplishments and explaining why the prize was given to him.

PAPERBOUND BOOK GUIDE FOR COLLEGES. *Bowker* 1976 pap. $2.00. Lists over 7,000 paperbacks in every subject area of interest suitable for use in college or by the serious reader. Sold in quantity lots at special low prices. Revised annually.

PAPERBOUND BOOKS IN PRINT. *Bowker* Subscription rate per year, including December base volume and May and September Supplements: $54.50. Provides an index to more than 123,000 paperback original and reprint editions, indexed by title, author and subject.

Paradis, Adrian A. THE RESEARCH HANDBOOK. *T. Y. Crowell* (Funk & Wagnalls) 1974 pap. $2.50

Peterson, Houston, Ed. A TREASURY OF THE WORLD'S GREAT SPEECHES. *Simon & Schuster* 1954 rev. ed. 1965 $9.95

POOLE'S INDEX TO PERIODICAL LITERATURE. *Peter Smith* 6 vols. bd. in 7 Vol. 1 (in 2 pts.) 1802–1881 Vol. 2 1882–1887 Vol. 3 1887–1892 Vol. 4 1892–1896 Vol. 5 1897–1902 Vol. 6 1902–1906 each $17.50 set $114.50

PUBLIC LIBRARY CATALOG. (Orig. "Standard Catalog for Public Libraries") *Wilson* 6th ed. 1973 with 4 annual supplements 1974–1977 $65.00

"The Sixth Edition of the *Public Library Catalog* is a selected, classified list of ,8,765 nonfiction titles chosen by a representative group of practicing librarians. There are 15,852 analytical entries, in addition to author, title, and subject entries for each book listed. . . . *Public Library Catalog* is designed to be used as a tool in book selection, as a source of cataloging and classification information, and as an aid for the reference librarian. Editions of books are often compared, enhancing the Catalog's value as a selection aid for the readers' adviser and as a buying guide for the order librarian"—(Publisher's catalog).

PUBLISHERS' TRADE LIST ANNUAL. *Bowker* 6 vols. 1975 set $42.50. The PTLA is a collection of the catalogs of some 2,250 individual American publishers, bound together alphabetically in six volumes; published annually in September.

THE READER'S ADVISER. *Bowker* 3 vols. Vol. 1 The Best in American and British Fiction, Poetry, Essays, Literary Biography, Bibliography and Reference ed. by Sarah L. Prakken 12th ed. 1974 $23.50 Vol. 2 British and American Drama and Foreign Literature in Translation ed. by F. J. Sypher 1977 (in prep.) Vol. 3 General Biography, History, Bibles, World Religions, Philosophy, Psychology, the Sciences, Folklore, the Lively Arts, Communications and Travel ed. by Jack A. Clarke 1977 (in prep.)

READERS' GUIDE TO PERIODICAL LITERATURE. 1900–date. *Wilson* 34 cumulative vols. 1900– Feb. 1975 Vols. 1–34 available, each $39.50. Semimonthly from Sept. to June, monthly July–Aug. annual subscription $39.50. An index by subject and author to selected U.S. general and nontechnical periodicals. The "Abridged Readers' Guide to Periodical Literature" is available where the more extensive coverage of the unabridged Guide is unnecessary (Vols. 13–25 1960–75 each $17.00).

REPRINTS IN PRINT—Serials 1969. Comp. and ed. by Sam P. Williams *Oceana* 1970 $25.00

"Series are listed under the collective title; separate works in the series are listed under the author's name; and collective series titles are indicated under subject. Serials are listed under subject and title. Although serial title changes are noted in the full title entry, cross references are not made from former titles. . . . A significant contribution to the bibliographical control of reprints"—(*LJ*).

RESEARCH CENTERS DIRECTORY. Ed. by Archie M. Palmer *Gale Research Co.* 5th ed. 1975 $68.00

This comprehensive guide to 4,500 nonprofit research centers on college campuses and elsewhere in the U.S. and Canada is arranged alphabetically by subject fields such as Agriculture,

Home Economics and Nutrition, Engineering and Technology, Government and Public Affairs, the Social Sciences, the Humanities and Religion. It is indexed by Subject, Name of Research Center, Sponsoring Institutions and Names of Research Directors.

REVIEWS-ON-CARDS. *Bowker* full service (both *LJ* and *SLJ*) $125 annually for some 6,000 adult and 2,800 juvenile reviews; *LJ* (adult) reviews $95 a year; *SLJ* (juvenile) reviews $65 a year

"Now you can have every book review from *Library Journal* and/or *School Library Journal* reproduced in full on a 3 x 5 card and rushed to you as each issue goes to press. This flexible service can be adapted to serve dozens of library needs: a *cumulative file* to eliminate searching through back issues of *LJ*; a *'purchasing' file* for new acquisitions; a *subject file*; etc. Space on top and back for annotations"—(Publisher's catalog.)

Robert, Henry M. ROBERT'S RULES OF ORDER REVISED: Seventy-Fifth Anniversary Edition. *Morrow* 1971 pap. $1.45

SCHOOL LIBRARY JOURNAL. *Bowker* monthly Sept. through May annual subscription $15.00. Articles, news, and a comprehensive review service of children's books. Includes approximately 2,800 reviews a year, written by professional librarians.

SENIOR HIGH SCHOOL LIBRARY CATALOG. (Orig. "Standard Catalog for High School Libraries") *Wilson* 10th ed. 1972 including five annual supplements to appear through 1977 $30.00. With the Catholic Supplement $35.00

Shores, Louis. BASIC REFERENCE SOURCES. Ed. by Lee Ash. 1954. Library Reference Ser. *Gregg* 1972 $13.25

Shove, Raymond H., and others. THE USE OF BOOKS AND LIBRARIES. *Univ. of Minnesota Press* (Minnesota University Library School) 10th ed. 1963 pap. $1.75

SPEECH INDEX: An Index to Collections of World Famous Orations and Speeches for Various Occasions. Comp. by Roberta B. Sutton. 1935. *Scarecrow Press* 4th ed. 1966 $22.50 Supplement 1966–1970 (1972) $8.50

THE STANDARD PERIODICAL DIRECTORY. *Oxbridge Pub. Co.* 1974 $60.00. The complete guide to more than 62,000 U.S. and Canadian periodicals. Alphabetical subject arrangement with author index and subject guide. Gives name and address of publisher, editorial content and scope, year founded, subscription rate, etc.

Sturgis, Alice F. STURGIS STANDARD CODE OF PARLIAMENTARY PROCEDURE. 1950. *McGraw-Hill* 2nd ed. 1966 $6.35 text ed. $4.95

SUBJECT COLLECTIONS: A Guide to Special Book Collections in Libraries, Including Indexes, Catalogs, Pictorial Material. Ed. by Lee Ash *Bowker* 4th ed. 1975 $38.50

This vastly enlarged edition provides all the data needed to locate, evaluate, and use 70,000 special book and manuscript collections—about 30,000 more than in the 3rd edition. The book covers collections housed in more than 15,000 academic, public and special libraries as well as those located in nearly 1,000 museums in the U.S., Canada, and Puerto Rico.

SUBJECT COLLECTIONS IN EUROPEAN LIBRARIES. Ed. by Richard C. Lewanski *Bowker* 2nd ed. Fall 1976 $36.00

"This revised and greatly expanded volume identifies about 12,000 collections in libraries throughout Europe. Entries are arranged by Dewey Decimal Classification and provide such useful information as name and location, director's name, date of foundation, brief history, present holdings, specially named collections and bequests, special subject collections, and unique items. Data can also be found on manuscript collections, readers' services, restrictions and reader qualifications, and a brief bibliography of publications on or about each library itself"—(Publisher's catalog).

SUBJECT GUIDE TO BOOKS IN PRINT. *Bowker* 2 vols. 1975 set $55.00

"An ideal bookfinder, *Subject Guide* lists nearly 375,000 books from over 3,000 U.S. publishers, and indexes them under 62,500 LC subject headings, with numerous cross references. Both old and new books, if available from the publishers, are listed here. Numerous forthcoming books are also listed by publishers as 'in prep.' Each entry includes full bibliographical information: author, title, publisher, current price and year of publication"—(Publisher's catalog).

SUBJECT GUIDE TO FORTHCOMING BOOKS. *Bowker* annual subscription $11.00 with "Forth-coming Books" $32.00 single copies each $4.00

"This bi-monthly companion to *Forthcoming Books* lists what books are coming in nearly 450 different subject areas. The comprehensive index covers the coming five-month season, with each issue overlapping and updating its predecessor"—(Publisher's catalog).

SUBSCRIPTION BOOKS BULLETIN REVIEWS: Reprinted from *The Booklist and Subscription Books Bulletin. American Lib. Assn.* 1962–1964 (1964) pap. $2.00 1964–1966 (1967) pap. $2.25 1966–1968 (1968) pap. $2.25

Times Literary Supplement (London). ESSAYS AND REVIEWS FROM THE TIMES LITERARY SUPPLEMENT. *Oxford* 10 vols. Vols. 1–2 o.p. Vol. 3 1964 (1965) $8.50 Vol. 4 1965 (1966) o.p. Vol. 5 1966 (1967) $10.25 Vol. 6 1967 (1968) $11.00 Vol. 7 1968 (1969) $11.00 Vol. 8 1969 (1970) $11.00 Vol. 9 1970 (1971) $12.00 Vol. 10 1971 (1972) $12.00 Vol. 11 1972 (1973) $14.50 Vol. 12 1973 (1974) $17.75

"An excellent record of the literary world"—(*LJ*).

THE TIMES LITERARY SUPPLEMENT (London), 1902–1964. Reprints of annual bound vols. *Kraus* 63 vols. 1967–1969 including the indexes for each vol. each $42.50 set $2,200.00. The complete record, in reprint, of this influential weekly.

TITLES IN SERIES. By Eleanora A. Baer. *Scarecrow Press* 2 vols. 2nd ed. 1964 set $42.50 Supplement 1967 $10.00 Supplement 1971 $15.00 Supplement 1974 $17.50

"A work of this kind has been badly needed. . . . It should pay for itself in time saved and books found by dealer and librarian"—(*Antiquarian Bookman*).

ULRICH'S INTERNATIONAL PERIODICALS DIRECTORY. *Bowker* 16th ed. 1975 $50.00

"In-depth information is provided here on some 62,000 periodicals from all over the world which are alphabetically arranged according to 249 subject headings. With this edition, coverage of publications on microform is extended, as is abstracting and indexing information. International Standard Serial Number (ISSN) with country code and Dewey Decimal Classification numbers are noted in the main entries together with subscription price, frequency of issue, name and address of publisher, circulation, languages used in text, year first published, and whether advertisements, reviews, bibliographies, illustrations, etc. are carried"—(Publisher's catalog).

UNION LIST OF SERIALS IN LIBRARIES OF THE UNITED STATES AND CANADA. Ed. by Edna Brown Titus *Wilson* 5 vols. 3rd ed. 1965 set $120.00

THE UNITED STATES CATALOG. Books in Print January 1928. *Wilson* o.p. Continued by the "Cumulative Book Index" (*see above*)

THE UNIVERSAL REFERENCE SYSTEM. A continuing series of computerized bibliographies for political and behavioral scientists. Ed. by Joan Bergholt and Alfred De Grazia. Political Science, Government and Public Policy Ser. *Plenum Pub.* 3 vols. 1973 $200.00 Supplement 1974 $250.00

VERTICAL FILE INDEX. 1932 to date. Issued monthly (except Aug.) with annual cumulations. *Wilson* annual subscription $11.00. Subject and title index to selected pamphlets.

Walford, Albert John, Ed. GUIDE TO REFERENCE MATERIAL. London, *Library Association* 1970–1975. Vol. 1 3rd ed. (1973) $20.00 Vol. 2 3rd ed. (1975) $20.00 *American Library Assn.* (Bowker) Vol. 3 2nd ed. (1970) $14.50. An annotated British list of leading worldwide reference books and bibliographies, with emphasis on current material published in Britain.

THE WELLESLEY INDEX TO VICTORIAN PERIODICALS 1824–1900. Ed. by Walter E. Houghton *Univ. of Toronto Press* 2 vols. Vol. 1 1966 $95.00 Vol. 2 1972 $125.00 set $195.00

WHITAKER'S FIVE-YEAR CUMULATIVE BOOK LIST 1968–1972. *Whitaker*, London (dist. by Bowker) 2 vols. 1974 set $45.00

A complete list of the new books and new editions published in the United Kingdom arranged by author and title, with details as to subtitle, size, number of pages, price, date, classification and publisher. In one alphabetical index, this gives a complete record of British publishing in the years 1968–1972. Based on lists printed weekly in *The Bookseller*, monthly in "Current Literature" and quarterly and annually in *Whitaker's Cumulative Book List*.

WHITAKER'S CUMULATIVE BOOK LIST. *Whitaker*, London annual vol. £ 5.50. A complete record of British publishing each year, with details as to title, subtitle, author, size, number of pages, price, month of publication, publisher and classification. In two indexes, one in 46 subject classifications; the other alphabetical by author and title, with full details on each entry.

Wiener, Philip P., Ed. DICTIONARY OF THE HISTORY OF IDEAS: Studies of Selected Pivotal Ideas. *Scribner* 4 vols. 1973 each $35.00

"Studies of seminal and recurring ideas in Western thought, in 311 original, signed articles by scholars from many countries"—*(Choice)*.

Wilcox, Dennis L. ENGLISH LANGUAGE NEWSPAPERS ABROAD: A Guide to Daily Newspapers in 56 Non-English Speaking Countries. *Gale Research Co.* 1967 $11.75

WILLING'S PRESS GUIDE—BRITISH EDITION. *IPC America, Inc.* (205 E. 42nd St., New York, N.Y.) $25.00. A directory to newspapers, magazines and annuals published in the United Kingdom.

Winchell, Constance M. GUIDE TO REFERENCE BOOKS. *American Lib. Assn.* 8th ed. 1967 $15.00 Supplements 1965–66 $3.50, 1967–68 $4.00, 1969–70 $4.50, all comp. by Eugene P. Sheehy. A selection aid, reference manual and textbook for study of reference books, describing titles in various languages arranged by subjects. (*For extended comment, see Chapter 3, Reference Books—Literature,* Reader's Adviser, *Vol. 1.*)

Wynar, Bohdan S., Ed. AMERICAN REFERENCE BOOKS ANNUAL. *Libraries Unlimited* 1975 $25.00. An indispensable guide to current reference books.

United States Government Publications

Some 27,000 different government publications are available to the public by purchase from the Office of the Superintendent of Documents, Government Printing Office, Washington, D.C. 20402. Sold at nominal prices (from $.05 and up), the topics covered in these books and pamphlets include a tremendous variety of subjects such as agriculture, child care, housing, finance, wildlife, American history, science, Army, geology, etc. The availability of these publications is publicized by means of catalogs and price lists. Lists of selected publications, issued biweekly, can be obtained without charge on request. The "Monthly Catalog of U.S. Government Publications," containing from 1,200 to 2,200 entries each month, lists all publications issued during the month and is sold on a subscription basis at $27.00 a year. In addition, the *Carrollton Press* publishes the 15-volume "Cumulative Subject Index to the Monthly Catalog of United States Government Publications, 1900–1971" for $1,160.

AMERICAN STATISTICS INDEX 1975. *Congressional Information Service* price varies based on size and character of the institution

"A comprehensive guide and index to the statistical publications of the United States Government"—(Publisher's catalog).

Ames, John G. COMPREHENSIVE INDEX TO THE PUBLICATIONS OF THE UNITED STATES GOVERNMENT, 1881–1893. 1905. *Johnson Reprint* 2 vols. 1971 set $105.00. Immediate successor to Poore's Catalog.

Andriot, John L. GUIDE TO U.S. GOVERNMENT PUBLICATIONS. *Documents Index* annual subscription $95.00. An up-to-date annotated guide to the serials and periodicals currently being published by the hundreds of U.S. Government agencies.

GUIDE TO U.S. GOVERNMENT STATISTICS. *Documents Index* 1974 $45.00

Body, Alexander C. ANNOTATED BIBLIOGRAPHY OF BIBLIOGRAPHIES ON SELECTED PUBLICATIONS AND SUPPLEMENTARY GUIDES TO THE SUPERINTENDENT OF DOCUMENTS CLASSIFICATION SYSTEM. *Press of Case Western* (available from Edwards Bros., Inc., P.O. Box 1007, Ann Arbor, Mich. 48104) Fourth Supplement 1967 $2.80 other prices available upon request

Boyd, Anne M., and Rae E. Rips. UNITED STATES GOVERNMENT PUBLICATIONS. *Wilson* 3rd ed. 1949 rev. ed. 1952 o.p. Primarily a textbook for library school students.

CHECKLIST OF UNITED STATES PUBLIC DOCUMENTS, 1789–1909. 1911. *Kraus* 3rd rev. and enl. ed. $45.00. Divided in three sections, (1) numbered Congressional publications, (2) departmental publications, and (3) miscellaneous publications of Congress. Is of greatest value to someone who already has considerable familiarity with government publications.

CHECKLIST OF UNITED STATES PUBLIC DOCUMENTS, 1789–1970. *U.S. Historical Documents Institute* 118 microfilm cartridges $2,550 index volumes $212.50

"A dual media collection of the active and inactive shelf list of the Superintendent of Documents"—(Publisher's catalog).

CIS INDEX AND ANNUAL. *Congressional Information Service* price available upon request. Covers significant Congressional publications issued by nearly 300 House, Senate and Joint Committees and subcommittees.

CUMULATIVE SUBJECT GUIDE TO UNITED STATES GOVERNMENT BIBLIOGRAPHIES 1924–1973. *Carrollton Press* 7 vols. 1975 set $620.00

"More than 40,000 complete entries describing bibliographies were taken from 50 years of the "Monthly Catalog of United States Government Publications" arranged alphabetically by subject, indexed by Su Docs Classification Numbers and keyed to a separate microfiche collection of bibliographies themselves"—(Publisher's catalog).

DOCUMENTS CATALOG, 1894–1940. *Government Printing Office.* Issued biennially, and discontinued with Vol. 25, covering 1939–1940. 1947. o.p. Replaced in 1947 by the expanded "Monthly Catalog," this successor to Ames' "Comprehensive Index" was an analytical dictionary catalog with entries under subject matter, individual author and governmental author.

INDEX TO UNITED STATES GOVERNMENT PERIODICALS, 1973. Ed. by Allan Carpenter *Infordata International* (175 East Delaware Place, Chicago, Ill. 60611) 1975 $150.00 per year. A quarterly index with an annual cumulation to 114 major periodicals. Coverage starts from 1970.

Jackson, Ellen. SUBJECT GUIDE TO MAJOR UNITED STATES GOVERNMENT PUBLICATIONS. *American Library Assn.* 1968 $6.00

Kerbec, Matthew J. LEGALLY AVAILABLE UNITED STATES GOVERNMENT INFORMATION: As a Result of the Public Information Act. *Van Nostrand-Reinhold* 2 vols. 1970 set $65.00

Leidy, W. Philip. A POPULAR GUIDE TO GOVERNMENT PUBLICATIONS. *Columbia* 3rd ed. 1968 $13.50

A selected list of 3,000 publications are arranged by subject headings. Each entry includes complete bibliographical data including price and ordering information. "There's a vast bibliographical maze in Washington, and one of the few ways to solve it is to follow the thread unreeled by W. Philip Leidy"—(David Glixon, in *SR*).

Morehead, Joe. INTRODUCTION TO UNITED STATES PUBLIC DOCUMENTS. *Libraries Unlimited* 1975 $10.00

NATIONAL ARCHIVES MICROFILM PUBLICATIONS. *National Archives and Records Service* (Publications Sales Branch 36, Washington, D.C. 20408) each roll $12.00. Over 100,000 rolls of microfilm covering American, Latin American, Asian, European and African History; Diplomatic, Military and Local History; Ethnology, Sociology, Genealogy, Economics and Law.

Poore, Benjamin Perley. POORE'S DESCRIPTIVE CATALOGUE OF THE GOVERNMENT PUBLICATIONS OF THE UNITED STATES, Sept. 5, 1774–March 4, 1881. 1885. *Johnson Reprint* 2 vols. set $105.00. The first and only attempt to list completely all government publications. Entries are arranged chronologically and are annotated.

Schmeckebier, Laurence F., and Roy B. Eastin. GOVERNMENT PUBLICATIONS AND THEIR USE. *Brookings* rev. ed. 1969 $10.95

For United Nations Publications, see this Chapter: Year Books and Almanacs, and Chapter 9, History, Government and Politics—Modern and World: International Relations and the United Nations.

BIOGRAPHICAL REFERENCE WORKS

General Directories

Basic reference books on special subjects are to be found within the related chapters.

BIOGRAPHICAL DICTIONARIES AND RELATED WORKS: An International Bibliography of Collective Biographies. Ed. by Robert B. Slocum *Gale Research Co.* 1967 $25.00 Supplement 1972 $25.00. Some 4,500 biographies listed from 108 countries or areas. Divided into three sections: Universal Biography; National or Area Biography; Biography by Vocation.

BIOGRAPHY INDEX: A Cumulative Index to Biographical Material in Books and Magazines. *Wilson* 9 vols. 1946–1973 each $50.00. Started in 1946, the "Biography Index" is issued quarterly, annually and in a three-year cumulative volume. It consists of a main or "name" alphabet and an index by professions and occupations. Current books of biography, periodical material and even references to chapters in books are included. Material covers individuals both living and dead. Obituaries of national and international interest listed.

CHAMBERS'S BIOGRAPHICAL DICTIONARY: The Great of All Nations and All Times. Ed. by William and J. L. Geddie and J. Liddell. 1897. A British book, orginally compiled by David Patrick and F. Hindes Groome. New ed. 1951 1953 1956 1962 ed. by J. O. Thorne *St. Martin's* 1969 $20.00. Facts and anecdotes of over 15,000 of history's famous and infamous figures of all nations and all times are included here, with such diverse personalities as Cleopatra, Cyrano de Bergerac and Eisenhower.

CURRENT BIOGRAPHY: Who's News and Why. *Wilson* Monthly 1943–   Yearbooks 1946–1973 each $12.00. A cumulative monthly featuring national and international names in the news of the day and covering some 40 subject fields from archeology to technology. Each issue contains a cumulated index to previous issues. Monthly issues are replaced by a bound annual volume of the entire year's material in one alphabet.

DICTIONARY OF AMERICAN BIOGRAPHY. Ed. by Allen Johnson and Dumas Malone. *Scribner* 20 vols. 1927–1936 o.p. popular ed. on thin paper with index and supplement vols. 1 and 2, 22 vols. in 11 o.p. subscription ed., 1927–1972 14 vols. with index and supplement vols. 3 and 4 $475.00

A monumental undertaking on the same scale as the English Dictionary of National Biography; Adolph S. Ochs contributed $500,000 to the American Council of Learned Societies for this purpose. Professor Allen Johnson of Yale was chosen as editor. After Professor Johnson's death in 1931, Dumas Malone completed the work. The biographies range in length from 500 to 16,000 words depending upon the significance and importance of the subject. In Vol. 20 there is a "Brief Account of the Enterprise" and an obituary sketch of Mr. Ochs by Elmer Davis. The 13,633 biographies of Americans no longer living are related in eleven million words. The enterprise cost $650,000.

The 11-volume edition has been culled into a one volume "Concise Dictionary of American Biography" edited by Joseph G. E. Hopkins (*Scribner* 1964 $25.00), which contains almost 15,000 biographies of prominent Americans from Colonial days to about 1940. The current edition contains 15,919 biographies.

DICTIONARY OF AMERICAN LABOR LEADERS. Ed. by Gary M. Fink and Milton Cantor *Greenwood* 1974 $19.95

"Biographical sketches of 500 or so individuals who have left their imprint upon the labor movement in the United States"—*(RQ)*.

THE DICTIONARY OF BIOGRAPHY. By Herbert Spencer Robinson. *Littlefield* 1975 pap. $4.95

"Only three to twelve lines describe each of the 3,500 subjects . . . but the range is vast and the identifications, though in telegraphic style, are rather more satisfying than those in a standard dictionary. There are useful indexes under fifty-five categories"—(David Glixon, in *SR*).

DICTIONARY OF CANADIAN BIOGRAPHY. Ed. by George W. Brown, David Hayne, Frances
Halpenny, Marc La Terreur, Marcel Trudel, and Andre Vachon *Univ. of Toronto
Press* Vol. 1 1000–1700 (1966) Vol. 2 1701–1740 (1969) Vol. 3 1741–1770 (1974) Vol.
10 1871–1880 (1972) each $20.00 Laurentian ed. each $60.00

"There is no better introduction to Canada, no reference work on early American history that
can rival it. Every library that pretends to any reference section needs it"—(*LJ*).

DICTIONARY OF NATIONAL BIOGRAPHY. Ed. by Sir Leslie Stephen and Sir Sidney Lee
Oxford 22 vols. 1938 set $395.00. Incorporates Supplement I as Vol. 22.

The D.N.B. is the largest of all national collections of biography, containing more than 30,000
biographies of persons no longer living. It was founded in 1882 by George M. Smith and issued
first in 66 volumes, 1885–1901. In 1908–09 these 66 volumes were reissued in 22 volumes. There
was a reissue of these 22 volumes in 1921–22 and again in 1938. The D.N.B. is national but not
international. It is wholly British and its chief value, as Sir Leslie Stephen said, "lies not in the long
article upon famous names but in the minor biographies of less conspicuous people." This policy
of the first editor has not always been carried out. Famous names have been treated at unnecessary
length and some have been published separately in book form, *e.g.* Lee's Shakespeare and
Stephen's Swift and Scott. It is *the* reference work for English biography.

SECOND SUPPLEMENT, Vol. 23 1901–11. Ed. by Sir Sidney Lee *Oxford* 3 vols. in 1 1912
reissue 1937 $27.25

THIRD SUPPLEMENT, Vol. 24 1912–21. Ed. by H. W. C. Davis and J. R. H. Weaver
Oxford 1927 reissue 1939 $18.75

FOURTH SUPPLEMENT, 1922–30. Ed. by J. R. H. Weaver *Oxford* 1937 $18.75. With an
Index covering all Supplements 1901–30.

FIFTH SUPPLEMENT, 1931–40. Ed. by L. G. W. Legg *Oxford* 1949 $22.50. With an Index
covering all Supplements 1901–40.

SIXTH SUPPLEMENT, 1941–50. Ed. by L. G. W. Legg and E. T. Williams *Oxford* 1959
$27.25. With an Index covering all Supplements 1901–50.

SEVENTH SUPPLEMENT, 1951–60. Ed. by E. T. Williams and Helen M. Palmer. *Oxford
Univ. Press* 1971 $32.25. With an index covering all supplements 1901–1960.

THE CONCISE DICTIONARY OF NATIONAL BIOGRAPHY FROM THE BEGINNINGS TO 1950.
Oxford 1939 Pt. 1 to 1900 (reprint 1953) $26.00 Pt. 2 1901–1950 $24.50

This is an epitome of the 22 volumes of the main work and its supplement. It appeared first in
1930, including then only the second and third supplements. In the present editions the
supplements are combined in one alphabet. The articles are abridged to one-14th of their original
length. This is an excellent two-volume dictionary of biography for the small library.

A DICTIONARY OF UNIVERSAL BIOGRAPHY. Ed. by Albert M. Hyamson. 1916. *Dutton* 2nd
rev. ed. 1951 o.p. This is actually a guide to biographies of people no longer living,
supplying brief information (birth and death dates, nationality, profession) and
indicating sources where further information can be found. Over 109,000 names are
included from all countries and all times. This second edition has been entirely
rewritten.

ENCYCLOPEDIA OF AMERICAN BIOGRAPHY. Ed. by John A. Garraty *Harper* 1974 $22.50

"Includes about 1000 well-written accounts of both historical and living persons selected by the
editors on the criteria of significance, achievement, fame, and topicality"—(*LJ*).

HALL OF FAME FOR GREAT AMERICANS AT NEW YORK UNIVERSITY. Ed. by Theodore
Morello *New York Univ. Press* 1967 $6.00. A guidebook which contains brief biogra-
phies of the 93 famous American artists, humanists, scientists and politicians en-
shrined at New York University's Hall of Fame.

INTERNATIONAL WHO'S WHO. Revised annually. *Europa Publications* (dist. by Int. Pubns.
Service) 38th rev. ed. 1974–75 $46.50. Published annually since 1936, this includes
over 15,000 entries, representing living internationally famous personages in all
countries, with emphasis on names prominent in politics, science, and the arts.

THE McGRAW-HILL ENCYCLOPEDIA OF WORLD BIOGRAPHY. Ed. by David I. Eggenberger *McGraw-Hill* 12 vols. 1973 set $250.00 for schools and libraries $275.00 for individuals. Contains 5,000 biographies of "universally" important persons. Each article has bibliographical references to works in English.

THE MACMILLAN DICTIONARY OF CANADIAN BIOGRAPHY. Ed. by Stewart W. Wallace *St. Martin's* 1964 $20.00

Biographies of over 600 Canadians who died before 1961. "The information is succinct, readable, . . . and authoritative"—*(LJ)*.

NATIONAL CYCLOPEDIA OF AMERICAN BIOGRAPHY. Ed. by John Dickson *James T. White & Co.* 1892 Vol. 50 and current vols. with loose-leaf index each $35.75; *University Microfilms* Vols. 1–50 rpt. each $22.50 set $980.00

This is a continuing series, beginning in 1892 with Volume 1. The biographies are not arranged alphabetically but are classified according to professions. The lists include Presidents of the United States, Cabinet officers, governors, generals, physicians, lawyers, editors, etc. Each volume has its own index and an additional loose-leaf Index containing three different indexes covering Vols. 1–50 (others in prep.) and cumulated supplements to date (*White* $35.75). The index is both personal and topical and includes subject headings by means of which organizations, businesses, industries and other activities can be referred to. *White's* "Conspectus of American Biography" (1937, o.p.) was compiled by the editorial staff of the "National Cyclopedia" and is still useful as an independent reference book as well as a classified index to the main work.

NEW CENTURY CYCLOPEDIA OF NAMES. Ed. by Clarence L. Barnhart, with the assistance of William D. Halsey and others. 1954. *Prentice-Hall* 3 vols. each $26.65 set $79.95

Originally the last volume of the famous "Century Dictionary and Cyclopedia," published in the '90's, this reference book had been out of print since World War I until the present edition. The new edition provides in an alphabet of more than 100,000 entries, under proper names, information on all kinds of subjects—biographical, literary, geographical, scientific, military, business, etc. A major reference work, especially for small libraries.

NOTABLE AMERICAN WOMEN, 1607–1950: A Biographical Dictionary. Ed. by Edward T. James *Harvard Univ. Press* 3 vols. 1972 set $75.00

"These volumes . . . represent the first reference work on 1,354 American women which goes beyond the suffragettes and the 'wives of famous men'—all kinds of women are treated in well written articles which range from 400 to 700 words"—*(Choice)*.

TAYLOR'S ENCYCLOPEDIA OF GOVERNMENT OFFICIALS, FEDERAL AND STATE. *Political Research, Inc.* (Dallas, Texas 75201) 1975–76 biennially with quarterly supplements price upon request. Some 20,000 names, addresses and phone numbers of government officials throughout the U.S.; 850 photographs; 51 detailed maps.

WEBSTER'S AMERICAN BIOGRAPHIES. *Merriam* 1974 $15.00. Includes over 3,000 brief biographies from Aaron, Henry to Zworkin, Vladimir.

WEBSTER'S BIOGRAPHICAL DICTIONARY. *Merriam* o.p. The 1972 edition contains more than 40,000 entries, approximately one-third of which are of living men and women.

WHO: Sixty Years of American Eminence; The Story of Who's Who in America. By Cedric A. Larson. *Astor-Honor* 1958 $7.50

"The author has gleaned from the archives a rich bounty of previously unpublished material. This he has skillfully blended together with a generous sprinkling of anecdotes about some of more than 127,000 greats and near greats who have made the pages of 'Who's Who' during the past 60 years"—*(Christian Science Monitor)*.

WHO WAS WHEN? A Dictionary of Contemporaries. By Miriam A. de Ford. *Wilson* 2nd ed. 1950 o.p. The subtitle, "A Dictionary of Contemporaries" means, in this case, a dictionary of the contemporaries of famous people from 500 B.C. to the present. The book is arranged in tabular form under such heads as Literature, Painting & Sculpture, Government & Law, Science & Medicine, etc. There is an alphabetical index.

WHO WAS WHO, 1951–1960. (English) *St. Martin's* 1961 $30.00. Information about people not living has been cumulated in these volumes available from *St. Martin's*: "Who Was

Who, 1897–1915" rev. with addenda and corrigenda 1920 1953 $30.00; "Who Was Who, 1916–1928" 1929 1962 $30.00; "Who Was Who, 1929–1940" 1941 $17.00; "Who Was Who, 1941–1950" 1952 1958 $30.00 set $180.00

WHO WAS WHO IN AMERICA. *Marquis* 6 vols. Vol. 1 1897–1942 Vol. 2 1943–1950 Vol. 3 1951–1960 Vol. 4 1961–1968 Vol. 5 1969–1973 Vol. 6 Historical Volume each $44.50 set $195.00

WHO WAS WHO IN AMERICA (Historical Volume, 1607–1896). *Marquis* 1963 rev. ed. 1967 $44.50. A compilation of sketches of individuals, both of the United States and other countries, who have made contribution to, or whose activity was in some manner related to, the history of the United States, from the founding of Jamestown Colony to the year of continuation of Volume I of "Who Was Who in America."

WHO'S WHO: Annual Biographical Dictionary. (English) *St. Martin's* 1977 $52.50. An annual publication which incorporates "Men and Women of the Time," giving brief biographical facts about living men and women, with a chronological list of their publications if they are writers.

WHO'S WHO IN AMERICA. *Marquis* 2 vols. 38th ed. 1974 set $69.50. A biennial publication begun by Albert Nelson Marquis. Modeled on the English "Who's Who" and first published in 1899–1900. In "Who's Who in America" there is not complete repetition of information in earlier volumes, and it is therefore necessary to keep the series from year to year.

WHO'S WHO IN THE ARAB WORLD. *Int. Pubns. Service.* 5th ed. 1974 $50.00

WHO'S WHO OF AMERICAN WOMEN (and Women of Canada). *Marquis* 9th ed. 1975 $47.50

WORLD WHO'S WHO OF WOMEN: 1974. *Rowman* 1975 $49.50

For regional and professional "Who's Who's," see next listing: Reference Tools and Directories in Special Fields.

Reference Tools and Directories in Special Fields

In addition to general biographical reference books there is an ever-growing list of trade rolls, catalogs, special biographical works and directories covering every conceivable profession and industry, country and city, international organization and local society. Compilations of public defenders or private detective agencies, purchasing guides or inland waterways do not lie within the province of *"The Reader's Adviser."* The following selection of titles, however, bears upon the fields dealt with in this volume. Directories in the field of the theater, other than "Who's Who," will be found in *"The Reader's Adviser,"* Volume 2, Chapter 1, Drama.

AMERICAN LIBRARY ASSOCIATION MEMBERSHIP DIRECTORY. *American Lib. Assn.* annual 1974 pap. $10.00

AMERICAN LIBRARY DIRECTORY, 1976–1977. Ed. by Jaques Cattell Press *Bowker* 30th ed. 1976 $45.00

Biennially revised, this covers over 25,950 U.S. libraries and 2,000 Canadian of every type; includes names of key personnel, addresses, number of volumes, special collections and much other useful material.

AMERICAN MEDICAL DIRECTORY. *American Medical Assn.* 4 vols. 26th ed. 1974 set $125.00

AMERICAN MEN AND WOMEN OF SCIENCE (orig. "American Men of Science" first published in 1906). Edited by Jaques Cattell Press *Bowker* 11 vols. Agricultural, Animal and Veterinary Sciences 1974 $25.00 Economics 1974 $25.00 Physical and Biological Sciences 6 vols. 12th ed. 1971–1973 each $37.50 Discipline Index 12th ed. 1973 $27.50 Social and Behavioral Sciences 2 vols. 12th ed. 1973 each $42.50 Discipline Index 12th ed. 1974 $25.00 Urban Community Science 1974 $22.50

THE AMERICAN NEGRO REFERENCE BOOK. Ed. by John P. Davis *Prentice-Hall* 1966 $24.95

Traces the Negro in America from past to present and offers much statistical and documented material on all facets of Negro life as well as informative articles by authoritative contributors. "Well worth the money"—(*Christian Century*).

AMERICAN SOCIETY OF COMPOSERS, AUTHORS AND PUBLISHERS: A biographical directory. *ASCAP* (575 Madison Ave., New York, N.Y.) 1966 $5.25

BIOGRAPHICAL DIRECTORY OF THE AMERICAN PSYCHIATRIC ASSOCIATION. *Bowker* 6th ed. 1973 $38.50. Detailed biographical sketches of some 20,000 members.

BURKE'S GENEALOGICAL HERALDIC HISTORY OF THE PEERAGE, BARONETAGE AND KNIGHT-AGE. *Burke's Peerage, Ltd.* (dist. by Arco) 105th ed. 1970 with abr. supplement $95.00. Lists the titled nobility of the United Kingdom including information on the current holder of the title, the title's origin and history.

DeBono, Edward, Ed. EUREKA: An Illustrated History of Inventions from the Wheel to the Computer. *Holt* 1974 $25.00

"The 500 paintings, drawings, diagrams and photographs (half of them in color) in this large-format book each illustrate a short, signed article on the origin of some technical device or process"—(*LJ*).

DIRECTORY OF AMERICAN SCHOLARS. Ed. by Jaques Cattell Press *Bowker* 4 vols. 6th ed. 1974 each $39.50 set $148.50. A companion to "American Men and Women of Science," it offers detailed biographical sketches of scholars in the humanities. Vol. 1 History Vol. 2 English, Speech and Drama Vol. 3 Foreign Languages, Linguistics, and Philology Vol. 4 Philosophy, Religion, and Law, and Name Index to all four volumes.

DIRECTORY OF ASSOCIATIONS IN CANADA. Ed. by Brian Land *Univ. of Toronto Press* 2nd ed. 1973 $35.00. Authoritative information on approximately 800 voluntary non-government nonprofit Canadian organizations.

DIRECTORY OF BRITISH SCIENTISTS 1966–1967. 1963. 2 vols. 3rd ed. 1967 o.p. About 50,000 entries with biographical information, also given by subject category. Includes research establishments with directors' names, scientific societies and their journals.

DIRECTORY OF SCIENCE INFORMATION SOURCES: International Biography. *Int. Pubns. Service* 2nd ed. 1967. $15.00. National and international directories of sources of scientific, technical and economic information; learned societies, professional associations, technical and research institutes, etc.

THE EBONY HANDBOOK (orig. "The Negro Handbook"). Comp. by Editors of *Ebony* and Doris E. Saunders *Johnson Pub.* 1974 $20.00

ENCYCLOPEDIA OF ASSOCIATIONS. Ed. by Margaret Fisk *Gale Research Co.* 3 vols. 9th ed. 1975 $55.00. Vol. 1 National Organizations of the U.S. Vol. 2 Geographic and Executive Index Vol. 3 New Associations and Projects. Carries a total of 14,563 organizations, grouped in 17 basic categories, such as trade, business, commercial, scientific, educational, religious, etc. Vol. 2 lists organizations by state and city and provides a list of association executives. Vol. 3 periodically updates the information contained in Vol. 1.

ENCYCLOPEDIA OF ENVIRONMENTAL SCIENCE. *McGraw-Hill* 1974 $24.00

"The 300 articles in this special encyclopedia are for the most part chosen from the more comprehensive 'McGraw Hill Encyclopedia of Science and Technology' and its yearbooks"—(*LJ*).

ENCYCLOPEDIA OF INDIANS OF THE AMERICAS. Ed. by Keith Irvine *Scholarly Press* 20 vols. 1974 set $775.00

ENCYCLOPEDIA JUDAICA. *Macmillan* 16 vols. 1972 set $500.00

"A landmark of creative endeavor and certainly the major Jewish publishing event of the decade"—(*Choice*).

ENCYCLOPEDIC DICTIONARY OF JUDAICA. Ed. by Geoffrey Wegoder *Leon Amiel Pub.* 1974 $29.95

"This concise, contemporary, and comprehensive work gives basic facts and figures on Jewish topics of interest particularly to the Western world: the Bible, Israel, Jewish communities, and famous Jews"—(*LJ*).

THE FOUNDATION DIRECTORY. Ed. by The Foundation Center *Columbia* 5th ed. 1975 $30.00. Basic information on nongovernmental, nonprofit foundations.

HUMANITIES INDEX (orig. "Social Sciences and Humanities Index" until mid-1974). Published quarterly with bound annual cumulations. *Wilson* service basis. An author-subject index to 260 periodicals covering such fields as archaeology, area studies, broadcasting, film, history, literature, music, philosophy, popular culture, religion, etc.

THE LIBRARIES, MUSEUMS AND ART GALLERIES YEARBOOK 1971. *Bowker* 1971 $19.25. The standard directory of the British library world. It covers 500 public libraries and 2,000 branches in the United Kingdom and Eire, 1,200 special (including academic) and industrial libraries, and 800 museums.

MARTINDALE-HUBBELL LAW DIRECTORY. *Martindale-Hubbell* (1 Prospect St., Summit, N.J.) annual 6 vols. 1975 price available upon request. Consolidation of "Martindale's American Law Directory," 1868–1930, and "Hubbell's Legal Directory," 1870–1930.

SOCIAL SCIENCES INDEX. Replaces "Social Sciences and Humanities Index" after mid-1974. Published quarterly with bound annual cumulations. *Wilson* service basis. An author-subject index to 263 periodicals covering such fields as anthropology, area studies, economics, environmental science, gerontology, law & criminology, nursing, political science, public administration, public health, etc.

Thompson, Kenneth. A DICTIONARY OF TWENTIETH CENTURY COMPOSERS (1911–1971). *St. Martin's* 1973 $30.00

"An excellent new reference work produced in England that is certain to become a standard source for all libraries as well as musical scholars. Thompson has selected 32 influential composers who all died within the period 1911–1971"—*(Choice)*.

Untermeyer, Louis. MAKERS OF THE MODERN WORLD. *Simon & Schuster* 1955 $12.50 pap. 1962 $3.95. The lives of 92 writers, artists, scientists, statesmen, inventors, philosophers, composers, and other creators who formed the pattern of our century.

WHO'S WHO IN AMERICAN POLITICS: A Biographical Directory of United States Political Leaders. *Bowker* 5th ed. 1975 $48.50

"This revised and updated edition lists over 18,000 notables covering the entire spectrum of American political life—from the President and key federal, state and local officials to non-office-holders who are politically active and influential and for the first time, to all state legislators. Each alphabetically arranged entry includes legal and mailing addresses; birthplace and date; party affiliation; present and previous political, governmental and business positions; achievements; and published books and articles. In addition, there is a geographical index to all biographies"—(Publisher's catalog).

WHO'S WHO IN LIBRARIANSHIP AND INFORMATION SCIENCE. Ed. by Thomas Landau *Int. Pubns. Service* 1972 $17.50

WHO'S WHO IN MUSIC: Musicians International Directory. *Hafner* 1972 $27.95

WHO'S WHO IN THE EAST. *Marquis* 14th ed. 1973 $45.00. Some 20,000 entries from the Middle Atlantic States, New England and Eastern Canada.

WHO'S WHO IN THE MIDWEST. *Marquis* 14th ed. 1974 $44.50. Contains 18,500 entries from the American Midwest and western Ontario and Manitoba.

WHO'S WHO IN THE SOUTH AND SOUTHWEST. *Marquis* 14th ed. 1975 $45.50. Lists over 18,500 Americans from the District of Columbia to Texas.

WHO'S WHO IN THE THEATRE. Ed. by Robert Finley and John Parker *Pitman* 15th ed. 1974 $32.50

WHO'S WHO IN THE WEST. *Marquis* 14th ed. 1974 $45.50. Lists over 18,500 individuals from New Mexico north to Saskatchewan and westward to Alaska and Hawaii.

WORLD GUIDE TO LIBRARIES. *Bowker* 2 vols. 4th ed. 1974 set $59.50. A listing of 37,000 special, university, and public libraries from 157 countries in Europe, Africa, America, Asia, Oceania.

THE WORLD OF LEARNING. *Gale Research Co.* 2 vols. 25th ed. 1974–75 $65.00

The indispensable guide to the academic, scientific and cultural life of every country in the world lists universities, colleges, libraries, museums, learned societies, professional associations, and research institutions; gives names of professors, deans and principals, curators and librarians as well as other important information in great detail.

WORLD WHO'S WHO IN FINANCE AND INDUSTRY. *Marquis* 19th ed. 1975–76 $47.50. Brief biographies of 30,000 international business leaders; index which lists the executives by company.

WORLD WHO'S WHO IN SCIENCE: From Antiquity to the Present. *Marquis* 1968 $60.00

ZIP CODE DIRECTORY. *U.S. Post Office Dept.* (Order from the Supt. of Documents, U.S. Government Printing Office, Washington, D.C. 20402) 1974 $15.65

REFERENCE BOOKS FOR ART AND MUSIC

This is a highly selective list of Art and Music reference books for general libraries.

Art and Architecture

AMERICAN ARCHITECTS DIRECTORY. Ed. by Jaques Cattell Press *Bowker* 3rd ed. 1970 o.p. Offers biographical information on some 15,000 architects.

THE AMERICAN ART DIRECTORY. *Bowker* rev. triennially 46th ed. 1976 $37.50 (in prep.). Sponsored by the American Federation of Arts.

THE ART INDEX. *Wilson* 1950– service basis. A cumulative author and subject index to a selected list of fine arts periodicals and museum bulletins published quarterly with bound annual and permanent two-year cumulations.

Boger, Louise Ade, and H. Batterson Boger. THE DICTIONARY OF ANTIQUES AND THE DECORATIVE ARTS. *Scribner* 1967 $19.95

Cheney, Sheldon. A NEW WORLD HISTORY OF ART. *Viking* 1937 rev. ed. 1956 $15.95. Includes 500 illustrations; 8 pages of full color; index; a new edition of a basic historical and critical work.

SCULPTURE OF THE WORLD: A History. *Viking* 1968 $15.00

"An excellent, comprehensive history . . . solid, attractive, profusely illustrated and well-organized"—*(PW)*.

Cummings, Paul. DICTIONARY OF CONTEMPORARY AMERICAN ARTISTS. *St. Martin's* rev. ed. 1971 $25.00

THE DIRECTORY OF WORLD MUSEUMS. Ed. by Kenneth Hudson and Ann Nicholls *Columbia* 1975 $65.00

"A listing of 22,000 museums throughout the world"—*(LJ)*.

ENCYCLOPEDIA OF WORLD ART. *McGraw-Hill* 15 vols. 1959–67 each $50.00 set $597.00 guide $1.00

This joint enterprise of *McGraw-Hill* and the Institute for Cultural Collaboration, an agency established in Rome by the G. C. Sansoni Publishing Co. of Florence and the Georgio Cini Foundation of Venice, is now complete. "There is nothing even remotely like this encyclopedia in its field. . . . I am all for it. . . . It is full of wonders"—(John Canaday, in the *N.Y. Times*). Vol. 15 is the index.

Fielding, Mantle. DICTIONARY OF AMERICAN PAINTERS, SCULPTORS AND ENGRAVERS. *Assoc. Booksellers* enlarged ed. 1974 $17.50

Fletcher, Banister Flight. A HISTORY OF ARCHITECTURE. *Scribner* 18th ed. 1975 $24.95

Gardner, Helen. ART THROUGH THE AGES. 1926. Rev. by Horst de la Croix and Richard G. Tansey *Harcourt* 5th ed. $13.95 6th ed. 1975 $14.95

Gombrich, Ernst H. THE STORY OF ART. *N.Y. Graphic Soc.* Phaidon Bks. 1972 $15.00 pap. $7.95

"Most lucid, most inspiring short story of art in the English language"—*(N.Y. Herald Tribune)*.

Haftmann, Werner. PAINTING IN THE TWENTIETH CENTURY. *Praeger* 2 vols. enl. ed. 1965 Vol. 1 An Analysis of the Artists and Their Work trans. from the German by Ralph Manheim pap. $3.95 Vol. 2 A Pictorial Survey with 1011 Reproductions Including

50 Plates in Full Color, 80 Pages of Text. 1961. Trans. from the German by Janet Seligman pap. $6.95

Short biographies with bibliographical references for nearly 500 artists. The new edition, smaller in format than the expensive 1961 edition, but with double the illustrations, includes painters of the 1960's. "Highly recommended as a survey of the painting of the western world of this century, and it has been sufficiently expanded to recommend it to collections owning the earlier edition"—(*LJ*).

Hatje, Gerd, Ed. ENCYCLOPEDIA OF MODERN ARCHITECTURE. *Harry N. Abrams* 1964 $17.50 rev. ed. pap. 1967 $7.95

Jaffe, Hans Ludwig C., Ed. 20,000 YEARS OF WORLD PAINTING. Trans. by R. E. Wolf *Harry N. Abrams* 1967 $30.00. Divided into six sections, each containing reproductions with comments and general introductions.

Janson, Horst W. HISTORY OF ART. *Harry N. Abrams* 1962 $22.50; *Prentice-Hall* 1969 $13.95

A "superior one-volume survey"—(*Choice*).

LAROUSSE ENCYCLOPEDIAS. Gen. Ed. René Huyghe; trans. from the French by Emily Evershed and others:

LAROUSSE ENCYCLOPEDIA OF PREHISTORIC AND ANCIENT ART. *Putnam* 1962 o.p.

LAROUSSE ENCYCLOPEDIA OF BYZANTINE AND MEDIEVAL ART. *Putnam* 1963 o.p.

LAROUSSE ENCYCLOPEDIA OF RENAISSANCE AND BAROQUE ART. *Putnam* 1964 o.p.

LAROUSSE ENCYCLOPEDIA OF MODERN ART: From 1800 to the Present Day. *Putnam* 1965 $20.00

Levey, Michael. A HISTORY OF WESTERN ART. *Praeger* 1968 $8.50 pap. $4.95

"An *extremely* useful single-volume history. . . . Elegant and witty as well as learned"—(*PW*).

Lucas, E. Louise. ART BOOKS: A Basic Bibliography on the Fine Arts. *N.Y. Graphic Soc.* 1968 $5.00 pap. $2.50

Organized in sections such as History and Theory, Architecture, Sculpture; monographs on famous artists. "Louise Lucas has an almost universal oversight of art scholarship. This is the best and most up-to-date one-volume art bibliography I have seen"—(*LJ*).

McGRAW-HILL DICTIONARY OF ART. Bernard S. Myers, Ed. Shirley D. Myers, Asst. Ed. *McGraw-Hill* 5 vols. 1969 boxed set $89.50. Contains 15,000 entries, alphabetically arranged, encompassing all areas of architecture, painting, sculpture, and the decorative and graphic arts. Illustrated with 2,100 halftones (400 in full color) and 200 line drawings.

McLanathan, Richard. ART IN AMERICA: A Brief History. *Harcourt* 1975 $8.50 paper $4.95

"A concise survey of American architecture, painting, and sculpture, from beginning of settlement to the present day. With some 170 illustrations in black and white and full color"— (Publisher's catalog).

Mayer, Ralph. DICTIONARY OF ART TERMS AND TECHNIQUES. *T. Y. Crowell* 1969 $8.95

Murray, Peter, and Linda Murray. DICTIONARY OF ART AND ARTISTS. *Penguin* rev. ed. pap. $2.65; *Gannon* 3rd ed. lib. bdg. $6.00

Phillips, Phoebe. COLLECTOR'S ENCYCLOPEDIA OF ANTIQUES. *Crown* 1973 $20.00

Savage, George, and Harold Newman. ILLUSTRATED DICTIONARY OF CERAMICS. *Van Nostrand-Reinhold* 1973 $18.95

VISUAL DICTIONARY OF ART. *N.Y. Graphic Soc.* 1973 $30.00

Walker, John A. GLOSSARY OF ART, ARCHITECTURE, AND DESIGN SINCE 1945. *Clive Bingley* 1973 $10.50

WHO'S WHO IN AMERICAN ART. Sponsored by the American Federation of Arts; ed. by Jaques Cattell Press *Bowker* 1976 $37.00

This indispensable tool includes biographical information on the activities of about 7,000 American artists in all fields of creative art, as well as a section devoted to Canadian artists. New categories in this edition include the names and activities of museum directors, art historians, critics, lecturers, collectors and educators. Other sections are obituaries; a geographical cross-index; a geographically arranged listing of national and regional open exhibitions in the United States.

WORLD ARCHITECTURE: An Illustrated History. Ed. by Trewin Cobblestone *Int. Pubns. Service* 1973 $15.00

It is "probably the best aid to the understanding and appreciation of the art of architecture through the ages as yet bound into one book"—*(LJ)*.

See also Chapter 15, Essays and Criticism, Reader's Adviser, Vol. 1, for the critical works on art by Walter Pater and Sir Herbert Read; Chapter 2, General Biography and Autobiography, this Volume, for Leonardo da Vinci, Benvenuto Cellini, Vincent Van Gogh, Frank Lloyd Wright and Paul Klee.

Music

Apel, Willi. HARVARD DICTIONARY OF MUSIC. *Harvard Univ. Press* 1969 $20.00

(With Ralph T. Daniel) THE HARVARD BRIEF DICTIONARY OF MUSIC. *Harvard Univ. Press* 1960 $6.95; *Simon & Schuster* Pocket Bks. 1961 pap. $1.25

Baines, Anthony, Ed. MUSICAL INSTRUMENTS THROUGH THE AGES. Pref. by the editor. Illus. *Walker & Co.* rev. ed. 1974 $12.50; *Penguin* Pelican Bks. 1961 pap. $2.85.
"A joy to handle, to read, and to study"—*(LJ)*.

BAKER'S BIOGRAPHICAL DICTIONARY OF MUSIC. Ed. by Nicolas Slonimsky *Schirmer* 5th ed. 1958 including supplement 1971 $35.00; supplement only $7.50

Barlow, Harold, and Sam Morgenstern. A DICTIONARY OF MUSICAL THEMES. *Crown* 1948 $6.95

Bernstein, Leonard. THE INFINITE VARIETY OF MUSIC. *Simon & Schuster* 1966 $6.50
"A Bernstein grab bag, highly enjoyable"—*(LJ)*. Includes his television scripts, analyses of four popular symphonies and musical illustrations.

Bookspan, Martin. 101 MASTERPIECES OF MUSIC AND THEIR COMPOSERS. *Doubleday* 1968 $8.95
"This book is an expansion of the [author's] magazine articles [in *Hi Fi/Stereo Review*] to include fairly detailed material on 36 composers and 101 of their most frequently played symphonic works. His descriptions and recommendations of the best recordings are sensible, nondogmatic and allow for divergence in taste"—(Raymond Erickson, in the *N.Y. Times*).

Bull, Storm. INDEX TO BIOGRAPHIES OF CONTEMPORARY COMPOSERS. *Scarecrow Press* 1964 $12.50. Some 6,000
"Tremendously useful"—*(LJ)*.

Chase, Gilbert. AMERICA'S MUSIC: From the Pilgrims to the Present. *McGraw-Hill* 2nd rev. ed. 1966 $15.00 rev. text ed. $10.50
"Indispensable"—*(LJ)*.

(Ed.). THE AMERICAN COMPOSER SPEAKS: A Historical Anthology, 1770–1965. *Louisiana State Univ. Press* 1967 $7.50
"A compilation of excerpts from the writings of thirty American composers, ranging (chronologically) from Francis Hopkinson (1737–1797) to Earle Brown (b. 1926). It is a most rewarding and valuable collection; rewarding because of what the composers themselves have to say, valuable because there is no other book like it"—*(LJ)*.

CONCISE ENCYCLOPEDIA OF JEWISH MUSIC. *McGraw-Hill* 1974 $14.95. The most comprehensive one-volume general reference work on Jewish music ever published.

Copland, Aaron. THE NEW MUSIC, 1900–1960. (Orig. "Our New Music") 1943. *Norton* rev. ed. 1968 $5.50; pap. $2.45
"This balanced survey of important musical ideas and the men who originated them is a useful summary of developments in our century"—*(LJ)*.

Cross, Milton, and David Ewen. MILTON CROSS' ENCYCLOPEDIA OF THE GREAT COMPOSERS AND THEIR MUSIC. *Doubleday* 2 vols. 1953 rev. ed. 1962 set $14.95. A listener's source book to the lives and music of 78 great composers; glossary; bibliography; index.

DICTIONARY OF CONTEMPORARY MUSIC. Ed. by John Vinton *Dutton* 1974 $25.00

Ewen, David. THE WORLD OF TWENTIETH CENTURY MUSIC. *Prentice-Hall* 1968 $14.95
    Mr. Ewen views this book as a "replacement" for his "The Complete Book of 20th Century Music," 1952. He "presents brief biographical sketches of almost 150 composers and even briefer discussions of approximately 1000 works, most of them orchestral"—(*LJ*).

Farish, Margaret K. STRING MUSIC IN PRINT. *Bowker* 2nd ed. 1973 $34.95. Covering ensemble music for all stringed instruments and solo music for violin, viola, cello and bass. An expansion of "Violin Music in Print" (1963, o.p.)

GREAT COMPOSERS 1300–1900. Ed. by David Ewen *Wilson* 1966 $10.00. The 198 most frequently sought.

Grout, Donald J. A HISTORY OF WESTERN MUSIC. *Norton* rev. ed. 1973 text ed. $11.50 abr. and rev. ed. 1973 text ed. $9.95

Grove, Sir George. GROVE'S DICTIONARY OF MUSIC AND MUSICIANS. 1879. Ed. by Eric Blom *St. Martin's* 1879 5th ed. enl. 10 vols. including supplement 1954 each $20.00 set $200.00 pap. each $7.95 set $79.50

Hentoff, Nat, and Albert J. McCarthy, Eds. JAZZ: New Perspectives on the History of Jazz. 1959. *Da Capo* 1974 lib. bdg. $13.50

Jacobs, Arthur. A NEW DICTIONARY OF MUSIC. *Penguin* pap. $1.75

KINGS OF JAZZ. Rev. and ed. by Stanley Green *A. S. Barnes* 1975 $17.50

Kinkle, Roger D. THE COMPLETE ENCYCLOPEDIA OF POPULAR MUSIC AND JAZZ, 1900–1950. *Arlington House* 1974 $75.00
    "This is a fine general music reference set conceived from much research and knowledge"—(*LJ*).

Lloyd, Norman. THE GOLDEN ENCYCLOPEDIA OF MUSIC. *Western Pub. Co.* Golden Bks. 1968 $14.95. Stories of operas, symphony analyses, biographies, etc.
    "Should bring joy to the world of the non-professional music-lover"—(David Glixon, in *SR*).

Marcuse, Sibyl. MUSICAL INSTRUMENTS: A Comparative Dictionary. 1964. *Norton* 1975 pap. $6.95. The only dictionary of its kind in English contains information on instruments from ancient times to the present, with bibliography.

THE MUSIC INDEX. Monthly and cumulated annually since 1949 *Information Coordinators, Inc.* (1435 Randolph St. Detroit, Mich. 48226) annual cumulations 1949–date at various prices, annual subscription (incl. subject heading list, 12 monthly issues and annual cumulation) $345.00. This excellent reference tool to over 270 current periodicals, compiled by skilled librarians, has a wide coverage of everything from the most popular subjects to the most "rarefied." With this volume the size has been enlarged because of a new feature, the incorporation of author entries (those of leading articles and books) into a dictionary arrangement.

THE NEW OXFORD HISTORY OF MUSIC. General Eds. J. A. Westrup, Gerald Abraham, E. J. Dent, Dom Anselm Hughes, Egon Wellesz, Martin Cooper *Oxford* 11 vols. projected 1954–
    Vol. 1 Ancient and Oriental Music ed. by Egon Wellesz 1957 $19.00 Vol. 2 Early Medieval Music up to 1300 ed. by Dom Anselm Hughes 1954 $18.50 Vol. 3 Ars Nova and the Renaissance, c. 1300–1540 ed. by Gerald Abraham and Dom Anselm Hughes 1960 $22.50 Vol. 4 The Age of Humanism, 1540–1630 ed. by Gerald Abraham 1968 $30.00 Vol. 5 Opera and Church Music, 1630–1750 ed. by Nigel Fortune and Anthony Lewis 1975 $49.50 Vol. 7 The Age of Enlightenment 1745–1790 ed. by Egon Wellesz and Frederick Sternfeld 1974 $32.50 Vol. 10 Modern Music 1890–1960 ed. by Martin Cooper 1974 $32.50. Under the editorship of Gerald Abraham, "The History of Music in Sound" is being prepared. This is a series of records planned as a supplement to "The New Oxford History of Music," each volume of recordings corresponding to a volume of the *History*. Volumes of recordings are accompanied by handbooks containing, in modern

notation, the whole or part of each composition recorded, annotations, translations of all texts, and a short bibliography. Recordings are available from RCA-Victor, and the handbooks (for vols. 1–10) are available separately from *Oxford* at $3.00 each.

Robertson, Alec, and Denis Stevens, Eds. THE PELICAN HISTORY OF MUSIC. *Penguin* Pelican Bks. 3 vols. pap. Vol. 1 Ancient Forms to Polyphony 1963 $3.75 Vol. 2 Renaissance to Baroque 1964 $2.25 Vol. 3 Classical and Romantic by Hugh Ottaway and Arthur Hutchings 1968 $1.65

Salzman, Eric. TWENTIETH-CENTURY MUSIC: An Introduction. History of Music Ser. *Prentice-Hall* 1974 $8.95 pap. $4.50

"Mr. Salzman covers an immense amount of material in a small space, but the condensation puts the revolutionary events of this century in vivid perspective"—(Raymond Ericson, in the *N.Y. Times*).

Scholes, Percy A. THE CONCISE OXFORD DICTIONARY OF MUSIC: With 125 Pictorial and Musical Illustrations. *Oxford* 1952 2nd ed. by J. O. Ward 1964 $7.50 pap. $3.95

THE LISTENER'S GUIDE TO MUSIC: With a Concert-Goer's Glossary. *Oxford* 1919 10th ed. 1942 1961 pap. $1.75

THE OXFORD COMPANION TO MUSIC. *Oxford* 1938 10th ed. 1970 $25.00

Schonberg, Harold C. THE GREAT CONDUCTORS. *Simon & Schuster* 1967 $7.50 pap. $3.95

Mr. Schonberg is the music critic for the *New York Times*. "In tracing the emergence of the conductor from his sometimes murky beginnings to the exalted position he now occupies in orchestral halls and opera houses, [he] has given us a history of musical tastes and values, especially from 1800 on"—(Thomas Lask, in the *N.Y. Times*). "This will undoubtedly remain the standard book on the subject for many years to come"—(*LJ*).

Simpson, Robert, Ed. THE SYMPHONY. *Drake* 2 vols. 1972 Vol. 1 Haydn to Dvorak $6.95 Vol. 2 Elgar to the Present Day $5.95; *Penguin* 2 vols. 1968 pap. Vol. 1 $1.85 Vol. 2 $1.65

Stambler, Irwin. THE ENCYCLOPEDIA OF POP, ROCK AND SOUL. *St. Martin's* 1974 $20.00

"Reflects the new roads popular music has taken since the mid-sixties"—(*LJ*).

Thompson, Oscar, Ed. THE INTERNATIONAL CYCLOPEDIA OF MUSIC AND MUSICIANS. *Dodd* 1938 10th rev. ed. by Bruce Bohle 1975 $49.95. Signed articles have been contributed by many authorities. In the new edition, biographies have been extended, new entries added, new compositions listed and evaluated.

Westrup, J. A., and F. L. Harrison, Eds. THE NEW COLLEGE ENCYCLOPEDIA OF MUSIC. *Norton* 1960 $10.00 pap. $3.95

See also Chapter 10, The Lively Arts and Communications: Opera, this Volume.

DATES AND FACTS

Arnold-Baker, C., and Anthony Dent. DICTIONARY OF DATES. *Dutton* Everyman's Ref. Lib. 1954 6th ed. rev. by Audrey Butler 1972 $7.50

Carruth, Gorton and others. THE ENCYCLOPEDIA OF AMERICAN FACTS AND DATES. *T. Y. Crowell* 1956 6th ed. 1972 $9.95. Classified in four parallel columns according to subject and arranged in chronological order from A.D. 1000 to the present, this records American facts, dates and events: vital statistics, awards, records, famous firsts, fads, fashions, slogans, sayings.

Douglas, George W. THE AMERICAN BOOK OF DAYS. Ed. by Helen Douglas Compton *Wilson* 2nd ed. 1948 $10.00. Gives the origin, history and observance of holidays, festivals, religious days, anniversaries, etc. The arrangement is chronological by month and day.

McWhirter, Norris, and Ross McWhirter, Eds. THE GUINNESS BOOK OF WORLD RECORDS. *Sterling Pub.* rev. ed. 1975 $6.95 deluxe ed. $8.95 lib. bdg. $6.89

Mirkin, Stanford M. What Happened When: A Noted Researcher's Almanac of Yesterday. (Orig. "When Did It Happen?") *Ives Washburn* (dist. by McKay) 1957 enl. ed.
1966 $7.95. A dictionary of dates of memorable events arranged chronologically
under days of the year and by a separate subject index.

Robertson, Patrick. The Book of Firsts. *Crown* 1974 $10.00
". . . the purpose of this book is to provide a chronology of a wide range of 'firsts' that have
contributed to life as it is lived today"—(Preface).

Wasserman, Paul, and Joanne Paskar, Eds. Statistics Sources. *Gale Research Co.* 4th ed.
1974 $45.00. Lists 21,000 sources for information on 11,800 topics in alphabetical
order.

*See Chapter 9, History, Government and Politics, this Volume, for additional reference books in this
field.*

YEAR BOOKS AND ALMANACS

Many organizations now issue year books. Those of general literary and historical use are
selected for this listing. Year books uniform with sets are published by most of the current
encyclopedias.

The Almanac of American Politics. Ed. by Michael Barone and Grant Ujifusi *Dutton*
1976 $15.95 pap. $7.95

Almanacs of the United States. Comp. by Milton Drake *Scarecrow Press* 2 vols. 1962 set
$35.00. This checklist includes 14,300 entries, including almanacs and calendars
published from 1639 on, with the arrangement geographical by state, then chronological by year of title.

The American Jewish Year Book. Ed. by Morris Fine and Milton Himmelfarb; Assoc.
Ed. Martha Jelenko. *The Jewish Publication Society of America* annual $13.95. Published
since 1899 and since 1909 issued in the office of the American Jewish Committee, it
contains an almanac, statistical and directory material and special articles prepared
primarily for Jewish readers.

The Annual Register of World Events: 1973. Ed. by Ivison S. Macadam. *St. Martin's*
1974 $27.50. Previously published with title "Annual Register: A Review of Public
Events at Home and Abroad"; other volumes available: 1965–69 each $25.00. Over
two centuries since first publication. This is a valuable reference.

Britain: An Official Handbook. Prepared by the Great Britain Central Office of
Information, London. *British Information Services* 1975 $8.00
An "excellent handbook . . . it is a factual account of the administration and the national
economy of the United Kingdom"—(LJ).

Canadian Almanac and Directory. 1847–   Ed. by Susan Walters *Pitman* 1974 $24.50.
Contains authentic legal, commercial, statistical, astronomical, departmental, ecclesiastical, educational, financial, and general information; over 50,000 listings.

Europa Year Book 1975. *Europa Publications*, London (dist. by Int. Pubns. Service) 2 vols.
16th ed. 1975 $84.00 Vol. 1 International Organizations and Europe including the
U.S.S.R. and Turkey Vol. 2 Africa, the Americas, Asia and Australasia
This survey and directory provides economic and statistical data as well as details of the
constitution, government, political parties, legal system and education; a directory section for each
country lists newspapers and periodicals, publishers, radio and television, banks, insurance
companies, chambers of commerce, trade associations and unions, transport companies, learned
societies, research institutes, libraries, museums and universities. Special sections give extensive
information about prominent international organizations. Vol. 1 has up-to-date information
about the European Common Market, the Outer Seven Free Trade Area, etc. Vol. 2 similarly
covers international organizations in Africa, the Americas, Asia and Australasia.

EUROPEAN FINANCIAL ALMANAC, 1974–1975. *Bowker* 1975 $50.00

"Brings together in an easy-to-use volume information on approximately 1300 financial institutions and their major executives in 13 European nations"—*(LJ)*.

FACTS ON FILE YEARBOOK. 1941– *Facts on File* 1941–1968 each $40.00 1969 $45.00 1970–1973 each $52.50 1974 $58.50

At the close of each year the 52 valuable weekly issues of *Facts on File Weekly News Reference Service* (with computer-processed cumulative index) are published in a single volume (with an annual index) to make up the "Yearbook." Yearbooks from 1941 to 1974 are presently available. Facts and nothing but facts in terse, unopinionated language provide the source materials from which future histories will be written. This series, each volume of which contains all the news of the world for its year, is of first importance as a reference work. *Facts on File* also publishes an annual "News Dictionary," covering the news of each year alphabetically. Volumes from 1964 to 1973 are available. (*See also title entry for "News Dictionary" below*). In both these publications it is possible to trace any event by person, subject, organization or country.

HANDBOOK ON INTERNATIONAL STUDY. *Inst. of International Education* 2 vols. 5th ed. 1970 pap. $7.00. Excellent guide for foreign students on study in the U.S. and for American students on study abroad. Another helpful book is "Study Abroad and Vacation Studies" Vol. 19 1973–74, a *UNESCO* publication (1975 pap. $6.00).

INFORMATION PLEASE, ALMANAC. 1947– Ed. by Dan Golenpaul *Simon & Schuster* 1974 $4.95 pap. $2.45

A project of the Dan Golenpaul Associates; well-planned use of material and excellent index.

THE MIDDLE EAST AND NORTH AFRICA. *Int. Pubns. Service* 21st ed. 1974 $36.00. Similar to "Europa Year Book" (*see above*), it covers Middle Eastern and North African countries with a Who's Who.

THE NEGRO ALMANAC. Comp. and ed. by Harry A. Ploski and Warren Marr. *Bellwether* (167 E. 67th St., New York, N.Y.) 1976 $59.95

"An indispensable reference work . . . a model of attractive presentation and clear, accurate writing"—*(Choice)*.

NEW GEOGRAPHY, 1970–71. By John Laffin. *Abelard-Schuman* 1971 $6.95

This biennial "is a welcome addition to the reference shelf. There are about 200 entries, in alphabetical order, ranging from Aden to Zambia (area statistics), and from Air Transport to Weather forecasting (subjects). If an area or subject is static it is omitted, as this book covers new geography, assessed and selected for educational value and general interest. It supplements existing textbooks by assembling vital current information drawn from a multitude of official sources"—*(LJ)*.

NEWS DICTIONARY 1975: An Encyclopedic Summary of Contemporary History. Ed. by Lester A. Sobel *Facts on File* annual since 1965 $9.50 pap. $6.75

"Designed to make available an inexpensive, authoritative, unbiased reference work that would provide brief yet detailed accounts of the major events of the year"—(Preface).

THE OFFICIAL ASSOCIATED PRESS ALMANAC, 1975. Successor to the "New York Times Encyclopedic Almanac." *Hammond Almanac* 1975 $5.95. Contains facts, statistics, colored maps and flags of the major nations.

THE OLD FARMER'S ALMANAC. 1791– *Yankee, Inc.* (Dublin, N.H., 03444) 1975 pap. $.75. Perhaps overshadowed by the size of its more stalwart brothers this little publication, "established in 1792 by Robert B. Thomas," has delighted New Englanders for its 178 years of continuous publication, in the same format.

THE POLITICAL HANDBOOK AND ATLAS OF THE WORLD: Parliaments, Parties and Press. *Simon & Schuster* 1971 $9.95. The annual edition gives information about all the countries of the world; composition of government, leaders and programs of political parties, political affiliations and editors of leading publications.

READER'S DIGEST ALMANAC AND INFORMATION YEARBOOK. 1966– *Reader's Digest Association* (dist. by Norton) 1975 $3.95

Ruffner, James A., and Frank E. Blair. THE WEATHER ALMANAC: A Reference Guide to Weather and Climate of the United States and Its Key Cities. *Gale* $17.50

"Descriptions of weather conditions and tables of climactic data for many American cities make this a valuable resource for persons embarking on a visit or a move to a new location."—(*LJ*).

THE STATESMAN'S YEARBOOK. *St. Martin's* 6 vols. available ed. by S. H. Steinberg 1961–1962 and 1962–1963 each $9.50 1964–1965 $10.00 1966–1967 $12.50; ed. by John Paxton 1973–1974 $13.95 1974–1975 $15.95. A standard manual which gives information about the governments of the world, but is especially full in its coverage of British history. It has appeared annually since 1864.

STATISTICAL YEARBOOK. Comp. by the United Nations Statistical Office *Int. Pubns. Service* vols. available 1960–1973 except 1971 and 1972 1960–1966 each $15.00 1967 and 1968 each $17.50 1969 $19.00 1970 $22.00 1973 $35.00. The fields of population, energy, forestry, public finance and others are treated.

WHITAKER'S ALMANACK. Vol. 106, 1974, London. *Whitaker* 1869– $12.50

The best almanac for the British Isles. Besides giving information on the events of the year, this almanac also gives complete lists of royalty, nobility, clergy, members of Parliament, etc.

WORLD ALMANAC: An Almanac and Book of Facts, 1975. 1868–   Ed. by Edward Kennedy *Doubleday* 1974 $5.95

Published without interruption since 1868. An almanac so inclusive it is worthy to be called an encyclopedia of current events and statistics. It is strongest in its record of United States history but touches other countries as well.

YEARBOOK OF INTERNATIONAL ORGANIZATIONS, 1974. *Int. Pubns. Service* 15th ed. $48.00

THE YEARBOOK OF THE UNITED NATIONS 1972. *United Nations Publications* $35.00

The 1972 volume of the complete and authoritative account of the organization includes a record of activities in many fields, among them: peaceful uses of outer space; questions concerning the uses of atomic energy; questions with respect to particular areas of the world with which the UN is concerned; economic development of underdeveloped areas; international commodity trade; human rights; freedom of information; UNICEF; non-self-governing territories and the international trusteeship system.

THE YEAR BOOK OF WORLD AFFAIRS, 1973. Ed. by George W. Keeton and George Schwarzenberger. Published under the auspices of the London Inst. of World Affairs. *Praeger* 1973 $22.50

This annual contains information about and interpretation of world problems by eminent specialists. The "Reports on World Affairs" section contains reviews of about 600 books on economics, geography, institutions, law, literature, psychology, sociology and strategy.

YEARBOOK ON HUMAN RIGHTS. Comp. by The United Nations, Dept. of Social Affairs. *Int. Pubns. Service* vols. available: 1961 1962 each $5.00 1963 $5.75 1964 $6.00 1965 $5.75 1966 $4.75 1967 $5.00 1968 $6.50 1970 $10.00 1971 $18.00

Chapter 2

General Biography and Auto-biography

"There is properly no History; only Biography."
—EMERSON

The emphasis in the first section of this Chapter—which forms a continuation and supplement to Chapter 16 of *"The Reader's Adviser,"* Volume I, on Literary Biography and Autobiography—has always been on the remarkable biographers—those who have made a name for themselves chiefly in this field. There are many excellent life histories to be found in both our volumes under other categories; one thinks immediately of the biographies by André Maurois, Nancy Mitford, Antonia Fraser and others; in autobiography Sean O'Casey, James Baldwin and Bertrand Russell leap to mind. Some have been cross-referenced here—together with the biographers and autobiographers in Volume I—but it is impossible to take account of all. This Chapter has again been divided into the two Sections, Biography and Autobiography, with a Section on "collective" works for each and with the addition of a new Selected List of Recent Biographies and Autobiographies (by authors other than those treated at length) just preceding the first main entries of the Chapter.

The interest in factual and interpretive accounts of significant lives or of personal records of remarkable events continues to grow, as seen in the present popularity of the documentary drama of Peter Weiss, Rolf Hochhuth and Heinar Kipphardt ("In the Matter of J. Robert Oppenheimer"), and of the "nonfiction novel" of the Truman Capote "In Cold Blood" genre. Thousands of pages of print are expended on the mysteries and controversies of the John Kennedy assassination. Autobiography (see introduction to that Section) puts us inside the skin of those who have accomplished much, witnessed great events, or known interesting people and enables us to share their experience vicariously; its great interest is attested to by the popularity of Albert Speer's memoirs and those of George Kennan, Dean Acheson, Harold Nicolson and Thomas E. Dewey to mention only a few. Recent White House assistants and government officials rush to jot down their memories while these are still "hot" and openly to speak their minds on past events. The emergence of the black American has brought a flood of autobiographies, often of very great interest—by Martin Luther King, Malcolm X, Eldridge Cleaver and Claude Brown, among others. These will be found grouped together or under main entries in Chapter 8, The Social Sciences, this Volume (consult the index for individual authors).

In recent years a growing number of biographers have begun to employ "psychoanalytic concepts in an effort to explain individual and group behaviour in history." Psycho-biography, or psycho-history as this method has come to be called, asks deeply probing questions about personal burdens, conflicts, complexes, and inhibitions. It seeks to provide insights into the human condition that will "contribute to [our] understanding of historical personages" (Joseph M. Woods in *The Historian* August, 1974). Several works employing this controversial technique are listed below and in Chapter 9, History, Government and Politics, this Volume.

Among the important biographical series are *Little-Brown's* Library of American Biography edited by Oscar Handlin (which now numbers 16 volumes, each $5.00, many of which are available in paper, each $2.95), *Washington Square's* Great American Thinkers Series and *Skira's* Who Was Series.

It should be noted that in this Chapter the works shown in the main entries for each author generally represent his biographical and/or autobiographical writings, not necessarily all of his works in print.

ON THE WRITING OF BIOGRAPHY

Altick, Richard D. LIVES AND LETTERS: A History of Literary Biography in England and America. *Knopf* 1965 $10.00

Bottrall, Margaret. EVERYMAN A PHOENIX: Studies in Seventeenth-Century Autobiography. *Bks. for Libraries* $8.75

Bowen, Catherine Drinker. ADVENTURES OF A BIOGRAPHER. *Little* 1959 $5.95

BIOGRAPHY: The Craft and the Calling. *Little* 1969 $5.95

"A joy to read, a real treat, should soon become a classic"—*(Chicago Sun-Times)*. *(See also her main entry below.)*

Clifford, James L. FROM PUZZLES TO PORTRAITS: Problems of a Literary Biographer. *Univ. of North Carolina Press* 1970 $6.00

Cockshut, A. O. J. TRUTH TO LIFE: The Art of Biography in the Nineteenth Century. *Harcourt* 1974 $7.50

Daghlian, Philip B., Ed. ESSAYS IN EIGHTEENTH-CENTURY BIOGRAPHY. Introd. by the editor *Indiana Univ. Press* 1968 $6.95

Kendall, Paul Murray. THE ART OF BIOGRAPHY. *Norton* 1965 pap. $1.45

"A comparison of the types and eras of biographical writings"—*(LJ)*.

Lee, Sidney. PRINCIPLES OF BIOGRAPHY. *Folcroft* 1973 $4.50

Nicolson, Sir Harold. THE DEVELOPMENT OF ENGLISH BIOGRAPHY. 1928. *Hillary House* $2.75; *Folcroft* 1973 $12.50

Stuart, Duane Read. EPOCHS OF GREEK AND ROMAN BIOGRAPHY. 1928. *Biblo & Tannen* 1967 $7.50

REFERENCE WORKS ON COLLECTIVE AND HISTORICAL BIOGRAPHY

BIOGRAPHY INDEX. *Wilson* 1946–   Vol. 1 Jan. 1946–July 1949 Vol. 2 Aug. 1949–Aug. 1952 Vol. 3 Sept. 1952–Aug. 1955 Vol. 4 Sept. 1955–Aug. 1958 Vol. 5 Sept. 1958–Aug. 1961 Vol. 6 Sept. 1961–Aug. 1964 Vol. 7 Sept. 1964–Aug. 1967 Vol. 8 Sept. 1967–Aug. 1970 each $50.00 U.S. and Canada $60.00 foreign. Issued quarterly (in Nov., Feb., May and Aug.) with bound annual and permanent three-year cumulations; annual subscription $25.00 U.S. and Canada $30.00 foreign

"Covers biographical material appearing in approximately 1,500 periodicals indexed in other Wilson indexes; current books of individual and collective biography in the English language; obituaries, including those of national interest published in the *New York Times*; and incidental biographical material in otherwise nonbiographical books. Bibliographies and portraits and other illustrations are noted when they appear in connection with indexed material. Biography Index consists of a main or 'name' alphabet and an index by professions and occupations"—(Publisher's catalog).

BIOGRAPHY NEWS. *Gale Research Co.* 1974–   Bimonthly issues $75.00; cumulates in annual clothbound volumes called BIOGRAPHY YEARBOOK $75.00

"This bimonthly periodical brings together in permanent form biographical profiles and personality feature stories gleaned from nearly 50 leading U.S. daily newspapers"—(Publisher's note).

CURRENT BIOGRAPHY. *Wilson* 1940–   11 monthly issues ($12.00 U.S. and Canada $15.00 foreign) Yearbooks 1940–43 ($24.00 each U.S. and Canada $28.00 foreign), 1944 and 1945 ($20.00 each U.S. and Canada $24.00 foreign), 1946–72 ($10.00 each U.S. and Canada $15.00 foreign), Cumulated Index 1940–70 ($6.00 U.S. and Canada $7.50 foreign)

Hyamson, Albert M. DICTIONARY OF UNIVERSAL BIOGRAPHY OF ALL AGES AND OF ALL PEOPLES. 1916. *Dutton* 2nd ed. 1951 $19.50

Kinsman, Clara D., Ed. CONTEMPORARY AUTHORS: A Bio-Bibliographical Guide to Current Authors and Their Work. *Gale Research Co.* 1962– 2 vols. per year, annual subscription $25.00

Shaw, Thomas Shuler, Comp. INDEX TO PROFILE SKETCHES IN *The New Yorker* MAGAZINE: Feb. 21, 1955 to Feb 21, 1970, Vols. 1–45. *Faxon* 2nd rev. ed. 1972 $12.00

See also Chapter 1, Reference Books—General: Biographical Reference Works, this Volume, for additional titles.

SELECTED RECENT COLLECTIVE BIOGRAPHIES

Plutarch's "Parallel Lives of Greeks and Romans" (*q.v.*) was probably the first collective biography. Other famous early ones are: Giorgio Vasari (1512–1574), a minor artist contemporary of Michelangelo and da Vinci and acquainted with all the artists of his time, "Lives of the Artists" (trans. by G. Bull *Penguin* pap. $1.95); "Lives of the Painters, Sculptors and Architects" (1908 *Dutton* Everyman's 4 vols. $3.95 each); "Lives of the Most Eminent Painters, Sculptors and Architects" (1912. *AMS Press* 10 vols. $42.50 each); John Aubrey (1626–1697), "Brief Lives, Chiefly of Contemporaries, Set Down between the Years 1669 and 1696", a racy picture of the time (*Univ. of Michigan Press* 1957 $5.95 pap. $2.25); "Brief Lives or Minutes of Lives" (*Oxford* 2 vols. 1972 $80.00); Izaak Walton (1593–1683, *q.v.*), "Lives of John Donne, Sir Henry Wotton, Richard Hooker, George Herbert, and Robert Sanderson" (*Oxford* $4.25); Samuel Johnson (1709–1784, *q.v.*), "The Lives of the English Poets" (1783. *Oxford* World Classics 2 vols. $3.75 each; *Adler's* 3 vols. 1968–69 set $102.00; *Octagon* 3 vols. set $47.50), critical biographies, some now considered minor, but important Johnson essays; and Alban Butler (1711–1773), "Lives of the Principal Saints" (1756–59 *Christian Classics* 5 vols. 1962 $29.50).

Arendt, Hannah. MEN IN DARK TIMES. Trans. by Clara and Richard Winston and others *Harcourt* 1968 $6.50 Harvest Bks. 1970 pap. $2.45

> A collection of 11 essays and addresses written over the past 12 years on Gotthold Ephraim Lessing, Rosa Luxemburg, Pope John XXIII, Karl Jaspers, Isak Dinesen, Hermann Broch, Walter Benjamin, Bertolt Brecht, Waldermar Gurian and Randall Jarrell. "The keynote of the book is set by its first essay, 'Humanity in Dark Times,' an address given in Hamburg in 1959 on the eighteenth-century playwright Lessing. After a few thorny pages of academic ritual, this is the most touching and desperately pertinent of all the essays.... Miss Arendt pleads, through the example of Lessing, that we keep talking, keep the discourse alive and political; that we remain silent about nothing. For, in the definition of this eloquent and anxious woman, independent but intensely political, 'humanity' consists of intelligent men conversing freely on public affairs"— (*SR*).

Brockway, Wallace, and Herbert Weinstock. MEN OF MUSIC. *Simon & Schuster* rev. ed. 1950 $9.95 1958 pap. $3.95

Butler, Alban. LIVES OF THE SAINTS. Ed. by Bernard Kelly *Christian Classics* 5 vols. 1962 $29.50

Canning, John, Ed. 100 GREAT KINGS, QUEENS AND RULERS OF THE WORLD. *Taplinger* $8.50

Cook, Fred J. THE DEMAGOGUES. Macmillan 1972 $4.95

> "Profiles of would-be despots from Samuel Parris to Joe McCarthy"—(Publisher's note).

Ebenstein, William, Ed. GREAT POLITICAL THINKERS: Plato to the Present. *Holt* (Rinehart) 4th ed. 1969 $12.95

Ewen, David, Comp. GREAT COMPOSERS 1300–1900: A Biographical and Critical Guide. *Wilson* 1966 $12.00

> "Indispensable for all libraries"—(*LJ*) as a companion volume to Mr. Ewen's 1937 work "Composers of Yesterday." Contains 200 biographies.

POPULAR AMERICAN COMPOSERS FROM REVOLUTIONARY TIMES TO THE PRESENT. *Wilson* 1962 $8.00 1st supplement 1972 $6.00

Ford, Ford Madox. PORTRAITS FROM LIFE. 1936. *Greenwood* 1974 $13.50. Memories and criticisms of Henry James, Conrad, Hardy, Wells, Stephen Crane, D. H. Lawrence, Galsworthy and others.

Fraser, Antonia, Ed. THE LIVES OF THE KINGS AND QUEENS OF ENGLAND. *Knopf* 1975 $17.50

"A collection of biographical sketches, replete with excellent illustrative material, written for a popular audience"—(*LJ*).

Goertzel, Victor, and Mildred G. Goertzel. CRADLES OF EMINENCE. *Little* 1962 $8.95. Thought-provoking study of the childhoods of over 400 famous 20th century men and women.

Gridley, Marion E. CONTEMPORARY AMERICAN INDIAN LEADERS. *Dodd* 1972 $4.95

"Twenty-six Indian leaders ranging from the young to the elder statesmen in tribal affairs"—(Publisher's note).

Kennedy, John Fitzgerald. PROFILES IN COURAGE. *Harper* 1956 memorial ed. 1964 $3.95 lib. bdg. $3.79 pap. $.95; *Franklin Watts* lg.-type ed. 1965 $8.95

In a thoughtful and enlightening book the late President of the United States wrote of "those men who had the courage, on matters of principle, to defy the angry power of an overwhelming majority of voters, in spite of unbounded calumny and vilification"—(*LJ*). It won for him the Pulitzer Prize in Biography in 1957 and a Christopher Award in 1956.

McPhee, John A. A ROOMFUL OF HOVINGS AND OTHER PROFILES. *Farrar, Straus* 1969 $5.95

"Five profiles of interesting persons, originally published in *The New Yorker*"—(Publisher's note).

Means, Marianne. THE WOMAN IN THE WHITE HOUSE. *Random* 1963 $8.95. Brief biographies of 12 First Ladies who directly or indirectly influenced the conduct of the Presidency.

Smith, Bradford. MEN OF PEACE. *Lippincott* 1964 $6.95

Biographies of Ikhnaton, Buddha, Asoka, Jesus, St. Augustine, St. Francis, William Penn, Thoreau, Tolstoy, Nobel, Carnegie, Angell, Wilson, Gandhi and Hammarskjöld. "Recommended"—(*LJ*). By a Quaker who spent some years in Asia and wrote many works of fiction and nonfiction before his premature death.

Snow, C. P. A VARIETY OF MEN. *Scribner* 1971 pap. $2.95. Nine influential statesmen, scientists and writers of the 20th century.

Thomas, Norman. GREAT DISSENTERS. *Norton* 1961 pap. 1970 $1.95

Socrates, Galileo, Paine, Wendell Phillips, and Gandhi—"men whose heresies have been the growing point of society"—(*Virginia Kirkus Service*).

Toynbee, Arnold J. ACQUAINTANCES. *Oxford* 1967 $7.95. Portraits of 24 public figures, close personal friends and relations.

Untermeyer, Louis. MAKERS OF THE MODERN WORLD: The Lives of Ninety-Two Writers, Artists, Scientists, Statesmen, Inventors, Philosophers, Composers and Other Creators Who Formed the Pattern of Our Century from Darwin to Dylan Thomas. *Simon & Schuster* 1955 $12.50 pap. 1962 $3.95

A SELECTED LIST OF RECENT BIOGRAPHIES AND AUTOBIOGRAPHIES

Many excellent biographies appear within author entries throughout this volume and *"The Reader's Adviser,"* Vols. 1–2. In general, these titles do not appear elsewhere, and all are of recent publication.

Acheson, Dean. PRESENT AT THE CREATION: My Years in the State Department. *Norton* 1969 $15.00. His memoirs of the years 1941–53; winner of the Pulitzer Prize for History in 1970.

THIS VAST EXTERNAL REALM. *Norton* 1973 $9.95

"This compilation of Acheson speeches, articles, and papers deals . . . with the period from the end of the Truman administration until Acheson's death in 1971"—(*LJ*).

Ardoin, John, and Gerald Fitzgerald. CALLAS: The Art and the Life and the Great Years. *Holt* 1974 $22.95

"Their impressions of '*La Divina*' are vivid and usually generous. They are aware they're discussing a living legend but they do not seem intent on building up or breaking down the myth. Rather they want very much to humanize that myth, to fill it out with significant anecdotes which contribute to our understanding of Callas the person and the artist"—*(LJ)*.

Barnett, Corelli. THE FIRST CHURCHILL: Marlborough, Soldier and Statesman. *Putnam* 1974 $14.95

"The outstanding military achievements of the Duke of Marlborough, set against 17th century English and European court intrigue, serve as the background to a penetrating portrayal of the personality of John Churchill"—*(Booklist)*.

Beaver, Ninette, B. K. Ripley and Patrick Trese. CARIL. *Lippincott* 1974 $10.00

"A starkly provocative narrative concerning the case of Caril Fugate, involved in 1958 with mass murderer Charles Starkweather. The bleak course of Caril's 16 years' imprisonment and all the legal ramifications are carefully examined"—*(Booklist)*.

Bedford, Sybele. ALDOUS HUXLEY. *Knopf* 1974 $15.00

"Bedford's great biography reveals Huxley through a moving narrative assembled from the documentary testimony of friends, admirers, even semi-distant viewers. Often carefully non-committal about Huxley's works, Bedford (herself a family friend) pointedly analyses his labrinthine family affairs and coolly surveys the question of his influence on the contemporary worship of hallucinogenic mind-openers"—*(LJ)*.

Bishop, Morris. SAINT FRANCIS OF ASSISI. *Little* 1974 $6.95

"The author reviews the historical evidence about Francis of Assisi and places him within the context of his 13th century society"—*(LJ)*.

Blunt, Wilfred. THE COMPLETE NATURALIST: A Life of Linnaeus. *Viking* 1971 $14.95
"A very readable yet scholarly biography of Linnaeus"—*(TLS)*.

Brough, James. PRINCESS ALICE: A Biography of Alice Roosevelt Longworth. *Little* 1975 $10.00

"An engaging re-creation celebrates the most audacious member of the Roosevelt clan, giving a richly anecdotal glimpse into period politics and society"—*(Booklist)*.

Caro, Robert A. THE POWER BROKER: Robert Moses and the Fall of New York. *Knopf* 1974 $17.95

"The portrait of New York's master planner, Robert Moses, a ruthless visionary who built toward a city of the future and found that power corrupts and so does the internal-combustion engine"—*(Time)*. Pulitzer Prize for Biography 1975.

Childs, Marquis. WITNESS TO POWER. *McGraw-Hill* 1975 $8.95. The recollections of a prominent newspaper columnist.

Clive, John. MACAULAY: The Shaping of the Historian. *Knopf* 1973 $15.00

"Clive's well written study . . . undertakes to explain the shaping of Macaulay's ideas and the directions which his energies took. It is as much a history of the pre-Victorian social and political thought and action as it is of Macaulay himself"—*(Atlantic)*.

Dewey, Thomas E. TWENTY AGAINST THE UNDERWORLD. *Doubleday* 1974 $12.50

"This first volume, which ends with Dewey's first (unsuccessful) try for New York governor in 1938, skillfully interweaves memoirs with key speeches that are used as convenient summaries"—*(LJ)*.

Donaldson, Frances. EDWARD VIII: A Biography of the Duke of Windsor. *Lippincott* 1975 $15.00

"Edward VIII, Duke of Windsor, had a lifetime that consisted of one event. He abdicated. . . . From the abdication on, the family treated him as an outsider, and his wife as a non-person, and for nearly 40 years the beastliness—arising chiefly from Edward's obsessive desire that the Duchess should be classified as 'Her Royal Highness', and curtsied to—continued with unremitting ferocity. . . . It is a sad story but a fascinating one"—*(LJ)*.

Dykhuizen, George. THE LIFE AND MIND OF JOHN DEWEY. *Southern Illinois Univ. Press* 1973 $15.00

"Drawing upon both published and unpublished sources, Dykhuizen has written an outstanding scholarly, yet highly readable, overview of the life of this great scholar and philosopher (1859–1952)"—(*LJ*).

Erikson, Erik H. GANDHI'S TRUTH: On the Origins of Militant Nonviolence. *Norton* 1969 $10.00 pap. $3.95

The author describes Gandhi's first Satyagraha campaign when he lead "a strike of textile workers in the city of Ahmedabad in 1918 . . . [He] reviews Gandhi's childhood and youth and discusses ways in which his personal history may have prepared him to be the revolutionary innovator of militant nonviolence"—(Publisher's note).

Fraser, Antonia. CROMWELL: The Lord Protector. *Knopf* 1974 $12.50; *Dell* 1975 pap. $1.95

The author portrays "the young radical agitator on behalf of the poor commoners, the . . . victorious general during the Great Civil War . . . and the soldier storming Drogheda to crush the Irish rebellion"—(Publisher's note).

Goldman, Peter. THE DEATH AND LIFE OF MALCOLM X. *Harper* 1973 $8.95 1974 pap. $1.95

"A great deal of research, especially through interviews, went into the making of this book; and the results justify [the author's] painstaking labors. Nowhere else in print has such a detailed, objective account of Malcolm X's last tragic years appeared"—(*LJ*).

Green, Martin. THE VON RICHTOFEN SISTERS: The Triumphant and Tragic Modes of Love. *Basic Bks.* 1974 $12.50

"This book is many things: biography, history of ideas, study of culture, and source of literary criticism. . . . Fascinating, rich in material that is otherwise hard to come by"—(*Choice*).

Griffiths, Richard. PÉTAIN: A Biography of Marshal Philippe Pétain of Vichy. *Doubleday* 1972 $10.00

"In the author's view, Pétain's career was of a single piece . . . Griffiths demonstrates that a close examination of his life up to that time eventually shows us that he would hardly have been expected to act in any other way"—(*LJ*).

Harlan, Louis R. BOOKER T. WASHINGTON: The Making of a Black Leader. *Oxford* 1972 $10.95

"The present work covers Washington's life from his birth as a slave in western Virginia up to the famous dinner with Theodore Roosevelt at the White House, an event signifying white recognition of Washington as the chief spokesman for black interests in the period before World War I"—(*LJ*).

Hartley, William, and Ellen Hartley. OSCEOLA: The Unconquered Indian. *Hawthorn* 1973 $6.95

"More than any other native American leader, Osceola personifies the spirit of Indian resistance to white domination"—(*LJ*).

Hendricks, Gordon. THE LIFE AND WORK OF THOMAS EAKINS. *Grossman* 1974 $37.50

"This full-scale biography offers a careful presentation of Eakins' life and surroundings"—(*LJ*).

Herr, Friedrich. CHARLEMAGNE AND HIS WORLD. *Macmillan* 1975 $15.00

According to *Library Journal*, "the profuse illustrations of Carolingian art and objects alone make this book worth the price. Couple these to the lively yet insightful prose of Herr, the well-known Austrian historian of ideas, and you have a valuable popular introduction to the life, times, and significance of the Father of Europe"—(*LJ*).

Hibbert, Christopher. GEORGE IV, Prince of Wales, 1762–1811. *Harper* 1972 $10.00

"The first of a two volume biography covers George IV's life before he became regent"—(*LJ*).

GEORGE IV, Regent and King, 1811–1830. *Harper* 1975 $15.00

"Extensive research includes the Royal Archives and many private manuscript collections. The book deserves a place in any solid English history collection"—(*LJ*).

Johannsen, Robert W. STEPHEN A. DOUGLAS. *Oxford* 1973 $19.95

"Johannsen is content to tell a full and impartial story, balancing the evidence as he has found it. He has made good use of the relevant monographs, but has relied mainly on manuscript and other primary sources. From these he has put together a well-organized and marvelously detailed account"—(*N.Y. Times*).

Josephson, Harold. James T. Shotwell and the Rise of Internationalism in America. *Fairleigh Dickinson Univ. Press* 1975 $14.50

"Josephson's biography offers the definitive charting of Shotwell's long career. Written in a clear and effective style, the study is sensibly, admirably comprehensive, and conveyed in a critically sympathetic spirit"—*(LJ)*.

Kalb, Marvin, and Bernard Kalb. Kissinger. *Little* 1974 $12.50

This is "the most detailed, comprehensive and readable study to date on Kissinger and his diplomacy"—*(LJ)*.

Kennedy, David M. Birth Control in America: The Career of Margaret Sanger. Yale Pubns. in American Studies *Yale Univ. Press* 1970 $12.50 pap. $3.45

"A biography of the woman who organized the first American Birth Control Conference in Nov. 1921 . . . formally established the American Birth Control League and was president of the American League from its inception in 1921 until 1928"—*(Choice)*.

Kokoschka, Oskar. My Life. *Macmillan* 1974 $10.00

"Kokoshka's record of his inner life is as richly volatile as his work and similarly marked by a private intensity of vision"—*(Booklist)*.

Langer, Walter C. The Mind of Adolf Hitler: The Secret Wartime Report. *Basic Bks.* 1972 $10.00; *New Am. Lib.* pap. $1.50

"This wartime report, previously available to only a handful of top American and British officials . . . emerges as a masterpiece of probing and understanding. . . . Langer surmises that Hitler was a neurotic psychopath with schizophrenic tendencies"—*(New Republic)*.

Lawrence, Jerome. Actor: The Life and Times of Paul Muni. *Putnam* 1973 $10.00

"A really three dimensional portrait of a major performing artist . . . his rise to stardom in the American Yiddish theater . . . his debut in films . . . the decline of his career and his resurrection in 'Inherit the Wind' "—*(PW)*.

Martin, Ralph G. The Woman He Loved. *Simon & Schuster* 1974 $9.95. A dual biography of the Duke and Duchess of Windsor.

Mazlish, Bruce. James and John Stuart Mill: Father and Son in the Nineteenth Century. *Basic Bks.* 1975 $16.95

"In his most impressive psychohistorical venture yet, Mazlish demonstrates that even an apparently worked out lode can yield riches anew when sophisticated tools are imaginatively applied"—*(LJ)*.

Morison, Samuel Eliot. Samuel de Champlain: Father of New France. *Little* 1971 $10.00

"The author does more than merely chronicle [his] hero's deeds for he provides a succinct and shrewd appraisal of French activities in North America until the mid-17th century"—*(N.Y. Times)*.

O'Connor, Richard. Heyward Broun: A Biography. *Putnam* 1975 $8.95

"O'Connor's colorful portrait of Broun and his times captures his days at Harvard, and his introduction to the rough-and-tumble school of journalism in pre–World War I as a sportswriter and as part of the intellectual ferment that became the Algonquin Round Table"—*(LJ)*.

Palmer, Alan. Metternich. *Harper* 1972 $12.50

"A well-researched sprightly life which provides new insight into Metternich's kaleidoscopic character . . . this biography becomes the standard on the subject"—*(LJ)*.

Parkinson, Roger. Zapata. *Stein & Day* 1975 $10.00

"Of all the figures of the Mexican Revolution of 1910, Emiliano Zapata holds particular interest for historians. Zapata found his strength in his fight for the land and the people of the state of Morelos"—*(LJ)*.

Pusey, Merlo John. Eugene Meyer. *Knopf* 1974 $15.00

"Pusey . . . , a former associate editor of the *Washington Post*, has written a distinguished study of the character and career of a singular man. When Eugene Meyer transformed a failing newspaper into the influential *Washington Post*, he was already seasoned by success in a phenomenal number of important early ventures, and was to serve briefly, as a coda, in yet another: as President of the World Bank"—*(Booklist)*.

Reid, B. L. The Man from New York: John Quinn and His Friends. *Oxford* 1968 $13.75. The biography of a New York lawyer, famous as an art collector. This book won the Pulitzer Prize for Biography in 1969.

Rose, Madeline Belkin. THE LIFE AND TIMES OF MY MOTHER AND ME. *Feminist Press* 1974 $2.50

This is "an oral history of a working class Brooklyn woman"—(Publisher's note).

Rowden, Maurice. LORENZO THE MAGNIFICENT. *Regnery* 1974 $14.95

"A vivid picture of this great Renaissance patron of the arts . . . the Medici family, Florence, and the intense rivalry between the city-states . . . Very readable . . . enhanced by the inclusion of many illustrations, paintings, and portraits"—(*LJ*).

Royko, Mike. Boss: Richard J. Daley of Chicago. *Dutton* 1971 $6.95; *New Am. Lib.* Signet Bks. pap. $1.25

"Daley emerges from Royko's cutting appraisal as an egotistical dictator, insensitive to government corruption and social evils in his city but above all perversely loyal to his machine . . . an immensely readable book, deserving a wide readership"—(*LJ*).

Speer, Albert. INSIDE THE THIRD REICH: Memoirs of Albert Speer. *Macmillan* 1970 $12.50; *Avon* 1974 pap. $1.95

"This is by far the most important and most startling book to come from the pen of one of Hitler's close collaborators. . . . While Hitler had no real friends, Speer knew him more intimately than most of his cronies and often talked to him frankly"—(*LJ*).

Spender, Stephen, Ed. W. H. AUDEN: A Tribute. *Macmillan* 1975 $14.95

"This is a lovely book: a collection of essays by friends about Auden at different periods of his life. This approach gives one the feeling of watching Auden develop and adds much to an understanding of the man who produced the poetry"—(*LJ*).

Thomas, Donald. CARDIGAN: A Life of Cardigan of Balaclava. *Viking* 1975 $12.50

"In this well-written and scholarly account, of interest to both the historian and the general reader, Cardigan appears as a yardstick by which the changing mores of Victorian England may be measured"—(*LJ*).

Tomalin, Claire. THE LIFE AND DEATH OF MARY WOLLSTONECRAFT. *Harcourt* 1974 $8.95

"Revolutionary, commune planner, advocate of free love, and author of the first book on Women's Lib all almost 200 years ago"—(*PW*).

Vaughan, Alden T. AMERICAN GENESIS: Captain John Smith and the Founding of Virginia. *Little* 1975 $6.95

"Vaughan's sympathetic account draws on the best in recent scholarship to provide a lucid, balanced, thoughtful, and credible reassessment"—(*LJ*).

Wain, John. SAMUEL JOHNSON. *Viking* 1975 $10.00

"Poet, critic, and writer of fiction, Wain also shares with Dr. Johnson a native attachment to the Midlands and the struggle through Oxford to Grub Street. . . . Wain has a taste for the essential fabric and detail of this special life, which he tells richly, mingling dignity with compassion, humor, and a leavening of wry insight into our own sad times"—(*LJ*).

Wechsberg, Joseph. VERDI. *Putnam* 1974 $15.00

"Wechsberg indicates that from Verdi's peasant upbringing to the fame and fortune of his mature years, the Italian composer's contradictory nature imparted much color to his personal affairs as well as to the operatic stage. The tastes and temper of 19th-century Italy are here hospitably re-created"—(*Booklist*).

Williams, T. Harry. HUEY LONG. *Knopf* 1969 $12.50; *Bantam* 1970 pap. $1.95

"A brilliant, bawdy and unforgettable picture of the most colorful as well as the most dangerous man ever to engage in American politics"—(*Book World*).

Woodham-Smith, Cecil. QUEEN VICTORIA: From Her Birth to the Death of the Prince Consort. *Knopf* 1972 $10.00

"Mrs. Woodham-Smith has given us an informative book, beautifully written, with the whole story developed into a memorable and convincing picture against a singularly vivid background of the times"—(*TLS*).

Wyndham, Francis, and David King. TROTSKY: A Documentary. *Praeger* 1972 $12.50; *Penguin* 1973 pap. $4.95

"A well-written documentary account, with plenty of pictures—many new to this reviewer—of a man who for a few years stood at the head of the most significant event of the century: the Russian Revolution"—(*LJ*).

BIOGRAPHY

PLUTARCH.   c. 46–c. 125 A.D.   *See Chapter 9, History, Government and Politics, this Volume.*

WALTON, IZAAK.   1593–1683.   *See Chapter 7, Science, this Volume.*

JOHNSON, SAMUEL.   1709–1784.   *See Chapter 16, Literary Biography and Autobiography, under Boswell*, Reader's Adviser, *Vol. I.*

BOSWELL, JAMES.   1740–1795. *See Chapter 16, Literary Biography and Autobiography* Reader's Adviser, *Vol. I.*

LOCKHART, JOHN GIBSON.   1794–1854.   *See Chapter 16, Literary Biography and Autobiography*, Reader's Adviser, *Vol. I.*

GASKELL, MRS. ELIZABETH (CLEGHORN STEVENSON). 1810–1865. *See Chapter 11, British Fiction: Middle Period, and Chapter 16, Literary Biography and Autobiography*, Reader's Adviser, *Vol. I.*

SANDBURG, CARL.   1878–1967.

When the poet Sandburg published the first two volumes of his life of Lincoln it was hailed as a deeply sympathetic study based on diligent research. The publication of the last four volumes, "The War Years," brought the author the 1940 Pulitzer Prize for History, as biographies of Lincoln were not then eligible for the biography award, and established the work as one of the great American biographies.

ABRAHAM LINCOLN: The Prairie Years. *Harcourt* 2 vols. 1926 boxed $40.00. Biography of Lincoln up to his inauguration.

ABE LINCOLN GROWS UP. Ed. by Max J. Herzberg; ill. by James Daugherty *Harcourt* 1931 $6.95 text ed. $1.80. Chapters on Lincoln's boyhood from "Abraham Lincoln: The Prairie Years."

ABRAHAM LINCOLN: The War Years. *Harcourt* 4 vols. 1936–39 Vols. I–2 boxed set $40.00, Vols. 3–4 boxed set $40.00, 4 vols. boxed set $80.00. Story of Lincoln's life from his inauguration to his death and funeral in 1865.

ABRAHAM LINCOLN: The Prairie Years and The War Years. *Harcourt* 6 vols. 1926–39 boxed set $120.00 definitive abridgement of the 6 vols. 1954 $12.95 Harvest Bks. pap. $5.95; *Dell* 3 vols. pap. each $.75, 3 vols. boxed set $2.95

MARY LINCOLN: Wife and Widow. 1932. *Harcourt* new ed. 1940 $5.95

LINCOLN COLLECTOR: The Story of Oliver R. Barrett's Great Private Collection. *Harcourt* 1949 $7.50. A source book of Lincolniana and Americana with a text by Sandburg on how the Barrett collection was amassed.

ALWAYS THE YOUNG STRANGERS. *Harcourt* 1953 $9.95. Autobiography.

LETTERS. Ed. by Herbert Mitgang *Harcourt* 1968 $12.50

Some 640 letters covering 64 years. The "editing is informative and unobtrusive . . . The letters do not diminish Carl Sandburg"—(*SR*).

See also Chapter 9, Modern American Poetry, Reader's Adviser, *Vol. I.*

JONES, ERNEST.   1879–1958.

Ernest Jones began in 1944 to write his autobiography and then abandoned it to write his three-volume life of Freud (*q.v.*). The 11 chapters that were written about his life up to 1918 and partially revised before his death were published as "Free Associations: Memoirs of a Psychoanalyst" (epilogue by Mervyn Jones 1959, o.p.). It is "an unemotional, carefully organized story of a famous man's intellectual adventures and professional growth," with little of the usual human-interest personal material. Its chief value lies in its description of the schools of medicine in London at the turn of the century. Among other titles by Jones which are available: "On the Nightmare" (1931. *Liveright* text ed. 1971 $8.95 pap. $2.95) and his very interesting "Hamlet and Oedipus" (1949. *Doubleday* Anchor Bks. 1954 pap. $1.45), the revision of an essay published in 1910 in the *American Journal of Psychology* entitled "The Oedipus Complex as an Explanation of Hamlet's Mystery." Dr. Jones also edited Freud's "Collected Papers" (*Basic Bks.* 5 vols. 1959 each $7.65 boxed set $37.50). Further professional works are published by *Schocken* and *Int. Univs. Press.*

THE LIFE AND WORKS OF SIGMUND FREUD. *Basic Bks.* 3 vols. 1953–57 Vol. 1 The
Formative Years and the Great Discoveries, 1856–1900 (1953) Vol. 2 Years of Maturity, 1901–1919 (1955) Vol. 3 The Last Phase, 1919–1939 (1957) each $11.00 set $31.75

THE LIFE AND WORKS OF SIGMUND FREUD. Abr. by Lionel Trilling and Steven Marcus
Basic Bks. 1961 $11.00 1974 pap. $4.95

See also Chapter 6, Psychology, this Volume, under Sigmund Freud.

STRACHEY, (GILES) LYTTON.   1880–1932.

Lytton Strachey was a member of the Cambridge-Bloomsbury intellectual circle of 1903 to 1930
which included E. M. Forster, Leonard and Virginia Woolf, and Clive Bell. Leon Edel has
described him "as the master of human character, of brevity and lucidity, of paradox and irony."
Strachey regarded history as Gibbon did, "not as the accumulation of facts but the relation of
them." His widespread influence upon other biographers may be attributed to his tendency to
emphasize what a man was rather than what he did, and to seize upon the uneventful parts of life
as the more interesting. His masterpiece, "Queen Victoria," is the first biography of English
royalty written with complete candor. British rulers—and, indeed, kings and queens in general—
had seldom if ever been subjects of humor. Strachey describes Queen Victoria with unflinching
frankness and unending amusement. The writing of biography, he felt, should be a creative art;
"in his hands it was lucid, subtle, elegant, ironic, disillusioning." Michael Holroyd's detailed
biography has revealed Strachey's homosexuality and other unusual personal foibles with contemporary frankness—and somewhat alters the reading public's previous view of the extraordinary
Bloomsbury group. Strachey was also author of "Landmarks in French Literature" (*Oxford* 1912
pap. 1969 $1.95).

EMINENT VICTORIANS. 1918. *Collins-World* $3.95; *Harcourt* Harbrace Pap. Lib. 1969
$1.45; *Putnam* Capricorn Bks. 1963 pap. $3.95; *Peter Smith* $4.25

QUEEN VICTORIA. 1921. *Harcourt* 1949 $2.95 Harbrace Pap. Lib. 1966 $.75

ELIZABETH AND ESSEX: A Tragic History. 1928. *Harcourt* Harvest Bks. 1969 pap. $2.45

BIOGRAPHICAL ESSAYS. *Harcourt* 1949 Harvest Bks. 1969 pap. $2.45

Books about Strachey

Lytton Strachey. By Max Beerbohm. 1943. *Haskell* 1974 $7.95; *Richard West* 1973 $10.00
Lytton Strachey: His Mind and Art. By Charles R. Sanders. 1957. *Kennikat* 1973 $17.50
The Psychological Milieu of Lytton Strachey. By Martin Kallich. *College & Univ. Press* $6.00
    1961 pap. $1.75
Lytton Strachey and the Bloomsbury Group: His Work, Their Influence. By Michael Holroyd.
    1967. *Penguin* 1972 pap. $2.25
Mentor of the "Bloomsbury Group": Lytton Strachey. By Michael Holroyd. 1968. *Roy* 2 vols.
    $3.98

MAUROIS, ANDRÉ (pseud. of Émile Herzog).   1885–1967. *See Chapter 9, French
Literature, Reader's Adviser, Vol. 2, and Chapter 16, Literary Biography and Autobiography, Vol. 1.*

VAN DOREN, CARL.   1885–1950. *See his main entry in Chapter 9, History, Government
and Politics—American, this Volume.*

FREEMAN, DOUGLAS SOUTHALL.   1886–1953.

Dr. Douglas Freeman is considered "one of the greatest biographers and military historians of
our time." Born in Lynchburg, Virginia, he was editor of the Richmond, Virginia, *News Leader*
from 1915 to 1949, when he retired to devote most of his time to writing. He was an authority on
military strategy and on military history of the Civil War. His biographies are notable for their
"almost incredibly detailed research . . . remorseless analysis of the reliability of testimony . . .
steady holding of the balances of judgment." "R. E. Lee" won the 1935 Pulitzer Prize for
Biography; in 1958, "George Washington: A Biography" (7 vols.) was awarded the Loubat Prize
and the Pulitzer Prize. Dr. Freeman was chosen by Princeton University and the Jefferson
Bicentennial Commission as chairman of the advisory committee and budget subcommittee in
charge of the definitive edition of "The Papers of Thomas Jefferson" (*see following Section on
Autobiography, this Chapter*). "Douglas Southall Freeman closed his useful and busy life dramatically
when he died at his desk after having written the last paragraph of the sixth volume of his
biography of George Washington"—(*N.Y. Times*). After Dr. Freeman's death the completion of his
great work was entrusted to John Alexander Carroll, who had carried on the necessary research in

the Library of Congress, and Mary Wells Ashworth, who had assisted the author at his home in Richmond. They followed "their master's style and approach so religiously that one can scarcely detect that there has been a change in authorship."

R. E. LEE. *Scribner* 4 vols. 1935 each $17.50; (with title "Lee" abr. by Richard B. Harwell) 4 vols. in 1 1961 $17.50

LEE'S LIEUTENANTS. *Scribner* 3 vols. 1942–44 Vol. I Manassas to Malvern Hill Vol. 2 Cedar Mountain to Chancellorsville Vol. 3 Gettysburg to Appomattox each $17.50

GEORGE WASHINGTON: A Biography. *Scribner* 7 vols. 1948–58 Vols. I and 2 Young Washington Vol. 3 Planter and Patriot Vol. 4 Leader of the Revolution Vol. 5 Victory with the Help of France Vol. 6 Patriot and President (by John Alexander Carroll and Mary Wells Ashworth) Vol. 7 First in Peace; (with title "Washington" abr. by Richard B. Harwell) 7 vols. in 1 1968. Both editions are out of print at present.

NICOLSON, SIR HAROLD (GEORGE). 1886–1968. *See Section on Autobiography, this Chapter.*

MORISON, SAMUEL ELIOT. 1887– *See Chapter 9, History, Government and Politics— American, this Volume.*

PEARSON, HESKETH. 1887–1964. *See Chapter 16, Literary Biography and Autobiography, Reader's Adviser, Vol. I.*

NEVINS, ALLAN. 1890– *See Chapter 9, History, Government and Politics—American, this Volume.*

BEMIS, SAMUEL FLAGG. 1891– *See Chapter 9, History, Government and Politics— American, this Volume.*

RENOIR, JEAN. 1894–

While recovering from war wounds in 1915, Jean Renoir, playwright, film director and second son of the great impressionist painter, listened to his father's reminiscences of his youth. These formed the basis of the warm biography "Renoir, My Father," enhanced by the recollections of Gabrielle, Renoir's model and housekeeper, and Jean's own youthful memories. Renoir, who died in 1919, is portrayed in the intimate world of his family, neighbors and friends, in this book, rich in anecdote, which is a delight to read. His life story, says *Time*, "is a powerful antidote to the notion—acquired perhaps from reading biographies of Van Gogh and Gauguin—that art must spring from anguish."

RENOIR, MY FATHER. *Little* 1962 $10.00 pap. $2.95

MY LIFE AND MY FILMS. *Atheneum* 1974 $10.00

"The filmmaker son of French painter Pierre Auguste Renoir defines his life in terms of the concepts of cinematic art he cultivated at an early age and strived to implement on the screen throughout his career"—*(Booklist)*.

Books about Renoir

Jean Renoir. By Pierre Leprohon. Trans. By Brigid Elson *Crown* 1972 pap. $3.50
Jean Renoir: The World of His Films. By Leo Braudy. *Doubleday* 1972 $8.95
Jean Renoir. By André Bazin. Ed. By Francois Truffaut *Simon & Schuster* 1973 $10.00; *Dell* Delta Bks. 1974 pap. $3.25
Jean Renoir. By Raymond Durgnat. *Univ. of California Press* 1974 $16.50

BOWEN, CATHERINE (SHOBER) DRINKER. 1897–1973.

Coming from a family that insisted that "music is an accomplishment, not a profession," Catherine Drinker Bowen did some free-lancing on musical subjects and became known first for a delightful volume of autobiographical essays for amateur music lovers called "Friends and Fiddlers" *(Little-Atlantic* 1935 $5.95). She studied the violin at Juilliard and frequently plays in a string quartet with friends.

"Yankee from Olympus" *(Little* 1944, o.p.), written with sympathy and imagination, is a study of three generations of the Holmes family in Massachusetts:—Abiel, the minister, born in 1763; Oliver Wendell, the doctor and "The Autocrat," born in 1809; and Mr. Chief Justice Holmes, who died in 1935. In her triad on lawyers, the third, "The Lion and the Throne: The Life and Times of Sir Edward Coke," about the champion of civil rights, may well prove the most significant. Turning her attention to Coke's chief rival and bitterest enemy, Francis Bacon, Mrs. Bowen presents that many-sided genius "in all his complexity. The great and near great of his age are all here in telling incidents and sharp vignettes"—(*LJ*).

Mrs. Bowen spent three years gathering facts for "Miracle at Philadelphia," a study of the 55 men who assembled during the hot summer of 1787 to work out the details of the Constitution of the United States. " 'Everyone is interested in how such wonderful men came out of the Revolution,' [she has] said. 'These men had just shared a tremendous experience together. They were absolutely convinced of the necessity of what they were doing in Philadelphia. They began to develop a tremendous sense of responsibility, to feel that the eyes of the world were indeed on them' "—(*PW*). *Library Journal* said of her book: "As Mrs. Bowen narrates, with her admirable skill as biographer-historian, . . . she vividly evokes the tensions and dramatic confrontations of conflicting personalities at that epochal event. There are brilliant characterizations of the famous delegates, the agonizing frustrations of endless debates and uncertainty as to the outcome."

In the delightful series of essays "The Adventures of a Biographer," she explains why she wrote her books and tells something of the problems and adventures she encountered along the way. "During her searches for biographical material she has visited Moscow, Boston, Washington, and London. She has interviewed Beacon Hill dowagers and Fleet Street lawyers in her quest for pertinent data." "An indefatigable worker, a researcher with a passion for accuracy," she writes with vivacious enthusiasm. Among her many honors are the 1958 National Book Award for Nonfiction, election to the National Institute of Arts and Letters, the Sarah Josefa Hale Award and the Constance Lindsay Skinner Award of the Women's National Book Association.

JOHN ADAMS AND THE AMERICAN REVOLUTION. *Little-Atlantic* 1950 $10.00; *Grosset* Univ. Lib. 1957 pap. $3.45

THE LION AND THE THRONE: The Life and Times of Sir Edward Coke. *Little-Atlantic* 1957 $10.00 pap. $3.45. This eminent English lawyer (1552–1634) prosecuted Sir Walter Raleigh.

FRANCIS BACON: The Temper of a Man. *Little-Atlantic* 1963 $7.50 pap. $1.95

(With others). FOUR PORTRAITS AND ONE SUBJECT: Bernard DeVoto. *Houghton* 1963 $4.00

MIRACLE AT PHILADELPHIA: The Story of the Constitutional Convention, May to September 1787. *Little-Atlantic* 1966 $11.95

BIOGRAPHY: The Craft and the Calling. *Little-Atlantic* 1969 $5.95

A discussion of her views on biographical writing. "As informative and charming and elegant a bit of shoptalk as I have read"—(Katherine Gauss Jackson, in *Harper's*).

THE ADVENTURES OF A BIOGRAPHER. *Little-Atlantic* 1959 $5.95. An intimate reminiscence.

FAMILY PORTRAIT. *Little-Atlantic* 1970 $8.95

"A delightfully written book about a group of sensitive, gifted people (The Bowens) who lived and contributed positively in the trying times of two wars, a depression and other 20th century trials"—(*LJ*).

THE MOST DANGEROUS MAN IN AMERICA: Scenes from the Life of Benjamin Franklin. *Little-Atlantic* 1974 $8.95

"After a biographical sketch of Franklin's youth, essays written with precision and humor review his scientific experimentation, describe his efforts to pacify the Indians, and illuminate the lengthy diplomatic career that saw Franklin at his best in an increasingly unsympathetic England"—(*Booklist*).

THARP, LOUISE HALL. 1898–   *See Chapter 16, Literary Biography and Autobiography, Reader's Adviser, Vol. I.*

CHAPMAN, HESTER W(OLFERSTAN). 1899–

Miss Chapman, an Englishwoman, has a long list of distinguished novels and biographies to her credit. However, it is her expert and entertaining studies of Tudor-Stuart figures, major and minor, which first made her American reputation. Of "Two Tudor Portraits" (1963, o.p.), Charles Poore said in the *N.Y. Times*: "Her pages are alive with interesting detail and she recreates the Tudor era with sharp, selective mastery." Other biographies published by *Little* and now out of print are: "Eugenie" (1961), "Lady Jane Grey" (1963), and "The Tragedy of Charles II in the Years 1630–1660" (1964). Miss Chapman had a varied early career of fashion modeling, secretarial work and teaching before her writing seriously got underway. Two of her novels now out of print in the United States are "Lucy" (*Morrow*, 1966), a portrayal of the world of Restoration theater, and "Fear No More" (*Morrow*, 1968).

GREAT VILLIERS: A Study of George Villiers, 2nd Duke of Buckingham, 1628–1687. 1949. *Richard West* $25.00

THE LAST TUDOR KING: A Study of Edward VI (1537–1553). *Macmillan* 1959 $4.95

PRIVILEGED PERSONS: Four Seventeenth-Century Studies. *Reynal* (dist. by Morrow) 1967 $6.00. Essays on the private lives of Sophia, Electress of Hanover; Hortense Mancini, a famous beauty; Louis XIII; and Thomas Bruce, Earl of Ailesbury.

THE THISTLE AND THE ROSE. *Coward* 1971 $6.95; *Pyramid Pubns.* 1972 pap. $1.25

CAROLINE MATILDA: Queen of Denmark. *Coward* 1972 $6.95

LIMMERSTON HALL. *Coward* 1973 $6.95; *Fawcett* Crest Bks. 1974 pap. $1.25

THE CHALLENGE OF ANNE BOLEYN. *Coward* 1974 $7.95

"This well-written, chatty and sympathetic account portrays Anne Boleyn not as a 'calculating' siren but rather as a gracious woman, interested in the new learning and completely over-shadowed by the king"—(*LJ*).

JOSEPHSON, MATTHEW. 1899–

The choice of subjects for "The Robber Barons" and "The Politicos" has given Josephson a special position as the chronicler of the last half of the 19th century. In reviewing "Edison" the *Nation* said: " 'America's ablest biographer' as Josephson was called by John Erskine, can recreate a great technological figure just as vividly as he portrayed the robber barons, politicos and novelists of his earlier book." Josephson was elected to the National Institute of Arts and Letters in 1948.

ZOLA AND HIS TIME: The History of His Martial Career in Letters; with an Account of His Circle of Friends, His Remarkable Enemies, Cyclopean Labors, Public Campaigns, Trials, and Ultimate Glorification. 1928. *Russell & Russell* 1969 $14.50

JEAN-JACQUES ROUSSEAU. 1931. *Russell & Russell* 1970 $21.00; *Richard West* $21.00

THE ROBBER BARONS 1861–1901. 1934. *Harcourt* Harvest Bks. 1962 pap. $2.85. A study of the giant American capitalists like Rockefeller, Morgan, Vanderbilt, Carnegie, Gould and Frick who flourished after the Civil War.

THE POLITICOS, 1865–1896. 1938. *Harcourt* Harvest Bks. 1963 pap. $4.95. About the American political leaders of the same period.

THE PRESIDENT MAKERS, 1896–1919. 1940. *Ungar* Am. Class. Ser. $12.00. An analysis of the political reform incited by the wealthy and talented men of the times.

EMPIRE OF THE AIR: Juan Trippe and the Struggle for World Airways. 1944. *Arno* 1972 $11.00

STENDHAL, or The Pursuit of Happiness. 1946. *Russell & Russell* 1969 $14.50

EDISON: A Biography. 1959. *McGraw-Hill* 1963 pap. $2.95

PORTRAIT OF THE ARTIST AS AN AMERICAN. *Octagon* 1964 $11.50. The fate of various artists in the United States.

INFIDEL IN THE TEMPLE. *Knopf* 1967 $10.00

"An eyewitness account of the controversial 1930's and their financiers and politicians"—(Publisher's note).

(With Hannah Josephson). HERO OF THE CITIES: A Political Portrait of Alfred E. Smith. *Houghton* 1969 $7.95

THE MONEY LORDS: The Great Financial Capitalists 1925–1950. *Weybright & Talley* (dist. by McKay) 1972 $10.00; *New Am. Lib.* pap. $1.95

The author "reminisces about the Wall Street of 50 years ago when he broke in 'at the top' of a long established Stock Exchange firm. From that beginning Josephson goes on to tell the story of the 'great capitalists' who were America's money lords between 1925 and 1950"—(*PW*).

WINWAR, FRANCES. 1900– *See Chapter 16, Literary Biography and Autobiography,* Reader's Adviser, *Vol. I.*

CECIL, LORD DAVID. 1902– *See Chapter 16, Literary Biography and Autobiography,* Reader's Adviser, *Vol. I.*

QUENNELL, PETER (COURTNEY). 1905– *See Chapter 16, Literary Biography and Autobiography,* Reader's Adviser, *Vol. I.*

EDEL, (JOSEPH) LEON. 1907– *See Chapter 16, Literary Biography and Autobiography,* Reader's Adviser, *Vol. I.*

JENKINS, ELIZABETH. 1907–

One of England's outstanding women biographers, Elizabeth Jenkins became known in this country for "Elizabeth the Great," the especial value of which is that "it is written by a woman, and by a particularly sensitive, perceptive, subtle one at that. . . . A clever woman herself, she is just the right person to write about one of the cleverest women who ever lived." Of "Elizabeth and Leicester," the *N.Y. Times* said: "Miss Jenkins is now the author of the most readable biography of Elizabeth available and also of a more specialized sequel." Elizabeth Jenkins, who was educated at St. Christopher School, Letchworth, and Newnham College, Cambridge, received the Femina Vie Heureuse Prize for her "Harriet" (1934, *New Am. Lib.* pap. $.95). "Brightness" (1964), "a sociopsychological novel with a religious theme running through it like a slender but strong thread"—*(LJ)* is now o.p. Other novels she has written are "Honey" (*Coward* 1968 $4.95) and "Dr. Gully's Story" (*Coward* 1972 $7.95; *Dell* 1973 pap. $1.50).

HENRY FIELDING. 1948. *Folcroft* $10.00

SIX CRIMINAL WOMEN. 1949. *Bks. for Libraries* $11.50. Six erring Englishwomen are the subjects of these studies.

ELIZABETH THE GREAT. *Coward* 1959 $8.95; *Putnam* Capricorn Bks. 1967 pap. $2.45

ELIZABETH AND LEICESTER. *Coward* 1962 $6.95

JANE AUSTEN. 1949. *T. Y. Crowell* (Funk & Wagnalls) Minerva Bks. 1969 pap. $2.95

CHUTE, MARCHETTE (GAYLORD). 1909– *See Chapter 16, Literary Biography and Autobiography,* Reader's Adviser, *Vol. I.*

CHURCHILL, RANDOLPH S(PENCER). 1911–1968. *See under Winston Churchill, Section on Autobiography, this Chapter.*

HEROLD, J(EAN) CHRISTOPHER. 1919–1964.

J. Christopher Herold's "Mistress to an Age" (*Bobbs* 1958, o.p.) won the National Book Award in 1959 as "a witty, beautifully controlled and highly entertaining account of one of the most remarkable women in history"—Germaine de Staël (1765–1817), the militant Swiss bluestocking. His "Bonaparte in Egypt" deals with a phase of Napoleon's career about which little has been written in English. "The Horizon Book of the Age of Napoleon" is a panorama of a tumultuous age, 1793 to 1815, with 400 illustrations, more than a third in color. The regular edition carries Mr. Herold's text in full but with a limited number of pictures. He edited and translated "The Mind of Napoleon," a collection of Napoleon's written and spoken words. Born in Czechoslovakia of Austrian parents, he was a grandson of Artur Schnabel, the pianist. Educated at German colleges and the University of Geneva, he emigrated in 1939 and finished his studies at Columbia University, New York. He served in World War II with Army Intelligence and later joined the editorial staff of *Columbia University Press.* Mr. Herold once said that he "rewrote some 10 million articles" for the *Columbia Encyclopedia*: "I learned everything from Turkish history to the genealogical tables of defunct monarchies." In 1956 Mr. Herold became editor in chief of the *Stanford University Press* while he continued his writing.

BONAPARTE IN EGYPT. *Harper* 1963 $8.95

THE AGE OF NAPOLEON. *Harper* 1963 $8.95

(Ed. and Trans.). THE MIND OF NAPOLEON: A Selection of His Written and Spoken Words. *Columbia* 1955 pap. $2.50

(With the Editors of *Horizon*). THE HORIZON BOOK OF THE AGE OF NAPOLEON. *Harper* 1963 $18.95

"Herold's book is essentially an attack on the view of Napoleon as a bearer of the Enlightenment. Though, according to Herold, Napoleon entered the stage of history through a door the Enlightenment opened, the part he played was a flat rebuttal of all the arguments for opening it . . . [Napoleon] exercised a reactionary influence, especially in laws affecting the family and women"—(*Harper's Magazine*).

AUTOBIOGRAPHY

The last few years have seen a great revival of interest in the autobiographical writings of statesmen and political leaders. It is fortunate for our national heritage that, under the sponsorship of foundations and private enterprise and issued by university presses, such distinguished projects as the publication of the "Papers" of such leaders as Franklin, the Adams Family, Jefferson, Madison and Hamilton have been undertaken. Churchill's unique record of the Second World War has been included in this chapter because of its great revelation of the personality of its author. Also in this section are the writings of American presidents and other world leaders, although certain ones (such as Hitler, Lenin and Stalin) have seemed, from the nature of their writings, more appropriate to the History Chapter and are here cross-referenced.

Brockway, Wallace, and Bart Keith Winer, Eds. *See under M. Lincoln Schuster below.*

Brooks, John, Ed. THE AUTOBIOGRAPHY OF AMERICAN BUSINESS. *Doubleday* 1974 $10.00

"The emergence of U.S. business from the nineteenth century to the present is profiled in excerpts from autobiographies of Andrew Carnegie, Henry Ford, Helena Rubinstein and others whose writings are also of value as curiosities in the genre of the self portrait"—*(Booklist)*.

Kaplan, Louis, and others, Eds. A BIBLIOGRAPHY OF AMERICAN AUTOBIOGRAPHIES. *Univ. of Wisconsin Press* 1961 $20.00. Selective list of 6,377 American autobiographies published before 1945.

Matthews, William, Comp. BRITISH AUTOBIOGRAPHIES: An Annotated Bibliography of British Autobiographies Published or Written before 1951. *Shoe String Press* 1968 $11.00

Padover, Saul K., Ed. CONFESSIONS AND SELF-PORTRAITS: 4600 Years of Autobiography, Assembled and Edited With an Introduction. 1957. *Bks. for Libraries* $12.50

Ross, Lillian, and Helen Ross. THE PLAYER: A Profile of an Art. *Simon & Schuster* 1962 pap. 1968 $2.95. Fascinating insight to the theatre as 55 actors and actresses individually discuss their lives and craft.

Saturday Review. WHAT I HAVE LEARNED: A Collection of Twenty Autobiographical Essays by Great Contemporaries from the *Saturday Review. Simon & Schuster* 1968 $6.50

"Brimful of ideas, makes most stimulating reading"—*(LJ)*. Cardinal Bea, Buckminster Fuller, Eric Hoffer, Reinhold Niebuhr, Alan Paton and Harry Golden are among the contributors.

Schuster, M. Lincoln, Ed. A TREASURY OF THE WORLD'S GREAT LETTERS: From Ancient Days to Our Own Time. 1940. *Simon & Schuster* 1960 pap. $3.45

A SECOND TREASURY OF THE WORLD'S GREAT LETTERS. Ed. by Wallace Brockway and Bart Keith Winer *Simon & Schuster* 1941 $5.00

AUGUSTINE, SAINT, Bishop of Hippo. 354–430. *See Chapter 4, World Religions, this Volume.*

LEONARDO DA VINCI. 1452–1519.

"The versatility and creative power of Leonardo mark him as a supreme example of Renaissance genius. The richness and originality of intellect expressed in his notebooks reveal one of the great minds of all time"—*(Columbia Encyclopedia)*. Leonardo, who was painter, sculptor, architect, musician, engineer and scientist, wrote the greater part of his "Treatise on Painting" and his extensive "Notebooks" during the 16 years that he spent in Milan at the court of Lodovico Sforza.

Some 700 "lost manuscript pages of Leonardo's were accidentally uncovered at the National Library in Madrid in 1965 by Dr. Jules Piccus (professor of Romance languages at the University of Massachusetts) in the course of some unrelated research. The manuscript includes pages of mirror-image text and many drawings of machines and technical devices conceived by Leonardo but not actually invented until long after his time. Among these were sketches of a chain drive, not unlike that now used on bicycles, and gears and hooks for hauling and releasing automatically like those on today's cranes. Dr. Miguel Bordonau, director of the library, disputed the contention that manuscripts had been "lost"; in fact, he said, they were on public display during the spring of 1965. An antiquated cataloging system appears to have been part of the trouble; the existence of the manuscripts seems, in any case, to have been unknown abroad. In July, 1967, *McGraw-Hill* and

Taurus Editions of Madrid announced an agreement to publish jointly popular, worldwide editions of the "Madrid Codices" which appeared in 1974.

"Ginevra deBenci" (c. 1477), the only painting generally acknowledged to be by Leonardo now outside Europe, was bought by the National Gallery of Art, Washington, D.C., in 1967 for $5–$6 million from Prince Franz Josef II of Liechtenstein—making it the "world's costliest painting" (*N.Y. Times*). Its official escorts maintained strict secrecy about their mission, not announced until the work had safely arrived. They sent a cable to Washington before leaving Europe: "The bird cooked at 45 degrees and was 55 per cent wet," which meant that these were its temperature and humidity requirements.

THE NOTEBOOKS. Ed. by Jean-Paul Richter. 1883. *Dover* 2 vols. 1970 pap. each $5.00; *Peter Smith* 2 vols. set $15.00; ed. by Pamela Taylor *New Am. Lib.* $3.95

SELECTIONS FROM THE NOTEBOOKS. Ed. by Irma A. Richter *Oxford* World's Class. 1952 $3.50

CODEX ATLANTICUS: A Facsimile of the Restored Manuscript. *Johnson Reprint* 12 vols. set $10,000

THE MADRID CODICES. Trans. by Ladislao Reti *McGraw-Hill* 1974 $400.00, deluxe ed. $750.00. This, together with "The Unknown Leonardo" (*see below*) was awarded the Carey-Thomas Award in 1975.

LITERARY WORKS. Ed. by Jean-Paul Richter *Phaidon* (dist. by N.Y. Graphic) 2 vols. 3rd ed. 1970 set $45.00

DRAWINGS. Ed. by Giorgio Castelfranco; trans. by Florence H. Phillips *Dover* 1968 pap. $2.00; *Gannon* lib. bdg. $6.00

LEONARDO DA VINCI ON PAINTING: A Lost Book (Libro A); reassembled from the Codex Vaticanus Urbinas 1270 and from the Codex Leicester; with a Chronology of Leonardo's "Treatise on Painting." Reassembled, trans. and ed. by Carlo Pedretti; fwd. by Sir Kenneth Clark *Univ. of California Press* 1964 $17.50

"About 1530, using Leonardo's manuscripts and separating them by subject matter, Francesco Melzi, Leonardo's pupil and assistant, compiled the *Codex Vaticanus Urbinas 1270*. Fragments of these manuscripts still exist, but nothing remains of *Libro A*. In his complex and richly documented book, Mr. Pedretti has reconstructed and dated the missing book. Scholars can now chronologically follow the development of Leonardo's art theories between 1508 and 1515"—(*LJ*).

Books about Leonardo da Vinci

Leonardo da Vinci. By Walter Pater. 1873. Color Bk. Ser. *Phaidon* (dist. by N.Y. Graphic) 1971 $5.95

Leonardo da Vinci: An Account of His Development as an Artist. By Sir Kenneth Clark. 1939. *Gannon* lib. bdg. $5.50; *Penguin* Pelican Bks. rev. ed. pap. $2.25. "The best single book on Leonardo."

Codex Huygens and Leonardo da Vinci's Art Theory. By Erwin Panofsky. 1940. *Greenwood* 1971 $12.25

Leonardo da Vinci—Life and Work, Paintings and Drawings: With the Leonardo Biography by Vasari (1568), Newly Annotated. Ed. by Ludwig Goldscheider. 1943. *Phaidon* (dist. by N.Y. Graphic) 8th ed. 1967 $13.50. This classic has Vasari's life as the main text, with da Vinci's letters, other documents concerning him, a chronology and bibliography. Reproduces all Leonardo's paintings and 80 drawings; 62 text illustrations; 135 large plates of which 43 are in color.

Leonardo da Vinci: A Study in Psychosexuality. By Sigmund Freud. 1947. *Random* Vintage Bks. 1955 1966 pap. $1.95

Leonardo da Vinci: Psychoanalytic Notes on the Enigma. By K. R. Eissler *Int. Univs. Press* 1961 $13.50. A study into the validity of criticism of Freud's book.

Leonardo da Vinci. By V. P. Zubov. 1962. Trans. from the Russian by David H. Kraus *Harvard Univ. Press* 1968 $11.00

"An interpretive biography of Leonardo's intellect. . . . A work of scholarship based on a profound knowledge of a wide variety of basic sources; there is no Marxist viewpoint stated or implied"—(*LJ*).

The World of Leonardo da Vinci: Man of Science, Engineer, and Dreamer of Flight. By Ivor B. Hart. 1962. *Kelley* $22.50

"This interesting book will long remain a standard work on Leonardo as scientist and engineer"—(*N.Y. Times*).

The Mechanical Investigations of Leonardo da Vinci. By Ivor B. Hart. *Univ. of California Press* 1963 pap. $1.95

Leonardo da Vinci and a Memory of His Childhood. By Sigmund Freud. Trans. by Alan Tyson; ed. by James Strachey *Norton* 1964 $3.50 pap. $1.55

Leonardo da Vinci: Aspects of the Renaissance Genius. Sel. and ed. with introd. by Morris Philipson. *Braziller* 1966 $8.95

Thirteen studies on Leonardo. Contributors include Bernard Berenson, Herbert Read, George Sarton, Giorgio de Santillana, Kenneth Clark and K. R. Eissler. Chronology; notes on contributors. "Should be useful for many years to come"—*(LJ)*.

The World of Leonardo. By Robert Wallace. *Time-Life* 1966 $8.95

Images of the Universe: Leonardo da Vinci, the Artist as Scientist. By Richard B. McLanathan. *Doubleday* 1966 $2.49

Leonardo da Vinci. By Hellmut Wohl. *McGraw-Hill* 1967 $8.95

Inventions of Leonardo da Vinci. By Margaret Cooper. *Macmillan* 1968 $6.95

Leonardo and the Age of the Eye. By Ritchie Calder. *Int. Pubns. Service* 1970 $21.00

Sublimations of Leonardo da Vinci: With a Translation of the Codex Trivulzianus by Pierina B. Castiglione. By Raymond S. Stites and M. Elizabeth Stites. *Smithsonian* 1970 $14.95

Leonardo: A Study in Chronology. By Carlo Pedretti. *Univ. of California Press* 1973 $10.95

The Unknown Leonardo. Ed. by Ladislao Reti. *McGraw-Hill* 1974 $39.95

CELLINI, BENVENUTO. 1500–1571.

Cellini today is more famous for his autobiography than for his statue of "Perseus." His autobiography has been called the most unflinching in all literature. His unhesitating confession of hate, theft, murder and sensuality has sometimes seemed shocking. The story of his many dishonorable adventures reads like a picaresque novel. Yet this autobiography is a valuable picture of its time. The manuscript of Cellini's autobiography was circulated for over 150 years before it was printed in 1730. During that time it was frequently copied, and many different texts of it exist at the present day. The translators listed have used different texts. Roscoe (*Oxford* World's Class.) omits certain unedifying passages. John Addington Symonds' is considered the best. (He also wrote a biography of Cellini, 1927, o.p.) Miss Macdonnell's spirited translation is made from the original manuscript, long thought lost. Cellini's "Treatises on Goldsmithing and Sculpture" (trans. by C. R. A. Ashbee *Dover* 1966 pap. $3.00; *Peter Smith* $4.50) is now in print.

THE LIFE OF BENVENUTO CELLINI: Written by Himself. Published first in 1730 in Italian. Trans. by Anne Macdonnell *Dutton* pap. $3.95; trans. by John A. Symonds *Liveright* Black & Gold Lib. $6.95

THE AUTOBIOGRAPHY OF BENVENUTO CELLINI. Trans. by John Addington Symonds *Doubleday* 1960 Anchor Bks. pap. $1.25; trans. by George Bull *Penguin* pap. $2.00

MEMOIRS: Written by Himself. *Oxford* World's Class. $2.50

TERESA OF JESUS, ST. 1515–1582. *See Chapter 11, Spanish Literature,* Reader's Adviser, *Vol. 2.*

EVELYN, JOHN. 1620–1706. *See Chapter 16, Literary Biography and Autobiography,* Reader's Adviser, *Vol. I.*

SÉVIGNÉ, MME DE. 1626–1696. *See Chapter 9, French Literature,* Reader's Adviser, *Vol. 2*

PEPYS, SAMUEL. 1633–1703. *See Chapter 16, Literary Biography and Autobiography,* Reader's Adviser, *Vol. 1.*

MONTAGU, LADY MARY WORTLEY. 1689–1762. *See Chapter 16, Literary Biography and Autobiography,* Reader's Adviser, *Vol. 1.*

CHESTERFIELD, (PHILIP DORMER STANHOPE), 4th Earl. 1694–1773. *See Chapter 16, Literary Biography and Autobiography,* Reader's Adviser, *Vol. 1.*

WESLEY, JOHN. 1703–1791. *See Chapter 4, World Religions, this Volume.*

FRANKLIN, BENJAMIN. 1706–1790.

Franklin's Autobiography was first printed in a French translation in 1791. The four different parts of the manuscript were written at various times and places, in England, in France and in Philadelphia. John Bigelow secured possession of the original manuscript discovered in France, and edited the only unmutilated and correct version of it. This was first published by *Lippincott* in 1867, with a second edition in 1884. The fifth edition (1905) continues the life of Franklin from the point where the Autobiography ends (1757) through the remaining 33 years of his life. This was compiled by means of his correspondence and other writings. The first translations of the Autobiography appeared in London in 1793, one published by J. Parsons, the other by G. C. and J. Robinson. William Temple Franklin, the grandson of Benjamin Franklin, who was in possession of the original manuscript, brought out his English edition of it in 1817, very much expurgated.

Franklin signed the name Richard Saunders to his shrewd maxims and proverbs in "Poor Richard's Almanack" (*McKay* $2.25; *Peter Pauper Press* 1939 $2.95). It was undoubtedly derived from and follows the pattern of the English "Poor Robin's Almanac" started in 1663. "Franklin's Wit and Wisdom" (vest pocket ed. $1.25) is published by *Peter Pauper Press*; *Teachers College* issued "Benjamin Franklin on Education" edited by John Hardin Best (1962 $5.95 pap. $2.50). Two other works in print are: "The Political Thought of Benjamin Franklin" (ed. by Ralph Ketcham *Bobbs* 1965 $7.50 pap. $2.75) and "Advice to a Young Man on the Choice of a Mistress" (*Gordon Press* $19.95).

AUTOBIOGRAPHY. *Assoc. Booksellers* Airmont Bks. pap. $.60; (and "Selections from Other Writings") ed. by Herbert W. Schneider *Bobbs* 1967 pap. $2.00; *Dodd* Gt. Ill. Class. 1963 $5.50; *Dutton* pap. $3.95; (and "Selected Writings") ed. by Dixon Wecter and Larzer Ziff *Holt* (Rinehart) 1954 pap. $1.95; (and "Other Writings") ed. by Russel B. Nye *Houghton* Riv. Eds. 1958 pap. $2.95; *Macmillan* Collier Bks. 1966 pap. $.65; (and "Selected Writings") ed. by Henry S. Commager *Modern Library* pap. $1.75; (and "Other Writings") ed. by L. Jesse Lemisch *New Am. Lib.* Signet 1961 pap. $.60; (and "Other Pieces") ed. by Dennis Welland *Oxford* 1970 pap. $6.50; *Franklin Watts* lg.-type ed. $7.95

AUTOBIOGRAPHY. Ed. by Leonard W. Labaree and others *Yale Univ. Press* 1964 $17.50 1967 pap. $3.75

The editors used Max Farrand's 1949 text based on the original manuscript, carefully rechecking it in the process. Likely to become the standard edition. "This is one of those rarest of historiographical achievements: a publication of the original text of a historical and literary classic in which the bookmaker's art and the historian's best technical editorial skill are combined to produce a work that is both a dependable scholar's source, a reader's delight, and a thing of beauty"—(*Am. Hist. Review*).

PAPERS. Ed. by Leonard W. Labaree; Whitfield J. Bell, Jr., Assoc. Ed.; Helen C. Boatfield and Helene H. Fineman, Asst. Eds. *Yale Univ. Press* 18 vols. 1959–74 each $20.00

Vol. 1 Jan. 6, 1706–Dec. 31, 1734 (1959) Vol. 2 Jan. 1, 1735–Dec. 31, 1744 (1960) Vol. 3 Jan. 1, 1745–June 30, 1750 (1961) Vol. 4 July 1, 1750–June 30, 1753 (1961) Vol. 5 July 1, 1753–Mar. 31, 1755 (1962) Vol. 6 Apr. 1, 1755–Sept. 24, 1756 (1963) Vol. 7 Oct. 1, 1756–Mar. 31, 1758 (1963) Vol. 8 Apr. 1, 1758–Dec. 31, 1759 (1965) Vol. 9 Jan. 1, 1760–Dec. 31, 1761 (1966) Vol. 10 Jan. 1, 1762–Dec. 31, 1763 (1966) Vol. 11 Jan. 1, 1764–Dec. 31, 1764 (1967) Vol. 12 Jan. 1, 1765–Dec. 31, 1765 (1968) Vol. 13 Jan. 1, 1766–Dec. 31, 1766 (1969) Vol. 14 Jan. 1, 1767–Dec. 31, 1767 (1970) Vol. 15 Jan. 1, 1768–Dec. 31, 1768 (1971) Vol. 16 Jan. 1, 1769–Dec. 31, 1769 (1971) Vol. 17 Jan. 1, 1770–Dec. 31, 1770 (1972) Vol. 18 Jan. 1, 1771–Dec. 31, 1771 (1974)

WORKS. Ed. by Bigelow *Somerset Pub.* 12 vols. $180.00

WRITINGS. Coll. and ed. by Albert H. Smyth. 1907. *Haskell* 10 vols. 1969 Vol. 1 Bibliographical Introduction and the "Autobiography" Vols. 2–10 Writings and Correspondence set $199.00

THE PENNSYLVANIA GAZETTE, 1728–1789. *Scholarly Press* 25 vols. $875.00

LETTERS TO THE PRESS, 1758–1775. Ed. by Verner W. Crane *Univ. of North Carolina Press* 1950 $8.95

HISTORICAL REVIEW OF THE CONSTITUTION AND GOVERNMENT OF PENNSYLVANIA, FROM ITS ORIGIN. 1759. *Arno* 1972 $28.00

THE BAGATELLES FROM PASSY: The first full Facsimile of the Literary Works written for his Lady Friends and Colleagues & privately printed on his own Press at Paris while he was America's Minister to the Court of France. Trans. by Willard R. Trask *Eakins* 1967 $7.50

Between 1905 and 1910, quite by chance, a clerk in a New York rare book dealer's shop discovered and ordered Franklin's "Bagatelles," lost for 100 years, when he found it listed in a French bookseller's catalog for 50 cents. What arrived from Paris was the only known copy extant, presumably one of the set of pamphlets Franklin printed for his associates at the French court, "personal, witty vignettes . . . written with a characteristically light Franklinesque touch" (*PW*). It is now part of the William Smith Mason Collection at the Yale University Library, valued at several thousand dollars. Leslie Katz, of *Eakins Press*, has observed: "These works take him out of the realm of the thrifty penny-pincher, and show him to be not only a rich personality and a warm human being, but a first-rate literary mind as well."

BENJAMIN FRANKLIN: Some Account of the Pennsylvania Hospital. A facsimile edition of Franklin's description, ed. with introd. by I. Bernard Cohen *Johns Hopkins Press* 1954 $5.00

ESSAYS ON GENERAL POLITICS, COMMERCE AND POLITICAL ECONOMY. Ed. by Jared Sparks and W. Phillips. 1836. *Kelley* 1966 $12.50

PREFACES, PROVERBS AND POEMS. Ed. by Paul L. Ford. 1889. *Richard West* $20.00

A BENJAMIN FRANKLIN READER. Ed. by Nathan G. Goodman *Apollo* 1971 pap. $3.95

AN APOLOGY FOR PRINTERS. Ed. by Randolph Goodman *Acropolis* 1973 pap. $1.95

Books about Franklin

Franklin Bibliography: A List of Books Written by or Relating to Benjamin Franklin. By Paul L. Ford. 1889. *Burt Franklin* 1966 $22.50. Over 1,000 entries.

Franklin: The Apostle of Modern Times. By Bernard Fay. 1929. *Richard West* $15.00

Two Franklins, Fathers of American Democracy. By Bernard Fay. 1933. *AMS Press* 1969 $11.00; *Scholarly Press* 1971 $19.00

Benjamin Franklin: A Biography. By Carl Van Doren. 1938. *Greenwood* 1973 $27.50. The definitive life, winner of the Pulitzer Prize.

Benjamin Franklin and a Rising People. By Verner W. Crane. Ed. by Oscar Handlin. *Little* 1954 $5.00 pap. $2.95
"The finest book on Benjamin Franklin, with the single exception of Carl Van Doren's biography."

Benjamin Franklin and American Foreign Policy. By Gerald Stourzh. *Univ. of Chicago Press* 2nd ed. 1969 $10.00 pap. $3.25

Benjamin Franklin. By Richard E. Amacher. U.S. Authors Series *Twayne* $6.50; *College & Univ. Press* 1962 pap. $2.45

Benjamin Franklin. By Ralph L. Ketcham. Great American Thinkers Ser. *Twayne* $7.50

Man Who Dared the Lightning: A New Look at Benjamin Franklin. By Thomas J. Fleming. *Morrow* 1971 $10.00

Code Number 72: Ben Franklin, Patriot or Spy? By Cecil B. Currey. *Prentice-Hall* 1972 $7.95

Franklin and Newton: An Inquiry into Speculative Newtonian Experimental Science and Franklin's Work in Electricity as an Example Thereof. By I. Bernard Cohen. *Harvard Univ. Press* rev. ed. 1973 $15.00

The Most Dangerous Man in America: Scenes from the Life of Benjamin Franklin. By Catherine Drinker Bowen. *Little-Atlantic* 1974 $8.95

Benjamin Franklin and the Politics of Liberty. By Thomas Wendel. Ed. by I. E. Cadenhead Shapers of History Ser. *Barron's* 1974 pap. $2.95

Men of Physics: Benjamin Franklin. By R. Seeger. *Pergamon* 1974 $9.00

Benjamin Franklin: His Wit, Wisdom, and Women. By Seymour S. Block. *Hastings House* 1975 $12.50

Benjamin Franklin and the Zealous Presbyterians. By Melvin H. Buxbaum. *Pennsylvania State Univ. Press* 1975 $14.50

The Private Franklin: The Man and His Family. By Claude-Ann Lopez and Eugenia W. Herbert. *Norton* 1975 $11.95

ROUSSEAU, JEAN JACQUES. 1712–1778. *See Chapter 9, French Literature*, Reader's Adviser, *Vol. 2.*

GARRICK, DAVID. 1717–1779.

"That young man never had his equal and he never will have a rival," said Alexander Pope of the brilliant actor and theater manager of 18th-century England. Although his family wanted him to be a lawyer, Garrick remained enchanted with the theater from childhood and abandoned his law studies when the chance came. He went to London in 1737 with Samuel Johnson and "three-halfpence in his [pocket]" and supported himself as a wine merchant there until October 1741, when he achieved his first success as Richard III at Goodman's Fields. From 1747 to 1776 he was a partner and manager at the Drury Lane Theater. Garrick sought to restore Shakespeare to the stage; he cared little for the bawdiness and sentimentality of Restoration drama. He acted brilliantly in both comedy and tragedy and made many innovations in staging technique at Drury Lane. "His daringly naturalistic style discredited forever the singsong elocution and formalized movements of the older tragedians"—(*Encyclopaedia Britannica*). Garrick's original works were mainly farces such as "The Lying Valet" (1741) and "Bon Ton, or, High Life Above Stairs" (1775). "Three Plays by David Garrick," edited by Elizabeth P. Stein (*Blom* 1967 $8.75), contains "Harlequin's Invasion," "The Jubilee" and "The Meeting of the Company, or Bayes' Art of Acting." He also collaborated with other playwrights and adapted many plays by Shakespeare and Jonson. Garrick is buried in the Poets' Corner of Westminster Abbey.

DIARY. Ed. by R. C. Alexander 1928 *Blom* $7.50

THE JOURNAL DESCRIBING HIS VISIT TO FRANCE AND ITALY IN 1763. Introd. and notes by G. W. Stone, Jr.; printed from the original ms. in the Folger Shakespeare Library. 1939 *Kraus* pap. $4.00

PINEAPPLES OF FINEST FLAVOUR: A Selection of Sundry Unpublished Letters of the English Roscius, David Garrick. Ed. by David M. Little 1930 *Russell & Russell* 1967 $8.00

Books about Garrick

Memoirs of the Life of David Garrick. By Thomas Davies. Ed. by Stephen Jones 1808 *Blom* 2 vols. $18.75
David Garrick, Dramatist. By Elizabeth P. Stein. 1937 *Blom* $12.50; *Kraus* 1938 pap. $14.00
Theatre in the Age of Garrick. By Cecil Price. *Rowman* 1973 $8.50

WALPOLE, HORACE, 4th Earl of Oxford. 1717–1797. *See Chapter 16, Literary Biography and Autobiography*, Reader's Adviser, *Vol. 1.*

WOOLMAN, JOHN. 1720–1772.

Like William Penn's "Fruits of Solitude" and Ben Franklin's "Autobiography," says Kenneth Rexroth, the journal of John Woolman is infused with the American Quaker ethic—a form of the business ethic but devoid of greed. "Even in Franklin, the main emphasis was on social responsibility, and in Penn and Woolman, the source of responsibility was found in contemplation, the highest form of prayer." John Woolman was a very early Quaker opponent of slavery, as an abuse which denied George Fox's recognition "of that of God in every man." He gave up his prosperous business as a merchant and spent 30 years voicing his "concern" to Meetings of Friends, some of whom—less enlightened than he—clung to their human property. He traveled extensively in the 13 colonies and eventually in England. It was largely because of Woolman's simple "witness in life and person" that the Society of Friends came to renounce slavery and "became the earliest, most powerful single force in the antislavery movement" (says Rexroth), eventually working illicitly in the Underground Railroad, which got slaves to Canada and freedom in the 19th century.

His journal, Rexroth continues, "is the simplest possible record of his ever widening travels and his ever deepening interior life, two aspects of one reality. He came, he spoke, he conquered, solely by the power of an achieved spiritual peace, a perfectly clear personality through which that Quaker Inner Light shone unimpeded from Friend to Friend. It is this moral quality, once called humility in days before our terminology of the virtues became hopelessly confused, that elevates Woolman's writing to the level of great prose. . . . All that Woolman needed to achieve greatness of style in language and life was perfect candor"—(in *SR*). We are much indebted to this fine essay in Kenneth Rexroth's "Classics Revisited" series.

WORKS. 1774. *Bks. for Libraries* $14.00; *Somerset Pub.* $14.50

JOURNAL (1774) and A PLEA FOR THE POOR (1763). Introd. by Frederick B. Tolles *Citadel Press* 1972 pap. $2.95; *Peter Smith* $4.25

JOURNAL AND MAJOR ESSAYS. Ed. by Phillips P. Moulton *Oxford* 1971 $10.50

SOME CONSIDERATIONS ON THE KEEPING OF NEGROES. 1800. *Arno* 1969 $7.00

Books about Woolman

John Woolman: The Mind of the Quaker Saint. By Edwin H. Cady. Great American Thinkers Ser. *Twayne* 1966 $6.95
John Woolman. By Paul Rosenblatt. U.S. Authors Ser. *Twayne* 1969 $6.50
Woolman and Blake: Prophets of Today. By Mildred B. Young. *Pendle Hill* 1971 pap. $.70
The Living Witness of John Woolman. By Phillips P. Moulton. *Pendle Hill* 1973 $.70

CASANOVA (or Casanova de Seingalt, or Giovanni Jacopo [or Giacomo] Casanova de Seingalt). 1725–1798. *See Chapter 16, Literary Biography and Autobiography*, Reader's Adviser, *Vol. 1.*

WASHINGTON, GEORGE. 1732–1799.

The definitive edition of Washington's writings, edited by John C. Fitzpatrick, includes his journals (that of his Journey to the West) and his diaries in four volumes, all of which have been edited separately. His "Farewell Address" (Sept. 17, 1796) is considered a monument of American oratory. It contains the famous passage warning the United States against "entangling alliances" with foreign powers. A confirmed diarist, his records of his public life furnish most of the material for the many biographies. But he also gives us glimpses of his less familiar private life as a comfortable Virginia squire with his family and 216 slaves at Mount Vernon. The last entry was written only a few hours before his death.

"No man in our history, not even Lincoln, has had so many distinguished biographers as Washington," said J. Donald Adams in the *N.Y. Times.* "They include John Marshall, Jared Sparks, Washington Irving, Edward Everett, Henry Cabot Lodge and Woodrow Wilson. There have been lives by William Roscoe Thayer, Owen Wister, Paul Leicester Ford, Rupert Hughes, W. E. Woodward and Douglas Freeman . . . and we need add only Parson Weems, the author of the first biography."

WRITINGS FROM THE ORIGINAL MANUSCRIPT SOURCES, 1745–1799. Ed. by John C. Fitzpatrick. 1931–44. *Greenwood* 39 vols. 1968 set $850.00

THE WASHINGTON PAPERS. Ed. by Saul K. Padover *Grosset* Univ. Lib. pap. $2.95. A selection from his speeches, writings, letters and personal papers.

DIARIES, 1748–1799. Ed. by John C. Fitzpatrick. 1925. *Kraus* 4 vols. set $60.00

JOURNAL OF MAJOR GEORGE WASHINGTON, 1754. Ed. by James R. Short and Thaddeus W. Tate, Jr. *Holt* 1959 facsimile ed. $2.50; *Univ. Press of Virginia* 1963 pap. $2.50; *Univ. Microfilms* 1966 $3.55

THE DIARY: From 1789 to 1791: Embracing the Opening of the First Congress, His Tours Through New England, Long Island and Southern States, Together With His Journal of a Tour to the Ohio, in 1753. Ed. by Benson J. Lossing 1860 *Bks. for Libraries* $9.75

FAREWELL ADDRESS. 1796. Ed. by Victor Hugo Paltsits 1935 *N.Y. Public Lib.* $35.00; *Arno* 1971 $35.00

GEORGE WASHINGTON: A Biography in His Own Words. Ed. by Ralph Andrist The Founding Fathers Ser. *Harper* 1973 $15.00

Books about Washington

The Life of Washington. By Mason L. Weems. 1800. Ed. by Marcus Cunliffe *Harvard* 1962 $7.50 pap. $3.25

Bibliotheca Washingtoniana: A Descriptive List of the Biographies and Biographical Sketches of George Washington. By William Spohn Baker. 1889. *Gale Research Co.* $9.00; *Gordon Press* $25.00. An annotated chronological listing of 502 American and foreign titles, 1777–1889.

George Washington. By Paul L. Ford. 1896. American Bicentennial Ser. *Kennikat* 1970 $13.50

George Washington. By Henry Cabot Lodge. Ed. by John T. Morse, Jr. 1898. *AMS Press* 2 vols. set $29.50

George Washington as the French Knew Him. By Gilbert Chinard. 1940. *Greenwood* $11.50

Washington and the Revolution, a Reappraisal. By Bernhard Knollenberg. 1940. *Shoe String Press* 1968 $7.50

George Washington: A Biography. By Douglas Southall Freeman (Vol. 7 by J. A. Carroll and M. W. Ashworth). *Scribner* 7 vols. 1948–54; abr. ed. by Richard B. Harwell 7 vols. in 1 1968 (both editions out of print). The definitive biography, awarded the Pulitzer Prize in 1958.

Washington and the American Revolution. By Esmond Wright. 1957. *Macmillan* Collier Bks. 1962 pap. $.95

George Washington: The Virginia Period, 1732–1775. By Bernhard Knollenberg. *Duke Univ. Press* 1964 $6.00

"Mr. Knollenberg is a formidable scholar and controversialist, not a 'debunker' . . . He is firm and convincing in his opinions"—*(TLS,* London).

George Washington. By James Thomas Flexner. *Little* 4 vols. 1965–72 Vol. 1 The Forge of Experience, 1732–1775 (1965) Vol. 2 In the American Revolution, 1775–1783 (1968) Vol. 3

And the New Nation, 1783–1793 (1970) Vol. 4 Anguish and Farewell, 1793–1799 (1972) each $15.00

George Washington, 1732–1799: Chronology, Documents, Bibliographical Aids. Ed. By Howard F. Bremer. *Oceana* 1967 $4.50

George Washington. Ed. by Morton Borden. Great Lives Observed Ser. *Prentice-Hall* 1969 $5.95 pap. $1.95

George Washington's Expense Account. By Marvin Kitman. *Simon & Schuster* 1970 $5.95

George Washington: The Image and the Man. By W. E. Woodward. *Liveright* 1972 $7.95 pap. $3.95

The Presidency of George Washington. By Forrest McDonald. American Presidency Ser. *Univ. Press of Kansas* 1974 $10.00

Washington, the Indispensable Man. By James Thomas Flexner. *Little* 1974 $12.50

"The personal, indelible imprint that the general/president stamped on a fledgling nation impresses Flexner as he presents Washington from early years building a fortune and respectable reputation as a colonial planter to the last years as a grand embodiment of the American nation"—*(Booklist)*.

George Washington and the American Revolution. By Burke David. *Random* 1975 $15.00

The author "has digested a vast amount of information on the Revolutionary War and has retold an engrossing story with a general focus on Washington"—*(PW)*.

ADAMS, JOHN, 1735–1826, ADAMS, JOHN QUINCY, 1767–1848, and ADAMS, CHARLES FRANCIS, 1807–1886.

The publication of the "great archive of Adams family papers long considered the most important collection of American historical manuscripts in private hands," sponsored by the Massachusetts Historical Society, financed by *Time, Inc.*, and edited by a distinguished staff of scholars, is a major publishing event. The papers were transferred to the Massachusetts Historical Society in 1956 by Thomas Boylston Adams and John Quincy Adams, members of the 10th American generation. The Adamses guarded their papers well and "have always hung on to every scrap of paper that seemed to have any historical value. The mammoth diary of John Quincy Adams is today regarded as one of his greatest achievements. Charles Francis Adams had a strong bent toward writing history and tending archives. He built the 'Stone Library' at Quincy to preserve the family papers and edited portions of them for publication. Charles Francis had four sons—John Quincy the 2nd, Charles Francis the 2nd, Henry and Brooks Adams. The last three were all historians and took a keen interest in the family records, besides adding considerably to their bulk. . . . In 1905 the three historian brothers and their nephew Charles Francis the 3rd (who later became Secretary of the Navy under President Hoover) created the 'Adams Manuscript Trust,' to take over the ownership and care of the family papers, as well as the Old House and Library. . . . For nearly 50 years the papers—neatly bound and boxed in tempting array—reposed on shelves in a double-locked room at the Massachusetts Historical Society, where they had been placed for safekeeping. Only a few researchers were permitted to see them and then only for limited studies."

The Adams Papers. Ed. by Lyman Henry Butterfield and others *Harvard Univ. Press* with *Atheneum* paperbound eds. as noted:

Series I Diaries: Diary and Autobiography of John Adams (1755–1804) 4 vols. 1961 set $35.00; *Atheneum* 4 vols. 1964 pap. each $2.65 set $9.95 The Earliest Diary of John Adams (1753–1759) 1966 $5.00 Diary of John Quincy Adams (1779–1848) 30 vols. (in prep.) Diary of Charles Francis Adams (1820–1880) Vols. 1 and 2 (1820–1829) 2 vols. 1964 set $30.00; *Atheneum* 1967 pap. each $3.95 Vols. 3 and 4 (1829–1832) 2 vols. 1968 set $30.00 Vols. 5 and 6 (1833–1836) 2 vols. 1974 set $40.00 18 further vols. in prep.

Series II Adams Family Correspondence (1761–1889) Vols. 1 and 2 (1761–1778) 2 vols. 1963 set $17.50; *Atheneum* 1965 pap. each $2.95 Vols. 3 and 4 (1778–1783) 2 vols. 1973 set $32.50 18 further vols. in prep.

Series III General Correspondence and Other Papers of the Adams Statesmen: Legal Papers of John Adams 3 vols. 1965 set $35.00; *Atheneum* 1968 pap. each $3.95

"A major feat in American historical scholarship"—(John F. Kennedy). Series IV consists of Adams Family Portraits (*see Books about the Adamses below for the first of these, 1967*). The "Adams Family Genealogy" is in prep. (also by *Harvard Univ. Press*). Projected volumes include a volume of "Autobiographical Writings of Louisa Catherine Adams and Diaries of Minor Adamses," "Papers of John Adams," "Papers of John Quincy Adams," "Papers of Charles Francis Adams."

Works of John Adams. Ed. by Charles Francis Adams. 1850–1856. *AMS Press* 10 vols. 1972 each $22.50 set $215.00

Familiar Letters of John Adams and His Wife Abigail Adams, During the Revolution. 1875. *Bks. for Libraries* facs. ed. $14.50

SPUR OF FAME: Dialogues of John Adams and Benjamin Rush, 1805–1813. Ed. by John A. Schutz and Douglass Adair *Huntington Library* 1966 $6.00

ADAMS-JEFFERSON LETTERS: The Complete Correspondence between Thomas Jefferson and Abigail and John Adams. Ed. by Lester J. Cappon *Univ. of North Carolina Press* 2 vols. 1959 set $12.50; *Simon & Schuster* pap. $5.95

POLITICAL WRITINGS OF JOHN ADAMS. Ed. by George A. Peek, Jr. *Bobbs* 1954 $6.50 pap. $1.75

DEFENSE OF THE CONSTITUTION OF GOVERNMENT OF THE UNITED STATES OF AMERICA. By John Adams. 1797. *Adler* 3 vols. in prep.; *Da Capo* 3 vols. 1969 $85.00

DISCOURSES ON DAVILA. By John Adams. 1805 *Da Capo* 1973 $15.00

NOVANGLUS and MASSACHUSETTENSIS, or Political Essays, Published in the Years 1774 and 1775 on the Principal Points of Controversy Between Great Britain and Her Colonies. By John Adams and Jonathan Sewall. 1819. *Russell & Russell* 1968 $10.00

WARREN-ADAMS LETTERS: Being Chiefly a Correspondence among John Adams, Samuel Adams, and James Warren. 1917–1925. *AMS Press* 2 vols. each $16.50 set $32.50

WRITINGS OF JOHN QUINCY ADAMS. Ed. by Worthington Chauncey Ford. 1913–17. *Greenwood* 7 vols. 1968 set $154.00; *Scholarly Press* 7 vols. each $24.50 set $149.00

THE DIARY OF JOHN QUINCY ADAMS 1794–1845. Ed. by Allan Nevins. 1928. *Ungar* 1969 $12.50

MEMOIRS OF JOHN QUINCY ADAMS: Comprising Portions of His Diary from 1795 to 1848. Ed. by Charles Francis Adams. 1874. *AMS Press* 12 vols. 1970 each $25.00 set $280.00; *Bks. for Libraries* 12 vols. set $300.00

SPEECH OF JOHN QUINCY ADAMS OF MASSACHUSETTS, Upon the Right of the People, Men and Women, to Petition. 1838. *Arno* 1969 $7.50

JOHN QUINCY ADAMS AND THE AMERICAN CONTINENTAL EMPIRE: Letters, Papers and Speeches. Ed. by Walter LaFeber *Quadrangle Bks.* 1965 pap. $2.25

LECTURES ON RHETORIC AND ORATORY. By John Quincy Adams. 1810. *Russell & Russell* 2 vols. 1962 set $17.50

ARGUMENT OF JOHN QUINCY ADAMS BEFORE THE SUPREME COURT OF THE UNITED STATES IN THE CASE OF THE UNITED STATES VS. CINQUE AND OTHERS, AFRICANS CAPTURED IN THE SCHOONER AMISTAD. 1841. *Arno* 1969 $5.50; *Negro Univ. Press* $7.75

JOHN ADAMS: A Biography in His Own Words. Ed. by James B. Peabody Founding Fathers Ser. *Harper* 1973 $15.00

THE BOOK OF ABIGAIL AND JOHN: Selected Letters of the Adams Family, 1762–1784. Ed. by Lyman Butterfield, Marc Friedlaender, and Mary-Jo Kline *Harvard Univ. Press* 1975 $15.00

Books about the Adamses

The Life of John Adams. By John Quincy and Charles Francis Adams. 1871. *Haskell* 2 vols. 1969 $39.95; *Scholarly Press* 2 vols. 1971 $47.50

Charles Francis Adams, 1807–1886. By His Son. Ed. by John T. Morse, Jr. 1900. *AMS Press* $15.00; *Richard West* $14.50

The Adams Family. By James Truslow Adams. 1930. *Greenwood* 1974 $16.00

Honest John Adams. By Gilbert Chinard. *Little* 1933 pap. $2.45; *Peter Smith* $5.50

John Quincy Adams. By Samuel Flagg Bemis. *Knopf* 2 vols. 1949–56 Vol. 1 John Quincy Adams and the Foundations of American Foreign Policy (1949) Vol. 2 John Quincy Adams and the Union (1956) each $12.50 boxed set $25.00
"In the depths of its insights and the restrained passion of its presentation, this is one of the great biographical studies of our time"—(*N.Y. Times*).

John Adams and the American Revolution. By Catherine Drinker Bowen. *Little* 1950 $10.00; *Grosset* Univ. Lib. 1957 pap. $3.45

Charles Francis Adams, 1807–1886. By Martin B. Duberman. *Stanford Univ. Press* 1961 $12.50 pap. $2.95

John Adams. By Page Smith. 1962. *Greenwood* 2 vols. set $39.00

Portraits of John and Abigail Adams. By Andrew Oliver. *Harvard Univ. Press.* 1967 $12.50
  Excellent plates and text which "traces the often complex history of each portrait.... Forming a leitmotiv of this book is the ambivalent tension between John Adams' Puritan distrust of portraiture and his obvious fascination with it, particularly those examples of art that depicted himself"—*(LJ)*.

John Adams, 1735–1826: Chronology, Documents, Bibliographical Aids. Ed. by Howard F. Bremer. Presidential Chronologies Ser. *Oceana* 1967 $4.50

John Quincy Adams: A Personal History of an Independent Man. By Marie B. Hecht. *Macmillan* 1972 $14.95

See also Adams, Henry, in Chapter 9, History, Government and Politics—American, this Volume.

GIBBON, EDWARD. 1737–1794.

Gibbon wrote no less than six autobiographies and a seventh fragmentary sketch. The first account has only to do with the history of his family; the second covers 27 years of his life; the third carries the story to 35 years of age; the fourth retells the same story to 35 years of age; the fifth, to 52 years of age; and the sixth tells his early life until 16 years of age. The first editor, the Earl of Sheffield, Gibbon's literary executor, wove these separate narratives into one and greatly condensed them (1796). Later editors, Milman in 1839, John Murray in 1896, and Birkbeck Hill in 1900 have printed the manuscript verbatim with various additions to it from the Journals and Letters. "Gibbon's Journal to January 28, 1763. My Journal I, II and III and Ephemerides, with introductory essays by D. M. Low" (1930, o.p.) was the first complete publication of the journal—which must be distinguished from his autobiography and his memoirs. "Among the books in which men have told the story of their own lives it stands in front rank. It is a striking fact that one of the first of autobiographies and the first of biographies were written in the same year. Boswell was still working at his life of Johnson when Gibbon began those memoirs from which his autobiography, in the form in which it was given to the world, was so skilfully pieced together"—(G. B. Hill).

Miss J. E. Norton has done "brilliant editorial work," in the "Letters." "Here at last is the personal Gibbon, as complete as he is every likely to be, three volumes of consummate care and scholarship . . . Here is some charming, witty, often even wise, observation, in a prose no less noble for being intimate. Here is all the editorial information and apparatus anybody could desire"—(Kenneth Rexroth, in the *Nation*).

AUTOBIOGRAPHY. *Oxford* World's Class. 1907 $3.50; ed. by M. M. Reese *Routledge & Kegan Paul* 1970 $5.25 pap. $2.25

MEMOIRS OF MY LIFE. Ed. by George B. Hill. 1900. *Richard West* $30.00

LETTERS. Ed. by J. E. Norton. 1956. *Hillary House* 3 vols. set $35.25. Some letters written from 1750 to 1794.

MISCELLANEOUS WORKS. Ed. by John, Earl of Sheffield. 1844. *AMS Press* 5 vols. each $22.50 set $105.00

PRIVATE LETTERS. Ed. by Rowland E. Prothero. 1896. *AMS Press* 2 vols. set $45.00

LIFE AND LETTERS. *Richard West* $20.00

ENGLISH ESSAYS. Ed. by Patricia B. Craddock. *Oxford* 1972 $33.75

GIBBONIANA. The Life and Times of Seven Major British Writers Ser. *Garland Pub.* 17 vols. 1974 each $22.00

Books about Gibbon

Edward Gibbon and His Age. By Edmund C. Blunden. 1935. *Folcroft* 1974 $5.50

The Transformation of the Roman World: Gibbon's Problem After Two Centuries. By Lynn T. White, Jr. *Univ. of Calif. Press* 1966 $10.00 1973 pap. $3.65

Edward Gibbon and His World. By Sir Gavin R. deBeer. *Viking* 1968 $6.95
  "A concise, beautifully written, compassionate account of the life and work of the unhappy, fat little author of 'The Decline and Fall' "—*(New Yorker)*. Copious illustrations.

Gibbon. By Cicely V. Wedgwood. Writers and Their Work Ser. *British Bk. Centre* $2.95 pap. $1.20

Gibbon and His Roman Empire. By David P. Jordan. *Univ. of Illinois Press* 1971 $8.95
  "Jordan's contribution is a serious attempt to place Gibbon in the age in which he lived and worked, the 18th-century, without denigrating his character as an historian or as a scholar. The result is a forthright account of what made Gibbon a typical intellectual product of the 18th-century Enlightenment"—*(Choice)*.

See also Chapter 9, History, Government and Politics—Ancient, this Volume, for other works of Gibbon.

JEFFERSON, THOMAS. 1743–1826.

Thomas Jefferson, third President of the United States (1801–1809), was chairman of the committee that prepared the Declaration of Independence. He wrote and presented the first draft to Congress July 2, 1776 (available in "Jefferson Drafts of the Declaration of Independence" ed. by Gerald D. Force *Acropolis Bks.* 1963 pap. $1.25). He was a man of outstanding curiosity, industry and versatility, and among other activities, the first American architect of his generation. His original designs (237 drawings) in the Coolidge Collection of the Massachusetts Historical Society have again become available with the reprinting of Fiske Kimball's "Thomas Jefferson, Architect" (1916, *Scholarly Press* $14.50). After his retirement from the Presidency, he lived at "Monticello," near Charlottesville, Va., which is still preserved as a memorial. The "Books from the Americana Collections of Thomas Jefferson" have been cooperatively microcarded for a group of American libraries from the originals or their replacements in the Library of Congress: 2,500 Microcards comprising approx. 750 selected titles (*Louisville Free Public Library* $500.00). The Jefferson "Bible," "Life and Morals of Jesus of Nazareth: Extracted Textually from the Gospels of Matthew, Mark, Luke and John" is available (introd. by Henry Wilder Foote 1904. *Folcroft* $25.00). He was fascinated by science, literature and music and was instrumental in founding the University of Virginia (chartered 1819). Although poor at speech-making, he wrote with great ease and vigor.

THE PAPERS OF THOMAS JEFFERSON. Ed. by Julian P. Boyd and others *Princeton Univ. Press* 60 vols. to be published 1950– Vols. 1–18 each $16.00 except Vols. 3, 8, 9, 11 & 18 each $20.00 index to Vols. 1–6 $4.00 index to Vols. 7–12 $4.00 index to Vols. 13–18 $6.00

Vol. 1. 1760–1776 (1950) Vol. 2. 1777–1779 (1950) Vol. 3. 1779–1780 (1951) Vol. 4. 1780–1781 (1951) Vol. 5. 1781 (1952) Vol. 6. 1781–1784 (1952) Vol. 7. 1784–1785 (1953) Vol. 8. 1785 (1953) Vol. 9. 1786 (1954) Vol. 10. 1786–1787 (1954) Vol. 11. 1787 (1955) Vol. 12. 1787–1788 (1955) Vol. 13. Mar.–Oct. 1788 (1956) Vol. 14. Oct. 1788–Mar. 1789 (1958) Vol. 15. Mar.–Nov. 1789 (1958) Vol. 16. Nov. 1789–Aug. 1790 (1961) Vol. 17. July–Dec. 1790 (1965) Vol. 18. Nov. 1790– Mar. 1791 (1971)

The huge storehouse of material, "The Papers of Thomas Jefferson," now being edited, is expected to be many years in production. One of the most monumental editorial tasks ever undertaken in this country, it is "eminently deserving the commendation not only of Americans but of the world, for free people everywhere owe more to Jefferson's fertile brain and active hand than they may realize"—(*Yale Review*).

AUTOBIOGRAPHY. With introd. by Dumas Malone *Putnam* 1959 Capricorn Bks. pap. $1.25

COMPLETE JEFFERSON. Ed. by Saul K. Padover *Bks. for Libraries* 1943 facsimile ed. $42.00

POLITICAL WRITINGS. Ed. by Edward Dumbauld *Bobbs* 1955 $5.00 pap. $1.60

FAMILY LETTERS. Ed. by Edwin M. Betts and James A. Bear *Univ. of Missouri Press* 1966 $11.00

ADAMS-JEFFERSON LETTERS: The Complete Correspondence between Thomas Jefferson and Abigail and John Adams. Ed. by Lester J. Cappon *Univ. of North Carolina Press* 2 vols. 1959 set $12.50; *Simon & Schuster* pap. $5.95

NOTES ON THE STATE OF VIRGINIA. 1785. Ed. by Thomas P. Abernethy *Harper* Torchbks. pap. $1.95; *Peter Smith* $4.00; ed. by William Peden *Univ. of North Carolina Press* 1955 $6.00; *Norton* 1972 pap. $1.95. A description of his native state, first published in Paris.

CRUSADE AGAINST IGNORANCE: Thomas Jefferson on Education. Ed. by Gordon C. Lee *Teachers College* 1961 $4.95 pap. $2.50

PAPERS RELATIVE TO GREAT BRITAIN 1791–1793. 1791. *Burt Franklin* $13.50

CORRESPONDENCE BETWEEN THOMAS JEFFERSON AND PIERRE SAMUEL DU PONT DE NEMOURS, 1798–1817. Ed. by Dumas Malone and trans. from the French by Linwood Lehmann. 1930. *Da Capo* 1970 $17.50; *Burt Franklin* 1972 $16.50

LIFE AND SELECTED WRITINGS. *Modern Library* 1944 $2.95

ON DEMOCRACY. Ed. by Saul K. Padover. 1939. *Greenwood* $15.00

COMPLETE ANAS. Ed. by Franklin B. Samuel. 1903. *Da Capo* $17.50

THE JEFFERSONIAN CYCLOPEDIA. 1900. Ed. by John P. Foley; new introd. by Julian P. Boyd *Russell & Russell* 2 vols. 1967 set $37.50. A comprehensive collection of Jefferson's views on government, politics, law, education, finance, art, religion, freedom, etc.

(With William Dunbar) DOCUMENTS RELATING TO THE PURCHASE AND EXPLORATION OF LOUISIANA. 1904. *Kelley* $12.50

THOMAS JEFFERSON: A Biography in His Own Words. Ed. by *Newsweek* Books Editors. Founding Fathers Ser. *Harper* 1974 $15.00

"Emphasis is understandably on the role played by Jefferson in the founding of the United States, not only as the draftsman of the Declaration of Independence but as a statesman, diplomat, humanist and multifaceted intellectual"—(*Booklist*).

Books about Jefferson

Jefferson and Hamilton. By Claude G. Bowers. *Houghton* 1925 $8.50 1967 pap. $2.65

Declaration of Independence: A Study in the History of Political Ideas. By Carl L. Becker. *Knopf* 1942 $5.95; *Random* Vintage Bks. pap. $1.95; *Peter Smith* $4.00

Thomas Jefferson: American Humanist. By Karl Lehmann. Fwd. by Dumas Malone. 1947. *Univ. of Chicago Press* 1974 pap. $6.50

Thomas Jefferson and American Democracy. By Max Beloff. 1948. *Macmillan* Collier Bks. 1966 pap. $1.25; *Verry* $4.00

Jefferson and His Time. By Dumas Malone. *Little* 5 vols. 1948–1974 Vol. I Jefferson the Virginian: From His birth in 1743 to His Departure for France in 1784 (1948) Vol. 2 Jefferson and the Rights of Man: From His First Ministry to France to the Beginnings of His Struggle with the Federalists (1951) Vol. 3 Jefferson and the Ordeal of Liberty (1969) Vol. 4 Jefferson the President: First Term, 1801–1805 (1970) Vol. 5 Jefferson the President: Second Term, 1805–1809 (1974) each $14.50 pap. each $2.95. This work won the Pulitzer Prize for 1975.

Thomas Jefferson: The Apostle of Americanism. By Gilbert Chinard. *Univ. of Mich. Press* 1957 pap. $2.95

Jeffersonian Tradition in American Democracy. By Charles M. Wiltse. *Farrar, Straus* (Hill & Wang) 1960 pap. $2.65

Lost World of Thomas Jefferson. By Daniel J. Boorstin. *Beacon Press* 1960 pap. $2.95; *Peter Smith* $4.75

Thomas Jefferson and the Development of American Public Education. By James B. Conant. *Univ. of California Press* 1962 $7.50

Jefferson and Madison: The Great Collaboration. By Adrienne Koch. *Oxford* 1964 pap. $2.95; *Peter Smith* $5.00

Thomas Jefferson and the Foundations of American Freedom. By Saul K. Padover. *Van Nostrand-Reinhold* Anvil Bks. 1965 pap. $2.95

Man from Monticello: An Intimate Life of Thomas Jefferson. By Thomas J. Fleming. *Morrow* 1969 $12.50

Thomas Jefferson and the New Nation: A Biography. By Merrill D. Peterson. *Oxford* 1970 $17.50

Jefferson Himself. By Bernard Mayo. *Univ. Press of Virginia* 1970 $6.75 pap. $3.00

Mr. Jefferson, Architect. By Desmond Guinness and Julius T. Sadler, Jr. *Viking* 1973 $14.95

Thomas Jefferson: An Intimate History. By Fawn M. Brodie. *Norton* 1974 $12.50

"The author seeks to draw a portrait of [Jefferson correlating] his public and private lives. . . . In probing the man's personal ambiguities—attitudes toward the church, slavery, women, revolution—she constructs an . . . inner portrait, one that surfaces in his relationships"—(*PW*).

Jefferson, Nationalism and the Enlightenment. By Henry Steele Commager. *Braziller* 1974 $7.50

"Philosophical concepts idealized in the writings of Jefferson and other founders of the nation are scrutinized in essays by a noted historian concerned with the effect of the myths of superiority and uniqueness enunciated by period thinkers"—(*Booklist*).

MADISON, JAMES.   1751–1836.

The fourth president of the United States, Virginia-born James Madison, was the chief architect of the Constitution. His journals provide our principal source of knowledge about the Constitutional Convention of 1787. With Alexander Hamilton and John Jay he wrote the famous

"Federalist Papers," although he later broke with Hamilton when the latter assumed leadership of the Conservative Party. Madison himself was a steadfast disciple of the liberal policies of Thomas Jefferson. When Jefferson became president, Madison was made Secretary of State. Succeeding as president, he faced the intricate problems in American trade relations with Europe that resulted in the War of 1812. In 1817, Madison and his wife, Dolly, the famous hostess, retired to their beautiful home "Montpelier" in Orange County, Va. In his last years Madison served as rector of Jefferson's University of Virginia.

PAPERS. Ed. by William T. Hutchinson, Robert A. Rutland, and William M. Rachal *Univ. of Chicago Press* 9 vols. 1962–74 Vol. I Mar. 16, 1751–Dec. 16, 1779 (1962) Vol. 2 Mar. 20, 1780–Feb. 23, 1781 (1962) Vol. 3 Mar.–Dec. 1781 (1963) Vol. 4 Jan. 1–July 31, 1782 (1965) Vol. 5 Aug. 1–Dec. 31, 1782 (1967) Vol. 6 Jan. 1–Apr. 30, 1783 (1969) Vol. 7 May 3, 1783–Feb. 20, 1784 (1971) Vol. 8 Mar. 10, 1784–Mar. 28, 1786 (1973) Vol. 9 (1974) Vols. I–2 $14.00 Vol. 3 $15.00 Vol. 4 $17.50 Vols. 5–8 each $20.00 Vol. 9 $18.50

COMPLETE MADISON: His Basic Writings. Ed. by Saul K. Padover. 1953. *Kraus* $12.50

NOTES OF DEBATES IN THE FEDERAL CONVENTION OF 1787. Ed. by Adrienne Koch *Ohio Univ. Press* 1966 $13.50; *Norton* 1969 pap. $4.45

THE VIRGINIA REPORT OF 1799–1800, TOUCHING THE ALIEN AND SEDITION LAWS, and VIRGINIA RESOLUTIONS OF DEC. 21, 1789. *Da Capo* $15.00

JOURNAL OF THE FEDERAL CONVENTION. Ed. by E. H. Scott. 1893. *Bks. for Libraries* $19.50

JAMES MADISON: A Biography in His Own Words. Ed. by Merrill D. Peterson. Founding Fathers Ser. *Harper* 1974 $15.00

Books about Madison

The Life of James Madison. By Gaillard Hunt. 1902. *Russell & Russell* 1968 $10.00
The Fourth President: The Life of James Madison. By Irving Brant. *Bobbs* 1941 $12.95
Jefferson and Madison: The Great Collaboration. By Adrienne Koch. *Oxford* 1964 pap. $2.95; *Peter Smith* $5.00
James Madison: A Biography. By Ralph Ketcham. *Macmillan* 1971 $17.50
James Madison. By Harold S. Schultz. Rulers and Statesmen of the World Ser. *Twayne* $6.95

MOZART, WOLFGANG AMADEUS. 1756–1791.

Emily Anderson's edition of the letters of this musical prodigy—who died at 35 and remains a giant of every kind of repertoire—is an "extraordinary piece of scholarship, the result of many years of trained and painstaking research. It is the only complete, wholly unexpurgated edition . . . in any language, since its German predecessors, the Schiedermair edition and less complete ones, were expurgated and drastically cut. The Mozart family were copious, indefatigable letter-writers, expressing themselves with such startling freedom, frankness, and coarseness of humor that every previous editor of their correspondence felt called upon to bowdlerize it. Miss Anderson has given us in English exactly what Mozart and his family wrote, and in doing so has presented a more perfect likeness of Mozart than any biographer has ever drawn"—(Marcia Davenport).

THE LETTERS OF MOZART AND HIS FAMILY. Trans. and ed. by Emily Anderson. 1938. *St. Martin's* 2 vols. 2nd ed. with new material prepared by A. Hyatt King and Monica Carolan 1966 each $21.50 boxed set $40.00

LETTERS. Ed. by Hans Mersman; trans. by M. M. Bozman. 1928. *Dover* 1972 pap. $3.50

MOZART: The Man and the Artist as Revealed in His Own Words. Ed. and trans. by Henry E. Krehbiel. 1926. *Peter Smith* $4.50

Books about Mozart

Mozart. By Marcia Davenport. 1932. *Scribner* rev. ed. 1956 $10.00; *Franklin Watts* lg.-type ed. 1965 $9.95
" 'Mozart,' Marcia Davenport's now-classic biography of the great eighteenth-century composer, was her first book. In the truest sense it was a labor of love. Mozart's life occupied her for years, during which, as she herself relates, she 'retraced every journey he made, saw every dwelling then extant in which he had ever lived, every theatre where his works were first performed, every library and museum where his manuscripts were then to be seen.' . . . A realistic, moving and engrossing biography, which at the same time is a loving and brilliant piece of psychography"—(SR).

Mozart. By Eric Blom. 1935. *Octagon* 1949 $8.50; *Macmillan* Collier Bks. pap. $1.50

Mozart: His Character, His Work. By Alfred Einstein. Trans. by Arthur Mendel and Nathan Broder *Oxford* 1945 $12.50 Galaxy Bks. 1965 pap. $3.95

Mozart and His Times. By Erich Schenk. *Knopf* 1959 $12.50

Mozart: The Man and His Works. Ed. by Christopher Raeburn. 1966. *Vienna House* 1974 pap. $4.95

Mozart: A Documentary Biography. By Otto E. Deutsch. *Stanford Univ. Press* 1966 $20.00

HAMILTON, ALEXANDER.   1757–1804.

The publication of the papers of Hamilton again focus attention on this interesting personality. "No one did more for all Americans," wrote Dorothie Bobbe in the *N.Y. Times*, "yet long-standing misconceptions about his character—his ambition, his supposed aristocratic leanings and opportunism—frequently prevent our appreciation of his extraordinary achievements." After West Indian birth and boyhood, he served in the American Revolution, rising to the rank of Lieutenant-Colonel at not much more than 20 years of age and became General Washington's chief aide. One of his colleagues called him "the pen of our army." His great service to the new Constitution was made by his contributions (with Madison and Jay) to *The Federalist* (1787–88). Our first Secretary of the Treasury, he was killed in the famous duel with Aaron Burr on Weehawken Heights.

WORKS. Ed. by Henry Cabot Lodge. 1904. *Haskell* 12 vols. 1969 set $250.00; *Scholarly Press* 12 vols. 1972 set $225.00

PAPERS. Ed. by Harold C. Syrett and Jacob E. Cooke, Assoc. Ed. *Columbia* 21 vols. 1961– 1974 each $17.50

Vol. 1 1768–1778 (1961) Vol. 2 1779–1781 (1961) Vol. 3 1782–1786 (1962) Vol. 4 1787–May 1788 (1962) Vol. 5 June 1788–Nov. 1789 (1963) Vol. 6 Dec. 1789–Aug. 1790 (1963) Vol. 7 Sept. 1790–Jan. 1791 (1963) Vol. 8 Feb.–July 1791 (1965) Vol. 9 Aug.–Sept. 1791 (1965) Vol. 10 Dec. 1791–Jan. 1792 (1966) Vol. 11 Feb.–June 1792 (1966) Vol. 12 July–Oct. 1792 (1967) Vol. 13 Nov. 1792–Feb. 1793 (1967) Vol. 14 Feb.–June 1793 (1969) Vol. 15 June 1793–Jan. 1794 (1969) Vol. 16 Feb.–July 1794; Vol. 17 Aug.–Dec. 1794; Vol. 18 Jan.–July 1795 (1973) Vol. 19 Aug.–Dec. 1795 (1973) Vol. 20 and 21 (1974)

THE FEDERALIST, 1787–1788. Ed. by Benjamin F. Wright *Harvard Univ. Press* 1961 $12.50; *Dutton* Everyman's $3.95; (Selections) ed. by Henry Steele Commager *AHM Pub.* Crofts Class. 1949 pap. $.85; *Random* Modern Lib. pap. $1.95

THE FEDERALIST PAPERS. Ed. by Clinton Rossiter *New Am. Lib.* Mentor Bks. 1961 pap. $1.95; (Selections) ed. by Ralph Gabriel *Bobbs* 1954 $5.00 pap. $2.25. (*See also Chapter 9, History, Government and Politics—American, this Volume, under "The Federalist Papers."*)

A NEW ACCOUNT OF THE EAST INDIES. Ed. by William Foster. 1930. *DaCapo* $31.50

THE ALEXANDER HAMILTON READER. Ed. by Margaret E. Hall *Oceana* 1957 $6.00

REPORTS. Ed. by Jacob E. Cooke *Harper* Torchbks. pap. $1.95; *Peter Smith* $4.25

ALEXANDER HAMILTON: Selections Representing His Life, His Thought, and His Style. Ed. by Bower Aly *Bobbs* 1957 $1.25

ALEXANDER HAMILTON: A Biography in His Own Words. Ed. by Mary-Jo Kline. Founding Fathers Ser. *Harper* 1973 $15.00

Books about Hamilton

Alexander Hamilton and the Growth of the New Nation (orig. "Alexander Hamilton: Portrait in Paradox"). By John C. Miller. *Harper* Torchbks. 1959 pap. $4.45

Interview in Weehawken: The Burr-Hamilton Duel as Told in the Original Documents. Ed. by Harold C. Syrett and Jean G. Cooke. *Wesleyan Univ. Press* 1960 $7.50

Alexander Hamilton. By Nathan Schachner. *A. S. Barnes* 1961 pap. $2.95

Alexander Hamilton and the Constitution. By Clinton Rossiter. *Harcourt* 1964 $7.50

"A respected political scientist and an authentic conservative, Rossiter appreciates the audacity of his claim [that] 'in a dozen ways that count heavily, this is clearly and perhaps fortunately a Hamiltonian rather than a Jeffersonian country' "—(*LJ*).

Alexander Hamilton: A Profile. Ed. by Jacob E. Cooke. *Farrar, Straus* (Hill & Wang) 1967 $5.95 pap. $2.45. Essays, concerned mostly with his political and economic philosophy, by Claude Bowers, Richard Morris, John C. Miller, Vernon Parrington, Adrienne Koch and others.

Jefferson and Hamilton. By Claude G. Bowers. *Houghton* 1967 $8.50 Sentry Bks. pap. $2.65

Alexander Hamilton. By Stuart G. Brown. Great American Thinkers Ser. *Twayne* $6.95

Alexander Hamilton: The Revolutionary Years. By Broadus Mitchell. *T. Y. Crowell* 1970 $10.00

NAPOLEON I (full French name Napoleon Bonaparte). 1769–1821.

Alan Moorehead has remarked in the *New York Times* that "the Napoleonic library has become so vast in the past 150 years that any new work on the great man . . . has to be of exceptional merit to make a mark. The standard biography by August Fournier is now o.p. Some standard and recent books on Napoleon and his widespread family are listed below.

LETTERS. Trans. by J. M. Thomson *Dutton* Everyman's $3.95

"In the opinion of the best French judges—Sainte-Beuve, for example, Napoleon was a great master of words. He wrote—for the most part, actually, dictated—an enormous quantity of letters, notes, proclamations, Orders of the Day, memoranda, very few of which have ever before been made available in English"—*(LJ)*.

Books about Napoleon

Napoleon. By Jacques Bainville. Trans. by Hamish Miles. 1932. *Kennikat* 1970 $15.00

Napoleon: From Tilsit to Waterloo, 1807–1815. 1935. Trans. from French by J. E. Anderson. *Columbia* 1969 $15.00

Napoleon. By Emil Ludwig. *Liveright* Black and Gold Lib. 1940 $7.95; *Pocket Bks.* 1973 pap. $1.25

Napoleon Bonaparte: His Rise and Fall. By James M. Thompson. *Oxford* 1952 $9.50

Napoleon. By Herbert Butterfield. *Macmillan* Collier Bks. 1962 pap. $.95

Empress Josephine. By Ernest John Knapton. *Harvard Univ. Press* 1963 $10.00

This impartial portrayal adds much to the understanding of Josephine's character and to the manners of her day. The author has evaluated records carefully and quotes liberally from them. "The most rewarding source is letters, notably Napoleon's ardent letters to Josephine and her letters to her children."

Horizon Book of the Age of Napoleon. By J. Christopher Herold and the editors of *Horizon*. *Harper* 1963 $18.95

"Splendidly illustrated" account *(LJ)* of Napoleon's political and military career—which involves the political and military history of the whole Western world.

Napoleon: A Biography with Pictures. By André Maurois. Trans. by D. J. Thomson *Viking* 1964 $6.95

Napoleon and Josephine: The Biography of a Marriage. By Frances Mossiker. *Simon & Schuster* 1964 $6.95

"A fine scholarly immensely readable 'biography of a marriage' which should stand as the definitive study"—*(LJ)*.

Napoleon. By Felix Markham. *New Am. Lib.* Mentor Bks. 1964 pap. $1.25

Napoleon's Battles: A History of his Campaigns. By Henry Lachouque. Trans. by Roy Monkcom *Dutton* 1966 $11.50

"Deserves a wide readership despite [Commandant Lachouque's] romantic attachment to an imagined image of the Emperor and towards the armies he commanded"—*(TLS*, London).

Napoleon's Marshals. By Ronald F. Delderfield. *Chilton* 1966 $5.95

The Bonapartes. By David Stacton. *Simon & Schuster* 1966 $7.95

From Napoleon's mother to present-day descendants, the Napoleonic drama is presented in a "trenchant style . . . as an immense and mordant Molièresque comedy"—*(Time)*.

Napoleon in Russia. By Alan Palmer. *Simon & Schuster* 1967 $7.50. A modest but very readable contribution.

Waterloo: Day of Battle. By David Howarth. *Atheneum* 1968 $7.95

"Re-creating the day as a dramatist rather than as a military analyst he has evoked an exciting panorama [in] the most balanced, realistic and valuable account of the struggle I have yet read"—(John Toland, in the *N.Y. Times*).

Napoleon. By André Castelot. Trans. from the French by Guy Daniels *Harper* 1971 $12.50

Napoleon Bonaparte: An Intimate Biography. By Vincent Cronin. *Morrow* 1972 $12.50; *Dell* 1973 pap. $1.95

"This well-written, eloquent book is a pleasure to read and will probably find many readers . . . Cronin will have rendered a service if he makes us stand back and reconsider our personal assessments of Napoleon, and he may help to dispel some lingering prejudices"—*(TLS*, London).

Napoleon. By David Chandler. *Saturday Review Press* (dist. by Dutton) 1974 $12.50

BEETHOVEN, LUDWIG VAN. 1770–1827.

"For a reluctant writer of letters, Beethoven turned out a considerable number. . . . His vein was characteristically one of desperate seriousness—direct, bludgeoning, uncompromising, intent upon attaining some goal or other: a good fish from the fishmonger or an appropriate sum of money from a publisher or nobleman—broken now and again by punning"—*(LJ)*. The composer emerges from his letters as a man "of great force and vigor, of wonderful verve. He is angry, moody, enraged, abusive, passionate, dejected, humorously buoyant, suspicious or misanthropic, but he is always alive"—(*N.Y. Times*).

LETTERS, 1790–1826. 1868. *Bks. for Libraries* 2 vols. in 1 $19.50; ed. by A. Eaglefield-Hull; trans. from the German by J. S. Shedlock 1926. *Dover* 1972 pap. $4.00

LETTERS: A Critical Edition with Explanatory Notes. Ed. by Alf C. Kalischer. 1909. *Bks. for Libraries* 2 vols. set $42.50

NEW BEETHOVEN LETTERS. Trans. and ed. by Donald W. MacArdle and Ludwig Misch *Univ. of Oklahoma Press* 1957 $15.00

BEETHOVEN: The Man and the Artist as Revealed in His Own Words. Trans. and ed. by H. E. Krehbiel. 1905. *Dover* pap. $1.25; *Peter Smith* $4.00

Books about Beethoven

Beethoven as I Knew Him: A Biography. By Anton Felix Schindler. 1860. Ed. by Donald W. MacArdle; trans. by Constance S. Jolly *Univ. of North Carolina Press* 1966 $12.50; *Norton* 1972 pap. $4.45
"Neither the new and straightforward translation, nor the clear, scholarly contributions of the editor . . . can relieve the stodginess of Schindler's prose. Nevertheless, serious students of Beethoven can hardly be without this book, which also stands as a memorial to MacArdle, who died shortly after delivering the manuscript to his publishers"—(*N.Y. Times*).

Beethoven and His Nine Symphonies. By George Grove. 1898. *Dover* 3rd ed. pap. $2.75; *Peter Smith* 3rd ed. $4.75

Beethoven: A Critical Biography. By Vincent D'Indy. Trans. from the French by Theodore Baker. 1913. *Bks. for Libraries* $11.50; *Da Capo* 1970 $8.50; *Scholarly Press* $9.50

Life of Beethoven. By Alexander Wheelock Thayer. Rev. and ed. by Elliot Forbes *Princeton Univ. Press* 2 vols. rev. ed. 1967 $40.00 pap. $6.95. Brought up to date factually since it appeared in 1921, this classic biography retains its delightfully antiquated style.

Beethoven: Impressions by His Contemporaries. Ed. by O. G. Sonneck. 1926. *Dover* 1966 pap. $2.00; *Peter Smith* $4.25

Beethoven: His Spiritual Development. By John W. Sullivan. 1927. *Knopf* 1960 $4.95; *Random* Vintage Bks. pap. $1.65

Beethoven the Creator. By Romain Rolland. Trans. by Ernest Newman. 1929. *Dover* pap. $3.50; *Peter Smith* $5.50

Beethoven. By Alan Pryce-Jones. 1933. *Dufour* rev. ed. 1968 pap. $2.95; *Macmillan* Collier Bks. 1962 pap. $.95

Beethoven: Biography of a Genius. By George R. Marek. *T. Y. Crowell* (Funk & Wagnalls) 1969 $12.50; *Apollo* 1972 pap. $4.95

Ludwig van Beethoven. By Hans C. Fischer and Eric Kock. *St. Martin's* 1971 $12.50

Creative World of Beethoven. Ed. by Paul H. Lang. *Norton* 1971 $7.95 pap. $2.25

The Interior Beethoven: A Biography of the Music. By Irving Kolodin. *Knopf* 1975 $12.50

CLAY, HENRY. 1777–1852.

"In 1957 the United States Senate recognized Henry Clay, along with his contemporaries, Daniel Webster and John C. Calhoun, as one of its five most outstanding members of all time." As Speaker of the House of Representatives, as Senator, as Secretary of State under the second Adams, and as three-time candidate for the Presidency, Henry Clay of Kentucky was rarely, if ever, during his career far from the center of the stage in American politics. "Clay the public man is revealed in many of his papers. So is Clay the high-living gentleman of Ashland (here are some of his liquor bills), the lawyer busy with land titles and bill collections, the horse trader, the speculator in real estate and the public-spirited citizen promoting higher education"—(*N.Y. Times*). The Clay papers are also important for the other subjects covered; arrangement is chronological; editorial comment is supplied where necessary; location of documents in the original is given.

PAPERS. Ed. by James F. Hopkins and Mary W. M. Hargreaves *Univ. Press of Kentucky* 4 vols. 1959–1973 Vol. I The Rising Statesman, 1797–1814 (1959) Vol. 2 The Rising Statesman, 1815–1820 (1961) Vol. 3 Presidential Candidate, 1821–1824 (1963) Vol. 4 Secretary of State, 1825 (1973) each $20.00. The first four of 10 projected vols.

PRIVATE CORRESPONDENCE. Ed. by Calvin Colton. 1855. *Bks. for Libraries* $20.75

Books about Clay

Henry Clay. By Carl Schurz. 1887. Ed. by John T. Morse, Jr. 1899. *AMS Press* 2 vols. set $29.50; *Ungar* 2 vols. 1968 set $17.50

The Life of Henry Clay. By Glyndon Van Deusen. 1937. *Little* pap. $2.95; *Peter Smith* $5.50
Henry Clay, Spokesman of the New West. By Bernard Mayo. 1937. *Shoe String Press* 1966 $13.00
Henry Clay and the Art of American Politics. By Clement Eaton. *Little* 1957 $5.00 pap. $2.95
Henry Clay and the Whig Party. By George R. Poage. *Peter Smith* 1965 $5.25

CALHOUN, JOHN CALDWELL. 1782–1850.

More than 30,000 Calhoun papers, discovered and organized in the South Caroliniana Library, will form the new edition of the "Papers," the first major compilation of his letters in more than 50 years, the first comprehensive collection of his speeches and other writings in more than a century. The "cast-iron man" who championed the rights of the minority in a democratic government, and supported State Rights, served more than 40 years in the government of the State and the Nation. Born of Scotch-Irish forebears and a native of South Carolina, he was a graduate of Yale, a member of the South Carolina Legislature and the National Congress, became Secretary of War, Secretary of State and Vice President of the United States (1825–1832).

WORKS. Ed. by Richard K. Crallé. 1851–56. *Russell & Russell* 6 vols. 1968 set $85.00

PAPERS. Ed. by Robert L. Meriwether and W. Edwin Hemphill *Univ. of South Carolina Press* 7 vols. 1959–73 Vol. I 1801–1817 (o.p.) Vol. 2 1817–1818 (o.p.) Vol. 3 1818–1819 (1967) Vol. 4 1819–1820 (1969) Vol. 5 1820–1821 (1971) Vol. 6 1821–1822 (1972) Vol. 7 1822–1823 (1973) each $25.00. The first 7 of 12 to 15 projected vols.

CALHOUN: Basic Documents. Ed. by John M. Anderson. 1952. *Bald Eagle Press* $5.00

A DISQUISITION ON GOVERNMENT. *Peter Smith* 1958 $3.00; (and "Selections from the Discourse") ed. by C. Gordon Post *Bobbs* 1953 $5.00 pap. $1.65

Books about Calhoun

John C. Calhoun. By Charles M. Wiltse. 1944–1951. *Russell & Russell* 3 vols. Vol. 1 Nationalist, 1782–1828 Vol. 2 Nullifier, 1829–1839 Vol. 3 Sectionalist, 1840–1850 1968 set $55.00
John C. Calhoun: An American Portrait. By Margaret L. Coit. *Houghton* 1950 $8.50 pap. $4.95
John C. Calhoun. By Richard N. Current. Great American Thinkers Series. *Twayne* $6.95
John C. Calhoun: A Profile. Ed. by John L. Thomas. *Farrar, Straus* (Hill & Wang) 1968 pap. $1.75. A collection of essays by various hands.
The Political Theory of John C. Calhoun. By August O. Spain *Octagon* 1968 $10.50
John C. Calhoun, Opportunist: A Reappraisal. By Gerald M. Capers. *Univ. Presses of Florida* 1968 $6.75; *Quadrangle Bks.* 1969 pap. $2.95

WEBSTER, DANIEL. 1782–1852.

Daniel Webster was born at Franklin, New Hampshire in 1782, was graduated from Dartmouth College in 1801, and was admitted to the bar four years later. In 1816 he moved to Boston where he practiced law and represented Massachusetts in the House of Representatives, vigorously championing that state's mercantile and shipping interests. Elected to the U.S. Senate in 1828, Webster became the country's best known political orator. He favored the Compromise of 1850 and helped secure its passage for which he was reviled as a traitor by many members of his own party. Webster's reputation as an orator is based on his legal and political debates as well as the many public addresses he delivered on patriotic occasions.

PAPERS. Ed. by Charles M. Wiltse and Harold D. Moser *Univ. Press of New England* 1974 Vol. I Correspondence, 1798–1824 $17.50

The first of 14 volumes planned in several series such as correspondence, legal papers, diplomatic papers. "This first volume covers Webster's education (at Dartmouth, in the law, and in local politics), his first election to Congress in 1812, and his stunning emergence as a constitutional lawyer and figure of high national visibility during the next dozen years. It includes a detailed chronology and a calendar of the papers"—(*LJ*).

LETTERS. Ed. by C. H. Van Tyne. 1902. *Greenwood* 1969 $19.75; *Haskell* 1969 lib. bdg. $24.95; *Scholarly Press* $29.75

SPEECHES AND ORATIONS. 1902. *Richard West* $50.00

Books about Webster

Daniel Webster and the Rise of National Conservatism. By Richard N. Current. Library of American Biography *Little* 1962 pap. $2.95
Daniel Webster and a Small College. By John C. Sterling. *Univ. Press of New England* 1965 $10.00

Daniel Webster and the Supreme Court. By Maurice G. Baxter. *Univ. of Massachusetts Press* 1966 $12.50

"This is a thoroughly researched, well-written study of Webster's arguments before the Supreme Court. After describing his development as a lawyer, Baxter devotes a chapter each to Webster's briefs in cases concerning Supreme Court jurisdiction, the contact clause, the rights and uses of property, and the commerce clause"—*(Am. Hist. Rev.)*.

Daniel Webster and the Politics of Availability. By Norman D. Brown. *Univ. of Georgia Press* 1969 $6.50

"In this short and clearly written book Norman D. Brown focuses on the years between the Webster-Hayne debate and the election of 1836, the period in which the 'godlike' Daniel was bitten most severely by the presidential bug"—*(Am. Hist. Rev.)*.

NEWMAN, JOHN HENRY, CARDINAL. 1801–1890. *See Chapter 4, World Religions, this Volume.*

LINCOLN, ABRAHAM. 1809–1865.

The publication of "The Lincoln Papers" (1948, o.p.) opened "a veritable treasury of source materials for the Civil War era" and gave us a deeply moving record of an intensely real man. "Shortly after Lincoln's death all the papers which had accumulated in his office files during the presidency, plus many more which he had brought with him from Springfield, were removed from the White House by his son. From that time until July 26, 1947, when the collection was first opened to the public, these papers were shrouded in secrecy"—(Publisher's note). The selection includes more than 500 vital documents from the monumental collection now in the Library of Congress. Under the terms of the will of Robert Todd Lincoln, who died July 26, 1926, the collection of some 10,000 Lincoln documents, which he had given to the Library of Congress in 1921, was to remain unopened for 21 years after his death. When the collection was opened, David C. Mearns, director of the reference department at the Library started work on these invaluable papers.

The biographies and interpretations of this great President continue to be written. Two noteworthy early ones are now out of print: "Life of Abraham Lincoln" by William Dean Howells (1860 1917) and "Abraham Lincoln" by Lord Charnwood (1916). The books about Lincoln below have been chosen from the mass of writings because of their value as discoveries of fresh material or authoritative earlier sources. "You will hear about many different Abraham Lincolns—for we all create our own from the promptings of our hearts and minds"—(Charles Poore, in the *N.Y. Times*).

COLLECTED WORKS. Ed. by Roy P. Basler; Asst. Eds. Marion Dolores Pratt and Lloyd A. Dunlap *Rutgers Univ. Press* 9 vols. 1953 set $115.00

FAMOUS SPEECHES. 1935. *Bks. for Libraries* facs. ed. $7.75

SPEECHES AND WRITINGS. Ed. by Roy P. Basler. 1946. *Kraus* $27.00

SELECTED WRITINGS AND SPEECHES. Ed. by T. Harry Williams *Hendricks House* 1943 $3.50

SELECTED SPEECHES, MESSAGES, AND LETTERS. Ed. by T. Harry Williams *Holt* (Rinehart) 1957 pap. $1.75

THE LIFE AND WRITINGS. Ed. by Philip Van Doren Stern and Allan Nevins *Random* Modern Lib. Giants 1942 $4.95

FOUR SPEECHES HITHERTO UNPUBLISHED OR UNKNOWN. Introd. by E. W. Wiley. 1927. *Kraus* $4.00

THE WIT AND WISDOM OF ABRAHAM LINCOLN. *Peter Pauper Press* vest-pocket ed. $1.95; *Revell* 1965 $1.95

THE LINCOLN-DOUGLAS DEBATES OF 1858. Ed. by Robert Johannsen *Oxford* 1965 pap. $2.95

THE POLITICAL THOUGHT OF ABRAHAM LINCOLN. Ed. by Richard N. Current. American Heritage Ser. *Bobbs* 1967 $7.50 pap. 3.25

COLLECTED POETRY. *Southern Illinois Univ. Press* 1972 $5.00

Books about Lincoln

Life of Lincoln. By William H. Herndon. 1889. Abr. ed. by David F. Hawkes. *Bobbs* 1971 $7.50 pap. $2.95; (with title "Abraham Lincoln") *Harcourt* Harvest Bks. 1974 pap. 5.95. The savagely attacked life by Lincoln's law partner.

Abraham Lincoln: A History. By John G. Nicolay and John Hay. Originally pub. in 10 vols. 1890. Ed. and abr. by Paul M. Angle *Univ. of Chicago Press* 1966 $10.00 pap. $3.45

The Life of Abraham Lincoln. By Ida M. Tarbell. 1908. *Richard West* 2 vols. 1973 $45.00

Abraham Lincoln: The Prairie Years and the War Years. By Carl Sandburg. *Harcourt* 6 vols. 1926–39 boxed $120.00; definitive 1-vol. abr. ed. 1954 $12.95; *Dell* 3 vols. pap. each $.75 boxed set $2.95 *(see also Sandburg's main entry, this Chapter)*

Lincoln Papers: The Story of the Collection with Selections to July 4, 1861. By David C. Mearns. 1948. *Kraus* 2 vols. in 1, 1968 $22.00

The Emergence of Lincoln. By Allan Nevins. Ordeal of the Union Series. *Scribner* 2 vols. 1950 Vol. I Douglas, Buchanan and Party Chaos, 1857–1859 Vol. 2 Prologue to Civil War, 1859–1861 each $15.00

Lincoln: A Picture Story of His Life. By Stefan Lorant. 1952. *Norton* 1969 $10.00

Abraham Lincoln: A Biography. By Benjamin Platt Thomas. *Knopf* 1952 $8.95; *Random* Modern Library 1968 $4.95

Abraham Lincoln. By Herbert Agar. 1952. Makers of History Ser. *Shoe String Press* 1965 $4.00

Life of Abraham Lincoln: An Illustrated Biography. By Stefan Lorant. 1954. *New Am. Lib.* Mentor Bks. pap. $.95. Compact yet comprehensive.

The Day Lincoln Was Shot. By Jim Bishop. *Harper* 1955 $7.95 Perennial Lib. 1964 pap. $.95

Lincoln, the President: Springfield to Gettysburg. By James Garfield Randall. 1955. *Peter Smith* 2 vols. set $11.00. Randall, who died in 1953, was the undisputed academic authority on Lincoln.

Lincoln, the Liberal Statesman. By James Garfield Randall. *Peter Smith* $4.75

Mr. Lincoln. By James Garfield Randall. Ed. by Richard N. Current *Peter Smith* $4.75

Six Months with Lincoln in the White House. By F. B. Carpenter. Ed. by John Crosby Freeman *Century House Americana* 1961 $6.00. An abridged edition of the book subtitled "The Inner Life of Lincoln" (1869. *Richard West* 1973 $35.00) which went through 16 editions. Written by the author-artist who painted "The First Reading of the Emancipation Proclamation" now hanging in the Capitol.

Citizen of New Salem. By Paul Horgan. *Farrar, Straus* 1962 $3.75. Lincoln's years of self-discovery.

Prelude to Greatness: Lincoln in the 1850's. By Don E. Fehrenbacher. *Stanford Univ. Press* 1962 $7.50 pap. $2.75

Lincoln and the Negro. By Benjamin Quarles. *Oxford* 1962 $8.95. An examination of Lincoln's changing views.

Statesmanship of the Civil War. By Allan Nevins. *Macmillan* Collier Bks. enl. ed. 1962 pap. $.95

The Lincoln Nobody Knows. By Richard N. Current. *Farrar, Straus* (Hill & Wang) 1963 pap. $2.45

Abraham Lincoln. By D. W. Brogan. *Schocken Bks.* 1963 pap. $1.75; *Richard West* 1973 $10.00

Mr. Lincoln and the Negroes: The Long Road to Equality. By William O. Douglas. *Atheneum* 1963 $4.95

Lincoln in Photographs: An Album of Every Known Pose. By Charles Hamilton and Lloyd Ostendorf. *Univ. of Oklahoma Press* 1963 $25.00. Some 119 photographs of Lincoln with 108 previously unpublished portraits of his contemporaries.

Two Roads to Sumter. By William and Bruce Catton. *McGraw-Hill* 1963 pap. $2.95. The "two roads" of Abraham Lincoln and Jefferson Davis to the Civil War.

Lincoln and the First Shot. By Richard N. Current. Critical Periods of History Ser. *Lippincott* 1964 pap. $2.45 "An excellent basic Civil War book" (*LJ*) by one of the foremost Lincoln scholars of our generation.

Lincoln and the Gettysburg Address: Commemorative Papers. Ed. by Allan Nevins *Univ. of Illinois Press* 1964 $2.95. Papers and poems presented in Washington in 1963 by Reinhold Niebuhr, John Dos Passos, Robert Lowell, Senator Paul H. Douglas, David C. Mearns and Arthur Lehman Goodhart.

Lincoln's Preparation for Greatness: The Illinois Legislative Years. By Paul Simon. *Univ. of Illinois Press* 1965 pap. $2.95

A Portion of that Field: The Centennial of the Burial of Lincoln. *Univ. of Illinois Press* 1967 $3.50. Contributions by Gwendolyn Brooks, Otto Kerner, Allan Nevins, Paul M. Angle, Mark Van Doren, Paul H. Douglas, Bruce Catton and Adlai Stevenson.

Lincoln's Plan of Reconstruction. By William B. Hesseltine. *Quadrangle Bks.* 1967 pap. $1.95; *Peter Smith* $4.00

See also Biography Section, this Chapter, under Sandburg, Carl, and Chapter 9, History, Government and Politics—American, Section on Civil War, this Volume.

RUSKIN, JOHN. 1819–1900. *See Chapter 16, Literary Biography and Autobiography, Reader's Adviser, Vol. 1.*

GRANT, U(LYSSES) S(IMPSON). 1822–1885.

Grant's "Personal Memoirs" (1885–1886, rev. with annot. and copious notes by Frederick D. Grant 1909 2 vols. o.p.) was written when he had retired and was in his last sickness. It ranks among the best of military autobiographies. The work showed a great gift of writing, presenting the life of a key figure in those crucial years. It was published in two volumes by Mark Twain's publishing firm, *Charles L. Webster and Co.*, and after its publication quickly ran to an enormous sale, said to have been the largest nonfiction sale of American publishing history. Grant's style has recently been compared to Churchill's (*q.v.*): "Here we find the sonorous, amiable periods suddenly punctuated by a wry crack. Perhaps this is accounted for by the similarity of the two careers, since both greatly gifted men had the experience, in the prime of life, of being put on the shelf—presumably forever"—(*SR*).

PAPERS. Ed. with introd. by John Y. Simon; prefs. by Bruce Catton and Allan Nevins *Southern Illinois Univ. Press* 5 vols. 1967–1973 Vol. 1 1837–1861 (1967) Vol 2 Apr.–Sept. 1861 (1969) Vol. 3 Oct. 1, 1861–Jan. 7, 1862 (1970) Vol. 4 Jan. 8–Mar. 31, 1862 (1972) Vol. 5 Apr. 1–Aug. 31, 1862 (1973) each $15.00. The first five of a projected 15 volume definitive collection; some 80 percent of the letters have never before been published.

PERSONAL MEMOIRS. Ed. by E. B. Long. 1952. *AMS Press* 2 vols. in 1 $30.00; *Grosset* Univ. Lib. pap. $2.95; *Peter Smith* abr. ed. $6.00

LETTERS OF ULYSSES S. GRANT TO HIS FATHER AND HIS YOUNGEST SISTER, 1857–1878. Ed. by J. G. Cramer, his nephew. 1912. *Kraus* $6.50

LETTERS TO A FRIEND. Ed. by James G. Wilson. 1897. *AMS Press* $6.00

Books about Grant

General Grant. By Matthew Arnold. 1887. With Mark Twain's "A Rejoinder." Ed. by John Y. Simon *Southern Illinois Univ. Press* 1966 $4.25

Captain Sam Grant. By Lloyd Lewis. *Little* 1950 $10.95. "The finest study of Grant's early years yet written"; painstaking documentation.

A Stillness at Appomattox. By Bruce Catton. *Doubleday* 1953 $6.95; *Pocket Bks.* pap. $1.50 (*See Chapter 9, History, Government and Politics—American, this Volume, for comment*).

U. S. Grant and the American Military Tradition. By Bruce Catton. *Little* 1954 $5.00 pap. $2.95. A straightforward, sympathetic biography (*see also Chapter 9, History, Government and Politics—American, this Volume*).

Ulysses S. Grant: Politician. By William B. Hesseltine. *Ungar* American Classics Ser. 1957 $11.00

Grant Moves South. By Bruce Catton. *Little* 1960 $10.95

Ulysses S. Grant. By J. A. Carpenter. Rulers & Statesmen of the World Ser. *Twayne* $6.95

Grant Takes Command. By Bruce Catton. *Little* 1969 $10.00

The Last Campaign: Grant Saves the Union. By Earl Schenck Miers. Great Battles of History Ser. *Lippincott* 1972 $7.95

"This is the study of people and not of forces . . . concentrated heavily upon four principals—Lincoln, Grant, Lee, and Davis. For the first three he showed admiration and compassion . . . With Davis, Miers is not so generous"—(*Journal of American History*).

ADAMS, HENRY (BROOKS). 1838–1918. *See Chapter 16, Literary Biography and Auto-biography*, Reader's Adviser, *Vol. 1*.

HOLMES, OLIVER WENDELL, JR. 1841–1935.

Mr. Justice Holmes, the American jurist, was born in Boston, the son of Oliver Wendell Holmes (*q.v.*, Reader's Adviser, *Vol. 1*, 1809–1894). He graduated from Harvard (A.B. 1861, LL.B. 1866), and served with distinction in the Union Army in the Civil War. He was professor of law at the Harvard Law School, Chief Justice of the Supreme Court of Massachusetts and Associate Justice of the U.S. Supreme Court (1902–1932). In addition to letters, diaries, speeches and judicial decisions, he was the author of "The Common Law" (1881, *Little* rev. ed. 1923 $12.50 pap. $2.45). "Touched with Fire: Civil War Letters and Diary of Oliver Wendell Holmes, Jr. 1861–1864" (ed. by Mark DeWolfe Howe, 1946) is now o.p. His dissenting opinions, "The Dissenting Opinions of Mr. Justice Holmes" (1929, o.p.), "many of them masterpieces of clear, forceful legal writing, were hailed by the nation's liberals," and he became known as "the great dissenter."

In 1967 Mark DeWolfe Howe, Holmes' biographer and frequent editor, died suddenly, leaving us the first two volumes (*see below*) of what was to be a full-length definitive biography. Professor Howe's long and devoted relationship with Justice Holmes had begun in 1933 when, fresh out of law school, he went to work for the Associate Supreme Court Justice. Of this experience, he later wrote in the *N.Y. Times*: "Those young men who went to Holmes, in the example of their employer, learned that professional capacity achieves the highest fruitfulness only when it is combined with energy of character and breadth of learning. For the first time, in other words, they saw their professional competence in perspective." (Howe became an authority on Constitutional law and was Harvard's first Charles Warren Professor in the History of American Law. He was an early and active opponent of the late Senator Joseph McCarthy.)

COLLECTED LEGAL PAPERS. *Peter Smith* $5.00

REPRESENTATIVE OPINIONS OF MR. JUSTICE HOLMES. Comp. by Alfred Lief. 1931. Greenwood 1972 $14.50

OCCASIONAL SPEECHES OF JUSTICE OLIVER WENDELL HOLMES. Comp. by Mark DeWolfe Howe *Harvard Univ. Press* 1962 $5.50. "Chance utterances of faith and doubt," as Holmes termed them.

THE HOLMES READER. Ed. by Julius J. Marke *Oceana* 1964 $6.00 pap. $2.50. Life, writings, speeches and judicial decisions.

(With Frederick Pollock) THE HOLMES-POLLOCK LETTERS: The Correspondence of Mr. Justice Holmes and Sir Frederick Pollock, 1874–1932. Ed. by Mark DeWolfe Howe *Harvard Univ. Press* 2nd ed. 1961 $13.50

(With Harold J. Laski) THE HOLMES-LASKI LETTERS: The Correspondence of Mr. Justice Holmes and Harold J. Laski, 1916–1935. 1953. Abr. ed. by Alger Hiss *Atheneum* 2 vols. 1963 pap. each $2.65

JUSTICE OLIVER WENDELL HOLMES: His Book Notices and Uncollected Letters and Papers. Ed. by Harry C. Shriver 1936. *DaCapo* 1973 $12.50

Books about Holmes

Justice Oliver Wendell Holmes: A Biography. By Silas Bent. 1932. *AMS Press* 1969 $14.50
Yankee from Olympus: Justice Holmes and His Family. By Catherine Drinker Bowen. *Little-Atlantic* 1944 o.p.
Justice Oliver Wendell Holmes. By Mark DeWolfe Howe. *Harvard Univ. Press* 2 vols. Vol I The Shaping Years, 1841–1870 (1957) Vol. 2 The Proving Years, 1870–1882 (1963) each $8.50
Mr. Justice Holmes and the Supreme Court. By Felix Frankfurter. *Atheneum* 2nd ed. 1965 pap. $1.25 Two well-known studies of Holmes again available: Frankfurter's 1938 series of Harvard lectures and the biographical essay for the 1944 *Dictionary of American Biography*.

GAUGUIN, PAUL. 1848–1903.

One of the most celebrated rebels from bourgeois life, and one of the most seductive examples of amateur turned professional, is Paul Gauguin, who until his mid-30's was a banker comfortably settled in Paris with his wife and children. Painting was his hobby. The story of how his hobby became his life, his flight to Tahiti and the deprivations he suffered for the sake of his painting has been a favorite subject of novels and film. His youngest son, Pola, who was two years old when his parents separated and who saw his father only once five years afterwards when Gauguin visited his family in Denmark, wrote "My Father, Paul Gauguin" (1937, o.p.).

INTIMATE JOURNALS. Trans. by Van Wyck Brooks *Liveright* 1970 pap. $2.25

NOA NOA: A Journal of the South Seas. 1924. *Farrar, Straus* 1957 pap. $1.95. His life in the South Pacific, important for its discussion of his aesthetic principles.

Books about Gauguin

The Moon and Sixpence. By W. Somerset Maugham. 1919. *Pocket Bks.* pap. $1.25
Gauguin's Paradise Lost. By Wayne Andersen. *Viking* 1971 Compass Bks. 1974 pap. $3.95
Gauguin and the Pont-Aven School. By Wladyslawa Jaworska. *N.Y. Graphic Soc.* 1972 $35.00
"The attempt to adjudicate the complicated issues surrounding the individual and collective contributions of Gauguin and his associates at Pont-Aven is seriously pursued and carefully documented"—(*Choice*).
Gauguin. By Daniel Wildenstein and Raymond Cogniat. Great Impressionists Ser. *Doubleday* 1974 $9.95

VAN GOGH, VINCENT. 1853–1890.

Van Gogh joined his younger brother Théo in Paris in 1886 and met Toulouse-Lautrec, Degas and Gauguin. He began then to paint the brilliant pictures that made him famous. In ill health, he went to Arles two years later and his art developed rapidly before his attacks of insanity and finally, his death. Irving Stone novelized his life in "Lust for Life" and edited "Dear Théo," 600 letters to his younger brother, in which he revealed himself. The "Complete Letters" is a monumental work, "edited with care and devotion, presented in attractive format, and destined to be the prime source for all writings about Vincent van Gogh hereafter"—(Sheldon Cheney, in *SR*).

DEAR THÉO: The Autobiography of Vincent Van Gogh. Ed. by Irving Stone. 1937. *Doubleday* 1958 $5.00; *New Am. Lib.* Signet Bks. 1969 pap. $1.50

COMPLETE LETTERS: With Reproductions of all the Drawings in the Correspondence. Trans. by C. de Dood *N.Y. Graphic Soc.* 3 vols. 1958 ltd. ed. lea. $300.00 slipcased $75.00

"Nothing that one can say about the quality of these letters is enough. They are the most important documents connected with modern art in existence"—(*New Statesman*).

VAN GOGH, A SELF-PORTRAIT: The Letters of Vincent van Gogh. Sel. by W. H. Auden; trans. by Cornelius de Dood and Mrs. J. van Gogh-Bonger *N.Y. Graphic Soc.* 1961 $12.50. Over 140 letters revealing his life as an artist; 8 paintings and 28 drawings.

LETTERS. Ed. with introd. by Mark Roskill *Antheneum* 1963 pap. $3.95

Books about van Gogh

Vincent van Gogh. By Osjkar Hagen. *Gordon Press* $28.00
Lust for Life: A Novel of Vincent van Gogh. By Irving Stone. 1934. *Doubleday* 1954 $7.95; *Simon & Schuster* (Washington Square) 1972 pap. $.95
Van Gogh. By Solveig Williams. *St. Martin's* 1972 pap. $4.95
Stranger on the Earth: A Psychological Biography of Vincent Van Gogh. By Albert J. Lubin. *Holt* 1972 $8.95
Van Gogh. By Jacques Lassaigne. Great Impressionists Ser. *Doubleday* 1974 $9.95

HARRIS, FRANK (JAMES THOMAS). 1856–1931. *See Chapter 16, Literary Biography and Autobiography,* Reader's Adviser, *Vol. I.*

WASHINGTON, BOOKER T(ALIAFERRO). 1856–1915.

This son of a mulatto slave and a white man became the leading educator of Negroes, an able public speaker in the interests of his work and an inspiration to Americans of all colors. After graduation from the Hampton Normal and Industrial Institute he taught there and was chosen to found the coeducational Tuskegee Normal and Industrial Institute in Alabama. Highly respected both as an educator and as a spokesman for the Negro, he was granted honorary degrees from both Harvard and Dartmouth and was officially received by the King of Denmark. Of his dozen books, two are autobiographies: "Up From Slavery," which has been translated into 18 languages, and "My Larger Education" (1911, *Mnemosyne* pap. $3.50) which describes his philosophy of education and of life.

PAPERS. Ed. by Louis R. Harlan, John W. Blassingame and Pete Daniel *Univ. of Illinois Press* 3 vols. 1972–74 Vol. I The Autobiographical Writings Vol. 2 1860–1889 Vol. 3 1889–95 Vols. 1–2 each $15.00, Vol. 3 $17.50

UP FROM SLAVERY. 1901. *Assoc. Booksellers* Airmont Bks. pap. $.60; *Bantam* 1970 pap. $.75; *Corner House* 1971 $9.50; *Dell* pap. $.75; *Dodd* 1972 $5.50; *Doubleday* 1933 $5.50; *Heritage Conn.* deluxe ed. $12.50; *Western Islands* 1965 pap. $1.00

WORKING WITH THE HANDS: Being a Sequel to "Up From Slavery." 1904. *Arno* 1970 $11.00; *Negro Univ. Press* $13.75

FUTURE OF THE AMERICAN NEGRO. 1899. *Greenwood* $9.25; *Haskell* 1969 $12.95; *Metro Bks.* 1969 $10.00; *Negro Univ. Press* $9.25

NEGRO IN THE SOUTH: His Economic Progress in Relation to His Moral and Religious Development. 1907. *AMS Press* $10.00; *Metro Bks.* 1972 $11.50

FREDERICK DOUGLASS. 1907. *Argosy-Antiquarian* 1969 $10.00; *Greenwood* $14.25; *Haskell* 1969 $16.95; *Negro Univ. Press* $14.25

NEGRO IN BUSINESS. 1907. *AMS Press* 1971 $12.50; *Johnson Reprint* $17.50; *Metro Bks.* 1969 $16.00

STORY OF THE NEGRO: The Rise of the Race from Slavery. 1909. *Negro Univ. Press* 2 vols. $25.00; *Peter Smith* 2 vols. $12.00

Books about Washington

Booker T. Washington's Own Story of His Life and Work: The Original Autobiography Brought up to Date with a Complete Account of Dr. Washington's Sickness and Death. By Albon L. Holsey. 1915. *Negro Univ. Press* $19.00

Booker T. Washington: The Master Mind of a Child of Slavery. By Frederick E. Drinker. 1915. *Negro Univ. Press* $14.75

Booker T. Washington and the Negro's Place in American Life. By Samuel R. Spencer, Jr. Introd. by Oscar Handlin. Library of American Biography Ser. *Little* 1955 $5.00 pap. $2.95. Compact and readable account of this educator's influence on America, Negro education and the life of his time.

Booker T. Washington and His Critics: The Problems of Negro Leadership. Ed. by Hugh Hawkins. *Heath* 1962 pap. $2.50 2nd ed. 1974 pap. $2.95

Negro Thought in America, 1880–1915: Racial Ideologies in the Age of Booker T. Washington. By August Meier. *Univ. of Michigan Press* 1963 $8.95 pap. $2.25

Booker T. Washington: The Making of a Black Leader, 1856–1901. By Louis R. Harlan. *Oxford* 1972 $10.95

"[This] book is a thoughtful re-evaluation of one of the most important black leaders who emerged in the 20th century and is highly recommended to both academicians and general readers. It adds vividly to our understanding of the complexities of racial ideology"— (*America*).

WILSON, WOODROW.   1856–1924.   (Nobel Peace Prize 1919)

World War II and the founding of the United Nations caused a revival of interest in Woodrow Wilson and his League of Nations. At the library of Princeton University, where he had served as president, the project of compiling and publishing his papers has been underway under the editorship of Arthur S. Link (*see below*). This is the first such massive work covering a 20th-century American statesman. Mr. Link has had access to Ray Stannard Baker's (1870–1946) invaluable collection of documents which were used in the latter's "Woodrow Wilson: Life and Letters" (1927–1940 *Greenwood* 8 vols. 1968 set $222.00) for which Baker, the Amherst essayist "David Grayson" as well as Wilson's personal friend and authorized biographer, received the 1940 Pulitzer Prize.

The first volume of the "Papers" includes a letter by Wilson the law student at the University of Virginia, who wrote: "As for myself, I suspect that one might find out almost, if not quite, as much about me from my letters as by associating with me, for I am apt to let my thoughts and feelings slip more readily from the end of my pen than from the end of my tongue." Still in print are his studies of American politics, "Congressional Government" (1885, *Peter Smith* $4.50) and "Constitutional Government" (1908. *Columbia* 1961 pap. $1.75), as well as "Division and Reunion: 1829–1889" (1893. *Peter Smith* $4.00). His "History of the American People" (1902. *Finch Press* 10 vols. 1918, in prep.) deals with people rather than with political events.

Papers. Ed. by Arthur S. Link and others. *Princeton Univ. Press* 1966–   Vol. 1 1856–1880 Vol. 2 1881–1884 Vol. 3 1884–1885 Vol. 4 1885 Vol. 5 1885–1888 Vol. 6 1888–1890 Vol. 7 1890–1892 Vol. 8 1892–1894 Vol. 9 1894–1896 Vol. 10 1896–1898 Vol. 11 1898–1900 Vol. 12 1900–1901 Vol. 13 o.p. Vol. 14 1901–1902 Vol. 15 1903–1905 Vol. 16 1905–1907 Vols. 1–7, 12, 15–16 each $22.50 Vols. 8–11 each $16.00 Vol. 14 $20.00

Public Papers. Ed. by Ray Stannard Baker and W. E. Dodd. 1925–27. *Kraus* 6 vols. set $120.00

Mere Literature and Other Essays. 1896. *Bks. for Libraries* $9.50; *Richard West* 1973 $9.45

The Case for the League of Nations. Ed. by Hamilton Foley. 1923. *Kennikat* 1967 $8.50; *Kraus* 1969 $10.00

Books about Wilson

Wilson. By Arthur S. Link. *Princeton Univ. Press* 5 vols. 1947–65 Vol. I Road to the White House (1947) $15.00 Vol. 2 The New Freedom (1956) $17.50 Vol. 3 The Struggle for Neutrality, 1914–1915 (1960) $17.50 Vol. 4 Confusions and Crises, 1915–1916 (1964) $16.50 Vol. 5 Campaigns for Progressivism and Peace, 1916–1917 (1965) $17.50. The definitive biography, to be completed with the addition of several more volumes. Professor Link, of Princeton University, is editor-in-chief of the Wilson papers and has written several other books about

Wilson including "Woodrow Wilson: A Brief Biography" (*Franklin Watts* 1972 pap. $2.45).
His "The New Freedom" (*Peter Smith* $4.95) received the Bancroft Prize in 1958.

Woodrow Wilson and the Politics of Morality. By John M. Blum. Library of American
Biography Ser. *Little* 1956 $5.00 1962 pap. $2.95

Woodrow Wilson and the World Settlement. By Ray Stannard Baker. *Peter Smith* 3 vols. 1958 set
$21.00

Mr. Wilson's War. By John Dos Passos. Mainstream of America Ser. *Doubleday* 1962 $7.50.
Covering the time between the presidency of Princeton and his death.

When the Cheering Stopped: The Last Years of Woodrow Wilson. By Gene Smith. Introd. by
Allan Nevins. 1964. *Morrow* 1971 $6.95 pap. $2.95

Thomas Woodrow Wilson: A Psychological Study. By William Bullitt and Sigmund Freud.
1967. *Avon* pap. $1.25

Completed in 1939 and kept in a vault until after Mrs. Wilson's death, this "psychological
analysis" caused a furor upon publication. A collaborative effort by Dr. Freud and the late
American diplomat who resigned as adviser to Wilson in Paris, 1919, its main thesis is that
Wilson suffered from severe personality problems (domination by his father, identification
with Christ) which thwarted his efforts to secure a lasting peace after World War I. The book
was generally criticized for its lack of objectivity and for the omission of much contradictory
evidence. "It is essentially a curiosity, of prime and probably temporary interest only to Freud
scholars"—(*N.Y. Times*).

Woodrow Wilson: The Academic Years. By Henry Wilkinson Bragdon. *Harvard Univ. Press*
1967 $12.50

The result of 28 years of work by a distinguished educator. "Wilson's life achievement and
torment as academic man has no better monument than this full and judicious study"—(*New
Republic*).

Woodrow Wilson: A Profile. Ed. by Arthur S. Link. American Profiles Ser. *Farrar, Straus* (Hill &
Wang) 1968 $5.95 pap. $2.25. An anthology of 14 articles or excerpts written between 1912
and 1929, plus three recent essays.

Woodrow Wilson and World Politics: America's Response to War and Revolution. By N.
Gordon Levin, Jr. *Oxford* 1968 $9.50 pap. 1970 $2.50

"Mr. Levin, in this sophisticated and complex, but unfailingly interesting study, leaves little
doubt that Woodrow Wilson inaugurated a new style and tone in American diplomacy.
Under the ideological banner of liberal internationalism, he insisted that America had a
moral obligation, a liberal mission to keep the 'world safe for democracy' "—(*LJ*). Winner of
the 1969 Bancroft Prize.

Woodrow Wilson: The Early Years. By George C. Osborn. *Louisiana State Univ. Press* 1968
$10.00

Righteous Conquest: Woodrow Wilson and the Evolution of New Diplomacy. By Sidney Bell.
Kennikat 1972 $10.95

"Tracing the origin of Wilson's ideas and their application in Mexico, Latin America, and
Europe, Bell builds a persuasive analysis that is clearly presented and adequately supported
by evidence. His brief is marred, however, by its excessive brevity; and it strangely neglects
the seminal work of N. Gordon Levin, Jr. whose ideas complemented Bell's in a great many
places"—(*LJ*).

Power and Grace: The Life of Mrs. Woodrow Wilson. By Ishbel Ross. *Putnam* 1974 $8.95

ROOSEVELT, THEODORE.   1858–1919.   *See Chapter 9, History, Government and Politics—American, and Chapter 12, Travel and Adventure, this Volume.*

YEATS, WILLIAM BUTLER.   1865–1939.   *See Chapters 7, Modern British Poetry, and
16, Literary Biography and Autobiography,* Reader's Adviser, *Vol. 1; and Chapter 4, Modern
British Drama,* Reader's Adviser, *Vol. 2.*

GANDHI, MOHANDAS K(ARAMCHAND) (also Mahatma Gandhi).   1869–1948.

The great Hindu nationalist leader wrote his "Autobiography" while he was in prison in the
early 20's. It appeared first as weekly articles in the Gujarati magazine *Navajioan* and is his "own
story of himself during the formative period of his early maturity." "It will never be possible to
deify Mohandas Gandhi behind a fine mist of ignorance so long as there are copies of his
autobiography available. For in this remarkable book of self-revelation, Gandhi writes with a
candor about things which no man can permit to a deity. . . . In this story of his 'experiment with
truth,' written about a quarter of a century ago, partly in prison, partly from a sickbed, Gandhi
exposes with characteristic frankness all the frailties he knew he had and some of which he may
have been less well aware"—(*N.Y. Herald Tribune*). In 1969 India was celebrating the centennial of
his birth, with the holding of commemorative exhibitions, lectures and shows of various kinds
throughout the nation.

COLLECTED WORKS. *Int. Pubns. Service* 53 vols. 1958–1974. Now in progress, the 55–60 volume set will contain all that Gandhi wrote and spoke. each $10.00

AUTOBIOGRAPHY: The Story of My Experiences with Truth. Trans. from the original in Gujarati by Mahadev Desai. 1924. *Beacon* 1957 pap. $3.95; *Heinman* 1969 $5.00; *Public Affairs Press* 1948 $6.00

GANDHI READER: A Source Book of His Life and Writing. Ed. by Homer Jack. 1956. *AMS Press* 1970 $25.00

ALL MEN ARE BROTHERS: Life and Thoughts of Mahatma Gandhi. *Columbia* 1969 $10.00; *UNESCO* $6.50; ed. by K. Kripalani *Verry* $2.75

NON-VIOLENCE IN PEACE AND WAR. 1944. *Verry* 2 vols. $9.50

ECONOMIC AND INDUSTRIAL LIFE AND RELATIONS. Ed. by V. B. Kher *Verry* 3 vols. 1957 $13.75

Books about Gandhi

Mahatma Gandhi, the Journalist. By S. N. Bhattacharya. *Asia Pub. House* 1966 $5.00

The Revolutionary Personality: Lenin, Trotsky, and Gandhi. By E. Victor Wolfenstein. *Princeton Univ. Press* 1967 $12.50 pap. 1971 $2.95

Gandhi's Truth: On the Origins of Militant Nonviolence. By Erik H. Erikson. *Norton* 1969 $10.00 pap. $3.95

Gandhi Remembered. By Horace Alexander. *Pendle Hill* 1969 pap. $.70

Mohandas Gandhi. By George Woodcock. Ed. by Frank Kermode *Viking* 1971 $6.50 pap. $1.95

Gandhi the Man. Ed. by Joanne Black and others. *Glide Urban Center Pubns.* 1972 $7.95 pap. $3.95

Mao Tse-Tung and Gandhi: Perspectives on Social Transformation. By Jayantanuya Bandyopadhyaya. *Int. Pubns. Service* 1974 $7.50; *Paragon Reprint* 1973 $6.00

Mahatma Gandhi. By Jawaharlal Nehru. *Asia Pub. House* 1974 $3.95

Mahatma Gandhi: Political Saint and Unarmed Prophet. By Dhananjay Keer. *Int. Pubns. Service* 1974 $17.00

"Among its many excellent features are the wealth of personal information it furnishes about Gandhi which is not generally known, the presentation of his ideas as reflected in his writings, given in running summaries by Keer, and the wide ranging discussion of the Indian political context"—(*Choice*).

See also Chapter 4, World Religions, this Volume.

GIDE, ANDRÉ (PAUL GUILLAUME). 1869–1951. *See Chapter 9, French Literature, Reader's Adviser, Vol. 2, and Chapter 16, Literary Biography and Autobiography, Reader's Adviser, Vol. I.*

WRIGHT, FRANK LLOYD. 1869–1959.

The volumes of Frank Lloyd Wright, America's great architect, are almost all autobiographical and are written with great literary charm and distinction. They set forth his philosophy, which revolutionized private and commercial building both here and abroad. He received the gold medal of the American Institute of Architects in 1948. "Drawings for a Living Architecture" is a glorious tribute, a representative selection of his drawings, which he himself supervised.

AN AUTOBIOGRAPHY. 1932. rev. ed. 1943. *Horizon Press* 1976 $17.50. His life and discussion of his buildings with 20 pages of photographs.

EARLY WORK. 1911. Introd. by Edgar Kaufmann *Horizon Press* 1969 $17.50. The first translation into English from the German in which it was first published. Photographs and plans.

ON ARCHITECTURE. Selected Writings 1894–1940. Ed. by Frederick Gutheim. 1941. *Grosset* Univ. Lib. 1960 pap. $2.45. All the famous concepts expressed in unique, poetic style.

WRITINGS AND BUILDINGS. Sel. by Edgar Kaufmann and Ben Raeburn. 1960. *New Am. Lib.* pap. $3.95. A selection from his writings and designs from the early 1890s to 1959; with 150 illustrations.

THE FUTURE OF ARCHITECTURE. *Horizon Press* 1953 $12.50; *New Am. Lib.* Mentor Bks. pap. $2.95. A collection of his later major writings. Beginning with the widely discussed "Conversation" (1953) in which he explains his aims and contributions, it includes several rare works originally published in separate editions.

AN AMERICAN ARCHITECTURE. Ed. by Edgar Kaufmann. *Horizon Press* 1955 $17.50

THE NATURAL HOUSE. *Horizon Press* 1957 $8.95; *New Am Lib.* Mentor Bks. pap. $2.95. An infinite variety of houses for people of limited means; with practical comments; a restatement of Wright's principles and beliefs.

A TESTAMENT. *Horizon Press* 1957 $17.50; *Avon* 1972 pap. $1.65. Sets forth his memories, his ideas, his hopes for the future.

THE LIVING CITY. *Horizon Press* 1958 $12.50; *New Am. Lib.* Mentor Bks. pap. $2.95. A lyrical and completely rewritten version of his "When Democracy Builds" (1945 o.p.).

DRAWINGS FOR A LIVING ARCHITECTURE. *Horizon Press* 1959 $17.50

SOLOMON R. GUGGENHEIM MUSEUM. *Horizon Press* 1960 $4.95

Books about Wright

> The Shining Brow: Frank Lloyd Wright. By Olgivanna Lloyd Wright (Mrs. Frank Lloyd Wright). *Horizon Press* 1960 $4.50. Mrs. Wright has also written "The Struggle Within" (1955. *Horizon Press* 1971 $5.00 pap. $2.50); "Our House" (*Horizon Press* 1959 $5.95); "The Roots of Life" (*Horizon Press* 1963 $5.50); and "Frank Lloyd Wright: His Life, His Work, His Words" (*Horizon Press* $8.50).
>
> Frank Lloyd Wright. By Vincent Scully, Jr. *Braziller* 1960 $5.95 pap. $2.95
>
> The Imperial Hotel: Frank Lloyd Wright and the Architecture of Unity. By Cary James. *Tuttle* 1968 $8.25. A tribute to the early Tokyo masterpiece, now unfortunately razed in its most original part.
>
> Two Chicago Architects and Their Clients: Frank Lloyd Wright and Howard Van Doren Shaw. By Leonard K. Eaton. *M.I.T. Press* 1971 $10.00 pap. $3.95
>
> Prairie School: Frank Lloyd Wright and His Midwest Contemporaries. By H. Allen Brooks. *Univ. of Toronto Press* 1972 $27.50
> "In this account of the work of the 'Architects of the Prairie School'. . . [Brooks] interweaves the careers of over two dozen architects active in the Middle West in the late nineteenth and early twentieth century"—(*BRD*).

LENIN (born Vladimir Ilyich Ulyanov).   1870–1924.   *See Chapter 9, History, Government and Politics—Modern and World, this Volume.*

CHURCHILL, SIR WINSTON (LEONARD SPENCER). 1874–1965. (Nobel Prize 1953)

Following the death of England's distinguished elder statesman, many books were published both as memorial tributes and commentaries on his long and influential career. In May of 1963 he announced that he would not run again for Parliament, having been in the House of Commons for more than 60 years. It was in 1940 that he became prime minister, holding the reins through the most critical years Britain had ever faced. Voted out in 1945, he and his party were recalled in 1951 and he was once more prime minister, stepping down in 1955 in favor of Anthony Eden. Queen Elizabeth II knighted Churchill, April 24, 1953, and presented him with the insignia of the Most Noble Order of the Garter. He had declined a knighthood proposed by King George VI because he felt so keenly the repudiation of his leadership when the Labor Party was victorious in 1945.

Prime Minister Sir Winston Churchill was awarded the 1953 Nobel Literature Prize (the first statesman to receive it for literature) for his brilliant and monumental war memoirs: "The Second World War." The *N.Y. Times* commented when the first volume of his memoirs was published: "Few books belong to the category of great events, and this is one of them. Few books make history in the sense that the epoch they depict will always live as they saw it. This is such a book." In April 1963, Congress agreed and the late President Kennedy proclaimed Sir Winston the first "honorary citizen" of the United States.

RANDOLPH S(PENCER) CHURCHILL (1911–1968) was at work on the third volume of his father's official biography when he died on June 6, 1968, three years after the death of Sir Winston. "When you are living under the shadow of a great oak tree," Randolph once said, "the small sapling, so close to the parent tree, does not perhaps receive enough light." Randolph did achieve prominence in his own right, however, as his father's principal, and excellent, biographer; as a journalist; as a politician who lost six elections for a seat in the House of Commons; and as a commando who parachuted into Yugoslavia in 1944 to act as liaison officer with Marshal Tito. Other works of Randolph, all o.p., are "The Six Day War" (1967), written with his son, the young Winston, on the Arab-

Israeli conflict; "The Fight for the Tory Leadership" (1964); and "Twenty-One Years" (1965), an account of his early life. His son Winston is author of "First Journey" (1965), describing a student trip to Africa; his sister Sarah (Sir Winston's second daughter) has written a book of poems, "The Empty Spaces" (*Dodd* 1967 $4.00). The success of "Jennie" in 1969 (*see list below*) indicates that Churchills will continue to occupy the literary spotlight for some time to come.

COMPLETE SPEECHES 1897–1963. Ed. by Robert Rhodes James *Bowker* 8 vols. 1975 set $185.00

"All libraries which support and encourage serious research programs and the use of original material will find the work indispensable"—(*Choice*).

MY EARLY LIFE: A Roving Commission. 1930. Introd. by Dorothy Thompson *Scribner* 1941 $7.95 1960 pap. $1.95; *Manor Bks.* 1972 pap. $1.50

AMID THESE STORMS: Thoughts and Adventures. 1932. *Bks. for Libraries* 1972 $12.50

MARLBOROUGH: His Life and Times. 1933. *Kelley* 6 vols. in 3 $125.00; abr. ed. by Henry Steele Commager *Scribner* 1968 $17.50

GREAT CONTEMPORARIES. 1937. *Bks. for Libraries* $14.75; *Univ. of Chicago Press* 1974 $7.95

CHURCHILL IN HIS OWN WORDS: The Years of Adventure. (Orig. "Great Destiny") *Putnam* Capricorn Bks. 1966 pap. $2.25

CHURCHILL IN HIS OWN WORDS: The Years of Greatness (orig. "Blood, Sweat and Tears"). *Putnam* Capricorn Bks. 1966 pap. $1.95

THE SECOND WORLD WAR. *Houghton* 6 vols. 1948–53 Vol. I The Gathering Storm Vol. 2 Their Finest Hour Vol. 3 The Grand Alliance Vol. 4 The Hinge of Fate Vol. 5 Closing the Ring Vol. 6 Triumph and Tragedy each $8.50 boxed set $50.00; *Bantam* 6 vols. pap. each $2.25

MEMOIRS OF THE SECOND WORLD WAR. Ed. by Denis Kelly *Houghton* 6 vols. 1959 each $10.00

HEROES OF HISTORY: A Selection of Churchill's Favorite Historical Characters. Ill. by Robert MacLean *Dodd* 1968 $4.95. Appropriate text has been selected from his four-volume "History of the English-Speaking Peoples." Profiles include Alfred the Great, Joan of Arc, Henry VIII, Washington, Lincoln, Queen Victoria and Churchill himself.

Books about Churchill

The Churchills: The Story of a Family. By Alfred Leslie Rowse. 1958. *Greenwood* 1974 $20.00
"The symphony of language, the well-turned anecdote, the sweep of a great family's history is all there"—(Ray A. Billington, Henry E. Huntington Library). "Rowse writes with unfailing verve and brilliance"—(Henry Steele Commager). One volume ed. of "The Churchills" (1956, o.p.) and "The Early Churchills" (1958 *Greenwood* $19.00).

Winston Churchill: A Biography. By Lewis Broad. 1963. *Greenwood* 2 vols. 1972 $40.00

Winston S. Churchill. By Randolph S. Churchill. *Houghton* 3 vols. 1966–71 Vol. I Youth, 1874–1900 (1966) $10.00 companion vols. containing the Churchill papers Pt. I 1874–1896 $12.50 Pt. 2 1896–1900 (1967) $12.50; Vol. 2 Young Statesman, 1901–1914 (1967) $10.00 companion vols. Pt. I 1901–1907 $15.00 Pt. 2 1907–1911 $15.00 Pt. 3 1911–1914 $15.00; Vol. 3 The Challenge of War, 1914–1916 By Martin Gilbert (1971) $15.00 companion vols. Pt. I July 1914–Apr. 1915 (1973) Pt. 2 May 1915–Dec. 1916 set $37.50
Due to the death of Randolph Churchill in 1968, Martin Gilbert, historian, Oxford scholar and research assistant to the author, has been chosen to complete the last three volumes. Of "Youth" Charles Poore said: It "will rivet our delighted attention for a long time. . . . Immensely rich revelation and surprises. . . . We have here the wildly explosive story of a very young man in a tearing hurry. He wants to be illustrious. He will be great." The companion volumes "show Winston as he really was, not as hagiographers would have us believe he was. But they have a secondary virtue in their portrayal of England in the plenitude of power"—(Drew Middleton, in the *N.Y. Times*).

Churchill: Taken From the Diaries of Lord Moran: The Struggle for Survival 1940–1965. By Churchill's private physician and constant companion after 1940. *Houghton* 1966 $10.00

Churchill and Beaverbrook: A Study in Friendship and Politics. By Kenneth Young. *James H. Heineman* 1967 $6.50

An account of the 55-year-old friendship based on the largely unpublished Beaverbrook archives. "Adds little new historical knowledge, but the narrative is well constructed and of sustained interest"—(*LJ*). "Full of fascinating detail and anecdotes"—(*Choice*).

Churchill. Ed. by Martin Gilbert. Great Lives Observed Ser. *Prentice-Hall* 1967 pap. $1.95
A view of Churchill through his papers and speeches, contemporaries' appraisals and assessments by recent historians. "A well-rounded collection, giving a good over-all perspective"—(*PW*). Mr. Gilbert teaches at Merton College, Oxford.

Churchill and the Montgomery Myth. By Reginald W. Thompson. *Evans* (dist. by Lippincott) 1968 $5.95
"For those who like revisionist histories, especially those who fiercely attack seemingly secure myths, and for those who enjoy military histories, this work will be immensely appealing"—(*LJ*).

Winston Churchill. By John Connell. *British Bk. Centre* $2.95 pap. $1.20

Bibliography of the Works of Sir Winston Churchill. Ed. by Frederick Woods. *Univ. of Toronto Press* 2nd ed. 1969 $27.50

Jennie: The Life of Lady Randolph Churchill: The Romantic Years 1854–1895. By Ralph G. Martin. 1969. *New Am. Lib.* 1970 pap. $1.75
Winston Churchill's glamorous mother was the American, Jennie Jerome. This is her story, in which "not only Jennie, but the world in which she lived dance before the reader in magnificent display. . . . The best documented and most readable account possible of this fascinating woman"—(Martin Gilbert, in *Book World*).

Winston Churchill 1874–1965. By Martin Gilbert. *Grossman* 1969 $3.95

War Ministry of Winston Churchill. By Maxwell P. Schoenfeld. *Iowa State Univ. Press* 1972 $9.95
"The author analyzes Churchill's wartime service from the standpoint of administrative history. [He sees him as] a man who placed political values ahead of military values: who was, contrary to popular belief, a good administrator and a faithful follower of the Chiefs of Staff in military matters"—(Publisher's note).

Winston Churchill. By Victor L. Albjerg. Rulers and Statesmen of the World Ser. *Twayne* 1973 $6.95

Churchill as War Lord. By Robert Lewin. *Stein & Day* 1974 $10.00
"Lewin has prepared a most estimable study of Churchill as a war leader . . . [This splendid study] evinces a wealth of detail and anecdote. It is scholarly writing at its best"—(*LJ*).

Winston Churchill. By Henry Pelling. *Dutton* 1974 $12.95
"[This] is the best birth-to-death biography of Churchill that has yet been written, although in its forthright, scrupulous way it is too much an account of the events of the life—setting the record straight—to do justice to the complexities, shadows and depths of the man himself"—(*N.Y. Times*).

See also Chapter 9, History, Government and Politics—British Commonwealth, this Volume.

HOOVER, HERBERT (CLARK). 1874–1964.

The first volume of the late President Hoover's "Memoirs" is an account of his early life from his birth in a Quaker family in Iowa, his adventurous life as an engineer and relief administrator in World War I to 1920 when he became Secretary of Commerce in the Harding cabinet. The second volume covers many public issues of the years 1920 to 1933 when he served eight years as Secretary of Commerce and four as President. The third volume is a defense of his Administration, an answer to the many who talked of "Hoover's depression." The *N.Y. Times* called the series "fascinating." Mr. Hoover's "The Ordeal of Woodrow Wilson" (1968, o.p.) is an important study. "An American Epic" is an account of American action to relieve suffering overseas during and after the World Wars.

PUBLIC PAPERS OF THE PRESIDENTS OF THE UNITED STATES, HERBERT HOOVER for 1929. *U.S. Govt. Printing Office*, Washington, D.C. 1975 $13.50

STATE PAPERS AND OTHER PUBLIC WRITINGS. Ed. by W. S. Myers 1934 *Kraus* 2 vols. $40.00

PROCLAMATIONS AND EXECUTIVE ORDERS, 1929–1933. *U.S. Govt. Printing Office*, Washington, D.C. 2 vols. 1974 set $24.55

MEMOIRS. *Macmillan* 3 vols. 1951–52 Vol. I Years of Adventure, 1874–1920 Vol. 2 The Cabinet and the Presidency, 1920–1933 Vol. 3 The Great Depression, 1929–1941. Out of print at present.

AMERICAN IDEALS VERSUS THE NEW DEAL. 1936. *Scholarly Press* 1971 $9.50

ADDRESSES UPON THE AMERICAN ROAD, 1933–1938. 1938. *Bks. for Libraries* 1972 $14.00

FURTHER ADDRESSES UPON THE AMERICAN ROAD, 1938–1940. 1940. *Bks. for Libraries* 1972 $11.50

(With H. Gibson). PROBLEMS OF LASTING PEACE. 1942. *Kraus* 1969 $10.00

THE CHALLENGE TO LIBERTY. *Da Capo* 1973 $8.95

AN AMERICAN EPIC. *Regnery* 2 vols. 1959–1960 Vol. I The Relief of Belgium and Northern France, 1914–1930 (1959) Vol. 2 Famine in Forty-Five Nations: Organization Behind the Front, 1914–1923 (1960) each $7.50

Books about Hoover

Herbert Hoover and the Great Depression. By Harris Gaylord Warren. 1959. *Norton* 1967 pap. $3.15

The Poverty of Abundance: Hoover, the Nation, the Depression. By Albert U. Romasco. *Oxford* 1965 $7.95 Galaxy Bks. 1968 pap. $2.50

The Interregnum of Despair: Hoover, Congress and the Depression. By Jordan A. Schwarz. *Univ. of Illinois Press* 1970 $7.95
"Schwarz has written a first-rate study of the attempts and failures of President Hoover and the Congress to deal with the Great Depression. . . . While this volume covers much the same ground as H. G. Warren's 'Herbert Hoover and the Great Depression', [it] includes enough new material to make it a necessity for every college and university library"—*(Choice)*.

Shattered Dream: Herbert Hoover and the Great Depression. By Gene Smith. *Morrow* 1970 $6.95
"Smith paints in harrowing detail a poignant picture of depression days, the ill-fated Bonus Expeditionary March, and the government's unavailing efforts to turn the tide"—*(LJ)*.

The Life and Accomplishments of Herbert Hoover. By Walter L. Miller. *Moore Pub. Co.* 1970 $6.95

Herbert Hoover's Latin American Policy. By Alexander De Conde. *Octagon* 1970 lib. bdg. $9.00

Herbert Hoover and the Crisis of American Capitalism. Ed. by J. Joseph Huthmacher and Warren Susman. *General Learning Corp.* 1973 $7.65; *Schenkman* pap. $2.95

The Hoover Presidency: A Reappraisal. Ed. by Martin Fausold and George Mazuzan. *State Univ. of N.Y. Press* 1974 $12.00

The President and Protest: Hoover, Conspiracy and the Bonus Riot. By Donald J. Lisio. *Univ. of Missouri Press* 1974 $12.00
"Lisio seeks to correct widely held misconceptions about Herbert Hoover's role in dealing with the 1932 bonus march. . . . His work makes a significant contribution to the reevaluation, indeed rehabilitation of Hoover's reputation presently underway by historians"— *(Choice)*.

FOSDICK, HARRY EMERSON. 1878–1969. *See Chapter 4, World Religions, this Volume.*

JONES, ERNEST. 1879–1958. *See preceding Section on Biography and Chapter 6, Psychology, under Freud, this Volume.*

KLEE, PAUL. 1879–1940.

The German artist, brought up in Switzerland, is known for his inventive and deceptively childlike drawings—often abstract, often witty, always exquisite. He had studied art and dabbled in writing and music until World War I when his German citizenship sent him to the Army for two years, after which he dedicated himself seriously to his art. He was, with Gropius, Bauer and Kandinsky, an early teacher at the remarkable art institute known as the Bauhaus in Weimar. His extraordinary genius was not fully appreciated until after World War II. Edited by his son, the Diaries are "a careful record of the maturation of their author, from the melodramatic, probing introspections of his youth to the determined calm of his 37th year. . . . That deliberate serenity . . . is a reflection of the astounding personal detachment achieved by Klee which, of course, influenced his art and which, in his writing, lends authority to his observations on himself, on the other modern masters like Kandinsky, Macke, Ensor, and Marc, and on the world of music and literature which profoundly affected his thinking"—*(Commonweal)*. His war experience, at the end of the Diaries, led him to make the classic observation: "The more horrible the world, the more abstract our art."

DIARIES, 1898–1918. Ed. with introd. by Felix Klee *Univ. of California Press* 1964 $15.00 pap. $4.95. Four notebooks, plus a brief autobiography written in 1940. Originally published in German in 1957.

PEDAGOGICAL SKETCHBOOK. *Praeger* 1960 pap. $1.75

ON MODERN ART. *Heinman* 1967 pap. $2.50

NOTEBOOKS. Ed. by Jurg Spiller and Bernard Karpel *Wittenborn* 2 vols. 1973 Vol. I The Thinking Eye $32.50 Vol. 2 The Nature of Nature $37.50

DRAWINGS. Ed. by Max Huggier. *Borden* $4.97 pap. $2.25

Books about Klee

　Klee: Study of His Life and Work. By Gualtieri de San Lazzaro. Trans. by Stuart Hood *Praeger* 1964 pap. $3.95
　Paul Klee. Ed. by Will Grohmann. Library of Great Painters Ser. *Abrams* 1967 $22.50 (with title "Klee") Great Art of the Ages Ser. 1969 $5.65 1970 pap. $1.95. The late Will Grohmann, distinguished German art critic and a long-time friend of Klee, became a leading authority on the artist and his work.
　Paul Klee. By Werner Schmalenbach. Folio Art Book Ser. *Crown* 1969 pap. $1.45
　Paul Klee and the Bauhaus. By Christian Geelhaar. *N.Y. Graphic Soc.* 1973 $25.00

STALIN, JOSEPH (VISSARIONOVICH).　1879–1953.　*See Chapter 9, History, Government and Politics—Modern and World, this Volume.*

WOOLF, LEONARD.　1880–　　*See Chapter 16, Literary Biography and Autobiography,* Reader's Adviser, *Vol. I.*

ROOSEVELT, FRANKLIN D(ELANO).　1882–1945.

　Franklin Delano Roosevelt, 32nd president of the United States, was one of the most controversial personalities of our times, yet one of the most admired. Born to wealth and a family of distinction at Hyde Park, New York, he came to office in 1932 in the depth of the economic depression the country was suffering, having served as Assistant Secretary of the Navy in the Wilson administration, as an unsuccessful candidate for vice-president with Cox, and as a successful governor of New York State. His "New Deal" policies have had a lasting influence on the country, which owes a continuing debt to his courage and vision as our leader in the days preceding and during World War II.

PUBLIC PAPERS AND ADDRESSES, 1928–1945. Ed. by Samuel Rosenman; with special introd. and explanatory notes by President Roosevelt. 1938–50. *Russell & Russell* 13 vols. 1969 each $30.00 set $325.00

COMPLETE PRESIDENTIAL PRESS CONFERENCES, 1933–1945. *Da Capo* 12 vols. each $40.00 set $450.00

DEVELOPMENT OF UNITED STATES FOREIGN POLICY. 1943. *Kraus* $5.00. Addresses and messages compiled from official sources to show the chronological development of U.S. foreign policy from F.D.R.'s announcement of the Good Neighbor Policy in 1933.

RENDEZVOUS WITH DESTINY: Addresses and Opinions. Arr. by J. B. Hardman. 1944. *Kraus* 1968 $15.00

NOTHING TO FEAR, SELECTED ADDRESSES. Ed. by Ben D. Zevin. 1946. *Bks. for Libraries* $17.50; *Popular Library* pap. $.75

F.D.R.: His Personal Letters. Ed. by Elliott Roosevelt; fwd. by Eleanor Roosevelt. 1947–50. *Kraus* 4 vols. set $98.50

LOOKING FORWARD. 1933. *Da Capo* 1973 $10.00

ON OUR WAY. 1934. *Da Capo* 1973 $10.00

AMERICA ORGANIZES TO WIN THE WAR: A Handbook on the American War Effort. 1942. *Bks. for Libraries* $14.50

THE AMERICAN WAY. *Citadel Press* pap. $.95

Books about Roosevelt

　As He Saw It. By Elliott Roosevelt. 1946. *Greenwood* 1974 $13.00
　The Roosevelt I Knew. By Frances Perkins. 1946. *Harper* pap. $2.75; *Peter Smith* $4.75
　President Roosevelt and the Coming of the War, 1941: A Study in Appearances and Realities. By Charles A. Beard. 1948. *Shoe String Press* 1968 $15.00
　Roosevelt and Hopkins: An Intimate History. By Robert E. Sherwood. 1949. *Harper* rev. ed. 1950 $15.00

Working with Roosevelt. By Samuel I. Rosenman. 1952. *Da Capo* 1972 $15.00

Franklin D. Roosevelt. By Frank Burt Freidel. *Little* 4 vols. 1952–1973 Vol. I The Apprenticeship (1952) Vol. 2 The Ordeal (1954, o.p.) Vol. 3 The Triumph (1956) Vol. 4 Launching the
New Deal (1973) Vols. 1, 3 and 4 each $15.00

Roosevelt: The Lion and the Fox. By James MacGregor Burns. *Harcourt* 1956 $12.50 Harvest
Bks. 1963 pap. $3.45
"If we exclude works of personal reminiscence, this book is easily the best. . . . It is thorough,
scholarly, incisive in its analysis, and highly readable"—(*Commonweal*). It received the Woodrow Wilson Foundation Award in 1957.

New Age of Franklin Roosevelt 1932–1945. By Dexter Perkins. *Univ. of Chicago Press* 1957 $6.75
pap. $1.95. A balanced evaluation of the Roosevelt era from the bank failures to Hiroshima.

The Age of Roosevelt. By Arthur M. Schlesinger, Jr. *Houghton* 3 vols. 1957–60 Vol. I The Crisis
of the Old Order (1957) Vol. 2 The Coming of the New Deal (1959) Vol. 3 The Politics of
Upheaval (1960) each $10.00 Vol. 1 pap. $2.65 Vol. 2 pap. $3.95

Sunrise at Campobello. By Dore Schary. *Random* 1958 $5.50. This documentary drama follows
F.D.R.'s formative years (1921–1924) from just before he was stricken with polio until he
conquers his physical failings.

Roosevelt and Howe. By Alfred B. Rollins, Jr. *Knopf* 1962 $6.95. A sophisticated history of the
relationship between F.D.R. and his most intimate aide during Roosevelt's early career until
Howe's death in 1936.

Franklin D. Roosevelt and the New Deal. By William Leuchtenberg. *Harper* 1963 Torchbks.
pap. $2.45. A readable one-volume survey of this important era.

Franklin Roosevelt. By Charles Peter Hill. *Oxford* 1966 $2.00

F.D.R.'s Undeclared War: 1939–41. By T. R. Fehrenbach. *McKay* 1967 $7.95
"A sympathetic portrayal of a President hampered by lack of public support for his planned
entry into a war that was more than a European power struggle"—(*LJ*).

Franklin Delano Roosevelt. Ed. by Gerald D. Nash. *Prentice-Hall* 1967 $5.95. A collection of
excerpts from published sources, including pieces by Arthur Schlesinger, Jr., Richard
Hofstadter, E. E. Robinson, Walter Lippmann, Winston Churchill, Adolf Hitler, Huey Long
and Herbert Hoover.

Franklin D. Roosevelt: A Profile. Ed. by William E. Leuchtenburg. American Profile Ser. *Hill &
Wang* 1967 $5.95 pap. $2.95. Essays by major Roosevelt biographers and critics representing
the different viewpoints in the major controversies.

Franklin D. Roosevelt and Foreign Affairs. Ed. by Edgar B. Nixon. *Harvard Univ. Press* 3 vols.
1969 Vol. I Jan. 1933–Feb. 1934 Vol. 2 Mar. 1934–Aug. 1935 Vol. 3 Sept. 1935–Jan. 1937
each $12.50 set $32.50

Roosevelt: The Soldier of Freedom. By James MacGregor Burns. *Harcourt* 1970 $12.50 Harvest
Bks. 1973 pap. $4.45
"For all his admiration of the courage and *sang-froid* of this 'soldier of freedom' Burns has
written a harshly critical assessment. He perceives the President as a deeply divided man. . .
who gave inadequate leadership to a fragmented nation"—(*N.Y. Times Book Review*).

Roosevelt and Pearl Harbor. By Leonard Baker. *Macmillan* 1970 $8.95

In Search of Roosevelt. By Redford G. Tugwell. *Harvard Univ. Press* 1972 $12.95
"The essays in this collection were written over the past 20 years and most have been
previously published. Tugwell, one of the original members of F.D.R.'s brain trust, uses each
essay to delve into Roosevelt's response to a particular set of circumstances or to a specific
problem in an attempt to understand some aspect of the President's character"—(*LJ*).

F.D.R., the Beckoning of Destiny: 1882–1928. By Kenneth S. Davis. *Putnam* 1972 $15.00

The F.D.R. Memoirs. By Bernard Asbell. *Doubleday* 1973 $10.00
"The major part of this book is written as though F. D. Roosevelt himself were speaking. It
covers the years from the Inauguration in 1933 to the declaration of war in 1941 in two dozen
first-person narratives describing the events as F.D.R. might have experienced them: the
bank crisis, launching N.R.A., handling the Supreme Court [and] expediting public works
projects"—(*PW*).

F.D.R.'s Last Year: April 1944–April 1945. By Jim Bishop. *Morrow* 1974 $12.50

Roosevelt and Churchill: Their Secret Wartime Correspondence. Ed. by Francis L. Lowenheim
and others. *Saturday Review Press* (dist. by Dutton) $17.50
"The top secret messages exchanged during World War II between Roosevelt and Churchill,
not previously available for publication"—(*Booklist*).

See also Roosevelt, (Anna) Eleanor, this Chapter.

O'CASEY, SEAN. 1884–1964. *See Chapter 4, Modern British Drama,* Reader's Adviser,
Vol. 2.

ROOSEVELT, (ANNA) ELEANOR.   1884–1962.

Born in New York City, the niece of Theodore Roosevelt and married to a distant cousin, Franklin Delano Roosevelt, this distinguished First Lady made a unique place for herself not only in the United States but in the world. Undaunted by critics, she followed her wide interests and "her tireless dedication to the cause of human welfare won her affection and honor." Her service as delegate to the General Assembly of the United Nations from 1945 to 1953 and again in 1961 and as first chairman of that body's Human Rights Commission was outstanding. Her travels to all parts of the globe are reflected in her writings. Her belief in the power of books was evidenced in many ways: she was, for example, a member of the board of the Junior Literary Guild. After her death the Eleanor Roosevelt Memorial Foundation was established, created by Congress but supported by the people of United States to serve the vital and unmet needs of the humanitarian causes she espoused. As Adlai E. Stevenson said of her, "She would rather light a candle than curse the darkness, and her glow has warmed the world."

Among her many books are several for young people including "Your Teens and Mine" (*Doubleday* 1961 $1.69) and "The Book of Common Sense Etiquette" (*Macmillan* 1962 $7.95). Her last book "Tomorrow Is Now" is a testament of faith in American traditions.

AUTOBIOGRAPHY. *Harper* 1961 $10.00. The first three parts are condensations of her three earlier books published by *Harper*: "This Is My Story" (1937), "This I Remember" (1949), and "On My Own" (1958), all out of print. The fourth part, "The Search for Understanding" is new material discussing her hopes for world peace.

(With William S. DeWitt). U.N. TODAY AND TOMORROW. *Harper* 1953 $5.95

YOU LEARN BY LIVING. *Harper* 1960 $7.95

TOMORROW IS NOW. *Harper* 1963 $6.95

Books about Eleanor Roosevelt

Eleanor and Franklin: The Story of Their Relationship Based on Eleanor Roosevelt's Private Papers. By Joseph P. Lash. *Norton* 1971 $12.50; *New Am. Lib.* 1973 pap. $1.95

Eleanor: The Years Alone. By Joseph P. Lash. *Norton* 1972 $9.95; ed. by Walter Pitkin *New Am. Lib.* 1973 pap. $1.95
    "This is the personal story of Eleanor Roosevelt's conquest of her own insecurity, and a documentation of her substantial contribution to the achievements of the Roosevelt era"—(*LJ*).

An Untold Story: The Roosevelts of Hyde Park. By Elliott Roosevelt and James Brough. *Putnam* 1973 $8.95; *Dell* 1974 pap. $1.75
    Elliott Roosevelt writes of "the father we loved and the mother we respected, portraying Franklin and Eleanor in . . . the context of their family relationships"—(*PW*).

Eleanor Roosevelt: Her Day. By A. David Gurewitsch. *Quadrangle* 1974 $7.95 pap. $3.95

See also Roosevelt, Franklin Delano, this Chapter.

TRUMAN, HARRY S.   1884–1972.

Mr. Truman, who became the 33rd President at the death of Franklin D. Roosevelt in 1945, was elected president in 1948. His "second volume [of "Memoirs"] is even more important than the first. Covering six years instead of one, and a wide variety of topics from the hydrogen bomb to Adlai Stevenson's 1952 campaign, it is less tightly organized and hence less absorbing; but again, it is a record of a series of crises courageously faced, and its scope adds to its impressiveness"—(Allan Nevins, in the *N.Y. Times*). "Mr President" by William Hillman (1952, o.p.) presented an honest, lifelike picture of a President in office, based on personal diaries, private letters and revealing interviews.

THE PUBLIC PAPERS OF THE PRESIDENTS OF THE UNITED STATES, HARRY S TRUMAN. 8 vols. covering 1945–1953. *U.S. Government Printing Office*, Washington, D.C. 1962–63 $5.50–$9.00

MEMOIRS. *Doubleday* 2 vols. 1955–56 Vol. I Years of Decisions Vol. 2 Years of Trial and Hope set $8.95

TRUMAN SPEAKS: The Principal Speeches and Addresses of President Harry S Truman. Ed. by Cyril Clemens. 1946. *Kraus* $7.50

THE TRUMAN PROGRAM. Ed. by M. B. Schnapper. 1949. *Greenwood* 1972 $13.00

THE QUOTABLE HARRY S TRUMAN. Ed. by T. S. Settel *Droke-Hallux* 1967 $2.95

THE WIT AND WISDOM OF HARRY S TRUMAN. Comp. by George S. Caldwell. 1966. *Stein & Day* 1972 $4.95 pap. $1.50. Selections from lectures, speeches, diaries and letters.

THE TRUMAN ADMINISTRATION: Its Principles and Practice. Ed. by Louis William Koenig *New York Univ. Press* 1956 $10.00. An admirable and informing selection from official papers, speeches and press conferences.

FREEDOM AND EQUALITY: Addresses by Harry S Truman. Ed. by David Horton *Univ. of Missouri Press* 1960 $2.95

MR. CITIZEN. 1960. *Popular Lib.* 1973 pap. $1.25

FREE WORLD AND FREE TRADE. *Southern Methodist Univ. Press* 1963 $5.00

Books about Truman

Man of Independence. By Jonathan Daniels. 1950. *Kennikat* 1971 $12.75

The Truman Administration: A Documentary History. Ed. by Barton J. Bernstein and Allen J. Matusow. 1966. *Harper* 1968 pap. $3.95
"The choice of documents is admirable and especially so as they pay attention to the occasionally unfortunate or ineffective economic policy of the first term. The notes are models of relevance and brevity. . . It is possible to trace here the history of American illusion and disillusion"—(*TLS*, London).

The Truman Presidency: The History of a Triumphant Succession. By Cabell Phillips. 1966. *Penguin* Pelican Bks. 1969 pap. $2.95
Written by a Washington journalist on the *N.Y. Times* staff, this account is "fast-moving, anecdotal and interesting, but also lacking in perceptive analysis, poorly organized and loosely written. Two advantages are Mr. Phillips' personal acquaintance with Truman plus his chapter notes"—(*LJ*).

Politics of Civil Rights in the Truman Administration. By William C. Berman. *Ohio State Univ. Press* 1970 $8.00
"Berman examines the motives of the Truman Administration with respect to civil rights and concludes it was forced to act because of the fear of losing the black vote in the 1948 election"—(*Choice*).

Truman and the 80th Congress. By Susan Hartmann. *Univ. of Missouri Press* 1971 $9.00
This is a "study of the . . . relationship between President Truman and the Republican 80th Congress elected in 1946. . . . The author concludes [that] the Truman leadership probably achieved what he set out to accomplish"—(*Annals of the American Academy*).

The Awesome Power: Harry S Truman as Commander in Chief. By Richard F. Haynes. *Louisiana State Univ. Press* 1973 $12.95
"A cautious and carefully circumscribed study of Truman's assertion and employment of power in his constitutional role as Commander-in-Chief. . . . Truman is praised as 'dedicated' and 'faithful' to his country and his conscience—if not always wise"—(*Choice*).

The Truman and Eisenhower Years: 1945–1960: A Selective Bibliography. By Margaret L. Stapleton. *Scarecrow Press* 1973 $6.50

Harry S Truman. By Margaret Truman. *Morrow* 1973 $10.95; *Pocket Bks.* 1974 pap. $1.95. A personal portrait of her father from his early days to his retirement in Independence, Mo.

Plain Speaking: An Oral Biography of Harry S Truman. By Merle Miller. *Putnam* 1974 $8.95
"Parts of this book deal with the memories of people who knew the president before 1935, the year he first went to Washington as Senator from Missouri. Other parts deal with his presidency and the period following it. The work is based on tapes Miller compiled from interviews with Truman and others in 1961–62 in Independence, Missouri"—(*BRD*).

NICOLSON, SIR HAROLD (GEORGE). 1886–1968.

Sir Harold Nicolson was the son of Lord Carnock and the husband of the late Victoria Sackville-West. Like Lord Carnock he devoted his life to the English diplomatic service. "Portrait of a Diplomatist" (1930 1939, o.p.), his biography of his father, is really part of a trilogy of diplomatic history (*see Chapter 9, History, Government and Politics—British Commonwealth, this Volume*). Sir Harold became a Fellow of the Royal Society of Literature and in 1953 was created Knight Commander of the Victorian Order by Queen Elizabeth II. "Journey to Java" (1958, o.p.) is his travel diary during a two months' cruise in 1957.

Sir Harold claimed that he had never written a *pure* biography, a life of an individual conceived solely as a work of art. His biographies are often fully as critical as biographical. "Some People" is delightful biographical fiction, which he called the most *impure* form of biography. His "Tennyson" (1923), "Byron" (1924) and "Swinburne" (1926) are back in print. "The English Sense of Humour and Other Essays" (1968 $4.95) has been published by *Funk & Wagnalls*.

"The Diaries and Letters" have been skillfully edited by Sir Harold's son, who is founder and director of the British publishing firm of Weidenfeld and Nicolson. Charles Poore said of Volume I: "Reading Sir Harold Nicolson's diaries is exhilarating. It is like being pelted by confetti made from Burke's 'Peerage,' Hansard's Parliamentary reports, and the British 'Who's Who.' . . . His book . . . is personal history at its best." Commenting on Volume 3, Mr. Poore wrote: "In many ways, this volume is the best. It balances Sir Harold's ventures in literature and politics, broadcasting, gardening, living spaciously, and tuft-hunting. Also, it chants one of the better current requiems for empires lost and manners gone to hell." John Mason Brown said of Volume 2: "None of the accounts that I have read of Britain during World War II equals this one in grace, perception and immediacy. . . . Closely following great events, Nicolson never fails to recognize the human, hence historical, importance of trivia. It is the past of more than twenty years ago, so near and yet so distant, which he makes wonderfully present on a daily basis in entry after entry. His ferreting eye for significant detail, his sense of character and scene, his civilized mind, his alert and remembering ear, and the ease and charm of his writing place his very personal record in the forefront of English diaries."

VICTORIA SACKVILLE-WEST (1892–1962) was Sir Harold's wife. She was born at Knole, the greatest private house in England, which she described—with its seven courts to correspond with the days of the week, its 52 staircases to match the weeks of the year, and its 365 rooms for every day in the year—in "Knole and the Sackvilles" (1923, o.p.). "All Passion Spent" (1931, o.p.) was her most successful novel. Sackville-West is distinguished for the modest and subtle perfection to be found in all her writings. *For her main entry, see Chapter 12, Modern British Fiction, Reader's Adviser, Vol. 1.*

DIARIES AND LETTERS. Ed. by Nigel Nicolson *Atheneum* 3 vols. 1966–68 Vol. 1 1930–1939 (1966) Vol. 2 The War Years: 1939–1945 (1967, o.p.) Vol. 3 The Later Years: 1945–1962 (1968) Vol. 1 $10.00 Vol. 3 $8.50

SOME PEOPLE. 1927. *Popular Lib.* 1974 pap. $1.25

THE DEVELOPMENT OF ENGLISH BIOGRAPHY. 1928. *Folcroft* 1973 $12.50; *Hillary House* $2.75; *Richard West* $10.00

See also Chapter 9, History, Government and Politics—British Commonwealth, this Volume.

SASSON, SIEGFRIED (LORRAINE). 1886–1967. *See Chapter 16, Literary Biography and Autobiography, Reader's Adviser, Vol. 1.*

MACAULAY, DAME ROSE. 1887–1958. *See Chapter 16, Literary Biography and Autobiography, Reader's Adviser, Vol. 1.*

HITLER, ADOLF. 1889–1945. *See Chapter 9, History, Government and Politics—Modern and World, this Volume.*

NEHRU, JAWAHARLAL. 1889–1964. *See Chapter 9, History, Government and Politics—Modern and World, this Volume.*

EISENHOWER, DWIGHT D(AVID). 1890–1969.

As Commander-in-Chief of Allied Forces in Western Europe, Dwight David Eisenhower was a World War II hero with a faultless record of success. After a brief stint as president of Columbia University, he accepted the supreme command of NATO, and the following year successfully ran against Democrat Adlai Stevenson to become the 34th President of the United States. To his post as first Republican President in a generation, Eisenhower brought "the full and affectionate confidence of a people who would have followed him toward any conceivable military enterprise"—(Sidney Hyman, in the *N.Y. Times*). Politically inexperienced, Eisenhower, as President, relied on the counsel of men of greater experience, especially John Foster Dulles, whom he called "my great Secretary of State." The appraisal of Eisenhower's Presidency is still being written. When he died in March, 1969, President Richard Nixon said in his eulogy: "Many leaders are known and respected outside their own countries. Very few are loved outside their own countries. Dwight Eisenhower was one of those few. He was probably loved by more people in more parts of the world than any President America has ever had." And the President quoted his former chief as having once said to an English audience shortly after V-E Day: "I come from the heart of America." "[He came] from its spirited heart," said Mr. Nixon. "He exemplified what millions of parents hoped that their sons would be—strong and courageous and honest and compassionate." The World War II generation will remember him as a man strong in battle who loathed war and sought always to keep the world at peace. His story of World War II was told in "Crusade in Europe" (1948, o.p.).

THE PUBLIC PAPERS OF THE PRESIDENTS OF THE UNITED STATES: DWIGHT D. EISENHOWER. 8 vols. covering 1953–61. *U.S. Government Printing Office*, Washington, D.C. $6.75–$8.25

PAPERS: THE WAR YEARS. Ed. by Alfred D. Chandler, Jr. and Stephen Ambrose *Johns Hopkins Press* 5 vols. 1970 set $85.00

Under the general editorship of Alfred D. Chandler, a group of historians at the Johns Hopkins University began the ten-year project of publishing "The Eisenhower Papers." "Their work involves letting the record speak for itself by arranging Eisenhower's official papers, culled of extraneous detail. It will be a day-by-day, month-by-month account of Eisenhower's rise to leadership, told in letters, papers, memoranda, reports and official documents, illuminated by the general's personal recollections. . . . To put the record in perspective they must: sift through 15 million documents ranging from classified government papers to letters and memorabilia from the general's friends and associates; review official documents and reports more voluminous than the combined papers of all U.S. Presidents before Franklin D. Roosevelt; hear Eisenhower's own views in personal interviews; maintain fidelity to the historian's craft without violating national security or compromising individuals still prominent in American life"—(*Johns Hopkins Journal*).

THE WHITE HOUSE YEARS. *Doubleday* 2 vols. Vol. 1 Mandate for Change, 1953–1956 o.p. Vol. 2 Waging Peace, 1956–1961 1965 $7.95 2 vol. ltd. ed. $100.00

PEACE WITH JUSTICE. *Columbia* $9.00

AT EASE: Stories I Tell to Friends. *Doubleday* 1967 $7.95. Reminiscing over a crowded lifetime, from Abilene to the White House.

THE QUOTABLE DWIGHT D. EISENHOWER. Ed. by Elsie Gollagher *Droke-Hallux* 1967 $2.95

IN REVIEW: Pictures I've Kept. *Doubleday* 1969 $2.49

GENERAL EISENHOWER ON THE MILITARY CHURCHILL: A Conversation with Alastair Cooke. *Norton* 1970 $4.95

Books about Eisenhower

Eisenhower. By John Gunther. *Harper* 1952 $5.95
Eisenhower as President. Ed. by Dean Albertson. *Farrar, Straus* (Hill & Wang) 1963 pap. $2.25. An anthology evaluating the historic and social significance of his administration.
Eisenhower and Berlin, 1945: The Decision to Halt at the Elbe. By Stephen E. Ambrose. *Norton* 1967 $4.00 pap. $1.25
Eisenhower: The President Nobody Knew. By Arthur Larson. 1968. *Popular Library* 1969 pap. $.75
An "affectionate and quite informative memoir of his years near the center of the Eisenhower circle"—(*N.Y. Times*). The author was President Eisenhower's speech writer and executive assistant.
Bitter Woods: A Comprehensive Study of the War in Europe. By John S. Eisenhower. *Putnam* 1969 $10.00; *Ace Bks.* 1970 pap. $1.95
Eisenhower: American Hero. By Keith Davis. *McGraw-Hill* 1969 $4.95
The Eisenhower Administration 1953–1961: A Documentary History. Ed. by Lawrence H. Larsen and Robert L. Branyan. *Random* 2 vols. 1971 set $62.00
Eisenhower and the American Crusades. By Herbert S. Parmet. *Macmillan* 1972 $12.95
"This thoroughly researched and well-written book is political history at its best. Parmet has written an integrated, chronological synthesis of Eisenhower's major political decisions, both overt and implicit, as they relate to the issues and personalities of the 1950's. The book is based on Presidential papers, oral history projects, private and public papers of the President's advisers and members of his cabinet, diverse journalistic accounts, and many personal interviews"—(*LJ*).
Eisenhower. By Martin Blumenson. *Ballantine Bks.* 1972 pap. $1.00
Eisenhower: Portrait of the Hero. By Peter Lyon. *Little* 1974 $15.00
Strictly Personal. By John S. Eisenhower. *Doubleday* 1974 $10.95
President Eisenhower's son shares the experiences of his "privileged" life. "Much of [it] involves the story of two lives—father and son, and the book is best when Ike comes on the scene. Though [it] will not change opinions about the senior Eisenhower, it does offer a son's view of a famous father"—(*LJ*).
The Eisenhower Era. By R. and Holbo Sellen. *Holt* 1974 pap. $3.00 2nd. ed 1975 $7.95
The President is Calling. By Milton S. Eisenhower. *Doubleday* 1974 $12.50. The President's brother tells of his public service years under various presidents and of his views of the role of the presidency.
Holding the Line: The Eisenhower Era 1952–1961. By Charles C. Alexander. *Univ. of Indiana Press* 1975 $12.50

"Alexander, a professor of history at Ohio University, offers a picture of the Eisenhower years which sees them less as a bland interlude between strong Democratic administrations than as a valiant struggle to hold ground in the Cold War arena without inordinate military expansion or open military conflict"—(*LJ*).

DE GAULLE, CHARLES (ANDRÉ JOSEPH MARIE). 1890–1970.

"The War Memoirs" of Charles de Gaulle, former President of France's Fifth Republic, has been called a classic and a literary masterpiece. "The austerity of the prose, the economy of words, the classic beauty of the images call to mind the finest passages of Caesar's Commentaries. Generations of present and future historians will read and weigh every word of these revelations"—(David Schoenbrun, in *SR*). It is important not only as a revelation of an enigmatic and brilliant man but for the comments about such men as Roosevelt, Churchill, Eden, Macmillan, Pope Pius, Cardinal Spellman, Eisenhower, Willkie, Hull, Forrestal, Pétain, Smuts and many others.

France without the leadership of Charles de Gaulle was an unlikely political reality for a decade. But as a result of a referendum in the spring of 1969, France *sans* de Gaulle became a political fact. The authoritarian President of the Fifth Republic did not get the mandate he deemed necessary to continue and so he abruptly retired on April 27, 1969. The man who had restored France as an international power amid continuous controversy and fanfare departed calmly from the political scene.

COMPLETE WAR MEMOIRS. *Simon & Schuster* 1958–1960 Touchstone-Clarion Bks. 1964 pap. 3 vols. in I Vol. I The Call to Honor, 1940–1942, trans. by Jonathan Griffin Vol. 2 Unity, 1942–1944 Vol. 3 Salvation, 1944–1946 trans. by Richard Howard set $4.95

DOCUMENTS TO THE WAR VOLUMES. *Simon & Schuster* 2 vols. 1960 set $10.00

MEMOIRS OF HOPE: Renewal and Endeavor. *Simon & Schuster* 1971 $10.00

Books about de Gaulle

France, Troubled Ally. By Edgar S. Furniss, Jr. 1960. *Greenwood* 1974 $20.00

De Gaulle and the French Army: A Crisis in Civil Military Relations. By Edgar S. Furniss, Jr. 1964. *Kraus* $4.00

The King and His Court. By Pierre Viansson-Ponté. Trans. by Elaine Halperin *Houghton* 1965 $5.00

A hilarious "power study . . . cast as a court chronicle"—(*N.Y. Times*). De Gaulle's own comment to the author, now political editor of *Le Monde:* "Everything considered, and whether you wish or not, your book partakes of the Gaullist mystique."

De Gaulle: A Political Biography. By Alexander Werth. *Simon & Schuster* 1966 $7.50

"Mr. Werth has instinctive understanding of politics and enormous first-hand knowledge of European affairs"—(*N.Y. Herald Tribune*).

Sons of France: Pétain and de Gaulle. By Jean-Raymond Tournoux. Trans. by Oliver Coburn *Viking* 1966 $5.95. Joint biography of the two proud, obstinate men who were lifelong friends until World War II, when they clashed as bitter enemies. Anecdotes and citations were collected by M. Tournoux over a 30-year period.

The Three Lives of Charles de Gaulle. By David Schoenbrun. *Atheneum* 1968 pap. $3.95. His career as soldier, as wartime leader in exile and as statesman, by an American correspondent in Paris.

De Gaulle's Foreign Policy: 1944–1946. By Anton W. De Porte. *Harvard Univ. Press* 1968 $9.00

The General. By Pierre Galante. *Random* 1969 $5.95. An informal and very human portrait.

Felled Oaks: Conversation with de Gaulle. By André Malraux. *Holt* (Rinehart) 1972 $6.95

The record of a day's talks which "ranged over French and world history, politics, art, great men, past and present, life and death itself"—(Publisher's note).

The Other de Gaulle: Diaries 1944–1954. By Claude Mauriac. Trans. by Moura Budberg and Gordon Latta *John Day* 1973 $12.95

"The author received a secretarial position with de Gaulle soon after the liberation of Paris. Via his diaries of the following ten years, we catch an informal glimpse of the general, with special attention given to the pivotal 1944–1947 period"—(*LJ*).

De Gaulle. By Brian Crozier. *Scribner* 1974 $12.50

"Crozier covers the whole range of de Gaulle's career—as writer, soldier, politician, statesman—in this account of his entire life from 1890 to 1970, and [seeks to] place his achievement in the context of contemporary history. [He draws] on hitherto unavailable sources, both documents and personal reminiscences. . . . In his final assessment Crozier writes that the fame of de Gaulle far outstrips his achievements"—(Publisher's note).

SITWELL, SIR OSBERT, 5th Bart. 1892–1969. *See Chapter 16, Literary Biography and Autobiography*, Reader's Adviser, *Vol. I.*

MAO TSE-TUNG. 1893–1976.

Both a brilliant theorist and a practical politician of extraordinary power, Mao Tse-Tung participated in planning and carrying out the Communist Revolt against the Kuomintang in 1927. It was then that he founded the Red Army with which he vanquished Chiang Kai-shek and the Kuomintang after World War II. In 1949, Mao assumed an official government position and in 1954 took virtual control of all China as Chairman of the People's Republic.

"A sharp sense of humor and a mastery of epigram combined with a happy facility in winning arguments is one of Mao's secrets of successful leadership. . . . Like most educated Chinese, Mao is a poet. Also master of a lucid prose style, he is the author of books and pamphlets which place him among the great revolutionary pamphleteers of all time"—(*Current Biography*). His handbook on guerrilla strategy (1962, o.p.) has become the blueprint for revolution in China, Cuba and Vietnam.

Mao's works have been massively produced within China and many distributed abroad, with translations into 23 languages. Extraordinarily successful in bookstores around the world has been a small volume, bound in red plastic, of Mao's "Quotations"—the "little red book" brandished at Red Guard demonstrations. Beginning in 1966, it was distributed from Peking in English, French and Chinese, and soon sold out in New York, Tokyo, Rome, London and Paris; it became a worldwide best seller.

SELECTED WORKS. *China Bks.* 4 vols. 1961 Vol. 1 1924–1937 Vol. 2 1937–1941 Vol. 3 1941–1945 Vol. 4 1945–1949 each $4.25 pap. each $2.75

SELECTED WORKS. From the Authorized-Peking-Edition; abr. ed. by Bruno Shaw *Harper* 1970 pap. $2.95; *Peter Smith* $5.00

SELECTED WORKS. Books 1 & 2. Committee for the Publication of the Selected Works of Mao, ed. by the Central Committee Staff. *Great Wall Press* 1972 $35.00

SELECTED READINGS. *China Bks.* 1971 $2.25 pap. $1.75

QUOTATIONS FROM CHAIRMAN MAO. 1966. *Bantam* 1967 pap. $1.25; ed. by Stuart R. Schram *China Bks.* 2nd ed 1967 plastic bdg. $.60; *Praeger* 1968 $5.00. The "Little Red Book" of the Chinese Red Guards.

MAO TSE-TUNG: An Anthology of His Writings. Ed. by Anne Freemantle *New Am. Lib.* 1962 1971 pap. $1.25

CHAIRMAN MAO TALKS TO THE PEOPLE: Talks and Letters 1956–1971. Ed. by Stuart R. Schram *Pantheon* 1974 $10.00 pap. $2.95

ON CONTRADICTION. *China Bks.* 4th ed. 1967 $.50

POLITICAL THOUGHT. Ed. by Stuart R. Schram *Praeger* rev. ed. 1969 pap. $4.95

FOUR ESSAYS ON PHILOSOPHY. *China Bks.* 1968 pap. $.60

POEMS. Trans. by Willis Barnstone and Ko Ching-Po. 1972. Ed. by Paul Engle *Dell* Delta Bks. 1973 pap. $2.45

Other titles are published in translation by China Bks.

Books about Mao Tse-Tung

Chinese Communism and the Rise of Mao. By Benjamin I. Schwartz. *Harvard Univ. Press* 1951 $7.50; *Harper* Torchbks. 1967 pap. $2.45. An excellent pioneer study of the Chinese Communist Party in the 1920s and early 1930s until Mao became its master.

The Communism of Mao Tse-Tung. By Arthur A. Cohen. *Univ. of Chicago Press* 1964 $7.50 pap. $2.95

"A careful, painstaking and pedantic work on Mao's real and/or claimed contributions to the theory and practice of Communism"—(*LJ*).

Mao Tse-Tung in Opposition, 1927–1935. By John E. Rue. *Stanford Univ. Press* 1966 $10.00 An "extraordinarily interesting volume. It treats of the time when Mao was just one Communist leader among many, and when neither he nor his comrades knew that one day he would be China's Communist emperor. . . . This history is highly germane to the present"—(*N.Y. Times*).

Mao and the Chinese Revolution. By Jerome Ch'en. *Oxford* 1967 pap. $3.50 With 37 poems trans. by M. Bullock and Jerome Ch'en. "Mr. Ch'en's biography is . . . the work of a pioneer. As such it has great merit and should be heartily welcomed by all those interested in contemporary history. The author has employed a very considerable number of Chinese sources, some of them quite rare"—(*TLS*, London).

Mao Tse-Tung. By Stuart R. Schram. *Simon & Schuster* 1967 $7.95; *Penguin* Pelican Bks. 1968 pap. $1.65
"The best appraisal of Mao to date . . . will no doubt stand the test of time"—(*N.Y. Times*).
China after Mao. By A. Doak Barnett. *Princeton Univ. Press* 1967 $8.50 pap. $3.95
Based on lectures given at Princeton University. "Certainly the most readable yet sound primer on present-day China available in book form"—(*Christian Science Monitor*).
Revolutionary Immortality: Mao Tse-Tung and the Chinese Cultural Revolution. By Robert Jay Lifton. *Random* 1968 $4.95 pap. $1.95; *Peter Smith* $4.00
"An essential study of Communist China; more than that, it is an original, intellectually exciting, gracefully written and wholly accessible essay on an aspect of human individual and mass psychology as it operates in contemporary revolutionary circumstances around the world"—(*N.Y. Times*). By the winner of the 1969 National Book Award for Science.
Protracted Game: A Wei-Ch'i Interpretation of Maoist Revolutionary Strategy. By Scott A. Boorman. *Oxford* 1971 pap. $2.95.
An examination of the Asian game of wei-ch'i "to discover what Westerners can learn about the strategy of Chinese Communist armies and of other Asian revolutionary forces"— (Publisher's note).
Mao's Way. By Edward E. Rice. *Univ. of California Press* 1972 $12.95 1974 pap. $4.95
"Rice relies on an enormous amount of primary and secondary sources to describe in a systematic and chronological fashion the contending groups in the upheaval in China. Though Rice has broken no new ground in the explanation of this movement, his account is the most comprehensively documented"—(*Annals of the American Academy*).
Mao and China: From Revolution to Revolution. By Stanley Karnow. *Viking* 1972 $15.00 Compass Bks. 1973 pap. $3.95
"Karnow's Mao is viewed 'in collision' with his own country, thwarted by the Chinese people, and opposed by most of his own Communist party colleagues for over two decades. That collision for Karnow is . . . rooted in Mao's opposition to the imperatives of 'administrative routine and technical specialization'. Mao, the poet of revolution, cannot adjust to the 'prose of stable administration' "—(*N.Y. Times Bk. Rev.*).
On the Long March with Chairman Mao. By Chen Chang-Feng. *China Bks.* 1972 pap. $.75
History and Will: Philosophical Perspectives of Mao Tse-Tung's Thought. By Frederic Wakeman, Jr. *Univ. of California Press* 1973 $12.75
"In this analysis of Mao's thought, Wakeman deals with a variety of historical and philosophical subjects . . . which provide the intellectual background of Maoism. The central theme of the book is the . . . contradiction between objective history and subjective will, which converge, according to the author, in the single focus of the Cultural Revolution"—(*LJ*).
Mao Tse-Tung and Gandhi: Perspectives on Social Transformation. By Jayantanuja Bandyopadhyaya. *Int. Pubns. Service* 1974 $7.50; *Paragon Reprint* 1973 $6.00
Mao Tse Tung. By Jack Gray. Makers of Modern Thought Ser. *Judson Press* 1974 pap. $1.95

See also Chapter 19, Asian Literature, Reader's Adviser, *Vol. 2.*

KHRUSHCHEV, NIKITA S(ERGEEVICH).   1894–1971.

After Nikita Krushchev's sudden elimination as Premier and First Deputy of the Soviet Union in October 1964, he practically disappeared from public view. The Soviet press began immediately to behave as if he had never existed, but the West continues to be interested in this enigmatic man who began life as a poor shepherd boy, became a loyal Stalinist henchman and after Stalin's death and his own rise to power turned against his former "great leader" with the massive de-Stalinization campaign which Harrison Salisbury considered his "greatest feat." He was interviewed regularly by the *N.Y. Times* when he went to vote. Preliminary biographies, studies of his rise and fall, have already begun to appear, but current biographers are greatly handicapped by the unavailability of the usual source material such as private letters and diaries. Much is left to speculation.

Of Krushchev's own writings translated into English most are now out of print including "For Victory in Peaceful Competition with Capitalism" (1960) which was his first book to be published in the United States. In 1961, the *N.Y. Times* reported the surprising fact that Krushchev had become the "most-translated author in the world" according to UNESCO's annual compendium of translations. However, this statistic is misleading, for though his speeches and writings had been published in translation from the Russian 198 times, 180 of these translations "never passed beyond Soviet borders, appearing in some of the two dozen other major languages of the Soviet Union."

KHRUSHCHEV SPEAKS: Selected Speeches, Articles and Press Conferences, 1949–1961.
Ed. By Thomas P. Whitney *Univ. of Michigan Press* 1963 $7.50. An illuminating collection of major public statements, including Khrushchev's debate with Walter

Reuther, interview during the U-2 crisis, eulogy and later condemnation of Stalin, and address to the Party Congress.

KHRUSHCHEV REMEMBERS. Ed. and trans. by Strobe Talbot; with an introd., commentary and notes by Edward Crankshaw *Little* 1971 $12.95

A "Hogarthian picture of Russian life at the top under Stalin, under Khrushchev, and as it is today. . . . [It] is on its own special terms a formidable document, a valuable testament in the history of Russian Communism . . . Surely no work on Russia in our times has raised so many questions"—(H. E. Salisbury, in the *N.Y. Times Bk. Rev.*). "Primarily [these memoirs] are Khrushchev's effort to justify himself and his career. . . . [He] emerges . . . as one of the most complex and contradictory major figures of the mid-twentieth century"—(*SR*).

Books about Khrushchev

Khrushchev: A Career. By Edward Crankshaw. *Viking* 1966 $7.50 Compass Bks. pap. $2.75
"It is too early for a deep or comprehensive study of Khrushchev, but Mr. Crankshaw has provided a lively working guide"—(Harrison Salisbury, in the *N.Y. Times*).
Khrushchev and the Soviet Leadership, 1957–1964. By Carl A. Linden. *Johns Hopkins Press* 1966 $11.00 pap. $2.95
"Professor Linden's study is an extremely useful contribution to the field"—(*TLS*, London).
Khrushchev. By Mark Frankland. Introd. by Harry Schwartz *Stein & Day* 1967 $6.95 pap. $2.95
A popular biography by a former Moscow correspondent of the London *Observer* which "avoids the all-black and all-white approach; shows that Khrushchev was neither a saint nor an archvillain; and places the Stalin period in good historical perspective"—(Alexander Werth, in the *Nation*).
The Berlin Crisis of 1961. By Robert M. Slusser. *Johns Hopkins Press* 1973 $17.50 pap. $8.50

MACMILLAN, SIR (MAURICE) HAROLD. 1894–

In 1963, Harold Macmillan retired from political life after seven years as Britain's Prime Minister. A decade before, one London writer had commented: "He may be the last of the suave, almost courtly British statesmen . . . who can turn up in Moscow wearing an astrakhan cap, or sit cross-legged talking oil with a Middle-Eastern sheik without loss of dignity." Born in London, the son of a Scotsman, he had studied classics and mathematics at Oxford; with characteristic British unflappability, as he lay wounded in No Man's Land during World War I he read a pocket copy of Homer in the original Greek. From 1920 to 1940 he was director of his family's publishing house, Macmillan & Co. Though he became a Conservative member of Parliament in 1924, it was not until World War II that his political career blossomed. "Under titles that changed as his responsibilities grew, he was, from January, 1943, to the end of the war in Europe, *the* British politician . . . acting for the British government in the Mediterranean Theatre of Operations"— (*New Yorker*). In 1950 the London *Sunday Times* observed: "He has an Edwardian charm and courtesy, as well as an Edwardian mustache. He is a political philosopher, as well as a practical statesman." His memoirs, which he began after a cancer operation in 1963, are marked by no little humor—"I have reached the age of indiscretion," he remarked on a recent visit to New York for publication of the second volume.

MIDDLE WAY. *St. Martin's* rev. ed. 1966 pap. $5.95

WINDS OF CHANGE: 1914–1939. The first volume of his memoirs. *Harper* 1966 $15.00

"In the first volume, Macmillan made progress; he got himself born, educated, wounded in action, married, into the family publishing business and into Parliament, but for the most part he was recalling a sad procession of failures. He spent the years between the two World Wars in political isolation, with hardly anybody to talk to about economics except Keynes, and hardly anybody to talk to about foreign policy except Churchill. These two prophets were widely regarded as cranks during that period of depression and appeasement"—(*New Yorker*).

THE BLAST OF WAR: 1939–1945. The second volume of memoirs. *Harper* 1968 $15.00

"In the guise of autobiography, Harold Macmillan has written a vivid, inside and thoroughly engrossing history of a major sector of World War II: the Mediterranean. . . . The scope of the book is as wide as the Mediterranean war itself: the conquest of North Africa and the divisions between the prickly de Gaulle and the politically bland Giraud, the question of whether to treat Italy after her surrender to the Allies as friend or foe, the rivalry between Tito and Mihailovic, the Greek civil war and much else. . . . There are any number of superb portraits of minor and major figures"—(*N.Y. Times*).

TIDES OF FORTUNE: 1945–1955. The third volume of memoirs. *Harper* 1969 $15.00

"This third volume of the memoirs of the former Prime Minister of Great Britain covers his political life from 1945 when Labor swept to power . . . to 1955, when with the Tories entrenched in office under Sir Anthony Eden, Macmillan left the Foreign Office to become Chancellor of the Exchequer, the last step on his road to 10 Downing Street"—(*LJ*).

RIDING THE STORM: 1956–1959. The fourth volume of memoirs. *Harper* 1971 $15.00

"This volume deals with his prime-ministership and with the events which occupied the international scene from 1956 until 1959"—(*LJ*).

POINTING THE WAY: 1959–1961. The fifth volume of memoirs. *Harper* 1972 $15.00

"The years covered in this volume were filled with great events and moments of historical drama. Macmillan provides an able and useful account but despite the welcome details he offers, we get little of the feel and vividness of the time"—(*LJ*).

AT THE END OF THE DAY. The sixth volume of memoirs. *Harper* 1974 $16.50

"Among the crises dealt with in the final volume of Macmillan's memoirs, which covers his last years as British Prime Minister, are the Cuban missile crisis, the French veto of the United Kingdom's entry into the European Common Market and domestic security scandals"—(*BRD*).

Books about Macmillan

Macmillan: A Study in Ambiguity. By Anthony Sampson. *Simon & Schuster* 1967 $6.50
"Harold Macmillan served longer than any other postwar Prime Minister of Great Britain, but his achievements are uncertain. In this most readable short book, Mr. Sampson tries to explain the reasons for this uncertainty—to examine the personality of a man who was both a Tory and a rebel, and to describe his policies, which often seem to have been the deepest expression of the man's personality and, at the same time, a collection of vote-catching improvisations. Mr. Sampson, in effect, is briskly and brightly telling us that it is too soon to say anything definitive about Harold Macmillan's place in history"—(*New Yorker*).

EDEN, SIR (ROBERT) ANTHONY, Earl of Avon.   1897–

"The man who succeeded Churchill" as Prime Minister of England emerges as "one of Europe's most prescient and effective spokesmen for freedom" in his autobiographical reports on the historic times he has lived through in positions of responsibility. He was Churchill's Foreign Secretary and succeeded him as Prime Minister in 1955, retiring in 1957 after the Suez débacle. As co-chairman of the 1954 Geneva Conference on Far Eastern Affairs, he had withstood both French and American pressure to escalate the Indochinese war. "He refused, as he said in his memoirs, 'to endorse a bad policy for the sake of unity.' It is precisely this profound honesty of the man that makes his words [on Vietnam] worth listening to today," said the *Saturday Review* of his "Toward Peace in Indochina" (1966, op.). In it he offers a 12-point settlement program for the Vietnam war. "Neutrality" he writes, "is not a crime; it is a risk. Indochina would be an example where neutrality could also be the way through to peace." The biography by Randolph Churchill, "The Rise and Fall of Sir Anthony Eden" (1959), is unfortunately out of print.

FOREIGN AFFAIRS. 1939. *Kraus* $16.00

FREEDOM AND ORDER: Selected Speeches, 1939–1946. 1948. *Kraus* $15.00

FACING THE DICTATORS. *Houghton* 1962 $8.50

The second volume of his memoirs tells the great and tragic story of the years from 1923 to 1938 "when dictators, defying the League of Nations, the sanctity of treaties and the ordinary decency of political and personal behavior rode whirlwind toward war"—(*N.Y. Times*).

THE RECKONING. *Houghton* 1965 o.p. This third volume of memoirs covers the war years, 1938–1945, during which Sir Anthony was Foreign Secretary, at the side of Winston Churchill and at the center of events.

STEVENSON, ADLAI E(WING).   1900–1965.

After Adlai Stevenson's sudden death in a London street in 1965, Walter Lippmann wrote that he represented "the kind of American that Americans themselves, and the great mass of mankind, would like to think that Americans are." Democratic Governor of Illinois, twice Presidential candiate, and Ambassador to the United Nations under Kennedy and Johnson, Stevenson was a self-styled "egghead" who was particularly admired by students and intellectual liberals but not always by his more "realistic" fellow politicians. "He was always disposed to thought; often he gave indications of seeing another side to the question even where the Communists were involved. He was also, it was privately alleged, somewhat moral; he always worried openly about world opinion; he viewed force as a last resort; and he seemingly believed in the United Nations. Not speeches but real belief"—(John Kenneth Galbraith, in the *N.Y. Times*). His nomination at the 1952 Democratic National Convention was one of the few genuine drafts in American political history. Unlike many politicians, he wrote most of his own speeches—speeches marked by eloquence and self-deprecatory wit. Stevenson's papers are now being edited by Walter Johnson and Carol Evans. The Adlai

Stevenson Institute of International Affairs was established in Chicago in 1967 as a permanent memorial.

PAPERS. Ed. by Walter Johnson and Carol Evans *Little-Atlantic* 1972 Vol. I Beginnings of Education, 1900–1941 $15.00

NEW AMERICA. Ed. by Seymour E. Harris and others. 1957 *Kennikat* 1971 $11.00

CALL TO GREATNESS. *Atheneum* 1962 pap. $1.25. An affirmation of democracy's will to survive and its ability to cope with totalitarianism.

LOOKING OUTWARD: Years of Crisis at the United Nations. Ed. by Robert and Selma Schiffer; pref. by John F. Kennedy *Harper* 1963 $5.95

A collection of his speeches both in the United Nations and outside. "The eloquence and wit of Adlai Stevenson give them unique savor"—(*N.Y. Times*).

AN ETHIC FOR SURVIVAL: Adlai Stevenson Speaks on International Affairs, 1936–1965. Ed. by Michael Prosser; fwd. by Hubert Humphrey *Morrow* 1969 $15.00. A collection of 50 speeches.

Books about Stevenson

Slanted News. By Arthur E. Rowse. 1957. *Greenwood* 1973 $10.00

Conscience in Politics: Adlai E. Stevenson in the 1950's. By Stuart G. Brown. *Syracuse Univ. Press* 1961 $4.50

Adlai Stevenson: Citizen of the World. By Bill Severn. *McKay* 1966 $4.75

"Since Stevenson was involved in many of America's domestic and foreign relations from the 1930's on, this book will also be valuable for supplementary reading.... Excerpts from Stevenson's sayings and speeches are incorporated in the text"—(*LJ*).

Adlai Stevenson: A Study in Values. By Herbert J. Muller. *Harper* 1967 $7.95

"Concentrating on analysis of Stevenson's ideas and a calculation of their impact on our political history, [Mr. Muller] adds a somewhat sardonic humor of his own which enhances the reader's pleasure and eases the weight of his formidable learning"—(*New Republic*).

The Remnants of Power: The Tragic Last Years of Adlai Stevenson. By Richard J. Walton. *Coward* 1968 $5.95

"A saddening account of the tragic effect of the dissemblances and hypocrisies of diplomacy as practiced by the United States upon a man of integrity"—(*LJ*). The author is a member of the U.N. press corps.

Adlai: The Springfield Years. By Patricia Harris. *Aurora Pub.* 1974 $7.95

CLARK, KENNETH MACKENZIE, Baron. 1903–

Born in 1903, the only child of a wealthy Scotch family, Kenneth Clark was educated at Winchester and Trinity College, Oxford. "After Oxford, Clark became a protegé of the art collector and critic Bernard Berenson.... Before he was 30 he had been appointed director of the National Gallery, and was on his way to becoming Lord Clark of Saltwood, the most influential tastemaker in the London art world"—(*Time*). He has presented the two highly acclaimed BBC television series "Civilisation" and "The Romantic Rebellion".

ANOTHER PART OF THE WOOD. *Harper* 1975 $11.00. His autobiography, from birth to the eve of World War II.

"By almost any standards, here is a story of privilege and deserved success. But there are more than cracks in Clark's golden bowl—the usual hint of sublime dissatisfaction successful men feel obliged to point out. A vein of self-contempt—sometimes but not always playful—runs through-out the book"—(*Time*).

REMBRANDT AND THE ITALIAN RENAISSANCE. *New York Univ. Press* 1966 $12.50; *Norton* 1968 pap. $2.65

CIVILISATION: A Personal View. *Harper* 1970 $17.95 1972 pap. $6.95

"Gathered here are thirteen lectures which the author originally presented on a BBC television series in the spring of 1969. The result is a history of western Europe from the fall of Rome to the present, constructed from the evidence of visible artifacts"—(*New Statesman*).

HENRY MOORE DRAWINGS. *Harper* 1974 $40.00. Clark is one of Henry Moore's closest friends.

THE ROMANTIC REBELLION: Romantic Versus Classic Art. *Harper* 1974 $15.00. This text was the basis for his BBC television series.

KENNAN, GEORGE F(ROST). 1904–   *See Chapter 9, History, Government and*
Politics—Modern and World, this Volume.

HAMMARSKJÖLD, DAG (HJALMAR AGNE CARL). 1905–1961. (Nobel Peace
Prize 1961)

Primarily a political economist, Hammarskjöld was Sweden's leading monetary expert and a
brilliant diplomat. He was elected Secretary-General to the United Nations in 1953 by nearly
unanimous vote, having previously been considered "the darkest of dark horses for the post"—
(*N.Y. Herald Tribune*).

He brought to this office an ideal of a truly international civil service, a passion for the rule of
decency and reason, and extended the scope of the Secretariat to a diplomatic and executive
position of unique importance. He was killed in a plane crash in 1961 while on an official mission
to the strife-torn Congo.

In 1964 "Markings" (from the Swedish *"Vägmärken"*) was posthumously published in a joint
English translation by Leif Sjöberg, assistant professor of Swedish language and literature at
Columbia, and the poet W. H. Auden. Hammarskjöld himself had described this (best-selling)
diary of religious and philosophical reflections "as a sort of *white book* concerning my negotiations
with myself and with God." This "journal of a soul" not only startled the world, but even his friends
"expressed amazement at the disclosure by the book of a profoundly religious and mystical inner life
about which they had known nothing." Others however felt that "his religious side, as revealed by the
diary, was only one of many facets of a brilliant, complicated person."

PUBLIC PAPERS OF THE SECRETARIES-GENERAL OF THE UNITED NATIONS. Ed. by Andrew
W. Cordier and Wilder Foote *Columbia* vols. 2–5 1972–1975 Vol. 2 Dag Hammarskjöld (1972) Vol. 3 Dag Hammarskjöld 1956–1957 (1973) Vol. 4 Dag Hammarskjöld 1958–1960 (1974) Vol. 5 Dag Hammarskjöld 1960–1961 (1975) each
$22.50. Vol. I of this series is concerned with Trygve Lie

MARKINGS. Trans. from the Swedish by Leif Sjöberg and W. H. Auden; fwd. by W. H.
Auden *Knopf* 1964 deluxe ed. $10.00

THE LIGHT AND THE ROCK: The Vision of Dag Hammarskjöld. Ed. by Trudy S. Settel
Dutton 1966 $4.50. A selection of his thoughts on many subjects, under four
headings: The Individual; Nature, Art, Writing, Religion; The World's Condition;
and the United Nations.

Books about Hammarskjöld

Dag Hammarskjöld: Custodian of the Brushfire Peace. By Joseph P. Lash. 1961. *Greenwood*
1974 $13.25. Not a definitive biography, but highly informative, by a veteran among United
Nations reporters.
Dag Hammarskjöld and Crisis Diplomacy. By Richard I. Miller. *Oceana* 1962 $7.50
The Quest for Peace: The Dag Hammarskjöld Memorial Lectures. Ed. by Andrew W. Cordier
and Wilder Foote. *Columbia* 1964 $12.50 pap. $2.95
Hammarskjöld: The Dangerous Man. By Emery Kelen. *Putnam* 1966 $5.95. A popular
biography by the caricaturist and U.N. television director who was also a close friend of the
late Secretary-General.
Dag Hammarskjöld's United Nations. By Mark W. Zacher. *Columbia* 1969 $9.00
"Zacher's study systematically analyzes the strategies and tactics utilized by Hammarskjöld to
promote pacific settlement of disputes, control and use of force, promote disarmament, and
to build a more peaceful world order"—(*Choice*).
Hammarskjöld. By James L. Henderson. Makers of the Modern World Ser. *Int. Pubns. Service*
1969 $6.25
Hammarskjöld. By Brian Urguhant. *Knopf* 1972 $12.50
"In this book, a comprehensive political analysis of Dag Hammarskjöld's seven years 1952–
1961 as the U.N.'s Secretary-General, Urguhant . . . chronicles in precise detail how close one
man often came to making the curious organization do what it was supposed to. . . .
Urguhant does not much deal with Hammarskjöld's private life, though he squelches for
good the rumors of his alleged homosexuality"—(*Time*).

JOHNSON, LYNDON B(AINES). 1908–1973.

It will be many years before history can pronounce final judgment on the Presidency of Lyndon
Johnson. We are much too close to evaluate the effectiveness of his Great Society programs and
too involved for dispassionate analysis of his relationship to contemporary problems. Most analysts
agree on one point: that Lyndon Johnson knew how to wield power. Assuming office after
President Kennedy's assassination in 1963, he accomplished the seemingly impossible task of

pushing Kennedy's then-stagnated New Frontier programs on civil rights, poverty and aid to education through Congress. However, his tragic involvement in Vietnam now overshadows in many people's minds the good accomplished by his massive civil rights and antipoverty legislation.

THE PUBLIC PAPERS OF THE PRESIDENTS OF THE UNITED STATES, LYNDON B. JOHNSON. 10 vols. covering 1963–1969. *United States Government Printing Office*, Washington, D.C. $6.25–$7.00

THE VANTAGE POINT: Perspectives of the Presidency, 1963–1969. *Holt* 1971 $15.00; *Popular Lib.* 1972 pap. $1.95

"The real story of the Johnsonian Presidency is not to be found in this book. It is his story as he would like things to be. It is straightforward enough from that viewpoint, and the writing is good, simple expository prose. . . . It is all tidied up, antiseptic, ordered, very calm; there are no villains, no personal opinions on people, no judgments, there is no anger, precious little intimacy"—(*N.Y. Times Bk. Rev.*).

INAUGURAL ADDRESS. *St. Onge* lea. $5.00

THE JOHNSON HUMOR. Ed. by Bill Adler. *Simon & Schuster* 1965 $2.95

QUOTABLE LYNDON B. JOHNSON. Ed. by Sarah H. Hayes *Droke-Hallux* 1968 $2.95

Books about Johnson

Lyndon B. Johnson and the World. By Philip Geyelin. *Praeger* 1966 $5.95
"The best book thus far written on the Presidency of Lyndon B. Johnson"—(Hans Morgenthau, *N.Y. Review of Books*). The author, a *Wall Street Journal* correspondent, calls it "an interim report on . . . how he approaches foreign affairs and the making of foreign policy."

A Very Personal Presidency: Lyndon Johnson in the White House. By Hugh Sidey. *Atheneum* 1968 $5.95
An "excellent" book (*New Yorker*) distilled from two million words of "raw material"—his weekly column on the Presidency in *Life* magazine.

JFK and LBJ: The Influence of Personality upon Politics. By Tom Wicker. 1968. *Penguin* Pelican Bks. 1969 pap. $2.25
The chief of the *N.Y. Times* Washington bureau offers his explanations for "Kennedy's inability to push through Congress his domestic programs and Johnson's loss of consensus in relation to the Vietnam war"—(*LJ*).

The Tragedy of Lyndon Johnson. By Eric F. Goldman. *Knopf* 1969 $8.95; *Dell* pap. $1.50
The author is a Princeton professor, president of the Society of American Historians, and was a White House aide for three years under the Johnson administration. "Probably one of the best of the journalistic accounts of L.B.J."—(Max Frankel, in the *N.Y. Times*).

The President Steps Down (orig. "L.B.J.: The Last Hundred Days"). By George Christian. *Macmillan* 1970 $6.95. A memoir of the last 100 days of his administration, written by the man who was Johnson's press secretary at the time.

No Hail, No Farewell. By Louis Heren. *Harper* 1970 $7.95
"This knowledgeable British reporter has written about the Johnson years with a degree of sympathy for the President's dilemma which no American writer may be able to summon for another 20 years"—(*LJ*).
"Mr. Heren clearly feels that denigration of President Johnson has been carried to such atrocious lengths that something must be done to rehabilitate him. What he has written is far from a eulogy, or even an apology, but it is at least a reasoned apologia"—(*TLS*, London).

LBJ: 37 Years of Public Life. By Joe B. Frantz. *Shoal Creek Pub. Co.* 1974 $10.00

BRAITHWAITE, E(DWARD) R(ICARDO).   1912–

E. R. Braithwaite was educated at New York University and Cambridge and spent ten years in London as a teacher and social worker—experiences warmly and movingly recounted in his best-selling "To Sir, With Love" and "Paid Servant." The former, which became a movie starring Sidney Poitier, is the story of his first teaching assignment at a secondary school in London's East End, a challenge—especially because of his color—which he faced with firmness, good sense and love. (The title was the inscription on his pupils' parting gift.) After nearly nine years of teaching, Braithwaite was transferred to London's Department of Child Welfare to help deal with problems involved in the heavy influx of colonial immigrants. "Paid Servant" concentrates on his efforts, in this capacity, to find a home for Roddy Williams, a mulatto rejected by both white and Negro families—with illuminating commentary on his colleagues' racial attitudes. Mr. Braithwaite has also written a novel, "Choice of Straws" (1966 *Pyramid Pubns.* 1972 pap. $.95), about adolescents caught up in the complexities of racial prejudice.

TO SIR, WITH LOVE. *Prentice-Hall* 1960 $5.30; *Pyramid Pubns.* 1973 pap. $.95

PAID SERVANT. *Pyramid Pubns.* pap. $.75

RELUCTANT NEIGHBORS. *McGraw-Hill* 1972 $6.95

"An articulate and moving examination of how his blackness has affected his life. . . . Braithwaite's reminiscences are vivid and the book is a dramatic, thought-provoking picture of the gap in understanding between black and white"—*(LJ)*.

KENNEDY, JOHN FITZGERALD. 1917–1963.

With the tragic assassination of the brilliant 35th President of the United States on a Dallas street in 1963, the books appraising his place in history will be written from many points of view and for many years to come. Articulate, forward-looking but with a great sense of the past, Kennedy was the only American President to be also a Pulitzer Prize winner, his "Profiles in Courage" have received that honor in 1957.

Born in Brookline, Mass., he was a Harvard graduate. He wrote "Why England Slept" (1940, *Funk & Wagnalls* 1961) while still an undergraduate. An expanded version of a pamphlet earlier published by the Anti-Defamation League has been republished as "A Nation of Immigrants" (1958, *Harper* 1964 lib. bdg. $5.49 1970 pap. $1.25). Of this Allan Nevins has said: "President Kennedy expounds the need for an enlargement of our narrow laws. His moving book expresses an ideal defined by Washington in the first years of the Republic: that America should always be a 'propitious asylum for the unfortunates of other countries.' " PT boat commander, Senator from Massachusetts, he brought to the White House not only youth but a vision, and his brutal death shocked the world. Dignitaries from many foreign countries, led by his brave and lovely widow, followed his funeral cortege on foot to the cathedral, in dramatic and impressive testimony to the respect and admiration he had gained during his two and a half years as President.

Helpful in approaching the vast accumulation of print about President Kennedy is James T. Crown's "The Kennedy Literature: A Bibliographical Essay" (*New York Univ. Press* 1968 $6.95)—"a well-written, carefully researched, scrupulously fair, and very interesting annotated bibliography"—*(LJ)*. Also available is a nonannotated Library of Congress bibliography (*United States Government Printing Office* 1964 pap. $.30).

THE PUBLIC PAPERS OF THE PRESIDENTS OF THE UNITED STATES, JOHN F. KENNEDY. *United States Government Printing Office*, Washington, D.C. 3 vols. each $9.00 Public messages, speeches and statements covering 1961–63.

MEMORABLE QUOTATIONS. Comp. by Maxwell Meyersohn. *T. Y. Crowell* 1965 $6.95. An excellent collection, with all sources cited, arranged under broad headings such as freedom and totalitarianism, civil liberties, education, space.

THE QUOTABLE MR. KENNEDY. Ed. by Gerald Gardner. 1962. *Popular Lib.* 1964 pap. $1.40. Short quotations on national and international topics taken from Kennedy speeches, 1957–62.

PROFILES IN COURAGE. *Harper* 1956 memorial ed. with fwd. by Robert F. Kennedy 1964 $8.95 pap $.95; *Franklin Watts* lg.-type ed. $8.95

THE STRATEGY OF PEACE. Ed. with introd. by Allan Nevins *Harper* 1960 $5.00; *Popular Lib.* pap. $.50

TO TURN THE TIDE. Ed. by John W. Gardner; fwd. by Carl Sandburg *Harper* 1962 $5.00. Statements and addresses of his first legislative year, up to the 1961 adjournment of Congress.

INAUGURAL ADRESS. *Acropolis* 1965 pap. $1.00; *St. Onge* lea. $5.00

THE BURDEN AND THE GLORY. Ed. by Allan Nevins; fwd. by Lyndon Johnson *Harper* 1964 $6.00. Selection of speeches and statements from the fall of 1961 until November 22, 1963.

Books about John F. Kennedy

John Kennedy: A Political Profile. By James MacGregor Burns. *Harcourt* 1959 $6.75

Portrait of a President: John F. Kennedy in Profile. By William Manchester. 1962. *Little* rev. ed. 1967 $5.95; *Manor Bks.* 1967 pap. $.75

"An effort to picture a man rather than a public figure"—*(New Republic)*. An expansion of a series of articles which originally appeared in *Holiday*. The 1967 edition includes a lengthy epilogue.

J. F. K.: The Man and the Myth. By Victor Lasky. 1963. *Arlington* 1966 $8.95. A highly controversial portrait, withdrawn from sale briefly upon his death.

John F. Kennedy, President. By Hugh Sidey. *Atheneum* 1963 $6.95

A Day in the Life of President Kennedy. By Jim Bishop. *Random* 1964 $5.95

Kennedy without Tears: The Man beneath the Myth. By Tom Wicker. Fwd. by Arthur Krock *Morrow* 1964 $2.95. Brief, witty and sensitive, this originally appeared in *Esquire.*

Kennedy. By Theodore C. Sorensen. *Harper* 1965 $12.50; *Bantam* 1966 pap. $1.95
  Kennedy's top aide and adviser covers the years 1953–1963. "Likely to remain the one, essential text on the Kennedy administration"—(*Book Week*).

A Thousand Days: John F. Kennedy in the White House. By Arthur M. Schlesinger, Jr. *Houghton* 1965 $9.00 ltd. ed. $50.00; *Fawcett* Premier Bks. 1971 pap. $1.95
  "A remarkable feat of scholarship and writing, set in the widest historical and intellectual frame. . . . A great President has found—perhaps he deliberately chose—a great historian"— (*N.Y. Times*).

The Pleasure of His Company. By Paul B. Fay, Jr. *Harper* 1966 $6.95
  "The author and JFK met at a PT-boat training base in 1942 and formed a friendship that lasted 21 years. . . . This book is mainly a collection of anecdotes about the late President"— (*LJ*).

John F. Kennedy and the New Frontier. Ed. with introd. by Aida D. Donald. *Farrar, Straus* (Hill & Wang) 1966 pap. $2.95. An anthology drawn from periodicals and excerpted from the books by Schlesinger, Sorensen and Koenig.

With Kennedy. By Pierre Salinger. *Doubleday* 1966 $5.95
  "An amiable and entertaining but not very penetrating memoir"—(*N.Y. Times*) by the former Presidential press secretary.

To Move a Nation: The Politics of Foreign Policy in the Administration of John F. Kennedy. By Roger Hilsman. 1967. *Dell* Delta Bks. 1968 pap. $2.95
  "A remarkable book, worth the wait. Part history, part memoir, and part political theory, it is precisely what the subtitle claims"—(*New Republic*). The author, who was Assistant Secretary of State for Far Eastern Affairs in 1963, describes seven crises from the Bay of Pigs to Vietnam.

Johnny, We Hardly Knew Ye: Memories of John Fitzgerald Kennedy. By Kenneth P. O'Donnell and David Powers. *Little* 1972 $8.95
  "A memoir by two close associates, focusing on Kennedy's development as a total politician from his first race for Congress in 1946 to his death"—(*LJ*).

The Best and the Brightest. By David Halberstam. *Fawcett* Crest Bks. 1973 pap. $1.95

Conversations with Kennedy. By Benjamin C. Bradlee. *Norton* 1975 $7.95
  "Personal reminiscences of Kennedy 'the man' rather than historical insights on Kennedy as President"—(*LJ*) by a close personal friend, now Executive Editor of the *Washington Post.*

Books about the Assassination

The Torch Is Passed. By the Associated Press. *Pocket Bks.* 1963 pap. $.75

Four Days: The Historic Record of the Death of President Kennedy. Comp. by United Press International and *American Heritage. Simon & Schuster* 1964 $2.95. Includes the newspaper account of the assassination, eulogies, comments from the world press, photographs.

The Official Warren Commission Report on the Assassination of President John F. Kennedy. With an analysis and commentary by Louis Nizer and a historical afterword by Bruce Catton *Doubleday* 1964 $4.95; introd. by Harrison E. Salisbury *Bantam* 1964 pap. $1.00; *Popular Lib.* pap. $.75; *U.S. Govt. Printing Office* 1964 $3.25 pap. $2.50

Hearings, Exhibit Materials and Depositions. Comp. by the Warren Commission, the basis of their Report. *U.S. Govt. Printing Office* 1964 26 vols. (*consult publisher for price*)

Portrait of the Assassin. By Gerald R. Ford and John R. Stiles. *Simon & Schuster* 1965 $6.95

Kennedy Assassination and the American Public. Ed. by Bradley S. Greenberg and Edwin B. Parker. *Stanford Univ. Press* 1965 $11.50

Whitewash: The Report on the Warren Report. By Harold Weisberg. Available from Mr. Weisberg (Hyattstown, Md. 20734) 1965 $4.95. Purports to describe government suppression of photographic evidence.

Whitewash II: The FBI-Secret Service Coverup. By Harold Weisberg. Available from Mr. Weisberg (*address in previous entry*) 1966 $4.95. Further "evidence" on the same subject.

Inquest: The Warren Commission and the Establishment of Truth. By Edward Jay Epstein. Introd. by Richard H. Rovere *Viking* 1966 $5.00 Compass Bks. pap. $1.75. One of the more responsible critques of the Warren Commission Report; it does not rule out the conspiracy theory.

A Mother in History. By Jean Stafford. *Farrar, Straus* 1966 $3.95. A book by the well-known writer of fiction based on interviews with Lee Oswald's mother, which illuminates the Oswald tragedy, whatever his guilt.

The Death of a President: November 20–25, 1963. By William Manchester. *Harper* 1967 $12.50
  The originally "authorized" biography whose general critical reception is summed up in the

Saturday Review's comment: "An infinity of detail . . . trivia and tragedy." It was finally published after a much publicized dispute between Manchester and the Kennedy family, which wanted to have certain passages (relating to President Johnson) deleted.

Presumed Guilty: Lee Harvey Oswald in the Assassination of President Kennedy. By Howard Roffman. *Fairleigh Dickinson* $10.00

The Day Kennedy Was Shot. By Jim Bishop. *T. Y. Crowell* (Funk & Wagnalls) 1968 $9.95; *Bantam* 1973 pap. $1.25

Three Assassinations: The Deaths of John and Robert Kennedy and Martin Luther King. Ed. by Janet Knight. *Facts on File* 1971 pap. $4.45

KENNEDY, ROBERT F(RANCIS).   1925–1968.

Senator Robert F. Kennedy's tragic assassination on June 6, 1968, just after his California primary triumph in his campaign for the U.S. Presidential nomination, left the nation stunned in the wake of his brother's assassination and that of Martin Luther King. Senator from New York and Attorney General in his brother's administration, he had represented, especially for the black citizens of America, a hope for justice, unity and peace. He left behind a manuscript, originally intended for eventual publication in the *N.Y. Times Magazine*. The article—his memoir of the Cuban missile crisis—was offered to bidders and sold to the McCall Corporation for an unprecedented $1,000,000; it appeared in the November 1968 issue of *McCall's* magazine on the 6th anniversary of those terrifying days of decision. Now published by *Norton*, it "may be one of the most important books of our time. . . . The main story is well known, but as a principal figure in resolving the crisis Robert Kennedy brings to it extraordinary authority with his own insights, perspectives and very important revelations of the decision-making process at the highest level, on the brink of nuclear holocaust. Robert Kennedy shows us what happens to the most competent men under stress. Above all, perhaps his most valuable contribution is the way he recounts the events of what superficially seems to have been exclusively a military crisis, while constantly posing moral and philosophical problems"—problems such as "the myths of national sovereignty, the infallibility of experts, notions of vital national interests as distinct from the interests of all humanity"—(David Schoenbrun, in the *N.Y. Times*).

THE ENEMY WITHIN. *Harper* 1960 $8.95

His inside account of the McClellan Committee Hearings. "An exciting, valuable and honest book. . . . Kennedy's story and views of how [the labor leader James] Hoffa won acquittal of a charge of bribing a committee investigator is revealing"—(*N.Y. Times*).

JUST FRIENDS AND BRAVE ENEMIES. 1962 *Popular Lib.* pap. $.60

An engaging report of his 28-day world tour in February 1962. "He highlights his public speeches, . . . and his free-wheeling give-and-take with students, labor leaders and the press, particularly in Japan, Indonesia and West Germany"—(*N.Y. Herald Tribune*). The title is taken from an 1806 letter of Thomas Jefferson to Andrew Jackson: "We must meet our duty and convince the world that we are just friends and brave enemies."

QUOTABLE ROBERT F. KENNEDY. Ed. by Sue G. Hall. *Droke-Hallux* 1967 $2.95

THIRTEEN DAYS: A Memoir of the Cuban Missile Crisis. Ed. by Richard Neustadt and Allison Graham; introds. by Robert S. McNamara and Harold Macmillan. 1969. *Norton* 1971 $5.50 pap. $1.95; *Franklin Watts* lg-type ed. $8.95; *New Am. Lib.* pap. $.95

The posthumously published inside account of the crucial days of the 1962 Cuban missile crisis as he lived through them with his brother and his administration. "One hopes that [all world leaders] with the personal power to end human history, will read this definitive text on atomic confrontation. It should be basic reading for all citizens everywhere, beginning at the seventh or eighth grades of elementary schools"—(David Schoenbrun, in the *N.Y. Times*).

Books about Robert F. Kennedy

An Honorable Profession: A Tribute to Robert F. Kennedy. Ed. by Pierre Salinger, Edwin Guthman, John Seigenthaler, and Frank Mankiewicz. *Doubleday* 1968 $5.95 ltd. ed. $100.00. Photographs, and contributions by John Glenn, Theodore C. Sorensen, Harold Macmillan, Andrei Voznesensky and others.

The Unfinished Odyssey of Robert Kennedy. By David Halberstam. *Random* 1969 $4.95

A study of his campaign for the Democratic Presidential nomination by an outstanding writer on current events. "Halberstam's extremely readable book shows him to be an admirer of the late Bobby Kennedy who does not demean his memory by any attempt to nourish a 'legend' or to paint out the warts in the portrait"—(*PW*).

Robert Kennedy: A Memoir. By Jack Newfield. *Dutton* 1969 $7.50

Kennedy Justice. By Victor Navasky. *Atheneum* 1971 $10.00

"An intricate and thorough study of Robert Kennedy's tenure as Attorney General, a scholarly work"—(*New Republic*).

Presidency on Trial: Robert Kennedy's 1968 Campaign and Afterwards. By Stuart G. Brown. *Univ. Press of Hawaii* 1971 $6.95

"By piecing together statements made in campaign speeches [he describes] how Robert Kennedy held out a promise for presidential leadership, and how a consequence of his death has been a return to 'politics as usual'. Against this background, the author analyzes the performance of President Nixon in handling the Vietnam war, civil rights, welfare and other matters"—(Publisher's note).

The Kennedys and Vietnam. Ed. by John Galloway. *Facts on File* 1971 pap. $2.95

The Kennedy Promise: The Politics of Expectation. By Henry Fairlie. *Doubleday* 1973 $7.95

"Fairlie, an English journalist who lives in the U.S., examines the campaigns and the administration of John F. Kennedy and the campaigns of his brother, Robert, and decides that both men (along with the staffs they selected) raised hopes in the American people that no one could fulfill. Mr. Fairlie thinks that in foreign and military affairs the Kennedys tended to invent crises or to exaggerate incidents into emergencies so as to be always agog and always acting"—(*New Yorker*).

FRANK, ANNE. 1929–1945.

When Anne Frank wrote in her diary, "I hope I shall be able to confide in you completely, as I have never been able to do in anyone before . . .," she did not realize that she would become an imperishable symbol of courage all over the Western World. This journal of a German-Jewish girl, who for two years lived with her parents in a warehouse in Holland in hiding from the Nazis, is one of the most moving stories of World War II. After the Nazis discovered their hiding place the members of the family were sent to concentration camps and Anne died in Bergen-Belsen in 1945. The diary, which was discovered and saved by friends, covers the years 1942 to 1944, three days before the arrival of the Nazis. "Anne, like any true writer, was at her best when, without self-consciousness or elaborate device, she poured out her personality. Such enormously difficult simplicity is the hallmark of her journal. Not even terror or the most painful constraint could deprive her of a wonderfully feminine, young, vital responsiveness. Somehow she preserved enough of the teenager's normal frivolities and irresponsibilities—enough to make her abnormal plight comprehensible. . . . She has shown us that it is possible to remain human as long as we are alive"—(*N.Y. Times*).

WORKS, 1959. *Greenwood* 1974 $13.50. A new edition of the "Diary" including an introd. by Ann Birstein and Alfred Kazin, line cuts and a group of fables, essays and personal reminiscences not previously published.

ANNE FRANK: The Diary of a Young Girl. Trans. from the Dutch by B. M. Mooyart; introd. by Eleanor Roosevelt. 1952. *Doubleday* rev. ed. 1967 $6.95; *Franklin Watts* lg.-type ed. $8.95; *Modern Library* $2.95; *Pocket Bks.* pap. $.95; *Washington Square* 1972 pap. $.95

Books about Anne Frank

The Diary of Anne Frank. A dramatization by Frances Goodrich and Albert Hackett of "Anne Frank: The Diary of a Young Girl." Fwd. by Brooks Atkinson *Random* 1956 $5.50; *Dramatists* acting ed. $1.25. Winner of the 1956 Pulitzer Prize and the N.Y. Drama Critics Circle Award.

Anne Frank: A Portrait in Courage. By Ernst Schnabel. Trans. by Richard and Clara Winston *Harcourt* 1958 $6.95 pap. $.65. A documentation of the "Diary" which tells of Anne's normal childhood, the Amsterdam hideaway, the arrest and the horrors of the Nazi concentration camp.

Tribute to Anne Frank. Ed. by Anneke Steenmeijer. *Doubleday* 1971 $8.95

The Obsession. By Meyer Levin. *Simon & Schuster* 1974 $8.95

"This is an account of Levin's twenty-year battle over the rejection and suppression of his dramatization of 'The Diary of Anne Frank'. . . . [his book is also] a self-analysis of an artist confronted with hostility, censorship and ideological hatred"—(Publisher's note).

Chapter 3

Bibles and Related Texts

"Of course the Bible is not a book. Because it is all bound together a literature covering seven or eight centuries is mistaken for a single volume. This is Christianity's fault. The only book the Bible resembles is an anthology."

—ISRAEL ZANGWILL

The Bible continues to be the most influential book that has ever been published in the English language. Each year new or revised editions, translations, commentaries, concordances, and handbooks pour from the world's presses in an attempt to throw new light on its ancient message. In this edition of *"The Reader's Adviser"* we have followed the previous pattern of listing religious material in two Chapters, one entitled "Bibles and Related Texts" and the other, which follows it immediately, on "World Religions." Since the word Bible usually connotes the Christian Old and New Testaments taken together (in Catholic Bibles only, the Apocrypha is included), this Chapter is in general confined to the texts of that Bible and the works relating to it, with the inclusion of the section on (Christian) Prayer Books and on (mainly Christian) Religious and Contemplative Anthologies. Since the Old Testament provided the Scriptures of the Jews long before Christ, however, there is much here pertaining to Judaism as well.

The King James Version, for Protestants, and, for Roman Catholics, the Douay Version continue to be the most widely read Bibles throughout Christendom, but "no century has seen the appearance of more modernized Bibles than has the twentieth century." In the past decade many more new translations for Roman Catholics, Protestants and Jews have appeared. In 1947, the discovery of the priceless Dead Sea Scrolls (*q.v.*), part of the library of a Jewish monastic community living before and during the time of Christ, opened the way for even more revisions. Other important documents, chiefly in Coptic translations from Greek, were found in 1945 at Nag Hammadi (Chenoboskion) in Egypt. These include such works as "The Gospel of Thomas" and "The Gospel of Philip," which may in time prove to be as important for the history of the second Christian century as the Scrolls have been for an earlier period—*(see Chapter 4, World Religions: Gnosticism, this Volume)*. Further and more recent discoveries are reflected in the Sections of this Chapter on Archeology and on the Dead Sea Scrolls.

For its period, the definitive bibliography of Bibles in all languages, with extensive notes and full indexes, is T. H. Darlow and H. F. Moule's "Historical Catalogue of the Printed Editions of Holy Scripture in the Library of the British and Foreign Bible Society" (London 1903–11, *Kraus* 4 vols. $117.00). An essential bibliography is "The English Bible in America: A Bibliography of Editions of the Bible and New Testament Published in America, 1777–1957," edited by Margaret T. Hills, Librarian of the American Bible Society (*American Bible Society* and *N. Y. Public Library* 1961 rev. ed. 1962 $10.50). Begun under Dagney Hansen as a revision of Darlow and Moule, it drew upon and collated four previous American Bible bibliographies. Titles were searched in the Library of the American Bible Society, the Union Catalog of the Library of Congress, and the larger Eastern university libraries. "Included are polyglot editions and commentaries which reproduce the Bible text. Annotations for important and offbeat printings are very full and include frequently fascinating biographical material on translators, printers and so forth." Another valuable resource is the *American Bible Society's* "Historical Catalog of Printed Editions of the English Bible, 1525–1961," edited by A. S. Herbert ($10.50). All known editions between 1824 and 1961, except reprints, are listed "unless they present some new feature of importance or interest." Various Bibles in reprint in a microformat are listed in the "Guide to Reprints 1975" Microcard Editions annual.

The first Bible in German with woodcut illustrations, from Augsburg (c. 1475), and a rare Latin Bible on vellum of Nicolaus Jenson, printed in Venice (1476) were in 1964 donated to the Library of Congress by Lessing G. Rosenwald ("its greatest benefactor," says the *N.Y. Times*). "Project 20" was a superb American television trilogy in 1967. Produced in color by Donald B. Hyatt for NBC, it presented the Bible in the visual expression of the great artists against a background of readings from it and music by Robert Russell Bennett. The Jerusalem Bible, the New Scofield Reference Bible, and the first facsimiles of the Aitken and Geneva Bibles are important new editions published in America since our tenth edition and are duly recorded in the pages following.

An event of great interest to Bible scholars, students, clergy and laymen was the publication, in the spring of 1966, of a new Greek text of the New Testament prepared by four scholars, including the Americans Bruce M. Metzger and Allen Wikgran, with 43 consultants over a period of ten years and published jointly by American, English, Scottish, German and Dutch Bible societies. It is presently in its second edition. ("The Greek New Testament," *American Bible Society*, $4.80). According to the *N.Y. Times*, "It is based on a detailed examination of what the scholars consider to be the best 100 known manuscripts and fragments. The total cost of the project before printing was more than $250,000. Since 1898 the standard Greek text has been the one first prepared by Eberhard Nestle, which is now in its 25th edition. The Nestle text refers to 200 different manuscripts and contains many more variants, or citations of places where manuscripts differ from one another, than the new Greek text. However, the latter includes references to early manuscripts that were not discovered until recently, and it contains more detailed lists of variants on controversial passages." It is from this new text that "Good News for Modern Man: The New Testament in Today's English Version" was translated into modern English (*see Section on Bibles in Modern English: American Bible Society*).

But the most important new development—an outgrowth of Vatican II and the developing consensus of the (chiefly Protestant) United Bible Societies—is the project which began to take shape about 1963 and was first publicly announced in 1966—that of producing a joint Catholic-Protestant Bible; it has enlisted the aid of Judaism as well. In 1965 Pope Paul VI promulgated the Constitution of Divine Revelation, first permitting interfaith versions. (The information and quotations that follow are from the *N.Y. Times*.) The Catholic editor for the project is an American Jesuit, the Reverend Walter M. Abbott, assistant for Bible matters to the late Augustin Cardinal Bea in the latter's capacity as head of the Vatican Secretariat for the Promotion of Christian Unity. Father Abbott has been editor of the Jesuit periodical *America* and is the author of "Documents of Vatican II" (*see Chapter 4, World Religions, Section on Modern Catholicism, this Volume*). He is also editor of *New Testament Abstracts*, "a record of current periodical literature in the field of New Testament studies, published three times a year." With him as co-editors were Rabbi Mark Tannenbaum of the American Jewish Committee, the Reverend J. Carter Swaim of the Presbyterian Church and the Reverend Rolfe Laier Hunt of the National Council of Churches, U.S.A. The group of editors and experts for the new translation met in Rome for preliminary talks in January 1967.

"In his speech of welcome, Cardinal Bea called production and distribution of a common Bible 'a work that is basic and vital to the future of Christianity.' The Cardinal apparently was referring to the belief, held by many Catholic and Protestant missionaries, that their failure to approach the non-Christian world with a common version of the Scriptures confuses their message. Partly as a result of this, and also as a result of the 'dispersed order' in which Catholics and Protestants work for converts, world population is growing much faster than the Christian part of it, [the main reason for Vatican II's approval of vernacular and cooperative Bible versions]. The Rev. Laton E. Holmgren, chairman of the United Bible Societies' executive committee and general secretary of the American Bible Society from 1963 to 1972, said response to the overtures from the

Catholic Church was consonant with the societies' 150-year-old tradition of collaboration with 'all who are devoutly concerned with the Christian world mission.' 'Of course there will be difficulties,' [he said, and described some of them]. But, he· continued, the unspoken question for all of Christianity is 'whether, in the fulfillment of His command to preach the Gospel in all the world, there will be shameful competition or joyful cooperation.' Among the practical difficulties are differing Protestant and Catholic views on the need for interpretive notes to Biblical texts and on the books that make up the Apocrypha, which are recognized as part of the Bible by Catholics but not by Protestants."

By June 1968, the Roman Catholic Church and the United Bible Societies had produced a document called "Guiding Principles for Interconfessional Cooperation in Translating the Bible," which "paves the way for a joint effort by the two bodies in preparation of the Bible. The work will include new translations and analyses of basic ancient texts, and production of complete common Bibles in all of the world's 2,200 languages and dialects, including almost 1,000 in which no translation exists."

The several years of ecumenical scholarship produced the "Oxford Annotated Bible with the Apocrypha" in 1965. It was the first edition of the English Bible to be accepted by both Protestants and Catholics. In 1973 a second edition was published ("The New Oxford Annotated Bible with the Apocrypha" $9.95–$14.95).

THE BIBLE IN THE MAKING

Barclay, William. THE MAKING OF THE BIBLE. *Abingdon* Bible Guide No. I (orig.) 1961 pap. $1.95

Barr, James. THE BIBLE IN THE MODERN WORLD. *Harper* 1973 $5.95

"The author attempts to explore the role of the Bible today by dealing with such issues as the authority of the Bible"—*(Choice)*.

Berkowitz, David Sandler. IN REMEMBRANCE OF CREATION: Evolution of Art and Scholarship in the Medieval and Rennaissance Bible. *Univ. Press of New England* 1968 $15.00

"This catalog of an exhibit at Brandeis University to celebrate the 20th anniversary of the library is in four parts: manuscripts, incunabula, 16th-Century scholarly editions, and 16th- and 17th-Century translations of the Bible. Mr. Berkowitz, professor of history and the history of ideas at Brandeis, contributes an illuminating introduction relating Hebrew and Christian tradition and textual scholarship"—*(LJ)*. Valuable information is also found in the appendixes.

Bratton, Fred Gladstone. A HISTORY OF THE BIBLE: An Introduction to the Historical Method. *Beacon* 1959 $4.25 pap. $2.95

Quite complete and wide-ranging, this emphasizes the relationship of the Bible to other religious writings of the Near East and traces the formation of the Testaments, with their subsequent translations and editions to our own time.

Bruce, Frederick F. THE BOOKS AND THE PARCHMENTS: Some Chapters on the Transmission of the Bible. 1950 1953. *Revell* 3rd rev. ed. 1963 $5.95

The Rylands Professor of Biblical Criticism and Exegesis at the University of Manchester, England, presents here for students and laymen "the results of the latest research and discovery in such fields as the languages of the Bible, the scripts in which they were written, the chief surviving manuscripts (including the Dead Sea Scrolls), the Canon of Scripture, the original text, the ancient versions, and the story of the English Bible, including some account of the New English Bible."

THE ENGLISH BIBLE: A History of Translations from the Earliest English Versions to the New English Bible. *Oxford* 1961 new and rev. ed. 1970 $6.95

"A comprehensive study of the various translations of the Bible into the English language"— (Publisher's catalog). "This version deals with the new editions of the RSV which have appeared since 1961, a fuller treatment of recent Roman Catholic versions with special attention given to the Jerusalem Bible, a section on Jewish translations and new works such as the American Bible Society's 'Good News for Modern Man' and William Barclay's 'The New Testament' "—*(Choice)*.

Foreman, Kenneth Joseph, and others. INTRODUCTION TO THE BIBLE. (Vol. I of Layman's Bible Commentary—*see Section on Bible Commentaries*). *John Knox Press* 1959 1967

$3.50. This first volume contains five general articles: What Is the Bible? by Kenneth J. Foreman; The History of the People of God, by Balmer H. Kelly; The Message of the Bible, by Arnold B. Rhodes; How We Got the Bible, by Bruce M. Metzger; How to Study the Bible, by Donald G. Miller.

Grant, Robert M. THE FORMATION OF THE NEW TESTAMENT. *Harper* 1965 text ed. $3.00
"This book is concerned strictly with the early decisions which went into accepting or rejecting Christian writings for inclusion in the 'recollections' of Jesus: anonymous writings, Hellenistic literature, and the Apocrypha. It identifies, by language and style, the possible authors of what, at the end of the second century, was not yet called 'the New Testament.' . . . Highly recommended"—(*LJ*). Bibliography.

Greenslade, S. L., General Ed. THE CAMBRIDGE HISTORY OF THE BIBLE. *Cambridge* 3 vols. Vol. 1 From the Beginnings to Jerome, ed. by P. R. Ackroyd and C. F. Evans 1970 $25.00 pap. $9.95 Vol. 2 The West from the Fathers to the Reformation, ed. by G. W. H. Lampe 1969 $25.00 pap. $9.95 Vol. 3 The West from the Reformation to the Present Day, ed. by S. L. Greenslade 1963 $25.00 pap. $9.95 set $65.00. A three-volume encyclopedia covering all aspects of the Bible from the history of its printing to its influence on present-day culture and traditions.

Herbert, A. S., Ed. HISTORICAL CATALOG OF PRINTED EDITIONS OF THE ENGLISH BIBLE, 1525–1961. *American Bible Society* 1962 $10.50
"Every known edition of the English Bible from 1525–1961 is listed in this Catalog. Reprints between the years 1824 and 1961 are omitted, however, unless they present some new feature of importance or interest. Up to 1640 the locations of copies in various libraries are indicated. After 1640 the volume described is the copy in the library of the British and Foreign Bible Society, London, unless otherwise stated. Commentaries with new translations are also cataloged"—(Publisher's catalog).

Hills, Margaret T., Ed. THE ENGLISH BIBLE IN AMERICA. *American Bible Society* 1962 $10.50
"A scholarly bibliography of editions of the Bible and New Testament published in America from 1777 to 1957, based on the American Bible Society's collection of American printings of the Scriptures in English, checked against similar holdings in the New York Public Library and a microfilm of the English Bible Section of the Library of Congress Union Catalog of Bibles. It includes descriptions of copies and their locations"—(Publisher's catalog).

Leishman, Thomas Linton. OUR AGELESS BIBLE. *Nelson* 1960 $3.25
A discussion of the development from the most ancient Hebrew manuscript to the RSV Bible, with an evaluation of the importance of recent discoveries such as the Dead Sea Scrolls.

MacGregor, Geddes. A LITERARY HISTORY OF THE BIBLE. *Abingdon* 1968 o.p. Dr. MacGregor deals with biblical interpretation in the Middle Ages before there was a printed English Bible, and with the early versions of the Bible including the Douay-Reims; he also discusses the development of modern versions.

Metzger, Bruce M. THE TEXT OF THE NEW TESTAMENT: Its Transmission, Corruption and Restoration. *Oxford* 2nd rev. ed. 1968 $7.50
The first edition was praised as "the most complete and up-to-date treatment of the subject in English"—(*The Critic*). The second cites over 150 additional books and articles on Greek manuscripts, early versions and critical studies of recent discoveries.

Neill, Stephen. THE INTERPRETATION OF THE NEW TESTAMENT 1861–1961. *Oxford* 1964 $7.75 pap. $4.50
"A survey of New Testament criticism showing its historical development, movements of thought, the contrasting personalities of scholars, and the permanent contributions made by various scholars"—(Publisher's catalog).

Nida, Eugene A., Ed. THE BOOK OF A THOUSAND TONGUES. *United Bible Societies* 2nd ed. 1972 $15.95
"A historical compendium of Scripture translations, showing an actual sample of Scripture in 1399 languages and dialects—the written languages of more than 97% of the world's population. Includes a brief history of Scripture publications in each language, information on Scriptures for the blind, and a chronological list of languages in which the Bible Societies have published"—(American Bible Society's catalog).

O'Callaghan, Edmund Bailey. A List of Editions of the Holy Scriptures and Parts
   thereof, Printed in America Previous to 1860. 1861. *Gale Research Co.* 1967
   $15.00

Rylaarsdam, J. Coert, Ed. Transitions in Biblical Scholarship. Vol. 6 in the 8-vol.
   Essays in Divinity Ser. *Univ. of Chicago Press* 1968 $10.50

   "Representative selections of alumni or of teachers in the Divinity School, University of
   Chicago. The essays cover a wide range of interests including biblical studies, textual criticism, and
   early church history. Especially recommended for theological collections"—(*LJ*).

Scriptures of the World. *United Bible Societies* 1974 pap. $2.00

   "A compilation of information about 1500 languages and dialects in which at least one complete
   book of the Bible has been published. Data concerning these languages and the publication history
   of Scriptures in them are presented in alphabetical, chronological, and geographical arrangement.
   There are 41 maps showing the areas in which these languages are spoken"—(American Bible
   Society's catalog).

THE HOLY BIBLE

Versions

Douay Version. 1582–1610. (Roman Catholic)

   This was a translation published at the English College in the town of Douai in northern France.
   Modern editions differ somewhat from the original, but the Bible used by Roman Catholics at the
   present day is, on the whole, the Douay translation. The new Confraternity Edition (*see below*) is
   intended to replace the Douay Version in the United States. The Roman Catholic Bible differs
   from the Protestant Bible not only in rendering but also in the *order* of the books, the *titles* of the
   books, and the *number* of the books. The books of the *Aprocrypha* are accepted as canonical and
   appear in the Roman Catholic Bible scattered among the various books of the Old and New
   Testaments.
   The peculiarity of the Douay Version, by which it is distinguished from Protestant versions, is
   the fact that it was translated from a Latin manuscript. The earliest manuscripts of the Old
   Testament are in Hebrew, and of the New Testament in Greek. When Rome conquered the
   world, and Latin became the speech of the people, there was need of a translation of the Bible into
   Latin, into the vulgar language—the language of the *vulgus*, the crowd. The Douay Version is a
   translation of the Latin translation called the Vulgate. The Vulgate (c. 383–405) was the work of
   Saint Jerome (Eusebius Hieronymous c. 340–420), one of the four Doctors of the Church, who
   spent most of his life in a monastery in Bethlehem, writing a large number of ecclesiastical works.
   John Wycliffe (or Wyclif, Wiclif, Wickliffe) (1320?–1384) initiated the first complete translation of
   the Bible from the Vulgate into English in order to reach the people directly. He himself
   translated the Gospels and probably the rest of the New Testament and part of the Old
   Testament. He entrusted the editing to John Purvey, who completed the translation (c. 1388).

Confraternity Edition. 1941–   (Roman Catholic)

   Generally known as the "Confraternity Edition," the Confraternity Version is a new translation, the first made from the original languages for Roman Catholics, and is intended to replace
   the Douay Version for public reading in the United States. The Confraternity revision of the New
   Testament translation was made in 1941 and is available from Catholic Bible publishers in
   volumes with the Old Testament in the Douay Version, the Psalms and the New Testament in the
   new Confraternity text.
   The new translation of the Old Testament, made in accordance with directives of the late Pope
   Pius XII in his Encyclical Letter of Sept. 30, 1943, is sponsored by the Bishops' Committee of the
   Confraternity of the Christian Doctrine.

King James Version. 1611. (Authorized)

   The King James Version is known as the Authorized Version, although, as a matter of fact, it
   was never authorized by the King. It was, however, initiated by him as the result of a Puritan
   complaint that the Coverdale Authorized Version, revised as the Bishops' Bible (1568), was not
   accurate. He appointed a group of scholars to undertake the task of fresh translation. Later
   editions had printed on their title pages, "Appointed to be read in the churches," which probably
   gave rise to the legend of authorization. The King James Version was made in 1607–1611 during
   the lifetime of Shakespeare—the Golden Age of English literature. It was translated by 54 scholars
   and is the most famous English Bible. Dwight Macdonald (like many who value the Bible as
   literature) regrets the fact that those who, with justice, have set out to *correct* this translation have
   usually gone too far and bowdlerized great passages. For many the King James, with all its

imperfections, can never be surpassed for poetry, religious feeling and majesty and loveliness of utterance. In "Against the American Grain" (1952, o.p.) in his essay on the Revised Standard Version called "Updating the Bible," Mr. Macdonald writes: "The King James Version is probably the greatest translation ever made. It is certainly 'The Noblest Monument of English Prose,' as the late John Livingston Lowes called his essay on the subject. 'Its phraseology,' he wrote, 'has become part and parcel of our common tongue.... Its rhythms and cadences, its turns of speech, its familiar imagery, its very words are woven into the texture of our literature.... The English of the Bible ... is characterized not merely by a homely vigor and pithiness of phrase but also by a singular nobility of diction and by a rhythmic quality which is, I think, unrivalled in its beauty.' ... The speed with which it was accomplished was possible only because it was not so much a new translation as a synthesis of earlier efforts, the final form given to a continuous process of creation, the climax to the great century of English Bible translation."

REVISED VERSION. 1881–1885. (The American Revised Version was published in 1901.)

The Revised Version of the King James was begun in 1870 at the Convocation of Canterbury by two committees, British and American, the latter advisory only. The New Testament was issued in 1881, and the whole Bible in 1885, by the *Oxford* and *Cambridge University Presses*. In 1901 the surviving members of the American committee published through *Nelson* in New York the American Revised Version embodying the readings they had previously suggested and other improvements. The revisions had been undertaken for two reasons:

1. Because of the discovery of fresh Bible manuscripts. When the King James Version of the Bible was made, there had not yet been discovered three early manuscripts of the Bible: the Vatican manuscript, 4th century (in the Vatican library, Rome); the Sinaitic manuscript, 4th century (discovered on Mt. Sinai, and long in Leningrad; purchased in 1934 by the Trustees of the British Museum for £100,000 from the Soviet Government, the price was the highest ever paid for a manuscript or printed book); the Alexandrian manuscript, 5th century (in British Museum). The discovery of these three manuscripts gave to translators a Bible text older and more accurate than any they had had before, and so much new light was thrown on obscure passages in the Scriptures that a fresh translation was not only warranted but demanded.

2. The second reason for revision was the archaic character of the language of the King James Version; so many words in the King James Version are obsolete, or have lost their original meaning that modern readers no longer understand them in their intended sense. For instance: David prays the Lord to enlarge his feet. In the Revised Version, the word "enlarge" is changed to "set free." This original meaning of the word survives today in the phrase "at large" meaning "free."

The translators of the Revised Version did not put the Bible into modern English—other translators have done that—but they did revise archaic words which are misleading in sense at the present day, and they corrected many mistranslations.

THE REVISED STANDARD VERSION. 1946–1952. (Authorized revision of the American Standard Version. There is also a Catholic edition.)

Important manuscripts and fragments became available that were not known in 1611 or even in 1901 when the American Standard Version appeared. An old Syriac version of the Gospels, probably of the second century, was found in a monastery on Mount Sinai; in 1933, a fragment of Tatian's Harmony of the Four Gospels was discovered at Dura on the Euphrates; and most important of all was the discovery of fragments of 12 manuscripts, now known as the Chester Beatty manuscripts, 3 of them from the New Testament, which may date as early as the first half of the third century. In addition to the biblical documents, a great number of Greek papyri and papyrus fragments were unearthed in Egypt. These writings were contemporary with the New Testament and, together with inscriptions, they furnished new meaning to Greek words and phrases, as they were used in the years when the New Testament was written.

In 1928, a committee of 15 scholars was appointed by the International Council of Religious Education, with which the educational boards of 44 of the major Protestant denominations of the United States and Canada are associated, and to which the copyright of the American Standard Version had been transferred. Lack of funds delayed the work, which was finally begun in 1937. The committee was divided into two sections, one for the Old Testament and one for the New. Dean Luther A. Weigle of the Yale Divinity School served as chairman of the whole committee and the executive secretary, from 1937 until his death in 1944, was the beloved scholar, James Moffatt. The New Testament appeared in 1946, the Old Testament in 1952, and the Apocrypha in 1957.

A delightful article appeared in the August 1946 issue of the *Atlantic Monthly*: "The New Testament, a New Translation" by W. Russell Bowie, one of the nine revision scholars. The resulting translation in English is as near as possible to what the writers of the original text set down and is a triumph of modern biblical knowledge.

The publication of the Revised Standard Version of the Holy Bible in September 1952, aroused great public interest and a new sales record was set: 1,600,000 copies in the first six weeks after publication. There is also a Catholic edition of the Revised Standard Version; however, it is no longer in general use.

THE NEW ENGLISH BIBLE (sometimes called the Oxford Bible).

An entirely new translation from the original Greek into current English, this version was prepared under the direction of all leading Protestant churches in the British Isles. The New Testament first appeared in 1961 and was published in its second edition in 1970. A new translation of the Old Testament and the Apocrypha was published in 1970. Scholars of different denominations and from a number of British universities have taken part in the work. They made a faithful rendering of the best available Greek texts and made use of the most recent biblical scholarship. The new translation was directed by the Joint Committee of the Churches which consisted of representatives of the Church of England, the Church of Scotland, the Methodist Church, the Congregational Union, the Baptist Union, the Presbyterian Church of England, the Churches in Wales, the Churches in Ireland, the Society of Friends, the British and Foreign Bible Society, and the National Bible Society of Scotland. "In assessing the evidence, the translators have taken into account (a) ancient manuscripts of the New Testament in Greek, (b) manuscripts of early translations into other languages, and (c) quotations from the New Testament by early Christian writers. . . . In particular, our knowledge of the kind of Greek used by most of the New Testament writers has been greatly enriched since 1881 by the discovery of many thousands of papyrus documents in popular or nonliterary Greek of about the same period as the New Testament. . . . Taken as a whole, our version claims to be a translation, free, it may be, rather than literal, but a faithful translation nevertheless, so far as we could compass it. . . . But always the overriding aims were accuracy and clarity. . . . The translators are as conscious as anyone can be of the limitations and imperfections of their work. No one who has not tried it can know how impossible an art translation is. . . . Yet we may hope that we have been able to convey to our readers something at least of what the New Testament has said to us during these years of work, and trust that under the providence of Almighty God this translation may open the truth of the scriptures to many who have been hindered in their approach to it by barriers of language"— (Introduction).

There was simultaneous publication worldwide jointly by *Cambridge University Press* and *Oxford University Press*.

THE JEWISH VERSION. 1917. (Revised Jewish Version begun 1955)

Published by the *Jewish Publication Society of America*, this is practically the first Jewish Bible in English. An earlier translation, made by Isaac Leeser in 1853, in Philadelphia, was a single-handed effort and was never widely read by Jews. Up to this time the English Bible used by those professing Judaism has been either the King James Version or the Revised. Orthodox Jews have preferred the King James Version because it does not use the name Jehovah, the ineffable name that never occurs in the Jewish Version. The Hebrew Bible (Old Testament only) is not called the Holy Bible, but the Holy Scriptures. The word "Bible" does not occur in the Bible itself. It came from the Latin *biblia*, from the Greek *biblia*, plural of *biblion*, the diminutive of *biblos*, "book"— "little book."

The paragraphing of the Jewish Version follows that of the Revised Version. Verse divisions, uniform with those of the King James Version, are indicated in small type. The correspondence is in some cases approximate rather than identical, because the Hebrews divide the Old Testament into 24 books, while the Protestants divide it into 39 books. The order of the Hebrew Bible is also slightly different from the order of the Protestant. The Hebrew Bible ends with an incomplete sentence, the 23rd verse of II Chronicles, "let him go up." In the Protestant Bible the Book of Ezra follows after II Chronicles and completes the sentence, "let him go up to Jerusalem which is in Judah."

The Revised Translation of the Holy Scriptures for Jews was undertaken in 1955 by the *Jewish Publication Society*. It is a complete revision of the 1917 Version and embodies all the latest findings of modern biblical scholarship for all people, together with a modern text which is free from all archaism of language and which, therefore, is more understandable to Jewish laymen.

Early Editions of the Bible

THE GUTENBERG BIBLE.

Printing from movable type was invented in the middle of the 15th century by Johannes Gutenberg (1400?–1468) at Mainz, Germany. The first book to be printed by Gutenberg was the Latin *Vulgate* translation of the Bible (c. 383–405) made by St. Jerome (c. 340–420). The first known copy of it was discovered at the Mazarin Library in Paris in 1760. Forty-seven copies of the Gutenberg Bible are extant, 12 printed on vellum and 35 on paper. According to St. Bonaventure University (1968) there are 14 copies in the United States (3 vellum and 11 paper). Some of the best-known in America are the copies bought by: James Lenox (1847) $2,500, in the New York Public Library; George D. Smith (1911) $50,000, for the Hoe copy now in the Huntington

Library; A. S. W. Rosenbach (1926) $106,000 for the Melk copy from the Melk monastery now in Yale University; U.S. Government (1930) $1,500,000, for the Abbey of St. Paul in Carinthia copy, 3 vols. printed on vellum (one of four known perfect copies on vellum) and 3,000 other incunabula now in the Library of Congress.

The 500th anniversary of Gutenberg's death was marked by a celebration in Mainz, Germany, on Feb. 2, 1968, which included the opening of a new and comprehensive exhibition at Mainz's Gutenberg Museum. At the same time the Grolier Club of New York held a large special exhibition of Gutenberg materials; three copies of his Bible were shown. (For the American facsimile edition, *see the Section on Special Editions of the Bible, under Gutenberg Bible*.)

TYNDALE, WILLIAM, version published 1525–1566.

The first printed English Bible was Tyndale's New Testament. His translation of the Pentateuch was issued in 1530 and revisions of both in 1534–35. Tyndale began his translation of the New Testament from Greek into the vernacular and, finding publication impossible in England, left for Hamburg (1524) and visited Luther (*q.v.*). He began printing his translation of Matthew and Mark at Cologne (1525); he completed printing at Worms of 3,000 New Testaments in small octavo, which were smuggled into England and there suppressed by bishops (only five or six copies are now extant). Constantly harassed, he was finally imprisoned, strangled and burned at the stake, in spite of intercession by Thomas Cromwell. An exact reprint of the edition of 1534, with the translator's prefaces and notes, has been edited for the Royal Society of Literature by N. Hardy Wallis (*Cambridge* $27.50).

COVERDALE, MILES, version published 1535–1537. First complete English Bible.

THE GREAT BIBLE. 1539–1569.

Authorized by Henry VIII, it is sometimes called the Cranmer Bible or the Cromwell Bible. The Psalms in the Protestant Episcopal Prayer Book through the revision of 1928 followed this translation.

THE GENEVA BIBLE. 1560–1644.

The first Bible in Roman type, it became therefore very popular. It was also the first English Bible to use marginal notes and verse divisions. It is often known as the "Breeches" Bible because of the rendering of Genesis 3:7: "They sewed figge-tree leaves together, and made themselves breeches." It was published by English exiles in Geneva and brought to America by the Pilgrims. An edition of this version was the first Bible printed at the *Cambridge University Press* in 1591; its publication broke the monopoly in Bible production in England, held up to that time by the King's printer in London. It was the favored Bible in England for half a century because of its excellent translation, though its Calvinist slant was a source of irritation to King James I. The first facsimile edition of this Bible was published in October 1969, by the *Univ. of Wisconsin Press*.

THE BISHOPS' BIBLE. 1568–1606.

A revision of the Great Bible, each book bears the initials of the Bishop who translated it. The 1602 edition was made the basis of the King James Bible.

THE UNIVERSITY OF CAMBRIDGE BIBLE. 1638.

"Since printing plates had not been invented, the printer had to re-set the Bible every time a reprint was needed. This led to thousands of misprints. The University of Cambridge was asked to produce an edition free from errors. . . . The printers were so proud of this Bible that they nailed a notice to the door of Great St. Mary's Church, challenging scholars to find a mistake in it."

THE ALGONQUIN BIBLE. 1663. Translated for the Indians, it was the first Bible printed in America.

THE BASKERVILLE BIBLE. 1763.

One of the most beautifully printed Bibles of all time, this was produced by John Baskerville (1706–1775), who was appointed Cambridge University Printer for the express purpose of producing a fine folio Bible and Prayer Books. He "designed the typeface which carries his name and which is still one of the best."

Nickname Bibles

There are a number of Bibles which have been given nicknames owing to some accident in their printing. These Bibles are not other versions of the Bible, but simply certain printings of the versions listed above.

"Treacle Bible." "Is there no treacle in Gilead?"—for "balm."

"Wicked Bible," omitting "not" in the seventh commandment, and reading "Thou shalt commit adultery."

"Vinegar" Bible, "vineyard" being printed as "vinegar."

"He" Bible and "She" Bible. Ruth 3:15, in its correct version, reads, "and she went into the city"; in the "He" Bible, "and he went into the city."

"Ears to ear" Bible. "Who hath ears to ear let him hear."

"Bugge Bible." "Afraid of bugges by night."

"Camels Bible." "And Rebekah arose, and her camels."

"Place-Makers Bible." "Blessed are the Place-Makers."

"Judas Bible." Contains misprints of "Judas" for "Jesus."

"Standing fishes Bible." "The fishes shall stand."

"Affinity Bible." The table of affinity has the error "A man may not marry his grandmother's wife."

"Lions Bible" was distinguished for its typographical errors among which was "Out of thy lions" instead of "loins."

"Sin On Bible." "Sin no more" is printed "Sin on more."

Bible Publishing Houses

Every bookseller should keep in his Bible section the current "Bible and Testament" catalogs of the publishers listed below. Most of them contain valuable selling information in addition to illustrations of the Bibles, specimen type pages and full descriptions. There have been, since our last edition, many mergers of Bible and other religious publishers, which we show now in corrected version, unless the publisher in question continues to issue an independent catalog under his old name.

American Bible Society

Since its founding in 1816, this missionary organization had issued to the end of 1961 49,779,992 complete Bibles and 542,827,985 Testaments, Portions and Selections of the Bible, a total of 592,607,977 including foreign editions. By 1968 the Society had distributed Scriptures in more than 600 languages and dialects. The inexpensive Scripture Portions, some illustrated, are available in the following languages: Chinese, Dutch, English, French, German, Greek, Italian, Japanese, Korean, Norwegian, Portuguese, Spanish, Serbo-Croation, Swedish and Tagalog.

> Text, Reference, Concordance, Lectern and Pulpit Bibles mainly in the King James Version with American spelling; Zipper Bibles in English and in Spanish (Valera Revised); Testaments; Scripture Portions in Foreign Languages (*see above*); Large Type Sight-Saving Portions; Study Eds.; Talking Bibles (recordings); Braille Bibles. The Society also publishes some issues in the Revised Standard Version. (*For Today's New English Version, see Section on Bibles in Modern English.*)

Benziger Brothers

THE NEW AMERICAN BIBLE. 1970 $9.95 pap. $5.28

THE NEW TESTAMENT FROM THE NEW AMERICAN BIBLE. 1970 pap. $1.95 (orders to *Macmillan*)

Cambridge University Press

The world's oldest Bible publisher, *Cambridge* published its first Bible in 1591, an edition in the Geneva Version. All are now in the King James Version except for the New English Bible published jointly with *Oxford*. (*See also Section on Bibles in Modern English for the New English Bible New Testament.*)

> Apocrypha, Bride's, Cambridge Compact, Cameo, Concordance, Family, Illustrated, Interleaved, Pew, Pulpit, Red Letter, Reference, Text, Paperback, Vest Pocket, Pocket, and Zipper Bibles. (*See also Section on Bibles in Modern English.*)

Christian Classics

DOUAY VERSION. 1964 $8.95

Wm. Collins-World Pub. Co. Inc.

Founded in 1819, *Collins* published a wide range of Bibles and Testaments in the Authorized King James Version, first printed under license in 1839. Merged with *World*

Publishing Company, they publish a complete line of Bibles in the King James and Revised Standard Versions. A recent publication is the illustrated New American Standard Bible (1974 $7.95 ref. ed. $15.95).

Concordant Publishing Concern

THE CONCORDANT LITERAL NEW TESTAMENT. Comp. by A. E. Knoch. Rev. 1966 various bindings $1.95–$9.95

Harper & Row—Harper & Brothers

Established in 1817, they published a wide range of Bibles and Testaments in the King James Version; the Revised Standard Version was added in 1962. In 1966 most of *Harper*'s line of Bibles was transferred to *Zondervan*.

A. J. Holman Co.

The oldest Bible publishing house in America. Bibles in both King James and Revised Standard Versions:

Revised Standard Version Bibles—Pulpit, New Testaments; King James Version Bibles— Family, Pulpit and Lectern, Fraternal Alter, White Fraternal, Masonic, New Testaments; New American Standard. (*See following Section—Bibles in Modern English and Section on Special Editions of the Bible and Parts of the Bible.*)

Holt, Rinehart and Winston, Inc.—The John C. Winston Co.

A large publisher of all types of Bibles merged to become this corporation in 1960. Its Bibles are now handled by *Zondervan*.

The Jewish Publication Society of America

The Society publishes the authoritative English translation of The Holy Scriptures used by Jews throughout the English-speaking world. In 1955 a revision of the 1917 translation was begun. For The Torah, newly translated and published in 1963, *see Section on Special Editions of the Bible and Parts of the Bible.*

THE HOLY SCRIPTURES ACCORDING TO THE MASORETIC TEXT. 1917. Various bindings, ranging from cloth $5.00 to Pulpit leatherette $27.50.

The Judson Press

THE MONTGOMERY NEW TESTAMENT IN MODERN SPEECH (*see following Section—Bibles in Modern English*).

P. J. Kenedy and Sons

NEW AMERICAN BIBLE. 1970 $9.95 deluxe ed. $17.95 text ed. $4.68 pap. $4.95 (orders to *Macmillan*)

Moody Press

NEW AMERICAN STANDARD BIBLE. $8.50–$26.95 pap. $1.25

Nelson-National

In 1962, the *National Bible Press*, makers of fine Bibles since 1863, merged with *Thomas Nelson & Sons* to become the new *Nelson-National* marketing organization. The House of Nelson was founded in 1798 in Edinburgh. The American branch was established in 1854. Always prominent as publishers of the King James Version, they were selected in 1901 to publish the American Standard Version. Their American Standard Bible is the Standard American Edition of the Revised Version. Embodied in the text are the preferred readings offered by the American members of the Revision Committee (*see Section on Versions—Revised Version*).

Nelson published the Revised Standard Version of the complete Bible on September 30, 1952, one of the greatest events in publishing history. This climaxed 16 years of work by a committee of America's foremost Bible scholars. The New Testament was completed and published in 1946 (*see Section on Versions—Revised Standard Version*).

Again in 1956, *Nelson* made the news when they announced a new Complete Concordance to the Revised Standard Version of the Holy Bible. Remington Rand's Univac Electronic Computing System was used to do 23 years' work in 1,000 hours. The Concordance was published on February 1, 1957 (*see Section on Bible Concordances*). Recent publications include The Common Bible with Apocrypha/Deuterocanonical Books RSV (2nd ed. $8.95–$12.95 pap. $5.95) and The Open Bible KJV (1975 $12.95–$38.95). (*See Section on Special Editions of the Bible and Parts of the Bible.*)

King James Version—Giant Print Bibles and Testaments, Pocket Bibles and Vest Pocket Testaments, Family, Brides', Young Readers' Bibles, Deluxe Gift, Special Award, Special Gift, Deluxe Award Bibles, Study, Pew, Reference, Large Print Reference Bibles, Special Cassette Bibles; Revised Standard Version, 2nd ed.—Lectern and Small Pulpit Bibles, Vest Pocket Testaments, Gift and Award Bibles, Pew, Study, Reference and Large Print Reference Bibles. New American Version for Catholics—Family and Brides' Bibles, Compact Bibles, Gift and Study Bibles; Today's English Version; American Standard Version.

Oxford University Press

The *Oxford* line of Bibles is the most extensive on the market. The Oxford Bible paper, used in their finer editions, is made by a secret process, and is the most opaque India paper made. *Oxford* prints mainly the King James Version, but has some Bibles in the Revised Standard Version. "Oxford—America's Gift Bible since 1675" is no idle advertising slogan. Their separate current catalog of Bibles and Prayer Books containing "Oxford's Aids for Easy Bible Sales" is equally valuable for the seasoned bookseller and his bewildered assistant.

Oxford celebrated the Golden Anniversary of the Scofield Reference Bible in 1959. Dr. Frank E. Gaebelein, son of Dr. Arno C. Gaebelein, one of the Reverend C. I. Scofield's consulting editors in 1909, has written a booklet on the 50-year history. After the 1917 publication of a "New and Improved Edition," it became, in 1930, the first book ever published by *Oxford* (New York) to sell a million copies. Since then, sales "have several times exceeded the million mark." In 1954 nine biblical scholars were selected to make a thorough revision in the light of modern biblical and archeological findings. It was published in 1967 as The New Scofield Reference Bible under the editorial direction of Dr. E. Schuyler English. (*See Section on Special Editions of the Bible and Parts of the Bible.*) In 1961 *Oxford* published jointly with *Cambridge* the New Testament of The New English Bible (*see Section on Bibles in Modern English*). The Old Testament and the Apocrypha have been translated and published with the revision of the New Testament in 1970 to form the New English Bible. A verse-by-verse examination of the completed translation of the Old Testament and Apocrypha has been undertaken "to ensure that the meaning of the original Hebrew and Greek in the best available texts and versions is fully and accurately represented"—(Publisher's note).

Text, Reference, Concordance, Red Letter, Family and Teachers' Bibles; Brides', Loose Leaf, Pew, Presentation, Text, Wide Margin, Pulpit, Lodge, and Lectern Bibles; Fraternal Bibles; Bibles with Apocrypha, Bibles with Prayer Book; Scofield Reference Bible; Pilgrim Edition annotated by E. Schuyler English; Bibles in blue, red, brown, maroon, purple, tan and green in addition to white and the traditional black; New Testaments; Prayer Books. (*See also Sections on Bibles in Modern English, Shorter Bibles, Special Editions of the Bible and Parts of the Bible and The New Testament.*)

The Seabury Press

Prayer Books and Hymnals.

Sheed & Ward. See Section on Bibles in Modern English.

University of Chicago Press. See Sections on Bibles in Modern English and Shorter Bibles.

Zondervan Publishing House

Since 1966 their list of Bibles has included editions formerly carried by *Harper & Row.*

Apocrypha, Award, Bride's, Children's, Clearblack Reference, Compact, Companion, Concordance, Family, Illustrated, Imperial Pica, Large Print, Marked Reference, New Encyclopedic Reference, Pew, Pulpit, Red Letter, Study, Teacher's, Text, White and Zipper Bibles in the King James Version. Award, Brevier Reference, Bride's, Children's, Compact, Concordance, Illustrated, Pew, Red Letter, Reference, Study, Teacher's, Text, White and Zipper Bibles in the Revised Standard Version.

Bibles in Modern English

The 20th-century translations or revisions include several notable examples: for Protestants, the American Standard Version (1901); the Weymouth (1909), the Smith-Goodspeed (1923–27), the Moffatt (1924), the Montgomery (1924), the Williams (1937), the Phillips Translations (1947–1958); the Revised Standard Version (1952); the New English Bible (1970); and 22 volumes of a projected 43 of an interfaith project, a new rendering by scholars from many countries, The Anchor Bible (*see under Doubleday*). For Roman Catholics there have appeared the Confraternity Revision of the New Testament (1941) and the Confraternity Version of the entire Bible (1952–1955); the Knox Translation of the whole Bible (1944–1956), the Kleist-Lilly Translation of the New Testament (1954), the New American Bible (1970) and the New American Standard Bible (1974). For Jews there are The Holy Scriptures According to the Masoretic Text (1917), the projected Revised Translation of The Holy Scriptures and the new (1963) translation of The Torah, the first five books of the Bible.

Earlier attempts to write the Bible in the language of the man in the street produced such shocking translations as "The Lord is my shepherd, I should not worry." Dwight Macdonald has a most interesting essay on this question in "Against the American Grain" (*see discussion in Section on Versions: King James Version, preceding*). The new translations are not attempts at rewriting the Authorized Version; they are entirely fresh translations from the original languages and in many cases from better texts newly discovered. The Basic English New Testament is scholarly and musical despite its limited 800-word vocabulary.

There is great similarity in these Bibles in modern English, as they are all made with the same idea and purpose. The changes are of this character: "Glad tidings" is translated "good news"; "suffer the little children" is "let the little children"; "begat" is modernized to "was the father of"; "ye" becomes "you"; "to thee and to thy seed" is "to you and your descendants." Measures of time and space and of the values of coins, as well as official titles, are given in their nearest English equivalents.

American Bible Society

GOOD NEWS FOR MODERN MAN: The New Testament in Today's English Version. Trans. by Robert G. Bratcher from the latest available Greek texts; ill. by Annie Vallotton pap. $1.95; *Broadman* 1967 pap. $1.25

The rendering is into "common English," as that used by the Voice of America and the U.N. is called. It avoids colloquialisms and archaisms that might be misunderstood by the reader knowing little English. This excellent bargain (599 pages) includes attractive line drawings by the Swiss artist Annie Vallotton. Since 1966 it has sold over 46 million copies and is presently in its 3rd edition and available with the imprimatur of the Roman Catholic Archbishop John Francis Whealon. "Good News for Modern Man" also appears as today's English version New Testament with more than 200 color photographs of biblical lands. $4.00 pap. $2.50.

Cambridge University Press

The New Testament of the English Bible was published jointly with the *Oxford University Press* in 1961 and in 1970 was revised and published with the Old Testament and Apocrypha to form the New English Bible, "a new translation of the Bible into modern English. Enriched by the most recent Biblical scholarship, the New English Bible has been acclaimed throughout the English speaking world for its faithful rendering of the ancient tongues into the language of today"—(Publisher's catalog). It is available in various

bindings with or without the Apocrypha—$5.45–$55.00 lib. bdg. Old Testament $8.95
New Testament $5.95 Apocrypha $4.95

Concordia (member of *Lutheran Pubs. Group*)

THE NEW TESTAMENT IN THE LANGUAGE OF TODAY. Trans. by the Lutheran scholar,
William F. Beck 1963 $5.95 pap. $2.50. A "lively, readable and accurate translation,"
of particular value to young people.

Doubleday

THE ANCHOR BIBLE.

Now available are the first 22 vols. of a projected 43 vols. under the editorial supervision of Dr.
William Foxwell Albright, for many years professor of Semitic languages at Johns Hopkins, and
Dr. David Noel Freedman, professor of Near Eastern Studies at the University of Michigan–Ann
Arbor and director of the program on studies in religion; to be published first in hardcovers
followed by paperbacks. The first 22 vols.: Vol. 1 Genesis, ed. by A. Speiser 1964 $8.00 Vol. 7A
Lamentations, trans. by Delbert R. Hillers 1972 $6.00 Vol. 7B Esther, ed. by Carey A. Moore 1975
$6.00 Vol. 12 I Chronicles, ed. by Jacob M. Myers 1965 $6.00 Vol. 13 II Chronicles, ed. by Jacob
M. Myers 1965 $6.00 Vol. 14 Nehemiah, ed. by Jacob M. Myers 1965 $7.00 Vol. 15 Job, rev. ed. by
Marvin H. Pope 1973 $8.00 Vol. 16 Psalms I, 1–50, ed. by Mitchell Dahood 1966 $8.00 Vol. 17
Psalms II, 51–100, ed. by Mitchell Dahood 1966 $7.00 Vol. 17A Psalms III, 101–150, ed. by
Mitchell Dahood $8.00 Vol. 18 Proverbs and Ecclesiastes, ed. by R. B. Scott 1965 $6.00 Vol. 20
Second Isaiah, ed. by John L. McKenzie 1968 $7.00 Vol. 21 Jeremiah, ed. by John Bright 1965
$8.00 Vol. 26 Matthew, ed. by William F. Albright and C. S. Mann 1971 $8.00 Vol. 29 The Gospel
According to John I—XII, ed. by Raymond E. Brown 1966 $8.00 Vol. 29A The Gospel According
to John XIII—XXI, ed. by Raymond E. Brown 1970 $8.00 Vol. 31 The Acts of the Apostles, ed. by
Johannes Munck 1967 $7.00 Vol. 34 Ephesians: Introduction, Translation and Commentary on
Chapters 1—3, Markus Barth 1974 $8.00 Vol. 34A Ephesians: Introduction, Translation and
Commentary on Chapters 4—6, Markus Barth 1974 $8.00 Vol. 36 To the Hebrews, ed. by George
W. Buchanan 1972 $7.00 Vol. 37 The Epistles of James, Peter, and Jude, ed. by Bo I. Reicke 1964
$6.00 Vol. 42 Esdras I and II, trans. by Jacob M. Myers 1974 $8.00

An interfaith project, with Protestant, Catholic and Jewish scholars from many countries
contributing individual volumes; the translation is "a new rendering . . . not intended to be a
slavishly literal word-for-word translation, nor a freehand paraphrase, but faithful in word and
phrase to the underlying Semitic and Greek texts, designed to catch their tone and spirit and
rhythm"; it is a "distinguished series"—*(LJ)*.

Harper and Row

THE MOFFATT BIBLE: A New Translation. By Dr. James Moffatt 1925 $8.50–$10.95

The Jewish Publication Society of America

For the Revised Translation of the Holy Scriptures begun in 1955, *see Section on Versions;*
for the new 1963 translation of The Torah, *see Section on Special Editions of the Bible and
Parts of the Bible.*

The Judson Press

THE NEW TESTAMENT IN MODERN ENGLISH. Translated by Helen Barrett Montgomery.
1924 $5.00–$10.00. Published on the centennial of the American Baptist Publication
Society.

The Macmillan Co.

LETTERS TO YOUNG CHURCHES: A Translation of the New Testament Epistles. By John B.
Phillips 1968 pap. $1.45

THE NEW TESTAMENT IN MODERN ENGLISH. Trans. by John B. Phillips 1965 rev. ed.
1972 $2.95–$5.95 pap. $1.45

FOUR PROPHETS. A translation of Amos, Hosea, Isaiah and Micah by John B. Phillips (his
first translation of the Old Testament) 1963 $3.95 pap. $1.45

Of the Phillips "Four Prophets," *Library Journal* said, "An Anglican minister has succeeded to a
remarkable degree in getting the sense and considerable of the spirit of the original into good
English idiom without departing too far from the exalted level of prophetic utterance."

Nelson-National

A complete line of Bibles in the American Standard Version and the Revised Standard Version.

Oxford University Press

A full line of Revised Standard Version Bibles including The Oxford Annotated Bible, the only RSV Bible of its kind, edited by Herbert G. May and Bruce M. Metzger with 16 contributors, including introductory material to the 66 books, annotations, cross-references and supplementary articles, new maps 1962 $7.50–$10.95; The Oxford Annotated Apocrypha (1965 $2.75, $3.95) has been combined with this Bible to produce the Oxford Annotated Bible with the Apocrypha 1965 $9.95–$14.95. "The high level of scholarship, meticulous care, clarity of style and practical helpfulness of the materials have been beautifully matched by the superb printing and binding of Oxford Press. The introductory article on the 'Number, Order and Names of the Books of the Bible' should be particularly useful to both Catholics and Protestants in understanding their divergent views of the canon of Scripture"—(LJ). The Oxford Annotated Bible and Apocrypha received the *imprimatur* of Richard Cardinal Cushing in 1966, and thus became acceptable for Roman Catholics. The New Testament of the New English Bible was published jointly with *Cambridge University Press* in 1961 (2nd edition 1970 $8.50–$12.50 pap. $2.95). The complete New English Bible was published in 1970. It is available in various bindings with or without the Apocrypha ($4.95–$75.00, lib. bdg. in 3 vols. Old Testament—introduction is longer and notes are more numerous than in other editions—$5.95 Apocrypha $2.95 New Testament 2nd ed. $4.95 set in slipcase $12.95).

Sheed and Ward

THE NEW TESTAMENT. Trans. by Msgr. Ronald Knox 1953 $4.50 pap. $1.95

THE HOLY BIBLE: A Translation by Msgr. Ronald Knox. 1950 $6.00

University of Chicago Press

THE NEW TESTAMENT: An American Translation by Edgar J. Goodspeed. 1923 o.p.

THE GOODSPEED PARALLEL NEW TESTAMENT (Goodspeed and King James Version in parallel columns) 1943 $8.00

THE HARPER STUDY BIBLE. Ed. with introd. by Harold Lindsell 1964 $13.95–$37.95

"Each book is preceded by a brief introduction . . . the annotations have their own index; there are maps and a concordance"—(LJ)

THE LAYMAN'S PARALLEL BIBLE. 1973 $17.95–$42.95 New Testament alone $5.95–$25.95

Four translations in parallel form—King James Version, Revised Standard Version, Modern Language Bible: The New Berkeley Version in Modern English, and the Living Bible, an interpretive translation or paraphrase.

THE NEW INTERNATIONAL VERSION.

This is "an entirely new translation . . . the result of a vast 10 year effort by an interdenominational team of Bible scholars sponsored by the New York International Bible Society"—(Publisher's catalog).

Small Bibles with Large Type

The bookseller quails most often before the Bible customer who demands "large, clear type in a small handy Bible." "As the Bible has three-quarters of a million words, it just can't be done, any more than you can put a quart of milk in a pint bottle"—(*Cambridge University Press* catalog). The suggestions that follow however attempt to answer that perennial question. The most recent Bible catalogs should also be consulted. *Unless otherwise noted, the King James Version is listed.*

American Bible Society

Good News for Modern Man—Large Print Edition 18-point type (6 ⅛″ × 9 ¼″) Today's English Version $2.16; Large Print New Testaments (6 ¼″ × 9 ½″) black leatheroid $2.34; hard cloth cover $2.40; Large Size New Testaments (5 ¾" × 8 ¼") hard black cloth $2.04; simulated black leather $1.60

Cambridge University Press

Turquoise Bible (5 ¾" × 9 ¹/₁₆") various bindings $26.95–$65.00

Collins + World

Large Print New Testament and Psalms red letter editions 5 ½" × 7 ⅝" × ½" $4.95–$7.95 black letter editions 5 ½" × 7 ¼" × ⅝" $6.95–$7.95; Longprimer Reference Bibles 6 ⅜" × 11 ½" × 1 ¼" red letter editions $12.95–$31.95 black letter editions $18.00–$31.95; text Bibles 6 ½" × 9 ¼" × 1 ¹/₁₆" red letter editions $12.95–$18.95 black letter edition $12.50. These are available thumb-indexed for an additional $3.00 each. Heritage Bibles red letter editions 6 ½" × 9 ½" × 1 ¼" $13.95–$29.95 special anniversary editions $25.00 thumb indexed $3.00 more

Nelson-National

Giant Print Bibles (6 ⅜" × 9 ¼" ×1 ¼") $9.50–$26.95; Giant Print New Testaments with Psalms $8.50–$17.95; Large Print Reference Bibles $10.00–$36.95; Large Print Reference Bibles RSV 2nd ed. gift boxes $22.95–$48.95

Oxford University Press

New Long Primer Concordance Bible (5 ¾" × 8 ⅝") red letter and black letter editions, various bindings $17.95–$45.00

Franklin Watts

New Testament. In the Revised Standard Catholic Version. 1967 $15.00; The King James Version 1967 $8.95

Shorter Bibles

A Beginner's Bible: A Shortened Bible in Modern English. Ed. by Margherita Fanchiotti with the advice and assistance of Nathaniel Micklem; ill.; maps Oxford 1958 $4.25

"In this 'Shorter Bible' the meaning of the original text is re-expressed in simpler language for those who find traditional Bible English too difficult"—(Publisher's Catalog).

New Testament in Shorter Form. (Orig. "Reader's New Testament") ed. by Samuel Terrien Macmillan 1970 $4.95 pap. $2.95

Shorter Books of the Apocrypha. By J. C. Dancy. New English Bible Commentaries: Old Testament. Cambridge 1972 $10.95 pap. $3.95

The Shorter Oxford Bible. Ed. and abr. by G. W. Briggs, G. B. Caird and N. Micklem. Oxford 1951 $4.25. The King James Version used for the canonical books and the Revised Version for the Apocrypha.

Special Editions of the Bible and Parts of the Bible

Most of the Bible Publishing Houses (q.v.) publish separate Testaments, Testaments with Psalms and Books of Psalms. (See also following Sections on The New Testament, Harmonies of the Gospels and The Apocrypha.) The most extraordinary special edition of a Bible to come to our attention is that of the Vulgate (in Latin, of course, and therefore included here mainly as a curiosity) published in 1969 by the Italian firm of Rizzoli (New York office at Rizzoli's bookstore). It is illustrated by Salvadore Dali in a number of sumptuous limited editions, some of which include an original illustration, some a sculptured mold, hand-worked in gold, of Mr. Dali's hand. Prices range from $1,800 to $17,500.

The Amplified Bible. Zondervan 1958–65 $12.95–$24.95

A conservative translation with added clarifying words (not in the Greek text) which elicited the following criticism from Library Journal: "Actually, under the guise of translation, a commentary has been produced with a consequent sacrifice of smoothness of rendering and most literary values. In the New Testament, footnotes usually give bibliographic documentation of the amplified text, but in the Old Testament, they are usually homiletical, devotional, or apologetic with a moralizing and dogmatic tone."

The Amplified New Testament. Zondervan 1958 $6.95 pap. $1.95; 1968 Pyramid Pubns. pap. $1.25. This new and conservative translation is said to be based on 27 translations including the Greek and indicates clarifying and connective words not in the Greek text. This has been a best-selling version.

Ballou, Robert O., Ed. THIS HE BELIEVED: The Religion of Jesus of Nazareth as Revealed by Readings from the Old and New Testaments and Other Sources. *Viking* 1959 $3.00. Selections from the King James Version and pre-Christian Jewish sources trace the growth of the religion of Jesus; 32 line drawings by Valenti Angelo. By the editor of "The Living Bible" (1952, o. p.).

BLUE DENIM BIBLE: The New Translation in Today's English Version. World Arts Foundation. *Holman* 1973 pap. $1.95

COMMON BIBLE WITH APROCRYPHA/DEUTEROCANONICAL BOOKS RSV. 2nd ed. *Nelson* $8.95–$12.95 pap. $5.95

"The result of 10 years of ecumenical scholarship, the first Bibles to be accepted by Roman Catholic, Protestant, and Greek Orthodox authorities"—(Publisher's catalog).

THE DAILY STUDY BIBLE SERIES. Ed. by William Barclay. *Westminster Press* 17 vols. 1957 set $52.50. Separate books annotated for study of the entire New Testament.

THE ENGLISH BIBLE: Translated out of the Original Tongues by the Commandment of King James the First. Anno 1611. *AMS Press* 6 vols. 1967 set $90.00

"Many great works of collaborative scholarship were produced at the turn of this century, but none is perhaps so well-known and so highly regarded as *The Tudor Translations*. The 56 volumes produced under the general editorship of William Ernest Henley and Charles Whibley between 1892 and 1927 are an honor roll of the language's most golden prose works introduced by some of our greatest scholars and critics"—(Publisher's note). This is a reprint from a 1903–04 edition in this series.

THE ENGLISH REVISED BIBLE. The text of the revisions of 1881–85. *Oxford* moroccoette $4.50

Graves, Robert. THE SONG OF SONGS. *Potter* 1973 $5.95

"A book of poetry and pictures, this is a new translation of the Canticle by an eminent classics scholar and poet"—(*Choice*).

THE GUTENBERG BIBLE: The Cooper Square Facsimile. Includes 97 full-color illuminated leaves. *Cooper* ltd. ed. 2 vols. $450.00 half lea. $600.00 lea. $750.00

THE HOLY BIBLE: Containing the Old and New Testaments; Translated out of the Original Tongues and with the Former Translations Diligently Compared and Revised. King James Version, 1611; a reference edition with concordance. *American Bible Society* 1963 $1.90–$3.70; *Pyramid Pubns.* 1973 pap. $1.95

"This is the first special reference Bible to be published by the American Bible Society in its almost 150-year history. It has been in preparation since 1946. All references, which appear at the bottom of the pages or under sectional headings, are to other Biblical passages. Of help to the general reader will be the list of more than 500 words which have changed meaning since the King James Version was issued. . . . There is also a section listing nearly 300 alternative readings for certain texts, based on newly discovered older manuscripts that were not available to the original King James translators. The concordance of more than 400 pages should be adequate for most purposes"—(*LJ*).

Hurlbut, Jesse Lyman. HURLBUT'S STORY OF THE BIBLE. *Revell* 1966 pap. $1.25; *Pyramid Pubns.* pap. $1.25. A great favorite for family libraries, it has sold over 1,800,000 copies; retells 168 stories.

THE JERUSALEM BIBLE. Ed. by Alexander Jones *Doubleday* 1966 $16.95 thumb-indexed $19.95; 2 vols. $15.90; Readers' Edition 1971 $9.95 pap. $5.95

Winner of the Thomas More Association Medal for "the most distinguished contribution to Catholic literature in 1966," this Bible contains introductions and notes translated from the French "*Bible de Jérusalem*," newly translated by French Dominicans at L'École Biblique in Jerusalem. The one-volume edition published in France in 1956 has been a best seller there. The English edition has been translated afresh from the ancient texts directly into modern English, with reference to the French edition, to the Dead Sea Scrolls and other newly accessible materials. "The numerous cross-references, the index of Biblical themes, and the modern, single-column arrangement of the text, all add to the value of this outstanding translation which should be considered for every library where there is a serious call for literature on the Bible"—(*LJ*). This, too, has become a best seller—in the United States. The editor, a leading biblical scholar, is Senior Lecturer in Divinity at Christ's College, Liverpool, and has studied at Upholland College, the Gregorian University, the Biblical Institute of Rome, and L'École Biblique of Jerusalem, where the French edition was born. "Welcome and useful . . . showing how closely Catholic, Protestant, and Jewish scholars agree in matters of textual, literary, and historical criticism, and thus affording an excellent instrument of the 'ecumenical dialogue' now being undertaken. . . . The translation is couched in idiomatic, modern English, clear, extraordinarily vivid, even colloquial, but not commonplace"—(Millar Burrows, Professor Emeritus of Biblical Theology, Yale Divinity School). "The scholarly notes and articles that give special character to this edition of the Bible are a monument to the progress of Roman Catholic biblical scholarship in recent years"—(*N.Y. Times*).

THE OLD TESTAMENT OF THE JERUSALEM BIBLE. $8.95; Readers' Edition 4 vols. pap. ea. $1.95

THE NEW TESTAMENT OF THE JERUSALEM BIBLE. 1967 $7.95; Readers' Edition 1969 pap. $1.75

THE PSALMS OF THE JERUSALEM BIBLE. 1970 pap. $1.45

Kallen, Horace M. THE BOOK OF JOB AS A GREEK TRAGEDY. *Farrar, Straus* (Hill & Wang) new ed. 1959 pap. o.p.

The authorized version is arranged as a Greek tragedy in the manner of Euripides. Long out of print, this edition was up to date with a new introduction. It should be compared with Archibald MacLeish's poetic drama "J.B." (*q.v.*, Reader's Adviser, *Vol. 1*). Another approach is Margaret B. Crook's "The Cruel God" (1959, o.p.). She sees the author of Job as introducing a broad, new concept of the nature of God.

Lamsa, George M., Trans. THE HOLY BIBLE FROM THE PESHITTA: The Authorized Bible of the Church of the East. *Holman* (dist. by Lippincott) 1958 $10.95 lea. $23.95 New Testament only $6.95 pap. $2.25. Several ancient manuscripts were compared by the translator, born in Kurdistan, where Syriac, a literary dialect of Aramaic, is still retained. The Peshitta was universally spoken in the Near East at the beginning of the Christian era. This English version is smooth and readable.

THE LORSCH GOSPELS. Latin text. Introd. by Wolfgang Braunfels *Braziller* ltd. ed. 1967 boxed $200.00

This Latin Bible, (10 ½″ × 14 ½″), facsimile of an illuminated manuscript of the Carolingian era—from about 810, is included here because of its special interest. It "unites in a single volume the scattered portions of the manuscript: the first two Gospels in the *Biblioteca Documentara Batthayneum* at Alba Julia, Rumania, the last two Gospels . . . and the carved ivory Christ cover, [which is elsewhere]. . . . The whole is sumptuously and meticulously reproduced [including 54 pages in four colors and silver and gold]. Wolfgang Braunfels's introduction comments on the history and makeup of the volume and provides a useful bibliography"—(*LJ*).

THE MARKED CHAIN-REFERENCE BIBLE. Ed. by J. Gilchrist Lawson *Zondervan* 1963 various bindings $18.95–$46.95

This is a new edition of the former "Marked Bible," acquired from *Holt, Rinehart and Winston*. The main features are the printings in four colors of four major themes—salvation, the Holy Spirit, temporal blessings and prophetic subjects. There are also 60,000 center-column cross-references, a 400-page combination Bible encyclopedia, 5,500 questions and answers on the content of the Bible, and 16 pages of full-color maps.

THE MASTERPIECE BIBLES. *Harry N. Abrams* Abradale Press 1959–1970 o.p. Each one contains 95 great biblical paintings, in full color and gold, by such artists as Michelangelo, Titian, Raphael, Rembrandt and Memling; the King James Version for Protestants, the Confraternity-Douay for Catholics.

THE MICHELANGELO BIBLE. o.p. Illustrated with color plates of 84 of Michelangelo's sculptures and marvelous Sistine Chapel frescoes. In Protestant and Catholic versions.

MODERN READER'S BIBLE. Ed. by Richard G. Moulton *Macmillan* 1-vol. ed. 1907 1943 $9.95

This is not a new version but a combination of several versions. It is the work of a distinguished biblical scholar and is based upon the Revised Version. The usual order of the books is changed.

They are grouped according to subject, as narrative, prophetical and poetical books. Three books of the Apocrypha are included: Ecclesiasticus, Tobit and the Wisdom of Solomon. Its unique feature is that it presents the books of the Bible in modern literary form—that is, in the typographical form in which lyrics, sonnets and dramatic dialogues are presented. When the text is in dialogue, the speakers are indicated. When a refrain occurs, it is entitled "Refrain." The acrostic Psalms are arranged as acrostics. When a book has a prologue and an epilogue, these parts are separated from the body of the context.

THE NEW OXFORD ANNOTATED BIBLE, REVISED STANDARD VERSION. Ed. by Herbert G. May and Bruce M. Metzger *Oxford* 1973 $7.50–$12.50

"Laymen, clergymen, teachers and students who want an accurate, scholarly, modern translation combined with outstanding study feature will find it in this Bible. These new and thoroughly updated editions contain the 2nd edition of the R.S.V. New Testament text. The many reading and study aids have been meticulously . . . revised. Supplementary articles have been updated, and three new ones have been added. The map section has been carefully revised in the light of the most recent archaelogical developments"—(Publisher's catalog).

THE NEW OXFORD ANNOTATED BIBLE WITH THE APOCRYPHA: An Ecumenical Study Bible. *Oxford* $9.95–$14.95

"When the original edition was published in 1965, it was widely hailed as a common Bible and was the first edition of the English Bible to receive both Protestant and Catholic approval"— (Publisher's catalog).

THE NONESUCH PRESS HOLY BIBLE: Authorized Version, with Apocrypha. Designed by Sir Francis Meynell; printed jointly by *Oxford University* and *Cambridge University Press;* with 105 sixteenth-century woodcuts of Bernard Salomon. 1963, o.p.

THE OPEN BIBLE. King James Version, red letter. *Nelson* $12.95–$38.95 thumb indexed $4.00 extra

"The most complete KJV study Bible in 40 years. 'The Open Bible' is the combined 1975 scholarship of 23 world-renowned editors and contributors"—(Publisher's catalog).

THE OXFORD ILLUSTRATED OLD TESTAMENT: With Drawings by Contemporary Artists. *Oxford* 5 vols. Vol. I Pentateuch 1968 Vol. 2 Historical Books 1968 Vol. 3 Poetical Books 1968 Vol. 4 Prophets 1969 Vol. 5 Apocrypha 1969 set $60.00

A five-volume edition of the King James Version of the Bible illustrated with nearly 700 drawings by 22 contemporary British artists, including Edward Ardizzone and Brian Wildsmith. "The drawings vary in style from realistic to abstract to pop. Job's daughters are front-view nudes, Susannah tempts the elders by removing the top half of her bikini and a couple in close embrace illustrate the Song of Solomon. . . . Oxford University Press said the new edition was an attempt to get away from traditional, sentimental Bible illustrations"—(*N.Y. Times*). When the Most Reverend Arthur Michael Ramsey, Archbishop of Canterbury, visited a London exhibition of the drawings he commented (according to the *Times*): "My mind had to make more mental jumps than it has ever had to do before on looking at the different media in the exhibition. . . . The Old Testament depicts human life, warts and all. I am not here to make judgment on the pictures."

PENTATEUCH AND HAFTORAHS. Hebrew text; English trans. and commentary. Ed. by J. H. Hertz *Oxford* 5 vols. 1929–36 Vol. I Genesis Vol. 2 Exodus Vol. 3 Leviticus Vol. 4 Numbers Vol. 5 Deuteronomy Vols. 2 and 4 o.p. Vols 1, 3 and 5 each $3.00

Phillips, J. B., Trans. *See Section on Bibles in Modern English under Macmillan.*

THE PILGRIM BIBLE. The complete Authorized King James text, ed. by Dr. E. Schuyler English assisted by 37 Evangelical contributors; notes, references and special helps. *Oxford* 1948 $9.50–$29.50

PSALMS FOR MODERN MAN: In Today's English Version. *American Bible Society* 1972 pap. $.95

THE REMBRANDT BIBLES. *Harry N. Abrams* Abradle Press 1959 o.p. Each one contains 116 of Rembrandt's works—44 paintings reproduced in full color; 72 etchings and drawings in gravure. The Protestant version is the King James, the Catholic the Confraternity-Douay.

THE SCOFIELD REFERENCE BIBLE. Ed. by C. I. Scofield, D.D. *Oxford* 1909 rev. ed. 1917 $8.95–$19.95

THE NEW SCOFIELD REFERENCE BIBLE. The original Scofield Bible newly revised by an editorial committee under the chairmanship of E. Schuyler English *Oxford* 1967 large size red letter ed. $27.95–$31.95; handy size red letter ed. $23.50–$29.95; large size black letter ed. $9.50–$42.50; handy size black letter ed. $19.95–$33.00; wide margin ed. $37.50; looseleaf ed. $15.00–$39.95, refills $3.50 per 96 pages (48 sheets)

Dr. Scofield was a Kansas lawyer, state legislator and U.S. attorney who, in his 37th year (1879) decided to devote the rest of his life to the Bible and in 1882 became a Congregational pastor. In 1902 he joined the Southern Presbyterian Church and undertook the Bible version which bears his name, much used by fundamentalists. He used the King James Version "with some words altered to help the reader" and provided an elaborate system of subheadings, cross-references, subject chain references, book introductions, footnotes, Concordance, maps, Special Helps, chronological information, all newly brought up to date in this edition, according to the latest scholarship, by Dr. English (who also edited the Pilgrim Bible) and his committee. "By far the most important, the most carefully constructed, and the most helpful reference Bible"—(*Moody Monthly*).

Sidney, Sir Philip, and the Countess of Pembroke, Trans. THE PSALMS OF SIR PHILIP SIDNEY AND THE COUNTESS OF PEMBROKE. Ed. by J. C. A. Rathmell. *New York Univ. Press* 1963 $10.00 A verse translation of which 43 Psalms are by Sidney, the rest by his sister. "This volume must rank . . . as one of the outstanding translations into English"—(*LJ*).

THE SONCINO BOOKS OF THE BIBLE. 14 vols. *Soncino* Chumash, Joshua and Judges, Samuel I and II, Kings I and II, Isaiah, Jeremiah, Ezekiel, Twelve Prophets, Psalms, Proverbs, Job, Five Megilloth, Daniel, Ezra and Nehemiah, Chronicles I and II. *Soncino Press* set $82.00

"The Soncino Books of the Bible series consists of the entire [Jewish Holy Scriptures, or Old Testament] in fourteen volumes. Each volume contains the complete Hebrew text with the corresponding English translation verse by verse, and extensive introductions, notes and commentaries. This vast work, prepared by Jewish scholars under the general editorship of the Rev. Dr. Abraham Cohen, although essentially a Jewish commentary, has included the . . . work of non-Jewish Bible scholars and expositors. Its primary object is to present in the English language a Jewish interpretation of the Hebrew Bible whether for Jewish or non-Jewish readers and students. It is the first English commentary on the whole Bible with this object in view. . . . Especially prepared for the general reader"—(Publisher's note).

Taylor, Kenneth. THE LIVING BIBLE REVISED STANDARD VERSION. *Doubleday* 1971 $10.95; *Tyndale* $10.95–$24.95

LIVING BIBLE: Holman Illustrated Edition. *Holman* (dist. by Lippincott) new ed. 1973 $14.95

THE TORAH: The First Five Books of the Bible. A New Translation of the Holy Scriptures According to the Masoretic Text. *The Jewish Publication Society of America* 1963 $6.00 lea. $12.00

As the first translation made directly from the traditional Masoretic text into English, the new Torah excels in "prosaic accuracy," according to one reviewer, at some expense of rhythm and beauty of language. "Where [in the King James Bible] Joseph once 'found grace in Pharaoh's eyes' we see 'Pharaoh taking a liking to Joseph,' " writes Abba Eban in the *N. Y. Times*; "where 'the spirit of God' once 'moved upon the face of the waters,' we now have 'a wind . . . sweeping over the water.' " Nevertheless, the new Torah does achieve fluency and legibility. The translators drop the archaic "thee" and "thou," and omit the ubiquitous "and" at the beginning of sentences. Throughout they aim for idiomatic rendering of text rather than the old word-for-word translation. Their abandonment of the customary two-column printing is a further aid to smooth reading. This Torah is the first fruit of a twenty-year project begun in 1955 by the *Jewish Publication Society*, which plans a full translation of the Old Testament to be published in English and Hebrew-English editions, plus commentaries and concordances. The translation is prepared by a committee of scholars headed by Harry M. Orlinsky, Professor of Bible at the Hebrew Union-Jewish Insitute of Religion in New York.

WILLIAM TYNDALE'S FIVE BOOKS OF MOSES CALLED THE PENTATEUCH: Being a Verbatim Reprint of the Edition of 1530, Compared with Tyndale's Genesis of 1534 and the

Pentateuch in the Vulgate, Luther and Matthew's Bible with Various Collations and Prolegomena by the Rev. J. I. Mombert. Introd. by F. F. Bruce *Southern Illinois Univ. Press* 1967 $22.50

The New Testament

Listed in this section, for easy reference and often under the translators' names, are unusual editions and New Testaments in modern English. Most of the Bible Publishing Houses (*q.v.*) publish Testaments in the standard versions. Editions of the New Testament may be found in the Section on Bibles in Modern English which covers both the Old and New Testaments.

Albright, William Foxwell, and David Noel Freedman, General Eds. THE ANCHOR BIBLE. *See Section on Bibles in Modern English under Doubleday.*

THE AMPLIFIED NEW TESTAMENT. *See Section on Special Editions of the Bible and Parts of the Bible.*

Barclay, William, Trans. THE NEW TESTAMENT: A New Translation. *Collins-World* 2 vols. Vol. 1 The Gospels and The Acts of the Apostles (1968) Vol. 2 Letters and the Revelation (1970) pap. each $1.95 set $3.95

> The translator, preacher and author of best-selling New Testament Commentaries, was professor of divinity and biblical criticism at Glasgow University. Of him the *Times Literary Supplement* (London) has said: "Dr. Barclay is a distinguished theologian, but he has always been a person who believes that the work of the theologian should have in mind people who are outside the profession." His translation has the clarity one would expect.

Beck, William F., Trans. THE NEW TESTAMENT IN THE LANGUAGE OF TODAY: An American Translation. *See Section on Bibles in Modern English under Concordia.*

Ellison, H. L. NEW TESTAMENT. Scripture Union Bible Study Books. *Eerdmans* 10 vols. 1974 pap. $11.95 with slipcase

Goodspeed, Edgar J. THE PARALLEL NEW TESTAMENT. *See Section on Bibles in Modern English under Univ. of Chicago Press.*

Jones, Alexander, Ed. THE NEW TESTAMENT OF THE JERUSALEM BIBLE. *See Section on Special Editions of the Bible and Parts of the Bible under Jerusalem Bible.*

Knox, Ronald, Trans. THE NEW TESTAMENT. *See Section on Bibles in Modern English under Sheed & Ward.*

Lamsa, George, Trans. THE NEW TESTAMENT. Trans. from the Peshitta. *See Section on Special Editions of the Bible and Parts of the Bible.*

LAYMAN'S PARALLEL NEW TESTAMENT. *See Section on Bibles in Modern English under Zondervan.*

Moffatt, James, Trans. THE MOFFATT NEW TESTAMENT: A New Translation. *See Section on Bibles in Modern English under Harper & Row.*

Montgomery, Helen Barrett, Trans. THE NEW TESTAMENT IN MODERN ENGLISH. Centenary Translation. *See Section on Bibles in Modern English under Judson Press.*

THE NEW ENGLISH BIBLE NEW TESTAMENT. *See Section on Versions and also under Oxford in Section on Bibles in Modern English.*

NEW INTERNATIONAL VERSION. New Testament. *See Section on Bibles in Modern English under Zondervan*

THE NEW TESTAMENT CATHOLIC EDITION. Revised Standard Translation. *Nelson* pap. $2.50 $3.00

Weust, Kenneth S., Trans. THE NEW TESTAMENT: An Expanded Translation. *Eerdmans* 1961 $6.95 pap. $3.95

Williams, Charles B. THE NEW TESTAMENT IN LANGUAGE OF THE PEOPLE. *Moody Press* 1937 1972 pap. $2.50

Harmonies of the Gospels

Another part or combination of parts of the Bible for which a bookseller is sometimes asked is that known as a Diatesseron, or Harmony of the Gospels. This is a combination of the Gospels into a single and consecutive narrative. Such an interweaving of the words of the four Evangelists presents the story of the life of Jesus without the repetition and without the conflicting chronology of the separate accounts of the Gospels.

HARMONY OF THE GOSPELS. Trans. by T. H. Parker; ed. by David W. Torrance and Thomas F. Torrance Calvin's New Testament Commentaries *Eerdmans* 3 vols. 1960 each $6.95

A HARMONY OF THE GOSPELS FOR STUDENTS: According to the Texts of the Revised Standard Version. By Ralph D. Heim. *Fortress* 1974 $4.75

THE JEFFERSON BIBLE: The Life and Morals of Jesus of Nazareth. By Thomas Jefferson. *McKay* reissue 1946 Pocket Class. $1.50

> A harmony of the King James Gospels made by Thomas Jefferson, the original manuscript of which is in the Library of Congress. He selected the extracts and put them together in sequence in a notebook for his own private spiritual use. He wrote to friends, "I have made for my own satisfaction, an extract from the Evangelists of His morals, selecting those only whose style and spirit proved them genuine and His own."

A HARMONY OF THE GOSPELS. By John H. Kerr. *Revell* $5.95. Uses text of the American Standard Revision.

THE HARMONY OF THE GOSPELS. By Ronald Knox. *Sheed & Ward* 1944. $6.00 pap. $2.50

A HARMONY OF THE GOSPELS. By Archibald T. Robertson. *Harper* 1922 $4.95

The Apocrypha

The Apocrypha is the name given to 14 books which were written between 200 B.C. and 100 A.D., the period between the Old and the New Testament. The word *apocrypha* comes from the Greek word meaning "hidden," or "spurious." The Roman Church accepts the books of the Apocrypha as of the same inspiration as the other books of the Bible; the Protestant Church considers them of lesser inspiration, and excludes them from the accepted canon. There is no doubt that Protestants have, in the past, greatly undervalued the beauty and the wisdom of the Apocrypha, but they are coming to a better appreciation of it.

In recent years, biblical scholars have been turning their attention more and more to the study of the Apocrypha. The work of the Reverend Dr. R. H. Charles, Canon of Westminster, is noteworthy in the field. His book, "Religious Development between the Old and the New Testament" (1914, o.p.) is a most informing and interesting study. "The Apocrypha, Bridge of the Testaments: A Reader's Guide to the Apocryphal Books of the Old Testament" by R. C. Dentan (*Seabury Press* 1954 pap. $1.95) is a "guide for the ordinary reader, by a teacher at the General Theological Seminary, that shows the importance of these often neglected books linking in time and content the Jewish and Christian Scriptures." Bruce M. Metzger's "An Introduction to the Apocrypha" (*Oxford* 1957 $5.75) is a comprehensive and concise examination of the books, their history and their significance, based on the Revised Standard Version. Of the greatest importance is the new translation of the German "New Testament Apocrypha," Vols. 1 and 2, by Edgar Hennecke (*see below*).

There are the Old Testament and the New Testament apocryphal writings. The latter are not included in the Bible, and there are few calls for them, except from those who are studying the works of early Italian painters, who used many of the stories from the New Testament Apocrypha in their works. Recent archeological discoveries, however, have increased the interest in apocryphal books.

Among the 13 leather-bound papyrus volumes of a long-lost Coptic Library discovered in the sands of Egypt was a work containing "the secret words which the Living Jesus spoke and Didymos Judas Thomas wrote," an anthology of 114 "sayings of Jesus," many of which reflect or parallel the words of Christ as recorded in the Gospels. Five Coptic and Hebrew scholars have translated it from the original Coptic, "The Gospel According to Thomas "(*Harper* 1959 $5.00). Discovered in the same tomb in Egypt was "The Gospel of Philip," translated from the photographic edition of the Coptic text and published for the first time in English (trans. with introd. and notes by R. McL. Wilson *Harper* 1963, o.p.). These Gnostic manuscripts are "of unexcelled importance in the reconstruction of the history of Christianity in the first and second centuries A.D."

See also Sections on Biblical Archeology and The Dead Sea Scrolls; and Chapter 4, World Religions, this Volume, for Gnosticism.

THE APOCRYPHA. *American Bible Society.* $1.00

THE APOCRYPHA. Ed. by E. J. Goodspeed *Random* Vintage Bks. pap. $2.45. (*See also "The Story of the Apocrypha" by E. J. Goodspeed.* Univ. of Chicago Press *1939 $4.95.*)

THE APOCRYPHA. King James Version. *Oxford* $2.95 and $3.50. The 14 books of the Old Testament included in the Septuagint and Vulgate, but not originally written in Hebrew.

THE LOST BOOKS OF THE BIBLE: And the Forgotten Books of Eden. *Collins-World* 1950 $3.95 pap. $1.50

NEW TESTAMENT APOCRYPHA. By Edgar Hennecke; English trans. by R. McL. Wilson; ed. by Wilhelm Schneemelcher. *Westminster* 2 vols. Vol. I Gospels and Related Writings 3rd ed. 1963 $10.00 Vol. 2 Writings Relating to the Apostles, Apocalypses, and Related Subjects 1966 $10.00

This world-famous reference book is now available in English for the first time: the first German edition came out in 1904, the second in 1924 and this is a translation of the completely revised 3rd German edition of 1959. "It collects translations and extracts from the great body of apocryphal material, often of heretical origins, which grew up around Jesus and other New Testament figures during the early centuries of the church yet remained outside the canon. . . . The English edition also includes a translation of the Gospel of Thomas and a precis of the Gospel of Truth."

THE OXFORD ANNOTATED APOCRYPHA. Ed. by Bruce M. Metzger. Revised Standard Version. *Oxford* $2.75 text ed. $3.95. (*See also Section on Special Editions of the Bible and Parts of the Bible for Oxford Annotated Bible with Apocrypha and comment.*)

BIBLE CONCORDANCES

A concordance is an alphabetical index of principal words in partial contexts, showing the places where the words occur in their full contexts, and is sometimes limited to common words, exclusive of proper names. There are concordances to the works of Shakespeare, Wordsworth, Tennyson, and others, but the Bible concordance is the most frequent. One Bible concordance differs from another in completeness, the number of words included; in the version of the Bible concorded; and in the inclusion or exclusion of the books of the Apocrypha.

Cruden, Alexander. A COMPLETE CONCORDANCE TO THE OLD AND NEW TESTAMENTS. 1737. Ed. by John Eadie *Revell* $8.95 pap. $1.50

The author of this famous work was a London bookseller, who was repeatedly confined in an insane asylum. He devoted all his lucid moments to the composition of this book. The concordance has been thoroughly revised by William Youngman. It is divided into three alphabets: common words; proper names; and the apocryphal books.

CRUDEN'S CONCORDANCE. *Baker Bk. House* unabridged ed. $8.95 reference ed. $4.95; *Broadman* $6.95

Hatch, E., and H. A. Redpath. A CONCORDANCE TO THE SEPTUAGINT AND OTHER GREEK VERSIONS OF THE OLD TESTAMENT (INCLUDING THE APOCRYPHAL BOOKS). 1897–1906. *Int. Pubns. Service* 2 vols. and supplement. 1954 $65.00

HOLMAN'S TOPICAL CONCORDANCE. *Holman* 1973 $5.95. An index to the Bible arranged by subjects in alphabetical order.

Joy, Charles R., Comp. HARPER'S TOPICAL CONCORDANCE. *Harper* 1940 rev. and enl. ed. 1962 $10.95

"This considerable enlargement of what has become a standard reference work for Bible students should be purchased by all but the smallest libraries, regardless of whether or not they have the first edition. Both subjects and texts listed have been increased by about 25 per cent. . . . Many of the new topics, integration and unemployment for example, reflect the current social involvement of Christianity"—(*LJ*).

NELSON'S COMPLETE CONCORDANCE OF THE REVISED STANDARD VERSION OF THE BIBLE. Comp. by Univac under the supervision of John W. Ellison *Nelson* 1957 $29.50

This is the concordance produced by one of the new miracle devices of science—Remington Rand's Univac Electronic Computing System, which did 23 years' work in 1,000 hours. It is a 1,900-page volume listing alphabetically every principal word in the RSVB. Under each word is a reference to the passage in which it appears and a few words from the passage itself. There are some 350,000 biblical contexts.

NEW COMBINED BIBLE DICTIONARY AND CONCORDANCE. *Baker Bk. House* new ed. 1973 pap. $1.95

THE OXFORD CONCISE CONCORDANCE TO THE REVISED STANDARD VERSION OF THE HOLY BIBLE. Comp. by Bruce M. Metzger and Isobel M. Metzger. *Oxford* 1962 $3.50. More than 25,000 references; entries under proper names are listed chronologically.

THE OXFORD POCKET CONCORDANCE. *Oxford* $3.50. King James Version. Includes a Dictionary of Scripture Proper Names, Subject Index, Concordance, Indexed Scripture Atlas, and eight pages of New Oxford Bible maps.

Strong, James. STRONG'S EXHAUSTIVE CONCORDANCE OF THE BIBLE. 1894. *Abingdon* 1958 $16.95. A concordance of the canonical books of the Old and New Testaments and a comparative concordance of the Authorized and Revised versions, which took 30 years to compile.

Young, Robert. ANALYTICAL CONCORDANCE TO THE BIBLE. *Eerdmans* rev. ed. 1955 indexed $15.95 thumb-indexed $18.50; *T. Y. Crowell* (Funk and Wagnalls) $13.75 thumb-indexed $15.50

A comprehensive concordance, giving 311,000 references. It is called "analytical" because it gives the various shades of meaning of related words represented in the English by one word, and gives the original Hebrew or Greek of such words. There are valuable supplements in the form of index lexicons to the Old and New Testaments for those unacquainted with Hebrew and Greek.

BIBLE COMMENTARIES

ABINGDON BIBLE COMMENTARY. Ed. by David G. Downey and Edwin Lewis *Abingdon* thumb-indexed $14.50–$16.50

"As a resource for church school teachers and as a textbook for teacher-training classes . . . it can hardly be surpassed"—(Luther A. Weigle). It is the work of 66 outstanding scholars.

Alleman, Herbert C., and Elmer E. Flack, Eds. OLD TESTAMENT COMMENTARY. *Fortress Press* 1948 $9.95

BROADMAN BIBLE COMMENTARY. Ed. by Clifton J. Allen *Broadman* new ed. 1969 $7.50

Bultmann, Rudolf. THE JOHANNINE EPISTLES: A Commentary on the Johannine Epistles. Tr. by R. P. O'Hara *Fortress Press* 1973

"Bultmann [is] regarded by many as the most significant figure in New Testament studies in the past half century. This study . . . is indispensable for the serious scholar"—(*Choice*).

THE CAMBRIDGE COMMENTARY ON THE NEW ENGLISH BIBLE. *Cambridge* $6.95–$14.95 pap. $2.95–$5.95. Includes the Old and New Testaments and the Apocrypha.

Clarke, Adam. ADAM CLARKE'S COMMENTARY ON THE ENTIRE BIBLE. Ed. by Ralph Earle *Baker Bk. House* rev. ed. 1968 $14.95

DAILY STUDY BIBLE SERIES. William Barclay, Ed. and Commentator. *Westminster Press* 17 vols. available 1957–61 each $3.25 set $52.50

This series is intended for daily use by the average layman for meditation and study, so only a few verses at a time are covered. Rev. Mr. Barclay is lecturer in New Testament Language and Literature and in Hellenistic Greek at the University of Glasgow. Does not cover the complete New Testament. (*Consult publisher's catalog for titles.*)

Drury, John. LUKE. New Testament Commentaries by J. B. Phillips. *Macmillan* 1973 pap. $1.50

"This commentary attempts to convey the Gospel of Luke in a contemporary idiom"—(*Choice*).

Dummelow, J. R. COMMENTARY ON THE HOLY BIBLE. *Macmillan* 1969 $7.95

ELLICOTT'S BIBLE COMMENTARY. Ed. by Donald Bowdle *Zondervan* 1971 $8.95

Erdman, Charles R. COMMENTARIES ON THE NEW TESTAMENT BOOKS. *Westminster Press* 17 vols. 1916–1936 pap. each $1.95 set $30.00. An older but respected series. (*Consult publisher's catalog for titles.*)

HARPER'S BIBLE COMMENTARY. By William Neil. *Harper* 1963 1975 pap. $3.95. Designed as a companion resource work to "Harper's Bible Dictionary," this excellent one-volume work is a reading companion to the RSV and the KJV Bibles. It has been highly praised by J. B. Phillips, who calls it "a book so good that we want all our friends to possess it."

HARPER'S NEW TESTAMENT COMMENTARIES. *Harper* 5 vols. Vol. I The Epistle to the Romans, by C. K. Barrett (1958) $7.50 Vol. 2 The First Epistle to the Corinthians, by C. K. Barrett (1968) $8.50 Vol. 3 The Johannine Epistles, by J. L. Houlden (1974) $6.95 Vol. 4 The Revelation of Saint John the Divine, by G. B. Caird (1966) $7.50 Vol. 5 The Second Epistle to the Corinthians, by C. K. Barrett (1974) $8.95

Harvey, A. E. THE NEW ENGLISH BIBLE COMPANION TO THE NEW TESTAMENT. *Oxford* 1970 $14.95; *Cambridge* pap. $3.95. This guide is intended to be read along with the New English Bible New Testament. The first half is available as "Companion to the Gospels" *Oxford* 1972 pap. $3.95

Hendrikson, William. NEW TESTAMENT COMMENTARY SERIES. *Baker Bk. House* To be completed in 14 vols. 8 vols. published. 1953– $5.95–$14.95. (*Consult publisher's catalog for titles.*)

Henry, Matthew. COMMENTARY ON THE WHOLE BIBLE. *Revell* new ed. 6 vols. 1953 each $9.00 set $49.95. A new biographical edition of a work first published nearly 200 years ago.

(With Thomas Scott). CONCISE COMMENTARY ON THE WHOLE BIBLE. *Moody Press* $10.95

INTERNATIONAL CRITICAL COMMENTARY. Samuel Rowles, Alfred Plummer and Charles A. Briggs, General Eds. *Allenson* 40 vols. bound in 39 $450.00; Old Testament 21 vols. bound in 20 $232.00 New Testament 19 vols. $218.00

A distinguished series of commentaries by the most eminent scholars of the late 19th and early 20th centuries. Each individual volume was prepared by one or more specialists and was published by *Scribner's* over the years from 1895 to 1937. Some titles in the series have had two and three editions.

THE INTERPRETER'S BIBLE. Ed. by George A. Buttrick *Abingdon* 12 vols. 1951–57 each $9.95 set $99.50

This comprehensive commentary by 146 biblical scholars and preachers was begun in 1945 and the first volume (Vol. 7) was published in 1951. With its general articles and introductions for every book, it is designed to be used by the general reading public as well as students and clergy. "This undertaking brings together outstanding work of modern research and scholarship"— (American Library Association).

THE INTERPRETER'S ONE VOLUME COMMENTARY. Ed. by Charles M. Laymon *Abingdon* 1971 $17.50 thumb-indexed $19.50

Irwin, C. H., Ed. IRWIN'S BIBLE COMMENTARY. *Zondervan* 1967 $5.95. Some 25,000 text references and an introduction to each of the books of the Bible.

JEROME BIBLE COMMENTARY. Ed. by R. E. Brown, J. A. Fitzemyer and R. E. Murphy *Prentice-Hall* 1968 $36.00

"Produced by the Catholic Biblical Association in England and representative of the best recent scholarship whether Roman Catholic or not"—(*Living Church*).

THE LAYMAN'S BIBLE COMMENTARY. *John Knox Press* 25 vols. 1959–64 each $3.50 set $77.50

This commentary gives for each book of the Bible, a brief introduction covering authorship, date, background, and purpose or message; an outline; and comments. The series "does for the Protestant layman what the Interpreter's Bible does for the clergy." "One of the newest and best of [Bible commentaries]. The authors are well-known Protestant Biblical scholars of this country and abroad; the writing is clear and aimed at the non-scholar. The volumes are trim, almost pocket size. It is a series that should prove exceedingly popular with many readers"—(*N.Y. Times*). (*Consult publisher for titles and authors.*)

Laymon, C. M., Ed. THE INTERPRETER'S ONE VOLUME COMMENTARY. *See The Interpreter's Bible Commentary.*

Lenski, Richard C. H. COMMENTARY ON THE NEW TESTAMENT. *Augsburg* 12 vols. 1933 set $92.00

McKenzie, J. L., Ed. THE NEW TESTAMENT FOR SPIRITUAL READING. *Seabury* 25 vols. each $6.00 set $119.00

"A translation of a German series by a variety of Roman Catholic scholars"—(*Living Church*).

A NEW CATHOLIC COMMENTARY ON HOLY SCRIPTURE. Ed. by Reginald C. Fuller; produced by the Catholic Biblical Association *Nelson* rev. ed. 1969 $29.95

This edition is not only a reworking of the 1953 edition by Bernard Orchard; four fifths of it is an entirely new commentary. "It would be hard to think of a better one-volume commentary for . . . an up-to-date introduction to the Bible not only as a literary text . . . but as the living source of a true theology"—(*TLS*, London).

NEW CENTURY BIBLE SERIES. *Attic Press*

This series "uses the RSV and is detailed without being heavily technical and has much worth for the non-specialist"—(*Living Church*).

NEW CLARENDON BIBLE SERIES. *Oxford* $2.50–$10.25

"The nine volumes . . . examine various sections of the Old and New Testaments with a view to a better understanding of their historic foundation and the spirit which inspired their composition. Texts are taken from the RSV except where noted"—(Publisher's catalog).

THE NEW INTERNATIONAL COMMENTARY ON THE NEW TESTAMENT. F. F. Bruce, Gen. Ed. *Eerdmans* 17 vols. 13 vols. ready 1951– $5.95–$12.95

THE NEW INTERNATIONAL COMMENTARY ON THE OLD TESTAMENT. Edward J. Young, Gen. Ed. *Eerdmans* 3 vols. 1964 each $9.95

Orlinsky, Harry Meyer. ESSAYS IN BIBLICAL AND JEWISH CULTURE AND BIBLE TRANSLATION. *KTAV* 1974 $15.00

"Every article reveals a novel approach and a deep respect for the traditional commentaries along with Orlinsky's cultural analysis"—(*LJ*).

PEAKE'S COMMENTARY ON THE BIBLE. Matthew Black, Gen. Ed. and New Testament Ed.; H. H. Rowley, Old Testament Ed. *Nelson* 1936 rev. ed. 1962 $19.50

This exhaustive and highly recommended commentary is intended for use with the Revised Standard Version. "Biblical material as it is there presented is commented on by more than 60 church scholars. Forty general articles, clearly written and backed by the latest scholarship, form an excellent background to Biblical studies. . . . The book is well furnished with maps, bibliographies of further readings, and a good glossary. It should have a wide public; the scholar, the preacher, and indeed every earnest and open-minded student of the Bible will find it valuable"— (*LJ*). " 'Revision' is hardly the right word to use in these circumstances. Of the sixty-two contributors listed . . . only one contributed to the old—Professor S. H. Hooke; and even then his contributions are different. The new Peake is a brand new book"—(*TLS*, London).

THE PELICAN GOSPEL COMMENTARIES. *Penguin* Pelican Bks. pap. The Gospel of St. Luke by G. B. Caird $2.50; The Gospel of St. Mark by D. E. Nineham (1964) $2.95; The Gospel of St. Matthew by J. Fenton (1964) $3.95; The Gospel of St. John by John Marsh (1968) $4.75

"These admirable volumes are scholarly, lucid and fully intelligible to the general reader without ever playing down to him. They give the right sort of information, without being overloaded with detail. . . . To be commended as an excellent introduction for students"—(*Church Times*). The series' general editor, Professor D. E. Nineham of Cambridge University, "gives to his commentary on Mark a long introduction which is intended to set the stage for our approach to all three synoptic gospels. This introduction is outstandingly good, for while it is thoroughly scholarly it is free from all the weaknesses of the academic mind"—(Roger Lloyd, in the *Guardian*, Manchester, England).

THE TYNDALE COMMENTARY. R. V. G. Tasker, Gen. Ed. of The New Testament; Edward J. Young, Gen. Ed. of The Old Testament *Eerdmans* 20 vols. $44.50

Van Doren, Mark, and Maurice Samuel. IN THE BEGINNING, LOVE: Dialogues on the Bible. *Day* 1973 $8.95

"This book demonstrates anew that biblical studies constitute an integral part of a liberal arts education"—(*Choice*).

WESLEYAN BIBLE COMMENTARY. *Eerdmans* 6 vols. 1965–69 each $9.95

BIBLE ATLASES, DICTIONARIES, ENCYCLOPEDIAS AND HANDBOOKS

The increased number of archeological discoveries and researches into the life of biblical times, as well as the newer revised modern versions of the Bible, has made necessary revised editions and several new titles among these basic reference books. A Bible dictionary contains short descriptive articles about people, places, things, and customs mentioned in the Bible. It explains the meaning of such terms as *phylactery, prophet, ark, Nazarite, Apocalypse,* etc. It differs from a concordance in that it lists many words and phrases that do not occur in the Bible itself; as, *Bible, Ten Commandments, Lord's Prayer.* A dictionary defines; a concordance locates words.

Aharoni, Yohanan, and Michael Avi-Yonah. THE MACMILLAN BIBLE ATLAS. *Macmillan* 1968 $14.95

"The two fine atlases by Professors Yohanan Aharoni and Michael Avi-Yonah of the Hebrew University, covering respectively the period of the Bible (1964) and the Intertestamental Period (1966) and originally published by Carta of Jerusalem, have now been happily brought together in an English version to form an excellent handbook. Through 264 maps—all of them clear and attractive, with pertinent captions and usually with an illustration or two—the reader is given an interesting and instructive guide to the significant events of the Bible from about 2000 B.C. to 200 A.D. . . . A necessary purchase"—(*LJ*).

Baly, Denis. THE GEOGRAPHY OF THE BIBLE. *Harper* 1974 $12.00

Berrett, LaMar C. DISCOVERING THE WORLD OF THE BIBLE. *Brigham Young Univ. Press.* 2nd ed. 1973 $14.95 pap. $10.95

Blaiklock, E. M. ZONDERVAN PICTORIAL BIBLE ATLAS. *Zondervan* 1969 $11.95

Buttrick, George Arthur, and others, Eds. THE INTERPRETER'S DICTIONARY OF THE BIBLE: An Illustrated Encyclopedia Identifying and Explaining all Proper Names and Significant Terms and Subjects in the Holy Scriptures, Including the Apocrypha, with Attention to Archaeological Discoveries and Researches into the Life and Faith of Ancient Times. *Abingdon* 4 vols. 1962 set $49.95

In preparation since 1955 and the work of over 250 top biblical scholars, both Christian and Jewish, this is an essential purchase for every library. It is one of the few titles which really deserves the description "a major work." "Without question, it is the most comprehensive and authoritative Bible dictionary to appear in English in over half a century. . . . Articles of 10 pages and more are not uncommon. The term 'Bible' is interpreted broadly to include not only Scriptural terms, but Biblical concepts and the historical setting in which the Scriptures were written. It includes words and subjects from the Apocrypha and the Pseudepigrapha as well as the traditional canon. . . . All articles are signed, and the major ones have excellent bibliographies"—(*LJ*). "Many of the 7,500 entries are long and beautifully written articles, frequently illustrated with helpful photos, detail maps, and drawings. Every idea is explored, with full objectivity, to its utmost implications"—(*SR*).

Cornfeld, Gaalyahu, Ed. A PICTORIAL BIBLICAL ENCYCLOPEDIA. *Macmillan* 1965 $17.50. Text by Israeli scholars.

Davis, John D. DICTIONARY OF THE BIBLE. *Baker Bk. House* 4th rev. ed. 1954 $8.95; *Broadman* $8.95; *Revell* 1972 $8.95

Douglas, J. D., Organizing Ed., and others. THE NEW BIBLE DICTIONARY. *Eerdmans* 1962 $14.95

"All of its 2300 articles were specially written for this publication. Every one of them is signed with the initials of its author or authors, and the list includes more than 100 distinguished names in the field of Biblical scholarship. Specialists in classical studies, Assyriology, Egyptian and Coptic philology, geography, even medical pathology are represented among the contributors along with those in Near-Eastern archaeology and the disciplines specializing in Hebraic, Aramaic and Greek literatures. . . . The principal editor . . . is associated with Cambridge University, his consulting editors with Oxford and the universities of Manchester and London. . . . This work of modern Biblical scholarship conceived within the framework of Protestant orthodoxy will be of particular interest to the Protestant layman"—*(LJ)*.

Finegan, Jack. HANDBOOK OF BIBLICAL CHRONOLOGY: Principles of Time Reckoning in the Ancient World and Problems of Chronology in the Bible. *Princeton Univ. Press* 1964 $14.50

The author records in his "customary scholarly and thorough manner" the method of counting time in the ancient world and applies it to the Old and New Testaments. "Highly recommended as an outstanding work"—*(LJ)*.

Gehman, Henry S., Ed. NEW WESTMINSTER DICTIONARY OF THE BIBLE. *Westminster* 1970 $10.95

Greenslade, S. L., Gen. Ed. THE CAMBRIDGE HISTORY OF THE BIBLE. *See entry in Section, The Bible in the Making, this Chapter.*

Halley, H. H. HALLEY'S BIBLE HANDBOOK. *Zondervan* $4.95. A best seller of which by late 1968 there were 2,500,000 copies in print.

Halverson, Marvin, and Arthur A. Cohen, Eds. A HANDBOOK OF CHRISTIAN THEOLOGY. 1965. *New Am. Lib.* pap. $3.95. A compact reference with brief subject entries written by eminent authorities.

Hastings, James, Ed. DICTIONARY OF THE BIBLE. 1930. Rev. ed. by Frederick C. Grant and H. H. Rowley *Scribner* new ed. rev. and reset 1963 $17.50

Brought up to date in accordance with the latest research, this standard reference work is based on the Revised Standard Version with cross-references to the King James Version and the Revised Versions.

"There are many new articles—the Scrolls of course, but one on 'Myth and Ritual' was a pleasant discovery. Many articles have been so complete rewritten that the original author's initials have had to be dropped; but others have been so amended that the initials of each author can appear, and always the *sortes* lit upon articles that had gained in the process. At that same time the calm balance of the original book has been preserved"—*(TLS*, London).

Jacobus, M. W., and A. C. Zenos, Eds. A NEW STANDARD BIBLE DICTIONARY. *T. Y. Crowell* (Funk & Wagnalls) 1936 $8.50. A cooperative work of high excellence.

Kittel, Gerhard, and Gerhard Friedrich, Eds. THEOLOGICAL DICTIONARY OF THE NEW TESTAMENT. *Eerdmans* 9 vols. 1964–1975 Vol. 1 1964 $20.50 Vol. 2 1965 $22.50 Vols. 3–5 1966–68 each $25.00 Vol. 6 1969 $15.00 Vol. 7 1970 $25.00 Vol. 8 1972 $18.50 Vol. 9 1973 $22.50

An unabridged English translation by Geoffrey Bromiley of the monumental German work. "There is nothing else quite like 'Kittel' in authority"—*(N.Y. Times)*.

Leon-Dufour, Xavier. DICTIONARY OF BIBLICAL THEOLOGY. Trans. by Joseph P. Cahill *Seabury Press* 1973 $19.50

"Seventy scholars have collaborated to produce this landmark dictionary of biblical themes. Already an acclaimed classic, it is destined to enrich the theological understanding of the world"— (Publisher's catalog).

McFarlan, Donald M. WHO AND WHAT AND WHERE IN THE BIBLE. *John Knox* 1974 pap. $3.45.

McKenzie, John L., S.J. DICTIONARY OF THE BIBLE. *Macmillan* (Bruce) 1965 $17.95 pap. $5.95

This "second single-volume Bible dictionary by a Catholic Biblical scholar to be written in English . . . is usable by the intelligent layman. . . . One can only marvel at the depth, breadth, and accuracy of the scholarship involved in this massive achievement. . . . The heavy dependence on archaeological research and interest in a theological understanding of the Biblical materials, brings this dictionary into the mainstream of current Biblical studies"—*(LJ)*. *Choice* (Sept. 1966) also gave this a favorable review.

May, Herbert G., and G. H. Hunt, Eds. OXFORD BIBLE ATLAS. *Oxford* 1962 2nd ed. 1974 $9.95 pap. $3.95

"Although most of its material is in the original 1962 issue, there is also a fair amount of new geographic, historical and archeological data from the last decade's many remarkable finds and refinements"—*(Christian Science Monitor)*.

Miller, Madeleine S., and J. Lane Miller. HARPER'S BIBLE DICTIONARY. *Harper* 3rd ed. 1944 rev. 1955 1973 $12.50 thumb-indexed $14.50

Pfeiffer, Charles F. BAKER'S BIBLE ATLAS. *Baker Bk. House* 1961 $8.95. Maps and text give location and data on significant geography.

(With Howard F. Vos). THE WYCLIFFE HISTORICAL GEOGRAPHY OF BIBLE LANDS. *Moody Press* 1967 $10.95

Rowley, Harold H., and Thomas W. Manson. A COMPANION TO THE BIBLE. *Allenson* 2nd ed. 1963 $12.00

Smith, William. SMITH'S BIBLE DICTIONARY. *Holman* rev. ed. with Concordance $4.95 thumb-indexed $7.50; *Revell* pap. $1.25; *Zondervan* 1955 $5.95

THE NEW SMITH'S BIBLE DICTIONARY. Rev. by Reuel Lemmons and others *Doubleday* rev. ed. 1966 $5.95 thumb-indexed $6.95

For popular use, "this newest revision has been 'completely rewritten' by a panel of American scholars; the editors are Southern Baptists, Presbyterians, and members of the Church of Christ. . . . Clearly written, [but] the fullness of reference and occasional argumentation of the *New Smith* could confuse the average reader"—*(LJ)*.

Stevenson, Burton Egbert. THE HOME BOOK OF BIBLE QUOTATIONS. *Harper* 1949 $13.50; *Dodd* rev. ed. 1967 $40.00. Based on the King James Version and including Apocrypha of both the Old and the New Testaments, this book arranges 20,000 quotations by subject with many cross-references and a word-concordance index.

Tenney, Merrill C., Gen. Ed. THE ZONDERVAN PICTORIAL BIBLE DICTIONARY. *Zondervan* 1963 rev. ed. 1969 $11.95 indexed $13.95

"This should be among the most popular and valuable one-volume Bible dictionaries. The more than 5000 entries range in length from two lines to several pages. All of the longer and many shorter articles are signed by one of the 65 cooperating Bible scholars. Almost without exception these men are theological conservatives or Fundamentalists. Many are on the Staff of Wheaton College, where the general editor serves as dean of the Graduate School of Theology. . . . The excellent map section is from the latest edition of the *Rand McNally Bible Atlas*. Recommended without reservation"—*(LJ)*.

THE ZONDERVAN PICTORIAL ENCYCLOPEDIA OF THE BIBLE. *Zondervan* 5 vols. 1975 $79.95

Unger, Merrill F. UNGER'S BIBLE DICTIONARY. *Moody Press* 1958 $10.95

This scholarly, readable, easily used reference tool is based on that edited by C. B. Barnes in 1900. The author, an expert, has brought the material up to date in the light of recent discoveries. The Dead Sea Scrolls information is outstanding. Many points have been clarified with concise data supplemented by 500 excellent photographs, maps and drawings.

UNGER'S BIBLE HANDBOOK. *Moody Press* 1966 $4.95

Vine, William Edwyn. AN EXPOSITORY DICTIONARY OF NEW TESTAMENT WORDS WITH THEIR PRECISE MEANINGS FOR ENGLISH READERS. *Revell* 5th imp. 4 vols. in 1 1953 $13.95 thumb-indexed $15.50

Westermann, Claus. HANDBOOK TO THE OLD TESTAMENT. Trans. and ed. by Robert H. Boyd *Augsburg* 1967 $5.95

"Knowledge of the Old Testament is vital to a proper understanding of the New Testament, contends Dr. Claus Westermann of Heidelberg. This . . . reference volume traces primary Biblical themes, includes four full-color maps and a time-table of Old Testament events"—(Publisher's note).

HANDBOOK TO THE NEW TESTAMENT. *Augsburg* 1969 $4.95

A companion volume to the above, this "concentrates on the message of each book, and traces themes and relationships between sections"—(*LJ*).

BIBLICAL ARCHEOLOGY

Archeology has become of increasing importance in tracing the history of biblical peoples. "Archaeology is gradually building up evidence of the development of the Hebrew script. Finds such as the Samaria ostraca, the Lachish letters and stamped jar handles from known archaeological contexts have given much help to epigraphists in dating the development of the script. The most important recent finds, the Dead Sea Scrolls, have not only helped in this, but also throw much light on the history of the books of the OT"— (*see article on "Archaeology" in Hastings' "Dictionary of the Bible"*). Some biblical scholars have felt that the finding in Egypt of the Coptic manuscript of the "Gospel of Thomas" in 1946 has the importance for the New Testament that the Dead Sea Scrolls have had for the Old. The Arab-Israeli Six-Day War left Sinai in the hands of Israel, and since its capture new investigations—of the route of the Exodus and other matters—have been pursued by Israeli archeologists.

In December 1968, the Mayor of Jerusalem announced the acquisition of the tombstone of King Uzziah of Judah, who reigned 2,700 years ago, though the tombstone itself only goes back 2,000 years and was placed there at his reburial, according to the inscription. It is the only such inscription extant (said the *N.Y. Times*) "relating directly to a king of the house of David."

See also Section on The Dead Sea Scrolls, following, and Chapter 4, World Religions—Gnosticism, this Volume.

Aharoni, Yohanan. THE LAND OF THE BIBLE: A Historical Geography. Trans. from the Hebrew by A. F. Rainey *Westminster Press* 1967 $7.95

"An authoritative, original and well written book [by the former] senior lecturer in Archaeology, Hebrew University. . . . In the first part he begins with the pertinent facts concerning the Land of Israel: its place in the ancient Near East, its boundaries, its economic features, and so on. He then deals with the history of Palestinology, methods of research, archaeology, and other pertinent matters. The second section is devoted to presenting Palestine's historical development from the protohistoric period to the Persian Empire. Useful maps, appendixes which include chronological tables, lists of site identification and abbreviations, and an index of Biblical references and geographical names increase the value of the book. Not everyone will agree with Dr. Aharoni's assumptions or conclusions"—(*LJ*). Maps, indexes and appendixes.

Albright, William Foxwell. ARCHAEOLOGY AND THE RELIGION OF ISRAEL. *Johns Hopkins Press* 5th ed. 1956 $9.00

ARCHAEOLOGY, HISTORICAL ANALOGY, AND EARLY BIBLICAL TRADITION. *Louisiana State Univ. Press* 1966 $2.75

THE ARCHAEOLOGY OF PALESTINE. 1960. *Peter Smith* rev. ed. $5.50

Anati, Emmanuel. PALESTINE BEFORE THE HEBREWS; A History of the Earliest Appearance of Man to the Conquest of Canaan. *Knopf* 1963 $10.00

Avi-Yonah, Michael, and others, Eds.; Benjamin Mazar, Editorial Board Chairman; English ed. trans. by Merton Dagut. ILLUSTRATED WORLD OF THE BIBLE LIBRARY *Daniel Davey* 5 vols. 1961 Vol. 1 The Laws Vol. 2 The Early Prophets Vol. 3 The Late Prophets Vol. 4 The Writings Vol. 5 New Testament each $20.00 Old Testament Ed. 4 vols. set $80.00 New Testament Ed. 5 vols. set $100.00

This five-volume "archaeological commentary," the result of an eight-year project, is "a luxury item; but few libraries which can afford it will want to be without it. The editors, who are Biblical archaeologists, take selected verses from each Biblical book and accompany them with full-color reproductions of inscriptions, seals, reliefs, maps, or modern photographs of the area, as the case may be"—(*LJ*). The first four volumes were published in both Hebrew and English and printed in Israel. The fifth volume was printed in England.

Blaiklock, Edward M. ARCHEOLOGY OF THE NEW TESTAMENT. *Zondervan* 1974 pap. $3.95

Browning, Iain. PETRA. *Noyes Press* 1974 $15.00

   "It brings again to notice the beautiful and still enigmatic city hidden away in the Wadi Moussa, in Jordan"—(*Choice*).

THE DEAD SEA SCROLLS. *See following Section.*

de Vaux, Roland. ANCIENT ISRAEL: Its Life and Institutions. *McGraw-Hill* 1965 Vol. 1 Social Institutions pap. $2.95 Vol. 2 Religious Institutions pap. $2.95

Duckat, Walter. BEGGAR TO KING: All the Occupations of Biblical Times. *Doubleday* 1968 $5.95; *Abingdon* 1971 pap. $2.95

   The director of vocational guidance of the Federation Employment and Guidance Service, New York City, draws on the Bible and rabbinic literature for his sources of information concerning the occupations he treats. "Mr. Duckat has performed a useful service in gathering his information from scattered sources in a number of books"—(*LJ*). Selected bibliography; cross-references.

Eissfeldt, Otto, Ed. THE OLD TESTAMENT: An Introduction; Including the Apocrypha and Pseudepigrapha, and also the Works of Similar Type from Qumran, the History of the Formation of the Old Testament. Trans. from the 3rd German ed. by Peter R. Ackroyd *Harper* 1965 $11.00

   "The translation into English of this well-balanced and authoritative work is of supreme importance. . . . Professor Eissfeldt details the literary and historical criticism of each book in canonical order. . . . The massive learning, the judicious scholarship, and the encyclopedic coverage of all points of view will make this 'introduction' a basic necessity for every scholarly O.T. collection"—(*LJ*).

Finegan, Jack. LIGHT FROM THE ANCIENT PAST: The Archeological Background of Judaism and Christianity. 1946. *Princeton Univ. Press* 2nd ed. 1960 Vol. 1 $16.50 pap. $3.95 Vol. 2 pap. $4.45

   This survey is "now presented in a revised edition, which incorporates the results of 13 more years of archaeological discovery and discussion. A completely new section is added on the Dead Sea Scrolls"—(*Christian Century*).

Frank, Harry Thomas. BIBLE, ARCHAEOLOGY, AND FAITH. *Abingdon* 1971 $12.50

   "After a brief examination of the history and provenance of archaeology in reconstructing and bringing to life the course of ancient history and culture, Frank . . . carries the reader through the whole course of biblical history"—(*LJ*).

Gaster, Theodor H. MYTH, LEGEND, AND CUSTOM IN THE OLD TESTAMENT: A Comparative Study with Chapters from Sir James Frazer's "Folklore in the Old Testament." *Harper* 1969 $20.00

Gray, John. ARCHAEOLOGY AND THE OLD TESTAMENT WORLD. 1962. *Gannon* $9.50

   Dr. Gray's "chief interest is in ancient Middle Eastern texts and their affinity with the writings of the Old Testament, and with the institutions, conventions and beliefs which they illustrate." His "account of what archaeology does and does not confirm in the Old Testament is informed, responsible, and extraordinarily fascinating"—(*New Yorker*).

Grosvenor, Melville Bell, and Frederick G. Vosburgh, Eds. EVERYDAY LIFE IN BIBLE TIMES. *National Geographic Society* 1967 $9.95

   "This is a good example of the National Geographic Society's bookmaking. Popular, widely endorsed, written largely by staff members of the Society, the book contains many essays by some of the world's leading authorities. The editors aim to 'bring Bible times to life.' There are hundreds of illustrations from photographs, old masters, and paintings commissioned for this book; some are superb, many are very unusual and would be hard to find elsewhere. The text has its merits. [One authority], for example, gives the reader a good idea of what archaeology is all about and warns that it 'is 99 per cent drudgery' "—(*LJ*).

Holt, John Marshall. THE PATRIARCHS OF ISRAEL. *Vanderbilt Univ. Press* 1964 $6.95

"Interestingly written, scientifically sound and, overall, reverent in point of view, this study of the patriarchal period of the Bible will be of great interest to general readers of all faiths and to Bible students.... An Episcopal priest ... has studied the times of the Patriarchs ... and here relates archaeological and historical findings from their period ... to the text of Genesis.... A fascinating and well-documented book"—(LJ). Bibliography.

Hunt, Ignatius, O.S.B. THE WORLD OF THE PATRIARCHS. Ed. by Bruce Vawter *Prentice-Hall* 1967 $7.50

"Professor Hunt ... has organized an amazing amount of up-to-date factual data from a vast array of authoritative sources. He has done this in a manner that is logical, readable, and the ultimate in brevity. The text is completely documented; each chapter is supplemented by readings for further study and there is a final general bibliography"—(LJ). In the Background to the Bible Series.

Kapelrud, Arvid S. THE RAS SHAMRA DISCOVERIES AND THE OLD TESTAMENT. Trans. from the Norwegian by G. W. Anderson *Univ. of Oklahoma Press* 1963 $4.95

These lectures which were given at the University of Oslo in the early 1950's have been supplemented to provide "a brief introduction to one of the most exciting and revolutionary archaeological discoveries of the early 20th century. The author displays the accuracy and judicious moderation of a competent scholar.... A stimulating survey"—(LJ). Bibliography.

Keller, Werner. THE BIBLE AS HISTORY: A Confirmation of the Book of Books. Trans. from the German by William Neil *Morrow* 1964 $9.95; *Apollo* 1969 pap. $3.50

This book has been a great success in Germany. Dr. Keller gathered a mass of archeological evidence to reveal the historical foundations of the Old and New Testaments; excellent photographs, maps, diagrams, bibliography and index.

THE BIBLE AS HISTORY IN PICTURES. *Morrow* 1964 $10.95

A companion to the book above. "The most recent discoveries of the archaeologist and historian are captured in 329 photographs and eight color plates that, together with accompanying Biblical passages and expository material by Mr. Keller, give a fresh and lively view of the people, places and events of these ancient times"—(N.Y. Times).

Kramer, Samuel Noah. THE SUMERIANS: Their History, Culture, and Character. *Univ. of Chicago Press* 1963 $10.00 1971 pap. $2.95

"Less than a century ago not only was nothing known of Sumerian culture" but "the very existence of a Sumerian people and language was unsuspected." Due to the advances of archeology, this work brimming with factual data and with quotations from Sumerian writings was made possible. Most interesting to biblical students are the numerous parallels found between biblical literature and Sumerian traditions (e.g., the flood story, the Cain-Abel motif, the Job motif and so on). Sumerian influence must have penetrated the Bible through the Canaanite, Hurrian, Hittite and Akkadian literature. Professor Kramer, an uncontested authority, writes with grace and urbanity.

Longstreth, Edward. DECISIVE BATTLES OF THE BIBLE. *Lippincott* 1962 $4.50

Historical narration in the Bible has long been considered as somewhat allegorical, but the author shows that archeological findings have verified the accounts of some of the great battles of the Israelites from the time of Abraham to the crucifixion of Christ.

Moscati, Sabatino. ANCIENT SEMITIC CIVILIZATIONS. *Putnam* 1958 Capricorn Bks. 1960 pap. $2.95

This is the first English edition of a well-written important book, revised and brought up to date. It appeared first in Italian in 1949. Chapters are devoted to the history, religion, literature and art of the Babylonians and Assyrians, the Canaanites, the Hebrews, the Aramaeans, the Arabs and the Ethiopians.

Negev, Avraham, Ed. ARCHAEOLOGICAL ENCYCLOPEDIA OF THE HOLY LAND. *Putnam* 1972 $15.95

"A mine of up-to-date information on archaeological discoveries in the Holy Land.... The content is, on a whole, excellent"—(Choice).

Parrot, André. LAND OF CHRIST. Trans. by James H. Farley. *Fortress Press* 1968 $6.95

"In his inimitable, fascinating style ... following a harmony of the life of Christ, the author applies his knowledge of archaeology, anthropology, psychology, history, and other disciplines to carry the reader back to the days of Our Lord.... The book has some useful tables, a brief bibliography, a list of illustrations, and indexes of scripture references, names and subjects. Highly recommended!"—(LJ).

Pfeiffer, Charles F., Ed. THE BIBLICAL WORLD: A Dictionary of Biblical Archaeology. *Baker Bk. House* 1966 $8.95

(With Howard F. Vos, Eds.). THE WYCLIFFE HISTORICAL GEOGRAPHY OF BIBLE LANDS. *Moody Press* 1967 $10.95

Two evangelical scholars show their love and knowledge of "biblical lands, pertinent archaeological discoveries, the history and geography of the Near East, and of the Bible itself"—(*LJ*). Preface, index, illustrations and photographs.

Pritchard, James Bennett. ARCHAEOLOGY AND THE OLD TESTAMENT. *Princeton Univ. Press* 1958 $9.50. A "mind-loosening book," this is careful and authoritative, covering excavations up to 1957.

GIBEON, WHERE THE SUN STOOD STILL: The Discovery of a Biblical City. *Princeton Univ. Press* 1962 $9.50 1973 pap. $3.45

Dr. Pritchard has become known for his expert accounts of modern biblical archeology. He "writes engagingly and knows how to explain new finds without burying his readers in superfluous detail." He has edited "Ancient Near East: An Anthology of Text and Pictures" (*Princeton Univ. Press* 1958 $9.50 pap. $3.95), which presents "to the student and general reader the raw material with which historians and Biblical scholars reconstruct the world in which the Old Testament was written."

Raphael, Chaim. THE WALLS OF JERUSALEM: An Excursion into Jewish History. *Knopf* 1968 $6.95

"For nearly 2000 years Jews have built their way of life, and way of looking at life, around a legend; but recent interpretations and decipherings of the Dead Sea Scrolls have turned that legend into real, inscribed facts. That is the view of Mr. Raphael, a Briton who combines a career in Her Majesty's Civil Service (Treasury) with writing"—(*Atlantic*).

Saggs, H. W. F. THE GREATNESS THAT WAS BABYLON: A Survey of the Ancient Civilization of the Tigris-Euphrates Valley. *New Am. Lib.* Mentor Bks. 1968 pap. $2.25; *Praeger* 1969 $13.00

Due in part to the clay-tablets which were used by the scribes and which are virtually indestructible, there is a prodigious amount of archeological and documentary evidence preserved in the ancient soil of Mesopotamia. "Written with consummate literary skill and enriched with well-chosen illustrations, this book combines authoritative scholarship with a more direct appeal to the informed lay reader"—(*LJ*).

Thompson, J. A. THE BIBLE AND ARCHAEOLOGY. *Eerdmans* 1962 $7.95

This accurate and well-documented book is a revision of three earlier and smaller books by Professor Thompson devoted to three separate periods of biblical history and "constitutes a popular but authoritative and satisfying survey of the archaeological contributions to Biblical interpretation."

Wright, G. Ernest, BIBLICAL ARCHAEOLOGY. *Westminster Press* 1957 new rev. and expanded ed. 1963 $12.95 abr. ed. 1961 pap. $2.25. An account of the most recent excavations and finds at Megiddo, Schechem and elsewhere.

Yadin, Yigael. ENCYCLOPEDIA OF ARCHAEOLOGICAL EXCAVATIONS IN THE HOLY LAND. *Prentice-Hall* 4 vols. 1973 each $25.00 Vol. 2 ed. by Michael Avi-Yonah

MASADA: Herod's Fortress and the Zealots' Last Stand. Trans. from the Hebrew by Moshe Pearlman *Random* 1966 $12.95

Dr. Yadin was the director of the excavation of Masada. "In 73 A.D., some three years after the rest of Palestine had been conquered, Masada fell to the Romans. Its surviving defenders, unwilling to become slaves of the conquerors, committed suicide. Nineteen centuries later, as a result of a joint excavation of the Hebrew University, the Israel Exploration Society, and the Israeli Antiquities Department, Masada has been excavated and restored. Next to Jerusalem itself, this fortress, perched on top of a mountain in the Judean wilderness and overlooking the Dead Sea, has perhaps the most emotional and nationalistic significance for the Jew. Yadin's book is the popular account of the excavation of Masada, its history and importance. No one is better qualified to write this account. . . . Structure by structure he relates the story of Masada in text and in pictures. The text, lucid and informative as it is, does not half as well reveal Masada to the reader as do the illustrations, which are magnificent"—(*LJ*).

THE DEAD SEA SCROLLS

The Bible was written during some 1,400 years (1300 B.C.–100 A.D.). Very few of its many authors have been identified. There are no known original manuscripts, only copies of copies and translations. Scholars had used Hebrew manuscripts of the Old Testament dating from the 9th to 11th centuries A.D. and the earliest complete New Testament manuscripts dating from the 4th century A.D. The oldest Gospel text in scholars' possession had been a papyrus fragment from John 18:31–33, written in Greek, probably early in the 2nd century, which describes the arraignment of Jesus before Pontius Pilate. Most of the present-day versions had been based on these manuscripts.

The most important archeological discoveries, described by sober and distinguished scholars as "sensational" and "phenomenal," began in the spring of 1947 when a Bedouin shepherd boy stumbled upon the entrance to a cliff cave at Qumrân near the northeast end of the Dead Sea. Scrolls of sheep and goatskin, carefully wrapped in linen and coated with wax, were preserved in tall clay jars in the cave. The boy, not suspecting that he had found the book of Isaiah copied in Hebrew, finally sold five scrolls through intermediaries to the Syrian Metropolitan Samuel at the monastery of Saint Mark in Old Jersualem. Since that time in adjacent caves hundreds of manuscripts have been found, some perfect, some reduced to "tens of thousands of fragments." Most of these are of leather, some of papyrus, and one of copper. They had been carefully inscribed in Hebrew, Greek and Aramaic, the last being the language of Jesus.

Scholars and archeologists almost all agree that the scrolls are to be dated between the years 200 B.C. and 70 A.D.—"biblical documents probably a thousand years older than the earliest important manuscripts previously known." Almost all agree, too, that the scrolls are the work of an ascetic heretical Jewish sect called by some the Essenes, or, by others, the Sons of Zadok. These men wrote the scrolls and hid them when the Romans destroyed Jerusalem and dispersed the Jews in 70 A.D. The ruins of a monastery have been excavated less than a mile from the caves. This building seems to have contained a scriptorium where the sacred writings were copied.

"In 1949 the cave was scientifically excavated by the Department of Antiquities of Jordan and the French School of Archaeology at Jerusalem, and hundreds of fragments of manuscripts were unearthed. The excavation of Khirbet Qumrân followed in 1951–56. . . . During the course of these discoveries another and quite unconnected collection of fragments was found in another valley some miles to the south, the Wadi Murabba 'at. These came from the 2nd cent. A.D. and consisted of letters, contracts, and similar documents, as well as biblical manuscripts, from the period of the revolt of Bar Cochba (132–35 A.D.). A third body of material, coming from later Christian centuries, appeared in the excavation of Khirbet Mird, the ruins of a Byzantine monastery farther up in the hills. All three collections are included under the term Dead Sea Scrolls in its widest sense, and all have their own importance"—(See article in Hastings' "Dictionary of the Bible").

On Nov. 1, 1961, the N.Y. Times reported that first-century documents found in remote caves along the western shore of the Dead Sea had been described as the most important discovery of the period next to the Dead Sea Scrolls. "The documents, said to be the largest collection found in the Holy Land so far, deal with the years 88 to 135 A.D. They focus on the last rebellion of the Jews against the Romans; the revolt was crushed in 135 A.D." Yigael Yadin, Professor of Archeology at the Hebrew University of Jerusalem, was quoted as saying that one significant aspect of the collection was that most of the documents are dated. "These dates, he said, 'provide a firm basis for evaluating the Dead Sea Scrolls on paleographic grounds.' The documents give the latest possible dating for the scrolls—the first century, he said. . . . All the documents are on papyrus, except for two Biblical fragments on parchment. Dr. Yadin said the parchment fragments were from the Book of Numbers and the Book of Psalms, and among the earliest known from the traditional or Masoretic, text of the Old Testament." In his interesting article, "The Battle of the Scrolls" (Atlantic, May 1967) Chaim Raphael says: "Looking back over the twenty years, we have seen not one but three dramas of discovery played out in this area—Qumran itself, Masada, and the astonishing finds of the Bar Kokhbah period (132–135 A.D.) in the Judaean desert close by. Though separate, they overlap in content and are unified in significance. Taken together they emerge as a celebration of history, almost as much in the way the discoveries were made as by what they reveal to us." An expansion of Mr. Raphael's discussion has appeared as a book: "The Walls of Jerusalem: An Excursion into Jewish History" (Knopf 1968 $6.95).

Israel announced, in October 1967, the discovery of a new, 26 foot Qumrân scroll, the longest ever found, half of it dealing with a temple and its accoutrements; the other half with rules on ritual matters and on preparedness for war. Professor Yigael Yadin, the Israeli archeologist who has played a major role in discovering and assessing these finds (see list below), in making the announcement did not disclose how the scroll had been acquired, but by November the N.Y. Times reported that the Israelis had seized it from a Bethlehem dealer after the capture of Bethlehem in the 1968 Six-Day War. Scholars voiced alarm. " 'I'm afraid this will close the door so far as any future scrolls are concerned,' the Rev. Roland de Vaux, the French Dominican priest who was editor in chief of the technical publication of the original scrolls, said recently"—(*N.Y. Times*). Edmund Wilson (*see list below*) in 1969 fully updated his original treatment of the subject—in as fascinating a manner as his first volume exhibited.

Allegro, John Marco. THE DEAD SEA SCROLLS. *Penguin* (orig.) 1956 pap. $2.25

Barthélemy, D., and J. T. Milik. DISCOVERIES IN THE JUDAEAN DESERT. Pub. under the auspices of the Jordan Dept. of Antiquities. In French, English and Aramaic. *Oxford* 5 vols. 1955–   Vol. 1 QUMRÂN CAVE I ed. by D. Barthélemy and J. T. Milik with contributions by R. de Vaux and others (1955) $17.00 Vol. 2 LES GROTTES DE MURABA'AT in 2 pts. ed. by P. Benoit and others (1961) $41.00 Vol. 3 LES PETITES GROTTES DE QUMRÂN in 2 pts. ed. by M. Baillet and others (1962) $41.00 Vol. 4 THE PSALMS SCROLL OF QUMRÂN CAVE XI ed. by J. Sanders (1965) $13.95 Vol. 5 QUMRÂN CAVE 4 ed. by John M. Allegro and Arnold A. Anderson (1968) $17.00

Black, Matthew, Ed. THE SCROLLS AND CHRISTIANITY. *Allenson* 1969 pap. $4.50

Brownlee, William Hugh. THE MEANING OF THE QUMRÂN SCROLLS FOR THE BIBLE: With Special Attention to the Book of Isaiah. *Oxford* 1964 $10.00

Bruce, Frederick Fyvie. SECOND THOUGHTS ON THE DEAD SEA SCROLLS. *Eerdmans* 1957 rev. ed. 1961 pap. $1.95

"Succinct and discriminating in choice of facts, fair-minded in interpretation, sensible and scholarly in his conclusions, Professor Bruce has produced the best and most readable book on the subject in England"—(*Spectator*). The author is professor of biblical history and literature in the University of Sheffield, England.

Burrows, Millar. MORE LIGHT ON THE DEAD SEA SCROLLS: New Scrolls and New Interpretations. *Viking* 1958 $6.95

Driver, G. R. THE JUDAEAN SCROLLS: The Problem and a Solution. *Schocken* 1966 $14.50

"The most comprehensive and thorough study of the Dead Sea scrolls yet to appear [and perhaps] the most controversial. [The] emeritus professor of Semitic philology at Oxford . . . challenges the mainstream of critical, scholarly opinion [with] this very cogent presentation of a minority view. . . . There is no other work in English which is as factually complete. It is carefully documented, has a very extensive bibliography, and is completely indexed"—(*LJ*).

Dupont-Sommer, André. THE ESSENE WRITINGS FROM QUMRAN. Trans. by G. Vermes. 1962. *Peter Smith* $6.50

Farmer, William R. MACCABEES, ZEALOTS, AND JOSEPHUS: An Inquiry into Jewish Nationalism in the Greco-Roman Period. 1956. *Greenwood* 1974 $11.25

Dr. Farmer analyzes the relationship of Jewish politics and religion. He discusses why Josephus (*q.v.*), historian of the Judeo-Roman war, expressed admiration for the Maccabees as pious patriots, but condemned the Zealots as a fanatic sect with no authentic connection to Jewish religion. The concluding chapters examine the bearing of the Dead Sea Scrolls upon this study of Jewish nationalism and the implications of the author's findings for New Testament studies.

Gaster, Theodor H., Trans. and ed. THE DEAD SEA SCRIPTURES IN ENGLISH TRANSLATION. *Doubleday* 1956 Anchor Bks. pap. $2.50

"The purpose of this book is to provide a complete and reliable translation . . . insofar as the original Hebrew texts have yet been published. Everything that is sufficiently well preserved to make connected sense has been included"—(Preface). Contents: Manual of Discipline; Zadokite Document; Formulary of Blessings; Hymn of the Initiants; Book of Hymns; Oration of Moses; Commentary on the Book of Micah; Commentary on the Book of Nahum; Commentary on the Book of Habakkuk; Commentary on Psalm 37; War of the Sons of Light and the Sons of Darkness; Manual of Discipline for the Future Congregation of Israel; New Covenant; Coming Doom; Sources; for Further Reading; Analytical Index; Biblical Quotations and Parallels.

LaSor, William S. THE DEAD SEA SCROLLS AND THE NEW TESTAMENT. *Eerdmans* 1967 pap. $3.95

Leaney, A. R. C. THE RULE OF QUMRAN AND ITS MEANING: Introduction, Translation and Commentary. *Westminster Press* 1966 $7.50

Called also the "Manual of Discipline" by other scholars who have published editions and translations, this is "the most important single scroll from the Dead Sea caves for a study of the thought and life of the Qumran community. Two-thirds of the present volume is a translation and detailed critical analysis and exegesis of this vital document with emphasis on its Biblical relevance, especially for the New Testament. . . . This constitutes the most extensive study of this ancient manuscript to appear"—(*LJ*). Bibliography. In the New Testament Library Series.

Mowry, Lucetta. THE DEAD SEA SCROLLS AND THE EARLY CHURCH. *Univ. of Notre Dame Press* 1966 pap. $2.25

Pfeiffer, C. F. THE DEAD SEA SCROLLS AND THE BIBLE. *Baker Bk. House* rev. ed. 1969 pap. $2.95

Roth, Cecil. DEAD SEA SCROLLS: A New Historical Approach. *Norton* 1965 pap. $2.25

Schubert, Kurt. THE DEAD SEA COMMUNITY: Its Origins and Teachings. 1959. *Greenwood* 1974

This is a well-balanced appraisal and concise summary of the life and thought of the sect which produced the Scrolls. It re-creates a vivid picture of the daily life of the Community and its relation to the Sadducees and Pharisees.

Vermes, Geza. THE DEAD SEA SCROLLS IN ENGLISH. Trans. with introd. by Geza Vermes *Penguin* Pelican Bks. (orig.) 1962 pap. $1.65; *Peter Smith* $5.00

Wilson, Edmund. THE DEAD SEA SCROLLS 1949–1969. *Oxford* 1969 $7.50

"A thorough revision of Edmund Wilson's famous account of the discovery, origins and significance of the Dead Sea Scrolls. . . . The new material includes the story of what happened to the Scrolls during the Arab-Israeli War of 1967"—(*PW*). "Among the recent discoveries Mr. Wilson discusses are an Aramaic version of Genesis, the controversial 'copper scrolls,' a 'new' manuscript of the Psalms, and the results of excavations at the site of the pre-Christian Essene monastery near the caves where the first scrolls were found. He offers also a fascinating interpretation of the historical events that may lie behind the scroll 'The War of the Children of Light against the Children of Darkness'; and he reviews the contributions, and their significance for biblical study, of a number of scholars at work on the scrolls. He also includes conversations with many people who have been directly involved, and, in a final chapter, offers some general reflections that clarify his own viewpoint"—(Publisher's note).

Yadin, Yigael. MESSAGE OF THE SCROLLS. *Grosset* Univ. Lib. pap. $2.25; *Simon & Schuster* 1957 $5.95 Touchstone-Clarion pap. $1.75

The author, an experienced archeologist, is "the son of the late Professor Sukenik, into whose hand some of the Scrolls from the first cave found their way soon after their discovery. By the use of his father's diaries he is able to shed new light on the confused story of what happened in Jerusalem at that time. Dr. Yadin took the initiative in the purchase for Israel of the manuscripts which had come into the possession of St. Mark's Monastery, and he is able to tell the story at first hand." His book is "scholarly, readable, accurate and nontechnical"—(*Spectator*).

(Ed.). THE SCROLL OF THE WAR OF THE SONS OF LIGHT AGAINST THE SONS OF DARKNESS. Trans. from the Hebrew by Batya and Chaim Rabin; introd. and commentary by the author *Oxford* 1962 $13.75

CRITICISM AND INTERPRETATION

This is a selected list of some of the standard and more recent works. Because of the vast numbers of commentaries on individual books of the Bible, we have in general limited this selection to books on the Bible as a whole or on the larger sections. *(See also Section on Bible Commentaries.)*

Altmann, Alexander, Ed. BIBLICAL AND OTHER STUDIES. *Harvard Univ. Press* 1963 $7.50

Anderson, Bernhard W. UNDERSTANDING THE OLD TESTAMENT. *Prentice-Hall* 1957 3rd ed. 1975 $11.95

Anderson, G. W. THE HISTORY AND RELIGION OF ISRAEL. *Oxford* 1966 $5.25

This volume is part of the revision of the books of the Old Testament in the Clarendon Bible Series. "The first volume differs from the earlier Clarendon volume in that it integrates the history and the religion of Israel, and in that it does not end with Ezra, but with the Maccabean Revolt. . . . This is a useful book, which presents the material from the liberal, scholarly viewpoint. Indexes and an attached chronological table increase its value. Every library should consider its purchase"—(*LJ*).

Asimov, Isaac. ASIMOV'S GUIDE TO THE BIBLE. Vol. 1 The Old Testament. *Doubleday* 1968
$12.50; *Avon* pap. 1971 $3.95

Isaac Asimov (*q.v.*) is the well-known science writer and author of science fiction, who here ventures into new territory. He "does not pretend to be a Biblical scholar. . . . The book is intended for readers who are already familiar with the Bible in a general way and have a grasp of its religious and ethical teaching. The book's only purpose is to set the various parts of Scripture in their proper historical milieu and explain the many puzzling allusions to persons, places and events. . . . Serious, in view of the author's concern for historical background, is his almost complete neglect of the whole field of Biblical archeology, which has contributed so much in the past generation toward a more adequate understanding of the world of the Bible. . . . One has the right to expect something better . . . in a book professing to deal with the Bible as a part of secular history—and which costs as much as this does. That is not to say the book is without value. There are those who will find it a useful, and fairly reliable, compendium of historical facts and curiosities"—(Robert C. Dentan, in the *N.Y. Times*).

Bewer, Julius A. THE LITERATURE OF THE OLD TESTAMENT. 1922. Third ed. completely rev. by Emil G. Kraeling. *Columbia* 3rd ed. 1962 $15.00. An older classic of criticism considered indispensable by many biblical scholars.

Bickerman, Elias. FOUR STRANGE BOOKS OF THE BIBLE: Jonah, Daniel, Koheleth, Esther. *Schocken* 1967 $7.50

A well-known scholar and teacher at Columbia University has written "partly exegesis, partly history of exegesis, and most of all a determination of historical setting. . . . His style is excellent. . . . The paucity of footnotes would indicate that he hoped for a general rather than an academic audience—yet the biblical erudition he assumes is considerable"—(*LJ*).

Blair, Edward P. ABINGDON BIBLE HANDBOOK. *Abingdon* 1975 $15.95

"No other handbook includes such a thorough and knowledgeable examination of each book in the Bible (including the Apocrypha)"—(Publisher's note).

Bornkamm, Gunther. THE NEW TESTAMENT: A Guide to Its Writings. *Fortress* 1973 $3.25

Buber, Martin. ON THE BIBLE: Eighteen Studies. Ed. by Nahum N. Glatzer *Schocken* 1968 $5.95. *(See also his main entry in Chapter 4, World Religions, this Vol.)*

Burrows, Millar. AN OUTLINE OF BIBLICAL THEOLOGY. *Westminster Press* 1946 $6.50

Charles, R. H. ESCHATOLOGY: The Doctrine of a Future Life in Israel, Judaism, and Christianity. 1899. With a new introd. and bibliography by George Wesley Buchanan *Schocken* new ed. 1963 pap. $3.95

This is the standard work on "Eschatology"—the concern about last things. The author describes the prophetic and apocalyptic views of "the end": judgment, life after death, and the messianic Kingdom. The new introduction and bibliography by George Wesley Buchanan of Wesley Theological Seminary gives a detailed review of work done since Charles' time.

Chase, Mary Ellen. THE BIBLE AND THE COMMON READER. *Macmillan* 1944 rev. ed. 1952 Collier Bks. 1962 pap. $1.45. A delightful book, written with simplicity and charm, but with sound scholarship. The King James Version is the basis for this interpretation of the Scriptures as literature and as history.

LIFE AND LANGUAGE IN THE OLD TESTAMENT. *Norton* 1955 pap. $2.25. An invaluable and charmingly written consideration of the Old Testament as a work of literary art is as well a keen analysis of the mind of the ancient Jewish people. The author's devotion to and understanding of the Bible is everywhere evident.

THE PSALMS FOR THE COMMON READER. *Norton* 1962 $5.95

"This estimable little book . . . is divided into three sections—descriptions of the psalms, outline of how they should be read, and a supplement with the psalms grouped by type—as well as a short history of Israel. . . . Highly recommended for its clarity of presentation, colorful detail, and unusually perceptive, spiritual qualities"—(*LJ*).

THE PROPHETS FOR THE COMMON READER. *Norton* 1963 o.p.

Cullmann, Oscar. THE NEW TESTAMENT: An Introduction for the General Reader. *Westminster Press* 1968 (orig.) pap. $2.95

"Concentrating more on the history than the theology of the New Testament, this 144-page book gives the non-specialized reader a look at 'scientific' Bible study, an approach that is usually found only in advanced, more technical works. . . . A lot of information is gathered into compact form here"—(PW).

Danker, F. W. MULTIPURPOSE TOOLS FOR BIBLE STUDY. *Concordia* 3rd ed. 1970 $6.95

Deen, Edith. ALL THE WOMEN OF THE BIBLE. *Harper* 1955 $8.95

This delightful volume contains biographies of *all* the women—saints and concubines, faithful wives and mothers, queens, sorceresses, business women and those who are nameless. Scholarship as well as deep insight characterizes this series of portraits written without sentimentality.

Dentan, Robert Claude. THE DESIGN OF THE SCRIPTURES: A First Reader in Biblical Theology. *Seabury Press* 1965 pap. $2.45. A "helpful well-organized work for the Protestant reader" by the Professor of Old Testament at the General Theological Seminary.

PREFACE TO OLD TESTAMENT THEOLOGY. *Seabury Press* 1963 $3.50

DeWolf, L. Harold. THE ENDURING MESSAGE OF THE BIBLE. 1960. *John Knox Press* rev. ed. 1965 pap. $1.45. The key ideas presented in everyday language.

Dodd, Charles H. THE BIBLE TODAY. *Cambridge* 1946 $7.50 1960 pap. $1.95

HISTORICAL TRADITION IN THE FOURTH GOSPEL. *Cambridge* 1963 $23.50

INTERPRETATION OF THE FOURTH GOSPEL. *Cambridge* 1958 $9.50 pap. $5.95

THE PARABLES OF THE KINGDOM. *Scribner* rev. ed. 1961 $5.95 pap. $2.25

Doty, William G. CONTEMPORARY NEW TESTAMENT INTERPRETATION. *Prentice-Hall* 1972 $7.95 pap. $3.95

"This is a very crowded, well informed, proper-name-burdened, and unusually helpful summary of the New Testament criticism field"—(*Christian Century*).

EERDMANS'S HANDBOOK TO THE BIBLE. Ed. by David Alexander and Pat Alexander *Eerdmans* 1973 $12.95

Ehrlich, Jacob W. THE HOLY BIBLE AND THE LAW. *Oceana* 1962 $8.95

This book is "eminently readable." As valuable as the wealth of biblical quotations are "the concise and informative introductions to each group of quotations. In these we are given the law of the subject as it existed in Biblical times, and an interpretation of that law"—(*LJ*).

Eichrodt, Walther. THE THEOLOGY OF THE OLD TESTAMENT. Trans. by John Baker *Westminster Press* 2 vols. Vol. 1 1961 $8.50 Vol. 2 1967 $7.95

Eller, Meredith Freeman. BEGINNINGS OF THE CHRISTIAN RELIGION: A Guide to the History and Literature of Judaism and Christianity. *College & Univ. Press* 1962 $9.50 pap. $4.50

Fosdick, Harry Emerson. A GUIDE TO UNDERSTANDING THE BIBLE. *Harper* 1938 Torchbks. 1956 pap. $2.75. The development of biblical ideas based on the chronological order of the books.

THE MODERN USE OF THE BIBLE. 1924. *Richard West* $10.00

Fuller, Reginald H. A CRITICAL INTRODUCTION TO THE NEW TESTAMENT. *Allenson* 1966 pap. $9.45

INTERPRETING THE MIRACLES. 1963. *Allenson* pap. $2.25. A companion volume to Hunter's "Interpreting the Parables" (*see under Hunter, A. M., following*).

Good, Edwin M. IRONY IN THE OLD TESTAMENT. *Allenson* 1965 $6.50

This is the first time irony has been analyzed as a literary device in the Old Testament. "The literary sophistication of the Old Testament writers which this study reveals will come as a surprise to some, but to all it will be a fresh and exciting insight into the high drama of some of the world's greatest literature"—(*LJ*).

Goodspeed, Edgar J. HOW CAME THE BIBLE? *Abingdon* 1940 pap. $1.50

THE STORY OF THE APOCRYPHA. *Univ. of Chicago Press* 1939 $4.95

THE STORY OF THE BIBLE. *Univ. of Chicago Press* 1936 $5.00. A one-volume edition of the two following titles.

THE STORY OF THE NEW TESTAMENT. *Univ. of Chicago Press* 2nd ed. 1931 $4.50

THE STORY OF THE OLD TESTAMENT. *Univ. of Chicago Press* 1934 $4.00

THE TWELVE: The Story of Christ's Apostles. 1957. *Macmillan* Collier Bks. 1962 pap. $.95. A universally respected and renowned scholar, Dr. Goodspeed (1871–1962) popularized biblical studies. His books are as readable as they are sound.

Gordis, Robert. THE BOOK OF GOD AND MAN: The Study of Job. *Univ. of Chicago Press* 1965 $12.00

Because of the special significance the Book of Job holds for contemporary readers, we break our rule concerning the exclusion of critical works on separate books of the Bible. "This magnificent study of one of the greatest literary masterpieces of all time cannot fail to thrill every serious student of the *Book of Job* or anyone deeply concerned about the enigmas of human existence.... The book includes a critical introduction and exposition, an original translation, detailed critical and bibliographical notes, and detailed bibliography. Rabbi Gordis' own critical point of view is in strong but informed reaction to the hyper-criticism which by its methods of dissection has so often missed the whole spirit and point of ancient literatures. As translator, he proves himself a sensitive literary artist"—(*LJ*).

Gottswald, Norman K. A LIGHT TO THE NATIONS: An Introduction to the Old Testament. *Harper* 1959 $11.95

Grant, Robert M. A HISTORICAL INTRODUCTION TO THE NEW TESTAMENT. 1963. *Simon & Schuster* 1972 pap. $3.95

Professor Grant of the University of Chicago uses a threefold approach: literary, historical and theological. "The result is a well-organized and brilliantly written book." *(See added comment in Section on Biblical Archeology.)*

A SHORT HISTORY OF THE INTERPRETATION OF THE BIBLE. *Macmillan* 1963 pap. $1.45

Guthrie, Donald, Ed. NEW TESTAMENT INTRODUCTION. *Inter-Varsity* 1971 $12.95

Guthrie, Harvey Henry. GOD AND HISTORY IN THE OLD TESTAMENT. 1960. *Allenson* $5.75

Some critics feel that too much has been attempted in this book by the Assistant Professor of Old Testament at the Episcopal Theological Seminary, Cambridge, Mass. "None the less, Dr. Guthrie's book is a most stimulating one and worthy of serious attention by all students of the Old Testament"—(*TLS*, London).

Heaton, Eric W. EVERYDAY LIFE IN OLD TESTAMENT TIMES. *Scribner* 1956 $8.95

"Exactly what readers and students of the Old Testament have been waiting for. Indeed, I know of no other book now in print which gives us what we need and want to know and which, moreover, supplies both necessity and desire in so lively and fascinating a manner"—(Mary Ellen Chase, in the *N.Y. Times*).

THE HEBREW KINGDOMS. *Oxford* 1968 $6.25

"Covering the central Old Testament period, from the legacy of Solomon's reign to the crisis of the Babylonian exile, this study uses literature of the period to clarify distinctive traditions in the religion and theology of Israel"—(Publisher's note). In the New Clarendon Bible Series. The Revised Standard Version is used. Illustrations and maps.

Heschel, Abraham J. THE PROPHETS. *Harper* 1963. Vol. 1 1969 pap. $2.95 Vol. 2 1971 pap. $3.25

This analysis of the significance of prophecy in the history of religion, and the nature and meaning of prophetic inspiration may be hard going for the average reader. But it is "soundly traditional yet fresh with new insight, compassionate of its subject but also provocative. There is not a dull page in it"—(*America*).

Hunt, Ignatius. UNDERSTANDING THE BIBLE. *Sheed & Ward* 1962 $3.95 pap. $2.95

Because the "renaissance of Catholic biblical scholarship has created some confusion and uncertainty in the minds of non-specialists ... who are unable to follow the new developments with any consistency," Father Hunt has provided this straightforward introduction. It is an "excellent example of popularization achieved without loss of scientific reliability"—(*Commonweal*).

Hunter, Archibald M. INTERPRETING THE PARABLES. *Westminster Press* 1961 $3.50

"Pastors and theological students have long since learned that A. M. Hunter of the University of Aberdeen can pack more biblical information into an attractive, functional style than any other scholar now at work.... This is a lucid, sensible interpretation"—(*LJ*).

INTRODUCING THE NEW TESTAMENT. 1945. *Westminster Press* 3rd ed. rev. and enl. 1973 $3.50

Nine new chapters have been added to this readable book.

Hyatt, J. Philip. THE HERITAGE OF BIBLICAL FAITH: An Aid to Reading the Bible. *Bethany* 1964 $5.95

"In this excellent volume" the professor of Old Testament at Vanderbilt University "uses the historical approach to Biblical studies although he does not neglect literary values. . . . Clear, sound, and exceptionally well written"—(*LJ*).

Jackson, Warren W. THE NEW TESTAMENT IN THE CONTEMPORARY WORLD. *Seabury Press* (orig.) 1968 pap. $2.50

Jeremias, Joachim. REDISCOVERING THE PARABLES. *Scribner* rev. ed. 1966 pap. $2.95

This is a simplified revision of a more scholarly work by the German theologian. He "deals concisely and in popular style with the problems of translation from the Greek text and the Aramaic. . . . An interesting glossary of historical terms relating to parables and an index to synoptic parables are included in the appendix. There is a valuable literary analysis of these great but simply-told narratives"—(*LJ*).

Kluger, Rivah Scharf. SATAN IN THE OLD TESTAMENT. Trans. by Hildegard Nagel *Northwestern Univ. Press* 1967 $5.50

Originally published in 1948 this book by a practising Jungian analyst "was considered so valuable by Jung himself that he included it in one of his own works. . . . Dr. Kluger's rich background in Semitic languages makes the book an authoritative one for experts, but too technical for the casual or general reader. . . . A fascinating book for those who know either Jung or the Old Testament"—(*LJ*).

Lindblom, Johannes. PROPHECY IN ANCIENT ISRAEL. *Fortress Press* 1972 $15.00

The *Times Literary Supplement* (London) said that this authoritative and comprehensive volume is "unlike any other work in Old Testament prophecy in its approach and organization, and it offers a rich feast to the reader."

Lockyer, Herbert. The All Ser. *Zondervan* 14 Bks. Bk. 1 All the Apostles of the Bible Bk. 2 All the Books and Chapters of the Bible Bk. 3 All the Doctrines of the Bible. Bks. 2–3 Set $12.90 Bk. 4 All the Children of the Bible Bk. 5 All the Holy Days and Holidays Bk. 6 All the Kings and Queens of the Bible Bks. 5–6 Set $12.90 Bk. 7 All the Men of the Bible Bk. 8 All the Women of the Bible Bks. 7–8 Set $12.90 Bk. 9 All the Miracles of the Bible Bk. 10 All the Parables of the Bible Bks. 9–10 Set $12.90 Bk. 11 All the Prayers of the Bible Bk. 12 All the Promises of the Bible Bks. 11–12 Set $12.90 Bk. 13 All the Trades and Occupations of the Bible Bk. 14 All the Messianic Prophecies of the Bible. Bks. 1–13 each $6.95 Bk. 14 $8.95 set $99.30

MacKenzie, J. G., S.J. FAITH AND HISTORY IN THE OLD TESTAMENT. *Univ. of Minnesota Press* 1963 $3.75; *Macmillan* pap. $1.45. An absorbing account for laymen as well as clergy.

Mackie, Annebeth. THE BIBLE SPEAKS AGAIN. Trans. from the Dutch title "Clear Wine." *Augsburg* 1969 $3.75

"I believe that this is the best and most inclusive book on the Bible available"—(William Barclay).

Mead, Frank S. WHO'S WHO IN THE BIBLE. *Revell* 1973 pap. $1.25

Metzger, Bruce M. THE TEXT OF THE NEW TESTAMENT: Its Transmission, Corruption and Restoration. *Oxford* 1964 2nd ed. 1968 $7.50

The author, one of the compilers of the 1966 new Greek text (*see introduction to this Chapter*) "discusses the transmission and the writing of ancient manuscripts, the description of the more important witnesses to the text of the New Testament, the history of New Testament textual criticism, and the different schools of textual methodology. . . . The most comprehensive, up-to-date, usable book available on this subject"—(*LJ*).

Minear, Paul S. IMAGES OF THE CHURCH IN THE NEW TESTAMENT. *Westminster Press* 1960 1970 pap. $2.95

This work was assigned to the author by the Faith and Order Department of the World Council of Churches. *Library Journal* has said of it: "One of the most significant theological books of the year. . . . Until this book there has been no one volume which has adequately studied in a scholarly way all the biblical pictures of the church. It is a masterful work, carefully planned, well organized, and brilliantly presented."

Moldenke, H. N., and A. L. Moldenke. PLANTS OF THE BIBLE. *Ronald* 1952 $10.50

Moody, Dale. THE SPIRIT OF THE LIVING GOD: Biblical Concepts Interpreted in Context. *Westminster Press* 1968 $6.00

"The book reveals Mr. Moody's competence and scholarship as well as his eclectic selectivity of conservative and liberal theology. Both liberal and conservative students can profit from this study. The indexes of Scripture references, names and subjects increase the value of this work"— *(LJ).*

Moule, C. F. D. THE BIRTH OF THE NEW TESTAMENT. *Harper* 2nd rev. ed. 1966 $9.00; *Allenson* pap. $5.50. This book was designed as a general introduction to "Harper's New Testament Commentaries." In a thorough and scholarly manner, Professor Moule presents his "analytical investigation of the social, religious, and intellectual circumstances which led to the writing of the New Testament."

MAN AND NATURE IN THE NEW TESTAMENT. *Fortress Press* 1967 pap. $1.00

THE PHENOMENON OF THE NEW TESTAMENT. *Allenson* 1967 $5.35 pap. $2.85

Moulton, Richard G. THE LITERARY STUDY OF THE BIBLE. 1899. *AMS Press* $11.00; *Folcroft* 1973 $25.00; *Richard West* 1905 $20.00. A most helpful account of the Bible's leading forms of literature.

Mowinckel, Sigmund. THE PSALMS IN ISRAEL'S WORSHIP. Trans. from the Norwegian by D. R. Ap-Thomas *Abingdon* 2 vols. 1962 set $16.95. The outstanding critical study of the Psalms and their usage by the world's authority in this field.

Neill, Stephen. THE INTERPRETATION OF THE NEW TESTAMENT, 1861–1961. *Oxford* $7.75 pap. $4.50

"In an interesting, fascinating manner, with many personal notations, [Bishop Neill] discusses the movements of thought and the permanent contributions made by the different schools. An invaluable conclusion assesses the position today. Highly recommended"—*(LJ).*

Noth, Martin. THE HISTORY OF ISRAEL. *Harper* 1958 2nd ed. 1960 $7.50. Perhaps the most comprehensive of all modern attempts to reconstruct the history of Israel.

Palmer, Humphrey. THE LOGIC OF GOSPEL CRITICISM. *St. Martin's* 1968 $13.95. A lecturer in Philosophy at University College, Cardiff, Wales, discusses the four types of modern New Testament criticism: textual, documentary, source and form. Bibliography.

Perrin, Norman. A MODERN PILGRIMAGE IN NEW TESTAMENT CHRISTOLOGY. *Fortress Press* 1974 $6.25

THE NEW TESTAMENT: An Introduction. *Harcourt* 1974 $5.95

REDISCOVERING THE TEACHING OF JESUS. *Harper* 1967 $6.95

This expands upon the work listed just above and revises it somewhat. "The book reflects Dr. Perrin's teacher, T. W. Manson, and represents a developed synthesis of Manson's methodology and form criticism in light of the advances made by liberal, critical scholarship. . . . It is enlightening and provocative and will be of value to both conservative and liberal religion collections"—*(LJ).* Contains an important preface, indexes and an annotated bibliography.

Phillips, J. B. RING OF TRUTH: A Translator's Testimony. *Macmillan* 1967 $2.95

"This is essentially a personal testimony to what the Bible, and particularly the New Testament, can bring of insight and renewal to the person who lives with it and takes it seriously. [The writer is] the gifted Anglican cleric who for the last 25 years has been translating the New Testament into modern English with such singular success and all but universal acceptance"—*(LJ).*

Price, James L. INTERPRETING THE NEW TESTAMENT. *Holt* 1962 2nd ed. 1971 $10.95. A descriptive analysis of the contents of each book of the New Testament placed in historical context plus interpretation and bibliography.

Rad, Gerhard von. GENESIS: A Commentary. Trans. by John Marks *Westminster Press* 1961 1973 $9.00

Without ignoring the standard patterns of literary and historical criticism, Professor von Rad, now of the University of Heidelberg, "goes beyond the atomistic results so often characteristic of source analysis techniques to a pre-eminently theological interpretation.... Here is superb commentary with a carefully written, nontechnical, critical introduction"—(*LJ*).

OLD TESTAMENT THEOLOGY. Trans. from the German by D. M. G. Stalker *Harper* 2 vols. Vol. 1 The Theology of Israel's Historical Traditions (1962) Vol. 2 The Prophets (1966) each $10.00

"Von Rad's style is commendable, his treatment profound and often stirring"—(*Christian Century*).

Richardson, Alan. AN INTRODUCTION TO THE THEOLOGY OF THE NEW TESTAMENT. *Harper* 1959 $7.50

Samuel, Maurice. CERTAIN PEOPLE OF THE BOOK. *Knopf* 1955 $5.95. A fine study of Old Testament characters from the point of view of their everyday motives and the historical forces guiding them.

Sanders, Paul S., Ed. TWENTIETH CENTURY INTERPRETATIONS OF THE BOOK OF JOB. *Prentice-Hall* 1968 $4.95 pap. $1.25

"The biblical Book of Job is examined from many angles in this collection of 11 scholarly essays by theologians, historians, and professors of English, Greek and Hebrew. Gilbert Murray compares Job with Prometheus and U. Milo Kaufmann contrasts Greek with Hebrew piety. Arnold Toynbee looks for mythological clues to the book's meaning, while Eugene Goodheart seeks meanings applicable to the modern world. Edward J. Kissane makes a close examination of the metrical structure of the original Hebrew verses. Selections, as usual with this series, are expertly chosen for a well-rounded survey"—(*PW*).

Schultz, Samuel J. THE OLD TESTAMENT SPEAKS. *Harper* 1970 $7.50. A complete survey of Old Testament history and literature.

Scott, R. B. Y. THE RELEVANCE OF THE PROPHETS. *Macmillan* rev. ed. 1969 $6.95 pap. $2.45

A Princeton University professor provides "one of the most practical and satisfying studies of Old Testament prophetic tradition now available"—(*LJ*).

THE WAY OF WISDOM IN THE OLD TESTAMENT. *Macmillan* 1971 $7.95

This book "will interest both the specialist and the general reader. Anyone with questions about the relevance of such a study of ancient wisdom for today's world owes it to himself to read Scott's epilogue"—(*LJ*).

Sherwin-White, Adrian Nicholas. ROMAN SOCIETY AND ROMAN LAW IN THE NEW TESTAMENT. *Oxford* 1963 $5.25. Lectures on the legal, administrative and municipal backgrounds of Acts and the synoptic gospels.

Shires, Henry M. FINDING THE OLD TESTAMENT IN THE NEW. *Westminster Press* 1974 $7.50

Spivey, Robert A., and D. Moody Smith, Jr. ANATOMY OF THE NEW TESTAMENT: A Guide to Its Structure and Meaning. *Macmillan* 2nd ed. 1974 $9.95

Swanston, Hamish F. G. THE COMMUNITY WITNESS: An Exploration of Some of the Influences at Work in the New Testament Community and Its Writings. *Sheed & Ward* 1967 $4.95

"This difficult but rewarding study by an English Oratorian priest, shows how the Old Testament writings, the preaching of the Resurrection, and the awareness of Christ's presence in the community, especially in its liturgical and sacramental life, not only influenced the formation of the early Christian community, but are evident everywhere in the pages of the New Testament.... His book should give serious students of Scripture and the early Church many new insights"—(*LJ*).

Terrien, Samuel. THE BIBLE AND THE CHURCH: An Approach to Scripture. *Westminster Press* 1963 $1.50

Trawick, Buckner B. THE BIBLE AS LITERATURE. College Outline Ser. *Harper* (Barnes & Noble) 2nd ed., 2 vols. Vol. 1 Old Testament and the Apocrypha (1970) pap. $2.50 Vol. 2 The New Testament (1968) pap. $1.75

Vawter, Bruce. THE CONSCIENCE OF ISRAEL: Pre-exilic Prophets and Prophecy. *Sheed &* *Ward* 1961 1969 pap. $2.45

"A book that is at once superbly written and theologically perceptive. The author, a well-known Roman Catholic scholar, undertakes to elucidate the pre-exilic prophets of Israel in language that can be understood by the average man"—(*Christian Century*).

Weiser, Artur. THE OLD TESTAMENT: Its Formation and Development. Trans. by Doro-thea M. Barton *Association Press* 1961 $5.95

"Particularly helpful is the inclusion of a carefully done treatment of the Apocrypha and the Pseudepigrapha ... to which has been added a general survey of the Qumran literature but without neglect of the Dead Sea materials"—(*LJ*).

Whyte, Alexander. WHYTE'S BIBLE CHARACTERS. *Zondervan* 1968 $11.95

Wolff, Hans Walter. THE OLD TESTAMENT: A Guide to Its Writings. Trans. by Keith R. Grim *Fortress* 1973 pap. $3.25

Wolff "introduces the reader to the categories of Old Testament literature and their major themes"—(*Choice*).

Worden, Thomas. THE PSALMS ARE CHRISTIAN PRAYER. *Sheed & Ward* 1961 $3.95

"Father Worden, Editor of *Scripture*, the quarterly of the English Catholic Biblical Association, has written what amounts to a short Biblical theology of the Old Testament based on the best modern Scripture scholarship in order to show the relevance of the Psalms for modern Chris-tians"—(*LJ*).

Wright, G. Ernest, and Reginald H. Fuller. THE BOOK OF THE ACTS OF GOD: An Introduction to the Bible. *Doubleday* 1957 Anchor Bks. pap. $2.95

Two eminent biblical authorities, writing primarily for laymen, take full benefit of the insights of recent scholarship to produce an extremely stimulating guide. "Interweaves scholarship and piety quite gracefully and achieves an astounding brevity"—(*SR*). In the Christian Faith Series.

PRAYER BOOKS

The first complete English Book of Common Prayer used in the Church of England and other Anglican churches was published in 1549 under Edward VI, and made compulsory by an Act of Uniformity. After several suppressions during changes in the English official religion, it was again revised and declared the only legal service book in 1662. No further revision of importance was adopted, although a revised form submitted to Parliament in 1927 was passed by the House of Lords but rejected by the House of Commons. Revised forms were issued in 1892 and 1929 in the United States. The Book of Common Prayer with the New Lectionary is paged according to the Standard Prayer Book as authorized and approved by the General Convention of the Protestant Episcopal Church in 1928. *Nelson-National*, *Oxford* and *Seabury Press* have the most extensive lists. Valuable for serious users of the Episcopal Prayer Book is "The Oxford American Prayer Book Commentary" by Massey Hamilton Shepherd, Jr. (*Oxford* 1950 $13.50), which gives the historical development and the religious significance of devotional forms. Brigid Brophy extolled this prayer book (in the *N.Y. Times*, 1968) as one of the great examples of English prose.

The Revised Hymnal with the Melodies was authorized by the General Convention in 1940 and contains 600 hymns, of which 201 are new. The Book of Common Prayer and the Hymnal are sometimes combined in one volume. On April 1, 1953, the Church Pension Fund of the Protestant Episcopal Church withdrew from all commercial publish-ing houses the right to print and sell the Protestant Episcopal Hymnal in combination with the Book of Common Prayer. This publishing right was at that time transferred to the *Seabury Press*, the official publishing house of the Protestant Episcopal Church, which now has an extensive list.

In the Roman Catholic Church, the use of the Roman Missal as a prayer book is much more widespread than it once was among laymen. As the Catholic Church has no authorized prayer book, various Missals—including contemporary Masses as well as arrangements and compilations of prayers, hymns and meditations—have been published. The Missal contains all the directions and texts necessary for the performance of Mass throughout the year. *Benziger Brothers, The Catholic Book Publishing Company, Liturgical Press, P. J. Kenedy* and *St. Anthony Guild Press* publish Catholic Missals.

Until 1966 the Mass was almost universally celebrated in Latin. A tremendous change has taken place since our last edition, brought about by the decision of the Sacred Congregation of Rites, acting on the directive of the Constitution on the Sacred Liturgy of the Second Vatican Council, that the Mass should from November 1965, be celebrated in the vernacular—except for a small portion still in Latin. (The English version of the canon, the most sacred portion of the Mass, after a period devoted to its careful translation, was first introduced in the U.S. in 1967.) In 1960 the late Pope John XXIII had issued a "Rubric" requesting this change. The new Mass involves more active participation by laymen in the act of worship, called for by the late Pope Pius X as early as 1903, and it now includes vocal responses in place of congregational silence. Another revision is in the greater choice and variation now allowed in the readings of Scripture at Mass. Also approved by American church officials, but not celebrated on a large scale, are "folk" Masses in which hymns resembling folksongs are sung to guitar accompaniment. The informal atmosphere makes these Masses popular with young people. *(See also introduction to Section on Modern Catholicism in Chapter 4, World Religions, this Volume.)* New editions of the Missal containing the liturgical changes of 1965 and after are available from the publishers noted above.

RELIGIOUS AND CONTEMPLATIVE ANTHOLOGIES

It is not within the scope of *"The Reader's Adviser"* to include individual books of "inspirational religious literature." Forty-six best sellers in this field from Hannah W. Smith's "The Christian's Secret of a Happy Life" (1875) to Fulton Sheen's "Life Is Worth Living" (1953) have been examined in "Popular Religion: Inspirational Books in America" by Louis Schneider and Sanford M. Dornbusch *(Univ. of Chicago Press* 1958 pap. $5.00). The study tends to show "that this literature is, in the main, conservative, worldly, preoccupied with man rather than with God, with health and success rather than spiritual salvation, with traces of the 'magical' "—*(LJ)*. Such standard works of inspiration as those by Saint Francis of Assisi and Thomas à Kempis will be found in the new Chapter 4, World Religions, this Volume. Listed here are some outstanding collections of spiritual and philosophic thought.

Adams, J. Donald. THE TREASURE CHEST: An Anthology of Contemplative Prose. 1946. *Bks. for Libraries* $14.50

Baillie, John. A DIARY OF READINGS: Being an Anthology of Pages Suited to Engage Serious Thought, One for Every Day of the Year, Gathered from the Wisdom of Many Centuries. *Scribner* 1955 $4.50

> The length and breadth of Dr. Baillie's reflections and his reading in literature and theology are shown also in his own small book, "Christian Devotion" *(Scribner* 1962 $3.50). Written with quiet grace and eloquence, it consists of 12 short, self-contained chapters on such diverse subjects as "Ways of Listening," "Christian Vigilance," and "Night Thoughts." "Baillie is particularly concerned with the Christian's role in a society that is almost as pagan as that of classical antiquity."

Barclay, William. THE BEATITUDES AND THE LORD'S PRAYER FOR EVERYMAN. *Harper* 1968 pap. $2.95

> An eminent British scholar interprets each phrase of the Lord's Prayer and some of the Beatitudes. "His main theme is that a Christian ethic is impossible without a Christian dynamic and that each person, in praying, must begin with what he knows and will then go on to fresh understanding. The book is highly recommended for biblical scholars and for informed laymen"—*(LJ)*.

Berrigan, Daniel, S.J. LOVE, LOVE AT THE END: Parables, Prayers and Meditations. *Macmillan* 1971 pap. $1.45

Protester-poet-priest Daniel Berrigan's prayers and meditations "redeem" the vagueness of the parables and provide "a way out of the darkness in a plea for a simple faith that finds Christ simply"—(LJ).

Brantl, George, Ed. THE RELIGIOUS EXPERIENCE. *Braziller* 2 vols. 1964 boxed set $17.50

"A collection of some 131 representative selections, from theory, personal narrative, and fiction, selected to illustrate the varieties of man's religious experiences. . . . Selections range in spirit from Thomas Aquinas to Philip Roth and in time from Aeschylus to Paul Tillich. . . . A fine collection"—(LJ).

Buechner, Frederick. THE MAGNIFICENT DEFEAT. *Seabury Press* 1966 pap. $1.65

"Reverend Buechner here gives us an admirable collection of meditations upon various aspects of the religiously meaningful life, grouped about the ideas of surrender, love, and grace. . . . They pierce the soul of contemporary man with the sword of religious relevance"—(LJ).

Cecil, David. THE OXFORD BOOK OF CHRISTIAN VERSE. *Oxford* 1940 $9.00

Clark, Thomas Curtis and Ester Gillespie. ONE THOUSAND QUOTABLE POEMS: An Anthology of Modern Religious Verse. 1937. *Bks. for Libraries* 1973 $27.50

Curtis, Charles Pelham, and Ferris Greenslet. THE PRACTICAL COGITATOR, or The Thinker's Anthology. *Houghton* 1945 1950 3rd ed. 1963 $6.95; *Dell* 1975 pap. $2.75

A rare, highly personal selection of excerpts from thoughtful writers of all ages, to "provide pegs, stout and well driven in, on which you can hang your own further thoughts."

Garvey, Robert. A CONCISE TREASURY OF BIBLE QUOTATIONS. *Jonathan David* 1974 $8.95

Gasztold, Carmen Bernos de. PRAYERS FROM THE ARK. Trans. by Rumer Godden *Viking* 1962 $5.95 boxed with "The Creatures' Choir" $7.95

This is not an anthology, but a small book of prayers of such unusual quality and appeal that it is included here. Written by a French poet who lives in a Benedictine *Abbaye* in France, the "poems seem to enter into the feelings of animals of the ark, expressing for each of them, very simply and feelingly, what might be his short intense prayer to God."

THE CREATURES' CHOIR. Trans. from the French (with fwd.) by Rumer Godden; ill. by Jean Primrose *Viking* 1965 $3.95 pap. $1.65

"The poems are as good as their predecessors and the book as beautifully designed. Free of sentimentality, the poems are true, simple and charming. Here animals, birds, fish, insects and reptiles speak to the Lord of their condition, giving thanks for what they are or expressing their yearning for what they would be"—(LJ).

Hammond, Emily V., Comp. THE GOLDEN TREASURY OF THE BIBLE. *Pyramid Bks.* 1968 pap. $.95

Kauffman, Donald T. THE TREASURY OF RELIGIOUS VERSE. *Pyramid Bks.* pap. $.95. Six hundred selections arranged under 33 topics.

Kilmer, Joyce, and James E. Tobin. AN ANTHOLOGY OF CATHOLIC POETS. 1917 1926. *Liveright* 1939 new rev. enl. ed. 1947 $6.95

Luccock, Halford E. 365 WINDOWS. *Abingdon* 1960 $2.75. These devotions originally appeared in the *Christian Herald*; they are very brief meditations with a suggested verse of Scripture and a one-sentence prayer—one selection for each day of the year.

Martin, Hugh, Ed. TREASURY OF CHRISTIAN VERSE. *Allenson* 1959 $2.50

Mead, Frank S., Ed. THE ENCYCLOPEDIA OF RELIGIOUS QUOTATIONS. *Revell* 1965 $8.95

"Brilliant [in] . . . its comprehensiveness, scholarship, and obvious usefulness, [it includes] objective and even antireligious quotations as well as the expected devout ones"—(David Glixon, in *SR*). The nearly 12,000 quotations are arranged alphabetically by subject.

Neil, William, Ed. CONCISE DICTIONARY OF RELIGIOUS QUOTATIONS. *Eerdmans* 1974 $7.95

Nettinga, James Z. QUOTATIONS FROM THE BIBLE FOR MODERN MAN. *Simon & Schuster* (Pocket Bks.) 1973 pap. $.95

Nichols, William. A NEW TREASURY OF WORDS TO LIVE BY. *Simon & Schuster* 1959 $4.50. Brief essays by many famous people including Adenauer, Margaret Mead and Mary Martin; a group of prayers is also included.

Nicholson, D. H. S., and A. H. E. Lee. THE OXFORD BOOK OF ENGLISH MYSTICAL VERSE. *Oxford* 1917 $9.75

Nola, Alfonso M. di. THE PRAYERS OF MAN: From Primitive Peoples to Present Times. Ed. by Patrick O'Connor; trans. by Rex Benedict *Astor-Honor* 1960 $12.50

"Both the immense labor of compiling this remarkable anthology and the difficulties of preparing an English-language edition will be gratefully appreciated by librarians and all readers interested in comparative religion and human expression of the idea of God. The Italian original . . . appeared in Parma in 1957. . . . By the prayers gathered here—after many years of research and selection—we are able to envision rites, festivals, liturgies and other forms of communal expression from antiquity to the present"—(*LJ*).

Phillips, Dorothy Berkeley, and others. THE CHOICE IS ALWAYS OURS: An Anthology on the Religious Ways; Chosen from Psychological, Religious, Philosophical and Bio-graphical Sources. 1948. *Pyramid Bks*. 1975 pap. $1.75

This carefully compiled volume "provides sources for regular reflection, methods for spiritual discipline leading to spiritual growth, insights into the interaction of body, mind and soul." "A valuable contribution to a very important kind of literature"—(Aldous Huxley).

Prochnow, Herbert V. TREASURY OF INSPIRATION: Illustrations, Quotations, Poems, and Selections. *Baker Bk. House* 1970 pap. $1.95

Thomas, R. S. THE PENGUIN BOOK OF RELIGIOUS VERSE. *Penguin* (orig.) 1963 pap. $.85; *Peter Smith* $4.00

Wallis, Charles L. A TREASURY OF POEMS FOR WORSHIP AND DEVOTION. *Baker Bk. House* 1974 pap. $3.95

Weatherhead, Leslie D. TIME FOR GOD. *Abingdon* 1968 $3.25

Meditations of the prominent British preacher that "reflect a conservative view of Christianity and of moral issues"—(*LJ*).

Chapter 4

World Religions

"Religion always has a dual relation to culture. . . . In reality, religion is never able to do without cultural forms. In the most profound act of religious introspection forms of cultural creation are operative."

—PAUL TILLICH

Religion continues to be one of the most powerful and creative forces in human history. There has never been a society, no matter how small, remote, or isolated, that did not have some form of religious faith to bind its people together. In the United States the major denominations are flourishing in both membership and income despite a severe economic depression. The recent canonization of Mother Seaton by the Roman Catholic Church attracted wide and favorable publicity in the mass media. A large reading public eagerly welcomes the increasing number of books from American publishers dealing with religious ideas, institutions, and leaders of all faiths. This chapter includes both popular and scholarly works on the chief religions of mankind—Christianity, Buddhism, Islam, and Judaism—as well as books on more recently established "cults" that offer alternative values to the alienated and the unchurched.

ANTHOLOGIES

Abernethy, George L., and T. A. Langford, Eds. THE PHILOSOPHY OF RELIGION: A Book of Readings. *Macmillan* 2nd ed. 1968 $10.95

Ballou, Robert Oleson, Ed. THE BIBLE OF THE WORLD. 1939. *Avon* 1973 pap. $4.95

> THE PORTABLE WORLD BIBLE. *Viking* Portable Library 1944 $5.95 1957 pap. $3.95. Both these titles contain selections from the world's great religions, with excellent introductions to each section.

Bouquet, A. C. SACRED BOOKS OF THE WORLD. 1954. *Folcroft* $10.00

Browne, Lewis, Comp. THE WORLD'S GREAT SCRIPTURES: An Anthology of the Sacred Books of the Ten Principal Religions. *Macmillan* 1946 1962 pap. $3.95. Historical introductions, interpretive comments, decorations and maps for the scriptures of Babylonia, Egypt, Hinduism, Buddhism, Confucianism, Jainism, Zoroastrianism, Judaism, Christianity and Mohammedanism.

Editors of *Life*. THE WORLD'S GREAT RELIGIONS. 1957. *Western Pub.* (Golden Press) de luxe ed. $6.95 lib. bdg. $7.50 pap. $3.95. The late Dr. Paul Hutchinson says in his introduction: "In this presentation of the great living religions . . . there is no attempt to force the faiths into ideological compartments that can be more deceptive than informative. What is here being sought is to show them as their followers know and practice them, with enough reference to the contents of the holy books, the sacred legends and myths and the traditional teachings which lie behind these practices to make them intelligible." Almost half of this magnificent book is devoted to Christianity. Judaism, Hinduism, Buddhism, Taoism, Confucianism and Islam are also thoroughly presented by beautiful color photography and a carefully chosen anthology drawn from scriptural writings. The book is presented as a great plea for religious tolerance. "In their religious aspirations men do not differ much from one another, no matter where they live or when."

Mandelbaum, Bernard, Ed. CHOOSE LIFE: A Philosophy for Today, Including Selections from the Writings of the World's Great Religious and Secular Thinkers. *Random* 1968; *Bloch* 1972 pap. $3.95. Selections that illuminate human life, taken from many

sources, including Isaiah, Buber, Gibran, Maimonides, the Torah, Midrash and
Hasidic lore.

Martin, Alfred Wilhelm. SEVEN GREAT BIBLES: The Sacred Scriptures of Hinduism,
Buddhism, Zoroastrianism, Confucianism (Taoism), Mohammedanism, Judaism,
and Christianity. 1930. *Cooper* 1975 $7.50

GENERAL HISTORIES AND COMPARATIVE STUDIES

Adams, Charles J., Ed. A READER'S GUIDE TO THE GREAT RELIGIONS. Pref. by the editor
Macmillan (Free Press) 1955 1965 $10.95

Aletrino, L. SIX WORLD RELIGIONS. *Morehouse* 1968 pap. $2.50
"An objective analysis by a well-known Dutch journalist of the major non-Christian religions of
the world"—*(PW)*.

Archer, John Clark, and C. E. Purinton. ASPECTS OF RELIGION IN THE SOVIET UNION,
1917–1967. *Univ. of Chicago Press* 1971 $22.00
"This collection of essays by qualified authors enhances our understanding of religion in the
Soviet Union"—*(LJ)*.

FAITHS MEN LIVE BY. 1934. *Bks. for Libraries* $17.50. An excellent reference.

Bach, Marcus. HAD YOU BEEN BORN IN ANOTHER FAITH. *Prentice-Hall* 1961 pap. 1973
$2.45. Dr. Bach is a professor of the School of Religion, State University of Iowa.
This is a useful, popular guide, not intended as a profound study. But it gives the
general reader a simply and agreeably written accurate account of the major
religions. The sacred books of each are mentioned.

MAJOR RELIGIONS OF THE WORLD. *Abingdon* 1959 $1.25

STRANGERS AT THE DOOR. *Abingdon* 1971 $3.95

Belford, Lee A., Gen. Ed. RELIGIOUS DIMENSIONS IN LITERATURE SERIES. *Seabury Press*
1968 pap. each $.85
These booklets of "instruction and commentary" each contain a brief biography of the author
and an outline and interpretation of one of his works. They are "designed to help the reader
discover himself as he faces inwardly the spiritual dilemmas that confront all human beings."
Among the writers treated are T. S. Eliot, Nathanael West, Iris Murdoch, Walker Percy. "Excellent introductions to important writers"—*(PW)*.

Bliss, Frederick Jones. THE RELIGIONS OF MODERN SYRIA AND PALESTINE. 1912. *AMS Press*
1972 $20.00

Bouquet, A. C. COMPARATIVE RELIGION. *Penguin* Pelican Bks. pap. $1.95. By an out-
standing authority.

Bowker, John. PROBLEMS OF SUFFERING IN RELIGIONS OF THE WORLD. *Cambridge* 1970
$15.95 pap. $4.95
"Penetrating and moving study"—*(LJ)*.

Braden, Charles S. THE WORLD'S RELIGIONS: A Short History. *Abingdon* 1939 rev. ed.
1954 Apex Bks. pap. $2.25

Bradley, David G. A GUIDE TO THE WORLD'S RELIGIONS. *Prentice-Hall* Spectrum Bks. 1962
pap. $2.45. A superb job of condensation and clarification, this little book is both
sympathetic and measured; an excellent quick reference; very useful "Bibliography
of Paperbound Books on the World's Religions."

Browne, Lewis. THIS BELIEVING WORLD: A Simple Account of the Great Religions of
Mankind. *Macmillan* 1944 $5.95 pap. 1962 $2.95

Burch, George Bosworth. ALTERNATIVE GOALS IN RELIGION: Love, Freedom, Truth.
McGill-Queen's Univ. Press 1973 $7.75 pap. $2.75
"As a dialogue the book is superb. A model of clarity and a delightful challenge to settled
patterns of thought about religions"—*(Choice)*.

Bush, Richard C. RELIGION IN COMMUNIST CHINA. *Abingdon* 1970 $9.50

"A well-researched book and nowhere else can one become familiar with so many facets of the religious problems of the world's most populous nation"—*(Critic)*.

Comstock, W. Richard, and others. RELIGION AND MAN: An Introduction. *Harper* 1971 $12.95

"Six areas of religion are analyzed for the reader with limited religious background"—*(WLB)*.

Cutler, Donald R., Ed. THE RELIGIOUS SITUATION: 1968. *Beacon* 1968 $15.00

This was the first in what was to be an annual series. "Contributors (numbering 58 in all) include outstanding writers from four continents who analyze and discuss the massive, often hidden impact of 'the religious situation' on the affairs of men and the nature of society"—*(PW)*. *Library Journal* found many essays to be of a high level, others less so; international coverage is somewhat uneven. But its nearly 1,000 pages contain much that cannot be found together elsewhere and it is useful on the religious reference shelf.

THE RELIGIOUS SITUATION: 1969. The second annual volume of the series. *Beacon* 1969 $15.00

Davidson, Gustav. THE DICTIONARY OF ANGELS. *Macmillan* (Free Press) 1967 $15.00 pap. $4.95

An illustrated source book containing 3,000 entries which identify and describe the angels of Judaism, Christianity and Mohammedanism. "The discipline of angelology . . . has just received a shot in the arm in the form of this unique reference work that the devotees of erudition will have a hard time putting down"—*(LJ)*.

Dewdney, Selwyn. THE SACRED SCROLLS OF THE SOUTHERN OJIBWAY. *Univ. of Toronto Press* 1975 $12.50

A DICTIONARY OF COMPARATIVE RELIGION. Ed. by S. G. F. Brandon *Scribner* 1970 $20.00

"This authoritative work, which fills the need for an up-to-date concise dictionary of the subject . . . is very highly recommended"—*(LJ)*.

Dumoulin, Heinrich. CHRISTIANITY MEETS BUDDHISM. *Open Court* 1974 $7.95

"Dumoulin, a world-renowned authority on Zen Buddhism and an active Catholic priest (a member of the Jesuit order), has lived for the past 40 years in Japan and teaches at the Jesuit-founded Sophia University in Tokyo. . . . Dumoulin discusses the encounters between Buddhism and Christianity that have taken place and are taking place in a growing number of countries—*(Choice)*.

Dunne, John S. THE WAY OF ALL THE EARTH: Experiments in Truth and Religion. *Macmillan* 1972 $6.95 pap. $2.95

"This is an extremely provocative reflection upon the importance of interreligious dialogue for our time . . . a theological achievement of the first order"—*(LJ)*.

Eliade, Mircea. PATTERNS IN COMPARATIVE RELIGION. Vol. 1 Trans. from the French by Rosemary Sheed. 1958. *New Am. Lib.* Meridian Bks. pap. $4.95

This important and "quite beautiful" work has gone into its third French edition and has been translated into German, Spanish and Italian. It is a detailed study of manifestations of the sacred in world religions.

THE SACRED AND THE PROFANE. 1959. *Harcourt* Harvest Bks. 1968 pap. $1.75

(With Joseph M. Kitagawa, Eds.). THE HISTORY OF RELIGIONS: Essays in Methodology. *Univ. of Chicago Press* 1959 $7.25 1973 pap. $2.45

Ellwood, Robert S. HISTORICAL ATLAS OF THE RELIGIONS OF THE WORLD. Ed. by Isma'il Ragi al Farugi *Macmillan* 1974 $15.00

The 65 maps "cover such subjects as origins and distribution of religions, spread of the sects, and locations of shrines and temples, sites and cities, as well as unusual topics such as stimulants and narcotics in religious use and pilgrim traffic to Mecca"—*(LJ)*.

RELIGIOUS AND SPIRITUAL GROUPS IN MODERN AMERICA. *Prentice-Hall* 1973 $8.95 pap. $4.95

"The author gives the reader a fascinating account of contemporary American cults and culture-change religious movements"—*(WLB)*.

Finegan, Jack. THE ARCHAEOLOGY OF WORLD RELIGIONS. *Princeton Univ. Press* 1952 $22.50. Treats primitive religions for the scholar and the general reader.

Frazier, Allie M., Ed. READINGS IN EASTERN RELIGIOUS THOUGHT. *Westminster Press* 3 vols. 1969 Vol. 1 Hinduism Vol. 2 Buddhism Vol. 3 Chinese and Japanese Religions pap. each $3.50. Selections from the sacred writings of the major Oriental religions with interpretative essays by scholars such as Eliade, Suzuki, Joseph Campbell, Heinrich Zimmer. Glossaries.

Gaer, Joseph. HOW THE GREAT RELIGIONS BEGAN. *Dodd* new and rev. ed. 1956 $6.00; *New Am. Lib.* $.95

WHAT THE GREAT RELIGIONS BELIEVE. *Dodd* 1963 $6.00; *New Am. Lib.* Signet pap. $1.25

"In an easy-to-read and understandable style he explains the major beliefs of 11 religions: Hinduism, Buddhism, Jainism, Confucianism, Taoism, Shintoism, Judaism, Christianity, Islam, Zoroastrianism, Zen-Buddhism. Following the explanations or brief biography of the founder of each religion, he presents selections from its sacred literature."

Gard, Richard A., Gen. Ed. GREAT RELIGIONS OF MODERN MAN. *Braziller* 6 vols. 1961 each $6.95. Rituals, prayers, and dogmas with commentary of the great world religions: Catholicism ed. by Dr. George Brantl; Protestantism ed. by Dr. Leslie Dunstan; Buddhism ed. by Richard A. Gard; Judaism ed. by Arthur Hertzberg; Hinduism ed. by Louis Renou; Islam ed. by John Alden Williams.

Gaskell, G. A. DICTIONARY OF ALL SCRIPTURES AND MYTHS. *Julian Press* 1960 $15.00. Deals with the sacred language—on the origin, nature and meaning of the scriptures and myths attached to the various world religions.

Graham, Aelred. THE END OF RELIGION: Autobiographical Explorations. *Harcourt* 1971 $7.95 1973 pap. $2.85

"Graham is a compassionate, civilized, literate, and witty man, and this sharing of his journey toward the truth of God is a document which deserves a wide audience"—(*LJ*).

Greenfield, Robert. THE SPIRITUAL SUPERMARKET. *Saturday Review Press* (dist. by Dutton) 1975 $11.50 pap. $3.95

"A thoughtful, entertaining account of a writer's year trailing the gurus of the East who've captured the allegiance of some of America's young. Wild, witty, and weird"—(*LJ*).

Hackin, J., and others. ASIATIC MYTHOLOGY. *T. Y. Crowell* 1963 $12.50. The history of the various religions, sects and mythologies outlined and explained within a historical setting.

Haddad, Robert M. SYRIAN CHRISTIANS IN MUSLIM SOCIETY: An Interpretation. *Princeton Univ. Press* 1970 $7.50

"Haddad . . . has made a significant contribution to several areas. The summing-up is an interpretative essay which will be well used by all those studying minority groups, whether within or without the Middle East"—(*Choice*).

Hardon, John A. RELIGIONS OF THE WORLD. *Doubleday* 2 vols. 1968 Image Bks. pap. Vol. 1 $1.95 Vol. 2 $1.45

Haydon, Albert Eustace. BIOGRAPHY OF THE GODS. 1941. *Bks. for Libraries* $13.75

Head, Joseph, and S. L. Cranston, Eds. and Comps. REINCARNATION: An East-West Anthology. *Theosophical Pubs.* 1968 pap. $2.25; *Causeway Bks.* 1973 $10.00

"This noble anthology proves that belief in reincarnation or some transformation after death is, or has been, held in all parts of the world, and from the most primitive times. . . . The quotations, many of considerable length, begin in the East with excellently chosen passages from the Buddhist, Hindu, Sikh, Egyptian, Judaic and other scriptures or from pertinent commentaries. Then follow, Christian, Mohammedan, and other texts, including the early Christian, the Druses, Roman Catholic, Masonic and 20th-century clerics of various faiths. In Part 2, 'Western Thinkers on Reincarnation,' the editors have collected a remarkable anthology from poets and other noted writers of Europe and America, grouped by country. Part 3 comprises quotations from scientists and psychologists on the subject. . . . An essential item for all large religious collections and useful in a library of any size, this book should be invaluable to clergymen and to professional writers and speakers"—(*LJ*).

Hick, John. GOD AND THE UNIVERSE OF FAITHS: Essays in the Philosophy of Religion. *St. Martin's* 1974 $12.95

THE HISTORICAL STUDY OF AFRICAN RELIGION. Ed. by T. O. Ranger and I. N. Kunambo *Univ. of California Press* 1972 $12.95

Hume, Robert Ernest. THE WORLD'S LIVING RELIGIONS: An Historical Sketch. 1925. *Scribner* rev. ed. 1959 $5.95 1964 pap. $4.95

"An exceedingly compact summary of the lives of the founders, the literature, the tenets, the strengths and the weaknesses of all the major faiths"—*(LJ)*.

Hutchison, John A., and James Alfred Martin, Jr. THE WAYS OF FAITH: An Introduction to Religion. *Ronald* 1953 2nd ed. 1960 $8.50

Idowu, E. Bolaji. AFRICAN TRADITIONAL RELIGION: A Definition. *Orbis* 1973 $6.95

"This important book is the first to place the study of African religion in the larger context of religious studies. The author is well qualified by his competence in the history of religions, Christian theology, and the religion of the Yoruba. There is no comparable work"—*(Choice)*.

Judah, J. Stillson. HARE KRISHNA AND THE COUNTERCULTURE. *Wiley* 1974 $12.95

"This informative book presents the most accurate description to date of the Krishna Consciousness Movement and its historical roots"—*(LJ)*.

Jurji, Edward J. THE MIDDLE EAST: Its Religion and Culture. 1956. *Greenwood* 1973 lib. bdg. $9.50

Keen, Sam. VOICES AND VISIONS. *Harper* 1974 $6.95

"Nine prominent 'gurus' explain different ways of understanding altered consciousness and the transformations they have undergone in their quests for comprehension"—*(Booklist)*.

Kellett, E. E. A SHORT HISTORY OF RELIGIONS. 1934. *Bks. for Libraries* facsimile ed. $21.50; *Folcroft* 1973 lib. bdg. $15.00

Kitagawa, Joseph M. RELIGIONS OF THE EAST. *Westminster Press* 1960 enl. ed. 1968 pap. $3.95

(Ed.) THE HISTORY OF RELIGIONS. 1935. Introd. by Joachim Wach *Univ. of Chicago Press* 1967 $11.00

"This volume inaugurates a new series on contemporary theology, written by graduates or faculty members of the University of Chicago Divinity School, to be published under the general title Essays in Divinity. It marks the 100th anniversary of the founding of the Divinity School and the 75th for the University. . . . This initial volume, edited by Professor Kitagawa of the Divinity School, consists of 11 essays on the problem of religious understanding or hermeneutics as seen by a group of specialists in the history of religions. . . . Very well written"—*(LJ)*. Among the contributors are Tillich, Eliade and Altizer. In the Essays in Divinity Series: Vol. 1.

Koller, John M. ORIENTAL PHILOSOPHIES. *Scribner* 1970 $8.95 pap. text ed. $3.75

"While a certain exuberance allied with an over-reliance on Western or "Westernized" Asian source material flaws the author's attempt at a complete summary of Asian philosophical-religious thought, Koller's approach has nobility and a valuable distinction—he has a gift for succinct definition that most readers will appreciate"—*(PW)*.

Kotturan, George. AHIMSA: Guatama to Gandhi. *Verry* 1973 $9.00

"In this unique study, Kotturan views the history of India through the perspective of *ahimsa*. Kotturan notes that it implies a positive life of compassion, tolerance and austerity"—*(Choice)*.

Landis, Benson Y. WORLD RELIGIONS: A Brief Handbook for the Layman. *Dutton* Everyman's 1957 rev. ed. 1965 $4.50

Benson Y. Landis of the National Council of Churches has edited a most useful reference work. In the new edition "only the statistics have been updated, but in many instances even these have not been changed. . . . It does not outdate your copy of the [still valuable] first edition"—*(LJ)*.

Langguth, A. J. MACUMBA: White and Black Magic in Brazil. *Harper* 1975 $8.95

"This is the fascinating first person account of a novelist reporter's research into the spirit-oriented religions in modern Brazil"—*(LJ)*.

Leacock, Seth, and Ruth Leacock. SPIRITS OF THE DEEP: A Study of an Afro-Brazilian Cult. *Doubleday* Natural History Press 1972 $9.95 Anchor Bks. pap. $3.95

"This study provides a rich opportunity to experience vicariously the life and traditions of modern members of a 'voodoo' cult in the environs of Belem, Brazil"—*(LJ)*.

Ling, Trevor. A HISTORY OF RELIGION EAST AND WEST: An Introduction and Interpretation. *Harper* 1970 $10.00

"This book will be most helpful to the nonspecialist. What it lacks in depth and variety of interpretation it provides in scope and general information"—*(Choice)*.

MacInnis, Donald E., Comp. RELIGIOUS POLICY AND PRACTICE IN COMMUNIST CHINA: A Documentary History. *Macmillan* 1972 $8.95

"This will be a useful sourcebook for all who are interested in the fate of religion in China. MacInnis, director of the China program of the National Council of Churches, has performed a great service by perceptively and painstakingly excerpting the most revealing passages from the vast body of source material on the subject"—*(LJ)*.

Marriott, Alice, and Carol K. Rachlin. PEYOTE. *T. Y. Crowell* 1971 $5.95; *New Am. Lib.* pap. $1.25

"The authors try to clear up a lot of half-truths and misconceptions about the religious and spiritual practices of American Indians who have fostered the use of Peyote since the last century"—*(LJ)*.

Mbiti, John S. AFRICAN RELIGIONS AND PHILOSOPHY. *Doubleday* Anchor Bks. 1970 pap. $2.50

"The book is written in easily understood English, clearly presenting that the African reality is a total life experience . . . highly recommended"—*(Choice)*.

NEW TESTAMENT ESCHATOLOGY IN AN AFRICAN BACKGROUND: A Study of the Encounter Between New Testament Theology and African Traditional Concepts. *Oxford* 1971 $8.00

"It is the most impressive African contribution to an African theology yet to be published and also contains much of interest to the student of religious change in Africa"—*(Choice)*.

Merton, Thomas. THE ASIAN JOURNALS OF THOMAS MERTON. Ed. by Naomi Burton and others *New Directions* 1973 $12.50 pap. $3.45

"Chiefly a day-to-day record of Merton's observations, conversations, readings, and reflections"—*(Choice)*.

Mitchell, Henry H. BLACK BELIEF: Folk Beliefs of Blacks in America and West Africa. *Harper* 1975 $7.95

"Mitchell, a professor of Black Church Studies at Rochester, argues that Black American Christianity was, from the earliest days of slavery, something more than voodoo and Black magic grafted on to the theology of Rome and Geneva"—*(Kirkus)*.

Moffitt, John. JOURNEY TO GORAKHPUR: An Encounter with Christ beyond Christianity. *Harper* 1972 $7.95

"This beautifully written book should appeal to people with religious commitments, to those who feel a need for spiritual uplift, and to those who are interested in a meeting ground between East and West"—*(LJ)*.

Murphy, Gardner, and Lois B. Murphy, Eds. ASIAN PSYCHOLOGY. *Irvington* 1968 $19.95

"An introduction—admittedly selective—to the great psychological systems of the Far East. These systems—Hinduism, Buddhism, Taoism, Confucianism, and Zen—are, of course, religions as well, but the purpose of their presentation here is to tell us something about how the Asian people regard the world around them and the nature of man. The editors have relied chiefly on selections from such fundamental writings as the Upanishads, the Bhagavad-Gita, the I Ching, and the works of patriarchs of Zen, but they do not leave us to wander alone in a wilderness of quotations; they have enlisted the aid of specialist scholars to elucidate and expand upon the texts, and to show us what to look for. A very useful book; there is no other like it"—*(New Yorker)*.

Needleman, Jacob. THE NEW RELIGIONS. *Doubleday* 1970 $6.95; *Simon & Schuster* Pocket Bks. pap. $1.50

"An important book in which the chairman of the philosophy department at San Francisco State examines six of the major new religions that have become fashionable in America lately. . . . The style is refreshing and lively"—*(Choice)*.

Neill, Stephen, Bishop. CHRISTIAN FAITHS AND OTHER FAITHS. *Oxford* 1961 2nd ed. 1970 $7.95 Galaxy Bks. pap. $2.95

Noss, John Boyer. MAN'S RELIGIONS. *Macmillan* 5th ed. 1974 $10.95. A most valuable book that offers a fine sympathetic introduction to all of the major religions.

Oman, John Campbell. THE BRAHMANS, THEISTS, AND MUSLIMS OF INDIA. 1907. *AMS Press* 1973 $22.50; *South Asia Bks.* $12.50

Parrinder, Geoffrey. A BOOK OF WORLD RELIGIONS. *Dufour* 1967 $6.00

"This book by an eminent British authority on the comparative study of religions, is divided into four parts—'Men at Prayer,' 'The Founders,' 'Holy Books and their Teachings,' and 'Growth and Present State of Religions' with many cross-references. Many maps and charts, an outline of religious teachers and their writings, dates and statistics of the world's religions, symbols for each sect, and numerous photographs add to its value and interest"—*(LJ)*.

A DICTIONARY OF NON-CHRISTIAN RELIGIONS. *Westminster Press* 1973 $10.95

"A timely and authoritative dictionary"—*(LJ)*.

Parsons, Elsie W. C. RELIGIOUS CHASTITY: An Ethnological Study. 1913. *AMS Press* 1975 $22.50

Prabhavananda, Swami, with the assistance of Frederick Manchester. THE SPIRITUAL HERITAGE OF INDIA. *Vedanta Press* 1963 $3.75 pap. $1.95

This is a compact but comprehensive volume, which is a "chronological survey with ample quotations and comments, illustrating the great works of Indian thought (the *Vedas*, the *Gita*, Jainism, Buddhism, the six systems of Hindu thought) and of the expounders of Vedanta, including Sri Ramakrishna. . . . Immensely informative, readable, and moving, this book is an excellent introduction to Vedanta for the layman as well as an outstanding reference work for the scholar"—*(LJ)*.

Rácz, István. THE UNKNOWN GOD. Photos by István Rácz; text by Carl A. Keller and others *Sheed & Ward* 1970 $19.50

"This is an outstanding introduction to world religions for the general reader and for young people"—*(LJ)*.

Radhakrishnan, Sir Sarvepalli. EASTERN RELIGIONS AND WESTERN THOUGHT. *Oxford* 2nd ed. 1940 $8.25 1975 pap. $3.95

RELIGION AND CHANGE IN CONTEMPORARY ASIA. Ed. by Robert F. Spencer *Univ. of Minnesota Press* 1971 $6.95

"This book is rather remarkable for the consistent clarity and in-depth approach of all its essays"—*(LJ)*.

Ross, Nancy Wilson. THREE WAYS OF ASIAN WISDOM: Hinduism, Buddhism, Zen and their Significance for the West. *Simon & Schuster* 1966 $7.50 pap. $2.95

An excellent book, warmly praised by Lewis Mumford, Sir Herbert Read and Justice William O. Douglas, among many. "The description of each 'way' in very clear and very interesting prose and the presentation of related and beautiful pictures combine to bring together essential points in history, main points in doctrine, and outstanding examples of expression in art. A discerning exposition of meanings is coupled with a delineation of connections but also of contrasts with Western philosophy, religion, art and science. . . . It is a beautiful book, and made both to enjoy and to ponder"—*(N.Y. Times)*.

Rowley, Peter. NEW GODS IN AMERICA: An Informal Investigation into the New Religions of American Youth Today. *McKay* 1971 $6.95

"Rowley's book is a sort of Baedeker through the labyrinth of the cults of experiential religion . . . an excellent introduction to the religious faiths of today's youth"—*(LJ)*.

SACRED TRADITION AND PRESENT NEED. Ed. by Jacob Needleman and Dennis Lewis *Viking* 1975 $10.00

"These essays . . . present authoritative spokesmen for Christianity (in dialogue with Zen, and as traditional contemplative Christianity), the Samkhya of India, Sufism, Vedanta, and mythology. The book aims to show that traditional religions . . . are more reliable guides for today's spiritual questing than substitute panaceas"—*(LJ)*.

Schmidt, Wilhelm. THE ORIGIN AND GROWTH OF RELIGION: Facts and Theories. 1931. *Cooper* 1972 $9.50

Schoeps, Hans-Joachim. THE RELIGIONS OF MANKIND. Trans. from the German by Richard Winston and Clara Winston *Doubleday* 1966 pap. $2.50

"Dr. Schoeps . . . is widely recognized as a leading authority in the field of comparative religion and religious history. With a smoothly flowing translation, the book reads well and easily, furthered by Dr. Schoeps' decision to concentrate on the broad sweep rather than the minute details of historical developments. . . . This book should become a basic work"—(*LJ*).

Seligmann, Kurt. MAGIC, SUPERNATURALISM, AND RELIGION. 1948. *Pantheon* 1972 $10.00 pap. $3.95

"Originally published in 1948, this classic is now reissued in a new format"—(*WLB*). "If a well-rounded library were to save space for just one book on magic and the occult, this might well be the one"—(*PW*).

Slater, Robert H. L. WORLD RELIGIONS AND WORLD COMMUNITY. *Columbia* 1963 $13.50. An examination of the major religions, their common elements and differences, and the contributions they may make towards the survival of the race.

Smart, Ninian. THE RELIGIOUS EXPERIENCE OF MANKIND. *Scribner* 1968 pap. $5.50

Professor Smart "traces and describes the continuing drama of the concepts of man's relation to God. . . . A remarkably comprehensive overview of the human religious experience [including the] philosophies, the rituals, the ethics of religion in ancient China and Japan, in the Mediterranean world . . . in Islam and in the unique Hebrew experience and the early Christian as well— Smart explores them thoroughly, always writing with severe objectivity . . . and sustained insight and interest"—(*PW*). His survey, "a basic foundation for laymen as well as a standard text" comes all the way up to Christian Science and Jehovah's Witnesses.

Smith, Ethel S. GOD AND OTHER GODS: Essays in Perspective on Persisting Religious Problems. *Exposition Press* 1973 $7.50

Smith, Howard D. CHINESE RELIGIONS: From 1000 B.C. to the Present Day. *Holt* 1968 $7.95 pap. 1971 $2.45

"A comprehensive, general introduction to the development of religious ideas in China [in which] the author discusses Confucianism, Taoism and Buddhism, as well as a . . . popular religion that has grown up over the past 700 years"—(*PW*). Mr. Smith served as a missionary in China for 24 years and more recently as lecturer in comparative religion at the University of Manchester, England.

Smith, Huston. THE RELIGIONS OF MAN. *Harper* 1958 $9.95 Colophon Bks. pap. $2.95 Perenn. Lib. pap. $1.25. A most helpful book on Hinduism, Buddhism, Confucianism, Taoism, Islam, Judaism and Christianity.

Smith, Wilfred Cantwell. THE FAITH OF OTHER MEN. 1963. *Harper* Torchbks. pap. 1972 $2.25

Professor Smith, who was director of the Center for the Study of World Religions at Harvard (1964–1973) "is one of the few Christian theologians truly capable of approaching other religions with humility, reverence, and genuine cross-cultural insights. He expresses most forcefully the feeling that in the age of nuclear weapons human brotherhood is no longer a matter of free choice"—(*PW*).

Soper, Edmund D. THE RELIGIONS OF MANKIND. *Abingdon* 3rd rev. ed. 1951 $3.95

Spencer, Sidney. MYSTICISM IN WORLD RELIGION. 1963. *Peter Smith* $6.00

Starkloff, Carl F. THE PEOPLE OF THE CENTER: American Indian Religion and Christianity. *Seabury Press* 1974 $5.95

Stevens, Edward. ORIENTAL MYSTICISM. *Paulist-Newman* 1974 pap. $1.95

"In all, this is a good book for the beginner"—(*Choice*).

Streeter, Burnett Hillman. THE BUDDHA AND THE CHRIST: An Exploration of the Meaning of the Universe and of the Purpose of Human Life. 1932. *Kennikat* 1970 $12.00; *Gordon Press* $35.00

Stroup, Herbert. FOUNDERS OF LIVING RELIGIONS. *Westminster Press* 1974 pap. $4.25

Tedlock, Dennis, and Barbara Tedlock, Comps. TEACHINGS FROM THE AMERICAN EARTH: Indian Religion and Philosophy. *Liveright* 1975 $9.95

"Balanced scholarly insight into the 'double vision' of American Indian religion and philosophy . . . a valuable compilation"—(*LJ*).

Tillich, Paul. CHRISTIANITY AND THE ENCOUNTER OF THE WORLD RELIGIONS. *Columbia* 1963 $9.00 pap. $1.75

"A clear and succinct analysis of the contemporary religious scene. Above all, it makes us aware of the tremendous impact the quasi-religions such as Communism are having on modern man, especially on non-Western man . . . immensely provocative and important"—(*Christian Century*).

Turner, Victor W. THE DRUMS OF AFFLICTION: A Study of Religious Processes Among the Ndembu of Zambia. *Oxford* 1968 $16.00

"No short summary can do justice to the quality and suggestiveness of Turner's ideas. A most original book which every scholarly library ought to possess"—(*Choice*).

Van Over, Raymond, Comp. CHINESE MYSTICS. *Harper* 1973 pap. $2.45

"The pieces represented are the essential core of early Chinese philosophical spirit. A reliable introductory work"—(*LJ*).

Wach, Joachim. COMPARATIVE STUDY OF RELIGIONS. Ed. by J. M. Kitagawa *Columbia* 1958 pap. 1961 $1.95

Watts, Alan. BEHOLD THE SPIRIT: A Study in the Necessity of Mystical Religion. 1947. *Pantheon* 1971 $5.95; *Random* Vintage Bks. 1972 pap. $1.95

BEYOND THEOLOGY: The Art of Godmanship. 1964. *Random* Vintage Bks. 1973 pap. $1.95

Weber, Max. THE RELIGION OF CHINA: Confucianism and Taoism. Trans. and ed. by Hans H. Gerth *Macmillan* (Free Press) 1951 $7.95 1964 1968 pap. $2.95. A brilliant, illuminating study.

THE RELIGION OF INDIA. *Macmillan* (Free Press) 1958 $7.95 pap. 1967 $2.95

THE WISDOM OF THE EAST SERIES. Cranmer-Byng, J. L., Gen. Ed. *Paragon Reprint* 51 vols. $1.75–$4.50 (*see publisher's catalog for titles*). This standard series, available once more in this country, includes authoritative translations of world-famous texts in the fields of philosophy, art, religion, poetry and science, from China, Japan, India, Persia and the Islamic cultures.

Wolfson, Harry Austryn. PHILO: Foundations of Religious Philosophy in Judaism, Christianity and Islam. *Harvard Univ. Press* 1947 2 vols. rev. 1962 $25.00

Worsley, Peter. THE TRUMPET SHALL SOUND: A Study of "Cargo" Cults in Melanesia. *Schocken* 1968 pap. $3.45

Younger, Paul. INTRODUCTION TO INDIAN RELIGIOUS THOUGHT. *Westminster Press* 1972 $4.95 pap. $2.45

Zaehner, R. C., Ed. THE CONCISE ENCYCLOPEDIA OF LIVING FAITHS. *Beacon* pap. $4.95. A large scholarly, well-illustrated description of the world's major religions: the prophetic group includes Judaism, Christianity, Islam and Zoroastrianism; the mystical or immanent Hinduism, Jainism, Buddhism, Shinto, Confucianism and Taoism.

CONCORDANT DISCORD: The Interdependence of Faiths. *Oxford* 1970 $15.00

"Zaehner's jumping from one cultural-religious expression to another is fascinating although sometimes disconcerting. His radical interpretations are refreshing and intriguing"—(*Choice*).

ZEN, DRUGS, AND MYSTICISM. *Pantheon* 1973 $6.95; *Random* Vintage Bks. pap. $1.95

"Relative compactness makes the main lines of Zaehner's thought more accessible here than in his most comprehensive work, *Concordant Discord*"—(*Choice*).

Zaretsky, Irving I., and Mark P. Leone, Eds. RELIGIOUS MOVEMENTS IN CONTEMPORARY AMERICA. *Princeton Univ. Press* 1975 $25.00

"These papers drawn largely from conferences in 1970 and 1971, present the most recent empirical and theoretical analyses of such movements as Pentecostalism, 19th-Century Protestant cults, and such contemporary phenomena as Hare Krishna"—(*LJ*).

EARLY RELIGIONS

Of the early religions that have vanished from the world much has been written. "Little wonder," writes John B. Noss in "Man's Religions," because these religions "were the vital agents of transition from primitive animism and polytheism to the higher religions." One can profitably study the fragments remaining of ancient belief to place in original context primitive elements that persist in the high religions, and to assess the qualitative difference between "early" and "late" use of certain material. The flood story, for instance, appears in the Babylonian Gilgamesh epic and in the Hebrew Noah story. One of the results of recent interest in the occult has been the reprinting of older works on ancient religions, many of them classics, yet outdated by more recent scholarly publications.

Bailey, Cyril. PHASES IN THE RELIGION OF ANCIENT ROME. 1932. *Greenwood Press* 1972 lib. bdg. $15.25

Bevan, Edwyn Robert, Ed. LATER GREEK RELIGION. 1927. *AMS Press* 1973 $12.50. A compilation of extracts in English from Greek authors.

THE BOOK OF THE DEAD: An English Translation of the Chapters, Hymns etc. of the Theban Recension (c. 4250–c. 2000 B.C.). By E. A. W. Budge. 1923. *Routledge & Kegan Paul* 1969 $25.50

"A poignant record of human hopes, fears and futility in the ages-old effort to deny the fact of death. Unlike some other religious documents, this most ancient of them—its ultimate derivation is pre-historic—has elements of the genius of the race which make it of concern not only to all educated people, but of particular concern to all involved in the study of the human mind or soul"—(*Psychiatric Quarterly*).

The basic Egyptian religious work was intended, with its charms, formulas and other funerary instructions, to guide souls on their journey to the Land of the Dead. There are many parallels to the Ten Commandments and the proverbs, the most famous section being the song of praise to the Sun God, "The Hymn to Ra." Samuel Birch made the first English translation and the most celebrated is by Sir Peter Le Page Renouf. Some of the significant chapters are illustrated in "Mythological Papyri: Texts and Plates," translated by Alexandre Piankoff and edited with a chapter on the Symbolism of the Papyri by N. Rambova (*Princeton Univ. Press* Bollingen Ser. 1957 boxed $40.00). Another discussion will be found in "The Book of the Dead" by E. A. W. Budge (with subtitle "The Papyrus of Ani" *Dover* pap. $4.95; *Peter Smith* $7.50; *University Bks.* 1960 $12.50).

Branston. Brian. THE LOST GODS OF ENGLAND. *Oxford University Press* new ed. 1974 $10.00

"The present volume traces, with care and much learning and charm, the relation of the English, via their Germanic ancestors, with the people who worshipped the northern gods, and it establishes . . . considerable similarity between their religious and cosmological notions and those of the northern branch"—(*Choice*).

Breasted, James H. THE DEVELOPMENT OF RELIGION AND THOUGHT IN ANCIENT EGYPT. *Peter Smith* 1959 $5.50; *Univ. of Pennsylvania Press* 1972 pap. $4.95

Budge, E. A. Wallis. FROM FETISH TO GOD IN ANCIENT EGYPT. 1934. *Blom* 1972 $17.50

GODS OF THE EGYPTIANS, or Studies in Egyptian Mythology. *Dover* 2 vols. 1968 pap. each $5.00; *Peter Smith* 2 vols. set $16.00

OSIRIS: The Egyptian Religion of Resurrection. 1911. *Dover* 2 vols. pap. Vol. I $5.00 Vol. 2 $4.00; *Peter Smith* 2 vols. $16.00

Burriss, Eli Edward. TABOO, MAGIC, SPIRITS: A Study of Primitive Elements in Roman Religion. 1931. *Greenwood Press* 1972 lib. bdg. $11.25

Cumont, Franz. THE AFTER-LIFE IN ROMAN PAGANISM. 1922. *Peter Smith* $5.25

ASTROLOGY AND RELIGION AMONG THE GREEKS AND ROMANS. 1912. *Dover* 1960 pap. $2.00; *Peter Smith* 1960 $5.25

THE MYSTERIES OF MITHRA. Trans. from the 2nd rev. French ed. by Thomas J. McCormack. 1911. *Dover* 1957 pap. $2.50; *Peter Smith* $5.25

Dumezil, Georges. ARCHAIC ROMAN RELIGION: With an Appendix on the Religion of the Etruscans. *Univ. of Chicago Press* 2 vols. 1970 set $32.00

"In the anthropology of primitive religion there are few scholars who can match the brilliance and insight of Dumezil. This is the first English translation of one of his major works, first published in France in 1966 . . . a seminal study for the student of ancient Roman religion"— (*Choice*).

GODS OF THE ANCIENT NORTHMEN. *Univ. of California Press* 1973 $10.00

"The scholarship, as always in Dumezil's work, is formidable and the abundant and informative notes and references will be a comfort to students"—(*Choice*).

Dunne, John S. THE CITY OF THE GODS: A Study in Myth and Mortality. *Macmillan* 1965 pap. 1973 $2.95

"A profound study of the myths of the afterlife in the ancient world . . . from the perspective of the Christian myth"—*(LJ)*.

Ferguson, John. THE RELIGIONS OF THE ROMAN EMPIRE. *Cornell Univ. Press* 1970 $10.75

"Using the latest historical and archaeological evidence, Ferguson, whose writings in the classical field have earned him a scholarly reputation, gives us a most comprehensive picture of the forms of religious beliefs, the new cults that emerged during this period, and how they conflicted and sometimes emerged with traditional beliefs"—*(Choice)*.

Ferm, Vergilius T. A. FORGOTTEN RELIGIONS, INCLUDING SOME LIVING PRIMITIVE RELIGIONS. 1950. *Bks. for Libraries* 1970 $16.00

Fowler, William Warde. THE RELIGIOUS EXPERIENCE OF THE ROMAN PEOPLE, FROM THE EARLIEST TIMES TO THE AGE OF AUGUSTUS. 1911. *Cooper* 1971 lib. bdg. $13.50

Frankfort, Henri. ANCIENT EGYPTIAN RELIGION: An Interpretation. *Harper* Torchbks. 1961 pap. $1.75; *Peter Smith* $5.25

BEFORE PHILOSOPHY. *Penguin* Pelican Bks. pap. $1.75; *Gannon* lib. bdg. $6.00

KINGSHIP AND THE GODS: A Study of Ancient Near Eastern Religion as the Integration of Society and Nature. *Univ. of Chicago Press* 1948 $12.50

Frazer, Sir James (George). THE GOLDEN BOUGH: A Study in Magic and Religion. 1890–1915. *For the many editions, see his main entry in Chapter 8, The Social Sciences, this Volume.*

ADONIS, ATTIS, OSIRIS: Studies in the History of Oriental Religion. 1914. Vols. 5 and 6 of "The Golden Bough." *St. Martin's* ea. $15.40

THE WORSHIP OF NATURE, Vol. I. 1926. *AMS Press* 1974 $35.00

Freund, Philip. MYTHS OF CREATION. Ill. by Milton Charles. *Transatlantic* 1975 pap. $2.95

"This work analyzes the main outline of ancient and primitive myths relating to creation. . . . Freund shows the numerous contradictions and divergent explanations of the same event or process held by astronomers, paleontologists and biologists. . . . Highly recommended"—*(LJ)*.

Grant, Frederick C., Ed. ANCIENT ROMAN RELIGION. *Bobbs* Lib. Arts 1957 $8.50 pap. $3.50

HELLENISTIC RELIGIONS: The Age of Syncretism. *Bobbs* Lib. Arts 1953 $6.00 pap. $2.00

Guthrie, W. K. C. THE GREEKS AND THEIR GODS. *Beacon* 1955 pap. $4.95. An often-quoted reference. Major figures of Greek mythology and their relation to Greek thought.

ORPHEUS AND THE GREEK RELIGION: A Study of the Orphic Movement. 1935. *Norton* 1967 $6.50

Heidel, Alexander. THE BABYLONIAN GENESIS. *Univ. of Chicago Press* 2nd ed. 1951 Phoenix Bks. pap. 1963 $2.45

THE GILGAMESH EPIC AND OLD TESTAMENT PARALLELS. *Univ. of Chicago Press* 2nd ed. 1949 $7.50 Phoneix Bks. pap. 1963 $3.75

Jaeger, Werner. EARLY CHRISTIANITY AND GREEK PAIDEIA. 1961. *Oxford* 1969 pap. $1.95

THE THEOLOGY OF THE EARLY GREEK PHILOSOPHERS. *Oxford* 1947 $9.50 pap. $3.95

James, Edwin Oliver. SEASONAL FEASTS AND FESTIVALS. *Harper* (Barnes & Noble) 1961 1963 pap. $1.75. Festivals in Ancient Egypt, Mesopotamia, Canaanite and Hebrew Palestine.

WORSHIP OF THE SKY-GOD: A Comparative Study of Semitic and Indo-European Religion. 1963. *Humanities Press* $7.50

The author, known for his many works "conceived in the spirit of detached scholarship based on vast erudition," was Professor of the History of Religion in the University of London, and Chaplain of All Souls College, Oxford.

Kramer, Samuel Noah, Ed. MYTHOLOGIES OF THE ANCIENT WORLD. *Doubleday* Anchor Bks. 1961 pap. $1.95

Lawson, John Cuthbert. MODERN GREEK FOLKLORE AND ANCIENT GREEK RELIGION: A Study in Survivals. 1910. Fwd. by A. N. Oikonomides *University Bks.* 1964 $10.00

"This work . . . was the outcome of research undertaken in Greece from 1898 to 1900. Mr. J. C. Lawson, Pembroke College, Cambridge, was among the first scholars to transcend the restrictions of philhellenic classical purism which had encapsulated the glory and greatness of ancient Greece in an insulated academic realm. Lawson went to Greece hoping to find survivals of classical mythology and folklore. The present work is a testimony to the correctness of his hunch.

"[Its value lies] in its overall emphasis on the continuities of cultural history and in the influence [the author] has had on the classical scholars of his and of subsequent generations"—*(LJ).* "A landmark in the history of folklore and ethnography"—*(TLS,* London). Includes an up-to-date bibliography.

Linforth, Ivan M. THE ARTS OF ORPHEUS. 1941. *Arno* 1973 $18.00

Morenz, Siegfried. EGYPTIAN RELIGION. *Cornell Univ. Press* 1973 $19.50

"This meticulous but readable translation should provide *the* replacement for the current plethora of obsolete reprints on Egyptian religiousness—like those of Wallis Budge"—*(Choice).*

Murray, Margaret Alice. THE WITCH-CULT IN WESTERN EUROPE: A Study in Anthropology. *Oxford* 1963 Galaxy Bks. pap. $2.75

Mylonas, George. ELEUSIS AND THE ELEUSINIAN MYSTERIES. *Princeton Univ. Press* 1961 $16.00 pap. $6.95. The history of the cult traced in the archeological remains.

Nilsson, Martin P. GREEK FOLK RELIGION. *Peter Smith* $5.00; *Univ. of Pennsylvania Press* 1972 pap. $2.95

Nock, Arthur Darby. ESSAYS ON RELIGION AND THE ANCIENT WORLD. *Harvard Univ. Press* 2 vols. 1972 set $35.00

"Since the turn of the century the religious life of the ancient world has become an important area of classical scholarship. One of the towering figures in the development of this field was the late Arthur Darby Nock, whose writings were remarkable for their wide erudition and consistent objectivity. This collection . . . affords an overall view of the progress of the field between 1925 and 1963"—*(LJ).*

Oakes, Maud van Cortlandt. THE TWO CROSSES OF TODOS SANTOS: Survivals of Mayan Religious Ritual. Bollingen Ser. *Princeton Univ. Press* 1951 1969 $8.50 pap. $3.45

"Nonscientists will find the broad, human picture fascinating while scientists will rejoice at the rich context"—*(N.Y. Times).*

Parrinder, Geoffrey. WITCHCRAFT: European and African. *Harper* (Barnes & Noble) 1958 rev. enl. ed. 1970 $7.00 pap. $3.25. The standard book on witchcraft, unique in bringing together the former European and American beliefs with those of Africa today.

Petrie, Sir Flinders. RELIGIOUS LIFE IN ANCIENT EGYPT. 1924. *Cooper* 1972 lib. bdg. $6.50

Piggott, Stuart. THE DRUIDS. *Praeger* 1975 $8.50

"A most eminently qualified scholar of British and classical antiquities . . . has here produced a serious, readable, and delightfully entertaining book"—*(LJ).* "First published in 1968, this is a thorough, non-technical study useful for reference as well as the general reader"—*(Booklist).*

Rahner, Hugo. GREEK MYTHS AND CHRISTIAN MYSTERY. Trans. by Brian Battershaw. 1963. *Biblo & Tannen* 1971 $13.50

"Nothing less than a paean of praise is in order for this splendid translation of an important work first published in 1945"—*(LJ).*

Seznec, Jean. THE SURVIVAL OF THE PAGAN GODS: The Mythical Tradition and Its Place in Renaissance Humanism and Art. Bollingen Ser. *Princeton Univ. Press* 1953 1972 pap. $3.95. The re-emergence of the ancient gods after the fall of Rome.

Steiner, Rudolf. CHRISTIANITY AS MYSTICAL FACT AND THE MYSTERIES OF ANTIQUITY. 1902 2nd ed. 1910. Trans. from the German and with notes by E. A. Frommer, Gabrielle Hess and Peter Kandler; ed. by Paul N. Allen; introd. by Alfred Heidenreich. (Major Writings of Rudolf Steiner, published in commemoration of the One Hundredth Anniversary of his birth, Vol. 5). *Anthroposophic Press* $5.50 pap. $2.95; *Multimedia* (Steiner) 1962 $8.95

The Austrian philosopher and founder of anthroposophy, in tracing his thesis, "presents interesting details about ancient Egypt, the Greek Mysteries, the Gospels, Plato, Plotinus, the Fourth Gospel and the Apocalypse and other matters."

Tylor, E. B. PRIMITIVE CULTURE. *Gordon Press* 2 vols. $100.00; *Peter Smith* 2 vols. 1958 each $6.00

Witt, R. E. ISIS IN THE GRAECO-ROMAN WORLD. *Cornell Univ. Press* 1971 $13.50

"It is an important contribution to an understanding of the religious attitudes of ordinary men and women who lived under the rule of the Caesars"—(*TLS,* London).

See also Chapter 3, Reference Books—Literature: Classical and Mythological Dictionaries, Reader's Adviser, *Vol. 1.*

ZOROASTRIANISM

One of the most influential religions of the ancient world was that ascribed to Zoroaster (*see his main entry, this Chapter*). Numerous references to it abound in Greek and Roman literature, and Plato (*q.v.*) was reportedly prevented from going to Persia to study Zoroastrianism at first hand "only by the outbreak of the War of Sparta with Persia in 396 B.C."—(John B. Noss, "Man's Religions"). The Magi who sought the infant Jesus in the Christian nativity story are supposed to have been priests of Zoroastrianism. Its beliefs influenced Judaeo-Christian theology and the later, "heretical" Gnostic religion, chiefly through its elaboration of the dual principle of good and evil, its belief in bodily resurrection, and its description of "last things" (eschatology). Years after the death of Zoroaster, there began within the religion a slow process of relapse into the old polytheism he had opposed—the old Aryan polytheism that developed in India into Vedic Hinduism. The religion turned to means of thwarting evil and daunting demons. Stamped out by the Muslims who overran Persia in the seventh century, Zoroastrianism survives today only among the Parsis of India and the Gabars of Iran. Its sacred book, the Avesta, reflects but little of a larger body of lost literature.

Cumont, Franz. THE MYSTERIES OF MITHRA. Trans. from the 2nd rev. French ed. by Thomas J. McCormack *Dover* 1957 pap. $2.50; *Peter Smith* $5.25

Dawson, Miles Menander. THE ETHICAL RELIGION OF ZOROASTER. 1931. *AMS Press* 1969 $9.50

Pavry, Jal D. C. THE ZOROASTRIAN DOCTRINE OF A FUTURE LIFE FROM DEATH TO THE INDIVIDUAL JUDGMENT. *AMS Press* $14.00

HINDUISM

Hinduism "is not one religion," writes John B. Noss in "Man's Religions," "but a family of religions. . . . Orthodox Hindus have an extraordinarily wide selection of beliefs and practices to choose from: they can be pantheists, polytheists, monotheists, agnostics, or even atheists; they may follow a strict or loose standard of moral conduct, or they may choose instead an amoral emotionalism or mysticism; they may worship regularly at a temple or go not at all. Their only universal obligation, if they are orthodox, is to abide by the rules of their caste and trust that by so doing their next birth will be a happier one." Hinduism comprises the whole complex of beliefs and institutions which have appeared from the time of the ancient "Vedas" until now. The sacred scriptures are the "Vedas," the hymns of the Aryans dating from earliest times and collected around 1000 B.C. When used as prayers and combined with ritual observances, the "Vedas" were thought to release a power of great efficacy, the Brahma. "The Brahmanas" is an extensive collection of formulas for the correct performance of sacrifice. Priests are Brahmans, highest of the four castes. "The Upanishads" date somewhat later than the "Vedas." They constitute a series of philosophic speculations on the nature of reality, and are extremely various in view. In revulsion from the inexorable process of birth, death, rebirth, death, the poets of the "Upanishads" developed a world-denying philosophic idealism.

Later Hinduism sought other ways to solve the pain of existence. Three ways of release are recognized in orthodox Hinduism: the Way of Works, outlined in the "Code of Manu," the Way of Knowledge, also elaborated in the "Code of Manu," and the Way of Devotion (*bhakti*). This latter is most beautifully expressed in the famous "Bhagavad Gita," which forms one episode in the "Mahabharata." Thomas Merton has said: "The Bhagavad Gita can be seen as the great treatise on the 'Active Life.' But it is really something more, for it tends to fuse worship, action and contemplation in a fulfillment of daily duty which transcends all three by virtue of a higher consciousness: a consciousness of acting passively, of being an obedient instrument of a transcendent will"—(in "The Bhagavad Gita as It Is").

Two other major historical solutions to the problem of suffering and rebirth are found in Jainism and Buddhism, both offshoots of Hinduism. (*For Buddhism see following.*) Newly available sacred literature of Jainism is to be found in *Dover's* "Jaina Sutra" (trans. by Hermann Jacobi, ed. by Max Müller, 2 vols. 1967 pap. each $3.50; *Peter Smith* each $6.50).

According to tradition Jainism was founded by Mahavira (599–527 B.C.). Legends of his life closely parallel those of Buddha. He was born into the noble caste; about the age of 30, he left wife, child and parents to seek wisdom: he practised the most severe asceticism and finally experienced release. Thereafter he was called *Jina* (conqueror) and his followers Jains. They number about two million today and are highly respected in India. The great Hindu philosophic systems took form during the millennium from 500 B.C. to 500 A.D. They include Yoga and Vedanta, both of which have enjoyed popularity in the West.

Translations of Texts

THE BEGINNINGS OF INDIAN PHILOSOPHY: Selections from the Rig Veda, Atharva Veda, Upanisads, and Mahabharata. Trans. and ed. by Franklin Edgerton *Harvard Univ. Press* 1965 $12.50

HINDU SCRIPTURES. Trans. and ed. by Robert C. Zaehner *Dutton* Everyman's rev. ed. $3.95

PRAYERS AND MEDITATIONS FROM THE SCRIPTURES OF INDIA. Ed. by Clive Johnson and Swami Prabhavananda *Vedanta Press* 1967 $3.75. More than 100 selections from Hindu sources.

THE VEDAS, C. 1300–1000 B.C.

The "Vedas" (*veda* means knowledge) were the earliest sacred scriptures of the Hindus comprising more than one hundred extant books. There are four collections of hymns, prayers and liturgical formulas, of which the "Rig-Veda" is the oldest and most important, the others being in part derived from it. The "Rig-Veda" is made up of hymns of praise, joyful and vigorous, resembling the Psalms, and contains 1,028 poems of some 10,000 stanzas.

THE UPANISHADS. C. 600 B.C. Trans. by F. Max Müller *Dover* 2 vols 1962 pap. Vol. 1 $4.00 Vol. 2 $3.50; trans. by Juan Mascaró *Gannon* lib. bdg. $5.00; trans. by Juan Mascaró *Penguin* pap. $1.25; trans. by F. Max Müller *Peter Smith* 2 vols. each $6.00; trans. by Swami Prabhavananda *Vedanta Press* 1967 $3.75. More than 100 selections from Hindu sources.

"The Upanishads" is a series of 108 mystical and philosophical prose works designed to guide the Hindu hermit to a union with Brahma. The Hindu belief is explained in the form of prayers, narratives, dialogues and observations. "The Upanishads" brought to Hindu philosophy "a new emphasis on Brahma as the supreme creating God, a conception that approaches monotheism." All the works postulate one fundamental truth, that the ground of all being, whether material or spiritual, is an all-inclusive reality, ultimate, infinite and self-sufficient. This reality is called Brahma. They also tend to agree on the belief in *transmigration of souls*, the doctrine of *Karma* (the law that one's thoughts and deeds have an ethical consequence in one's future existence), and on the concept of *Nirvana* (the passionless peace of release from *Karma* and the endless cycle of rebirth). Known in Europe during the 18th century, the work has influenced Schopenhauer, Carlyle, Emerson and Yeats. For a general introduction with a detailed study of the Isha, Kena and the Taittiriya texts, *see* M. P. Pandit's "The Upanishads: Gateway of Knowledge (*Vedanta Press* 1960 $3.00).

THE UPANISHADS: The Thirteen Principal Upanishads. Trans. from the Sanskrit, with an outline of the philosophy of the Upanishads by R. E. Hume *Oxford* 2nd rev. ed. 1931 Galaxy Bks. 1971 pap. $3.95

EIGHT UPANISHADS. Trans. by Swami Gambhiranda *Vedanta Press* bilingual ed., Sanskrit and English 2 vols. 1957–1958 Vol. 1 The Isha, Kena, Katha, and Taittiriya Vol. 2 Aitareya, Mundaka, Mandukya, and Prasna set $8.00

THE UPANISHADS: Breath of the Eternal. Trans. by Swami Prabhavananda and Frederick Manchester *New Am Lib.* Mentor Bks. pap. $.95

THE UPANISHADS. Trans. and ed. by Swami Nikhilananda *Harper* Torchbks. (abr.) $2.95

THE BRAHMA SUTRAS (Vedanta Sutras). Badarayana. Trans. by Swami Vireswarananda *Vedanta Press* bilingual ed., Sanskrit and English 2nd ed. 1948 $4.00. The basis of Vedanta.

THE VEDANTA SUTRAS [of Badarayana]. Trans. by George Thibaut; ed. by F. Max Müller *Dover* Sacred Books of the East 2 vols. pap. Vol. 1 $5.00 Vol. 2 $4.00; *Peter Smith* 2 vols. each $6.50

Vedanta is a system of monistic or pantheistic philosophy, based on the Upanishads; an investigation of the latter part of the Vedas, afterwards interpreted as embodying the ultimate aim or end of the Vedas.

THE RAMAYANA (c. 500 B.C.–c.200 A.D.). *See Chapter 19, Asian Literature, Section on South Asia: India and Pakistan*, Reader's Adviser, *Vol. 2*.

THE MAHABHARATA. Trans. from the Sanskrit by Chakravarthi V. Narasimhan *Columbia* 1964 $12.50 pap. $3.95. An English version based on selected verses

The Bhagavad Gita is the most influential of all the many scriptures of the Hindu religion and is contained in the enormous 200,000-line Mahabharata, the older and more remarkable of the two great Indian epics. It began as the story of two feuding families (around 500 B.C.), but later revisions concentrated on the epic of Krishna. In Kenneth Rexroth's most interesting article, "The Mahabharata," in the *Saturday Review* of Sept. 30, 1967, to which the reader is referred, he says: "For a person with Western standards there is only one way to read the *Mahabharata*—a complete suspension of not just disbelief, but of all critical faculties. There are modern prose versions, tremendously abridged, which are easy reading. Chakravarthi B. Narasimhan's is the most recent, but it reduces the jungle of the original to a small, cultivated field. Perhaps the best idea is to read such an abridgment for the "story" and then sample a complete version at leisure, for the *Mahabharata* is as inexhaustible and as exhausting as India itself. India has no written history until Muslim times, but the *Mahabharata* is a kind of written archeology and the reader can dig down, like Schliemann through the nine towns of Troy, encapsulated like a golden onion—down from the latest, something very like the Indian present."

THE MAHABHARATA, Bks. 1 and 2. Trans. and ed. by J. A. B. van Buitenen *Univ. of Chicago Press* 1975 $29.50

Contains "The Book of the Assembly Hall" and "The Book of the Forest." "Van Buitenen's volume is a scholarly translation—accompanied by an elaborate introduction and notes—of the first of the 18 major books which make up the epic. The translation is based on the Poona critical edition of 1933–66. It inaugurates van Buitenen's project of rendering the entire critical edition into English; the remaining 17 books are to be published in six succeeding volumes over the next decade or so"—(*Choice*).

THE BHAGAVAD GITA (200 B.C.–200 A.D.). Trans. by Mohini M. Chatterji, pref. by Ainslie Embree *Causeway* $7.95; trans. by Juan Mascaró *Gannon* lib. bdg. $5.00; trans. and interpreted by Franklin Edgerton *Harvard Univ Press* 2 vols. 1944 set $9.00 pap. each $1.95; ed. by Robert Charles Zaehner *Oxford* 1968 $16.25 Galaxy Bks. pap. $3.95; trans. by Juan Mascaró *Penguin* 1962 pap. $1.25; trans. by Swami Nikhilananda *Ramakrishna* $4.95 pocket ed. $3.00; trans. by Annie Besant *Theosophical Pubs.* Quest Bks. 1968 $2.50; trans. by Swami Prabhavananda and Christopher Isherwood, introd. by Aldous Huxley 1944 *Vedanta Press* $2.95; trans. by Swami Swarupananda *Vedanta Press* bilingual ed., Sanskrit and English $3.50; trans. by Swami Vireswarananda *Vedanta Press* bilingual ed., Sanskrit and English $4.25

"The Bhagavad Gita, which means 'Song of the Lord,' one of the world's greatest religious classics, . . . has been more admired and used for devotional needs than any other Hindu work. The poem tells the story of warrior Arjuna, who suddenly hesitates as he is about to lead his brothers into battle with their own kinsmen, wondering whether one should perform an act injurious to others. At this time, Krishna appears to him and speaks at length about the way of *bhakti*, the true way to man's salvation and release from suffering"—(*LJ*). "Sometime around the third century before the Christian era, an unknown author inserted into the epic story of *The Mahabharata* [*see entry above*] a comparatively short religious document, not only small in comparison to the immense size of the epic itself—which was already becoming the gatherall for Hinduism—but far shorter than any of the scriptures of the other world religions. This is the *Bhagavad Gita*, or "The Lord's Song," one of the three or four most influential writings in the history of man. . . . The unknown author intended . . . the resolution and sublimation of the contradictions of the religious life in the great unity of prayer"—(Kenneth Rexroth, in *SR*).

THE BHAGAVAD GITA: The Song Celestial. A translation in Victorian verse by Sir Edwin Arnold; ill. by Y. G. Srimati *Inter-Culture* pap. $1.25; *Routledge & Kegan Paul* $1.25; *Theosophical Pubs.* $1.00

THE BHAGAVAD GITA. Trans. with introd. by Elliot Deutsch *Holt* 1968 $4.95

This includes critical essays by the translator, who is a professor of philosophy at the University of Hawaii and editor of *Philosophy East and West.* His translation is especially designed for Western students of philosophy and religion. "Highly recommended"—(*LJ*).

THE BHAGAVAD GITA AS IT IS: A New Translation, with Commentary. By Swami A. C. Bhaktivedanta; with appreciations by Allen Ginsberg, Denise Levertov, and Thomas Merton *Bhaktivedanta Bk. Trust* $12.95 pap. $7.95; *Macmillan* 1972 $10.95

KRISHNA: Myths, Rites, and Attitudes. Ed. by Milton Singer. 1966. *Univ. of Chicago Press* 1969 pap. $2.95

"Westerners have long been interested in the legends of Krishna, a field almost as vast as India itself. Historically there are three Krishnas, or three aspects of one Krishna: the tribal chief; the god incarnate; and Krishna of Gokula—the divine herdsman, the mischievous child, the endearing lover, the eternal paradox of flesh and spirit. It is the third Krishna that is the subject of this book. Six American and three Indian scholars have joined to examine the steady stream of poetry, legend, myth, and rite which since about A.D. 200 have dramatized the deeds and described the world of Krishna of Gokula—a land where every object if rightly seen is a key to truth and eternity"—(Publisher's note). Includes "studies, text and context."

IN PRAISE OF KRISHNA: Songs from the Bengali. Trans. by Edward C. Dimock, Jr., and Denise Levertov; introd. by Edward C. Dimock, Jr.; ill. by Anju Chaudhuri *Doubleday* Anchor Bks. pap. $1.95

"Mr. Dimock, a linguist and anthropologist by training, is an expert on Bengali language and literature. On the poetic aspects of the English translation, Denise Levertov, who is herself a poet of repute, has done an excellent job of reproducing the feeling of the original. The illustrations by contemporary Bengali artist Anju Chaudhuri add to the appeal of the volume"—(Dhirendra Sharma, in the *N.Y. Times*).

Krishna is the eighth incarnation of the Lord Vishnu in Hindu mythology, who as preacher of the Bhagavad Gita, which proclaims his divine sovereignty, came to earth thousands of years ago as man's saviour. He is the object of many forms of devotional worship and is traditionally dark-skinned.

Books about Hinduism

Abbott, John. THE KEYS OF POWER: A Study of Indian Ritual and Belief. 1932. *University Books* 1974 $10.00

Akhilananda, Swami. SPIRITUAL PRACTICES. *Claude Stark* Memorial ed. 1974 $8.50

"Swami Akhilananda . . . was active in the Vedanta movement from 1926 to his death in 1962. *Spiritual Practices* . . . is a simple guide to developing one's spiritual life as a preparation to a direct experience of God"—(*Choice*).

Banerjee, Akshaya Kumar. DISCOURSES ON HINDU SPIRITUAL CULTURE. *Verry* 1967 $6.50

Barborka, Geoffrey A. THE PEARL OF THE ORIENT: The Message of the Bhagavad-Gita for the Western World: A New Commentary. *Theosophical Pubs.* Quest Bks. 1968 (orig.) pap. $1.95

Bouquet, Alan C. HINDUISM. *Humanities Press* 1949 2nd ed. 1962 pap. $2.25

Brown, Cheever Mackenzie. GOD AS MOTHER: A Feminine Theology in India. *Claude Stark* 1974 $15.00

"The first full-length monograph in English on the feminine symbolism of an Indian purana (devotional compilation of myths), this Harvard doctoral thesis is an important contribution both to the study of medieval Hinduism and to the growing interest in feminine theologies . . . this work will reward determined undergraduates and specialists. Recommended"—(*Choice*).

Carman, John B. THE THEOLOGY OF RAMANUJA: An Essay in Interreligious Understanding. *Yale Univ. Press* 1974 $17.50

"Attractive and competent book"—(*Choice*). "A scholarly and reliable guide to . . . the theology of one of India's greatest religious thinkers"—(*TLS*, London).

Chinmoy, Sri. COMMENTARY ON THE BHAGAVAD GITA: The Song of the Transcendental Soul. *Multimedia* (Steiner) pap. $1.95

"Sri Chinmoy, known as an ardent propagator of peace of mind realized through spirituality, feels that understanding the Bhagavad Gita's wisdom is central to transcendental awakening. This commentary transmits the Gita's simplicity and profundity"—(*LJ*).

Danielou, Alain. HINDU POLYTHEISM. Bollingen Ser. *Princeton Univ. Press* 1964 $13.50. A comprehensive study of the faith of one-tenth of mankind.

Dasgupta, Surendra Nath. HINDU MYSTICISM. 1929. *Ungar* 1960 pap. $2.25

Eliade, Mircea. YOGA: Immortality and Freedom. Trans. by Willard R. Trask Bollingen Ser. *Princeton Univ. Press* 2nd ed. 1968 $16.00 pap. $3.95. An admirable study, highly recommended.

Eliot, Charles. HINDUISM AND BUDDHISM: An Historical Sketch. 1921. *Routledge & Kegan Paul* 3 vols. 1968 set $49.50

Fausset, Hugh l'Anson. THE FLAME AND THE LIGHT: Meanings in Vedanta and Buddhism. 1958. *Greenwood* 1969 $11.75

"A graceful blending of the scholarly and the personal"—(*S.R.*).

Feuerstein, George, and Jeanine Miller. YOGA AND BEYOND: Essays in Indian Philosophy. *Schocken* 1972 $5.95

"Heady and discerning . . . delving into classical yoga and the Vedas as the life source of all later Indian philosophy"—(*LJ*).

Gopalan, S. OUTLINES OF JAINISM. *Halsted Press* 1973 pap. $4.95

"Highly recommended to fill the gap in most library collections of books in English on Jainism"—(*Choice*).

Gopi, Krishna. THE SECRET OF YOGA. *Harper* 1972 $6.95

"A finely reasoned correlation of Indian Yogic philosophy together with a clear statement of the basis of Kundalini Yoga"—(*LJ*).

Isherwood, Christopher, Ed. VEDANTA FOR MODERN MAN: A Symposium. 1951. *New Am. Lib.* 1972 pap. $1.50

VEDANTA FOR THE WESTERN WORLD: A Symposium on Vedanta. 1945. *Vedanta Press* 1946 3rd ed. 1961 $4.25; *Viking* Compass Bks. 1960 pap. $3.45

Judah, J. Stillson. HARE KRISHNA AND THE COUNTERCULTURE. *Wiley* 1974 $12.95

"This informative book presents the most accurate description to date of the Krishna Consciousness Movement and its historical roots"—(*LJ*).

Kirk, James A., Comp. STORIES OF THE HINDUS: An Introduction through Texts and Interpretation. *Macmillan* 1972 $7.95 pap. $2.95

"Kirk introduces us to Hindu culture in the manner that a Hindu would be introduced to it—by word of mouth. An excellent introduction"—(*LJ*).

Krishnamurti, Jiddu. *See his main entry, this Chapter.*

Menen, Aubrey. THE MYSTICS. *Dial* 1974 $15.00

"Menen has zeroed in on the background of Hindu religious thought. . . . This book is a first-hand, discriminating evocation of the mystical spirit alive in the India of today"—(*LJ*).

Morgan, Kenneth. RELIGION OF THE HINDUS. *Ronald* 1953 $6.95. An excellent study voicing the comments of leading Hindu thinkers.

Nikhilananda, Swami. HINDUISM: Its Meaning for the Liberation of the Spirit. 1958. *Ramakrishna* 1959 $3.95

Nivedita, Sister. COMPLETE WORKS. *Vedanta Press* 4 vols. each $6.00

Prabhavananda, Swami. THE SERMON ON THE MOUNT ACCORDING TO VEDANTA. *Vedanta Press* $2.95; *New Am. Lib.* Mentor Bks. 1972 pap. $1.25

> Commentary on the Sermon, pointing out the common spiritual bases underlying Christianity and the great faiths of the East.

THE SPIRITUAL HERITAGE OF INDIA. *Vedanta Press* $3.75 pap. $1.95

> A history of India's philosophy and religion, including discussions of the Vedas, Upanishads, Bhagavad-Gita, Buddhism, and Jainism, which touches on the lives of great Indian thinkers.

VEDIC RELIGION AND PHILOSOPHY. *Vedanta Press* $2.25

> A text on the Vedas, the Upanishads, and the Bhagavad-Gita including a general description of Indian philosophy.

Radhakrishnan, Sir Sarvepalli. *See his main entry, this Chapter.*

Raju, P. T. THE PHILOSOPHICAL TRADITIONS OF INDIA. *Univ. of Pittsburgh Press* 1972 $7.95

> "A most informative and clear survey . . . extremely well written"—(*LJ*).

Renou, Louis, Ed. HINDUISM. *Braziller* 1961 $6.95; *Simon & Schuster* (Washington Square) 1963 pap. $.95. One of the volumes in the Great Religions of Man series, this contains a history of Hinduism, a selection from its literature, classical and modern, and a final section on the role of Hinduism as a force in Indian society.

RELIGIONS OF ANCIENT INDIA. *Schocken* 1968 $4.50 pap. $1.75

> Renou, a professor of Sanskrit and Indian literature at the Sorbonne, "offers a brief survey of the religious movements in India . . . based upon the Jordan Lectures in Comparative Religion delivered at the School of Oriental and African Studies at the University of London in 1951"—(*PW*). Hinduism is emphasized and Buddhism omitted; the author finds much promise in the increase of Western interest in Indian thought—as an antidote to Western materialism.

Reymond, Lizelle. SHAKTI: A Spiritual Experience. *Knopf* 1974 $5.00

> "First published in France in 1951, this brief, readable, and well-translated book brings to English readers the perceptive insights of an author well schooled in Hindu thought"—(*LJ*).

Rutledge, Dom Denys. IN SEARCH OF A YOGI. Pref. by Thomas Merton. 1963. *Gordon Press* $34.95. This describes an exploration in search of the holy men of India undertaken by a Benedictine monk; starting from Poona, he travelled to the source of the Ganges, finding not only many Hindu holy men, but Catholics, both Indian and Western, as well.

Satprem. SRI AUROBINDO: or The Adventure of Consciousness. *Harper* 1974 $7.95 pap. $3.95

> "Put simply Aurobindo's Yoga aims at the reconciliation of spirit and matter—an intriguing idea that provides insight into the nature of man"—(*LJ*).

Sen, Kshitimohan. HINDUISM. *Penguin* Pelican Bks. 1962 pap. $1.50; *Gannon* lib. bdg. $5.50

Singh, Gopal. THE RELIGION OF THE SIKHS. *Asia Pub. House* 1971 $4.75

> "Neither an introduction to the Sikh religion nor a systematic analysis of its main teachings . . . the book has an attractively poetic quality"—(*Choice*).

Stark, Claude Alan. GOD OF ALL: Sri Ramakrishna's Approach to Religious Plurality. *Claude Stark* 1974 $12.00

> "Stark's book is a solid scholarly work, fully documented. . . . Stark's fluid style of writing makes it an excellent book"—(*Choice*).

Stevenson, Margaret Sinclair. THE HEART OF JAINISM. 1915. *Verry* 1970 $10.00

Stroup, Herbert. LIKE A GREAT RIVER: An Introduction to Hinduism. *Harper* 1972 $5.95

> "The author, a sociologist, aims to give the beginning reader in the subject a glimpse of the depth and breadth of the Hindu way. Stroup's analysis . . . will give the reader not only a better idea of Indian culture, but of his own as well"—(*LJ*).

Weber, Max. THE RELIGION OF INDIA: The Sociology of Hinduism and Buddhism. Trans. and ed. by Hans H. Gerth and Don Martindale *Macmillan* (Free Press) 1958 pap.

$3.95. The noted sociologist (1864–1920) analyzes the Hindu social system and discusses the character and significance of castes and the orthodox and heterodox holy teaching of the intellectuals.

Zaehner, Robert C. HINDUISM. *Oxford* Galaxy Bks. 1962 pap. $2.50

Zimmer, Heinrich. PHILOSOPHIES OF INDIA. Ed. by Joseph Campbell Bollingen Ser. *Princeton Univ. Press* 1951 $14.50 pap. $4.95. A presentation of all the philosophical traditions of India.

BUDDHISM

Out of the spiritual dilemma of Hinduism and its belief in the endless cycle of pain and rebirth grew a method of salvation which comprises one of mankind's highest ethical achievements. "The Way" taught by Guatama the Buddha (*see his main entry, this Chapter*) was a way of ethical self-culture and moral reconstitution of personality. Buddhism retains from Hinduism the belief in the law of *Karma*, the transmigration of souls and the necessity of freeing oneself from the web of desire of any kind. Its great goal is *Nirvana*, "a state of perfectly painless peace and joy." But in Buddhism *Nirvana* becomes a psychologically achieved freedom from desire and thus from misery. Buddha in his own life tested and found inadequate the Hindu method of salvation through extreme asceticism, philosophic speculation, and religious devotion. He taught a "Middle Way" of self-knowledge and self-control.

The teachings of Buddha were ethical rather than religious. His followers turned it into a religion based on devotion to the compassionate figure of the Enlightened One himself. There developed through the years an extreme variety of Buddhist organizations and cults. The chief division is between Mahayana and Hinayana Buddhism. Mahayana started in northern India and spread to China and Japan. Distinctive to Mahayana is the veneration of Bodhisattvas, a great, even innumerable, company of spiritual beings, who hear prayers and come actively to man's aid.

Hinayana, or Southern Buddhism, is an older more conservative form that still exists in Southeast Asia. It stems from the third century A.D., when the great king Asoka sent a Buddhist mission to Ceylon. Since Ceylon was for centuries unaffected by any of the catastrophic changes that went on in India, the Buddhist doctrine there remained true to the earliest tenets. The oldest Buddhist texts were preserved there also, later to be retranslated back into Hindu, the famous Pali texts. (In 1967 scholars found in Korea the text of a well-known 'sutra,' or Buddhist scripture, translated by Mi T'o-hsien, who lived in Changan, the ancient Chinese capital, from 680 to 704 A.D. Authorities date the scroll as having been made between 704 and 751. It is believed to be the oldest *printed* text ever discovered.) Hinayana Buddhism, which is also called Theravada and The Old School of Wisdom, is centered in the figure of the monk: for the monastic life of solitary meditation is the road to sainthood. It is this form of Buddhism that has offered to the world such a startling picture of courage in the suicides of the Vietnamese monks, who immolated themselves in 1963 in protest over the persecution of the Buddhist church by the government of Ngo Dinh Diem.

Another form of Buddhism that has attracted worldwide attention, although not important to the historical development of Buddhism, is the Tantric Buddhism of Lamaism practiced in Tibet. Probably the most familiar form of Buddhism to Western thinkers is the Japanese Mahayana school of Zen. Many well-known intellectuals have been drawn by its mysticism in recent years. It is the Zen school of Buddhism that appealed to the "Hippie" movement in the U.S.A.

Translations of Texts

BUDDHIST MAHAYANA TEXTS. Trans. by E. Cowell; ed. by Max Müller *Dover* 1967 pap. $4.00

BUDDHIST MONASTIC DISCIPLINE: The Sanskrit Pratimoksa Sutras of the Mahasamghikas and Mulasarvastivadins. Ed. by Charles S. Prebish *Pennsylvania State Univ. Press* 1974 $13.50

"The *Pratimoksa* . . . a monastic code of offenses, is a great noncanonical Buddhist text of great antiquity, antedating the Buddhist canon. It is of great importance apart. The beginning student as well as the scholar will find much here that is useful"—(*Choice*).

THE LION'S ROAR OF QUEEN SRIMALA. Trans. by Alex Wayman and Hideko Wayman *Columbia* 1973 $12.50

This Buddhist scripture "was widely influential in Indian and later Buddhism . . . Happily, the cooperative effort of two extraordinarily capable scholars has yielded a reliable and readable version"—(*Choice*).

THE PLATFORM SUTRA OF THE SIXTH PATRIARCH: The Text of the Tun-huang Manuscript. Trans. with introd. by Philip B. Yampolsky *Columbia* 1967 $13.50

This is a basic text of Zen Buddhism, originating in China in the 9th century. "Dr. Yampolsky, a lecturer in Japanese at Columbia, presents the history of the sutra, varying versions, the biography of Hui-neng, and extensive critical comment. . . . Indispensable"—(*LJ*).

Books about Buddhism

Anesaki, Masaharu. NICHIREN, THE BUDDHIST PROPHET. 1916. *Peter Smith* $5.25. Deals with the alleged inspirer of Soka Gakkai, the "militant" Buddhists of Japan.

Arguelles, José and Miriam. MANDALA. *Shambhala* 1972 $12.50 pap. $5.95

"A mandala is a circular diagram used in several Eastern traditions as an aid to meditation . . . the book is the best and certainly the most readable introduction to the concept of the mandala and the techniques centered around it"—(*LJ*).

Ashvagosha. THE AWAKENING OF FAITH. Trans. by Timothy Richard; ed. with introd. by Alan Hull Walton; fwd. by Aldous Huxley 1907. *University Books* 1967 $5.00. The fundamental doctrines of the Mahayana school of Buddhism by an Indian poet of the first or second century A.D. The translator is a British scholar who spent most of his life in China.

Bell, Sir Charles. THE RELIGION OF TIBET. 1931. *Krishna Press* $29.95

Blofeld, John. THE TANTRIC MYSTICISM OF TIBET: A Practical Guide. *Causeway* 1973 $6.95; *Dutton* pap. 1970 $2.75

"Blofeld's well-written and erudite book . . . should find its readers among many of our contemporaries whose motivation is not so much scholarly curiosity as the pursuit of personal spiritual progress"—(*LJ*).

Buddhadasa, Bhikkhu. TOWARD THE TRUTH. *Westminster* 1971 pap. $2.95

"This is a very welcome effort, bringing to our attention an example of the creative interpretation of orthodox Buddhist doctrines by a highly respected and learned Thai monk. . . . This is an important publication in the field of modern Theravada thinking"—(*LJ*).

Bunnag, Jane. BUDDHIST MONK, BUDDHIST LAYMAN: A Study of Urban Monastic Organization in Central Thailand. *Cambridge* 1973 $16.50

"Valuable book"—(*Choice*).

Ch'en, Kenneth K. S. BUDDHISM IN CHINA: A Historical Survey. *Princeton Univ. Press* 1964 $20.00 1972 pap. $3.95

"The professor of religion and Oriental studies at Princeton . . . traces in a lucid and authoritative fashion the vicissitudes of Buddhism in China from its arrival during the Han dynasty 2000 years ago to present times. . . . His volume . . . will be standard reading on the subject for many years to come"—(*LJ*). Bibliography.

BUDDHISM: The Light of Asia. *Barron's* 1968 $7.25 pap. $2.25

THE CHINESE TRANSFORMATION OF BUDDHISM. *Princeton Univ. Press* 1973 $15.00 pap. $9.50

"Well-written and well-researched, this book includes abundant passages translated from primary materials, and makes available in English the results of much Japanese scholarship. Most of the book is eminently readable"—(*Choice*).

Conze, Edward, Trans. BUDDHISM: Its Essence and Development. *Harper* Torchbks. pap. $1.95; *Peter Smith* $5.00

BUDDHIST SCRIPTURES. *Penguin* (orig.) 1959 pap. $1.25. Contains useful introductory and explanatory notes.

BUDDHIST THOUGHT IN INDIA. *Univ. of Michigan Press* Ann Arbor Bks. 1967 pap. $3.25

Coomaraswamy, Ananda. BUDDHA AND THE GOSPEL OF BUDDHISM. 1917. *Folcroft* $40.00; *Harper* Torchbks. pap. $3.25; *South Asia Bks.* $14.00; *University Bks.* $10.00; *Verry* $14.00

"One of the classic descriptions in English of the origins, development, theology, terminology, and influence of Buddhism"—*(LJ)*.

Dasgupta, Shashi Bhushan. AN INTRODUCTION TO TANTRIC BUDDHISM. 1958 *Shambhala* 1974 pap. $3.95

David-Neel, Alexandra. MAGIC AND MYSTERY IN TIBET. *Dover* 1971 pap. $3.00; *Penguin* pap. $1.65; *Peter Smith* $5.50; *University Bks.* 1965 $7.50. By one of the few Westerners who lived in Tibet, a Buddhist scholar of recognized standing.

Dogen. A PRIMER OF SOTO ZEN: A Translation of Dogen's Shobogenzo Zuimonki. *Univ. Press of Hawaii* (East-West Ctr.) 1971 $6.00 pap. $2.45

"Zen Buddhism has produced a flood of trashy literature . . . This little book, a careful and attractive translation . . . is welcome contrast that should stand high on the priority list for acquisition by any library"—*(Choice)*.

Dumoulin, Heinrich, S.J. A HISTORY OF ZEN BUDDHISM. 1963. *Beacon* 1969 pap. $3.45

Eliot, Charles. HINDUISM AND BUDDHISM: An Historical Sketch. 1954. *Routledge & Kegan Paul* 3 vols. 1968 set $49.50

JAPANESE BUDDHISM. 1959. *Routledge & Kegan Paul* 1967 $21.00

Fa-Hien. A RECORD OF BUDDHISTIC KINGDOMS: Being an Account by the Chinese Monk Fa-Hien of his Travels in India and China (A.D. 399–414) in Search of the Buddhist Books of Discipline. Trans. by James Legge, in 1886. *Dover* pap. $2.00; *Int. Pubns. Serv.* $9.00; *Paragon Reprint* 1965 $8.00

Fox, Douglas A. THE VAGRANT LOTUS: An Introduction to Buddhist Philosophy. *Westminster Press* 1973 pap. $3.50

"A thorough exposition, admirable for its constructive clarity"—*(LJ)*.

Glasenapp, Helmuth von. BUDDHISM, A NON-THEISTIC RELIGION: With a Selection from Buddhist Scriptures. *Braziller* 1970 $7.50

"Von Glasenapp was a recognized expert on Indian religion and philosophy and the author of many books on the subject. In this work, originally published in Germany in 1954, and the first of his books to be translated into English, he analyzes the Buddhist scriptures to ascertain whether Buddhism can be called a religion despite its denial of a personal God. Recommended"—*(LJ)*.

Goddard, Dwight, Ed. A BUDDHIST BIBLE. 1938. *Beacon* pap. $5.95 1970

"This first appeared in 1938; it has been revised to include new and better translations . . . it provides the general reader with an overall view of the many schools of Buddhist thought as well as a handbook of the major documents of that belief"—*(PW)*.

Grimm, George. THE DOCTRINE OF THE BUDDHA. Ed. by M. Keller-Grimm and Max Hoppe *Verry* 1965 rev. 1973 $11.50

Grousset, René. IN THE FOOTSTEPS OF THE BUDDHA. Trans. by J. A. Underwood. 1932. *Bks. for Libraries* $14.25

"A useful popularization"—*(Choice)*.

Guenther, Herbert V. THE TANTRIC VIEW OF LIFE. *Shambhala* 1972 $8.50

"This is a new book concerned with Buddhist Tantrism, which the author takes care to distinguish from the Hindu forms. . . . Although often difficult, this is a strikingly insightful book"—*(Choice)*.

(With Choggam Trungjia). THE DAWN OF TANTRA. *Shambhala* 1975 $7.95 pap. $3.50

"The author's discussion of such themes as the meaning of tantra principles, the level of the tantra commitment and the place of tantra within the Buddhist tradition is generally clear and comprehensible"—(*LJ*).

Herrigel, Eugen. THE METHOD OF ZEN. Trans. by R.F.C. Hull; ed. by Hermann Tausend. 1953. *Random* Vintage Bks. 1974 pap. $1.95. Probably the most lucid popular account of the teaching and practice.

ZEN IN THE ART OF ARCHERY. *Pantheon* 1953 $4.95; *Random* Vintage Bks. 1971 pap. $1.95. A fascinating discussion of a single skill, showing how Zen can, according to those who follow it, make easier anything one does.

Humphreys, Christmas. BUDDHISM. *Penguin* Pelican Bks. pap. $2.25. An excellent primer.

ZEN: A Way of Life. 1965. *Little* 1971 pap. $2.65

"This work presents an account of the nature of Zen, and the ultimate goal of its teaching; the latter portion of the book offers a practical system of training for the Zen way of life"—(*LJ*).

Hyers, Conrad. ZEN AND THE COMIC SPIRIT. *Westminster Press* 1974 $6.95 pap. $3.95

"Anyone who has had any contact with Zen knows that it delights in humor. Hyers does a creditable job. Zen humor is approached from several points of view in an attempt to show how Zen profanes the sacred in order to destroy the concept of any difference between the two"—(*LJ*).

Johnston, William. THE STILL POINT: Reflections on Zen and Christian Mysticism. *Fordham Univ. Press* 1970 $7.50; *Harper* pap. $1.25

While non-Catholics, and certainly non-Christians, will take issue with some of the basic assumptions, this is not crucial to the message of the book as a whole, which has much of great weight to offer not only to the Christian but to the Westerner who wishes to understand Zen better"—(*LJ*).

Kennett, Jiyu. SELLING WATER BY THE RIVER: A Manual of Zen Training. *Pantheon* 1972 $10.00

"The book is primarily addressed to the Western reader and is lucidly written . . . he will . . . find the work interesting and also instructive"—(*LJ*).

Lassalle, H. M. Enomiya. ZEN MEDITATION FOR CHRISTIANS. *Open Court* new ed. 1974 $7.95

"The value of Lassalle's book lies in his comparison of similar thoughts and expressions in the two traditions. He seems not to force either into the mold of the other; he lets each reflect the genuineness of the other's mystical experience"—(*Choice*).

Levy, Paul. BUDDHISM: A "Mystery Religion"? 1957. *Humanities Press* $5.00; *Schocken* 1968 $5.00

This book is based on the Jordan Lectures in Comparative Religion given at the School of Oriental and African Studies, University of London in 1953 by Mr. Levy. It "penetrates Buddhism through the back door of rituals, analyzing the initiation rites of present day monasteries, deducing from them what primitive Buddhism may have been. . . . This book contributes to the demythologizing of Buddhism and is a highly provocative, important contribution"—(*LJ*).

Ling, Trevor. THE BUDDHA: Buddhist Civilization in India and Ceylon. *Scribner* 1973 $10.00

"This work should be welcomed as a challenge to the generally accepted view that sees the Theravadin tradition as being almost entirely individualistic in orientation. Ling's style is highly readable"—(*Choice*).

McGovern, William M. AN INTRODUCTION TO MAHAYANA BUDDHISM, WITH SPECIAL REFERENCE TO CHINESE AND JAPANESE PHASES. 1922. *AMS Press* 1971 $9.50

MacQuitty, William. BUDDHA. *Viking* 1969 $10.00

Contains both color and black and white photographs "of unusual pictorial and verbal beauty. Factually accurate, yet poetic in a calm persuasive manner"—(*LJ*).

Merton, Thomas. MYSTICS AND ZEN MASTERS. 1967. *Dell* 1969 pap. $2.75

ZEN AND THE BIRDS OF APPETITE. *New Directions* (dist. by Lippincott) $6.50 pap. $1.75

See also his main entry, this Chapter.

Mitchell, Elsie P. Sun Buddha, Moon Buddha: Zen Quest. *Weatherhill* 1973 $6.95

"A wise book, bringing together many significant comparisons of Christian and Buddhist viewpoints, but not denigrating either"—(*LJ*).

Morgan, Kenneth W., Ed. The Path of the Buddha: Buddhism Interpreted by Buddhists. *Ronald* 1956 $6.95. Eleven leading Buddhists describe beliefs and practices of their faith.

Murata, Kiyoaki. Japan's New Buddhism: An Objective Account of Soka Gakkai. *Weatherhill* 1969 $5.95

"A brief and clear presentation, well illustrated with photographs"—(*Choice*).

Nhat Hanh, Thich. Zen Keys. *Doubleday* Anchor Bks. 1974 pap. $1.95

"An introduction to Zen by a noted Vietnamese Zen monk"—(*LJ*).

Ogata, Sohaku. Zen for the West. 1959. *Greenwood* 1973 lib. bdg. $10.50

Pirsig, Robert M. Zen and the Art of Motorcycle Maintenance: An Inquiry into Values. *Morrow* 1974 $7.95; *Bantam* pap. $2.25

"The author's motorcycle trip with his young son from Minnesota to Bozerman, Montana and on to the Pacific sets an everchanging scene for this unusual autobiography . . . This work should be accessible to a wide audience since it deals with meaning and values not only on an abstract level but in a very personal way as well"—(*LJ*).

Rahula, Walpola. What the Buddha Taught. *Dufour* 1967 $4.95; *Grove* Evergreen Bks. 1962 rev. ed. 1975 pap. $1.75

Ross, Nancy Wilson, Ed. The World of Zen. *Random* 1969 Vintage Bks. pap. $3.95. The editor wrote "Three Ways of Asian Wisdom" (*see General Histories list, this Chapter*).

Saddhatissa, H. The Buddha's Way. *Braziller* 1972 $6.95

"This is a short book, but a clear and concise one in which each word counts. The author, an ordained Buddhist priest, is a proficient scholar who has researched and taught his subject in the U.S., Canada, and England as well as India"—(*LJ*).

Buddhist Ethics: Essence of Buddhism. 1971 *Braziller* $6.50 pap. $2.95

"Certainly ethics does not form the whole of Buddhism, but the author indicates its wide extent within the larger structure. This is a book of lasting importance for the serious inquirer, whether scholar, student or practitioner"—(*LJ*).

Sato, Giei. Unsui: A Diary of Zen Monastic Life. Text by Eshin Nishimura. *Univ. Press of Hawaii* 1973 $8.95 pap. $4.95

"The core of this perfectly delightful book is a collection of 97 watercolor sketches drawn by the Zen monk Sato. These often humorous sketches depict the daily life in a Japanese Zen monastery . . . The book provides a useful introduction to the daily regimen in a Zen monastery"—(*Choice*).

Saunders, E. Dale. Buddhism in Japan: With an Outline of Its Origins in India. *Univ. of Pennsylvania Press* 1964 $9.00 pap. $3.45

"The history and doctrines of Buddhism are clearly sketched from the time of Gautama himself until the arrival of the religion in the Japanese islands 1000 years later. . . . [Professor] Saunders also carries the evolution of Buddhism in Japan forward to the new sects of the mid-20th century. . . . Recommended"—(*LJ*).

Shaftel, Oscar. An Understanding of the Buddha. *Shocken* 1974 $8.50

"An unusual introduction to the wide scope of Buddhist thought. Shaftel skillfully integrates some of the best-known general studies in Buddhism . . . with judicious selections from primary sources in translation"—(*Choice*).

Shibayama, Zenkei. Zen Comments on the Mumonkan. *Harper* 1974 $10.95; *New Am. Lib.* Signet pap. $2.25

"The reader can now read . . . the actual presentation of koans and their interpretations. The book is more useful to understanding the core of Zen discipline than the many popular descriptive books on today's market"—(*Choice*).

Spiro, Melford E. Buddhism and Society: A Great Tradition and Its Burmese Vicissitudes. *Harper* 1970 Torchbks. pap. $5.95

"Here is a book that is unexpectedly rich and is worthy of the widest acclaim"—(*LJ*).

Steinilber-Oberlin, Emile. The Buddhist Sects of Japan: Their History, Philosophical Doctrines and Sanctuaries. 1938. *Greenwood* 1970 lib. bdg. $14.00

Stryk, Lucien, and T. Ikenoto, Eds. Zen: Poems, Prayers, Sermons, Anecdotes, Interviews. *Doubleday* Anchor Bks. 1965 pap. $1.95

"A noteworthy contribution to our understanding of this elusive and fascinating subject. . . . The selections are most illuminating; the translations almost always successful, and in the case of the poetry, exceptionally fine. . . . Highly recommended"—(*LJ*).

Suzuki, Beatrice Lane. Mahayana Buddhism. Fwd. by Christmas Humphreys. 1959. *Macmillan* 1969 pap. 1.45

Suzuki, Daisetz T. The Essentials of Zen Buddhism: An Anthology of the Writings of Daisetz T. Suzuki. Ed. with introd. by Bernard Phillips *Greenwood* 1973 $23.50

This convenient and authoritative volume is "recommended particularly for those libraries, which do not need Suzuki's complete works, but which have a demand for a good volume on Zen."

Introduction to Zen Buddhism. *Grove* Black Cat Bks. 1964 pap. $1.95; *Causeway* 1974 $10.00

Manual of Zen Buddhism Rev. ed. 1950. *Grove* Evergreen Bks. 1960 pap. $2.95

An anthology from original sources; reproductions of Buddhist paintings, drawings and religious statues. Dr. Suzuki, who was 97 at his death in 1966, wrote more than 100 volumes on Zen and Buddhism in Japanese and English and was widely recognized as their leading interpreter to the Western World. He discusses these elusive teachings in clear and precise language and gives an account of other leading Buddhist sects in Japan.

Outlines of Mahayana Buddhism. Introd. by Alan W. Watts. 1907. *Harper* Torchbks. 1968 $2.45; *Shocken* 1963 $8.00 pap. $2.95. The basic introduction to the main tradition of Buddhism.

Studies in Zen. *Dell* 1963 pap. $2.45

The Training of the Zen Buddhist Monk. 1934. *University Books* 1965 $6.00; *Wingbow Press* 1974 pap. $3.00

"A straightforward description of Zen monastic life [which] presumes a prior knowledge of Zen and acceptance of its basic tenets. . . . Charming illustrations of monastery activities by Zenchu Sato"—(*LJ*). It includes a description of the author's own initiation into Zen.

Zen and Japanese Culture. Bollingen Ser. *Princeton Univ. Press* 1959 $14.50 pap. $4.95

Zen Buddhism: Selected Writings of D. T. Suzuki. Ed. by William Barrett *Doubleday* Anchor Bks. 1956 pap. $2.50

Swearer, Donald K. Buddhism in Transition. *Westminster Press* 1970 $5.50 pap. $2.65

"Swearer of Oberlin College has chosen to examine Buddhism in transition within its South-east Asian cultural context. Well documented. Highly recommended"—(*LJ*).

Secrets of the Lotus: Studies in Buddhist Meditation. *Macmillan* 1971 $6.95 pap. $1.95

"Since meditation is now an in thing, this book is timely. It results from a month-long experiment in 1969 at Oberlin College in which 28 students of varied backgrounds were exposed to both Theravada and Zen meditation techniques. No significant conclusions as to the results of the experiment can be drawn; but the material is a distinctly useful addition to the literature"— (*LJ*).

Watts, Alan W. The Book: On the Taboo against Knowing Who You Are. *Pantheon* 1966 $5.95; *Random* Vintage Bks. $1.65

Certain aspects of Zen are here drawn upon as a guide for young people in particular; this has had a wide sale as an "underground" work. It offers a philosophy for the "alienated." The individual is urged to consider himself not as an "ego" but as a part of a great cosmic, harmonious design, needing his cooperation rather than his continual striving to better it as a world "outside" him. We *are* our world, says Watts, we must accept it and fall in with its rhythm and change it in spirit, becoming loving instruments of something greater than ourselves. We destroy ourselves and our society by material desires that drive us to unworthy and ultimately self-defeating goals.

The Spirit of Zen: A Way of Life, Work and Art in the Far East. 1955 *Grove* rev. ed. 1959 Evergreen Bks. 1960 pap. $2.45; *Paragon Reprint* $3.50

THIS IS IT AND OTHER ESSAYS ON ZEN AND SPIRITUAL EXPERIENCES. *Pantheon* 1960 $5.95;
Random Vintage Bks. $1.95

THE WAY OF ZEN. *Pantheon* 1957 $6.95; *Random* Vintage Bks. pap. $1.95

"Mr. Watts's book is certainly the most explicit and orderly account of Zen Buddhism that has yet appeared in English"—(*New Statesman*). Alan Watts received a grant from the Bollingen Foundation to write this study and has achieved a distinguished career as an exponent—and a detached one—of Zen in particular, and also of Christianity. He is today much read by American young people. He knows Chinese; his immaculate scholarship is matched by his clarity and grace of style.

Weber, Max. THE RELIGION OF INDIA: The Sociology of Hinduism and Buddhism. Trans. and ed. by Hans H. Gerth and Don Martindale *Macmillan* (Free Press) 1958 pap. $3.95

Welch, Holmes. THE PRACTICE OF CHINESE BUDDHISM, 1900–1950. *Harvard Univ. Press* 1967 $17.50 pap. $6.95

Professor Welch uses oral sources in his research for this volume. "His transcription of these interviews with elderly practitioners has added immeasurably to the sparse literature of this subject. . . . Recommended"—(*LJ*). In the Harvard East Asian Series.

THE BUDDHIST REVIVAL IN CHINA. *Harvard Univ. Press* 1968 $15.00

Professor Welch, a research associate at the East Asian Research Center and assistant director of the Center for the Study of World Religions, Harvard, plans a three-volume series, of which this is the first. The second will deal with a history of the Buddhist revival and the third with Buddhism in Communist China. In the Harvard East Asian Series.

BUDDHISM UNDER MAO. *Harvard Univ. Press* 1972 $16.00

"The third book in Welch's trilogy on Buddhism in 20th-Century China is, like its predecessors . . . the last word on its subject"—(*LJ*).

Wetering, Janwillem vande. THE EMPTY MIRROR: Experiences in a Japanese Zen Monastery. *Houghton* 1974 $5.95 pap. $3.95

"Another book of a Westerner's Zen monastery experiences, but this one's different . . . it's an excellent one. His naive and unscholarly approach makes all the old Zen tales and aphorisms new and all the old ritual fresh"—(*LJ*).

Wright, Arthur Frederick, Ed. BUDDHISM IN CHINESE HISTORY. *Stanford Univ. Press* 1959 $6.00; pap. $1.95. "Dynamic," clear and readable.

STUDIES IN CHINESE THOUGHT. *Univ. of Chicago Press* 1953 $10.00. With contributions by Derk Bodde and others. Discerning studies based upon mature use of original sources.

TAOISM

Taoism (pronounced "dhowism") is "the vehicle of beliefs and practices which, during a long emergence from the soil of popular faith and superstition, have expressed the philosophical and mystical aspects of Chinese thought and life"—(John B. Noss, "Man's Religions"). There had existed since the earliest times in China a concept of the *Tao*, the Way, the operative force of harmony and order within the universe. About the fifth century B.C., according to ancient tradition, the book of the Tao Teh Ching was composed by the (legendary?) seer Lao-Tzu (*see his main entry, this Chapter*). It describes the Tao as the one all-embracing life process with which man must attune himself if he is to achieve harmony in this life. The method of attainment is one of yielding, of mystical union. In its later phases, the mysticism of Taoism was debased to magic, the Tao Teh Ching was used as a treasury of powerful formulas and charms, and the religion accumulated numberless folk gods, fairies and spirits.

Blofeld, John. THE SECRET AND SUBLIME: Taoist Mysteries and Magic. *Verry* 1973 $13.75; *Dutton* pap. $2.45

"Most of the incidents are culled from seventeen years of living in China, primarily in the 1930's, and from his many subsequent trips to the East . . . intended as an introduction to popular Taoism for the non-specialist"—(*Choice*).

Huai-Han-Tzu. TAO: The Great Luminant. Trans. by E. Morgan. 1935. *Paragon Reprint* 1966 $11.00. Essays.

Legge, James, Trans. THE TEXTS OF TAOISM. Ed. by F. Max Müller 1891. *Dover* 2 vols. pap. each $3.50; *Peter Smith* 2 vols. each $6.00. Works of Lao Tse, Chuang Tse, etc.; annotated.

Lu, Yen. THE SECRET OF THE GOLDEN FLOWER: A Chinese Book of Life. Trans. by Richard Wilhelm; commentary by C. G. Jung. 1931. *Causeway* 1975 $7.95; *Harcourt* Harvest Bks. 1970 pap. $2.35; *Wehman* $6.95

This volume contains a translation of an ancient Chinese text which deals with Chinese Yoga or mystical philosophy. The text was discovered and the translation made by the famous German authority on Chinese thought, Richard Wilhelm who has added an introduction and comments on the text. The relationship between Eastern mysticism and Western practical psychology is the subject of an appended commentary by C. G. Jung.

T'ao Ch'ien. TAO THE HERMIT. Trans. by W. Acker *Vanguard* $3.50

Waley, Arthur. THE WAY AND ITS POWER: A Study of the Tao Te Ching and Its Place in Chinese Thought. 1934. *Harper* (Barnes & Noble) 1956 $6.50; (and translation of the "Tao Te Ching") *Grove* Evergreen Bks. 1958 pap. $2.95

Watts, Alan W. NATURE, MAN AND WOMAN. 1958. *Random* Vintage Bks. pap. $1.95 A discussion of man's relation to woman and to nature in light of the Chinese philosophy of the Tao.

Welch, Holmes. TAOISM: The Parting of the Way. *Beacon* 1966 $5.00 pap. $3.95

This book "clarifies a large area of literature and history that up to now has been a mystery to the West, and it makes fascinating reading even for those whose interest may be casual"—(*New Yorker*).

CONFUCIANISM

For 2,500 years Confucianism has been the most powerful single influence on the culture and history of China. It structured the form of Chinese society, politics and education. It exerted almost equal influence on the cultures of Japan and Korea. A wonderfully rationalistic and humanistic ethic, Confucianism begins with the premise that all men are born good. It teaches that wayward individuals and corrupt societies can regain their original goodness by emulating the virtues of ancient heroes. An individual can become truly noble, both in terms of character and social position, through proper education and right conduct. Thus anyone can be a member of the nobility. The highest of all social positions is reserved for the scholar. In common with Taoism, Confucianism believes in the Tao (the force of order and harmony within the universe) and in the dual cosmic principle of yang-yin (the "male" and "female" properties of energy and matter).

Certain scholars have contended that Confucianism is an ethical philosophy and not a religion. Nonetheless it has fulfilled a religious function throughout the centuries. It seems evident that Confucius himself *(see his main entry, this Chapter)* was agnostic but did not oppose customary beliefs. Later, Confucianism developed a complex system for the appeasement of harmful spirits. It placed central emphasis on the ancestor cult. Indeed, until recent years, veneration for the family has been the basis for all social order in China: one's place and duty in society matched one's place and duty within the family. There is within Confucianism no concept of the "good life" apart from the good of the entire social order.

Baynes, Cary F., and R. Wilhelm, Trans. THE I CHING, or Book of Changes. Fwd. by C. G. Jung and new introd. by Helmut Wilhelm Bollingen Ser. *Princeton Univ. Press* 3rd ed. 1967 $8.50. One of the Five Classics of Confucianism, the I Ching is one of the oldest and most important works of Chinese philosophy.

Chai, Ch'u, and Winberg Chai, Eds. LI CHI, BOOK OF RITES: An Encyclopedia of Ancient Ceremonial Usages, Religious Creeds and Social Institutions. Trans. by James Legge; introd. by the editors *University Bks.* 2 vols. boxed set $25.00

Chang, Carsun. The Development of Neo-Confucian Thought. *College & Univ. Press* 1957 Vol. 1 pap. $2.95

> This is a history of modern Chinese thought, roughly from 1500–1870, with a brief survey bringing the narrative to the 1960s. "The abundance of original source quotations, while they may impair the style, are a welcome factor in the volume for the Western reader."

Collis, Maurice. The First Holy One. 1948. *Greenwood* 1970 lib. bdg. $14.25

Creel, Herrlee G. Confucius and the Chinese Way. *Harper* Torchbks. 1960 pap. $3.25; *Peter Smith* $5.00

Confucius: The Man and the Myth. 1949. *Greenwood* 1972 $17.00

Dhiegh, Khigh. The Eleventh Wing: An Expostition of the Dynamics of I Ching for Now. *Nash Pub. Corp.* 1973 $8.95; *Dell* pap. $3.25

> "The *I ching's* relevance to contemporary Western civilization is investigated by the director of the International I Ching Studies Institute who provides an extension of traditional interpretation of this classic Chinese book of wisdom beyond the customary references of the 10 wings or commentaries"—*(Booklist)*.

Legge, James, Trans. The I Ching. Writings of King Wan, Duke of Chou, with 10 Appendixes by Confucius, Notes and Introduction. Ed. by F. Max Müller *Bantam* pap. $1.50; *Causeway Press* $10.00; *Citadel Press* pap. $4.95; *Dover* pap. $3.50; *Peter Smith* $6.00; *Wehman* $5.95

Liu, Wu-chi. Confucius: His Life and Time. 1955. *Greenwood* 1972 lib. bdg. $11.50

Nivison, David S., and Arthur F. Wright. Confucianism in Action. *Stanford Univ. Press* 1959 $10.00. Twelve papers by experts on various aspects of Confucianism and Neo-Confucianism.

Shyrock, John K. The Origin and Development of the State Cult of Confucius. 1932. *Paragon Reprint* $11.50

Siu, R. G. H. The Man of Many Qualities: A Legacy of the I Ching. *M.I.T. Press* 1968 $8.95; (with title "Portable Dragon") pap. $1.95

See also Chapter 5, Philosophy: Ancient and Oriental Philosophy, this Volume.

Wang, Yang-Ming (Wang Shou-jên). Instructions for Practical Living and Other Neo-Confucian Writings (Chu'uan-hsi lu). Trans. with notes by Wing-tsit Chan *Columbia* 1963 $13.50. A book for the specialist and those general readers with a deep interest in Chinese thought.

Wilhelm, Helmut. Change: Eight Lectures on the I Ching. Trans. from the German by Cary F. Baynes Bollingen Ser. *Princeton Univ. Press* 1960 $6.50 pap. $2.45. Studies on the Book of Changes.

Wilhelm, Richard. Confucius and Confucianism. 1931. *Harcourt* Harvest Bks. 1971 pap. $1.65; *Kennikat* 1970 $7.50

Wright, Arthur Frederick, Ed. The Confucian Persuasion. *Stanford Univ. Press* 1960 $10.00 pap. $3.45. Ten distinguished scholars explore Confucianism in widely different spheres of thought and action.

(Ed.). Confucianism and Chinese Civilization. *Stanford Univ. Press* 1975 $10.00 pap. $3.95

(With Denis Twitchett, Eds.). Confucian Personalities. *Stanford Univ. Press* 1962 $12.50 pap. $3.45

SHINTO

The indigenous religion of Japan, Shinto, is usually practised along with Buddhism and Confucianism. Basically a folk religion involving ancestor worship, the basic Shinto concept of deity is that of *Kami*. *Kami* is holy spiritual power present to a greater or lesser degree in every living thing. Men possess more *Kami* than animals; the emperor possesses more *Kami* than other men. Departed spirits are *Kami*. Westerners became familiar with the *kamikaze* pilots during World II: the invulnerable warriors who achieved victory through suicide. Thus they became *Kami*, illustrious spirits worthy of great veneration. Their courage expressed in an extreme form the gratitude and loyalty the Shintoist feels for his national and family heritage.

Anesaki, Masaharu. HISTORY OF JAPANESE RELIGION: With Special Reference to the Social and Moral Life of the Nation. 1930. *Tuttle* 1963 $10.50. One of the standard surveys, somewhat dated, but highly recommended.

Aston, W. G. SHINTO: The Way of the Gods. 1905. *Krishna Press* 1974 $34.95

Bunce, William K., Ed. RELIGIONS IN JAPAN. *Tuttle* 1959 pap. $2.95

Casal, U. A. THE FIVE SACRED FESTIVALS OF ANCIENT JAPAN: Their Symbolism and Historical Development. *Tuttle* 1967 $6.60

"Mr. Casal has succeeded in throwing light on the origins of five important Japanese festivals. . . . His discussion of the accompanying ceremonies is detailed but lucid"—(*LJ*).

Hearn, Lafcadio. JAPAN'S RELIGIONS: Shinto and Buddhism. Ed. by Kazumitsu Kato *University Bks.* 1966 $10.00. Hearn, a distinguished lover of the East, was born in 1850 and died in 1904, but this is still of value.

MODERN JAPAN AND SHINTO NATIONALISM. *Paragon Reprint* 2nd rev. ed. 1947 $12.00

Holtom, Daniel C. THE NATIONAL FAITH OF JAPAN. 1938. *Paragon Reprint* $12.00

Hori, Ichiro. FOLK RELIGION IN JAPAN: Continuity and Change. Ed. by Joseph Kitagawa and Alan L. Miller *Univ. of Chicago Press* 1968 $12.00 pap. 1974 $4.25

Based on the Haskell Lectures given by the author in 1965 at the University of Chicago, this points out the blending that occurs among many religions in Japan, including folk religion, and "stresses the relationship between Japanese folk-religion and the social structures of Japanese life—family, kinship, village community, and so on. A splendid contribution"—(*LJ*).

Kitagawa, Joseph M. RELIGION IN JAPANESE HISTORY. *Columbia* 1966 $15.00

Mason, Joseph T. W. THE MEANING OF SHINTO: The Primaeval Foundations of Creative Spirit in Modern Japan. 1935. *Kennikat* $8.50

Ono, Sokyo, in collaboration with William P. Woodward. SHINTO: The Kami Way. *Tuttle* 1962 $4.50

"Here at last is an excellently rounded introduction to the subject by an eminent Shinto scholar. Dr. Ono has compressed a wealth of fundamental information into his brief volume. . . . Useful for all public, college, and university collections"—(*LJ*).

Stiskin, Nahum. THE LOOKING-GLASS GOD: Shinto, Yin-Yang, and a Cosmology for Today. *Autumn Press* 1972 $4.95

"In this version the author has enlarged and revised the original text and included new illustrations and diagrams. The author posits a unifying cosmology for man . . . An enthralling and well-written book"—(*LJ*).

ISLAM

By a conservative estimate, there are now 600 million people within the faith of Islam, and the number is steadily increasing. The religion founded by Mohammed (*see his main entry, this Chapter*) has had direct impact upon the Western world from its beginning, both by warfare and through Islam's great medieval scholars.

Islam is a strict monotheism. The basic beliefs necessary to the faithful are contained in the Five Doctrines: there is one true God, Allah; there are angels, including Gabriel and a fallen angel, Iblis (Satan), whose minions are the djinn (demons); there are four inspired books including the Torah, the Psalms of David, the Evangel of Jesus, and the Qu'ran, which is Allah's final message; there are 28 prophets including Adam, Noah, Abraham, Moses, Jesus and John the Baptist, but the greatest and last is Mohammed; there will be an end of this world, a bodily resurrection and a final judgment. The doctrine of *Kismet* (fate) is also taught but is not necessary to the faith. The faithful believer responds to Allah by the Five Pillars of Faith: repetition of the creed; prayer; almsgiving; fasting; and pilgrimage to Mecca. The development of Moslem thought has been marked by countless complex theological differences often accentuated by bitter political dissension.

Abbott, Nabia. AISHAH: The Beloved of Mohammed. 1942. *Arno Press* 1973 $15.00

Ali, Ameer. THE SPIRIT OF ISLAM. 1922. *Humanities Press* $10.50

Attar, Farid al-Din. MUSLIM SAINTS AND MYSTICS: Episodes from the Tadkhkirat al-Auliya ("Memorial of the Saints"). Trans. by A. J. Arberry. 1965. Persian Heritage Ser. *Routledge & Kegan Paul* 1973 $13.25

> A prose work by one of the great poets of 13th-century Islamic literature. This is "the first volume of a series aimed at making major works of Persian literature more generally available to the interested Western reader"—(*LJ*). Bibliography. In the UNESCO Collection of Representative Works.

> *See also Chapter 18, Middle Eastern Literature, Section on Persian Literature*, Reader's Adviser, *Vol. 2.*

Bell, Richard. THE ORIGIN OF ISLAM IN ITS CHRISTIAN ENVIRONMENT: The Gunning Lectures, Edinburgh University, 1925. *International Scholarly Bk. Services* 1968 $18.50

Bodley, R. V. C. THE MESSENGER: The Life of Mohammed. 1946. *Greenwood* 1969 lib. bdg. $14.75

Cragg, Kenneth. THE HOUSE OF ISLAM. *Dickenson Pubs.* 2nd ed. 1975 pap. $4.95

> "A valuable supplementary text ... strongly recommended as a follow-up to Gibb" (*see below*)—(*Choice*).

Gabrieli, Francesco. MUHAMMAD AND THE CONQUESTS OF ISLAM. Trans. from the Italian by Virginia Luling and Rosamund Linell *McGraw-Hill* 1965 pap. $2.95

> The author is an Italian specialist on Islam. "His style is compact and economical and the translation reads well. The story is well connected and impressive without a burdensome emphasis on dates and historical background. This book is for the general reader interested in one of the world's significant and astonishing historical eras"—(*LJ*). In the World University Library Series.

Geertz, Clifford. ISLAM OBSERVED: Religious Development in Morocco and Indonesia. Terry Lecture Ser. *Yale Univ. Press* 1968 $8.50; *Univ. of Chicago Press* pap. $1.95. A study of Islam as it has developed in divergent cultures.

Gibb, Hamilton A. R. MODERN TRENDS IN ISLAM. 1947. *Octagon Bks.* 1972 lib. bdg. $10.00

MOHAMMEDANISM: An Historical Survey. *Oxford* 2nd ed. 1953 pap. $2.50

STUDIES IN THE CIVILIZATION OF ISLAM. Ed. by Sanford J. Shaw and William R. Polk *Beacon* 1962 pap. $2.95; *Peter Smith* $5.50. Sir Hamilton Gibb was a world-renowned Islamic authority and a University Professor at Harvard. The third book contains 15 major essays on Islamic history and culture selected by two young Harvard professors.

(With J. H. Kramer, Eds.). SHORTER ENCYCLOPEDIA OF ISLAM. *Cornell Univ. Press* 1953 $32.50

Glubb, John Bagot. THE LIFE AND TIMES OF MUHAMMAD. *Stein & Day* 1970 pap. $2.95

> The book "should have a special place among the biographies of Muhammad since its author is thoroughly familiar with the Bedouin Arabs, having lived among them a good portion of his life. This familiarity with the setting ... makes the work particularly valuable"—(*Choice*).

Guillaume, Alfred. ISLAM. *Penguin* Pelican Bks. 2nd ed. pap. $1.35

Hodgson, Marshall G. S. THE VENTURE OF ISLAM: Conscience and History in a World Civilization. *Univ. of Chicago* 3 vols. 1975 set $60.00

> "Perhaps the best interpretive history of the development of the Muslim world"—(*LJ*).

Kaba, Lansine. THE WAHHABIYYA: Islamic Reform and Politics in French West Africa. *Northwestern Univ. Press* 1974 $13.50

> "A significant addition to the literature on African Islam"—(*Choice*).

Katsh, Abraham I. JUDAISM AND THE KORAN. *A. S. Barnes* 1962 pap. $2.45

JUDAISM IN ISLAM: Biblical and Talmudic Backgrounds of the Koran and Its Commentaries. 1954. *KTAV* 1954 $12.50

Kritzeck, James, Ed. ANTHOLOGY OF ISLAMIC LITERATURE: From the Rise of Islam to Modern Times. *New Am. Lib.* $4.95. The more than 40 selections include newly translated sections from the Koran and essays, poetry, and proverbs on the favorite Islamic themes of love, beauty, death and God; a basic book. Professor Kritzeck is Professor of Oriental Languages and History at the University of Notre Dame.

MODERN ISLAMIC LITERATURE: From Eighteen Hundred to the Present. *New Am. Lib.* 1972 pap. $1.95

Lewis, Bernard, and Joseph Schacht, Eds. ENCYCLOPEDIA OF ISLAM. *Humanities Press* 5 vols. 1960–   Vol. 1 A–B: Fasc. 1–22 (1960) $110.00 Vol. 2 C–G: Fasc. 23–40 (1965) $125.00 Vol. 3 H–Iram: Fasc. 41–55 (1969) $166.50 Vols. 4–5 (in prep.). This monumental reference contains articles by leading scholars from all over the world. Produced under the patronage of the International Union of Academies, its general editors are Professor Lewis of the University of London and Professor Schacht of Columbia.

Lings, Martin. A SUFI SAINT OF THE TWENTIETH CENTURY: Shaikh Ahmad al-'Alawi; His Spiritual Heritage and Legacy. *Univ. of California Press* 2nd ed. rev. and enl. 1973 $10.00 pap. $2.95

WHAT IS SUFISM? *Univ. of California Press* 1975 $8.50

"The basic themes of Sufism are brought out in a way that considers its historical development, its ties with Islam, and its mysticism. A substantive introduction which will not only expand the reader's spiritual awareness, but also widen his perspective of the Islamic world"—*(LJ)*.

Morgan, Kenneth W. ISLAM: The Straight Path. *Ronald* 1958 $6.95

Planhol, Xavier de. THE WORLD OF ISLAM. *Cornell Univ. Press* 1959 pap. $3.50

Rahman, Fazlur. ISLAM. *Holt* 1967 $8.95; *Doubleday* Anchor Bks. 1968 pap. $2.50

Professor Rahman is the Director of the Central Institute for Islamic Research, Karachi, Pakistan. "The best general introduction to, and interpretation of, the Islamic religion which has yet been written"—(Professor James Kritzeck, University of Notre Dame). In the History of Religion Series.

Rosenthal, Erwin I. J. ISLAM IN THE MODERN NATIONAL STATE. *Cambridge* 1966 $13.50

"A thorough, competent study based upon firsthand acquaintance with the people, and with leaders and native scholars in each country. For the specialist and advanced student"—*(LJ)*.

Saunders, J. J. A HISTORY OF MEDIEVAL ISLAM. *Routledge & Kegan Paul* 1965 $7.00

Schacht, Joseph, and C. E. Bosworth, Eds. THE LEGACY OF ISLAM. *Oxford* 1974 $11.25

This work "has a two-fold purpose; to analyze the contribution of Islamic civilization to the achievements of mankind and to depict the contacts of Islam with the Non-Islamic world"— (*Choice*).

Schuon, Frithjof. UNDERSTANDING ISLAM. Trans. from the French by D. M. Matheson 1963. *Penguin* 1972 pap. $1.45; *Peter Smith* $4.50

A closely argued commentary "designed to 'explain why Moslems believe in [Islam]' "—*(LJ)*.

DIMENSIONS OF ISLAM. *Humanities Press* 1970 $6.75

"A sequel to his earlier and more basic *Understanding Islam*"—*(LJ)*.

Smith, Wilfred C. ISLAM IN MODERN HISTORY. *Princeton Univ. Press* 1957 $12.50; *New Am. Lib.* Mentor Bks. 1959 pap. $1.25

Stewart, Desmond, and Eds. of Time-Life Books. EARLY ISLAM. Great Age of Man Ser. *Time-Life Bks.* (Silver) 1967 $7.95

"Mr. Stewart, who has lived and taught in the Middle East, accomplishes what is an extremely difficult task—presenting the background and early theological and political development of Islam coupled with a series of chapters devoted to the culture, science, and art of the early Islamic world"—*(LJ)*.

Trimingham, J. Spencer. THE INFLUENCE OF ISLAM UPON AFRICA. Arab Background Series. *Praeger* 1968 $6.00

"Dr. Trimingham, former head of the Department of Arabic and Islamic Studies at the University of Glasgow, describes the penetration of Islam into the African continent, interpreting the implications of this still unfinished process upon the life and thought of Africa"—(*PW*). "Excellent"—(*LJ*).

THE SUFI ORDERS IN ISLAM. *Oxford* 1973 $11.00 pap. $2.95

"This book contains a very valuable account of the historical development of the Islamic, mystic, Sufi orders . . . until a more adequate historical account of the Sufi orders is written, this work is the most informative text available in English"—(*Choice*).

Watt, W. Montgomery. MUHAMMAD: Prophet and Statesman. *Oxford* 1974 $10.25 pap. $3.95

"Essentially an abridgement of the . . . [author's] *Muhammad at Mecca* and *Muhammad at Medina*"—(*Choice*).

JUDAISM

"Any ancient library is hard to read and understand," Samuel Sandmel has said. The history of Jewish religion is the history of that group of Semitic people who chose to and were chosen to enter into a covenant relationship with the One God, Yahweh, maker of the world and its inhabitants. Their interaction with Yahweh—and His activity within the social and natural order of the world—formed the basis of those events which were remembered and recounted from generation to generation. Eventually, and over a period of centuries, Hebrew historians wrote down this oral tradition. Their records, dating from about the eighth century B.C., are preserved in a small library of 39 books that form Hebrew Scripture. It exists as the Old Testament of the Christian Bible and is called the "Tanak" in Hebrew. The Tanak is arranged in three divisions: the "Torah" (or "Law"); the "Neviim" (or "Prophets"); and the "Kesuvim" (or "Writings").

The Torah consists of Genesis, Exodus, Leviticus, Numbers and Deuteronomy. It is also called "The Five Books of Moses," the "Humash" and the "Pentateuch," and forms the earliest canon of Hebrew scripture. About 250 B.C. a translation was made of the Torah into Greek, according to legend, by 70 or 72 men. Thus the name "Septuagint." To this Greek version of the Laws subsequently were added the other "accepted" books as well as some not accepted in the Hebrew canon. The Greek Tanak, then, differs somewhat from the Hebrew, and the Catholic canon of Scripture (based on the Greek) differs from the Protestant Bible (based on the Hebrew text). The marginal books are preserved in the Apocrypha. Writings which failed of approval everywhere are termed "pseudepigrapha." *See* Bamberger's "The Bible: A Modern Jewish Approach" and Sandmel's "The Hebrew Scriptures: An Introduction to Their Literature and Religious Ideas" (*under History, Criticism and Commentary below*). The Jewish Seminary of America, New York, has in its library on microfilm ("reproducing documents from library and university collections from Moscow to the Vatican"), "one of the greatest collections of Hebrew manuscripts in the world"—(*N.Y. Times*).

THE TORAH: The Five Books of Moses. (c. 13th–8th cent. B.C.) *Jewish Publication Society of America* 1963 buckram $6.00 lea. $12.00

This translation of the Pentateuch, prepared by a committee of eminent scholars, is drawn directly from ancient Hebrew texts. It "takes cognizance of the linguistic and archaeological advances made in recent years, and transmits the meaning and intent of the original Hebrew in a simple English style." It is expected that new translations of "The Prophets" and "The Writings" will follow as part of a 20-year project. The story of the Torah and its later interpretations in the Talmud is told by Max I. Dimont in "Jews, God and History" (*Simon & Schuster* 1962 $7.50; *New Am. Lib.* Signet 1964 pap. $.95).

See also main entry for Moses, this Chapter.

NOTES ON THE NEW TRANSLATION OF THE TORAH. Ed. by Harry M. Orlinsky for the Committee on the Translation of the Torah *Jewish Publication Society of America* 1969 $6.00

THE TALMUD. (2nd–6th centuries A.D.).

The Talmud is the great rabbinical thesaurus of opinions and views–the Oral Law of the Jews reduced to written form. "The Oral Law had its origins in Babylonia during the captivity of the

Jews in the sixth century B.C. The theater of Jewish life was shifted from Palestine in the West to Babylonia in the East and the old Hebrew religion was profoundly changed into Judaism." There is a Palestinian Talmud, completed in the 4th century and a Babylonian one—much longer— finished in Babylonia in the 6th century. The Talmud (Hebrew, meaning *teaching, learning*) is in direct line of descent from the Old Testament and represents the orthodox rabbinical literature connecting the Old Testament with medieval and modern Judaism. It consists of Mishnah (Hebrew, *oral repetition, teaching*), a systematic collection of religious-legal decisions developing the laws of the Old Testament, and Gemara (Aramaic, *completion, decision*) which contains supplementary material, legal and otherwise. As in the Koran, there is "great irregularity of treatment, variations of style, abrupt transitions from the spiritual to the crude and trivial and from superstition to the purest insight."

The first known printing of the Talmud was in Spain about 1475, just before the Spanish Inquisition, and in the succeeding 400 years about 70 editions were issued in Spain, Italy, Portugal, Poland, Switzerland, Holland, Germany, Austria, Russia and Lithuania. The Talmud is the accepted authority for orthodox Jews everywhere. In April 1968, Dr. Louis Finkelstein, Chancellor of the Jewish Theological Seminary of America (New York) announced that a concordance to the Babylonian Talmud was now half finished; 18 volumes have been published in Israel—the first such work ever to have been attempted. A concordance to the Palestinian Talmud will also be published. The Seminary, with financial assistance from private individuals, is supporting these publications.

THE SONCINO TALMUD. Ed. by Rabbi Dr. Isidore Epstein; fwd. by Dr. J. H. Hertz. *Bloch Pub. Co.* (Soncino Press) 18 vols. 1961 set $330.00

Separate volumes are available as follows: Seder Zeraim 1 vol.; Seder Moed 4 vols.; Seder Nashim 4 vols.; Seder Nezikin 4 vols.; Seder Kodashim 3 vols.; Seder Tohoroth 1 vol.; Index 1 vol. (various prices)

This first complete and unabridged English translation of the Babylonian Talmud, prepared by a large committee of experts under the direction of Dr. Epstein, has been hailed as a "monument of modern scholarship."

THE BABYLONIAN TALMUD. *Rebecca Bennet Pubs.* 64 vols. each $6.00 set $384.00. Each Tractate is one to three bilingual volumes with Hebrew and English versions beginning at either end of each book.

THE SONCINO HEBREW AND ENGLISH TALMUD. *Bloch Pub. Co.* (Soncino Press) 10 vols. 1962–   Vol. 1 Tractate Berakoth $15.75 Vol. 2 Tractate Baba Mezia $23.00 Vol. 3 Tractate Gittin $19.00 Vol. 4 Tractate Baba Kamma $23.00 Vol. 5 Tractate Kiddushin $19.00 Vol. 6 Tractate Pesahim $23.00 Vol. 7 Tractate Sanhedrin $24.75 Vol. 8 Tractate Kethuboth $26.75 Vols. 9–10 Tractate Shabbath set $39.50. Other volumes are projected for this edition of the Talmud. The translation is identical with that of "The Soncino Talmud" *above*.

THE LIVING TALMUD: The Wisdom of the Fathers. Trans. and ed. by Judah Goldin *New Am. Lib.* 1957 pap. $.95

THE TALMUD: Selections from the Contents of That Ancient Book, Its Commentaries, Teachings, Poetry and Legends. With brief sketches of the men who made and commented on it, by H. Polano *Warne* $3.95

THE MINOR TRACTATES OF THE TALMUD. Trans. by Eli Cashdan; ed. by A. Cohen; fwd. by Chief Rabbi Israel Brodie. With introd., commentary and index. *Bloch Pub. Co.* (Soncino Press) 2 vols. 1963 $25.00

Complete and in English for the first time, these 15 minor or extracanonical tractates (here presented with adequate notes) are often considered "apocrypha" because their great value to rabbis has allowed their inclusion in the printed editions of the Talmud. "Highly recommended as a basic reference source"—(*LJ*).

PIRKE ABOTH: The Sayings of the Fathers. Ed. by Joseph H. Hertz *Behrman* $2.95. A canonical tractate of the Talmud.

MAFTEHOTH HATALMUD (Keys to the Talmud). Hebrew-English. *Rebecca Bennet Pubs.* 2 vols. $12.00 thumb-indexed $18.00. Six indexes provide an invaluable help in reading even a few of the Tractates.

Books about the Talmud

The Talmud. By Isaac Unterman. *Bloch Pub. Co.* pap. $4.95

The Ethics of the Talmud: Sayings of the Fathers. By R. Travers Herford. Preface by John J. Tepfer. Hebrew-English text. *Schocken* 1962 $3.50 pap. $1.95. A comprehensive guide for the English reader.

Invitation to the Talmud: A Teaching Book. By Jacob Neusner. *Harper* 1973 $7.95

"A well-known Judaic scholar invites the reader to enter the world of Talmudic study"—(*LJ*).

THE MAIN INSTITUTIONS OF JEWISH LAW. By Rabbi Dr. Isaac Herzog. *Bloch Pub. Co.* (Soncino Press) 2 vols. Vol. 1 The Law of Property Vol. 2 The Law of Obligations set $21.00

"Even a cursory glance through the book is sufficient to arouse admiration for the extraordinary erudition displayed by the author [former Chief Rabbi of Israel]"—(*Jewish Chronicle*).

THE MIDRASH RABBAH. Ed. by Rabbi Dr. H. Freedman and Maurice Simon *Bloch Pub. Co.* (Soncino Press) 10 vols. set $165.00

The "Midrash," much of which has never been translated, is that branch of Talmudic literature compiled as a loose commentary of Scripture rather than, like the Talmud itself, in subject order. It contains the homiletical, ethical and moral interpretation of the Scriptures as expounded by the Rabbis in the synagogues and colleges. The Hebrew word *midrash* does not mean exactly what we understand by a commentary. "It is 'an imaginative development of a thought or theme suggested by Scripture, especially a didactic or homiletic exposition or an edifying religious story' "— ("Dictionary of the Bible"). "The Midrash on Psalms" has been well translated from the Hebrew and Aramaic by William G. Braude (*Yale Univ. Press* 1959 2 vols. $45.00).

HAMMER ON THE ROCK, A MIDRASH READER: Wisdom and Poetry of the Talmud and Midrash. Ed. by Nahum N. Glatzer *Schocken* 1962 $4.00 pap. $2.25

From the Talmud and its companion work, the Midrash, the editor has selected over 200 representative passages to give a lively account of great religious thinking and law at the level of life and experience.

THE KABBALAH: The Religious Philosophy of the Hebrews. By Adolphe Franck; introd. by John C. Wilson 1926. *University Bks.* 1967 $6.95; *Arno* $17.00. This translation from the second French edition of 1892 provides the text of the Kabbalah in simple and understandable terms.

THE ZOHAR (13th century A.D.). Ed. by Maurice Simon. *Bloch Pub. Co.* (Soncino Press) 5 vols. $75.00. The first complete translation into English.

THE ZOHAR. R-B Edition. *Rebecca Bennet Pubs.* 5 vols. set $36.00. In English, these volumes are part of the R-B Edition 64-vol. Babylonian Talmud.

ZOHAR—THE BOOK OF SPLENDOR: Basic Readings from the Kabbalah. Ed. with introd. by Gershom G. Scholem *Schocken* 1949 1963 pap. $1.95

THE ALPHABET OF CREATION: An Ancient Legend from the Zohar. Drawings and text by Ben Shahn 1963. *Schocken* 1965 pap. $2.25

This strange and beautiful book was first published in 1954 by *Spiral Press* in a limited edition; this is an offset reproduction. In this allegorical exposition of the 22 letters of the Hebrew alphabet, each letter pleads with God that the earth be created through Him. "The illustrations for each letter are distinctively Shahn, but also have an ancient mystical flavor."

The "Zohar," the 13th-century cabalistic classic by the Spaniard Moses de Leon, is supposedly based on the 2nd-century mystical writings of Rabbi ben Yohai. It is in essence a commentary of the Pentateuch. Kabbalah (or Cabbalah) is the name of a medieval Jewish theosophical system of scriptural interpretation that bears similarities to Neoplatonism, Gnosticism and the Vedanta philosophy of Hinduism. The books of speculative theology and mystical number symbolism that comprised the Kabbalah revealed the "hidden" or occult meanings of the Scriptures. At its highest, the Kabbalah expressed a deeply mystical religion and influenced many Christian scholars. In its debased form, however, it became associated with sorcery and magic.

THE ANATOMY OF GOD: The Book of Concealment. The Great Holy Assembly and The Lesser Holy Assembly of the Zohar, with The Assembly of the Tabernacle. Comp. by Roy A. Rosenberg *KTAV* 1973 $10.00

"This is the first complete English translation of some of the most fundamentally important sections in the Zohar, the single most important text in the history of Jewish mysticism. . . . Libraries should not resist acquiring this volume"—(*Choice*).

THE PASSOVER HAGGADAH. Traditional translation. *Shulsinger Bros.* $.40–$25.00

THE PASSOVER HAGGADAH: With English Translation. Revised edition, ed. by Nahum N. Glatzer; extensive commentary on the Seder by E. D. Goldschmidt; ill. from the famous Prague Haggadah of 1526 *Schocken* 1953 2nd ed. 1968 pap. $2.25

THE PASSOVER HAGGADAH. English trans. ed. by Rabbi Morris Silverman *Hartmore House* (dist. by Assoc. Booksellers) $4.95 pap. $1.95; *Prayer Bk. Press* $4.95 pap. $2.45

"The Haggadah is the book of the Jewish Passover; it is used during the service to acquaint the participant with the events of the Exodus and the Passover, salient points of Jewish history and tradition and commentaries from sages through the ages, songs, stories, legends, etc. It also explains the meaning and use of traditional Passover dishes like the bitter herbs and the bread of affliction, the *charoseth* or the mortar (made of apples, nuts and wine) with which Pharaoh made the captive Jews of Egypt build the walls and pyramids (bricks without straw), the heroical adventures of Moses, the ten plagues, etc."—(*PW*).

THE NEW HAGGADAH. Ed. by Mordecai Kaplan. 1941. *Behrman House* $2.50

THE FREEDOM SEDER: A New Haggadah for Passover. By Arthur I. Waskow *Holt* 1970 $3.95 pap. $1.50

"The Freedom Seder in English and transliterated Hebrew, follows the traditional order of more orthodox versions. What Waskow (a fellow of the Institute for Policy Studies, Washington, D.C.) has done however, is connect contemporary struggles toward freedom with the efforts of the past . . . this Haggadah is of much current interest for Jews and non-Jews alike"—(*LJ*).

AN ISRAEL HAGGADAH FOR PASSOVER. Adapted by Meyer Levin *Abrams* special ed. 1970 $35.00 pap. $12.95

"Presented in a lavish layout, illustrated with color photographs . . . this is a pleasant, beautiful book, not as vital as A. Waskow's, *The Freedom Seder*, but of interest in its own way"—(*LJ*).

A FEAST OF HISTORY: Passover through the Ages as a Key to Jewish Experience; with a New Translation of the Haggadah for Use at the Seder. By Chaim Raphael *Simon & Shuster* 1972 $12.50

"A lavish and beautifully illustrated book"—(*LJ*).

A PASSOVER HAGGADAH: The New Union Haggadah. Ed. by Herbert Bronstein for the Central Conference of Americh Rabbis *Grossman* 1974 $17.50

"This beautifully produced new edition and translation of the Passover Haggadah is the work of the American Reform movement. . . . The work is generally very well and very sensitively done. An interesting feature of this work is to note how the Reform movement, having discarded traditional elements in Judaism in the 19th century, is now moving back towards them"—(*Choice*).

HAGGADAH AND HISTORY: A Panorama in Facsimile of Five Centuries of the Printed Haggadah from the Collections of Harvard University and the Jewish Theological Seminary of America. By Yosef Hayim Yerushalmi *Jewish Publication Society of America* 1974 $27.50

"This handsomely produced volume traces the Passover Haggadah through place and time, illustrating highlights from printed Haggadahs of the past 500 years with 200 full page plates (each accompanied by an always intriguing commentary)"—(*LJ*).

THE HOREB: A Philosophy of Jewish Laws and Observances. Presented with commentary by Samuel Raphael Hirsch; trans. from German by Dayan Dr. I. Grunfeld *Bloch Pub. Co.* (Soncino Press) 2 vols. $25.00

THE SERVICE OF THE HEART: A Guide to the Jewish Prayer Book. By Evelyn Garfiel *A. S. Barnes* $5.95; *Wilshire* pap. $3.00. A comprehensive guide to the *Siddur*.

These prayers were collected and set down for the first time by Amran Gaon, the head of the academy of Sura in the 9th century, upon request of the Jews of Spain. "The Siddur is today the most known, the most read, the most directly affecting religious book of the Jews"—(Harry Gersh, in "The Sacred Books of the Jews"). It is constantly being changed to modernize the translations and in some editions to include prayers for the Jews slaughtered by the Nazis.

Collections

Adler, Morris, Comp. JEWISH HERITAGE READER. Ed. by L. Edelman *Taplinger* 1965 pap. $5.95

Ginzberg, Louis. THE LEGENDS OF THE JEWS. *Jewish Publication Society of America* 7 vols. 1956 each $6.00 set $42.00; *Simon & Schuster* rev. ed. 1961 $6.00 pap. $2.45

"The most oustanding work on Jewish folklore and legends ever published," this collection has been culled from Talmudic-Midrash literature and from the Apocrypha and Pseudepigrapha. This is a new edition of "The Legends of the Bible" (1956, o.p.).

Glatzer, Nahum N., Ed. A JEWISH READER: In Time and Eternity. *Schocken* 1946 rev. and enl. ed. 1963 pap. $2.95. Selections from postbiblical Jewish literature, theology, faith, philosophy, folklore, practical law. This is a revised edition of "In Time and Eternity."

(Ed.) THE LANGUAGE OF FAITH: A Selection of the Most Expressive Jewish Prayers. *Schocken* standard ed. $10.00 deluxe ed. $10.00; abr. ed. $4.95

Hertzberg, Arthur, Ed. JUDAISM: A Selection of Writings. Great Religions of Modern Man Ser. *Braziller* $6.95

"In a degree seldom achieved, Rabbi Arthur Hertzberg is able to make clear to the non-Jew what it is that is the continuing strength and essence of the Jewish faith"—(*N.Y. Times*).

Konvitz, Milton R., Ed. JUDAISM AND HUMAN RIGHTS. *Viking* 1972 $7.50

"This is a thoughtful, sometimes penetrating work that clarifies and gives contemporary resonance to the major role of Judaism in developing and preserving basic concepts and practices that are fundamental to modern philosophical, religious, and political thinking"—(*PW*).

Leiman, Sid Z., Ed. THE CANON AND MASORAH OF THE HEBREW BIBLE: An Introductory Reader. *KTAV* 1974 $29.50

"Leiman and KTAV have cooperated to produce an extraordinarily fine anthology on the formation of the Hebrew Bible.... This anthology, drawing on the very best scholarhsip, surpasses any other work on the formation and canonization of Hebrew scripture"—(*Choice*).

Leslau, Wolf, Trans. FALASHA ANTHOLOGY: The Black Jews of Ethiopia. *Yale Univ. Press* 1951 $11.50

Montefiore, C. G., and H. Loewe. A RABBINIC ANTHOLOGY. *Schocken* $20.00 pap. $7.50. Numerous selections from the nonlegal passages of rabbinic literature with commentary on each. Two introductions, one representing a Reform and one an Orthodox approach.

Newman, Louis I. and Samuel Spitz, Eds. THE HASIDIC ANTHOLOGY: Tales and Teachings of the Hasidim. 1954. Trans. from the Hebrew, Yiddish and German *Schocken* rev. ed. 1963 pap. $3.95

Noveck, Simon, and Abraham Ezra Millgram, Eds. B'NAI B'RITH GREAT BOOKS SERIES. *Bloch Pub. Co.* 5 vols. (Vols. 1 to 4 ed. by Noveck, Vol. 5 by Millgram.) Vol. 1 Great Jewish Personalities in Ancient and Medieval Times Vol. 2 Great Jewish Personalities in Modern Times Vol. 3 Great Jewish Thinkers of the Twentieth Century Vol. 4 Contemporary Jewish Thought: A Reader Vol. 5 Great Jewish Ideas. 1963 each $5.95 pap. $3.95

Rappoport, Angelo S. MYTH AND LEGEND OF ANCIENT ISRAEL. 1928. Introd. by Raphael Patai *KTAV* 1965 rev. ed. 1966 3 vols. set $27.50

The author, a well-known authority on Jewish folklore, brings together, in topical arrangement, the "legends, preserved and scattered throughout the apocryphal, midrashic, and related rabbinic literature.... Highly recommended as a basic reference"—(*LJ*).

Riemer, Jack, Ed. JEWISH REFLECTIONS ON DEATH. *Schocken* 1975 $7.95

"This volume delivers what it promises. Riemer has collected two dozen essays, each a personal statement drawn from the author's unique Jewish background.... The entire collection provokes thought and discussion"—(*LJ*).

Roth, Cecil. GLEANINGS: Essays in Jewish History, Letters and Art. *Bloch Pub. Co.* 1967 $7.95

> A collection of articles by the prominent Jewish historian, published over a period of 40 years in various periodicals. The book is "easy to read except for some included Hebrew documents. . . . Contains material likely to be unfamiliar as yet to many students of religious history. In the last section of the book Mr. Roth discusses the Kennicott Bible, considered by some to be the finest illuminated Hebrew manuscript in existence. The 22 pages of black-and-white illustrations show the beauty of the Spanish codex"—(LJ).

See also Chapter 15, Other European Literature, Section on Yiddish Literature, and Chapter 18, Middle Eastern Literature, Section on Hebrew Literature, Reader's Adviser, Vol. 2.

Reference Works

Abrahams, I., and C. G. Montefiore, Eds. THE JEWISH QUARTERLY REVIEW: 1889–1908. *KTAV* 1966 21 vols. $400.00

> "A goldmine of material. . . . No journal in the field has ever surpassed this Series in the quality and lasting value of its articles and reviews. . . . Highly recommended"—(LJ). Includes an index with subject guide which make it an excellent reference tool on all aspects of Judaism.

Ausubel, Nathan. THE BOOK OF JEWISH KNOWLEDGE. *Crown* 1964 $12.95

> "An engrossing, well-written and well-organized one-volume encyclopedia arranged alphabetically, this covers all areas of Jewish life and thought from Biblical times to the present. . . . A very worthwhile reference tool"—(LJ). There are 604 pages with good cross-referencing, an index of persons and a general index of 10,000 entries; 750 illustrations.

Ben-Asher, Naomi, and Hayim Leaf, Eds. THE JUNIOR JEWISH ENCYCLOPEDIA. *Shengold Pub.* 1957 rev. ed. 1974 $10.95

> Intended for a general introductory, rather than "juvenile," readership, this one-volume encyclopedia has received many awards including one from the Jewish Book Council of America.

Carmin, I. Ed. WHO'S WHO IN WORLD JEWRY. *Pitman* 3rd ed. 1972 $45.00

Donin, Hayim. TO BE A JEW: A Guide to Jewish Observance in Contemporary Life. Selected and compiled from the Shulhan arukh and Responsa literature, and providing a rationale for the laws and the traditions. *Basic Bks.* 1972 $10.95

> "Primarily factual and only secondarily theological, it will be valuable for reference"—(Choice).

Freedman, Seymour E. THE BOOK OF KASHRUTH: A Treasury of Kosher Facts and Frauds. *Bloch Pub. Co.* 1970 $6.50

> "Until the appearance of this book no comprehensive popular treatment was available. The book is ably written, filled with practical information, and very readable"—(LJ).

Jacobs, Louis. WHAT DOES JUDAISM SAY ABOUT . . .? *Quadrangle* 1973 $7.95

> "Rabbi Jacobs, the outstanding contemporary British Jewish scholar, has written an interesting and useful book. He attempts to provide a quick brief, yet authoritative summary of what Judaism has to say about major issues of general concern. . . . It will be a helpful reference work"—(Choice).

Patai, Raphael, Ed. ENCYCLOPEDIA OF ZIONISM AND ISRAEL. *McGraw-Hill–Herzl Press* 1971 2 vols. $44.50. A reference work devoted to the history of Zionism and of Israel up to the Six-Day War, published in commemoration of the 20th anniversary of the establishment of the State of Israel.

Roth, Cecil, and Geoffrey Wigoder, Eds. THE NEW STANDARD JEWISH ENCYCLOPEDIA. *Doubleday* 4th ed. 1970 $19.95

Shulman, Albert M. GATEWAY TO JUDAISM: Encyclopedia Home Reference. *A. S. Barnes* 2 vols. 1971 $25.00

> "In this encyclopedic guide to Judaism, the author has created a reference tool that will be useful and interesting to the layman, student, and teacher"—(LJ).

Singer, Isadore, Ed. THE JEWISH ENCYCLOPEDIA: A Descriptive Record of the History, Religion, Literature, and Customs of the Jewish People From the Earliest Times. 1904. *KTAV* 12 vols. 1964 set $125.00

> "The first serious reference work of its kind in any language, it has maintained its position—and not only in the English-speaking world. . . . With its . . . faults . . . it is still highly recommended"—

(*LJ*). The latest revised edition, though revisions were minor, was dated 1925; it is the 1904 edition which is reprinted here.

STUDY OF JUDAISM: Bibliographical Essays. By Richard Bavier. *KTAV* 1972 $12.50

"An entirely new work which is very up-to-date, including material published in 1972, it supplies a long-felt need for bibliographic aids in the areas it covers"—(*Choice*).

Werblowsky, R. J. Zwi, and Geoffrey Wigoder, Eds. THE ENCYCLOPEDIA OF THE JEWISH RELIGION. *Holt* 1966 $18.00

This was "prepared in Israel for the benefit of the inquiring layman. Its 3,000 entries in A–Z order embrace all phases and periods of Jewish life and thought that are 'relevant to the exposition of religious ideas.' Concise accounts are given of such subjects as dietary laws, ancient tribes of the eastern Mediterranean, current religious groups and practices, the books of the Old Testament, the holidays, the Talmud, the calendar, teachers and sages, towns famed for their Jewish people or events, philosophical concepts. The material is conscientiously cross-referenced, and the 415 large two-column pages are supplemented by a number of black-and-white halftone plates"—(David Glixon, in *SR*).

See also Chapter 9, History, Government and Politics–Jewish History, Reader's Adviser, *this Volume.*

History, Criticism, and Commentary

Ackroyd, Peter R. ISRAEL UNDER BABLYLON AND PERSIA. *Oxford* 1970 $6.00

"It is a clear, precise, and fascinatingly written account"—(*Choice*).

Agus, Jacob B. THE EVOLUTION OF JEWISH THOUGHT. 1959. *Arno* 1973 $22.00

Albright, William Foxwell. YAHWEH AND THE GODS OF CANAAN: An Historical Analysis of Two Contrasting Faiths. 1968. *Humanities Press* $10.50

An analysis of the Canaanite, the Phoenician and Israelite religions that influenced the ancient Jews. "The author offers archeological and linguistic evidence that the seeds of Judaic mono-theism were sown among the Israelites much earlier than is generally assumed"—(*PW*).

Anderson, Bernhard W. UNDERSTANDING THE OLD TESTAMENT. *Prentice-Hall* and ed. 1966 $11.95 3rd ed. 1975 $11.95

Arzt, Max. JUSTICE AND MERCY: Commentary on the Liturgy of the New Year and the Day of Atonement. *Hartmore House* (dist. by Assoc. Booksellers) 1963 $4.95. Perhaps the first such extensive commentary in English, this is primarily for the Conservative worshipper.

Baeck, Leo. THE ESSENCE OF JUDAISM. 1905. *Schocken* 1948 1961 pap. $3.75

Leo Baeck (1873–1956) was a remarkable young rabbi who, in this book, "stated that there must be a dialogue between Jew and Christian, but it can be authentic only if the Jewish sources of Christianity are fully and consciously acknowledged. The Jewishness of Jesus may not be denied. This also explains why, in the dark days of 1933, German Jewry chose Baeck to be their leader to negotiate with the Nazis. His empathy with all segments of the community, including the Zionists, his insistence that all Jewish denominations expressed the essence of Judaism, made him the ideal spokesman for all factions. This was his life as well as his philosophy. Baeck could have left Germany at any time in the Thirties. He deliberately chose to remain with his flock. Five times he was imprisoned; finally he was sent to Theresienstadt where, under incredible conditions of degradation, he continued to function as a rabbi and teacher. By a remarkable quirk of fate the Nazis believed that, with the death of a certain Moravian rabbi named Beck shortly after Baeck's arrival in Theresienstadt, they had rid themselves of their arch-antagonist. 'Herr Baeck, are you still alive?' asked an unbelieving Eichmann in April 1945. ... He survived the war to teach Judaism in many parts of the world, and died in London in 1956. A distinguished German social psychologist, H. G. Adler, who endured the camp with Baeck, wrote of him later: 'He was a shining beacon in the salt-tear ocean of despair' "—(Alan W. Miller, in *SR*). A recent brief biography of Baeck by his translator Albert H. Friedlander is "Leo Baeck: Teacher of There-sienstadt" (*Holt* 1968 $8.95), written, says Alan W. Miller, "pellucidly and with consummate skill"—(in *SR*).

Bamberger, Bernard J. THE BIBLE: A Modern Jewish Approach. *Schocken* 1963 pap. $2.25. A concise introduction to the Hebrew Scriptures, their literary structure, their concepts of God, man and society.

THE STORY OF JUDAISM. *Schocken* rev. 3rd ed. 1970 $8.50 pap. $4.50

A history of Judaism from its beginnings through the 20th century. "Written from a Reform viewpoint, this book links the evolution of religious ideas and practices to the developments of Jewish history"—(American Council for Judaism). "A formidable task ... admirably accomplished"—*(LJ)*.

Baron, Salo W. SOCIAL AND RELIGIOUS HISTORY OF THE JEWS. *Columbia* 2nd rev. and enl. ed. 15 vols. and index: Vols. 1 and 2 (1952) Vols. 3, 4, 5 (1957) Vol. 6, 7, 8 (1958) Vols. 9, 10 (1965) Vols. 11, 12, (1967) Index (1960) Vols. 13, 14 (1969) Vol. 15 (1973) each $17.50

The author is a professor emeritus of Jewish history, literature, and institutions at Columbia University. The 80-year old scholar was recently honored by the B'nai B'rith Heritage Award for his "positive contribution to contemporary literature by his authentic interpretation of Jewish life and values." This series is "a landmark for scholars and specialists in the field of Judaic history. . . . At the same time, it must be said that the information is [given] in a very arid and colorless style"— *(LJ)*.

(With Joseph L. Blau, Eds.) JUDAISM: Postbiblical and Talmudic Period. *Bobbs* Lib. Arts 1954 $6.50 pap. $3.25

Bauer, Yehuda. MY BROTHER'S KEEPER: A History of the American Jewish Joint Distribution Committee 1929–1939. *Jewish Publication Society of America* 1974 $7.95

"The first of a projected three volume history meticulously reviews the history of JDC Financial disbursement begun in 1914 to alleviate the plight of overseas Jewry"—*(Booklist)*.

"One of the most important books on modern Jewish history which has appeared in many years"—*(Choice)*.

Bermant, Chaim. THE WALLED GARDEN: The Saga of Jewish Family Life and Tradition. *Macmillan* 1975 $12.95

"In clear and nontechnical language, Bermant thoroughly covers all possible grounds of Jewish human affairs; all the Jewish holidays, both major and minor; the Sabbath, of course; and the dietary laws. . . . The book will undoubtedly appeal to Jews and non-Jews alike"—*(LJ)*.

Bernstein, Herman. THE TRUTH ABOUT THE PROTOCOLS OF ZION: A Complete Exposure. 1935. *KTAV* 1971 $19.95

Bickerman, Elias. FROM EZRA TO THE LAST OF THE MACCABEES: Foundations of Postbiblical Judaism. *Schocken* 1962 pap. $2.95. This "intelligent interpretation" examines the elements that shaped the Jewish people after their return from the Babylonian Exile in 538 B.C.

Blau, Joseph L. THE STORY OF JEWISH PHILOSOPHY. *KTAV* 1962 $5.95. Intended more for the general reader than the scholar, this is "an excellent well-written survey, highly recommended."

(Ed.) REFORM JUDAISM, A HISTORICAL PERSPECTIVE: Essays from the Yearbook of the Central Conference of American Rabbis. *KTAV* 1973 $15.00

"This anthology ... helps to fill an enormous void. It is a superb example of selection ... an absolutely indispensable volume"—*(Choice)*.

Bowker, John. THE TARGUMS AND RABBINIC LITERATURE: An Introduction to Jewish Interpretations of Scripture. *Cambridge* 1969 $22.50

"This carefully researched and documented study ... serves very well as an introduction to rabbinic thought and literature. Students of the New Testament will welcome it, since a knowledge of rabbinic Judaism is essential to an understanding of the New Testament"—*(LJ)*.

Bright, John. THE HISTORY OF ISRAEL. *Westminster Press* 2nd. ed. 1972 $10.95

Bruce, F. F. ISRAEL AND THE NATIONS: From the Exodus to the Fall of the Second Temple. *Eerdmans* 1963 pap. $3.25 A detailed account of Israel's history from the Exile to 73 A.D.; especially useful for Scripture teachers.

Buber, Martin. *See his main entry, this Chapter.*

Chill, Abraham. THE METZVOT: The Commandments and Their Rationale. *Bloch Pub. Co.* 1975 $15.95

"Chill, a modern traditionalist rabbi living in Israel, concentrates on the divine commandments as interpreted by the major classical commentators of Judaism"—(*LJ*).

Chouraqui, Andre. THE PEOPLE AND THE FAITH OF THE BIBLE. *Univ. of Massachusetts Press* 1975 $12.50

"A comprehensive, informative, accurate survey of the life, customs, practices and beliefs of ancient Israel . . . . The sweep of the author's vision and the profundity of his understanding give the work an inspirational quality unusual in a book so full of information"—(*LJ*).

Comay, Joan. THE TEMPLE OF JERUSALEM. *Holt* 1975 $15.00

"Comay's thesis in this informative history of one of Judaism's central sanctums is primarily that the holiest shrine in Judaism and, by extension, the Jewish ideas of God, Torah, people of Israel, and land of Israel are absolute necessities in the continuity, identity, and survival of the Jewish people"—(*LJ*).

Dimont, Max. JEWS, GOD AND HISTORY. *Simon & Schuster* 1963 $10.95; *New Am. Lib.* Signet 1964 pap. $1.50. Will Burant (*q.v.*) calls this "a lucid, spirited survey of one of the most fascinating subjects in history."

Dubnov, Simon M. HISTORY OF THE JEWS. 1939. Trans. by Moshe Spiegel from the Russian; introd. by Oscar Handlin *A. S. Barnes* (Yoseloff) 5 vols. 1939–73 Vol. I From the Beginning to Early Christianity (1939) Vol. 2 From 70 A.D. to the Early Middle Ages Vol. 3 European Jews from 1215 to 1648 (rev. ed. 1967) Vol. 4 From Cromwell's Commonwealth to the Napoleonic Era (1971) Vol. 5 From the Congress of Vienna to the Emergence of Hitler (1973) each $15.00

First written in Russia, it appeared in Germany between 1925 and 1929. The present translation is from the definitive Russian version of 1939. "This massive work is a classic of Jewish historiography, vast in scope, sound in scholarship, and scientific in methodology. A broad sociological approach, singularly free from theological preconceptions, has made it an indispensable reference for scholars despite the accumulation of new information on Jewish history in the decades since its composition"—(*LJ*).

Eisenberg, Azriel. JEWISH HISTORICAL TREASURES. *Bloch Pub. Co.* 1969 $10.00

"The author is to be congratulated upon his choice of materials; he succeeds in providing us with a pictorial chain of significant Jewish historical development—(*LJ*).

THE SYNAGOGUE THROUGH THE AGES. *Bloch Pub. Co.* 1974 $12.50

"A thoroughly engaging survey which illustrates the effect of changes in Judaism on the structure and purposes of the synagogue"—(*Booklist*).

Epstein, Rabbi Dr. Isidore. THE FAITH OF JUDAISM: An Interpretation for Our Times. *Bloch Pub. Co.* (Soncino Press) $8.95. The well-known Hebrew scholar expounds the religious faith on which the social doctrine of Judaism is founded.

Feldman, David M. BIRTH CONTROL IN JEWISH LAW: Marital Relations, Contraception and Abortion As Set Forth in the Classic Texts of Jewish Law. *New York Univ. Press* 1968 $9.95; *Schocken* 1974 pap. $3.95

Finkelstein, Louis, Ed. THE JEWS. *Schocken* 4th ed. 3 vols. 1970–71 pap. Vol. I Their History (1970) $4.95 Vol. 2 Their Religion and Culture (1971) $5.95 Vol. 3 Their Role in Civilization (1971) $5.95

Gersh, Harry. THE SACRED BOOKS OF THE JEWS. *Stein & Day* 1968 1972 pap. $2.95

"Harry Gersh, author of several previous books relating to Judaism, [attempts] a survey of all the classic Jewish literature, of which the Bible is the fountainhead, with the Talmud and medieval and modern Jewish books its far-flung tributaries. In a lucid and well-written foreword, Mr. Gersh discusses the unique role that the book has occupied in Jewish life and the veneration that was accorded the written word through the ages: 'For the Jews, every change in belief and practice grew out of a piece of writing; every quarrel was tied to a chapter or a book; many a martyrdom was for a scroll.' . . . The book may be recommended to a reader seeking a well-written, brief vademecum to classic Jewish literature"—(Robert Gordis, in the *N.Y. Times*).

Godbey, Allen H. THE LOST TRIBES, A MYTH: Suggestions towards Rewriting Hebrew History. *KTAV* 1974 $25.00

Goldberg, Israel. ÍSRAEL: A History of the Jewish People. 1949. *Greenwood* 1972 $25.00

Grant, Michael. THE JEWS IN THE ROMAN WORLD. *Scribner* 1973 $10.00
   "A lucid analysis"—*(Booklist)*.

Graves, Robert, and Raphael Patai. HEBREW MYTHS: The Book of Genesis. *McGraw-Hill* 1966 pap. $2.95
   Some 60 stories of creation and what followed, distilled from Old Testament sources, and presented in the light of modern anthropology and mythology. "A well-written, illuminating, often humorous account, particularly strong in putting things into historical, geographical, etymological focus, and, above all, in comparative mythology and religion"—*(LJ)*.

Greenstone, Julius H. THE MESSIAH IDEA IN JEWISH HISTORY. 1906. *Greenwood* 1972 $13.75

Guttman, Julius. PHILOSOPHIES OF JUDAISM: The History of Jewish Philosophy from Biblical Times to Franz Rosenzweig. 1933. Introd. by R. J. Werblowsky; trans. by David W. Silverman *Schocken* 1973 $5.50
   The life, work and teaching of every significant thinker from the Bible, Philo of Alexandria, and the rabbis of the Talmud through the great medieval thinkers, to those of the 20th century. Originally published in German in 1933, this was called by *Library Journal* "the best history of Jewish philosophy to date."

Heaton, E. W. THE HEBREW KINGDOMS. *Oxford* 1967 $6.25. A study of the central period of the Old Testament, from the legacy of Solomon's reign to the crisis of the Babylonian exile; based on new archeological discoveries.

SOLOMON'S NEW MEN: The Emergence of Ancient Israel as a National State. *Universe* 1975 $15.00
   "Heaton's discussions of the life and culture of the first Israel that flourished some nine centuries B.C. is rich in insights"—*(PW)*.

Hengel, Martin. JUDAISM AND HELLENISM: Studies in Their Encounter in Palestine During the Early Hellenistic Period. *Fortress* 2 Vols. 1974 set $34.00
   "Hengel, a leading German scholar, whose work here appears in a fine English translation, presents an excellent, comprehensive study of the impact of Hellenism on Judaism in the inter testamental period. . . . This is no mere re-hash, but a fundamental rethinking of the subject"—*(Choice)*.

Heschel, Abraham. GOD IN SEARCH OF MAN: A Philosophy of Judaism. 1955. *Octagon* 1972 lib. bdg. $14.50

ISRAEL: An Echo of Eternity. *Farrar, Straus* 1969 $5.50 pap. $3.25
   "Herschel . . . explains ably the reasons and meanings behind this mystical attachment of the Jewish people to Israel"—*(LJ)*.

MAN IS NOT ALONE: A Philosophy of Religion. 1951. *Octagon* 1972 $11.75

A PASSION FOR TRUTH. *Farrar, Straus* 1973 $8.95 pap. $3.65
   "It is probably the best book on Hasidism to appear in the English language"—*(LJ)*.

Hirsch, Rabbi Samson Raphael. JUDAISM ETERNAL. Selected essays trans. from the German, with introd. and biography, by Dayan Dr. I. Grunfeld *Bloch Pub. Co.* (Soncino Press) 2 vols. 3rd ed. 1967 set $22.00

Jacobs, Louis. HASIDIC PRAYER. *Schocken* 1973 $10.00
   "The book is well written and extensively documented, but its technical nature restricts it to libraries with an interest in Judaica, religion, and mysticism"—*(LJ)*.

JEWISH BIBLICAL EXEGESIS. *Behrman House* 1973 $4.50 pap. $3.95
   "Jacobs . . . here presents a highly instructive collection of translations, introductions, and clarifications of Jewish biblical exegesis from the 11th to the 20th centuries"—*(Choice)*.

Josephus, Flavius. *See his main entry in Chapter 9, History, Government, and Politics—Ancient, this Volume.*

Kadushin, Max. THE RABBINIC MIND. *Bloch Pub. Co.* 3rd ed. 1972 $9.75 pap. $4.95. Interpretations of rabbinical texts by a rabbi who is a theologian and professor of the psychology of religion.
   "Rich in insights and in erudition"—*(LJ)*.

Kahn, Robert I. THE TEN COMMANDMENTS FOR TODAY. *Pyramid Bks.* 1974 pap. $1.25

"Rabbi Kahn makes the Ten Commandments live for all today by his interesting use of Talmudic anecdotes and materials and pertinent, timely references to current living . . . . A valuable book for all Jews and Christians"—*(LJ)*.

Kanof, Abram. JEWISH CEREMONIAL ART AND RELIGIOUS OBSERVANCE. *Harry N. Abrams* 1970 $32.50

"Kanof's lavishly illustrated survey of Jewish ceremonial art has the merit, rare in such surveys, of being thorough and authoritative. The richly detailed yet lucidly written narrative encompasses the entire field of Jewish ceremonial art"—*(LJ)*.

Kaufmann, N. Yehezkel. THE RELIGION OF ISRAEL. Trans. and ed. by Moshe Greenberg *Schocken* $12.50 pap. $4.95; *Univ. of Chicago Press* 1960 $12.50

Kohler, Kaufmann. THE ORIGINS OF THE SYNAGOGUE AND THE CHURCH. 1929. *Arno* 1973 $18.00

Lamm, Norman. FAITH AND DOUBT: Studies in Traditional Jewish Thought. *KTAV* 1972 $12.50

"While Lamm draws on all Jewish philosophy, he is one of the first to translate into English and interpret the great 19th century Halakic thinkers. These thought provoking studies will be of interest to the student and the informed layman"—*(LJ)*.

Leslie, S. Clement. THE RIFT IN ISRAEL: Religious Authority and Secular Democracy. *Schocken* 1971 $7.50

"This is a thoughtful, compellingly written interpretive essay on the background, nature, and problems of the religious-secular dichotomy of Israeli nationhood"—*(LJ)*.

Liber, Maurice. RASHI. 1906. *Greenwood* $12.00; *Sepher–Hermon Press* 1970 $8.75

Lods, Adolphe. THE PROPHETS AND THE RISE OF JUDAISM. 1937. *Greenwood* 1971 $17.25

McKenzie, John L. A THEOLOGY OF THE OLD TESTAMENT. *Doubleday* 1974 $8.95

"McKenzie's treatment is competent, thorough, lucid, and stimulating"—*(LJ)*.

Mintz, Jerome R. LEGENDS OF THE HASIDIM: An Introduction to Hasidic Culture and Oral Tradition in the New World. *Univ. of Chicago Press* 1968 $12.50 1974 pap. $5.95

"Mr. Mintz, associate professor, Folklore Institute, Indiana University, presents both a detailed history and scholarly anthroposociological study"—*(LJ)*.

Moore, George Foot. JUDAISM IN THE FIRST CENTURIES OF THE CHRISTIAN ERA: The Age of the Tannaim. *Harvard Univ. Press* 3 vols. 1927–1930 set $25.00; *Schocken* 2 vols. 1971 pap. $8.00

Muilenburg, James. THE WAY OF ISRAEL: Biblical Faith and Ethics. *Harper* 1961 Torchbks. pap $1.75; *Peter Smith* $4.75

Myers, J. M. THE WORLD OF THE RESTORATION. Backgrounds to the Bible Ser. *Prentice-Hall* 1968 $7.50

Jewish history from the 6th century B.C. to the last half of the 4th century B.C. Bibliographies. "Well-documented . . . an eminently readable book"—*(LJ)*.

Netanyahu, B., Ed. THE WORLD HISTORY OF THE JEWISH PEOPLE. *Rutgers Univ. Press* Vol. 1 At the Dawn of Civilization: A Background of Biblical History, ed. by E. A. Speiser (1965) Vol. 2 The Dark Ages 700–1096, ed. by Cecil Roth (1966) each $20.00

"The second volume of "The World History of the Jewish People," which will be 11th in the 20-volume series when it is completed . . . , "The Dark Ages: Jews in Christian Europe 700–1096" . . . presents studies by 13 scholars under the editorship of Cecil Roth, reader emeritus in Jewish studies of Oxford University and professor of Jewish history of Bar-Ilan University in Israel. The series, which was planned 15 years ago by Israeli and American committees, is being published in Israel . . . England . . . and the United States"—*(N.Y. Times)*. The *N.Y. Times* critic, Thomas Lask, feels, in reviewing Vol. 2, that a unified approach would have been preferable to the separate essays by eminent scholars, since many use the same material, and that some of the scholarly apparatus might have been transferred to the "excellent" notes. Joseph Bram (in *LJ*) found Vol. 1 to promise a "unique work of history" at a high level. Each is self-contained and valuable for its own sake.

Neusner, Jacob. FIRST CENTURY JUDAISM IN CRISIS. *Abingdon* 1975 pap. $4.50

"A beautiful book for the general reader. Enthusiastically recommended"—*(Choice)*.

THERE WE SAT DOWN: Talmudic Judaism in the Making. *Abingdon* 1971 pap. $2.95

"A 'brief recapitulation' of Neusner's five volume work *A History of the Jews in Babylonia* (*Humanities* each $23.50–$35.25), is offered in this readable and useful introduction to the social and religious history of Babylonian Jewry from 100 B.C. to 1640 A.D."—(*Choice*).

(Ed.). UNDERSTANDING RABBINIC JUDAISM FROM TALMUDIC TO MODERN TIMES. *KTAV* 1974 $12.50 pap. $5.95

"Neusner, Professor of Religion at Brown and an important contributor to the critical study of Talmudic Judaism, has edited an interesting anthology of some of the most significant secondary sources on rabbinic Judaism. . . . The material has been selected to give an insight into the variety of rabbinic experience and the manifold nature fo rabbinic Judaism"—(*Choice*).

Oesterley, William O. E., and T. H. Robinson. THE HEBREW RELIGION. *Allenson* 2nd ed. 1937 $14.00. Two great scholars present an analysis of Old Testament religion.

(With G. H. Box). A SHORT SURVEY OF THE LITERATURE OF RABBINICAL AND MEDIAEVAL JUDAISM. 1920. *Burt Franklin* 1973 lib. bdg. $20.50

Pearlman, Moshe. THE MACCABEES. *Macmillan* 1973 $12.95

"While superb scholarship is evident, this is not a dry text, but a dramatization of the times and events of the second century B.C. The many illustrations recreate the setting for these events, while the maps permit the reader to follow the campaign in detail"—(*Choice*).

Plaut, W. Gunther. THE GROWTH OF REFORM JUDAISM: American and European Sources. Fwd. by Rabbi Jacob K. Shankman *Union of American Hebrew Congregations* 1965 $8.75

More than 200 selections from the writings of leaders of Judaism. "The author's technique of splicing a writer's thoughts and grafting them on to dozens of subjects runs the risk of presenting an incomplete, if not a confusing picture of a man's position. Nevertheless, Rabbi Plaut has succeeded admirably in presenting an abundance of useful source material"—(*LJ*).

Pritchard, James B., Ed. SOLOMON AND SHEBA. *Phaidon* (dist. by Praeger) 1974 $17.50

"In this work, six scholars examine the literature arising from the brief biblical accounts, of Sheba's visit to Israel which have been embellished in various ways by the different cultures"—(*LJ*).

Rabinowitsch, Wolf Zeev. LITHUANIAN HASIDISM. *Schocken* 1971 $7.00

"Unquestionably a definitive study"—(*LJ*).

Radin, Max. THE JEWS AMONG THE GREEKS AND ROMANS. 1915. *Arno* 1973 $23.00

Rankin, O. S. ISRAEL'S WISDOM LITERATURE: Its Bearing on Theology and the History of Religion. 1935. *Allenson* 1936 $6.00; *Schocken* 1969 pap. $2.45

Roth, Cecil. HISTORY OF THE JEWS. 1954. *Schocken* rev. ed. 1961 pap. $3.95

Widely regarded as the best one-volume history of the Jews in English, this book combines high scholarship with popular appeal.

A HISTORY OF THE MARRANOS. 1932. *Sepher-Hermon Press* 4th ed. 1974 $14.50; *Arno* 1975 $26.00; *Schocken* pap. $5.50

"The late Cecil Roth (Oxford) was one of the outstanding Jewish historians of the 20th century. Among his many valuable works is this detailed study of the Marranos, those Spanish Jews who, when forced to accept either Christianity or exile, chose, at least outwardly, to embrace Christianity while inwardly and secretly remaining true to their Jewish faith. . . . This remains the standard introductory work on the subject"—(*Choice*).

A SHORT HISTORY OF THE JEWISH PEOPLE. *Hartmore House* (dist. by Assoc. Booksellers) 1969 $14.95

"Although it is not now the most popular one-volume history, it remains eminently readable and reliable. . . . Although there are revisions, the work remains substantially the same. . . . Roth's history is still among the best of the one-volume treatments of the Jewish experience"—(*Choice*).

Roth, Leon. JUDAISM: A Portrait. *Schocken* 1972 pap. $2.75; *Viking* 1961 $4.00

Rowley, H. H. WORSHIP IN ANCIENT ISRAEL: Its Forms and Meaning. *Allenson* 1967 $14.00

A narrative description by the distinguished scholar of the Old Testament on the development of worship in early Israel as he sees it. "Valuable and stimulating"—(*LJ*).

Rubenstein, Richard L. THE RELIGIOUS IMAGINATION: A Study in Psychoanalysis and Jewish Theology. *Beacon* 1971 pap. $2.95

The oral traditions of the rabbis that were embodied in commentaries and explanations of the Torah are viewed by this lecturer in the humanities at the University of Pittsburgh as "a kind of projective test of centuries of rabbinic thought. [His book is the product] of careful analysis and penetrating understanding"—(*LJ*).

Rudavsky, David. MODERN JEWISH RELIGIOUS MOVEMENTS: A History of Emancipation and Adjustment. (Orig. "Emancipation and Adjustment") *Behrman House* 1972 $6.95 pap. text ed. $3.95

"Professor Rudavsky, of the New York University Institute of Hebrew Studies, presents the 18th and 19th Century backgrounds of contemporary Jewish thought and analyzes the major developments in contemporary Judaism stressing personalities and ideas in Orthodoxy, Reform, Conservation and Reconstructionism. . . . Wisely historical"—(*LJ*).

Russell, D. S. THE JEWS FROM ALEXANDER TO HEROD. New Clarendon Bible Ser. *Oxford* 1967 pap. $8.00. A survey of Jewish history and religion.

Sachar, Abram Leon. A HISTORY OF THE JEWS. *Knopf* 1938 4th rev. ed. 1965 $10.00 pap. text ed. $7.95

A one-volume history from biblical times to the present, by the first president of Brandeis University. "There is no better one-volume history of the Jews available"—(*Nation*).

Sandmel, Samuel. THE HEBREW SCRIPTURES: An Introduction to Their Literature and Religious Ideas. *Knopf* 1963 text ed. $10.95

Dr. Samuel Sandmel, Provost of the Hebrew Union College and a distinguished scholar in the field of Bible, Hellenistic Judaism and early Christianity, has written "an introduction to the Hebrew Scriptures intended for the general reader which scholars also will find stimulating and rewarding, both when they agree and when they disagree with him." Rabbi Sandmel is "not interested in setting forth doctrine but in illuminating texts. . . . In the process a whole cornucopia of learning is made available to the reader: the nature of Old Testament prophecy, the characteristics of Hebrew poetry, the complicated but fascinating problem of the authorship of the Pentateuch, and much more. . . . It will fascinate all those who would like even a glimpse into the deep, deep well of the past"—(*N.Y. Times*).

Schechter, Solomon. ASPECTS OF THE RABBINIC THEOLOGY: Major Concepts of the Talmud. 1909. *Schocken* 1961 pap. $2.95. A trustworthy statement of those ideas which form the religious consciousness of the Jewish people.

Scholem, Gershom. KABBALAH. *Quadrangle* 1974 $9.95

"Scholem (Hebrew University) is one of the greatest Jewish scholars of this century. His work on Jewish mysticism has, in effect, single-handedly created the academic study of this esoteric but important subject. . . . On almost every topic covered in this volume Scholem's views are definitive. . . . The material in this volume is demanding; it is not for beginners who would do better with Scholem's classic *Major Trends in Jewish Mysticism* (*Schocken* 3rd ed. 1954 $10.00 pap. $3.95)"—(*Choice*).

THE MESSIANIC IDEA IN JUDAISM AND OTHER ESSAYS ON JEWISH SPIRITUALITY. *Schocken* 1971 $15.00 pap. $3.95

"The book is an authoritative contribution to the study of Jewish mysticism and is highly recommended for scholar and layman alike"—(*LJ*).

SABBATAI SEVI: The Mystical Messiah. 1626–1676. *Princeton Univ. Press* 1973 $27.50 pap. $9.50

"Unknown material from the Sabbatians themselves, shedding new light on the career of the false Messiah from Smyrna who stirred up hope for Jewish redemption, is authoritatively researched by the foremost scholar in the field. Scholem stresses the impact of the Cabbalistic movement. . . . An outstanding and fascinating work on an important epoch in Jewish history. This English edition completely revises the 1957 Hebrew original and incorporates numerous newly discovered sources"—(*LJ*).

Schürer, Emil. HISTORY OF THE JEWISH PEOPLE IN THE TIME OF JESUS. 1890. Ed. by N. N. Glatzer. *Schocken* 1961 pap. $3.45. A new abridged version of the monumental work on Palestine from the Maccabean revolt to the fall of Jerusalem.

Schwarz, Leo W., Ed. GREAT AGES AND IDEAS OF THE JEWISH PEOPLE. *Random* Modern Lib. $5.95. A definitive cultural history dealing with the major themes of Jewish intellectual and spiritual tradition.

Silver, Daniel J., and Bernard Martin. A HISTORY OF JUDAISM. *Basic Bks.* 2 vols. 1974 set $37.00

"These two large, elegantly written, lucid, and comprehensive volumes supply the best single history of Judaism. They are thorough, balanced, and a pleasure to read. . . . A masterpiece of erudition, taste, judgment, and intelligent narrative"—(*Choice*). "A two volume cultural history of Judaism intended for the interested but not necessarily informed general reader"—(*Booklist*).

Sklare, Marshall. CONSERVATIVE JUDAISM: An American Religious Movement. *Schocken* new augmented ed. 1955 1972 $10.00 pap. $3.95

Wiesel, Elie. SOULS ON FIRE: Portraits and Legends of Hasidic Masters. *Random* 1972 $8.95 Vintage Bks. pap. $1.65

"In this very enjoyable volume, the author has succeeded in transporting us into the world of Hasidism, while, at the same time, making it relevant to our own times"—(*LJ*).

Zucker, Norman L. THE COMING CRISIS IN ISRAEL: Private Faith and Public Policy. *M.I.T. Press* 1973 $15.00

"The relationship of Judaism to Israel is portrayed with great simplicity and understanding"—(*LJ*).

Jews, Christians, and Their Joint Heritage

Bishop, Claire H. HOW CATHOLICS LOOK AT JEWS: Inquiries into Italian, Spanish, and French Teaching Materials. *Paulist-Newman* 1974 pap. $4.50

"A major part of the European research concerning Christian anti-Semitism is here presented and evaluated"—(*Choice*). "Analysis of religious teaching as a source of bias has been furthered by the present study"—(*Booklist*).

Daim, Wilfried. CHRISTIANITY, JUDAISM, AND REVOLUTION. *Ungar* 1973 $7.50

"Daim's theme is that revolutionary movements in the West take their original impulse from the Old Testament vision of a God who liberates people. . . . A good introductory study of the relationship of Christianity to society's attempts to find more constructive foundations"—(*LJ*).

Littell, Franklin H. THE CRUCIFIXION OF THE JEWS. *Harper* 1975 $7.95

"Littell's book confronts Christendom with its massive betrayal of the Jewish people when the Holocaust came upon them"—(*LJ*).

Maritain, Jacques. A CHRISTIAN LOOKS AT THE JEWISH QUESTION. 1939. *Arno* 1973 $7.00

Montefiore, Claude G. JUDAISM AND ST. PAUL: Two Essays. 1914. *Arno* 1973 $15.00

Sobel, B. Zvi. HEBREW CHRISTIANITY: The Thirteenth Tribe. Contemporary Religions Movements Ser. *Wiley* 1974 $12.50

"The latest addition to this series is also the first book-length account of its subject, Jews who have been converted to Christianity. In certain respects the book is quite comprehensive. . . . Generally, the book is interesting, informative, and highly readable. . . . The only evident fault of any magnitude is the author's penchant for value judgments"—(*Choice*).

Vermes, Geza. JESUS THE JEW: A Historian's Reading of the Gospels. *Macmillan* 1974 $6.95

"Vermes, Reader in Jewish Studies at Oxford University and a well-known scholar in the field of inter-testamental Judaism, has written an interesting new book on Jesus. Vermes' main objective is to try to renew the investigation into the question of the 'historical Jesus' against the background of Judaism in Palestine in the time of Jesus. . . . His primary contention and conclusion is that Jesus is best understood as a Galilean Hasid (pious wonder-worker) rather than as either a zealot, Essene, Pharisee, or Sadducee!"—(*Choice*).

Walker, Thomas. JEWISH VIEWS OF JESUS: An Introduction and an Appreciation. 1931. *Arno* 1973 $9.00

Wilken, Robert L. JUDAISM AND THE EARLY CHRISTIAN MIND: A Study of Cyril of Alexandria's Exegesis and Theology. *Yale Univ. Press* 1971 $12.50

"A very competent and clearly written scholarly work. . . . Recommended"—(*LJ*).

Modern Jewish Thought—A Selection of Recent Books

Berkovits, Eliezer. MAJOR THEMES IN MODERN PHILOSOPHIES OF JUDAISM: A Critical Evaluation. *KTAV* 1974 $12.50 pap. $4.95

Winner of the Jewish Book Council Award for the best book on Jewish thought in 1974. "The essays are of an extremely high standard of scholarship and intellectual acumen. . . . Very highly recommended for its readability and fine sense of intellectual discrimination"—(*Choice*).

Cohen, Arthur A. THE MYTH OF THE JUDEO-CHRISTIAN TRADITION. *Schocken* 1969 1971 pap. $2.75

"Cohen's main point is well taken: historically and theologically there is no single 'Judeo-Christian' tradition, and the confrontation of synagogue and church has been characterized far more by mutual ignorance and hostility than by recognition of a common heritage . . . [his] book is both lively and significant and should be read by anyone concerned with Jewish-Christian contacts"—(*Choice*).

Fackenheim, Emil L. QUEST FOR PAST AND FUTURE: Essays in Jewish theology. *Beacon* 1968 1970 pap. $3.45

"Provides a highly unified insight into Judaism seen from the perspective of an intensely committed Jew oriented toward existentialism. The essays reveal a genuine and dauntless wrestling with some of the great dilemmas of theology and the human condition in general"—(*LJ*).

Gordis, Robert, and Ruth B. Waxman, Eds. FAITH AND REASON: Essays in Judaism. *KTAV* 1973 $15.00

An anthology of articles that have appeared in *Judaism*. "Generally the quality of the essays in this collection is high; some of the best pieces written on Jewish thought since 1952 have been included"—(*Choice*).

Jospe, Alfred, Ed. TRADITION AND CONTEMPORARY EXPERIENCE: Essays on Jewish Thought and Life. *Schocken* 1970 $8.50 pap. $3.45

"The compilation should interest a wide range of library patrons"—(*LJ*).

Kaplan, Mordecai M., and Arthur A. Cohen. IF NOT NOW, WHEN: Toward a Reconstitution of the Jewish People; Conversations between Mordecai M. Kaplan and Arthur A. Cohen. *Schocken* 1973 $5.95

"Kaplan was born in 1881 in Lithuania and Cohen was one of his students at the Jewish Theological Seminary of America. . . . The book was edited by the authors from the tape scripts of conversations they had during two weeks in 1971. A most stimulating and well written dialogue"— (*LJ*).

Miller, Alan W. THE GOD OF DANIEL S.: In Search of the American Jew. *Dell* 1972 pap. $2.45

"A brilliant book, eminently quotable, it will add clarity to understanding the Jew in our society"—(*LJ*).

Neusner, Jacob, Comp. UNDERSTANDING JEWISH THEOLOGY: Classical Issues and Modern Perspectives. *KTAV* 1973 $7.95

"Once again the prolific and eminent historian of Judaism . . . at Brown University has made an important contribution to the academic study of Jewish life and thought. . . . This anthology first presents a reliable picture of classical Jewish theological reflection and then proceeds to show what happens when traditional categories are refracted through contemporary events and thinking"— (*Choice*).

Plotkin, Frederick. JUDAISM AND TRAGIC THEOLOGY. *Schocken* 1973 $7.95

"A genuinely important and original contribution to the philosophy of religion out of the resources of Judaism. . . . Well-written and straightforward, the book's argument is worked out with great clarity and passion"—(*Choice*).

Rawidowicz, Simon. STUDIES IN JEWISH THOUGHT. *Jewish Publication Society of America* 1974 $6.95

"Simon Rawidowicz (1896–1957) was one of the more original thinkers on the modern Jewish scene. . . . A number of essays in this volume deal with his unconventional philosophy of Jewish history. Others address themselves to medieval Jewish philosophy and to Jewish thought in the modern period"—(*Choice*).

Wouk, Herman. THIS IS MY GOD: The Jewish Way of Life. *Doubleday* 1959 $6.95

GNOSTICISM

At the time the Christian sect appeared, the entire eastern Mediterranean world was in a state of profound spiritual ferment. Innumerable Gnostic sects appeared. For four centuries Gnostic thought presented a major challenge to Christian belief. It was finally suppressed however, and virtually disappeared from the world. Recently a number of original Gnostic writings have come to light. "The discovery about 1945, at Nag Hammadi in Egypt (the ancient Chenoboskion), of what was probably the complete sacred library of a gnostic sect, is one of those sensational events in the history of religious-historical scholarship which archaeology and accident have so lavishly provided since the beginning of this century. It was preceded ... by the enormous find, early in the century, of Manichaean writings at Turfan in Chinese Turkestan; by the further unearthing, about 1930 in the Egyptian Fayum, of parts of a Manichaen library in Coptic; and was closely followed by the discovery of the Dead Sea Scrolls in Palestine"—(Hans Jonas, "The Gnostic Religion"). Because of political intrigue on the part of governments claiming rights to the finds, and professional jealousy on the part of scholars working with the Chenoboskion material, only the smallest part of the find has been translated and published. From this, however, and from the description of Gnosticism found in the writings of the early Church Fathers, it is possible to sketch a brief outline of Gnostic belief. Although various in emphasis, the Gnostic sects shared a belief in an utterly transcendent God, radically alien to this world, and a conviction that the material, historical world is utterly evil and depraved. This dualism characterized their thought about God and the world, matter and spirit, soul and body, good and evil, life and death. They conceived of salvation as escape from the prison of this world: the means of salvation was "Gnosis" (Knowledge). Gnostic "Knowledge" was a nonrational and supranatural state of awareness closely bound with mystical experience. Those who were "Knowing Ones," or Gnostics, tended to live out their historical existences as ascetics or as amoral beings, free from the "enslaving" laws of morality whether Mosaic, Christian or Greek. Early Christian thinkers found this nihilism dangerously wrong-headed and declared its Christian version heretical.

See Section on Religious Leaders, Reformers and Thinkers, this Chapter, for Mani (founder of Manichaeism).

Doresse, Jean. THE SECRET BOOKS OF THE EGYPTIAN GNOSTICS: An Introduction to the Gnostic Coptic Manuscripts Discovered at Chenoboskion. Trans. and critical evaluation of the Gospel according to Thomas. 1960. *AMS Press* 1972 $19.50

Drower, E. S., Trans. CANONICAL PRAYERBOOK OF THE MANDAEANS. *Humanities Press* 1959 $35.25

"In Mandaean poetry the gnostic soul pours forth its anguish, nostalgia and relief in an unending stream of powerful imagery"—(Hans Jonas, in "The Gnostic Religion").

Foerster, Werner, Comp. GNOSIS: A Selection of Gnostic Texts. Trans. by R. M. Wilson *Oxford* 2 vols. 1972–74 Vol. 1 Patristic Evidence (1972) $19.25 Vol. 2 Coptic and Nandaic Sources (1974) $24.00

"This translation of Foerster's important collection of Gnostic texts is an invaluable aid to scholarship in the history of religion"—(*Choice*).

Goodspeed, Edgar Johnson. STRANGE NEW GOSPELS. 1931. *Bks. for Libraries* 1971 $8.75

Grant, Robert M. GNOSTICISM AND EARLY CHRISTIANITY. *Columbia* 1959 2nd ed. 1966 $12.50. This important book clarifies the history of Gnosticism, stressing its roots in Jewish thought.

Hennecke, Edgar. NEW TESTAMENT APOCRYPHA. Ed. by Wilhelm Schneemelcher; English trans. by R. McL. Wilson *Westminster Press* 2 vols. 1963–66 Vol. 1 Gospels and Related Writings (1963) Vol. 2 Writings Relating to the Apostles, Apocalypses and Related Subjects (1966) each $10.00

This English version of a world-famous German work will be indispensable to all students of the New Testament and the early Church. It collects translations and extracts from the great body of apocryphal material, often of heretical origins, which grew up during the early centuries of the church. There is a translation of the Gospel of Thomas and a précis of the Gospel of Truth. (*See additional comment in Chapter 3, Bibles and Related Texts: The Apocrypha, this Volume.*)

Jonas, Hans. GNOSTIC RELIGION: The Message of the Alien God and the Beginnings of Christianity. *Beacon* 1958 2nd enl. ed. 1963 pap. $2.45; *Peter Smith* $5.50. A beautifully organized and lucid exposition by an eminent authority.

Puech, Henri-Charles, and others. THE GOSPEL ACCORDING TO THOMAS. Trans. from the Coptic *Harper* 1959 $5.00

CHRISTIANITY

We have divided our lists of selected readings on Christian thought and the Christian Church into five chronological groups corresponding more or less to major phases of Church development: the Early Church of Saints, Heretics and Fathers; the Medieval Church of Monks and Scholars; the Renaissance and Reformation Church of Reformers and Humanists; the Post-Reformation Church; and Modern Christianity. The latter topic has been much expanded in this edition to keep pace with the vast changes that have taken place in the "exploding" churches of the mid-sixties. Our broad topics under Modern Christianity (*for further subdivisions, see table of contents*) are now Modern Protestantism and Modern Catholicism where the treatment of Ecumenism will be found.

General Histories and Reference Works

Ahlstrom, Sydney E. A RELIGIOUS HISTORY OF THE AMERICAN PEOPLE. *Yale Univ. Press* 1972 $25.00 1974 pap. text. ed. $8.95; *Doubleday* Image Bks. 2 vols. 1975 pap. each $3.50

"A carefully researched and documented analysis of the American religious consciousness"—(*LJ*).

Belloc, Hilaire. THE CRISIS OF CIVILIZATION. 1937. *Greenwood* 1973 $10.75

Bettenson, Henry, Ed. DOCUMENTS OF THE CHRISTIAN CHURCH. *Oxford* 1947 2nd ed. 1968 $7.95 pap. $3.95. Important documents of the early Church plus more recent additions.

Brock, Peter. PACIFISM IN EUROPE TO 1914. *Princeton Univ. Press* 1972 $8.75

Brock deals "almost exclusively with Christian pacifism, tracing its development from the early Church through the pacifism sectarians to the increasingly secular peace movements of the later 19th century"—(*Choice*).

Buechner, Frederick. WISHFUL THINKING: A Theological ABC. *Harper* 1973 $4.95

"This short introduction to religious language is really a lexicon of significant religious words. The orientation is Protestant Christianity. . . . The entries are sometimes long, sometimes brief; they are also both witty and serious"—(*LJ*).

Burkill, T. A. THE EVOLUTION OF CHRISTIAN THOUGHT. *Cornell Univ. Press* 1971 $15.00 text ed. $10.75

"By far the most comprehensive one volume survey of the major trends in Christian thought to have been published recently"—(*Choice*).

Catholic University of America. THE NEW CATHOLIC ENCYCLOPEDIA: An International Work of Reference on the Teachings, History, Organization and Activities of the Catholic Church, and on All Institutions, Religions, Philosophies, and Scientific and Cultural Developments Affecting the Catholic Church from Its Beginning to the Present. *McGraw-Hill* 15 vols. and Index 1967 set $550.00

This reference work includes articles by scholars and theologians of all religions and replaces the 1909–1914 edition, which has long been out of print. It is profusely illustrated. "The New Catholic Encylopedia, which consists of 15 green, black and gold volumes, contains 17,000 articles on subjects ranging from the Doctrine of Atonement and St. Paul to Comic Books and International Trade. It incorporates the decrees of the Ecumenical Council and pronouncements by Pope Paul VI, and reflects in its editorial policies contemporary themes such as ecumenism, theological development and the role of the laity in the church. The Rev. John P. Whalen, the managing editor, said yesterday that the new encyclopedia reflected a 'healthy liberalism' "—(*N.Y. Times*). "Obviously not all the articles are masterpieces, but they are uniformly excellent both in scholarship and readability"—(*LJ*). The Editor-in-Chief was the Most Reverend William J. McDonald, D.D.

THE CHRISTIAN FAITH: Essays in Explanation and Defence. Ed. by W. R. Matthews. 1936. *Bks. for Libraries* 1971 $14.25

Constantelos, Demetrios J. THE GREEK ORTHODOX CHURCH: Faith, History, and Practice. Fwd. by Archbishop Jakovas *Seabury Press* 1967 pap. $1.95

A "well-written, authoritative" (*LJ*) interpretation of the teachings of the Greek Church.

Dunney, Joseph A. CHURCH HISTORY IN THE LIGHT OF THE SAINTS. 1944. *Bks. for Libraries* 1974 $21.50

ENVIRONMENTAL FACTORS IN CHRISTIAN HISTORY. Ed. by John Thomas McNeill, Matthew Spinka and Harold R. Willoughby. 1939. *Kennikat* 1970 $15.00

Florovsky, Georges. BIBLE, CHURCH, TRADITION: An Eastern Orthodox View. *Nordland* 1972 $6.95

"Florovsky is one of the greatest Russian Orthodox theologians of this century. . . . Whatever [he] writes is usually sound in scholarship and challenging because of his creative imagination"— (*Choice*).

CHRISTIANITY AND CULTURE. *Nordland.* 1974 $9.95

"This . . . volume . . . by the man who through common consent has been the leading spokesman for Orthodox thought is a major contribution to theological literature"—(*Choice*).

Forell, George Wolfgang. THE PROTESTANT FAITH. *Fortress* 1960 rev. ed. 1975 $5.95

Gonzalez, Justo L. A HISTORY OF CHRISTIAN THOUGHT. *Abingdon* 3 vols. 1970–1975 Vol. 1 From the Beginnings to the Council of Chalcedon in A.D. 451 (1970) $10.00 Vol. 2 From Augustine to the Eve of the Reformation (1971) $9.00 Vol. 3 From the Protestant Reformation to the Twentieth Century (1975) $13.95

"Originally written for seminarians in Latin America, [this work] incorporates corrections suggested by Protestant and Catholic scholars in its English revisions"—(*Choice*).

Guitton, Jean. GREAT HERESIES AND CHURCH COUNCILS. 1965. *Bks. for Libraries* 1971 $10.50

Harkness, Georgia. WOMEN IN CHURCH AND SOCIETY: A Historical and Theological Inquiry. *Abingdon* 1971 $4.75

The author brings the authority of personal experience as well as scholarship to her discussion. . . . Highly recommended"—(*LJ*).

Harvey, Van A. A. HANDBOOK OF THEOLOGICAL TERMS. *Macmillan* 1966 $5.95 pap. $1.45

A listing of 350 theological terms which help to differentiate "Roman Catholic, Protestant and Eastern Orthodox interpretation"—(*LJ*) by a Professor of Theology at Southern Methodist University.

Hudson, Winthrop S. RELIGION IN AMERICA. *Scribner* 1965 2nd ed. 1973 $12.50 pap. $4.95

This is "an excellent introduction and summary of American religious studies which will become the standard text in the field, especially at the undergraduate level"—(*Choice*). It is not, of course, confined to Christianity.

Kepler, Thomas S. A JOURNEY WITH THE SAINTS. 1951. *Bks. for Libraries* 1971 $10.50

Kerr, Hugh T., Ed. READINGS IN CHRISTIAN THOUGHT. *Abingdon* 1966 $10.95

"An excellent source book for all interested in the history and development of Christian thought. . . . Selections, beginning with Justin Martyr and ending with current living theologians"—(*LJ*).

Latourette, Kenneth Scott. CHRISTIANITY THROUGH THE AGES. *Harper* 1965 $3.50; *Peter Smith* $5.75

"The outline and development of the paragraphs in this work closely parallel the chapters of his larger *History of Christianity* ... and the multi-volume *History of the Expansion of Christianity* [*Zondervan* 7 vols. each $4.95 set $32.95]. Besides the inevitable compression, the emphases on worship and missions which distinguished the *History* are largely absent here. The final chapter briefly outlines developments since the *History*. The author validly insists that this is not simply an abridgment; the opening and final chapters illustrate his continually developing philosophy of history"—(*LJ*). Dr. Latourette, a prolific writer and former professor at the Yale Divinity School, as well as a former president of the American Historical Association and of the American Baptist Convention, was 84 when he was struck and killed by a car in front of his home in Oregon City, Ore., in 1968.

A HISTORY OF CHRISTIANITY. *Harper* 1953 rev. ed. 2 vols. 1975 Vol. 1 Beginnings to 1500 Vol. 2 The Reformation to the Present pap. each $6.95

McGinley, Phyllis. SAINT-WATCHING. *Viking* 1969 pap. $1.95; *Doubleday* Image Bks. 1974 pap. $1.75

"A warm, humorous, and affectionate book of prose about the saints she likes. . . . Here is an ecumenical book written for all people who like people"—(*LJ*).

McLean, George F., O.M.I., Ed. PHILOSOPHY IN THE 20TH CENTURY: Catholic and Christian. *Ungar* 2 vols. 1968 Vol. 1 An Annotated Bibliography of Philosophy in Catholic Thought: 1900–1964 Vol. 2 A Bibliography of Christian Philosophy and Contemporary Issues each $7.50 set $15.00

Magill, Frank, Ed., with Ian McGreal, Assoc. Ed. MASTERPIECES OF CHRISTIAN LITERATURE IN SUMMARY FORM. *Harper* 1963 $15.00

Essay-reviews of 300 important writings from the early Church to the present. This collection chosen from a poll of works "most influential to the development of Protestantism," contains a surprising emphasis on contemporary thought.

Manschreck, Clyde L. A HISTORY OF CHRISTIANITY IN THE WORLD: From Persecution to Uncertainty. *Prentice-Hall* 1974 $8.95

Marchant, Sir James, Ed. THE COMING-OF-AGE OF CHRISTIANITY. 1950. *Greenwood* 1971 $11.00

Marrin, Albert, Ed. WAR AND THE CHRISTIAN CONSCIENCE: From Augustine to Martin Luther King, Jr. *Regnery* 1971 $12.50 pap. $3.95

"Marrin has shown good historical scholarship in making his selections and has written an excellent and knowledgeable introduction to each, placing the writer and his writing into proper historical perspective"—(*LJ*).

Marty, Martin E., and Dean G. Peerman, Eds. A HANDBOOK OF CHRISTIAN THEOLOGIANS. *New Am. Lib.* Meridian 1976 pap. $3.95

This discusses the thought of 26 theologians. "The treatment biographically, atmospherically, and theologically of each is of an unusually high calibre"—(*LJ*).

More, Paul Elmer. THE CATHOLIC FAITH. 1931. *Kennikat* 1972 $12.00

Neill, Stephen Charles. THE CHRISTIAN SOCIETY. 1952. *Greenwood* 1972 $15.25

(With Hans-Ruedi Weber, Eds). THE LAYMAN IN CHRISTIAN HISTORY. *Westminster Press* 1963 $7.50

A History of laymen in the church from the earliest times to the present; sponsored by the World Council of Churches, it includes Protestant, Catholic and Orthodox contributions.

Nevins, Albert J., Comp. and ed. with introd. THE MARYKNOLL CATHOLIC DICTIONARY. Pref. by Donald Attwater *Grosset* 1965 $9.95

"Well planned and well executed"—(*LJ*).

THE OXFORD DICTIONARY OF THE CHRISTIAN CHURCH. Ed. by F. L. Cross and E. A. Livingstone *Oxford* 1957 2nd ed. 1974 $35.00

"This complete revision and updating has kept the high standards of the original publication. It has now brought within the scope of the *Dictionary* the work of the Second Vatican Council and the attendant changes in the Roman Catholic Church, as well as the continuing developments in ecumenical work, theological modernization, and the emergence of new leadership since that time"—(*Choice*).

Pelikan, Jaroslav. THE CHRISTIAN TRADITION: A History of the Development of Doctrine. *Univ. of Chicago Press* 5 vols. 1971– Vol. 1 The Emergence of the Catholic Tradition, 100–600 (1971) $15.00 pap. $4.95 Vol. 2 The Spirit of Eastern Christendom, 600–1700 (1974) $16.50

> When complete this will be a 5-volume historical evaluation of Christian doctrine and tradition, to which the volume "Historical Theology" (*see Section on Creeds and Doctrines below*) serves as an introductory prolegomenon. "Endowed with up-to-date scholarship, based mainly on primary sources, relevant to the concerns of contemporary readers, and writing with a flowing style, Pelikan has produced what is by far the best English introduction to the first six centuries of Christian doctrine"—(*Choice,* on Vol. 1).

Rahner, Karl, Cornelius Ernst and Kevin Smyth, Eds. SACRAMENTUM MUNDI: An Encyclopedia of Theology. *Seabury Press* 6 vols. 1969 set $125.00

> A scholarly compendium of modern Catholic theological thought. "The clarity of the writing, the sensitivity to contemporary debates, and the thoroughness of its coverage make this an extremely valuable reference work"—(Daniel Callahan).

Richardson, Alan. A DICTIONARY OF CHRISTIAN THEOLOGY. *Westminster Press* 1969 $8.50

> "This is a handy, authoritative reference work"—(*LJ*).

Rogier, L. J., R. Aubert, M. M. Knowles and John Tracy Ellis, Eds. THE CHRISTIAN CENTURIES: A New History of the Catholic Church. *McGraw-Hill* 2 vols. 1963–1969 Vol. 1 The First Six Hundred Years by Jean Danielou and Henri Marrou (1963) $12.50 Vol. 2 The Middle Ages by M. M. Knowles and D. Obolensky (1969) $15.00

St. Joseph's Seminary. THE CATHOLIC ENCYCLOPEDIA FOR SCHOOL AND HOME. *Grolier* 13 vols. (consult publisher for prices)

Schaff, Philip. HISTORY OF THE CHRISTIAN CHURCH. 1960. *Eerdmans* 8 vols. Vol. 1 Apostolic Christianity Vol. 2 Ante-Nicene, 100–325 Vol. 3 Nicene and Post-Nicene, 311–600 Vol. 4 Medieval Christianity, 590–1073 Vol. 5 Middle Ages, 1049–1294 Vol. 6 Middle Ages, 1294–1517 Vol. 7 German Reformation Vol. 8 Swiss Reformation each $9.50 set $74.50

Schamoni, Wilhelm. THE FACE OF THE SAINTS. Trans. by Anne Fremantle. 1947. *Bks. for Libraries* 1972 $20.50

Thomas, George F., Ed. THE VITALITY OF THE CHRISTIAN TRADITION. 1944. *Bks. for Libraries* 1971 $15.25

Tillich, Paul. A HISTORY OF CHRISTIAN THOUGHT. Ed. by Carl E. Braaten. 1968. *Simon & Schuster* Touchstone-Clarion Bks. pap. $4.95

Walker, Williston. GREAT MEN OF THE CHRISTIAN CHURCH. 1908. *Bks. for Libraries* 1968 $16.00

A HISTORY OF THE CHRISTIAN CHURCH. Ed. by R. T. Handy. *Scribner* 3rd ed. 1970 $9.95

THE WESTMINSTER DICTIONARY OF CHURCH HISTORY. Ed. by Jerald C. Brauer *Westminster Press* 1971 $17.50

THE WESTMINSTER LIBRARY OF CHRISTIAN CLASSICS. *Westminster Press* 26 vols. 1953–1963 each $5.00–$7.50 (consult publisher's catalog for individual titles and editors). This superb achievement of religious publishing makes available translations of original writings of the most important thinkers in Christian history.

Wood, Herbert George. CHRISTIANITY AND CIVILIZATION. 1943. *Octagon* 1973 $8.50. Based on six lectures delivered at Cambridge University in 1942.

The Early Church: Saints, Heretics and Fathers

"The first Christian century has had more books written about it than any other comparable period of history"—(John B. Noss' "Man's Religions"). The men who built the Christian Church from Gospel into a world organization, who actively participated in the amalgam of the Judeo-Christian tradition with the Graeco-Roman, left a fascinating body of written documents. For individual titles of their writings, and for the new series of the lives of the saints, see the following publishers' catalogs: *Alec Allenson* distributes translations of Clement of Rome, Dionysius the Areopagite, Athanasius, Cyril of Jerusalem, Ignatius of Antioch, and Tertullian. Catholic University of America, through *Consortium Press*, publishes the "Fathers of the Church" series in 67 vols. (each $12.00–$29.00). *Eerdmans* has reprinted "The Writings of the Nicene and Post-Nicene Fathers" with 14 vols. in the first series (the works of St. Augustine and St. John Chrysostom, each $6.00 set $80.00) and 14 vols. in the second series (each $6.00 set $80.00). *Harvard Univ. Press* Loeb Library has 2 vols.: "The Apostolic Fathers" (includes Clement, Ignatius, Polycarp, Didache, Barnabas), and "The Shepherd of Hermas." *Paulist-Newman* has been producing since 1946 their series "Ancient Christian Writers: The Works of the Fathers in Translation." The volumes now available include writings of Clement of Rome, St. Cyprian, St. Augustine, Arnobius, Tertullian, Jerome, Methodius, Athenagoras and others (each $2.50–$8.75). *Regnery* publishes in 4 vols. new translations of "The Sunday Sermons of the Great Fathers" (each $4.50 set $18.00 de luxe ed. each $7.50 set $30.00). Other translations, not parts of series, are also available, such as "Early Christian Writings: The Apostolic Fathers" (trans. by Max Staniforth *Penguin* Class. pap. $2.95), and "A Source Book for Ancient Church History" by Joseph C. Ayer (1913. *AMS Press* 1970 $18.00). *See main entries, this Chapter, for Paul, Jesus, Saint Augustine, and Saint Bede.*

Arnold, Eberhard. THE EARLY CHRISTIANS AFTER THE DEATH OF THE APOSTLES: Selected and Edited from All the Sources of the First Centuries. *Plough* 1970 $12.50. Originally published in Germany in 1926, it represents a free-church interpretation of and a collection of readings from the early church.

Attwater, Donald. THE PENGUIN DICTIONARY OF SAINTS. *Penguin* pap. $2.50; *Peter Smith* $4.75

Bainton, Roland H. EARLY CHRISTIANITY. *Van Nostrand-Reinhold* Anvil Bks. 1960 pap. $3.25

Bauer, Walter. ORTHODOXY AND HERESY IN EARLIEST CHRISTIANITY. Ed. by Robert Kraft and Gerhard Krodel *Fortress* 1971 $12.50

"In 1934, Bauer suggested a radical revision of the classical theory of orthodoxy.... Bauer argued that orthodoxy triumphed at a relatively late date after a long period of tentative efforts, with early formulations in certain areas that were later declared heretical.... [A] classical study in the history of Christian thought"—*(Choice)*.

Bettenson, Henry, Ed. EARLY CHRISTIAN FATHERS: A Selection from the Writings of the Fathers from St. Clement of Rome to St. Athanasius. *Oxford* 1956 1969 pap. $4.95

THE LATER CHRISTIAN FATHERS: A Selection from the Writings of the Fathers from St. Cyril of Jerusalem to St. Leo the Great. *Oxford* 1970 $5.00 pap. 1973 $2.95

Brown, Peter. RELIGION AND SOCIETY IN THE AGE OF SAINT AUGUSTINE. *Harper* 1972 $12.00

"The great value of Brown's work is the immense number of detailed insights both of other scholars and his own. This is an excellent and important book for scholars in the field of history of religion"—*(Choice)*.

Brownrigg, Ronald. THE TWELVE APOSTLES. *Macmillan* 1974 $12.95

"An engaging, generally well-documented, and thorough study"—*(LJ)*.

Carrington, Philip. THE EARLY CHRISTIAN CHURCH. *Cambridge* 2 vols. 1957 Vol. 1 o.p. Vol. 2 $22.50

Chadwick, Henry. THE EARLY CHURCH. Pelican History of the Church Ser., Vol. 1. *Penguin* Pelican Bks. (orig.) pap. $2.25; *Eerdmans* 1968 $6.95

"Volume 1 in the Pelican History of the Church series takes the story of the fledgling Christianity ... from the death of Christ to the papacy of Gregory the Great. The author is Regius Professor of Divinity at Oxford University"—*(PW)*.

Cochrane, Charles Norris. CHRISTIANITY AND CLASSICAL CULTURE: A Study of Thought and Action from Augustus to Augustine. *Oxford* 1944 Galaxy Bks. pap. $4.95

Conzelmann, Hans. THE HISTORY OF PRIMITIVE CHRISTIANITY. *Abingdon* 1973 $8.50 pap. $4.50.

"Conzelmann, a leading scholar on this subject, examines the origins and early development of Christianity from the time following the life and ministry of Jesus Christ to the end of the first century. . . . This book will probably become a classic"—(*Choice*).

Danielou, Jean. THE GOSPEL MESSAGE AND HELLENISTIC CULTURE. Trans. and ed. by John Austin Baker. A History of Early Christian Doctrine before the Council of Nicaea, Vol. 2 *Westminster Press* 1973 $17.50

"The book is well-written, well-organized, and well-translated. Part of a three-volume work, it maintains the same high standards as its predecessor, "The Theology of Jewish Christianity" (*Regnery*, 1964 [o.p.]). When completed the set will be the standard work in the field"—(*LJ*).

Davies, J. G. THE DAILY LIFE OF EARLY CHRISTIANS. 1953. *Greenwood* 1969 $12.00

Delehaye, Hippolyte. THE LEGENDS OF THE SAINTS. First ed. Brussels 1905; 4th ed. 1955. Trans. from the French by Donald Attwater, with a memoir of the author by Paul Peeters. *Fordham Univ. Press* 1961 $10.00; *Univ. of Notre Dame Press* 1961 pap. $1.95. A translation by the English scholar of a famous and scholarly treatment of hagiography.

Downey, Glanville. GAZA IN THE EARLY SIXTH CENTURY. *Univ. of Oklahoma Press* 1963 $3.95

"This is a scholarly but very readable account of how a former stronghold of the Philistines and a home of paganism developed into a prominent Christian center of intellectual and literary activity." Extremely well conceived and carried out, this will be of service to scholars, specialists and general and informed readers.

Edwards, O. C., Jr. HOW IT ALL BEGAN: Origins of the Christian Church. *Seabury Press* 1973 $5.95

"A well-documented account based primarily on the Bible and patriotic writings"—(*LJ*).

Enslin, Morton Scott. CHRISTIAN BEGINNINGS. *Harper* Torchbks. 1956 pap. $2.75

Gager, John G. KINGDOM AND COMMUNITY: The Social World of Early Christianity. *Prentice-Hall* 1975 $6.95 pap. $4.50

"A fascinating and provocative study of early Christianity by an outstanding New Testament scholar now teaching at Princeton"—(*Choice*).

Goguel, Maurice. THE PRIMITIVE CHURCH. Trans. from the French by H. C. Snape. 1947. *Humanities Press* 1964 $11.00

The third part of a trilogy by the leading French liberal theologian and historian, who died in 1955. "Goguel viewed the apostle Paul as the most important figure in the emergence of Christianity"—(*LJ*).

Goodspeed, Edgar J. THE HISTORY OF EARLY CHRISTIAN LITERATURE. Ed. by Robert M. Grant *Univ. of Chicago Press* rev. and enl. ed. Phoenix Bks. 1966 pap. $1.95
"An up-to-date survey, worthy of the original"—(*Journal of Biblical Literature*).

Harnack, Adolf. THE MISSION AND EXPANSION OF CHRISTIANITY IN THE FIRST THREE CENTURIES. 1905. *Bks. for Libraries* 2 vols. 1972 $43.25; *Peter Smith* $6.75

Lebreton, Jules, and Jacques Zeiller. THE HISTORY OF THE PRIMITIVE CHURCH. 1949. *Gordon Press* $80.00

Loisy, Alfred F. ORIGINS OF THE NEW TESTAMENT. Trans. by L. P. Jacks *Humanities Press* 1950 $4.25; (with "The Birth of the Christian Religion") *University Bks.* 1962 $10.00

Mayr-Harting, Henry. THE COMING OF CHRISTIANITY TO ENGLAND. Fabric of British History Ser. *Schocken* 1972 $12.50
"Recommended"—(*Choice*).

O'Connor, Daniel William. PETER IN ROME. Fwd. by Frederick C. Grant *Columbia* 1969 $20.00

The professor of religion at St. Lawrence University deals with "the literary, liturgical, and archaeological evidence for Peter's presence, martyrdom, and burial in Rome. . . . Recommended"—(*LJ*).

Pothan, S. G. THE SYRIAN CHRISTIANS OF KERALA. *Asia Pub. House* 1963 $6.50

To a historian of Christianity the province of Kerala on the southwest coast of India should be of great interest as one of the oldest seats of the developing Christian church. The accepted tradition maintains that Christianity reached the shores of India before the end of the first century A.D. The author, himself an erudite Syrian Christian, makes it clear that this church is Syrian in its liturgy and sacred language, but Indian in ethnic composition, daily speech and all other respects.

Prestige, G. L. FATHERS AND HERETICS. *Allenson* 2nd ed. 1952 pap. $10.00

Quasten, Johannes. PATROLOGY. *Paulist-Newman* 3 vols. 1950–1961 Vol. 1 The Beginnings of Patristic Literature (1950) $10.50; Vol. 2 The Ante-Nicene Literature After Irenaeus (1953) $10.50; Vol. 3 The Golden Age of Greek Patristic Literature (1961) $13.50

Richardson, Cyril C., Ed. EARLY CHRISTIAN FATHERS. *Westminster Press* 1953 $7.50; *Macmillan* 1970 pap. $2.95

Ryan, John. IRISH MONASTICISM: Origins and Early Development. *Cornell Univ. Press* 1931 1972 $16.50

Stevenson, James, Ed. THE NEW EUSEBIUS: Documents of the Church to A.D. 337. *Seabury Press* 1957 1963 pap. $8.25

Strachey, Marjorie. THE FATHERS WITHOUT THEOLOGY. *Braziller* 1958 $4.00. Iconoclastic discussion of the writings of the great Church Fathers.

Tyson, Joseph B. A STUDY OF EARLY CHRISTIANITY. *Macmillan* 1973 $9.50

"A masterful treatment of the opening decades in the history of Christianity, from the life of Jesus to the period just prior to the Emperor Constantine's reign. . . . Tyson [is] an associate professor and chairman of the religion department at Southern Methodist University"—(*Choice*).

Waddell, Helen. THE DESERT FATHERS. *Harper* (Barnes & Noble) 1936 1974 $7.50; *Univ. of Michigan Press* Ann Arbor Bks. 1957 pap. $2.25

Weiss, Johannes. EARLIEST CHRISTIANITY: A History of the Period A.D. 30–150. Ed. by F. C. Grant *Peter Smith* 2 vols. 1959 Vol. 1 Primitive Community: The Gentile Mission and Paul, the Missionary Vol. 2 Paul the Christian and Theologian: The Missionary Congregation and the Beginnings of the Church, the Separate Areas set $12.00

Wilken, Robert L. THE MYTH OF CHRISTIAN BEGINNINGS: History's Impact on Belief. *Doubleday* Anchor Bks. 1971 pap. $1.45

"Wilken writes in an easy style, and his presentation is warm and enthusiastic. He evaluates the 4th-Century writer, Eusebius of Caesarea, who set standards for all future church history"—(*LJ*).

Wolfson, Harry Austryn. THE PHILOSOPHY OF THE CHURCH FATHERS. Vol. 1 Faith, Trinity, Incarnation. (Harvard University Press Faculty Prize—1956) *Harvard Univ. Press* 1956 1964 3rd rev. ed. 1970 $12.50

The Medieval Church: Monks and Scholars

In the Middle Ages Western civilization and the Church were one. Theology and philosophy served the same end. Further philosophic readings are to be found in *Chapter 5, Philosophy: Medieval Philosophy, this Volume.*

See main entries for Saint Francis of Assisi, Saint Thomas Aquinas, Thomas à Kempis, and Saint Anselm, this Chapter; see Chapter 9, French Literature, Reader's Adviser, Vol. 2, for Abélard and Héloïse; see Chapter 5, Philosophy: Medieval Philosophy, this Volume, for Duns Scotus.

Bainton, Roland H. THE MEDIEVAL CHURCH. *Van Nostrand-Reinhold* Anvil Bks. (orig.) 1962 pap. $3.25

Barraclough, Geoffrey. THE MEDIEVAL PAPACY. *Harcourt* 1968 pap. $4.95

"The author, who taught at both Oxford and Cambridge before succeeding Arnold Toynbee at the University of London, assembles the best recent French, German, and Italian scholarship in this interpretation"—(*PW*).

Cohn, Norman. THE PURSUIT OF THE MILLENNIUM: Revolutionary Messianism in Medieval and Reformation Europe and Its Bearing on Modern Totalitarian Movements.

Oxford 1957 rev. ed. 1970 $12.50 pap. $3.95. A history of popular religious and social movements in Europe from the 11th to the 16th century.

Coulton, George G. FIVE CENTURIES OF RELIGION. *Cambridge* 1950 Vol. 4 Last Days of Medieval Monachism $29.50. (Vol. 1–3, o.p.).

THE INQUISITION AND LIBERTY. 1929. *Peter Smith* 1969 $6.00; *Richard West* 1973 $10.00

LIFE IN THE MIDDLE AGES. *Cambridge* 2 vols. 1930 pap. each $6.95

Cusa, Nicholas de. UNITY AND REFORM: Selected Writings of Nicholas de Cusa. Ed. by John P. Dolan *Univ. of Notre Dame Press* 1962 $7.95

Daly, Lowrie, S. J. BENEDICTINE MONASTICISM: Its Formation and Development Through the 12th Century. *Sheed & Ward* 1965 $7.50; *Guild Bks.* 1970 pap. $3.45

By a professor of history at St. Louis University. "An excellent overview"—(*LJ*).

Deanesly, Margaret. A HISTORY OF THE MEDIEVAL CHURCH, 590–1500. *Harper* (Barnes & Noble) 9th ed. 1969 $9.00 pap. $5.50

Duckett, Eleanor. MONASTICISM. The Gateway to the Middle Ages Vol. 3 *Univ. of Michigan Press* 1938 $4.95 Ann Arbor Bks. 1961 pap. $2.45

Fairweather, E. R. A. SCHOLASTIC MISCELLANY: Anselm to Ockham. *Westminster Press* 1956 $7.50; *Macmillan* Collier Bks. 1970 pap. $2.95

Fremantle, Anne. THE AGE OF FAITH. Introd. by Robert S. Lopez Great Ages of Man Ser. *Time-Life Bks.* 1965 $7.95

"One of the best productions in this . . . series. . . . The illustrations are superb. . . . The essay on religious communities is made up of photographs from current monastic life. The text is lucid, sometimes graceful"—(*LJ*).

Hinnebusch, William A. THE HISTORY OF THE DOMINICAN ORDER. *Alba House* 2 vols. 1966–73 Vol. 1 Origins and Growth to 1500 (1966) Vol. 2 Intellectual and Cultural Life to 1500 (1973) each $9.75

"Monumental . . . highly recommended"—(*Choice*).

Knowles, David, and Dimitri Obolensky. THE MIDDLE AGES. The Christian Centuries, Vol. 2 *McGraw-Hill* 1969 $15.00

"An unusually fine work, recommended for the general reader as well as the student of history"—(*LJ*).

Lerner, Robert E. THE HERESY OF THE FREE SPIRIT IN THE LATER MIDDLE AGES. *Univ. of California Press* 1972 $12.50

"A sound study of the movement which many historians have considered the most significant Continental heresy of the 14th Century. The Brethren of the Free Spirit were accused of many types of crimes. . . . The book is written with unusual sophistication and charm"—(*LJ*).

MacCulloch, John Arnott. MEDIEVAL FAITH AND FABLE. 1932. *Bks. for Libraries* 1973 $15.00; *Finch Press* $18.00

McNeill, John T. THE CELTIC CHURCHES: A History A.D. 200 to 1200. *Univ. of Chicago Press* 1974 $10.00

"A professor emeritus of Union Theological Seminary, . . . McNeill has mingled narration and evaluation in recounting the lives and accomplishments of the individualistic personalities who left such an indelible mark on Celtic institutions"—(*Choice*).

Morrison, Karl F. TRADITION AND AUTHORITY IN THE WESTERN CHURCH, 300–1140. *Princeton Univ. Press* 1969 $15.00

"This is a fine piece of scholarship. . . . It has enriched like few other works our understanding of the thought of the early Middle Ages in western Europe and it demonstrates how closely that world was linked to its Roman and Byzantine past"—(*TLS*, London).

Oberman, Heiko A. THE HARVEST OF MEDIEVAL THEOLOGY: Gabriel Biel and Late Medieval Nominalism. 1963. *Eerdmans* rev. ed. 1968 pap. $3.95. This book received the first $3,000 Robert Troup Paine Prize.

Renouard, Yves. THE AVIGNON PAPACY, 1305–1403. *Shoe String Press* 1970 $7.50

"This title was originally published in French in 1954. . . . Students of the period will find it extremely helpful"—(*LJ*).

Robson, John A. WYCLIF AND THE OXFORD SCHOOLS. *Cambridge* 1961 $16.50

Rogers, Francis M. THE QUEST FOR EASTERN CHRISTIANS: Travels and Rumor in the Age of Discovery. *Univ. of Minnesota Press* 1962 $4.75

"The Renaissance explorations of the Portuguese in the Far East were motivated not merely by a thirst for knowledge and a desire for economic gain but also by the dream of discovering Christians beyond the Islamic crescent." In examining pertinent literature of the 4th to 16th centuries, Professor Rogers shows that the West hoped to find allies in the fabled lands of Prester John—in India, Ethiopia, and Cathay.

Runciman, Steven. THE EASTERN SCHISM: A Study of the Papacy and the Eastern Churches during the XIth and XIIth Centuries. *Oxford* 1955 $7.00

Russell, Jeffrey. DISSENT AND REFORM IN THE EARLY MIDDLE AGES. *Univ. of California Press* 1965 $8.95

"This detailed work treats the nature and origins of heresies of the 8th to 12th centuries. [A] very well written contribution to intellectual and religious history"—(*LJ*). By an associate professor of history at the University of California (Riverside).

THE HISTORY OF MEDIEVAL CHRISTIANITY: Prophecy and Order. 1968. *AHM Pub. Corp.* pap. $5.25. An investigation of church history from the early fourth century to the later Middle Ages.

Seward, Desmond. THE MONKS OF WAR: The Military Religious Orders. *Shoe String Press* 1972 $13.50

"This is the only general introduction and survey of all of the orders published in the past century in English"—(*Choice*).

Smith, A. Lionel. CHURCH AND STATE IN THE MIDDLE AGES. 1913. *Int. Scholarly Bk. Service* 1964 $15.00

Six lectures on "the relationship between England and the Papacy in the middle of the 13th century. . . . A valuable source"—(*LJ*).

Turberville, Arthur S. THE SPANISH INQUISITION. 1932. *Shoe String Press* 1968 $8.50

Waddell, Helen. PETER ABELARD. *Peter Smith* 1959 $4.50; *Viking* Compass Bks. 1959 pap. $1.95. (*See also Abélard and Héloïse, Chapter 9, French Literature,* Reader's Adviser, *Vol. 2.*)

Wakefield, Walter L. HERESY, CRUSADE, AND INQUISITION IN SOUTHERN FRANCE, 1100–1250. *Univ. of California Press* 1974 $14.50

"The best brief work on the subject in any language"—(*LJ*).

(With Austin P. Evans, Eds.). HERESIES OF THE HIGH MIDDLE AGES: Selected Sources. *Columbia* 1969 $25.00

"Both the general reader and the scholar will be grateful for this work"—(*Choice*).

The Church of the Renaissance and Reformation: Reformers and Humanists

The Renaissance and the Reformation are inextricably linked. Since Abélard, scholars fired by fresh contact with classical thought had questioned assumptions of the established church. Early radical attempts at reform failed and the challenges for change, voiced by many men, blended into the general intellectual ferment. With Martin Luther (*q.v.*), Melanchthon (*q.v.*) and others, the protest broke out into vigorous activity.

See main entries, this Chapter, for Erasmus, Luther, Menno Simons, Melanchthon, John Knox, and John Calvin. In Reader's Adviser, *Vol. 1, see Chapter 10, British Fiction: Early Period, for Saint Thomas More, and in Vol. 2, see Chapter 11, Spanish Literature, for Saint Teresa of Jesus and Saint John of the Cross.*

Adam, Karl. ONE AND HOLY. 1951. *Greenwood* 1969 $8.50

Bainton, Roland H. HUNTED HERETIC: The Life and Death of Michael Servetus, 1511–1553. *Peter Smith* 1960 $6.00

THE REFORMATION OF THE SIXTEENTH CENTURY. *Beacon* 1965 pap. $2.95; *Peter Smith* $5.25

STUDIES ON THE REFORMATION. *Beacon* 1963 pap. $2.25

(With Eric W. Gritsch). BIBLIOGRAPHY OF THE CONTINENTAL REFORMATION: Materials Available in English. 1935. *Shoe String Press* 2nd ed. rev. and enl. 1973 $10.00

"No better collection of materials in English on the Continental Reformation exists than this revised, greatly enlarged edition of a 1935 publication which includes Catholic reform and Erasmus"—(*Choice*).

Bangert, William V. A HISTORY OF THE SOCIETY OF JESUS. *Institute of Jesuit Sources* 1972 $14.75

"By far the best one-volume history of the Society of Jesus available to the contemporary reader in any language"—(*America*).

Beard, Charles. THE REFORMATION OF THE 16TH CENTURY. 1883. Introd. by Ernest Barker; fwd. by Joseph Dorfman *Univ. of Michigan Press* Ann Arbor Bks. 1962 pap. $2.95

Belloc, Hilaire. HOW THE REFORMATION HAPPENED. 1928. *Peter Smith* 1970 $4.50

Bradshaw, Brendan. THE DISSOLUTION OF THE RELIGIOUS ORDERS IN IRELAND UNDER HENRY VIII. *Cambridge* 1974 $16.50

"Father Bradshaw provides an irenic perspective for a topic that has often been and continues to be treated in a prejudicial and controversial fashion"—(*Choice*).

Brodrick, James. THE ORIGIN OF THE JESUITS. 1940. *Greenwood* 1971 $13.50

Bromiley, G. W., Ed. ZWINGLI AND BULLINGER. *Westminster Press* 1953 $7.50. Huldreich (or Ulrich) Zwingli (1484–1531) was a Swiss religious reformer and Heinrich Bullinger (1504–1575), his disciple, became head of the Reformation in German Switzerland after Zwingli's death.

Courvoisier, Jacques. ZWINGLI: A Reformed Theologian. *John Knox Press* 1963 pap. $1.00

Cuthbert, Father. THE CAPUCHINS: A Contribution to the History of the Counter-Reformation. 1928. *Kennikat* 2 vols. 1971 set $19.50

Davies, Horton. WORSHIP AND THEOLOGY IN ENGLAND. Vol. 1: From Cranmer to Hooker. *Princeton Univ. Press* 1970 $17.50

It "will be a standard volume"—(*TLS*, London).

Dickens, A. G. THE COUNTER REFORMATION. History of European Civilization Library *Harcourt* 1969 pap. $4.95

"This is an admirable book, full of insight"—(*TLS*, London).

THE ENGLISH REFORMATION. *Schocken* 1964 $8.50 pap. $3.45

"Mr. Dickens, professor of history at the University of London, has written a clear and fascinating account of the men and movements that brought dramatic changes to the life and religion of England in the period from the Middle Ages to the years of Elizabeth I"—(Nash K. Burger, in the *N.Y. Times*).

REFORMATION AND SOCIETY IN SIXTEENTH-CENTURY EUROPE. History of European Civilization Library. *Harcourt* 1966 $5.50 pap. $4.95

"An impressive essay [which] synthesizes modern scholarship while remaining firmly rooted in the society and thought from which the Reformation emerged"—(*LJ*).

Donaldson, Gordon. THE SCOTTISH REFORMATION. *Cambridge* 1972 $19.50

Dunstan, J. Leslie. PROTESTANTISM. Great Religions of Modern Man Ser. *Braziller* 1961 $6.95; *Washington Square* 1962 pap. $.75

Fenlon, Dermot. HERESY AND OBEDIENCE IN TRIDENTINE ITALY: Cardinal Pole and the Counter Reformation. *Cambridge* 1972 $19.50

"This book . . . serves as an excellent introduction to Italian reform movements in the first half of the 16th century . . . pleasant, clear reading"—(*Choice*).

Haller, William. THE RISE OF PURITANISM. 1938. *Univ. of Pennsylvania Press* 1972 pap. $5.95; *Peter Smith* $6.50

Hillerbrand, Hans J. CHRISTENDOM DIVIDED: The Protestant Reformation. *Westminster Press* 1971 $9.95

Hutchinson, Francis E. CRANMER AND THE ENGLISH REFORMATION. 1951. *Macmillan* Collier Bks. 1962 pap. $.95

Jones, Rufus M. SPIRITUAL REFORMERS OF THE 16TH AND 17TH CENTURIES. *Peter Smith* 1959 $6.00

Knowles, David. RELIGIOUS ORDERS IN ENGLAND. *Cambridge* 3 vols. 1948–59 Vol. 1 The Old Orders (1948) $26.50 Vol. 2 End of the Middle Ages (1955) $23.50 Vol. 3 The Tudor Age (1959) $26.50

Léonard, Émile G. A HISTORY OF PROTESTANTISM: Vol. 1, The Reformation. Ed. by H. H. Rowley *Bobbs* 1968 $12.50
   "This work is the first volume of a definitive history of the Protestant movement from its roots in the medieval period to the present time. Émile Léonard, professor emeritus of Hebrew language and literature, Manchester University, emphasizes nonreligious factors involved in the Reformation. His thesis is that the Reformation was the final development of Roman Catholicism. . . . Extensive, classified bibliography and a detailed index"—*(LJ)*.

McFarlane, Kenneth B. JOHN WYCLIFFE AND THE BEGINNING OF ENGLISH NON-CONFORMITY. 1952. *Verry* $5.50

McGiffert, A. C. PROTESTANT THOUGHT BEFORE KANT. 1911. *Peter Smith* $5.25

Mosse, George L. THE REFORMATION. 1953 3rd ed. 1963. *Peter Smith* $5.00

Nugent, Donald. ECUMENISM IN THE AGE OF THE REFORMATION: The Colloquy of Poissy. *Harvard Univ. Press* 1974 $14.00
   "Nugent's study . . . sheds new light on the characters and events of 16th-century France immediately prior to the Wars of Religion"—*(Choice)*.

O'Connell, Marvin R. THE COUNTER REFORMATION, 1559–1610. Ed. by William R. Langer The Rise of Modern Europe Ser. *Harper* 1974 $10.00 Torchbks. 1974 pap. $4.95
   "It is a vigorous, spritely, and authoritative account doubtless destined to become a standard"—*(LJ)*.

Olin, John C., Comp. THE CATHOLIC REFORMATION: Savonarola to Ignatius Loyola, Reform in the Church 1495–1540. *Christian Class.* 1969 $8.50
   "A remarkable choice of documents . . . a valuable source book"—*(Choice)*.

(With others, Eds.). LUTHER, ERASMUS, AND THE REFORMATION: A Catholic-Protestant Reappraisal. *Fordham Univ. Press* 1970 $8.00
   "This volume is a monument to the new spirit of Reformation scholarship"—*(Choice)*.

Ozment, Steven E., Ed. THE REFORMATION IN MEDIEVAL PERSPECTIVE. *Franklin Watts* 1971 $12.50 pap. $3.45
   "A collection of important scholarly articles . . . a representative selection of the very significant scholarly work done recently on the Reformation"—*(Choice)*.

Pollen, John H. THE ENGLISH CATHOLICS IN THE REIGN OF QUEEN ELIZABETH: A Study of Their Politics, Civil Life, and Government, 1558–1580, from the Fall of the Old Church to the Advent of the Counter-Reformation. 1920. *Burt Franklin* 1971 $20.50

Porter, H. C., Ed. PURITANISM IN TUDOR ENGLAND. History in Depth Ser. *Univ. of South Carolina Press* 1970 $9.95 pap. $4.95. Document selections and commentaries.

Smith, Preserved. THE AGE OF THE REFORMATION. *Macmillan* Collier Bks. 2 vols. 1962 Vol. 1 The Reformation in Europe Vol. 2 The Social Background of the Reformation each $1.50

Spinka, Matthew, Ed. JOHN HUS AT THE COUNCIL OF CONSTANCE. *Columbia* 1965 $13.50

Steinmetz, David C. REFORMERS IN THE WINGS. *Fortress* 1971 $8.50. Portraits of 20 individuals who were lesser known leaders of the Reformation, divided into four groups: late medieval Catholic reformers, Lutherans, Calvinists, and Radicals.

Tawney, R. H. RELIGION AND THE RISE OF CAPITALISM. *Peter Smith* $5.50. An important study of the roots of Protestant thought.

Trinterud, Leonard J., Ed. ELIZABETHAN PURITANISM. Library of Protestant Thought. *Oxford* 1971 $12.50

A selection of documents. "Highly recommended"—(*LJ*).

Williams, George H. THE RADICAL REFORMATION. *Westminster Press* 1962 $19.50

Wilson, Derek. A TUDOR TAPESTRY: Men, Women and Society in Reformation England. *Univ. of Pittsburgh Press* 1972 $10.95

"A rare and most admirable acheivement"—(*LJ*).

The Post-Reformation Church

See main entries for Pascal, George Fox, Swedenborg, Jonathan Edwards, John Wesley and Cardinal Newman, this Chapter.

Andrewes, Lancelot. THE COMPLETE WORKS. Ed. by J. P. Wilson and J. Bliss *Oxford* 11 vols. 1841–54 set $300.00. The Bishop of Chichester, Ely and Winchester, Lancelot Andrewes (1555–1626), a good and devout man, was known as a theologian and was one of the first men authorized to create a new English version of the Bible. He was royal chaplain to Elizabeth, James I and Charles I.

Barbour, Hugh, and Arthur O. Roberts, Eds. EARLY QUAKER WRITINGS, 1650–1700. *Eerdmans* 1973 $9.95

"No other single volume has incorporated such a broad selection of early Quaker classics"— (Publisher's note).

Brauer, Jerald C., Ed. REINTERPRETATION IN AMERICAN CHURCH HISTORY. *Univ. of Chicago Press* 1968 $9.50

"Various experts state and document the changes which have occurred in the study of American church history. The contributors note new methodical and interpretive trends. Some deal with general, overall changes; others with changes related to more specific problems, for example, missionary motivation, or with persons of major importance such as Jonathan Edwards. All students of church history, especially of the American Church will find this volume stimulat- ing"—(*LJ*).

Brodie, Fawn M. NO MAN KNOWS MY HISTORY: The Life of Joseph Smith, the Mormon Prophet. *Knopf* 1946 2nd ed. rev. and enl. 1971 $12.50

"Twenty-five years have passed since the first edition of Brodie's excellent interpretive biogra- phy. . . . The valuable biography is enhanced in its original usefulness by this second edition"— (*Choice*).

Bushman, Richard L., Ed. THE GREAT AWAKENING: Documents on the Revival of Religion, 1740–1745. *Univ. of North Carolina Press* 1970 $9.25; *Norton* 1972 pap. $4.25

Carter, Paul Allen. THE SPIRITUAL CRISIS OF THE GILDED AGE. *Northern Illinois Univ. Press* 1971 $8.50

The author "concentrates on the years from 1865 to 1895 and discusses the tensions related to the crisis of faith brought about by the rise of modern science, especially Darwinism, both biological and social. . . . [He] demonstrates great breadth and depth of understanding, and he tells his story with verve and style"—(*LJ*).

Church, Richard William. THE OXFORD MOVEMENT: Twelve Years, 1833–1845. Ed. with introd. by Geoffrey Best *Univ. of Chicago Press* 1970 $9.00 Phoenix Bks. pap. $3.25

"Church's history of the Oxford Movement continues to be the classic account of the movement by an active participant and close friend of J. H. Newman. . . . The present edition reproduces the edition of 1891, adding a map of Oxford (1837) and an introduction by editor Best"—(*Choice*).

Coulson, John. NEWMAN AND THE COMMON TRADITION: A Study of the Church and Society. *Oxford* 1970 $8.50

"Mr. Coulson explores and compares the reflections on this subject of three . . . religious thinkers of the nineteenth century, Coleridge, Newman, and F. D. Maurice . . . no one who gives thought to these questions should miss [this book]"—(*TLS*, London).

Cragg, Gerald R. THE CHURCH AND THE AGE OF REASON, 1648–1789. Pelican Church History, Vol. 4. *Penguin* Pelican Bks. pap. $2.75; *Eerdmans* 1964 $5.00

Crowther, M. A. THE CHURCH EMBATTLED: Religious Controversy in Mid-Victorian England. *Shoe String Press* 1970 $9.25

"A welcome addition to the small but growing literature concerning church history in England during the Victorian era"—(*Choice*).

Desroche, Henri. THE AMERICAN SHAKERS: From Neo-Christianity to Presocialism. *Univ. of Massachusetts Press* 1971 $15.00

"In this scholarly and readable work, first published in France in 1955, [the author, who teaches at the Sorbonne] analyzes the Shaker movement from the 18th Century to its demise in the 20th in terms of religious, political, and social phenomena . . . this is a topical book that should appeal to serious readers"—(*LJ*).

Garrison, Winfred Ernest. THE MARCH OF FAITH: The Story of Religion in America since 1865. 1933. *Greenwood* 1971 $15.25

Gaustad, Edwin Scott. THE RELIGIOUS HISTORY OF AMERICA. *Harper* 1966 pap. $3.95

(Ed.). THE RISE OF ADVENTISM: Religion and Society in Mid-Nineteenth Century America. *Harper* 1974 $12.50

Lectures delivered during 1972–73 at Loma Linda University Church in California. "This collection of essays . . . brings together the work of distinguished students of religion in American history and focuses upon the neglected but crucial decades of the 1840s and 1850s"—(*Choice*).

Gay, Peter, Ed. DEISM: An Anthology. *Van Nostrand* Anvil Bks. (orig.) pap. $3.25

"The Deist movement, based on an heretical philosophy that espoused natural religion and rejected revelation and the Christian god, flourished in England from the 1690's to the 1740's and resulted in a rash of pamphleteering. . . . Samples of their many shades of opinion are given in this anthology"—(*PW*). Deism was also the "creed" of many early Americans, such as Benjamin Franklin. Peter Gay won the National Book Award for "The Enlightenment: The Rise of Modern Paganism" (*Knopf* 1966 $10.95; *Random* Vintage Bks. 1968 pap. $2.95).

Handy, Robert T., Ed. THE SOCIAL GOSPEL IN AMERICA, Gladden, Ely and Rauschenbusch. Library of Protestant Thought *Oxford* 1966 $11.95. Selections from the writings of each of these turn-of-the-century Protestant leaders, a Congregationalist, an Episcopalian and a Baptist, who had in common a strong commitment to social justice and whose work is attracting renewed attention today.

Isicher, Elizabeth. VICTORIAN QUAKERS. *Oxford* 1970 $13.75

Jones, Rufus M. THE LATER PERIODS OF QUAKERISM. 1921. *Greenwood* 2 vols. 1970 $35.00

Knox, Ronald. ENTHUSIASM: A Chapter in the History of Religion with Special Reference to the Seventeenth and Eighteenth Centuries. *Oxford* 1950 $19.25; *Christian Class.* $16.50

This book deals "with the many aspects of enthusiasm and its history in the special sense of the word as used here—believing oneself to be the recipient of special divine communications resulting in extravagant and visionary opinions, usually ill-regulated."

Latourette, Kenneth Scott. CHRISTIANITY IN A REVOLUTIONARY AGE: A History of Christianity in the Nineteenth and Twentieth Centuries. 1958. *Greenwood* 5 vols. 1973 set $95.00; *Zondervan* each $4.95 set $23.75

Lekai, Louis J. THE RISE OF THE CISTERCIAN STRICT OBSERVANCE IN SEVENTEENTH CENTURY FRANCE. *Catholic Univ. of America Press* 1968 $11.95

"Richly informative. . . . This book may be read in full confidence and benefit by all historians, theologians, and general readers"—(*Choice*).

Lovejoy, David S. RELIGIOUS ENTHUSIASM AND THE GREAT AWAKENING. *Prentice-Hall* 1969 pap. $2.95

Manuel, Frank E. THE RELIGION OF ISAAC NEWTON. *Oxford* 1974 $11.25

"These Fremantle Lectures of 1973 reflect extensive knowledge of the period and serve as a very readable introduction to the late 17th century as well as to the style of Newton's religious search"—(*Choice*).

Merwick, Donna. BOSTON PRIESTS, 1848–1910: A Study of Social and Intellectual Change. *Harvard Univ. Press* 1973 $12.00

Middlekauff, Robert. THE MATHERS: Three Generations of Puritan Intellectuals, 1596–1728. *Oxford* 1971 $12.50

Miller, David W. CHURCH, STATE, AND NATION IN IRELAND, 1898–1921. *Univ. of Pittsburgh Press* 1973 $14.95

"Nothing in its field and period is comparable to this work"—(*Choice*).

Mossner, Ernest Campbell. BISHOP BUTLER AND THE AGE OF REASON: A Study in the History of Thought. 1936. *Blom* 1971 $12.50

O'Connell, Marvin R. THE OXFORD CONSPIRATORS: A History of the Oxford Movement 1833–45. *Macmillan* 1969 $9.95

Peterson, Charles S. TAKE UP YOUR MISSION: Mormon Colonizing along the Little Colorado River, 1870–1900. *Univ. of Arizona Press* 1973 $9.50 pap. $5.95

"Peterson has produced the definitive work on the Mormon migration to the Little Colorado River in Arizona"—(*Choice*).

Posey, Walter Brownlow. THE DEVELOPMENT OF METHODISM IN THE OLD SOUTHWEST, 1783–1824. 1933. *Porcupine Press* 1974 $10.00

Sandeen, Ernest R. THE ROOTS OF FUNDAMENTALISM: British and American Millenarianism, 1800–1930. *Univ. of Chicago Press* 1970 $13.50

This book "will be read by every serious student of American religion"—(*Choice*). "First-rate historical study"—(*LJ*).

Smith, H. Shelton. IN HIS IMAGE, BUT—Racism in Southern Religion, 1780–1910. *Duke Univ. Press* 1972 $9.75

"This scholarly study . . . is an important contribution to understanding the complications of racism"—(*LJ*).

Smith, Timothy L. REVIVALISM AND SOCIAL REFORM: American Protestantism on the Eve of the Civil War. *Peter Smith* $5.00

Sykes, Norman. CHURCH AND STATE IN ENGLAND IN THE EIGHTEENTH CENTURY. 1934. *Octagon* 1975 $15.50

Thompson, David M., Ed. NON-CONFORMITY IN THE NINETEENTH CENTURY. *Routledge & Kegan Paul* 1972 $12.00 pap. $5.00

"A most useful collection of documentary extracts illustrating the fortunes of non-conformity in the 19th century"—(*Choice*).

Trinterud, Leonard J. THE FORMING OF AN AMERICAN TRADITION: A Reexamination of Colonial Presbyterianism. 1949. *Bks. for Libraries* 1970 $14.25

Turner, Frank Miller. BETWEEN SCIENCE AND RELIGION: The Reaction to Scientific Naturalism in Late Victorian England. *Yale Univ. Press* 1974 $13.50

"The search for some alternative to Christianity as the basis for personal and social values has been brilliantly illuminated in this book"—(*Choice*).

Vaughan, Alden T., Ed. THE PURITAN TRADITION IN AMERICA, 1620–1730. *Harper* 1972 pap. $3.25; *Univ. of South Carolina Press* $9.95

"Vaughan here attempts to survey all aspects of the Puritan experience through well-chosen documentary selections . . . the result is an excellent introduction to American Puritanism"—(*Choice*).

Vidler, Alexander R. THE CHURCH IN AN AGE OF REVOLUTION: 1789–Present. *Penguin Pelican Bks.* 1962 rev. ed. 1971 pap. $3.25

Watkins, Owen C. THE PURITAN EXPERIENCE: Studies in Spiritual Autobiography. *Schocken* 1972 $12.00

"An important contribution to the history of ideas. . . . Highly recommended"—(*Choice*).

Welch, Claude. Protestant Thought in the Nineteenth Century: Vol. 1 1799–1870.
  Yale Univ. Press 1972 $15.00

  "[This] projected two-volume work . . . promises to be one of the finest studies on Protestant
  thought in the 19th century"—*(Choice)*.

Creeds and Doctrines

The creeds and confessions developed at various times by the Christian Church are basic
to an understanding of church history, theology and the emergence of major branches of
Christendom. Adolf Harnack (1851–1930) wrote the monumental "History of Dogma"
(1900), available from *Peter Smith* (trans. from the 3rd German edition by Neil Buchanan
7 vols. bound as 4 set $27.00).

Gerrish, B. A., Ed. The Faith of Christendom. *Peter Smith* $4.75. This "source book of
  creeds and confessions" contains the basic official statements of faith, each with
  historical and explanatory comment. The period covered is from the earliest days,
  through the reformation and up to the present.

Kelly, John N. D. The Athanasian Creed. *Allenson* 1965 $5.00

Early Christian Doctrines. *Harper* 1959 $6.00

Leith, John H., Ed. Creeds of the Churches: A Reader in Christian Doctrine from the
  Bible to the Present. 1963. *John Knox Press* rev. ed. 1973 pap. $3.95. This source book
  contains all the major theological affirmations from the ancient faith of the Hebrews
  to the Batak Creed of 1951, in which the Indonesian Christians expressed their
  belief, in the idiom of their own culture.

Pannenberg, Wolfhart. The Apostles' Creed: In the Light of Today's Questions.
  Westminster Press 1972 $5.95

  "This is a laudable attempt to interpret the archaic language of the Apostles' Creed for the 20th
  Century man who may find parts of the Bible and creeds contradictory or irrelevant"—*(LJ)*.

Pelikan, Jaroslav. Historical Theology: Continuity and Change in Christian Doctrine.
  Westminster Press 1971 $9.95

  "It treats the nature of doctrinal change and its historical study, the relationship of historical
  theology to other disciplines, its main practitioners, and especially the significance of Harnack's
  interpretation of the history of dogma"—*(LJ)*.

Richardson, Alan. Creeds in the Making. *Macmillan* (Free Press) 2nd ed. 1959 pap.
  $1.95

Routley, Erik. Creeds and Confessions: From the Reformation to the Modern Church.
  Allenson 1963 $4.95. A history of the interrelationship of the attempts by the
  Reformed Churches, over the centuries, to define and codify their doctrines.

Thompson, Bard. Liturgies of the Western Church. *New Am. Lib.* 1961 pap. $3.95;
  Peter Smith $6.00

Whale, J. S. Christian Doctrine. *Cambridge Univ. Press* 1941 $10.95 pap. $2.45

Modern Christianity

The trials and tribulations of Christian churches as well as their successes inevitably
reflect the vicissitudes of the general society. Most denominations are suffering from a
marked decrease in donations these days while inflation eats away at their fixed income.
Consequently, many churches are curtailing their religious and educational programs
and cutting administrative staff positions. Missionary activities are at an all-time low partly
because of the shortage of funds and partly due to local political reactions against foreign
"intrusion." On the positive side, however, the controversies centered around radical
interpretations of the Bible appear to be lessening and sizeable increases in attendance
are reported by many denominations. The ecumenical spirit, though considerably
diminished, continues to exist in most American communities.

Baltazar, Eulalio R. The Dark Center: A Process Theology of Blackness. *Paulist-Newman*
  1974 pap. $4.95

"This has all the ingredients of a controversial book. Baltazar (Federal City College, Washington, D.C.) . . . demonstrates that darkness really plays an ambivalent role in both scripture and tradition, that it can be positive as well as negative. Focusing on that positive role, especially in the Western mystical tradition, he delineates the outline of a positive theology of darkness in which darkness becomes the central symbol of the Christian faith"—*(Choice)*.

Baum, Gregory. MAN BECOMING: God in Secular Experience. *Seabury Press* 1970 $7.95

"Deserves the widest reading and discussion by all thoughtful adults"—*(LJ)*. The author is a professor of theology at St. Michael's College, Toronto.

Blanshard, Brand. REASON AND BELIEF. *Yale Univ. Press* 1975 $30.00

"A diligently reasoned yet fascinating treatment of Western beliefs"—*(Choice)*. By Yale's emeritus idealist philosopher.

Burr, Nelson R., Comp. RELIGION IN AMERICAN LIFE. *AHM Pub. Corp.* 1971 $5.95 pap. $2.95. A bibliography.

Butterfield, Herbert. CHRISTIANITY AND HISTORY. *Scribner* 1950 $5.95

Capon, Robert Farrar. HUNTING THE DIVINE FOX: Images and Mystery in Christian Faith. *Seabury Press* 1974 $5.95

"Written in an up-to-date, lively, and highly readable style, it sheds light on many issues likely to have been pondered by thoughtful lay persons"—*(Choice)*. The author is an Episcopal priest and theologian.

Cox, Harvey. *See his main entry, this Chapter.*

Cullmann, Oscar. CHRIST AND TIME. *Westminster Press* 1950 rev. ed. 1964 $8.00

DeWolf, L. Harold. THEOLOGY OF THE LIVING CHURCH. *Harper* rev. ed. 1960 $8.95

Dunne, John S. A SEARCH FOR GOD IN TIME AND MEMORY. *Macmillan* 1969 $6.95 pap. $1.95

"This volume is a profound interpretation of the meaning of time, memory, myth, and death for individuals confronted with the complexities of modern life"—*(LJ)*.

Earle, William, James M. Edie and John Wild. CHRISTIANITY AND EXISTENTIALISM. *Northwestern Univ. Press* 1963 pap. $2.50

These six essays were first presented as public lectures. "The stance of the book is unique because of the excellent treatment given the Punic fathers, the radical criticism given the 'existentialism' of St. Thomas and Maritain, and the hopes expressed for a renewal of Christianity under new forms and symbols."

Ellul, Jacques. THE MEANING OF THE CITY. Trans. by D. Pardee *Eerdmans* 1970 pap. $2.45

The author "has struck a responsive cord in the U.S. and it is another strong reflection of Ellul's conviction that only by refusal 'to compromise with the forms and forces of our society can we recover the hope of human freedom' "—*(Choice)*.

PRAYER AND MODERN MAN. Trans. by C. E. Hopkins *Seabury Press* 1970 1973 pap. $2.95

"This book, in a style and theology reminiscent of Kierkegaard and Barth, is distinguished by constant concern with technological men and social involvement"—*(Choice)*.

Feuerbach, Ludwig. THE ESSENCE OF CHRISTIANITY. Trans. by George Eliot; ed. by E. Graham Waring and F. W. Strothmann *Peter Smith* $5.00; *Ungar* pap. $1.25; introd. by Karl Barth, fwd. by H. Richard Niebuhr *Harper* Torchbks. 1957 pap. $1.95

Fromm, Erich. THE DOGMA OF CHRIST AND OTHER ESSAYS ON RELIGION, PSYCHOLOGY AND CULTURE. *Holt* 1963 $3.95. The long title essay, comprising almost half the book, is appearing for the first time in English, translated by James Luther Adams. *(See also Fromm's main entry in Chapter 6, Psychology.)*

Gilkey, Langdon. CATHOLICISM CONFRONTS MODERNITY: A Protestant View. *Seabury Press* 1975 $8.95

"A thoroughly provocative and professional piece of writing"—*(LJ)*.

NAMING THE WHIRLWIND: The Renewal of God-Language. *Bobbs* 1969 $7.50 pap. $3.75

"In both length and quality this is a substantial volume. . . . Well written, fully documented, and displaying an enviable range of wide reading in both theological and philosophical thought, it ranks at the top of contemporary theological exploration. . . . Highly recommended for all readers"—*(Choice)*.

Graef, Hilda. MYSTICS OF OUR TIME. *Paulist-Newman* 1962 pap. $1.95. A brilliant clarification of a misunderstood subject; examines 10 modern men and women.

Graham, W. Fred. PICKING UP THE PIECES. *Eerdmans* 1975 pap. $3.95
"This clearly written study analyzes the challenge of secularization to the Christian faith"—(*LJ*).

Greeley, Andrew M. COME BLOW YOUR MIND WITH ME. *Doubleday* 1971 $5.95
"This thought-provoking, timely, and exciting book is . . . honest and factual. . . . [The author] has looked at the hard facts without prejudice and has discovered the disappointments of the time together with the continuing deterioration of organized religion in the U.S."—(*LJ*).

THE DENOMINATIONAL SOCIETY: A Sociological Approach to Religion in America. *Scott, Foresman* 1973 pap. $5.95
"A valuable contribution to a field badly in need of a theoretical base"—(*Choice*).

UNSECULAR MAN: The Persistence of Religion. *Schocken* 1972 $7.95
"Greely is a highly respected sociologist, a Catholic priest and the director of the Center for the Study of American Pluralism at the National Opinion Research Center in Chicago. His attempt to refute the 'conventional wisdom' which alleges a religious decline in contemporary society results in an erudite, highly readable, and often politically controversial analysis"—(*Choice*).

Hamilton, Michael P., Ed. THE CHARISMATIC MOVEMENT. *Eerdmans* 1975 pap. $3.95
"This volume is . . . a helpful and generally fair overview of what will prove to be an increasingly important movement in the Christian church"—(*LJ*).

Hartshorne, Charles. THE DIVINE RELATIVITY: A Social Conception of God. Terry Lectures Ser. *Yale Univ. Press* 1948 new ed. 1964 $8.75

THE LOGIC OF PERFECTION AND OTHER ESSAYS IN NEOCLASSICAL METAPHYSICS. *Open Court* 1962 pap. $3.95

A NATURAL THEOLOGY FOR OUR TIME. *Open Court* $4.50 pap. $1.95

(With William L. Reese). PHILOSOPHERS SPEAK OF GOD. *Univ. of Chicago Press* 1953 $12.00

Hollenweger, W. J. THE PENTECOSTALS: The Charismatic Movement in the Churches. Trans. by R. A. Wilson *Augsburg* 1972 $9.95
"Hollenweger has written a complex and valuable study of the world-wide Pentecostal movement"—(*Choice*).

Kaufman, Gordon D. RELATIVISM, KNOWLEDGE AND FAITH. *Univ. of Chicago Press* 1960 $7.00

SYSTEMATIC THEOLOGY: A Historical Perspective. *Scribner* 1969 pap. $6.50

Kline, George L. RELIGIOUS AND ANTI-RELIGIOUS THOUGHT IN RUSSIA. *Univ. of Chicago Press* 1969 $8.50
A short study by a professor of philosophy at Bryn Mawr, who "attempts to capture the flavor and excitement" of Russian religious and philosophical thought at the turn of the century. "Quite catholic . . . neatly arranged . . . well-researched"—(*LJ*).

Lepp, Ignace. ATHEISM IN OUR TIME. Trans. from the French by Bernard Murchland, C.S.C. *Macmillan* 1963 pap. $1.45. A distinguished critique.

Macquarrie, John. CONTEMPORARY RELIGIOUS THINKERS: From Idealist Metaphysicians to Existential Theologians. Fwd. by Martin E. Marty *Harper* 1968 pap. $4.50. A selection of excerpts from some two dozen 20th-century theologians and philosophers.

THE FAITH OF THE PEOPLE OF GOD: A Lay Theology. *Scribner* 1972 pap. $2.45

STUDIES IN CHRISTIAN EXISTENTIALISM. *Westminster Press* 1966 $6.00; *McGill-Queens Univ. Press* $7.00
"The most valuable survey of the meaning of existentialism for Christianity"—(*LJ*).

THINKING ABOUT GOD. *Harper* 1975 $8.95

TWENTIETH CENTURY RELIGIOUS THOUGHT: The Frontiers of Philosophy and Theology, 1900–1970. 1963. *Allenson* rev. ed. 1971 pap. $6.65. This invaluable introduction to the major thinkers and ideas of our time is by a professor of theology at Oxford, who formerly taught systematic theology at Glasgow University and then at Union Theological Seminary in New York.

Marty, Martin E. THE FIRE WE CAN LIGHT: The Role of Religion in a Suddenly Different World. *Doubleday* 1973 $5.95

"The work abounds with observations of current religious phenomena. . . . Well-written and timely"—*(LJ)*.

(With Dean G. Peerman, Eds.). HANDBOOK OF CHRISTIAN THEOLOGIANS. *New Am. Lib.* Meridian Bks. 1967 pap. $3.95

Mays, Benjamin Elijah. THE NEGRO'S GOD AS REFLECTED IN HIS LITERATURE. 1938. *Atheneum* pap. $2.75; *Negro Univ. Press* $11.50; *Russell & Russell* 1968 $8.00

"A pioneering work by the President Emeritus of Morehouse College, first published in 1938 when he was Dean of Religion at Howard University"—*(Choice)*.

Modras, Ronald E. PATHS TO UNITY: American Religion Today and Tomorrow. *Sheed & Ward* 1968 pap. $4.95

"A clear and comprehensive presentation of the beliefs and practices of the major faiths in America, set in historical context. Modras, a priest of the Archdiocese of Detroit, writes with a knowledge gained from personal experience as a teacher of ecumenism in the Detroit Institute for Continuing Education"—*(Choice)*.

Phillips, J. B. GOD OUR CONTEMPORARY. *Macmillan* 1960 pap. $1.45

RELIGION IN AMERICAN LIFE. Ed. by James W. Smith and A. L. Jamison *Princeton Univ. Press* 4 vols. 1961 set $50.00 *(see below for editors and separate volume prices)*

Vol. 1 The Shaping of American Religion $12.50 pap. $3.45 Vol. 2 Religious Perspectives in American Culture $13.50 Vol. 3 Religious Thought and Economic Society: The European Background, by J. Viner o.p. Vol. 4, parts 1 and 2 and Vol. 4, parts 3, 4, and 5 A Critical Bibliography of Religion in America, by Nelson R. Burr in collab. with James Ward Smith and A. Leland Jamison 2 vols. set $30.00 "An outgrowth of Princeton University's Special Program in American Civilization, this series makes available to the public a rounded and stimulating appraisal of the influences of religion on American culture, and the influence of America on religion generally. Every library of whatever type should find this set useful."

Rosten, Leo, Ed. RELIGIONS OF AMERICA. *Simon & Schuster* rev. ed. 1975 $12.95 pap. $5.95. Each article on the major religious groups has been brought up to date and approved by the church concerned for this revised edition.

Russell, Bertrand. WHY I AM NOT A CHRISTIAN AND OTHER ESSAYS ON RELIGION AND RELATED SUBJECTS. Ed. by Paul Edwards *Simon & Schuster* 1957 $6.95 pap. $1.95. This offers much insight on what Christianity might be. Whether or not one shares his views, this master of English prose is brilliant and thought-provoking. Includes appendix on "The Bertrand Russell Case."

Santmire, H. Paul. BROTHER EARTH: Nature, God and Ecology in Time of Crisis. *Nelson* 1970 $4.95

"This is perhaps the best general presentation of a balanced study of the relationship between theology and ecology"—*(Choice)*.

Shinn, Roger L. MAN: The New Humanism. New Directions in Theology Today, Vol. 6. *Westminster Press* 1968 $4.50 pap. $2.85. A survey of the effects of recent developments in the social sciences on Christianity.

Smith, John E. REASON AND GOD: Encounters of Philosophy with Religion. *Yale Univ. Press* 1961 pap. $2.95

Dr. Smith, Clark Professor of Philosophy at Yale University, examines in five successive chapters the religious implications of the philosophy of Kant, Rousseau, Nietzsche, Peirce, and John Dewey. "Their influence on contemporary religious thought and particularly on such theologians as Bultmann, Heidegger, and Tillich is brilliantly outlined."

Sperry, Willard L. RELIGION IN AMERICA. *Peter Smith* $5.25

Thielicke, Helmut. BETWEEN HEAVEN AND EARTH. 1965. *Greenwood* 1975 $12.00. By the theologian and rector of Hamburg University.

Tsanoff, Radoslav A. AUTOBIOGRAPHIES OF TEN RELIGIOUS LEADERS: Alternatives in
Christian Experience. *Trinity Univ. Press* 1968 $7.00

"A brilliant book, using the lives of people to tell of their own experiences"—(*Choice*).

Walhout, Donald. INTERPRETING RELIGION. *Prentice-Hall* 1963 $11.50. Controversial prob-
lems in current religious thought discussed by the author and by the outstanding
theologians and philosophers, including Buber, Gilson, Niebuhr, and Barth.

White, Andrew D. HISTORY OF THE WARFARE OF SCIENCE WITH THEOLOGY IN CHRISTEN-
DOM. 1896. *Dover* 2 vols. pap. each $3.50; *Macmillan* (Free Press) 1965 pap. $2.95;
Peter Smith 2 vols. set $12.00

Wieman, Henry Nelson. THE SOURCE OF HUMAN GOOD. *Southern Illinois Univ. Press* 1964
pap. $2.95

Modern Protestantism

The liberalization of Protestant theology continues, but at a much slower pace than in the
1960's. Conservatives and moderates have been able to slow theological changes in several
denominations and in the Lutheran Church Missouri Synod the conservatives have
succeeded in returning theology to a more fundamentalist position. The ecumenical
movement is slowly slackening as most denominations are more and more preoccupied
with their internal problems.

Ahlstrom, Sydney E., Ed. THEOLOGY IN AMERICA: The Major Protestant Voices from
Puritanism to Neo-Orthodoxy. *Bobbs* Lib. Arts. 1967 pap. $5.50

"Selections from 13 American theologians make up this compendium. The editor offers them
in proof of his assertion, that, in spite of the activism that has characterized the church in America,
a substantial theological tradition has taken shape in our culture. . . . A useful source book for the
student of church history and of general development of the American mind"—(*Virginia Kirkus
Service*).

Bloesch, Donald G. THE EVANGELICAL RENAISSANCE. *Eerdmans* 1973 pap. $2.95

"Modern conservative evangelicals, says Bloesch, are participating in a religious revival that
surpasses old-time evangelical and Protestant churches in soundness of faith, vitality, and future
prospects. . . . [The author] is convinced that evangelical vitality requires . . . historical and
ecumenical sensitivity"—(*Choice*).

Brown, Robert McAfee. THE SPIRIT OF PROTESTANTISM. *Oxford* 1961 Galaxy Bks. 1965
pap. $2.95

Cleage, Albert B., Jr. BLACK CHRISTIAN NATIONALISM: New Directions for the Black
Church, Including Papers Presented to the First Black Christian Nationalist Convention. *Morrow* 1972 $8.95 pap. $3.45

"Even for those who might disagree violently with Cleage's often repetitive prose, this book
offers a wealth of insights into the struggle of blacks for the control of their lives"—(*LJ*).

THE BLACK MESSIAH. *Sheed & Ward* 1968 pap. $3.95

"Beginning with Scripture and closing with prayers, these 20 orations from Detroit's Shrine of
the Black Madonna are more angry, eloquent prophecies than sermons . . . The style, from
generations of black preachers, will remind readers of Martin Luther King; the content will not"—
(*LJ*). God to Mr. Cleage is black, and he speaks the language of Black Power, but he is being heard
and attended to by white churchmen who seek to understand the roots of militance.

Clebsch, William A. AMERICAN RELIGIOUS THOUGHT: A History. *Univ. of Chicago Press*
1973 $10.00 pap. $3.95

"This tough-minded, well-written, somewhat unorthodox book can excite the reader"—(*Choice*).

Cobb, John B., Jr. LIVING OPTIONS IN PROTESTANT THEOLOGY. *Westminster Press* 1962
$7.95

THE STRUCTURE OF CHRISTIAN EXISTENCE. *Westminster Press* 1967 $4.95

Cone, James H. BLACK THEOLOGY AND BLACK POWER. *Seabury Press* 1969 pap. $2.95

"Cone (Union Seminary) provides a theological grounding for Black Power and propounds a
sophisticated Black Theology. . . . This harsh little volume is suggestive, perceptive, provocative,
readable, and needed"—(*Choice*).

A Black Theology of Liberation. *Lippincott* 1970 $5.95 pap. $2.95

"Although it is addressed primarily to black Americans, this thoughtful analysis of the black religious experience in America should have a much wider appeal"—*(LJ)*.

Cowan, Wayne H., Ed. Witness to a Generation: Significant Writings from "Christianity and Crisis," 1941–1966. Pref. by Herbert Butterfield; introd. by the author *Bobbs* Liberal Arts 1966 $5.95 pap. $1.95

An "interestingly varied collection of articles and editorials . . . well-organized and well-edited [from] a superior journal of opinion"—(Robert Lekachman, in the *N.Y. Times*).

Davis, Lawrence B. Immigrants, Baptists, and the Protestant Mind in America. *Univ. of Illinois Press* 1973 $8.95

"This volume is a substantial contribution to knowledge, revising many commonly accepted interpretations and presenting a wealth of new information besides"—*(Choice)*.

Dickinson, Eleanor, and Barbara Benziger. Revival! *Harper* 1974 $7.95 pap. $4.95

"A coffee table book that combines the drawings of Dickinson with the text of Benziger . . . it is excellent social documentary as well as delightful art that sympathetically encapsulates the spirit of the revival meeting"—*(LJ)*.

Enroth, Ronald M., and others. The Jesus People: Old-Time Religion in the Age of Aquarius. *Eerdmans* new ed. 1972 pap. $2.95

"Surely the best book yet on the Jesus movement, though the concluding evaluation is of less value"—*(LJ)*.

Frazier, E. Franklin. The Negro Church in America. 1963. *Schocken* new ed. 1973 $7.50 pap. $2.95

"Frazier's book, first published in 1963, has been reprinted nine times to become a sort of classic not only in religious studies, but also in sociology with a historical perspective"—*(PW)*. (*See also C. Eric Lincoln, below.*)

Handy, Robert T. A Christian America: Protestant Hopes and Historical Realities. *Oxford* 1971 $7.95 1974 pap. $2.95

An "excellent and authoritative study"—*(LJ)*. "It will prove to be an important source for the study of the history of religion in America"—*(Choice)*.

Hordern, William E. A Layman's Guide to Protestant Theology. *Macmillan* 1955 rev. ed. 1968 pap. $1.95

"Clear insights, the brief pungent and accurate evaluative descriptions of different theological viewpoints in the total Christian spectrum from the extreme right to the extreme left make this book a valuable asset"—*(LJ)*.

Hudson, Winthrop S. The Great Tradition of the American Churches. 1953. *Peter Smith* 1970 $5.25

Jones, Charles Edwin. A Guide to the Study of the Holiness Movement. *Scarecrow Press* 1974 $27.50

"One of the most complex and little understood facets of American religious life is the 'holiness movement' that emerged primarily from Methodism in the late 19th century. In this massive bibliography of over 7,300 entries, Jones (Brown University Library) provides sketches of 150 distinct holiness groups, lists the associated literature, and attempts a classification scheme"—*(Choice)*.

Jones, William R. Is God a White Racist? A Preamble to Black Theology. *Doubleday* 1973 $7.95 Anchor Bks. pap. $3.50

"Jones (Yale Divinity School) provides what is clearly the most significant of the spate of recent works in black theology. . . . This clearly written, closely reasoned book is a major work of humanistic theological criticism"—*(Choice)*.

King, Martin Luther, Jr. *See his main entry in Chapter 8, the Social Sciences, this Volume.*

Kroner, Richard. Between Faith and Thought. 1966. *Greenwood* 1975 $12.00

An examination of the relationship between revelation and speculation and faith and reason by a Professor Emeritus of Philosophy at the University of Kiel, Germany, and Professor Emeritus of the Philosophy of Religion, Union Theological Seminary, New York. John E. Smith of Yale calls the work "an acute, relevant, and moving defense of the primacy of faith."

Lincoln, C. Eric. THE BLACK CHURCH SINCE FRAZIER. *Schocken* 1973 $10.00 pap. $2.95

"Lincoln's premise is that the new Black church of the 1960s and 1970s rose from the ashes of the Negro church, that it has been a vitally important voice of freedom and social change and that with it has come the new black theology"—*(PW)*.

Marty, Martin E. PROTESTANTISM. *Holt* (Rinehart) 1972 $8.95; *Doubleday* Image Bks. 1974 pap. $2.45

"While doing full justice to the diversities existing within the great families of Protestantism, Marty, winner of the 1972 National Book Award in philosophy and religion for his "Righteous Empire," demonstrates several patterns of orientation, which provide a discernable consistency to the Protestant phenomenon"—*(LJ)*.

RIGHTEOUS EMPIRE: The Protestant Experience in America. *Dial* 1970 $8.95 pap. $2.95

"This illuninating contribution to American history deserves a place in most libraries"—*(LJ)*.

Miller, William Robert. CONTEMPORARY AMERICAN PROTESTANT THOUGHT, 1900–1970. *Bobbs* 1973 $9.50 pap. $4.75

Moltmann, Jürgen. THE CRUCIFIED GOD: The Cross of Christ as the Foundation and Criticism of Christian Theology. *Harper* 1974 $10.00

"This is a serious work of theology, showing a powerful and first-rate mind at work. It breaks new ground in showing the relation of the cross to the transformation of the world"—*(LJ)*.

Niebuhr, H. Richard. *See his main entry, this Chapter.*

Pittenger, W. Norman. RECONCEPTIONS IN CHRISTIAN THINKING, 1817–1967. *Allenson* 1968 $4.50

"The author informatively traces scientific-psychosocial concepts of the God/man relationship, paying tribute to the contribution of such Anglican Church fathers as William Temple.... Worthwhile"—*(LJ)*.

Rauschenbusch, Walter. *See his main entry, this Chapter.*

Robinson, John A. T. *See his main entry, this Chapter.*

Smith, John E. EXPERIENCE AND GOD. *Oxford* 1968 $5.95 1974 pap. $2.95

"A persuasive defense of the convictions of religious faith. This book by a professional philosopher makes a timely contribution to the debate about God, and brings to the debate a logical rigor that has been lacking in too many of the popular theological presentations"—(John Macquarrie).

Von Rohr, John. PROFILE OF PROTESTANTISM: An Introduction to Its Faith and Life. *Dickenson Pubs.* 1969 pap. $6.95

"Only positive acclaim can be credited to Von Rohr, with his skills of analysis, his ability to summarize, and his superb knowledge of the Reformation period.... The material is substantial, the scope inclusive, and the style adequate although tinctured with generalizations and some special personal pleadings"—*(Choice)*.

Wilmore, Gayraud S. BLACK RELIGION AND BLACK RADICALISM. *Doubleday* 1972 $7.95 Anchor Bks. pap. $3.50

"The author, a professor of social ethics at Boston University, is splendidly equipped to write this superior account of the complex interrelationships of black religion and radicalism in America from the earliest slavery period to 1970"—*(Choice)*.

Protestant Denominations

Block, Marguerite Beck. THE NEW CHURCH IN THE NEW WORLD: A Study of Swedenborgianism in America. 1932. New introduction by Robert H. Kirven *Octagon* 1968 $13.50

"Reprint of a standard history . . . Kirven's introduction to the reprint reports on responses to the original publication and brings the work chronologically up to date"—*(Choice)*. (*See also Swedenborg's main entry, this Chapter.*)

Bodensieck, Julius, Ed. THE ENCYCLOPEDIA OF THE LUTHERAN CHURCH. Pref. by the editor; fwd. by Fredrik A. Schiotz *Augsburg* 3 vols. 1965 set $25.00

Contributions by scholars and specialists, arranged alphabetically, this reference "covers all the important names and places pertinent to Lutheranism, describes the work of the Church, and even interprets Lutheran doctrine"—(*LJ*). The editor is a professor at Wartburg Seminary, Dubuque, Iowa.

Brinton, Howard. FRIENDS FOR 300 YEARS. *Pendle Hill* 1952 pap. $2.50. On the Quakers, or Religious Society of Friends.

Dawley, Powel Mills. THE EPISCOPAL CHURCH AND ITS WORK. *Seabury Press* rev. ed. 1955 $3.50 pap. $1.95. A well-founded, easy-to-read introduction.

Durnbaugh, Donald F. THE BELIEVERS' CHURCH: The History and Character of Radical Protestantism. *Macmillan* 1968 $7.95 pap. $2.95

"Mr. Durnbaugh, associate professor of church history, Bethany Theological Seminary, Illinois, explains, protests, drops names, constructs a history of the heretic groups, and splits the atom. . . . Well written and shows merit as a study of the modern church in contrast to its antecedents"—(*LJ*).

Hoekema, Anthony A. THE FOUR MAJOR CULTS: Christian Science, Jehovah's Witnesses, Mormonism, Seventh-Day Adventism. *Eerdman's* 1963 $6.95

Professor Hoekema gives "an analysis of the doctrinal teachings. . . . [Although he is] outspoken in his negative attitude toward the four 'cults,' as he labels them, [he] has done a remarkable job of examining their respective publications"—(*LJ*).

Hostetler, John A. AMISH SOCIETY: Fulfillment and Stress in the Little Community. *Johns Hopkins Press* 1963 rev. ed. 1970 $12.00 pap. $2.95

John, DeWitt, and Erwin D. Canham. THE CHRISTIAN SCIENCE WAY OF LIFE and A CHRISTIAN SCIENTIST'S LIFE. 1962. *Christian Science Publ. Co.* 1971 pap. $1.95

This comprehensive discussion is an introduction to the organizational framework of the church, its board of lectureship, its publishing society, and other outstanding activities and information about the Christian Science Practitioner and the Christian Science method of healing, as well as the Church's attitude toward the medical profession. The book closes with a short, incisive autobiographical discussion by Erwin Canham, editor of the *Christian Science Monitor*.

Loetscher, Lefferts A. A BRIEF HISTORY OF THE PRESBYTERIANS. *Westminster Press* rev. ed. 1958 pap. $1.85

Mendelsohn, Jack. WHY I AM A UNITARIAN UNIVERSALIST. 1964. *Beacon* 1966 pap. $2.95. A prominent Unitarian minister defines his philosophy of life.

More, Paul E., and F. L. Cross. ANGLICANISM: The Thought and Practice of the Church of England. *Allenson* 1935 1957 $23.00

Mulder, William, and A. Russell Mortensen, Eds. AMONG THE MORMONS: Historic Accounts by Contemporary Observers. 1958. *Univ. of Nebraska Press* Bison Bks. 1973 pap. $4.95

Nelson, E. Clifford. LUTHERANISM IN NORTH AMERICA, 1914–1970. *Augsburg* 1972 $7.50

Norwood, Frederick A. THE STORY OF AMERICAN METHODISM: A History of the United Methodists and their Relations. *Abingdon* 1974 $17.95 pap.$9.95

"Norwood (Garrett Theological Seminary) traces the impact of Methodism on America (and vice versa) from the 18th century to 1974. . . . This is the best single-volume history of American Methodism now available"—(*Choice*).

O'Dea, Thomas F. THE MORMONS. *Univ. of Chicago Press* 1957 $12.50 Phoenix Bks. pap. $3.95

Schmid, Heinrich. THE DOCTRINAL THEOLOGY OF THE EVANGELICAL LUTHERAN CHURCH. Trans. from the German by Charles A. Hay and Henry E. Jacobs *Augsburg* 1961 $6.50. A reprint of the classic work as formulated by scholars of the 16th and 17th centuries.

Simcox, Carroll E. THE HISTORICAL ROAD OF ANGLICANISM. *Regnery* 1967 $6.25

Sykes, Norman. OLD PRIEST AND NEW PRESBYTER. *Cambridge* 1956 $16.50. The background of Presbyterianism.

Thompson, Ernest Trice. PRESBYTERIANS IN THE SOUTH. *John Knox Press* 3 vols. 1963–73 Vol. 1 1607–1861 (1963) Vol. 2 1861–1890 (1973) Vol. 3 1890–1972 (1973) each $15.00 set $39.95

"The authoritative text on a specific religious tradition, giving in addition a stimulating interpretation of its place in the larger context of American Christianity. Highly recommended"— (*Choice*).

Trueblood, D. Elton. THE PEOPLE CALLED QUAKERS. 1966. *Friends United Press* 1971 pap. $2.50

Dr. Trueblood describes the development of Quakerism, its beliefs, practices, and its original contributions to religious thought. . . . Recommended"—(*LJ*).

Woodcock, George, and Ivan Avakumovic. THE DOUKHOBORS. *Oxford* 1968 $8.95

The authors, professors at British Columbia, "have produced a volume that will become a standard reference"—(*Choice*).

Modern Catholicism

These are troubled times for the Catholic Church all over the world. Its enormous membership continues to be divided by disputes over abortion, birth control, and divorce. Priests and nuns are leaving the active ministry in great numbers, while many parishes and parochial schools are seriously understaffed. In the Third World many bishops have begun to insist on the need for an indigenous and independent church administered by local clergy. Other churchmen have vigorously supported human liberation which has resulted in serious conflicts with authoritarian regimes in Latin America and Africa. The Catholic Church retains an immense vitality, however, and a vast fund of talent as the titles on this list show convincingly.

Abell, Aaron, I., Ed. AMERICAN CATHOLIC THOUGHT ON SOCIAL QUESTIONS. American Heritage Ser. *Bobbs* 1968 $8.50 pap. $5.25

"A superb anthology" (*LJ*) with introductory notes, bibliography and index.

Amato, Joseph. MOUNIER AND MARITAIN: A French Catholic Understanding of the Modern World. *Univ. of Alabama Press* 1975 $9.50

"Successful both as significant efforts at 20th-century self-understanding and also as attempts to teach French intellectuals to grasp their place in modern times, Maritain and Mounier respond to the contemporary problem of the alienation of man from his own personhood, other men, nature, and God"—(*LJ*).

Bea, Augustin Cardinal. THE UNITY OF CHRISTIANS. Ed. by Bernard Leeming. *Christian Classics* 1963 $5.95

"The book is probably the clearest statement of the Roman position that has yet appeared in English."

Berrigan, Daniel. LOVE, LOVE AT THE END: Parables, Prayers and Meditations. *Macmillan* 1968 1971 pap. $1.45

"Father Berrigan might be called the poet laureate of those who announce the failure of the institutional church. His commitment to life and to the spirit that expands without drugs, his unswerving pursuit of love and justice, are a bracing tonic. in *Love, Love at the End* short meditations, free verse, and startling parables pour out with velocity, verve, and a deep love for Creation. Berrigan knows life and can write of it with a mixture of humor and holiness. The church ought always to have such critics"—(David Poling, in *SR*).

NIGHT FLIGHT TO HANOI: Daniel Berrigan's War Diary. *Macmillan* 1968 $4.95

This book, which includes 11 poems and a "Letter from Three Jails," "records the author's reflections about his mission to secure the release of three American fliers, his impressions of North Vietnam under war conditions, and his conclusions about the nature and consequences of the use of American power in Asia"—(*PW*).

THEY CALL US DEAD MEN: Reflections on Life and Conscience. Introd. by William Stringfellow *Macmillan* 1966 1968 pap. $1.45

A "penetrating series of essays on various aspects of contemporary religion and civilization. . . . Father Berrigan sees an increasing growth in understanding and community awareness in which the actively religious must play a leading part. Highly recommended"—(*LJ*).

(With Robert Coles). THE GEOGRAPHY OF FAITH: Conversations between Daniel Berrigan, When Underground, and Robert Coles. *Beacon* 1971 $7.50 pap. $2.95

The discussions took place between Harvard psychiatrist Coles and anti-war Jesuit Berrigan while the latter was still a fugitive. "Highly recommended"—(*LJ*).

Berrigan, Philip. PRISON JOURNALS OF A PRIEST REVOLUTIONARY. *Holt* (Rinehart) 1970 $5.95

"Philip Berrigan is the elder of the two Berrigan brothers. This book is basically a record of his second imprisonment at Baltimore and at the Federal penitentiaries at Lewisburg and Allenwood, Pennsylvania for destroying government draft files. . . . Indispensable reading for an understanding of new trends within the American Roman Catholic Church"—(*Choice*).

Brown, Raymond E. BIBLICAL REFLECTIONS ON CRISES FACING THE CHURCH. *Paulist-Newman* 1975 pap. $2.45

Cogley, John. CATHOLIC AMERICA. *Dial* 1973 $9.95; *Doubleday* Image Bks. 1974 pap. $1.75

"A layman's view of the history of Catholicism in the U.S. with an appraisal of its current status as an institution"—(*Choice*).

Corita, Sister. FOOTNOTES AND HEADLINES: A Play-Pray Book. Foreword by Daniel Berrigan, S.J. *Seabury Press* 1967 $6.00 pap. $3.45. Marshall McLuhan called this prayer book in "swinging" color "an x-ray of human thought and social institutions."

Cornell, Thomas C., and James H. Forest, Eds. A PENNY A COPY: Readings from the Catholic Worker. *Macmillan* 1968 $6.95

A selection of articles from the radical monthly founded in 1933, edited by Dorothy Day and still a penny a copy. The journal reflects the concern of this deeply religious anarchist-pacifist group for the outcasts of society, whom it feeds and shelters near New York's Bowery and in other "houses of hospitality" throughout the country. Many of its ideals are increasingly being taken up by a broader segment of Catholicism, though it has never had the wholehearted approval of the Church. "What is most remarkable about many of these articles is first, that they speak so directly to the needs of our own time and second, that they avoid the sentimentality which is, apparently, a constant temptation to small, radical groups. . . . I have neither faith nor hope that the ideals of the Catholic Worker will soon prevail in this world. It is their fate to be the leaven, the salt of the earth. But if we are not nourished with their impossible ideals we will die"—(James Finn, in the *New Republic*).

Curran, Charles E. CONTEMPORARY PROBLEMS IN MORAL THEOLOGY. *Fides Pubs.* 1970 pap. $1.95

The author, on the theology faculty at Catholic University of America, "focuses on the inadequacies of past theological approaches. . . . Useful insights into current thinking of a liberal Catholic writing in the field of moral theology"—(*Choice*).

D'Arcy, Martin C. DIALOGUE WITH MYSELF. Introd. by Ruth Nanda Anshen *Simon & Schuster* 1966 pap. $2.95

The English Jesuit "outlines, in beautiful prose, his solution to problems raised by . . . modern [theological] scholars"—(*LJ*).

Davis, Charles. TEMPTATIONS OF RELIGION. *Harper* 1974 $5.95

Mr. Davis, the leading Catholic theologian in Great Britain, left both the priesthood and the Church in 1967 and wrote "A Question of Conscience: Why I Left the Roman Catholic Church" (*Harper* 1967, o.p.). In this book "Davis continues his gentle debate with the Church through his form of the common current insistence that one can, and must, determine for oneself the parameters of religious obedience, rather than simply capitulate to traditional norms. . . . Deftly bringing together the personal sins with ecclesiastical issues, he also makes clear that the temptations can lure any religious view into non-religion"—(*Choice*).

Dewart, Leslie. THE FOUNDATIONS OF BELIEF. *Seabury Press* 1969 $9.50 pap. $4.95. Here he pursues the subject treated in the entry below and provides a detailed critique on what he sees as the insufficiencies of Thomism.

THE FUTURE OF BELIEF: Theism in a World Come of Age. *Seabury Press* 1966 pap. $2.45

Dr. Dewart, theologian at St. Michael's College of the University of Toronto, "undertakes in a 'tentative and exploratory' way . . . nothing less than a complete reformulation of the philosophic basis of Christianity. It is an important book if only for the fact that it goes straight to the only question that can rescue contemporary theology from its present confused state: How do you speak about God in a technological society? [Dewart] understands healthy religious faith as the ability to interpret both God and human experience in the same terms. The problem, he maintains, is that it is difficult for modern man to relate his '*ordinary* Christian religious experience and the *trivial* experiences of every day, like reading a newspaper' "—(Edward B. Fiske, in the *N.Y. Times*).

Fitzsimons, M. A., Ed. THE CATHOLIC CHURCH TODAY: Western Europe. *Univ. of Notre Dame Press* 1969 $10.00

"An analysis of post-Vatican II Catholicism in Holland, Germany, Austria, Switzerland, Italy, Portugal, Spain, France, Belgium, Ireland, Scotland, and England"—*(Choice)*.

Gleason, Philip, Ed. CONTEMPORARY CATHOLICISM IN THE UNITED STATES. *Univ. of Notre Dame Press* 1969 $10.00

"These penetrating essays deal with external relations and social context more than with doctrinal teachings. The book will be of value not only for Catholic thinkers but for all who have a concern for the place of religion in American life"—*(Choice)*.

Goergen, Donald. THE SEXUAL CELIBATE. *Seabury Press* 1975 $8.95

"In this thoughtful and illuminating book a Catholic professor of theology argues that the celibate life can be properly sexual, just as the married life can be properly chaste. The difference is that the celibate chooses to abstain from *genital* sexuality, which is particular, but not from *affective* sexuality, which is universalizing"—*(Choice)*.

Greeley, Andrew M. A FUTURE TO HOPE IN: Socio-Religious Speculations. *Doubleday Image Bks.* 1970 pap. $1.25

"Father Greeley of the University of Chicago here presents his analyses of some of the major problems facing the American Catholic Church today. . . . He makes excellent use of modern sociological and theological data and is a refreshing contrast to the prophets of doom and the naive liberals who are so vocal today"—*(LJ)*.

Hardon, John A. THE CATHOLIC CATECHISM. *Doubleday* 1975 $9.95 pap. $5.95

"This work will fill the place long ago vacated by the venerable Baltimore catechism as a definitive statement of the teachings of the Roman Catholic Church. Although called a catechism, it is not a simple question-and-answer arrangement but a scholarly study which explores every facet of Catholic belief in a clear, readable style"—*(LJ)*.

Häring, Bernard. THE CHRISTIAN EXISTENTIALIST: The Philosophy of Self-Fulfillment in Modern Society. *New York Univ. Press* 1968 $6.95; *Christian Classics* $4.50

This book is yet another collection, this time from Father Häring's Deems Lectures given at New York University in 1966 "on personalism . . . existentialism in Christian ethics . . . and socialism. . . . Well-written"—*(LJ)*.

SHALOM: Peace, the Sacrament of Reconciliation. *Farrar, Straus* 1968 $6.50; *Doubleday Image Bks.* pap. $1.95

Drawing on lectures and seminars he gave in the U.S., the eminent German theologian "attempts to solve present problems within the sacrament of Penance"—*(LJ)*.

John XXIII, Pope. *See his main entry, this Chapter*.

Küng, Hans. *See his main entry, this Chapter*.

McAvoy, Thomas T. A HISTORY OF THE CATHOLIC CHURCH IN THE UNITED STATES. *Univ. of Notre Dame Press* 1969 $14.00

"It is probably the finest recent one-volume treatment available which also achieves relative objectivity"—*(Choice)*.

McBrien, Richard P. THE REMAKING OF THE CHURCH: An Agenda for Reform. *Harper* 1973 $6.95

"The author is a well-established and highly respected younger theologian of the Roman Catholic Church, having come to prominence since Vatican Council II"—*(Choice)*. "All in all, the book is a clear and well-documented study"—*(LJ)*.

McKenzie, John L. THE ROMAN CATHOLIC CHURCH. *Holt* 1969 $6.95 pap. $4.95; *Doubleday* Image Bks. pap. $1.95

"Can the Church become an ecumenical Christian Church, 'truly Catholic in the etymological sense of the word?' " is the question asked and looked into by Father McKenzie. A Thomas More Book Club August 1969, selection.

McNamara, William. THE HUMAN ADVENTURE: Contemplation for Modern Man. *Doubleday* 1974 $5.95 Image Bks. 1976 pap. $1.75

"This is a lucid, simple, profound, and witty explanation of Christian mystical experience. It offers fresh examples and new language for Classic mystical insights, relating Christian contemplations to Oriental methods"—*(LJ)*.

Maritain, Raissa. RAISSA'S JOURNAL: Presented by Jacques Maritain. *Magi Bks.* 1975 $12.95
This book "is primarily a record of her inner, mystical, contemplative life of prayer"—*(LJ)*.

Milhaven, John G. TOWARD A NEW CATHOLIC MORALITY. *Doubleday* Image Bks. 1972 pap. $1.45
"This is one of the best introductions to Catholic ethics to be published recently"—*(Choice)*.

Murray, John Courtney. THE PROBLEM OF GOD: Yesterday and Today. *Yale Univ. Press* 1964 $7.50 pap. $1.95. From lectures given by the distinguished Jesuit at Yale in 1962.

A NEW CATECHISM: Catholic Faith for Adults. Trans. from the Dutch by Kevin Smyth *Seabury Press* 1967 $7.95

This is the first English edition of the controversial "Dutch Catechism," commissioned by the Dutch bishops and prepared by the Higher Catechetical Institute in Nijmegen. Given its original imprimatur by Bernardus Cardinal Alfrink, ranking prelate of the Dutch hierarchy, it is designed for adults who seek "to enunciate God's ineffable mystery in the language of our times." Conversational and informal in tone, it challenges traditional dogmas, such as those on birth control, the concept of hell and other matters. On Dec. 1, 1968, the *N.Y. Times* reported that "a commission of Cardinals, backed by Pope Paul VI, demanded today that the progressive Dutch catechism be modified to reflect strict Roman Catholic Orthodoxy on at least 10 disputed points. Publication of the declaration by six Cardinals named by the Pope to study the catechism brought a long-standing dispute into the open and threatened to widen the already significant breach between the Vatican and the ultraprogressive Dutch Church. The practical effect of the action is uncertain." An American imprimatur had been granted, then withdrawn. By the end of 1968 the Catechism had sold 250,000 copies in the U.S. It received the Thomas More Medal for Catholic publishing before the commission's decision. Early in 1969 Herder announced it had sold a quarter of a million copies in English and now stocked the Catechism in Dutch, French, German, Spanish and Portuguese.

Noonan, John T., Jr. POWER TO DISSOLVE: Lawyers and Marriages in the Courts of the Roman Curia. *Harvard Univ. Press* 1972 $15.00
"A masterpiece of historical, legal, and theological scholarship"—*(Choice)*.

Nouwen, Henri J. M. CREATIVE MINISTRY. *Doubleday* 1971 $5.95
"The author's style is engagingly unpretentious, and his text is sprinkled with anecdotal illustrations drawn from experience"—*(Kirkus Service)*.

THE WOUNDED HEALER: Ministry in Contemporary Society. *Doubleday* 1972 $5.95
"An interestingly effective work"—*(Kirkus Service)*.

(With Walter J. Gaffney). AGING: The Fulfillment of Life. *Doubleday* 1974 $6.95 1976 pap. $2.45
"A much needed book as well as a salutary one, and so unemphatic that it is all the more readily accepted"—*(Kirkus Reviews)*.

Novak, Michael. A TIME TO BUILD. *Macmillan* 1967 $8.95
"In one essay after another Novak presents the views of today's young liberal Catholics, who are badly frightening many of their bishops but who are in most cases moving the more enlightened members of the hierarchy to recognize them, if for no other reason than that the future seems to be cast in their language and style"   (Paul Cuneo, *SR*).

O'Brien, David J. AMERICAN CATHOLICS AND SOCIAL REFORM: The New Deal Years. *Oxford* 1968 $8.95. An examination of the American Catholic interpretation of the New Deal and Depression era.

Ong, Walter J. IN THE HUMAN GRAIN: Further Explorations of Contemporary Culture. *Macmillan* 1967 $5.95
A selection of essays, by a distinguished Catholic writer, on electronic communication as it relates to the Judeo-Christian heritage today. "A marvelous, perhaps major, testament of Christian optimism," by "one of the most learned and lucid interpreters of the totality of contemporary culture"—*(N.Y. Times)*.

Rahner, Karl. *See his main entry, this Chapter.*

Rhodes, Anthony R. E. THE VATICAN IN THE AGE OF THE DICTATORS, 1922–1945. *Holt* (Rinehart) 1974 $10.00

"On the basis of new sources of information derived mainly from documents recently published by the German Foreign Office, the British Foreign Office, and the Vatican, Rhodes dispels several misinformed criticisms of the Vatican's quest for power"—*(Choice)*.

Ryan, Mary Perkins, and John Julian Ryan. LOVE AND SEXUALITY: A Christian Approach. 1967. *Doubleday* Image Bks. 1969 pap. $1.45

Two Catholic laymen express a "positive and idealistic, but not unrealistic" approach to Christian love, marriage and procreation—*(LJ)*.

Schillebeeckx, Eduard. CELIBACY. Trans. by C. A. L. Jarrott. *Sheed & Ward* 1968 $3.95

"A brief, solid study of celibacy in the Latin-rite Catholic Church, treating both the history of the legislation and the scriptural doctrine behind it. The author believes that celibacy ought to be a voluntary part of the priesthood"—*(PW)*.

THE EUCHARIST. *Sheed & Ward* 1968 $3.95

"Truly creative theologizing which aids rather than confuses the Church in its continuous attempt to understand its God-given faith and life"—*(Living Church)*. The eminent Dutch theologian had an improtant part in formulating the controversial Dutch "New Catechism."

Schmitt, Karl M., Ed. THE ROMAN CATHOLIC CHURCH IN MODERN LATIN AMERICA. *Knopf* 1972 pap. $3.50

Shuster, George N. CATHOLIC EDUCATION IN A CHANGING WORLD. 1967. *Univ. of Notre Dame Press* pap. $2.95

The concern of this prominent educator is that Catholics should support a program of "religiously based humanistic education. Suggestions include a gradual cutback in Catholic primary schools, upgrading and expansion of Catholic high schools, concentration on a reduced number of liberal arts colleges, and a major effort to develop a few first-rate universities"—*(PW)*.

Teilhard de Chardin, Pierre. *See his main entry, this Chapter.*

Trent, James W., and Jenette Golds. CATHOLICS IN COLLEGE: Religious Commitment and the Intellectual Life. *Univ. of Chicago Press* 1967 $12.00

"The study concludes that Catholic college students whether in Catholic or secular colleges are more anti-intellectual and more authoritarian than non-Catholic students. . . . Nonflattering but hopeful view of Catholic intellectual life. . . . Trent is a competent research psychologist and a Catholic"—*(Choice)*.

Turner, Frederick C. CATHOLICISM AND POLITICAL DEVELOPMENT IN LATIN AMERICA. *Univ. of North Carolina Press* 1971 $9.25

"The book is an excellent and well-researched account of the changing role of the Church in Latin America"—*(LJ)*.

Ulanov, Barry, Ed. CONTEMPORARY CATHOLIC THOUGHT. *Sheed & Ward* 1962 $6.00

This very distinguished introduction to some of the best modern Catholic writing on theology may be too advanced for some general readers, but any anthology which includes such writers as Josef Jungmann, Gabriel Marcel, Jacques Maritain, Henri di Lubac and Pierre Teilhard de Chardin will be of great interest to clergymen, professors and students of theology, and informed laymen.

Van der Meer, Haye. WOMEN PRIESTS IN THE CATHOLIC CHURCH?: A Theological-Historical Investigation. *Temple Univ. Press* 1973 $12.50

The author's "thorough research represents a solid base and unique effort to explore and to open the way for the ordination of women"—*(Choice)*.

Van der Plas, Michel, and Henk Suer, Eds. THOSE DUTCH CATHOLICS. Trans. from the Dutch by Theo Westow *Macmillan* 1968 $4.95. An anthology of stimulating essays by six Dutch Catholics sympathetic to change within the Church.

Vanier, Jean. BE NOT AFRAID. *Paulist-Newman* 1975 pap. $2.95

VATICAN COUNCIL II. *Farrar, Straus* 1968 $10.00 pap. $2.65. A new one-volume revision of the four reports that have become the standard source books on the subject. It omits chronologies, lists of speakers and documentary appendixes.

The Church in State and Society

Bates, Miner Searle. RELIGIOUS LIBERTY: An Inquiry. 1945 *Da Capo* 1972 $17.50

"This volume remains basic"—*(Choice)*.

Bellah, Robert N. THE BROKEN COVENANT: American Civil Religion in Time of Trial. *Seabury Press* 1975 $7.95

"The topics covered include our unhappy experiment with slavery from which spring our current racial problems, our conflicting ideas of just what democracy is, and the long debate about the Protestant ethic. Bellah's method is to combine social criticism with humanistic scholarship in order to examine the views of a wide variety of American voices"—*(LJ)*.

Biéler, André. THE POLITICS OF HOPE. Trans. by D. Pardee *Eerdmans* 1974 pap. $3.95

"Though the book is now a little dated (the French original appeared in 1970), the result is a broadly based statement that should have wide appeal"—*(LJ)*.

Bock, Paul. IN SEARCH OF A RESPONSIBLE WORLD SOCIETY: The Social Teachings of the World Council of Churches. *Westminster Press* 1974 $10.00

"An amazingly compact, comprehensive, astute, and fair history of the development since 1920 of the social teachings of the World Council of Churches and its predecessors"—*(Choice)*. "A thoroughly researched, well-edited, tightly written, and significant study"—*(LJ)*.

Boles, Donald E. THE TWO SWORDS: Commentaries and Cases in Religion and Education. *Iowa State Univ. Press* 1967 $10.95

"Boles is professor of government at Iowa State University and this book is a companion volume to his earlier publication, *The Bible, Religion, and the Public Schools* (3rd ed. 1965 $6.95). . . . It is a valuable source"—*(Choice)*.

Callahan, Daniel, and others. THE ROLE OF THEOLOGY IN THE UNIVERSITY. *Macmillan* (Bruce Bks.) 1967 pap. $3.25

"A balanced reexamination of theology as an academic discipline. The publication is a hopeful sign"—*(Choice)*.

Dean, Thomas. POST-THEISTIC THINKING: The Marxist Christian Dialogue in Radical Perspective. *Temple Univ. Press* 1975 $12.95

"Dean (Temple) makes a significant contribution to radical theology and to the Marxist-Christian dialogue"—*(Choice)*.

Girardi, Giulio. MARXISM AND CHRISTIANITY. *Macmillan* 1968 $5.95. A comparison for Christians.

Griffin, John Howard. THE CHURCH AND THE BLACK MAN. *Pflaum-Standard* pap. $2.95. The author of "Black Like Me" examines the record of the Church in racial matters and interviews well-known writers on the subject. Included is a recording of some voices of Black America.

Holbrook, Clyde A. RELIGION: A Humanistic Field. *Prentice-Hall* 1963 $8.95

"This study of the place of religion in our educational systems is the most important one on the subject to have appeared in the last several years"—*(LJ)*.

Hook, Sidney. RELIGION IN A FREE SOCIETY. *Univ. of Nebraska Press* 1967 $5.95.

The well-known Professor of Philosophy at New York University discusses current social issues. Says Hook, "Theological dogma introduced to control public policy is a dagger thrust at the very heart of the political democratic process."

Hough, Joseph C., Jr. BLACK POWER AND WHITE PROTESTANTS: A Christian Response to the New Negro Pluralism. *Oxford* 1968 $6.95 pap. $2.95

The chairman of the faculty of religion at Claremont Graduate School discuss race relations in the U.S. and the ethics of pluralism. "This is an objective and sympathetic reading of the message of Black Power to the white churches. Mr. Hough refuses to see the Black Power movement purely as a disaster and feels that a Christian should be able to admit its necessity at the present time. The situation is however critical: violence cannot be avoided. If a way can be found to translate the Gospel into political action the crisis may be ultimately fruitful, not purely destructive. The book is a plea for Christian sanity and a refusal of despair. As such it should be read not only by Protestants but by all Americans whether Christians or not"—(Thomas Merton).

Konvitz, Milton R. RELIGIOUS LIBERTY AND CONSCIENCE. *Viking* 1968 $4.50 pap. $1.35

"Mr. Konvitz, professor of law and of industrial labor relations, Cornell, argues for the Constitutional recognition of conscience by adding the words 'or of conscience' to the first amendment. . . . He concludes that conscience is primary; religion, a derivative of conscience"—*(LJ)*. A brilliant book.

Meland, Bernard Eugene. THE SECULARIZATION OF MODERN CULTURES. 1966. *Seminary Co-op* $3.50. This book, based on the Barrows Lectures (1964–65) delivered at the University of Calcutta and the University of Poona, examines the rejection of historic guidelines of religious sanctions by modern day societies in India and the West.

Millea, Thomas. GHETTO FEVER. *Macmillan* (Bruce Bks.) 1968 $3.95. Stresses the role of the Church in Chicago's ghetto.

Miller, William Robert. NONVIOLENCE: A Christian Interpretation. *Schocken* 1966 pap. $2.95

A study by the former editor of the *United Church Herald* which documents cases such as those of the Moravian Indians, 1782, the South African movement of the 1950's, the U.S. struggle in the South, and others. "The documentation is scholarly; the book is well-organized and the topic is timely"—*(LJ)*.

Mindszenty, Jozsef, Cardinal. MEMOIRS. Trans. by Richard and Clara Winston *Macmillan* 1974 $10.00

"The bulk of Mindszenty's memoirs is concentrated on his imprisonment and continuing bitterness toward the Russians and Communism"—*(Booklist)*.

Morgan, Richard E. THE POLITICS OF RELIGIOUS CONFLICT: Church and State in America. *Pegasus* 1968 $5.95 pap. $1.95

"Morgan (Columbia) has written a very useful and stimulating book"—*(Choice)*.

Muggeridge, Malcolm. SOMETHING BEAUTIFUL FOR GOD: Mother Teresa of Calcutta. *Harper* 1971 $6.95; *Ballantine Bks.* 1973 pap. $2.00

"This slender volume is the outcome of the author's TV interview with Mother Teresa in London . . . it is a moving account of the nun's work"—*(LJ)*.

Muir, William K., Jr. PRAYER IN THE PUBLIC SCHOOLS: Law and Attitude Change. *Univ. of Chicago Press* 1968 $7.50

"A sociological study of the effect of a Supreme Court decision on public, and some private, school officials. . . . Mr. Muir concludes that law can be effective"—*(LJ)*.

Novak, Michael. A THEOLOGY FOR A RADICAL POLITICS. 1969 *Seabury Press* pap. $1.95. Written with sympathy for America's young revolutionaries by this Catholic author.

Ogletree, Thomas W., Ed. OPENINGS FOR MARXIST-CHRISTIAN DIALOGUE. *Abingdon* 1969 $3.75

"Recommended"—*(LJ)*.

Paupert, Jean-Marie. THE POLITICS OF THE GOSPEL. *Holt* (Rinehart) 1969 $4.95

"Written with profound commitment and convincing arguments, this book [by a French Catholic] seeks to describe the logic which today drives many Christians into political involvement"—*(Choice)*.

Pfeffer, Leo. CHURCH, STATE AND FREEDOM. 1953. *Beacon* rev. ed. 1967 $15.00

Dr. Pfeffer "examines here the implications and consequences of the First Amendment. . . . An extremely important reference book on a vital subject"—*(LJ)*.

Ruether, Rosemary Radford. THE RADICAL KINGDOM: The Western Experience of Messianic Hope. *Paulist-Newman* 1970 1975 pap. $3.95

"A book deeply concerned with understanding our present situation and the principles and alternatives involved in it. An analysis such as this is . . . indispensable for such an understanding"—*(Choice)*.

Simon, Gerhard. CHURCH, STATE, AND OPPOSITION IN THE U.S.S.R. *Univ. of California Press* 1974 $12.00

The author "shows how religion has survived under a fiercely atheistic regime, either as an officially tolerated and complaisant body or as a persecuted and hunted prey. The most interesting part of the book, supplemented by some fascinating documentary material, analyzes attempts made by believers of every religious persuasion . . . to enjoy the freedom of worship that is their legal right"—*(LJ)*.

Sleeper, C. Freeman. BLACK POWER AND CHRISTIAN RESPONSIBILITY: Some Biblical Foundations for Social Ethics. *Abingdon* 1969 $4.50

"An excellent example of clear, honest Biblical study and interpretation as related to urgent contemporary issues—in this instance, racial conflict and the emergence of the 'black power' concept"—(*PW*).

Smart, Ninian. SECULAR EDUCATION AND THE LOGIC OF RELIGION. *Humanities Press* 1969 $4.50

"Can religion be taught in a secular educational system in a manner acceptable to the Christian *and* the Humanist? Smart, professor of religious studies, University of Lancaster, and well known as a sensitive scholar of world religions, answers the question in an affirmative, provocative, and refreshing way"—(*Choice*).

Stackhouse, Max L. ETHICS AND THE URBAN ETHOS: An Essay in Social Theory and Theological Reconstruction. *Beacon* 1972 $7.95 1974 pap. $3.95

"Scholarly and lucidly written, this book is intended for readers seriously interested in our society and with some background in theology"—(*LJ*).

Stringfellow, William. DISSENTER IN A GREAT SOCIETY: A Christian View of America in Crisis. *Holt* 1967 $4.95; *Abingdon* pap. $1.45

Mr. Stringfellow "is concerned with the whole of what he regards as the *malaise* in American life: the continuing struggle between the races, the enshrinement of property and the desecration of people, the meaning of the rise of rightist groups, and the gospel of Goldwaterism. . . . What makes his work interesting is that he writes as a radical Christian. . . . His favorite targets, like those of Jesus, are religious hypocrites who wash their hands in innocence of the wounds inflicted on the world"—(Philip Scharper, in *Harper's*).

Stroup, Herbert. CHURCH AND STATE IN CONFRONTATION. *Allenson* 1967 $6.95

An official of the National Council of Churches surveys the history of his subject and urges a "cordial and cooperative relationship" between the two, with mutually protective safeguards. "Very helpful and informative"—(*LJ*).

Strout, Cushing. THE NEW HEAVENS AND NEW EARTH: Political Religion in America. *Harper* 1974 $12.50

"This extremely important study of the relationship between religion and American democracy is a gold mine of fresh insights and lively analysis"—(*Choice*). "An important book on a highly significant subject"—(*LJ*).

Wolf, Donald J. TOWARD CONSENSUS: Catholic-Protestant Interpretations of Church and State. *Peter Smith* 1968 $4.50

"A scholarly treatment. . . . Father Wolf's . . . position . . . is well taken and shows a remarkable lack of bias"—(*LJ*).

Radical Theology

Altizer, Thomas J. J. THE GOSPEL OF CHRISTIAN ATHEISM. *Westminster Press* pap. $1.75

"A clear and succinct statement of Altizer's revisionist position. He believes that 'we are now entering a period in which Christianity must confront the most radical challenge that it has faced since the time of the beginning' "—(*LJ*).

THE NEW APOCALYPSE. *Michigan State Univ. Press* 1967 $8.50

(With William Hamilton). RADICAL THEOLOGY AND THE DEATH OF GOD. *Bobbs* 1966 $5.00

The authors are leading exponents of the "Death of God" theology. Their essays are "often brilliant and deep, [and] bristle with linguistic, logical, and theological difficulties. . . . The articles have many good insights, but they are not too clear on the details of God's so-called death, and they don't really explain how Christian atheism is possible"—(*LJ*).

Berton, Pierre. THE COMFORTABLE PEW. *Lippincott* 1965 $3.50 pap. $1.95. The important and quite devastating critique which resulted when an agnostic was asked to write the Anglican Church of Canada's Lenten book for 1965.

Bloch, Ernst. ATHEISM IN CHRISTIANITY: The Religion of the Exodus and the Kingdom. *Seabury Press* 1972 $12.50

The reader "will definitely be challenged, provoked, and infuriated by this strange and complex book. . . . The style is highly demanding but well worth the effort needed"—(*Choice*).

Bonhoeffer, Dietrich. *See his main entry, this Chapter.*

Boyd, Malcolm. *See his main entry, this Chapter.*

Callahan, Daniel. ABORTION: Law, Choice, and Morality. *Macmillan* 1970 $14.95 pap. $4.95

Cooper, John Charles. THE ROOTS OF THE RADICAL THEOLOGY. *Westminster Press* 1967 $4.95

"Professor Cooper, of the philosophy department at Newberry College, South Carolina, has ably attempted 'to *understand* the genetic development of this new trend in Christian thought in a positive way [and] to lay bare some of the reasons why radical theology has arisen in our time.'... Highly recommended"—*(LJ)*.

Cousins, Ewert H., Ed. HOPE AND THE FUTURE OF MAN. *Fortress* new ed. 1972 pap. $3.95

"This provocative volume ... is an excellent introduction to contemporary theology and its potential resources for relating the gospel of hope to despairing man"—*(Choice)*.

Cox, Harvey. *See his main entry, this Chapter.*

Daly, Mary. BEYOND GOD THE FATHER: Toward a Philosophy of Women's Liberation. *Beacon* 1973 $8.95 pap. $3.95

"An excellent book"—*(Choice)*.

Deloria, Vine, Jr. GOD IS RED. *Dell* 1975 pap. $2.95

"His most mature and perceptive work to date"—*(Choice)*.

Durandeaux, Jacques. LIVING QUESTIONS TO DEAD GODS. Pref. by Gabriel Vahanian *Sheed & Ward* 1968 $3.95

"An intense intellectual and spiritual examination of the possibility of faith in God under contemporary conditions"—*(PW)*.

Gearhart, Sally Miller, and William R. Johnson. LOVING WOMEN/LOVING MEN: Gay Liberation and the Church. *Glide Urban Center Pubns.* 1974 pap. $6.95

Gish, Arthur G. THE NEW LEFT AND CHRISTIAN RADICALISM. *Eerdmans* 1970 pap. $2.45

"This is a brave, thought-provoking book about what is called 'The New Left', which Gish heralds as a third alternative to acquiescence to injustice on one side and violent revolution on the other"—*(Choice)*.

Hamilton, Kenneth. TO TURN FROM IDOLS. *Eerdmans* 1973 pap. $3.95

An argument "for a theology capable of relating the living God to relevance, change, and liberation"—*(Choice)*.

Heyer, Robert J., Ed. WOMEN AND ORDERS. *Paulist-Newman* 1974 pap. $1.45

"A lively compendium of the major arguments for the ordination of women" by Roman Catholics and Episcopalians—*(Choice)*.

Holmes, William A. TOMORROW'S CHURCH—A COSMOPOLITAN COMMUNITY: A Radical Experiment in Church Renewal. *Abingdon* 1968 $3.75

An examination of the Northhaven Methodist congregation in Dallas which is experimenting in church renewal. "A good blueprint [for] the hope for renewal in the church. . . . The author has the advantage of speaking from experience born of experiment"—(David Poling, in *SR*).

Howard, Thomas. CHRIST THE TIGER: A Postscript to Dogma. *Lippincott* 1967 $4.50 pap. $2.45

This is written "out of a background in the conservative evangelical end of the Protestant spectrum; [Mr. Howard] has known the spiritual security and thus sterility which afflicts so many who make their home there. He has also shown how he can take the raw material of their vision and at once transcend and transform it"—(Martin E. Marty).

Lascaris, Andrew. THE THEOLOGY OF GOD. *Fides Pubs.* 1973 pap. $1.25

"A new apologetics with an energy and freshness commensurate with the depth of real convictions and the solid historical seriousness of Catholic scholarship. The effect is ecumenical indeed"—*(Choice)*.

McLoughlin, William G., and Robert Bellah, Eds. RELIGION IN AMERICA. *Beacon* 1968 pap. $3.45. Essays on 'civil religion' in America by Harvey Cox, Martin E. Marty, Harold Sutherland, Daniel Callahan and others.

Marty, Martin E., and Dean G. Peerman. THE NEW THEOLOGY. *Macmillan* (orig.) Nos. 1–10 pap. each $1.95. An annual paperback.

Meeks, M. Douglas. ORIGINS OF THE THEOLOGY OF HOPE. *Fortress* 1974 $8.50

Miller, William Robert. GOODBYE, JEHOVAH: A Survey of the New Directions in Christianity. 1969. *Avon Bks.* pap. $1.45. A valuable assessment, consisting of essays on "The Comfortable Pew," "The Secular City," "Situation Ethics," Christian Atheism, Malcolm Boyd, Bishop Robinson and the like. By an expert in the field. Bibliography.

(Ed.) THE NEW CHRISTIANITY. *Dell* Delta Bks. 1968 pap. $2.45

An anthology of selections, in chronological arrangement, from William Blake on, of the thinkers who were at the roots of the present ferment. With Mr. Miller's "skillful introductions and careful editing, [this] is an excellent introduction to one stream of contemporary Christian thought"—(*LJ*). "An excellent anthology—the best currently available [on the subject]"—(*SR*).

Moltmann, Jürgen. RELIGION, REVOLUTION, AND THE FUTURE. *Scribner* 1969 $7.95. Lectures and essays on the "Theology of Hope."

THE THEOLOGY OF HOPE. *Harper* 1967 $10.00

Dr. Moltmann, a well-known German theologian of Tübingen University, who was visiting professor at Duke University and lecturer at Union Theological Seminary in 1968, "holds that God is to be regarded not as a supreme and static being but as the One who is coming to man. God's most important characteristic in this theory is not that He acted in the past, but that He has promised to act in the future. For the German theologian, the primary religious experience for the individual is not faith or love but hope. The implication of this focus on the future, however, is not withdrawal from the world in the hope that a better world will somehow evolve, but radical and revolutionary involvement in order to participate in its coming"—(Edward B. Fiske, in the *N.Y. Times*). This quotation is from the *Times'* front-page story of March 1968, indicating that emphasis on the "Death of God" was now, through the writings of Dr. Moltmann and others, giving way to his concept of "Hope."

Muggeridge, Malcolm. JESUS THE MAN WHO LIVES. *Harper* 1975 $17.95

"This book is an able antidote to the dismissal of God of some recent theology, and is a desperately needed oasis in the vast desert of avant-garde ethical pronouncements"—(*Choice*). By the well-known British journalist.

Ogletree, Thomas W. THE DEATH OF GOD CONTROVERSY. *Abingdon* 1966 pap. $1.45

Dr. Ogletree examines the writings of the American theologians Van Buren, Altizer and Hamilton, "giving the necessary background for and explanations of radical theology.... Although Dr. Ogletree neither agrees nor refutes the 'God is dead' theology, the book makes an important contribution to this debate"—(*LJ*). Bibliography.

Paoli, Arturo. FREEDOM TO BE FREE. *Orbis* 1973 pap. $4.95

"A timely, interesting, and unusual book on the theology of liberation, revolution, and peacemaking, as reflected in the thought of an activist. Paoli is a member of the Congregation of the Little Brothers at Fortin Olmos in Argentina"—(*Choice*).

Peerman, Dean, Ed. FRONTLINE THEOLOGY. Introd. by Martin E. Marty *John Knox Press* 1967 $4.50

"A collection of autobiographical essays in which 18 theologians ... address themselves to the subject of 'How I am Making Up My Mind.' The articles originally appeared in 'The Christian Century.' ... The recurring concern of 'Frontline Theology,' of course, is how to deal with 'the secular,' and in a helpful introductory essay Martin E. Marty puts the issue in perspective"—(*N.Y. Times*).

Petulla, Joseph M. CHRISTIAN POLITICAL THEOLOGY: A Marxian Guide. *Orbis* 1972 pap. $4.95

"A breath of fresh air in theology"—(*Choice*).

Richardson, Herbert W. TOWARD AN AMERICAN THEOLOGY. 1967. *E. Mellen* 1974 $6.95

"Discussing the relationships of society, technology, and faith, and philosophical aspects of theological enquiry, Professor Richardson, of Harvard's Divinity School, brings a penetrating, synthetic, and analytic mind to bear upon a variety of concerns"—(*LJ*).

Robinson, John. A. T. HONEST TO GOD. *Westminster Press* 1963 (orig.) pap. $1.65. The book by the Anglican Bishop that startled England in 1963 and prepared the way for the many current works of Protestant self-criticism and radical theology.

THE HUMAN FACE OF GOD. *Westminster Press* 1973 $7.95

"Ten years after *Honest to God*, Bishop Robinson has given to the English-speaking world what may well prove to be the most relevant volume of the 20th century on the nature of God"—(*Choice*).

See also his main entry, this Chapter.

Ryan, Michael D., Comp. THE CONTEMPORARY EXPLOSION OF THEOLOGY: Ecumenical Studies in Theology. *Scarecrow Press* 1975 $7.50

"Highly recommended"—(*Choice*).

Schilling, S. Paul. GOD INCOGNITO. *Abingdon* 1974 $5.95

"Schilling is widely read, organizes his material beautifully, and writes lucidly"—(*Choice*).

Schoonenberg, Piet. COVENANT AND CREATION. *Univ. of Notre Dame Press* 1969 $5.95

"Schoonenberg, one of the contributors to the famous Dutch Catechism, offers here an incisive commentary on an important contemporary theme"—(*Choice*).

Smart, Ninian. THE PHENOMENON OF RELIGION. *Seabury Press* 1973 $6.95

"This book provides a needed antidote to the postwar secularized movements that have monopolized much contemporary thinking toward religion"—(*Choice*).

Thielicke, Helmut. HOW TO BELIEVE AGAIN. *Fortress* 1972 pap. $3.95

"These sermons by one of the foremost living German theologians are a powerful and moving presentation of Jesus as the word of God who calls men to faith in him"—(*Choice*).

Vahanian, Gabriel. THE DEATH OF GOD. *Braziller* 1961 $6.95 pap. $2.95. The title caught on—but Dr. Vahanian was later led to disavow the more extreme interpreters of his phrase in "No Other God" (*see entry below*).

NO OTHER GOD. *Braziller* 1964 $5.95 pap. $2.50

WAIT WITHOUT IDOLS. *Braziller* 1964 $6.95 pap. $2.95

Dr. Vahanian "takes as his thesis the belief that Western literature from Saint Augustine to the present has been Christian literature (with a small 'c'). . . . Vahanian writes extremely well and his book will prove rewarding reading for anyone concerned with the life of the spirit"—(*LJ*).

Van Buren, Paul. THEOLOGICAL EXPLORATIONS. *Macmillan* 1968 $4.95

The professor of religion at Temple University "explores the nature of theology and its role in the plurality and relativism of our contemporary culture"—(*PW*).

Watts, Alan. BEYOND THEOLOGY: The Art of Godmanship. *Random* Vintage Bks. pap. $1.95

Mr. Watts "recognizes that Christianity has many objectionable facets in its uncompromising, imperious and invincibly self-righteous attitudes and its emphasis on everlasting damnation"—(*LJ*). "This witty little book is a large theological event; an Olympian laugh that will set 'kings to cutting capers and priests to picking flowers' "—(Joseph Campbell). The prolific author is a scholarly authority on Zen Buddhism and an Episcopal clergyman expert at interpreting Eastern and Christian philosophies, whose "The Book" (*see Section on Buddhism*) has been a paperback best seller to young people.

Williams, Daniel Day. THE SPIRIT AND THE FORMS OF LOVE. *Harper* 1968 $7.00

"In a day of pop theology, methodological uncertainty, and religious experimentation, this book is a rare piece of convincing theological scholarship. . . . It is *the* authority in the field and will remain such for years to come"—(*Choice*).

Wills, Gary. BARE RUINED CHOIRS: Doubt, Prophecy, and Radical Religion. *Doubleday* 1972 $7.95

Woelfel, James W. BORDERLAND CHRISTIANITY: Critical Reason and the Christian Vision of Love. *Abingdon* 1973 $5.75

"A challenging and scholarly collection of essays"—(*Choice*).

Personal and Social Ethics

Barbour, Ian G., Ed. EARTH MIGHT BE FAIR: Reflections on Ethics, Religion, and Ecology. *Prentice-Hall* 1972 pap. $3.95

"A serious effort to articulate an 'ecological theology' and an 'ecological ethic' "—(*Choice*).

Ellul, Jacques. To WILL AND TO DO: An Ethical Research for Christians. *United Church* (Pilgrim) 1969 $10.00

> "An excellent book for anyone whose concern is for the preservation of the transcendental God in the contemporary discussion of ethics"—(*Choice*).

Fletcher, Joseph Francis. MORAL RESPONSIBILITY: Situation Ethics at Work. *Westminster Press* 1967 pap. $2.85

> Mr. Fletcher develops his contention that what is "Right" depends on the specific situation. "A most stimulating, controversial, and opinion-shaking book to ponder and discuss"—(*PW*).

SITUATION ETHICS: The New Morality. *Westminster Press* 1966 $4.50 pap. $2.25

> A best-selling discussion of morality which seeks a middle way between legalism and license. "The situationist." says Mr. Fletcher, "follows a moral law or violates it according to love's need." And: "Everything else without exception, all laws and rules and principles and ideals and norms, are only *contingent*, only valid *if they happen* to serve love in any situation. . . . It is the strategy of love."

Macquarrie, John, Ed. DICTIONARY OF CHRISTIAN ETHICS. *Westminster Press* 1967 $10.00

> "This unique reference book, compiled by a foremost theologian, professor of systematic theology at Union Theological Seminary, brings together the significant thinking currently being done on Christian ethics. Eighty Christian and Jewish scholars have contributed articles dealing with basic ethical concepts, biblical and theological ethics and substantial ethical problems. The articles are short; the major ones have bibliographies; and all are signed. There are good cross references"—(*LJ*).

Outka, Gene. AGAPE: An Ethical Analysis. *Yale Univ. Press* 1972 $15.00

> "Outka, an assistant professor of religion at Princeton University, reviews the Christian authors (both Roman Catholic and Protestant) of the past 40 years who have treated agape, or love, as referred to in the two-fold biblical command of love of God and neighbor. . . . A clear and perceptive analysis"—(*Choice*).

Robinson, John A. T. *See his main entry, this Chapter.*

Sellers, James. THEOLOGICAL ETHICS. *Macmillan* 1966 $5.95 pap. $2.45

> The ethics of the professor of theology at Vanderbilt University are based on the Judeo-Christian heritage, emphasizing human activity. "Very well organized, richly annotated and written in a clear, simple style which belies its erudition"—(*LJ*).

Spurrier, William A. NATURAL LAW AND THE ETHICS OF LOVE: A New Synthesis. *Westminster Press* 1974 $5.95

Wood, Frederic C., Jr. SEX AND THE NEW MORALITY. *Association Press* 1968 pap. $2.25

> The author, as chaplain at Goucher College, achieved newspaper headlines when he candidly explained to undergraduates the "new" sexual morality. In this book he "analyzes and gives guidelines for applying the ethical attitude or 'situation ethics' to troubled sex questions of today"—(*PW*).

Ecumenism

Brown, Robert McAfee. FRONTIERS FOR THE CHURCH TODAY. *Oxford* 1973 $5.95

> "A rather unusual but very timely book . . . can be read with confidence and comfort. Recommended to all scholars and students of ecumenism and to everybody who is interested in updating his church"—(*Choice*).

Cavert, Samuel McCrea. THE AMERICAN CHURCHES IN THE ECUMENICAL MOVEMENT, 1900–1968. *Association Press* 1968 $9.95

> This is the first of two projected volumes sponsored by the Union Theological Seminary and "bound to become a standard work"—(*LJ*). The second volume will be a reference guide for specific areas of ecumenism.

Congar, Yves, O.P. ECUMENISM AND THE FUTURE OF THE CHURCH. *Christian Class.* 1967 $4.95. Historical study of the conflicts among Christians with an essay on the future prospects for ecumenism.

Goodall, Norman. ECUMENICAL PROGRESS: A Decade of Change in the Ecumenical Movement, 1961–71. *Oxford* 1972 $10.25

> "A definitive work which deals with the major developments of the World Council of Churches during the turbulent decade of 1961–71"—(*Choice*).

Küng, Hans. *See his main entry, this Chapter.*

Neill, Stephen. THE CHURCH AND CHRISTIAN UNION: The Bampton Lectures for 1964. *Oxford* 1968 $12.00

"Neill rethinks his own ecumenical position in the light of 40 years' experience and attempts to estimate the differences between the theological climate of the 1920's and that of our own era. . . . Neill makes it clear that the path of Christian unity is far more thorny and difficult than originally supposed"—(*Choice*).

Oosthuizen, G. C. THEOLOGICAL BATTLEGROUND IN ASIA AND AFRICA: The Issues Facing the Churches and the Efforts to Overcome Western Divisions. *Humanities Press* 1972 $27.50

"Warmly recommended for any scholar or general reader interested in how much Asia and Africa have contributed to ecumenical awareness"—(*Choice*).

Rouse, Ruth, and Stephen C. Neill, Eds. A HISTORY OF THE ECUMENICAL MOVEMENT, 1517–1948. *Westminster Press* 2nd ed. 1967 $12.50. A reference work which includes biographies and bibliographies.

Vajta, Vilmos, Ed. THE GOSPEL AND THE AMBIGUITY OF THE CHURCH. *Fortress* 1974 $8.95

"Seven leading Lutheran theologians (East and West Europeans and Americans) associated with the Institute for Ecumenical Research at Strasbourg, France, contribute a chapter each to this volume. . . . A substantial contribution to ecumenical discussion"—(*Choice*).

THE GOSPEL AND UNITY. *Augsburg* 1971 $5.95

"The book says something new and important. . . . The six essays . . . are all written from a Lutheran confessional perspective, and precisely because they take the theology of their own tradition seriously they raise the level of ecumenical dialogue to a level which might make it relevant again"—(*Choice*).

Visser't Hooft, Willem A. MEMOIRS. *Westminster Press* 1973 $15.00

"The author was at the center of the development of the World Council of Churches from the mid-twenties through the World War II period of a Provisional Committee and held office as General Secretary from the inception of the Council in 1948 until his retirement in 1966. He is the leading authority on the Council"—(*Choice*).

RELIGIOUS LEADERS, REFORMERS AND THINKERS

MOSES. c. 1300 B.C.

"Although Judaism is the religion of a people who trace their origins back to Abraham (1750 B.C.), its real beginnings are linked with Moses, the 'Lawgiver' "—(David Bradley, in "A Guide to the World's Religions"). Born of Israelite parents dwelling in Egypt, Moses was adopted by a daughter of Pharaoh and raised in a luxury unavailable to his own kinsmen at that time. (In earlier years, the Israelites had filled favored positions of great influence. The mad king, Rameses II, however, feared their power, and, needing large forces of labor to execute his fantastic building program, enslaved them.) The story of Moses' murder of an Egyptian, his flight, his encounter with Yahweh and his leading of his people out of Egypt is told in the Old Testament books of Exodus, Leviticus, Numbers and Deuteronomy. His great contribution to the Hebrew religion was in mediating the Covenant that Yahweh desired to make with his people, the terms of which were set forth in the Ten Commandments.

In the 19th century, scholars began to doubt the existence of Moses; he was disposed of by one witty critic as "the greatest man who never lived." By the end of the 19th century, very few scholars still maintained the traditional beliefs regarding the authorship of the biblical books. "According to the dominant school of the Higher Criticism, the Pentateuch was the result of an elaborate and complex amalgam of at least five distinct literary sources, which were written over a period of six centuries. All these documents were substantially later than Moses. . . . The past few decades have undermined the central position of this Documentary Theory in biblical studies. The rich archeological discoveries in the Middle East since World War I, which have brought untold artifacts and documents to light, have not 'proved' the Bible to be 'true,' but they have been highly significant nevertheless"—(*N.Y. Times*). "Moses and the Original Torah" by Abba Hillel Silver is now o.p. Two fictional biographies of Moses are "The Tables of the Law" by Thomas Mann (*Knopf* 1945 $4.50) and "Moses" by Sholem Asch (1951, o.p.).

THE TORAH. The Five Books of Moses. *Jewish Publication Society* 1962 $6.00 lea. $12.00.
See comment in Section on Judaism, this Chapter.

Books about Moses

In the Steps of Moses the Lawgiver. By Louis Golding. 1937. *Folcroft* $15.00

Moses and Monotheism. By Sigmund Freud. *Random* Vintage Bks. 1955 pap. $1.95

Moses: The Revelation and the Covenant. By Martin Buber. *Harper* Torchbks. 1958 pap. $2.45

Moses in the Fourth Gospel. By Francis T. Glasson. *Allenson* 1963 $5.35 pap. $2.85

This Man Moses. By Israel H. Weisfeld. *Bloch Pub. Co.* $7.50

Moses and Joshua. By Henri B. Gaubert. *Hastings House* 1968 $5.95

Moses: Where It All Began. By Moshe Pearlman. *Abelard-Schuman* 1974 $8.95

ZOROASTER (ZARATHUSTRA). fl. 6th century B.C.

The great prophet Zoroaster is thought to have been born in Media, Persia, the son of a wealthy Aryan landowner. He left his parents and wife when he was 20 to wander in search of wisdom. After years of meditation, at the critical age of 30 he received a revelation: the archangel Vohu Manah led him into the dazzling presence of the Supreme Being, Ahura Mazda (the god of light from whom comes the name "Mazda lamp"). Ahura Mazda called Zoroaster to be his prophet and instructed him in the doctrines and duties of religion. Zoroaster's early preaching brought little success. Later, however, he converted an Aryan prince, Vishtaspa, through his remarkable cure of the prince's beloved black horse, and the entire court followed in embracing the new religion.

Zoroaster's teachings, which differed in many respects from later Zoroastrianism, or Mithraism, are thought to be contained in that portion of the sacred book, the "Avesta," called the "Gathas." He proclaimed a strong ethical monotheism and squarely opposed the popular polytheism. (This widespread nature religion of Aryan origin also formed the background of Vedic Hinduism.) Frederic Nietzsche's (*q.v.*) "Thus Spake Zarathustra" bears little or no relationship to the life and teachings of Zoroaster.

AVESTA: The Religious Books of the Parsees. Ed. by Arthur H. Bleeck *Krishna Press* $34.95

Books about Zoroaster

The Life of Zoroaster in the Words of His Own Hymns, the Gathas. Trans. by Kenneth S. Guthrie. 1914. *AMS Press* $9.50

Zoroaster: Prophet of Ancient Iran. By Abraham V. Jackson. 1928. *AMS Press* $17.50

Ethical Religion of Zoroaster. By Miles M. Dawson. 1931. *AMS Press* 1969 $9.50

Zoroaster and His World. By Ernst Herzfeld. 1947. *Octagon* 2 vols. 1974 $37.50

The Western Response to Zoroaster. By Jacques Duchesne-Guillemin. 1958. *Greenwood* 1973 $7.75

For books on Zoroastrianism, see Section on Zoroastrianism, this Chapter.

LAO-TZU (also Lao-tse or Lao-tsze; orig. Li Erh). c. 604–531 B.C.

"Legend ascribes the beginning of the Taoist movement to a shadowy figure called Lao-Tzu," writes David G. Bradley in "A Guide to the World's Religions." Very little is known of his life: his very existence is a matter of debate among scholars. The dates assigned to him are unconfirmed, though there is a strong Confucian tradition that the young Confucius met the Old Master at least once. According to legend, Lao-Tzu was a public official and sage who came to question the vanity of all human institutions and efforts. He is said to have renounced the world of deluded, corrupt men, and to have set forth for the West in a cart drawn by two black oxen. At the "Western Gate," the gatekeeper prevailed upon him to set down his philosophy of life. Lao-Tzu obliged, wrote down the Tao Têh Ching, and went upon his way, never to be heard from again.

THE LIGHT OF CHINA: Selections. *Krishna Press* $29.95

THE WISDOM OF LAOTSE. Trans. by Lin Yu-t'ang *Random* (Modern Lib.) 1948 $2.95

TAO TE CHING: The Book of the Way and Its Virtue. (With title "The Way of Life: Tao Te Ching") trans. by R. B. Blakney *New Am. Lib.* Mentor Bks. 1955 pap. $1.25

TAO TE CHING. Trans. by D. C. Lau *Knopf* 1972 $7.95; *Penguin* 1964 pap. $.95

THE WAY OF LAO TZU. Trans. by Wing-t'sit Chan *Bobbs* Lib. Arts. 1963 $6.50 pap. $1.95

THE WAY OF LIFE ACCORDING TO LAOTZE. By Witter Bynner. 1944. *Putnam* 1962 Capricorn Bks. pap. $.95. The poet's version of the reflections of Lao-Tzu.

THE CANON OF REASON AND VIRTUE (Tao Teh King). Ed. by Paul Carus *Open Court* bilingual ed., Chinese-English rev. ed. $5.00 1973 pap. $1.95; (with title "Tao Teh King: Nature and Intelligence") ed. by Archie J. Bahm *Ungar* 1958 pap. $1.95

TREATISE ON RESPONSE AND RETRIBUTION (Tai-Shang Kan-Ying P'ien). Trans. by Daisetz Teitaro Suzuki and Paul Carus 1906; ed. by Paul Carus *Open Court* 1944 1973 $2.50 pap. $1.95. Contains Chinese text and explanatory notes.

THE SAYINGS OF LAO TZU. Trans. with introd. by Lionel Giles. *Paragon Reprint* 1950 $3.50

SELECTIONS FROM THE UPANISHADS AND THE TAO TE KING. (Orig. "Sayings of Lao Tzu") trans. by Charles Johnston and Lionel Giles. 1897. *Cunningham Press* 1951 $3.00

Books about Lao-Tzu

Zen for the West. By Sohaku Ogata. 1959. *Greenwood* 1973 $9.50
Homage to the Ancient Child: An Essay on the Tao Te Ching of Lao Tzu. By Eugene H. Sloane. *Owl* 1968 pap. $.75
The Way of Chuang Tzu. By Thomas Merton. *New Directions* 1969 $6.50 pap. $1.75
Lao-Tzu and Taoism. By Max Kaltenmark. Trans. by Roger Greaves *Stanford Univ. Press* rev. ed. 1969 $5.95 pap. $1.95
Lao-Tzu and the Te Ching. By Bennett B. Sims. *Franklin Watts* 1971 lib. bdg. $4.33

For books on Taoism, see Section on Taoism, this Chapter.

BUDDHA: "The Enlightened One" (Gautama Buddha, orig. Prince Siddhartha). c. 563–483 B.C.

The Indian philosopher and founder of Buddhism was born at Kapilavastu near the border of Nepal. Of noble birth, Prince Siddhartha became weary of his luxurious life, renounced it (c. 533 B.C.) and became a hermit and wanderer. In his search for relief from life's suffering and pain, he rejected both hedonism and asceticism. According to legend, a great emancipation of the spirit came to him under a pipal tree (the sacred Bo tree) at Buddh Gaya (hence his title, Buddha, the Enlightened One). Once "enlightened," he devoted the rest of his life to teaching the attainment of peace with oneself (Nirvana) by means of "right" living and mental discipline. To perpetuate his teachings, he formed the first group of Buddhist monks from among his disciples. Sir Edwin Arnold's poem "The Light of Asia" (1879. *Inter-Culture* 1949 pap. $1.00; *Routledge & Kegan Paul* 1971 pap. $1.25; *Theosophical Pub. House* 1969 pap. $1.25) tells a romantic story of his life.

THE GOSPEL OF BUDDHA. Trans. by Paul Carus *Open Court* 1917 rev. & enl. ed. 1973 $15.00 pap. $2.95; *Gordon Press* $26.00; *Omen Press* 1972 pap. $3.65

BUDDHIST WISDOM BOOKS: The Diamond Sutra, The Heart Sutra. Trans. by Edward Conze *Hillary House* 1958 $5.00; *Harper* Torchbks. pap. $2.45

BUDDHISM IN TRANSLATIONS: Passages Selected from the Buddhist Sacred Books and Translated from the Original Pali into English. Trans. by Henry Clarke Warren. 1896. *Atheneum* 1963 pap. $3.95

BUDDHIST TEXTS THROUGH THE AGES. Ed. by Edward Conze and others *Harper* Torchbks. pap. $2.45

BUDDHIST SCRIPTURES. Trans. by Edward Conze *Penguin* pap. $1.25. A reader in the most important Buddhist literature from Buddha to Zen.

BUDDHIST SUTRAS TRANSLATED FROM PALI. Trans. by T. W. Rhys Davids; ed. by F. Max Müller. 1881. Sacred Books of the East Ser. *Dover* 1969 pap. $3.00; *Krishna Press* $20.00; *Peter Smith* $6.00; *Verry* $8.25

THE DHAMMAPADA (c. 1–100 B.C.). *Cunningham Press* 1955 $3.00; trans. by P. Lal from Pali *Farrar, Straus* 1967 $5.50 Noonday pap. $2.95; trans. by Irving Babbitt *New Directions* 1965 pap. $1.50; trans. by Swami Sarvepalli Radhakrishnan *Oxford* 1950 $3.20; trans. by Narada Thera *Paragon Reprint* $4.00; (with the "Sutta-Nipata") trans. by Juan Mascaro *Penguin* 1973 pap. $1.25; ed. by F. Max Müller, trans. by T. W. Rhys Davids *Verry* $8.25. The "Dhammapada" is one of the ancient books of Buddhism.

THE LION'S ROAR: An Anthology of the Buddha's Teachings Selected from the Pali Canon. Ed. by David Maurice *Citadel Press* 1967 $4.95

"A quiet, unpretentious attempt by Mr. Maurice himself a Buddhist, to bring the teachings of Buddha to the ordinary reader. A highly significant book"—(*LJ*).

WORLD OF THE BUDDHA: A Reader. Ed. by Lucien Stryk *Doubleday* 1968 Anchor Bks. 1969 pap. $2.95

A selection of Buddhist scripture from "Three Baskets" to Zen poetry with an introduction and commentaries by the editor. "The best available translations have been used"—(*LJ*).

SAYINGS OF BUDDHA: The Ita-Vuttaka. Trans. by J. H. Moore II. 1908. *AMS Press* $12.50. A Pali work of the Buddhist Canon.

SOME SAYINGS OF THE BUDDHA: According to the Pali Canon. Trans. by Frank Lee Woodward *Oxford* 1939 Galaxy Bks. 1973 pap. $1.95; *Gordon Press* $29.95

THE TEACHINGS OF THE COMPASSIONATE BUDDHA. Ed. by Edwin A. Burtt *New Am. Lib.* (orig.) Mentor Bks. 1955 pap. $1.25

BUDDHIST MEDITATION. Trans. and ed. by Edward Conze. 1956. *Harper* Torchbks. pap. $1.60

THE QUESTIONS OF KING MILINDA. Trans. by T. W. Rhys Davids; ed. by F. Max Müller. 1890–94. *Dover* 2 vols. pap. Vol. 1 $3.00 Vol. 2 $3.50; *Peter Smith* 2 vols. $10.50; *Verry* 2 vols. each $8.25

BUDDHIST LOGIC. Trans. by Theodore Stcherbatsky. 1930. *Dover* 2 vols. pap. each $4.00; *Humanities Press* 2 vols. 1958 set $44.75; *Peter Smith* 2 vols. each $5.50

BUDDHACARITA, or Acts of the Buddha. Trans. by E. H. Johnston. 1936. *Verry* 2 vols. in 1 1973 $11.50

BUDDHIST LEGENDS. Trans. by Eugene W. Burlingame. Harvard Oriental Series. *Verry* 3 vols. 1969 $27.50

BUDDHIST TEXTS FROM JAPAN. Trans. by F. Max Müller. 1881. *AMS Press* 1973 $22.50

BUDDHIST MAHAYANA TEXTS. Trans. by E. B. Cowell and others; ed. by F. Max Müller Books of the East Ser. *Dover* 1969 pap. $3.50; *Krishna Press* $23.95; *Peter Smith* $6.00; *Verry* $8.25

BUDDHIST PARABLES. Trans. by Eugene W. Burlingame *Gordon Press* $25.00; *Krishna Press* $29.00

Books about Buddha

Buddha: His Life, His Doctrine and His Order. By Hermann Oldenburg. *Gordon Press* $29.00

The Life of Buddha as Legend and History. By Edward J. Thomas. 1949. *Routledge & Kegan Paul* 1969 $10.00

The Life of Buddha According to the Legends of Ancient India. By André Ferdinand Herold. *Tuttle* 1954 pap. $2.95

The Creed of Buddha. By Edmond Holmes. 1957. *Greenwood* 1973 $11.50

The Life of the Buddha. By Alfred C. Foucher. Trans. by Simone Boas. 1963. *Greenwood* 1972 $14.75

The Footprints of Gautama the Buddha. By Marie B. Byles. *Theosophical Pub. House* 1967 pap. $1.75

Gautama-Buddha. By J. Kashyap. *Inter-Culture Assocs.* 1968 pap. $.50

The God of Buddha. By Jamshed Fozdar. *Asia Pub. House* 1973 $10.00

For books on Buddhism, see Section on Buddhism, this Chapter.

CONFUCIUS (also K'ung Fu-tze or K'ung Tzu). 551–478 B.C.

Celebrated as a philosopher and founder of a Chinese religion, Confucius lived in the feudal state of Lu in what is now the province of Shantung. He edited four of the "Five Classics" (Wu Ching). They are the "Book of History" (Shu Ching); the "Book of Poetry" (Shih Ching); the "Book of Changes" (I Ching, used for divination); the "Book of Rites" (Li Chi); and the "Spring and Autumn Annals" (the Ch'un Ch'iu, which is thought to have been actually written by him). The "Book of Filial Piety" (Hsiao Ching) is sometimes included. Books by Confucius' disciples, called the "Four Books" (Ssu Shu) include the "Book of Mancius," the most renowned interpreter of Confucius' thought, who lived c. 372–289 B.C. Our best information about Confucius' life comes from the "Analects," the famous collection of his sayings. The obscurity of the ancient Chinese ideograms makes translation of Confucian scriptures most difficult. Thus any two English versions of the same text may differ widely. He is noted mainly for his ethics; his religious thought was tenacious of ancient rites and customs, introduced no innovations. Virtue, according to this philosophy, consists of *li*, or rules for proper conduct, i.e., etiquette and ethical principles, and *ren*, or benevolent love of mankind. His precepts apply to the here and now rather than the forever after.

THE SACRED BOOKS OF CONFUCIUS AND OTHER CONFUCIAN CLASSICS. Ed. by Ch'u Chai and Winberg Chai *University Books* 1965 $6.50

Excellent translations by two professors of American universities of "the basic copies of Confucian writings and ideas," which present "an integrated view of the evolution of Confucian thought"—(*LJ*).

THE WISDOM OF CONFUCIUS. Ed. by Miles M. Dawson *Branden* pap. $.95; trans. and ed. by Lin Yutang *Random* Modern Lib. 1943 $2.95; *Peter Pauper Press* $1.95

CONFUCIAN ANALECTS. Trans. and ed. by James Legge. 1893. *Dover* pap. $4.00; ed. by W. Jennings *Gordon Press* $25.00; trans. by Ezra Pound 1956 *Hillary House* 1970 $7.25; *Peter Smith* $6.25

THE ANALECTS, or The Conversations of Confucius with His Disciples and Certain Others. Trans. by William E. Soothill; ed. by D. S. Hosie. 1937. *Paragon Reprint* 1968 $15.00 pap. $7.50

THE ANALECTS. Trans. and annot. by Arthur Waley. 1938. *Hillary House* 1964 $9.25; *Random* Vintage Bks. pap. $1.95

THE SAYINGS OF CONFUCIUS. Trans. by James R. Ware. 1939. *New Am. Lib.* Mentor Bks. pap. $.75

THE CONFUCIAN ODES: The Classic Anthology Defined by Confucius. Trans. by Ezra Pound. 1954. *New Directions* 1959 pap. $2.45

"Mr. Pound's work on Confucius has introduced a new element into the literary context of our time. As with Chapman's Homer or Dryden's Virgil, Pound's Confucius is to be read as much in relation to its translator as to its original author; it is a twentieth century reading of Confucius"— (*New Republic*).

CONFUCIUS: The Great Digest, the Unwobbling Pivot, the Analects. Trans. by Ezra Pound *New Directions* 1969 pap. $2.45

Books about Confucius

Confucius and Confucianism. By Richard Wilhelm. 1931. *Harcourt* Harvest Bks. 1971 pap. $1.65; *Kennikat* 1970 $7.50

The First Holy One. By Maurice Collis. 1948. *Greenwood* 1970 $14.25

Confucius and the Chinese Way. By Herrlee Glessner Creel. 1949. *Harper* Torchbks. 1960 pap. $3.25; *Peter Smith* $4.50. A reprint of "Confucius, the Man and the Myth" (*Greenwood* 1973 $14.75).

Confucius, His Life and Time. By Wu-Chi Liu. 1955. *Greenwood* 1972 $11.50

Confucius. By Shigeki Kaizuka. Trans. by Geoffrey Bownas. 1956. *Fernhill* $3.25

The Heart of Confucius: Interpretations of *Genuine Living* and *Great Wisdom*. By Archie J. Bahm. *Walker & Co.* 1970 $4.50

"This attractive little book tells what all Western readers should know about Confucius and why his teachings are important. . . . These teachings [are presented] in a lively, accessible prose"—(*N.Y. Times Bk. Review*). Almost half of the book is a translation of major passages; the rest an explanation of key Confucian concepts.

Confucius: The Secular as Sacred. By Herbert Fingarette. *Harper* 1972 $5.00 Torchbks. pap. $2.75

For books about Confucianism, see Section on Confucianism, this Chapter.

PAUL THE APOSTLE (orig. Saul). c. 10 B.C.–c. 10 A.D.—64 A.D.

Frequently called "the second founder of Christianity," this remarkable man was born a free Roman citizen in Tarsus of a Pharisaical Hebrew family. In his devotion to the teachings of Pharisaism, he became the most fanatical scourge of those heretical Jews who followed Jesus. Traveling to Damascus to root out believers who had fled northward, he experienced an astonishing conversion to the very teachings he had so vehemently opposed. Christ appeared in a vision and called Paul to serve Him. Paul immediately began to proclaim the Christian teachings, developing and elaborating doctrine, and transforming the scope of the missionary work. He brought his deep knowledge of Old Testament law to the elucidation of the concept of the Logos.

His doctrine of justification by faith has been one of the most enriching of all Christian ideas and directly influenced Martin Luther's thinking to a measureless degree. Paul was the first to develop the meaning of the Lordship of Christ for the whole world (as opposed to the idea of Christ as the Messiah for the Hebrews). Paul found in Christ the power to unite Greek, Jew and Roman; to fuse the legal, mystic and rational. He carried the teachings of Christianity to the whole world of his day. Evidence indicates that he died in Rome following a period of imprisonment—probably executed as a disturber of Roman peace.

THE NEW TESTAMENT: The Epistles of Paul. (Romans, 1st and 2nd Corinthians; Galatians; Philippians; Colossians; 1st and 2nd Thessalonians; Philemon, "now almost universally recognized as genuine"; the authenticity of Ephesians still a matter of dispute.)

Books about Paul the Apostle

Epochs in the Life of Paul. By Archibald T. Robertson. 1909. *Baker Bk. House* 1974 pap. $3.45
Paul and Paulism. By James Moffatt. 1910. *Folcroft* $10.00
The Life of Paul. By Benjamin W. Robinson. 1918. *Univ. of Chicago Press* 2nd ed. 1928 pap. $6.50; *Folcroft* $15.00
Paul. By Edgar J. Goodspeed. 1948. *Abingdon* 1959 pap. $1.95
Chapters in the Life of Paul. By John Knox. *Abingdon* Apex Bks. 1950 pap. $2.50
Paul. By Martin Dibelius. Ed. by W. G. Kümmel. *Westminster Press* 1953 $3.50. The great German scholar presents an influential analysis.
The Mysticism of Paul the Apostle. By Albert Schweitzer. 1955. *Seabury Press* 1968 pap. $2.95
The Genius of Paul: A Study in History. By Samuel Sandmel. 1958. *Schocken* 1970 $6.50 pap. $2.45
The Story of Paul. By James Kallas. *Augsburg* 1966 pap. $1.95
The Spiritual Journey of St. Paul. By Lucien Cerfaux. Trans. by John C. Guinness. *Sheed & Ward* 1968 $5.50
"An outstanding authority on the life and letters of St. Paul, presents here, the whole body of Pauline thought, based on Paul's letters, and on the writings of others associated with him"— (*LJ*).
Paul: Messenger and Exile. By John J. Gunther. *Judson Press* 1971 $6.95
Reapproaching Paul. By Morton S. Enslin. *Westminster Press* 1972 $5.95
My Brother Paul. By Richard L. Rubenstein. *Harper* 1972 $5.95
"The excellence of this book is that the author has ably combined the results of scholarly biblical research and the findings of depth psychology to portray effectively the profundity of Paul's religious genius"—(*Commonweal*).
Paul: Envoy Extraordinary. By Malcolm Muggeridge and Alec Vidler. *Harper* 1972 $5.95
Much of the book is the television script for the dialogue the two authors held on five 1971 BBC programs. "The dialogue . . . describes the places Paul visited and . . . attempts to bring out his personality and ministry"—(*LJ*).
Ambassador for Christ. By William Barclay. *Judson Press* 1974 pap. $1.95

JESUS (or Jesus Christ, Christ Jesus, Jesus of Nazareth).   c. 8/4 B.C.–c. 30 A.D.

It is paradoxical that the exact dates of that life from which we date time should be a question for scholars. The present error in reckoning the earthly life of Jesus Christ stems from a sixth-century mistake. No attempt will here be made to sketch the life of Jesus. It is cogent to remark that no other life or death has so affected human history, no other subject has been so tirelessly written of. Jesus himself wrote no books; his teaching was entirely by word of mouth and by the manner of his life. It was some years after his death that his followers wrote down from memory some of his sayings and certain facts of his ministry. Biblical scholars since the last century have worked to distinguish the early from the late material written about him. Today it appears possible to make certain distinctions between the Jesus of history and the Christ of Christian faith.

THE NEW TESTAMENT: The Four Gospels.

Books about Jesus

The Life of Jesus. By Ernest Renan. 1863. *Belmont-Tower* 1972 pap. $1.25
The Life and Morals of Jesus of Nazareth, Extracted Textually from the Gospels of Matthew, Mark, Luke and John. By Thomas Jefferson. *Folcroft* 1904 $25.00
The Quest of the Historical Jesus. By Albert Schweitzer. 1906. *Macmillan* 1948 pap. $3.95
Christ of the New Testament. By Paul E. More. 1924. *Greenwood* $12.50
The Teaching of Jesus. By Thomas W. Manson. *Cambridge Univ. Press* 2nd ed. 1935 pap. $2.95
The Christ of the Gospels. By John W. Shepard. *Eerdmans* rev. ed. 1946 $7.95
A Psychiatric Study of Jesus. By Albert Schweitzer. 1948. *Peter Smith* 1963 $4.00

Jesus. By Martin Dibelius. *Westminster Press* 1949 $3.50. A famous study by one of the world's leading biblical scholars.

The Greatest Story Ever Told: The Life of Christ. By Fulton Oursler. *Doubleday* 1949 $6.95 pap. $1.75

The Life of Jesus. By Edgar J. Goodspeed. 1950. *Harper* Torchbks. 1968 pap. $1.95; *Franklin Watts* lg.-type ed. $8.95

The Work and Words of Jesus. By Archibald Hunter. *Westminster Press* 1951 rev. ed. 1973 pap. $3.50

Lord. By Romano Guardini. *Regnery* 1954 $7.50

Jesus. By Charles Guignebert. *University Bks.* 1956 $10.00
"There is no book which will give the interested layman a more comprehensive account of what has been written and said about the life of Jesus and a fairer estimate of conflicting evidence"—(Reinhold Niebuhr).

The Life of Christ. By Fulton J. Sheen. 1958. *Popular Lib.* pap. $.95

This He Believed: The Religion of Jesus of Nazareth as Revealed in Readings from the Old and New Testaments and Other Sources. Ed. by Robert O. Ballou. *Viking* 1959 $3.00

The Christology of the New Testament. By Oscar Cullmann. *Westminster Press* 1959 rev. ed. 1964 $6.50

The New Quest of the Historical Jesus. By James M. Robinson. *Allenson* 1959 $7.25 pap. $4.75

The Message of Jesus. Ed. by Harvie B. Branscomb. Rev. ed. by Ernest W. Saunders *Abingdon* rev. ed. 1960 pap. $1.75

Jesus of Nazareth. By Gunther Bornkamm. Trans. by Irene and Fraser McLuskey *Harper* 1960 $6.00

The Son of Man. By Francois Mauriac. Trans. by Bernard Murchland. 1960. *Macmillan* (Collier Bks.) 1961 pap. $.95

The Prophet From Nazareth. By Morton S. Enslin. 1961. *Schocken* 1968 $6.00 pap. $1.95

The Earliest Lives of Jesus. By Robert M. Grant. *Allenson* 1961 $3.50

Life and Teachings of Jesus. By Charles M. Laymon. *Abingdon* rev. ed. 1962 $4.95

To Know Jesus Christ. By Francis J. Sheed. *Sheed & Ward* 1962 $5.00

Christ the Center. By Dietrich Bonhoeffer. Trans. by John Bowden *Harper* 1966 $3.95. By the eminent German theologian, martyred for defending his ethic during World War II. Based on lectures at the University of Berlin in 1933.

The Christ. By Charles Guignebert. Trans. by Peter Ouzts and Phyllis Cooperman; ed. and rev. by Sonia Volochova *University Books* 1966 $10.00
"Guignebert (1867–1939) is representative of that generation of French scholars whose writings and ideas dominated New Testament studies in the period between the two World Wars"—(*LJ*).

The Life of Jesus. By Marcello Craveri. Trans. from the Italian by Charles Lam Markmann *Grove* 1967 pap. $1.95
Dr. Craveri uses scholarly evidence to support his conclusions about the life and history of Jesus Christ, always distinguishing between the known facts and the constructions men have built about him. It caused considerable controversy on first publication in Italy. "A completely rewarding and absorbing investigation"—(Thomas Lask, in the *N.Y. Times*). Craveri is "just the one to set the whole problem of the life of Jesus in proper historical perspective"—(Frederick C. Grant, Professor Emeritus, Union Theological Seminary).

Jesus. By Hugh Anderson. Great Lives Observed Ser. *Prentice-Hall* Spectrum Bks. 1968 pap. $5.95
A collection of readings by well-known authorities from the 19th century to the present day on the Jesus of history, with an interesting introductory discussion by the editor, a professor at Duke University.

The Cosmic Christ: From Paul to Teilhard. By George A. Maloney, S.J. *Sheed & Ward* 1968 $6.95
"A Jesuit scripture scholar, in this beautifully literate and scholarly book, traces the concept of Christ the Logos, the incarnate Word as the point at which the sacred intercepts the profane"—(*LJ*).

The Real Jesus: How He Lived and What He Taught. By Louis Cassels. *Doubleday* 1968 $4.95

MANI (also Manes or Manichaeus). 215/216–274?

Raised in a religious community in southern Babylonia, Mani in youth had a vision of an angel calling him to found a new religion. As he traveled to India and around the Persian Empire making converts, he acknowledged that there had been many true prophets (including Adam, Enoch, Buddha, Zoroaster and Jesus), but conceived of himself as the "seal of the prophets" bearing the universal message. Previous religions, he felt, had suffered the limitations of being localized in one language and one people and their original truths had soon become distorted.

Hoping to preserve the purity of his new faith, Mani wrote seven major works in his native dialect and encouraged their translation into other languages. These books, which became the Manichaean canon, disappeared during the persecutions of the Middle Ages, but recently portions have been unearthed in archeological excavations in Turfan and Egypt. Mani himself eventually fell foul of the civil authorities and died in prison after a brief captivity.

The mythology of Manichaeism is based on the imagery of Light and Darkness, seen as Good and Evil. These are separate and opposing principles, but in the world they have become mixed. Human bondage is light imprisoned in matter, and man's salvation lies in his protection of this light and in the soul's conscious rejection of the evil impulses of the body. In practice, the ideal life meant withdrawal from the world in strict chastity, poverty and abstinence from meat and wine.

From the center in Babylonia, Manichaean missionaries spread throughout the ancient world from Spain to China. (St. Augustine [q.v.] was converted to Manichaeism for about a dozen years during his youth in Carthage in the 4th century.) But the Manichaean spirit was felt to be a threat to the values of other religions and it was vigorously persecuted as a heresy by Christians in the 6th century, by the Chinese in the 9th century and by Muslims in the 10th. It managed to survive in the western Mediterranean, among the Cathars, who settled in Languedoc, centered around the town of Albi—hence they were known as Albigenses. (The word Cathar refers properly to the "pure" or celibate order of Manichaeans—a distinction similar to that of Catholic monks.) For a fascinating consideration of the possible hidden and pervasive influence of Manichaeism on Western literature, see Denis de Rougemont's "Love in the Western World" (*Pantheon* 1956 $7.95; *Harper* 1974 pap. $3.25).

Books about Mani

Against the Manichees. By Saint Serapion. *Kraus* 1931 pap. $3.50
Anthropos and Son of Man: A Study in the Religious Syncretism of the Hellenistic Orient. By Carl H. Kraeling. *AMS Press* 1927 $12.50
Researches in Manichaeism, with Special Reference to the Turfan Fragments. By Abraham V. Williams Jackson. *AMS Press* 1932 $18.00
Medieval Manichee. By Steven Runciman. *Cambridge* 1947 $9.50
Gospel of the Prophet Mani. By Duncan Greenlees. *Theosophical Pub. House* $3.75

AUGUSTINE, SAINT, Bishop of Hippo.   354–430.

St. Augustine's "Confessions," a beautifully written apology for the Christian convert, is a classic of Christian mysticism. It tells of his being brought up a Christian by his mother, St. Monica; of his conversion to Manichaeism in Carthage; and of his great doubt and mental agony before his re-conversion to Christianity and baptism in Milan on Easter, 387. Roman Catholic and Protestant theologians consider him the founder of theology. Next to the "Confessions," his best-known work is the "City of God," an apology for Christianity. Although he preferred a studious, contemplative life, he was urged by the congregation of Hippo to be ordained as a priest and four years later, in 395, he was consecrated bishop. For the next 34 years he rarely left the small coastal city, but his influence spread throughout the Christian world through the letters which he dispatched to congregations in many lands. About 250 of these, written to admonish, explain or encourage, still survive. Couched in a colloquial style, they are nonetheless powerful and persuasive. He was killed when the Vandals besieged Hippo.

BASIC WRITINGS. Ed. by Whitney J. Oates *Random* 2 vols. 1948 each $11.00 boxed set $20.00

SELECTED WRITINGS. Ed. by Roger Hazelton *Peter Smith* $5.50

EARLIER WRITINGS. Ed. by J. H. S. Burleigh Library of Christian Classics, Vol. 6. *Westminster Press* 1953 $6.50

THE CONFESSIONS. 397–401. *Assoc. Booksellers* (Airmont Bks.) 1968 pap. $.75; Fathers of the Church Ser. *Catholic Univ. of America Press* $25.00; trans. by Francis J. Sheed *Christian Class.* $5.95; trans. by Edward B. Pusey *Dutton* Everyman's $3.95; *Harvard Univ. Press* Loeb 2 vols. 1912 each $7.00; trans. by J. G. Pilkington *Liveright* Black & Gold Lib. $7.95; trans. by Edward B. Pusey *Macmillan* (Collier Bks.) 1961 pap. $.65; trans. by Rex Warner *New Am. Lib.* Mentor Bks. pap. $1.25; trans. by R. S. Pine-Coffin *Penguin* 1961 pap. $1.95; ed. by J. M. Campbell and M. P. McGuire *Prentice-Hall* 1941 $5.25; trans. by Francis J. Sheed *Sheed & Ward* 1969 Bks. I–13 each $3.50 Bks. I–10 pap. each $1.75

THE CITY OF GOD AGAINST THE PAGANS. 413–426. Fathers of the Church Ser. *Catholic Univ. of America Press* Bks. I–7 $24.00 Bks. 8–16 $28.00 Bks. 17–22 $28.00; trans. by

John Healey, ed. by R. V. Tasker *Dutton* Everyman's 2 vols. each $3.95; *Harvard Univ. Press* Loeb 7 vols. each $7.00; trans. by J. W. Wand *Oxford* 1963 $5.00; *Random* (Modern Lib. Giants) $4.95

ON THE TWO CITIES: Selections from the City of God. Ed. by F. W. Strothmann *Ungar* $4.50 pap. $1.45

POLITICAL WRITINGS. Ed. by Henry Paolucci *Regnery* pap. $1.95

SAINT AUGUSTINE: On Education. Trans. and ed. by George Howie *Regnery* 1969 $12.50 pap. $3.95

SERMONS ON THE LITURGICAL SEASONS. Fathers of the Church Ser., *Catholic Univ. of America Press* $23.00

THE TEACHER and TWO WORKS ON FREE WILL. Fathers of the Church Ser., *Catholic Univ. of America Press* $17.00

TREATISES ON MARRIAGE AND OTHER SUBJECTS. Fathers of the Church Ser., *Catholic Univ. of America Press* $23.00

TREATISES ON VARIOUS MORAL SUBJECTS. Fathers of the Church Ser., *Catholic Univ. of America Press* $24.00

THE TRINITY. Fathers of the Church Ser., *Catholic Univ. of America Press* $27.00

LETTERS. Fathers of the Church Ser., *Catholic Univ. of America Press* Nos. I–82 $22.00; 83–130 $20.00; 131–164 $20.00; 165–203 $21.00; 204–272 $16.00

SELECT LETTERS. *Harvard Univ. Press* Loeb $7.00

Other titles are published by Bobbs, Catholic Univ. of America Press, Macmillan (Free Press), Marquette Univ. Press, Paulist-Newman, Regnery, Peter Smith, and Ungar.

Books about St. Augustine

Saint Augustine and French Classical Thought. By Nigel Abercrombie. 1938. *Russell & Russell* 1972 $9.00

Companion to the Study of St. Augustine. Ed. by Roy W. Battenhouse. *Oxford* 1955 $6.95

Guide to the City of God. By Marthinus Versfeld. *Humanities Press* (Fernhill) 1958 $3.75

The Christian Philosophy of Saint Augustine. By Étienne Henry Gilson. Trans. by L. E. Lynch *Random* 1960 $10.00

The Political and Social Ideas of St. Augustine. By Herbert A. Deane. *Columbia* 1963 pap. $3.95. In this basic work, Dr. Deane has succeeded "in outlining Augustine's thought on man, society, and the state. His use of many direct quotations enables the reader to judge accuracy of the interpretations for himself."

Christian Faith and the Interpretation of History: A Study of St. Augustine's Philosophy of History. By G. L. Keyes. *Univ. of Nebraska Press* 1966 $5.95

Plato and Augustine. By Karl Jaspers. *Harcourt* Harvest Bks. 1966 pap. $1.65

Augustine of Hippo: A Biography. By Peter Brown. *Univ. of California Press* 1967 $11.00 pap. $2.95
"Scholarly, strong in bibliography and references and yet readable and interesting"—(*LJ*).

Saint Augustine's Confessions: The Odyssey of Soul. By Robert J. O'Connell. *Harvard Univ. Press* 1969 $7.50

The Light of the Mind: St. Augustine's Theory of Knowledge. By Ronald H. Nash. *Univ. Press of Kentucky* 1969 $6.50

Saeculum: History and Society in the Theology of St. Augustine. By R. A. Markus. *Cambridge* 1970 $14.50

The Mysticism of St. Augustine. Ed. by Francis J. Sheed. *Sheed & Ward* 1972 pap. $2.95

Religion and Society in the Age of Saint Augustine. By Peter Brown. *Harper* 1972 $12.00
"The great value of Brown's work is the immense number of detailed insights both of other scholars and his own. This is an excellent and important book for students in the field of history of religions"—(*Choice*).

Augustine. Ed. by R. A. Markus. *Doubleday* Anchor Bks. 1972 pap. $2.50

MOHAMMED (or Muhammad).   570–632.

When Mohammed was born in Mecca, the great trade center was already the center of the religious piety attached to the Kaaba, the Holy Rock, and its pantheon of tribal deities, of whom Allah was one. The future Prophet of Islam was orphaned at an early age, and was raised by his grandfather and uncle. Both men were prominent members of the Quraysh, the tribe responsible for maintaining the Kaaba and its lands and sacred well. Under their guardianship, Mohammed grew up in an atmosphere of religious excitement.

Possibly from the Jews and Christians who dwelt in or visited Mecca, possibly from contacts made on later trips, Mohammed learned something of the biblical faith. In his twenties he married the wealthy widow Khadijah, who freed him from financial concern, supported his meditations, bore him seven children and became his first and most fervent follower. In a cave in Mount Hira near Mecca, where Mohammed frequently withdrew for meditation, he experienced a vision of the angel Gabriel calling him to prophesy. When he felt convinced that the revelation was genuine, Mohammed began to preach, proclaiming Allah as the one true God, the same God who had revealed himself to Abraham, Moses and Jesus. It was his monotheism that aroused the fury of the inhabitants of Mecca, whose livelihood depended in part upon pilgrims who came to worship the Gods of the Kaaba.

Mohammed was forced to flee Mecca in 622. From this event, the Hegira, Islam dates its calendar. It marks the beginning of the Mohammedan era. The Prophet found refuge in Medina and there established his theocracy. There too, he began to develop his theory of Holy War. He assembled an army, and, in 630, marched against Mecca. He readily conquered the city, purged the Kaaba of pagan gods, and pronounced the brotherhood of all Moslems. He was well on his way to unifying the divergent Arab tribes when he died suddenly (poisoned, according to one legend, by a woman who sought to test his ability to prophesy the future).

The sacred book of Islam was, according to its tenets, revealed by God to the Prophet Mohammed. It is written in classical Arabic and considered the most influential book in the world after the Bible. Sale's English translation is a classic, but his notes are out of date.

THE KORAN (Qur'ân). 651–52. Trans. by J. M. Rodwell *Dutton* Everyman's $3.95; trans. by George Sale *Folcroft* $10.00; abr. ed. trans. by N. J. Dawood *Penguin* Class. 1964 pap. $1.95; *Peter Pauper Press* (dist. by Van Nostrand-Reinhold) deluxe ed. $4.95; trans. by George Sale *Warne* 1909 $4.95

THE KORAN: A New Translation and Presentation. Ed. by H. Mercier; trans. by L. Tremlett from the French *Verry* 1973 text ed. $12.50 pap. $6.50

THE MEANING OF THE GLORIOUS KORAN. Trans. by Mohammed M. Pickthall *New Am. Lib.* Mentor Bks. pap. $1.50

THE KORAN INTERPRETED. By Arthur J. Arberry. *Macmillan* 1955–56 1964 pap. $4.95. Professor Arberry of Cambridge University aims in this work "to present to English readers what Muslims the world over hold to be the meaning of the words of the Koran, and the nature of that Book, in not unworthy language and concisely, with a view to the requirements of English Muslims."

Books about Mohammed

Mohammed and the Rise of Islam. By David S. Margoliouth. 1905. *AMS Press* 1973 $24.50; *Bks. for Libraries* 1973 $23.50

The Spirit of Islam: A History of the Evolution and Ideals of Islam with a Life of the Prophet. By Syed A. Ali. *Hillary House* 1922 text ed. $8.75

Aishah: The Beloved of Mohammed. By Nabia Abbott. 1942. *Arno* 1973 $15.00

Muhammad at Mecca. By W. Montgomery Watt. *Oxford* 1953 $9.50. This deals with the first part of his career with special attention to the economic and sociological background.

Mohammed: The Man and His Faith. By Tor Andrae. Trans. by Theophil Menzel. 1956. *Bks. for Libraries* $12.00; *Harper* Torchbks. 1960 pap. $1.95

Muhammad at Medina. By W. Montgomery Watt. *Oxford* 1956 $13.75. A study of the second part of his career from the standpoint of the modern historian.

Islam: Muhammad and His Religion. Ed. by Arthur Jeffery. *Bobbs* Lib. Arts 1958 $6.00 pap. $2.25

Muhammad, Prophet and Statesman. By W. Montgomery Watt. *Oxford* 1961 $10.25 pap. $2.95. This short account is a good introduction to the religion.

The Eternal Message of Mohammed. By Abdul-Rahman Azzam. Trans. by Caesar E. Farah; pref. by Vincent Sheean *Devin-Adair* 1964 $6.50; *New Am. Lib.* Mentor Bks. pap. $.75 This study, by the first Secretary General of the Arab League, emphasizes Islam as both a culture and a religion; a life of the Prophet is included.

The Life of Muhammad: A Translation of Ibn Ishaq's 'Sirat Rasaul Allah.' Trans. and ed. by Alfred Guillaume. *Oxford* 1967 pap. $7.50

The Prophet Muhammed and His Mission. By Athar Husain. *Asia Pub. House* 1968 $5.25

The Life and Times of Muhammad. By John Glubb. *Stein & Day* 1970 pap. $2.95

For books about Islam, see Section on Islam, this Chapter.

BEDE (or Baeda, Beda), SAINT.   673–735.

The "Venerable Bede," English scholar, historian and theologian, was associated with the monastery at Jarrow throughout his life where he taught Greek, Latin, Hebrew and theology. His famous ecclesiastical history, in Latin, describes Celtic Britain and Saxon England, and all that is known of his life comes to us from a short autobiography appended to it.

HISTORICAL WORKS. *Harvard Univ. Press* Loeb 2 vols. each $7.00

A HISTORY OF THE ENGLISH CHURCH AND PEOPLE. 731. New and unabridged trans. with introd. by Leo Sherley-Price *Gannon* $5.00; *Penguin* 1955 pap. $1.95

THE ECCLESIASTICAL HISTORY OF ENGLAND. Ed. by John A. Giles. 1849. *AMS Press* 1971 $15.00

THE ECCLESIASTICAL HISTORY OF THE ENGLISH NATION. Trans. by John Stevens *Dutton* Everyman's $3.95

THE ECCLESIASTICAL HISTORY OF THE ENGLISH PEOPLE. Ed. by Bertram Colgrave and R. A. Minors *Oxford* 1969 $25.75

Books about Bede

The Venerable Bede: His Life and Writings. By G. F. Browne. 1919. *Folcroft* 1972 $12.50
Concordance to the *Historia Ecclesiastica* of Bede. Ed. by Putnam F. Jones. 1929. *Mediaeval* $10.00
Bede: His Life, Times and Writings: Essays in Commemoration of the Twelfth Centenary of His Death. Ed. by Alexander Hamilton Thompson. *Oxford* 1935 $6.25; *Russell & Russell* 1966 $8.00
Hand-List of Bede Manuscripts. By Max L. W. Laistner and H. H. King. *Cornell Univ. Press* 1943 $7.50
Anglo-Saxon Saints and Scholars. By Eleanor S. Duckett. 1947. *Shoe String Press* 1967 $11.00
Bede and Dunstan. By Mary R. Price. *Oxford* 1968 $2.00
The World of Bede. By Peter H. Blair. *St. Martin's* 1971 $12.95
"A most useful, even indispensable, companion to the text of Bede for every serious student. Criticism of some of its details must not be allowed to outweigh appreciation of its general excellence. It will be long before it is superseded"—(*TLS*, London).

ANSELM, SAINT (Archbishop of Canterbury).   1033?–1109.

St. Anselm, the Italian churchman, was born of noble parents in Piedmont and entered the Benedictine monastery of Bec in Normandy. During his abbotship there he conceived of the ontological argument for the existence of God—that the very conception of a God implies His existence, since one cannot conceive of anything more perfect.

In thus combining theology and philosophy, Anselm held that faith presupposed reason. Theologically, Anselm reinterpreted the doctrine of the Atonement, insisting that man's redemption is with Christ in the Eucharist, a concept which quickly gained general acceptance. Admired by William the Conqueror, who took Britain in 1066, Anselm later became Archbishop of Canterbury.

BASIC WRITINGS: Proslogium; Monologium; On Behalf of the Fool by Gaunilon; and Cur Deus Homo. Trans. from the Latin by Sidney Norton Dean; with an introd., bibliography and reprints of the opinions of the leading philosophers and writers on ontological argument. 1903. New introd. to 1962 ed. by Charles Hartshorne *Open Court* 1948 new ed. 1962 $10.00 pap. $3.95

PROSLOGION, WITH 'A REPLY ON BEHALF OF THE FOOL' BY GAUNILO AND 'THE AUTHOR'S REPLY TO GAUNILO.' Trans. with introd. by M. J. Charlesworth *Oxford* 1955 1965 $7.75

THE DE GRAMMATICA OF ST. ANSELM: The Theory of Paronymy. Trans. by Desmond P. Henry *Univ. of Notre Dame Press* 1964 $7.95

TRUTH, FREEDOM, AND EVIL: Three Philosophical Dialogues. Trans. and ed. with introd. by Jasper Hopkins and Herbert W. Richardson *Harper* Torchbks. 1967 pap. $2.25

ANSELM OF CANTERBURY: Why God Became Man and the Virgin Conception and Original Sin. *Magi Bks.* 1969 lib. bdg. $10.50 pap. $6.50

TRINITY, INCARNATION AND REDEMPTION: Theological Treatises. Ed. by Jasper Hopkins and Herbert W. Richardson *Harper* Torchbks. 1970 pap. $2.75

Books about St. Anselm

Anselm: Communion and Atonement. By George H. Williams. *Concordia* 1960 pap. $1.50

Life of St. Anselm: Archbishop of Canterbury. By Eadmer. Ed. by Richard W. Southern. 1962. *Oxford* 1972 $15.25

St. Anselm and His Biographer. By Richard W. Southern. *Cambridge* 1963 $19.50

Anselm's Discovery: A Re-examination of the Ontological Proof for God's Existence. By Charles Hartshorne. *Open Court* 1965 $10.00 pap. $3.95

The Many-Faced Argument. By John Hick and Arthur McGill. *Macmillan* 1967 $8.95 pap. $2.95

The Logic of Saint Anselm. By Desmond P. Henry. *Oxford* 1967 $9.50

Memorials of Saint Anselm. Ed. by Richard W. Southern and F. S. Schmitt. *Oxford* 1969 $19.25

A Companion to the Study of St. Anselm. By Jasper Hopkins. *Univ. of Minnesota Press* 1972 $10.50

MAIMONIDES (or Rabbi Moses ben Maimon).   1135–1204.

The most celebrated of medieval Hebrew philosophers, Moses ben Maimon, was born in Cordova, Spain, when it was already under Moslem influence. A man of extraordinary learning, he absorbed from Arab scholars their Aristotelian and neo-Platonic philosophy. When the Moslems captured Cordova in 1148, Maimonides moved to Cairo, where he became Rabbi of the Cairo synagogue and physician to Saladin, Sultan of Egypt. He wrote in both Arabic and Hebrew. Notable among his works are his commentary on the Mishnah, the "Guide for the Perplexed" and various works on medicine, mathematics, theology, law and logic. His genius for applying the techniques of Greek (via Arabic) philosophy to the revelation of the Old Testament faith exerted a profound influence on the 12th-century Christian philosophers, especially St. Thomas Aquinas.

Several critics attacked Maimonides' rationalism. Nahmanides (1195–1270) was one of the ablest spokesman of those Rabbis who preferred to think of religion as nonrational and mystical, accessible only to the devout. More famous was Rabad—Rabbi Abraham ben David (1125–1198) of Posquières, France—who won the title the "Critic" for his searching criticism of Maimonides' "Mishnah Torah." Rabad's life and thought are extensively presented in the recent study by Isadore Twersky, "Rabad of Posquières: A Twelfth-Century Talmudist" (*Harvard Univ. Press* 1962 $8.50). "Rashi and the Christian Scholars" by Herman Hailperin (*Univ. of Pittsburgh Press* 1963 $15.00) is a further study in medieval Jewish theology. Maimonides' medical writings in 3 volumes are available from *Lippincott* (Vol. 1 "Treatise on Asthma" (1963) $5.00; Vol. 2 "Treatise on Poisons and Their Antidotes" (1966) $6.50; Vol. 3 "Treatise on Hemorrhoids: Responsa" (1969) $5.00 ed. by Suessman Muntner and Fred Rosner).

THE CODE OF MAIMONIDES. Yale Judaica Ser. *Yale Univ. Press* 12 vols. 1949–72 (*consult catalog for translators, titles and prices*)

COMMANDMENTS. *Bloch Pub. Co.* 2 vols. set $30.00

THE GUIDE FOR THE PERPLEXED. Trans. by M. Friedlander 1904. *Dover* 1957 pap. $3.50; *Peter Smith* 1957 2nd rev. ed. $5.50; trans. by Shlomo Pines *Univ. of Chicago Press* 1963 $18.00 1974 2 vols. pap. Vol. 1 $7.25 Vol. 2 $7.95

COMMENTARY TO MISHNAH ABOTH: Ethics of the Fathers. 1168. Trans. with introd., notes and a translation of Mishnah Aboth by Rabbi Arthur David *Bloch Pub. Co.* 1968 $6.00

"First translation into English [to celebrate] 800th anniversary of Maimonides' first publication of his commentary"—(*PW*).

EPISTLE TO YEMEN. *Kraus* 1952 $10.00

REASON OF THE LAWS OF MOSES. Trans. by James Townley. 1827. *Greenwood* $16.75

MEDICAL APHORISMS. Trans. and ed. by Fred Rosner *Bloch Pub. Co.* 2 vols. in 1 1973 $12.50

Books about Maimonides

Spinoza, Descartes and Maimonides. By Leon Roth. 1924. *Russell & Russell* 1963 $5.75

Essays on Maimonides. Ed. by Salo W. Baron. 1941. *AMS Press* $10.00

The Teachings of Maimonides. By Abraham Cohen. *KTAV* rev. ed. 1969 $10.00

Maimonides and Abrabanel on Prophecy. By Alvin J. Reines. *KTAV* 1971 $12.50

Maimonides: His Life and Works. By David Yellin and Israel Abrahams. *Sepher-Hermon* rev. ed. 1973 $7.95

Sex Ethics in the Writings of Moses Maimonides. By Fred Rosner. *Bloch Pub. Co.* 1974 $7.95

FRANCIS OF ASSISI, SAINT (orig. Giovanni Francesco Bernardone). 1182–1226.

St. Francis founded the Franciscan Order in 1208 in Assisi, Italy, and was one of the most beloved of the saints. From "The Little Flowers" the reader gains insight into the personality of the man and his companions. The simple anecdotes exemplify his great love of nature, of man and of God. He lived in poverty and with the friars of his newly formed order went about the countryside preaching. Among the work they undertook was the repair and restoration of churches, including the famous St. Mary's of the Angels near Assisi.

WRITINGS. Ed. by Benen Fahy and Placid Hermann *Franciscan Herald Press* 1964 $4.95

WORDS OF ST. FRANCIS. Ed. by J. Meyer *Franciscan Herald Press* pap. $1.95

THE LITTLE FLOWERS. Trans. by Raphael Brown *Doubleday* 1971 pap. $1.75; (and "The Mirror of Perfection" and "Life of St. Francis") *Dutton* Everyman's 1908 $3.95; *Peter Pauper Press* (dist. by Van Nostrand-Reinhold) $1.95

Books about St. Francis

St. Francis of Assisi: First and Second Life of St. Francis With Selections from Treatise on the Miracles of Blessed Francis. By Brother Thomas of Celano. Trans. from the Latin with introd. and footnotes by Placid Hermann, O.F.M. *Franciscan Herald Press* 1962 $11.95
"Brother Thomas of Celano, a contemporary and follower of St. Francis, was his first biographer. His two lives and a portion of his "Treatise on the Miracles of Blessed Francis" are now translated for the first time in over half a century.... Father Hermann includes in his commentaries copious notes and evaluations of the literary and historical aspects of Brother Thomas's legacy.... This long overdue modern translation is an important and fascinating addition to Franciscan literature"—*(LJ)*.

Saint Francis of Assisi: Social Reformer. By Leo L. Dubois. 1906. *Folcroft* $15.00

Saint Francis of Assisi: A Biography. By Johannes Jorgensen. Trans. by T. O'Conor Sloane. 1912 *Doubleday* Image Bks. 1955 pap. $1.45

Saint Francis of Assisi. By Gilbert K. Chesterton. *Doubleday* new ed. 1927 Image Bks. 1957 pap. $1.25

Francis of Assisi. By Ray C. Petry. 1941. *AMS Press* $6.50

St. Francis, Nature Mystic: The Derivation and Significance of the Nature Stories in the Franciscan Legend. By Edward A. Armstrong. *Univ. of California Press* 1963 $12.00

St. Francis of Assisi. By Abbé Omer Englebert. *Franciscan Herald Press* 1965 $8.50

St. Francis of Assisi: A Great Life in Brief. By E. M. Almedingen. *Knopf* 1967 $4.95
"In telling Francis' story [the author] recreates the world and the church of the time, thereby clarifying the unique character that was Francis.... His youthful problems, his spiritual crises, and the role played by [Saint] Clare are all included in this biography and help to give even greater stature to this universally loved Saint. Highly recommended"—*(LJ)*.

St. Francis of Assisi. By T. S. R. Boase. *Indiana Univ. Press* 1968 $7.50
"Among the numerous lives of St. Francis this one ... is a small masterpiece.... More important than the clear picture of the life and times of the 13th Century is the affectionate and reverent insight into the heart of Brother Francis. This gracious retelling of the fact and fable that make up the legend can be enjoyed by all kinds of readers of all shades of belief"—*(LJ)*.

Saint Francis. By Nikos Kazantzakis. *Simon & Schuster* Touchstone-Clarion Bks. pap. $2.95

St. Francis of Assisi: Patron of the Environment. By Warren N. Hansen. *Franciscan Herald Press* 1971 $4.95

St. Francis of Assisi. By John Holland-Smith. *Scribner* 1972 $8.95

Brother Francis: An Anthology of Writings by and about St. Francis Assisi. Ed. by Lawrence Cunningham. *Harper* 1972 $5.95

St. Francis of Assisi: Writings and Early Biographies Omnibus of Sources for Life of St. Francis. Ed. by Marion A. Habig and others. *Franciscan Herald Press* 1973 $18.95

Francis of Assisi. By John H. Smith. *Scribner* 1974 pap. $1.95

St. Francis of Assisi. By Morris Bishop. Library of World Biography Ser. *Little* 1974 $6.95
"Bishop does not deny the spiritual and poetic genius of the saint, but he puts these qualities into focus along with Francis' less saintly emotions.... Bishop does not debunk Francis, but tries to understand him in the light of our current insights into behavior and motivation"—*(LJ)*.

THOMAS AQUINAS, SAINT. 1225?–1274.

The study of philosophy has as an end, Thomas Aquinas said, not the knowledge of what others have thought, but objective truth. This Italian philosopher and Doctor of the Church, the greatest figure of medieval Scholasticism, is one of the principal saints of the Roman Catholic Church (canonized in 1323) and the founder of the system declared by Leo XIII to be its official philosophy. His two most important works are his "*Summa Contra Gentiles*," which "defends Christianity in the area of natural theology," and "*Summa Theologica*," a work whose "three divisions are related to God, Man, and Christ and in which Thomas attempted to summarize all human knowledge." "St. Thomas's magnificent synthesis is now recognized generally as one of the greatest works of human thought. His wide-embracing philosophy is applied to every realm of human life. Thomism is a complete structure in itself, not simply a collection of theories"— (*Columbia Encyclopedia*).

SUMMA THEOLOGIAE. c. 1265–1274. Thomas Gillby, O.P. (Cambridge), P. K. Meagher, O.P. (Cambridge) and T. C. O'Brien, O.P. (American supervising editor, Washington), Gen. Eds. *McGraw-Hill* 60 vols. 1964–74 (*consult catalog for titles and prices*)

Ranking among the greatest documents of the Christian church, providing the framework for Catholic studies in theology and for a classical Christian philosophy, the publication of this new edition is of major importance. Each volume is a self-contained treatise. Each page of the Latin text (newly revised) is faced by a fresh English translation which is explanatory rather than literal; glossary of technical terms.

SUMMA THEOLOGICA. Trans. by the Fathers of the English Dominican Province; with 50 articles by scholars *Christian Class.* 3 vols. set $60.00

BASIC WRITINGS. Ed. and annot. with introd. by Anton C. Pegis *Random* 2 vols. 1945 boxed set $25.00

THE WRITINGS OF ST. THOMAS AQUINAS. Trans. by Thomas Gilby *Heritage Press* deluxe ed. $10.00

SELECTED WRITINGS. Trans. by Robert P. Goodwin *Bobbs* 1965 $6.00 pap. $1.60; ed. by M. C. D'Arcy *Dutton* Everyman's 1939 $3.95

INTRODUCTION TO ST. THOMAS AQUINAS. Ed. by Anton C. Pegis *Random* Modern Lib. 1948 pap. $1.95

THE POCKET AQUINAS. Ed. by Vernon J. Bourke *Simon & Schuster* Washington Square (orig.) 1960 pap. $1.25

AN AQUINAS READER. Ed. by Mary T. Clark *Doubleday* Image Bks. 1972 pap. $2.45

SELECTED POLITICAL WRITINGS. Trans. by J. G. Dawson *Harper* (Barnes & Noble) 1959 $6.50; *Macmillan* 1960 pap. $2.75

COMMENTARY ON THE METAPHYSICS OF ARISTOTLE. Trans. by John P. Rowan *Regnery* 2 vols. 1961 set $25.00. The first translation into English of this monumental work.

Other titles are published by AMS Press, Doubleday, Hafner, Magi Bks., Marquette Univ. Press, Prentice-Hall, and Regnery.

Books about St. Thomas Aquinas

The Philosophy of St. Thomas Aquinas. By Étienne Gilson. 1924. *Folcroft* $20.00
Saint Thomas Aquinas. By Gilbert Keith Chesterton. 1933. With an appreciation by Anton C. Pegis *Doubleday* Image Bks. 1974 pap. $1.45
The Spirit in the World. By Karl Rahner. 1939 rev. 1957. Trans. by William Dych *Seabury Press* 1968 $9.50
   "This work is very profound and would be of benefit mainly to readers on the graduate level"—(*Choice*).
St. Thomas and the Problem of Evil. By Jacques Maritain. *Marquette Univ. Press* 1942 $2.50. One of the Aquinas Lecture series.
Aquinas. By Frederick C. Copleston, S.J. *Penguin* Pelican Bks. (orig.) 1955 pap. $1.45; *Gannon* $4.50
The Christian Philosophy of St. Thomas Aquinas. By Étienne Gilson. With a Catalogue of St. Thomas's Works by I. T. Eschmann; trans. by L. K. Shook *Random* 1956 1960 $10.00
The Political Thought of Thomas Aquinas. By Thomas Gilby. *Univ. of Chicago Press* 1958 pap. $9.50

Thomism: An Introduction. By Paul Grenet. Trans. from the French by James F. Ross *Christian Class.* 1960 $4.95
> An examination, by a philosophy professor at the Institut Catholique of Paris, of Aquinas' philosophy of nature and metaphysics. "Recommended"—*(LJ).*

A Philosophy of God: The Elements of Thomist Natural Theology. By Thomas Gornall, S.J. *Sheed & Ward* 1962 $3.95
> Father Gornall, lecturer in philosophy at Heythrop College in England, "has taken St. Thomas's thoughts relating to God, His existence and his attributes and re-emphasized them in a very readable style to combat present-day misunderstandings of basic Thomist concepts."

Saint Thomas and Philosophy. By Anton C. Pegis. *Marquette Univ. Press* 1964 $2.50

Thomism in an Age of Renewal. Ed. by Ralph M. McInerny. 1966. *Univ. of Notre Dame Press* 1968 pap. $2.45
> Professor McInerny of Notre Dame concludes that "St. Thomas's clarity of thought and the intellectual discipline which his philosophy provides is as relevant now as it was in the 13th century. This book has the carefully reasoned development and pedagogical wit one expects from a good philosophy teacher"—*(LJ).*

DUNS SCOTUS, JOHANNES (John). c. 1265–1308. *See Chapter 5, Philosophy: Medieval Philosophy, this Volume.*

THOMAS à KEMPIS (Thomas van Kempen). 1380–1471.

Thomas van Kempen was born in the German town of Kempen, from which came the name he is known by. He was educated at a school founded by Gerhard Groote and later entered a monastery established by him. There Thomas spent the rest of his long life. The "Imitation of Christ" is usually attributed to him, although there has been dispute as to whether he was merely the copyist for the manuscript.

IMITATIO CHRISTI (Of the Imitation of Christ). Trans. by Sr. Simone Inkel *Abbey Press* 1973 pap. $3.95; *Bruce Pub. Co.* 1940 1959 $2.25; ed. by Harold Gardiner *Doubleday Image Bks.* 1955 pap. $1.45; *Dutton* Everyman's $3.95; *Moody Press* pap. $1.25; ed. by Albert J. Nevins *Our Sunday Visitor* 1973 pap. $1.50; trans. by Leo Sherley-Price *Penguin* Class. pap. $1.45; *Peter Pauper Press* (dist. by Van Nostrand-Reinhold) $1.95 deluxe ed. $4.95; *Revell* 1963 $1.95; trans. by Msgr. Ronald Knox and Michael Oakley *Sheed & Ward* 1959 $3.00 imit. lea. $3.50; *Wehman* 1969 $2.95; trans. by George Stanhope 1886 *Richard West* $10.00
> This classic book of meditation and admonition attributed to the Dutch monk, Thomas van Kempen, but possibly written by another member of his circle, the *"Devotio Moderna,"* is often published as a prayer book. Its gentle piety and unworldliness have made it popular with Christians of all denominations. It was written in Latin and has been translated into many editions. The anonymous translation used in the Everyman's edition is the earliest one in English (1440).

Books about Thomas à Kempis

Thomas à Kempis. By S. Kettlewell. 1882. *Richard West* 2 vols. $85.00

Thomas à Kempis: His Age and Book. By J. E. De Montmorency. 1906. *Kennikat* 1970 $12.50

ERASMUS, DESIDERIUS (Erasmus of Rotterdam). 1469–1536.

Erasmus, the great Dutch scholar and humanist, is regarded as the leader in the renaissance of learning in northern Europe. He was a friend and correspondent of every notable figure of his day. During his third trip to England (1509–14), he taught Greek at Cambridge and completed his scholarly Latin translation from the Greek New Testament, which for centuries remained the basis of New Testament scholarship. In a single week at the home of Sir Thomas More (*q.v.*), Erasmus wrote his satirical monologue in Latin, "The Praise of Folly." Folly praises herself and proclaims her superiority over Wisdom. The author's argument, of course, is "that it is folly not to see things as they really are; scholars should not abandon ideals just because they cannot be fully realized but should apply their learning and reason as best they can to daily living."

Erasmus was born in Rotterdam, the son of Gerard, priest at Gouda, and Margaretha, a woman of Rotterdam. Their love story is told in Charles Reade's "The Cloister and the Hearth" (*q.v.*). He was educated at the universities of Paris, Turin and Bologna, ordained a priest and became Bachelor and Doctor of Theology. With the other humanists he sought to integrate classical and biblical knowledge. During the great turbulence of the Reformation he tried not to take sides but, disliking Luther's violence, finally took his stand against his friend and with the Roman Catholics. When the Reformation was triumphant in 1529 he went into exile. One of his most popular works was the "Adages," (*see note below*), which went into 120 editions before 1570. It contains over 3,000 apothegms with·explanations which show an appreciation of classical rhetoric. His influence was felt in the works of Luther, Rabelais and Montaigne, and his educational theories took root in English schools.

THE ESSENTIAL ERASMUS. Ed. by John P. Dolan *New Am. Lib.* Mentor Bks. 1964 pap. $1.25

CHRISTIAN HUMANISM AND THE REFORMATION: Selected Writings. With "The Life of Erasmus" by Beatus Rhenanus. Ed. by John C. Olin *Peter Smith* 1967 $4.25

ERASMUS ON HIS TIMES: A Shortened Version of the Adages (1500). Ed. by Margaret Mann Phillips *Cambridge* 1964 1967 pap. $3.95

"The Adages" was one of the earliest "best sellers" and went through many reprints in its author's lifetime. Influential in its age, it consists of Latin or Greek popular sayings (the latter Erasmus translated into Latin) followed by Erasmus' philosophical comments. "Necessary evil," "a rare bird" and "a dog in the manger" are expressions found here. Mrs. Phillips, a Fellow of the (English) Royal Society of Literature, provides a lengthy introductory section and translates most of Erasmus' original Latin essays.

ENCHIRIDION. 1503. Trans. and ed. by Raymond Himelick. 1963. *Peter Smith* 1967 $4.50

THE PRAISE OF FOLLY. 1511. Trans. and ed. by Leonard F. Dean *Hendricks House* 1969 $3.00 pap. $1.95; *Univ. of Michigan Press* 1958 $4.40 Ann Arbor Bks. 1958 pap. $1.95; trans. by Betty Radice *Penguin* pap. $1.95; trans. by Hoyt H. Hudson *Princeton Univ. Press* 1970 $7.50 pap. $2.95

THE EDUCATION OF A CHRISTIAN PRINCE. 1515. Ed. by Lester K. Born *Octagon* 1965 $12.50; *Norton* 1968 pap. $2.95

COLLOQUIES. 1516. Trans. by Craig R. Thompson *Univ. of Chicago Press* 1965 $22.50

This eminently "browsable" work is presented here in its "first full-length translation . . . since the 18th century . . . handsomely printed and fully introduced. Originally intended as aids to learning Latin, the dialogues were soon discovered as vehicles for their author's reforming notions and personal attitudes and reflect him accordingly—by turns biting, tolerant, amused, provocative, and sober. Best of all the translator manages to stay out of his author's way"—*(LJ)*.

THE JULIUS EXCLUSUS. 1518. Trans. by Paul Pascal; introd. and notes by J. Kelly Sowards *Indiana Univ. Press* 1968 $6.95

The dialogue between Pope Julius II (1443–1513) and St. Peter "written just after the pope's death [but not published until later] and here translated for the first time in its entirety, is a trenchant and bitterly amusing criticism-from-within of the Renaissance church and at the same time supports the conciliar movement in passages of deep idealism"—*(LJ)*.

TEN COLLOQUIES. Ed. by Craig R. Thompson *Bobbs* 1957 $5.00 pap. $1.50

THE COMPLAINT OF PEACE. (And the "Adages") trans. by Margaret Mann Phillips *Garland Pub.* $23.50; trans. by T. Paynell *Open Court* 1974 $5.00 pap. $1.45

EPISTLES OF ERASMUS: From His Earliest Letters to His Fifty-first Year, Arranged in Order of Time, Translated from the Early Correspondence, with a Commentary Confirming the Chronological Arrangement and Supplying Further Biographical Matter. Trans. by Francis M. Nichols, with introd., notes and critical commentary. 1918. *Russell & Russell* 3 vols. 1962 set $50.00

ERASMUS AND CAMBRIDGE: The Cambridge Letters of Erasmus. Ed. by H. C. Porter and D. F. Thomson *Univ. of Toronto Press* 1963 $12.50

CORRESPONDENCE. Ed. by Beatrice Corrigan *Univ. of Toronto Press* 2 vols. 1974–75 Vol. I Letters 1–141: 1484–1500 (1974) Vol. 2 Letters 142–297: 1501–1514 (1975) each $25.00

(With Martin Luther). DISCOURSE ON FREE WILL. 1524. Trans. by Ernst F. Winter *Ungar* 1960 $5.00 pap. $1.95. Erasmus' attack and Luther's reply.

Books about Erasmus

Bondage of the Will. By Martin Luther. Trans. by J. L. Packer and O. R. Johnston. *Revell* 1970 $5.95

The Age of Erasmus. By Percy S. Allen. 1914. *Russell & Russell* 1963 $10.00

Erasmus: A Study of His Life, Ideals and Place in History. By Preserved Smith. 1923. *Peter Smith* $4.25

A Key to the Colloquies of Erasmus. By Preserved Smith. 1927. *Kraus* pap. $3.50

The Youth of Erasmus. By Albert Hyma. 1931. *Russell & Russell* 2nd ed. 1968 $16.00

Erasmus of Rotterdam. By Stefan Zweig. Trans. by Eden and Cedar Paul. 1934. *Richard West* $20.00

Erasmus and the Northern Renaissance. By Margaret Mann Phillips. 1949. *Macmillan* Collier Bks. 1965 pap. $1.25; *Verry* 1949 $4.00

Erasmus and the Age of Reformation. By Johan Huizinga. *Harper* Torchbks. 1957 pap. $1.95

Erasmus of Christendom. By Roland H. Bainton. *Scribner* 1969 pap. $2.65; *Christian Class.* $6.95
This "will probably become the standard work on Erasmus in English. . . . Recommended for all libraries which seek interesting and important holdings in religion or church history"—(*Choice*).

Erasmus. Ed. by T. A. Dorey. *Univ. of New Mexico Press* 1970 $6.00
This volume by British and Canadian scholars "contains chapters on the importance of Erasmus as an interpreter of the Classics, as a satirist, and as a writer of letters. There is an account of his work as a Biblical scholar and religious reformer, an examination of his linguistic style, and a discussion of the Medieval background and the significance of Erasmus to our own times"—(Introduction).

MORE, SIR THOMAS, SAINT. 1478–1535. *See Chapter 10, British Fiction: Early Period*, Reader's Adviser, *Vol. I.*

LUTHER, MARTIN. 1483–1546.

Luther, the great religious reformer, was also "a literary genius whose services to German literature cannot be overestimated." His three great literary monuments are the German Bible, his hymns and his polemical prose writings. His translation of the New Testament (1522) based on the Greek version of Erasmus (*q.v.*) and of the Old Testament (1523–1534) from the Hebrew of Reuchlin was called by Nietzsche (*q.v.*) "*das Meisterstück der Deutschen Prosa*" (the masterpiece of German prose). Using a "vivid, homely German salted with popular phrases and colloquialisms," Luther's Bible went into 377 editions during his lifetime and remains the standard Protestant version in German, comparable to the King James version in English. The hymns combine piety with a popular spirit and rhythm suitable for congregational participation. The most famous is "*Ein' feste Burg ist Unser Gott*" (A Mighty Fortress is Our God). His Reformation tracts, sermons, commentaries and catechisms, all written in a homely racy idiom for popular appeal in his time, are now read mostly by specialists.

The father of the German Reformation was born in Eisleben, became an Augustinian friar and was ordained a priest. Luther was early to recognize that his spiritual views were in conflict with those of the Pope and the Church. He held that a man's sins could be forgiven through his own faith. After a mission to Rome (1510–1511), he attacked the sale of indulgences, or priestly forgiveness of sin, by which money was being raised for the construction of St. Peter's. In 1517 he is said to have nailed to the church door in Wittenberg his 95 "theses" against the sale of such indulgences. After three years in which he defended his stand in speeches and writings, he was excommunicated and his works were burned in Rome in 1520. In 1521 he refused to recant before the Diet of Worms, was put under the ban of the empire and hidden by his friend Frederick of Saxony in Wartburg castle. Here he began his translation of the New Testament. He returned to Wittenberg in 1522 and married a former nun in 1525. The term, "Protestants" was given to his followers, who "protested" against the Edict of Worms.

LUTHER'S WORKS. *Concordia* and *Fortress* 56 vols. 1958–   (*consult publishers' catalogs for titles, prices, and various editors and translators*)

This edition is making available large bodies of material hitherto accessible only in the original tongues. The translations are being made by those who know German (including Luther's German of the 16th century), and also Latin, Greek and Hebrew in order to deal with the biblical quotations.

SELECTED WRITINGS. Ed. by Theodore G. Tappert *Fortress* 4 vols. pap. 1967 each $3.50 set $12.00

MARTIN LUTHER: Selections from His Writings. Ed. with introd. by John Dillenberger *Doubleday* Anchor Bks. 1961 pap. $2.95

GREAT THOUGHTS FROM LUTHER. *Collins-World* $1.95

NINETY-FIVE THESES (With the Pertinent Documents from the History of the Reformation). Ed. by Kurt Aland *Concordia* 1967 $3.50; ed. by E. G. Schwiebert *Concordia* 1948 pap. $.50; ed. by G. W. Sandt *Fortress* 1957 pap. $3.00

LUTHER'S LARGE CATECHISM. Trans. by J. M. Lenker *Augsburg* 1967 $2.75; *Fortress* 1961 $4.50

THE SMALL CATECHISM IN CONTEMPORARY ENGLISH. *Augsburg* 1963 pap. $.30; *Fortress* 1963 pap. $.30

THE BONDAGE OF THE WILL. Trans. by J. I. Packer and O. K. Johnston *Kregel* $3.75; *Revell* 1970 $5.95

THREE TREATISES. Trans. by Charles M. Jacobs and others *Fortress* 1943 pap. $2.75

CHRISTIAN LIBERTY. *Fortress* 1943 pap. $.60

Books about Luther

Luther and the German Reformation. By Thomas M. Lindsay. 1900. *Folcroft* $20.00; *Richard West* $25.00

Luther's Table Talk. By Preserved Smith. 1907. *Columbia* 1970 $7.50

Life and Letters of Martin Luther. By Preserved Smith. 1911. *Richard West* 1973 $20.00

Three Reformers: Luther, Descartes, Rousseau. By Jacques Maritain. 1928. *Greenwood* $10.50; *Kennikat* 1970 $8.75; *Peter Smith* $4.25

Here I Stand: A Life of Martin Luther. By Roland H. Bainton. *Abingdon* 1951 $6.95 pap. $2.25; *New Am. Lib.* Mentor Bks. pap. $1.25

The Revolt of Martin Luther. By Robert Herndon Fife. *Columbia* 1957 $15.00. A searching biography of Luther's life up to and including the Diet of Worms—the crucial period during which his theological views were molded. His youthful impressions, formative experiences and influential associations are told dramatically.

Young Man Luther. By Erik H. Erikson. *Norton* 1958 $6.50 pap. $1.95

Luther the Expositor. Ed. by Jaroslav Pelikan. *Concordia* 1959 $9.00

Luther. By John Osborne. *New Am. Lib.* Signet 1961 pap. $.95

A moving and effective British play about this haunted and neurotic mover of men, with the emphasis on his physical, mental and spiritual trials.

The Age of the Reformation. By Preserved Smith. *Macmillan* Collier Bks. 2 vols. pap. 1962 each $1.50

Studies on the Reformation. By Roland H. Bainton. *Beacon* 1963 pap. $2.25. Deals especially with Martin Luther and his struggle with some radical interpreters of the Reformation.

Luther's Progress to the Diet of Worms. By Gordon Rupp. *Harper* Torchbks. 1964 pap. $1.45

Luther and the Reformation. By Vivian H. H. Green. *Putnam* Capricorn Giants 1964 pap. $1.95

A "concise, balanced history" (*LJ*) with chronology and bibliography.

Martin Luther: A Biographical Study. By John M. Todd. *Paulist-Newman* 1964 pap. $2.95

"Well-written" biography (*LJ*) by a scholarly Roman Catholic layman.

Luther for an Ecumenical Age: Essays in Commemoration of the 450th Anniversary of the Reformation. Ed. by Carl S. Meyer. *Concordia* 1967 $9.00

Martin Luther. Ed. by Brian Tierney and others. *Random* 1968 pap. $1.25

The Trial of Luther. By James Atkinson. *Stein & Day* 1971 $7.95

Atkinson "scrutinizes the juridical skirmishing and also dissects the theological and ecclesiastical issues at stake. One of the more useful features of the presentation is the author's translation of several conflicting eyewitness stenographic accounts of the proceedings at Worms. The book's perspective is decidedly pro-Luther; however the evaluation of all principal personalities is fair. Facsimiles of pertinent documents and portrait engravings enhance the appeal of the narrative"—(*LJ*).

The Ethics of Martin Luther. By Paul Althaus. Trans. from German by Robert C. Schultz. *Fortress* 1972 $8.95

The German Nation and Martin Luther. By Arthur G. Dickens. *Harper* 1974 $12.50

MENNO SIMONS. c. 1496–1561.

Born in Friesland, Menno Simons became an ordained priest who studied the New Testament and the teachings of Martin Luther. He questioned the rite of infant baptism; nor was he satisfied with the answers given him by the leaders of the new Protestant movement. In 1556 he left the Catholic Church and joined a branch of the Anabaptists, whose leader he became. The Mennonites are survivors of this group.

COMPLETE WRITINGS OF MENNO SIMONS. Ed. by John C. Wenger; trans. by Leonard Verduin *Herald Press* 1956 $15.95

Books about Menno Simons

A Tribute to Menno Simons. By Franklin H. Littell. *Herald Press* 1961 pap. $1.25

Bibliography of Menno Simons. By Irvin B. Horst. *Herald Press* 1962 $17.00

Mennonites and Their Heritage. By Harold S. Bender and C. Henry Smith. *Herald Press* 1964 pap. $1.50

Introduction to Mennonite History. Ed. by Cornelius J. Dyck. *Herald Press* 1967 $6.95 pap. $3.95

String of Amber: The Heritage of the Mennonites. By B. Davies. *Heinman* 1973 $10.00

MELANCHTHON, PHILIPP (Schwarzed or Schwartzerd, Philipp).   1497–1560.

Melanchthon (the Greek translation of his German name) was Luther's collaborator. A brilliant scholar from his youth, he became professor of Greek at the newly founded University of Wittenberg when he was only 21. His systematic exposition of Luther's theology, *"Loci Communes Rerum Theologicarum"* (1521), was the first great scholarly treatise of the Protestant Reformation. Melanchthon also drafted the Augsburg confession. A moderate, Melanchthon tried to settle the differences between Luther and Calvin and to find a position of agreement for Protestants and Catholics. He was noted for his vast learning, his skill in dialectics and exegesis.

SELECTED WRITINGS. Ed. by Elmer E. Flack and Lowell Satre; trans. by Charles L. Hill *Augsburg* 1962 o.p.

MELANCHTON AND BUCER. Ed. by Wilhelm Pauck Library of Christian Class. *Westminster Press* 1969 $7.50

Translations of Melanchthon's *Loci Communes Theologici* (1521) and Bucer's "On the Kingdom of Christ." "Reformation expert Wilhelm Pauck, ably assisted by translators Lowell Satre and Paul Larkin, has provided the authoritative introductions [and] explanatory notes"—(*Christian Century*).

Books about Melanchthon

Philipp Melanchthon, The Protestant Preceptor of Germany. By James W. Richard. 1898. *Burt Franklin* 1974 $21.50

Melanchthon: Alien or Ally?. By Franz Hildebrandt. 1946. *Kraus* 1968 $10.00

Melanchthon: The Quiet Reformer. By Clyde L. Manschreck. 1958. *Greenwood* 1975 $17.50

A New Look at the Lutheran Confession. By Holsten Fagerberg. Trans. by Gene J. Lund *Concordia* 1972 $12.50

KNOX, JOHN. 1505–1572.

Little is known of the early life of the founder of Scottish Presbyterianism. He entered the Roman Catholic Church as priest and became sympathetic toward some of the new reformation theories sweeping the continent. By 1545 he was an acknowledged Protestant and allied himself with the reformer George Wishart shortly before Wishart was burned for heresy. John Knox was called to the Ministry and preached for reformed religion in 1547. Captured at St. Andrews when it was forced to surrender, he was sent to France and was thrown into a French prison galley, 1548–1549. Rescued by the Protestant Government of King Edward VI, he went to England where he was appointed a royal chaplain in 1551. At the ascension of the Catholic Mary Tudor to the English throne, he fled to Geneva. There he studied and conferred with John Calvin. Knox returned to Scotland in 1559 and preached widely against Catholicism and especially against Mary, Queen of Scots, whom he called Jezebel. Under Knox's tireless leadership, Presbyterianism became the official religion of Scotland.

His writings included the "First Blast of the Trumpet against the Monstrous Regiment of Women" (1558), a fiery tract aimed at Mary Tudor and the Scottish Regent, Mary of Guise, but published only in time to offend Elizabeth I; and the "History of the Reformation of Religion within the Realme of Scotland," finished in 1564, but not published until after his death, in 1584. He is not to be confused with the modern writer on religion of the same name.

WORKS. Ed. by David Laing. 1846–64. *AMS Press* 6 vols. each $28.00 set $205.00

GREAT THOUGHTS FROM KNOX. *Collins-World* imitation lea. $1.95

Books about Knox

John Knox and the Reformation. By Andrew Lang. 1905. *Folcroft* 1973 $9.95; *Kennikat* 1966 $10.00

John Knox: The Hero of the Scottish Reformation. By Henry Cowan. 1905. *AMS Press* 1970 $16.00

John Knox and John Knox's House. By Charles J. Guthrie. 1905. *Richard West* 1973 $25.00

John Knox: Portrait of a Calvinist. By Edward Muir. 1929. *Bks. for Libraries* $12.50; *Norwood Editions* $11.45

John Knox. By G. R. Pearce. 1936. *Richard West* $12.50

John Knox. By Eustace Percy. 1937. *Attic Press* 1964 $4.00; *John Knox Press* 1965 $3.00; *Richard West* $4.00

The Life of John Knox. By George R. Preedy. 1940. *Richard West* $25.00

Plain Mr. Knox. By Elizabeth Whitley. *John Knox Press* 1961 $1.00
Trumpeter of God. By W. Stanford Reid. *Scribner* 1974 $12.50

CALVIN, JOHN (orig. Jean Chauvin or Caulvin). 1509–1564.

Next to Luther (*q.v.*) the most commanding figure of the Reformation is John Calvin. He is the only one of the great reformers who can justly be called international. Although he lived in exile from his native France, he directed the French reformation, he advised the English Archbishop Thomas Cranmer when Cranmer, as regent to the youthful Edward VI, was preparing the Prayer Book in the English language, and he counselled John Knox (*q.v.*) during the latter's residence in Geneva. It was in Geneva, of course, that Calvin established the theocracy he governed for 23 years.

"The Institutes of the Christian Religion" was the first theological treatise in French prose. Calvin's style is "clear and precise," with all the forcefulness of Latin oratory. The French Protestant theologian and scholar was well educated at the University of Paris and the law schools of Orléans and Bourges. He was thoroughly trained in law and logic and in Latin, Greek and Hebrew. After he had accepted many of Martin Luther's ideas he was forced to flee from France to Basle, Switzerland. "The Institutes" was written originally in Latin and published first in 1536. Calvin later expanded it and translated it into French in 1541. It was responsible for the spread of Protestantism in non-Lutheran countries and "shaped the ideas of the Huguenots in France, the Puritans in England, and through them the early culture of America." It influenced Milton, John Bunyan and Jonathan Edwards.

JOHN CALVIN: Selections from His Writings. Ed. by John Dillenberger *Doubleday* Anchor Bks. (orig.) 1971 pap. $2.45

THEOLOGICAL TREATISES. Ed. by John K. S. Reid *Westminster Press* 1954 $6.00

THE INSTITUTES OF THE CHRISTIAN RELIGION. 1536. 1541. Ed. by John T. McNeill; trans. by Ford Lewis Battle *Westminster Press* 2 vols. 1949 1960 set $15.00

ON GOD AND MAN: Selections from The Institutes of the Christian Religion. Ed. by F. W. Strothmann *Ungar* 1965 $3.75 pap. $.95

ON THE CHRISTIAN FAITH: Selections from the Institutes, Commentaries and Tracts. Ed. by John T. McNeill *Bobbs* 1958 pap. $1.45

ON GOD AND POLITICAL DUTY. *Bobbs* 1956 pap. $1.25

CONCERNING THE ETERNAL PREDESTINATION OF GOD. Trans. by J. K. S. Reid *Attic Press* 1961 $6.50

CALVIN: Commentaries. Ed. by Joseph Haroutunian *Westminster Press* 1958 $7.50

COMMENTARIES ON THE OLD TESTAMENT. *Eerdmans* 30 vols. 1948 each $5.50–$7.95. Reprint of an 1845 edition.

NEW TESTAMENT COMMENTARIES. Various editors and translators. *Eerdmans* 9 vols. 1959–64 $5.00–$7.95

CALVIN'S NEW TESTAMENT COMMENTARIES. Trans. by Thomas H. L. Parker *Eerdmans* 1972 $7.95

LETTERS. Compiled from the original manuscripts and edited with historical notes by Jules Bonnet; trans. by M. R. Gilchrist and David Constable. 1858. *Burt Franklin* 4 vols. 1973 set $85.00

(With Jacopo Sadoleto). REFORMATION DEBATE. Ed. By John C. Olin *Harper* Torchbks. pap. $1.45; *Peter Smith* $4.00

Books about Calvin

John Calvin: The Organiser of Reformed Protestantism, 1509–1564. By Williston Walker. 1906. *AMS Press* $8.50; *Schocken* 1969 $8.50 pap. $2.95

The Rise and Development of Calvinism. By John H. Bratt. *Eerdmans* 1959 pap. $2.45

Word and Spirit: Calvin's Doctrine of Biblical Authority. By H. Jackson Forstman. *Stanford Univ. Press* 1962 $6.50
    This praiseworthy collation of Calvin's concepts is somewhat marred for the general reader by its dissertation style. Numerous examples are drawn from the "Institutes" and the "Commentaries." An Epilogue summarizes contemporary attitudes towards the Calvinistic heritage.

Studies in John Calvin. Ed. by Gervase E. Duffield. *Eerdmans* 1966 $5.95

John Calvin, the Church and the Eucharist. By Kilian McDonnell. *Princeton Univ. Press* 1967 $15.00

Calvin and Calvinism: Sources of Democracy. Ed. by Robert M. Kingdon and Robert D. Lindner. *Heath* 1970 pap. $2.50

Calvinism and the Religious Wars. By Franklin C. Palm. *Howard Fertig* 1971 $8.50

Constructive Revolutionary: John Calvin and His Socio-Economic Impact. By W. Fred Graham. *John Knox Press* 1971 $7.95

"This is a study of Calvin's 'secular' thought. It analyzes Calvin's social and economic influence on the Geneva of his time and on the Western world today"—(Publisher's note). "A useful book for Reformation and Calvinism collections"—(*LJ*).

The Heritage of John Calvin: Lectures. By John H. Bratt. *Eerdmans* 1973 $5.95

TERESA (or Theresa) OF JESUS, SAINT. 1515–1582. *See Chapter 11, Spanish Literature*, Reader's Adviser, *Vol. 2.*

JOHN OF THE CROSS, SAINT (San Juan de la Cruz; real name Juan de Yepis y Alvarez). 1542–1591. *See Chapter 11, Spanish Literature*, Reader's Adviser, *Vol. 2.*

PASCAL, BLAISE. 1623–1662.

"Blaise Pascal . . . was a passionate, many-sided genius, whose intellectual vigor triumphed over physical infirmity so severe as to occasion the admission that he had 'never passed a day without pain.' Respected as a creative mathematician even today, he was also an amateur physicist and the inventor of the first workable calculating machine. His stinging *Provincial Letters* in defense of the Jansenists infuriated the powerful Jesuits; best known for his *Pensées,* he will never be forgotten as a spiritual writer." So John K. Amrein, a librarian of Penn State University, describes this many-sided man (in *LJ*). "*Pensées*" is an attempt to show the necessity of Christian belief. In his famous "bet" or wager, Pascal concludes that since one cannot prove or disprove God's existence, one may lose by not believing and can only gain by believing. Pascal's style is still considered one of the finest in French literature.

PROVINCIAL LETTERS. 1656–57. Trans. by A. J. Krailsheimer *Penguin* 1968 o.p. This title is available in French.

PENSÉES. 1670. Trans. by W. F Trotter, ed. with introd. and notes by Louis Lafuma *Dutton* Everyman's 1931 new ed. 1960 $3.95; introd. and notes by H. F. Stewart *Random* (Modern Lib.) 1967 pap. $1.45; trans. by H. F. Stewart *Pantheon* 1965 $8.95; trans. with introd. by A. J. Krailsheimer *Penguin* 1961 pap. $1.65

First published in 1670, after his death, the "*Pensées*" "is, in reality, the skeleton of an Apologia for Christianity which Pascal was preparing." Because of the religious biases of Pascal's friend, the Duc de Roanez, and the committee of Jansenists who prepared the copy, this and other early editions fail to do justice to Pascal. *Choice* (June 1967) says of the *Penguin* Krailsheimer translation: "The best English translation of the *Pensées* yet, and replaces in the Penguin Classics series the translation by J. M. Cohen, which was already quite good. Krailsheimer's version also compares favorably with that of Turnell—probably the best previous one—in that it so frequently achieves Pascal's pungency or eloquence with less departure from the literal meaning. Krailsheimer has also had the intelligence to base his translation on the Lafuma major edition (not the case of any other translation) which is probably the best and certainly the most useful for reference. And the translator . . . has provided an introduction which is a model: concise, well written, and so judicious and perceptive that specialists as well as novices to Pascal studies will find much of interest. As interest in Pascal seems to be at an all-time high, this book should certainly be in every library; one could almost wish it to replace all other versions, for none other will lead students to such a true appreciation of Pascal, and some others (e.g. the Trotter version, which is generally available) will positively mislead them."

THE HEART OF PASCAL. by H. F. Stewart. 1945. *Folcroft* 1974 $17.50; *Richard West* $10.00. His meditations and prayers, notes for his anti-Jesuit campaign, remarks on language and style, etc. drawn from the "*Pensées*."

THE THOUGHTS: A Selection of Blaise Pascal. Ed. and trans. by Arthur H. Beattie *AHM Pub. Corp.* Crofts Class. 1965 pap. $.85

THOUGHTS ON RELIGION AND OTHER SUBJECTS. Trans. by W. F. Trotter; ed. by Elizabeth B. Thayer and Horace S. Thayer *Simon & Schuster* (Washington Square) 1965 pap. $.75

Books about Pascal

Pascal and the Port Royalists. By William Clark. 1902. *Richard West* $20.00
Pascal's Philosophy of Religion. By C. J. Webb. 1929. *Kraus* $5.50
Pascal, the Life of Genius. By Morris Bishop. 1936. *Greenwood* 1968 $19.75
Blaise Pascal. By H. F. Stewart. 1942. *Richard West* 1973 $5.00
Pascal: The Emergence of Genius. By Émile Cailliet. 1961. *Greenwood* 2nd ed. $14.75
Pascal. By Jean Mesnard. *Univ. of Alabama Press* 1969 $6.50
Strange Contrarieties: Pascal in England During the Age of Reason. By John C. Barker. *McGill-Queens Univ. Press* 1974 $15.00
Blaise Pascal: The Genius of His Thought. By Roger Hazelton. *Westminster Press* 1974 $7.50
"This short and very readable work investigates the motivating forces in Pascal's development and presents a holistic view of a complex personality. In addition to the necessary biographical data and descriptions of Pascal's scientific experiments there is a brilliant chapter on the literary style of the *"Pensées"* and "Provincial Letters"—(*LJ*).

FOX, GEORGE. 1624–1691.

The English founder of the Society of Friends (Quakers) was an extraordinary man and a mystic who sought to realize the presence of God within the human community. His life was marked by imprisonments, beatings and revilement, yet his spirit of steadfast courage and joy is evident throughout his voluminous writings. He was by nature serious and contemplative and at the age of 19 he "entered upon a wandering quest for spiritual enlightenment." When he was 22 he "underwent a mystical experience which taught him that Christianity is not an outward profession but an inner light by which Christ directly illumines the believing soul." Dissatisfied with the teachings of the established church and even the nonconformist groups of the time, Fox began preaching what he believed on his own in the country, in private houses and barns and in the open air. He began to preach in 1647, won many followers in spite of violent opposition, traveled in the West Indies and America and twice visited Holland. His "Journal," with a preface by his friend, William Penn, was published after his death.

A very valuable collection has been edited by Jessamyn West (*q.v.*), herself a lifelong Friend: "The Quaker Reader" (*Viking* 1962 $7.95). "Beginning with the writings of George Fox and his friend and follower William Penn, this anthology, through selections from diaries, journals and essays, traces the origins and spread of Quakerism, the increasing wealth and influence of Quaker communities on both sides of the Atlantic, their battle against slavery, led by John Woolman, and their world-wide achievements in the service of humanity"—(Publisher's note).

Works. 1831. *AMS Press* 8 vols. 1975 each $17.50 set $135.00

The Journal. 1694. Ed. by Norman Penney; introd. by Rufus Jones *Dutton* Everyman's $3.95; ed. by Norman Penney 1911 *Octagon* 2 vols. 1973 set $41.00; ed. by Rufus M. Jones with essay by Henry J. Cadbury *Putnam* Capricorn Bks. 1963 pap. $1.95

George Fox's Book of Miracles. Ed. by Henry J. Cadbury. 1948. *Octagon* 1973 $11.00

Books about Fox

Voice of the Lord: A Biography of George Fox. By Harry E. Wildes. *Univ. of Pennsylvania Press* 1964 $11.50
The Religion of George Fox as Revealed in His Epistles. By Howard H. Brinton. *Pendle Hill* 1968 pap. $.70
The Atonement of George Fox. By Emilia Fogelklou-Norlind. Ed. by Eleanore P. Mather. *Pendle Hill* 1969 pap. $.70
George Fox: Man and Prophet. By Hanna D. Monaghon. *Franklin Pub. Co.* (2047 Locust St., Philadelphia, Pa. 19103) 1970 $5.95

SWEDENBORG, EMANUEL. 1688–1772.

Swedenborg was a distinguished scientist who became assessor on the Swedish board of mines in 1716. Queen Ulrika Eleonora made him a nobleman in 1719 and he took his place in the House of Peers. He wrote many scientific and mathematical works in Latin and foresaw many modern inventions and scientific theories. About 1743 he began having visions and after resigning his position as assessor in 1747, he devoted the rest of his life to physical and spiritual research, writing voluminously in Latin on the interpretation of the Scriptures. Swedenborg believed in the absolute unity of a God who embraces infinite love and divine wisdom. He foresaw a Second Coming and believed himself divinely appointed to reveal Christian truth. He did not preach or try to found a sect himself, but after his death his followers organized the Swedenborgian Church known as New Jerusalem Church or Church of the New Jerusalem. "The True Christian Religion," his last and crowning work, provides a comprehensive summary of his teachings.

THE GIST OF SWEDENBORG. Ed. by Julian K. Smyth and William F. Wunsch *Swedenborg Foundation* 1962 $1.00

ARCANA COELESTIA (Heavenly Secrets). *Swedenborg Foundation* 12 vols. each $4.75 set $48.00 student ed. each $3.00 set $30.00

SPIRITUAL DIARY. *Krishna Press* 6 vols. $210.00; *Swedenborg Foundation* 5 vols. set $26.00

APOCALYPSE EXPLAINED. *Swedenborg Foundation* 6 vols. 1972 each $4.75 set $24.00 student ed. each $3.00 set $15.00

INDEX TO APOCALYPSE EXPLAINED. *Swedenborg Foundation* 2 vols. 1972 set $10.00

APOCALYPSE REVEALED. *Swedenborg Foundation* 2 vols. 1971 set $8.50

FOUR LEADING DOCTRINES OF THE NEW CHURCH. 1882. *AMS Press* 1972 $11.50; (with title "Four Doctrines") ed. by Alice S. Sechrist *Swedenborg Foundation* 1971 $4.75 text ed. $3.00 pap. $1.00

DIVINE PROVIDENCE. Trans. by William F. Wunsch *Swedenborg Foundation* 1961 rev. ed. 1970 $4.75 text ed. $3.00 pap. $1.00

HEAVEN AND HELL. 1758. *Swedenborg Foundation* 1971 $4.75 student ed. $3.00 pap. $1.00

THE TRUE CHRISTIAN RELIGION (Vera Christiana Religio): Containing the Universal Theology of the New Church Foretold by the Lord in Daniel VII 13, 14; and in Revelation XXI 1, 2. 1771. Trans. from the original Latin; ed. by John C. Ager *Swedenborg Foundation* 2 vols. 1963 1972 each $4.75 set $8.50 student ed. each $3.00 set $5.00

DIVINE LOVE AND WISDOM. *Swedenborg Foundation* 1969 $4.75 text ed. $3.00 pap. $1.00

MISCELLANEOUS THEOLOGICAL WORKS. 1857. *Swedenborg Foundation* 2nd ed. 1970 $4.75 student ed. $3.00

POSTHUMOUS THEOLOGICAL WORKS. *Swedenborg Foundation* 2 vols. 1972 each $4.75 set $8.50 student ed. each $3.00 set $5.00

Books about Swedenborg

Swedenborg: Life and Teachings. By George Trobridge. *Swedenborg Foundation* 1913 4th ed. 1968 $1.95 pap. $1.00. Biography with summaries of his theological, scientific and philosophical works.

My Religion. By Helen Adams Keller. 1927. *Pyramid Bks.* 1974 pap. $1.25; *Swedenborg Foundation* 1962 1972 $2.50 pap. $1.00

Emanuel Swedenborg, Scientist and Mystic. By Signe Toksvig. 1948. *Bks. for Libraries* 1972 $18.50

The Swedenborg Epic. By Cyriel O. Sigstedt. 1952. *AMS Press* 1971 $20.00

The Essential Swedenborg. By Sig Synnestvedt. *Swedenborg Foundation* 1970 $5.95

Emanuel Swedenborg. By Inge Jonsson. World Authors Ser. *Twayne* $6.95

Introduction to Swedenborg's Religious Thought. By John Howard Spalding. *Swedenborg Foundation* 1973 pap. $1.25

The Presence of Other Worlds: The Journey of Emanuel Swedenborg. By Wilson Van Dusen. *Harper* 1974 $6.95

"Van Dusen has done an admirable job of distilling the often obscure thought of this complex and unusual thinker"—*(LJ)*.

EDWARDS, JONATHAN. 1703–1758.

After graduating from Yale at 17, the precocious youth studied theology, and a few years later, joined his grandfather in the ministry at Northampton, Mass. After his grandfather's death he took over the congregation. A forceful preacher of powerful logic, Edwards was an ardent Calvinist. His favorite themes were predestination and the absolute dependence of humble man upon God and upon divine grace, which alone could save man. He rejected with fire the Arminian modification of these Calvinist doctrines. In 1734–1735 he held a religious revival in Northampton which in effect brought the "Great Awakening" to New England. Stern in demanding strict orthodoxy and fervent zeal from his congregation, Edwards was unbending in a controversy over tests for church membership. In 1750 his congregation dismissed him. He then moved to Stockbridge, Mass., where he went to care for the Indian mission and to minister to a small white congregation. There he completed his theological masterpiece, "The Freedom of the Will" (1754), which sets forth metaphysical and ethical arguments for determinism. In 1757 he was called to be President of the College of New Jersey (now Princeton) but he died a few months later.

WORKS. Ed. by Edward Williams and Edward Parsons. 1847. *Burt Franklin* 10 vols. 1968 set $185.00

WORKS. Ed. by Perry Miller. *Yale Univ. Press* 4 Vols. 1957–1972 Vol. 1 The Freedom of the Will, ed. by Paul Ramsey (1957) Vol. 2 Religious Affections, ed. by John E. Smith (1959) Vol. 3 Original Sin, ed. by Clyde A. Holbrook (1970) Vol. 4 The Great Awakening, ed. by C. C. Goen (1972) Vols. 1–3 each $22.50 Vol. 4 $27.50

JONATHAN EDWARDS: Basic Writings. Ed. by Ola Winslow *New Am. Lib.* Signet 1965 pap. $.95

JONATHAN EDWARDS: Representative Selections. Rev. ed. by Clarence H. Faust and Thomas H. Johnson. 1935. *Peter Smith* 1962 $5.00

SELECTED WRITINGS. Ed. by Harold P. Simonson *Ungar* 1970 $5.75 pap. $2.45

THE PHILOSOPHY OF JONATHAN EDWARDS. Ed. by Harvey G. Townsend. 1955. *Greenwood* 1973 $13.25

CHRISTIAN LOVE AND ITS FRUITS. 1751. *Kregel* $4.50

ON FREEDOM OF THE WILL. 1754. Ed. by Arnold S. Kaufman and William Frankena *Bobbs* 1969 $6.50 pap. $2.45

THE NATURE OF TRUE VIRTUE. 1765. Fwd. by William A. Frankena *Univ. of Michigan Press* 1960 $4.40 Ann Arbor Bks. pap. $1.75

A DISSERTATION CONCERNING LIBERTY AND NECESSITY. 1797. *Burt Franklin* 1974 $16.50

TREATISE ON GRACE AND OTHER POSTHUMOUS WRITINGS INCLUDING OBSERVATIONS ON THE TRINITY. Ed. by Paul Helm *Attic Press* 1971 $5.00

Books about Edwards

Printed Writings of Jonathan Edwards, 1703–1758: A Bibliography. By Thomas H. Johnson. 1940. *Burt Franklin* 1970 $15.00

Jonathan Edwards, 1703–1758. By Ola E. Winslow. 1940. *Octagon* 1972 $15.00

Jonathan Edwards. By Perry Miller. 1949. *Greenwood* 1973 $14.25

Jonathan Edwards: The Narrative of a Puritan Mind. By Edward Hutchins Davidson. *Harvard Univ. Press* 1968 $6.00; *Houghton* 1965 pap. $4.95
A "brief important, but difficult study" which is "beautifully written"—(*Choice*).

The Theology of Jonathan Edwards: A Reappraisal. By Conrad Cherry. 1966. *Peter Smith* $4.50
"Scholarly" and "thoroughly documented" (*LJ*), this seeks to show that to Edwards "religious faith was inseparable from one's active, practical life in the world," in the words of the author.

Jonathan Edwards. By Alfred Owen Aldridge. Great American Thinkers Ser. *Twayne* 1966 $7.95

Jonathan Edwards: His Life and Influence. Ed. by Charles Angoff. *Fairleigh Dickinson Univ. Press* $4.50

Jonathan Edwards. By Edward M. Griffin. *Univ. of Minnesota Press* 1971 pap. $1.25

The Ethics of Jonathan Edwards: Morality and Aesthetics. By Clyde A. Holbrook. *Univ. of Michigan Press* 1973 $10.00

Jonathan Edwards: Theologian of the Heart. By Harold Simonson. *Eerdmans* 1974 $7.95
"In this highly interpretive study Simonson . . . bases his analysis on Edwards' 'sense of the human heart' "—(*Choice*).

WESLEY, JOHN. 1703–1791.

The English evangelical leader never considered himself a man of letters but his great literary activity was a part of his religious zeal. He joined his brother Charles' group of earnest philanthropic "methodists" at Oxford and became the leader of the Methodist Society in 1729. "With his picked band of helpers he preached to the poor, the outcast and the desperate, ministering to their spiritual and social needs. . . . For the use of his followers he wrote concise grammars of English and classical languages; handbooks of medicine, physics, logic, and of ecclesiastical, Roman and English history; edited the works of Bunyan, Law and others . . . and produced Bible commentaries and 50 works of divinity." In 1735, accompanied by his brother Charles and a companion, Wesley set out for the colony of Georgia to teach Christianity to the Indians and to give spiritual leadership to the colony. Although his effort was not highly successful, Wesley regarded this period as the "second rise of Methodism." The hymns which he wrote in collaboration with his brother influenced English religious poetry as their simple statements replaced the earlier involved metaphysical imagery. His "Journal," in which he recorded the daily course of his long, devoted life, is written with frankness, ironic humor, unfailing faith and personal humility. It presents a vivid picture of the man and of the manners and conditions of his time. The "Letters" edited by John Telford in 8 vols. is now o.p.

John's youngest brother, CHARLES WESLEY (1707–1788), is justly famed as a hymn writer. An edition of his poetry, "Representative Verse of Charles Wesley" (ed., sel., and with introd. by Frank Baker *Abingdon* 1962, o.p.), serves to promote Charles Wesley's importance as a secular poet as well. It was Charles who was called "methodist" by his fellow students because of his methodical habits of study.

SELECTIONS FROM THE WRITINGS. Ed. by Herbert Welch *Abingdon* 1942 $5.00

THE MESSAGE OF THE WESLEYS: A Reader of Instruction and Devotion. Comp. with introd. by Philip S. Watson *Macmillan* 1964 pap. $1.95. Excerpts compiled from a Methodist point of view by the Harris F. Roll professor emeritus of systematic theology at Garrett Theological Seminary.

FORTY-FOUR SERMONS. *Allenson* new ed. 1944 $4.75

EXPLANATORY NOTES UPON THE NEW TESTAMENT. 1755. *Allenson* 1950 $4.75

A PLAIN ACCOUNT OF CHRISTIAN PERFECTION. *Allenson* rev. ed. 1952 pap. $2.00

LENT WITH JOHN WESLEY. Ed. by Gordon S. Wakefield *Morehouse* 1965 pap. $1.25

JOHN WESLEY IN WALES. 1739–1790. Ed. by A. H. Williams *Verry* 1971 $13.00

PRIMITIVE REMEDIES (orig. "Primitive Physick"). *Woodbridge Press* 1973 pap. $1.95

THE JOURNAL. Ed. by Percy L. Parker *Moody Press* 1951 pap. $1.35

Books about Wesley

The Life and Times of the Rev. John Wesley. By Luke Tyerman. 1872. *Burt Franklin* 3 vols. 1973 set $72.50

The Lord's Horseman. By Humphrey Lee. 1928. *Abingdon* 2nd ed. 1954 Apex Bks. 1970 pap. $1.75
"The chancellor of Southern Methodist University has written a warm, moving biography of the founder of Methodism as his 18th century contemporaries saw him and reacted to his teachings. Index"—(*Bookmark*).

The Wesleyan Movement in the Industrial Revolution. By Wellman J. Warner. 1930. *Russell & Russell* 1967 $8.00

John Wesley. By Ingvar Haddall. *Abingdon* 1961 $3.50

John Wesley: A Theological Biography. By Martin Schmidt. Trans. from the German by Norman P. Goldhawk *Abingdon* 2 vols. 1963–1973 Vol. 1 (1963) $6.50 Vol. 2 Pt. 1 (1973) $12.95 Pt. 2 trans. by Denis Inman (1973) $12.95

John Wesley and the Christian Ministry. By Albert B. Lawson. *Allenson* 1963 $8.00

John Wesley. By Albert C. Outler. *Oxford* 1964 $9.95

John Wesley. By Dorothy Marshall. *Oxford* 1965 pap. $1.50

John Wesley: His Puritan Heritage. By Robert C. Monk. *Abingdon* 1966 $5.50

John Wesley and the Church of England. By Frank Baker. *Abingdon* 1969 $14.50

For books on Methodism see Section on Protestant Denominations, this Chapter.

WOOLMAN, JOHN. 1720–1772. *See Chapter 2, General Biography and Autobiography, this Volume.*

NEWMAN, JOHN HENRY, CARDINAL. 1801–1890.

The great English theologian, Anglican leader of the Oxford Movement, later became a Cardinal of the Roman Catholic Church. His "Apologia," a masterpiece of English autobiographical writing, is a defense of the religious convictions which led him to abandon the Church of England for the Church of Rome. Newman's integrity had been attacked by Charles Kingsley (*q.v.*). "Change in belief is one of the most frequent causes for autobiography. . . . There are two forms of Apologia, one written entirely to convince outsiders, the other partially, if not wholly, to convince oneself"—(Anna Robeson Burr). The earlier *Oxford* edition of the "Apologia" (1931, o.p.) contains the versions of 1864 and 1865, preceded by Newman's and Kingsley's pamphlets, with an introduction by Wilfrid Ward. The "Apologia" was widely read and it served an immediate purpose by assuring Newman's position in the Church.

As a young man he wrote the hymn "Lead, Kindly Light" (1833) on the boat from Palermo to Marseilles, and, in Rome, other poems published as "Lyra Apostolica" (1834, o.p.). His essays retain their vitality and are still widely read. In "The Idea of a University" he maintains that the duty of a university is the training of the mind, rather than the diffusion of useful knowledge. Newman ranks as one of the masters of English prose; his style is simple, lucid, clear, and unusually convincing. The fine, inclusive two-volume biography, which won the 1962 James Tait Black Award—Meriol Trevor's "Newman: The Pillar of the Cloud" together with "Newman: Light in Winter"—(1962, 1963), is now o.p.

PAROCHIAL AND PLAIN SERMONS. 1834–42. *Christian Class.* 8 vols. 1966–68 each $8.75

OXFORD UNIVERSITY SERMONS. *Christian Class.* 1966 $8.75

UNIVERSITY SERMONS. 1843. *Allenson* 1970 pap. $5.65

LECTURES ON JUSTIFICATION. 1838. *Christian Class.* 1966 $8.75

ESSAY ON THE DEVELOPMENT OF CHRISTIAN DOCTRINE. 1845. Ed. by J. M. Cameron *Christian Class.* 1968 $8.75; *Penguin* Pelican Bks. 1974 pap. $3.45

ON THE SCOPE AND NATURE OF UNIVERSITY EDUCATION (1859), and SCIENTIFIC INVESTIGATION (1852). Ed. by William C. Brown; introd. by Wilfrid Ward *Dutton* Everyman's 1933 $3.95

APOLOGIA PRO VITA SUA: Being a History of His Religious Opinions. 1864. *Christian Class.* 1973 $8.75; ed. by A. D. Culler *Houghton* 1956 pap. $2.95; ed. by David De Laura *Norton* Critical Eds. 1968 pap. $1.95; ed. with introd. and notes by Martin J. Svaglic *Oxford* 1967 $21.00 introd. by Basil Willey World's Class. 1964 $3.00

THE HEART OF NEWMAN'S APOLOGIA. Ed. by Margaret R. Grennan. 1934. *Russell & Russell* 1970 $10.00

THE IDEA OF A UNIVERSITY. 1873. *Christian Class.* 1973 $8.75; ed. by Martin Svaglic *Holt* (Rinehart) 1960 pap. $3.95. The same as "The Scope and Nature of University Education" enlarged by Lectures and Essays.

THE USES OF KNOWLEDGE: Selections from "The Idea of a University." Ed. by Leo L. Ward. 1948. *AHM Pub. Corp* Crofts Class. pap. $.85

MEDITATIONS AND DEVOTIONS. 1893. *Christian Class.* $5.95

A NEWMAN COMPANION TO THE GOSPELS: Sermons. *Christian Class.* 1966 $7.50

ESSAYS ON MIRACLES. *Christian Class.* 1969 $8.75

NEWMAN, THE ORATORIAN: His Unpublished Oratory Papers. Ed. by P. Murray *Christian Class.* 1969 $9.75

HISTORICAL SKETCHES. *Christian Class.* 3 vols. 1970 each $8.75

PHILOSOPHICAL NOTEBOOK. Ed. by Edward Sillem and A. J. Boekraed *Humanities Press* 2 vols. 1969–70 each $10.50; *Learned Pubns.* 2 vols. 1969–70 set $23.00

(With William E. Gladstone). NEWMAN AND GLADSTONE: The Vatican Decrees. Ed. by Alvan S. Ryan *Univ. of Notre Dame Press* 1962 $6.95 pap. $1.95

LETTERS AND DIARIES. Ed. by Charles S. Dessain and Thomas J. Gornall *Oxford* Vols. 23–26 1973–74 Vol. 23 Defeat at Oxford, Defence at Rome. Jan. to Dec. 1867 (1973) Vol. 24 Grammar of Ascent. Jan. 1868 to Dec. 1869 (1973) Vol. 25 The Vatican Council Jan. 1870 to Dec. 1871 (1973) Vol. 26 Jan. 1872 to Dec. 1873 (1974) Vols. 23–24 each $29.00 Vols. 25–26 each $38.50

Books about Cardinal Newman

Newman's Way: The Odyssey of John Henry Newman. By Sean O'Faolain. *Devin-Adair* 1952 $5.00

The Imperial Intellect: A Study of Newman's Educational Ideal. By Arthur Dwight Culler. 1955. *Greenwood* $13.50. A thoughtful study and re-evaluation based "as much as possible on manuscript materials."

God and Myself: The Spirituality of John Henry Newman. By Hilda Graef. 1957. *Christian Class.* $5.95

The author traces Newman's spiritual development through his writings, making clear "the long, slow soul-searching that changed his religious views and brought him into the Roman Catholic church"—(*PW*). "A most valuable supplement to the numerous biographies"—(*LJ*).

The Acton-Newman Relations: The Dilemma of Christian Liberalism. By Hugh A. MacDougall. *Fordham Univ. Press* 1962 $8.00

The Consecration of Learning: Lectures on Newman's Idea of a University. By Fergal McGrath. *Fordham Univ. Press* 1963 $9.00

Newman's Apologia: A Classic Reconsidered. Ed. by Vincent F. Blehl, S.J., and Francis X. Connolly. *Harcourt* 1964 $4.50

These eight papers, presented at the symposium of Fordham University's Center of Newman Studies to commemorate the centenary of the publication of "Apologia Pro Vita Sua," are "an excellent contribution to Newman studies"—(*LJ*). It includes a bibliography.

The Newman Brothers: An Essay in Comparative Intellectual Biography. By William Robbins. *Harvard Univ. Press* 1966 $6.00

The letters of the Newman brothers John and Francis, are "often sharp in expression but obviously sincere." Francis became an unbeliever. "Selections from the *Apologia*, from letters of the Cardinal, some not yet published, and from other sources are here quoted in contrast to excerpts from Francis' published works. . . . A reader quite familiar with the Cardinal and his times might find this study in contrasts stimulating, provocative, if not irritating"—(*LJ*).

John Henry Newman. By Charles S. Dessain. *Christian Class.* 1966 $4.95; *Stanford Univ. Press* 2nd ed. 1971 $6.95

Boundaries of Fiction: Carlyle, Macaulay, Newman. By George Levine. *Princeton Univ. Press* 1968 $11.50

Newman and the Common Tradition: A Study in Language of Church and Society. By John Coulson. *Oxford* 1970 $8.50

Witness to the Faith: Cardinal Newman on the Teaching Authority of the Church. By Gary Lease. *Duquesne Univ. Press* (dist. by Humanities Press) 1972 $7.50

Cardinal Newman in His Age: His Place in English Theology and Literature. By Harold C. Weatherby. *Vanderbilt Univ. Press* 1973 $11.50

EDDY, MARY BAKER. 1821–1910.

Ill all her life, Mary Baker Eddy experienced a miraculous "cure" as the result of reading the New Testament, or so she felt. She extended to others her method of Christian healing and developed a wide following. The Church of Christ Scientist, or Christian Science, which she founded, rests on her teachings in "Science and Health," considered by her followers to be divinely inspired and therefore unalterable. Mrs. Eddy also founded three periodicals, the *Christian Science Monitor*, the *Christian Science Journal* and the *Christian Science Sentinel*.

PROSE WORKS. *First Church of Christ Scientist* standard ed. $12.00

SCIENCE AND HEALTH WITH KEY TO THE SCRIPTURES. 1875. *First Church of Christ Scientist* standard ed. $5.50 other eds. $2.25–$38.00

A COMPLETE CONCORDANCE TO SCIENCE AND HEALTH WITH KEY TO THE SCRIPTURES. *First Church of Christ Scientist* $12.50

THE FIRST CHURCH OF CHRIST, SCIENTIST, AND MISCELLANY. *First Church of Christ Scientist* pap. $1.85

POEMS INCLUDING CHRIST AND CHRISTMAS. *First Church of Christ Scientist* $3.50

RETROSPECTION AND INTROSPECTION. *First Church of Christ Scientist* pap. $1.25

THE UNITY OF GOOD: Rudimental Divine Science. *First Church of Christ Scientist* pap. $1.25

Books about Eddy

Mrs. Eddy: The Biography of a Virginal Mind. By Edwin F. Dakin. *Peter Smith* $6.50

Mental Healers: Franz Anton Mesmer, Mary Baker Eddy, Sigmund Freud. By Stefan Zweig. *Ungar* 1962 $8.50 pap. $2.95

Mary Baker Eddy. By Robert Peel. *Holt* 1966 2 vols. 1971–1972 Vol. I The Years of Discovery, 1821–1875 (1972) $7.50 pap. $3.45 Vol. 2 The Years of Trial (1971) $8.95

"Mr. Peel has supplied the reader with much background information that has not been published before. . . . This title is the most complete biographical study of the religious leader to date"—(*LJ*).

The Life of Mary Baker Eddy and the History of Christian Science. By Georgine Milmine. *Baker Bk. House* 1971 repr. $5.95

RAUSCHENBUSCH, WALTER.   1861–1918.

A liberal American theologian of Lutheran background and socialist leanings, Walter Rauschenbusch looked upon his time as one of both hope and danger. The Christian task, he wrote in his first and very influential book, "Christianity and the Social Crisis," is "to transform human society into the Kingdom of God by regenerating all human relations and reconstituting them in accordance with the will of God." Through the book he became known as the chief proponent of the "social gospel."

Newly graduated from the Rochester Theological Seminary, the young, optimistic minister accepted the pastorate of the Second German Baptist Church in a slum section of New York City then known as "Hell's Kitchen." Here he learned to contend with the social and political problems of urban and industrial America and sought—with others—to bring Christian involvement to their solution. It was a time of American political and social ferment, when Lincoln Steffens and the muckrakers were active under the Presidency of Theodore Roosevelt, the labor movement was gathering force and the ideas of the British Fabians were beginning to cross the Atlantic.

Rauschenbusch was convinced that the individual must save himself through his society. "He envisioned the masses of the common people extending the principles of democracy into the socio-economic order and establishing a cooperative commonwealth. To motivate and inspire this effort, a religious revival was needed. Asceticism, dogmatism and ceremonialism had no place in such a revival, however; it was to be rather a 'social awakening'—a spiritual and ethical renewal centered on 'the fundamental convictions of Jesus' regarding the value of life and human solidarity. He credited his typical reader with sound moral instincts and an elementary grasp of 'Christ's law of love and the golden rule'; it was his task to probe further 'in the direction toward which Jesus led' and 'to bring to a point what we all vaguely know' "—(William Robert Miller, in "Contemporary American Protestant Thought"). He was not alone, for the churches too were taking up the social gospel—under the influence of his thought and of the socialist theories then permeating American intellectual circles and American reform politics. The Federal Council of Churches, one of the early Protestant ecumenical efforts, was founded in 1908.

Rauschenbusch interpreted the growth of industrialism and the consequent rise of the labor movement as evolution working for Christianity in the "Kingdom of God." As the needs of society changed, he modified his outlook and saw socialization as necessary only in those areas which had become monopolistic. One of his important books was "Christianizing the Social Order" (1912, o.p.). World War I saddened him and he died at its end, of cancer. He had suffered much of his life from deafness, but traveled widely and taught for many years at the Rochester Theological Seminary.

CHRISTIANITY AND THE SOCIAL CRISIS. 1907. Ed. by Robert D. Cross *Peter Smith* $4.75

"A factually and theologically sturdy presentation of the vital issues of the day, . . . boldly prophetic and general"—(William Robert Miller).

PRAYERS OF THE SOCIAL AWAKENING. 1909. *Folcroft* $7.50

CHRISTIANIZING THE SOCIAL ORDER. 1913. *Folcroft* $7.50; *Kelley* $15.00

A THEOLOGY FOR THE SOCIAL GOSPEL. 1917. *Abingdon* Apex Bks. 1961 pap. $2.95. The standard work of a major movement in American theology.

THE SOCIAL PRINCIPLES OF JESUS. 1920. *Folcroft* $7.50

THE RIGHTEOUSNESS OF THE KINGDOM. Ed. with introd. by Max L. Stackhouse; fwd. by Dr. Robert T. Handy *Abingdon* 1968 $5.95

Written during his eleven years as a Baptist minister in New York's "Hell's Kitchen," and now published for the first time, in this book Rauschenbusch directly confronts the social problems that concerned him—poverty, race and social status.

Books about Rauschenbusch

The Social Gospel in America: Gladen, Ely and Rauschenbusch. Ed. by Robert T. Handy. Library of Protestant Thought *Oxford* 1966 $8.95

GANDHI, MOHANDAS K(ARAMCHAND)   (sometimes called Mahatma Gandhi). 1869–1948.

In "Makers of the Modern World," Louis Untermeyer (*q.v.*) wrote: "Until the early years of the twentieth century India, to the average Occidental, was as far removed in concern as it was remote in distance. By 1940, however, it had violently intruded itself and its incalculable possibilities upon the attention of the entire world. This was due almost wholly to one man, Mohandas Karamchand Gandhi, an undersized, unpretentious, and deeply religious Hindu, sometimes described as a saint attempting to be a politician, although Gandhi insisted the truth was the other way round." It has been said that Gandhi spent 2,089 days in Indian jails and it was in jails that "he did his most concentrated reading and much of his meditating." It was in jail in the early 20's that he wrote his "Autobiography," a remarkable book of self-revelation.

In South Africa (1893), because of his mistreatment for his defense of Asiatic immigrants, he instituted his first *Satyagraha*, a campaign of civil disobedience expressed in nonviolent resistance to the laws, "passive resistance." He was given the title "Mahatma" ("great-souled") by the common people about 1920. "Asserting the unity of mankind under one God, Gandhi throughout his life preached Christian and Moslem ethics along with Hindu." He was, of course, the initiator of the struggle for Indian independence and a perennial worker for peace between Hindu and Moslem—indeed, for peace among the nations of the world as well. His campaigns of nonviolent disobedience have been adopted by protagonists of civil rights in the United States and by some colonial peoples in other parts of the world.

COLLECTED WORKS. *Int. Pubns. Service* 53 vols. 1958–74 each $10.00. An expected 60 volumes are being published by the Government of India; editions in English and in Hindi are available.

ESSENTIAL WRITINGS. Ed. by V. V. Murti *Int. Pubns. Service* 1973 $8.50

GANDHI: Selected Writings. Ed. by Ronald Duncan *Harper* Colophon Bks. 1972 pap. $2.75

THE ESSENTIAL GANDHI: An Anthology. Ed. by Louis Fischer *Random* Vintage Bks. 1962 pap. $2.45

Gandhi's "intimate struggles, intensive moral search and ruthless honesty" are revealed here through his own words. These extracts are woven into a chronological sequence and are supplied with connecting links. The research was done by Deirdre Randall, "who has carried out her task with balance and discrimination."

THE WISDOM OF GANDHI. *Philosophical Lib.* 1967 $3.75

NON-VIOLENT RESISTANCE (Satyagraha). Ed. by Bharatan Kumarappa *Schocken* 1961 $8.00 pap. $2.75; *Verry* bds. $3.25

GANDHI ON NON-VIOLENCE: Selected Texts from "Non-Violence in Peace and War." Ed. by Thomas Merton *New Directions* 1965 pap. $1.50

IN SEARCH OF THE SUPREME. Ed. by V. B. Kher *Verry* 3 vols. bds. $11.00

THE WAY TO COMMUNAL HARMONY. Ed. by U. R. Rao *Verry* bds. $5.50

Books about Gandhi

Mahatma Gandhi's Ideas. By C. F. Andrews. 1929. *Hillary House* 1949 $3.75

The Life of Mahatma Gandhi. By Louis Fischer. 1959. (With title "Gandhi") *New Am. Lib.* Mentor Bks. 1960 pap. $1.25; *Macmillan* Collier Bks. 1962 pap. $1.95

The Philosophy of Mahatma Gandhi. By Dhirendra M. Datta. *Univ. of Wisconsin Press* 1973 $7.50 pap. $2.50

Mahatma Gandhi: A Great Life in Brief. By Vincent Sheean. *Knopf* 1955 $3.95

Mahatma Gandhi, a Descriptive Bibliography. By Jagdish S. S. Sharma. *Verry* 1955 2nd ed. 1968 $13.50

Mahatma Gandhi: Essays and Reflections on His Life and Work. Ed. by Sarvepalli Radhakrishnan. *Inter-Culture* 3rd ed. 1964 pap. $2.80

Conquest of Violence: The Gandhian Philosophy of Conflict. By Joan Valérie Bondurant. *Univ. of California Press* rev. ed. 1965 $8.50 pap. $2.45

Gandhi and the Nuclear Age. By Arne Naess. *Bedminster* 1965 $5.00

Mahatma Gandhi. By Bal R. Nanda. Shapers of History Ser. *Barron's* 1965 pap. $1.25

Gandhi. By Geoffrey Ashe. *Stein & Day* 1968 1969 pap. $3.95

The British historian in this biography "is concerned with the personality of the man and with his influence upon his followers and the world. . . . Highly recommended"—(*LJ*). "A mighty fine portrait and . . . a very moving one of the man who was in the opinion of many as near to a saint as our century has produced"—(Thomas Lask, in the *N.Y. Times*).

Gandhi and Modern India. By Penderel Moon. *Norton* 1968 $6.95

"The author, a Fellow of All Souls, Oxford, [and] an authority on India . . . brings some fresh insights to this smooth retelling of the life of Mahatma Gandhi, although some of his more political conclusions seem to contradict his stress on Gandhi's immense influence as a personality whose power was rooted in religion"—(*PW*). Bibliography.

Mahatma Gandhi. By Romain Rolland. *Garland Pub. Co.* $11.00

Mahatma Gandhi, One Hundred Years. By Sarvepalli Radhakrishnan. *Int. Pubns. Service* 1968 $6.00; *Kennikat* 1968 $12.50

Non-Violence and Aggression: A Study of Gandhi's Moral Equivalent of War. By H. J. Horsburgh. *Oxford* 1968 $6.00

Gandhi: A Life. By Krishna Kripalani. *Verry* 1968 $6.75

Truth and Nonviolence: A UNESCO Symposium on Gandhi. Ed. by T. K. Mahadevan. *Kennikat* 1970 $10.00

The Quest for Gandhi. Ed. by G. Ramachandran and T. K. Mahadevan. *Verry* 1970 $5.50

The Meanings of Gandhi. Ed. by Paul F. Power. *Univ. Press of Hawaii* 1971 $7.75

The Moral and Political Thought of Mahatma Gandhi. By Raghavan Iyer. *Oxford* 1973 $12.50

See also Chapter 2, General Biography and Autobiography: Autobiography, this Volume.

SCHWEITZER, ALBERT. 1875–1965. (Nobel Peace Prize 1952)

This "all-round" genius, recalling Leonardo da Vinci for his achievements in medicine, music, literature, philosophy, theology, religion and the practical application of Christianity, has been described as "the greatest man in the world" and "the most civilized man of the 20th century." He was an Alsatian and the son of a Lutheran pastor. After studying theology and philosophy at the University of Strasbourg, Schweitzer began to pursue his interest in the Synoptic Gospels and the life and teachings of Jesus. His interpretation of the life of Christ led him to believe and practice what he considered the spirit of Jesus—the kingdom of God on earth among men. In 1913, he went to French Equatorial Africa as a medical missionary. During World War I he was interned in France, but later returned to his hospital at Lambaréné, which he and a group of Africans had built by hand. Over the years the village grew and his hospital gained international recognition. In his later years he suffered a certain amount of criticism and one hostile book ("Verdict on Schweitzer," by Gerald McKnight) for his somewhat paternalistic attitude toward Africans—as though they were perhaps children—but his dedication to their medical needs continued to the end of his life. He is noted for his "Philosophy of Civilization," which will be completed with the publication of a third volume. He stresses the "mutual enrichment of the humanities and the sciences," his ethics centering in "reverence for life." In three appeals broadcast from Oslo in 1958, he called for the immediate renunciation of nuclear bomb tests and nuclear weapons. He has written the definitive biography of Bach: "J. S. Bach" (trans. by Ernest Newman 1911 *Dover* 2 vols. pap. each $3.00 *Macmillan* 2 vols. 1962 set $15.00; *Peter Smith* 2 vols. $11.00), and "Goethe: Five Studies" (*Beacon* 1961, o.p.).

Except for visits to the Continent to raise money, he left Africa very infrequently. In 1949 he came to the United States to address the Goethe Festival in Colorado. In 1951, he was elected to the seat on France's Academy of Moral and Political Science that was vacated by the death of Marshal Pétain and received the Peace Prize of the German book trade. The German Physicians' Congress presented him with the first Paracelsus Medal, in honor of the 16th-century alchemist and physician (1952). In 1953 he won the Nobel Peace Prize, held over from 1952, for forsaking fame to spend 40 years of his life discharging "the greatest unpaid debt of Western civilization." An impressive documentary film of his life and work at Lambaréné was released early in 1957. In 1959 he received the $2,000 Joseph Lemaire Humanitarian Foundation Prize, Brussels, Belgium. On his death at the age of 90, Norman Cousins wrote (in *SR*) that Schweitzer "proved that although a man may have no jurisdiction over the fact of his existence, he can hold supreme command over the meaning of existence for him. Thus, no man need fear death; he need fear only that he may die without having known his greatest power—the power of his free will to give his own life for others."

A TREASURY OF ALBERT SCHWEITZER. Ed. by Thomas Kiernan *Bks. for Libraries* 1965 $12.50

ALBERT SCHWEITZER: An Anthology. Ed. by Charles R. Joy. 1947. *Beacon* 1955 pap. $2.45

THE QUEST OF THE HISTORICAL JESUS. 1906. Trans. by W. Montgomery *Macmillan* 1910 1968 pap. $3.95

A PSYCHIATRIC STUDY OF JESUS. *Peter Smith* 1963 $4.00

THE PHILOSOPHY OF CIVILIZATION. Trans. by Charles Thomas Campion; rev. by Mrs. C. E. B. Russell *Humanities Press* 2 vols. 1923–47 Pt. I Decay and Restoration of Civilization (1923) 2nd ed. 1971 pap. $6.50 Pt. II Civilization and Ethics (1923–47) 3rd ed. $11.50

THE MYSTICISM OF PAUL THE APOSTLE. 1931. *Seabury Press* 1968 pap. $2.95

THE LIGHT WITHIN US. 1959. *Citadel Press* pap. $.95; *Greenwood* 1971 $7.00

THE ESSENCE OF FAITH. *Citadel Press* pap. $.95

THE TEACHING OF REVERENCE FOR LIFE. *Holt* 1965 $3.95; (with title "Reverence for Life") trans. by Reginald H. Fuller *Harper* 1971 $4.95

MEMOIRS OF CHILDHOOD AND YOUTH. American ed. trans. by Charles Thomas Campion *Macmillan* 1925 1963 pap. $.95. Informally written memoirs of home and school life up to nineteen years of age.

OUT OF MY LIFE AND THOUGHT: An Autobiography. Trans. by Charles Thomas Campion. 1933. *Holt* 1972 pap. $2.95; with postscript 1932–1949 by Everett Skillings *New Am. Lib.* Mentor Bks. 1953 pap. $1.25

AFRICAN NOTEBOOK: Reminiscences Including Hospital Life and Scenes. 1938. Trans. by Mrs. C. E. B. Russell *Peter Smith* $4.00

Books about Schweitzer

The Albert Schweitzer Jubilee Book. Ed. by Abraham A. Roback. 1945. *Greenwood* $20.00
The Challenge of Schweitzer. By J. Middleton Murry. 1948. *Richard West* $12.50
Music in the Life of Albert Schweitzer (with selections from his writings). Ed. by Charles R. Joy. 1951. *Bks. for Libraries* $12.00
Albert Schweitzer: Man of Mercy. By Jacquelyn Berrill. *Dodd* 1956 $3.95
Days with Albert Schweitzer. By Frederick Franck. 1959. *Greenwood* 1974 $9.50
Dr. Schweitzer of Lambaréné. By Norman Cousins. 1960. *Greenwood* 1973 $12.50. Based upon extraordinary conversations and correspondence.
Schweitzer: Prophet of Radical Theology. By Jackson Lee Ice. *Westminster Press* 1971 $7.50
The author "seeks to demonstrate the relevance of Albert Schweitzer for contemporary theology.... In Ice's opinion, although Schweitzer was not a Christian atheist as such, his philosophy implies the death of the absolute or traditional God of Christianity"—(*Christian Century*).
Schweitzer: A Biography. By George Marshall and David Poling. *Doubleday* 1971 $7.95
"An interesting, well-written work commended for authenticity in a foreword by Rhena Schweitzer, the doctor's daughter. Except for a few final chapters probing the inner man and considering controversy, it is chiefly a chronological report of events and accomplishments"—(*LJ*).

UNDERHILL, EVELYN. 1875–1941.

This Anglican religious leader is relatively unknown in America, but during her lifetime she exerted wide influence in England through her writings and by conducting retreats. In private life the wife of a London barrister, Hubert Stuart Moore, she wrote poetry and novels in addition to her many books on the devotional life and Christian experience. She was "a woman of intelligence, humor and understanding." Her writing is characterized by a depth of insight and a radiance of spirit that drew clergymen and laymen alike into the band of her devoted followers. "Concerning the Inner Life" (1926), "House of the Soul" (1929), and "Worship" (1936) are o.p.

MYSTICISM. 1911. *Dutton* 1931 pap. $2.95; *New Am. Lib.* Merit 1955 $4.95

THE MYSTIC WAY. 1913. *Richard West* $15.00

THE MYSTICS OF THE CHURCH. 1920. *Schocken* 1964 $7.00

This survey takes the most important figures in Christian religious history and describes "with simplicity" (*LJ*) their beliefs, struggles and efforts to make mysticism fundamental to Christianity.

THE FRUITS OF THE SPIRIT (1942), LIGHT OF CHRIST, and ABBA: Meditations Based on the Lord's Prayer (1940). *McKay* 1956 $3.50

PRACTICAL MYSTICISM. 1951. *Dutton* Everyman's 1960 pap. $1.75

THE ESSENTIALS OF MYSTICISM AND OTHER ESSAYS. *Dutton* pap. $1.95

BUBER, MARTIN. 1878–1965.

The Jewish theologian-philosopher, teacher and writer was born in Vienna. In 1938 he emigrated from Germany to Palestine and joined the faculty of the Hebrew University in Jerusalem, where he remained until his retirement in 1951. He was "in the truest sense the living embodiment of the ancient *Zaddik* tradition" and served as an interpreter of modern Jewish thought to the non-Jewish world; he worked for both the development of Hasidism and the recognition of the cultural significance of Judaism. Reinhold Niebuhr (*q.v.*) called him "the greatest living Jewish philosopher." In his classic, the prose poem "I and Thou," from which his later work sprang, Buber conceived the individual as in permanent relationship with all forms of life, finding his fulfillment in the reciprocity of the relationship—the "Thou" being God. His theology, Will Herberg says, "falls in with the general movement of religious existentialism," of which he was one of the main contemporary sources. In his lifetime Buber received many honors. The citation accompanying the Goethe prize awarded him by the University of Hamburg stated that it was intended "to honor your great scholarly work, but, more than that, your activity in the spirit of a genuine humanity." He had once said, "I know nothing of death, but I know that God is eternal and I know this too, that he is my God." Honored and much beloved, Buber died in Jerusalem in 1965.

WRITINGS. Ed. by Will Herberg *New Am. Lib.* Meridian Bks. $3.95; *Peter Smith* 1958 $5.50

THE WAY OF RESPONSE: Selections From His Writings. Ed. by Nahum N. Glatzer *Schocken* 1966 1971 pap. $2.25

An "anthology of short, paragraphic excerpts" which presents "Buber's understanding of an essential uniqueness in man"—*(LJ)*.

THE KNOWLEDGE OF MAN: Selected Essays. Trans. by Maurice Friedman and Ronald Gregor Smith; ed. with introd. by Maurice Friedman *Harper* Torchbks. 1966 pap. $1.95; *Humanities Press* 1965 $8.75

THE PHILOSOPHY OF MARTIN BUBER. Ed. by Paul A. Schilpp and Maurice Friedman *Open Court* 1967 $15.00. Selections from Buber's writings with critical essays and a bibliography.

ON THE BIBLE: Eighteen Studies. Ed. by Nahum N. Glatzer *Schocken* 1968 $5.95

Including some translated into English for the first time, these studies "acquaint the reader with the central themes in Buber's works on the Bible and his endeavor to elucidate Biblical ideas, concepts, values, and their concrete meaning now and in the past"—*(PW)*.

I AND THOU. 1937. Trans. by Walter Kaufman *Scribner* 2nd ed. with a postscript by the author 1958 1970 $5.95 pap. $1.95

A "philosophic prose-poem about the meaning of personal existence"—*(SR)*.

MAMRE: Essays in Religion. 1946. Trans. by Greta Hort *Greenwood* 1972 $11.00

BETWEEN MAN AND MAN. Trans. by Ronald Gregor Smith. 1947. *Macmillan* 1965 pap. $1.45

FOR THE SAKE OF HEAVEN: A Chronicle. Trans. by Ludwig Lewisohn. 1953. *Atheneum* 1969 pap. $3.45; *Greenwood* $11.50

GOOD AND EVIL: Two Interpretations. *Scribner* 1953 pap. $1.95

TALES OF RABBI NACHMAN. 1956. Trans. and ed. by Maurice Friedman *Avon Bks.* Discus 1970 pap. $1.45; *Horizon Press* 1968 $4.95; *Peter Smith* 1962 $4.00

PROPHETIC FAITH. *Harper* Torchbks. 1960 pap. $2.75

TWO TYPES OF FAITH: The Interpretation of Judaism and Christianity. *Harper* Torchbks. 1961 pap. $1.75

ON JUDAISM. Ed. by Nahum N. Glatzer *Schocken* 1972 $5.95 pap. $2.95

"Anyone who shares [with Buber] this passionate demand for justice . . . will find in these prophetic pages more than an ally or an exemplar, although he will find at least that. . . . He will also . . . learn a good deal about himself, reflected in the visage of a bearded sage who confronted the world in all its complexity, neither with tragic resignation nor facile optimism but with the tough temerity of an imperishable and illusionless hope"—(William Robert Miller, in *SR*).

THE ECLIPSE OF GOD: Studies in the Relation between Religion and Philosophy. *Harper* Torchbks. pap. $2.25

HASIDISM AND MODERN MAN. Trans. by Maurice Friedman *Harper* Torchbks. pap. $2.50

MOSES: The Revelation and the Covenant. *Harper* Torchbks. pap. $2.45

THE KINGSHIP OF GOD. *Harper* Torchbks. 1972 pap. $2.95

THE ORIGIN AND MEANING OF HASIDISM. *Horizon Press* 1972 $6.95 pap. $3.45

ON ZION: The History of an Idea. Trans. by Stanley Godman 1952 *Schocken* 1973 $7.00

A BELIEVING HUMANISM: My Testament, 1902–1965. Trans. with introd. and commentary by Maurice Friedman *Simon & Schuster* 1968 $5.95 Touchstone Bks. 1969 pap. $1.95

"Buber tries to define his own faith based . . . upon . . . his own understanding of man and nature"—(*LJ*). In the Credo Perspectives Series.

Other titles are published by Beacon, Harper, Horizon Press, Humanities Press, Schocken, Scribner and Peter Smith.

Books about Buber

Martin Buber. By Arthur A. Cohen. *Hillary House* 1957 $2.75
Martin Buber: Jewish Existentialist. By Malcolm L. Diamond. 1960. *Gannon* $8.50
Martin Buber: The Life of Dialogue. By Maurice Friedman. *Harper* Torchbks. 1960 pap. $2.25
Martin Buber. By Ronald G. Smith. *John Knox Press* 1967 pap. $1.25
The Wanderer and the Way: The Hebrew Tradition in the Writings of Martin Buber. By Roy Oliver. *Cornell Univ. Press* 1968 $6.50
The Promise of Buber. By Lowell D. Streiker. The Promise of Theology Ser. *Lippincott* 1969 $3.50 pap. $1.50
The Holy Spirit in the Theology of Martin Buber (orig. "Martin Buber, a Theologian of the Spirit"). By W. D. Stephens. *Cambridge* 1970 $16.50
Martin Buber: An Intimate Portrait. By Aubrey Hodes. *Viking* 1971 $7.95 Compass Bks. pap. $2.25
The Hebrew Humanism of Martin Buber. By Grete Schaeder. Trans. by Noah J. Jacobs *Wayne State Univ. Press* 1973 $17.50
Martin Buber. By Werner Manheim. *Twayne* 1974 $6.95
Analytical Interpretation of Martin Buber's "I and Thou." By Alexander Kohanski. *Barron's* 1975 pap. $1.95

FOSDICK, HARRY EMERSON. 1878–1969.

From 1915 to 1946 Dr. Fosdick was professor of practical theology at Union Theological Seminary. He became pastor in 1926 of the Park Avenue Baptist Church (later the Riverside Church) in New York, where he served until 1946. He won wide recognition as a modernist leader in the fundamentalist controversy of the 1920s. Many of his forceful and practical sermons were published, and his books have had a long and continuous popularity. Dr. Fosdick was the author of several religious books for young people: "Martin Luther" (*Random* 1956 $3.87), "Jesus of Nazareth" (*Random* 1959 $2.95), and "The Life of St. Paul" (*Random* 1962 $2.95). A number of his books and his autobiography "The Living of These Days" (*Harper* 1956) are o.p.

THE SECOND MILE. 1912. *Folcroft* $5.00

THE MEANING OF PRAYER. 1915. *Association Press* 1962 pap. $2.50; *Folcroft* $5.00

THE CHALLENGE OF THE PRESENT CRISIS. 1917. *Folcroft* $5.00

THE MODERN USE OF THE BIBLE. 1925. *Richard West* $10.00

SUCCESSFUL CHRISTIAN LIVING. 1937. *Folcroft* $5.00

A GUIDE TO UNDERSTANDING THE BIBLE. 1938. *Harper* 1956 pap. $2.75

ON BEING A REAL PERSON. *Harper* 1943 $5.50 pap. $1.50

A GREAT TIME TO BE ALIVE: Sermons on Christianity in Wartime. 1944. *Bks. for Libraries* $10.50

ASSURANCE OF IMMORTALITY. *Attic Press* 1958 $2.50

DEAR MR. BROWN: Letters to a Person Perplexed about Religion. *Harper* 1961 pap. $1.95. This series of letters to a hypothetical Mr. Brown has grown from many letters seeking advice, and personal conferences with men and women seeking guidance. Dr. Fosdick's treatment of some major theological problems is clear and cogent.

Books about Fosdick

Preaching as Counseling. By Edmund H. Linn. *Judson Press* $4.95

JOHN XXIII, Pope (born Angelo Giuseppe Roncalli). 1881–1963.

As "Good Pope John" lay dying in 1963, he spoke with the simple and absolute faith which had characterized his life: "Every day is a good day to be born, every day is a good day to die." This rare man—a true Christian—born a peasant, had inherited St. Peter's chair by accident, elected as a "provisional" Pope when the Cardinals failed to reach agreement after the death of Pius XII. Son of farmers near Bergamo in northern Italy, Roncalli early decided to become a priest and to take Christ literally as his model, despite his realization at the age of 18 that to be "similar to the good Jesus" was to be "treated as a madman." After nearly 20 years serving in minor posts in Bulgaria, Turkey and Greece, he was sent in 1944 to Paris as Papal Nuncio, where, according to *Time*, "during his 8 years' stay, Nuncio Roncalli became one of the most popular men in Paris." His papacy (1958–1963) was marked by a spirit of liberalism and unusual informality and by his initiative in calling the Second Vatican Council.

From his unwavering faith came Roncalli's strengths—his humility before God (which he never confused with meekness before men), his easy familiarity with everyone (workmen, peasants, criminals, dignitaries), his surprisingly vigorous papal leadership, his splendid freedom from convention, and even his sense of humor. He won the hearts of many outside the Catholic fold with his precedent-breaking encyclical of 1963, *"Pacem in Terris,"* which offered radical wisdom to a world still torn with strife. In a fine essay included in her "Men in Dark Times" (*Harcourt* 1968 $6.50, Harvest Bks. 1970 pap. $2.45), Hannah Arendt (*q.v.*) wrote of Angelo Roncalli: "What set him free was that he could say without reservation, mental or emotional: 'Thy will be done.' In the 'Journal,' it is not easy to discover, under the layers and layers of pious language which has become for us, but never for him, platitudinous, this simple basic chord to which his life was tuned. Even less would we expect from it the laughing wit he derived from it. But what else except humility did he preach when he told his friends how the new awesome responsibilities of the pontificate had at first worried him greatly and even caused him sleepless nights—until one morning he said to himself: 'Giovanni, don't take yourself that seriously!' and slept well ever after."

On November 18, 1965, his successor Paul VI announced the initiation of formal proceedings toward the recognition of Pope John's sainthood.

JOURNAL OF A SOUL. Trans. by Dorothy White *McGraw-Hill* 1965 deluxe ed. $50.00. Pope John's notebooks of spiritual reflections, meditations, prayers and some notes for his planned autobiography. The moving record of the Pope who never failed to be human.

AN INVITATION TO HOPE. Trans. and arr. by Msgr. John Gregory Clancy, Pope John's confessor. Credo Perspective Ser. *Simon and Schuster* 1967 $3.95 pap. $1.95. Personal writings which form a spiritual autobiography.

PEACE ON EARTH. *Our Sunday Visitor* pap. $4.50. His encyclical of 1963 concerning relations among men, their rights and duties as citizens of the state.

MY BISHOP: A Biography. 1916. *McGraw-Hill* new ed. 1969. The life of Giacomo Tedeschi, Bishop of Bergamo, to whom Angelo Roncalli was secretary as a young priest.

Books about Pope John XXIII

Call Me John. By Richard J. Cushing. *Daughters of St. Paul* $4.00 pap. $3.00
Everybody's Pope: The Life of John 23rd. *New City* 1966 pap. $1.00
John Twenty Third: Simpleton or Saint. By Giacomo Lercaro. *Franciscan Herald* 1968 $3.50
Pope John XXIII. By Paul Johnson. *Little* 1974 $6.95
"Perhaps the most valuable contribution of the book is that it brings into focus the political, theological, and economic realities of the Church which shaped Pope John and which he in turn influenced"—(*LJ*).

TEILHARD DE CHARDIN, PIERRE, S.J. 1881–1955.

Teilhard de Chardin, the Jesuit theologian, paleontologist and anthropologist, "has forced theologians to view their ideas in the new perspective of evolution and scientists to see the spiritual implications of their knowledge. He has both clarified and unified our vision of reality." Thus—introducing "The Phenomenon of Man"—wrote Sir Julian Huxley, grandson of Thomas Huxley, who 100 years ago had defended his friend Charles Darwin (*q.v.*), the original controversial evolutionist, against opposition from both the scientific and theological camps of the time. Teilhard in his lifetime knew similar trials and remains controversial among conservative churchmen and scientists. Since the posthumous appearance of the many works which his Church prevented his publishing in his lifetime, he is, on the other hand, now recognized as a giant in both their worlds by a vast group of each.

Teilhard was born into a pious, aristocratic and wealthy French family, distantly descended from the atheist Voltaire. The devout Teilhard spent many years wrestling with the problem of reconciling his strong religious bent with his equally strong and determined curiosity about the development and future of man, which he studied in archeology, geology and paleontology. He eventually achieved the synthesis expressed in his greatest books, "The Phenomenon of Man" (mainly scientific) and "The Divine Milieu" (in which the synthesis is clearly set forth). He saw the process of evolution as preconceived and moved by God—a personal God in a personal and mystical universe, a God far removed from "that old man up there." The process began with the "pre-life" stage and advanced from the stage of physical "life" alone to one tempered by *thought*— which makes man unique in the animal world. The logical consummation is the stage, not yet achieved, of "hyper-life." (He invented his own vocabulary for these concepts, for which the words given here are rough approximations.) It is toward this last, convergent stage which Teilhard believed man to be moving; it is in this stage, through the love of Christ, that man has it in his power to reach a perfect union with God and complete the plan of the Universe.

Evolution and religion to Teilhard were two sides of the same coin. "Evolution is a general condition to which all theories, all hypotheses, all systems must bow and which they must satisfy if they are to be thinkable and true," he wrote. The imperfections in the infallible system of evolution as it advanced were merely temporary deviations from the scheme, necessary "because His perfections cannot run counter to the nature of things, and because a world, assumed to be progressing towards perfection, is of its nature precisely still partially disorganized."

The conflict between his obedience to the Church and adherence to his own glowing religio-scientific concepts was at times great. "If I rebelled (humanly, it would be so easy and so sweet)," he wrote, "I would betray my belief that Our Lord activates all events. . . . It is essential I show, by my example, that if my ideas are novel, they make me no less faithful." The ban on his writings, and eventually on his teaching at the Catholic Institute in Paris, led him to spend much of his life in the East, particularly China, on paleontological digging expeditions, and he contributed to the discovery and assessment of Peking Man. Eventually he settled in New York, where he spent the last years of his life doing scientific work for the Wenner-Gren Foundation for Anthropological Research and where in 1955 he died. As a man of science, he had been affiliated with such institutions as the Paris Museum of Natural History, the Academy of Sciences and the French National Center for Scientific Research. He became a member of the French Legion of Honor. His stature among his many admirers continues to increase and his books have sold phenomenally throughout the world.

THE PHENOMENON OF MAN. Pub. in France 1955. Trans. from the French by Bernard Wall; introd. by Sir Julian Huxley *Harper* 1959 $5.95 Torchbks. 1961 pap. $1.95. His major work.

MAN'S PLACE IN NATURE: The Human Zoological Group. 1956. Trans. by René Hague; introd. by Bernard Wall; pref. by Jean Piveteau *Harper* 1966 Colophon Bks. 1973 pap. $2.45. In this technical discussion of evolution and paleontology Teilhard's aim was, as he said, "to study the structure of the human zoological group and the evolutionary directions it follows."

THE DIVINE MILIEU: An Essay on the Interior Life. Trans. by Bernard Wall; introd. by Pierre Leroy, S.J. *Harper* 1960. Torchbks. pap. $1.50

"The spiritual testament of one of the greatest scientists, thinkers and mystics of our twentieth century, this . . . deserves the praise given it by numerous scholars in widely varied fields"— (*Commonweal*).

THE ACTIVATION OF ENERGY. 1963. Trans. by René Hague *Harcourt* 1971 $7.50 Harvest Bks. 1972 pap. $2.95

THE FUTURE OF MAN. Trans. by Norman Denny *Harper* 1964 Torchbks. 1969 pap. $1.95

This, which won the Catholic Book Award for general nonfiction in 1965, shows Teilhard as "at once both a fervent Catholic and a thinker who sought to express the old truths in new language. . . . Love is the real center of his thinking"—(*N.Y. Times*). Where "The Phenomenon of Man" looks backward upon past evolution, "The Future of Man" sets its sights on man's further development by erecting "philosophical projections of both religion and science beyond their present boundaries, and [viewing] these projections as aiming at an ultimate point of convergence in cosmic history. This breathtaking enterprise has made Teilhard de Chardin a bearer of hope to those men who look forward to an eventual reconciliation between traditional religion and scientific naturalism"—(*LJ*).

BUILDING THE EARTH. Trans. from the French by Noel Lindsay; fwd. by Max H. Bégouën; ill. by Sister Rose Ellen. 1965. *Avon Bks.* 1969 pap. $1.25

The five texts here, written between 1931 and 1941, were first printed as part of the first *Cahier* of the Association of Friends of Pierre Teilhard de Chardin. Together "they form a good [brief] summary of Teilhard's religious, political, and moral thought on man's future, a kind of epitome of his cosmic vision"—(*LJ*).

HYMN OF THE UNIVERSE. *Harper* 1965 $3.50 Colophon Bks. 1969 pap. $1.95

"A poet's as well as a mystic's book, a book of unfolding radiance. Even a non-religious person cannot help but be moved"—(Louis Untermeyer). "A passionate, powerful work—priceless"— (*LJ*).

THE MAKING OF A MIND: Letters from a Soldier-Priest 1914–1919. Trans. by René Hague; introd. by Marguerite Teilhard-Chambon *Harper* 1965 $5.00

Written from the front to his closest friend and cousin Marguerite, these letters "not only describe his reactions to the war and show its decisive effect on his development, but they are also filled with plans for writing"—(*LJ*).

THE PRAYER OF THE UNIVERSE (orig. "Writings in Time of War"). Trans. by René Hague *Harper* 1968 abr. ed. 1973 pap. $1.25

Essays written from the front between 1916 and 1919, "primarily for himself to set down clearly the philosophical ideas he had been developing—to serve perhaps as his testament, or possibly as the basis for expansion later on"—(*PW*). "A remarkable tribute to the strength of Teilhard's personality . . . should increase the understanding of his thought"—(*TLS*, London).

HOW I BELIEVE. *Harper* 1969 pap. $.75

CHRISTIANITY AND EVOLUTION. Trans. by René Hague *Harcourt* 1971 $5.95 Harvest Bks. 1974 pap. $2.95

"Superbly translated. . . . What Teilhard is calling for is a new theology which views Christ as universal, a radical energy suffusing the totality of being. . . . Highly recommended"—(*Choice*).

HUMAN ENERGY. *Harcourt* 1971 $5.95 Harvest Bks. 1972 pap. $1.95

LET ME EXPLAIN. Ed. by J. P. Demoulin *Harper* 1972 pap. $2.45

ON LOVE. *Harper* 1973 $3.95

ON HAPPINESS. Trans. by René Hague *Harper* 1974 $3.95

LETTERS FROM A TRAVELLER. *Harper* 1962 Torchbks. 1968 pap. $2.45

Books about Teilhard de Chardin

The Religion of Teilhard de Chardin. By Henri de Lubac, S.J. Trans. by René Hague. Pub. in France 1962. *Christian Class.* 1967 $5.00
  An interpretation of Teilhard's religion as it influenced his thought, this includes several letters to and from Teilhard published here for the first time. The author, a distinguished French theologian, was a personal friend of Teilhard.
Teilhard de Chardin: The Man and his Meaning. By Henri de Lubac. Trans. by René Hague. Pub. in France 1964. *New Am Lib.* Mentor Bks. 1967 pap. $.95
Teilhard de Chardin: Pilgrim of the Future. Ed. by Neville Braybrooke. 1964. *Fernhill* 1968 pap. $1.75
  A symposium which includes Teilhard's "The Meaning and Constructive Value of Suffering" and "Christ in Matter" as well as essays by George Barbour, Canon Charles E. Raven, D. M. MacKinnon, Karl Stern and Bernard Towers. "An important collection"—(*PW*).
Teilhard de Chardin and the Mystery of Christ. By Christopher F. Mooney. 1966. *Doubleday* Image Bks. 1968 pap. $1.45
Teilhard de Chardin's Theology of the Christian World. By Robert Faricy, S.J. *Sheed & Ward* 1967 $6.00
  "A synthesis of Teilhard's thought on 'the place of man's endeavor in a universe that is centered on Christ.' [Father Faricy considers] Teilhard's writings from this aspect of the meaning of human activity [and] accomplishes his task magnificently"—(*LJ*).
Science and Faith in Teilhard de Chardin. By Claude Cuenot and others. *Humanities Press* 1967 $3.25
From Science to Theology: The Evolutionary Design of Teilhard de Chardin. By Georges Crespy. Trans. by George H. Shriver *Abingdon* 1968 $4.00. A discussion of Teilhard's concepts of man, God and evil.
The Spirituality of Teilhard de Chardin. By Thomas Corbishley. *Paulist-Newman* 1972 pap. $1.45
Pierre Teilhard de Chardin's Philosophy of Evolution. By H. James Birx. *C. C. Thomas* 1972 $9.75
Teilhard de Chardin: In Quest of the Perfection of Man. Ed. by Geraldine O. Browning, Joseph L. Aliota and Seymour M. Farber *Fairleigh Dickinson Univ. Press* 1973 $13.50. Papers presented at a symposium in San Francisco, May 1971.

TEMPLE, WILLIAM (Archbishop of Canterbury). 1881–1944.

William Temple, Archbishop of Canterbury from 1942 until his early death in 1944, was an outstanding figure in the movement to found the World Council of Churches. The first son of an Archbishop of Canterbury ever to reach his father's high office (Frederick Temple held the office from 1896 to 1902), he spent much of his youth in Lambeth Palace. His upbringing was most conservative, but William Temple himself became a distinguished 'low church' liberal and champion of progressive social and ecclesiastical ideas. O.p. are "Mens Creatrix" (*St. Martin's* 1917), "Christus Veritas" (*St. Martin's* 1924), "Nature, Man and God" (*St. Martin's* 1934), "Readings in St. John's Gospel" (*St. Martin's* 1934) and "Some Lambeth Letters" (*Oxford* 1963).

FIVE MISCELLANEOUS ESSAYS. Ed. by Samuel H. Monk. *Univ. of Michigan Press* 1963 $5.00

HOPE OF A NEW WORLD. 1940. *Bks. for Libraries* 1974 $7.00

RELIGIOUS EXPERIENCE AND OTHER ESSAYS AND ADDRESSES. 1958 *Allenson* 1959 $4.50 *Attic Press* $4.00

WHAT CHRISTIANS STAND FOR IN THE SECULAR WORLD. *Fortress* 1965 pap. $1.00

Books about Temple

William Temple, Archbishop of Canterbury: His Life and Letters. By Frederic A. Iremonger. 1948. Abr. ed. by David C. Somervell. *Oxford* 1963 pap. $2.25

William Temple's Philosophy of Religion. By Owen C. Thomas. *Allenson* 1961 $5.50

Social Concern in the Thought of William Temple. By Robert Craig. *Allenson* 1963 $5.50

William Temple's Political Legacy. By John D. Carmichael and Harold S. Goodwin. *Allenson* 1963 $5.50

William Temple, Twentieth-Century Christian. By Joseph F. Fletcher. *Allenson* 1963 $7.50

BULTMANN, RUDOLF (KARL). 1884–

American theologians have recently become more than ever interested in the achievement of Rudolf Bultmann. The son of a German Evangelical-Lutheran pastor, he studied in Marburg, Tübingen and Berlin. He was associated with Karl Barth (*q.v.*) and others in the revolt against Adolf Harnack and that branch of 19th-century theology devoted to discovering the "Jesus of history." Using the tools of criticism that Harnack (and Weiss) had developed, Bultmann came to very skeptical conclusions about the New Testament documents as records of historical fact. Much of the material attached to the figure of Jesus seemed to belong to the realm of "myth," "the undifferentiated discourse of a prescientific age, when events both in the world of men and in the world of nature were assigned to the direct agency of occult forces whether divine or demonic"— (*See* John Macquarrie's "Twentieth Century Religious Thought" *Allenson* rev. ed. 1971 pap. $6.65).

If Christianity is inseparably tied to ancient mythology and cosmology, how can one hold to it? Bultmann replied that the New Testament must be "demythologized," translated and disengaged from a framework that obscures its truth from men of the post-mythical age. The hidden truth buried within myth is the *kerygma*, the divine word God has addressed to man. The demythologized *kerygma* can elucidate our understanding of our own existence. Bultmann finds the most valuable framework for this understanding in existentialism, specifically that of Martin Heidegger (*q.v.*), a position that brought him into opposition to Barth.

HISTORY OF THE SYNOPTIC TRADITION. 1921. *Harper* 1963 $10.50

JESUS AND THE WORLD. *Scribner* 1934 pap. $2.45

THEOLOGY OF THE NEW TESTAMENT. *Scribner* 1951 1955 1970 $10.00 pap. $4.95. A basic work.

(With others). KERYGMA AND MYTH. 1953. Ed. by Hans W. Bartsch *Harper* Torchbks. 1961 pap. $1.45. An influential work.

PRIMITIVE CHRISTIANITY. Trans. by R. H. Fuller *New Am. Lib.* Meridian Bks. 1956 $3.95

HISTORY AND ESCHATOLOGY: The Presence of Eternity. 1957. *Harper* Torchbks. 1962 pap. $1.95

JESUS CHRIST AND MYTHOLOGY. *Scribner* 1958 $3.50 pap. $1.95

(With Karl Jaspers). MYTH AND CHRISTIANITY. *Farrar, Straus* Noonday 1958 pap. $2.45

OLD AND NEW MAN. Trans. by Keith Crim *John Knox Press* 1967 pap. $1.50

FAITH AND UNDERSTANDING. Trans. by Louise P. Smith; ed. by Robert W. Funk *Harper* 1969 $7.50

THE GOSPEL OF JOHN: A Commentary. *Westminster Press* 1971 $15.00

Books about Bultmann

The Scope of Demythologizing: Bultmann and His Critics. By John Macquarrie. 1961. *Peter Smith* $4.50

Kerygma and History. Trans. and ed. by Carl E. Braaten and R. A. Harrisville. *Abingdon* 1962 $5.00. A critical appraisal of Bultmann theology in essays by outstanding European scholars representing a variety of theological orientations.

The Divided Mind of Modern Theology, Karl Barth and Rudolf Bultmann 1908–1933. By James D. Smart. *Westminster Press* 1967 $7.50
"This examination of their early works is designed not to reconcile their viewpoints but to clarify them, and to foster a healthy dialogue among their supporters"—*(PW)*.

An Introduction to the Theology of Rudolf Bultmann. By Walter Schmithals. Trans. by John Bowden *Augsburg* 1968 $6.50
Bultmann himself calls this the best book to have been written on his thought. "Very readable" *(LJ)*, with bibliography and indexes.

Existentialist Theology: A Comparison of Heidegger and Bultmann. By John Macquarrie. *Harper* Torchbks. pap. $2.25

Jaspers and Bultmann: A Dialogue between Philosophy and Theology in the Existentialist Tradition. By Eugene T. Long. *Duke Univ. Press* 1968 $6.50

History and Existential Theology: The Role of History in the Theology of Rudolf Bultmann. By Norman J. Young. *Westminster Press* 1969 $5.95

The Thought of Rudolf Bultmann. By André Malet. Trans. by Richard Strachan *Doubleday* 1971 $8.95

Rudolf Bultmann. By Morris Ashcraft. Ed. by Bob E. Patterson *Word Bks.* 1972 $4.95

Political Theology. By Dorothee Soelle. Trans. from the German by John Shelley *Fortress* 1974 pap. $3.50

BARTH, KARL. 1886–1968.

Probably the most famous theologian of this century though essentially a conservative in today's raging debates, Karl Barth was an explosive figure in the world from 1919, when he published his revolutionary "The Epistle to the Romans," until his death in 1968. This epoch-making work took him from his pastorate in a small Swiss village to professorships at the universities of Göttingen, Münster and Bonn. His impact gave rise to the theological tag "Barthianism" (still a more or less misunderstood term), and to the widespread use of his equally controversial metaphor for God as "Utterly Other." A dialectic theologian, his views modified as his thought progressed. Nevertheless he is consistent in his repudiation of natural theology and its implication of man's discovery of God. Barth's theology is unalterably centered in the idea that God encounters man, "the word of Christ" comes from God to man; there is no other "way" from man to God. Neither is valid knowledge of God available through philosophic speculation or in religions other than Christian. He vigorously denied the assumptions of humanism.

"Church Dogmatics" was his *magnum opus*, which the *N.Y. Times* described at his death as "one of the monuments of 20th-century scholarship. . . . It grew to more than 6 million words on 7,000 pages in 12 volumes. It still lacked several volumes when he retired in 1962 and abandoned the project. The title was carefully chosen and reflected Dr. Barth's conviction that theology must be deeply rooted in the life of the Christian churches. . . . 'The theologian who has no joy in his work is not a theologian at all,' he said. 'Sulky faces, morose thoughts and boring ways of speaking are intolerable in this science.' " A kindly man with a sense of humor who had been a courageous opponent of Hitler on behalf of the German churches and was deported from Germany by the Nazis, he once wrote: "The angels laugh at old Karl. They laugh at him because he tries to grasp the truth about God in a book of Dogmatics. They laugh at the fact that volume follows volume, and each is thicker than the previous one. . . . And they laugh about the men who write so much about Karl Barth instead of writing about the things he is trying to write about"—*(N.Y. Times)*. Passionately fond of Mozart, he used to play two or three of the composer's records every morning before starting work. Two of his sons have become theologians. One of them, Markus Barth, teaches in this country at the Pittsburgh Theological Seminary.

Opponents attacked Barth as heretical, as pessimistic, anticultural and theologically rigid. Adherents have valued his insistence on the qualitative uniqueness of Christianity and his claim that "theology is a free science" with no obligation to harmonize its findings with secular thought. His great power was readily acknowledged by leaders of almost all camps. No Evangelical theologian since the Reformation has received so much attention from the Roman Catholic Church. Indeed, Barth's system has been likened to that of St. Thomas Aquinas *(q.v.)*. His work opened new areas for discussion in the Ecumenical-Roman Catholic debate.

THE EPISTLE TO THE ROMANS. 1919. Trans. from the German of the 6th ed. by Edwyn C. Hoskyns *Oxford* 1933 $9.75 Galaxy Bks. 1968 pap. $3.50

THEOLOGY AND CHURCH: Shorter Writings, 1920–1928. *Allenson* 1962 $8.50

THE WORD OF GOD AND THE WORD OF MAN. 1925. Trans. by Douglas Horton *Harper* Torchbks. 1957 pap. $2.95; *Peter Smith* 1958 $4.25

CHRISTIAN LIFE. 1930. *Allenson* 1962 $4.00

CHURCH DOGMATICS, 1936–69. *Allenson* 4 vols. in 13 pts. Vol. I Doctrine of the Word of God 2 pts. The Revelation of God Vol. 2 The Doctrine of God Pt. I Knowledge and Reality of God Pt. 2 Election and Command of God Vol. 3 Doctrine of Creation Pt. I Work of Creation Pt. 2 The Creature Pt. 3 The Creator and His Creature Pt. 4 Command of God the Creator Vol. 4 Doctrine of Reconciliation Pt. I Jesus Christ: the Lord as Servant Pt. 2 The Servant as Lord Pt. 3 Jesus Christ the True Witness, and Sects. 1–2 Pt. 4 Sects. 3–5 Pt. 4 Baptism as Foundation of Christian Life each $18.50 except Vol. 4 Pt. 4 $11.50 set $233.50

CHURCH DOGMATICS: A Selection. Sel. by Helmut Gollwitzer: trans. and ed. by G. W. Bromily *Harper* Torchbks. 1962 pap. $2.75; *Peter Smith* $4.50

DOGMATICS IN OUTLINE. 1947 *Harper* Torchbks. 1959 pap. $2.25

THE HUMANITY OF GOD. 1956. *John Knox Press* 1960 pap. $2.45

PROTESTANT THOUGHT: From Rousseau to Ritschl. 1959. *Bks. for Libraries* $14.00; *Simon & Schuster* Touchstone Clarion Bks. 1969 pap. $2.95

CREDO. Trans. by J. Strathhearn McNab; fwd. by Robert M. Brown *Scribner* 1962 pap. $1.45. A more simple and popular statement of the faith of the Church.

EVANGELICAL THEOLOGY: An Introduction. Trans. by Grover Foley. 1963. *Doubleday* Anchor Bks. pap. $2.50. Originally a valedictory course of 17 lectures at the University of Basel, this volume contains the restatement of his neo-orthodox position.

GERMAN CHURCH CONFLICT. Trans. by T. H. Parker *John Knox Press* 1965 pap. $1.95

ON MARRIAGE. Ed. by Franklin Sherman Social Ethics Ser. *Fortress* 1968 pap. $1.00

CHRIST AND ADAM. *Macmillan* Collier Bks. 1968 pap. $1.95

REVOLUTIONARY THEOLOGY IN THE MAKING: Barth-Thurneysen Correspondence, 1914–1925. Trans. by James D. Smart *John Knox Press* 1964 $3.95. Fragments from the letters between Barth and Thurneysen at a time when both were young pastors in Switzerland. First published as a Festschrift, they are too elliptical to be understood except by specialists.

HOW I CHANGED MY MIND. Introd. by John D. Godsey *John Knox Press* 1966 $2.00
This "delightful little book . . . can serve as a useful introduction to the man and his work"—
(*LJ*). "A bracing demi-autobiography, essentially composed of three self-descriptive articles Barth wrote for the *Christian Century* in 1938, 1948, and 1958. . . . Actually, in the three decades considered, Barth changed his mind rather little. . . . The dominant impression these pages leave is of Barth's heroic stubbornness, the reasoned yet pugnacious refusal to let others think for him; when political relativism was fashionable, he implacably opposed Hitler, and when political absolutism prevailed, he took a mediating attitude toward Communism"—(*New Yorker*).

Books about Barth

Barthian Theology. By John McConnachie. 1933. *Bks. for Libraries* 1972 $12.50
Christianity and Barthianism. By Cornelius Van Til. *Presbyterian & Reformed* 1960 pap. $4.95
The Pacifism of Karl Barth. By John H. Yoder. *Herald Press* 1964 pap. $.25. A pamphlet.
The Theology of Karl Barth: An Introduction. By Herbert Hartwell. *Allenson* 1964 $4.95
Karl Barth's Theological Method. By Gordon H. Clark. *Presbyterian & Reformed* $5.00
The Divided Mind of Modern Theology: Karl Barth and Rudolf Bultmann, 1908–1933. By James D. Smart. *Westminster Press* 1967 $7.50
"The central position of the book is to show that the present 'Divided Mind' is largely attributable to a lack of understanding [by partisans] of these two theologians, and will continue as long as the two sectors fail to consider each other's view. . . . Very readable"—
(*LJ*). Professor Smart teaches philosophy at Union Theological Seminary; he bases his discussion on a study of the early thought of both his subjects.

Bultmann-Barth-Catholic Theology. By Heinrich Fries. Trans. and ed. by Leonard Swidler *Duquesne Univ. Press* 1967 text ed. $5.50

Karl Barth and the Problem of War. By John H. Yoder. *Abingdon* 1970 pap. $2.95

Karl Barth. By John S. Bowden. *Allenson* 1971 pap. $1.95

The Theology of Karl Barth. By Hans Von Balthasar. Trans. by J. Drury *Doubleday* Anchor Bks. 1972 pap. $2.50

TILLICH, PAUL (JOHANNES).   1886–1965.

"Dr. Paul Tillich, the Protestant theologian, once said, 'I was thinking about infinity at the age of 8.'" At an advanced age he was still thinking, and teaching and preaching all around the country, in many places with the biggest audience of the local lecture season. Dr. Tillich, who had until late in his life a small office in Swift Hall at the University of Chicago Divinity School, told a visitor in 1963: "The important thing is not that people go more to church, listen to evangelists and join churches. The important thing is that the younger generation asks the right questions, and this is something which has not yet exhausted itself"—(Quotations from the *N.Y. Times*).

One of the greatest of modern theologians, he approximated in his theology the standard he suggested for Protestant theology in general: "To incorporate strictly scientific methods, a critical philosophy, a realistic understanding of man and society, and powerful ethical principles and motives." Though he became an American citizen, Tillich was born in Prussia and studied at Tübingen, Berlin and Halle. He was removed from his post as professor of philosophy at Frankfurt-am-Main in 1933 for outspoken opposition to National Socialism. "I had the great honor to be about the first non-Jewish professor dismissed from a German university," he said. He left Germany soon after and eventually began teaching at the Union Theological Seminary in New York. His great work, "Systematic Theology," was developed in America in the English language he learned at the age of 47. He died in 1965.

Starting as a Christian existentialist, Tillich went on to explore ontological structures of theology. His system of thought is derived from a "correlation" between the question of human existence and the answer of God's revelation. Unlike Barth (*q.v.*) he found natural theology meaningful because the question of God arises from man's awareness of his own finitude. Tillich employs the discoveries of psychoanalysis to depict the human condition. His concept of God is of suprapersonal, suprarational "depth," or "being." "Being" manifests itself to man through revelation within which reason is raised to an ecstatic, mystic level and the subject-object relationship is overcome. His popular books express his systematic theology in a graceful, vivid style readily available to nonspecialists. As he finished the third volume of his "Systematic Theology," the *N.Y. Times* reported his saying: "I hope every century will develop its own theology. Answers and questions come out of current situations and theology must always speak to them." As Roger Hazelton wrote in the *New Republic* of Jan. 6, 1968, "Tillich's greatness as a thinker, now as before, lies in the fact that he knows what man is made of, what he suffers from, and what he can hope for."

THE ETERNAL NOW. *Scribner* 1963 pap. $1.95

This collection of 16 sermons delivered over an 8-year period is a good introduction to Tillich's thought. "The language is precise, direct and colorful; the author's message is profound but clear. He discusses such modern dilemmas as isolation, lack of communication, and the pressure for conformity"—(*LJ*).

THE PROTESTANT ERA. Trans. with a Concluding Essay by James Luther Adams *Univ. of Chicago Press* 1948 (abr.) Phoenix Bks. 1957 pap. $2.95

THE SHAKING OF THE FOUNDATIONS. *Scribner* 1948 pap. $1.95

SYSTEMATIC THEOLOGY. *Univ. of Chicago Press* 3 vols. 1951–63 Vol. I (1951) o.p. 1973 pap. $2.95 Vol. 2 (1957) $4.95 Vol. 3 (1963) $6.95 3 vols. in I $15.00

These volumes make "Tillich's life work available in the form in which he himself envisaged it, a summing up of his reflections on the significance of modern culture and the Christian faith for one another"—(*New Republic*).

THE COURAGE TO BE. *Yale Univ. Press* 1952 $10.00 1959 pap. $2.95

LOVE, POWER AND JUSTICE. 1954. *Oxford* Galaxy Bks. 1960 pap. $1.95

NEW BEING. *Scribner* 1955 pap. $1.95

BIBLICAL RELIGION AND THE SEARCH FOR ULTIMATE REALITY. *Univ. of Chicago Press* 1955 $4.50 Phoenix Bks. 1955 pap. $1.50

THE DYNAMICS OF FAITH. 1957. *Harper* Torchbks. pap. $1.75

THE THEOLOGY OF CULTURE. 1959. Ed. by Robert C. Kimball *Oxford* Galaxy Bks. 1964 pap. $1.95

MORALITY AND BEYOND. *Harper* Torchbks. 1963 pap. $1.25

CHRISTIANITY AND THE ENCOUNTER OF THE WORLD RELIGIONS. *Columbia* 1963 $7.00
pap. $1.95

THE WORLD SITUATION. *Fortress* 1965 pap. $1.00. First published as a Chapter in the
symposium "The Christian Answer."

MY SEARCH FOR ABSOLUTES. Ill. by Saul Steinberg Credo Perspectives Ser. *Simon &
Schuster* 1967 $4.95 Touchstone Bks. 1969 pap. $1.95
This two-volume addition to Tillich's "Systematic Theology" is a clear and readable autobiography based on lectures given at the University of Chicago Law School which "gives the reader
insight into the man, his ideas, and the forces that aided in his search for absolutes which give life
meaning"—(*PW*).

A HISTORY OF CHRISTIAN THOUGHT. Ed. with introd. by Carl E. Braaten 1968. *Simon &
Schuster* Touchstone Bks. pap. $4.95
These are lectures, delivered in 1953 at the Union Theological Seminary, which "deal compre-
hensively with the developing history of Christianity from the pre-Christian era to the present"—
(*PW*).

WHAT IS RELIGION? Ed. by James Luther Adams *Harper* 1969 Torchbks. 1973 pap.
$2.45

Books about Tillich
The Theology of Paul Tillich. Ed. by Robert W. Bretall and Charles W. Kegley. *Macmillan* 1952
1961 pap. $2.45
The Existentialist Theology of Paul Tillich. By Bernard Martin. 1962. *College & Univ. Press* 1963
$7.50 pap. $2.45
This excellent book is a significant introduction to and summary of the principal themes of
philosophy and/or theology by an outstanding young Jewish scholar, Rabbi Martin of the Mt.
Zion Hebrew Congregation in St. Paul, Minnesota. Although the author differs from Tillich,
not only in detail but also in general principle, his book should be of great interest to college
and seminary students, informed laymen and scholars.
Paul Tillich's Philosophy of Culture, Science, and Religion. By James Luther Adams. *Schocken*
1970 pap. $2.95
"Valuable as a basic study"—(*LJ*). Includes a bibliography.
The Power of Self-Transcendence: An Introduction to the Philosophical Theology of Paul
Tillich. By Guyton B. Hammond. Library of Contemporary Theology Ser. *Bethany Press* 1965
pap. $2.45
"This study by . . . [an] associate professor at Virginia Polytechnic Institute, is an excellent
and useful introduction to Tillich's thought . . . and his impact upon contemporary American
thought"—(*LJ*).
Paul Tillich: An Appraisal. By J. Heywood Thomas. Ed. by D. E. Nineham and E. H. Robertson
John Knox Press 1966 pap. $1.25
This book illuminates the philosophical system without distorting it and explains Tillich's
thought without entering into controversy. After graduating in theology at the University of
Wales, the author did research in the philosophical theology of Kierkegaard at Cambridge
and later became Tillich's pupil at Union Theological Seminary. This volume should interest
intellectual Christians of all denominations.
Vision of Paul Tillich. By Carl J. Armbruster. *Sheed & Ward* 1967 $6.95
Religious Symbols and God: A Philosophical Study of Tillich's Theology. By William L. Rowe.
Univ. of Chicago Press 1968 $8.00
An associate professor of philosophy at Purdue University attempts "to decipher and
interpret the complex language of Tillich's theology. . . . Mr. Rowe writes exceedingly well
and has a gift for clarity and exact expression. . . . Recommended"—(*LJ*).
Reflection and Doubt in the Thought of Paul Tillich. By Robert P. Scharlemann. *Yale Univ. Press*
1969 $8.50
Paul Tillich's Dialectical Humanism: Unmasking the God above God. By Leonard Wheat. *Johns
Hopkins Press* 1970 $11.00
Paul Tillich: Basics in His Thought. By James F. Anderson. *Magi Bks.* 1972 $4.95
Paulus. By Rollo May. *Harper* 1973 $5.95
From Time to Time. By Hannah Tillich. *Stein & Day* 1974 pap. $1.95
"The author of this autobiography sketches . . . the course of her own life, her marriage to
Tillich, their flight from Naziism, and their final years at Union Theological Seminary,
Harvard and Chicago"—(*LJ*).
Tillich's System. By Wayne W. Mahan. *Trinity Univ. Press* 1974 $7.50

RADHAKRISHNAN, SIR SARVEPALLI. 1888–

The distinguished East Indian philosopher and statesman was professor of Eastern religions and ethics at Oxford from 1936 to 1952. He has been India's delegate to UNESCO and Indian ambassador to the U.S.S.R. In 1957 he became vice-president and from 1962 to 1967 was president of the Indian Republic. In addition to his many original works, he has edited several volumes on philosophy and translated and edited "The Dhammapada" (*Oxford* 1950 $3.20), "The Brahma Sutra: The Philosophy of Spiritual Life" (1960. *Greenwood* 1968 $28.25), "The Bhagavad-gita" (*Harper* Torchbks. pap. $2.75), and "The Principal Upanishads" (*Humanities Press* 1953 $13.25 pap. $10.00).

Radhakrishnan contends that all religion is essentially the same—"not a creed or code, but an insight into reality," a philosophy for mankind without conflict, dogma or authoritarianism. His philosophy of "absolute idealism" provides a possible basis for the fusion of Eastern and Western thought. Sir Sarvepalli has been awarded the 1959 Goethe Plaquette and the 1961 German Bookseller's Peace Prize.

INDIAN PHILOSOPHY. 1923. *Humanities Press* 2 vols. 1962 set $33.00

THE HINDU VIEW OF LIFE. *Macmillan* 1927 1939 $3.00 pap. $1.45

EASTERN RELIGIONS AND WESTERN THOUGHT. *Oxford* 1939 2nd ed. 1940 $8.25

THE RECOVERY OF FAITH. 1955. *Greenwood* $10.25; *Inter-Culture* 1969 pap. $1.50. Impartial and brilliant criticism of the faults of all our existing political, religious and social systems.

EAST AND WEST IN RELIGION. *Harper* (Barnes & Noble) 1958 $3.50

OCCASIONAL SPEECHES AND WRITINGS. *Verry* 3 vols. 1962–65 Vols. I–2 1952–59 $5.50 Vol. 3 July 1959–May 1962 $5.50

HISTORY OF PHILOSOPHY, EASTERN AND WESTERN. *Harper* (Barnes & Noble) 2 vols. 1962 set $18.50

RELIGION IN A CHANGING WORLD. *Humanities Press* 1967 $5.50

RELIGION AND CULTURE. *Inter-Culture* 1971 pap. $1.50

OUR HERITAGE. *Inter-Culture* 1974 pap. $1.60

Books about Radhakrishnan

The Philosophy of Sarvepalli Radhakrishnan. Ed. by Paul Arthur Schilpp. *Open Court* 1952 $15.00. Twenty-three descriptive and critical essays by American, British and Indian scholars; Radhakrishnan's own "fragments of a confession," "The Religion of the Spirit and the World's Need" and his reply to his critics.

Introduction to Radhakrishnan. By S. J. Samartha. *Association Press* 1964 pap. $2.25

Radhakrishnan and Integral Experience. By J. G. Arapura. *Asia Pub. House* 1966 $6.25

Sarvepalli Radhakrishnan: A Study of the President of India. Ed. by K. Iswara Dutt *Verry* 1966 $4.00

Radhakrishnan, the Portrait of an Educationalist. By R. P. Singh. *Verry* 1967 $5.50

Radhakrishnan: Comparative Studies in Philosophy Presented in Honor of His Sixtieth Birthday. *Humanities Press* 1968 $7.25

BRUNNER, (HEINRICH) EMIL. 1889–1966.

Second only to Barth (*q.v.*), the Swiss Protestant Brunner was an outstanding representative of "Continental theology." The neo-orthodoxy of both Barth and Brunner sought a continuing dialogue between theology and humanistic culture. Brunner broke with Barth, however, in the matter of "natural theology," Barth denying that revelation was possible except through Christ directly to man, Brunner finding a place in his own theology for revelation from sources derived from man's reason, culture and experience of nature. His originality centered in his exposition of the responsibility of the individual before God. He analyzed the "contradiction that every man knows between what he is and what he ought to be," and says that the contradiction "can truly be understood only in terms of a God who speaks to man and to whose word man responds." Brunner lectured and taught at many seminaries including Princeton Theological Seminary in America. He was Professor of Theology at the University of Zurich (1924–1953) and Christian University, Tokyo, Japan (1953–1955). In 1955 he returned to Switzerland to become a preacher at the Fraumünster Church in Zurich, where he died in 1966. A number of his titles are o.p.

THE MEDIATOR. 1927. Eng. trans. 1934. *Westminster Press* 1947 1965 pap. $3.25

OUR FAITH. *Scribner* 1936 pap. $2.45

The Christian Doctrine of Creation and Redemption. *Westminster Press* 1952 $6.50

Truth as Encounter. *Westminster Press* 1964 $5.00

The Scandal of Christianity. *John Knox Press* 1965 pap. $1.50

Books about Brunner

Emil Brunner: An Introduction to the Man and His Thought. By Paul K. Jewett. *Inter-Varsity Press* 1961 pap. $.95

The Theology of Emil Brunner. Ed. by Charles W. Kegley. The Library of Living Theology, Vol. 3. *Macmillan* 1962 $7.50

"In an age when theology is becoming increasingly controversial, he stands out as a great mediator who offers a practical alternative to the extreme positions of Barth and Bultmann. This collection is intended to assess Brunner's balanced middle way." Among the essays of more general interest are those by Niebuhr and Tillich. This is an essential book for theological libraries and is highly recommended for university and large public libraries.

Brunner's Dialectic. By Robert Reymond. *Presbyterian & Reformed* pap. $.75

NIEBUHR, REINHOLD. 1892–1971.

"The number one theologian of United States Protestantism," as *Time* called Mr. Niebuhr, was Professor of Applied Christianity at Union Theological Seminary, New York from 1930 to 1960. An influential and stimulating lecturer and teacher, through his books he "captured the attention of the literate and thoughtful not so much by his views about the nature and destiny of man as by the passionate moral integrity and intellectual keenness at once so alive to detail and so bold in perspective—with which he explored the great issues of our age"—(Sidney Hook, in the *N.Y. Times*). His liberalism, humanism and social idealism pervaded his thought on Christianity and provided considerable stimulus for the recent renaissance in American theology. Niebuhr was elected a member of the American Academy of Arts and Letters in 1958 and lectured at Union Theological Seminary during the 1960s.

The Contribution of Religion to Social Work. 1932. *AMS Press* 1972 $5.00

Moral Man and Immoral Society. *Scribner* Lyceum Ed. 1932 pap. $2.45

Beyond Tragedy: Essays on the Christian Interpretation of History. 1937. *Bks. for Libraries* $11.50

Christianity and Power Politics. 1940. *Shoe String Press* 1969 $7.00

The Children of Light and the Children of Darkness: A Vindication of Democracy and a Critique of its Traditional Defense. *Scribner* 1944 Lyceum Ed. 1960 pap. $2.45

The Nature and Destiny of Man: A Christian Interpretation. *Scribner* 2 vols. 1949 Vol. 1 Human Nature Vol. 2 Human Destiny pap. each $2.95

Faith and History: A Comparison of Christian and Modern Views of History. *Scribner* 1949 $8.95

Christian Realism and Political Problems. 1953. *Kelley* 1975 $11.00

Love and Justice: Selections from the Shorter Writings. Ed. by D. B. Robertson. 1957. *Peter Smith* $4.25

Pious and Secular America. 1958. *Kelley* $9.00

The Structure of Nations and Empires. 1959. *Kelley* 1972 $12.50

"A brilliant and profound orientation by one of the most creative thinkers of our time"—(*LJ*).

Faith and Politics: A Commentary on Religious, Social and Political Thought in a Technological Age. Ed. with introd. by Ronald H. Stone *Braziller* 1968 $6.50

Essays and interviews written after 1930. Dr. Niebuhr translates "his profoundly Christian faith and insights into terms that are contemporary, down-to-earth and relevant to the deepest values of religion"—(*PW*).

Justice and Mercy. Ed. by Ursula Niebuhr *Harper* 1974 $5.95

"Nine sermons and addresses, interspersed with collections of prayers, litanies, and other liturgical forms. Planned before Niebuhr's death in 1971, this work has been posthumously edited by his wife Ursula, who draws on her husband's own words in the introduction to sketch his understanding of both prayer and preaching"—(*LJ*).

Books about Niebuhr

Reinhold Niebuhr: Prophet from America. By D. R. Davies. 1945. *Attic Press* $1.50; *Bks. for Libraries* $7.50

Reinhold Niebuhr: His Religious, Social and Political Thought. Ed. by Robert W. Bretall and Charles W. Kegley. *Macmillan* 1956 1962 pap. $3.95. An important group of essays on Niebuhr's various points of view and his influence in the present day.

Sin and Science: Reinhold Niebuhr as Political Theologian. By Holtan P. Odegard. 1956. *Greenwood* 1973 $11.25

The Protestant Search for Political Realism, 1919–1941. By Donald B. Meyer. 1960. *Greenwood* 1973 $19.25

The Courage to Change: An Introduction to the Life and Thought of Reinhold Niebuhr. By June Bingham. 1961. *Kelley* $15.00; *Scribner* 1972 $8.95

Reinhold Niebuhr. By Nathan A. Scott, Jr. Pamphlets on American Writers *Univ. of Minnesota Press* 1963 pap. $1.25

The Promise of Reinhold Niebuhr. By Gabriel Fackre. *Lippincott* 1970 $3.50 pap. $1.75

"Fackre has done a remarkable job.... This little book can serve both as an excellent introduction to its subject and as a contribution to on-going discussions of Niebuhr's relevance.... Considerable biographical material, including Niebuhr's political involvements and shifts, is integrated into the exposition"—*(Choice)*.

Reinhold Niebuhr: Prophet to Politicians. By Ronald Stone. *Abingdon* 1972 $8.00

"An account of Niebuhr's ... public career and of the ethical and pragmatic convictions that shaped it.... The author ... writes very clearly and has organized his findings so well that the book will appeal to the general reader as well as to the philosopher or theologian"—*(LJ)*.

NIEBUHR, H(ELMUT) RICHARD. 1894–1962.

Though H. Richard Niebuhr, Protestant theologian, clergyman and professor at Yale, is less widely known and wrote fewer books than his brother Reinhold (*q.v.*), his own religious thinking was original and strongly influential in its field. Like his brother, he belonged to the movement known as Neo-orthodoxy, derived from Sören Kierkegaard, which found its expression between the World Wars in the lectures of Emil Brunner and Karl Barth. But he was strongly American—in his compatibility with the God of Jonathan Edwards and in his focus on the development of the Church in America.

Richard Niebuhr readily admits, in fact insists upon, the relativity of our knowledge of God as well as the inability of words adequately to define His reality. All doctrine, he says, is necessarily limited. "There is no greater barrier to understanding," (he wrote in "The Kingdom of God in America") "than the assumption that the standpoint which we happen to occupy is a universal one, while that of the object of our criticism is relative." Man's knowledge of God must begin with faith, even if faith at first is only a point of view; he then seeks to understand its limitations by studying the sociohistorical factors in its development. Faith is essential as an act of affirmation rather than as a reasoned conclusion, for it is from man's relationship with God that he derives his sense of moral responsibility, a human dignity and human community. Like Barth, Niebuhr was reacting against the diluted "middle-class" Christianity in which, as the latter described it, "a God without wrath brought men without sin into a kingdom without judgment through the ministrations of a Christ without a cross." As William Robert Miller has said (in "Contemporary American Protestant Thought," to which we are much indebted here), Richard Niebuhr "built no system but in his dealing with facts demonstrated a method and offered perspectives which transcend his own time."

THE SOCIAL SOURCES OF DENOMINATIONALISM. 1929. *New Am. Lib.* Meridian pap. $3.95; *Peter Smith* $6.00

THE KINGDOM OF GOD IN AMERICA. 1935. *Harper* Torchbks. pap. $1.95

THE MEANING OF REVELATION. *Macmillan* 1941 pap. 1967 $1.95

CHRIST AND CULTURE. 1951. *Harper* Torchbks. pap. $2.25; Peter Smith $4.00

THE RESPONSIBLE SELF: An Essay in Christian Moral Philosophy. Introd. by James M. Gustafson *Harper* 1963 $5.00

In this book, based on lectures delivered at Glasgow University, Niebuhr discusses responsibility and its relation to society, time, history, sin and salvation. "Illuminating and timely"—*(LJ)*.

RADICAL MONOTHEISM IN WESTERN CULTURE. *Harper* Torchbks. pap. $1.45

(With Waldo Beach, Eds.). CHRISTIAN ETHICS—Sources of the Living Tradition. *Ronald* 1955 rev. ed. 1973 $8.50

Books about Niebuhr

Faith and Ethics: The Theology of H. Richard Niebuhr. Ed. by Paul Ramsey. 1957. *Peter Smith* $4.25

The Theology of H. Richard Niebuhr. By Libertus Hoedemaker. *United Church* 1971 $10.00

To See the Kingdom: The Theological Vision of H. Richard Niebuhr. By James W. Fowler. *Abingdon* 1974 $10.95

KRISHNAMURTI, JIDDU.   1895–

The English social reformer and theosophist, Mrs. Annie Besant (1847–1933) met the Indian Krishnamurti in 1909 and proclaimed him a reincarnation of the messianic Buddha. After touring England and America with her in 1926 and 1927, he repudiated these claims. He finally settled in California and continued an active career of lecturing and writing.

EDUCATION AND THE SIGNFICANCE OF LIFE. *Harper* 1953 $3.00

THE FIRST AND LAST FREEDOM. *Harper* 1954 $5.00; *Theosophical Pub. House* 1968 pap. $1.95

LIFE AHEAD. 1963. *Theosophical Pub. House* 1967 pap. $1.45. Probes the multiple concerns of contemporary man to reveal the possibilities of a mature and intelligent life.

THINK ON THESE THINGS. *Harper* 1964 1970 pap. $1.50

COMMENTARIES ON LIVING: From the Notebooks of J. Krishnamurti. Ed. by D. Rajagopal *Fernhill* 3 vols. 1965–67 each $5.50; *Theosophical Pub. House* 3 series 1967 pap. each $2.25; *Verry* 1965 1st and 2nd series each $5.50 3rd series $6.75

FREEDOM FROM THE KNOWN. Ed. by Mary Lutyens *Harper* 1969 $4.95
"A synthesis of Krishnamurti's mature thought"—(*LJ*).

TALKS AND DIALOGUES. *Avon Bks.* 1970 pap. $1.45

AT THE FEET OF THE MASTER. *Theosophical Pub. House* 1970 pap. $1.25

THE ONLY REVOLUTION. Ed. by Mary Lutyens *Harper* 1970 $4.95
This book "is a series of short essays on meditation which all follow the same plan: some remarks on meditation (the leitmotiv of the book), a description of the landscape which gave rise to them, and a dialogue with some person or persons in the context of the landscape described"—(*TLS*, London).

THE URGENCY OF CHANGE. Ed. by Mary Lutyens *Harper* 1971 $4.95

YOU ARE THE WORLD. *Harper* 1972 pap. $2.25

BEYOND VIOLENCE. *Harper* 1973 pap. $2.25

THE IMPOSSIBLE QUESTION. *Harper* 1973 $4.95

TRADITION AND REVOLUTION. Ed. by Pupul Jayakar and Sunanda Patwardhan *Fernhill* 1973 $5.00

THE AWAKENING OF INTELLIGENCE. *Harper* 1974 $10.00

THE BEGINNINGS OF LEARNING. *Harper* 1975 $10.00
"Here are transcripts of conversations with students and teachers at the Brockwood Park School in England. . . . Throughout the book . . . Krishnamurti [expresses] deep concern for the problems of educating the young to become human beings who can yet survive in a competitive world"—(*LJ*).

Books about Krishnamurti

J. Krishnamurti and Awareness in Action. By Atmaram D. Dhopeshwarkar. *Humanities Press* 1967 $3.25

Candles in the Sun: Theology and Krishnamurti. By Emily Lutyens. *Gordon Press* $34.95

RAHNER, KARL, S.J.   1904–

Karl Rahner is the eminent German Catholic existentialist theologian whose thought derives in part from the non-Catholic Martin Heidegger (*q.v.*), under whom he studied from 1934 to 1936. Father Rahner's distinguished scholarly career has not kept him from speaking meaningfully to the educated layman. Of his many works (over 750 articles on theological, philosophical and religious subjects), "The Christian Commitment" was especially well received in the United States.

He was official theologian at the Second Vatican Council and has recently taught at the Universities of Innsbruck, Munich and Münster.

The complexity of Rahner's thought and language can be demanding and "sometimes obscure, but only because he himself is struggling to articulate the ideas that are teeming within him"— (Thomas A. Wassmer). His province has been the Church and her sacraments, priesthood, laity and mission in the world. He is critical of the Church but he loves her; he is "timely *and* traditional . . . original *and* orthodox . . . liberal *and* level-headed"—*(The Critic)*. He has addressed himself to abstruse theological and doctrinal questions; to the life of the Catholic layman, eating, sitting, walking—and doubting; to the vocation of the parish priest. He has urged the Church to get into the world and respond to the most crucial needs. Since he understands so well both the older generation of the Catholic hierarchy and the younger radicals, he has been able to play a special liberalizing role, in part through his prolific writings, as both mediator and proponent of innovation. He is always impatient (says the Rev. William T. Cunningham) with the "ghetto" that Catholic culture has constructed for itself, "with the Catholic universities, its support of laws against moral decline, and its pastors, high and low, who serve institutions rather than guide souls." With Cornelius Ernst and Kevin Smyth, he has edited a six-volume Catholic theological encyclopedia *"Sacramentum Mundi" (Seabury Press* 1969 set \$135.00), which was published simultaneously in English, Dutch, French, German, Italian and Spanish editions.

THE RAHNER READER. Ed. by Gerald McCool *Seabury Press* 1974 \$12.50 pap. \$4.95

THE CHRISTIAN COMMITMENT. *Sheed & Ward* 1963 \$4.50

"After [a] diagnosis of Catholic ills, Fr. Rahner reveals his understanding of Christian commitment in which the nature of man is permeated with the supernature of God and begins to exercise a Christ-like responsibility for the world in those areas in which the hierarchically constituted church is impotent"—(Rev. William T. Cunningham).

THEOLOGY FOR RENEWAL: Bishops, Priests, Laity. *Sheed & Ward* 1964 \$4.00

Collected articles and lectures "which all tend in the same direction, namely, toward the understanding that the church must have a sound theological basis . . . to endure in a changing world"—*(The Critic)*.

NATURE AND GRACE: Dilemmas in the Modern Church. *Sheed & Ward* 1964 \$3.50

CHRISTIAN IN THE MARKET PLACE. Trans. by Cecily Hastings *Sheed & Ward* 1966 \$4.00; *Christian Class.* 1966 \$4.00

More about the function of the Christian in his society; a companion to "The Christian Commitment." "Writing of this calibre is hard to match anywhere"—*(LJ)*.

BELIEF TODAY. Trans. by M. H. Heelan and others; ed. by Hans Küng. Theological Meditations Ser. *Sheed & Ward* 1967 \$3.50. Considers whether a Christian can believe and maintain his intellectual integrity; how faith affects everyday activities, and the like.

ON PRAYER. *Paulist-Newman* 1968 pap. \$1.45

SPIRIT IN THE WORLD. 1939. Trans. by William Dych *Seabury Press* 1968 \$9.50

The author "uses a Thomistic metaphysics of knowledge explained in terms of transcendental and existential philosophy to define man as that essence of absolute transcendence towards God insofar as man in his understanding and interpretation of the world respectfully 'preapprehends' towards God"—(Foreword).

HEARERS OF THE WORD. 1941. Trans. by Michael Richards *Seabury Press* 1969 \$6.50

"A metaphysical or ontological analysis of human knowing with the aim of showing human nature is open to possible revelation from God"— *(Christian Century)*. "This book is a key to the central theme of all of Rahner's later theology . . . and it is indispensable for a full appreciation of Rahner's work"—*(Commonweal)*.

GRACE IN FREEDOM. Trans. by Hilda Graef *Seabury Press* 1969 \$5.95

In these essays "the ground and modes of man's freedom in God . . . provide the focus for a series of reflections on . . . aspects of the present situation Catholics find themselves in"— (Publisher's note).

THE PRIESTHOOD. 1970. Trans. by Edward Quinn *Seabury Press* 1973 \$8.95

"These reflections on the Spiritual Exercises of St. Ignatius Loyola are based on retreat conferences given by Rahner in 1961 to candidates for ordination. . . . This presentation of the basic principles of the spiritual life provides insight into the psychology of a life with Christ in God"—*(LJ)*.

The Trinity. *Seabury Press* 1970 $4.95

Do You Believe in God? Trans. by Richard Strachan *Paulist-Newman* 1971 pap. $1.45

"According to the writer's thesis everyone believes in God at least implicitly.... Rahner's reflections are intended to help man existentially appreciate his true metaphysical status in the contemporary world"—(*Christian Century*).

Theological Investigations. *Seabury Press* Vols. 7–10 1972–73 Vols. 7–8 Further Theology of the Spiritual Life, trans. by David Bourke (1972) Vols. 9–10 Writings 1965–67 (1973) each $9.75

The Shape of the Church to Come. *Seabury Press* 1974 $6.95

Opportunities for Faith: Elements of a Modern Spirituality. 1970. Trans. by Edward Quinn *Seabury Press* 1975 $8.95

"Several published and unpublished sermons, addresses, and lectures delivered to a variety of audiences from 1968–1970"—(*Choice*).

(Ed.). Encyclopedia of Theology: The Concise Sacramentum Mundi. *Seabury Press* rev. abr. ed. 1975 $27.50

Books about Rahner

Karl Rahner: His Life, Thought and Work. By Herbert Vorgrimler. Trans. by Edward Quinn *Paulist-Newman* 1966 pap. $.95
The Philosophy of Karl Rahner. By Joseph Donceel. *Magi Bks.* 1969 pap. $.50
The Theology of Karl Rahner. By Gerald A. McCool. *Magi Bks.* 1969 pap. $.50
Death in Every Now. By Robert Ochs. *Sheed & Ward* 1969 $4.25. A very scholarly exposition of Rahner's philosophy of theology.

BONHOEFFER, DIETRICH. 1906–1945.

"In the grey dawn of an April day in 1945, in the concentration camp at Flossenburg shortly before it was liberated by the Allied forces, Dietrich Bonhoeffer was executed by the special order of Heinrich Himmler"—(John Doberstein's introduction to "Life Together"). Much of Bonhoeffer's published work was written during the years he was imprisoned. The German theologian and pastor left Germany in 1933 in protest against the anti-Jewish legislation forced on the churches. He returned in 1939 (from the U.S.), however, deliberately to help his colleagues in the resistance movement, though he was forbidden by the government to teach, write or speak in public. He saw the monstrosity of Hitlerism as requiring of him secular action and became a courier for the group of generals plotting Hitler's death. He was caught and arrested in 1943.

An extraordinary scholar who had earned a Ph.D. at the age of 21, Bonhoeffer drew from Kant (*q.v.*) and Heidegger (*q.v.*) to develop his understanding of the relation of revelation to the church. His "secular" Christianity brought him to maintain that man must assume full responsibility for his actions and commitments—to the Right and the Good, as Bonhoeffer saw them, exemplified by the life of Jesus. Clearly he did not exclude complicity with violence in those desperate times, as many of his successors would exclude it in our time. His ethic is based on situations of real life rather than abstract speculation. It was an ethic that could live out to full measure the "cost of discipleship." "I have had time [he wrote] to think and to pray about my situation and that of my nation.... I have come to the conclusion that I have made a mistake in coming to America. I must live through this difficult period of our national history with the Christian people of Germany.... Such a decision each man must make for himself. Christians in Germany will face the terrible alternative of either willing the defeat of their nation in order that Christian civilization may survive, or willing the victory of their nation and thereby destroying our civilization. I know which of these alternatives I must choose"—(Dietrich Bonhoeffer, in a letter to Reinhold Niebuhr, July 1939).

His heroism has caught the imagination of many and helped to strengthen the liberal wing of the German Lutheran Church. Union Theological Seminary published in 1967, in its *Quarterly Review*, a series of his poignant letters from prison to his fiancée, a German woman, now Mrs. Maria von Wedemeyer-Weller, who has lived for many years in the United States. Ved Mehta's "The New Theologian" (*Harper* 1966, o.p.) contains, among its interviews with live theologians, some interesting insights into Bonhoeffer as revealed by surviving friends and others who knew him.

Preface to Bonhoeffer: The Man and Two of His Shorter Writings. Ed. by John D. Godsey *Fortress* 1965 $2.95

Life Together. Trans. with introd. by John W. Doberstein *Harper* 1954 $3.95

ETHICS. Ed. by Éberhard Bethge *Macmillan* 1965 pap. $1.45

THE COST OF DISCIPLESHIP. Trans. by R. H. Fuller *Macmillan* 2nd rev. ed. 1967 $4.95 pap. $1.95

CREATION AND FALL and TEMPTATION. *Macmillan* 1965 pap. $.95

COMMUNICATION OF SAINTS. Harper 1964 $4.00

CHRIST THE CENTER. Trans. by John Bowden; introd. by Edwin H. Robertson *Harper* 1966 $3.95

"A translation of the compiled edition of students' notes from Bonhoeffer's Berlin lectures from 1933. . . . Incomplete, rough, disorganized and important"—(*LJ*).

PSALMS. *Augsburg* 1970 $2.75

LETTERS AND PAPERS FROM PRISON (orig. "Prisoner for God"). Ed. by Eberhard Bethge *Macmillan* 1953 1967 $4.95 enl. ed. 1972 $7.95 pap. $2.95

"This new edition, while omitting nothing found in the earlier editions, shifts the emphasis to the private sphere of Bonhoeffer's life. . . . References to his fiancée and to their plans for marriage, omitted in earlier editions, are now included, as is her recent article containing excerpts from his personal letters. . . . The book also contains hitherto inaccessible letters and legal papers referring to Bonhoeffer's trial, a reminiscence by Karl-Friedrick Bonhoeffer of the time spent in prison by members of his family, and a new introduction by Dietrich Bonhoeffer's close friend Eberhard Bethge"—(Publisher's note).

TRUE PATRIOTISM: Letters, Lectures and Notes, 1939–45. Ed. and trans. by Edwin H. Robertson and John Bowden *Harper* 1973 $6.95

These writings "reflect the agonies of conscience which Bonhoeffer experienced in his struggle for freedom during the German terror and demise"—(*Christian Century*).

Books about Bonhoeffer

Dietrich Bonhoeffer. By Edwin H. Robertson. *John Knox Press* 1966 pap. $1.25
The Life and Death of Dietrich Bonhoeffer. By Mary Bosanquet. *Harper* Colophon Bks. 1969 pap. $2.95
"A splendid biography, comprehensive, accurate and beautifully written"—(*LJ*).
The Steps of Bonhoeffer: A Pictorial Album. By J. Martin Bailey. *United Church* 1969 $6.95; *Macmillan* 1971 pap. $3.95
The Promise of Bonhoeffer. By Benjamin A. Reist. *Lippincott* 1969 $3.50 pap. $1.95
Bonhoeffer's Theology: Classical and Revolutionary. By James W. Woelfel. *Abingdon* 1970 $6.95
    In this volume "a professor of philosophy at the University of Kansas analyzes many of Bonhoeffer's best known ideas to show how they reflect the influence of Karl Barth, Rudolf Bultmann, and Paul Tillich as well as Martin Luther"—(*LJ*).
Memo for a Movie: A Short Life of Dietrich Bonhoeffer. By Theodore A. Gill. *Macmillan* 1970 $5.95
    "A selection and arrangement of facts which Gill has intended as the basis for a full-length film on Bonhoeffer's . . . career"—(*LJ*).
Dietrich Bonhoeffer: Man of Vision, Man of Courage. By Eberhard Bethge. Trans. from the German by Eric Mosbacher and others under the editorship of Edwin H. Robertson *Harper* 1970 $17.95
    "One of the major biographies of this century. Indispensable for theologians and modern historians of every kind, it will also fascinate and challenge every sensitive reader"—(*Christian Century*).
Dietrich Bonhoeffer: Theologian of Reality. By André Dumas. Trans. by Robert McAfee Brown *Macmillan* 1971 $7.95
    "In this analysis of Bonhoeffer's thought all the theological writings, spanning the years from 1927 to 1944, are examined developmentally and systematically, placed in their biographical and intellectual setting, and compared with other thinkers such as Barth, Heidegger and Bultmann. . . . Dumas's book is easily the best overall analysis of Bonhoeffer's thought which has yet appeared"—(*Commonweal*).
The Bonhoeffers: Portrait of a Family. By Sabine Liebholz-Bonhoeffer. *St. Martin's* 1972 $8.95
Dietrich Bonhoeffer: Reality and Resistance. By Larry L. Rasmussen. *Abingdon* 1972 pap. $4.95
Dietrich Bonhoeffer. By Dallas M. Roark. Makers of the Modern Theological Mind Ser. *Word Bks.* 1972 $4.95
Reality and Faith: The Theological Legacy of Dietrich Bonhoeffer. By Heinrich Ott. *Fortress* 1972 $11.50

"The net effect [of this work] is a creative interpretation and its usefulness lies perhaps as much in discovering Ott himself at work as in expanding the field of English language Bonhoeffer studies"—(*LJ*).

WEIL, SIMONE. 1909–1943.

The remarkable career of Simone Weil resembles the lives of some of the saints and mystics of the Middle Ages. T. S. Eliot felt that she had "a kind of genius akin to that of saints." Her influence on modern thought has been considerable. She was born in Paris, the daughter of a well-to-do doctor. But she identified herself early with the underprivileged and continued to do so. When Paris was occupied by the Germans in 1940, she went to Marseilles with her Jewish parents. There she met the Reverend Father Perrin, who interested her in the Roman Catholic Church. Although she never became a convert in fact, she practised Catholicism as closely as a non-Catholic can for the short remainder of her life. As William Robert Miller says in "The New Christianity" (*Dell* Delta Bks. 1968 pap. $2.45), "she refused to be baptized because she felt this would divide her from the rest of mankind." "Waiting for God" (U.S. 1951. *Harper* Colophon Bks. 1973 pap. $2.95) contains her letters to Father Perrin and her "spiritual autobiography." She described herself as the bell which tolls to bring others to church. She worked for the Free French while in England, refusing to eat any more than her countrymen were allowed in occupied territory. In 1943 she died of "voluntary starvation."

"This brilliant, difficult girl, who was a philosophical, mathematical and literary genius, was one of the greatest minds of our time. Everything she writes is new-minted, pure gold; she never had a stale thought or expression. . . . The 'Notebooks' she originally wrote in her clear, concise longhand have been ably translated. . . . They make stimulating reading for the dipper and the digger alike; no one can fail to find here something they need, and much they know but cannot quite express'—(*N.Y. Times*).

Germaine Brée has said of her (in *SR*): "Simone Weil first generated interest on this side of the Atlantic in the early Fifties, when a selection of her writings, *The Need for Roots* [1952. Trans. by Arthur Wills *Harper* Colophon Bks. 1971 pap. $2.95], was published here in translation. The very title appealed to people still haunted by World War II and the unsettling vistas opened by Hiroshima. But Simone Weil was not easy to read, nor does she mete out easy comfort. Powerful as are some of her insights, her writing itself is fragmentary, steeped in difficult concepts, in unexplained references to such widely diverse works as the *Upanishads,* the pre-Socratic Greek philosophers, the Bible, the French classics, Shakespeare. The interest in Simone Weil consequently waned. . . . Somehow one cannot help but feel that there is a kind of appalling, inverted correspondence between Simone Weil's tormented life and the apocalyptic, nightmarish world of the Thirties and Forties. It is as though the frail young woman with her relentless energy and intellectual drive had been designated to carry the cross of all the suffering of our contemporary world."

SELECTED ESSAYS 1934–1943. Trans. and ed. by Sir Richard Rees *Oxford* 1962 $8.00. Essays on philosophical, historical and political themes.

THE ILIAD, or The Poem of Force. 1940. Trans. by Mary McCarthy; rev. by Dwight Macdonald *Pendle Hill* 1956 pap. $.70. An analysis of Homer's work as one drenched in violence, in which much of Simone Weil is revealed as well. A pamphlet.

INTIMATIONS OF CHRISTIANITY AMONG THE ANCIENT GREEKS. 1951. Trans. and ed. by Elizabeth C. Geissbuhler *Humanities Press* 1957 $5.00

GRAVITY AND GRACE. *Humanities Press* 1952 $3.00 pap. $1.50

ON SCIENCE, NECESSITY AND THE LOVE OF GOD. Trans. by Richard Rees *Oxford* 1968 $8.50

OPPRESSION AND LIBERTY. Trans. by Arthur Wills and John Petrie *Univ. of Massachusetts Press* 1973 $8.50

SEVENTY LETTERS. Trans. by Richard Rees *Oxford* 1965 $7.00

FIRST AND LAST NOTEBOOKS. Trans. by Richard Rees *Oxford* 1970 $10.25

Books about Weil

Simone Weil. By Eric W. F. Tomlin. *Hillary House* 1954 $2.75

Simone Weil: A Sketch for a Portrait. By Sir Richard Rees. *Southern Illinois Univ. Press* 1966 $4.50. A useful basic study by her translator.

Simone Weil. By David Anderson. *Allenson* 1971 pap. $1.95

Approaching Simone. By Megan Terry. *Feminist Press* 1973 pap. $2.50

MERTON, THOMAS (known as Father M. Louis).   1915–1968.

Thomas Merton was already known as a poet before his autobiography, "The Seven Storey Mountain," became a best seller. This tells of his conversion to the Roman Catholic faith and of the profound spiritual experiences that led him to enter the severe discipline of the Trappist monastery of Gethsemani in Kentucky. Born in France, he grew up there and in England and the United States. He studied at Cambridge and Columbia, where he was graduated in 1938, taking his M.A. there in 1939. He entered the monastery in 1941 and was later ordained a priest. In his life of silence and withdrawal Merton continued to write, describing his life as a monk, providing a history of the Cistercian order and sharing his private meditations. His great humility and intense mysticism have influenced numbers of readers of all faiths. His interests were wide and deep, embracing Zen Buddhism, the theological revolution, the American racial crisis, America's role in the world and the crying need for international peace, all seen through the eyes of a profoundly spiritual and compassionate man. His accidental death at 53 in Bangkok left many with the feeling that a modern saint had passed from the world. Thomas Merton's "Selected Poems" is available (*New Directions* 1959 rev. and enl. 1967 pap. $1.75); another collection of poems is "Cables to the Ace, or Familiar Liturgies of Understanding" (*New Directions* 1968 pap. $1.25). "Life and Holiness" won the Catholic Press Association Award for spiritual writing in 1964.

A THOMAS MERTON READER. Ed. by Thomas P. McDonnell. 1962. *Doubleday* Image Bks. 1974 pap. $2.95

NEW SEEDS OF CONTEMPLATION. 1949. *New Directions* rev. ed. 1972 $6.50; (with title "Seeds of Contemplation") *Dell* 1953 pap. $.50

LAST OF THE FATHERS: Saint Bernard of Clairvaux and the Encyclical Letter, Doctor Mellifluus. 1954. *Greenwood* $9.00

NO MAN IS AN ISLAND. 1955. *Doubleday* Image Bks. 1967 pap. $1.45. Meditations on certain basic verities of the spiritual life.

LIVING BREAD. *Farrar, Straus* 1956 $3.00

LIFE AND HOLINESS. *Doubleday* Image Bks. 1964 pap. $.85. An excellent and much needed exposition of the theology of work.

SEEDS OF DESTRUCTION. *Farrar, Straus* 1964 $4.95; *Macmillan* 1967 pap. $1.45

In this collection of letters and essays, "with penetrating insight Father Merton examines two crucial issues of the 20th century: segregation and the Negro revolution, and nuclear war and Christian responsibility.... An important, timely book"—(*LJ*). Among his correspondents are James Baldwin, Mark Van Doren, the mayor of Hiroshima, a Cuban poet. The selection of both the Catholic Literary Foundation and Catholic Book Club.

SEASONS OF CELEBRATION. *Farrar, Straus* 1965 $4.95

A collection of essays and addresses, "all concerned with the liturgy and its feasts or seasons" written 1952–65, which are "thought provoking, inspirational, and written in elegant prose"— (*LJ*).

RAIDS ON THE UNSPEAKABLE. *New Directions* 1966 1970 pap. $2.25

A collection of pieces around the theme of the world of the 1960's; "they include parables, myths, essays, meditations, satires, a manifesto, and adaptations from the poems of a mediaeval Arab mystic. The themes include the myths of Prometheus and Atlas; atomic warfare; the writings of Flannery O'Connor, Julien Green, and Ionesco; and an address written for an international congress of poets. There are also some drawings called "signatures" or "abstract writings"—(*LJ*).

CONJECTURES OF A GUILTY BYSTANDER. *Doubleday* 1966 Image Bks. 1968 pap. $1.75

Notes, opinions, experiences, reflections and meditations from Merton's notebooks 1956–65, among them, "It suddenly dawned on me that anti-Americanism in the world today is a hatred as deep and as lashing and as all-inclusive as anti-Semitism.... We have hated our need for compassion and have suppressed it as a 'weakness' and our cruelty has far outstripped our sense of mercy." *Library Journal* described the book as "a new stage in the calmness, maturity and breadth of view which is the fruit of monastic life."

MYSTICS AND ZEN MASTERS. 1967. *Dell* Delta Bks. 1969 pap. $2.25

"Sixteen essays [which] explore the possibility of a common ground in mysticism.... A scholarly and masterly work, probably too tough to be read much outside theology collections; more's the pity"—(*LJ*).

ZEN AND THE BIRDS OF APPETITE. *New Directions* 1968 $6.50 pap. $1.75. Sympathetic essays on Zen Buddhism.

THOUGHTS IN SOLITUDE. *Doubleday* Image Bks. 1968 pap. $.95

FAITH AND VIOLENCE: Christian Teaching and Christian Practice. *Univ. of Notre Dame Press* 1968 pap. $2.45. Essays on a crucial question of our age, in which Merton takes the side of nonviolence.

THE CLIMATE OF MONASTIC PRAYER. Ed. by M. Basil Pennington. 1969. *Cistercian Pubns.* 1973 $4.95

THE WAY OF CHUANG TZU. *New Directions* 1969 $6.50 pap. $1.75

THE WISDOM OF THE DESERT. *New Directions* 1970 $6.50 pap. $1.50

CONTEMPLATIVE PRAYER. *Doubleday* Image Bks. 1971 pap. $1.25

THOMAS MERTON ON PEACE. *Saturday Review Press* 1971 $7.95

THOMAS MERTON ON PRAYER. Ed. by John J. Higgins *Doubleday* 1973 $5.95

CONTEMPLATION IN A WORLD OF ACTION. *Doubleday* Image Bks. 1973 pap. $1.95

THE SEVEN STOREY MOUNTAIN. 1948. *Doubleday* Image Bks. 1970 pap. $1.95; *New Am. Lib.* Signet pap. $1.25. His autobiography—his conversion.

THE SIGN OF JONAS. 1953. *Doubleday* Image Bks. 1973 pap. $1.95. His personal journal covering six years at the monastery.

THE SECULAR JOURNAL. *Farrar, Straus* 1959 $3.75

This is his pre-Trappist journal, which starts in Greenwich Village in 1939 and ends at Gethsemani in 1941. "It is of interest and value as the raw material of sanctity. The book is the diary of a young man in search of his identity, a recent convert to Catholicism, a voyager to the threshold of a Cistercian monastery. . . . In this chronicle a lonely soul gropes its uncharted way to fulfillment. Or was it uncharted?"—(*SR*).

THE ASIAN JOURNAL. Ed. by Naomi B. Stone and others *New Directions* 1973 $12.50

Books about Merton

Thomas Merton: A Bibliography. By Frank Dell' Isola. *Farrar, Straus* 1956 $3.50
"Christian scholars of the future will owe to Mr. Dell' Isola a great debt indeed. The least one can say of the bibliography is that it should have its place on the shelf of every reference department in every library of the land"—(*Catholic World*).
A Hidden Wholeness: The Visual World of Thomas Merton. Ed. by John Howard Griffin. *Houghton* 1970 $15.00
"During the last three years of his life Merton began to experiment with photography as another way of expressing his vision of reality. This book offers a selection of his pictures, explained by . . . brief quotations from his work. The second part contains photographs of Merton and his friends taken by Griffin at the monastery"—(*LJ*).
Thomas Merton: Social Critic. By James T. Baker. *Univ. Press of Kentucky* 1971 $8.00
Pray to Live: Thomas Merton, a Contemplative Critic. By Henri J. Nouwen. *Fides* 1972 pap. $2.95
Thomas Merton: A Different Drummer. By Robert J. Voight. *Liguori Pubns.* 1972 pap. $1.75
Thomas Merton: The Man and His Works. By Dennis McInerny. *Cistercian Pubns.* 1974 $7.95
Thomas Merton, Monk: A Monastic Tribute. Ed. by Brother Patrick Hart. *Sheed & Ward* 1974 $8.95
"This collection of remembrances . . . is the most intimate biography of this complex, simple man yet to be written. The notes on the contributors are in themselves fascinating"—(*LJ*). Winner of the Catholic Press Association Religious Book Award for Biography, in 1975.
Thomas Merton: Bibliography. By Marquita Breit. *Scarecrow Press* 1974 $6.00

ROBINSON, JOHN A(RTHUR) T(HOMAS), Bishop of Woolwich.   1919–

"When the theological history of our time is finally written, there is no doubt that a crucial chapter will be given to the little book, by J. A. T. Robinson, Bishop of Woolwich, entitled 'Honest to God,' not because it is a work of great depth or originality—which it isn't—but because it made theological discussion for the first time seem interesting and important to the contemporary layman"—(*N.Y. Times*). Though it is hard to remember that in 1963 it seemed shocking and disturbing for a clergyman to criticize openly his own Church, Bishop Robinson with "Honest to God" in 1963 released many inhibitions and let open the floodgates of the New Christianity. Without rejecting classic Christian doctrine, Bishop Robinson's main concern has been to find the *language* capable of relating theology to the dilemmas of modern man. In his most systematic work, "Exploration into God," he has described the religious challenge of our time as one of "theography" rather than theology—the need is not to question the existence of God, but to locate Him on the "map" of our existence. Rejecting the location of God "above man" (as "the Old Man in the Sky"), Robinson would place Him at the center of human life, in the spirit of Tillich, who saw God as the Ground of man's being. Bishop Robinson is discussed in many of the books on Radical Theology, such as William R. Miller's "Goodbye, Jehovah" (*Avon Bks.* Discus 1969 pap. $1.45). O.p. are "In the End God" (1950), "Jesus and His Coming" (1958), "On Being the Church in the World" (1962), "Liturgy Coming to Life" (1964), and "Christian Morals Today" (1964).

THE BODY: A Study in Pauline Theology. *Allenson* 1952 $4.85 pap. $2.35

TWELVE NEW TESTAMENT STUDIES. *Allenson* 1962 $6.00 pap. $3.50

HONEST TO GOD. *Westminster Press* 1963 pap. $1.65. His devastating critique of churchliness, which sold over a million copies.

THE NEW REFORMATION? *Westminster Press* 1965 pap. $1.65

EXPLORATION INTO GOD. Perspectives in Humanism Ser. *Stanford Univ. Press* 1967 $2.95 pap. $1.95. Lectures given in 1966, developing the theme of "Honest to God." A prologue describes the progress of his thinking.

THAT I CAN'T BELIEVE. 1967. *New Am. Lib.* (dist. by Norton) $5.95. A series of brief, popular essays on such controversial topics as miracles, Hell, the Second Coming, angels, the Trinity.

CHRISTIAN FREEDOM IN A PERMISSIVE SOCIETY. *Westminster Press* 1970 pap. $2.95

THE DIFFERENCE IN BEING A CHRISTIAN TODAY. *Westminster Press* 1972 pap. $1.50

THE HUMAN FACE OF GOD. *Westminster Press* 1973 $7.95

"The bishop's basic concern—to affirm the real humanity of Christ—results in reinterpretation of such doctrines as the virgin birth of Christ, his preexistence, the two natures, etc."—(*LJ*).

Books about Robinson

The Honest to God Debate. Ed. by David L. Edwards. *Westminster Press* 1963 pap. $2.25

BOYD, MALCOLM. 1923–

"I don't think I'm controversial. I think the Gospel is controversial," the Episcopal clergyman and chaplain-at-large to America's college students has said. An astonishing book of prayers which sold phenomenally under the title "Are You Running with Me, Jesus?" brought him fame and followers in 1965, and it soon appeared he was no thumping revivalist but a serious Christian critic of American society who had found a way to reach sophisticated young people. Nicknamed the "espresso priest" for his efforts to remove religion from the "ghettoized" churches and put it into places where the people are, including union halls, theaters and night clubs, Mr. Boyd often speaks candidly and offers his modern prayers to a new kind of "congregation." His appearance in 1966 with Dick Gregory at the hungry i night club in San Francisco outraged conservative clergymen, who saw him as a headline seeker. (Today in the wake of intervening events, he seems less surprising.) His commitment is to solving contemporary problems; his weapon for the struggle to revolutionize the status quo is Love—and a lot of it. "In my prayers," he has explained, "I'm relating to a great deal of suffering and pain in the world. I don't feel this is a very happy culture, whether you're on top or on the bottom." Freedom Rides took him from Alabama to Mississippi to Watts, and to an arrest in Chicago. Robert McAfee Brown has called him the "catalyst of ferment within the church, [but] a nuisance to its structure."

As a youngster, Malcolm Boyd was not interested in the church or the smug and pious religion he felt it had to offer, and his first career was that of a Hollywood public relations man. In 1951, long-sidetracked leanings led him to make a fresh start by entering divinity school: "I just pictured myself in an ivy-covered church, administering Communion." By 1959 he was chaplain at Colorado State University, where he first started his coffeehouse ministry. Since then he has written five plays which deal with racial conflict, one of which has been televised. These efforts, too, have met with criticism—for his choice of contemporary language. All his books have enjoyed immense popularity (much of the money received from their sales is donated to civil rights organizations), and through them he has proved, perhaps, to a new group of Americans that Christianity can be "relevant." "Free to Live, Free to Die" (1967) and "You Can't Kill the Dream" (1968) are o.p.

THE HUNGER AND THE THIRST. *Morehouse* 1964 pap. $.50

Three essays, one partly autobiographical, stress "the false values of modern life, [and] the resultant conformity that deadens men's souls"—(*PW*).

ARE YOU RUNNING WITH ME, JESUS? Afterword by William Robert Miller *Holt* 1965 $3.95; *Avon Bks.* Discus 1972 pap. $1.25

His revolutionary book of personal prayers close to contemporary life and daily speech. It became a runaway best seller. "This book destroys the conventional distance between prayer and 'ordinary life.' . . . There are few books of prayers I would give to a friend. This is one of them"— (Robert McAfee Brown). "The prayers are deeply personal, though their subjects range from civil rights to unwanted pregnancy to poverty. . . . Sometimes slangy, always eloquent . . . a very moving book"—(*N.Y. Times*).

MALCOLM BOYD'S BOOK OF DAYS. 1968. *Fawcett* Premier Bks. pap. $.95

This is "a collection of readings, quotations and 'straws of life' for each day of the year. Taken daily at breakfast, they will alternatively send you back to bed or charging out to remake the world. . . . Much of the material is taken from Father Boyd's own books, including the popular collection of prayers, 'Are You Running With Me, Jesus?' Some of it is trite rather than inspirational; much of it is self-conscious and even vain. Yet even here there is a refreshing spiritual honesty"—(Edward B. Fiske, in the *N.Y. Times*).

THE FANTASY WORLDS OF PETER STONE AND OTHER FABLES. 1969. *Avon Bks.* 1971 pap. $1.25

Here Mr. Boyd uses "the fable form—which closely parallels the Biblical parables (with down-to-earth contemporary subject matter). The fables are delightful and wise, lightly devastating, compassionate and understanding. . . . No heavy moralizing here; no sermonizing on sin. Boyd is lighter, brighter and fresher than he has ever appeared before in print"—(*PW*).

HUMAN LIKE ME, JESUS: Prayers with Notes on the Humanistic Revolution. *Simon & Schuster* 1971 $5.95

"This work includes Prayers of Personal Identity, for Liberation, for Sexual Humanness, Prayers in the Seasons, Prayers in a Black Student Center, Prayers on Curious Occasions, Prayers in Struggle"—(Publisher's note).

THE LOVER. *Word Bks.* 1972 $4.95

THE RUNNER. *Word Bks.* new ed. 1974 $5.95. About Jesus and his influence on modern man.

(With Paul Conrad). WHEN IN THE COURSE OF HUMAN EVENTS. *Sheed & Ward* 1973 $5.95

AS I LIVE AND BREATHE: Stages of an Autobiography. *Random* 1969 $6.95

KÜNG, HANS.   1928–

When the radical Catholic theologian and priest Hans Küng taught at the (nondenominational Protestant) Union Theological Seminary (New York) in 1967–1968, the *N.Y. Times* said that he was "praised by students and faculty members as one of the most profound and original thinkers on religion in the world"—and his scholarship is undisputed. Concerned for the present "credibility" of his Church, he has sought reform from within in ways that have offended conservative cardinals and caused his books on occasion to suffer Church censorship. His purpose, however, has been to broaden the institutional base of Catholicism toward being truly democratic, that it may ultimately become truly ecumenical. Among his stronger statements (quoted in the *N.Y. Times*) have been: "Soberly and without covering up, [we must say] that, alas, there have on innumerable occasions been sins against the freedom of the Children of God committed in our church and that they are countless to this day." On another occasion he likened Catholicism to Communism: "Are not both absolutist, centralist, totalitarian, in short, enemies of human freedom?" And he has advocated that laymen have a share in electing the Pope.

Nevertheless, he has been influential in some of the changes which emerged from Vatican II, especially through his 1962 "The Council, Reform and Reunion." Of his outstanding work, "The Church" (dedicated to the Archbishop of Canterbury!), *Library Journal* wrote: "His basic point is that 'the real Church is not an ideal, sacral, eternal phenomenon, floating somewhere between God and men. The real Church is rather the Church of God, composed of men, existing in the world for the world.' The church therefore always expresses itself in terms of a particular historical situation and must be studied in this light. He discusses the fundamental structure of the church as it has been conditioned by history from the New Testament time to the present; the dimensions of the church—one, catholic, holy, apostolic; and ecclesiastical offices, especially with regard to the need for reconciliation of the Christian churches."

Still trim and youthful, with an infectious smile, the Swiss-born Dr. Küng is dean of the Roman Catholic theology faculty at the University of Tübingen, Germany. He is editor of "Apostolic Succession" (*Paulist-Newman* $4.50), "The Church and Ecumenism" (*Paulist-Newman* $4.50), "Post-

Ecumenical Christianity" (*Seabury Press* 1970 pap. $3.95), and "The Plurality of Ministries" (*Seabury Press* 1972 pap. $3.95).

THE COUNCIL, REFORM AND REUNION. Trans. from the German by Cecily Hastings *Sheed & Ward* 1961 $3.95

"Appearing just before Vatican II, [this] established 'reform' as a Roman Catholic imperative, and . . . informed hundreds of thousands of Catholics (including bishops) about what was at stake at Vatican II"—(Michael Novak, in the *N.Y. Times*).

THE COUNCIL IN ACTION. Trans. by Cecily Hastings *Sheed & Ward* 1963 $4.50. Lectures and statements made by Küng during the first session of Vatican II.

THE STRUCTURES OF THE CHURCH. Trans. by Salvator Attanasio *Nelson* 1964 $7.50; *Univ. of Notre Dame Press* 1968 pap. $3.45

This is a preliminary study for "The Church." Dr. Küng's "thesis is that the church itself is like one vast ecumenical council convoked by God. . . . Very rewarding in its contribution to ecumenism and to renewal, but it requires careful reading"—(*A Guide to Catholic Reading*).

SACRAMENTS: An Ecumenical Dilemma. *Paulist-Newman* 1967 $4.50

THE CHURCH. Trans. by Ray and Rosaleen Ockenden *Sheed & Ward* 1967 $6.95

His major work. "Clear and well written, with full bibliographical references, and scripture, name and subject indexes"—(*LJ*).

TRUTHFULNESS: The Future of the Church. *Sheed & Ward* 1968 $4.50

Here "he preaches, at least by implication, a revolution in terms that will offend many but will inspire most. . . . Probably [his] most on-target work to date"—(*Virginia Kirkus Service*). "Four specific portions of the book deserve special mention: Küng's comments on the departure of Charles Davis from the church, the analysis of the traditionalist's minority position on the papal birth control commission, comments on the pastoral ministry as distinguished from the teaching ministry, his suggestions for a democratically elected, representative hierarchy"—(*LJ*).

THE FUTURE OF ECUMENISM. *Paulist-Newman* $4.50

THE PAPAL MINISTRY IN THE CHURCH. *Seabury Press* 1971 pap. $3.95

INFALLIBLE? An Inquiry. *Doubleday* Image Bks. 1972 pap. $1.45

"Clearly . . . a major contribution to the discussions on reform and renewal in the Catholic church today"—(*Choice*).

WHY PRIESTS? A Proposal for a New Church Ministry. Trans. by Robert C. Collins *Doubleday* 1972 $5.95

Küng suggests that "leader ministers need not be academically trained, celibate, male, full-time, or committed for life; in fact they would not even have to be ordained . . . since the sacraments do not require ordained ministers and even bishops are not essentially different from laymen"—(*LJ*).

COX, HARVEY (GALLAGHER, JR.). 1929–

Dr. Harvey Cox, of the Harvard Divinity School, a Baptist minister who caught the public imagination with "The Secular City," says in his book "On Not Leaving It to the Snake": "Man is that creature who is created to shape and enact his own destiny. Whenever he relinquishes that privilege to someone else, he ceases to be a man. We must be careful today with all our emphasis on the servant role of the church not to give the impression that the Gospel calls man to plebeian servility. It does not. It calls him to adult stewardship, to originality, to inventiveness and the governance of the world."

"The Secular City" in 1965 surprised its author by becoming a best seller and catapulting him into prominence. With the Bible as its base, it studies the increasing "secularization" of western religion. In his interesting essay on the book in "Goodbye, Jehovah," William Robert Miller says, "The concept of secularization has little to do with secularism; it does not apply to the neat medieval dichotomy, does not derive from the Greek idea of the secular. As Cox puts it, 'secularization implies a historical process, almost certainly irreversible, in which society and culture are delivered from tutelage to religion and closed metaphysical world views. For primitive, presecular man (and for medieval peasants in large measure), nature is alive with magic, impregnated with signs and portents which are inseparable from reality. The creation story of Genesis is not about how things originated but about the fact that man was given domination over them. Man is created in the image of God and inherits some of God's own creativity. . . . A de-divinization of nature is a precondition for the rise of natural science and for the matter-of-fact technology that gives man effective control over nature." Dr. Cox's demonstration of the desirability of this secularization was one of the mainstreams which pointed toward "Christian atheism" and the Death of God controversy, and "The Secular City" became itself controversial.

It is Dr. Cox's thesis that man must find solutions to his problems without the traditional form of religion, without metaphysics and in secular terms for our secular and technological world. "For too long our main strategy as churchmen in the society was to tell the world what to do," he has said. Now "we want to talk about how we can act as Christians on our hopes for society." For Dr. Cox God is not dead—He is ahead of most Christians today; it is man who has lost contact with what God is saying to him. "The biblical God calls man through events of social change, and . . . the church becomes the church by participating in the revolutionary work of God"—("God's Revolution and Man's Responsibility").

This "revolutionary work" means involvement in the world and the attempting to solve civilization's present social ills. Dr. Cox himself has been to jail for his part in civil rights demonstrations; he was a local chairman of the Americans for Democratic Action in Boston, a founder of the Boston Industrial Mission and, from 1963 to 1965, a fraternal worker for the Gossner Mission in East Berlin.

THE SECULAR CITY. *Macmillan* 1965 Collier Bks. 1966 pap. $1.45

"It is hard not to agree with a great deal of what he says as well as to applaud the liveliness and clarity with which he says it. . . . He interprets secularization as the sign of man's coming of age and advocates that instead of panicking and characteristically trying to arrest the process, the church should become the avant-garde in helping it along"—(*N.Y. Times*).

GOD'S REVOLUTION AND MAN'S RESPONSIBILITY. *Judson Press* 1965 pap. $1.50

Based on lectures delivered in 1965 to a student group at an American Baptist Assembly in Wisconsin, this "is a dissection of some theological verbiage in areas where Cox believes there is a need for some skin-grafting in order to convince the world that it is still the bearer of the Word made flesh"—(*The Christian Century*).

ON NOT LEAVING IT TO THE SNAKE. *Macmillan* 1968 $4.95

"Dr. Cox, in this brilliant series of essays, calls for man to cast off his slothfulness, 'his unwillingness to be everything man was intended to be,' and to become a decision-making creature"—(*LJ*). "The secular man about whom Cox has often written will find little in these essays that will greet him on his own terms. Cox insists on a Biblical perspective to throw the secularist off balance. Traditional Biblicists may find the Cox here influenced by the Marxist atheist Ernst Bloch and the Catholic evolutionist Teilhard de Chardin. . . . The shapers of the newer theology will find most of the writings here quite familiar"—(Martin E. Marty, in the *N.Y. Times*).

FEAST OF FOOLS: A Theological Essay on Festivity and Fantasy. *Harvard Univ. Press* 1969 $5.95; *Harper* 1972 pap. $1.50

"Drawing on the medieval Feast of Fools for his theme, [Cox] covers the full range of modern ceremonies and their social implications. . . . Well written and cogently argued, this is a delightful critique of Western civilization"—(*LJ*).

THE SEDUCTION OF THE SPIRIT: The Use and Misuse of People's Religion. *Simon & Schuster* 1973 $8.95 Touchstone Bks. 1974 pap. $2.95

(Ed.). THE SITUATION ETHICS DEBATE. Introd. by the editor *Westminster Press* 1968 pap. $2.65

An anthology of the reactions to Joseph Fletcher's "Situation Ethics: The New Morality" (*see Section on Personal and Social Ethics, this Chapter*). "Many of the authors, even the editor, take off from Fletcher's theories and carry them further. On the other hand, some of the reviewers denounce the Fletcher theories. This is not a calm book"—(*PW*).

Books about Cox

The Secular City Debate. Ed. by Daniel Callahan. *Macmillan* 1966 $5.95 pap. $1.45
Spirited, provocative criticisms of "The Secular City," with a vigorous rejoinder from Harvey Cox. A collection of articles, pro and con, about Harvey Cox and "The Secular City." "At several points throughout the text, Cox is permitted to clarify his intent. In several cases, he profits so much from his critics that he offers modifications of his theme. This compilation will be a valuable companion to the study of *The Secular City* and should aid the course of the 'debate' immeasurably"—(*LJ*).

The Ambiguity of Religion. By David Baily Harned. *Westminster Press* 1968 pap. $2.45. A discussion on views of modern religion as represented by Paul Tillich and Harvey Cox.

Chapter 5

Philosophy

"Between theology and science there is a No Man's Land, exposed to attack from both sides; this No Man's Land is philosophy. Almost all questions of interest to speculative minds are such as science cannot answer, and the confident answers of theologians no longer seem as convincing as they did in former centuries. . . . The circumstances of men's lives do much to determine their philosophy; but conversely, their philosophy does much to determine their circumstances. . . . To teach how to live without certainty, and yet without being paralyzed by hesitation, is perhaps the chief thing that philosophy, in our age, can still do for those who study it."
—BERTRAND RUSSELL

To the nonphilosopher who takes up the subject, the great creative minds of this discipline must often seem to be playing at intellectual games. One philosopher says "Life is this" and seems quite certain of it; he invents or builds a whole complex system on his original thought—possibly one as simple as Descartes' "I think; therefore I am." He may be an optimist, like Leibniz, who sees life as full of possibility and hope. Along comes another—this time a pessimist, like Hume—who draws quite different deductions from the same general set of phenomena. To a neophyte the philosophical structures of those who pursue Reason may, therefore, appear to be based in a fundamental absurdity. Who is right? Where lies the Truth? (But this is what those philosophers are trying to get *at*). Does outlook depend on temperament? on what the philosopher had for breakfast one morning? Perhaps—but they cannot be too lightly dismissed, for the reasons given above by Bertrand Russell. How men see the world has always been the mainspring of their actions and has deeply affected the course of history, as it will in the future. The ideas of Rousseau are said to have contributed to bringing about the French Revolution, those of Nietzsche to the rise of Hitlerism. The pen, as the adage has it, is mightier than the sword.

In a second way, too, the philosophers have been important. In examining their world they have often made scientific observations later drawn on by their successors. Aristotle dominated "science" until the Renaissance; the ideas of Leibniz are quoted by Norbert Wiener as seminal to his own discipline—Cybernetics, or Information Theory—which in its turn has been crucial to the advent of the modern computer. One can multiply the examples a hundredfold. The third great value of philosophy and its study for modern man is (again see Russell, above) in his own contemporary search for meaning and direction. Religion provides answers to life's riddles for some of us, but those who do not profess a religion develop a philosophy which keeps them going; the great philosophers can offer to inquirers, young and old, new insight on their own lives. There has always been an overlap between religion and philosophy, of course: in St. Thomas Aquinas, Sören Kierkegaard and Teilhard de Chardin (whose thinking was largely rejected by his own Church in his lifetime) we see examples of the interlocking of secular and religious thought.

The history of philosophy is divided into three main epochs. The first period is that of ancient or Greek philosophy; the second, medieval philosophy or scholasticism; the third, beginning with the Renaissance, modern philosophy. The first period includes two or three great Asian thinkers who are to be found in the Chapter on World Religions. The second period is marked by the Christian philosophy of the Middle Ages. The writings of the early Church fathers are today mainly of theological interest, and are also classified in *"The Reader's Adviser"* under Religion. To the Greeks, philosophy meant literally the love of wisdom. It has embraced Physics, once called "natural philosophy," and Psychology—the latest branch of learning to be separated from it. Philosophy in one definition has been described as "the science which investigates the most general facts and principles of reality and of human nature and conduct." It is now usually understood as being that

266

science which comprises Ethics, Aesthetics, Metaphysics and the Theory of Knowledge. Critical commentaries and histories now far outnumber the philosophical texts. They form a tributary literature that is truly auxiliary.

BIBLIOGRAPHY AND REFERENCE BOOKS

Aiken, Henry D., and William Barrett, Eds. PHILOSOPHY IN THE 20TH CENTURY. *Harper* 3 vols. 1971 pap. Vol. 1 $4.45 Vol. 2 $4.75 Vol. 3 o.p.

Bahm, Archie J., Ed. DIRECTORY OF AMERICAN PHILOSOPHERS No. 5 1970–71. *Archie J. Bahm* (Department of Philosophy, Univ. of New Mexico, Albuquerque, N.M.) 1970 $14.95

"The bulk of this [annual] directory consists of a list of U.S. colleges and their philosophy staffs arranged by states ... and an alphabetical list of American philosophers"—*(LJ)*. The present edition of this useful work is expanded well beyond the size of the original.

Baldwin, James Mark, Ed. DICTIONARY OF PHILOSOPHY AND PSYCHOLOGY. 1901–02 1910. *Peter Smith* 3 vols. 1940 Vols. 1 and 2 each $16.50 Vol. 3 Bibliography of Philosophy and Psychology and Cognate Subjects, comp. by Benjamin Rand 1949 2 pts. each $13.50 set $60.00

De George, Richard T. GUIDE TO PHILOSOPHICAL BIBLIOGRAPHY AND RESEARCH. *Prentice-Hall* 1971 $6.25

DIRECTORY OF AMERICAN SCHOLARS. Vol. 4, Philosophy, Religion, and Law. *Bowker* 6th ed. 1974 $39.50

Edwards, Paul, Ed. THE ENCYCLOPEDIA OF PHILOSOPHY. *Macmillan* (Free Press) 4 vols. 1973 set $99.50

This is the first major reference work in philosophy in the English language, produced under the general editorship of Professor Edwards of Brooklyn College and the New School for Social Research in New York. There are 1,450 signed articles by 500 authorities from 24 nations, under the direction of an editorial board of 153 international scholars. "With the publication of this multivolume set, the 'reference gap' for philosophy has been bridged in a most impressive manner. [The articles] are arranged alphabetically and they vary in length from half a column to over 50 pages. Each major article has its own bibliography, which includes recommendations for the general reader and more scholarly citations for professional philosophers. [There are] numerous cross references, placed immediately before the major articles. . . .

"Aesthetics, the great man theory of history, philosophy of the social sciences, and computing machines are among the major topics treated. . . . Oriental philosophy is covered as thoroughly and authoritatively as our own Western traditions; ancient and medieval philosophers receive a coverage at least equal to that of contemporary thinkers. . . . The *Encyclopedia of Philosophy* is characterized by a lively style and large attractive print. . . . The manner of presentation is orderly, logical, and authoritative. A detailed, easy-to-use subject index greatly enhances the usefulness of this set for non-specialists. . . . Under 'Concepts of God,' for instance, we find references to Abelard, Emil Brunner, Reinhold Neibuhr, and many other philosophers and theologians as well as a sprightly essay on 'Popular Arguments for the Existence of God.' . . . Here also students of science will find references to technical articles . . . and to numerous articles on individual scientists, such as Percy Bridgman, Robert Boyle, and Michael Faraday. Because of its broad coverage and sound scholarship, this encyclopedia is strongly recommended for college, university, and all but the smallest public libraries"—*(LJ)*. "It is inconceivable that any college library should not hasten to acquire it. . . . The only word for it is superb"—*(Classical World)*.

Gutmann, James, Ed. PHILOSOPHY A TO Z. *Grosset* 1963 $4.75. The editor is Professor Emeritus and former Chairman of Department of Philosophy, Columbia University.

Magill, Frank N., and Ian P. McGreal, Eds. MASTERPIECES OF WORLD PHILOSOPHY. *Harper* 1961 $15.00 lib. bdg. $12.69

"Two hundred classic works of philosophy, chiefly Western, are digested, each prefaced by a statement of the 'principal ideas advanced' and a brief identification of the author and the type of writing ... arranged in chronological order, with author and title indexes for quick reference. A glossary of 250 terms is given as a help to readers not familiar with concepts of technical philosophy. Critical comments are included within each digest, especially to point out the influences of earlier philosophers on the later. Recommended chiefly as a reference aid"—*(LJ)*.

Nauman, St. Elmo, Jr. DICTIONARY OF AMERICAN PHILOSOPHY. *Philosophical Lib.* 1973 $10.00

Runes, Dagobert David, Ed. DICTIONARY OF PHILOSOPHY. New Study Outline Ser. *Littlefield* 1955 1962 1971 pap. $3.50

(Ed.). PHILOSOPHY FOR EVERYMAN: From Socrates to Sartre. *Littlefield* 1974 $2.50

Russell, Bertrand. AN OUTLINE OF PHILOSOPHY. 1960. *New Am. Lib.* Meridian Bks. pap. $3.95

Steenbergen, G. J., and Johan Grooten. NEW ENCYCLOPEDIA OF PHILOSOPHY. Trans. and ed. by Edmond Van Den Bossche *Philosophical Lib.* 1972 $15.00

Urmson, J. O. THE CONCISE ENCYCLOPEDIA OF WESTERN PHILOSOPHY AND PHILOSOPHERS. *Hawthorn Bks.* 1960 $17.95. Plato to the Existentialists explained by leading scholars in 431 pages.

GENERAL HISTORIES AND CRITICISM

Some significant books on philosophical systems and schools of philosophy have been included in this section with the general histories and criticism.

For a reasonably short introduction, available in paperback, E. W. F. Tomlin's "The Western Philosophers" is recommended. A longer, brilliant but eminently clear and readable survey for the layman is Bertrand Russell's beautifully written "History of Western Philosophy," tempered with humor and a best seller since its first publication in 1946. Lord Russell has covered much of the same ground in a briefer and more recent work (it also begins "before Socrates") called "Wisdom of the West," which advances further into the 20th century; this one is available paperbound. Karl Jaspers, one of the most distinguished living scholars in European literature and thought, has published the first two volumes of his "The Great Philosophers," rewarding for layman and scholar alike. Existentialism, of major interest a few years ago, and influential through the writings of Jean-Paul Sartre and others, is well treated in "Irrational Man" by William Barrett (*see list on Modern Philosophy*). Those seeking an understanding of 20th-century American philosophy should consult two books by Andrew J. Reck which provide excellent coverage: "Recent American Philosophy" (1964, o.p.) and "The New American Philosophers: An Exploration of Thought since World War II" (1968). And for insight into a controversial "prophet" of the student New Left of the late 1960's (who is himself of an older generation), see Herbert Marcuse's "One-Dimensional Man," which takes philosophy where it has often ventured in the past—into the realm of political science. This and other works by Professor Marcuse will be found under his main entry, this Chapter.

See also additional titles and lists in Sections following on Ancient and Oriental Philosophy; Medieval Philosophy; Modern Philosophy.

Allen, E. L. FROM PLATO TO NIETZSCHE: Ideas that Shape Our Lives. 1959. *Fawcett* pap. $1.25

Armstrong, A. H., Ed. THE CAMBRIDGE HISTORY OF LATER GREEK AND EARLY MEDIEVAL PHILOSOPHY. *Cambridge* 1967 $27.50

"This work of masterly scholarship contains eight parts: Greek philosophy from Plato to Plotinus, Philo and the beginnings of Christian thought, Plotinus, the later Neoplatonists, Marius Victorinus and Augustine, the Greek Christian Platonist tradition from the Cappadocians to Maximus and Eriugena, Western Christian thought from Boethius to Anselm, and early Islamic philosophy. The volume succeeds admirably [in its task]"—(*LJ*).

Avey, Albert E. HANDBOOK IN THE HISTORY OF PHILOSOPHY. 1954. *Harper* Barnes & Noble 2nd. ed. 1961 1971 pap. $2.25

Beck, R. N., Ed. PERSPECTIVES IN PHILOSOPHY: A Book of Readings. *Holt* 2nd. ed. 1969 pap. $6.95

Bréhier, Émile. THE HISTORY OF PHILOSOPHY. Trans. by Thomas Joseph (Vol. 1) and Wade Baskin (Vols. 2–7) *Univ. of Chicago Press* 7 vols. Vol. 1 The Hellenic Age (1963) $8.50 pap. $2.75 Vol. 2 The Hellenistic and Roman Age (1965) $8.50 pap. $2.75 Vol. 3 The Middle Ages and the Renaissance (1965) $9.00 pap. $1.95 Vol. 4 The Seventeenth Century (1966) $13.00 pap. $3.95 Vol. 5 The Eighteenth Century (1967) $9.00 pap. $2.45 Vol. 6 The Nineteenth Century (1968) $10.00 pap. $3.45 Vol. 7 Contemporary Philosophy—Since 1850 (1969) $9.75 pap. $2.95. "Large libraries which possess [other such histories] should also acquire Brehier"—(*LJ*).

Brennan, Joseph G. THE MEANING OF PHILOSOPHY: A Survey of the Problems of Philosophy and of the Opinions of the Philosophers. *Harper* 1953 2nd ed. 1967 $11.50. A lucid exposition.

Clark, Gordon Haddon. THALES TO DEWEY: A History of Philosophy. *Houghton* 1957 $11.95

Copleston, Frederick C. A HISTORY OF PHILOSOPHY. *Paulist-Newman* 8 vols. 1946–   Vol. 1 Greece and Rome (1946) $8.95 Vol. 2 Mediaeval Philosophy—Augustine to Scotus (1950) $8.95 Vol. 3 Mediaeval Philosophy—Ockham to Suárez (1953) $8.95 Vol. 4 Descartes to Leibniz (1959) $8.95 Vol. 5. Hobbes to Hume (1959) $8.95 Vol. 6 Wolff to Kant (1960) $8.95 Vol. 7 Fichte to Nietzsche (1963) $8.95 Vol. 8 Bentham to Russell $9.50; *Doubleday* Image Bks. pap. Vol. 1 Greece and Rome 2 pts. each $1.75 Vol. 2 Mediaeval Philosophy Pt. I $1.95 Pt. 2 $1.75 Vol. 3 Late Mediaeval and Renaissance Philosophy 2 pts. each $1.75 Vol. 4 Modern Philosophy; Descartes to Leibniz $1.95 Vol. 5 17th and 18th Century British Philosophers 2 pts. each $1.75 Vol. 6 Modern Philosophy: French Enlightenment to Kant Pt. I $1.45 Pt. 2 $1.75 Vol. 7 Pt. I Modern Philosophy: Fichte to Hegel $1.75 Pt. 2 Schopenhauer to Nietzsche $1.75 Vol. 8 Pt. I Modern Philosophy—Bentham to Russell: British Empiricism and the Idealist Movement in Great Britain $1.75 Pt. 2 Idealism in America, The Pragmatic Movement, The Revolt Against Idealism $1.75

"Fair, thorough, and essential for any good library"—(*Choice*). "The reason why Fr. Copleston is so good an historian of philosophy is that he manages to combine a capacity for clear and exact thinking with a range of sympathy which is able to include even the least clear and exact of thinkers. This is an unusual combination of qualities"—(*TLS*, London).

Durant, Will. THE STORY OF PHILOSOPHY: The Lives and Opinions of the Great Philosophers of the Western World. 1926. *Simon & Schuster* rev. ed. 1933 1950 $9.95 Touchstone-Clarion 1961 pap. $2.95 Pocket Bks. 1962 pap. $1.25

Feibleman, James K. UNDERSTANDING PHILOSOPHY. *Dell* Laurel Eds. 1975 pap. $1.50

Flew, Anthony. INTRODUCTION TO WESTERN PHILOSOPHY. *Bobbs* 1971 $8.00

Frost, S. E., Jr. BASIC TEACHINGS OF THE GREAT PHILOSOPHERS. *Doubleday* 1962 pap. $1.95. A comprehensive summary.

Hartnack, Justus. HISTORY OF PHILOSOPHY. *Humanities Press* 1973 pap. $7.50

Heidegger, Martin. THE END OF PHILOSOPHY. Trans. by J. Stambaugh *Harper* 1973 $4.95
"It is a highly condensed and difficult original attempt to think what Whitehead called the 'form of forms of thought' about being, from Plato to Nietzsche"—(Frederick J. Crosson).

Hook, Sidney, Ed. DIMENSIONS OF MIND. 1960. *Macmillan* Collier Bks. $1.50. Provocative discussion by Professor Hook, N. Wiener, B. F. Skinner, W. Köhler, J. B. Rhine and others on the mind, the formation of concepts and the possibility of a machine functioning as a brain.

Jaspers, Karl. THE GREAT PHILOSOPHERS. Trans. by Ralph Manheim; ed. by Hannah Arendt *Harcourt* 2 vols. Vol. I The Foundations (1962) Vol. 2 The Original Thinkers (1966) each $12.95 (*for complete information see his main entry, this Chapter*).

Joad, Cyril E. M. GUIDE TO PHILOSOPHY. 1936. *Dover* pap. $4.00; *Folcroft* 1973 $5.00

Jones, William Thomas. A History of Western Philosophy. *Harcourt* 1952 rev. ed. pap. 1969 4 vols. Vol. 1 The Classical Mind Vol. 2 The Medieval Mind Vol. 3 Hobbes to Hume Vol. 4 Kant to Wittgenstein and Sartre Vols. 1–3 each $5.50 Vol. 4 $5.95. Major figures with extensive quotations from sources.

Kaufman, Walter A., Ed. Philosophic Classics. *Prentice-Hall* 2 vols. 1961 2nd ed. 1968 Vol. 1 Thales to Ockham Vol. 2 Bacon to Kant each $10.95

Kirk, Russell. The Conservative Mind: From Burke to Santayana. 1953 *Avon* 1973 pap. $3.95

The Intemperate Professor and Other Cultural Splenetics. *Louisiana State Univ. Press* 1965 $5.00

The conservative Russell Kirk "writes effortlessly where others use jargon. . . . If there is a decadence, Kirk implies, we need not look for hidden sociological poisons, but for conscious individuals who make the wrong decisions or for institutions that fail in their tasks. . . . The cumulative effect is a quiet but persistent critique of the prevailing ideology"—(Thomas Molnar, in *National Review*).

Lovejoy, Arthur O. The Great Chain of Being. *Harvard Univ. Press* 1936 $10.00 pap. $2.75. His most significant work; on the conception of the world as accepted to the close of the 18th century.

Essays in the History of Ideas. *Johns Hopkins Press* 2nd ed. 1952 $12.50. Influential book which traces the unit ideas of philosophies through intellectual history.

McMullin, Ernan, Ed. The Concept of Matter in Greek and Mediaeval Philosophy. *Univ. of Notre Dame Press* 1963 pap. 1965 $3.00. The 27 essays and commentaries which constitute this volume chart the various conceptions of the material world held by philosophers and scientists since the Pre-Socratic era. This exhaustive study of an important philosophical issue is recommended to larger public and academic libraries.

Mason, Sr. M. Elizabeth. Active Life and Contemplative Life: A Study of the Concepts from Plato to the Present. Ed. by George E. Ganss *Marquette Univ. Press* 1961 pap. $2.50

Matson, Wallace J. Sentience. *Univ. of California Press* 1975 $7.95

O'Connor, D. J., Ed. A Critical History of Western Philosophy. *Macmillan* (Free Press) 1964 $11.95

"The contributors to this joint venture have made a real effort to go beyond a mere exposition of various philosophical systems and have tackled their subject matter in an evaluative and critical manner. . . . The purely historical analysis of philosophical doctrines, without being sacrificed completely, has been subordinated to the attempt 'to bring out whatever may be in them that is of permanent philosophical interest' "—(*LJ*). The authors are chiefly British and "on the highest level of competence."

Pap, Arthur. Elements of Analytic Philosophy. 1949. *Macmillan* (Hafner) 1972 $14.95

Parker, Francis H. The Story of Western Philosophy. *Indiana Univ. Press* 1967 $10.00 pap. $2.95

Polanye, Michael, and Harry Prosch. Meaning. *Univ. of Chicago Press* 1975 $12.50

This book "clearly and adroitly renders the complexities of various fields of knowledge accessible to any interested reader"—(*LJ*).

Radhakrishnan, Sir Sarvepalli, and others, Eds. History of Philosophy: Eastern and Western. 1953. *Harper* (Barnes & Noble) 2 vols. 1967 set $18.50

Randall, John Herman, Jr. The Career of Philosophy. *Columbia* 2 vols. Vol. 1 From the Middle Ages to the Enlightenment (1962) $22.50 pap. $5.00 Vol. 2 From the German Enlightenment to the Age of Darwin (1965) $17.50 pap. $3.45

Russell, Bertrand. A History of Western Philosophy. *Simon & Schuster* 1945 $12.95

"Readable, witty, incisive, challenging, paradoxical"—(*New Republic*).

See also his main entry, this Chapter.

Schiffer, Stephen R. MEANING. *Oxford* 1973 $10.50

"A brilliant analysis of the nature of language and communication"—*(Choice)*.

Singer, Marcus G., and Robert R. Ammerman, Eds. INTRODUCTORY READINGS IN PHILOSOPHY. *Scribner* 2nd ed. 1974 pap. $6.95

Smart, Harold R. PHILOSOPHY AND ITS HISTORY. *Open Court* 1963 $5.00 pap. $1.95. A critical examination of the permanent values to philosophy of its own history.

Stace, Walter T. MYSTICISM AND PHILOSOPHY. 1960. *Humanities Press* (Fernhill) $13.25

Stumpf, Samuel E. SOCRATES TO SARTRE. *McGraw-Hill* 1971 2nd ed. 1975 $9.95

Thomas, George F. RELIGIOUS PHILOSOPHIES OF THE WEST. *Scribner* 1965 pap. $4.95

"This is a well-written history of Western religious philosophies from Plato to Tillich, to each of whom a chapter is devoted. . . . Dr. Thomas [also covers] Whitehead, Dewey, Feuerbach, Kierkegard, Hegel, Kant, Hume, Spinoza, Eckhardt, Aquinas, Augustine, Plotinus, and Aristotle"—*(LJ)*.

Wedberg, Anders. HISTORY OF PHILOSOPHY. *Bedminster* 1974 $11.00

Weitz, Morris, Ed. PHILOSOPHY IN LITERATURE: Shakespeare, Voltaire, Tolstoy and Proust. *Wayne State Univ. Press* 1963 pap. $2.95

PROBLEMS IN AESTHETICS: An Introductory Book of Readings. *Macmillan* 1959 2nd ed. 1970 $11.50. A comprehensive anthology, of which the first two sections are surveys of some principal theories of art, including Plato, Aristotle, Fry, Maritain, Bosanquet, Croce and others. The third and longest section contains essays by art authorities Berenson, Matisse, Ivor Richards and others.

Whittemore, Robert C. MAKERS OF THE AMERICAN MIND: Three Centuries of American Thought and Thinkers. 1964. *Bks. for Libraries* 1972 $18.25

Whittemore "considers American thought and thinkers from the Puritans to Alfred North Whitehead. [He] discusses widely known individuals (Walt Whitman and Abraham Lincoln) and those less widely known (Abner Kneeland and William Torey Harris) and includes politicians, poets, scientists, educators, and others. It is a superbly done book . . . charm and grace of language wed to excellent balance of judgment, thought, and opinion"—*(LJ)*.

Windelband, Wilhelm. HISTORY OF ANCIENT PHILOSOPHY. Trans. by Herbert E. Cushman. 1899. *Dover* pap. $3.50; *Gannon* $8.00

A HISTORY OF PHILOSOPHY. Trans. by James H. Tufts Vol. 1 Greek, Roman and Medieval 2nd ed. 1910 *Harper* 1958 Torchbks. 1968 pap. $2.75 Vol. 2 o.p.

Zenkovsky, V. V. A HISTORY OF RUSSIAN PHILOSOPHY. Trans. by George L. Kline *Columbia* 2 vols. 1953 set $22.50. Comprehensive, thoroughly documented and clearly written by a Russian born and educated author, this is the first history of Russian philosophy ever published in English.

ANCIENT AND ORIENTAL PHILOSOPHY

Although we think first of our Graeco-Roman past when considering ancient philosophy, interest is growing in the Eastern philosophies and their contribution to Western culture. Zen Buddhism, in particular, has an appeal for modern poets and, together with the Hinduism of the Bhagavad Gita, for example, has attracted such religious-philosophical thinkers as Thomas Merton and Alan Watts.

In Oriental thought it is often very difficult to separate philosophy from the religions of Buddhism, Confucianism, Hinduism, Shinto, Taoism and Vedanta. A selected list of Works on Oriental or Eastern Philosophy has been included in this section, but the books on these religions of the East will be found in Chapter 4, World Religions, this Volume.

Works on Oriental or Eastern Philosophy

Brown, W. Norman. MAN IN THE UNIVERSE: Some Continuities in Indian Thought. Pref. by O. L. Chavarria-Aguilar *Univ. of California Press* 1966 $8.50. The 1965 Rabindranath Tagore Memorial Lectures.

Professor Brown analyzes "the particular answers India has fashioned to the universal question of man's relationship to man and his universe. . . . The search for reality as opposed to the phenomenal world, the recognition of all life as a unity, and the interpretation of time as a destructive agent are themes which . . . Brown traces . . . from [their] earliest appearances through the *Rig Veda, Upanishads, Bhagavad Gita*, and their embodiment in Jainism and Buddhism. A small but excellent work"—*(LJ)*.

Chai, Ch'u, and Winberg Chai, Eds. I CHING: Book of Changes. Trans from the Chinese by James Legge; introd. and study guide with drawings, appendixes and notes. 1899. *University Bks.* 1965 $10.00

"One of the world's most ancient, most mysterious, and yet most rational documents, *I Ching*, did not escape the attention of the 18th-century European philosophers, who learned about it through the Jesuits then active in China. These Jesuits hopefully saw a common ground in this work for Chinese tradition and Christianity, as the work shows both the roots of Confucian humanism and the mysticism of Lao-Tzu. It was not until the 19th century that full translations appeared. Among these were Legge's in 1882, together with other Chinese classics, in Max Müller's "Sacred Book of the East Series," which has long been out of print"—*(LJ)*. *(See also Siu, R. G. H., below.)*

Chan, Wing-Tsit, Trans. and comp. A SOURCE BOOK IN CHINESE PHILOSOPHY. Fwd. by Charles A. Moore *Princeton Univ. Press* 1963 $17.50 pap. $3.95. This collection of translated philosophical pieces with helpful commentaries, ranging from Confucius to Mao Tse-tung, is the work of a Chinese "elderly scholar" in this country; a significant contribution.

Creel, Herrlee Glessner. CHINESE THOUGHT FROM CONFUCIUS TO MAO TSE-TUNG. *Univ. of Chicago Press* 1953 $10.00 pap. $3.25. This informal and very readable account from the earliest times to the present is by the Professor of Chinese Literature and Institutions at the University of Chicago.

Dasgupta, Surendra Nath. INDIAN IDEALISM. *Cambridge* 1962 $9.50 pap. $1.65

INDIAN PHILOSOPHY. *Cambridge* 5 vols. 1922–1955 Vol. 1 1922 $23.50 Vol. 2 1933 $27.50 Vol. 3 1940 $23.50 Vol. 4 1949 $23.50 Vol. 5 1955 $14.50 set $95.00

Fakhry, Majid. A HISTORY OF ISLAMIC PHILOSOPHY. *Columbia* 1970 $4.75

"This is the only modern, comprehensive, integrated history in English and will be the basic text for some time to come"—*(LJ)*.

Fung Yu-lan (or Fêng Yu-lan). HISTORY OF CHINESE PHILOSOPHY. *Princeton Univ. Press* 2 vols. Vol. 1 The Period of the Philosophers from the Beginnings to Circa 100 B.C. trans. by Derk Bodde (rev. 1952) $16.50 Vol. 2 The Period of Classical Learning From the Second Century B.C. to the Twentieth Century A.D. (1953) $20.00

A SHORT HISTORY OF CHINESE PHILOSOPHY. Ed. by Derk Bodde. 1958. *Macmillan* (Free Press) pap. $2.95

Koller, John. ORIENTAL PHILOSOPHIES. *Scribner* 1970 $8.95

"An excellent overview of Oriental philosophy for the beginning student or lay reader"—*(Choice)*.

Moore, Charles A., with assistance from Aldyth V. Morris, Eds. THE CHINESE MIND: Essentials of Chinese Philosophy and Culture. *Univ. of Hawaii Press* (East-West Center) 1967 $12.00 pap. $3.95

The papers in this volume were presented at the four University of Hawaii East-West Philosophers' Conferences held between 1939 and 1964. They "deal with the ethics and personal philosophy of traditional China. . . . [An] attractive book"—*(LJ)*. The contributors, including the Chinese (Hu Shih and others), are generally from non-Communist backgrounds.

THE INDIAN MIND: Essentials of Indian Philosophy and Culture. *Univ. of Hawaii Press* (East-West Center) 1967 $12.00 pap. $3.95

Also presented at the East-West Philosophers' Conferences, these papers deal with "metaphysical matters, epistemological concerns, problems in ethical and social philosophy, topics such as religion, politics, economics and the philosophical basis of the law. . . . All were written by specialists in the field [mostly Indian]. . . . Highly recommended"—*(LJ)*.

THE JAPANESE MIND: Essentials of Japanese Philosophy and Culture. *Univ. of Hawaii Press* (East-West Center) $12.00 pap. $4.95

Radhakrishnan, Sir Sarvepalli. EASTERN RELIGIONS AND WESTERN THOUGHT. *Oxford* 2nd ed. 1940 $8.25 1975 pap. $3.95

INDIAN PHILOSOPHY. 1931. *Humanities Press* 2 vols. 1962 set $33.00

Siu, R. G. H. THE MAN OF MANY QUALITIES: A Legacy of the I Ching. *M.I.T. Press* 1968 $8.95

"In this collection of about 700 quotations by more than 650 writers from nearly 60 countries over a period of [many] centuries, R. G. Siu . . . attempts to interpret in varied degrees the principles of the I Ching, one of the most important Chinese classics"—(*LJ*). (*See also Chai, Ch'u, above.*)

Waley, Arthur. THREE WAYS OF THOUGHT IN ANCIENT CHINA. 1939. *Harper* (Barnes & Noble) 1953 $8.50; *Doubleday* Anchor Bks. 1956 pap. $1.95

Watt, W. Montgomery. ISLAMIC PHILOSOPHY AND THEOLOGY. *Aldine* 1962 $5.00

Zimmer, Heinrich Robert. PHILOSOPHIES OF INDIA. Ed. by Joseph Campbell *Princeton Univ. Press* 1969 $14.50 pap. $3.95. Valuable study of Hindu thought.

See also Chapter 4, World Religions, this Volume.

Oriental Philosophers

LAO-TZU   (also Lao-tse or Lao-tsze; orig. Li Erh).   c. 604–531 B.C.   *See Chapter 4, World Religions, this Volume.*

BUDDHA: "The Enlightened One" (Gautama Buddha, orig. Prince Siddhartha).   c. 563–483 B.C.   *See Chapter 4, World Religions, this Volume.*

CONFUCIUS.   551–478 B.C.   *See Chapter 4, World Religions, this Volume.*

Works on Ancient Philosophy

Boas, George. RATIONALISM IN GREEK PHILOSOPHY. *Johns Hopkins Press* 1961 $14.00

"Some 2500 years ago in Greece men began to wonder about the ultimate and original substance underlying the world of appearance. . . . With great clarity and wit Boas describes this growth and the ultimate demise of the rule of reason in Greek philosophy from Thales to Plotinus. . . . It is not technical and is easily understood by the interested layman"—(*LJ*).

Bolton, J. D. P. GLORY, JEST AND RIDDLE. *Harper* (Barnes & Noble) 1973 $10.00

"A rich and stimulating chronicle of the nature and growth of the individual. . . . With thoroughness the author shows what various writers, philosophers and others, have contributed to the concept and expression of the self. . . . This is in every way a richly rewarding work"—(*Classical Outlook*).

Boman, Thorleif. HEBREW THOUGHT COMPARED WITH GREEK. Trans. by Jules L. Moreau. 1961. *Norton* 1970 pap. $2.95. This book "challenges every preacher, student of the faith, and philosopher, even at the secular level, to come to grips with its implications."

Brumbaugh, Robert. THE PHILOSOPHERS OF GREECE. 1964. *Apollo* 1970 pap. $2.65

Burnet, John. EARLY GREEK PHILOSOPHY. 1908. *Harper* (Barnes & Noble) 4th ed. repr. of 1930 ed. $9.00 Entirely rewritten in its third edition, it has superseded all other works on the subject.

Clarke, Martin Lowther. THE ROMAN MIND: Studies in the History of Thought from Cicero to Marcus Aurelius. 1956. *Norton* 1968 pap. $1.75

"A quite admirable book, distinguished not only by its brevity and lucidity . . . but by an incisive historical judgment"—(*TLS*, London).

Cornford, Francis. FROM RELIGION TO PHILOSOPHY: A Study of Western Speculation. 1912. *Harper* 1957 pap. $2.75; *Peter Smith* 1958 $4.50

Diogenes Laertius. LIVES OF EMINENT PHILOSOPHERS. *Harvard Univ. Press* Loeb 2 vols. each $7.00. The oldest history of Greek philosophy in existence is doubly valuable in that it quotes freely from earlier works no longer extant.

Dover, K. J. GREEK POPULAR MORALITY IN THE TIME OF PLATO AND ARISTOTLE. *Univ. of California Press* 1975 $16.00

"Doubtlessly, the work will become a standard reference: it is philological spadework for philosophical reflection"—(*LJ*).

Edelstein, Ludwig. THE MEANING OF STOICISM. Pub. for Oberlin College by *Harvard Univ. Press* 1966 $3.00

"This book contains the Martin Classical Lectures for 1956 by the late Professor Edelstein. Without delving too deeply into controversial points of detail, he confines himself to a broad outline of the basic characteristics of Stoicism.... An admirable tribute to the late author's perceptiveness and scholarship"—(*LJ*). In the Martin Classical Lectures Series.

Gomperz, Theodor. GREEK THINKERS: A History of Ancient Philosophy. 1931. *Humanities Press* 4 vols. 1953 each $8.75 text ed. each $7.50

Guthrie, William Keith Chambers. THE GREEK PHILOSOPHERS: From Thales to Aristotle. 1950. *Harper* 1960 pap. $1.95

A HISTORY OF GREEK PHILOSOPHY. *Cambridge* 4 vols. 1962 1975 Vol. 1 Earlier Presocratics and the Pythagoreans Vol. 2 The Presocratic Tradition from Parmenides to Democritus Vol. 3 The Fifth Century Enlightenment Vol. 4 Plato—The Man and His Dialogues: Earlier Period each $34.50

Havelock, Eric A. A HISTORY OF THE GREEK MIND: Vol. 1 Prefaces to Plato. *Harvard Univ. Press* 1962 $10.00; *Grosset* pap. $2.95. "This scholarly, original, debatable work should be read by classicists." In a stimulating analysis of Plato's attack on poetry (*Republic*), the Harvard professor retraces early Greek thought.

Heidegger, Martin. EARLY GREEK THINKING. *Harper* 1975 $10.50

Hussey, Edward. THE PRESOCRATICS. *Scribner* 1973 $7.95 lyceum ed. pap. $2.95

"Comprehensive picture of Greek thinkers of the 6th and 5th centuries B.C."—(Publisher's catalog). "Recommended"—(*Choice*).

Hyland, Drew A. THE ORIGINS OF PHILOSOPHY: Rise in Myth and the Pre-Socratics. *Putnam* 1973 $6.95 1975 pap. $3.95

"Highly recommended to all undergraduate libraries"—(*Choice*).

Kirk, Geoffrey Stephen, and J. E. Raven. PRESOCRATIC PHILOSOPHERS: A Critical History with a Selection of Texts. *Cambridge* 1957 $15.50 pap. $4.95

Long, A. A. HELLENISTIC PHILOSOPHY. *Scribner* 1974 $10.00

"A study of the dominant intellectual movements from 323 B.C. to the end of the Roman Republic"—(Publisher's catalog).

Mourelato, Alexander P. D., Ed. THE PRE-SOCRATICS: A Collection of Critical Essays. *Doubleday* Anchor Bks. pap. $5.95

"Heartily recommended"—(*Choice*).

Nietzsche, Friedrich Wilhelm. PHILOSOPHY IN THE TRAGIC AGE OF THE GREEKS. *Regnery* 1962 pap. $1.25

Parker, G. F. A SHORT ACCOUNT OF GREEK PHILOSOPHY: From Thales to Epicurus. *Harper* Perenn. Lib. 1969 pap. $1.25

Peters, F. E. GREEK PHILOSOPHICAL TERMS: A Historical Lexicon. *New York Univ. Press* 1967 $8.95 pap. $2.95

"Heady, handy reference.... Peters has tried, with diacritical terms and over citing and cross-referencing, to construct a facile handbook.... Recommended for philosophy collections"—(*Choice*).

Robinson, John M. INTRODUCTION TO EARLY GREEK PHILOSOPHY. *Houghton* 1968 pap. $6.95

Sandbach, F. H. THE STOICS. *Norton* 1975 $7.95

"Sandbach has written an original study which will be of enormous value to undergraduates and graduate students alike, as well as to the intelligent general reader"—(*Choice*).

Singer, Irving. THE NATURE OF LOVE: Plato to Luther. *Random* 1966 $10.00

"Telling of idealization in Freud and Santayana, [Singer] then describes the views of Plato, Aristotle, Plotinus, Ovid, and Lucretius. Finally, he discusses elements of Christian love—*eros, philia, nomos, agape*—in the Middle Ages and in Luther. A later volume is to discuss courtly, Romantic, and modern love. . . . Recommended highly"—(*LJ*).

Smith, Thomas Vernor, Ed. PHILOSOPHERS SPEAK FOR THEMSELVES. *Univ. of Chicago Press* Phoenix Bks. 1956 Vol. 1 From Thales to Plato. Representative writings of the major pre-Socratic philosophers pap. $4.45 Vol. 2 From Aristotle to Plotinus pap. $2.45

Windelband, Wilhelm. HISTORY OF ANCIENT PHILOSOPHY. 1899. Trans. by Herbert Ernest Cushman. 3rd ed. 1925. *Dover* 1957 pap. $3.50

Zeller, Eduard. OUTLINES OF THE HISTORY OF GREEK PHILOSOPHY. 13th ed. rev. by W. Nestle and trans. by L. R. Palmer *Humanities Press* 13th ed. rev. 1969 $15.00

THE STOICS, EPICUREANS AND SCEPTICS. *Russell & Russell* rev. ed. 1962 $12.50

Ancient Philosophers

The greatest philosophers of ancient times were Socrates, Plato and Aristotle. Plato was a young man of thirty at Socrates' death, and still in his prime when Aristotle was born.

SOCRATES. 469 B.C.–399 B.C.

Socrates, like Jesus, left no writings of his own behind him. His teachings were entirely oral. What knowledge we have of his philosophy comes to us entirely through the writings of his disciples, Plato (*see following*) and Xenophon (*q.v.*). Plato wrote four dialogues in which Socrates is the chief speaker. These are known as the Socratic Dialogues. The "Euthyphro" discusses holiness and piety; the "Apology" is Socrates' defense before his judges; "Crito" is Socrates' answer to a proposal that he attempt escape from jail; "Phaedo" is the story of how he drank the hemlock and died.

Socrates introduced a new, personal approach to philosophy when he taught that "virtue . . . was the consequence of self-knowledge; and moral goodness was the greatest value in the universe"—(E. W. F. Tomlin). "Know thyself" became his motto. When his friend Chaerephon asked the Delphic Oracle if any man were wiser than Socrates, the reply was that Socrates was the wisest of living men because he knew that he knew nothing. Socrates' questioning of many traditional beliefs caused him to be tried for his alleged corruption of Athenian youth and for his refusal to worship the gods of the city-state (Socrates reverenced spiritual values, but held that the mythological tales of gods and goddesses were poetic creations rather than acceptable religious tenets). He welcomed the court's death sentence in his reply to the judges, recorded by Plato in "Phaedo": "I shall then be able to continue my search into true and false knowledge, as in this world so also in the next; and I shall find out who is wise, and who pretends to be wise and is not."

Xenophon (*q.v.*) in his "Memorabilia," or "Memoirs of Socrates," tells of the last years of his master's life. Both Plato and Xenophon knew Socrates only as an old man. The Platonic Socrates and the Socrates of Xenophon are often very different. Xenophon, the historian, is usually considered to be the more accurate witness. Plato did not profess to delineate the opinions of an actual Socrates. Xenophon's "Symposium," or "Banquet," is a philosophical treatise on love and friendship in which Socrates is one of the speakers. Plato also wrote a "Symposium" on the same subjects.

EUTHYPHRO, APOLOGY, CRITO, PHAEDO, PHAEDRUS. Trans. by Harold N. Fowler *Harvard Univ. Press* Loeb $7.00

PORTRAIT OF SOCRATES. Trans. by R. W. Livingstone *Oxford* 1938 $3.50 pap. $1.95. The Apology, Crito, and Phaedo. The introduction deals with the life, times and work of Socrates.

EUTHYPHRO, CRITO, APOLOGY, SYMPOSIUM. Trans. by Benjamin Jowett; rev. ed. with introd. by Moses Hadas *Regnery* Gateway Eds. 1953 1960 pap. $.95

PLATO ON THE TRIAL AND DEATH OF SOCRATES: Euthyphro, Apology, Crito, Phaedo. Trans. by L. Cooper. 1941 *Burt Franklin* $13.50; *Cornell Univ. Press* 1967 pap. $1.95

THE TRIAL AND DEATH OF SOCRATES: Apology, Crito and Closing Scene of the Phaedo. Trans. with introd. by John Warrington *Dutton* Everyman's $3.95

THE LAST DAYS OF SOCRATES: Apology, Crito, Phaedo. Trans. by Hugh Tredennick *Penguin* Class. pap. $1.25

PHAEDO. Trans. by F. J. Church *Bobbs* Lib. Arts 1951 pap. $.65

LACHES AND CHARMIDES. Trans. by Rosamund Kent Sprague *Bobbs* Lib. Arts 1973 pap. $2.50

Books about Socrates

Socrates and the Socratic Schools. By Eduard Zeller. Trans. from the 3rd German edition by Oswald J. Reichel. 1885. *Russell & Russell* 1962 $10.00

Socratic Method and Critical Philosophy: Selected Essays. By Leonard Nelson; trans. by Thomas Kite Brown; fwd. by Brand Blanshard; introd. by Julius Kraft. 1949. *Dover* 1965 pap. $2.00; *Peter Smith* $4.50

Socrates. By Alfred Edward Taylor. 1952. *Doubleday* Anchor Bks. pap. $1.45. Good biography reconstructed from fragments.

Socratic Humanism. By Laszlo Versényi. Fwd. by Robert S. Brumbaugh *Yale Univ. Press* 1963 $5.00 pap. $1.75

"An intelligent, readable and attractive book. [Dr. Versényi believes] that the early philosophers of nature neglected the human condition but it was the Sophists that reintroduced the problem of man thus preparing the grounds for Socrates' humanism"—*(Classical World)*.

The Socratic Enigma. Ed. by Herbert Spiegelberg and B. Q. Morgan. *Bobbs* Lib. Arts 1964 $6.50 pap. $2.00

The Philosophy of Socrates. By Norman Gulley. *St. Martin's* 1968 $12.95

The Concept of Irony: With Constant Reference to Socrates. By Sören Kierkegaard. Trans. by Lee M. Capel *Indiana Univ. Press* 1968 pap. $2.95

Socrates. By William Keith Chambers Guthrie. *Cambridge* 1971 pap. $3.95. Extracted from Vol. 3 of his "A History of Greek Philosophy" *(see above)*

Philosophy of Socrates. Ed. by Gregory Vlastos. *Doubleday* 1971 pap. $2.45

Nietzsche's View of Socrates. By Werner J. Dannhauser. *Cornell Univ. Press* 1974 $15.00

"A useful and instructive addition to the growing critical literature on Nietzsche in English"— *(Choice)*.

For Xenophon on Socrates, see Xenophon's main entry in Chapter 9, History, Government and Politics—Ancient, this Volume.

PLATO. 429 B.C.–347 B.C.

Plato studied with Socrates from the age of 20 and was the chief recorder of his master's work. He also founded the Academy in an Athens garden, of which Aristotle became a student member. Plato "left behind him the first systematic body of literature the ancient world had produced"— (E. W. F. Tomlin).

Plato's Dialogues number 35, of which seven are considered spurious. The best known, after the Socratic Dialogues are: "Lysis," on Friendship; "Phaedrus," on Love; "Laches," on Valor; "Charmides," on Temperance; "Gorgias," on Rhetoric; "Ion," on Homer and Poetic Inspiration. The "Republic," in ten books, pictures an ideal state and is the earliest of Utopias. The "Republic" was the first of a trilogy; the "Timaeus," a project for world reformation, and the "Critias," a fragment, being the sequels. Jowett's translations are masterpieces; he made Plato an English classic. The Loeb versions are noteworthy, particularly the volumes of "Dialogues" translated by H. N. Fowler with their "easy, flowing rendering." *St. Martin's Press* Golden Treasury "Republic" translated by Davies and Vaughan is recommended, as are all translations by I. A. Richards and W. H. D. Rouse.

WORKS. *Harvard Univ. Press* Loeb 12 vols. each $7.00; trans. by Benjamin Jowett, sel. and ed. by Irwin Edman *Random* (Modern Lib.) 1930 pap. $3.95

THE PORTABLE PLATO. Ed. with introd. by Scott Buchanan *Viking* Portable Lib. 1948 $6.95 pap. $3.95. Contains the Republic, The Symposium, Protagoras and Phaedo, in the Jowett translation; excellent introduction.

THE COLLECTED DIALOGUES OF PLATO: Including the Letters. Ed. by Edith Hamilton and Huntington Cairns. 1961 *Princeton Univ. Press* $10.00

This handy edition, less than two inches thick, has been made possible by the use of good Bible paper. The editors have tried, quite successfully, to select the best translation of each dialogue. "This edition should be a boon to students and teachers who must refer simultaneously to several of the dialogues. It is also an excellent buy for the small library that does not have a good multivolume translation."

THE DIALOGUES OF PLATO. Trans. by B. Jowett; 4th ed. rev. by D. J. Allan and H. E. Dale *Oxford* 4 vols. 4th rev. ed. 1953 Vol. 1 $9.75 Vol. 2 $10.25 Vol. 3 o.p. Vol. 4 $10.25

SELECTIONS. Ed. by Raphael Demos *Scribner* 1927 pap. 1972 $3.95

SELECTED PASSAGES. Ed. by R. W. Livingstone *Oxford* World's Class. 1940 $2.50

A PLATO READER. Trans. by B. Jowett; ed. by R. B. Levinson *Houghton* Riv. Eds. 1953 pap. $3.75. Includes the complete Euthyphro, Apology, Crito and Phaedo; selections from the Symposium, Phaedrus, Republic and other dialogues.

THE WISDOM AND IDEAS OF PLATO. Ed. by E. Freeman and D. Appel *Fawcett* Premier Bks. 1966 pap. $.95. Contains introductory explanations to passages from several dialogues.

FIVE GREAT DIALOGUES: Apology, Crito, Phaedo, Symposium, Republic. Trans. by Benjamin Jowett; ed. with introd. by Louise Ropes Loomis *Van Nostrand–Reinhold* 1942 $3.95

DIALOGUES: Euthyphro, Apology, Crito, Phaedo, Phaedrus. Trans. by Harold North Fowler; introd. by W. R. M. Lamb *Harvard Univ. Press* Loeb 1914 1953 $7.00. First volume of "Works" *above*.

GREAT DIALOGUES OF PLATO. Trans. by W. H. D. Rouse. *New Am. Lib.* Mentor Bks. pap. $1.75. Contains: Ion, Meno, Symposium (The Banquet), The Republic (Bks. 1–10 and Summary), Apology (Defense of Socrates), Crito, Phaedo (Phaidon), Greek Alphabet and a pronouncing index.

DIALOGUES. Trans. by Benjamin Jowett from the 3rd trans. ed. by W. C. Greene *Liveright* 1927 $7.95; trans. by Benjamin Jowett unabr. ed. *Random* 2 vols. 1937 each $15.00 boxed set $30.00; ed. by J. D. Kaplan *Simon & Schuster* (Washington Square) 1961 pap. $.95

PARMENIDES, THEAITETOS, THE SOPHIST, THE STATESMAN. Trans. with introd. by John Warrington *Dutton* Everyman's 1961 $3.95. These dialogues form a single group and illustrate Plato's theory of knowledge.

EUTHYPHRO, APOLOGY, CRITO. Trans. by F. J. Church; introd. by Robert D. Cumming *Bobbs* Lib. Arts 1956 pap. $.90. Includes the death scene from Phaedo.

THE SOCRATIC DIALOGUES. *See also preceding entry on Socrates.*

THE REPUBLIC AND OTHER WORKS. Trans. by Benjamin Jowett *Doubleday* Dolphin Bks. pap. $2.50

THE REPUBLIC. Trans. by Benjamin Jowett, introd. by F. Gemme *Assoc. Booksellers* Airmont Bks. 1968 pap. $.95; ed. by Allan Bloom *Basic Bks.* 1968 $15.00 pap. $5.75; trans. and ed. by I. A. Richards *Cambridge* 1966 $12.50 pap. $3.75; trans. by A. D. Lindsay *Dutton* Everyman's 1950 New Am. ed. pap. $2.95; *Harvard Univ. Press* Loeb 2 vols. each $7.00; trans. from Burnet's text by F. M. Cornford *Oxford* 1945 pap. $2.50; trans. by H. D. P. Lee *Penguin* Class. pap. $1.50; trans. by Benjamin Jowett *Random* (Modern Lib.) 1941 $3.95 Vintage Bks. pap. $1.95; trans. by Davies and Vaughan *St. Martin's* Golden Treasury $4.95

EUTHYDEMUS. Ed. by Rosamund Kent Sprague *Bobbs* Lib. Arts 1969 pap. $1.75

TIMAEUS. Trans. by Francis Cornford; ed. by Oskar Piest *Bobbs* Lib. Arts pap. $1.50. (*See note for next entry.*)

TIMAEUS. Trans. with introd. by H. D. P. Lee *Penguin* (orig.) 1966 pap. $1.50
  In the excellent Penguin Classics series. "Cornford remains the standard work, but a Greekless reader may . . . be helped by a peek at Lee"—(*Choice*).

PROTAGORAS and MENO. Trans. by W. K. C. Guthrie *Penguin* Class. 1957 pap. $1.45

MENO. Trans. by Benjamin Jowett *Bobbs* Lib. Arts 1949 pap. $.75

THE SYMPOSIUM AND OTHER DIALOGUES. Trans. and ed. by Michael Joyce, Michael Oakley and John Warrington *Dutton* Everyman's 1964 $3.95

THE SYMPOSIUM. Trans. by Benjamin Jowett; introd. by F. H. Anderson *Bobbs* Lib. Arts 1948 1956 pap. $.75; trans. by W. Hamilton *Penguin* (orig.) 1952 pap. $1.25;

dramatized by F. Kobler and E. Müller *Ungar* $4.50 pap. $1.95; trans. by Suzy Gordon, ed. by John Brentlinger *Univ. of Massachusetts Press* 1970 $10.00 pap. $4.00

PHAEDRUS. Trans. by W. C. Helmbold and W. G. Rabinowitz *Bobbs* Lib. Arts 1956 pap. $.95; trans. and ed. by R. Hackforth *Cambridge* 1952 1972 $5.50

GORGIAS. Trans. with introd. by W. C. Helmbold *Bobbs* Lib. Arts 1952 pap. $1.10. A comparatively early work—a dialogue between Socrates and Callicles.

PLATO'S STATESMAN. Trans. by J. B. Skemp. 1952. *Bobbs* Lib. Arts. 1957 pap. $2.00

EPISTLES. Trans. by Glenn R. Morrow *Bobbs* Lib. Arts 1962 pap. $1.75

Additional separate titles are published by Bobbs Lib. Arts.

Books about Plato

The Unity of Plato's Thought. By Paul Shorey. 1903. *Shoe String Press* $5.00

What Plato Said. By Paul Shorey. 1933. *Univ. of Chicago Press* 1957 $15.00 abr. ed. 1965 pap. $3.45

Plato's Thought. By G. M. A. Grube. 1935. *Beacon* 1958 pap. $2.45

The Philosophy of Plato. By Guy Cromwell Field. *Oxford* Home Univ. Lib. 1969 pap. $2.50

Plato's Earlier Dialectic. By Richard Robinson. *Oxford* 1953 2nd ed. 1954 $7.75

An Interpretation of Plato's Doctrines. By I. M. Crombie. *Humanities Press* 2 vols. Vol. 1 Plato on Man and Society (1962) Vol. 2 Plato on Knowledge and Reality (1963) each $18.75

Preface to Plato. By Eric A. Havelock. *Harvard Univ. Press* 1963 $12.50
> The first of the author's projected series on the Greek mind, and an excellent study. Professor Havelock "attempts to explain Plato's vehement attack upon poets and poetry. . . . The target was an educational procedure and a whole way of life, the effect of which was the poetic state of mind, which constituted the chief obstacle to scientific rationalism"—*(Yale Review)*.

Plato's Republic: A Philosophical Commentary. By Robert C. Cross and A. D. Woozley. *St. Martin's* 1964 $8.95
> The authors have attempted, they say, "to produce a book that will serve as something of an introduction to philosophy via the Republic, rather than a specialised Platonic study." "Students at all university levels (and perhaps some professional scholars . . .) will benefit from these clear and unexcited discussions of the main themes of moral and metaphysical philosophy, and of Plato's treatment of them"—*(TLS*, London). The writing is of "a clarity that is most striking. In fact, supreme lucidity may be singled out as primary among the virtues of this distinguished scholarly work"—*(Virginia Quarterly Review)*.

New Essays on Plato and Aristotle. Ed. by Renford Bambrough. *Humanities Press* 1965 $6.50
> "A brilliant, if rather uneven, set of essays which breaks important new ground"—*(TLS*, London).

Plato's Thought in the Making: A Study of the Metaphysics. By J. E. Raven. *Cambridge* 1966 $13.50

Plato's Progress. By Gilbert Ryle. *Cambridge* 1966 $15.95 pap. $5.95
> "Ryle brings erudite scholarship and vivid imagination to the question of the development of Plato's thought. He throws out the traditional Socratic/post-Socratic division of the dialogues and introduces a number of adventuresome theses in its place"—*(Choice)*.

The Socratic Paradoxes and the Greek Mind. By Michael J. O'Brien. *Univ. of North Carolina Press* 1967 $8.25
> "This important book reexamines Plato's analysis of moral experience, and the rational and irrational influences that contribute to its being what it is"—*(LJ)*.

The Great Thinkers on Plato. Ed. By Barry Gross. *Putnam* 1969 pap. $2.25
> The technique of recording weighty opinions "is adroitly followed in the present volume of essays, chapters, and lectures on Plato, selected by Barry Gross. He provided illuminating introductions to the 27 well-chosen discussions included in the volume, with a general introduction on problems in understanding Plato"—*(LJ)*.

Plato Manuscripts: A New Index. Ed. by Robert S. Brumbaugh and Rulon Wells. Plato Microfilm Project of the Yale Univ. Library. *Yale Univ. Press* 1968 $8.50

Plato and the Individual. By H. D. Rankin. *Harper* (Barnes & Noble) 1969 pap. $3.00

Plato's Psychology. By T. M. Robinson. *Univ. of Toronto Press* 1971 $10.00
> "Robinson soberly discusses modern European, British, and American scholarship in the light of ancient evidence (tends to reject the neo-Platonic readings by Proclus and Plutarch in favor of Aristotle's more liberal ones)"—*(Choice)*.

Plato. By J. C. B. Gosling. *Routledge and Kegan Paul* 1973 $16.50
> "This book should be very helpful to upper-division undergraduates, graduate students, and teachers of philosophy and classics"—*(Choice)*.

Plato on Man. By A. Zakopoulos. *Philosophical Lib.* 1975 $7.50

Plato's "Sophist": A Commentary. By Richard S. Bluck. *Harper* 1975 $14.00
"Bluck studies 'The Sophist' as a way of interpreting Plato, notably his theory of forms, developed after the Republic"—*(LJ)*.

The Argument and the Action of Plato's Laws. By Leo Strauss. *Univ. of Chicago Press* 1975 $10.75

ARISTOTLE.   384 B.C.–322 B.C.

The great philosopher and scientist was the son of a doctor, to whom he probably owed his interest in biology. At the age of 17 he joined Plato's *(q.v.)* Academy and remained there 20 years. After Plato died Aristotle went to Assos, then to Mytilene, where he remained until he accepted an invitation from Philip of Macedon to become tutor to the 13 year-old Alexander. When Philip was assassinated, Aristotle returned to Athens and decided to start a new school in the Lyceum, a grove sacred to Apollo Lyceius. "Because of Aristotle's custom of walking up and down under a covered court, or *peripatos* while lecturing or discussing some philosophic or scientific matter, his group became known as the 'Peripatetics.' " The emphasis was on biology, history, and philosophy. Aristotle "classified the sciences, added scientific data in many fields, particularly in biology, encouraged and developed ideas in ethics and politics, and developed logic as a science of reasoning."

Owing to a series of accidents, nearly everything he wrote has been lost. The surviving works are in the form of elaborate lecture-notes. His cosmology, which was accepted in Europe in modified form until the time of Galileo, is explained in the "Physics" and "Metaphysics." The most important of his more humanistic studies is the "Nicomachean Ethics," in which he tries to analyze happiness. The "Politics" is a discussion of the nature, aims and methods of the city-state. In the "Rhetoric" and "Poetics" he turns his attention to the arts. His method is "tentative, undogmatic and amazingly conscientious." He influenced profoundly the course of medieval philosophy and science. "No Greek can claim greater importance in the history of European thought." Older studies (from the late 19th and early 20th century) by Bhandari and Sethi, R. Chance, and T. Davidson have recently been reprinted by *Verry, Kennikat,* and *Burt Franklin* respectively.

WORKS: The Oxford Translation. Trans. under the editorship of J. A. Smith and W. D. Ross by J. I. Beare, Ingram Bywater and others *Oxford* 12 vols. 1908–1952 various prices *(consult publisher's catalog for individual titles)*.

The *Oxford* Aristotle was issued in parts over a period of years. The work was undertaken at the desire of Benjamin Jowett whose translation of the "Politics" appears in Vol. 10. The 11th volume to be published was Vol. 3, which contains the original preface of 1908 and a preface commemorative of the completion of the series. Vol. 12, published in 1952, contains Select Fragments. This monumental translation supersedes all others and contains such great classics as the Jowett "Politics" and the "Poetics" by I. Bywater.

WORKS. *Harvard Univ. Press* Loeb 23 vols. each $7.00

BASIC WORKS OF ARISTOTLE. Ed. with introd. by Richard P. McKeon *Random* 1941 $12.50

INTRODUCTION TO ARISTOTLE. Ed. with a general introd. and introds. to the particular works by Richard P. McKeon *Random* (Modern Lib.) 1947 pap. $2.25

SELECTIONS. Trans. and ed. by P. Wheelwright *Bobbs* (Odyssey) $4.00 pap. $3.50; ed. by William D. Ross *Scribner* 1971 Lyceum Ed. $2.95

THE PHILOSOPHY OF ARISTOTLE. New selection with introd. and commentary by Renford Bambrough *New Am. Lib.* (orig.) pap. $1.50

THE POCKET ARISTOTLE. Trans. by W. D. Ross; ed. by Justin D. Kaplan *Simon & Schuster* (Washington Square) pap. $.95

THE NICOMACHEAN ETHICS. Trans. with introd. by Martin Ostwald *Bobbs* Lib. Arts 1962 $6.00 pap. $2.50

ETHICS: The Nicomachean Ethics. Trans. by John Warrington *Dutton* Everyman's $3.95; trans. by W. David Ross *Oxford* World's Class. 1954 $5.75; newly trans. with introd. by J. A. K. Thomson *Penguin* Class. 1955 pap. $1.45

POETICS. Trans. with introd. by John Warrington *Dutton* Everyman's 1963 $3.95; trans. by S. H. Butcher *Farrar, Straus* (Hill & Wang) 1961 pap. $1.50; trans. by Gerald F.

Else *Univ. of Michigan Press* 1967 $4.50 pap. $1.95; trans. by Preston H. Epps *Univ. of North Carolina Press* 1942 pap. $1.25

POETICS: A Translation and Commentary for Students of Literature. By L. Golden and O. B. Hardison, Jr. *Prentice-Hall* 1968 $7.95 pap. $4.50

ARISTOTLE ON THE ART OF POETRY. By Lane Cooper *Cornell Univ. Press* rev. ed. 1962 $2.45

ON THE ART OF POETRY. Trans. by S. H. Butcher *Bobbs* Lib. Arts 1958 pap. $1.50; trans. by I. Bywater *Oxford* 1920 pap. $1.95

ART OF POETRY: A Greek View of Poetry and Drama. Based on Bywater's translation, with introd. and explanations by W. H. Fyfe *Oxford* 1940 $2.50. A volume designed for the general reader who knows no Greek.

ON THE ART OF FICTION: Translation of the Poetics. Trans. with introd. essay and explanatory notes by L. J. Potts *Cambridge* 1953 $5.95 1966 pap. $1.95

ON POETRY AND STYLE. Trans. with introd. by G. M. A. Grube *Bobbs* Lib. Arts 1958 $4.00 pap. $.85

THEORY OF POETRY AND FINE ART. Trans. by S. H. Butcher; introd. by John Gassner *Peter Smith* $5.25

POLITICS AND POETICS. Trans. by Benjamin Jowett and Thomas Twining; introd. by Lincoln Diamant *Viking* Compass Bks. 2 vols. in 1 1957 pap. $2.25

POLITICS and THE CONSTITUTION OF ATHENS. Trans. and ed. by John Warrington *Dutton* Everyman's 1959 $3.95

POLITICS. Trans. by H. Rackham *Harvard Univ. Press* Loeb 1933 $7.00; trans. by J. A. Sinclair *Penguin* Class. (orig.) 1962 pap. $1.65

RHETORIC (trans. by W. Rhys Roberts) and POETICS (trans. by Ingram Bywater). Introd. by Friedrich Solmsen *Random* Mod. Lib. 1955 $3.95

METAPHYSICS. Trans. and ed. by John Warrington; introd. by Sir David Ross *Dutton* Everyman's 1956 $3.95

This translation was called, on publication, "the most accurate and usable text of the 'Metaphysics' which is now available" by John Wild of Harvard University. It has been rearranged to give a more logical sequence to the exposition and to make the text as easily comprehensible as possible to the general reader. It is Volume No. 1000 in the Everyman's Library, one which helped to celebrate the 50th anniversary of that eminent series.

METAPHYSICS. Newly translated as a postscript to natural science, with an analytical index of technical terms, by Richard Hope. 1952. *Univ. of Michigan Press* Ann Arbor Bks. 1960 pap. $3.95

METAPHYSICS. Trans. by H. G. Apostle *Indiana Univ. Press* 1966 $18.95 pap. $5.95

"This is the first of a projected series of volumes comprising the complete works of Aristotle in translation, each volume with its own notes on the translation it contains. . . . The translator appears to have achieved a fairly happy balance"—(*LJ*).

PRIOR AND POSTERIOR ANALYTICS. Trans. by John Warrington *Dutton* Everyman's 1964 $3.95

ARISTOTLE'S PHYSICS. Trans. by Richard Hope. *Univ. of Nebraska Press* 1961 pap. $1.75

THE CONSTITUTION OF ATHENS AND RELATED TEXTS. Trans. with introd. and notes by Kurt von Fritz and Ernst Kapp *Hafner* 1950 pap. $2.95

ARISTOTLE'S DE ANIMA WITH THE COMMENTARY OF ST. THOMAS AQUINAS. Trans. by K. F. Foster and S. Humphries *Yale Univ. Press* 1951 $10.00

DE ANIMA. Trans. by D. W. Hamlyn. Bks. 2 and 3, with excerpts from Bk. 1. Clarendon Aristotle Series *Oxford* 1968 pap. $7.25

PROTREPTICUS: A RECONSTRUCTION. Ed. by Anton-Hermann Chroust *Univ. of Notre Dame Press* 1964 pap. $1.45. Essay attempts to reconstruct likely content of an early Aristotelian work.

ARISTOTLE ON HIS PREDECESSORS. Trans. and ed. by A. E. Taylor *Open Court* 2nd ed. $8.00 pap. $1.95

Books about Aristotle

The Political Thought of Plato and Aristotle. By Ernest Barker. 1906. *Russell & Russell* $17.00; *Peter Smith* $5.50; *Dover* 1959 pap. $3.50

Aristotle. By Sir William David Ross. 1924. *Barnes & Noble* 5th rev. ed. 1955 pap. $3.75

Aristotle: Fundamentals of the History of His Development. By Werner Jaeger. Trans. from the German by Richard Robinson *Oxford* 1934 2nd ed. 1948 pap. $2.85

Aristotle's Criticism of Plato and the Academy. By Harold F. Cherniss. 1944. *Russell & Russell* 1962 $17.00

Aristotle: The Nicomachean Ethics: A Commentary. By Harold Henry Joachim. Ed. by D. A. Rhees *Oxford* 1951 $10.25
"Rich in specific insights, in textual interpretation . . . and a deep systematic knowledge."

The Philosophy of Aristotle. By D. J. Allan. *Oxford* 1952 2nd ed. 1970 pap. $2.50

Aristotle's Theory of Poetry and Fine Art. By Samuel H. Butcher. Introd. by John Gassner *Dover* 4th rev. ed. 1955 pap. $2.25

The Poetics of Aristotle, Its Meaning and Influence. By Lane Cooper. 1956. *Cooper* 1972 $8.75

Aristotle's Poetics: The Argument. By Gerald Frank Else. *Harvard Univ. Press* 1957 $17.50. A "monumental contribution."

Aristotle. By John Herman Randall, Jr. *Columbia* 1960 $13.00 1962 pap. $2.95
"In a clear and lively language the author presents the man as well as his works and thoughts, his Hellenic background as well as his ageless embodiment of man's urge and ability to know"—(*LJ*).

On Aristotle and Greek Tragedy. By John Jones. *Oxford* 1962 pap. $2.95
This book aims to discover what Aristotle was really saying about the drama in his "Poetics," and to test these discoveries upon plays by Aeschylus, Sophocles and Euripides.

Rational Man: A Modern Interpretation of Aristotelian Ethics. By Henry B. Veatch. *Indiana Univ. Press* 1962 pap. $2.65
Dr. Veatch, professor of philosophy at Indiana University, argues the need for a return to studies in normative ethics. The book "commends itself to thoughtful general readers because of its moral insights and simple style."

A Portrait of Aristotle. By Marjorie Grene. *Univ. of Chicago Press* 1963 $10.00 1967 pap. $2.95
"A successful presentation of the workings of Aristotle's philosophy so that the student of classics or of philosophy can absorb Aristotle's most difficult thoughts in some sort of order and with a plan"—(*PW*).

New Essays on Plato and Aristotle. Ed. by Renford Bambrough. *Humanities Press* 1965 $5.50
"The essays . . . are written by authors who believe that the study of the classical philosophers has a lesson for the philosophers of today"—(*New Statesman*). "This attractive [book] will be read with great interest by all students of Plato and Aristotle"—(*Classical World*).

Aristotle's Poetics and English Literature: A Collection of Critical Essays. Ed. with introd. by Elder Olson. *Univ. of Chicago Press* 1965 $6.50 pap. $2.45

Aristotle: A Collection of Critical Essays. Ed. by J. M. Moravcsik. *Doubleday* Anchor Bks. (orig.) 1967 pap. $1.45; *Univ. of Notre Dame Press* 1968 $6.95. Contains 14 essays; "Will certainly be welcomed by philosophers and obviously deserves an index" (*LJ*), which it lacks.

Aristotle: His Thought and Its Relevance Today. By Cyril Winn and Maurice Jacks. *Harper* (Barnes & Noble) 1967 $5.00

Aristotle: The Growth and Structure of His Thought. By G. E. Lloyd. *Cambridge* 1968 $7.00 pap. $2.45

Aristotle's Ethical Theory. By W. R. Hardie. *Oxford* 1968 $7.00

Aristotle. By John Ferguson. *Twayne* $6.95
"There is no small compendium to Aristotle in English more useful than this one. It is not intended as a work for scholarly reference. It is written nevertheless, for serious students in the style of a genial teacher, proceeding, text by text, through the entire scope of Aristotle's work."—(*Choice*).

Aristotle and His School. By Felix Grayeff. *Harper* (Barnes & Noble) 1974 $11.50

Time and Necessity: Studies in Aristotle's Theory of Modality. By Jaakko Hintikka. *Oxford* 1974 $17.75
Concentrates "on the logical modalities in Aristotle and their consequences for his ideas on time, determinism and infinity"—(Frederick J. Crosson).

Aristotle: A Contemporary Appreciation. By Henry B. Veatch. *Indiana Univ. Press* 1974 $7.95 pap. $2.95
"Good books for undergraduates on classical philosophy are so rare that this book should probably be acquired by all college libraries"—(*Choice*).

Aristotle's Man: Speculations upon Aristotelian Anthropology. By Stephen R. Clark. *Oxford* 1975 $19.25

"A unique interpretation of Aristotle . . . which makes the biological conception of devolution—opposed to evolution—crucial to Aristotle's biology"—(*Choice*).

EPICURUS.   342? B.C.–270 B.C.

The founder of Epicureanism was born at Samos. He taught in several towns in Asia Minor before going to Athens and establishing a school about 306 B.C. A generous and genial man, he defined philosophy as the art of making life happy, but that a life of pleasure must also be a life of prudence, honor and justice. Of his voluminous writings, only fragments remain. Cyril Bailey's "Extant Remains," with short critical apparatus and notes (1926, o.p.) is the preferred translation. The finest exposition of Epicurus's ideas is given by the Roman poet Lucretius (*q.v.*) in his "De Rerum Natura" ("On the Nature of Things").

THE EPICUREAN LETTERS. Trans. by Russell M. Geer *Bobbs* Lib. Arts 1964 $5.00 pap. $1.25. Also includes "Principal Doctrines" and "Vatican Sayings."

Books about Epicurus

The Stoics, Epicureans and Sceptics. By Eduard Zeller. Trans. by Oswald J. Reichel. 1879. *Russell & Russell* rev. ed. 1962 $12.50

Stoic and Epicurean. By Robert Hicks. 1910. *Russell & Russell* 1962 $13.00

The Greek Atomists and Epicurus. By Cyril Bailey. 1928. *Russell & Russell* 1964 $16.50

St. Paul and Epicurus. By Norman W. DeWitt. *Univ. of Minnesota Press* 1954 $6.00

Epicurus and His Philosophy. By Norman W. DeWitt. 1954. *Greenwood* 1972 $15.00

Two Studies in the Greek Atomists. By David J. Furley. *Princeton Univ. Press* 1966 $10.00

"These studies combine intensive analysis of textual evidence and an effort to see each problem in the context of earlier and contemporary philosophical discussion. Aristotle's contributions are pivotal: he criticized earlier atomism and was answered in turn by Epicurus. . . . A rich, rewarding book"—(*Classical World*).

Epicurus: An Introduction. By J. M. Rist. *Cambridge* 1972 $12.50

LUCRETIUS (Titus Lucretius Carus).   c. 99 B.C.–c. 55 B.C.   *See Chapter 8, Latin Literature*, Reader's Adviser, *Vol. 2*.

PHILO JUDAEUS (Philo of Alexandria).   fl. c. 1 A.D.

Called "the Jewish Plato," Philo sought to harmonize a philosophy of religion from his study of Greek philosophers with the doctrines of the Old Testament Pentateuch. His belief in the *logos* or "word" as the creative force in the world is thought to have influenced the Gospel of St. John. He knew of and wrote about the heretical sect of Jewish Essenes or holy men, whose manuscripts, found in 1947, are now known as the "Dead Sea Scrolls." (*See Chapter 3, Bibles and Related Texts—Section on The Dead Sea Scrolls.*)

PHILOSOPHICAL WORKS. Trans. by Francis Henry Colson and George Herbert Whitaker *Harvard Univ. Press* Loeb 10 vols. 1929–1939 each $7.00

WORKS: Supplements 1–2. Trans. from the ancient Armenian version of the original Greek by Ralph Marcus. *Harvard Univ. Press* Loeb 2 vols. Suppl. 1 Questions and Answers on Genesis Suppl. 2 Questions and Answers on Exodus each $7.00

Books about Philo

Philo and the Oral Law. By Samuel Belkin. 1940. *Johnson Reprint* $17.50

Philo: Foundations of Religious Philosophy in Judaism, Christianity, and Islam. By Harry A. Wolfson. *Harvard Univ. Press* 2 vols. 1947 set $25.00

"We have here not only by far the best and most detailed treatise on Philo that has ever appeared but also an invaluable presentation of the subject matter of the philosophy of religion"—(*American Historical Review*).

EPICTETUS.   60 A.D.–138 A.D.

"Epictetus was a Stoic philosopher, a slave who later gained his freedom. His maxims were collected in a manual, or enchiridion, by his pupil, Arrian, who also published his discourses. But Epictetus—the impoverished, majestic, and witty cripple—commends both my esteem and my affection. . . . He taught that if a man desired contentment he must 'make the best of his own faculties and take everything else as it happens to occur.' What really matters is not what we do but the way in which we do it"—(Sir Harold Nicolson). The Matheson translation (1916) is excellent and was called "a most pleasant and graceful version" by W. A. Oldfather (*see Loeb ed. below*).

DISCOURSES, MANUAL, AND FRAGMENTS. Trans. by W. A. Oldfather *Harvard Univ. Press* Loeb 2 vols. 1926 each $7.00

MORAL DISCOURSES, THE ENCHIRIDION AND FRAGMENTS. Trans. with introd. by Elizabeth Carter; ed. by W. H. D. Rouse *Dutton* Everyman's 1955 $3.95

DISCOURSES. Trans. by P. E. Matheson. 1968 *Heritage, Conn.* $11.95

GOLDEN SAYINGS and THE HYMN OF CLEANTHES. Trans. by Hastings Crossley 1903. *Richard West* 1912 $10.00

ENCHIRIDION. (And "Meditations of Marcus Aurelius Antoninus") trans. by George Long *Regnery* 1956 pap. $1.25; trans. by Higginson *Bobbs* Lib. Arts pap. $.80

MARCUS AURELIUS (ANTONINUS). 121 A.D.–180 A.D.

Marcus Aurelius was Emperor of Rome from 160 to 180. Although a Roman, he wrote his "Meditations" in Greek, preferring the tongue for the "propriety and facility of his expressions," since "the Latin tongue in matter of philosophy comes as short of the Greek as the English doth of Latin." Aurelius was a Stoic, and his "Meditations" are the flower of the Stoic philosophy. Long's was once the familiar and most widely read translation (1862) but it is now surpassed by the more recent Loeb Library translation. Meric Casaubon did the first English translation in 1634, which C. R. Haines in his preface to the Loeb edition has described as "albeit involved and periphrastic, not without dignity or scholarship."

THE MEDITATIONS. Trans. by G. M. A. Grube *Bobbs* Lib. Arts 1962 $5.00 pap. $2.40; trans. by Meric Casaubon *Dutton* Everyman's 1935 $3.95; trans. by C. R. Haines *Harvard Univ. Press* Loeb $7.00; trans with commentary by A. S. L. Farquharson *Oxford* 1944 2 vols. $23.50; trans. by George Long *Peter Pauper Press* 1942 new ed. 1956 $4.95 pocket ed. $1.95; trans. by J. H. Staniforth *Penguin* 1964 pap. $1.50

MEDITATIONS. (And Epictetus' "Enchiridion") trans. by George Long; introd. by Russell Kirk *Regnery* 1956 $1.25

THOUGHTS. Trans. by John Jackson *Oxford* World's Class. 1940 $5.00

Books about Marcus Aurelius

Marcus Aurelius Antoninus. By P. B. Watson. 1884. *Books for Libraries* $12.50. Treats Marcus Aurelius' career as emperor and philosopher.

Marcus Aurelius: A Biography. By Henry D. Sedgwick. *AMS Press* 1921 $8.00

PLOTINUS. 205 A.D.–270 A.D.

Plotinus belonged to the Neo-Platonic school. His system was the last of the old Greek philosophies; he is generaly grouped today with the mystics. Plotinus' philosophy has a moral basis. To him "everything happens by necessity, ultimately by the inward necessity of the One or the Good. The One must, by the necessity of its own nature, emanate Reason; Reason must emanate Soul; and Soul must emanate Body"—(Francis H. Parker, in "The Story of Western Philosophy"). The Stephen MacKenna translation won scholarly recognition and is "always lucid and pleasant to read." The more recent version by Professor Katz, assistant professor of philosophy at Vassar, is a "valuable contribution to the stock of English translations"—(*Ethics*).

WORKS. Trans. by H. Armstrong *Harvard Univ. Press* Loeb 6 vols. 1966 1967 vols. 1, 2 and 3 each $7.00 vols. 4, 5 and 6 (in prep.)

THE ENNEADS. Trans. by Stephen MacKenna *Pantheon* 1956 rev. ed. 1957 $20.00

THE PHILOSOPHY OF PLOTINUS. Trans. and ed. with introd. by Joseph Katz. 1950. *Prentice-Hall* 1960 pap. $5.25. Selected books of the Enneads.

Books about Plotinus

The Philosophy of Plotinus. By Émile Bréhier. Trans. by Joseph Thomas *Univ. of Chicago Press* 1958 $5.50. A highly recommended, clear and readable presentation.

Nature, Contemplation, and the One: A Study in the Philosophy of Plotinus. By John N. Deck. *Univ. of Toronto Press* 1967 $6.50

Plotinus: The Road to Reality. By J. M. Rist. *Cambridge* 1967 $16.50

Plotinus' Philosophy of the Self. By G. J. O'Daly. *Harper* (Barnes & Noble) 1973 $12.00

LONGINUS (Cassius?). c. 213 A.D.–273 A.D.

The chief fame of the eminent Greek rhetorician and philosopher of the Platonic school, Cassius Longinus, rests on the treatise, traditionally but probably erroneously attributed to him,

"On the Sublime." It is one of the great works of literary criticism and extolls sincerity and loftiness of style. The identity of the author remains undetermined; the manuscripts name a "Dionysius Longinus." Cassius Longinus taught rhetoric in Athens and wrote "Philological Discourses," "On First Principles," "On the Chief End." His last years were spent in Palmyra, where he tutored the children of Queen Zenobia. He became her political advisor and encouraged her to resist Rome. After Zenobia's fall, Longinus was beheaded as a traitor by the Emperor Aurelian. "On the Sublime" was much admired by the English poets of the Augustan age.

ON THE SUBLIME. (And Aristotle's "Poetics" and Demetrius' "On Style") trans. by W. H. Fyfe *Harvard Univ. Press* Loeb 1927 $7.00

ON GREAT WRITING (On the Sublime). Trans. with introd. by George M. Grube *Bobbs* Lib. Arts 1957 pap. $1.25

ON SUBLIMITY. Trans. by D. A. Russell *Oxford* 1965 $1.70

MEDIEVAL PHILOSOPHY

Only in recent years have the opinions of philosophers changed in regard to medieval thought, following the revolt and prejudice against scholasticism during the 16th and 17th centuries. Medieval philosophers were without exception clerics, for it was only with the protection of the Church, especially in monasteries, that there was any cultivation of learning. The religious philosophers of this period, therefore, are to be found in Chapter 4, World Religions, this Volume.

When the 11th century opened, Christian philosophers had only an odd assortment of reference works besides the writings of the early Christians: Plato's "Timaeus" with a commentary and two logical works of Aristotle. St. Anselm (d. 1109, *q.v.*) has been called "the father of scholasticism." Peter Abélard (d. 1143, *q.v.*, Reader's Adviser, *Vol. 2*) of the tragic pair, Héloïse and Abélard, was noted for his dialectical skill. When he raised the question of faith versus reason he was brought to trial for it. The reconciliation of faith and reason was the chief problem of the scholastics Albertus Magnus (d. 1280), St. Thomas Aquinas (d. 1274, *q.v.*), and St. Bonaventure (d. 1274). The hopeless confusion in the writings of the 11th and 12th centuries gave way then to the first manifestations of systematic thought—the great philosophical synthesis of the Middle Ages. For in the 13th century the founding of the universities gave scholars a greater opportunity to gather and to reach a wider public. The universities at Oxford and Paris were the most prominent in philosophy; it was to Paris that the Italian St. Thomas Aquinas went in 1252. John Duns Scotus (d. 1308, *see following*), "the Subtle Doctor," studied and taught at Oxford and taught at Paris and Cologne; his school of Scotists opposed the Thomists, or followers of St. Thomas.

Because of recent scholarly research, more translations into English and increased interest in mystical works, some of the most significant, though almost forgotten, developments of philosophic thought of the 1200 years between St. Augustine (354–430, *q.v.*) and the 17th century are again being read. There has been a new translation of one of the most celebrated documents of Western mysticism—"The Cloud of Unknowing" by an English mystic of the 14th century (trans. from archaic to modern English with an introd. by Ira Progoff *Julian Press* 1957 $5.00). Other editions, one ed. by Justin McCann (*Christian Classics* 1973 $5.95) and another trans. by Clifton Wolters (*Penguin* 1968 pap. $1.50) are available.

Selected List of Works on Medieval Philosophy

Armstrong, A. H., Ed. THE CAMBRIDGE HISTORY OF LATER GREEK AND EARLY MEDIEVAL PHILOSOPHY. *Cambridge* 1967 $27.50. "Outstanding"—(*Choice*).

Bréhier, Émile. THE MIDDLE AGES AND THE RENAISSANCE. Trans. from the French by Wade Baskin History of Philosophy Ser. *Univ. of Chicago Press* 1965 $9.00 pap. $1.95

By the late professor of philosophy at the Sorbonne. "Neo-platonism, Abélard's ethics, 12th-century heresies, and the diffusion of Aristotelian thought, are all clearly and succinctly explained"—(*LJ*). Bibliography, index, footnotes.

Burch, George B. EARLY MEDIEVAL PHILOSOPHY. 1951. *Bks. for Libraries* $10.50. Concise and readable.

Copleston, Frederick C. A HISTORY OF MEDIEVAL PHILOSOPHY. *Harper* 1972 $11.00 Torchbks. pap. $3.45

"One of the most comprehensive and judicious one-volume presentations of an extremely diverse and difficult period of thought, this book is moreover, gracefully written"—(*Choice*).

Fremantle, Anne Jackson, Ed. THE AGE OF BELIEF: The Medieval Philosophers. With introd. and interpretive commentary. 1955. *New Am. Lib.* 1955 pap. $1.50

Gilson, Étienne Henry. HISTORY OF CHRISTIAN PHILOSOPHY IN THE MIDDLE AGES. *Random* 1955 $15.00. A Catholic philosopher's monumental study.

Leff, Gordon. MEDIEVAL THOUGHT FROM ST. AUGUSTINE TO OCKHAM. *Penguin* Pelican Bks. 1963 pap. $1.45

McKeon, Richard. SELECTIONS FROM MEDIEVAL PHILOSOPHERS. *Scribner* Mod. Student's Lib. 2 vols. 1929 1959 pap. each $2.95 Vol. 1 Augustine to Albert the Great Vol. 2 Roger Bacon to William of Ockham

Maurer, Armand A. MEDIEVAL PHILOSOPHY. Pref. by Étienne Gilson *Random* 1962 $12.50

This work selects about 20 leading philosophers of the period from Augustine to Suarez and gives a clear description of their most important doctrines. It will not replace the more detailed histories but is easier reading for the nonspecialist.

Petry, Ray C. LATE MEDIEVAL MYSTICISM. *Westminster Press* 1957 $7.50. A noteworthy collection of examples of mystical and contemplative writings (11th–18th centuries).

Pieper, Josef. SCHOLASTICISM: Personalities and Problems of Medieval Philosophy. Trans. by Richard and Clara Winston. 1960. *McGraw-Hill* 1964 pap. $1.95. A survey by the German Thomist philosopher.

Rand. E. K. FOUNDERS OF THE MIDDLE AGES. 1928. *Dover* pap. $3.50; *Peter Smith* $5.00

"Thoughtful, beautifully written"—(*American Historical Review*).

Randall, John Herman, Jr. THE CAREER OF PHILOSOPHY: From the Middle Ages to the Enlightenment. *Columbia* 1965 $22.50 pap. $5.00

"Professor Randall has crowned his 40-odd years of teaching and research with a work staggering in its depth of erudition and remarkable in its readability. Written from the viewpoint of a humanist and a rationalist, it surveys the development of modern philosophic concepts from the early Middle Ages to Hume and Rousseau." This ambitious work is an encyclopedic and extraordinarily lucid exposition of the ideas which have shaped the contemporary consciousness and should appeal to all literate, inquiring readers.

Taylor, Henry Osborn. THE MEDIEVAL MIND: A History of the Development of Thought and Emotion in the Middle Ages. 4th ed. 1925. *Harvard Univ. Press* 2 vols. 1949 1959 set $25.00

Weinberg, Julius. A SHORT HISTORY OF MEDIEVAL PHILOSOPHY. *Princeton Univ. Press* 1964 $10.00 pap. $3.45

Wolfson, Harry A. THE PHILOSOPHY OF THE CHURCH FATHERS. *Harvard Univ. Press* 1956 3rd rev. ed. 1970 $15.00. Vol. 1 Faith, Trinity, Incarnation. Awarded the Harvard University Press Faculty Prize in 1956.

Medieval Philosophers

AUGUSTINE, SAINT (Bishop of Hippo). 354–430. *See Chapter 4, World Religions, this Volume*.

BOËTHIUS, ANICIUS MANLIUS SEVERINUS (also Boetius and Boece). c. 480–524.

Boëthius, Roman philosopher and statesman, is a link between the ancient world and the Middle Ages. A translator of Aristotle into Latin, he was the last of the Romans, born of a Christian family, and the first of the Scholastics. His father had been a consul, and Boëthius himself was made a consul in 510. Late in Theodoric's reign he was falsely charged with treason and was imprisoned and later put to death. While in prison he wrote "The Consolation of Philosophy," in prose and verse, a work derived from Plato and Aristotle. "In one dialogue, an attempt to find why evil exists in a world where God is the highest good and the truest happiness, Lady Philosophy tells him that the absence of self-knowledge is the source of his weakness. She also comments on the practices of the Goddess Fortuna." The "Consolation" has influenced thinking ever since it was first written. King Alfred translated it into Anglo-Saxon (published at Oxford in 1698). Chaucer made an English version of part of this dialogue, and Queen Elizabeth tried her hand at translating it. Before the invention of printing, translations existed in a dozen languages. The earliest English versions are by George Colville (London, 1550) and by Viscount Preston (London, 1695).

THE CONSOLATION OF PHILOSOPHY. Trans. with introd. by Richard H. Green *Bobbs* Lib. Arts 1962 $5.00 pap. $1.50; ed. and abr. by James J. Buchanan, introd. by Whitney J. Oates *Ungar* 1957 pap. $1.45; introd. by William Anderson *Southern Illinois Univ. Press* 1964 $12.00; in King Alfred's Anglo-Saxon, trans. by Martin F. Tupper (1864) and S. Fox *AMS Press* $12.50

TRACTATES and DE CONSOLATIONE PHILOSOPHIAE. Trans. by H. F. Stewart and E. K. Rand *Harvard Univ. Press* Loeb 1918 1926 $7.00

Books about Boëthius

Chaucer and the Consolation of Philosophy of Boëthius. By Bernard L. Jefferson. 1917. *Gordian* 1967 $6.00; *Haskell* $11.95

Boëthius: Some Aspects of His Times and Works. By Helen M. Barrett. 1940. *Russell & Russell* 1965 $7.50

King Alfred and Boëthius. By F. Anne Payne. *Univ. of Wisconsin Press* 1968 $11.50

ANSELM, SAINT. 1033?–1109. *See Chapter 4, World Religions, this Volume.*

THOMAS AQUINAS, SAINT. 1225?–1274. *See Chapter 4, World Religions, this Volume.*

DUNS SCOTUS, JOHANNES (JOHN). c. 1265–1308.

A Scottish philosopher and scientist—and a Franciscan—Scotus taught at Oxford, Paris and Cologne. "The exact canon of Duns Scotus' work is unknown; hence it is not possible to state fully and positively what were his own beliefs. He followed St. Bonaventure in putting Aristotelian thought to the service of Christian theology"—(*Columbia Encyclopedia*). The Scholastic group called (after him) Scotists opposed the Thomism of the followers of St. Thomas Aquinas (*q.v.*). The Scotists reject matter as the principle of individuality (the Thomist theory) in favor of form. Scotus was a "moderate realist" (in the words of Bertrand Russell), one to whom experience and evidence were important as determiners of knowledge. "The subtleties and refinements of Scotism were later attacked; and in the 16th century the name Duns or Dunce gained its present ignominious meaning." However, the Franciscans even today are in general Scotists rather than Thomists.

PHILOSOPHICAL WRITINGS. *Bobbs* Lib. Arts 1964 pap. $2.75

TREATISE ON GOD AS FIRST PRINCIPLE. *Franciscan Herald Press* pap. $2.50

MODERN PHILOSOPHY

Modern philosophy begins with the Renaissance, which revolutionized philosophic thought with its new revelations in physics and astronomy. Descartes is considered the founder of modern philosophy because he was the first to be profoundly affected by the new attitude. Various schools of philosophy were developed in Europe during the following centuries. One of the most important modern movements is that of the logical analysis of science developed by Whitehead and Bertrand Russell. The German Husserl, founder of modern phenomenology, influenced Heidegger, his pupil, and the most prominent French existentialists of our time, Merleau-Ponty and Sartre. "In America and England philosophy is largely pragmatism, positivism, logical empiricism, linguistic analysis, and philosophy of science; in Europe it is mainly phenomenology, metaphysics, and existentialism"—(Reuben Abel in *SR*, June 15, 1963).

The Austrian philosopher, Ludwig Wittgenstein (1889–1951), who spent his life analyzing the language that philosophers use in writing about the world, is a dominant influence on American philosophy today. The technical language and narrow scope of so much academic writing represents a form of elitism that has failed to reach a broad reading public. As Reuben Abel has noted: "Books on philosophy in America do not now usually have the wide audience they once commanded. The problems are often too technical, the language too specialized, the issues too remote from the ordinary affairs of men." In recent years, however, the number of new titles (including popularizations) and reprints in this field seems to indicate that intelligent laymen are again turning for insights to philosophers.

"Readings in Twentieth Century Philosophy," edited by Alston and Nakhnikian, gives representative selections with excellent explanations of basic approaches, concepts, and theses of modern works on Western philosophic thought that have become prominent since 1900.

Works on Modern Philosophy

Adams, E. M. PHILOSOPHY AND THE MODERN MIND. *Univ. of North Carolina Press* 1975 $12.95

Adams, G. P., and W. P. Montague, Eds. CONTEMPORARY AMERICAN PHILOSOPHY. 1930. *Russell & Russell* 2 vols. 1962 $25.00

Adler, Mortimer J. THE DIFFERENCE OF MAN AND THE DIFFERENCE IT MAKES. *Holt* 1967 $7.95; *New Am. Lib.* 1968 pap. $3.95

> Based on the Encyclopaedia Britannica Lectures delivered at the University of Chicago. Not since Aquinas has a question been so completely stated, the answers to it so fairly presented and then so adequately tested. The book may be read for the esthetic pleasure that belongs to perfect works in logic and mathematics no less than to perfect works of art"—(Sir Herbert Read, in *SR*). "An original and important work. . . . A triumph of logic, of fairness, of lucid exposition, and of imaginative foresight about human consequences"—(Jacques Barzun).

Aiken, Henry D., and William Barrett, Eds. PHILOSOPHY IN THE TWENTIETH CENTURY. *Harper* 3 vols. 1971 Vol. 1 $4.45 Vol. 2 $4.75 Vol. 3 $4.75

Alston, William P., and George Nakhnikian, Eds. READINGS IN TWENTIETH CENTURY PHILOSOPHY. *Macmillan* (Free Press) 1963 $11.95

> Representative selections from the major works of many of this century's most important British, Continental and American philosophers cover metaphysics, theory of knowledge, ethics, philsophy of religion, philosophy of mind, logic and philosophy of language; introductions to sections, brief biographies of the philosophers, annotated bibliographies; very valuable.

Bahm, Archie J. ETHICS AS A BEHAVIORAL SCIENCE. *C. C. Thomas* 1974 $9.75. An eloquent plea for the recognition of ethics as a distinct social science.

Barfield, Owen. WORLDS APART. *Wesleyan Univ. Press* 1964 $6.00 pap. $1.95

> "This excellent dialogue is a stimulating contribution to the promising exchange among various compartmentalized intellectual disciplines and invites comparison to Plato on several points. More bold than Plato, who usually discusses only one or two views in each dialogue, Barfield ranges seven views over against each other. . . . Like Plato, the dialogue has no positive result except illumination. . . . This book is *necessary* for high school, public, and college libraries"—(*LJ*).

Barnes, Hazel. AN EXISTENTIALIST ETHICS. *Knopf* 1967 $7.95

> The author first "expands on the need for an ethic that will allow existentialist thinking to be applied to ordinary life decisions, [then] she contrasts existential thinking—usually Sartre's brand of existential philosophy—with the other current American intellectual fashions (beatniks and hipsters, the New Left, and various Eastern philosophies) and then attempts to outline the life responsibilities of anyone who claims to be an existentialist"—(*PW*). A "highly creative and brilliantly critical work"—(*LJ*).

Barrett, William. IRRATIONAL MAN: A Study in Existential Philosophy. *Doubleday* 1958 Anchor Bks. pap. $2.95. A "most lucid exposition."

WHAT IS EXISTENTIALISM? *Grove* 1963 pap. $2.95

> "The first half is a reprinting of Barrett's excellent but out-of-print 1947 *Partisan Review* pamphlet; the second part discusses the contribution to modern existentialist philosophy by the German Martin Heidegger, whom Barrett considers to be the most important thinker in the group which includes Kierkegaard, Hegel, Jaspers, Husserl, and Sartre. His treatment of complex and difficult material is in a modern idiom, well paced, clear, and straightforward"—(*LJ*).

Bayles, Michael D., Ed. CONTEMPORARY UTILITARIANISM. *Doubleday* Anchor Bks. 1968 pap. $1.45

"Old-fashioned utilitarianism, the view that the right action is the one which produces the greatest net benefit to all concerned, was challenged by the question: Is it right to torture an innocent man if by so doing one can save a community from harm? A new view, 'rule-utilitarianism,' answers the question thus: Yes, if the greatest net benefit would result not only in this case but in all comparable cases, cases coming under the same 'rule.' Ten appraisals of this new view, all written in the last 20 years, are here presented. . . . A valuable book for even a small collection on philosophical ethics"—(*LJ*). Bibliography.

Beauchamp, Tom L., Ed. Ethics and Public Policy. *Prentice-Hall* 1975 $12.50

"A thorough and discriminating anthology for problems-oriented ethics or social philosophy courses or for any concerned layman who wishes to know what contemporary philosophers have to say on pressing social concerns"—(*LJ*).

Black, Max. Caveats and Critiques: Philosophical Essays in Language, Logic, and Art. *Cornell Univ. Press* 1975 $15.00

"The writing is a model of clarity and the thought is stimulating; but the middle six essays are not for the general reader whom Black claims to include in his audience"—(*LJ*).

Blackham, Harold John. Six Existentialist Thinkers. *Humanities Press* 1952 1961 $6.00; *Harper* Torchbks. 1959 pap. $1.25

Bochénski, Innocentius Marie. Contemporary European Philosophy. Trans. from the 2nd rev. German ed. by Donald Nicholl and Karl Aschenbrenner *Univ. of California Press* 1956 $10.00 pap. $3.45

Bontempo, Charles J., and S. Jack Odell, Eds. The Owl of Minerva: Philosophers on Philosophy. *McGraw-Hill* 1975 $10.00

"The tone, style, and competence of [these] papers vary greatly: from seriousness in K. R. Popper's and P. Lorenzen's to frivolousness in P. Ziff's, from pellucidly clear writing by A. J. Ayer and B. Blanchard to H. Marcuse's muddiness"—(*LJ*).

Bronowski, Jacob, and Bruce Mazlish. The Western Intellectual Tradition from Leonardo to Hegel. *Harper* 1960 1962 pap. $4.25

Burr, John R., and Milton Goldinger. Contemporary Issues in Philosophy. *Macmillan* 1972 pap. $5.95

Care, Norman S., and Charles Landesman, Eds. Readings in the Theory of Action. *Indiana Univ. Press* $12.50 pap. $4.25

"Before one can adequately answer the question as to what human actions are justified, one must have an adequate understanding of the concept of action and of what constitutes a justification. This book edited by Norman S. Care, assistant professor of philosophy, Oberlin College, and Charles Landesman, associate professor of philsophy, Hunter College, attempts to provide such an understanding. The readings are intellectually exciting and are recommended for college libraries"—(*LJ*). Contains bibliography.

Carr, David. Phenomenology and the Problem of History: A Study of Husserl's Transcendental Philosophy. *Northwestern Univ. Press* 1974 $13.00

"Carr is to be commended for the exceptionally high caliber of his analysis and his suggestive insights into transcendental phenomenology and this much-neglected problem"—(*LJ*).

Cassirer, Ernst, and others, Eds. Renaissance Philosophy of Man. Sel. trans. from Petrarca and others. *Univ. of Chicago Press* 1948 $12.50 Phoenix Bks. pap. $3.45

Castaneda, Hector-Neri, and George Nakhnikian, Eds. Morality and the Language of Conduct. *Wayne State Univ. Press* 1962 pap. $4.95

This is a collection of nine essays by contemporary American philosophers that have to do with problems in moral judgments. "The introductory essay on 'Recent Conceptions of Morality' by William K. Frankena is especially helpful in giving the reader his bearings in the terra incognita of modern moral philosophy. . . . While clearly intended for the specialist, this book will yield much that is of value to the diligent layman."

Castell, Alburey. Introduction to Modern Philosophy. *Macmillan* 3rd ed. 1975 $9.75

Caton, Charles E., Ed. Philosophy and Ordinary Language. *Univ. of Illinois Press* Illini Bks. 1963 pap. $1.95

An anthology presenting 12 essays on language by philosophers of the movement which has come to be known as "ordinary-language" philosophy. The need for such a collection seems especially pressing in view of the fact that the distinguishing characteristic of this group of analytic philosophers is their taking special and systematic account of the role played by ordinary language in the genesis and resolution of philosophical problems.

Cioran, E. M. THE TEMPTATION TO EXIST. Trans. by Richard Howard; introd. by Susan Sontag *Quadrangle Bks.* 1968 pap. $2.95

A well-known French-Rumanian essayist "examines the existential themes of nationalism, death, and religion with the depth and imagination of both philosopher and poet. He is an interesting writer, and his presentation is often as illuminating as his ideas"—*(LJ)*.

Collins, James. INTERPRETING MODERN PHILOSOPHY. *Princeton Univ. Press* 1972 $14.00 pap. $7.50

"A tightly reasoned and well-documented study which does illuminate the methodology and epistemology of history of modern philosophy"—*(Choice)*.

Copleston, Frederick C. CONTEMPORARY PHILOSOPHY: Studies of Logical Positivism and Existentialism. *Paulist-Newman Press* 1956 pap. 1972 $4.25

Coreth, Emerich. METAPHYSICS. Trans. and ed. by Joseph Donceel; critique by Bernard J. F. Lonergan. 1968. *Seabury Press* $4.95 pap. 1972 $4.95

Dresden, Sam. HUMANISM IN THE RENAISSANCE. Trans. from the French. *McGraw-Hill* 1968 (orig.) pap. $2.45

A professor of French literature at the University of Leyden, the author is presented in "a crystalline translation"—*(PW)*.

Ewing, A. C. IDEALISM: A Critical Survey. 1934. *Harper* (Barnes & Noble) $20.00

"This book evaluates and, through criticism, reaches some positive conclusions regarding the characteristic doctrines of the idealism which dominated philosophy during the last century. The author takes an uncommon approach in seeking to combine realism with a greater appreciation of views which emphasize the unity and rationality of the universe"—(Publisher's catalog).

Ferrater Mora, José María. PHILOSOPHY TODAY. *Columbia* 1960 $7.50

Fingarette, Herbert. ON RESPONSIBILITY. *Basic Bks.* 1967 $5.00

Mr. Fingarette "analyzes responsibility in terms of care, concern, acceptance, commitment, choice, and 'the creativity in choice.' He discusses the 'forms of life,' that is, forms 'socially given' and 'socially realized,' which 'constitute the form and content of responsibility.' His questions are clear and challenging; his answers, although fertile, are less clear and less well organized"—*(LJ)*.

THE SELF IN TRANSFORMATION: Psychoanalysis, Philosophy and the Life of the Spirit. *Harper* Torchbks. pap. 1963 $3.25

This is a penetrating study of many relationships from an essentially 'existential' point of view. For the greater part "the volume is a high-powered microscope used by a brilliant philosopher to bring profound illumination into psychoanalysis—not only to its basic theoretical underpinnings, but to its relationships in the whole scheme of man's being"; not only required reading for specialists but of great value to the informed layman.

Frankel, Charles, Ed. THE GOLDEN AGE OF AMERICAN PHILOSOPHY. *Braziller* 1960 $8.50. Selections from the works of 9 philosophers who wrote in the period between the Civil War and the Great Depression.

French, Peter A. INDIVIDUAL AND COLLECTIVE RESPONSIBILITY: Massacre at My Lai. *Schenkman* 1973 $2.95

(Ed.). CONSCIENTIOUS ACTIONS: The Revelations of the Pentagon Papers. *Schenkman* 1974 $2.95

Friedman, Maurice, Ed. THE WORLDS OF EXISTENTIALISM: A Critical Reader. *Random* 1964 $12.50

"A lively introduction. . . . There is no book of introductory readings that is so versatile, cosmopolitan and exhaustive. . . . Recommended generally"—*(LJ)*.

Gardiner, Patrick, Ed. NINETEENTH CENTURY PHILOSOPHERS. *Macmillan* (Free Press) 1969 pap. $3.95

Gay, Peter. THE ENLIGHTENMENT: An Interpretation. *Knopf* 2 vols. Vol. 1 The Rise of Modern Paganism (1966) $10.95 Vol. 2 The Science of Freedom (1969) $10.00; *Random* Vintage Bks. Vol. 1 1968 pap. $2.95

"Mr. Gay's eloquence and drive and immense good humor cannot help but draw one into what is unquestionably an intellectually important reinterpretation of the Enlightenment and of the genesis and significance of the three-generation 'little flock of philosophers' . . . who gave the 18th century its unique intellectual flavor and fervor. Mr. Gay, a professor of history at Columbia, argues that it was unique and delimitable; in effect, he argues that there was an Enlightenment, and that its convergent rationalism, critical skepticism and anticlericalism marked the birth of modern thought"—(Eliot Fremont-Smith, in the *N.Y. Times*). Winner of the 1967 National Book Award for History and Biography.

THE PARTY OF HUMANITY: Essays in the French Enlightenment. *Knopf* 1963 $7.95

"Professor Gay is an enthusiastic champion of Voltaire, Rousseau, Diderot, and the other members of that energetic band of philosophers and men of letters. He expounds their ideas with skill and defends them with spirit against detractors"—(LJ).

Gill, Jerry H., Ed. PHILOSOPHY TODAY. *Macmillan* 3 nos. 1968–1970 pap. each $1.95

Hancock, Roger N. TWENTIETH CENTURY ETHICS. *Columbia* 1974 $10.00

"This book surveys the main types of 20th century Anglo-American metaethical theories, questions the rigid separation of metaethics from normative ethics, and defends a naturalistic metaethics"—(LJ).

Harman, Gilbert, Ed. ON NOAM CHOMSKY: Critical Essays. *Doubleday* 1974 pap. $5.95

"This collection of essays by philosophers, psychologists, and an anthropologist treats methodological issues, rationalism and the theory of innate ideas, and questions of syntax and semantics"—(LJ).

Heiss, Robert. HEGEL, KIERKEGAARD, MARX. *Delacorte* 1975 $12.50 pap. $3.25

Heiss "usefully illuminates the dialectic in the voluminous writings of three major 19th century philosophers"—(LJ).

Hirst, R. J., Ed. PERCEPTION AND THE EXTERNAL WORLD. Problem of Philosophy Ser. *Macmillan* (orig.) 1965 pap. $1.95

This "treats as the main problems of perception the study of its nature and of the processes involved in it, and the investigation of 'how far, if at all, it can be regarded as a true source of knowledge about the world.' . . . The 23 selections, from 5 historic thinkers and 12 20th-century philosophers, are excellently chosen"—(LJ). Bibliography.

Höffding, Harald. A HISTORY OF MODERN PHILOSOPHY. 1900. Trans. by B. E. Meyer *Dover* 2 vols. 1955 Vol. 1 Renaissance to Rousseau Vol. 2 Kant to German Philosophers of 1850–1880 pap. each $4.00; *Peter Smith* 2 vols. 1962 $12.00. By the great Danish historian of modern philosophy.

Hook, Sidney. THE QUEST FOR BEING. 1961. *Greenwood* 1971 $12.75

In presenting his philosophy of naturalistic humanism, this Professor of Philosophy at New York University "attributes the religious renaissance of our time to an irrational movement in modern thought, triggered by a loss of nerve in the face of present-day social and political crises."

(Ed.). NEW YORK UNIVERSITY INSTITUTE OF PHILOSOPHY SYMPOSIA. Art and Philosophy *New York Univ. Press* $9.00; Determinism and Freedom in the Age of Modern Science *New York Univ. Press* $8.00; *Macmillan* pap. $1.50; Dimensions of Mind *New York Univ. Press* $8.50; *Macmillan* pap. $1.50; Human Values and Economic Policy *New York Univ. Press* 1967 $8.50; Law and Philosophy *New York Univ. Press* $9.40; Philosophy and History *New York Univ. Press* $9.50; Psychoanalysis, Scientific Method, and Philosophy *New York Univ. Press* $10.00; Religious Experience and Truth *New York Univ. Press* $9.50

Hospers, John. HUMAN CONDUCT: Problems of Ethics. *Harcourt* 1972 $6.95

Huxley, Julian, Ed. THE HUMANIST FRAME. 1961. *Bks. for Libraries* 1972 $16.25

Sir Julian called on 25 notable humanists, chiefly English, for essays on the implications of the new "Evolutionary Humanism," which promises to integrate all human activities and bridge ideological, and, even, political gaps. The level of the essays is generally high and their appeal will be to students and more serious readers.

Joad, Cyril E. M. Introduction to Modern Philosophy. *Oxford* 1924 $2.50

Kaplan, Abraham. The New World of Philosophy. *Random* 1961 pap. $2.95

Abraham Kaplan of the University of Michigan "achieves a triumph in these interpretive studies of some of the main movements of modern philosophic thought.... The writing is marked by a wit and pungency unwonted in philosophic prose"—(*N.Y. Times*).

Kaufmann, Walter. Critique of Religion and Philosophy. 1958. *Harper* pap. $3.75. A wise and witty book.

Existentialism from Dostoevsky to Sartre. *New Am. Lib.* Meridian Bks. 1975 pap. $3.95

Kenner, Hugh. The Counterfeiters: An Historical Comedy. *Indiana Univ. Press* 1968 $6.95

"Sketching the rise of modern man from his roots in 17th-Century empiricism, Mr. Kenner shows him trapped in a universe of objects and machines which begin to get the upper hand. And in charting the course of philosophical, linguistic, artistic, and technical counterfeiting, Mr. Kenner uses such unlike materials as Swift, Pope, Defoe, Buster Keaton . . . Andy Warhol [and others. The author] here displays his usual perspicacity and wit"—(*LJ*). Mr. Kenner is Professor of English at The Johns Hopkins University.

Kiralyfalvi, Bela. The Aesthetics of Gyorgy Lukács. *Princeton Univ. Press* 1975 $9.00

This is "the first monograph in English devoted wholly to 'The Specific Nature of Aesthetics' (1963)"—(*LJ*).

Knight, Alice Valle. The Meaning of Teilhard de Chardin: A Primer. *Devin-Adair* 1974 $7.50 pap. $3.95

Knight, Isabel F. The Geometric Spirit: The Abbé de Condillac and the French Enlightenment. *Yale Univ. Press* 1968 $15.00

Mrs. Knight, of the History Department of Pennsylvania State University, "shows Condillac as a political conservative seeking 'a wiser more humane version of the Ancien Régime.' . . . For a long time this will be an important book for the study of the whole enlightenment, not merely of Condillac"—(*LJ*). Contains an index and annotated bibliography.

Koch, Adrienne, Ed. Philosophy for a Time of Crisis: An Interpretation with Key Writings by Fifteen Great Modern Thinkers. *Dutton* 1959 pap. $1.95. A vigorous defense of the Western liberal tradition.

Kolakowski, Leszek. Toward a Marxist Humanism: Essays on the Left Today. Trans. from the Polish by Jane Peel *Grove* 1968 pap. $2.40

"With considerable justice the publisher calls this book one of the most important philosophical statements to break through the Iron Curtain.... Kolakowski's thrust, explained in his title, progresses in a series of thoroughly reasoned essays which result, in effect, in a basic revision of 'Marxism' along lines of individual freedom"—(*PW*).

Koster, Donald. Transcendentalism in America. *Twayne* 1975 $7.50

This book "traces the background and influence [of transcendentalism], examines its spread in this country, and investigates at length the positions held by its chief exponents Emerson, Thoreau, Whitman"—(*LJ*).

Lee, Edward N., and Maurice Mandelbaum, Eds. Phenomenology and Existentialism. *Johns Hopkins Press* 1967 $13.50 pap. $2.95

The editors, both professors of philosophy at Johns Hopkins University, "show how continental philosophers are dealing with problems that occupy their English-speaking counterparts" in this collection of lectures delivered at Johns Hopkins in the spring of 1966. "The volume deserves to be available in every good academic library and in the larger public collections"—(*LJ*).

Levi, Albert William. Philosophy and the Modern World. 1959. *Peter Smith* $10.00

Lovejoy, Arthur O. The Thirteen Pragmatisms and Other Essays. *Johns Hopkins Press* 1963 $13.50. The nine essays deal with pragmatism in relation to realism, theology and materialism.

Mack, Mary Peter, Ed. A Bentham Reader: Selections. *Pegasus* 1969 pap. $2.95

Mandelbaum, Maurice. History, Man, and Reason: A Study in Nineteenth-Century Thought. *Johns Hopkins Press* 1971 $16.50 pap. $3.95

Manuel, Frank E., Ed. THE ENLIGHTENMENT. *Prentice-Hall* 1965 $4.95 pap. $2.95; *Peter Smith* $5.25

"A selection of popular writings from the Enlightenment [that] . . . emphasize the natural and social sciences and admirably summarize the essence of that time. [It] will be useful in courses in intellectual history and in the history of philosophy"—(*LJ*).

Martin, Bernard. GREAT TWENTIETH-CENTURY JEWISH PHILOSOPHERS: Buber, Rosenzweig and Sestov. *Macmillan* 1969 $8.95 pap. $2.95

Mead, George Herbert. MOVEMENTS OF THOUGHT IN THE NINETEENTH CENTURY. Ed. by Merritt H. Moore. *Univ. of Chicago Press* 1936 $15.00 pap. $3.45. This treats romanticism, utilitarianism, mechanism, realism and pragmatism.

Montague, Richard. FORMAL PHILOSOPHY: Selected Papers of Richard Montague. Ed. by R. Thomason *Yale* 1974 $12.00

These essays "develop the theory that the syntax and semantics of natural languages—specifically English—are part of mathematics and hence can be formalized"—(Publisher's note).

Morris, Bertram. PHILOSOPHICAL ASPECTS OF CULTURE. *Kent State Univ. Press* (Antioch Press) 1961 $7.00

This is an ambitious book in which the author, a Professor of Philosophy at the University of Colorado, attempts, and to a large extent, succeeds in formulating a new synthesis by which men can evaluate the world in which they live.

Mourant, John A., and others. ESSAYS IN PHILOSOPHY. *Pennsylvania State Univ. Press* 1962 $8.50

The authors of these essays, members of the Philosophy Department of the Pennsylvania State University, dissatisfied with the trend of American thinking, have turned once more to the classical tradition of Western philosophy in an effort to understand, in terms of the Western spirit, the various expressions of human life and history.

Muirhead, John Henry, Ed. CONTEMPORARY BRITISH PHILOSOPHY. *Humanities Press* 1924–1926 2 vols. in 1 1953 $13.75

Naess, Arne. FOUR MODERN PHILOSOPHERS: Carnap, Wittgenstein, Heidegger, Sartre. Trans. from the Norwegian by Alastair Hannay *Univ. of Chicago Press* 1968 $11.50

The professor of philosophy at the University of Oslo distinguishes between Carnap and Wittgenstein's philosophy of linguistics and Sartre and Heidegger's philosophy of existentialism. He includes biographical information.

Northrup, F. S. C. MAN, NATURE AND GOD: A Quest for Life's Meaning. *Simon & Schuster* Trident Press 1962 $4.50 Touchstone-Clarion Bks. 1972 pap. $2.95. The eminent philosopher discusses his intellectual adventures through various disciplines with such great modern thinkers as Whitehead, Hocking, Einstein and Wittgenstein and others. His autobiography of ideas "makes for fascinating, even inspiring reading."

Parrington, Vernon L. MAIN CURRENTS IN AMERICAN THOUGHT. *Harcourt* 3 vols. 1954 Vol. 1 The Colonial Mind (1620–1800) Vol. 2 Romantic Revolution in America (1800–1860) Harvest Bks. pap. each $3.45 Vol. 3 Beginnings of Critical Realism in America (1860–1920) Harbinger Bks. pap. $3.85

Patka, Frederick. EXISTENTIALIST THINKERS AND THOUGHT. 1962. *Citadel Press* pap. $2.45

Philipson, Morris, Ed. AESTHETICS TODAY: Selected Readings. *Peter Smith* $6.50; *New Am. Lib.* Meridian Bks. 1961 pap. $3.95. Essays by "art historians, a music critic, social scientists, and at least one theologian."

Pols, Edward. THE RECOGNITION OF REASON. *Southern Illinois Univ. Press* 1963 $6.00

"Professor Pols's primary thesis is that the present revolutionary situation in philosophy demands a new and radical beginning. . . . His peculiar task is the identification and validation of reason as an autonomous activity. To do this he develops his own concepts, among which are 'subjective dynamism,' 'transformation of subjectivity,' and, most importantly, 'radically originative reflection' "—(*LJ*). Bibliography.

Pompa, Leon. VICO: A Study of the "New Science." *Cambridge* 1975 $14.95

"Pompa's study supplies a much needed analytic introduction to and interpretation of the main philosophical theories of Vico's somewhat obscure and confused *New Science*"—(*LJ*).

Prosch, Harry. THE GENESIS OF TWENTIETH CENTURY PHILOSOPHY: The Evolution of Thought from Copernicus to the Present. 1964. *Apollo* 1972 $2.95

Reck, Andrew J. THE NEW AMERICAN PHILOSOPHERS: An Exploration of Thought Since World War II. *Louisiana State Univ. Press* 1968 $8.95; *Dell* pap. $2.65

> The new American philosophers are C. I. Lewis, Stephen Pepper, Brand Blanshard, Ernest Nagel, John Herman Randall, Jr., Justus Buchler, Sidney Hook, F. C. S. Northrop, James Kern Feibleman, John Wild, Charles Hartshorne and Paul Weiss. "What history will do with these men is not yet clear, but Professor Reck has declared himself at this point. The essays in the volume are of relatively equal length, survey the basic positions of each of the writers, never enter into long criticism and analysis"—(LJ).

Reese, William L. ASCENT FROM BELOW: An Introduction to Philosophical Inquiry. *Houghton* 1959 $10.95. Tries to clarify basic problems such as those concerning freedom, value, beauty and ethics.

Reinhardt, Kurt F. THE EXISTENTIALIST REVOLT. 1952. *Ungar* 2nd ed. 1960 $8.50 pap. $3.75. Covers themes and phases in the work of Kierkegaard, Nietzsche, Heidegger, Jaspers, Sartre, Marcel.

Salk, James. THE SURVIVAL OF THE WEST. *Harper* 1973 $6.95

Schneider, Herbert W. A HISTORY OF AMERICAN PHILOSOPHY. *Columbia* 1946 2nd ed. 1963 $15.00 pap. $7.50. A companion volume is Joseph L. Blau's "American Philosophic Addresses 1700–1900" (*Columbia* 1946 $15.00).

Smith, John E. THE SPIRIT OF AMERICAN PHILOSOPHY. *Oxford* 1963 Galaxy Bks. pap. $2.95

Smith, Thomas V., and Marjorie Grene, Eds. PHILOSOPHERS SPEAK FOR THEMSELVES: Berkeley, Hume, and Kant. *Univ. of Chicago Press* Phoenix Bks. 1957 pap. $3.95

> PHILOSOPHERS SPEAK FOR THEMSELVES: Descartes to Locke. *Univ. of Chicago Press* Phoenix Bks. 1957 $11.50 pap. $3.45

Sontag, Frederick. THE EXISTENTIALIST PROLEGOMENA. *Univ. of Chicago Press* 1969 $9.00

> "In this truly outstanding and significant work, Professor Sontag of Pomona College and Claremont Graduate School has taken his point of departure from Kant's *Prolegomena to Any Future Metaphysics*"—(LJ). He treats mainly Kierkegaard, Heidegger, Wittgenstein.

Sosa, Ernest, Comp. CAUSATION AND CONDITIONALS. *Oxford* 1975 pap. $4.95

Stich, Stephen P., Comp. INNATE IDEAS. *Univ. of California Press* 1975 $12.50

> "The work will be of value for teachers and students, as well as researchers who want to find these materials in one place"—(Choice).

Teilhard de Chardin, Pierre. TOWARD THE FUTURE. Trans. by René Hague *Harcourt* 1975 $6.95

> "These 14 essays (written between 1929 and 1954) evoke the progressive unification of mankind, intensification of our collective consiousness, and the movement toward the convergent structure of evolution seeking its cosmic center"—(LJ).

Thayer, H. S. MEANING AND ACTION: A Critical History of Pragmatism. *Bobbs* Lib. Arts 1968 $10.00

Thevenaz, Pierre. WHAT IS PHENOMENOLOGY? AND OTHER ESSAYS. Trans. and ed. with introd. by James M. Edie *Quadrangle Bks.* 1962 pap. $2.45

> Phenomenology as a minor but lively current of thought was first stated 50 years ago by Husserl, a Jewish mathematician who died in oblivion in Nazi Germany. It is a science of human experience, a study of phenomena called "essences," and was developed through Heidegger and Sartre.

Tomlin, E. W. F. THE WESTERN PHILOSOPHERS. *Harper* 1963 Perenn. Lob. pap. $1.25

Tymieniecka, Anna-Teresa. PHENOMENOLOGY AND SCIENCE IN CONTEMPORARY EUROPEAN THOUGHT. Fwd. by I. M. Bochenski *Polish Institute of Arts & Sciences in America* (59 E. 66 St., New York, N.Y. 10021) 1962 $2.50. This is a survey of the European point of view on phenomenology, which has now become an important movement (*see Thevenaz, above*). Its impact has been felt on such disparate fields as psychotherapy, anthropology and art criticism.

Unger, Peter. IGNORANCE: A Case For Skepticism. *Oxford* 1975 $19.50

White, Alan R. MODAL THINKING. *Cornell Univ. Press* 1975 $12.50

White, Morton Gabriel. SCIENCE AND SENTIMENT IN AMERICA: Philosophical Thought from Jonathan Edwards to John Dewey. *Oxford* 1972 $8.95

"An interpretive study of the major American philosophers from Edwards to Dewey, presenting the thesis of a strong dualistic tendency deeply ingrained in early American philosophy and interpreting this dualism both as a basis for an anti-intellectualism and as indicative of a concern to make philosophy relevant to all of the concern of civilization"—(*Choice*).

TOWARDS REUNION IN PHILOSOPHY. *Atheneum* 1963 pap. $1.65

"Possibly the best critical history of the important problems in the development of philosophy since the publication in 1912 of Bertrand Russell's 'The Problem of Philosophy' "—(*Harvard Law Review*).

(Ed.) THE AGE OF ANALYSIS: 20th Century Philosophers. Sel. with introd. and interpretive commentary. 1955. *New Am. Lib.* pap. $1.50

Wild, John. THE CHALLENGE OF EXISTENTIALISM. *Indiana Univ. Press* Midland Bks. 1955 pap. $2.50; *Peter Smith* $5.00

Wolff, R. PHILOSOPHY: A Modern Encounter. *Prentice-Hall* 1971 $11.95 pap. $6.75

Modern Philosophers

ERASMUS. 1466?–1536. *See Chapter 4, World Religions, this Volume.*

LUTHER, MARTIN. 1483–1546. *See Chapter 4, World Religions, this Volume.*

CALVIN, JOHN. 1509–1564. *See Chapter 4, World Religions, this Volume.*

BRUNO, GIORDANO. 1548–1600.

Bruno was born near Naples and was for a period a Dominican monk. He fled the order when he became disillusioned with Catholicism. Since Protestant tenets did not satisfy him either, he incurred the hostility of religious leaders throughout Europe and was constantly on the move, teaching for short periods at Paris, Oxford and Wittenberg. To escape persecution he fled to England, where he composed some of his most important works. His doctrine is relativist and pantheistic; influenced by Copernicus (*q.v.*), he formulated what is now known as the "cosmic" theory—God, in many forms but essentially One, pervades all things in the universe. In 1591 he returned to Venice where he was accused of heresy by the Inquisition and eventually burned to death. He influenced later philosophy greatly, especially that of Spinoza (*q.v.*) and Leibniz (*q.v.*).

THE EXPULSION OF THE TRIUMPHANT BEAST. Trans. by Arthur D. Imerti *Rutgers Univ. Press* 1964 $9.00. The first translation into English of one of his daring and heretical books.

HEROIC ENTHUSIASTS. Pt. I. Trans. by L. Williams. 1887. *Scholarly Press* $14.50. An ethical poem.

SELECTED WORKS. *Gordon Press* $30.00

THE ASH WEDNESDAY SUPPER. *Humanities Press* 1975 $12.00

Books about Bruno

The Renaissance Theory of Love: The Context of Giordano Bruno's *Eroici Furori*. By John Charles Nelson. *Columbia* 1958 $11.00. This aims to further the understanding of Bruno through an analysis of his major work "De Gli Eroici Furori."

Giordano Bruno and the Hermetic Tradition. By Frances A. Yates. *Univ. of Chicago Press* 1964 $12.50; *Random* pap. $2.45

"Miss Frances Yates's book is an important addition to our knowledge of Giordano Bruno. But it is even more important, I think, as a step toward understanding the unity of the sixteenth century, when the late Renaissance turned into the scientific revolution"— (J. Bronowski, in the *N.Y. Review of Books*).

The Infinite in Giordano Bruno. Ed. by Sidney Greenberg. *Octagon* 1971 $10.50

The Cosmology of Giordano Bruno. By Paul-Henri Michel. Trans. from the French by R. E. W. Maddison *Cornell Univ. Press* 1973 $13.50

BACON, FRANCIS, Baron Verulam, Viscount St. Albans. 1561–1626.

Sir Francis Bacon, son of the Lord Keeper of England's Great Seal, lived a stormy political life in the reigns of Elizabeth I and James I. Lawyer and member of Parliament, he eventually became

Lord Chancellor for James I, but a trial for bribery ultimately stripped him of office. He was fined £40,000, imprisoned in the Tower of London for a short time and was banished from court and public office for the remainder of his life. During his exile "he commenced a digest of the laws of England, a history of England under the princes of the House of Tudor, a body of natural history, a philosophical romance, and a Latin translation of *The Advancement of Learning*, with seven new parts added, including *The New Atlantis*"—(Jack Valenti, in *SR*). In 1626, Bacon's intellectual curiosity caused his death when he caught pneumonia stuffing a hen with snow in a refrigeration experiment.

Bacon's philosophy is founded upon empiricism, the doctrine that the origin of knowledge is either experience or experiment. He is called "the Father of Experimental Philosophy" because, rejecting Aristotle, he was the first to systematize and popularize the experimental method. He owes his important place in the history of thought to his use of his inductive method. "The Advancement of Learning" is his survey of the purpose and method of his whole work. "The Novum Organum," or "Indications Concerning the Interpretation of Nature," is the most important expression of his fundamental principles. He wrote all his important works in Latin, as he believed the Latin tongue would outlive the English and would be the international tongue of learning. The greatest edition of Bacon's complete works is that editied by James Spedding, again in print. (In the past certain works of Shakespeare have sometimes been attributed to Bacon, but with little support from serious modern scholars.)

THE WORKS OF FRANCIS BACON. Ed. by James Spedding and others. 1857–74. *Adler's* 14 vols. set $475.00; *Scholarly Press* 1968 14 vols. set $225.00; *Somerset Pubs.* 14 vols. set $375.00

THE ADVANCEMENT OF LEARNING. 1605. Ed. by G. W. Kitchin; introd. by Arthur Johnson *Rowman* 1973 $6.50 pap. $3.00; ed. by Arthur Johnson *Oxford* 1974 $11.25; (and "The New Atlantis") World's Class. 1938. $5.00

THE NEW ORGANON. 1620. Ed. by Fulton H. Anderson *Bobbs* Lib. Arts 1960 $5.00 pap. $1.95

Books about Bacon

Francis Bacon on Communication and Rhetoric. By Karl R. Wallace. *Univ. of North Carolina Press* 1943 $7.50

The Philosophy of Francis Bacon. By Fulton H. Anderson. 1948. *Octagon* 1970 $12.00

Francis Bacon: The Temper of a Man. By Catherine Drinker Bowen. *Little* 1963 $7.50 pap. $1.95

"The portrait that the author presents here is both more appealing and more perceptive than usual. . . . It is a tribute not only to genius . . . but to the quality of his genius. Mrs. Bowen puts her finger on the qualities of mind which were so prophetic of the future in him: his preoccupation with things, rather than with useless systems of thought, his careful observation of objects and of natural phenomena; his insistence on the importance of the mechanical, the value he set on utility and experimentation for the benefit of man, the practical effects of men's knowledge"—(*N.Y. Times*).

Sir Francis Bacon. By A. Wigfall Green. English Authors Ser. *Twayne Pub.* 1966 $6.50

The discussions in this book are arranged according to the genres which Bacon wrote in, rather than the order in which he wrote. "The sole purpose of this study is to whet the appetite of the student to read every written word of this man of the Renaissance who took all knowledge to be his province and who, like the man of the modern world, would know all and be all"—(Author's preface).

The Philosophy of Francis Bacon. By Benjamin Farrington. *Univ. of Chicago Press* 1967 pap. $1.95

Francis Bacon: From Magic to Science. By P. Rossi. Trans. by Sacha Rabinovitch *Univ. of Chicago Press* 1968 $8.00

Essential Articles for the Study of Francis Bacon. Ed. by Brian Vickers. *Shoe String Press* 1969 $8.50

Bacon. By Charles Williams. *Folcroft* 1973 $20.00

Bacon. By J. M. Patrick. *British Bk. Centre* $3.95 pap. $1.50

Francis Bacon: Discovery and the Art of Discourse. By Lisa Jardine. *Cambridge* 1975 $15.50

See also Chapter 15, Essays and Criticism, Reader's Adviser, *Vol. I.*

HOBBES, THOMAS. 1588–1679.

Hobbes, the first English philosopher to challenge theological orthodoxy, developed a striking system of materialism. He is better known, however, for his teaching concerning ethics and politics. Like Bacon, he drew his theories from sensory observation. During his earlier years he traveled in Europe. In 1640 he left England again in fear of the Parliament and lived among the philosophers in Paris. "Leviathan," his great defense of the authoritarian state, "turned even the exiled Royalists against him because of its irreligion. Hobbes fled for his life back to London, where Parliament chose to let him alone."

A fundamental thesis of the "Leviathan" is that in their natural state, the lives of men are "solitary, poor, nasty, brutish, and short," a fact which "induces them to put voluntary restraint upon themselves in the common interest. This self-denying ordinance is the social covenant which ends the State of Nature and inaugurates the Civil State or Commonwealth," said Hobbes. On the Restoration, Hobbes became friendly with Charles II. When he was 84 he wrote a humorous autobiography in Latin verse. He translated "The Iliad" and "The Odyssey" a few years before his death. The studies by George C. Robertson (1886), John Laird (1934) and Clarence D. Thorpe (1940) have recently been reprinted by *Reprint House International* (Robertson) and *Russell & Russell* (both the others).

LEVIATHAN. 1651. Ed. by Herbert W. Sneider *Bobbs* Lib. Arts 1958 $6.00 pap. $2.00; ed. by Michael Oakeshott *Dutton* Everyman's 1973 $3.95; *Macmillan* Collier Bks. 1962 pap. $1.25; repr. of 1751 ed. *Oxford* $6.50; ed. by Crawford B. MacPherson *Penguin* 1975 pap. $5.95; *Peter Smith* $4.95; ed. by Francis Randall *Simon & Schuster* (Washington Square) 1969 pap. $.90

MAN (1658) and CITIZEN (1651). Ed. by Bernard Gert *Doubleday* Anchor Bks. 1972 pap. $2.95; *Peter Smith* $6.00

BEHEMOTH: The History of the Causes of the Civil War in England. 1679. *Burt Franklin* 1963 $16.50

Books about Hobbes

Hobbes. By Sir Leslie Stephen. *Univ. of Michigan Press* 1961 Ann Arbor Bks. pap. $1.75

Idea and Essence in the Philosophies of Hobbes and Spinoza. By Albert G. A. Balz. 1918. *AMS Press* $7.50

The Aesthetic Theory of Thomas Hobbes. By Clarence D. Thorpe. 1926. *Russell & Russell* 1964 $8.50

The Political Philosophy of Hobbes: Its Basis and Its Genesis. By Leo Strauss. Trans. from the German by Elsa M. Sinclair *Univ. of Chicago Press* 1952 $6.00 Phoenix Bks. 1963 pap. $2.25

The Political Philosophy of Hobbes: His Theory of Obligation. By Howard Warrender. *Oxford* 1957 $10.25

Hobbes. By T. E. Jessop. 1961. *British Bk. Centre* $3.95 pap. $1.50

The Political Theory of Possessive Individualism: Hobbes to Locke. By C. B. Macpherson. *Oxford* 1962 $10.25 pap. $3.25

Hobbes' Science of Politics. By M. M. Goldsmith. *Columbia* 1966 $10.00

A Columbia assistant professor "sees in the work of the 17th-century philosopher much meaning for today's social and political world. Hobbes developed a general philosophical system, based on the deductive method of physical inquiry, in which all social and political order, to be effective, must be based on the natural physical order. For men to live in productive, peaceful harmony with one another, the commonwealth he posited, among other things, should be based on a monarchy in which all citizens would have contractually placed their safety and well-being under the power of a sovereign. The sovereign's authority (and responsibility) would be complete. Mr. Goldsmith has carefully reviewed primary as well as secondary sources for this study"—(*LJ*).

Hobbes's System of Ideas. By J. W. N. Watkins. *Hillary House* 1965 2nd ed. 1973 $9.00 pap. $5.00

The Anatomy of Leviathan. By F. S. McNeilly. *St. Martin's* 1968 $11.95

The Logic of Leviathan: The Moral and Political Theory of Thomas Hobbes. By David P. Gauthier. *Oxford* 1969 $7.75

Hobbes on Civil Association. By Michael Oakeshott. *Univ. of California Press* 1975 $8.50

DESCARTES, RENÉ. 1596–1650.

Descartes, a Frenchman, is the "Father of Modern Philosophy" by universal consent. His system of philosophy is called "Cartesian," from the Latinized form of his name Cartesius. It was Descartes who formulated the memorable statement, "*Cogito, ergo sum*," "I think; therefore I am."

"Like Bacon, Descartes was convinced that the traditional Aristotelian logic which he had been taught in school was inadequate as a method of demonstration; at best it was good only for pedagogical purposes, for displaying what had already been demonstrated to be true. Unlike Bacon, however, Descartes found the key to his new method in the procedures of mathematics rather than those of the empirical sciences"—(Francis H. Parker). He became interested in mathematics and studied law. After a period of military service, he is said to have had a mystical experience which revealed a new thought system to him. "He conceived in a flash of inspiration the outlines of what he believed to be an entirely new science of nature and thought. An experience very similar to that which befell Archimedes, when he exclaimed 'Eureka' ('I have found it!'), followed. This moment of intense exhilaration in turn gave place to a series of prophetic dreams"—(E. W. F. Tomlin).

His "Discourse on Method" was written in 1637. It was his systematization of how one arrives at truth. "The Method which Descartes proposed to apply to every sphere of knowledge was that which was best exemplified in analytical geometry. The stages and procedure used in a geometrical problem could surely be made to yield results of equal certitude in the sphere of metaphysics, logic, and ethics"—(Tomlin). He established four rules to follow in the pursuit of truth. "The first rule is to accept nothing except what is so clear and distinct that it connot be doubted: . . . [I think; therefore I am.] The second and third rules say that a problem must be broken up into parts and the parts arranged in a deductive order beginning with what is axiomatically true"—(Parker). The last rule is to review all material that is being examined so that nothing has been left out.

Although solitary by inclination, Descartes knew many of the great thinkers and their royal patrons of his day—late in his life he tutored Queen Christina of Sweden in the New Philosophy. His influence was vast in the thought of his time and in the centuries following. Earlier studies by Norman K. Smith (1902) and Alexander B. Gibson (1932) have recently been reprinted by *Russell & Russell*.

PHILOSOPHICAL WORKS. Trans. by E. S. Haldane and G. R. T. Ross. *Cambridge* 2 vols. Vol. I $17.95 pap. $4.95 Vol. 2 $15.00 pap. $4.95

THE PHILOSOPHICAL WRITINGS. *Random* (Modern Lib.) $3.95; *Bobbs* Lib. Arts 1971 $4.75

PHILOSOPHICAL ESSAYS. Trans. by L. J. Lafleur. *Bobbs* Lib. Arts $5.00 pap. $2.25

DISCOURSE ON METHOD (1637); MEDITATIONS ON THE FIRST PHILOSOPHY (1641); and PRINCIPLES OF PHILOSOPHY (1644). Trans. by J. Veitch 1850. *Dutton* Everyman's $3.95

DISCOURSE ON METHOD AND MEDITATIONS. (In "The Rationalists") *Doubleday* Dolphin Bks. 1962 pap. $2.50

DISCOURSE ON METHOD. Trans. by L. J. Lafleur *Bobbs* Lib. Arts 1956 pap. $.75; trans. by John Veitch *Open Court* (abr.) $2.25 pap. $1.25; trans. by Arthur Wollasten *Penguin* 1968 pap. $1.25

DISCOURSE OF METHOD FOR THE WELL GUIDING OF REASON. 1966. *Humanities Press* (Fernhill) $15.50

DISCOURSE ON METHOD, OPTICS, GEOMETRY, AND METEOROLOGY. Trans. by P. Olscamp *Bobbs* Lib. Arts 1965 $7.50 pap. $5.00

MEDITATIONS AND SELECTIONS FROM THE PRINCIPLES OF RENÉ DESCARTES. Trans. by John Veitch *Open Court* 1950 1966 $6.00 pap. $1.25

MEDITATIONS. Trans. by L. J. Lafleur *Bobbs* Lib. Arts 1951 pap. $.85 (and "Discourses on Method") 1960 pap. $1.25

RULES FOR THE DIRECTION OF THE MIND. Trans. by L. J. Lafleur *Bobbs* Lib. Arts pap. $2.00

LA GÉOMÉTRIE (The Geometry). 1637. Trans. by D. E. Smith and M. L. Latham 1925. *Dover* pap. $3.00; French-English ed. trans. by Latham and Smith *Open Court* $10.00; *Peter Smith* $4.50

Books about Descartes

The Principles of Descartes' Philosophy. By Benedictus de Spinoza. Trans. from the Latin by Halbert Hains Britan *Open Court* 1974 pap. $2.95

The Dream of Descartes. By Jacques Maritain. *Kennikat* 1945 $7.50

Descartes and the Modern Mind. By Albert G. A. Balz. *Shoe String Press* 1952 1967 $12.50. Descartes seen as the first of the modern philosophers in a scholarly work by the Corcoran Professor of Philosophy at the University of Virginia.

Bibliographia Cartesiana: A Critical Guide to the Descartes Literature. By Gregor Sebba. *Heinman* 1964 $25.00

The Metaphysics of Descartes: A Study of the Meditations. By L. J. Beck. *Oxford* 1965 $8.50

From Beast Machine to Man Machine. By Leonora Rosenfield. *Octagon* 1967 $14.50
Descartes: A Study of His Philosophy. By Anthony Kenny. *Random* (orig.) 1968 pap. $2.95;
  Peter Smith $4.50
Descartes: A Collection of Critical Essays. Ed. by Willis Doney. 1974. *Univ. of Notre Dame Press*
  $8.95 pap. $3.45
Descartes. By S. V. Keeling. *Oxford* 2nd ed. pap. $4.50
An Approach to Descartes' Meditations. By Frederick Brodie. *Humanities Press* 1970 $12.75
Cartesian Studies. Ed. by Ronald J. Butler. *Harper* (Barnes & Noble) 1972 $7.00
Descartes. By Jonathan Ree. *Universe Bks.* 1975 $8.50
  "Ree presents a nuanced and balanced evaluation of the whole of Descartes's works and
  affirms Descarte's right to the title of founder of the new philosophy which was to be carried
  on by Newton and later scientists"—(*LJ*).

PASCAL, BLAISE. 1623–1662. *See Chapter 4, World Religions, this Volume.*

SPINOZA, BARUCH (or BENEDICTUS de). 1632–1677.

Spinoza was a Spanish-Jewish philosopher born in Amsterdam, who renounced Judaism, was
excommunicated from his synagogue and spent most of his life in Holland. His romantic and
tragic career has made him one of the most beloved of the philosophers. Israel Zangwill in his
"Dreamers of the Ghetto" (1898, o.p.) has drawn a memorable portrait of Spinoza as "The Maker
of Lenses," a profession of his youth. The deep piety of Spinoza's mind won for him the title of
"God-intoxicated." He changed his name from Baruch to Benedictus, the Latin form of Baruch,
which means "blessed." He developed the Cartesian system of philosophy, bringing to it a
mathematical precision of thought which Descartes (*q.v.*) had lacked. "The Ethics" and other titles
were posthumously published.

Bertrand Russell says of Spinoza (in his "History of Western Philosophy"), that he "is the noblest
and most lovable of the great philosophers. . . . The problem for Spinoza is easier than it is for one
who has no belief in the ultimate goodness of the universe. Spinoza thinks that, if you see your
misfortunes as they are in reality, as part of the concatenation of causes stretching from the
beginning of time to the end, you will see that they are only misfortunes to you, not to the
universe, to which they are merely passing discords heightening an ultimate harmony."

THE CHIEF WORKS. Trans. by R. H. M. Elwes with a bibliog. note by Francesco
  Cordasco *Dover* 3rd ed. 2 vols. 1952 1955 pap. each $3.50; *Peter Smith* 2 vols. set
  $12.00

THE POLITICAL WORKS: The Tractatus Theologico-Politicus in part, and the Tractatus
  Politicus in full. Trans. and ed. by A. G. Wernham *Oxford* 1958 $13.75

EARLIER PHILOSOPHICAL WRITINGS. Trans. by F. A. Hayes *Bobbs* Lib. Arts $6.00 pap.
  $2.50

ETHICS (1677) and ON THE CORRECTION OF THE UNDERSTANDING (1687). Trans. by
  Andrew Boyle; introd. by T. S. Gregory *Dutton* Everyman's reissue 1955 $3.95

ETHICS. (And "The Improvement of Understanding") trans. by William H. White; ed.
  by James Gutman *Hafner* 1953 pap. $3.95

THE PRINCIPLES OF DESCARTES' PHILOSOPHY. 1663. Trans. from the Latin by Halbert H.
  Britan *Open Court* pap. $2.95

THE ETHICS. 1677. (In "The Rationalists") *Doubleday* Dolphin Bks. 1962 pap. $2.50

A SHORT TREATISE ON GOD, MAN, AND HIS WELL-BEING. Trans. and ed. by A. Wolf
  Russell & Russell 1963 $8.50

Books about Spinoza

Spinoza, Descartes, and Maimonides. By Leon Roth. 1924. *Russell & Russell* 1963 $5.75
Spinoza. By Stuart Hampshire. 1951. *Harper* (Barnes & Noble) 1961 $3.50; *Penguin* Pelican Bks.
  rev. ed. 1962 pap. $1.95
Spinoza's Critique of Religion. By Leo Strauss. *Schocken* 1965 $8.50
The Political Philosophy of Spinoza. By Robert J. McShea. *Columbia* 1968 $10.00
  "Mr. McShea, who is assistant professor of government at Boston University, persuasively
  shows how Spinoza's political thought 'is yet alive and relevant to our concerns' "—(*LJ*).
Spinoza and the Rise of Liberalism. By L. S. Feuer. *Peter Smith* $4.75
  "A masterful fusion of history, psychology and philosophy"—(*Nation*).
The Philosophy of Spinoza: Unfolding the Latent Processes of His Reasoning. By Harry
  Austryn Wolfson. *Schocken* 2 vols. 1969 $2.95

Spinoza. By Dan Levin. *McKay* 1970 $8.50

Spinoza's Theory of Truth. By Thomas C. Mark. *Columbia* 1972 $7.00

Spinoza: A Collection of Critical Essays. Ed. by Marjorie Grene. *Doubleday* 1973 pap. $4.95

Salvation from Despair: A Reappraisal of Spinoza's Philosophy. By Errol E. Harris. *Humanities Press* 1973 $24.00

Spinoza. By Karl Jaspers. Trans. from the German by Ralph Manheim; ed. by Hannah Arendt *Harcourt* 1974 pap. $2.95

Studies in Spinoza: Critical and Interpretive Essays. By S. Paul Kashap. *Univ. of California Press* 1974 $12.75 pap. $3.45

LOCKE, JOHN. 1632–1704.

The English rationalist philosopher, Locke, is the "Founder of Modern Psychology." Other philosophers before him were content to deal with ideas objectively. Locke regarded ideas subjectively, inquired into their origin, and examined the operations of the mind. He peered into reason itself, sought to define the nature and limitations of our understanding. How we come by knowledge was the great question that he tried to answer. Basic to his theories was the concept of the human mind as a *tabula rasa*, the blank slate on which all we learn and become is written by experience. His monumental "Essay on Human Understanding" is one of the most popular works of philosophy ever written. It attracted great attention when first published and passed through six editions in 14 years. It "was to furnish basic premises, not only for the coming eighteenth century Age of Reason and the deistic theology upon which many of its ideas were based, but also for the incipient Industrial Revolution with its rising entrepreneur class, and for political revolution in America." The first "Treatise of Civil Government" was written in answer to a work called "Patriarcha," in defense of the divine right of kings, by Sir Robert Filmer. Locke attacked the "divine right" tradition on rational grounds. His second treatise on government discusses the "state of nature," in which the individual can only take the law into his own hands. In a developed society this is impractical, and rational men must, by the will of the majority, enact laws for the protection of property and other individual rights—a philosophy, says Bertrand Russell, that was "on the whole adequate and useful until the industrial revolution." Santayana (*q.v.*) has said of Locke: "Father of psychology, father of the criticism of knowledge, father of theoretical liberalism, godfather at least of the American political system, of Voltaire and the Encyclopedia, at home he was the ancestor of that whole school of polite moderate opinion which can unite liberal Christianity with mechanical science and with psychological idealism."

Works. Reprint of the 1823 London edition. *Adler's* 10 vols. 1963 $300.00

The Educational Writings of John Locke. Ed. with introd. by James L. Axtell *Cambridge* 1968 $19.50

Essay Concerning Human Understanding. 1690. Ed. by A. C. Fraser 1894. *Dover* 2 vols. 1959 pap. each $4.50; *Dutton* 1909 Everyman's 2 vols. each $3.95; ed. by A. D. Woozley *New Am. Lib.* Meridian Bks. abr. pap. $4.95; ed. with an introd., critical apparatus and glossary by Peter H. Nidditch *Oxford* 1975 $39.50 abr. and ed. by A. S. Pringle-Pattison 1924 $4.95; ed. by Alexander C. Fraser *Peter Smith* 2 vols. set $12.50

Of the Conduct of the Understanding. Ed. by F. W. Garforth *Teachers College Press* $5.95 pap. $2.50

Essays on the Law of Nature. The Latin text with a trans., introd. and notes, together with transcripts of Locke's shorthand in his journal for 1676; ed. by W. von Leyden *Oxford* 1954 $6.50

Two Treatises of Government. 1690. Ed. by Peter Laslett *Cambridge* 1960 $19.50; *Macmillan* (Hafner) 1974 $2.95; *New Am. Lib.* pap. $1.95

This critical edition by a Fellow of Trinity College and Lecturer in History at Cambridge University is reconstituted from Locke's own corrected copy and set in its context in Locke's life and thought with the help of the Lovelace papers.

Two Treatises of Civil Government. *Dutton* Everyman's reissue 1953 $3.95; (with Robert Filmer's "Patrarchia") ed. by T. I. Cook *Macmillan* (Hafner) 1947 1956 pap. $2.95

Two Tracts on Government. Ed. by P. Abrams. *Cambridge* $11.50

Second Treatise of Civil Government, and Letter on Toleration. Ed. by John Wiedhofft Gough *Harper* (Barnes & Noble) 3rd ed. 1966 $7.50

SECOND TREATISE OF GOVERNMENT. Ed. by Thomas P. Peardon *Bobbs* Lib. Arts pap. $1.25

TREATISE OF CIVIL GOVERNMENT and A LETTER CONCERNING TOLERATION. Ed. by Charles L. Sherman. *Irvington Bks.* pap. $4.95

OF CIVIL GOVERNMENT, SECOND ESSAY. Introd. by Russell Kirk *Regnery* Gateway Eds. 1960 pap. $.90

SEVERAL PAPERS RELATING TO MONEY, INTEREST AND TRADE. *Kelley* 1968 $15.00

A LETTER CONCERNING TOLERATION. Ed. by P. Romanell *Bobbs* Lib. Arts pap. $1.75

THE REASONABLENESS OF CHRISTIANITY, A DISCOURSE OF MIRACLES and part of A THIRD LETTER CONCERNING TOLERATION. Ed. and abr. with introd. by I. T. Ramsey *Stanford Univ. Press* 1958 pap. $1.45

ON EDUCATION. Ed. by P. Gay *Teachers College Press* $5.95 pap. $2.50

SOME THOUGHTS CONCERNING EDUCATION. Ed. by F. W. Garforth *Barron's* 1964 $6.00 pap. $1.95

Books about Locke

The Life of John Locke. By H. R. Bourne. 1876. *International Pubns.* 2 vols. set $65.00

Bibliographical Introduction to the Study of John Locke. By Hans O. Christophersen. 1930. *Burt Franklin* $12.50

John Locke and English Literature of the Eighteenth Century. By Kenneth MacLean. 1936. *Russell & Russell* 1962 $7.00

John Locke and the Doctrine of Majority-Rule. By Willmoore Kendall. 1941. *Univ. of Illinois Press* 1962 pap. $1.25; *Peter Smith* $4.00. Out-of-print for almost 10 years, this book received wide attention when it was first published.

John Locke's Political Philosophy: Eight Studies. By John Wiedhofft Gough. *Oxford* 2nd ed. 1973 $13.00

John Locke. By Richard I. Aaron. *Oxford* 1954 3rd ed. 1971 $11.25

John Locke: A Biography. By Maurice Cranston. *Verry* 1957 $20.00. The author received the James Tait Black Memorial Prize for this in 1958.

Locke. By Maurice Cranston. *British Bk. Centre* 1961 $.75. A pamphlet.

The Political Theory of Possessive Individualism: Hobbes to Locke. By C. B. Macpherson. *Oxford* 1962 $10.25 pap. $3.25

John Locke. By D. J. O'Connor. *Dover* 1966 pap. $1.75; *Peter Smith* $4.00

Locke and Berkeley: A Collection of Critical Essays. By David M. Armstrong and C. B. Martin. *Univ. of Notre Dame Press* 1968 $7.95

"The essays, well chosen and covering a wide range of ideas, have been written for the most part by distinguished men in the field of philosophy; the writing is generally good"—(*LJ*).

Political Thought of John Locke. By John Dunn. *Cambridge* 1969 $14.50

Locke and the Compass of Human Understanding. By John W. Yolton. *Cambridge* 1970 $12.50

John Locke and Education. By John W. Yolton. *Philadelphia Bk. Co.* 1971 pap. $2.95

John Locke. By J. D. Mabbott. *Schenkman* 1973 $3.95

John Locke. By Mabel Sahakian and William S. Sahakian. *Twayne* 1975 $6.50

LEIBNIZ (or Leibnitz), GOTTFRIED WILHELM, Baron VON. 1646–1716.

The German philosopher and mathematician was also prominent in public affairs. He developed new notations of calculus, published in 1684 before Newton's (*q.v.*) and the subject thereafter of long controversy. He tried to find a common ground for the Catholic and Protestant faiths in his "*Systema Theologicum*" written in 1686 but not published until 1819. He spent his last 30 years in the study of many philosophical and scientific subjects and has left no complete and finished exposition of his philosophy. Most of his writing was in the form of essays and treatises. His principal theological work, "Théodicé" (1710) is a discussion of the problem of evil and a defense of optimism, or the "preestablished harmony" of all things. Voltaire (*q.v.*) ridiculed it in "Candide." Leibniz was one of the great system-builders, who posited a complex system of "monads"—independent entities—and of "worlds." Voltaire's Leibniz-figure says after every catastrophe (in "Candide") that "everything is for the best in the best of all possible worlds." Leibniz endeavored, among other things, to prove the existence of God. Bertrand Russell (in his "History of Western Philosophy") thinks Leibniz most important for his pioneering in mathematics and in mathematical logic, though Russell finds Leibniz's very clearly expressed philosophical tenets "fantastic."

PHILOSOPHICAL WRITINGS. Trans. by Mary Morris; ed. by G. H. Parkinson *Rowman* $4.00

New Essays Concerning Human Understanding. Trans. by A. G. Langley. 1894. *Open Court* $20.00

Monadology. 1714. (And Other Philosophical Essays) trans. by P. and A. M. Schrecker *Bobbs* Lib. Arts 1965 $6.00 pap. $2.00; (and Other Philosophical Writings) trans. by Robert Latta *Oxford* 1898 $7.75

Discourse on Metaphysics and The Monadology. (In "The Rationalists") *Doubleday* 1962 pap. $2.50

Discourse on Metaphysics; Correspondence with Arnauld; and Monadology. Trans. by G. R. Montgomery *Open Court* $10.00 pap. $3.95

Logical Papers. Trans. and ed. by G. H. R. Parkinson *Oxford* 1966 $7.00

Theodicy. Ed. by Diogenes Allen *Bobbs* Lib. Arts 1966 pap. $3.25

Philosophical Papers and Letters. Ed. by Leroy E. Loemker *Humanities Press* 1970 repr. $48.00

Books about Leibniz

Leibniz's New Essays Concerning Human Understanding. By J. Dewey. 1888. *Humanities Press* 1961 $6.50

Leibnitz and the 17th Century Revolution. By. R. W. Meyer. Trans. by J. P. Stern *Hillary House* 1952 $6.50

A Critical Exposition of the Philosophy of Leibnitz. By Bertrand Russell. *Humanities Press* 2nd rev. ed. $12.00

Logic and Reality in Leibniz's Metaphysics. By G. H. R. Parkinson. *Oxford* 1965 $7.75

The Philosophy of Leibniz. By N. Rescher. *Prentice-Hall* (orig.) 1966 pap. $3.95

Leibniz's Philosophy of Logic and Language. By Hide Ishiguro. *Cornell Univ. Press* 1972 $8.50

Leibniz and Dynamics. By Pierre Costabel. Trans. from the French by R. E. Madison *Cornell Univ. Press* 1973 $8.50

The Philosophy of Leibniz and the Modern World. Ed. by Ivor Leclerc. *Vanderbilt Univ. Press* 1973 $15.00

Leibnitz: An Introduction. By C. D. Broad and C. Lewey. *Cambridge* 1975 $14.95 pap. $4.95

Leibniz: A Collection of Critical Essays. Ed. by Harry G. Frankfurt. *Peter Smith* $5.25

VICO, GIAMBATTISTA. 1668–1744. *See Chapter 10, Italian Literature*, Reader's Adviser, *Vol. 2*.

BERKELEY, GEORGE, Bishop. 1685–1753.

Berkeley, the Anglo-Irish philosopher, sometime Bishop of Cloyne, formulated the system of immaterialism, denying the existence of a material external world and stating that the mind alone exists as a thinking being. His subjective idealism was a development of Locke's philosophy. His two works explaining this idea, "A New Theory of Vision" and "A Treatise Concerning the Principles of Human Knowledge," were publicly neglected despite their revolutionary contents, much to Berkeley's surprise. Hoping to reach a wider audience, Berkeley rewrote his theories in more palatable form as "Three Dialogues between Hylas and Philonous." "They are in some respects a reversion to the Platonic form of dialogues, except that they assume a rather more propagandist air. . . . Berkeley did not try to bewilder and astonish; he was out to combat what he believed to be the most dangerous tendency of his age, namely, the drift towards materialism"— (E. W. F. Tomlin). Most of his works were published before he was 30.

A friend of such literary figures as Addison, Pope, Steele, and Swift, "Berkeley conceived the plan of bringing Christian civilization to America by establishing a college in Bermuda, [or by a later plan, on Berkeley's arrival in the New World, in Rhode Island. Neither was realized.] But on the long view Berkeley's efforts were not in vain. Yale and Harvard benefited directly by his visit; Columbia University and the University of Pennsylvania had the advantage of his counsel in their early days. The University of Berkeley, California, and the Berkeley Divinity School, New Haven, commemorate his name"—(A. A. Luce).

Philosophical Writings. Ed. by D. M. Armstrong *Macmillan* Collier Bks. pap. $1.95

Philosophical Works: Including the Works on Vision. Ed. by M. R. Ayers *Rowman* 1975 $16.75

A New Theory of Vision (1709) and Other Writings. Introds. by Thomas E. Jessup *Dutton* Everyman's repr. 1954 $3.95

THE PRINCIPLES OF HUMAN KNOWLEDGE and THREE DIALOGUES BETWEEN HYLAS AND PHILONOUS. Introd. by G. J. Warnock *Peter Smith* $6.00

A TREATISE CONCERNING THE PRINCIPLES OF HUMAN KNOWLEDGE. 1710. *Bobbs* Lib. Arts 1957 pap. $1.10; *Open Court* $5.00 pap. $1.50

THREE DIALOGUES BETWEEN HYLAS AND PHILONOUS. 1713. *Bobbs* Lib. Arts 1954 pap. $1.25; *Open Court* 1935 $5.00 pap. $1.25

WORKS ON VISION. Ed. by C. M. Turbayne *Bobbs* Lib. Arts 1963 $6.00 pap. $2.25

PRINCIPLES, DIALOGUES, AND PHILOSOPHICAL CORRESPONDENCE. Trans. by C. M. Turbayne *Bobbs* Lib. Arts 1965 $6.00 pap. $2.50

Books about Berkeley

The Development of Berkeley's Philosophy. By George A. Johnston. 1923. *Russell & Russell* $10.00

Bibliography of George Berkeley. By Thomas E. Jessop. 1934. *Burt Franklin* $9.50

George Berkeley: A Study of His Life and Philosophy. By John Wild. 1936. *Russell & Russell* 1962 $12.00

Berkeley's Immaterialism: A Commentary on His "A Treatise Concerning the Principles of Human Knowledge." By Arthur Aston Luce. 1945. *Russell & Russell* 1968 $8.00

Berkeley. By T. E. Jessop. *British Bk. Centre* 1962 $2.95. A pamphlet.

Locke and Berkeley: A Collection of Critical Essays. Ed. by David M. Armstrong and C. B. Martin. *Univ. of Notre Dame Press* 1968 $7.95. (*See note under Locke.*)

Berkeley. By Harry M. Bracken. *St. Martin's* 1974 $9.95

Berkeley: The Philosophy of Immaterialism. By Ian C. Tipton. *Harper* (Barnes & Noble) 1974 $18.50

VOLTAIRE (François-Marie Arouet de Voltaire). 1694–1778. *See Chapter 9, French Literature,* Reader's Adviser, *Vol. 2.*

HUME, DAVID. 1711–1776.

Hume, the Scotsman, is the chief skeptic in modern philosophy. He "reached the extreme limit of skepticism without crossing it into credulity or creed," although he "had his own sort of faith: faith in the unchanging order of the universe"—(Basil Willey, in "The English Moralists"). Josiah Royce (*q.v.*) ranked him next to Hobbes as the greatest of speculative thinkers. Bertrand Russell calls him "one of the most important among philosophers because he developed to its logical conclusion the empirical philosophy of Locke and Berkeley, and by making it self-consistent made it incredible: in his direction, it is impossible to go further. To refute him has been, ever since he wrote, a favorite pastime among metaphysicians." Russell finds "none of their refutations convincing" but hopes that Hume's pessimism is not the last word. Hume's "Treatise of Human Nature" consists of three parts: Understanding; Passions; Morals. Hume is well known as a historian. Sir Harold Nicolson (*q.v.*) has said that he finds Hume "invigorating, being fortified by his massive Scottish sense and his firm Scottish style. . . . He was a calm brand of rationalist who denied faith 'as more properly an art of the sensitive than of the cogitative part of our nature' and who asserted that 'all knowledge degenerates into probability.' "

PHILOSOPHICAL WORKS. 1882–86. Ed. by T. H. Hill Green and T. H. Hodge Gross *Adler's* 4 vols. 1964 half-lea. set $150.00

HUME'S MORAL AND POLITICAL PHILOSOPHY. Ed. by Henry D. Aiken *Hafner* 1948 text ed. pap. $3.95

POLITICAL ESSAYS. Ed. by Charles W. Hendel *Bobbs* Lib. Arts 1953 $5.00 pap. $3.50

ESSAYS: Moral, Political and Literary. *Oxford* 1963 $6.00

PHILOSOPHY. *Modern Library* 1963 $2.45 lib. bdg. $2.95

A TREATISE OF HUMAN NATURE. 1739–40. Introd. by A. D. Lindsay *Dutton* Everyman's reissue 2 vols. 1956 each $3.95; ed. by L. A. Selby-Bigge *Oxford* 1902 1941 $5.00 pap. $3.95

According to Bertrand Russell ("History of Western Philosophy"), the "Treatise," his major work, was later shortened "by leaving out the best parts and most of the reasons for Hume's conclusions; the result was the *Inquiry into Human Understanding.*"

ABSTRACT OF A TREATISE OF HUMAN NATURE, 1740: A Pamphlet Hitherto Unknown. 1938. *Shoe String Press* $4.00

ENQUIRIES CONCERNING HUMAN UNDERSTANDING. *Open Court* 1901 $10.00 pap. $2.95; ed. by L. A. Selby-Bigge *Oxford* 2nd ed. 1902 $6.00 pap. $3.75

AN INQUIRY CONCERNING HUMAN UNDERSTANDING. Ed. by Charles W. Hendel *Bobbs* Lib. Arts 1955 $5.00 pap. $1.50

HUME ON HUMAN NATURE AND THE UNDERSTANDING. Introd. by Antony Flew *Macmillan* Collier Bks. 1962 pap. $1.25

AN ENQUIRY CONCERNING THE PRINCIPLES OF MORALS. 1751. *Open Court* $8.00 pap. $1.25

AN INQUIRY CONCERNING THE PRINCIPLES OF MORALS. 1751. Introd. by Charles W. Hendel *Bobbs* Lib. Arts 1957 pap. $1.25

DIALOGUES CONCERNING NATURAL RELIGION. First pub. 1779, after his death. Ed. by N. K. Smith *Bobbs* Lib. Arts 1962 pap. $1.75; ed. by Henry D. Aiken *Macmillan* (Hafner) 1953 1972 pap. $1.95

NATURAL HISTORY OF RELIGION. Ed. by H. E. Root *Stanford Univ. Press* 1957 1967 pap. $1.25

ON RELIGION. Ed. by Richard Wollheim *Peter Smith* $5.50

OF THE STANDARD OF TASTE AND OTHER ESSAYS. Ed. by J. Lenz *Bobbs* Lib. Arts 1965 $6.00 pap. $2.00

THE PHILOSOPHICAL HISTORIAN. Ed. by R. H. Popkin and D. Norton *Bobbs* Lib. Arts 1965 $8.50 pap. $4.50

Books about Hume

Hume's Philosophy of Human Nature. By John Laird. *Shoe String Press* 1932 $10.00
Hume's Theory of the External World. By H. H. Price. *Oxford* 1940 $7.00
The Forgotten Hume: Le Bon David. By Ernest Mossner. 1943. *AMS Press* $10.00
Hume's Philosophy of Belief. By Antony G. N. Flew. *Humanities Press* 1961 $8.75
The Moral Philosophy of David Hume. By R. Broiles. *Humanities Press* 1964 pap. $4.50
Hume. By Montgomery Belgion. *British Bk. Centre* 1965 $2.95 pap. $1.20. A pamphlet.
The Ironic Hume. By John V. Price. *Univ. of Texas Press* 1965 $6.75. "This is [an original and] significant study of the ironic in the expression or form of Hume's philosophy"—*(LJ)*.
Hume. Ed. by V. C. Chappell. Modern Studies in Philosophy Ser. *Univ. of Notre Dame Press* 1968 $10.95 pap. $3.95
A collection of critical essays. "The philosophy of David Hume has become of increasing interest to modern philosophers, and these essays serve to reinforce the view that the ideas of Hume are still important for us to ponder in the 20th century"—*(LJ)*.
David Hume: His Theory of Knowledge and Morality. By D. G. C. MacNabb. *Shoe String Press* 1966 1973 $6.00
David Hume. By John Price. *Twayne Pub.* 1968 $6.50
The Philosophy of David Hume. By Norman K. Smith. *St. Martin's* $11.95 pap. $6.95
Ethical Naturalism: Hobbes and Hume. By John Kemp. *St. Martin's* 1970 pap. $2.95
Hume's Philosophical Development: A Study of His Methods. By James Noxon. *Oxford* 1973 $8.00
Hume's Philosophical Politics. By Duncan Forbes. *Cambridge* 1975 (in prep.)
Probability and Hume's Inductive Scepticism. By D. C. Stove. *Oxford* 1973 $9.75
Hume, Precursor of Modern Empiricism. By Farhang Zabeeh. *Humanities Press* rev. ed. 1973 $12.75
Human Nature and Utility in Hume's Social Philosophy. By W. Gordon Ross. 1942. *Russell & Russell* 1975 $10.00

ROUSSEAU, JEAN JACQUES. 1712–1778. *See Chapter 9, French Literature, Reader's Adviser, Vol. 2.*

DIDEROT, DENIS. 1713–1784.

"Diderot's collected works total twenty volumes, ranging from a delightful farce-comedy, to tragedy, poetry, philosophy, aesthetics, criticism, politics, and religion. He made numerous translations [and his works] inspired all his French contemporaries, as well as Lessing and Goethe in Germany. He was not the atheist his detractors said, but believed only in religious tolerance and speculative freedom"—*(Cyclopedia of World Authors)*.

The *"Encyclopédie"* was probably the most important achievement of the French Enlightenment. Diderot worked at this task from 1751 to 1772, aided by Voltaire, Montesquieu, Rousseau and others, all of whom became known as philosophers, men believing it their "mission to apply reason to the problems of society"—(E. W. F. Tomlin). It was published under the title *"Encyclopédie; ou Dictionnaire Raissonné des Sciences, des Arts et des Métiers"* in 28 volumes, increased by a 6-volume supplement, 1776–1777, and by two volumes of tables (1780). His enlightened views made him the object of all manner of persecution. "He wrote some extraordinary dialogues on science, philosophy and morals, which anticipate so much of Romanticist doctrine that though they have been twice forgotten they are now re-emerging; and he produced three works of fiction which develop a psychology so close to ours that they are now beginning to be enjoyed by a growing body of readers"—(*N.Y. Times*). An informative biography, now o.p., and praised as "the most complete, the most impartial, and the most carefully documented biography of Diderot in any language" (*American Historical Review*) is Arthur McCandless Wilson's "Diderot: The Testing Years, 1713–1759" (1957). It treats Diderot's life up until the critical year of 1759.

DIDEROT'S EARLY PHILOSOPHICAL WORKS. Ed. by Margaret Jourdain. 1916. *AMS Press* $15.00; *Burt Franklin* 1972 $12.50

A DIDEROT PICTORIAL ENCYCLOPEDIA OF TRADES AND INDUSTRY MANUFACTURING AND THE TECHNICAL ARTS: In Plates Selected from *"L'Encyclopédie; ou Dictionnaire Raisonné des Sciences, des Arts et des Métiers."* 1751–1772. Ed. with introd. and notes by Charles Coulston Gillispie *Dover* 2 vols. 1959 each $15.00

ENCYCLOPEDIA: Selections. Trans. by Nelly S. Hoyt and Thomas Cassier *Bobbs* Lib. Arts 1965 $7.50 pap. $4.25

Books about Diderot

Diderot as a Disciple of English Thought. By R. L. Cru. 1925. *AMS Press* $15.00
Diderot's Imagery. By E. M. Steel. 1941. *Haskell* $13.95
The Censoring of Diderot's Encyclopédie and the Re-established Text. By Douglas H. Gordon and Norman L. Torrey. *AMS Press* 1947 $9.00
    "The patience of Diderot in the composition of his Encyclopedia found an unfortunate match in the over-cautious censoring of the publisher, Le Breton. The fascinating study of that betrayal, its implications at a time when freedom of expression was fighting for its very voice, and the text as restored constitute this vital book whose significance is belied by a slender appearance"—(Publisher's note).
The Encyclopédie of Diderot and D'Alembert. By John Lough. *Cambridge* 1954 $7.50
Francis Bacon and Denis Diderot. By Lilo K. Luxembourg. *Humanities Press* 1967 $7.25
Diderot. By Arthur M. Wilson. *Oxford* 1972 $25.00
Diderot: The Virtue of a Philosopher. By Carol Blum. *Viking* 1974 $8.95
    "Hero of that successful counter-culture which was the Enlightenment, Diderot had an acute lifelong need to appear, to be, and especially to feel virtuous. Blum traces the expression and self-examination of that need"—(Frederick J. Crosson).

KANT, IMMANUEL. 1724–1804.

Josiah Royce (*q.v.*) spoke of Kant as "the thinker upon whom, more than upon any other center, modern thought turns as upon a fulcrum." Many critics consider Kant the greatest name in the history of philosophy. "I cannot myself agree with this estimate," says Bertrand Russell (in the "History of Western Philosophy"), "but it would be foolish not to recognize his great importance." Kant's system of philosophy was the most extensive and voluminous that had yet been formulated, and the vast bulk of commentaries upon his writings testify to their profundity. He invented so many new philosophical terms that his German offers many difficulties to translators. He was the founder of the Critical Philosophy, as he called it, and the founder of that German idealism whose effects, modified by Fichte and Hegel, persisted into the 20th century. Mind with him reasserted itself over matter. His greatest work is the "Critique of Pure Reason." "It is an examination of the mind with a view to detect its *a priori* principles. He calls them pure because they are *a priori*, because they are above and beyond experience." Kant lent hope again to a body of philosophical thought dessicated by Hume's dead-end determinism; he again set man "free."

THE PHILOSOPHY OF KANT. Ed. and trans. with introd. by Carl Joachim Friedrich *Random* (Modern Lib.) 1949 $2.95

CRITIQUE OF PURE REASON. 1781. Trans. by F. Max Müller *Doubleday* Anchor Bks. 2nd rev. ed. pap. $2.95; trans. by J. M. D. Meiklejohn, introd. by A. D. Lindsay *Dutton* Everyman's 1934 1955 $2.50; trans. by Norman Kemp Smith *St. Martin's* 1929 1952 $18.95 pap. $4.95

KANT'S PROLEGOMENA TO ANY FUTURE METAPHYSICS. Trans. with introd. and notes by P. G. Lucas *Harper* (Barnes & Noble) 1954 $3.50 trans. by L. Beck and P. Carus *Bobbs* Lib. Arts $3.00 pap. $1.20

FUNDAMENTAL PRINCIPLES OF THE METAPHYSICS OF ETHICS. 1785. Trans. by Otto Manthey-Zorn *Irvington Bks.* $3.95

FOUNDATIONS OF THE METAPHYSICS OF MORALS. Trans. by Lewis Beck; ed. by Robert Paul Wolff *Bobbs* Lib. Arts 1959 pap. $3.00

THE FUNDAMENTAL PRINCIPLES OF THE METAPHYSICS OF MORALS. Trans. by T. K. Abbott *Bobbs* Lib. Arts 1949 pap. $1.00

MORAL LAW, or Kant's Groundwork of the Metaphysics of Morals. Trans. by H. J. Paton *Harper* (Barnes & Noble) 1948 1958 1967 $5.00 Torchbks. pap. $2.25

METAPHYSICAL PRINCIPLES OF VIRTUE. Trans. by J. Ellington *Bobbs* Lib. Arts $5.00 pap. $2.50

CRITIQUE OF PRACTICAL REASON. 1788. Trans. by Lewis W. Beck *Bobbs* Lib. Arts 1956 pap. $2.00

CRITIQUE OF JUDGMENT. 1790. Trans. by J. H. Bernard; ed. by Irwin Edman *Macmillan* (Hafner) 1951 text ed. pap. $3.95; trans. by J. C. Meredith *Oxford* 2 vols. in 1 1928 1952 $7.25

FIRST INTRODUCTION TO THE CRITIQUE OF JUDGMENT. Trans. by J. Haden *Bobbs* Lib. Arts 1965 pap. $2.00

RELIGION WITHIN THE LIMITS OF REASON ALONE. 1793. Trans. by T. M. Greene and H. H. Hudson; introds. by T. M. Greene and John Silber 1934 *Harper* Torchbks. 1960 pap. $2.95

PERPETUAL PEACE. 1795. Trans. by Lewis W. Beck *Bobbs* Lib. Arts 1957 pap. $1.65

EDUCATION. *Univ. of Michigan Press* 1960 $4.40 Ann Arbor Bks. pap. $1.65

EDUCATIONAL THEORY OF IMMANUEL KANT. Trans. by Edward F. Buchner. 1904. *AMS Press* 1972 $9.00; *Gordon Press* $29.95; *Scholarly Press* $9.00

LECTURES ON ETHICS. Introd. by Lewis W. Beck. 1963. *Peter Smith* $4.75

KANT ON HISTORY. Trans. by L. W. Beck and others; ed. by L. W. Beck *Bobbs* Lib. Arts 1963 $5.00 pap. $1.50

METAPHYSICAL ELEMENTS OF JUSTICE. Trans. by J. Ladd *Bobbs* Lib. Arts 1965 $6.50 pap. $2.50

OBSERVATIONS ON THE FEELING OF THE BEAUTIFUL AND SUBLIME. Trans. by J. T. Goldthwait *Univ. of California Press* 1960 pap. $2.25

THE ANALYTIC OF THE BEAUTIFUL and THE FEELING OF PLEASURE AND DISPLEASURE. Trans. by W. Cerf *Bobbs* Lib. Arts $5.00 pap. $2.00

PHILOSOPHICAL CORRESPONDENCE, 1759–1799. Trans. and ed. by Arnulf Zweig *Univ. of Chicago Press* 1967 $9.00

METAPHYSICAL FOUNDATION OF NATURAL SCIENCE. Trans. by James Ellington *Bobbs* Lib. Arts 1970 $7.50 pap. $4.25

LOGIC. Trans. by Robert S. Hartman and Wolfgang Schwarz. *Bobbs* Lib. Arts 1974 $10.00 pap. $3.95

Books about Kant

Kant's Metaphysics of Experience. By H. J. Paton. 2 vols. 1936 set $22.00

Kant's Pre-Critical Ethics. By Paul Arthur Schilpp. *Northwestern Univ. Press* 1938 rev. ed. 1960 $7.50. Helps clarify Kant's later ethics.

The Heritage of Kant. Ed. by G. T. Whitney and D. F. Bowers. 1939. *Russell & Russell* 1962 $10.00

Introduction to Kant's Critique of Pure Reason. By T. D. Weldon. *Oxford* 1945 2nd ed. 1958 $7.75

Kant's First Critique: An Appraisal of the Permanent Significance of Kant's Critique of Pure
Reason. By Heinrich Walter Cassirer. 1955. *Humanities Press* $8.25

A Commentary on Kant's Critique of Pure Reason. By Lewis White Beck. *Univ. of Chicago Press*
1960 $6.00 pap. $1.95. A historical, literary and philosophical examination which considers
his work in relation to the 18th century background.

Kant for Everyman. By Willibald Klinke. Trans. by Michael Bullo *Macmillan* Collier Bks. 1962
pap. $.95

Kant and the Problem of Metaphysics. By Martin Heidegger. Trans. by J. S. Churchill *Indiana
Univ. Press* 1962 pap. $2.45; *Peter Smith* $5.00

Immanuel Kant. By F. Paulsen. *Ungar* 1963 $9.00

Kant's Theory of Mental Activity. By Robert P. Wolff. 1963 *Peter Smith* $6.00

Kant and the Southern New Critics. By William J. Handy. *Univ. of Texas Press* 1963 $5.00
This book examines, somewhat elliptically, the thesis that "John Crowe Ransom, Allen Tate,
Cleanth Brooks, and others have all been influenced by the Kantian generative idea that a
work of art is the celebration of man's qualitative experience"—*(LJ)*.

Kant's Analytic. By Jonathan Bennett. *Cambridge* 1966 $13.50 pap. $4.95
"Bennett's scholarship and [thoroughly modern] point of view combine to make this book of
prime importance for students of modern philosophy"—*(Choice)*. It is a commentary, by a
lecturer in moral science at Cambridge, on the first half of the "Critique of Pure Reason."

Kant. By Karl Jaspers. *Harcourt* 1966 pap. $1.35

The Bounds of Sense: An Essay on Kant's Critique of Pure Reason. By P. F. Strawson. *Harper*
(Barnes & Noble) 1966 $8.50
This is an "attempt to disentangle Kant's major theses and to show what is used as a reason
for what, as well as to identify points of permanent interest as opposed to mere philosophical
curiosities.... Lucid and well argued, [it] is sure to become a classic; it is suitable for
advanced undergraduates"—*(Choice)*.

Kant: A Collection of Critical Essays. Comp. by Robert Wolff. *Univ. of Notre Dame Press* 1968
$6.95 pap. $3.95

Immanuel Kant. By Lucien Goldman. *Humanities Press* 1972 $9.50

The Autonomy of Reason: A Commentary on Kant's "Groundwork of the Metaphysics of
Morals." By Robert Paul Wolff. *Harper* (Barnes and Noble) 1972 $12.50

The Harmony of Reason: A Study in Kant's Aesthetics. By Francis X. Coleman. *Univ. of
Pittsburgh Press* 1974 $12.50

Kant's Aesthetic Theory. By Donald W. Crawford. *Univ. of Wisconsin Press* 1974 $12.50

Kant. By Stephan Korner. *Penguin* 1975 pap. $2.50

Kant and the Problem of History. By William A. Galston. *Univ. of Chicago* 1975 $13.50
"Galston does an excellent job in integrating Kant's philosophy of history with his other
philosophical doctrines as well as situating him in the whole philosophic tradition"—*(LJ)*.

Acting on Principle: An Essay on Kantian Ethics. By Onora Nell. *Columbia* 1975 $10.00
"Nell envisions the categorical imperative as a practical as well as theoretical principle.... He
argues that Kant's tests of contradiction in conception and contradiction as well are fruitful
tests of the maxim relating to the formula and provide the necessary synthesis of the
universal and particular"—*(LJ)*.

Kant's Critique of Metaphysics. By W. H. Walsh. *Rowman* 1975 $14.50

FICHTE, JOHANN GOTTLIEB. 1762–1814.

Fichte, the German philosopher and metaphysician, was at first an ardent disciple of Kant (*q.v.*),
whom he visited in 1791. He was the "exponent of a system of transcendental idealism emphasizing the self-activity of reason and setting forth a perfected Kantian system." The Ego was the
center of Fichte's universe. He was professor and first rector of the newly founded University of
Berlin from 1810 to 1814. "Fichte is not important as a pure philosopher, but as the theoretical
founder of German nationalism, by his *Addresses to the German Nation*, which were intended to
rouse the Germans to resistance to Napoleon after the battle of Jena. The Ego as a metaphysical
concept easily became confused with the empirical Fichte; since the Ego was German, it followed
that the Germans were superior to all other nations.... On this basis he worked out a whole
philosophy of nationalistic totalitarianism"—(Bertrand Russell, in the "History of Western Philosophy").

THE VOCATION OF MAN. 1800. Trans. by W. Smith and R. M. Chisholm *Bobbs* Lib. Arts
1956 pap. $2.00; trans. by William Smith. 1906. *Open Court* $4.95 pap. $1.45

ADDRESSES TO THE GERMAN NATION. 1808. Ed. by George Kelly *Harper* Torchbks. pap.
$2.75

Books about Fichte

Johann Gottlieb Fichte. By H. C. Engelbrecht. 1933. *AMS Press* $12.50

Novalis' Fichte Studies: The Foundations of His Aesthetics. By Geza von Molnar. *Humanities Press* 1970 $7.75

HEGEL, GEORG WILHELM FRIEDRICH. 1770–1831.

Hegel was "the culmination of the movement in German philosophy that started from Kant"—(B. Russell). The work of Fichte and Schelling, the other two important figures, has had no complete English translation. Hegel introduced the dialectic method in philosophy, in which an element called the "thesis" is pitted against an opposing element, the "antithesis," to result in a "synthesis." He used this concept to illuminate many aspects of human experience. Though a Platonist, Hegel accepts "as philosophically significant the Christian doctrines of the Fall, the Incarnation and the Redemption. . . . Hegel's Christianity is not merely a private conviction but an integral element in his philosophical system"—(E. W. F. Tomlin, in "The Western Philosophers"). Josiah Royce (*q.v.*) says of Hegel's style that it "is notoriously one of the most barbarous, technical, and obscure in the whole history of philosophy." His influence has been wide, affecting, among others, Marx, Bosanquet and Croce.

THE PHILOSOPHY OF HEGEL. Ed. by C. J. Friedrich *Random* Modern Lib. 1953 pap. $3.95

SELECTIONS. Ed. by Jacob Loewenberg *Scribner* Mod. Student's Lib. 1975 pap. $3.95

SCIENCE OF LOGIC. 1812–1816. Trans. by Johnston and Struthers *Humanities Press* 2 vols. 1929 1952 set $15.00

PHENOMENOLOGY OF THE MIND. Trans. by J. B. Baillie *Harper* introd. by George Lichtheim, Torchbks. 1967 pap. $5.45; *Humanities Press* 1964 $25.50

LECTURES ON THE HISTORY OF PHILOSOPHY. Vol. 1 trans. and ed. by E. S. Haldane; Vols. 2-3 trans. and ed. by E. S. Haldane and F. H. Simson *Humanities Press* 3 vols. 1912 1954 set $45.00

LECTURES ON THE PHILOSOPHY OF HISTORY. 1831. Prefs. by Charles Hegel and the translator J. Sibree; new introd. by C. J. Friedrich *Dover* 1956 pap. $3.00. His students brought together these notes after his death.

LECTURES ON THE PHILOSOPHY OF RELIGION. *Humanities Press* 3 vols. 1962 $35.00

REASON IN HISTORY: A General Introduction to the Philosophy of History. Trans. by R. S. Hartman *Bobbs* Lib. Arts 1953 pap. $1.25

THE PHILOSOPHY OF RIGHT. Trans. with notes by T. M. Knox *Oxford* 1942 $7.25 pap. $2.95

ON CHRISTIANITY: Early Theological Writings. Trans. by T. M. Knox; ed. by Richard Kroner and T. M. Knox *Peter Smith* $5.00

POLITICAL WRITINGS. Trans. by T. M. Knox *Oxford* 1964 $9.50

THE PHILOSOPHY OF NATURE. Trans. by A. V. Miller *Oxford* 1970 $16.00 pap. $8.00

THE PHILOSOPHY OF MIND. Trans. by William Wallace *Oxford* 1971 $13.75 pap. $6.50

THE LOGIC OF HEGEL. Trans. by William Wallace *Oxford* 3rd ed. 1975 $19.25 pap. $4.95

AESTHETICS: Lectures on Fine Art. Trans. by T. M. Knox *Oxford* 2 vols. 1975 set $96.00

Books about Hegel

The Philosophy of Hegel: A Systematic Exposition. By Walter Terence Stace. *Dover* 1955 pap. $4.00; *Gannon* $7.50. An unabridged and unaltered republication of the excellent first edition (1924).

Introduction to Hegel. By G. R. G. Mure. *Oxford* 1940 $7.00

A Study of Hegel's Logic. By G. R. G. Mure. *Oxford* 1950 $9.50

Reason and Revolution: Hegel and the Rise of Social Theory. By Herbert Marcuse. 2nd ed. with supplementary chapter. *Humanities Press* 1955 $9.25; *Beacon* 1960 pap. $3.95

Hegel: A Re-Examination. By J. N. Findlay. 1958. *Humanities Press* $13.75; *Macmillan* (Collier Bks.) 1962 pap. $1.50

Hegel on Art: An Interpretation of Hegel's Aesthetics. By Jack Kaminsky. *State Univ. of N.Y. Press* 1962 $6.00 pap. $2.45

Professor Kaminsky's work is the most extensive study of the subject available in English. He "succeeds in the difficult task of summarizing Hegel's aesthetics in a clear, well-balanced text which follows the historical lines set down by the philosopher."

High Tide of Prophecy: Hegel, Marx, and the Aftermath. By Karl R. Popper. Volume 2 of
"The Open Society and Its Enemies." *Princeton Univ. Press* 1963 $10.00 pap. $3.45
The Philosophy of Hegel. By G. R. G. Mure. *Oxford* 1965 $3.50
The Philosophical Foundations of Marxism. By Louis K. Dupré. *Harcourt* 1966 pap. $4.40
Hegel: Reinterpretation, Texts, and Commentary. Ed. by Walter Kaufmann. *Peter Smith* $5.00
   This "is the first time in any language that the entire Hegel canon has been reviewed in one
   place, and Professor Kaufmann has done this enormous task deftly. . . . An important
   contribution to his field"—*(LJ)*.
Hegel: A Reinterpretation. By Walter Kaufmann. *Doubleday* Anchor Bks. pap. $2.50. Omits the
   texts and commentary of the hardback just above.
Hegel's First American Followers. By Loyd D. Easton. *Ohio Univ. Press* 1967 $10.00
   "From 1848 to 1860, three energetic, now all-but-forgotten thinkers in Cincinnati (J. B.
   Stallo, Moncure Conway, and August Willich) and one in Canton (Peter Kaufmann) ex-
   pounded, interpreted, and defended Hegel's philosophy for the American public. [Their]
   lives and thoughts, . . . and their place in the growth of American philosophy, are here
   perceptively analyzed and evaluated"—*(LJ)*.
The Religious Dimension in Hegel's Thought. By Emil L. Fackenheim. *Indiana Univ. Press* 1968
   $9.50; *Beacon* pap. $3.45
   This work "reveals the years of study which underlie it." Professor Fackenheim of the
   University of Toronto "discussses knowledge, the 'Hegelian middle,' the religious basis for
   Hegel's philosophy. . . . He believes that Hegel offers a means of resolving the modern
   tension between revelation and rationality"—*(LJ)*.
Hegel. By Franz Wiedman. Trans. by Joachim Neugroschel. *Pegasus* 1968 $5.00 pap. $1.75
   By the head of the philosophy department at the Philosophical-Theological Institute at
   Dillingen, Germany, this contains "very little discussion about significances except in regard
   to the 'right-' and 'left-wing' interpreters," and has other drawbacks. "Still, since this is
   probably the only biography in English, there is a use for this book, at least until there is a
   translation, or, better, a continuation, of such books as George Lukàcs' *Der Junge Hegel*"—
   (LJ).
New Studies in Hegel's Philosophy. By W. E. Steinkraus. *Holt* 1971 $7.00
Hegel. By Raymond Plant. *Indiana Univ. Press* 1973 $7.95
Hegel. By G. Taylor. *Cambridge* 1975 $36.00
Hegel on Reason and History. By George D. O'Brien. *Univ. of Chicago* 1975 $18.50
   "A very welcome and needed contribution to Hegelian scholarship"—*(LJ)*.
Hegel, Kierkegaard, Marx. By Robert Heiss. *Delacorte* (dist. by Dial) 1975 $12.50; Dell 1975 pap.
   $3.95

SCHELLING, FRIEDRICH (WILHELM JOSEPH) von. 1775–1854.

Schelling was with Kant (*q.v.*), Fichte (*q.v.*), and Hegel (*q.v.*), one of the four great German
philosophers responsible for providing the philosophic basis for the German Romantic movement, which had profound repercussions in literature and the other arts and spread throughout
Europe. In his youth he studied theology at the University of Tübingen and later became a
professor at Jena, where he knew and collaborated with Fichte. He held a number of other
professorships and government posts. Hegel was originally his pupil and disciple but the three—
Schelling, Fichte and Hegel—eventually went their separate ways. Schelling began his philosophical career as a mystic and developed what he called a "Philosophy of Nature," which soon gave way
to a "Philosophy of Identity," moving by thesis and antithesis toward the Absolute. In time this
came to seem to him abstract and fruitless and he concentrated on a philosophy of history, which
he expressed in "Of Human Freedom" and "Ages of the World."

On University Studies. 1802. Trans. by E. S. Morgan; rev. with introd. by Norbert
   Guterman *Ohio Univ. Press* 1966 $7.00

   "It is valuable less as a study in the philosophy of higher education than as a relatively short and
readable introduction to the whole of Schelling's thought. Until now this work has not been
available in English in book form. The skillful translation, the good general introduction, and the
very useful editorial notes make this a publication which should be welcomed by advanced
students of philosophy"—*(LJ)*.

Of Human Freedom. 1809. Trans. by James Gutmann *Open Court* $6.00 pap. $1.95

Ages of the World. 1854. Trans. by Frederick W. Bolman, Jr., in 1942. *AMS Press* $7.50

SCHOPENHAUER, ARTHUR. 1788–1860.

The brilliance and clarity of Schopenhauer's style make him one of the best known of
philosophers to the general public. He is the great German pessimist whose theory of the primacy
of the will was developed later by Nietzsche and others. "In proportion as will has gone up in the

scale," says Bertrand Russell, "knowledge has gone down. [This preeminence of the will] was prepared by Rousseau and Kant, but was first proclaimed in its purity by Schopenhauer. For this reason, in spite of inconsistency and a certain shallowness, his philosophy has considerable importance." The philosopher found happiness to be only the absence of pain, the cessation of desire. He was a far from pleasant person. Russell recounts the story of his annoyance with an elderly seamstress, whom he threw downstairs; he had to pay her damages as long as she lived and expressed only relief at her ultimate demise.

WORKS. Ed. and abr. by Will Durant; introd. by Thomas Mann *Ungar* 1962 $8.50 pap. $3.25

THE WILL TO LIVE: Selected Writings. Ed. by Richard Taylor. 1962. *Ungar* $8.50 pap. $3.25

THE WORLD AS WILL AND REPRESENTATION. 1819. Trans. by E. F. J. Payne 1955. *Dover* 2 vols. 1966 pap. each $4.50; *Peter Smith* 2 vols. set $12.00

ESSAYS ON THE FREEDOM OF THE WILL. Trans. by K. Kolenda *Bobbs* Lib. Arts 1960 $1.50

STUDIES IN PESSIMISM. *Scholarly Press* $9.00

THE BASIS OF MORALITY. Trans. by E. F. J. Payne *Bobbs* Lib. Arts 1965 $6.00 pap. $2.75

COUNSELS AND MAXIMS. Trans. by T. Bailey Saunders, in 1899. *Scholarly Press* $9.00

PARERGA AND PARALIPOMENA: Short Philosophical Essays. 1851 *Oxford* 2 vols. 1974 Vol. 1 $30.50 Vol. 2 $40.00 set $65.00

Books about Schopenhauer

The Life of Arthur Schopenhauer. By William Wallace. 1890. *Scholarly Press* $14.50
The Aesthetic Theories of Kant, Hegel and Schopenhauer. By I. Knox. *Humanities Press* $7.50
Schopenhauer. By Patrick Gardiner. 1963. *Gannon* $4.50; *Peter Smith* $4.25
Arthur Schopenhauer. By Helen Zimmern. *Haskell* 1974 $13.95

COMTE, AUGUSTE. 1798–1857.

The French philosopher, Comte, was the originator of the philosophy of positivism. This system makes a résumé of all preceding philosophies and classifies them according to three historical stages of development: the supernatural, the metaphysical or abstract, and the positive or scientific. According to Comte's own view "the crown of his labors" was "the institution of the science of sociology and of the religion of humanity." He is generally considered the founder of sociology. "Humanism" as a kind of religion developed throughout Europe as a result of his teachings.

THE POSITIVIST LIBRARY. Trans. and ed. by Frederick Harrison 1886. *Burt Franklin* 1971 $9.50; *Somerset Pubs.* $5.00

GENERAL VIEW OF POSITIVISM. Trans. by J. H. Bridges *Speller* 1957 $6.00. Official Centenary ed. of the Int. Auguste Comte Centenary Comm.

INTRODUCTION TO POSITIVE PHILOSOPHY. Ed. with introd. and revised trans. by Frederick Ferré *Bobbs* Lib. Arts 1970 pap. $1.50

THE ESSENTIAL COMTE. Trans. and annot. by Margaret Clarke; ed. by Stanislav Andreski *Harper* (Barnes & Noble) 1974 $18.75 pap. $5.25

AUGUSTE COMTE AND POSITIVISM: The Essential Writings. Ed. by Gertrud Lenzer *Harper* pap. $7.25

SYSTEM OF POSITIVE POLITY. 1851. Trans. by John Henry Bridges, 1875–1877. *Burt Franklin* 4 vols. 1966 set $90.00

Books about Comte

Auguste Comte and Positivism. By John Stuart Mill. 1865. *Univ. of Michigan Press* 1961 Ann Arbor Bks. pap. $2.45
Comte, the Founder of Sociology. By Francis S. Marvin. 1936. *Russell & Russell* 1965 $7.50
European Positivism in the Nineteenth Century: An Essay in Intellectual History. By Walter M. Simon. 1963. *Kennikat* 1971 $13.50
This work contains "essays on Comte and the organized Positivist movement after his death [and] analysis of the extent to which Comte's doctrine actually influenced thought in France, England, and Germany in the nineteenth century, outside the small circle of his avowed

followers. In general, the author feels, that influence has been much overrated"—(*American Historical Review*).

EMERSON, RALPH WALDO. 1803–1882. *See Chapter 15, Essays and Criticism*, Reader's Adviser *Vol. 1*.

MILL, JOHN STUART. 1806–1873.

Introduced to Jeremy Bentham's theory of utilitarianism by his father, the social reformer James Mill, John Stuart Mill became its chief exponent. This modern theory of hedonism, or happiness, declared that "the criterion of right and wrong is the tendency of an action to produce the happiness of mankind." Primitive hedonisms, like Epicureanism, were concerned with the happiness of the individual. Utilitarianism is the doctrine of "universal hedonism," the greatest happiness of the greatest number. Mill's "Essay on Liberty" and his autobiography have become classics. From him stemmed many of the ideas for social and political reform that are today common property, particularly in England and the United States.

COLLECTED WORKS. *Gordon Press* $159.00

UTILITARIANISM (1863); ON LIBERTY (1859); REPRESENTATIVE GOVERNMENT (1861). *Bobbs* Lib. Arts pap. $1.00; introd. by A. D. Lindsay *Dutton* Everyman's 1950 $3.95

UTILITARIANISM; ON LIBERTY; ESSAY ON BENTHAM. Together with sel. writings by Jeremy Bentham and John Austin. Ed. with introd. by Mary Warnock *New Am. Lib.* Meridian Bks. 1962 pap. $4.95

ON LIBERTY; REPRESENTATIVE GOVERNMENT; THE SUBJUGATION OF WOMEN. *Oxford* World's Class. $5.95

ON LIBERTY. *AHM Pub. Corp.* Crofts Class. pap. $.85; *Bobbs* Lib. Arts 1956 pap. $1.50; ed. by David Spitz *Norton* Critical Eds. 1975 $8.95 pap. $2.95

CONSIDERATIONS ON REPRESENTATIVE GOVERNMENT. 1861. Ed. by Currin V. Sheilds *Bobbs* Lib. Arts 1958 $2.50

THE SUBJUGATION OF WOMEN. 1869. *MIT Press* 1970 pap. $1.95

AUTOBIOGRAPHY (from the original ms.). *Columbia* 1924 1944 $2.45; *Oxford* World's Class. $2.75; *Bobbs* Lib. Arts 1958 $5.00 pap. $2.00; ed. by Jack Stillinger *Houghton* 1964 pap. $2.95

Books about Mill

English Utilitarians: Jeremy Bentham, James Mill, John Stuart Mill. By Sir Leslie Stephen. *Peter Smith* 3 vols. in 1 1950 $15.00; *Kelley* 1968 3 vols. set $37.50
The Philosophy of J. S. Mill. By R. P. Anschutz. *Oxford* 1953 $5.00
Bibliography of the Writings of J. S. Mill. By J. S. Mill. *AMS Press* $10.00
Poetry and Philosophy: A Study in the Thought of John Stuart Mill. By Thomas Woods. *Humanities Press* 1961 $6.00
John Stuart Mill. By John B. Ellery. English Authors Ser. *Twayne* 1964 $6.50
Carlyle and Mill. By Emery Neff. *Octagon* 1964 $14.50
John Stuart Mill. By Maurice Cranston. *British Bk. Centre* $2.95 pap. $1.20
Matthew Arnold and John Stuart Mill. By Edward Alexander. *Columbia* 1965 $10.00
   This is "a very thorough and scholarly analysis of the mainstream of Victorian thought by comparing the philosophies of that age's two leading thinkers . . . who represented humanism and liberalism"—(*LJ*).
John Stuart Mill. By Alexander Bain. *Folcroft* 1973 $20.00
Marx and Mill: Two Views of Social Conflict and Social Harmony. By G. Duncan. *Cambridge* 1973 $15.50
On Liberty and Liberalism: The Case of John Stuart Mill. By Gertrude Himmelfarb. *Knopf* 1974 $8.95
John Stuart Mill: A Mind at Large. Ed. by Eugene August. *Scribner* 1975 $10.00
   "The first complete survey of the works of the 19th century philosopher and political economist"—(Publisher's catalog).
John Stuart Mill. By Alan Ryan. *Routledge and Kegan Paul* 1975 $6.25
   "This guide to Mill's best known writings presents him as a public thinker, someone who sought to improve mankind by addressing any part of the educated public who might listen to him"—(*LJ*).

KIERKEGAARD, SÖREN (AABYE). 1813–1855.

The great Danish philosopher and theologian, one of whose legs was shorter than the other and who was "an oddity . . . given to high spirits and sharp talk in public and melancholia in private" (Malcolm Muggeridge), laid the foundation of "existential" philosophy over a hundred years ago. So modern is his point of view that he became the guide of the writers of the French Resistance and postwar France who are known as "existentialists." "The existent individual, as Kierkegaard defines him, is . . . he who is in an infinite relationship with himself and has an infinite interest in himself and his destiny"(Jean Wahl, in introd. to "Essays in Existentialism" by Jean-Paul Sartre). His personal life was often combative; W. H. Auden found it impossible to imagine him as a *child* and felt that "something [went] badly wrong with [his] affective life." He won the heart of Regine Olsen, with whom he was in love, only to renounce her as a fiancée; he thereupon dedicated all his future works to her. Kierkegaard did important work in esthetics and greatly influenced Danish literature.

Modern critics, philosophers and theologians continue to be fascinated by his philosophy. A sampling from several of them provides a rounded picture of his message and influence: "Kierkegaard saw the reintroduction of Christianity into Christendom as his life's work. He was of the opinion that it was impossible in the present secularized state of Christendom to gain any impression whatsoever of the passion of the Christian faith. A wealth of information about Christianity had caused men to forget what it means to *exist* as a Christian. At the same time, men had also lost the necessary passion for existing as *human beings.* Both therefore had to be restored at the same time; for a Christianity that does not live by the passion of faith is invariably also a deeply inhuman affair"—(Hermann Diem). Malcolm Muggeridge writes: "As he continually points out, all that is most mediocre and contemptible in human beings derives from the pursuit of earthly happiness. It is the glory of Christianity to have denounced and defied this pursuit; the Christian who none the less goes crawling on his stomach to make his peace with happiness earns Kierkegaard's particular contempt"—(*Observer,* London).

"*Philosophical Fragments* (1844) and *Concluding Unscientific Postscript* (1846) are the central works in the development of Kierkegaard's life-purpose. Together, the two books present as directly and methodically as can be expected the philosophical thinking of a man whose method is indirect and whose philosophy is not a system. The titles are in themselves characteristic hits at the elaborate system established under the rule of Hegel ('the System'). Existentialism begins as a voice raised in protest against the absurdity of Pure Thought"—(H. J. Blackham). (Kierkegaard himself wrote, "One might say that I am the moment of individuality, but I refuse to be a paragraph in a system.") W. H. Auden (in the *New Yorker*): "His essential warning is directed not to the man-in-the-street, not to the bourgeois man, not even to the clergyman, but to the gifted man, the individual endowed with an exceptional talent for art or science or philosophy. The fact that such a gift is granted to one and not to all means that it is ethically neutral, for only those demands are ethical which apply to all human beings. . . . He is a prophet, calling the talented to repentance. No person of talent who has read him can fail to realize that the talented man, even more than the millionaire, is the rich man for whom it is so difficult to enter the Kingdom of Heaven. On this subject, Kierkegaard speaks with absolute authority; one may doubt his theological orthodoxy, one may question his right to demand of others a martyr's death which he did not suffer himself, but one can have no doubt whatsoever that he was a genius."

A KIERKEGAARD ANTHOLOGY. Ed. by Robert Bretall. 1946. *Random* Modern Lib. 1959 $2.95. Fifty selections from 16 of the most important works.

THE LIVING THOUGHTS OF KIERKEGAARD. Ed. by W. H. Auden *Indiana Univ. Press* Midland Bks. 1963 pap. $2.75. Selected from "Fear and Trembling," "The Works of Love," "The Concept of Dread," "Sickness unto Death" and other works.

SELECTIONS FROM THE WRITINGS OF KIERKEGAARD. Ed. by Lee M. Hollander *Doubleday* Anchor Bks. pap. $1.95

THE PRAYERS OF KIERKEGAARD. Ed. with a new interpretation of his life and thought by Perry D. LeFevre *Univ. of Chicago Press* 1956 Phoenix Bks. pap. $2.50

WORKS OF LOVE. *Harper* 1962 Torchbks. pap. $2.95; *Peter Smith* $4.50

THE CONCEPT OF IRONY WITH CONSTANT REFERENCE TO SOCRATES. 1841. Trans. with introd. and notes by Lee M. Capel. 1966. *Indiana Univ. Press* 1968 pap. $2.95

"With a single stroke Mr. Capel has established himself in the forefront of Kierkegaard's American interpreters and translators"—(*LJ*).

REPETITION: An Essay in Experimental Psychology. 1843. Trans. and ed. by Walter Lowrie 1941. *Harper* Torchbks. pap. $1.60; *Gannon* 1970 $6.50

EITHER/OR. 1843. Trans. by W. Lowrie *Princeton Univ. Press* 2 vols. 1971 Vol. 1 $15.00 pap. $2.95 Vol. 2 $13.50 pap. $2.45

FEAR AND TREMBLING (1843) and THE SICKNESS UNTO DEATH (1848). Trans. by Walter Lowrie *Princeton Univ. Press* 1941 $9.50 pap. $2.45

THE CONCEPT OF DREAD. 1844. Trans. by Walter Lowrie *Princeton Univ. Press* 1944 2nd ed. 1957 $7.50 pap. $1.95

PHILOSOPHICAL FRAGMENTS. 1844. Trans. by David Swenson; ed. by Niels Thulstrup *Princeton Univ. Press* 2nd ed. 1962 rev. trans. by H. V. Hong $11.50 pap. $2.95

STAGES ON LIFE'S WAY. 1845. Trans. by Walter Lowrie; introd. by Paul Sponheim *Schocken Bks.* 1967 $10.00 pap. $3.45

CONCLUDING UNSCIENTIFIC POSTSCRIPT. 1846. Trans. by David F. Swenson, completed after his death by Walter Lowrie *Princeton Univ. Press* American-Scandinavian Foundation 1941 $15.00 pap. $3.95

EDIFYING DISCOURSES. 1847. Introd. by Paul Holmer *Harper* 1958 Torchbks. pap. $1.95

WORKS OF LOVE. 1847. Trans. by Howard and Edna Hong *Harper* 1962 Torchbks. pap. $2.95; *Peter Smith* $5.00

CHRISTIAN DISCOURSES (1848); THE LILIES OF THE FIELD AND THE BIRDS OF THE AIR; and THREE DISCOURSES ON COMMUNION ON FRIDAYS. Trans. with introd. by Walter Lowrie *Oxford* 1940 $5.75; *Princeton Univ. Press* 1971 pap. $3.45

THE POINT OF VIEW FOR MY WORK AS AN AUTHOR. 1851. Ed. by Benjamin Nelson *Harper* Torchbks. pap. $1.95; *Peter Smith* $5.00

ATTACK UPON CHRISTENDOM. 1854–55. Trans. with introd. by Walter Lowrie *Princeton Univ. Press* 1944 $8.50 pap. $3.45

ON AUTHORITY AND REVELATION: The Book on Adler, or A Cycle of Ethico-Religious Essays. Trans. with introd. and notes by Walter Lowrie. 1955. *Gannon* 1970 $7.00. The first translation of "The Book on Adler" which contains the author's convictions about Christian authority in the case of the defrocking of a priest.

CRISIS IN THE LIFE OF AN ACTRESS AND OTHER ESSAYS ON THE DRAMA. *Gannon* 1970 $7.50; *Humanities Press* 1967 $5.50

ARMED NEUTRALITY and AN OPEN LETTER. Trans. and ed. by Howard V. Hong and Edna H. Hong; commentaries by Gregor Malantschuk. 1968. *Simon & Schuster* Touchstone-Clarion Bks. pap. $1.95
Mr. Malantschuk's notes and article "are themselves serious contributions to Kierkegaard studies"—(*LJ*).

PURITY OF HEART. Trans. by Douglas Steere *Harper* Torchbks. pap. $2.25

THE JOURNALS OF SÖREN KIERKEGAARD: A Selection. Trans. and ed. by Alexander Dru. 1938. *Harper* Torchbks. pap. $1.95

JOURNALS AND PAPERS. Trans. and ed. by Howard V. and Edna H. Hong, assisted by Gregor Malantschuk *Indiana Univ. Press* Vol. 1 (1967) $17.50 Vol. 2 (1970) $13.95. These are the first of five proposed volumes of Kierkegaard's journals to be translated from the Danish edition. The Hongs have arranged the volumes topically and within the topics, chronologically. Volume I received the National Book Award for Translation in 1968.

Books about Kierkegaard

Kierkegaard. By Walter Lowrie. 1938. *Peter Smith* 2 vols. $10.00
A Short Life of Kierkegaard. By Walter Lowrie. 1942 1958. *Princeton Univ. Press* 1965 $9.95 pap. $2.95

The Mind of Kierkegaard. By James Daniel Collins. *Regnery* Gateway Eds. 1953 1965 pap. $1.45. A sympathetic young Roman Catholic scholar presents a valuable and often brilliant study.

A Kierkegaard Critique. Ed. by Howard A. Johnson and Niels Thulstrup. *Regnery* Gateway Eds. 1967 pap. $2.25

Kierkegaard's Authorship: A Guide to the Writings of Kierkegaard. By George E. Arbaugh and George B. Arbaugh. *Augustana College Library Pubs.* 1968 $6.95

"This excellent volume will reward study for years to come. The authors' object is to examine the individual works of Kierkegaard in their internal structure, literary form, and philosophic and/or theological significance"—*(LJ)*. The works are studied chronologically.

On Becoming the Truth: An Introduction to the Life and Thought of Sören Kierkegaard. By Walter W. Sikes. *Bethany Press* 1968 pap. $2.95

"Each of Kierkegaard's categories related to becoming a Christian is herein examined in a thoroughly competent fashion. . . . He might possibly have overemphasized the importance of Hegelianism in Copenhagen at the time and it is not at all certain that the few judgments he makes about Hans Larsen Martensen are completely balanced. This work should be in every theological library and most serious philosophy collections"—*(LJ)*.

Kierkegaard and the Existential Philosophy. By Lev Shestov. Trans. by E. Hewitt *Ohio Univ. Press* 1968 1970 $11.00

Essays on Kierkegaard. By Jerry H. Gill. *Burgess* 1969 pap. $3.50

Kierkegaard and Heidegger: The Ontology of Existence. By Michael Wyschogrod. 1954. *Humanities Press* 1970 $7.25

Kierkegaard and Consciousness. By Adi Shmueli. *Princeton Univ. Press* 1971 $9.50

Kierkegaard's Presence in Contemporary American Life: Essays from Various Disciplines. Ed. by Lewis A. Lawson. *Scarecrow Press* 1971 $7.50

Kierkegaard: A Collection of Critical Essays. By Josiah Thompson. *Doubleday* Anchor Bks. 1972 pap. $2.95; *Peter Smith* $6.00

Kierkegaard. By Josiah Thompson. *Knopf* 1973 $8.95

Kierkegaard: A Fiction. By Barbara Anderson. *Syracuse Univ. Press* 1974 $8.75

SPENCER, HERBERT. 1820–1903.

This English philosopher called his philosophy the "Synthetic Philosophy" because it attempted "to combine all the sciences into a connected whole." This most comprehensive system, which aimed to unify and to systematize all knowledge, was outlined in "First Principles" published in 1862, and developed in the successive volumes on the principles of biology, of psychology, of sociology and of ethics. Spencer is "the one true prophet of the philosophy of evolution." He anticipated in broad outline the theory of evolution, "the survival of the fittest," which Darwin developed in detail in the "Origin of the Species" in 1859. His works out of print include "Principles of Biology" (2 vols. 1864–1867).

WORKS, 1884–1904. *Adler's* 21 vols. set $900.00; *Int. Pubns. Service* 21 vols. $900.00

PRINCIPLES OF SOCIOLOGY: Selections. 1868–1896. Ed. by Stanislav Andreski *Shoe String Press* 1969 $25.00

HERBERT SPENCER ON SOCIAL EVOLUTION. Ed. by J. D. Y. Peel *Univ. of Chicago Press* 1972 $11.50 Phoenix Bks. pap. $2.95

ESSAYS ON EDUCATION. 1861. *Littlefield* 1963 pap. $1.95; *Norwood Editions* repr. of 1896 ed. $15.00

SOCIAL STATICS: The Conditions Essential to Human Happiness Specified, and the First of Them Developed. 1851. *Kelley* $15.00; pref. by Frances Neilson *Schalkenbach* 1954 $6.00

PRINCIPLES OF PSYCHOLOGY. 1870–1872. *Milford House* repr. of 1881 2 vols. 1973 $65.00

PRINCIPLES OF SOCIOLOGY. *Greenwood* 3 vols. 1975 $90.00

THE EVOLUTION OF SOCIETY: Selections from Herbert Spencer's Principles of Sociology. Ed. with introd. by Robert J. Caneiro *Univ. of Chicago Press* 1967 $10.50

THE STUDY OF SOCIOLOGY. 1928. New introd. by Talcott Parsons *Univ. of Michigan Press* 1961 $5.95 Ann Arbor Bks. pap. $3.25

Books about Spencer

Kant and Spencer: A Critical Exposition. By Borden P. Browne. 1912. *Gordon Press* $28.00

Spencer: The Evolution of a Sociologist. By J. D. Y. Peel. *Basic Bks.* 1971 $10.00
The Philosophy of Herbert Spencer. By W. H. Hudson. *Haskell* 1974 $12.95
Herbert Spencer: Structure, Function and Evolution. Ed. by Stanislav Andreski. *Scribner* 1975 $8.95

PEIRCE, CHARLES S(ANTIAGO) S(ANDERS). 1839–1914.

Peirce has been called the master of American philosophy. He published so few works in his lifetime that recognition of his importance was long delayed. He first came to public attention when his article "How to Make Our Ideas Clear" appeared in the *Popular Science Monthly* of January 1878. Though he was an "ingenious philosopher of vast erudition, consistently fresh in his systematic approach to his work," some critics feel that he failed, since he produced no philosophical system. He influenced Josiah Royce and John Dewey and was the first to employ the term "pragmatism," later used with acknowledgment by William James. He regarded logic as the beginning of all philosophical study and established the foundations of symbolic logic. "To find the meaning of an idea, said Peirce, we must examine the consequences to which it leads in action; otherwise dispute about it may be without end, and will surely be without fruit"—(Will Durant, in "The Story of Philosophy").

COLLECTED PAPERS. *Harvard Univ. Press* 1935 8 vols. in 4 bks. 1959–1960 Vols. 1–6 ed. by Charles Hartshorne and Paul Weiss Vol. 1 Principles of Philosophy (1931) Vol. 2 Elements of Logic (1932) Vol. 3 Exact Logic (1933) Vol. 4 The Simplest Mathematics (1933) Vol. 5 Pragmatism and Pragmaticism (1934) Vol. 6 Scientific Metaphysics (1935) 3 bks. each $30.00 Vols. 7 and 8 ed. by Arthur W. Burks Vol. 7 Science and Philosophy (1958) Vol. 8 Reviews, Correspondence, and Bibliography (1958) $20.00

PHILOSOPHICAL WRITINGS. Sel. and ed. by Justus Buchler *Dover* 1956 pap. $4.00; *Peter Smith* $5.25

ESSAYS IN THE PHILOSOPHY OF SCIENCE. Ed. with introd. by Vincent Tomas *Bobbs* Lib. Arts 1957 pap. $2.75

SELECTED WRITINGS, 1839–1914. (Orig. "Values in a Universe of Chance") ed. by Philip P. Wiener *Dover* pap. $4.00; *Peter Smith* pap. $5.50

ESSENTIAL WRITINGS. Ed. by Edward C. Moore *Harper* 1972 pap. $3.95

Books about Peirce

Thought of Charles S. Peirce. By Thomas A. Goudge. 1950. *Dover* 1969 pap. $3.00; *Peter Smith* $6.00
The Development of Peirce's Philosophy. By Murray G. Murphey. *Harvard Univ. Press* 1961 $11.00
   Basing his book on unpublished Peirce manuscripts, Mr. Murphey sought insight into Peirce's thought through the events of the philosopher's life. "The biographical clues reveal many an aspect that eluded earlier commentators. . . . The chronological examination of facts leads to a factually inevitable conclusion for which Mr. Murphey deserves every praise; he has the courage to state that Peirce's manuscripts 'are the ruins of a once great structure . . . the grand design was never fulfilled' "—(*LJ*).
The Origins of Pragmatism: Studies in the Philosophy of Charles Sanders Peirce and William James. By A. J. Ayer. *Freeman, Cooper* 1969 $8.80. (*For comment, see under William James.*)

JAMES, WILLIAM. 1842–1910.

Someone has said that Henry James was a novelist who wrote like a philosopher and his brother William a philosopher who wrote like a novelist. He is eminently readable and persuasive to the layman, though philosophers have tended to find inconsistencies in his theories. Bertrand Russell says of him (in the "History of Western Philosophy"): "James was primarily a psychologist, but he was important in philosophy on two accounts: he invented the doctrine which he called 'radical empiricism,' and he was one of the three protagonists of the theory called 'pragmatism' or 'instrumentalism.' In later life he was, as he deserved to be, the recognized leader of American philosophy. He was led by the study of medicine to the consideration of psychology; his great book on the subject, published in 1890, had the highest possible excellence. . . . There were two sides to [his] philosophical interests, one scientific, the other religious. On the scientific side, the study of medicine had given his thoughts a tendency toward materialism, which, however, was held in check by his religious emotions. His religious feelings were very Protestant, very democratic, and very full of the warmth of human kindness. He refused altogether to follow his brother Henry into fastidious snobbishness. 'The prince of darkness,' he said, 'may be a gentleman, as we are told he is, but whatever the God of earth and heaven is, he can surely be no gentleman.' That is a very characteristic pronouncement."

James' pragmatic method is to test any speculation by asking what the practical consequences will be to ourselves if it be true. Popularly stated, it defines truth as "anything that works." John J. McDermott, Professor of Philosophy at Queens College, says (in his preface to the "Writings") that James' philosophy "can best be approached in terms of his personal confrontation with nihilism; his belief in a continuous, intelligible, but unfinished universe; and his attempt to develop a method of inquiry which does justice to the processive quality of both nature and man while providing for the fruitful realization of human 'interest.' James's preoccupation with individualized energies, psychic states, religious experience, extrasensory perception and the problem of truth, should be viewed as a function of these larger concerns." On the religious side, James' "Will to Believe" is still widely read. Since the existence of God is not provable by scientific method, says James, the skeptic must decide if belief in God will make the world for him a happier, more constructive place, with creative effects in his own life—if so, he may will to believe; he can only gain thereby; belief *works* for him. Russell says: "James' doctrine is an attempt to build a superstructure of belief upon a foundation of scepticism, and like all such attempts it is dependent on fallacies . . . [and] only part of the subjective madness which is characteristic of most modern philosophy." Nonetheless, some of James' readers who are not professional philosophers have been led to belief from arguments such as his, and his "religious" influence, says William Robert Miller (in the *N.Y. Times*), is reappearing among the radical theologians of the late 1960's. "The Varieties of Religious Experience" also remains popular as the account by a psychologist deeply respectful of religion while not himself a man of religion in the conventional sense. His fascinating prose style and cosmopolitan outlook made him the most influential American thinker of his day. "The great use of a life," he once said, "is to spend it for something that outlasts it."

"From his eighteenth year until his death at sixty-eight, James's life was a struggle to overcome crippling neuroses. He knew he was neurotic, as were his sister Alice and the two younger brothers . . . but he kept sane by admitting his condition and fighting his symptoms. His scientific training and his honesty with himself enabled him to make contributions of permanent value to the literature of neurology"—(Gay Wilson Allen).

THE WRITINGS OF WILLIAM JAMES: A Comprehensive Edition. Ed. with introd. by John J. McDermott, including "Annotated Bibliography" of James' works *Random* 1967 (Modern Lib. Giant) $5.95

"The vast selection of pieces represents the diversity in James' thinking that most collections miss; there is a bibliography of James' writings, and a learned introduction that . . . provides a good account of James' ideas, particularly his changing ideas of consciousness"—(*New Republic*).

SELECTED PAPERS ON PHILOSOPHY. Introd. by C. M. Bakewell *Dutton* Everyman's 1918 1956 $3.95

MORAL PHILOSOPHY OF WILLIAM JAMES. Ed. and introd. by John K. Roth *Apollo* 1960 pap. $2.95

A WILLIAM JAMES READER. Ed. by Gay W. Allen *Houghton* 1972 pap. $4.25

THE WILL TO BELIEVE AND OTHER ESSAYS IN POPULAR PHILOSOPHY (1898) and HUMAN IMMORTALITY (1898). *Dover* 1955 pap. $2.75; *Peter Smith* $5.00

ESSAYS ON FAITH AND MORALS. (Orig. "The Will to Believe"). Sel. by Ralph Barton Perry. 1943. *New Am. Lib* Meridian Bks. pap. $3.95; *Peter Smith* 1962 $6.00; *Richard West* $10.00

ON SOME OF LIFE'S IDEALS. 1899. *Folcroft* $6.50

TALKS TO TEACHERS ON PSYCHOLOGY AND TO STUDENTS ON SOME OF LIFE'S IDEALS. 1899. 1914. *Dover* 1962 pap. $1.25; *Norton* pap. $1.25; *Peter Smith* $4.75

THE VARIETIES OF RELIGIOUS EXPERIENCE. 1902. new ed. 1928. *Macmillan* Collier Bks. pap. $1.25; *New Am. Lib.* pap. $1.50; *Random* (Modern Lib.) 1936 $3.95

PRAGMATISM: A New Name for Some Old Ways of Thinking. 1907. Ed. by Frederick Burkhardt; textual ed. Fredson Bowers, assisted by Ignas K. Skrupskelis *Harvard* 1975 $12.50; (and four essays from "The Meaning of Truth") ed. by Ralph Barton Perry *New Am. Lib.* Meridian Bks. 1943 pap. $3.95; *Simon & Schuster* (Washington Square) pap. $.95; *Peter Smith* $5.00

ESSAYS ON PRAGMATISM. Ed. with introd. by Alburey Castell *Macmillan* (Hafner) 1948 1954 pap. $1.95

THE MEANING OF TRUTH: A Sequel to Pragmatism. 1909. *Greenwood* 1968 $13.00; *Univ. of Michigan Press* 1970 $6.95 Ann Arbor Bks. pap. $3.95

A PLURALISTIC UNIVERSE. 1909. *Folcroft* 1973 $20.00; (and "Essays in Radical Empiricism" 1911) *Peter Smith* $7.00

MEMORIES AND STUDIES. 1911. Ed. by Henry James *Folcroft* 1973 $16.00; *Greenwood* 1968 $16.25; *Scholarly Press* 1971 $14.50

LETTERS OF WILLIAM JAMES AND THEODORE FLOURNOY. Trans. and ed. by R. C. LeClair *Univ. of Wisconsin Press* 1966 $12.50. Professor Flournoy was a Swiss psychologist.

Books about James

> Annotated Bibliography of the Writings of William James. By Ralph Barton Perry. 1920. *Christian F. Verbeke* $9.50
>
> The Three Jameses. By C. Hartley Grattan. 1932. *New York Univ. Press* reissue 1962 $10.00 pap. $2.75
>
> The Thought and Character of William James. By Ralph Barton Perry. 1935. *Harvard Univ. Press* abr. ed. 1948 $11.00. Pulitzer Prize-winning biography.
>
> In Commemoration of William James, 1842–1942. 1942. *AMS Press* $7.50. A collection of essays about James.
>
> The James Family. By F. O. Matthiessen. *Knopf* 1947 $10.00
>
> In the Spirit of William James. By Ralph Barton Perry. *Indiana Univ. Press* 1958 pap. $1.50; *Peter Smith* $4.00
>
> William James: A Biography. By Gay Wilson Allen. *Viking* 1967 pap. $3.45
> The first thorough biography in 30 years, and an excellent one. "Using a wealth of sources, more than any previous author has had at his disposal for this subject, and tracing with skill and understanding the relationship between William James' emotional and intellectual life, Gay Wilson Allen has written a lucid and important biography"—*(PW)*.
>
> Introduction to William James. By Andrew J. Reck. *Indiana Univ. Press* 1967 $6.95 $6.50
>
> William James. By Bernard P. Brennan. United States Authors Ser. *Twayne* 1968 pap. $2.45
>
> The Origins of Pragmatism: Studies in the Philosophy of Charles Sanders Peirce and William James. By A. J. Ayer. *Freeman, Cooper* 1969 $8.80
> The British philosopher has "focused all of his attention of these figures [and] limited himself to their pragmatism and allied doctrines.... We can be grateful for an illuminating and challenging study, which allows us to witness the impact of two of our most distinguished philosophical minds on one of the most lucid and least insular of present-day English philosophical writers"—(Morton White, in the *N.Y. Review of Books*).
>
> Freedom and Moral Life: The Ethics of William James. By John K. Roth. *Westminster Press* 1969 $5.00
>
> Unifying Moment: The Psychological Philosophy of William James and Alfred North Whitehead. By Craig R. Eisendrath. *Harvard Univ. Press* 1971 $10.00

See also Chapter 6, Psychology, this Volume.

NIETZSCHE, FRIEDRICH. 1844–1900.

The German, Nietzsche, began his career as an advocate of Schopenhauer's philosophy. He rejected, however, Schopenhauer's "will-to-live" theory, and substituted the "will-to-power." This led to Nietzsche's famous doctrine of the superman, his protest against the excesses of humanitarianism. "His work has had considerable influence on Nazi and totalitarian type political thinkers." Nietzsche's greatest work, "Thus Spake Zarathustra," was made the basis of a tone poem by Richard Strauss. "Ecce Homo" is autobiographical. Among writers of philosophy, especially among German writers, Nietzsche stands out for the clarity and charm of his style. Much of his writing reads like "prose-poetry," so exalted and rhapsodical is it in tone.

His father was a Lutheran pastor, and after his early death the young Friedrich was brought up in the midst of five women: his mother, his grandmother, two aunts and his sister. It is not surprising that some of the most bitter language of his later work is directed against women. In 1882 he had a disillusioning experience with Lou Andreas-Salomé (1861–1937), a young Finnish woman who was interested in his intellectual pursuits but not in marriage. Her own works— fiction, essays, and treatises on psychoanalysis—are hardly read any more. For the first full-length biography of this remarkable woman, "My Sister, My Spouse: A Biography of Lou Andreas-Salomé" (*Norton* 1962 $5.00 pap. $3.95), the author, H. F. Peters, had access to her papers and has interpreted her writings not so much in their own right, but chiefly as sources for her life and ideas. "The emphases in his book are on the fateful parts she played in the lives of Nietzsche, Rilke, and a considerable number of other men." A more recent and most interesting "psychoanalytic" biography is Rudolph Binion's "Frau Lou: Nietzsche's Wayward Disciple" (*Princeton Univ. Press* 1968 $15.00 pap. $5.95) which contains an important bibliography.

James Gutman wrote of the philosopher (*Nation,* April 8, 1968): "Nietzsche's thought and vision are increasingly relevant. His analyses of human weakness and his vision of the possibilities of human power, his awareness of the dissolution of traditional values of Christendom, his sense of urgency of a revaluation of traditional values, the almost apocalyptic anticipation of wars to come, make his writings singularly topical."

COMPLETE WORKS. Ed. by Oscar Levy *Gordon Press* 18 vols. 1964 ltd. ed. set $640.00

BASIC WRITINGS. *Random* (Modern Lib. Giants) $5.95

THE PORTABLE NIETZSCHE. Sel. and trans. with introd., pref. and notes by Walter Kaufmann *Viking* 1954 $5.50 pap. $3.50

New translations in their entirety of: Thus Spake Zarathustra; Twilight of the Idols; the Antichrist; Nietzsche Contra Wagner; also selections from 12 other works, many notes and letters, a chronology, a bibliographical note and an informative introduction.

THE BIRTH OF TRAGEDY. 1872. (And the "Genealogy of Morals," 1887) trans. by Francis Golffing *Doubleday* Anchor Bks. 1956 pap. $1.95; (and "The Case of Wagner") *Random* Vintage Bks. 1967 pap. $1.95

THUS SPAKE ZARATHUSTRA. 1883–1891. *Dutton* Everyman's $3.95; *Gordon Press* 1974 $39.95; trans. by R. J. Hollingdale *Penguin* 1961 pap. $1.25; *Random* (Modern Lib.) $3.95; trans. by Walter Kaufmann *Viking* Compass Bks. rev. ed. 1966 pap. $1.95

BEYOND GOOD AND EVIL. 1886. Trans. by Walter Kaufmann *Random* Vintage Bks. 1966 pap. $2.45; trans. with introd. by Marianne Cowan *Regnery* 1955 pap. $1.95

THE USE AND ABUSE OF HISTORY. Trans. by A. Collins *Bobbs* Lib. Arts 1957 pap. $.90

PHILOSOPHY IN THE TRAGIC AGE OF THE GREEKS. Trans. with introd. by Marianne Cowan *Regnery* 1962 pap. $1.25

ON THE GENEALOGY OF MORALS (1887) and ECCE HOMO (1908). Trans. by Walter Kaufmann *Random* Vintage Bks. pap. $1.95

JOYFUL WISDOM. Trans. by Thomas Common *Ungar* $9.50 pap. $3.25

THE WILL TO POWER. 1901. Trans. by Walter Kaufmann and R. J. Hollingdale *Random* 1967 Vintage Bks. 1968 pap. $2.95

"Beginning in 1901 . . . various editors published versions of *The Will to Power*, grouping under appropriate topic headings selected notebook entries, ranging from 483 in the 1901 edition to over a thousand in the 1911 edition. The present translation follows the arrangement of the 1911 edition and includes extensive annotations"—*(LJ)*.

NIETZSCHE: A SELF PORTRAIT FROM HIS LETTERS. Ed. by Peter Fuss and Henry Shapiro *Harvard Univ. Press* 1971 $8.00

Books about Nietzsche

Nietzsche. By Crane Brinton. *Harper* Torchbks. pap. $2.25

Nietzsche: Philosopher, Psychologist, Antichrist. By Walter Arnold Kaufmann. 1950. *Random* Vintage Bks. pap. $2.45. A reappraisal that "may be the definitive study of Nietzsche's life and thought."

The Tragic Philosopher: A Study of Friedrich Nietzsche. By F. A. Lea. *Harper* (Barnes and Noble) 1957 $16.50

"Any college or research library interested in Nietzsche in depth would be interested in this"—*(Reprint Bulletin)*.

Nietzsche. By Martin Heidegger. *Adler's* 2 vols. 1961 set $34.00

Whitman and Nietzsche. By C. N. Stavrou. *AMS Press* 1964 lib. bdg. $12.50

Nietzsche: An Introduction to the Understanding of His Philosophical Activity. By Karl Jaspers. Trans. by Charles F. Wallraff and Frederick D. Schmitz *Univ. of Arizona Press* 1965 $12.00; *Regnery* Gateway Eds. pap. $3.95

"In [Dr. Jaspers'] view, Nietzsche must be placed alongside Kierkegaard as a major influence on contemporary philosophy. . . . The book is equipped with the full scholarly apparatus of footnotes, an extensive bibliography, and chronological tables"—*(LJ)*. Dr. Jaspers is, of course, the philosophy professor of Heidelberg and Basel who was one of the founders of existentialism. A closely reasoned, scholarly work of "almost overpowering detail"—*(LJ)*.

Nietzsche As Philosopher. By A. Danto. *Macmillan* 1965 $5.95 pap. $2.45

[The author aims] "to display the philosopher as a systematic thinker, and in paying special attention to the epistemological and logical elements in Nietzsche's writings he presents an interestingly unfamiliar picture of Nietzsche's work"—(*N.Y. Review of Books*).

Nietzsche: The Man and His Philosophy. By R. J. Hollingdale. *Louisiana State Univ. Press* 1967 pap. $2.45

"Mr. Hollingdale has written a scholarly and attractive study of both the man and his work. It enables us to see Nietzsche against his own background: to see the real originality of his philosophy; and to see how far he was in truth, and how he was converted into being, a prophet of the Nazi movement"—(*New Statesman*).

Friedrich Nietzsche: An Illustrated Biography. By Ivo Frenzel. Trans. from the German by Joachim Neugroschel *Pegasus* 1967 pap. $1.00

This book's "usefulness as an introduction to the philosopher will certainly be considerable"—(*LJ*).

Nietzsche the Thinker: A Study. By William Mackintire Salter. *Ungar* $11.00

Dostoevsky, Tolstoy and Nietzsche. By Lev Shestov. *Ohio Univ. Press* 1970 $11.00

Nietzsche: A Biographical Introduction. By Janko Lavrin. *Scribner* 1972 $6.95 pap. $2.95

Nietzsche. By R. J. Hollingdale. *Routledge and Kegan Paul* 1973 $9.25 pap. $4.75

Truth and Value in Nietzsche: A Study of His Metaethics and Epistemology. By John T. Wilcox. *Univ. of Michigan* 1974 $9.00

Friedrich Nietzsche: Philosopher of Culture. By Frederick Copleston. *Harper* (Barnes and Noble) 2nd ed. 1975 $10.95

"Copleston's book on Nietzsche is one of the best expositions and discussions of that philosopher in the English language"—(*The Sunday Times,* London).

Index to Nietzsche. Ed. by Robert Guppy; trans. by Paul V. Cohn *Gordon Press* 1975 $39.95

BOSANQUET, BERNARD. 1848–1923.

Bosanquet, an English philosopher, was educated at Oxford, where he later lectured. His works have been called the ripest fruit of the idealistic development in England. Patriotism he considered to be a sober loyalty toward fellow citizens. Influenced by Hegel, Bosanquet eventually "arrived at the conviction of an indispensable reality beyond and behind experience, a reality which determines the true mutual relations of all beings"—(*Encyclopaedia Britannica*).

THREE LECTURES ON AESTHETIC. Ed. with introd. by Ralph G. Ross *Bobbs* Lib. Arts 1963 pap. $1.25; *Kraus* 1968 $10.00

KNOWLEDGE AND REALITY. 1885. *Kraus* $19.00

LOGIC, or The Morphology of Knowledge. 1888. *Kraus* 2nd ed. 2 vols. in 1 $38.00

HISTORY OF AESTHETIC. 1892. *Humanities Press* 1956 $11.50

THE ESSENTIALS OF LOGIC. 1895. *St. Martin's* $4.95; *Kraus* 1968 $11.00

THE PHILOSOPHICAL THEORY OF THE STATE. 1899. *St. Martin's Press* 1920 4th ed. 1923 $5.95

THE PRINCIPLE OF INDIVIDUALITY AND VALUE. 1911. *Kraus* $24.00

THE VALUE AND DESTINY OF THE INDIVIDUAL. 1912. *Kraus* $20.00

SOCIAL AND INTERNATIONAL IDEALS. 1917. *Bks. for Libraries* 1967 $13.75; *Kraus* $19.00

SOME SUGGESTIONS IN ETHICS. 1918. *Kraus* 1968 $14.00

IMPLICATION AND LINEAR INFERENCES. 1920. *Kraus* 1968 $12.00

THREE CHAPTERS ON THE NATURE OF THE MIND. 1923. Ed. by Helen Bosanquet *Kraus* 1968 $11.00

SCIENCE AND PHILOSOPHY, AND OTHER ESSAYS. *Bks. for Libraries* $13.00

CROCE'S AESTHETICS. *Haskell* 1972 pap. $2.95; *Gordon Press* 1974 $25.00

ROYCE, JOSIAH. 1856–1916.

Royce stands next to William James as an American philosopher of international repute. He has been called "a philosopher of imagination" because he "reinstated in philosophical thinking the element of imagination." Charles M. Bakewell (in the *Nation*) has pointed out that the philosophies of James and of Royce were complementary rather than antagonistic. James was a pragmatist, Royce an absolute idealist. Ethical and religious interests predominate in the work of both men. Royce's delightful style makes easy reading. His pages contain abundant incident, anecdote, quotation and illustration. Santayana (*q.v.*) treats Royce, among others, in his "Character and Opinion in the United States" (*Norton* $1.95).

Royce, like James, was also a psychologist. "Of the two branches of psychology, philosophical and experimental, Royce was really interested in the former. . . . *The World and the Individual* is largely philosophical psychology. . . . He served as president of the American Psychological Association, and as chairman of its Committee on Apparitions and Haunted Houses, which, at his prompting changed its title to the Committee on Phantasms and Presentments"—(Vincent Buranelli). Royce also wrote a novel and literary criticism.

BASIC WRITINGS. Ed. by John J. McDermott *Univ. of Chicago Press* 2 vols. 1969 each $17.50

THE PHILOSOPHY OF JOSIAH ROYCE. Ed. by John K. Roth *T. Y. Crowell* 1971 $8.95; *Apollo* 1971 $2.95

THE RELIGIOUS ASPECT OF PHILOSOPHY. 1885. *Folcroft* $17.50; *Peter Smith* $5.50

THE SPIRIT OF MODERN PHILOSOPHY. 1892. *Norton* 1967 pap. $2.65; *Peter Smith* $5.00

STUDIES OF GOOD AND EVIL: A Series of Essays upon Problems of Philosophy and Life. 1898. *Shoe String Press* $11.00

THE CONCEPTION OF GOD. 1898. *Scholarly Press* $14.50

THE CONCEPTION OF IMMORTALITY. 1900. *Greenwood* 1968 $5.25; *Scholarly Press* $5.00

THE WORLD AND THE INDIVIDUAL. 1900–1901. *Peter Smith* $12.00. Royce's most ambitious work (the Gifford lectures).

RACE QUESTIONS, PROVINCIALISM, AND OTHER AMERICAN PROBLEMS. 1908. *Bks. for Libraries* $11.00

THE PROBLEM OF CHRISTIANITY. 1913. *Univ. of Chicago Press* 1968 $14.00; *Regnery* Gateway Eds. 2 vols. 1968 pap. each $2.45

FUGITIVE ESSAYS. 1920. *Bks. for Libraries* $14.25

PRINCIPLES OF LOGIC. *Citadel Press* pap. $.95

LETTERS. Ed. by John Clendenning *Univ. of Chicago Press* 1970 $17.50

Books about Royce

Josiah Royce. By Vincent Buranelli. American Authors Ser. *Twayne* 1963 $7.95; *College & Univ. Press* 1964 pap. $2.45
This is "an attempt to present Josiah Royce as he has not been presented before—to describe him in the round and through his multifarious aspects from novelist and literary critic to logician and metaphysician"—(Author's preface).
The Moral Philosophy of Josiah Royce. By Peter Fuss. *Harvard Univ. Press* 1965 $8.00
"This is the first full-scale study of Royce's ethics. It applies with exceptional success the best canons of philosophical scholarship. Reporting the development of Royce's ethical theories from his earliest to his final writings, Mr. Fuss pauses at strategic points to examine the validity of Royce's salient contributions to the understanding of right and wrong. The examination is well-informed, penetrating, and fair"—(L.J).
Josiah Royce. By Thomas F. Powell. 1967. *Twayne* $7.95
Royce and Hocking: American Idealists. By Daniel S. Robinson. *Christopher Pub.* 1968 $5.00
"In this single volume there are compiled essays from various journals and books, many of which are practically inaccessible today. The letters of William Ernest Hocking and of Josiah Royce's son, Stephen, contain informative items nowhere else available in print"—(Publisher's note).
Josiah Royce: An Intellectual Biography. By Bruce Kuklick. *Bobbs* Lib. Arts 1972 $12.50
Self and the World in the Philosophy of Josiah Royce. By Bhagwah B. Singh. *C. C. Thomas* 1973 $7.95

BERGSON, HENRI (LOUIS). 1859–1941. (Nobel Prize 1927)

No other thinker at the beginning of the century succeeded so well in interesting the public in philosophy. His new theory of the universe was that evolution is due to an indwelling creative force which he called the *élan vital*, "vital energy," recalling the "will-to-live" of Schopenhauer. His work provoked a vast amount of controversy. He was born of Anglo-Jewish parents in Paris and was educated in the Paris public schools and French universities. He became a member of the French Academy in 1914 and received the Nobel Prize for Literature in 1927. Just the month before he died, he renounced all his posts and honors because of discrimination against the Jews, though the Vichy government had exempted him because of his "literary and artistic services to the Nation."

TIME AND FREE WILL. 1889. Trans. by F. L. Pogson *Harper* Torchbks. 1960 pap. $3.45; *Humanities Press* 1910 1971 $10.00

MATTER AND MEMORY. 1896. Trans. by Nancy Paul and W. Scott Palmer *Humanities Press* 1911 1970 $10.00

LAUGHTER. 1900. (And George Meredith's "Essay on Comedy") *Doubleday* Anchor Bks. 1956 pap. $1.95; *Peter Smith* $4.50

CREATIVE EVOLUTION. 1907. *Richard West.* repr. of 1911 ed. $20.00

CREATIVE MIND: An Introduction to Metaphysics. (With title "An Introduction to Metaphysics") trans. by T. E. Hulme *Bobbs* Lib. Arts 1949 pap. $.80; *Citadel Press* 1974 pap. $3.45; (with title "A Study in Metaphysics") trans. by Maybelle L. Andison *Littlefield* 1965 pap. $1.95

DURATION AND SIMULTANEITY. Trans. by L. Jacobson *Bobbs* Lib. Arts 1965 $6.00

Books about Bergson

The Philosophy of Bergson. By Bertrand Russell. 1914. *Folcroft* $10.00

Bergson: Philosopher of Reflection. By I. W. Alexander. *Hillary House* 1957 $2.75

The Bergsonian Heritage. Ed. by Thomas Hanna. *Columbia* 1962 $9.00
  To mark the centenary of his birth, 11 French and American scholars interpret Bergson's life and thought. "In the introduction, the editor assigns Bergson an important place in modern philosophy for the subtlety of his arguments and the wealth of insights, rather than for the endurance of specific doctrines." A bibliography of his chief works and recent full-length books on him is appended.

Bergson and the Stream of Consciousness Novel. By Shiv K. Kumar. *New York Univ. Press* 1963 $6.95 pap. $1.95. Uses his concepts to analyze the work of Dorothy Richardson, Virginia Woolf and James Joyce.

DEWEY, JOHN. 1859–1952.

John Dewey, while head of the philosophy department at Columbia, was the foremost authority on progressive education in America. In 1899 he published his revolutionary book, "The School and Society," "which is considered," says Bertrand Russell, "the most influential of all his writings." "Progressive" schools, embodying his concept of learning by *experiencing*—or becoming involved in the processes of knowledge, as opposed to mere book-learning and rote reproduction of the words of the teacher—burgeoned in this country in the 1920's. Though the broader forms of permissiveness (not sanctioned by Dewey), to which interpretations of progressive schooling sometimes led, have in general been avoided in U.S. public education, the taking of trips, the making of model African villages, the use of dramatization, the freer classroom with movable furniture are just a few of the elements in which Dewey's view of education as personal inquiry are still pursued in American education today.

In philosophy, says Bertrand Russell, "Dewey does not aim at judgments that shall be absolutely 'true' or condemn their contradictories as absolutely 'false.' In his opinion there is a process called 'inquiry,' which is one form of mutual adjustment between an organism and its environment." Russell agrees wholeheartedly with most of Dewey's educational doctrines but finds the degree of his philosophic relativism hard to digest. "Logic: The Theory of Inquiry," published when he was nearly 80, is Dewey's major philosophical work. He made his field the whole of human experience—including politics and psychology—following eagerly wherever the spirit of inquiry might lead him. Dewey derives more thoroughly from America than any other American philosopher, accepting democracy completely and believing that democracy is a primary ethical value. His original philosophy, called instrumentalism, holds that "the various modes and forms of human activity are instruments developed by man to solve his multiple individual and social problems"— (*Columbia Encyclopedia*). Instrumentalism is related to utilitarianism and pragmatism.

THE EARLY WORKS OF JOHN DEWEY, 1882–1898. *Southern Illinois Univ. Press* 5 vols. Vol. 1 1882–1888: Early Essays and Leibniz's New Essays Concerning the Human Understanding (1968) Vol. 2 1887: Psychology (1967) Vol. 3 1889–1892: Early Essays and Outline of a Critical Theory of Ethics (1969) Vol. 4 1893–1894: Early Essays and The Study of Ethics (1971) Vol. 5 1895–1898: Early Essays (1972) each $15.00 pap. $2.95. These are textual editions sponsored by the Cooperative Research on Dewey Publications Program at Southern Illinois University; they bear the seal of the Modern Language Assn. Center for Editions of American Authors.

THE MIDDLE WORKS OF JOHN DEWEY, 1889–1924. *Southern Illinois Univ. Press* 2 vols. Vol. 1 1889–1901 Vol. 2 1902–1903 (in prep). This is a continuation of "The Early Works" (*above*), which will bring together all of Dewey's works except correspondence. The first 2 vols. are also approved by MLA Center for Editions of American Authors.

ON EXPERIENCE, NATURE, AND FREEDOM: Representative Selections. Ed. by Richard J. Bernstein *Bobbs* Lib. Arts 1960 pap. $2.75

THE CHILD AND THE CURRICULUM (1902) and THE SCHOOL AND SOCIETY (1899). Introd. by Carmichael *Univ. of Chicago Press* $6.00 Phoenix Bks. 1956 pap. $2.25

HOW WE THINK. 1909. *Heath* 1933 $9.95

DEMOCRACY AND EDUCATION. *Macmillan* 1916 pap. $2.75

INTEREST AND EFFORT IN EDUCATION. 1913. With a new preface by James E. Wheeler *Southern Illinois Univ. Press* 1975 pap. $2.65

ESSAYS IN EXPERIMENTAL LOGIC. 1916. *Dover* 1953 pap. $3.50; *Peter Smith* $5.00

RECONSTRUCTION IN PHILOSOPHY. 1920. *Beacon* 1957 pap. $2.95

HUMAN NATURE AND CONDUCT. 1922. *Random* Modern Library $3.95

EXPERIENCE AND NATURE. *Open Court* 1925 $10.00 rev. ed. pap. $2.75; *Dover* pap $3.00; *Peter Smith* $5.00

THE QUEST FOR CERTAINTY. 1929. *Putnam* Capricorn Bks. 1960 pap. $1.95

ART AS EXPERIENCE. 1934. *Putnam* Capricorn Bks. 1959 pap. $2.35

A COMMON FAITH. *Yale Univ. Press* 1934 $7.50 1960 pap. $2.25

LOGIC: The Theory of Inquiry. *Holt* 1938 $10.50

ON EDUCATION. *Random* Modern Library $2.45

PHILOSOPHY AND CIVILIZATION. *Peter Smith* $5.00

FREEDOM AND CULTURE. *Putnam* Capricorn Bks. 1963 pap. $2.25

EXPERIENCE AND EDUCATION. *Macmillan* Collier Bks. pap. $1.25

PHILOSOPHY OF EDUCATION. (Orig. "Problems of Men"). 1946. Littlefield College Outline Ser. *Littlefield* 1958 pap. $2.50

Books about Dewey

John Dewey: Philosopher of Science and Freedom. Ed. by Sidney Hook. 1939. *Greenwood* $12.25

John Dewey: The Reconstruction of the Democratic Life. By Jerome Nathanson. 1951. *Ungar* $4.50 pap. $1.45. Excellent résumé of Dewey's ideas as philosopher, psychologist and educator.

John Dewey in Perspective. By George R. Geiger. 1958. *Greenwood* 1974 $12.00

John Dewey. Ed. by John Blewett. 1960. *Greenwood* 1973 $11.25

John Dewey: A Centennial Bibliography. By Milton Halsey Thomas. *Univ. of Chicago Press* 3rd ed. 1962 $10.00
The writings about Dewey have grown considerably since the first edition of this bibliography in 1929 and the second in 1939. The first part contains a chronological listing of the books, articles and miscellaneous writings from 1882 to 1960. Part 2 consists of a bibliography of writings about Dewey, arranged alphabetically by author. This book is well-edited and useful.

Dewey on Education: Appraisals. Ed. by Reginald Archambault. *Philadelphia Bk. Co.* 1966 $3.25; *Peter Smith* $4.50

John Dewey's Philosophy of Value. By James Gouinlock. *Humanities Press* 1972 $10.00

A Guide to the Works of John Dewey. Ed. by Jo A. Boydston. *Southern Illinois Univ. Press* 1972 $7.00 pap. $2.95
"A comprehensive survey of the entire corpus of Dewey's work—almost 1,000 items. [Now] we have all of Dewey—classified both chronologically and logically, except for stray pieces which perhaps this collection will eventually incorporate"—(*Choice*).

Young John Dewey: An Essay in American Intellectual History. By Neil Coughlan. *Chicago Univ. Press* 1975 $10.75

HUSSERL, EDMUND. 1859–1938.

Edmund Husserl, founder of modern phenomenology, influenced his pupil Heidegger and the most prominent French existentialists of our time, Merleau-Ponty and Sartre. "For Husserl, phenomenology was a discipline that attempts to describe what is given to us in experience without obscuring preconceptions or hypothetical speculations; his motto was 'to the things themselves'—rather than to the pre-fabricated conceptions we put in their place. . . . Instead of making intellectual speculations about the whole of reality, philosophy must turn, Husserl declared, to a pure description of what is"—(William Barrett, in "Irrational Man").

IDEAS: General Introduction to Pure Phenomenology. 1931. *Humanities Press* 1958 $10.50 pap. $2.75; *Macmillan* Collier Bks. pap. 1962 $1.50. Published in German 1913.

CARTESIAN MEDITATIONS: An Introduction to Phenomenology. Trans. by Dorion Cairns *Heinman* 1960 1970 pap. $4.50; *Humanities Press* 1960 pap. $4.25

PHENOMENOLOGY OF INTERNAL TIME-CONSCIOUSNESS. Trans. by James S. Churchill; ed. by Martin Heidegger *Indiana Univ. Press* 1964 $7.95 pap. $1.95

PARIS LECTURES. *Humanities Press* 1964 pap. $4.25

IDEA OF PHENOMENOLOGY. Trans. by William P. Alston and George Nakhnikian *Humanities Press* 1964 pap. $4.25

PHENOMENOLOGY AND THE CRISIS OF PHILOSOPHY. Trans. by Quentin Lauer *Harper* Torchbks. 1965 pap. $2.45. Published in German 1936.

LOGICAL INVESTIGATIONS. *Humanities Press* 2 vols. 1970 set $36.00. Published in German, 1900–1901.

Books about Husserl

Edmund Husserl's Theory of Meaning. By J. N. Mohanty. *Humanities Press* 1964 $8.25
Aims of Phenomenology. By Marvin Farber. *Harper* Torchbks. 1966 pap. $2.25; *Peter Smith* $4.50
Sensations and Phenomenology. By Harmon M. Chapman. *Indiana Univ. Press* 1966 $7.50
Husserl: An Analysis of His Phenomenology. By Paul Ricoeur. Trans. by E. G. Ballard and L. E. Embree *Northwestern Univ. Press* 1967 $8.50
    "From 'the best informed French historian of phenomenology' comes this superb collection of essays of interpretation and criticism of Husserl"—(*LJ*).
Foundations of Phenomenology: Edmund Husserl and the Quest for a Rigorous Science of Philosophy. By Marvin Farber. *State Univ. of New York Press* 3rd ed. 1967 $10.00 pap. $4.95
Phenomenology. By Quentin Lauer. *Harper* Torchbks. pap. $2.45
Phenomenology of Husserl: Selected Critical Readings. Ed. by R. O. Elveton. *Quadrangle* 1970 $15.00 pap. $2.95
Guide to Translating Husserl. By Dorion Cairns. *Humanities Press* 1973 $16.00 pap. $12.00
Edmund Husserl: Philosopher of Infinite Tasks. *Northwestern Univ. Press* 1973 $10.00
Husserl and the Search for Certitude. By Leszek Kolakowski. *Yale Univ. Press* 1975 $6.95
    "This slim book comprises the Cassirer lectures delivered at Yale University in 1974"—(*LJ*).

WHITEHEAD, ALFRED NORTH. 1861–1947.

It has been said that "the road to future metaphysical speculation will be *through* Whitehead and not round him." He criticized antireligious science, and his philosophy of "organism" is idealistic rather than materialistic. "He aimed at reconciling the discordant components of existence. The whole world, he declared, is a process of enduring, harmonious interaction. He looked for essential unity in the apparent diversity of things"—(*Biographical Encyclopedia of Philosophy*). After his graduation from Cambridge he lectured there and at the University of London on mathematics; from 1924 to 1937 he was professor of philosophy at Harvard and Emeritus Professor of Philosophy until his death. Like Bertrand Russell, he viewed philosophy at the start from the standpoint of mathematics, and, with Russell, he wrote "*Principia Mathematica*" (1910–1913, *Cambridge* 2nd ed. 3 vols. 1925–1927 set $95.00 Vol. 1 1962 pap. $1.95). Although the very nature of his subject makes his work abstruse, Edmund Wilson has called his style "not so much lucid as crystalline." Whitehead was a "master of vivid aphorism and subtle wit." In 1945 he received Britain's Order of Merit, considered the highest honor in the field of learning.

ALFRED NORTH WHITEHEAD: An Anthology. Ed. by F. S. C. Northrop and Mason Gross *Macmillan* 1953 1961 $6.95 pap. $2.95

"The editors have chosen excerpts so skillfully that this anthology of less than a thousand pages not only represents his diverse channels of thought comprehensively but manages to unify and relate them. . . . Several of his essays . . . are far too technical for the average reader, but the examples of Whitehead's thinking on such topics as religion, symbolism, scientific method, and thinking itself are readable with a little effort, and well worth that effort"—(*New Yorker*).

WHITEHEAD'S INTERPRETATION OF SCIENCE: Representative Selections. Ed. with introd. by A. H. Johnson *Bobbs* Lib. Arts 1961 pap. $2.50

WHITEHEAD'S AMERICAN ESSAYS IN SOCIAL PHILOSOPHY. 1959. *Greenwood* 1975 $12.25

THE CONCEPT OF NATURE. *Cambridge* 1919 $12.50 pap. $4.75

SCIENCE AND THE MODERN WORLD. *Macmillan* 1925 $6.95 pap. $1.95. His best non-technical book.

SYMBOLISM: Its Meaning and Effect. 1927. *Putnam* Capricorn Bks. 1959 pap. $1.65

THE AIMS OF EDUCATION. 1928. *Macmillan* 1959 $5.00 pap. $2.45

PROCESS AND REALITY: An Essay in Cosmology. 1929. *Macmillan* 1967 $6.50 pap. $3.95

ADVENTURES OF IDEAS. *Macmillan* 1933 $6.95 pap. $1.95

RELIGION IN THE MAKING. 1936. *New Am. Lib.* Meridian Bks. 1960 pap. $2.95

MODES OF THOUGHT. *Macmillan* (Free Press) 1968 pap. $1.95. Eight lectures.

SCIENCE AND PHILOSOPHY. 1947. *Littlefield* 1964 pap. $1.95; *Philosophical Lib.* 1968 pap. $1.65

ESSAYS IN SCIENCE AND PHILOSOPHY. 1947. *Greenwood* 1968 pap. $18.50

AN INTRODUCTION TO MATHEMATICS. *Oxford* 1948 rev. ed. 1959 Galaxy Bks. pap. $2.50

THE PHILOSOPHY OF ALFRED NORTH WHITEHEAD. Ed. by P. A. Schilpp. 1941. *Open Court* $15.00. Contains the only existing Whitehead autobiography, critical essays and an excellent bibliography of his works.

Books about Whitehead

Whitehead's Theory of Knowledge. 1941. By John W. Blyth. *Kraus* 1973 $8.00

Whitehead's Philosophy of Time. By William W. Hammerschmidt. 1947. *Russell & Russell* 1975 $8.00

Whitehead's Theory of Reality. 1952. By A. H. Johnson. 1962 *Peter Smith* $4.75

Whitehead's Philosophy of Civilization. 1958. By A. H. Johnson. *Dover* 1962 pap. $2.50; *Peter Smith* $4.75

An Interpretation of Whitehead's Metaphysics. By William A. Christian. *Yale Univ. Press* 1959 1967 pap. $2.95. Based mainly on the later writings beginning with "Science and the Modern World" (1925), this discusses theological implications.

Whitehead's Philosophy of Science. By Robert M. Palter. *Univ. of Chicago Press* 1960 $8.50

Understanding Whitehead. By Victor Lowe. *Johns Hopkins Press* 1962 $11.00 pap. $3.45

The author of this little book has been "remarkably successful in helping the more general reader to understand Whitehead's philosophy. . . . The opening chapter entitled 'Whitehead's Way' serves as a general introduction. Successive chapters on the first, second and third periods of Whitehead's work grow increasingly complex but never incomprehensible."

Whitehead's Philosophy of Organism. By D. Emmet. *St. Martin's* 2nd ed. 1966 $10.95

Whitehead's Metaphysics: A Critical Examination of Process and Reality. By Edward Pols. *Southern Illinois Univ. Press* 1967 $6.50

Whitehead's Philosophy: Selected Essays, 1935–1970. By Charles Hartshorne. *Univ. of Nebraska Press* 1972 $7.95

The Civilization of Experience: A Whiteheadian Theory of Culture. By David L. Hall. *Fordham Univ. Press* 1973 $12.50

SANTAYANA, GEORGE. 1863–1952.

A gentle and famous philosopher-poet, born and reared in Spain, educated at Harvard and later Professor of Philosophy there, Santayana resided abroad after 1914. Most of his later work was done in England and Italy. At the beginning of World War II he entered the nursing home in Rome, of the nuns known as the Blue Sisters, and remained there until his death. He was still a Spanish subject. His last book "The Poet's Testament" (1953, o.p.) contains a few unpublished lyrics, several translations and two plays in blank verse. The title comes from the poem read at his funeral, which begins: "I give back to the earth what the earth gave/ All to the furrow, nothing to the grave."

"Nineteenth-century England and America, according to Santayana, constitute the most barbarous civilization in history. . . . The nineteenth-century emphasis on the material left no room for universality in poetry. The poetry of barbarism, represented by the works of Browning and Whitman, yielded a whimsical and flickering retrospective fancy, negative and partial ideals, and a moral strength possessed of 'blind and miscellaneous vehemence.' . . . Browning and Whitman proved to Santayana that in the nineteenth century the growing order in the spheres of science and industry was paralleled by a growing chaos in the sphere of the imagination"—(James Ballowe, in introd. to "George Santayana's America").

His first published philosophical book, "The Sense of Beauty," was an important contribution in the field of aesthetics. His great early classic, "The Life of Reason," states the essence of his attitude toward nature, life and society. It was published in 5 volumes: "Introduction and Reason in Common Sense" (1905, o.p.), "Reason in Society" (*see below*), "Reason in Religion" (1905, o.p.) and "Reason in Science" (1966, o.p.) "Scepticism and Animal Faith" serves as an introduction to "Realms of Being," published in 4 volumes, which discusses the themes of man's knowledge. His ideas were "popularized" in his only novel, "The Last Puritan," which became a surprise best seller overnight. "He came into a changing American scene with a whole group of concepts that enormously enriched our thinking. He gave a moving vitality to what had often been obscure abstractions . . . he made the whole relationship of reason and beauty, each to the other, come alive and stay alive"—(*N.Y. Times*). Santayana's "Complete Poems" are available from *Bucknell Univ. Press* (1975 $35.00).

THE PHILOSOPHY OF GEORGE SANTAYANA: Selections. Ed. by Irwin Edman. 1953. *Richard West* $20.00

SELECTED CRITICAL WRITINGS. Ed. by Norman Henfrey *Cambridge* 2 vols. 1968 Vol. I $16.50 pap. $5.95 Vol. 2 $14.50 pap. $4.95

THE GENTEEL TRADITION: Nine Essays. Ed. with introd. and notes by Douglas L. Wilson *Harvard Univ. Press* 1967 $6.50. Includes bibliography.

LITTLE ESSAYS DRAWN FROM THE WRITINGS OF GEORGE SANTAYANA. Ed. by L. P. Smith. 1920. *Bks. for Libraries* $13.00

GEORGE SANTAYANA'S AMERICA: Essays on Literature and Culture. Comp. with introd. by James Ballowe *Univ. of Illinois Press* 1967 pap. $2.25

SANTAYANA ON AMERICA. Ed. by Richard C. Lyon. 1968. *Harcourt* Harbinger Bks. pap. $3.75

PHYSICAL ORDER AND MORAL LIBERTY. Ed. by John and Shirley Lachs *Vanderbilt Univ. Press* 1969 $7.95. Previously unpublished essays.

THE SENSE OF BEAUTY: Being the Outline of Aesthetic Theory. 1896 rev. ed. 1938. *Dover* 1955 pap. $1.50; *Macmillan* Collier Bks. pap. $1.50; *Peter Smith* $4.75

INTERPRETATIONS OF POETRY AND RELIGION. 1900. *Peter Smith* 1958 $5.25

REASON IN SOCIETY. 1905. *Macmillan* Collier Bks. 1962 pap. $.95

WINDS OF DOCTRINE (1913) and PLATONISM AND THE SPIRITUAL LIFE (1927). *Peter Smith* 1958 $5.25

EGOTISM IN GERMAN PHILOSOPHY. 1916. *Haskell* 1971 $11.95; (with title "The German Mind: A Philosophical Diagnosis") *Apollo* 1968 pap. $1.95; *Peter Smith* $5.00

CHARACTER AND OPINION IN THE UNITED STATES. 1920. 1934. *Norton* 1967 pap. $1.95

SCEPTICISM AND ANIMAL FAITH: Introduction to a System of Philosophy, 1923. *Dover* 1955 pap. $3.50; *Peter Smith* $5.00

SOLILOQUIES IN ENGLAND AND LATER SOLILOQUIES. 1925. *Univ. of Michigan Press* Ann Arbor Bks. 1967 pap. $2.25

DIALOGUES IN LIMBO (1925): With Three New Dialogues. 1926. *Kelley* $11.50

REALMS OF BEING. *Cooper* 4 bks. in 1 The Realm of Essence (1927) The Realm of Matter (1930) The Realm of Truth (1937) The Realm of Spirit (1940) 1942 $19.95

THE REALM OF ESSENCE. 1928. *Greenwood* 1974 $9.75

THE REALM OF MATTER. 1930. *Greenwood* 1974 $10.25

SOME TURNS OF THOUGHT IN MODERN PHILOSOPHY. 1933. *Bks. for Libraries* $8.25

THE LAST PURITAN: A Memoir in the Form of a Novel. *Scribner* 1935 $10.00

OBITER SCRIPTA: Essays, Lectures and Reviews. 1936. Ed. by Justus Buchler and Benjamin Schwartz *Richard West* $17.50

DOMINATIONS AND POWERS: Reflections on Liberty, Society and Government. 1951. *Kelley* repr. of 1954 ed. $16.50

THE LETTERS OF GEORGE SANTAYANA. Ed. by Daniel Cory. 1955. *Richard West* 1973 $20.00

Books about Santayana

The Mind of Santayana. By Richard Butler. 1955. (With title "The Life and World of George Santayana") *Regnery* Gateway Eds. 1960 pap. $1.45. Father Butler's scholarly book is also a warmly affectionate portrait of the philosopher in his last years.

Santayana and the Sense of Beauty. By Willard Eugene Arnett. 1955. *Peter Smith* 1960 $5.00. A discerning analysis of Santayana as artist-philosopher.

Moral Philosophy of Santayana. By Milton Munitz. 1958. *Greenwood* 1973 $8.00

Santayana's Aesthetics. By Irving Singer. 1957. *Greenwood* 1973 $11.25

The Essential Wisdom of George Santayana. By T. N. Munson. *Columbia* 1962 $10.00

Santayana: The Later Years. A Portrait with Letters. By Daniel Cory. *Braziller* 1963 $7.50

This important book marks the centennial year of Santayana's birth. Daniel Cory was Santayana's secretary who became his close friend and, eventually, his literary executor. His book is a portrait of the philosopher over a 25-year period and includes some 300 Santayana letters not published before.

The Rational Society: A Critical Reading of Santayana's Social Thought. By Beth J. Singer. *Press of Case Western* 1970 $6.95

Santayana: An Examination of His Philosophy. By Timothy Sprigge. *Routledge and Kegan Paul* 1974 $15.00

CROCE, BENEDETTO. 1866–1952. *See Chapter 10, Italian Literature,* Reader's Adviser, *Vol. 2.*

SHESTOV, LEV (born Lev Isaakovich Schwarzmann). 1866–1938.

"Athens and Jerusalem is the culmination of Shestov's entire lifetime of intellectual inquiry and spiritual striving. . . . In it he set himself the task of critically examining the pretension of human reason to possession of the capacity for attaining ultimate truth. . . . Shestov was haunted for years by the biblical legend of the fall. As he interpreted it, when Adam ate the fruit of the tree of knowledge, faith was displaced by reason and scientific knowledge. The sin of Adam has been repeated by his descendants, whose relentless pursuit of knowledge has led not to ultimate truth but to the choking of the springs of life and the destruction of man's primordial freedom"— (Bernard Martin, in the preface to that work).

Shestov belongs in the stream of the religious existentialists and was deeply interested in the work of Nietzshe and of Kierkegaard; he knew and was close to Berdyaev and in touch with Husserl, Heidegger and Buber. In his own strong voice, however, deeply reliant on the God, not of the conventional churches, but of the Old Testament as he interpreted it, he denounced conventional metaphysics and the domination of a rigidly structural world view in which man is governed by Necessity. Men, he cried, have fettered themselves with crutches and limits and made themselves puny; we must seek a new God—with God "all things are possible." "All Things Are Possible" was the 1920 English version of the title of his most important early "existential" work, an attack on traditional metaphysics: "The Apotheosis of Groundlessness" (1905), to which D. H. Lawrence provided the introduction. The novelist wrote: " 'Everything is possible'—this is his really central cry. It is not nihilism. It is only a shaking free of the human psyche from old bonds. The positive central idea is that the human psyche or soul, really believes in itself. . . . No ideal on earth is anything more than an obstruction, in the end, to the creative issue of the spontaneous soul." Bernard Martin says, in his excellent introduction (already quoted) to "Athens Jerusalem": "Shestov suggests . . . that modern man can perhaps reach the God of the Bible only by first passing through the experience of his own nothingness, and by coming to feel, as Nietzsche did, that God is not. . . . 'Sometimes [says Shestov] this is the sign of the end and of death. Sometimes of the beginning and of life. As soon as man feels that God is not, he suddenly comprehends the frightful horror and the wild folly of human temporal existence . . . [and] awakens. . . . Was it not so with Nietzsche, Spinoza, Pascal, Luther, Augustine, even with St. Paul?' "

Lev Shestov was the son of Jewish parents and studied at Kiev and the University of Moscow. He received the title of Candidate of Laws from the University of Kiev, but was denied the doctor of law title because his dissertation on the Russian working class was judged "revolutionary" by the Committee of Censors in 19th-century Moscow. Shestov worked for a while in his father's textile firm and began writing for avant-garde periodicals in Kiev. In 1898 his first book appeared,

"Shakespeare and His Critic Brandes," in which "he attacked the positivism and skeptical rationalism of the famous Danish critic and essayist in the name of a vague moral idealism"— (Martin). In "Good in the Teaching of Tolstoy and Nietzsche: Philosophy and Preaching" (1900, *Ohio Univ. Press* 1969, o.p.) "Shestov contrasted Nietzsche's supposedly cruel, unpitying and amoral philosophy with the pretentious moralistic preaching of Tolstoy" (Martin) and thus clearly in Nietzsche's favor.

Shestov spent a number of years abroad—in Switzerland or Germany, before World War I. From 1918 to 1919 he taught Greek philosophy at the People's University of Kiev, but dissatisfaction with the Bolshevik regime caused him to settle in Paris in 1920, where he taught at the Sorbonne and moved in a circle of Russian émigrés, including Berdyaev. He became increasingly interested in religion and the work of the great religious philosophers and finished his great "Athens and Jerusalem" just before his death.

Shestov was deeply concerned philosophically with Russian literature—particularly Dostoyevsky and Chekhov—and wrote many essays on the subject. As Sidney Monas says in his valuable introduction to "Chekhov and Other Essays" (which, taken with Martin's long piece, provides a fine complementary survey of Shestov's life), he was also a "witty, trenchant and supple writer whom it is a *pleasure* to read."

CHEKHOV AND OTHER ESSAYS. 1908. New introd. by Sidney Monas *Univ. of Michigan Press* 1966 pap. $1.95; (with title "Penultimate Words and Other Essays") introd. by John Middleton Murry *Bks. for Libraries* 1966 $7.25. Contents: Anton Chekhov; The Gift of Prophecy [Dostoyevsky]; Penultimate Words; The Theory of Knowledge.

POTESTAS CLAVIUM. 1919. Trans. by Bernard Martin *Ohio Univ. Press* 1967 $11.00; *Regnery* pap. $3.45

A "striking assault on rationalist metaphysics"—(*PW*).

KIERKEGAARD AND THE EXISTENTIAL PHILOSOPHY. 1939. Trans. by Elinor Hewitt *Ohio Univ. Press* 1970 $11.00

ATHENS AND JERUSALEM. Written in 1938, first published in Paris in 1951. Trans. with lengthy, "brilliant" (*LJ*) introduction by Bernard Martin *Ohio Univ. Press* 1966 $11.00; *Simon & Schuster* 1968 pap. $2.45

"In this long, closely-reasoned examination of the roots and development of the Judaeo-Christian tradition, Shestov makes clear his passionate anti-rationalism, persuasively denying the claims to truth made by speculative philosophy (Athens)"—(*LJ*).

(With others). ESSAYS IN RUSSIAN LITERATURE: The Conservative View. Trans. by Spencer Roberts *Ohio Univ. Press* 1968 $10.50

IN JOB'S BALANCES. Trans. by Camilla Coventry and C. A. Macartney *Ohio Univ. Press* 1974 $12.00

Books about Shestov

Two Russian Thinkers: An Essay in Berdyaev and Shestov. By James C. Wernham. *Univ. of Toronto Press* 1968 $5.50

Wernham emphasizes the two philosophers' "common bond as existentialist thinkers under a strong influence of Dostoevski and their common concern for religious metaphysics. He shows Shestov as having had the sharper critical faculty"—(*LJ*).

RUSSELL, BERTRAND (ARTHUR WILLIAM RUSSELL), 3rd Earl. 1872–1970. (Nobel Prize 1950)

Bertrand Russell was the philosophical and mathematical giant of our age. His publishers wrote: "It has been said that 'his admirable and lucid English style may be attributed to the fact that he did not undergo a classical education at a public school.' " As an English stylist Lord Russell had the extraordinary gift of understanding and pioneering in the most abstruse fields of human knowledge and of being able to make at least their broader outlines crystal-clear to the layman. (In this connection he described the title of a course he wished to give at an American university as "Words and Facts." But not until he had made the title five times as long and heavy with philosophic "jargon" did he feel it would be acceptable to the authorities.) Though a scientist, his life was also political and passionate; one may have disagreed on occasion with his political judgment and deplored some of his personal foibles and yet have recognized him as one of the greatest logical minds mankind has produced—one with the wit of a wicked angel, a vast concern for the human race and an essentially Christian kind of morality (he rejected Christianity as such) which denies religious modes of thought, in large part, because religion does not live up to its claims. In the first volume of his "Autobiography" he said: "Three passions, simple but overwhelmingly strong, have governed my life: the longing for love, the search for knowledge, and unbearable pity for the sufferings of mankind." And elsewhere: "Often I feel that religion, like the sun, has extinguished the stars of less brilliancy but not less beauty, which shine upon us out of the darkness of a godless universe. The splendour of human life, I feel sure, is greater to those who are not dazzled by the divine radiance; and human comradeship seems to grow more intimate and more tender from the sense that we are all exiles on an inhospitable shore." After a lonely childhood Russell went to Cambridge, the university with which he was chiefly associated throughout his long and productive life.

Russell succeeded to an earldom in 1931 and took his seat in the House of Lords. During World War I he was imprisoned as a pacifist. He wrote *"Principia Mathematica"* in collaboration with A. N. Whitehead (*q.v.*), his greatest and probably most enduring work. In 1940 he lectured at the University of Chicago, Harvard University and at the University of California and in April was appointed professor of philosophy at the College of the City of New York. Later the appointment was revoked by a Supreme Court Justice on the ground that certain passages in his books carried moral contamination for the youth of New York City. *See* "The Bertrand Russell Case," edited by John Dewey and H. M. Kallen (1941, o.p.). He returned to England in 1944 as Fellow and Lecturer of Trinity College, Cambridge. Here he completed his "philosophical testament"— "Human Knowledge," a book of enormous scope. "All the central issues in contemporary philosophy, from the theory of meaning to the nature of space-time are discussed with . . . characteristic incisiveness, technical skill and imagination"—(Sidney Hook). A rationalist, a materialist, a great mathematician, to him science was truth. His books were always provocative and highly personal, reflecting his immense knowledge and zest for life. The later titles are marked by the same qualities that distinguished the earlier—"a witty, lucid, and urbane style, a vigorous intellect, and an erudition that can be simultaneously graceful and leviathan." He was awarded the 1950 Nobel Prize for Literature, sharing it with William Faulkner (*q.v.*).

Always a crusader for pacificism, his dread of nuclear war colored his attitude in most of his later writings. In "Unarmed Victory" (1963, o.p.) he tried to influence leaders and public opinion on both sides.

In 1967 Russell sponsored a "Vietnam war crimes tribunal" which he declared to be in the legal tradition of the international trials at Nuremberg after World War II. President de Gaulle refused France as a meeting place and after further difficulties the site selected was Stockholm, where a group of intellectuals, led by Jean-Paul Sartre, attempted to demonstrate that the United States was guilty of war crimes in Vietnam. Too old to travel to Stockholm for the meetings, Russell provided most of the financial support and said of his purpose, as reported in the *N.Y. Times:* "What I hope is that the Americans will arouse so much opposition against themselves in the world that in their own minds they will start to think it is not worth the trouble." The tribunal examined America's use of antipersonnel bombs in raids on North Vietnam, heard accounts from North Vietnamese victims of bomb and chemical warfare and saw films of bombed areas. Accused of genocide, the United States refused to comment on the tribunal's conclusion. His own articles on the general subject, "War Crimes in Vietnam" were published in 1967 by the *Monthly Review Press.* Early in 1969 a conference called by the Bertrand Russell Peace Foundation (again without the philosopher in attendance at Stockholm) found the Soviet Union similarly blameworthy for its 1968 invasion of Czechoslovakia.

The first two volumes of his "Autobiography" have sometimes been found frivolous and "scrappy" but by most critics are admired as the eminently readable—and often very funny— outline of an incredibly rich experience, in constant contact with the great and near-great, of a fearless iconoclast who often found himself discharged or willingly let go for his unorthodox activities and opinions—particularly in this country—and often in financial straits as a result. Malcolm Muggeridge (in *Esquire*) said: "The second volume is even better than the first. . . . Russell is an authentic hero of our time, and posterity will value, as we do, his honest, truthful and accomplished account of himself"—a sentiment echoed many times over. He wrote an average of a letter every 30 hours of his life and some 100,000 of these (mostly to other great or powerful men of his age) were privately sold in the summer of 1967, together with some 400 manuscripts. This treasure trove has yet to be published—books by Russell, therefore, may be expected to appear for a generation or more to come. Because of his longevity, his acquaintances spanned nearly a century. He "debated philosophy with Wittgenstein and fiction with Conrad and D. H. Lawrence, he . . . argued economics with Keynes and civil disobedience with Gandhi, his open letters . . . provoked Stalin to a reply and Lyndon Johnson to exasperation"—(George Steiner, in the *New Yorker*).

THE BASIC WRITINGS OF BERTRAND RUSSELL, 1903–1959. Ed. by Robert E. Egner and Lester E. Denonn; preface by the author *Simon & Schuster* 1961 $12.50 Touchstone-Clarion Bks. pap. $3.85

"This anthology, authorized and introduced by the author himself, consists of 81 essays and chapters or passages from longer works and has been selected to represent Lord Russell as philosopher, mathematician, man of letters, historian and analyst of international affairs." The book is addressed to the informed layman and the "selections, in addition to illustrating the astounding range of Lord Russell's interest and knowledge, demonstrate his 'ability to discuss any problem in a scientific, objective and dispassionate way.' "

BERTRAND RUSSELL'S BEST. Ed. by R. E. Egner *New Am. Lib.* (orig.) pap. $.95

LOGIC AND KNOWLEDGE: Essays 1901–50. Ed. by Robert Charles Marsh. 1956. *Putnam* Capricorn Giants 1971 pap. $3.45

PRINCIPLES OF MATHEMATICS. 1903. *Norton* 1938 pap. $3.25

THE PROBLEMS OF PHILOSOPHY. 1912. *Oxford* Galaxy Bks. 1959 pap. $1.95

(With Alfred North Whitehead). PRINCIPIA MATHEMATICA. *Cambridge* 1910–13 2nd ed. 3 vols. 1925–27 set $95.00 abr. ed. pap. $1.95

MYSTICISM AND LOGIC. 1918. *Harper* (Barnes & Noble) 1954 $8.50

ANALYSIS OF MIND. 1921. *Humanities Press* 1961 $10.50

THE ABC OF RELATIVITY. 1925. *Humanities Press* 1969 $5.50; *New Am. Lib.* Signet 1970 pap. $.75

EDUCATION AND THE GOOD LIFE. *Liveright* 1926 $5.95 pap. $3.95

SCEPTICAL ESSAYS. 1928. *Harper* (Barnes & Noble) repr. of 1935 ed. 1960 $8.50

OUR KNOWLEDGE OF THE EXTERNAL WORLD. 1929. *Humanities Press* rev. ed. 1953 $9.00

EDUCATION AND THE SOCIAL ORDER. 1932. *Humanities Press* 1967 $7.50 pap. $2.00

POWER. 1938. *Norton* 1969 pap. $3.25

INQUIRY INTO MEANING AND TRUTH. 1940. *Humanities Press* $9.75

A HISTORY OF WESTERN PHILOSOPHY: And Its Connection with Political and Social Circumstances from the Earliest Times to the Present Day. *Simon & Schuster* 1945 $6.95 Touchstone Bks. pap. $4.95

HUMAN KNOWLEDGE: Its Scope and Limits. *Simon & Schuster* 1948 $6.95 Touchstone Bks. pap. $3.95

AUTHORITY AND THE INDIVIDUAL. 1949. *AMS Press* $8.50. The Reith Lectures.

UNPOPULAR ESSAYS. *Simon & Schuster* 1951 $6.95 Touchstone Bks. pap. $1.95

COMMON SENSE AND NUCLEAR WARFARE. *Simon & Schuster* 1959 pap. $1.00; *AMS Press* $8.50

HAS MAN A FUTURE? *Penguin* 1961 pap. $.95; *Simon & Schuster* 1962 $3.00

THE SCIENTIFIC OUTLOOK. *Norton* 1962 pap. $1.95

THE ART OF PHILOSOPHIZING AND OTHER ESSAYS. 1968. *Littlefield* 1974 pap. $1.50

"The three essays in this book, 'The Art of Rational Conjecture,' 'The Art of Drawing Inferences,' and 'The Art of Reckoning,' were written in 1942 for Hademan-Julius and are now printed in book form for the first time. The pieces respectively tell how to be a philosopher, a logician, and a mathematician"—(*LJ*).

PORTRAITS FROM MEMORY AND OTHER ESSAYS. *Simon & Schuster* 1956 $6.50 Touchstone Bks. pap. $1.95. Shaw, Wells, Conrad, Santayana, Whitehead and D. H. Lawrence appear in the "brilliant, mellow and many-faceted little autobiography."

MY PHILOSOPHICAL DEVELOPMENT. *Simon & Schuster* 1959 $3.75. With appendix "Russell's Philosophy" by Alan Wood. An intellectual autobiography—beginning when he was 16 and written with his usual clarity and wit.

THE AUTOBIOGRAPHY OF BERTRAND RUSSELL. 3 vols. Vols. 1–2 *Little-Atlantic* Vol. 1 1872–1914 $7.95 Vol. 2 1914–1944 $8.95 Vol. 3 *Simon & Schuster* 1944–1969 $8.50

Books about Russell

Bertrand Russell: The Passionate Skeptic. By Alan Wood. *Simon & Schuster* 1958 $3.50
"A most exhilarating book"—(*New Yorker*).

Bertrand Russell's Philosophy of Morals. By Lillian W. Aiken. *Humanities Press* 1963 $6.00

Bertrand Russell, A. S. Neill, Homer Lane, W. H. Kilpatrick: Four Progressive Educators. Comp. by Leslie R. Perry. *Macmillan* 1967 pap. $1.95

Bertrand Russell and the British Tradition in Philosophy. By D. H. Pears. *Random* 1971 pap. $1.95

Professor Pears attempts "to place Russell in the evolving tradition of British empircism while at the same time explicating many of Russell's seminal concepts. He treats cogently ... Russell's debt to Hume; ... his reaction against 19th-Century idealists; and his important interaction with Wittgenstein. [Not an easy book, it] is surely one of the most important books to appear on Russell's ideas"—*(LJ)*.

Bertrand Russell. Ed. by A. J. Ayer. *Viking* 1972 $6.95 pap. $2.25

The Development of Bertrand Russell's Philosophy. By Ronald Jager. *Humanities Press* 1973 $17.50

Bertrand Russell's Philosophy. Ed. by George Nakhnikian. *Harper* (Barnes and Noble) 1974 $19.50

The Life of Bertrand Russell. By Ronald W. Clark. *Knopf* 1975 $17.50

The Tamarisk Tree. By Dora Russell. *Putnam* 1975 $9.95

My Father Bertrand Russell. By Katharine Tait. *Harcourt* 1975 $8.95

HOCKING, WILLIAM ERNEST. 1873–1966.

Influenced by both William James and Josiah Royce, as well as by early initiation into science and engineering, Hocking described his philosophical thinking as composed of "realism ... mysticism ... idealism also, its identity not broken." "I wish," he once said, "to discern what character our civilizations, now unsteadily merging into a single world civilization, are destined to take in the forseeable future, assuming that we have a forseeable future."

The Harvard "President's Report" for 1965–66 said of him: "William Ernest Hocking, Alford Professor of Natural Religion, Moral Philosophy and Civil Polity, *Emeritus,* died June 12, 1966 in his ninety-third year. Professor Hocking, like R[alph] B[arton] Perry, was a scholar who bridged the years from the admired era of Santayana, Palmer, Royce and James to our own times. His school of thought has been called objective idealism or, in his own words 'nonmaterialistic realism,' a kind of blend of the pragmatic and the idealistic. His first book, *The Meaning of God in Human Experience* (1912), established his reputation and became a classic in the region between philosophy and theology. This was the beginning of a long line of books and articles which for half a century brought his characteristic 'warmth, clarity and insight' (in the words of a colleague) to a variety of human problems ranging from ethics to education. A sampling of [his] titles will suggest the reach of his 'ecumenical temper.' ... Mr. Hocking graduated from the College in 1901 and took his doctorate in 1904. After a period at Berkeley and at New Haven, he returned here as Professor of Philosophy in 1914 and five years later was elected to the Alford chair. Although he became *Emeritus* in 1943, he remained active and intellectually alert to the end of his life, conducting a large and lively correspondence with friends, colleagues and students the world over and lending the kindly sagacity of a great teaching mind to countless admiring younger men and women."

THE MEANING OF GOD IN HUMAN EXPERIENCE. 1912. *Folcroft* $10.00

MAN AND THE STATE. 1926. *Shoe String Press* 1968 $15.00

THE COMING WORLD CIVILIZATION. *Greenwood* $10.00. A searching analysis for serious readers, which received the Lecomte du Noüy Award in 1957.

Books about Hocking

Royce and Hocking: American Idealists. By Daniel S. Robinson. *Christopher Pub.* 1968 $5.00

Within Human Experience: The Philosophy of William Ernest Hocking. By Leroy S. Rouner. *Harvard Univ. Press* 1969 $10.00

BERDYAEV, NICHOLAS (also written Berdiav, Berdiaev; Nikolai). 1874–1948.

The great Russian Orthodox religious philosopher was born in Kiev. After the Revolution he founded the Free Academy of Spiritual Culture and was given the chair of philosophy at the University of Moscow. He was imprisoned for his defense of religion and was driven into exile, first to Berlin (1922), then to Paris (1934). There he was director of the Academy of the Philosophy of Religion that he had founded in Berlin. "The Realm of Spirit and the Realm of Caesar" (1953) was his last testament found after his death and put into publishable form by a group of his friends. It shows "no sign of decay of mental power or spiritual force." His "lucid thought and luminous style give his work an almost compulsive force."

Berdyaev's early interest was in Marxism but "it was a deviation from orthodox Marxism in that it insisted that only transcendental critical idealism can solve the problem of truth"—(Louis J. Shein, in "Readings in Russian Philosophical Thought"). He later became interested in mystical and religious ideas.

THE RUSSIAN REVOLUTION. 1933. *Univ. of Michigan Press* 1960 $4.40 pap. $1.75

DOSTOEVSKY. 1934. Trans. by Donald Attwater *New Am. Lib.* pap. $2.95

THE BOURGEOIS MIND AND OTHER ESSAYS. 1934. Trans. by Donald Attwater and others *Bks. for Libraries* 1967 $7.00. Includes also "Man and Machine," "Christianity and Human Activity," "The Worth of Christianity and the Unworthiness of Christians."

THE FATE OF MAN IN THE MODERN WORLD. 1935. *Univ. of Michigan Press* 1961 $4.40

FREEDOM AND THE SPIRIT. 1935. *Bks. for Libraries* 1972 $15.00

SLAVERY AND FREEDOM. *Scribner* 1944 1960 pap. $3.45; *Association Press* 1973 pap. $7.00

THE ORIGIN OF RUSSIAN COMMUNISM. 1948 1955. *Univ. of Michigan Press* 1960 pap. $2.25

TOWARDS A NEW EPOCH. 1949. *Folcroft* $10.00

THE BEGINNING AND THE END. Trans. by R. M. French 1952. *Peter Smith* $4.50

THE REALM OF SPIRIT AND THE REALM OF CAESAR. 1953. *Greenwood* 1975 $10.75

THE MEANING OF HISTORY. Trans. by George Reavey *Peter Smith* $4.50

Books about Berdyaev

Rebellious Prophet. By Donald A. Lowrie. 1960. *Greenwood* 1974 $13.50

Berdyaev's Philosophy: The Existential Paradox of Freedom and Necessity. By Fuad Nucho; with introd. by Richard Kroner *Peter Smith* $3.00
"Dr. Nucho (a Lutheran pastor and scholar) has presented a systematic exposition of Berdyaev's progress from what might be termed a Marxist-Christian synthesis (in 1901) to a strongly anti-Marxist, Christian-existentialist position in his later years. In his concepts of freedom and responsibility, Berdyaev has certain affinities with Kierkegaard, Heidegger, and Tillich, but his reconciliation of these opposites is his own. Exiled from Russia in 1922, he lived in Berlin and Paris, writing voluminously (some 30 books), most of them now translated into English. Dr. Nucho's analysis of this significant body of work is a lucid, informative contribution recommended for all collections of contemporary philosophy"—(*LJ*).

Two Russian Thinkers: An Essay in Berdyaev and Shestov. By James C. S. Wernham. *Univ. of Toronto Press* 1968 $5.50

Freedom in God: A Guide to the Thought of Nicholas Berdyaev. By E. L. Allen. *Folcroft* $5.00

CASSIRER, ERNST.   1874–1945.

This German philosopher was a professor at the University of Hamburg 1919–1933, then became a lecturer at Oxford University. He taught in Sweden, later in the United States. He was regarded as the leading representative of the Neo-Kantian Marburg School, and extended inquiries in the fields of psychology and science by his detailed studies. He was a humanist, "one of the great historians of ideas."

SUBSTANCE AND FUNCTION. And Einstein's "Theory of Relativity." Authorized trans. by W. C. and M. C. Swabey. 1923. *Dover* 1953 pap. $4.00; *Peter Smith* $5.75

THE INDIVIDUAL AND THE COSMOS IN RENAISSANCE PHILOSOPHY. 1927 Trans. with introd. by Mario Domandi. 1964. *Univ. of Pennsylvania Press* 1972 pap. $2.95
"A book for scholars. . . . One of the standard works on Renaissance philosophy"—(*LJ*).

THE LOGIC OF THE HUMANITIES. Trans. by Clarence S. Howe *Yale Univ. Press* 1961 $12.50 pap. $2.95. A treatise on language and its symbolic structures, written in 1942, ranges over language, poetry, art and religion.

AN ESSAY ON MAN. *Yale Univ. Press* 1944 $12.50 pap. $3.25

THE MYTH OF THE STATE. Ed. by C. W. Hendel *Yale Univ. Press* 1946 $15.00 pap. $2.95

LANGUAGE AND MYTH. 1946 Trans. by Susanne K. Langer 1946. *Dover* 1953 pap. $1.25; *Peter Smith* $3.50

THE PROBLEM OF KNOWLEDGE. Trans. by W. H. Woglom and C. W. Hendel *Yale Univ. Press* 1950 $17.50 pap. $3.45. A standard work.

THE PHILOSOPHY OF SYMBOLIC FORMS. Trans. by Ralph Manheim *Yale Univ. Press* 3 vols. 1953–57 Vol. 1 Language (1953) $17.50 pap. $3.45 Vol. 2 Mythical Thought (1955) $15.00 pap. $3.95 Vol. 3 Phenomenology of Knowledge (1957) $20.00 pap. $4.95

THE QUESTION OF JEAN-JACQUES ROUSSEAU. Trans. and ed. by Peter Gay. 1954. *Indiana Univ. Press* 1963 pap. $1.65; *Peter Smith* $4.00

DETERMINISM AND INDETERMINISM IN MODERN PHYSICS: Historical and Systematic Studies of the Problem of Causality. Trans. by O. Theodor Benfey *Yale Univ. Press* 1956 $12.50

ROUSSEAU, KANT AND GOETHE. *Princeton Univ. Press* 1970 $8.50 pap. $1.95

Books about Cassirer

The Philosophy of Ernst Cassirer. Ed. by Paul A. Schilpp. *Open Court* 1949 $15.00 1973 pap. $8.95

Symbol and Reality: Studies in the Philosophy of Ernst Cassirer. By Carl H. Hamburg. *Humanities Press* 1956 $6.25

Ernst Cassirer: Scientific Knowledge and the Concept of Man. By Seymour W. Itzkoff. *Univ. of Notre Dame Press* 1971 $9.95

SCHWEITZER, ALBERT. 1875–1965. *See Chapter 4, World Religions, this Volume.*

BUBER, MARTIN. 1878–1965. *See Chapter 4, World Religions, this Volume.*

COHEN, MORRIS R(APHAEL). 1880–1947.

Cohen, who taught philosophy at the City College of New York and who began life as the son of Russian-Jewish immigrants, is one of the most important American philosophers since William James. He had great influence through his books and his teaching. In a review of "A Dreamer's Journey," his autobiography (1949, o.p.), Perry Miller wrote (in the *Nation*): "It is both ironic and fitting that with the posthumous publication of his autobiography, even though it was left unfinished and the last chapters are fragments, there appears the book by which Morris Cohen will be longest and most widely remembered. It will demand a permanent place among the classics of immigrant narrative, and one not too far behind the greater classics of intellectual biography. And because it reveals in human terms, with humility and yet with a touch of vanity, the sources from which his strength is gathered, it explains why he conspicuously succeeded in writing philosophy that can be read as literature."

LAW AND THE SOCIAL ORDER: Essays in Legal Philosophy. 1933. *Shoe String Press* $12.50

(With Ernest Nagel). AN INTRODUCTION TO LOGIC AND SCIENTIFIC METHOD. *Harcourt* 1934 $7.50 (first part, "An Introduction to Logic") 1962 pap. $2.35

FAITH OF A LIBERAL. 1946. *Bks. for Libraries* $19.25

THE MEANING OF HUMAN HISTORY. *Open Court* 1947 $10.00 pap. $3.95

REASON AND LAW: Studies in Juristic Philosophy. 1950 *Greenwood* 1972 $12.25

(With Felix S. Cohen) READINGS IN JURISPRUDENCE AND LEGAL PHILOSOPHY. *Little* 1951 $16.00

A DREAMER'S JOURNEY: The Autobiography of Morris Raphael Cohen. 1949. *Arno* 1975 $22.00

Books about Cohen

Mind and Nature: A Study on the Naturalistic Philosophies of Cohen, Woodbridge and Sellers. By Cornelius F. Delaney. *Univ. of Notre Dame Press* 1969 $9.95

MARITAIN, JACQUES. 1882–1973.

T. S. Eliot once called Maritain "the most conspicuous figure and probably the most powerful force in contemporary philosophy." His wife and devoted intellectual companion, the late Raïssa Maritain, was of Jewish descent but joined the Catholic Church with him in 1906. He studied under Bergson (*q.v.*) but was dissatisfied with his teacher's philosophy, eventually finding certainty in the system of St. Thomas Aquinas (*q.v.*). He has lectured widely in Europe, in North and South America and lived and taught in New York during World War II. He was appointed French ambassador to the Vatican in 1945, but resigned in 1948 to teach philosophy at Princeton, where he remained until his retirement as professor emeritus, in 1953. He was prominent in the Catholic intellectual resurgence. He had a keen perception of modern French literature and a definite political philosophy. "His metaphysical position is that of a Thomist, but his Thomism is a vital reinterpretation and application of the principles of Scholasticism." In November 1963, Maritain was honored by the French literary world with the national Grand Prize for letters, which includes a cash award of 5,000 francs (about $1,000). He "learned of the award at his retreat in a small

monastery near Toulouse where he has been living in ascetic retirement for the last few years"—
(*N. Y. Times*). In 1967 the publication of "The Peasant of the Garonne" disturbed the French
Roman Catholic world. In it, Maritain attacks the "neo-modernism" which he saw develop in the
Church "in the past decade or two and especially in the years since the Second Vatican
Council. . . . He laments that in avant-garde Roman Catholic theology today he can 'read nothing
about the redeeming sacrifice or the merits of the Passion.' In his interpretation, the whole of the
Christian tradition has identified redemption with the sacrifice of the cross. But now all of that is
being discarded, along with the idea of hell, the doctrine of creation out of nothing, the infancy
narratives of the Gospels, and belief in the immortality of the human soul"—(Jaroslav Pelikan, in
SR).

THE SOCIAL AND POLITICAL PHILOSOPHY OF JACQUES MARITAIN. Selected writings ed. by
   Joseph W. Evans and Leo R. Ward in consultation with the author. 1955. *Kelley* 1974
   pap. $13.50

CHALLENGES AND RENEWALS. Ed. by J. Evans and L. Ward *Univ. of Notre Dame Press* 1966
   $8.50; *New Am. Lib.* Meridian Bks. 1968 pap. $2.65
   "Included in this anthology of the philosophical writings of Jacques Maritain are chapters from
   almost all of his major works, arranged under the broad headings of 'Theory of Knowledge,'
   'Metaphysics,' 'Ethics,' 'Esthetics,' 'Politics,' and 'Philosophy of History' "—(*LJ*). Complementary
   volume to that above.

AN INTRODUCTION TO PHILOSOPHY. *Sheed & Ward* 1930–37 text ed. $3.00

ART AND SCHOLASTICISM AND THE FRONTIERS OF POETRY. 1935. Trans. by Joseph W.
   Evans *Univ. of Notre Dame* Press 1974 $9.95 pap. $3.25

INTEGRAL HUMANISM. 1936. Trans. by Joseph W. Evans *Univ. of Notre Dame Press* 1973
   $10.95 pap. $3.95

SCHOLASTICISM AND POLITICS. 1940. *Bks. for Libraries* $11.00

RANSOMING THE TIME. Trans. by Harry L. Binsse. 1941. *Gordian* 1972 $10.00

EDUCATION AT THE CROSSROADS. *Yale Univ.* Press 1943 $7.50 1960 pap. $1.95

ART AND POETRY. 1943. *Kennikat* $6.25

CHRISTIANITY AND DEMOCRACY. Trans. by Doris C. Anson. 1944. *Bks. for Libraries* 1972
   $9.50

EXISTENCE AND THE EXISTENT. 1948. Trans. by Lewis Galantière and Gerald B. Phelan
   Greenwood 1975 $10.25

MAN AND THE STATE. *Univ. of Chicago Press* 1951 $7.00 1955 pap. $2.45. Received the
   Catholic Literary Award (1952).

CREATIVE INTUITION IN ART AND POETRY. *New Am. Lib.* Meridian Bks. 1955 pap. $4.95

REFLECTIONS ON AMERICA. 1958. *Gordian* 1975 $8.50. An optimistic tribute to the
   American way.

ON THE USE OF PHILOSOPHY: Three essays. *Princeton Univ. Press* 1961 $6.00; *Atheneum*
   1965 pap. $1.65

THE RESPONSIBILITY OF THE ARTIST. 1962. *Gordian* 1972 $7.50. On the relationship
   between art and morality.

THE PEASANT OF THE GARONNE: An Old Layman Questions Himself About the Present
   Time. Trans. by Michael Cuddihy and Elizabeth Hughes. 1968. *Macmillan* 1969 pap.
   $1.95
   "On the surface this book is a bitter and caustic attack on the 'new theology' and its forefathers,
   Teilhard, Marx, the existentialists and phenomenologists [but] beneath the subtle insinuating
   style, Maritain has raised real philosophical and theological questions"—(*LJ*).

*Other titles are published by Harper, Hillary House, Kennikat, Kraus, Macmillan, Marquette
Univ. Press, New American Library, Sheed & Ward and Univ. of Notre Dame Press.*

Books about Maritain

   Jacques Maritain: The Man and His Achievement. Ed. with introd. by Joseph W. Evans. *Twin
   Circle* 1963 $5.00. Essays on Maritain by contemporaries, requiring some philosophic back-
   ground.

The Foundation of Jacques Maritain's Political Philosophy. By Hwa Jol Jung. *Univ. of Florida Press* 1960 pap. $2.00

Jacques Maritain: Homage in Words and Pictures. By John H. Griffin and Yves R. Simon. *Magi Bks.* 1974 $14.95

Mounier and Maritain: A French Catholic Understanding of the Modern World. By Joseph A. Amato. *Univ. of Alabama Press* 1974 $8.50

Our Friend, Jacques Maritain. By Julie Kernan. *Doubleday* 1975 $6.95

Recent Studies in Philosophy and Theology. By David H. Freeman. *Presbyterian & Reformed Pub. Co.* $3.95

JASPERS, KARL. 1883–1969.

The German psychiatrist-philosopher Jaspers was the originator of German existentialism. His was "a lucid and flexible intelligence in the service of a genuine and passionate concern for mankind." He was removed from his professorship at the University of Heidelberg by the Nazis in 1937, but was reinstated in 1945 on the approval of the American Occupation Army. In 1949 he went to the University of Basel. The *N.Y. Times* wrote of him in his lifetime: "Jaspers shows himself . . . to be one of the most diligent and sensitive students of contemporary history. He has a good eye for the present because he knows what to fear in it—particularly the loss of individual freedom."

"*The Future of Mankind* is characteristic of his work. . . . Here again he is concerned about the fate of man and wants to arouse conscience in face of the deadly danger of atomic warfare. At the same time he attempts to apply the principles of his philosophy to a new field, and to lay the foundations of a political philosophy"—(*TLS*, London). After the German publication of this book, he was awarded the German Peace Prize at the 1958 Frankfurt Book Fair, presented by Hannah Arendt, who urged the English translation. "Philosophy Is for Everyman," based on a series of television lectures, "is a finished work, rigorously outlined, lucidly written, and forcefully argued. . . . [Jaspers says that in the 20th century] a total revaluation of ideas is necessary. Briefly he surveys, in turn, history and its pertinence to the present, politics and its connection with freedom [and other factors]. In each case, Jaspers draws the reader . . . to the root of things—to the true meaning and goal of existence. In doing so, he deliberately . . . points to the limitations of knowledge based on reason. . . . Philosophy [he argues] has ceased to be an integral, all encompassing system which explains the universe and informs men with assurance what is true and false, right and wrong. Philosophy rather is a mode of thinking, the substantive conclusions of which [Jaspers says] are rarely stated with precision. It reflects [for Jaspers] the state of knowledge in the modern world—fragmented, tentative, and shadowed by large areas of doubt"—(Oscar Handlin, in the *Atlantic*).

His *N.Y. Times* obituary brought out Professor Jaspers' great personal courage. "As professor of philosophy at the University of Heidelberg he was outspoken against Hitlerism. The Nazis retired him in 1937, but they could not silence him short of killing him. And this they planned to do. Indeed, on the eve of the departure of Dr. Jaspers and his wife for a concentration camp, they were saved by the American Army's capture of Heidelberg in 1945. Restored to his professorship after the war, he was unsparing in criticism of Germans for their war guilt and for their genocidal campaigns against Jews and other minorities. . . . As for moral guilt, he argued that every individual is morally accountable for his deeds. 'It is never simply true that orders are orders,' he declared. . . . Dr. Jaspers's wife was Gertrud Mayer, whom he married in 1910. She was a Jew, and her husband's refusal to part from her was among the Nazis' indictments of Dr. Jaspers. The couple had no children. Mrs. Jaspers, also a philosopher, is 90." The *Times* said in assessing him: "With Sören Kierkegaard, Martin Heidegger and Jean-Paul Sartre, Karl Jaspers was one of the makers and shapers of existentialist philosophy. For almost 50 years, in books, essays and lectures, he strove to give a personalist answer to modern man's questions about his own nature and the nature of existence."

MAN IN THE MODERN AGE. 1933. *Doubleday* 1957 Anchor Bks. pap. $1.95

THE WAY OF WISDOM: An Introduction to Philosophy. *Yale Univ. Press* 1951 $10.00 pap. $2.95. A summary of his philosophical beliefs; "a beautiful and puzzling book."

REASON AND ANTI-REASON IN OUR TIME. Trans. by Stanley Godman. 1952. *Shoe String Press* 1971 $5.00

REASON AND EXISTENZ: Five Lectures. Trans. with introd. by William Earle *Farrar, Straus* Noonday 1955 pap. $2.45. Profound inquiry into the possibility and limits of reason in penetrating the meaning of human existence.

PHILOSOPHY OF EXISTENCE. Trans. by Richard F. Grabau *Univ. of Pennsylvania Press* 1971 $5.00 pap. $1.95

THE FUTURE OF MANKIND. Trans. by E. B. Ashton *Univ. of Chicago Press* 1961 $9.50
Phoenix Bks. 1963 pap. $2.95

THE GREAT PHILOSOPHERS. Trans. by Ralph Manheim; ed. by Hannah Arendt *Harcourt*
2 vols. Vol. 1 The Foundations; The Paradigmatic Individuals: Socrates, Buddha,
Confucius, Jesus; The Seminal Founders of Philosophical Thought: Plato, Augustine, Kant (1962) Vol. 2 The Original Thinkers (1966) each $12.95 Harvest Bk. pap.
eds. of separate chapters of each volume are available: From Vol. 1, Kant $1.35 Plato
and Augustine $1.65 Socrates, Buddha, Confucius, Jesus $1.75; from Vol. 2,
Anaximander, Heraclitus, Parmenides, Plotinus, Lao-tzu, Nagarjuna $3.25 Anselm
and Nicholas of Cusa $3.50 Spinoza $2.75

Library Journal said of Vol. 1: "This is a major work, a brilliant book, difficult in parts, and to be
recommended for all libraries except the very small." It is not a history of philosophy. "Jaspers
defends the unity of philosophy and his aim is to make philosophy available to all, to provide the
serious reader with a guide 'to the thinking of the great philosophers and to a personal encounter
with them.' " The second volume "consists of long essays on the pre-Socratics, Plotinus, Anselm,
Nicholas of Cusa, Spinoza, the Chinese Lao Tzu and the Indian Nazariuna. Jaspers' own ideas are
found in the brief introduction. . . . This book is original, difficult and important. It will appeal to
both the professional philosopher and to the student of thought and culture"—(*LJ*).

TRUTH AND SYMBOL: From *Von der Wahrheit*. Trans. with introd. by Jean T. Wilde and
others *College & Univ. Press* (orig.) 1962 pap. $1.95

THE FUTURE OF GERMANY. 1966. Trans. and ed. by E. B. Ashton; introd. by Hannah
Arendt *Univ. of Chicago Press* 1967 pap. 1970 $6.50

"Jaspers, renowned philosopher at the University of Basel and formerly at Heidelberg, has not
lost his intellectual vigor and fighting spirit at the age of 84. The Bonn 'establishment' did not like
this book, when it was first published in Germany last year, but the young generation was grateful
for his forthrightness; the book sold more than 80,000 copies in less than a year. In the American
version those chapters are wisely omitted which were made obsolete by the end of the Erhard
regime. The book retains Jaspers' still valid basic criticism of the West German democracy and the
serious condition in which the whole nation finds itself. In 'Postscript 1967' he brings his analysis
up to date"—(*LJ*). The *New Republic* found the book "uneven. . . . Jaspers knows nothing about
politics. . . . Yet [it] concludes with a spate of good ideas."

PHILOSOPHY IS FOR EVERYMAN. Trans. by R. F. C. Hull and Grete Wels *Harcourt* 1967
$4.95

THE PERENNIAL SCOPE OF PHILOSOPHY. Trans. by Ralph Manheim *Shoe String Press* 1968
$7.50

PHILOSOPHY. Trans. by E. B. Ashton *Univ. of Chicago Press* 3 vols. 1969–1971 Vol. I
$11.50 Vol. 2 $15.00 Vol. 3 $10.00

Jaspers "takes his place among the major expositors of existential philosophy on the American
scene"—(*Choice*).

Books about Jaspers

Karl Jaspers: An Introduction to His Philosophy. By Charles F. Wallraff. *Princeton Univ. Press*
1970 $9.50 pap. $2.95
Existence, Existenz and Transcendence: An Introduction to the Philosophy of Karl Jaspers. By
Oswald O. Schraz. *Duquesne Univ. Press* (dist. by Humanities Press) 1971 $10.00
Reason Revisited: The Philosophy of Karl Jaspers. By Sebastian Samay. *Univ. of Notre Dame
Press* 1971 $10.00
The Philosophy of Karl Jaspers. Ed. by Paul A. Schilpp. *Open Court* new ed. 1974 pap. $8.95
Karl Jaspers: Philosophy as Faith. By Leonard H. Ehrlich. *Univ. of Massachusetts Press* 1975
$12.50
". . . Ehrlich carefully delineates Jasper's notion of philosophical faith and religious faith, and
then mirrors Jasper's basic concepts in the thought of religious thinkers such as Buber and
Tillich"—(*LJ*).

*Other titles are published by Putnam, Regnery, Shoe String Press, Peter Smith, Univ. of Arizona
Press, Univ. of Chicago Press and Univ. of Pennsylvania Press.*

ORTEGA Y GASSET, JOSÉ. 1883–1955.

The essayist and philosopher, a thinker influential in and out of the Spanish world, is known chiefly through "The Revolt of the Masses," showing the two very disparate influences of Nietzsche and of Bergson. Salvador de Madariaga called him "a refined humanist strongly influenced by German contemporary neo-Kantian schools of thought." Ortega's predominant thesis is the need of an intellectual aristocracy governing in a spirit of enlightened liberalism. After Franco's victory in the Civil War the dictator offered to make Ortega Spain's "official philosopher" and publish a de luxe edition of his works—with certain parts deleted. The philosopher refused, became a voluntary exile in Argentina and in 1941 was appointed professor of philosophy in the University of San Marcos in Lima, Peru. He returned to Spain in 1945 and died in Madrid.

"His thinking emphasizes man's situation in history and society, and he formulated early in his career the phrase 'I am myself and my circumstances.' Complementary to this, he developed a theory of perspective which attempts to bring together nationalism and relativism. 'Each life is a point of view directed upon the universe.... Every age has its own distinctive standards and values, absolute for itself, but invalid for other epochs.' This doctrine is the philosophical justification for his insistent concern with the present.... The specific need of our times, as Ortega sees it, is the vitalism of Bergson and Dilthey reconciled to rationalism by the fact that reason is our only tool in the process of existence: Ortega's formula is, therefore, *Cogito Quia Vivo*.... The 'theme of our time' consists of subordinating reason to vitality, localizing it within the biological, submitting it to the spontaneous.... Pure reason has to yield up its dominion to vital reason"—("Modern World Literature").

MEDITATIONS ON QUIXOTE. 1914. Trans. from the Spanish by Evelyn Rugg and Diego Marin; introd. and notes by Julian Marias *Norton* 1961 pap. $2.45. Ortega's first book, in which he uses "Quixote" only as a springboard to build up an aesthetic, is fashioned from a multiplicity of topics, and presents a kind of aggregate philosophy of literature.

THE MODERN THEME. 1923. *Peter Smith* $4.50

THE REVOLT OF THE MASSES. 1930. Trans. by the author *Norton* 1932 1957 $5.95 pap. $1.95

HISTORY AS A SYSTEM. *Norton* 1941 1961 pap. $1.85

THE DEHUMANIZATION OF ART (1925) and NOTES ON THE NOVEL. Trans. by Helene Weyl. 1948. *Princeton* rev. ed. 1968 $7.50 pap. $2.45

ON LOVE: Aspects of a Single Theme. Trans. by Tony Talbot *New Am. Lib.* Meridian Bks. 1957 pap. $2.95

MAN AND PEOPLE. Trans. by Willard R. Trask *Norton* 1957 1963 pap. $3.95. "The book will remain a vivid recounting of some of the chief features of the topography, flora and fauna of live human experience"—(*N.Y. Herald Tribune*).

MAN AND CRISIS. Trans. by Mildred Adams *Norton* 1958 pap. $2.95. "This book will not only be widely read. It will also be remembered"—(*N.Y. Times*).

WHAT IS PHILOSOPHY? Trans. by Mildred Adams *Norton* 1961 pap. $1.85

THE MISSION OF THE UNIVERSITY. Trans. and ed. by Howard Lee Nostrand *Norton* 1966 pap. $1.95

CONCORD AND LIBERTY. *Norton* 1963 pap. $2.45. Some essays on the nature of political freedom; intellectualism and the crisis of the intellect in the modern world; the history of philosophy.

This posthumous volume consists of a series of lectures begun in 1929 at the University of Madrid. "Interrupted when the university was closed as a result of political troubles, they were resumed in a Madrid theatre. Part of the lectures had been given earlier in Buenos Aires." "Coming upon these ideas thirty years later, after existentialism and phenomenology have made them commonplace, may impair the sense of freshness, but it will not prevent one from rereading Ortega with admiration and pleasure"—(*SR*).

THE ORIGIN OF PHILOSOPHY. Trans. by Tony Talbot *Norton* 1968 $4.00 pap. $1.50

"Stimulating insights sparkle here like gems; that philosophy was a fruit of the entrance of Greece into a period of freedom, that freedom involves enlargement of the circle of possibilities beyond immediate needs, that contact with foreigners expands the circle of one's choices, that 'vital wealth' results in part from emancipation from myth and tradition"—(LJ).

SOME LESSONS IN METAPHYSICS. *Norton* 1970 $5.50 pap. $2.45

AN INTERPRETATION OF UNIVERSAL HISTORY. *Norton* 1975 $8.95 pap. $4.95

Books about Ortega

Ortega y Gasset. By José Ferrater Mora. *Hillary House* $2.25. A summary and critical analysis of the thought, writings and cultural contributions.

Major Themes of Existentialism in the Works of Ortega y Gasset. By Janet W. Diaz. *Int. Scholarly Bk. Services* 1970 pap. $6.50

José Ortega y Gasset: Philosophy of European Unity. By Harold Raley. *Univ. of Alabama Press* 1971 $8.75

José Ortega y Gasset. By Franz Niedermayer. Trans. by Peter Tirner *Ungar* 1973 $6.00

GILSON, ÉTIENNE. 1884–

Like his fellow countryman, Jacques Maritain, Étienne Gilson is a neo-Thomist for whom Christian revelation is an indispensable auxiliary to reason. *Why* anything exists is a question science cannot answer and may even deem senseless. Gilson finds the answer to be "each and every particular existing thing depends for its existence on a pure Act of existence." God is the supreme Act of existing. An authority on the Christian philosophy of the Middle Ages, Gilson has lectured widely on theology, art, the history of ideas and the medieval world. He was a founder of the Pontifical Institute of Medieval Studies in Toronto.

REASON AND REVELATION IN THE MIDDLE AGES. 1938. *Scribner* Lyceum Ed. $1.95

GOD AND PHILOSOPHY. *Yale Univ. Press* 1941 $8.50 pap. 1959 $2.45

HISTORY OF PHILOSOPHY AND PHILOSOPHICAL EDUCATION. *Marquette Univ. Press* 1947 $3.00

WISDOM AND LOVE IN ST. THOMAS AQUINAS. *Marquette Univ. Press* 1951 $2.50

HISTORY OF CHRISTIAN PHILOSOPHY IN THE MIDDLE AGES. *Random* 1955 $12.95; *Christian Class.* $27.50. A monumental study of medieval scholastic theology.

THE CHRISTIAN PHILOSOPHY OF ST. THOMAS AQUINAS. *Random* 1956 $10.00

PAINTING AND REALITY. *Princeton Univ. Press* 2nd ed. 1957 $17.50. A. W. Mellon Lectures in the Fine Arts.

THE CHRISTIAN PHILOSOPHY OF SAINT AUGUSTINE. *Random* 1960 $10.00

HELOÏSE AND ABELARD. *Univ. of Michigan Press* 1960 $4.40 Ann Arbor Bks. pap. $4.95

FORMS AND SUBSTANCES IN THE ARTS. *Scribner* 1966 $6.95

"A panoramic view of the conditions [of] existence of fine art. . . . Architecture, painting, music, dance, poetry, and theatre comprise the large divisions of the book. A distinct philosophical reserve pervades the work, and very little praise is meted out for contemporary art: always it is the complaint that the new materials have not found an esthetic form"—(LJ).

Books about Gilson

Recent Studies in Philosophy and Theology. By David H. Freeman. *Presbyterian & Reformed* $3.75

An Étienne Gilson Tribute. Ed. by Charles J. O'Neil. *Marquette Univ. Press* 1959 $7.00

"Twenty-one contributions on twenty-one phases of philosophical thought form this tribute. Each is an expression of the esteem held for Étienne Gilson by his students from the Pontifical Institute of Medieval Studies over 30 years"—(Publisher's note).

Other titles are published by Bks. for Libraries, Burt Franklin, Christian Classics, Folcroft, Franciscan Herald, Marquette Univ. Press, Scribner and Peter Smith.

RADHAKRISHNAN, SIR SARVEPALLI. 1888–   *See Chapter 4, World Religions, this Volume.*

COLLINGWOOD, R(OBIN) G(EORGE). 1889–1943.

A remarkable thinker who sought to bridge the gulf which Darwin's discoveries appeared to have set up between science and religion in the 19th century, Collingwood began to study Latin at the age of four, Greek at six and the natural sciences shortly afterwards. He attended Oxford University, where he studied philosophy, classics, archeology and history; later he taught philosophy there. Participation in numerous archeological excavations allowed him to see, he said, "the importance of the questioning activity in life" and he became a respected scholar on the subject of Britain under the Roman conquest. But he was also an artist by nature—a fine, disciplined writer who was actively interested in music and the pictorial arts. He deplored the divisiveness of increasing specialization and sought a philosophy which would harmonize all knowledge, and a religion "scientific" in nature in which faith and reason each played a role. He felt that the Renaissance had mistakenly drawn lines of separation among the various disciplines of study, that a close unity existed among them.

In *"Speculum Mentis"* Collingwood saw "the development of the human mind from imaginative gropings to complete self-consciousness . . . as the dialectical development of art, or imagination, into successively religion, science, history, and philosophy: where by 'dialectical' he meant what Plato and Hegel meant, namely, the pitting of a thesis against its antithesis out of which developed a synthesis, which in turn provided the thesis for further development"—(E. W. F. Tomlin). "Collingwood believed that to restore the unity of life . . . is simply to fulfill the fundamental principle of Christianity, according to which 'the only life worth living is the life of the whole man, every faculty of body and soul unified into a single organic system' "—(Lionel Rubinoff, in introd. to "Faith and Reason"). His earlier work, "Religion and Philosophy" (1916, o.p.), saw philosophy as "the basis from which all diversity in knowledge both proceeds and returns" and "as the basis through which the unity of Christianity may be restored"—(Rubinoff). His "Essay on Metaphysics" and "The Idea of History" express a philosophy of history that regards metaphysics as a historical science. Collingwood also developed esthetic theories influenced by his study of Benedetto Croce (*q.v.*).

"The importance of Collingwood's work has yet to be appreciated, for it represents one of the most far-reaching attempts of modern times to demonstrate how philosophy can become of immediate use to men of action: this being possible, in Collingwood's view, by abandoning its three-hundred-year subservience to the method of natural science, which has led to increasing chaos in practical affairs as a result of the assumption that 'science is power,' and its adoption of a method of understanding human affairs from the only point of view likely to shed light upon them, namely, by submitting them to the scrutiny of the historical imagination"—(E. W. F. Tomlin).

His works on archeology include the following: "Roman Britain" (1921, *Oxford* $6.00); (with Ian Richmond) "The Archaeology of Roman Britain" (1930, *Harper* (Barnes & Noble) 1968 $21.00); (with J. N. Myres) "Roman Britain and the English Settlements" (*Oxford* 2nd ed. 1937 $9.75); and (with R. P. Wright) "Roman Inscriptions of Britain" (*Oxford* 1965, o.p.).

ESSAYS IN THE PHILOSOPHY OF ART. Ed. by Alan Donagan. 1964. *Peter Smith* $5.00

ESSAYS IN THE PHILOSOPHY OF HISTORY. Ed. by W. Debbins *Univ. of Texas Press* 1965 $6.50

SPECULUM MENTIS, or The Map of Knowledge. *Oxford* 1924 $10.25

OUTLINES OF A PHILOSOPHY OF ART. 1925. *Somerset Pubs.* $7.50

AN ESSAY ON PHILOSOPHICAL METHOD. *Oxford* 1933 $7.00

THE PRINCIPLES OF ART. *Oxford* 1938 $13.75 Galaxy Bks. pap. $2.95

AN ESSAY ON METAPHYSICS. *Oxford* 1940 $9.50; *Regnery* 1972 pap. $3.45

THE NEW LEVIATHAN, or Man, Society, Civilization and Barbarism. 1942. *Apollo* 1971 pap. $2.65

THE IDEA OF NATURE. 1945. *Oxford* 1960 $7.25 Galaxy Bks. pap. $1.95

THE IDEA OF HISTORY. 1956. *Oxford* Galaxy Bks. pap. $2.95

HUMAN NATURE AND HUMAN HISTORY. *Haskell* 1972 pap. $2.95

AN AUTOBIOGRAPHY. *Oxford* 1939 $5.00 pap. $1.95

Books about Collingwood

Neo-Idealistic Aesthetics: Croce-Gentile-Collingwood. By Merle E. Brown. Ed. by Barbara Woodward *Wayne State Univ. Press* 1966 $9.95
"Brown has avoided arbitrary terminology as it is used by the philosophers he studies and has utilized a subtle dramatic approach in his working out of the conflict of ideas which will appeal to those who have some foundation in the history of philosophy generally and in aesthetics in particular"—(*Choice*). "A detailed historical study, with the benefit of much untranslated material in journals hard to find, with a lively sense of the give and take spurring Croce and Gentile in their mutual development"—(*Journal of Aesthetics*).
R. G. Collingwood. By E. W. F. Tomlin. *British Bk. Centre* $2.95 pap. $1.20. A pamphlet.
Collingwood and the Reform of Metaphysics. By Lionel Rubinoff. *Univ. of Toronto* 1970 $17.50

Critical Essays in the Philosophy of Robin George Collingwood. Ed. by Michael Krausz. *Oxford* 1972 $15.25

HEIDEGGER, MARTIN.   1889–

The German religious existentialist trained in scholastic philosophy and became interested in Husserl's phenomenology. He taught at Freiburg and returned there from Marburg as successor to Husserl. In 1933 he became the first National-Socialist rector at Freiburg. He "is everyman's conception of a German philosopher: ascetic, withdrawn, a trifle eccentric and virtually impossible to understand. . . . He has been described as a mixture of scholar and Black Forest peasant and he still favors breeches and heavy woolen stockings. From time to time he shows up at the University of Freiburg to hold crowd-attracting lectures. . . . Almost a recluse, Heidegger has been known to abuse callers who have gotten him on the phone, and to follow it up with an unfriendly letter. This does not happen often because Heidegger has no phone of his own"—(*N.Y. Times*).

Heidegger distinguishes between *Sein and Dasein. Dasein* implies that "man is possibility, he has the power to be. His existence is in his choice of the possibilities which are open to him, and since this choice is never final, once for all, his existence is indeterminate because not terminated. . . . The mode of existence of the human being . . . is being-in-the-world . . . the being of a self in its inseparable relations with a not-self, the world of things and other persons in which the self always and necessarily finds itself inserted"—(H. J. Blackham, in "Six Existentialist Thinkers").

BEING AND TIME. 1927. Trans. from the 7th German ed. with pref. by John Macquarrie and Edward Robinson *Harper* 1962 $15.00

This is the first translation into English of a book often called untranslatable. *"Sein and Zeit"* is one of the great classics of modern philosophy and a basic work in existentialism. It is a very difficult book even for a German reader, "full of coined expressions, puns, and resurrected obsolete terms. Nevertheless, the translation accurately reflects the original style and spirit as well as the substance, with a marked consistency of vocabulary aided by a glossary of German expressions and several indexes"—(*LJ*).

EXISTENCE AND BEING. *Regnery* Gateway Eds. 1950 pap. $1.95

AN INTRODUCTION TO METAPHYSICS. 1953 German ed. trans. by Ralph Manheim *Yale Univ. Press* 1959 $10.00 1974 pap. $2.95. The reworked text of lectures delivered at the University of Heidelberg in 1935.

WHAT IS PHILOSOPHY? Trans. by William Kluback and Jean T. Wilde *College & Univ. Press* 1956 pap. $1.95; *Twayne* $4.00

THE QUESTION OF BEING. Ed. by William Kluback and Jean T. Wilde *College & Univ. Press* 1958 pap. $1.95

KANT AND THE PROBLEM OF METAPHYSICS. Trans. by James S. Churchill *Indiana Univ. Press* Midland Bks. 1962 pap. $2.45; *Peter Smith* $6.00

DISCOURSE ON THINKING. Trans. by John M. Anderson and E. Hans Freund; introd. by John M. Anderson *Harper* 1966 Torchbks. 1969 pap. $3.25

"Can be recommended to the lay reader who wants a brief introduction to Heidegger"—(*LJ*).

WHAT IS A THING? Trans. by W. B. Barton, Jr., and Vera Deutsch, with an analysis by Eugene T. Grendlin *Regnery* 1968 $8.50 pap. $3.95

"The book is quite important in its own right, without reference to the clarification on the history of Heidegger's thought which it can provide: the sorts of 'thing' he investigates include tools, man, works of art, the state, and the world. It is a pity then that the production is so second-rate, the translation so often unclear or inappropriate, the indexes so unhelpful. But the content wins out: the reinterpretation of the *cogito sum* in the light of the mathematization of metaphysics, alone, is worth the book's price"—(*LJ*).

WHAT IS CALLED THINKING? Trans. by J. Glenn Gray and Fred D. Wieck Religious Perspectives Ser. *Harper* 1968 Torchbks. 1972 pap. $3.45

"A translation of lectures from 1952 that are as near a definitive statement of Heidegger's new period that can be found. . . . A careful reading of this [wise] work can reveal far more to the philosophically uninitiated . . . than can most of his other works"—(*LJ*).

ESSENCE OF REASONS. Trans. by Terrence Malick *Northwestern Univ. Press* bilingual ed. 1969 $5.00

On the Way to Language. Ed. by J. Glenn Gray and Fred Wieck; trans. by Peter Hertz *Harper* 1971 $7.95

Poetry, Language and Thought. Trans. by Albert Hofstadter *Harper* 1971 Colophon Bks. 1975 pap. $3.45

This is an "indispensable addition to Heidegger in English and required reading for anyone interested in philosophy. . . . Heidegger, in short, is here not merely philosophizing but thinking. The translation is adequate and at times insightful and felicitous"—(*Choice*).

On Time and Being. Trans. by Joan Stambaugh *Harper* 1972 $4.95

This book "contains 4 items: a 1962 lecture, 'Time and Being'; a seminar report on it by Alfred Guzzani; a 1969 lecture, 'The End of Philosophy and the Task of Thinking'; a 1963 Festschrift essay, 'My Way to Phenomenology' "—(*LJ*).

The End of Philosophy. *Harper* new ed. 1973 $4.95

"A key to the later Heidegger, this condensation of his thought on Being is jampacked; it will strike non-Heideggerians as being dense, bewildering, near-Germanic gibberish. Those in the fold will welcome it"—(*Christian Century*).

Identity and Difference. Trans. by Joan Stambaugh *Harper* Torchbks. 1974 pap. $2.95

Early Greek Thinking. Trans. by David Krell and Frank Capuzzi *Harper* 1975 $10.50

Schelling's Treatise on the Essence of Human Freedom. Trans. by Joan Stambaugh *Northwestern Univ. Press* (in prep.)

Books about Heidegger

The Meaning of Heidegger: A Critical Study of an Existentialist Phenomenology. By Thomas Langan. *Columbia* 1959 $12.50 1961 pap. $2.45

Martin Heidegger: A First Introduction to His Philosophy. By Joseph Kockelmans. *Duquesne Univ. Press* (dist. by Humanities Press) 1965 $5.50

Anatomy of Disillusion: Martin Heidegger's Notion of Truth. By W. B. Macomber. *Northwestern Univ. Press* 1967 $8.00

Heidegger and the Quest for Truth. Ed. with introd. by Manfred S. Frings. *Quadrangle* 1968 pap. $2.45

Essays on Heidegger by various hands. "The theme present throughout the present study is that of the simultaneous revealment and concealment of Being as the dominant feature both of philosophizing and of the history of thought"—(*LJ*).

Being, Man and Death: A Key to Heidegger. By James M. Demske. *Univ. Press of Kentucky* 1970 $8.95

This book "is nearly indispensable for the serious student of Heidegger and will be useful for the beginner despite its limited focus and theme. Good bibliography of the relevant works in German and English. . . . Certainly belongs in all libraries"—(*Choice*).

Commentary on Heidegger's Being and Time. By Michael Gelven. *Harper* Torchbks. 1970 pap. $3.50 lib. bdg. $6.00

Heidegger's Metahistory of Philosophy: Amor Fati, Being and Truth. By Bernd Magnus. *Humanities Press* 1970 pap. $8.75

Heidegger and the Path of Thinking. Ed. by John Sallis. *Duquesne Univ. Press* (dist. by Humanities Press) 1970 text ed. $8.50

Heidegger and the Tradition. By Werner Marx. *Northwestern Univ. Press* 1971 $10.00

On Heidegger and Language. By Joseph J. Kockelmans. *Northwestern Univ. Press* 1972 $12.00

Humanism and Ethics: An Introduction to the Letter on Humanism by Heidegger. By Robert H. Cousineau. *Humanities Press* 1972 $13.75

The Tradition via Heidegger: An Essay on the Meaning of Being in the Philosophy of Martin Heidegger. By John W. Deely. *Humanities Press* 1972 pap. $14.00

Philosophy of Martin Heidegger. By J. L. Mehta. *Harper* Torchbks. 1972 pap. $3.75

Heidegger on the Divine: The Thinker, the Poet and God. By James L. Perotti. *Ohio Univ. Press* 1974 $7.50

"Not for the beginning student of Heidegger, although the well-done second, third and fourth chapters rehearsing Heidegger's 'destruction' of metaphysics should prove hopeful to those struggling with it for the first time. The book does not advance Heidegger scholarship greatly, but it is a succinct alternative to some of the more weighty standard works of Heidegger"—(*Choice*).

Language and the World: A Methodological-Structural Synthesis Within the Writings of Martin Heidegger and Ludwig Wittgenstein. By George F. Sefler. *Humanities Press* 1974 $6.50

MARCEL, GABRIEL.   1889–1973.

"The label 'Christian existentialism' is an expression coined by others in describing the philosophy of Gabriel Marcel. . . . He has said: 'All my effort can be described as a straining towards the production of currents by which life is restored to certain areas of the mind which have sunk into torpor and begun to decay.' . . . Music and playwriting have been lifelong vocations of Marcel. From Bach he acknowledges his concern for the vitality and pervasiveness of religious experience. And to dramatic writing with its cast of characters caught up in the enactment of life's symphonies, Marcel found himself indebted for the inspiration to depict the immediate, the spontaneous, and the unpredictable in human interaction. . . . The key to his epistemology and for that matter his whole philosophy lies in an understanding of what he means by participation. To be is to participate in being . . . man can either become insular or engage himself to the rest of being. Since self and that which self participates in cannot be separated, man is organic with the world and it to him"—(See Frederick Patka's "Existentialist Thinkers and Thought").

THE MYSTERY OF BEING. Regnery Gateway Eds. 2 vols. 1960 Vol. 1 Reflections and Mystery, trans. by G. Fraser pap. $1.85 Vol. 2 Faith and Reality, trans. by R. Hague pap. $1.65

PHILOSOPHY OF EXISTENCE. Trans. by Manya Harai. 1949. Essay Index Reprint Ser. Bks. for Libraries facs. ed. $8.75

HOMO VIATOR. 1951. Trans. by Emma Craufurd. 1962. Peter Smith $5.25

ROYCE'S METAPHSICS. Trans. by Virginia Ringer and Gordon Ringer. 1956. Greenwood 1975 $11.50

THE PHILOSOPHY OF EXISTENTIALISM. Citadel Press 1961 pap. $1.95

MAN AGAINST MASS SOCIETY. Regnery Gateway Eds. 1962 pap. $1.95

CREATIVE FIDELITY. Trans. by Robert Rosthal. From his French work of 1940, "Du Refus à l'Invocation." Farrar, Straus 1964 Noonday pap. $3.45

THE EXISTENTIALIST BACKGROUND OF HUMAN DIGNITY. Harvard Univ. Press 1963 $7.00. The William James Lectures, delivered at Harvard University, 1961–62. A retrospective account of his development as a dramatist, philosopher and human being; his polemic is against Marxism, bureaucracy and technology.

PHILOSOPHICAL FRAGMENTS: 1901–1914 and THE PHILOSOPHER AND PEACE. Univ. of Notre Dame Press 1965 pap. $1.75

A METAPHYSICAL JOURNAL. Trans. by Bernard Wall Regnery Gateway Eds. 1967 pap. $2.65

BEING AND HAVING: An Existentialist Diary. Trans. by Katherine Farrer Peter Smith $5.25

TRAGIC WISDOM AND BEYOND. Trans. by Stephen Jolin and Peter McCormick. Studies in Phenomenology and Existential Philosophy Northwestern Univ. Press text. ed. 1973 $9.00

Books about Marcel

The Philosophy of Gabriel Marcel. By Kenneth T. Gallagher. Fwd. by Gabriel Marcel Fordham Univ. Press 1962 rev. ed. 1975 pap. $5.00
Marcel has been for nearly four decades one of the world's most influential thinkers "underivative and unclassifiable though he may be. This book is the first study in the U.S. of Marcel's work in its entirety. Marcel himself, in the foreword, approves Gallagher's results, especially the latter's identification of 'participation' as the leitmotif of his thought"—(LJ).
Gabriel Marcel. By Thomas J. M. van Ewijk. Paulist-Newman 1965 pap. $1.25
Gabriel Marcel. By Sam Keen. John Knox Press 1967 pap. $1.75

WITTGENSTEIN, LUDWIG.   1889–1951.

The Austrian-born Wittgenstein is probably the most eminent philosopher of that branch of the neorealist movement known as "logical empiricism." Trained as an engineer, Wittgenstein settled in England, where his teaching exerted wide influence. His first book, "Tractatus Logico-Philosophicus," published in 1922, contained the predominant attitude of his thought, summarized in the oft-quoted sentence, "Whereof one cannot speak, thereon one must be silent." George Steiner's "Language and Silence: Essays on Language, Literature, and the Inhuman" (Atheneum 1970 $8.00

text ed. pap. $3.95)—like so much of the "new" drama—is deeply concerned with the pauses in language, the use of language to *avoid* communication, the need for silence in a world flooded with "information." Of Wittgenstein he says: "The greatest of modern philosophers was also the one most profoundly intent on escaping from the spiral of language. Wittgenstein's entire work starts out by asking whether there is any verifiable relation between the word and the fact. That which we call fact may well be a veil spun by language to shroud the mind from reality. Wittgenstein compels us to wonder whether reality can be *spoken of,* when speech is merely a kind of infinite regression, words being spoken of other words. . . . The famous closing proposition of the *Tractatus* is not a claim for the potentiality of philosophic statement such as Descartes advanced. On the contrary; it is drastic retreat from the confident authority of traditional metaphysics. It leads to the equally famous conclusion: 'It is clear that Ethics cannot be expressed.'. . . . The silence, which at every point surrounds the naked discourse, seems, by virtue of Wittgenstein's force of insight, less a wall than a window. With Wittgenstein, as vith certain poets, we look out of language not into darkness but light. Anyone who reads the *Tractatus* will be sensible of its odd, mute radiance."

Like Wittgenstein, the philosophers of the logical empirical movement abandon the investigation of empirical facts to the various special sciences; they tend to regard the investigation of a transcendent realm of allegedly "transempirical fact" as fruitless or illusory; and they see the task of philosophy as that of analyzing and clarifying logical procedures involved in what we *say* about the world. Logical empiricism is much interested in the limits of language and the meaning of meaning.

TRACTATUS LOGICO-PHILOSOPHICUS. 1921 German. First Eng. trans. 1922 by D. F. Pears and B. F. McGuinness. *Humanities Press* 1961 corrected ed. 1963 without German text $6.00 1974 pap. $3.00

PHILOSOPHICAL INVESTIGATIONS. Ed. by Kenneth Scott *Macmillan* 1953 3rd ed. 1973 text ed. pap. $4.25

PHILOSOPHICAL REMARKS. Ed. by Rhees Rush *Harper* (Barnes & Noble) text ed. $18.50

REMARKS ON THE FOUNDATIONS OF MATHEMATICS. Trans. by G. E. M. Anscombe; ed. by G. H. von Wright and others. 1956. *M.I.T. Press* 2nd ed. 1967 pap. $3.95

WITTGENSTEIN ON THE FOUNDATIONS OF MATHEMATICS: Notes from His Cambridge Lectures, 1939. Ed. by Cora Diamond *Cornell Univ. Press* 1975 $18.50

THE BLUE AND BROWN BOOKS: Preliminary Studies for the Philosophical Investigations. *Harper* (Barnes & Noble) 1958 2nd ed. 1969 $6.00 Torchbks. pap. $2.25

NOTEBOOKS NINETEEN FOURTEEN-NINETEEN SIXTEEN. Ed. by G. E. Anscombe and G. H. von Wright *Harper* 1961 Torchbks. 1969 pap. $2.45

LECTURES AND CONVERSATIONS ON AESTHETICS, PSYCHOLOGY, AND RELIGIOUS BELIEF. Ed. by Cyril Barrett *Univ. of California Press* 1967 pap. $1.50

"In 1938 Wittgenstein delivered a short course of lectures on aesthetics to a small group of students at Cambridge. The present volume has been compiled from notes taken down at the time by three of the students . . . supplemented by notes of conversations on Freud . . . and by notes of some lectures on religious belief"—(Publisher's note).

PROTOTRACTATUS: An Early Version of *Tractatus Logico-Philosophicus.* Ed. by B. F. McGuinness, T. Nyberg and G. H. von Wright; trans. by D. F. Pears and B. F. McGuinness *Cornell Univ. Press* 1971 $24.50

ON CERTAINTY. *Harper* Torchbks. 1972 pap. $2.95

PHILOSOPHICAL GRAMMAR. Trans. by A. J. Kenny *Univ. of California Press* 1974 $18.00

LETTERS FROM LUDWIG WITTGENSTEIN. With a memoir by Paul Engelmann; trans. by L. Furtmuller *Horizon Press* pap. 1974 $2.95

LETTERS TO C. K. OGDEN. Ed. by G. H. von Wright *Routledge and Kegan Paul* 1973 $6.25

LETTERS TO RUSSELL, KEYNES, AND MOORE. Ed. by G. H. von Wright *Cornell Univ. Press* 1974 $9.75

Books about Wittgenstein

Terms in Their Propositional Contexts in Wittgenstein's Tractatus: An Index. By G. K. Plochmann and J. B. Lawson. *Southern Illinois Univ. Press* 1962 $7.00. The Index is in English, based on a new rendering of the terms, but is keyed to references to the C. K. Ogden version.

Wittgenstein and Modern Philosophy. By Justus Hartnack. Trans. from the Danish and ed. by
  Maurice Cranston *New York Univ. Press* 1965 $6.95
  The Danish Professor Hartnack "analyzes the key ideas found in [the *"Tractatus Logico-
  Philosophicus"* and "Philosophical Investigations"] and traces Wittgenstein's influence on the
  schools of logical positivism and analytical philosophy and some contemporary British
  philosophers"—*(LJ)*.
Language, Persons, and Belief. By Dallas M. High. *Oxford* 1967 $6.95
  "Not only does it present a revolutionary yet sound understanding of the later philosophy of
  Wittgenstein, but it does so in a well-documented and clearly argued manner.... What
  specifically sets this book off from so many others in the field of 'religious language' is its
  happy combination of an authentic understanding of language philosophy with profound
  theological insight"—(Jerry H. Gill).
Ludwig Wittgenstein: A Memoir. By Norman Malcolm and George H. von Wright. *Oxford* 1967
  pap. $1.95
Wittgenstein: The Philosophical Investigations. Ed. by George Pitcher. *Univ. of Notre Dame Press*
  1968 $10.95 1974 pap. $3.95. An essay collection on the philosopher by contemporaries.
Studies in the Philosophy of Wittgenstein. Ed. by Peter Winch. *Humanities Press* 1969 text ed.
  $8.75
Wittgenstein's Conception of Philosophy. By K. T. Fann. *Univ. of California Press* 1969 $7.75
  pap. $2.45. Based on the author's doctoral dissertation and provides an introduction to the
  work of Wittgenstein.
Strict Finitism: An Examination of Ludwig Wittgenstein's Remarks on the Foundations of
  Mathematics. By Charles F. Kielkopf. *Humanities Press* 1970 pap. text ed. $13.50
Introduction to Wittgenstein's Tractatus. By G. E. M. Anscombe. *Humanities Press* 3rd ed. text
  ed. $5.00 pap. $2.00; *Univ. of Pennsylvania Press* 1971 pap. $2.45
Essays on Wittgenstein. Ed. by E. D. Klemke. *Univ. of Illinois Press* 1971 $10.95 pap. $4.50
Wittgenstein, The Early Philosophy: An Exposition of the Tractatus. By Henry L. Finch.
  Humanities Press 1971 text ed. $10.00
Language Learning in Wittgenstein's Later Philosophy. By Charles S. Hardwick. *Humanities
  Press* 1971 text ed. pap. $7.75
  "A clearly written critical work on the later Wittgenstein's doctrines of language and
  learning"—*(Choice)*.
Wittgenstein's Philosophy of Language: Some Aspects of Its Development. By James Bogen.
  Humanities Press 1972 text ed. $13.50
Wittgenstein and Justice: On the Significance of Ludwig Wittgenstein for Social and Political
  Thought. By H. Pitkin. *Univ. of California Press* 1972 $13.50 pap. $3.95
  "Though both title and subtitle mention Wittgenstein, this book is more broadly based on
  Wittgensteinianism as developed not only by Wittgenstein but by such philosophers as
  Austin, Ziff and Cavell—the last being quoted almost as much as the master himself.... The
  book requires some sophistication from its readers.... It is recommended as a good, clear
  survey of the Wittgensteinian position for qualified students"—*(Choice)*.
The Doctrine of the Tyranny of Language: An Historical and Critical Examination of the Blue
  Book. By Morris S. Engel. *Humanities Press* 1972 pap. text ed. $10.00
Ludwig Wittgenstein: Philosophy and Language. Ed. by Alice Ambrose and Morris Lazerowitz.
  Humanities Press 1972 text ed. $18.50
  "This collection of essays on Wittgenstein's philosophy ... consists of previously unpublished
  essays, several of which have been contributed by former students and close friends of
  Wittgenstein.... While the essays vary considerably in range of subject matter and degree of
  difficulty, the collection is a suitable acquisition for an undergraduate library and appropriate
  reading for students engaged in advanced work in philosophy at an undergraduate level"—
  (*Choice*).
Wittgenstein on Philosophy and the Metaphysics of Experience. By P. M. Hacker. *Oxford* 1972
  $14.50
  "Hacker's analysis is thorough and probably the most sympathetic we have to date. The book
  is brilliantly written and is an excellent companion guide to and beyond the writings of
  Wittgenstein"—*(LJ)*.
Induction and Deduction: A Study in Wittgenstein. By Ilham Dilman. *Harper* (Barnes and
  Noble) 1973 $11.50
  "The discussions are skillful, and part two will especially interest readers of Wittgenstein. A
  useful and stimulating book"—*(LJ)*.
Language and Being in Wittgenstein's "Philosophical Investigations." By Jeffrey T. Price.
  Humanities Press 1973 pap. $8.00
Essays after Wittgenstein. By John F. M. Hunter. *Univ. of Toronto Press* 1973 $15.00
  "Intended for the use of graduate and upper-level undergraduate students, this is a valuable
  addition to libraries"—*(Choice)*.

Wittgenstein. By Anthony Kenny. *Harvard Univ. Press* 1973 text ed. $7.50 pap. $2.95
This book "is a masterpiece of both scholarship and criticism. It tracks the development and interplay of the many themes that have given Wittgenstein a central place in contemporary philosophy"—*(Choice)*.

Wittgenstein's Vienna. By Allan Janik and Stephen Toulmin. *Simon & Schuster* 1973 $8.95
"This very important book will prove indispensable to both historians and philosophers. It will also stir a great deal of controversy because it overthrows the conventional view of Wittgenstein. . . . The aim of the book is to set us right about Wittgenstein's intentions, which were cultural and ethical rather than narrowly linguistic. Essential for all academic libraries, this book is suitable for general libraries, as well, despite a number or difficult sections"—*(LJ)*.

Wittgenstein. By W. W. Bartley, III. *Lippincott* 1973 $6.95
This "is a sensitive and exceptionally interesting account of a philosopher even more enigmatic than Sartre. . . . Bartley's emphasis on the moral thrust of the philosophy provides a new perspective, as does the apparently well-documented description of Wittgenstein's experience as a schoolteacher in lower Austria. His treatment is non-technical, lucid, and concise"—*(LJ)*.

Architecture of Ludwig Wittgenstein: A Documentation with Excerpts from the Family Recollections by Hermine Wittgenstein. By Bernhard Leitner. Trans. by Richard Ilgner *Press of Nova Scotia* (dist. by Jaap Rietman) 1973 $9.95

Understanding Wittgenstein. Ed. by Godrey Vesey. Royal Institute of Philosophy Lectures, 1972–73 vol. 7. *St. Martin's* 1974 text ed. $15.95

Language and the World: A Methodological Synthesis within the Writings of Martin Heidegger and Ludwig Wittgenstein. By George F. Sefler. *Humanities Press* 1974 text ed. $6.50

Wittgenstein's Language. By Timothy Binkley. *Humanities Press* text ed. pap. $15.50

NIEBUHR, REINHOLD. 1892–1971. *See Chapter 4, World Religions, this Volume.*

LANGER, SUSANNE K(ATHERINA KNAUTH). 1895–

As friend and pupil of Alfred North Whitehead, Susanne Langer was led into a long and profound study of symbolic logic. In her first published work, "The Practice of Philosophy," she established her position. "Philosophical Sketches" is valuable as an introduction to the work of this outstanding American philosopher. This collection of nine short articles, some previously published, some delivered as papers, is intended as preliminary thought for "Mind: An Essay on Human Feeling," the first of three projected volumes—to be her *magnum opus*. In the "Sketches," "Mrs. Langer is committed to philosophy as the systematic study of meanings. She deals here mainly with feelings and symbols both broadly interpreted and considered in their many relationships and their impact on civilization and culture"—*(LJ)*. Her thesis in "Mind" is that the mind's "function is possessed to a greater or lesser extent by all organic life, from the unicellular organism to man, and that all life is permeated with acts that are influenced by it. . . . Professor Langer propounds two opposed and complementary functional principles by which organic life proceeds—individuation and involvement. A cell or an organ inhibits its own growth at a certain point. This is an example of individuation. On the other hand, involvement has been present in organic life since the very beginning. Not only are cells involved with other cells but all acts are to some extent involved with other acts. And acts tend to recur, forming rhythmic patterns. Professor Langer is fascinated by rhythm—by what she refers to as "dialectical concatenation into rhythmic series," which is to be observed in the acts of organisms. She even suggests a rhythmic origin for life . . . though she quickly dismisses this idea as speculative. . . . The references to art are also continually cropping up. Growth—the perpetual trend of life—is compared with melody, which always moves (or, rather, grows) to its point of climax and then recedes, often to gather impetus toward a succeeding climax. In our apprehension of the world around us, 'feeling' is basic. 'Where nothing ever is felt,' Professor Langer states (and few would disagree), 'nothing matters' "—(Winthrop Sargeant, in the *New Yorker*). Mrs. Langer, who has taught at Wellesley, Smith, and has been on the faculty of the University of Delaware and New York University, is Professor Emeritus of Philosophy and recently a research scholar at Connecticut College.

INTRODUCTION TO SYMBOLIC LOGIC. 1937 1953 3rd ed. 1967. *Dover* pap. $4.00

PHILOSOPHY IN A NEW KEY: A Study in the Symbolism of Reason, Rite and Art. *Harvard Univ. Press* 1942 3rd ed. 1957 $11.50 pap. $3.50

FEELING AND FORM: A Theory of Art. *Scribner* 1953 pap. $4.95

PROBLEMS OF ART. *Scribner* 1957 pap. $2.95. Ten philosophical lectures.

(Ed.). REFLECTIONS ON ART: A Source Book of Writings by Artists, Critics and Philosophers. With the editor's interpretations. *Johns Hopkins Press* 1958 1961 pap. $3.95 *Oxford* 1961 pap. $2.50

MIND: An Essay on Human Feeling. *Johns Hopkins Press* 2 vols. Vol. 1 1967 $15.00 pap.
1970 $3.95 Vol. 2 1973 $12.50 pap. 1974 $3.95

"The second volume and fourth part of a six-part study on the conceptual foundations of
biology. . . . The study traces the continuous evolution of life from its simplest forms to the most
complex phenomena of mind. . . . For advanced students of philosophy of biology, aesthetics, and
philosophy of mind"—(*Choice*).

EDMAN, IRWIN. 1896–1954

Professor of Philosophy at Columbia, Irwin Edman was a philosopher as well as a professor of
philosophy, according to his own distinction. "Philosopher's Holiday" (1938, o.p.), an autobiography of a sort, made the author well known to the general reading public. His love of music, travel,
and poetry and his unusual contacts with curious human beings, "philosophers without portfo-
lios," give his books a wide interest. He followed in the direction of William James and John
Dewey, guided by Platonism.

ADAM, THE BABY AND THE MAN FROM MARS. 1929. Essay Index Reprint Ser. *Bks. for
Libraries* 1968 $12.75

THE CONTEMPORARY AND HIS SOUL. 1931. *Kennikat* $7.00

ARTS AND THE MAN. *Norton* 1939 pap. 1960 $1.85

PHILOSOPHER'S QUEST. 1947. *Greenwood* 1973 lib. bdg. $13.50

MARCUSE, HERBERT. 1898–

At a recent lecture in a Yale Philosophy Department series on "Revolution" Professor Marcuse
lauded the graffiti of French students in May 1968 as an incisive slogan for his own vision of
revolution: "All power to the imagination!" and "Be reasonable: ask the impossible." Herbert
Marcuse, whom some blame for the worldwide wave of student rebellion but who is more likely
merely the newly discovered longstanding expression of it, is, says the *N.Y. Times*, "dapper, relaxed
and [radiates] philosophical benignity." "He tears us apart if we don't think analytically," say his
students—"if we come out sounding like Marcuse. . . . He insists on the questioning spirit." He was
born in Germany and attended the Universities of Freiburg and of Berlin. A Social Democrat in
Germany, he migrated to the United States in 1934, became a citizen in 1940 and was a high U.S.
government consultant during World War II. "Dr. Marcuse is a professed philosophical Marxist,
in that he sees contemporary life as a class struggle in which suppressed and exploited segments of
society should act to revamp the socio-economic order. . . . Soviet spokesmen, however, disown
and denounce Dr. Marcuse because he rejects Karl Marx's cherished 'working class' as the instrument of revolutionary change and thinks it must come from groups like oppressed minorities
and freethinking youth"—(*N.Y. Times*). Professor Marcuse has said, "I have tried to show that
any change would require a total rejection or, to speak the language of the students, a perpetual
confrontation of [contemporary] society." By late 1968 Professor Marcuse had become, again
according to the *N.Y. Times*, the "idol" of "restive college students from Berkeley to Bologna"
and an apostle of the "New Left." He has lectured at Harvard and Columbia and has taught
philosophy and political science at Brandeis; he is now a professor of philosophy at the University
of San Diego, where his position has been challenged by San Diego conservatives to the extent
of threats on his life.

"One-Dimensional Man" is a "critique of modern technological societies. . . . One-dimensional-
ity refers to a tendency to flatten our diverse and conflicting levels of existence and experience and
make them consistent. . . . Art and literature no longer provide a refuge for oppositional
personalities who do not fit into the dominant scheme of things; even the most avant-garde and
'shocking' cultural products are accepted by the benign establishment. They not only siphon off
discontent, they too have market value. Since all forms of potential opposition can be accepted
within the status quo, their revolutionary and critical character is deflated. In a series of brilliant
analyses that probe deeply into language, popular culture, science, and philosophy, Marcuse
traces how multi-dimensional criticism has been collapsed into one-dimensional ideology"—
(Robert Blauner, in *Trans-action*). Sidney Hook has accused Marcuse of wanting to deny freedom
of speech to extremists, or even to those who would "choose 'middle-class values.' He replied [said
Hook]: 'Well, since I have already gone out on a limb, I may as well go all the way. I would prefer
that they did not have the right to choose wrongly.' " Marcuse feels that Hitler was allowed too
much latitude under German democracy, the situation that made his rise to power possible.

The reader is referred to the very interesting article in the *N.Y. Times Magazine* of Oct. 27, 1968,
an interview by three French journalists in which Marcuse defines what he believes to be his
relationship to the student movement. Some of the sympathizers with the students would deplore
the use of violence; on this point Marcuse was questioned in the article mentioned: "*And to try to
destroy this society which is guilty of violence, you feel that violence is both legitimate and desirable. Does this*

mean that you think it impossible to evolve peacefully and within the democratic framework toward a nonrepressive, freer society? Marcuse: The students have said it: a revolution is always just as violent as the violence it combats. I believe they are right. *But you still think it is possible, in spite of the judgment of Freud, to whom yor refer frequently in 'Eros and Civilization,' to create a free society. Doesn't this betray a remarkable optimism?* Marcuse: I am optimistic, because I believe that never in the history of humanity have the resources necessary to create a free society existed to such a degree. I am pessimistic because I believe that the established societies—capitalist society in particular—are totally organized and mobilized against this possibility."

"Not only is there no revolution in the offing [Marcuse] says, but the final crisis of capitalism may be a century away. . . . Evil is absolute and total on one side only. On the 'socialist' side, evil is merely a rather unfortunate aberration from the true path. Civil liberties do not strengthen a country's defenses against totalitarianism, according to Dr. Marcuse, they only succeed in bringing about fascism. Let's not worry, however, it's all a century away," says Arnold Beichman in the *Christian Science Monitor* of Marcuse's latest essays.

EROS AND CIVILIZATION: A Philosophical Inquiry into Freud. *Beacon* 1955 $8.95 pap. 1966 1974 $3.95

REASON AND REVOLUTION: Hegel and the Rise of Social Theory. *Humanities Press* 1955. 2nd ed. 1968 $13.50; *Beacon* 1960 pap. $3.95

SOVIET MARXISM. *Columbia* 1958 $13.50; *Random* Vintage Bks. 1968 pap. $2.45

ONE-DIMENSIONAL MAN: Studies in the Ideology of Advanced Industrial Society. *Beacon* 1964 $7.50 pap. $3.95

"His virtuoso presentation spans a remarkably wide range of thinking—the social sciences, philosophy (especially philosophy of science and logic), linguistics, and literature and the arts. . . . A brilliant book"—*(LJ)*.

NEGATIONS: Essays in Critical Theory. With translations from the German by J. J. Shapiro *Beacon* 1969 $7.50

"These essays from the mid-1930's and 1960's fit together in two ways: their common subject is 'freedom, peace, and happiness'; and the 'handle' for getting hold of this subject is the history of philosophy. [Marcuse] argues that 'the real fight [however, is] the political fight.' In the foreword he reveals his attitude up to the present and this is worth the book's price alone"—*(LJ)*.

AN ESSAY ON LIBERATION. *Beacon* 1969 pap. $1.95

"In this explorative essay he presses beyond Marxist 'critical analysis' to offer utopian speculations made necessary by the inchoate anarchism of student 'activists' who know what they are *against* but need a vision of a truly free society to sustain them in a long struggle against overwhelming odds. Marcuse only approximates that vision, at best. . . . But his critique of the brutalizing effects of what he considers our conservative-capitalist Establishment is powerful. [The] book may in time prove a prophetic and noble statement"—*(PW)*.

FIVE LECTURES. *Beacon* 1970 $7.50 pap. $1.95

"The unity of the book stems from the development of Marcuse's thought. Three of the lectures deal with Marcuse's Freudianism"—*(LJ)*.

COUNTERREVOLUTION AND REVOLT. *Beacon* 1972 $7.50 pap. $2.45

"Marcuse brings together aesthetics, the study of nature, and the prospects of world revolution"—*(Christian Century)*.

STUDIES IN CRITICAL PHILOSOPHY. Trans. by Joris DeBres *Beacon* 1973 $7.95 pap. $2.95. Contains "Freedom and the Historical Imperative," a lecture delivered in 1969 after the May events and campus revolts. Also includes critique of Sartre's existentialism and a review of Marx's Economical-Philosophical Manuscripts.

Books about Marcuse

Freudian Left: Wilhelm Reich and Geza Roheim and Herbert Marcuse. By Paul Robinson. *Harper* Colophon Bks. 1969 pap. $1.95

Critical Interruptions: New Left Perspectives on Herbert Marcuse. By Paul Breines. *Seabury Press* 1970 $5.50 pap. $2.95

Herbert Marcuse: An Exposition and a Polemic. By Alasdair MacIntyre. *Viking* 1970 $4.95 pap. $1.65

Contra Marcuse. By Eliseo Vivas. *Arlington* 1971 $8.95 pap. $2.45. A very critical but unscholarly account by an author who self-admittedly has not thoroughly surveyed Marcuse.

New Theories of Revolution: A Commentary on the Views of Franz Fanon, Regis Debray and Herbert Marcuse. By Jack Woddis. *International Pubs.* 1972 $10.00 pap. $3.65
The author "seeks to show that Fanon, Debray and Marcuse . . . grossly underestimate the importance of the working class"—*(Choice).*
Critique of Herbert Marcuse. By Jurgen Habermas. *Dutton* 1974 $9.95
Herbert Marcuse: From Marx to Freud and Beyond. By Sidney Lipshires. *General Learning Corp.* 1974 pap. $2.85

HOOK, SIDNEY. 1902–

Dr. Hook was born and educated in New York City and taught, very early in his career, in the city's public schools. Morris Cohen *(q.v.)* was among his teachers at City College; he later studied under John Dewey at Columbia University, where he received his Ph.D. in 1927. He immediately began teaching at New York University, where he has served as chairman of the philosophy department at the Washington Square College, head of the graduate department and head of the all-university department, retiring from this post in May 1968. On that occasion one of his colleagues recalled Hook's remark, "I've had a wonderful week, a fight every day"—(quoted in the *N.Y. Times*). The philosopher Brand Blanshard has called Hook "that inexhaustible geyser of books, lectures, and essays, a philosopher who scents the smell of battle from afar and is soon in the midst of it, giving as well as he gets, and usually somewhat better."

An early Marxist in his fervent desire for social reform, Dr. Hook was deeply impressed by his teachers Cohen and Dewey. He still passionately espouses a form of Marxism which Andrew J. Reck describes as properly "democratic socialism," but of his own brand; he early denounced communism as practised in the Soviet Union and remains one of its most dogged and vocal opponents. "As a philosopher, Hook's most distinctive contribution is his theory of democracy. . . . On occasions too numerous to count Hook has attempted to elucidate the objective meaning of democracy, to canvas the objections raised against it, to marshal the arguments in its behalf, and, as behooves the philosopher, to examine the kinds of theroretical justifications which from time to time come forth in its support. . . . His early books, *Towards the Understanding of Karl Marx* and *From Hegel to Marx*, are by far the best expository, interpretive, historical, and critical studies of Marx's thought ever written by an American philosopher.

". . . Persistently criticizing the historical determinism of orthodox Marxism, Hook argues that history contains the contingent and the unforeseen and, further, that individual men play important roles in the making of history"—(*See* Andrew J. Reck, "The New American Philosophers"). "The Hero in History" concerns this idea. The *N.Y. Times* has said of him: "A pragmatist who believes that all viable reform must come from within, he has had few rivals in his ability to launch and sustain a dialogue on the great issues of our time. He has made those dialogues memorable for their fireworks, whether the subject was nuclear physics or psychoanalysis, civil disobedience or the Bill of Rights—or a new form of tyranny over the mind of man." He has recently defended the right of the scholar to remain "disengaged" in his search for truth, and has attacked Herbert Marcuse *(q.v.)* for what Hook considers a new dogmatism.

Professor Hook received Guggenheim Fellowships in 1928 and 1953 to study European philosophy, traveling to Russia and Germany, and was granted a Ford Foundation Fellowship in 1958 to study Asian philosophy and culture. A Fellow of the American Academy of Arts and Sciences, he was president of the Eastern Division of the American Philosophical Association in 1959. He delivered the Montgomery Lectures in Contemporary Civilization at the University of Nebraska in 1964 and has edited a series of volumes which record symposia conducted by New York University's Institute of Philosophy *(for a detailed description, see the list of Works on Modern Philosophy, earlier in this Chapter).*

In a recent address at the Hoover Institute at Stanford, Hook stated, "survival is not the be-all and end-all of a life worthy of man. Sometimes the worst thing we can know about a man is that he survived. . . . Man's vocation should be the use of the art of intelligence in behalf of freedom."

FROM HEGEL TO MARX: Studies in the Intellectual Development of Karl Marx. 1936. *Humanities Press* 1958 $7.50; *Univ. of Michigan* Ann Arbor Bks. pap. $2.95

JOHN DEWEY: An Intellectual Portrait. 1939 *Greenwood* 1973 $12.25

REASON, SOCIAL MYTHS, AND DEMOCRACY. 1940. *Humanities Press* $6.00

THE HERO IN HISTORY: A Study in Limitation and Possibility. 1943. *Humanities Press* 1955 $6.50; *Beacon* 1955 pap. $2.95

HERESY, YES—CONSPIRACY, No. 1953. *Greenwood* 1973 $13.75

(Ed.). MARX AND THE MARXISTS: The Ambiguous Legacy. *Van Nostrand-Reinhold* Anvil Bks. 1955 pap. $3.95

COMMON SENSE AND THE FIFTH AMENDMENT. 1957. *Constructive Action* 1963 pap. $1.75

POLITICAL POWER AND PERSONAL FREEDOM: Critical Studies in Democracy, Communism and Civil Rights. 1959. *Macmillan* Collier Bks. pap. $1.50

THE QUEST FOR BEING AND OTHER STUDIES IN NATURALISM AND HUMANISM. 1959 1961. *Greenwood* 1971 $12.75

THE PARADOXES OF FREEDOM. *Univ. of California Press* 1962 pap. $1.95

EDUCATION FOR MODERN MAN. 1963. *Humanities Press* 1973 $8.50

RELIGION IN A FREE SOCIETY. *Univ. of Nebraska Press* 1967 $5.95

ACADEMIC FREEDOM AND ACADEMIC ANARCHY. 1970. *Dell* 1971 pap. $2.45

EDUCATION AND THE TAMING OF POWER. *Open Court* 1973 $8.95

PRAGMATISM AND THE TRAGIC SENSE OF LIFE. *Basic Bks.* (dist. by Harper) 1975 $12.50

"This collection of 13 essays—including two not published previously—ranges over law, ethics, religion, politics, history, education, and metaphysics"—*(LJ)*.

Books about Hook

Sidney Hook and the Contemporary World: Essays on the Pragmatic Intelligence. Ed. by Paul Kurtz. *John Day* 1968 $10.95

"Eleven of the [difficult] essays in the book deal with Hook's life and philosophical career, or with the doctrines he has espoused in such fields as moral philosophy, politics, religion, metaphysics and the theory of knowledge. The other 12 essays are independent contributions to these fields by a number of scholars. [The book] strikes too uncritically laudatory a tone.... Of 23 contributions to this volume, only three ... directly challenge Hook's positions"—*(N.Y. Times)*. There is an extensive bibliography.

SARTRE, JEAN-PAUL. 1905–   (Nobel Prize refused 1964)

Sartre is the chief prophet of Existentialism, that bleak philosophy of despair that grew from the defeat of France. When the intellectuals of the Left Bank felt abandoned and helpless, it offered both a personal and a social answer. There are two types of Existentialists, those who follow the mystical Danish pastor of the nineteenth century, Sören Kierkegaard (*q.v.*), and Sartre's atheistic followers, who reject Kierkegaard's belief in God but accept his idea of man's existence in a hostile, disordered world, trying to make the best of things, fulfilling his life and achieving final freedom. In "Existentialism," he denies that his philosophy is one of despair, and says: "Man is nothing else but what he makes of himself. You're free, choose, that is, invent." But many find his formula full of paradoxes. "Being and Nothingness," the "Critique of Dialectical Reason" (1960, o.p.) and "Search for a Method" provide the core of his thought and its development. In the latter two volumes he answered his critics by setting the existentialist "man alone" in his social and world context.

Sartre was for 13 years an obscure teacher of philosophy. He was mobilized as a private at the beginning of the war; was taken prisoner and spent nine months in a German war prison. When released, he returned to Paris to take an active part in the Communist resistance organization. He abandoned teaching for writing and formulated his philosophy.

"It isn't usual that you can say of an acknowledged playwright or novelist that a book of his essays ["Literary and Philosophical Essays"] may be as valuable as anything he has done. But Sartre has always seemed to me an idea man, an intellectual first, only afterward an artist; his novels and plays come alive where he touches upon the idea, where the idea is directly on stage or hanging around very close in the wings; the center of his power as a writer is neither in philosophy nor literature separately, but in their curious point of intersection. This is why, paradoxical though it may sound, these essays seem to me the most vital and significant Sartre that we have yet been given in English"—(William Barrett, in the *N.Y. Times*).

In 1964 Sartre published the autobiography of his early years, "The Words" (*Fawcett* Premier Bks. pap. $.95), in which he "declared that he had derived his metaphysical yearnings from the upbringing he had had, in his bookish grandfather's world of words, and that he had been cured of his idealistic hankerings, not by existentialism, but by the impact of Marxism"—(Philip Rahv). "The Ghost of Stalin" (*Braziller* 1968 $4.50) written at the time of the Soviet Hungarian invasion, warned the French Communist Party against Stalinism; "The Communists and Peace" (*Braziller* 1968 $6.95) analyzed the structure of the French party and its relation with the workers.

Sartre was interviewed on the occasion of his seventieth birthday by Michel Contat in the *New York Review of Books*. In the interview he discussed his general staisfaction with his life but also his disappointment at losing his eyesight and his ability to work. He claims that he is still interested in music, politics and philosophy, but that nothing really excites him anymore.

THE TRANSCENDENCE OF THE EGO: An Existentialist Theory of Consciousness. 1937. Trans. and annot. with introd. by Forrest Williams and Robert Kirkpatrick *Farrar, Straus* Noonday 1957 pap. $1.95; *Octagon* 1972 lib. bdg. $7.00

First published in France in 1937, this marks his break with the German phenomenological movement originating with Husserl, by which he had been greatly influenced, and led to the full existentialist expression of "Being and Nothingness." A "brilliant polemic against the pure Ego"— (*Journal of Philosophy*).

ANTI-SEMITE AND JEW. 1948 *Schocken Bks.* 1965 $5.00 pap. $1.95. His contribution to the literature on the Jewish problem.

EXISTENTIAL PSYCHOANALYSIS. Trans. by Hazel E. Barnes. 1953. *Regnery* Gateway Eds. 1962 pap. $1.10. A new psychoanalysis based on the principles of existentialism.

LITERARY AND PHILOSOPHICAL ESSAYS. Trans. by Annette Michelsen. 1955. *Macmillan* Collier Bks. pap. $1.50

EXISTENTIALISM AND HUMAN EMOTIONS. 1957. *Citadel Press* 1971 pap. $1.95. Contains "Existentialism" as well as parts of "Being and Nothingness."

SEARCH FOR A METHOD. 1957. Trans. with introd. by Hazel E. Barnes. 1963. *Random* Vintage Bks. 1968 pap. $1.65

Sartre clarifies his view of the nature of history and its effect on the individual's search for freedom and rediscovery of himself, both central concerns of existentialism. It provides an introduction to Sartre's second great philosophical work after "Being and Nothingness"—the "Critique of Dialectical Reason," and demonstrates how Sartre has reconciled his existentialism and Marxism as aspects of the same world view.

BEING AND NOTHINGNESS. *Citadel Press* abr. ed. 1965 pap. $4.95; trans. by Hazel E. Barnes *Simon & Schuster* (Washington Square) pap. $1.45

This great work, in French *"L'Être et le Néant,"* is, together with Sartre's *"Critique de la Raison Dialectique"* ("Critique of Dialectical Reason," obtainable here only in French, *French and European* pap. $10.50) basic to an understanding of his existentialism. The *"Critique,"* says Hazel Barnes in her introduction to "Search for a Method" (*see above*) "presented a carefully worked out social and political philosophy . . . a total view of man's position-in-the-world"; it was published in France in 1960.

TO FREEDOM CONDEMNED: A Guide to the Philosophy of Jean-Paul Sartre. 1960. *Citadel Press* 1973 pap. $1.95. The essence of his philosophy presented in an alphabetically organized manner by Justus Streller.

SARTRE ON CUBA. 1961. *Greenwood* 1974 $9.00

PSYCHOLOGY OF IMAGINATION. *Citadel Press* 1961 pap. $2.75

IMAGINATION: A Psychological Critique. Trans. with introd. by Forrest Williams *Univ. of Michigan Press* 1962 $3.95 pap. $2.25

In this book, of great importance to philosophers and psychologists and of interest to the informed layman, he continues his examination of the bases of psychology-philosophy with studies of images and imagination.

LITERATURE AND EXISTENTIALISM. Trans. by Bernard Frechtman. *Citadel Press* 1962 pap. $2.25

ESSAYS IN AESTHETICS: Art and Philosophy, an Existentialist Approach. Trans. by W. Baskin *Bks. for Libraries* 1963 $8.75; *Simon & Schuster* (Washington Square) 1966 pap. $.90

THE PHILOSOPHY OF JEAN-PAUL SARTRE. Ed. by R. D. Cumming *Random* 1965 $10.00 Modern Lib. $2.95 Vintage Bks. 1972 pap. $2.45

Selections from 15 of Sartre's works arranged in logical order—"the only single-volume compendium of Sartre's work available"—brings together "the basic ideas heretofore scattered in many volumes and covering an astonishing variety of subjects. In the process Dr. Cumming has offered a particularly lucid introduction, has organized the material under clarifying subject headings (often provided by himself), and has attempted to reach a standard usage for Sartre's difficult and highly semantic vocabulary"—(*LJ*).

SITUATIONS: The Artist and His Conscience (*Situations* IV). Trans. by Benita Eisler *Braziller* 1965 $5.95; *Fawcett* Premier Bks. 1974 pap. $1.25

A collection of essays on many subjects, including the "Reply to Albert Camus"—which explains the cooling of their friendship—and a poignant brief tribute to Camus after his death. The book provides interesting insights into his broad view of man.

ESSAYS IN EXISTENTIALISM. Ed. with fwd. by Wade Baskin *Citadel Press* 1967 pap. $4.95

ON GENOCIDE. *Beacon* 1969 $4.95

Sartre's conclusion is that the U.S. is practicing genocide in Vietnam. The introduction by Sartre's daughter Arlette El Kain-Sartre, includes a summary of the evidence and the judgments of the International War Crimes Tribunal, established through the suggestion of Bertrand Russell.

THE COMMUNISTS AND PEACE. *Braziller* 1968 $6.95

THE GHOST OF STALIN. *Braziller* 1968 $4.50

BETWEEN EXISTENTIALISM AND MARXISM. Trans. by John Matthews *Pantheon* 1975 $10.00

"Such topics as genocide in Vietnam, the philosophy of Kierkegaard, psychoanalysis, and definitions of an intellectual provide Sartre with expansive opportunity to exercise his wide range of knowledge and viewpoints"—(*Booklist*).

Books about Sartre

Sartre: His Philosophy and Existential Psychoanalysis. By Alfred Stern. 1953. *Dell* Delta Bks. rev. & enlarged ed. 1968 pap. $1.95
"This new edition of Professor Stern's book is a welcome addition to the literature currently available on Sartre. Unfortunately, the changes in Sartre's thought indicated in the *Critique de la raison dialectique* . . . are only hinted at. . . . Recommended for libraries with a demand for popular work on philosophy"—(*LJ*).

Sartre: Romantic Rationalist. By Iris Murdoch. *Yale Univ. Press* 1953 pap. $1.95. A "remarkably intelligent and penetrating introduction to and commentary upon Sartre."

Tragic Finale: An Essay in the Philosophy of Jean-Paul Sartre. By Wilfrid Desan. 1954. *Harper* 1960 pap. $2.45. A critique of "Being and Nothingness."

An Existentialist Aesthetic: The Theories of Sartre and Merleau-Ponty. By Eugene Kaelin. *Univ. of Wisconsin Press* 1962 $20.00

To Be and Not to Be: An Analysis of Jean-Paul Sartre's Ontology. By Jacques Salvan. *Wayne State Univ. Press* 1962 pap. $3.95

Jean-Paul Sartre: The Existentialist Ethic. By Norman N. Greene. *Univ. of Michigan Press* 1960 pap. $1.75

The Philosophy of Existentialism. By Gabriel Marcel. *Citadel Press* 1961 pap. $1.95
Henri Peyre has called this study of Sartre's philosophy, in contrast to the dominant orthodoxies of our time (Catholicism, Liberalism, Marxism), "one of the fairest, most dispassionate and yet most searching and enlightening studies on Sartre which has yet appeared in English."

The Marxism of Jean-Paul Sartre. By Wilfrid Desan. *Doubleday* Anchor Bks. 1965 *Peter Smith* $4.00
"Professor Desan's [study of Sartre's 'Critique of Dialectical Reason'] is not only a brilliant analysis of Sartre's work, but is invaluable for its exposition of Marxism in several manifesta-tions, its practical application to questions such as the Negro revolution, and for its meticulous and always scrupulous objections to the Sartrean position as regards Marxism"—(*LJ*).

Emotion in the Thought of Sartre. By Joseph P. Fell. *Columbia* 1965 $10.00
"Professor Fell draws primarily from Sartre's *The Emotions, Outline of a Theory* and *Being and Nothingness*. In the second part of the book he analyzes Sartre's idea in the light of other theories—those of William James, Janet, and others—and shows Sartre's specific innovations and his debts to Hegel"—(*LJ*). For the reader with a thorough grounding in Sartre's work; indispensable for the student.

Sartre: A Philosophic Study. By Anthony Manser. *Oxford* 1966 Galaxy Bks. pap. $2.95
"The work manifests an almost intuitive awareness of the vital meaning of Sartre's words; yet this is not a matter of easy insight, but of serious, painstaking study, into which the reader is carefully drawn. Perhaps the only full-length study of Sartre in English, which begins adequately to judge Sartre as a philosopher, and at the same time place him literarily"—(*Choice*).

Sartre's Ontology: À Study of Being and Nothingness in the Light of Hegel's Logic. By Klaus Hartmann. *Northwestern Univ. Press* 1966 $5.95. "An outstanding interpretation of Sartre for specialists"—*(LJ)*.

Sartre: The Theology of the Absurd. By Régis Jolivet. Trans. by Wesley C. Piersol *Newman Press* 1967 $3.50

"M. Jolivet [in a brief, church-approved work] analyzes the meaning and development of Sartre's anti-theology and the implications of his universe in which God is a void and the void is the milieu in which we move absurdly, condemned to failure. The book is also concerned with Marxist influences on Sartre, his disillusionment with official Communism, and his deeprooted sympathy for all the oppressed"—*(PW)*.

Scandalous Ghost: Sartre's Existentialism as Related to Vitalism, Humanism, Mysticism, Marxism. By Jacques Salvan. *Wayne State Univ. Press* 1967 $8.95

Existentialist Ethics. By Hazel Barnes. *Knopf* 1967 $7.95

Four Modern Philosophers: Carnap, Wittgenstein, Heidegger, Sartre. By Arne Naess. Trans. by Alastair Hannay *Univ. of Chicago Press* 1968 $11.50 pap. $3.25

Jean-Paul Sartre. By Henri Peyre. *Columbia* 1968 pap. $1.00

Reason and Violence. By R. D. Laing and David Cooper. Fwd. by Sartre *Random* 1971 pap. $1.95

Humans Being: The World of Jean-Paul Sartre. By Joseph H. McMahon. *Univ. of Chicago Press* 1971 $15.50

Sartre: A Collection of Critical Essays. Ed. by Mary Warnock. *Doubleday* Anchor Bks. 1971 pap. $2.50; *Peter Smith* $4.50

Camus and Sartre: Crisis and Commitment. By Germaine Brée. *Delacorte* 1972 $7.95

"Meticulous in the account she gives of the friendship of the two men, of the controversies that separated them, and particularly of the very great differences in their temperament and outlook and philosophy"—*(Nation)*.

Quintessence of Sartrism. By Maurice Cranston. *Harper* 1972 pap. $3.95

Sartre: A Biographical Outline. By Philip Thody. *Scribner* 1972 $6.95 pap. $2.45

Sartre. By Hazel Barnes. *Lippincott* 1973 $6.95

"Recommended for public library collections and lower level academic ones"—*(Choice)*.

Adventures of the Dialectic. By Maurice Merleau-Ponty. Trans. by Joseph J. Bien *Northwestern Univ. Press* 1973 $8.50

Jean-Paul Sartre: The Philosopher as a Literary Critic. By Benjamin Suhl. *Columbia* 1973 $12.50 pap. $3.45

"One of the best books on Sartre"—*(Choice)*.

Commentary on Sartre's Being and Nothingness. By Joseph S. Catalano. *Harper* Torchbks. 1974 pap. $3.95

Sartre and the Sacred. By Thomas M. King. *Univ. of Chicago Press* 1974 $8.95

From Sartre to the New Novel. By Betty T. Rahv. *Kennikat* 1974 $8.95

Jean-Paul Sartre. By Arthur C. Danto. *Viking* 1975 $7.95 pap. $2.95

"A provocative reading of Sartre's early philosophy"—*(LJ)*.

MERLEAU-PONTY, MAURICE. 1908–1961.

Merleau-Ponty "studied carefully not only Husserl's published works. He was for a long time closely associated with Sartre and deeply influenced by him. He read widely in Scheler, as well as Heidegger, and was intimately familiar with the Gestalt psychology of the 1920's and 1930's. Nurtured on this ground, he made important contributions to the phenomenological investigation of human existence in the life-world and its distinctive structures. He was a revolutionary, and his philosophy, even more than that of his French contemporaries, was a philosophy of the evolving, becoming 'historical present.' Merleau-Ponty views man as an essentially historical being and history as the dialectic of meaning and non-meaning which is working itself out through the complex, unpredictable interaction of men and the world. Nothing historical ever has just one meaning; meaning is ambiguous and is seen from an infinity of viewpoints. He has been called a philosopher of ambiguity, of contradiction, of dialectic. His search is the search for 'meaning.' 'In Praise of Philosophy' is his Inaugural Lecture at the College de France. This lecture was delivered in 1953 after Merleau-Ponty was elected to the chair of Philosophy, the youngest man ever to hold that chair"—*(See* the foreword to "In Praise of Philosophy"). The philosophic movement to which Merleau-Ponty most closely belongs is that of "phenomenological existentialism," whose study, as implied above, starts from human perception.

The Phenomenology of Perception. *Humanities Press* 1962 $19.50

In Praise of Philosophy. Trans. with a fwd. by John Wild and James M. Edie *Northwestern Univ. Press* 1963 $4.50

THE STRUCTURE OF BEHAVIOR. *Beacon* 1963 $8.50 pap. $3.45

Here the philosopher shows "that man relates to his own existence as a totality which moves from this wholeness in ways which favor his own particular growth tendencies rather than as a mere reactor to the world as an imposer of determined responses"—*(LJ)*.

SIGNS. Trans. by Richard McCleary *Northwestern Univ. Press* 1964 $12.50 pap. $3.95

"In *Signs* he leaves no important area of inquiry untouched—the philosophical, political, anthropological, the sociological or the artistic—in his search for that which can be understood from within even as "personal intentions" are tending toward progresses which are themselves "mediated by things." The mythical is not a past fact, but a means "of resolving some local, present tension, and is re-created in the dynamics of the present"—*(LJ)*.

SENSE AND NON-SENSE. Trans. by Hubert L. Dreyfus *Northwestern Univ. Press* 1964 $7.50 pap. $3.25

THE PRIMACY OF PERCEPTION. Trans. by William Cobb and others; ed. by James M. Edie *Northwestern Univ. Press* 1964 $8.00 pap. $3.25

"In *The Primacy of Perception* he uses the phenomenological approach to reexamine the basis of humanity: 'human relations are able to grow, to change their avatars into lessons, to pick out the truth of their past in the present, to eliminate certain mysteries which render them opaque and thereby make themselves more translucent.' Of special significance is the correlation which Merleau-Ponty finds between linguistic phenomenon and the emergence of the sense of self-identity"—*(LJ)*.

THE VISIBLE AND THE INVISIBLE. Trans. by Alphonso Lingis *Northwestern Univ. Press* 1968 $11.00

HUMANISM AND TERROR. *Beacon* 1969 $7.50 pap. $2.95

"Merleau-Ponty has a faith in the proletariat that is beautiful in the abstract but that sees in revolutionary reality what simply isn't there"—*(America)*.

THEMES FROM THE LECTURES AT THE COLLEGE DE FRANCE, 1952–60. *Northwestern Univ. Press* 1970 $5.00

ADVENTURES OF THE DIALECTIC. Trans. by Joseph J. Bien *Northwestern Univ. Press* 1973 $8.50

CONSCIOUSNESS AND THE ACQUISITION OF LANGUAGE. Trans. by Hugh J. Silverman *Northwestern Univ. Press* 1973 $6.25

The author "synthesizes the works of Paul Guillaume, Edmund Husserl, and Max Scheler, and then . . . [attacks] Piaget's approach. Many American scholars would view this material as a strange blend of philosophy and psychology"—*(Choice)*.

THE PROSE OF THE WORLD. Trans. by John O'Neill; ed. by Claude Lefort *Northwestern Univ. Press* 1973 $6.00

Books about Merleau-Ponty

An Existentialist Aesthetic: The Theories of Sartre and Merleau-Ponty. By Eugene F. Kaelin. *Univ. of Wisconsin Press* 1962 $20.00

Merleau-Ponty: Existentialist of the Social World. By Albert Rabil. *Columbia* 1967 $7.50

This study, "which won the Ansley award, is a lucid exposition of the development of [his] political thought. Mr. Rabil's thesis is that the influence of Sartre on Merleau-Ponty was pernicious and tended to lead Merleau-Ponty into fruitless bypaths away from his own more fundamental insights. One of the principal merits of Rabil's book is its facts about the political situation in France immediately after World War II, in the context of which Merleau-Ponty worked out his political and social philosophy"—*(LJ)*.

The Philosophy of Merleau-Ponty. By John F. Bannan. *Harcourt* 1967 pap. $3.50

This work examines Merleau-Ponty's "arguments, their documentation, and what it is they strive to accomplish"—(Author's preface). It is a well-written, well-organized discussion whose many clear subdivisions will assist the student and interested layman. Mr. Bannan teaches at Loyola University.

Marxism and the Existentialists. By Raymond Aron. *Harper* 1969 $6.95

"These five essays, 1946–64, bring up to date Aron's long standing dispute with the Marxists and, more especially, with the Marxist sympathies of Sartre and Merleau-Ponty"—*(Choice)*.

Phenomenology of Expression. By Remy C. Kwant. *Duquesne Univ. Press* (dist. by Humanities Press) 1969 $6.50

Perception, Expression and History: The Social Phenomenology of Maurice Merleau-Ponty. By
  John O'Neill. *Northwestern Univ. Press* 1970 $4.50
The Horizons of the Flesh: Critical Perspectives on the Thought of Merleau-Ponty. By Garth
  Gillan. *Southern Illinois Univ. Press* 1973 $7.95
Once More from the Middle: A Philosophical Anthropology. By James Sheridan. *Ohio Univ.
  Press* 1973 $8.50

Chapter 6

Psychology

"Mental life or behavior is too complex and comprehensive to be seen through one window, even if it be a bay window. Just because there are so many facets, it behooves us to be stationed at various points to be on the watch for unexpected developments."

—A. A. ROBACK

No one living in our complex industrial society can afford to ignore the findings and insights of psychologists. Since the early years of this century their rigorous study of rational and irrational patterns of human behavior has enabled reformers, social planners, and political leaders to reshape our evolving institutions. After the days of William James—the first American psychologist of prominence—the greatest single impact on American psychology was that of Sigmund Freud and his theory of psychoanalysis (exploration of the unconscious to discover the roots of a patient's trouble and deliver him of it) with its emphasis on sexual motivations and the importance of early childhood experience. He had a revolutionary—and therapeutic—impact for his day on the study of human behavior and the treatment of pathological "mental" cases. Jung and Adler broke away from him, founding their own schools of psychology—Freudianism with a difference.

In America after World War I, the behaviorists, led by John B. Watson, revolted against Freudian forms of "mental manipulation" and urged the study and treatment of human behavior from the outside. Their particular views have ceased to be a force, but their successors, B. F. Skinner and others, today pursue a similar direction. Skinner and his followers have challenged some of our most cherished beliefs about human behavior, emotion and the nature of learning. E. L. Thorndike (and the educator John Dewey, *q.v.*) made important discoveries in the psychology of learning which profoundly affected the course of American education. Psychiatry became a respectable branch of medicine, and the entire medical profession has recently been made aware of psychological factors which can cause or aggravate—or cure—illness.

Two world wars led to many discoveries in the treatment of the shell-, bomb- and battle-shocked, particularly in the area of psychopharmacology—the use of drugs to modify behavior and reduce anxiety. We are still uncertain, however, whether hallucinogenic drugs and even tranquilizers produce irreversible physical changes in the brain. Psychologists are deeply divided over the extent to which we should use drugs to create radically different states of being and consciousness. Whether "tranquilizers" are not now over-used is, of course, still an open question. Electrical shock treatments—(still controversial in some quarters—as described in Millen Brand's novel "Savage Sleep" [*Crown* 1968 $6.95]) have been found to relieve cases of severe or suicidal depression by banishing memory for a time and so to bring about the restructuring of thought patterns. Group therapy—the exchange of experiences and problems through conversation among small groups of the similarly afflicted—has been found to help relieve neuroses and more serious difficulties. Other fields of development and exploration include those on the control of behavior; on the control of intelligence (with its somewhat sinister possibilities); on the teaching (conditioning was Pavlov's term) of animals and human beings by mechanical means such as "Skinner boxes" and teaching machines; on information theory in its psychological applications; on personality, perception, many aspects of learning and creativity; on the phenomena of sleep, dreams and sensory deprivation; on the functioning of the brain and nervous system; on social psychology—the study of group behavior and of the interactions of people within groups; on face-to-face behavior. All these make of modern psychology a vast and disparate field, but one of converging perspectives, in which no one theory or area of study can claim to have all the answers and most of which are contributing at an extraordinary rate to our knowledge of ourselves. Psychology interacts more and more with other fields—the sciences, commerce and industry (industrial psychology), courts of law, the arts, even (see, for example, Fromm and Laing) with politics, government and international relations in problems of social organization, social justice, and of war and peace.

One of the dominant current trends is that which opposes itself both to the lengthy and expensive methods of (originally Freudian) psychoanalysis and to what many see as the mechanistic bias of the B. F. Skinner behaviorists. It is called sometimes the "third force" in psychology, sometimes "humanist" or "existentialist" psychology. Its emphasis on the whole man in the whole world seeks to develop value, purpose and self-fulfillment through the encouragement of creativity and the discovery of the maximum potential of each unique human being. It is not uncritical of society; it does not ask the individual to "adapt," all smoothed at the edges, but rather to become a person capable of standing up to the society and helping to mold it, through his own actions, in constructive ways. It demonstrates that "man is the captive neither of heredity nor environment, but is part of an 'echo system' between himself and his society—which influences him (even physiologically) as he influences it"—(Edwin Giventer). It emphasizes health rather than illness, looks forward rather than back. Erich Fromm, Bruno Bettelheim, Gardner and Lois Murphy, Erik Erikson, Fritz Redl, Abraham Maslow, Rollo May and R. D. Laing all hold in one way or another this optimistic, creative view of man. They attempt to set man in humane and compassionate perspective—to heal the world as well as the troubled human being, realizing as perhaps never before, that the two are interdependent. The psychologists of this trend encompass most of our new author entries.

Particularly helpful for the preparation of this Chapter have been the latest edition (4th) of the "Harvard List of Books in Psychology" (*Harvard Univ. Press* 1971 pap. $2.75) and two histories of psychology that are available in paperback: "The Pelican History of Psychology" (*Penguin* 1968 pap. $1.95) by Robert Thomson, and A. A. Roback's "A History of American Psychology" (*Macmillan* Collier Bks. 2nd ed. 1964 pap. $1.95).

Among the journals valuable to laymen, *Psychology Today, Contemporary Psychology* (official publication of the American Psychological Association) and the *Psychiatry and Social Science Review* can be recommended.

BIBLIOGRAPHY AND REFERENCE BOOKS

Alexander, Franz. FUNDAMENTALS OF PSYCHOANALYSIS. *Norton* 1948 pap. 1963 $2.25. A well-organized, readable and compact outline.

> (With Samuel Eisenstein and Martin Grotjahn, Eds.). PSYCHOANALYTIC PIONEERS. *Basic Bks.* 1966 $15.00
>
> "The editors try to give as rounded a view as is possible. . . . Ferenczi, Rank, Jung, Federn, Briehl, W. Reich, M. Klein, K. Horney, H. Hartmann, E. Kris, Anna Freud and others are among the workers described. Contributors in addition to the editors are such excellent analysts as M. Romm, N. Loewenstein, E. Pumpian-Mindlin and others. The volume unreservedly belongs in all collections in the psychological and psychiatric-psychoanalytic fields"—(*LJ*).

American Psychiatric Association. BIOGRAPHICAL DIRECTORY OF THE AMERICAN PSYCHIATRIC ASSOCIATION. Published for the American Psychiatric Association. *Bowker* 1958 6th ed. 1973 $38.50

> This authoritative biographical record of active psychiatrists in the United States and Canada is the only up-to-date guide to the 20,000 members of the American Psychiatric Association. Members are listed alphabetically with a geographical index for convenient cross-reference. An excellent source book and "essential for all libraries."

Arieti, Silvano, and others, Eds. AMERICAN HANDBOOK OF PSYCHIATRY. *Basic Bks.* 6 vols. 1959–66 rev. 2nd ed. 1974–75 Vol. 1 $28.50 Vols. 2–6 each $22.50 Vols. 1–3 set $73.50 Vols.4–6 set $67.50

Baldwin, James Mark, Ed. DICTIONARY OF PHILOSOPHY AND PSYCHOLOGY: Including Many of the Principal Conceptions of Ethics, Logic, Aesthetics. 1901–1902 1910. *Peter Smith* 3 vols. 1940 Vols. 1 and 2 each $16.50; Vol. 3 Bibliography of Philosophy, Psychology and Cognate Subjects, comp. by Benjamin Rand in 2 parts 1949 each $13.50 set $60.00

Battro, Antonio M. PIAGET: Dictionary of Terms. Trans. by Elizabeth Rutschi-Herrmann and Sarah F. Campbell. *Pergamon* 1973 $14.00

Beigel, Hugo G. DICTIONARY OF PSYCHOLOGY AND RELATED FIELDS: German-English. *Ungar* 1971 $9.00

"Indispensable for those doing research based on original works of Freud, Jung, Adler, Binswanger, Bleuler, *et al*"—*(Choice)*.

Berne, Eric. LAYMAN'S GUIDE TO PSYCHIATRY AND PSYCHOANALYSIS (Orig. "The Mind in Action"). *Simon & Schuster* rev. ed. 1968 $8.95 pap. $1.95

Borgatta, Edgar F., and William W. Lambert, Eds. HANDBOOK OF PERSONALITY THEORY AND RESEARCH. *Rand McNally* 1967 $25.00

Braga, Laurie, and Joseph Braga. LEARNING AND GROWING: A Guide to Child Development. *Prentice-Hall* 1975 $7.95 pap. $2.95

"Packed with facts, this book should be helpful to parents, informative for students, useful even to specialists. It discusses in full detail behaviors which may be expected of children at each yearly age level from birth to five years"—*(LJ)*.

Brenner, Charles. ELEMENTARY TEXTBOOK OF PSYCHOANALYSIS. *Doubleday* Anchor Bks. 1957 pap. $1.25; *International Univs. Press* rev. & enl. ed. 1973 $8.95

Brussell, James Arnold. LAYMAN'S GUIDE TO PSYCHIATRY. *Harper* (Barnes & Noble) 2nd ed. 1967 $5.00 pap. $1.95

(With George La Fond Cantzlaar). THE LAYMAN'S DICTIONARY OF PSYCHIATRY. *Harper* (Barnes & Noble) Everyday Handbks. 1967 $5.00

"The approximately 1,500 descriptive psychiatric terms (including names of famous psycho-analysts and psychiatrists) found in this dictionary are defined in an understandable, jargon free style"—*(Choice)*.

Caplan, Gerald, Ed. AMERICAN HANDBOOK OF PSYCHIATRY: Child and Adolescent Psychiatry—Sociocultural and Community Psychiatry. *Basic Bks.* 2nd ed. 1974 $22.50

Chess, Stella. INTRODUCTION TO CHILD PSYCHIATRY. *Grune* 2nd ed. 1969 $7.00

Deutsch, Morton, and Robert M. Krauss. THEORIES IN SOCIAL PSYCHOLOGY. Fwd. by Edwin G. Boring Basic Topics in Psychology Ser. *Basic Bks.* 1965 $5.00

"Mr. Deutsch and Mr. Krauss have systematically and critically examined the backgrounds and modern developments of this diffuse and rapidly expanding field and have written a praiseworthy book, one that will guide, not overwhelm"—*(LJ)*.

Drever, James. DICTIONARY OF PSYCHOLOGY. *Penguin* 1952 rev. ed. 1964 pap. $1.65; *Gannon* $4.50

Eidelberg, Ludwig, Ed. ENCYCLOPEDIA OF PSYCHOANALYSIS. *Macmillan* (Free Press) 1968 $27.50

"Dr. Eidelberg and his associates, who are largely affiliated with the psychoanalytic group of the Downstate Medical College, have prepared a fairly comprehensive compendium of the more important concepts of the classical or orthodox Freudian school. The book is also liberally sprinkled with non-Freudian originated concepts which bear upon the theories of Freud. There are 643 entries . . . a bibliography of 1500 titles, and an index of 6000 items. The material is clearly and concisely written"—*(LJ)*.

Ellis, Albert, and Albert Abarbanel, Eds. THE ENCYCLOPEDIA OF SEXUAL BEHAVIOR. 1961. *Jason Aronson* rev. ed. 1973 $25.00

Under the editorship of two well-known psychotherapists, national and international authorities contribute over 100 articles on the biology, physiology and anatomy of sex for "professional people and intelligent laymen." "This mammoth opus . . . with its liberal-to-conservative viewpoints, has both a scholarly reference and a general reading nature. Absolutely essential for medical, academic, and many categories of special libraries. Highly informative in all large branches of public library systems"—(*LJ*).

English, Horace Bidwell, and Ava C. English. A Comprehensive Dictionary of Psychological and Psychoanalytical Terms: A Guide to Usage. *McKay* 1958 $10.75 text ed. $8.00

Eysenck, H. J., and others, Eds. Encyclopedia of Psychology. *Seabury* 3 vols. 1972 set $75.00

"Contributors are from 22 countries. Bibliographies are included. Intended for professional psychologists, students, and the intelligent layman"—(Publisher's note).

Flugel, John Carl. A Hundred Years of Psychology, 1833–1933. With supplementary material for 1933–1963 by Donald J. West. 1964. *International Univs. Press* rev. ed. 1970 $15.00

"This very short overview of psychology is a pithy and sharp account of most of the ways . . . psychology has arrived at its present forms of existence. . . . The approach is clearly not exhaustive, but it manages to encompass the larger movements as well as the smaller offshoots, thereby conveying a sense of continuity seldom achieved in works of this kind. This work should prove of immense value to any one desiring an historical perspective on psychology to the present day"—(*LJ*).

Freeman, Harrop A. Counseling in the United States. *Oceana* 1967 $12.00

Freemon, Frank R. Sleep Research: A Critical Review. *C. C Thomas* 1973 $14.50

"An excellent book: exhaustive, yet concise presentation and explanation of sleep as a phenomenon and the current state of research make it invaluable as a reference work as well as a source book"—(*Choice*).

Frosch, John, and Nathaniel Ross, Eds. The Annual Survey of Psychoanalysis: A Comprehensive Survey of Current Psychoanalytic Theory and Practice. *International Univs. Press* 10 vols. 1952–1971 Vol. 1 1952 Vol. 2 1953 Vol. 3 1956 Vol. 4 1958 Vol. 5 1959 Vol. 6 1961 Vol. 7 1963 Vol. 8 1965 Vol. 9 1967 Vol. 10 1971 each $15.00. Contains summaries of articles, studies and books on the history, critique, theory and applications of psychoanalytic psychiatry, therapy and training. The best single source of information about psychoanalytic literature.

Golann, Stuart E., and Carl Eisdorfer, Eds. Handbook of Community Mental Health. *Prentice-Hall* (Appleton) 1972 $29.95

Goldenson, Robert M. The Encyclopedia of Human Behavior: Psychology, Psychiatry, and Mental Health. *Doubleday* 2 vols. 1970 $24.95. Contains over 1,000 articles on such diverse topics as dream interpretation, phobia, and Parkinson's disease, arranged in alphabetical order.

Greenfield, Norman S., and Richard Sternbach, Eds. Handbook of Psychophysiology. *Holt* 1973 $25.95

Grinstein, Alexander. The Index of Psychoanalytic Writings. Pref. by Ernest Jones. *International Univs. Press* 14 vols. 1956–1973 Vols. 1–5 (1956–1960) set $150.00 Vols. 6–9 (1963–1966) set $150.00 Vols. 10–14 (1973) set $150.00. A revision and bringing up to date of John Rickman's "Index Psychoanalyticus." 1893–1926.

Harriman, Philip L. Dictionary of Psychology. *Citadel Press* 1971 pap. $3.95

Handbook of Psychological Terms. *Littlefield* 1965 pap. $2.50; *Rowman* 1965 lib. bdg. $5.95

The handbook is "intended to speed the reader through the maze of technical vocabulary in scientific psychology"—(Preface).

The Harvard List of Books in Psychology. Comp. and ed. by the psychologists in Harvard University *Harvard Univ. Press* 4th ed. 1971 pap. $2.75

"744 entries arranged in 31 basic subject areas, selected by 40 specialists who chose the best books in their respective fields"—(Publisher's note).

Hendrick, Ives. Facts and Theories of Psychoanalysis. *Knopf* 1934 3rd ed. 1958 $7.95; *Dell* 1966 pap. $.95

Herrnstein, Richard J., and Edwin G. Boring, Eds. A SOURCE BOOK IN THE HISTORY OF PSYCHOLOGY. Pref. by Edward H. Madden Source Books in the History of the Sciences Ser. *Harvard Univ. Press* 1965 $15.00 pap. $5.95

"Excellent as far as it goes, but the editors have omitted the histories of social and clinical psychology.... Considering these omissions, it is safe to say that interested readers and scientists will have accessible, in this text, the selected writings of most of the important Europeans who have contributed to the history of psychology"—*(LJ)*.

Hinsie, Leland, and Robert Campbell. PSYCHIATRIC DICTIONARY. *Oxford* 4th ed. 1970 $19.95

The material of this dictionary "has been drawn from words and concepts current in the field of psychiatry—with definitions and illustrative quotations that aim to give these vital, clinical meaning"—(Preface).

Kanner, Leo. CHILD PSYCHIATRY. *C. C. Thomas* 4th ed. 1972 $16.50

Kiell, Norman, Ed. PSYCHOANALYSIS, PSYCHOLOGY, AND LITERATURE: A Bibliography. *Univ. of Wisconsin Press* 1963 $15.00

Krech, David, Richard S. Crutchfield and Norman Livson. ELEMENTS OF PSYCHOLOGY. *Knopf* 1958 2nd ed. 1969 $13.95 text ed. $10.95 (with subtitle "A Briefer Course") 1970 pap. $8.95. A stimulating introduction for the beginner.

Lingeman, Richard R. DRUGS FROM A TO Z: A Dictionary. *McGraw-Hill* 1969 $6.95 pap. $2.95

"The whole history of drugs and addicts [is] given from amphetamines to zonked, from Milltown to STP"—*(Choice)*.

MENTAL HEALTH BOOK REVIEW INDEX: An Annual Bibliography of Books and Book Reviews in the Behavioral Sciences. Editorial Committee, Ilse Bry and Lois Afflerbach, Chairmen *Counsel on Research in Bibliography* (Paul Klapper Library, Queens College, Flushing, N.Y.) 17 vols. 1956–72 pap. set $132.00

Mental Health Materials Center. A SELECTIVE GUIDE TO MATERIALS FOR MENTAL HEALTH AND FAMILY LIFE EDUCATION. *Perennial Education* 1973 $35.00

Morgan, Clifford T., and R. A. King. INTRODUCTION TO PSYCHOLOGY. *McGraw-Hill* 4th ed. 1971 $11.95 (with title "Brief Introduction to Psychology") ed. by John Hendry 1973 pap. $6.50

Nordby, Vernon J., and Calvin S. Hall. A GUIDE TO PSYCHOLOGISTS AND THEIR CONCEPTS. *Scribner* 1975 $8.00

Perlin, Seymour, Ed. A HANDBOOK FOR THE STUDY OF SUICIDE. *Oxford* 1975 $9.95 pap. $5.95

"This work comprises 11 contributions which examine suicidal behavior in the context of history, literature, philosophy, anthropology, sociology, biology, psychiatry, and epidemiology"—*(LJ)*.

PSYCHOSOURCES: A Psychology Resource Catalog. *Bantam* 1973 pap. $5.00

Roback, Abraham A. A HISTORY OF AMERICAN PSYCHOLOGY. 1952. *Macmillan* Collier Bks. 2nd ed. 1964 pap. $1.95. An excellent survey.

HISTORY OF PSYCHOLOGY AND PSYCHIATRY. 1961. *Greenwood* $17.75

(With T. P. Kiernan). PICTORIAL HISTORY OF PSYCHOLOGY AND PSYCHIATRY. *Philosophical Lib.* $12.50

Storz, Anne, Ed. PSYCHOLOGY 73/74 ENCYCLOPEDIA. *Dushkin* 1973 pap. $5.95

Tarczan, Constance. AN EDUCATOR'S GUIDE TO PSYCHOLOGICAL TESTS: Descriptions and Classroom Implications. *C. C. Thomas* 1972 $6.95 pap. $3.95

Thomson, Robert. THE PELICAN HISTORY OF PSYCHOLOGY. *Penguin* Pelican Bks. (orig.) 1968 pap. $1.95; *Gannon* lib. bdg. $5.00. An excellent overview of the subject from the early 19th century to Jerome Bruner; clear and broad in scope. Dr. Thomson, an Englishman, has taught at Durham and Leicester Universities.

U.S. National Institute of Mental Health. MENTAL HEALTH AND CHANGE: An Annotated Bibliography. *U.S. Government Printing Office* (Washington, D.C.) 1973 pap. $3.00

Watson, Robert I. EMINENT CONTRIBUTORS TO PSYCHOLOGY: A Bibliography of Primary References. *Springer Pub.* 1974 $24.00

THE GREAT PSYCHOLOGISTS: From Aristotle to Freud. *Lippincott* 1963 2nd ed. 1968 $10.00 text ed. $6.95 pap. $7.50

(With Henry C. Lindgren). PSYCHOLOGY OF THE CHILD. *Wiley* 3rd ed. 1973 $11.95

Wolman, Benjamin B. DICTIONARY OF BEHAVIORAL SCIENCE. *Van Nostrand-Reinhold* 1973 $19.95

"Contains 1,200 concise entries to terms, persons, and tests on psychology, psychiatry, and neurology"—(Publisher's note).

(Ed.) HANDBOOK OF GENERAL PSYCHOLOGY. *Prentice-Hall* 1973 $45.00

Zusne, Leonard. NAMES IN THE HISTORY OF PSYCHOLOGY: A Biographical Sourcebook. *Wiley* 1975 $17.95

Zusne "presents biographical information about the most eminent psychologists"—(*LJ*).

Works on Modern Psychology and Psychoanalysis

The titles below have been chosen with the layman in mind.

Adelson, Edward T., Ed. SEXUALITY AND PSYCHOANALYSIS. *Brunner/Mazel* 1975 $13.95

"This collection of essays presents the latest physiological, anatomical, biochemical, and psychological research in sexuality and relates it to classical and modern psychoanalytic thinking . . . it helps formulate the directions contemporary psychoanalysis can follow"—(*LJ*).

Aichhorn, August. DELINQUENCY AND CHILD GUIDANCE: Selected Papers. Ed. by Otto Fleischmann and others. Menninger Foundation Monograph Ser. *International Univs. Press* 1967 $10.00

WAYWARD YOUTH. 1935. Introd. by Sigmund Freud *Viking* Compass Bks. 1965 pap. $1.45

Albert, Ethel M., and others, Eds. GREAT TRADITIONS IN ETHICS: An Introduction. *Van Nostrand-Reinhold* 2nd ed. 1969 pap. $6.50

Alvarez, Walter C. MINDS THAT CAME BACK. Introd. by Dr. Hervey M. Cleckley *Lippincott* 1961 $6.95

The editor of *Modern Medicine* and Emeritus Professor of Medicine, University of Minnesota, offers here "a unique project to physicians, psychiatrists, jurists, clergymen, social workers, and to 'thoughtful adults'—his own reviews of outstanding autobiographies of about 75 abnormal personages. He quotes from, comments on, and summarizes the memoirs of Beers, Dostoevsky, Lucy Freeman, Maupassant, Nietzsche . . . and others, who successfully returned from the strange limbo of insanity, alcoholism, neurosis, epilepsy, phobia, or psychoanalysis"—(*LJ*).

(With Sue March). HOMOSEXUALITY VS. GAY LIBERATION: A Confrontation Doublebook. *Pyramid Pubns.* (orig.) 1974 pap. $1.75

Angyal, Andras. NEUROSIS AND TREATMENT: A Holistic Theory. Trans. and ed. by Eugenia Hanfmann and Richard M. Jones. 1965. *Viking* Compass Bks. 1974 pap. $3.75

Argyris, Chris. INTERVENTION THEORY AND METHOD: A Behavioral Science View. *Addison-Wesley* 1970 $11.95. By an authority on industrial psychology.

Arieti, Silvano. INTERPRETATION OF SCHIZOPHRENIA. *Basic Bks.* 1975 $22.50. Awarded a 1975 National Book Award "for its scientific content and profound humanism."

THE WILL TO BE HUMAN. *Quadrangle Bks.* 1972 $8.95

Axline, Virginia M. DIBS: In Search of Self. *Houghton* 1965 $5.95; *Ballantine* 1969 pap. $1.25

PLAY THERAPY. 1965. *Ballantine* rev. ed. 1969 pap. $1.25

Back, Kurt W. BEYOND WORDS: The Story of Sensitivity Training and the Encounter Movement. *Russell Sage* (dist. by Harper) 1972 $7.95; *Penguin* Pelican Bks. 1973 pap. $1.75

An "excellent attempt at appraising sensitivity training as a social movement without uncritically accepting it or irrationally denouncing it. Back puts sensitivity training into historical perspective"—(*Choice*).

Bandura, Albert, Ed. PSYCHOLOGICAL MODELING: Conflicting Theories. *Aldine* 1972 $7.95 pap. $2.95

"This book is made up of nine chapters, each written by an expert scientist well known for his research in modeling . . . The reference features are exceptionally good with each article having its own bibliography"—(*Choice*).

Barker, Roger G. ECOLOGICAL PSYCHOLOGY: Concepts and Methods for Studying the Environment of Human Behavior. *Stanford Univ. Press* 1968 $7.50

Barron, Frank. CREATIVE PERSON AND CREATIVE PROCESS. *Holt* 1969 pap. text ed. $4.15

CREATIVITY AND PERSONAL FREEDOM. *Van Nostrand-Reinhold* rev. ed. 1968 pap. $4.95

Baruch, Dorothy W. ONE LITTLE BOY. *Dell* Delta Bks. pap. $2.25

Bell, John F. FAMILY THERAPY. *Jason Aronson* 1975 $20.00

Bell "surveys findings yielded from practice, values in therapy, special types of family work, and . . . preventive intervention on the community level"—(*LJ*).

Bellak, Leopold. OVERLOAD: The New Human Condition. *Human Sciences Press* 1975 $9.95

"Bellak attempts to integrate clinical and research psychiatry into a method by which the crises faced by contemporary society may be treated, in much the same manner as a psychiatrist treats a patient"—(*LJ*).

Berelson, Bernard, Ed. THE BEHAVIORAL SCIENCES TODAY. *Basic Bks.* 1963 $5.95; *Harper* Torchbks. pap. $2.25 The authors of these 20 brief papers include most of the leading American scholars in these fields. The papers are "generally excellent, clearly presented, and sometimes stimulating," and will interest specialists and laymen.

(With Gary A. Steiner). HUMAN BEHAVIOR: An Inventory of Scientific Findings. *Harcourt* 1967 pap. text ed. $2.55

Berne, Eric. *See his main entry, this Chapter.*

Bertalanffy, Ludwig von. ROBOTS, MEN AND MINDS: Psychology in the Modern World. *Braziller* 1967 $5.00

"In this brilliant tour de force, the eminent biologist and general systems theorist looks at psychology, biology, science in general, and, from there, proceeds to discuss the state of the world. He sees fundamental, even preposterous contradictions, best exemplified in psychology, where eminent investigators make pompous generalizations based on trivial experiments. . . . His goals are important, his arguments sound, and his writing is not only scientifically accurate but exciting and even inspirational"—(*LJ*).

Bettelheim, Bruno. *See his main entry, this Chapter.*

Blum, Eva M., and Richard H. Blum. ALCOHOLISM: Modern Psychological Approaches to Treatment. *Jossey-Bass* 1967 $12.50

Blum, Richard H., and others. THE DREAM SELLERS: Perspectives on Drug Dealers. Behavioral Science Ser. *Jossey-Bass* 1972 $12.50

Bowlby, John. ATTACHMENT. *Basic Bks.* 1969 $12.50

CHILD CARE AND GROWTH OF LOVE. *Penguin* (orig.) Pelican Bks. pap. $1.25

SEPARATION: Anxiety and Anger. *Basic Bks.* 1973 $12.50

(With others). MATERNAL CARE AND MENTAL HEALTH and THE DEPRIVATION OF MATERNAL CARE. *Schocken* 1966 pap. $2.45

Brecher, Edward M. THE SEX RESEARCHERS. *Little* 1970 $6.95

"As a medical journalist specializing in sex research, Brecher has written an historical account of sex research. This account combines a readable, nontechnical style with scientific accuracy"— (*Choice*).

Brown, James A. THE SOCIAL PSYCHOLOGY OF INDUSTRY. *Penguin* Pelican Bks. (orig.) pap. $1.45; *Gannon* lib. bdg. $4.50

TECHNIQUES OF PERSUASION—From Propaganda to Brainwashing. *Penguin* Pelican Bks. (orig.) 1963 pap. $1.45; *Peter Smith* $5.00

Brown, Roger. A FIRST LANGUAGE: The Early Stages. *Harvard Univ. Press* 1973 $15.00

SOCIAL PSYCHOLOGY. *Macmillan* (Free Press) 1965 $10.95

Bugental, James F. T. CHALLENGE OF HUMANISTIC PSYCHOLOGY. *McGraw-Hill* 1967 $9.95 pap. $6.92

THE SEARCH FOR AUTHENTICITY: An Existential-Analytic Approach to Psychotherapy. *Holt* 1965 $12.00

Burton, Arthur, and others. TWELVE THERAPISTS. *Jossey-Bass* 1973 $12.50

"For the first time a group of well known psychotherapists have made available biographical material which affords important insights into the art of mental healing and those who practice it. This is a rare event in an otherwise fairly obscure and private undertaking"—(*Choice*).

Caplan, Gerald. SUPPORT SYSTEMS AND COMMUNITY MENTAL HEALTH. *Human Sciences Press* 1973 $13.95

THEORY AND PRACTICE OF MENTAL HEALTH CONSULTATION. *Basic Bks.* 1970 text ed. $10.75

(With Serge Lebovici, Eds.). ADOLESCENCE: Psychosocial Perspectives. *Basic Bks.* 1969 $12.50

"A group of clinicians and researchers, including Anna Freud, Jean Piaget, and Fritz Redl, met in 1966 to discuss the adolescents who must face a nuclear-space age, often from a better educated vantage point than their adult authority figures. This well-edited compilation of updated papers left an impression that the contributors enjoyed themselves working at this congress and their frequent intellectual asides and speculative flights will provide material for graduate research for many years to come. . . . An extraordinary book"—(*LJ*).

Chess, Stella, M.D., Alexander Thomas, M.D., and Herbert G. Birch, M.D., Ph.D. YOUR CHILD IS A PERSON: A Psychological Approach to Parenthood without Guilt. *Viking* 1965 Compass Bks. 1972 pap. $1.95

Child, Irvin L. HUMANISTIC PSYCHOLOGY AND THE RESEARCH TRADITION: Their Several Virtues. *Wiley* 1973 $8.95

"An appreciative look at both hard and soft psychology, each from the viewpoint of the other. In doing so, Child points out significant complementaries"—(*Choice*).

Church, Joseph. UNDERSTANDING YOUR CHILD FROM BIRTH TO THREE: A Guide to Your Child's Psychological Development. *Random* 1973 $6.95

Clarke, Ann M., and Alan D. Clarke, Eds. MENTAL DEFICIENCY: The Changing Outlook. *Macmillan* (Free Press) 3rd ed. 1975 $25.00

"The definitive work on mental deficiency"—(*Choice*).

Coles, Robert. CHILDREN OF CRISIS. *Little-Atlantic* 3 vols. 1967–1973 Vol. 1 A Study of Courage and Fear (1967) $10.00 Vol. 2 Migrants, Mountaineers and Sharecroppers (1972–1973) $12.50 pap. $4.95; Vol. 3 The South Goes North (1972–1973) $12.50 pap. $4.95; *Dell* Delta Bks. pap. Vol. 1 $3.45

THE MIND'S FATE: Ways of Seeing Psychiatry and Psychoanalysis. *Little* 1975 $10.00

"A collection of occasional pieces, book reviews, articles, etc"—(*N.Y. Times*).

Colman, Arthur D., and Libby Lee. LOVE AND ECSTASY. *Seabury Press* 1975 $7.95

"A psychiatrist and a professor of English literature here explore in detail the role that the experience of ecstasy plays in human life"—(*LJ*).

Cornsweet, Tom N. VISUAL PERSPECTIVE. *Academic Press* 1970 $15.00

"Written by a well-known researcher in psychology, this is a textbook by which the student is guided to an understanding of the physics of light, optics of the eye, structure of the visual system, and behavior of the organism as a psycho-physical observer"—(*Choice*).

Corsini, Raymond J., and Genevieve Painter. THE PRACTICAL PARENT: ABCs of Child Discipline. *Harper* 1975 $10.00

This book presents "the Dreikurs/Alderian method of family living and child rearing"—(*LJ*).

DeBold, Richard C. MANUAL OF CONTEMPORARY EXPERIMENTS IN PSYCHOLOGY. *Prentice-Hall* 1968 pap. (orig.) $5.95

Dement, William C. SOME MUST WATCH WHILE SOME MUST SLEEP. *Scribner* 1974 $5.95

"By far, the best exposition of the mysteries of sleep written for the layperson"—(*LJ*).

Deutsch, Helen. CONFRONTATIONS WITH MYSELF. *Norton* 1973 $6.95

"A psychiatrist who received her training from Freud and then went on to become the first director of the Vienna Training Institute, Deutsch reminisces about her experiences and insights over a long career in analysis"—(*LJ*).

Deutsch, Morton. THE RESOLUTION OF CONFLICT: Constructive and Destructive Processes. *Yale Univ. Press* 1973 $15.00

Diamond, Edwin. THE SCIENCE OF DREAMS. *Manor Bks.* 1968 pap. $.75

This up-to-date summary, written by a *Newsweek* feature writer, is "science reporting at its best, information-packed and eminently readable with no sacrifice of accuracy or overstress on the sensational." It ranges from the beliefs of primitive man to the theories of psychoanalysis. It will be "useful in university as well as general collections and is highly recommended"—(*LJ*).

Ellenberger, Henri F. THE DISCOVERY OF THE UNCONSCIOUS: The History and Evolution of Dynamic Psychiatry. *Basic Bks.* 1970 $15.00

"Ellenberger has produced the new standard account of the rise of the dynamic psychologies of Freud, Jung, Adler, and Janet, and for unspecialized libraries the book can serve in lieu of much monographic material. . . . A monumental work of almost unbelievable erudition"—(*Choice*).

Ellis, Albert. *See his main entry, this Chapter*.

Erikson, Erik H. *See his main entry, this Chapter*.

Faber, Nancy W. THE RETARDED CHILD. *Crown* 1968 $5.95

"This book by a former teacher in the public schools speaks not only to parents and professionals but to the general public as well. Written with poignancy, understanding, and acute perception, it offers a uniquely useful and practical approach to the highly complex field of mental retardation"—(*LJ*). The first half of her book studies case histories in 12 foreign countries; the second half deals with the U.S.A.

Fancher, Raymond E. PSYCHOANALYTIC PSYCHOLOGY: The Development of Freud's Thought. *Norton* 1973 $8.95 pap. $2.95

Felix, Robert H. MENTAL ILLNESS: Progress and Prospects. Bampton Lectures in America Ser. *Columbia* 1967 $7.00

"This is an optimistic book. Dr. Felix, Dean of the School of Medicine at St. Louis University, believes that an accelerated revolution is taking place in the United States toward the ultimate conquest of mental illness. . . . The material is well documented throughout. Problems are posed clearly and the solutions proposed are feasible. Dr. Felix's language is colorful, and he expresses his convictions without being unduly subjective"—(*LJ*).

Fincher, Jack. HUMAN INTELLIGENCE. *Putnam* 1976 $14.95

This book "presents the latest research, experiments, and controversies that are leading to an entirely new and expanded definition of human intelligence"—(Publisher's note).

Fingarette, Herbert. THE MEANING OF CRIMINAL INSANITY. *Univ. of California Press* 1972 $11.50 pap. 1974 $3.25

ON RESPONSIBILITY. *Basic Bks.* 1967 $5.00

SELF-DECEPTION. Studies in Philosophical Psychology Ser. *Humanities Press* 1969 $6.00

Flugel, John Carl. MAN, MORALS AND SOCIETY. *International Univs. Press* 1970 $12.00 pap. $3.45

PSYCHOANALYTIC STUDY OF THE FAMILY. *Hillary House* $8.75

THE PSYCHOLOGY OF CLOTHES. *International Univs. Press* 1969 $10.00 pap. $2.95

Foucault, Michel. MADNESS AND CIVILIZATION: A History of Insanity in the Age of
Reason. Trans. from the French by Richard Howard; introd. by José Barchilon
Pantheon 1965 $7.95; *Random* Vintage Bks. pap. $2.45

"Mr. Foucault attacks the myth of mental illness and presents the concept of madness as it must
have existed at the time. He shows how madness and non-madness and reason and non-reason are
inextricably involved. . . . A difficult but rewarding book, beautifully written, and subtle in its
development"—*(LJ)*.

MENTAL ILLNESS AND PSYCHOLOGY. *Harper* 1974 $9.00 Torchbks. pap. $2.95

Frank, Jerome D. PERSUASION AND HEALING: A Comparative Study of Psychotherapy.
Johns Hopkins Press 1963 2nd rev. ed. 1973 $12.50; *Schocken* 1974 pap. $4.75

SANITY AND SURVIVAL: The Psychological Aspects of War and Peace. *Random* 1967
$5.95 Vintage Bks. pap. $1.95

"Dr. Frank, widely-published practising psychiatrist and commentator on public affairs, has
written a readable book which forces the reader to correlate and rethink a whole range of life-
death issues in this post-atomic world. . . . 'The Predicament—Genocidal Weapons,' [is a chapter]
in which he points out that there are enough nuclear weapons extant to detonate three million
Hiroshimas and one Denver arsenal stockpiles enough nerve gas to destroy all mankind. [In the
chapter] 'Why Nations Fight: The Image of the Enemy' . . . Dr. Frank is at his professional
best. . . . In the 12th chapter he explores conflict without violence—making an impressive if not
finally convincing case for the efficacy of non-violent survival if only man's 'moral sense' can
control his drive to power"—*(LJ)*.

Frank, Lawrence K. THE IMPORTANCE OF INFANCY. *Random* 1966 pap. (orig.) $2.95; *Peter
Smith* $4.50

Frankl, Viktor E. THE DOCTOR AND THE SOUL: From Psychotherapy to Logotherapy.
Knopf 1955 rev. ed. 1965 $6.95; *Random* Vintage Bks. 1973 pap. $1.95

MAN'S SEARCH FOR MEANING: An Introduction to Logotherapy. *Beacon* rev. ed. 1963
$5.95; *Simon & Schuster* (Pocket Bks.) pap. $1.25 Touchstone-Clarion Bks. 1970 pap.
$1.95

PSYCHOTHERAPY AND EXISTENTIALISM. *Simon & Schuster* Touchstone-Clarion Bks. 1968
pap. $2.95

Freud, Sigmund. *See his main entry, this Chapter*.

Frey-Rohn, Liliane. FROM FREUD TO JUNG: A Comparative Study of the Psychology of the
Unconscious. *Putnam* 1975 $16.00

The author "shows a keen interest in historical perspective and immense familiarity with her
subject matter as she traces in detail the contrasting theories of Freud and Jung from earliest
conceptual beginnings to fully developed formulations. Among the fundamental issues she deals
with are the hypothesis of sexual libido versus total psychic energy"—*(LJ)*.

Fromm, Erich, and Michael Maccoby. SOCIAL CHARACTER IN A MEXICAN VILLAGE: A
Sociopsychoanalytic Study. *Prentice-Hall* 1970 $8.95 pap. $3.45

"An empirical study of Mexican peasants by two distinguished psychoanalysts"—*(Choice)*.

See also his main entry, this Chapter.

Gardner, Howard. THE QUEST FOR MIND: Piaget, Lévi-Strauss, and the Structuralist
Movement. *Knopf* 1973 $6.95

"Gardner has brilliantly summarized and interrelated the ideas of Piaget and Lévi-Strauss in a
readable manner. The foundations of structuralism . . . and 'discovering the overall organization
between parts and wholes' . . . are explained"—*(Choice)*.

Garrett, Henry Edward. I.Q. AND RACIAL DIFFERENCES. *Howard Allen Enterprises* 1973 pap.
$1.00

Geba, Bruno. VITALITY TRAINING FOR OLDER ADULTS: A Positive Approach to Growing
Older. *Random* 1975 $5.95

The author "outlines his particular form of therapy (with conversational case histories) against a philosophic backdrop of the conflict between a youth-oriented society and the very real need for a positive psychic identity for the older person"—(LJ).

Gibson, Eleanor J. PRINCIPLES OF PERCEPTUAL LEARNING AND DEVELOPMENT. *Prentice-Hall* (Appleton) 1970 $11.95

"This volume covers the entire spectrum of the ways in which development and learning can affect perception"—(*Choice*).

Gilkey, Langdon B. SHANTUNG COMPOUND: The Story of Men and Women under Pressure. *Harper* 1966 $5.95

Observations, recorded daily by the well-known American theologian, in his Japanese internment camp during World War II. "The thing that differentiates this personal account from others is that it tells what the residents did and did not do as individuals, not what the Japanese did to them. What makes it distinguished, though, is Mr. Gilkey's penetrating observations on the behavior of individuals when they are stripped of social status, wealth, and freedom, and put under protected, confining, and crowded conditions"—(LJ).

Glasser, William. THE IDENTITY SOCIETY. *Harper* rev. ed. 1975 $8.95 Colophon Bks. pap. $2.95

MENTAL HEALTH OR MENTAL ILLNESS: Psychiatry for Practical Action. *Harper* 1961 $5.95 Perenn. Lib. 1970 pap. $1.50

REALITY THERAPY: A New Approach to Psychiatry. *Harper* 1965 $6.95 Perenn. Lib. 1975 pap. $1.95 Colophon Bks. 1975 pap. $2.95

Dr. Glasser attacks the Freudian method of concentrating on the past life of an individual in therapy and builds his new therapy on showing patients how to manage their present and future. He has wide experience as a psychiatrist in Los Angeles and a consultant to school systems. His book has sold over 100,000 copies.

SCHOOLS WITHOUT FAILURE. *Harper* 1969 $6.95 Perenn. Lib. 1975 pap. $1.95 Colophon Bks. 1975 pap. $2.95

Glock, Charles Y., Robert Wuthnow, Jane Piliavin and Metta Spencer. ADOLESCENT PREJUDICE. *Harper* 1975 $15.00

This volume is "based on a 1963 University of California study of anti-semitism in the United States"—(LJ).

Goffman, Erving. FRAME ANALYSIS: An Essay on the Organization of Experience. *Harvard Univ. Press* 1974 $12.50; *Harper* Colophon Bks. 1974 pap. $3.95

INTERACTION RITUAL: Six Essays on Face-to-Face Behavior. *Aldine* 1967 $10.95; *Doubleday* Anchor Bks. 1967 pap. $2.95

"Mr. Goffman, author of *The Presentation of Self in Everyday Life* (Doubleday, 1959), is a serious student of the games people play; he urges the development of a 'sociology of occasions.' He feels psychotic behavior is overemphasized, and that there should be more study of the rules for public conduct"—(LJ).

Goldenson, Robert M. MYSTERIES OF THE MIND: The Drama of Human Behavior. *Doubleday* 1973 $7.95; *Harper* (Barnes & Noble) 1974 pap. $1.50

Grant, Brian W. SCHIZOPHRENIA: A Source of Social Insight. *Westminster Press* 1975 $10.00

A "scholarly work, written with an exceptional understanding"—(LJ).

Griffith, Edward F. MARRIAGE AND THE UNCONSCIOUS. *C. C. Thomas* 2nd ed. 1967 $8.50

Grinker, Roy R. PSYCHIATRY IN BROAD PERSPECTIVE. *Human Sciences Press* 1974 $14.95

"This book is largely a personalized, multidisciplinary overview of aspects of psychiatric research by a psychiatrist who has spent 40 years in the field. It considers topics such as the qualities of a researcher, designing a research program [and] aspects of biological, psychoanalytic, and clinical research"—(LJ).

PSYCHOSOMATIC CONCEPTS. *Jason Aronson* 1974 $10.00

Group for the Advancement of Psychiatry, Committee on Adolescence. NORMAL ADOLESCENCE: Its Dynamics and Impact. Introd. by Katherine B. Oettinger *Scribner* 1968 $5.95 Headline Ed. pap. $1.65

Haber, Ralph N., and Maurice Hershenson. THE PSYCHOLOGY OF VISUAL PERCEPTION. *Holt* 1973 $12.50

"Much valuable information in an exceptionally clear manner"—*(Choice)*.

Halleck, Seymour L. THE POLITICS OF THERAPY (orig. "Uses of Psychotherapy"). *Jason Aronson* 1971 $12.50; *Harper* Perenn. Lib. 1972 pap. $1.95

PSYCHIATRY AND THE DILEMMAS OF CRIME: A Study of Causes, Punishment and Treatment. Fwd. by Karl Menninger *Harper* 1967 $10.95; *Univ. of California Press* 1971 pap. $3.95

From a point of view that does not absolve society of blame for its criminals, "Professor Halleck, of the University of Wisconsin, has written a scholarly and thorough work on the relationship of psychiatry to criminology"—*(LJ)*.

(With Walter Bromberg). PSYCHIATRIC ASPECTS OF CRIMINOLOGY. *C. C. Thomas* 1968 $5.50

Harding, M. Esther. THE I AND THE NOT-I: A Study in the Development of Consciousness. Bollingen Ser. *Princeton Univ. Press* 1965 $9.50 pap. 1973 $2.95

PSYCHIC ENERGY: Its Source and Its Transformation. Bollingen Ser. *Princeton Univ. Press* 2nd rev. ed. 1963 $16.50 pap. $3.95. One of the most influential source books.

WOMAN'S MYSTERIES: Ancient and Modern. Jung Foundation Ser. *Putnam* 1972 $7.50; *Bantam* 1973 pap. $1.95

Harris, Irving. EMOTIONAL BLOCKS TO LEARNING. *Macmillan* (Free Press) 1961 $6.95 pap. $2.45

Havemann, Ernest. THE AGE OF PSYCHOLOGY. *Simon & Schuster* (Fireside) 1957 pap. $1.00

Heidbreder, Edna. SEVEN PSYCHOLOGIES. *Prentice-Hall* (Appleton) 1963 pap. (orig.) $4.95. An important introduction for the beginner.

Herrnstein, Richard J. BEHAVIOR: An Introduction to Comparative Psychology. *Holt* 1967 pap. $9.50

I.Q. IN THE MERITOCRACY. *Little-Atlantic* 1973 $7.95

Hess, Walter R. THE BIOLOGY OF MIND. Trans. from the German by Gerhardt von Bonin *Univ. of Chicago Press* 1964 $7.50

"Dr. Hess, the world-renowned Swiss physiologist (Nobel Prize, 1949), here presents a running commentary, based on his long lifetime of work and reflection, of all that he considers significant in the recent findings of psychophysiology or biology of mind—the interrelationship of brain and behavior. . . . [His] bringing together, [his] melding of the important findings of animal experimentation and human development and behavior studies is Dr. Hess's great contribution"—*(LJ)*.

Hillman, James. RE-VISIONING PSYCHOLOGY. *Harper* 1975 $10.00

"As an explorer of the imaginal realm of the psyche faithful to the reality of the archetypes rather than to any one theory about them, Hillman has no living peer"—*(LJ)*.

Homan, William E. CHILD SENSE: A Pediatrician's Guide for Today's Families. *Basic Bks.* 1969 $7.95; *Bantam* 1970 pap. $1.25

Isaacs, Susan. THE NURSERY YEARS: The Mind of the Child from Birth to Six Years. *Schocken* 1968 $5.50 pap. $2.45; *Vanguard* $2.75

Joint Commission on Mental Health of Children. CHILD MENTAL HEALTH: A Reader. *Harper* 1975 $10.00

MENTAL HEALTH FROM INFANCY THROUGH ADOLESCENCE. *Harper* 1973 $15.00

Joint Commission on Mental Illness and Health. ACTION FOR MENTAL HEALTH. *Basic Bks.* 1961 $12.00

Jones, Maxwell. BEYOND THE THERAPEUTIC COMMUNITY: Social Learning and Social Psychiatry. *Yale Univ. Press* 1968 $7.50

Jung, Carl Gustav. *See his main entry, this Chapter*.

Kagan, Jerome, Robert McCall, and others. CHANGE AND CONTINUITY IN INFANCY. *Wiley* 1971 $11.95

"Informative report of a longitudinal study of 180 infants who came to Kagan's Harvard laboratory at 4, 8, 13 and 27 months for a series of assessment procedures centered on four themes: early *anlage* of conceptual tempo, class and sex differences in attentional processes, and continuities in cognitive development"—(*Choice*).

Kagan, Jerome, and Robert Coles, Eds. TWELVE TO SIXTEEN: Early Adolescence. *Norton* 1973 $15.00 pap. $3.95

"In this very uncommon collection of essays, a group of experts from a variety of social science disciplines talk about the young adolescent. It is an uncommon collection both because of the uniformly high quality of the contributions and because of the way in which diverse pieces nonetheless hang together as a meaningful whole"—(*Choice*).

Kanner, Leo. CHILDHOOD PSYCHOSIS: Initial Studies and New Insights. *Halsted Press* 1973 $10.95

A HISTORY OF THE CARE AND STUDY OF THE MENTALLY RETARDED. *C. C. Thomas* 1967 $7.50 pap. 1974 $4.75

Keen, Samuel. VOICES AND VISIONS. *Harper* 1974 $6.95

"The author . . . here brings together interviews he conducted with nine figures in the humanistic psychology movement . . . they were originally published in *Psychology Today*"—(*LJ*).

Keller, Fred S. THE DEFINITION OF PSYCHOLOGY. *Prentice-Hall* (Appleton) 2nd ed. 1973 $4.95

"A brief, interesting, well-written history of scientific psychology"—(*Choice*).

Kiell, Norman. VARIETIES OF SEXUAL EXPERIENCE (orig. "Psychosexuality in Literature"). *International Univs. Press* 1973 $25.00

(Ed.). THE PSYCHOLOGY OF OBESITY: Dynamics and Treatment. *C. C. Thomas* 1973 $13.95

Klein, Melanie. CONTRIBUTIONS TO PSYCHOANALYSIS, 1921–1945. *Hillary House* 1950 text ed. $13.25. By a woman who in her lifetime and even today has been the acknowledged leader in psychology on the South American continent.

NARRATIVE OF A CHILD ANALYSIS. *Delacorte* 1974 $20.00. A fascinating case study of a ten year old boy.

THE PSYCHOANALYSIS OF CHILDREN. *Delacorte* 1975 $17.50

"A classic work which revolutionized child analysis"—(Publisher's note).

Kline, Nathan S. FROM SAD TO GLAD: Kline on Depression. *Putnam* 1974 $7.95; *Ballantine Bks.* 1975 pap. $1.95

Klineberg, Otto. THE HUMAN DIMENSION IN INTERNATIONAL RELATIONS. *Holt* 1964 pap. (orig.) $5.00

RACE AND PSYCHOLOGY. *Unipub* 1965 pap. $.75

Kris, Ernst. PSYCHOANALYTIC EXPLORATIONS IN ART. *International Univs. Press* 1962 $13.50; *Schocken* 1964 pap. $3.45

Kubie, Lawrence S. NEUROTIC DISTORTION OF THE CREATIVE PROCESS. 1958. *Farrar, Straus* Noonday 1961 pap. $2.45

PRACTICAL AND THEORETICAL ASPECTS OF PSYCHOANALYSIS. *International Univs. Press* 1971 rev. ed. 1975 $15.00 pap. $2.95

Kuiper, Pieter C. THE NEUROSIS. *International Univs. Press* 1972 $10.00

Laing, Ronald D. *See his main entry, this Chapter.*

Landreth, Catherine. EARLY CHILDHOOD: Behavior and Learning. *Knopf* rev. ed. 1967 $10.95 text ed. $9.95

"A revision of *The Psychology of Early Childhood* [1958, o.p.], this book is written primarily as a basic text for students in courses concerned with the behavior and learning of children from the prenatal period through age six. Catherine Landreth's purpose is: to give a balanced presentation of what is known about the behavior and learning of this age group; to stimulate meaningful inquiry into complex problems rather than to search for simple answers; and to encourage *use* of facts rather than *memorization*. . . . Valuable"—(*LJ*).

Lecky, Prescott. SELF-CONSISTENCY: A Theory of Personality. 1951. *Shoe String Press* 1973 $5.00; *Island Press* 1973 $4.95

Lesse, Stanley, Ed. MASKED DEPRESSION. *Jason Aronson* 1975 $12.50

"The 20 articles here collected present symptom patterns, hypotheses of origin, relation to suicide, and psychological therapies"—(*LJ*).

Levinson, Harry, EXCEPTIONAL EXECUTIVE: A Psychological Conception. *Harvard Univ. Press* 1968 $8.00; *New Am. Lib.* 1971 pap. $1.50

EXECUTIVE STRESS. *Harper* 1970 $7.95

THE GREAT JACKASS FALLACY. *Harvard Univ. Press* 1973 $7.00. About executive goals and achievements, motivational psychology in personnel management.

Lidz, Theodore. ORIGIN AND TREATMENT OF SCHIZOPHRENIC DISORDERS. *Basic Bks.* 1973 $6.95

THE PERSON: His Development Throughout the Life Cycle. *Basic Bks.* 1968 $10.75

Professor Lidz is a psychiatrist and the chairman of the Department of Psychiatry at Yale University's School of Medicine. "With admirable thoroughness, [he] starts his exploration of the nature of human nature by examining the human endowment, as differentiated from that of the animal, and the function of the family as the setting within which the human personality evolves. . . . *The Person* reveals the process by which man is made an individual and a *human* being. . . . Nothing so clearly reveals how individual and how human a person can become than the portrait of the man who emerges from between the lines of the book—the author himself"—(George Krupp, in *SR*).

Lifton, Robert Jay. BOUNDARIES: Psychological Man in Revolution. *Random* 1970 $5.95 Vintage Bks. 1970 pap. $1.95

DEATH IN LIFE: Survivors of Hiroshima. *Random* 1968 $12.50

With this Dr. Lifton of Yale won the 1969 National Book Award in the Sciences. His citation read: "To Dr. Robert Jay Lifton for *Death in Life*, a distinguished study of wide human interest. This perceptive analysis in depth by a psychiatrist of the survivors of the first atomic bomb serves to remind us of an event too easily forgotten. It establishes that the tragedy of Hiroshima did not end with the destruction of the city but had a profound and lasting effect on the lives of all those involved in it. It makes vivid to us in literary form the social and ethical consequences of a single act of war."

Lorenz, Konrad. STUDIES IN ANIMAL AND HUMAN BEHAVIOUR: Vol. 1. Trans. by R. Martin *Harvard Univ. Press* 1970 $10.00

"Vol. I covers six translated essays of Lorenz, the founding father of ethology. . . . It will appeal to [all] . . . concerned with the development and emergence of the science of animal behavior"—(*Choice*).

Lowenthal, Majorie Fiske. LIVES IN DISTRESS: The Paths of the Elderly to the Psychiatric Ward. *Basic Bks.* 1964 $6.95

This is "the first of a projected series of four works to deal with the aging process as it reveals itself in psychological, sociological and physiological terms. The study, which summarizes research conducted at the Langley Porter Neuropsychiatric Institute, San Francisco, applies the usual approaches to research and is done with care, precision, and an abiding interest in minute documentation and correlation of their findings"—(*LJ*).

(With Paul L. Berkman). AGING AND MENTAL DISORDER IN SAN FRANCISCO: A Social Psychiatric Study. *Jossey-Bass* 1967 $12.50

Lowry, Richard. THE EVOLUTION OF PSYCHOLOGICAL THEORY: 1650 to the Present. *Aldine* 1971 $8.95

"Designed for advanced undergraduate psychology majors"—(*Choice*).

Lundberg, Margaret J. THE INCOMPLETE ADULT: Social Class Constraints on Personality Development. *Greenwood* 1974 $12.50

"Lundberg argues that degree of personality development is directly related to social class membership"—(*LJ*).

Lunde, Donald T., and Herbert Katchadourian. FUNDAMENTALS OF HUMAN SEXUALITY. *Holt* 1972 $7.50

"A scholarly, accurate, nonsensational work—one of the best of its kind"—(*LJ*).

Lynd, Helen Merrill. On SHAME AND THE SEARCH FOR IDENTITY. *Harcourt* 1958 Harvest Bks. 1970 pap. $2.95

Maas, Henry S., and Joseph A. Kuypers. FROM THIRTY TO SEVENTY: A Forty-Year Longitudinal Study of Adult Life Styles and Personality. *Jossey-Bass* 1974 $10.95

McClelland, David C., and others. THE DRINKING MAN. *Macmillan* (Free Press) 1972 $10.00

(With Robert S. Steele, Eds.). HUMAN MOTIVATION: A Book of Readings. *General Learning Corp.* 1973 text ed. $11.95 pap. $7.95

Masters, William H., and others. PLEASURE BOND: A New Look at Sexuality and Commitment. *Little* 1975 $8.95
"Considers in a more personal way, the values of sexual relations"—(*Booklist*).

May, Rollo. *See his main entry, this Chapter.*

Milne, Lorus, and Margery Milne. THE ANIMAL IN MAN. *McGraw-Hill* 1973 $8.95
"By demonstrating the numerous instances of parallel behavior patterns, as well as the differences, between man and animal, the authors raise the question as to how free *is* man—or are all his actions predetermined"—(*LJ*).

Mitchell, Marjorie E. THE CHILD'S ATTITUDE TO DEATH. *Schocken* 1967 $4.95

Morris, Desmond. INTIMATE BEHAVIOR. *Random* 1972 $6.95
"Here he focuses on man's social and sexual touching activities. An elementary book, perhaps much of it has been said before, but Morris entertains as he instructs, and psychology students will be reminded to keep an eye on the physical side of man"—(*Choice*).

Moustakas, Clark E. THE CHILD'S DISCOVERY OF HIMSELF. *Jason Aronson* 1974 $10.00; *Ballantine* 1974 pap. $1.25

PORTRAITS OF LONELINESS AND LOVE. *Prentice-Hall* 1974 $6.95 pap. $2.95

Muensterberger, Warner, and Aaron H. Eastman. THE PSYCHOANALYTIC STUDY OF SOCIETY. *International Univs. Press* $15.00
"The wide area of applicability of psychoanalytic concepts and the vitality of contemporary psychoanalytic thinking are well documented in this volume"—(*LJ*).

Munroe, Ruth L. SCHOOLS OF PSYCHOANALYTIC THOUGHT. *Holt* 1955 $13.00

Murphy, Gardner. *See his main entry, this Chapter.*

Neisser, Edith G. MOTHERS AND DAUGHTERS: A Lifelong Relationship. *Harper* 1967 rev. ed. 1973 $10.00
A "thoroughly documented, painstakingly researched and completely fascinating work"—(*LJ*).

Neumann, Erich. DEPTH PSYCHOLOGY AND A NEW ETHIC. Trans. by E. Rolfe. *Putnam* 1970 $7.00
"Neumann has dealt very effectively with the ethical implications of the unconscious, noting the old and new ethic, the stages of ethical development, and the aims and values of the new ethic"—(*Choice*).

Paul, Norman L., and Betty Paul. A MARITAL PUZZLE: Trans-Generational Analysis in Marriage Counseling. *Norton* 1975 $8.95
Includes "eight transcripts of therapy sessions"—(*LJ*).

Piaget, Jean. *See his main entry, this Chapter.*

Pines, Maya. THE BRAIN CHANGERS: Scientists and the New Mind Control. *Harcourt* 1973 $7.95

REVOLUTION IN LEARNING: The Years from Birth to Six. *Harper* 1967 $8.95 Harrow Bks. pap. $.95

Poussaint, Alvin, and James Comer. BLACK CHILD CARE. *Simon & Schuster* 1975 $9.95
"This book, written in question-and-answer format, is a stage-by-stage study of the black child's development from infancy through adolescence"—(*Time*).

Renshon, Stanley A. PSYCHOLOGICAL NEEDS AND POLITICAL BEHAVIOR: A Theory of Personality and Political Efficacy. *Macmillan* (Free Press) 1974 $10.95

"Renshon argues that the motivation to participate in political activities arises from what he identifies as the need for personal control"—*(Choice)*.

Rogers, Carl R. *See his main entry, this Chapter*.

Rolo, Charles J., Ed. PSYCHIATRY IN AMERICAN LIFE. 1963. *Bks. for Libraries* $10.50; *Dell* 1968 pap. $1.95

"Lay readers who have been both bothered and fascinated by the subject will find in this symposium much information about what psychiatry is, its accomplishments, its limits, and its current status in the medical profession." Sixteen contributors, including Alfred Kazin, who notes the impact of psychiatry on literature, and Royden C. Astley, who analyzes the conflicts between psychiatry and religion; useful bibliography—*(Book of the Month Club News)*.

Rosen, George. MADNESS IN SOCIETY: Chapters in the Historical Sociology of Mental Illness. *Univ. of Chicago Press* 1968 $9.50; *Harper* Torchbks. (orig.) 1967 pap. $2.95

"With the improbable cunning of the sociologist, Rosen takes a long view of the history of madness in hopes of finding the wisdom that may be stored in previous ages. He has found, among other things, that every period has had its ways of distinguishing true madness from behavior that varied widely from prevailing norms"—(Donald M. Kaplan, in the *N.Y. Times*).

Ruesch, Jurgen. DISTURBED COMMUNICATION. *Norton* 1972 pap. $3.95

THERAPEUTIC COMMUNICATION. *Norton* 1973 pap. $4.95

Rycroft, Charles. ANXIETY AND NEUROSIS. *Penguin* 1970 $6.50 pap. $1.25

A CRITICAL DICTIONARY OF PSYCHOANALYSIS. *Littlefield* 1973 pap. $2.95

IMAGINATION AND REALITY. *International Univs. Press* 1968 $10.00

Salzman, Leon. THE OBSESSIVE PERSONALITY. *Jason Aronson* 1968 text ed. $10.00

"Dr. Leon Salzman, professor of clinical psychiatry, Georgetown University School of Medicine, merits a prize for his jargon-free discussion of the obsessive-compulsive personality, 'today's most prevalent neurotic character structure' "—*(LJ)*.

Sampson, Ronald V. THE DISCOVERY OF PEACE. *Pantheon* 1973 $6.95

THE PSYCHOLOGY OF POWER. 1965. *Pantheon* 1966 $7.95; *Random* Vintage Bks. pap. $1.95

"A Freudian and Adlerian rationale lies in the heart of this remarkable book. The work revolves about man's interminable attempt to achieve power (superiority) in the social, political, economic, and psychological dimensions of experience, and focuses down hard on the ensuing dialectic (conflict) between . . . antithetical behaviors. . . . While not a psychologist, Sampson [a political scientist] nonetheless writes with psychological acumen. . . . It appears that in order to achieve a true state of superiority, in the sense of actualizing and maximizing human integrative potential, man has to learn to love beyond himself with compassion and empathy and concern for all life— much in keeping with Schweitzer's concept of 'reverence for life,' a cardinal criterion of psycholog- ical maturity. As Sampson points out, this proposal is scarcely new but was set forth articulately nearly 2,000 years ago. . . . Essential to college and university collections in the behavioral sciences"—*(Choice)*.

Sanford, Nevitt. ISSUES IN PERSONALITY THEORY. Behavioral Science Ser. *Jossey-Bass* 1970 $9.75

SELF AND SOCIETY: Social Change and Individual Development. *Aldine* 1966 $12.50

"In this major review by the distinguished Stanford psychologist, the theory and practice of social psychology is discussed in an effort to develop practical guidelines for the more effective use of this science in our world. Professor Sanford's key concept is the 'change-promoting institution,' the institution that is evolved by society to bring about the socialization of its members"—*(LJ)*.

(With Craig Comstock, Eds.). SANCTIONS FOR EVIL: Sources of Social Destructiveness. Behavioral Science Ser. *Jossey-Bass* 1971 $10.75; *Beacon* 1972 pap. $3.95

Scientific American Resource Library. READINGS IN PSYCHOLOGY, Vol. 3. *W. H. Freeman* 1973 $10.00. A collection of readings from various issues of the *Scientific American*.

Seabrook, Jeremy. LONELINESS. *Universe Bks.* 1975 $7.00

"A collection of edited transcripts based on conversations the author had with 'two or three hundred people' in England"—*(LJ)*.

Seeley, John. THE AMERICANIZATION OF THE UNCONSCIOUS. *Jason Aronson* $12.50

"A brilliant and persuasive argument against this overconfident 'boxing off' of disciplines because their approaches seem to dictate mutual exclusion. Seeley's address here is to sociology (his own specialty) and psychoanalysis, two bodies of thinking with an apparent polarity in the explanation of man's behavior"—(John Bright, in *SR*). The author's thesis is that revolutionary changes in American psychiatry and sociology are producing a "distinctly American Unconscious."

Shostrom, Everett L. FREEDOM TO BE: Experiencing and Expressing Your Total Being. *Prentice-Hall* 1972 $5.95; *Bantam* 1974 pap. $1.50

MAN, THE MANIPULATOR: The Inner Journey from Manipulation to Actualization. *Abingdon* 1967 $5.95; *Bantam* 1968 pap. $1.25

Dr. Shostrom, director of the Institute of Therapeutic Psychology at Santa Ana, Calif., discusses the difference between "manipulation," or the exploitation involved in relationships to which one does not give oneself, and "actualization," its opposite, with a discussion of the application of these concepts to various forms of psychotherapy.

Skinner, Burrhus F. *See his main entry, this Chapter.*

Smith, Henry C. PERSONALITY DEVELOPMENT. *McGraw-Hill* 2nd ed. 1974 $11.95

SENSITIVITY TRAINING: The Scientific Understanding of Individuals. *McGraw-Hill* 1973 $10.50

(With John H. Wakeley). PSYCHOLOGY OF INDUSTRIAL BEHAVIOR. *McGraw-Hill* 3rd ed. 1972 $10.95

Stein, Morris I., Ed. CONTEMPORARY PSYCHOTHERAPIES. *Macmillan* (Free Press) 1961 $8.95

Ten of the leading exponents of various types of psychotherapies are contributors to this authoritative volume which belongs in any collection where such a book is desired by either informed lay persons or workers in the sociological, psychological or psychiatric fields.

Stone, L. Joseph, Lois B. Murphy and Henrietta T. Smith, Eds. THE COMPETENT INFANT: Research and Commentary. *Basic Bks.* 1974 $32.00

Strecker, Edward Adam. BASIC PSYCHIATRY. *Random* 1952 $6.95. An excellent survey for the layman.

Taylor, Calvin W., Ed. CLIMATE FOR CREATIVITY. *Pergamon* 1972 $14.50

Thass-Thienemann, Theodore. THE INTERPRETATION OF LANGUAGE. *Jason Aronson* 2 vols. rev. ed. 1973 Vol. 1 Understanding the Symbolic Meaning of Language Vol. 2 Understanding the Unconscious Meaning of Language each $15.00

Ulanov, Ann B. THE FEMININE IN JUNGIAN PSYCHOLOGY AND IN CHRISTIAN THEOLOGY. *Northwestern Univ. Press* 1972 $10.50

"Ulanov has dealt with one of the most current issues in our culture—the feminine—producing one of the finest substantive studies on the topic for many years. . . . Her work revolves around Jung's approach to and the structure of the psyche"—(*Choice*).

Vgotsky, Lev S. THE PSYCHOLOGY OF ART. *M.I.T. Press* $12.50 pap. $3.95

THOUGHT AND LANGUAGE. Trans. by Eugenia Hanfmann and Gertrude Vakar. *M.I.T. Press* 1962 $7.50 pap. $2.45

Wallerstein, Robert S. PSYCHOTHERAPY AND PSYCHOANALYSIS: Theory, Practice, Research. *International Univs. Press* 1975 $17.50

"Sixteen previously published papers [which] demonstrate meticulous erudition in psychoanalysis and psychotherapy"—(*LJ*).

Wallis, Robert. TIME: Fourth Dimension of the Mind. Trans. from the French by Betty B. Montgomery and Denis B. Montgomery; introd. by Marshall McLuhan *Harcourt* 1968 $6.95

"Out of his investigations in neurology and medical psychology, Wallis has come up with some new interpretations of mental illness and some new approaches to its treatment. He explores profoundly the role of the senses, especially sight and hearing, in the construction of the notion of time"—(*PW*). "A remarkable study"—(*LJ*). Dr. Wallis is a French physician now practising in New York.

Watts, Alan W. THE BOOK: On the Taboo Against Knowing Who You Are. *Pantheon* 1966 $5.95; *Random* Vintage Bks. 1972 pap. $1.65

This authority on comparative religions brings "insights from the Eastern religions . . . to bear upon the problems of Western man's misuse of his technological knowledge to the point of his imminent destruction. A timely, thoughtful, relevant book"—*(LJ)*. By 1968 it had become one of great interest to young people—to whom, in general, it is addressed. A best seller.

PSYCHOTHERAPY EAST AND WEST. *Pantheon* 1961 $6.95; *Ballantine Bks.* 1969 pap. $.95

Wepman, Joseph M., and Ralph W. Heine, Eds. CONCEPTS OF PERSONALITY. *Aldine* 1963 $8.95

This highly-recommended, nearly encyclopedic collection of 17 essays by proponents of various points of view in personality study results from a special series of lectures at the University of Chicago sponsored by their Interdepartmental Committee on Clinical and Counseling Psychology.

Werner, Heinz. COMPARATIVE PSYCHOLOGY OF MENTAL DEVELOPMENT. 1940. *International Univs. Press* rev. ed. 1970 $13.50 pap. $3.95

White, Robert W., and Norman F. Watt. THE ABNORMAL PERSONALITY. *Ronald* 1964 4th ed. 1973 $11.50

Whiting, Beatrice, and John Whiting in collaboration with Richard Longabaugh. CHILDREN OF SIX CULTURES: A Psycho-Cultural Analysis. *Harvard Univ. Press* 1975 $10.00

"A study of the observed social behavior of 134 children from the ages of three to eleven in Okinawa, Kenya, India, Mexico, and the United States"—*(LJ)*.

Wolf, Theta H. ALFRED BINET. *Univ. of Chicago Press* 1973 $13.75

"This book is unique and should be a standard reference for some time"—*(Choice)*.

Wyss, Dieter. PSYCHOANALYTIC SCHOOLS FROM THE BEGINNING TO THE PRESENT. Trans. from the German by Gerald Onn *Jason Aronson* 1973 $15.00

PSYCHOLOGISTS

LOCKE, JOHN. 1632–1704. *See Chapter 5, Philosophy, this Volume.*

GALTON, SIR FRANCIS. 1822–1911. *See Chapter 7, Science, this Volume.*

JAMES, WILLIAM. 1842–1910.

William James, the brilliant and readable Harvard "pragmatic" philosopher and the first Harvard Professor of Psychology (1889–1897), is one of the "fathers" if not *the* father of American psychology. After brief personal investigation of the work of Helmholtz, Hering and Wundt in Germany, he introduced experiments in psychology in a Harvard graduate course on "The Relations Between Physiology and Psychology" in 1875. His "Principles of Psychology" (1890) became a standard textbook. James saw human psychology as a biological adjustment to changing environment—with the state of consciousness as a "selecting agency." His student G. Stanley Hall, later himself a pioneer of distinction in the field, recalled (says Gay Wilson Allen) how in the early days James kept "in a tiny room under the staircase of the Agassiz museum . . . a metronome, a device for whirling a frog" and other novel research tools for the period. His philosophical and psychological studies had each an effect on the other, but in 1897 he took the Harvard Chair in Philosophy and devoted the rest of his life to that discipline.

THE WRITINGS OF WILLIAM JAMES: A Comprehensive Edition. Ed. with introd. by John J. McDermott, including "Annotated Bibliography" of James' works *Random* Modern Lib. Giant $4.95

"A valuable contribution to the current William James revival. . . . Mr. McDermott has chosen not only the well-known James classics but has also drawn from unpublished papers and from newspaper interviews, and combined all into a comprehensive portrait of our greatest American philosopher"—*(LJ)*.

WILLIAM JAMES READER. Ed. by Gay W. Allen *Houghton* 1972 pap. (orig.) $4.25

WILLIAM JAMES ON PSYCHICAL RESEARCH. Ed. by Gardner Murphy and Robert Ballou. 1960. *Kelley* $13.50; *Viking* Compass Bks. 1969 pap. $2.25

PRINCIPLES OF PSYCHOLOGY. 1890. *Dover* 2 vols. 1950 pap. Vol. 1 $4.00 Vol. 2 $4.50; *Peter Smith* 2 vols. set $13.00. Authorized unabridged editions.

TALKS TO TEACHERS ON PSYCHOLOGY AND TO STUDENTS ON SOME OF LIFE'S IDEALS. 1899. *Dover* 1962 pap. $1.25; *Norton* 1958 pap. $1.25; *Norwood Editions* $10.00; *Peter Smith* $4.75

THE VARIETIES OF RELIGIOUS EXPERIENCE. 1902 new ed. 1928. *Macmillan* Collier Bks. 1961 pap. $1.25; *Random* Modern Lib. 1936 $2.95; *New Am. Lib.* pap. $1.50

PSYCHOLOGY: The Briefer Course. 1892. Ed. by Gordon Allport *Harper* Torchbks. 1961 pap. $2.45; fwd. by Gardner Murphy *Macmillan* Collier 1962 pap. $1.50

Books about James

On the Way Toward a Phenomenological Psychology: The Psychology of William James. By Hans Linschoten. Trans. from the Dutch and ed. by Amedeo Giorgi *Duquesne Univ. Press* (dist. by Humanities Press) 1968 $9.50
The Professor of Experimental and General Psychology at the University of Utrecht (until his early death in 1964) "finds multitudes [of contradictions] in the philosophy of William James but insists that, transcending ostensible internal contradictions, a synthesis of a great philosophy may nevertheless be detected. . . . Notwithstanding that this is a psychologist writing for psychologists and his book is by no means a bedside reader, a certain freshness breaks through. Hans Linschoten's study leaves no doubt that a brilliant if controversial career, perhaps not yet at its height, was tragically halted"—(Alan W. Miller, in *SR*).
William James and Phenomenology: A Study of the Principles of Psychology. By Bruce Wiltshire. *Indiana Univ. Press* 1968 $12.50
Unifying Moment: The Psychological Philosophy of William James and Alfred North White-head. By Craig R. Eisendrath. *Harvard Univ. Press* 1971 $10.00

See also Chapter 5, Philosophy, this Volume.

PAVLOV, IVAN PETROVITCH. 1849–1936. (Nobel Prize 1904)

This Russian physiologist and experimental psychologist received, in 1904, the Nobel Prize in Physiology and Medicine for his work on the digestive glands. Pavlov's objective (rather than subjective) approach to research greatly influenced the field of experimental psychology. He is known especially for his chief work, "Conditioned Reflexes" (1926, Eng. trans. 1927).

SELECTED WORKS. *S. F. Book Imports* 1955 $5.00

THE ESSENTIAL WORKS OF PAVLOV. Ed. by Michael Kaplan *Bantam* (orig.) pap. $1.25

CONDITIONED REFLEXES: An Investigation of the Physiological Activity of the Cerebral Cortex. 1926. Trans. and ed. by G. V. Anrep. 1927. *Dover* 1960 pap. $3.00; *Peter Smith* 1960 $5.00

LECTURES ON CONDITIONED REFLEXES. Trans. by W. Horsley Gantt. 1928. *International Pubs.* 1963 pap. $3.25

CONDITIONED REFLEXES AND PSYCHIATRY. Trans. by W. Horsley Gantt. 1941. *International Pubs.* 1963 pap. $1.95

ESSAYS IN PSYCHOLOGY AND PSYCHIATRY. 1957. *Citadel Press* 1962 pap. $1.95

Books about Pavlov

Pavlov and His School. By Yurii P. Frolov. Trans. from Russian by C. P. Dutt. 1937. *Johnson Reprint* 1970 $16.75
Pavlov: A Biography. By Boris P. Babkin. *Univ. of Chicago Press* 1949 $10.50
Pavlovian Approach to Psychopathology. By W. Horsley Gantt and others. *Pergamon* 1970 $18.00

FREUD, SIGMUND. 1856–1939.

"Few men can claim a wider or deeper influence on their age" than Sigmund Freud. His was the revolutionary theory of the unconscious, that strange submerged part of the human mind. His was the new method of treating mental and emotional illness, which he called psychoanalysis—the beginning of modern psychiatry. His theories and concepts have influenced anthropology, education, art and literature. He was born in Moravia of a middle-class Jewish family and lived most of his life in Vienna. He died in London, a refugee from Hitlerism.

With his collaborator Josef Breuer, Freud worked originally toward curing patients of hysteria by uncovering their "unconscious" through hypnosis. He later substituted his own method of free association for the same end. His theories of personality were not well received by the medical profession or the general public until about 1909, when he first explained himself in the U.S., and many of Freud's contemporaries (such as Adler, Jung and later Karen Horney and Erich Fromm) disagreed with his emphasis on the infantile sexual instinct and the Oedipus complex. But whatever the developments, Freud's work will remain basic. A play about Freud, "A Far Country," by Henry Denker (*Random* 1961, o.p.), was presented on Broadway in the early 1960s.

Note: Where two dates are given below directly after the title, the first is for first publication in German, the second in English.

COMPLETE PSYCHOLOGICAL WORKS, STANDARD EDITION. Trans. under general editorship of James Strachey, advised and assisted by Freud's daughter, Anna Freud (*q.v.*). (23 vols. of text and an index vol.) *Macmillan* standard ed. 24 vols. 1953 1964 set $210.00; abstracts by Robert R. Holt *Jason Aronson* 1974 $15.00

PSYCHOLOGICAL WORKS, STANDARD EDITION. Ed. by James Strachey *Norton*

Following vols. available: The Psychopathology of Everyday Life. 1904, 1914. Trans. by Alan Tyson pap. 1971 $2.95 Jokes and Their Relation to the Unconscious. 1905. Trans. by James Strachey 1961 pap. $2.75 Totem and Taboo. 1913, 1918. Trans. by James Strachey 1952 $6.00 pap. $1.95 Leonardo da Vinci and A Memory of His Childhood. 1916. Trans. by Alan Tyson 1964 $3.50 pap. $1.95 Beyond the Pleasure Principle. 1920. Trans. by James Strachey 1975 $6.95 pap. $1.95 Group Psychology and the Analysis of the Ego. 1922. Trans. by James Strachey 1975 $6.95 pap. $1.95 The Ego and the Id. 1923, 1927. Trans. by Joan Riviere 1961 pap. $1.25 The Question of Lay Analysis: An Introduction to Psychoanalysis. 1926, 1948. Trans. by James Strachey 1950 1969 pap. $1.95 The Future of an Illusion. 1927. Trans. by James Strachey 1975 $5.95 An Autobiographical Study. 1927. Trans. by James Strachey 1963 pap. $1.95 Civilization and Its Discontents. 1930. Trans. by James Strachey 1962 $4.50 pap. $1.95 New Introductory Lectures on Psychoanalysis. 1933. Trans. by James Strachey 1965 $6.95 pap. $2.95 An Outline of Psycho-Analysis. Trans. by James Strachey 1949 pap. $1.25 On Dreams. Trans. by James Strachey 1952 pap. 1962 $1.25 Complete Introductory Lectures on Psychoanalysis. Trans. by James Strachey 1966 $14.95 ["A representative compilation of the whole range of Freud's ideas"—(*LJ*).] On the History of the Psycho-Analytic Movement. Trans. by Joan Riviere 1966 $3.50 pap. $2.25

THE COLLECTED PAPERS. Trans. by Joan Riviere and others; ed. by Ernest Jones *Basic Bks.* 5 vols. 1959 each $7.65 set $37.50

This is the first American edition of this valuable set, previously only available from England. The collection was made by various editors from 1924 to 1950. These reports of Freud's theoretical and clinical investigations formed the base on which he erected his larger, more famous works. A necessity for young psychoanalysts, it is also very stimulating reading for laymen interested in the field.

THE COLLECTED PAPERS. Ed. with introd. by Philip Reiff. *Macmillan* Collier Bks. 10 vols. 1963 pap. various prices as follows:

Vol. 1 History of the Psychoanalytic Movement $1.25 Vol. 2 Early Psychoanalytic Writings o.p. Vol. 3 Therapy and Technique $1.50 Vol. 4 Dora—An Analysis of a Case of Hysteria $1.25 Vol. 5 Sexual Enlightenment of Children $1.50 Vol. 6 General Psychological Theory $1.25 Vol. 7 Three Case Histories $1.50 Vol. 8 Sexuality and the Psychology of Love $1.50 Vol. 9 Character and Culture o.p. Vol. 10 Studies in Parapsychology $.95. The paperback edition of the *Basic Bks.* "Collected Papers," immediately above.

THE BASIC WRITINGS. Trans. and ed. with introd. by Abraham A. Brill *Random* Modern Lib. Giants 1938 $4.95

GENERAL SELECTION FROM THE WORKS OF SIGMUND FREUD. Ed. by John Rickman *Doubleday* 1957 Anchor Bks. pap. $1.95; *Liveright* $6.95

FREUD AND PSYCHOLOGY: Selected Readings. Ed. by S. G. Lee and M. Herbert *Penguin* 1971 pap. $1.75; *Peter Smith* $4.00

THE INTERPRETATION OF DREAMS. 1900 1913. *Random* Modern Lib. 1950 $2.95

THE INTERPRETATION OF DREAMS. Trans. and ed. by James Strachey *Basic Bks.* 1955 $10.00; *Avon Bks.* 1967 pap. $1.95

A variorum edition "incorporating all the alterations, additions, and deletions made by the author in the German text over a 30-year period, copiously annotated by the translator, with completely recast bibliographies, new appendixes, indexes of dreams, and a massive general index. . . . An essential acquisition"—(LJ).

THE PSYCHOPATHOLOGY OF EVERYDAY LIFE. 1904 1914. *New Am. Lib.* Mentor Bks. 1952 pap. $1.25

THREE ESSAYS ON THE THEORY OF SEXUALITY. 1905. Trans. and newly ed. by James Strachey *Basic Bks.* rev. ed. 1962 $7.95; *Avon Bks.* 1971 pap. $1.65; (with title "Three Contributions to the Theory of Sex") trans. by Abraham A. Brill 1910 *Dutton* Everyman's 1962 pap. $1.25; *Johnson Reprint* repr. of 1930 ed. $14.00

SELECTED PAPERS ON HYSTERIA AND OTHER PSYCHONEUROSES. Trans. by Abraham A. Brill. 1909. *Johnson Reprint* $14.00

A GENERAL INTRODUCTION TO PSYCHOANALYSIS. 1910. Authorized English trans. of the rev. ed. by Joan Riviere, 1920. *Liveright* Black & Gold. Lib. 1935 $9.95; *Simon & Schuster* Pocket Bks. pap. $1.25 Touchstone-Clarion Bks. rev. ed. 1969 pap. $2.95

TOTEM AND TABOO. 1913 1918. Trans. by Abraham A. Brill *Random* Vintage Bks. pap. $1.65. Freud attempts to trace the origins of religion and morality.

HISTORY OF THE PSYCHO-ANALYTIC MOVEMENT. Trans. by Abraham A. Brill. 1917. *Johnson Reprint* $10.50

BEYOND THE PLEASURE PRINCIPLE. 1920. Trans. by James Strachey *Liveright* 1922 new ed. 1970 $3.95 pap. $1.95

GROUP PSYCHOLOGY AND THE ANALYSIS OF THE EGO. Trans. by James Strachey *Liveright* 1922 $3.95

THE FUTURE OF AN ILLUSION. 1927. Trans. by W. D. Robson-Scott *Liveright* 1949 $4.95; *Doubleday* Anchor Bks. 1957 pap. $1.45

LEONARDO DA VINCI: A Study in Psychosexuality. 1932. *Random* Vintage Bks. 1966 pap. $1.95

PROBLEM OF ANXIETY. *Norton* 1936 pap. $1.25

MOSES AND MONOTHEISM. 1939. Ed. by Katherine Jones *Random* Vintage Bks. 1955 pap. $1.95

FREUD: A Dictionary of Psychoanalysis. Ed. by Nandor Fodor and Frank Gaynor; introd. by Theodor Reik. 1950. *Greenwood* $9.50

ON APHASIA. Trans. by E. Stengel *International Univs. Press* 1953 $7.50

CIVILIZATION, WAR AND DEATH. Ed. by John Rickman *Hillary House* 1953 $25.00

ORIGIN AND DEVELOPMENT OF PSYCHOANALYSIS. *Regnery* 1960 pap. $1.45

THE COCAINE PAPERS. Ed. by Robert Byck *New Am. Lib.* Meridian Bks. pap. $4.95; *Spring Pubns.* 1963 $3.00; *Stonehill Pub. Co.* 1974 $14.95
"Provides access to some psycho-pharmacologic notes of 19th century authors who first studied cocaine"—(LJ).

DELUSION AND DREAM AND OTHER ESSAYS. *Beacon* 1966 pap. $2.95

INFANTILE CEREBRAL PARALYSIS. Trans. by Lester A. Russin *Univ. of Miami Press* 1968 $15.00

CREATIVITY AND THE UNCONSCIOUS: Papers on the Psychology of Art, Literature, Love, Religion. *Harper* Torchbks. pap. $2.75

A YOUNG GIRL'S DIARY. *Gordon Press* $29.95

LETTERS. Trans. by James and Tania Stern; ed. by Ernst L. Freud *Basic Bks.* 1960 $12.75 pap. 1975 $5.95
From about 4,000 letters, Freud's youngest son selected 315 of a personal kind to present a portrait of the man. The letters are arranged chronologically from June 1873, to September 1939. Recipients include friends and disciples, members of Freud's family, and such noted persons as Einstein, Thomas Mann, Rolland, Schnitzler, H. G. Wells, and Arnold and Stefan Zweig. "There is a greatness, a consistency of style. Those virtues which mark Freud's genius—his

manifold curiosity; his swiftness of judgment, his tenacity—are exhibited throughout his letters, though in a minor, private key"—(*Nation*).

THE ORIGINS OF PSYCHOANALYSIS: Sigmund Freud's Letters to Wilhelm Fliess, Drafts and Notes (1887–1902). Ed. by Marie Bonaparte, Anna Freud and Ernst Kris *Basic Bks.* 1954 $10.00

PSYCHOANALYSIS AND FAITH: The Letters of Sigmund Freud and Oskar Pfister. Trans. by Eric Mosbacher *Basic Bks.* 1963 $5.95. The correspondence between Freud, the "unrepentant heretic," and a Protestant clergyman; published for the first time.

A PSYCHO-ANALYTIC DIALOGUE: The Letters of Sigmund Freud and Karl Abraham, 1907–1926. Trans. by Bernard Marsh and Hilda C. Abraham; ed. with pref. by Hilda C. Abraham and Ernst L. Freud; introd. by Edward Glover *Basic Bks.* 1966 $7.50

"In their letters—which Dr. Glover points out read 'like the index to a textbook of abnormal (and normal) psychology'—the two analysts traded ideas about many of the principal ideas and subjects Freud was investigating. . . . Richly rewarding"—(*LJ*).

LETTERS OF SIGMUND FREUD AND ARNOLD ZWEIG. Ed. by Ernst L. Freud *Harcourt* 1971 pap. $2.35

SIGMUND FREUD AND LOU ANDREAS-SALOME: Letters. Ed. by Ernst Pfeiffer *Harcourt* 1972 $7.95

THE FREUD-JUNG LETTERS: The Correspondence Between Sigmund Freud and C. G. Jung. Ed. by William McGuire; trans. by Ralph Manheim and R. F. C. Hull. Bollingen Ser. *Princeton Univ. Press* 1974 $17.50

Books about Freud

Sigmund Freud: His Personality, His Teaching and His School. By Fritz Wittels. Trans. from the German by Eden and Cedar Paul. 1924. *Bks. for Libraries* $11.50

Freud and His Time. By Fritz Wittels. *Liveright* (dist. by Norton) 1931 $6.95

The Life and Works of Sigmund Freud. By Ernest Jones. *Basic Bks.* 3 vols. 1953–1957 Vol. 1 The Formative Years and the Great Discoveries: 1856–1900 (1953) Vol. 2 Years of Maturity: 1901–1919 (1955) Vol. 3 The Last Phase: 1919–1939 (1957) each $11.00 boxed set $31.75; ed. and abr. by Lionel Trilling and Steven Marcus with introd. by Lionel Trilling 3 vols. in 1 1961 $11.00 abr. ed. pap. 1974 $4.95

The author of this great biography, "a dauntingly stupendous task," was a member of Freud's small circle of co-workers, his close friend for 40 years, Permanent President of the International Psycho-Analytic Association and founder and former editor of the *International Journal of Psychoanalysis.* Dr. Jones had at his disposal from the Freud family all the personal records and correspondence including 2,500 letters, among them the 1,500 love letters written by Freud to his future wife. Upon the publication of the last volume, Charles Rolo of the *Atlantic* said: "Dr. Jones's great achievement is that—in addition to setting on record so detailed, lucid and informed a study of Freud's personal history and his work—he has projected to the layman the inner drama that pervades Freud's life, the excitement of a revolutionary adventure of the mind." In their laudable attempt to make the three-volume monumental work more accessible to the general reader, Trilling and Marcus "have eliminated the documentation and deleted various whole chapters, most of the excursive footnotes, and some letters, but have retained whatever material is relevant to an understanding of Freud's life and character." (*See also Jones' main entry, Chapter 2, General Biography and Autobiography, this Volume.*)

Freud's Contribution to Psychiatry. By Abraham A. Brill. 1944. *Norton* 1962 pap. $1.45; *Peter Smith* $5.00; *Washington Square* 1968 pap. $.75

Sigmund Freud: Man and Father. By Martin Freud. *Vanguard* 1958 $5.00. Freud's eldest son recalls events of his childhood in a refreshing series of episodes.

Sigmund Freud's Mission: An Analysis of His Personality and Influence. By Erich Fromm. 1959. *Peter Smith* $4.75

"Brilliantly written"—(*N.Y. Times*).

Freud and Psychoanalysis. By Carl G. Jung. Vol. 4 of Jung's "Collected Works." Ed. by Herbert Read, G. Adler and others. Bollingen Ser. *Princeton Univ. Press* 1961 $11.00

Psychoanalysis: The First Ten Years 1888–1898. By Walter A. Stewart. *Macmillan* 1967 $5.95

"A delineation of Freud's theories which led to his blind alleys and an outlining of how Freud resolved his difficulties. Dr. Stewart is scholarly, detached, and dedicated to the task he has assigned himself"—(*LJ*).

Beyond the Chains of Illusion. By Erich Fromm. *Simon & Schuster* 1967 $5.95

Reich Speaks of Freud. Ed. by Mary Higgins and Chester M. Raphael. Trans. by Therese Pol Farrar, Straus 1967 $5.95 pap. $2.95

Wilhelm Reich, a student of Freud, made many contributions of his own to the field of psychoanalysis and later founded his own cult. "Amidst some of Reich's hyperbolic exaggerations, one finds here pungent descriptions of Freud's courage, his intellectuality, his Jewishness, his marriage, as well as his inner harshness and lack of interest in saving the world. . . . Much the most interesting part of [the book] consists of tape-recorded interviews which Dr. Kurt Eissler conducted in 1952 on behalf of the Freud archives [with] the surviving early analysts about their contact with Freud"—(Nation).

Freud and His Early Circle. By Vincent Brome. 1968. Apollo 1969 pap. $2.25

Mr. Brome's book concentrates not on the theoretical divergences between rival schools, though he handles them competently enough, but on the tangle of motives, temperaments, and misunderstandings of which this complex story is composed. On a subject that has generated much heat he writes with the dispassion of a historian. . . . He has produced an excellent book"—(J. W. Burrow, in SR).

Freud: Political and Social Thought. By Paul Roazen. Knopf 1968 $6.95 text ed. $4.85; Random Vintage Bks. 1970 pap. $1.95

A political scientist, in "an endeavor to develop the relationship between psychoanalysis and political science [examines] Freud's own application of his concepts and their political and social implications"—(LJ).

Freud and the Americans: The Origin and Foundation of the Psychoanalytic Movement in America 1876–1918. By Nathan G. Hale, Jr. Oxford 1971 $15.00

"In this first of a series of volumes dealing with the impact of Freud on the American scene, the author proposes to deal with . . . the state of psychiatry, neurology and sexual morality in this country before Freud's appearance at the Clark University Conference in September 1909"—(America).

Sigmund Freud. By Michael H. Duke. Makers of Modern Thought Ser. Judson Press 1972 pap. (orig.) $1.50

Fact and Fantasy in Freudian Theory. By Paul Kline. Harper (Barnes & Noble) 1972 $17.50

Freud: A Biographical Introduction. By Penelope Balogh. Scribner 1972 $6.95 pap. $2.45

Freud—The Man, His World, His Influence. Ed. by Jonathan Miller. Little 1972 $14.95

"Portrayed are Freud's Vienna—sensual, anti-Semitic, a crucible of intellect and art; as well as Freud's relationship to Marx, philosophy, child rearing, anthropology, aesthetics, morality, and surrealist art"—(LJ).

Development of Freud's Thought: From the Beginnings (1886–1900) through Id Psychology (1900–1914) to Ego Psychology (1914–1939). By Reuben Fine. Jason Aronson rev. ed. 1973 $10.00

Freud as We Knew Him. Ed. by Hendrik M. Ruitenbeek. Wayne State Univ. Press 1973 $17.50

Psychoanalytic Psychology: The Development of Freud's Thought. By Raymond E. Fancher. Norton 1973 $8.95 pap. $2.95

Sigmund Freud. By Paul Roazen. Makers of Modern Social Science Ser. Prentice-Hall Spectrum Bks. 1973 $6.95 pap. $2.95

Freud and His Followers. By Paul Roazen. Knopf 1975 $15.00

[Roazen's] book is "scholarly but not forbidding, well-written, of importance to specialists, but also fascinating for anyone interested in the history of psychology or in the personalities of Freud's circle"—(LJ).

ROYCE, JOSIAH. 1856–1916. See Chapter 5, Philosophy, this Volume.

DEWEY, JOHN. 1859–1952. See Chapter 5, Philosophy, this Volume.

ELLIS, HAVELOCK. 1859–1939.

Ellis's works fall under many heads: science, art, travel, poetry, essays. "It is doubtful whether any [recent] writer has attained equal eminence in fields so widely differentiated." His most important work was his "Studies in the Psychology of Sex," which, when first published in England, was the subject of legal battles as to its "obscenity." However, the book helped to change public attitudes toward sex and greatly contributed to the study of sexual problems. Ellis interpreted his data from a biological rather than a clinical viewpoint. Freud, who drew from his material, regarded Ellis's conclusions as "happy anticipations of our own deductions." Ellis's most popular philosophical work is "The Dance of Life," a survey of modern civilization giving the author's own outlook on life. Many of the earlier books are out of print. The son of a British ship's captain, he spent much of his childhood in the Pacific. He became a teacher in New South Wales, then studied medicine in London, eventually devoting himself to research and writing in England. His autobiography "My Life" (1939), "On Life and Sex" and "Sex and Marriage" (1952) are out of print.

STUDIES IN THE PSYCHOLOGY OF SEX. 1898. *Random* 2 vols. 1936 each $13.50 boxed set
$25.00

WORLD OF DREAMS. 1922. *Gale Research Co.* 1971 $13.50

THE DANCE OF LIFE. 1923. *Greenwood* 1973 $15.00

PSYCHOLOGY OF SEX: A Manual for Students. 1933. *New Am. Lib.* Mentor Bks. pap. $.95

FROM ROUSSEAU TO PROUST. 1935. *Bks. for Libraries* 1968 $11.75

WOODWORTH, ROBERT SESSIONS.   1869–1962.

"Dynamic" psychology, as interpreted and developed by the former professor of psychology at
Columbia, is a "modest unaggressive system," and the result of the contributions of many
schools—a psychology of cause and effect. "What the psychologist really wants to know, he
maintains, is why people do the things they do—how they learn and think, why they feel as they
feel and act as they act." In 1956 Professor Woodworth received the Gold Medal from the
American Psychological Foundation; his "Psychology: A Study of Mental Life" written with
Donald George Marquis (*Holt* 1921) is out of print.

DYNAMIC PSYCHOLOGY. 1918. Classics in Psychology Ser. *Arno* $11.00

(With Harold Schlosberg). EXPERIMENTAL PSYCHOLOGY. *Holt* 1938 rev. ed. 1954 $14.75

HEREDITY AND ENVIRONMENT: A Critical Survey of Recently Published Material on
Twin and Foster Children. 1941. *Social Science Research Council* pap. $.90

(With M. R. Sheehan). CONTEMPORARY SCHOOLS OF PSYCHOLOGY. *Ronald* 1948 3rd ed.
1964 $8.50

ADLER, ALFRED.   1870–1937.

This Austrian psychiatrist founded the school of individual psychology. He was associated with
the early group of Freud's followers; he later left it, rejecting Freud's emphasis on the (biological)
sexual drives as the chief psychological determinants of personality. Adler saw personality
disorders as arising from feelings of inferiority or inadequacy in the ability to reach one's life
goals. For Adler the processes of socialization within one's culture are the important factors in
determining a character style.

After his break with Freud in 1911, Adler founded his own school. In 1919 he set up the first
child guidance clinic within the Vienna school system. In 1935 he moved to the United States,
where he spent the rest of his life in psychiatric practice and the giving of lectures. He, with Jung,
was one of the two most important contemporary dissenters from Freud. Rudolf Dreikurs'
"Fundamentals of Adlerian Psychology" (with a foreword by Adler, 1950, o.p.) is an excellent
summary for the layman; it was originally published in German in 1933.

THE INDIVIDUAL PSYCHOLOGY OF ALFRED ADLER: A Systematic Presentation in Selections from His Writings. Ed. and annotated by Heinz L. and Rowena R. Ansbacher
Basic Bks. 1956 $12.50; *Harper* Torchbks. pap. $4.45

SUPERIORITY AND SOCIAL INTEREST: A Collection of Later Writings. Ed. by Heinz L. and
Rowena R. Ansbacher *Northwestern Univ. Press* 1964 2nd rev. ed. 1970 $15.00; *Viking*
Compass Bks. 1973 pap. $3.95

THE PRACTICE AND THEORY OF INDIVIDUAL PSYCHOLOGY. 1923. Trans. by P. Radin
Humanities Press rev. ed. 1971 $13.25; *Littlefield* 2nd ed. 1969 pap. $2.95

THE NEUROTIC CONSTITUTION. 1926. *Bks. for Libraries* 1972 $15.75

UNDERSTANDING HUMAN NATURE. 1927. Trans. by W. B. Wolfe *Humanities Press* 1962
text ed. $10.50; *Fawcett* Premier Bks. 1968 pap. $.95

THE PROBLEMS OF NEUROSIS: A Book of Case Histories. 1929. *Harper* Torchbks. pap.
$2.25

THE SCIENCE OF LIVING. 1929. Ed. by Heinz L. Ansbacher *Doubleday* Anchor Bks. (orig.)
1969 pap. $1.50

THE EDUCATION OF CHILDREN. 1930. Trans. by E. F. Jensen. *Regnery* 1970 pap. $2.95

WHAT LIFE SHOULD MEAN TO YOU. 1931. *Putnam* Capricorn Bks. 1959 pap. $2.25

SOCIAL INTEREST: A Challenge to Mankind. *Putnam* 1939 Capricorn Bks. 1964 pap.
$1.85

EDUCATION OF THE INDIVIDUAL. 1958. *Greenwood* $9.00

THE PROBLEM CHILD. *Putnam* Capricorn Giant 1963 pap. $1.95

Books about Adler

Inferiority Feelings in the Individual and the Group. By F. Oliver Brachfeld. Trans. from the French by Marjorie Gabain. 1951. *Greenwood* 1970 $12.25

Alfred Adler: The Man and His Work. By Hertha Orgler. *Liveright* 1963 $6.95; *New Am. Lib.* 1972 pap. $1.75

Alfred Adler: His Influence on Psychology Today. Ed. by the American Society of Adlerian Psychology and Harold Mosak. *Noyes Press* 1973 $12.50

Masks of Loneliness: Alfred Adler in Perspective. By Manes Sperber. *Macmillan* 1974 $7.95

McDOUGALL, WILLIAM. 1871–1938.

At one time the foremost psychologist in all the English-speaking countries, McDougall was an American, born in England, who taught at Harvard and later at Duke University. An early interest in the relationship of physiology to psychology influenced the experiments he conducted for 17 years on the heredity of acquired characteristics. McDougall understood social psychology as being chiefly determined by instinct. His "Introduction to Social Psychology," when first published, received wide praise from the medical and lay world alike. By the 1920's however, the strong reaction against instinctual theories of behavior had reduced the stature of his work, and his later books are now o.p.

AN INTRODUCTION TO SOCIAL PSYCHOLOGY. 1908. *Harper* (Barnes & Noble) 30th ed. 1961 pap. $3.75; *Milford House* 1973 $40.00

BODY AND MIND. 1911. *Greenwood* 1974 $16.25

THE GROUP MIND. 1920. Classics in Psychology Ser. *Arno* 2nd ed. $20.00

RELIGION AND THE SCIENCES OF LIFE: With Other Essays on Allied Topics. 1934. *Bks. for Libraries* $11.75

BRILL, A(BRAHAM) A(RDEN). 1874–1948.

Brill was the founder of psychoanalysis in America. He first brought Freud's teaching to this country, and first translated his works into English. He also translated Jung. He was born in Austria and came to the United States alone at the age of 13. He graduated from New York University, took his medical degree at Columbia, taught at both universities and was a practicing psychoanalyst. "Basic Principles of Psychoanalysis" is the classic handbook of psychoanalysis for laymen.

PSYCHOANALYSIS: Its Theories and Practical Applications. 1913. *Arno* 1972 $15.00

FUNDAMENTAL CONCEPTIONS OF PSYCHOANALYSIS. 1921. *Arno* 1973 $16.00

FREUD'S CONTRIBUTION TO PSYCHIATRY. 1944. *Norton* 1962 pap. $1.45; *Peter Smith* $5.00

BASIC PRINCIPLES OF PSYCHOANALYSIS. 1949. *Simon & Schuster* (Washington Square) 1968 pap. $1.25

THORNDIKE, EDWARD LEE. 1874–1949.

Educational psychologist and author of the intelligence test bearing his name, Thorndike is also known for his work in educational statistics. He studied under William James at Harvard and carried out experiments on animal intelligence with some chickens he kept in the basement of James's house—his landlady having refused to let him keep them in his room! He took his M.A. at Harvard. Thorndike's first papers were on "The Psychology of Fishes" and "The Mental Life of Monkeys." When he took his doctor's degree at Columbia in 1898 the statistical treatment of test results in psychology was a novelty. He went to Teachers College in 1899 as instructor in genetic psychology. He believed that "everything that exists exists in quantity" and could be measured as a key to scientific progress in education. He devised scales for measuring excellence of reading, English composition, handwriting and drawing and intelligence tests for various grade levels. The former Dean of Teachers College, James E. Russell, said of him: "His service to pedagogical procedure has revolutionized educational administration." Thorndike's Law of Effect, which had its origin in his early tests on animals, was strengthened by his later experiments in human learning. He concluded that the important factors in learning are repetition and reward. His techniques of animal experiment and his methods of psychological measurement were important advances in American psychology before World War I. Back in print are his books about words: "A Teacher's Word Book of the Twenty Thousand Words Found Most Frequently and Widely in General Reading for Children and Young People" (1932. *Finch Press* $12.00; *Gale Research Co.* $12.00) and "Teaching of English Suffixes" (1941. *AMS Press* $17.50).

PSYCHOLOGY AND THE SCIENCE OF EDUCATION: Selected Writings. Ed. by Geraldine M. Joncich *Teachers College Press* 1962 $5.95 pap. $2.50

SELECTED WRITINGS FROM A CONNECTIONIST'S PSYCHOLOGY. 1949. *Greenwood* $14.75

EDUCATIONAL PSYCHOLOGY. 1903. *Arno* $40.00; *Greenwood* 3 vols. 1913–1914 set $56.25; *Norwood Editions* $20.00

ANIMAL INTELLIGENCE: Experimental Studies. 1911. *Hafner* 1965 $11.95

INDIVIDUALITY. 1911. *Norwood Editions* $10.00

EDUCATION: A First Book. 1912. Classics in Psychology Ser. *Arno* $14.00; *Norwood Editions* $15.00

(With others). VENTILATION IN RELATION TO MENTAL WORK. 1916. *AMS Press* 1971 $17.50

(With others). THE MEASUREMENT OF INTELLIGENCE. 1927. Classics in Psychology Ser. *Arno* $29.00

HUMAN LEARNING. 1931. *Johnson Reprint* $10.50; *M.I.T. Press* 1967 $6.50 pap. $2.95

FUNDAMENTALS OF LEARNING. 1932. *AMS Press* 1971 $19.50

(With Institute of Educational Research, Teachers College, Columbia University). EXPERIMENTAL STUDY OF REWARDS. 1933. *AMS Press* 1974 $17.50

PSYCHOLOGY OF WANTS, INTERESTS AND ATTITUDES. 1935. *Johnson Reprint* 1970 $16.75

MAN AND HIS WORKS. 1943. *Kennikat* 1969 $7.50

HUMAN NATURE AND THE SOCIAL ORDER. Ed. and abr. by Geraldine J. Clifford *M.I.T. Press* 1970 text ed. $15.00 pap. $3.95

Books about Thorndike

Sane Positivist: A Biography of Edward L. Thorndike. By Geraldine M. Joncich. *Wesleyan Univ. Press* 1968 $25.00

JUNG, C(ARL) G(USTAV). 1875–1961.

The Swiss Dr. Jung was one of the most famous of modern psychologists and psychiatrists. Jung met Freud (*q.v.*) first in 1907 and became his foremost associate and disciple. The break came with the publication of Jung's "Psychology of the Unconscious" in 1916, which did not follow Freud's theories of the libido and the unconscious. Jung eventually rejected Freud's system of psychoanalysis for his own "Analytical Psychology." This emphasizes present conflicts rather than those from childhood; it also takes into account the conflicts arising from what Jung called the "collective unconscious"—evolutionary and cultural factors determining individual development. Jung was considered by Freud's followers as a "deserter" and a "mystic"; his theories have continued to be the topic of heated discussions. He invented the association word test and contributed the word "complex" to psychology. He first described the "introvert" and "extrovert" types. Jung's interest in the human psyche, past and present, led him to study mythology, alchemy, oriental religions and philosophies and primitive peoples. Later he became interested in parapsychology and the occult. He considered those unidentified flying objects in "Flying Saucers: A Myth of Things Seen in the Skies" (1960, o.p.). He felt that these might be a psychological projection of modern man's anxieties.

Dr. Jung was elected a fellow of the Royal Society of Medicine and given an honorary D.Sc. by Oxford University, the first psychologist to receive such an honor in England. He received honorary degrees from Harvard, the University of Calcutta, the Banaras Hindu University, the University of Allahabad in India and the University of Geneva.

COLLECTED WORKS. Ed. by Sir Herbert Read, M. Fordham and Gerhard Adler; trans. from the German by R. F. C. Hull. Bollingen Ser. *Princeton Univ. Press* 20 vols. 1953–

Vol. 1 Psychiatric Studies (1957 2nd ed. 1970) $8.50 Vol. 2 Experimental Researches, trans. by Diana Riviere (1971) $17.50 Vol. 3 Psychogenesis of Mental Disease (1960) $9.50 Vol. 4 Freud and Psychoanalysis (1961) $11.00 Vol. 5 Symbols of Transformation (1956 2nd ed. 1967) $16.00 Vol. 6 Psychological Types (1971) $15.00 Vol. 7 Two Essays on Analytical Psychology (1953 2nd ed. 1972) $11.00 pap. $3.95 Vol. 8 The Structure and Dynamics of the Psyche (1960 2nd ed. 1970) $15.00 Vol. 9 Pt. 1 Archetypes and the Collective Unconscious (1959 2nd ed. 1969) $15.00 Vol. 9 Pt. 2 Aion: Researches into the Phenomenology of the Self (1958 2nd ed. 1968) $10.00 Vol. 10 Civilization in Transition (1964) $15.00 Vol. 11 Psychology and Religion: West and East (1958 2nd ed. 1970) $15.00 Vol. 12 Psychology and Alchemy with previously unpublished pref. by Jung

(1953 2nd ed. 1968) $15.00 Vol. 13 Alchemical Studies (1968) $12.50 Vol. 14 Mysterium Coniunctionis (1963 2nd ed. 1970) $15.00 Vol. 15 The Spirit in Man, Art, and Literature (includes essays on Joyce and Picasso) (1966 2nd ed. 1971) $7.50 pap. $1.95 Vol. 16 The Practice of Psychotherapy (1954 2nd ed. 1966) $11.50 Vol. 17 The Development of Personality (1954) $7.50 Vol. 18 The Symbolic Life (1975) $20.00 Vol. 19 Bibliography of Jung's Writings and Vol. 20 General Index (in prep.)

Extracts of some of the volumes of the Bollingen edition of "The Collected Works" are available from Princeton Univ. Press in paper editions as follows:

On the Nature of the Psyche. Extracted from Vol. 8 1969 $2.95
The Psychology of the Transference. Extracted from Vol. 16 $2.95
Psychology and Education. Extracted from Vol. 17 $2.95
Four Archetypes. Extracted from Vol. 9 Pt. 1 $2.45
Mandala Symbolism. Extracted from Vol. 9 Pt. 1 1972 $3.95
Answer to Job. Extracted from Vol. 11 1972 $2.95
Synchronicity: An Acausal Connecting Principle. Extracted from Vol. 8 1973 $2.45
Dreams. Extracted from Vols. 4, 8, 12 and 16 1973 $3.95
The Psychoanalytic Years. Extracted from Vols. 2, 4 and 17 1974 $2.95
The Psychology of Dementia Praecox. Extracted from Vol. 3 1974 $2.95
Critique of Psychoanalysis. Extracted from Vols. 4 and 18 1975 $2.95
Psychology and the Occult. Extracted from Vols. 1, 8 and 18 (in prep.)

BASIC WRITINGS. Ed. by Violet de Laszlo *Random* Modern Lib. 1959 $3.95

PSYCHOLOGICAL REFLECTIONS: A New Anthology of His Writings, 1905–1961. Ed. by Jolande Jacobi and R. F. C. Hull Bollingen Ser. *Princeton Univ. Press* 1953 1970 $10.00 pap. $2.95

PSYCHE AND SYMBOL: A Selection from the Writings of C. G. Jung. Ed. by Violet de Laszlo *Doubleday* Anchor Bks. (orig.) 1958 pap. $2.95

THE PORTABLE JUNG. Ed. by Joseph Campbell *Viking* 1971 $7.95 pap. $3.25

THE PSYCHOLOGY OF DEMENTIA PRAECOX. 1909. *Johnson Reprint* $10.50

THEORY OF PSYCHOANALYSIS. 1915. *Johnson Reprint* $10.50

MODERN MAN IN SEARCH OF A SOUL. Trans. by W. S. Dell and C. F. Baynes *Harcourt* 1933 Harvest Bks. 1955 pap. $1.75

ANALYTICAL PSYCHOLOGY: Its Theory and Practice. 1935. *Pantheon Bks.* 1968 $6.95; *Random* Vintage Bks. 1970 pap. $1.95

(With Carl Kerényi). ESSAYS ON A SCIENCE OF MYTHOLOGY: The Myths of the Divine Child and the Divine Maiden. 1949. Bollingen Ser. *Princeton Univ. Press* 1969 $8.50 pap. $2.95

THE UNDISCOVERED SELF. Trans. by R. F. C. Hull *Little-Atlantic* 1958 $4.75 pap. $2.45; *New Am. Lib.* 1974 pap. $.95. An essay on modern man's predicament. "Most profound and stimulating little book."

THE FREUD-JUNG LETTERS: The Correspondence Between Sigmund Freud and C. G. Jung. Ed. by William McGuire; trans. by Ralph Manheim and Richard F. C. Hull Bollingen Ser. *Princeton Univ. Press* 1974 $17.50

LETTERS 1906–1950. Ed. by Gerhard Adler and Aniela Jaffé; trans. by Richard F. C. Hull Bollingen Ser. *Princeton Univ. Press* 1973 $17.50

"Over 900 letters have been selected from over 1600 written between 1906 and 1950 to more than 500 different persons of prominence. The letters were often the medium for communicating his ideas to the outside world and for rectifying misinterpretations that might have no other means of correction"—*(Choice)*.

MEMORIES, DREAMS, REFLECTIONS. Recorded and ed. by Aniela Jaffé; trans. by Richard and Clara Winston *Pantheon Bks.* 1963 rev. ed. 1973 $10.00; *Random* Vintage Bks. pap. $2.95

This long, profound, absorbing autobiographical book, described as an "interior biography," is now accessible, in its language and its thought, to the layman as well as to psychologists. It is mostly written from thorough interviews, which the editor began with Jung in 1957, but four chapters, including those on his childhood and his skepticism about theology, were written by Jung himself.

Books about Jung

The Psychology of C. G. Jung. By Jolande F. Jacobi. Trans. from the German by Ralph Manheim *Yale Univ. Press* 1943 new ed. 1963 $10.00 pap. $3.25

What Jung Really Said. By E. A. Bennet. *Schocken* 1967 $6.00 pap. $1.95

"Mr. Bennet, a psychotherapist and friend of the late Dr. Jung, reviews Jung's work as it developed: first, with Bleuler and Janet; then with Freud, who had the most influence on him; and finally, his own independent work, as creator and leader of a new and influential school of thought and therapy. . . . A well-written book, highly recommended"—*(LJ)*.

The Way of Individuation. By Jolande Jacobi. Trans. by R. F. C. Hull *Harcourt* 1967 $4.75

"Dr. Jacobi is well known as a systematic expositer of Jung's ideas. This book presents in nontechnical fashion for the educated layman a discussion of Jung's concept, individuation, the innate tendency of an individual to realize himself as a unique, whole person"—*(LJ)*.

Jung's Contribution to Our Time: The Collected Papers of Eleanor Bertine. Ed. by Elizabeth C. Rohrbach *Putnam* 1968 $6.50

Reveal "the distillate of a life's dedication to psychotherapy . . . framed in Jung's analytical psychology"—*(LJ)*.

Modern Psychology: The Teachings of Carl Gustav Jung. By David Cox. Everyday Handbooks Ser. *Harper* (Barnes & Noble) 1968 pap. $1.95

From the Life and Work of C. G. Jung. By Aniela Jaffé. Trans. from the German by Richard F. C. Hull *Harper* 1971 $8.50 pap. $2.25

The Myth of Meaning. By Aniela Jaffé. Trans. by R. F. C. Hull *Putnam* 1971 $7.00

"The author, an analytical psychologist and personal secretary to Carl Jung during his last years, devotes herself to the problem of explaining Jung's main interest—the meaning and aim of human existence"—*(LJ)*.

The Feminine in Jungian Psychology and in Christian Theology. By Ann Belford Ulanov. *Northwestern Univ. Press* 1971 $10.50

The author's work "revolves around Jung's approach to and the structure of the psyche, his polaric but common concern for the symbols and functions of the psyche, his concept of the feminine in both male and female, and the concept of the feminine as it relates to the religious function and the doctrine of man, God and Christ, and the Spirit"—*(Choice)*.

The Great Mother: An Analysis of the Archetype. By Erich Neumann. Trans. by Ralph Manheim Bollinger Ser. *Princeton Univ. Press* 1972 $13.50 pap. $3.95

A Primer of Jungian Psychology. By Calvin S. Hall and Vernon J. Nordby. *Taplinger* 1973 $5.95; *New Am. Lib.* Mentor Bks. 1973 pap. $1.50

"The aim of this little book is 'to present Jung's concepts and theories clearly, simply, and accurately.' This the authors have done—and very competently"—*(LJ)*.

C. G. Jung. By Anthony Storr. Ed. by Frank Kermode *Viking* 1973 $5.95 pap. $1.95

This book "explains Jung's complex theories of analytical psychology in a clear, simple, understandable prose . . . Storr refers to the Collected Works frequently and in this way provides a guide to them on such topics as individuation, self, archetype, and other Jungian formulations. Enjoyable reading for the layman or the beginning student"—*(Choice)*.

C. G. Jung and the Scientific Attitude. By Edmund D. Cohen. *Philosophical Lib.* 1974 $7.50

Jung. By Laurens Van der Post. *Pantheon* 1975 $10.00

"Loaded with rich perceptions. . . . A most stimulating book"—*(PW)*.

RANK, OTTO. 1884–1939.

Considered one of the most gifted psychotherapists of his time, Rank investigated matters "beyond psychology," and became known for his energy, intellectual curiosity and self-awareness. In the years of his association with Freud (*q.v.*) from 1905 to 1925, he served as secretary to the psychoanalytic movement and it was generally assumed that Freud regarded him as his successor. Rank, however, eventually came to see the roots of all psychoneuroses in the experience of birth. This theory he described in "The Trauma of Birth." Such differences caused his break with Freud in the middle 20's, after which he lived in Paris (1926–1934) and in New York (1934–1939). He first formulated his theories about art and neurosis in the series of remarkable daybooks (1903–1904), selections from which were published for the first time in Jessie Taft's "Otto Rank" (1958, o.p.). In 1912 he helped to found *Imago*, the first European journal of psychoanalysis.

ART AND THE ARTIST: The Creative Urge and Personality Development. 1907 rev. 1932. Trans. by Charles F. Atkinson *Agathon Press* 1968 $15.00

THE MYTH OF THE BIRTH OF THE HERO: A Psychological Interpretation of Mythology. 1909. Trans. by F. Robbins and Smith Ely Jelliffe. 1914. *Johnson Reprint* $14.00; (and "Other Essays") ed. by Philip Freund *Random* Vintage Bks. 1959 pap. $1.95

(With Hans Sachs). SIGNIFICANCE OF PSYCHOANALYSIS TO THE MENTAL SCIENCES. Trans. by Charles R. Rayne. 1916. *Johnson Reprint* $14.00

THE DON JUAN LEGEND. 1924. Trans. and ed. by David G. Winter *Princeton Univ. Press* 1975 $8.50. The first English translation.

THE TRAUMA OF BIRTH. 1924. English trans. 1929. *Harper* Torchbks. 1973 pap. $2.95

MODERN EDUCATION: A Critique of Its Fundamental Ideas. 1932. Trans. by Mabel E. Moxon *Agathon Press* 1968 $9.00

WILL THERAPY and TRUTH AND REALITY. 1936. *Knopf* 1945 $7.95

BEYOND PSYCHOLOGY. 1941. *Dover* 1959 pap. $2.50; *Gannon* lib. bdg. $6.00

PSYCHOLOGY AND THE SOUL. 1950. *A. S. Barnes* Perpetua Bks. 1961 pap. $1.65

DOUBLE: A Psychoanalytic Study. Ed. by Harry Tucker, Jr. *Univ. of North Carolina Press* 1971 $5.00

HORNEY, KAREN. 1885–1952.

Dr. Horney was born in Hamburg, Germany, the daughter of a Norwegian father and a Dutch mother. While studying at medical school at the University of Berlin she became interested in psychoanalysis. She came to this country in 1932 to be assistant director of the Chicago Institute of Psychoanalysis. She then became a practicing analyst and lecturer at the New School for Social Research in New York. In 1941 she helped to found the American Institute for Psychoanalysis and held the post of dean until her death. She edited "Are You Considering Psychoanalysis?" (*Norton* 1946 pap. $2.25). Like that of other analysts, much of her work involved a restatement of Freudian theory. "I believe," she wrote in her first book, "that deference for Freud's gigantic achievements should show itself in building on the foundations that he has laid, and that in this way we can help to fulfill the possibilities which psychoanalysis has for the future, as a theory as well as a therapy." The *N.Y. Times* has said of her, however: "Much of Karen Horney's psychological theorizing has passed into common currency. . . . During the thirties and forties, [she] was a revolutionary thinker, pitting her culturally embedded, female-accented psychology against what she considered Freud's excessively male, materialistic and biologically determined theories." "New Perspectives in Psychoanalysis: Contributions to Karen Horney's Holistic Approach" (ed. with introd. by Harold Kelman, *Norton* 1965 $5.00) is a collection of her papers and edited lecture notes which emphasize the clinical and technical aspects of her theory. Some formal papers by her students and associates are also included.

THE NEUROTIC PERSONALITY OF OUR TIME. *Norton* 1937 $6.75 pap. $2.95

NEW WAYS IN PSYCHOANALYSIS. *Norton* 1939 $5.95 pap. $1.55

SELF-ANALYSIS. *Norton* 1942 $6.50 pap. $2.25

OUR INNER CONFLICTS: A Constructive Theory of Neurosis. *Norton* 1945 $6.45 pap. $1.95

NEUROSIS AND HUMAN GROWTH: A Study of Self-realization. *Norton* 1950 $6.50 pap. 1970 $2.95

FEMININE PSYCHOLOGY. Ed. with introd. by Harold Kelman *Norton* 1967 $6.95 pap. 1973 $2.95

Dr. Horney's "humanism, her ability to reason clearly and write simply are evident in this collection, which reveals her gradually evolving ideas about feminine psychology and her level-headed solutions to the problems created by distrust between the sexes. Those familiar with her books will want to add 'Feminine Psychology' to their collection. Those unfamiliar will find this an admirable introduction"—(*N.Y. Times*).

Books about Horney

Helping People: Karen Horney's Psychoanalytic Approach. By Harold Kelman. *Jason Aronson* 1971 $20.00

Development in Horney Psychoanalysis: A Selection of Articles from the *American Journal of Psychoanalysis* 1950–1970. Ed. by Rubins. *Krieger* $12.50 pap. $6.50

WERTHEIMER, MAX. 1886–1943.

Considered a "genius" by Einstein, Max Wertheimer was one of the founders of Gestalt psychology—a school strong in the 20's and 30's which has since been absorbed into other groups. It dealt with the psychology of perception—*Gestalt* in German means "shape" or "form." Wertheimer's experiments with the perception of motion "led him to the simple thesis that the perception of movement is given 'whole' in experience, and cannot be reduced to compounded sensory elements"—(Robert Thomson, in "The Pelican History of Psychology"). He and others of the school, using their backgrounds in physics and biology, made discoveries and formulated laws useful to later psychological studies of learning, remembering, thinking and judging.

Born in Prague, Wertheimer did important research at the University of Frankfurt and Berlin. He came to the United States during the rise of Hitler and joined the faculty at the New School for Social Research in New York. During his career he worked with his fellow Gestaltists Wolfgang Köhler, author of "Gestalt Psychology" (*Liveright* 1947 $8.95 pap. 1970 $3.45; *New Am. Lib.* Signet Bks. 1974 pap. $1.25), and Kurt Koffka, who wrote "Principles of Gestalt Psychology" (1935. *Harcourt* Harbinger Bks. 1967 pap. $3.95) and "The Growth of the Mind" (*Humanities Press* 2nd rev. ed. 1928 text ed. $13.75). Wertheimer's later work was in learning and learning theory.

PRODUCTIVE THINKING. Ed. by Michael Wertheimer. 1945. *Harper* rev. ed. 1959 $6.95 Torchbks. 1971 pap. $2.25

REIK, THEODOR. 1888–1969.

The Viennese-born psychoanalyst became Freud's pupil in 1910, completed the first doctor's dissertation on psychoanalysis in 1911 and took his Ph.D. in psychology at the University of Vienna in 1912. He lectured at the Vienna Psychoanalytic Institute, in Berlin and at The Hague, Holland. He came to the United States in 1938 and became an American citizen. He was the founder of the National Psychological Association for Psychoanalysis, which accepts lay analysts for membership and has programs for their training. Dr. Reik himself never had medical training. "The Question of Lay Analysis" of Freud (*q.v.*) was written to defend Reik for this lack. Dr. Reik's "Listening With the Third Ear" is a stimulating discussion of Freud's discovery of psychoanalysis, and describes in detail his own cases during 37 years of active practice. His books show great erudition and, written with literary skill, sparkle "with insights and witty profundities." He may be regarded as "the founding father of *archeological psychoanalysis*, a branch of depth psychology dedicated to the probing of archaeological and anthropological data from psychoanalytic viewpoints. The ultimate objective of this approach is to reach the 'hidden core' of prehistoric society and religion."

Out of print are: "Masochism in Sex and Society" (*Grove* 1949), "Sex in Man and Woman" (*Farrar, Straus* 1960), "The Psychology of Sex Relations" (*Grove* 1961), "The Temptation" (*Braziller* 1961), "Pagan Rites in Judaism" (*Farrar, Straus* 1963), "Voices from the Inaudible" (*Farrar, Straus* 1964), "Curiosities of the Self" (*Farrar, Straus* 1965), and "The Many Faces of Sex" (*Farrar, Straus* 1966).

LISTENING WITH THE THIRD EAR. 1948. *Pyramid Bks.* 1972 pap. $1.95

DOGMA AND COMPULSION. 1951. *Greenwood* 1973 $13.25

THE SECRET SELF. 1953. *Greenwood* 1973 $13.50

OF LOVE AND LUST. 1957. *Jason Aronson* 1974 $12.50

COMPULSIONS TO CONFESS: On the Psychoanalysis of Crime and Punishment. 1959. *Bks. for Libraries* $17.50

THE CREATION OF WOMAN: A Psychoanalytic Inquiry into the Myth of Eve. 1960. *McGraw-Hill* 1973 pap. $1.95

JEWISH WIT. 1962. *Taplinger* $6.00 pap. $2.45

Reik "has written . . . a kind of analytic joke book to illustrate a comparative social psychology of [the Jewish] people. . . . The book is fascinating reading and at the very least gives some unusual insights into the psychological aspects of the cultural heritage of a people"—(*LJ*).

THE NEED TO BE LOVED. 1963. *Bantam* 1964 pap. $.95. An examination of the many aspects of the problem from infancy to old age.

FRAGMENT OF A GREAT CONFESSION. 1965. *Greenwood* 1973 $17.50

THE SEARCH WITHIN: The Inner Experiences of a Psychoanalyst. *T. Y. Crowell* (Funk & Wagnalls) 1968 $8.95 pap. $3.95; *Jason Aronson* 1974 $12.50

MYTH AND GUILT. *Grosset* 1970 pap. $2.95

LEWIN, KURT. 1890–1947.

A Gestalt psychologist (*see Wertheimer, above*) and pioneer in social psychology, Kurt Lewin was born in Germany, studied and taught at the University of Berlin and in 1932 came to the U.S. to escape the rise of Hitlerism. His great contribution to psychology was in the field of group dynamics. He found that "it is usually easier to change individuals formed into a group than to change any one of them separately." A famous study is his comparison of autocratic and democratic group behavior, to which his experience of Nazism contributed. He made extensive use of charts and diagrams to illustrate the interactions of persons within a group or groups; this general field and practice became important in the training of American teachers. He was director of the Child Welfare Research Station at the University of Iowa and shortly before his early death helped establish the Research Centre for Group Dynamics, originally at M.I.T.—now moved to the University of Michigan.

A DYNAMIC THEORY OF PERSONALITY. 1935. *McGraw-Hill* 1945 pap. $3.45. An extension of Gestalt concepts.

THE PRINCIPLES OF TOPOLOGICAL PSYCHOLOGY. 1936. *Johnson Reprint* 1969 $24.50

CONCEPTUAL REPRESENTATION AND THE MEASUREMENT OF PSYCHOLOGICAL FORCES. 1938. Psychology Ser. *Johnson Reprint* 1968 $10.50

RESOLVING SOCIAL CONFLICTS. Ed. by Gertrude Weiss Lewin *Harper* 1948 $6.95

Books about Lewin

Practical Theorist: The Life and Work of Kurt Lewin. By Alfred J. Marrow. *Basic Bks.* 1969 $8.50

SULLIVAN, HARRY STACK. 1892–1949.

"Conceptions of Modern Psychiatry" was originally published as articles in the periodical *Psychiatry* of which Sullivan was an editor. He contributed greatly to the understanding of schizophrenia and obsessional states. As head of both the William Alanson White Foundation and the Washington School of Psychiatry he brought his view to public and professional attention that psychoanalysis "needed to be supplemented by a thoroughgoing study of the impact of cultural forces upon the personality."

CONCEPTIONS OF MODERN PSYCHIATRY. With fwd. by the author and a critical appraisal of the theory by Patrick Mullahy. 1940. *Norton* 1953 $8.50 pap. $3.95

THE INTERPERSONAL THEORY OF PSYCHIATRY. Ed. by Helen S. Perry and Mary L. Gawel; introd. by Mabel Blake Cohen *Norton* 1953 pap. $2.95

PSYCHIATRIC INTERVIEW. *Norton* 1954 $7.50 pap. 1970 $2.95

SCHIZOPHRENIA AS A HUMAN PROCESS. Introd. and commentaries by Helen Swick Perry *Norton* 1962 pap. 1974 $3.65

The contents of this volume, posthumously gathered, consist of the early work of Dr. Sullivan when he was associated with the Sheppard and Enoch Pratt Hospital. He was thoroughly familiar with Freud, "but he had the freedom to go beyond and to apply and to originate new approaches to mental illness."

THE FUSION OF PSYCHIATRY AND SOCIAL SCIENCE. Introd. by Helen Swick Perry *Norton* 1964 pap. 1971 $3.45

Here Sullivan "makes some sorties into sociology and tries to tie his psychoanalytic theories into the workings of society as a culture made up of subcultures with interaction of one on the other and vice versa"—(*LJ*).

PERSONAL PSYCHOPATHOLOGY: Early Formulations. *Norton* 1972 $12.50

CLINICAL STUDIES IN PSYCHIATRY. Ed. by Helen S. Perry *Norton* 1973 pap. $3.65

Books about Sullivan

Psychoanalysis and Interpersonal Psychiatry: The Contributions of Harry Stack Sullivan. Ed. by Patrick Mullahy. *Jason Aronson* 1967 $6.95

The Conditions of Human Growth. By Jane Pearce, M.D. and Saul Newton. *Citadel Press* 1969 $6.95 pap. $3.95

Dr. Jane Pearce and Saul Newton, Directors of the Sullivan Institute for Research in Psychoanalysis, bring together in this volume most of the basic theory of Harry Stack Sullivan, as well as their own experiences and formulations. It "should prove stimulating, not only to the followers of Sullivan's evolution, but to non-Sullivanians as well. The volume suffers from the lack of an index, a curious omission from an otherwise careful and thoughtful piece of work. It is recommended for all collections in the psychiatric and clinical psychological fields, as well as general collections for the informed layman who wants an overview of the interpersonal theory of the Sullivan school"—(*LJ*).

The Beginnings of Modern American Psychiatry: The Ideas of Harry Stack Sullivan. By Patrick Mullahy. *Houghton* Sentry Bks. 1973 pap. $4.95

MENNINGER, KARL (AUGUSTUS). 1893–

The Menninger Clinic was founded in Topeka, Kansas in 1920 by Karl and his father, Charles, and in 1926 they were joined by Karl's brother, William (1899–1966, author of "A Psychiatrist for a Troubled World: Selected Papers," *Viking* 1967, o.p.). The Menninger Foundation for the purpose of research, training and public education in psychiatry, started in 1941, has become a psychiatric center of the United States. "The Menninger Story," written with vividness and grace by Walker Winslow (1956, o.p.), shows how "the members of this Kansas family built up their Foundation, became individually famous in the process, and influenced the practice and development of psychiatry throughout the world." Karl Menninger was instrumental in founding the Winter Veterans' Administration Hospital at the close of World War II. It functioned not only as a hospital but as the center of the largest psychiatric training program in the world. "The Crime of Punishment" attracted much attention (and some controversy) in 1968. A former professor of criminology and an officer of the American League to Abolish Capital Punishment, Dr. Menninger feels that there may be less violence today than there was 100 years ago, but better reported. "We need criminals to identify ourselves with," he has said, "to secretly envy and to stoutly punish." His plea is for humane, constructive treatment in place of vengeance, and an end to public apathy. The "controlling" of crime by "deterrence," he says, makes "getting caught the unthinkable thing" for offenders—(as quoted in the *N.Y. Times*).

Professional works by Dr. Menninger include "A Manual for Psychiatric Case Study" (*Grune* 1952, o.p.); (with Philip S. Holzman) "Theory of Psychoanalytic Technique" (*Basic Bks.* 1958 2nd ed. 1973 $7.95; *Harper* Torchbks. pap. $2.25); and (with Seward Hiltner) "Constructive Aspects of Anxiety" (*Abingdon* 1963, o.p.). With G. Devereux, Dr. Menninger prepared a "Guide to Psychiatric Books: With a Suggested Basic Reading List" (*Grune* 1920 3rd ed. 1972 $11.50). The books of both brothers are written with great clarity and human sympathy. They have done much to dispel "public misunderstanding and doubt about the wisdom of looking into mental and emotional states as an essential approach to the healing of disease, both organic and functional."

THE HUMAN MIND. *Knopf* 1930 3rd rev. and enl. ed. 1945 $10.00

MAN AGAINST HIMSELF. *Harcourt* 1938 $12.50 Harvest Bks. 1956 pap. $2.15

(With Jeannetta L. Menninger). LOVE AGAINST HATE. *Harcourt* 1942 1959 $9.50 Harvest Bks. pap. $2.45

(With Martin Mayman and Paul Pruyser). THE VITAL BALANCE: The Life Process in Mental Health and Illness. *Viking* 1963 Compass Bks. 1967 pap. $2.65

With two psychologists at the Menninger Clinic, Dr. Menninger presents to the layman his hopeful new unitary concept of mental illness, which treats all mental health problems as aspects of the same basic disorder.

THE CRIME OF PUNISHMENT. *Viking* 1968 $6.95 Compass Bks. pap. $1.95

This, an expansion and rewriting of the Isaac Ray Award lectures given by Dr. Menninger at Columbia University in 1963 and 1964, and at the University of Kansas in 1966, indicts the U.S. penal system and presents proposals for its reform. Menninger speaks out persuasively against this system with facts about police, courts, judges, jails, lawyers, psychiatrists, many case histories and, above all, with the immense background and mature wisdom of an eminent psychiatrist"— (*LJ*).

FREUD, ANNA. 1895–

Anna Freud, daughter of the famous Sigmund, has been instrumental in carrying on the work and studies of her father. An exponent of orthodox Freudian theory, she wrote "Psychoanalysis for Teachers and Parents" to explain his basic theory to the general public and layman. It is a charming exposition and reminds us, in part by the fact that we recognize so much of it as familiar, of the tremendous impact Freud has had on the general culture of the 20th-century Western world as well as the understanding and healing his work made possible for troubled human beings. Deeply interested in the problems of children, Anna Freud organized a residential war nursery for homeless youngsters during World War II and has for many years directed the Hampstead Child Therapy Clinic in London, England, where she makes her home.

Although she lacks medical training, her vast experience and lucid writing have earned her the respect of many physicians and medical institutions. Some of her most important work has been done on the functioning of the ego in normal as well as disturbed children.

WRITINGS. *International Univs. Press* 7 vols. 1937–74 Vol. 1 Introduction to Psychoanalysis: Lectures for Child Analysts and Teachers, 1922–35 (1974) $7.50 Vol. 2 The Ego and the Mechanism of Defense (1937 rev. ed. 1967) $6.50 Vol. 3 Infants without Families: Reports on the Hampstead Nurseries (1973) $17.50 Vol. 4 Indications for Child Analysis and Other Papers (1968) $15.00 Vol. 5 Research at the Hampstead Child-Therapy Clinic and Other Papers, 1956–1965 (1969) $17.50 Vol. 6 Normality and Pathology in Childhood: Assessments of Development (1966) $8.00 Vol. 7 Problems of Psychoanalytic Training, Diagnosis and the Techniques of Therapy (1971) $12.50

PSYCHOANALYSIS FOR TEACHERS AND PARENTS. Trans. by Barbara Low *Emerson Bks.* 1935 $4.25; *Beacon* 1960 pap. $2.95

(With Dorothy T. Burlingham). WAR AND CHILDREN. Ed. by Philip R. Lehrman. 1943. *Greenwood* 1973 $9.25

THE PSYCHOANALYTICAL TREATMENT OF CHILDREN: Lectures and Essays. 1946. *International Univs. Press* 1965 $7.00; *Schocken* 1964 pap. $1.75

(With Thesi Bergmann). CHILDREN IN HOSPITAL. *International Univs. Press* 1966 $7.50 pap. $2.45

DIFFICULTIES IN THE PATH OF PSYCHOANALYSIS: A Confrontation of Past with Present Viewpoints. Freud Anniversary Lecture Ser. *International Univs. Press* 1969 $5.00

MURPHY, GARDNER. 1895–

"Although Gardner Murphy has never been a popularizer of psychology, he is one of the best-known psychologists in the United States"—("Current Biography," 1960). His "Historical Introduction to Modern Psychology" is a standard work, and other books of his are widely used as textbooks. His interests have been broad and varied. He taught psychology for 21 years at Columbia, from which he received the Butler Medal in 1932, and he was chairman of the psychology department at the City College of New York. Since 1952 he has been director of research at the Menninger Foundation, Topeka, Kansas (*see Karl Menninger*), where he himself has been especially active in the study of perceptual learning. Other projects he has supervised have been in the fields of psychotherapy and the study of infancy.

Two of his important earlier books are "Personality" and "Human Potentialities." In these he did important work toward "the new view of man"—the humanistic view sometimes referred to as the "third force" in psychology and exemplified today by Laing, Maslow, May and others. Robert Thomson writes of "Human Potentialities": "Data from almost every department of psychology were synthesized and related by Murphy to produce an eclectic, functional, 'field' theory of personality. Murphy has been concerned, after considering all the determinants of behaviour, to emphasize potentials for growth and fulfillment"—(in the "Pelican History of Psychology"). As was true of William James, Gardner Murphy has been deeply interested in psychical research and "has steadfastly maintained a sympathetic attitude [to it] on the basis of experimental data"—(Thomson). "The Challenge of Psychical Research" gives his views on the subject; it received generally favorable reviews and is a responsible work in a debatable field. He is a former president of the American Psychological Association and of the British Society for Psychical Research, London.

Also working at Menninger, sometimes in collaboration with him, is his wife, LOIS BARCLAY MURPHY, who made the Sarah Lawrence College Nursery School famous and whose work in child psychology from an affirmative approach is well known. Among her most important books are "The Widening World of Childhood" (*Basic Bks.* 1962 $10.00 pap. $3.95), based on the "coping" project at Menninger, and "Personality in Young Children" (1956, o.p.).

A wide interest in public affairs took Dr. Murphy and his wife to New Delhi as consultants for UNESCO to the Indian Ministry of Education. "In the Minds of Men" (1953, o.p.) is an account of their mission. Another fruit of their Asian experience was "Asian Psychology," an anthology of excerpts from the classics of Hinduism, Buddhism, Confucianism and other Eastern religions which seem to them related to the Asian concept of "mind" in a philosophical sense. He now lives in Washington, D.C.

HISTORICAL INTRODUCTION TO MODERN PSYCHOLOGY. 1929. *Harcourt* rev. ed. 1949 $9.50; (with Joseph K. Kovach) 3rd ed. 1972 $12.95

EXPERIMENTAL SOCIAL PSYCHOLOGY. 1937. *Greenwood* $37.75

(With Rensis Likert). PUBLIC OPINION AND THE INDIVIDUAL: A Psychological Study of Student Attitudes on Public Questions, with a Retest Five Years Later. 1938. *Russell & Russell* 1967 $10.00

PERSONALITY: A Biosocial Approach to Origins and Structure. 1947. *Basic Bks.* 1966 $15.00 pap. $4.95

INTRODUCTION TO PSYCHOLOGY. 1951. *Greenwood* $34.50

HUMAN POTENTIALITIES. *Basic Bks.* 1958 $7.50

An affirmation of man's ability to change and to find self-fulfillment through self-discovery and understanding. "An inspiring, beautifully written credo"—*(LJ)*.

THE CHALLENGE OF PSYCHICAL RESEARCH: A Primer of Parapsychology. *Harper* 1961 Colophon Bks. 1970 pap. $1.95

PSYCHOLOGICAL THOUGHT FROM PYTHAGORAS TO FREUD: An Informal Introduction. *Harcourt* Harbinger Bks. 1968 pap. $3.65

(With Herbert E. Spohn). ENCOUNTER WITH REALITY: New Forms for an Old Quest. International Ser. in the Behavioral Sciences *Houghton* 1968 $7.95

(With Lois B. Murphy, Eds.). ASIAN PSYCHOLOGY. *Basic Bks.* 1968 $7.50 pap. $3.95

(With Lois B. Murphy, Eds.). WESTERN PSYCHOLOGY FROM THE GREEKS TO WILLIAM JAMES. *Basic Bks.* 1969 $8.95

(With Morton Leeds). OUTGROWING SELF-DECEPTION. *Basic Bks.* 1974 $6.95

PIAGET, JEAN. 1896–

The Swiss psychologist Jean Piaget is a modern giant—to some a controversial one—in the study of intelligence and its development through childhood to maturity. A prolific writer on the results of his studies and their application to educational theory, he is also a director of the study of child psychology at the Institut de Psychologie et des Sciences de l'Éducation at the University of Geneva, devoted to child study and teacher training. His books have been printed in six languages and he regularly packs lecture halls in many countries, in spite of language barriers and translation difficulties. Piaget's approach to learning combines philosophy, biology and psychology, and consequently has been of interest to psychologists, philosophers and educators.

Piaget began by attempting to see the world with all its contradictions and changes through the eyes of a growing child—by interviewing children and analyzing the concepts behind their often surprising or "amusing" answers. Jerome Bruner (*q.v.*), who has done much to make Piaget known in the U.S., has said: "What he has done is to write the implicit logical theory on which the child proceeds in dealing with intellectual tasks." For Piaget, intellectual growth is a gradual, spontaneous development through four roughly divided chronological (physiological) stages, each stage bringing its own more advanced mode of thinking until, at maturity, the individual is able to cope with an adult environment. The recent American publication in English translation of more than a dozen of Piaget's difficult works is testimony as to how great is present interest in him in this country. An excellent and readable summary of his theories is to be found in David Elkind's introduction to "Six Psychological Studies."

Dr. Piaget has been a professor at the Universities of Geneva, Lausanne, Paris and Neuchâtel, where he took his doctorate in science in 1918. He is founder and director of the International Center of Genetic Epistemology in Geneva, devoted to philosophic and psychological studies. He has been affiliated with the International Office of Education and the executive council of UNESCO. A charming person—with what David Elkind has called "great intellectual presence"—Dr. Piaget is of a shaggy appearance reminiscent of Einstein. He has, not surprisingly, remarkable rapport—and is instantly popular—with children of every age.

THE PSYCHOLOGY OF INTELLIGENCE. 1950. *Littlefield* 1966 pap. $1.95; *Routledge & Kegan Paul* 1971 $7.50

(With Bärbel Inhelder). THE PSYCHOLOGY OF THE CHILD. Trans. by Helen Weaver *Basic Bks.* 1969 $7.95 pap. $3.50

"A clear, concise summary of Piaget's theoretical orientation and supporting research in child psychology"—*(Choice)*.

SCIENCE OF EDUCATION AND THE PSYCHOLOGY OF THE CHILD. Trans. by D. Coltman *Grossman* 1970 $7.50; *Viking* Compass Bks. 1971 pap. $1.95

"In this modestly sized book Piaget looks at the educational enterprise from a broad historical and international perspective ... Piaget is an innovator who should be heeded by all who are looking for new directions in education"—*(Choice)*.

STRUCTURALISM. Trans. by C. Maschler *Basic Bks.* 1970 $5.95

"In this extremely scholarly work, Piaget elaborates on the three defining marks of structuralism: wholeness, transformation, and self regulation. Structuralism is viewed as a method, not a doctrine, arrived at by a special effort of reflective abstraction"—*(Choice)*.

GENETIC EPISTEMOLOGY. Trans. by Eleanor Duckworth *Columbia* 1970 $7.00; *Norton* 1971 pap. $1.65

"By far the most helpful aid in understanding other volumes of Piaget that has been published"—(*Choice*).

PSYCHOLOGY AND EPISTEMOLOGY. Trans. by Arnold Rosin *Grossman* 1971 $7.95; *Viking* Compass Bks. 1972 pap. $1.95

(With Bärbel Inhelder). MENTAL IMAGERY IN THE CHILD: A Study of the Development of Imaginal Representation. Trans. by P. A. Chilton *Basic Bks.* 1971 $12.50

"Their first book on the topic of mental imagery . . . [provides] an avenue to understanding Piagetian concepts and procedures"—(*Choice*).

TO UNDERSTAND IS TO INVENT: The Future of Education. *Grossman* 1973 $7.50

"Consists of two essays written for UNESCO. . . . The first essay is mainly about learning science; the second on the right to free and universal education, parents' responsibilities, broad personality development, and social obligations"—(*Choice*).

THE CHILD AND REALITY: Problems of Genetic Psychology. Trans. from the French by Arnold Rosin *Grossman* 1973 $7.95; *Viking* Compass Bks. 1974 pap. $1.95

UNDERSTANDING CAUSALITY. Trans. by Donald and Marguerite Miles *Norton* 1974 $10.00

Piaget "summarizes the complete research in the relations between causality and Piagetian operations"—(*Choice*).

MAIN TRENDS IN PSYCHOLOGY. *Harper* Torchbks. 1974 pap. $1.95

(With Bärbel Inhelder). MEMORY AND INTELLIGENCE. *Basic Bks.* 1974 $12.50

"A major new work. . . . Herein the authors extend their study of children's developing ability to understand logical, numerical, and causal structures"—(*Choice*).

JEAN PIAGET: The Man and His Ideas. By Richard I. Evans. Trans. by Eleanor Duckworth *Dutton* 1973 $8.95 pap. $2.95. Transcripts of filmed and audiotaped interviews, a summary of his theories of the developing individual, Paiget's autobiography, and an essay "Genetic Epistemology" by Piaget.

Books about Piaget

The Developmental Psychology of Jean Piaget. By John H. Flavell. *Van Nostrand Reinhold* 1963 1973 pap. $6.95

This "represents the only available thorough survey of the developmental psychology of Piaget. Flavell has clearly and concisely presented the theoretical position which Piaget has developed, and has also included evidence used in formulating this stand"—(James J. Gallagher, in the *Journal of Research in Science Teaching*).

An Outline of Piaget's Developmental Psychology for Students and Teachers. By Ruth M. Beard. *Basic Bks.* 1969 $6.50; *New Am. Lib.* 1972 pap. $1.50

Piaget's Theory of Intellectual Development. By Herbert Ginsburg and Sylvia Opper. *Prentice-Hall* 1970 $6.95

The authors "manage to present Piaget clearly and interestingly, while covering the work in more depth than in most brief presentations: for instance they explain Piaget's interests in genetic epistemology, and include a fair amount of detail on his use of logic"—(*Choice*).

Understanding Piaget: An Introduction to Children's Cognitive Development. By Mary A. Pulaski. *Harper* 1971 $7.95

Introduction to Piaget. By P. G. Richmond. *Basic Bks.* 1971 $5.45 pap. $2.45

Piaget's Theory of Cognitive Development: An Introduction for Students of Psychology and Education. By Barry J. Wadsworth. *McKay* 1971 pap. $2.50

"Wadsworth uses a simple easy-to-read style to explain his interpretation of Piaget's theory of cognitive development . . . his purpose is to entice the reader to do his own research of Piaget's writings"—(*Choice*).

Brief Introduction to Piaget. By Nathan Isaacs. *Agathon Press* (dist. by Schocken) 1973 $4.95 pap. $2.75

Piagetian Research: A Handbook of Recent Studies. By Sohan Modgil. *Fernhill* 1974 $19.50

Thinking Goes to School: Piaget's Theory in Practice. By Hans G. Furth and Harry Wachs. *Oxford* 1974 $8.95

ALLPORT, GORDON W(ILLARD). 1897–1967.

Dr. Allport, professor of psychology at Harvard from 1942 until his death, did important work in the study of social attitudes and in the study of personality and its measurement. In youth he visited Sigmund Freud in Vienna, and, according to the *N.Y. Times*, was not so impressed by him as to feel there was not "room for one more behavioral scientist in the world." "It was Dr. Allport's belief that the Freudian personality theories were fitted for only a small minority of individuals. He explained his theories in 'Personality: A Psychological Interpretation' [1937, o.p.]. He once called his own ideas a form of 'empiricism restrained by reason.' 'But I've always been a maverick,' he added."

Dr. Allport was especially concerned with—and outspoken against—religious and racial prejudice. He shared "with William James and John Dewey the resolute capacity to see man as human regardless of whatever particular scientific trends may hold sway at any given moment. Allport helps fulfill his own prediction, that 'soon . . . psychology will offer an image of man more in accord with the democratic ideals by which psychologists as individuals live' "—(Rollo May, in SR). He served as president of the American Psychological Association in 1937, receiving the Gold Medal Award from that organization in 1963. Dr. Allport was editor of the *Journal of Abnormal and Social Psychology* for 12 years.

(With P. E. Vernon). STUDIES IN EXPRESSIVE MOVEMENT. 1933. *Macmillan* (Hafner) 1967 $8.95

(With Hadley Cantril). PSYCHOLOGY OF RADIO. 1935. *Arno* 1971 $15.00

USE OF PERSONAL DOCUMENTS IN PSYCHOLOGICAL SCIENCE. *Social Science Research Council* 1942 pap. $1.50

(With Leo Postman). THE PSYCHOLOGY OF RUMOR. 1946. *Russell & Russell* 1965 $8.50

THE INDIVIDUAL AND HIS RELIGION: A Psychological Interpretation. *Macmillan* 1950 pap. 1962 $1.95

THE NATURE OF PREJUDICE. *Addison-Wesley* 1954 $10.95; *Doubleday* Anchor Bks. abr. ed. 1958 pap. $2.95·

BECOMING: Basic Considerations for a Pyschology of Personality. *Yale Univ. Press* 1955 $8.50 pap. 1960 $2.25

PATTERN AND GROWTH IN PERSONALITY. *Holt* 1961 $13.00

PERSONALITY AND THE SOCIAL ENCOUNTER. *Beacon* 1964 $7.50 pap. $2.95

(Ed.). LETTERS FROM JENNY. *Harcourt* 1965 $3.50 pap. $2.45

THE PERSON IN PSYCHOLOGY. *Beacon* 1968 $9.95 pap. $2.95

Essays (1939–67) "dealing with the applications of varieties of psychological theories, the influence and relationship between personality development and social institutions, prejudice as a personality trait, and finally a biographical section which provides a biographical approach to the psychological theories of individual psychologists. The separate parts are held together by Mr. Allport's consistent interest in individual development"—(LJ).

Books about Allport

Gordon Allport: The Man and His Ideas. By Richard I. Evans. *Dutton* 1971 pap. $1.95
Gordon W. Allport's Ontopsychology of the Person. By Joseph P. Ghougassian. *Philosophical Lib.* 1972 $8.75

FROMM, ERICH. 1900–

Born in Frankfurt, Germany, Erich Fromm studied sociology and psychology at the Universities of Heidelberg, Frankfurt and Munich and received a Ph.D. from Heidelberg in 1922. After training in psychoanalysis in Munich and Berlin, he has devoted himself to consultant psychology and theoretical investigation. He first visited the United States in 1933 and is now an American citizen. His "Man for Himself" brought a "new trend in the study of man." "Escape from Freedom" studies the causes of totalitarianism. In "The Art of Loving," he discusses love generally and comes to the conclusion that although the "principle underlying capitalistic society and the principle of love are incompatible. . . . Love is the only sane and satisfactory answer to the problem of human existence." In "May Man Prevail?" he says that what is required above all is a drastic change in the U.S. attitude: "What can save us and what can help mankind is a renaissance of the spirit of humanism, of individualism, and of America's anticolonist tradition." Dr. Fromm is a humanist and a socialist in the pure sense. In "Beyond the Chains of Illusion," he shows that socialism has been badly distorted from its Marxian ideals. "He believes that our only chance to avoid the probability of nuclear war is bureaucratic capitalism toward which the West seems to be heading."

He has written brilliantly on "Sigmund Freud's Mission: An Analysis of His Personality and Influence" (*Harper* 1959 pap. 1972 $1.60; *Peter Smith* $3.75; *see under Freud*). "Zen Buddhism and Psychoanalysis" (*Harper* 1970 pap. $1.95) was written with D. T. Suzuki and Richard de Martino.

Thomas Harvey Gill has said of Fromm that he "has brilliantly performed a difficult and important task. For to translate psychiatric concepts into language intelligible to a lay audience while preserving scientific integrity is a job whose difficulty becomes apparent only to those who attempt it. Dr. Fromm has done this admirably." No longer a practicing analyst, Dr. Fromm has maintained an interest in his profession and teaches at New York University as well as at the National University of Mexico.

ESCAPE FROM FREEDOM. *Holt* (Rinehart) 1941 $7.00 1963 $7.95; *Avon Bks.* 1971 pap. $1.65

MAN FOR HIMSELF: An Inquiry into the Psychology of Ethics. *Holt* (Rinehart) 1947 $7.95 $7.00; *Fawcett* Premier Bks. 1973 pap. $1.50

PSYCHOANALYSIS AND RELIGION. *Yale Univ. Press* 1950 $8.75 pap. 1959 $1.95; *Bantam* 1967 pap. $.95

THE FORGOTTEN LANGUAGE: An Introduction to the Understanding of Dreams, Fairy Tales and Myths. *Holt* (Rinehart) 1951 $7.95; *Grove* Evergreen Bks. 1956 pap. $2.45

SANE SOCIETY. *Holt* 1955 $7.95; *Fawcett* Premier Bks. 1973 pap. $1.25

THE ART OF LOVING: An Enquiry into the Nature of Love. *Harper* 1956 $4.95 lg.-type ed. $6.95 Perenn. Lib. 1974 pap. $.95; *Bantam* 1970 pap. $.75

MARX'S CONCEPT OF MAN. *Ungar* 1961 $6.75 pap. $3.45

BEYOND THE CHAINS OF ILLUSION: My Encounter with Marx and Freud. *Simon & Schuster* 1962 $5.95 Touchstone-Clarion Bks. pap. $1.95

THE DOGMA OF CHRIST AND OTHER ESSAYS ON RELIGION, PSYCHOLOGY AND CULTURE. *Holt* 1963 $3.95. His projection of the concept of fatherhood found in psychoanalysis to the experience of early Christianity, with its emphasis on the role of the Son and the doctrine of a God made man.

YOU SHALL BE AS GODS: A Radical Interpretation of the Old Testament and Its Traditions. *Holt* 1966 $5.95; *Fawcett* Premier Bks. 1973 pap. $1.25

THE REVOLUTION OF HOPE: Toward a Humanized Technology. *Harper* 1968 $5.95 Perenn. Lib. 1974 pap. $1.25; *Bantam* 1968 pap. $.95

HEART OF MAN. *Harper* Colophon Bks. 1968 pap. $1.45 Perenn. Lib. 1971 pap. $1.25

(With Ramón Xirau, Eds.). THE NATURE OF MAN: A Reader. *Macmillan* 1968 $7.95 pap. $2.95

Selections, some 70, ranging from the Upanishads to David Riesman. "After analyzing past efforts to identify the essence of man, [the editors] put forward their own provocative suggestion, that man's capacity 'to become aware, to give account to himself of himself and of his existential situation . . . is fundamentally his nature' "—(LJ).

THE CRISIS OF PSYCHOANALYSIS. *Holt* 1970 $5.95; *Fawcett* Premier Bks. 1971 pap. $.95

(With Michael Maccoby). SOCIAL CHARACTER IN A MEXICAN VILLAGE. *Prentice-Hall* 1970 $8.95 pap. $3.45

"An empirical study of Mexican peasants by two distinguished psychoanalyists"—(*Choice*).

THE ANATOMY OF HUMAN DESTRUCTIVENESS. *Holt* new ed. 1973 $10.95; *Fawcett* Crest Bks. 1975 pap. $2.25

Books about Fromm

Man in Estrangement: Paul Tillich and Erich Fromm Compared. By Guyton B. Hammond. *Vanderbilt Univ. Press* 1965 $6.50

Dialogue with Erich Fromm. By Richard I. Evans. *Harper* 1966 $5.95
His ideas as elicited by a professor from the University of Houston "in an eminently readable manner"—(LJ).

Personality: The Need for Liberty and Rights. By Rubin Gotesky. *Libra* 1967 $3.50

Erich Fromm. By Don Hausdorff. U.S. Authors Ser. *Twayne* $6.50

ERIKSON, ERIK H(OMBURGER). 1902–

American youth by the thousands have taken up Dr. Erikson's concern with their "identity" and "identity crisis." He is a practising psychoanalyst whose theory of human development views the ego as evolving through the classical Freudian stages, which are each affected by cultural and social, as well as biological, factors. In adolescence, according to Erikson, the search for an "identity" becomes crucial. The conflicts between the self and its new view of parents as well as the world at large cause an "identity crisis"—which Erikson finds a phenomenon affecting whole peoples in ways analogous to its effect on single individuals. Most of his writings explore this theme and its ramifications.

Born in Germany, Dr. Erikson was graduated from the Vienna Psychoanalytic Institute and came to the United States in 1933. He holds an honorary degree from Harvard, where he was Professor Emeritus of Human Development and Lecturer on Psychiatry. He has done extensive research at various American universities and was for a decade a senior staff member of the Austen Riggs Center, an institute in Stockbridge, Mass., for the study and treatment of neurosis. He now lives in southern California.

CHILDHOOD AND SOCIETY. *Norton* 1950 rev. ed. 1968 $10.00 pap. $2.95

"Erikson's approach is basically that of psychoanalysis, but of psychoanalytic theory sophisticated with the insight of cultural anthropology and with a keen sense for history"—(Clyde Kluckhohn).

YOUNG MAN LUTHER: A Study in Psychoanalysis and History. *Norton* 1958 $6.50 pap. $1.95

"A unique integration of psychoanalysis, history, and the problem of the Great Man"—(Margaret Mead).

(Ed.). YOUTH: Change and Challenge. *Basic Bks.* 1963 $7.50; (with title "Challenge of Youth") *Doubleday* Anchor Bks. pap. $2.50

INSIGHT AND RESPONSIBILITY. *Norton* 1964 $7.95 pap. $1.95. Six lectures dealing with the ethical implications of psychoanalytic insight and man's responsibility to succeeding generations.

IDENTITY AND THE LIFE CYCLE. *International Univs. Press* 1967 $20.00

IDENTITY: Youth and Crisis. *Norton* 1968 $8.95 pap. $2.95

An adaptation of major essays over the last 20 years, this "offers a tremendous richness of ideas. It illuminates the striving for identity—one of the fundamentals of personality growth. It analyzes the influences on the youthful individual of social conditions and mores which create norms and tensions often harmful to psychic development. It discusses the 'inexorable standardization of American adolescence' and pinpoints *identity confusion* as leading young people into pseudo-intimacies, intellectual stagnation and impoverished interpersonal relationships"—(Hillel A. Schiller, *Book-of-the-Month Club News*).

(With Huey P. Newton). IN SEARCH OF COMMON GROUND. Ed. by Kai T. Erikson *Norton* 1973 $6.95

LIFE HISTORY AND THE HISTORICAL MOMENT. *Norton* 1975 $9.95

"A collection of previously published essays which cover a wide range of Erikson's interests . . . most date from the late 1960's and early 1970's"—(*LJ*).

Books about Erikson

Three Theories of Child Development. By Henry W. Maier. *Harper* 1965 2nd ed. 1969 $9.50
Dialogue with Erik Erikson. By Richard I. Evans. *Harper* 1967 $5.95
"A psychologist and teacher of psychology at the University of Houston has attempted to extract [Erikson's] underlying philosophies and conceptualizations by utilizing the Socratic method—that is, teaching his audience through questioning his subjects. As a corollary to Erikson's work the dialogue has value; read without previous knowledge of Erikson's theories it would be more frustrating than fruitful"—(*N.Y. Times*).
Erik H. Erikson: The Growth of His Work. By Robert Coles. *Little-Atlantic* 1970 $10.00

REDL, FRITZ. 1902–

This Austrian-born, Freudian-trained psychologist came to the United States in 1936. An advocate of "milieu therapy"—the treatment of disturbed children in groups in a permissive atmosphere—Fritz Redl is the founder and former director of the Detroit Group Project and its summer camp. He is director of Detroit's Pioneer House, a residential home for disturbed children, and Distinguished Professor of Behavioral Sciences at Wayne State University.

Much of his writing is for the professional concerned with disturbed children, but the interested teacher, parent or layman will enjoy him too, perhaps particularly his selected writings in "When We Deal with Children." He writes in a manner of his own—of "kids," "toughies," "my thieves at camp"—which sometimes irritates his professional readers but more often amuses them. He has, writes Professor Maxine Greene of Teachers College (in *SR*), "the bad manners to refuse ordinary categorization. Like the children's mental disorders he describes, he is not 'well-adjusted' in the sense of fitting into one of the standard professional slots. For one thing, he is more interested in mental health than he is in mental sickness. For another, he is preoccupied with the 'improvement' of disturbed children and with the identification of the kinds of supportive life experiences which enable such children to 'choose' their better selves. . . . Throughout ['When We Deal with Children'] there is a consciousness of continuing crisis which gives the book—for all its vitality and good humor—a tone of urgency." A psychiatric colleague writes of the same work in the *American Journal of Psychiatry:* "This book is a delight to read. For anyone who has been fortunate enough to know Professor Redl, or to have heard him present material at scientific meetings, one can relive the pleasure of the charm, wit, and highly specialized terminology of the author. He challenges, startles, and stimulates as he educates. His writings are provocative, amusing, logical, and not easily forgotten." Fritz Redl was awarded a White House citation in 1965 "for services to the mental health of the children of the United States."

(With David Wineman). CHILDREN WHO HATE: The Disorganization and Breakdown of Behavior Controls. *Macmillan* (Free Press) 1951 $6.50 pap. $2.45. A study of aggressive children.

(With David Wineman). CONTROLS FROM WITHIN: Techniques for the Treatment of the Aggressive Child. *Macmillan* (Free Press) 1952 $5.95 pap. $2.95. For leaders and professionals.

(With David Wineman). THE AGGRESSIVE CHILD. *Macmillan* (Free Press) 1957 $8.95

(With William Wattenberg). MENTAL HYGIENE IN TEACHING. *Harcourt* 2nd ed. 1959 $9.95

(With David Wineman). WHEN WE DEAL WITH CHILDREN: Selected Writings. *Macmillan* (Free Press) 1966 pap. $3.95

PRE-ADOLESCENTS: What Makes Them Tick. *Child Study Press* 1972 pap. $.75

ROGERS, CARL RANSOM.   1902–

Educated at the University of Wisconsin and Columbia University (Ph.D. 1931), Carl Rogers taught at several large universities for many years and conducted a private practice as a counseling psychologist. *Current Biography* states that "He is best known as the originator of the nondirective 'client centered' theory of psychotherapy. This prescribes a person-to-person, rather than a doctor-patient relationship between therapist and client, and allows the client to control the course, pace, and length of his own treatment." Rogers has recently incorporated many of the elements of this theory into the basic structure of encounter groups.

The author of many books and articles, Rogers has received many professional awards in official recognition of his high achievements, most notably the presidency of the American Psychological Association in 1946–1947. Presently, he is a resident fellow at the Center for Studies of the Person at La Jolla, California.

MEASURING PERSONALITY ADJUSTMENT IN CHILDREN NINE TO THIRTEEN YEARS OF AGE. 1931. *AMS Press* $17.50

COUNSELING AND PSYCHOTHERAPY. *Houghton* 1942 text ed. $9.95

CLIENT CENTERED THERAPY. *Houghton* 1951 pap. $6.95

(With Rosalind F. Dymond, Eds.). PSYCHOTHERAPY AND PERSONALITY CHANGE. *Univ. of Chicago Press* 1954 $10.75

THERAPIST'S VIEW OF PERSONAL GOALS. *Pendle Hill* 1960 (orig.) pap. $.70

ON BECOMING A PERSON. *Houghton* 1961 $8.50 pap. 1970 $3.25

(With Barry Stevens). PERSON TO PERSON: The Problem of Being Human. *Real People Press* 1967 $4.50 pap. $3.00; *Simon & Schuster* (Pocket Bks.) 1971 pap. $1.25

FREEDOM TO LEARN: A View of What Education Might Become. *Bobbs* Lib. Arts 1969 $8.95

CARL ROGERS ON ENCOUNTER GROUPS. *Harper* 1970 $5.95 pap. 1973 $2.50

BECOMING PARTNERS: Marriage and Its Alternatives. *Delacorte* 1972 $7.95; *Dell* Delta Bks. 1973 pap. $2.65

BETTELHEIM, BRUNO.   1903–

Dr. Bruno Bettelheim has had remarkable success in treating very deeply emotionally disturbed children. He is a vehement opponent of the "operant conditioning" methods of B. F. Skinner (*q.v.*) and other behaviorists. He himself once studied with Sigmund Freud. Austrian-born, Dr. Bettelheim was profoundly influenced by the year he spent in a German concentration camp during World War II. His famous "Individual and Mass Behavior" (1943, o.p.), first published in a scientific periodical and then in pamphlet form, is a study of the human personality under the stress of totalitarian terror and concentration camp living. Bettelheim sees a relationship between the disturbances of the concentration camp survivors and those of the autistic (rigidly withdrawn) children he describes in "The Empty Fortress"—because both have lived through "extreme situations."

"The Children of the Dream" describes with considerable enthusiasm the absence of neurosis in children brought up in a group of other children and cared for by adults not their parents in the Israeli *kibbutz*. Dr. Bettelheim believes that American ghetto children would benefit from this kind of experience in preference to the at best partial benefits of present Head Start and other programs designed to accelerate educational progress for the deprived.

Dr. Bettelheim was the principal of the Sonia Shankman Orthogenic School, a residential laboratory for the treatment of disturbed children at the University of Chicago, where he was Rowley Professor of Education and Professor of Psychology and Psychiatry until his retirement. Most of his books reflect his school experience.

LOVE IS NOT ENOUGH: The Treatment of Emotionally Disturbed Children. *Macmillan* (Free Press) 1950 $7.95; *Avon Bks.* pap. $1.50

Bettelheim points out in this study that parents, besides loving their children, should "create a setting in which both their own legitimate needs and the needs of their children can be satisfied with relative ease"; he describes the methods of his own school (*see his biographical note*) in this light.

SYMBOLIC WOUNDS: Puberty Rites and the Envious Male. *Macmillan* 1954 Collier Bks. rev. ed. 1962 pap. $1.50. Points out the need for a revision of Freudian theories in light of recent knowledge.

TRUANTS FROM LIFE: The Rehabilitation of Emotionally Disturbed Children. *Macmillan* (Free Press) 1955 $9.95 pap. 1964 $3.50. Case studies of four psychotics successfully treated at Dr. Bettelheim's school.

THE INFORMED HEART: Autonomy in a Mass Age. *Macmillan* (Free Press) 1960 $7.95; *Avon Bks.* 1971 pap. $1.50. How man can achieve self-realization in spite of present barriers.

PAUL AND MARY: Two Case Histories of Truants from Life. *Doubleday* Anchor Bks. 1961 pap. $1.95

DIALOGUES WITH MOTHERS. *Macmillan* (Free Press) 1962 $7.95; *Avon Bks.* 1971. pap. $1.25

(With M. Janowitz). SOCIAL CHANGE AND PREJUDICE. *Macmillan* (Free Press) 1964 $6.95

THE EMPTY FORTRESS: Infantile Autism and the Birth of the Self. *Macmillan* (Free Press) 1967 $10.50 pap. $3.95

In this "striking combination of casebook, plea for charity, and medical polemic, Bettelheim analyzes the nature of infantile autism with exhaustive care, describes (only to dismiss) rival theories of its origins, explodes some myths that have arisen about this form of psychosis, charts courses of treatment, and offers some tentative theories of his own. The most beautiful, most heart-rending, and . . . most enduring part of his book consists of three case histories"—(Peter Gay, in the *New Yorker*).

THE CHILDREN OF THE DREAM. *Macmillan* (Free Press) 1969 $7.95; *Avon Bks.* 1971 pap. $1.50. An appraisal of child-rearing in the Israeli *kibbutz*.

A HOME FOR THE HEART. *Knopf* 1973 $12.50

SKINNER, B(URRHUS) F(REDERIC).   1904–

B. F. Skinner, Edgar Pierce Professor of Psychology at Harvard, is a behaviorist whose accomplishments are admired by many colleagues and feared by others. Like the earlier behaviorists J. B. Watson and others, he believes that psychology should not be a matter of mental manipulation but must concern itself from the outside with the study and influencing of human behavior. His theory of "operant conditioning" as a teaching method, on which his famous teaching machine is based, asserts that reward should follow spontaneous desirable behavior and provide it with reinforcement until the desired learning occurs. With his method and the use of the "Skinner box" which automatically provides reinforcement to learning (often in the form of food) for the animal performing within it, he originally trained animals and birds to perform unusual tasks. His teaching machines have produced some remarkable results with both children and adults—both "normal" and psychotic. While at the University of Minnesota during World War II, he trained pigeons to pilot missiles, and he once devised an "Air-Crib," as an "ideal" environment—scientifically regulated—for the development of infants. His own daughter spent almost two of her earliest years in one of these. His opponents, not unnaturally, fear the dehumanizing aspects of such a mechanistic approach, but his devices have nevertheless proved, at the very least, valuable and ingenious adjuncts to other methods of education. Skinner himself has been at pains to deny the "mechanistic" tag, and his achievements as a creative writer show an imaginative power that implies considerable human sensitivity.

Professor Skinner, who once intended to *become* a writer, is the author of a novel, "Walden Two," a description of a systematized utopia run on behaviorist lines. The book received both praise and adverse criticism. He has won the Howard Cosby Warren Award of the Society for Experimental Psychology (1942), the American Psychological Association Award for distinguished contribution to science (1958), and its gold medal, its highest honor (1971).

THE BEHAVIOR OF ORGANISMS: An Experimental Analysis. 1938. *Prentice-Hall* (Appleton) 1966 $5.40 pap. $3.80. His explanation of his theory of "operant conditioning."

WALDEN TWO. *Macmillan* 1948 1960 pap. $2.50. Skinner's idea of utopia in the form of a novel.

SCIENCE AND HUMAN BEHAVIOR. *Macmillan* (Free Press) 1953 $7.50 pap. 1965 $3.45. A discussion of his behaviorism.

VERBAL BEHAVIOR. *Prentice-Hall* (Appleton) 1957 $10.50. Skinner's William James Lectures at Harvard.

(With Charles B. Ferster). SCHEDULES OF REINFORCEMENT. *Irvington Pubns.* 1957 $22.95

CUMULATIVE RECORDS: A Selection of Papers. 1959. *Prentice-Hall* (Appleton) 3rd ed. 1972 $14.95

(With James Holland). THE ANALYSIS OF BEHAVIOR: A Program for Self-Instruction. *McGraw-Hill* 1961 $9.50 pap. $6.50

THE TECHNOLOGY OF TEACHING. *Prentice-Hall* (Appleton) 1968 pap. (orig.) $4.50

BEYOND FREEDOM AND DIGNITY. *Knopf* 1971 $6.95; *Bantam* 1972 pap. $1.95
"Intensely provocative in that it challenges two of man's cherished attributes—his individual freedom and his self-dignity"—*(Choice)*.

CONTINGENCIES OF REINFORCEMENT: A Theoretical Analysis. *Prentice-Hall* 1972 pap. $6.50

ABOUT BEHAVIORISM. *Knopf* 1974 $6.95

Books about Skinner
B. F. Skinner: The Man and His Ideas. By Richard I. Evans. *Dutton* 1968 pap. $1.65
"Highly recommended as an excellent introduction to Skinner and as an extremely valuable complement to his published writings"—*(LJ)*.
A Walden Two Experiment. By Kathleen Kinkade. *Morrow* 1974 pap. $3.25
The Pseudo Science of B. F. Skinner. By Tibor R. Machan. *Arlington House* 1974 $9.95
An Introduction to Behavior Theory and Its Applications. By Robert L. Karen. *Harper* 1974 $11.95
The Skinner Primer: Behind Freedom and Dignity. By Finley Carpenter. *Macmillan* (Free Press) 1974 $7.95 pap. $2.45

MASLOW, ABRAHAM H(AROLD). 1908–1970.
Abraham Maslow's "Toward a Psychology of Being" sold in its first edition over 100,000 copies. Like R. D. Laing (*q.v.*) he questioned the old psychoanalytic notions of being well or ill "adjusted" to the world and spoke from a broadly human base. Human nature—the inner nature of every individual which is uniquely his own—"seems not to be . . . necessarily evil; . . . the basic human capacities are on their face either neutral, pre-moral or positively 'good.' What we call evil behavior appears most often to be a secondary reaction to frustration of this intrinsic nature." On this foundation he built an affirmation of man and man's potentialities for self-fulfillment and

psychological health. He considered his "humanistic" or "Eupsychian" approach to be part of the revolution now taking place in psychology, as in other fields, toward a new view of man as a sociable, creative and loving being whose welfare lies not in the cure of "neurosis" or other ills but on the development of his most socially and personally constructive potential.

Professor Maslow was Chairman of the Psychology Department at Brandeis. He taught for 14 years at Brooklyn College and was President of the American Psychological Association in 1967–1968. His wife, Bertha, helped edit his journals and last papers after his death as well as a memorial volume about him.

(Ed.). MOTIVATION AND PERSONALITY. *Harper* 1954 2nd ed. 1970 pap. $7.50

(Ed.). NEW KNOWLEDGE IN HUMAN VALUES. *Harper* 1959 $7.95; *Regnery* 1970 pap. $2.65

TOWARD A PSYCHOLOGY OF BEING. *Van Nostrand Reinhold* 1962 2nd ed. 1968 $5.95 pap. $3.50. Reflects his optimism and faith in man.

RELIGIONS, VALUES, AND PEAK-EXPERIENCES. 1964. *Viking* Compass Bks. 1970 pap. $1.75

EUPSYCHIAN MANAGEMENT: A Journal. *Dow Jones-Irwin* 1965 $7.95 text ed. $5.95 1973 $8.50

THE PSYCHOLOGY OF SCIENCE: A Reconnaissance. *Harper* 1966 $7.95; *Regnery* Gateway Eds. 1969 pap. $1.95

"A criticism of Western science, especially psychology, with its focus on solving problems that are often of trivial value"—(*LJ*).

(With Hung-Min Chiang). HEALTHY PERSONALITY READINGS. *Van Nostrand-Reinhold* 1969 pap. $3.25

FARTHER REACHES OF HUMAN NATURE. *Viking* 1971 $12.50 Compass Bks. pap. $2.95

DOMINANCE, SELF-ESTEEM, SELF-ACTUALIZATION: Germinal Papers of A. H. Maslow. Ed. by Bertha G. Maslow and International Study Project, Inc. *Brooks-Cole* 1973 pap. $5.95

JOURNALS. Ed. by Bertha G. Maslow and International Study Project, Inc. *Brooks-Cole* 1973 $37.50

Books about Maslow

Abraham H. Maslow: A Memorial Volume. Ed. by Bertha G. Maslow and the International Study Project, Inc. *Brooks-Cole* 1972 $12.50

A. H. Maslow: An Intellectual Portrait. By Richard J. Lowry. *Brooks-Cole* 1973 $5.95

MAY, ROLLO. 1909–

"The development of an existential psychology in America is in good part the work of Rollo May. He helped bring existentialism to psychology some fifteen years ago, and since then his impact has increased each year. As he says here, he isn't an existentialist in a 'cultist' sense. In American psychology the existential approach is part of a wider trend which includes many views." So writes Eugene T. Gendlin in *Psychology Today*. May's psychology is sometimes referred to as humanistic—he is one of the affirmative, "third force" American psychologists who are also critical of the society in which we live. Professor Gendlin writes further: "In . . . *Psychology and the Human Dilemma*, May offers a wealth of valid and stimulating ideas in a totally engaging and readable fashion. [The human dilemma is that] man is always both an active subject and a passive object. . . . May [says]: 'Only in knowing ourselves as the determined ones are we free.' This last sentence and his many similar discussions seem to mean that we can't help what happens, but only what attitude we take toward what happens. In fact, he means more than this—in taking an attitude toward what happens we change what happens. . . ." Dr. May was in late 1968 the subject of an article in the *N.Y. Times* in which he was said to feel that "one sign that the modern age is dying is that its myths are dying." We are at present in a "limbo" between myths—the situation in which people become disoriented and "alienated." "In the new myths," he said, "I would think that racial variation will be seen as a positive value, that emphasis on one world will replace fragmented nationalism, and that things will be valued more for their intrinsic worth rather than in use—what they can be banked for."

As a young man Professor May taught for a period at the American college in Saloniki, Greece. He took his Ph.D. at Columbia in 1949. Among his present activities are his work as Supervisory and Training Analyst at the William Alanson White Institute in New York City and Adjunct Professor of Clinical Psychology at the New York University Graduate School of Arts and

Sciences. He has lectured at many other colleges and universities and was Visiting Professor at Harvard in its 1964 summer session and at Yale in 1972.

THE MEANING OF ANXIETY. *Ronald* 1950 $8.95

MAN'S SEARCH FOR HIMSELF. *Norton* 1953 $5.95; *Dell* Delta Bks. 1973 pap. $2.65

THE ART OF COUNSELING. *Abingdon* Apex Bks. pap. $1.50

(With others, Eds.). EXISTENCE—A New Dimension in Psychiatry and Psychology. *Basic Bks.* 1958 $12.00; *Simon and Schuster* Touchstone-Clarion Bks. 1967 pap. $2.95

(Ed.). SYMBOLISM IN RELIGION AND LITERATURE. *Braziller* 1960 $5.00 pap. $2.95

(Ed.). EXISTENTIAL PSYCHOLOGY. *Random* 2nd ed. 1961 pap. $2.25

PSYCHOLOGY AND THE HUMAN DILEMMA. *Van Nostrand-Reinhold* 1966 pap. $3.95

An "existential discussion of the dichotomy between reason and emotion and the resulting isolation of the individual"—(*LJ*).

(With Leopold Caligor). DREAMS AND SYMBOLS: Man's Unconscious Language. *Basic Bks.* 1969 $9.95

LOVE AND WILL. *Norton* 1969 $7.95; *Dell* 1974 pap. $1.75 Delta Bks. 1973 pap. $2.95

The "focus is man vis-a-vis his contemporary world. And he finds that man is a very troubled soul, not because of his world but because of himself"—(*Choice*).

POWER AND INNOCENCE: A Search for the Sources of Violence. *Norton* 1972 $7.95

PAULUS. *Harper* 1973 $5.95

THE COURAGE TO CREATE. *Norton* 1975 $7.95

BERNE, ERIC LENNARD. 1910–1970.

Eric Berne was a practicing psychiatrist and the author of the best selling work "Games People Play" which was published by *Grove Press* in 1964 and remained on the best seller lists until 1967. It sold approximately 650,000 hardcover copies. In it, Berne argued that people tend to play games with each other in their interpersonal relationships for a number of reasons, namely to escape from reality, to hide ulterior motives, and to avoid actual participation in real life. A few of these games are destructive but most are desirable and necessary. Dr. Berne demonstrated to his readers how to recognize these games and how to play the most socially useful roles.

A native of Montreal, Canada, Berne had a medical degree from McGill University and later studied at the New York City Psychiatric Institute. At the time of his fatal heart attack in 1970, Berne was a Lecturer in group therapy at the Langley-Porter Neuropsychiatric Institute and a Consultant at the McAuley Clinic in San Francisco.

LAYMAN'S GUIDE TO PSYCHIATRY AND PSYCHOANALYSIS (orig. "The Mind in Action") 1957. *Simon & Schuster* rev. ed. 1968 $8.95 pap. $1.95

TRANSACTIONAL ANALYSIS IN PSYCHOTHERAPY: A Systematic Individual and Social Psychiatry. *Grove* Evergreen Bks. 1961 (orig.) pap. $3.95; *Ballantine Bks.* 1973 pap. $1.95

GAMES PEOPLE PLAY: The Psychology of Human Relationships. *Grove* 1964 $6.50 Black Cat Bks. pap. $1.50

"A compendium of unconscious maneuvers nearly everyone makes in his relationships with other people, and its forthright language and somewhat acid style understandably appeal to laymen who may easily recognize themselves as adept life-game players"—(*Newsweek*).

STRUCTURE AND DYNAMICS OF ORGANIZATIONS AND GROUPS. *Grove* Evergreen Bks. 1966 pap. $2.95; *Ballantine Bks.* 1973 pap. $1.95

PRINCIPLES OF GROUP TREATMENT. *Oxford* 1966 $7.50; *Grove* Evergreen Bks. 1968 pap. $4.95

HAPPY VALLEY. *Grove* 1968 $4.95

SEX IN HUMAN LOVING. *Simon & Schuster* 1970 $6.95 Pocket Bks. 1971 pap. $1.50

WHAT DO YOU SAY AFTER YOU SAY HELLO? The Psychology of Human Destiny. *Grove* 1972 $10.00; *Bantam* 1973 pap. $1.95

"As a psychiatrist, Dr. Berne found that each person—under the powerful influences of his parents—writes in early childhood his own script that will determine the general course of his life.

... [Dr. Berne] demonstrates how each life script gets written, how it works, and how each of us can break free of it to help us attain real autonomy and true fulfillment"—(Publisher's note).

ELLIS, ALBERT. 1913–

Albert Ellis is a clinical psychologist and a marriage counselor. "I usually work with psychotherapy and marriage counseling," he told the editors of *Contemporary Authors*, "from 9:45 A.M. to 11 P.M., including the holding of six different psychotherapy groups every week." Dr. Ellis originated the Rational-Emotive Psychotherapy movement, which ignores Freudian theories and advocates the belief that emotions come from conscious thought "as well as internalized ideas of which the individual may be unaware."

Ellis was educated at the City College of New York and at Columbia University where he received a Ph.D. in psychology in 1943. He taught for a number of years at Rutgers and the Union Graduate School. Presently, he is the Executive Director of the Institute for Rational Living, Inc.

THE ART AND SCIENCE OF LOVE. *Lyle Stuart* 1969 $7.95; *Bantam* pap. $1.50

(With Robert Harper). GUIDE TO RATIONAL LIVING. *Prentice-Hall* 1961 $7.50; *Wilshire* pap. $2.00

(With Robert Harper). CREATIVE MARRIAGE. *Lyle Stuart* 1961 $5.00

(With Robert Harper). GUIDE TO SUCCESSFUL MARRIAGE. *Wilshire* 1962 pap. $3.00

REASON AND EMOTION IN PSYCHOTHERAPY. *Lyle Stuart* 1962 $12.00

SEX AND THE SINGLE MAN. *Lyle Stuart* $5.95; *Dell* 1966 pap. $.75

SEX WITHOUT GUILT. *Lyle Stuart* rev. ed. 1966 $4.95; *Wilshire* pap. $2.00

IS OBJECTIVISM A RELIGION? *Lyle Stuart* 1968 $5.95

(With Roger O. Conway). THE ART OF EROTIC SEDUCTION. *Lyle Stuart* 1968 $4.95; *Ace Bks.* 1972 pap. $1.25

HOW TO LIVE WITH A NEUROTIC. 1969. *Crown* rev. ed. 1974 $6.95

(With John M. Gullo). MURDER AND ASSASSINATION. *Lyle Stuart* 1971 $10.00

GROWTH THROUGH REASON: Verbatim Cases in Rational-Emotive Therapy. *Science & Behavior Bks.* 1971 $8.95

EXECUTIVE LEADERSHIP: A Rational Approach. *Citadel Press* 1972 $6.95

HOW TO MASTER YOUR FEAR OF FLYING. *Curtis Bks.* 1972 pap. $.95

HUMANISTIC PSYCHOTHERAPY: The Rational-Emotive Approach. Ed. by Edward Sagarin *Julian Press* 1973 $8.95; *McGraw-Hill* 1974 pap. $2.95

(With Albert Abarbanel, Eds.). ENCYCLOPEDIA OF SEXUAL BEHAVIOR. *Jason Aronson* rev. ed. 1973 $25.00

THE SENSUOUS PERSON: Critique and Connections. *Lyle Stuart* 1973 $6.95; *New Am. Lib.* Signet Bks. 1974 pap. $1.50

HOW TO RAISE AN EMOTIONALLY HEALTHY, HAPPY CHILD. *Wilshire* pap. $2.00

BRUNER, JEROME S(EYMOUR). 1915–

Bruner, a writer on education and promoter of Piaget (*q.v.*), has said—in direct opposition to Piaget's theories of natural readiness—that "any subject can be taught effectively in some intellectually honest form to any child at any stage of development." (The conflict may, however, be one of terminology rather than physiology or psychology.) Bruner's studies have been principally concerned with the nature of perception and the effects of motivation and personality on learning. Professor Bruner was director of the Harvard Center for Cognitive Studies from 1961 to 1972. He received the award for Distinguished Scientific Contribution from the American Psychological Association in 1962. Since 1972 he has been Watts Professor of Psychology at Oxford University.

THE PROCESS OF EDUCATION. *Harvard Univ. Press* 1960 $2.75; *Random* Vintage Bks. pap. $1.65

"Already ranks as one of the most important and influential works on education"—(*Fortune*). A "lovely book. . . . In my opinion it will be a classic, comparable for its philosophical centrality and humane concreteness to some of the essays of Dewey"—(Paul Goodman, in the *N.Y. Herald Tribune*).

ON KNOWING: Essays for the Left Hand. *Harvard Univ. Press* 1962 $4.95 *Atheneum* 1965 pap. $2.65

"There is much wisdom in these essays, much shrewdness, excellent advice on education, and an awareness of the arts and of literary values which is not often to be found in books by psychologists or by educators. It is elegantly written and the printing and illustrations are a joy to the reader"—(Henri Peyre).

(With J. J. Goodnow and G. A. Austin). A STUDY OF THINKING. *Wiley* 1956 pap. $6.50

TOWARD A THEORY OF INSTRUCTION. *Harvard Univ. Press* Belknap Press 1966 $4.95 pap. 1974 $1.95

(With R. Olver and G. A. Austin). STUDIES IN COGNITIVE GROWTH. *Wiley* 1966 $11.95

PROCESSES OF COGNITIVE GROWTH: Infancy. *Barre* (dist. by Crown) 1968 $4.50

RELEVANCE OF EDUCATION. *Norton* 1971 $5.95 1973 pap. $2.45

BEYOND THE INFORMATION GIVEN: Studies in the Psychology of Knowing. Ed. by Jeremey M. Anglin *Norton* 1973 $13.95 pap. $4.50

PATTERNS OF GROWTH. *Oxford* 1974 pap. $1.60

LAING, R(ONALD) D(AVID). 1927–

R. D. Laing is a prominent British psychoanalyst who has won wide attention in this country, especially among young people, for his questioning of many of the old concepts of what is "normal" and what is "insane" in a world which he sees as infinitely dangerous in the hands of "normal" men. In "The Politics of Experience," an excellent introduction to his thinking, he writes: "A little girl of seventeen in a mental hospital told me she was terrified because the Atom Bomb was inside her. That is a delusion. The statesmen of the world who boast and threaten that they have Doomsday weapons are far more dangerous, and far more estranged from 'reality' than many of the people on whom the label 'psychotic' is affixed."

Much of his work has been done in the field of schizophrenia. Philosophical and humanist in approach, he questions many of the cut-and-dried classifications for the mentally ill, whom he regards with great compassion; he looks beyond the "case" to the man or woman trying to come to grips with life in the broadest human context. He is a compelling writer of great literary skill who brings to his studies a world view that reaches far beyond the confines of his profession. Born in Glasgow, Dr. Laing practices at the Tavistock Institute of Human Relations and directs the Langham Clinic—both in London, England. He has been chairman of the Philadelphia Association Ltd. (London) since 1964.

THE DIVIDED SELF: An Existential Study in Sanity and Madness. 1960. *Pantheon* 1969 $5.95

THE SELF AND OTHERS: Further Studies in Sanity and Madness. 1961. *Pantheon* 2nd ed. 1970 $5.95; *Penguin* Pelican Bks. 1972 pap. $2.50

(With David G. Cooper). REASON AND VIOLENCE: A Decade of Sartre's Philosophy, 1950–1960. Fwd. by Jean-Paul Sartre. 1964. *Pantheon* 1971 $5.95; *Random* Vintage Bks. 1971 pap. $1.95

(With Herbert Phillipson and A. Russell Lee). INTERPERSONAL PERCEPTION. 1966. *Springer Pub.* $5.50; *Harper* Perenn. Lib. pap. $1.50

THE POLITICS OF EXPERIENCE. 1967. *Ballantine Bks.* pap. $1.75 A most interesting discussion of his psychological theories—for laymen—in the context of the modern world. Brief and beautifully written.

THE POLITICS OF THE FAMILY AND OTHER ESSAYS. *Pantheon* 1971 $4.95; *Random* Vintage Bks. 1972 pap. $1.95

Books about Laing

R. D. Laing and Anti-Psychiatry. Ed. by Robert Boyers and Robert Orrill. *Octagon* 1971 1974 $12.00

Going Crazy: The Radical Therapy of R. D. Laing. Ed. by Hendrik Ruitenbeek, *Bantam* (orig.) 1972 pap. $1.65

R. D. Laing. By Edgar Z. Friedenberg. Modern Masters Ser. *Viking* 1974 $5.95 pap. $1.95

Chapter 7

Science

"The fairest thing we can experience is the mysterious. It is the fundamental emotion which stands at the cradle of true art and true science. He who knows it not, can no longer wonder, no longer feel amazement, is as good as dead, a snuffed-out candle."

—ALBERT EINSTEIN

"Man must not be turned into a chicken or a rat as in the well-known experiments in which elation is induced electrically through electrodes inserted into the brain."

—ANDREI D. SAKHAROV

Science continues to capture the popular imagination with its dramatic successes in outer space. The linking of the Apollo-Soyuz space vehicles in the summer of 1975 and two recent Soviet space probes of Venus (Venera 9 and 10) bear witness to its phenomenal accomplishments. At home, modern technology has transformed every aspect of our daily lives. "Through the application of science, human beings in America and other parts of the world have been liberated from plagues, pestilences, threats of famine, hardship and torment that once seemed an unalterable part of the human condition," Robert Nesbit wrote in the *New York Times Magazine* (September 28, 1975). "It is hard to think of an area of modern physical welfare that cannot be traced in some way to science and technology."

Despite these triumphs, science and scientists have not escaped severe criticism for their glowing and sometimes rash predictions. "In the past few years," Nesbit continues, "disenchantment has set in, with the public concluding that the postwar promises of learning were inflated and misleading." We need only think of the DDT fiasco, nuclear reactors, chemical pollution, and the newly discovered dangers of aerosol propellants to realize the truth of these remarks. "For whatever reasons, however improperly held, the sense of failure of [scientific] knowledge begins to hover over the landscape." Public distrust of the massive projects carried out by physical scientists in the 1960s has prompted severe cuts in funding for nearly all branches of science. NASA is struggling to keep together its once superb cadre of engineers and technicians until a time when public opinion will again support a bold, new program. Even medical researchers complain bitterly of their lack of funds.

Problems of communication between humanists and scientists remain alive and worrisome. The wide "gulf of prejudice" between these two groups of intellectuals, which C. P. Snow once called the "two cultures," remains unbridged. "Although there is some public awareness of what science and scientists are really like, their stereotyped images remain powerful." In a poll of their readers recently conducted by Philip Hills and Michael Shalles for *New Society* (August 28, 1975) it appeared that non-scientists have little gratitude for what science has done for the material advancement of mankind. Scientists are seen as remote, withdrawn, secretive people with little humanity in their nature. They have narrow interests and are described as fat, balding and shabbily dressed. Fortunately, Hills and Shalles indicate, in a concluding paragraph, some ways in which this unsatisfactory relationship between science and society might be improved.

In an effort to combat these stereotypes many American scientists have begun to display a public-spirited concern for the dire consequences of unbridled technological growth. Men of science frequently testify at legislative hearings on the health problems caused by the careless use of pharmacologically active ingredients and the growing necessity for population controls. They organize research teams in order to preserve vanishing species of wildlife and they investigate reckless advertising claims for new wonder drugs and food additives. Over the past decade many of their colleagues have promoted "pure" research, particularly biomedical research, as an almost holy cause. Still other scientists and science writers have authored books and articles in which they discuss the consequences of industrial pollution in a language that the layman can easily understand.

"Scientists must communicate to the public that their profession is a human activity," writes University of Wisconsin physics professor Robert March, author of "Physics for Poets" (*McGraw-Hill* 1970 $7.95), "carried out by people who experience the same emotions, intuitions and prejudices as everyone else. Also, it must be made clear that science can and must be understood by the layman so he can cope with a society which is depending more and more on science as a way of life."

Through the efforts of scientific journalists, the popular understanding of science has so increased as to render obsolete many of the standard works by an earlier generation. A wide range of popularized works incorporating the latest scientific findings are included in this Chapter.

GENERAL REFERENCE WORKS

The "American Book Publishing Record" (*Bowker* $19.00 a year; *see Chapter 1, Reference Books—General, this Volume*), a montly publication, lists all books appearing in the "Weekly Record" by Dewey Decimal arrangement. Science titles, formerly published in "American Scientific Books" (*Bowker*), are now incorporated in BPR, as only back volumes of ASB are still available (*consult publisher's catalog for years and prices*).

AMERICAN MEN AND WOMEN OF SCIENCE. First published in 1906. *Bowker* 7 vols. 13th ed. 1976 each $50.00. The 13th edition of this indispensable reference work for academic, public and special libraries contains over 110,000 biographies of U.S. and Canadian scientists, alphabetically arranged.

Asimov, Isaac. ASIMOV'S BIOGRAPHICAL ENCYCLOPEDIA OF SCIENCE AND TECHNOLOGY. *Doubleday* 1965 rev. ed. 1972 $12.95

"This book is a compilation of more than 1000 vignettes of scientists from early Greek times to the present day. The entries are arranged chronologically according to the birth date of each major scientist, followed by biographies of other scientists who were closely related to his school of thought. The index is organized by biography number to help give an idea of the interrelation of the sciences"—(*LJ*).

ASIMOV'S GUIDE TO SCIENCE. *Basic Bks.* rev. ed. 1972 $15.50

See also his main entry, this Chapter.

THE BASIC DICTIONARY OF SCIENCE. Ed. by E. C. Graham for the Orthological Institute. *Macmillan* 1966 $6.95 pap. $2.95. Covers, in Basic English, more than 25,000 terms in science and technology.

Bausum, Harold T. SCIENCE FOR SOCIETY: A Bibliography. *American Assn. for the Advancement of Science* 3rd ed. 1972 pap. $1.00

Bernal, John D. THE SOCIAL FUNCTION OF SCIENCE. *M.I.T. Press* 1967 $12.50 pap. $3.95

Brown, Peter, and George B. Stratton, Eds. THE WORLD LIST OF SCIENTIFIC PERIODICALS PUBLISHED IN THE YEARS 1900–60. *Shoe String Press* 3 vols. 4th ed. 1963 set $90.00

Burnham, J. C. SCIENCE IN AMERICA: Historical Selections. *Holt* (Rinehart) 1971 pap. $6.00

CHAMBERS DICTIONARY OF SCIENCE AND TECHNOLOGY. Ed. by T. C. Collocott and A. B. Dobson *A.S. Barnes* 1972 rev. ed. 1974 $22.50

Cohen, Morris R., and Israel E. Drabkin, Eds. A SOURCE BOOK IN GREEK SCIENCE. *Harvard Univ. Press* 1948 text ed. $15.00

DICTIONARY OF SCIENTIFIC BIOGRAPHY. Ed. by C. C. Gillespie *Scribner* 9 vols. 1971– each $35.00. Published under the auspices of the American Council of Learned

Societies, this work is modelled on the prestigious *Dictionary of National Biography*. Twelve volumes are projected.

Dresner, Stephen. UNITS OF MEASUREMENT: An Encyclopaedic Dictionary of Units Both Scientific and Popular and the Quantities They Measure. *Hastings House* 1972 $15.00

ENCYCLOPEDIA OF THE LIFE SCIENCES. Ed. by Herman Gregoire and others *Doubleday* 8 vols. 1965–1968 Vol. 1 The Living Organism Vol. 2 The Animal World Vol. 3 The World of Plants Vol. 4 The World of Microbes Vol. 5 The Human Machine: Mechanisms Vol. 6 The Human Machine: Disorders Vol. 7 The Human Machine: Adjustments Vol. 8 Man of Tomorrow each $4.95

Fishlock, David, Ed. THE NEW SCIENTISTS. *Oxford* 1971 pap. $3.25

Gray, Peter, Ed. THE ENCYCLOPEDIA OF MICROSCOPY AND MICRO TECHNIQUE. *Van Nostrand-Reinhold* 1973 $32.50

Grogan, Denis. SCIENCE AND TECHNOLOGY: An Introduction to the Literature. *Shoe String Press* new and rev. ed. 1973 $9.00

Hogben, Lancelot Thomas. VOCABULARY OF SCIENCE. *Stein & Day* 1971 $6.95 pap. $1.95

INDEX TO SCIENTISTS OF THE WORLD FROM ANCIENT TO MODERN TIMES: Biographies and Portraits. Ed. by Norma O. Ireland *Faxon* 1962 $13.00

INTERNATIONAL CATALOGUE OF SCIENTIFIC LITERATURE, 1901–1914. *Johnson Reprint* 32 vols. set $1100.00; *Scarecrow Press* various sections each $12.00

Jones, Bessie Zaban, Ed. THE GOLDEN AGE OF SCIENCE: Thirty Portraits of the Giants of 19th-Century Science by Their Scientific Contemporaries. Introd. by Everett Mendelsohn. Published in cooperation with the Smithsonian Institute by *Simon & Schuster* 1967 $12.00

"The material is arranged in the order of the birth dates of the biographees. As a collection the book gives an excellent idea of the development of the sciences during the 19th-century"—(*LJ*).

Klein, H. Arthur. THE WORLD OF MEASUREMENTS. *Simon & Schuster* 1974 $14.95

This is an "immensely valuable reference work about each of the myriad units of measurement"—(*LJ*).

McGRAW-HILL DICTIONARY OF SCIENTIFIC AND TECHNICAL TERMS. Ed. by Daniel N. Lapedes *McGraw-Hill* 1974 $39.50. Contains almost 100,000 terms currently in use.

McGRAW-HILL ENCYCLOPEDIA OF ENVIRONMENTAL SCIENCE. *McGraw-Hill* 1974 $19.95

McGRAW-HILL ENCYCLOPEDIA OF SCIENCE AND TECHNOLOGY: An International Reference Work. *McGraw-Hill* 1960 15 vols. 3rd ed. 1971 each $27.35 set $410.00

The basic "jewel"—(*LJ*).

YEARBOOK 1971–1973 each $27.50 1974 $28.00 Comprehensive annual coverage to supplement and update the original.

Meisel, Max., Ed. A BIBLIOGRAPHY OF AMERICAN NATURAL HISTORY: The Pioneer Century, 1769–1865. 1924–1929. *Hafner* 3 vols. facsimile ed. 1967 set $65.00

"The work is essentially divided into two parts: Part A, bibliographic material dealing with the historical, biographical and bibliographical aspects of the Colonial Period and the Pioneer Century; and Part B, a bibliographical portrait of those institutions which aided the development of natural history during this period"—(*LJ*).

Newman, James Roy, Ed. THE HARPER ENCYCLOPEDIA OF SCIENCE. *Harper* 1963 4 vols. in 1 rev. ed. 1967 $40.00

"An exposition of all branches of science and technology in a single alphabetic sequence of more than 4,000 entries. . . . The principles of New Mathematics, the courtship of fishes, the analysis of quasars, the definition of definition, the seeding of clouds, the rules of scientific method, and the inclusion of a thousand biographies hint at the book's scope. The authenticity and clarity of the writing and illustrations, and the thoroughness of the encyclopedia's cross references and index, make it an epochal research facility"—(David Glixon, in *SR*).

NOBEL LECTURES. *For those volumes that concern the Sciences, see Chapter 1, Reference Books— General: Bibliographic and Reference Tools, this Vol.*

THE PENGUIN BOOK OF TABLES. *Penguin* rev. & abr. ed. 1974 pap. $.95

THE PENGUIN DICTIONARY OF SCIENCE. Ed. by E. B. Uvarov and D. R. Chapman *Schocken* 4th ed. 1972 $11.95

SCIENTIFIC AND TECHNICAL BOOKS IN PRINT 1975: Subject Index, Author Index. *Bowker* 1975 $38.50. Nearly 60,000 titles of in-print U.S. books are listed.

Turkevich, John, and Ludmilla B. Turkevich, Eds. PROMINENT SCIENTISTS OF CONTINENTAL EUROPE. *American Elsevier* 1968 $16.00. Collection of short biographies.

VAN NOSTRAND'S SCIENTIFIC ENCYCLOPEDIA. *Van Nostrand-Reinhold* 1938 4th rev. ed. 1968 $42.75

"One of the best and most reliable one-volume scientific encyclopedias in the market"—*(LJ)*. A useful work for both the scientist and the layman, it contains in a single alphabetical list the terms used in science and technology. "Monumental"—*(SR)*.

Walford, A. J. GUIDE TO REFERENCE MATERIAL. Vol. 1 Science and Technology. *Bowker* 1966 3rd ed. 1973 $17.95

Winchell, Constance M., and O. A. Johnson. GUIDE TO REFERENCE BOOKS. *American Library Assn.* 8th ed. 1967 $15.00 Ed. by Eugene P. Sheehy Supplement 1 1965–1966 1968 pap. $3.50 Supplement 2 1967–1968 1970 pap. $4.00 Supplement 3 1969–1970 1972 pap $4.50

WORLD WHO'S WHO IN SCIENCE: A Biographical Dictionary of Notable Scientists from Antiquity to the Present. *Marquis* 1968 $60.00

Zuckerman, Sir Solly. BEYOND THE IVORY TOWER: The Frontiers of Public and Private Science. *Taplinger* 1971 $7.95

GENERAL HISTORIES, STUDIES, PHILOSOPHY

Asimov, Isaac. *See his main entry, this Chapter.*

Barbour, Ian G. MYTHS, MODELS, AND PARADIGMS: A Comparative Study in Science and Religion. *Harper* 1974 $6.95

Ben-David, Joseph. THE SCIENTIST'S ROLE IN SOCIETY: A Comparative Study. *Prentice-Hall* 1971 $6.95 pap. $2.95

"A unique and unquestionably important book for students of science and society"—*(Choice)*.

Bernal, John Desmond. SCIENCE IN HISTORY. *M.I.T. Press* 4 vols. 1971 Vol. 1 The Emergence of Science Vol. 2 The Scientific and Industrial Revolution Vol. 3 The Natural Sciences in our Time Vol. 4 The Social Sciences: A Conclusion each $12.50 boxed set $40.00 pap. each $3.95 boxed set $15.00

Boffey, Philip M. THE BRAIN BANK OF AMERICA: An Inquiry into the Politics of Science. *McGraw-Hill* 1975 $10.95

Boffey "presents a brief history of the [National] Academy [of Sciences], describes its relationships with closely connected institutions . . . and makes recommendations for reform"—*(Choice)*.

Boyko, Hugo, Ed. SCIENCE AND THE FUTURE OF MANKIND. *Indiana Univ. Press* 1964 $12.50; *Hillary House* 1964 $13.75. Papers by 21 famous scientists published for the World Academy of Art and Science.

Bradbury, Savile. THE MICROSCOPE PAST & PRESENT. *Pergamon* 1967 $5.00 pap $3.00

Braithwaite, Richard B. SCIENTIFIC EXPLANATION: A Study of the Function of Theory, Probability and Law in Science. *Cambridge* 1953 $17.50 pap. $5.95

Breurer, Hans. COLUMBUS WAS CHINESE: Discoveries and Inventions of the Far East. *McGraw-Hill* 1972 $8.95

"That Chinese science was thousands of years ahead of western science is well known from early records, which are cited in chapters on astronomy and mathematics; maps on paper, silk, and stone; the oldest seismograph; the compass, kites and parachutes; gunpowder and cannons, even the Great Wall"—*(LJ)*.

Brody, Baruch A., and Nicholas Capaldi, Eds. SCIENCE: Men, Methods, Goals. *Addison-Wesley* (Benjamin) 1968 pap. $5.00. A collection of readings representing many of the major views on the methodology of the psysical sciences.

Bronowski, Jacob. *See his main entry, this Chapter.*

Brooks, Harvey. THE GOVERNMENT OF SCIENCE. *M.I.T. Press* 1968 $10.00. Essays by the Harvard Dean of Engineering and Applied Physics, 1960–1967.

Bruce, Robert V. ALEXANDER GRAHAM BELL AND THE CONQUEST OF SOLITUDE. *Little* 1973 $12.50
"This is a long overdue, in-depth, and carefully researched biography of the inventor"—*(LJ)*.

Burnham, Jack. BEYOND MODERN SCULPTURE: The Effects of Science and Technology on the Sculpture of this Century. *Braziller* 1968 $20.00 pap. $5.95

Bush, Vannevar. SCIENCE IS NOT ENOUGH. 1967. *Apollo* 1969 pap. $1.95
"Ten essays that reflect the philosophy and opinions of Dr. Bush . . . on science, culture, and management, information retrieval and data processing, medicine, and the actual impact science has made on man's way of life"—*(LJ)*.

Butterfield, Herbert. ORIGINS OF MODERN SCIENCE. *Macmillan* (Free Press) rev. ed. 1965 pap. $1.95

(With others). A SHORT HISTORY OF SCIENCE: A Symposium. *Doubleday* 1959 pap. $1.45

Calder, Ritchie (now Lord Ritchie-Calder). MAN AND THE COSMOS: The Nature of Science Today. 1968. *New Am. Lib.* Signet 1969 pap. $1.25
"Mr. Calder emphasizes cosmology, nuclear and quantum physics, relativity theory, geophysics, and molecular biology. . . . A readable and useful summary for the layman"—*(LJ)*.

Cardwell, Donald S. FROM WATT TO CLAUSIUS: The Rise of Thermodynamics in the Early Industrial Age. *Cornell Univ. Press* 1972 $11.50
"In this pathbreaking book, Cardwell demonstrates in detail that the growth of thermodynamic science had its roots in the development of machines, especially the steam engine"—*(Choice)*.

Clagett, Marshall. GREEK SCIENCE IN ANTIQUITY. 1955. *Bks. for Libraries* $10.50. From its primitive origins through its high points in Euclid, Archimedes, Appollonius of Perga and others; "lucid, concise and trenchant."

THE SCIENCE OF MECHANICS IN THE MIDDLE AGES, 1200–1400. *Univ. of Wisconsin Press* 1959 $8.00

(Ed.). CRITICAL PROBLEMS IN THE HISTORY OF SCIENCE. *Univ. of Wisconsin Press* 1959 $12.50 pap. $4.95. Sixteen major papers presented at an international meeting, covering the Scientific Revolution, teaching of the history of science, science and the French Revolution, conservation of energy, evolution, and the structure of matter and chemical and physical theory.

Commoner, Barry. SCIENCE AND SURVIVAL. *Viking* 1966 Compass Bks. 1967 pap. $1.65; *Ballantine Bks.* 1970 pap. $1.25. On the biological consequences of scientific progress.

Conant, James B. MODERN SCIENCE AND MODERN MAN. *Columbia* 1952 $7.50; *Doubleday* Anchor Bks. 1959 pap. $1.45. The philosophical and spiritual implications of the new insight into the nature of the universe.

SCIENCE AND COMMON SENSE. *Yale Univ. Press* 1951 $15.00 pap. $3.45; *Franklin Watts* lg.-type ed. $9.95. Through selected case histories the author explains the methods of science for the layman.

(With others, Eds.). HARVARD CASE HISTORIES IN EXPERIMENTAL SCIENCE. *Harvard Univ. Press* 2 vols. 1957 set $15.00
"Gives the general reader a perspective of the relationship between the sciences and other forms of human activity."

Cottrell, Sir Alan. PORTRAIT OF NATURE: The World as Seen by Modern Science. *Scribner* 1975 $8.95

Dampier, William Cecil. THE HISTORY OF SCIENCE AND ITS RELATIONS WITH PHILOSOPHY AND RELIGION. *Cambridge* rev. ed. 1949 $14.50 pap. $6.95

(With Margaret Dampier, Eds.). READINGS IN THE LITERATURE OF SCIENCE. 1959. *Peter Smith* $4.50

Daniels, George H. SCIENCE IN AMERICAN SOCIETY: A Social History. *Knopf* 1971 $10.00

"A comprehensive study of science and its interaction with American society, the social, cultural, political, and religious institutions from the 15th Century to the 1970s"—(*LJ*).

Davis, Douglas. ART AND THE FUTURE: A History/Prophecy of the Collaboration between Science, Technology and Art. *Praeger* 1974 $20.00

"Beginning with Leonardo da Vinci, the author traces the development of movements and leaders on a worldwide basis up to the present, including experiments with lasers and computers"—(*LJ*).

Dubos, René Jules. *See his main entry, this Chapter.*

Eakin, Richard M. GREAT SCIENTISTS SPEAK AGAIN. *Univ. of California Press* 1975 $6.95

The author "appears in period dress as one of six great biologists . . . who expound on their own work"—(*LJ*).

Eiseley, Loren. THE FIRMAMENT OF TIME. *Atheneum* 1960 pap. $2.65

THE IMMENSE JOURNEY. *Random* 1951 Vintage Bks. 1957 pap. $1.95; *Franklin Watts* lge.-type ed. $7.95

See also his main entry in Chapter 8, The Social Sciences, this Vol.

Elliott, Lawrence. GEORGE WASHINGTON CARVER: The Man Who Overcame. Fwd. by Frederick D. Patterson *Prentice-Hall* 1966 $6.40

Gillespie, Charles C. GENESIS AND GEOLOGY: A Study in the Relations of Scientific Thought, Natural Theology and Social Opinion in Great Britain, 1790–1850. *Harper* 1959 $4.50

Glass, Bentley, and others, Eds. FORERUNNERS OF DARWIN: 1745–1859. *Johns Hopkins Press* 1959 pap. $4.95

Greenberg, Daniel S. THE POLITICS OF PURE SCIENCE. *New Am. Lib.* Plume 1968 $3.95

"A prodigious amount of searchingly analyzed information about the political structure and working of American basic science, with side-glances at developments in Europe and the U.S.S.R."—(*N.Y. Times*).

Hall, Alfred Rupert. SCIENTIFIC REVOLUTION, 1500–1800: The Formation of the Modern Scientific Attitude. 1954. *Beacon* 1956 rev. ed. 1966 pap. $3.95

"A trustworthy and well-written account of the factual history of science" with interpretation of various movements.

Haskins, Caryl P., Ed. THE SEARCH FOR UNDERSTANDING. *M.I.T. Press* 1969 $10.00 pap. $2.95; *Walker & Co.* 1967 $6.00

"Selections from writings of scientists associated with the Carnegie Institution, beamed toward a much wider audience than the writers' scientific peers. Written with vigor and clarity, aurthoritative and precise, they cover numerous subjects: pulsating stars, geochemistry, archaeology in Guatemala, the first heart beats, mutations, large telescopes. Many are important contributions to scientific literature"—(*LJ*).

Hellman, Geoffrey T. THE SMITHSONIAN: Octopus on the Mall. *Lippincott* 1967 $5.95

"The character and careers of the men who ran the Smithsonian, the rocky road to acquisitions, money and personality troubles, dealings with Congress—Mr. Hellman tells about in his wry and amusing way"—(*N.Y. Times*).

Hesse, Mary. STRUCTURE OF SCIENTIFIC INFERENCE. *Univ. of California Press* 1974 $15.00

Hindle, Brooke. THE PURSUIT OF SCIENCE IN REVOLUTIONARY AMERICA, 1735–1789. *Univ. of North Carolina Press* 1956 $7.50; *Norton* 1974 pap. $3.95

Hutchings, Edward, and Elizabeth Hutchings, Eds. SCIENTIFIC PROGRESS AND HUMAN VALUES: Proceedings of the Conference Celebrating the 75th Anniversary of the

California Institute of Technology in Pasadena, California, October 25–27, 1966. *American Elsevier* 1967 $7.50

Jachim, Anton G. SCIENCE POLICY MAKING IN THE UNITED STATES AND THE BATAVIA ACCELERATOR. *Southern Illinois Univ. Press* 1975 $8.95

"A really interesting analysis of science as a social system"—(*LJ*).

Keenan, Boyd R., Ed. SCIENCE AND THE UNIVERSITY. *Columbia* 1966 $9.00

Klaw, Spencer. THE NEW BRAHMINS: Scientific Life in America. *Morrow* 1968 $6.95; *Apollo* 1969 pap. $2.50

"A meritorious contribution to non-reverential but responsible scrutiny of the scientific community. . . . The impression that emerges is that for many of the community's inhabitants, scientific life today can be quite unpleasant—dull and dreary in places, brutally competitive in others and, again contrary to the popular image, not particularly rewarding financially or intellectually for the bulk of its practitioners"—(*N.Y. Times*).

Koning, John W., Jr. THE SCIENTIST LOOKS AT RESEARCH MANAGEMENT. *American Management Assn.* 1975 pap. $7.50

Leigh, Egbert G., Jr. ADAPTATION AND DIVERSITY: Natural History and the Mathematics of Evolution. *Freeman, Cooper, Co.* 1972 $7.75

Leigh's book "should please both the student of natural history and the mathematician of evolutionary studies"—(*Choice*).

Martin, Charles-Noel. THE UNIVERSE OF SCIENCE. Trans. by T. Schoeters *Farrar, Straus* (Hill & Wang) 1963 $3.95

As a French journalist for *Figaro* and a nuclear physicist, the author is conversant with the latest findings of physicists, astronomers, astrophysicists, biologists, chemists and geologists. He writes plainly and often stimulatingly for the educated layman. "He *does* admit that 'intelligence' cannot be explained by means of molecules of amino acids alone."

Merton, Robert K. THE SOCIOLOGY OF SCIENCE: Theoretical and Empirical Investigations. *Univ. of Chicago Press* 1973 $12.50

"Merton's philosophy of the nature of scientific investigations in a social context is well stated in this collection of his writings"—(*LJ*).

Michaelis, Anthony R., and H. Harvey, Eds. SCIENTISTS IN SEARCH OF THEIR CONSCIENCE. *Springer-Verlag* 1973 $18.90

The proceedings of the Symposium on the Impact of Science on Society, Brussels 1971. "The major topics are the relationship of science and society as well as the increasing responsibility of scientists for the uses of science"—(*LJ*).

Needham, Joseph. THE GRAND TITRATION: Science and Society in East and West. *Univ. of Toronto Press* 1970 $15.00

(Ed.). SCIENCE AND CIVILIZATION IN CHINA. *Cambridge* To be in 7 vols. 1954–   Vol. 1 Introductory Orientation (1954) $27.50 Vol. 2 History of Scientific Thought (1956) $43.50 Vol. 3 Mathematics and the Sciences of the Heavens and the Earth (1959) $47.50 Vol. 4 Physics and Physical Technology, Pt. 1 Physics (1962) $27.50 Pt. 2 Mechanical Engineering (1965) $49.50 Pt. 3 Engineering and Nautics (1970) $55.00 Vol. 5 Chemistry and Chemical Technology Pt. 2 Spagyrical Discovery and Invention: Magisteries of Gold and Immortality (1974) $35.00

Orlans, Harold, and others, Eds. SCIENCE POLICY AND THE UNIVERSITY. *Brookings* 1968 $7.95 pap. $2.95. Papers from Brookings symposia on the use of federal funds for university research.

Pantin, Carl F. A. THE RELATIONS BETWEEN THE SCIENCES. Ed. with introd. and notes by A. M. Pantin and W. H. Thorpe *Cambridge* 1968 $9.50. The physical and biological sciences compared and examined.

Popkin, Roy. THE ENVIRONMENTAL SCIENCE SERVICES ADMINISTRATION. *Praeger* 1967 $8.50. On government agencies such as the Coast and Geodetic Survey, the Weather Bureau, the Institute of Telecommunication Sciences and Aeronomy.

Price, Derek J. de Solla. LITTLE SCIENCE, BIG SCIENCE. *Columbia* 1963 pap. $1.95

SCIENCE SINCE BABYLON. *Yale Univ. Press* 1961 $6.50 enl. ed. 1974 $11.00 pap. $2.95

In the first title, which contains his 1962 Pegram Lectures, the author discusses the changes in the state of science from the "Little Science" of yesterday through the "Big Science" of today into an inevitable "New Scientific Maturity" of tomorrow. The second title, also originally a series of lectures, deals with what the author considers the diseases of science. Together, the two books form companion pieces.

Reingold, Nathan, Ed. SCIENCE IN NINETEENTH-CENTURY AMERICA: A Documentary History. *Farrar, Straus* (Hill and Wang) 1964 pap. $2.45

Richter, Maurice N., Jr. SCIENCE AS A CULTURAL PROCESS. *Schenkman* 1975 pap. $3.75

Rossi, Paolo. FRANCIS BACON: From Magic to Science. Newly trans. by Sacha Rabinovitch *Univ. of Chicago Press* 1968 $8.00. (*See also Bacon's main entry in Chapter 5, Philosophy, this Vol., and in Chapter 15, Essays and Criticism, Reader's Adviser, Vol. 1.*)

Sarton, George. THE APPRECIATION OF ANCIENT AND MEDIEVAL SCIENCE DURING THE RENAISSANCE (1450–1600). 1955. *A. S. Barnes* 1961 pap. $1.65

Very useful for reference work, this is largely "a bibliographical catalogue of early printed editions . . . enriched with biographical notes . . . and brief comments."

A HISTORY OF SCIENCE. *Harvard Univ. Press* 2 vols. 1952–1959 Vol. 1 Ancient Science through the Golden Age of Greece (1952) Vol. 2 Hellenistic Science and Culture in the Last Three Centuries B.C. (1959) each $15.00; *Norton* 2 vols. pap. 1970 each $3.25

These are the first two volumes of a projected series by the most distinguished historian of science of our time (*see also his main entry, this Chapter*). Professor Sarton, who died in 1956, planned to extend this history down to modern times. The first volume ranges from pre-history through the civilizations of Egypt and Mesopotamia to Plato and Aristotle; the second is concerned with the Hellenistic world which ranged from Alexandria, Israel, India and Parthia to Rome and Carthage.

INTRODUCTION TO THE HISTORY OF SCIENCE. 1948. *Krieger* 5 vols. Vol. 1 From Homer to Omar Khayyam Vol. 2 2 pts. From Rabbi Ben Ezra to Roger Bacon Vol. 3 Pt. 1 First Half of the Fourteenth Century Pt. 2 Second Half of the Fourteenth Century set $175.00

"An important reference history, covering European and Asiatic countries, rich in biography and bibliography"—("Guide to Reference Books").

Shapley, Harlow, Samuel Rappaport and Helen Wright, Eds. THE NEW TREASURY OF SCIENCE. Introd. by Harlow Shapley *Harper* 1965 $10.95. A complete revision of "The Treasury of Science" (1943 5th ed. 1963); contains over 90 selections by famous scientists.

See also Shapley's main entry, this Chapter.

Singer, Charles. A SHORT HISTORY OF SCIENTIFIC IDEAS TO 1900. *Oxford* 1941 rev. ed 1959 $15.25 pap. $5.75

Snow, C. P. THE TWO CULTURES AND A SECOND LOOK. *Cambridge* 1964 1969 $3.95 pap. $1.75

A discussion of the perilous split between art and science, by a scientist who is also a successful novelist. The original text of this controversial work, together with relevant criticisms and Sir Charles's challenging replies. (*See also his main entry in Chapter 12, Modern British Fiction, Reader's Adviser, Vol. 1, for further comment.*)

Steneck, Nicholas H., Ed. SCIENCE AND SOCIETY: Past, Present, and Future. *Univ. of Michigan Press* 1975 $15.00

"The contents of this volume augment the recent celebratory notice taken of Copernicus' 500th anniversary"—(*Choice*).

Taton, René, Ed. A HISTORY OF SCIENCE. French ed. pub. 1957. *Basic Bks.* 4 vols. 1963–66 Vol. 1 Ancient and Medieval Science (1963) Vol. 2 The Beginnings of Modern Science from 1450 to 1800 (1964) Vol. 3 Science in the Nineteenth Century (1965) Vol. 4 Science in the Twentieth Century (1966) Vols. 1–3 each $17.50 Vol. 4 o.p. A definitive history by many fine authorities.

Taylor, Sir James. THE SCIENTIFIC COMMUNITY. *Oxford* 1973 pap. $3.50

"A wide-ranging account of the development of the technical and scientific establishment in the world"—*(LJ)*.

Thorndike, Lynn. A HISTORY OF MAGIC AND EXPERIMENTAL SCIENCE. *Columbia* 8 vols. 1923–58 each $15.00. A scholarly work which covers the subject to Sir Isaac Newton.

SCIENCE AND THOUGHT IN THE FIFTEENTH CENTURY. *Macmillan* (Hafner) 1929 1967 $9.95. Studies in the history of medicine and surgery, natural and mathematical science, philosophy and politics.

Weinberg, Alvin M. REFLECTIONS ON BIG SCIENCE. *M.I.T. Press* 1968 $6.95 pap. $1.95

The director of Oak Ridge National Laboratory "believes that technology increasingly can be harnessed to the service of man and to the solution of most of his basic social problems. He tends to underestimate the darker side of science and technology with its unforeseen consequences, and misses the critical fact that we have not really learned to adequately control modern technology. Important and recommended"—*(Choice)*.

Whitehead, Alfred North. SCIENCE AND THE MODERN WORLD. *Macmillan* 1926 $6.95 (Free Press) 1967 pap. $1.95. Science, philosophy and life through the eyes of an eminent mathematician and philosopher.

See also his main entry in Chapter 5, Philosophy, this Vol.

Whitrow, G. J. THE NATURE OF TIME. *Holt* 1973 $6.95

The author "discusses a variety of measurements of time, including biological clocks, a comparatively new concept; man's early definitions of time; the relationship between relativity and time"—*(LJ)*.

Wightman, William P. D. THE GROWTH OF SCIENTIFIC IDEAS. 1951. *Greenwood* 1974 $20.50. A well-organized and intelligently interpreted history of the part played by physical and biological science in the creation of culture up to about 1900.

Zuckerman, Sir Solly. SCIENTISTS AND WAR: The Impact of Science on Military and Civil Affairs. *Int. Pubns. Service* 1966 $5.25

The chief scientific adviser to the British Government "is well worth listening to"—*(New Yorker)*.

ASTRONOMY. *See under Physics.*

ATOMIC ENERGY. *See under Physics.*

BIOLOGY AND ECOLOGY

Abercrombie, M., and others. A DICTIONARY OF BIOLOGY. 1960. *Penguin* 6th ed. 1973 pap. $1.95

Beckmann, Peter. ECO-HYSTERICS AND THE TECHNOPHOBES. *Golem* 1974 $6.95

"Beckmann presents a strong case for continued growth and development in the areas of science and technology, in the conviction that only through further advances in these areas can practical solutions be found that will ultimately solve our environmental problems"—*(LJ)*.

Bernal, J. D. THE ORIGIN OF LIFE. 1967. *Universe Bks.* $12.50

"An interesting book which gives the present set of opinions relating to the origin of life on this planet. . . . An excellent appendix"—*(Choice)*.

Brainerd, John W. WORKING WITH NATURE: A Practical Guide. *Oxford* 1973 $15.00

"An introductory manual to environmental management. . . . The various types of habitats—wetlands, deserts, coastal marshes, etc.—are given a nontechnical yet knowledgeable treatment"—*(LJ)*.

Bridges, William. GATHERING OF ANIMALS: An Unconventional History of the New York Zoological Society. *Harper* 1974 $12.50

"An entertaining, anecdotal narrative of the New York Zoological Society from its opening in the late nineteenth century to the present"—*(Booklist)*.

Brook, Alan J. THE LIVING PLANT: An Introduction to Botany. *Aldine* 1964 $12.50
"Excellent"—*(LJ)*.

Carlson, Elof Axel, Ed. MODERN BIOLOGY: Its Conceptual Foundations. Introd. by the editor Science Ser. *Braziller* 1967 $7.50
"An annotated anthology of articles basic to the science of biology, [some] by the founders of the science"—*(LJ)*. Includes pieces by Darwin, J. D. Watson, Francis Crick.

Chauvin, Rémy, ANIMAL SOCIETIES FROM THE BEE TO THE GORILLA. Trans. from the French by George Ordish *Farrar, Straus* (Hill & Wang) 1968 $6.95
The distinguished biologist-entomologist examines "the social behavior of insects, with emphasis on bees, and higher animals including birds and such mammals as the gorilla. His thesis, developed in detail, is that a colony or group is best considered as a whole organism"—*(PW)*.

Chedd, Graham. NEW BIOLOGY. *Basic Bks.* 1974 $7.50
"Easily read by the layman, the book provides an understanding of molecular biology and its practical applications"—*(LJ)*.

Christensen, Clyde M. MOLDS, MUSHROOMS AND MYCOTOXINS. *Univ. of Minnesota Press* 1975 $11.50

Coleman, William. BIOLOGY IN THE NINETEENTH CENTURY: Problems of Form, Function, and Transformation. *Wiley* 1971 pap. $3.00

Collis, John Stewart. THE VISION OF GLORY: The Extraordinary Nature of the Ordinary. *Braziller* 1973 $8.95
"This insightful book translates the world of scientific formulas into language through which the lay naturalist can appreciate the beauties and physical sustenance that natural chemical reactions produce for humankind"—*(LJ)*.

Commoner, Barry. CLOSING CIRCLE: Nature, Man, and Technology. *Knopf* 1971 $6.95; *Bantam* 1972 pap. $1.95
"A factual presentation and clear analysis that goes straight to the heart of the fix in which we find ourselves. The overlaying thesis is that of technology expanding at the expense of our natural environment"—*(LJ)*.

Cosslett, V. E. MODERN MICROSCOPY, or Seeing the Very Small. *Cornell Univ. Press* 1967 pap. $1.95
"An eminently readable and factual introduction to (and review of) the science of microscopy"—*(LJ)*.

Crosby, Alfred W., Jr. THE COLUMBIAN EXCHANGE: Biological and Cultural Consequences of 1492. *Greenwood* 1972 $9.50
"Crosby's view is that the most significant changes brought on by the Columbian voyages were biological in nature, and that colonization contributed . . . to the extinction or near-extinction of many forms of plant and animal life . . . until what once had been biologically discrete continents had become 'two Europes and two Africas, one on either side of the Atlantic' "—*(LJ)*.

De Bach, Paul. BIOLOGICAL CONTROL BY NATURAL ENEMIES. *Cambridge* 1974 $14.95 pap. $5.95 Presents a strong, well-documented case for the emphasis on pest control by natural means, particularly the introduction of a variety of insect predators.

De Witt, H. C. D. PLANTS OF THE WORLD. Trans. by A. J. Pomerans *Dutton* 3 vols. 1966–1969 each $19.95

Dobzhansky, Theodosius. THE BIOLOGY OF ULTIMATE CONCERN. *New Am. Lib.* 1967 Meridian 1969 pap. $2.95. An examination of man's place in the universe as affected by biology and genetics.

GENETICS OF THE EVOLUTIONARY PROCESS. *Columbia* 1971 $15.00 pap. $4.95

HEREDITY AND THE NATURE OF MAN. 1964. *New Am. Lib.* Signet pap. $.95
Professor Dobzhansky "deals with the molecular discoveries of genetic mechanisms which cast new light on the possible origin of life, but more important, provides the necessary background to deal intelligently with such concepts as race, equality of opportunity, human rights, and to understand the processes of evolution as they apply not only to our past but to our future"—*(LJ)*.

Douglas, William O. THREE HUNDRED YEAR WAR: A Chronicle of Ecological Disaster. *Random* 1972 $5.95

"In this silent spring approach to saving the good earth, [Douglas] views the problems that arise from the drive for profits and technical advances . . . This factual review is often shocking, but it offers solutions, explains what is being done, what must be done, what the costs will be"—*(LJ)*.

Dubos, René J. SO HUMAN AN ANIMAL. *Scribner* 1968 $8.95 pap. $2.45

The biologist views man individually as "a unique combination of genetic, social and individual 'memories' allowing for a greater repertoire of choices than either physiologists or psychoanalysts admit"—(John Leonard, in the *N.Y. Times*). Winner of the 1969 Pulitzer Prize for general nonfiction.

See also his main entry, this Chapter.

Emmel, Thomas C. AN INTRODUCTION TO ECOLOGY AND POPULATION BIOLOGY. *Norton* 1973 $6.95

"The ecology of plant and animal communities and the consequences of environmental alteration; problems generated by pollution of waterways, the land, and air; implications of continued population growth and the difficulties of its regulation are major topics of concern"— *(LJ)*.

Etherington, John R. ENVIRONMENT AND PLANT ECOLOGY. *Wiley* 1975 $22.50

Evans, A. GLOSSARY OF MOLECULAR BIOLOGY. *Wiley* 1975 $6.95

Gittelson, Bernard. BIORHYTHM: A Personal Science. *Arco* 1976 $6.95

Goldstein, Philip. GENETICS IS EASY. *Lantern Press* new rev. ed. $8.00; *Viking* Compass Bks. 1970 pap. $1.95

A "complex" subject in which "the discussion progresses from the historical developments to more difficult topics. . . . Bibliography"—*(LJ)*.

Headstrom, Birger Richard. NATURE IN MINIATURE. *Knopf* 1968 $10.00

An "approach to the mysterious world that can be seen only through the magnifying glass or microscope . . . arranged according to what may be observed throughout the months of the year in backyards, woods, and fields"—*(LJ)*.

Howells, William. EVOLUTION OF THE GENUS *HOMO*. *Addison-Wesley* 1973 pap. $3.95

MANKIND IN THE MAKING: The Story of Human Evolution. *Doubleday* rev. ed. 1967 $7.95

Hull, David L. DARWIN AND HIS CRITICS: The Reception of Darwin's Theory of Evolution by the Scientific Community. *Harvard Univ. Press* 1973 $18.50

"According to the author, Darwin's theory of evolution did not measure up to the standards of contemporary scientific philosophy. . . . Extensive use is made of European and American reviews of Darwin's work, providing some stimulating insights into scientific thought of the Victorian era"—*(LJ)*.

Hutchinson, Peter. EVOLUTION EXPLAINED. *David & Charles* 1975 $12.50

Huxley, Anthony. PLANT AND PLANET. *Viking* 1975 $12.50

Hynes, H. B. N. THE ECOLOGY OF RUNNING WATERS. *Univ. of Toronto Press* 1971 $25.00

"An essential handbook for advanced studies concerned with freshwater biology"—*(Choice)*.

Kendrew, John C. THE THREAD OF LIFE: An Introduction to Molecular Biology. *Harvard Univ. Press* 1966 $5.00. A study of DNA by a 1962 Nobel Prize winner based on his B.B.C. television lectures.

Ley, Willy. THE DAWN OF ZOOLOGY. Nature and Natural History Ser. *Prentice-Hall* 1968 $9.95

An "excursion into the beginnings of zoology, [which] concentrates on the attitudes of men towards animals and their ideas of zoology during earlier periods. Legends, lore, writings, and discoveries of prehistoric hunters, Greek philosophers, priests, explorers, and others are examined. Included is the background for our modern knowledge of animals and for beliefs in such mysterious creatures as the Waldrapp, Urus, Tree-geese, and Legless Bird of Paradise"—*(LJ)*.

Luria, S. E. LIFE, THE UNFINISHED EXPERIMENT. *Scribner* 1973 $7.95

"Luria concentrates on the critical need of any species to be able to adapt or evolve to survive radical changes in his environment, regardless of the origin of those changes; he questions whether man is capable of such change. . . . A very thought-provoking contribution to an area of current strong interest"—*(LJ)*.

McClary, Andrew. BIOLOGY AND SOCIETY: The Evolution of Man and His Technology. *Macmillan* 1975 $7.95

McHale, John. THE ECOLOGICAL CONTEXT. *Braziller* 1971 $7.95 pap. $3.95

McHale "deals with the life support systems of the physical environment (energy and materials) on a global scale"—*(Choice)*.

Milne, Lorus, and Margery Milne. THE AGES OF LIFE. *Harcourt* 1968 $6.95

Here they "trace the growth processes and prospects of human beings, using analogies drawn from plant and animal life from all parts of the world"—*(PW)*.

ARENA OF LIFE: The Dynamics of Ecology. *Doubleday* (Natural History Press) 1972 $15.00

"They trace evolution as well as the impact of the various geologic epochs on the earth's ecosystems"—*(LJ)*.

LIVING PLANTS OF THE WORLD. *Random* 1967 $15.00

This able writing team discuss the "major higher plant families of the world and their most interesting and fascinating representatives. . . . They present 150 of the most important families, stressing their values and uses in providing man with medicines, foods, narcotics, perfumes, incense, lumbers, gums, rubbers, waxes, spices, and many other products. . . . [A] fine book"— *(LJ)*.

PATTERNS OF SURVIVAL. Nature and Natural History Ser. *Prentice-Hall* 1967 $8.95

"A panorama of adaptations of living organisms to their various environments. . . . Highly recommended"—*(Choice)*.

Mines, Samuel. LAST DAYS OF MANKIND: Ecological Survival or Extinction. *Simon & Schuster* 1971 $7.95

"With life in the balance, Samuel Mines advocates the development of a new land ethic and a comprehensive politics of ecology so that the creatures of the world may survive"—*(LJ)*.

Moen, Aaron N. WILDLIFE ECOLOGY: An Analytical Approach. *W. H. Freeman* 1973 $17.50

Nilsson, Lennart, and Jan Lindberg. BEHOLD MAN: A Photographic Journey of Discovery Inside the Body. *Little* 1974 $25.00

"A masterful exploration of the mysteries of the human body through the art of photography. A view of the world through a human retina and a single cell of the cerebellum are just two of the photographic gems. . . . The accompanying text is well done and scientifically accurate"—*(LJ)*.

Owen, D. F. WHAT IS ECOLOGY? *Oxford* 1974 $7.95

"An introduction to the science of ecology which does not presume background in biology"— *(Booklist)*.

Pennak, R. W. THE COLLEGIATE DICTIONARY OF ZOOLOGY. *Ronald* 1964 $11.50

Pfeiffer, John E., and the editors of *Life*. THE CELL. Introd. by René Dubos Science Library Ser. *Time-Life Bks.* 1964 rev. ed. 1969 $8.80

A "rich summary" *(LJ)* of the developments in molecular biology. Illustrated.

Phillips, J. G., Ed. ENVIRONMENTAL PHYSIOLOGY. *Wiley* 1975 $9.95

"This book is concerned with the ways in which animals are adapted physiologically to the physical stresses of their environment"—*(LJ)*.

Rapport, Samuel, and Helen Wright, Eds. BIOLOGY. New York University Library of Science Ser. *New York Univ. Press* 1967 $6.95; *Simon & Schuster* (Washington Square) 1968 pap. $.90

"This collection of articles and excerpts from books by noted scientists and science writers offers a readable introduction to the history of biological concepts, including those of the cell, the origin of life, evolution, and genetics"—*(LJ)*.

Romer, Alfred S. THE PROCESSION OF LIFE. *Universe Bks.* 1968 $12.50; *Doubleday* Anchor Bks. 1972 pap. $2.95. The evolution of the chief animal groups is traced by the Harvard professor of zoology.

Rosenfeld, Alfred. THE SECOND GENESIS: The Coming Control of Life. 1968. *Pyramid Bks.* 1972 pap. $1.95. Discussion of this rather frightening prospect. Illustrated.

Rostand, Michael. HUMANLY POSSIBLE: A Biologist's Notes on the Future of Mankind. *Saturday Review Press* (dist. by Dutton) 1974 $6.95

Salthe, Stanley N. EVOLUTIONARY BIOLOGY. *Holt* 1973 $11.50

"A superlative treatise on evolution with a strong philosophical bent. . . . There is a gentle, relentless flow of information, argument, and theory from the opening paragraph to the end"— (*Choice*).

Sargent, Frederick. HUMAN ECOLOGY. *American Elsevier* 1975 $34.75

Shepard, Paul. THE TENDER CARNIVORE AND THE SACRED GAME. *Scribner* 1973 $9.95. A controversial view of man's behavior and ecology in the light of a million years as hunter-gatherer.

(With Daniel McKinley, Eds.). ENVIRON-MENTAL: Essays on the Planet as a Home. *Houghton* 1971 pap. $5.95

(With Daniel McKinley, Eds.). THE SUBVERSIVE SCIENCE: Essays Toward an Ecology of Man. *Houghton* 1969 pap. $6.95. Some 36 essays by eminent scientists with commentary on each by the editors.

Simpson, George Gaylord. BIOLOGY AND MAN. *Harcourt* 1969 $5.95 Harvest Bks. 1971 pap. $1.95

THE MEANING OF EVOLUTION: A Study of the History of Life and of Its Significance for Man. *Yale Univ. Press* rev. ed. 1967 $12.50 pap. $3.95

Smith, Anthony. THE BODY. *Avon Bks.* 1969 pap. $1.25

"This book of practical physiology offers about as much information about the care and operation of the human body as one is likely to find between the covers of a single volume"— (*National Observer*).

Taylor, Gordon Rattray. THE BIOLOGICAL TIME BOMB. 1966. *New Am. Lib.* Mentor 1969 pap. $1.25

"This book is intentionally and quite properly devoted almost exclusively to biological science as a generator of problems; and the last few pages briefly review the possibility that research is doing us more harm than good"—(Robert S. Morrison, in the *N.Y. Times*).

Thomas, Lewis. THE LIVES OF A CELL: Notes of a Biology Watcher. *Viking* 1974 $6.95

Wagner, Richard H. ENVIRONMENT AND MAN. *Norton* 1971 $7.50

"This introduction to man's relationship with, and his place within, the natural ecological system presents a vast amount of material calculated to encourage participation in the attack upon man-environment problems and to create a sensitivity for the quality of the environment"—(*LJ*).

Wasserman, Aaron O. BIOLOGY. *Prentice-Hall* (Appleton) 1973 $11.80

"The book introduces a variety of biological points of view—phylogenetic, behavioral, ecological, physiological—integrating all most successfully"—(*LJ*).

Watson, James D. THE DOUBLE HELIX: Being a Personal Account of the Discovery of the Structure of DNA. *Atheneum* 1968 $7.95; *New Am. Lib.* Signet 1969 pap. $.95

Wilentz, Joan Steen. THE SENSES OF MAN. *T. Y. Crowell* 1968 $6.95; *Apollo* 1971 pap. $2.45

"A fascinating account of current and older experimental and theoretical work on the senses, the nervous system, and the brain"—(*LJ*).

Wilson, Edward O. SOCIOBIOLOGY: The New Synthesis. *Harvard Univ. Press* 1975 $20.00

"*Sociobiology* is the study of the biological basis for social behavior in all species of animals. . . . This definitive book is certain to become a classic in its field"—(*LJ*).

Zuckerman, Sir Solly, Ed. CLASSICS IN BIOLOGY. 1960. *Kennikat* 1971 $12.75

THE CONCEPTS OF HUMAN EVOLUTION. *Academic Press* 1974 $29.00

The Naturalist's World: A Selected List

Abbey, Edward. CACTUS COUNTRY. American Wilderness Ser. *Time-Life* 1973 $7.95

Adams, Alexander B. ETERNAL QUEST: The Story of the Great Naturalists: From Aristotle to Thomas Huxley. *Putnam* 1969 $10.95

Allen, Durward L. THE LIFE OF PRAIRIES AND PLAINS. Our Living World of Nature Ser. *McGraw-Hill* 1967 $5.50

Beston, Henry. ESPECIALLY MAINE: The Natural World of Henry Beston. Ed. by Elizabeth Coatsworth *Stephen Greene Press* 1970 $6.95

THE OUTERMOST HOUSE. 1928. *Ballantine Bks.* 1971 pap. $.95; *Viking* Compass Bks. 1961 pap. $1.45. A charming classic, written while the author lived for a year in a cottage on the sand dunes of Cape Cod.

Blunt, Wilfred. THE COMPLETE NATURALIST: A Life of Linnaeus. *Viking* 1971 $14.95

"A very readable yet scholarly biography of Linnaeus"—(*TLS*, London).

Borland, Hal G. BORLAND COUNTRY. *Lippincott* 1971 $7.95

HILL COUNTRY HARVEST. *Lippincott* 1967 $6.95

Winner of the John Burroughs Medal. Mr. Borland is the nature editorial writer for the *N.Y. Times* Sunday edition. "He shares with Joseph Wood Krutch the gift of being able to endow the least and most common aspects of nature with excitement, meaning, and value. It is an uncommon gift, and Mr. Borland is an uncommon man"—(*SR*).

HOMELAND: A Report from the Country. *Lippincott* 1969 $4.50

"Borland sets us quietly turning with the globe itself from spring to summer to autumn to winter and back again, as he plays his subtle variations on the great seasonal themes"—(*LJ*).

THE SEASONS. Photographs by Les Line. *Lippincott* 1973 $14.95

"In *Seasons* writer and photographer [editor of *Audubon Magazine*], have collaborated in a magnificent evocation of the reality and the mystery, the inherent beauty of life on this planet"—(Publisher's note).

Botting, Douglas. HUMBOLDT AND THE COSMOS. *Harper* 1973 $15.00

"A smoothly written biography of an unusual figure in the history of the natural sciences"—(*LJ*).

Brown, Leslie. THE LIFE OF THE AFRICAN PLAINS. *McGraw-Hill* 1972 $4.95

"A brief natural history of the savannas"—(*LJ*).

Carrighar, Sally. HOME TO THE WILDERNESS. *Houghton* 1973 $7.95; *Penguin* 1974 pap. $1.95

"An autobiographical study of a rather unique relationship the author has established with the world of nature over many years"—(*LJ*).

Clement, Roland C. THE LIVING WORLD OF AUDUBON. *Grosset* 1974 $25.00

"Juxtaposing colorplates of 64 of Audubon's illustrations for *The Birds of America* with striking color photographs of the same species in natural settings, this is a fine alliance which works to the advantage of both artist and photographer"—(*Booklist*).

Costello, David F. THE DESERT WORLD. *T. Y. Crowell* 1972 $7.95

"This book presents the curious and dramatic extremes of the great North American desert lands"—(*LJ*).

THE PRAIRIE WORLD. *T. Y. Crowell* 1969 $7.95

"The seasons, plants, mammals, birds, insects, reptiles and amphibians, the patterns of drought and renewal and of fire and renewal [on the western prairie]"—(*N.Y. Times Bk. Review*).

Davis, Millard C. THE NEAR WOODS. *Knopf* 1975 $10.00

"Observes in fascinating detail the ecology of the woods—the relationships of trees to other plants, to insects, animals and man; and to the soil where they grow"—(*LJ*).

Dillard, Anne. PILGRIM AT TINKER CREEK. *Harper* 1974 $7.95. A chronicle of her life with nature in the Roanoke Valley of Virginia; awarded the Pulitzer Prize for general nonfiction in 1975.

Farb, Peter. THE FACE OF NORTH AMERICA: The Natural History of a Continent. Introd. by Marston Bates; ill. by Jerome Connolly *Harper* 1963 $10.00 Colophon Bks. pap. $2.95

Graustein, Jeannette E. THOMAS NUTTALL, NATURALIST: Explorations in America, 1808–1841. *Harvard Univ. Press* 1967 $13.50

This "is scarcely Boswellian in style or gusto and suffers much from the ritual strictures of academic naiveté, but it is nonetheless a significant addition to American letters. Aside from a few regrettable lapses into the suppositions that must tempt all biographers, it is a work of sound scholarship and exceedingly high standards of research"—(*SR*).

Heckman, Hazel. ISLAND IN THE SOUND. *Univ. of Washington Press* 1967 $5.95. Nature on a remote island in Puget Sound.

ISLAND YEAR. *Univ. of Washington Press* 1972 $7.95

"This second book by Hazel Heckman on her adopted wilderness island in Puget Sound is a touching plea for keeping our unspoiled corners of land from being turned into additional bulldozed developments"—(*LJ*).

Hoover, Helen. A PLACE IN THE WOODS. *Knopf* 1969 $5.95

"This is an account of how the author and her husband quit Chicago, bought a cabin, and settled in for year-round life on the fringe of Minnesota's northernmost wilderness. Neither of them was experienced in rural living—(*Natural History*).

THE YEARS OF THE FOREST. *Knopf* 1973 $6.95. An account of her sixteen years in the north woods of Minnesota.

Hutchins, Ross E. ISLAND OF ADVENTURE. *Dodd* 1968 $6.00. The animal and plant life of a semi-tropical marshland area in Mississippi near the Gulf of Mexico.

Johnson, E. D. H., Ed. THE POETRY OF EARTH: A Collection of English Nature Writings. Introd. by the author *Atheneum* 1965 pap. 1974 $4.25. Fourteen prose selections. A most attractive grouping, including Gilbert White, Richard Jefferies, G. M. Hopkins and others.

Kirk, Ruth. DESERT: The American Southwest. The Naturalists' America Ser. *Houghton* 1973 $10.00

Krutch, Joesph Wood. *See his main entry, this Chapter.*

Leopold, Aldo. SAND COUNTY ALMANAC: With Other Essays on Conservation from Round River. *Oxford* 1966 $7.95; *Ballantine Bks.* 1970 pap. $1.95. The seasons in nature in central Wisconsin; a classic in the field of conservation.

ROUND RIVER: From the Journals of Aldo Leopold. Ed. by Luna B. Leopold *Oxford* Galaxy Bks. 1972 pap. $1.75

Ogburn, Charlton, Jr. THE CONTINENT IN OUR HANDS. *Morrow* 1971 $8.95

"Mr. Ogburn, naturalist-author, set out in a camper-bus on a 22-day, 9,600 mile tour across America. . . . One might call him a Thoreau of the road, for his gaze is inward and on nature in a way that makes civilization almost alien"—(*N.Y. Times Bk. Review*).

THE WINTER BEACH. Ill. by Edward and Marcia Norman *Morrow* 1966 $7.95; *Simon & Schuster* Pocket Bks. 1971 pap. $1.25 Touchstone Bks. pap. $3.95

Winner of the John Burroughs Medal. The author "gives us the look and sound of that sea in every shift of wind. . . . It is an eloquent, and an elegant, depiction"—(*New Yorker*).

Olson, Sigurd F. OPEN HORIZONS. *Knopf* 1969 $5.95

"The author tells of his youth in the Great Lakes country, his experience as a wilderness guide . . . [his] studies and teaching in biology and geology, the long process of personal discovery that led him to writing in an effort to interpret wilderness and all its complex meanings, and to defend its vulnerable cause"—(*LJ*).

Russell, Andy. THE HIGH WEST. *Viking* 1974 $12.95

TRAILS OF A WILDERNESS WANDERER. *Knopf* 1971 $6.95. Autobiographical experiences with nature.

Sheldrick, Daphne J. ANIMAL KINGDOM: The Story of Tsavo, the Great African Game Park. *Bobbs* 1974 $7.95. The story of the establishment of a game park in Kenya.

Sierra Club. For information on the outstanding publications—mostly photographs and text—of this organization which does valiant work for the conservation of America's wilderness, write to the Sierra Club (Mills Tower, San Francisco, Calif. 94104) for catalog. Most books are $25.00 or more, but there are a number of less expensive titles. Some have been reprinted as *Sierra Club-Ballantine* paperbacks.

Sutton, Ann, and Myron Sutton. THE AMERICAN WEST: A Natural History. *Random* 1969 $20.00

WILDERNESS AREAS OF NORTH AMERICA. *T. Y. Crowell* (Funk & Wagnalls) 1974 $10.00

Symons, R. D. SILTON SEASONS: From the Diary of a Countryman. *Doubleday* 1975 $6.95. Rural life on the prairies of Saskatchewan.

Teale, Edwin Way. *See his main entry, this Chapter.*

Terres, John K. FROM LAUREL HILL TO SILER'S BOG: The Walking Adventures of a Naturalist. *Knopf* 1969 $6.95

Welker, Robert Henry. NATURAL MAN: The Life of William Beebe. *Indiana Univ. Press* 1975 $11.50

Woodin, Ann. HOME IS THE DESERT. Introd. by Joseph Wood Krutch *Macmillan* 1964 $6.95 Collier Bks. 1970 pap. $2.95

"Fascinating and altogether wonderful, rich with sound natural history and warm with the human touch. . . . She has made the desert country and its natives, both plant and animal, vividly alive"—(Hal Borland).

IN THE CIRCLE OF THE SUN (orig. "Home Is the Microbus"). *Macmillan* 1964 1971 $7.95

Living Creatures: A Selected List

Bourne, Geoffrey H., and Maury Cohen. THE GENTLE GIANTS: The Gorilla Story. *Putnam* 1975 $10.00

"A general introduction to the largest of man's close relatives"—(LJ).

Box, Hilary V. ORGANIZATION IN ANIMAL COMMUNITIES: Experimental and Naturalistic Studies of the Social Behavior of Animals. *Crane Russak* 1973 $12.75

Brown, Theo W. SHARKS: The Silent Savages. *Little* 1975 $7.95

"How sharks behave and how man might control them—this is the subject of a spellbinding new book by a veteran diver and researcher"—(Publisher's note).

Budker, Paul. LIFE OF SHARKS. *Columbia* 1971 $12.50

"An authoritative survey of the biology of sharks"—(LJ).

Burton, John A. OWLS OF THE WORLD: Their Evolution, Structure, and Ecology. *Dutton* 1973 $17.95

"This attempt to write about and illustrate every known species of owl is highly successful"—(LJ).

Burton, Robert. THE LIFE AND DEATH OF WHALES. *Universe Bks.* 1973 $6.95

"A great deal of information has been packed into this highly recommended little book"—(LJ).

Carr, Archie. So EXCELLENT A FISHE: A Natural History of Sea Turtles. *Doubleday* Natural History Press 1967 $5.95 Anchor Bks. 1973 pap. $2.95. On the work of experimental stations which investigate the mysterious life cycle of these turtles. Most interesting and entertaining.

Clark, Eleanor. THE OYSTERS OF LOCMARIAQUER. Ill. by Leonid Berman *Pantheon* 1964 $5.95; *Random* Vintage Bks. pap. $1.65. Robert Penn Warren's wife, herself a distinguished writer, tells about the oysters and the customs of this town in Brittany; a National Book Award winner.

Clarkson, Ewan. WOLF COUNTRY: A Wilderness Pilgrimage. *Dutton* 1975 $8.95

"Clarkson recounts his observations from several seasons spent at Isle Royale in Lake Superior, and in the wilderness area of northern Minnesota"—(LJ).

Cosgrove, Margaret. MESSAGES AND VOICES: The Communication of Animals. *Dodd* 1974 $4.95

Dorst, Jean. THE LIFE OF BIRDS. Trans. by C. Galbraith *Columbia* 2 vol. 1974 set $35.00

"Exhaustive scientific study of avian behavior"—(*Booklist*). "In this excellent study, one of the world's leading ornithologists discusses the biology of birds and their place in the ecosystems of the world"—(*LJ*).

Douglas-Hamilton, Iain, and Oria Douglas-Hamilton. AMONG THE ELEPHANTS. *Viking* 1975 $14.95

The author "has closely observed his animal subjects in their natural environment for several years, recording every detail"—(*LJ*).

Eakin, Richard M. THE THIRD EYE. *Univ. of California Press* 1974 $7.50

"Eakin discusses the distribution of 'the third eye' [the pineal eye] among animals, its purpose and form, and uses it as a stepping stone to a broader treatment of light-sensitive organs as found in a number of species"—(*LJ*).

Eaton, Randall L. THE CHEETAH: The Biology, Ecology, and Behavior of an Endangered Species. *Van Nostrand-Reinhold* 1973 $12.95

"Eaton's purpose is to demonstrate the significant role this animal plays in a much larger ecological drama being staged today on the African plains"—(*LJ*).

Evans, Howard E. WASP FARM. *Doubleday* Anchor Bks. 1973 pap. $2.50; *Peter Smith* $4.50

(With Mary L. Eberhard). THE WASPS. *Univ. of Michigan Press* 1970 $7.95 Ann Arbor Bks. 1970 pap. $3.45

Evans, William F. COMMUNICATION IN THE ANIMAL WORLD. Ill. by Nancy Lou Gahan *T. Y. Crowell* 1968 $5.95; *Apollo* 1971 pap. $1.95

Fogden, Michael, and Patricia Fogden. ANIMALS AND THEIR COLORS: Camouflage, Warning Coloration, Courtship and Territorial Display, Mimicry. *Crown* 1974 $9.95

"On the biological significance of coloration in animals, and how it has developed to insure the survival of numerous species"—(*LJ*).

Frisch, Karl von. THE DANCE LANGUAGE AND ORIENTATION OF BEES. Trans. by Leigh E. Chadwick *Harvard Univ. Press* Belknap Press 1967 $17.00

"Delightfully well written"—(*LJ*).

See also his main entry, this Chapter.

Gardiner, Mary S. THE BIOLOGY OF INVERTEBRATES. *McGraw-Hill* 1973 $16.95

"A comprehensive treatment of all invertebrate groups except protochorodates"—(*Choice*).

Geist, Valerius. MOUNTAIN SHEEP: A Study in Behavior and Evolution. *Univ. of Chicago Press* 1972 $14.50

"The theory of mountain sheep evolution is integrated through social behavior, population dynamics, bioenergetics, zoogeography, and ecology into a functional whole, and Geist compares sheep ecology with moose ecology in a functional way"—(*Choice*).

MOUNTAIN SHEEP AND MAN IN THE NORTHERN WILDS. *Cornell Univ. Press* 1975 $10.00

Goodall, Jane. *See her main entry: Lawick-Goodall, Jane, Baroness van, this Chapter.*

Guggisberg, C. A. W. CROCODILES: Their Natural History, Folklore and Conservation. *Stackpole* 1972 $7.95

"Here is a wealth of scientific information, beliefs, superstitions, and tales about sizes, shapes, and dispositions of saurians in different parts of the world"—(*LJ*).

Harrison, Hal H. A FIELD GUIDE TO BIRDS' NESTS: Of 285 Species Found Breeding in the United States East of the Mississippi River. Peterson Field Guide Ser. *Houghton* 1975 $8.95

Hvass, Hans. FISHES OF THE WORLD IN COLOR. Trans. by Gwynne Vevers *Dutton* 1965 $5.95

REPTILES AND AMPHIBIANS IN COLOUR. *Int. Pubns. Service* 1974 $7.50

Jensen, Albert C. COD. *T. Y. Crowell* 1972 $7.95

"The life and natural history of *Gadus morhua*, the Atlantic Cod"—(*LJ*).

Koch, Thomas J. THE YEAR OF THE POLAR BEAR. *Bobbs* 1975 $8.95

"Koch gives us all the latest information that is available, in a now familiar format: mother animal gives birth to cub (male of course) and we follow them through their year, pausing often for bits of history and scientific information"—(LJ).

Kruuk, Hans. THE SPOTTED HYENA: A Study of Predation and Social Behavior. *Univ. of Chicago Press* 1972 $15.00

"An outstanding treatise on the spotted hyena based on several years of field work in the Serengeti Plains and Ngorongoro Crater. This study is fundamentally one on the predation and social behavior of this animal"—(*Choice*).

Lawick, Hugo, Baron van, and Jane Lawick-Goodall. INNOCENT KILLERS. *Houghton* 1971 $10.00

"The present book describes the behavior of the Cape Hunting Dog (*Lycaon pictus*), the Golden Jackal (*Canis aureus*), and the Spotted Hyena (*Crocuta crocuta*). . . . Popular myths are exploded, both hyenas and wild dogs attack zebras, a pack of strolling wild dogs does not panic a herd of ungulates. . . . The style is popular, absorbing, sympathetic"—(*Choice*).

Leftwich, A. W. A DICTIONARY OF ZOOLOGY. *Crane, Russak* 3rd ed. 1973 $13.50

Leviton, Alan E. REPTILES AND AMPHIBIANS OF NORTH AMERICA. *Doubleday* 1972 $9.95

"These interesting creatures, many relatively unknown and seemingly strange, are described in this informative handbook. It provides information on their physiology and anatomy, habits and behavior, reproduction, life cycles, longevity, foods, habitats, and other details"—(LJ).

Lockley, Ronald M. THE PRIVATE LIFE OF THE RABBIT: An Account of the Life History and Social Behavior of the Wild Rabbit. *Macmillan* 1974 $6.95

McIntyre, Joan, Comp. MIND IN THE WATERS: A Book to Celebrate the Consciousness of Whales and Dolphins. *Scribner* 1974 $14.95

"As head of Project Jonah, McIntyre's purpose is to establish recognition of cetaceans both as an endangered species and in their unique relationship to mankind"—(*Booklist*).

McMillan, Ian. MAN AND THE CALIFORNIA CONDOR. *Dutton* 1968 $6.95

McNulty, Faith. THE GREAT WHALES. *Doubleday* 1974 $4.95

Matthews, Leonard Harrison. LIFE OF MAMMALS. Natural History Ser. *Universe Bks.* 2 vols. 1970–71 each $12.50

Matthiessen, Peter. THE SHOREBIRDS OF NORTH AMERICA. Ed. by Gardner D. Stout; ill. by Robert Verity Clem; species accounts by Ralph S. Palmer *Viking* 1967 $22.50

See also his main entry, this Chapter.

Michener, Charles D. THE SOCIAL BEHAVIOR OF THE BEES: A Comparative Study. *Harvard Univ. Press* 1974 $25.00

"The division of labor, mechanisms of communication, the structure and care of nests by members of a single hive are considered here, as is the natural evolution of the numerous groups of social bees"—(LJ).

Milne, Lorus, and Margery Milne. THE INVERTEBRATES OF NORTH AMERICA. *Doubleday* 1972 $9.95

Moss, Cynthia. PORTRAITS IN THE WILD: Behavior Studies of East African Mammals. *Houghton* 1975 $12.50

The author "has assembled the latest reports on 15 mammals: elephant, giraffe, black rhinoceros, zebra, baboon, spotted hyena, six antelopes, and three cats"—(*PW*).

Neill, Wilfred T. LAST OF THE RULING REPTILES: Alligators, Crocodiles, and Their Kin. *Columbia* 1971 $15.95

"A definitive work, bolstered with a lengthy bibliography that directs the reader to numerous intriguing titles"—(LJ).

Nicolai, Jürgen. BIRD LIFE. Introd. by Konrad Lorenz *Putnam* 1974 $25.00

"A treatise on bird behavior illustrated with striking colorplates"—(*Booklist*).

North, Sterling. RACCOONS ARE THE BRIGHTEST PEOPLE. *Dutton* 1966 $6.95

Ordish, George. THE YEAR OF THE BUTTERFLY. *Scribner* 1975 $8.95

"The complete life history of the monarch butterfly in a readable, narrative form ... an extraordinary amount of information is included here"—(*LJ*).

Roots, Clive. Animals in the Dark. *Praeger* 1974 $8.95. The Winnipeg Zoo director describes the activities of nocturnal and subterranean creatures.

Rugoff, Martin, and Ann Guilfoyle, Eds. The Private Lives of Animals. *Grosset* 1974 $17.95

"Covers almost every aspect of the behavior of wild animals, from the largest mammals to minute invertebrates"—(Kirtley F. Mather).

Russell, Andy. Grizzly Country. *Knopf* 1967 $7.95. Photographs and 40 years' worth of observations of the bears' habits and antics.

Horns in the High Country. *Knopf* 1973 $6.95

"An account of the wild sheep and the mountain goat and the spacious and natural world in which they live"—(Publisher's note).

Ryden, Hope. God's Dog. *Coward* 1974 $12.50

"The coyote in its natural surroundings is closely observed and described in a personalized study"—(*Booklist*).

Schaller, George B. The Deer and the Tiger: A Study of Wildlife in India. *Univ. of Chicago Press* 1967 $12.50 Phoenix Bks. 1974 pap. $6.95. His results of a detailed investigation of the tiger as a predator.

Golden Shadows, Flying Hooves. *Knopf* 1973 $8.95. A popular account of his three years' experience in the Serengeti with lions, wild dogs, leopards, and hyenas.

The Mountain Gorilla: Ecology and Behavior. *Univ. of Chicago Press* 1963 $12.50

Serengeti: A Kingdom of Predators. *Knopf* 1972 $12.95

"With text and photographs the author presents the life of the five great African predators—lion, leopard, cheetah, wild dog, hyena—and the species on which they prey, observed close up in their natural habitat during three and a half years in Africa"—(Publisher's note).

The Serengeti Lion: A Study in Predator-Prey Relations. *Univ. of Chicago Press* 1972 $12.50

This "is the most comprehensive scientific study yet published on the behavior of free-living lions"—(*SR*). "The main body of the book presents factual material on the lion, its social group structure and movements, behavior within the group, population dynamics, food habits, and hunting methods. There are chapters on other predators: leopard, cheetah, wild dog, hyena, jackals, reptiles, birds, and man"—(*LJ*). National Book Award winner in science for 1973.

The Year of the Gorilla. *Univ. of Chicago Press* 1964 $10.00 Phoenix Bks. pap. $2.95; *Ballantine Bks.* pap. $.75

Schwiebert, Ernest G. Trout. *McKay* 3 vols. 1975 set $35.00

Scott, Peter, and the Wildfowl Trust. Swans. *Houghton* 1972 $15.00

"Although intended as a scientific study, *Swans* has been written with such skill and verve that it provides good reading for the layman, for birders, or for scientists in other fields"—(*LJ*).

Sheldon, William. The Wilderness Home of the Giant Panda. *Univ. of Massachusetts Press* 1975 $10.00. The field journal of an expedition to Szechwan province, China, 41 years ago.

Solem, Alan. The Shell Makers: Introducing Mollusks. *Wiley* 1974 $9.95

"Solem reviews their evolution, adaptations to specific habitats, feeding patterns, etc., using much of the recent scientific literature. A worthwhile addition to basic zoology collections"—(*LJ*).

Sparks, John, and Tony Soper. Owls: Their Natural and Unnatural History. *Taplinger* 1970 $7.95

Stadtfeld, Curtis K. Whitetail Deer: A Year's Cycle. *Dial* 1975 $7.95

"Well researched and beautifully written, with recent data on population and other ecological factors"—(*LJ*).

Stenuit, Robert. The Dolphin, Cousin to Man. Trans. from the French by Catherine Osborne *Bantam* 1972 pap. $.95

Topsell, Edward. THE FOWLES OF HEAVEN OR HISTORY OF BIRDES. Ed. by Thomas P. Harrison and F. David Hoeniger *Univ. of Texas Press* 1972 $15.00. An edition of Topsell's ms. of his translation and abridgement of Ulisse Aldrovandi's (1522–1605) "Ornithologiae." Covers A–C, except book 14.

THE HISTORY OF FOUR-FOOTED BEASTS AND SERPENTS AND INSECTS. Introd. by Willy Ley *Da Capo* 3 vols. 2nd ed. 1967 set $65.00 Vol. I The History of Four-Footed Beasts (1607) Vol. 2 The History of Serpents, both by Edward Topsell, taken principally from the *Historiae Animalium* by Conrad Gesner (1608) Vol. 3 The Theatre of Insects, by Theodore Muffet (1658)

Willy Ley writes of Topsell's work in the introduction: "It was the first major book on animals printed in Great Britain in English; and it appeared at the last moment in history when all zoological knowledge since antiquity could be summarized sympathetically, before it was rendered a curiosity by the many new discoveries soon to come." "An exceptionally handsome job, luxuriously produced, and will delight anyone interested in old and/or beautiful books"—(*N.Y. Times*).

Walker, Ernest P., and others. MAMMALS OF THE WORLD. *Johns Hopkins Press* 2 vols. 3rd ed. 1975 set $37.50

"New material provided includes 270 photographs, ten genera, and updated information supplied by zoologists"—(*LJ*).

Walker, Lewis Wayne. THE BOOK OF OWLS. *Random* 1974 $12.50

"A snappy capsulation of the natural history of owls"—(*Booklist*).

Williamson, H. D. THE YEAR OF THE KOALA. *Scribner* 1975 $8.95

"The scene of this beautifully written narrative is New South Wales and the koala's year begins in December"—(*PW*).

CHEMISTRY

Asimov, Isaac. A SHORT HISTORY OF CHEMISTRY. *Doubleday* Anchor Bks. 1965 pap. $1.95

See also his main entry, this Chapter.

Borrow, Gordon M. GENERAL CHEMISTRY. *Wadsworth* 1974 $14.95

UNDERSTANDING CHEMISTRY. *Addison-Wesley* (Benjamin) 5 vols. 1967 Vol. 1 Chemical Quantities Vol. 2 Chemical Bonding Vol. 3 Chemical Reactions Vol. 4 Chemical Equilibria Vol. 5 Chemical Systems pap. each $2.95

Baum, Stuart J., and Charles Scaife. CHEMISTRY: A Life Science Approach. *Macmillan* 1975 $13.95

Billmeyer, Fred W., Jr. SYNTHETIC POLYMERS: Building the Giant Molecule. *Doubleday* 1972 $6.95

"A detailed survey of the high polymer molecule ranging from basic structure to latest application"—(*LJ*).

Clark, George L., and Gessner G. Hawley, Eds. ENCYCLOPEDIA OF CHEMISTRY. *Van Nostrand-Reinhold* 2nd ed. 1966 $28.95

Cottrell, T. L. CHEMISTRY. *Oxford* 2nd ed. 1970 pap. $1.95

Dewar, Michael J. INTRODUCTION TO MODERN CHEMISTRY. *Oxford* 1965 pap. $3.95

MOLECULAR ORBITAL THEORY OF ORGANIC CHEMISTRY. *McGraw-Hill* 1969 $18.50

Eubanks, I. D., and O. C. Dermer. CHEMISTRY IN CIVILIZATION. *Ronald* 1974 $9.50

Fleming, Ian. SELECTED ORGANIC SYNTHESIS: A Guidebook for Organic Chemists. *Wiley* 1973 $18.95

Goldwater, Leonard J. MERCURY: A History of Quicksilver. *York Press* 1972 $15.00. The origins and uses, properties and behavior, etc. of mercury from Aristotle to the present.

Gregory, Richard P. THE BIOCHEMISTRY OF PHOTOSYNTHESIS. *Wiley* 1971 $10.25

"Stimulating comparisons between analogous systems in plant and animal life, *e.g.* processes in the chloroplast and in the mitochondrion"—*(Choice)*.

Gymer, Roger G. CHEMISTRY: An Ecological Approach. *Harper* 1973 $12.95

"An ecological approach to chemistry without excluding the topics traditionally found in texts for science majors (quantum theory, molecular orbitals etc.)"—*(Choice)*.

Jones, Mark M., and others. CHEMISTRY, MAN AND SOCIETY. *Saunders* 1972 $12.95

Kirk, R. E., and D. F. Othmer. ENCYCLOPEDIA OF CHEMICAL TECHNOLOGY. Anthony Stander, Executive Ed. *Wiley* 22 vols., suppl. and index 2nd ed. 1963–72 each $55.00 complete set $1200.00

Leicester, Henry Marshall. THE HISTORICAL BACKGROUND OF CHEMISTRY. 1956. *Dover* 1971 pap. $3.00; *Peter Smith* $5.50

(With Herbert S. Klickstein, Eds.). SOURCE BOOK IN CHEMISTRY 1900–1950. *Harvard Univ. Press* 1968 $12.50

An addendum to "Source Book in Chemistry, 1400–1900," edited by Mr. Leicester and Herbert S. Klickstein (*Harvard Univ. Press* 1952 $15.00). Seclections from 90 "classic" papers with illustrations; "a fine 10-page bibliography of biographies. . . . The range of appeal for readers should be from students to emeriti!"—*(Choice)*.

Metzger, Norman. MEN AND MOLECULES. 2nd Ser. *Crown* 1966 2nd ed. 1972 $5.95

Miall, Lawrence Mackenzie, and D. W. A. Sharp, Eds. A NEW DICTIONARY OF CHEMISTRY. 1940. *Halsted Press* 4th ed. 1968 $15.50

Multhauf, Robert P. THE ORIGINS OF CHEMISTRY. 1967. *Univ. of Chicago Press* $9.50

A "most engaging book" (*LJ*) on the history of scientific knowledge to the 17th century.

Nechamkin, Howard. CHEMISTRY OF THE ELEMENTS. *McGraw-Hill* 1968 $3.95. Studies individually each element of the periodic table.

Needham, Dorothy M. MACHINA CARNIS: The Biochemistry of Muscular Contraction in Its Historical Development. *Cambridge* 1972 $55.00

"A monumental work by a distinguished biochemist"—*(Choice)*.

Nordmann, Joseph. WHAT IS CHEMISTRY: A Chemical View of Nature. *Harper* 1974 $12.95

Pierce, James B. THE CHEMISTRY OF MATTER. *Houghton* 1970 $12.95

Pimentel, George C., and Richard D. Spratley. CHEMICAL BONDING CLARIFIED THROUGH QUANTUM MECHANICS. *Holden-Day* 1969 pap. $7.95

Porterfield, William W. CONCEPTS OF CHEMISTRY. *Norton* 1972 $12.95

"A must for all college libraries, public libraries, and collections dealing with chemistry"— *(Choice)*.

Richardson, J. F., J. M. Coulson, and D. G. Peacock. CHEMICAL ENGINEERING. *Pergamon* 4 vols. 1968–74 Vol. 1 (1968) $9.00 Vol. 2 (1968) $11.50 Vol. 3 (1971) $14.00 Vol. 4 (1974) $15.00

Sherwood, Martin. THE NEW CHEMISTRY. *Basic Bks.* 1973 $9.50

"Much is quite readable without even a moderate prior knowledge of the subject. Accounts of the discovery of industrial chemical products, such as nylon, plastics, and food products, are fascinating"—*(LJ)*.

Smith, Richard Furnald. CHEMISTRY FOR THE MILLION. *Scribner* 1972 $7.95 pap. 1974 $2.95

"Chapters cover such themes as ancient origins and alchemy, metals, Lavoisier, oxygen, inert gases, the Periodic Table, halogens, nonmetals, and carbon"—*(LJ)*.

Stevens, B. CHEMICAL KINETICS: For General Students of Chemistry. *Wiley* Halsted Press 2nd ed. 1970 pap. $2.50

"An excellent review and condensation of the material related to chemical equilibrium and rates of reaction . . . sufficient to give a student an understanding of the factors that determine the nature and course of a reaction between molecules under a set of specific conditions"—*(Choice)*.

Williams, Roger J., and Edwin M. Lansford, Jr., Eds. THE ENCYCLOPEDIA OF BIOCHEMIS-
TRY. *Van Nostrand-Reinhold* 1967 $27.50. 876 pages; 800 articles

EARTH SCIENCES

American West Editors. THE MAGNIFICENT ROCKIES: Crest of a Continent. *American West*
1973 $18.50

"This volume traces their natural history, exploring their vast plant and animal resources . . . a
comprehensive survey of one of the most beautiful areas of our country"—*(LJ)*.

Barrett, E. C. CLIMATOLOGY FROM SATELLITES. *Barnes & Noble* 1974 $27.50

Berry, W. B. N. THE GROWTH OF A PREHISTORIC TIME SCALE: Based on Organic Evolution. *W. H. Freeman* 1968 pap. $2.50. Discusses the methods of measuring prehistoric
time.

Blatt, Harvey. ORIGIN OF SEDIMENTARY ROCKS. *Prentice-Hall* 1972 $16.50

Bolt, Bruce A. GEOLOGICAL HAZARDS: Earthquakes, Tsunamis, Volcanoes, Avalanches,
Landslides, Floods. *Springer Verlag* 1974 $14.00

Brunsden, Denys, and John C. Doornkamp, Eds. THE UNQUIET LANDSCAPE. *Indiana Univ.
Press* 1975 $15.00

"A profusely illustrated introduction to geomorphology"—*(LJ)*.

Bullard, Fred M. VOLCANOES IN HISTORY, IN THEORY, IN ERUPTION. *Univ. of Texas Press*
1962 $10.00

Burchfield, Joe D. LORD KELVIN AND THE AGE OF THE EARTH. *Science History Pubns.* 1975
$15.00

"A history of an idea, tracing the acceptance of Kelvin's theory in terms of the scientific and
philosophical milieu in which it was conceived"—*(LJ)*.

Calder, Nigel. RESTLESS EARTH: A Report on the New Geology. *Viking* 1972 $10.00

"Using his gift for clearly presenting concise explanations of complex scientific concepts, Nigel
Calder tells of the 'dynamic forces at work in plate tectonics' or continental drift"—*(LJ)*.

THE WEATHER MACHINE. *Viking* 1974 $14.95. How weather patterns have changed and
continue to change.

Clement, Roland C. NATURE ATLAS OF AMERICA. *Hammond* 1973 $17.95

"Beautifully illustrated with close to 250 color photographs and an impressive number of maps,
this book offers a factual, concise survey of the North American continent—its flora, fauna, and
geology . . . it describes our deciduous forests, prairie soil, minerals, and climate that have
nourished an incredible variety of trees, mammals, birds, and fishes. Highly recommended"—
(LJ).

Cloud, Preston, Ed. ADVENTURES IN EARTH HISTORY. *W. H. Freeman* 1970 pap. $9.95

"A collection of 83 significant papers on geology and related topics in oceanography, climatology, origin of the universe and solar system, organic evolution . . . that span the period from the
time of Nicolaus Steno (1669) to the present"—*(LJ)*.

Colbert, Edwin H. MEN AND DINOSAURS. *Dutton* 1968 $8.95. A history of the unearthing of
both in fossil form.

WANDERING LANDS AND ANIMALS. *Dutton* 1974 $12.50

"Drawing on his own observations and collections of fossil material in the Antarctic, Colbert has
put together a volume that supports the concept of continental drift through the evidence of
paleontological findings. . . . A highly readable, authoritative review of present knowledge in the
field"—*(LJ)*.

Court, Arthur, and Ian Campbell. MINERALS: Nature's Fabulous Jewels. *Harry N. Abrams*
1974 $35.00

This book is to be "treasured for the wealth of information it contains about minerals in general
and in particular"—(Kirtley F. Mather).

Craig, Richard A. THE EDGE OF SPACE: Exploring the Upper Atmosphere. Ill. by Joyce A. Lake. Science Study Ser. *Doubleday* 1968 $4.50 Anchor Bks. pap. $1.25

Darden, Lloyd. THE EARTH IN THE LOOKING GLASS. *Doubleday* 1974 $7.95

"Describes in non-technical language the newly developing technology of 'remote sensing' whereby much valuable knowledge may be economically secured about the surface of the earth and its resources by the use of low-flying satellites"—(Kirtley F. Mather).

Deming, H. G. WATER: The Fountain of Opportunity. *Oxford* 1975 $12.50

Desautels, Paul E. THE GEM KINGDOM. *Random* 1971 $17.95

THE MINERAL KINGDOM. *Grosset* 1968 $7.95. A historical study of the discovery and use of minerals.

ROCKS AND MINERALS. *Grosset* 1974 $12.95

"A breathtaking color survey of some outstanding minerals, with information on their physical properties, from the famous collection of the Smithsonian Institution"—(*LJ*).

Dineley, David. EARTH'S VOYAGE THROUGH TIME. *Knopf* 1974 $8.95

Dineley "discusses the evolution of life, geological cycles, natural history, and continental drift"—(*Booklist*).

Eagleman, Joe R., and others. THUNDERSTORMS, TORNADOES, AND BUILDING DAMAGE. *Heath* 1975 $23.00

"An in-depth analysis of tornadoes and their devastation to building structures in their path"—(*LJ*).

Fairbridge, Rhodes W., Ed. ENCYCLOPEDIA OF GEOCHEMISTRY AND ENVIRONMENTAL SCIENCES. *Van Nostrand-Reinhold* 1972 $49.50

"A valuable reference work"—(*Choice*).

Frye, Keith. MODERN MINERALOGY. *Prentice-Hall* 1974 $12.50

Halacy, D. S. EARTHQUAKES: A Natural History. *Bobbs* 1974 $7.95

Hallam, A. A REVOLUTION IN THE EARTH SCIENCES: From Continental Drift to Plate Tectonics. *Oxford* 1974 $10.00

Hapgood, Charles H. MAPS OF THE ANCIENT SEA KINGS: Evidence of Advanced Civilization in the Ice Age. Fwd. by John K. Wright *Chilton* 1966 $14.50

An "amazing and exciting book," in which "careful study of ancient maps [points] to a vanished civilization of over 6000 years ago, well versed in science, with a knowledge of technology that we did not begin to obtain until the 18th century"—(*LJ*).

Helm, Thomas. HURRICANES: Weather at Its Worst. *Dodd* 1967 $6.00. Treats their causes and forecasting and describes the most disastrous storms of the 20th century.

Hodgson, John H. EARTHQUAKES AND EARTH STRUCTURE. *Prentice-Hall* 1964 $6.50

Hurlbut, Cornelius S., Jr. MINERALS AND MAN. *Random* 1968 $17.95

Kauffmann, John M. FLOW EAST: A Look at Our North Atlantic Rivers. *McGraw-Hill* 1973 $7.95

"A thoughtful discussion of the rivers of the northeastern United States and their courses through rural and urban areas"—(*LJ*).

LAROUSSE ENCYCLOPEDIA OF THE EARTH. Fwd. by Vivian Fuchs and Fenton Carroll *Crown* 1972 pap. $6.95

Lewis, Richard S. A CONTINENT FOR SCIENCE: The Antarctic Adventure. Fwd. by Thomas O. Jones *Viking* 1965 $7.95. Records the work, mostly of American scientists, on exploring the nature of this continent.

(With Philip M. Smith, Eds.). FROZEN FUTURE: A Prophetic Report from Antarctica. *Quadrangle* 1974 $12.50

"Contributions from noted scientists who are citizens of the 12 countries represented [in Antarctica] discuss prehistoric glaciation, the need for conservation of the resources of this inhospitable-to-man region, etc."—(*LJ*).

Macan, T. T. PONDS AND LAKES. *Crane, Russak* 1974 $10.50

MacDonald, Gordon A. VOLCANOES. *Prentice-Hall* 1972 $18.00

"A long awaited and virtually complete compendium of information about an interesting subject"—*(Choice)*.

(With Agatin T. Abbott). VOLCANOES IN THE SEA: The Geology of Hawaii. *Univ. of Hawaii Press* 1971 $15.00

"Excellent volume by the foremost authority on Hawaiian geology, giving a complete and readable account of the interesting geologic history of the Hawaiian Islands"—*(Choice)*.

Marvin, Ursula B. CONTINENTAL DRIFT: The Evolution of a Concept. *Smithsonian Institution* 1973 $12.50

"The volume traces the ideas and explores the personalities that have influenced the development of geology"—*(LJ)*. The author is a member of the Smithsonian Astrophysical Observatory.

Mason, Brian, and Leonard G. Berry. ELEMENTS OF MINERALOGY. *W. H. Freeman* 1968 $11.95

Mather, Kirtley F., Ed. SOURCE BOOK IN GEOLOGY, 1900–1950. *Harvard Univ. Press* 1967 $15.00. Important historical record of 20th-century discoveries.

Moore, Ruth E. MAN, TIME AND FOSSILS. *Knopf* rev. ed. 1961 $8.95

Moore, Wilfred George. A DICTIONARY OF GEOGRAPHY: Definitions and Explanations of Terms Used in Physical Geography. 1952. *Penguin* 1963 pap. $1.75; *Praeger* rev. and enl. ed. 1967 $6.50

Ogburn, Charlton, Jr. THE FORGING OF OUR CONTINENT. 1968. *Hale* $4.95. A geologic history of North America.

Phillips, Owen M. THE HEART OF THE EARTH. *Freeman, Cooper & Co.* 1968 $4.75. How the earth's interior is studied.

Ranwell, D. S. ECOLOGY OF SALT MARSHES AND SAND DUNES. *Wiley* 1973 $14.50

"A timely book as the public becomes increasingly concerned about the artificial erosion of our coastal areas by real estate developers, and the subsequent pollution of one of the most valuable natural areas we have"—*(LJ)*.

Riley, D., and L. Spalton. WORLD WEATHER AND CLIMATE. *Cambridge* 1974 $7.95

Rittmann, Alfred. VOLCANOES AND THEIR ACTIVITY. *Wiley* 1962 $15.75

Scorer, Richard. CLOUDS OF THE WORLD: A Complete Color Encyclopedia. *Stackpole* 1972 $29.95

Shepard, Francis P., and Harold R. Wanless. OUR CHANGING COASTLINES. *McGraw-Hill* 1971 $39.50

"An outstanding compilation of information on the U.S. coastline and its occurring changes, including Alaska and Hawaii. Excellent descriptions of various coastal landforms are included"—*(Choice)*.

Shimer, John A. FIELD GUIDE TO LANDFORMS IN THE UNITED STATES. *Macmillan* 1972 $10.95

A "professional geologist and writer, [Shimer] points out the common conditions and forces that produced the mountains, shaped the hills, cut the valleys, modified the slopes, and arranged the streams and lakes"—*(LJ)*.

THIS CHANGING EARTH: An Introduction to Geology. *Harper* 1968 $7.95 (Barnes & Noble) 1969 pap. $1.75

Simpson, George Gaylord. THE LIFE OF THE PAST: An Introduction to Paleontology. *Yale Univ. Press* 1953 $8.75

Stephenson, T. A., and Anne Stephenson. LIFE BETWEEN TIDEMARKS ON ROCKY SHORES. *W. H. Freeman* 1973 $15.00 pap. $6.95

"A synoptic account of the life-long studies of T. A. (deceased) and Anne Stephenson, outstanding authorities on global intertidal ecology. In a very readable, lucid form it characterizes the rocky shores of the earth, their zonational patterns, and descriptions of key intertidal populations"—*(Choice)*.

Sullivan, Walter. Continents in Motion: The New Earth Debate. *McGraw-Hill* 1974 $17.95

"Theories of continental drift offered since the early years of the twentieth century to explain the present state of the planet are chronologized and clarified by the science editor of the *New York Times*"—*(Booklist).*

Tazieff, Haroun. The Making of the Earth: Volcanoes and Continental Drift. *Atheneum* 1975 $7.00

"The style recommends this book to public collections, but its content makes it equally appropriate for scientific libraries"—*(LJ).*

Todd, David K., Ed. The Water Encyclopedia: A Compendium of Useful Information on Water Resources. *Water Information Center* 1971 $27.50

A "unique publication endeavoring to assemble information on the many aspects of water"—*(Choice).*

Vitaliano, Dorothy B. Legends of the Earth: Their Geologic Origins. *Indiana Univ. Press* 1973 $12.50

Ward, Barbara, and René Dubos. Only One Earth: The Care and Maintenance of a Small Planet. *Norton* 1972 $6.00

The Weather Almanac: A Reference Guide to the Weather and Climate of the United States and Its Key Cities, Including Reference Data on Storms and Weather Extremes. Ed. by James A. Ruffner and Frank E. Blair. *Gale Research Co.* 1974 $12.50

Winkless, Nels, and Iben Browning. Climate and the Affairs of Men. *Harper* 1975 $8.95

"Using tidal forces as a controlling element, the authors have related just about every world event or phenomenon to weather patterns"—*(LJ).*

Wyckoff, Jerome. Rock, Time, and Landforms. *Harper* 1966 $10.00

"A wonderful foundation book" in geology—*(LJ).*

Conservation

Adams, Alexander B. Eleventh Hour: A Hard Look at Conservation and the Future. *Putnam* 1970 $7.95

Allen, Thomas B. Vanishing Wildlife of North America. *National Geographic Soc.* 1974 $4.25

"An encyclopedic approach to a sad subject—the potential for extinction of many reptiles, fish, birds, and mammals in North America"—*(LJ).*

Amory, Cleveland. Man Kind? Our Incredible War on Wildlife. *Harper* 1974 $8.95

"Outraged at the decimation of animals by hunters, Amory laces his documented polemic with ironic humor"—*(Booklist).*

Atkinson, J. Brooks. This Bright Land. *Doubleday* Natural History Press 1974 $5.95

"As much a naturalist as a Pulitzer Prize winner and drama critic, Brooks Atkinson demonstrates a real concern for the plight of America's natural beauty and wildlife heritage . . . This is not a long book but one that should be required reading for every person in America"—*(LJ).*

Clepper, Henry E., Ed. Leaders of American Conservation. *Ronald* 1971 $10.95

Origins of American Conservation. *Ronald* 1968 $5.95

"A valuable historical handbook"—*(LJ).*

Curry-Lindahl, Kai. Let Them Live: A Worldwide Survey of Animals Threatened with Extinction. *Morrow* 1972 $9.95 pap. $3.95

The author "deals with all known vertebrate species and subspecies that have become extinct or are declining so rapidly that they soon may be. Continent by continent, region by region, these animals and their problems are surveyed and discussed"—*(LJ).*

Ehrenfeld, David W. Conserving Life on Earth. *Oxford* 1972 $10.00

"My role in writing this book," the author says, "has been that of an advocate for the natural world." As such, Ehrenfeld has examined in depth the problems of overpopulation, technology, the extinction of animal and plant species, pollution, urban blight, the gradual decay and destruction of our environment"—*(LJ).*

Evans, Howard Ensign. LIFE ON A LITTLE-KNOWN PLANET. *Dutton* 1968 $8.50; *Dell* Delta Bks. pap. $2.45

"The 'little-known planet' of the title is the earth; and Evans is pleading for a greater understanding of earth life—even unto the smallest bug. Seldom, if ever, has the case for the natural sciences—and for conservation—been presented with such reasoned, convincing eloquence"—*(N.Y. Times)*.

Fitter, Richard. VANISHING WILD ANIMALS OF THE WORLD. Introd. by Peter Scott of the World Wildlife Fund; fwd. by the Duke of Edinburgh; 43 color plates *Franklin Watts* 1969 $7.95

Graham, Frank, Jr. MAN'S DOMINION: The Story of Conservation in America. *M. Evans* 1971 $8.95

"The author of *Since Silent Spring* tells the troubled story of the conservation movement. . . . It is obvious from the book that the battles of the past, once considered over and won, will continually reoccur"—*(LJ)*.

WHERE THE PLACE CALLED MORNING LIES: A Personal View of the American Environment. *Viking* 1973 $6.95

"The book is a plea for controlling the inroads that industry is making on the rural areas of Maine, and the problems that modern technology has brought"—*(LJ)*.

Hallet, Jean-Pierre, and Alex Pelle. ANIMAL KITABU. *Random* 1968 $6.95; *Fawcett* 1972 pap. $1.25

A plea for the conservation of African game. "Twelve years of intimate contact with the animals and people of the African bush provide a firm basis for this intriguing discussion of animal behavior"—*(Choice)*.

Harwood, Michael. THE VIEW FROM HAWK MOUNTAIN. *Scribner* 1973 $6.95

"Near Reading, Pennsylvania, Hawk Mountain Sanctuary has long been the site of hawk counts, in an effort to awaken the public to the danger of agricultural pesticides to birds . . . Harwood also discusses the problems of shrinking nesting areas as land use for recreation and housing expands, and of man's often illegal hunting of birds of prey"—*(LJ)*.

McHenry, Robert, and Charles Van Doren. A DOCUMENTARY HISTORY OF CONSERVATION IN AMERICA. *Praeger* 1972 $13.50

"A selection of 211 documents recording the historical development of conservation in America . . . It is an excellent and important contribution that gets to the heart of our environmental problems—human attitudes"—*(Choice)*.

Marsh, George Perkins. MAN AND NATURE. 1864. Ed. with introd. by David Lowenthal *Harvard Univ. Press* 1965 pap. $5.95. The first American book on conservation—admired by James Russell Lowell, Stewart Udall and Lewis Mumford.

Milne, Lorus, and Margery Milne. THE COUGAR DOESN'T LIVE HERE ANYMORE. *Prentice-Hall* 1971 $10.70

"An overall view of the present state of the world's rapidly disappearing wildlife. . . . Emphasis is placed on the fact that although extinction is a feature of evolution, it has been distorted by man who has transformed the earth so drastically that he is rapidly destroying plant and animal species"—*(LJ)*.

Murphy, Robert. WILD SANCTUARIES: Our National Wildlife Refuges—A Heritage Restored. Fwd. by Stewart L. Udall *Dutton* 1968 $22.50

Myers, Norman. THE LONG AFRICAN DAY. *Macmillan* 1972 $25.00

"The melancholy theme, that African animals may have reached the twilight of their many millenia long African day, recurs throughout the book. Most of it, however, is a chronicle of the colorful, typical 24 hour day in the fascinating savannah wilds of East Africa. The author discusses measures that have been and can be taken to conserve these animals and their land"—*(LJ)*.

Perry, John. OUR POLLUTED WORLD: Can Man Survive? *Franklin Watts* rev. ed. 1972 $5.95

"Although he is often pessimistic, still it is reassuring to know that research, new discoveries, and the increased awareness of industry, government, politicians, and the general public hold forth a promise for the future"—*(LJ)*.

Regenstein, Louis. THE POLITICS OF EXTINCTION: The Shocking Story of the World's Endangered Wildlife. *Macmillan* 1975 $9.95

Rienow, Robert, and Leona Train Rienow. MOMENT IN THE SUN: A Report on the Deteriorating Quality of the American Environment. *Dial* 1967 $7.95; *Ballantine Bks.* 1969 pap. $.95

> The Rienows plead for the development of a conservation ethic which places emphasis on the quality rather than the quantity of life. "Highly recommended for the layman"—*(Choice).*

Sax, Joseph. DEFENDING THE ENVIRONMENT: A Strategy for Citizen Action. *Knopf* 1971 $6.95

> "The main thrust of this book is toward the use of the courts and litigation by private citizens to protect public rights, rather than leave this protection to bureaucratic agencies and forums that have been content to give away our land, air, and waterways to vested interests"—*(LJ).*

Stevens, Leonard A. CLEAN WATER: Nature's Way to Stop Pollution. *Dutton* 1973 $10.00

> "Stevens offers an alternative to the traditional dumping of sewage into our streams and oceans. . . . He proposes the recycling of sewage by disposing of it on land, and letting soil bacteria and green plants break down the waste materials"—*(LJ).*

Stewart, George R. EARTH ABIDES. *Hermes* 1974 $8.95; *Fawcett* Crest Bks. 1974 pap. $1.25

Udall, Stewart L. AMERICA'S NATURAL TREASURES. *Rand McNally* 1971 $14.95

Oceanography

Bardach, John E. HARVEST OF THE SEA. *Harper* 1968 $7.95 Colophon Bks. 1970 pap. $1.95

> "Summarizes present-day knowledge of the oceans, the problems of utilizing their resources, and what advances can be expected in the years ahead"—*(LJ).*

(With others). AQUACULTURE: The Farming and Husbandry of Freshwater and Marine Organisms. *Wiley* 1972 $37.50

Bellamy, David. THE LIFE-GIVING SEA. *Crown* 1975 $15.95

> "A British scientist's remarkable view of the evolution of the oceans and their place in man's world"—(Publisher's note). Based on the author's BBC television series.

Bennett, Isabel. THE GREAT BARRIER REEF. *Scribner* 1974 $17.50. The ecology, marine life, natural history, and future of the Australian reef.

Carson, Rachel L. *See her main entry, this Chapter.*

Cousteau, Jacques Yves. *See his main entry, this Chapter.*

Fairbridge, Rhodes Whitmore, Ed. THE ENCYCLOPEDIA OF OCEANOGRAPHY. *Van Nostrand-Reinhold* 1966 $29.95

> "Short, selective bibliographies follow most articles. . . . It offers a clear, direct presentation of a field which is becoming increasingly popular and more important. . . . Entries range from introductory material written for the layman to articles requiring substantial background"—*(LJ).*

Gaskell, T. F. THE GULF STREAM. *T. Y. Crowell* (John Day) 1973 $5.95

> "Gaskell traces its history from the first definitive discovery (by none other than Benjamin Franklin) through to the present in terms of its own characteristics as well as the influence the Gulf Stream has exerted on climate, navigation, etc."—*(LJ).*

(Ed.). USING THE OCEANS. *Beekman Pub.* 1970 $6.00

Gross, M. Grant. OCEANOGRAPHY: A View of the Earth. *Prentice-Hall* 1972 $13.95

Hass, Hans. CHALLENGING THE DEEP: Thirty Years of Undersea Adventure. Trans. from the German by Ewald Osers *Morrow* 1972 $11.95

> The author "narrates his experiences among the fauna and flora of the deep. . . . There is also an interesting recounting of the increasing sophistication of underwater equipment to facilitate man's exploration of the mysteries of the ocean bottom"—*(LJ).*

Hentze, Carl. THE BOTTOM OF THE SEA AND BEYOND. *Nelson* 1975 $5.95

> This is "a clear, readable account of some of man's efforts to explore the land beneath the sea"—*(LJ).*

Hidy, George M. THE WAVES: The Nature of Sea Motion. *Van Nostrand-Reinhold* 1971 $7.00 pap. $3.95

> "A very lucid, authoritative but nontechnical, conceptual review of dynamical oceanography"—*(Choice).*

Horsfield, Brenda, and Peter B. Stone. THE GREAT OCEAN BUSINESS. *Coward* 1972 $12.95; *New Am. Lib.* Mentor Bks. 1974 pap. $1.95

"Horsfield and Stone consider the ocean a place of business which has great potential for development. They discuss the possibility of exploitation of mineral resources, ocean mining, undersea oil well drilling, and sea farming"—(*LJ*).

Howse, Derek, and Michael Sanderson. THE SEA CHART: An Historical Survey. *McGraw-Hill* 1973 $12.95

"A beautifully illustrated history of navigational charts and maps, this volume contains 60 reproductions, many in color, of sea charts in the famous collection of the National Maritime Museum of Greenwich, England, from 1420 to the present"—(*LJ*).

Idyll, C. P., Ed. EXPLORING THE OCEAN WORLD: A History of Oceanography. *T. Y. Crowell* 1972 $14.95

"Expert contributors deal with underwater landscapes and archeology; the biology, chemistry, and physics of the oceans, food from and farming the sea, and mineral resources and power"—(*LJ*).

Moorcraft, Colin. MUST THE SEAS DIE? *Gambit* 1973 $6.95

"Presents a graphic picture of the growing contamination of our oceans and its devastating effect on plant and animal life within. A plan of action to reverse the deterioration is given, as well as suggestions as to what the individual can do to improve conditions"—(*LJ*).

Parry, John H. THE DISCOVERY OF THE SEA. *Dial* 1974 $20.00

"Parry discusses the history of ship design, the gradual sophistication of the art of navigation, refinements in mapmaking, even the impact of astrology on man's reasons and needs to venture forth upon the world's seas and oceans"—(*LJ*).

Penzias, Walter, and M. W. Goodman. MAN BENEATH THE SEA: A Review of Underwater Ocean Engineering Technology. *Wiley* 1973 $35.75

"Bound to become the standard reference on the subject, this volume consists of 19 chapters that explore every aspect of man's descent beneath the surface of the oceans"—(*LJ*).

Perry, Richard. THE UNKNOWN OCEAN. *Taplinger* 1971 $7.95

"Waters below a few hundred feet of the surface have barely been explored, and the natural history of creatures living there is largely a mystery.... Perry attempts to answer questions about this strange environment and its inhabitants"—(*LJ*).

Ross, David A. INTRODUCTION TO OCEANOGRAPHY *Prentice-Hall* (Appleton) 1971 $9.50

"This volume is beautiful. It reads well, has lots of lovely pictures, and it covers those areas which would constitute an introduction to oceanography.... Almost anyone would find something of interest in this book"—(*Choice*).

Schlee, Susan. THE EDGE OF AN UNFAMILIAR WORLD: A History of Oceanography. *Dutton* 1973 $10.95

The author "follows the main lines of ocean research during the 19th and 20th centuries ... describes the scientific issues clearly for a lay audience"—(*Choice*).

Shenton, Edward H. DIVING FOR SCIENCE: The Story of the Deep Submersibles. *Norton* 1972 $8.95. The history and design of such craft from 1953 and August Piccard's *Trieste* to recent search and recovery missions for science.

Smith, F. G. Walton. THE SEAS IN MOTION. *T. Y. Crowell* 1973 $7.95

"Ocean currents, waves, and tides are what this book is all about, and there will be few who will not learn something new by reading it"—(*LJ*).

Soule, Gardner. GREATEST DEPTHS: Probing the Seas below Twenty Thousand Feet. *Macrae Smith* 1970 $5.95

Stewart, Harris B., Jr. DEEP CHALLENGE. *Van Nostrand-Reinhold* 1966 $5.95

"Dr. Stewart, the qualified director of the Institute for Oceanography, Environmental Science Services Administration, U.S. Department of Commerce, has written a fascinating and timely book. The chapters cover undersea topography, tides, currents, waves, sea life, sea water, territorial ownership and what we can expect from the future. The implications are of extreme importance to all of us"—(*LJ*).

Vetter, Richard C., Ed. OCEANOGRAPHY: The Last Frontier. *Basic Bks.* 1973 $10.00

"Written by leading oceanographers, the chapters compact an impressive array of facts on the exploration of the seas"—*(LJ)*.

Wertenberger, William. The Floor of the Sea: Maurice Ewing and the Search to Understand the Earth. *Little* 1974 $10.00

"A tribute to the late Maurice Ewing, marine geophysicist and founder of a major U.S. oceanographic research organization"—*(Booklist)*.

Zeiller, Warren. Tropical Marine Invertebrates of Southern Florida and the Bahama Islands. *Wiley* 1974 $37.50

MATHEMATICS

Adler, Irving. Mathematics and Mental Growth. Diagrams by Ruth Adler and Ellen Viereck. *John Day* 1968 $6.50. Eight essays in defense of the new math, originally published in professional journals for teachers.

The New Mathematics. *John Day* rev. and enl. ed. 1972 $7.95

Amstadter, Bertram L. Reliability Mathematics: Fundamentals, Practices, Procedures. *McGraw-Hill* 1971 $18.50

"This book is essentially self-contained since the background information, criteria, examples, and tables are all there. Theory is not neglected, but the emphasis is upon applications. Special attention is given to logic diagrams, mathematical models, [and] system prediction"—*(Choice)*.

Asimov, Isaac. The Realm of Algebra. *Houghton* 1961 $5.95; *Fawcett* Premier Bks. 1970 pap. $.95

See also his main entry, this Chapter.

Beckmann, Petr. A History of Pi. *Golem Press* 2d ed. 1971 $6.30

"A popular history of the discovery and measurement of the constant ratio of the circumference of a circle to its diameter from very early times to the recent calculations by digital computer"—*(LJ)*.

Boyer, Carl B. A History of Mathematics. *Wiley* 1968 $15.75

"Detailed and comprehensive, the subject is examined from primitive number concepts to the new math"—*(LJ)*.

Crossley, J. N., and others. What Is Mathematical Logic? *Oxford* 1973 pap. $1.95

"An honest introduction to mathematical logic unencumbered by ordinarily unavoidable technical details"—*(Choice)*.

Deming, Richard. Metric Power: Why and How We Are Going Metric. *Nelson* 1974 $5.95

"Schools and many segments of industry are making progress in this area, so more and more general readers will be taking an interest also. Contains definitions, some history, and methods of conversion. A useful, readable work"—*(LJ)*.

Fuchs, Walter R. Mathematics for the Modern Mind. Trans. from the German by Dr. H. A. Holstein *Macmillan* 1967 $6.95

"In this book Walter Fuchs, who is in charge of the science study programs over the Bavarian television network, allows the educated layman to peer behind the curtain of modern mathematics and gain some understanding of what the modern mathematician is attempting to do. Although he tries to ease the way with many simple examples and excellent illustrations from everyday life, the concepts in themselves are not simple and require a great deal of mental effort to grasp"—*(LJ)*.

Gardner, Martin. Mathematical Carnival. *Knopf* 1975 $8.95

"This is a vintage collection [of mathematical games] from recent *Scientific American* columns"—*(LJ)*.

Gilbert, Thomas F., and Marilyn B. Gilbert. Thinking Metric. *Wiley* 1973 pap. $2.95

"Chapters are devoted to such topics as distance and speed, volume, weight and mass, temperature, work and power, conversion to metric units, etc."—*(LJ)*.

Hogben, Lancelot Thomas. Mathematics for the Million. *Norton* 1951 4th ed. rev. with additional material and new illustrations 1968 $10.00

STATISTICAL THEORY: The Relationship of Probability, Credibility and Error. *Norton* rev. ed. 1968 $15.00

A critical examination of "statistical theory from the point of view of the non-mathematician"—*(LJ)*.

See also his main entry, this Chapter.

James, Glenn, and Robert C. James, Eds. MATHEMATICS DICTIONARY. *Van Nostrand-Reinhold* 1959 3rd ed. 1968 $15.95. A valuable reference work which has been revised in accordance with recent developments in the teaching of mathematics. 8,000 entries, 446 pages, Dictionary of Symbols; tables.

Kline, Morris. MATHEMATICAL THOUGHT FROM ANCIENT TO MODERN TIMES. *Oxford* 1973 $35.00

A "comprehensive historical survey of the conceptual development of mathematics"—*(Choice)*.

MATHEMATICS IN WESTERN CULTURE. *Oxford* 1953 $12.50 Galaxy Bks. 1964 pap. $3.95.
A historical look at the contribution of mathematics to Western societies.

(Ed.). THE UNIVERSAL ENCYCLOPEDIA OF MATHEMATICS. Fwd. by James R. Newman *Simon & Schuster* 1964 $9.95

"A new, complete, and compact encyclopedia of mathematics from the elementary high school level through college calculus"—*(LJ)*.

Newman, James R., Ed. THE WORLD OF MATHEMATICS. *Simon & Schuster* 4 vols. 1956–60 Vol. 1 Men and Numbers Vol. 2 The World of Laws and the World of Chance Vol. 3 The Mathematical Way of Thinking Vol. 4 Machines, Music and Puzzles set $30.00 pap. set $14.95

"The editor (formerly consultant on the literature of mathematics to the Library of Congress) has spent fifteen years in preparing this work ... Mr. Newman freely admits that his own prejudices have strongly influenced his choice. But the resulting collection promises to be the most frequently used reference book on mathematics, as well as a delight to readers with a wide range of background"—*(N.Y. Times)*.

Osen, Lynn M. WOMEN IN MATHEMATICS. *M.I.T. Press* 1973 $5.95

"A perceptive and intriguing account of the lives and scientific contributions of female mathematicians through the ages"—(Kirtley F. Mather).

Owen, George E. THE UNIVERSE OF THE MIND. *Johns Hopkins Press* 1971 $15.00 pap. $4.95

"A knowledge of college mathematics is presupposed in this history of mathematical thought. The discussion is oriented to the chronological order in which contributors provided the milestones upon which mathematics and physics are based"—*(LJ)*.

Phillips, Esther R. AN INTRODUCTION TO ANALYSIS AND INTEGRATION THEORY. *T. Y. Crowell* Intext 1971 $12.95

"An excellent book on the construction of an integral by completing a space of elementary functions which surpasses the standard work ... in clarity and completeness of the treatment"—*(Choice)*.

Reichmann, W. J. CALCULUS EXPLAINED. *Wiley* (Halsted Press) 1969 $7.25 pap. $3.50

THE SPELL OF MATHEMATICS. *Wiley* (Halsted Press) 1967 $5.95

"Mr. Reichmann, a practicing statistician in British commerce and industry for many years, translates into easily readable prose the sense of poetry that he feels mathematics contains. His treatment is outstanding of the unexpected relationships between one branch of mathematics and another, the applicability to the world around us of many esoteric pure theories, and the many diverse ways in which many mathematical theorems can be proved"—*(LJ)*.

Sarton, George A. THE STUDY OF THE HISTORY OF MATHEMATICS and THE STUDY OF THE HISTORY OF SCIENCE. 1936 *Dover* pap. $2.25

See also his main entry, this Chapter.

Stanley, Julius C., and others, Eds. MATHEMATICAL TALENT. *Johns Hopkins Press* 1973 $10.00 pap. $2.95. Treats of the discovery and training of exceptional mathematical talent among high school and college students.

Ulam, S. M. ADVENTURES OF A MATHEMATICIAN. *Scribner* 1975 $14.95

"A mathematician recollects some of the great scientists of our time"—*(PW)*.

Wilder, Raymond L. THE EVOLUTION OF MATHEMATICAL CONCEPTS: An Elementary Study. 1968. *Wiley* (Halsted Press) pap. $2.95

"Professor Wilder, University of Michigan . . . attempts to determine how and why mathematical concepts were created and developed from the viewpoint of an anthropologist"—*(LJ)*.

INTRODUCTION TO THE FOUNDATIONS OF MATHEMATICS. *Wiley* 2nd ed. 1965 $12.25

Wilson, Robin J. INTRODUCTION TO GRAPH THEORY. *Academic Press* 1973 $7.50

"The many illustrations and graphs are a great help, and there are numerous exercises, many of which are used to introduce new ideas and topics. The writing style is excellent, clear but concise"—*(Choice)*.

Young, Frederick H. THE NATURE OF MATHEMATICS. *Wiley* 1968 $11.25. A good introduction to the subject for the layman.

MEDICINE AND HEALTH

AMERICAN MEDICAL BIOGRAPHY, or Memoirs of Eminent Physicians. 1828–45. *Milford House* 2 vols. 1967 Vol. 1 by James Thacher Vol. 2 by Stephen Williams set $40.00; *Da Capo* 2 vols. set $32.50

Amosoff, Nicolai. THE OPEN HEART. Trans. by George St. George *Simon & Schuster* 1967 $4.95

The Soviet Union's noted cardiac surgeon and inventor of the artificial lung and the Extracorporeal Heart-Lung Circulation machine, both used in heart transplant operations, recalls some vital operations he performed—in a "marvellously frank and moving book"—*(PW)*.

Andrewes, Sir Christopher H. THE NATURAL HISTORY OF VIRUSES. *Norton* 1967 $10.00

Baldry, P. E. THE BATTLE AGAINST HEART DISEASE. *Cambridge* 1971 $10.00

"This book provides an opportunity to view recent advances against the backdrop of past discoveries"—*(LJ)*.

Barnard, Christiaan. HEART ATTACK: You Don't Have to Die. *Delacorte* 1972 $6.95; *Dell* 1973 pap. $1.95

Benet, Sula. HOW TO LIVE TO BE 100: The Life-Style of the People of the Caucasus. *Dial* 1976 $8.95

Bourne, Gordon, and David N. Danforth. PREGNANCY. *Harper* 1975 $15.00

An "excellent reference source, which provides clear, thorough information on female anatomy and physiology"—*(LJ)*.

Brown, Barbara B. NEW MIND, NEW BODY BIOFEEDBACK: New Directions for the Mind. *Harper* 1974 $9.95

Burgess, Louise Bailey. ALCOHOL AND YOUR HEALTH. *Charles Pub.* (dist. by Hawthorn) 1973 $12.50

"One of the best-documented treatises on the problems of alcohol abuse and its impact on American life. Explores the multiple theories and interpretations that have been offered on the subject of alcoholism and its potential for treatment with authority and scholarship"—*(LJ)*.

Cartwright, Frederick F. THE DEVELOPMENT OF MODERN SURGERY. *T. Y. Crowell* 1968 $6.95. This covers 150 years and includes discussion of transplanted organs.

(With Michael D. Biddiss). DISEASE AND HISTORY. *T. Y. Crowell* 1972 $7.95; *New Am. Lib.* Mentor Bks. 1974 pap. $1.75

"The authors examine the effects that disease, both epidemic and personal, has had upon the history of peoples"—*(TLS,* London).

Cushing, Harvey. *See his main entry, this Chapter.*

Dubos, René Jules. THE MIRAGE OF HEALTH: Utopias, Progress, and Biological Change. *Harper* 1971 pap. $1.25

See also his main entry, this Chapter.

Field, Mark G. Soviet Socialized Medicine: An Introduction. *Macmillan* (Free Press) 1967 $7.95

Glemser, Bernard. Man against Cancer. *T. Y. Crowell* (Funk & Wagnalls) 1969 $7.95

Goodfield, June. The Siege of Cancer. *Random* 1975 $8.95

"An exciting and thought-provoking look at what kinds of human beings cancer researchers are, how they work and think, how they look at themselves and their colleagues, and what the possibilities are for the future"—*(LJ)*.

Gotzsche, Anne-Lise. The Fluoride Question. *Stein & Day* 1975 $8.95

Horrobin, David F. International Handbook of Medical Science. *Putnam* 1970 $16.00

Klaw, Spencer. The Great American Medical Show: The Unhealthy State of U.S. Medical Care and What We Can Do. *Viking* 1975 $10.00

"This closely reasoned, thoroughly researched book mounts a devastating critique of American medicine"—*(PW)*.

Lasagna, Louis. The VD Epidemic: How It Started, Where It's Going, and What to Do About It. *Temple Univ. Press* 1975 $6.95

Lausch, Erwin. Manipulation: Dangers and Benefits of Brain Research. Trans. by Oliver Coburn *Viking* 1974 $8.95

A "fascinating, controversial study"—*(Booklist)*.

Lenihan, John. Human Engineering: The Body Re-Examined. *Braziller* 1975 $7.95

An "unusual book written by a distinguished bioengineer"—*(LJ)*.

Locke, David M. Viruses: The Smallest Enemy. *Crown* 1974 $10.95

"A basic, readable study of viruses for the nonprofessional"—*(Booklist)*.

Longmore, Donald. The Heart. *McGraw-Hill* 1971 $4.95 pap. $2.45

Machines in Medicine. *Doubleday* 1970 $6.95

McKay, Clive. Notes on the History of Nutrition Research. *Hans Huber* (dist. by Williams & Wilkins) 1973 $22.25

Provides "information on how to track down research that has been done in a wide variety of areas, and how to become familiar with the advancements in the science of nutrition, beginning with the 18th Century. . . . A good source book for students of nutrition"—*(LJ)*.

Majno, Guido. The Healing Hand: Man and Wound in the Ancient World. *Harvard Univ. Press* 1975 $25.00

"This fascinating and attractively produced book is the product of eight years of literary and laboratory research . . . [it] discusses the medical, archeological, and literary evidence of man's knowledge of wounds and their treatment"—*(LJ)*.

Marine, Gene, and Judith Van Allen. Food Pollution: The Violation of Our Inner Ecology. *Holt* 1972 $8.95

"Numerous horrifying accounts of the synthetic or poisoned foods and untested chemicals we consume are related in detail. A bleak picture of the food industry emerges as the decisions of careless officials, blunders of the Food and Drug Administration, and the greedy actions of big business are exposed"—*(LJ)*.

Marks, Geoffrey, and William K. Beatty. The Story of Medicine in America. *Scribner* 1974 $10.00

"Provides an excellent summary of developments in medical research and the elevation of the art of healing from its most primitive form and quackery to a respected profession. . . . An organized, carefully researched and documented approach to a subject of broad interest"—*(LJ)*.

Mayo, Charles W. Mayo: The Story of My Family and My Career. *Doubleday* 1968 $7.50. About the Mayo brothers and their famous Clinic in Rochester, Minn.

Mowbray, Alan Q. Transplant: A True Account of a Modern Surgical Miracle. *McKay* 1974 $8.95

Murray, D. Stark. Blueprint for Health. *Schocken* 1974 $7.50

Based on "a survey of current health needs and systems of health care in more than 20 countries"—*(LJ)*.

Nilsson, Lennart. Behold Man: A Photographic Journey of Discovery Inside the Body. *Little* 1974 $25.00

Osler, Sir William. *See his main entry, this Chapter.*

Pool, J. Lawrence. Your Brain and Nerves. *Scribner* 1973 $6.95

Pool presents a detailed, careful review of brain and nerve activity for the general reader. He concentrates in particular on nervous disorders, outlining their causes, how to recognize them, methods of diagnosing them, and the latest methods of treatment.

Prescott, David M. Cancer: The Misguided Cell. *Bobbs* (Pegasus) 1973 $6.95 pap. $1.95

"Prescott, internationally known for his research in cell biology, has described the disease in terms of the physiology of the individual cell, how the disease affects the body, and the latest methods of treatment"—(*LJ*).

Reid, Robert. Microbes and Men. *Dutton* 1975 $8.95

"A popularization of the lives of the men who founded such sciences as bacteriology, immunology, and chemotherapy"—(*LJ*).

Restak, Richard M. Premeditated Man: Bioethics and the Control of Future Human Life. *Viking* 1975 $8.95

The author is a "practicing neurologist who believes that science is too serious a business to be left to the scientists"—(*N.Y. Times*).

Rosebury, Theodore. Microbes and Morals: The Strange Story of Venereal Disease. *Viking* 1971 $7.95

"Considered are the spread of VD, control, diagnosis, treatment, penicillin resistance, clinics and other problems which affect people today"—(*LJ*).

Selzer, Arthur. The Heart: Its Function in Health and Disease. *Univ. of California Press* 1968 $7.95

Shryock, Richard Harrison. Medicine in America: Historical Essays. Fwd. by Merle Curti *Johns Hopkins Press* 1966 $12.50

Covers Cotton Mather, Benjamin Rush and others; "an unusually interesting book"—(*LJ*).

Singer, Charles, and Ashworth E. Underwood. A Short History of Medicine. *Oxford* 2nd ed. 1962 $15.00

Sorkin, Alan L. Health Economics: An Introduction. *Heath* 1975 $12.00

"A textbook for undergraduates enrolled in health economics courses"—(*Choice*).

Stedman, Thomas L., and others. Stedman's Medical Dictionary. *Williams & Wilkins* 22nd ed. 1972. $18.50

Thomas, John A., and others. Drugs, Medicines and Other Agents: An Introduction to Our Chemical Environment. *Kent State Univ. Press* 1976 $9.00 pap. $4.95

"An illustrated handbook for the lay person"—(Publisher's note).

Waksman, Selman A. The Conquest of Tuberculosis. *Univ. of California Press* 1965 $9.50. By the Nobel laureate who discovered streptomycin.

Watson, Lyall. The Romeo Error: A Matter of Life and Death. *Doubleday* Anchor Bks. 1975 pap. $7.95

Watson states that "death is a nebulous state differing from life only by the absence of a coordinating pattern to keep cells in their organized units"—(*Booklist*).

Young, James Harvey. The Medical Messiahs: A Social History of Health Quackery in Twentieth Century America. *Princeton Univ. Press* 1967 $13.50

The Toadstool Millionaires: A Social History of Patent Medicines in America before Federal Regulations. *Princeton Univ. Press* 1972 $11.00 pap. $3.45

Zimmerman, David R. Rh: The Intimate History of a Disease and Its Conquest. Introd. by James Watson *Macmillan* 1973 $8.95

"Zimmerman takes a personal approach to the story, focusing his attention on the individuals who contributed to the control of this tragic disease caused by antigen incompatibility between mother and fetus"—(*LJ*).

PHYSICS

Alfven, Hannes. The Atom, Man and the Universe: The Long Chain of Complications. Trans. from the Swedish by John Hoberman *W. H. Freeman* 1969 $3.95

Worlds-Antiworlds: Antimatter in Cosmology. *W. H. Freeman* 1966 $3.95

A distinguished scientist, specializing in hydromagnetics and plasma physics, proposes the formulation of cosmological principles based on recent advances in elementary particle physics. . . . The book is written for the nonscientist but will also be of interest to specialists in astronomy and physics. . . . This is an essential acquisition for all science collections"—*(LJ)*.

Angrist, Stanley W., and Loren G. Hepler. Order and Chaos: Laws of Energy and Entropy. *Basic Bks.* 1967 $5.95

"The authors, both professors at Carnegie Institute of Technology, have aimed this brief work on thermodynamics at the intelligent nonspecialist. Although the book demands little mathematical knowledge of the reader, there is plenty of intellectual meat here"—*(LJ)*.

Baldwin, George C. Introduction to Nonlinear Optics. *Plenum Pub.* 2nd ed. 1974 pap. $5.95

Bergmann, Peter G. The Riddle of Gravitation. *Scribner* 1968 pap. 1969 $2.65

"One of the world's leading experts on the theory of relativity and gravitation explains past and present theories of gravitation in language that an intelligent, reasonably well-informed lay reader can understand"—*(LJ)*.

Bernal, John D. The Extension of Man: A History of Physics before the Quantum. *M.I.T. Press* 1972 $12.50

"This survey of the history of physics, dealing with the earliest phases, explains how its experimental state developed to the end of the 19th Century"—*(LJ)*.

Blakemore, J. S. Solid State Physics. *W. B. Saunders* 1974 $16.95

Brillouin, Léon. Relativity Reexamined. *Academic Press* 1970 $11.00

"A tantalizing, unique, and rather brief monograph by a very distinguished physicist which poses a large number of questions and gives rather small attention to possible procedures for their solution"—*(Choice)*.

Cassidy, Harold G. Science Restated: Physics and Chemistry for the Non-Scientist. *Freeman, Cooper & Co.* 1970 $8.75

"This is a rare text that goes into considerable depth, presents an open-ended modern view, preserves breadth without making the hopeless effort of covering the whole waterfront"—*(Choice)*.

Cohen, Bernard L. Concepts of Nuclear Physics. *McGraw-Hill* 1971 $14.95

"One of the few books that manages to be sophisticated without demanding more background in quantum mechanics than many students can muster"—*(Choice)*.

Cooper, Leon N. An Introduction to the Meaning and Structure of Physics. *Harper* 1968 1970 $15.95

"Prepared for college students not majoring in science, this introductory text, illustrated with numerous sketches, diagrams, and photographs, is admirably suited for the intelligent layman"— *(LJ)*.

Feurer, Lewis S. Einstein and the Generations of Science. *Basic Bks.* 1974 $12.95

"The changes wrought in the world of physics by the concepts of relativity and quantum physics are at the base of this well-written analysis of the physicists and the events happening at the time of these developments"—*(LJ)*.

Frisch, Otto R. The Nature of Matter. *Dutton* 1972 $7.95 1973 pap. $3.95

"Beginning with the early history of the concepts of elements and atoms, gases, liquids, and solids, [Frisch] progresses through the ideas of energy and heat to the quantum theory"—*(LJ)*.

Fuchs, Walter R. Physics for the Modern Mind. *Macmillan* 1967 $6.95

Gamow, George. Biography of Physics. *Harper* 1961 $7.50

Thirty Years That Shook Physics. *Doubleday* 1966 $5.95 pap. $1.95

"A potent, pocket-sized history full of facts, fun, and fancy; Planck, Pauli, and puns; neutrons, name dropping, and nonsense"—*(LJ)*.

See also his main entry, this Chapter.

Gottleib, Milton, Max Garbuny, and Werner Emmerich. SEVEN STATES OF MATTER. Ed. by Sharon Banigan; fwd. by Leonard Carmichael *Walker & Co.* 1966 $7.95

"The 'Westinghouse Search Books' comprise an outstanding collection of books presenting modern science at the level of the student and layman. This volume is a superb discussion of the nature of matter, written by three leading Westinghouse scientists. . . . The treatment is generally nonmathematical. . . . This is a well-written well-edited volume and is highly recommended"— *(LJ)*.

Gray, H. J., and Alan Isaacs, Eds. A NEW DICTIONARY OF PHYSICS. (Orig. "Dictionary of Physics") *Longman* 2nd ed. 1974 $25.00

"Intermediate between a strict dictionary . . . and an encyclopedia"—*(Choice)*.

Guillemin, Victor. THE STORY OF QUANTUM MECHANICS. *Scribner* 1968 $9.95 pap. $3.95

"Admirably told by Professor Guillemin of Harvard"—*(LJ)*.

Heisenberg, Werner. PHYSICS AND BEYOND: Encounters and Conversations. Trans. from the German by Arnold J. Pomerans; ed. by Ruth N. Anshen *Harper* 1971 $7.95 Torchbks. pap. $2.95

"The author is a Nobel Prize Winner and Director of the Max Planck Institute for Physics and Astrophysics. Based on his reminiscences, notes, conversations, and talks—or 'encounters'—with such men as Planck, Bohr, Pauli, Einstein, Schrodinger, Rutherford, Hahn, and others who were largely responsible for the development of atomic physics during the first half of this century, the author reveals some of the creative processes of science at work, the roots, and the conditions in which creativity flourishes"—*(LJ)*.

Jauch, Josef M. ARE QUANTA REAL? A Galilean Dialogue. *Indiana Univ. Press* 1973 $6.95

"Both physicists and people interested in modern tendencies in philosophy need to understand how the development of quantum physics has affected the meanings that can be given to the word 'reality' and both groups frequently get it wrong"—*(Choice)*.

THE FOUNDATIONS OF QUANTUM MECHANICS. 1967. *Addison-Wesley* 1973 $15.00

Jeans, Sir James Hopwood. *See his main entry, this Chapter.*

Karplus, Martin, and Richard N. Porter. ATOMS AND MOLECULES: An Introduction for Students of Physical Chemistry. *W. A. Benjamin* 1971 $17.50 pap. $7.95

"Discusses the structure of one electron and many electron atoms, interatomic interactions, diatomic and polyatomic molecules, and molecular spectra"—*(Choice)*.

Khuon, Ernst von. THE INVISIBLE MADE VISIBLE: The Expansion of Man's Vision of the Universe through Technology. Trans. by Paula Arno *N.Y. Graphic Society* 1973 $22.50

"Certain aspects of optics have not often been the subject of books aimed at the non-specialist, so this treatment of a number of special topics in this field at a popular level is especially welcome. Included are such subjects as x-rays, electron photomicroscopy, polarized light photomicroscopy, and ultra-high-speed photography. The splendid photographs (some in color) are noteworthy"— *(LJ)*.

Koslow, Arnold, Ed. THE CHANGELESS ORDER: The Physics of Space, Time and Motion. *Braziller* 1967 $7.50

"Well done. The introductory essays to the two parts are very nicely written, although possibly too brief. . . . Overall, an excellent book"—*(Choice)*.

Lapp, Ralph E. THE LOGARITHMIC CENTURY. *Prentice-Hall* 1973 $7.95

"The author, a noted physicist, gives a great deal of emphasis to the energy problems of the country, yet includes warnings about environmental problems"—*(LJ)*. "Lapp is one of the best explainers of technological crises issues, and this book [on the energy crisis] does him particular credit"—*(N.Y. Times Bk. Review)*.

Lenchek, Allen M., Ed. THE PHYSICS OF PULSARS. *Gordon & Breach* 1972 $14.50

"Radio, optical, and X-ray observations, pulsar periods, pulsar searches, and pulsar distances are some of the topics descussed"—*(Choice)*.

Magie, William F., Ed. A SOURCE BOOK IN PHYSICS. *Harvard Univ. Press* 1963 $15.00

An important reference for the history; "an excellently chosen collection"—*(New Scientist)*.

March, Robert H. PHYSICS FOR POETS. *McGraw-Hill* 1970 $7.95

Marion, Jerry B. PHYSICS: The Foundations of Modern Science. *Wiley* 1973 $12.00

THE UNIVERSE OF PHYSICS: A Book of Readings. *Wiley* 1970 $7.75

National Research Council. Physics Survey Committee. PHYSICS IN PERSPECTIVE, Vol. 1.
National Academy of Sciences 1972 $20.00

"Detailed and comprehensive, the report offers numerous recommendations along with a balanced picture of the outstanding achievements in this discipline [physics] and its contributions to science as a whole"—(*LJ*).

Oppenheimer, J. Robert. *See his main entry, this Chapter.*

Samburksy, Samuel, Ed. PHYSICAL THOUGHT FROM THE PRE-SOCRATICS TO THE QUANTUM PHYSICISTS. *Universe Bks.* 1974 $20.00

"This anthology is possibly the best collection of this type ever to be published"—(*LJ*).

Thewlis, J., Ed. CONCISE DICTIONARY OF PHYSICS. *Pergamon* 1973 text ed. $16.50

(With others, Eds.). ENCYCLOPAEDIC DICTIONARY OF PHYSICS. *Pergamon* 9 vols., 5 suppl. 1965–75 Supplement 1 (1966) $20.00 Supplement 2 (1967) $25.00 Supplement 3 (1969) $25.00 Supplement 4 (1971) $35.00 Supplement 5 (1975) $40.00

"This work is the most significant contribution to the reference literature of physics since 1923, when 'Glazebrook's Dictionary of Applied Physics' appeared. In general, the articles are at the graduate level, although a few of them, highly mathematical in character, may be most useful to the specialist"—(*LJ*).

Wieder, Sol. THE FOUNDATIONS OF QUANTUM THEORY. *Academic Press* 1973 $13.95

"[This] book starts with a historical review and a chapter on classical dynamics; then comes an introduction to linear vector spaces and on page 60 commences the development of the theory from mathematical axioms. . . . It is probably the best book of its kind"—(*Choice*).

The Atom and Nuclear Energy

Boorse, Henry A., and Lloyd Motz, Eds. THE WORLD OF THE ATOM. Fwd. by I. I. Rabi *Basic Bks* 2 vols. 1966 set 38.50

More than 100 selections of writings on the atom, from Lucretius to the moderns, with biographical notes. . . . Highly recommended to all science libraries and collections"—(*LJ*).

Cochran, Thomas B. THE LIQUID METAL FAST BREEDER REACTOR: An Environmental and Economic Critique. *Johns Hopkins Press* 1974 pap. $6.50

"The author is one of those who questions the credentials of this type of reactor, as well as the planning for a multi-million dollar demonstration project associated with it"—(*LJ*).

Cohen, Bernard L. CONCEPTS OF NUCLEAR PHYSICS. *McGraw-Hill* 1971 $15.95

NUCLEAR SCIENCE AND SOCIETY. *Doubleday* Anchor Bks. (orig.) 1974 pap. $2.95

Davis, George E. RADIATION AND LIFE. *Iowa State Univ. Press* 1967 $7.95

"A most comprehensive popular coverage of nuclear radiations and their application to life, it provides the layman with an explanation not only of atoms and isotopes, but also of basic energy relations, computational methods, and types of reactors. . . . The explanations are clear and proceed from the known to the unknown"—(*Choice*).

Foreman, Harry, Ed. NUCLEAR POWER AND THE PUBLIC. *Univ. of Minnesota Press* 1970 $9.00; *Doubleday* 1972 pap. $2.50

"Authoritative proponents and opponents of nuclear power here present their views in well reasoned, calm, and technically correct papers so that readers can better judge how clean or unclean, how hazardous or safe, how necessary or unnecessary this form of power may be"—(*LJ*).

Gofman, John W., and Arthur R. Tamplin. POISONED POWER: The Case Against Nuclear Power Plants. *Rodale Press* 1971 $6.95 pap. $2.95

"A strongly worded polemic against the Atomic Energy Commission, public utilities, and manufacturers of nuclear power plants. The authors, themselves employed at the AEC funded Lawrence Radiation Laboratories, argue that nuclear power has not proved to be clean, safe, or even cheap"—(*LJ*).

Graetzer, Hans G., and David L. Anderson, Eds. THE DISCOVERY OF NUCLEAR FISSION: A Documentary History. *Van Nostrand-Reinhold* 1971 $6.50 pap. $2.95

"Consists primarily of original reports from scientific journals which are given continuity by editorial comment and explanatory notes. The story begins in 1934 and ends with the first successful chain reaction experiment by Enrico Fermi in December 1942"—(*LJ*).

Green, Philip. DEADLY LOGIC: The Theory of Nuclear Deterrence. Fwd. by Edgar S. Furniss, Jr. *Ohio State Univ. Press* 1966 $6.00; *Schocken* 1968 pap. $2.45

"Professor Green destroys . . . the rationalization of prominent writers that the consequences of nuclear attack need not leave a country totally devastated. . . . He proves with stringent logic and thorough research that the attempt to make a predictable science of deterrence has failed. This book should be on every shelf"—(*LJ*).

Greenway, Frank. JOHN DALTON AND THE ATOM. *Cornell Univ. Press* 1966 $8.00. Early discoveries by the British chemist (1776–1844).

Groueff, Stephane. MANHATTAN PROJECT: The Untold Story of the Making of the Atomic Bomb. *Little* 1967 $8.95

"Absorbing history of the atomic bomb, how it was built, problems involved, conditions and circumstances under which the work was carried out. Brings together and clarifies much of the vast, scattered information and minute details (some of it only recently declassified), while at the same time personalities—especially Leslie R. Groves—are brought into focus. An essential book"—(*SR*). By the New York bureau chief of the French weekly *Paris Match*. One of *Library Journal's* "100 best" sci-tech books of 1967.

Inglis, David Rittenhouse. NUCLEAR ENERGY: Its Physics and Its Social Challenge. *Addison-Wesley* 1973 $6.95 pap. $4.95

This book "will be particularly valuable as a reference text for the many environmental physics and chemistry courses now appearing in college and university curricula"—(*Choice*).

Irving, David. THE GERMAN ATOMIC BOMB: The History of Nuclear Research in Nazi Germany. *Simon & Schuster* 1968 $6.95

"Mr. Irving, a British writer, has produced a fascinating and meticulously documented account of the German attempt to manufacture an atomic bomb in the Second World War"—(*New Yorker*).

Jungk, Robert. BRIGHTER THAN A THOUSAND SUNS: A Personal History of the Atomic Scientists. Trans. by James Cleugh *Harcourt* 1958 pap. 1970 $3.45. The inside story of events leading to the construction of the atomic and hydrogen bombs as revealed through conversations with the physicists responsible for them and a study of their works. The author was alternately praised for his restraint and damned for his biased judgment.

Lapp, Ralph E., and Howard Andrews. NUCLEAR RADIATION PHYSICS. *Prentice-Hall* 4th ed. 1972 $14.50

Lilienthal, David. CHANGE, HOPE AND THE BOMB. *Princeton Univ. Press* 1963 $8.50 pap. $1.95

The first chairman of the Atomic Energy Commission wrote this book before the Geneva Treaty was initialed, "and possibly he'd shade a phrase or two today. But not much. His basic thesis remains, at once the most devastating and the most hopeful comment yet made on the nuclear crisis"—(*Book-of-the-Month Club News*).

Marion, Jerry B. ENERGY IN PERSPECTIVE. *Academic Press* 1974 pap. $4.95

"Chemical and physical principles of energy are discussed, along with the environmental effects of energy usage and the availability of fuel supplies. The controversy over nuclear reactors as power sources is also covered"—(*LJ*).

Moss, Norman. MEN WHO PLAY GOD: The Story of the Hydrogen Bomb and How the World Came to Live with It. *Harper* 1969 $8.95

Newman, James R. THE RULE OF FOLLY. Preface by Erich Fromm *Simon & Schuster* rev. ed. 1962 pap. $1.25. Some of the author's papers on the frightening dangers of atomic warfare.

Novick, Sheldon. THE CARELESS ATOM. *Houghton* 1969 $5.95

The Program Administrator of the Center for the Biology of Natural Sciences at Washington University in St. Louis, with passionate concern, "expolores the nature of the public's risk, both from reactor explosion . . . and radioactive pollution of the environment"—(*N. Y. Times*).

Seaborg, Glenn T. NUCLEAR MILESTONES. *W. H. Freeman* 1972 $7.50

(With W. R. Corliss). MAN AND ATOM: Shaping a New World Through Nuclear Technology. *Dutton* 1971 $10.00

"The authors' views on utilizing the atom's power are entirely optimistic. [They] attempt to bridge the gap of understanding between those working with nuclear matters and the general public by giving a 'comprehensive picture of man's relationship with the atom' "—(*LJ*).

Sherwin, Martin J. A WORLD DESTROYED: The Atomic Bomb and the Grand Alliance. *Knopf* 1975 $10.00

"A dispassionate, richly detailed account that promises for the present, at least, to be the definitive book on the formation of atomic energy policy during World War II"—(*Time*).

Strickland, Donald A. SCIENTISTS IN POLITICS: The Atomic Scientists Movement, 1945–1946. *Purdue Univ. Press* 1968 $4.95

"This study emphasizes the factionalism, division of ideologies, diffusion, and misgivings that characterized the scientific movements of the Manhattan Project scientists during the Truman Administration in 1945 and the mobilization of scientists for the McMahon atomic energy bill of 1946"—(*LJ*).

Thackray, Arnold. JOHN DALTON: Critical Assessments of His Life and Science. *Harvard Univ. Press* 1972 $11.50

Space and Astronomy

Alter, Dinsmore. A PICTORIAL GUIDE TO THE MOON. *T. Y. Crowell* 1963 3rd ed. 1973 $8.95
An illustrated guide to the moon's surface.

(With others). PICTORIAL ASTRONOMY. *T. Y. Crowell* rev. ed. 1974 $10.00

Asimov, Isaac. ASIMOV ON ASTRONOMY. *Doubleday* 1974 $8.95

"A collection of 17 essays selected from his earlier works, now out of print"—(*LJ*).

THE UNIVERSE: From Flat Earth to Quasar. *Walker & Co.* rev. ed. 1971 $7.95

"Using his special gifts for presenting clear, concise explanations, imaginative comparisons, and apt analogies, Asimov brings up to date this brilliant survey of the universe"—(*LJ*).

See also his main entry, this Chapter.

THE ASTRONAUTS: We Seven. *Simon & Schuster* 1962 $7.50. The inside story of the preparation for and launching of Project Mercury as told by Carpenter, Grissom, Glenn, Cooper, Shepard, Schirra and Slayton.

Bedini, Silvio A., and others, Eds. THE MOON: Man's Greatest Adventure. *Harry N. Abrams* 1971 $45.00

"A thick folio-sized volume of photographs, many of which are in color and frequently occupy an entire page"—(*LJ*).

Bracewell, Ronald Newbolt. THE GALACTIC CLUB: Intelligent Life in Outer Space. *W. H. Freeman* 1975 $6.95 pap. $3.95

This book "presents in a readable and colorful style the many aspects of this fascinating probe of ever-widening interest and possibilities"—(*Choice*).

Bradbury, Ray, and others. MARS AND THE MIND OF MAN. *Harper* 1973 $7.95

"In 1971 a panel of scientists and writers was held at the California Institute of Technology to discuss Mars and what the Mariner 9 spacecraft might see photographically . . . Their discussion constitutes the first part of this book. The other part is made up of some of the outstanding pictures of Mars taken from the spacecraft as well as comments by the participants"—(*LJ*).

Brow, Peter Lancaster. COMETS, METEORITES AND MEN. *Taplinger* 1974 $12.50

"Known scientific facts are blended with accounts of events and scientists associated with the subject"—(*LJ*).

Cade, C. Maxwell. OTHER WORLDS THAN OURS. *Taplinger* 1967 $7.50

"A fast-paced, accurate and factual survey of current knowledge in astronomy [with] speculative thoughts on exobiology or life beyond the earth and problems in extra-terrestrial communication"—*(LJ)*.

Caidin, Martin. DESTINATION MARS. *Doubleday* 1972 $7.95. Current knowledge about Mars, based on the Mariner 9 photographs.

PLANETFALL. *Coward* 1974 $7.95

"An interesting account of space exploration, including manned and unmanned flights to the planets as well as the moon. Possibilities of life on other planets, the origin of the solar system and future space flights are among the topics covered"—*(LJ)*.

Cherrington, Ernest H., Jr. EXPLORING THE MOON THROUGH BINOCULARS. *McGraw-Hill* 1969 $10.00

"A handbook meant to help the amateur astronomer using binoculars to recognize lunar features"—*(PW)*.

Clarke, Arthur C. THE PROMISE OF SPACE. *Harper* 1968 $8.95

A "lucid, matter-of-fact and amazingly convincing book"—(Eliot Fremont-Smith, in the *N.Y. Times*).

REPORT ON PLANET THREE AND OTHER SPECULATIONS. *Harper* 1972 $7.95; *New Am. Lib.* 1973 pap. $1.25

"Beginning with a 'translation' of a Martian's supposed view of life on earth with its poisonous atmosphere, the book continues with some 20 essays on its technical future, space travel, and the frontiers of science. . . . This thought-provoking book is filled with facts and ideas"—*(LJ)*.

(Ed.). THE COMING OF THE SPACE AGE: Famous Accounts of Man's Probing of the Universe. *Hawthorn* 1967 $6.95

"There is no more interesting or convincing guide to the worlds beyond the earth than Arthur C. Clarke"—*(N.Y. Herald Tribune)*.

Cole, Franklyn. FUNDAMENTAL ASTRONOMY: The Solar System and Beyond. *Wiley* 1974 $10.95

Cooper, Henry S. F., Jr. APOLLO ON THE MOON. *Dial* 1969 $4.50

Written before the landing of July 20, 1969, this will be followed by many books on the actual events of that day. "Witty and irreverent," Mr. Cooper is "gracefully literate and offers a pleasant contrast to the technical jargon, the crackling voices and electronic beeps" of some other writers— (Christopher Lehmann-Haupt, in the *N.Y. Times*).

THIRTEEN: The Flight That Failed. *Dial* 1973 $5.95

"A near-disaster in space is the theme of this readable account of Apollo 13's flight. . . . The account includes not only the astronauts but also the ground controllers and their differing concepts of the exciting events taking place"—*(LJ)*.

Corliss, William R. MYSTERIES OF THE UNIVERSE. *T. Y. Crowell* 1967 $5.95

"Several of the most interesting aspects of current cosmological research are discussed for the adult layman"—*(LJ)*.

Cornell, James, and E. N. Hayes, Eds. MAN AND COSMOS: Nine Guggenheim Lectures on the Solar System Sponsored by the Smithsonian Institution. *Norton* 1975 $8.95

"The authors, all top-flight specialists in various aspects of solar system research, have done a fine job of summarizing the latest (as of late 1972) research findings in their respective fields"— *(LJ)*.

Cousins, Frank W. THE SOLAR SYSTEM. *Universe Bks.* 1972 $20.00

"Bridging the gap between scientist and layman, this book brings together data and information gleaned from a vast amount of literature, some of it widely scattered, that has been generated over hundreds of years. . . . More than 150 photographs and drawings supplement the text"—*(LJ)*.

Flammarion, Camille. THE FLAMMARION BOOK OF ASTRONOMY. 1880. Trans. from the French by Annabel and Bernard Pagel; prepared under the direction of Gabrielle Camille Flammarion and André Danjon. Illus. *Simon & Schuster* expanded and modernized ed. 1964 $22.95

Gamow, George. THE CREATION OF THE UNIVERSE. *Viking* rev. ed. 1961 $5.75. A discussion of the arguments for and against the "big bang" and "steady state" theories of the origin of the universe.

See also his main entry, this Chapter.

Grissom, Virgil (Gus). GEMINI: A Personal Account of Man's Venture into Space. Ed. by Jacob Hay *Macmillan* 1968 $5.95

"Modestly, smoothly and with touches of humor and human interest, the late 'Gus' Grissom has written about the Gemini missions and the way they were planned to work into a trip to the moon"—*(PW)*.

Guest, John, Ed. EARTH AND ITS SATELLITE. *McKay* 1971 $15.00

"Earth and Moon are considered together in an attempt to show how they evolved and developed in space and to explain their differences and geological properties"—*(LJ)*.

Hartmann, William K. MOONS AND PLANETS: An Introduction to Planetary Science. *Bogden & Quigly* 1972 $17.25

"An artistic and philosophical success, as well as the most comprehensive introductory account available of our present knowledge of the solar system"—*(Choice)*.

Heide, Fritz. METEORITES. 1957. Trans. from the German by Edward Anders and Eugene R. DuFresne *Univ. of Chicago Press* 1964 $6.50 Phoenix Bks. pap. $2.25

Hess, Wilmot N. WEATHER AND CLIMATE MODIFICATION. *Wiley* 1974 $29.95

(With Gilbert D. Mead, Eds.). AN INTRODUCTION TO SPACE SCIENCE. *Gordon & Breach* 1965 rev. and enl. ed. 1968 $54.00. A compilation of writings by scientists affiliated with NASA's Goddard Space Flight Center.

Howard, Neale E. THE TELESCOPE HANDBOOK AND STAR ATLAS. *T. Y. Crowell* 1967 $12.95

"A basic handbook . . . for the amateur astronomer"—*(LJ)*.

Hynek, J. Allen. THE UFO EXPERIENCE: A Scientific Inquiry. *Regnery* 1972 $6.95; *Ballantine Bks.* 1974 pap. $1.50. Hynek investigated UFO problems for the Air Force for more than 20 years and criticizes the findings of the Condon Report.

Jackson, Joseph H., III. PICTORIAL GUIDE TO THE PLANETS. *T. Y. Crowell* 2nd ed. 1973 $12.50

This is "informative and written in a descriptive rather than a highly technical style. It discusses features of each planet as well as space exploration, life on other planets, etc."—*(LJ)*.

Jastrow, Robert. RED GIANTS AND WHITE DWARFS: Man's Descent from the Stars. *Harper* 1967 rev. ed. 1970 $6.95; *New Am. Lib.* Signet 1971 pap. $1.50

"Extensive revisions in this edition, including new chapters on the moon, Mars, and Venus, were the result of recent space exploration. . . . It follows the sequence of cause and effect that runs through the creation and evolution of the universe, galaxies, stars, planets, and life itself . . . Dr. Jastrow is Director of the Goddard Institute for Space Research"—*(LJ)*.

(With Malcolm H. Thompson). ASTRONOMY: Fundamentals and Frontiers. *Wiley* 2nd ed. 1974 $14.50

Jobes, Gertrude, and James Jobes. OUTER SPACE: Myths, Name Meanings and Calendars From the Emergence of History to the Present Day. *Scarecrow Press* 1965 $11.00

An index which makes "fascinating reading"—*(LJ)*.

Keyhoe, Donald E. ALIENS FROM SPACE: The Real Story of Unidentified Flying Objects. *Doubleday* 1973 $7.95; *New Am. Lib.* Signet 1974 pap. $1.50. The author was director of the National Investigations Committee on Aerial Phenomena which analyzed nearly 11,000 UFO reports by the mid-sixties.

King, Henry C. PICTORIAL GUIDE TO THE STARS. *T. Y. Crowell* 1967 $8.95

Kopal, Zdenek. MAN AND HIS UNIVERSE. *Morrow* 1974 $7.95 pap. $2.95

"Kopal, a noted astronomer, guides the reader to a fundamental understanding of the universe, the sun and stars, and the distant galaxies"—*(LJ)*.

Levitt, Israel M. BEYOND THE KNOWN UNIVERSE: From Dwarf Stars to Quasars. *Viking* 1974 $10.95

"White dwarfs, pulsars, quasars—terms like these often confuse the layman trying to understand current research in astronomy. This book, aimed at the nonspecialist, provides a readable explanation of recent work in this field"—*(LJ)*.

Lewis, Richard S. APPOINTMENT ON THE MOON: The Full Story of Americans in Space from Explorer One to the Lunar Landing and Beyond. *Viking* rev. ed. 1969 $10.00. By the science editor of the *Chicago Sun-Times*.

THE VOYAGES OF APOLLO: The Exploration of the Moon. *Quadrangle* 1974 $10.00
"A fascinating and valuable summation"—*(Booklist)*.

Ley, Willy. *See his main entry, this Chapter.*

Lovell, Sir Bernard. *See his main entry, this Chapter.*

McLaughlin, Charles, Ed. THE SPACE AGE DICTIONARY. *Van Nostrand-Reinhold* 2nd ed. 1963 $11.95

Macvey, John W. WHISPERS FROM SPACE. *Macmillan* 1973 $8.95
"A very readable discussion of the possibility of using radio astronomy as a key to the question of whether or not life exists in other parts of the univese"—*(LJ)*.

Mason, Brian, and William G. Melson. LUNAR ROCKS. *Wiley* 1970 $11.00

Menzel, Donald H., and others. SURVEY OF THE UNIVERSE. *Prentice-Hall* 1970 $16.95

Moore, Patrick. *See his main entry, this Chapter.*

Motz, Lloyd. THE UNIVERSE. *Scribner* 1975 $14.95
"Professor Motz skillfully blends astrophysics and cosmology to outline the probable history of the universe to date"—*(LJ)*.

THE NEW SPACE ENCYCLOPEDIA: A Guide to Astronomy and Space Exploration. *Dutton* rev. ed. 1974 $14.95

Page, Thornton, and Lou William Page, Eds. SKY AND TELESCOPE LIBRARY OF ASTRONOMY. *Macmillan* 8 vols. 1965–1969 Vol. 1 Wanderers in the Sky (1965) Vol. 2 Neighbors of the Earth (1965) Vol. 3 Origin of the Solar System (1966) Vol. 4 Telescopes: How to Make and Use Them (1966) Vol. 5 Starlight (1967) Vol. 6 Evolution of Stars (1967) Vol. 7 Stars and Clouds of the Milky Way (1968) Vol. 8 Beyond the Milky Way (1969) each $7.95 except Vol. 2 $8.95

Rohr, Hans. BEAUTY OF THE UNIVERSE. Trans. by Arthur Beer *Viking* 1971 $10.00
"Composed largely of photographs with a commentary, this outstanding book reveals such splendors as the Pleiades, solar and lunar eclipses, planets . . . the Milky Way, etc."—*(LJ)*.

Ronan, Colin A. ASTRONOMY. *Harper* (Barnes & Noble) 1973 $10.50

DISCOVERY OF THE GALAXIES. *Grossman* 1969 $3.95

INVISIBLE ASTRONOMY. *Lippincott* 1972 $7.95
An "excellent and most up-to-date summary of the methods and results of all the astronomical techniques which do not rely on visible light"—*(Choice)*.

Sagan, Carl, and Thornton Page, Eds. UFOs—A Scientific Debate. *Cornell Univ. Press* 1974 $12.50 pap. $3.95
"Consists of papers given in 1969 at a symposium on UFOs held at a prestigious conference, the annual meeting of the American Association for the Advancement of Science"—*(LJ)*.

Shapley, Harlow. *See his main entry, this Chapter.*

Shelton, William R. MAN'S CONQUEST OF SPACE. *National Geographic Soc.* 1968 $4.25

Sklar, Lawrence. SPACE, TIME, AND SPACETIME. *Univ. of California Press* 1973 $15.00

Smolders, Peter L. THE SOVIETS IN SPACE. Trans. by Marian Powell *Taplinger* 1974 $9.95
This book "is based on the author's personal interviews with many cosmonauts and Russian engineers. It is a useful account of the Soviet space program"—*(LJ)*.

Struve, Otto, and Velta Zebergs. ASTRONOMY OF THE 20TH CENTURY. *Macmillan* 1962
$12.50. A contemporary astronomer reviews the astronomical discoveries of the 20th
century and the personalities behind them; authoritative and lucidly written.

Taylor, L. B. FOR ALL MANKIND: America's Space Programs in the 1970s and Beyond.
Dutton 1974 $8.95
"An introductory overview of aerospace capabilities"—*(Booklist)*.

Vladimirov, Leonid. THE RUSSIAN SPACE BLUFF: The Inside Story of the Soviet Drive to
the Moon. Trans. by David Floyd *Dial* 1973 $5.95
"An interesting view of the Soviet space program as seen by the author, a former Russian
engineer who defected to the West several years ago"—*(LJ)*.

von Braun, Wernher, and Frederick I. Ordway III. THE HISTORY OF ROCKETRY AND
SPACE TRAVEL. Introd. by Frederick C. Durant III; ill. by Harry H.-K. Lange *T. Y.
Crowell* 1967 3rd rev. ed. 1975 $19.95
"The coverage is international and ample, even exploring such fascinating side paths as science
fiction and firecrackers"—*(PW)*. "Brilliantly conceived and written"—Sir Bernard Lovell.
See also von Braun's main entry, this Chapter.

Weigert, A., and H. Zimmermann. A CONCISE ENCYCLOPEDIA OF ASTRONOMY. Trans. by J.
Home Dickson from *"ABC der Astronomie;"* ill. *American Elsevier* 1968 $9.00
"Accurate, clearly written"—*(LJ)*. 368 pages; includes about 1,500 definitions and articles.

Whipple, Fred L. EARTH, MOON, AND PLANETS. *Harvard Univ. Press* 3rd ed. 1968 $8.75
pap. $2.75

Whitney, Charles A. DISCOVERY OF OUR GALAXY. *Knopf* 1971 $10.00. Professor of
Astronomy at Harvard and a physicist at the Smithsonian Astrophysical Observatory,
Dr. Whitney has written the history of man's concept of our galaxy, the Milky Way,
from the 6th century B.C. to 1970.

TECHNOLOGY AND ENGINEERING

Adler, Irving. THINKING MACHINES: A Layman's Introduction to Logic—Boolean Algebra and Computers. *T. Y. Crowell* (John Day) rev. ed. 1974 $6.95

Arnold, Tom and Frank S. Vaden. INVENTION PROTECTION FOR PRACTICING ENGINEERS.
Beekman Pub. 1971 $10.95
"Discussed are the problems of what is patentable and what is not, patent searching, securing a
patent, evaluating patents for purchase or sale, litigation and enforcement, licensing, the function
of a patent attorney, and trends in patent law"—*(LJ)*.

Barbour, Ian G. SCIENCE AND SECULARITY: The Ethics of Technology. *Harper* 1971 $4.95
This book "has to do with knowledge and survival yoked by the desperate need for individual
and corporate decision and action"—*(Choice)*.

Brier, Alan, and Ian Robinson. COMPUTERS AND THE SOCIAL SCIENCES. *Columbia* 1974
$12.50 pap. $6.00

Brinkworth, B. J. SOLAR ENERGY FOR MAN. *Wiley* 1973 $8.95

Brown, John A., and Robert S. Workman. HOW A COMPUTER SYSTEM WORKS. *Arco* 1974
$8.95 pap. $5.95

Brown, Ronald. LASERS: A Survey of Their Performance and Applications. *Beekman Pub.*
1969 $18.00

Clark, John D. IGNITION: An Informal History of Liquid Rocket Propellants. *Rutgers
Univ. Press* 1972 $10.00
"This chronicle of men, rocketry, and chemical engineering has a magnetic authenticity, and
manages to combine literary color and scientific nomenclature with remarkable élan"—*(Choice)*.

Collier, Basil. The Airship: A History. *Putnam* 1974 $12.95

This is the "record of the evolution of lighter-than-air flight from the earliest experimental attempts through the advances made by the Zeppelin"—(*Booklist*).

Cuadra, Carlos A., and Ann Luke, Eds. The Annual Review of Information Science and Technology: Vol. 8. *American Society for Information Science* 1973 $22.00

"Workers in the physical, biological and social sciences, especially those who must struggle with the literature deluge, will find much of interest and needed help in this review"—(*Choice*).

De Camp, L. Sprague. The Ancient Engineers. 1963. *Ballantine Bks.* 1974 pap. $1.75; *M.I.T. Press* 1970 pap. $2.95. A most readable popular history of technology.

Diebold, John. Ed. The World of the Computer. *Random* 1973 $12.50

"A fine collection of 33 essays whose authors include . . . John von Neumann, John Mauchly, Norbert Wiener, John Eckert, Margaret Mead and Arthur C. Clarke . . . which treat all aspects of computers"—(*LJ*).

Duffie, John A., and William A. Beckman. Solar Energy/Solar Processes. *Wiley* 1974 $16.95

Eames, Charles, and Ray Eames. A Computer Perspective. Ed. by Glen Fleck *Harvard Univ. Press* 1973 $15.00

"A collection of photographs and drawings plus a brief, running explanatory text which together describe the history of computers. The book covers the period 1890–1950"—(*LJ*).

Etkin, Bernard. Dynamics of Atmospheric Flight. *Wiley* 1972 $19.95

"This work has excited great interest and appreciation among leaders in the field"—(*Choice*).

Feldzamen, Alvin N. Intelligent Man's Easy Guide to Computers. *McKay* 1971 $7.95

"The author's easily read style imparts a feeling for the principles and functioning of computers and a basic understanding of the mechanisms in use, their applications for the small business-man, and the work of the systems analyst"—(*LJ*).

Florman, Samuel C. The Existential Pleasures of Engineering. *St. Martin's* 1975 $7.95

A "valuable reading for engineers given to self scrutiny"—(*Time*).

Fromm, Erich. The Revolution of Hope: Toward a Humanized Technology. *Harper* 1968 $5.95 pap. 1970 $1.95; *Bantam* pap. $.95. By a distinguished psychologist.

Fuchs, Walter R. Cybernetics for the Modern Mind. *Macmillan* 1971 $6.95

A "guided tour through the mathematical world of information processing. . . . Considerable emphasis is placed on the mathematics of information transmission, the electronic machines involved, and computer technology to carefully explain what computers can and cannot do"—(*LJ*).

Georgano, G. N. Encyclopedia of American Automobiles. *Dutton* 1971 $14.95

Gibbs-Smith, Charles H. Flight through the Ages: A Complete Illustrated Chronology from the Dreams of Early History to the Age of Space Exploration. *T. Y. Crowell* 1974 $17.95

"An informative digest of the chronology of flight from the beginnings of the dream to the present involvement with speed and space"—(*Christian Science Monitor*).

Goldstine, Herman H. The Computer from Pascal to von Neumann. *Princeton Univ. Press* 1972 $12.50

The author "deals briefly with the development of the computer from the 17th century to the 1930s, and extensively with the work of the author, John von Neumann, and others"—(*LJ*).

Hamilton, David. Technology, Man and the Environment. *Scribner* 1973 $9.95

"The author writes of the nature and implications of technical progress, and all that it has brought: new materials such as plastics and metals; a variety of energy sources; new modes of transportation; a revolution in food production; exploration of the seas; development of computer hardware and software and their uses in society"—(*LJ*).

Handel, S. A Dictionary of Electronics. *Gannon* 3rd ed. $5.00; *Penguin* rev. ed. 1971 pap. $2.50; *Peter Smith* 3rd ed. $4.50

Harmon, Margaret. STRETCHING MAN'S MIND: A History of Data Processing. *Mason & Charter* 1975 $8.95

"A general view of computers and their development written for the layman"—(*Choice*).

Hine, Charles R. MACHINE TOOLS AND PROCESSES FOR ENGINEERS. *McGraw-Hill* 1971 $17.50

"The author covers all the important tools with a descriptive and analytical treatment that shows how they should be used, what they can and cannot be expected to do"—(*LJ*).

Hoenig, Stuart A. HOW TO BUILD AND USE ELECTRONIC DEVICES WITHOUT FRUSTRATION, PANIC, MOUNTAINS OF MONEY, OR AN ENGINEERING DEGREE. *Little* 1973 $9.95

Howard, Frank, and William B. Gunston. CONQUEST OF THE AIR. *Random* 1972 $25.00

"This extensive collection of pictures, sketches, and color photographs, presented with an informative nontechnical text, gives a broad overview of how aircraft have developed in less than 70 years"—(*LJ*).

Johnson, Olaf A. DESIGN OF MACHINE TOOLS. *Chilton* 1971 $8.50

"Techniques and stages for designing machine tools described by an expert. . . . There are details for making a market survey, preparing designs, developing prototypes, and mass production"—(*LJ*).

Katzan, Harry, Jr. INFORMATION TECHNOLOGY: The Human Use of Computers. *Petrocelli Bks.* (dist. by Mason & Charter) 1974 $11.95

"It discusses not only the application of computers in several areas of society but also the basics of computer operations and programming"—(*LJ*).

Kranzberg, Melvin, and William H. Davenport, Eds. TECHNOLOGY AND CULTURE: An Anthology. *Schocken* 1972 $10.00

Kranzberg, Melvin, and Carroll W. Pursell Jr., Eds. TECHNOLOGY IN WESTERN CIVILIZATION. *Oxford* 2 vols. 1967 Vol. 1 The Emergence of Modern Industrial Society, Earliest Times to 1900 Vol. 2 Technology in the Twentieth Century each $9.95

"This comprehensive survey preserves the individual styles, emphases and interpretations of the various scholar-contributors, while molding them into a coherent, unified narrative"—(*LJ*).

Kuhns, William. THE POST-INDUSTRIAL PROPHETS: Interpretations of Technology. *Weybright & Tally* (dist. by McKay) 1971 $6.95

"An important book that compares the interpretations of a number of well-known commentators on current technological society"—(*Choice*).

Kursunoglu, Behram, and Arnold Perlmutter, Eds. IMPACT OF BASIC RESEARCH ON TECHNOLOGY. *Plenum* 1973 $16.50. Seven essays on scientific and technical developments by contributors like Vladimir Zworykin, Edward Teller, John Bardeen, P. A. M. Dirac, Lamb, Schawlow and Biondi.

Lawless, Edward W. TECHNOLOGY AND SOCIAL SHOCK. *Rutgers Univ. Press* 1975 $17.50 pap. $5.95

"This book is about the increasingly wary reaction of people to the revelation that many of our technological innovations have shown that there are a lot of snakes in our garden of affluence"—(Publisher's note).

Layton, Edwin T., Jr., Ed. TECHNOLOGY AND SOCIAL CHANGE IN AMERICA. *Harper* 1975 pap. $4.50

Liptak, Bela G., Ed. ENVIRONMENTAL ENGINEERS' HANDBOOK. *Chilton* 3 vols. 1975 set $75.00

Liptak "brings together in one source all the technical and scientific information needed for pollution abatement"—(Publisher's note).

McCullough, David. THE GREAT BRIDGE. *Simon & Schuster* 1972 $10.95

"This dramatic history of the Brooklyn Bridge is based on solid research involving not only general and technical literature, but also original papers and letters never before examined. . . . McCullough writes also of the times, of the politics, of the economic and social conditions of New York and of America during the period of the bridge's conception and construction"—(*LJ*).

May, George. A MOST UNIQUE MACHINE: A History of the Automobile Industry in Michigan. *Eerdmans* 1974 $6.95

"A thorough, consistently enjoyable introduction for the general reader and students of the growth of modern enterprise"—*(Booklist)*.

Morison, Elting E. FROM KNOW-HOW TO NOWHERE. *Basic Bks.* 1974 $8.95

MEN, MACHINES, AND MODERN TIMES. *M.I.T. Press* 1968 $6.95 pap. $1.95

"A series of essays and lectures giving historical perspective on technological change"—*(LJ)*.

Nitske, W. Robert. THE LIFE OF WILHELM CONRAD ROENTGEN: Discoverer of the X-Ray. *Univ. of Arizona Press* 1971 $8.50

Pacey, Arnold. THE MAZE OF INGENUITY: Ideas and Idealism in the Development of Technology. *Holmes & Meier* 1975 $12.50

Plowden, David. BRIDGES: The Spans of North America. *Viking* 1974 $27.50

"Both bridges and their builders are brought to life by this book"—*(LJ)*.

Ronan, Colin A. LOST DISCOVERIES: The Forgotten Science of the Ancient World. *McGraw-Hill* 1973 $10.95

"A highly readable account of the scientific achievements of the ancient world"—*(LJ)*.

Sanders, Donald H. COMPUTERS IN SOCIETY: An Introduction to Information Processing. *McGraw-Hill* 1973 $10.95

"Written in terms the nontechnical person can understand, the author presents a survey of the history of information processing, the role and features of computers, operation of computer systems, and applications of computers in a wide spectrum of uses"—*(LJ)*.

Sheahan, Richard. NON-TECHNICALLY SPEAKING: Energy and Environment. *St. Martin's* 1976 $6.95

"This book, written for the layman, describes how contemporary and future energy and environmental processes work"—*(PW)*.

Simonson, G. R., Ed. THE HISTORY OF THE AMERICAN AIRCRAFT INDUSTRY: An Anthology. *M.I.T. Press* 1968 $12.95

"This collection brings together some of the important 'classic selections' on the industry, many [of which] are out of print or available in scattered copies only"—*(LJ)*.

Singer, Charles, and others, Eds. A HISTORY OF TECHNOLOGY. *Oxford* 5 vols. 1954–1958 Vol. 1 From Early Times to Fall of Ancient Empires (1954) Vol. 2 The Mediterranean Civilization and the Middle Ages, c. 700 B.C.–C. A.D. 1500 (1956) Vol. 3 From the Renaissance to the Industrial Revolution, c. 1500–c. 1750 (1957) Vol. 4 The Industrial Revolution, c. 1750–c. 1850 (1958) Vol. 5 The Late Nineteenth Century, c. 1850–c. 1900 (1958) each $40.00

Slade, Edward. METALS IN THE MODERN WORLD: A Study in Materials Development. Science Ser. *Doubleday* 1968 $6.95 pap. $2.45

The nontechnical style keeps this within the range of the layman. Enhanced by many fine illustrations and drawings, a good number in color, it covers the nature of metals, the extraction, shaping and forming of metals, the role of automation in metallurgical industries and related topics.

Smith, Philip H. WHEELS WITHIN WHEELS. *T. Y. Crowell* (Funk & Wagnalls) 1968 $5.95

"An historical study of the American automobile industry . . . from 1895 to the present"—*(LJ)*.

Steadman, Philip. ENERGY, ENVIRONMENT AND BUILDING. *Cambridge* 1975 $14.95 pap. $5.95

"A thorough and readable compendium of current work [addressed] to energy-conservation professionals and energy saving designers-builders"—*(LJ)*.

Susskind, Charles. UNDERSTANDING TECHNOLOGY. *Johns Hopkins Press* 1973 $6.95

"It discusses how technology developed, how inventions like electronic equipment and the computer ushered in a new era, and the relationship of society to the technologist. Many modern inventions and processes are described in terms the reader with little technical background could easily grasp"—*(LJ)*.

Teller, Edward. *See his main entry, this Chapter.*

Tomeski, Edward A., and Harold Lazarus. PEOPLE ORIENTED COMPUTER SYSTEMS: The Computer in Crisis. *Van Nostrand-Reinhold* 1975 $13.95
"A well-organized, clearly expressed book"—*(LJ)*.

Van Tassel, Dennis. COMPUTER SECURITY MANAGEMENT. *Prentice-Hall* 1972 $12.50
"This is an absorbing study of problems of security in computer operation and procedure"—*(LJ)*.

Weik, Martin H., Jr., Ed. THE STANDARD DICTIONARY OF COMPUTERS AND INFORMATION PROCESSING. *Hayden* 1969 $13.75

Wempner, Gerald. THE MECHANICS OF SOLIDS: With Applications to Thin Bodies. *McGraw-Hill* 1973 $24.50

Whitt, Frank Rowland, and David Gordon Wilson. BICYCLING SCIENCE: Ergonomics and Mechanics. *M.I.T. Press* 1975 $12.95

Wiener, Norbert. THE HUMAN USE OF HUMAN BEINGS: Cybernetics and Society. 1950 rev. ed. 1954 *Avon Bks.* 1967 pap. $1.65

SCIENTISTS

Included in this group are, in general, the great—or early—scientists who are known primarily for their own discoveries or conclusions, and who have at least one work in print which a layman would find not entirely beyond him. In the section following this will be found Naturalists and Science Writers. There are inevitably some overlaps: Laura Fermi, though not herself a scientist, has explained the work of her husband, Enrico Fermi, who wrote little for laymen; she is treated, therefore, in his entry. Lancelot Hogben and George Gamow, to take two examples, are themselves scientists but are best known for their excellent writing for laymen; so they appear in the "Writers" section.

HIPPOCRATES.   c. 460 B.C.–c. 370 B.C.
The "father of medicine" was the first to separate medicine from superstition and guesswork and to place it on a scientific basis. The Greek physician held the fallacious theory that disease was the result of "humors" or disorders of the body fluids. His keen observation of his patients resulted in his noting many signs of disease such as the "facial expression in approaching death known as the 'facies Hippocratica' and the succussion sound of fluid in the chest." He saw the promotion of cleanliness and proper diet as the most important duty of the physician. The "Hippocratic oath," administered to many graduates of medicine, cannot be credited to him, but certainly represents his ideals of medical service. The well-known translation by Francis Adams (1886) is generally good but occasionally misleading; the later one by W. H. S. Jones and E. T. Withington is now preferred.

THE MEDICAL WORKS. *Harvard Univ. Press* Loeb 4 vols. 1923–27 Vols. 1, 2 and 4 trans. by W. H. S. Jones, Vol. 3 trans. by E. T. Withington (Vol. 4 with Heracleitus' "On the Universe") each $7.00

THE GENUINE WORKS. Trans. and ed. by Francis Adams. 1886. *Robert E. Krieger* 1971 $15.00 lea. $27.00

Books about Hippocrates
Hippocrates: Father of Medicine. By Herbert S. Goldberg. *Franklin Watts* 1962 lib. bdg. $4.33
Hippocrates. By Edwin B. Levine. *Twayne* $6.95
Hippocrates Revisited: A Search for Meaning. Ed. by Roger J. Bulger. *Medcom* (dist. by McKay) 1973 $13.95

ARISTOTLE.   384 B.C.–322 B.C.   *See Chapter 5, Philosophy, this Vol.*

EUCLID.   c. 323 B.C.–285 B.C.
The "Elements" was first translated by Sir Henry Billingsley in 1570 and is a collection of geometrical theorems and problems which forms the basis for geometry. Almost nothing is known of the life of this important Greek mathematician. The standard translation from the standard text of Heiberg is that of Sir T. L. Heath.

THE ELEMENTS OF EUCLID. Trans. with introd. and commentary by Sir Thomas L. Heath. 1926. 1956. *Dover* 3 vols. 2nd ed. rev. and enl. pap. Vols. 1 and 3 each $3.50 Vol. 2 $3.00; ed. by Isaac Todhunter, introd. by Sir Thomas Heath *Dutton* Everyman's 1933 $3.95

Books about Euclid

Commentary of Pappus on Book X of Euclid's Elements: Arabic Text and Translation. Trans. by William Thomson; ed. by Gustav Junge and William Thomson. 1930. *Johnson Reprint* $17.50. Pappus was a Greek mathematician of the fourth century.

Ancient Science and Modern Civilization: Euclid and His Time; Ptolemy and His Time; The End of Greek Science and Culture. By George A. L. Sarton. *Univ. of Nebraska Press* 1954 Bison Bks. pap. $1.65

Euclid and Geometry. By Estelle A. DeLacy. *Franklin Watts* 1963 lib. bdg. $4.33

The Story of Euclid. By F. W. Frankland. *Gordon Press* $28.00

Proclus' Commentary on the First Book of Euclid's Elements. Trans. by Glenn R. Morrow. *Princeton Univ. Press* 1970 $15.00

PTOLEMY (Claudius Ptolemaseus).   fl. c. 127 A.D.–141 or 151 A.D.

A Graeco-Egyptian astronomer, mathematician and geographer, Ptolemy is known primarily for the geocentric theory of the universe expounded in his important "System of Mathematics," a 13-volume textbook on astronomy based on the mathematical and astronomical systems already developed by the Greeks. According to the Ptolemaic view, sun, moon and stars all revolved in circular orbits around a stationary earth. This theory remained the standard one until the 16th century, when it was finally disproved by Copernicus (*q.v.*). Despite Ptolemy's original observations, his contributions to science rest in his work as a collator and expounder of the contemporary knowledge of Alexandrian scientists.

TETRABIBLIOS. (And Manetho's "Aegyptiaca, etc.") *Harvard Univ. Press* Loeb 1940 $7.00; *Symbols & Signs* 1974 $6.95 pap. $3.50

GEOGRAPHY OF CLAUDIUS PTOLEMY. Trans. and ed. by Edward L. Stevenson. *AMS Press* 1932 $147.50

Books about Ptolemy

Ancient Science and Modern Civilization: Euclid and His Time; Ptolemy and His Time; The End of Greek Science and Culture. By George A. Sarton. *Univ. of Nebraska Press* 1954 Bison Bks. 1964 pap. $1.65

GALEN.   c. 130 A.D.–C. 200 A.D.

Galen was born in Pergamum of Greek parents. He served as physician to the gladiatorial school there and after about 162 lived in Rome, where he became physician to Marcus Aurelius (*q.v.*). He is known as a pioneer in anatomy and wrote extensively on medical subjects; some 80 of his treatises survive, but many more have been lost. He showed that the arteries contain blood (rather than air) and made many discoveries about the circulatory systems. He dissected animals (particularly the Barbary ape) and learned much from his treatment of injured gladiators. For some 13 centuries he remained the standard authority on medicine for the Western world, though Vesalius (*q.v.*) corrected a number of his assumptions. A. J. Brock's translation of the "Natural Faculties" was called "spirited, idiomatic, scholarly, and often happy; thus it is very readable by itself"—(*Classical Review*). Now o.p. are Galen's "On Anatomical Procedures," a translation of the surviving books with an introduction by Charles Singer (1962), the "Later Books" of the "Procedures" edited by B. Towers and M. C. Lyons, translated by W. L. H. Duckworth (1956), "On Usefulness of Parts of the Body" trans. by M. T. May (1968), and "Galen's Hygiene" trans. by R. M. Green and others (1951).

ON THE NATURAL FACULTIES. Trans. by A. J. Brock *Harvard Univ. Press* Loeb 1916 $7.00

GALEN'S INSTITUTIO LOGICA: English Translation, Introduction and Commentary. Ed. by John S. Kieffer *Johns Hopkins Press* 1964 $6.50

ON THE PASSIONS AND ERRORS OF THE SOUL. Trans. by Paul W. Harkins *Ohio State Univ. Press* 1964 $4.75

Books about Galen

Galen and the Syllogism. By Nicholas Rescher. *Univ. of Pittsburgh Press* 1966 $6.95

Galenism: Rise and Decline of a Medical Philosophy. By Owsei Temkin. *Cornell Univ. Press* 1973 $15.00

COPERNICUS, NICOLAUS (Latinized form of Mikolaj Kopernik or Niklas Koppernigk). 1473–1543.

A churchman like many learned men of his day, Copernicus received a doctorate in canon law from the University of Ferrara in Italy and returned to his native Poland in 1506; he eventually settled in East Prussia, where he became a canon of the cathedral at Frauenberg. The work that immortalized this Polish astronomer is the treatise setting forth his belief that the sun is the center of a great system, with the earth, one of the planets, revolving about it. This work, *"De Revolutionibus Orbium Coelestium,"* dedicated to Pope Paul III, was probably completed by 1530. Because of the controversies it aroused, it was not published until 1543, when its author lay dying. The Copernican System replaced the Ptolemaic System and displaced man from the position at the center of the universe which he had held for over a millennium. Copernicus is regarded as the founder of modern astronomy.

ON THE REVOLUTION OF THE HEAVENLY SPHERES. Trans. from the Latin by A. M. Duncan *Wiley* (Halsted Press) 1974 $32.50

THREE COPERNICAN TREATISES. Ed. by Edward Rosen. 1939 2nd rev. ed. (with annotated Copernicus bibliography, 1939–58) 1959. *Octagon* 1971 $21.00; *Peter Smith* 2nd rev. ed. $4.50. Contains an early version of his theory.

Books about Copernicus

Copernicus: The Founder of Modern Astronomy. By Angus Armitage. 1938. *A. S. Barnes* 1962 pap. 1971 $1.95
Nicholas Copernicus, 1543–1943. By Stephen P. Mizwa. 1943. *Kennikat* 1969 $5.00. An assessment on the 400th anniversary of his birth.
The Copernican Revolution. By Paul S. Goodman. *Gotham Bookmart* 1947 pap. $4.50
The World of Copernicus (orig. "Sun, Stand Thou Still"). By Angus Armitage. 1947. *Beekman Pubs.* 1972 pap. $4.95
The Copernican Revolution: Planetary Astronomy in the Development of Western Thought. By Thomas S. Kuhn. *Harvard Univ. Press* 1957 $9.00 pap. $2.75
The Heritage of Copernicus: Theories "Pleasing to the Mind." Ed. by Jerzy Neyman. *M.I.T. Press* 1974 $30.00
The Astronomical Revolution. By Alexandre Koyré. *Cornell Univ. Press* 1973 $17.50
Nicolaus Copernicus: An Essay on His Life and Work. By Fred Hoyle. *Harper* 1973 $5.95
The World of Copernicus. By H. Bietkowski and W. Zonn. *Heinman* 1973 $15.00
The Scientific World of Copernicus. Ed. by B. Bienkowska. Trans. from the Polish by K. Cekalska *Reidel Pub.* 1973 $19.50
Nicolaus Copernicus and His Epoch. By Jan Adamczewski. *Scribner* 1974 $7.95
"This brief scholarly volume . . . displays the context of Copernicus's lifetime in good color and velvety gravure, and in a meticulously detailed text"—(*Scientific American*).
Copernicus—Yesterday and Today. Ed. by Arthur Beer and K. A. Strand. *Pergamon* (In prep.)

VESALIUS, ANDREAS. 1514–1564.

The work of the Flemish professor of anatomy at the University of Padua controverted Galen in many particulars and provoked an outcry. Vesalius left Padua and became the physician of Charles V and his son Philip II. He died at Zante, Greece, when returning from a pilgrimage to Jerusalem. Vesalius' remarkable studies and drawings (said to be by another hand than his but certainly done under his direction)—the illustrations to his important work, *"De Humanis Corporis Fabrica"* ("The Fabric of the Human Body," o. p.)—were based on direct observation through dissection. Vesalius' great book, published in 1543, within weeks of Copernicus' (*q.v.*) similarly epoch-making treatise on astronomy, provided, with Galen's work, the basis for modern anatomy.

THE ILLUSTRATIONS FROM THE WORKS OF ANDREAS VESALIUS OF BRUSSELS. Ed. by J. B. Saunders and Charles D. O'Malley. 1950. *Dover* pap. $4.00; *Peter Smith* $8.00

Books about Vesalius

Andreas Vesalius Bruxelsensis. By Moritz Roth. 1892. *Hafner* 1965 $29.50
A Bio-bibliography of Andreas Vesalius. By Harvey W. Cushing. *Shoe String Press* 2nd ed. 1962 $22.50
Andreas Vesalius of Brussels, 1514–1564. By Charles D. O'Malley. *Univ. of California Press* 1964 $15.00
"On the eve of the tetracentenary of his death comes this definitive biography . . . by a professor of the history of medicine at U.C.L.A., long a student of this important figure in the history of anatomy and science. The first biography of this kind since Roth's work in 1892, it incorporates the Vesalian research of the last 70 years. The book is not only a study of 16th-century anatomy and medicine, but also of Renaissance education and society, for

Vesalius, a wide-ranging member of the republic of letters, sojourned in Louvain, Paris, Padua, and Basel. Vesalius's great achievement, the *De humani corporis fabrica* (1543), a monument of printing and of science, is thoroughly explored in his own words and in the context of the Galenic anatomy of the times. The appendix contains extensive translations from the *Fabrica,* several of Vesalius's consilia or medical opinions, and Vesalian correspondence. . . . An outstanding work of scholarship"—*(LJ).*

Vesalius: Father of Modern Anatomy. By Jerome Tarshis. *Dial* 1969 $3.95

BACON, FRANCIS, Baron Verulam, Viscount St. Albans. 1561–1626. *See Chapter 5, Philosophy, this Vol., and Chapter 15, Essays and Criticism,* Reader's Adviser, *Vol. 1.*

GALILEI, GALILEO. 1564–1642.

By his persistent investigation of natural laws the great Italian astronomer, mathematician and physicist laid the foundations for modern science. Through his construction and use of astronomical telescopes he greatly enlarged the scope of man's vision and conception of the universe. He discovered, too, the important principle that bodies of different weights fall at the same rate of speed and acceleration. Galileo was a professor of mathematics at the Universities of Pisa and Padua (1589–1610) and later Chief Mathematician and Philosopher to the Grand Duke of Tuscany. He was tried in Rome (1633) by the Inquisition for upholding the system of Copernicus (*q.v.*) and made to deny his belief that the sun was the central body with the earth and other planets revolving about it. The legendary account of the trial now states that after his abjuration Galileo rose from his knees muttering, *"E pur si muove"* (nevertheless it does move). After a short period of imprisonment and an enforced residence in Siena, he was allowed to live in seclusion near Florence where he continued his pursuit of scientific truth until his death.

THE ACHIEVEMENT OF GALILEO. Ed. by James Brophy and Henry Paolucci *College & Univ. Press* 1962 $7.50 pap. 1963 $2.45

Some selected basic writings are presented in good translations, as are a very few pieces by the Catholic hierarchy in the "Galileo Case." Twentieth-century commentary on Galileo's work and his significance are added, and the editors have appended their own rather popular evaluation of Galileo. "His contributions to man's knowledge have been studied for many years but this book gives us a manageable, handy, single volume with which to see him in today's meaning"—*(LJ).*

ON MOTION (c. 1590) and ON MECHANICS (c. 1600). Trans. and ed. by I. A. Drabkin and Stillman Drake *Univ. of Wisconsin Press* 1960 $12.50

DIALOGUE CONCERNING THE TWO CHIEF WORLD SYSTEMS, PTOLEMAIC AND COPERNICAN. 1632. Trans. by Stillman Drake; fwd. by Albert Einstein *Univ. of California Press* 1953 2nd rev. ed. 1967 $15.00 pap. $2.95

Completely unabridged and translated from the definitive Italian text into modern English this includes Galileo's handwritten additions. The "Dialogue" is concerned with arguments for and against the motion of the earth and is primarily astronomical and philosophical in content.

DIALOGUES CONCERNING TWO NEW SCIENCES. 1638. *Dover* 1914 pap. $3.00; *Peter Smith* $4.25; trans. by Henry Crew and Alfonso de Salvio *Northwestern Univ. Press* 1950 $9.50

DISCOURSE ON BODIES IN WATER. Trans. by Thomas Salusbury. 1665. *Univ. of Illinois Press* 1960 $5.00

DISCOVERIES AND OPINIONS OF GALILEO. Trans. by Stillman Drake *Doubleday* Anchor Bks. 1957 pap. $1.95; *Peter Smith* 1959 $4.25

Books about Galileo

The Crime of Galileo. By George de Santillana. *Univ. of Chicago Press* 1955 $10.00 pap. 1959 $2.25

"A masterly intellectual whodunit, this brilliant and exciting book gives the fullest account yet of the difference of opinion between Galileo Galilei and the Holy Inquisition"—a controversy of profound religious and political import; absorbing for general reader, historian or scientist.

Galileo and the Scientific Revolution. By Laura C. Fermi and Gilberto Bernardini. *Basic Bks.* 1961 $5.50

Homage to Galileo. Ed. by Morton F. Kaplon. *M.I.T. Press* 1965 $6.00

Galileo Galilei: A Biography and Inquiry Into His Philosophy of Science. By Ludovico Geymonat. 1957 Trans. from the Italian with notes by Stillman Drake; fwd. by Giorgio de Santillana *McGraw-Hill* 1965 pap. $2.95

The author, an Italian Marxist philosopher and historian of science, forcefully contends that "Galileo's greatness lay in his appeal to empiricism rather than to a kind of Platonism"—(*LJ*). "Admirably translated" and "very readable," this book "may be followed throughout by the nonscientist, while the extensive notes and references ensure its usefulness to the serious student of scientific history"—(*N.Y. Times*).

Galileo Reappraised. Ed. by Carlo L. Golino. *Univ. of California Press* 1966 $7.25

Galileo. By Bertolt Brecht. Trans. by Charles Laughton; ed. by Eric Bentley *Grove* Black Cat Bks. 1966 pap. $1.65
A version which Brecht rewrote in 1947, after Hiroshima, in which he saw Galileo's recantation as the step by which science became irresponsible (enabling such later horrors to take place). Eric Bentley calls it "a Marxist defense of a social conception of science against the 'liberal' view that truth is an end in itself." A fine play, whether or not one accepts the playwright's thesis.

Galileo, Science and the Church. By Jerome J. Langford. 1966. *Univ. of Michigan Press* Ann Arbor Bks. rev. ed. 1971 pap. $2.45

Galileo Studies: Personality, Tradition, and Revolution. By Stillman Drake. *Univ. of Michigan Press* 1970 $8.50

The Natural Philosophy of Galileo: Essay on the Origins and Formation of Classical Mechanics. By Maurice Clavelin. Trans. from the French by A. J. Pomeranz *M.I.T. Press* 1974 pap. $22.50

Galileo: A Philosophical Study. By Dudley Shapere. *Univ. of Chicago Press* 1974 $9.75 pap. $2.95

Galileo. By Colin Ronan. *Putnam* 1974 $14.95
"An informative yet simply written look at Galileo and his world"—(*Booklist*).

KEPLER, JOHANNES (also John).   1571–1630.

Johannes Kepler was the German astronomer and friend of Galileo who first formulated the laws of planetary motion, of which the first and best known is that the orbit of every planet is an ellipse, the plane of which passes through the center of the sun. As a young man he was an assistant to Tycho Brahe, another early astronomer and mathematician. Later Kepler held several posts as government mathematician in German principalities. His life was shadowed by illness and religious persecution. Kepler had a mystical approach to the marvels of the universe, apparent in his writings, which were purchased in manuscript after his death by Catherine II of Russia. His "*Somnium*" seems relevant today—it describes an imaginary trip to the moon. "*Weltharmonik*" trans. by M. Casper (1939) and "The Six-Cornered Snowflake" trans. by C. Hardie (1966) are o.p.

EPITOME OF COPERNICAN ASTRONOMY. Bks. 4 and 5 1939. *Kraus* 2 vols. in 1 $15.50

SOMNIUM: The Dream, or Posthumous Work on Lunar Astronomy. Trans. and ed. by Edward Rosen *Univ. of Wisconsin Press* 1967 $15.00

KEPLER'S DREAM: With the Full Text and Notes of *Somnium, sive Astronomia Lunaris*. Ed. by John Lear; trans. from the Latin by Patricia Kirkwood *Univ. of California Press* 1965 $8.75. A good translation which includes Kepler's own footnotes; commentary by Mr. Lear.

Books about Kepler

An Account of the Astronomical Discoveries of Kepler. By Robert Small. 1804. *Univ. of Wisconsin Press* 1963 $15.00

Watershed: A Biography of Johannes Kepler. By Arthur Koestler. *Doubleday* 1960 pap. $2.50

John Kepler. By Angus Armitage. 1966. *Roy Pubs.* 1967 $6.95
An interesting, attractively produced and readable short work (194 pages) first published in England. "Highly recommended"—(*LJ*).

The Astronomical Revolution. By Alexandre Koyré. *Cornell Univ. Press* 1973 $17.50

Kepler: Four Hundred Years. Ed. by Arthur Beer. *Pergamon* (in prep.)

HARVEY, WILLIAM.   1578–1657.

The English physiologist and physician demonstrated that the blood flows in one stream through veins and arteries with the heart acting as a muscular pump, a revolutionary discovery for his day which was only finally substantiated in 1827. He studied at Cambridge and under Hieronymus Fabricius in Padua. He was court physician to James I and Charles I and president of the Royal College of Physicians.

WORKS. 1847. Trans. from the Latin with a life of the author by Robert Willis *Johnson Reprint* 1965 $35.00

LECTURES ON THE WHOLE OF ANATOMY: An Annotated Translation of William Harvey's *Prelectiones Anatomiae Universalis.* Trans. and ed. by Charles O'Malley, F. N. L. Poynter and K. F. Russell *Univ. of California Press* 1961 $11.50

"These lecture notes, available now for the first time in English, give some fascinating glimpses into the development of Harvey's understanding of the circulation of the blood and into the anatomical and medical practices of his time." This is a scholarly work which fills a gap in the literature of medical history.

DE MOTU LOCALI ANIMALIUM. 1627. Trans. and ed. by Gweneth Whitteridge *Cambridge* 1959 $13.50

In his work on the motion of the heart and blood Harvey referred to a projected work on the local movement of animals. Written as a series of notes, and probably never put into a final literary form, this is the first Latin-English edition.

DE MOTU CORDIS: Anatomical Studies on the Motion of the Heart and Blood. 1628. Trans. and ill. by Chauncey D. Leake *C. C. Thomas* 1928 5th ed. 1970 pap. $4.50. This first presented Harvey's important thesis.

THE CIRCULATION OF THE BLOOD. *Dutton* Everyman's 1963 $3.95

Books about Harvey

The Life of William Harvey. By Geoffrey Keynes. *Oxford* 1966 $20.50
Harvey and the Circulation of the Blood. By Jonathan Miller. *Grossman* 1968 $3.95
William Harvey and the Circulation of the Blood. By Gweneth Whitteridge. Ed. by M. A. Hoskin. History of Science Lib. *American Elsevier* 1970 $12.75

DESCARTES, RENÉ.   1596–1650.   *See Chapter 5, Philosophy, this Vol.*

BOYLE, ROBERT.   1627–1691.

Boyle was the first to distinguish between a chemical element and a compound. He defined the nature of a chemical reaction and of chemical analysis. His important "Boyle's law" of gases demonstrated that their volume and pressure vary inversely if the temperature is constant. He was born in Ireland, son of the 1st Earl of Cork, and became a Fellow of the Royal Society.

ROBERT BOYLE ON NATURAL PHILOSOPHY: An Essay with Selections from his Writings. By Marie Boas Hall. Fwd. by Norman Russell Hanson *Indiana Univ. Press* 1965 $12.50

"A distinguished historian of science, Mrs. Hall has devoted most of her scholarly research to Boyle, and she is uniquely prepared to write the long introductory essay which opens the book and places Boyle's contributions in the stream of scientific thought. This essay also serves as a prelude to the wide selection of Boylean writings which constitute the second part of the volume"—(*LJ*).

THE SCEPTICAL CHYMIST. 1661. *Dutton* Everyman's 1911 $3.95. Expounds his "mechanical philosophy" of chemistry.

EXPERIMENTS IN PNEUMATICS. Ed. by James Bryant Conant *Harvard Univ. Press* 1950 pap. $1.50

EXPERIMENTS AND CONSIDERATIONS TOUCHING COLOURS. c. 1664. *Johnson Reprint* 1964 $17.50

ORIGIN AND VIRTUES OF GEMS. 1672. Contributions to the History of Geology Ser. *Macmillan* (Hafner) 1972 $14.95

Books about Boyle

Robert Boyle and Seventeenth-Century Chemistry. By Marie Boas Hall. 1958. *Kraus* 1968 $12.00
Robert Boyle: Father of Chemistry. By Roger Pilkington. *Saifer* 1959 $4.00

HUYGENS, CHRISTIAAN.   1629–1695.

This Dutch mathematician and physicist was the son of the poet and musician, Constantijn Huygens. Christiaan has many "firsts" and discoveries to his credit: he discovered an improved method of grinding and polishing lenses: discovered a satellite of Saturn and the rings of Saturn; improved telescopes; developed the wave theory of light; enunciated his (Huygens') principle according to which the surface constituting a wave front is determined; investigated the polarization of light; was the first to use the pendulum to regulate the movement of clocks. In 1673

Huygens published his major work, the *"Horologium Oscillatorium,"* on the physical dynamics of the pendulum. Long resident in Paris, he became one of the first members of the French Academy. He was also a Fellow of the (English) Royal Society. In 1681 he returned to Holland and on his death bequeathed his manuscripts to the university of Leyden.

CELESTIAL WORLDS DISCOVER'D, or Conjectures Concerning the Inhabitants, Plants and Productions of the Worlds in the Planets. 1698. Facsimile edition. *Int. Scholarly Bk. Services* 1968 $15.00

Books about Huygens

Codex Huygens and Leonardo da Vinci's Art Theory. By Erwin Panofsky. 1940. *Greenwood* 1971 $12.25

On A Research Program in Early Modern Physics. By Paul Elzinga. Studies in the Theory of Science Ser. *Humanities Press* 1972 $11.50

NEWTON, SIR ISAAC. 1642–1727.

The great Sir Isaac Newton, most of whose epoch-making work occurred in his middle 20's, is best known for his formulation of the laws of gravity and motion. He also discovered that white light may be broken up into the colors of the spectrum by the use of a glass prism and invented a reflecting telescope. As an innovator he aroused controversy, like so many other changers of the status quo. In 1669 he was appointed professor at Cambridge, where he had formerly studied; he represented that University in Parliament. After moving to London in 1701, he became president of the Royal Society in 1703 and was knighted in 1705. Newton devoted much time in his later years to research on historical and religious matters and to secret experiments in alchemy. His writings on these, published posthumously, caused heated debate, but were not taken seriously. He is buried in Westminster Abbey. Voltaire said of him that "if all the geniuses of the universe assembled, he should lead the band."

UNPUBLISHED SCIENTIFIC PAPERS: A Selection from the Portsmouth Collection in the University Library, Cambridge. Chosen, trans. and ed. by Alfred Rupert Hall and Marie Boas Hall *Cambridge* 1962 $19.50

The Portsmouth collection is so extensive (about three million words) that it is unlikely that it will ever be printed in its entirety. The 20 papers which constitute this volume are divided into six sections: mathematics; mechanics; theory of matter; manuscripts relating to the "Principia"; education; and notes on Hooke's "Micrographia." Each section is preceded by a critical introduction which provides the historical, intellectual and technical background necessary for the understanding of the documents.

MATHEMATICAL PAPERS. Ed. by Derek T. Whiteside and M. A. Hoskin *Cambridge* 6 vols. 1967–74 Vol. 1 1664–1666 (1967) Vol. 2 1667–1670 (1968) Vol. 3 1670–1673 (1968) each $45.00 Vol. 4 1674–1684 (1971) $55.00 Vol. 5 (1972) $65.00 Vol. 6 1684–1691 (1974) $72.50

An "outstanding" work—*(Choice)*.

MATHEMATICAL WORKS. Ed. by Derek T. Whiteside *Johnson Reprint* 2 vols. 1967 Vol. 1 $20.25 Vol. 2 $24.50

NEWTON'S PHILOSOPHY OF NATURE: Selected Writings. Ed. by H. Standish Thayer *Macmillan* (Hafner) 1953 pap. $2.95

MATHEMATICAL PRINCIPLES OF NATURAL PHILOSOPHY (1687) and SYSTEM OF THE WORLD (1704) *(Principia)*. Trans. by Andrew Motte, c. 1729. Ed. by Florian Cajori *Univ. of California Press* 1934 $15.00 2 vols. pap. 1962 Vol. 1 The Motions of Bodies $3.85 Vol. 2 The System of the World $3.25; *Greenwood* 1962 $22.00; *Humanities Press* 2 vols. 1968 set $49.50 trans. by Robert Thorp 1777 $32.50

NEW THEORY ABOUT LIGHT AND COLORS. 1672. *Hafner* 1965 $2.95

OPTICKS. 1704. *Dover* 1931 4th ed. 1952 pap. $4.00

TREATISE OF THE SYSTEM OF THE WORLD. 1731. *Beekman Pub.* 1969 $18.00

CORRESPONDENCE. Ed. by H. W. Turnbull and J. F. Scott *Cambridge* 4 vols. 1959–61 Vol. 1 1661–1675 (1959) Vol. 2 1676–1687 (1960) Vol. 3 1688–1694 (1961) Vol. 4 1694–1709 (1961) each $39.50. As far as possible, letters are presented in their original form.

CORRESPONDENCE OF SIR ISAAC NEWTON AND PROFESSOR COTES. Ed. by James Edelston *Int. Scholarly Bk. Services* 1969 $19.00

Books about Newton

Demonstration of Some of the Principal Sections of Sir Isaac Newton's Principles of Natural Philosophy. By John Clarke. 1730. *Johnson Reprint* 1972 $21.00

The Elements of Sir Isaac Newton's Philosophy. By Voltaire. 1738. Trans. by J. Hanna *Int. Scholarly Bk. Services* 1967 $14.00

An Account of Sir Isaac Newton's Philosophical Discoveries. By Colin Maclaurin. 1748. *Adler's* 1970 $34.00; *Johnson Reprint* 1967 $24.50

Analytical Review of Sir Isaac Newton's *Principia*. By Henry Brougham and E. J. Routh. *Johnson Reprint* 1972 $31.50

Memoirs of the Life, Writings and Discoveries of Sir Isaac Newton. By David Brewster. 1855. *Johnson Reprint* 2 vols. 1965 $49.00

Bibliography of the Works of Sir Isaac Newton. By George J. Gray. 2nd ed. 1907. *Beekman Pub.* 1966 $9.95

Sir Isaac Newton. By S. Brodetsky. 1927. *Richard West* $20.00

Metaphysical Foundations of Modern Physical Science. By Edwin A. Burtt. 2nd ed. 1932 *Doubleday* Anchor Bks. 1954 pap. $1.95; *Humanities Press* 1967 $12.00

Isaac Newton: A Biography. By Louis T. More. 1934. *Peter Smith* $5.50

Newton Demands the Muse: Newton's Opticks and the Eighteenth Century Poets. By Marjorie Hope Nicolson. *Princeton Univ. Press* 1946 pap. $2.95

Sir Isaac Newton: His Life and Work. By Edward N. Andrade. 1954. *Doubleday* Anchor Bks. 1958 pap. $1.95

A "leading British physicist and historian of research writes simply and with keen insight."

Franklin and Newton. By I. Bernard Cohen. *Harvard Univ. Press* 1956 rev. ed. 1973 $15.00

Background to Newton's *Principia*. By John Herivel. *Oxford* 1965 $18.50

Newtonian Studies. By Alexandre Koyré. 1965. *Univ. of Chicago Press* Phoenix Bks. pap. $2.45

A Portrait of Isaac Newton. By Frank E. Manuel. *Harvard Univ. Press* Belknap Press 1968 $13.50

From a modern psychological vantage point Professor Manuel studies the character, temperament and life style of Newton from his boyhood in Lincolnshire to his powerful maturity in London. The biographer "presents all this with his customary zest for ideas and lucidity of style; which makes an exciting book for a wide circle of readers"—(*LJ*).

Newton and Gravitation. By Colin Ronan. *Grossman* 1968 $3.95

Methodological Heritage of Newton. Ed. by R. E. Butts and J. W. Davis. *Univ. of Toronto Press* 1970 $6.50

Introduction to Newton's *Principia*. By I. Bernard Cohen. *Harvard Univ. Press* 1971 $30.00

"This very readable volume, conceived by two renowned historians of science and executed by one of them, presents a fascinating introduction to [the *Principia*]"—(*Choice*).

Newtonian Mechanics. By Anthony P. French. *Norton* 1971 $10.00 pap. $5.95

"Newtonian mechanics is enthusiastically presented with thoughtful discussions of the fundamental ideas, their range of applicability, and their relation to experiment, together with many clearly presented examples"—(*Choice*).

Visionary Physics: Blake's Response to Newton. By Donald Ault. *Univ. of Chicago Press* 1974 $12.50

"Though not the first book to discuss Newton's literary influence, Visionary Physics may be the most insightful"—(*LJ*).

BERKELEY, GEORGE, Bishop. 1685–1753. *See Chapter 5, Philosophy, this Vol.*

FRANKLIN, BENJAMIN. 1706–1790. *See Chapter 2, General Biography and Autobiography, this Vol.*

LAMARCK, JEAN BAPTISTE (PIERRE ANTOINE DE MONET, Chevalier de). 1744–1829.

Lamarck was a French biologist and naturalist, who did early classification of invertebrates. He laid the foundation for modern invertebrate paleontology and for Darwin's theory of evolution, a debt which Darwin readily acknowledged. "Zoological Philosophy" describes his evolutionary theory. He maintained that acquired characteristics could be inherited, a theory later discredited but now being reconsidered on evidence that some lower forms of life do inherit traits artificially induced in their parents.

HYDROGEOLOGY. Trans. by Albert V. Carozzi *Univ. of Illinois Press* 1964 $4.75

ZOOLOGICAL PHILOSOPHY. Trans. by Hugh Elliot. 1941. *Macmillan* (Hafner) 1963 $10.95

FARADAY, MICHAEL. 1791–1867.

The physicist-chemist Faraday was a brilliant experimenter whose inventions and discoveries were among the most significant in the history of science. As a boy of 13, the son of a blacksmith, he was an apprentice to a bookseller. He educated himself by reading and by listening to the lectures of the scientist Humphry Davy, with whom he later began his career as a laboratory assistant. Faraday's discoveries on the nature of electricity and of electric and magnetic forces provided impetus to the Industrial Revolution and much of the basis for modern technology: he invented the first electric dynamo and established the laws of electrolysis. In 1825 he became director of the laboratory and of the Royal Society. A lucid and exciting speaker (and writer), he lectured regularly, often to audiences of young people. Faraday refused a knighthood as well as the presidency of the Royal Society. His "Diary" (ed. by T. Martin 3 vols., 1932–1936) is o.p.

CHEMICAL MANIPULATION. 1827. *Wiley* (Halsted Press) 1974 $35.00

EXPERIMENTAL RESEARCHES IN ELECTRICITY. Orig. published in 3 vols. 1839–1855. *Dover* 3 vols. in 2 1962 each $12.50

EXPERIMENTAL RESEARCHES IN CHEMISTRY AND PHYSICS. 1859. *Int. Pubns. Service* 1969 $35.00

ON THE VARIOUS FORCES OF NATURE. (Orig. "A Course of Six Lectures on the Forces of Matter and Their Relations to Each Other") 1860. *T.Y. Crowell* 1961 $2.75. Lectures for young people on gravity, electricity and magnetism.

THE CHEMICAL HISTORY OF A CANDLE. Ed. by William Crookes; ill. by Jeanyee Wong *T.Y. Crowell* 1957 $3.50; *Macmillan* Collier Bks. 1962 pap. $.95. Lectures for young people, given at the Royal Institute.

THE ACHIEVEMENTS OF MICHAEL FARADAY. Ed. by L. Pearce Williams *Johnson Reprint* 1973 $35.00. Letters and other writings.

Books about Faraday

Michael Faraday: His Life and Work. By Silvanus P. Thompson. 1901. *Russell & Russell* 1974 $17.00

Michael Faraday: A List of His Lectures and Published Writings. Ed. by Alan E. Jeffreys. *Academic Press* 1960 $12.00

Faraday as a Discoverer. By John Tyndall. *T. Y. Crowell* 1961 $2.75; *Apollo* pap. $1.75

Faraday, Maxwell, and Kelvin. By David K. C. MacDonald. *Doubleday* 1964 pap. $1.45

Michael Faraday: A Biography. By L. Pearce Williams. 1965. *Simon & Schuster* Touchstone Bks. 1971 pap. $4.95

"Dr. Williams has written a definitive study of the man and his work. Although the subject matter is necessarily of a technical nature, the book's clear and vivid prose style should make it appealing to a wider audience"—(*LJ*).

The Contribution of Faraday and Maxwell to Electrical Science. By R. A. R. Tricker. *Pergamon* 1966 $8.00 pap. $5.50

Faraday and Electricity. By Colin Ronan. *Grossman* 1968 $3.95

Faraday as a Natural Philosopher. By Joseph Agassi. *Univ. of Chicago Press* 1971 $12.50

AGASSIZ, (JEAN) LOUIS (RODOLPHE). 1807–1873.

"The exact description of things seen, on which so much 20th century writing is founded, was a craft developed as recently as the 19th century, and not by men of letters but by scientists. Agassiz was quite possibly the greatest master of this art who ever lived"—(Hugh Kenner). As a penurious student and professor in Paris, this Swiss naturalist and geologist studied fish classification and produced the monumental treatise on extinct life forms of the sea, *"Recherches sur les Poissons Fossiles"* (1833–34). His second period of research was devoted to the study of Swiss glaciers; he made important discoveries about the Ice Age in Europe. The widespread hunger for scientific knowledge in the early 19th century brought him to this country (in 1846), where he became a professor of zoology and geology at Harvard. A skillful lecturer and popular and devoted teacher, he revolutionized the study of natural history by urging and practising the fresh observation and interpretation of nature as opposed to reliance on traditional classification systems. The Agassiz approach was adopted by an entire generation of scientists. With his usual industry and enthusiasm he established the museum of comparative zoology, now the "Agassiz Museum," at Harvard. His second wife, Elizabeth Cabot Cary, a pioneer in the higher education of women, played a major role in the founding of Radcliffe College. His famous "Essay on Classification" is included in his "Contributions to the Natural History of the United States" (4 vols. 1857–1862, o.p.). Ezra Pound (*q.v.*) once said of him: "Agassiz, apart from his brilliant achievements in natural science, ranks as a writer of prose, precise knowledge of his subject leading to great exactitude of expression."

ESSAY ON CLASSIFICATION. Ed. by Edward Lurie *Harvard Univ. Press* 1962 $7.50

STUDIES ON GLACIERS. (1840). Trans. and ed. by Albert V. Carozzi. (And "Discourse of Neuchatel") *Macmillan* (Hafner) 1967 $30.95

(With Augustus Gould). PRINCIPLES OF ZOOLOGY. 1848. American Environmental Studies Ser. *Arno* 1970 $10.00

LAKE SUPERIOR: Its Physical Character, Vegetation and Animals as Compared with Those of Other and Similar Regions. 1850. American Environmental Studies Ser. *Arno* 1970 $17.00; *Robert E. Krieger Pub. Co.* $16.50

METHODS OF STUDY IN NATURAL HISTORY. 1863. American Environmental Studies Ser. *Arno* 1970 $13.00

LOUIS AGASSIZ: His Life and Correspondence. 1885. *Somerset Pubs.* 2 vols. set $29.50

(With Elizabeth Agassiz). JOURNEY IN BRAZIL. Ed. by Curtis Wilgus *Praeger* 1969 $22.50

Books about Agassiz

Louis Agassiz. By Alice Bache Grould. 1900. *Folcroft* $10.00
Louis Agassiz as a Teacher. By Lane Cooper. 1917. *Norwood Editions* $10.00
Runner of the Mountain Tops: The Life of Louis Agassiz. By Mabel L. Robinson. 1939. *Gale Research Co.* 1973 $14.00
Louis Agassiz: A Life in Science. By Edward Lurie. *Univ. of Chicago Press* 1960 $12.00 Phoenix Bks. abr. ed. 1967 pap. $2.95

DARWIN, CHARLES ROBERT. 1809–1882.

Darwin's interest in the study of evolution began when he was official naturalist on the H.M.S. *Beagle*, which sailed around the world from 1831 to 1836. After his return he continued his research on animal and plant forms, concluding that "selection was the key to man's success." His theory of evolution, soon known as Darwinism, held that beneficial variations of a species were preserved, while others, unfavored by their environments, were eliminated in the struggle for existence. Darwin used as support the findings of anatomy, geology, embryology and paleontology. Although later research made it necessary to modify some of Darwin's statements, his discoveries corroborated by Mendelian genetics, became the "prime cornerstone of modern scientific teaching." The storm aroused by the first publication of "On the Origin of Species" in 1859, and its sequel "The Descent of Man" 11 years later, is still raging in some parts of the world between the evolutionists and fundamentalists. The famous 1925 "monkey trial" of John T. Scopes for teaching Darwinism was repeated in 1968 in Arkansas; Mrs. Jon O. Epperson, a biology teacher, was the defendant. This time the decision reversed a state's antievolution law. Darwin is remembered as a warm and modest man. Always poor in health, he spent the last 40 years of his life studying and writing at his home in Down, Sussex. Darwin had the faculty of writing simply about abstruse matters, and his use of reminiscence or a discursive anecdote lends great color to his scientific expositions. National Education Television in 1968 presented a fascinating BBC documentary on his life and work, and in 1969 five young students from Harvard and McGill followed Darwin's *Beagle* voyage—with many adventures and misadventures—to make a film.

WORKS. 1897. *AMS Press* 18 vols. each $27.50 set $485.00

THE DARWIN READER. Ed. by Marston Bates and Philip S. Humphrey *Scribner* 1956 pap. $3.95

This carefully edited selection from his best-known works shows "his genius at its most arresting, revolutionary, and pertinent." There are excerpts from the "Autobiography," "The Voyage of the Beagle," "The Origin of Species," "The Descent of Man" and "The Expression of the Emotions"; bibliography of critical appraisals of Darwin and his work.

THE ORIGIN OF SPECIES and THE DESCENT OF MAN. *Random* Modern Lib. Giants 1949 $4.95

THE DESCENT OF MAN and SELECTIONS IN RELATION TO SEX. 1871. *Gale Research Co.* 1974 $23.00; *Int. Pubns. Service* 2 vols. 1969 $55.00; *Richard West* 1902 $6.50

THE ORIGIN OF SPECIES BY MEANS OF NATURAL SELECTION. 1859. *Macmillan* Collier Bks. 1962 pap. $.95; *New Am. Lib.* Mentor pap. $1.25; *Oxford* World's Classics 1929 $4.50; ed. by J. W. Burrow *Penguin* 1969 pap. $1.45; ed. and abr. by Charlotte and William Irvine *Ungar* 1956 pap. $1.45; *Richard West* 2 vols. in 1 1914 $20.00

THE ORIGIN OF SPECIES: A Variorum Text. Ed. by Morse Peckham *Univ. of Pennsylvania Press* 1959 $19.00

Six editions of "The Origin" were issued under Darwin's direction between 1859 and 1872. Each edition embodied the author's own revision of his theory as new evidence presented itself. By 1872 about 75 per cent of the first edition had been rewritten. This variorum edition presents the text of the first edition with the variants of other editions printed directly beneath the relevant sentences.

THE VOYAGE OF THE "BEAGLE." 1860. Ed. by Leonard Engle *Dutton* Everyman's 1907 1955 $3.95; *Bantam* 1972 pap. $1.25; *Doubleday* 1962 pap. $2.95; ed. by Nora Barlow 1933. *Kraus* 1969 $49.50

ON THE MOVEMENTS AND HABITS OF CLIMBING PLANTS. 1865. *Int. Pubns. Service* 1973 $9.50

THE VARIATION OF ANIMALS AND PLANTS UNDER DOMESTICATION. 1868. *Int. Pubns. Service* 2 vols. 1969 $57.50

THE EXPRESSION OF THE EMOTIONS IN MAN AND ANIMALS. 1872. *AMS Press* 1972 $27.50; *Greenwood* 1973 $14.50; *Univ. of Chicago Press* 1965 $10.00 Phoenix Bks. pap. $2.45; *Richard West* $20.00

THE POWER OF MOVEMENT IN PLANTS. 1880. *Da Capo* 2nd ed. 1966 $17.50; *Richard West* 1892 $20.00

DARWIN ON HUMUS AND THE EARTHWORM: The Formation of Vegetable Mould. 1881. *Humanities Press* 4th ed. 1966 $4.50; *Int. Pubns. Service* 1969 $22.50

FOUNDATIONS OF THE ORIGIN OF SPECIES. Ed. by Francis Darwin. 1909. *Kraus* 1969 $11.00. Two essays written in 1842 and 1844.

NATURAL SELECTION. Ed. by Robert C. Stauffer *Cambridge* 1975 $49.50

"This book is probably the publishing event of the decade in history of science. . . . I cannot praise highly enough the meticulous work of Stauffer and a staff of assistants in rendering the text right down to the details of Darwin's misspellings. And it was no easy task. . . . Natural Selection is a joy to read. It is full of insights and subtle observations"—(*Science*). Dr. Stauffer is Professor of History of Science at the University of Wisconsin-Madison.

DARWIN AND HENSLOW, THE GROWTH OF AN IDEA: Letters 1831–1860. Ed. by Nora Barlow *Univ. of California Press* 1967 $10.00. John Stevens Henslow was a professor of botany who introduced Darwin to the field and made possible his voyage on the *Beagle*.

LIFE AND LETTERS OF CHARLES DARWIN. Ed. by Francis Darwin. 1888. *Finch Press* 2 vols. $45.00; *Johnson Reprint* 3 vols. 1969 set $70.00; *Richard West* 1973 $30.00

MORE LETTERS OF CHARLES DARWIN: A Record of His Work in a Series of Hitherto Unpublished Letters. Ed. by Francis Darwin and A. C. Seward. 1903. *Johnson Reprint* 2 vols. 1971 set $63.00

AUTOBIOGRAPHY, 1809–1882. Ed. by Nora Barlow, 1959. With original omissions restored. *Norton* 1969 pap. $2.45

This edition restores Darwin's comments on religion, omitted from the original version of 1887 because of family sentiment. "Some of the passages formerly suppressed are the most revealing he ever wrote concerning his own estimate of the bearing of his famous theory on religion, morals and philosophy"—(J. W. Krutch, in the *N.Y. Times*). The editor is the granddaughter of Charles Darwin.

AUTOBIOGRAPHY AND SELECTED LETTERS. Ed. by Francis Darwin, 1892. *Dover* 1959 pap. $2.50; *Peter Smith* 1960 $5.00. An unabridged and unaltered republication of the work first published in 1892 with the title "Charles Darwin: His Life Told in an Autobiographical Chapter."

Books about Darwin

Darwiniana: Essays and Reviews Pertaining to Darwinism. By Asa Gray. 1877. Ed. and annotated with introd. by A. Hunter Dupree *Harvard Univ. Press* 1963 $10.00 pap. $2.95; *Richard West* 1973 $30.00. The introduction provides background material for the essays.

Darwinism and What It Implies. By Sir Arthur Keith. 1928. *Richard West* $10.00

Darwin, Marx, and Wagner: Critique of a Heritage. By Jacques Barzun. 1941. *Doubleday* Anchor Bks. rev. ed. 1958 pap. $2.50

"A thought-provoking and stimulating book"—(*SR*). Barzun portrays these three and analyzes their thought in an attempt to show that they "really established the mechanistic, pseudo-scientific 'system' which is the root of all Communism and Fascism"—(Publisher's note).

Darwin: Before and After. By Robert E. Clark. 1948. *Richard West* $15.00

Doctor Darwin. By Hesketh Pearson. 1949. *Folcroft* $20.00

Darwin: Competition and Cooperation. By Ashley Montagu. 1952. *Greenwood* 1973 $8.50

Apes, Angels and Victorians. By William Irvine. 1955. *McGraw-Hill* 1972 pap. $2.95; *New Am. Lib.* Meridian $3.95. A skillful blending of information and humor about Charles Darwin, T. H. Huxley and the impact of Darwinism on the 19th-century world.

Charles Darwin. By Ruth E. Moore. *Knopf* 1955 $3.95

A "wonderfully lucid account of his intellectual achievements and their revolutionary consequences."

Darwin's Century: Evolution and the Men Who Discovered It. By Loren C. Eiseley. *Doubleday* Anchor Bks. 1958 pap. $2.95

"A triumph of intelligent popularization"—(*New Yorker*).

A Book That Shook the World: Anniversary Essays on Charles Darwin's 'Origin of Species.' Ed. by Ralph Buchsbaum. *Univ. of Pittsburgh Press* 1958 pap. $1.95

Darwin and the Darwinian Revolution. By Gertrude Himmelfarb. 1958. *Norton* 1968 pap. $3.95

"The book will place in clearer perspective the role of Darwin in nineteenth-century thought"—(*N.Y. Times*).

Evolution after Darwin. Ed. by Sol Tax and C. Callender. *Univ. of Chicago Press* 3 vols. 1960 Vol. 1 Evolution of Life: Its Origin, History and Future $15.00 Vol. 2 Evolution of Man: Mind, Culture and Society $12.00 Vol. 3 Issues in Evolution $10.00

Charles Darwin: Founder of the Theory of Evolution and Natural Selection. By Gerhard Wichler. *Pergamon Press* 1961 $8.00

Darwin and the Modern World View. By John C. Greene. *Louisiana State Univ. Press* 1961 pap. 1973 $1.95. An interesting study of the problems confronting two major modern schools of thought concerning evolution: the antitheological and the fundamentalist religions.

The Tangled Bank: Darwin, Marx, Frazer and Freud as Imaginative Writers. By Stanley E. Hyman. *Atheneum* 1962 pap. 1974 $4.25

The Quest for the Father: A Study of the Darwin-Butler Controversy. By Phyllis Greenacre. *International Univs. Press* 1963 $7.00

What Darwin Really Said. By Benjamin Farrington. *Schocken* 1966 $3.50 pap. $1.75

Charles Darwin. By Robert C. Olby. *Oxford* 1967 $2.00

The Great Monkey Trial. By L. Sprague de Camp. *Doubleday* 1968 $8.95

"The most comprehensive book on the Scopes Trial, and much the best. Mr. de Camp's principal interest, beyond telling a dramatic story, lies in correcting the Menckenite distortions in the popular image of the case: Bryan's opposition to evolution was really quite moderate; the trial was mainly amiable and the town of Dayton surprisingly open-minded; Bryan did not die of a broken heart but from cheating on his diabetes diet. Only on one issue does Mr. de Camp take an extreme position: Darrow and the defense were quite right to turn the trial into a circus, as the most effective way of exposing fundamentalist absurdity"—(*New Yorker*).

The Triumph of the Darwinian Method. By Michael T. Ghiselin. *Univ. of California Press* 1969 $8.95 pap. $3.25

Darwin and His Critics: The Reception of Darwin's Theory of Evolution by the Scientific Community. By David L. Hull. *Harvard Univ. Press* 1973 $18.50

"Writing clearly and cogently, [Hull] skillfully combines five of his own brief essays with an anthology of 16 contemporary reviews of "The Origin of Species" and adds helpful comments"—(*Choice*).

Comparative Reception of Darwinism. Ed. by Thomas F. Glick. *Univ. of Texas Press* 1975 $15.00

GALTON, SIR FRANCIS. 1822–1911.

The founder of the science of eugenics, Galton established and endowed a laboratory at the University of London. His great work was the application of exact quantitative methods, chiefly mathematical, to biology. From the publication of "The Origin of Species" in 1859, he was a convert to the theory of Darwin (*q.v.*), who was his first half-cousin. His many scientific contributions included his introduction of the use of finger printing, invented by the astronomer, Sir William Herschel; composite photographs and the first meteorological charts. His mechanical ingenuity and personal resourcefulness led him to carry a sort of periscope which he used to see over the heads of others in a crowd.

Galton's work on the measurement of ability and the relationship of ability to other factors deeply influenced the new discipline of psychology. Through his student J. M. Cattell, later the teacher of E. L. Thorndike (*q.v.*), his intelligence and other psychometric tests provided the basis for modern psychological testing. Galton's "hereditary" bias prevented him, however, from taking adequate account of environmental factors affecting human and animal intelligence. His writing on difficult subjects is clear and simple. For a good account of his impact on American psychology, see "The Pelican History of Psychology" by Robert Thomson (*Penguin* Pelican Bks. [orig.] 1968 pap. $2.75).

NARRATIVE OF AN EXPLORER IN TROPICAL SOUTH AFRICA. 1853. *Johnson Reprint* 1971 $20.25

HEREDITARY GENIUS: An Inquiry into Its Laws and Consequences. 1869. *Peter Smith* $6.75. Analyzes men of famous families.

FRANCIS GALTON'S ART OF TRAVEL. 1872. *David & Charles* $8.95

NATURAL INHERITANCE. 1889. *AMS Press* $14.00

FINGER PRINTS. 1892. *Da Capo* 2nd ed. 1966 $9.50

INQUIRIES INTO HUMAN FACULTY AND ITS DEVELOPMENT. 1901. *AMS Press* $11.25

ENGLISH MEN OF SCIENCE: Their Nature and Nurture. *International Scholarly Bk. Services* 1970 $13.50

MEMORIES OF MY LIFE. 1908. *AMS Press* $21.50

Books about Galton

Rustic Sounds and Other Studies in Literature and Natural History. By Francis Darwin. 1917. *Bks. for Libraries* $9.00

Eugenics: Galton and After. By C. P. Blacker. *Hillary House* 1952 $4.50

Francis Galton: The Life and Work of a Victorian Genius. By D. W. Forrest. *Taplinger* 1974 $14.95

MENDEL, GREGOR JOHANN. 1822–1884.

Mendel, the Austrian biologist, was a Roman Catholic priest whose classic article (*see below*) on the breeding of peas (1865) was only reprinted posthumously as a pamphlet. It described Mendel's crucial discoveries, based on intensive experimentation, in genetics, which made their impact only at the turn of the century. These, now known as Mendel's laws, concern the incidence of dominant and recessive characteristics and other factors in the offspring of plant and animal families. Besides their importance for the understanding of human biological inheritance, they have been of great practical assistance in the breeding of animals and plants.

EXPERIMENTS IN PLANT-HYBRIDISATION. 1886. Fwd. by Paul Christopher Mangelsdorf *Harvard Univ. Press* 1965 pap. $1.00

Books about Mendel

The Mechanism of Mendelian Heredity. By Thomas H. Morgan. 1915. *Johnson Reprint* 1972 $28.00

Mendelism and Evolution. By E. B. Ford. *Wiley* Halsted Press 8th ed. 1965 $3.50

The Matter of Mendelian Heredity. By Kenneth R. Lewis and John B. Lewis. *Williams & Wilkins* 1964 $10.00

The Origin of Genetics: A Mendel Source Book. Ed. by Curt Stern and Eva R. Sherwood. *W. H. Freeman* 1966 pap. $2.25

Origins of Mendelism. By Robert C. Olby. *Schocken* 1966 $6.95 pap. $2.45

Heritage from Mendel: Proceedings of the Mendel Centennial Symposium Sponsored by the Genetics Society of America, Fort Collins, 1965. Ed. by R. Alexander Brink with the assistance of E. Derek Styles; fwd. by Robert P. Wagner. *Univ. of Wisconsin Press* 1967 $20.00 pap. $5.50

Gregor Mendel: Father of the Science of Genetics. By Harry Sootin. *Vanguard* 1958 $4.50 "Although Mr. Sootin has written his biography for teen-age readers, he has done a job worth the attention of anyone, explaining even complicated genetic principles simply and well"— (*New Yorker*).

PASTEUR, LOUIS. 1822–1895.

This many-sided scientific genius spent most of his life teaching at various universities throughout France, including the Sorbonne and the École Normale in Paris. He had a passion for work, whose virtues he liked to extol, and was able to combine his teaching with research of tremendous consequence. His discoveries about bacteria demolished once and for all the ancient theory of the "spontaneous generation" of disease; his "pasteurization" process became the widely used method of decontaminating milk; with it, among other services to his country, he saved the wine and beer industries of France from endemic souring. He did valuable work on diseases of the silkworm (which threatened the French silk industry) and on rabies, to which the Pasteur Institute in Paris, of which he became the first director, was devoted. He lived to receive many honors but declined all temptations to wealth.

STUDIES ON FERMENTATION. 1879. Trans. and ed. with commentary by James Bryant Conant *Harvard Univ. Press* 1952 pap. $1.50; *Kraus* $18.50

Books about Pasteur

The Life of Pasteur. By René Vallery-Radot. 1906. Trans. by R. L. Devonshire *Finch Press* $14.00

Louis Pasteur. By Albert Keim and Louis Lumet. Trans. by Frederic T. Cooper. 1914. *Folcroft* $10.00

Pasteur: The History of a Mind. By Emile Duclaux. 1920. *Scarecrow Press* 1973 $12.50

Louis Pasteur. By Samuel J. Holmes. 1924. *Gannon* $5.00

Pasteur's and Tyndall's Study of Spontaneous Generation. Ed. by James Bryant Conant. *Harvard Univ. Press* 1953 pap. $1.50

Pasteur and the Invisible Giants: A Biography. By Edward F. Dolan, Jr. *Dodd* 1958 $3.95

Louis Pasteur: A Great Life in Brief. By Pasteur Vallery-Radot. *Knopf* 1958 $3.95
"Pasteur was really great, and his grandson . . . makes him so appealing that the book's lack of critical shading does not matter much"—(*N.Y. Times*).

Louis Pasteur: The Man and His Theories. By Hilaire Cuny. *Eriksson* 1966 $5.00

Louis Pasteur: The Germ Killer. By L. Mann. *Macmillan* 1966 $2.95

Pasteur and the Germ Theory. By J. K. Crellin. *Grossman* (dist. by Viking) 1968 $3.95

FABRE, JEAN HENRI CASIMIR. 1823–1915.

The French entomologist worked directly from nature. After a period of teaching at French universities he spent all his time observing and writing about insect behavior. His well-known essays on the life and habits of various insects are imaginative and charming. Now o.p. is "The Marvels of the Insect World" (1938), selected translations from his main work "*Souvenirs Entomologiques*" (10 vols., 1879–1907).

THE LIFE OF THE SPIDER. 1912. *Horizon Press* 1971 $7.50

SOCIAL LIFE IN THE INSECT WORLD. 1912. Trans. by Bernard Miall *Bks. for Libraries* $14.75; *Gale Research Co.* 1972 $14.00

THE INSECT WORLD OF J. HENRI FABRE. Ed. with notes by Edwin Way Teale *Dodd* 1949 $4.00; *Apollo* 1961 pap. $1.95; *Fawcett* Premier Bks. 1964 pap. $.60

Books about Fabre

The Life of Jean Henri Fabre 1823–1915. By Augustin Fabre. 1921. *Folcroft* $10.00

Fabre: Poet of Science. By G. V. Legros. *Horizon Press* 1971 $7.50

HUXLEY, THOMAS HENRY. 1825–1895.

Huxley, "the great Agnostic," the living example of the high ethical standards of the true evolutionist and the true rationalist, devoted himself almost exclusively to the defense and exposition of Darwin's theory of evolution. Like Darwin he started his scientific investigations while on a voyage to far places. He was assistant surgeon on the S.S. *Rattlesnake*, sent to explore Australia and the Great Barrier Reef, and stayed with the ship throughout the voyage (1846–50). Although he was one of the foremost anatomists of his time, his lectures and books were almost entirely on Darwinism. He had "the gift for the apt and acid phrase" and his "pure, rapid, athletic English" has stood as a model for all scientific writers. Huxley was later active as secretary and president of the Royal Society and as a member of many Royal Commissions. His period on the London school board had an important impact on British educational reform.

COLLECTED ESSAYS. 1902. *Greenwood* 9 vols. 1969 set $126.00

SELECTIONS FROM THE ESSAYS OF THOMAS HENRY HUXLEY. Ed. by Alburey Castell *AHM Pub. Corp.* Crofts Class. 1948 pap. $.85.

CRITIQUES AND ADDRESSES. 1873. *Bks. for Libraries* 1972 $12.00

AMERICAN ADDRESSES. 1877. *Bks. for Libraries* 1973 $9.50

ESSAYS UPON SOME CONTROVERTED QUESTIONS. 1892. *Bks. for Libraries* 1973 $21.50

DARWINIANA. 1896. *AMS Press* $11.50

EVOLUTION AND ETHICS AND OTHER ESSAYS. 1896. *AMS Press* 1970 $7.50; *Scholarly Press* $9.50

(With Julian S. Huxley). TOUCHSTONE FOR ETHICS, 1893–1943. 1947. *Bks. for Libraries* 1974 $11.00; (with title "Evolution and Ethics, 1893–1943") *Kraus* $10.50

T. H. HUXLEY ON EDUCATION. Ed. by Cyril Bibby *Cambridge* 1971 $10.50

ON THE ORIGIN OF SPECIES, or The Causes of the Phenomena of Organic Nature. (Orig. "On Our Knowledge of the Causes of the Phenomena of Organic Nature") 1862. Introd. by Ashley Montagu *Univ. of Michigan Press* 1968 $4.40 Ann Arbor Bks. pap. $1.75

MAN'S PLACE IN NATURE. 1863. *Univ. of Michigan Press* 1959 $4.95 pap. $2.25. Contests the anatomist Richard Owen's view that man differs from other animals in the structure of his brain.

THE CRAYFISH: An Introduction to the Study of Zoology. Am. ed. 1880. *M.I.T. Press* 1974 $12.50

DIARY OF THE VOYAGE OF H.M.S. RATTLESNAKE. Ed. by Julian Huxley 1936. *Kraus* $18.00

ON A PIECE OF CHALK. Ed. with introd. and notes by Loren Eiseley; ill. by Rudolf Freund *Scribner* 1965 $4.95; *Oriole Eds.* 1971 pap. $.65

"Huxley takes a simple piece of chalk found in a carpenter's pocket and proceeds from its study back into the mist of long-vanished geological eras"—(Publisher's note). "The utter charm of Huxley's Lay Lectures remains . . . . The ability of a first-class scientist to write well and interestingly for the public is rare, and no one has had it in a greater degree than Huxley. This beautiful book also contains excellent notes by Loren Eiseley, and superb illustrations by Rudolf Freund"—(*LJ*).

AUTOBIOGRAPHY AND ESSAYS. Ed. by Brander Matthews. 1919. *Kraus* 1969 $14.00

Books about Huxley

Thomas Henry Huxley. By Edward Clodd. 1902. *Folcroft* $15.00; *Richard West* 1973 $15.00
Thomas H. Huxley. By James R. Ainsworth-Davis. 1907. *AMS Press* $11.50
Thomas Henry Huxley. By Leonard Huxley. 1920. *Bks. for Libraries* $10.00
Freethinkers of the Nineteenth Century. By Janet E. Courtney. 1920. *Bks. for Libraries* $11.50; *Folcroft* $11.00; *Richard West* $11.45
Apes, Angels and Victorians: The Story of Darwin, Huxley and Evolution. By William Irvine. 1955. *McGraw-Hill* 1972 pap. $2.95; *New Am. Lib.* Meridian $3.95 "A surprisingly fresh and lively account of the two men who did more than any other Englishmen of their time to create the intellectual atmosphere in which we still live."
Thomas Henry Huxley. By William Irvine. *British Bk. Centre* 1960 $2.95 pap. $1.20. A pamphlet.
Thomas Henry Huxley. By Albert Ashforth. *Twayne* 1970 $6.50
Darwin and Huxley in Australia. By A. J. Marshall. *Verry* 1971 $11.00
Scientist Extraordinary: T. H. Huxley. By Cyril Bibby. *St. Martin's* 1972 $8.95
An "account for the ordinary reader of his scientific and public work, with biographical detail cut to the minimum. It is well worth reading"—(*Economist*).

OSLER, SIR WILLIAM, Bart. 1849–1919.

The distinguished and beloved Canadian physician, teacher and medical historian wrote an accomplished prose. Dr. Joseph Collins once wrote of him as "the most widely-known and best-loved physician in the world." From the time of his call to his alma mater, McGill Medical School, to his going to the Univeristy of Pennsylvania, then to Johns Hopkins and on to Oxford University, his career was a steady rise to fame and success. The one dark page in his story was the loss of his only son in World War I. He was knighted in 1911. His most important research was on diseases of the circulatory system.

A WAY OF LIFE AND OTHER SELECTED WRITINGS. (Orig. "Selected Writings" 1951) *Dover* 1951 pap. $2.75; *Peter Smith* 1950 $4.75

AEQUANIMITAS. 1904. *McGraw-Hill* 3rd ed. 1932 $9.00. Essays.

A WAY OF LIFE: An Address Delivered to Yale Students Sunday Evening, April 20, 1913. *Harper* 1937 $1.50: *C. C. Thomas* 1969 $3.95

The Evolution of Modern Medicine: A Series of Lectures Delivered at Yale University on the Silliman Foundation in April, 1913. 1922. *Arno* 1972 $15.00

Student Life and Other Essays. 1931. *Bks. for Libraries* 1967 $8.00

Osler's Textbook Revisited: Reprint of Selected Sections with Commentaries. Ed. by A. McGehee Harvey and Victor A. McKusick *Prentice-Hall* 1967 $14.25 pap. $7.10

Continual Remembrance: Letters from Sir William Osler to His Friend Ned Milburn. 1865–1919. Comp. by Howard L. Holley *C. C. Thomas* 1968 $6.75. Letters between Osler and a boyhood friend.

Books about Osler

Life of Sir William Osler. By Harvey Cushing (*q.v.*). *Oxford* 2 vols. 1925 1940 boxed $30.00

Osler, and Other Papers. By William S. Thayer. 1931. *Bks. for Libraries* $12.75

Sir William Osler: Historian and Literary Essayist. By William White. *Wayne State Univ. Press* 1951 pap. $2.95

William Osler Commemorative Issue. Ed. by John H. Talbott. *American Medical Association* 1970 pap. $2.00

Humanism in Medicine. by John P. McGovern and Chester R. Burns. *C. C. Thomas* 1973 $9.75

BAILEY, LIBERTY HYDE. 1858–1954.

This American botanist and horticulturist is noted for his basic works in both fields. He was instrumental in raising the stature of horticulture to that of an applied science and in bettering the living conditions and education of farmers. A professor of horticulture at Cornell, he also held many administrative positions. "Bailey was a man of driving energy. As a diversion from administrative burdens and research in science he wrote two volumes of poetry and nine in the fields of rural sociology, religion and philosophy"—(*Encyclopaedia Britannica*). He wrote over 60 books on botany, horticulture and agriculture.

Sketch of the Evolution of Our Native Fruits. 1898. *Scholarly Research, Inc.* 1973 $22.25

Cyclopedia of Horticulture. *Gordon Press* 4 vols. $299.95

(Ed.). The Standard Cyclopedia of Horticulture. *Macmillan* 6 vols. 1914–17 o.p. 3 vols. rev. ed. 1935 each $22.00 set $65.00

Manual of Cultivated Plants. *Macmillan* 1924 rev. ed. 1949 $19.95

How Plants Get Their Names. 1933. *Dover* pap. $1.50; *Peter Smith* $4.50; *Gale Research Co.* 1973 $8.00

(With Ethel Z. Bailey). Hortus Second. *Macmillan* 1941 1958 $14.95

Pruning Manual. Rev. by E. P. Christopher *Macmillan* 1954 $8.95

Nursery Manual. *Macmillan* rev. ed. 1967 $7.95

The Holy Earth. *Gordon Press* $25.00

Books about Bailey

Liberty Hyde Bailey. By Andrew D. Rodgers, III. 1949. *Hafner* 3rd ed. 1965 $11.95

"Mr. Rodgers alternates between the romantic and the pedantic. Documents and letters are lavishly quoted and footnoted. But through this musty material steals the soft breath of orchards in bloom and of fields turning green in the spring. Especially is this true in the description of Bailey's Michigan boyhood"—(*N.Y. Times*).

WHITEHEAD, ALFRED NORTH. 1861–1847. *See Chapter 5, Philosophy, this Vol.*

CURIE, MARIE (SKLODOWSKA). 1867–1934. (Nobel Prize 1903, 1911)

The story of Marie Curie—the poor Polish girl who became a governess for five years and by hard work and single concentration of purpose trained herself as a scientist and became co-discoverer of the new element radium—is a dramatic one. On her savings she had managed to get to Paris in 1891 for further study and there met Pierre, a physicist, then 35, whom she married in 1895. Two daughters were born of this union: Irène—who with her husband Frédéric Joliot-Curie (*see Enrico Fermi*) was to make further discoveries in her parents' field and with him also to receive the Nobel Prize in 1935—and Eve, musician and journalist, who has written her mother's biography. Marie and Pierre worked with tremendous determination against considerable hardship to isolate the element emitting even stronger rays than those of uranium; the fact that uranium was radioactive had been discovered in 1896 by Henri Becquerel, who shared with them their 1903 Nobel Prize in Physics. (The Curies' work had involved reducing some eight tons of pitchblende to produce a decigram of pure radium.) Fame from then on pursued them. After Pierre was hit by a wagon and killed in 1906, Mme Curie continued her work in radioactivity and received the 1911 Nobel Prize in Chemistry. She had taken over her husband's professorship at the Sorbonne and was the director of the Radium Institute from 1914 until 1932 (when her daughter Irène succeeded her); she did heroic war work in World War I. When an American woman, Mrs. William Brown Meloney, learned that Mme Curie lacked a supply of radium for her further research, she rallied American women to purchase a gram for $100,000, presented to the frail scientist by President Harding at the White House in 1921. In 1934 Mme Curie died of leukemia, brought on by her exposure to radiation over many years of unremitting effort.

Her story of her husband and their life together has a simplicity, clarity and quietness in the telling, through which its author's personality shines luminously, that put it among the most fascinating works in the history of science. Sixty-two pages are her memoir of him and forty her own autobiography. Professor Emeritus Le Corbeiller of Harvard has said: "I know of no scientist's biography as moving as the two that are united in this book." (In addition to the adult works below there are many books for young people on Mme Curie which do not fall within the province of *"The Reader's Adviser."*)

PIERRE CURIE. 1923. Trans. by Charlotte and Vernon Kellogg; introd. by Mrs. William Brown Meloney *Dover* pap. $1.25; *Peter Smith* $3.75. Includes Mme Curie's autobiography as well.

RADIOACTIVE SUBSTANCES: A Translation from the French of the Classical Thesis Presented to the Faculty of Sciences in Paris. 1961. *Greenwood* 1971 $11.00

Books about Curie

Madame Curie. By Eve Curie. *Doubleday* 1949 $5.95; *Pocket Bks.* 1969 pap. $1.25
Marie Sklodowska-Curie: Centenary Lectures. Comp. by the International Atomic Energy Agency. *UNIPUB* 1968 pap. $5.00
Marie Curie. By Robert Reid. *Saturday Review Press* (dist. by Dutton) 1974 $8.95
"A well written narrative summarizing the total record of a persistent disciple of pure science, a pioneer in the intellectual recognition of social and political forces in her native Poland, and an indomitable woman in fields then normally closed to women. . . . This objective account draws upon familiar and obscure sources, and is highly recommended"—*(LJ)*.

CUSHING, HARVEY (WILLIAM). 1869–1939.

Cushing, the great Boston surgeon who founded a new school of neuro-surgery, had a rare literary talent and it is regrettable that his books of essays and a journal ("From a Surgeon's Journal, 1915–1918," 1936) are now out of print. His Life of Osler won the 1925 Pulitzer Prize in Biography. He taught at Johns Hopkins University, Harvard and Yale. Cushing is the author of many monographs on brain surgery.

HARVEY CUSHING: Selected Papers on Neurosurgery. Ed. by Donald D. Matson and others *Yale Univ. Press* 1969 $30.00

TUMORS OF THE NERVOUS ACUSTIOUS AND THE SYNDROME OF THE CEREBELLOPONTILE ANGLE. 1917. *Hafner* 1963 $17.95

LIFE OF SIR WILLIAM OSLER. *Oxford* 2 vols. 1925 1940 boxed $30.00

CONSECRATIO MEDICI AND OTHER PAPERS. 1928. *Bks. for Libraries* 1970 $12.50

(With L. Eisenhardt). MENINGIOMAS: Their Classification, Regional Behavior, Life History and Surgical End Results. 1938. *Macmillan* (Hafner) 2 vols. 1969 $29.95

A BIO-BIBLIOGRAPHY OF ANDREAS VESALIUS. 1943. *Shoe String Press* 2nd ed. rev. 1962 $22.50

Books about Cushing

Genius with a Scalpel: Harvey Cushing. By Justin F. Denzel. *Messner* 1971 $3.95

RUTHERFORD, ERNEST, 1st Baron. 1871–1937. (Nobel Prize 1908)

As one investigates the lives and writings of the foremost atomic scientists of our day, a single name occurs in connection with the early careers of many of them—that of Lord Rutherford. Peter Kapitza, the Russian physicist, spent 13 years working under and with him at the Cavendish Laboratory, Cambridge, and has provided a vivid and affectionate portrait of him in three chapters of "Peter Kapitsa on Life and Science" (*q.v.*), which remarkably convey Lord Rutherford as the brilliant chemist and physicist to whom young scientists from all over the world flocked to learn from (if they could qualify)—first at McGill (Montreal, 1898–1907), then at Manchester (1907–1919) and finally at Cambridge, where he was from 1919 until his death director of the Cavendish.

Lord Rutherford's own discoveries developed from that of the French scientist Henri Becquerel, who had established in 1896 that uranium salts steadily emitted waves of unvarying intensity which produced an image of themselves when left in contact with a photographic plate in total darkness. Rutherford proved that the atoms of the uranium, hitherto supposed to be unchangeable, were in a state of constant decomposition as they produced the rays and were in fact emitting energy from sources within themselves of tremendous potential. For this discovery he received the Nobel Prize in 1908. Working on a theory of Niels Bohr, he established the fact that the atom was a kind of small "solar system" made up of a nucleus and revolving particles called protons and electrons; later his theory of the presence of neutrons as well was proved by others. He also discovered that the rays emitted could be separated into alpha and beta types (there are also gamma rays). Bombardment by alpha rays could cause the decomposition of more stable atoms—could in fact "smash the atom," releasing its energy with tremendous consequences for the world. His theories led indirectly to the development of the atom- and hydrogen-bombs, in which many of his students later found themselves involved.

Lord Rutherford was the son of a New Zealand farmer and a graduate of Canterbury College, N.Z., who won a scholarship for scientific study in England and worked at the Cavendish until offered the chair of physics at McGill. Not the least of his abilities was as the inspirer of the scientific imaginations of other men, such as Bohr, Hahn and Kapitza.

THE COLLECTED PAPERS OF LORD RUTHERFORD OF NELSON. Ed. by J. Chadwick *Wiley* 3 vols. 1962–1965 Vol. 1 (1962) o.p. Vol. 2 (1963) $18.95 Vol. 3 (1965) $16.25

(With Bertram B. Boltwood). RUTHERFORD AND BOLTWOOD: Letters on Radioactivity. Ed. by Lawrence Badash *Yale Univ Press* 1969 $17.50

Books about Rutherford

Giant of the Atom: Ernest Rutherford. By Robin McKown. *Simon & Schuster* (Messner) 1962 $3.34

Rutherford Jubilee International Conference, Manchester, 1961. Proceedings. Ed. by J. B. Birks. *Academic Press* 1962 $39.50

Rutherford at Manchester. Ed. by J. B. Birks. *Addison-Wesley* (Benjamin) 1963 $17.50

Rutherford and the Nature of the Atom. By Edward N. Andrade. 1964. *Peter Smith* $3.75

Ernest Rutherford: Architect of the Atom. By Peter Kelman and A. Harris Stone. *Prentice-Hall* 1968 $4.50

Rutherford—Recollections of the Cambridge Days. By Margaret Oliphant. *American Elsevier* $8.95

Lord Rutherford. By Norman Feather. *Crane, Russak* 1973 $10.50

RUSSELL, BERTRAND (ARTHUR WILLIAM RUSSELL) 3rd Earl. 1872–1970.
See Chapter 5, Philosophy, this Vol.

CARREL, ALEXIS. 1873–1944. (Nobel Prize 1912)

"Man the Unknown" and "Reflections on Life" contain the essence of Dr. Carrel's experiences and philosophy as surgeon, experimental biologist and as a man living in the modern world. While a medical student at the University of Lyon, this French scientist acquired his great surgical dexterity not only by dissection and anatomical study but also by carpentry and sewing. During his service as a major in World War I he perfected the famed Carrel-Dakin antiseptic solution for the treatment of infected wounds. In 1938, Dr. Carrel and Charles Lindbergh (*q.v.*) published their "Culture of Organs" on the use of Lindbergh's perfusion pump, or artificial heart, in a new technique of tissue culture perfected by the surgeon. He experimented with tissues living outside the body and developed methods of cultivating them. Dr. Carrel won the Nobel Prize in 1912 for success in suturing blood vessels and transplanting organs. In the 1940's he was a leader of the *Fondation Française pour l'Étude des Problèmes Humains*.

MAN THE UNKNOWN. 1935. *Harper* rev. ed. 1939 $6.95

REFLECTIONS ON LIFE. 1952. Trans. by Antonia White. 1965 o.p.

Books about Carrel

Alexis Carrel: Visionary Surgeon. By W. Sterling Edwards and Peter D. Edwards. *C. C. Thomas* 1974 $5.00

JEANS, SIR JAMES (HOPWOOD). 1877–1946.

Few modern men of science have achieved such popular literary success as Sir James Jeans. He was "a master of English and of mathematical physics" who, with his "incomparable gifts of lucid exposition, persuades even the non-mathematical mind that it can probe the secrets of inter-stellar space." Such books as "The Mysterious Universe" (*Cambridge* 1930, o.p.) and "The Universe Around Us" (*Cambridge* 1929, o.p.) sold in the thousands. He is known for his important work in the application of mathematics to the problems of physics and astronomy. He taught for four years at Princeton in response to an invitation of Woodrow Wilson (*q.v.*), then president of the university. Later Jeans lectured at Cambridge and Oxford and was research associate at Mt. Wilson Observatory. He was showered with honors among them the Order of Merit, held by only 24 Englishmen. He was knighted by the King in 1928.

AN ELEMENTARY TREATISE ON THEORETICAL MECHANICS. 1907. *Dover* 1968 pap. $2.75; *Peter Smith* $4.50

THE MATHEMATICAL THEORY OF ELECTRICITY AND MAGNETISM. 1908. *Cambridge* $19.50 pap. 1961 $5.95

DYNAMICAL THEORY OF GASES. 4th ed. 1925. *Dover* pap. $4.00

ASTRONOMY AND COSMOGONY. 1928. With a new preface by Lloyd Motz. *Dover* 2nd ed. 1961 pap. $3.50; *Peter Smith* 1962 $5.50

EOS: On the Wider Aspects of Cosmogony. 1928 *Bks. for Libraries* $9.75

STARS IN THEIR COURSES. *Cambridge* 1931 $8.00

THE NEW BACKGROUND OF SCIENCE. 1933. *Univ. of Michigan Press* Ann Arbor Bks. 1959 pap. $1.95

SCIENCE AND MUSIC. 1937. *Dover* 1968 pap. $2.50

PHYSICS AND PHILOSOPHY. 1942. *Univ. of Michigan Press* Ann Arbor Bks. 1958 pap. $1.75

EINSTEIN, ALBERT. 1879–1955. (Nobel Prize 1921)

"What is really beautiful is science!" Einstein said. "It is a great gift if one is permitted to work in science for his whole life." The genius who changed the entire concept of the universe became a citizen of the United States in 1940. Despite his preeminence and personal popularity in his native Germany, he was forced as a Jew to seek exile by Adolf Hitler in 1933. Einstein abandoned his home in Berlin, a gift to him from its citizens, and escaped to America. He settled in Princeton, N.J., at the Institute for Advanced Study near Princeton University. In 1939 he wrote the historic letter to President Franklin Delano Roosevelt, advising him on the possibilities of atomic warfare. Einstein received the 1921 Nobel Prize in Physics and gave his prize money to charity. His death at Princeton was mourned around the world. President Eisenhower declared that "no other man contributed so much to the vast expansion of twentieth century knowledge." There have been several biographies of this great scientist, but "Einstein the man is as unknown as Einstein the philosopher and scientist"—(Allan Keller, in the *N.Y. World-Telegram*). Einstein in his later years brooded much about the applications of his own work to the making of atomic and hydrogen bombs and of the general responsibility for Hiroshima and Nagasaki of the American scientific community. In his "Open Letter to the General Assembly of the United Nations" (1947) he advocated world government.

EINSTEIN ON PEACE. Ed. by Otto Nathan and Heinz Norden; pref. by Bertrand Russell. 1960. *Schocken* 1968 $10.00 pap. $3.95

RELATIVITY: The Special and General Theory. 1920. Trans. by Robert W. Lawson *Crown* 1961 pap. $.95; *Peter Smith* $3.50

THE MEANING OF RELATIVITY. Trans. by E. P. Adams *Princeton Univ. Press* 1923 5th ed. 1956 $7.50 pap. $2.45

(With Hendrik A. Lorentz, H. Minkowski, and Hermann Weyl). THE PRINCIPLE OF RELATIVITY. Trans. by W. Perrett and G. B. Jeffrey; notes by Arthur Sommerfeld. 1924. *Dover* pap. $2.25

INVESTIGATIONS ON THE THEORY OF THE BROWNIAN MOVEMENT. Ed. by R. Furth; trans. by A. D. Cowper. 1926. *Dover* pap. $1.50

(With Leopold Infeld). THE EVOLUTION OF PHYSICS. *Simon & Schuster* 1938 $6.95
Touchstone-Clarion Bks. 1961 pap. $2.75

ALBERT EINSTEIN: Philosopher-Scientist. Ed. by Paul A. Schilpp. 1950. *Open Court* 2 vols.
1973 set $15.00 pap. set $6.90. Contains Einstein's reply to his critics and his informal
autobiography.

IDEAS AND OPINIONS. *Crown* 1954 $5.00; *Dell* 1973 pap. $1.50. On topics of general
interest.

OUT OF MY LATER YEARS. 1950. *Citadel Press* 1973 pap. $2.95; *Greenwood* 1970 $11.00

A most interesting collection of writings including many of autobiographical interest. It is
divided into the following sections: Convictions and Beliefs; Science; Public Affairs (including his
"Open Letter" to the U.N.—*see biographical note above*); Science and Life; Personalities (nine,
including fellow scientists and Gandhi); and My People (the Jews).

(With others). LETTERS ON WAVE MECHANICS. *Philosophical Lib.* $6.00

Books about Einstein

Einstein Theory of Relativity. By Lillian R. Lieber. *Holt* 1945 $3.95
Einstein: His Life and Times. By Philipp Frank. *Knopf* 1947 1953 $7.95
The Universe and Dr. Einstein. By Lincoln Barnett. 1948. *Morrow* rev. ed. 1957 $6.00; *Bantam*
1974 pap. $.95
Albert Einstein. By Leopold Infeld. *Scribner* 1950 pap. $2.25
Einstein's Theory of Relativity. By Max Born. 1962. *Dover* rev. ed. pap. $2.75; *Peter Smith* 1962
$4.75. By a fellow physicist and Nobel Prize-winner (*see his main entry below*).
Bibliographical Checklist and Index of the Published Writings of Albert Einstein. By Nell Boni.
Cooper $6.00
Einstein. By Boris G. Kuznetsov. 1965. *Gannon* 1970 $7.50
Einstein: The Man and His Achievement. Ed. by G. J. Whitrow. 1967. *Dover* 1973 pap. $1.50
Einstein: The Life and Times. By Ronald W. Clark. *T. Y. Crowell* 1971 $15.00; *Avon Bks.* 1972
pap. $1.95
Einstein and the Generations of Science. By Lewis S. Feuer. *Basic Bks.* 1972 $12.95
"An excellent study of the philosophical, psychological, and sociological roots of the 20th
century 'revolution' in physics, encompassing relativity and quantum mechanics"—(*LJ*).
Albert Einstein: Creator and Rebel. By Banish Hoffmann and Helen Dukas. *Viking* 1972 $8.95;
New Am. Lib. Plume 1973 pap. $2.95. Helen Dukas was Einstein's private secretary from 1928
until his death in 1955.
Albert Einstein: The Man and His Theories. By Hilaire Cuny. *Fawcett* Premier Bks. 1973 pap.
$.95
The Einstein Decade: 1905–1915. By Cornelius Lanczos. *Academic Press* 1973 $12.50
Albert Einstein. By Peter N. Hamilton. Makers of Modern Thought Ser. *Judson Press* 1973 pap.
$1.50
Conversations with Einstein. By Alexander Moszkowski. *Horizon Press* 1973 $8.50
Einstein. By Jeremy Bernstein. Ed. by Frank Kermode. Modern Masters Ser. *Viking* 1973 $6.95
pap. $2.75
"This unpretentious little book explains, in simple words but with complete scientific
accuracy, what Einstein did and what sort of man he was"—(*N.Y. Times Bk. Review*).

HAHN, OTTO.   1879–1968.   (Nobel Prize 1944)

Otto Hahn's Nobel Prize in Chemistry was won (with Fritz Strassmann) for their "discovery of
the fission of heavy nuclei"—or the splitting of the uranium atom, which led to the development of
the atom bomb. Much of his early work was done with Lise Meitner, physicist, who died in
England a few months after Hahn. In the 1930s the Jewish Lise Meitner was forced to flee
Germany and carried on her work in Sweden. (She later shared in the U.S. Atomic Energy
Commission's $50,000 1966 Enrico Fermi Award—for her own work on the atom—with Hahn
and Strassmann.) In 1938 Drs. Hahn and Strassmann, in the course of bombarding uranium with
a stream of neutrons, found that the products of the bombardment were the elements barium,
lanthanum and cerium, whose atomic weight was only half that of uranium. Unable to believe that
they had split the atom, then thought to be impossible, they published their results without
claiming their obvious *coup*. It was Lise Meitner in Sweden who confirmed their feat. The Danish
Niels Bohr (*q.v.*) took the news to America.

Of Hahn's autobiography, *Library Journal* said: "Dr. Seaborg in his excellent introduction gives a
brief summary of nuclear power history which resulted from this discovery. The autobiography
concentrates on Dr. Hahn's scientific work leading to his discovery. Regrettably the book does not
touch on his work during W.W. II, his role in preventing Hitler's Germany from getting the atom

bomb, and his sense of social guilt, when America dropped the bomb, that almost led to his suicide. The translation is very good and the format and directness will make the book of value to young people. Translations of three original papers proving nuclear fission will make the book of value to the serious student."

Max Born (*q.v.*) wrote of the book: "Otto Hahn began his scientific work at a time when 'Big Science' was still unknown. He made his apparatus with his own hands and did his measurements without the help of electronic gadgets. Thus he became a great scientist and laid the foundations of the atomic age through his discovery of nuclear fission. . . . Here is the fascinating story of his scientific life, written by himself in a most charming manner."

Born in Frankfurt-am-Main, Dr. Hahn pursued his postgraduate studies in England with Sir William Ramsay and in Canada with Ernest Rutherford (later Lord Rutherford). He returned to Germany to the Kaiser Wilhelm Institute and became its director (1928–1944). He continued his research throughout the war years (and was thought to be working on an atom bomb for Germany, but—whether through his own preventive efforts or not—this never materialized). In 1945 he was taken prisoner by the Allies and sent to detention in England—secretly—at a farm near Cambridge. It was here that he learned that he had won the 1944 Nobel Prize in Chemistry. (He was able to claim it only in 1946.) Here, too, he was at the news of Hiroshima.

After the war, free again, he remained in Germany, pursuing his work at Göttingen. His book includes reminiscences of many well-known scientists such as Max Planck, the Joliot-Curies and Enrico Fermi.

OTTO HAHN: A Scientific Autobiography. Trans. and ed. by Willy Ley; introd. by Glenn T. Seaborg *Scribner* 1966 $9.95

STEFANSSON, VILHJALMUR. 1879–1962. *See Chapter 12, Travel and Adventure, this Vol.*

BORN, MAX. 1882–1970. (Nobel Prize 1954)

Max Born, who received the Nobel Prize for Physics in 1954 for his work in quantum mechanics, was as a Jew forced to flee Hitler's Germany in 1933. He himself played no direct part in work toward the atom bomb, but he had had among his students at Göttingen, brilliant young physicists such as Oppenheimer, Teller and Fermi, and much of his writing concerns itself with the moral and ethical implications of science in our day. He had enjoyed having "such clever and efficient pupils," he says, but he wishes "they had shown less cleverness and more wisdom"; I feel that I am to blame "if all they learned from me were methods of research."

Elsewhere in "My Life and My Views" (from which we have quoted) he says: "[Only] after Hiroshima did clear convictions begin to take shape in me. Otherwise, an awareness of the scientist's social responsibility would certainly have found expression in my earlier educational work and perhaps not so many of my pupils would have been ready to collaborate on the atom bomb." He has devoted considerable energy (like Linus Pauling) to bring the world of scientists and statesmen to sanity on the subject of the awful weapons science has fathered, the human questions involved in space exploration, the making of a better world and the maintenance of peace. He is, however, pessimistic. As he wrote in the *Bulletin of Atomic Scientists* in November 1965: "I am haunted by the idea that this break in human civilization, caused by the discovery of the scientific method, may be irreparable. Though I love science I have the feeling that it is so much against history and tradition that it cannot be absorbed by our civilization. The political and military horrors and the complete breakdown of ethics which I have witnessed during my life may be not a symptom of an ephemeral social weakness but a necessary consequence of the rise of science—which in itself is one of the highest intellectual achievements of man. If this is so, there will be an end to man as a free, responsible being."

Dr. Born became a British subject in 1939 and worked (1933–36) at Cambridge, becoming Professor of Natural Philosophy at Edinburgh thereafter, until his retirement in 1953, when he returned to live in Bad Pyrmont, Germany.

EINSTEIN'S THEORY OF RELATIVITY. 1924. *Dover* rev. ed. 1962 pap. $2.75; *Peter Smith* rev. ed. $4.75

THE RESTLESS UNIVERSE. 1935 2nd ed. 1951. *Dover* pap. $3.50; *Peter Smith* $4.25

ATOMIC PHYSICS. Trans. by John Dougal *Macmillan* (Hafner) 8th ed. 1969 $13.95

THE NATURAL PHILOSOPHY OF CAUSE AND CHANCE. 1949. *Peter Smith* $4.50

PHYSICS IN MY GENERATION. 1956. *Springer-Verlag* 2nd rev. ed. 1969 pap. $3.80

MECHANICS OF THE ATOM. Trans. by J. W. Fisher *Ungar* 1960 $7.50

PROBLEMS OF ATOMIC DYNAMICS. Trans. by W. P. Allis and others *Ungar* 1960 $6.00; *M.I.T. Press* 1970 pap. $2.95

BORN-EINSTEIN LETTERS. *Walker & Co.* 1970 $8.50

MY LIFE AND MY VIEWS. *Scribner* 1968 $6.95. Essays, many autobiographical.

EDDINGTON, SIR ARTHUR (STANLEY). 1882–1944.

Eddington and Jeans (*q.v.*) were the first among the scientists to interpret the universe for the modern layman. Eddington understood Einstein's theory of relativity at an early stage and made many discoveries of his own about the stars and their nature, origin and composition. After 25 years of study he began to translate the abstractions of science into lay terms. His "The Nature of the Physical World" explains relativity; the *Saturday Review* declared that "to any intelligent and thoughtful reader who would know something of . . . the bearings of the new [scientific] theories . . . on the eternal problems of philosophy and theology, it would be difficult to suggest a better or nobler introduction than this brilliant book." Eddington was the son of a Quaker schoolmaster and he remained a Quaker, refusing on religious principle to take part in World War I. He received many honors including a knighthood and the Order of Merit, but remained a modest "man of profound culture, a skilled dialectician, a pretty wit."

THE MATHEMATICAL THEORY OF RELATIVITY. 3rd ed. 1924. *Chelsea Pub.* 1974 $9.95

SPACE, TIME AND GRAVITATION: An Outline of the General Relativity Theory. 1920. *Cambridge* 1960 $11.50

THE NATURE OF THE PHYSICAL WORLD. 1928 1932. *Univ. of Michigan Press* Ann Arbor Bks. 1958 pap. $2.45

THE EXPANDING UNIVERSE. *Cambridge* 1933 $5.95; *Univ. of Michigan Press* Ann Arbor Bks. 1958 pap. $1.75

NEW PATHWAYS IN SCIENCE. 1935 1938. *Univ. of Michigan Press* Ann Arbor Bks. 1959 pap. $1.95

THE PHILOSOPHY OF PHYSICAL SCIENCE. 1939. *Univ. of Michigan Press* Ann Arbor Bks. 1958 pap. $2.45

Books about Eddington

The Sources of Eddington's Philosophy. By Herbert Dingle. *Cambridge* 1954 $.75
Men of Physics: Sir Arthur Eddington. By Clive W. Kilmister. *Pergamon* 1966 $7.00 pap. $5.00

GODDARD, ROBERT HUTCHINGS. 1882–1945.

Dr. Goddard, born in Worcester, Mass., is known as the father of the rocketry which has led to space exploration. *Library Journal* has described him as "the American rocket pioneer whose vision often outdistanced his achievement. Goddard, the taciturn, secretive Clark University professor, developed prior to World War II a rocket almost identical to the German V-2; long before the War he had worked out designs for recoilless rifles, military rockets, liquid rocket fuels, the principle of multistage rockets, and a host of inventions incorporated into modern missiles." His "Papers" include his journal of his personal and technical activities.

PAPERS. Ed. by Esther C. Goddard and G. Edward Pendray *McGraw-Hill* 3 vols. 1967 Vol. 1 1898–1924 Vol. 2 1925–1937 Vol. 3 1938–1945 set $160.00

BOHR, NIELS. 1885–1962. (Nobel Prize 1922)

Niels Bohr was a remarkable Danish physicist, the student of Lord Rutherford's (*q.v.*) at Manchester who suggested to Rutherford a theory on which the latter based his experimental model of the atom in 1911—this defined the atom as a nucleus around which particles revolved in an infinitesimal solar system. Refined and proved accurate by Bohr in 1915, it was called the Bohr-Rutherford model and won Bohr the 1922 Nobel Prize in Physics. In World War II he predicted to American physicists, on the basis of what he had heard of Otto Hahn's (*q.v.*) work in Germany, that the nucleus of the uranium atom was capable of being divided in two nearly equal halves—also soon borne out.

In his early career he studied at the Cambridge Cavendish Laboratory and then with Rutherford at Manchester. In 1920 he became director of the Copenhagen Institute of Theoretical Physics, which he had helped establish. In the 1930s he was instrumental in assisting Jewish scientists to escape from Germany and Italy; and it was he, on a sojourn at Princeton, who persuaded Einstein to warn Franklin Roosevelt of the likelihood of atomic warfare. He returned to Nazi-occupied Denmark and worked against the Germans until obliged to escape to avoid imminent arrest. He then joined the U.S. atomic effort at Los Alamos and played an important part in scientific discussions with Churchill and Roosevelt, but after the war sent two letters to the United Nations, in 1950 and 1956, pleading for openness and cooperation among nations for the avoidance of nuclear suicide. In later years he devoted considerable time to promoting the peaceful uses of atomic energy. He received the first U.S. Atoms for Peace Prize from President Eisenhower in 1957—one of the many honors bestowed on him.

"The Atomic Theory and the Description of Nature" (1934) and "Essays on Atomic Physics and Human Knowledge, 1958–1962" (1964) are o.p.

COLLECTED SCIENTIFIC WORKS. Vol. 1 *American Elsevier* 1971 $62.50

Books about Bohr

    Niels Bohr: The Man, His Science, and the World They Changed. By Ruth Moore. *Knopf* 1966 $7.95. An attractive, clear and interesting study for the general reader by a fine science writer.

    Niels Bohr: His Life and Work as Seen by His Friends and Colleagues. Ed. by S. Rozental. *Wiley* 1967 pap. $5.95. A clear analysis for student and layman.

SHAPLEY, HARLOW. 1885–1972.

It has been said of Harlow Shapley, probably America's best-known astronomer, that he "has almost as many awards and medals as the stars he has discovered." He was astronomer at Mt. Wilson Observatory (1914–1921), director of the Harvard Observatory (1921–1952), and Paine Professor of Astronomy at Harvard University. His first work was on the "enigmatical short-period variables known as Cepheids" and in 1914 he advanced his "pulsation theory" of these stars. Then he discovered that variable stars held the key to stellar distances. This discovery gave the world a totally new conception of the immensity of the universe. His writings and lectures are particularly illuminating for the layman. Charles Poore has called him "an irrepressible volunteer counselor to the universe." In "The View from a Distant Star," he raises basic questions about man's ability to survive both terrestrially and extraterrestrially. "He ranges from the origin and evolution of our galaxy to water dowsing, from the possibility of cosmical obliteration of man to the boredom of scientific meetings." His writing is always crystal clear. "He revels in awesome statistical expositions of our fly-speck size on the great picture windows of infinity."

He edited "Source Book in Astronomy, 1900–1950" (*see below*) and "Science in Progress, Third Series" (1942. *Bks for Libraries* $19.75); in collaboration with others he edited "Climate Change: Evidence, Causes, and Effects" (*Harvard Univ. Press* 1953 $10.00) and "The New Treasury of Science" (*Harper* 5th rev. ed. 1965 $10.95), based on "The Treasury of Science" (1943, o.p.). He is one of the most human of the scientists and never dramatizes what he has done. In talking of the heavens and other astronomers, he has said: "We make all this funny fury about things as old as the stars. Sometimes I suspect I know what they're twinkling at."

GALAXIES. *Harvard Univ. Press* 1943 rev. ed. 1961. 3rd ed. rev. by Paul W. Hodge 1972 $10.00; *Atheneum* 1967 pap. $2.45

"The book is well apportioned among the various branches of the subject: it is clear, interesting and very well illustrated. Much of the material is treated briefly, but this is inevitable if it is to be kept within bounds, and there is compensation in the extensive references to the work of others. There is a good index"—(*Science Progress*).

OF STARS AND MEN: The Human Response to an Expanding Universe. *Beacon* 1958 $5.95

(Ed). SOURCE BOOK IN ASTRONOMY, 1900–1950. *Harvard Univ. Press* 1960 $11.95. One of an important series in the history of the sciences.

(With others). TIME AND ITS MYSTERIES. *Macmillan* Collier Bks. 1962 pap. $.95

THE VIEW FROM A DISTANT STAR: Man's Future in the Universe. 1963. *Dell* pap. $.75

BEYOND THE OBSERVATORY. *Scribner* 1967 pap. 1972 $2.65

"One of the most stimulating and provocative collections of scientific essays to appear in recent years"—(*LJ*).

THROUGH RUGGED WAYS TO THE STARS. *Scribner* 1969 $6.95. His reminiscences.

FRISCH, KARL von. 1886– (Nobel Prize 1973)

" 'Man and the Living World,' " wrote Ruth Moore in the *N.Y. Times*, "is at once a broad, scientific summary of biology and a book to engage and delight the mind." Written for the general reader, but with the authority of a lifetime of study and original research, these are "captivating and memorable accounts of the form and development of many of the world's myriad plants, insects, and animals, including man."

The Austrian zoologist "has acheived international recognition for his pioneer research on sense functions in fish and for his discovery of the 'language' of the bees which he describes in his great book, 'The Dancing Bees.' " In this book he explains how these insects are able to communicate to their fellow colonists the direction, distance, quantity and quality of food by means of dances.

As a student von Frisch studied medicine and zoology in Vienna, his birthplace, and Munich. Later he was appointed Director of the Zoological Institutes in Rostock, Breslau and Munich, where he held the chair for Zoology until his retirement. He has lectured in the United States, is a member of the National Academy of Science, Washington, of the Royal Society of London, and of the Austrian Academy of Science, Vienna. In 1959 he was awarded the Kalinga Prize and in 1963 a Balzan Prize.

"Ten Little Housemates" (1960), a nontechnical book on the insects found in the house, and "A Biologist Remembers" (1967) are o.p.

MAN AND THE LIVING WORLD. 1949. Trans. by Elsa B. Lowenstein *Harcourt* 1963 $8.95 Harvest Bks. pap. $1.65

THE DANCING BEES: An Account of the Life and Senses of the Honey Bee. Trans. from the German by Dora Ilse and Norman Walker *Harcourt* 1955 1961 rev. ed. 1965 $6.95 Harvest Bks. pap. $3.25

THE DANCE LANGUAGE AND ORIENTATION OF BEES. Trans. by Leigh E. Chadwick *Harvard Univ. Press* Belknap Press 1967 $17.00

BEES: Their Vision, Chemical Senses, and Language. *Cornell Univ. Press* rev. ed. 1971 $8.75 pap. $3.45

(With Otto Von Frisch). ANIMAL ARCHITECTURE. Trans. by Lisbeth Gembrich *Harcourt* 1974 $12.95

HUXLEY, SIR JULIAN (SORELL). 1887–1975.

Sir Julian, elder brother of Aldous Huxley (*q.v.*) was born in London, the eldest son of Leonard Huxley, biographer and historian; the "nephew of Mrs. Humphry Ward; the grand-nephew of Matthew Arnold (*q.v.*); and the grandson of the great scientist, Thomas Henry Huxley (*q.v.*)." Julian Huxley began gathering honors while at Balliol College, Oxford, where he took a first in natural science (zoology) and where he lectured on zoology for two years. He is a gifted master of lucid prose and has written innumerable articles and books, many on science for the unscientific, on subjects ranging from "the evolutionary conception of God to the politics of ants." He has advocated a scientific humanism as a substitute for the mysticism of the past. He has interested himself in politics as science, was Director-General of UNESCO (1940–1948) and wrote "UNESCO: Its Purpose and Its Philosophy" (1947 o.p.). He has edited "The Humanist Frame" (1961. *Bks. for Libraries* 1972 $14.75) and "The New Systematics" (1940. *Scholarly Press* $29.50). In January 1960, Sir Julian received the New York University Medal following his lecture entitled "Evolution in Our Time." "My final belief is in life," he has written.

THE INDIVIDUAL IN THE ANIMAL KINGDOM. 1912. *Scholarly Press* $9.50; *Somerset Pub.* $7.50

ESSAYS OF A BIOLOGIST. 1923. *Bks. for Libraries* 1972 $11.00; *Kraus* $15.00

ANTS. 1930. *AMS Press* 1969 $5.00

AFRICA VIEW. 1931. *Greenwood* 1968 $23.75

(With others). SCIENCE AND RELIGION. 1931. *Bks. for Libraries* 1975 $7.75

(With Gavin de Beer). ELEMENTS OF EXPERIMENTAL EMBRYOLOGY. 1934. *Macmillan* (Hafner) 1963 $14.95

SCIENCE AND SOCIAL NEEDS. 1935. *Kraus* $15.00

EVOLUTION: The Modern Synthesis. 1942. *Macmillan* (Hafner 3rd ed. 1974 $15.95

HEREDITY, EAST AND WEST: Lysenko and World Science. 1949. *Kraus* 1969 $10.50

EVOLUTION IN ACTION. *Harper* 1953 $4.95

FROM AN ANTIQUE LAND: Ancient and Modern in the Middle East. New introd. by Huxley. 1954 2nd ed. 1967. *Beacon* pap. $2.95

"He is prepared to consider, knowledgeably, the whole long and astonishing development of the region, plus its birds, animals, geological structure, unlikely visitors, ruins, buildings, waterworks, literature, and current problems, but he will not be bound by chronology or by anyone's formal historical theory, least of all the pessimistic views of Toynbee, which irritate him"— (*Atlantic*).

(With others). EVOLUTION AS A PROCESS. 1954 2nd ed. 1958. *Macmillan* Collier Bks. 1963
pap. $1.50

(With W. Suschitzky). KINGDOM OF THE BEASTS. *Vanguard* 1956 $15.00

MEMORIES. *Harper* 1971 $10.00

MEMORIES TWO. *Harper* 1974 $8.95

SINNOTT, EDMUND W(ARE).   1888–1968.

One of the world's leading botanists, Dr. Sinnott was particularly interested in problems of
biological philosophy. In "The Biology of the Spirit," his main thesis is "that protoplasm, the basic
stuff of plant and animal life, has 'biological purpose.' In man, this 'goal seeking' protoplasm,
which seems to direct human motivation, is an extension of a universal reality—'God' ('Spirit',
'Force' or 'Personality')." In "Matter, Mind and Man," he "provides answers for man's perennial
questions—about himself and his world 'that will form a unified and logically harmonious
framework of concepts about man and his relation to his life and to the universe.' 'Our aim,' he
writes, 'has been to fit man into the universe of matter, mind, and spirit without the necessity of
dismembering him.' He sees man steadily and sees him whole, and believes that only in God can
man be fulfilled"—(*SR*). He is the author of many textbooks.

THE BIOLOGY OF THE SPIRIT. 1955. *Science of Mind* 1973 pap. $3.00

MATTER, MIND AND MAN: The Biology of Human Nature. *Atheneum* 1962 pap. $2.75

THE BRIDGE OF LIFE: From Matter to Spirit. *Simon & Schuster* 1966 $4.95 Touchstone
1972 pap. $3.45

Professor Sinnott "is a humanist of mellow learning. He writes in a style that takes the reader
gently by the arm and conducts him in a straight line across the bridge. Indeed the writing at times
sprouts wings"—(Brand Blanshard, in the *N.Y. Times*).

BUSH, VANNEVAR.   1890–1974.

Dr. Vannevar Bush contributed much to the development of the high-speed computer in his
capacity as a brilliant engineer; he had a long career in important posts as administrator in the
field of science, particularly government science. He has been, among many other activities,
professor at M.I.T. and dean of its School of Engineering, president of the Carnegie Institution
(for scientific research) in Washington, D.C., director of the U.S. Office of Scientific Research and
Development during World War II and chairman of the Corporation, M.I.T. (After his retirement in 1959 he was honorary chairman.) He was a staunch defender of Oppenheimer (*q.v.*) at the
time of the latter's security hearing.

Of "Modern Arms and Free Men" the *Atlantic* wrote: "Dr. Bush has written a book of
transparent candor based on a full knowledge of what happened before his eyes and under his
direction. I believe that his sincere, refreshing faith in the democratic scheme of life springs from
experience and observation. He has seen it at work and found it good. And in this book he has said
so nobly. It is a book which should be read wherever doubts persist and faith falters. It is not an
opiate. It is a call to free men to be worthy of their heritage." Charles Poore said (in the *N.Y. Times*)
of "Science Is Not Enough": "I hope future man [whether produced in a test tube or not] may
have the kind of a mind honored by Vannevar Bush." As the interpreter of government science
with thoughts of his own on the subject, Vannevar Bush is imperative reading for those who wish
to understand and come to grips with the crucial role of science in American society today.

MODERN ARMS AND FREE MEN: A Discussion of the Role of Science in Preserving
Democracy. *M.I.T. Press* 1948 rev. ed. with new introd. by the author 1967 $12.50
pap. $2.95

SCIENCE IS NOT ENOUGH: Reflections for the Present and the Future. 1967. *Apollo* 1969
pap. $1.95. Essays.

PIECES OF THE ACTION. *Morrow* 1970 $8.95 pap. $2.95. Autobiographical volume.

COMPTON, ARTHUR HOLLY.   1892–1962.   (Nobel Prize 1927)

Arthur Holly Compton came of a distinguished family. His father, Elias Compton, was an early
child psychologist; his brother Karl, a physicist of note, became president of M.I.T.; his brother
Wilson became well known in the field of conservation. Dr. Compton himself won the Nobel Prize
in Physics in 1927 for his discovery of the Compton Effect in atomic physics, a complicated concept
for the layman, but one which disproved classical theory and was a significant contribution to the
field. He was one of the workers on the atomic bomb who became deeply concerned about its
potential for the world and signed the "Mainau Declaration of Nobel Laureates" (*see Linus Pauling*)
asking that nations renounce the use of nuclear weapons. Dr. Compton taught throughout most of

his life—at Washington University (St. Louis) and the University of Chicago. Of his "Cosmos" (*Knopf* 1967, o.p.) *Publishers' Weekly* wrote: "Arthur Holly Compton believed that science is a search for truth, and that scientific truths must be applied in the service of humanity, for the general welfare of all mankind, in the interest of order and peace. Dr. Compton is at his charming best when he addresses himself warmly to students; his delight in creativity and experimentation, his love for his work, is contagious. Cosmic rays, scattered X-rays, are fascinating, not forbiddingly technical subjects in this book. There are lively profiles of many eminent scientists here, too." *Choice*, which praised "the depth and quality of his insights," went on to say: "Though most of the book deals with the meaning of science, and the impact (past and future) of science on society, there is also a very lucid presentation called 'The Nature of Things,' which allows the nonscientist to grasp the significant physical problems and their unfolding in time. Throughout the book, one message is foremost; science is a humanizing and spiritual endeavor. It comes through loud and clear."

"The Human Meaning of Science" (1940) and "The Atomic Quest" (1956) are o.p.

SCIENTIFIC PAPERS. Ed. by Robert S. Shankland *Univ. of Chicago Press* 1973 $27.50

FREEDOM OF MAN. 1935. *Greenwood* 1970 $9.00

(With Samuel K. Allison). X-RAYS IN THEORY AND EXPERIMENT. *Van Nostrand-Reinhold* 2nd ed. 1935 $24.50

MAN'S DESTINY IN ETERNITY. 1949. *Bks. for Libraries* 1975 $11.00

Books about Compton

> The House on College Avenue: The Comptons at Wooster, 1891–1913. By James R. Blackwood. *M.I.T. Press* 1968 $10.00 pap. $2.95
> "Their intellectual, physical and moral growth is discussed with charm and insight in this model cultural-biographical study"—(*LJ*).

BROGLIE, LOUIS (VICTOR PIERRE RAYMOND), Prince DE. 1892–   (Nobel Prize 1929)

This French physicist was a professor at the Sorbonne, a member of the French Academy and permanent secretary of the French Academy of Sciences. In 1929 he received the Nobel Prize in Physics for his work on the wave theories of electrons. Now o.p. are his "New Perspectives in Physics" (1961), a collection of papers and essays on various aspects of physics written between 1950 and 1956, and "Current Research in Astronautical Sciences" (1961). He is an authority on quantum physics and on the structure of matter as well as an excellent writer on science.

MATTER AND LIGHT: The New Physics. Trans. by W. H. Johnston. 1939. *Gannon* $6.00

REVOLUTION IN PHYSICS: A Non-Mathematical Survey of Quanta. Trans. by Ralph W. Niemeyer. 1953. *Greenwood* $12.50

NON-LINEAR WAVE MECHANICS: A Causal Interpretation. *American Elsevier* 1960 $16.50

INTRODUCTION TO THE VIGIER THEORY OF ELEMENTARY PARTICLES. *American Elsevier* 1963 $12.50

CURRENT INTERPRETATION OF WAVE MECHANICS. *American Elsevier* 1964 $13.50

WAVE MECHANICS AND MOLECULAR BIOLOGY. *Addison-Wesley* 1966 $13.50

PHYSICS AND MICROPHYSICS. *Grosset* pap. $2.25

HALDANE, J(OHN) B(URDON) S(ANDERSON). 1892–1964.

J. B. Haldane, an eccentric genuis, was once described as "the last man who might know all there was to know." A student of classics at Oxford, he became a brilliant biochemist, physiologist and geneticist—and Marxist revolutionary (until he broke with the Communist Party over its uncritical reverence for the Russian biologist Lysenko). During his (openly) Communist period he did important work in science for the British government. An officer in World War I, he later taught at the University of London and made remarkable discoveries in the application of mathematics and statistics to biology. Upset by the British attack on Egypt over Suez, Haldane spent his last years pursuing his research and holding various scientific posts in India, though he traveled back to England on several occasions and on one of these read his own obituary on BBC television.

Haldane was known for trying dangerous experiments on himself and for his lucid and enthusiastic expositions of his science for the layman. "This ability to entrance," writes Ronald W. Clark in "JBS," "was due partly to his own humble wonder at the world around him [and partly to] his facility for linking the facets of one science with those of all the rest; beneath this there lay . . .

the touchstones of personal integrity, honesty and courage. It was perhaps these qualities above all which throughout his long life enabled him to exhibit the qualities of the *guru*. When he said 'Rise up and follow me,' men did."

POSSIBLE WORLDS: And Other Papers. 1928. *Bks. for Libraries* 1975 $12.00

ENZYMES. 1930. *M.I.T. Press* 1965 $10.00 pap. $2.95

THE CAUSES OF EVOLUTION. 1932. *Cornell Univ. Press* 1966 pap. $1.95

SCIENCE AND HUMAN LIFE. 1933. *Bks. for Libraries* 1972 $11.00

FACT AND FAITH. 1936. *Folcroft* $5.00

MARXIST PHILOSOPHY AND THE SCIENCES. 1939. *Bks. for Libraries* $8.00

SCIENCE ADVANCES. 1948. *Verry* $2.75

CALLINICUS: A Defence of Chemical Warfare. *Garland Pub.* $11.00

Books about Haldane

Haldane and Modern Biology. Ed. by K. R. Dronamraju. *Johns Hopkins Press* 1968 $12.00
"A truly fascinating" collection (*LJ*) of essays by an international group of scientists.
JBS: The Life and Work of J. B. S. Haldane. By Ronald W. Clark. *Coward* 1969 $6.95
"J. B. S. Haldane loomed larger than life in so many ways that it is difficult to compress his accomplishments and personality into a brief biography. Ronald Clark, who based his work on primary sources . . . has met the challenge, however, in this delightful, balanced, well-written study of both the man and his work. He presents scientific explanations with a lucidity likely to have pleased Haldane himself. He includes the details of Haldane's often flamboyant life without sensationalism but also without sloughing over highly controversial works. . . . I cannot recommend this book too highly"—(*LJ*).

KAPITZA, PETER L(EONIDOVICH) (also Pyotr, Kapitsa). 1894–

Peter Kapitza, Russian physicist, has had an extraordinary scientific career in two worlds. He graduated from the Polytechnic Institute in Moscow in 1918 when his homeland was in turmoil, and in 1921, when it was difficult for his countrymen to leave the Soviet Union, the intervention of the writer Maxim Gorky allowed his departure to England, where he was able to work with Lord Rutherford (*q.v.*) at the Cavendish Laboratory of Cambridge University from 1921 to 1934. Here, with the aid of large equipment, he did important work in nuclear physics and in the behavior of matter at low temperatures and under the influence of powerful magnetic fields. He received the James Clark Maxwell Prize in 1923, the first of many honors, and soon became a full professor at Cambridge. In 1934 he returned with his wife to Moscow for a visit and was prevented by Stalin from leaving the Soviet Union. There he was required to stay; the Soviet government purchased his Cambridge equipment for him; and he eventually became director of the Institute for Problems in Physics of the Soviet Academy of Sciences. He has received the Order of Lenin and enjoys the status of Hero of Socialist Labor. He was confined to the East-bloc nations until 1965, when once again he was allowed to venture to West Europe to receive the Niels Bohr International Gold Medal in Denmark; in 1966 he rejoined old friends on a visit to Cambridge and addressed the Royal Society.

"Important as the contributions of the 74-year-old Peter Kapitza the scientist have been, the contributions of Peter Kapitza the humanist have been at least as great," says Harrison Brown—for he has not hesitated to criticize the weaknesses he has found in Soviet science or to speak his mind on other matters while managing "to inject the needle under the skin in just the right way, so that the patient is helped without being unduly irritated." "Peter Kapitsa on Life and Science" reveals a scientist with a generous world view combined with a sensitive understanding of human beings, a man whom it is a delight to know.

THE COLLECTED PAPERS OF P. L. KAPITZA. Trans. by Dr. Nikolic; ed. by Dirk Ter Haar *Pergamon* 2 vols. 1965 Vol. 1 1916–1934 $32.50 Vol. 2 1938–1964 $29.50

PETER KAPITSA ON LIFE AND SCIENCE: Addresses and Essays Collected, Translated and Annotated with an Introduction by Albert Parry. 1968 o.p. Addresses and essays; Albert Parry teaches Russian at Colgate.

FERMI, ENRICO, 1901–1954 (Nobel Prize 1938), and LAURA FERMI, 1907–

Enrico Fermi, the brilliant Italian atomic physicist, built on the work of the Joliot-Curies (*see Marie Curie*), who had discovered that the nucleus of the stable aluminum atom could be altered by bombardment with alpha rays and thereafter remained radioactive as a new element. Fermi found, in 1934, that bombardment with the atomic particles called neutrons, especially when slowed (by parafin or water in his original experiments) was far more effective than alpha rays. In the course of his research he also discovered elements 93, now known as neptunium, and 94, plutonium—though without realizing it at the time. His neutron-bombardment achievement led to the awesome proof, at the University of Chicago in 1942, that with graphite in great quantity (the atomic pile) as the neutron-slowing medium a chain reaction could be set in motion for the explosion of a uranium bomb. He later participated in the work at Los Alamos under J. Robert Oppenheimer.

With the encouragement of one of his father's friends this prodigy, son of an inspector of railways, learned elementary physics in boyhood from books and from experiments of his own. He studied at the University of Pisa and in Germany and taught at a number of Italian universities. In 1939 he learned, at the moment Mussolini was beginning to persecute the Jews in earnest, that he had won the Nobel Prize for the two early feats described above. Since his wife, Laura, was Jewish, he used the trip to Stockholm, together with his prize money, to escape to the United States, where he had already arranged a position teaching at Columbia University. Later he and his family went to the University of Chicago and Los Alamos, where he played a crucial role in the wartime atomic bomb project, though as an enemy alien he had no official title other than that of trusted consultant. Fatalistic, he was not one of those who looked back with horror on the making of the bomb; he felt that warfare was endemic with the human race and that the consequences of nuclear weapons lay in other hands than his. He died of cancer at the age of 53. Element 100 has been called fermium after him and the Atomic Energy Commission has named its highest award for him.

LAURA FERMI made the personal side of the atom discoveries vivid in her "Atoms in the Family," following it with other science books for the general reader. She is also the author of "Mussolini" (*Univ. of Chicago Press* 1961 $12.00 Phoenix Bks. pap. $2.95) and "Illustrious Immigrants: The Intellectual Migration from Europe, 1930–1941" (*Univ. of Chicago Press* 1968 2nd ed. 1971 $12.50 Phoenix Bks. 1972 pap. $3.95), about the distinguished refugees who found the U.S. a haven from Hitler's anti-Semitism, among which her husband and other scientists were numbered.

An excellent primer on atomic theory for the layman as well as a most clear and interesting short discussion of Fermi and his work, with index and selections from cogent writings by and about him, is "Enrico Fermi: The Man and His Theories" by Pierre de Latil (trans. from the French by Len Ortzen 1966 and now unfortunately o.p.).

Books by Enrico Fermi

COLLECTED PAPERS. Ed. by Emilio Segrè and others *Univ. of Chicago Press* 2 vols. 1962
    Vol. 1 Italy 1921–1938 (1962) Vol. 2. United States 1939–1954 (1965) each $25.00

Much is technical, but where it is not, his own writing is "gracefully clear," even to the layman. "Notes by [his friends] provide illuminating comments about Fermi's habits and characteristics, his apparent indifference to politics, economics, philosophy and the visual fine arts, his extraordinary physical insights, his vigor and competitiveness, his gaiety and informality. Altogether this is a most likable work as well as an invaluable one, skillfully and imaginatively edited and worthy of the man it memorializes"—(*Scientific American*).

THERMODYNAMICS. 1937. *Dover* pap. $2.00; *Gannon* $5.50

NUCLEAR PHYSICS. *Univ. of Chicago Press* 1950 rev. ed. 1974 pap. $8.00

NOTES ON QUANTUM MECHANICS. *Univ. of Chicago Press* Phoenix Bks. 1961 pap. $2.25. A
    facsimile reproduction of the manuscript for a course at the University.

MOLECULES, CRYSTALS AND QUANTUM STATISTICS. Ed. by L. Motz; trans. by M. Ferro-
    Luzzi *Addison Wesley* (Benjamin) 1966 pap. $15.00

NOTES ON THERMODYNAMICS AND STATISTICS. *Univ. of Chicago Press* Phoenix Bks. (orig.)
    1966 pap. $1.50. A facsimile reproduction of the author's manuscript notes for a
    course given in 1950–1951.

Books by Laura Fermi

ATOMS IN THE FAMILY: My Life with Enrico Fermi. *Univ. of Chicago Press* 1954 $8.50
    Phoenix Bks. pap. $2.45

ATOMS FOR THE WORLD. *Univ. of Chicago Press* 1957 pap. 1974 $8.50

THE STORY OF ATOMIC ENERGY. *Random* 1961 $2.95

(With Gilberto Bernardini). GALILEO AND THE SCIENTIFIC REVOLUTION. *Basic Bks.* 1961
    $5.50

Books about Enrico Fermi

　　Enrico Fermi, Physicist. By Emilio Segre. *Univ. of Chicago Press* 1970 $8.50 Phoenix Bks. 1972
　　　　pap. $2.95
　　Enrico Fermi: Father of the Atomic Bomb. By Robert Lichello. Ed. by Steve Rahmas *SamHar
　　　　Press* 1972 lib. bdg. $1.98 pap. $.98

LAWRENCE, ERNEST ORLANDO. 1901–1958. *See under* OPPENHEIMER, J.
ROBERT, 1904–1967, *this Chapter.*

PAULING, LINUS (CARL). 1901–　　(Nobel Prize 1954, 1963)

　　This American winner of two Nobel Prizes, the first in Chemistry for his discoveries on the
structure of the molecule and nature of the chemical bond, did pioneering work in many areas of
his field including its medical applications; his books on chemistry are basic to present-day
understanding of the subject. He did his research and taught at the California Institute of
Technology 1922–1964, was research professor at the Center for the Study of Democratic
Institutions (Calif.) 1963–67 and is now at the University of California (San Diego). Understanding as he did the threat to the human system from radioactive fallout in the postwar days of
indiscriminate atomic-bomb testing, he conducted a personal crusade in the fifties and early sixties
seeking a halt to the tests, for which he suffered considerable persecution at the hands of the U.S.
government in the form of denial of passport and the like—as a dangerous radical. He was
certainly one of those most responsible for the change in American public opinion which resulted
in the present international ban (of 1963) on above-ground testing. He received the Nobel Prize
for Peace in recognition of his efforts—from an international community which had admired him
throughout, threatened as it felt itself from fallout experiments by the two major nuclear powers.
His "No More War!" (*T. Y. Crowell* 1958, o.p.), written in this cause, is still a valuable primer on the
nature of the three giant bombs of which we know—the atomic, hydrogen and thermonuclear—
and of the effects of radiation on human beings. He was instrumental in procuring the signatures
of some 52 Nobel Laureates for the "Mainau Declaration of Nobel Laureates" in 1955 which
ended: "In extreme danger no national will deny itself the use of any weapon that scientific
technology can produce. All nations must come to the decision to renounce force as a final resort
of policy. If they are not prepared to do this they will cease to exist."
　　Dr. Pauling plays an offstage role in James D. Watson's "The Double Helix" (*Atheneum* 1968
$7.95; *New Am. Lib.* Signet 1969 pap. $.95), as the American who was competing with Watson and
his colleague Francis Crick to be the first to establish the structure of the DNA molecule in 1953.
Crick and Watson won.

　　(With E. B. Wilson, Jr.). INTRODUCTION TO QUANTUM MECHANICS. *McGraw-Hill* 1935
　　　　$13.95

　　THE NATURE OF THE CHEMICAL BOND AND THE STRUCTURE OF MOLECULES AND CRYS-
　　　　TALS: An Introduction to Modern Structural Chemistry. 1939. *Cornell Univ. Press* 3rd
　　　　ed. 1960 $17.50

　　THE CHEMICAL BOND: A Brief Introduction to Modern Structural Chemistry. *Cornell
　　　　Univ. Press* (abr.) 1967 $7.50 pap. $3.95. An abridgement of his 1939 classic, "The
　　　　Nature of the Chemical Bond."

　　(With H. A. Itano). MOLECULAR STRUCTURE AND BIOLOGICAL SPECIFICITY—A Sympo-
　　　　sium. *Macmillan* (Hafner) 3rd ed. 1961 $5.75

　　COLLEGE CHEMISTRY. *W. H. Freeman* 3rd ed. 1964 $9.25

　　(With Roger Hayward). THE ARCHITECTURE OF MOLECULES. *W. H. Freeman* 1970 pap.
　　　　$4.95

　　GENERAL CHEMISTRY. *W. H. Freeman* 3rd ed. 1970 $12.50

　　VITAMIN C AND THE COMMON COLD. *W. H. Freeman* 1970 $3.95 pap. $1.95; *Bantam* 1971
　　　　pap. $1.25

OPPENHEIMER, J. ROBERT. 1904–1967.

　　The story of J. Robert Oppenheimer is a dramatic one. An American physicist, teacher and
director (1943–1945) of the Los Alamos Scientific Laboratory, where he was the major figure in
the development of the atomic bomb, he knew Sanskrit, the religions of the East, art, literature
and music; his career was one of contradiction, triumph, tragedy and partial restitution. Although
he clung to his government posts (he chose to become a government "consultant," only, in 1952),

after Hiroshima he was a strong believer and speaker in favor of international control of atomic energy and an opponent of the arms race.

In 1954, after a controversial Atomic Energy Commission Security hearing which unearthed his earlier association with American radicals, he was declared a "security risk" and denied further access to classified government information. The hearing brought out several not yet clearly explained instances which made him appear somewhat irresponsible in past statements, one of which, regarding Haakon Chevalier, he later retracted. The scientific community at large, however, was distressed and disturbed by Oppenheimer's treatment at the hands of the A.E.C., and at least a dozen distinguished scientists came warmly to his defense, including Karl Compton, Hans Bethe (q.v.) and Vannevar Bush (q.v.), who testified: "My faith [in Dr. Oppenheimer] has not been in the slightest degree shaken by . . . anything. But I think this board or no board should sit on a question in this country of whether a man should serve his country or not because he expressed strong opinions. If you want to try that case, you can try me. I have expressed strong [and unpopular] opinions . . . and I intend to do so. When a man is pilloried for doing that, this country is in a severe state."

In Haakon Chevalier's bitter account, "Oppenheimer: The Story of a Friendship" (Braziller 1967, o.p.), Oppenheimer appears something of a devil; in Nuel Pharr Davis's brilliant "Lawrence and Oppenheimer" he is seen as a kind of saint; still another view is presented in the fascinating play by the German Heinar Kipphardt, which opened in New York to general acclaim early in 1969: "In the Matter of J. Robert Oppenheimer," much of it drawn from actual testimony at his hearing. The mysteries of his enigmatic personality remain.

Oppenheimer was a remarkable physicist, to whom students flocked, and a remarkable administrator. A short time after his "fall" at the hands of the A.E.C., he was unanimously elected to the post of director of the Institute for Advanced Study at Princeton. And in 1963 he received, in what many felt was a justified but surprising reversal, the A.E.C.'s highest honor, its Enrico Fermi Award for his contributions to the peaceful uses of atomic energy.

Oppenheimer's colleague at the University of California (Berkeley), where he taught for nearly 20 years, was ERNEST ORLANDO LAWRENCE (1901–1958), whose own contributions to nuclear physics were greater than those of Oppenheimer and won him the Nobel Prize for Physics in 1939. Lawrence developed the first cyclotron, or giant atom-smasher. Nuel Pharr Davis makes much of the contrast between Lawrence's narrower fields of interest and role as an "organization man" (who, like Teller, favored the construction of the fission-fusion-fission superbomb and clashed bitterly with Oppenheimer after World War II) and Oppenheimer's complexity and torment, born of his wider sympathies. Perhaps the key to the fascination of Oppenheimer, neither saint nor devil, is that he found himself at the heart of the conflicts and great decisions that can mean life or extinction for modern man. His post-Hiroshima sense of guilt, foreboding, victimization and bewilderment are, in the end, those of a whole generation.

SCIENCE AND THE COMMON UNDERSTANDING. 1954. *Simon & Schuster* Touchstone Bks. 1966 pap. $1.25

THE OPEN MIND. *Simon & Schuster* 1955 Touchstone Bks. 1960 pap. $1.00

The discussion centers on "the two themes of atomic weapons and the relationship between science and culture." "Others can write with comparable cogency about atomic issues, but no one can match the eloquence and sensitiveness with which Dr. Oppenheimer conveys the characteristics and the dilemmas of scientific activity to the layman"—(*Yale Review*).

THE FLYING TRAPEZE: Three Crises for Physicists. 1964. Ed. by M. A. Preston *Harper* 1969 pap. $1.25

LECTURES ON ELECTRODYNAMICS. *Gordon Press* 1970 $21.00

Books about Oppenheimer and Lawrence

In the Matter of J. Robert Oppenheimer. By Heinar Kipphardt. Trans. by Ruth Speirs *Farrar, Straus* (Hill & Wang) 1968 pap. $.95. A play.

The Oppenheimer Affair: A Political Play in Three Acts. By Joseph Boskin and Fred Krinsky. *Macmillan* (Glencoe) 1968 pap. $2.95

An American Genius: The Life of Ernest Orlando Lawrence. By Herbert Childs. *Dutton* 1968 $12.95

"Ernest Lawrence, who died in 1958, is perhaps best known today by the general public for the laboratory which bears his name—the Lawrence Radiation Laboratory of the University of California. . . . This extensive biography, intended for the general reader, is primarily a personal rather than a scientific treatment. Herbert Childs, a free-lance writer, has based his book on more than 800 interviews which he conducted with Dr. Lawrence's family, friends, and colleagues. Despite immense detail, this is a highly readable, fascinating story and will be of interest to a wide range of readers"—(*LJ*).

Lawrence and Oppenheimer. By Nuel Pharr Davis. *Simon & Schuster* 1968 $7.50 Touchstone Bks. 1969 pap. $2.95; *Fawcett* Premier Bks. 1969 pap. $1.25

"This book is a triumph . . . as a character study of scientists in action; as the story of the creation of the atom bomb; as a reminder of a national disgrace; and as a trenchant analysis of the growth of 'big science,' its Byzantine relationship with government and the policies arising from that reltionship. Nuel Pharr Davis weaves these worthy themes into a glittering whole cloth"—(*N.Y. Times*).

Swift Years: Robert Oppenheimer's Story. By Peter Michelmore. *Dodd* 1969 $6.95

Story of J. Robert Oppenheimer. By D. Royal. *St. Martin's* 1969 $5.95

Oppenheimer Case: Security on Trial. By Philip M. Stern and Harold P. Green. *Harper* 1969 $10.00

Great Weapons Heresy. By Thomas W. Wilson, Jr. *Houghton* 1970 $5.95

Oppenheimer Hearing. By John Major. *Stein & Day* 1971 $8.95

In the Matter of J. Robert Oppenheimer: Transcript of Hearing before Personnel Security Board. Ed. by U.S. Atomic Energy Commission. 1954. *M. I. T. Press* 1971 $17.50 pap. $5.95

BETHE, HANS (ALBRECHT). 1906– (Nobel Prize 1967)

Hans Bethe was awarded the Nobel Prize in 1967 for his "discovery of the carbon cycle, by which stars convert hydrogen into helium"—(*Harper Encyclopedia of Science*). In the *N.Y. Times Magazine* of March 10, 1968, Lee Edson called him a "scientific man for all seasons. To the physicists, this shy, simple man from Cornell, hardly known to the public, is one of the most impressive scientists of our times, author of a score of theories that have enlarged our scientific horizons, a man who can, in the words of a colleague, 'crunch a problem by the sheer force of his mental artillery,' and the only living scientist, it is said further, who knows the whole of theoretical physics. To Washington politicians Bethe's credentials are more awesome still. He is one of the leading architects of the atom bomb and the hydrogen bomb and, if it can be included in the same package, of the nuclear test-ban treaty. . . . 'Presidents Eisenhower and Kennedy consulted him regularly,' says a highly placed Government official. 'What's more important, they listened to his advice.' . . . The final Bethe—and indeed perhaps the real man after all—is America's most outstanding and influential advocate of nuclear disarmament. Since 1945, when he saw the consequences of that dire scientific deed, the A-bomb, he has written articles and pamphlets, signed petitions (selectively, he hastens to say), held press conferences, lectured and debated throughout the world, and occasionally buttonholed important Government officials on behalf of any sensible move that would limit and control the terrible weaponry of total destruction."

Dr. Bethe was born in Strasbourg and taught theoretical physics at various German universities until, as another remarkable Jewish refugee from Nazism, he came to the U.S. in 1935 and joined the faculty of Cornell University. He has continued to teach there ever since except for an intermission during World War II when he was head of the Theoretical Physics Division of the Los Alamos Laboratory under Oppenheimer. He has received many honors beside the Nobel—among them the Max Planck Medal of the German Physical Society (1955), the Atomic Energy Commission's 1961 Enrico Fermi Award and the 1961 Eddington Medal of the British Royal Astronomical Society.

(With E. E. Salpeter). QUANTUM MECHANICS OF ONE AND TWO ELECTRON ATOMS. *Springer-Verlag* 1957 $19.70

(With Roman W. Jackiw). INTERMEDIATE QUANTUM MECHANICS. Ed. by J. David Jackson and David Pines *Addison-Wesley* (Benjamin) 1968 $17.50 pap. $9.95

Books about Bethe

Perspectives in Modern Physics. By R. E. Marshak. *Wiley* 1966 $25.50

LANDAU, LEV (DAVIDOVICH). 1908–1968. (Nobel Prize 1962)

This Moscow theoretical physicist received the Nobel Prize for his work on gases. "A key figure in Soviet space technology, he helped make the first Soviet atomic bomb [and] for his contributions to low-temperature physics he was voted the Fritz London Award at the 1960 International Congress of Physics held in Toronto"—(*Columbia Encyclopedia*).

A child prodigy, Landau earned his doctorate from the University of Leningrad at the age of 21. Later he studied with Niels Bohr (*q.v.*) in Copenhagen for a period. He was imprisoned for a year as a "German spy" in the Stalin purges of the 1930s and released through the efforts of Peter Kapitza (*q.v.*), in whose Institute for Problems of Physics he later served in an official capacity. (Kapitza is said to have threatened his own resignation if Landau were not freed.) He became a leading Soviet physicist and professor at the University of Moscow. In January 1962, he had a near-fatal automobile accident which left him in a coma for seven weeks. He was saved by the efforts of neurosurgeons summoned from all over the world. "Collected Papers" ed. by Dirk ter Haar (*Pergamon* 1965) is o.p.

(With Y. Smorodinsky). Lectures on Nuclear Theory. *Plenum Pub.* 1959 $15.00

(With Eugene M. Lifshitz). Fluid Mechanics. *Addison-Wesley* 1959 $16.50

(With G. B. Rumer). What Is Relativity? Trans. by N. Kemmer *Basic Bks.* 1961 $4.25; *Fawcett* Premier Bks. 1972 pap. $.75

(With Eugene M. Lifshitz). Electrodynamics of Continuous Media. *Addison-Wesley* 1960 $15.50

(With Eugene M. Lifshitz). Quantum Mechanics: Non-Relativistic Theory. *Addison-Wesley* 2nd ed. 1965 $16.50

(With Eugene M. Lifshitz). Statistical Physics. *Addison-Wesley* 2nd ed. 1969 $16.50

(With Eugene M. Lifshitz). Theory of Elasticity. *Addison-Wesley* 2nd ed. 1971 $9.00

(With Eugene M. Lifshitz). Classical Theory of Fields. Trans. by Morton Hammermesh *Addison-Wesley* 1971 $16.00

(With Eugene M. Lifshitz). Shorter Course of Theoretical Physics: Vol. 2 Quantum Mechanics *Pergamon* 1975 $12.00

(With others). General Physics: Mechanics and Molecular Physics. *Pergamon* 1967 $9.50

Books about Landau

The Man They Wouldn't Let Die. By Alexander Dorozynski. *Macmillan* 1965 $4.95
  "This is the story of Lev Davidovich Landau, Russian physicist, Nobel Prize winner, a great teacher, a tireless debater, and a great wit. It is the story of an act of humanity—the collaboration of Russian, French, Czech, and Canadian physicians to save Landau after an automobile accident had mangled his body and crushed his spirit. It is also one of the rare accounts of the conditions under which scientific research is carried on in the Soviet Union"—(*LJ*).
Soviet Leaders. Ed. by George W. Simmonds. *T. Y. Crowell* 1967 $10.00. Contains a biography of Landau by Albert Parry.

TELLER, EDWARD. 1908–

Edward Teller was born in Hungary, came to the U.S. in 1935 and became an American citizen in 1941. Known as one of the scientists who favored the development of a nuclear arsenal, he has clashed with Oppenheimer, with whom he worked at the University of California and Los Alamos, and others who have warned against the danger of the nuclear arms race. During World War II he worked under Fermi at Columbia on research toward the construction of the atom bomb. He then taught (1946–52) at the University of Chicago, while associated with the Los Alamos project (*see J. Robert Oppenheimer*), and at the University of California, where he directed a section of its radiation laboratory for the Atomic Energy Commission. He now devotes full time to research. His view of science as expressed in his books is important education for the layman, whether or not one shares Dr. Teller's outlook. He was the 1962 winner of the A.E.C.'s Enrico Fermi Award.

The Reluctant Revolutionary. *Univ. of Missouri Press* 1964 $2.50

(With others). The Education of the Scientist in a Free Society. Ed. by A. Bernard Drought *Marquette Univ. Press* 1959 pap. $2.50

VON BRAUN, WERNHER. 1912–

Wernher von Braun, after earlier studies and experiments in rocketry, became (1937–45) technical director of German research in this field at Peenemünde, where he was responsible for the development and production of the V-2 rockets, which were directed against England particularly, in World War II. He was invited to the U.S. after the war and became an American citizen in 1955. He has held many important posts in the U.S. missile and space-flight programs and was director of NASA's George C. Marshall Space Flight Center, Huntsville, Ala. He is now vice-president, Engineering and Development, Fairchild Industries, Germantown, Md.

The Mars Project. *Univ. of Illinois Press* 1953 pap. $.95

First Men to the Moon. *Holt* 1960 $3.95

(With Frederick I. Ordway). The History of Rocketry and Space Travel. *T. Y. Crowell* 1966 3rd ed. 1975 $19.95

SPACE FRONTIER. *Holt* 1967 rev. ed. 1971 $6.95; *Fawcett* Premier Bks. 1969 pap. $.95

Books about von Braun

Wernher von Braun. By Heather M. David. Lives to Remember Ser. *Putnam* 1967 lib. bdg. $4.29

Wernher von Braun: Space Pioneer. By John C. Goodrum. Heroes of Space Ser. *Strode* 1969 $3.95

LOVELL, SIR (ALFRED CHARLES) BERNARD (sometimes listed as A. C. or Alfred C.). 1913–

Sir Bernard Lovell has become well known in this country particularly as a tracker of satellites and spacecraft, Soviet and American, in his capacity as director of the Nuffield Radio Astronomy Laboratories, Jodrell Bank, Cheshire, England. He can usually tell us what is doing "up there" and "out there," since his laboratories boast the world's largest radio telescope. How it was built and other matters of interest are told in "The Story of Jodrell Bank" (1968, o.p.). "The Explosion of Science" (1967, o.p.) was listed by *Library Journal* as one of the 100 best sci-tech books of 1967. Also o.p. are his "Radio Astronomy" written with J. Clegg (1952), "Meteor Astronomy" (1954), and "Discovering the Universe" (1964) done with Lady Joyce Lovell, his wife. Sir Bernard has been at Jodrell Bank since 1951, and has been professor of radio astronomy at the University of Manchester for the same period.

OUR PRESENT KNOWLEDGE OF THE UNIVERSE. *Harvard Univ. Press* 1967 $4.00 pap. $1.80.

Three popular lectures, rewritten in lucid form, with diagrams and other material.

ORIGINS AND INTERNATIONAL ECONOMICS OF SPACE EXPLORATION. *Aldine* 1973 $3.75; *Halsted Press* (dist. by John Wiley) 1974 $4.50

"An extremely useful and concise summary of the state of international space research"—(*TLS*, London).

OUT OF THE ZENITH: Jodrell Bank, 1957–1970. *Harper* 1974 $12.50

"A detailed account of the dozen or so years when this famous radio telescope installation was in 24-hour use. . . . The discovery of quasars, pulsars, and collaboration with the U.S. and Russia are among those events fully described"—(*LJ*).

(With Patrick Moore). CONCISE ATLAS OF THE UNIVERSE. *Rand McNally* 1974 $16.95

SAKHAROV, ANDREI D(MITRIEVICH). 1921– (Nobel Prize 1975)

Andrei Sakharov of the Soviet Union "is, in a sense, a kind of Oppenheimer, Teller, and Hans Bethe all rolled into one. He speaks with a voice at least equal to the sum of all three and, perhaps, even more powerfully, since his achievement was greater and more critical. In 1945 the Soviet Union lay at the mercy of the American A-bomb. Less than a decade later she had matched the United States in nuclear weaponry and produced the first H-bomb ahead of her rival for world power. The debt of the Kremlin to Soviet physics and, specifically, to Sakharov is immeasurable." So writes Harrison Salisbury in his introduction to "Progress, Coexistence and Intellectual Freedom," which astounded the world (it is dated June 1968) when it appeared in full in the *N.Y. Times* in July 1968. It had been circulated clandestinely in typescript among the rebellious artistic and scientific circles in Moscow. The work of a loyal citizen and Communist who is nevertheless deeply disturbed at trends within his own country (the imprisonment of the writers Sinyavsky and Daniel, for example), in ours (the war in Vietnam) and in the world at large (poverty, the population explosion, the bomb), he dares to offend his government to avert what he sees as the almost certain annihilation of the human race if cooperative steps, which he outlines, are not taken between East and West before it is too late. This brief book, with copious and enlightening notes by Mr. Salisbury, long the Moscow correspondent of the *N.Y. Times*, is worth its weight in gold.

In the early 1960s Mr. Sakharov was one of those who fought the brief return to grace (under Khrushchev) of the discredited biologist Lysenko, whose forcibly imposed theories had, under Stalin, brought Soviet science into disrepute throughout the world. He is a graduate of Moscow University and has won the order of Lenin and the Stalin Prize. With Peter Kapitza (*q.v.*), the other prominent but outspoken Soviet physicist, he shares a concern for the effects of science on the future of all mankind.

Selected for the Nobel Peace Prize in 1975 for his leadership of the human rights movement within the Soviet Union during the past decade, his citation reads in part, "a firm believer in the brotherhood of man, in genuine coexistence as the only way to save mankind. . . . As a nuclear physicist he has, with his special insight and responsibility, been able to speak out against the dangers inherent in the armaments race between states."

SAKHAROV SPEAKS. *Random* Vintage Bks. pap. $1.65

MY COUNTRY AND THE WORLD. *Knopf* 1975 $5.95

"Sakharov begins his essay with a stinging, detailed indictment of Soviet domestic and foreign policy . . . and concludes with a 12-point program for reform of the Soviet system"—(*Time*).

NATURALISTS AND SCIENCE WRITERS

LUCRETIUS (Titus Lucretius Carus). c. 99 B.C.–c. 55 B.C. *See Chapter 8, Latin Literature*, Reader's Adviser, *Vol. 2*.

PLINY THE ELDER (Gaius Plinius Secundus). 23 A.D.–79 A.D.

This Roman scholar and naturalist wrote many works in the fields of history, rhetoric, natural science and military tactics. Only his great work, the "Natural History," the oldest encyclopedia (in 37 books) is extant. It deals with the nature of the physical universe: geography, anthropology, zoology, botany, mineralogy and other allied subjects. Pliny was credulous; his "History" contains many unsubstantiated marvels and many, many errors of fact. He hated to waste time, and his prolific output was considered authoritative for several centuries after his lifetime. It offers information on ancient art and general culture which is to be found nowhere else. He died of asphyxiation near Naples during a massive eruption of Vesuvius.

THE ELDER PLINY'S CHAPTERS ON THE HISTORY OF ART. Trans. and ed. by K. Jax-Blake and Eugenie Sellers *Ares* 1974 $12.50

NATURAL HISTORY. *Harvard Univ. Press* Loeb 10 vols. 1938– each $7.00. The first 5 vols. and Vol. 9 trans. by Harris Rackham, Vols. 6–8 trans. by W. H. S. Jones, Vol. 10 trans. by D. E. Eichholz; (selections) trans. by Philemon Holland (1601), ed. by Paul Turner *Southern Illinois Univ. Press* 1962 $17.50

WALTON, IZAAK. 1593–1683.

"The Compleat Angler," one of the most famous books in English, was written by a self-educated ironmonger. Walton wrote it for his own pleasure as well as that of others; it not only describes the technique of angling, but is a contemplative essay on the peace and quietude attained by the fisherman. After its first appearance in 1653 there were frequent revisions adding new material during the author's lifetime. George Saintsbury called Walton's style one of a "singular and golden simplicity." In spite of Walton's background he became recognized as a "gentleman" of cultured tastes and learning. An Anglican and Royalist, he was overjoyed with the Restoration. In his own time, Walton was known as a biographer, author of the "Lives of John Donne, Sir Henry Wotton, Richard Hooker, George Herbert and Robert Sanderson" (*Oxford* $4.25).

Kenneth Rexroth wrote a charming essay on "The Compleat Angler" in the *Saturday Review* of Sept. 16, 1967, which catches the secret of its enduring appeal—and that of its author shining through it: "Izaak Walton, above all other writers in English, owes his enormous popularity to his virtues as a man, and these virtues are what condition his style and give his work its fundamental meaning. Millions have read him with joy who have never caught a fish since childhood, if at all. Indeed, . . . in America at least, most of the kinds of fish he talks about are left to small boys. The second half of the *Compleat Angler* was added in late editions and written by Charles Cotton as a guide to trout fishing in rough water. Those who want to know how to catch fish can learn most from Cotton's additions. We read Izaak Walton for a special quality of soul . . . for his tone, for his perfect attunement to the quiet streams and flowered meadows and bosky hills of the Thames valley long ago. . . . It may sound outrageous to say that Izaak Walton wrote one of the Great Books—and that about catching fish—because he was a saint, but so it is. . . . He is, in fact, an unusual embodiment of a quietly powerful tradition, that of the contemplative laymen, St. Thomas More, Nicholas Ferrer, William Law, Gilbert White. After the eighteenth century this type is more commonly found in the sciences than in religion. And like Gilbert White's *Natural History and Antiquities of Selborne*, Walton's *The Compleat Angler* is in a sense, a scientific work, an outstanding example of the piety of science."

THE COMPLEAT ANGLER, or The Contemplative Man's Recreation. 1653–1676. *Dutton* Everyman's 1906 $3.95 pap. $1.50; ed. by John Buchan *Oxford* 1914 World's Classics 1935 $4.25; *Rowman* 1962 1974 $7.50

Books about Walton

Walton and Some Earlier Writers on Fish and Fishing. By R. B. Marston. 1894. *Richard West* $30.00

Thomas Ken and Izaak Walton: A Sketch of Their Lives and Family Connection. By E. Marston. 1908. *Richard West* $35.00

Making of Walton's Lives. By David Novarr. *Cornell Univ. Press* 1958 $17.50
Izaak Walton. By Margaret Bottrall. *British Bk. Centre* $2.95 pap. $1.20. Pamphlet.
The Art of "The Compleat Angler." By John R. Cooper. *Duke Univ. Press* 1968 $6.00. Professor
Cooper teaches English and the humanities at the University of Chicago.

BARTRAM, JOHN. 1699–1777. *See* BARTRAM, WILLIAM, 1739–1823, *this Chapter.*

WHITE, GILBERT. 1720–1793.

"The Natural History of Selborne" has been called "the solitary classic of natural history in English literature." White was born and died in the place he immortalized, Selborne, in the county of Hampshire, England. He was a graduate, then junior proctor and dean, of Oriel College, Oxford. Ordained deacon in 1747, he eventually became curate in his own village, where he inherited from an uncle "The Wakes," the house in which he had been born. He started his famous book as a sort of garden calendar, as early as 1751 and it took shape in a series of letters to other naturalists between 1767 and 1787. It was popular from the first.

In another of Kenneth Rexroth's superb essays on "The Classics Revisited" (in *SR*, May 11, 1968), he writes of White's "Natural History": "From 1789 to 1901 the book went through ninety editions in the British Isles alone, as well as others in the United States and translations on the Continent. Since then, every few years have seen a new edition illustrated, lavishly produced, or published in cheap pocketbook form. Meanwhile, the entire scientific age has gone by and Gilbert White's observations have been superseded, some of his theories have been proved wrong, and his taxonomy—the naming and classification of species—has long been out of date. Yet his book holds its own. No other work of early science is still so widely read. . . . Only Audubon can compare with Gilbert White in popularity. . . . If anyone had told [him] he was one of the greatest masters of English prose, White would have doubted his flatterer's sanity. He did not even consider himself a scientist—just a country clergyman making observations in letters to his scientist friends, now long forgotten, whom he thought incomparably more important than himself. . . . As we follow White's patient, day-by-day chronicle of the drama of living beings played on the tiny stage of a small section of eighteenth-century Hampshire, we are in fact witnesses to a major drama in the life of mankind: the birth of natural science, and the exciting practice of a new-found virtue, the scientific method. . . . There are few other books that communicate so well the first law of scientific research: the practice of a humility from which springs both personal integrity and the discovery of facts and laws which are revelations of the integrity of nature. . . . On the *Natural History of Selborne* is formed the whole English tradition of amateur natural history—the birdwatching and botanizing and passionate devotion to hedgehogs in the hedgerows. . . . Finally, White communicates the beauty and quiet drama of the English countryside through the seasons. He does this by careful, concrete, accurate description, but also by intimacy—by a special talent for unobtrusive companionship. He takes us with him, person with person."

THE NATURAL HISTORY OF SELBORNE, 1789. Ed. with introd. by James Fisher *Dufour* 1960 $5.25; *Dutton* 1921 Everyman's 1949 $3.95 pap. 1972 $1.95; *Oxford* World's Classics 1937 $3.50

THE PORTRAIT OF A TORTOISE: Extracted from the Journals and Letters of Gilbert White. 1846. *Scholarly Press* $6.00

JOURNALS. *Taplinger* 1970 $15.00

Books about White

Life and Letters of Gilbert White of Selbourne. By Rashleigh Holt-White. 1901. *AMS Press* 2 vols. 1970 set $37.00
Gilbert White and Selborne. By Henry C. Shelley. *Richard West* $30.00
Bibliography of Gilbert White. By Edward A. Martin. *Richard West* $14.95

BARTRAM, WILLIAM, 1739–1823, and JOHN BARTRAM, 1699–1777.

"The Travels of William Bartram," published first in Philadelphia in 1791, describes travels through North and South Carolina, Georgia, and East and West Florida by the son of the great botanist, John Bartram. The Bartrams, father and son, were America's earliest naturalists, friends of Benjamin Franklin and founders of the first American botanical garden. They write of plants, animals and primitive Indian life in our 18th-century wilderness. William was also a nature artist who influenced the English Romantics. John Bartram was a self-educated liberal Quaker. In a number of posts, including that of botanist to George III for the American colonies, he introduced many new plants in Europe and the New World.

JOHN AND WILLIAM BARTRAM'S AMERICA: Selections from the Writings of the Philadelphia Naturalists. Ed. by Helen Gere Cruikshank. ill. by Francis Lee Jacques. 1957. *Devin-Adair* $10.00

OBSERVATIONS ON THE INHABITANTS, CLIMATE, SOIL, RIVER, PRODUCTIONS, ANIMALS AND OTHER MATTERS WORTHY OF NOTICE. By John Bartram. 1751. *Scholarly Press* $9.50; *Univ. Microfilms* 1966 $5.75

THE TRAVELS OF WILLIAM BARTRAM. 1791. Ed. with introd. by Mark Van Doren 1928. *Dover* pap. $3.50; (with title "Travels through North and South Carolina") *Gordon Press* $29.95; *Peter Smith* 1963 $5.50; ed. by Francis Harper *Yale Univ. Press* 1958 $27.50

Books about the Bartrams

Exploring with the Bartrams. By Ann and Myron Sutton. 1963. *Hale* lib. bdg. $3.27
Two professional naturalists have written a book for young people discussing the Bartrams' various trips in detail. Father and son are examined to show the differences in their personalities and attitudes, especially toward the American Indians. Illustrated with drawings by William Bartram, photographs and additional maps.

Memorials of John Bartram and Humphry Marshall. Sel. by William Darlington. 1849. Ed. with introd. by Joseph Ewan. *Macmillan* (Hafner) 1967 $25.95. A collection of the letters of Humphry Marshall, John Bartram and others.

AUDUBON, JOHN JAMES. 1785–1851.

The great American ornithologist was born in Haiti, educated in France and came to the Audubon estate "Mill Grove" near Philadelphia in 1803. As a youth his favorite occupations were observing birds and organizing bird-banding flights, the first in this country. He began by painting portraits and teaching drawing, then conceived the idea of painting every species of American bird in its native habitat. He spent years traveling through the wilderness and enduring incredible hardships. His drawings and paintings of bird life "represent a rare combination of artistic talent and scientific observation and remain one of the great achievements of American intellectual history"—(*Columbia Encyclopedia*). Despondent at being unable to provide for his family, he went to Great Britain in search of a publisher in 1826 and "The Birds of America" in elephant folio size, was published in parts between 1827 and 1838. The accompanying text, called "Ornithological Biography" (5 vols. 1831–1839) was prepared largely in Edinburgh in collaboration with William MacGillivray. "The Viviparous Quadrupeds of North America," which he began in collaboration with John Bachman, was completed by his two sons.

THE BIRDS OF AMERICA. 1827–1838. *Dover* 7 vols. pap. 1967 each $3.00; *Peter Smith* 7 vols. each $5.50 set $37.50

SYNOPSIS OF THE BIRDS OF NORTH AMERICA. 1839. *Johnson Reprint* $14.00

AUDUBON WATERCOLORS AND DRAWINGS. Ed. by Edward H. Dwight *Pierpont Morgan Lib.* 1965 pap. $2.50

AUDUBON AND HIS JOURNALS. Ed. by Maria R. Audubon. 1897. *Bks. for Libraries* 2 vols. set $36.50; *Gordon Press* 2 vols. set $70.00; *Peter Smith* 2 vols. set $15.00

THE 1826 JOURNALS OF JOHN JAMES AUDUBON. Transcribed with introd. and notes by Alice Ford *Univ. of Oklahoma Press* 1967 $12.50

This is the first unabridged version to be published of Audubon's journal describing his search in England and Scotland for a publisher for "Birds of America." "Audubon was a painstaking diarist, and this eight-month memoir, written in the form of letters to his wife in Louisiana, shows him at his best—naïve, sincere, proud, and, above all, ebullient: 'I was asked to imitate the Wild Turkey call, and I did, to the surprise of all the circle. Hooted like a Barred Owl, and cooed like the doves.' Miss Ford's notes . . . are excellent, but it should be added that the index is not perfectly reliable. Illustrated with sketches and drawings done by Audubon during his trip"—(*New Yorker*).

AUDUBON IN THE WEST. Ed. with introd. by John Frederic McDermott *Univ. of Oklahoma Press* 1965 $6.95

"In twenty letters [all but two of which are first published here] John James Audubon describes his last expedition, in 1843, up the Missouri River [in search of material for "Quadrupeds of North America"]. Will be prized as much by historians as by bird lovers"—(*Journal of American History*). "Their value as a first-hand account of the bustling frontier can not be doubted. . . . Very detailed and utterly necessary notes and a copious bibliography"—(*LJ*).

DELINEATIONS OF AMERICAN SCENERY AND CHARACTER. 1926. *Arno* 1970 $16.00

(With John Bachman). THE QUADRUPEDS OF NORTH AMERICA. 1848. Ed. with new text by Victor H. Cahalane; fwd. by Fairfield Osborne; ill. in color by John James Audubon and John Woodhouse Audubon *Arno* 3 vols. 1974 $75.00

LETTERS, 1826–1840. Ed. by H. Corning. 1930. *Kraus* 2 vols. in 1 $20.00

Books about Audubon

Audubon the Naturalist: A History of His Life and Time. By Francis Hobart Herrick. 1917. *Dover* 2 vols. 1968 pap. each $3.50; *Peter Smith* 2 vols. set $12.00

John James Audubon. By Alice E. Ford. *Univ. of Oklahoma Press* 1965 $15.00 pap. $4.95
"A definitive biography, probably containing all the important information we are ever likely to have about his life from his birth ... until his death.... The result of long years of research"—(*N.Y. Times*). Miss Ford contributes much on Audubon's family background and early years and reappraises the many legends about him. Includes chronology, listing of his work, bibliography of his work and sources.

Audubon. By Constance Rourke. *Franklin Watts* lg.-type ed. 1965 $9.95

The Living World of Audubon. By Roland C. Clement. *Grosset* new ed. $17.95

THOREAU, HENRY DAVID. 1817–1862. *See Chapter 15, Essays and Criticism, Reader's Adviser, Vol. 1.*

BURROUGHS, JOHN. 1837–1921.

John Burroughs, the son of a New York farmer, was the friend of such well-known contemporaries as John Muir, Theodore Roosevelt, Henry Ford, Thomas Edison and Walt Whitman. Burroughs met Whitman in Washington, became his friend and wrote two books about him: "Notes on Walt Whitman as Poet and Person" (1867. *Haskell* 1969 $9.95) and "Walt Whitman: A Study" (1896. *AMS Press* $8.50; *Scholarly Press* 1970 $14.50; *Richard West* 1973 $8.45). In 1871 Burroughs retired from his varied career as teacher, farmer, clerk and journalist and became the "Hudson River naturalist." He spent the next 50 years of his life writing on the wildlife he (like Thoreau) observed from his cabin, "Slabsides"—now a public shrine—and the surrounding areas. The John Burroughs Memorial Association was established in his memory; it concerns itself with conservation and presents an annual John Burroughs Medal for the best book of nature writing published the preceding year.

WRITINGS. 1871–1922. *Russell & Russell* 23 vols. 1968 each $7.50 set $150.00. Many of the titles are also published by *Bks. for Libraries, Finch Press, Folcroft, Scholarly Press* and *Richard West.*

Vol. 1 Wake Robin (1871) Vol. 2 Winter Sunshine (1879) Vol. 3 Birds and Poets and Other Papers (1877) Vol. 4 Locusts and Wild Honey (1879) Vol. 5 Prepacton (1881) Vol. 6 Fresh Fields (1884) Vol. 7 Signs and Seasons (1886) Vol. 8 Indoor Studies: Thoreau, Arnold Johnson (1889) Vol. 9 Riverby (1896) Vol. 10 Literary Values and Other Papers: Emerson, Thoreau (1903) Vol. 11 Far and Near (1904) Vol. 12 Ways of Nature (1905) Vol. 13 Leaf and Tendril (1908) Vol. 14 Time and Change (1912) Vol. 15 Summit of the Years Vol. 16 Whitman: A Study (1896) Vol. 17 Light of Day Vol. 18 Breath of Life Vol. 19 Under the Apple Trees (1916) Vol. 20 Field and Study Vol. 21 Accepting the Universe (1920) Vol. 22 Under the Maples (1921) Vol. 23 Last Harvest (1922)

JOHN BURROUGHS' AMERICA. Ed. with introd. by Farida A. Wiley; fwd. by Julian Burroughs; drawings by Francis Lee Jaques *Devin-Adair* 1951 $7.50. Selections from his writings.

THE HEART OF JOHN BURROUGHS' JOURNALS. Ed. by Clara Barrus. 1928. *Kennikat* $11.00

STUDIES IN NATURE AND LITERATURE. 1875. *Folcroft* $15.00

SQUIRRELS AND OTHER FUR-BEARERS. 1900. *Finch Press* $8.00; *Folcroft* $15.00

SONGS OF NATURE. 1901. *Folcroft* $15.00; *Richard West* $12.00

A YEAR IN THE FIELDS. 1901. *Folcroft* $15.00

CAMPING AND TRAMPING WITH ROOSEVELT. 1906. *Arno* 1970 $7.50

NATURE NEAR HOME AND OTHER PAPERS. 1919. *Scholarly Press* $9.00

AFOOT AND AFLOAT. 1923. *Scholarly Press* $9.00

Books about Burroughs

Our Friend, John Burroughs. By Clara Barrus. 1914. *Haskell* 1970 $15.95; *Richard West* 1973 $17.75

The Real John Burroughs. By William Sloane Kennedy. 1924. *Richard West* $20.00

The Life and Letters of John Burroughs. By Clara Barrus. 1925. *Russell & Russell* 2 vols. 1968 set $27.50

The Slabsides Book of John Burroughs. By H. A. Haring. 1931. *Richard West* $20.00

Whitman and Burroughs, Comrades. By Clara Barrus. 1931. *Kennikat* 1967 $12.50

Edge of April: A Biography of John Burroughs. By Hildegarde Hoyt Swift. *Morrow* 1957 $5.95. A book for young people.

John Burroughs, Naturalist. By Elizabeth B. Kelley. *Exposition Press* 1959 $6.00. A biography by the grand-daughter of the naturalist, with much previously unpublished material from letters and journals.

John Burroughs. By Perry D. Westbrook. *Twayne* 1974 $6.50

MUIR, JOHN. 1838–1914.

This Scottish-born American naturalist traveled over much of this country—from Canada to the Gulf of Mexico—keeping a diary of his thoughts and observations. His specialties were glaciers, woodlands and horticulture, interests that sent him to Australia, South America and Africa. His studies of the Yosemite Valley revealed much about its geological origins. He was a great conservationist and a crusader for national parks and reservations. He gained President Theodore Roosevelt's (*q.v.*) support, while on a camping trip with him, and was influential in setting aside additional forest reserves.

THE WILDERNESS WORLD OF JOHN MUIR. With introd. and interpretive comments by Edwin Way Teale *Houghton* 1954 $7.95

A "superb collection" of some 50-odd selections "chronologically arranged so that they come close to providing a biography of the famous Scot, or at least a 'biography' of his view of life."

SOUTH OF YOSEMITE: Selected Writings of John Muir. Ed. with fwd. by Frederic R. Gunsky; ill. by Philip Hyde and John Muir *Doubleday* National History Press 1968 $7.50

STUDIES IN THE SIERRA. Ed. by William E. Colby *Sierra Club* 1949 rev. ed. 1960 $3.75. First published in 1874 as articles in the *Overland Monthly*.

THE MOUNTAINS OF CALIFORNIA. 1894. *Doubleday* Natural History Press pap. $1.95

OUR NATIONAL PARKS. 1901. *AMS Press* 1970 $11.50; *Scholarly Press* $7.95

MY FIRST SUMMER IN THE SIERRA. 1911. *Norman S. Berg* 1972 $12.50

THE YOSEMITE. 1912. *Doubleday* Natural History Press 1962 pap. $1.25

TRAVELS IN ALASKA. 1915. *AMS Press* 1971 $9.50; *Scholarly Press* $9.50

A THOUSAND MILE WALK TO THE GULF. 1916. *Norman S. Berg* 1969 $12.95. The journal of a trek from Indiana to Mexico.

CRUISE OF THE CORWIN. 1917. *Norman S. Berg* new ed. 1974 $12.50

STEEP TRAILS. 1918. Ed. by William F. Rade *Norman S. Berg* 1970 $12.50

(With Richard Kauffman). GENTLE WILDERNESS: The Sierra Nevada. Ed. with fwd. by David Brower *Sierra Club* 1964 $30.00

"Not even the time-distance of 100 years can prevent the combined talents of two observing men from producing 'a large, impressive contemporary tribute to California's Sierra Nevada mountains.' The brief text consists of edited excerpts from John Muir's 'My First Summar in the Sierra.' . . . The principal feature of this large-format volume is the precision color photography of Richard Kauffman. Mr. Kauffman is a rare combination of photographer, mountaineer and commercial printer"—(*LJ*).

THE STORY OF MY BOYHOOD AND YOUTH. 1913. *Univ. of Wisconsin Press* 1965 pap. $2.50

LETTERS TO A FRIEND. *Norman S. Berg* new ed. 1973 $10.00

Books about Muir

Alaska Days with John Muir. By S. Hall Young. 1915. *Blom* 1974 $12.75

Life and Letters of John Muir. By William F. Bade. 1924. *AMS Press* 2 vols. each $23.50 set $45.00

The Wilderness World of John Muir. By Edwin Way Teale. *Houghton* 1954 $7.95

Muir of the Mountains. By William O. Douglas. *Houghton* 1961 $2.95

John Muir. By Herbert F. Smith. *Twayne* 1964 $6.50; *College & Univ. Press* 1964 pap. $2.45

John Muir and the Sierra Club: The Battle for Yosemite. By Holway R. Jones. *Sierra Club* 1964 $10.00

John Muir. By Thomas J. Lyon. *Boise State College Press* 1972 pap. $1.00

HUDSON, W(ILLIAM) H(ENRY). 1841–1922.

Besides his novels, with their vivid passages on nature, particularly that of South America, his birthplace, Hudson wrote on the English countryside in "Hampshire Days" (1903), "The Land's End" (1908) and "Afoot in England" (1909). His prose is magically evocative of field, forest and jungle. He also studied the birds of his two favorite areas in the "Letters" (*see below*), "British Birds" (1895), "Birds in London" (1898), "Birds of La Plata," and other books.

THE COLLECTED WORKS OF W. H. HUDSON. 1922–23. *AMS Press* 24 vols. 1968 each $15.00 set $360.00

LETTERS ON THE ORNITHOLOGY OF BUENOS AYRES. Ed. by David R. Dewar; fwd. by Herbert F. West; published by permission of the Zoological Society of London *Cornell Univ. Press* 1951 $7.50

ONE HUNDRED FIFTY-THREE LETTERS OF W. H. HUDSON. Ed. by Edward Garnett. 1923. *Richard West* $30.00

FAR AWAY AND LONG AGO. 1918. *AMS Press* 1968 $15.00; *Dutton* pap. $2.75; *Folcroft* 1973 $14.00. Autobiographical.

Books about Hudson

Bibliography of the Writings of W. H. Hudson. By G. F. Wilson. 1922. *Haskell* 1972 $8.95; *Kennikat* 1968 $5.00

W. H. Hudson: A Portrait. By Morley Roberts. 1924. *Haskell* 1974 $15.95; *Richard West* $17.50

W. H. Hudson: The Vision of Earth. By Robert Hamilton. 1946. *Kennikat* 1970 $6.50; *Norwood Editions* $6.25

W. H. Hudson. By Ruth Tomalin. *Dufour* 1954 $3.95; *Greenwood* $8.00

W. H. Hudson. By J. T. Frederick. English Authors Ser. *Twayne* $6.50

See also Chapter 6, British Fiction: Middle Period, Reader's Adviser, *Vol. 1.*

JEFFERIES, RICHARD. 1848–1887. *See Chapter 15, Essays and Criticism,* Reader's Adviser, *Vol. 1.*

ROOSEVELT, THEODORE. 1858–1919. *See Chapter 12, Travel and Adventure, this Vol., for his work as a naturalist.*

SARTON, GEORGE (ALFRED LÉON). 1884–1956.

This Belgian-American historian and philosopher of science devoted his life to bridging the gap between science and the humanities and to making the history of science an academic discipline in itself. He wrote, in "The History of Science and the New Humanism," "We shall be true humanists only to the extent of our success in combining the historical and the scientific spirit" and "We all live in the present, but the present of the uneducated is narrow and mean, while that of the true humanist is catholic and generous." Elsewhere he said, "Science is progressive and therefore ephemeral; art is nonprogressive and eternal." The fine quality of his writing can be judged from these excerpts. He possessed a "rather frightening erudition," but in a series of essays for the *New Yorker* his daughter, May Sarton (*q.v.*), the novelist and poet, added to our picture a man of great charm and total dedication. He came to the United States in 1918, was associated with the Carnegie Institution of Washington for many years and taught at Harvard University. He held many honorary degrees, twice received the Prix Binoux from the Académie des Sciences of Paris, and was decorated Knight of the Order of Leopold, Belgium, in 1940.

THE STUDY OF THE HISTORY OF MATHEMATICS and THE STUDY OF THE HISTORY OF SCIENCE. 1936. *Dover* 2 vols. in 1 pap. $2.25

LIFE OF SCIENCE: Essays in the History of Civilization. 1948. *Bks. for Libraries* 1970 $9.50

INTRODUCTION TO THE HISTORY OF SCIENCE. 1950. *Williams & Wilkins* 2 vols. 1927–1931 Vol. 1 $27.50 Vol. 2 $42.50 5 vols. 1974 $175.00

A HISTORY OF SCIENCE. *Harvard Univ. Press* 2 vols. 1952–1959 Vol. 1 Ancient Science through the Golden Age of Science (1952) Vol. 2 Hellenistic Science and Culture in the Last Three Centuries B.C. (1959) each $15.00; *Norton* 2 vols. pap. each $3.25

ANCIENT SCIENCE AND MODERN CIVILIZATION: Euclid and His Time; Ptolemy and His Time; The End of Greek Science and Culture. *Univ. of Nebraska Press* 1954 Bison Bks. 1964 pap. $1.65

THE HISTORY OF SCIENCE AND THE NEW HUMANISM. 3rd ed. 1956. *Indiana Univ. Press* 1962 pap. $1.95; *Peter Smith* $4.25

APPRECIATION OF ANCIENT AND MEDIEVAL SCIENCE DURING THE RENAISSANCE. *A. S. Barnes* 1961 pap. $1.65

KRUTCH, JOSEPH WOOD. 1893–1970.

In the 1950s "Mr. Krutch became desert-stricken on his first view of New Mexico. He went back four more times for brief spells, and finally, upon being granted a sabbatical leave by Columbia University—where he [was then] Professor of Dramatic Literature—he returned to spend it in Arizona, a mile from a mountain and surrounded by desert. He stayed a year, and communed with three dimensions of desert life—the intimate, that showed him insects, birds, animals and plants; the vast, that showed him sky, distance, climate and season; and the illimitable, that allowed him his own speculations. In prose that holds something of the clear, dry light of the land he loves, he shares with us his discoveries and his associations. They are richly worth sharing"—(Paul Horgan, in the *N.Y. Times*). So was the literary critic and well-known authority on the drama transformed into one of our best nature writers.

He retired from teaching in 1950 and gave up his post as drama critic of the *Nation* (which he had held since 1924). In 1954 he received the John Burroughs Medal for "The Desert Year" and in 1955 the National Book Award for nonfiction for "The Measure of Man." It is an arresting discussion of man in a mechanistic age, "a courageous statement of the humanist position, and an inquiry into the fundamentals at a moment when the world is distracted by superficialities." In 1964 Mr. Krutch received a Richard Prentice Ettinger Medal for creative writing in science and literature. The *N.Y. Times* called "The Great Chain of Life" "the best introduction to natural history that has yet been written." He also edited "The Gardener's World" (1960, o.p.), an anthology of "plant lore and gardening from Homer to Thoreau, from Boccaccio to Edwin Way Teale"; "The World of Animals: A Treasury of Lore, Legend and Literature by Great Writers and Naturalists from the 5th Century B.C. to the Present" (*Simon & Schuster* 1961 $10.00); and with Paul S. Eriksson "Treasury of Birdlore" (1962. *Eriksson* 1969 $7.95).

"Mr. Krutch's own explanation of himself makes an unusual, unheroic, but deeply thought-provoking autobiography," the *Christian Science Monitor* writes of "More Lives than One." "It is unheroic not so much because Mr. Krutch is modest as because he is detached, analytical, amused at the man he sees as he looks backward through the telescope of his career. It is deeply thoughtful because that same less-than-giant man has for decades been looking outward with equal detachment and growing perspective on the purpose and nature of mankind in modern times."

BEST NATURE WRITING OF JOSEPH WOOD KRUTCH. *Morrow* 1970 $8.50

KRUTCH OMNIBUS: Forty Years of Social and Literary Criticism. *Morrow* 2nd ed. 1970 $8.50

HENRY DAVID THOREAU. 1948. *Greenwood* 1973 $13.00; *Morrow* 1974 pap. $2.95

THE TWELVE SEASONS: A Perpetual Calendar for the Country. Ill. by Armin Landeck. 1949. *Bks. for Libraries* $9.75

THE DESERT YEAR. 1952. Decorations by Rudolph Freund *Viking* 1960 Compass Bks. 1963 pap. $1.85

THE MEASURE OF MAN: On Freedom, Human Values, Survival and the Modern Temper. 1954. *Grosset* Univ. Lib. 1956 pap. $1.95; *Peter Smith* $3.75

THE VOICE OF THE DESERT: A Naturalist's Interpretation. *Morrow* 1955 pap. $1.95

THE GREAT CHAIN OF LIFE. Ill. by Paul Landacre *Houghton* 1957 $5.95

GRAND CANYON: Today and All Its Yesterdays. 1958. *Morrow* 1971 pap. $2.25; *Peter Smith* $4.25

"This book is a nicely calculated introduction, much more than a guide book, readable on its own merits, a temper to the virtue of really looking"—(*N.Y. Times*).

HUMAN NATURE AND THE HUMAN CONDITION. *Random* 1959 $6.95

"What Mr. Krutch has done in the present book is to take us gently along with him from one obvious point to another until the cumulative effect is such that halfway through we suddenly become aware that here is an indictment of modern civilization so powerful that we are tempted to run off and join Thoreau (one of the author's favorite heroes) in the woods of Walden"—(*N.Y. Times*).

FORGOTTEN PENINSULA: A Naturalist in Baja California. *Apollo* 1961 pap. $2.25

BIRDSONGS IN LITERATURE. *Houghton* 1967 $6.00

IF YOU DON'T MIND MY SAYING SO: Essays on Man and Nature. Introd. by J. K. Hutchens *Apollo* pap. $2.75

MORE LIVES THAN ONE: An Autobiography. *Morrow* Sloane 1962 $5.95

HOGBEN, LANCELOT (THOMAS). 1895–1975.

"Mathematics for the Million" and "Science for the Citizen" were two great successes in making difficult scientific knowledge popular. Professor Hogben is known best among scientists for his work in endocrinology and genetics. He was professor of zoology at the University of Birmingham (1941–1947) then became professor of medical statistics there. His "Essential World English" (*Norton* 1962, o.p.) contains a program based on semantic principles to help people of all nationalities for whom English will be a medium of communication, particularly in the teaching and learning of science. His style has been described as "reminiscent of that of Bertrand Russell or of J. B. S. Haldane. He falls somewhat short of them in wit and lucidity, though not in sheer vigor." Three of his engrossing and clearly written books for older children, now o.p., are "The Wonderful World of Mathematics" (1955), "The Wonderful World of Energy" (1957) and "The Wonderful World of Communication" (1959).

MATHEMATICS FOR THE MILLION. *Norton* 1937 rev. ed. 1968 $10.00

SCIENCE FOR THE CITIZEN. *Norton* 1938 rev. ed. 1957 $15.00

STATISTICAL THEORY. *Norton* 1955 rev. ed. 1968 $15.00

VOCABULARY OF SCIENCE. *Stein & Day* 1971 $6.95 pap. $1.95

BEGINNINGS AND BLUNDERS. *Grosset* 1971 $4.95

MAPS, MIRRORS AND MECHANICS. *St. Martin's* 1974 $4.95

ASTRONOMER, PRIEST AND ANCIENT MARINER. *St. Martin's* 1974 $4.95

JAFFE, BERNARD. 1896–

This American popularizer of science and its history has an easy style most interesting for general readers. His first great success, which is still widely read, was "Crucibles." The revised and expanded "Men of Science in America" (1944 rev. ed. 1958, o.p.) has an added chapter devoted to Enrico Fermi and America's contribution to atomic and nuclear physics, as well as revised and rewritten essays on the spirit and future of American science. "Michelson and the Speed of Light" (*Doubleday* 1960) is o.p.

CRUCIBLES: The Story of Chemistry. 1934. *Fawcett* Premier Bks. rev. & abr. ed. 1960 pap. $.95

CHEMISTRY CREATES A NEW WORLD. *T. Y. Crowell* 1957 $5.95

MOSELEY AND THE NUMBERING OF THE ELEMENTS. *Doubleday* 1971 pap. $1.95

TEALE, EDWIN WAY. 1899–

This American literary naturalist has been described by the *Saturday Review* as a writer, naturalist and photographer who "excels in all three branches of his art." He has been awarded the John Burroughs Medal for distinguished nature writing and in 1957 received the Christopher Award for "Autumn Across America." His books have been published in England and in French, Spanish, Finnish and Braille editions. He is a past president of the N.Y. Entomological Society, a Fellow of the N.Y. Academy of Sciences and an Associate of the Royal Photographic Society. His "American Seasons" volumes are fascinating accounts of his trips across America in pursuit of seasonal changes, observed in sensitive detail. His "Strange Lives of Familiar Insects" is absorbing and delightful.

ADVENTURES IN NATURE. *Apollo* 1961 pap. $1.95. Thirty-one selections chosen from half a dozen of his earlier works, several of which are now out of print.

GRASSROOTS JUNGLES. *Dodd* rev. ed. 1937 $6.95

NEAR HORIZONS. *Dodd* 1942 $6.95; *Pyramid Bks.* pap. $.75

NORTH WITH THE SPRING. *Dodd* 1951 $10.00; *Apollo* 1969 pap. $2.50

AUTUMN ACROSS AMERICA. *Dodd* 1956 $10.00; *Apollo* 1969 pap. $2.50

JOURNEY INTO SUMMER. *Dodd* 1960 $10.00; *Apollo* 1969 pap. $2.50

WANDERING THROUGH WINTER: A Naturalist's Record of a 20,000 Mile Journey
through the North American Winter from California to Maine. *Dodd* 1965 $10.00;
Apollo 1969 pap. $2.50

THE AMERICAN SEASONS. *Dodd* 4 vols. 1966 set $40.00. The four volumes above in a
boxed set, with a biography of Teale by Edward H. Dodd, Jr.

THE STRANGE LIVES OF FAMILIAR INSECTS. 1962. *Apollo* 1968 pap. $2.25

THE LOST WOODS: Adventures of a Naturalist. Photographs by the author. *Dodd* 1961
$6.95

SPRINGTIME IN BRITAIN. *Dodd* 1970 $7.50

EDWIN WAY TEALE'S PHOTOGRAPHS OF AMERICAN NATURE. *Dodd* 1972 $17.50

A NATURALIST BUYS AN OLD FARM. *Dodd* 1974 $10.00

"After living on the south shore of Long Island for 30 years, the Teales moved to a farm in
Connecticut with more or less 130 acres"—(Publisher's note).

DUBOS, RENÉ JULES. 1901–

René Dubos is a famous microbiologist and emeritus professor at Rockefeller University,
formerly the Rockefeller Institute, New York City. Born and educated in France, he came to the
United States in 1924 to join the research staff at Rutgers University and is now a naturalized citizen.
"I am a microbiologist," he once told a reporter for the *New Yorker* (April 8, 1961), "one of those
specialized scientists whose professional jargon is almost meaningless to the rest of mankind. . . .
Yet never in my professional life do I find myself far removed from the man of flesh and blood."
Dr. Dubos has served as president of several professional associations and has been awarded more
than a score of prizes and medals by the world scientific community.

DREAMS OF REASON: Science and Utopias. *Columbia* 1961 $10.00 pap. $1.95

TORCH OF LIFE. *Simon & Schuster* 1962 $3.95

THE UNSEEN WORLD. *Rockefeller Univ. Press* 1962 $6.00

"The story of microorganisms, both disease producing agents and 'domesticated' microbes that
yield beer, cheese, antibiotics, etc."—(*N.Y. Times Bk. Review*).

MAN ADAPTING. *Yale Univ. Press* 1965 $17.50 pap. $3.75

"An incisive analysis of the situation in organized medicine, which continues to define all the
minute particulars of life without adapting to the new problems posed by the modern social
conflict"—(Oscar Handlin, *Atlantic*).

SO HUMAN AN ANIMAL. *Scribner* 1968 $8.95 pap. $2.45

Dubos "asserts that we are as much the product of our total environment as of our genetic
endowment. . . . that we can change our suicidal course by learning to deal scientifically with the
living experience of man"—(Publisher's note).

REASON AWAKE: Science for Man. *Columbia* 1970 $10.00 pap. $3.45

"Dubos attempts to determine the role of science in human life and the growth of civilization . . .
[and] indicates new attitudes and directions that could help man to find his place within nature"—
(*LJ*).

MIRAGE OF HEALTH. *Harper* 1971 pap. $1.25

A GOD WITHIN. *Scribner* 1972 $8.95 pap. 1973 $2.95

"He is less fearful of the end of life on earth as the result of the current technologically-rooted
environmental crisis than he is of the degradation of human life as we know it. . . . He believes
men have not done enough in their stewardship of the earth, but can create a new 'scientific
theology' out of a sense of *'en theos'*—the ancient belief that each place has its deity or spirit"—
(*PW*).

(With Barbara Ward). ONLY ONE EARTH: The Care and Maintenance of a Small Planet.
Norton 1972 $6.00

A study done for the United Nations giving background information on the "fact of environmental interrelationships—air, water, land, energy resources—and the consequences of policies which ignore these interrelationships"—(*America*).

BEAST OR ANGEL? Choices That Make Us Human. *Scribner* 1974 $8.95

"Dubos emphasizes those unique qualities of man that have enabled him through socialization and acculturation to adapt to the environment"—(*Booklist*).

OF HUMAN DIVERSITY. *Barre* (dist. by Crown) 1974 $5.95

GAMOW, GEORGE. 1904–1968.

The Russian-American nuclear physicist, born in Odessa, stands at the top of modern popularizers of science. In 1956 UNESCO awarded him the Kalinga Prize in scientific writing for the nonscientist. His "Mr. Tompkins" series used the figure of a bank clerk curious about science as an intriguing protagonist. He did his earlier research at the University of Copenhagen, Cambridge University and the University of Leningrad, where he was professor (1931–1933). He came to the United States, taught at George Washington University (1934–1956) and at the University of Colorado (1956–1968). He served with several U.S. government agencies. His books are stimulating and extremely well written for the general reader.

Dr. Gamow also did important work in nuclear physics—on nuclear fission and fusion and related research—which contributed to the present state of scientific knowledge in this field. He was unusual in combining the "charming cocksureness and buoyancy" (*N.Y. Times*) of his popular writing with significant original scientific discovery. O.p. is "A Planet Called Earth" (1963), his "biography of earth" based on the latest research from Van Allen belts to the Mohole project.

MR. TOMPKINS IN PAPERBACK. *Cambridge* 1967 $8.50 pap. $1.95. Based on "Mr. Tompkins in Wonderland" (1939) and "Mr. Tompkins Explores the Atom" (1945); part of a popular series.

ONE, TWO, THREE—INFINITY: Facts and Speculations of Science. 1947. *Viking* rev. ed. 1961 Compass bks. pap. 1963 $2.45; *Bantam* 1971 $1.25

THE CREATION OF THE UNIVERSE. 1952. *Viking* rev. ed. 1961 $5.75

MATTER, EARTH AND SKY. *Prentice-Hall* 1958 2nd ed. 1965 $12.50 answers to uneven-numbered questions pap. $.50. Though designed for the instruction of college students, this excellent introductory text is well suited for the general reader.

THE BIOGRAPHY OF PHYSICS. *Harper* 1961 $7.50

THE ATOM AND ITS NUCLEUS. *Prentice-Hall* 1961 Spectrum Bks. pap. $1.95. A survey of the growth of human knowledge of the atom from the time of the Greeks to the present.

GRAVITY: Classic and Modern Views. *Doubleday* Anchor Bks. 1962 pap. $2.50

A STAR CALLED THE SUN. *Viking* 1964 $7.95

A revision of his 1940 "The Birth and Death of the Sun" (*New Am. Lib.* pap. $.60). "There are numerous photographs and a number of excellent line drawings which are the hallmark of this author's work"—(*LJ*).

THIRTY YEARS THAT SHOOK PHYSICS: The Story of Quantum Theory. *Doubleday* 1966 $5.95 Anchor Bks. pap. $1.95

A second work, after "Gravity," in the Science Study Series. "The author has again displayed the ability to interweave technology with interesting biographical summaries of the contributors, making this writing enjoyable as well as most informative"—(*LJ*).

(With John Cleveland). PHYSICS: Foundations and Frontiers. *Prentice-Hall* 2nd ed. 1969 $13.50

SNOW, SIR C(HARLES) P(ERCY). 1905–ᅠᅠ*See Chapter 12, Modern British Fiction, Reader's Adviser, Vol. 1.*

LEY, WILLY. 1906–1969.

This scientist, born in Berlin, was a citizen of the U.S. from 1944, a consultant to the office of technical services of the U.S. Department of Commerce and a research engineer for the Washington Institute of Technology, 1944–48. "In all my books," he once wrote, "whether on extinct or living animals, or on rockets and space travel, I have always acted on the belief that my readers will be interested if the story is well told." This belief led him to some delightful ramblings in the fields of paleontology and natural history. "With customary zeal and thoroughness he [sought] to determine the extent to which early accounts of unusual animals and plants were based on fact or fantasy." His first book was a small paper-backed volume published in Germany in 1926, "Trip into Space," and in 1927 he was among the founders of the German Society for Space Travel. An early predicter of moon travel and a writer on the Apollo missions, he died on June 25, 1969, less than a month before man's first landing on the moon. His "Rockets, Missiles and Men in Space" (1951 rev. ed. 1968) is o.p.

EXOTIC ZOOLOGY. *Viking* rev. ed. 1959 $5.95; *Putnam* Capricorn Bks. 1966 pap. $2.65

A selection, reworking and revision of material which appeared in the author's "The Lungfish, The Dodo, and the Unicorn" (1941, 1958), "Dragons in Amber" (1951), and "Salamanders and Other Wonders" (1955).

POLES. *Time-Life Bks.* 1962 $8.80

WATCHERS OF THE SKIES: An Informal History of Astronomy from Babylon to the Space Age. *Viking* 1963 $8.50 Compass Bks. pap. $2.95

BORDERS OF MATHEMATICS. *Pyramid Bks.* pap. $.75

FOR YOUR INFORMATION: On Earth and in the Sky. 1967. *Ace Bks.* 1968 pap. $.95

"An engaging miscellany: among the best articles are speculation about the temperature and size of various stars and a lively summary of Russian scientists' excitement over meteorites, past and present"—*(PW)*.

THE DAWN OF ZOOLOGY. *Prentice-Hall* 1968 $9.95

EVENTS IN SPACE. *McKay* 1969 $5.95; *Popular Lib.* 1970 pap. $.75. A history of space exploration to Apollo 9.

CARSON, RACHEL LOUISE.   1907–1964.

It is not often that there occurs that "publishing phenomenon as rare as a total solar eclipse"— two titles by the same author appearing on the best-seller list at the same time. It is not often that the *N.Y. Times* comments upon this phenomenon editorially as it did on April 27, 1952, when Miss Carson's only two books (the first two in the listing below) appeared there. The editorial stated further: "Great poets from Homer, with his sonorous hexameters on the 'loud-sounding sea,' down to Masefield, with his poignant verses about sailing, have tried to evoke the deep mystery and endless fascinations of the ocean; but the slender, gentle lady who is editor of the United States Fish and Wildlife Service seems to have the best of it. Once or twice in a generation does the world get a physical scientist with literary genius." "The Sea Around Us" won the National Book Award in 1951 and the John Burroughs Medal in 1952. In "The Edge of the Sea," *Time* reported, she has again "shown her remarkable talent for catching the life breath of science on the still glass of poetry."

"Silent Spring," written as she was dying of cancer, was a passionate and reasoned attack on the widespread indiscriminate use of pesticides. It, too, became a worldwide best seller and was a prime mover in arousing the present American concern to end or bring under control man's rapid destruction of his environment (*see the list on Conservation in the Earth Sciences Section, this Chapter*).

Miss Carson began her serious study of biology at Pennsylvania College for Women and continued at Johns Hopkins and the Marine Biological Laboratory at Woods Hole, Massachusetts. She became editor-in-chief of the U.S. Fish and wildlife Service but resigned in 1952 to devote full time to writing. In 1953 she was elected to the National Institute of Arts and Letters, the first science writer elected to the group in 13 years. In 1963 she received for "Silent Spring," the Founders Award, highest prize of the Izaak Walton League; and the first "Woman of Conscience" citation of the National Council of Women in the United States for "the courage to express her convictions in the face of powerful opposition." She received many other honors and awards. In 1968 she was the subject of a moving television documentary (ABC), in which Helen Hayes narrated material from her life and works.

UNDER THE SEA-WIND: A Naturalist's Picture of Ocean Life. *Oxford* 1941 new ed. 1952 $7.50; *New Am. Lib.* Signet 1962 pap. $1.25

THE SEA AROUND US. *New Am. Lib.* Mentor Bks. 1954 pap. $1.50; *Oxford* 1951 rev. ed 1961 $7.95; *Franklin Watts* lg.-type ed. 1966 $8.95; *Western Pub. Co.* Golden Press 1958 $6.95

THE EDGE OF THE SEA. *Houghton* 1955 $7.95; *New Am. Lib.* Signet 1971 pap. $.95

SILENT SPRING. *Houghton* 1962 $6.95 Sentry Eds. 1973 pap. $2.95; *Fawcett* Crest Bks. 1973 pap. $1.25

A SENSE OF WONDER. *Harper* 1965 $7.95 pap. $3.95. Her exploration of the natural world with a child.

Books about Carson

Since Silent Spring. By Frank Graham, Jr. *Houghton* 1970 $6.95

Sea and Earth: The Life of Rachel Carson. By Philip Sterling. *T. Y. Crowell* 1970 $4.95; *Dell* 1974 pap. $.95

The House of Life: Rachel Carson at Work. By Paul Brooks. *Houghton* 1972 $8.95; *Fawcett* Crest Bks. 1974 pap. $1.75

FERMI LAURA. 1907–   *See under* FERMI, ENRICO, 1901–1954, *in Section on Scientists, this Chapter*.

BRONOWSKI, JACOB. 1908–1974.

Born in Poland and educated in England, Dr. Bronowski was a mathematician, a philosopher of science, and a gifted writer on scientific topics. He served for many years as a researcher and official working for various departments in the British government and UNESCO. His broadcasts for the BBC from 1948 to the mid-1960s won him a wide popular following and led to his award-winning series "The Ascent of Man" that has recently appeared on American TV networks. Dr. Bronowski has often been a visiting lecturer and professor at British, Canadian, and American universities. At the time of his death in 1974 Bronowski was on the staff of the Salk Institute for Biological Studies at La Jolla, California.

WILLIAM BLAKE: A Man without a Mask. 1947. *Haskell* 1969 $11.95

COMMON SENSE OF SCIENCE. *Harvard Univ. Press* 1953 $4.50; *Random* Vintage Bks. pap. $1.65. Brief and important essays on translating science for the layman.

SCIENCE AND HUMAN VALUES. 1958. (And "The Abacus and the Rose") *Harper* Torchbks. rev. and enl. ed. 1972 pap. $1.25

This book "offers more information and light about the sciences and their relation to the progress of the human spirit than many a book ten times as large"—(*N.Y. Herald Tribune*).

THE IDENTITY OF MAN. 1966. *Doubleday* rev. ed. 1972 $5.95 pap. $1.95

"Four lectures on Man and Nature given at the American Museum of Natural History in which he reviews recent discoveries in physics and biology and their implication for a humanistic philosophy for men"—(Publisher's note).

THE ASCENT OF MAN. *Little* 1974 $15.00. Thirteen essays on the development of science from prehistory to the present, derived from the television series.

(With Bruce Mazlish). WESTERN INTELLECTUAL TRADITION: From Leonardo to Hegel. 1960. *Bks. for Libraries* 1970 $17.50; *Harper* Torchbks. pap. $3.25

(With others). IMAGINATION AND THE UNIVERSITY. *Univ. of Toronto Press* 1964 $5.00

PETERSON, ROGER TORY. 1908–

This American ornithologist, who received the John Burroughs Medal in 1950 for "Birds Over America," has been engaged in bird painting and illustration of bird books since 1934. "Wild America" is the record of a 30,000-mile journey around the continent by the distinguished naturalist and his British colleague, who was seeing the continent for the first time. Peterson's illustrations are outstanding. He has been editor of the Field Guide Series for *Houghton Mifflin Co.* since 1946 (*see catalog for these titles*). He edited "The Bird Watcher's Anthology" (*Harcourt* 1957 o.p.). His work is imaginative and trustworthy; he is the acknowledged dean of American nature guide editors. "Wildlife in Color" (1949) and "The World of Birds" done with James Fisher (1964) are o.p.

BIRDS OVER AMERICA. *Dodd* 1948 rev. ed. 1964 $7.50

HOW TO KNOW THE BIRDS. *Houghton* 1949 1962 $5.95; *New Am. Lib.* Signet 1971 pap. $.95

(With James Fisher). WILD AMERICA. *Houghton* 1955 $7.95 Sentry Eds. pap. $4.25

(With Russell Bourne and Alma D. MacConomy, Eds.). GARDENING WITH WILDLIFE. *National Wildlife* new ed. 1974 $12.95

BIRDS. Time-Life Nature Library Ser. *Time-Life Bks.* 1968 lib. bdg. $8.80 1969 $3.95

COUSTEAU, JACQUES YVES. 1910–

"The Silent World" "is a book whose interest, wonder, excitement, and perhaps value it would be difficult to exaggerate. It is new on every page. It supplements the newness with photographs of things never seen before. . . . Its style has the French clarity and wit"—(*Christian Science Monitor*). The senior author of this story of undersea discovery and adventure is a "French naval officer who with two companions invented the aqualung, which enables them to dive without the usual impedimenta, to 200 and 300 feet below the surface of the sea." "We have tried to find the entrance to the great hydrosphere because we feel that the sea age is soon to come," the authors say.

M. Cousteau has conducted experiments with underwater colonies in "Conshelf" (Continental Shelf) 1 and 2 (*see note on "A World without Sun"*). He intends to occupy progressively greater depths, predicting that "peopled reefs will become as commonplace on the Continental Shelf as oil-drilling towers have in recent decades"—(*LJ*). In 1968 ABC began a television series entitled "The Undersea World of Jacques Cousteau" (of which M. Cousteau is executive producer) and marked by the "excellent photography that characterizes the work of Captain Cousteau and his associates"—(*N.Y. Times*). The fascination of the underwater world for man and his inventions for its exploration are discussed in "The Coast of Coral" by Arthur C. Clarke (*Harper* 1956 $6.95). "Captain Cousteau's Underwater Treasury" (*Harper* 1959 $11.50), edited by Jacques Yves Cousteau and James Dugan, represents a varied collection of true stories of undersea adventures and exploration. At present, Cousteau, his 18-man crew and electronically equipped ship *Calypso* are searching for the legendary city of Atlantis around the island of Santorini and its sunken volcanic crater.

THE OCEAN WORLD OF JACQUES COUSTEAU. *Harry N. Abrams* 12 vols. 1972–   each $7.95

A projected 20-volume "encyclopedia of the sea." Volumes will include "photographs and diagrams of the inhabitants of the deep as well as . . . facts concerning their life styles and some . . . theories about the future uses that man can make of the oceans"—(*Best Sellers*).

Available titles are: Oasis in Space 1972 The Quest for Food 1973 Window in the Sea 1973 The Challenge of the Sea 1973 Guide to the Sea 1975 Instinct and Intelligence 1975 Mammals in the Sea 1975 Man Reenters the Sea 1975 Pharaohs of the Sea 1975 Provinces of the Sea 1975 Riches of the Sea 1975 The Sea in Danger 1975 A Sea of Legends 1975

(With Frédéric Dumas). THE SILENT WORLD. Ed. by James Dugan *Harper* 1953 $8.95 lib. bdg. $5.39 pap. $.95

(With James Dugan). THE LIVING SEA: A Sequel to "The Silent World." *Harper* 1963 $10.00; *Ballantine Bks.* 1973 pap. $2.00; *Simon & Schuster* Pocket Bks. 1972 pap. $.95

"Some academic oceanographers have found it fashionable to discount [Cousteau's] exploits. But the years of effort that have been compressed into the pages of this book speak for themselves of the great contribution Captain Cousteau has made to oceanographic science. . . . In 'The Living Sea,' as in his earlier best seller 'The Silent World,' Captain Cousteau conveys the sense of adventure and the vision that continue to inspire his work"—(*Christian Science Monitor*).

A WORLD WITHOUT SUN. Ed. by James Dugan *Harper* 1965 $15.00

"Cousteau fans will be delighted with this account (published last year in French by Hachette) of Conshelf 2, the underwater colony established and maintained in the Red Sea, 25 miles off Port Sudan, by the Office Française de Recherches Sous-Marines, during the spring and summer of 1963. . . . The purpose of the underwater colony was to determine if men could live, work, and maintain health while continuously subject to great pressure. . . . The photography is outstanding"—(*LJ*).

(With Philippe Cousteau). THE SHARK: Splendid Savage of the Sea. Trans. by F. Price *Doubleday* 1970 $7.95

Their observations and experiences studying sharks in the Red Sea and western Indian Ocean. "Outstanding for its photographs and very well translated from the French, this is a report for scuba divers working where sharks occur and a book for nature lovers"—(*Choice*).

(With Philippe Diole). THE WHALE: Mighty Monarch of the Sea. *Doubleday* 1972 $9.95

(With Philippe Diole). OCTOPUS AND SQUID: The Soft Intelligence. *Doubleday* 1973 $9.95. The intelligence, behavior, mating habits, etc. of octopuses, squid and other cephalopods.

(With Philippe Diole). DIVING COMPANIONS: Sea Lions—Elephant Seal—Walrus. *Doubleday* 1974 $10.95

(With Philippe Diole). DOLPHINS AND FREEDOM. Trans. by J. F. Bernard *Doubleday* 1975
   $12.95

"Observations, experiments, and personal encounters interwoven with historical accounts of
dolphin behavior and speculation about the future of man's relationship with the dolphins"—
(Publisher's note).

SANDERSON, IVAN (TERRANCE).   1911–1973.

Sanderson was a British zoologist who became an American citizen. He had a gift for describing
rare and unusual small animals, as well as illustrating his own books with delightful drawings.
"Animal Treasure" contains an account of adventure in the deep forests of West Africa. "The
Continent We Live On" is a most effective argument for conservation in North America,
illustrated by the author's photographs. "The book begins in the Arctic (black and white of two
polar bears crossing an endless expanse of floe); it ends in the Mexican Sierra (color photo of a
magnificent, snarling jaguar)." For his book about those mysterious creatures, "The Abominable
Snowmen," he scanned "a thousand years of literature, and found 'some hundred separate and
isolated areas in the world where . . . ABSMs have been reported,' including U.S.A. Sanderson, a
student of plant and animal distribution, essays a pseudoscientific approach, basing his research
on the theory that such vegetation-eating creatures must live in montane forest areas, noting that
reports of ABSMs occur only in such places. He classifies all data found in a mass of reports, myth,
legend, folklore and tradition, supporting his point with a multitude of maps. His conclusion is
that ABSMs are 'a valid . . . concrete subject for investigation' "—(*LJ*). He edited "Animal Tales:
An Anthology of Animal Literature of All Countries" (*Knopf* 1946 $8.95).

ANIMAL TREASURE. 1937. *Pyramid Bks.* pap. $.75

HOW TO KNOW THE AMERICAN MAMMALS. *Little* 1951 $6.95

LIVING MAMMALS OF THE WORLD *Doubleday* 1955 $15.95

THE CONTINENT WE LIVE ON. *Random* 1961 $20.00

THE ABOMINABLE SNOWMEN: Legend Come to Life. *Chilton* 1961 $7.50

THE DYNASTY OF ABU: A History and Natural History of the Elephants and Their
   Relatives Past and Present. *Knopf* 1962 $6.95. A thorough and learned history.

THE MONKEY KINGDOM. *Chilton* 1963 $6.50

(With David Loth). IVAN SANDERSON'S BOOK OF GREAT JUNGLES. *Simon & Schuster* 1965
   $9.95 pap. $2.95

"This book is one sense the culmination of his learning; in another, a memoir of his excitement
and experience. In any case, he has parted the green veil to permit an extended glimpse into its
variety and mystery at all levels—plant, animal and human, i.e., pygmy life. The result for the
reader is a coherent, intriguing picture of a much befogged subject. More than 100 photographs,
drawings, and engravings, some by Sanderson himself, in large and handsome format"—(*LJ*).

UNINVITED VISITORS: A Biologist Looks at UFO's. *Regnery* (Cowles) 1967 $6.95

LIVING TREASURE. *Pyramid Bks.* pap. $.75

CARIBBEAN TREASURE. *Pyramid Bks.* pap. $.95

INVISIBLE RESIDENTS: A Disquisition upon Certain Matters Maritime, and the Possibility
   of Intelligent Life under the Waters of this Earth. *T. Y. Crowell* 1970 $7.50; *Avon Bks.*
   1973 pap. $.95

INVESTIGATING THE UNEXPLAINED: A Compendium of Disquieting Mysteries of the
   Natural World. *Prentice-Hall* 1972 $7.95

GREEN SILENCE: Travels through the Jungles of the Orient. Ed. by Sabina Sanderson
   McKay 1974 $7.95

"This posthumous memoir records Sanderson's travels and observations made during a trip he
took in 1928"—(*Best Sellers*).

ADAMSON, JOY.

"Born Free," the amazing story of Elsa, the lioness which Mrs. Adamson brought up and then
trained for wild life, and its sequel, "Living Free," which tells the story of Elsa and her cubs, have
sold nearly two million copies and have been translated into 16 languages. The third book, "Forever
Free," opens sadly with the death of Elsa from an infection, then tells the exciting story of how the
cubs went through many dangers before they could be rescued and finally released in the Serengeti

Park in Tanganyiká. "The story is a fascinating one," wrote Gerald Durrell of "Living Free," "not only for anyone interested in animals, but for the serious student of zoology as well. Her style is pleasantly terse and factual, without any of the anthropomorphic frills that usually attend books of this sort. . . . This is a wonderful and enchanting book."

Joy Adamson, who was born in Austria, has spent over 35 years in Kenya. As a well-known painter, she was commissioned by the Government there to paint Africans of various tribes wearing their traditional costume. In order to make this record she had the unique experience of living for eight years alone among the tribes. She has told this story, with her own African portraits as illustration, in "The Peoples of Kenya" (1967, o.p.). These pictures, together with her pictures of the flowers of Kenya (for which she received the Grenfell Gold Medal of the Royal Horticultural Society), now hang in the Coryndon Museum, Nairobi; while her pictures of the local fish of the African coast of the Indian Ocean have been bought by the municipality of Mombasa. Mrs. Adamson is reticent about her date of birth.

BORN FREE: A Lioness of Two Worlds. *Pantheon* 1960 $6.95; *Random* Vintage Bks. 1974 pap. $1.25

LIVING FREE: The Story of Elsa and Her Cubs. Introd. by Sir Julian Huxley *Harcourt* 1961 $9.50; *Bantam* pap. $.75

FOREVER FREE. *Harcourt* 1963 $9.50; *Bantam* pap. $.75

SPOTTED SPHINX. *Harcourt* 1969 $9.50. Her experiences in changing an eight-month old cheetah, Pippa, from a house pet to one able to fend for herself in the wild.

PIPPA'S CHALLENGE. *Harcourt* 1972 $9.50; *Ballantine Bks.* 1973 pap. $2.00. Close range observations of the development and behavior of two cheetahs from Pippa's litters.

JOY ADAMSON'S AFRICA. *Harcourt* 1972 $13.95

Books about Adamson

A Lifetime with Lions. By George Adamson. *Doubleday* 1968 $6.95
An autobiography of George Adamson, her husband. Mr. Adamson was a Kenya game warden who came to prefer observing animals to hunting them. A third of the book is devoted to his career with his wife since their marriage in 1944, their raising of Elsa and the making of the movie "Born Free." "A great story of a rough, adventurous, rewarding life, told modestly, with gleams of humor and passages of tremendous excitement"—*(PW)*.

HOYLE, FRED. 1915–

The *New Yorker* described "The Nature of the Universe" as a "worthy successor to, and to some extent an intentional revision of, Sir James Jeans' (*q.v.*) 'The Mysterious Universe' and Arthur Eddington's (*q.v.*) 'The Nature of the Physical World.' " The author, head of the Institute of Theoretical Astrophysics at Cambridge University, broadcast these popular lectures over the BBC in England. In a clear and simple style, he discusses great questions of space and time for the general reader and includes some revolutionary speculations as to where we may go tomorrow. He has also written many books of superior science fiction.

THE NATURE OF THE UNIVERSE. *Harper* 1951 rev. ed. 1960 $4.95

FRONTIERS OF ASTRONOMY. *Harper* 1955 $7.50

MAN AND MATERIALISM. 1956. *Bks. for Libraries* $9.50

OF MEN AND GALAXIES. *Univ. of Washington Press* 1966 $2.95 pap. $1.45

GALAXIES, NUCLEI AND QUASARS. *Harper* 1965 $5.95

MAN IN THE UNIVERSE. *Columbia* 1966 $6.00
A monograph of five lectures. "This is a provocative, controversial and stimulating book which should arouse much comment both *pro* and *con*. Highly recommended"—*(LJ)*.

THE NEW FACE OF SCIENCE. *Norton* 1971 $6.95; *New Am. Lib.* Meridian pap. $3.95

FROM STONEHENGE TO MODERN COSMOLOGY. *W. H. Freeman* 1972 $4.95

ENCOUNTER WITH THE FUTURE. Ed. by Ruth N. Anshen *Simon & Schuster* 1965 $4.95. His intellectual autobiography.

ASIMOV, ISAAC. 1920–

An American Associate Professor of Biochemistry at the Boston University School of Medicine and author of over 100 books, Asimov is a noted scientist. When reviewing "The Wellsprings of

Life," the *N.Y. Times* said: "One of the best serious-popular writers about biology is Isaac Asimov, who is that phenomenon, a professional scientist . . . who handles words skillfully. He also realizes that to present a difficult science to intelligent lay readers calls for strategy as well as tactics. . . . Asimov's strategy is to start his book with the age of biological innocence a little more than 100 years ago. . . . With his readers still in a glow of effortless understanding, Asimov hits them with ideas, such as Mendelian inheritance, that call for closer attention. Before they get discouraged, he lets them relax again and hear how leopards got their spots. This alternation of hard and soft material is one of the most effective strategies of popular scientific writing." Born in Russia, he is a graduate of Columbia University (B.S. 1939 M.A. 1941 Ph.D. 1953).

Asimov is also an accomplished writer of science fiction, most of which is published by *Doubleday*, and of books in the field of history as well as books for young people. Many of his collections of serious essays are made up of articles which originally appeared in the *Magazine of Fantasy and Science Fiction*.

THE BEST OF ISAAC ASIMOV. *Doubleday* 1974 $6.95

ASIMOV ON CHEMISTRY. *Doubleday* 1974 $8.95

Essays originally published in the *Magazine of Fantasy and Science Fiction*. "Popular exploration of basic scientific data"—(*Booklist*).

ASIMOV ON ASTRONOMY. *Doubleday* 1974 $8.95. Seventeen essays from earlier o.p. works on all aspects of astronomy.

THE MARVELS OF SCIENCE (orig. "Only a Trillion"). 1958. *Macmillan* Collier Bks. 1962 pap. $.95

Explains how elementary arithmetic can help scientists speculate and arrive at complex conclusions about atoms, hemoglobin, protein structure, and life on other planets. "For those who enjoy Asimov's rather simplified style and anything but simplified imagination—most people do— there is no need for justification"—(*San Francisco Chronicle*).

THE WELLSPRINGS OF LIFE. 1960. *New Am. Lib*. Signet pap. $.95. A popular treatment of evolutionary theory.

LIFE AND ENERGY. 1962. *Avon Bks*. 1972 pap. $1.25

"The author has a lucid style and a sure sense for the logical development of his subject. He uses effective analogies and helpful diagrams. This is not a watered-down treatment, and it does require some study. It is heartily recommended for all public and college libraries."

THE HUMAN BODY: Its Structure and Operation. *Houghton* 1963 $8.95; *New Am. Lib*. Signet 1964 pap. $.95

THE HUMAN BRAIN. *Houghton* 1963 $6.95; *New Am. Lib*. Signet pap. $.95. Companion volume to "The Human Body."

THE GENETIC CODE. 1963. *New Am. Lib*. Signet pap. $.95

This authoritative and exciting book, written for the layman, explains the significance of the new discoveries about deoxyribonucleic acid, commonly known as DNA, and the light cast, by these findings, upon the very nature of life. RNA (ribonucleic acid) is also discussed. "Highly recommended for all school, academic, and public libraries"—(*LJ*).

A SHORT HISTORY OF BIOLOGY. *Doubleday* 1964 pap. $1.25

"Sound in its subject matter and very well written"—(*LJ*).

ASIMOV'S BIOGRAPHICAL ENCYCLOPEDIA OF SCIENCE AND TECHNOLOGY. *Doubleday* 1964 rev. ed. 1972 $12.95

THE UNIVERSE: From Flat Earth to Quasar. *Walker & Co*. 1966 rev. ed. 1971 $7.95; *Avon Bks*. 1965 pap. $.95

A history of astronomy. "The second half requires an understanding of certain phenomena in physics and chemistry. . . . A tremendous amount of material in a clear and orderly fashion"— (*LJ*).

UNDERSTANDING PHYSICS. *Walker & Co*. 3 vols. 1966 Vol. 1 Motion, Sound, and Heat Vol. 2 Light, Magnetism, and Electricity Vol. 3 The Electron, Proton, and Neutron each $7.95; *New Am. Lib*. Signet 3 vols. 1969 pap. each $1.25

"These three volumes should be a valuable addition to the libraries of secondary schools especially. Beginning students in physics should find the lucid explanations most helpful; and the layman desirous of understanding our 'atomic age' could find no better introduction"—(Benjamin Bold, Chairman, Department of Mathematics, Stuyvesant High School).

THE STARS IN THEIR COURSES. *Doubleday* 1971 $5.95; *Ace Bks.* 1972 pap. $1.25. Seventeen essays on various topics in astronomy, physics, chemistry and sociology.

THE LEFT HAND OF THE ELECTRON. *Doubleday* 1972 $6.95; *Dell* 1974 pap. $1.25

ASIMOV'S GUIDE TO SCIENCE. *Basic Bks.* rev. ed. 1972 $15.50

MORE WORDS OF SCIENCE. *Houghton* 1972 $5.95. Defines 250 new terms.

THE ENDS OF THE EARTH: The Polar Regions of the World. *McKay* 1975 $15.00

"Asimov, in another quite fascinating work, describes the basic astronomical conditions of Earth's climates and seasons"—(*LJ*).

EYES ON THE UNIVERSE: A History of the Telescope. *Houghton* 1975 $8.95

"An eminently readable and informative history, intended for the general reader"—(*LJ*).

OF MATTER GREAT AND SMALL. *Doubleday* 1975 $6.95

"A collection of 17 short factual essays"—(*LJ*).

SCIENCE PAST—SCIENCE FUTURE. *Doubleday* 1975 $8.95

Books about Asimov

Isaac Asimov: A Checklist of Work Published in the United States. By Marjorie M. Miller. *Kent State Univ. Press* 1972 $6.50

MOORE, PATRICK (ALFRED).   1923–

"Patrick Moore writes for the mature and ambitious reader, and does it so simply and smoothly that the reader can start with no scientific knowledge whatever and come out as something of an expert"—(Harlow Shapley). A leading astronomer, Patrick Moore, F.R.A.S., F.R.S.A., is also general editor of "The Amateur Astronomer's Library" (*consult Norton catalog for authors and prices*).

SUNS, MYTHS AND MEN. (Orig. "The Story of Man and the Stars") *Norton* 1955 rev. ed. 1969 $7.95. A history of astronomy from the cave man to modern times.

SCIENCE AND FICTION. 1957. *Folcroft* $15.00

SPACE IN THE SIXTIES. 1963. *Gannon* $6.50

A SURVEY OF THE MOON. *Norton* 1963 $6.95

This is a fully revised and expanded edition of "A Guide to the Moon" (*Norton* 1953 $6.50). Some of the earlier material has been kept, but most has been rewritten, and many new findings incorporated. There is an added chapter on "the other side of the moon," including the photographs as released by Russia.

NAKED-EYE ASTRONOMY. *Norton* 1966 $6.50

(With Francis Jackson). LIFE ON MARS. *Norton* 1966 $4.50

"A survey and analysis of the present state of knowledge, theory and research on the Martian atmosphere and surface"—(*LJ*).

(With Peter J. Cattermole). CRATERS OF THE MOON: An Observational Approach. *Norton* 1967 $5.95

THE AMATEUR ASTRONOMER'S GLOSSARY. *Norton* 1967 $5.95

"A basic reference tool"—(*Choice*).

THE SUN. *Norton* 1968 $4.95

AMATEUR ASTRONOMY. (Orig. "The Amateur Astronomer") Amateur Astronomer's Library *Norton* 1956 rev. ed. 1968 $6.95

"A fine, up-to-date handbook for the beginning amateur"—(*LJ*).

SPACE: The Story of Man's Greatest Feat of Exploration. *Doubleday* Natural History Press 1969 $12.95

SEEING STARS. *Rand McNally* 1971 $3.95

THE PICTURE HISTORY OF ASTRONOMY. 1964. *Grosset* rev. ed. 1972 $7.95

"The story of astronomy is told from ancient times up to the moon flights of 1972. . . . This oversized volume is crammed with facts and can be quite useful on both the technical and popular levels"—(*LJ*).

New Guide to the Planets. *Norton* 3rd ed. 1972 $7.95

Challenge of the Stars. *Rand McNally* 1972 $6.95

Can You Speak Venusian? A Guide to Independent Thinkers. *Norton* 1973 $6.95

"Moore writes of people who are firm believers in the flatness of the earth and in visitors from Venus, among others. . . . The author simply presents the reader with some unusual notions, perhaps held by a larger number of persons than we may know, in a delightfully lively and humorous style"—*(LJ)*.

(With Charles A. Cross). Mars. *Crown* 1973 $7.95

Patrick Moore's Color Star Atlas. *Crown* 1974 $7.95

Watchers of the Stars. *Putnam* 1974 $15.95

(Ed.). The Atlas of the Universe. *Rand McNally* 1970 $35.00

(Ed.). Astronomical Telescopes and Observatories for Amateurs. *Norton* 1973 $7.95

"Consists of a collection of 14 essays on the construction of various types of telescopes and related devices. Although a vast amount of detailed instructions on making the equipment is presented, the style is easy to follow"—*(LJ)*.

(Ed.). Yearbook of Astronomy, 1975. *Norton* 1975 $8.95 1976 ed. (in prep.) Published annually. Back editions for 1970 and 1971 available at $4.95 each.

MATTHIESSEN, PETER. 1927–

This naturalist and novelist, who was born in New York City, was graduated from Yale and attended the Sorbonne, has had a career as varied as his books. He taught creative writing at Yale; was one of the founders of the *Paris Review*; engaged in commercial fishing and operated a charter boat out of Montauk, Long Island; has lived in Europe, chiefly in Paris; has accompanied expeditions into the Canadian Northwest Territories and the rain forests of Peru, and has visited wild areas of all five continents.

"Wildlife in America" is a "survey of the white man's effect on the fishes, amphibians, reptiles, birds and mammals of North America, from the earliest records to the present day." The *Chicago Tribune* said of it: "Thoroughness is one of the many virtues of this book. [Another] is its style. . . . It is vigorous and resourceful, equally able to convey factual information and to evoke a mood." Of "The Cloud Forest," the *N.Y. Times* wrote: "Mr. Matthiessen . . . is master of a clean, dry, straightforward prose that is yet vivid and often aptly picturesque. Beneath this prose, there is an extraordinary perception." "Under the Mountain Wall" combines "documentary value with a haunting literary quality." The author was a member of the Peabody-Harvard Expedition, the first white men to contact and observe the Kurelu. This "account of the daily life, work, play, war and death among the Kurelu tribe of Central New Guinea—living survivors of the Stone Age" is "a precious record of a way of life doomed to disappearance."

Wildlife in America. Ill. by Bob Hines *Viking* 1959 Compass Bks. 1964 pap. $2.25

The Cloud Forest: A Chronicle of the South American Wilderness. *Viking* 1961 $6.50; *Ballantine Bks.* 1973 pap. $1.65; *Pyramid Bks.* pap. $.75

Under the Mountain Wall: A Chronicle of Two Seasons in the Stone Age. *Viking* 1962 $7.50

Oomingmak: The Expedition to the Musk Ox Island in the Bering Sea. *Hastings House* 1967 $3.95

The Shorebirds of North America. Ed. by Gardner D. Stout *Viking* 1967 $22.50

Blue Meridian: The Search for the Great White Shark. *New Am. Lib.* 1973 pap. $1.50. His experiences on a world expedition in 1969 and 1970 with Peter Gimbel and a crew of professional divers to find and film underwater the great white shark.

The Wind Birds. *Viking* 1973 $9.95

Far Tortuga. *Random* 1975 $10.95. His account of the men and life on a turtle boat out of Grand Cayman in the Caribbean to a remote island south of Cuba.

(With Eliot Porter). The Tree Where Man was Born. *Dutton* 1972 $17.50; (and "The African Experience") *Avon Bks.* 1974 pap. $6.95. His travels and observations in Africa from 1960 to 1970, with color photography by Eliot Porter.

LAWICK-GOODALL, JANE, Baroness VAN.   1934–

An ethologist and writer, Jane Goodall began her scientific career as an assistant to Dr. Louis Leakey in Nairobi. After returning to England to secure financial backing, she conducted a field study in Kenya on the behavior of chimpanzees that brought her worldwide fame. Miss Goodall discovered that chimps are not exclusively vegetarians and that they often make and use simple tools for food gathering. Her method of lengthy observations of a small number of animals has been very influential in the scientific behavioral community. She was the eighth person to receive a Ph.D. from Cambridge University without having previously earned a B.A.

Her husband, Baron Hugo Van Lawick, does all the color photography for her television programs and books, and has written "Solo: The Story of the African Wild Dog" (*Houghton* 1974 $6.95) which has detailed information on the hunting, mating, and pup-rearing behavior of wild dogs.

MY FRIENDS THE WILD CHIMPANZEES. *National Geographic Soc.* 1968 $4.25

"Her field observations of chimps in the Gombe Stream Game Reserve cover family structure and social interactions"—(*Natural History*).

IN THE SHADOW OF MAN. *Houghton* 1971 $10.00; *Dell* 1972 pap. $1.50 Delta Bks. 1974 pap. $2.95. A report of ten years of field observation of the chimpanzee group—their individual personalities, family patterns, behavior, etc.

(With Hugo Van Lawick). INNOCENT KILLERS. *Houghton* 1971 $10.00; *Ballantine Bks.* 1973 pap. $2.00

"Wild dogs, jackals and hyenas have a bad name, but the authors, studying them in Serengeti Park, found the creatures no meaner than any other animals who make an honest living by eating their neighbors"—(Phoebe Adams in *Atlantic*).

(With Hugo Van Lawick). GRUB: The Bush Baby. *Houghton* 1972 $4.95. The story of their son who was born in Africa and reared close to the chimpanzees.

Chapter 8

The Social Sciences

"Since he came down from the trees, man has faced the problem of survival, not as an individual but as a member of a social group. His continued existence is testimony to the fact that he has succeeded in solving the problem; but the continued existence of want and misery, even in the richest of nations, is evidence that his solution has been, at best, a partial one."

—ROBERT L. HEILBRONER

"Social Science is still quite fashionable today," Marc Roberts noted in a recent essay in *Daedalus* (Summer, 1974). "Public interest and support continue at high levels." At the same time, however, many liberal and radical intellectuals question its usefulness to society in the light of rising crime, unemployment, poverty, and inflation. The much vaunted "professional detachment" of social scientists toward these pressing social problems has been denounced as immoral if not anti-social. Social scientists have responded to this criticism by undertaking more applied research projects and by reporting their findings to an increasingly large nonspecialist public. They have also accepted an expanded public role "by way of the mass media, opinion polls, and the popular representation of specialized research." Works by such respected scholars as John K. Galbraith, David Riesman, Erving Goffman and Desmond Morris have even turned into best sellers.

In this edition of *"The Reader's Adviser"* we have continued the organization of the previous volume with a few changes. A glance at the table of contents will show this organization clearly. There are now five selected lists: Anthropology, Economics, Education, Sociology, and Society in Modern America. This last category includes works on the major social and economic problems of the day, particularly those arising from our recent Recession and its impact on the general population.

The number of entires in these book lists has increased significantly, and they have been broken down into pertinent subject categories. Works reporting basic research are listed alongside well-written popularizations of empirical studies. A number of "modern classics," still in print, have been included because social science research has always been a collective endeavor and the works of pioneer social scientists are still frequently cited in the classroom and consulted in faculty study rooms.

See also Chapter 6, Psychology, this Vol.

GENERAL HISTORIES AND REFERENCE WORKS

Various volumes of value to trained social workers and for reference use in academic libraries are published by *Columbia* for the National Conference on Social Welfare (1949– $2.25–$6.00; *consult publisher's catalog for individual titles.*)

See also special Reading Lists which follow and Chapter 1, Reference Books—General: Biographical Reference Works, Yearbooks, Almanacs, this Vol., for reference works in specific areas.

AMERICAN MEN AND WOMEN OF SCIENCE. Ed. by Jaques Cattell Press *Bowker* 7 vols. 13th ed. 1976 each $50.00

Six biographee volumes, alphabetically arranged, contain profiles of some 110,000 U.S. and Canadian scientists now working and teaching in 1,000 areas of science, including selected social sciences. Each entry includes full name, discipline, education, professional experience, memberships, areas of research and specialization, and address. The seventh volume is the geographic and disciplinary index, which indexes all of the scientists listed in Volumes 1–6 by both location and areas of professional specialization.

Beals, Ralph L. THE POLITICS OF SOCIAL RESEARCH: An Inquiry into the Ethics and Responsibilities of Social Scientists. *Aldine* 1969 $8.95

Becker, Howard, and Harry E. Barnes. SOCIAL THOUGHT FROM LORE TO SCIENCE. 1961. *Dover* 3 vols. rev. ed. 1966 pap. each $3.50; *Peter Smith* 3 vols. 3rd ed. 1961 each $6.00

Denzin, Norman K., Ed. THE VALUES OF SOCIAL SCIENCE. *Transaction Bks.* rev. 2nd ed. 1973 $9.95 pap. $3.95

ENCYCLOPEDIA OF SOCIAL WORK. Ed. by Robert Morris *National Assn. of Social Workers* 1971 $22.50. Published at 3-year intervals.

Freides, Thelma K. LITERATURE AND BIBLIOGRAPHY OF THE SOCIAL SCIENCES. *Wiley* (Melville Press) 1973 $12.95

Ginger, Ray, Ed. AMERICAN SOCIAL THOUGHT. *Farrar, Straus* (Hill & Wang) 1961 $4.00. Twelve selections from the individuals who formulated American social thought, including William James, John Dewey, Charles S. Peirce, Oliver Wendell Holmes, Jr., C. H. Cooley, Eugene V. Debs, Samuel Gompers, Jane Addams and others.

Goode, William J., and others. SOCIAL SYSTEMS AND FAMILY PATTERNS: A Propositional Inventory. *Bobbs* 1971 $30.00

"It places at [our] fingertips a vast mine of organized material that would not otherwise be accessible without great effort"—(*Choice*).

Hasenfeld, Yeheskal, and Richard A. English, Eds. HUMAN SERVICE ORGANIZATIONS: A Book of Readings. *Univ. of Michigan Press* 1974 $15.00

Hoselitz, Berthold F., Ed. A READER'S GUIDE TO THE SOCIAL SCIENCES. *Macmillan* (Free Press) rev. ed. 1970 $9.25

"Each chapter discusses the type of literary output for the field and the nature and use of available tools such as books, journals, pamphlets, and reference works"—(Publisher's note).

INTERNATIONAL BIBLIOGRAPHY OF THE SOCIAL SCIENCES. Ed. by UNESCO International Comm. for Social Sciences Documentation *Aldine* 4 vols. Vol. 1 Social and Cultural Anthropology Vol. 2 Economics Vol. 3 Political Science Vol. 4 Sociology each $25.00 back vols. 1960–1970 each $15.00

INTERNATIONAL ENCYCLOPEDIA OF THE SOCIAL SCIENCES. Ed. by David L. Sills and others *Macmillan* (Free Press) 17 vols. 1968 each $55.00 set $495.00

The "IESS" was designed, according to the editors, "to complement, not to supplant its predecessor, the 'Encyclopaedia of the Social Sciences' " (*see below under Seligman, Edwin R. A.*). The new work "consists of 17 volumes, with 1716 signed original articles written especially for it by 1505 social science scholars from 33 different countries"—(*PW*). In its review, *Choice* said: "The 'IESS' represents the most significant publishing event in the field of social sciences in the last 25 years. It fills a keenly felt need of the postwar generation of students and scholars for a truly modern synthesis of all important scholarly achievements in 10 distinct and several related subfields of contemporary social science. Reference departments of college and research libraries . . . cannot afford not to acquire this . . . set that will remain a valuable and indispensable research tool for some time to come."

Kister, Kenneth. SOCIAL ISSUES AND LIBRARY PROBLEMS: Case Studies in the Social Sciences. *Bowker* 1968 $12.95

"A work designed to help librarians with the problems that arise in dealing with the literature of the social sciences. Using actual case studies, it explores such broad areas as censorship, politics, civil rights, etc., as they are related to library collections"—(Publisher's note).

Kolb, William J., and Julius Gould, Eds. UNESCO DICTIONARY OF THE SOCIAL SCIENCES. Comp. under the auspices of UNESCO; fwd. by the Secretariat of UNESCO *Macmillan* (Free Press) 1964 $19.95

"Undoubtedly the best one-volume dictionary of the language of the social scientist available today"—(*LJ*).

Levitas, Gloria B., Ed. CULTURE AND CONSCIOUSNESS: Perspectives in the Social Sciences. *Braziller* 1967 $7.50. An anthology of selections from the works of 31 authors including Freud, Marx, Herbert Spencer, Durkheim, Weber, Mannheim, MacIver, Lorenz, Parsons and others.

Lynd, Robert S. KNOWLEDGE FOR WHAT: The Place of Social Science in American Culture. 1939. *Princeton Univ. Press* 1969 $10.00 pap. $2.95

McInnis, Raymond G., and James W. Scott. SOCIAL SCIENCE RESEARCH HANDBOOK. *Harper* (Barnes & Noble) 1974 $10.00

"The aim of this book is to provide students and others doing research in the social sciences with an integrated and analytical guide to sources of information available in most academic libraries"—(Preface).

MAIN TRENDS OF RESEARCH IN THE SOCIAL AND HUMAN SCIENCES: Part One, Social Sciences. *Mouton* (dist. by Humanities Press) 1971 $25.50

"This well planned, authoritative study is the best up-to-date general treatment of social science research capabilities currently available"—(*Choice*).

Mason, John Brown. RESEARCH RESOURCES: Annotated Guide to the Social Sciences. *American Bibliographical Center-Clio Press* 2 vols. 1968–1971 Vol. 1 International Relations and Recent History: Indexes, Abstracts, and Periodicals (1968) pap. $4.50 Vol. 2 Official Publications: U.S. Government, United Nations, International Organizations, and Statistical Sources (1971) $11.95 pap. $5.95

Parsons, Talcott, and Edward A. Shils, Eds. TOWARD A GENERAL THEORY OF ACTION: Theoretical Foundations for the Social Sciences. *Harvard Univ. Press* 1951 $13.50; *Harper* Torchbks. pap. $3.25

Rosenberg, Marie Barovic, and Len V. Bergstrom, Eds. WOMEN AND SOCIETY: A Critical Review of Literature with a Selected Annotated Bibliography. *Russell Sage* (dist. by Harper) 1975

Saveth, Edward N., Ed. AMERICAN HISTORY AND THE SOCIAL SCIENCES. *Macmillan* (Free Press) 1964 $10.95

Seligman, Edwin R. A., Ed. ENCYCLOPAEDIA OF THE SOCIAL SCIENCES. *Macmillan* 15 vols. 1930–1935 o.p. popular ed. 8 vols. 1937 each $40.00 set $195.00

The outstanding, basic reference book for the social sciences as a whole, projected and prepared under the auspices of ten learned societies. It "aims to cover all important topics in the fields of political science, economics, law, anthropology, sociology, penology and social work, and the social aspects of ethics, education, philosophy, psychology, biology, geography, medicine, art, etc." It is international in scope but the emphasis is on the English-speaking world and western Europe. The articles are by specialists and signed with full names.

Sessions, Vivian S., Ed. DIRECTORY OF DATA BASES IN THE SOCIAL AND BEHAVIORAL SCIENCES. *Science Associates* 1974 $35.00

"Although the preponderance of entries is for the United States, institutions in about forty other countries are [also] listed"—(*College & Research Libraries*).

Showers, Victor. THE WORLD IN FIGURES. *Wiley* 1973 $12.50

"A digest of significant, authoritative and comparable statistical information about 250 countries, 1600 cities, and 200 other geographic and cultural features completely cross-referenced and indexed"—(Publisher's note).

Tipple, John, Ed. THE PRAGMATIC NATION: A History of American Social Thought Since 1865. *Pegasus* 4 vols. projected 1967–   Vols. 1 & 4 (in prep.); Vol. 2 The Capitalist Revolution: A History of American Social Thought, 1890–1919 (1970) $7.95 pap. $2.95 Vol. 3 The Crisis of the American Dream: A History of American Social Thought 1920–1940 (1967) pap. $2.95

"This study by Professor Tipple is lucid, urbane, and thoroughly documented. Although it only occasionally includes material not available in standard histories of the period, it synthesizes and updates the conclusions of older accounts. Much more important, Mr. Tipple supplements his own record of the era with primary source comments by such writers and speakers as Warren Harding, Eugene Debs, John L. Lewis, Walter Lippmann, Lewis Mumford, Lincoln Steffens, F. Scott Fitzgerald, and Alfred North Whitehead. The dual approach of publishing contemporary records in the same books with Mr. Tipple's historical interpretations is very commendable and welcome"—(*LJ*, reviewing Vol. 3).

U.S. Library of Congress. National Referral Center. A DIRECTORY OF INFORMATION RESOURCES IN THE UNITED STATES: Social Sciences. *U.S. Library of Congress* rev. ed. 1973 $10.00

White, Carl M., and associates. SOURCES OF INFORMATION IN THE SOCIAL SCIENCES: A Guide to the Literature. *American Lib. Assn.* 2nd ed. 1973 $25.00

"An annotated bibliography of basic books and reference works in history, economics and business administration, sociology, anthropology, education, psychology, and political science. Each subject is covered by a specialist in the field"—(Publisher's note).

White, Morton. SOCIAL THOUGHT IN AMERICA. 1949. *Beacon* 1957 pap. $2.45; *Peter Smith* $4.50

ANTHROPOLOGY

The American Museum Source Books in Anthropology Series of *Doubleday* Natural History Press is a noteworthy one in this area.

Alland, Alexander. WHEN THE SPIDER DANCED. *Doubleday* 1975 $8.95. About the Abron people on the Ivory Coast.

Ardrey, Robert. AFRICAN GENESIS. *Atheneum* 1961 $9.95; *Dell* Laurel Bks. pap. $.95 Delta Bks. pap. $1.95

"Fascinating stuff"—(*PW*).

THE TERRITORIAL IMPERATIVE: A Personal Inquiry into the Animal Origins of Property and Nations. Ill. by Berdine Ardrey *Atheneum* 1966 $10.95; *Dell* Delta Bks. 1968 pap. $2.45 Laurel Bks. 1971 pap. $1.25

"Recommended with elation. . . . *The Territorial Imperative* will be attacked as well as defended, for it dares to go out on many an anthropological and biological limb. . . . It is a pioneer, trail-blazing effort. . . . There is hardly a page from which the intelligent reader will not learn something new"—(Clifton Fadiman). *See* Ashley Montagu's main entry, this Chapter, however, for a dissenting opinion shared by many scholars.

Bicchieri, M. G., Ed. HUNTERS AND GATHERERS TODAY: A Socioeconomic Study of Eleven Such Cultures in the Twentieth Century. *Holt* (Rinehart) 1972 $10.00

"The 11 original chapters written for this book testify to the considerable current interest in people who up to recently survived entirely through hunting, fishing, and gathering"—(*Choice*).

Boas, Franz. *See his main entry, this Chapter.*

Boyd, Doug. ROLLING THUNDER: A Personal Exploration into the Secret Healing Powers of an American Indian Medicine Man. *Random* 1975 $8.95

"This work is at once a fascinating chronicle of a shaman's power—whether it is used to heal an infected leg or to cause rain and thunder to appear out of nowhere—and at the same time a major document of Indian culture and society"—(*LJ*).

Brill, Charles. INDIAN AND FREE: A Contemporary Portrait of Life on a Chippewa Reservation. *Univ. of Minnesota Press* 1974 $9.75

Bushnell, G. H. S. THE FIRST AMERICANS: The Pre-Columbian Civilizations. Library of the Early Civilizations Ser. *McGraw-Hill* 1968 $5.50 pap. $3.95

Campbell, Joseph. THE MASKS OF GOD. *Viking* 4 vols. 1959–1968 Vol. 1 Primitive Mythology (1959) $8.95 pap. $3.25 Vol. 2 Oriental Mythology (1962) $8.95 pap. $3.75 Vol. 3 Occidental Mythology (1964) $8.95 pap. $3.75 Vol. 4 Creative Mythology (1968) $12.50 pap. $4.50 boxed set $32.95

Cohen, David Steven. THE RAMAPO MOUNTAIN PEOPLE. *Rutgers Univ. Press* 1974 $15.00

"This book is about a group of people who have no name for themselves. They are known to their neighbors as the Jackson whites, a name that is offensive to them. . . . They are found today principally in three communities where the Ramapos cross the border between southeastern New York and northern New Jersey"—(*LJ*).

Cooley, Charles Horton. *See his main entry, this Chapter.*

Coon, Carleton S. *See his main entry, this Chapter.*

Durkheim, Émile, and Marcel Mauss. PRIMITIVE CLASSIFICATION. Trans. by Rodney Needham *Univ. of Chicago Press* 1963 $5.00 Phoenix Bks. pap. $1.95

See also Durkheim's main entry, this Chapter.

Frantz, Charles. THE STUDENT ANTHROPOLOGIST'S HANDBOOK: A Guide to Research Training and Career. *Schenkman* 1972 pap. $2.95

Fried, Morton H. THE STUDY OF ANTHROPOLOGY. *T. Y. Crowell* 1972 pap. $3.95

(Ed.). READINGS IN ANTHROPOLOGY. *T. Y. Crowell* 1959 2 vols. 2nd ed. 1968 pap. each $5.95

Gans, Herbert J. THE URBAN VILLAGERS: Group and Class in the Life of Italian-Americans. *Macmillan* (Free Press) 1962 $8.95 pap. $2.95

Geertz, Clifford. THE INTERPRETATION OF CULTURES: Selected Essays. *Basic Bks.* 1973 $15.00

"A collection of essays by one of the most articulate cultural anthropologists of this generation. . . . This volume is important for specialists in anthropology, and it would also be useful for advanced students in the social sciences"—*(Choice)*.

Glob, P. V. THE MOUND PEOPLE: Danish Bronze-Age Man Preserved. *Cornell Univ. Press* 1974 $12.50

"Numerous photographs and drawings support a stimulating and fascinating text that offers new insights on early Scandinavian settlements"—*(LJ)*.

Goldman, Irving. ANCIENT POLYNESIAN SOCIETY. *Univ. of Chicago Press* 1970 $17.50

This book "focuses particularly upon a concept of status system as central to social and cultural description and analysis"—*(Choice)*.

Harris, Marvin. COWS, PIGS, WARS AND WITCHES: The Riddles of Culture. *Random* 1974 $7.95

"An anthropology professor and author explores the reasons for such cultural phenomena as pig hate and cow love, and attempts to shed some light on riddles of culture ranging from potlatch to pot head"—*(LJ)*.

CULTURE, MAN AND NATURE: An Introduction to General Anthropology. *T. Y. Crowell* 1971 $10.95

Hatch, Elvin. THEORIES OF MAN AND CULTURE. *Columbia* 1973 $12.50

"Hatch provides the profession with the first comprehensive and dispassionate history of the discipline since . . . 1937"—*(Choice)*.

Herskovits, Melville J. CULTURAL ANTHROPOLOGY. *Knopf* 1955 $10.95

ECONOMIC ANTHROPOLOGY. (Orig. "Economic Life of Primitive Peoples") *Norton* 1965 pap. $3.95

Hibben, Frank C. THE LOST AMERICANS. 1946. *T. Y. Crowell* rev. ed. 1968 $5.95; *Apollo* pap. $1.25; *Peter Smith* $4.25

Hoben, Alan. LAND TENURE AMONG THE AMHARA OF ETHIOPIA: The Dynamics of Cognatic Descent. *Univ. of Chicago Press* 1973 $9.50

Howells, William W. THE PACIFIC ISLANDERS. *Scribner* 1974 $12.50 pap. $4.95

"Howells makes an admirable effort to outline the prehistory of Oceania from the earliest appearance of man in Australia 30,000 years ago through the settlement and occupation of the various island groups. . . . Howells is a most capable author and this is an excellent review of Oceania"—*(Choice)*.

Hymes, Dell, Ed. REINVENTING ANTHROPOLOGY. *Pantheon* 1972 $12.95

"What is anthropology? If it didn't exist would it be invented now? And if so, what form would it take? In this provocative book, 16 anthropologists pose these questions and others, and offer their viewpoints on what anthropology is and what it should be doing. . . . This study should be read by all anthropologists"—*(LJ)*.

Jorgensen, Joseph G. THE SUN DANCE RELIGION: Power for the Powerless. *Univ. of Chicago Press* 1972 $20.00

"Here is ethnohistory at its best, but with a bit more detail on Sun Dance rituals than the average historian may want to read"—*(American Historical Review)*.

Klein, Richard G. ICE-AGE HUNTERS OF THE UKRAINE. *Univ. of Chicago Press* 1973 $6.50
    pap. $2.95

> Klein "reveals substantial information gathered by Russian scientists concerning Neanderthal
> and early modern man that has been unknown to Western scholars"—(*LJ*).

Kluckhohn, Clyde. *See his main entry, this Chapter.*

Kroeber, Alfred Louis. *See his main entry, this Chapter.*

Leakey, L. S. B. *See his main entry, this Chapter.*

Levison, Michael, and others. THE SETTLEMENT OF POLYNESIA: A Computer Simulation.
    Univ. of Minnesota Press 1973 $10.75

> "From shores as far east as the Americas, as far west as Melanesia, and from Hawaii down to
> New Zealand 101,106 simulated drift voyages and 8,052 crew-directed voyages were launched,
> after the input of such data as winds and surface currents of the Pacific"—(*LJ*).

Lévi-Strauss, Claude. AN INTRODUCTION TO A SCIENCE OF MYTHOLOGY. Trans. by J. and
    D. Weightman *Harper* 4 vols. projected 1969–   Vol. 1 The Raw and the Cooked
    (1969) $12.50 Torchbks. 1970 pap. $2.95 Vol. 2 From Honey to Ashes (1973) $16.00

> This translation, "the first of a projected four volume *Mythologiques* (three have now been
> published in France) by Lévi-Strauss, professor of social anthropology (College de France) . . .
> constitutes the first full-scale demonstration of the methodology developed and called by the
> author, structural anthropology"—(*Choice*).

Levy, Jerrold Edgar, and Stephen J. Kunitz. INDIAN DRINKING: Navajo Practices and
    Anglo-American Theories. *Wiley* 1974 $12.50

> "Why Indians drink is a question Levy and Kunitz, an anthropologist and a medically trained
> sociologist, approach with data they collected among four groups of Navajo . . . and from the Hopi
> and White Mountain Apache. They found no single answer"—(*Choice*).

Liebow, Elliot. TALLEY'S CORNER: A Study of Negro Streetcorner Men. Fwd. by Hylan
    Lewis *Little* 1967 $6.95 pap. $2.75

> "An eloquent vindication of, and plea for, anthropological investigations of Black Ghetto life"—
> (Publisher's note).

Linton, Ralph. *See his main entry, this Chapter.*

Littlewood, Robert. PHYSICAL ANTHROPOLOGY OF THE EASTERN HIGHLANDS OF NEW
    GUINEA. *Univ. of Washington Press* 1973 $10.00

> "The present volume is superb in style, coverage, illustrations, and authority. It seems suitable
> for senior-level students with some background in genetics, statistics, and physical anthropolo-
> gy"—(*Choice*).

Lorenz, Konrad. *See his main entry, this Chapter.*

Mails, Thomas E. THE PEOPLE CALLED APACHE. *Prentice-Hall* 1974 $25.00

> "This combination of history, anthropology and art describes the four branches of the Apaches:
> Western, Chiricahua, Mescalero, and Jicarilla. . . . An obvious labor of love, this beautiful book will
> instill a new appreciation of the rich Apache heritage of the Southwest"—(*LJ*).

Mair, Lucy. AFRICAN SOCIETIES. *Cambridge* 1974 $12.50 pap. $3.95

> "Mair draws upon published ethnographies of 18 tropical African societies, using each society
> to illustrate a different problem posed by social anthropologists"—(*LJ*).

Mead, Margaret. *See her main entry, this Chapter.*

Milner, Christina, and Richard Milner. BLACK PLAYERS: The Secret World of Black
    Pimps. *Bantam* 1973 pap. $1.50

Montagu, M. F. Ashley. *See his main entry, this Chapter.*

Murphy, Yolanda, and Robert F. Murphy. WOMEN OF THE FOREST. *Columbia* 1975 $10.00
    pap. $3.45

> "Years of learning to know and to write about the Amazonian Mundurucu assuredly explains
> the simple excellence of this theme"—(Earl W. Count).

Nance, John. THE GENTLE TASADAY: A Stone Age People in the Philippine Rain Forest.
    Harcourt 1975 $15.00

Oliver, Douglas L. ANCIENT TAHITIAN SOCIETY. *Univ. Press of Hawaii* 3 vols. 1975 set
   $55.00
   An "important publication in anthropology"—(*Choice*).

Pinney, Roy. VANISHING TRIBES. *T. Y. Crowell* 1968 $8.95

Pospisil, Leopold. ANTHROPOLOGY OF LAW: A Comparative Theory. *Harper* 1971 $9.95
   "By a major scholar in the field, this book is an important, eminently readable contribution to
   legal anthropology and to the comparative study of law in society"—(*Choice*).

Radcliffe-Brown, Alfred R. METHOD IN SOCIAL ANTHROPOLOGY. Ed. by M. R. Srinivas.
   Univ. of Chicago Press 1958 $7.00

   STRUCTURE AND FUNCTION IN PRIMITIVE SOCIETY. *Macmillan* (Free Press) 1952 $7.95
   pap. $1.95

Rainwater, Lee. BEHIND GHETTO WALLS: Black Family Life in a Federal Slum. *Aldine* 1970
   $12.50 pap. $4.95

Rapport, Samuel, and Helen Wright, Eds. ANTHROPOLOGY. Fwd. by Joseph Bram *New
   York Univ. Press* 1967 $6.95; *Simon & Schuster* (Washington Square) 1968 pap. $.90. A
   compilation of papers by L. S. B. Leakey, J. Gunnar Andersson, Bronislaw Malinowski, Claude Lévi-Strauss, Ruth Benedict and others.

Redfield, Robert. THE PRIMITIVE WORLD AND ITS TRANSFORMATIONS. *Cornell Univ. Press*
   1957 1967 $6.50 pap. $1.95

Reichel-Dolmatoff, G. THE SHAMAN AND THE JAGUAR: A Study of Narcotic Drugs among
   the Indians of Colombia. *Temple Univ. Press* 1975 $15.00
   "A beginning for further investigation by anthropologists and ethnobiologists"—(*LJ*).

Reiter, Rayna, Ed. TOWARD AN ANTHROPOLOGY OF WOMEN. *Monthly Review* 1975 $15.00
   These "papers present a very different, yet not radically feminist look at human evolution, the
   origin of the family, and the role of women in a variety of cultural settings"—(*LJ*).

Rosaldo, Michelle Z., and Louise Lamphere, Eds. WOMAN, CULTURE, AND SOCIETY.
   Stanford Univ. Press 1974 $12.50 pap. $3.95
   "[These] essays . . . begin to fill a void in the field of anthropology by asking new questions about
   sex roles and the relationship of women to economics, politics, reproduction, and socialization. . . . For the most part the essays are parts of larger studies, and the volume serves a useful
   purpose . . . as an introduction to recently completed work or work in progress"—(*Choice*).

Schneider, Harold K. ECONOMIC MAN: The Anthropology of Economics. *Macmillan* (Free
   Press) 1974 $8.95
   "For a subject fraught with debate, [the author] provides a *vade mecum* indispensable for any
   advanced undergraduate or graduate student taking a course in the subject"—(*Choice*).

Seibel, H. D., and A. Massing. TRADITIONAL ORGANIZATIONS AND ECONOMIC DEVEL-
   OPMENT: Studies of Indigenous Cooperatives in Liberia. *Praeger* 1974 $10.00

Shapiro, Harry L., Ed. MAN, CULTURE AND SOCIETY. *Oxford* 1956 Galaxy Bks. rev. ed.
   1971 pap. $3.50. Essays for the general reader by the most eminent scholars in the
   field of social anthropology.

Southall, Aidan, Ed. URBAN ANTHROPOLOGY: Cross-Cultural Studies of Urbanization.
   Oxford 1973 pap. $4.95

Tax, Sol, Ed. HORIZONS OF ANTHROPOLOGY. *Aldine* 1964 pap. $3.45
   Twenty-one essays serving as "a guide to what we know and what we have yet to learn about
   human nature and behavior"—(Publisher's note).

   SERIAL PUBLICATIONS IN ANTHROPOLOGY. *Univ. of Chicago Press* 1973 $5.95 pap. $2.95

Teilhard de Chardin, Pierre. THE PHENOMENON OF MAN. Introd. by Julian Huxley *Harper*
   1959 Torchbks. 1961 pap. $1.95
   Father Teilhard, philosopher, paleontologist and discoverer of Peking Man, has presented us
   "with a humanism that is at once scientific in its grounding and religious in its last implication."—
   (James Collins).

   See also his main entry in Chapter 4, World Religions, this Vol.

Turnbull, Colin M. THE MOUNTAIN PEOPLE. *Simon & Schuster* 1972 $7.95

U.S.S.R. Academy of Sciences. VILLAGE OF VIRIATINO: An Ethnographic Study of a Russian Village from the Revolution to the Present. Ed. by Sula Benet *Doubleday* 1971 pap. $1.95

"An ethnographic study of a collective-farm village in central Russia, conducted by a group of researchers from the Institute of Ethnography of the U.S.S.R. Academy of Sciences in the mid-1950's"—*(Choice)*.

Vayda, Andrew P., Ed. ENVIRONMENT AND CULTURAL BEHAVIOR: Ecological Studies in Cultural Anthropology. *Doubleday* Natural History Press 1969 $7.95 pap. $4.50

PEOPLES AND CULTURES OF THE PACIFIC: An Anthropological Reader. *Doubleday* Natural History Press 1968 $9.95 pap. $4.50. Twenty-four essays on the South Pacific by Mead, Grace, Goodenough, Malinowski and others.

Washburn, Sherwood L., and Ruth Moore. APE INTO MAN: A Study of Human Evolution. *Little* 1973 pap. $3.95

Worth, Sol, and John Adair. THROUGH NAVAJO EYES: An Exploration in Film Communication and Anthropology. *Indiana Univ. Press* 1973 $12.50

"A valuable pioneer study in an important area of research"—*(Choice)*.

Yoors, Jan. THE GYPSIES. *Simon & Schuster* 1967 $6.95 Touchstone-Clarion Bks. 1969 pap. $1.75

At the age of 12, Jan Yoors joined a Romany Gypsy family as their adopted son and traveled with them for ten years throughout Europe. His account is "an exciting first hand impression of life in a Gypsy camp forever on the move. A most valuable and original contribution"—*(N.Y. Times)*.

THE GYPSIES OF SPAIN. *Macmillan* 1974 $12.95

ECONOMICS

An important series is Industry and the American Economy, published by the *National Association of Manufacturers*. The *United Nations* publishes a number of annual economic surveys such as the "Economic Survey of Europe," "Economic Survey of Africa" and "World Economic Survey" *(consult publisher's catalog for individual titles and prices)*. *Augustus M. Kelley's* publisher's catalog contains an extensive list of reprints of economic classics.

Adams, Walter. THE STRUCTURE OF AMERICAN INDUSTRY. *Macmillan* 4th ed. 1971 pap. $7.95. Selected articles which analyze specific industries.

Adelman, Irma, and Cynthia T. Morris. ECONOMIC GROWTH AND SOCIAL EQUITY IN DEVELOPING COUNTRIES. *Stanford Univ. Press.* 1974 $10.00

"An elaborate and statistically sophisticated effort to review the process of political, economic, and social development by examining the records of 74 underdeveloped countries for the period 1957–1968. . . . An outstanding work in the development field"—*(Choice)*.

Adelman, Morris A. THE WORLD PETROLEUM MARKET. *Johns Hopkins Press* 1973 $22.50

"Adelman offers a provocative and controversial analysis of the economic factors underlying recent developments in the oil industry, especially the changing relationships between oil producing countries and companies"—*(Choice)*.

Agarwala, Amar N., and S. P. Singh, Eds. ACCELERATING INVESTMENT IN DEVELOPING ECONOMICS. *Oxford* 1969 $8.50

Alexander, Herbert E. MONEY IN POLITICS. *Public Affairs Press* 1972 $10.00

This book "is by far the most thorough, comprehensive study of financing American politics and the ramifications of various methods of finance"—*(Choice)*.

Bach, George L. MAKING MONETARY AND FISCAL POLICY. *Brookings* 1971 $7.50

"Bach is a professor of economics at Stanford University and the author of a widely used textbook in basic economics. In this new work he discusses the tensions or power struggles that exist between various fiscal policy-making entities"—*(LJ)*.

Baldwin, Robert E. NONTARIFF DISTORTIONS OF INTERNATIONAL TRADE. *Brookings* 1971 $6.95

> Baldwin gives us "the first complete treatment of nontariff barriers to international trade to be found in the literature"—(*Choice*).

Barnet, Richard J., and Ronald E. Müller. GLOBAL REACH: The Power of the Multinational Corporations. *Simon & Schuster* 1975 $11.95

> The authors indict the multinational corporations "for committing a crime against a rational, equitable, and settled world order"—(*SR*).

Bauer, Peter T. DISSENT ON DEVELOPMENT: Studies and Debates in Development Economics. *Harvard Univ. Press* 1972 $15.00

Beard, Miriam. A HISTORY OF BUSINESS. *Univ. of Michigan Press* Ann Arbor Bks. 2 vols. 1962–1963 pap. Vol. 1 From Babylon to the Monopolists (1962) $2.95 Vol. 2 From the Monopolists to the Organization Man (1963) $2.25. Discusses the relationship of the businessman to the state and society.

Berle, Adolf A. THE AMERICAN ECONOMIC REPUBLIC. *Harcourt* 1963 $5.75 Harvest Bks. 1965 pap. $1.65

(With Gardiner C. Means). THE MODERN CORPORATION AND PRIVATE PROPERTY. *Harcourt* rev. ed. 1968 $12.50 Harvest Bks. 1969 pap. $3.25

Boulding, Kenneth E. BEYOND ECONOMICS: Essays on Society, Religion, and Ethics. *Univ. of Michigan Press* 1968 $9.50 Ann Arbor Bks. 1970 pap. $2.95

> "This collection of some twenty essays, most of them papers read to non-economists, shows Dr. Boulding's emergence as a social philosopher rivaling two other economists, Milton Friedman and John Kenneth Galbraith"—(Spencer Pollard, in *SR*).

ECONOMICS AS A SCIENCE. *McGraw-Hill* 1970 $6.95 pap. $4.95

BUSINESS PERIODICALS INDEX. *Wilson* 1958–   Monthly with an annual cumulative issue. Service basis.

Chamberlain, John. THE ENTERPRISING AMERICANS: A Business History of the United States. *Harper* 1963 new ed. 1974 $8.95

Childs, Marquis, and Douglass Cater. ETHICS IN A BUSINESS SOCIETY. 1954. *Greenwood* 1973 $9.25. An analysis of Christian ethics as applied to economic goals.

Cipolla, Carlo M., Ed. THE ECONOMIC DECLINE OF EMPIRES. *Harper* (Barnes & Noble) 1970 $12.00 pap. $6.00

Cochran, Thomas C. BUSINESS IN AMERICAN LIFE: A History. *McGraw-Hill* 1972 $12.50

> "Written by the dean of American business historians, this book is not a business history but rather a broad, synthetic study of the impact of business as an institution on various aspects and institutions in American society"—(*Choice*).

Demaris, Ovid. DIRTY BUSINESS: The Corporate-Political Money-Power Game. *Harper's Magazine Press* 1974 $10.95

> "An eye-opening account of the widespread nature of graft and corruption in American politics and business"—(*LJ*).

Derber, Milton. THE AMERICAN IDEA OF INDUSTRIAL DEMOCRACY, 1865–1965. *Univ. of Illinois Press* 1971 $7.50

> The author "traces the development of industrial democracy in the governance of an enterprise or industry in the U.S. through five stages from 1865 to the present"—(*Choice*).

Dorfman, Joseph. THE ECONOMIC MIND IN AMERICAN CIVILIZATION, 1606–1933. *Kelley* 5 vols. 1946–1959 Vols. 1 and 2 1606–1865 (1946) Vol. 3 1865–1918 (1949) Vols. 4 and 5 1918–1933 (1959) Vols. 1, 2, 4 and 5 each $12.50 Vol. 3 $15.00 set $57.50

Douglas, Paul H. IN OUR TIME. *Harcourt* 1968 $6.95

> "A sound, constructive and sometimes controversial exposition of American economic problems and related subjects such as political ethics and our national resources"—(*PW*).

Drucker, Peter F. THE AGE OF DISCONTINUITY: Guidelines to Our Changing Society. *Harper* 1969 $10.00. A discussion of the new shape of the world's economy. .

Dymsza, William A. MULTINATIONAL BUSINESS STRATEGY. *McGraw-Hill* 1972 $6.95

"This book develops a rational and systematic guide for companies operating on a multinational basis"—*(LJ)*.

Edwin, Ed. FEAST OR FAMINE: Food, Farming, and Farm Policies in America. *McKay* (Charterhouse) 1974 $9.95

A discussion of "the production and processing of the world food supply"—*(Booklist)*.

Ehrlich, Paul, and Anne H. Ehrlich. THE END OF AFFLUENCE: A Blueprint for Your Future. *Ballantine Bks.* 1975 pap. $1.95

Einzig, Paul. THE DESTINY OF THE DOLLAR. *St. Martin's* 1972 $8.95

Farrar, David. THE WARBURGS: The Story of a Family. *Stein & Day* 1975 $8.95

"An internationalized version of "Our Crowd" zeros in on the rich and influential Warburg family"—*(Booklist)*.

Flash, Edward S., Jr. ECONOMIC ADVICE AND PRESIDENTIAL LEADERSHIP: The Council of Economic Advisers. *Columbia* 1965 $13.50

"Mr. Flash gives ample consideration to the political and social necessities that contribute to economic determinations. . . . A valuable study"—*(LJ)*.

Frazer, William J., Jr. CRISIS IN ECONOMIC THEORY: A Study of Monetary Policy, Analysis, and Economic Goals. *Univ. Presses of Florida* 1974 $20.00 pap. $14.50

"A well-written and comprehensive review of the current status of monetary theory and policy"—*(Choice)*.

Galbraith, John Kenneth. *See his main entry, this Chapter.*

Gist, Ronald R. MARKETING AND SOCIETY. *Holt* 1971 $10.95

Gist "places emphasis on the effect of marketing practices on society and the environment"—*(LJ)*.

Green, Timothy. THE WORLD OF GOLD TODAY. (Orig. "The World of Gold") *Walker & Co.* 1968 rev. ed. 1973 $8.95

Greenleaf, William, Ed. AMERICAN ECONOMIC DEVELOPMENT SINCE 1860. Documentary History of the United States Ser. *Univ. of South Carolina Press* 1968 $9.95; *Harper* Torchbks. 1968 pap. $3.45

Handlin, Oscar, and Mary F. Handlin. WEALTH OF THE AMERICAN PEOPLE: A History of American Affluence. *McGraw-Hill* 1975 $10.00

"Rejecting the 'Cliometric' approach as unsuited to the understanding of the intricate intertwining of people, events, and institutions, the Handlins concentrate on a theoretic narrative enlivened with vivid vignettes and illuminating examples"—*(LJ)*.

Hansen, Alvin H. BUSINESS CYCLES AND NATIONAL INCOMES. *Norton* expanded ed. 1964 $9.50

FISCAL POLICY AND BUSINESS CYCLES. *Norton* 1941 $8.50

Harrod, Roy F. ECONOMIC DYNAMICS. *St. Martin's* 1973 $8.95

ECONOMIC ESSAYS. *St. Martin's* new 2nd ed. 1972 $12.95

Hayek, Friedrich August. THE ROAD TO SERFDOM. *Univ. of Chicago Press* 1944 $7.00 Phoenix Bks. pap. $2.95

Heesterman, A. FORECASTING MODELS FOR NATIONAL ECONOMIC PLANNING. *Gordon & Breach* 1970 $9.00

"Excellent book on the linear econometric models, with a special stress of macroeconomic models. There is a clear and reasonable coverage of the existing models and submodels"—*(Choice)*.

Heilbroner, Robert L. THE LIMITS OF AMERICAN CAPITALISM. *Harper* 1966 $5.95 Torchbks. pap. $1.25

"Dr. Heilbroner has written a book about which there will be some controversy. . . . The general theme is that the future will be planned, for just as capitalism succeeded feudalism, so too will science probably succeed capitalism. . . . A thought-provoking book, well-written, and with good examples of the basis of Heilbroner's thought"—(LJ).

THE MAKING OF ECONOMIC SOCIETY. *Prentice-Hall* 1962 4th ed. 1972 $8.95 pap. $5.00. An interesting account by this brilliant writer on economics for the layman.

THE WORLDLY PHILOSOPHERS. *Simon & Schuster* 1953 rev. ed. 1972 $7.95 Touchstone-Clarion Bks. 1972 pap. $2.45; *Franklin Watts* lg.-type ed. $12.50. A "multi-faceted" biography: the personal and professional lives of the great economists.

(With others). IN THE NAME OF PROFIT: Profiles in Corporate Greed. *Doubleday* 1972 $6.95; *Paperback Lib.* 1972 pap. $1.50
"Six cases of corporate wrongdoing are presented in this collection of factual exposés"—(LJ).

Heller, Walter W. NEW DIMENSIONS OF POLITICAL ECONOMY. *Harvard Univ. Press* 1966 $5.50; *Norton* 1967 pap. $1.75
"A delightful, winsome, and significant book. In this expanded form of his Godkin Lectures, delivered at Harvard University in 1966, the author reviews his experiences as a policy-maker and their implications for the discipline of economics and for the political economy of economic policy. . . . Professor Heller writes with a sprightliness and piquancy rare and refreshing in a profession justly famous for arid, formalistic, and turgid prose. Indeed, the reader may find himself swept along by the sheer contagion of the author's own enthusiasm and persuasiveness"—(*Political Science Quarterly*).

Hicks, John R. A THEORY OF ECONOMIC HISTORY. *Oxford* 1970 $5.00 pap. $1.95
"A highly learned, unique and readable set of essays . . . that deserve the widest possible readership"—(*Choice*).

Jacoby, Neil H. CORPORATE POWER AND SOCIAL RESPONSIBILITY: A Blueprint for the Future. *Macmillan* 1971 $10.00
Jacoby "concludes that corporations will have to respond to changing social values"—(LJ).

Johnson, Arthur M., Ed. THE AMERICAN ECONOMY: An Historical Introduction to the Problems of the 1970's. *Macmillan* (Free Press) 1974 $10.00
"A well-timed collection of readings on selected contemporary issues . . . [the book] points up the challenge facing all thoughtful people and attempts to put modern day problems in historical perspective"—(LJ).

Johnson, Harry G. ASPECTS OF THE THEORY OF TARIFFS. *Harvard Univ. Press* 1972 $12.00
"This book brings together in convenient form many of the papers normally assigned to students in advanced international economic courses. A must for all college and research libraries"—(*Choice*).

Keynes, John Maynard. *See his main entry, this Chapter*.

Knorr, Klaus. POWER AND THE WEALTH: The Political Economy of International Power. *Basic Bks.* 1973 $7.95
"Knorr dissects the concept of power into categories of actual and potential capabilities relating both to the economics of the state and the linkage to the international political system"—(*Choice*).

Kochanek, Stanley A. BUSINESS AND POLITICS IN INDIA. *Univ. of California Press* 1974 $16.50
"An extraordinarily well-written, lucid, and scholarly contribution to the growing literature on the Indian political system . . . [with] a thorough review of the literature on business groups in India"—(*Choice*).

Krooss, Herman E., and Charles Gilbert. AMERICAN BUSINESS HISTORY. *Prentice-Hall* 1972 $10.00 pap. $5.95
"This excellent text will fill a definite need as a balanced survey of business history in its broadest sense and as a new, standard definitive work on the subject for general readers"—(*Choice*).

Lev, Baruch. FINANCIAL STATEMENT ANALYSIS: A New Approach. *Prentice-Hall* 1974 $9.95 pap. $4.95
"A marvel of clarity and scholarly thoroughness, this book shows the way to getting financial statement analysis out of the doldrums it has been in for some decades. Lev attempts to bridge the gap between the traditional focus on financial ratios and the recent advances in accounting, economics, and finance theory"—(*Choice*).

Little, Jane Sneddoń. EURO-DOLLARS: The Money Market Gypsies. *Harper* 1975 $12.50

"An expert from Boston's Federal Reserve Bank describes the workings of the Euro-dollar market"—(*Booklist*).

MCGRAW-HILL DICTIONARY OF MODERN ECONOMICS: A Handbook of Terms and Organizations. By Douglas Greenwald and others *McGraw-Hill* 1965 2nd ed. 1973 $19.95

Manley, John F. THE POLITICS OF FINANCE: The House Committee on Ways and Means. *Little* 1971 $7.50

"Data and theory are woven together in chapters on committee recruitment, committee integration, the leadership of Chairman Wilbur Mills, and the committee's relationships with the House, Senate, and executive branch"—(*Choice*).

Mason, Edward S., and Robert E. Asher. THE WORLD BANK SINCE BRETTON WOODS. *Brookings* 1973 $17.50

"The prestige of Mason and Asher made it possible for them to draw on sources outside as well as within the Bank and to make objective judgments on its accomplishments and problems. . . . This volume is indispensable to every serious student of finance and development"—(*Choice*).

Mayer, Martin. THE BANKERS. *Weybright & Talley* (dist. by McKay) 1975 $15.00

Meadows, Donella H., Dennis L. Meadows, Jorgen Randers, and William W. Behrens. THE LIMITS TO GROWTH: A Report for the Club of Rome's Project on the Predicament of Mankind. *Universe Bks.* 1973 $6.50

"This volume will probably be one of the most stimulating books of the 1970's. The Club of Rome has taken the concept of exponential growth and applied it to the interrelationship between 5 variables: industrial growth, pollution, depletion of natural resources, depletion of arable land, and population growth"—(*Choice*).

Melman, Seymour. AMERICAN CAPITALISM IN DECLINE: The Cost of a Permanent War Economy. *Simon & Schuster* 1974 $8.95

"Melman discusses the illusory prosperity of a war economy which masks its basically unproductive nature"—(*Booklist*).

(Ed.). WAR ECONOMY OF THE UNITED STATES: Readings in Military Industry and Economy. *St. Martin's* 1971 $10.00

Mosley, Leonard. POWER PLAY IN THE MIDDLE EAST. *Random* 1973 $10.00

The author "attempts to answer many of the questions that serious men and women have been asking everywhere. Is the West losing in its fight to hold on to its Middle East oil concessions?"—(*LJ*).

Moussa, Pierre. THE UNDERPRIVILEGED NATIONS. *Beacon* 1963 (orig.) pap. $1.95; *Peter Smith* $4.00. The French economist discusses the effective use of resources of underdeveloped countries and the economics and politics of their growth.

Myrdal, Gunnar. *See his main entry, this Chapter.*

Narver, John C. CONGLOMERATE MERGERS AND MARKET COMPETITION. *Univ. of California Press* 1967 $8.50

"A scholarly and detailed study . . . technical . . . but because of the wide-spread interest in and importance of this type of merger in the present economy, it will be of interest to a [wide] audience"—(*LJ*).

(With R. Savitt). THE MARKETING ECONOMY: An Analytical Approach. *Holt* 1971 $11.00

Neufeld, E. P. THE FINANCIAL SYSTEM OF CANADA: Its Growth and Development. *St. Martin's* 1972 $20.00

This is "a comprehensive review of the development and changing relative importance of all forms of financial intermediation in Canada"—(*Choice*).

Nielsen, Waldemar A. THE BIG FOUNDATIONS. *Columbia* 1972 $12.50

"An investigation of the 33 largest foundations—how they spend their money, what impact they have, who runs them, etc."—(*LJ*).

North, Douglass C., and Robert P. Thomas. THE RISE OF THE WESTERN WORLD: A New Economic History. *Cambridge* 1973 $7.95

"This volume will undoubtedly become one of the most widely read sources for European economic history. . . . North and Thomas have authored a significant addition to our knowledge of the early economic history of Europe"—(*Choice*).

O'Brien, D. P. THE CLASSICAL ECONOMISTS. *Oxford* 1975 $19.25

The author presents "an outstanding exposition of the classical economists and their theories"—(*LJ*).

Orsagh, Thomas, Ed. ECONOMIC HISTORY OF THE UNITED STATES PRIOR TO 1860. *American Bibliographical Center-Clio Press* 1974 $7.95

Parkinson, Cyril Northcote. BIG BUSINESS. *Little* 1974 $3.95

Parkinson "sets aside wit in favor of a sober, factual exposition of the workings of the business and industrial establishment, its relations with government and unions, and the pervasive influences on daily life"—(*Booklist*).

Passell, Peter, and Leonard Ross. THE RETREAT FROM RICHES: Affluence and Its Enemies. *Viking* 1972 $6.95

"This book, by two economists, sets out to formulate a new way of thinking to supplant the theory of antigrowth which has been widely touted in recent years and which, the authors declare, is self-defeating"—(*LJ*).

Pryor, Frederic L. PROPERTY AND INDUSTRIAL ORGANIZATION IN COMMUNIST AND CAPITALIST NATIONS. *Indiana Univ. Press* 1974 $17.50

"A very scholarly mix of institutionalism, theoretical analysis, and empiricism is the better way of characterizing the latest work by Pryor. . . . The volume verges on a reference work"—(*Choice*).

Ridgeway, James. THE LAST PLAY: The Struggle to Monopolize the World's Energy Resources. *Dutton* 1970 $10.00

The author presents "a searching examination of the monopolistic trends of the so-called energy companies"—(*LJ*).

Robinson, Joan. ECONOMIC HERESIES: Some Old-Fashioned Questions in Economic Theory. *Basic Bks.* 1971 $6.95

The author, "one of the most renowned Keynesian economists . . . is revolting against the now orthodox Keynesian or New Economics"—(*Choice*).

Rosen, Sumner M., Ed. ECONOMIC POWER FAILURE: The Current American Crisis. *McGraw-Hill* 1975 $8.95

"This book is a collection of essays by an assortment of economists . . . the writers seem in the main younger men with what would at one time have been called a strong left-wing bias . . . the unifying theme of the book is implicit in its title"—(*SR*).

Rubner, Alex. THREE SACRED COWS OF ECONOMICS. *Harper* (Barnes & Noble) 1971 $8.50

"An attempt to give the public a realistic view of three economic items that are often taken more seriously than they should be: gross national product, forecasting, and planning"—(*LJ*).

Sampson, Anthony. THE SEVEN SISTERS: The Great Oil Companies and the World They Made. *Viking* 1975 $10.00

The author "has performed one of the higher functions of journalism. He has entered an area of baffling complexity and made sense of it"—(*N.Y. Times*).

Schoenfeld, David, and Arthur A. Natella. THE CONSUMER AND HIS DOLLARS. Fwd. by Esther Peterson *Oceana* 1966 2nd rev. ed. 1970 $6.00. For the beginning student and general reader.

Servan-Schreiber, Jean-Jacques. THE AMERICAN CHALLENGE. Trans. from the French by Ronald Steel *Atheneum* 1968 $6.95; *Avon Bks.* Discus pap. $1.65

The editor of the popular French *L'Express* "urges Europe to meet the challenge of American superiority in technology and business management. The author contends that without urgent political and educational changes and without the creation of a European federation which includes Britain, 'the third industrial power in the world, following the United States and the Soviet Union could well be in 15 years, not Europe, but the American industry in Europe.' According to the international edition of the *Herald Tribune*, the book 'has touched off reaction on every level of French society' "—(*PW*). It was a best seller in the United States. In no sense anti-American, it urges Europeans to meet the American challenge before it is too late.

Sethi, S. Prakash. Up Against the Corporate Wall: Modern Corporations and Social Issues of the Seventies. *Prentice-Hall* 1971 $9.95 pap. $7.50 2nd ed. 1974 $10.00 pap. $7.50

"Actual case histories (20 in all) are used to illustrate the conflict between major corporations and various groups: environmentalists, consumers, minorities [and] labor unions"—(*LJ*).

Sloan, Harold Stephenson, and A. J. Zurcher. Dictionary of Economics. *Harper* (Barnes & Noble) 5th ed. 1970 $8.50 pap. $2.95. Describes basic economic principles as well as new legislation and interpretation.

Sobel, Robert. Amex: A History of the American Stock Exchange, 1921–1971. *Weybright & Talley* (dist. by McKay) 1973 $10.95

The Great Bull Market: Wall Street in the 1920's. Essays in American History Ser. *Norton* 1968 pap. $1.95

"A perceptive study not only of the 1929 panic, but also of the entire decade"—(*LJ*).

The Money Manias: The Eras of Great Speculation in America, 1770–1970. *Weybright & Talley* (dist. by McKay) 1973 $9.95

Panic on Wall Street: A History of America's Financial Disasters. *Macmillan* 1968 $8.95 Collier Bks. 1972 pap. $2.95

Starr, Roger. Housing and the Money Market. *Basic Bks.* 1975 $10.95

A "book about the production costs and financing of housing"—(*N.Y. Times*).

Tawney, Richard H. *See his main entry, this Chapter.*

Theobald, Robert. An Alternative Future for America II. *Swallow* 1968 rev. and enl. ed. 1970 $6.00 pap. $2.00

Futures Conditional. *Bobbs* 1972 $6.95 pap. $3.25

Weisskopf, Walter A. Alienation and Economics. *Dutton* 1971 $7.95

The author "discusses GNP fetishism and states that keeping overabundance as our goal may lead ultimately to destruction or dissolution"—(*LJ*).

Woytinsky, Emma S. Profile of the U.S. Economy: A Survey of Growth and Change. Fwd. by Ewan Clague *Praeger* 1967 $15.00

"Encyclopedic in its coverage and . . . a valuable research tool" (*LJ*) by the Russian-born economist.

Zerden, Sheldon. Best Books on the Stock Market: An Analytical Bibliography. *Bowker* 1972 $12.95

"Under such subject headings as fundamental analysis, technical analysis, mutual funds, options, psychology and speculation, 150 alphabetically arranged titles are surveyed for the methods and techniques they propose or for their portrayal of Wall Street people and events"—(Publisher's note). Chosen as the American Library Association's Reference Book of the Year.

EDUCATION

Armytage, W. H. G. Four Hundred Years of English Education. *Cambridge* 1964 3rd ed. 1969 pap. $5.75

Ashton-Warner, Sylvia. Spearpoint: Teacher in America. *Knopf* 1972 $5.95; *Random* Vintage Bks. pap. $1.95. Her experiences in a new experimental school in the Rockies.

Teacher. *Simon & Schuster* 1963 $6.50 Touchstone-Clarion Bks. 1971 pap. $2.95; *Bantam* 1971 pap. $1.25

Bailyn, Bernard. Education in the Forming of American Society: Needs and Opportunities for Study. *Univ. of North Carolina Press* 1970 $4.50; *Norton* 1972 pap. $1.45

Barzun, Jacques. The American University: How It Runs, Where It Is Going. *Harper* 1968 $7.95

"Spirited, urgent, 'The American University' admirably mingles overview and detail, ranges clearly and forcefully over faculty recruitment, student unrest, the Ph.D. octopus, rising tuition costs, intervention in research by government and industry, and above all the paradox of burgeoning programs and growing dissatisfaction, of affluence and the threat of poverty, even bankruptcy"—(*Book-of-the-Month Club News*).

See also his main entry in Chapter 15, Essays and Criticism, Reader's Adviser, *Vol. 1.*

Beggs, David W., III. TEAM TEACHING: Bold New Venture. Bold New Venture Ser. *Indiana Univ. Press* 1964 $7.95

(With Edward G. Buffie, Eds.). INDEPENDENT STUDY: Bold New Venture. Bold New Venture Ser. *Indiana Univ. Press* 1965 $8.95

"This material should provide 'grist' for educational theorists and educational practictioners and should be of interest to a variety of persons in the teaching field"—(*LJ*).

Bennis, Warren. THE LEANING IVORY TOWER. Higher Education Ser. *Jossey-Bass* 1974 $7.75

Bergevin, Paul. A PHILOSOPHY FOR ADULT EDUCATION. *Seabury Press* 1967 1970 $4.95 pap. $2.45

Bird, Caroline. THE CASE AGAINST COLLEGE. *McKay* 1975 $9.95. A discussion of student dissatisfaction with college, as documented by random interviews.

Bowen, James. A HISTORY OF WESTERN EDUCATION. *St. Martin's* 2 vols. 1972– set $35.00
"A monumental work"—(*Choice*).

Bronfenbrenner, Urie, and John C. Condry, Jr. TWO WORLDS OF CHILDHOOD: U.S. and U.S.S.R. *Russell Sage* (dist. by Harper) 1970 $7.95
"A very important book. The American reader will be shocked by the clearly documented evidence that child rearing in the U.S.S.R. is distinctly challenging to that in the U.S.A. in terms of the behavior and values of its product"—(*Choice*).

Brown, William E., and Andrew M. Greeley. CAN CATHOLIC SCHOOLS SURVIVE? *Sheed & Ward* 1971 $6.00
"The purpose of this book is to impel the Catholic community to do the good it can [do] and should be done now about the crisis in Catholic education"—(*Choice*).

Brubacher, John S. THE COURTS AND HIGHER EDUCATION. *Jossey-Bass* 1971 $8.75

(With Willis Rudy). HIGHER EDUCATION IN TRANSITION: A History of American Colleges and Universities, 1636–1968. *Harper* 2nd rev. and enl. ed. 1968 $12.00

Bruner, Jerome S. THE RELEVANCE OF EDUCATION. *Norton* 1971 $5.95 new ed. 1973 pap. $2.45

See also his main entry in Chapter 6, Psychology, this Vol.

Buetow, Harold A. OF SINGULAR BENEFIT: The Story of Catholic Education in the United States. *Macmillan* 1970 $12.50

Bullock, Henry Allen. A HISTORY OF NEGRO EDUCATION IN THE SOUTH: From 1619 to the Present. *Harvard Univ. Press* 1967 $9.95; *Praeger* 1970 pap. $3.45
"A highly readable book that reflects an enormous amount of thorough research. . . . Every true educator will want to read this book"—(*LJ*).

Carnoy, Martin. EDUCATION AS CULTURAL IMPERIALISM. *McKay* 1974 $8.95 pap. $3.95
The author is "one of a small group of revisionist historians who are reinterpreting the history of schooling as the record of economic determination by the elite. . . . Carnoy convincingly documents his thesis that schooling exists to fit children into social and economic roles in the capitalist structure"—(*Choice*).

Chall, Jeanne S. LEARNING TO READ: The Great Debate. *McGraw-Hill* 1967 $9.65 pap. $2.95
"More nearly a reference book than a text, [this book] is based on secure research techniques and extensive study of the most basic aspects of reading instruction. Complete bibliographies of several kinds and a good index make it valuable for use in the library"—(*LJ*).

Chickering, Arthur W. EDUCATION AND IDENTITY. *Jossey-Bass* 1970 $9.50
"A massive sociopsychological enquiry into student development which evolved from Chickering's 'Project on Student Development at Small Colleges,' a longitudinal research and action program which studied personality change and attrition"—(*Choice*).

Cohen, Sol, Ed. EDUCATION IN THE UNITED STATES: A Documentary History. *Random* 5 vols. 1974 set $165.00

"The documents in this primary source reference work detail the history of American education from its English antecedents to the present. Topics include educational theory and practice, teacher education, textbooks, education of minorities, and the development of the common school"—(Publisher's note).

Commager, Henry Steele. THE COMMONWEALTH OF LEARNING. *Harper* 1968 $6.95

Cordasco, Francesco, and William W. Brickman. A BIBLIOGRAPHY OF AMERICAN EDUCATIONAL HISTORY: An Annotated and Classified Guide. *AMS Press* 1975 $12.50

Cremin, Lawrence A. AMERICAN EDUCATION: The Colonial Experience, 1607–1783. *Harper* 1971 $15.00

"The first of a projected three-volume history of American education begun in the mid-1960's, funded with a generous grant from the Carnegie Corporation"—*(Choice)*.

Decter, Midge. LIBERAL PARENTS, RADICAL CHILDREN. *Coward* 1975 $7.95

This book "is, the author says, 'an essay in fictionalized sociology' and it addresses what she considers an urgent question: what has gone wrong with the children?"—*(SR)*.

Dentler, Robert A., and others, Eds. THE URBAN R's: Race Relations as the Problem in Urban Education. Published for the Center for Urban Education. *Praeger* 1967 pap. $3.25

Dewey, John. *See his main entry in Chapter 5, Philosophy, this Vol.*

EDUCATION INDEX. *Wilson* 1929–   published monthly from September to June with permanent bound annual cumulations. Service basis.

Engelmann, Siegfried. PREVENTING FAILURE IN THE PRIMARY GRADES. *Simon & Schuster* 1969 $10.75 pap. $5.88

Epstein, Leon D. GOVERNING THE UNIVERSITY. *Jossey-Bass* 1974 $10.50

The author "explores the complex character of university government in a clear and straightforward manner. The contents expose and analyze the conflicting claims and roles of the many diverse interests in and around the university"—*(Choice)*.

Eurich, Alvin C., Ed. CAMPUS 1980: The Shape of the Future in American Higher Education. *Delacorte* 1968 $6.95 *Dell* pap. $2.45. Sixteen essays by eminent educators such as John W. Gardner, David Riesman, William Arrowsmith and Clark Kerr.

HIGH SCHOOL NINETEEN EIGHTY. *Pitman* 1970 $8.50

Fantini, Mario D. PUBLIC SCHOOLS OF CHOICE. *Simon & Schuster* 1974 $8.95

WHAT'S BEST FOR THE CHILDREN? Resolving the Power Struggle between Parents and Teachers. *Doubleday* 1974 $7.95

Fuchs, Estelle, and Robert J. Havighurst. TO LIVE ON THIS EARTH: American Indian Education. *Doubleday* 1973 $8.95

"This volume, essentially a digest of the National Study of American Indian Education (1971), describes where Indians live today and where they attend school, the Indian students' mental attitudes, and their perceptions of the schools themselves"—*(Choice)*.

Ginzberg, Eli. CAREER GUIDANCE: Who Needs It, Who Provides It, Who Can Improve It? *McGraw-Hill* 1971 $7.95

Goodman, Paul. *See his main entry, this Chapter.*

Gorman, Alfred H. TEACHERS AND LEARNERS: The Interactive Process of Education. *Allyn & Bacon* 2nd ed. 1974 $9.95 pap. $4.95

Herbst, Jurgen, Comp. THE HISTORY OF AMERICAN EDUCATION. *AHM Pub. Corp.* 1973 pap. $2.95

Highet, Gilbert. THE ART OF TEACHING. *Knopf* 1950 $6.95; *Random* Vintage Bks. pap. $1.95

Hofstadter, Richard, and Wilson Smith. AMERICAN HIGHER EDUCATION: A Documentary History. *Univ. of Chicago Press* 2 vols. 1961 set $17.50 Phoenix Bks. pap. Vol. 1 $2.95 Vol. 2 $3.45

Holt, John. How CHILDREN LEARN. *Pitman* 1969 $5.95; *Dell* pap. $.95 Delta Bks. 1972 pap. $2.45

> John Holt's "book, a poetic, humane, perceptive account of some of his own teaching experiences with the very young, should be made required reading for every teacher in America"— *(Nation)*.

THE UNDERACHIEVING SCHOOL. *Pitman* 1969 $5.95; *Dell* 1972 pap. $.95 Delta Bks. 1970 pap. $2.25

WHAT DO I DO ON MONDAY? *Dutton* 1970 $7.50; *Dell* 1974 pap. $1.50 Delta Bks. pap. $2.45

Hook, Sidney, Ed. THE PHILOSOPHY OF THE CURRICULUM: The Need for General Education. *Prometheus Bks.* (dist. by Hawthorn) 1975 $10.95. Hook argues against "relevant" education.

Hughes, John F. EDUCATION AND THE STATE. *American Council on Education* 1975 $12.00

> Hughes is "largely concerned with the issues of financing educational goals, equalizing educational justice, management and governance in higher education and educational reform"—*(LJ)*.

Illich, Ivan. DESCHOOLING SOCIETY. *Harper* 1972 pap. $1.25

Jacoby, Susan. INSIDE SOVIET SCHOOLS. *Farrar, Straus* 1974 $8.95

Jencks, Christopher, and David Riesman. THE ACADEMIC REVOLUTION. *Doubleday* 1968 Anchor Bks. pap. $4.95

> "A whopping sociological and historical analysis of American higher education"—*(New Yorker)*.

Jencks, Christopher, and others. INEQUALITY: A Reassessment of the Effect of Family and Schooling in America. *Basic Bks.* 1972 $12.50

Kazamias, Andreas, and Byron G. Massialas. TRADITION AND CHANGE IN EDUCATION: A Comparative Study. *Prentice-Hall* 1965 pap. $3.45

Kerr, Clark, and others. THE UNIVERSITY IN TRANSITION. Ed. by Festus J. Viser *Memphis State Univ. Press* 1971 $3.50

Kohl, Herbert R. MATH, WRITING AND GAMES IN THE OPEN CLASSROOM. *Random* 1974 $6.95 pap. $2.45

THE OPEN CLASSROOM. *Random* 1970 $4.95 pap. $1.65

THIRTY-SIX CHILDREN. *Norton* 1968 $5.95; *New Am. Lib.* Signet Bks. 1973 pap. $.95

> "A teacher's experiences in a New York City ghetto school. "Required reading for everyone . . . concerned with meaningful education"—*(LJ)*.

Kozol, Jonathan. FREE SCHOOLS. *Houghton* 1972 $4.95; *Bantam* 1972 pap. $1.50

Krug, Edward A. THE SHAPING OF THE AMERICAN HIGH SCHOOL. *Univ. of Wisconsin Press* 2 vols. 1969–1972 Vol. 1 1880–1920 (1969) pap. $4.95 Vol. 2 1920–1941 (1972) $15.00. A history of the secondary school in America and the development of its curriculum.

Lawlor, John, Ed. HIGHER EDUCATION: Patterns of Change in the 1970's. *Routledge & Kegan Paul* 1972 $7.50

Livesy, Herbert. THE PROFESSORS: Who They Are, What They Do, What They Really Want and What They Need. *Charterhouse* 1975 $9.95

> "In more than 20 profiles of representative professors—from teaching assistants to university presidents—Livesy explores the services, rewards, self-seeking myths, ambitions, and traditions of the profession"—*(LJ)*.

Lortie, Dan C. SCHOOL TEACHER: A Sociological Study. *Univ. of Chicago Press* 1975 $10.95

> "The first full length study of teachers within the context of the sociology of occupations"—*(LJ)*.

McCarthy, Donald J., and others. NEW PERSPECTIVES ON TEACHER EDUCATION. *Jossey-Bass* 1973 $8.75

McGee, Reece J. ACADEMIC JANUS. *Jossey-Bass* 1971 $8.75

"A study of the liberal arts college . . . this is probably the best single study on its topic now available"—*(Choice)*.

Marks, Barbara S., Ed. THE NEW YORK UNIVERSITY LIST OF BOOKS IN EDUCATION. *Scholastic Bk. Services* 1968 pap. $8.00. A selected, annotated bibliography containing 2,857 entries classified under 175 subject headings.

Marland, Sidney P., Jr. CAREER EDUCATION: A Proposal for Reform. *McGraw-Hill* 1974 $7.95

Suggests "a program that would prepare students for a well-integrated life in which work plays an important part"—*(LJ)*.

Mayer, Frederick. A HISTORY OF EDUCATIONAL THOUGHT. *Charles E. Merrill* 3rd ed. 1973 $10.95

(Ed., with introd.). GREAT IDEAS OF EDUCATION. *College & Univ. Press* 3 vols. 1966 Vol. 1 The Bases of Ancient Education Vol. 2 The Road to Modern Education Vol. 3 The Foundations of Contemporary Education each $7.50 set $22.50

Messerli, Jonathan. HORACE MANN: A Biography. *Knopf* 1972 $15.00

This is "the most important biography of Mann yet undertaken"—*(Choice)*.

Meyer, Adolph. AN EDUCATIONAL HISTORY OF THE AMERICAN PEOPLE. *McGraw-Hill* 2nd ed. 1967 $10.50

AN EDUCATIONAL HISTORY OF THE WESTERN WORLD. *McGraw-Hill* 1965 2nd ed. 1972 $10.95

Montessori, Maria. *See her main entry, this Chapter.*

Park, Joe. THE RISE OF AMERICAN EDUCATION: An Annotated Bibliography. *Northwestern Univ. Press* 1965 $8.00 pap. $3.50

Parsons, Talcott, and Gerald M. Platt. THE AMERICAN UNIVERSITY. *Harvard Univ. Press* 1973 $15.00

"This book is without question one of the most important books to be published in the last few years concerning American higher education. Not only is its senior author America's most influential sociologist, but the volume provides one of the very few efforts to place the university in its societal context"—*(Choice)*.

Peterson, Alexander D. C. A HUNDRED YEARS OF EDUCATION: A Comparative Study of Educational Patterns in Western Europe and the United States. *Humanities Press* 2nd rev. ed. 1960 $6.00

Piaget, Jean. *See his main entry, Chapter 6, Psychology, this Vol.*

Pines, Maya. REVOLUTION IN LEARNING: The Years from Birth to Six. *Harper* 1967 $7.95 Harrow Bks. pap. $.95

Ravitch, Diane. THE GREAT SCHOOL WARS. *Basic Bks.* 1975 $12.95

"A detailed untendentious, quietly authoritative historical inquiry into the political struggles that wracked the New York schools between 1805 and 1973 as successive immigrant waves passed through them"—*(N.Y. Times Bk. Review)*.

Reischauer, Robert D., and others. REFORMING SCHOOL FINANCE. *Brookings* 1973 $6.95 pap. $2.50

Here's "a concise and discriminating analysis . . . The authors display the customary literary skills of Brookings researchers. Clarity and parsimony in developing arguments are the hallmarks of the book"—*(Choice)*.

Ridgeway, James. THE CLOSED CORPORATION: American Universities in Crisis. *Random* 1968 $5.95

The university's entanglement with big business and government. "This very readable book may set a few mountains trembling"—*(PW)*.

Riesman, David. *See his main entry, this Chapter.*

Riessman, Frank. THE CULTURALLY DEPRIVED CHILD. *Harper* 1962 $6.95

HELPING THE DISADVANTAGED PUPIL TO LEARN MORE EASILY. *Prentice-Hall* 1966 pap.
$2.25

Rist, Ray C. THE URBAN SCHOOL: A Factory for Failure: A Study of Education in
American Society. *M.I.T. Press* 1973 $12.50

Rogers, David. 110 LIVINGSTON STREET: Politics and Bureaucracy in the New York City
School System. *Random* 1968 $8.95 Vintage Bks. 1969 pap. $2.45

Roszak, Theodore, Ed. THE DISSENTING ACADEMY. Anti-Textbook Ser. *Pantheon* 1968
$8.95

Sale, Kirkpatrick. S. D. S. *Random* 1973 $15.00

Schultz, Stanley K. THE CULTURE FACTORY: Boston Public Schools, 1789–1860. *Oxford*
1973 $11.50

"Schultz has written a full and colorful history of Boston public schools in the early national
period. Horace Mann and Massachusetts pioneered the extension of public schooling, and Boston
led the state"—(*Choice*).

Scribner, Harvey B., and Leonard B. Stevens. MAKE YOUR SCHOOLS WORK: Practical
Imaginative and Cost-Free Plans to Turn Public Education Around. *Simon & Schuster*
1975 $7.95

The authors present "ten innovative programs for improving the scope and quality of
American education"—(*LJ*).

Silberman, Charles E. CRISIS IN THE CLASSROOM: The Remaking in American Education.
Random 1970 $10.00

(Ed.). THE OPEN CLASSROOM READER. *Random* 1973 $12.50 Vintage Bks. pap. $2.95

Skinner, B. F. *See his main entry, Chapter 6, Psychology, this Vol.*

STANDARD EDUCATION ALMANAC, 1973–1974. Ed. by Jerry I. Reitman and Jon S. Greene
Marquis $25.00

Information on student enrollment, faculty salaries, state education expenditures, educational
research, etc. "This and subsequent volumes should be considered by any person or library having
to answer statistical questions about education in the United States"—(*LJ*).

Stoddard, George Dinsmore. THE OUTLOOK FOR AMERICAN EDUCATION. *Southern Illinois
Univ. Press* 1974 $8.95

Taylor, Harold. THE WORLD AS TEACHER. *Southern Illinois Univ. Press* 1974 pap. $3.95

Tunstall, Jeremy, Ed. THE OPEN UNIVERSITY OPENS. *Univ. of Mass. Press* 1975 $10.00 pap.
$4.00. An interim report of Britain's Open University.

Tyack, David B. THE ONE BEST SYSTEM: A History of American Urban Education.
Harvard Univ. Press 1974 $15.00

"This excellent analysis by one of the new revisionist historians of education, concentrates on
the decision-making processes and organization of urban schools during the last 15 years"—(*LJ*).

Ulich, Robert. THE EDUCATION OF NATIONS: A Comparison in Historical Perspective.
Harvard Univ. Press rev. ed. 1967 $11.00

THE HISTORY OF EDUCATIONAL THOUGHT. *Van Nostrand* 2nd ed. 1968 pap. $6.50

Vaizey, John. EDUCATION IN THE MODERN WORLD. *McGraw-Hill* 1967 pap. $2.45

"This effective book is a welcome addition to the rather sparse literature on international
education. . . . Recommended for laymen and educators interested in the subject"—(*LJ*).

(With others). THE POLITICAL ECONOMY OF EDUCATION. *Int. Pubns. Service* 1972 $20.00;
Halsted Press 1973 $14.95

Van Til, William, Ed. CURRICULUM: Quest for Relevance. *Houghton* 2nd ed. 1974 $7.50

Wattenbarger, James, and Bob N. Cage. MORE MONEY FOR MORE OPPORTUNITY. *Jossey-
Bass* 1974 $8.95

The author "surveys the theory, history and resources of financing the public community
college"—(*Choice*).

Wilson, Robert C., and others. COLLEGE PROFESSORS AND THEIR IMPACT ON STUDENTS. *Wiley* 1975 $12.95. Data from 1,000 college teachers at six institutions.

Wolff, Robert Paul. THE IDEAL OF THE UNIVERSITY. *Beacon* 1970 $5.95 pap. $1.95

Woodring, Paul. THE HIGHER LEARNING IN AMERICA: A Reassessment. *McGraw-Hill* 1968 $6.95 pap. $2.95

   "This is a superbly argued, excellently written presentation of higher education in America today—its historical antecedents, its present state, its problems, and its probable lines of future development. . . . As one of the best discussions of American higher education . . . this volume is enthusiastically recommended for all serious readers"—(*LJ*).

Ziegler, Harmon, and Karl Johnson. THE POLITICS OF EDUCATION IN THE STATES. *Bobbs* 1972 $8.00

   "An important monograph . . . whose concerns deal with areas of public policy as an output of political systems"—(*Choice*).

SOCIOLOGY

The following list covers books of a general sociological nature. Among the useful series are *Pantheon's* Report from a Village Series and the *Univ. of Chicago Press's* Heritage Sociology Series. *See also Section on Society in Modern America.*

Aron, Raymond. MAIN CURRENTS IN SOCIOLOGICAL THOUGHT. *Basic Bks.* 2 vols. 1965–1967 Vol. 1 Montesquieu, Comte, Marx, Tocqueville, the Sociologists, and the Revolution of 1848 (1965) $8.95 Vol. 2 Durkheim, Pareto, Weber (1967) $8.50; *Doubleday* Anchor Bks. 2 vols. 1968–1970 pap. Vol. 1 $2.50 Vol. 2 $1.95

Bales, Robert F., and others, Eds. SMALL GROUP STUDIES IN SOCIAL INTERACTION. *Knopf* rev. ed. 1965 $11.95

Barnes, Harry Elmer, Ed. AN INTRODUCTION TO THE HISTORY OF SOCIOLOGY. *Univ. of Chicago Press* 1948 $17.50 Phoenix Bks. abr. ed. 1966 pap. $3.45

Bell, Daniel. THE COMING OF POST-INDUSTRIAL SOCIETY: A Venture in Social Forecasting. *Basic Bks.* 1973 $12.50

   "Bell argues that we are entering a post-industrial era, the defining characteristic of which is the centrality of theoretical knowledge as the source of innovation and policy formulation"—(*Choice*).

   THE CULTURAL CONTRADICTIONS OF CAPITALISM. *Basic Bks.* 1975 $12.95

Bendix, Reinhard. EMBATTLED REASON: Essays on Social Knowledge. *Oxford* 1971 $9.75

   "Twelve essays on social knowledge forming, in part, a brief intellectual autobiography by one of the great names in modern sociology"—(*Choice*).

Blau, Peter M. ON THE NATURE OF ORGANIZATIONS. *Wiley* 1974 $14.50

   (With Otis D. Duncan). THE AMERICAN OCCUPATIONAL STRUCTURE. *Wiley* 1967 $16.75

Blau, Zena S. OLD AGE IN A CHANGING SOCIETY. *Franklin Watts* 1973 $9.95 pap. $2.95

   "This is a thoughtful attempt to conceptualize the aging process in terms of role exit, and to see it as part of a lifelong process defined by the social structure and social mechanisms"—(*Choice*).

Bottomore, T. B. SOCIOLOGY AS SOCIAL CRITICISM. *Pantheon* 1975 $8.95

   "These are powerful thoughts from a powerful thinker, and the collection is of sufficient depth and scope to instruct the historian, sociologist, or political scientist"—(*LJ*).

Braude, Lee. WORK AND WORKERS: A Sociological Analysis. *Praeger* 1975 $10.00

   Intended "as an introductory analysis for the beginning student in the sociology of occupations"—(*LJ*).

Butler, Robert M. WHY SURVIVE: Being Old in America. *Harper* 1975 $15.00

   Butler "reviews the panoply of ugly social facts which add up to 'ageism' . . . meaning prejudice against old persons"—(*LJ*).

Carter, Hugh, and Paul Glick. MARRIAGE AND DIVORCE: A Social and Economic Struggle. *Harvard Univ. Press* 1970 $8.50

"A convenient source of social data on American families in the 1960's based on large nationwide samples . . . a much needed updating of Glock's American Families, [o.p.]"—*(Choice)*.

Cottle, Thomas J. A FAMILY ALBUM: Portraits of Intimacy and Kinship. *Harper* 1975 $7.95

These portraits are "vignettes of life's crucibles in a stream-of-consciousness technique"—*(Choice)*.

Dahrendorf, Ralf. CLASS AND CLASS CONFLICT IN INDUSTRIAL SOCIETY. *Stanford Univ. Press* 1959 $10.00 pap. $2.95

Denzin, Norman K., Ed. THE RESEARCH ACT: A Theoretical Introduction to Sociological Methods. *Aldine* 1970 $9.50

"Destined to be a standard reference in sociological methodology for years to come"—*(Choice)*.

SOCIOLOGICAL METHODS: A Sourcebook. *Aldine* 1970 $15.50 pap. $5.95

Dollard, John A. CASTE AND CLASS IN A SOUTHERN TOWN. *Doubleday* Anchor Bks. 1957 pap. $1.95; *Peter Smith* $4.25. A classic.

Elliott, Philip. THE SOCIOLOGY OF THE PROFESSIONS. *Seabury Press* 1972 $8.95

"A must purchase for libraries for their sociology of professions work and organization collections"—*(Choice)*.

Friedlander, Walter A. INTERNATIONAL SOCIAL WELFARE. *Prentice-Hall* 1975 $9.95

This volume "surveys international social welfare agencies which have developed in response to world-wide need for such services"—*(LJ)*.

Glazer, Myron. THE RESEARCH ADVENTURE: Promise and Problems of Field Work. *Random* 1973 pap. $2.95

"An unusual and important contribution to the literature on social scientists' concerns with personal ethics, those of his profession, and those of the subjects of the investigation. Very readable, highly recommended for undergraduates"—*(Choice)*.

Glock, Charles Y., and Rodney Stark. RELIGION AND SOCIETY IN TENSION. *Rand McNally* 1965 pap. $5.95

Goffman, Erving. *See his main entry, this Chapter*.

Hollander, Paul. SOVIET AND AMERICAN SOCIETY: A Comparison. *Oxford* 1973 $12.50

"A comparative study of two supernations, their similarities and differences"—*(Choice)*.

Homans, George C. SOCIAL BEHAVIOR: Its Elementary Forms. *Harcourt* rev. ed. 1974 $11.95

Kadushin, Alfred. THE SOCIAL WORK INTERVIEW. *Columbia* 1972 $12.50

"Kadushin deals with cross-cultural interviewing, including the aged and children, non-verbal communications, and the group interview as well as a detailed analysis of process"—*(Choice)*.

Lachenmeyer, Charles W. THE LANGUAGE OF SOCIOLOGY. *Columbia* 1972 $7.50

"From the bold beginning statement that 'sociology is not a science' to an ending that expresses hope that it might be, this analysis of the failings of sociology is loaded with insights, practical suggestions, and brilliant analyses"—*(Choice)*.

Lazarsfeld, Paul F. MAIN TRENDS IN SOCIOLOGY. *Harper* Torchbks. 1973 pap. $1.95

(With others, Eds.). THE USES OF SOCIOLOGY. *Basic Bks.* 1967 $15.00

Lenski, Gerhard E. POWER AND PRIVILEGE: A Theory of Social Stratification. *McGraw-Hill* 1966 $11.50

Lindenfeld, Frank. RADICAL PERSPECTIVES ON SOCIAL PROBLEMS: Readings in Critical Sociology. Ed. by Kenneth Scott *Macmillan* 2nd ed. 1973 pap. $3.25

(Ed.). READER IN POLITICAL SOCIOLOGY. *T. Y. Crowell* (Funk & Wagnalls) 1968 $6.95 Minerva Press pap. $3.95. Contributors include William Kornhauser, Samuel P. Huntington, Seymour M. Lipset and Daniel Bell.

Lipset, Seymour M., and Reinhard Bendix. SOCIAL MOBILITY IN INDUSTRIAL SOCIETY: A Study of Political Sociology. *Univ. of California Press* 1959 pap. $1.95

Merton, Robert K. ON THEORETICAL SOCIOLOGY: Five Essays, Old and New. *Macmillan* (Free Press) 1967 pap. $2.45

SOCIAL THEORY AND SOCIAL STRUCTURE. *Macmillan* (Free Press) 1968 $9.95

(With others, Eds.). SOCIOLOGY TODAY: Problems and Prospects. *Basic Bks.* 1959 $7.50; *Harper* Torchbks. 2 vols. pap. Vol. 1 $1.95 Vol. 2 $2.45

Mitchell, G. Duncan. A HUNDRED YEARS OF SOCIOLOGY. *Aldine* 1968 $8.95

(Ed.). A DICTIONARY OF SOCIOLOGY. *Aldine* 1967 $8.75

Moore, Wilbert E. THE PROFESSIONS: Roles and Rules. *Russell Sage* 1971 $8.95

"Coherent and well balanced overview of the structure and functions of the organized professions in modern society"—*(Choice)*.

Nadel, Siegfried F. THE THEORY OF SOCIAL STRUCTURE. *Routledge & Kegan Paul* 1969 $6.25

Nisbet, Robert A. THE SOCIOLOGICAL TRADITION. *Basic Bks.* 1967 $7.95 pap. $4.45

"Perhaps the most significant thing about this many-sided and many-valued book is that it constitutes a major step in the ongoing reform of the history of social theory. It is one further milestone, and an important one at that, in the transition of the history of social theory to a more serious and complex genre. Substantively, Professor Nisbet's work focuses on the intellectual contributions of Tocqueville, Marx, Weber, Durkheim, and Simmel, with strong references to their supporting epigoni, which are organized in terms of what he takes to be the five core ideas of sociology: community, authority, status, the sacred, and alienation"—*(Political Science Quarterly)*.

Ossenberg, Richard J., Ed. CANADIAN SOCIETY: Pluralism, Change, and Conflict. *Prentice-Hall* 1972 $5.50 pap. $3.50

"This small volume might well be rated among the top of the recent sociological studies of Canada. It grew out of the 1967 Summer Institute on Canadian Society at the University of Calgary. . . . The essays cover the Canadian dialectic, hinterland versus metropolis, urbanization and industrialization, pluralism and conflict in ethnic relations"—*(Choice)*.

Parsons, Talcott. SOCIAL STRUCTURE AND PERSONALITY. *Macmillan* (Free Press) 1964 $9.50 pap. $3.45

"A brilliant collection of essays that will have great interest for all social scientists, psychologists, physicians, and clergymen"—*(LJ)*.

SOCIOLOGICAL THEORY AND MODERN SOCIETY. *Macmillan* (Free Press) 1967 $12.95

(Ed.). THEORIES OF SOCIETY. *Macmillan* (Free Press) 1961 1965 $14.95. A basic reference source containing selections from social theorists from Machiavelli, Locke, and John Stuart Mill to Freud, Durkheim and Cassirer, with introductory essays.

Peel, J. D. Y. HERBERT SPENCER: The Evolution of a Sociologist. *Basic Bks.* 1971 $10.00

"This beautifully written and thoroughly documented book should stimulate a renewed interest in Spencer, and more significantly in social evolution"—*(Choice)*.

Perlman, Robert. CONSUMERS AND SOCIAL SERVICES. *Wiley* 1975 $9.95 pap. $5.50

"Examines in detail the interaction between consumer and supplier with consideration of the types of consumers, their expressed needs, the results expected, the cost to the consumer, etc."—*(LJ)*.

Popper, Karl R. THE OPEN SOCIETY AND ITS ENEMIES. *Princeton Univ. Press* 2 vols. 5th rev. ed. 1966 Vol. 1 The Spell of Plato Vol. 2 The High Tide of Prophecy: Hegel, Marx and the Aftermath each $10.00 pap. each $3.45

Pumphrey, Ralph E., and Muriel W. Pumphrey, Eds. THE HERITAGE OF AMERICAN SOCIAL WORK. *Columbia* 1961 $15.00 pap. $7.00

"This is the first general comprehensive published selection of original source materials in the field of social work. The 112 documents which are quoted range from the Poor Law of 1601 to the Supreme Court decision of 1937 upholding the Social Security Act. . . . Not only have the editors done a good job of choosing and arranging their materials, but they have also added long chapter introductions and frequent notes of explanation"—*(LJ)*.

Rabb, Theodore K., and Robert I. Rotberg, Eds. THE FAMILY IN HISTORY: Interdisciplinary Essays. *Harper* Torchbks. (orig.) 1973 pap. $3.95

Riley, Matilda W., and Edward E. Nelson, Eds. SOCIOLOGICAL OBSERVATION: A Strategy for New Social Knowledge. *Basic Bks.* 1974 $10.95

"This pioneering work brings together 28 readings from the past 40 years, representing some of the American Sociological Association's most important publications"—*(LJ)*.

Rosow, Irving. SOCIALIZATION TO OLD AGE. *Univ. of California Press* 1975 $9.00

"This is a book on adult socialization theory . . . not a treatise on aging"—*(LJ)*.

Ruitenbeek, Hendrik M., Ed. VARIETIES OF CLASSIC SOCIAL THEORY. *Dutton* 1963 pap. $2.95. Important statements by 17 social theorists.

(Ed.). VARIETIES OF MODERN SOCIAL THEORY. *Dutton* 1963 pap. $2.75. Eighteen essays by such leading moderns as Fromm, Hartmann, Tillich, and Riesman.

Sanders, William B., Ed. THE SOCIOLOGIST AS DETECTIVE: An Introduction to Research Methods. *Praeger* 1974 $9.00

Scanzoni, John H. CHANGING PATTERNS IN MARRIAGE AND THE FAMILY. *Macmillan* (Free Press) 1975 $12.95

"The book is intended as a resource for sociologists and social psychologists interested in the family and population growth"—*(LJ)*.

Schwartz, Mildred A. POLITICS AND TERRITORY: The Sociology of Regional Persistence in Canada. *McGill-Queen's Univ. Press* 1974 $14.75

"No single study has ever delved as deeply or as thoroughly into the political and social ramifications of Canadian regional diversity as this one"—*(Choice)*.

Szczepanski, Jan. POLISH SOCIETY. *Random* 1971 pap. $3.25

"In a space of 200 pages the author tackles and handles with notable expertise the major characteristics of present-day Polish socialist society—political, economic, cultural, and social—in the context of an historical approach which counterposes the Poland of the interwar years to its present successor"—*(Choice)*.

Taylor, James B., and Jerry Randolph. COMMUNITY WORKER. *Jason Aronson* 1975 $7.50

The authors' "observations on skills a community worker needs but which are not learned in school"—*(LJ)*.

Thibaut, John W., and H. H. Kelley. THE SOCIAL PSYCHOLOGY OF GROUPS. *Wiley* 1959 $11.75

Tiger, Lionel. MEN IN GROUPS. *Random* 1969 $6.95 Vintage Bks. pap. $1.95

"This monograph, written for the sophisticated layman, attempts to integrate a fantastic quantity of related literature from virtually all of the disciplines, focusing upon the biological basis for the male bond as a significant social characteristic of human groups"—*(Choice)*.

Tiryakian, Edward A. ON THE MARGIN OF THE VISIBLE: Sociology, the Esoteric and the Occult. *Wiley* 1974 $9.95

(Ed.). PHENOMENON OF SOCIOLOGY: A Reader in the Sociology of Sociology. *Irvington Bks.* 1971 pap. $9.95

Turner, Jonathan H. AMERICAN SOCIETY: Problems of the Structure. *Harper* 1973 pap. $5.95

"This book is well-organized and written, and its relevance for contemporary American society should make it an excellent text for freshmen college students"—*(Choice)*.

Westley, William A., and Margaret W. Westley. THE EMERGING WORKER: Equality and Conflict in the Mass Consumption Society. *McGill-Queen's Univ. Press* 1971 $7.50

An "important book which significantly updates the field of industrial sociology"—*(Choice)*.

Zetterberg, Hans L. ON THEORY AND VERIFICATION IN SOCIOLOGY. *Bedminster* 3rd ed. 1965 $4.50

SOCIETY IN MODERN AMERICA

This selected list covers the broad spectrum of American society today and is supplementary to the succeeding sublistings on specific topics of present concern. Among the noteworthy series are *Braziller's* The American Image Series and *Washington Square's* Problems of American Society Series.

Aron, Raymond. The Industrial Society: Three Essays on Ideology and Development. *Praeger* 1967 $4.95

See also his main entry, this Chapter.

Bennis, Warren G., Ed. American Bureaucracy. *Transaction Bks.* 2nd ed. 1972 $7.95 pap. $2.95

(With Philip E. Slater). The Temporary Society. *Harper* 1968 $6.50 pap. $1.60. An examination of the effects of rapid change upon American society.

Bernard, Jessie. Women and the Public Interest: An Essay on Policy and Protest. *Aldine* 1971 $10.25 pap. $3.95

Brooks, John. The Go-Go Years. *Weybright & Talley* (dist. by McKay) 1973 $10.00; ed. by George Young *Ballantine Bks.* 1974 pap. $1.95

The Great Leap: The Past Twenty-Five Years in America. *Harper* 1966 $7.95 Colophon Bks. pap. $2.50

Drucker, Peter F. The Age of Discontinuity: Guidelines to Our Changing Society. *Harper* 1969 $10.00

Galbraith, John Kenneth. The Affluent Society. *Houghton* 1958 2nd ed. 1969 $6.95 Sentry Bks. 1971 pap. $2.95; *New Am. Lib.* Mentor Bks. rev. ed. 1970 pap. $1.25

(With Mohinder S. Randhawa). The New Industrial State. *Houghton* 1967 2nd rev. ed. 1971 $8.95 Sentry Bks. 1972 pap. $3.25

For further comment on both, see Galbraith's main entry, this Chapter.

Ginzberg, Eli, and Robert M. Solow, Eds. The Great Society. *Basic Bks.* 1974 $8.95 pap. $3.95

Hofstadter, Richard. Anti-Intellectualism in American Life. *Knopf* 1963 $7.95; *Random* Vintage Bks. pap. $2.95

See also his main entry, Chapter 9, History, Government and Politics, this Vol.

Lader, Lawrence. Abortion Two: Making the Revolution. *Beacon* 1974 $7.95 pap. $3.95

Lipset, Seymour M., and Earl Raab. The Politics of Unreason: Right Wing Extremism in America, 1790–1970. *Harper* 1970 $12.50 Torchbks. pap. $4.95

The authors "blend social science technique and analytical categories with historical materials in an analysis that begins with the . . . pre Civil War era"—(*Choice*).

Long, Edward V. The Intruders: The Invasion of Privacy by Government and Industry. Fwd. by Hubert H. Humphrey *Praeger* 1967 $5.95. By the former Senator from Missouri, who was Chairman of the Senate Subcommittee on Administrative Practice and Procedure, and in 1965 instigated hearings on activities of governmental agencies using wiretapping and other eavesdropping devices.

Lundberg, Ferdinand. The Rich and the Super-Rich: A Study in the Power of Money Today. *Lyle Stuart* 1968 $15.00; *Bantam* 1969 pap. $1.95. A modern successor to the author's controversial classic, "America's Sixty Families" (1937, o.p.).

Lynd, Robert S., and Helen Merrell Lynd. Middletown: A Study in Contemporary American Culture. *Harcourt* 1937 1939 1959 Harvest Bks. pap. $3.85

Middletown in Transition: A Study in Cultural Conflicts. *Harcourt* 1937 1939 Harvest Bks. 1963 pap. $4.45

"Middletown" (commonly supposed to be Muncie, Ind.) is the result of Dr. Lynd's work as director of the Small City Study of the Institute for Social and Religious Research (1923–26). Its sequel, "Middletown in Transition," is a re-evaluation of the town after the depression. Both books are pioneer works in the objective study of a modern city and R. L. Duffus has called them "the most valuable record we shall ever have of an American community of that period," a "magnificent piece of work which should interest all thoughtful readers," and a work "recognized instantly as a classic."

Packard, Vance (Oakley). A NATION OF STRANGERS. *McKay* 1972 $7.95; *Simon & Schuster* (Pocket Books) 1974 pap. $1.75. Because of the increasing mobility of Americans, Packard states that many people do not even know their neighbors.

THE PYRAMID CLIMBERS. *Fawcett* Crest Bks. 1968 pap. $.95

In this work intended for mass consumption, Mr. Packard "covers many aspects of the organization man's trip up the ladder to 'executive status,' or better, to the rarefied upper reaches of the corporate pyramid. . . . Strongly and generally recommended"—*(LJ)*.

THE SEXUAL WILDERNESS: The Contemporary Upheaval in Male-Female Relationships. *McKay* 1968 $6.95; *Pocket Bks.* 1970 pap. $1.25

"A well-written and conscientiously researched study"—*(LJ)*. "A serious study of sexual and social change, written for laymen and in laymen's language"—*(PW)*.

Phillips, Cabell. THE 1940s: Decade of Triumph and Trouble. *N.Y. Times* Chronicle of American Life Ser. *Macmillan* 1974 $12.95

"Cabell Phillips uses little theoretical analysis and conjectural explanation in telling this story, but he does develop the theme that the 1940s was a transitional decade that brought the country into what we call the modern era; that in the 1970s we are living in a well-defined continuum that grew directly out of the social and economic upheaval of World War II, and that what went before is obsolete and irrelevant"—*(N.Y. Times)*.

Prewitt, Kenneth. THE RECRUITMENT OF POLITICAL LEADERS: A Study of Citizen-Politicians. *Bobbs* 1971 $8.50

A "major work on the theory and data of political socialization and recruitment"—*(Choice)*.

Samuel, Howard D., Ed., with introd. TOWARD A BETTER AMERICA. *Macmillan* 1968 $5.95. Essays by contributors such as Carl Rowan, Eric Sevareid, Alan Barth, Edward R. Murrow, Leon Keyserling, Dwight Macdonald, George F. Kennan, T. H. White and Adlai E. Stevenson deal with racial problems, the McCarthy era, poverty and foreign affairs.

Schoenberger, Robert A., Ed. THE AMERICAN RIGHT WING: Readings in Political Behavior. *Holt* 1970 pap. $3.95

"Valuable anthology to all students of political sociology"—*(Choice)*.

Terkel, Studs. DIVISION STREET: America. *Pantheon* 1966 $7.95; *Avon Bks.* 1968 pap. $1.50

"This book, the work of a Chicago radio journalist, consists of the more or less autobiographical reflections of seventy Chicagoans of various ages, races, and classes. It is not intended to be a portrait of Chicago, and it isn't; it is far too random and inconclusive. It is, however, a totally absorbing book, a book of revelations—numbing, maddening, exhilarating—about mid-twentieth-century Americans"—*(New Yorker)*.

HARD TIMES: An Oral History of the Great Depression in America. *Pantheon* 1970 $8.95; *Avon Bks.* 1971 pap. $1.50

Westin, Alan F. PRIVACY AND FREEDOM. *Atheneum* 1967 $12.50. Winner of the 1968 George Polk Memorial Book Award.

(With Michael A. Baker). DATABANKS IN A FREE SOCIETY. *Quadrangle Bks.* 1974 $12.50 pap. $4.95

Yarmolinsky, Adam. THE MILITARY ESTABLISHMENT: Its Impact on American Society. *Harper* 1971 $10.00

"This book documents the cost, size, and influence of the military establishment and the weakness of countervailing institutions"—*(Choice)*.

Labor, Automation and Management

Among the series are those on Industrial Relations and Personnel, *Prentice-Hall*, and the Problems of the Modern Economy, *Norton. See also Chapters 7, Science: Technology and Engineering, and 10, Communications and the Lively Arts: Communications, this Vol.*

Ashenfelter, O., and A. Rees, Eds. DISCRIMINATION IN LABOR MARKETS. *Princeton Univ. Press* 1975 $9.00

"Ashenfelter found that craft unions tend to increase white-black wage differentials while industrial unions tend to narrow them"—(Earl W. Count).

Bernstein, Irving. THE LEAN YEARS: A History of the American Worker 1920–1933. *Houghton* 1960 $10.00 pap. 1972 $2.95

THE TURBULENT YEARS: A History of the American Worker 1933–1941. *Houghton* 1970 $12.95 pap. 1971 $4.95

Bird, Caroline. EVERYTHING A WOMAN NEEDS TO KNOW TO GET PAID WHAT SHE'S WORTH. *McKay* 1973 $8.95

The author "advises women on how to handle themselves in a male-oriented job world"—*(LJ)*.

Brink, Victor Z. COMPUTERS AND MANAGEMENT; The Executive Viewpoint. *Prentice-Hall* 1971 $7.95

Brink "tells what the view from the top should be with regard to the computer activities of a business organization"—*(LJ)*.

Brooks, Thomas R. TOIL AND TROUBLE: A History of the American Labor Movement. Fwd. by A. H. Raskin *Delacorte* 1965 rev. ed. 1971 $7.95 *Dell* Delta Bks. 1972 pap. $2.65

"An excellent and relatively brief history of the American labor movement from colonial times to the present day"—*(LJ)*.

Coles, Flournoy A., Jr. BLACK ECONOMIC DEVELOPMENT. *Nelson Hall* 1975 $9.95

Cross, Wilbur. JOHN DIEBOLD: Breaking the Confines of the Possible. Introd. by Karl A. Hill. Future Makers Ser. *James H. Heineman, Inc.* 1966 $6.50. An account of the career of the man known as "Mr. Automation."

Drucker, Peter F. MANAGEMENT: Tasks, Responsibilities, Practices. *Harper* 1974 $15.00

"The book is a lengthy manager's handbook on selected topics. The material covered, as indicated by the subtitle, is important to all managers regardless of functional area and size of the organization"—*(Choice)*.

Foster, James C. THE UNION POLITIC: The C.I.O. Political Action Committee. *Univ. of Missouri Press* 1975 $12.00

"The author argues convincingly that the political invincibility of the CIO:PAC was a myth"—*(LJ)*.

Ginzberg, Eli, and Alice M. Yohalem, Eds. CORPORATE LIB: Women's Challenge to Management. *Johns Hopkins Press* 1973 $6.50 pap. $2.50

"Thirteen contributors, male and female, explore the role of women in management"—*(LJ)*.

Goodwin, Leonard. DO THE POOR WANT TO WORK? A Social-Psychological Study of Work Orientations. *Brookings* 1972 $6.50

"The book focuses on the author's attempts to discover whether the unemployed and under-employed have different orientations toward work than regularly employed persons"—*(LJ)*.

Granick, David. MANAGERIAL COMPARISONS OF FOUR DEVELOPED COUNTRIES: France, Britain, United States, and Russia. *M.I.T. Press* 1973 $15.00

Granick "compares French and British styles of management of large manufacturing enterprises, chiefly with each other but also to some extent with practice in the U.S. and the Soviet Union"—*(Choice)*.

Grindley, C. B., and John W. Humble. THE EFFECTIVE COMPUTER: A Management by Objectives Approach. *American Management Assn.* 1974 $10.95

An "attempt to overcome computer waste and inefficiency by employing the basic tenets of MBO management"—*(LJ)*.

Hamermesh, Daniel S., Ed. LABOR IN THE PUBLIC AND NONPROFIT SECTORS. *Princeton Univ. Press* 1975 $11.50

Herling, John. RIGHT TO CHALLENGE: People and Power in the Steelworker's Union. *Harper* 1972 $12.50

"This book is a probing and scrupulously researched account of the steelworker's intra-organizational crisis of the fifties and sixties"—*(LJ)*.

Heyel, Carl, Ed. THE ENCYCLOPEDIA OF MANAGEMENT. *Van Nostrand-Reinhold* 2nd ed. 1973 $32.50

Hodson, Bernard A. MODERN DATA PROCESSING FOR MANAGEMENT: A Basic Systems Approach. *Cahners* 1971 $17.50

The book is "designed to serve as an introduction to the field of advanced technology"—*(LJ)*.

Jaffe, Abram J., and Joseph Froomkin. TECHNOLOGY AND JOBS. *Praeger* 1968 $8.00

Jay, Anthony. MANAGEMENT AND MACHIAVELLI: An Inquiry into the Politics of Corporate Life. *Holt* 1968 $4.95 pap. $3.40

"Though Mr. Jay thinks there is a lot wrong with today's corporations, he offers his readers pearls of wisdom instead of grapes of wrath"—*(New Yorker)*.

Jenkins, David. JOB POWER: Blue and White Collar Democracy. *Doubleday* 1973 $8.95

"A frontal attack on the traditional, pyramidal, authoritarian management structures"—*(LJ)*.

Korda, Michael. POWER! HOW TO GET IT, HOW TO USE IT. *Random* 1975 $8.95

Laslett, John H. M. LABOR AND THE LEFT: A Study of Socialist and Radical Influences in the American Labor Movement, 1881–1924. *Basic Bks.* 1970 $10.00

The author "seeks to determine the factors responsible for the failure to build a labor-based socialist political movement [in the U.S.]"—*(Choice)*.

Lawless, David J. EFFECTIVE MANAGEMENT: Social Psychological Approach. *Prentice-Hall* 1972 $10.95

"A solid attempt to bridge the gap between the findings of social and behavioral psychologists on such topics as motivation, incentives, leadership, social skills and the managers of people for whom the findings are intended"—*(LJ)*.

Le Masters, E. E. BLUE-COLLAR ARISTOCRATS. *Univ. of Wisconsin Press* 1975 $8.95. A study of the patrons of a small town (Middleton, Wis.) tavern.

Lens, Sidney. THE LABOR WARS: From the Molly Maguires to the Sitdowns. *Doubleday* 1973 $9.95

"This scholarly, continually absorbing history of the labor movement in the United States attempts to show the kinship between the demonstrators of today and the protestors of yesterday"—*(LJ)*.

Levison, Andrew. THE WORKING CLASS MAJORITY. *Coward* 1974 $8.95

Levison "challenges currently popular assumptions about the social and political values and the economic status of blue-collar workers and comes up with strong disagreements"—*(Booklist)*.

Lloyd, Cynthia B., Ed. SEX DISCRIMINATION AND THE DIVISION OF LABOR. *Columbia* 1975 $17.50 pap. $6.00

"The 17 papers in this volume explore the economic role of women with particular emphasis on female wages, employment, and income"—(Earl W. Count).

London, Joan, and Harry Anderson. SO SHALL YE REAP. *T. Y. Crowell* 1971 $6.95 pap. $2.45

A "carefully written account of the California Farm Labor Movement, including the story of the best known participant in the movement, Cesar Chavez"—*(LJ)*.

Longmate, Norman. THE WORKHOUSE. *St. Martin's* 1974 $8.95

A "social history of attitudes toward poverty as embodied in the existence of the workhouse"—*(Booklist)*.

Lubove, Roy. THE STRUGGLE FOR SOCIAL SECURITY, 1900–1935. *Harvard Univ. Press* 1968 $8.00

McConnell, Grant. PRIVATE POWER AND AMERICAN DEMOCRACY. 1966. *Random* Vintage Bks. 1970 pap. $2.45

Merrill, Harwood F., Ed. CLASSICS IN MANAGEMENT. *American Management Assn.* 1960 1970 $12.50

O'Brien, James J. MANAGEMENT WITH COMPUTERS. *Van Nostrand* 1972 $10.95

O'Brien "investigates the relationship between managers and computer specialists"—*(LJ)*.

Parker, R. H. MANAGEMENT ACCOUNTING: An Historical Perspective. *Kelley* 1969 $10.00

This book "fills a gap in our literature on accounting history, tracing the development of cost control and decision-making functions neglected by accountant-historians"—*(Choice)*.

Rees, Albert, and others. Workers and Wages in an Urban Labor Market. *Univ. of Chicago Press* 1970 $10.00

"A study of the Chicago labor market by two eminent labor economists and a team of well-known associates"—(*Choice*).

Renshaw, Patrick, The Wobblies: The Story of Syndicalism in the United States. *Doubleday* 1967 $5.95 Anchor Bks. 1968 pap. $1.45

"Big Bill Haywood and the countless million who held IWW cards live again in these pages as they fight the good fight against oppression and even militarism"—(*LJ*).

Seligman, Ben B. Most Notorious Victory: Man in an Age of Automation. Fwd. by Robert L. Heilbroner *Macmillan* (Free Press) 1966 $7.95

"A critique, a perspective, and a philosophy of action without which life under cybernation will become intolerable"—(*LJ*).

Somers, Gerald G., Ed. Retraining the Unemployed. *Univ. of Wisconsin Press* 1968 $17.50

Sprinkel, Beryl W. Money and Markets: A Monetarist View. *Richard D. Irwin* 1971 $8.95

Sprinkel "tells how to put monetary theory to work in practical ways"—(*LJ*).

Stogdill, Ralph Melvin. Handbook of Leadership: A Survey of Theory and Practice. *Macmillan* (Free Press) 1974 $19.95

"Using approximately 30 categories [the author] cites better than 1,000 studies of leadership . . . he provides clear, operational statements of findings and summarizes the unit at the end"—(*Choice*).

Taft, Philip. The Rights of Union Members and the Government. *Greenwood* 1975 $14.95

"A comprehensive examination of the effects of the 1959 Labor Management Reporting and Disclosure Act, which represents the most detailed regulation of internal union affairs ever undertaken by the Federal government"—(*LJ*).

Tannenbaum, Arnold S., and others. Hierarchy in Organizations. *Jossey-Bass* 1974 $12.50

"What are some of the alternatives to hierarchial management? Must we accept hierarchial structure as an indispensable element in human society?"—(*LJ*).

Terkel, Studs. Working People Talk about What They Do All Day and How They Feel about What They Do. *Pantheon* 1974 $10.00; *Avon* 1975 pap. $2.25

Tunnard, Christopher, and Boris Pushkarev. Man-Made America: Chaos or Control? *Yale Univ. Press* 1963 $25.00. Winner of the National Book Award in 1964.

Tyler, Gus. Labor in the Metropolis. *Charles E. Merrill* 1972 pap. $3.95

Uris, Auren. The Frustrated Titan: Emasculation of the Executive. *Van Nostrand-Reinhold* 1972 $8.95

Uris "identifies the ways of increasing effectiveness and improving productivity through greater use of people's abilities"—(*LJ*).

Whyte, William H., Jr. The Organization Man. *Simon & Schuster* 1956 $8.95 Touchstone-Clarion Bks. 1972 pap. $2.45

Wight, Oliver. The Executive's New Computer: Six Keys to Systems Success. *Prentice-Hall* (Reston) 1972 $9.00

Wight presents "a general view of computers and programming, and then offers practical advice to executives who wish to use computers successfully and avoid the all too frequent failures"—(*LJ*).

Wren, Daniel A. The Evolution of Management Thought. *Ronald* 1972 $10.00

The author "follows the development from its earliest beginnings to the present. It shows how economic, social, and political values have influenced the assumptions that men have made about men and organizations"—(*LJ*).

Integration, Racial Problems, Minorities

A particularly valuable series on these subjects is *Twayne's* The Immigrant Heritage in America. Two important series specializing in reprints of Afro-American Literature are

The Black Experience in America series, *Negro Universities Press*, and The Negro Now series, *McGrath Pub. Co.* Also important is *Arno's* The American Immigration Collection (Oscar Handlin, Gen. Ed.), a series of reprints covering the years 1620 to 1920. *See also Chapters 9, History, Government and Politics—American: Afro-American History, and 11, Folklore and Humor: Afro-American Folklore, this Vol.*

Amfitheatrof, Frank. THE CHILDREN OF COLUMBUS: An Informal History of the Italians in the New World. *Little* 1973 $8.95

Bailey, Ronald W., Ed. BLACK BUSINESS ENTERPRISE: Historical and Contemporary Perspectives. *Basic Bks.* 1971 $12.50

"A collection of reprints by 30 distinguished authors"—(*LJ*).

Baldwin, James. THE FIRE NEXT TIME. *Dial* 1963 $5.95; *Dell* 1970 pap. $.95; *Franklin Watts* lg.-type ed. $7.95

NOBODY KNOWS MY NAME. *Dial* 1954 1961 $6.95; *Dell* pap. $.60

NOTES OF A NATIVE SON. *Dial* 1955 $6.95; *Bantam* 1971 pap. $1.45; *Beacon* 1957 pap. $2.45

For comment on all three, see his main entry in Chapter 14, Modern American Fiction, Reader's Adviser, Vol. 1.

Baroe, Niels Winther. INDIAN AND WHITE: Self-Image and Interaction in a Canadian Plains Community. *Stanford Univ. Press* 1975 $8.50

A "study of Cree Indians and their white neighbors. . . . [This] book will excite students and professionals alike with its insights"—(*Choice*).

Barton, Josef J. PEASANTS AND STRANGERS: Italians, Rumanians, and Slovaks in an American City, 1890–1950. Studies in Urban History Ser. *Harvard Univ. Press* 1975 $12.00

"Barton traces the origins, migration, settlement patterns, community development, and social mobility of three ethnic groups in Cleveland"—(*LJ*).

Brink, William, and Louis Harris. BLACK AND WHITE: A Study of U.S. Racial Attitudes Today. *Simon & Schuster* 1967 $5.95 Touchstone-Clarion Bks. 1969 pap. $1.95. Public opinion samplings of racial attitudes in 1967.

Brown, Claude. MANCHILD IN THE PROMISED LAND. *Macmillan* 1965 $7.95; *New Am. Lib.* Signet 1971 pap. $1.50. A best seller. The life of a Negro youth in Harlem in the late 1940s and 1950s.

Brown, H. Rap. DIE, NIGGER, DIE. *Dial* 1970 $5.95; *Dell* Delta Bks. pap. $2.25

Carmichael, Stokely. STOKELY SPEAKS: Black Power to Pan-Africanism. *Random* 1971 $6.95 Vintage Bks. pap. $1.95

(With Charles V. Hamilton). BLACK POWER: The Politics of Liberation in America. *Random* 1968 $5.95 Vintage Bks. pap. $1.95. The origins, history and future of the Black Power movement described by two of its more prominent figures.

Clark, Kenneth B. *See his main entry, this Chapter.*

Cleaver, Eldridge. *See his main entry, this Chapter.*

Coles, Robert. CHILDREN OF CRISIS. *Little-Atlantic* 3 vols. 1967–1973 Vol. 1 A Study of Courage and Fear (1967) $8.50 *Dell* 1968 pap. $2.65 Vol. 2 Migrants, Mountaineers and Sharecroppers (1972–1973) $12.50 pap. $4.95 Vol. 3 The South Goes North (1972–1973) $12.50 pap. $4.95

Volume 1, winner of a 1968 Anisfield-Wolf Award, is "a compassionate inquiry into interracial attitudes in the South, conducted not in the academic cloister, but in neighborhoods—white and black—of a South torn by desegregation"—(*SR*).

Conot, Robert. RIVERS OF BLOOD, YEARS OF DARKNESS. *Morrow* 1968 $7.50; *Bantam* pap. $1.25

Cordasco, Francesco. ITALIANS IN THE UNITED STATES: A Bibliography of Reports, Texts, Critical Studies, and Related Materials. *Oriole Edns.* 1972 $6.95

Cruse, Harold. THE CRISIS OF THE NEGRO INTELLECTUAL. *Morrow* 1967 $10.00 pap. $3.50

"Harold Cruse has written an angry, bitter and intemperate book, and the response of the engaged reader is going to be the same. It's a book that will provoke finger-waving rebuttal, shouting arguments, name-calling accusations. So lofty and demanding are his own standards that he stands in opposition to the broadest possible spectrum of workers in the cause of the American Negro, both white and colored, from reformist integrationists to the most violent advocates of black power. In almost 600 pages, Mr. Cruse finds no one he agrees with wholeheartedly, with the possible exception of the late C. Wright Mills, the only white man he thinks he might have had as an ally"—(Thomas Lask, in the *N.Y. Times*).

REBELLION OR REVOLUTION? *Morrow* 1968 1972 pap. $1.95

Fánon, Frantz. BLACK SKIN, WHITE MASKS. Trans. from the French by Charles L. Markmann *Grove* 1967 $5.00 Black Cat Bks. pap. $1.65

THE WRETCHED OF THE EARTH. Trans. from the French by Constance Farrington; pref. by Jean-Paul Sartre *Grove* Black Cat Bks. 1965 pap. $1.95. The late black psychiatrist analyzes the "Negro neurosis"; these two titles have had immense impact throughout the black world.

Fermi, Laura. ILLUSTRIOUS IMMIGRANTS: The Intellectual Migration from Europe, 1930–1941. *Univ. of Chicago Press* 1968 2nd. ed. 1971 $12.50 Phoenix Bks. 1972 pap. $3.95

Frazier, E. Franklin. BLACK BOURGEOISIE: The Rise of a New Middle Class in the United States. *Macmillan* (Free Press) 1957 pap. $2.95 Collier Bks. pap. $.95

NEGRO YOUTH AT THE CROSSWAYS: Their Personality Development in the Middle States. *Schocken* 1967 $6.50 pap. $2.45

Gambino, Richard. BLOOD OF MY BLOOD: The Dilemma of the Italian-Americans. *Doubleday* 1974 $7.95

Ginzberg, Eli, Ed. BUSINESS LEADERSHIP AND THE NEGRO CRISIS. *McGraw-Hill* 1968 $6.95. Essays by Kenneth Clark, John McKnight, Bayard Rustin, Nathan Wright and others.

Glazer, Nathan, and Daniel P. Moynihan. BEYOND THE MELTING POT: The Negroes, Puerto Ricans, Jews, Italians and Irish of New York City. *M.I.T. Press* 1963 rev. 2nd ed. 1970 $15.00 pap. $1.95. The first edition won the Anisfield-Wolf Award in 1964.

Grebler, Leo, and others. THE MEXICAN AMERICAN PEOPLE: The Nation's Second Largest Minority. *Macmillan* (Free Press) 1970 $14.95

"Combining insightful analysis of Spanish surname census data with data from sample surveys conducted in San Antonio and Los Angeles, this book in its author's words attempts to . . . present a portrait of the Mexican-American minority in relation to the dominant society"—(*Choice*).

Greeley, Andrew M. WHY CAN'T THEY BE LIKE US? Facts and Fallacies about Ethnic Differences and Group Conflicts in America. *Dutton* 1971 $7.50

Gregory, Dick. THE SHADOW THAT SCARES ME. Ed. by James R. McGraw *Doubleday* 1968 $4.95; *Pocket Bks.* 1969 pap. $.75

"Some humorous yet very serious lay sermons about the black-white situation in America and some of the things that have to be done"—(*PW*).

Grier, William H., and Price M. Cobbs. BLACK RAGE. Prefs. by Senator Fred R. Harris and Gunnar Myrdal *Basic Bks.* 1968 $5.95; *Bantam* 1969 pap. $.95

Two black psychiatrists at the University of California Medical Center, San Francisco, present, through their own case studies, a theory that the causes for Negro neuroses lie more in American society than in the personality of the individual. Christopher Lehmann-Haupt in the *N.Y. Times* considered this work to be "among the most important books on the Negro to appear in the last decade."

Handlin, Oscar. THE UPROOTED. *Little-Atlantic* 1951 2nd. enl. ed. 1973 $8.95 pap. $3.95; *Grosset* Univ. Lib. 1957 pap. $2.50

See also his main entry in Chapter 9, History, Government and Politics—American, this Vol.

Hapgood, Hutchins. The Spirit of the Ghetto: Studies of the Jewish Quarter of New York. Ed. with introd. by Moses Rischin; ill. by Jacob Epstein *Harvard Univ. Press* Belknap Press 1967 $8.50; pref. and notes by Harry Golden, ill. by Jacob Epstein *Schocken* pap. $2.95

Hentoff, Nat. The New Equality. *Viking* 1964 Compass Bks. 1965 pap. $1.45

Our Children Are Dying. Introd. by John Holt *Viking* 1966 Compass Bks. 1967 pap. $1.35. An account of the unconventional administration of a Harlem elementary school by its courageous principal, Elliott Shapiro.

Hughes, Langston. I Wonder as I Wander: An Autobiographical Journey. *Farrar Straus* (Hill & Wang) Am. Century 1964 pap. $3.95 Noonday pap. $3.95. The author tells of his travels to Russia, China, Japan and Spain, among other experiences.

See also his main entry in Chapter 9, Modern American Poetry, Reader's Adviser, Vol. 1.

Jackson, Kenneth T. The Ku Klux Klan in the City, 1915–1930. Urban Life in America Ser. *Oxford* 1967 $8.95 pap. $2.95

"The movement of the Negroes from the rural South to the urban South and North during and after World War I met a violent racist response. Accordingly, Jackson's commendable study of the K.K.K. in the cities nicely complements the work being done on the ghettos. The Klan during 1915–30 was largely an urban organization, feeding off working- and lower-middle-class unrest. It rose as an enormous political power, electing mayors and even higher officials, and dominating cities and occasionally states. For the most part it was less anti-Negro than anti-Catholic; not racism but anti-foreignism occupied most of its attention. The slogan was 100 percent Americanism, and most of the ingredients of a Fascist movement were there"—*(Nation)*.

Johnson, Henry S., and W. J. Hernandez-M., Eds. Educating the Mexican American. *Judson Press* 1971 pap. $6.95

"Thirty-four articles by leading Mexican American educators which deal with various aspects of the education of Mexican Americans of all ages . . . provides a multifaceted articulate view of their educational needs throughout the U.S."—*(Choice)*.

Kane, Michael B. Minorities in Textbooks: A Study of Their Treatment in Social Studies Texts. *Quadrangle Bks.* 1971 $5.95 pap. $1.95

"A consistently objective, fair-minded, and skillfully handled new study of the extent to which Jewish, Black, Indian, Oriental, and Spanish speaking Americans are included in representative secondary school social studies textbooks"—*(Choice)*.

Kelly, Lawrence C. The Navajo Indians and Federal Indian Policy, 1900–1935. *Univ. of Arizona Press* 1968 $7.50

Navajo Roundup. *Pruett* 1970 $9.95

Killens, John Oliver. Black Man's Burden. *Simon & Schuster* (Trident Press) 1966 $4.95 Touchstone Bks. 1976 pap. $1.95. The author of "And Then We Heard the Thunder" (*Knopf* 1963 $7.95), a novel on the Negro G.I. in World War II, expresses some thoughts on the racial situation.

King, Martin Luther, Jr. *See his main entry, this Chapter.*

Kornblum, William. Blue Collar Community. *Univ. of Chicago Press* 1975 $8.95

Kovel, Joel. White Racism: A Psychohistory. *Pantheon* 1971 $7.95

This is "a readable, reasonable, and very persuasive application of clinically validated psychological theory to the long standing and ubiquitous phenomenon of racism"—*(Choice)*.

Kozol, Jonathan. Death at an Early Age: The Destruction of the Hearts and Minds of Negro Children in the Boston Public Schools. *Houghton* 1967 $5.95; *Bantam* 1970 pap. $1.25

The author, a graduate of Harvard and a Rhodes Scholar, taught fourth grade in a school in the predominantly black Roxbury section of Boston until he was fired for reading a poem by Langston Hughes to his students. His book is a scathing indictment of the Boston school system. Nat Hentoff writes in the *New Yorker*: "Whatever its effects on the Boston public-school system (so far they appear to be nonexistent), I expect that 'Death at an Early Age' will be read in the future, as 'Nicholas Nickleby' is now, by those whose habit it is to look back in wonder at the barbarisms of past civilizations." The book won the National Book Award in Science, Philosophy and Religion in 1968.

Landes, Ruth. THE MYSTIC LAKE SIOUX: Sociology of the Mdewakantonwan Santee. *Univ. of Wisconsin Press* 1969 $14.00

THE PRAIRIE POTAWATOMI: Tradition and Ritual in the Twentieth Century. *Univ. of Wisconsin Press* 1970 $17.50

"An excellent contribution to our understanding of the problems of minority groups"—*(LJ)*.

Lester, Julius. LOOK OUT, WHITEY! BLACK POWER'S GON' GET YOUR MAMA! *Dial* 1968 $5.95; *Grove* 1969 pap. $1.50

"An oratorical, hortatory, angry, and sometimes humorous history and explication of the black power movement"—*(LJ)*.

Levitan, Sar A., and others. STILL A DREAM: The Changing Status of Blacks Since 1960. *Harvard Univ. Press* 1975 $15.00

A "comprehensive and up-to-date statistical analysis of black economic and social status"—(Publisher's note).

Lincoln, Charles Eric. BLACK MUSLIMS IN AMERICA. *Beacon* 1961 rev. ed. 1973 $12.50 pap. $3.95

McKissick, Floyd, and W. Worthy. BLACK POWER AND THE WORLD REVOLUTION. *Holt* 1972 $6.95

Malcolm X. THE AUTOBIOGRAPHY OF MALCOLM X. Ed. and epilogue by Alex Haley; introd. by M. S. Handler *Grove* 1965 $7.50 Black Cat Bks. pap. $1.95

"A remarkable testimony of a man who experienced utter pathos as a child and a young man, but within a very few years transformed his life to impeccable piety"—*(LJ)*.

MALCOLM X SPEAKS: Selected Speeches and Statements. Ed. with notes by George Breitman *Grove* Black Cat Bks. pap. $.95

Marden, Charles F., and Gladys Meyer. MINORITIES IN AMERICAN SOCIETY. *Van Nostrand-Reinhold* 4th ed. 1973 pap. $7.95

Marquis, Arnold, A GUIDE TO AMERICA'S INDIANS: Ceremonials, Reservations, and Museums. *Univ. of Oklahoma Press* 1975 $7.50

A "brief general introduction to Indians"—*(LJ)*.

Marshall, Burke. FEDERALISM AND CIVIL RIGHTS. Fwd. by Robert F. Kennedy *Columbia* 1964 $5.00. A former prominent Justice Department official discusses the need for federal involvement in civil rights.

Meyer, Roy W. HISTORY OF THE SANTEE SIOUX: United States Indian Policy on Trial. *Univ. of Nebraska Press* 1967 $8.95

Miller, Elizabeth W., and Mary Fisher, Eds. THE NEGRO IN AMERICA: A Bibliography. Compiled for the American Academy of Arts and Sciences. *Harvard Univ. Press* 1966 rev. ed. 1970 $10.00 pap. $4.95

Moody, Ann. COMING OF AGE IN MISSISSIPPI: An Autobiography. *Dial* 1968 $7.95; *Dell* Laurel Eds. 1970 pap. $1.25 Delta Bks. 1970 pap. $2.45

Moore, Joan W., and Alfredo Cuellar. MEXICAN AMERICANS. *Prentice-Hall* 1970 $5.95 pap. $3.50

"No better introduction to Mexican-Americans can be recommended"—*(Choice)*.

Moquin, Wayne, and Charles Van Doren, Eds. A DOCUMENTARY HISTORY OF THE ITALIAN-AMERICANS. *Praeger* new ed. 1974 $15.00 pap. $4.95

A DOCUMENTARY HISTORY OF THE MEXICAN AMERICANS. *Bantam* 1972 pap. $1.25

Myrdal, Gunnar. AN AMERICAN DILEMMA. *Harper* rev. ed. 1962 $18.50. *For comment, see his main entry, this Chapter.*

Novak, Michael. THE RISE OF THE UNMELTABLE ETHNICS. *Macmillan* 1972 $8.95

Parks, Gordon. BORN BLACK. *Lippincott* 1971 $10.00

A CHOICE OF WEAPONS. Ed. by Virginia F. Allen and Florette Henri *Harper* 1966 $7.95 Perenn. Lib. 1973 pap. $1.25

Porter, Judith D. BLACK CHILD, WHITE CHILD: The Development of Racial Attitudes. *Harvard Univ. Press* 1971 $8.95

"An ingenious and detailed study into the origins of racial attitudes among three-to-five year old black and white children in integrated and segregated play schools"—*(Choice)*.

Powledge, Fred. BLACK POWER, WHITE RESISTANCE: Notes on the New Civil War. *Simon & Schuster* Touchstone-Clarion Bks. 1971 pap. $2.95. A white Southern reporter argues for interracial cooperation.

Ryan, Joseph A., Ed. WHITE ETHNICS: Life in Working Class America. *Prentice-Hall* 1974 $7.95 pap. $2.95

A "good introduction to a central issue in contemporary American society"—*(LJ)*.

Schrag, Peter. DECLINE OF THE WASP. *Simon & Schuster* 1971 $6.95

Seder, Joan, and Berkeley G. Burrell. GETTING IT TOGETHER: Black Businessmen in America. *Harcourt* 1971 $6.95

"These are the stories of 16 black businessmen who have become successful and made a lot of money despite humble beginnings and rampant prejudice"—*(LJ)*.

Shannon, William V. THE AMERICAN IRISH: A Political and Social Portrait. *Macmillan* rev. ed. 1966 $9.95 Collier Bks. 1974 pap. $4.95

Shockley, John S. CHICANO REVOLT IN A TEXAS TOWN. *Univ. of Notre Dame Press* 1974 $9.95 pap. $3.95

"The town is Crystal City and the time is the 1960s. The revolt consists of the victories at the ballot box and in the council chambers for the town's Mexican-American population. It is an interesting and at times exciting story"—*(Choice)*.

Silberman, Charles E. CRISIS IN BLACK AND WHITE. *Random* 1964 $7.95 Vintage Bks. pap. $1.95

Simpson, George E., and J. M. Yinger. RACIAL AND CULTURAL MINORITIES: An Analysis of Prejudice and Discrimination. *Harper* 4th ed. 1972 $13.95

Steiner, Stan. THE ISLANDS: The Worlds of the Puerto Ricans. *Harper* 1974 $12.50

THE NEW INDIANS. *Harper* 1968 $8.95; *Dell* Delta Bks. 1969 pap. $2.45

"The American Indian is demanding Red Power. He is having a tough fight with a short stick. But reports that he is vanishing have been grossly exaggerated. That is the story told in Stan Steiner's 'The New Indians,' a magnificent blockbuster of a book"—(Charles Poore, in the *N.Y. Times*).

LA RAZA: The Mexican Americans. *Harper* 1970 $8.95

"Steiner traveled throughout the Southwest going into the barrios, seeking firsthand information on Chicano movements. The result is a series of readable and informative conversations with Mexican-Americans. Steiner faithfully reproduces Chicano views on gringos, governmental officials, Texas Rangers, and public school teachers among others"—*(Choice)*.

Strober, Gerald. AMERICAN JEWS: Community in Crisis. *Doubleday* 1974 $7.95. The author argues that Judaism is today under assault from both internal weaknesses and external pressure.

Tannenbaum, Frank. SLAVE AND CITIZEN: The Negro in the Americas. 1948. *Random* Vintage Bks. 1962 pap. $1.65. A brief but important comparison of the slave systems of North and South America.

Thomas, Piri. DOWN THESE MEAN STREETS. *Knopf* 1967 $7.95; *New Am. Lib.* Signet 1971 pap. $1.25

The autobiography of a Puerto Rican youth growing up in East Harlem's el Barrio. "Charged with high voltage. . . . The words jump right out of the page. . . . It is every bit as shocking an eyeopener as Brown's memorable book, 'Manchild in the Promised Land' "—(John Barkham, in *SR Syndicate*).

Tussman, Joseph, Ed. THE SUPREME COURT ON RACIAL DISCRIMINATION. *Oxford* 1963 pap. $2.95. Transcripts of important recent rulings.

Vivo, Paquita, Ed. THE PUERTO RICANS: An Annotated Bibliography. *Bowker* 1973 $15.50
Produced by the Puerto Rican Research and Resource Center, this bibliography was
compiled from a number of major United States and Puerto Rican library catalogs.
Its purpose is to offer the English-speaking reader "a complete bibliographic overview of Puerto Ricans."

Weed, Perry. THE WHITE ETHNIC MOVEMENT AND ETHNIC POLITICS. *Praeger* 1973 $16.50

Wilhoit, Francis M. THE POLITICS OF MASSIVE RESISTANCE. *Braziller* 1974 $8.95 pap. $3.95
"His lucid and fact-based explanation of the counter-revolutionary tactics of the white suprem-
acists [opposing civil rights for blacks] . . . expertly sums up a sad chapter in American history"—
(*Choice*).

Wright, Nathan, Jr. BLACK POWER AND URBAN UNREST: Creative Possibilities. *Hawthorn
Bks.* 1967 pap. $1.95
"In July 1966 the National Committee of Negro Churchmen met in New York to examine the
positive implications of the Black Power concept. Nathan Wright, Jr., explains their position in
Black Power and Urban Unrest: Creative Possibilities. 'While pushing and participating in the
absolutely worthwhile interracial program in the field of civil rights, the black people of America,'
he writes, 'ought long ago to have been addressing themselves to the far more basic business of the
development by black people of black people for the growth into self-sufficiency and self-respect
of black people. This is the main and previously neglected business to which we must address
ourselves. It is to this top priority concern of self-development that the issue of Black Power calls
the black people of America today' "—(*SR*).

LET'S WORK TOGETHER. *Hawthorn Bks.* 1968 pap. $1.95
"Dr. Wright . . . has not written a Pollyanna call for unity as his title might suggest, but rather
. . . a hardheaded delineation of areas in which the white liberal and black militant might each
work independently and occasionally together toward the common end of a just society"—(*LJ*).

Young, Whitney M., Jr. BEYOND RACISM: Building an Open Society. *McGraw-Hill* 1969
$6.95 pap. $2.95

Women in Society

This list includes books on the women's movement as well as women in our society. Many
other books on women are found in the appropriate subject lists throughout the book
such as Anthropology, History, and Science. See also a bibliography "Feminists Feast" by
Sheila Tobias in *Choice* September 1973 (Vol. 10: 928–934).

Ahlum, Carol, and Jacqueline M. Fralley. FEMINIST RESOURCES FOR SCHOOLS AND COL-
LEGES: A Guide to Curriculum Materials. *Feminist Press* 1973 pap. $1.00. An anno-
tated bibliography.

Banner, Lois W. WOMEN IN MODERN AMERICA: A Brief History. *Harcourt* 1974 pap. $4.25
"The book will be useful to the general reader and as a supplement to college courses in U.S.
history which often underemphasize women's role and activities"—(*Choice*).

Beauvoir, Simone de. THE SECOND SEX. Trans. by H. M. Parshley *Knopf* 1953 $12.95;
Random Vintage Bks. 1974 pap. $2.95

Bird, Caroline. BORN FEMALE: The High Cost of Keeping Women Down. *McKay* 1968 rev.
ed. 1970 $8.95 pap. $3.95; *Simon & Schuster* (Pocket Bks.) 1974 pap. $1.25
"This is a worthwhile addition to the growing literature on the problems faced by working
women and the adjustments both society and women are making to meet those problems. The
book is recommended for public and academic libraries"—(*LJ*).

Brownmiller, Susan. AGAINST OUR WILL: Men, Women, and Rape. *Simon & Schuster* 1975
$10.95
This book "deserves a place on the shelf next to those rare books about social problems which
force us to make connections we have too long evaded, and change the way we feel about what we
know"—(*N.Y. Times*).

Bullough, Vern L., and Bonnie Bullough. THE SUBORDINATE SEX: A History of Attitudes
Toward Women. *Univ. of Illinois Press* 1973 $10.95; *Penguin* 1974 pap. $2.95

De Crow, Karen. SEXIST JUSTICE: How Legal Sexism Affects You. *Random* 1974 $7.95

"A woman lawyer and officer of N.O.W. examines the ways in which women are discriminated against by the legal system and how this discrimination maims society at large"—*(American Libraries)*.

Decter, Midge. THE NEW CHASTITY AND OTHER ARGUMENTS AGAINST WOMEN'S LIBERATION. *Coward* 1972 $5.95; *Putnam* Capricorn Giants 1974 pap. $2.65

A "slashing critique of the women's liberation movement"—*(American Libraries)*.

Ellmann, Mary. THINKING ABOUT WOMEN. *Harcourt* 1968 Harvest Bks. 1970 pap. $2.65

Firestone, Shulamith. THE DIALECTIC OF SEX: The Case for Feminist Revolution. *Morrow* 1974 pap. $2.95

Freeman, Jo. THE POLITICS OF WOMEN'S LIBERATION: A Case Study of an Emerging Social Movement and Its Relation to the Policy Process. *McKay* 1975 $8.95 pap. $4.95

"A scholarly yet completely absorbing history of the second wave of feminism, with emphasis on the relationship between the women's movement and public policy"—*(LJ)*.

Friedan, Betty. THE FEMININE MYSTIQUE. *Norton* 1963 $7.95 2nd ed. 1974 $8.95; *Dell* 1975 pap. $1.25

Greer, Germaine. THE FEMALE EUNUCH. *McGraw-Hill* 1971 $6.95; *Bantam* 1972 pap. $1.95

Hahn, Emily. ONCE UPON A PEDESTAL: An Informal History of Women's Lib. *T. Y. Crowell* 1974 $6.95

Harrison, Cynthia E. WOMEN'S MOVEMENT MEDIA: A Source Guide. *Bowker* 1975 $13.95

"A well organized listing of more than 500 groups, this source book covers both print and nonprint information"—*(LJ)*.

Janeway, Elizabeth. MAN'S WORLD, WOMAN'S PLACE: A Study in Social Mythology. *Morrow* 1971 $8.95

The author "presents the most sophisticated, integrated, and intelligent analysis of women's place since Beauvoir's 'The Second Sex' (1953)"—*(Choice)*.

Johnston, Jill. THE LESBIAN NATION. *Simon & Schuster* 1973 $7.95 pap. $2.95

An "engrossing and wildly honest account of her emergence as a revolutionary, a lesbian, [and] a feminist"—*(American Libraries)*.

Kanowitz, Leo. WOMEN AND THE LAW: The Unfinished Revolution. *Univ. of New Mexico Press* 1969 $8.95 pap. $3.95

Korda, Michael. MALE CHAUVINISM: How It Works. *Random* 1973 $6.95

Kraditor, Aileen S., Ed., with introd. UP FROM THE PEDESTAL: A Documentary History of the Rise of the American Women. *Quadrangle Bks.* 1968 pap. $2.95

"This brilliantly edited anthology of basic documents generated in the struggle for women's rights is a major contribution to American social history"—*(LJ)*.

Lerner, Gerda. BLACK WOMEN IN WHITE AMERICA. *Pantheon* 1972 $12.95

Martin, M. Kay, and Barbara Voorhies. FEMALE OF THE SPECIES. *Columbia* 1974 $15.00 pap. $6.00

The author "commences with biology, cross-refers to the non-human primates, then proceeds to the status of womanness in horticultural, agricultural, pastoral, and industrial societies"—(Earl W. Count).

Millett, Kate. FLYING. *Knopf* 1974 $8.95

This is a "record of one decisive year in Kate Millett's life—her struggle to live out her personal ideas in the face of the demands made on her as a Women's movement spokeswoman"—*(American Libraries)*.

SEXUAL POLITICS. *Avon Bks.* 1971 pap. $2.95

Morgan, Robin, Ed. SISTERHOOD IS POWERFUL: An Anthology of Writings from the Women's Liberation Movement. *Random* 1970 $8.95 Vintage Bks. pap. $2.45

Rosen, Marjorie. PopČorn Venus. *Coward* 1973 $9.95

"A gifted young film critic chronicles the evolving image of women on film"—*(American Libraries)*.

Rossi, Alice S., Ed. The Feminist Papers: From Adams to Beauvoir. *Columbia* 1973 $12.95; *Bantam* 1974 pap. $1.95

Roszak, Betty, and Theodore Roszak, Eds. Masculine Feminine: Readings in Sexual Mythology and the Liberation of Women. *Harper* 1970 pap. $2.95

Rowbotham, Sheila. Hidden From History: Rediscovering Women in History from the 17th Century to the Present. *Pantheon* 1974 $7.95

Schneir, Miriam, Ed. Feminism: The Essential Historical Writings. *Random* 1971 $7.95 pap. $2.45

Scott, Anne Firor. The Southern Lady: From Pedestal to Politics, 1830–1930. *Univ. of Chicago Press* 1972 $7.50 pap. $2.45

Sochen, June. Herstory: A Woman's View of American History. *Alfred Pub. Co.* 1974 $10.00 pap. $5.95

"Informal replay of American history this time focusing primarily on women"—*(Booklist)*.

Theodore, Athena, Ed. The Professional Woman. *Schenkman* 1971 $12.50 pap. $5.95

"Fifty four readings that explore the economic, social, and personal realities (and myths) of the female professional in America"—(Publisher's note).

Urbanization

The following list includes books which not only elucidate our urban crisis, but also offer some resourceful and creative solutions to its problems. Good series on this subject are *Oxford's* Urban Life in America Series (Richard C. Wade, Gen. Ed.) and *Braziller's* Planning and Cities Series. The *American Jewish Committee* (165 E. 56th St., New York, N.Y. 10022) publishes an array of pamphlets, articles and bibliographies designed to promote better understanding of urban problems. Catalog, "Cities in Crisis," on request.

Abrams, Charles. The City Is the Frontier. *Harper* 1965 Colophon Bks. pap. $1.95

The Language of Cities: A Glossary of Terms. *Viking* 1971 $10.00; *Avon Bks.* 1972 pap. $3.95

"As well as definitions of urban affairs terms . . . [this book] also gives explanations . . . of the philosophical and theoretical backgrounds of the terms"—*(LJ)*.

Bacon, Edmund N. The Design of Cities. *Viking* 1966 rev. ed. 1974 $20.00. An eminent city planner discusses the city as a work of art.

Bellush, Jewel, and Murray Hausknecht, Eds. Urban Renewal: People, Politics and Planning. *Doubleday* Anchor Bks. 1967 pap. $2.45

A "valuable collection" (*LJ*) of essays.

Berry, Brian J. L. Growth Centers in the American Urban System. *Ballinger Pub.* 2 vols. 1973 Vol. 1 Community Development and Regional Growth in the Sixties and Seventies $9.50 Vol. 2 Working Materials on the U.S. Urban Hierarchy and on Growth Center Characteristics Organized by Economic Regions $19.50

The Human Consequences of Urbanization. *St. Martin's* 1973 $9.95 pap. $3.95

"One of the foremost authorities on urbanization has produced an outstanding short survey of its impact during this century, both in the urban-industrial West and less-developed countries . . . . At last there is a small volume on urbanization worth its high cost. The value lies in the considerable work the author devoted to saying important things briefly"—*(Choice)*.

(With Frank E. Horton). Urban Environmental Management: Planning for Pollution Control. *Prentice-Hall* 1974 $14.95

(With Jack Meltzer, Eds.). Goals for Urban America. *Prentice-Hall* Spectrum Bks. 1967 pap. $1.95. Essays on urban renewal.

Clawson, Marion, and Peter Hall. Planning and Urban Growth: An Anglo-American Comparison. *Johns Hopkins Press* 1973 $12.50

Cowan, Peter, Ed. DEVELOPING PATTERNS OF URBANIZATION. *Sage Pubns.* 1970 $7.00

Eldredge, H. Wentworth, Ed. TAMING MEGALOPOLIS. *Praeger* 1967 2 vols. Vol. 1 What Is and What Could Be Vol. 2 How to Manage an Urbanized World each $9.25; *Doubleday* Anchor Bks. 2 vols. pap. Vol. 1 $2.50 Vol. 2 $3.50. Volume 1 contains articles on present urban renewal projects, city politics, pollution, etc. and plans for improvement. Contributors include Pope Paul VI, Lyndon Johnson, Jane Jacobs and August Heckscher. Volume 2 consists of more specialized articles on city planning.

Elkins, T. H. THE URBAN EXPLOSION. *Humanities Press* 1973 pap. $2.25

ENCYCLOPEDIA OF URBAN PLANNING. Ed. by Arnold Whittick *McGraw-Hill* new ed. 1974 $29.50

This is "an encyclopedia of international scope [and] . . . a work of collaboration of numerous contributors, of the publisher, and of the editor"—(Preface).

Faltermayer, Edmund K. REDOING AMERICA: A Nationwide Report on How We Can Make Our Cities and Suburbs Livable. *Macmillan* Collier Bks. 1969 pap. $1.95

"He has prepared a blueprint here that every library should have. Every urban dweller should read it as a litany of hope"—(*LJ*).

Frieden, Bernard J., and Robert Morris, Eds. URBAN PLANNING AND SOCIAL POLICY. *Basic Bks.* 1968 pap. $5.75

Includes writings of more than 30 specialists, including Charles Silberman and Bayard Rustin. "Its bibliographies are excellent and current. . . . It is not a book on physical planning, but rather one about the political and social handling of poverty and segregation"—(*LJ*).

Friedmann, John. URBANIZATION, PLANNING AND NATIONAL DEVELOPMENT. *Sage Pubns.* 1973 $12.50

Germani, Gino. MODERNIZATION, URBANIZATION AND THE URBAN CRISIS. *Little* 1973 pap. $5.95

Gottman, Jean. MEGALOPOLIS: The Urbanized Northeastern Seaboard of the United States. 1961. *Kraus* $10.00; *M.I.T. Press* 1964 pap. $4.95

Green, Constance M. AMERICAN CITIES IN THE GROWTH OF THE NATION. *Harper* Colophon Bks. pap. $2.25

THE RISE OF URBAN AMERICA. *Harper* 1965 $7.95 Colophon Bks. pap. $2.25

Greer, Scott. THE URBANE VIEW: Life and Politics in Metropolitan America. *Oxford* 1972 $9.50 Galaxy Bks. 1973 pap. $2.95

Hacker, Andrew. THE NEW YORKERS: A Profile of an American Metropolis. *Mason* 1975 $10.00

Hacker "manages to weave a stylish and easily understandable tapestry of the comings and goings of some eight million people"—(*LJ*).

Halprin, Lawrence. CITIES. *M.I.T. Press* rev. ed. 1972 $12.50 pap. $4.95

FREEWAYS. *Van Nostrand-Reinhold* 1966 $16.95

Handlin, Oscar. THE NEWCOMERS: Negroes and Puerto Ricans in a Changing Metropolis. *Harvard Univ. Press* 1959 $5.00; *Doubleday* Anchor Bks. pap. $1.95

(With John Burchard, Eds.). THE HISTORIAN AND THE CITY. *M.I.T. Press* 1963 $12.50 pap. $2.95

This book resulted from a conference held at Cambridge, Mass., in 1961 which "attempted to relate to the present changing status of the city. The essays still contain some of the flavor and vitality of oral delivery, but the footnotes and bibliographies indicate the depth of study upon which each is founded. This excellent study of current opinion about the city commends itself to university and public libraries." Professor of History at Harvard University since 1954, Handlin won the Pulitzer Prize for History in 1952 for his book, "The Uprooted" (*Little-Atlantic* 1951 $5.50; *Grosset* Univ. Lib. 1957 pap. $1.65).

Hawley, Amos H. URBAN SOCIETY: An Ecological Approach. *Ronald* 1971 $8.50

Higbee, Edward. A QUESTION OF PRIORITIES: New Strategies for Our Urbanized World. Introd. by R. Buckminster Fuller *Morrow* 1970 pap. $2.25

"This interesting, very readable book closely examines the problems of local government, budgets, societal interaction, and psychological studies and offers new insights into urban problems. Informed laymen as well as specialists in many fields will want to read it"—*(LJ)*.

Hollingshead, August B. ELMTOWN'S YOUTH. *Wiley* 1949 pap. $5.50. One of the most famous sociological studies.

Jacobs, Jane. THE DEATH AND LIFE OF GREAT AMERICAN CITIES. *Random* 1961 $10.00 Vintage Bks. pap. $1.95; *Modern Library* 1969 $2.95

THE ECONOMY OF CITIES. *Random* 1969 $5.95 Vintage Bks. 1970 pap. $1.95

Le Corbusier. THE RADIANT CITY. *Grossman* 1967 $22.50

McKelvey, Blake. AMERICAN URBANIZATION: A Comparative History. *Scott, Foresman* 1973 pap. $2.50

THE CITY IN AMERICAN HISTORY. *Harper* (Barnes & Noble) 1969 $8.50

"[The author's introduction] constitutes the most extensive essay on the city in American history yet produced . . . a helpful introduction to the study of urban history"—*(Journal of American History)*. The documents section ranges from Jefferson's letters to the Commission on Civil Disorders of 1968.

THE EMERGENCE OF METROPOLITAN AMERICA, 1915–1966. *Rutgers Univ. Press* 1968 $10.00

This book begins where "The Urbanization of America" *(see below)* ended. "Each of the six chapters covers a single decade, from the Great War through the Great Society. The emphasis is on the growth of metropolitan consciousness, and on political and institutional efforts to find new methods of dealing with . . . migration and such attendant problems as housing, employment, and ethnic conflict"—*(American Historical Review)*.

THE URBANIZATION OF AMERICA, 1860–1915. *Rutgers Univ. Press* 1963 $10.00

"The city historian of Rochester, New York, paints here on a broad canvas the history of American cities in what he regards as the half century in which they flowered, ending with the beginning of the transition to the metropolis." Comprehensive in scope, the book is "recommended for public and academic libraries as a general overview of a tangled skein"—*(LJ)*.

Meltsner, Arnold J. THE POLITICS OF CITY REVENUE. *Univ. of California Press* 1971 $10.00

"While this book is devoted specifically to the city of Oakland, California, the principles studied and elaborated are applicable to almost any city. Data for the book were collected while Meltsner was serving as participant-observer in the city manager's office"—*(Choice)*.

Miller, Zane L. URBANIZATION OF MODERN AMERICA: A Brief History. *Harcourt* 1973 pap. $3.95

Moynihan, Daniel Patrick, Ed. TOWARD A NATIONAL URBAN POLICY. *Basic Bks.* 1970 $8.95

"A collection of papers on such topics as poverty, education, population make-up, transportation, housing, urban design, crime, pollution, urban renewal, health planning, land use, and government"—*(LJ)*.

Mumford, Lewis. *See his main entry, this Chapter.*

Reps, John W. THE MAKING OF URBAN AMERICA: A History of City Planning in the United States. *Princeton Univ. Press* 1965 $37.50

"The first comprehensive documentary of its kind. It is a fascinating study and is not likely to be surpassed for a long time"—*(LJ)*.

Saarinen, Eliel. THE CITY, ITS GROWTH, ITS DECAY, ITS FUTURE. *M.I.T. Press* 1965 $12.50 pap. $2.95

Schwartz, Barry, Ed. THE CHANGING FACE OF THE SUBURBS. *Univ. of Chicago Press* 1975 $16.00

Simon, Arthur R. STUYVESANT TOWN, U.S.A.: Pattern for Two Americas. *New York Univ. Press* 1970 $6.95

"Simon, rector of Trinity Lutheran Church in the Lower East Side of Manhattan, has studied the first project of slum clearance and redevelopment attempted by private enterprise with public assistance. Stuyvesant Town, a precursor of the urban renewal movement, became a testing ground for the civil rights struggle"—(*LJ*).

Suttles, Gerald D. THE SOCIAL CONSTRUCTION OF COMMUNITIES. *Univ. of Chicago Press* 1972 $9.50 1973 pap. $2.45

> After identifying various types of communities Suttles "suggests some individual strategies, alliances and public programs to improve communities, ending with a not too hopeful analysis of the local geographic community as 'communion' "—(*Choice*).

THE SOCIAL ORDER OF THE SLUM: Ethnicity and Territory in the Inner City. *Univ. of Chicago Press* rev. ed. 1968 $8.95 Phoenix Bks. 1970 pap. $2.45

Taylor, William L. HANGING TOGETHER: Equality in an Urban Nature. *Simon & Schuster* 1971 $7.95 pap. $3.95

> Taylor, in "this well written volume competently surveys the past, present, and future of urban blacks in the U.S."—(*Choice*).

Tice, George A. URBAN LANDSCAPES: A New Jersey Portrait. *Rutgers Univ. Press* 1975 $20.00 pap. $12.50

Von Eckardt, Wolf. A PLACE TO LIVE: The Crisis of the Cities. Fwd. by August Heckscher *Delacorte* 1967 $9.95; *Dell* Delta Bks. 1969 pap. $2.65

> Von Eckardt reasons that the deplorable state of architecture in our cities is one of the major factors contributing to the urban crisis in an "intelligent, knowledgeable [and] journalistic style. . . . Hundreds of well-chosen photographs illustrating the text sensitively illustrate the points he makes"—(*LJ*).

Wakstein, Allen M., Ed. URBANIZATION OF AMERICA: An Historical Anthology. *Houghton* 1970 pap. (orig.) $6.95

Weaver, Robert C. DILEMMAS OF URBAN AMERICA. *Harvard Univ. Press* 1965 $3.50; *Atheneum* 1967 pap. $1.95

THE URBAN COMPLEX: Human Values in Urban Life. *Doubleday* Anchor Bks. 1964 pap. $1.95

> The former Secretary for Housing and Urban Development presents seven essays on urban renewal on the Federal level. "A significant book. . . . It should be considered basic in its area"— (*LJ*).

Weicher, John C. URBAN RENEWAL: National Programs for Local Problems. *American Enterprise Pubns.* 1973 $3.00

Wilson, James Q., Ed. METROPOLITAN ENIGMA: Inquiries into the Nature and Dimensions of America's Urban Crisis. *Harvard Univ. Press* 1968 $9.95; *Doubleday* Anchor Bks. 1970 pap. $2.95

> The twelve chapters of essays by different contributors "concern the distribution of urban jobs and industry, urban transportation, finance, housing, race and migration, crime, schools, rioting, poverty, pollution and urban beauty"—(*Choice*).

URBAN RENEWAL: The Record and the Controversy. *M.I.T. Press* 1967 $12.50 pap. $4.45

Poverty and Unemployment

Blaustein, Arthur I., and Roger R. Woock, Eds. MAN AGAINST POVERTY: World War III. *Random* 1968 $10.00. A collection of writings on the question of poverty by such authors as Michael Harrington, Paul Goodman, Robert Coles, Barbara Ward Jackson, Oscar Lewis, William A. Williams, Amitai Etzioni, Martin Luther King, Jr., and Senator William Fulbright.

Bloomberg, Warner, Jr., and Henry J. Schmandt, Eds. URBAN POVERTY: Its Social and Political Dimensions. *Sage Pubns.* 1970 pap. $4.95

Brager, George A., and Francis P. Purcell, Eds. COMMUNITY ACTION AGAINST POVERTY: Readings from the Mobilization Experience. *College & Univ. Press* 1967 $7.00 pap. $3.45. Papers dealing with the history of Mobilization for Youth, a demonstration project for motivating the poor to deal with their own problems.

The Citizens' Board of Inquiry into Hunger and Malnutrition in the United States. HUNGER, U.S.A. Introd. by Robert F. Kennedy *Beacon* 1958 pap. $3.95

Coles, Robert, and Al Clayton. STILL HUNGRY IN AMERICA. Introd. by Edward M. Kennedy; photographs by Al Clayton *Norton* 1969 $7.95 pap. $2.95

> "This photographic essay, including interviews with the poor themselves and accompanied by 110 photographs . . . taken in rural Mississippi, in Appalachia, and in the . . . center of Atlanta, Georgia, conveys . . . the plight of the millions of poor [in America]"—(Publisher's note).

Coombs, Philip H., and Manzoor Ahmed. ATTACKING RURAL POVERTY: How Nonformal Education Can Help. *Johns Hopkins Press* 1974 $15.00 pap. $3.95

> This is "the first systematic study of nonformal education *i.e.* programs outside the standard school system, designed to increase the skills and productivity of farmers, artisans, craftsmen, and entrepreneurs"—(*Choice*).

Donovan, John C. THE POLITICS OF POVERTY. American Government Policy Studies *Pegasus* 2nd ed. 1973 pap. $1.95. The chairman of the department of government and legal studies at Bowdoin College analyzes the political factors impeding government poverty programs.

Dugan, Dennis J., and William H. Leahy. PERSPECTIVES ON POVERTY. *Praeger* 1973 $13.50

Eames, Edwin, and Judith Granich Goode. URBAN POVERTY IN A CROSS-CULTURAL CONTEXT. *Macmillan* (Free Press) 1973 $8.95

> "Two anthropologists seek to present an historical perspective of the culture of poverty, as it has existed in the evolution of society, from primitive to technological"—(*LJ*).

Elman, Richard M. THE POORHOUSE STATE: The American Way of Life on Public Assistance. *Dell* Delta Bks. 1968 pap. $2.25

Ferman, Louis, Joyce L. Kornbluh and Alan Haber, Eds. POVERTY IN AMERICA: A Book of Readings. Introd. by Michael Harrington *Univ. of Michigan Press* 1968 $12.50 pap. $6.95. Essays on poverty by such writers as Martin Deutsch, Leon Keyserling, Dwight Macdonald, Oscar Ornati and Bayard Rustin.

Fishman, Leo, and Betty G. Fishman. EMPLOYMENT, UNEMPLOYMENT AND ECONOMIC GROWTH. *T. Y. Crowell* 1966 $6.00 pap. $2.95

Ginsburg, Helen, Ed. POVERTY, ECONOMICS AND SOCIETY. *Little* 1972 pap. $5.95

Gladwin, Thomas. POVERTY U.S.A. *Little* 1967 $4.75 pap. $1.95

> This "invaluable work is neither optimistic nor pessimistic, and it neither blames nor preaches; it just tells, and tells brilliantly"—(*New Yorker*).

Good, Paul. THE AMERICAN SERFS: A Report on Poverty in the Rural South. *Putnam* 1968 $5.95

Harrington, Michael. THE OTHER AMERICA: Poverty in the United States. *Macmillan* 1962 rev. ed. 1970 $7.95; *Penguin* Pelican Bks. 1962 pap. $1.45

See also his main entry, this Chapter.

Hazlitt, Henry. THE CONQUEST OF POVERTY. *Arlington* 1973 $8.95

> "Viewing poverty as an individual problem, the author attacks social welfare expenditures, guaranteed income plan, job programs, labor unions, minimum wage laws, and progressive income taxes because they interfere with the free enterprise system"—(*LJ*).

Huber, Joan, and Paul Chalfant. SOCIOLOGY OF AMERICAN POVERTY. *Schenkman* 1974 $11.25 pap. $4.50; *General Learning Corp.* 1974 pap. $5.95

James, Dorothy. POVERTY, POLITICS AND CHANGE. *Prentice-Hall* ref. ed. 1972 $6.95 pap. $3.25

Leacock, Eleanor, Ed. CULTURE OF POVERTY: A Critique. *Simon & Schuster* Touchstone Bks. 1971 pap. $3.95

Lewis, Oscar. *See his main entry, this Chapter.*

Meissner, Hanna H. POVERTY IN THE AFFLUENT SOCIETY. *Harper* rev. ed. 1973 pap. $4.50

Minuchin, Salvador, and others. FAMILIES OF THE SLUMS. *Basic Bks.* 1967 $13.50. A report by a team of social caseworkers from the Wiltwyck School for Boys on disadvantaged families in urban areas.

Moynihan, Daniel Patrick. MAXIMUM FEASIBLE MISUNDERSTANDING: Community Action of the War on Poverty. *Macmillan* (Free Press) 1969 $5.95 pap. $2.95. A criticism of the poverty program for its inefficiency in involving the poor people themselves in antipoverty efforts.

(Ed.). ON UNDERSTANDING POVERTY: Perspectives from the Social Sciences. *Basic Bks.* 1969 $10.00 pap. $4.95

These articles "make a significant contribution to understanding the nature of poverty and the various programs that have been developed in an attempt to eliminate it in the United States. They represent the conclusions of a number of eminent social scientists and persons who have actually been involved in the creation, implementation, and evaluation of antipoverty programs"—*(LJ)*.

Myrdal, Gunnar. THE CHALLENGE OF WORLD POVERTY: A World Anti-Poverty Program in Outline. *Pantheon* 1970 $8.95; *Random* Vintage Bks. 1971 pap. $2.95

"This work is a sequel to his "Asian Drama" and contains the policy prescriptions which grew out of that earlier work. Radical reforms in the underdeveloped countries are called for to reduce social inequality and to encourage attitudes which promote economic progress"—*(Choice)*.

See also his main entry, this Chapter.

Okun, Arthur M., Ed. THE BATTLE AGAINST UNEMPLOYMENT. *Norton* rev. ed. 1972 $7.95 pap. $2.45

Padfield, Harland, and Roy Williams. STAY WHERE YOU WERE: A Study of Unemployables in Industry. *Lippincott* 1973 $7.50 pap. $3.25

Palmer, John L. INFLATION, UNEMPLOYMENT, AND POVERTY. *Lexington Bks.* 1973 $12.50

Piven, Frances F., and Richard A. Cloward. REGULATING THE POOR: The Functions of Public Welfare. *Pantheon* 1971 $10.00

"This work is outstanding for its presentation and analysis of Great Society programs of the 1960's, including their political aspects"—*(Choice)*.

Roach, Jack, and Janet Roach, Eds. POVERTY: Selected Readings. *Gannon* $7.00; *Penguin* 1972 pap. $3.95

Roby, Pamela, Ed. THE POVERTY ESTABLISHMENT. *Prentice-Hall* 1974 $7.95 Spectrum Bks. 1974 pap. $2.95

"The basic thesis of this collection of essays . . . is that the power structure organized poverty programs to regulate the poor so that economic inequality might be maintained in the United States"—*(Best Sellers)*.

Rothman, David J., and Sheila M. Rothman. ON THEIR OWN: The Poor in Modern America. *Addison Wesley* 1972 pap. $3.50

Simon, Arthur R. BREAKING BREAD WITH THE HUNGRY. Venture Ser. *Augsburg* 1971 pap. $2.50

Solow, Robert M. THE NATURE AND SOURCES OF UNEMPLOYMENT IN THE UNITED STATES. *Int. Pubns. Service* (orig.) 1971 pap. $2.50

Theobald, Robert, Ed. DIALOGUE ON POVERTY. *Bobbs* (orig.) pap. $1.50

SOCIAL POLICIES FOR AMERICA IN THE SEVENTIES: Nine Divergent Views. *Doubleday* 1968 Anchor Bks. 1969 pap. $1.45

Ulmer, Melville J. UNEMPLOYMENT: The Problem of Prosperity. Ed. by Mary E. Dillon *Barron* 1974 pap. $1.25

Wilber, George L., Ed. POVERTY: A New Approach. *Univ. Press of Kentucky* 1974 $13.50

Zimpel, Lloyd, and Daniel Panger. BUSINESS AND THE HARDCORE UNEMPLOYED: A Management Guide to Hiring, Training and Motivating Minority Workers. *Fell* 1970 $9.95

A "working manual specifying ways and means of meeting the problem economically, effectively, and to the mutual benefit of employer and employee. . . [It] will be of interest to public libraries and special collections that are oriented toward labor management and minority issues"—*(LJ)*.

Crime and Justice

Adler, Freda. SISTERS IN CRIME: The Rise of the New Female Criminal. *McGraw-Hill* 1975 $8.95

"The theme of this study is that the civil rights movement and the women's liberation movement have given impetus to a change in female criminal behavior"—*(LJ)*.

Asch, Sidney H. POLICE AUTHORITY AND THE RIGHTS OF THE INDIVIDUAL. Know Your Law Books Ser. *Arco* 2nd ed. 1968 $4.95 Arc Bks. 2nd ed. 1968 pap. $1.45

Association of the Bar of the City of New York. FREEDOM OF THE PRESS AND FAIR TRIAL: The Final Report with Recommendations of the Special Committee on Radio, Television, and the Administration of Justice, Judge Harold R. Medina, Chairman. *Columbia* 1967 $7.00

Bailey, F. Lee. FOR THE DEFENSE. *Atheneum* 1975 $10.95

"The true horrors of our criminal justice system—especially of one of its grossest manifestations, the conspiracy trial—are devastatingly chronicled in the last third of the account"—*(LJ)*.

Becker, Harold K. ISSUES IN POLICE ADMINISTRATION. *Scarecrow Press* 1970 $7.50

(With George T. Felkenes). LAW ENFORCEMENT: A Selected Bibliography. *Scarecrow Press* 1968 $7.00

Bedau, Hugo Adam. JUSTICE AND EQUALITY. *Prentice-Hall* 1971 $7.95 pap. $1.95

(Ed.). THE DEATH PENALTY IN AMERICA. *Aldine* 2nd ed. 1968 $12.50. A collection of essays by writers including J. Edgar Hoover and Jacques Barzun.

Black, Charles Lund. CAPITAL PUNISHMENT: The Inevitability of Caprice and Mistake. *Norton* 1974 $5.95 pap. $1.95

"Black's thesis argues that there are two critical problems inherent in the death penalty—the possibility of mistake and the arbitrariness in its administration—that are insoluble by presently conceived legal methods"—*(Booklist)*.

Carte, Gene E., and Elaine H. Carte. POLICE REFORM IN THE UNITED STATES. *Univ. of California Press* 1975 $10.00

THE CHALLENGE OF CRIME IN A FREE SOCIETY: A Report by the President's Commission on Law Enforcement and Administration of Justice. Ed. by H. Ruth and others. 1968. *Da Capo* 1971 $12.50; *Avon Bks.* pap. $2.45

Chevigny, Paul. COPS AND REBELS: A Study of Provocation. *Pantheon* 1972 $7.95; *Curtis Bks.* 1973 pap. $1.25

"A New York A.C.L.U. lawyer defending three Black Panthers accused of criminal conspiracy in 1970 describes the use of [Wilbert Thomas], a black undercover policeman in apprehending the accused Panthers; tells the story of the youths' radicalization in their Brooklyn ghetto; and narrates their trial"—*(PW)*.

POLICE POWER: Police Abuses in New York City. *Pantheon* 1969 $6.95; *Random* Vintage Bks. 1969 pap. $1.95

Clark, Leroy D. THE GRAND JURY: The Use and Abuse of Political Power. *Harper* 1975 $7.95

Clark "examines the use and abuses of federal grand juries . . . and suggests strengthening . . . [their] independence by giving them the authority to initiate investigations"—*(LJ)*.

Coffey, Alan, and others. HUMAN RELATIONS: Law Enforcement in a Changing Community. *Prentice-Hall* 1971 $9.95

The author "focuses upon police and community relations"—*(Choice)*.

Cray, Ed. THE BURDEN OF PROOF: The Case of Juan Corona. *Macmillan* 1973 $8.95

"Cray's well-written narrative charges that the state of California hastily convinced itself of Corona's guilt [the alleged murders of 25 migrant workers] and then shaped its investigation and prosecution to convict him, rather than honestly attempting to find out what actually happened"— (*LJ*).

THE ENEMY IN THE STREETS: Police Malpractice in America. *Doubleday* Anchor Bks. 1972 pap. $2.50

Davis, Kenneth Culp. DISCRETIONARY JUSTICE: A Preliminary Inquiry. *Louisiana State Univ. Press* 1969 $8.50; *Univ. of Illinois Press* 1971 pap. $2.45. The John P. Wilson Professor of Law at the University of Chicago investigates the lack of uniformity in the sentencing of convicted persons throughout the United States.

Dodge, Calvert R., Ed. A NATION WITHOUT PRISONS: Alternatives to Incarceration. *Heath* 1975 $16.00

Gaddis, Thomas E., and James O. Long. KILLER: A Journal of Murder. *Macmillan* 1970 $7.95

A "remarkable case history built around the autobiographical writings and letters of Carl Panzram (1891–1930), alleged killer of 21 people"—(*Choice*).

Glaser, Daniel, Ed. HANDBOOK OF CRIMINOLOGY. *Rand McNally* 1975 $12.50

Glueck, Sheldon S., and Eleanor T. Glueck. OF DELINQUENCY AND CRIME. *C. C. Thomas* 1974 $12.75

Goldfarb, Ronald. JAILS: The Ultimate Ghetto. *Doubleday* 1975 $9.95

The author "has studied and written extensively about the criminal justice system. In this book he describes objectively and with impressive detail the use and misuse of jails in this country"— (*LJ*).

Harris, Sara. HELLHOLE: The Shocking Story of the Inmates and Life in the New York City House of Detention for Women. 1967. *Tower* 1970 pap. $.95

Hazelrigg, Lawrence, Ed. PRISON WITHIN SOCIETY: A Reader in Penology. *Doubleday* 1968 Anchor Bks. 1969 pap. $2.95

Helfer, Ray E., and C. Henry Kempe, Eds. THE BATTERED CHILD. *Univ. of Chicago Press* 1968 2nd ed. 1974 $15.00. A study of child abuse in the United States.

Henshel, Richard L., and Robert A. Silverman, Eds. PERCEPTION IN CRIMINOLOGY. *Columbia* 1975 $15.00

"This largely exploratory treatment encourages us to reevaluate our beliefs about the definition and control of crime"—(*LJ*).

Hibbert, Christopher. THE ROOTS OF EVIL: A Social History of Crime and Punishment. 1963. *T. Y. Crowell* (Funk & Wagnalls) 1968 pap. $3.95. Addressed primarily to the uninformed, this book is in effect "the careful reduction of a criminological library to a single volume."

Hoenig, Gary. REAPER: The Inside Story of a Gang Leader. *Bobbs* 1975 $6.95

"A case study of a Bronx gang leader which reads almost like a fictionalized treatment"—(*LJ*).

Horne, Peter. WOMEN IN LAW ENFORCEMENT. *C. C. Thomas* 1975 $12.75

The author "summarizes the role played by female police officers in law enforcement"—(*LJ*).

Hosford, Ray, and C. S. Moss, Eds. THE CRUMBLING WALLS: Treatment and Counseling of Prisoners. *Univ. of Illinois Press* 1975 $8.95

"Ten essays and reports of seven case studies ... intended as a text for training prison professionals"—(*LJ*).

Inciardi, James A. CAREERS IN CRIME. *Rand McNally* 1975 pap. $3.95

The author's "research on crime as a profession"—(*Choice*).

James, Howard. CRISIS IN THE COURTS. Fwd. by Earl F. Morris *McKay* 1968 $6.95 pap. $2.95. A critique of America's defective court system based on a series of articles published in the *Christian Science Monitor* in 1967, for which Mr. James was awarded the Pulitzer Prize in National Reporting in 1968.

Kirkendall, Jack L., and Peter C. Unsinger. COMMUNITY POLICE ADMINISTRATION. *Nelson* 1975 $14.00

> Provides "a fine road map for this sometimes confusing area of management theory"—(*LJ*).

Lester, David, and Gene Lester. CRIME OF PASSION, MURDER AND THE MURDERER. *Nelson-Hall* 1975 $10.00

> "Statistics, patterns of murder, theories of violence, and case histories are discussed'—(*LJ*).

Lewis, Anthony. GIDEON'S TRUMPET. *Random* 1964 $6.95 Vintage Bks. pap. $1.95. A stirring account of the historic Gideon vs. Wainwright case in which the Supreme Court ruled that all defendants are entitled to legal counsel.

Maas, Peter. SERPICO. *Viking* 1973 $7.95; *Bantam* 1974 pap. $1.75

> "Called a 'psycho' by some of his superiors in the New York Police Department, a 'rat—and worse'—by many of his fellow policemen, Patrolman Frank Serpico spent many of his 11 years on the force pushing for exposure of widespread corruption. Eventually his efforts resulted in the now-famous Knapp Commission hearings"—(*Christian Science Monitor*). The book was made into a successful movie.

> THE VALACHI PAPERS. *Putnam* 1968 $6.95; *Bantam* 1969 pap. $1.25. The story of Joseph Valachi, Mafia informer.

Masotti, Louis H., and Don R. Bowen, Eds., with introd. RIOTS AND REBELLION: Civil Violence in the Urban Community. *Sage Pubns.* 1968 $10.00 pap. $4.50. The authors are political scientists at Case Western Reserve University and consultants to the National Commission on Civil Disorders.

Matzner, Dorothe, and Margaret English. VICTIMS OF JUSTICE. *Atheneum* 1973 $10.00

> "This book graphically portrays the emotional and financial ordeal of a criminal trial resulting in what has been called the damnation of acquittal"—(*Choice*).

Mayer, Martin. THE LAWYERS. *Harper* 1967 $10.00; *Dell* 1968 pap. $.95. This scathing analysis received the Scribes Book Award in 1968 as the best book interpreting the legal profession to the layman.

Menninger, Karl. THE CRIME OF PUNISHMENT. *Viking* 1968 $6.95 Compass Bks. pap. $1.95. *For comment see his main entry in Chapter 6, Psychology, this Vol.*

Mitford, Jessica. KIND AND USUAL PUNISHMENT: The Prison Business. *Knopf* 1973 $7.95 Vintage Bks. pap. $2.45

> "An incisive critique of contemporary corrections as practiced in the U.S. Mitford's pen is indeed a sharp sword that slashes at the established penal structure in no uncertain terms . . . this book should crack correctional walls"—(*Choice*).

Niederhoffer, Arthur. BEHIND THE SHIELD: The Police in Urban Society. *Doubleday* 1967 Anchor Bks. 1969 pap. $1.95

Packer, Herbert L. THE LIMITS OF THE CRIMINAL SANCTION. *Stanford Univ. Press* 1968 $8.95. A Stanford law professor analyzes the definition of crime as a community value judgment.

Podgorecki, Adam. LAW AND SOCIETY. *Routledge & Kegan Paul* 1975 $18.75

> Makes "a valuable addition to the literature about the acceptance, rejection, or modification of law by various social elements"—(*LJ*).

Radano, Gene. WALKING THE BEAT: A New York Policeman Tells What It's Like on His Side of the Law. 1968. *Macmillan* Collier Bks. 1969 pap. $1.25

Ratcliffe, James M., Ed., with introd. THE GOOD SAMARITAN AND THE LAW. 1966. *Peter Smith* $4.75

Rawls, John. A THEORY OF JUSTICE. *Harvard Univ. Press* 1972 $15.00

> "A book of unquestioned importance . . . [which reassesses] the social contract and natural rights theories upon which most modern regimes are based"—(*Choice*).

Richardson, James F. THE NEW YORK POLICE: Colonial Times to 1901. *Oxford* 1970 $8.50

> "Richardson, a trained urban historian, adds indispensable background material for understanding such issues as conflict between law and custom, the role of politics in police work, and the police response to riots, immigrants, and social change"—(*Choice*).

Stark, Rodney. POLICE RIOTS: Collective Violence and Law Enforcement. *Wadsworth* 1972 $6.95 pap. $3.95

"Every now and then in certain fields of social sciences a one-of-a-kind book comes along which ought to be widely read both inside and outside its discipline. This very readable book on violence by American policemen is just that type"—*(Choice)*.

Taylor, Ian, and others. CRITICAL CRIMINOLOGY. *Routledge & Kegan Paul* 1975 $18.75

In this book are combined "valid critiques of the old conservatism (belief in hierarchy and dominance on the basis of law and order) and the newer liberal concern with institutional reform and cultural change"—*(LJ)*.

THE NEW CRIMINOLOGY: For a Social Theory of Deviance. *Routledge & Kegan Paul* 1973 $19.95

"A radical critique of the major contributions to criminological thought"—*(Choice)*.

Taylor, Telford, and others. PERSPECTIVES ON JUSTICE. *Northwestern Univ. Press* 1975 $6.50

Trojanowicz, Robert C., and Samuel Dixon. CRIMINAL JUSTICE AND THE COMMUNITY. *Prentice-Hall* 1974 $10.50

The author "provides a refreshing approach to the analysis of the factors relating to criminal justice and community relations"—*(Choice)*.

Wilson, James Q. THINKING ABOUT CRIME. *Basic Bks.* 1975 $10.95

"[This book] should be read by a very large segment of the population. Here is wisdom, clarity of language, thoughtful alternatives for public policy and broad erudition"—*(N.Y. Times)*.

VARIETIES OF POLICE BEHAVIOR: The Management of Law and Order in Eight Communities. *Harvard Univ. Press* 1968 $10.00; *Atheneum* 1970 pap. $2.95

Young, Leontine. WEDNESDAY'S CHILDREN: A Study of Child Neglect and Abuse. *McGraw-Hill* 1964 pap. 1971 $2.45

This report is "not a dull, statistical study but highly readable. . . . Recommended for immediate reading"—*(LJ)*.

Zimring, Franklin E., and Gordon J. Hawkins. DETERRENCE: The Legal Threat in Crime Control. *Univ. of Chicago Press* 1973 $13.50

"In this first full-length effort Zimring and a British criminologist analyze the crucial issues and purposes of deterrence and punishment and provide the reader with a synthesis of research and theoretical writings on this crucial aspect of criminal justice"—*(Choice)*.

Zinn, Howard, Comp. JUSTICE IN EVERYDAY LIFE: The Way It Really Works. *Morrow* 1974 $10.00

"Daily injustices afflicting citizens in the Boston area are reported in everyday language and assembled by a university professor who offers suggestions for people power"—*(Booklist)*.

Alcoholism, Drugs and Related Problems

Ajami, Alfred M. DRUGS: An Annotated Bibliography and Guide to the Literature. *Hall* 1973 $15.00

Ashley, Richard. COCAINE: Its History, Uses, and Effects. *St. Martin's* 1975 $7.95

"An interesting, readable book"—*(Choice)*.

Barber, Bernard. DRUGS AND SOCIETY. *Russell Sage* 1967 $6.50

"Mr. Barber, professor of sociology at Barnard, has written an informative survey of some of the major problems in the relationships between drugs, the health professions, the public, and the law"—*(LJ)*.

Barber, Theodore X. LSD, MARIJUANA, YOGA, AND HYPNOSIS. *Aldine* 1971 $8.95

Explores "the psychological processes which underlie the phenomena of drug usage, yoga, and hypnosis . . . [and] makes specific recommendations about drug legislation"—*(Choice)*.

BIBLIOGRAPHY ON DRUG ABUSE: Prevention, Treatment, Research. *Human Service Press* 1973 pap. $8.95. Compiled by the Center for Human Services, National Institute for Drug Programs.

Block, Marvin A. ALCOHOL AND ALCOHOLISM: Drinking and Dependence. *Wadsworth* (orig.) 1970 pap. $1.95

ALCOHOLISM: Its Facets and Phases. *John Day* 1965 $7.95

"The book is written in non-technical language, from the viewpoint of a physician who sees the alcoholic as no different from many of his other patients who are sick, unhappy, and in need of help"—*(LJ)*.

Brenner, Joseph H., Robert Coles, and Dermot Meagher. DRUGS AND YOUTH: Medical, Psychiatric, and Legal Facts. *Liveright* 1972 $5.95

"A reasoned, concise, and unemotional appraisal of a subject which usually makes tempers flare and nerves fray"—(Publishers's note).

Bruun, Kettil, Lynn Pan, and Ingemar Rexed. THE GENTLEMEN'S CLUB: International Control of Drugs and Alcohol. *Univ. of Chicago Press* 1975 $12.50

Cohen, Sidney. BEYOND WITHIN: The LSD Story. *Atheneum* rev. ed. 1967 $6.95

THE DRUG DILEMMA. *McGraw-Hill* 1969 $5.95 pap. $3.95

A "tersely written, clear-headed study" *(LJ)* by a psychiatrist who deals with young drug users.

Glasscote, Raymond M., and others. THE TREATMENT OF ALCOHOLISM: A Study of Programs and Problems. *American Psychiatric Assn.* 1969 pap. $3.00. A report on public and private agencies and their existing programs.

THE TREATMENT OF DRUG ABUSE: Programs, Problems, Prospects, 1972. *American Psychiatric Assn.* 1972 pap. $7.00

Hentoff, Nat. A DOCTOR AMONG THE ADDICTS. *Rand McNally* 1968 $5.95; *Grove* Black Cat Bks. 1970 pap. $.95

"In a concise, clear account Mr. Hentoff traces the dedicated work of [psychiatrist Dr. Marie Nyswander] and the growing acceptance of the methadone treatment"—*(LJ)*.

Lennard, Henry L., and others. MYSTIFICATION AND DRUG MISUSE: Hazards in Using Psychoactive Drugs. *Jossey-Bass* 1971 $6.75

"The book is a courageous attack on the pestilence delivered on mankind by the drug conspiracy"—*(Choice)*.

Lindesmith, Alfred R. ADDICTION AND OPIATES. *Aldine* 1968 $10.95

Louria, Donald B. THE DRUG SCENE. *McGraw-Hill* 1968 $6.50

"Dr. Louria, long associated with Bellevue in addition to being president of the New York State Council on Drug Addiction [has written] a dispassionate survey of the drug problem in this country, backed up with historical data, a survey of the current medical and sociologic literature, and two excellent chapters on drug use in England and Sweden. Dr. Louria makes careful distinction between users and sellers, L.S.D. and marijuna, marijuana and heroin. He makes specific recommendations for changes in the penal code that would acknowledge these distinctions"—(Michael Halberstam, in the *N.Y. Times*).

OVERCOMING DRUGS: A Program for Action. *McGraw-Hill* 1972 $15.00

Plaut, Thomas F. A., Ed. ALCOHOL PROBLEMS: A Report to the Nation by the Cooperative Commission on the Study of Alcoholism. *Oxford* 1967 $5.75 pap. $1.95

"This report reminds us that not all drinking is harmful; rather, there are harmful attitudes toward drinking which need rethinking while effort is made to discourage harmful drinking"—*(LJ)*.

Szasz, Thomas S. CEREMONIAL CHEMISTRY: The Ritual Persecution of Drugs, Addicts, and Pushers. *Doubleday* 1974 $6.95

"Szasz argues that anti-drug laws and sentiments are not so much medically as politically and morally motivated"—*(LJ)*.

Tart, Charles T. ON BEING STONED: A Psychological Study of Marijuana Intoxication. *Science & Behavior Bks.* 1972 $7.95

"A 300 page report of a federally financed study concerning the subjective effects of marijuana intoxication. The text discusses the results of this study in great depth. The methodology is sound, the reasoning is tight, the conclusions justified by the data"—*(Choice)*.

Trice, Harrison M., and Paul Roman. SPIRITS AND DEMONS AT WORK: Alcohol and Other Drugs on the Job. *Cornell Univ. Press* 1972 $5.00

"This book focuses on the relationship between use and abuse of mind-altering substances and the performance of work roles"—*(LJ)*.

White, William, and Ronald F. Albano, Eds. NORTH AMERICAN SYMPOSIUM ON DRUGS AND
  DRUG ABUSE. *North American Pub. Co.* $27.50

SOCIAL SCIENTISTS, EDUCATORS, AUTHORS

BACON, FRANCIS. 1561–1626. *See Chapter 15, Essays and Criticism*, Reader's Adviser, *Vol. 1, and Chapter 5, Philosophy, this Vol.*

HOBBES, THOMAS. 1588–1679. *See Chapter 5, Philosophy, this Vol.*

LOCKE, JOHN. 1623–1704. *See Chapter 5, Philosophy, this Vol.*

HUME, DAVID. 1711–1776. *See Chapter 5, Philosophy, this Vol.*

ROUSSEAU, JEAN JACQUES. 1712–1778. *See Chapter 9, French Literature*, Reader's
  Adviser, *Vol. 2.*

SMITH, ADAM. 1723–1790.

  The Scottish professor of moral philosophy at the University of Glasgow was a well-known
absent-minded professor. While traveling in France as tutor to the Duke of Buccleuch he began
his most famous work, "An Inquiry into the Wealth of Nations," which has been called "the
outpouring not only of a great mind, but of a whole epoch." An excellent summary of Smith's
inquiry and its results is to be found in Robert L. Heilbroner's "The Worldly Philosophers" (*see
Section on Economics*). In brief, he studied the buying, selling and manufacturing world of his time
and formulated the laws of the market—those of supply and demand and of competition; each
element he saw acting upon the others (and each entrepreneur acting from self-interest) in such a
way as to make the system self-regulating. This concept, true for its time, led to the school of
laissez-faire economics of the 19th century and early 20th; by that time other factors had entered
the picture—which the crash of 1929 devastatingly revealed. Smith saw economics as a changing
"organism," however, and could not, of course, predict the whole course of economic history. He
"wrote before the Industrial Revolution was well launched, and some of his theories were voided
by its developments, but as an analyst of institutions and an influence on later economists he has
never been surpassed."

WORKS. Ed. by Dugald Stewart *Adler's* 5 vols. 1963 set $250.00

EARLY WRITINGS. Ed. by J. Ralph Lindgren *Kelley* 1967 $10.00

THE THEORY OF MORAL SENTIMENTS. 1759. *Arlington* 1969 $8.00; *Kelley* 1966 $15.00

LECTURES ON RHETORIC AND BELLES LETTRES. 1762–1763. Ed. by John M. Lothian
  Humanities Press 1963 $6.50; *Southern Illinois Univ. Press* 1971 $7.50

LECTURES ON JUSTICE, POLICE, REVENUE AND ARMS. 1763. Ed. with an introd. and notes
  by Edwin Cannan. 1896. *Kelley* 1964 $10.00. Lectures delivered at the University of
  Glasgow and reported by a student in 1763.

THE WEALTH OF NATIONS. 1776. *Dutton* Everyman's 2 vols. 1910 each $3.95; (with title
  "Inquiry into the Nature and Causes of the Wealth of Nations") *Kelley* 2 vols. 1966 set
  $67.50; *Random* (Modern Library Giants) 1937 $4.95; ed. by Andrew Skinner *Penguin* Pelican Bks. 1970 pap. $2.45; *Peter Smith* bks. 1–3 $4.50

SELECTIONS FROM THE WEALTH OF NATIONS. Ed. by George J. Stigler *AHM Pub. Corp.*
  Crofts Class. 1957 pap. $.85

THE WEALTH OF NATIONS: Representative Selections. Ed. by Bruce Mazlish *Bobbs* Lib.
  Arts 1961 pap. $1.75

Books about Smith

  A Biographical Memoir of Adam Smith. By Dugald Stewart. 1793. *Kelley* 1966 $15.00
  The Essential Principles of the Wealth of Nations Illustrated. By John Gray. 1797. *Kelley* 1968
    $10.00
  The Ethical and Economic Theories of Adam Smith. By Glen R. Morrow. 1923. *Kelley* 1966
    $8.50
  Adam Smith, 1776–1926. By John M. Clark and others. 1928. *Kelley* $8.50
  Adam Smith Today. Ed. by Arthur H. Jenkins. 1948. *Kennikat* 1969 $15.00
  Adam Smith: A Bibliographical Checklist. By Burt Franklin and Francesco Cordasco. *Burt
    Franklin* 1950 $10.00

The House of Adam Smith. By Eli Ginzberg. *Octagon* 1964 $10.00

The Individual in Society: Papers on Adam Smith. By A. L. Macfie. *Humanities Press* 1967 $10.00

Adam Smith's Moral and Political Philosophy. By Herbert L. Schneider. *Harper* Torchbks. 1970 pap. $3.45; *Peter Smith* $5.50

The Economics of Adam Smith. By Samuel Hollander. *Univ. of Toronto Press* 1973 $15.00

PAINE, THOMAS. 1737–1809.

Paine was born in England, the son of a Quaker corset maker. He came to America in 1774 with letters of introduction from Benjamin Franklin (*q.v.*). His "Common Sense" published early in 1776 had a tremendous effect in helping to bring about the Declaration of Independence. He went to London and while there wrote "The Rights of Man" directed against the detractors of the French Revolution, especially Edmund Burke. Paine's sharp criticism of the British government caused his exile to France, where he became involved in French politics; he was later imprisoned there in 1793–94. His antibiblical tract "The Age of Reason" and his critical "Letter to George Washington" caused a furor in this country, to which, however, he returned in 1802 to endure the general opprobrium. He died impoverished and embittered.

WRITINGS. Ed. by Moncure D. Conway. 1894–1896. *AMS Press* 4 vols. each $9.00 set $33.50; *Burt Franklin* 4 vols. in 2 set $33.50

THOMAS PAINE: Key Writings. *Peter Smith* $6.00

THOMAS PAINE: Selections. Ed. by Harry H. Clark *Farrar, Straus* (Hill & Wang) 1961 pap. $3.45

COMMON SENSE (1776) and OTHER POLITICAL WRITINGS. Ed. by Nelson F. Adkins. *Bobbs* 1953 pap. $1.60

COMMON SENSE and THE CRISIS (1776). 1960. *Doubleday* Anchor Bks. 1970 pap. $1.25

THE RIGHTS OF MAN. 1791. *Dutton* Everyman's 1935 $3.95 pap. 1972 $1.75

THE AGE OF REASON. In 2 pts., 1794 and 1795. Pt. 1 ed. by Alburey Castell *Bobbs* Lib. Arts pap. $1.40 Pt. 2 o.p.

SIX NEW LETTERS OF THOMAS PAINE. Ed. by Harry H. Clark *Univ. of Wisconsin Press* 1939 $2.50

Books about Paine

The Life of Thomas Paine. By Moncure D. Conway. 1892. *Blom* 1968 $15.75; *Folcroft* 1973 $15.50; *Norwood Editions* $20.00; *Richard West* $15.50

Tom Paine. by Hesketh Pearson. 1937. *Richard West* $25.00

Thomas Paine: His Life, Work and Times. By Audrey Williamson. *St. Martin's* 1973 $12.50 "This is a sympathetic, but somewhat pedantic work, superior in its coverage of Paine's earlier years in England and the later period in France throughout the Revolution and Directoire, but rather simplistic in the treatment of his involvement with the American Revolution"— (Alfred Stern, in *LJ*).

Rebel: A Biography of Tom Paine. By Samuel Edwards. *Praeger* new ed. 1974 $9.95

Paine. By David Freeman Hawke. *Harper* 1974 $15.00 "By far the finest biography of Paine I've ever read. . . . This is also a superb psycho-history, a tragicomic study of a manic genius, writer, engineer, and gadfly. Because virtually none of Paine's private papers survive, Hawke's painstaking research is remarkable; and history aside, as a character study along, Paine is a completely fascinating work"—(Alfred Stern, in *LJ*).

YOUNG, ARTHUR. 1741–1820.

Young, "the greatest of English agriculturalists and the poorest of practical farmers," wrote some 70 volumes on his travels in England, France and Italy, observing the practice of agriculture and industry at first hand. His books were very famous and exerted great influence in his day, especially his "Course of Experimental Agriculture" and his "Farmer's Calendar." Now o.p. is his "Letters Concerning the Present State of the French Nation" (1769).

A SIX WEEKS TOUR THROUGH THE SOUTHERN COUNTIES OF ENGLAND AND WALES. 1769. *Kelley* $17.50

A SIX MONTHS TOUR THROUGH THE NORTH OF ENGLAND: Containing an Account of the Present State of Agriculture, Manufactures and Population, in Several Counties of

This Kingdom. 2nd rev. ed. 1771. *Kelley* 4 vols. 1967 set $75.00. Data on the conditions and effects of the early Industrial Revolution as observed by Young on his tour.

A FARMER'S TOUR THROUGH THE EAST OF ENGLAND. 1771. *Kelley* 4 vols. $75.00

POLITICAL ESSAYS CONCERNING THE PRESENT STATE OF THE BRITISH EMPIRE. 1772. *Gregg Press* 1971 $30.00

POLITICAL ARITHMETIC: Containing Observations on the Present State of Great Britain; and the Principles of Her Policy in the Encouragement of Agriculture. Addressed to the Economical Societies Established in Europe. To which Is Added, a Memoir on the Corn Trade: Drawn up and Laid before the Commissioners of the Treasury of Governor Pownall. 1774. *Kelley* 1967 $15.00

TOUR IN IRELAND (1776–1779). 1780. Ed. with introd. by A. W. Hutton 1892; bibliography by John P. Anderson *Irish Univ. Press* 2 vols. 1971 set $22.80

TRAVELS IN FRANCE DURING THE YEARS 1787, 1788 AND 1789. 1792–1794. (Selections) Ed. by Constantia E. Maxwell. 1929. *Kelley* $15.00; ed. by Jeffry Kaplow *Peter Smith* $6.00

THE AUTOBIOGRAPHY OF ARTHUR YOUNG: With Selections from His Correspondence. Ed. by M. Bentham-Edwards. 1898. *Kelley* 1967 $15.00

BENTHAM, JEREMY.   1748–1832.

A close friend of James Mill, father of John Stuart Mill (*q.v.*), Jeremy Bentham was the founder of Utilitarianism. He wrote books in many fields, including philosophy, economics, law and political science. His greatest work, "Principles of Morals and Legislation," describes his utilitarian philosophy and asserts that the greatest good for the greatest number is the primary goal of social ethics.

WORKS. Ed. by John Bowring, 1838–1843. *Russell & Russell* 11 vols. 1962 set $225.00

ECONOMIC WRITINGS. Ed. by W. Stark. 1952–1954. *Burt Franklin* 3 vols. set $37.50; *Humanities Press* 3 vols. Vol. 1 $8.25 Vol. 2 $9.50 Vol. 3 $9.25

INTRODUCTION TO THE PRINCIPLES OF MORALS AND LEGISLATION. 1789. (In "The Utilitarians" with Mill's "Utilitarianism" and "On Liberty") *Doubleday* Anchor Bks. 1961 pap. $1.95; *Peter Smith* 1962 $4.00; ed. by Laurence J. Lafleur *Macmillan* (Hafner) 1935 pap. 1948 $2.95; ed. by J. H. Burns and H. L. Hart *Humanities Press* 1970 $21.50

NOT PAUL, BUT JESUS. 1823. *Kelley* $15.00

BENTHAM'S HANDBOOK OF POLITICAL FALLACIES. 1824. Ed. by Harold A. Larrabee. 1952. *Apollo* 1971 pap. $2.95

RATIONALE OF PUNISHMENT. 1830 *Finch Press* $26.00

LIMITS OF JURISPRUDENCE DEFINED. First printed from the author's manuscript with introd. by Charles Warren Everett. 1945. *Greenwood* 1970 $16.25; (with title "Of Laws in General") ed. by H. L. A. Hart *Humanities Press* (Athlone Press) 1970 $21.50

CORRESPONDENCE. Ed. by Timothy L. Sprigge *Humanities Press* 3 vols. 1968–1971 Vols. 1–2 1752–1780 (1968) Vol. 3 Jan. 1781–Oct. 1788 (1971) each $34.25

Books about Bentham

On Bentham (1838) and Coleridge (1840). By John Stuart Mill. *Humanities Press* 1950 $4.25; *Peter Smith* 1963 $4.00

The English Utilitarians. By Leslie Stephen. 1900. *Kelley* 3 vols. set $37.50; *Peter Smith* 3 vols. in 1 $15.00. Vol. 1 Jeremy Bentham Vol. 2 James Mill Vol. 3 John Stuart Mill. An aid to the understanding of utilitarianism and the 19th-century intellectual climate in England.

Jeremy Bentham: His Life and Work. By Charles M. Atkinson. 1905. *AMS Press* $8.50; *Greenwood* $10.75; *Kelley* 1968 $10.00

The Growth of Philosophic Radicalism. By Elie Halévy. 1928 rev. ed. 1952. Trans. by Mary Morris; pref. by A. D. Lindsay *Kelley* 3 pts. $16.50. Pt. 1 The Youth of Bentham (1776 to 1789) Pt. 2 The Evolution of the Utilitarian Doctrine from 1789 to 1815 Pt. 3 Philosophic Radicalism (1901). Bibliography.

Bentham and the Ethics of Today. By David Baumgardt. *Octagon* 1967 $18.00

In the Interest of the Governed: A Study in Bentham's Philosophy of Utility and Law. By David Lyons. *Oxford* 1973 $8.00

Bentham's Political Thought. Ed. by Bhikhu C. Parekh. *Harper* (Barnes & Noble) 1973 $15.00 pap. $4.95

Jeremy Bentham: Ten Critical Essays. Ed. by Bhikhu C. Parekh. *International Scholarly Bk. Services* 1974 $15.00

WOLLSTONECRAFT, MARY.   1759–1797.

Mary Wollstonecraft was an early rebel against society and an ardent feminist whose "Vindication of the Rights of Women" was extraordinary for its day. She began her independent career as a governess and later became literary consultant to a London publisher. The promise of the French Revolution drew her to Paris in 1792; there a love affair brought her a daughter. She returned to London in 1795 and in 1797 married William Godwin, the philosopher, writer and social thinker. She died giving birth to her second daughter, Mary, who married the poet Shelley (*q.v.*).

THOUGHTS ON THE EDUCATION OF DAUGHTERS. 1787. Ed. by Gina Luria *Garland Pub.* 1974 $22.00; *Kelley* 1973 $10.00

A VINDICATION OF THE RIGHTS OF WOMEN. 1792. *Collectors Edns.* 1971 $18.00; *Garland Pub.* 1974 $22.00; ed. by Charles W. Hagelman, Jr. *Norton* 1967 pap. $1.95; (with J. S. Mill's "Subjugation of Women") *Dutton* Everyman's 1929 $3.95

POSTHUMOUS WORKS. Ed. by William Godwin. 1798. *Garland Pub.* 4 vols. 1974 each $22.00; *Kelley* 4 vols. in 2 1970 $27.50

THE LOVE LETTERS OF MARY WOLLSTONECRAFT TO GILBERT IMLAY. Ed. by Roger Ingpen. 1908. *Folcroft* 1974 $17.50

GODWIN AND MARY: Letters of William Godwin and Mary Wollstonecraft. Ed. by Ralph M. Wardle *Univ. Press of Kansas* 1964 $4.00

LETTERS TO GILBERT IMLAY. 1879. *Haskell* 1971 $13.95

LETTERS WRITTEN DURING A SHORT RESIDENCE IN SWEDEN, NORWAY AND DENMARK. *Branden* $15.00; *British Bk. Centre* 1973 $27.50

MEMOIRS. Ed. by William Godwin *Gordon Press* 1973 $29.95; *Haskell* 1969 $17.95; ed. by Gina Luria *Garland Pub.* 1974 $22.00

Books about Wollstonecraft

A Study of Mary Wollstonecraft and the Rights of Women. By Emma R. Clough. 1898. *Folcroft* $30.00; *Gale Research Co.* $12.50; *Gordon Press* 1972 $29.95

Mary Wollstonecraft: A Study in Economics and Romance. By George R. Taylor. 1911. *Greenwood* $8.75; *Haskell* 1969 $11.95

Mary Wollstonecraft and the Beginnings of Female Emancipation in England and France. By Jacob Bouten. 1922. *Gordon Press* $29.95; *Porcupine Press* 1975 $12.00

Mary Wollstonecraft. By Madeline Linford. 1925. *Folcroft* $17.50; *Gordon Press* 1972 $25.00

Mary Wollstonecraft: A Critical Biography. By Ralph M. Wardle. *Univ. of Nebraska Press* Bison Bks. 1966 pap. $2.45

"Any reader who wants all the available facts about [Mary Wollstonecraft] will have to refer to this book"—(*Nation*).

One Woman's Situation: A Study of Mary Wollstonecraft. By Margaret George. *Univ. of Illinois Press* 1970 $6.50

Mary Wollstonecraft. By Eleanor Flexner. *Coward* 1972 $8.95; *Penguin* 1973 pap. $2.50

The Life and Death of Mary Wollstonecraft. By Claire Tomalin. *Harcourt* 1974 $8.95

"For an interpretation of [Mary Wollstonecraft's] life there is no better book than Claire Tomalin's, or likely to be in the foreseeable future. It is a wise, penetrating, sympathetic biography of a remarkably complex woman"—(*New Statesman*).

SAINT-SIMON, CLAUDE HENRI DE ROUVROY, Comte de.   1760–1825.

The "giant" of French social thought of the 18th century, Saint-Simon proposed the establishment of a science devoted to the systematic study of changes in social and economic conditions that resulted from the Industrial Revolution. The new discipline should take into account the discoveries of "pure" science, and should be aimed at uncovering general principles of "social happiness." Auguste Comte (*q.v.*), Saint-Simon's disciple, gave the designation "sociology" to the

Count's field of study and discovery. Saint-Simon's great work was *"Le Nouveau Christianisme"* ("The New Christianity," 1825), not now available here in translation. In it he related the Christian ideals of love and brotherhood to his vision of a society reorganized on rational principles. He is not to be confused with the earlier writer of memoirs, Louis, Duc de Saint-Simon (*q.v.*).

SOCIAL ORGANIZATION, THE SCIENCE OF MAN, AND OTHER WRITINGS. Trans. and ed. by Felix Markham *Harper* Torchbks. pap. $1.95; *Peter Smith* $4.00

Books about Saint-Simon

The Saint-Simonian Religion in Germany. By E. M. Butter. 1926. *Howard Fertig* 1968 $15.00

Socialism and Saint-Simon. By Emile Durkheim. Trans. by Charlotte Sattler; ed. by Alvin W. Gouldner *Antioch Press* (dist. by Kent State Univ. Press) 1958 $5.00

The New World of Henri Saint-Simon. By F. E. Manuel. 1956. *Univ. of Notre Dame Press* 1963 pap. $2.25

Saint-Simonism in the Radicalism of Thomas Carlyle. By David B. Cofer. 1931. *Haskell* 1970 pap. $4.95; *Richard West* $4.50

The Doctrine of Saint-Simon: An Exposition. By George G. Iggers. *Schocken* new ed. 1972 $7.50 pap. $3.95

MALTHUS, THOMAS ROBERT. 1766–1834.

The English parson, economist and sociologist was a pioneer in the modern study of the growth of population. Thomas Carlyle, after he read Malthus, called economics "the dismal science." Malthus maintained that poverty was the unavoidable consequence of the fact that food and goods increase only in arithmetical progression, while population multiplies by geometrical progression. He tended to view disaster and disease as saviors of mankind from general want, therefore, and to regard charity toward the poor as antisocial. He outraged a generation, but his theories have in many instances been supported by later economists and social thinkers, on whom he exercised great influence.

OCCASIONAL PAPERS OF T. R. MALTHUS ON POPULATION AND POLITICAL ECONOMY: From Contemporary Journals. Written anonymously and hitherto uncollected. Ed. with introd. essay by Bernard Semmel. *Burt Franklin* 1963 $17.50

PAMPHLETS 1800–1817. *Kelley* $12.50

AN ESSAY ON THE PRINCIPLE OF POPULATION. 1798. *Kelley* $15.00; ed. by Anthony Flew *Penguin* Pelican Bks. 1971 pap. $1.45; *Peter Smith* $4.50

POPULATION: The First Essay. Fwd. by Kenneth F. Boulding *Univ. of Michigan Press* 1959 $4.40 pap. $1.75; (with title "The First Essay on Population") 1926. *Kelley* $15.00

INQUIRY INTO THE NATURE AND PROGRESS OF RENT AND THE PRINCIPLES BY WHICH IT IS REGULATED. 1815. *Greenwood* $7.75

PRINCIPLES OF POLITICAL ECONOMY. 1820. 2nd ed. 1836. *Kelley* $16.50

THE MEASURE OF VALUE: Stated and Illustrated, with an Application of It to the Alterations in the Value of the English Currency Since 1790. 1823. *Kelley* $7.50

DEFINITIONS IN POLITICAL ECONOMY: Preceded by an Inquiry into the Rules Which Ought to Guide Political Economists in the Definitions and Use of their Terms with Remarks on the Deviations from These Rules in Their Writings. 1827. With a new introd. by Morton Paglin *Kelley* $10.00

Books about Malthus

Reply to the Essay on Population by the Rev. T. R. Malthus. By William Hazlitt. 1807. *Kelley* $12.50

Inquiry Concerning the Population of Nations. By George Ensor. 1818. *Kelley* 1967 $15.00

Of Population: An Enquiry Concerning the Power of Increase in the Numbers of Mankind, Being an Answer to Mr. Malthus' Essay on That Subject. By William Godwin. 1820. *Kelley* $17.50

Malthus and His Work. By James Bonar. 1885 2nd ed. 1924. *Kelley* 2nd ed. $15.00

Population: A Study in Malthusianism. By Warren S. Thompson. 1914. *AMS Press* 1969 $12.50

Population Problems of the Age of Malthus. By Grosvenor T. Griffith. 1926. *Kelley* 1967 $12.50

Illustrations and Proofs of the Principle of Population. By Francis Place. 1930. *Kelley* 1967 $12.50

Malthus and Lauderdale: The Anti-Ricardian Tradition. By Morton Paglin. 1961. *Kelley* $10.00

OWEN, ROBERT.   1771–1858.

This British social reformer was an important initiator of the cooperative movement, still in existence today. He believed that mankind was no better than its environment and that if environment were changed a real Utopia might be achieved. (*See list of famous Utopias under Sir Thomas More in Chapter 10, British Fiction: Early Period,* Reader's Adviser, *Vol. 1.*) A wealthy man, who expended most of his fortune in social experiment, he started the cooperative community of New Lanark, Scotland, his own version of Utopia—complete with mills and worker housing— which achieved some degree of success, and later one in New Harmony, Ind. (U.S.A.), which failed disastrously. An advocate of trade unionism, he worked for protective legislation for laborers and played a major role in achieving passage of the British Factory Act of 1819.

SELECTED WRITINGS OF ROBERT OWEN: A Collection of Pamphlets 1819–1850. *Kelley* 1974 $20.00

ROBERT OWEN ON EDUCATION. Ed. by Harold Silver *Cambridge* 1969 $10.50

A NEW VIEW OF SOCIETY, or Essays on the Formation of the Human Character. 1816. *AMS Press* $12.50; *Kelley* $10.00; (and "Report to the County of Lanark") *Peter Smith* $4.75

A NEW VIEW OF SOCIETY AND OTHER WRITINGS. Introd. by G. D. H. Cole 1853. *Dutton* Everyman's 1927 $3.95

REPORT TO THE COUNTY OF LANARK; Of a Plan for Relieving Public Distress, and Removing Discontent, by Giving Permanent Productive Employment to the Poor and Working Classes. 1821. *AMS Press* 1972 $15.00

BOOK OF THE NEW MORAL WORLD, Vols. 1–13 1834–1845. *Greenwood* set $395.00; Pts. 1– 7 1842. *Kelley* 1971 $15.00

A DEVELOPMENT OF THE PRINCIPLES AND PLANS ON WHICH TO ESTABLISH SELF-SUPPORT-ING HOME COLONIES. 1841. *AMS Press* 1972 $21.50

REVOLUTION IN THE MIND AND PRACTICE OF THE HUMAN RACE. 1849. *Kelley* 1974 $15.00

ROBERT OWEN'S JOURNAL, Nos. 1–104. 1852. *Kelley* $50.00

ROBERT OWEN'S MILLENIAL GAZETTE. 1858. *AMS Press* $27.50

THE LIFE OF ROBERT OWEN. Written by himself, with selections from his writings and correspondence. 1857–1858. *Gordon Press* 2 vols. set $29.00; *Kelley* 2 vols. in 1 $22.50

Books about Owen

The Life, Times and Labours of Robert Owen. By Lloyd Jones. 1890. *AMS Press* 2 vols. in 1 1972 $17.00

Robert Owen: A Biography. By Frank Podmore. 1906. *Haskell* 1971 $29.95; *Kelley* 2 vols. in 1 $22.50

Robert Owen, 1771–1858: A New Bibliographical Study. By Shigeru Goto. 1934. *Kelley* 2 vols. in 1 $25.00

Robert Owen of New Lanark. By Margaret Cole. 1953. *Kelley* 1975 $10.00

Utopianism and Education: Robert Owen and the Owenites. Ed. by John F. Harrison. Classics in Education Ser. *Teachers College Press* 1969 $6.95 pap. $3.50

Robert Owen, Aspects of His Life and Work. Ed. by J. Butt. *Humanities Press* 1971 $12.75

Co-Operation and the Owenite Socialist Communities in Britain 1825–1845. By R. C. Garnett. *Humanities Press* 1972 $16.95

Robert Owen at New Lanark: 1824–1838. *Arno* 1972 $13.00

RICARDO, DAVID.   1772–1823.

The British economist, as a young Jew turned Quaker, made a fortune in brokerage at 25 and retired to develop his economic theories and write about them. A close friend of Malthus (*q.v.*), he had many intellectual arguments with him, highly productive for the development of both. He is known for his "iron law of wages" and for his labor theory of value; his principles dominated 19th-century economic thinking, and he is known today as the father of the conservative, as opposed to the Keynesian school of economics. It has been said that between them Malthus and Ricardo did one astonishing thing—they changed the world from an optimistic to a pessimistic one.

WORKS AND CORRESPONDENCE. Ed. by P. Sraffa *Cambridge* 10 vols. 1951–1957 each $12.50 Vol. 11: Index. Ed. by P. Sraffa & M. H. Dobb 1973 $10.95

THE PRINCIPLES OF POLITICAL ECONOMY AND TAXATION. 1817. *Dutton* Everyman's 1912 1933 $3.95 pap. 1973 $2.25

ECONOMIC ESSAYS. Ed. with introd. by Sir Edward C. Gonner. 1923 *Kelley* $10.00

Books about Ricardo

David Ricardo: A Centenary Estimate. By Jacob H. Hollander. 1910. *Kelley* 1968 $8.50. Three lectures "to mark the centenary of the appearance of Ricardo's first important publication, 'The High Price of Bullion, a Proof of the Depreciation of Bank Notes,' " 1810.

Analysis and Review of the Peculiar Doctrine of the Ricardo, or New School of Political Economy. By William H. Sleeman. 1837. *Kelley* 1968 $7.50

Ricardian Socialists. By Esther Lowenthal. 1911. *Kelley* 1968 $7.50

Ricardian Rent Theory in Early American Economics. By John R. Turner. 1921. *Burt Franklin* $12.50

David Ricardo and Ricardian Theory: A Bibliographical Checklist. By Burt Franklin and G. Legman. *Burt Franklin* 1949 $10.00

The Key to Ricardo. By Oswald St. Clair. 1957. *Kelley* $12.50

COMTE, AUGUSTE. 1798–1857. *See Chapter 5, Philosophy, this Vol.*

MILL, JOHN STUART. 1806–1873. *See Chapter 5, Philosophy, this Vol.*

MARX, KARL. 1818–1883.

The German genius Karl Marx produced works of incalculable influence on the modern world, an influence which has been compared to that of the Gospels, of the Koran, or of Newton's (*q.v.*) "*Principia*." "The history of Marx's teachings is a study in irony. His theories have become official doctrine in just those parts of the world which he thought farthest removed from the opportunity for socialism, and they arouse the most skepticism in those parts of the world which he thought ripe for the application of his views"—(Charles Frankel, in *SR*). He repudiated all existing socialist theories as either utopian or unsocialistic. He developed his own dynamic theory of social change (dialectical materialism) which became the basis of what he called "scientific socialism," from which most modern forms of socialism and communism are derived. An important addition to the early history of Marxism is "The First International: Minutes of the Hague Congress 1872 with Related Documents" (trans. and ed. by Hans Gerth *Univ. of Wisconsin Press* 1958 $15.00). Daniel Norman Jacobs has edited "The New Communist Manifesto and Related Documents" (*Harper* 1961 2nd ed. 1962 Torchbks, 3rd rev. ed. pap. $2.45; *Peter Smith* 1963 $4.50).

In May 1968, the 150th anniversary of the birth of Marx was celebrated in London (where he is buried), Moscow and West Germany. Of the latter tribute, the *N.Y. Times* wrote: "Although his name has been anathema in West Germany, Marx was acclaimed today in this [city of Trier] near the Luxembourg border as one of Germany's greatest sons. A permanent exhibition of his letters, works and related materials was formally opened in the house where he was born, at 10 Brücke Strasse. A symposium on 'Karl Marx Today,' sponsored by the United Nations Educational, Scientific and Cultural Organization, was opened with delegates from 20 lands. A commemorative Marx stamp was issued by the West German Post Office." A student demonstration against Willy Brandt and the Social Democrats added excitement to this occasion, and East and West German Communists held their own separate celebration nearby, with the Soviet ambassador to Bonn in attendance.

In East Berlin "*Der Herr Schmidt:* A German Spectacle with Police and Music," a satire on Marx by the East German playwright Günther Rücker, became immensely popular after its opening early in February 1969. The play deals with the political trials of Communists held on the order of King Friedrich Wilhelm IV of Prussia in Cologne in 1852. It is "based on historical record and on Marx's own 'Revelations Concerning the Communist Trial at Cologne.' But unlike his mentor, Mr. Rücker aims for the laughs, and on the way he takes daring digs at Walter Ulbricht's German Democratic Republic in the current Socialist Realist mania for painting portraits, the cult of a Socialist Goethe and the dialect of Mr. Ulbricht's native Saxony"—(*N.Y. Times*).

Harry Schwartz has written (in the *N.Y. Times*): "In terms of his impact on the 20th century, Karl Marx is regarded by many as the most influential thinker who ever lived. Communist-ruled countries with populations totaling a billion people hail him as the founder of their fundamental ideology. In non-Communist nations, his ideas are supported in whole or in part by millions of Communists and Socialists, while even non-Marxist historians, economists and other social scientists agree that his ideas have profoundly shaped the modern world and influenced much accepted academic thinking. [Yet in his day he was a relatively minor figure. His] classic work, 'Das Kapital,' was considered so boring and difficult to read that the Russian censors approved a translation for publication on the ground that so few people could understand the book that it posed no threat to the Czarist regime."

THE COLLECTED WORKS OF MARX AND ENGELS. *International Pubs.* 3 vols. 1974 Vol. 1
  1835–1843 The Early Writings of Marx Vol. 2 1835–1843 The Early Writings of
  Engels Vol. 3 1843–1844 Articles and Works by Marx and Engels each $7.50

"The first of a projected 50 volume English translation of published works, manuscripts, and
private correspondence of Marx and Engels"—*(LJ)*.

KARL MARX LIBRARY. Ed. by Saul K. Padover *McGraw-Hill* 1971–

The Works of Marx collected and arranged topically. To be published in a multi-volume set.
The following volumes are currently available: On Revolution (1972 $4.95); On the First
International (1973 $20.00 pap. $4.95); On America and the Civil War (1973 $10.00 pap. $3.50);
Sources of Democracy: Voices of Freedom, Hope and Justice (1973 $150.00); On Freedom of the
Press and Censorship (1974 $10.00 pap. $3.95); On Religion (1974 $10.00 pap. $6.95); On
Education, Women and Children ($10.00 pap. $5.95)

EARLY WRITINGS. *McGraw-Hill* 1963 $6.00 pap. $2.45

POLITICAL WRITINGS. Ed. by David Fernbach *Random* 3 vols. 1974 Vol. 1 The Revolution
  of 1848 Vol. 2 Surveys from Exile Vol. 3 The First International and After Vols. 1–2
  each $10.00 Vol. 3 $12.95 Vintage Bks. 3 vols. pap. Vols. 1–2 each $2.45 Vol. 3 $2.95

ESSENTIAL WRITINGS. Ed. by Frederic L. Bender *Harper* Torchbks. 1972 pap. $3.95;
  Peter Smith $6.00

SELECTED WRITINGS IN SOCIOLOGY AND SOCIAL PHILOSOPHY. Ed. by T. B. Bottomore
  and M. Rubel *McGraw-Hill* 1964 pap. $2.45

(With Friedrich Engels). SELECTED WORKS OF MARX AND ENGELS. *International Pubs.* 1968
  $8.50 pap. $4.25

(With Friedrich Engels). BASIC WRITINGS ON POLITICS AND PHILOSOPHY. Ed. by Lewis
  S. Feuer *Doubleday* Anchor Bks. 1959 pap. $2.95; *Peter Smith* $5.00

WRITINGS OF THE YOUNG MARX ON PHILOSOPHY AND SOCIETY. Trans. and ed. by Lloyd
  D. Easton and Kurt H. Guddat *Doubleday* 1967 Anchor Bks. pap. $3.95

"This translation and editing of the writings of the young Marx by two scholars, one an
outstanding philosopher, the other, a specialist in German literature, marks a significant contribution to Marxian studies. The book is significant in that it seeks to convey what Marx 'actually said in
the dozen years prior to the *Communist Manifesto.*' The material used is taken from Marx-Engels
Historisch-Kritische Gesamtausgabe and covers the writings from 'Reflections of a Youth on Choosing
an Occupation,' 1835, to criticism of 'The Poverty of Philosophy,' 1847"—*(LJ)*. There is a valuable
introduction.

KARL MARX ON SOCIETY AND SOCIAL CHANGE: With Selections by Friedrich Engels. Karl
  Marx introd. by Neil J. Smelser. Heritage of Sociology Ser. *Univ. of Chicago Press* 1973
  $11.00

ECONOMIC AND PHILOSOPHICAL MANUSCRIPTS OF 1844. Trans. by Martin Milligan; ed.
  with introd. by Dirk J. Struik *International Pubs.* 1932 rev. ed. 1964 pap. $2.45

"The editor's introduction is a very useful clarification and note on the context and environ-
ment which made up the background against which Marx wrote. Also included is Frederick
Engel's 'Outlines of a Critique on a Political Economy' which serves as a historic analysis of the
Marxian concept of the then existing social order"—*(LJ)*.

THE POVERTY OF PHILOSOPHY. 1847. *International Pubs.* pap. $2.25. Marx's answer to
  Proudhon's "The Philosophy of Poverty" (1846).

(With Friedrich Engels). COMMUNIST MANIFESTO. 1848. Ed. by Samuel H. Beer *AHM
  Pub. Corp.* Crofts Class. 1955 pap. $.85; *International Pubs.* pap. $.40; (with Engels's
  "Principles of Communism" and "The Communist Manifesto after One Hundred
  Years") ed. by Paul M. Sweezy and Leo Huberman *Monthly Review Press* 1968 $4.00
  pap. $1.45; ed. by Harold J. Laski *Pantheon* 1967 $4.95; *Pathfinder Press* 1968 pap.
  $.75; introd. by A. J. P. Taylor *Penguin* Pelican Bks. 1968 pap. $.95; *Regnery* Gateway
  Eds. 1960 pap. $.35; ed. by D. Ryazanoff *Russell & Russell* 1913 1963 $13.00; trans. by
  Samuel Moore, ed. by Joseph Katz and F. B. Randall *Washington Square* 1965 pap.
  $.75

CAPITAL. 1867–1894. (With title "Das Kapital") trans. by Eden and Ceder Paul; introd. by G. D. H. Cole *Dutton* Everyman's 2 vols. 1930 each $3.95; ed. by Friedrich Engels *International Pubs.* 3 vols. 1925 1939 1948 1967 Vol. 1 The Process of Capitalist Production Vol. 2 The Process of Circulation of Capital Vol. 3 The Process of Capitalist Production as a Whole set $25.00 pap. boxed $13.50; ed. by Max Eastman *Modern Library* Giants $5.95; abr. ed. by Serge Levitsky *Regnery* Gateway Eds. 1960 pap. $3.45

CAPITAL AND OTHER WRITINGS. Ed. by Max Eastman *Random* (Modern Lib.) 1932 $2.95

THEORIES OF SURPLUS VALUE. *Beekman Pub.* 3 vols. 1964–1972 Vol. 1 $10.00 Vols. 2–3 each $12.00; (Selections) trans. by G. A. Bonner and E. Burns *Kelley* 1952 $7.50

CRITIQUE OF HEGEL'S "PHILOSOPHY OF RIGHT." Ed. by I. O'Malley *Cambridge* 1970 $9.50

CONTRIBUTION TO THE CRITIQUE OF POLITICAL ECONOMY. Ed. by Maurice Dobb *International Pubs.* 1971 $7.50 pap. $3.25

(With Friedrich Engels). CIVIL WAR IN THE UNITED STATES. *International Pubs.* 1937 rev. ed. 1961 pap. $2.65

(With Friedrich Engels). GERMAN IDEOLOGY. Ed. by C. J. Arthur *International Pubs.* 1939 1947 1970 $6.95 pap. $2.25

(With Friedrich Engels). LETTERS TO AMERICANS. *International Pubs.* 1953 1962 $6.95 pap. $2.45

Other titles are published by Beekman Pub., Bks. for Libraries, China Bks., Doubleday, Burt Franklin, Harper, Humanities Press, International Pubs., Kelley, McGraw-Hill, Macmillan (Free Press), Random and Schocken.

Books about Marx

Historical Materialism and the Economics of Karl Marx. By Benedetto Croce. Trans. by C. M. Meredith. 1914. *Russell & Russell* 1966 $7.50

Marx, Lenin and the Science of Revolution. By Max F. Eastman. 1926. *Hyperion Press* 1973 $13.00

Karl Marx's Interpretation of History. By Mandell M. Bober. *Harvard Univ. Press* 1927 2nd rev. ed. 1948 $11.00; *Norton* 1965 pap. $3.95

Essays on Marx and Russia. By Benedetto Croce. Trans. and ed. by Angelo A. DeGennaro *Ungar* 1966 pap. $1.45

The Teachings of Karl Marx. By Vladimir I. Lenin. *International Pubs.* rev. ed. 1964 pap. $.75

Karl Marx: The Story of His Life. By Franz Mehring. Trans. by Edward Fitzgerald *Humanities Press* 1936 $14.75; *Univ. of Michigan Press* Ann Arbor Bks. 1962 pap. $3.95

Karl Marx: His Life and Environment. By Sir Isaiah Berlin. *Oxford* 1939. Galaxy Bks. 3rd ed. 1963 pap. $1.95

From Hegel to Marx: Studies in the Intellectual Development of Karl Marx. By Sidney Hook. *Humanities Press* 1950 1958 $9.25; *Univ. of Michigan Press* Ann Arbor Bks. 1962 pap. $2.95

Marx and the Marxists: The Ambiguous Legacy. By Sidney Hook. *Van Nostrand-Reinhold* Anvil Bks. 1955 pap. $3.50; *Peter Smith* $3.25. An excellent evaluation, with the views of orthodox Marxists, revisionists and Communists.

Darwin, Marx and Wagner: Critique of a Heritage. By Jacques Barzun. *Doubleday* Anchor Bks. rev. ed. 1958 pap. $2.50; *Peter Smith* 2nd ed. $4.25

Philosophy and Myth in Karl Marx. By Robert C. Tucker. *Cambridge* 1961 2nd ed. 1972 $9.50 pap. $2.95

Marx, Proudhon and European Socialism. By John Hampden Jackson. *Macmillan* Collier Bks. 1962 pap. $1.25; *Verry* $4.00

Beyond the Chains of Illusion. By Erich Fromm. *Simon & Schuster* 1962 1967 $5.95

Marx and the Western World. Ed. by Nicholas Lobkowicz. *Univ. of Notre Dame Press* 1967 $10.95 pap. $3.95
This is the record of an international symposium held at the University of Notre Dame to assess "the new writings on Marx that see him as part of the Western tradition, rather than as an alien contrivance from the East. . . . The compilation is both wide of scope and intensive in inquiry"—(*LJ*).

What Marx Really Said. By H. B. Acton. What They Really Said Ser. *Schocken* 1967 1971 $6.00 pap. $2.45

"This small book achieves Professor Acton's purpose, to elucidate some of Marx's thinking"—
(*LJ*).

The Social and Political Thought of Karl Marx. By Shlomo Avineri. *Cambridge* 1968 1971
$14.50 pap. $3.95

Marx. By Robert Payne. *Simon & Schuster* 1968 $10.00

"The Marx pictured in Robert Payne's biography . . . is a Marx described not through the
eyes of the true believer, but a Marx who, as an isolated scholar and would-be revolutionary
concerned with alienation and injustice, attempts to convert those around him and change
the course of world history. It is a Marx who is one among many jealous and competing
revolutionaries, a man whose theories and judgments often seem incongruous to his personal
and public life. It is a Marx who, in stark contrast to his ideal of the Communist man, turns
violently upon his friends, pursues the very bourgeois vices he vehemently condemns, and
exploits those around him. It is a Marx who suffers mightily from his inability to establish
intimate, lasting personal relations"—(Steven Warnecke, in *SR*).

Theory of Capitalist Development. By Paul M. Sweezy. *Monthly Review Press* 1968 pap. $3.95

The Sociology of Marx. By Henri Lefebvre. Trans. by Norbert Guterman *Random* Vintage Bks.
1969 pap. $1.95

"A study of Marx's conception of the dialectical movement of reality and truth. . . . A
stimulating work, meant to convince, and to develop in depth the faithful follower's
awareness of Marxism"—(*LJ*).

Karl Marx. By Murray Wolfson. *Columbia* 1969 pap. $1.45

Marxism and the Existentialists. By Raymond Aron. World Perspectives Ser. *Harper* 1969 $6.95

Marshall, Marx and Modern Times. By Clark Kerr. *Cambridge* 1969 $6.95

Young Hegelians and Karl Marx. By David McLellan. *Praeger* 1969 $8.50

Marx before Marxism. By David McLellan. *Harper* 1970 $7.95 Torchbks. 1971 pap. $2.75

For Marx. By Louis Althusser. *Random* Vintage Bks. 1970 pap. $1.95

Karl Marx: Early Texts. Ed. and trans. by David McLellan. *Harper* (Barnes & Noble) 1971 $9.00

Reading Capital. By Louis Althusser and Etienne Balibar. Trans. by Ben Brewster *Pantheon*
1971 $10.00

Unknown Karl Marx. Ed. by Robert Payne. *New York Univ. Press* 1971 $9.75

From Marx to Hegel. By George Lichtheim. *Seabury Press* 1971 $7.95

The Formation of the Economic Thought of Karl Marx, 1843 to "Capital." By Ernest Mandel.
Trans. by B. Pearce *Monthly Review Press* 1971 $7.95 pap. $3.25

"A remarkable compression of both an exploration of the maturation of ideas on the part of
Karl Marx himself and a survey of current theoretical revaluations of Marxian concepts"
—(*Choice*).

Birth of the Communist Manifesto. Ed. and annotated by Dirk J. Struik. *International Pubs.* 1971
$7.50 pap. $3.25

An "excellent analysis of the intellectual and socio-political origins of the 'Communist
Manifesto' "—(*Choice*).

The Thought of Karl Marx. By David McLellan. *Harper* 1972 $7.95

Marx's Theory of Alienation. By Istvan Meszaros. *Harper* Torchbks. 1972 pap. $3.25; *Humanities Press* 1973 $7.50; *Peter Smith* $6.50

Marx's Paris Writings: An Analysis. By John Maguire. *Harper* (Barnes & Noble) 1973 $9.00

Karl Marx. Ed. by Tom Bottomore. Makers of Modern Social Science Ser. *Prentice-Hall* 1973
$6.95 Spectrum Bks. pap. $2.45

Marx and Mill: Two Views of Social Conflict and Social Harmony. By G. Duncan. *Cambridge*
1973 $15.50

Marxism and History. By Helmut Fleischer. Trans. by E. Mosbacher *Harper* 1974 $8.00
Torchbks. pap. $3.95

"Fleischer's succinct analysis and convincing exposition of Marx's philosophy make this work
the most valuable recent effort in this field"—(*Choice*).

Karl Marx: His Life and Thought. By David McLellan. *Harper* 1974 $12.50

Karl Marx: His Life and Teachings. By Ferdinand Tonnies. *Michigan State Univ.* 1974 $8.50

Karl Marx: Economy, Class and Social Revolution. Ed. by Z. A. Jordan. *Scribner* 1975 $10.00

Marx's Daughters: Eleanor Marx, Rosa Luxemburg, Angelica Balabanoff. By Ronald Florence.
Dial 1975 $10.00

MORGAN, LEWIS HENRY. 1818–1881.

Lewis Henry Morgan, a lawyer by occupation, was greatly interested in Indian culture; in 1847
the Senecas made him an honorary member of their tribe. His books were major contributions to
the creation of scientific anthropology, and earned for him the title of "father of American
Anthropology." "The League of the Iroquois" was the first scientific account of an Indian tribe to
be published and to this day remains the best work on the Iroquois. . . . "I think it can safely be

predicted that generations of Americans will read Lewis Henry Morgan's 'Indian Journal,' with much the same kind of pleasure and interest that they have read the journals of Lewis and Clark"—(Ashley Montagu, in the *N.Y. Times*).

LEAGUE OF THE HO-DE-SAU-NEE OR IROQUOIS. 1851. Ed. by Henry M. Lloyd *Burt Franklin* 2 vols. rev. ed. 1966 set $27.50; (with title "The League of the Iroquois") *Citadel Press* 1972 pap. $3.95; *Peter Smith* 1962 $6.75

THE AMERICAN BEAVER AND HIS WORKS. 1868. *Burt Franklin* 1970 $18.50

THE SYSTEMS OF CONSANGUINITY AND AFFINITY OF THE HUMAN FAMILY. 1870. *Humanities Press* 1966 $41.25. A pioneer work in the scientific study of kinship.

ANCIENT SOCIETY, or Researches in the Line of Human Progress from Savagery through Barbarism to Civilisation. 1877. Ed. by L. A. White *Harvard Univ. Press* 1964 $13.50; ed. by E. B. Leacock *Peter Smith* $8.00

HOUSES AND HOUSE: Life of the American Aborigines. 1881. Ed. with introd. by Paul Bohannan *Univ. of Chicago Press* 1966 $11.00 Phoenix Bks. pap. $2.95

Studies the relationship between the domestic architecture and social organization of the Indians of North and Central America. "A fascinating book full of unexpected incidents, descriptions and surprise interpretations of Amerind ethnographical and archaeological patterns. Today the book is of historic value for its insight and clarity of statement, and for providing a picture of cultures mostly long since gone. Professor Bohannan's stimulating introductory essay will suggest new ways of looking at Morgan's accomplishments"—(*LJ*).

THE INDIAN JOURNALS, 1859–1862. By Leslie A. White *Univ. of Michigan Press* 1959, o.p.

Books about Morgan

Lewis Henry Morgan, Social Evolutionist. By Bernhard J. Stern. 1931. *Russell & Russell* 1966 $7.50
Lewis Henry Morgan: American Scholar. By Carl Peter Resek. *Univ. of Chicago Press* 1960 $7.00

ENGELS, FRIEDRICH. 1820–1895.

Friedrich Engels is known chiefly through his collaboration with Karl Marx (*q.v.*), whom he met in Paris in 1844; together they laid the foundations of modern communism, notably, in 1848, through their joint authorship of the Communist Manifesto. Born into a wealthy manufacturing family, Engels helped finance the political activities and publications of the two friends. Following the unsuccessful revolution in Germany in 1848, which he and Marx had been active in organizing, Engels moved to England, where he spent the rest of his life.

Both men contributed to the development of the First International—Engels was secretary for Spain, Portugal and Italy in its General Council, After the death of Marx, Engels saw that his friend's posthumous works were published, and edited those left unfinished, including the final two of the three volumes of "*Das Kapital*." Engels continued his political activity by taking an active role in the Second International. Engels' ideas of history as evolutionary process and his application of Marx's dialectical materialism to natural science were influential in the thought of later political radicals, notably Lenin (*q.v.*).

SELECTED WRITINGS. Ed. by William O. Henderson *Penguin* Pelican Bks. (orig.) 1967 pap. $1.95

THE CONDITION OF THE WORKING CLASS IN ENGLAND, 1844. 1845. Trans. from the German by W. O. Henderson and W. H. Challoner. 1887. *Stanford Univ. Press* 1958 $10.00 pap. $3.45

SOCIALISM: Utopian and Scientific. 1878. *International Pubs.* 1935 pap. $1.00; *Pathfinder Press* 1972 pap. $.95. An exposition of the principles of scientific communism.

THE ORIGIN OF THE FAMILY, PRIVATE PROPERTY AND THE STATE. 1884. English 1902. Ed. by Eleanor B. Leacock *International Pubs.* 1942 1972 $7.50 pap. $2.45

THE PEASANT WAR IN GERMANY. English 1926. *International Pubs.* 1966 pap. $1.95. A study of the 1525 peasant revolt, its role in the Reformation and a comparison of Muenzer and Luther.

GERMAN REVOLUTIONS: The Peasant War in Germany; Germany: Revolution and Counter-Revolution. *Univ. of Chicago Press* 1967 $8.75 Phoenix Bks. pap. $2.95

GERMANY: Revolution and Counter-Revolution. *International Pubs.* rev. ed. 1969 $5.95 pap. $1.95

DIALECTICS OF NATURE. *International Pubs.* 1940 $7.50 pap. $2.85. Marxism and the natural sciences.

THE ROLE OF FORCE IN HISTORY: A Study of Bismarck's Policy of Blood and Iron. Trans. and ed. by Ernst Wangermann. *International Pubs.* 1968 $4.25 pap. $1.85. Published in English for the first time.

ENGELS ON CAPITAL. *International Pubs.* new ed. 1974 $6.00 pap. $1.75

For works written with Karl Marx, see Marx's main entry, this Chapter. Other titles are published by International Pubs.

Books about Engels

Marx and Engels through the Eyes of Their Contemporaries. *Beekman Pub.* $7.50

Leon Trotsky on Engels and Kautsky. By Leon Trotsky. *Pathfinder Press* pap. $.50

Karl Marx and Friedrich Engels. By David Riazanov. Trans. from the Russian by Joshua Kunitz. 1927. *Monthly Review Press* 1974 $8.95 pap. $3.45

Friedrich Engels: A Biography. By Gustav Mayer. 1936. *Howard Fertig* 1969 $12.50

Friedrich Engels: The Shadow Prophet. By Grace Carlton. 1965. *Fernhill* $7.50

Interpretation of the Political Ideas of Marx and Engels. By J. B. Sanderson. *Fernhill* (orig.) 1969 pap. $3.75

Marx-Engels. By Melvin Cherno. Ed. by I. E. Cadenhead *Barron's* 1974 pap. $2.95

Engels, Manchester and the Working Class. By Steven Marcus. *Random* 1974 $8.95

The Life of Friedrich Engels. By William O. Henderson. *International Scholarly Bk. Services* 2 vols. 1974 Vol. 1 The Young Revolutionary $22.50 Vol. 2 Marx's Alter Ego, 1850–1896 $25.00

SPENCER, HERBERT. 1820–1903. *See Chapter 5, Philosophy, this Vol.*

TYLOR, SIR EDWARD BURNETT. 1832–1917.

"Tylor's is the first great name in anthropology—perhaps the greatest to date," writes A. L. Kroeber, "and 'Primitive Culture' is his greatest book." His pioneering work, "Anthropology," is still "essentially modern in its cultural theories and concepts." After traveling in the U.S. and Mexico, this English anthropologist first became famous with "Researches into the Early History of Mankind" (1865). In 1896 he became the first professor of anthropology at Oxford University. His most original contribution to anthropology lies in his analysis of religion as behavior motivated by value.

ANAHUAC, or Mexico and the Mexicans, Ancient and Modern. 1861. *Bergman* $6.95; *Gordon Press* $25.00. Observations from a trip to Mexico in 1856.

RESEARCHES INTO THE EARLY HISTORY OF MANKIND AND THE DEVELOPMENT OF CIVILIZATION. 1865. Ed. by Paul Bohannan *Univ. of Chicago Press* abr. ed. 1964 $8.50 Phoenix Bks. pap. $2.95

PRIMITIVE CULTURE. 1871. *Gordon Press* 2 vols. $100.00; *Peter Smith* 2 vols. 1958 Vol. 1 Origins of Culture Vol. 2 Religion in Primitive Culture each $6.00

ANTHROPOLOGY. 1881. Ed. by Leslie A. White *Univ. of Michigan Press* (abr.) 1960 $4.95 Ann Arbor Bks. pap. $2.25

GEORGE, HENRY. 1839–1897.

"Progress and Poverty," by an American, sold millions of copies all over the world. It was written by a man who had worked at a number of trades and experienced desperate poverty. He pointed out the paradox of poverty in the midst of wealth and laid it entirely to the evils of rent. The rich, he said, because they owned good land, ground the faces of the poor in the extraction of unearned rent. A "single tax" on land—the only one to be levied—would relieve the rich of their rents for the good of the entire community. His theories have influenced tax legislation in many countries, and his "single tax" has today its ardent advocates. To the sophisticated economist there can be, alas, no one simple solution to man's economic ills, though George is acknowledged to have recognized an important element among them.

COMPLETE WORKS. 1906–1911. *AMS Press* 10 vols. 1904 each $17.50 set $175.00

PROGRESS AND POVERTY. 1879. *Schalkenbach* 75th anniv. abr. ed. 1954 $3.00 deluxe ed. $5.00 pap. $2.00

A Perplexed Philosopher. *Schalkenbach* $2.00

Protection or Free Trade. 1886. *Schalkenbach* $2.00

The Science of Political Economy. 1897. *Schalkenbach* $2.00

Social Problems. *Schalkenbach* $2.00

Schalkenbach publishes several other titles, including "Progress and Poverty" translated into a number of languages.

Books about George

The Life of Henry George. By Henry George, Jr. 1911. *Schalkenbach* $3.00; *Gordon Press* $29.95
Henry George. By John H. Holmes. *Gordon Press* $29.95
The Prophet of San Francisco: Henry George. By Louis F. Post. 1930. *Gordon Press* $27.00
Henry George, Citizen of the World. By Anna G. De Mille. Ed. by Don C. Shoemaker. 1950.
   Greenwood 1972 $22.75
Henry George in the British Isles. By Elwood P. Lawrence. *Michigan State Univ. Press* 1957 $5.00
Henry George. By Edward J. Rose. *Twayne* 1968 $6.50; *College & Univ. Press* 1968 pap. $2.45
Henry George. By Jacob Oser. *Twayne* 1974 $6.95

SUMNER, WILLIAM GRAHAM. 1840–1910.

Of William Graham Sumner it has been said, "his sociology bridged the gap between the economic ethic set in motion by the Reformation and the thought of the nineteenth century"— (Richard Hofstadter, in "Social Darwinism in America"). His "science of society" represented a synthesis of the three great traditions of Western capitalistic culture: the Protestant ethic, the doctrine of the classical economics of *laissez faire* and Darwinian natural selection. He was a vigorous champion of the disappearing middle class (whose members he called "Forgotten Men") against the rising mastodons of Big Business, Big Labor and Big Government. Few sociological works have had the vast attraction and continuing fascination of his classic, "Folkways," first published in 1906 (o.p.).

Essays. Ed. by Albert G. Keller and Maurice R. Davie. 1934. *Gordon Press* 2 vols. $70.00; *Shoe String Press* 2 vols. 1969 $27.50

Sumner Today: Selected Essays. Ed. by Maurice R. Davie. 1940. *Greenwood* 1971 $12.50

Forgotten Man's Almanac: Rations of Common Sense from William Graham Sumner. Ed. by Albert G. Keller. 1943. *Greenwood* 1971 $17.75

History of American Currency. 1874. *Greenwood* 1968 $15.50; *Kelley* 1968 $15.00

Andrew Jackson as a Public Man: What He Was, What Chances He Had, and What He Did with Them. 1882. Ed. by John T. Morse, Jr. 1899. *AMS Press* $18.50; *Greenwood* $13.50; *Haskell* $17.95; *Scholarly Press* $12.50

What Social Classes Owe to Each Other. 1883. *Arno* 1972 $7.00; *Caxton* 1947 pap. $1.75

The Financier and the Finances of the American Revolution. 1891. *Burt Franklin* 2 vols. set $18.50; *Kelley* 2 vols. set $25.00

War and Other Essays. Ed. by Albert G. Keller. 1911. *AMS Press* 1970 $12.50; *Bks. for Libraries* $17.25

Earth-Hunger and Other Essays. 1913. *Bks. for Libraries* $15.00

Forgotten Man and Other Essays. Ed. by Albert G. Keller. 1919. *Bks. for Libraries* $19.75

Challenge of Facts and Other Essays. 1914. *AMS Press* $14.50

Books about Sumner

Society and Social Change in the Writings of St. Thomas, Ward, Sumner, and Cooley. By Sr. Mary E. Healy. 1948. *Greenwood* 1972 $10.75
American Conservatism in the Age of Enterprise, 1865–1910. By Robert G. McCloskey. *Harper Torchbks.* 1951 pap. $1.60

WARD, LESTER FRANK. 1841–1913.

The "dean of American sociologists" lived to see sociology become an academic discipline which he himself taught at Brown University, beginning 1906. He maintained that "human society, rather than being merely the passive product of unconscious forces, may be shaped by human intelligence" (*Collier's Encyclopedia*), a theory first expressed in "Dynamic Sociology." Ward approached sociology from a psychological viewpoint. With William Graham Sumner (*q.v.*) he dominated American social thought before the turn of the century.

LESTER FRANK WARD: Selections from His Work. Ed. by Israel Gerver, with critical and biographical introd. Major Contributors to Social Science Ser. *T. Y. Crowell* 1963 pap. $2.75

DYNAMIC SOCIOLOGY. 1883. *Greenwood* 2 vols. 1968 set $48.00; *Johnson Reprint* 2 vols. 1968 $42.00

APPLIED SOCIOLOGY: A Treatise on the Conscious Improvement of Society by Society. 1906. *Arno* 1974 $21.00

PSYCHIC FACTORS OF CIVILIZATION. 2nd ed. 1908. *Johnson Reprint* $16.75

PURE SOCIOLOGY. 2nd ed. 1909. *Kelley* 1974 $16.50

Books about Ward

Sociology and Education: Analysis of the Theories of Spencer and Ward. By Elsa P. Kimball. 1932. *AMS Press* $12.50

Society and Social Change in the Writings of St. Thomas, Ward, Sumner, Cooley. By Sr. Mary E. Healy. 1948. *Greenwood* 1972 $10.75

Lester F. Ward: The American Aristotle. By Samuel Chugerman. *Octagon* 1965 $18.50

PARETO, VILFREDO. 1848–1923.

The great Italian social theorist published his monumental *"Trattato di Sociologia Generale"* in 1916. It was soon translated into most of the major European languages, and in 1935 into English under the title "The Mind and Society." Pareto is celebrated for his vast encyclopedic system and for his original delineation of rational and nonrational factors in social action. His theory of the cyclical rise and fall of elite governing groups was used by the Italian Fascists to justify their ideology.

MANUAL OF POLITICAL ECONOMY. 1909. Trans. by Ann Schweir; ed. by Alfred N. Page. *Kelley* 1969 $25.00

LETTERS FROM LIBERTY. *Revisionist Press* $35.00

THE MIND AND SOCIETY: A Treatise on General Sociology. 1935. Trans. from the Italian by Andrew Bongiorno, Arthur Livingston and James H. Rogers; ed. by Arthur Livingston. 4 vols. o.p. Vol. 1 Nonlogical Conduct Vol. 2 Theory of Residues Vol. 3 Theory of Derivations Vol. 4 The General Form of Society

THE RULING CLASS IN ITALY BEFORE 1900. 1950. *Howard Fertig* 1974 $9.50

THE RISE AND FALL OF ELITES. *Bedminster* 1962 1968 $4.50

Books about Pareto

An Introduction to Pareto: His Sociology. By George C. Homans and Charles P. Curtis, Jr. 1934. *Howard Fertig* 1970 $12.00

Pareto's General Sociology: A Physiologist's Interpretation. By Lawrence J. Henderson. 1935. *Russell & Russell* 1967 $6.00

Pareto and Mosca. Ed. by James H. Meisel. *Prentice-Hall* 1965 $4.95 Spectrum Bks. pap. $2.45

Pareto's Methodological Approach to Economics: A Study in the History of Some Scientific Aspects of Economic Thought. By Vincent J. Tarascio. *Univ. of North Carolina Press* 1968 $6.00 .

FRAZER, SIR JAMES (GEORGE). 1854–1941.

Sir James Frazer is known chiefly as the author of "The Golden Bough." No study of mythology and folklore is complete without reference to this monumental masterpiece which builds up an account of the evolution of religion, tracing many myths and rites to the prehistoric beginnings of agriculture. It is based on a remarkably broad and reliable knowledge and written with great imagination and literary skill. Sir James was a Scottish anthropologist and classical scholar, writing many books and receiving many honors during his long life. He held the chair of social anthropology at Liverpool, 1907–1922. He edited and translated the classics and was a critic of English literature of the 18th century. At the time of his death the *N.Y. Herald Tribune* said editorially: "The impact of his extraordinary labor seems certain to be felt for decades to come."

"The Golden Bough" appeared originally in 16 volumes (1890–1915); the 12-volume popular edition was brought out in 1935, the first abridged one-volume edition in 1922 and another one-volume abridgment in 1959.

THE GOLDEN BOUGH: A Study in Magic and Religion. 1890. *St. Martin's* 13 vols. 3rd ed. each $15.40 set $200.00; *Macmillan* 1 vol. abr. ed. $7.95 pap. 1960 $3.95

Vols. 1–2 Magic Art and the Evolution of Kings (1911) Vol. 3 Taboo and the Perils of the Soul (1911) Vol. 4 The Dying God (1911) Vols. 5–6 Adonis, Attis, Osiris: Studies in the History of Oriental Religion (1914) Vols. 7–8 Spirits of the Corn and the Wild (1912) Vol. 9 Scapegoat (1913) Vols. 10–11 Balder the Beautiful: Fire Festivals of Europe and the Doctrine of the External Soul (1913) Vol. 12 Bibliography and General Index (1915) Vol. 13 Aftermath: Supplement (1936)

THE NEW GOLDEN BOUGH: A New Abridgment of the Classic Work. Ed. by Theodore H. Gaster. *Phillips* 1959 $15.95; *New Am. Lib.* Mentor Bks. pap. $1.95

This one-volume abridgement is based on the original 12 volumes and the supplementary "Aftermath." It includes Frazer's notes (not previously included in a one-volume edition) and Dr. Gaster's own supplementary notes and comments. The critic David Glixon, however, has warned that Gaster's edition "throws many of Frazer's main concepts out the window"—*(PW)*.

LECTURES ON THE EARLY HISTORY OF THE KINGSHIP. 1905. *AMS Press* 1973 $16.50

THE DEVIL'S ADVOCATE: A Plea for Superstition. (Orig. "Psyche's Task," 1909.) 1927. *Finch Press* $15.00

TOTEMISM AND EXOGAMY: A Treatise on Certain Early Forms of Superstition and Society. 1910. *Harper* (Barnes & Noble) Vols. 1–4 set $90.00

PSYCHE'S TASK: A Discourse Concerning the Influence of Superstition on the Growth of Institutions. 1913. *Harper* (Barnes & Noble) 2nd rev. ed. 1968 $12.50

THE BELIEF IN IMMORTALITY AND THE WORSHIP OF THE DEAD. 1913–1924. *Harper* (Barnes & Noble) 3 vols. 1968 Vol. 1 Belief among the Aborigines of Australia, Torres Straits Islands, New Guinea and Melanesia (1913) Vol. 2 Belief among the Polynesians (1922) Vol. 3 Belief among the Micronesians (1924) set $65.00

THE MAGICAL ORIGIN OF KINGS. 1920. *Harper* (Barnes & Noble) 1968 $13.50

MYTHS OF THE ORIGIN OF FIRE. 1930. *Hacker Art Bks.* 1971 $17.50

GARNERED SHEAVES: Essays, Addresses, Reviews. 1931. *Bks. for Libraries* 1967 $13.75

CREATION AND EVOLUTION IN PRIMITIVE COSMOGONIES AND OTHER PIECES. 1935. *Bks. for Libraries* 1967 $9.00

ANTHOLOGIA ANTHROPOLOGICA. Ed. by Robert A. Downie from a selection of the ms. notebooks. 1938–1939. *AMS Press* 4 vols. Vol. 1 The Native Races of Africa and Madagascar (1938) $67.50 Vol. 2 The Native Races of America (1939) $67.50 Vol. 3 The Native Races of Australasia (1939) $47.50 Vol. 4 The Native Races of Asia and Europe (1939) $47.50

Books about Frazer

A Bibliography of Sir James George Frazer, O.M. Ed. by Theodore Besterman. 1934. *Fernhill* 1968 $11.00

A Scientific Theory of Culture and Other Essays. By Bronislaw Malinowski. *Univ. of North Carolina Press* 1944 $4.95

The Tangled Bank: Darwin, Marx, Frazer and Freud as Imaginative Writers. By Stanley Edgar Hyman. *Atheneum* 1962 pap. 1974 $4.25

Frazer and the Golden Bough: A Personal Memoir Together with an Appraisal of Sir James Frazer's Work. By Robert Angus Downie. *Humanities Press* 1970 $6.50

The Literary Impact of the Golden Bough. By John B. Vickery. *Princeton Univ. Press* 1973 $16.50 pap. $8.50

VEBLEN, THORSTEIN (BUNDE). 1857–1929.

Lewis Mumford (*q.v.*) called Veblen "one of the half-dozen important figures in scholarship that America has produced since the Civil War, . . . grimly whimsical, . . . a stick of dynamite wrapped up . . . to look like a stick of candy." His parents were Norwegian farmers of intellectual disposition, and Veblen was born on a farm in Wisconsin but reared in Minnesota. He was educated at Carleton College Academy and Carleton College, went to Johns Hopkins for graduate study but transferred to Yale for his Ph.D. He had majored in philosophy but in the years of waiting for a teaching appointment, which he spent in study and writing, he developed into an economist. When the University of Chicago was founded in 1892, he went there as instructor and became associate professor of economics. He taught at Stanford University, the University of Missouri, and the New School for Social Research; edited the *Journal of Political Economy* and was one of the editors of the *Dial*. Eccentric, tubercular, bitter (yet at the same time attractive to many women, his affairs with whom he rarely bothered to conceal), the man Veblen "was a tragic failure." But "the economist and philosopher and author Thorstein Veblen was one of the shining triumphs of our age." At times he wrote with deliberate obscurity; his sesquipedalian words, said Mumford, constituted "desperately accurate circumlocutions." But his thinking is clear and incisive and much of his writing wittily brilliant and readable. From him came the now-familiar phrases "conspicuous waste," "absentee ownership," the "price system." He was "the man who shook the world with his irony and who opened the way to new social systems." His sharp criticism of American materialism and his disdain of the social niceties make him seem particularly "relevant" to the rebellious youth of today.

WRITINGS. *Kelley* 11 vols. set $100.00

THE PORTABLE VEBLEN: Including Selections from Nine Books. Ed. by Max Lerner *Viking* 1958 $5.95 pap. $3.25

VEBLEN ON MARX, RACE, SCIENCE AND ECONOMICS. *Putnam* Capricorn Bks. 1969 pap. $2.65

THE THEORY OF THE LEISURE CLASS. 1899. *T. Y. Crowell* (Funk & Wagnalls) Minerva Press 1967 pap. $1.95; *Houghton* 1973 $6.95; *Kelley* 1965 $12.50; *New Am. Lib.* Mentor Bks. 1954 pap. $1.25

THE THEORY OF BUSINESS ENTERPRISE. 1904. *Kelley* 1965 $12.50

INSTINCT OF WORKMANSHIP. 1914. rev. ed. 1918. *Kelley* $12.50

IMPERIAL GERMANY AND THE INDUSTRIAL REVOLUTION. 1915. *Univ. of Michigan Press* Ann Arbor Bks. 1966 pap. $2.65; *Viking* rev. ed. 1968 $5.00

INQUIRY INTO THE NATURE OF PEACE. 1917. *Kelley* 1963 $12.50

THE HIGHER LEARNING IN AMERICA. 1918. *Farrar, Straus* (Hill & Wang) 1957 pap. $1.95; *Kelley* 1965 $10.00

THE PLACE OF SCIENCE IN MODERN CIVILISATION AND OTHER ESSAYS. 1919. *Russell & Russell* 1961 $18.00

ON THE NATURE AND USES OF SABOTAGE. 1919. *Oriole Edns.* 1971 pap. $.75

THE INDUSTRIAL SYSTEM AND THE CAPTAINS OF INDUSTRY. 1919. *Oriole Edns.* 1971 pap. $.75

VESTED INTERESTS AND THE COMMON MAN. 1920. *Kelley* 1963 $8.50; *Putnam* Capricorn Bks. 1969 pap. $1.65

THE ENGINEERS AND THE PRICE SYSTEM. 1921. *Kelley* 1965 $8.50

ABSENTEE OWNERSHIP. 1923. *Beacon* pap. $2.95; *Kelley* 1963 $12.50

ESSAYS IN OUR CHANGING ORDER. 1934. Ed. by Leon Ardzrooni *Viking* $5.75; *Kelley* 1963 $12.50

Books about Veblen

Thorstein Veblen and His America. By Joseph Dorfman. 1934. *Kelley* 1964 $15.00
What Veblen Taught. Ed. by Wesly C. Mitchell. 1936. *Kelley* 1963 $15.00
Thorstein Veblen. By Douglas F. Dowd. Great American Thinkers Ser. *Twayne* $7.95
"A readable text by a leading Veblen specialist that may inspire 'digging' into Veblen's originals"—(*LJ*).
Thorstein Veblen: The Carleton College Veblen Seminar Essays. Ed. by Carlton C. Qualey. *Columbia* 1968 $9.00. Essays by students and scholars.
Thorstein Veblen: Essays, Reviews and Reports. Ed. by Joseph Dorfman. *Kelley* 1975 $35.00
"Professor Dorfman's new volume will be a browser's delight to all true Veblenians and is a necessary supplement to the great life"—(*TLS*, London).

Thorstein Veblen and the Institutionalists: A Study in the Social Philosophy of Economics. By David Seckler. *Macmillan* 1975 $25.00
   A "good book from the orthodox point of view. [It] provides a substantial guide to the perplexed"—(*TLS*, London).

BOAS, FRANZ.   1858–1942.
   This American anthropologist was born in Westphalia, Germany. He came to the U.S. in 1886 and carried on anthropological research in North America, Mexico and Puerto Rico. He became Professor of Anthropology at Columbia University in 1899, and was Curator of Anthropology at the American Museum of Natural History (1901–1905). Boas was an authority on anthropometry and on linguistics of North American Indians. He was enormously influential in his field and rigorously scientific in his collection of data.

THE SHAPING OF AMERICAN ANTHROPOLOGY, 1883–1911: A Franz Boas Reader. Ed. by George W. Stocking, Jr. *Basic Bks.* 1973 $12.95
   "The editor's aim has been to publish some of the work Boas did when he was in his prime and to present the man in his totality. . . . In addition to an introductory essay by the editor, there are nearly 50 selections, many of them pleasant surprises to find in a single volume"—(*Choice*).

THE CENTRAL ESKIMO. 1888. Introd. by Henry B. Collins *Univ. of Nebraska Press* Bison Bks. 1964 pap. $2.45; *Peter Smith* $4.50

SOCIAL ORGANIZATION AND SECRET SOCIETIES OF THE KWAKIUTL INDIANS. 1895. *Johnson Reprint* 1970 $42.00

THE ESKIMO OF BAFFIN LAND AND HUDSON BAY. 1901. *AMS Press* 1974 $38.00

THE MIND OF PRIMITIVE MAN. *Macmillan* (Free Press) 1911 rev. ed. 1938 1965 pap. $2.45

INTRODUCTION TO HANDBOOK OF AMERICAN INDIAN LANGUAGES. (With J. W. Powell's "Indian Linguistic Families of America North of Mexico") ed. by Preston Holder *Univ. of Nebraska Press* Bison Bks. 1966 pap. $1.85; *Peter Smith* $4.75

KWAKIUTL ETHNOGRAPHY. Ed. with introd. by Helen Codere *Univ. of Chicago Press* 1966 $13.75

(Ed.). HANDBOOK OF AMERICAN INDIAN LANGUAGES. 1911. *Humanities Press* 2 vols. 1969 set $82.50

(Ed.). GENERAL ANTHROPOLOGY. 1938. *Johnson Reprint* 1965 $12.50

PRIMITIVE ART. 1927. *Dover* pap. $3.00; *Peter Smith* 1962 $5.50

ANTHROPOLOGY AND MODERN LIFE. 1928. *Norton* 1962 pap. $1.85

BELLA BELLA TEXTS. 1928. *AMS Press* 1969 $15.00

RACE, LANGUAGE AND CULTURE. *Macmillan* (Free Press) 1940 pap. 1966 $3.95

ETHNOGRAPHY OF FRANZ BOAS: Letters and Diaries of Franz Boas Written on the Northwest Coast from 1886–1931. Ed. by Ronald P. Rohner *Univ. of Chicago Press* 1969 $13.00

Books about Boas
   Franz Boas: 1858–1942. By Alfred Louis Kroeber. 1943. *Kraus* pap. $5.00
   Franz Boas. By Melville Herskovits. 1953. *Kelley* 1970 $8.50

DURKHEIM, ÉMILE.   1858–1917.
   The greatest of French sociologists, Émile Durkheim, has probably exerted more influence on modern social theory than has any other man. His system of thought is tantamount to social and moral philosophy. "Sociologism," the concept most closely associated with his name, might be defined as "the viewpoint of those sociologists who, making sociology completely irreducible to psychology, consider it as necessary and sufficient for the total explanation of social reality" (Edward Tiryakian, in "Sociologism and Existentialism"). Durkheim's thought, which stems from Claude Henri Saint-Simon (*q.v.*) and Auguste Comte (*q.v.*), and which is liked to the theories of Karl Marx (*q.v.*), provides a valuable statement of the nature of socialist thought before Lenin. Durkheim is at present viewed with increasing interest here and abroad. *Library Journal* has said of him: "He developed his own independent and remarkable concept of sociology which stressed the collective mind of society, recognized authority as a moral force, and ascribed a vital role to the

science of statistics. Although Durkheim strongly believed in the 'non-rational' element of sociology, he did not discount the impact of philosophy on [that discipline]." Durkheim's pioneer study of "Suicide" (1897) remains one of the matchless achievements of theoretical research. The contemporary French scholar, Maurice Halbwachs, has summarized Durkheim's final work in "Sources of Religious Sentiment" (*Macmillan* [Free Press] 1962 $4.95).

ÉMILE DURKHEIM: Selected Writings. Ed. and trans. by Anthony Giddens *Cambridge* 1972 $11.50 pap. $3.95

"The book contains a lucid and informed 50 page introduction and 13 well chosen, newly translated selections (some for the first time) drawn from the entire breadth of Durkheim's important works. . . . Probably the single most valuable collection of Durkheim's work presently available in English"—(*Choice*).

ÉMILE DURKHEIM: Ed. by George Simpson *T. Y. Crowell* 1963 pap. $2.75. Selections from his work with commentary.

THE DIVISION OF LABOR IN SOCIETY. 1893. 1933. Trans. by George Simpson *Macmillan* (Free Press) 1947 $5.50 pap. $2.95. The first great work of the famous French sociologist; "a book that must be read by all those who profess some knowledge of social thought."

THE RULES OF SOCIOLOGICAL METHOD. 1895. Trans. by Sarah A. Solovay and John H. Mueller; ed. by George E. G. Catlin *Macmillan* (Free Press) 8th ed. 1950 $4.95 pap. $1.95. A classic of sociology and of the methodology of political science.

SUICIDE: A Study in Sociology. 1897. Trans. by John A. Spaulding and George Simpson *Macmillan* (Free Press) 1951 $8.95 pap. $2.95

(With Marcell Mauss). PRIMITIVE CLASSIFICATION. 1903. Trans. from the French and ed. with introd. by Rodney Needham *Univ. of Chicago Press* 1963 $5.00 Phoenix Bks. pap. $1.95

This is one among several French sociological classics made available in English by the members of the department of social anthropology at Oxford University. "In their essay the two authors deal with the relationship which they claim exists between the subdivisions of primitive societies into clans, moieties, and other social segments and the conceptual categories used by these societies in ordering the world of nature."

THE ELEMENTARY FORMS OF RELIGIOUS LIFE. 1912. Trans. by Joseph W. Swain. *Macmillan* (Free Press) 1954 $7.95 pap. $3.50; *Humanities Press* 1964 text ed. $7.25

SOCIOLOGY AND PHILOSOPHY. Trans. by D. F. Pocock *Macmillan* (Free Press) 1953 $4.50 pap. 1974 $1.95. His theory of society as a dynamic system which is the real source of moral life.

EDUCATION AND SOCIOLOGY. Trans. by Sherwood D. Fox; fwd. by Talcott Parsons. *Macmillan* (Free Press) 1956 $5.95. The statement of his original theory regarding the problems of education.

SOCIALISM AND SAINT-SIMON. Ed. by Alvin W. Gouldner; trans. by Charlotte Sattler *Antioch Press* (dist. by Kent State Univ. Press) 1958 $5.00

MONTESQUIEU AND ROUSSEAU: Forerunners of Sociology. Trans. by Ralph Manheim. 1960. *Univ. of Michigan Press* Ann Arbor Bks. pap. $1.95

MORAL EDUCATION. Trans. by Herman Schnurer; ed. by Everett K. Wilson *Macmillan* (Free Press) 1961 $7.95 pap. 1973 $3.45. His convincing and provocative argument for establishing a strong secular morality via the public schools.

SOCIALISM. *Macmillan* Collier Bks. 1962 pap. $.95

ON MORALITY AND SOCIETY. Ed. by Robert N. Bellah *Univ. of Chicago Press* 1973 $10.50

Books about Durkheim

Émile Durkheim and His Sociology. By Harry Alpert. 1939. *Russell & Russell* 1961 $12.00
Émile Durkheim, 1858–1917: A Collection of Essays, with Translations and a Bibliography. Ed. by Kurt H. Wolff. *Ohio State Univ. Press* 1960 $7.50
Social Meanings of Suicide. By Jack D. Douglas. *Princeton Univ. Press* 1970 $15.00 pap. $3.95

Capitalism and Modern Social Theory: An Analysis of the Writings of Marx, Durkheim and Max
  Weber. By Anthony Giddens. *Cambridge* 1971 $14.50 pap. $4.95
Émile Durkheim: Sociologist and Philosopher. By Dominick La Capra. *Cornell Univ. Press* 1972
  $12.50
  "It may well be the best intellectual portrait of Durkheim currently available in English"—
  (*Choice*).
Images of Society: Essays on the Sociological Theories of Tocqueville, Marx and Durkheim. By
  Gianfranco Poggi. *Stanford Univ. Press* 1972 $8.95
Durkheim: Morality and Milieu. By Ernest E. Wallwork. *Harvard Univ. Press* 1972 $10.00
Émile Durkheim: His Life and Work, a Historical and Critical Study. By Steven Lukes. *Harper*
  1973 $17.50
  Lukes "develops a sophisticated treatment of Durkheim's biography and works"—(*Choice*).
The Sociology of Émile Durkheim. By Robert A. Nisbet. *Oxford* 1973 $9.95 pap. $2.95

SIMMEL, GEORG. 1858–1918.

The "enormously influential" theorist and teacher was largely responsible for establishing
sociology as an independent discipline in Germany. He was chiefly concerned with defining the
processes of human interaction that frequently recur, such as competition, subordination and
superordination; he drew general principles from the isolated phenomena per se rather than
from one context of their meaning or historical setting.

GEORG SIMMEL ON INDIVIDUALITY AND SOCIAL FORMS. Ed. by Donald N. Levine.
  Heritage of Sociology Ser. *Univ. of Chicago Press* 1971 $15.75 Phoenix Bks. 1972 pap.
  $4.25

THE SOCIOLOGY OF GEORG SIMMEL. Trans. by Kurt H. Wolff *Macmillan* (Free Press)
  1950 $9.50 pap. $3.50

CONFLICT AND THE WEB OF GROUP AFFILIATIONS. *Macmillan* (Free Press) 1955 $6.50
  pap. $2.45

(With others). ESSAYS ON SOCIOLOGY, PHILOSOPHY AND AESTHETICS. Ed. by Kurt H.
  Wolff *Gannon* $9.50

Books about Simmel

The Social Theory of Georg Simmel. By Nicholas J. Spykman. 1925. *Aldine* 1966 pap. $3.50;
  Russell & Russell 1964 $8.50
Georg Simmel, 1858–1918: A Collection of Essays, with Translations and a Bibliography. Ed. by
  Kurt H. Wolff. *Ohio State Univ. Press* 1959 $7.50
Experience and Culture: The Philosophy of Georg Simmel. By Rudolph Weingartner. *Wesleyan
  Univ. Press* 1962 $7.50
Georg Simmel. Ed. by Lewis A. Coser. Makers of Modern Social Science Ser. *Prentice-Hall* 1965
  $4.95
  "Lewis Coser had drawn on his knowledge of the work of Georg Simmel to assemble a
  collection of essays about the sociologist that presents a rounded picture of the work and
  character of this brilliant but controversial theorist"—(*LJ*).

WEBB, BEATRICE, 1858–1943, and SIDNEY (JAMES) WEBB, Baron Passfield,
  1859–1947.

The unusual partnership of Beatrice and Sidney Webb affected most of the major social and
political reforms in the England of their era. Together they were the chief factor of the Fabian
Society and of the budding English Labor Party. Early in their marriage they wrote "The History
of Trade Unionism" and "Industrial Democracy." Before undertaking their great study of English
local government, they visited the United States, New Zealand and Australia. "Beatrice Webb's
American Diary" records their 100-day tour across this country in 1898. "Many of her comments
anticipate those of Lincoln Steffens; she was even more prescient in her fear of the bureaucratic
power of a civil service of experts. The Webbs' interviews . . . with Theodore Roosevelt and
Woodrow Wilson, each relatively unknown at that time, are of value as the observations of an
informed mind from outside America. . . . Mrs. Webb had serious limitations; she was provincial
to a high degree, with both British and social-class prejudices which mar the value of the work"—
(*LJ*).
Sidney Webb was a member of Parliament, became Secretary of State in 1929, and was created
Baron Passfield. Beatrice Webb stuck to her socialist guns and refused to share the title with him.

THE HISTORY OF TRADE UNIONISM. 1894. rev. ed. 1920. *AMS Press* rev. ed. $12.50;
  Kelley rev. ed. $18.50

INDUSTRIAL DEMOCRACY. 1897. rev. ed. 1920. *AMS Press* $35.00; *Kelley* rep. of 1897 ed. 1965 $18.50

BEATRICE WEBB'S AMERICAN DIARY, 1898. Ed. by David A. Shannon *Univ. of Wisconsin Press* 1963 $10.00

PROBLEMS OF MODERN INDUSTRY. 1902. *Bks. for Libraries* 1970 $12.00

PREVENTION OF DESTITUTION. 1911. *Kelley* $12.50

ENGLISH LOCAL GOVERNMENT. 6 vols. 1906–1922. *International Scholarly Bk. Services* 11 vols. 2nd ed. set $110.00

DECAY OF CAPITALIST CIVILIZATION. 1923. *Bks. for Libraries* $9.50; *Greenwood* $13.50

DEVELOPMENT OF ENGLISH LOCAL GOVERNMENT, 1689–1835. *Oxford* 1963 $3.50

METHODS OF SOCIAL STUDY. 1932. *Kelley* 1967 $11.50

Books about the Webbs

The History of the Fabian Society. By Edward Reynolds Pease. New introd. by Margaret Cole *International Scholarly Bk. Services* 1962 $10.00; *Richard West* 1973 $25.00

Beatrice Webb: A Life (1858–1943). By Kitty Muggeridge and Ruth Adam. *Knopf* 1968 $7.95 "Very few people have ever 'done' more with and in their lives than Beatrice and Sidney. They lived a terrifyingly active life in a number of different spheres, and they left several monuments of their activity behind them. . . . It was impossible to write a life of Beatrice without dealing continually and at length with these activities and their results, and they are given their adequate place in this book. But the authors had to decide what exactly the place should be. . . . This book takes a firm line. It deals with the life of action and the nature and value of its achievements only in so far as they are part of the life of Aunt Bo and throw light upon her character. . . . Mrs. Muggeridge and Mrs. Adam have written an extremely good biography"—(Leonard Woolf, in the *New Statesman*).

DEWEY, JOHN. 1859–1952. *See Chapter 5, Philosophy, this Vol.*

ADDAMS, JANE. 1860–1935. (Nobel Peace Prize 1931)

The founder of Hull House in Chicago in 1889, Jane Addams was a world leader in social settlement work and foremost in the struggle for women's rights, woman suffrage and world peace. In 1915, during World War I, she got together a small band of energetic women from several countries and founded the pacifist Women's International League for Peace and Freedom, still in existence today, with Pearl Buck and Mrs. Martin Luther King, Jr., among its members. Hull House in its early days drew artists, intellectuals, writers and social reformers, many of whom stayed there for a time and later wrote of the excitement it generated. In 1931 Miss Addams was co-winner (with Nicholas Murray Butler) of the Nobel Prize.

SOCIAL THOUGHT OF JANE ADDAMS. Ed. by Christopher Lasch *Bobbs* 1965 $7.50 pap. $4.35

DEMOCRACY AND SOCIAL ETHICS. 1902. Ed. by Anne Firor Scott *Harvard Univ. Press* 1964 pap. $1.95; (and "Other Essays") *Scholarly Press* $14.50

NEWER IDEALS OF PEACE. 1907. Peace Movement in America Ser. *Jerome S. Ozer* 1972 $10.95

TWENTY YEARS AT HULL HOUSE. 1910. *Macmillan* 1912 1966 $6.95; *New Am. Lib.* Signet pap. $.95

A NEW CONSCIENCE AND AN ANCIENT EVIL. 1912. Family in America Ser. *Arno* 1972 $11.00

SPIRIT OF YOUTH AND THE CITY STREETS. 1909. 1912. *Univ. of Illinois Press* 1972 $6.95 pap. $2.45; *McGrath* repr. of 1930 ed. 1972 $12.00; *Norwood* $10.00

PEACE AND BREAD IN TIME OF WAR. 1922. *Finch Press* $14.00; *Jerome S. Ozer* 1972 $10.95; (and "Patriotism and Pacifists in Wartime") *Garland Pub.* $19.00

THE EXCELLENT BECOMES THE PERMANENT. 1932. *Bks. for Libraries* $8.75

MY FRIEND, JULIA LATHROP. 1935. Children & Youth Ser. *Arno* 1974 $14.00

Books about Addams

Jane Addams of Hull House. By Winifred E. Wise. *Harcourt* 1935 $5.75   •
Jane Addams: A Biography. By James W. Linn. 1935. *Greenwood* 1968 $22.25
Beloved Lady: A History of Jane Addams' Ideas on Reform and Peace. By John C. Farrell. *Johns
Hopkins Press* 1967 $8.50
Jane Addams and the Liberal Tradition. By Daniel Levine. *State Historical Society of Wisconsin*
1971 $8.50
American Heroine: The Life and Legend of Jane Addams. By Allen F. Davis. *Oxford* 1973
$10.95

WHITEHEAD, ALFRED NORTH.   1861–1947.   *See Chapter 5, Philosophy, this Vol.*

COOLEY, CHARLES HORTON.   1864–1929.

A sociologist with a deep interest in psychology, the American Charles Horton Cooley is known
for his pioneer work in the field of social psychology. He opposed the tendency among sociologists
to study individual behavior apart from its social context, and to look at institutions apart from
individuals. He coined the phrases "the looking-glass self" and "primary groups," and his concepts
of the interaction of the individual and society and of primary social groups have had wide
influence.

HUMAN NATURE AND THE SOCIAL ORDER. 1902 rev. ed. 1922. *Schocken* 1964 pap. $2.95

SOCIAL ORGANIZATION: A Study of the Larger Mind. 1909. Introd. by Philip Rieff
Schocken 1962 pap. $2.95

SOCIAL PROCESS. 1918. Perspectives in Sociology Ser. *Southern Illinois Univ. Press* 1966
$10.00 pap. $3.45

SOCIOLOGICAL THEORY AND SOCIAL RESEARCH. 1930. *Kelley* 1969 $12.50

Books about Cooley

Charles Horton Cooley: His Life and His Social Theory. By Edward C. Jandy. 1942. *Octagon*
1969 $12.00
Society and Social Change in the Writings of St. Thomas, Ward, Sumner, and Cooley. By Sr.
Mary E. Healy. 1948. *Greenwood* 1972 $10.75

WEBER, MAX.   1864–1920.

The outstanding German sociologist opposed the Marxian interpretation of historical change in
terms of man's rational economic interest. He held that it is not "material" economic conditions
that constitute the major driving force in social life, but rather the spirit of the community, which
he described in terms of "common value orientation." In his most famous work, "The Protestant
Ethic and the Spirit of Capitalism," Weber argues that Calvinism was prerequisite to the
development of capitalism. Because the Calvinist refuses to adapt to a sinful world, because he
strives ceaselessly to transform it, disciplined conduct and hard work acquire moral virtue, thus
producing the "value orientation"—involving social approval of competitive production for
private gain—necessary to workable capitalism. In his studies of Oriental religions, Weber
demonstrated that although economic factors in the Orient at the time of the Reformation were
not dissimilar to economic factors in Western Europe, capitalism did not similarly develop because
the Eastern religions did not produce "favorable" value systems.

MAX WEBER: Selections from His Work. Introd. by S. M. Miller. Major Contributors to
Social Science Ser. *T. Y. Crowell* 1963 pap. $2.75

FROM MAX WEBER: Essays in Sociology. Trans. from the German and ed. with introd.
by Hans H. Gerth and C. Wright Mills *Oxford* 1946 pap. $3.50

THE PROTESTANT ETHIC AND THE SPIRIT OF CAPITALISM. 1920. *Scribner* 1930 1948 $5.95
pap. $2.45

MAX WEBER ON LAW IN ECONOMY AND SOCIETY. 1921. Trans. by Edward Shils; ed. by
Max Rheinstein *Harvard Univ. Press* 1954 $11.00; *Simon & Schuster* Clarion Bks. 1967
pap. $2.95. Selected passages.

MAX WEBER ON THE METHODOLOGY OF THE SOCIAL SCIENCES. 1922. *Macmillan* (Free
Press) 1949 $5.95

THE THEORY OF SOCIAL AND ECONOMIC ORGANIZATION. 1922. Trans. by Talcott Parsons
Macmillan (Free Press) 1947 $8.95 pap. $3.50

RELIGION OF CHINA. *Macmillan* (Free Press) 1951 $7.95 pap. $2.95

RELIGION OF INDIA. *Macmillan* (Free Press) 1958 $7.95 pap. $2.95

THE CITY. Trans. and ed. by Don Martindale and Gertrude Neuwirth *Macmillan* (Free Press) 1958 $5.95 pap. $2.45

THE RATIONAL AND SOCIAL FOUNDATIONS OF MUSIC. Ed. by Don Martindale and Johannes Riedel *Southern Illinois Univ. Press* 1958 1969 $7.00 pap. $2.25

GENERAL ECONOMIC HISTORY. 1923. Trans. by Frank H. Knight. 1927. *Macmillan* Collier Bks. 1961 pap. $1.50

BASIC CONCEPTS IN SOCIOLOGY. Trans. by H. P. Secher *Citadel Press* 1962 pap. $2.25; *Greenwood* $7.50

THE SOCIOLOGY OF RELIGION. Trans. by Ephraim Fischoff *Beacon* 1964 $7.50 pap. $2.75
"There can be hardly any doubt that Max Weber is the most eminent sociologist of all time. His vast literary legacy is to this day of utmost interest to all serious students of society. At the same time many a professional sociologist has been made uncomfortable by his fabulous erudition and unique sophistication, which defies all emulation. Max Weber's German style is an additional handicap to those whose knowledge of German is limited. . . . Talcott Parsons' introductory essay is probably one of his best statements on Max Weber, whose exegete he has been for several decades"—(*LJ*).

POLITICS AS A VOCATION. *Fortress Press* 1965 pap. $1.00

ECONOMY AND SOCIETY: An Outline of Interpretive Sociology. Trans. by Ephraim Fischoff; ed. by Guenther Roth and Claus Wittich *Bedminster* 3 vols. 4th ed. 1968 boxed set $40.00

MAX WEBER ON CHARISMA AND INSTITUTION BUILDING. Ed. by S. N. Eisenstadt. Heritage of Sociology Ser. *Univ. of Chicago Press* 1968 $12.00 Phoenix Bks. pap. $4.95

MAX WEBER ON UNIVERSITIES. Trans. and ed. by Edward Shils *Univ. of Chicago Press* 1974 pap. $2.95

Books about Weber

Max Weber's Political Ideas in the Perspective of Our Time. By Karl Lowenstein. *Univ. of Mass. Press* 1966 pap. $4.50

The Sociology of Max Weber. By Julian Freund. Trans. from the French by Mary Ilford. 1966. *Pantheon* 1968 $7.95; *Random* Vintage Bks. 1969 pap. $1.95
"Mr. Freund, a sociologist, discusses the ideas and vision of Max Weber, who places sociology on a scientific basis. He proceeds to explain Weber's methodology, his interpretative sociology, and a number of his special sociologies, such as the sociology of economics, religion, politics, law, art, and music. In his interpretation of Weber's sociology, Mr. Freund relies primarily on Weber's works, but occasionally he refers also to the ideas of other scholars in the field, for example, Émile Durkheim and Georg Simmel, and provides his own examples to clarify further Weber's theories"—(*LJ*).

Iron Cage: An Historical Interpretation of Max Weber. By Arthur Mitzman. *Knopf* 1970 $7.95; *Grosset* 1971 pap. $2.95

Max Weber. Ed. by Dennis Wrong. Makers of Modern Social Science Ser. *Prentice-Hall* 1970 $5.95 Spectrum Bks. pap. $2.45
"A collection of papers by various authors, evaluating Weber's thoughts on capitalism, the sociology of religion, his theory of bureaucracy, his ideas on authority, charismatic leadership, and his philosophy of history and politics"—(*BRD*).

Max Weber and Sociology Today. Ed. by Otto Stammer. *Harper* 1971 $7.50 Torchbks. 1972 pap. $2.95

Scholarship and Partisanship: Essays on Max Weber. By Reinhard Bendix and Guenther Roth. *Univ. of California Press* 1971 $12.50 pap. $3.25

A Critique of Max Weber's Philosophy and Social Science. By Walter G. Runciman. *Cambridge* 1972 $6.50

Max Weber. By Donald G. Macrae. Modern Masters Ser. *Viking* 1974 $5.95 pap. $2.25
"A general critique which seeks to replace the canonization accorded Weber with a more moderated perspective"—(*Booklist*).

Max Weber and the Theory of Modern Politics. By David Beetham. *Humanities Press* 1974 $20.00

STEFFENS, (JOSEPH) LINCOLN. 1866–1936.

The "Autobiography" is a vital account of the place Steffens held in the American radical movement and of its leaders and activities. Steffens, a great muckraker, wrote sensational articles and exposés of municipal corruption while he held editorial positions on *McClure's*, the *American* and *Everbody's* magazines. His articles, with those of others, in a period when reform was in the air, did much to bring about social amelioration in the U.S. In his later years Steffens became increasingly convinced that the hope of a future of social justice lay in communism.

THE WORLD OF LINCOLN STEFFENS. Ed. by Herbert Shapiro and Ella Winter; introd. by Barrows Dunham *Farrar, Straus* (Hill & Wang) 1962 pap. $2.45. An anthology containing much previously uncollected material. "Steffens wrote in the past but he talks to the present and future whatever the date."

THE SHAME OF THE CITIES. 1904. *Farrar, Straus* (Hill & Wang) 1957 pap. $2.65; *Peter Smith* 1959 $4.00. A collection of articles from *McClure's Magazine* in the early 1900s exposing corruption.

THE STRUGGLE FOR SELF-GOVERNMENT. 1906. Introd. by David W. Noble *Johnson Reprint* 1969 $21.00

THE UPBUILDERS. 1909. *Univ. of Washington Press* 1969 $9.50 pap. $2.95

BOY ON HORSEBACK. *Harcourt* 1935 $5.50

AUTOBIOGRAPHY. *Harcourt* 1931 1967 $12.00 Harvest Bks. 2 vols. 1968 pap. Vol. 1 $2.55 Vol. 2 $2.95

Books about Steffens

The Muckrakers: The Era in Journalism that Moved America to Reform— the Most Significant Magazine Articles of 1902–1912. Ed. and with notes by Arthur and Lila Weinberg. 1961. *Putnam* Capricorn Bks. 1964 pap. $3.60. A "rich slice of social history."

And Not to Yield: An Autobiography. By Ella Winter. *Harcourt* 1963 $5.95

This is a candid and entertaining story of an emancipated woman, her adventures around the literary world and her marriages to two extraordinary men: Lincoln Steffens, and Donald Ogden Stewart, playwright, philosopher, and humorist. We learn much of Steffens, the man and father, here.

Lincoln Steffens. By Justin Kaplan. *Simon & Schuster* 1974 $10.00

This "is a brilliant biography of a man and an age—shot through with political and moral contradictions, a weaving together of a vast amount of complicated material . . . Kaplan has pulled Steffens not only from the shadows of the Autobiography but also from the bowdlerized version of history where most of us first learned about him"—(*SR*).

MONTESSORI, MARIA. 1870–1952.

Maria Montessori, Italian educator and the first woman doctor granted a degree in Italy, is a name often heard since the early 1900s in the field of childhood education. Dissatisfied with the educational methods of her time, she developed her own theories in systematic fashion. The "Montessori Method," as it became known, involves allowing the child to develop at his own pace through the manipulation of materials. This and other of her concepts have had considerable influence on modern education.

She first worked with retarded children, then classified as "untrainable," most of whom she succeeded in teaching to read and write. She established a number of "Houses of Children" in Italy devoted to providing new opportunities for slum children; recent American efforts in this direction have led to a strong revival of interest in her work. In his introduction to the *Schocken* "Montessori Method" (*see below*), Professor Hunt points out that she provided "a splendid beginning precisely adapted to this purpose of counteracting deprivation." Her *Association Montessori Internationale*, established in 1929 to promote her ideas and to sell her special learning equipment, exists today, run by her adopted son (Miss Montessori never married).

COLLECTED WORKS. *Gordon Press* $125.95

THE MONTESSORI METHOD: The Education of Children from Three to Six. 1912. Trans. from the Italian by Anne E. George·*Bentley* 1964 $6.50; *Norwood* $15.00; introd. by J. McV. Hunt *Schocken* rev. ed. 1964 $6.00 pap. $2.45

DR. MONTESSORI'S OWN HANDBOOK. 1914. *Bentley* 1964 $5.00; *Norwood* $10.00; introd. by Nancy McCormick Rambusch *Schocken* 1965 $4.95 pap. $1.95

THE ADVANCED MONTESSORI METHOD. 1917–1918. *Bentley* 2 vols. 1964 Vol. 1 Spontaneous Activity in Education $6.50 Vol. 2 Montessori Elementary Material $8.50

THE SECRET OF CHILDHOOD. 1936. *Ballantine Bks.* 1972 pap. $1.50; *Fides* 1966 pap. $1.50; *Norwood* $12.50

THE ABSORBENT MIND. 1949. Trans. by Claude A. Claremont *Holt* 1967 $6.95; *Dell* Delta Bks. 1969 pap. $2.25

SPONTANEOUS ACTIVITY IN EDUCATION. *Schocken* 1965 $6.00 pap. $2.95

THE DISCOVERY OF THE CHILD. *Ballantine Bks.* 1972 pap. $1.50; *Fides* 1967 pap. $3.95

THE CHILD IN THE FAMILY. Trans. by Nancy Circillo *Regnery* 1970 $5.95; *Avon Bks.* 1970 pap. $1.25

EDUCATION AND PEACE. *Regnery* 1973 $6.50

FROM CHILDHOOD TO ADOLESCENCE. *Schocken* 1973 $6.95

THE MONTESSORI ELEMENTARY MATERIAL. Trans. by Arthur Livingston *Schocken* 1973 $7.50 pap. $3.45

CHILDHOOD EDUCATION. Trans. by A. M. Joosten *Regnery* 1974 $5.95

Books about Montessori

The Montessori Revolution in Education. By E. Mortimer Standing. 1962. *Schocken* 1966 $4.50 pap. $1.95
    "This work is among the best available for an overview of Montessori's philosophy"—*(Choice)*.
Maria Montessori. By E. Mortimer Standing. *New Am. Lib.* Mentor Bks. pap. $1.50
Montessori for Parents. By Dorothy C. Fisher. *Bentley* 1965 $5.95
Montessori for the Disadvantaged. Ed. by R. Calvert Orem. *Putnam* 1967 $5.95
Children of the Dream. By Bruno Bettelheim. *Avon Bks.* 1971 pap. $1.50
Montessori: A Modern Approach. By Paula P. Lillard. *Schocken* 1972 $6.95 pap. 1973 $1.95
The Hidden Hinge. By Rosa C. Packard. *Fides* 1972 $6.50; *Ballantine Bks.* 1973 pap. $1.50
Let My Children Work. By John P. Blessington. *Doubleday* 1974 $5.95
Maria Montessori. By Rita Kramer. *Putnam* 1976 $10.00

KROEBER, A(LFRED) L(OUIS). 1876–1960.

A. L. Kroeber was "an anthropologist's anthropologist. He made original contributions to almost every subdivision of this vast field of knowledge (ethnology, social organization, linguistics, archeology, et al.) and tackled every vital issue within it. No one could match his enormous erudition, and not many among his professional peers possessed his intellectual level-headedness and equanimity." A student of Franz Boas (*q.v.*), he focused his study on the Indians of North and South America. Kroeber looked for the patterns of culture which mold a society and the individual within it. He founded and taught (1901–1946) in the department of anthropology at the University of California (Berkeley), directed its anthropological museum, and was an initiator of the American Anthropological Association. In 1945 Kroeber was awarded the Huxley Memorial Medal of the Royal Anthropological Institute and in 1946 the Viking Medal of the Wenner-Gren Foundation for Anthropological Research.

His wife, THEODORA KROEBER, has written that "beautiful and compelling book," "Ishi in Two Worlds: A Biography of the Last Wild Indian in North America" (fwd. by Lewis Gannett *Univ. of California Press* 1961 $7.95 pap. $2.45) and "Ishi, Last of His Tribe" (*Parnassus* 1964 $5.50 lib. bdg. $5.35; *Bantam* 1973 pap. $.95). Her late husband, says the *Atlantic*, was "one of the anthropologists into whose hands Ishi was lucky enough to fall when he came down out of the California hills in 1911. He was the last member of a small tribe of Indians [the Yahi, the southernmost tribe of Yana] who had been so mauled by white settlers that they finally took to complete concealment as the only possible means of survival. . . . The anthropologists of the museum of the University of California, hearing that a small-town sheriff had a wild man in custody, went and rescued the captive. . . . Since there was no precedent for dealing with a case like Ishi's, the ingenious museum staff converted him into a live exhibit. . . . This . . . was actually a mutually satisfactory arrangement." Mrs. Kroeber has retold in "simple, supple style," nine authentic stories from the native Indian literature of California—"The Inland Whale" (*Univ. of California Press* 1959 pap. $2.45; *Peter Smith* $4.00). For adults, "the stories all succeed as stories; they please, engage, move, or divert without depending for their effect on their exotic source"—*(New Yorker)*. She has written (with Robert F. Heizer) "Almost Ancestors: The First Californians" (*Sierra Club* 1968 $15.00; *Ballantine Bks.* 1970 pap. $3.95).

ANTHROPOLOGY: Race, Language, Culture, Psychology, Prehistory. 1923. *Harcourt* rev. ed. 1948 $13.50

ANTHROPOLOGY: Biology and Race. *Harcourt* Harbinger Bks. 1963 pap. $2.45. A reissue of the chapters from the 1923 publication concerned with biology and race.

ANTHROPOLOGY: Culture Patterns and Processes. *Harcourt* Harbinger Bks. 1963 pap. $2.45. A reissue of the chapters from the 1923 publication concerned with culture patterns and processes.

HANDBOOK OF THE INDIANS OF CALIFORNIA. 1925. *Scholarly Press* 1972 $49.50

CULTURAL AND NATURAL AREAS OF NATIVE NORTH AMERICA. 1939. *Kraus* $25.00

CONFIGURATIONS OF CULTURE GROWTH. *Univ. of California Press* 1944 $15.00

THE NATURE OF CULTURE. *Univ. of Chicago Press* 1952 $15.00

ANTHROPOLOGY TODAY: An Encyclopedic Inventory. *Univ. of Chicago Press* 1953 $22.50 Selections ed. by Sol Tax 1962 pap. $3.95

STYLE AND CIVILIZATIONS. 1957. *Greenwood* 1973 $9.50

Books about Kroeber

Alfred Kroeber: A Personal Configuration. By Theodora Kroeber. *Univ. of California Press* 1970 $10.00

Alfred Kroeber. By Julian Steward. Leaders of Modern Anthropology Ser. *Columbia* 1973 $10.00 pap. $2.95

TROTSKY, LEON. 1879–1940. *See Chapter 9, History, Government and Politics— Modern and World, this Vol.*

TAWNEY, R(ICHARD) H(ENRY). 1880–1962.

The two major works of the English economist are "The Acquisitive Society" and "Religion and the Rise of Capitalism." He was a leading Fabian Socialist who had a leading role, through his writings, in defining the economic and other policies of the British Labor Party. His ideas of society are "founded on common sense and knowledge of how human beings can reasonably be expected to behave." "While urging the socialization of the economic system, he also emphasizes the need for guarding the political and civil liberties of the individual: 'The serious danger is . . . not that democracy may be sacrificed to the reckless pursuit of economic freedom,' he said in 1944. 'It is that the establishment of the conditions of such freedom may be too long delayed, and that the failure to achieve it may discredit democracy.' " In "Business and Politics under James I" (1958, o.p.), "Professor Tawney provides us with a fascinating case study in the interrelation of economics and politics . . . and does so with that command of historical evidence and that felicity of phrase which have made him one of the great masters of his craft"—(*The Annals*).

THE AGRARIAN PROBLEM IN THE SIXTEENTH CENTURY. 1912. *Burt Franklin* $22.50; *Gannon* 1970 $7.50; *Harper* Torchbks. pap. $3.95

THE ACQUISITIVE SOCIETY. 1920. *Harcourt* 1946 Harvest Bks. 1955 pap. $1.95. A classic analysis of individual property rights.

THE BRITISH LABOR MOVEMENT. 1925. *Greenwood* 1969 $11.50

RELIGION AND THE RISE OF CAPITALISM. 1926. *New Am. Lib.* Mentor Bks. pap. $.95; *Peter Smith* 1963 $4.75

EQUALITY. 1931. *Harper* (Barnes & Noble) 1964 pap. $1.75

LAND AND LABOR IN CHINA. 1932. *Octagon* 1964 $10.00

SOCIAL HISTORY AND LITERATURE. 1950. *Folcroft* 1973 $4.50; *Humanities Press* pap. $1.25; *Richard West* 1973 $4.50

THE W.E.A. AND ADULT EDUCATION. *Humanities Press* 1953 $1.25

THE ATTACK: And Other Papers. 1953. *Bks. for Libraries* 1970 $9.50

BUSINESS AND POLITICS UNDER JAMES THE FIRST: Lionel Cranfield as Merchant and Minister. 1958. *Russell & Russell* 1975 $18.00

THE RADICAL TRADITION: Twelve Essays on Politics, Education, and Literature. Ed. by Rita Hinden; fwd. by A. Creech Jones; postscript by Hugh Gaitskell. 1964. *T. Y. Crowell* (Funk & Wagnalls) Minerva Press 1967 pap. $1.95

These are papers Tawney himself assembled before his death; "mostly addressed to situations in Britain, they all bear the stamp of Tawney's genius, and his faith in the educability of human beings"—(*LJ*).

HARRINGTON'S INTERPRETATION OF HIS AGE. Studies in History Ser. *Haskell* 1972 pap. $2.95

COMMONPLACE BOOK. Ed. by J. M. Winter and D. M. Joslin *Cambridge* 1972 $6.50

TEILHARD DE CHARDIN, PIERRE, S.J. 1881–1955. *See Chapter 4, World Religions, this Vol.*

KEYNES, JOHN MAYNARD, 1st Baron of Tilton. 1883–1946.

Lord Keynes, now recognized as a very great economist (at least by those of liberal persuasion), has had a profound effect on the Western economic thought and practice of this century. The liberal branch of economics, indeed, is generally known as "Keynesian." As British Treasury representative at the Versailles Peace Conference, following World War I, he saw clearly the grave consequences of the vengeful economic terms imposed on defeated Germany and resigned his post. His book "The Economic Consequences of the Peace" scourged those responsible—chiefly Lloyd George and Woodrow Wilson—and made his reputation, if a controversial one. Controversial he was to remain, but after the crash of 1929 his theories influenced government economic policy throughout the Western world.

Though his famous "General Theory" contained some revolutionary concepts, "the policy recommendations derived from it were largely prompted by conservative considerations. Keynes hoped that the essential features of the capitalist system could be preserved. [But] *laissez-faire*, as he had demonstrated, was essentially a fair weather system.... Governments had a major responsibility for regulating the economic climate in ways that would permit the market system to achieve its full potential"—(William L. Barber). This was his message to Franklin Roosevelt as the latter strove to bring the U.S. out of the Great Depression; when private capital could not move, government, he said must undertake projects to provide work and therefore buying power to set the economy in motion again. This has often meant deficit financing. Keynes found the element of *stimulus* to the flow of goods and services most important in time of stagnation or breakdown, rather than the "balanced budget" policy of the conservatives, and Roosevelt's New Deal showed that his theories could work. As British delegate to the 1944 Bretton Woods Monetary Conference, he had a part in the founding of the World Bank and the International Monetary Fund—new projects for keeping the economy reasonably stable on an international scale which are still, of course, in existence.

Keynes was brilliant and versatile in many fields. A graduate of Eton and Cambridge, where he later taught, he had a profound interest in the arts, played a part in the Bloomsbury literary circle, collected paintings, married a ballet dancer and actress—Lydia Lopokova—played a leading part in a number of British arts projects and generally managed to lead an exceptionally active life in many fields beside the economic. As an investor he made himself a fortune; he was able to make money for the British government as well. A fascinating account of him is to be found in Robert L. Heilbroner's "The Worldly Philosophers" (*Simon & Schuster* rev. ed. 1972 $7.95 Touchstone-Clarion Bks. 1972 pap. $2.25; *Franklin Watts* lg.-type ed. $12.50); Roy Harrod's excellent work is the definitive biography to date.

COLLECTED WRITINGS. *St. Martin's* 16 vols. 1971–1973 each $9.50

Vol. 1 Indian Currency and Finance (1971) repr. of 1913 ed. Vol. 2 The Economic Consequences of the Peace (1971) repr. of 1919 ed. Vol. 3 Revision of the Treaty (1972) Vol. 4 Tract on Monetary Reform (1972) Vols. 5–6 Treatise on Money (1972) Vol. 7 General Theory (1973) Vol. 8 Treatise on Probability (1972) Vol. 9 Essays in Persuasion (1972) Vol. 10 Essays in Biography (1972) Vols. 11–12 o.p. Vols. 13–14 The General Theory and After, ed. by Donald Moggridge (1973) Vol. 15 Activities and Associated Writings: India and Cambridge (1971) Vol. 16 Activities and Associated Writings: The Treasury and Versailles (1971)

SCOPE AND METHOD OF POLITICAL ECONOMY. 4th ed. 1917. *Kelley* $12.50

INDIAN CURRENCY AND FINANCE. 1913. *Burt Franklin* 1971 $9.50

ECONOMIC CONSEQUENCES OF THE PEACE. 1919. *Harper* Torchbks. 1971 pap. $3.25

A REVISION OF THE TREATY. 1922. *Bks. for Libraries* 1973 $9.75

END OF LAISSEZ-FAIRE. 1927. *William C. Brown* $3.50

ESSAYS IN PERSUASION. 1931. *Norton* 1963 pap. $2.95

ESSAYS IN BIOGRAPHY. 1933. *Dufour* 1950 $3.00; *Norton* 1963 pap. $2.25

THE GENERAL THEORY OF EMPLOYMENT, INTEREST, AND MONEY. *Harcourt* 1936 $9.50
Harbinger Bks. 1965 pap. $3.45

TWO MEMOIRS: Doctor Melchior, a Defeated Enemy and My Early Beliefs. 1949. *Kelley*
$7.50

Books about Keynes

The Life of John Maynard Keynes. By Roy F. Harrod. 1952. *Kelley* 1968 $17.50; *Avon Bks.* 1971
pap. $2.45

A Guide to Keynes. By Alvin H. Hansen. *McGraw-Hill* 1953 pap. $2.95. An excellent guide to
Keynes' General Theory by a leading American Keynesian.

The Failure of the New Economics: An Analysis of the Keynesian Fallacy. By Henry Hazlitt.
Arlington 1975 $9.95
"In his criticism of Keynes' 'General Theory,' Mr. Hazlitt has shaken by his challenges what
may justly be called an important vested interest; he will be attacked in general and in detail.
But he will be discussed—and it may well be that economists will begin to scrutinize the whole
body of Keynesian doctrine"—(*N.Y. Times*).

What Keynes Means. By Anatol Murad. *College & Univ. Press* 1962 pap. $2.45

The Keynesian System. By David McCord Wright. *Fordham Univ. Press* 1962 $5.00

Keynes' General Theory: Reports of Three Decades. Ed. by Robert Lekachman. *St. Martin's*
1964. rev. ed. 1968 $4.95 pap. $2.95

The Age of Keynes. By Robert Lekachman. *Random* 1966 $8.95 Vintage Bks. pap. $2.45
"Mr. Lekachman, an economist by profession and the chairman of the economics department
at the State University of New York at Stony Brook, has written an illuminating biography of
an idea. It is an idea that today has so thoroughly permeated Western economic thought and
conduct that Lekachman must devote the last third of his book to events that have occurred
since Keynes's death in 1946"—(Christopher Lehmann-Haupt, in the *N.Y. Times*).

Keynes and After. By Michael Stewart. 1967 *Peter Smith* 1969 $4.50

The Indigent Rich: A Theory of General Equilibrium in a Keynesian System. By J. W. Cumes.
Pergamon 1972 $9.00

Keynes and the Monetarists. By Sidney Weintraub. *Rutgers Univ. Press* 1973 $12.50

Keynes: Aspects of the Man and His Work. Ed. by D. E. Moggridge. *St. Martin's* 1974 $10.95

Reconstruction of Political Economy: An Introduction to Post-Keynesian Economics. By J. A.
Kregel. *Halsted Press* 1974 $14.95

Keynesian Kaleidics: The Evolution of a General Political Economy. By G. L. Shackle. *Univ. of
Edinburgh Press* (dist. by Aldine) 1974 $5.00

The New Economics One Decade Older. By James Tobin. *Princeton Univ. Press* 1974 $6.50

The Crisis in Keynesian Economics. By Sir John Hicks. *Basic Bks.* 1975 $5.95

Essays on John Maynard Keynes. Ed. by Milo Keynes. *Cambridge* 1975 $16.50

ORTEGA Y GASSET, JOSÉ. 1883–1955.   *See Chapter 5, Philosophy, this Vol.*

MALINOWSKI, BRONISLAW (KASPER). 1884–1942.

This Anglo-Polish anthropologist was born in Cracow, Poland, and subsequently became
naturalized as a British subject. Malinowski went on early expeditions to New Guinea and North
Melanesia. He became Professor of Anthropology at the University of London in 1927; he made
further field studies among the Pueblo Indians and the Bantu tribes of South and East Africa. He
came to the U.S. in 1938 and died here in 1942. "As a founder of the so-called functional school of
anthropology, he insisted on studying human culture as a pragmatically connected whole and in
examining human institutions in the light of their functioning within the framework of that
whole"—("Twentieth Century Authors"). It would be difficult to overstate his influence on
contemporary social science. "He had a unique way of clearing the terminological jungle of
superfluous growth and of approaching his object of study boldly and directly. There was no room
for antiquarianism in his analysis of primitive societies, nor did he ever mistake outward social
forms (of kinship, clanship, or types of marriage) for the ultimate *reality* of human behavior.
Everything he wrote or lectured about was clear, forthright, and challenging to his contemporaries"—(*LJ*).

Out of print are: "The Dynamics of Culture Change: An Inquiry into Race Relations in Africa"
(1945); "Freedom and Civilization" (1960); "Coral Gardens and Their Magic" (1965) and his New
Guinea journals, "A Diary in the Strict Sense of the Term" (1963).

ARGONAUTS OF THE WESTERN PACIFIC. *Dutton* 1922 pap. $2.75

MYTH IN PRIMITIVE PSYCHOLOGY. 1926. *Negro Univs. Press* 1972 $8.00

CRIME AND CUSTOM IN SAVAGE SOCIETY. 1926. *Humanities Press* 1970 $7.25; *Littlefield* 1969 pap. $1.75

SEX AND REPRESSION IN SAVAGE SOCIETY. 1927. *Humanities Press* 1953 $9.00; *New Am. Lib.* 1955 pap. $3.95

THE SEXUAL LIFE OF SAVAGES IN NORTH-WESTERN MELANESIA: An Ethnographic Account of Courtship, Marriage and Family Life among the Natives of the Trobriand Islands, British New Guinea. 1929 3rd ed. 1948. Pref. by Havelock Ellis *Harcourt* Harvest Bks. 1962 pap. $5.25

FOUNDATIONS OF FAITH AND MORALS. 1936. *Folcroft* $6.50

A SCIENTIFIC THEORY OF CULTURE. *Univ. of North Carolina Press* 1944 $4.95

MAGIC, SCIENCE AND RELIGION AND OTHER ESSAYS. 1948. *Doubleday* Anchor Bks. 1954 pap. $1.95

THE FAMILY AMONG THE AUSTRALIAN ABORIGINES: A Sociological Study. Introd. by J. A. Barnes *Schocken* 1963 $8.00 pap. $2.95

METHODS OF STUDY OF CULTURE CONTACT IN AFRICA. *Int. Pubns. Service* 1965 $5.00

THE FATHER IN PRIMITIVE PSYCHOLOGY. *Norton* 1966 pap. $1.75

Books about Malinowski

Politics of the Kula Ring: An Analysis of the Findings of Malinowski. By J. P. S. Uberoi. *Humanities Press* 1962 2nd ed. 1971 $6.00
Order and Rebellion in Tribal Africa. By Max Gluckman. *Macmillan* (Free Press) 1963 $8.95
The London School of Linguistics: A Study of the Linguistic Theories of B. Malinowski and J. R. Firth. By D. Terence Langendoen. *M.I.T. Press* 1968 $7.95
Man and Culture: An Evaluation of the Work of Bronislaw Malinowski. Ed. by Raymond Firth. *Humanities Press* 1970 text ed. $8.25 pap. $3.25

BENEDICT, RUTH (FULTON).   1887–1948.

Ruth Benedict did not begin to study anthropology until 1919. Prior to that she had taught English in a girl's school in California. Studying and working closely with Franz Boas at Columbia University, she made her first of many field studies among the Serrano Indians in California in 1922. She received her Ph.D. in 1923 and advanced from lecturer to full professor at Columbia University in 1948. "She was a scientist who had focused her analytic gifts on the differences between people . . . not in order to forge weapons of discrimination . . . but in order to understand the crowning purpose of being individual and different." Dr. Alfred Kroeber called "Patterns of Culture" a "milestone in the development of anthropology." Margaret Mead, writing of the same work, said that "Dr. Benedict's work is based upon a scholarly knowledge of the sources, combined with firsthand experience of American Indian tribes, but she has taken her material and reworked it, simplifying it to a more universal context, the philosophy of history." Ruth Benedict had her poems published in the *Nation* and *Poetry* under the name of Anne Singleton. "Race, Science and Politics" (1940) is o.p.

AN ANTHROPOLOGIST AT WORK: Writings of Ruth Benedict. 1959. Ed. by Margaret Mead *Avon* 1973 pap. $3.95

"Diaries, journal entries, an autobiographical fragment somehow blend with poetry, correspondence and anthropological writings of Mrs. Benedict. It all adds up to an almost embarrassingly intimate picture of a great woman"—(*N.Y. Times*).

THE CONCEPT OF THE GUARDIAN SPIRIT IN NORTH AMERICA. 1923. *Kraus* pap. $5.00

TALES OF THE COCHITI INDIANS. 1931. *Scholarly Press* $14.50

PATTERNS OF CULTURE. *Houghton* 1934 $7.95 pap. 1961 $2.25

ZUNI MYTHOLOGY. 1935. *AMS Press* 2 vols. 1969 each $25.00 set $47.50; *Finch Press* 2 vols. set $44.00

THE CHRYSANTHEMUM AND THE SWORD: Patterns of Japanese Culture. *Houghton* 1946 $6.95; *New Am. Lib.* Merit 1967 pap. $3.95

Books about Benedict

Ruth Benedict. By Margaret Mead. Leaders of Modern Anthropology Ser. *Columbia* 1974 $8.95
"A renowned student writes of her teacher, later her colleague and close friend. Portions of Mead's concise biography are taken from a larger work, An Anthropologist at Work

(1959). . . . The combined selections provide an exceptionally apt introduction to her work"—(*Booklist*).

CHASE, STUART. 1888–

The tragedy of waste—"waste in manpower, natural resources, money—and what to do about it, has been the lively concern of economist Stuart Chase," who writes most readably on economics from the point of view of the consumer. His many books and articles have contributed greatly to a popular understanding of the "economy of abundance." Not surprisingly, Stuart Chase has nine generations of thrifty New Englanders behind him. "The Tragedy of Waste" was his first important book in his own field. "He draws on his immense range of knowledge in contemporary social science to sharpen our wits about the political, social, and economic changes we have lived through," the *Library Journal* reported of "Guides to Straight Thinking." Mr. Chase's liberal and cogent views have had wide influence in his own field of economics and in those of semantics, communications and human relations. He has thought about society from a broad and humane base.

THE TRAGEDY OF WASTE. 1929. *Finch Press* $14.00

THE ECONOMY OF ABUNDANCE. 1934. *Bks. for Libraries* $12.50; *Kennikat* 1971 $12.50

MAN AND MACHINES. 1935. *Finch Press* $15.00

THE TYRANNY OF WORDS. *Harcourt* 1938 Harvest Bks. 1959 pap. $2.45

WHERE'S THE MONEY COMING FROM: Problems of Postwar Finance. 1943. *Greenwood* 1968 $11.25

FOR THIS WE FOUGHT: Guidelines to America's Future as Reported to the Twentieth Century Fund. 1946. *Greenwood* 1968 $9.25

THE PROPER STUDY OF MANKIND: An Inquiry into the Science of Human Relations. *Harper* 1948 2nd ed. 1962 $6.95 rev. ed. 1967 pap. $.95

(With Marian T. Chase). THE POWER OF WORDS. *Harcourt* 1954 $8.50

GUIDES TO STRAIGHT THINKING: With Thirteen Fallacies. *Harper* 1956 $6.95

THE MOST PROBABLE WORLD. *Harper* 1968 $5.95. A look at what life may be like in the next century; he sees a period of difficult adjustment followed by creative change and stabilization.

LIPPMANN, WALTER. 1889–1974. *See Chapter 9, History, Government and Politics—American, this Vol.*

SOROKIN, PITIRIM A(LEKSANDROVITCH). 1889–1968.

The internationally-known Russian-born sociologist and social philosopher, who had been secretary to the Premier in the Kerensky government, came to this country in 1923 and was naturalized in 1930. He was professor of sociology at the universities of Minnesota (1924–1930) and Harvard (1930–1935), where he was founder and first chairman of the department of sociology. At Harvard he began his studies in "creative altruism" to discover what made for peaceful, constructive human relations. After his retirement from Harvard in 1955, he continued this pursuit at his Research Center for Creative Altruism in Cambridge, Mass. As a sociologist he was a pioneer in the "all but impregnable" problem of social change. In his great four-volume work, "Social and Cultural Dynamics," he presents the course of history as a continuous but irregular fluctuation between two basically different kinds of culture, "sensate" and "ideational." The cause of the fluctuation he describes as "imminent causation," theorizing that societies change because it is their nature to change, somewhat as an acorn grows into an oak and not some other kind of tree because it is its nature to do so. Some critics have found Sorokin's "imminent causation" not a sufficient explanation, but acclaim his "assault" on the mystery of social mobility.

CONTEMPORARY SOCIOLOGICAL THEORIES: Through the First Quarter of the Twentieth Century. *Harper* 1928 Torchbks. pap. $3.95

SOCIAL AND CULTURAL DYNAMICS. 1937–1941. *Bedminster* 4 vols. 1962 boxed set $40.00; *Sargent* 4 vols. in 1 (abr.) 1957 1970 $10.00

THE CRISIS OF OUR AGE: The Social and Cultural Outlook. *Dutton* 1941 pap. $1.75

MAN-SOCIETY IN CALAMITY: The Effects of War, Revolution, Famine, Pestilence upon the Human Mind, Behavior, Social Organization and Cultural Life. 1942. *Greenwood* 1968 $16.75

SOCIETY, CULTURE AND PERSONALITY: Their Structure and Dynamics; a System of General Sociology. 1947. *Cooper* 1962 $12.50

MODERN HISTORICAL AND SOCIAL PHILOSOPHIES. 1950. (Orig. "Social Philosophies in an Age of Crisis") *Dover* 1964 pap. $2.75; *Peter Smith* $4.75

LEAVES FROM A RUSSIAN DIARY AND THIRTY YEARS AFTER. 1950. *Kraus* $14.50

EXPLORATIONS IN ALTRUISTIC LOVE AND BEHAVIOR. 1950. *Kraus* $14.50

ALTRUISTIC LOVE: A Study of American Good Neighbors and Christian Saints. 1950. *Kraus* 1968 $10.50

THE AMERICAN SEX REVOLUTION. *Sargent* 1956 $3.50

SOCIAL AND CULTURAL MOBILITY. *Macmillan* (Free Press) 1959 $10.00 pap. $3.95

(With Walter A. Lunden). POWER AND MORALITY. *Sargent* 1959 $3.50

BASIC TRENDS OF OUR TIMES. *College & Univ. Press* 1964 $5.00 pap. $2.25

THE SOCIOLOGY OF REVOLUTION. *Howard Fertig* 1967 $15.00

A LONG JOURNEY. *College & Univ. Press* 1963 $6.00

His autobiography begins with the early days in Russia when "he was jailed several times under the Tsarist regime and the Communist, thus giving ample evidence of his lifelong intellectual independence and militancy. Not many academic men can match Professor Sorokin's epic experiences or his immense erudition and intellectual productivity. His autobiography will be found exciting even by students of the social sciences whose theoretical preferences are in conflict with those of the eminent author"—*(LJ)*.

Books about Sorokin

The Sociology of Knowledge. By J. P. Maquet. Trans. from French by John F. Locke. 1951. *Greenwood* 1973 $13.50

Values in Human Society. By Frank R. Cowell. Extending Horizons Ser. *Sargent* 1970 $8.95

Sociological Theories of Pitirim A. Sorokin. By Carle C. Zimmerman. Ed. by T. K. N. Unnithan *Humanities Press* 1974 pap. $4.00

Love, Altruism and World Crisis. By Joseph Allen Matter. *Nelson-Hall* 1974 $9.95

LINTON, RALPH. 1893–1953.

"The Tree of Culture" is the major work of the great American anthropologist, although he himself was proudest of "The Study of Man." Born and reared as a Quaker, Ralph Linton's interest shifted from archeology to anthropology. He worked at the Field Museum of Natural History in Chicago and made field trips to Madagascar and East Africa. In 1928 he joined the faculty of the University of Wisconsin. He subsequently taught at Columbia University and in 1946 became Sterling Professor of Anthropology at Yale University. He was an adopted member of the Comanche tribe and accepted as a master carver by the Marquesan tribesmen. Furthermore, he became "a properly accredited *ombiasy nkazo* (medicine man) in Madagascar and was even invited to join the Rotary Club of a middle western city."

ARCHAEOLOGY OF THE MARQUESAS ISLANDS. 1925. *Kraus* $12.50

TANALA: A Hill Tribe of Madagascar. 1933. *Kraus* pap. $16.00

THE STUDY OF MAN: An Introduction. 1936. *Prentice-Hall* 1964 pap. $6.25

THE CULTURAL BACKGROUND OF PERSONALITY. 1945. *Prentice-Hall* 1961 pap. $3.50

(With Paul Wingert). ARTS OF THE SOUTH SEAS. 1946. *Arno* 1972 $24.00

(Ed.). MOST OF THE WORLD: The Peoples of Africa, Latin America and the East Today. 1949. *Greenwood* $34.00

THE TREE OF CULTURE. *Knopf* 1955 $10.95; abr. ed. by Adelin Linton *Random* Vintage Bks. 1959 pap. $1.95

ACCULTURATION IN SEVEN AMERICAN INDIAN TRIBES. *Peter Smith* $7.50

KINSEY, ALFRED C. 1894–1956.

The two books below from the Institute for Sex Research at Indiana University aroused tremendous interest on publication. Both, with their startling conclusions, were best sellers. They have been called "pioneer studies of great significance . . . part of the scientific heritage of the entire world." "Pregnancy, Birth and Abortion" (1958, o.p.), by Paul H. Gebhard and others, represents the third volume of the "Kinsey Reports," and is, like its predecessors, a publication of the Institute for Sex Research. The fourth volume appeared in 1965 as "Sex Offenders: An Analysis of Types" (*Harper* $15.00). "While it probably will not cause as much controversy as the first Kinsey Report, it will furnish ammunition for those who argue that 'what two or more consenting adults do sexually in private should not be governed by statute law' "—(*LJ*).

(With others). SEXUAL BEHAVIOR IN THE HUMAN MALE. *Saunders* 1948 $10.25

(With others). SEXUAL BEHAVIOR IN THE HUMAN FEMALE. *Saunders* 1953 $10.25; *Pocket Bks.* pap. $2.50

Books about Kinsey

Statistical Problems of the Kinsey Report of Sexual Behavior in the Human Male. By William G. Cochran and others. 1954. *Greenwood* 1968 $11.50
Kinsey: A Biography. By Cornelia V. Christenson. *Indiana Univ. Press* 1971 $7.95
Dr. Kinsey and the Institute for Sex Research. By Wardell B. Pomeroy. *Harper* 1972 $10.00; *New Am. Lib.* 1973 pap. $1.95

FULLER, R(ICHARD) BUCKMINSTER. 1895–

R. Buckminster Fuller, designer of the "geodesic dome" at the Expo 67 Montreal World's Fair, has, besides his revolutionary architectural design capabilities (he has never held a license as an architect, believing that the profession is stultified), an extraordinary vision of a world in which technology truly becomes the servant of man and produces—as it can well do—the solutions to man's problems through bold use of imagination combined with technical know-how. He believes that reformers err in depending on politics to bring a better world; politics, he says, never has: "I have undertaken the reform of the environment and have never tried to reform man." He proposes "doing more with less," and "a return to the universe as our starting point." The earth itself is a spaceship on which we have lived for millennia without realizing it; and we have survived. We can continue to survive, says "Bucky," the optimist always. Young people flock to hear his fascinating lectures; older people, who have found his geodesic constructions invaluable in many fields—the sturdy basic geodesic dome for something as large as a concert hall can be constructed from prefabricated components in less than a day—have had perforce to take him seriously. He also serves as a president and director of numerous companies that make use of his ideas.

Mr. Fuller was a dropout at Harvard, tried it again and was "tossed out" (says an article by David Jacobs in an April 1967 *N.Y. Times Magazine*) "for 'general irresponsibility.' As soon as World War I came along he enlisted in the Navy and reinforced his knowledge of ships and navigational principles. He married Ann Hewlett, whose father taught him a great deal about construction engineering. In 1922 Hewlett and Fuller founded the Stockade Building System to manufacture the father-in-law's invention, a fibrous concrete building block. When Fuller's daughter died of infantile paralysis that same year, Fuller sought relief from his grief in work; but his contacts with the 'sub-industry' of building, 'the most ignorant and most prodigious of men's fumbling activities,' only deepened his depression. In 1927 he lost financial control of the Stockade Company, and he contemplated suicide; another daughter had just been born, and he saw nothing in front of him to make life better for her. He elected instead to change the whole world."

Mr. Fuller dates his career from that moment in 1927, when at the age of 32, he began to formulate his ideas without regard to financial ambition. He had further setbacks, but the Marines, then Ford, then Henry Kaiser found uses for the domes he devised in the 1940's. By 1960 "Fuller had become, if not America's vanguard scientist, at least its master dome-maker; and his two associated companies began to make money"—(*N.Y. Times*). His own income grew correspondingly; much of it is spent on travel to all corners of the U.S. and of the world—at a killing pace which does not seem to bother him.

Mr. Fuller's prose style is complex, but it seems right for him, and the reader becomes accustomed to following his lightning mental processes in such sentences (most are longer) as "Priority of access to man's highest capability has thus far always gone to weaponry; the home front has always been the antipriority area." He writes with a puckish sense of humor, but the man once considered as a sort of Rube Goldberg and somewhat mad is as serious as he has always been, and offers, if not utopia, great hope to a bewildered world in which the necessity of harnessing technology for human use by human beings has become paramount.

NO MORE SECONDHAND GOD AND OTHER WRITINGS. 1963. *Doubleday* Anchor Bks. 1971 pap. $2.95. Prose and prose-poem essays, 1940–62.

EDUCATION AUTOMATION: Freeing the Scholar to Return to His Studies. 1962. *Doubleday* Anchor Bks. 1971 pap. $1.95. A lecture delivered in 1961.

NINE CHAINS TO THE MOON. 1963. *Doubleday* Anchor Bks. 1971 pap. $2.95. An adventure story for the mind.

IDEAS AND INTEGRITIES. 1963. *Macmillan* Collier Bks. 1969 pap. $1.95

OPERATING MANUAL FOR SPACESHIP EARTH. 1969. *Simon & Schuster* (Pocket Bks.) 1970 pap. $1.25 Touchstone-Clarion Bks. 1970 pap. $1.95

UTOPIA OR OBLIVION: The Prospects for Mankind. 1969. *Bantam* 1969 pap. $1.25; *Overlook Press* 1973 $11.95

UNTITLED EPIC POEM ON THE HISTORY OF INDUSTRIALIZATION. *Simon & Schuster* 1970 $4.95 Touchstone-Clarion Bks. 1971 pap. $1.95

(With others). I SEEM TO BE A VERB. *Bantam* 1970 pap. $1.65

(With Eric A. Walker and James R. Killian, Jr.). APPROACHING THE BENIGN ENVIRON-MENT. The Franklin Lectures in the Sciences and Humanities, Series I. Ed. by Taylor Littleton *Univ. of Alabama Press* 1970 $6.00; *Macmillan* Collier Bks. pap. $1.25

FOUR D TIME LOCK. *Gannon* $7.50

INTUITION. *Doubleday* Anchor Bks. 1973 pap. $2.95

EARTH, INC. *Doubleday* Anchor Bks. 1973 pap. $2.95; *Peter Smith* $5.00

SYNERGETICS: Explorations in the Geometry of Thinking. *Macmillan* 1975 $25.00

This volume is "intended to bring together in a concerted presentation the philosophy, logic and disputation of a long, productive, and controversial life"—(*SR*).

Books about Fuller

Wizard of the Dome: R. Buckminster Fuller, Designer for the Future. By Sidney Rosen. *Little* 1969 $4.95

Bucky: A Guided Tour of Buckminster Fuller. By Hugh Kenner. *Morrow* 1973 $7.95 pap. 1974 $3.95

MUMFORD, LEWIS. 1895–

Lewis Mumford, who has lived in New York City most of his life, did work at Columbia, New York University, and the New School for Social Research where he first met Thorstein Veblen (*q.v.*). He edited "Roots of Contemporary American Architecture: A Series of 37 Essays Dating from the Mid-Nineteenth Century to the Present (1952. *Dover* 1969 pap. $4.50; *Peter Smith* $7.50). He says of himself: "My political convictions have remained consistently Socialist from the beginning, but I have never been either a Marxian or a totalitarian. I am not one of those who suddenly became conscious of social disorder and wretchedness only after the stock market went to pieces in 1929; and as time has gone on I have become more, rather than less radical." In such works as "Technics and Civilization" and "The Culture of Cities" he has written of his ideas on "machines, cities, buildings, social life and people" with "insight and imaginative acuity." He has always been concerned with cities and buildings as fit habitations and working places for human beings. "I am an optimist about possibilities, a pessimist about probabilities," he has said. Mr. Mumford received a medal for "special achievement" from the Brandeis University Creative Arts Awards Commission in 1969. That year he was also appointed honorary consultant to the Library of Congress in American cultural history for a three-year term. In 1972 he was awarded the National Medal for Literature by the National Book Committee.

THE HIGHWAY AND THE CITY: Essays 1953–1963. *Harcourt* Harvest Bks. 1963 pap. $2.35

"Gathered in one volume, Mumford's sagacious challenges of certain clichés and misconceptions of modern architecture and city planning are even more powerfully persuasive than they were when these essays appeared piecemeal in *The New Yorker* and elsewhere over the past decade. . . . Mumford's consistent, specific, and constructive warnings are still far from being fully understood, let alone widely heeded. . . . This book, therefore, should be readily available to all"—(*LJ*).

THE STORY OF UTOPIAS. 1922. *Viking* Compass Bks. 1962 pap. $2.45; *Peter Smith* 1963 $4.50

STICKS AND STONES: A Study of American Architecture. 1924 rev. with new introd. 1955. *Dover* pap. $2.00; *Peter Smith* $4.25

THE GOLDEN DAY: A Study in American Literature and Culture. 1926 1968. *Peter Smith* $4.25

THE BROWN DECADES: A Study of the Arts in America, 1865–1895. 1931 2nd. rev. ed. 1955. *Dover* pap. $2.00; *Peter Smith* $4.25

TECHNICS AND CIVILIZATION. The Renewal of Life Ser. *Harcourt* 1934 Harbinger Bks. 1963 pap. $4.25

THE CULTURE OF CITIES. The Renewal of Life Ser. *Harcourt* 1938 Harvest Bks. 1970 pap. $5.75. An account of how the cities of the world have grown to be what they are, and an inquiry into the contemporary and future aspects of urban life.

THE CONDITION OF MAN. The Renewal of Life Ser. *Harcourt* 1944 with a new preface by the author Harvest Bks. 1973 pap. $3.95

THE CONDUCT OF LIFE. The Renewal of Life Ser. *Harcourt* 1951 Harvest Bks. 1960 pap. $3.45. On the ethical and religious issues that confront the modern man. Offers a new orientation, directed to the renewal of life and the reintegration of modern civilization.

ART AND TECHNICS. *Columbia* 1952 $8.00 pap. 1960 $1.95

THE HUMAN PROSPECT. Ed. by Harry T. Moore and Karl W. Deutsch. 1955. *Southern Illinois Univ. Press* 1965 pap. $2.65

THE TRANSFORMATIONS OF MAN. 1956. *Harper* Torchbks. 1972 pap. $2.95; *Peter Smith* $5.00

THE CITY IN HISTORY: Its Origins, Its Transformations and Its Prospects. *Harcourt* 1961 $15.00 Harbinger Bks. 1968 pap. $4.95. Winner, in 1961, of a National Book Award.

THE MYTH OF THE MACHINE. *Harcourt* 2 vols. Vol. 1 Technics and Human Development (1967) $12.00 Harvest Bks. 1971 pap. $5.25 Vol. 2 The Pentagon of Power (1970) $12.95 Harvest Bks. 1974 pap. $4.95

Volume 1 "examines the 'broad streak of irrationality that runs all through human history' and suggests an original and clarifying view of the relationship between man and technics in our own time—not so different from that of ancient Egypt—and in the future. It is a stimulating volume, informed both with an enormous range of knowledge and empathetic spirit, and hopeful at least in its broad, and perhaps corrective view of human evolution, ecology and aspiration"—(Eliot Fremont-Smith, in the *N.Y. Times*). The second volume is concerned with the regressive nature of the myth of the machine from earliest times to the nuclear age. "The most powerful pages . . . are those in which he demonstrates the limitations of orthodox scientific methods when applied to humanity"—(*N.Y. Review of Books*).

THE URBAN PROSPECT. *Harcourt* 1968 $7.95 Harvest Bks. 1969 pap. $2.75. Fourteen essays on urban problems and what to do about them.

INTERPRETATIONS AND FORECASTS, 1922–1972: Studies in Literature, History, Biography, Technics, and Contemporary Society. *Harcourt* 1973 $12.95. A personal selection reflecting 50 years of publication by the author.

MYRDAL, (KARL) GUNNAR. 1898–

"As a rather lonely explorer of the American dilemmas of poverty amid great wealth and discrimination against Negroes, Karl Gunnar Myrdal looked ahead 23 years ago and predicted this country's racial crisis in terms that today are common language among sociologists"—(*N.Y. Times*). His book was "An American Dilemma: The Negro Problem and Modern Democracy" and it has become a classic. The Swedish economist, sociologist, statesman and critic-at-large, has often visited this country and brought his powerful intellect to bear upon its problems. "I permit myself free opinions in America," he has said "—this is my second home. I'm a Swede who feels as much allegiance to America as Americans." In this capacity he has freely criticized American participation in the Vietnam war and in 1967 found it "shocking to see how much easier it is to get appropriations for war than to make a modest start on the development of a more wholesome urban life." The *N.Y. Times* says further of him: "Dr. Myrdal has not spared his own country from his penchant for the intellectual irritant. In Sweden's small, homogenous society he has provoked more indignation, admiration, criticism and enthusiasm than perhaps any other Swede in his lifetime. He has also been catholic in his influence, and many things at home bear his name: the Myrdal sofa (a very broad one); the Myrdal house (a tenement house for families with many children); Myrdal cycles (for two or three); and Myrdale (couples living together without marriage)."

Dr. Myrdal's "second magnum opus," more than ten years in the writing, is his "Asian Drama." *Choice* wrote of it: "This three volume vivisection of South Asia's (Pakistan, India, Ceylon, Burma, Malaya, Thailand, Indonesia, the Philippines, Laos, Cambodia, and South Viet-Nam) agony of poverty could very well serve as the main text for one-half dozen social science courses in as many disciplines. The regional focus is no mere conspectus but a brilliant tour de force detailing the social dynamics of underdevelopment over its entire spectrum. Myrdal is clear and forceful in rejecting the utility of conventional Western theories, analytical tools, models, and value premises. Instead, the proper understanding of the 'poverty of nations' requires an institutional approach which is nothing less than 'history and politics, theories and ideologies, economic structures and levels, social stratification, agriculture and industry, population developments, health and education . . . studied not in isolation but in their mutual relationships.' In over 2,200 pages of text and appendices Myrdal's claim and approach are stunningly made good. It is not too early to call this work a classic."

Dr. Myrdal is a graduate in law from the University of Stockholm who also took his doctorate in economics and began a teaching career, then becoming, at the age of 34, Lars Hierta Professor of Political Economy and Public Finance. He received a Rockefeller fellowship to do the American research that led to "An American Dilemma" and shortly thereafter was appointed Minister of Commerce in the Swedish government. In 1947 he became secretary general of the Council for Europe at Geneva. His wife, Alva Myrdal, herself a writer, meanwhile brought up three children and served her country in the Swedish parliament and as Swedish ambassador to India. He and she collaborated on a study of Sweden's falling birth rate which made a strong impact in that country.

Jan Myrdal, their son, did not find it easy to be the offspring of these forceful personalities and has told of his own rebellion and disillusion with the values of contemporary Europe in "Confessions of a Disloyal European" (*Pantheon* 1968 $5.95; *Random* Vintage Bks. 1969 pap. $1.65). This was generally considered the brilliant expression of a generation quite different from that of his parents—whose *generation* at least he attacks in such passages as "We describe how the poor are plundered by the rich. We live among the rich. Live on plunder and pander ideas to the rich." His earlier volume, "Report from a Chinese Village" (*Pantheon* 1965 $8.95; *Random* Vintage Bks. 1972 pap. $2.45) was also well received. He collaborated with his father on "Chinese Journey" in 1965 and has written a number of other books about China and Asia.

MONETARY EQUILIBRIUM. 1939. *Kelley* $8.50

POPULATION: A Problem for Democracy. *Peter Smith* $4.25

AN AMERICAN DILEMMA: The Negro Problem and Modern Democracy. 1942. *Harper* rev. ed. 1962 $18.50 Torchbks. 1962 pap. $3.95

THE POLITICAL ELEMENT IN THE DEVELOPMENT OF ECONOMIC THEORY. Trans. by Paul Streeten. 1953. *Humanities Press* 1971 $10.00; *Simon & Schuster* Touchstone-Clarion Bks. 1969 pap. $2.45

VALUE IN SOCIAL THEORY: A Selection of Essays on Methodology. 1958. *Routledge & Kegan Paul* 1968 $7.50

BEYOND THE WELFARE STATE. *Yale Univ. Press* 1960 pap. $2.95. A discussion of economic planning in the Western countries, the Soviet bloc and the underdeveloped nations of the world.

CHALLENGE TO AFFLUENCE. *Pantheon* 1963 $5.95; *Random* Vintage Bks. pap. $1.65

(With Jan Myrdal). CHINESE JOURNEY. *Pantheon* 1965 $9.95; *Beacon* pap. $2.95

ASIAN DRAMA: An Inquiry into the Poverty of Nations. 3 vols. 1968. *Kraus* 3 vols. $25.00; *Pantheon* 3 vols. pap. set $10.00; 1 vol. abr. ed. by Seth King *Pantheon* 1972 $10.00; *Random* Vintage Bks. 1971 pap. $2.45

"The incredibly detailed knowledge assembled in the three volumes of 'Asian Drama' by Mr. Myrdal and his international team of assistants will make the work a basic source not only for the study of that area, but for the whole field of economic development. . . . Gunnar Myrdal has earned the gratitude of both his colleagues and of the political leaders of the world"—(Thomas Balogh, in the *N.Y. Times*).

AN APPROACH TO THE ASIAN DRAMA: Selections from Asian Drama. *Random* Vintage Bks. pap. $3.95

OBJECTIVITY IN SOCIAL RESEARCH. *Pantheon* 1969 pap. $1.95

CHALLENGE OF WORLD POVERTY: A World Poverty Program in Outline. *Pantheon* 1970 $8.95

ECONOMIC THEORY AND UNDERDEVELOPED REGIONS. Ed. by Ruth N. Anshen *Harper* Torchbks. 1971 pap. $1.95

AGAINST THE STREAM: Critical Essays on Economics. *Pantheon* 1973 $10.00; *Random* Vintage Bks. 1975 pap. $2.95

HUTCHINS, ROBERT M(AYNARD). 1899–

Agreement on the basic purposes and methods of education is a will o' the wisp that continues to elude academic theorists. But for years, where the heat and dust of battle have been thickest, Robert Maynard Hutchins has wielded his intellectual weapons in the cause of liberal education. In the United States, education for life as opposed to training for a vocation has been upgraded and downgraded as the American mood changed (at present the profound dissatisfaction of the college generation with materialistic values has led to its very considerable upgrading), but in all its ups and downs the figure of Dr. Hutchins has stood as the chief opponent of specialized or vocationally oriented education for the intellectually able.

Liberal education, he says, "prepares the young for anything that may happen; it has value under any circumstances. . . . It gets them ready for a lifetime of learning. It connects man with man. It introduces all men to the dialogue about the common good of their own country and of the world community. It frees their mind of prejudice. It lays the basis of practical wisdom." The increasing complexities of American civilization are no justification, to Dr. Hutchins' mind, for modifying this approach. "The more technological the Society," he says in "The Learning Society," the less *ad hoc* education can be. The reason is that the more technological the society is, the more rapidly it will change and the less valuable *ad hoc* education will become. It now seems safe to say that the best practical education is the best theoretical one."

After serving as Dean of Yale Law School in 1929 Dr. Hutchins became (at 29) President, and in 1949 Chancellor, of the University of Chicago, remaining there until 1951. During this period he and Mortimer Adler introduced the Great Books program into the Chicago curriculum—on the theory that the best education is achieved through reading and understanding the work of the great minds of the past. He also abolished football at Chicago. Later he became Associate Director of the Ford Foundation and President of the Fund for the Republic—the latter in the face of the oppressive climate for free expression brought about by the Senator Joseph McCarthy witchhunts. But he saw to it that the Fund's projects included studies of the Federal loyalty-security program, of political blacklisting in the entertainment industries and of the nature of Communism in the United States. Dr. Hutchins survived—with the freedoms he had helped to preserve. He has recently retired as the chief executive officer of the Center for the Study of Democratic Institutions at Santa Barbara, Calif., a "community of scholars" under the aegis of the Ford Foundation. He remains as chairman of the Board of Editors of Encyclopaedia Britannica.

NO FRIENDLY VOICE. 1936. *Greenwood* $11.75

THE HIGHER LEARNING IN AMERICA. *Yale Univ. Press* 1936 rev. ed. 1961 $7.50 pap. $1.95

ST. THOMAS AND THE WORLD STATE. *Marquette Univ. Press* 1949 $2.50. An argument for world law, world government and a world state; based on the philosophy of St. Thomas Aquinas.

THE UNIVERSITY OF UTOPIA. *Univ. of Chicago Press* 1953 Phoenix Bks. pap. $2.25

THE CONFLICT IN EDUCATION IN A DEMOCRATIC SOCIETY. 1953. *Greenwood* 1972 $8.75

(With Mortimer J. Adler, Eds.). THE GREAT IDEAS TODAY. *Praeger* 1966 1973 $11.00

THE LEARNING SOCIETY. Britannica Perspectives Ser. *Praeger* 1968 $4.50; *New Am. Lib.* Mentor 1973 pap. $1.25

"An elegantly written, beautifully reasoned defense of liberal education, graceful, humane. Dr. Hutchins, an unpedantic pedant, an intellectually stimulating teacher, contends that good education produces men, not manpower; concerned critics of society, not conformists; valuable human beings aware of their own cultural heritage and committed to the idea of brotherhood. Dr. Hutchins does not promote education as a panacea; he convincingly argues that educational systems are a reflection of national culture—if the culture is shoddy and materialistic, the educational system will be shoddy and materialistic"—(*PW*).

Books about Hutchins

Humanistic Education and Western Civilization: Essays for Robert M. Hutchins. Ed. with introd. by Arthur A. Cohen. 1964. *Bks. for Libraries* $10.75

"This compilation of 14 original essays by an equal number of contributors . . . is a fitting tribute to Robert M. Hutchins on his 65th birthday. . . . Seldom does a reader have the pleasure of sampling the works of so many renowned individuals in one book"—(*LJ*). Contributors include Mortimer Adler, William O. Douglas, Milton Mayer, John Courtney Murray, S. J., David Riesman and F. Champion Ward.

FREYRE, GILBERTO DEMELLO. 1900–   *See Chapter 16, Latin American Literature—Brazilian Literature*, Reader's Adviser, *Vol. 2. For his books on Brazil, see listing on Latin America, Chapter 9, History, Government and Politics, this Vol.*

MEAD, MARGARET. 1901–

This American anthropologist is a graduate of Barnard College, where she studied under Franz Boas. She became assistant curator (1926), then associate curator (1942) and finally emeritus curater (1969) of ethnology in the American Museum of Natural History, New York City. Her studies of the cultures of many remote peoples have extended over 40 years, her first field work, in the Samoan Islands, having been undertaken in 1925–26, where she studied the development of the adolescent girl under primitive conditions. "Coming of Age in Samoa" was called "a remarkable contribution to our knowledge of humanity"—(*N.Y. Times*). Rebecca West described "Male and Female" as a "vast, turbulent book . . . turbulent because Margaret Mead is a genius of the prophetic sort." She is a specialist in what she herself describes as "conditioning of the social personalities of both sexes." Her subjects cover "comparative child psychology, oceanic ethnology, cooperation and competition among primitive peoples, and cross-cultural communications." "Margaret Mead's New Guinea Journal" was seen on television in December 1968. It was a report on her third trip to the area studied for one of her earliest books; recent years have brought change even to its remotest tribes, for which her affection and warmth were evident in the film. She has also recently testified before a U.S. Senate Committee on solving the problem of hunger in the United States.

She has edited several collections: "Cultural Patterns and Technical Change" (*New Am. Lib.* pap. $1.25); with Martha Wolfenstein, "Childhood in Contemporary Cultures" (*Univ. of Chicago Press* 1955 $11.50 Phoenix Bks. 1963 pap. $4.95); "Cooperation and Competition Among Primitive Peoples" (*Peter Smith* enl. ed. $5.25); with Ruth Bunzel, "The Golden Age of American Anthropology" (*Braziller* 1960 $12.50); and, with Frances B. Kaplan, "American Women: The Report of the President's Commission on the Status of Women and Other Publications of the Commission" (1965, o.p.).

COMING OF AGE IN SAMOA. 1928. *Dell* 1967 pap. $1.25; *Morrow* 1971 pap. $2.50; *Peter Smith* $4.75

GROWING UP IN NEW GUINEA. 1930. *Apollo* 1962 pap. $2.50; *Dell* pap. $1.25; *Peter Smith* $4.50

THE CHANGING CULTURE OF AN INDIAN TRIBE. 1932. *AMS Press* $14.50

SEX AND TEMPERAMENT IN THREE PRIMITIVE SOCIETIES. 1935. *Dell* 1967 pap. $1.25; *Morrow* pap. $2.95; *Peter Smith* $5.50

AND KEEP YOUR POWDER DRY: An Anthropologist Looks at America. 1942. *Bks. for Libraries* $11.50; *Morrow* 1971 pap. $2.95

MALE AND FEMALE: A Study of the Sexes in a Changing World. 1949. *Dell* 1968 pap. $1.25

THE SCHOOL IN AMERICAN CULTURE. *Harvard Univ. Press* 1951 $2.50

NEW LIVES FOR OLD: A Cultural Transformation—Manus, 1928–1953. *Morrow* 1956 1966 $8.50; *Apollo* pap. $3.25; *Dell* 1968 pap. $1.25

(With Ruth Benedict, Eds.). AN ANTHROPOLOGIST AT WORK. 1958. *Avon Bks.* 1973 pap. $3.95

ANTHROPOLOGY: A Human Science. *Van Nostrand-Reinhold* 1964 pap. $2.95. Selected papers, 1939–1960.

CONTINUITIES IN CULTURAL EVOLUTION. *Yale Univ. Press* 1964 $17.50 pap. $3.95

(With others, Eds.). SCIENCE AND THE CONCEPT OF RACE. *Columbia* 1969 $12.50 pap. $2.50

A symposium "on the present state of knowledge and research on problems and . . . the evolving concepts of race in [various] fields"—(*LJ*).

CULTURE AND COMMITMENT. *Doubleday* Natural History Press 1970 $5.00 pap. $1.95

BLACKBERRY WINTER: A Memoir. *Morrow* 1972 $8.95; *Simon & Schuster* (Pocket Bks.) 1975 pap. $1.95 Touchstone-Clarion Bks. 1973 pap. $2.95

HOFFER, ERIC. 1902–   *See Chapter 15, Essays and Criticism,* Reader's Adviser, Vol. 1.

LEAKEY, L(OUIS) S(EYMOUR) B(AZETT). 1903–1972.

Born in Kabete, Kenya, the British anthropologist was a leading authority on the peoples of East Africa, particularly the Kikuyu. He spoke "the Kikuyu language 'as well as, if not better than, English'; [was] an elder of the tribe; and [described] himself as "in so many ways a Kikuyu myself.' " He was Curator of the Coryndon Memorial Museum in Nairobi, Kenya, and Honorary Keeper of Paleontology and Prehistory there. He made major contributions to the study of prehistoric man. He unearthed Proconsul fossils. "Olduvai Gorge, 1951–1961, Vol. 1" presents the background evidence for future studies of what is probably the most important prehistoric site in the world. It was at Olduvai that the skull of *Zinjanthropus boisei*, the world's earliest tool-making man, was found. In 1967 Dr. Leakey discovered the fossil of what he called *Kenyapithecus africanus*, now recognized as the earliest man-like creature. "The new finds push the divergence of apes and men so far back that it is no longer a question of finding an ape-like ancestor for man but of finding a common ancestor for both"—(John Davy, in the *Observer*, London). He received many awards for his pioneer work. From 1960 to 1961 he was president of the South African Archeological Society. During this time he was also a Herbert Spencer Lecturer at Oxford University. In 1961 he was a Huxley Memorial Lecturer at Birmingham University. His wife, Dr. Mary Leakey, shared many of his anthropological diggings and discoveries. She returned to Laetolil in Tanzania after his death where she unearthed numerous human bones that have recently been dated from 3.35 million to 3.75 million years old.

"Mau Mau and the Kikuyu" (1952), "Defeating Mau Mau" (1954) and Leakey's story of his own and others' discoveries in "African Eden" (1963) are out of print.

THE STONE AGE RACES OF KENYA. 1931. *Humanities Press* 2nd ed. 1970 $22.00

ADAM'S ANCESTORS: The Evolution of Man and His Culture. 1934. *Harper* Torchbks. 4th ed. 1960 pap. $1.95; *Peter Smith* $4.25

STONE AGE AFRICA: An Outline of Prehistory in Africa. 1936. *Negro Univs. Press* 1973 $13.75

PROGRESS AND EVOLUTION OF MAN IN AFRICA. *Oxford* 1961 $2.75

OLDUVAI GORGE, 1951–1961. *Cambridge* 3 vols. 1965–72 Vol. 1 Preliminary Report: Geology and Fauna (1965) Vol. 2 (with P. V. Tobias) The Cranium of Australopithecus (Zinjanthropus) Boisei (1965) Vol. 3 Excavations in Beds I and II 1960–63, ed. by Mary D. Leakey (1972) Vol. 1 $32.50 Vols. 2–3 each $35.00

KENYA: Contrasts and Problems. *Schenkman* 1966 $5.95

(With others). ADAM OR APE: A Sourcebook of Discoveries About Early Man. *Schenkman* 1967 1971 $11.25 pap. $4.95; *General Learning Corp.* 1971 $11.95 pap. $5.40

(With Vance Morris Goodall). UNVEILING MAN'S ORIGIN. *General Learning Corp.* 1969 $7.50 pap. $4.25; *Schenkman* 1969 $6.95 pap. $3.95. A century of thought about human evolution.

(With R. J. Savage, Eds.). FOSSIL VERTEBRATES OF AFRICA. *Academic Press* 2 vols. 1969–1970 Vol. 1 $7.50 Vol. 2 $22.00

THE STONE AGE CULTURES OF KENYA COLONY. Ed. by Brian Fagan *International Scholarly Bk. Services* 1971 $25.00

ANIMALS OF EAST AFRICA. *National Geographic Society* $4.25

WHITE AFRICAN: An Early Autobiography. Fwd. by K. F. Mather *Schenkman* 1966 $7.95 pap. $3.95; *Ballantine Bks.* 1973 pap. $1.50

"The energy, enthusiasm, directness and iconoclasm of the famous explorer of man's African past are wholly displayed"—(*Scientific American*).

BY THE EVIDENCE: Memoirs 1932–1951. *Harcourt* 1974 $9.95

Books about Leakey

Leakey's Luck: The Life of Louis Seymour Bazett Leakey, 1903–1972. By Sonia Cole. *Harcourt* 1975 $14.95

The author, in "this excellent and entertaining view, combines familiarity with Leakey and access to all his papers with the independence of a forthright biographer"—(*LJ*).

LORENZ, KONRAD Z(ACHARIAS). 1903–

"Man Meets Dog," by the famous Austrian naturalist, is "a highly enlightening book by a scientific observer who has spent years watching and interpreting animal behavior." Of "King Solomon's Ring" the *N.Y. Times* said: "As a writer, he is endowed with a fine sense of humor . . . and he writes of his long and intimate association with the birds and beasts with charm, lightness and a felicity of style that carry the reader along with sustained and fascinated attention."

"On Aggression" became an American best seller. In it Dr. Lorenz argues that man is aggressive by nature and must understand himself if he is to bring human aggression under control. This, said Eliot Fremont-Smith, "is his masterwork and probably one of the most important books of our age. Dr. Lorenz offers what amounts to a revolutionary view of the functions of aggression within species and its natural checks in animals and man, and how, in the evolution of the latter, aggressive instincts have developed without properly balancing or inhibiting controls." His views are not unanimously accepted, but he has adduced much evidence for them in what Ashley Montagu has called an "exciting, informative, and stimulating" book. Konrad Lorenz is director of the Max Planck Institute for Behavioral Physiology in Bavaria, West Germany.

King Solomon's Ring: New Light on Animal Ways. 1949. Trans. by Marjorie Kerr Wilson; ill. by the author; fwd. by Julian Huxley *T. Y. Crowell* 1952 $6.95; *Apollo* 1961 pap. $1.95; *New Am. Lib.* pap. $1.25

Man Meets Dog. 1955. *Penguin* 1965 pap. $1.45

The Evolution and Modification of Behavior. *Univ. of Chicago Press* 1965 $6.00 Phoenix Bks. pap. $1.75

On Aggression. Trans. by Marjorie Kerr Wilson *Harcourt* 1966 $7.95 Harvest Bks. 1974 pap. $3.50; *Bantam* 1970 pap. $1.45

Studies in Animal and Human Behaviour. *Harvard Univ. Press* 2 vols. 1970–71 each $11.75

(With P. Leyhausen). Motivation of Human and Animal Behavior. *Van Nostrand-Reinhold* 1973 $15.95 pap. $6.95

Civilized Man's Eight Deadly Sins. Trans. by Marjorie Kerr Wilson *Harcourt* 1974 $4.95

Books about Lorenz

Man and Aggression. Ed. by Ashley Montagu. *Oxford* 2nd ed. 1973 $8.50 Galaxy Bks. pap. $2.95

COON, CARLETON S(TEVENS). 1904–

The *N.Y. Times* called Professor Coon's "Story of Man" the "first anthropological account of human history which is both readable and authoritative." The noted author was Curator of Ethnology and Professor of Anthropology at the (Univ. of Pennsylvania) University Museum in Philadelphia from 1948 to 1963 where he arranged the famous "Hall of Man" exhibit. He was born in Wakefield, Mass., and received his A.B., M.A. and Ph.D. from Harvard, where he taught before going to the University of Pennsylvania. He has traveled extensively in Africa, the Near and Middle East, and Europe. In "The Origin of Races," he presents what is said to be a new theory. In his introduction, he "tells us that the decision to write it was taken by him in 1939. 'For twenty years, in peace and war, at home and on expeditions, I collected material with this task in mind.' His task can be defined as an attempt to find out 'how far back in prehistoric antiquity . . . human racial groups can be traced.' He favors the view that the races of man are much older than has been assumed by most anthropologists, and that the 'moment of separation' among racial subspecies of mankind should be put back several hundred thousand years"—(*LJ*). The sequel to "The Origins" is "The Living Races of Man," which completes Coon's "comprehensive study. . . . He presents new findings and conclusions concerning race origins, distribution, biochemical and pathological peculiarities, as well as behavioral patterns of man based on recent serological and genetic research"—(*LJ*). Margaret Mead has described it as "an enormous, erudite, provocative, stimulating, zestful book."

Professor Coon has edited (with Edward E. Hunt, Jr.) "Anthropology, A to Z" (*Grosset* $4.75 pap. $2.95) and "A Reader in General Anthropology" (*Holt* 1948 $11.00) as well as (with J. M. Andrews) "Studies in the Anthropology of Oceania and Asia, Presented in Memory of Roland B. Dixon" (1943. *Kraus* pap. $15.00).

TRIBES OF THE RIF. 1931. *Kraus* $36.00

THE RACES OF EUROPE. 1939. *Greenwood* 1972 $31.50

MOUNTAINS OF GIANTS: A Racial and Cultural Study of the North Albanian Mt. Ghege. 1950. *Kraus* $8.50

CARAVAN: The Story of the Middle East. *Holt* 1951 rev. ed. 1958 $10.00

THE STORY OF MAN: From the First Human in Primitive Culture and Beyond. *Knopf* 1954 2nd rev. ed. 1962 $10.00

THE SEVEN CAVES: Archaeological Explorations in the Middle East. *Knopf* 1957 $6.95

THE ORIGIN OF RACES. Knopf 1962 $12.95 text ed. $10.95

(With Edward E. Hunt, Jr.). THE LIVING RACES OF MAN. *Knopf* 1965 $12.50 text ed. $10.95

YENGEMA CAVE REPORT. *University Museum* 1968 $3.50

THE HUNTING PEOPLES. *Little-Atlantic* 1971 $10.00 pap. $3.95

Coon "describes the unusual cultural customs of the living hunters of the world, points out their similarities and differences, and analyzes their social and political organizations, marriage customs, and ceremonies"—(*LJ*).

ARON, RAYMOND. 1905–

Library Journal wrote of "The Industrial Society": "Raymond Aron is one of France's most distinguished social theorists of the post war era. His works range from formal studies of sociological theory to international relations to current political and social commentary. In this book, Mr. Aron concludes his discussion of some crucial questions begun in earlier works: the nature of modern, industrial society; the ideological character of our era; and theories of development. . . . Mr. Aron's outlook will not be to everyone's liking, and one gets the impression from these essays that they consist largely of replies to his critics." Commenting on two of the earlier works, J. P. Nettl wrote in the *N.Y. Review of Books*: "His two big volumes of expository lectures published under the title *Main Currents in Sociological Thought*, as well as his earlier *German Sociology*, are masterly intellectual simplifications, clarifications, and demonstrations of consistency." Professor Aron has described contemporary society as "a sort of *commedia dell'arte* in which the actors have the right to improvise along prescribed lines."

THE OPIUM OF THE INTELLECTUALS. 1955. *Norton* 1962 pap. $2.25

(With August Heckscher). DIVERSITY OF WORLDS. 1957. *Greenwood* 1973 $9.25

(Ed.). WORLD TECHNOLOGY AND HUMAN DESTINY. *Univ. of Michigan Press* 1963 $5.95

(With Bert Hoselitz, Eds.). SOCIAL DEVELOPMENT. *Humanities Press* 1965 pap. $11.00

MAIN CURRENTS IN SOCIOLOGICAL THOUGHT. Trans. by Richard Howard and Helen Weaver *Basic Bks.* 2 vols. 1965–67 Vol. 1 Montesquieu, Comte, Marx, Tocqueville, the Sociologists and the Revolution of 1848 (1965) $8.95 Vol. 2 Durkheim, Pareto, Weber (1967) $8.50; *Doubleday* Anchor Bks. pap. Vol. 1 $2.50 Vol. 2 $1.95

THE INDUSTRIAL SOCIETY: Three Essays on Ideology and Development. *Praeger* 1967 $4.95

PROGRESS AND DISILLUSION: The Dialectics of Modern Society. *Praeger* 1968 $5.50

See also Chapter 9, History, Government and Politics—Modern and World, this Vol.

KLUCKHOHN, CLYDE. 1905–1960.

"Mirror for Man," a study of what anthropology can do for world peace, received the $10,000 Whittlesey House–*Science Illustrated* Award in 1949 as the best book of science for the layman and a book which "contributed most to man's understanding of the world today." Clyde Kluckhohn was born in LeMars, Iowa. Forced to leave Princeton because of an illness, he spent several months in New Mexico, where he came to know the Zuni and Navajo Indians. After four years at the University of Wisconsin and a period at Oxford as a Rhodes scholar, he studied anthropology in

Vienna, Paris, Oxford and Madrid. He taught at Harvard, made field trips to New Mexico and Arizona, and traveled in the Pacific Islands, Australia and New Zealand.

CULTURE AND BEHAVIOR: Collected Essays. Ed. by Richard Kluckhohn *Macmillan* (Free Press) 1962 $8.95 pap. $2.45

(With Katharine Spencer). BIBLIOGRAPHY OF THE NAVAJO INDIANS. 1940. *AMS Press* $7.50

(With L. C. Wyman). INTRODUCTION TO NAVAHO CHANT PRACTICE. 1940. *Kraus* pap. $10.00

NAVAHO WITCHCRAFT. 1944. *Beacon* 1962 pap. $2.95

(With Dorothea G. Leighton). THE NAVAHO. *Harvard Univ. Press* 1946 rev. ed. 1973 $10.00 pap. $3.95; rev. by Richard Kluckhohn and Lucy Wales *Doubleday* Natural History Press 1962 pap. $2.50

MIRROR FOR MAN. *McGraw-Hill* 1949 $6.95 pap. $1.95; *Fawcett* 1972 pap. $1.25

ANTHROPOLOGY AND THE CLASSICS. The Colver Lectures of 1960. *Brown Univ. Press* 1961 $5.00

(With W. W. Hill and Lucy Wales Kluckhohn). NAVAHO MATERIAL CULTURE. *Harvard Univ. Press* 1971 $25.00

MONTAGU, ASHLEY (Montague Francis Ashley Montagu).   1905–

Ashley Montagu, an Anglo-American anthropologist, prefers to call himself a "social biologist." David Manning White describes him (in *SR*), as "a quasi-ubiquitous peripatetic who strides with jet-age speed into the diverse areas of that problem child, Man." By November of 1975 he had written over 50 books—of which a number are collections of his essays—and edited 11. "The Natural Superiority of Women," one of his most popular works, is intended, he says, "to bring the sexes closer together, not to set them apart by placing one above the other." His outlook is optimistic, but his witty attack on all that cheapens and degrades in our civilization is unsparing. He upholds the dignity and infinite potentiality of all the races of man.

He "has long courted controversy by upsetting what he has called 'venerable errors' and [has often] ventured into such sensitive areas as race, the relations between the sexes, and child rearing"—(*Current Biography*). Professor Montagu, who became an American citizen in 1940, has made important contributions to anthropology and is known for the grace, insight and incisive humor of his writing. When one of his friends was asked what his specialty was, the friend replied, "I should say that Ashley Montagu's specialty is versatility."

MAN'S MOST DANGEROUS MYTH: The Fallacy of Race. 1942. *Oxford* 1974 $15.00 Galaxy Bks. pap. $3.95

ON BEING HUMAN. 1950. *Hawthorn Bks.* rev. ed. 1967 $4.95 pap. $1.95

Montagu's theme is that "cooperation rather than competition is the basic law of nature. . . . A most moving testament to human dignity"—(*LJ*). The new edition has been revised only enough to bring it up to date.

ON BEING INTELLIGENT. 1951. *Greenwood* 1973 $10.50

DARWIN: Competition and Cooperation. 1952. *Greenwood* 1973 $8.50

THE NATURAL SUPERIORITY OF WOMEN. *Macmillan* 1953 rev. ed. 1968 $6.95 pap. $1.95

ANTHROPOLOGY AND HUMAN NATURE. *Sargent* 1957 $6.00; *Brown Bk.* pap. $2.75. Practical uses of this justifiably popular field.

MAN, HIS FIRST TWO MILLION YEARS: A Brief Introduction to Anthropology. 1957. rev. ed. 1969. *Dell* Delta Bks. pap. $2.45

Montagu "paints a broad, comprehensive picture, without presenting his sometimes unique theories in any great detail"—(*PW*).

RACE, SCIENCE AND HUMANITY. *Van Nostrand-Reinhold* 1963 pap. $2.95. A collection of 12 of the author's most important writings on these subjects.

THE CONCEPT OF RACE. *Macmillan* (Free Press) 1964 $7.95 Collier Bks. 1969 pap. $2.45

(With Edward Darling). THE PREVALENCE OF NONSENSE. *Harper* 1967 $7.95; *Dell* Delta Bks. 1969 pap. $2.45

"A biting, satiric look at the human folly . . . embodied in institutionalized nonsense: customs, traditions, food use, taboos, religion, race theories and so on"—(*LJ*). "A contribution to the gaiety of the nation, at a moment when gaiety is in short supply"—(Gerald W. Johnson).

(Ed.). MAN AND AGGRESSION. *Oxford* 1968 2nd ed. 1973 $8.50 Galaxy Bks. pap. $2.95

SEX, MAN, AND SOCIETY. 1969. *Tower Press* 1970 pap. $1.25

(With Edward Darling). IGNORANCE OF CERTAINTY. *Harper* 1970 $7.95

TOUCHING: The Human Significance of the Skin. *Columbia* 1971 $10.00; *Harper* Perenn. Lib. 1972 pap. $1.50

(Ed.). CULTURE AND HUMAN DEVELOPMENT: Insights into Growing Human. *Prentice-Hall* 1974 $7.95

"Studies on the influence of environment as the dominant factor in the social acculturation of humans"—(*Booklist*).

(Ed.). THE ENDANGERED ENVIRONMENT. *Mason & Lipscomb* 1974 $9.95

Contains "brief quotations from more than 150 sources which deal with . . . pollution"—(*LJ*).

(Ed.). THE PRACTICE OF LOVE. *Prentice-Hall* 1975 $8.95 pap. $2.95

EISELEY, LOREN C(OREY). 1907–

"Like everything he writes it is eloquent, moving, and profound," said Joseph Wood Krutch of "The Mind as Nature" (1962, o.p.), an exploration of "the important role the teacher plays in the universal drama." "As a scientist Dr. Eiseley's general concern has been with the evolution of life—but more specifically with the emergence of the human experience. He has roamed the Western regions of this American continent to find clues of the earliest human life here and has published widely in the technical journals of his discipline. As a poet and a writer he has contributed to leading literary anthologies . . . and [many] magazines"—(Fwd. to "The Mind as Nature"). Two collections of his poetry are: "Notes of an Alchemist" (*Scribner* 1972 $6.95) and "The Innocent Assassins" (*Scribner* 1973 $6.95).

At the University of Pennsylvania he has been Chairman of the Department of Anthropology, University Professor of Anthropology and the History of Science, and Chairman of the Department of History and Philosophy of Science in the Graduate School.

The *New Yorker* called "The Firmament of Time" an "irresistible inducement to partake of the almost forgotten excitements of reflection." Of "The Immense Journey," the *N.Y. Times* wrote: "It proves to be a delightful journey, full of beautiful images and fascinating ideas. Often he leaves the narrow road of science to delve into the world of pure fantasy, for Mr. Eiseley is one of the rare scientists who can look beyond science into the realm of the spirit, beyond facts to the beauty that defies explanation." And from the *Christian Science Monitor:* "His style is beautiful, compelling in impact and poetic in its imagery. His subject is one of the epics of natural science—the 'immense journey' of life as known on this planet."

THE IMMENSE JOURNEY. *Random* 1957 Vintage Bks. pap. $1.95; *Franklin Watts* lg.-type ed. $7.95

"A collection of essays . . . about the recency of man, his development, genetic endowments and the enormous, interlinked complexity of life"—(*Virginia Kirkus Service*).

DARWIN'S CENTURY: Evolution and the Men Who Discovered It. *Doubleday* Anchor Bks. 1958 pap. $2.95. Winner of the Phi Beta Kappa Award.

THE FIRMAMENT OF TIME. *Atheneum* 1960 pap. $2.65. Essays, addresses and lectures on evolution; winner of the John Burroughs Medal.

FRANCIS BACON AND THE MODERN DILEMMA. 1962. *Bks. for Libraries* $8.00

UNEXPECTED UNIVERSE. *Harcourt* 1969 $6.95 Harvest Bks. 1972 pap. $1.95

Describes "a naturalist's encounter with unexpected and symbolic aspects of the universe. . . . Through it all, like a hidden thread, . . . runs the theme of desolation and renewal in the planet's history"—(Publisher's note).

THE NIGHT COUNTRY. *Scribner* 1971 $7.95 pap. $2.95

"These autobiographical tales keep illustrating the theses that wind through all his writing—the fallibility of science, the mystery of evolution, the surprise of life"—(*Time*).

THE INVISIBLE PYRAMID. *Scribner* 1972 $6.95 pap. $2.95

"Describing the rise of man as an organism devouring the environment and polluting his world space, [the author] charges that the wealth and inventive genius being poured into the Space Age constitutes a public sacrifice equivalent to the building of the Great Pyramid at Giza. . . . [He also] explores man's nature, his conception of time, and his first intrusion into space"—(Publisher's note).

THE MAN WHO SAW THROUGH TIME. (Orig. "Francis Bacon and the Modern Dilemma" *see above*) Scribner rev. ed. 1973 pap. $2.45

GALBRAITH, JOHN KENNETH. 1908–

John Kenneth Galbraith, Paul M. Warburg Professor of Economics at Harvard, is a remarkable figure in American economic, political and literary life. Six feet six in height and regarded in youth by his family as a prodigy, he has always stood out in the world, but his great intellectual abilities, combined with charm, wit, self-discipline and good judgment have enabled him to accomplish an extraordinary quantity of impressive work both serious and frivolous; even the frivolous has had a semiserious satirical purpose.

"The Affluent Society"—an examination written in Switzerland on a Guggenheim Fellowship and begun with the tentative title "Why People Are Poor" (in such a society)—ended as a caustic but brilliant dissection of America in the 1950s that became a widely quoted best seller—in 1969 reissued in a revised edition. "It brought," says the *Atlantic,* "wit and dream into the usually forbidding discussion of economics and contributed numerous words and phrases to the language of that inexact science. The book helped to get the country thinking about the true nature and disposition of its wealth."

His second magnum opus has been "The New Industrial State," which immediately made the bestseller lists on publication. This first burst upon the world as a series of Reith Lectures for the BBC in England; it analyzes what Galbraith sees as the "technostructure" of American economic life: the gigantic interacting mechanism comprised of the huge corporations and the national government, in which, says Galbraith, the consumer is the loser. Like his earlier book this has aroused both admiration and controversy; Galbraith's picture of the smooth and massive workings of the contemporary economic scene have been challenged in some quarters as oversimplified or out of focus. One such critic, Raymond J. Saulnier (writing in the *N.Y. Times*), who disagrees with Galbraith on many points, concludes his review with the statement: " 'The New Industrial State' deserves the widest possible attention and discussion. It will provoke much argument among economists; it may well inspire graduate schools of business to ask new questions about what they are doing; and, hopefully, it will provide a conversation piece in executive dining rooms. All in all, a constructive result." Adolf A. Berle wrote (in *SR*): "For some years, John Kenneth Galbraith has been poking, prodding, and irritating America toward a measure of understanding of its economic life. . . . This time he has tackled a more serious task of laying out an economic theory corresponding to its major facts. The book is long overdue. *The New Industrial State* will make economic history. . . . Galbraith deals with realities instead of fiction. This may not make him popular—but from here out no serious scholar will be able to skate along on past assumptions." Other reviewers have written in the same vein; the impact of "The New Industrial State" is certain to be felt for years to come.

Professor Galbraith was born in Ontario, Canada, to a family of Puritan tradition who were stockbreeders, and his undergraduate study was in animal husbandry at Ontario Agricultural College (now the University of Guelph). He soon switched to economics, receiving his M.A. from the University of Toronto and his Ph.D. from the University of California (Berkeley). From there he went to Harvard as an instructor under the economist Alvin Hansen. After five years he went to Princeton, from which in 1941, on the basis of his first book, he was recruited by President Franklin Roosevelt to become deputy administrator for the Office of Price Administration, an unpopular job whose pressures eventually brought his resignation. He became a writer for Henry Luce's *Fortune* for five years, then in 1948 returned to Harvard as a professor. In this period he became close to the group of liberal Democrats including Arthur M. Schlesinger, Jr. (*q.v.*), who were pressing the John F. Kennedy candidacy for President. After John Kennedy's election, Mr. Galbraith somewhat reluctantly left his economic studies and his writing and teaching for a period as Ambassador to India (1961–63), which he later said gave him time to develop perspective on the half-completed "New Industrial State." In recent years he has been active politically, particularly in opposition to the Vietnam war and in the traumatic 1968 Presidential campaign, when he became chairman of Americans for Democratic Action and supported the McCarthy and Humphrey efforts for the Presidency.

Between these many activities he has managed to write a number of peripheral works: the Signet Broadside "How to Get Out of Vietnam," which produced considerable impact at the height of the controversy (subtitled "A Workable Solution to the Worst Problem of Our Time" [1967, o.p.]); "The Triumph," a bright satirical novel—and best seller—about the U.S. State Department and the overthrow of a mythical dictatorship in South America (subtitled "A Novel of Modern Diplomacy" *Houghton* 1968 $4.95); (with Mohinder Singh Randhawa) "Indian Painting:

The Scene, Themes and Legends," which *Publisher's Weekly* called "a beauty of a book"—it contains reproductions of paintings from Mr. Galbraith's and other collections (*Houghton* 1968 $35.00). A book he wrote—a spoof—while Ambassador to India, and therefore pseudonymously as "Mark Epernay," is "The McLandress Dimension" (*Houghton* 1963 $3.75). "The McLandress Dimension of the title is a Parkinsonian formula for determining the length of time that any given politician or statesman can spend *not* thinking about himself. Naturally, it can measure very short intervals. Light and witty reading"—*(PW)*. This was said to have been taken seriously by one South American sociological journal, which gave it lengthy sociological analysis! "The Scotch" is his description of the community in southern Ontario where he grew up. "The book, a short one, is written with such grace, intimacy, and delightful anecdote [that] one is inclined to look upon it as a little classic"—*(LJ)*.

For all his lightness of heart, Mr. Galbraith is clearly yet another of the important small group of serious thinkers who want to make America human, compassionate and livable again. As such, with his intellectual gifts and his power of getting his ideas across to many people in attractive form, his value is incalculable.

THE THEORY OF PRICE CONTROL. *Harvard Univ. Press* 1952 $2.25 Mr. Galbraith thinks this may be his "best" book, though his earliest.

THE GREAT CRASH, 1929. *Houghton* 1955 3rd ed. 1972 $5.95 Sentry Eds. pap. $1.95

(With others). MARKETING EFFICIENCY IN PUERTO RICO. *Harvard Univ. Press* 1955 $4.50

AMERICAN CAPITALISM. *Houghton* 1956 $4.00 Sentry Eds. 1965 pap. $3.25

THE AFFLUENT SOCIETY. *Houghton* 1958 2nd ed. 1969 $6.95 Sentry Eds. 1971 pap. $2.95; *New Am. Lib.* Mentor Bks. 1970 pap. $1.25

ECONOMICS AND THE ART OF CONTROVERSY. *Random* Vintage Bks. 1959 pap. $1.25

THE LIBERAL HOUR. *Houghton* 1960 $3.50; *New Am. Lib.* Mentor Bks. pap. $.95

ECONOMIC DEVELOPMENT. (Orig. "Economic Development in Perspective," 1962) *Harvard Univ. Press* rev. and enl. ed. 1964 $2.95; *Houghton* Sentry Eds. 1964 pap. $2.25

THE NEW INDUSTRIAL STATE. *Houghton* 1967 2nd rev. ed. 1971 $8.95 Sentry Eds. 1972 pap. $3.25; *New Am. Lib.* Signet 1968 pap. $1.95

A CONTEMPORARY GUIDE TO ECONOMICS, PEACE AND LAUGHTER. *Houghton* 1971 $7.95

"These are 26 essays by a famous economist sometimes with economics as the subject, sometimes not. The period of time of the writing is 1960 to 1970"—*(LJ)*.

ECONOMICS AND THE PUBLIC PURPOSE. *Houghton* 1973 $10.00

"The theme of this book is: to the giant business corporations go the spoils, not to the consumer or the small businessman . . . This is Galbraith's most carefully developed book. . . . The book is bold, thought provoking, and controversial"—*(Choice)*.

MONEY: Whence It Came, Where It Went. *Houghton* 1975 $10.00

Galbraith draws some "useful lessons for us. One is that throughout history the men who have largely determined monetary action have been held in awe by the world, although they have rarely if ever known what they are doing"—*(N.Y. Times)*.

JOURNEY TO POLAND AND YUGOSLAVIA. *Harvard Univ. Press* 1958 $3.00

AN AMBASSADOR'S JOURNAL: A Personal Account of the Kennedy Years. *Houghton* 1969 $10.00

A CHINA PASSAGE. *Houghton* 1973 $5.95

"Professor Galbraith's journal of his recent visit to China is short, amusing and unpretentious. He clearly enjoyed what he saw while remaining well aware that much was not being shown"— *(Atlantic)*.

THE SCOTCH. *Houghton* 1964 $4.95; *New Am. Lib.* 1970 pap. $2.95. A memoir of his childhood in Canada.

Books about Galbraith

John Kenneth Galbraith and His Critics. By Charles H. Hession. *Norton* 1972 $6.95; *New Am. Lib.* Signet 1972 pap. $1.50

John Kenneth Galbraith and the Lower Economics. By Myron E. Sharpe. *International Arts and Sciences* 1973 $6.00

LÉVI-STRAUSS, CLAUDE. 1908–

"When we make the mistake of thinking that the Savage is governed solely by organic or economic needs, we forget that he levels the same reproach at us, and that to him his own desire for knowledge seems more balanced than ours." With these words the eminent social anthropologist Claude Lévi-Strauss goes to the root of his theory of the equal importance of the societies loosely labeled "primitive" and "civilized."

From his personal studies of "primitive" tribal structures among the Indians of North and South America, Professor Lévi-Strauss demonstrates that each culture has its own system of concepts and categories derived from experience and imposed by the surrounding natural world. The structural patterns, family relationships and social myths that result may vary widely according to whether they develop in an isolated Amazon tribe or in our Western "advanced" society, but the difference is one of kind rather than one of quality. This approach has brought Professor Lévi-Strauss into sharp controversy with other social philosophers such as Jean-Paul Sartre, who trace a historical development, with an implied concept of progress, between primitive and civilized societies.

"The Elementary Structures of Kinship," first published in 1949 but not available in translation from the French until 1969, has long been regarded by anthropologists in all parts of the world as a basic text on the structural development of societies through family relationships and the mores surrounding them. "The Savage Mind" (in French, *"La Pensée Sauvage"*), Lévi-Strauss's exposition of his original theories of mental development in "primitive" societies, bore on the cover of its French edition a picture of the wild pansy, the other meaning of its French title, and included an appendix with a description of the plant. Geoffrey Gorer, reviewing the book for the London *Observer,* says: "This is not merely intellectual playfulness; the contrast between wild uncultivated plants and man-made cultivated varieties underlies much of his argument about the nature of primitive thought and its contrasts with historical logical systems of causality which were developed after the Neolithic revolution, itself founded on cereals selected from the wild varieties."

Lévi-Strauss has spent very little time in the field beyond the few years in Brazil in his youth and some time spent in the United States, and has written only one research monograph; he prefers to compare the structures of societies in his study. His emphasis on the horizontal comparative study of structures is explained in a most interesting article by Sanche de Gramont in the *N.Y. Times Magazine* (Jan. 28, 1968) as follows: "Structuralism, as Lévi-Strauss has used it in his ethnological research, is essentially a way of answering the question, 'How do you play this game?' Imagine someone who has never seen a playing card watching a rubber of bridge. By observing the way the cards are played, he should be able to reconstruct, not only the rules (or structure) of bridge, but the composition (or structure) of a deck of cards. In the same way, the ethnologist observes how marriages are arranged within a tribe and is able to extrapolate certain laws, or structures, that govern the tribe's social organization. 'Structuralism,' says Lévi-Strauss, 'is the search for unsuspected harmonies. It is the discovery of a system of relations latent in a series of objects.' It is based on the idea that human behavior can be classified scientifically, like a plant or a chemical element. There is nothing arbitrary in nature. Why should there be anything arbitrary in man? There must be laws governing human behavior just as there are laws governing pollenization or cellular growth. Lévi-Strauss believes you can study a tribe the same way a biolgist studies an amoeba."

This method, as M. de Gramont points out, "has flowered into the movement called Structuralism with many exotic blossoms. It is being applied indiscriminately to areas for which Lévi-Strauss never intended it. From an ethnological method, it has sprouted into a full-fledged philosophical doctrine whose impassioned partisans insist that all of human knowledge must be re-examined in its light." M. Lévi-Strauss disowns this use of his theory as what he regards as a cultural plaything, but novels and plays are now called "structuralist" and he has found it a term hard to escape.

Professor Lévi-Strauss worked from 1942 to 1945 at the New School for Social Research and the École Libre des Hautes Études, both in New York, and spent a year as Cultural Attaché at the French Embassy in Washington. He is an Honorary Fellow of the Royal Anthropological Institute of Great Britain and Ireland, Foreign Fellow of the American Philosophical Society, and affiliated with learned societies in several other countries. Since 1960 he has been Professor of Social Anthropology at the Collège de France, Paris.

THE ELEMENTARY STRUCTURES OF KINSHIP. 1949. Trans. from the French by James H. Bell and John Von Sturmer; ed. by Rodney Needham. 1962. *Beacon* 1969 pap. $5.95

TRISTES TROPIQUES: An Anthropological Study of Primitive Societies in Brazil. 1955. Trans. by John and Doreen Weightman *Atheneum* 1st complete ed. 1974 $12.50 pap. $3.95

STRUCTURAL ANTHROPOLOGY. 1958. Trans. by C. Jacobson and B. G. Schoepf *Basic Bks.* 1963 $10.75

THE SAVAGE MIND. 1962. *Univ. of Chicago Press* 1966 $5.95 Phoenix Bks. pap. $3.45

TOTEMISM. *Beacon* 1963 pap. $2.95

THE SCOPE OF ANTHROPOLOGY. Trans. and ed. by Sherry D. Paul and Robert A. Paul *Grossman* 1968 $3.00 pap. $1.45

AN INTRODUCTION TO A SCIENCE OF MYTHOLOGY. Trans. by John and Doreen Weightman *Harper* 2 vols. 1969–1973 Vol. 1 The Raw and the Cooked (1969) $12.50 Torchbks. 1970 pap. $2.95 Vol. 2 From Honey to Ashes (1973) $16.00 Torchbks. pap. $3.95. The first volumes available in English; Vol. 3 The Origin of Table Manners and Vol. 4 Man Naked have been published in France.

Books about Lévi-Strauss

Claude Lévi-Strauss: An Introduction. By Octavio Paz. Trans. by J. S. and Maxine Bernstein *Cornell Univ. Press* 1970 $6.95; *Dell* Delta Bks. 1974 pap. $2.25

Claude Lévi-Strauss: The Anthropologist as Hero. Ed. by Nelson E. Hayes and Tanya Hayes. *M.I.T. Press* 1970 $12.50 pap. $2.95

From Symbolism to Structuralism: Lévi-Strauss in a Literary Tradition. By James A. Boon. *Harper* 1972 $11.00 Torchbks. 1972 pap. $3.95

Elementary Structures Reconsidered: Lévi-Strauss on Kinship. By Francis Korn. *Univ. of California Press* 1973 $8.50

"[A] relentless critique of Lévi-Strauss [which] questions not only the theoretical significance, but also the carefulness and correctness of the ethnographic interpretations of that work"— (*Choice*).

Claude Lévi-Strauss. By Edmund Leach. *Viking* rev. ed. 1974 $7.50 pap. $2.95

The Unconscious in Culture: The Structuralism of Claude Lévi-Strauss in Perspective. Ed. by Ino Rossi. *Dutton* 1974 pap. $6.95

RIESMAN, DAVID. 1909–

David Riesman made a national reputation overnight with "The Lonely Crowd," a study of psychological and sociological factors in human gregariousness which is still a classic. "Riesman is utterly prolific with ideas. Where some sociologists need six articles to elaborate one idea, he reverses the proportion. It may be that we shall have to use these ideas as catalysts rather than as conclusions. In any event, we have in Riesman a sociologist with 'style,' a moralist with a new vocabulary, a critic whose judgments illuminate some of the darker corners of the contemporary scene, and a writer whose insights are often spectacular"—(*SR*). After graduating from Harvard Law School, he lived in Washington working as law clerk to Mr. Justice Brandeis in Georgetown. He practised in Boston, Buffalo and New York. He was Professor of Social Science at the University of Chicago and is now Henry Ford II Professor of Social Science at Harvard University. "Culture and Social Character: The Work of David Riesman Reviewed," edited by Seymour M. Lipset and Leo Lowenthal (1961, o.p.), is a discussion by 26 scholars of the theories of Professor Riesman, particularly as expressed in "The Lonely Crowd."

Out of print are: "Individualism Reconsidered" (1954), "Constraint and Variety in American Education" (1957), and "Abundance for What? and Other Essays" (1963).

THE STORY OF MEDICINE IN THE MIDDLE AGES. 1935. *Kelley* $15.00

THE LONELY CROWD: A Study of the Changing American Character. *Yale Univ. Press* 1950 abr. ed. 1960 1969 $12.50 pap. $3.75

(With Nathan Glazer). FACES IN THE CROWD: Individual Studies in Character and Politics. *Yale Univ. Press* 1952 rev. ed. 1964 $25.00 abr. ed. pap. $4.95

(With Christopher Jencks). THE ACADEMIC REVOLUTION. *Doubleday* 1968 $10.00 Anchor Bks. pap. $4.95

Mr. Jencks is a former editorial board member of the *New Republic* now at the Harvard Graduate School of Education. The authors discuss here "the rise to power of professionalism in the universities, particularly on the graduate level, and its effects on higher education generally, graduate and undergraduate, on college policies, programs and goals, and on the structure and expectations of American society as a whole. The main thesis of the volume is that the graduate school, through its growing prestige in the community at large, its intimate connections with government, foundations and business, and its control of teacher appointments in the colleges, has become the determining factor in the shaping, running and philosophy of higher education in America today"—(Eliot Fremont-Smith, in the *N.Y. Times*).

GOODMAN, PAUL.   1911–1972.

In his *N.Y. Times* review of "Like a Conquered Province" (*Random* 1960 Vintage Bks. 1965 pap. $1.95) Thomas Lask called Paul Goodman "the ombudsman of our morality." (Paradoxically, of course, by bourgeois standards his manner of life was outrageously *im*moral.) Throughout his prolific career as novelist, poet, dramatist and social scientist, Mr. Goodman set up his own visionary goals and, since he found our society falling so far short of them, was a drastic, often iconoclastic social critic.

Among his works of fiction (in part autobiographical) are the novels "The Empire City" (*Macmillan* 1964 pap. $2.95), "Making Do" (o.p.), "Adam and His Works: Collected Stories" (*Random* Vintage Bks. 1968 pap. $2.45), and the short stories "Our Visit to Niagara" (1967, o.p.). Books of verse are "The Lordly Hudson" (1962, o.p.), "Hawkweed" (*Random* 1967 $5.95 Vintage Bks. 1967 pap. $1.65), "The Open Look" (*T. Y. Crowell* Funk & Wagnalls 1969 $5.95), "Homespun of Oatmeal Gray" (*Random* 1970 $5.00 Vintage Bks. 1970 pap. $1.95), and "Collected Poems" (*Random* 1974 $12.50). His other literary works include "The Structure of Literature" (*Univ. of Chicago Press* 1954 Phoenix Bks. pap. $2.45), "Three Plays: The Young Disciple, Johan and Faustina" (1965, o.p.) and "Speaking and Language: Defense of Poetry" (*Random* 1972 $6.95 Vintage Bks. 1972 pap. $1.95).

Mr. Goodman's caustic but constructive views of the American establishment, particularly modern American education, have made him what "Current Biography" (1968) calls "the father figure of the New Left." He wrote (in the *N.Y. Review of Books*): "There are, of course, two opposite interpretations of why pedagogy wants to indoctrinate, and in my opinion both are correct. On the one hand, the elders, priests, and schoolteachers are instilling an ideology to support their system of exploitation, including the domination of the old over the young, and they have to make a special effort to confuse and mystify because the system does not recommend itself to common sense. At present, when formal education swallows up so much time of life and pretends to be practical preparation for every activity, ideological processing is especially deadly. Those who succumb to it have no wits of their own left and are robots."

He suggested a permissive "Summerhill" education to the age of 12 and then a chance for children to work at something useful to the community which they themselves can organize, "poking around" in spare time or on the job at what interests them—the only way anyone really learns, he said, and added, "I have often spelled out this program of incidental education and found no takers." Of his seriousness as a social critic, there can be no doubt; clearly some adaptation of his thinking is one way in which education needs to go, providing "at an earlier stage of life than is now possible the qualities of relevance," visible social contribution and the motivation to learn what one is capable of learning and wishes or needs to know while directing one's own activity.

GROWING UP ABSURD. *Random* 1960 $6.95 Vintage Bks. pap. $1.95. The critique of American life and education which first brought him wide public attention.

UTOPIAN ESSAYS AND PRACTICAL PROPOSALS. *Random* 1962. Vintage Bks. pap. $1.95

COMPULSORY MIS-EDUCATION. (And "The Community of Scholars," 1962) *Random* Vintage Bks. pap. $1.95. Students as "the major exploited class." "The Community of Scholars" suggests that colleges retreat from bureaucracy by breaking up into small, intimate units.

PEOPLE OR PERSONNEL. (And "Like a Conquered Province") *Random* 1965 Vintage Bks. pap. $1.95

THE FEDERALIST VERSUS THE JEFFERSONIAN REPUBLICANS. 1967. *Peter Smith* $4.75

(Ed.). ESSAYS ON AMERICAN COLONIAL HISTORY. 1967. *Bks. for Libraries* $20.50; *Holt* (Dryden) 2nd ed. 1972 pap. $6.00; *Peter Smith* $6.00

(With F. O. Gatell). THE AMERICAN COLONIAL EXPERIENCE: An Essay in National Origins. *Peter Smith* $5.50

THE AMERICAN CONSTITUTION. *Wiley* 1970 $7.75 pap. $3.75

(With F. O. Gatell). AMERICA IN THE TWENTIES: The Beginning of Contemporary America. *Holt* 1972 $4.00

(With F. O. Gatell). USA: An American Record. *Holt* (Dryden) 1972 2 vols. pap. each $4.95

FIVE YEARS: Thoughts During a Useless Time. *Random* Vintage Bks. 1969 pap. $1.95. A spiritual autobiography.

NEW REFORMATION: Notes of a Neolithic Conservative. *Random* Vintage Bks. 1971 pap. $1.95

McLUHAN, (HERBERT) MARSHALL. 1911–

Herbert Marshall McLuhan's sudden "rise," in 1966, from years of quiet academic retreat in Toronto to nationwide prominence, television appearances and a prestigious professorship at Fordham, followed several years of popularity with young people as author of "Understanding Media," which became an underground best seller. The theory expounded in this and his other major work, "The Gutenberg Galaxy," is, briefly, that the form of communication used by man at different stages in his progress through history determines his thinking processes and thus the shape and course of society itself. With the invention of the alphabet and the proliferation of the printed word human thought became fixed in linear patterns. As new methods of communication have come along, notably radio and television, fresh concepts have been introduced and new influences brought to bear on human reactions—influences have to do with the mere proliferation of meanings bombarding each of us, rather than their content. Hence Dr. McLuhan's basic dogma, "The medium is the message." By 1967 enough of *his* message (often contradictory and smothered in verbiage) had got through to the general public to make him a general conversation piece. He had, of course, hit upon some timely and astonishing truths.

Beginning conventionally enough, Dr. McLuhan studied in Canada and at Cambridge, and subsequently taught English literature at a number of Catholic institutions in the United States and Canada. By the time his first book, "The Mechanical Bride," appeared in 1951 he had developed his characteristic intellectual style—the transmission of challenging and radical ideas through a rapid-fire series of aphorisms that, even when understood, seemed to admit of little discussion. In television round tables he has often confounded his fellow-discussants mainly by abandoning the rules of conventional logic altogether—an amusing situation for a little, but one which has its limits as communication with other minds and is apt very soon to pall. His appointment to an Albert Schweitzer Professorship at Fordham in 1966 was compounded by the controversy which arose when the State of New York, on legal advice, at the last minute withheld the funds for the professorship from Fordham as a sectarian institution (the University eventually financed the professorship itself). Since then, and the phenomenal success of the mainly visual paperback version of "The Medium Is the Massage," other events have distracted the fickle public and he has been less in the public eye.

Recently there has come a reassuring message from Mr. McLuhan that in spite of all the marvelous new electronic means of communication there will in the future still be room for books. They are, he says, "a very special form of communication" and "will persist." "Clear prose," he once stated, in reference to what goes inside books, "indicates an absence of thought." By this standard his own written work, which has nevertheless stimulated new ways of thinking about a changed and changing world, must be considered among the most thoughtful of the age.

He has written "The Interior Landscape: The Literary Criticism of Marshall McLuhan, 1934–1962" (*McGraw-Hill* 1969 $6.95 pap. $2.95), edited by Eugene McNamara, and with R. J. Schoeck "Voices of Literature: Sounds, Masks, Roles" (*Holt* 1972 pap. $5.25).

THE MECHANICAL BRIDE: Folklore of Industrial Man. *Vanguard* 1951 $12.50; *Beacon* pap. $2.95

An indignant attack on our culture—of media pressures, the life insurance man, the comicscript and the "Ballet Luce." McLuhan "brilliantly" blasts the "commercial magic" of a generation—(Hugh Dalziel Duncan).

(With Edmund Carpenter, Eds.). EXPLORATIONS IN COMMUNICATIONS: An Anthology. Contemporary Communications Ser. *Beacon* 1960 $4.00 pap. $1.95

Twenty-four articles reprinted from *Explorations*, a University of Toronto journal on communications published between 1953 and 1959. Contributors include David Riesman, Robert Graves, Gilbert Seldes, Northrop Frye and Ray Birdwhistell, among others.

THE GUTENBERG GALAXY: The Making of Typographic Man. *Univ. of Toronto Press* 1962 $12.50 pap. $2.75; *New Am. Lib.* 1969 Mentor Bks. pap. $1.50

"With enormous erudition, McLuhan has brought the whole Western intellectual tradition into a single hypothesis: that the basic experience of Western man has been shaped mainly by the invention of type"—(*Educational Leadership*). The bibliography, some 200 annotated entries, "is in every sense a tool that can be used to advantage by any symbol analyst, whatever his interests, and however much he may disagree with McLuhan's views"—(H. D. Duncan).

UNDERSTANDING MEDIA: The Extensions of Man. *McGraw-Hill* 1964 $7.95 pap. $1.95; *New Am. Lib* Mentor Bks. 1973 pap. $1.25

Greeted as revolutionary and "brilliant," if also "fuzzy" and disorganized, "Understanding Media" was for many months after publication an "underground" book among the young. It made Professor McLuhan "the oracle of the electric age." Here he finds that our bombardment by messages of every variety (in which, ultimately, the medium itself *becomes* the message) is transforming a "linear" to a "spatial" culture and making the globe itself a tribal village. Stimulating, irritating, often penetrating, often arguable—if you can climb that slippery pole.

(With others). VERBI-VOCO-VISUAL EXPLORATIONS. *Something Else* 1967 pap. $2.95

This takes its title from an essay by Dr. McLuhan originally published in 1958 in the Toronto magazine *Explorations*, of which he was an editor. In it he first developed the themes of much of his later work. Seven other essays on the same general topic by other hands are included.

(With Harley Parker). THROUGH THE VANISHING POINT: Space in Poetry and Painting. World Perspectives Ser. *Harper* 1968 $7.50 1969 pap. $1.95

"This 37th volume in the World Perspectives series reveals Marshall McLuhan and his co-author, Harley Parker, exploring poetry and painting in an entirely original manner. The book's premise is basic McLuhan—change the environment, change the man—and his perspectives"— (*PW*).

(With Quentin Fiore). WAR AND PEACE IN THE GLOBAL VILLAGE. *McGraw-Hill* 1968 $5.95

"Teaming up once again with his cohorts of the *Medium Is the Massage* . . . Marshall McLuhan has produced this visually and verbally provocative book liberally sprinkled with marginal quotes from *Finnegan's Wake*. He skims over the weighty problems of our troubled world: perplexing, new environments; war; communism; LSD. One of his themes is that violence is a quest for identity inspired by technical innovations. And according to McLuhan, war looms when this identity is threatened"—(*LJ*).

COUNTERBLAST. *Harcourt* 1969 $7.50 Harvest Bks. 1970 pap. $1.95

CULTURE IS OUR BUSINESS. *McGraw-Hill* 1970 $10.00

(With Barrington Nevitt). TAKE TODAY: The Executive as Dropout. *Harcourt* 1972 $9.95

Books about McLuhan

The Sense and Nonsense of Marshall McLuhan. By Sidney Finkelstein. *International Pubs*. 1968 $4.95 pap. $1.45
Marshall McLuhan. By Jonathan Miller. Ed. by Frank Kermode *Viking* 1971 $4.95 pap. $1.75

GARDNER, JOHN W(ILLIAM). 1912–

For his handling of controversial and critical issues in an era of turmoil John Gardner has been called "the calmest voice and coolest mind in American public life"—(James Reston, in the *N.Y. Times*). Mr. Gardner, indeed, has contributed to the search for solutions to America's problems from many points of view: he has been president (for ten years) of the Carnegie Corporation of New York and of the Carnegie Foundation for the Advancement of Teaching, a member of both the Kennedy and Johnson Special Task Forces on Education and Secretary of Health, Education and Welfare under President Johnson. His resignation early in 1968 from his cabinet post was said to have been due to the prospective curtailment of his ambitious programs for welfare and education because of increased government military expenditures. He is presently chairman of Common Cause and a consultant for the Carnegie Corporation.

EXCELLENCE: Can We Be Equal and Excellent Too? *Harper* 1961 $5.95 lg.-type ed. $6.95 Colophon Bks. pap. $1.45

"Mr. Gardner's book has the virtue of going directly to questions that are in the minds of educators, parents, teachers, and students in the schools and colleges and dealing with them sympathetically on the basis of his personal knowledge of the American system as it works"—(*SR*).

SELF-RENEWAL: The Individual and the Innovative Society. *Harper* 1964 $5.95 Colophon Bks. pap. $1.75

"John Gardner is the most perceptive living observer of American society. In warm, hard-hitting wisdom, he defends the major principles and rules by which individuals renew themselves and develop their own creativity, and, by this, develop a self-renewing society. In so doing, he smashes many clichés of the liberal and conservative, and must offend the cultists of decay, self-pity and chaos. No matter, it is high time these things were said and no one is in better position than John Gardner to say them"—(Adolf A. Berle).

No Easy Victories. Ed. by Helen Rowan *Harper* 1968 Colophon Bks. 1970

"Helen Rowan . . . chose aphoristic paragraphs from Mr. Gardner's best talks and articles. The result is the most readable foray into America's public affairs and private hangups I've seen this year. No one else on the national scene makes so much sense with such disarming grace"— (Charles Poore, in the *N.Y. Times*).

Recovery of Confidence. *Norton* 1970 $5.00

A "discussion of the ability of Americans to deal effectively with problems in the areas of peace, discrimination, poverty, and pollution control"—*(BRD)*.

In Common Cause. *Norton* 1972 $3.95

"In 1970 Gardner formed an organization called Common Cause which promised to lobby in the public's interest by attacking specific evils in the government and trying to make things more equitable for the average citizen"—*(LJ)*.

LEWIS, OSCAR. 1914–1970.

Called by different critics a work of "unique concentration and sympathy," "extraordinary," "gripping" and "burningly relevant to the world in which we live," "The Children of Sanchez" was thus reviewed by R. S. H. Crossman in the *New Statesman:* "Here at last is a social scientist who neither explains poverty nor sits in judgment on it. Here is a liberal free from that patronizing sympathy with which so many progressives vitiate their approach to 'backward' peoples. . . . Concentrating on the Sanchez family, he has narrowed his researches to a single drop in the turbulent waters of Mexican poverty. But a living understanding of one family teaches us far more about the nature of poverty than a tome of sociological generalizations about the Mexican working class. . . . Whether judged as literature or as sociology, 'The Children of Sanchez' is a masterpiece." The book received the Child Study Association of America Family Life Award in 1961 and the Brotherhood Award of the National Conference of Christians and Jews in 1962.

"*La Vida*," which won a 1966 National Book Award and the 1967 *Saturday Review*-Anisfield-Wolf Award for significant contributions to intergroup relations, is "the first complete portrait of a [large] Puerto Rican family in the slums of San Juan and in New York. [It has] an actuality, a vividness, and an impact that will reverberate in the mind . . . in the disturbing and complex ways in which characters in a superior novel keep coming back unbidden"—(Nat Hentoff, in the *New Yorker*). A social anthropologist specializing in the study of rural societies, Dr. Lewis was born in New York City, took his doctorate at Columbia, taught at Brooklyn College and Washington University, and was Professor of Anthropology at the University of Illinois.

The Big Four. *Knopf* 1938 $8.95; *Ballantine Bks*. 1974 pap. $1.65

Effects of White Contact Upon Blackfoot Culture, with Special Reference to the Role of the Fur Trade. *Univ. of Washington Press* 1942 $7.00

Silver Kings. *Knopf* 1947 $5.95

Tepoztián: Village in Mexico. *Holt* 1960 pap. $3.00

Life in a Mexican Village: Tepoztián Restudied. *Univ. of Illinois Press* 1951 1963 pap. $3.95; *Peter Smith* $6.00

Five Families: Mexican Case Studies in the Culture of Poverty. *Basic Bks.* 1959 $10.00 *New Am. Lib.* Mentor Bks. 1971 pap. $.95

The Children of Sanchez: Autobiography of a Mexican Family. *Random* 1961 $12.50 Vintage Bks. pap. $2.95

Pedro Martinez: A Mexican Peasant and His Family. *Random* 1964 Vintage Bks. 1964 pap. $3.45

"A moving tape-recorded story"—*(LJ)*.

San Francisco: Mission to Metropolis. *Howell-North Bks.* 1966 $6.95

La Vida: A Puerto Rican Family in the Culture of Poverty, San Juan and New York. *Random* 1966 $12.50 Vintage Bks. pap. $2.95

A Study in Slum Culture: Backgrounds for "*La Vida.*" *Random* 1968 $7.95. A statistical frame of reference.

Death in the Sanchez Family. *Random* 1969 $4.95 Vintage Bks. 1970 pap. $1.95

Anthropological Essays. *Random* 1970 $12.95

WARD, BARBARA. 1914–   *See Chapter 9, History, Government and Politics—*
Modern and World, this Vol.

CLARK, KENNETH BANCROFT. 1914–

"Today it has become fashionable, as the civil rights movement grows in fervor, to move from appeasement to a stance of defiance, a new fantasy of *militancy*. But . . . it is clear—or ought to be—that American society would not sustain a separate black nation." In his book "Dark Ghetto" Dr. Kenneth B. Clark thus epitomizes the position he has taken in the current struggles of white and black to understand one another in America.

A distinguished black teacher and psychologist, Dr. Clark has been a member of the Psychology Department of City College, New York, since 1942. He is also a member of the New York State Board of Regents and a founder of the Northside Center for Child Development and Harlem Youth Opportunities Unlimited (HARYOU). Some of the formative influences in his life have been his mother, a shop steward for the International Ladies Garment Workers Union in a New York sweatshop ("I guess my first contact with social issues was listening to Mama tell of her difficulties in organizing a union in her shop"); Dr. Ralph J. Bunche, under whom he studied political science at Howard University; and Gunnar Myrdal (*q.v.*), with whom he worked for two years on the study of the American Negro problem which resulted in Myrdal's "An American Dilemma."

As black power militancy has grown and positions have hardened, Dr. Clark has made himself increasingly known as one who, while totally committed to equality and justice for Afro-Americans, is totally opposed to any doctrine of separatism for black and white. In May 1969, Antioch College, of which Dr. Clark was a trustee, established a "racially organized and exclusionary" Afro-American Studies Institute—as Dr. Clark described it. In his resignation as trustee Dr. Clark wrote: "There is absolutely no evidence to support the contention that the inherent damage to human beings of primitive exclusion on the basis of race is any less damaging when demanded or enforced by the previous victims than when imposed by the dominant group."

PREJUDICE AND YOUR CHILD. *Beacon* 1963 pap. $1.95; *Peter Smith* $4.25

DARK GHETTO: Dilemmas of Social Power. Fwd. by Gunnar Myrdal *Harper* 1965 $6.95
Torchbks. pap. $1.75

"Dark Ghetto is based on Dr. Clark's personal experiences and a report he prepared while serving as chief consultant to Harlem Youth Opportunities Unlimited (HARYOU), which was financed by the President's Committee on Juvenile Delinquency and the city of New York. In probing the pathologies of Harlem, Dr. Clark, professor of psychology at the City College of New York, analyzes the poverty, crime, low aspirations, family instability, and exploitation of the degraded humans who are 'social victims' of a world for which they are not responsible. In using Harlem as the symbol of the dark ghetto, Dr. Clark presents facts about political, religious, economic, and intellectual leadership that raises many more questions about the effectiveness of social work agencies and public school teachers and administrators in dealing with problems of the ghetto. It is evident that research is only beginning to answer some of the many questions related to victims of poverty, who are ironically surrounded by an affluent society. The fallacy that inhabitants of the ghetto are responsible for their own condition is destroyed in this work. This in itself is a major contribution"—(*LJ*).

(With Talcott Parsons, Eds.). THE NEGRO AMERICAN. Introds. by the editors; fwd. by
Lyndon B. Johnson; sel. and introd. by Arthur Trottenberg; photographs by Bruce
Davidson. 1966. *Beacon* pap. $3.95

"The reviewer wants to state emphatically without any further ado that every library owes it to its readers to add this book to its collection. [This] offers one of the best and the most scholarly explorations of [the subject.] The editors have brought together a galaxy of experts on the historical, political, economic, educational, sociological and psychological aspects of this many-sided issue. In coverage this collection of 30 essays is equivalent to several books. In its up-to-dateness it has no rivals. The reader is spared all unnecessary appeals to his moral sense. He is assumed to be a person of goodwill already and possessed of an earnest outlook on our social world. This work could also serve as a basic textbook in a college course on the American Negro"—(*LJ*).

(With Jeannette Hopkins). RELEVANT WAR AGAINST POVERTY: A Study of Community
Action Programs and Observable Social Change. *Harper* 1969 $6.95

(With Alex C. Sherriffs). HOW RELEVANT IS EDUCATION IN AMERICA TODAY? *American
Enterprise* 1970 pap. $5.75

(With MARC Staff). A POSSIBLE REALITY. *Emerson Hall* 1972 $6.95

THE PATHOS OF POWER. *Harper* 1974 $7.95

"Clark's literate and readable reflections on social power ... are re-presented here. His examination of the dilemma of modern man is original and perceptive and leads to the real crux of the book: psychology and the social sciences have not yet fully accepted their responsibility for actively contributing to the creative use of power for humanity"—(*LJ*).

HEYERDAHL, THOR. 1914– *See Chapter 12, Travel and Adventure, this Vol.*

MILLS, C(HARLES) WRIGHT. 1916–1962.

"No American sociologist in this century has shaken the ivory towers of the conservative academicians more than the late C. Wright Mills, who, in his brief 45 years of life, brought the study of society out of cloud-cuckoo-land into the arena of practical politics and public concern. There is a wide popular acceptance of Mr. Mills's basic point—that America is run by a combination of 'the high military, the corporation executives, and the political directorate' "—(*LJ*). In "Power, Politics and People" the "essays are grouped around four central aspects of Mills' thought. First is the concept of power. Second is the matter of politics, especially the long-term implications of liberalism and conservatism, and liberalism and Marxism. Third is the question of people. Mills was fascinated by human society and wrote a number of articles and essays on love and marriage, the dilemma of the modern city, and the problems of today's intellectual. Finally, there is a section that presents Mills' important contributions to the sociology of knowledge"— (Publisher's note). At the time of his death, C. Wright Mills was Associate Professor of Sociology at Columbia University and widely recognized both here and abroad as one of the most stimulating critics of modern civilization.

POWER, POLITICS AND PEOPLE: The Collected Essays of C. Wright Mills. Ed. by Irving Louis Horowitz *Oxford* 1963 $12.50 Galaxy Bks. 1967 pap. $4.95

"This volume of collected essays points not only to the concreteness but also the range and depth of Mills' concern with the social world. . . . These selections are fine examples of the areas of Mills' interests; they reveal his clarity of thought and his precision of expression, two highly desirable virtues for a sociologist"—(*Commonweal*).

THE NEW MEN OF POWER. 1948. *Kelley* $10.00

(With Clarence Senior and Rose Kohn Goldsen). PUERTO RICAN JOURNEY: New York's Newest Migrants. 1950. *Russell & Russell* 1967 $13.50

WHITE COLLAR: The American Middle Classes. *Oxford* 1951 $10.00 Galaxy Bks. 1956 pap. $2.95. A complete documentation of the malaise of our time.

(With Hans Gerth, Eds.). CHARACTER AND SOCIAL STRUCTURE: The Psychology of Social Institutions. *Harcourt* 1953 Harbinger Bks. pap. $3.95

THE POWER ELITE. *Oxford* 1956 $10.50 Galaxy Bks. 1959 pap. $2.95. The style of life of the men and women at the pinnacles of fame and power in mid-century America.

THE SOCIOLOGICAL IMAGINATION. *Oxford* 1959 $7.59 Galaxy Bks. 1967 pap. $1.95

(Ed.). IMAGES OF MAN. *Braziller* 1960 $7.50

THE MARXISTS. *Dell* (orig.) 1962 Laurel Leaf Lib. pap. $1.50

SOCIOLOGY AND PRAGMATISM: The Higher Learning in America. Ed. by Irving L. Horowitz *Oxford* 1964 $12.50 Galaxy Bks. 1966 pap. $3.95

Books about Mills

The New Sociology: Essays in Social Science and Social Theory, in Honor of C. Wright Mills. Ed. by Irving L. Horowitz. *Oxford* 1964 $12.50 Galaxy Bks. pap. $3.95
C. Wright Mills and the Power Elite. Ed. by G. William Domhoff and Hoyt B. Ballard. *Beacon* 1968 $7.50 pap. $2.95
"Critical essays on C. Wright Mills' book, 'The Power Elite' (1956). The editors have followed Mills' classification of his critics as liberal, radical, or highbrow, and have added a reply to criticism written by Mills in 1957, as well as a summary essay by G. W. Domhoff. The result is an interesting cross-section of current thinking on an important subject"—(*PW*).

BELL, DANIEL. 1919–

With Carnegie Corporation support, Columbia's noted sociologist was appointed a "committee of one" to study and propose reforms for the practice and theory of general and liberal education at Columbia, Harvard and Chicago. The result of his year-long project is his award-winning "The Reforming of General Education," in which he asserts that general education must change according to the changing character of knowledge and of society since the American university now is a politico-social organism. "What Oxford and Cambridge were to England in the time of its greatness, so Harvard, California, Columbia, and other national universities are now to the world-powerful United States. The all-important difference is that the forms of education in which the English universities excelled—the individual tutorial, classical studies, humanistically oriented history and politics, and philosophy—are precisely the areas which seem least useful and relevant to the going concerns of our present national society"—(Henry David Aiken, in the *N.Y. Review of Books*).

Bell regards the understanding of self in a historical context as a necessary and fundamental result of liberal education. "An integrated mind, fully awake to its own more ultimate concerns and aware of its own human possibilities, is, at all stages of its educational development, more than an intra-cranial meeting place for the disciplining of disciplines. Knowledge of forms of scholarly inquiry and learning will serve at best only to relate those same investigations to each other. But the contemporary university student needs and demands something else as well. To be sure, he wants help toward an understanding of the connections between, say, the methods of physical science and those of sociology or between the findings of the economic historian and those of the historian of English literature. He wants also to know the wisdom that may lie in the study of such connections. He wants not only to tie the academic strands together, but to tie his knowledge of them and their methods back into his developing experience as a human being. He wants to know what they portend as forms of life, both for him and for his kind"—(Aiken).

Dr. Bell was a member of the committee which prepared and organized the inception of a faculty-student senate at Columbia, where he taught for ten years. He was the chairman of the American Academy of Arts and Sciences' Commission for the Year 2000. He has been a Professor of Sociology at Harvard since 1969. A former managing editor of the *New Leader* and labor editor of *Fortune* for ten years, Dr. Bell also serves on the editorial board of *The American Scholar* and *Daedalus*.

MARXIAN SOCIALISM IN THE U.S. Studies in American Civilization Ser. *Princeton Univ. Press* 1952 pap. $2.95

THE END OF IDEOLOGY: On the Exhaustion of Political Ideas in the Fifties. *Macmillan* (Free Press) 1960 $9.50 pap. $2.95

(Ed.). THE RADICAL RIGHT. 1963. *Bks. for Libraries* $14.50; *Doubleday* 1963 Anchor Bks. pap. $2.50

An expanded and updated version of "The New American Right" (1955), this book of essays examines the principles and people behind McCarthyism. Authors include the editor, Richard Hofstadter, David Riesman, Nathan Glazer, Peter Viereck, Talcott Parsons, Alan Westin, Herbert Hyman and Seymour Lipset.

THE REFORMING OF GENERAL EDUCATION: The Columbia College Experience in Its National Setting. Fwd. by David B. Truman *Columbia* 1966 $10.00

This "offers by far the most articulate presentation by a university . . . man of the problems and possibilities of liberal education in the university age. . . . Bell's major innovating idea . . . is that *the* indispensable education, which a liberally endowed university college alone can adequately provide—whether in courses conducted under general education auspices or in the more specialized offerings of academic departments—should be a continuous, increasingly sophisticated training in the methods of inquiry and learning which the (natural) sciences, the social sciences, and the humanities respectively exemplify"—(Henry David Aiken, in the *N.Y. Review of Books*). It received the 1966 Book Award from the American Council on Education for a significant contribution to the knowledge and advancement of higher education in the United States.

(Ed.). TOWARD THE YEAR 2000: Work in Progress. *Houghton* 1968 $7.95; *Beacon* 1969 pap. $3.95

In these essays, originally published in *Daedalus*, the members of the Commission for the Year 2000, of which Dr. Bell was chairman, speculate on problems in a variety of areas, suggesting ideas for "alternative futures." Among those represented are Herman Kahn, Anthony Wiener, Daniel Moynihan, Erik Erikson and Margaret Mead.

THE COMING OF POST-INDUSTRIAL SOCIETY: A Venture in Social Forecasting. *Basic Bks.* 1973 $12.50

GOFFMAN, ERVING. 1922–

"One of the greatest writers alive today is a man whom our culture hardly knows, the sociologist Erving Goffman. He was born in Toronto, educated at Chicago, taught at Berkeley in its Free Speech Movement days. Wherever he has been, he has been virtually anonymous. He has taken no part in political or cultural affairs. He does not speak at conferences or appear on talk shows. He almost never allows himself to be photographed. He has written eight books in the last 12 years, but they have all been organized in densely academic formats, written in a remote, pedantic style, and apparently aimed at limited, specialized audiences. In his books, as in his life, he projects a persona of utter impersonality. In fact, ironically, this apparent impersonality only heightens all that is most personal, and most powerful, in his vision of life"—(Marshall Berman, in the *N.Y. Times Bk. Review*). Since 1968 Goffman has been Benjamin Franklin Professor of Anthropology and Sociology at the University of Pennsylvania.

THE PRESENTATION OF SELF IN EVERYDAY LIFE. *Doubleday* Anchor Bks. (orig.) 1959 pap. $2.50; *Overlook Press* 1974 $10.00. A number of interpersonal games, set routines govern how people function.

ASYLUMS: Essays on the Social Situation of Mental Patients and Other Inmates. *Aldine* 1961 $12.95; *Doubleday* Anchor Bks. 1961 pap. $2.95

ENCOUNTERS: Two Studies in the Sociology of Interaction. *Bobbs* (orig.) 1961 pap. $2.95

BEHAVIOR IN PUBLIC PLACES: Notes on the Social Organization of Gatherings. *Macmillan* (Free Press) 1963 $7.95 pap. $2.95

STIGMA: Notes on the Management of Spoiled Identity. *Prentice-Hall* Spectrum Bks. (orig.) 1963 pap. $1.95; *Aronson* 1974 $7.50. The focus is on everyday social relations that cause discomfort and embarrassments.

INTERACTION RITUAL: Essays on Face-to-Face Behavior. *Doubleday* Anchor Bks. (orig.) 1967 pap. $2.95; *Aldine* 1967 $10.95

His earliest essays "On Face-Work," "The Nature of Deference and Demeanor" and "Embarrassment and Social Interaction" published in 1955 which undertake to interpret everyday life as a 'ritual order' "—(*N.Y. Times Bk. Review*).

RELATIONS IN PUBLIC: Micro Studies of the Public Order. *Basic Bks.* 1971 $8.65; *Harper* Colophon Bks. 1972 pap. $2.45. Observations of the ways people behave in public places, their social interactions and ritual enactments in everyday situations.

STRATEGIC INTERACTION. *Univ. of Pennsylvania Press* 1971 $8.50 pap. $2.95; *Ballantine Bks.* 1972 pap. $1.50

FRAME ANALYSIS: An Essay on the Organization of Experience. *Harvard Univ. Press* 1974 $12.50; *Harper* Colophon Bks. 1974 pap. $3.95

"A sophisticated description of what Goffman takes to be 'the basic frameworks of understanding available in our society for making sense out of events'. The book has the sensitivity and richness of detail and the exquisite moral vulnerability one expects from Goffman: it places these qualities . . . into a new psychological and philosophical framework of greatly expanded scope"—(*LJ*).

KAHN, HERMAN.   1922–

Variously thought of as the "Clausewitz of the nuclear age," "a ruthless mathematician," and one of the acknowledged models from which "Dr. Strangelove" was drawn, Herman Kahn is the director of the Hudson Institute, one of the best known of the 100 or so Federal Contract Research Centers or "think tanks." In the peaceful reaches of upper Westchester, New York, Mr. Kahn and his staff apply mathematical and scientific methods to the intensive study of "software"—the human element of military strategy—in an age of nuclear warfare.

According to Mr. Kahn, "Our primary focus . . . is on major policy issues, and we believe that our job is to emphasize rather speculative areas of study. . . . Our most basic objective is to stimulate the imagination." Studies of the feasibility of blast shelters and civil defense systems have led him to more fundamental considerations of nuclear rivalries, deterrence and ultimately of the predictable effects of nuclear warfare. To critics who contend, like Erich Fromm (*q.v.*), that such preoccupation with thermonuclear war makes its occurrence more likely, Mr. Kahn responds that thinking about peace has little effect on those responsible for making war, while thinking about war may possibly contribute to preserving peace. His essays in "Thinking About the Unthinkable" follow this line of thought. "You'll never get people to understand what's confusing," he says, "unless you make it stark." His "scenarios" conjure up various possibilities as the outcome of a given situation and develop each to provide alternatives for planning. "On Thermonuclear War" discusses the theory of deterrence—the theory that adequate knowledge of the enemy's capability for attack prevents hair-trigger nuclear response to "provocation." "A thermonuclear balance of terror," he says, "is equivalent to the signing of a nonaggression treaty which states that neither the Soviets nor the Americans will initiate an all-out attack, no matter how provoking the other side may become."

Mr. Kahn has been a close Presidential adviser and governmental consultant and is taken seriously even by the Russians, who saw in an article of his in *Fortune* "How to Think About the Russians," confirmation of an American threat against East Germany, Poland and Czechoslovakia. Elsewhere he and his institute have been the frequent butt of satire in the films "Dr. Strangelove," "Fail Safe" and "The War Game."

ON THERMONUCLEAR WAR. *Princeton Univ. Press* 1961 $20.00; *Macmillan* (Free Press) 2nd ed. 1969 pap. $3.95

THINKING ABOUT THE UNTHINKABLE. *Avon Bks.* 1964 pap. $1.65

ON ESCALATION: Metaphors and Scenarios. *Praeger* 1965 1969 $7.50

EMERGING JAPANESE SUPERSTATE: Challenge and Response. *Prentice-Hall* 1970 $8.55 Spectrum Bks. 1971 pap. $2.45

(With B. Bruce-Biggs). THINGS TO COME: Thinking about the Seventies and Eighties. *Macmillan* 1972 $6.95

(Ed.). THE FUTURE OF THE CORPORATION. *Mason & Lipscomb* 1974 $8.95

HARRINGTON, MICHAEL.   1928–

Michael Harrington's "The Other America" sold over half a million copies and brought its author into national prominence. It shocked the nation into realizing the extent to which its affluence was creating poverty—whose grim American face he painted in all-too-convincing detail. As the rich became richer, Mr. Harrington pointed out, the poor became poorer—and ever less able to escape from the vicious circle of want and ignorance and the accompanying disease, crime and degradation. "The Other America" has been credited with being the chief inspiration of the War on Poverty, and its author was (in 1964) consultant to Sargent Shriver's Task Force on Poverty; he later performed the same function for Mayor John V. Lindsay of New York. He has recently called the federal project a "highly inadequate, highly conditioned program [in which] poverty won." "The Accidental Century" is a study of the "accidental" revolutions of our age. Produced with the backing—moral and financial—of the Center for the Study of Democratic Institutions, it is "an exciting book on the history of ideas" which ends "on a note of hope," says *Library Journal.* Mr. Harrington, it continues, "notes the importance of the public service sector of the economy; the recognition that going to school is an economically productive function, and the realization that not working, for the young and the old, is becoming a social necessity. 'If there is to be a humane outcome to the contemporary Western adventure,' [says the author,] the 19th-century socialists 'will have to be right in their faith that the people can freely and democratically take control of their own lives and society.' "

In "Toward a Democratic Left," Mr. Harrington notes that the new priorities of President Johnson's Great Society program, or what is left of it, are actually a continuation of Franklin Roosevelt's New Deal policies, but that the Big Business complex which has emerged since World War II is becoming concerned about social problems: "What was considered 'socialism' only yesterday," he says, "is turning into sound business investment." Business must become a part of a New Democratic Left, which is largely to be welded from *all* the forces opposing the Congressional Conservative Republican-Dixiecrat bloc. But business must stop looking for a return on its investment: "The democratic Left must not only commit itself to 'uneconomic' investments in human beings but must do so in such a way as to increase the quality of the society." Mr. Harrington goes on: "What is needed in addition is action to create an environment in which it is more 'natural' to help one's fellow man than to profit from him. An analysis of international and domestic social issues shows over and over that there is an objective need for more public, as opposed to private, investment; for social, as opposed to individual, consumption; and for giving aesthetic and other non-commercial values a claim on material resources. For as the social, non-profit and aesthetic sectors of the society expand, more and more people will be able to live their lives and express themselves in the actual practice of a cooperative, rather than a competitive, ethic. And that fact will be the most powerful sermon of all."

Mr. Harrington is no newcomer to the field of helping the poor to help themselves; he has been actively working at it most of his adult life. After graduating from Holy Cross College he attended Yale Law School briefly, received his M.A. in English at the University of Chicago and joined Dorothy Day's Catholic Worker movement—a radical Catholic pacifist group which dedicates itself, among other activities, to living in poverty and providing food and hospitality for "bums," drug addicts and the outcasts of our society. He became an associate editor of its organ, the *Catholic Worker*, and later a contributing editor of *Dissent.* A resident of New York City, he has been since 1967 a board member of the A. Philip Randolph Institute and since 1965 has served as a consultant to the Fund for the Republic. He is chairman of the League for Industrial Democracy. Many articles by him have appeared in *Commentary, Commonweal, Harper's, Look* and the *Partisan Review*. In 1963 "The Other America" won him the George Polk and the Sidney Hillman Foundation Awards. He received the Riordan Award of the Washington Newspaper Guild in 1964 and an honorary Doctor of Humane Letters from Bard College in 1966. He is presently a Professor of Political Science at Queens College in New York City.

THE OTHER AMERICA: Poverty in the United States. *Macmillan* 1962 rev. ed. 1970 $7.95; *Penguin* Pelican Bks. 1962 pap. $1.45

"One of those rare books that directly influence political action"—(Eliot Fremont-Smith, in the *N.Y. Times*).

THE RETAIL CLERKS. *Wiley* (orig.) 1962 pap. $3.25

THE ACCIDENTAL CENTURY. *Macmillan* 1965 $7.95; *Penguin* Pelican Bks. pap. $1.45

TOWARD A DEMOCRATIC LEFT: A Radical Program for a New Majority. *Macmillan* 1968 $5.95; *Penguin* Pelican Bks. 1969 pap. $1.25

"A manifesto as well as a radical critique and polemic"—*(Newsweek)*.

SOCIALISM. *Saturday Review Press* 1972 $12.50; *Bantam* 1973 pap. $2.25

"Harrington here means to write a definition, history and prognosis of socialism and, except for the last, he has done this very well"—*(Newsweek)*.

(With Irving Howe). THE SEVENTIES: Problems and Proposals. *Harper* 1972 $12.50 Colophon Bks. 1973 pap. $4.45

FRAGMENTS OF THE CENTURY. *Saturday Review Press* 1974 $7.95

The author is concerned with "such varied 20th-Century phenomena as the death of God, the New Left, psychoanalysis, the SDS, racial violence, and the role that socialists and communists have played in our political process. His narrative is also filled with . . . sketches of numerous political and labor leaders"—*(LJ)*.

(With T. F. Lindsay). THE CONSERVATIVE PARTY, 1918–1970. *St. Martin's* 1974 $15.95

KING, MARTIN LUTHER, Jr.   1929–1968   (Nobel Peace Prize 1964)

The tragic assassination of the Rev. Dr. Martin Luther King, Jr. in April 1968, removed from the American scene the man of his time with the greatest potential for constructive solutions to the bitter problems of race in the American community. A strong and tireless fighter for black justice and equality, his principles rooted in nonviolence and a religion of brotherhood and tolerance, Dr. King had the confidence of the majority of blacks and whites alike. The voices raised against him came from extremists, few but vocal on both sides of the color barrier. The full tragedy of his death lies in the fact that it gave them rein and stilled forever that steadfast, rational, compassionate Christian voice, whose power to curb the violence it decried will not soon be equaled.

As minister of the Dexter Avenue Baptist Church in Montgomery, Ala., in the mid-fifties, Dr. King while still very young dramatically moved to the forefront of the civil rights movement through his leadership of the Montgomery bus boycott. By the time this particular fight was won and the Supreme Court, in 1956, declared the Alabama segregation laws unconstitutional, he was recognized as a national figure.

His further efforts to challenge unjust laws by peaceful means through the Southern Christian Leadership Conference, which he headed, put his personal stamp of nonviolent action on the entire civil rights movement. Far from passive, and closely modeled on Gandhi's theory of civil disobedience, his method was to bring pressure for racial justice by marches, sit-ins, pray-ins, consultations with government, even periods in prison. Perhaps his most triumphant moment was at the fine and peaceful 1963 March on Washington, when from the steps of the Lincoln Memorial Dr. King made the ringing "I have a dream" speech to the thousands of black and white citizens assembled there. The triumph, of course, was in the new *sharing* of the dream—a dream not yet fulfilled and still a matter of pain and struggle. The following year he was awarded the Nobel Peace Prize.

It was his passionate commitment to peaceful solutions, coupled with his increasing conviction that the civil and economic fate of black people was inextricably linked with those of that nation at large that led Dr. King eventually to make one of his chief objectives the ending of the war in Vietnam. He felt that while billions of dollars annually were being poured into controversial military expenditures the massive support required to make the "Great Society" poverty programs effective and end the ghetto slums could never be financed. He felt, too, that the war was sapping the American moral fiber and bringing untold cruelty to distant Asians at our hands and degrading America in the process.

It seemed for a while as though the shock of this great leader's assassination might actually accelerate some of the positive actions he had so long fought for. But memories are short, and these words, taken from one of Dr. King's addresses, are still all too relevant: "America, you've strayed away. You've trampled over nineteen millions of your brethren. All men are created equal. Not some men. Not white men. All men. America, rise up and come home."

STRIDE TOWARD FREEDOM: The Montgomery Story. *Harper* 1958 $4.95

THE MEASURE OF A MAN. 1959. *United Church* 1968 $2.95. A collection of meditations and prayers concerned with man and the essence of life. Published as a memorial edition.

WHY WE CAN'T WAIT. *Harper* 1964 $6.95; *New Am. Lib.* Signet pap. $.95

"This book might well be entitled 'From Birmingham to Washington' for it details the story of the Birmingham demonstrations and the March on Washington by America's Negroes. In a clear, lucid style, filled with facts, Dr. King spells out the reason for Negro demonstrations, the why of Freedom Now, and the frustration that breeds impatience"—(*LJ*).

WHERE DO WE GO FROM HERE: Chaos or Community. *Harper* 1967 $6.95; *Beacon* pap. $1.95

"Unlike some of his earlier writings, the strength and appeal of Martin Luther King's fourth book . . . lie in its moderate, judicious, constructive, pragmatic tone. In the place of fire there is the light of intelligence. In the place of a passionate '*J'accuse*' there is a reasoned plea for collaboration"—(Milton R. Konvitz, in *SR*).

THE TRUMPET OF CONSCIENCE. *Harper* 1968 $6.95

Five speeches originally given over the Canadian Broadcasting Corporation network in late 1967, dealing with Dr. King's view of the war in Vietnam, and advocating new, massive civil disobedience in protest.

Books about King

What Manner of Man: A Biography of Martin Luther King, Jr. By Lerone Bennett, Jr. *Johnson Pub.* 1964 1968 $5.95; *Simon & Schuster* (Pocket Books) 1968 pap. $.95
To Kill a Black Man. By Louis Lomax. *Holloway* 1968 pap. $.95
Martin Luther King, Jr. By William Robert Miller. *Avon Bks.* 1969 pap. $1.25
My Life with Martin Luther King, Jr. By Coretta S. King. *Holt* 1969 $6.95; *Avon Bks.* 1970 pap. $1.50. The moving account by his gifted widow, who has carried on his work.
I Have a Dream: The Life and Times of Martin Luther King, Jr. By Lenwood G. Davis. *Adams* (orig.) 1969 pap. $4.95; *Greenwood* 1973 $12.75
Martin Luther King, Jr.: A Profile. Ed. by C. Eric Lincoln. American Profiles Ser. *Farrar, Straus* (Hill & Wang) 1970 pap. $1.95
Marching to Freedom: The Life of Martin Luther King, Jr. Ed. by Robert M. Bleiweiss. *New Am. Lib.* Signet 1971 pap. $.95
An American Death. By Gerold Frank. *Bantam* 1973 pap. $1.95
The Search for the Beloved Community: The Thinking of Martin Luther King, Jr. By Kenneth L. Smith and Ira G. Zepp, Jr. *Judson Press* 1974 $6.95
The Trial of Martin Luther King. By Alan Westin and Barry Mahoney. *T. Y. Crowell* 1974 $5.95

CLEAVER, ELDRIDGE. 1935–

Of Eldridge Cleaver's "Soul on Ice" Kenneth B. Clark (*q.v.*) wrote: "Cleaver's explicit and implicit diagnoses of the moral dry rot which mocks our democracy may be an even more valid diagnosis of the nature and future of our civilization than all of the discussion of our affluence and our military power. The publication of this book might contribute to the understanding of our chronic urban eruptions—if we still have the capacity to understand and if we still have the ethical strength to do anything about our understanding." "Soul on Ice," a series of personal essays and letters written from a California prison, is "about being imprisoned in white America; about white women and black men, and above all about a tomorrow of black men and black women. [It] comes through as the manifesto of a revolution Eldridge Cleaver is leading"—(Maxwell Geismar, in the introduction).

This former minister of information for the militant group known as the Black Panthers, past candidate for the U.S. Presidential nomination of the Peace and Freedom Party, former convict and bail jumper, has been called by *Time* "an authentically gifted prose stylist capable of evoking picturesque images and fiery moods." As well as an author of books, Mr. Cleaver has been a staff writer for *Ramparts* magazine and has made numerous contributions to *Esquire*, *Black Dialogue*, the *Liberator* and *Mademoiselle*, but he considers his real vocation that of a "full-time revolutionary in the struggle for black liberation in America."

Mr. Cleaver's writing is uncompromising in the hatred it expresses for white oppression and he does not hesitate to say precisely what he means: "There's pain, there's suffering, there's death, and I see no justification for waiting until tomorrow to say what you could say tonight."

The public has had mixed reactions to this militant leader, and he was in September-October 1968 a controversial subject at the University of California, Berkeley, where a group of students and faculty members supported his participation in an experimental studies course in the face of opposition by Governor Reagan and the Board of Regents. The University, however, backed him and the Board of Regents overruled the Governor's attempt to force Berkeley to cancel the lectures. By late October 1968, however, he was about to be returned to jail as a violator of the parole granted him after a period of imprisonment, 1958–1966 (for assault and attempted murder), on the grounds that he had been a party to an April 1968 incident in which two people were killed. Associate Justice Thurgood Marshall handed down the Supreme Court opinion that he should be returned to jail, but Mr. Cleaver had in the meantime disappeared. After a self-imposed exile in Cuba, Algeria and France, he returned to this country in November 1975, prepared to face the old charges of parole violation and assault. "It's a new situation now," he said, according to *Time Magazine*, "Black people have undergone a fundamental change for the better. I've got two kids, I'm almost bald, I've got gray hair, and my political ideas have become refined. Living under dictatorships gives you a more balanced picture of what's going on in the world."

Cleaver was born in Little Rock, Arkansas, and raised in the Los Angeles ghettos. It was during his nine years in prison that he formulated his black power philosophy. Although he is not a stranger to violence, he is against it. "Guns are ugly," he said. "People are what's beautiful; and when you use a gun to kill someone, you're doing something ugly." Lindsay Patterson has described his views in the *N.Y. Times*: "Unlike some militants who have no plan or design other than to level society and kill off whites (and then what, another Biafra?), Cleaver realizes that a coalition of responsible persons is needed. . . . 'We start with the basic principle,' says Cleaver, 'that every man, woman and child on the face of the earth deserves the very highest standard of living that human knowledge and technology is capable of providing. Period. No more than that, no less than that.' " That he is a brilliant and powerful writer and interpreter of his people, there can be no doubt.

SOUL ON ICE. Introd. by Maxwell Geismar *McGraw-Hill* 1968 $6.50; *Dell* pap. $.95 Delta Bks. pap. $1.95. The book which brought him national attention.

BLACK PAPERS. *McGraw-Hill* 1969 $4.95

POST-PRISON WRITINGS AND SPEECHES. Ed. by Robert Scheer *Random* 1969 pap. $1.95

"A gut-churning account. The picture of Eldridge Cleaver that emerges is moving in the extreme: his dread of being hounded back to prison, his revolutionary assertion of manhood in the face of a white society he sees as castrating to his brothers; his savage contempt of 'talk' when only action matters; his terrors, frustrations and loneliness—even his love, which underlies his bitter eloquence"—(*PW*). "This book . . . reveals him as a humane, brave and wise man, wherever he may be and whatever the justness of his cause"—(Christopher Lehmann-Haupt, in the *N.Y. Times*).

(With others). WAR WITHIN: Violence or Nonviolence in the Black Revolution. Ed. by James R. Ross *Sheed & Ward* 1971 $6.50 pap. $3.95

Chapter 9

History, Government and Politics

"History is three-dimensional. It partakes of the nature of science, art, and philosophy."

—Louis Gottschalk

"Nobody can read, even in part, the histories of Caesar, Clarendon, Guizot, Ranke, Motley, Mommsen, Maitland, or Rostovtzeff and be the same person afterwards."

—Jacques Barzun

"The writing of history at its highest level is a combination of scientific and artistic genius." Very few historians reach this peak, the English librarian, F. Seymour Smith, points out in "An English Library" (*Academic Press* 1971 $7.50), his annotated guide to 1,300 classics. He continues: "The greatest history in English, 'The Decline and Fall of the Roman Empire' [of Gibbon], is a supreme example of the result of painstaking research and artistic understanding which time has corrected only in minor detail. Carlyle's 'French Revolution,' on the other hand, may not now be regarded as an adequate treatment of its subject, yet the exhilaration gained by reading it more than compensates for its subjective distortion. . . . Few histories equal these two in style."

Contemporary history was once synonymous with unscholarly history. The ideal of the academic historian was to keep history passionless, and to that end he argued that the times a man wrote of should not be the times a man lived in. Today the idea has changed. A new generation feels that the history that is passionless is bloodless, is but the ghost of history. The ancients wrote contemporary history for their contemporaries; the moderns would write all history, whether past or present, for their contemporaries.

Barbara Tuchman, author of the Pulitzer Prize-winning "Guns of August," wrote a most illuminating article, "Can History Be Served Up Hot?" for the *N.Y. Times Book Review* (March 8, 1964). Who are the historians, she asks, "contemporaries of the event or those who come after? The answer is obviously both." She differentiates between the "more or less unconscious sources" (autobiographies and memoirs, first-hand accounts by journalists, the books of "Active Participants or Axe-Grinders" among them) and the true latter-day historians, who can be "at least *relatively* objective, which is not the same thing as being neutral or taking no sides. There is no such thing as a neutral or purely objective historian. Without an opinion a historian would be simply a ticking clock, and unreadable besides." She speaks of the curious fact that poets "have done very well with history both of their own times and of times long ago." Who can forget Tennyson's "Charge of the Light Brigade," Macaulay's "Horatius at the Bridge," Longfellow's "Midnight Ride of Paul Revere" or Emerson who commemorated Concord Bridge, where "once the embattled farmers stood and fired the shot heard round the world"? "The primary duty of the historian is to stay within the evidence," she says, and concludes: "What his imagination is to the poet, facts are to the historian. His exercise of judgment comes in their selection, his art in their arrangement. His method is narrative. Narrative is the lifeblood of history; it is the vehicle that carries it, the medium through which the historian communicates what he has to tell. Macaulay said history should ideally be a compound of poetry and philosophy. Today they argue whether it is art or science. For myself I incline toward the first of both these choices, but primarily I think of the historian as a storyteller. His subject is the story of man's past. His function is to make it known."

Meanwhile, other historians are attempting to transform history into a rigorous social science through the collection and analysis of quantitative data. Having assembled mountains of statistical data from a wide variety of sources, these researchers then apply the behavioral models of the social sciences to the study of history. "Questions that have become the targets of concerted quantitative research . . . include the analysis of the black experience during the half century between the Civil War and World War I, legislative history in Europe and the Americas, popular voting behavior during the past century, and social histories of sex, marriage and the family; stretching back into medieval times for Great Britain and France and into the colonial period for the United States"—(Robert William Fogel, in *The American Historical Review*, April 1975). Representative works by cliometricians (as these historians call themselves) may be found under the appropriate period classifications.

BOOKS ON THE WRITING AND PHILOSOPHY OF HISTORY

Barzun, Jacques. CLIO AND THE DOCTORS: Psycho-History, Quanto-History and History. *Univ. of Chicago Press* 1974 $7.95

"Barzun wants to save history from its enemies, and its friends, and he argues his case with much art . . . he distinguishes between history proper and special studies set in the past, in which the techniques of a science or social science are deployed to explicate a problem which merely chances to be historical, *e.g.* Napoleon's health. . . . Barzun then asserts that grafting the social sciences on to history to form a 'new history' (*e.g.* psycho-history or quanto-history) can only fail"— (*LJ*).

Becker, Carl Lotus. EVERYMAN HIS OWN HISTORIAN: Essays on History and Politics. 1935. *Quadrangle Bks.* 1966 pap. $2.95

Braudy, Leo. NARRATIVE FORM IN HISTORY AND FICTION: Hume, Fielding, and Gibbon. *Princeton Univ. Press* 1970 $10.00

"This remarkable monograph is about the artistic element in historical method, the structure of narrative"—(*American Historial Review*).

Butterfield, Herbert. MAN ON HIS PAST: The Study of the History of Historical Scholarship. *Cambridge Univ. Press* 1955 $10.50 pap. $2.95

Carr, Edward H. WHAT IS HISTORY? The Trevelyan Lectures, 1961. *Knopf* 1962 $4.95; *Random* Vintage Bks. pap. $1.95

Collingwood, Robin G. THE IDEA OF HISTORY. Ed. by T. M. Knox *Oxford Univ. Press* 1946 $8.50 Galaxy Bks. 1956 pap. $2.50

See also his main entry in Chapter 5, Philosophy, this Vol.

Gay, Peter. STYLE IN HISTORY. *Basic Bks.* 1974 $8.95

"It can be read with profit and pleasure by anyone from the undergraduate level up who is interested in the history of historical thought"—(*Choice*).

Gottschalk, Louis. UNDERSTANDING HISTORY: A Primer of Historical Method. 1950 *Knopf* Vintage Bks. 1969 pap. $3.95

(Ed.). GENERALIZATION IN THE WRITING OF HISTORY. *Univ. of Chicago Press* 1963 $8.50

Guinsburg, Thomas N. THE DIMENSIONS OF HISTORY. *Rand McNally* 1971 pap. $3.50. A collection of articles dealing with various facets of historiography.

Halperin, S. William, Ed. ESSAYS IN MODERN EUROPEAN HISTORIOGRAPHY. *Univ. of Chicago Press* 1970 $12.50

"Analytical biographies of 16 important historians who lived roughly between 1880–1960. Each biography is written by a competent scholar"—(*Choice*).

Holborn, Hajo. HISTORY AND THE HUMANITIES. *Doubleday* 1972 $6.95

"Three themes run through this collection: the role of classical culture in modern history, the ideal of scientific history, and the understanding of human nature as the basis for moral action"— (*Choice*).

Iggers, Georg G. THE GERMAN CONCEPTION OF HISTORY. *Wesleyan Univ. Press* 1968 $15.00

> "An authority in the field ... demonstrates the development of German historicism from its origins through the impact of dictatorship on German historical thought; he carefully assesses each phase of the development"—*(LJ)*.

Landes, David and Charles Tilly, Eds. HISTORY AS A SOCIAL SCIENCE. *Prentice-Hall* 1971 $5.95

> "It treats the discipline of history in general and seeks to define the characteristics of social-scientific history in terms of ideal types ... describes some of the varieties of social-scientific history, their achievements, limitations, and promise"—(Preface).

Lewis, Bernard. HISTORY: Remembered, Recovered, Invented. *Princeton Univ. Press* 1975 $6.95

> "Three types of history are defined: traditional, the discovery and analysis of historical data by academic scholarship, and the construction of history for a particular end"—*(LJ)*.

Lifton, Robert J., and Eric Olson, Eds. EXPLORATIONS IN PSYCHOHISTORY: The Wellfleet Papers. *Simon & Schuster* 1975 $9.95 Touchstone pap. $3.95

> "This collection of papers by a most distinguished gathering of thinkers is an important and potentially influential contribution in the emergence of the new discipline of psychohistory ... [which] represents, for all the follies of its lesser practitioners, an attempted breakthrough into exploring the human condition"—*(LJ)*.

Meyerhoff, Hans, Ed. THE PHILOSOPHY OF HISTORY IN OUR TIME. *Doubleday* Anchor Bks. (orig.) 1959 pap. $1.95

Nevins, Allan. HISTORY AND HISTORIANS. *Scribner* 1975 $12.50

> "Appealing models of historical craftsmanship"—*(LJ)*.

See also his main entry, this Chapter.

Plumb, John H. THE DEATH OF THE PAST. *Houghton* 1971 $5.00 pap. $1.75

Rowse, Alfred Leslie. THE USE OF HISTORY. *Verry* rev. ed. 1963 $4.00; *Macmillan* 1966 Collier Bks. pap. $1.25

See also his main entry in Section on History of the British Commonwealth, this Chapter.

Smith, Page. THE HISTORIAN AND HISTORY. *Random* Vintage Bks. 1964 pap. $1.95

> "Professor Smith, author of the prize-winning biography of John Adams, now turns his efforts to a critical but constructive scrutiny of his own profession. Smith's purpose is not only to trace the already well delineated path of the development of historical writing, but to investigate many of the epistemological assumptions held by those currently engaged in historical research"—*(LJ)*.

SOCIAL HISTORIANS IN CONTEMPORARY FRANCE: Essays from *Annales*. Trans. and ed. by the Staff of *Annales Harper* 1972 $9.50 pap. $2.95

Tillinghast, Pardon E. THE SPECIOUS PAST: Historians and Others. *Addison-Wesley* 1972 pap. $2.75

> "A literate, accurate, well-documented study of the present dilemmas of history that seeks chiefly to learn whether history is still relevant despite relativity and a new moral climate and, if so why"—*(Choice)*.

Trevelyan, George Macaulay. CLIO: A Muse, and Other Essays. 1913. Richard West 1973 $12.50

See also his main entry in Section on History of the British Commonwealth, this Chapter.

Walsh, William H. INTRODUCTION TO THE PHILOSOPHY OF HISTORY. *Hillary House* 1964 $4.50; (with title "The Philosophy of History: An Introduction") *Harper* Torchbks. 1960 pap. $1.60

White, Morton. FOUNDATIONS OF HISTORICAL KNOWLEDGE. *Harper* 1965 pap. $2.25

REFERENCE AND IMPORTANT SERIES

Most of the reference books for this Chapter are included under the sections to which they apply, and many general reference works will be found under Modern and World History: Reference Books. Among the important history series available are the following *(consult publishers for individual titles and prices)*: Development of Western Civilization, *Cornell*; Mainstreams of the World, *Doubleday*; Mainstreams of America, *Doubleday*; Documentary History of Western Civilization, *Harper*; History of Europe, *Harper*; Rise of Modern Europe, *Harper*; History of Mankind, *Harper*; Great Battles of History, *Lippincott*; Ancient Peoples and Places, *Praeger*; Modern Nations in Historical Perspective, *Prentice-Hall*; Great Ages of Man, *Time-Life Bks.*; History of the Modern World, *Univ. of Michigan Press*; and The Great Histories, *Simon & Schuster* (Washington Square).

Black, Eugene C., and Leonard W. Levy, Gen. Eds. THE DOCUMENTARY HISTORY OF WEST-ERN CIVILIZATION. *Walker & Co.* 1968–   each $12.50. Projected for this series are 51 volumes, to cover: The Ancient and Medieval History of the West; Early Modern History; Revolutionary Europe, 1789–1848; Nationalism, Liberalism, and Socialism, 1850–1914; and The Twentieth Century. Each work provides editorial commentary; some material appears in English for the first time.

Boyd, Andrew Kirk Henry. AN ATLAS OF WORLD AFFAIRS. *Praeger* 1957 6th rev. ed. 1910 $5.00 pap. $2.25. Small, compact ready-reference atlas; well indexed.

Brock, Clifton. THE LITERATURE OF POLITICAL SCIENCE: A Guide for Students, Librarians and Teachers. *Bowker* 1969 $11.50

This is "a methodological and substantive guide to library resources relevant to the needs of political science students. It discusses reference tools and other documentary resources, with explanations and examples for their use. This book is more than a simple listing and description of resources; it points to the most important materials and demonstrates how to exploit them"—(Publisher's note).

AN ENCYCLOPEDIA OF WORLD HISTORY: Ancient, Medieval and Modern. Comp. and ed. by William Leonard Langer. *Houghton* 1940 5th ed. 1972 $17.50. A revised and modernized version of Ploetz's "Epitome."

EUROPA YEAR BOOK 1974. *Gale Research Co.* 2 vols. 1974 Vol. 1 International Organizations, Europe Vol. 2 Africa, the Americas, Asia, and Australasia each $35.00 set $70.00. A world directory of every country and international organization. *(For further comment see Chapter 1, Reference Books—General: Year Books, this Vol.)*

FOREIGN AFFAIRS BIBLIOGRAPHY. *Bowker* (with Council on Foreign Relations) Vol. 1, 1932–1942, ed. by Robert Gale Woodbert 1969 Vol. 2, 1942–1952, ed. by Henry L. Roberts 1969 (no Vol. No.) 1952–1962, ed. by Henry L. Roberts 4th ed. 1964 each $23.00 1962–1972 ed. by Janis A. Kreslins 1976 $42.50

Vols. 1 and 2 are "now reprinted for the first time since their original publication (in association with *Foreign Affairs* magazine of the Council on Foreign Relations). These annotated bibiographies list the most significant books in the field of international relations published throughout the world during the decades 1932–1942 and 1942–1952 respectively. Approximately 9,500 titles in at least 30 languages are listed—and in many instances appraised—in each volume. Each entry is followed by complete bibliographical data: author's full name, publisher, place and date of publication, number of pages. The books are entered according to subject matter and are generally cross referenced. There is a complete author index in each volume"—(Publisher's note). The 1952–1962 volume lists over 9,000 volumes in similar arrangement.

Howe, George Frederick, and others, Eds. THE AMERICAN HISTORICAL ASSOCIATION'S GUIDE TO HISTORICAL LITERATURE. *Macmillan* 1961 $16.50

A listing of the most important printed materials in the long history of mankind. This is a completely new reworking of the famous 1931 edition; organized into nine sections: Introduction and General History, Historical Beginnings, The World in Recent Times plus six geographical topics. In any given field the "researcher can find the most significant material in any language in this one convenient compendium." It "is meant to aid 'students, teachers, librarians and others who seek the most satisfactory works for historical studies'; it is not designed for the specialist, but is 'an instrument of education and general reference.' A committee of distinguished historians directed its preparation with the help of about 230 experts"—*(LJ)*.

LAROUSSE ENCYCLOPEDIA OF MODERN HISTORY: From 1500 to the Present Day. Ed. by Marcel Dunan; fwd. by A. J. P. Taylor *Harper* 1964 $30.00; *Crown* 1972 pap. $6.95 "Exceptionally well written"—*(LJ)*.

NEW YORK TIMES INDEX. *See Chapter 1, Reference Books—General: Yearbooks, this Vol.*

THE PRESS IN LATIN AMERICA $17.50; THE PRESS IN AFRICA $15.00; THE PRESS IN ASIA AND OCEANIA $19.50. 1973 *Rowman*

"Up-to-date information about more than 600 newspapers in 37 Latin American countries, 365 newspapers in 47 African countries, and 628 newspapers in 39 Asian countries is found in this compact, three-volume set. Published in Germany and written in English and German, all significant data is included: name, address, political trend, circulation, language, format, frequency of issue, price of advertising, kind of readers, etc. You'll find information about each country: area, population, type of government, national language, currency, religion, etc. There is also an International Press listing, and each volume is indexed alphabetically and geographically"—(Publisher's note). Some 800 pages is the total for the three volumes.

WORLDMARK ENCYCLOPEDIA OF THE NATIONS. Ed. by Moshe Y. Sachs and Louis Barron. 1960. *Harper* 5 vols. 4th rev. ed. 1971 set $69.95

A convenient reference for economic, political, geographic and historical information on Africa, the Americas, Asia-Australasia, Europe and the United Nations. Authoritative and up-to-date facts about all nations, their peoples and their relationships with each other. A one-volume version of the Worldmark Encyclopedia appeared in 1960 under the general editorship of Benjamin A. Cohen, formerly Undersecretary of the United Nations. . . . Leading historians, economists, political scientists, geographers and commercial and financial authorities have contributed articles. "For exhaustive, all-out treatment . . . the veritable last word is 'The Worldmark Encyclopedia of the Nations' "—(SR).

ANCIENT HISTORY

The great age of Greek history "is separated from our generation by more than two thousand years" but, Arnold Toynbee (*q.v.*) writes after World War I in "The Legacy of Greece": "These men had travelled along the road on which our feet were set; they had travelled it farther than we, travelled it to the end; and the wisdom of greater experience and the poignancy of greater suffering than ours was expressed in the beauty of their words." Francis Godolphin speaks in his preface to "The Greek Historians," published during World War II, of how these writers "succeeded in being astonishingly articulate in dealing with the problems of their own history. . . . Many of the fundamental problems of society are examined by them in terms which seem to be directly related to our present-day problems; forms of government, the nature of imperialism, the importance of military strategy, these and many other questions, to which we are still seeking answers, are dealt with by the Greek historians. . . ." Among worthy series in this field are Aspects of Greek and Roman Life, *Cornell Univ. Press*; The Library of Early Civilizations (Stuart Piggott, Gen. Ed.), *McGraw-Hill*; The "Daily Life" [of the Etruscans, etc.] Series, *Macmillan*; the Legacy Series, *Oxford*; and the Ancient Peoples and Places Series, *Praeger*.

In connection with this section the reader may wish to look at two chapters in *"The Reader's Adviser,"* Volume 2: Chapter 7, Classical Greek Literature, and Chapter 8, Roman Literature.

Adcock, Frank Ezra. THE ROMAN ART OF WAR UNDER THE REPUBLIC. 1960 *Harper* (Barnes & Noble) rev. ed. 1971 $5.00. A study of the art of war as an integral part of Roman statecraft.

ROMAN POLITICAL IDEAS AND PRACTICE. *Univ. of Michigan Press* Ann Arbor Bks. 1959 pap. $1.65

Traces the history of Rome from its inception to 200 A.D., with emphasis on political development. "Warmly recommended to scholar and layman alike"—(N.Y. Times).

Adkins, Arthur W. MORAL VALUES AND POLITICAL BEHAVIOUR IN ANCIENT GREECE: From Homer to the End of the Fifth Century. *Norton* 1973 $5.95

"This book advances our knowledge of the basic value system of ancient Greece by the careful analysis of Greek moral terminology"—(Choice).

Aldred, Cyril. AKHENATEN AND NEFERTITI. *Viking* 1973 $16.95

Alsop, Joseph. FROM THE SILENT EARTH: A Report on the Greek Bronze Age. Introd. by Sir Maurice Bowra; photographs by Alison Frantz *Harper* 1964 $7.50. Recreation of the Mycenaean civilization of ancient Greece for the general reader.

Andrewes, Antony. THE GREEKS. The History of Human Society Ser. *Knopf* 1967 $7.95. Stresses the social, economic and political life of Greece.

Badian, Ernst E. PUBLICANS AND SINNERS: Private Enterprise in the Service of the Roman Republic. *Cornell Univ. Press* 1972 $6.50

"An exhaustive study of government contracts and contractors (the publicans) from the third century B.C. to the death of Caesar"—*(Choice)*.

Bamm, Peter. ALEXANDER THE GREAT: Power as Destiny. Trans. from the German by J. Maxwell Brownjohn *McGraw-Hill* 1968 $9.95

Barker, Sir Ernest. THE POLITICAL THOUGHT OF PLATO AND ARISTOTLE. 1906. *Dover* 1959 pap. $3.50; *Russell & Russell* 1959 $17.00; *Peter Smith* $5.50; (with title "Greek Political Theory: Plato and His Predecessors") *Harper* (Barnes & Noble) 1960 pap. $4.50

Bengtson, Hermann. INTRODUCTION TO ANCIENT HISTORY. Trans. by R. I. Frank and Frank D. Gilliard *Univ. of California Press* 1970 $7.50

"Here we have chiefly superbly chosen selective bibliographies for each area of ancient history and the allied disciplines with . . . a brief introductory description for each field and a history of its scholarship"—*(Choice)*.

Bottero, Jean, and others, Eds. THE NEAR EAST: The Early Civilizations. Trans. by R. F. Tannenbaum. Delacorte World History Ser. *Delacorte* 1967 $9.95

"This is the most satisfactory work I have seen on its subject and level. . . . Highly recommended for the academic library"—*(LJ)*.

Brothwell, Don, and Patricia Brothwell. FOOD IN ANTIQUITY: A Survey of the Diet of Early Peoples. *Praeger* 1969 $8.50

"A book that will whet the appetite of any archeologist interested in the food habits of early man from the prehistoric period to classical Greece and Rome . . . It is a mine of information on every variety of food linked to the diet of early man"—*(Choice)*.

Burford, Alison. CRAFTSMEN IN GREEK AND ROMAN SOCIETY. Ed. by H. H. Scullard *Cornell Univ. Press* 1972 $11.75

"This book deals with such themes as the craftsman's working conditions, relations with his patron, what he did in his spare time, and how he and others regarded his work"—*(Choice)*.

Burn, A. R. THE PELICAN HISTORY OF GREECE. (Orig. "The Traveller's History of Greece) *Penguin* Pelican Bks. 1966 pap. $1.95

CAMBRIDGE ANCIENT HISTORY. J. B. Bury, S. A. Cook, F. E. Adcock and M. P. Charlesworth, Gen. Eds. of 2nd ed. *Cambridge* 12 vols. of text Vol. 1 Pt. I Prolegomena and Prehistory 3rd ed. 1970 Vol. 1 Pt. 2 Early History of the Middle East 3rd ed. 1971 Vol. 2 Pt. 1 History of the Middle East and the Aegean Region c. 1800–1380 B.C. 3rd ed. 1973 Vol. 2 Pt. 2 History of the Middle East and the Aegean Region c. 1380–1000 B.C. ed. by I. E. Edwards and others 3rd ed. 1975 Vol. 3 The Assyrian Empire 2nd ed. 1925 Vol. 4 The Persian Empire and the West 2nd ed. 1926 Vol. 5 Athens 478–401 B.C. 2nd ed. 1927 Vol. 6 Macedon 401–301 B.C. 2nd ed. 1927 Vol. 7 The Hellenistic Monarchies and the Rise of Rome 2nd ed. 1928 Vol. 8 Rome and the Mediterranean, 218–133 B.C. 2nd ed. 1930 Vol. 9 The Roman Republic, 133–44 B.C. 2nd ed. 1932 Vol. 10 The Augustan Empire, 44 B.C.–A.D. 70 2nd ed. 1934 Vol. 11 The Imperial Peace, A.D. 70–192 2nd ed. 1936 Vol. 12 The Imperial Crisis and Recovery, A.D. 193–324 2nd ed. 1939 (Vols. 1 and 2 ed. by E. S. Edwards, C. J. Gadd and N. G. L. Hammond in 2 pts.) each $32.50 5 vols. of plates (Vol. 1 in prep.) Vols. 2–5 each $17.50

Casson, Lionel. ANCIENT EGYPT. Great Ages of Man Ser. *Time-Life* 1965 $6.95 lib. ed. $8.80. An introduction to the civilization of ancient Egypt, recommended for the layman, done by the author and the Editors of Time-Life Bks.

SHIPS AND SEAMANSHIP IN THE ANCIENT WORLD. *Princeton Univ. Press* 1971 $22.50

"Utilizing literary and iconographic evidence, as well as the reports of underwater archeologists [Casson] presents carefully delineated solutions to the numerous complex questions raised by the fragmentary and often contradictory literary sources"—(*Choice*).

Cottrell, Leonard. THE QUEST FOR SUMER. *Putnam* 1965 $5.95. Discusses the art, music, religion, literature and myths of this oldest known civilization.

Desborough, Vincent R. THE GREEK DARK AGES. *St. Martin's* 1972 $14.95

"In this first general survey of the period from about 1125 B.C. to about 900 B.C., so much light is thrown on the causes for the decline of Mycenaean civilization, the nature of Submycenaean material culture and the part it played in the rise of what we call Greek civilization that we shall not for long be able to continue to use the term 'dark ages' "—(*Choice*).

Duncan-Jones, Richard. THE ECONOMY OF THE ROMAN EMPIRE. *Cambridge* 1974 $22.50

The author "has succeeded in compiling a remarkably large number of statistics . . . These have been gleaned from a very wide variety of sources (including Latin novels), and, most importantly, they are treated with considerable statistical and economic sophistication"—(*Choice*).

Durant, Will. *See his main entry in Section on Modern and World History, this Chapter.*

Ehrenberg, Victor. FROM SOLON TO SOCRATES: Greek History and Civilization during the Sixth and Fifth Centuries B.C. *Harper* (Barnes & Noble) 1973 $12.75 pap. $6.75

Ferguson, John. THE RELIGIONS OF THE ROMAN EMPIRE. *Cornell Univ. Press* 1970 $10.50

"It is a deeply penetrating study of every aspect of religious belief during the first three centuries of the Roman Empire, from the 'Great Mother' concept to ideas of death"—(*Choice*).

Finley, Moses I. THE ANCIENT GREEKS: An Introduction to Their Life and Thought. *Viking* 1963 Compass Bks. pap. $1.45

ASPECTS OF ANTIQUITY: Discoveries and Controversies. *Viking* 1969 pap. $1.65. Sixteen essays, scholarly appraisals of different aspects of ancient civilizations (Greece, the Middle East and Rome).

Garnsey, Peter. SOCIAL STATUS AND LEGAL PRIVILEGE IN THE ROMAN EMPIRE. *Oxford* 1970 $11.00

"A young Oxford scholar has brought together the political, economic, legal, social and linguistic strands of [Roman legal] development and has given us a masterful synthesis of the relevant scholarly literature"—(*Choice*).

Gelzer, Matthias. THE ROMAN NOBILITY. Trans. by Robin Seager *Harper* (Barnes & Noble) 1969 $7.00

"Distinguished as all Professor Gelzer's writing has been, this is perhaps his most important work"—(*TLS*, London).

Grant, Michael. THE CLIMAX OF ROME: The Final Achievements of the Ancient World, A.D. 161–337. *New Am. Lib.* 1970 pap. $3.95

"Largely a numismatist's history making much of coins which survive in abundance, and of coin-legends"—(*TLS*, London). From the reign of Marcus Aurelius to the death of Constantine.

ROMAN HISTORY FROM COINS. *Cambridge Univ. Press* 1968 $5.50 pap. $2.45

Hale, William Harlan. ANCIENT GREECE. (Orig. "The Horizon Book of Ancient Greece") *McGraw-Hill* 1970 $2.75

Hamblin, Dora Jane, and Mary Jane Grunsfeld. THE APPIAN WAY: A Journey. *Random* 1974 $12.50

The authors "have re-created the life and times of a road and its users and offered reasons for its well deserved place in history"—(*LJ*).

Hamilton, Edith. *See her main entry in the Section on Ancient History by Modern Writers, this Chapter.*

Hammond, Nicholas Geoffrey Lemprière. A HISTORY OF GREECE TO 322 B.C. *Oxford* 2nd ed. 1967 $11.00. A modern interpretation of Greek thought and culture.

Harvey, Sir Paul. THE OXFORD COMPANION TO CLASSICAL LITERATURE. *Oxford* 2nd ed. 1937 $8.50

Hawkes, Jacquetta, Ed. ATLAS OF ANCIENT ARCHEOLOGY. *McGraw-Hill* 1974 $19.50

"The time span covered is from 1,800,000 B.C. at Olduval Gorge to the 16th century at several new world sites; classical Greece and Rome which have been adequately covered elsewhere, are not included"—*(LJ)*.

Hinz, Walther. THE LOST WORLD OF ELAM: Recreation of a Vanished Civilization. Trans. by Jennifer Barnes *N.Y. Univ. Press* 1973 $10.95

The author, "a world authority on Elam, brings to the student almost everything known about the 'wicked Elamites' and their stubbornly conservative culture"—*(Choice)*. "One is left marveling at the quantities and quality of information pieced together from such slender sources"—*(TLS*, London).

Kagan, Donald. THE OUTBREAK OF THE PELOPONNESIAN WAR. *Cornell Univ. Press* 1969 $11.50

The book offers an "evaluation of the origins and causes of the Peloponnesian War, based on evidence produced by modern scholarship and on a . . . reconsideration of the ancient texts"—(Publisher's note).

Keller, Werner. THE ETRUSCANS. Trans. from the German by Alexander Henderson and Elizabeth Henderson *Knopf* 1974 $12.50

This is "a very knowledgeable and readable history that incorporates more recent discoveries"—*(LJ)*.

Kitto, Humphrey D. F. THE GREEKS. *Aldine* 1951 $9.95; *Penguin* Pellican Bks. 1951 pap. $1.25; *Peter Smith* $3.75. A classic work on the character and history of ancient Greece by a noted authority.

Lindsay, Jack, THE ANCIENT WORLD: Manners and Morals. *Putnam* 1968 $7.95

"Jack Lindsay writes a rich, nonprofessional prose that communicates a vast and fascinating amount of learning"—*(PW)*.

MEN AND GODS ON THE ROMAN NILE. *Fernhill* 1968 $12.00. An account of Roman Egypt; bibliography.

Lintott, Andrew William. VIOLENCE IN REPUBLICAN ROME. *Oxford* 1968 $11.25

"Dr. Lintott shows how, to Roman thinking, there was nothing objectionable in the use of force—murder to defend a man's life or property from assault or to preserve the liberty of the state"—*(TLS*, London).

THE LOEB CLASSICAL LIBRARY. *Harvard Univ. Press* each $7.00. A series of Greek and Latin texts—some 400 or more volumes—with parallel English translations. Various translators and editors (*see publisher's catalog for individual titles*).

MacMullen, Ramsay. CONSTANTINE. *Dial* 1969 $7.95

"The main events of Constantine's life are briefly sketched, and the main features of his administrative, military and religious policies are described with clarity and economy"—*(Choice)*.

Meiggs, Russell. THE ATHENIAN EMPIRE. *Oxford* 1972 $25.00

"For the first time we now have a full account of Athen's imperial experience that takes account both of the new data, provided by the numerous inscriptions discovered during the 20th century and by the results achieved by over 100 years of scholarly study"—*(Choice)*.

Mellart, James. EARLIEST CIVILIZATIONS OF THE NEAR EAST. *McGraw-Hill* 1966 $5.95 pap. $3.95

1000 B.C. and back. "Although popular, the book is excellent for undergraduates in history, art history, and anthropology"—*(Choice)*.

Momigliano, Arnaldo. THE DEVELOPMENT OF GREEK BIOGRAPHY: Four Lectures. *Harvard Univ. Press* 1971 $8.00

"After an introductory survey of modern theories concerning the origin of Greek biography, the author traces the biographical tradition from the fifth century to the reign of Augustus. . . . A small but elegantly written book whose interest is not limited to students of the classics"—*(Choice)*.

Mommsen, Theodor. *See his main entry in the Section on Ancient History by Modern Writers, this Chapter.*

Muir, Ramsay. MUIR'S ATLAS OF ANCIENT AND CLASSICAL HISTORY. Ed. by R. F. Treharne and Harold Fullard *Harper* (Barnes & Noble) 6th ed. 1963 $3.50. Shows geography for periods from the 15th century B.C. to the barbarian invasions.

Mylonas, George E. MYCENAE AND THE MYCENAEAN AGE. *Princeton Univ. Press* 1966 $27.50

Nims, Charles F. THEBES OF THE PHAROAHS: Pattern for Every City. *Int. Pubns. Service* 1965 $15.00. Includes photographs.

Oppenheim, A. Leo. ANCIENT MESOPOTAMIA: Portrait of a Dead Civilization. *Univ. of Chicago Press* 1964 $12.00 Phoenix Bks. 1958 pap. $3.95

An excellent work of "meticulous scholarship"—(*LJ*).

LETTERS FROM MESOPOTAMIA: Official, Business and Private Letters on Clay Tablets from Two Millennia. *Univ. of Chicago Press* 1967 $9.50. Offers an insight into the daily lives of ancient peoples.

OXFORD CLASSICAL DICTIONARY. Ed. by N.G. Hammond and H. H. Scullard *Oxford Univ. Press* 2nd ed. 1970 $35.00

Payne, Robert. ANCIENT ROME. (Orig. "The Horizon Book of Ancient Rome") *McGraw-Hill* rev. ed. 1970 pap. $2.95

Peck, Harry Thurston, Ed. HARPER'S DICTIONARY OF CLASSICAL LITERATURE AND ANTIQUI-TIES. 1897. *Cooper* 1962 lib. bdg. $25.00. A complete and well-illustrated encyclopedia in dictionary form; selected bibliography for most major articles.

Piggott, Stuart. ANCIENT EUROPE: From the Beginnings of Agriculture to the Classical Antiquity, a Survey. *Aldine* 1966 $12.50 pap. $3.95

"A readable report . . . highly recommended"—(*LJ*). About European prehistory.

Richardson, Emeline. THE ETRUSCANS: Their Art and Civilization. *Univ. of Chicago Press* 1964 $9.50

Roebuck, Carl. THE WORLD OF ANCIENT TIMES. *Scribner* 1966 $15.00 pap. $5.95

"Mr. Roebuck, head of the classics department at Northwestern University, is a distinguished authority. His new book, on the history of the Western World from Neolithic Man to Constantine, is the finest one-volume history of this period I have seen. Its synthesis of a large amount of detail is yet very readable. Illustrations and maps are numerous and well selected"—(*LJ*).

Rostovzeff, Mikhail Ivanovich. GREECE. Trans. from the Russian by J. D. Duff; ed. by Elias J. Bickerman *Oxford Univ. Press* 2nd ed. 1930 pap. 1963 $2.95

ROME. Trans. by J. D. Duff; ed. by Elias J. Bickerman *Oxford Univ. Press* 1927 pap. 1960 $2.95

THE SOCIAL AND ECONOMIC HISTORY OF THE HELLENISTIC WORLD. *Oxford Univ. Press* 3 vols. 1941 set $100.00

THE SOCIAL AND ECONOMIC HISTORY OF THE ROMAN EMPIRE. Ed. by P. M. Frazer *Oxford Univ. Press* 2 vols. 1926. 2nd ed. 1957 set $59.50

Siebert, Isle. WOMEN IN THE ANCIENT NEAR EAST. Image of Women Ser. *Abner Schram* 1974 $20.00

"An auspicious beginning for what promises to be an important series of studies. [This volume] . . . examines the social, legal, and religious status of women from many walks of life over some 2000 years"—(*LJ*).

Snowden, Frank M., Jr. BLACKS IN ANTIQUITY: Ethiopians in the Greco-Roman Experience. *Harvard Univ. Press* 1970 $12.50 pap. $2.45

"Snowden's thorough presentation of the data leaves no doubt that the Negro was a familiar figure in the ancient world without there being any development of a 'racist' attitude toward him on the part of the majority white population . . . an essential purchase for libraries"—(*Choice*).

Starr, Chester G. A HISTORY OF THE ANCIENT WORLD. *Oxford* 1964 2nd ed. 1974 $15.00 text ed. $9.95

A "readable survey of human history from the Paleolithic Age through the dissolution of the Roman Empire in the West"—(*LJ*). Includes chapters on India and China.

Sulimirski, Tadeusz. THE SARMATIANS. Ancient Peoples and Places Ser. *Praeger* 1971 $10.00

"The first book ever to be published on the Sarmatians. It is a comprehensive and well written work detailing the economy, social organization, and material remains of the Sarmatians"— (*Choice*).

Toynbee, J. M. DEATH AND BURIAL IN THE ROMAN WORLD. Ed. by H. H. Scullard *Cornell Univ. Press* 1971 $9.75

"Here for the first time is assembled the wealth of literary and archeological evidence for a penetrating and fascinating account of how the Romans thought of death and their burial customs"—(*Choice*).

Usher, Stephen. THE HISTORIANS OF GREECE AND ROME. *Taplinger* 1970 $6.50

"Amazingly, the first of its kind—a survey of classical historiography from beginning to end"— (*Choice*).

Webster, T. B. L. ATHENIAN CULTURE AND SOCIETY. *Univ. of Calif. Press* 1973 $10.00

"The best book in English on classical Athens for the general reader"—(*TLS*, London).

Wellard, James. THE SEARCH FOR THE ETRUSCANS. *Saturday Review Press* 1973 $16.95

White, K. D. ROMAN FARMING. *Cornell Univ. Press* 1970 $14.50

"The 14 chapters range topically from a thorough discussion of the sources of Roman farming, to the attitude of the Romans toward agriculture and the various methods used in maintaining soil fertility, drainage and irrigation, crop and animal husbandry, and the management of great estates"—(*Choice*).

Yadin, Yigael. BAR-KOKHBA: The Rediscovery of the Legendary Hero of the Second Jewish Revolt against Rome. *Random* 1971 $15.00

"Bar-Kokhba, history's first guerrilla fighter, hero of his people in the fight for survival against the might of the whole Roman empire, takes on modern dimensions: the history of modern Israel is then the re-enactment of the ancient events"—(*Choice*).

Ancient Greek Historians

The comparative merits of the various translations of the Greek and Latin historians are ably summarized in "The Classics in Translation" by Frank Seymour Smith (1930, *Burt Franklin* 1968 $15.00) and many of his evaluations are quoted.

Finley, Moses I., Ed. THE PORTABLE GREEK HISTORIANS: The Essence of Herodotus, Thucydides, Xenophon, Polybius. *Viking* 1959 $4.95 pap. $2.50. Selections from the historians with an introd. to their work and biographical notes.

Godolphin, Francis R. B., Ed. THE GREEK HISTORIANS. The complete and unabridged historical works, with an introduction, revisions and additional notes by the editor. *Random* 2 vols. 1942 set $25.00

Herodotus, translated by George Rawlinson; Thucydides, translated by Benjamin Jowett; Xenophon, translated by Henry G. Dakyns; Arrian, translated by Edward J. Chinnock.

Robinson, Charles Alexander, Jr., Ed. SELECTIONS FROM GREEK AND ROMAN HISTORIANS. *Holt* (Rinehart) 1957 pap. $2.95

HERODOTUS. 484 B.C.–424 B.C.

Herodotus was called "the father of history." His histories are divided into nine books, named after the nine Muses. They treat of the wars between the Greeks and the Orientals, extending from the accession of Croesus, 560 B.C. to 478 B.C., the capture of Lesbos or, as Kenneth Rexroth has said (in *SR*), "the successful defense of a democratic, rational, secular society against the onslaughts of what Gibbon in another context altogether was to call barbarism and superstition." It was the history of the invasion of Xerxes that first attracted Herodotus, and that part of his narrative has always been considered the most important and the most interesting. "Early Ionian Historians" (1939, *Greenwood* $11.75), by Lionel Pearson, is a scholarly study of his literary sources. Herodotus had no conception of the modern idea of investigating sources and evidence, but H. J. Rose has said that he was the first to handle his materials critically and "to make the subject truly philosophic by correlating causes and effects instead of merely setting down, more or less accurately, what had taken place." Modern research has proved Herodotus to be accurate "even in areas like Egypt, Scythia, and the outer barbarians, where skeptical 19th-century critics assumed that he was romancing"—(Rexroth). The histories form a delightful story book, written in the style of artless conversation. They are the fountain of history, from which countless histories have sprung. The George Rawlinson edition (1858) was long considered the standard version, highly praised by scholars as an English classic, but the later (1920–1924) translation by A. D. Godley is highly regarded.

HISTORIES. Trans. by Isaac Littlebury. 1709. *AMS Press* 2 vols. set $40.00; *Bks. for Libraries* repr. of 1847 ed. $19.50; trans. by George Rawlinson, ed. by E. H. Blakeney *Dutton* Everyman's 1964 2 vols. each $3.95; trans. by A. D. Godley *Harvard Univ. Press* Loeb 4 vols. 1920–24 each $7.00; trans. by Aubrey de Sélincourt *Penguin* 1954 pap. $2.95; trans. by George Rawlinson (1858) in Godolphin's "The Greek Historians" *Random* 2 vols. 1942 set $25.00

Books about Herodotus

Studies in Herodotus. By Joseph Wells. 1923. *Bks. for Libraries* $9.00
Herodotus. By Terrot R. Glover. 1924. *AMS Press* 1970 $9.00; *Bks. for Libraries* $15.50
A Commentary on Herodotus. Ed. by Walter W. How and Joseph Wells. *Oxford* 2 vols. rev. ed. 1928 Vol. I $5.00 Vol. 2 $6.00
Lexicon to Herodotus. By J. E. Powell. 1938. *Adler's* 1960 $24.00
Herodotus: Father of History. By John L. Myres. *Oxford* 1953 $9.50
The World of Herodotus. By Aubrey de Sélincourt. *Little* 1962 pap. $2.45
  "A masterly survey of Greek civilization down to the death of Alexander"—(E. V. Rieu).
Herodotus: An Interpretative Essay. By Charles W. Fornara. *Oxford* 1971 $6.00

THUCYDIDES.   c. 470 B.C.–400 B.C.

Thucydides was the founder of "political history." Political science was the great interest of his day, a day that saw the fall of the Athenian empire. The political causes leading to the decline of Athens are the chief interest of his history. He was also the first of the military historians. His chosen subject was the Peloponnesian War, which covered 27 years of his own lifetime, 431–404 B.C., and in which he fought as a commander of Athenian troops in Thrace. His ideal of history is said to have been first accuracy, and then relevancy. Unlike Herodotus (*q.v.*), he rarely digressed. His history is unfinished, breaking off in the middle of the year 411 B.C. Thucydides initiated the writing of contemporary history. Again, as with Plato and Aristotle, Benjamin Jowett's Thucydides (1881) is a "justly recognized" masterpiece. Second in importance is the translation by Richard Crawley.

COMPLETE WRITINGS: The Peloponnesian Wars. Trans. by Benjamin Jowett in Godolphin's "The Greek Historians" *Random* 2 vols. 1942 set $25.00 trans. by Richard Crawley; introd. by Joseph Gavorse (Modern Lib.) 1934 pap. $1.95

THE HISTORY OF THE PELOPONNESIAN WAR. Trans. by R. Whistler *Dufour* 1962 $7.25; trans. by Richard Crawley (1874) *Dutton* Everyman's 1910 1936 $3.95; trans. by C. F. Smith *Harvard Univ. Press* Loeb 4 vols. 1919 each $7.00; trans. by Sir Richard W. Livingstone *Oxford* World's Class. 1943 $6.00 Galaxy Bks. 1960 pap. $2.95; trans. by Rex Warner *Penguin* 1954 rev. ed. 1973 pap. $2.85

SPEECHES. Ed. by H. F. Harding *Coronado* 1974 $12.50 pap. $7.50

"Let it be said immediately, this book is unreservedly recommended to all students of Thucydides in general and of his speeches in particular"—(*Choice*).

Books about Thucydides

Thucydides and the Science of History. By Charles N. Cochrane. 1929. *Russell & Russell* 1965 $7.50
An Historical Commentary on Thucydides. By Arnold W. Gomme. *Oxford* 4 vols. 1945–1970 Vol. I Introduction and Commentary on Book I (1945) $12.75 Vols. 2 and 3 The Ten Years' War, Books 2–3 and 4–5 (1956) each $16.00 Vol. 4 Books 5–7 (1970) each $16.00. Scholarly and valuable, using both ancient and modern literature. A commentary on the Greek text.
Thucydides and the World War. By Louis E. Lord. 1946. *Russell & Russell* 1967 $8.50
Greek Political Theory: The Image of Man in Thucydides and Plato. (Orig. "Man in His Pride"). By David Grene. *Univ. of Chicago Press* 1950 Phoenix Bks. 1965 pap. $1.95
Thucydides and His History. By Frank E. Adcock. 1963. *Shoe String Press* 1973 $6.25
Thucydides. By John H. Finley, Jr. *Univ. of Michigan Press* 1963 pap. $2.25
Thucydides and the Politics of Bi-polarity. By Peter J. Fliese. *Louisiana State Univ. Press* 1966 $6.00

Three Essays on Thucydides. By John H. Finley, Jr. *Harvard Univ. Press* 1967 $6.00
  Articles originally published separately by a former Oxford professor and present professor of Greek Literature at Harvard "that are among the most important studies of [Thucydides] in the present century"—(G. W. Bowersock).
Individuals in Thucydides. By H. D. Westlake. *Cambridge* 1968 $13.50
  "The purpose of this book is to examine the treatment of leading individuals in the *History* and to try to show that in this single aspect of the work divergences may be observed between the first half and the second"—(Author's introduction).
The Speeches in Thucydides: A Collection of Original Studies with a Bibliography. Ed. by Philip A. Stadter. *Univ. of North Carolina Press* 1973 $10.95
Thucydides, the Artful Reporter. By Virginia J. Hunter. *A. M. Hakkert* 1974 $10.00
Chance and Intelligence in Thucydides. By Lowell Edmunds. *Harvard Univ. Press* 1975 $10.00
  Edmunds "analyzes the idea of chance in opposition to the complex of ideas surrounding notions of perception, planning, craft and the like"—(*LJ*).

XENOPHON. c. 434 b.c.–355 b.c.

Of the three ancient Greek historians whose work has survived, Xenophon is read most, but he is regarded by historians as hardly more than a dilettante. As a private individual he seems to have been a frank and sensible man of affairs and a great lover of outdoor life. His works consist of: "The Hellenica," a history of Greece (*Hellas*), which begins where Thucydides (*q.v.*) left off and carries the narrative down to 362 b.c., 50 years later. The "Anabasis," or the March of the Ten Thousand, is the story of the expedition of Cyrus the Younger and his 10,000 Greek mercenaries against Artaxerxes of Persia. Xenophon accompanied this expedition in person. The biographical works are the "Memorabilia" of Socrates and its companion volume, the "Symposium," the table talk of Socrates (*q.v.*). The Loeb edition is recommended first; Miller's translation has been called "really satisfying," Brownson's "admirable." The Dakyns version is "faithful to the tone and the spirit of the original" —(J. Hereford). Xenophon is the reputed author of essays on miscellaneous topics. In print is "The Art of Horsemanship" translated by Morris H. Morgan (*British Bk. Centre* 1972 $6.95).

COMPLETE WORKS. Trans. by Henry G. Dakyns in Godolphin's "The Greek Historians." *Random* 2 vols. 1942 set $25.00

CYROPAEDIA. Trans. by Walter Miller *Harvard Univ. Press* Loeb 2 vols. 1945 each $7.00

HELLENICA. Trans. by C. L. Brownson *Harvard Univ. Press* Loeb 2 vols. each $7.00

THE ANABASIS. Trans. by C. L. Brownson *Harvard Univ. Press* Loeb $7.00

THE MARCH UP COUNTRY: A Modern Translation of the Anabasis. Trans. by W. H. D. Rouse *Univ. of Michigan Press* 1958 pap. $2.45

"Xenophon has a thrilling tale to tell of how 10,000 Greeks almost overthrew the Persian Empire and of how they suffered on the return march through Armenia, until finally, when the Black Sea was sighted, the triumphant cry went up, 'The sea, the sea'—for the sea was an element with which Greeks could usually cope"—(*N.Y. Times*).

MEMORABILIA AND OECONOMICUS (trans. by E. C. Marchant) and SYMPOSIUM AND APOLOGY (trans. by O. J. Todd) *Harvard Univ. Press* Loeb 1914–1920 $7.00

SCRIPTA MINORA. Trans. by E. C. Marchant *Harvard Univ. Press* Loeb 1914–1920 $7.00

THE PERSIAN EXPEDITION. Trans. by Rex Warner *Penguin* 1949 rev. ed. 1973 pap. $2.95; *Gannon* $6.00

THE ECONOMIST OF XENOPHON. Trans. by Alexander D. O. Wedderburn and W. G. Collingwood. 1876. *Burt Franklin* $11.50

RECOLLECTIONS OF SOCRATES and SOCRATES' DEFENSE BEFORE THE JURY. Trans. by Anna Benjamin *Bobbs Lib. Arts* 1965 pap. $1.65

MEMOIRS OF SOCRATES and THE SYMPOSIUM. Trans. with introd. by Hugh Tredennick. 1970. *Peter Smith* $4.75

Books about Xenophon

On Tyranny. By Leo Strauss. *Cornell Univ. Press* 1968 pap. $1.95
Xenophon's Socratic Discourse: An Interpretation of the Oeconomicus. By Leo Strauss. Trans. by Carnes Lord *Cornell Univ. Press* 1971 $8.50 pap. $1.95
Xenophon. By J. K. Anderson. *Scribner* 1974 $10.00

POLYBIUS.   c. 201 B.C.–c. 120 B.C.

Polybius was a well-educated Greek gentleman and statesman who witnessed, helped in and wrote of the rise and triumph of the Roman Empire. After King Philip of Macedon was defeated in 168 B.C., a thousand Greeks of high station were sent to Rome for trial. Polybius became pro-Roman and warned his fellow hostages to submit to the inevitable. He associated with the leading Roman families and became the private tutor and friend of the younger Scipio Africanus. Polybius joined Scipio in Africa and was present at the siege and destruction of Carthage in 146 B.C. Of the 40 books of his Roman "Histories" only the first 5 have been preserved intact, with portions of the rest in excerpts. He is a scientific historian, valued for his objectivity, criticized for a rather dry and moralistic style. His information about the Roman army of his day, its tactics and strategy, the Roman government and the character of the people, is priceless.

THE HISTORIES. Trans. by W. R. Paton *Harvard Univ. Press* Loeb 6 vols. 1922–1927 each $7.00; trans. by Evelyn S. Schuckburgh. 1889 1962. *Greenwood* 2 vols. set $38.00

Books about Polybius

Historical Commentary on Polybius. By F. W. Walbank. *Oxford Univ. Press* 2 vols. 1957–1967 Vol. 1 Commentary on Books 1–6 (1957) $20.50 Vol. 2 Commentary on Books 7–18 (1967) $24.00

"Based upon prolonged study of the Greek text, it is in the great tradition of classical scholarship and will be an indispensable tool of the workshop for all those with a specialist interest in Hellenistic history and that of the earlier Republic of Rome. But it is more than this, for it is illumined throughout with an awareness of the larger issues involved which give Polybius's History its interest for us at the present day"—(*Manchester Guardian*).

The Manuscript Tradition of Polybius. By J. M. Moore. *Cambridge Univ. Press* 1966 $11.00
Polybius. By. F. W. Walbank. *Univ. of Calif. Press* 1973 $8.50

PLUTARCH.   c. 46–c. 125 A.D.

Plutarch's "Parallel Lives of Greeks and Romans" number 48, consisting of 22 pairs and 4 single biographies. They were originally written to kindle emulation in youth, but their chief value today is historical. Plutarch was an excellent biographer, although his history is not always trustworthy, especially in regard to the Romans. His "On Love, the Family, and the Good Life" has been translated by Moses Hadas (*New Am. Lib.* 1957 pap. $.60).

The earliest and most famous translation, by Sir Thomas North, of "Parallel Lives," made from the French of Amyot in 1579, was the version used by Shakespeare as the source of his Roman tragedies. Dryden's translation of Plutarch was revised by the poet Arthur Hugh Clough in 1864. The B. Perrin Loeb translation is faithful, "coming probably between North's and Clough's in order of merit." Philemon Holland's "Moralia," translated in 1603, has "a fresh and genuine literary value."

"To Plutarch life is activity; a man's actions reveal his character; his actions are initiated by himself or are reactions to the actions of other men. . . . [Therefore] the minor part of a life contains strictly moral sidelights on its subject, the major portion is given up to narrative; and, since the hero is a man who has played a big part in the events of his times, campaigns and politics, strategy and state-craft make up most of the narrative. There are times when Plutarch, like the good story-teller he is, is carried away by his story, and a life contains perhaps more of the setting than is strictly necessary. Moreover he is a philosopher, and there are passages of musing, often highly interesting, but not always relevant"—(R. H. Barrow).

PARALLEL LIVES. Trans. By Dryden and Clough *Dutton* Everyman's 3 vols. each $3.95; trans. by Bernadette Perrin *Harvard Univ. Press* Loeb II vols. 1914– each $7.00; Dryden trans. *Modern Library* Giants $4.95

PLUTARCH'S LIVES. Trans. by Sir Thomas North. 1579. *AMS Press* 6 vols. each $15.00; ed. by John S. White 1900 *Biblo & Tannen* $5.95; sel. and ed. with introd. by Paul Turner *Southern Illinois Univ. Press* 2 vols. 1963 set $30.00

EVERYBODY'S PLUTARCH. Trans. by John Dryden, corrected from the Greek and rev. by Arthur Hugh Clough; arr. and ed. for the modern adult reader by Raymond T. Bond *Dodd* Gt. Ill. Class. 1962 $5.95

NINE GREEK LIVES: Rise and Fall of Athens. Trans. by Ian Scott-Kilvert *Penguin* 1960 pap. $1.75

THE LIVES OF THE NOBLE GREEKS. Ed. by Edmund Fuller *Dell* abr. ed. pap. $.75

EIGHT GREAT LIVES. Trans. by Kevin Guinagh; ed. by Charles Alexander Robinson, Jr. *Holt* (Rinehart) 1960 $2.95

Six Roman Lives. (Orig. "Fall of the Roman Republic") trans. by Rex Warner *Penguin* 1958 pap. $2.75

Makers of Rome. Trans. by Ian Scott-Kilvert *Penguin* 1973 pap. $1.75

The Lives of the Noble Romans. Ed. by Edmund Fuller *Dell* abr. ed. pap. $.75

Moralia. *Harvard Univ. Press* Loeb 14 vols. of 16 ready. Vols. 1–5 trans. by F. C. Babbitt Vol. 6 trans. By W. C. Helmbold Vols. 7 and 14 trans. by P. H. Delacy and B. Einarson Vol. 8 trans. by P. A. Clement and H. B. Hoffleit Vol. 9 trans. by E. L. Minar, Jr., F. H. Sandbach and W. C. Helmbold Vol. 10 trans. by H. N. Fowler Vol. 11 trans. by L. Pearson and W. C. Helmbold Vol. 12 trans. by Harold Cherniss and W. C. Helmbold Vol. 15 trans. by F. H. Sandbach each $7.00

Books about Plutarch

Plutarch's Quotations. By William C. Helmbold and Edward N. O'Neil. *Press of Case Western* 1959 $4.00

Plutarch's Historical Methods: An Analysis of the Mulierum Virtues. By Philip A. Stadter. *Harvard Univ. Press* 1965 $4.00

"An admirable example of . . . the careful examination of a text in order to establish what earlier works it is based on," though it offers the scholar little that is new—(*Choice*). "An enjoyable work"—(*Classical World*).

Plutarch. By C. J. Gianakaris. *Twayne* $6.95

Plutarch: Alexander. By J. R. Hamilton. *Oxford* 1969 $11.00

Plutarch and Rome. By C. P. Jones. *Oxford* 1971 $11.25

Plutarch. By D. A. Russell. *Scribner* 1973 $8.95

ARRIAN (FLAVIUS ARRIANUS)   c. 95–c. 175 A.D.

A Roman by birth, who held government positions under the Emperor Hadrian, Arrian spent his retirement in Athens, where he wrote in Greek several geographical and historical works following in general the style of Xenophon. His principal work was his sober account of Alexander the Great's eastern campaigns, which, "deriving its facts from writers of Alexander's own date, and not to be followed blindly, is the best account of the matter antiquity has left us, and supremely readable"—(H. J. Rose). He also wrote two books on the philosophy of Epictetus (*q.v.*).

The Anabasis of Alexander and The Indica. Trans. by E. Iliff Robson *Harvard Univ. Press* Loeb 2 vols. 1921–33 each $7.00; trans. by Edward J. Chinnock in Godolphin's "The Greek Historians" *Random* 2 vols. 1942 set $25.00

The Campaigns of Alexander. Trans. by Aubrey de Sélincourt *Penguin* 1972 pap. $2.45; *Gannon* lib. bdg. $5.50; *Peter Smith* $4.50

Ancient Roman Historians

Laistner, Max L. The Greater Roman Historians. 1947. *Univ. of Calif. Press* pap. $2.25; *Peter Smith* $4.00

CAESAR, JULIUS (Caius Julius Caesar).   100 B.C.–44 B.C.

One of the most controversial characters of history is known to us mainly through Shakespeare's tragedy, "Julius Caesar," and Plutarch's (*q.v.*) "Parallel Lives." Caesar excelled in "war, in politics, in statesmanship, in letters, in oratory and in social grace." His literary works were highly esteemed by his contemporaries and only recently are again being read for their clear, beautiful and concise prose. His commentaries on the Gallic Wars ("*De Bello Gallico*") in seven books and on the Civil Wars ("*De Bello Civili*") in three books survive: classic military documents and among the most reliable of the histories of antiquity. His other works including two books on Latin usage, speeches, pamphlets, poetry and plays have perished. Arthur Golding's translation in 1565 is considered the "earliest and best." The translations made by A. G. Peskett of the "Civil Wars" and by H. J. Edwards of the "Gallic Wars" for the Loeb Library are recommended. The more recent renderings are those by John Warrington and Moses Hadas.

War Commentaries: De Bello Gallico and De Bello Civili. Trans. and ed. by John Warrington *Dutton* Everyman's 1953 $3.95

Commentaries. Trans. by Somerset de Chair with engravings by Clifford Webb *Golden Cockerel* $45.00; trans. by William Duncan 1753. *AMS Press* $49.50

Gallic War. Trans. by Joseph Pearl *Barron's* 1962 $5.50 pap. $1.95; trans. by H. J. Edwards *Harvard Univ. Press* Loeb $7.00

THE CIVIL WARS. Trans. by A. G. Peskett. *Harvard Univ. Press* Loeb $7.00

Books about Caesar

Julius Caesar. By Alfred L. Duggan. *Knopf* 1955 $3.95

Caesar as Man of Letters. By Frank E. Adcock. 1956. *Shoe String Press* 1969 $4.50; *Richard West* $4.45

Julius Caesar in Shakespeare, Shaw, and the Ancients. Ed. by George B. Harrison. *Harcourt* 1960 pap. $4.50. Includes Shakespeare's "Julius Caesar" and Shaw's "Caesar and Cleopatra."

Julius Caesar: Man, Soldier, and Tyrant. By John F. Fuller. 1965. *Funk & Wagnalls* 1969 pap. $2.95

"The approach of this book is determined by the trade of its author, a well-known British military historian. There are maps of the principal battles and interesting illustrations of contemporary weapons. Readers must be warned that they will find little of Shaw's Caesar here and nothing of Shakespeare's"—(*N.Y. Times*).

Caesar: Politician and Statesman. By Matthias Gelzer. *Harvard Univ. Press* 6th ed. 1968 $12.50

Divus Julius. By Stefan Weinstock. *Oxford* 1971 $30.75

LIVY (Titus Livius).   59 B.C.–17 A.D.

Livy's history consisted originally of 142 books, of which only 35 are extant. It begins with the founding of the city in 753 B.C. by Romulus, a legendary king, whom Livy accepts as historical. It extends down to his own time, the reign of the Emperor Augustus. Livy was the court historian. He desired to point out to the Romans moral lessons that might be drawn from their history. He is far from accurate in his facts, but his style is agreeable and easy. Macaulay (*q.v.*) said of Livy: "No historian with whom we are acquainted has shown so complete an indifference to truth. He seems to have cared only about the picturesque effect of his book, and the honor of his country."

WORKS. *McKay* $4.25

ROMAN HISTORY. *Harvard Univ. Press* Loeb 14 vols. 1919–1943 Vols. 1–5 trans. by B. O. Foster Vols. 6–7 trans. by F. G. Moore Vols. 9–11 trans. by Evan T. Sage Vol. 12 trans. by Evan T. Sage and Alfred C. Schlesinger each $7.00

THE EARLY HISTORY OF ROME. Trans. by Aubrey de Sélincourt *Penguin* (orig.) 1960 pap. $2.45; *Gannon* lib. bdg. $5.50

WAR WITH HANNIBAL. Trans. by Aubrey de Sélincourt *Penguin* (orig.) 1965 pap. $2.95; *Gannon* lib. bdg. $6.00

Books about Livy

Livy: His Historical Aims and Methods. By P. G. Walsh. *Cambridge* 1961 $13.50

"While [Dr. Walsh's] interpretation of Livy is not novel, it is marked by thoroughness, conservative good sense, and eminent readability. The last quality is heightened by the admirable typography"—(*American Historical Review*).

Livy. By K. Melbourne Sinclair. *International Scholarly Bk. Services* 1961 pap. $2.30

Commentary on Livy, Books 1–5. By R. M. Ogilvie. *Oxford* 1965 $25.75

Concordance to Livy. By David W. Packard. *Harvard Univ. Press* 4 vols. 1968 set $125.00

Livy. Ed. by T. A. Dorey. *Univ. of Toronto Press* 1971 $10.00. Essays on subjects related to Livy and his influence on later writers.

A Commentary on Livy, Books 31–33. By John Briscoe. *Oxford* 1973 $25.75

JOSEPHUS, FLAVIUS.   37–95 A.D.

Josephus was a Jew who wrote both in Greek and Hebrew. His histories are full of errors, but he was in the main honest and had a sincere liking for his countrymen. At one period he was governor of Galilee. The history often includes the "Antiquities of the Jew," the "History of Jewish Wars," and the "Life of Josephus by Himself." The standard translation by William Whiston, issued in 1737, and revised by A. R. Shilleto in 1888 (o.p.), first appeared in the Bohn Library. Through his writings we have some knowledge of the Essenes, who are supposed to have written the Dead Sea Scrolls (*see Chapter 3, Bibles and Related Texts, this Vol.*). There is a biographical trilogy by Lion Feuchtwanger, translated by Willa and Edwin Muir: Vol. 1 "Josephus" (1932), Vol. 2 "The Jew of Rome" (1936, o.p.), and Vol. 3 "Josephus and the Emperor" (1942, o.p.).

COMPLETE WORKS. *Baker Bk. House* 4 vols. $29.95; trans. by Henry St. John Thackeray and ed. by E. H. Warmington *Harvard Univ. Press* Loeb 9 vols. 1926–1943 each $7.00; trans. by William Whiston. 1936. *Kregel* lg.-type ed. 1970 $10.95 pap. $7.95

THE LIFE AND WORKS OF FLAVIUS JOSEPHUS. Trans. and ed. by William Whiston. 1936. *Holt* 1957 $15.95. The standard version.

THE JEWISH WAR. Trans. by Geoffrey A. Williamson *Penguin* 1959 pap. $1.95; *Peter Smith* $5.00

THE GREAT ROMAN-JEWISH WAR and THE LIFE OF JOSEPHUS. Trans. by William Whiston; ed. with introd. by William Farmer. 1960. *Peter Smith* $5.50

JERUSALEM AND ROME. Ed. by Nahum N. Glatzer *Peter Smith* $5.50

Books about Josephus

Josephus: The Man and the Historian. By Henry St. John Thackeray. 1929. *KTAV* rev. ed. 1968 $7.95

Five Men: Character Studies from the Roman Empire. By Martin P. Charlesworth. 1936. *Bks. for Libraries* $7.75

Maccabees, Zealots and Josephus: An Inquiry into Jewish Nationalism in the Greco-Roman Period. By William R. Farmer. 1956. *Greenwood* 1974 $11.25

Josephus: A Historical Romance. By Lion Feuchtwanger. *Atheneum* 1972 pap. $4.95

LUCAN (Marcus Annaeus Lucanus). 39–65 A.D.

The Latin poet, nephew of Seneca, at first a favored member of Nero's court circle, was later implicated in a plot to murder Nero and committed suicide. His only extant work, the unfinished *"Bellum Civile"* (often called the "Pharsalia"), is an epic in ten books of hexameters on the war between Pompey and Caesar. He was often flamboyant in manner and liked to digress, but Shelley, a later poet, admired him greatly for the force and beauty of much of his writing.

THE CIVIL WAR: Books 1-10. Trans. by J. D. Duff *Harvard Univ. Press* Loeb 1928 $7.00

PHARSALIA. Trans. by Robert Graves *Penguin* 1957 o.p.

Books about Lucan

The Poet Lucan: Studies in Rhetorical Epic. By M. P. O. Morford. *Harper* (Barnes & Noble) 1967 $3.00
"The book is short but well documented and thorough in what it attempts, and it is especially welcome because of the general lack of critical studies of Lucan: most valuable and original is probably the discussion of the description and function of storms in ancient epic. . . . The brief final chapter is a thoughtful picture of Lucan's place in the literature of his age"— *(Choice)*.

Transmission of the Text of Lucan in the Ninth Century. By Harold C. Gotoff. *Harvard Univ. Press* Loeb Monographs 1971 $8.50

TACITUS, CORNELIUS. 55–117 A.D.

The "Annals" of Tacitus cover the period from the foundation of the city to the fall of the Republic in 31 B.C. The "History" covers the reigns of the twelve Caesars, from Augustus to Domitian, 31 B.C.–96 A.D. *"Germania"* is a record of a visit to Germany. *"Agricola"* is a biography of his father-in-law, who was governor of Britain. Tacitus, like Livy, emphasized the ethical side of history, which he wrote in a very dramatic and oratorical style. He is regarded as the only historian of the ancient world worthy to stand beside Thucydides. Tacitus left us a gallery of portraits which remarkably convey the personalities of his subjects.

COMPLETE WORKS: The Annals; The History; The Life of Cnaeus Julius Agricola; Germany and Its Tribes; A Dialogue on Oratory. Trans. by Alfred John Church and William Jackson Brodribb; ed. with introd. by Moses Hadas *Modern Library* 1942 pap. $1.95

HISTORIES AND ANNALS. The Histories trans. by Clifford H. Moore, The Annals trans. by John Jackson *Harvard Univ. Press* Loeb 4 vols. 1925 each $7.00

HISTORIES. Trans. by W. Hamilton Fyfe *Oxford* 2 vols. 1912 set $5.00; trans. by Kenneth Wellesley *Penguin* pap. $2.95

DIALOGUS, AGRICOLA, GERMANIA. Trans. by Herbert W. Benario *Bobbs* Lib. Arts 1967 $6.00 pap. $1.95; trans. by W. Peterson and Maurice Hutton *Harvard Univ. Press* Loeb 1925 $7.00

AGRICOLA. Trans. by Alfred J. Church and William J. Brodribb. 1869. *St. Martin's* $2.50; (and the "Germania") trans. by Hugh Mattingly *Penguin* pap. $1.25

Books about Tacitus

Tacitus, the Man and His Work. By Clarence W. Mendell. 1957. *Shoe String Press* 1970 $12.00

Tacitus. By Ronald Syme. *Oxford* 2 vols. 1958 set $25.50

Ten Studies in Tacitus. By Ronald Syme. *Oxford* 1970 $9.50. (*See his main entry, this section, for comment.*)

An Introduction to Tacitus. By Herbert W. Benario. *Univ. of Georgia Press* 1975 $6.50 pap. $3.00

"This concise volume assumes no previous knowledge of Tacitus, but begins with a summary of the high points of Roman political and military history, working into Tacitus' life and times"—(*LJ*)

PROCOPIUS. d. 565?

The Byzantine historian was private secretary to Belisarius, whom he accompanied on his Persian, African and Italian campaigns. "His chief works are generally known as 'Procopius' History of His Own Time'— dealing mainly with the wars against the Goths, Vandals, and Persians—and 'Secret History of Procopius'—which is largely a scandalous and often scurrilous court chronicle. . . . In his polished style Procopius imitated the historians of the Greek classical period"—(*Columbia Encyclopedia*).

HISTORY OF THE WARS and SECRET HISTORY. Trans by B. H. Dowling *Harvard Univ. Press* Loeb 7 bks. in 4 vols. Vol. 1, Bks. 1–2 Persian War Vol. 2, Bks. 3–4 Vandalic War Vol. 3, Bks. 5–6 Gothic War Vol. 4, Bks. 6–7 Gothic War each $7.00

SECRET HISTORY (Anecdota). Trans. by Richard Atwater; fwd. by Arthur E. Boak *Univ. of Michigan Press* 1961 $4.50 pap. $1.75

Ancient History by Modern Writers

GIBBON, EDWARD. 1737–1794.

Gibbon's "Decline and Fall" bridges the abyss between the ancient and the modern world. It is the one historical work of the 18th century that is still accepted as authoritative. It covers the 13 centuries of history in which paganism was breaking down and Christianity taking its place. Kenneth Rexroth has said (in *SR*): "Gibbon's history is the perfect expression and fulfillment of the Age of Reason, the eighteenth century. . . . Even more than Toynbee's work, Gibbon's is a judgment, but a judgment achieved by the presentation of an integral work of art, the magnificent progress of a great story and the scenic aspect of marvelous events."

THE DECLINE AND FALL OF THE ROMAN EMPIRE. 1776–1828. Ed. by John B. Bury repr. of 1909 ed. 7 vols. *AMS Press* $260.00; ed. by Frank C. Bourne *Dell* abr. ed. 1963 pap. $1.75; *Dutton* Everyman's 6 vols. 1954 each $3.95; ed. by D. M. Lowe *Harcourt* abr. ed. 1960 $15.00; ed. by Jacob Sloan *Macmillan* Collier Bks. 2 vols. abr. ed. 1962 pap. each $.95; *Random* (Modern Lib.) 3 vols. each $4.95; (and "Other Selected Writings") ed. by Hugh Trevor-Roper *Simon & Schuster* (Washington Square) 3 vols. pap. $4.95

THE PORTABLE GIBBON: The Decline and Fall of the Roman Empire. Selections ed. with introd. by Dero A. Saunders; pref. by Charles Alexander Robinson, Jr. *Viking* 1952 $5.50 pap. $3.35

HISTORY OF CHRISTIANITY. 1883. *Arno* 1972 $37.00; *Gordon Press* $29.95

Books about Gibbon

Edward Gibbon's Antagonism to Christianity. By Shelby T. McCloy. 1933. *Burt Franklin* $17.50
A Bibliography of the Works of Edward Gibbon. By Jane E. Norton. 1940. *Oxford* $11.25
Edward Gibbon and His World. By Gavin R. deBeer. *Viking* 1968 $6.95
"Those readers looking for an intellectual portrait of Gibbon will not find it here . . . The writing is careful, and Sir Gavin is intimately familiar with his subject and his world. Lovers of Gibbon and the 18th Century will enjoy this handsome book"—(*LJ*).
Gibbon. By Cicely V. Wedgwood. *British Bk. Centre* $3.95 pap. $1.50
Edward Gibbon. By R. N. Parkinson. *Twayne* 1973 $6.50
Decline and Fall of the Roman Empire: A Reappraisal for Our Own Times. By Michael Grant. *Crown* 1975 $12.95

See also Chapter 1, General Biography and Autobiography, this Vol.

MOMMSEN, THEODOR. 1817–1903. (Nobel Prize 1902)

The German scholar Theodor Mommsen taught at universities in Leipzig, Zurich, Breslau and Berlin. He was known to the general public as the author of "The History of Rome" (1854–56, o.p.), a book of great literary merit. Originally published in three volumes, it described the political struggle which accomplished the fall of the republic with great vigor, and its modern interpretation brought to life the Roman statesmen of antiquity. He never finished the fourth volume, but the fifth was published in 1885. Mommsen received the Nobel Prize for literature in 1902, the first historian to be so honored.

THE HISTORY OF ROME: From the Conquest of Carthage to the End of the Republic. 1854–56. Trans. and rev. with introd. and notes by Dero A. Saunders and John H. Collins *World Pub.* 1958 o.p.

MEDIEVAL AND RENAISSANCE STUDIES. Ed. by Eugene F. Rice, Jr. *Cornell Univ. Press* 1959 $14.50

PROVINCES OF THE ROMAN EMPIRE: The European Provinces. Ed. by T. Robert Broughton *Univ. of Chicago Press* 1968 $13.50 Phoenix Bks. pap. $4.50; *Ares* 2 vols. 1974 set $30.00

IMPERIAL LIVES AND LETTERS OF THE ELEVENTH CENTURY. Trans by Karl F. Morrison *Columbia* 1962 $11.00

BURY, JOHN B(AGNELL).   1861–1927.
Bury was an Irish historian, one of the foremost modern authorities on the East Roman Empire. He considered history a science—"not less, and not more." "He stressed historical continuity, and he thought that accident was a frequent determinant in the history of premodern societies. His breadth of viewpoint is reflected in his attention to administration, institutions, topography, and the arts, which contributed to his unrivaled knowledge of late Roman and Byzantine times"—(*Columbia Encyclopedia*). Bury's edition of Gibbon's "Decline and Fall" superseded all earlier editions. His "Idea of Progress: An Inquiry Into Its Origin and Growth" was originally published in 1920 (with introd. by Charles A. Beard *Dover* 1932 pap. $2.75; *Peter Smith* 1960 $4.50). His "History of Freedom of Thought," originally published in 1912, is o.p.

HISTORY OF THE LATER ROMAN EMPIRE FROM THE DEATH OF THEODOSIUS I TO THE DEATH OF JUSTINIAN. 1889. *Dover* 2 vols. 1957 pap. each $3.50; *Peter Smith* 2 vols. each $5.50

A HISTORY OF GREECE TO THE DEATH OF ALEXANDER THE GREAT. 1900. *St. Martin's* 3rd rev. ed. 1951 $10.95

THE LIFE OF ST. PATRICK: His Place in History. 1905. *Bks. for Libraries* $15.00

SELECTED ESSAYS. Ed. by Harold Temperly. 1909. *Bks. for Libraries* 1930 $9.50

THE ANCIENT GREEK HISTORIANS. 1909. *Dover* 1957 pap. $3.00; *Peter Smith* $4.50

IMPERIAL ADMINISTRATIVE SYSTEM OF THE NINTH CENTURY. 1911. *Burt Franklin* $14.50

HISTORY OF THE EASTERN ROMAN EMPIRE. 1912. *Russell & Russell* 1965 $11.50

THE INVASION OF EUROPE BY THE BARBARIANS. 1928. *Norton* 1967 pap. $3.95; *Russell & Russell* 1963 $11.00

(With others). THE HELLENISTIC AGE: Aspects of Hellenistic Civilization. 1923. *Kraus* $10.00; *Norton* 1970 pap. $2.45

BREASTED, JAMES H(ENRY).   1865–1935.
Breasted, Director of the Oriental Institute and Professor of Egyptology and Oriental History, University of Chicago, was a leading authority on Egyptian history. "The Dawn of Conscience," written for the general reader, points out how comparatively young the Age of Character is, dating back 5,000 years, while the Age of Force is probably a million years old or more. He edited and translated "Ancient Records of Egypt," historical documents from the earliest times to the Persian Conquest. His son Charles wrote his biography in "Pioneer to the Past" (1943. *Kelley* $15.00).

A HISTORY OF EGYPT FROM THE EARLIEST TIMES TO THE CONQUEST OF THE PERSIANS. 1905. *Scribner* rev. ed. 1909 $15.00

THE DEVELOPMENT OF RELIGION AND THOUGHT IN ANCIENT EGYPT. 1912. *Univ. of Pennsylvania Press* 1972 pap. $4.95; *Peter Smith* $5.25

THE CONQUEST OF CIVILIZATION. (Orig. "Ancient Times") 1916. *Harper* rev. ed. 1938 $10.00. New ed. including new text, author's own revisions and notes; ed. by Edith W. Ware.

ORIGINS OF CIVILIZATION. 1919. *Finch Press* $15.00

EDWIN SMITH SURGICAL PAPYRUS. *Univ. of Chicago Press* 2 vols. 1930 set $60.00

THE DAWN OF CONSCIENCE. *Scribner* 1933 $10.00

(Trans. and ed.). ANCIENT RECORDS OF EGYPT: Historical Documents from the Earliest Times to the Persian Conquest. 1906. *Russell & Russell* 5 vols. in 3 1962 set $65.00

HAMILTON, EDITH.   1867–1963.

Here are unusual accounts, written in a delightfully animated style, of the Greek and Roman ways of life in contrast with each other and with the modern world. The author touches on ancient literature, customs, philosophy, and art. Her translations from the literature are strikingly modern and amusing, illumined by her lucid style and imaginative scholarship. "Witness to the Truth" has for its subject the teachings of Jesus and the early Christians and with her work on Greek and Roman thought, rounds out "her study of the moral and intellectual sources of our modern society." Just "four days short of 90," in August 1957, on the stage of the ancient theater of Herodes Atticus at the foot of the Acropolis, in the presence of cabinet ministers, diplomats and Athenian intellectuals, she was decorated by King Paul of Greece and made an honorary Athenian citizen. She said in her address on that occasion: "Greece rose to the very height not because she was big, she was very small; not because she was rich, she was very poor; not even because she was wonderfully gifted. She rose because there was in the Greeks the greatest spirit that moves in humanity, the spirit that makes men free." At her death John Mason Brown said of her: "Nobility of mind, character and spirit is rare indeed. Wisdom, true wisdom, is no less rare. Edith, one of the most human of mortals, was the radiant possessor of both."

THE GREEK WAY. *Norton* 1930 $6.95; *Avon Bks.* 1973 pap. $1.50; *Franklin Watts* lg.-type ed. 1958 $9.95

THE ROMAN WAY. *Norton* 1932 $9.25 *Avon Bks.* 1973 pap. $1.50

MYTHOLOGY. *Little* 1942 $7.95; *Grosset* pap. $2.50; *New Am. Lib.* 1971 pap. $1.50; *Franklin Watts* lg.-type ed. 1966 $12.50. Greek, Roman and Norse myths.

WITNESS TO THE TRUTH: Christ and His Interpreters. *Norton* 1948 rev. ed. 1957 pap. $2.35

SPOKESMEN FOR GOD. *Norton* 1949 pap. $2.75

THE ECHO OF GREECE. *Norton* 1957 $6.95 pap. $2.45

THE EVER-PRESENT PAST. *Norton* 1964 $5.00 pap. $2.95

"Essays, addresses and book reviews by the author of 'The Greek Way' and 'The Roman Way' are presented in a posthumous collection, with a prolog by Boris Fielding Reid. Some of the literary essays are on the Greek tragedians, some on Corneille and Racine, and some on modern poetry and prose. In the *Saturday Review*, E. C. Dunn said, 'Drawing on the thinking of the undated ever-present past, Miss Hamilton offers a lively challenge to the present' "—(*PW*).

Books about Hamilton

Edith Hamilton: An Intimate Portrait. By Doris Fielding Reid. *Norton* 1967 $5.00

"This chatty, informal biography, based chiefly on the recollections of the author and of other friends, [is] an essential book"—(*LJ*).

SYME, SIR RONALD.   1903–

Born in New Zealand and educated at Oriel College, Oxford University, Syme had a long and distinguished career in teaching, diplomacy, and scholarship. From 1929 to 1949 he was a fellow at Trinity College, and from 1949 to 1970 he was Camden Professor of Ancient History at Oxford. Syme is generally regarded as one of the three greatest modern historians of ancient Rome.

THE ROMAN REVOLUTION. *Oxford* 1939 pap. $5.75

"The book is of a distinguished and erudite scholarship and of a remarkable depth. It is vigorously written and at the moment wears a topicality (though it is to the writer's credit that he never exploits it) which gives the story a profound significance to the student of modern Europe"—(*TLS*, London).

TACITUS. *Oxford* 2 vols. 1958 $25.50

SALLUST. Sather Classical Lectures *Univ. of California Press* 1964 $11.95

"This eagerly awaited volume . . . should be read by all seriously interested in Roman history. It starts with a careful analysis of Sallust's antecedents and the political situation of his age; this is followed by detailed consideration of Sallust as politician and historian"—(*American Historical Review*).

AMMIANUS AND THE HISTORIA AUGUSTA. *Oxford* 1968 $10.25

"Seldom has a scholarly enquiry conducted with such peremptory sobriety culminated in such pure delight"—(*TLS*, London).

TEN STUDIES IN TACITUS. *Oxford* 1970 $9.50

The author "displays again his right to a place in the triumvirate of modern masters of Roman history beside Gibbon and Mommsen"—(*American Historical Review*).

HISTORIA AUGUSTA: A Call of Clarity. 1971. *Int. Pubns. Service* $19.50

EMPERORS AND BIOGRAPHY: Studies in the Historia Augusta. *Oxford* 1971 $11.00

"As usual [the author's] style is terse, clear, entertaining and elegant: careful analysis of earlier scholarship and a concluding chapter on theoretical matters make this a valuable model for all students of source criticism"—(*Choice*).

HISTORY OF THE BRITISH COMMONWEALTH

The year 1800, which saw the birth of George Bancroft, the American historian, and of Thomas Babington Macaulay, marked the beginning of a new era in historical writing. The historians who lived before 1800 seldom went to original sources for their material, and their works have consequently been superseded by those of later historians who based their writings on scientifically conducted investigations. With the dawn of the 19th century, history became a science for specialists, and the methods of the older historians were discredited. George Peabody Gooch (*q.v.*) went so far as to say, "All eighteenth century historians are condemned except Gibbon."

Some of the older well-known English histories are: the eminently readable but unreliable "History of England from the Fall of Wolsey to the Defeat of the Spanish Armada 1529–1588" (1856–1870 *AMS Press* rev. ed. 12 vols. $175.00) by James Anthony Froude (1818–1894), who has been called England's National Historian; "The First Two Stuarts and the Puritans' Revolution, 1603–1660" (1895. *Norwood* $10.00) by Samuel Rawson Gardiner (1829–1902), the great political historian; Henry Thomas Buckle's (1821–1862) brilliant but unfinished "Introduction to the History of Civilization in England" (1857–61 *Somerset Pubs.* 1950 $24.50); and Albert F. Pollard's (1869–1948) very scholarly "History of England from the Accession of Edward VI to the Death of Elizabeth" (1910 *Greenwood* $20.00).

No one who is interested in English history should miss Walter Sellar and Robert Yeatman's amusing satire, "1066 and All That: A Memorable History of England, Comprising all the Parts You Can Remember, Including 103 Good Things, 5 Bad Kings and 2 Genuine Dates" (1931. *Dutton* 1950 $3.95 pap. $1.25).

Among series of note are the English Historical Documents Series (*see alphabetical listing*), *Knopf's* The British Empire before the Revolution, and the University of Chicago's Classics of British Historical Literature.

See also Section on Canada following American History, this Chapter.

Ashley, Maurice P. GREAT BRITAIN TO 1688. History of the Modern World Ser. *Univ. of Michigan Press* 1961 $7.50

GREATNESS OF OLIVER CROMWELL. *Macmillan* Collier Bks. 1966 pap. $1.50

Ashton, Thomas S., Gen. Ed. AN ECONOMIC HISTORY OF ENGLAND. 5 vols. 1955–61 Vol. 1 The Middle Ages by Ephraim Lipson, 12th ed. 1959 $6.75 Vols. 2–3 The Age of Mercantilism by Ephraim Lipson 2 vols. 6th ed. 1961 $22.00 Vol. 4 The Eighteenth Century by Thomas S. Ashton 1955 $8.00 pap. 1972 $4.00 Vol. 5 1870–1939 by William Ashworth 1960 pap. 1972 $3.75. There are many economic histories of England, but few cover the whole period of English history.

Ausubel, Herman. THE LATE VICTORIANS: A Short History. *Van Nostrand-Reinhold* Anvil
   Bks. 1955 pap. $3.25; *Peter Smith* $4.00

Baker, Timothy. MEDIEVAL LONDON. *Praeger* 1970 $11.95

   THE NORMANS. 1966. *Macmillan* Collier Bks. 1969 pap. $2.45

   "Uncluttered by scholarly paraphernalia, but carrying an extensive bibliography, this book
   provides a conservatively modern synthesis of the course and events of the Conquest and a rather
   full evaluation of its effects upon society, government, the church, language, architecture and the
   arts"—(*LJ*).

Battiscombe, Georgina. SHAFTESBURY: The Great Reformer, 1801–1885. *Houghton* 1975
   $15.00

   Shaftesbury's "efforts against the prevailing *laissez-faire* attitude of his age resulted in improved
   conditions in a veritable spectrum of human horrors ranging from treatment of lunatics to work in
   mines and factories by children . . . This is the first complete biography of Shaftesbury in modern
   times"—(*LJ*).

Beaglehole, J. C. THE LIFE OF CAPTAIN JAMES COOK. *Stanford Univ. Press* 1974 $18.50

   "A man of dauntless ambition, a restless doer, a skeptical and meticulous observer, [Cook]
   circumnavigated the globe two and a half times, explored the South Pacific, probed the Antarctic,
   charted endless seacoasts, and discovered numerous islands. . . . All in all, the standard work for
   decades to come, and a delight for the armchair admiral"—(*Choice*).

Beckett, James G. THE MAKING OF MODERN IRELAND, 1603–1923. *Knopf* 1966 $10.00

   "An entirely successful history of one of history's outstanding failures—English rule in Ireland.
   The author, who teaches at Queen's University, Belfast, has provided a narrative well stocked with
   data, tracing the sad succession of missteps—of errors and ill will, of exploitation and rebellion—
   that ended in the two nations' separation"—(*New Yorker*).

Beer, Samuel H. BRITISH POLITICS IN THE COLLECTIVIST AGE. 1965. *Random* Vintage Bks.
   1969 pap. $3.45

   "A subtle and scholarly analysis of the prevailing political culture and the patterns of interest,
   power, and policy"—(*LJ*).

Bell, J. Bowyer. THE SECRET ARMY: A History of the I.R.A. *M.I.T. Press* 1974 $4.95

   "A detailed, fascinating, grim account of the IRA's warfare against the British and those Irish
   who opposed the freedom of Ireland . . . ."—(Leonard W. Doob).

Bell, P. M. H. A CERTAIN EVENTUALITY: Britain and the Fall of France. *Atheneum* 1975
   $11.95

   "His chapters on British Opinion and on problems of opinion and propaganda are particularly
   valuable, while his analysis of British relations with the Vichy government and the emerging De
   Gaulle is thorough and well balanced"—(*LJ*).

BIBLIOGRAPHY OF BRITISH HISTORY. *Oxford* 4 vols. 1933–74 To 1485 ed. by Edgar P.
   Graves 2 vols. 2nd ed. 1974 set $40.00; Tudor Period 1485–1603 ed. by Conyers
   Read 1933 2nd ed. 1959 $13.75; Stuart Period 1603–1714 ed. by Mary F. Keeler
   2nd ed. 1970 $16.00

Borer, Mary Cathcart. BRITAIN—TWENTIETH CENTURY: The Story of Social Conditions.
   Warne 1967 $7.95

Bridenbaugh, Carl. VEXED AND TROUBLED ENGLISHMEN, 1590–1642. *Oxford* 1968 $12.50.
   An analysis of the causes of the emigration to America.

BRITISH HISTORY ATLAS. Ed. by M. Gibert *Macmillan* 1969 $4.95

Brooke, John. KING GEORGE III: America's Last Monarch. *McGraw-Hill* 1972 $12.50

   "Resolutely asserting that George III was neither mad nor bad, Brooke offers a defence of the
   King against every aspect of the Whig tradition. Legend and fable, at least those hostile to the
   King, are labeled as such"—(*Journal of Interdisciplinary History*).

Burton, Elizabeth. THE PAGEANT OF GEORGIAN ENGLAND. *Scribner* 1968 $6.95

   "A thoroughly readable social history of 18th-Century and early 19th-Century England"—(*LJ*).

Butler, D. E., and Jennie Freeman. BRITISH POLITICAL FACTS, 1900–1965. *St. Martin's* 3rd
   ed. 1968 $15.95

THE CAMBRIDGE HISTORY OF THE BRITISH EMPIRE. J. Holland Rose, A. P. Newton and
   E. A. Benians, Gen. Eds. *Cambridge* 8 vols. 1929–63 Vol. 1 The Old Empire, from the
   Beginnings to 1783 Vol. 2 The Growth of the New Empire, 1783–1870 $35.00 Vol. 3
   The Empire Commonwealth, 1870–1919 $35.00 Vol. 4 British India, 1479–1858
   Vol. 5 Indian Empire, 1858–1918 Vol. 6 Canada and Newfoundland Vol. 7, Pt. 1 Aus-
   tralia Vol. 7, Pt. 2 New Zealand Vol. 8 South Africa, Rhodesia and the High Commis-
   sion Territories. All vols. o.p. except vols. 2 and 3.

Cannon, John. THE FOX-NORTH COALITION: Crisis of the Constitution, 1782–84. *Cambridge* 1970 $13.50
   "An interesting study of a significant episode in late 18th century English politics"—*(Choice).*

PARLIAMENTARY REFORM, 1640–1832. *Cambridge* 1973 $18.50 pap. $6.95

Cantor, Norman F. THE ENGLISH: A History of Politics and Society to 1760. *Simon &
   Schuster* 1967 $10.00 pap. 1969 $3.95
   "In this first volume of a projected two, Mr. Cantor has written a highly personal book, and a
   rather mixed one. Ostensibly a conspectus of English history, it attends to that task in a series of
   careful, and carefully written, sections on the development of English government, law, and
   society. . . . He has written an almost old-fashioned account of an England governed by its
   monarchs and upper classes, a political history understood from within a developing system of
   rule. This does leave out more than is comfortable—especially the main part of the English
   nation—but it gives the book real coherence and a powerful sense of intelligent life"—(G. R. Elton,
   in *Political Science Quarterly*).

Churchill, Peregrine, and Julian Mitchell. JENNIE: Lady Randolph Churchill, a Portrait
   with Letters. *St. Martin's* 1975 $10.00

Clark, Sir George. ENGLISH HISTORY: A Survey. *Oxford* 1972 $10.00
   "This book is fresh, bright, urbane, witty and incorporates the latest findings of recent
   scholarship in English history"—*(Choice).*

Connery, Donald S. THE IRISH. *Simon & Schuster* 1968 $7.95 pap. 1970 $2.95

Costigan, Giovanni. A HISTORY OF MODERN IRELAND: With a Sketch of Earlier Times.
   Pegasus 1969 $7.95 pap. $2.95

Cross, Colin. THE FALL OF THE BRITISH EMPIRE: 1918–1968. *Coward* 1969 $8.95

Douglas, David C. WILLIAM THE CONQUEROR: The Norman Impact Upon England.
   English Monarchy Ser. *Univ. of California Press* 1964 $12.50 pap. $3.85
   "No modern study so well describes the consolidation of the Norman lands in the 11th century,
   the tribulations of the great duke, and his triumph on either side of the Channel as does David
   Douglas's mature, meticulous, and magisterial volume"—*(LJ).*

EDINBURGH HISTORY OF SCOTLAND. *Harper* (Barnes & Noble) 4 vols. 1968–   Vol. 1 The
   Making of the Kingdom by A. A. M. Duncan (in prep.) $35.00 Vol. 2 The Later
   Middle Ages by Ranald Nicholson (1974) $25.00 Vol. 3 James V to James VII by
   Gordon Donaldson (1971) $13.50 Vol. 4 1689 to the Present by William Ferguson
   (1968) $14.50

Ehrman, John. THE YOUNGER PITT: The Years of Acclaim. *Dutton* 1970 $14.95
   "Ehrman has mastered the period and sources, and his work will clearly be the definitive
   biography for a long time to come"—*(Choice).*

ENGLISH HISTORICAL DOCUMENTS SERIES. D. C. Douglas, Gen. Ed. *Oxford* 12 vols. 1953–
   1974
   The basic material of English history in the form of documents rendered in full. Vol. 1 c. 500–
   1042 ed. by Dorothy Whitelock (1955) $23.50 Vol. 2 1042–1189 ed. by D. C. Douglas and G. W.
   Greenaway (1953) $22.50 Vol. 3 1189–1327 ed. by D. C. Douglas and Harry Rothwell (1974)
   $56.00 Vol. 4 1327–1485 ed. by A. R. Myers (1969) $29.50 Vol. 5 1485–1558 ed. by C. H. Williams
   (1967) $29.00 Vol. 8 1660–1714 ed. by Andrew Browning (1953) $20.00 Vol. 10 1714–1783 ed. by
   D. B. Horn and Mary Ransome (1957) $22.50 Vol. 11 1783–1832 ed. by A. Aspinall and E.
   Anthony Smith (1959) $22.50 Vol. 12 Pt. 1 1833–1874 ed. by G. M. Young and W. D. Handcock
   (1956) $22.50. Vols. 6, 7 and 9 are o.p.

Ensor, Robert C. ENGLAND, 1870–1914. *Oxford* 1936 $9.95

Erickson, Arvel B., and Martin J. Havran, Eds. READINGS IN ENGLISH HISTORY. *Scribner* 1967 pap. $4.75

Fisher, John. THE AUSTRALIANS FROM 1788 TO MODERN TIMES. Taplinger 1968 $5.50

Flanner, Janet. LONDON WAS YESTERDAY, 1934–1939. *Viking* 1975 $9.95. Includes more than 75 black-and-white photographs.

Fraser, Antonia. CROMWELL. *Knopf* 1973 $12.50; *Dell* 1975 pap. $1.95

KING JAMES: VI of Scotland and I of England. *Knopf* 1975 $12.50
The author presents "a sympathetic and appreciative essay"—(*LJ*).

MARY, QUEEN OF SCOTS. *Delacorte* 1969 $10.00; *Dell* 1971 pap. $1.75
"No source of information has been neglected. . . . This is both a trustworthy chronicle and an absorbingly readable story"—(*TLS*, London).

Frere, Sheppard S. BRITANNIA: A History of Roman Britain. *Harvard Univ. Press* 1967 $15.00
"Because our knowledge of Roman Britain has increased greatly during the last three decades, this volume was designed to update earlier scholarly works. Professor Frere, of Oxford, who has played an important role in this historical research, has produced a well-written and organized book"—(*LJ*).

Geoffrey of Monmouth. HISTORY OF THE KINGS OF BRITAIN. Trans. by Sebastian Evans; rev. by Charles W. Dunn *Dutton* 1958 pap. $2.45; trans. by Lewis Thorp *Peter Smith* $4.00
Geoffrey of Monmouth (c. 1100–1154) was Bishop of St. Asaph. His "history," source of much of what we know of Arthurian legend, was compiled, it is now thought, from many earlier writings as well as from oral tales. He himself claimed this to be a translation from a single ancient work.

Gipson, Lawrence Henry. *See his main entry, this Section.*

Gladstone, William Ewart. THE GLADSTONE DIARIES, 1825–39. Ed. by M. R. Foot *Oxford* 2 vols. 1968 $47.00
"This meticulously researched edition of the heretofore virtually inaccessible diaries of one of Britain's greatest prime ministers is not only a fascinating account of the intense moralizing and constant self-examination that typified William Gladstone's mind, but it is an extremely useful bibliographical tool that no respectable library should overlook"—(*LJ*).

Gordon, Michael R. CONFLICT AND CONSENSUS IN LABOUR'S FOREIGN POLICY, 1914–1965. *Stanford Univ. Press* 1969 $8.95
"A first rate political essay on the foreign policy of the British Labour Party . . . No other work covers the field"—(*Choice*).

Green, John Richard. A SHORT HISTORY OF THE ENGLISH PEOPLE. 1874. Ed. by L. C. Jane. With surveys, by other hands, extending the period covered to 1960. *Dutton* Every-man's 2 vols. 1960 each $3.95; *Norwood* repr. of 1897 ed. $10.00
Green's "Short History" covers the years 607 to 1873. "A Political and Social Survey from 1815 to 1914," by R. P. Farley is included and further sections dealing with Britain from 1918 to 1939 and from 1945 to 1960, with chronological lists of military and political events of both World Wars, are included in the Dutton editon. "The hero of the book is the people. History was not only past politics to Green (1837–1883), history was religion, social life, art, literature." He divided his history, not according to reigns, but according to the governing feature of the periods and emphasized the years of peace far more than the years of war. This history has always been noted for its literary grace and vivid, lucid style.

Hall, H. Duncan. COMMONWEALTH: A History of the British Commonwealth of Nations. *Van Nostrand-Reinhold* 1971 $29.95
The author "has been close to many of the events he describes, and the air of authenticity, the very minuteness of knowledge which informs the text, and the balanced appraisals of once heated events, lend the work the weight, gravity, and value of an encyclopedia"—(*Choice*).

Hamer, David Alan. JOHN MORLEY: Liberal Intellectual in Politics. *Oxford* 1968 $16.25
"A minute examination of Morley's opinions, or rather a successful attempt to rescue them from oblivion"—(*TLS*, London).

LIBERAL POLITICS IN THE AGE OF GLADSTONE AND ROSEBERRY: A Study in Leadership and Policy. *Oxford* 1972 $16.25

Hill, Christopher. CHANGE AND CONTINUITY IN SEVENTEENTH-CENTURY ENGLAND. *Harvard Univ. Press* 1975 $12.00

REFORMATION TO INDUSTRIAL REVOLUTION. (Pelican Economic History of Britain, Vol. 2) *Penguin* 1970 pap. $1.95; *Peter Smith* $4.50

Hobsbawm, Eric J. INDUSTRY AND EMPIRE: From 1750 to the Present Day. (Pelican Economic History of Britain, Vol. 3) *Penguin* 1970 pap. $2.45; *Peter Smith* $4.25
"Mr. Hobsbawm is a historian of remarkable intelligence and erudition. This . . . economic history of Britain since 1750 is most welcome"—(*LJ*).

Holcombe, Lee. VICTORIAN LADIES AT WORK: Middle-Class Working Women in England and Wales 1850–1914. *Shoe String Press* 1973 $12.00
"Traces the evolution of proper, middle class women from their enforced status as mere social ornaments in mid-19th century to a position of recognized independence in the working world by the outbreak of World War I"—(*LJ*).

Howarth, David. SOVEREIGN OF THE SEAS: The Story of British Sea Power. *Atheneum* 1974 $14.95
"A readable, accurate general survey of British naval history"—(*LJ*).

Inglis, Brian. ROGER CASEMENT. *Harcourt* 1974 $8.95
"This splendid book tells the story of a troubled soul who surmounted his troubles and rose to greatness"—(*TLS*, London).

Jones, James Rees. THE REVOLUTION OF 1688 IN ENGLAND. *Norton* 1973 $11.95
"General readers will find the whole work uniquely intelligent, for compared with even the most recent works of Maurice Ashley and John Carswell, the Revolution is not treated as a working out of manifest destiny, nor are there any questions begged as in the classic coverage of G.M. Trevelyan"—(*Choice*).

Kealey, Edward J. ROGER OF SALISBURY: Viceroy of England. *Univ. of Claifornia Press* 1972 $13.50
"Kealey discusses Roger as man, as ecclesiastical administrator and politician, and as royal official with sympathy and insight. He is careful to place the events of Roger's career in broader historical context and to explain bureaucratic and administrative complexities"—(*Choice*).

Kellas, James G. MODERN SCOTLAND: The Nation since 1870. *Praeger* 1968 $8.00

Kirby, D.P. THE MAKING OF EARLY ENGLAND. Fabric of British History Ser. *Schocken* 1968 $10.00

Langford, P. THE FIRST ROCKINGHAM ADMINISTRATION 1765–66. *Oxford* 1973 $14.50
"A commentary that is lively throughout, and he [the author] loves to sally forth with fine, firm, general statements, some of which are beautifully provocative"—(*TLS*, London).

Leach, Douglas Edward. ARMS FOR EMPIRE: A Military History of the British Colonies in North America, 1607–1763. *Macmillan* 1973 $14.95
This is "a major undertaking to say the least. It covers the complex military events of the American colonies of Great Britain over a two and one-half century period ranging from 1607 to 1763"—(*The Historian*).

McFarlane, K.B. LANCASTRIAN KINGS AND LOLLARD KNIGHTS. *Oxford* 1972 $9.50
"A brilliant and important book for students and scholars alike, based upon an intimate familiarity with the history of late 14th and early 15th century England"—(*Choice*).

Macmillan, Harold. *See his main entry in Chapter 2, General Biography and Autobiography, this Vol.*

Mansergh, Nicholas. THE COMMONWEALTH EXPERIENCE: A Critical History of the British Commonwealth. History of Civilization Ser. *Praeger* 1969 $12.50

Mattingly, Garrett. THE ARMADA. *Houghton* 1959 $7.50 pap. 1962 $2.65. A classic account.

Mayhew, Henry. LONDON LABOUR AND THE LONDON POOR, 1861–62. 1865. *Dover* 4 vols. 1968 pap. each $4.00; *Peter Smith* 4 vols. set $26.00; *International Scholarly Bk. Services* 4 vols. 1967 set $70.00; *Kelley* 4 vols. 1967 set $10.00

Henry Mayhew (1812–1877), comic novelist and one of the original owners and editors of *Punch*, described himself as "a literary man, desirous of letting the rich know something more about the poor." In an objective and factual style Mayhew records his interviews with London's poor in this prodigious work. W. H. Auden writes of him (in the *New Yorker*): "Among social anthropologists Mayhew is unique, so far as I know, in his combination of a Fabian Society passion for statistics, a Ripley passion for believe-it-or-not facts as sheer oddities, and a passion for the idiosyncrasies of character and speech such as only the very greatest novelists have exhibited."

Melli, Frank J. GREAT BRITAIN AND THE CONFEDERATE NAVY, 1861–1865. *Univ. of Indiana Press* 1970 $7.50

Miller, John D. THE COMMONWEALTH IN THE WORLD. *Harvard Univ. Press* 3rd. ed. 1965 $8.00

Moore, Marianne. VICTORIAN WIVES. *St. Martin's* 1974 $8.50

"Marital roles available to nineteenth-century women in both England and the U.S. are compared. The relatively enlightened situation of women in America is contrasted to the expectations and assumptions of Victorian England"—(*Booklist*).

Morris, James. PAX BRITANNICA: The Climax of an Empire. *Harcourt* 1968 $9.50

"James Morris combines the techniques of a radio commentator with those of a descriptive travel writer in a successful portrayal of what the Empire looked and felt like in a variety of places at the end of the 19th century, how it ticked, who pulled the strings, and the practical ends and ideals it served"—(Sir Philip Magnus, in the *N.Y. Times*).

Mowat, Charles L. BRITAIN BETWEEN THE WARS: 1918–1940. *Univ. of Chicago Press* 1955 $13.50; *Beacon* 1971 pap. $4.95

Namier, Lewis, and John Brooke, Eds. THE HOUSE OF COMMONS, 1754–1790. *Oxford* 3 vols. 1964 $80.00

Nicolson, Harold. *See his main entry, this Section, and in Chapter 2, General Biography and Autobiography, this Vol.*

OXFORD HISTORY OF ENGLAND. Sir George N. Clark, Gen. Ed. *Oxford* 15 vols. (*consult publisher's catalog for authors, titles and prices*)

Poole, Austin Lane, Ed. MEDIEVAL ENGLAND. *Oxford* 2nd rev. ed. 1958 $17.00

Quinn, David B. ENGLAND AND THE DISCOVERY OF AMERICA, 1481–1620. *Knopf* 1974 $15.00

"Because this study is filled with so many new facts and interpretations it may well take years for its full significance to be appreciated"—(*LJ*).

Rabb, Theodore. ENTERPRISE AND EMPIRE: Merchant and Gentry Investment in the Expansion of England, 1575–1630. *Harvard Univ. Press* 1967 $12.50

"The author does not follow the usual historical methods in this study, but instead turns to computer data processing techniques. In studying each of the 6,000 persons who had a financial interest in any of the overseas enterprises in England during the period, Rabb 'programs' this information into the computer"—(*Choice*).

Schroeder, Paul W. AUSTRIA, GREAT BRITAIN, AND THE CRIMEAN WAR: The Destruction of the European Concert. *Cornell Univ. Press* 1973 $19.50

"An important revisionist study of the history of the Crimean War diplomacy, the product of extensive archival research in London, Paris, and Vienna, as well as a thorough examination of the voluminous secondary material"—(*Choice*).

Sears, Stephen W., Ed. HORIZON HISTORY OF THE BRITISH EMPIRE. *American Heritage* (dist. by McGraw-Hill) 1974 $25.00

"A series of essays by noted historians, journalists, and political scientists which outline the rise and fall of these empires in a scholarly and highly readable manner"—(*LJ*).

Skidelsky, Robert. OSWALD MOSLEY. *Holt* 1975 $15.00

"Biographer Skidelsky, who teaches at Johns Hopkins, works hard at creating a sympathetic and revealing study of the root of Mosley's fascism. A shameless elitism and a longing for an almost feudal sense of self-sufficient community, a revulsion against war caused by his experiences in 1914, and an aristocrat's disdain for the middle class are primary elements in Mosley's career"— (*Time*).

Smellie, K. B. GREAT BRITAIN SINCE 1688: A Modern History. *Univ. of Michigan Press* 1962 $7.50

Smith, Goldwin. A HISTORY OF ENGLAND. 1949. *Scribner* 4th ed. 1974 $12.50 pap. $9.95

Smith, Lacey Baldwin. THE ELIZABETHAN WORLD. *Houghton* 1967 $6.50 Sentry eds. 1971 pap. $2.25

Steinberg, S. H., Ed. DICTIONARY OF BRITISH HISTORY. *St. Martin's* 2nd ed. 1971 $10.95

Taylor, A. J. P. *See his main entry in Section on Modern and World History, this Chapter.*

Trevelyan, George M. *See his main entry, this Section.*

Uzoigwe, Godfrey N. BRITAIN AND THE CONQUEST OF AFRICA: The Age of Salisbury. *Univ. of Michigan Press* 1974 $14.00

Webb, Robert K. MODERN ENGLAND: From the 18th Century to the Present. *Dodd* 1968 pap. $7.50

Wedgwood, Cicely V. THE THIRTY YEARS WAR. 1939. *Doubleday* Anchor Bks. pap. $1.95; *Peter Smith* $6.00; *Humanities Press* (Fernhill) $16.50

Wilding, Norman, and Philip Laundy. AN ENCYCLOPEDIA OF PARLIAMENT. *Int. Pubns. Service* 4th rev. ed. 1972 $20.00

WILLING'S PRESS GUIDE, BRITISH EDITION. *IPC America, Inc.* (205 East 42 St., New York, N.Y.) 1976 $25.00. This is the famous guide to the British press that has been the reference source for names and addresses of the British publications for over 90 years. Includes all London, suburban, county and local newspapers, over 4,000 periodicals and some 1,500 annuals. Gives price, publisher, year of establishment and frequency of publication.

Wilson, Trevor. THE DOWNFALL OF THE LIBERAL PARTY: 1914–35. *Cornell Univ. Press* 1966 $11.50

"The English Liberal Party disintegrated at a time and over issues that are close enough for the reader to learn from this sensible, sensitive study not only particular facts but a good deal about what makes for modern party unity or fragmentation. Policies and leaders divided the Liberals, and since nothing fails like failure, the moment the Party looked like a loser it lost campaign contributions. Down through the nineteen-twenties, Mr. Wilson points out, the Liberal Party retained a distinctive character and following, but the decision of the Labour Party to contest every Parliamentary seat forced a series of sharp, three-cornered elections, which the impecunious Liberals could not afford. Mr. Wilson's postmortem, then, does not wholly blame the corpse; the Liberal Party, he makes clear, did not just fall—it was pushed. The author, by the way, offers portraits of those rivals, Asquith and Lloyd George, that are among the best—the most plausible and the most temperate—available"—(*New Yorker*).

Woodward, Sir Llewellyn. GREAT BRITAIN AND THE WAR OF 1914–1918. *Harper* (Barnes & Noble) 1967 $18.75; *Beacon Press* 1970 pap. $4.95

Ziegler, Philip. KING WILLIAM IV. *Harper* 1973 $12.50

"By far the best life of William IV of England that has yet appeared, superseding all previous biographies of the subject"—(*Choice*).

THE ANGLO-SAXON CHRONICLE. 450–1150. Trans. and ed. by G. N. Garmonsway. 1934. *Dutton* Everyman's $3.95; C-Text of the Old English Chronicles, ed. by H. A. Rositzke. 1940. *Johnson Reprint* pap. $5.50; ed. by Charles Plummer *Oxford* 2 vols. 1899 $17.00

The Chronicle recounts the history of the English to 1154. It was probably begun by monks at Winchester. Alfred the Great made a revision about 891, including material from Bede (*q.v.*) and others. The manuscripts of the Chronicle taken as a whole, form "the first national continuous history of a western nation in its own language," and "the first great book in English prose."

BEDE (or Baeda, Beda), SAINT. 673–735. *See Chapter 4, World Religions, this Vol.*

HOLINSHED, RAPHAEL. d. 1580?

Born in Cheshire, Holinshed worked as a translator for the printer and publisher Reginald Wolfe when he first came to London, and Wolfe is said to have had a hand in his "Chronicles," as did several other writers. Modern interest in Holinshed's work stems mainly from the fact that Shakespeare found in it the source of plots for such plays as "Macbeth" and "King Lear."

HOLINSHED'S CHRONICLES OF ENGLAND, SCOTLAND AND IRELAND. 1578. Ed. by Sir Henry Ellis. 1807–08. *AMS Press* 6 vols. each $45.00 set $240.00. The standard.

HOLINSHED'S CHRONICLE AS USED IN SHAKESPEARE'S PLAYS. Ed. with introd. by Allardyce Nicoll and Josephine Nicoll *Dutton* Everyman's $3.95

CLARENDON, EDWARD HYDE, 1st Earl.   1609–1674.

Edward Hyde was an ardent Royalist from the time he entered Parliament in 1640. During the Civil War he accompanied the young Charles II into exile and began his history. After Cromwell's death, Hyde helped restore the monarchy in 1660. The "Clarendon Code" was the harsh legislation passed against dissenters. One of the famous passages in his history described the Trial, Death and Character of King Charles I.

SELECTIONS FROM THE HISTORY OF THE REBELLION AND CIVIL WARS, AND THE LIFE BY HIMSELF. Ed. by G. Huehns *Oxford* World's Class. $3.75

BURKE, EDMUND.   1729–1797.

"Edmund Burke, 18th Century British politician and writer, is remembered chiefly for his eloquent and prophetic objections to the French Revolution, but throughout his writing one finds a political philosophy that appeals to today's intellectual conservatives"—(*LJ*). He is one of the immense figures of English political history and one of the great masters of English prose. His letters reveal a young man torn between choosing a career in literature or in politics, who finally emerged a towering figure in both.

WORKS OF THE RIGHT HONORABLE EDMUND BURKE. 1899. *Somerset Pubs.* 12 vols. set $220.00

SELECTED WRITINGS AND SPEECHES. Ed. by P. J. Stanlis. 1963. *Peter Smith* $6.50

SPEECHES. Ed. by F. G. Selby. 1956. *Greenwood* 1974 $15.00

SPEECHES AND LETTERS ON AMERICAN AFFAIRS. Introd. by Peter McKevitt *Dutton* Everyman's $3.95

SELECTED WRITINGS AND SPEECHES ON AMERICA. Ed. by Thomas H. Mahoney *Bobbs* 1964 $6.00 pap. $1.75

THE PHILOSOPHY OF EDMUND BURKE: A Selection from His Speeches and Writings. Ed. by Louis I. Bredvold and Ralph G. Ross *Univ. of Michigan Press* Ann Arbor Bks. 1961 $5.95 pap. $2.95

ON THE AMERICAN REVOLUTION. Ed. by E. R. Barkan *Peter Smith* 2nd ed. $6.00

ACCOUNT OF THE EUROPEAN SETTLEMENTS IN AMERICA. 1758. *AMS Press* 2 vols. repr. of 1808 ed. set $30.00; *Arno* 2 vols. in 1 repr. of 1777 ed. 1972 $40.00; *Gregg* 2 vols. repr. of 1758 ed. set $32.00

SPEECH ON CONCILIATION WITH THE COLONIES. 1775. *Regnery* Gateway Eds. 1964 pap. $.95

REFLECTIONS ON THE REVOLUTION IN FRANCE. 1790. Ed. by Thomas H. D. Mahoney *Bobbs* 1955 $5.00 pap. $2.00; *Doubleday* Anchor Bks. pap. $2.50; ed. with notes by A. J. Grieve *Dutton* Everyman's $3.95; ed. by William B. Todd *Holt* pap. $2.95

CORRESPONDENCE. Thomas W. Copeland, Gen. Ed. *Univ. of Chicago Press* 9 vols. 1958–1971 Vol. 1 1958 Vol. 2 1960 Vol. 3 1961 Vol. 4 1963 Vol. 5 1965 Vol. 6 1967 Vol. 7 1968 Vol. 8 1970 Vol. 9 1971 Vol. 1 $20.00 Vol. 2 $28.00 Vols. 3–6, 8–9 each $25.00 Vol. 7 $30.00

Books about Burke

Edmund Burke and His Literary Friends. By Donald C. Bryant. 1939. *Richard West* $25.00
Burke and the Nature of Politics. By Carl B. Cone. *Univ. Press of Kentucky* 2 vols. 1957–64 Vol. 1 The Age of the American Revolution (1957) Vol. 2 The Age of the French Revolution (1964) each $9.00

"This biography is typical of much sound American professional scholarship. There is little analysis, little judgment, but a steady, accurate, comprehensive narrative of Burke's life, interspersed with an excellent précis of what he said and wrote"—(J. H. Plumb, in the *New York Review of Books*).

The Political Reason of Edmund Burke. By Francis P. Canavan *Duke Univ. Press* 1960 $6.75

Burke, Disraeli and Churchill: The Politics of Perseverance. By Stephen R. Graubard. *Harvard Univ. Press* 1961 $7.50

Edmund Burke: The Practical Imagination. By Gerald W. Chapman. *Harvard Univ. Press* 1967 $9.00

"Each of five tightly argued chapters surveys the development of Burke's opinion on one of the great issues, or crises, with which he dealt. . . . The useful bibliography and very helpful notes introduce other interpretations, so that an interested student can here find a well defined thesis—that Burke's thinking typifies the union of 'perhaps the two greatest achievements of English culture to date—its literary imagination, and its success in practical politics'—and a critique of much recent work on Burke"—(*Choice*).

Burke. By. T. E. Utley. *British Bk. Centre* $2.95 pap. $1.20

Problem of Burke's Political Philosophy. By Burleigh Wilkins. *Oxford* 1967 $9.00

The "author concludes that Burke's political philosophy was a conservative version of the natural law and not a denial of the natural law in the name of either history or utility . . . This admirable book is good tempered, thoughtful, sensible, clear and concise"—(*American Historical Review*).

The Social Thought of Rousseau and Burke: A Comparative Study. By David Cameron. *Univ. of Toronto Press* 1973 $11.50

The author "first surveys the prevailing critical approach that emphasizes the differences between Burke and Rousseau. Then, in the two major parts of the book he delineates their considerable substantive agreement: first, on human nature and natural law and, second, on the notions of reason and of liberty in the political community"—(*Choice*).

Edmund Burke: His Political Philosophy. By Frank O'Gorman. *Indiana Univ. Press* 1973 $6.95

"One of the best recent studies of Burke. . . . [It] would be an excellent selection for a course in modern political theory and should be acquired by all undergraduate and research collections"—(*Choice*).

Marx and Burke: A Revisionist View. By Ruth A. Bevan. *Open Court* 1973 $7.95

The author "compares the historical and political theories of Marx and Burke. Both theorists are found to be relevant to modern substantive and methodological problems in politics. Similarities are discovered in their concepts of change and revolution, their rejection of philosophical rationalism of the Enlightenment, and their historical empiricism"—(*Choice*).

MACAULAY, THOMAS BABINGTON, 1st Baron. 1800–1859.

Macaulay's "History" covers a period of only 17 years. It begins with the accession of James II and extends to the death of William III: 1685–1702. Macaulay was a Whig, and his work attacks the Tory versions of English history. James Ford Rhodes says: "Macaulay's 'History' is a great book, shows extensive research, a sane method, and an excellent power of narration; and when he is a partisan, he is so honest and transparent that the effect of his partiality is neither enduring nor mischievous." Sir Charles Harding Firth's "Commentary on Macaulay's History of England" includes lectures on Macaulay's methods and errors, his treatment of Scotch and Irish history and his complete disregard of America.

SELECTED WRITINGS. Ed. by John Clive and Thomas Pinney. Classics of British Historical Literatue Ser. *Univ. of Chicago Press* 1972 $15.00 Phoenix Bks. 1973 pap. $4.25

CRITICAL AND HISTORICAL ESSAYS. 1843. Introd. by Douglas Jerrold *Dutton* Everyman's 2 vols. pap. each $3.95

THE HISTORY OF ENGLAND FROM THE ACCESSION OF JAMES II. 1849. Ed. by Charles H. Firth *AMS Press* 6 vols. 1913–15 set $120.00; *Dutton* Everyman's 4 vols. each $3.95

ESSAY ON FREDERIC THE GREAT. 1893. *AMS Press* $5.00; *Scholarly Press* $6.00

Books about Macaulay

Lord Macaulay: The Pre-eminent Victorian. By Sydney C. Roberts. 1927. *Folcroft* 1973 $5.00

Commentary on Macaulay's History of England. By Charles H. Firth. 1938. *Harper* (Barnes & Noble) 1965 $9.00

The Commentary "has dated [since first publication] but remains a classic in its kind"—(*TLS*, London).

Lord Macaulay, Victorian Liberal. By Richard C. Beatty. 1938. *Shoe String Press* 1971 $12.00

The Life and Letters of Lord Macaulay. By George O. Trevelyan. *Oxford* 2 vols. 1961 set $7.00

Macaulay. By G. R. Potter. *British Bk. Centre* 1962 $2.95 pap. $1.20

Macaulay. By Jane Millgate. *Routledge & Kegan Paul* 1973 $10.00 pap. $5.00

"This is an examination of Macaulay's intellectual heritage, his methods and techniques [and] the relationship of his . . . political career to his writing"—(*Economist*).

Macaulay: Shaping of the Historian. By John Clive. *Knopf* 1973 $15.00

"Clive's well-written study . . . undertakes to explain the shaping of Macaulay's ideas and the directions which his energies took. It is, therefore, as much a history of pre-Victorian social and political thought and action as it is of Macaulay himself"—(Phoebe Adams, in the *Atlantic*).

See also Chapter 15, Essays and Criticism, Reader's Adviser, *Vol. 1.*

GOOCH, GEORGE PEABODY. 1873–1968. *See Section on Modern and World History, this Chapter.*

BARKER, SIR ERNEST. 1874–1960.

The English political scientist wrote delightfully in "Age and Youth" (1953, o.p.), his autobiography and the record of his academic career. Sir Ernest's approach to his material on political theory is philosophical rather than historical or governmental. He is "concerned not so much with the historical development of institutions as with the ideas and ideologies behind them." His "Principles of Social and Political Theory" has been called "the author's most comprehensive statement of his own political theory." Other of his books still in print are "The Political Thought of Plato and Aristotle" (1906. *Russell & Russell* $17.00; *Dover* 1959 pap. $3.50; *Peter Smith* $5.50), "The Crusades" (1923. *Bks. for Libraries* $7.50), "Citizen's Choice" (1937. *Bks. for Libraries* $8.75), "The Development of Public Services in Western Europe, 1660–1930" (1944. *Shoe String Press* 1966 $4.00), "Greek Political Theory: Plato and His Predecessors" (orig. "Political Thought of Plato and Aristotle") (*Harper* (Barnes & Noble) rev. ed. 1960 pap. $4.50) and "Traditions of Civility" (1948. *Shoe String Press* 1967 $10.00). He edited "The Library of Greek Thought" (1923–34. *AMS Press* 9 vols. set $90.00) among other works.

POLITICAL THOUGHT IN ENGLAND: 1848–1914. 1915. *Oxford* 1947 $3.50

CHURCH, STATE AND STUDY. 1930. *Greenwood* 1974 $12.00

UNIVERSITIES IN GREAT BRITAIN. 1931. *Norwood Editions* $7.50

OLIVER CROMWELL AND THE ENGLISH PEOPLE. 1937. *Bks. for Libraries* 1972 $7.50

REFLECTIONS ON GOVERNMENT. 1942. *Oxford* 1967 pap. $2.95

ESSAYS ON GOVERNMENT. 1945. *Oxford* 2nd ed. 1965 $6.00 pap. $2.75

PRINCIPLES OF SOCIAL AND POLITICAL THEORY. *Oxford* 1951 $7.25 pap. $2.50

CHURCH, STATE AND EDUCATION. 1957. *Norwood Editions* $10.00

CHURCHILL, SIR WINSTON (LEONARD SPENCER). 1874–1965. (Nobel Prize 1953)

Sir Winston both made and wrote history during his country's gravest years. As soldier, statesman, orator and author he possessed humor, understanding and magnificent courage. He received the Nobel Literature Prize for "The Second World War" and *Houghton,* in 1953, received the Carey-Thomas Award for its publication. "A History of the English-Speaking Peoples" is a "brilliant and sustained piece of historical writing." Sir Harold Nicolson (*q.v.*) said of it in the *N.Y. Times:* "The narrative is so lucid, the treatment so unbiased, the events so vividly portrayed and the style so memorable, that the book leaves a fixed impress on the mind. It is a work of research and reflection; it is both massive and readable, authoritative and exciting, instructive and pleasurable, stimulating and abundantly fair."

WHILE ENGLAND SLEPT: A Survey of World Affairs, 1932–1938. 1938. *Bks. for Libraries* $14.50

THE SECOND WORLD WAR. *Houghton* 6 vols. 1948–1953 Vol. 1 The Gathering Storm (1948) Vol. 2 Their Finest Hour (1949) Vol. 3 Grand Alliance (1949) Vol. 4 Hinge of Fate (1950) Vol. 5 Closing the Ring (1952) Vol. 6 Triumph and Tragedy (1953) each $8.50 boxed set $50.00; (with title "Memoirs of the Second World War") abr. ed. by Denis Kelly *Houghton* 6 vols. 1959 each $10.00; *Bantam* 6 vols. 1962 each $2.25

A HISTORY OF THE ENGLISH-SPEAKING PEOPLES. *Dodd* 4 vols. 1956–1958 Vol. 1 The Birth of Britain (to 1485) Vol. 2 The New World (1485–1688) Vol. 3 The Age of Revolution (1688–1815) Vol. 4 The Great Democracies (1815–1901) each $6.95 set

$25.00; abr. ed. by Henry Steele Commager *Simon & Schuster* (Pocket Bks.) 1966 pap. $1.65

THE ISLAND RACE. *Dodd* 1968 $27.50 smaller format $9.95

The story of Britain extracted from the 4 vol. history. "Intended to celebrate the author's 90th birthday. Ordinarily such a condensation would have been unnecessary, but this lavish folio has truly superb illustrations, many in color, matching the grandeur of the text"—*(LJ)*.

THE RIVER WAR. *Universal Pub.* 1964 pap. $.75

Books about Churchill

Churchill, Roosevelt, Stalin: The War They Waged and the Peace They Sought. By Herbert Feis. 1957. *Princeton Univ. Press* 2nd ed. 1967 $15.00 pap. $3.95

Burke, Disraeli, and Churchill: The Politics of Perseverance. By Stephen R. Graubard. *Harvard Univ. Press* 1961 $7.50

"Dr. Graubard had the happy idea of reviving the long historical essay and in this book has carried it out with distinction. The three essays are agreeably written, and the reader is carried easily along by a blend of narrative and analysis informed by judgment, imagination, and good sense"—*(American Historical Review)*.

Churchill and the Montgomery Myth. By Reginald W. Thompson. *M. Evans* (dist. by Lippincott) 1968 $5.95

"This is a further attempt to cut Montgomery down to size, but the tough little man emerges still largely unscathed [despite] Mr. Thompson's case, well written and cogently set out"—*(Economist)*.

See also Chapter 2, General Biography and Autobiography, this Vol.

TREVELYAN, GEORGE MACAULAY. 1876–1962.

When George Macaulay Trevelyan died at the age of 86, he was known as "Britain's most eminent historian." Son of Sir George Otto Trevelyan and grandnephew of Thomas Babington Macaulay, he was Regius Professor of Modern History at Cambridge and from 1940 to his retirement in 1951 Master of Trinity College. His books, written from the point of view of an advanced Liberal, carried out his belief that history should be made interesting to the general reader and to the student. His monumental "English Social History" has been a standard text on both sides of the Atlantic for many years. He also wrote a number of biographies, studies and books of essays, including "Garibaldi and the Making of Italy" (1911. *Folcroft* 1973 $6.25; *Humanities Press* 1948 $7.25) and "Clio: A Muse and Other Essays" (1913. *Bks. for Libraries* 1968 $8.00; *Folcroft* 1973 $7.95; *Richard West* 1973 $12.50).

ENGLAND UNDER THE STUARTS. 1907. *Harper* (Barnes & Noble) 21st ed. 1961 $12.00 pap. $6.00

HISTORY OF ENGLAND. 1926. *Doubleday* Anchor Bks. 3 vols. Vol. 1 From the Earliest Times to the Reformation Vol. 2 The Tudors and the Stuart Era Vol. 3 From Utrecht to Modern Times. pap. Vols. 1 and 3 $2.50 Vol. 2 $1.45

THE ENGLISH REVOLUTION, 1688–1689. 1938. *Oxford* 1965 pap. $1.95

A SHORTENED HISTORY OF ENGLAND. 1943. *Penguin* 1960 pap. $3.75. From earliest times to World War II.

ENGLAND UNDER QUEEN ANNE. 1930–1934. *Humanities Press* 3 vols. 1948 Vols. 1–2 o.p. Vol. 3 $7.25

ENGLISH SOCIAL HISTORY: A Survey of Six Centuries, Chaucer to Queen Victoria. 1942. *Harper* (Barnes & Noble) 1961 $13.00; *McKay* 1965 pap. $2.95

ILLUSTRATED ENGLISH SOCIAL HISTORY. *McKay* 4 vols. 1949–1952 Vol. 1 Chaucer's England and the Early Tudors Vol. 2 The Age of Shakespeare and the Stuart Period Vol. 3 The Eighteenth Century Vol. 4 The Nineteenth Century each $11.95

ILLUSTRATED HISTORY OF ENGLAND. Ills. sel. by St. John Gore *McKay* 1956 $14.50; *Longman* 1973 deluxe ed. $35.00 text ed. $15.00

AUTOBIOGRAPHY AND OTHER ESSAYS. 1949. *Bks. for Libraries* $9.75; *Folcroft* 1973 $9.75

THE RECREATIONS OF AN HISTORIAN. *Folcroft* 1973 $15.00

Books about Trevelyan

Trevelyan Papers. 1856 1863 1872. Ed. by C. Payne Collier, Sir Walter C. Trevelyan and Charles E. Trevelyan *AMS Press* 3 vols. each $25.00; *Johnson Reprint* 3 vols. $28.00

G. M. Trevelyan. By John Harold Plumb. *British Bk. Centre* $2.95 pap. $1.20

GIPSON, LAWRENCE H(ENRY).   1880–

The tenth volume of Professor Gipson's magnum opus, "The Triumphant Empire: Thunder Clouds Gather in the West," won the Pulitzer Prize in History for 1962. After his return in 1907 from Oxford, where he was a Rhodes scholar, Professor Gipson followed a teaching career, and is currently Emeritus Resident Professor at Lehigh University. "The Coming of the Revolution, 1763–1775" (1954, $8.95 Torchbks. pap. $3.25) is part of *Harper's* New American Nation Series. He is also the author of "Jared Ingersoll: A Study of American Loyalism in Relation to British Colonial Government" (1920, *Russell & Russell* 1968 $12.50; *Yale Univ. Press* 1971 $17.50 pap. $3.95).

Professor Gipson held the Harmsworth Chair in American History at Oxford from 1951–52 and was Honorary Consultant in American Colonial History to the Library of Congress from 1965–67. Max Beloff has said of him: "The writing of history on the grand scale is out of fashion. It is generally regarded as unrewarding to the author and even more so to the publisher. To this rule Professor Gipson provides a shining exception. . . . Here indeed is an historian in the Macaulay tradition—with all the technical resources that Macaulay could not command."

THE BRITISH EMPIRE BEFORE THE AMERICAN REVOLUTION: Provincial Characteristics and Sectional Tendencies in the Era Preceding the American Crisis. *Knopf* 15 vols. 1954–1970 Vols. 1–13 each $12.50 Vols. 14–15 each $15.00

"The present volumes display . . . mastery of great detail, maintenance of the broad central course of the narrative, constant attention to the tremendously extensive literature of the subject without loss of contact with the primary sources"—*(LJ)*. "This is history on the grand scale, one of the most important historical enterprises of our generation, and historians to come will have cause to thank Professor Gipson for the mass of fresh information which he has gathered from original sources"—(Louis B. Wright). "The most distinguished multivolume work by any living American historian"—(A. L. Burt). Vol. 14 is a bibliographical guide and Vol. 15 is a guide to manuscripts.

NICOLSON, SIR HAROLD (GEORGE).   1886–1968.

"Sir Harold offers us the priceless gift of readable and lucid narrative expressed in gracious and flexible English prose"—(Review of "Congress of Vienna" in the London *Spectator*). His "Good Behavior" (*Peter Smith* 1960 $5.00) is a study of the social manners of 12 civilizations, from the early history of China to the present. "Portrait of a Diplomatist," the biography of his father, Lord Carnock, is out of print. He is an entertaining and original biographer of literary as well as diplomatic figures. His "Diaries and Letters" provide a valuable historical, day-by-day account of Britain in World War II. (*For comment, see cross-reference below.*)

PEACEMAKING, 1919. 1933. *Grosset* Univ. Lib. 1965 pap. $2.50; *Peter Smith* $4.50

DIPLOMACY. 1939. *Oxford* 3rd ed. 1963 Galaxy Bks. pap. $1.95

THE CONGRESS OF VIENNA: A Study of Allied Unity 1812–1822. 1946. *Harcourt* Harbinger Bks. 1970 pap. $2.35; *Peter Smith* $5.00

THE EVOLUTION OF DIPLOMACY. (Orig. "The Evolution of Diplomatic Method") 1954. *Macmillan* 1962 Collier Bks. pap. $.95

See also Chapter 2, General Biography and Autobiography, this Vol.

TOYNBEE, ARNOLD J(OSEPH).   1889–1975.   *See Section on Modern and World History, this Chapter.*

BRYANT, SIR ARTHUR.   1899–

Sir Arthur has had a most interesting and varied career. After leaving Harrow at 18 to serve in the RAF, he attended Oxford, taught school, read for the Bar, and produced pageants with great success. Since 1931 he has written histories, biographies and plays in addition to lecturing, broadcasting and contributing frequently to leading London periodicals. Some of his historical works now o.p. are "The Turn of the Tide: A History of the War Years Based on the Diaries of Field Marshal Lord Alanbrooke" (1939–43) and "The Fire and the Rose" (1965).

THE ENGLAND OF CHARLES II. 1934. *Bks. for Libraries* $9.75

TRIUMPH IN THE WEST. 1943–46. *Greenwood* 1974 $19.50

THE MAKERS OF ENGLAND. 1954. *New Am. Lib.* $3.50

THE AGE OF CHIVALRY. 1964. *New Am. Lib.* $3.95

"This volume contains a wealth of material masterfully shaped and moulded. Law and parliament, peer and peasant, every class and every aspect of the country's life receive generous and judicious treatment"—(*LJ*).

THE MEDIEVAL FOUNDATION OF ENGLAND. 1967. *Macmillan* Collier Bks. 1968 pap. $1.95

"This useful, easy, short social history by a well-known English historian opens into remote millennia when England was a damp melting pot for assorted migratory peoples. It closes at the end of the fourteenth century, when England had survived invasions by Romans, Danes, Saxons, and Normans (who nearly all became Englishmen) and had acquired a parliament, two universities, much of her legal system, and something of her national character. Sir Arthur, as usual, writes reliably well. He is a trifle insistent that England, B.C. or A.D., is the best of possible places, but that makes for happy history"—(*New Yorker*).

SET IN A SILVER SEA. *Doubleday* 1968 $5.95

"An attractively graphic and eloquent social history of England from the 17th through the 19th centuries, with a brief glance at the 20th century. . . . A spirited and immensely readable book of history"—(*PW*).

THE GREAT DUKE. *Morrow* 1972 $8.95. Primarily a study of Wellington as a soldier and commander.

ROWSE, A(LFRED) L(ESLIE). 1903–

Professor Rowse has defined history as "life looked back over in the perspective of time," and has always wished to avoid the "cold mutton" aspect of so many history books. He is a noted authority on the Elizabethan Age. The *Spectator* of London said of "The Expansion of Elizabethan England": "Mr. Rowse commands wide knowledge, a glowing and fearless exuberance, a gift of narrative, and a powerful imaginative insight which brings persons and events most vividly to life." He has translated and completed Lucien Romier's "History of France" (1953, o.p.).

ON HISTORY: A Study of Present Tendencies. 1927. *Folcroft* 1973 $10.00

THE USE OF HISTORY. 1946. *Verry* rev. ed. 1963 $4.00; *Macmillan* Collier Bks. 1966 pap. $1.25

THE ENGLAND OF ELIZABETH. (Orig. "The Elizabethan Age," Vol. 1). 1950. *Macmillan* 1961 pap. $2.95

A NEW ELIZABETHAN AGE. 1952. *Somerset Pubs.* $6.50

AN ELIZABETHAN GARLAND. 1953. *AMS Press* $9.50

THE EXPANSION OF ELIZABETHAN ENGLAND. (Orig. "The Elizabethan Age," Vol. 2). 1955. *Scribner* 1972 pap. $3.95

THE EARLY CHURCHILLS. 1956. *Greenwood* 1974 $19.00

THE CHURCHILLS. 1966. *Greenwood* 1974 $20.00. An abridgement of "The Early Churchills" and "The Later Churchills" (1958, o.p.).

THE ELIZABETHAN RENAISSANCE. *Scribner* 2 vols. 1972 Vol. 1 The Cultural Achievement Vol. 2 The Life of the Society each $12.50 pap. 1974 each $4.95

THE TOWER OF LONDON IN THE HISTORY OF ENGLAND. *Putnam* 1972 $12.95

WINDSOR CASTLE IN THE HISTORY OF ENGLAND. *Putnam* 1974 $14.95

BOWLE, JOHN. 1905– *See Section on Modern and World History, this Chapter.*

TAYLOR, A(LAN) J(OHN) P(ERCIVALE). 1906– *See Section on Modern and World History, this Chapter.*

PLUMB, J(OHN) H(AROLD). 1911–

Educated at Cambridge, Dr. Plumb has taught there for over two decades, and is Professor of Modern History there. His full-scale biography of the 18th-century statesman Walpole (father of Horace) is a portrait of the man and of his era, providing an authentic record of England and European political history of that time, based on diaries, letters and other first-hand documents. Says Crane Brinton: "Dr. Plumb writes firmly and well in the British academic tradition of his master, G. M. Trevelyan" (*q.v.*)—(*N.Y. Herald Tribune*). He is also the author of "The Italian Renaissance: A Concise Survey of Its History and Culture" (*Harper* Torchbks. pap. $1.60) and "The Horizon Book of the Renaissance" (*Doubleday* Am. Heritage Press 1961 $17.50 deluxe ed. $19.95). Dr. Plumb writes regularly and brilliantly for the *Saturday Review*.

G. M. Trevelyan. *British Bk. Centre* 1950 $2.95 pap. $1.20

England in the Eighteenth Century: 1714–1815. *Penguin* (orig.) 1950 Pelican Bks.
   pap. $1.65; *Gannon* $4.50

Chatham. 1953. *Shoe String Press* 1965 $4.00

Sir Robert Walpole. 1956–61. *Kelley* 2 vols. Vol. 1 The Making of a Statesman (1956)
   Vol. 2 The King's Minister (1961) set $30.00

The First Four Georges. *Franklin Watts* (Fontana) 1956 pap. $1.50

Men and Centuries. *Houghton* 1963 $6.00

"This volume of 25 reprinted essays and reviews deals with 'The Eighteenth Century Scene,'
'African Studies,' and 'Men and Books.' The first group possesses solid virtues; the essays on
Macaulay and Trevelyan are worthy tributes; the African sketches may serve to remind Americans
of their general ignorance of that vast subject"—(*LJ*).

The Origins of Political Stability: England, 1675–1725. *Houghton* 1967 $6.00;
   Penguin 1974 pap. $2.95

"Professor Plumb is the most accomplished of that small band of professional historians at
present working on the history of England under the later Stuarts. . . . This is a brilliant and
decisive restatement, sweeping aside the work of lesser men who have lately usurped a position of
authority in this field. The main argument . . . is coherent and severely logical, and presented with
a grace and precision which cannot disguise the author's inimitable style"—(*Observer*, London).

Death of the Past. *Houghton* 1970 $5.00 Sentry Eds. 1971 pap. $1.75

In the Light of History. *Houghton* 1973 $6.95; *Dell* Delta Bks. 1974 pap. $2.95. A
   collection of his essays dealing with the 18th century, the historical ancestry of some
   current problems, and popular misconceptions of Victorian and Edwardian England.

TREVOR-ROPER, HUGH R(EDWALD). 1914–

Professor Trevor-Roper was educated at Oxford University, where he is now Regius Professor
of Modern History; his maiden lecture at Oxford defined the function of history to be making
itself "useful and controversial"—an axiom he has observed in his own career. As an intelligence
officer in the British army during World War II, he was assigned to study the events surrounding
Hitler's death; he described the results of this foray in "The Last Days of Hitler" (*Macmillan* Collier
Bks. 3rd ed. 1966 pap. $1.25), praised by Arthur M. Schlesinger (in the *Nation*) as "a brilliant
professional performance." His collection "Historical Essays" ranges in topic from Home to Lytton
Strachey. Crane Brinton (*q.v.*) called it "a fine collection, a sort of personal anthology, displaying
fully [the author's] range, his scholarship and his sentiments." Discussing "The Crisis of the
Seventeenth Century" in the *N.Y. Review of Books*, J. P. Kenyon has described Professor Trevor-
Roper as "one of the most brilliant writers of English prose alive, in any sphere. His touch in minor
details is unerring, and his metaphors never swallow their referred subject; the image of
Cromwellian backbenchers as 'clumsy old bluebottles caught in the delicate web spun by nimble
radical spiders' is witty and accurate, yet it does not enmesh us in consideration of arachnidae and
insectae."

He has also written "The Rise of Christian Europe" (*Harcourt* 1965 pap. $3.95), which spans the
period from Charles Martel to the Medicis, and edited "Essays in British History" (1965, o.p.).

Historical Essays. 1956. (Orig. "Men and Events") *Gannon* 1970 $6.00; *Harper*
   Torchbks. 1957 pap. $2.45; *Peter Smith* $4.75

The European Witch Craze of the 16th and 17th Centuries and Other Essays.
   1968. (Orig. "The Crisis of the Seventeenth Century") *Harper* 1969 Torchbks. pap.
   $1.95

The Romantic Movement and the Study of History. *Humanities Press* 1969 $1.25

Blitzkrieg to Defeat. *Holt* 1971 pap. $1.95

Queen Elizabeth's First Historian: William Camden and the Beginnings of English
   Civil History. *Humanities Press* (Fernhill) 1971 pap. $2.25

Plunder of the Arts in the Seventeenth Century. *Transatlantic* 1972 $8.75

NORTH AND SOUTH AMERICA

American History

"The historian is peculiarly fitted to serve as mediator between man's limitations and his aspirations, between his dreams of what ought to be and the limits of what, in the light of what has been, can be," wrote C. Vann Woodward (*q.v.*), Sterling Professor of History at Yale, in his presidential address "The Future and the Past" (*American Historical Review*, February 1970). "There is no other branch of learning," he added, "better qualified to mediate between man's daydream of the future and his nightmare of the past, or, for that matter between his nightmare of the past and his daydream of the future." In the last decade revisionist historians have been preoccupied with a vast reinterpretation of America's past as it has been presented in the standard texts. These new readings of our history, often based on the same old evidence, range from Daniel Boorstin's "cheerful vision of the American past" to savage attacks on Franklin Roosevelt's New Deal and a devastating reassessment of Jacksonian Democracy. At the moment, another dominant concern among these revisionist scholars appears to be a re-evaluation of our revolutionary heritage and its impact on the greater Western society.

Other American historians have, meanwhile, addressed themselves to problems to which there are quantitative answers. "Historians too have adapted the new technology [of computers]," Robert Swierenga noted in a recent issue of the *Journal of American History* (March 1974), "but not without much soul searching." The computer revolution which engulfed the social sciences in the 1950's has now infiltrated the ranks of historians. Recent computer assisted work in American history has included studies of community structure, immigration, slavery, geographical mobility and the process of urbanization. A body of numerical data, drawn from both printed and manuscript sources, has been gathered and programmed to provide striking reinterpretation of many aspects of our social and political history. We have included in this section several recent works that are based, at least in part, on data quantification and statistical evidence.

It will be noted that many older works in American history, mentioned in our previous edition as o.p., are now back in print (owing to the indefatigable activities of the reprint firms)—if not in toto, at least in abridged form. These will now be found under the appropriate headings in the subject lists. Even the works of John Fiske (1842–1901), until recently limited to "The Critical Period of American History, 1783–1789" (1901. *Norwood Editions* $12.50), are now available complete in an expensive edition from *AMS Press*. Noted for his pleasing, lucid style, Fiske was the recognized authority on our pre-constitutional history. As one of the modern expositors of science, he interpreted the events of our history as being the results of revolutionary processes. His "Darwinism and Other Essays" (1913. *Kraus* $12.00) is again available separately.

The many new editions of the public and personal papers of our great men furnish the best source material of our historical heritage. *See Chapter 2, General Biography and Autobiography, this Vol. for: Franklin, Washington, The Adams Family (John, John Quincy and Charles Francis), Jefferson, Madison, Hamilton, Lincoln and other modern Presidents and statesmen.*

Our Federal Government has just passed through the greatest constitutional crisis in our history. The recent threat of a presidential impeachment has inspired many Americans to return to the study of our past so that they may better understand the probable direction of our future. American history offers the political background of our present dilemmas; Chapter 8, The Social Sciences (*q.v.*) provides the complementary discussion of their contemporary manifestations.

Books on the Writing of American History

Benson, Lee. TURNER AND BEARD: American Historical Writing Reconsidered. *Macmillan* (Free Press) 1965 pap. $1.95

Billias, George Athan. AMERICAN HISTORY: Retrospect and Prospect. *Macmillan* (Free Press) 1971 $8.95 pap. $5.50

Garraty, John A. INTERPRETING AMERICAN HISTORY: Conversations with Historians. *Macmillan* 1970 $10.95

"Garraty has tape-recorded long interpretive interviews with 29 eminent American historians. These conversations are edited to about 25 pages each, covering practically every aspect of American history . . . Garraty's subjects are all members of the 'academic establishment' and they all represent varying degrees of the consensus approach"—(*Choice*).

Hofstadter, Richard. THE PROGRESSIVE HISTORIANS: Turner, Beard, Parrington. *Knopf* 1968 $8.95; *Random* Vintage Bks. 1970 pap. $2.95. *See comment under his main entry, this Section.*

(With Seymour Martin Lipset, Eds.). SOCIOLOGY AND HISTORY: Methods. Sociology of American History Ser. *Basic Bks.* 1968 $7.95 pap. $3.95. Essays concerning the application of sociological methods to the study of history. Contributors include Bernard and Lotte Bailyn, Lee Benson, David Donald, Eric L. McKitrick and Paul F. Lazarsfeld.

(With others). THE STRUCTURE OF AMERICAN HISTORY. *Prentice-Hall* 2nd ed. 1973 pap. $6.50

Higham, John. WRITING AMERICAN HISTORY: Essays on Modern Scholarship. *Univ. of Indiana Press* 1972 pap. $2.95

"Writing beautifully and incisively, Higham outlines the growth of American historiography, analyses some of its methodological and philosophical problems, and suggests ways of overcoming confining limitations. He urges historians to move beyond the so-called consensus approach and be more evaluative"—(*Choice*).

Katz, Stanley, and Stanely Kutler, Eds. NEW PERSPECTIVES ON THE AMERICAN PAST. *Little* 2 vols. 2nd ed. 1972 Vol. 1 1607–1877 Vol. 2 1877 to the Present pap. each $5.95

Kraus, Michael. THE WRITING OF AMERICAN HISTORY. 1937 1953. *Univ. of Oklahoma Press* 1968 repr. of 1953 ed. $7.95

Lowenberg, Bert James. AMERICAN HISTORY IN AMERICAN THOUGHT: Christopher Columbus to Henry Adams. *Simon & Schuster* 1972 $15.00

Morton, Marian J. THE TERRORS OF IDEOLOGICAL POLITICS: Liberal Historians in a Conservative Mood. *Press of Case Western* 1972 $5.95

Saveth, Edward Norman. AMERICAN HISTORY AND THE SOCIAL SCIENCES. *Macmillan* (Free Press) 1964 $10.95

Skotheim, Robert Allen. AMERICAN INTELLECTUAL HISTORIES AND HISTORIANS. *Princeton Univ. Press* 1966 $12.00 pap. 1970 $3.95

Although this historiographical survey "ignores a great deal of what most people would think is American intellectual history [it] was worth writing and is worth reading. Even when he is dealing with an author now rightly almost totally unknown . . . he has a good deal of interest to say"—(*TLS*, London). Historians such as Charles A. Beard, Carl Becker, Merle Curti, Ralph Gabriel, Perry Miller, Samuel Eliot Morison, Vernon Louis Parrington and James Harvey Robinson are discussed.

Sternsher, Bernard. CONSENSUS, CONFLICT AND AMERICAN HISTORIANS. *Univ. of Indiana Press* 1975 $15.00

"American historiography has been characterized by a fundamental debate between those scholars who perceive our national existence to be one of broadscale democracy realized (attributable to either a pervasive Lockeian ideology or a unique geographical and cultural experience) and opponents who stress the persistence of deep-rooted social and economic conflict. Sternsher's excellent, authoritative and comprehensive marshaling of the data (containing little that is original) traces the historiography of the debate itself, and also weighs the validity of the evidence"—(*LJ*).

Van Tassell, David D. RECORDING AMERICA'S PAST: An Interpretation of the Development of Historical Studies in America, 1607–1884. *Univ. of Chicago Press* 1960 $7.95

A "significant . . . study of causes and trends"—*(American Historical Review)*.

Vitzthum, Richard C. THE AMERICAN COMPROMISE: Theme and Method in the Histories of Bancroft, Parkman, and Adams. *Univ. of Oklahoma Press* 1974 $8.95

Wish, Harvey. THE AMERICAN HISTORIAN: A Social-Intellectual History of the Writing of the American Past. *Oxford* 1960 $7.95 pap. 1962 $3.95. An evaluation of the men who have recorded the story of our history from Colonial times to the present.

Woodward, C. Vann, Ed. THE COMPARATIVE APPROACH TO AMERICAN HISTORY. *Basic Bks.* 1968 pap. $2.95

The Sterling Professor of American History at Yale University has edited "this collection of 24 essays by eminent American historians who test the uniqueness of American history by comparing it with the histories of other countries in similar stages of development. Contributors include Seymour Martin Lipset, John Higham, Richard Hofstadter, George E. Mowry, Ernest R. May, and David M. Potter. . . . Intended for the serious student, the book is highly recommended for college and large public libraries"—*(LJ)*.

Important Series

In each case, see publisher's catalog for editors and titles of individual volumes.

AMERICAN ASSEMBLY BOOKS. *Prentice-Hall* Spectrum Bks. 20 vols. each $5.95–$7.95 pap. $1.95–$2.45

AMERICAN HISTORICAL SOURCES: Research and Interpretation Series. Ed. by L. Ratner *Prentice-Hall* 7 vols. each $3.95 pap. $1.50–$1.60

AMERICAN IMMIGRATION COLLECTION. Oscar Handlin, Gen. Ed. *Arno* Series 1 41 vols. 1969 set $492.50 Series 2 33 vols. 1970 set $472.00. A series of reprints covering the history of immigration to America from 1620 to 1920. Oscar Handlin was the former Charles Warren Professor of American History at Harvard.

AMERICAN NATION SERIES. Albert Bushnell Hart, Gen. Ed. *Harper* 9 vols. each $5.00. Reissues of books of historical scholarship published between 1904 and 1908.

AMERICANA LIBRARY. Robert E. Burke, Gen. Ed. *Univ. of Washington Press* 28 vols. $7.50–$9.50 pap. $2.95–$3.45

BROADSIDES. *New Am. Lib.* Signet Bks. 10 vols. $.60–$1.25. Pamphlets offering critical examination of issues (Vietnam, civil disobedience and the like) vital to America today. Authors include John Kenneth Galbraith, Abe Fortas and Senator Eugene J. McCarthy.

CHICAGO HISTORY OF AMERICAN CIVILIZATION SERIES. Daniel J. Boorstin, Gen. Ed. *Univ. of Chicago Press* 28 vols. each $7.50 pap. $2.95

CLASSIC AMERICAN HISTORIANS SERIES. Paul M. Angle, Gen. Ed. *Univ. of Chicago Press* 6 vols. each $10.00 pap. $3.45–$3.95

EYEWITNESS ACCOUNTS OF AMERICAN HISTORY SERIES. *Prentice-Hall* 16 vols. each $4.95 pap. $1.95

EYEWITNESS ACCOUNTS OF THE AMERICAN REVOLUTION. Peter Decker, Gen. Ed. *Arno* 101 vols. $1190.00. Brings together firsthand accounts of the war by soldiers and civilians from both sides.

THE FIRST AMERICAN FRONTIER SERIES. Ed. by Dale Van Every *Arno* 61 vols. 1971 $1281.00

"Covers the period from 1750, when English traders first planted the seeds of the westward movement by threatening the French dominion of the Ohio, to 1815 when the last challenge to American sovereignty to the mid-continent was defeated"—(Publisher's note).

GREAT AMERICAN THINKERS SERIES. Arthur W. Brown and Thomas S. Knight, Gen. Eds. *Simon & Schuster* (Washington Square) 5 vols. pap. each $.60–$.95

A HISTORY OF AMERICAN LIFE. Ed. by Arthur M. Schlesinger and D. R. Fox. *Macmillan* 13 vols. set $100.00

LIBRARY OF AMERICAN BIOGRAPHY. Oscar Handlin, Gen. Ed. *Little* 16 vols. each $5.00 pap. $2.95

MAINSTREAM OF AMERICA SERIES. Ed. by Lewis Gannett *Doubleday* 1953–   9 vols. each $6.95–$7.95. A new approach, telling America's story in narrative form.

THE MAKING OF AMERICA. David Donald, Gen. Ed. *Farrar, Straus* (Hill & Wang) 6 vols. each $2.25–$5.75 pap. $1.95. Books of historical scholarship intended for the student and general reader.

NEW AMERICAN NATION SERIES. Henry Steele Commager and Richard B. Morris, Gen. Eds. *Harper* 44 vols. each $7.95–$10.00 pap. $2.45–$2.95

RESEARCH LIBRARY OF COLONIAL AMERICA. Ed. by Richard C. Robey. *Arno* 54 vols. 1972 set $1,412.00. Includes histories, personal narratives, and promotional literature.

URBAN LIFE IN AMERICA SERIES. Richard C. Wade, Gen. Ed. *Oxford* 15 vols. each $8.00– $10.00 pap. $2.50–$2.95

YALE CHRONICLES OF AMERICA. Ed. by Allen Johnson and Allan Nevins *Yale Univ. Press* (available from U.S. Pubs. Assn.) 56 vols. each $4.45 set $225.00. From the days of the early Red Man to the aftermath of World War II; in narrative prose.

YALE PAGEANT OF AMERICA. Ed. by Ralph Henry Gabriel *Yale Univ. Press* (available from U.S. Pubs. Assn.) 15 vols. each $12.75 set $175.00. A series of 11,500 pictures, rare charts and maps, linked by scholarly text; indexed.

Reference Books and Books of Documents

The U.S. Government Printing Office publishes the Public Papers of the Presidents of the United States and can provide a small catalog on this series. (*For guides and other information about U.S. Government publications, see Chapter 1, Reference Books—General, this Vol. See also special Reading Lists following and Chapter 1, Reference Books—General: Biographical Reference Works, Yearbooks and Almanacs, this Vol.*).

Adams, James Truslow, Ed. ALBUM OF AMERICAN HISTORY. *Scribner* 6 vols. new ed. 1969 $120.00 (by subscription only). Pictorial account of American society from Colonial times to the present.

ATLAS OF AMERICAN HISTORY. *Scribner* 1943 $20.00 (by subscription only). Companion volume to the "Dictionary" below.

DICTIONARY OF AMERICAN HISTORY. 1940. *Scribner* 7 vols. 2nd rev. ed. 1942 Vol. 7 Index 1961 $120.00 (by subscription only)

Adler, Mortimer J., and Charles Van Doren, Eds. THE ANNALS OF AMERICA. *Encyclopaedia Britannica* 23 vols. 1974 (*see publisher's catalog*). Twenty-one volumes, chronologically arranged, of original source materials from specific periods in American history, 1493–1973. The two-volume Conspectus provides a topical index to the great issues in American history and a bibliography of recommended reading and additional source material.

American Heritage. THE AMERICAN HERITAGE PICTORIAL ATLAS OF UNITED STATES HISTORY. *McGraw-Hill* 1966 $16.50. An attractive and fascinating work with commentary by Roger Butterfield.

American Historical Association. George Howe and others, Eds. GUIDE TO HISTORICAL LITERATURE. *Macmillan* 1961 $16.50

American Historical Review. Vols. 1-55 (1895–1950). *Kraus* set $1925.00 pap. set $1700.00

Andrews, Wayne, Ed., and Thomas C. Cochran, Advisory Ed. CONCISE DICTIONARY OF AMERICAN HISTORY. *Scribner* 1962 $25.00

This reference volume containing over 1,100 double-columned pages of 2,200 articles is a "masterly authority." Based on the six-volume set by James Truslow Adams (*see above*) which for two decades was the recognized leader in its field, this admirably edited concise version provides the essentials of the original in one volume. "An invaluable book," said the *N.Y. Times*—"Some of the articles . . . have been retained intact—after all, you can't beat the late Douglas Southall Freeman on the Battle of Gettysburg or Allan Nevins on the history of the Standard Oil Co. Others have been cut or have been brought up to date. Thomas C. Cochran of the University of Pennsylvania was the advisory editor . . . Wayne Andrews the editor at Scribner's end. Starting in 1956, many months were spent in finding which bits of history should be altered, due to change of emphasis or new material, the remainder of the time processing history as it came in from scholars across the land."

Andriot, John L. GUIDE TO U.S. GOVERNMENT STATISTICS. *Documents Index* 4th ed. 1973. An especially useful and comprehensive guide to the statistical content of Federal publications; arrangement primarily by government department or agency.

Bailey, Thomas A. THE AMERICAN SPIRIT: United States History as Seen by Contemporaries. *Heath* 2 vols. 3rd ed. 1973 pap. each $5.95

Bailyn, Bernard, and J. N. Barrett, Eds. PAMPHLETS OF THE AMERICAN REVOLUTION, 1750–1776. *Harvard Univ. Press* 1965 Vol. 1 1750–1765 $15.00

Beers, Henry Putney. BIBLIOGRAPHIES IN AMERICAN HISTORY: Guide to Materials for Research. 1942. *Octagon* 1973 $17.50. Lists more than 11,000 bibliographies in a classified arrangement.

Bemis, Samuel F., and G. G. Griffin. GUIDE TO THE DIPLOMATIC HISTORY OF THE U.S. 1775–1921. *Peter Smith* 1965 $13.50

Boatner, Mark M. III. THE CIVIL WAR DICTIONARY. *McKay* 1959 $17.50. Includes illustrations, maps and diagrams.

ENCYCLOPEDIA OF THE AMERICAN REVOLUTION. *McKay* 1966 rev. ed. 1974 $17.50

"All the important officers and statesmen are here, all the campaigns, all the battles, all the forts, described in a vivid style and easily found in their alphabetical location. . . . An amazingly thorough, illuminating, and authoritative work of reference"—(David Glixon, in *SR*).

Boorstin, Daniel J., Ed., with introd. AN AMERICAN PRIMER. *Univ. of Chicago Press* 2 vols. 1969 set $12.50. Eighty-three chronologically arranged documents, statements, essays, etc., beginning with the Mayflower Compact of 1620 to President Johnson's Address on Voting Rights of 1965.

Branyan, Robert L., and Lawrence H. Larsen, Eds. THE EISENHOWER ADMINISTRATION, 1953–1961: A Documentary History. *Random* 2 vols. 1971 set $55.00

Brown University. John Carter Brown Library. BIBLIOTHECA AMERICANA: Books of North and South America. 1870–71. *Kraus* 2 vols. set $49.50

Byrd, William. THE PROSE WORKS OF WILLIAM BYRD OF WESTOVER: Narratives of a Colonial Virginian. Ed. with introd. by Louis B. Wright *Harvard Univ. Press* Belknap Press 1966 $12.50. Fascinating picture of plantation life of the period. "One of the wealthiest and most prominent Virginians of his era, William Byrd II was a planter, merchant, scholar, lawyer, and government official."

Carman, Harry J., and Arthur William Thompson. A GUIDE TO THE PRINCIPAL SOURCES FOR AMERICAN CIVILIZATION, 1800–1900, IN THE CITY OF NEW YORK. *Columbia* Manuscripts, o.p. Printed Materials 1962 $20.00. The vast resources of New York City "have been made immeasurably more accessible with the publication of this guide."

Carruth, Gorton Veeder, and others, Eds. THE ENCYCLOPEDIA OF AMERICAN FACTS AND DATES. *T. Y. Crowell* 1956 6th ed. 1972 $8.95. Facts, dates and events from all departments of American life beginning with 1000 A.D.

Church, Elihu Dwight. CATALOGUE OF BOOKS RELATING TO THE DISCOVERY AND EARLY HISTORY OF NORTH AND SOUTH AMERICA. 1907. Comp. by G. W. Cole *Peter Smith* 5 vols. set $80.00

Commager, Henry Steele, Ed. DOCUMENTS OF AMERICAN HISTORY. 1934. *Prentice-Hall* (Appleton) 2 vols. 9th ed. 1974 pap. Vol. 1 $8.95 Vol. 2 $9.50 combined vol. $18.50

Evans, Charles. AMERICAN BIBLIOGRAPHY. 1903–34. *Scarecrow Press* 13 vols. in 1 Mini-Print vol. 1967 $42.00; *Peter Smith* 14 vols. Vols. 1–12 1639–1799 $135.00 Vol. 13 1799–1800 $20.00 Vol. 14 Index by R. P. Bristol $20.00

Fitzhugh, William. WILLIAM FITZHUGH AND HIS CHESAPEAKE WORLD, 1676–1701. Ed. with introd. by Richard Beale Davis *Univ. Press of Virginia* 1963 $9.75

Fitzhugh, (1651–1701), lawyer, successful colonist and prosperous planter-resident on the Potomac, wrote the 212 letters (May 15, 1679 to April 26, 1699) which cover a great variety of commercial, professional and personal subjects. His descendants were to play an important part during the founding of the Republic and after. Carefully edited with an excellent introduction, this will be the definitive edition, barring the discovery of many new letters.

Freidel, Frank, and Richard Showman, Eds. HARVARD GUIDE TO AMERICAN HISTORY. 1954. *Harvard Univ. Press* 2 vols. rev. ed. 1974 set $45.00. A comprehensive guide to American history. About one third of the entries are new. Includes practical suggestions on research, writing and publication.

A GUIDE TO THE STUDY OF THE UNITED STATES OF AMERICA: Representative Books Reflecting the Development of American Life and Thought. *U. S. Government Printing Office* (available from the Supt. of Documents, U. S. Government Printing Office, Washington, D.C. 20402, order number Z-1215. U53) $7.00

Harris, Seymour E., Ed. AMERICAN ECONOMIC HISTORY. *McGraw-Hill* 1961 $11.95. From about 1800 to the present, each chapter written by an expert, among them Arthur Schlesinger and John D. Black.

Hofstadter, Richard, and Michael Wallace, Eds. AMERICAN VIOLENCE: A Documentary History. *Knopf* 1970 $10.00

This book is "a collection of well-chosen, brief, primary accounts of incidents [which give] a good cumulative sense of the extent and variety of the nation's social violence"—(*American Historical Review*).

Hotten, John Campden, Ed. THE HOTTEN LIST: The Original Lists of Persons of Quality; Emigrants . . . and Others Who Went from Great Britain to the American Plantations, 1600–1700. *Genealogical Pub. Co.* repr. of 1874 ed. 1974 $15.00. More than 11,000 names are listed of "persons of quality, emigrants, religious exiles, political rebels, apprentices, servingmen sold, children stolen, and maids pressed." The authority for the lists is clearly stated.

Howes, Wright, Comp. U.S.–IANA (1650–1950). *Bowker* 2nd ed. 1962 $28.50. Bibliography of "rare and scarce books relating to human activities in the United States."

Hurwitz, Howard L. AN ENCYCLOPEDIC DICTIONARY OF AMERICAN HISTORY. *Simon & Schuster* (Washington Square Press) 1970 pap. $1.45

Johnson, Donald B., Comp. NATIONAL PARTY PLATFORMS, 1840–1972. *Univ. of Illinois Press* 5th ed. 1973 $20.00

Johnson, Thomas H., Ed. THE OXFORD COMPANION TO AMERICAN HISTORY. *Oxford* 1966 $17.50

"An incredibly good job . . . as comprehensive and authoritative in substance as one could possibly hope from so wide-ranging but highly condensed a work"—(Lyman H. Butterfield).

Kavenagh, W. Keith, Ed. FOUNDATIONS OF COLONIAL AMERICA: A Documentary History. *Bowker* 3 vols. 1973 set $96.00. Over 1,000 documents on American colonial history arranged by date, place and subject.

Leidy, W. Philip. A POPULAR GUIDE TO GOVERNMENT PUBLICATIONS. *Columbia* 3rd ed. 1968 $13.50. Bibliographical data for a selected list of government publications. (*For further comment, see Chapter 1, Reference Books—General: United States Government Publications, this Vol.*)

Leuchtenburg, William E., Ed. THE NEW DEAL: A Documentary History. *Harper* Torchbks. 1968 pap. $2.25; *Univ. of South Carolina Press* 1969 $9.95

Long, E. B., and Barbara Long. THE CIVIL WAR DAY BY DAY. *Doubleday* 1971 $17.50

McMasters, John Bach. HISTORY OF THE PEOPLE OF THE UNITED STATES. 9 vols. 1883– 1927. Ed. by Louis Filler *Farrar, Straus* (abr.) 1964 $5.50. A classic history, now back in print in abridged form.

Miller, Perry, and Thomas H. Johnson, Eds. THE PURITANS: A Sourcebook of Their Writings. 1938. *Harper* Torchbks. 2 vols. pap. each $2.95; *Peter Smith* 2 vols. each $6.00

Moquin, Wayne, Ed. GREAT DOCUMENTS IN AMERICAN INDIAN HISTORY. *Praeger* 1973 $13.50. Nearly 100 documents on tribal life, racial conflicts and the contemporary Indian movements.

Morris, Richard B., and Jeffrey B. Morris, Eds. ENCYCLOPEDIA OF AMERICAN HISTORY. *Harper* Bicentennial Ed. 1976 $28.50 lib. bdg. $19.76. Includes maps, charts, index.

(With James Woodress, Eds.) VOICES FROM AMERICA'S PAST. *Dutton* 3 vols. 1963 Vol. 1 Colonies and the New Nation Vol. 2 Backwoods Democracy to World Power Vol. 3 Twentieth Century each $4.95 set $12.95

Parrington, Vernon Louis. MAIN CURRENTS IN AMERICAN THOUGHT. 1927. *Harcourt* 3 vols. 1955 Vol. 1 The Colonial Mind, 1620–1800 Vol. 2 The Romantic Revolution in America, 1800–1860 Vol. 3 The Beginnings of Critical Realism in America, 1860– 1920 pap. Vol. 1 $2.65 Vol. 2 $2.85 Vol. 3 $3.85. Awarded the Pulitzer Prize for History in 1928.

Petersen, Svend. A STATISTICAL HISTORY OF THE AMERICAN PRESIDENTIAL ELECTIONS. Introd. by Louis Filler *Ungar* 1962 $9.50

"Like most statistical histories, these columnar tabulations are dry as dust until actually needed; then they become invaluable. Nowhere else in a single source can one find the answer to practically any question on Presidential elections.... Convenient, indispensable aid for political leaders, journalists, students, historians—and all libraries"—(*LJ*).

Poulton, Helen. THE HISTORIAN'S HANDBOOK: A Descriptive Guide to Reference Works. *Univ. of Oklahoma Press* 1971 $9.95 pap. $4.95

Sabin, Joseph, and others, Eds. DICTIONARY OF BOOKS RELATING TO AMERICA FROM ITS DISCOVERY TO THE PRESENT TIME. 1869–1892, 1928–1936. *Harper* (Barnes & Noble) 29 vols. in 15 1961 repr. of 1936 ed. set $450.00; *Scarecrow Press* 29 vols. in 2 Mini-Print vols. 1966 set $99.50

Schlissel, Lillian, Ed. CONSCIENCE IN AMERICA: A Documentary History of Conscientious Objection in America, 1757–1967. *Dutton* 1968 $6.50 pap. $2.75. The American tradition of dissent is illuminated in these pages.

Scott, John Anthony, Ed. LIVING DOCUMENTS IN AMERICAN HISTORY. *Simon & Schuster* (Washington Square) 1969 pap. $1.45

Shaw, Ralph, and Richard Shoemaker, Comps. AMERICAN BIBLIOGRAPHY, 1801–1819. *Scarecrow Press* 22 vols. 1958–1965 set $185.50

Smith, James Ward, and Albert Leland Jamison, Eds. RELIGION IN AMERICAN LIFE. *Princeton Univ. Press* 4 vols. 1961 Vol. 1 The Shaping of American Religion $12.50 Vol. 2 Religious Perspectives in American Culture $13.50 Vol. 3 Religious Thought and Economic Society: The European Background by J. Viner o.p. Vol. 4 Critical Bibliography of Religion in America, 2 vols. by N. R. Burr $30.00 set $50.00

Taken together, the contributors "form something of a roll call of the most distinguished observers of the American religious scene." "For years to come the bibliography will be indispensable" for all who wish to investigate the historical implications.

Sperber, Hans, and Travis Trittschuh. AMERICAN POLITICAL TERMS: An Historical Dictionary. *Wayne State Univ. Press* 1962 $14.50. Defines approximately 1,000 words and phrases, with information on usage.

STATISTICAL ABSTRACT OF THE UNITED STATES. 1879 to date, annually. *U.S. Government Printing Office* (Washington, D.C. 20402) $5.75. This outstanding compendium is a boon to librarians who have to answer a large volume of public inquiries for factual data. Both government and private data sources are reviewed and evaluated annually.

U.S. GOVERNMENT ORGANIZATION MANUAL. 1935 to date, annually. National Archives and Record Service, *U.S. Government Printing Office* (Washington, D.C. 20402) $3.00. This indispensable tool lists and describes the functions of all departments of the Federal Government, of their divisions, bureaus, commissions and services. Revised annually.

WEBSTER'S GUIDE TO AMERICAN HISTORY: A Chronological, Geographical Survey and Compendium. Ed. by Charles Van Doren and Robert McHenry *Merriam* 1971 $14.95

One- and Two-Volume Surveys

Among the various American histories, the bookseller will perhaps be more interested in shorter surveys than in the varied representation of special periods and aspects which the librarian will need. There are many such histories. Most are school or college texts. Some however are written for the general reader, or at least with his preference for literary style in view.

Distinct from straight event or political histories are the studies of intellectual and cultural history. Among the surveys in this field are: Merle Curti's "The Growth of American Thought" (*Harper* 1943 3rd ed. 1964 $14.95), which won the Pulitzer Prize in 1944; Perry Miller's "The New England Mind from Colony to Province" (*Harvard Univ. Press* 1953 $12.50; *Beacon* 1961 pap. $4.95); Vernon Parrington's classic "Main Currents in American Thought" (*Harcourt* 1955 3 vols. pap. Vols. 1 and 2 each $3.45 Vol. 3 $3.85); Philip Schaff's "America: A Sketch of its Political, Social and Religious Character" (ed. by Perry Miller *Harvard Univ. Press* 1961 $6.00); William Appleman Williams' "The Contours of American History" (1961. *Peter Smith* $5.50; *Franklin Watts* 1966 pap. $3.95), a perceptive analysis of the changing pattern of American thought; Winthrop Hudson's "Religion in America" (*Scribner* 2nd ed. 1973 $12.50 pap. $5.95); and Alan Heimert's "Religion and the American Mind: From the Great Awakening to the Revolution" (*Harvard Univ. Press* 1966 $15.00). (*See also Perry Miller's main entry, this Section.*)

Bancroft, George. A HISTORY OF THE UNITED STATES OF AMERICA FROM THE DISCOVERY OF THE CONTINENT. 1834–1874. 6 vols. rev. ed. 1885. *Kennikat* $110.00; ed. by Russell B. Nye *Univ. of Chicago Press* abr. ed. 1966 $10.00 pap. $3.45

Banner, Lois W. WOMEN IN MODERN AMERICA: A Brief History. *Harcourt* 1974 pap. $4.25
   "The book will be useful to the general reader and as a supplement to college courses in U.S. history which often underemphasize women's roles and activities"—(*Choice*).

Berkey, Andrew S., and James P. Shenton, Eds., with introd. THE HISTORIANS' HISTORY OF THE UNITED STATES. *Putnam* 2 vols. 1966 boxed set $16.95 pap. 1972 Vol. 1 $4.95 Vol. 2 $4.25. Excerpts from the writings of outstanding American historians.
   "Recommended for all general collections"—(*LJ*).

Blum, John M., and others. THE NATIONAL EXPERIENCE: A History of the United States. *Harcourt* 3rd ed. 1973 $13.95 pap. 2 vols. Pt. 1 to 1877 Pt. 2 Since 1865 each $8.50. A survey of political, economic, social and intellectual development in America.

Boorstin, Daniel J., Ed. AMERICAN CIVILIZATION. *McGraw-Hill* 1972 $35.00
   A big picture book on the new American way of life "ingeniously and intelligently planned"—(*TLS*, London).

Brock, William R. THE UNITED STATES 1789–1890. *Cornell Univ. Press* 1975

"Brock, [an eminent British scholar], has essayed an introductory survey of the sources that are basic to an understanding of American history in the years 1789–1890"—*(LJ)*.

Carman, Harry J., and others. A HISTORY OF THE AMERICAN PEOPLE. 1952. *Knopf* 2 vols. 3rd ed. 1967 Vol. 1 To 1877 Vol. 2 Since 1865 pap. each $6.95

The political, economic, social and intellectual forces that have influenced American life are all discussed. The story of the growth of the Republic retold with "all-round excellence"—*(LJ)*. The writing is clear if "a bit heavy"—*(N.Y. Herald Tribune)*.

Cooke, Alistair. ALISTAIR COOKE'S AMERICA. *Knopf 1973 $15.00*

"A panoramic book, traveling fast and high, and the view it gives of our land and the people below is exhilarating"—*(Atlantic)*.

Furnas, J. C. THE AMERICANS: A Social History of the United States, 1587–1914. *Putnam* 1969 $12.95

GREAT TIMES: An Informal Social History of the United States, 1914–1929. *Putnam* 1974 $15.00

Sequel to "The Americans." "It is a good narrative synthesis with some interpretive analysis"— *(LJ)*.

Garraty, John A., and the Editors of American Heritage. THE AMERICAN NATION. Introd. by Roger Butterfield *Harper* 1968 $15.95 2nd ed. 1971 2 vols. set $12.95

Handlin, Oscar. A HISTORY OF THE UNITED STATES. *Holt* 2 vols. 1968 Vol. 1 o.p. Vol. 2 $12.00

AMERICA: A History. *Holt* 1968 $13.00. A one-volume edition of "A History of the United States."

Hofstadter, Richard, William Miller and Daniel Aaron. THE UNITED STATES: A History of a Republic. *Prentice-Hall* 1957 3rd ed. 1972 $11.50 2 vols. pap. each $6.25

Written for college undergraduates, this text has sold over 110,000 copies since publication and is used in major colleges and universities. The authors have woven into the political narrative the significant developments in economic and cultural matters to provide a synthesis of American history for this generation. Bibliographies and maps are valuable additions.

Malone, Dumas, and Basil Rauch. EMPIRE FOR LIBERTY: The Genesis and Growth of the United States of America. *Prentice-Hall* (Appleton) 6 vols. 1964–1965 Vol. 1 American Origins to 1789 Vol. 2 The Republic Comes of Age, 1789–1841 Vol. 3 Crisis of the Union, 1841–1877 Vol. 4 The New Nation, 1865–1917 Vol. 5 War and Troubled Peace, 1917–1939 Vol. 6 America and World Leadership, 1940–1965 pap. each $4.25 except Vol. 2 $5.50 (Orig. 2 vol. ed. 1960, o.p.)

Professor Malone, the biographer of Thomas Jefferson and an editor of the *Dictionary of American Biography*, and Professor Rauch, an authority on the New Deal, span American history from the Norsemen to the present. It is above the average college text in style and readability. It possesses real literary distinction.

Morison, Samuel Eliot. THE OXFORD HISTORY OF THE AMERICAN PEOPLE. *Oxford* 1965 $17.50 text ed. $10.95; *New Am. Lib.* 3 vols. pap. each $1.95

A general history from prehistoric times to the assassination of President Kennedy. A "quick reference book for young people, and a really delightful book to read"—*(LJ)*.

(With Henry Steele Commager and William E. Leuchtenburg). THE GROWTH OF THE AMERICAN REPUBLIC. *Oxford* 2 vols. 6th enl. and rev. text ed. 1969 each $9.95 boxed set $35.00

Incorporating the material of the original 1930 single-volume edition, this new edition carries events up to 1968. Each volume has a bibliography and index. *The Christian Science Monitor* wrote of the 5th edition: "It constitutes the standard by which other inclusive American histories are to be judged."

Morris, Richard B., and William Greenleaf. U.S.A: The History of a Nation. *Rand McNally* 2 vols. 1969 each $4.95. From the ancient Indian civilizations to the Vietnam peace negotiations as of late Autumn 1968.

Nevins, Allan, and Henry Steele Commager. A SHORT HISTORY OF THE UNITED STATES. *Knopf* rev. and enl. ed. 1966 $10.00 pap. $2.95

Rhodes, James Ford. HISTORY OF THE UNITED STATES FROM THE COMPROMISE OF 1850 TO THE MCKINLEY-BRYAN CAMPAIGN of 1896. 1893–1919. *Kennikat* 8 vols. $135.00; ed. by Allan Nevins *Univ. of Chicago Press* abr. ed. 1966 $11.50 pap. $3.95

Supplementary General Reading List

This list is a miscellany of books which do not necessarily fit into the seven Selected Lists which follow. Most are on our early history. Many aspects of American life are covered in other chapters. *See Chapter 7, Science, for material on atomic energy, the space program, conservation; Chapter 8, Social Sciences, for material on education, social problems; Section of this Chapter on Modern and World History: Modern World at War, and Asia (for Vietnam War).*

Anderson, William. THE WILD MAN FROM SUGAR CREEK: The Political Career of Eugene Talmadge. *Louisiana State Univ. Press* 1975 $11.95

"This is a book of real interest"—(*TLS*, London).

Bell, Daniel. THE COMING OF POST-INDUSTRIAL SOCIETY: A Venture in Social Forecasting. *Basic Bks.* 1973 $12.50

Bernstein, Barton J., Ed. TOWARDS A NEW PAST: Dissenting Essays in American History. *Pantheon* 1968 $6.95; *Random* Vintage Bks. 1969 pap. $1.95. Contributors include Barton Bernstein, Michael Lebowitz, Jesse Lemisch, Staughton Lynd and Stephan Thernstrom. Their thesis is that we have been served "consensus" or "homogenized" history since World War II. These 12 young scholars proceed to revise it; a challenging book. In the Anti-Textbook Series.

Bettman, Otto L. THE GOOD OLD DAYS—THEY WERE TERRIBLE. *Random* 1974 $10.00

This book "presents some of the realistic and less pleasant aspects of the human conditions in the U.S. from the Civil War through the early 1900's"—(*LJ*).

Boorstin, Daniel J. THE AMERICANS. *Random* 3 vols. 1958–73 Vol. 1 The Colonial Experience (1958) Vol. 2 The National Experience (1965) Vol. 3 The Democratic Experience (1973) Vols. 1–2 each $12.50 Vol. 3 $10.00 pap. Vol. 1 $3.45 Vol. 2 $2.45 Vol. 3 $3.95

"Totally delightful . . . a profoundly arresting contribution to American history"—(*SR*). The story of how Europeans became Americans, Vol. 1 won a Bancroft Prize, Vol. 2 the 1965 Parkman Prize.

See also his main entry, this Section.

Bridenbaugh, Carl. CITIES IN REVOLT: Urban Life in America, 1743–1776. *Knopf* 1955 $10.95; *Oxford* 1970 pap. $4.50

VEXED AND TROUBLED ENGLISHMEN, 1590–1642. The Beginnings of the American People Ser. *Oxford* 1968 $12.50. A social, economic and cultural history of England at this time, describing some of the causes of the "Great Migration."

Brown, Roger H. THE REPUBLIC IN PERIL: 1812. 1964. *Norton* 1971 pap. $2.45

"A major revision of thinking about the War of 1812"—(*LJ*).

Chidsey, Donald Barr. THE FRENCH AND INDIAN WAR. *Crown* 1969 $4.50

THE LOUISIANA PURCHASE. *Crown* 1972 $4.95

THE SPANISH AMERICAN WAR. *Crown* 1971 $4.50

Davis, Allen F. AMERICAN HEROINE: The Life and Legend of Jane Addams. *Oxford* 1975 $12.50

"An impressively researched and splendidly written new biography . . . a major contribution both to urban and to intellectual history"—(*TLS*, London).

De Voto, Bernard. ACROSS THE WIDE MISSOURI. *Houghton* 1947 $12.50 pap. $3.95

THE COURSE OF EMPIRE. *Houghton* 1952 $8.50

YEAR OF DECISION: 1846. 1943. *Houghton* 1950 $7.95 pap. $3.95

See also his main entries, this Chapter, and in Chapter 15, Essays and Criticism, Reader's Adviser, *Vol. 1.*

Dick, Everett. THE LURE OF THE LAND: A Social History of the Public Lands from the Articles of Confederation to the New Deal. *Univ. of Nebraska Press* 1970 $9.50

"A specialist on the history of the West, Dick has written a social history of the public lands from the formation of the public domain in 1776 to 1935 when F. D. R. withdrew all lands from private entry"—*(Choice).*

Douglas, Paul H. IN THE FULLNESS OF TIME: The Memoirs of Paul H. Douglas. *Harcourt* 1972 $13.50

Eaton, Clement. THE GROWTH OF SOUTHERN CIVILIZATION, 1790–1860. *Harper* 1961 $8.95 Torchbks. pap. $3.00. This extensive and thorough study of the pre-Civil War South is fascinating reading and important as a background for an understanding of some of the conditions and problems in the Southern regions today.

HISTORY OF THE OLD SOUTH. *Macmillan* 3rd ed. 1975 $12.95

HISTORY OF THE SOUTHERN CONFEDERACY. *Macmillan* 1954 $7.95 (Free Press) 1965 pap. $2.45

Gay, Peter. A LOSS OF MASTERY: Puritan Historians in Colonial America. *Univ. of California Press* 1966 $7.00. Includes analyses of William Bradford, Cotton Mather and Jonathan Edwards.

Gordon, Michael, Ed. THE AMERICAN FAMILY IN SOCIAL-HISTORICAL PERSPECTIVE. *St. Martin's* 1973 $12.95 pap. $5.50

Hofstadter, Richard. THE AGE OF REFORM: From Bryan to F. D. R. *Knopf* 1955 $6.95. Winner of the Pulitzer Prize in History, 1955.

ANTI-INTELLECTUALISM IN AMERICAN LIFE. *Knopf* 1963 $7.95; *Random* Vintage Bks. pap. $2.95

This is "chiefly a history of movements in this country which, from the first broadsides against Jefferson through the preachings of Billy Sunday to the conformist training in our high schools today, have used the stereotype of the intellectual to knock down opponents"—*(N.Y. Times).*

Horowitz, David. THE FATE OF MIDAS AND OTHER ESSAYS. *Ramparts Press* 1972 $7.95 pap. $2.95

Jensen, Richard. THE WINNING OF THE MIDWEST: Social and Political Conflict, 1888–1896. *Univ. of Chicago Press* 1971 $12.50

"An appreciation of [President] McKinley's political genius is a major theme of Richard Jensen's superb study of Midwestern electoral politics in the 1890's"—*(American Historical Review).*

Laing, Alexander. THE AMERICAN HERITAGE HISTORY OF SEAFARING AMERICA. *McGraw-Hill* 1974 $25.00

Leckie, Robert. THE WAR NOBODY WON: 1812. *Putnam* 1974 $5.95

THE WARS OF AMERICA. Introd. by Richard B. Morris *Harper* 1968 $13.50

"A splendidly dramatic and fascinating panoramic narrative, and probably as good a popular access to the wars of America and the men who led them and fought them, all in a single volume"—*(N.Y. Times).*

Lerner, Max. AMERICA AS A CIVILIZATION. *Simon & Schuster* 1957 $12.00 Touchstone-Clarion 2 vols. 1961 Vol. 1 The Basic Frame Vol. 2 Culture and Personality pap. each $2.45. By the well-known political commentator and columnist.

Lloyd, Alan. THE SCORCHING OF WASHINGTON: The War of 1812. *Luce* (dist. by McKay) 1975 $8.95

"Designed for the popular reader, this compact, highly-readable history contains enough detail to tantalize but not so much as to overwhelm"—*(LJ).*

Manchester, William Raymond. THE GLORY AND THE DREAM: A Narrative History of America, 1932–1972. *Little* 1974 $20.00

"A 40 year era of vivid change is minutely unraveled beginning with the F. D. R. administration during the Depression through World War II, the Truman/McCarthy era, and the years of turmoil from Kennedy and Johnson to Nixon"—*(Booklist)*.

O'Neill, William L. COMING APART: An Informal History of America in the 1960's. *Quadrangle* 1973 $12.50 pap. $3.95

"Coming Apart is that rare thing—a work of true perspective on the contemporary scene"—(Publisher's note).

Perrett, Geoffrey. DAYS OF SADNESS, YEARS OF TRIUMPH: The American People, 1939–1945. *Coward* 1973 $10.00; *Penguin* 1974 pap. $2.95

"A first rate social history from an impressive new talent who writes with both flair and maturity"—*(LJ)*.

Phillips, Cabell. FROM THE CRASH TO THE BLITZ, 1929–1939. The New York Times Chronicle of American Life Ser. *Macmillan* 1969 $12.50

"A journalistic reprise of the revolutionary decade that ran from the stock market crash of 1929 to the onset of the Second World War in 1939"—(Publisher's note).

THE NINETEEN FORTIES: Decade of Triumph and Trouble. The New York Times Chronicle of American Life Ser. *Macmillan* 1974 $12.95. A sequel to the above title.

Schlesinger, Arthur M. THE BIRTH OF THE NATION: A Portrait of the American People on the Eve of Independence. Introd. by Arthur M. Schlesinger, Jr. *Knopf* 1968 $7.95. *See comment under his main entry, this Section.*

Schlesinger, Arthur M., Jr., Gen. Ed. HISTORY OF U.S. POLITICAL PARTIES. *Chelsea House* (with Bowker) 4 vols. 1973 set $135.00

Schwartz, Bernard. THE LAW IN AMERICA: A History. *McGraw-Hill* 1974 $12.50

Stott, William. DOCUMENTARY EXPRESSION AND THIRTIES AMERICA. *Oxford* 1973 $12.50

Terkel, Studs. HARD TIMES: An Oral History of the Great Depression. *Pantheon* 1970 $8.95; *Avon* 1971 pap. $1.50

"While there have been a number of recent accounts of the Depression published, these unusual and intriguing interviews deserve their own separate place in the essential historiography of the era"—*(Choice)*.

Thernstrom, Stephan. THE OTHER BOSTONIANS: Poverty and Progress in the American Metropolis, 1880–1970. Harvard Studies in Urban History *Harvard Univ. Press* 1973 $12.00

"This volume is a valuable contribution to what is known as quantitative history. Thernstrom uses modern statistical methods in studying the movement of a significant urban population"—*(Choice)*. This book was awarded a Bancroft Prize in American History in 1974.

Tindall, George B. THE EMERGENCE OF THE NEW SOUTH, 1913–1945. The History of the South Ser. *Louisiana State Univ. Press* 1967 $12.50 pap. $4.50

"A hefty, thorough, absorbing study"—*(New Yorker)*.

Vaughan, Alden T. NEW ENGLAND FRONTIER: Indians and Puritans, 1620–1675. *Little* 1965 $7.50 pap. $2.95. A most interesting study of relations between the two.

Weisberger, Bernard A. THE AMERICAN HERITAGE HISTORY OF THE AMERICAN PEOPLE. *McGraw-Hill* 1971 $19.95

Wyndette, Olive. ISLANDS OF DESTINY: A History of Hawaii. *Tuttle* 1968 $6.60

Seven Selected Lists

The American Revolution and Its Bicentennial Celebration

With the advent of the Bicentennial celebration of the American Revolution, there has been an outpouring of titles on that colorful era. Historians have reassessed the ideological conflicts and probed their social and economic origins. The general reader's interest in our early history is at an all time high as every state participates in honoring its revolutionary heritage. The following books were selected from several hundred titles recently published or brought back into print. For additional titles see "A Checklist of Bicentennial Books" in *Publisher's Weekly* August 1, 1975, pages 71–86.

Alden, John Richard. THE AMERICAN REVOLUTION: 1775–1783. *Harper* 1954 $7.95 Torchbks. pap. $2.75

    A HISTORY OF THE AMERICAN REVOLUTION. *Knopf* 1969 $10.00

    "Alden's narrative swings along at a sweeping pace. I know of no other single volume that revitalizes the era with such balance and candor"—(Charles Poore, in the *N.Y. Times*).

THE AMERICAN HERITAGE HISTORY OF THE AMERICAN REVOLUTION. Ed. by Richard M. Ketchum; narrative by Bruce Lancaster; introd. by Bruce Catton *McGraw-Hill* 1975 $22.50

Bailyn, Bernard. THE IDEOLOGICAL ORIGINS OF THE AMERICAN REVOLUTION. *Harvard Univ. Press* 1967 $9.50 pap. $2.95. Awarded the Pulitzer Prize in History and a Bancroft Prize in 1968.

    THE ORDEAL OF THOMAS HUTCHINSON. *Harvard Univ. Press* 1974 $12.50

    "A sympathetic picture of the much vilified Loyalist governor of Massachusetts at the time of the American Revolution"—(*Booklist*).

Balderston, Marion, and David Syrett. THE LOST WAR: Letters from British Officers during the American Revolution. Introd. by Henry Steele Commager *Horizon Press* 1975 $11.95

Berkin, Carol. JONATHAN SEWALL: Odyssey of an American Loyalist. *Columbia* 1974 $10.95

    "An excellent history of Sewall's involvement in the struggle for power in Massachusetts between 1761 and 1775"—(*LJ*).

Boatner, Mark M. III. LANDMARKS OF THE AMERICAN REVOLUTION: A Guide to Locating and Knowing What Happened at the Sites of Independence. *Stackpole* 1973 $10.00

    "The special strength of the book lies in the author's ability to relate each battle or landmark to local history"—(*LJ*).

Bowler, R. Arthur. LOGISTICS AND THE FAILURE OF THE BRITISH ARMY IN AMERICA, 1775–1783. *Princeton Univ. Press* 1975 $12.50

Bridenbaugh, Carl. THE SPIRIT OF '76: The Growth of American Patriotism before Independence. *Oxford* 1975 $6.95

    This book "invites the reader to discuss, question, and debate the origins of the American spirit, and thus, it should be required reading in the bicentennial era"—(*LJ*).

Brown, Wallace. THE GOOD AMERICANS: The Loyalists in the American Revolution. *Morrow* 1969 $7.95 pap. $2.50; *Peter Smith* $5.00

    "One of the virtues of Brown's book is that it restores a much-needed perspective to the active role of the Tories in the Revolution. . . . Based upon solid research in numerous archives and other relevant sources [this] is an excellent summary of the Loyalist dilemma"—(*Best Sellers*).

Carrington, Henry B. BATTLE MAPS AND CHARTS OF THE AMERICAN REVOLUTION. *Arno* 1974 $35.00

    "This book is living history. It will bring to life the excitement and drama—as well as the deep significance of those battles where men fought and died to wrest their nation out of the British Empire"—(Publisher's note).

Champagne, Roger J. ALEXANDER MCDOUGALL AND THE AMERICAN REVOLUTION IN NEW YORK. *Syracuse Univ. Press* 1975 $10.95. A probing study of one of Washington's inner circle of advisers during the war.

Davis, David Brion. THE PROBLEM OF SLAVERY IN AN AGE OF REVOLUTION, 1770–1823. *Cornell Univ. Press* 1975 $17.50

    Davis "explores the international impact and social significance of anti-slavery thought in a critical era"—(Publisher's note).

Dupuy, Trevor N., and Gay M. Hammerman, Eds. PEOPLE AND EVENTS OF THE AMERICAN REVOLUTION. *Bowker* 1974 $11.50

ENGLISH DEFENDERS OF AMERICAN FREEDOM 1774–1778. *U.S. Library of Congress* 1975 $4.75

"Six pamphlets attacking British Policy after the North Ministry turned to coercion, written by Jonathan Shipley, Bishop of St. Asaph; John Cartwright; Matthew Robinson-Morris, Baron Roheby; Catherine Macaulay; and Willoughby Bertie, Earl of Abingdon"—(Publisher's note).

Evans, Elizabeth. WEATHERING THE STORM: Women of the American Revolution. *Scribner* 1975 $12.50

"Colorful, exciting accounts of the American Revolutionary period as recorded in the journals of 11 women"—(*LJ*).

Fleming, Thomas. 1776: YEAR OF ILLUSIONS. *Norton* 1975 $12.50

Fowler, William M., Jr. REBELS UNDER SAIL: The American Navy during the Revolution. *Scribner* 1976 $15.00

Fritz, Jean. CAST FOR A REVOLUTION: Some American Friends and Enemies. *Houghton* 1972 $7.95

"Warm portraiture, encased in a soft-spoken narrative account with dramatic innuendos, rescues an unusual woman from oblivion and affords an intimate view of Massachusetts' moral . . . climate and tensions prior to, during, and after the Revolution"—(*Booklist*).

Gates, Ruth, and Diane Loewenson. BICENTENNIAL PHILADELPHIA: A Family Guide to the City and Countryside. *Lippincott* 1974 $8.95 pap. $4.95

"A marvelous job covering historic sites and museums; theatres, restaurants, and shops; sports and fairs; classes, clubs, and hobbies, etc. There is even a list of places accessible to the handicapped"—(*LJ*).

Hawke, David Freeman. PAINE. Harper 1974 $15.00

"Candid, knowledgeable biography of the incredibly diverse, brilliant propagandist and revolutionary idealist"—(*Booklist*).

Jackson, John W. THE PENNSYLVANIA NAVY 1775–1781: The Defense of the Delaware. *Rutgers Univ. Press* 1974 $12.50

Jensen, Merrill. THE FOUNDING OF A NATION: A History of the American Revolution, 1763–1776. *Oxford* 1968 $15.00 text ed. $10.95

Kammen, Michael. A ROPE OF SAND: The Colonial Agents, British Politics, and the American Revolution. *Random* Vintage Bks. 1974 pap. $1.95

Knollenberg, Bernhard. THE GROWTH OF THE AMERICAN REVOLUTION 1766–1775. *Macmillan* (Free Press) 1975 $15.00

"A detailed inventory of the elements that led to the Revolution"—(*LJ*).

Koenig, W. J., and S. L. Mayer. EUROPEAN MANUSCRIPT SOURCES OF THE AMERICAN REVOLUTION. *Bowker* 1975 $27.50

"An indispensable aid for study of the American Revolution [which] identifies repositories and provides summaries of their contents"—(*LJ*).

MacLeod, Duncan J. SLAVERY, RACE AND THE AMERICAN REVOLUTION. *Cambridge* 1975 $15.95 pap. $5.95

Marcus, Jacob R. THE COLONIAL AMERICAN JEW, 1492–1776. *Wayne State Univ. Press* 3 vols. 1970 set $45.00

Marion, John Francis. BICENTENNIAL CITY: Walking Tours of Historic Philadelphia. *Pyne Press* (dist. by Scribner) 1974 $14.95 pap. $4.95

"The attractions of Philadelphia from the historic to the idiosyncratic are given their due in an enjoyable guide for city lovers and travelers who have not lost their zeal for exploration"—(*Booklist*).

Miers, Earl Schenck. CROSSROADS OF FREEDOM: The American Revolution and the Rise of a New Nation. *Rutgers Univ. Press* 1971 $9.00

"Colorful vignettes of Molly Pitcher and unsung heroes and attention to the more imaginative of Washington's officers heightens the adventure . . . this brief military history does have the human touch and is enjoyable"—(*Choice*).

Mitchell, Broadus. The Price of Independence: A Realistic View of the American Revolution. *Oxford* 1974 $9.50

"This is a highly readable collection of nineteen essays [portraying] the non-heroic and ugly reality, the follies without the grandeur of 1776"—(*TLS*, London).

Morpurgo, J. E. Treason at West Point: The Arnold-André Conspiracy. *Masson/Charter* 1975 $6.95

"This enticing narrative provides a much needed British perspective into the extenuating circumstances behind the actions of the principals involved. Arnold is unmasked but not redeemed, while André is seen as the victim of circumstance"—(*LJ*).

Morris, Richard B. The American Revolution Reconsidered. *Harper* Torchbks. pap. $1.45

The Peacemakers: The Great Powers and American Independence. *Harper* 1965 $10.00 Torchbks. pap. $3.75

"The making of the peace that ended the American Revolution and gave independence to the United States was the most crucial engagement and most notable victory in American diplomatic history. This brilliant book, winner of the 1965 Bancroft Prize, is the first full account of how America's 'undisciplined marines,' Benjamin Franklin, John Adams, and John Jay, out-maneuvered the Great Powers to win that victory"—(*History Book Club Review*).

Seven Who Shaped Our Destiny: The Founding Fathers as Revolutionaries. *Harper* 1973 $8.95

"Mr. Morris has presented an entertaining and instructive examination of the Founding Fathers, one that elevates their humanity without demeaning their accomplishments"—(*American Historical Review*).

Muenchhausen, Friedrich von. At General Howe's Side, 1776–1778. Trans. by Ernst Kipping *Philip Freneau Press* 1974 $14.95

"Captain von Muenchhausen's diary . . . helps to fill a gap in our knowledge of the Howe campaign. . . . On matters that came under his direct observation, he was perceptive, honest, and lively. His diary is very useful in giving us a day-by-day account of routine at headquarters, the social life of the British high command and European attitudes toward America and its soldiers"—(*Choice*).

Neuenschwander, John A. The Middle Colonies and the Coming of the American Revolution. National University Publications Ser. in American Studies *Kennikat* 1974 $12.50

Palmer, David R. The Way of the Fox. *Greenwood* 1975 $12.50

This study "investigates in logical sequence . . . General Washington's strategic conduct of the war"—(Publisher's note).

Peckham, Howard H. The Toll of Independence Engagements and Battle Casualties of the American Revolution. *Univ. of Chicago Press* 1974 $7.50

Peoples Bicentennial Commission. America's Birthday: A Planning and Activity Guide for Citizens Participation during the Bicentennial Years. *Simon & Schuster* 1974 $8.95 pap. $3.95

"This useful manual presents alternatives to guidelines advocated by the establishment dominated Federal American Revolution Bicentennial Administration"—(*LJ*).

Rand McNally Atlas of the American Revolution. With a commentary by Kenneth Nebenzahl *Rand McNally* 1974 $35.00

"The core of this elegantly produced book is 54 battle and 'theatre of war' maps—mostly of British origin, some French, a few American—published during the American Revolution for the edification of participants and observers here and abroad"—(*N.Y. Times*).

Rezneck, Samuel. Unrecognized Patriots: The Jews in the American Revolution. *Greenwood* 1975 $13.95

Rice, Howard C., and Anne S. Broun, Eds. The American Campaigns of Rochambeau's Army, 1780–1783. *Princeton Univ. Press* 2 vols. 1972 set $100.00

Smith, Dwight L., Ed. Era of the American Revolution: A Bibliography. *American Bibliographical Center–Clio Press* 1974 $35.00

Stember, Sol. The Bicentennial Guide to the American Revolution. *Dutton* 3 vols. 1974 pap. each $12.85. A detailed travel guide to important touring sights on the American Revolution.

Trevelyan, George Otto. The American Revolution. 1899–1914. Ed. by Richard B. Morris *McKay* 1964 $12.50. A condensation into one volume of the six-volume work originally published at the beginning of the twentieth century.

U.S. News and World Report. 200 Years: A Bicentennial Illustrated History of the United States. *Simon & Schuster* 2 vols. 1974 set $32.95

Van Doren, Carl Clinton. The Secret History of the American Revolution. 1941. *Popular Library* 1973 pap. $1.50; *Viking* Compass Bks. 1968 pap. $2.95

Wood, Gordon S. The Creation of the American Republic, 1776–1787. *Univ. of North Carolina Press* 1970 $15.00; *Norton* 1972 pap. $3.45

"One of the half dozen most important books ever written about the American Revolution"— (*N.Y. Times*).

Young, Alfred F. The American Revolution: Explorations in the History of American Radicalism. *Northern Illinois Univ. Press* 1974 $15.00 pap. $5.00

The North American Indian and the Opening of the West

The history of the American Indian has been falsified, misrepresented, and distorted in many standard works on the colonization of the United States. The Indian's role has too often been depicted as a primitive warrior and hunter rather than as a civilized farmer and craftsman with a highly developed oral literature. Recently, a tremendous surge of anger has prompted Indian leaders to call for a thorough revision of their history. "Collectively the new volumes on Indian-white relations throw a fresh beam of light on our general history" Wilbur R. Jacobs noted in the *American Historical Review's* "Native American History: How It Illuminates Our Past" (June 1975 p. 595–609). "One also obtains a feeling of permanence, a greater appreciation of the Indian's long past—and the implication for his long future." The following titles, chosen from several score recent works, are an attempt to represent all sides in this continuing debate. A few titles about the modern Indian are to be found under Integration, Racial Problems, Minorities in Chapter 8, The Social Sciences. (*See also Chapter 11, Folklore and Humor: American Indian Folklore.*)

A valuable series, of which over 100 titles are still available, is that of the *University of Oklahoma Press:* The Civilization of the American Indian. *See publisher's catalog for titles and authors.* Related series are *Holt's* Histories of the American Frontier and *Yale University Press's* Western Americana Series.

Adams, Alexander B. Geronimo: A Biography. *Putnam* 1971 $7.95

"The author includes the entire history of the Apache wars, along with much material on Mangas Coloradas, Cochise, and other leaders . . . Adams is definitely on the side of the Indian and this reviewer has to agree with him in most cases"—(*LJ*).

The American Indian Reader: A History. *Indian Historian Press* 1972 $4.00

Bartlett, Richard A. New Country: A Social History of the American Frontier, 1776–1890. *Oxford* 1974 $12.50

Billington, Ray A. America's Frontier Heritage. *Univ. of New Mexico* 1973 pap. $4.95.

Westward Expansion: History of the American Frontier. *Macmillan* 4th ed. 1974 $11.95

Brandon, William. THE LAST AMERICANS: The Indian in American Culture. *McGraw-Hill* 1974 $12.95

This is a "work many judge to be the finest one-volume history. Brandon has narrative eloquence, blended with profundity of generalization, shrewd realism, moral dignity, sly humor, irony, and historic truth"—*(American Historical Review)*.

Brown, Dee. BURY MY HEART AT WOUNDED KNEE: An Indian History of the American West. *Holt* 1971 $10.95; *Bantam* 1972 pap. $1.95

Brown "has tried to describe the settlement of the West as the Indians saw it. The story is inevitably disjointed, sometimes hopelessly confusing despite the author's inclusion of brief chapter headings explaining what the U.S. government was really up to, and always no picture to be proud of"—*(Atlantic)*.

Catlin, George. LETTERS AND NOTES ON THE MANNERS, CUSTOMS AND CONDITIONS OF THE NORTH AMERICAN INDIAN. 1844. *Dover* 2 vols. 1973 each $8.00 pap. each $4.00

"Catlin's 'letters'—traveler's accounts sent to Eastern newspapers—are as vividly descriptive as his famous portraits of Western chiefs"—*(LJ)*.

Debo, Angie. A HISTORY OF THE INDIANS OF THE UNITED STATES. Civilization of the American Indians Ser. *Univ. of Oklahoma Press* 1970 $8.95

"An outstanding student of American Indian history has here synthesized her almost 50 years' research"—*(Choice)*.

Deloria, Vine, Jr. BEHIND THE TRAIL OF BROKEN TREATIES: An Indian Declaration of Independence. *Delacorte* (dist. by Dial) 1974 $8.95 pap. $2.95

"The Indian author and lawyer argues that the best solution to the Indian problem for Indians and the Federal government alike is to honor old treaties and to develop a new treaty relationship which gives tribes the status of quasi-international independence"—*(LJ)*.

CUSTER DIED FOR YOUR SINS: An Indian Manifesto. *Macmillan* 1969 $6.95; *Avon* 1970 pap. $1.25

An informative and angry catalog of abuses . . . [the author] is perceptive in his analysis of the differences between Indian problems and those of blacks and other minority groups and his commentary on Indian affairs is enlightening"—*(LJ)*.

Dial, Adolph L., and David K. Eliades. THE ONLY LAND I KNOW: A History of the Lumbee Indians. *Indian Historian Press* 1975 $9.75

"This is the first general history of the Lumbee Indians, a unique group residing mostly in North Carolina. Their Indian background is unknown, but they apparently absorbed the survivors of the 'lost colony' of Roanoke and became anglicized before further European contact"—*(LJ)*.

Dick, Everett. SOD HOUSE FRONTIER, 1854. 1890. *Johnson Reprint* 1954 $7.95

VANGUARDS OF THE FRONTIER: A Social History of the Northern Plains and Rocky Mountains from the Fur Traders to the Sod Busters. *Univ. of Nebraska Press* 1965 pap. $3.95

This book "seeks to discover the [pioneers'] manner of living, their dress, food, ways of enjoying themselves, methods of labor, and their mode of life in general"—(Preface).

Driver, Harold E. INDIANS OF NORTH AMERICA. *Univ. of Chicago Press* 1961. 2nd rev. ed. 1969 $15.00 pap. $6.85

Fehrenbach, T. R. COMANCHES: The Destruction of a People. *Knopf* 1974 $12.50

This author "places the Comanches in historical perspective (using considerable material on related subjects) and chronicles Comanche history from their origins to loss of independence on the reservation"—*(LJ)*.

Fite, Gilbert C. THE FARMER'S FRONTIER: 1865–1900. 1966. *Holt* 1969 pap. $3.10; *Univ. of New Mexico Press* 1973 pap. $4.95. The transformation of the American West from unoccupied wilderness into settled agricultural communities.

Gibson, Arrel M. THE CHICKASAWS. Civilization of the American Indian Ser. *Univ. of Oklahoma Press* 1971 $8.95

"In a straightforward narrative style, Gibson provides us a thorough description of the life of one of the major Southern tribes"—*(Choice)*.

Goetzmann, William H. EXPLORATION AND EMPIRE: The Explorer and the Scientist in the Winning of the American West. *Knopf* 1966 $12.50; *Random* 1972 pap. $3.95. This received the Pulitzer Prize in history, 1967.

Hagan, William T. AMERICAN INDIANS. Ed. by Daniel J. Boorstin. History of American Civilization Ser. *Univ. of Chicago Press* 1961 $6.50 pap. $1.95. In brief but vivid form, the author presents the story of a clash between two cultures—the American Indian Nations and the rising United States and shows that the conflict with the newcomers and the resulting defeat of the Indians were inevitable.

Hawgood, John A. AMERICA'S WESTERN FRONTIERS: The Exploration and Settlement of the Trans-Mississippi West. *Knopf* 1967 $12.50

"An English historian tells the whole grand story, from the earliest Spanish probes in the sixteenth century down to the West today. Mr. Hawgood knows the country better, by far, than most Americans, and he describes it beautifully"—(*New Yorker*). Winner of the Alfred A. Knopf Western History Prize in 1966.

Jennings, Francis. INDIANS, COLONIALISM, AND THE CANT OF CONQUEST. *Univ. of North Carolina Press* 1975 $12.00

Kirsch, Robert, and William S. Murphy. WEST OF THE WEST: Witnesses to the California Experience, 1540–1906. *Dutton* 1967 $10.00. An anthology of the most important writings on California's history. "Admirably edited"—(Allan Nevins).

Lewis, Meriwether, and William Clark. *See Chapter 12, Travel and Adventure, this Vol.*

Martin, Paul S., and others. INDIANS BEFORE COLUMBUS: Twenty Thousand Years of North American History Revealed by Archaeology. *Univ. of Chicago Press* 1947 $12.50

McDowell, William L., Jr., Ed. DOCUMENTS RELATING TO INDIAN AFFAIRS, 1754–1765. Colonial Records of South Carolina *Univ. of South Carolina Press* 1970 $20.00

"Faithfully reproducing the documents without annotation, the editor adds a thirty-four page introduction as historical background and includes a convenient calendar of documents listed chronologically"—(*American Historical Review*).

Monaghan, Jay, Ed. THE BOOK OF THE AMERICAN WEST. Clarence P. Hornung, Art Dir. *Simon & Schuster* 1963 $22.50. Material not usually found in books on the West is found here; 10 authorities have written chapters on their specialties; illustrations include more than 200 drawings, paintings, engravings, prints, woodcuts, and lithographs of the period.

National Geographic Society. THE WORLD OF THE AMERICAN INDIAN. *National Geographic Society* 1974 $9.95

Rogin, Michael P. FATHERS AND CHILDREN: Andrew Jackson and the Subjugation of the American Indian. *Knopf* 1975 $13.95

"Michael Rogin has written a richly complex work that will compel major reinterpretations of the Age of Jackson"—(*N.Y. Times Book Review*).

Steiner, Stanley. THE NEW INDIANS. *Harper* 1968 $8.95; *Dell* Delta Bks. pap. $2.45

This study "attempts to present the thoughts and attitudes of the Indian toward his past"—(*LJ*).

Turner, Frederick Jackson. THE FRONTIER IN AMERICAN HISTORY. Fwd. by Ray A. Billington *Holt* (Rinehart) reissue $5.95 pap. 1962 $5.50; *Peter Smith* $7.50

See also his main entry, this Section

VOICES FROM WOUNDED KNEE, 1973: In the Words of the Participants. *Akwesane Notes* (Mohawk Nation, via Rooseveltown, N.Y.) 1974 pap. $4.95

"Produced by the energetic staff of the Mohawk Nation's national newspaper and based on reports from the Wounded Knee Information Collective, this album documents the acceleration of conflict in last year's Wounded Knee action"—(*LJ*).

Washburn, Wilcomb E., Comp. THE AMERICAN INDIAN AND THE UNITED STATES: A Documentary History. *Random* 4 vols. 1973 set $125.00

"These four volumes of primary source material have been compiled to show how the relationship between the American Indian and the U.S. Government evolved"—*(Booklist)*.

THE INDIAN IN AMERICA. The New American Nation Ser. *Harper* 1975 $10.00

"The Director of the Office of American Studies at the Smithsonian Institution systematically ties together the history of North American Indian culture into three periods: first, the early years of confrontation with Europeans during which Indians maintained equal footing with white men; second, the period between the end of the colonial era and the second half of the nineteenth century, in which Indian equality was corroded; and third, the years that followed the organization of reservations"—*(Booklist)*.

Wissler, Clark. INDIANS OF THE UNITED STATES: Four Centuries of Their History and Culture. Ed. by Lucy W. Cluckhohn. 1946. *Doubleday* rev. ed. 1966 $7.95 Anchor Bks. pap. $2.50

The Civil War

The deluge of books that marked the national observance of the Civil War Centennial seems to be abating, but reader interest continues. Since 1957, the Civil War Round Table of New York has presented an annual Fletcher Pratt Award for the year's best nonfiction study of the period. The reader is referred to the Allan Nevins (and others) bibliography listed below.

Alexander, Thomas B., and Richard E. Beringer. THE ANATOMY OF THE CONFEDERATE CONGRESS: A Study of the Influences of Member Characteristics on Legislative Voting Behavior, 1861–1865. *Vanderbilt Univ. Press* 1972 $10.00

It "begins with a profile of the Confederate Congress [and then analyzes] the voting habits of the members"—*(Annals Am. Academy)*.

Boatner, Mark Mayo III. THE CIVIL WAR DICTIONARY. *McKay* 1959 $17.50

Brewer, James H. THE CONFEDERATE NEGRO: Virginia's Craftsmen and Military Laborers, 1861–1865. *Duke Univ. Press* 1969 $7.50

"Interesting details of the operation of such diverse institutions as a hospital, a tannery, railroads, and ordnance plants with much information akin to case histories make this a most readable book"—*(LJ)*.

Catton, Bruce. *See his main entry, this Section*.

Channing, Steven A. CRISIS OF FEAR: Secession in South Carolina. *Simon & Schuster* 1970 $7.95; *Norton* pap. $2.95

"A study of the months preceding [the] state's secession from the Union in December 1860 . . . it was fear of emancipation, or of black men not enslaved, that brought on secession"—*(LJ)*.

Cook, Adrian. THE ARMIES OF THE STREETS: The New York City Draft Riots of 1863. *Univ. Press of Kentucky* 1974 $14.50

"A vivid, exciting, hour-by-hour account of the bloody violence"—*(LJ)*.

Cox, Lawanda, and John H. Cox, Eds. RECONSTRUCTION: The Negro and the New South. *Univ. of South Carolina Press* 1973 $9.95; *Harper* Torchbks. pap. $5.95

Craven, Avery. THE COMING OF THE CIVIL WAR. *Univ. of Chicago Press* 2nd ed. 1957 $13.50 pap. $2.95

RECONSTRUCTION: The Ending of the Civil War. *Holt* 1969 $6.95

Danziger, Edmund J. ADMINISTERING THE RESERVATION POLICY DURING THE CIVIL WAR. *Univ. of Illinois Press* 1974 $7.95

Davis, Jefferson. *See his main entry, this Section*.

Donald, David. CHARLES SUMNER AND THE COMING OF THE CIVIL WAR. *Knopf* 1960 $8.95. Pulitzer Prize winner in biography, 1961.

CHARLES SUMNER AND THE RIGHTS OF MAN. *Knopf* 1970 $15.00

Dornbusch, Charles E., Comp. MILITARY BIBLIOGRAPHY OF THE CIVIL WAR. *N.Y. Public Lib.* 3 vols. 1967–72 Vol. 1 Regimental Publications and Personal Narratives of the Civil War: Northern States (1961–62) $25.00 Vol. 2 Regimental Publications and Personal Narratives: Southern, Border, and Western States and Territories; Federal Troops Union and Confederate Biographies (1967) $10.00 Vol. 3 General References, Armed Forces, Campaigns, Battles, and Index (1972) $20.00

Fogel, Robert William, and Stanley L. Engerman. TIME ON THE CROSS: The Economics of American Negro Slavery. *Little* 2 vols. incl. suppl. 1974 $12.50

This is "the first full scale treatment of American Negro slavery grounded in the quantitative method"—*(TLS*, London).

Foote, Shelby. THE CIVIL WAR: A Narrative. *Random* 3 vols. 1958–74 Vol. 1 Fort Sumter to Perryville (1958) Vol. 2 Fredericksburg to Meridian (1963) Vol. 3 Red River to Appomattox (1974) Vols. 1–2 each $15.00 Vol. 3 $20.00 set $60.00

A "recapitulation of both sides of the Civil War which weaves together political issues, military strategy, and the personalities of contemporaries"—*(Booklist)*.

Frassanito, William A. GETTYSBURG: A Journey in Time. *Scribner* 1975 $12.95

"In this unique combination of history and photography, Frassanito has collected all available photographs of Gettysburg which were taken just after that decisive battle was over. . . . [His aim] is to recreate the battle on a day-to-day basis using the photographs as illustrations enabling the reader to visualize the scene"—*(LJ)*.

Freeman, Douglas Southall. *See Chapter 2, General Biography and Autobiography: Biography, this Vol., for his life of Robert E. Lee.*

Freidel, Frank B., Ed. UNION PAMPHLETS OF THE CIVIL WAR, 1861–1865. *Harvard Univ. Press* 2 vols. 1967 set $25.00

Futch, Ovid L. HISTORY OF ANDERSONVILLE PRISON. *Univ. of Florida Press* 1968 $5.00

"The purpose of this study is to determine what happened at Andersonville, to examine the conditions which resulted in high mortality among the prisoners and to consider the question of responsibility for those conditions"—(Preface).

Grant, Ulysses S. *See Chapter 2, General Biography and Autobiography: Autobiographers, this Vol.*

Grossman, Julian. ECHO OF A DISTANT DRUM: Winslow Homer and the Civil War. *Abrams* 1974 $25.00

Hyman, Harold M., Ed. NEW FRONTIERS OF THE AMERICAN RECONSTRUCTION. *Univ. of Illinois Press* 1966 $4.95

"In the last couple of decades a growing number of 'revisionist' historians have challenged the traditional picture of the Reconstruction as an era of unmitigated evil, *i.e.* oppression of Southern whites. The modern viewpoint, espoused by W. E. B. Dubois as early as 1910, dominates all of the papers in this book, which contains the proceedings of the 1965 Reconstruction Conference at Illinois. A pair of papers devoted to the South American and Canadian views of Reconstruction provide unusual studies of the time, although the Canadian essay really has little to do with Reconstruction. Closest to the heart of the problem are two excellent articles by J. H. Franklin and C. Vann Woodward on Negro Reconstruction, amplified by commentary from other specialists"—*(LJ)*.

Kerby, Robert L. KIRBY SMITH'S CONFEDERACY: The Trans-Mississippi South, 1863–1865. *Columbia* 1972 $13.50

"Kerby strongly implies that the . . . Southerners did not have their hearts in the war, at least not fully and thus he agrees with E. M. Coulter on the Confederate States of America . . . that the South was not willing to sacrifice enough to win"—*(Choice)*.

Merrill, James M. WILLIAM TECUMSEH SHERMAN. *Rand McNally* 1971 $10.00

Presents "little-known insights into the powerful character of 'Cump' Sherman and the trials of his large family"—*(Booklist)*.

Myers, Robert Manson, Ed. THE CHILDREN OF PRIDE: A True Story of Georgia and the Civil War. *Yale Univ. Press* 1972 $25.00

"This is a collection of more than 1,000 letters written by the members of a large and prominent Georgia family in the years 1854–68"—(Publisher's note). This work won the Flethcher Pratt Award for 1972, for the best nonfiction book on the Civil War.

Nevins, Allan, and others, Eds. CIVIL WAR BOOKS: A Critical Bibliography. (For the U.S. Civil War Centennial Commission) *Louisiana State Univ. Press* 2 vols. 1967–68 each $11.50 set $20.00

See also his main entry, this Section.

Nichols, Roy F., Ed. BATTLES AND LEADERS OF THE CIVIL WAR. *A. S. Barnes* Yoseloff 4 vols. 1957. Vol. 1 From Sumter to Shiloh Vol. 2 North to Antietam Vol. 3 Retreat from Gettysburg Vol. 4 Way to Appomattox boxed set $50.00 ltd. ed. lea. $150.00

Oates, Stephen B. To PURGE THIS LAND WITH BLOOD: A Biography of John Brown. *Harper* 1970 $10.95 Torchbks. 1972 pap. $3.95

"Based on contemporary letters, diaries, journals, newspapers, published reports, and recollections of eyewitnesses [this is an account] of Brown's career before he went to Kansas—a period of misfortune, frustration and personal anguish which deeply influenced his character and later actions"—(Publisher's note).

Parish, Peter J. THE AMERICAN CIVIL WAR. *Holmes & Meier Pubs.* 1975 $25.00 pap. $12.50

"A judicious blend of social, political and military history covering every conceivable facet of the struggle"—(LJ).

Randall, James G., and David Donald. THE CIVIL WAR AND RECONSTRUCTION. *Heath* 1953 2nd rev. ed. 1969 $13.95; *Little* 2nd rev. ed. 1973 $15.00. A revision of the late Dr. Randall's work by one of his protegés at the University of Illinois.

Rawley, James A. TURNING POINTS OF THE CIVIL WAR. *Univ. of Nebraska Press* Bison Bks. 1974 pap. $2.95

Roland, Charles F. THE CONFEDERACY. *Univ. of Chicago Press* 1960 $6.75 pap. $2.45

Rose, Willie Lee. REHEARSAL FOR RECONSTRUCTION. 1964. *Random* Vintage Bks. pap. $2.40. Winner of the 1965 Francis Parkman Award.

Sherman, William Tecumseh. "WAR IS HELL!" William T. Sherman's Personal Narrative of His March through Georgia. *Beehive* 1974 $20.00

"Familiar material . . . attractively packaged for a popular audience"—(*Choice*).

Tucker, Glenn. HIGH TIDE AT GETTYSBURG. 1958. *Press of Morningside Bookshop* rev. ed. 1974 $9.00

LEE AND LONGSTREET AT GETTYSBURG. *Bobbs* 1968 $6.00

"Lucid, argument-provoking history, easily one of the best Civil War books of our times"—(LJ).

Van Deusen, Glyndon G. WILLIAM HENRY SEWARD. *Oxford* 1967 $15.00

Vandiver, Frank E. THEIR TATTERED FLAGS: The Epic of the Confederacy. *Harper* 1970 $10.95

The author examines "daily life in the South: the politics, the professions, the literature, the social groups and classes . . . the military campaigns and the soldiery"—(Publisher's note).

Wiley, Bell Irvin. CONFEDERATE WOMEN. Contributions in American History Ser. *Greenwood* 1975 $10.95

United States Government and Politics

Public interest in the workings of our federal government is at an all time high, perhaps because we now seek with such great urgency answers to the questions: "How did we get where we are now?" and "Where do we go from here?" Several hundred titles have been carefully considered in order to provide a balanced list of books, both scholarly and popular, on the current crises that threaten the future of our republic. A number of the titles listed below describe and analyze the crisis in Presidential authority during the Nixon administration, commonly known as the Watergate conspiracy.

Among series useful to students of the political process are *Little, Brown's* Study of Congress Series, *Praeger's* Library of U.S. Government Departments and Agencies and *Prentice-Hall's* American Assembly Series—papers from annual conferences of experts on matters of concern to this country. Many U.S. Presidents and statesmen are main entries in Chapter 2, General Biography and Autobiography. The U.S. Government Printing Office is an excellent source of material, and one's own senator or congressman, as well as those who are chairmen of Congressional committees dealing with particular topics of interest, will usually send verbatim records of Congressional hearings and the like free on request. (*See also Chapter 1, Reference Books—General, and listing on Reference Books and Books of Documents, this Section, above.*) A sublisting on Civil Liberties and Conscientious Objection will be found at the end of this list.

Bailey, Thomas A. DEMOCRATS VS. REPUBLICANS: The Continuing Clash. *Hawthorn* 1968 $4.95. A history of inter-party competition in American politics.

Bailyn, Bernard. THE ORIGINS OF AMERICAN POLITICS. *Knopf* 1968 $5.95; *Random* Vintage Bks. 1970 pap. $1.95. Three essays, given in 1965 as the Charles Colver Lectures at Brown University.

Berger, Raoul. EXECUTIVE PRIVILEGE: A Constitutional Myth. Studies in Legal History Ser. *Harvard Univ. Press* 1974 $14.95

> The author seeks to disprove "the Nixon Administration's view that the propriety of the use of executive privilege is a question solely for the President"—(*Christian Science Monitor*).

IMPEACHMENT: The Constitutional Problems. Studies in Legal History Ser. *Harvard Univ. Press* 1973 $14.95 pap. 1974 $3.95; *Bantam* 1974 pap. $2.25

Bernstein, Carl, and Bob Woodward. ALL THE PRESIDENT'S MEN. *Simon & Schuster* 1974 $8.95; *Warner* pap. $1.95

> "The *Washington Post* reporters whose investigative journalism first revealed the Watergate scandal tell the way it happened from the first suspicions . . . to the final moments when they were able to put the pieces of the puzzle together and write the series that won the *Post* a Pulitzer Prize"—(Publisher's note).

BIOGRAPHICAL DIRECTORY OF THE AMERICAN CONGRESS, 1774–1961. *U.S. Government Printing Office* 1961 $11.75. Short, concise, objective sketches of all congressmen during those years; a section on the officers of the executive branch and cabinets from Washington to Eisenhower; and a chronological listing by states of congressmen from the First to the 86th Congress.

BIOGRAPHICAL DIRECTORY OF THE UNITED STATES EXECUTIVE BRANCH, 1774–1971. Ed. by Robert Sobel *Greenwood* 1971 $27.50. Patterned on the above, it includes brief sketches of the Presidents, heads of state, and cabinet officers during those dates.

Bolling, Richard. POWER IN THE HOUSE: A History of the Leadership of the House of Representatives. 1968. *Putnam* 1974 pap. $3.25

Broder, David S. THE PARTY'S OVER: The Failure of Politics in America. *Harper* 1972 $7.95 Colophon Bks. pap. $2.95

> "This is a book about the erosion of public confidence in . . . the two party system. . . . Broder argues for a realignment of the two parties in such a way that the people through viable participation insure responsible party action"—(*LJ*).

Brogan, Denis W. POLITICS IN AMERICA. *Harper* Torchbks. 1969 pap. $3.95

> "A classic study of the political structure of the United States"—(NYPL).

Buckley, William F., Jr. THE JEWELER'S EYE: A Book of Irrestible Political Reflections. *Putnam* 1968 $6.95; *Berkley Pub.* 1969 pap. $.95. A collection of his essays on politics and society.

UP FROM LIBERALISM. *Arlington House* rev. ed. 1968 $5.00. An attack on liberalism by the publisher of the *National Review*.

Bunzel, John H. ANTI-POLITICS IN AMERICA: Reflections on the Anti-Political Temper and Its Distortions of the Democratic Process. 1967 *Random* Vintage Bks. 1970 pap. $1.95

Canan, James W. THE SUPER WARRIORS: The Fantastic World of Pentagon Super-Weapons. *McKay* 1975 $12.50

It "examines the inner workings of the Pentagon in its efforts to procure more weapons"—*(LJ)*.

Chomsky, Noam. AMERICAN POWER AND THE NEW MANDARINS. *Pantheon* 1969 $7.95; *Random* Vintage Bks. 1969 pap. $2.45

"Mr. Chomsky, a professor at M.I.T. and a linguistic scholar, is afraid that when history comes to judge this generation, it will be accused, as so many Germans have been accused elsewhere, of silently agreeing in the massacre of hundreds of thousands of innocent Vietnamese, of not protesting loudly and clearly enough and of not doing enough to stop it"—(Thomas Lask, in the *N.Y. Times*). Among those who were acquiescent by remaining in positions of power as the "new mandarins" he counts Arthur Schlesinger, Walt Rostow, Roger Hilsman and others.

Clark, Ramsay. CRIME IN AMERICA: Observations on Its Nature, Causes, Prevention, and Control. *Simon & Schuster* 1970 $6.95 Touchstone-Clarion Bks. 1971 pap. $1.50

The former U.S. Attorney General "discusses the crime problem, diagnoses the roots of antisocial behavior in American society, and proposes the specific measures the nation must take if we are to banish the causes of crime American style"—(Publisher's note).

Commager, Henry Steele. THE DEFEAT OF AMERICA: Presidential Power and the National Character. *Simon & Schuster* 1975 $7.95 pap. $2.95

This volume "assembles for the first time under a single cover a half dozen of Commager's articles (1968–72) on the growth and misuses of Presidential power and on the Vietnam war"—*(LJ)*.

See also his main entry, this Section.

Congressional Quarterly Service. THE COMPLETE WATERGATE: Chronology of a Crisis. *Congressional Quarterly Service* Washington, D.C. 1975 $35.00

CONGRESSIONAL QUARTERLY'S GUIDE TO THE CONGRESS OF THE UNITED STATES. *Congressional Quarterly Service* $35.00

THE WASHINGTON LOBBY. *Congressional Quarterly Service* 2nd ed. 1974 pap. $4.50

"An objective résumé of lobbying practices in the nation's capital from 1969 to 1974"—*(Booklist)*.

Dommel, Paul R. THE POLITICS OF REVENUE SHARING. *Univ. of Indiana Press* 1975 $8.50

Dommel "sets forth the political and legislative history of revenue sharing within the broad context of public policy making"—*(LJ)*.

Emerson, Thomas I., and others. POLITICAL AND CIVIL RIGHTS IN THE UNITED STATES. *Little* 2 vols. 3rd ed. 1967 Vol. 1 Individual Rights Vol. 2 Discrimination with 1973 supplements set $60.00; student ed. abr. 2 vols. Vol. 1 $14.50 Vol. 2 $13.50; supplements 2 vols. pap. Vol. 1 $9.75 Vol. 2 $8.95

Frye, Alton. A RESPONSIBLE CONGRESS: The Politics of National Security. *McGraw-Hill* 1975 $10.00

It "provides some first detailed documentation from the Senate side of the changing Congressional role in national security policy"—*(LJ)*.

Green, Mark J. THE OTHER GOVERNMENT: The Unseen Power of Washington Lawyers. *Grossman* 1975 $12.50

"In this book, Mark Green, a very literate lawyer and, in the past, an exceptionally valuable man on the Washington scene, examines two of the major firms of lawyer-lobbyists—Covington and Burling, and another somewhat more recent arrival on the scene, Wilmer, Cutler, and Pickering"—*(N.Y. Times Bk. Review)*.

Guttmann, Allen. THE CONSERVATIVE TRADITION IN AMERICA. *Oxford* 1967 $7.50

Hargrove, Erwin C. THE POWER OF THE MODERN PRESIDENCY. *Temple Univ. Press* 1974 $10.00

"Full-scale judgment of the contemporary presidency as it stands in the light of mid-twentieth century developments"—*(Booklist)*.

Hess, Stephen. THE PRESIDENTIAL CAMPAIGN: The Leadership Selection Process after Watergate. *Brookings* 1974 $2.50

The author "presents a concise, fairly comprehensive account of the role of the campaign in the Presidential selection process"—(*LJ*).

Hofstadter, Richard. THE AMERICAN POLITICAL TRADITION: And the Men Who Made It. *Knopf* 1948 new ed. 1973 $7.95; *Random* Vintage Bks. pap. $1.95. Biographical studies of the principal formers of American political thought.

See also his main entry, this Section.

Hughes, Emmet John. THE LIVING PRESIDENCY. *Coward* 1973 $10.50; *Penguin* 1974 pap. $2.95

"A professor of politics at Rutgers University seeks to show how men and moments have shaped presidential power"—(*Newsweek*).

Jackson, John E. CONSTITUENCIES AND LEADERS IN CONGRESS: Their Effects on Senate Voting Behavior. *Harvard Univ. Press* 1974 $10.00

"A sophisticated statistical model of the important influences upon individual U.S. Senators' voting"—(*LJ*).

Jaffe, Philip J. THE RISE AND FALL OF AMERICAN COMMUNISM. *Horizon Press* 1975 $6.95

"The career of Earl Browder, who led the Communist Party, U.S.A. from 1930 until 1945 when he was purged on Moscow's orders"—(*LJ*).

Kennedy, John F. PROFILES IN COURAGE. *Harper* 1956 memorial ed. 1964 $10.00 pap. $1.25; *Franklin Watts* lg.-type ed. $8.95. The late President's study of American statesmen who risked their political lives for a principle.

Kirkpatrick, Lyman B., Jr. THE REAL C.I.A. *Macmillan* 1968 $6.95. By the former executive director of the agency.

THE U.S. INTELLIGENCE COMMUNITY. *Farrar, Straus* (Hill & Wang) 1973 $7.95 pap. $2.95

Lasch, Christopher. THE AGONY OF THE AMERICAN LEFT. *Knopf* 1969 $5.95; *Random* Vintage Bks. pap. $1.95

THE NEW RADICALISM IN AMERICA, 1889–1963: The Intellectual as a Social Type. *Knopf* 1965 $7.95; *Random* Vintage Bks. pap. $1.95

Leuchtenburg, William E. FRANKLIN D. ROOSEVELT AND THE NEW DEAL, 1932–1940. *Harper* 1963 $8.95 Torchbks. pap. $2.45. Winner of the Bancroft Prize.

(Ed.). THE NEW DEAL. *Univ. of South Carolina Press* 1969 $9.95; *Harper* Torchbks. pap. $2.25

McCarthy, Mary. THE MASK OF STATE: Watergate Portraits. *Harcourt* 1974 $6.95

Ms. McCarthy provides "descriptions of the chief Watergate characters, based upon her immediate personal reactions as the hearings unfolded"—(*LJ*).

McGarvey, Patrick J. C.I.A.: The Myth and the Madness. *Saturday Review Press* (dist. by Dutton) 1972 $6.95

This study is "intended less as an exposé than an attempt to dispel self-perpetuated myths surrounding the CIA"—(*Booklist*).

McKay, Robert B. REAPPORTIONMENT: The Law and Politics of Equal Representation. Fwd. by August Heckscher. 1965. *Simon & Schuster* 1970 pap. $3.95. By the Associate Dean of the Law School of New York University.

Mankiewicz, Frank. U.S. VS. RICHARD M. NIXON. *Quadrangle* 1975 $8.95

"The author, a former campaign manager for George McGovern, argues that it was the law, not the press that accomplished Nixon's downfall"—(*Time*).

Mosher, Frederick C., and others. WATERGATE: Implications for Responsible Government. *Basic Bks.* 1975 $8.95

"The official commissioned report to the Senate Watergate Committee"—(*LJ*).

Osborne, John. THE LAST NIXON WATCH. *New Republic* 1975 $7.95. This book consists largely of reprints from the author's columns in the *New Republic*.

Peirce, Neal R. THE MEGASTATES OF AMERICA: People, Politics and Power in the Ten Great States. *Norton* 1972 $12.95. The first volume of a projected nine volume series which will cover all 50 states. Other titles now available are: "The Mountain States" (1972) $9.95; "The Pacific States" (1972); "The Deep South States" (1974) $12.95 and "The Border South States" (1974) $12.95

Pfeffer, Leo. THIS HONORABLE COURT: A History of the United States Supreme Court. *Beacon* 1965 $10.95 pap. $2.45. An ideological history of the Court as a group exerting liberal or conservative influence, as the pendulum swung.

Rather, Dan, and Gary Paul Gates. THE PALACE GUARD. *Harper* 1974 $8.95; *Warner* 1975 pap. $1.95

"An examination of the character and influence of the Cabinet members and presidential advisers in the White House during the Nixon administration. The authors [both CBS newsmen] seek to show how the better Cabinet officers and well-qualified White House staffers were pushed aside by Haldeman/Ehrlichmann and Co."—*(LJ)*.

Rosenberg, Kenyon C., and Judith K. Rosenberg. WATERGATE: An Annotated Bibliography. *Libraries Unlimited* 1975 $11.50

Rossiter, Clinton. CONSERVATISM IN AMERICA: The Thankless Persuasion. *Knopf* 2nd rev. ed. 1962 $6.95; *Random* Vintage Bks. pap. $1.95

Safire, William. BEFORE THE FALL: An Inside View of the Pre-Watergate White House. *Doubleday* 1975 $12.50

The author (a former speechwriter for the Nixon administration) "has provided a remarkably candid inside view of the Pre-Watergate White House. He focuses primarily on events in which he took part: he does not attempt a definitive, comprehensive account"—*(LJ)*.

THE NEW LANGUAGE OF POLITICS: A Dictionary of Catchwords, Slogans and Political Usage. *Random* 1968 $17.50; *Macmillan* Collier Bks. rev. ed. 1972 pap. $4.95

Schuck, Peter H. JUSTICE ON THE HILL: A Study of the House and Senate Judiciary Committees. *Grossman* 1975 $15.00 pap. $6.95

"A real contribution to the literature of political science and public affairs"—*(LJ)*. (Ralph Nader Congress Project)

Seidler, Murray B. NORMAN THOMAS: Respectable Rebel. *Syracuse Univ. Press* 2nd ed. 1967 $7.00

"Virtually a history of the American Socialist Party in a biography of its six-time presidential candidate"—(NYPL). (*See also Norman Thomas's main entry, this Section.*)

Sorensen, Theodore C. WATCHMEN IN THE NIGHT. *M.I.T. Press* 1975 $8.95

"Sorensen's solution [to the problem of Presidential power] is to preserve a constitutionally strong Presidency while urging Congress, the courts, and the people to hold the President more accountable"—*(LJ)*.

Sussman, Barry. THE GREAT COVERUP: Nixon and the Scandal of Watergate. *New Am. Lib.* 1974 Signet pap. $1.95

"Reconstruction of the Watergate affair by the city editor of the *Washington Post* proportionates with a retrospective telescoping effect the entire two-year crisis"—*(Booklist)*.

Theis, Paul A., and William P. Steponkus. ALL ABOUT POLITICS: Questions and Answers on the U.S. Political Process. *Bowker* 1972 $12.95

United States Congress. THE CONGRESSIONAL DIRECTORY. *U.S. Government Printing Office* Washington, D.C. $3.00 annually

U.S. GOVERNMENT ORGANIZATION MANUAL. 1935 to date. *U.S. Government Printing Office* $3.00 annually

Vaughan, Robert G. THE SPOILED SYSTEM: A Call for Civil Service Reform. *McKay* (Charterhouse) 1975 $12.95

This book "presents 53 detailed remedies on such issues as discipline, appeals, and equal employment"—*(LJ)*.

Weisband, Edward, and Thomas M. Franck. RESIGNATION IN PROTEST. *Grossman* (dist. by Viking) 1975 $10.00

"Unlike their counterparts in Britain, who often depart noisily for reasons of political principle, resigning American Cabinet members and high Washington bureaucrats tend to leave the government like guests who have been to a bad party but are too polite to say so. They smile gamely; they send the President thank-you notes"—*(Time)*.

White, Theodore H. BREACH OF FAITH: The Fall of Richard Nixon. *Atheneum* 1975 $10.00

White "retells the whole story of the President's fall, even dealing with his character as a rootless outsider who bitterly resented social slights offered him by men like Eisenhower and Rockefeller"—*(Time)*.

WHO'S WHO IN AMERICAN POLITICS. Ed. by Jaques Cattell Press *Bowker* 5th ed. 1975 $48.50

"This revised and updated edition lists over 18,000 notables covering the entire spectrum of American political life—from the President and key federal, state and local officials to non-office-holders who are politically active and influential and, for the first time, to all state legislators"—(Publisher's note).

Woodward, C. Vann, Comp. RESPONSES OF THE PRESIDENTS TO CHARGES OF MISCONDUCT. *Delacorte* (dist. by Dial) 1974 $10.00

"At the request of the Impeachment Inquiry Staff of the House Committee on the Judiciary, Woodward and 14 other historians prepared this 'factual account without evaluation' for the staff's use in studying grounds for impeachment of Richard Nixon"—*(Booklist)*.

Civil Liberties and Conscientious Objection

Abraham, Henry J. FREEDOM AND THE COURT: Civil Rights and Liberties in the United States. *Oxford* 1967 2nd ed. 1972 $12.50 pap. $3.95

A professor of political science at the University of Pennsylvania "suggests the point where a democratic society must draw the line between individual freedom and the rights of others, and in the process, he clearly and succinctly sets forth the historical background and the significance of the 1966–67 Supreme Court decisions in these areas"—*(LJ)*.

Aryeh, Neier. DOSSIER: The Secret Files They Keep on You. *Stein & Day* 1975 $7.95

"The ACLU executive director is rightfully outraged in this provoking, big-brotherish litany of invasions of privacy (intended or not) which come about through the overuse and misuse of too many records"—*(LJ)*.

Barker, Lucius, and Twiley W. Barker, Jr. FREEDOMS, COURTS, AND POLITICS: Studies in Civil Liberties. *Prentice-Hall* 1965 pap. 1972 $5.50

Bedau, Hugo Adams, Ed. CIVIL DISOBEDIENCE: Theory and Practice. *Pegasus* 1969 $7.50 pap. $2.25. Essays by Martin Luther King, Jr., A. J. Muste, Bertrand Russell and others.

Brock, Peter. PACIFISM IN THE UNITED STATES: From the Colonial Era to the First World War. *Princeton Univ. Press* 1968 $27.50

TWENTIETH CENTURY PACIFISM. *Van Nostrand-Reinhold* 1970 pap. $3.50

Chalidze, Valery. To DEFEND THESE RIGHTS: Human Rights and the Soviet Union. Trans. by Guy Daniels *Random* 1975 $8.95

"Chalidze, a well-known member of the U.S.S.R. human rights movement and now a U.S. resident after the 1972 revocation of his Soviet citizenship, has written a moving work concerning the defence of human rights"—*(LJ)*.

Cohen, Carl. CIVIL DISOBEDIENCE: Conscience, Tactics, and the Law. *Columbia* 1971 $7.50 pap. $2.95

"Cohen, an associate professor of philosophy at the University of Michigan, provides a timely and much-needed conceptual classification of civil disobedience"—*(LJ)*.

Dorsen, Norman. FRONTIERS OF CIVIL LIBERTIES. Pref. by Robert F. Kennedy; introd. by Louis H. Pollak *Pantheon* 1968 $8.95

A professor of law at New York University who is vice-chairman of the Board of Directors of the American Civil Liberties Union has produced "a collection of the raw materials with which civil liberties law is made—Dorsen's legal briefs, memos to the A.C.L.U. and other organizations, reports of strategy conferences, articles in legal and popular journals, testimony before governmental bodies, and similar items that play a vital role in the eventual issuing of judicial opinions, statutes, and executive orders"—(*N.Y. Times*).

(Ed.) RIGHTS OF AMERICANS: What They Are—What They Should Be. *Pantheon* 1971 $12.95; *Random* Vintage Bks. 1972 pap. $3.95

Douglas, William O. ANATOMY OF LIBERTY. *Simon & Schuster* 1967 $4.95

RIGHT OF THE PEOPLE. *Pyramid Bks.* 1972 pap. $1.25

Finn, James L., Ed. A CONFLICT OF LOYALTIES: The Case for Selective Conscientious Objection. *Bobbs* Pegasus 1968 $6.00 pap. $1.95

Fisher, Charles W. MINORITIES, CIVIL RIGHTS, AND PROTEST. *Dickenson Pubs.* 1970 pap. $2.95

Hall, Robert T. MORALITY OF CIVIL DISOBEDIENCE. *Harper* 1972 $9.50

"This book discusses such questions as the nature of civil disobedience, its relation to more obviously criminal conduct, and the competing obligation to obey the law"—(*LJ*).

Lloyd, Cynthia B., Ed. SEX, DISCRIMINATION, AND THE DIVISION OF LABOR. *Columbia* 1975 $15.00 pap. $6.00

"Fifteen original essays . . . which dramatize the discrepancy between what women and men earn and which also highlight the discrimination women face"—(*LJ*).

Mayer, Peter, Ed. THE PACIFIST CONSCIENCE. *Holt* 1965 $7.95; *Regnery* Gateway Eds. 1967 pap. $2.95. With an introduction by the editor and bibliography by William Robert Miller.

Reitman, Alan, Ed. THE PRICE OF LIBERTY: Perspectives on Civil Liberties by Members of the A.C.L.U. [American Civil Liberties Union] *Norton* 1969 $6.95

THE PULSE OF FREEDOM: American Liberties 1920s–1970s. *Norton* 1974 $10.00

Rosengart, Oliver. THE RIGHTS OF SUSPECTS: American Civil Liberties Union Handbook. *Dutton* 1973 $5.95

"A very helpful and detailed exposition of a much maligned group in our society, written by a law teacher and practitioner"—(*Choice*).

Rudovsky, David. RIGHTS OF PRISONERS: The Basic A.C.L.U. Guide to Prisoner Rights. *Dutton* 1973 $4.95

"A valuable and useful guide to the legal rights of those convicted of a crime and those awaiting trial and jailed (for want of bail in most instances)"—(*Choice*).

Schlissel, Lillian, Ed. CONSCIENCE IN AMERICA: A Documentary History of Conscientious Objection in America, 1757–1967. *Dutton* 1968 $6.50 pap. $2.75

Spinrad, William. CIVIL LIBERTIES. *Quadrangle* 1970 $7.95

"The findings of this pioneer work suggest specific areas in which supplementary study is still needed"—(*LJ*).

Westin, Alan F. PRIVACY AND FREEDOM. *Atheneum* 1967 $12.50

This "massive study of privacy in the United States—what it was meant to be and what is happening to it—may well rank among the most important books of this decade"—(*SR*).

Zinn, Howard. DISOBEDIENCE AND DEMOCRACY: Nine Fallacies on Law and Order. *Random* Vintage Bks. 1968 pap. $1.65

United States Foreign Policy

The hope continues that "through diplomacy, the instrument of policy, . . . new systems of international order can come peaceably into being and older ones can remain viable" (Paul Seabury, in "Power, Freedom, and Diplomacy"). A good series is the American Foreign Policy Library, co-edited by Crane Brinton and Lincoln Gordon, *Harvard Univ. Press*. The question of the Cold War has been treated in general here, that of the Vietnam war in a special listing on Vietnam under Modern and World History: Asia. The listings on The Modern World at War, International Relations and the U.N., and others under Modern and World History include titles touching on U.S. foreign relations.

Ambrose, Stephen E. RISE TO GLOBALISM: 1938–1970. *Penguin* 1970 pap. $2.45

Aron, Raymond. THE IMPERIAL REPUBLIC: The United States and the World 1945–1973. Trans. by Frank Jellinek *Prentice-Hall* 1974 $10.00

> "The book is not easy to read and understand because of its complex analyses and the difficulties of translation, but it is nevertheless of fundamental importance providing as it does relief from the bankrupt scholarly confrontation among American experts. Aron's analysis of the international economy is perhaps the most useful part of the book"—(*Choice*).

Bailey, Thomas A. THE ART OF DIPLOMACY: The American Experience. *Irvington Pubns.* 1968 $11.95 pap. $6.95

A DIPLOMATIC HISTORY OF THE AMERICAN PEOPLE. *Prentice-Hall* 8th ed. 1969 $11.50. A classic in its field.

Ball, George W. THE DISCIPLINE OF POWER: Essentials of a Modern World Structure. *Little* 1968 $7.50

> "Mr. Ball is a knowledgeable and forceful writer, and his book is intellectually stimulating and full of acute assessments and persuasive ideas, particularly on what power is and what nations require to exercise it now"—(*N.Y. Times*). The author is, of course, the former Under Secretary of State and U.S. Ambassador to the U.N.

Barnet, Richard J. INTERVENTION AND REVOLUTION: The United States in the Third World. *New Am. Lib.* 1972 pap. $1.75

> "A founder and co-director of the Institute for Policy Studies has written a calm, dispassionate book, perceptive and truthful, that quietly demolishes the basis of most American foreign policy since the war"—(*Nation*).

THE ROOTS OF WAR: The Men and Institutions behind U.S. Foreign Policy. *Atheneum* 1972 $10.00; *Penguin* 1973 pap. $1.65

Bemis, Samuel Flagg. THE LATIN AMERICAN POLICY OF THE UNITED STATES: An Historical Interpretation. 1943. *Norton* 1967 pap. $3.45

See also his main entry, this Section.

Clough, Ralph N. EAST ASIA AND U.S. SECURITY. *Brookings* 1975 $8.95 pap. $3.50

> "Former diplomat Clough systematically and perceptively analyzes current U.S. interests and argues for a continuation of détente with Mainland China and Russia"—(*LJ*).

Davis, Lynn E. THE COLD WAR BEGINS: Soviet-American Conflict over Eastern Europe. *Princeton Univ. Press* 1975 $15.00

> "In a dispute over who started the Cold War, Davis offers a thorough and scholarly argument in favor of acquitting the U.S."—(*LJ*).

De Conde, Alexander. A HISTORY OF AMERICAN FOREIGN POLICY. *Scribner* 1963 2nd ed. 1971 $15.00 pap. $5.95. Intelligent and fair, this readable survey deals with our diplomatic history from the Monroe Doctrine to Yalta.

De Novo, John A. AMERICAN INTERESTS AND POLICIES IN THE MIDDLE EAST, 1900–1939. *Univ. of Minnesota Press* 1963 $12.50

Divine, Robert A. AMERICAN FOREIGN POLICY: A Documentary History. *Peter Smith* $6.00

SECOND CHANCE: The Triumph of Internationalism in America during World War II. *Atheneum* 1967 1971 pap. $3.45

> "A first-rate history of the international organization movement and its effect upon American foreign policy before and during World War II"—(*LJ*).

DOCUMENTS ON AMERICAN FOREIGN RELATIONS. 1952–1966 ed. by C. W. Baier and others. *Verry* 1952 $5.00 1954, 1955, 1957 each $6.00 1958, 1959, 1960, 1961 each $6.95 1962 $7.50 1965, 1966 each $9.50; 1967 ed. by Richard P. Stebbins *Simon & Schuster* 1968 $11.95; 1968–69 ed. by Richard P. Stebbins and Elaine P. Adam 1972 $14.95; 1970 ed. by Elaine P. Adam and William Lineberry 1973 $14.95. Published for the Council on Foreign Relations.

Dulles, Foster Rhea. AMERICAN POLICY TOWARD COMMUNIST CHINA, 1949–1969. *T. Y. Crowell* 1972 $7.95

"Written in masterful prose Dulles' book should command the attention of scholars and laymen alike"—(*Choice*)

Fleming, D. F. AMERICA'S ROLE IN ASIA. *T. Y. Crowell* (Funk & Wagnalls) 1969 $6.95

THE UNITED STATES AND THE LEAGUE OF NATIONS, 1918–1920. 1932 *Russell & Russell* 2nd ed. with new final chapter 1968 $22.50

THE UNITED STATES AND THE WORLD COURT, 1920–1966. 1945 *Russell & Russell* 2nd ed. with new final chapter 1968 $10.00

Fontaine, André. HISTORY OF THE COLD WAR. *Pantheon* 2 vols. 1968–69 Vol. 1 From the October Revolution to the Korean War trans. by D. D. Paige Vol. 2 From the Korean War to the Present trans. by Bruce Renaud each $12.50

"The journalist's eye for the vivid anecdote and aphorisms brighten the text, and the pace is never dropped in a welter of detail, nor is there oversimplification"—(*Choice*).

Fulbright, J. William. THE CRIPPLED GIANT: American Foreign Policy and Its Domestic Consequences. *Random* 1972 $6.95

"Fulbright's plea for an end to the sacrificing of domestic tranquillity at the expense of questionable foreign adventures is a cogent admonition"—(*Choice*).

Gaddis, John L. THE UNITED STATES AND THE ORIGINS OF THE COLD WAR, 1941–1947. *Columbia* 1972 $15.00 pap. $4.45. Winner of the Bancroft Prize for 1972.

Griswold, A. Whitney. THE FAR EASTERN POLICY OF THE UNITED STATES. *Yale Univ. Press* 1962 pap. $3.95

Gustafson, Milton O., Ed. THE NATIONAL ARCHIVES AND FOREIGN RELATIONS RESEARCH. *Ohio Univ. Press* 1974 $10.00

Halberstam, David. THE BEST AND THE BRIGHTEST. *Random* 1972 $10.00

"This is a study of the decision-making process that got us into the Vietnam War and kept us there, a study of the nature of political power that concentrates on the men who made the critical decisions, the assumptions they brought to their various jobs, and the society that produced these assumptions"—(*Newsweek*).

Halle, Louis J. THE COLD WAR AS HISTORY. *Harper* 1967 $8.95 pap. 1971 $3.45

"The book is founded, diffidently but firmly, on the balance of power as the inescapable law of life, inside nations and among them"—(*Nation*).

DREAM AND REALITY: Aspects of American Foreign Policy. 1959. *Greenwood* 1973 $13.75; *Harper* Colophon Bks. 1974 pap. $3.75

Hilsman, Roger. THE CROUCHING FUTURE: International Politics and U.S. Foreign Policy, a Forecast. *Doubleday* 1975 $12.50

The author "attempts to predict the world's political, social, and economic development into the 21st Century"—(*LJ*).

THE POLITICS OF POLICY MAKING IN DEFENSE AND FOREIGN AFFAIRS. *Harper* 1971 pap. $4.50

TO MOVE A NATION: The Politics of Foreign Policy-Making in the Administration of John F. Kennedy. 1967. *Dell* 1968 pap. $2.95

"An account, based largely on the author's recollections as a participant, of the improvisation and implementation of American foreign policy during John Kennedy's time in the White House. . . . This is an important and engrossing work of diplomatic history; it is unfailingly lucid, reasonable, and humane, and—rare for a work in its genre—never self-serving"—(*New Yorker*).

Horowitz, David. EMPIRE AND REVOLUTION: A Radical Interpretation of Contemporary History. *Random* 1970 pap. $1.95

THE FREE WORLD COLOSSUS: A Critique of American Foreign Policy in the Cold War. *Farrar, Straus* (Hill & Wang) rev. ed. 1971 $8.50 pap. $2.95

"Most basically and in common with other 'new revisionists', he rejects not only the American Government's explanation of how the cold war developed, but the work of those who have relied on official records for their own analysis. He argues that American ambition, combined with domestic economic, social, and political interests, led to grave miscalculations concerning the nature of Communism and Russian Communist intentions"—(*Choice*).

(Ed.) CONTAINMENT AND REVOLUTION. *Beacon* 1968 $5.95 pap. $2.45. Excellent essays by various writers.

Houghton, Neal D., Ed. STRUGGLE AGAINST HISTORY: U.S. Foreign Policy in an Age of Revolution. *Simon & Schuster* 1968 pap. $2.95. Essays by scholars including Arnold J. Toynbee.

Jonas, Manfred. ISOLATIONISM IN AMERICA: 1935–1941. *Cornell Univ. Press* 1969 $11.50 pap. $3.45

Jones, Robert H. THE ROADS TO RUSSIA: United States Lend-Lease to the Soviet Union. *Univ. of Oklahoma Press* 1969 $9.95

Presents "a detailed and objective picture of the numerous personal, political, military, and economic difficulties in which Harry Hopkins was Roosevelt's effective and self-sacrificing helper"—(*LJ*).

Kahn, E. J., Jr. THE CHINA HANDS: America's Foreign Service Officers and What Befell Them. *Viking* 1975 $12.95

"A sensitive, knowing account of their ordeal"—(*Time*).

Kennan, George Frost. *See his main entry in Section: History: Modern and World, this Chapter.*

Kennedy, Robert F. THIRTEEN DAYS: A Memoir of the Cuban Missile Crisis. Introd. by Robert S. McNamara and Harold Macmillan *Norton* 1969 $5.50 pap. 1971 $2.50; *Franklin Watts* lg.-type ed. $8.95

Kolko, Joyce, and Gabriel Kolko. THE LIMITS OF POWER: The World and United States Foreign Policy, 1945–1954. *Harper* 1972 $15.00 pap. $6.95

"Conventional interpretations are challenged on every page with a cool iconoclasm"—(*Choice*).

La Feber, Walter. THE NEW EMPIRE: An Interpretation of American Expansion, 1860–1898. *Cornell Univ. Press* 1963 $14.50 pap. $3.45

Levin, N. Gordon, Jr. WOODROW WILSON AND WORLD POLITICS: America's Response to War and Revolution. *Oxford* 1970 pap. $2.50

May, Ernest R. IMPERIAL DEMOCRACY: The Emergence of America as a Great Power. 1961. *Harper* Torchbks. 1973 pap. $3.45

"This careful study by Professor May of Harvard traces the interplay of diplomacy, politics and jingoism that powered our imperial adventure . . . it is a masterful synthesis of diplomatic and political history which will serve scholars and informed general readers as the definitive story. . . . Highly recommended for all but small libraries"—(*LJ*).

(Ed.) AMERICAN FOREIGN POLICY. *Braziller* 1963 $5.00

Mee, Charles L., Jr. MEETING AT POTSDAM. *M. Evans* (dist. by Lippincott) 1975 $10.95

Here, "in this close and lively look at the three Potsdam participants, Charles Mee, the former editor of *Horizon* now turned popular historian, gives nobody credit for good intentions . . . [His] postrevisionist thesis is that all 'three men rescued discord from the threatened outbreak of peace' "—(*Time*).

Morgenthau, Hans J. A NEW FOREIGN POLICY FOR THE UNITED STATES. *Praeger* 1968 2nd ed. 1973 $7.95 pap. $3.50. A liberal view by one of the chief academic opponents of the Vietnam War.

POLITICS AMONG NATIONS: The Struggle for Power and Peace. *Knopf* 5th ed. 1974 $12.95 text ed. $10.95

Offner, Arnold. THE ORIGINS OF THE SECOND WORLD WAR: American Foreign Policy and World Politics, 1919–1941. *Praeger* 1975 $4.95

"A cogent, detailed, well-organized survey"—(*LJ*).

Simpson, Smith. RESOURCES AND NEEDS OF AMERICAN DIPLOMACY. Ed. by Thorsten Sellin *American Academy of Political and Social Science* 1968 $4.00 pap. $3.00

Tucker, Robert W. THE RADICAL LEFT AND AMERICAN FOREIGN POLICY. *Johns Hopkins Press* 1971 $7.50 pap. $2.75. Probably the best critique of the revisionist school.

Williams, William Appleman. AMERICAN-RUSSIAN RELATIONS, 1781–1947. *Octagon* 1971 $14.50

THE SHAPING OF AMERICAN DIPLOMACY. *Rand McNally* 2 vols. 1956 pap. $6.50

THE TRAGEDY OF AMERICAN DIPLOMACY. *Dell* Delta Bks. rev. 2nd ed. 1972 pap. $2.95

(Ed.) FROM COLONY TO EMPIRE: Essays in the History of American Foreign Relations. *Wiley* 1972 $10.95

Afro-American History

The call for Black Studies programs and greater educational opportunities for Afro-Americans has its roots in the interrelated causes of much of today's American unease; we have needed to understand our grave deficiency and to remedy it. That there has always been an Afro-American history is testified to by the hundreds of volumes from the past now being reprinted, but it is recognized, too, that American textbooks have been, until very recently, patronizing and have treated the Afro-American as an Invisible Man, in Ralph Ellison's telling phrase. The distortion is now being righted, but there is the danger, voiced by John Hope Franklin, Kenneth Clark, Arthur Schlesinger, Jr., and other responsible writers on history or social problems, that the pendulum may swing too far in the other direction and lose sight of scholarship. "Let us remember," Arthur Schlesinger has said, "that history has a purpose of its own and that we degrade history when we try to make it a weapon in political struggles." There is indeed little need to exaggerate when so many excellent books of high scholarly standard are now available which make an excellent case for the Afro-American; many of them are listed below.

There have been countless articles and bibliographies on this subject recently, of which some of the most helpful are: "The Negro in America: A Bibliography" edited by Elizabeth W. Miller and Mary L. Fisher (*Harvard Univ. Press* 2nd rev. ed. 1970 $10.00 pap. $4.95); Harry Alleyn Johnson's "Multimedia Materials for Afro-American Studies: A Curriculum Orientation and Annotated Bibliography of Resources" (*Bowker* 1971 $22.50); "A Working Bibliography on the Negro in the United States" edited by Dorothy B. Porter (*University Microfilms* 1969 $7.50) and for paperback editions "Selected Titles in Afro-American and African Culture" prepared by the Education Improvement Project Staff of the Southern Association of Colleges and Schools, 1969.

For the researcher there is "Directory of Afro-American Resources" compiled by Walter Schatz (*Bowker* 1970 $21.00) and S. F. Biddle's description of the "Schomburg Center for Research on Black Culture: Documenting the Black Experience" (*N.Y. Public Lib. Bulletin* 1972 76:21–35). Much of this famous collection is now available on microfilm from the 3M IM Press. Among the many series on this subject are studies in American Negro Life, *Atheneum;* The American Negro: His History and Literature, *Arno;* the Basic Afro-American Reprint Library, *Johnson Reprint;* The Ebony Classics, *Johnson Pub. Co.;* and Negro Periodicals Reprints, *Negro Universities Press. G. K. Hall* publishes annual and cumulative volumes of the "Index to Periodical Articles by and about Negroes" which indexes some 4,000 articles per year. (*Further information may be had from the publisher at 70 Lincoln St., Boston, Mass. 02111.*) The listing below is, in general, confined to material on the Afro-American past. Current developments are covered in Chapter 8, The Social Sciences: Integration, Racial Problems, Minorities, this Vol. (*See also Chapter 11, Folklore and Humor: Afro-American Folklore; Chapter 14, Modern American Fiction,* Reader's Adviser, *Vol. 1; and Chapter 17, African Literature,* Reader's Adviser, *Vol. 2.*)

Anderson, Marian. MY LORD, WHAT A MORNING. *Viking* 1956 $5.75; *Avon Bks.* 1964 pap. $.75. Inspirational autobiography of a great singer.

Aptheker, Herbert. A DOCUMENTARY HISTORY OF THE NEGRO PEOPLE IN THE UNITED
    STATES. 1951. *Citadel Press* 3 vols. 1962–1974 Vol. 1 From Colonial Times to 1910
    Vol. 2 1910–1932 (1973) Vol. 3 1933–1945 (1974) Vol. 1 $10.00 Vols. 2–3 each
    $17.50 2 vols. pap. 1962–64 Vol. 1 From Colonial Times through the Civil War
    (1962) Vol. 2 From the Reconstruction Years to the Founding of the N.A.A.C.P.,
    1910 (1964) each $4.95

    "Still an important source book"—*(Choice)*.

    NAT TURNER'S SLAVE REBELLION: The Environment, the Event, the Effects. *Humanities
    Press* 1966 $4.00; *Grove* Black Cat Bks. 1968 pap. $.95. Includes the full text of the
    "confessions" of Nat Turner made in prison in 1831.

Bennett, Lerone, Jr. BEFORE THE MAYFLOWER: A History of the Negro in America, 1619–
    1964. *Johnson Pub.* 1969 $6.95; *Penguin* Pelican Bks. 1962 pap. $2.65

    "Panoramic history of Negro life in America which dispels some popular notions and accepted
    myths"—(James E. Wright, in *LJ*).

    THE CHALLENGE OF BLACKNESS. *Johnson Pub.* 1972 $6.95

Berlin, Ira. SLAVES WITHOUT MASTERS: The Free Negro in the Antebellum South.
    Pantheon 1975 $15.00

    "Berlin poses new questions and offers revised analyses of the status, ideas and way of life of the
    free Negroes of the Antebellum South. At the same time, the study explores race relations as
    enunciated by whites in the differing Southern states"—*(Booklist)*.

Blassingame, John W. THE SLAVE COMMUNITY: Plantation Life in the Antebellum South.
    Oxford 1972 $8.95 pap. 1973 $2.50

    "Using a variety of sources, including the memoirs of former slaves, the author examines the
    ways that blacks became enslaved, their processes of acculturation in the American South, and
    their . . . ties to their African heritage. He shows how the slave was able to control parts of his own
    life while often wearing the mask of submissiveness"—(Publisher's note).

Bontemps, Arna. ONE HUNDRED YEARS OF NEGRO FREEDOM. *Dodd* 1961 $6.00; *Apollo* pap.
    $1.95

Buckmaster, Henrietta. LET MY PEOPLE GO: The Story of the Underground Railroad and
    the Abolition Movement. 1941. *Peter Smith* 1959 $4.75

Bullock, Henry Allen. A HISTORY OF NEGRO EDUCATION IN THE SOUTH: From 1619 to the
    Present. *Harvard Univ. Press* 1967 $9.95; *Praeger* 1970 pap. $3.45. Awarded a
    Bancroft Prize in 1968.

Butcher, Margaret J. THE NEGRO IN AMERICAN CULTURE. *Knopf* 1956 2nd ed. 1972 $7.95;
    New Am. Lib. 1971 pap. $1.50. Discusses black artists and writers in every field.

Clarke, John Henrik, Ed. MARCUS GARVEY AND THE VISION OF AFRICA. *Random* 1974
    $12.95 Vintage Bks. pap. $2.95

Conrad, Earl. THE INVENTION OF THE NEGRO. *Eriksson* 2nd ed. 1969 $5.95 pap. $1.95

    "Analyzes the historical development of the concept of the 'Negro,' which the author feels has
    been molded by white institutions, history, and conventions"—(NYPL).

Davidson, Basil. BLACK MOTHER: The Years of the African Slave Trade. *Little* 1961 $10.00
    (with title "The African Slave Trade: Precolonial History, 1450–1850") pap. $2.95.
    Examination of the African beginnings of the American slave trade.

Davis, David Brion. THE PROBLEM OF SLAVERY IN WESTERN CULTURE. *Cornell Univ. Press*
    1966 $15.00 pap. $2.95

    This indispensable volume won a 1967 Pulitzer Prize, an Anisfield-Wolf Award "for extraordi-
    nary contribution to intergroup understanding" and the National Mass Media Brotherhood
    Award. Eugene D. Genovese wrote of it in the *Journal of Southern History:* "It will remain a
    magnificent contribution to intellectual and social history. Its range and depth, its bold re-
    examination of old questions and exploration of new ones, and its urbane and unsentimental
    humanity guarantee that *The Problem of Slavery in Western Culture* will be studied for decades to
    come."

Davis, John Preston, Ed. THE AMERICAN NEGRO REFERENCE BOOK. *Prentice-Hall* 1966 $24.95. (*For comment, see Chapter 1, Reference Books—General: Reference Tools and Directories in Special Fields, this Vol.*)

Delany, Martin R. THE CONDITION, ELEVATION, EMIGRATION, AND DESTINY OF THE COLORED PEOPLE OF THE UNITED STATES. The American Negro: His History and Literature Ser. *Arno* 1968 $6.50 pap. $2.45. The author was called by Abraham Lincoln "this most extraordinary and intelligent black man."

Dobler, Lavinia, and Edgar Toppin. PIONEERS AND PATRIOTS: The Lives of Six Negroes of the Revolutionary Era. *Doubleday* 1965 Zenith pap. $1.45

Douglass, Frederick. MY BONDAGE AND MY FREEDOM. 1855. *Johnson Pub.* 1971 $7.95; *Dover* 1969 pap. $3.50

"The classic fugitive slave narrative and one of the classics of American autobiography"—(C. Vann Woodward, in *SR*).

Drewry, Henry, and Cecelia H. Drewry, Eds. AFRO-AMERICAN HISTORY: Past to Present. *Scribner* 1971 pap. $5.95

"A collection of fifty-four readings covering the history of Afro-Americans from their African heritage to present-day protests"—(Publisher's note.)

Du Bois, W. E. B. *See his main entry, this Chapter.*

Durham, Philip, and Everett L. Jones. NEGRO COWBOYS. *Dodd* 1965 $5.00

"Among the cowboys who rode the ranges from Texas to Montana . . . were more than 5,000 Negroes. This startling fact was uncovered by Univ. of California professor Philip Durham and Everett L. Jones, who plowed through 300 memoirs and histories in search of references to Negro cowboys"—(*Time*).

Ebony Editors. THE EBONY HANDBOOK. (Orig. "The Negro Handbook"). *Johnson Pub.* 1974 $20.00. (*For comment, see Chapter 1, Reference Books—General: Reference Tools and Directories in Special Fields, this Vol.*)

EBONY PICTORIAL HISTORY OF BLACK AMERICA. Ed. by Lerone Bennett, Jr. *Johnson Pub.* 4 vols. 1971 set $38.90

"A complete illustrated history of black people in America—more than 1,000 pictures"—(Publisher's note).

Fishel, Leslie H., Jr., and Benjamin Quarles. THE BLACK AMERICAN: A Documentary History. *Scott, Foresman* 1970 pap. $5.50

Franklin, John Hope. *See his main entry. this Section.*

Frazier, E. Franklin. BLACK BOURGEOISIE: The Rise of a New Middle Class in the United States. *Macmillan* (Free Press) pap. $2.95; Collier Bks. 1962 pap. $1.25

"Analysis of the life of the upper-middle-class American Negro, by an outstanding Negro sociologist"—(James E. Wright, in *LJ*).

THE NEGRO FAMILY IN THE UNITED STATES. *Univ. of Chicago Press* rev. ed. 1966 $7.50 pap. $2.95

Fry, Gladys-Marie. NIGHT RIDERS IN BLACK FOLK HISTORY. *Univ. of Tennessee Press* 1975 $9.50

"The night riders referred to are slave owners and their descendants who used various techniques to keep blacks in their quarters at night (and thus unable to get together to plan insurrections). . . . A patrol system was instituted whereby slaves would receive severe beatings if found away from home without a pass"—(*LJ*).

Garrison, William Lloyd. DOCUMENTS OF UPHEAVAL: Selections from William Lloyd Garrison's *The Liberator*, 1831–1865. Ed. with pref. by Truman Nelson. *Farrar, Straus* (Hill & Wang) 1966 $5.95 pap. $2.45

THOUGHTS ON AFRICAN COLONIZATION. The American Negro: His History and Literature Ser. *Arno* 1968 $9.00 pap. $3.25. By the outstanding white abolitionist of the 19th century.

Genovese, Eugene D. THE POLITICAL ECONOMY OF SLAVERY: Studies in the Economy and Society of the Slave South. *Pantheon* 1965 $7.95; *Random* Vintage Bks. pap. $1.95

ROLL, JORDAN, ROLL: The World the Slaves Made. *Pantheon* 1974 $17.50

"A Marxist account of slaves and their masters in the Old South"—(Publisher's note).

Goode, Kenneth G. FROM AFRICA TO THE UNITED STATES AND THEN: A Concise Afro-American History. *Scott, Foresman* rev. ed. 1975 pap. $2.95

Herskovits, Melville J. THE MYTH OF THE NEGRO PAST. *Beacon* 1958 pap. $2.95

"Anthropological study of the American Negro, from African origins to his position in contemporary society"—(James E. Wright, in *LJ*).

Holt, Rackham. GEORGE WASHINGTON CARVER: An American Biography. *Doubleday* 1964 $5.95

"Based on actual interviews and close association with many individuals at Tuskegee, this biography presents the life and work of the outstanding Negro scientist"—(James E. Wright, in *LJ*).

MARY MCLEOD BETHUNE: A Biography. *Doubleday* 1942 $6.95

"Accurately records the dynamic personality and accomplishments of a great woman who devoted her life to improving the social and educational position of her fellow Negroes, particularly the youth"—(James E. Wright, in *LJ*).

Hoover, Dwight W., Ed., with commentary. UNDERSTANDING NEGRO HISTORY. *Franklin Watts* 1968 pap. $2.95

Hughes, Langston. *See his main entry in Chapter 9, Modern American Poetry,* Reader's Adviser, *Vol. I.*

Jacques-Garvey, Amy, Ed. THE PHILOSOPHY AND OPINIONS OF MARCUS GARVEY. The American Negro: His History and Literature Ser. *Arno* 2 vols. 1968–69 Vol. I $4.50 Vol. 2 $10.00. By the originator of the "Back-to-Africa" Movement, edited by his wife.

Johnson, Harry A. MULTIMEDIA MATERIALS FOR AFRO-AMERICAN STUDIES. *Bowker* 1971 $22.50

Jordan, Winthrop W. THE WHITE MAN'S BURDEN: Historical Origins of Racism in the United States. *Oxford* 1974 $8.95 pap. $1.95. An abridgement of his "White over Black" (*see below*).

WHITE OVER BLACK: American Attitudes toward the Negro, 1550–1812. *Univ. of North Carolina Press* 1968 $12.50; *Penguin* Pelican Bks. 1969 pap. $2.95

"A major effort to distinguish and analyze the sources of American responses"—(*Choice*).

Kraditor, Aileen. MEANS AND ENDS IN AMERICAN ABOLITIONISM: Garrison and His Critics on Strategy and Tactics, 1834–1850. *Pantheon* 1968 $7.95; *Random* Vintage Bks. 1970 pap. $1.95

"William Lloyd Garrison, whose newspaper, the *Liberator*, led the crusade against slavery from 1834 right up to and through the Civil War, has received rough treatment from historians. Aileen Kraditor brings the issue into the open through careful research into existing records (letters, editorials, speeches) and quite reverses the verdict"—(*PW*).

As Fawn Brodie wrote in the *New Republic*, he was "the Dr. Spock of the nineteenth century. On October 21, 1835, he was led by a mob through Boston streets with a rope about his neck, and he was rescued by police barely in time to spare him a coat of tar and feathers. In 1854 in Framingham Grove he ceremoniously burned the U.S. Constitution, which he had long denounced as a pro-slavery document, a 'covenant with death and an agreement with hell.' The act made Americans shudder, as do the flag burnings of our own time. But Garrison, unlike Dr. Spock, was not sentenced to jail for conspiracy, or even for simple defilement of Holy Writ." These and other adventures are recounted in this excellent book.

Leckie, William H. THE BUFFALO SOLDIERS: A Narrative of the Negro Cavalry in the West. *Univ. of Oklahoma Press* 1970 $5.95

"Well written and thoroughly documented"—(*LJ*).

Levitan, Sar A. STILL A DREAM: The Changing Status of Blacks since 1960. *Harvard Univ. Press* 1975 $15.00

"An abundance of statistical data [intended] to demonstrate that in several key areas—such as income, health, and education—American blacks have made significant socioeconomic advances since the early 1960's"—(*LJ*).

McPherson, James M. THE NEGRO'S CIVIL WAR: How American Negroes Felt and Acted during the War for the Union. *Pantheon* 1965 $7.95. Documents assembled by Professor McPherson of Princeton.

Meltzer, Milton. IN THEIR OWN WORDS: A History of the American Negro. *Apollo* 3 vols. 1967 Vol. 1 1619–1865 Vol. 2 1865–1916 Vol. 3 1916–1966 pap. each $1.65

Miller, Elizabeth W., Comp. THE NEGRO IN AMERICA: A Bibliography. *Harvard Univ. Press* 1966 rev. ed. 1970 $10.00 pap. $4.95

"Compiled for the American Academy of Arts and Sciences, this selective, scholarly bibliography will be a welcome addition to the reference collections of both public and college libraries. Some older works are noted, but the main concentration is on titles appearing in the years 1954 to 1965. Topically arranged; many references are accompanied by brief, descriptive annotations. Author index"—(*LJ*).

Mintz, Sidney W. SLAVERY, COLONIALISM, AND RACISM. *Norton* 1975 $10.95

"Each of the 11 essays in this broad-ranging and important collection surveys a major aspect of the black experience in Africa and the Americas"—(*LJ*).

Mullin, Gerald. FLIGHT AND REBELLION: Slave Resistance in Eighteenth Century Virginia. *Oxford* 1972 $7.95

"Two features distinguish this from many similar studies: slavery is examined as a condition modified by time and circumstance rather than as a constant relationship to be morally condemned or practically excused: a further . . . attempt is made to assess the cultural and psychological effects of bondage upon the slaves"—(*TLS*, London).

Oates, Stephen B. THE FIRES OF JUBILEE: Nat Turner's Fierce Rebellion. *Harper* 1975 $7.95

Osofsky, Gilbert. BURDEN OF RACE: A Documentary History of Negro-White Relations in America. *Harper* 1967 $7.95 Torchbks. 1968 pap. $3.75

Pope-Hennessy, James. SINS OF OUR FATHERS: A Study of the Atlantic Slave Traders, 1441–1807. *Knopf* 1968 $7.95

"Mr. Pope-Hennessy, although not a specialist on this particular subject, has delved deeply into the primary sources to write a valuable history of the slave trade. This is the sad story of one of humanity's greatest crimes. Millions of Africans were captured, sold, and transported to strange lands—many of them dying en route (fortunate creatures!). The author has attempted to understand the slave-traders themselves—their motivation and their philosophy. He finds that the main incentive was profit, and that the British decision to end slavery also stemmed from changing economic factors which made the trade less profitable. . . . An authoritative, well-written book"— (*LJ*).

Porter, Kenneth Wiggins. THE NEGRO ON THE AMERICAN FRONTIER. *Arno* 1971 $15.00. A compilation of research done over a 40 year period by the foremost authority on the Negro on the frontier.

Quarles, Benjamin. THE NEGRO IN THE AMERICAN REVOLUTION. *Univ. of North Carolina Press* Inst. of Early American History and Culture 1961 $6.95; *Norton* 1973 pap. $1.95

"Written in a style that is easy to read and understand, the book demonstrates the historians' love of facts, while it fills a longtime gap." In addition to ten thoroughly documented chapters, there is a precise bibliography, denoting even primary sources, such as manuscripts and unpublished dissertations.

THE NEGRO IN THE CIVIL WAR. 1953. *Russell & Russell* 1968 $15.00; *Little* 1969 pap. $2.65

See also entry for Fishel, Leslie H., Jr., above, and for Sterling, Dorothy, below.

Redding, J. Saunders. THEY CAME IN CHAINS: Americans from Africa. 1950. *Lippincott* 1969 rev. ed. 1973 $6.25 pap. $3.25

"Covers 300 years of Afro-American history—from the despairing years in which they 'came in chains' to this country up to the period immediately preceding the Supreme Court's ruling on desegregation in schools. It focuses on the economic factors that kept the Negro in virtual chains even after the Emancipation Proclamation"—(*PW*).

Redkey, Edwin S. BLACK EXODUS: Black Nationalist and Back-to-Africa Movements, 1890–1910. *Yale Univ. Press* 1970 $10.00 pap. $2.45

"With careful authority Redkey explores the relationship between 'black nationalist' sentiment (which is defined with precision) and the desire of many American black 'peasants' to return to Africa in order to escape injustice, poverty, and discrimination"—(*Choice*).

Robinson, Armistead L., and others, Eds. BLACK STUDIES IN THE UNIVERSITY: A Symposium. *Yale Univ. Press* 1969 $10.00

Salk, Erwin A. A LAYMAN'S GUIDE TO NEGRO HISTORY. *McGraw* 1967 $6.95

"An outstanding guide to further study. Includes bibliographies, significant dates, and numerous sources for material and information"—(N.Y. *Public Lib*.).

Shaw, Nate. ALL GOD'S DANGERS: The Life of Nate Shaw. Ed. by Theodore Rosengarten *Knopf* 1974 $10.00. An oral autobiography of an 85 year old black tenant farmer, recorded over four years of taping by the editor.

Sloan, Irving J. THE BLACKS IN AMERICA, 1492–1970: A Chronology and Fact Book. *Oceana* 3rd ed. 1971 $5.00. Events significant to black Americans are listed.

Smith, Dwight L., Ed. AFRO-AMERICAN HISTORY: A Bibliography. *American Bibliographical Center—Clio Press* new ed. 1974 $45.00

Stampp, Kenneth M. THE PECULIAR INSTITUTION. *Knopf* 1956 $7.95; *Random* Vintage Bks. pap. $1.95. A very important discussion of slavery.

Sterling, Dorothy, Ed. SPEAK OUT IN THUNDER TONES: Letters and Other Writings by Black Northerners, 1787–1865. *Doubleday* 1973 $5.95

(With Benjamin Quarles). LIFT EVERY VOICE: The Lives of Booker T. Washington, W. E. B. Du Bois, Mary Church Terrell, and James Weldon Johnson. *Doubleday* 1965 pap. $1.45

Sterling, Philip, and Rayford W. Logan. FOUR TOOK FREEDOM: The Lives of Harriet Tubman, Frederick Douglass, Robert Smalls, and Blanche K. Bruce. *Doubleday* 1967 $3.75 pap. $1.45

Still, William. THE UNDERGROUND RAILROAD. The American Negro: His History and Literature Ser. *Arno* 1968 $25.00; *Johnson Pub.* 1970 $10.50

"William Still, son of ex-slave parents, kept full records of the Philadelphia Vigilance Committee for helping fugitive slaves in the 1850s and published them in his 800-page book, *The Underground Railroad* (1872). The stories he preserved of hundreds of fugitives are personal, detailed, and circumstantial, and with due allowance for the human proclivity for making a good story better, they can be read with profit"—(C. Vann Woodward, in *SR*).

Thorpe, Earl E. BLACK HISTORIANS: A Critique. (Orig. "Negro Historians in the U.S.") *Morrow* 1958 rev. ed. 1971 $7.95 pap. $3.85

Dr. Thorpe, chairman of the Department of History at North Carolina Central University, "has made an effort to be objective, pointing out weaknesses as well as strengths of various historians. This is a scholarly work, admirably documented"—(*LJ*).

THE MIND OF THE NEGRO: An Intellectual History of Afro-Americans. *Negro Univs. Press* 1961 $22.50

Williams, George W. THE HISTORY OF THE NEGRO RACE IN AMERICA FROM 1619 TO 1880. The American Negro: His History and Literature Ser. *Arno* 1968 $34.50

"A monument in American historiography"—(C. Vann Woodward, in *SR*).

A HISTORY OF THE NEGRO TROOPS IN THE WAR OF THE REBELLION, 1861–65. *Negro Univs. Press* 1968 $12.75

Woodward, C. Vann. *See his main entry, this Section.*

Work, Monroe N. A BIBLIOGRAPHY OF THE NEGRO IN AFRICA AND AMERICA. 1928. *Argosy-Antiquarian* $22.50; *Octagon* 1966 $23.50

Wright, Richard. BLACK BOY: A Record of Childhood and Youth. 1945. *Harper* 1969
$7.95 pap. $1.25

"Honest, shocking autobiography of one of America's most able writers"—(James E. Wright, in
LJ).

NATIVE SON. 1940. *Harper* 1969 $8.95 pap. $1.25

TWELVE MILLION BLACK VOICES: A Folk History of the Negro in the U.S. 1941. *Arno*
1969 $10.00

See also his main entry in Chapter 14, Modern American Fiction, Reader's Adviser, Vol. 1.

Canada

Americans have long known too little about their great neighbor to the north. Its colorful
Prime Minister, Pierre Trudeau, and the 1976 Olympic Games have aroused new
curiosity and interest. This list has been reviewed and many titles annotated by the
Reference Staff of the University of Manitoba Library at Winnipeg.

Berger, Carl. THE SENSE OF POWER: Studies in the Ideas of Canadian Imperialism, 1867–
1914. *Univ. of Toronto Press* 1970 $12.50 pap. $3.95

"An examination of the ideas of Canadian imperialists in the years from Confederation to the
First World War. As such it is very nearly the first scholarly intellectual history produced by a
Canadian historian. Certainly, it is the very best"—(*Choice*).

Braroe, Niels Winther. INDIAN AND WHITE: Self-Image and Interaction in a Canadian
Plains Community. *Stanford Univ. Press* 1975 $8.50

"Braroe's analysis of social interaction between a small group of Canadian Cree Indians and
their white neighbors is an important contribution to societal studies. Especially significant is the
persistence of ethnic identity which he finds. There is little evidence of 'melting pot' activities
between the Indians and the whites"—(*LJ*).

CANADA IN WORLD AFFAIRS. The Canadian Institute of International Affairs Ser. *Oxford*
12 vols. 1956–68 Vols. 1-4 o.p. Vol. 5 1946–1949 (1959) pap. $2.75 Vol. 6 1949–1950
(1957) pap. $2.50 Vol. 7 Sept. 1951–Oct. 1953 (1956) pap. $1.65 Vol. 8 1953–1955
(1959) pap. $1.95 Vol. 9 Oct. 1955–June 1957 (1959) pap. $1.95 Vol. 10 1957–1959
(1968) $7.50 Vol. 11 o.p. Vol. 12 1961–1963 (1968) $10.00. A narrative account by
various well-qualified authors.

Careless, James M. S., Ed. COLONISTS AND CANADIANS, 1760–1867. *Macmillan* (of Canada)
1971 $10.95 pap. $3.95; *St. Martin's* $9.95

(With R. Craig Brown, Eds.). THE CANADIANS, 1867–1967. *Macmillan* (of Canada) 1968
$13.50 pap. $4.95; *St. Martin's* pap. $5.95. Together these two volumes make a survey
history "as pleasing and interesting as is available." It is a decade by decade history,
with each decade treated by a different historian.

Chalmers, J. W., and W. J. Eccles. HISTORICAL ATLAS OF CANADA. *Moyer* Weston, Ontario
$2.75. High school level, comprehensive. Covers growth of Canada: wars affecting
Canada: Exploration: Settlement: Communications: Resources: Energy.

Classen, H. George. THRUST AND COUNTERTHRUST: The Genesis of the Canada–United
States Boundary. *Rand McNally* 1967 $6.95

Corbett, Edward M. QUEBEC CONFRONTS CANADA. *Johns Hopkins Press* 1967 $11.00

"From a study made under a Brookings Institution Federal Executive Fellowship, Edward
Corbett states why he considers that Quebec is having a social revolution supported by a dynamic
cultural and intellectual renaissance"—(*PW*). "For anyone interested in finding out what is going
on in Quebec these days, there can scarcely be a better source"—(*LJ*).

Craig, Gerald M. THE UNITED STATES AND CANADA. American Foreign Policy Library
Harvard Univ. Press 1968 $10.95

Professor Craig of the University of Toronto, "aims directly at the general American reader
whose knowledge of Canada is limited to the usual clichés. . . . Highly recommended"—(*LJ*).

Creighton, Donald. CANADA'S FIRST CENTURY, 1867–1967. *St. Martin's* 1970 $12.75

This is "a response by Canada's most eminent historian to the insecurities of the country in the 1960's. . . . The central argument is that the unity achieved in 1867 and solidified by the economic developments in the early years of this century has been progressively eroded until the very survival of the nation has become doubtful"—(*Choice*).

Eccles, William John. THE CANADIAN FRONTIER, 1534–1760. *Holt* 1969 $7.95 pap. $4.45

"Eccles [Canada's leading authority on Frontenac] provides the best, most succinct and freshest statement now available on the nature of society in New France"—(*Choice*).

Innis, Harold. ESSAYS IN CANADIAN ECONOMIC HISTORY. Ed. by Mary Quale Innis *Univ. of Toronto Press* 1956 pap. $4.50

Innis' major publications were heavy reading but it is possible to sample his work by reading these essays which deal with various aspects of the economy. Canada is seen as a hinterland serving external metropoles.

Kennedy, John H. JESUIT AND SAVAGE IN NEW FRANCE. 1950. *Shoe String Press* 1971 $7.50

The author draws on the "Jesuit Relations and Allied Documents" edited by Reuben G. Thwaites (*see entry below*) to give an image of the "noble savage" as described by immigrants to New France.

Kilbourn, William, Ed. CANADA: A Guide to the Peaceable Kingdom. *Macmillan* (of Canada) 1970 $10.95 pap. $4.95; *St. Martin's* 1971 $10.95. A collection of pieces by popular and scholarly writers on people, places, politics, mores, religion and life styles with the underlying theme of the Canadian identity.

MacEwan, Grant. BETWEEN THE RED AND THE ROCKIES. *Univ. of Toronto Press* 1952 pap. $3.50. Interesting stories bearing on the development of the West and recounting the revolution from a fur trading to an agricultural economy.

SITTING BULL: The Years in Canada. *Hurtig Pubs.* (10560 105 St. Edmonton Alta. T5H 2W7) 1973 $8.95. An important historical document showing the cultural shock experienced by the native people when the white man moved in on his land and threatened his whole life style. This book has done much to awaken the present day Westerner to the need to assist the Indian *now*.

MacKirdy, Kenneth A., and others. Eds. CHANGING PERSPECTIVES IN CANADIAN HISTORY. *Univ. of Notre Dame Press* 1967 $8.75

"This collection combines primary documents, accounts by earlier historians, and commentaries by recent scholars, to illustrate the development of thought on major problems in Canada's past and present"—(*LJ*).

Morton, William L. THE CANADIAN IDENTITY. *Univ. of Toronto Press* 2nd ed. rev. 1972 pap. $2.95; *Univ. of Wisconsin Press* 2nd ed. 1972 $12.50 pap. $2.95. An attempt to describe the character of Canadian nationhood in its peculiarly intimate association with the Commonwealth and the United States.

Mowat, Farley. THE DESPERATE PEOPLE. *Little-Atlantic* 1959 $6.95. This sensitive and well written book draws attention to the problems of Eskimo integration. It is an engrossing book which will shock and anger the reader. It shows clearly the plight of the people of Northland Canada.

THE NATIONAL ATLAS OF CANADA. *Macmillan* (of Canada) 4th ed. 1974 $67.50

Pearson, Lester B. MIKE: The Memoirs of the Right Hon. Lester B. Pearson. *Univ. of Toronto Press* 2 vols. 1972–73 Vol. 1 1897–1948 (1972) Vol. 2 1948–1957 (1973) each $12.50; *New Am. Lib.* 2 vols. pap. each $1.95; *Quadrangle* 2 vols. 1972–74 each $12.50

These two volumes outline Mr. Pearson's liberal political philosophy. Throughout his public life, first as career diplomat, and then as politician, he followed a political doctrine totally lacking in fanaticism but fully committed to gaining for Canada an independent voice in international affairs. No Prime Minister since Laurier has been so influential in shaping Canada's future and in freeing her from undue dominance from both the United States and Great Britain. Most strongly recommended.

Schull, Joseph. LAURIER: The First Canadian. *St. Martin's* 1965 $11.95

A biography of the man who led Canada to nationhood. "Author Schull deserves an accolade for this work"—(*LJ*).

Story, Norah, Comp. THE OXFORD COMPANION TO CANADIAN HISTORY AND LITERATURE. *Oxford* 1967 $18.50, 1967–72 suppl. ed. by William Toye pap. $9.50

Thorburn, Hugh G. PARTY POLITICS IN CANADA. *Prentice-Hall* 3rd ed. 1972 $7.50 pap. $3.95. The author describes some of Canada's lesser known political parties—the UFA, CCF, Social Credit etc. Colourful and interesting.

Thordarson, Bruce. LESTER PEARSON: Diplomat and Politician. *Oxford* 1974 pap. $4.95
"A well-balanced brief biography of Canada's 14th prime minister (1963–68) who as a career diplomat and foreign minister was a leading figure in the international organizations of the post 1945 world"—(*Choice*).

TRUDEAU AND FOREIGN POLICY: A Study in Decision-Making. *Oxford* 1972 pap. $3.25. This is a review of Canadian foreign policy (especially with regard to NATO) undertaken by the Trudeau government between 1968 and 1970. It provides a clear insight into the present government's political philosophy.

Thwaites, Reuben G., Ed. THE JESUIT RELATIONS AND ALLIED DOCUMENTS: The Travels and Explorations of the Jesuit Missionaries in New France, 1610–1791. *Rowman* 73 vols. in 36 1959 set $400.00

Trudeau, Pierre E. CONVERSATIONS WITH CANADIANS. *Univ. of Toronto Press* 1972 $8.50 pap. $1.95

FEDERALISM AND THE FRENCH CANADIANS. Introd. by John T. Saywell; pref. by Gerard Pelletier *St. Martin's* 1968 $6.50
Prime Minister Trudeau's "book on federalism is a collection of essays, a mosaic. It is a series of navigational markers and warnings for those who, like himself, delight in skilled and complicated action. [These essays] are written at the level of Edmund Burke's best meditations"—(Marshall McLuhan, in the *N.Y. Times*).

Walters, Susan, Ed. THE CANADIAN ALMANAC AND DIRECTORY FOR 1975. *Pitman* 1975 $24.50

Wilson, Edmund. O CANADA: An American's Notes on Canadian Culture. *Farrar, Straus* 1965 $4.95. Fascinating literary and political commentary on both the English and French sectors.

Winks, Robin W. THE BLACKS IN CANADA: A History. *Yale Univ. Press* 1971 $15.00
"The Canadian experience has been different, and there are some instructive contrasts (and analogies) with American life"—(*Choice*).

Woodcock, George. THE DOUKHOBORS. *Oxford* 1968 $7.50. Highly readable book by a professor of political science on the European background and the Canadian experience of this Russian pacifist sect which inhabits British Columbia.

Latin America

This list includes recent books on Latin America and U.S.–Latin American relations, with a few titles on individual countries. *See also Chapter 16, Latin American Literature*, which includes South American and Mexican works translated from the Spanish, with a supplementary list of Brazilian Novelists, translated from the Portuguese. Series include Borzoi Books on Latin America, *Knopf*; Studies in Contemporary Latin America, *Macmillan* (Free Press); Latin American Histories, *Oxford*; and the Texas Pan American Series, *Univ. of Texas Press*. The Latin American Center at the University of California (Los Angeles, Calif. 90024) publishes a number of reference works in series; *catalog available on request.*

Adams, Richard Newbold. CRUCIFIXION BY POWER: Essays on Guatemalan National Social Structure, 1944–1966. *Univ. of Texas Press* 1970 $10.00
"One of the three best works ever published on Latin America, [this] is certainly the best piece on Guatemala and is probably the best country study of any Latin American country"—(*Choice*).

Aguilar, Luis E., Ed. MARXISM IN LATIN AMERICA. *Knopf* 1968 $4.50 pap. $3.50
"A highly representative, but heretofore difficult to find, selection of Latin Marxist and Communist writers in the period 1890–1967"—(*LJ*).

Aguilar Monteverde, Alonso. Pan Americanism from Monroe to the Present: A View from the Other Side. Trans. by Asa Zantz *Monthly Review Press* 1969 pap. $2.95

Allende Gossens, Salvador. Chile's Road to Socialism. Ed. by John B. Garces *Penguin* 1973 pap. $2.45. Allende's speeches and press conferences constitute a valuable primary source for understanding Chilean socialism.

Blanco, Hugo. Land or Death: The Peasant Struggle in Peru. *Pathfinder* 1972 $6.95 pap. $2.45

"A most interesting personal account—necessary reading for those involved with contemporary Latin America"—(*LJ*).

Bourne, Richard. Political Leaders of Latin America. *Knopf* 1970 $8.95

Bourricaud, François. Power and Society in Contemporary Peru. Trans. by Paul Stevenson *Praeger* 1970 $11.00

"This work was originally published in France in 1967; in it, the author analyses the Peruvian Crisis concentrating upon the years 1956–1964. . . . He . . . postulates that a violent social crisis is not inevitable and that the process of modernization can be peaceable"—(*LJ*).

Brandenburg, Frank R. The Making of Modern Mexico. Introd. by Frank Tannenbaum *Prentice-Hall* 1964 $10.95

A senior economist of the National Planning Association "presents a major analytical study . . . invaluable for an understanding of present-day Mexico"—(*LJ*).

Burns, E. Bradford, Ed. A Documentary History of Brazil. *Knopf* 1966 $4.95 pap. $2.95

Carmack, Robert M. Quichean Civilization: The Ethnohistoric, Ethnographic and Archaeological Sources. *Univ. of California Press* 1973 $15.00

Castro, Fidel. The Cuban Revolution, National Liberation and the Soviet Union: Two Speeches. *New Outlook* 1974 pap. $.70

Ché Guevara, Ernesto. Bolivian Diaries: Nov. 7, 1966 to Oct. 7, 1967. Ed. by Robert Scheer; introd. by Fidel Castro *Bantam* 1968 pap. $1.45

Reminiscences of the Cuban Revolutionary War. *Monthly Review Press* 1968 pap. $3.25

Clissold, Stephen. Latin America: New World, Third World. *Praeger* 1972 $13.50

"Clissold covers five centuries of Latin American history in this useful tool for identifying political and historical trends"—(*LJ*).

Coe, Michael D. The Maya. *Praeger* 1966 $8.50 pap. $3.95

"An excellent survey"—(*LJ*).

Collier, Simon D. From Cortés to Castro: An Introduction to the History of Latin America, 1492–1973. *Macmillan* 1974 $12.95. An exercise in thematic history with events treated chronologically within each topic.

Connel-Smith, Gordon. The United States and Latin America: An Historical Analysis of Inter-American Relations. *Wiley* 1974 $16.75

"The author is obviously favorable to a realignment and reassessment of the U.S. view toward Latin America, and argues forcefully and idealistically for greater U.S. recognition of Latin America's equality and importance"—(*LJ*).

Culbert, T. Patrick. The Lost Civilization: The Story of the Classic Maya. *Harper* 1974 pap. $2.95. A readable thought provoking study of the Classic Maya with a reasoned explanation for their collapse.

Cumberland, Charles C. Mexican Revolution: The Constitutionalist Years. *Univ. of Texas Press* 1974 $10.00

Mexico: The Struggle for Modernity. *Oxford* 1968 $8.95 pap. $2.95

Mr. Cumberland "abandons the conventional political-biographical approach to examine, with a firm grasp of monographical material, the elements that gave structure to the nation's history. In a precise and analytical manner, he cogently summarizes and evaluates Spanish colonial policy, particularly its impact on the conquered Indians. His interpretation, clearly organized and richly documented, adds a new dimension to our knowledge of the colonial period"—(Ramon Eduardo Ruiz, in the *N.Y. Times*).

ENCYCLOPEDIA OF LATIN AMERICA. Ed. by Helen Delpar *McGraw-Hill* 1974 $29.95

"Various Latin Americanists provide concise articles on Latin America past and present (with emphasis on the national period of its development). Entries on subjects such as architecture, agrarian reform, political movements, and historical events often include bibliographies or illustrations; descriptions of geographical features and biographies of living and deceased Latin Americans are also provided"—(*LJ*).

Fernandes, Florestan. THE NEGRO IN BRAZILIAN SOCIETY. Trans. by J. D. Skiles and others; ed. by P. B. Eveleth *Columbia* 1971 $4.50

Freyre, Gilberto de Mello. THE MANSIONS AND THE SHANTIES: The Making of Modern Brazil. Trans. by Harriet de Onis *Knopf* 1963 $12.50

THE MASTERS AND THE SLAVES: A Study in the Development of Brazilian Civilization. 1933. Trans. from the Portuguese by Samuel Putnam *Knopf* 1964 $12.50 pap. $3.50. By the eminent Brazilian writer and sociologist.

NEW WORLD IN THE TROPICS: The Culture of Modern Brazil. *Knopf* 1959 $7.95; *Random* Vintage Bks. pap. $1.65

PORTUGUESE IN THE TROPICS. Trans. by H. M. D'O Matthew and F. de Mello Moser *Hafner* 1961 pap. $8.50

Furtado, Celso. ECONOMIC DEVELOPMENT OF LATIN AMERICA: A Survey from Colonial Times to the Cuban Revolution. Trans. by Suzette Macedo *Cambridge* 1971 $11.95 pap. $4.95

"An analysis of the historical roots of Latin American social and economic institutions, through the period of the industrial revolution"—(*Economist*).

Galeano, Eduardo. OPEN VEINS OF LATIN AMERICA: Five Centuries of the Pillage of a Continent. Trans. by Cedric Belfrage *Monthly Review Press* 1973 $8.95

"Galeano . . . spokesman for the Left has written a brilliant summary of five centuries of foreign exploitation of Latin America"—(*Choice*).

Galindez Suarez, Jesus de. THE ERA OF TRUJILLO, DOMINICAN DICTATOR. Ed. by Russell Fitzgibbon *Univ. of Airzona Press* 1973 pap. $4.50

Gil, Federico. LATIN AMERICAN–UNITED STATES RELATIONS. *Harcourt* 1971 pap. $4.25

Gonzalez, Edward. CUBA UNDER CASTRO: The Limits of Charisma. *Houghton* 1974 pap. $6.50

Goodsell, Charles T. AMERICAN CORPORATIONS AND PERUVIAN POLITICS. *Harvard Univ. Press* 1974 $14.00

Goodsell, James Nelson. FIDEL CASTRO'S PERSONAL REVOLUTION IN CUBA: 1959–1973. *Knopf* 1975 $7.95

Graham, Richard, and Peter H. Smith, Eds. NEW APPROACHES TO LATIN AMERICAN HISTORY. *Univ. of Texas Press* 1974 $8.75

Gray, Richard B. LATIN AMERICA AND THE UNITED STATES IN THE 1970'S. *F. T. Peacock Pubs.* 1971 $10.00 pap. $5.95

Griffin, Charles C., and Warren J. Benedict, Eds. LATIN AMERICA: A Guide to the Historical Literature. *Univ. of Texas Press* 1971 $25.00

Gutierrez, Carlos Maria. THE DOMINICAN REPUBLIC: Rebellion and Repression. *Monthly Review Press* 1972 $6.95

"This short, readable, journalistic account depicts the country from an anti-U.S. perspective, but it precisely and accurately presents the views of the opposition groups without interjecting the views of the author"—(*Choice*).

Hemming, John. THE CONQUEST OF THE INCAS. *Harcourt* 1973 $14.00 pap. $4.95

Hilton, Ronald. THE LATIN AMERICANS: Their Heritage and Their Destiny. *Lippincott* 1973 $7.50 pap. $3.25

"Both an overview of Latin America's past and a critical assessment of current trends in the area today"—(Publisher's note).

Hurwitz, Samuel J., and Edith F. Hurwitz. JAMAICA: A Historical Report. *Praeger* 1971 $9.50

"This work is not only a comprehensive history of Jamaica, but it is also the first one to analyze events in the 1960's in the light of broader historical themes"—(*Choice*).

Jagan, Cheddi. THE WEST ON TRIAL: My Fight for Guyana's Freedom. *International Pubs.* 1973 pap. $1.95

"The fiery leader of the leftist People's Progressive Party in British Guiana, now [independent] Guyana, gives a somewhat embittered account of his political fortunes"—(*LJ*).

James, Daniel. CHÉ GUEVARA: A Biography. *Stein & Day* 1970 $3.95

Johnson, John J. THE MILITARY AND SOCIETY IN LATIN AMERICA. *Stanford Univ. Press* 1964 $8.50 pap. $3.25

"John J. Johnson has added to his stature as one of our leading Latin-Americanists by this solid, thoughtful study"—(*N.Y. Times Bk. Rev.*).

Jorrin, Miguel, and John D. Marty. LATIN AMERICAN POLITICAL THOUGHT AND IDEOLOGY. *Univ. of North Carolina Press* 1971 $12.50

"For anyone interested in the development of Latin American political thought, this book is essential background reading. . . . The intellectuals included here appear to be the most interesting and important of their age"—(*Annals Am. Academy*).

Levine, Daniel H. CONFLICT AND POLITICAL CHANGE IN VENEZUELA. *Princeton Univ. Press* 1973 $13.00

Lipset, Sheldon B. THE CANAL ASPECTS OF UNITED STATES PANAMANIAN RELATIONS. *Univ. of Notre Dame Press* 1967 $5.95 pap. $2.25

Logan, Rayford W. HAITI AND THE DOMINICAN REPUBLIC. *Oxford* 1968 $6.75
"Highly recommended"—(*LJ*).

Malloy, James M. BOLIVIA: The Uncompleted Revolution. *Univ. of Pittsburgh Press* 1970 $12.95

Mariategui, José Carlos. SEVEN INTERPRETATIVE ESSAYS ON PERUVIAN REALITY. Trans. by Marjory Urquidi *Univ. of Texas Press* 1971 $8.50 pap. $3.45

Mitchell, Sir Harold. CONTEMPORARY POLITICS AND ECONOMICS IN THE CARIBBEAN. *Ohio Univ. Press* 1968 $15.00

Munro, Dana Gardner. THE UNITED STATES AND THE CARIBBEAN REPUBLICS, 1921–1933. *Princeton Univ. Press* 1974 $17.50

Pescatello, Ann, Ed. FEMALE AND MALE IN LATIN AMERICA. *Univ. of Pittsburgh Press* 1973 $9.95

In these 12 essays "the authors examine the role of women in both traditional and modernizing Latin American societies [making] . . . comparisons of Latin American and North American attitudes [and] . . . machismo (or male dominance)"—(*LJ*).

Pike, Frederick B. SPANISH AMERICA: Tradition and Social Innovation. *Norton* 1973 $7.95 pap. $3.45

Prescott, William Hickling. *See his main entry, this Section.*

Russell-Wood, A. J. R. FROM COLONY TO NATION: Essays on the Independence of Brazil. *Johns Hopkins Press* 1975 $12.50

These "seven considered and penetrating essays, all written by respected academicians, treat the political, social, cultural and intellectual aspects of the situation"—(*LJ*).

Sater, William F. THE HEROIC IMAGE IN CHILE: Arturo Prat, Secular Saint. *Univ. of California Press* 1973 $10.50. Interesting study of the hero in Latin America and the way in which the Chilean government used Prat for its own ends.

Schneider, Ronald M. THE POLITICAL SYSTEM OF BRAZIL: Emergence of a "Modernizing" Authoritarian Regime, 1964–1970. *Columbia* 1971 $13.50

"This volume uses the Brazilian example to test theories on the role of the armed forces in Latin America and in other developing areas. Nine well documented chapters present theoretical considerations, outline background material, and treat events since 1964, while an appendix provides biographical data on military leaders"—*(LJ)*.

Smith, Peter H. ARGENTINA AND THE FAILURE OF DEMOCRACY: Conflict among the Political Elites, 1904–1955. *Univ. of Wisconsin Press* 1974 $12.50

POLITICS AND BEEF IN ARGENTINA: Patterns of Conflict and Change. Institute of Latin American Studies Ser. *Columbia* 1969 $10.00

"This study of the political climate in Argentina from 1900 to 1946 . . . examines the several interest groups affected by the cattle industry [and shows] how they articulated their demands"—*(LJ)*.

Tannenbaum, Frank. MEXICO: The Struggle for Peace and Bread. *Knopf* 1950 $6.95

TEN KEYS TO LATIN AMERICA. *Knopf* 1962 $6.95; *Random* Vintage Bks. pap. $1.95

Thomas, Hugh. CUBA: The Pursuit of Freedom 1762–1969. *Harper* 1971 $25.00

"This book is the only competent survey of Cuban history available in English, and it surpasses anything that has been done in the Spanish language"—*(Choice)*.

Thompson, J. Eric S. THE RISE AND FALL OF MAYAN CIVILIZATION. *Univ. of Oklahoma Press* 2nd ed. 1966 $5.95

"A standard, authoritative general book [that is] . . . pleasingly written, highly literate, and nicely illustrated"—*(Choice)*.

Tugwell, Franklin. THE POLITICS OF OIL IN VENEZUELA. *Stanford Univ. Press* 1975 $8.50

Tullis, F. La Mond. LORD AND PEASANT IN PERU: A Paradigm of Political and Social Change. *Harvard Univ. Press* 1970 $10.50

Villas Boas, Orlando, and Claudio Villas Boas. XINGU: The Indians, Their Myths. *Farrar, Straus* 1974 $12.95

This book "based on the brothers' journals treats some 14 tribes of the Alto Xingu of Central Brazil"—*(LJ)*.

Wagley, Charles. AN INTRODUCTION TO BRAZIL. *Columbia* 1963 rev. ed. 1971 $12.50 pap. $3.95

Webb, Kempton Evans. THE CHANGING FACE OF NORTHEAST BRAZIL. *Columbia* 1974 $20.00

"Webb treats Northeastern Brazil, one of the most troublesome geographic-social regions in the Americas, in an evolutionary light to determine the symptoms of its illness"—*(Choice)*.

Wiarda, Howard J., Ed. POLITICS AND SOCIAL CHANGE IN LATIN AMERICA: The Distinct Tradition. *Univ. of Mass. Press* 1974 $12.00 pap. $5.00

Williams, Eric. FROM COLUMBUS TO CASTRO: The History of the Caribbean, 1492–1969. *Harper* 1971 $10.95

The author "utilizes a comparative framework to treat 'internal' Caribbean historic and contemporary problems such as slavery, plantation economics, and political and economic fragmentation . . . [he] often verbally flogs imperialists and imperial historians for their distorted perspective on the region"—*(Choice)*.

Womack, John, Jr. ZAPATA AND THE MEXICAN REVOLUTION. *Knopf* 1969 $10.00; *Random* Vintage Bks. pap. $2.95

"John Womack, writing 'a study not in historical sociology but in social history,' very wisely sticks close to the nine years of revolution in Morelos (1910–19), and, in documenting and detailing it as has never been done before, he has, by his regional approach, immeasurably increased the possibilities of achieving a really satisfactory general history of the much written about but imperfectly understood Mexican Revolution, the most inchoate and incoherent of all the genuine revolutions in this century"—(Frank Jellinek, in the *N.Y. Times*).

Zea, Leopoldo. LATIN AMERICA AND THE WORLD. *Univ. of Oklahoma Press* 1969 $4.95

In these six essays a distinguished Latin American philosopher emphasizes three themes: "that nationalism is important to all non-Western lands (among which Zea includes Latin America), that nationalism must early solve the land problem in these less developed areas, and that nations not allied with the Soviet Union or the U.S. need to unite to prevent being exploited"—(*Choice*).

THE DECLARATION OF INDEPENDENCE, 1776, and THE CONSTITUTION OF THE UNITED STATES OF AMERICA, 1787–1788.

The full and formal Declaration of Independence, adopted July 4, 1776, by representatives of the 13 North American Colonies, announced the separation of the colonies from Great Britain and the birth of the United States. The Constitution of the United States, embodying the fundamental principles upon which the American republic is conducted, was drawn up at the Federal Constitutional Convention at Philadelphia in 1787, was signed on Sept. 17, 1787, and ratified by the required number of states (nine) by June 21, 1788.

THE DECLARATION OF INDEPENDENCE AND THE CONSTITUTION. Ed. by Earl Latham *Heath* 3rd ed. 1975 pap. $2.95

THE LIVING U.S. CONSTITUTION. Presented with historical notes by Saul K. Padover. 1953. *New Am. Lib.* rev. ed. 1968 pap. $1.50

THE CONSTITUTION OF THE UNITED STATES AND RELATED DOCUMENTS. Ed. by Martin Shapiro *AHM Pub.* Crofts Class. 1966 pap. $.85

THE CONSTITUTION OF THE UNITED STATES. Ed. by Edward C. Smith *Harper* Perenn. Lib. 1974 pap. $1.25 (Barnes & Noble) 9th ed. 1972 pap. $1.50; ed. by Floyd G. Cullop *New Am. Lib.* Signet 1969 pap. $.95

Books about the Declaration of Independence and the Constitution

Documentary History of the Constitution of the United States of America, 1786–1870. Derived from Records, Manuscripts, and Rolls Deposited in the Bureau of Rolls and Library of the Department of State. 1894. *Johnson Reprint* 5 vols. 1966 each $49.00 set $210.00

The Records of the Federal Convention of 1787. Ed. by Max Farrand. 1911. *Yale Univ. Press* 4 vols. 1966 Vols. I–3 each $25.00 Vol. 4 $10.00 pap. Vols. I–2 each $6.95 Vol. 3 $4.95 Vol. 4 $3.75

"Nothing official was published about the Convention which framed the Constitution until at least 30 years after its occurrence.... The documents are reprinted exactly from the originals and are presented in chronological sequence. The work presents statements of proceedings in the Convention rather than theoretical interpretations of clauses"—(*PW*).

The Declaration of Independence: Its History. By John H. Hazelton. 1906. American Constitutional and Legal History Ser. *Da Capo* 1970 $22.50

An Economic Interpretation of the Constitution of the United States. By Charles A. Beard. 1913. *Macmillan* 1935 $6.95 (Free Press) 1965 pap. $2.95

The Declaration of Independence: A Study in the History of Political Ideas. By Carl L. Becker. 1922. *Knopf* 1942 $6.95; *Random* Vintage Bks. pap. $1.95; *Peter Smith* $4.50. The definitive study.

The Growth of Constitutional Power in the United States. By Carl Brent Swisher. *Univ. of Chicago Press* 1946 Phoenix Bks. 1963 pap. $2.45. An excellent compilation.

The American Constitution. By Alfred H. Kelly and Winfred A. Harbison. *Norton* 1948 4th ed. 1970 $11.75

The Constitution and What It Means Today. By Edward S. Corwin. *Princeton Univ. Press* 13th rev. ed. 1973 $20.00 pap. $3.95. A definitive discussion of the law and practice of the Constitution and its interpretation by Congress, the Presidency and the courts over the years.

The Declaration of Independence and What It Means Today. By Edward Dumbauld. 1950. *Univ. of Oklahoma Press* 1968 $2.95

The Story of the Declaration of Independence. By Dumas Malone. Pictures by Hirst Milhollen and Milton Kaplan *Oxford* 1954 1974 $15.00. Gives the background of political events and a complete history of the actual document.

The Birth of the Bill of Rights, 1776–1791. By Robert Allen Rutland. *Univ. of North Carolina Press* 1955 $7.50; *Macmillan* Collier Bks. 1962 pap. $.95

We the People: The Economic Origins of the Constitution. By Forrest McDonald. *Univ. of Chicago Press* 1958 $10.50 pap. $2.95

The Antifederalists: Critics of the Constitution, 1781–1788. By Jackson Turner Main. *Univ. of North Carolina Press* 1961 $7.50; *Quadrangle* pap. $2.25

"First-rate scholarship"—(*LJ*).

Constitutions of the United States: National and State. By Columbia University, Legislative Drafting Research Fund. Loose-Leaf Service and Supplements. *Oceana* 1961 3 vols. 1967 set with supplements $175.00. An invaluable reference, accurate and clear.

A Commentary on the Constitution of the United States. By Bernard Schwartz. *Macmillan* 2 vols. 1962 Vol. 1 The Powers of Government: Federal and State Powers Vol. 2 Powers of Government each $12.50 boxed set $25.00. A basic reference work, and an erudite one, on Constitutional law.

A Biography of the Constitution of the United States. By Broadus Mitchell and Louise Pearson Mitchell. *Oxford* 1964 $10.50 pap. $3.50. Includes the document itself; the personalities and legal struggles are analyzed.

The Constitution of the United States. By Edward Dumbauld. *Univ. of Oklahoma Press* 1964 $9.95
A Federal judge and author of works on American legal history gives the "text of each clause of the Constitution of the United States; its history (that is, the background of its introduction and discussion in the Constitutional Convention of 1787); and the interpretations placed upon the clause by the Supreme Court through the years. . . . Highly recommended"—*(LJ)*.

Quarrels That Have Shaped the Constitution. Ed. by John A. Garraty. *Harper* 1964 $4.95 pap. $2.95
Sixteen major Supreme Court decisions presented in a most interesting manner by a group of "distinguished and competent" authors *(LJ)* in a compilation by Professor Garraty of Columbia. Civil rights cases loom large in it.

Alexander Hamilton and the Constitution. By Clinton Rossiter. *Harcourt* 1964 $7.50
"A skilled historian and political scientist, in sharp and ringing phrases . . . analyzes the importance of Hamilton's broad construction of the Constitution, his advocacy of a strong Presidency, and his insistence upon the supremacy of the Supreme Court over the courts of the States to the growth of a viable nation"—*(Book Week)*. "Mr. Rossiter's final chapter, . . . 'The Relevance of Hamilton,' a model of its kind—judicious, temperate, complete—is, at least to one reader, the finest thing in an excellent book"—(Louis M. Hacker, in the *N.Y. Times*).

The Ordeal of the Constitution: The Antifederalist and the Ratification Struggle of 1787–1788. By Robert Allen Rutland. *Univ. of Oklahoma Press* 1966 $8.95
"This is a valuable examination of the struggle for ratification of the Constitution of the United States especially with regard to those who opposed it. [Important are] its research of original sources and the casting of new light and shadows on this formative period"—*(LJ)*.

Miracle at Philadelphia. By Catherine Drinker Bowen. *Little* 1966 $11.95
An account by the distinguished biographer (*q.v.*) of the sessions originally held to amend the Articles of Confederation, which resulted, rather, in the drafting of the Constitution. "Mrs. Bowen has chosen just the right tone. She has not tried to make the scenes more theatrical or throw a Technicolor wash over the proceedings. Her writing is deliberately plain. Her judgments are balanced and respectful but far from idolatrous"—*(N.Y. Times)*.

1787: The Grand Convention. By Clinton Rossiter. *Macmillan* 1966 $7.95; *New Am. Lib.* 1968 pap. $1.50
"In this magnificent, scholarly book that is so well written it will be read by the high school as well as the graduate student, the entire history of the convention, the delegates, the finished work, and the story of ratification is told. . . . His bibliography is impressive in scope and depth. . . . Nothing of value has been omitted"—*(LJ)*.

With Liberty and Justice for All: The Meaning of the Bill of Rights Today. By Harold V. Knight. Introd. by Roger Baldwin *Oceana* 1967 $7.50
"An important reference book, elucidating problems concerning civil liberties. . . . Admirably adapted for the layman"—*(LJ)*.

Class Conflict, Slavery, and the United States Constitution: Ten Essays. By Staughton Lynd. *Bobbs* 1967 $8.25
"Staughton Lynd seeks to contribute to a new kind of history. He writes: 'The new (perhaps New Left) American history emphasizes economic causes while avoiding the caricature that limits "the economic factor" to conscious pursuit of pecuniary advantage. It insists on a comparative approach to the revolutions of 1776–1783 and 1861–65, without denying that American history has a variety of "exceptional features." ' For the most part, this is a collection of essays which have appeared in scholarly journals. [Professor Lynd] contends that C. A. Beard's version of the nature of strife in this constitutional period requires revision. Rather than a conflict between capitalists and farmers, Mr. Lynd argues, the conflict was between commercial and non-commercial interests"—*(LJ)*.

Origins of the Fifth Amendment. By Leonard W. Levy. *Oxford* 1968 $15.95 pap. $4.50
This won the 1969 Pulitzer Prize for History. It is the "first and only full-length study . . . definitive . . . and monumental. The clarity and flow of Dr. Levy's narrative is, in view of the complexity of the subject, almost unbelievably readable and intriguing"—*(Boston Herald)*.

The Bill of Rights: A Documentary History. By B. A. Schwartz. *McGraw-Hill* 2 vols. 1971 set $65.00

THE FEDERALIST PAPERS.   1787–1788.

The widely read "Federalist Papers," a series of 85 political essays, was initiated by Alexander Hamilton (*q.v.*) with the intention of persuading New York to approve the Federalist Constitution. He wrote 51 of the essays and of his two collaborators, James Madison wrote 14 and John Jay, 5. The authorship of 15 is in dispute (as between Hamilton and Madison). The essays "have been acclaimed from the time of their appearance to the present day with praise for their cogency of argument, exposition of American political philosophy, and literary quality"—(*Columbia Encyclopedia*).

THE FEDERALIST. By Alexander Hamilton, James Madison and John Jay. Ed. with introd. and notes by Jacob E. Cooke *Wesleyan Univ. Press* 1961 $25.00

Vital for scholarly reference and recommended for all academic and large public libraries, this is "the first accurate edition . . . to reconstruct the definitive text from the newspapers, from subsequent editions and from the authors' revisions. All versions have been collated and annotated, and the whole indexed completely with cross references. The disputed authorship of some numbers among the papers is discussed in a lengthy introductory essay"—(*LJ*).

THE FEDERALIST. By Alexander Hamilton, John Jay and James Madison. Ed. by Benjamin F. Wright *Harvard Univ. Press* 1961 $12.50; ed. by Henry Cabot Lodge. 1956. *Modern Library* pap. $1.95

THE FEDERALIST PAPERS. Ed. by Roy P. Fairfield *Doubleday* Anchor Bks. pap. $1.95; *Peter Smith* $4.25; *Dutton* Everyman's $3.95; ed. by Clinton L. Rossiter *New Am. Lib.* 1961 pap. $1.95; ed. by Andrew Hacker *Random* (Washington Square) 1971 pap. $.75

ON THE CONSTITUTION: Selections from The Federalist Papers. 1954. *Bobbs* $5.00 pap. $2.25

SELECTIONS FROM THE FEDERALIST. Ed. by Henry Steele Commager *AHM Pub.* Crofts Class. 1949 pap. $.85

Books about the Federalist Papers

The Federalist Era, 1789–1801. By John C. Miller. *Harper* 1960 $8.95 pap. $2.25
The Federalist: A Classic on Federalism and Free Government. By Gottfried Dietze. *Johns Hopkins Press* 1960 pap. $3.45
Inference and Disputed Authorship: The Federalist. By Frederick Mosteller and D. Wallace. *Addison-Wesley* 1964 $16.95
The Federalist vs. the Jeffersonian Republicans. By P. Goodman. *Peter Smith* $4.25

See also Alexander Hamilton in Chapter 2, General Biography and Autobiography, this Vol.

PRESCOTT, WILLIAM HICKLING.   1796–1859.

This great American historian, a native of Massachusetts and a Harvard graduate, injured his eye in youth and gave up his legal training. With his sight partially restored, he became interested in the writing of history and produced his historical classics in the constant struggle against blindness. All his books are marked by careful research, great narrative power and impartiality.

WORKS. Ed. by Wilfred H. Munroe and others. 1904. *AMS Press* 22 vols. each $21.00 set $450.00

PAPERS. Ed. by C. Harvey Gardiner *Univ. of Illinois Press* 1964 $10.00

"This book, consisting of items from 34 institutional and private holders of Prescott manuscripts, has been assembled with admirable diligence. And the manuscripts have been edited with an even, common-sensical hand. Somehow, though, the Prescott to be found here is not the revered historian at all but a New England dilettante who collected Spanish-language documents and engaged in endless crabbed exchanges over the publication of his books"—(*N.Y. Times*).

HISTORY OF THE REIGN OF FERDINAND AND ISABELLA THE CATHOLIC. 1838. Ed. and abr. by C. Harvey Gardiner *Heritage, Conn.* $11.95

THE CONQUEST OF MEXICO AND THE CONQUEST OF PERU. *Random* (Modern Lib. Giants) $5.95; ed. by Roger Howell (Washington Square) pap. $1.45

HISTORY OF THE CONQUEST OF MEXICO. 1843. *Dutton* Everyman's 2 vols. each $3.95; ed. and abr. by C. Harvey Gardiner *Univ. of Chicago Press* 1966 $10.00 Phoenix Bks. pap. $3.45

HISTORY OF THE CONQUEST OF PERU. 1847. *Dutton* Everyman's 1963 $3.95 pap. 1972 $2.50; abr. ed. by Victor von Hagen *New Am. Lib.* Mentor Bks. pap. $1.25

LITERARY MEMORANDA. Ed. by C. Harvey Gardiner *Univ. of Oklahoma Press* 2 vols. 1961 boxed set $12.50 pap. $5.95. These memoranda cover most of the historian's adult life, from 1823 to 1858.

CORRESPONDENCE, 1833–1847. Ed. by Roger Wolcott. 1925. *Da Capo* 1970 $29.50

Books about Prescott

Life of William Hickling Prescott. By George Ticknor. 1864. *Richard West* $25.00
William Hickling Prescott: American Historian. By Harry T. Peck. 1905. *AMS Press* 1970 $5.00; *Greenwood* $10.00; *Kennikat* $6.50
William Hickling Prescott: A Memorial. Ed. by Howard F. Cline and others. *Duke Univ. Press* 1959 $5.00
Prescott and His Publishers. By C. Harvey Gardiner. *Southern Illinois Univ. Press* 1959 $5.95
"Gardiner has given us in very readable fashion and on the basis of research in a wide range of sources a book that adds much insight into one of our greatest historians"—(*American Historical Review*).
William Hickling Prescott: A Biography. By C. Harvey Gardiner *Univ. of Texas Press* 1970 $8.50

TOCQUEVILLE, ALEXIS (CHARLES HENRI MAURICE CLEREL) DE. 1805–1859.

This French writer is best known in this country for "Democracy in America." In 1831 he was sent on a mission to the U.S. to study American penitentiaries. The results of his findings, written in collaboration with Gustave de Beaumont de La Bonnière, were published in 1833 under the title "*Du Système Penitentiaire aux États-Unis et de son Application en France*" (*see English version below*). It was this journey that inspired his more famous work, written soon after. He became French minister of foreign affairs in 1849. His "Journey to England and Ireland" (trans. by George Lawrence, ed. by J. P. Mayer) is available from *Peter Smith* ($4.75). He also wrote "The Old Regime and the French Revolution" (trans. by Stuart Gilbert *Doubleday* Anchor Bks. 1955 pap. $2.50; *Peter Smith* $5.00) and "The European Revolution and Correspondence with Gobineau" (trans. and ed. by John Lukacs 1959 *Greenwood* $17.25; *Peter Smith* $6.00).

(With Gustave de Beaumont) ON THE PENITENTIARY SYSTEM IN THE UNITED STATES. 1833. Trans. by Francis Lieber *Patterson Smith* $14.00; *Southern Illinois Univ. Press* 1964 $6.00

"This is a fascinating book from the point of view of social history; much is here that could have relevance to our so-called modern methods"—(*LJ*). It is based on a ten-month journey of investigation and study on which the two authors were sent by the French Minister of the Interior.

DEMOCRACY IN AMERICA. 1835–1840. Trans. by George Lawrence, ed. by J. P. Mayer *Doubleday* Anchor Bks. 1969 pap. $4.95; trans. by Phillips Bradley. 1926. *Knopf* 2 vols. 1944 set $15.00; ed. by Richard D. Heffner *New Am. Lib.* abr. ed. pap. $1.25; trans. by Henry Reeve, ed. by Henry Steele Commager *Oxford* 1947 $4.00; *Random* Vintage Bks. 2 vols. pap. Vol. 1 $1.95 Vol. 2 $2.45; *Schocken* 2 vols. 1961 set $7.00 pap. each $2.95; trans. by Henry Reeve, ed. by Andrew Hacker *Simon & Schuster* (Washington Square) abr. ed. 1971 pap. $.95

Of the excellent Lawrence translation, *Choice* said: "Lawrence's edition, based on the scholarly 1961 French edition prepared by J. P. Mayer, should . . . be warmly welcomed." In "a freer translation than Reeve's Lawrence's wonderful style has given us a work that will be standard for many years"—(*LJ*).

(With Gustave de Beaumont) TOCQUEVILLE AND BEAUMONT ON SOCIAL REFORM. Trans. and ed. with introd. by Seymour Drescher. *Gannon* 1970 $8.50; *Harper* Torchbks. 1968 pap. $2.95

"Both men chose to devote their energies to questions which were not only in the mainstream of contemporary humanitarian reform but were also the residue of a respectable notable tradition going back into the old regime"—(Introduction).

Books about de Tocqueville

Alexis de Tocqueville: A Biographical Study in Political Science. By J. P. Mayer. 1940. *Peter Smith* 1960 $4.25
Tocqueville in America. By George W. Pierson. 1959. *Peter Smith* 1960 $6.00

Tocqueville and the Old Regime. By Richard Herr. *Princeton Univ. Press* 1962 pap. $1.95
   This is an "account of the writing and arguments of Tocqueville's *Ancien Régime et la Révolution.* . . . Its basic theme is the growth of democracy in France"—(*American Political Science Review*). "There is much of interest and value in this concise study as Herr skillfully elaborates on his theme. [A] well-grounded, discerning, and lucid interpretation"—(*American Historical Review*).
Tocqueville and England. By Seymour Drescher. *Harvard Univ. Press* 1964 $10.00. Focused on the French parliamentarian's links with England, his second homeland.
De Tocqueville. By Edward T. Gargan. *Hillary House* 1965 $2.75
   "Gargan has given us a brief study that should be useful to undergraduates who are unfamiliar with the main outlines of Tocqueville's work. . . . Gargan somewhat modifies the fashionable view that Tocqueville was simply a pessimist whose prophecies concerning the development of democracy were delivered in tones of utter despair. There is a good bibliography, including editions and translations of Tocqueville's works and a list of 20 critical studies in four languages"—(*Choice*).
Tocqueville and the Problem of Democracy. By Marvin Zetterbaum. *Stanford Univ. Press* 1967 $6.95
   An excellent study and analysis, "informative, difficult, and challenging"—(*American Historical Review*).
Dilemmas of Democracy: Tocqueville and Modernization. By Seymour I. Drescher. *Univ. of Pittsburgh Press* 1968 $9.95
Tocqueville and America. By Max Lerner. *Harper* 1969 pap. $1.60
Liberty, Equality and Revolution in Alexis de Tocqueville. By Irving M. Zeitlin. *Little* 1971 pap. $3.95
De Tocqueville. By Hugh Brogan. *Franklin Watts* (Fontana) 1973 pap. $1.50

DAVIS, JEFFERSON. 1808–1889.

   Chosen by the provisional congress as President of the Confederate States of America in 1861, Davis's policies aroused serious opposition within the Confederacy. As the fortunes of war turned against the South, criticism of Davis increased in intensity. He was indicted for treason in May 1866. Released on bond, he spent the last years of life in retirement at his estate, "Beauvoir," on the Gulf of Mexico in Mississippi. There (1878–1881) he wrote "The Rise and Fall of the Confederate Government."
   Hudson Strode's 3-volume "Jefferson Davis" is valuable for its scholarly presentation of much hitherto unpublished material. "First Lady of the South: The Life of Mrs. Jefferson Davis" by Ishbel Ross (1958. *Greenwood* 1973 $17.50) is a skillfully written biography, the most valuable part being the account of her life after the fall of the Confederacy.

PAPERS. Ed. by Haskell M. Monroe, Jr. and James T. McIntosh Vol. 1 *Louisiana State Univ. Press* 1971 $17.50

JEFFERSON DAVIS, CONSTITUTIONALIST: His Letters, Papers and Speeches, Ed. by Dunbar Rowland. 1923. *AMS Press* 10 vols. each $27.50 set $275.00

THE RISE AND FALL OF THE CONFEDERATE GOVERNMENT. 1878–81. *A. S. Barnes* Yoseloff 2 vols. boxed set $25.00 ltd. lea. ed. $75.00; *Peter Smith* abr. ed. $7.50

THE CALENDAR OF THE JEFFERSON DAVIS POSTWAR MANUSCRIPTS IN THE LOUISIANA HISTORICAL ASSOCIATION COLLECTION. 1943. *Somerset Pub. Co.* $19.50

Books about Davis

Jefferson Davis: Ex-President of the Confederate States of America, a Memoir by His Wife. By Varina Davis. 1890. *Bks. for Libraries* 2 vols. $59.50
Jefferson Davis. By William E. Dodd. 1907. *Russell & Russell* 1966 $10.50
Jefferson Davis: The Unreal and the Real. By Robert M. M. McElroy. 1937. *Kraus* 2 vols. in 1 1969 $25.00
Jefferson Davis. By Hudson Strode. *Harcourt* 3 vols. 1955–64 Vol. 1 American Patriot, 1808–1861 (1955) $10.00 Vol. 2 Confederate President (1959) $6.75 Vol. 3 Tragic Hero (1964) $8.75
   "The magnificent documentation of all three volumes, the spirited style, and the careful and candid judgments . . . makes this trilogy a landmark in the writing of American biography"—(*Washington Star*).
Two Roads to Sumter. By William and Bruce Catton. *McGraw-Hill* 1963 pap. $2.95
Road to Appomattox. By Bell I. Wiley. *Atheneum* 1968 pap. $2.95

PARKMAN, FRANCIS. 1823–1893.

Parkman made seven trips to Europe to search French and English archives in order to verify the data upon which he based his remarkable histories. He chose for his general subject the rise and decline of France's power in North America. Kenneth Rexroth has written (in *SR*), of "France and England in North America": "Parkman's history is the story of our heroic age, and, like the *Iliad*, it is the story of the war between two basic types of personality. It is from this archetypal struggle that it derives its epic power. As Parkman works his history out in detail, the personal conflicts of its actors give it the intricacy and ambiguity of a psychological novel. That this struggle is echoed in the spiritual conflict of the author gives the book an intimacy and depth beyond that of factual history." Of the same book Edmund Wilson says: "The clarity, the momentum and color of the first volumes of Parkman's narrative are among the most brilliant achievements of the writing of history as an art." Wilson's section on Parkman in "O Canada" is rewarding indeed.

The Journals, rediscovered after almost 40 years, were started while he was a Harvard undergraduate, determined even then to write the histories in spite of poor health and eyesight. The early journals incude precise and dramatic descriptions of summer trips from 1841 to 1846 in the wilds of New England, New York State, Canada, the Northwest and Europe. Most interesting are his notes for "The Oregon Trail," which he dictated, after a breakdown in health, to a cousin.

WORKS. *AMS Press* 20 vols. each $20.00 set $395.00

THE PARKMAN READER. Sel. and ed. with an introd. and notes by Samuel Eliot Morison *Little* 1955 $8.50 pap. $2.95

From the nine-volume "France and England in North America," (*see below*) Professor Morison has chosen complete sections which have the greatest interest for present-day readers and which together give a coherent account of early North American colonial history.

SEVEN YEARS WAR: A Narrative Taken from "Montcalm and Wolfe," "The Conspiracy of Pontiac" and "A Half Century of Conflict." Ed. by John H. McCallum *Harper* Torchbks. 1968 pap. $3.25

THE OREGON TRAIL: Sketches of Prairie and Rocky Mountain Life. 1849. *Assoc. Booksellers* Airmont Bks. 1964 pap. $.60; *Holt* 1931 $5.50; ill. by James Daugherty *New Am. Lib.* 1950 pap. $.75; Franklin Watts lg.-type ed. 1967 $7.95; ed. by E. N. Feltskog *Univ. of Wisconsin Press* 1969 $20.00

THE CONSPIRACY OF PONTIAC. 1851. *Macmillan* Collier Bks. pap. $1.50; *Peter Smith* $4.00

FRANCE AND ENGLAND IN NORTH AMERICA. *Ungar* 9 vols. set $110.00

Single volumes of this history available are: Pioneers of France in the New World (1865) *Corner House* 1970 $12.50. The Jesuits in North America (1867) introd. by John Francis Bannon *Corner House* 1970 $12.50; *Peter Smith* $4.50. Count Frontenac and New France under Louis Fourteenth (1877) *Peter Smith* $5.00. Montcalm and Wolfe (1884) *Macmillan* Collier Bks. pap. $1.50; *Peter Smith* $4.25. A Half-Century of Conflict (1892) *Macmillan* Collier Bks. pap. $1.50; *Peter Smith* $4.00.

"The best way to lay a foundation for the understanding of Canada is to read Francis Parkman's great history. . . . An unrivalled work, fascinating as well as informative"—(Edmund Wilson in "O Canada").

JOURNALS. Ed. by Mason Wade *Kraus* 2 vols. in 1 1947 $25.00

LETTERS. Ed. by Wilbur R. Jacobs *Univ. of Oklahoma Press* 2 vols. 1960 boxed set $12.50. Over 400 letters that tell a romantic story of the Old West.

Books about Parkman

The Life of Francis Parkman. By Charles H. Farnham. 1901. *Folcroft* $10.00; *Greenwood* $13.75; *Scholarly Press* 1970 $13.95

Francis Parkman. By Henry D. Sedgwick. 1904. *Richard West* 1973 $12.45

Francis Parkman, Heroic Historian. By Mason Wade. 1942. *Shoe String Press* 1972 $15.00

Parkman's History: The Historian as Literary Critic. By Otis A. Pease. 1953. *Shoe String Press* 1968 $4.00

"Despite its brevity (86 pages), it is a work of genuine distinction"—(*SR*).

Francis Parkman. By Robert L. Gale. *Twayne* 1973 $6.50

ADAMS, HENRY (BROOKS). 1838–1918.

Henry Adams was the grandson of John Quincy Adams, the sixth President of the United States (*q.v.*). Adams' history was disappointing to historians, as they had looked to him to explain his ancestor's change from Federalism to Republicanism. He confined himself mainly to the political and constitutional history of two presidential administrations. His history is a brilliant one, illuminating politics and politicians, issues and struggles. He wrote a very good biography of an American statesman: "The Life of Albert Gallatin" (1879. *Peter Smith* 1943 $10.00).

HISTORICAL ESSAYS. 1891. *Adler's* $26.40

THE GREAT SECESSION WINTER OF 1860–61 AND THIRTEEN OTHER ESSAYS. Ed. by George Hochfield *A. S. Barnes* 1962 pap. $2.25

JOHN RANDOLPH OF ROANOKE. 1882. *AMS Press* $12.50; *Peter Smith* $4.25

HISTORY OF THE UNITED STATES. 1889–91. *Hillary House* 9 vols. 1962 o.p.

Vols. 1 and 2 First Administration of Thomas Jefferson, 1801–1805 Vols. 3 and 4 Second Administration of Thomas Jefferson, 1805–1809 Vols. 5 and 6 First Administration of James Madison, 1809–1813 Vols. 7–9 Second Administration of James Madison, 1813–1817

THE UNITED STATES IN 1800. *Cornell Univ. Press* 1955 pap. $1.95; *Peter Smith* $4.25. Rept. of first six chapters of "History of the United States" (*see above*), during the administrations of Jefferson and Adams.

HISTORY OF THE UNITED STATES DURING THE ADMINISTRATIONS OF JEFFERSON AND MADISON. Abr. ed. by Ernest Samuels *Univ. of Chicago Press* 1967 $12.50 Phoenix Bks. pap. $3.45. Much of the style and approach which gained the original 9-vol. history its high reputation has been retained. Does not include the famous first six chapters available in "The United States in 1800" (*see above*).

DEGRADATION OF THE DEMOCRATIC DOGMA. 1919. Introd. by Brooks Adams *Harper* Torchbks. 1969 pap. $2.95; *Peter Smith* $4.75

Books about Adams

Henry Adams. By James Truslow Adams. 1933. *Greenwood* $11.50; *Scholarly Press* 1970 $14.50; *Richard West* $11.00
Henry Adams. By Ernest Samuels. *Harvard Univ. Press* 3 vols. 1948–1964 Vol. 1 Young Henry Adams (1948) $10.00 Vol. 2 The Middle Years, 1877–1891 (1958) $12.00 Vol. 3 The Major Phase (1964) $15.00. Vol. 2 won for Dr. Samuels the Bancroft Prize for 1959 as well as the Francis Parkman Prize of the Society of American Historians.
"[This is] one of the great biographical achievements of our time . . . a joy to every intelligent reader"—(Edward Wagenknecht, in the *Chicago Tribune*).
Henry Adams: Scientific Historian. By William H. Jordy. 1952. *Shoe String Press* 1970 $10.50
Henry Adams. By Louis Auchincloss. Univ. of Minnesota Pamphlets on American Writers. *Univ. of Minnesota Press* 1971 pap. $1.25

See also Chapter 16, Literary Biography and Autobiography, Reader's Adviser, Vol. 1, and Chapter 2, General Biography and Autobiography, this Vol., under the Adams Family.

WILSON, WOODROW. 1856–1924. *See Chapter 2, General Biography and Autobiography, this Vol.*

ROOSEVELT, THEODORE. 1858–1919. (Nobel Peace Prize 1906)

In 1963 the two homes of Theodore Roosevelt, the Manhattan brownstone on East 20th Street where he was born, and Sagamore Hill, his Oyster Bay, Long Island, country house, were given to the nation by the Theodore Roosevelt Association, with $500,000 to maintain the shrines. It was at Sagamore Hill that Roosevelt accepted the nomination for the Governorship of New York, the Vice-Presidency and finally the Presidency of the United States, and it was here that he died. Through his efforts the Peace Conference that ended the Russo-Japanese War met at Portsmouth, New Hampshire, for which Roosevelt won the Nobel Peace Prize in 1906.

One of the important scholarly projects of our time is the publication of the remarkable collection of 10,000 Theodore Roosevelt letters in eight volumes, an undertaking "which will do more to restore Theodore Roosevelt to his rightful place in the gallery of American statesmen than anything else, and one which illuminates a whole epoch of our history"—(Henry Commager, in the *N.Y. Herald Tribune*). Roosevelt's "Letters to His Children" are endearing. They reveal the tender side of the Rough Rider, and the fun-loving disposition of a devoted father. "Theodore Roosevelt's Diaries of Boyhood and Youth" (1928) is out of print.

In 1967 an immense bronze and stone memorial to Theodore Roosevelt was unveiled on a wild island in the Potomac, a setting which would have pleased that hearty outdoorsman. President Johnson spoke at the ceremonies, calling him a "giant" of American history and recalling his words, "Woe to the country where a generation arises which . . . shrinks from doing the rough work of the world."

WRITINGS. Ed. by William H. Harbaugh *Bobbs* Lib. Arts 1967 $7.50 pap. $4.00

PRESIDENTIAL ADDRESSES AND STATE PAPERS. Introd. by Albert Shaw. 1905. *Kraus* 4
   vols. in 2 1968 set $46.00

ADDRESSES AND PRESIDENTIAL MESSAGES, 1902–1904. Introd. by Henry Cabot Lodge
   Kraus $15.00

THE ROOSEVELT POLICY: Speeches, Letters and State Papers, Relating to Corporate
   Wealth and Closely Allied Topics. Ed. by William Griffith. 1919. *Kraus* 3 vols. in 1
   $35.00

THE NAVAL WAR OF 1812; or The History of the United States Navy during the Last
   War with Great Britain. 1882. *Haskell* 1969 $23.95; *Scholarly Press* 1971 $15.95

GOUVERNEUR MORRIS. 1888. *AMS Press* $11.00; *Haskell* 1969 $16.95; *Scholarly Press* 1971
   $11.95

THE WINNING OF THE WEST. 1889–96. Ed. by Harvey Wish. 1962. *Peter Smith* $4.00;
   Somerset Pubs. 6 vols. $72.00

AMERICAN IDEALS AND OTHER ESSAYS, SOCIAL AND POLITICAL. 1897. *AMS Press* $10.00;
   Scholarly Press $9.50

HISTORY AS LITERATURE AND OTHER ESSAYS. 1913. *Kennikat* $9.00

THE NEW NATIONALISM. 1961. *Peter Smith* $5.00

LETTERS. Sel. and ed. by Elting E. Morison; John M. Blum, Assoc. Ed. *Harvard Univ.
   Press* 8 vols. 1951–54 Vol. 1 Years of Preparation, 1868–1898 Vol. 2 Years of
   Preparation, 1898–1900 Vol. 3 The Square Deal, 1901–1903 Vol. 4 The Square Deal,
   1903–1905 Vol. 5 The Big Stick, 1905–1907 Vol. 6 The Big Stick, 1907–1909 Vol. 7
   The Days of Armageddon, 1909–1914 Vol. 8 The Days of Armageddon, 1914–1919
   sold only in 2-vol. sets (Vols. 1–2, 5–6 o.p.) Vols. 3–4, 7–8 each set $25.00

LETTERS TO HIS CHILDREN. Ed. by Joseph B. Bishop. 1919. *Norwood Editions* $4.00

AUTOBIOGRAPHY. Ed. with introd. by Wayne Andrews *Octagon* 1973 $14.50. An
   abridged version of "Theodore Roosevelt: An Autobiography" (1913. *Scribner* 1929,
   o.p.).

*Other titles are published by AMS Press, Arno, Gregg, Haskell, Kraus, Scholarly Press and the
Theodore Roosevelt Association.*

Books about Roosevelt

   Theodore Roosevelt. By H. F. Pringle. *Harcourt* 1931 Harvest Bks. 1956 pap. $2.65. This
   biography won the Pulitzer Prize in 1932.
   Theodore Roosevelt and the Progressive Movement. By George E. Mowry. 1946. *Farrar, Straus*
   (Hill & Wang) 1960 pap. $2.95. "A scholarly, critical and original" work containing valuable
   material on America's political development.
   Republican Roosevelt. By John M. Blum. *Harvard Univ. Press* 1954 $5.00; *Atheneum* 1962 pap.
   $1.65
   "A fresh, well-written biographical treatment."
   The Roosevelt Family of Sagamore Hill. By Hermann Hagedorn. *Macmillan* 1954 $7.50. A
   graceful and refreshing account of the domestic felicity of the great "T. R." in the center of
   all activities, family and political.
   Theodore Roosevelt and the Rise of America to World Power. By Howard Kennedy Beale.
   Johns Hopkins Press 1956 $17.50; *Macmillan* Collier Bks. 1966 pap. $1.50. "A volume of
   thorough, solid scholarship."
   The Era of Theodore Roosevelt and the Birth of Modern America, 1900–1912. By George E.
   Mowry. *Harper* 1958 $8.95 Torchbks. 1963 pap. $2.75
   Roosevelt and the Russo-Japanese War. By Tyler Dennett. *Peter Smith* 1958 $5.50
   Theodore Roosevelt and the Japanese-American Crisis. By Thomas A. Bailey. *Peter Smith* 1964
   $5.50
   Theodore Roosevelt: A Profile. Ed. by Morton Keller. American Profiles Ser. *Farrar, Straus* (Hill
   & Wang) 1967 $5.95 pap. $2.95. Selections from William Allen White, John Blum, Stuart
   Sherman, H. L. Mencken, Hamilton Basso, John Chamberlain, Louis Filler, Dixon Wector,
   Richard Hofstadter and Howard K. Beale.

Theodore Roosevelt and Japan. By Raymond A. Esthus. *Univ. of Washington Press* 1967 $7.95
A "professor of history at Tulane University has used both Japanese and Russian sources
previously unavailable. . . . A clear and straightforward narrative of a complicated and
important period of American diplomatic history"—(*LJ*).

An Uncertain Friendship: Theodore Roosevelt and Japan, 1906–1909. By Charles E. Neu.
Harvard Univ. Press 1967 $9.00
"Neu omits any extensive treatment of the Russo-Japanese War of 1904–05 and tends to
place much more emphasis upon the domestic background of Roosevelt's foreign policy.
Roosevelt emerges from the pages of this book as a shrewd politician as well as diplomat.
Recommended"—(*Choice*).

Theodore Roosevelt and the Politics of Power. By G. Wallace Chessman. *Little* 1969 $5.00 pap.
$2.95
"Perhaps wisely, the author has shunned Roosevelt as a 'colorful' character, huntsman,
Rough Rider and all that, and set his direct, unadorned prose to the task of showing him in
political action"—(*PW*).

Roosevelt's Rough Riders. By V. C. Jones. *Doubleday* 1971 $10.00

Theodore Roosevelt. Ed. by Dewey Grantham. *Prentice-Hall* 1971 $5.95 pap. $1.95

Theodore Roosevelt. By David H. Burton. Rulers and Statesmen of the World Ser. *Twayne* 1973
$6.95

Departing Glory: Theodore Roosevelt as Ex-President. By Joseph L. Gardner. *Scribner* 1973
$12.50

See also Chapter 12, Travel and Adventure, this Vol.

TURNER, FREDERICK JACKSON. 1861–1932.

Born in Wisconsin, Frederick Jackson Turner graduated from the University of Wisconsin,
where he later taught, and received his Ph.D. from Johns Hopkins University. His estimate of the
importance of the frontier struggles in the development of the American character and consciousness was unique in his day. He once described American history as "a series of social
evolutions recurring in differing geographic basins across a raw continent." He was professor of
history at Harvard, 1910–24. Oscar Handlin has written of him (in the *N.Y. Times*): "Turner
himself best explained his role: 'My work really grew out of a preliminary training in Medieval
history, where I learned to recognize the reactions between a people in the gristle, and their
environment, and saw the interplay of economic, social and geographic factors in the politics,
institutions, ideals and life of a nation and its relations with its neighbors.' He did not set his
students to work on the frontier of the West in any narrow sense. He asked the best of them to deal
with the interplay he recognized, demanding of them also a commitment to precise methods; and
they did much to vitalize American historiography in the Progressive era."

"The Significance of Sections in American History" won him a posthumous Pulitzer Prize. His
doctoral dissertation "The Character and Influence of the Indian Trade in Wisconsin" (1891. *Burt
Franklin* $4.50) has recently been reprinted.

EARLY WRITINGS. 1938. *Bks. for Libraries* $11.50

AMERICA'S GREAT FRONTIERS AND SECTIONS: Unpublished Essays. Ed. by Wilbur R.
Jacobs *Peter Smith* $4.00

THE SIGNIFICANCE OF THE FRONTIER IN AMERICAN HISTORY. 1894. Ed. by Harold P.
Simonson *Ungar* pap. $1.25; *University Microfilms* 1966 $3.55. Essays delivered at the
1893 meeting of the American Historical Association.

THE RISE OF THE NEW WEST, 1819–1829. 1906. *Macmillan* Collier Bks. 1962 pap. $1.25;
Peter Smith $6.00

THE FRONTIER IN AMERICAN HISTORY. 1920. *Holt* $5.95 pap. $5.50; *Peter Smith* $7.50

THE SIGNIFICANCE OF SECTIONS IN AMERICAN HISTORY. 1932. *Peter Smith* $5.00

THE UNITED STATES, 1830–1850. 1935. *Norton* 1965 pap. $3.95; *Peter Smith* $6.50

THE HISTORICAL WORLD OF FREDERICK JACKSON TURNER WITH SELECTIONS FROM HIS
CORRESPONDENCE. Ed. by Wilbur R. Jacobs *Yale Univ. Press* 1968 pap. $3.45

Books about Turner

Turner and Beard: American Historical Writing Reconsidered. By Lee Benson. *Macmillan*
(Free Press) 1965 pap. $1.95

Frontier Thesis: Valid Interpretation of American History. By Ray A. Billington. *Holt* 1966
pap. $3.00; *Peter Smith* $5.50

The Progressive Historians: Turner, Beard, Parrington. By Richard Hofstadter. *Knopf* 1968 $8.95; *Random* Vintage Bks. 1970 pap. $2.95

"The sympathetic portrayal of the Progressive intellectual as underdog does not diminish from the objective, indeed clinical quality of Hofstadter's criticism, which is as full on the failings of his subjects as on their achievements. His discussion is incisive and lucid, written with grace and wit, unflaggingly interesting"—(Oscar Handlin, in the *N.Y. Times*).

Genesis of the Frontier Thesis: A Study in Historical Creativity. By Ray A. Billington. *Huntington Library* 1971 $8.50

Frederick Jackson Turner: Historian, Scholar, Teacher. By Ray A. Billington. *Oxford* 1973 $17.50

"This is the rich harvest of decades of fruitful study devoted to the thought and writings of Turner. It is not another analysis of the frontier and sectional hypotheses but rather a full account of the intellectual and professional life of this most eminent historian"—(*Choice*).

DU BOIS, W(ILLIAM) E(DWARD) B(URGHARDT).   1868–1963.

Truman Nelson, a personal friend of the Du Boises, wrote a most interesting review of Dr. Du Bois's "Autobiography" in the *Nation* of April 29, 1968, from which the quotations which follow are taken. This man of towering intellect was born in Great Barrington, Mass., five years after the Emancipation Proclamation was signed. "In the little New England town . . . there was a pride among the people that they had helped put down a wicked rebellion and thereby freed four million slaves. [As he grew up] they wanted the black Du Bois to succeed as proof that smashing the slave owner's rebellion was right." With their encouragement, and by working his own way, he achieved a B.A. from both Harvard and Fisk Universities, an M.A. and Ph.D. from Harvard and a period of study at the University of Berlin. He later said that these accomplishments made him "the most conspicuously trained young Negro of my day." He taught briefly at Wilberforce University before he became professor of history and economics at Atlanta University, 1896–1910. There to prove the fallacy of theories that raised racial barriers to intelligence, "he formed cadres of scholars to discover the relations of cause and effect among living persons, with the accuracy of first-rate historians working in areas of time-fixed facts." He put the results into a book, "The Souls of Black Folk," in which he expressed his conviction that "the problem of the twentieth century is the problem of the color line." In 1905 Dr. Du Bois became a major figure in the Niagara Movement, a crusading effort to end discrimination. This weak organization collapsed, but it prepared the way for the founding (in which Du Bois played a major role) of the National Association for the Advancement of Colored People. He became its director of publicity and research as well as editor of *The Crisis*, its official organ. "For twenty-four years he wielded an instrument of propaganda which created, almost single-handedly, a black intelligentsia and mass black awareness. Then, inexplicably to him, he was not allowed to conduct it as he thought he should."

He returned to Atlanta University and tried to implement a plan to make the Negro Land Grant Colleges "centers of black power. . . . Black people would be given back their history, their destiny, in a continuous flow of raw data and published studies." At first Atlanta approved of his idea, but later it retracted; when Du Bois tried to return to the NAACP, they too rejected him. "His grand design to unify the black intellectual community [made him] as dangerous as Karl Marx."

In 1961 President Kwame Nkrumah invited Dr. Du Bois, then well over 90, to Ghana as director of an *Encyclopedia Africana* project (Du Bois had organized the first Pan African Congress, which met in Paris in 1919). He died in Ghana after becoming a citizen of that country—and, at 93, a member of the Communist Party.

His posthumous autobiography (in spite of Herbert Aptheker's listing as editor) contains the "*unretouched* words of a 90-year-old man squaring himself with death, and expecting it every day from a heart beating against impossible odds. His writing is unbelievably strong and young, without self-pity and vibrant with righteous anger. He could not include everything. He barely touches on his peaks as a great writer, a great historian, the father of Pan Africanism." It has been said that had he not felt in the end (in Mr. Nelson's words) "that only a Communist revolution could contain him and use him as the embodiment of black millions fighting to be free," he would have been seen now as an American national hero after whom streets and libraries and schools would have been named. Besides the works cited above, Dr. Du Bois wrote a biography, "John Brown" (1909. *Kraus* $15.00); two novels, "The Quest of the Silver Fleece" (1911, *AMS Press* $12.50; *Arno* 1970 $13.00; *Bks. for Libraries* $14.75) and "Dark Princess" (1928. *AMS Press* $12.50); and edited "Atlanta University Publications" (reprinted in the series The American Negro: His History and Literature, *Octagon* 2 vols. 1968 set $29.50).

The Philadelphia Negro: A Social Study. 1899. *Blom* 1967; *Kraus* 1973 $18.00; *Schocken* 1967 $8.50 pap. $3.45

The Souls of Black Folk. 1903. *Dodd* 1970 $5.50; *Fawcett* Premier Bks. pap. $.95; *Johnson Reprint* $10.50; *New Am. Lib.* 1969 pap. $1.25; *Peter Smith* $2.50; *Simon & Schuster* (Washington Square) pap. $.95

GIFT OF THE BLACK FOLK. 1924. *AMS Press* 1972 $10.00; *Johnson Reprint* 1969 $14.00; *Simon & Schuster* (Washington Square) 1970 pap. $.95

BLACK RECONSTRUCTION IN AMERICA, 1860–1880. 1935. *Atheneum* 1969 pap. $4.95; *Russell & Russell* $16.50

THE DUSK OF DAWN: An Essay Toward an Autobiography of a Race Concept. 1940. *Schocken* 1968 $6.50

THE SUPPRESSION OF THE AFRICAN SLAVE TRADE. 1940. *Louisiana State Univ. Press* 1969 pap. $2.45; *Dover* 1970 pap. $2.50; *Russell & Russell* 1965 $8.50; *Schocken* 1969 $7.50 pap. $2.45. His doctoral thesis; *Current Biography* called it "the standard work on the subject."

THE WORLD AND AFRICA. 1955. *International Pubs.* enl. ed. 1965 $8.95 pap. $2.95

EDUCATION OF BLACK PEOPLES, 1906–1960: Ten Critiques. Ed. by Herbert Aptheker *Univ. of Mass. Press* 1973 $10.00

CORRESPONDENCE. Ed. by Herbert Aptheker *Univ. of Mass. Press* 1973 Vol. 1 Selections, 1877–1934 $20.00

AUTOBIOGRAPHY: A Soliloquy on Viewing My Life from the Last Decade of Its First Century. Ed. by Herbert Aptheker 1968. *International Pubs.* $10.00 pap. $3.45

Books about Du Bois

    W. E. B. Du Bois: Negro Leader in a Time of Crisis. By Francis L. Broderick. *Stanford Univ. Press* 1959 $6.75 pap. $2.95
    "Applying an easy style and a gift for trenchant analysis to a thorough knowledge of his material Broderick has produced a highly readable and scholarly intellectual biography"— (*American Historical Review*). "Broderick has effectively unravelled the complex facets of his subject's fascinating career"—(*The Annals*).
    W. E. B. Du Bois: Propagandist of the Negro Protest. By Elliott M. Rudwick. *Univ. of Pennsylvania Press* 2nd ed. 1969 $9.00; *Atheneum* 1968 pap. $3.25
    W. E. B. Du Bois: A Profile. Ed. by Rayford Logan. American Profile Ser. *Farrar, Straus* (Hill & Wang) 1971 $6.50 pap. $2.75
    W. E. B. Du Bois. Ed. by William M. Tuttle, Jr. Great Lives Observed Ser. *Prentice-Hall* 1973 $6.95 pap. $2.45

BECKER, CARL LOTUS. 1873–1945.

Few American historians have written as well as Becker, Cornell's famous professor of modern European history. "The Heavenly City of the Eighteenth Century Philosophers" (1932. *Yale Univ. Press* 1959 $9.50 pap. $2.95) has become a classic, as has "The Heavenly City Revisited" (ed. by Raymond O. Rockwood *Shoe String Press* 1968 $7.00). In "Detachment and the Writing of History," Mr. Snyder has gathered together Becker's little gems on historical writing, education and democracy from hitherto inaccessible sources. Other books are "Freedom and Responsibility in the American Way of Life," five lectures delivered at the University of Michigan (1945, o.p.) and "Progress and Power" (1930, o.p.). Freedom and democracy were Becker's themes as a leading historian and distinguished historical essayist.

A HISTORY OF POLITICAL PARTIES IN THE PROVINCE OF NEW YORK, 1760–1776. 1908. *Univ. of Wisconsin Press* 1960 pap. $3.95

THE BEGINNINGS OF THE AMERICAN PEOPLE. 1915. *Cornell Univ. Press* 1960 pap. $2.45

THE EVE OF THE REVOLUTION. Yale Chronicles of America. *U.S. Pubs. Assn.* $4.45

THE DECLARATION OF INDEPENDENCE: A Study in the History of Political Ideas. 1922. *Knopf* reissue with new pref. 1942 $5.95; *Random* Vintage Bks. pap. $1.95; *Peter Smith* $4.50

THE SPIRIT OF '76 AND OTHER ESSAYS. 1927. *William C. Brown* $6.50

SAFEGUARDING CIVIL LIBERTY TODAY. *Peter Smith* 1949 $3.50

DETACHMENT AND THE WRITING OF HISTORY: Essays and Letters. Ed. by Phil L. Snyder *Cornell Univ. Press* 1961 pap. $1.95; *Greenwood* 1972 $11.50

EVERYMAN HIS OWN HISTORIAN. *Quadrangle* 1966 pap. $2.95

WHAT IS THE GOOD OF HISTORY? Selected Letters, 1900–1945. Ed. by Michael Kammen *Cornell Univ. Press* 1973 $12.50

Books about Becker

Carl Becker: On History and the Climate of Opinion. By Charlotte Watkins Smith. *Cornell Univ. Press* 1956 $8.50; *Southern Illinois Univ. Press* 1973 pap. $2.65

Carl Becker: A Biographical Study in American Intellectual History. By Burleigh T. Wilkins. *M.I.T. Press* 1961 1967 $10.00 pap. $3.45
"Professor Wilkins' book must be regarded as the definitive work on Becker, as a personality and as a historian by virtue of both adequate coverage and admirable discretion and wisdom in appraisal. It is difficult to discern how anything of vital significance could be added or any of the cogent generalizations about Becker and his work successfully challenged"—*(The Annals).*

The Pragmatic Revolt in American History: Carl Becker and Charles Beard. By Cushing Strout. *Cornell Univ. Press* 1966 pap. $1.95

American Intellectual Histories and Historians. By Robert Allen Skotheim. *Princeton Univ. Press* 1966 $12.00 pap. 1970 $3.95. *(For comment, see listing at beginning of this Section under American History.)*

BEARD, CHARLES A(USTIN), 1874–1948, and MARY R. BEARD, 1876–1958.

Charles A. Beard, a political scientist whose histories were always written from the economic point of view, was an authority on American government and politics. "The Rise of American Civilization" (1927. *Macmillan* 1947, o.p.) treats of politics, economics, war, imperialism, literature, art, music, religion, sciences, the press, and woman's relation to social development. He described his collaboration with his wife on this book as "a division of argument." MARY R. BEARD (1876–1958) wrote "Women as a Force in History" (*Macmillan* Collier Bks. pap. $1.95), "On Understanding Women" (1931. *Greenwood* 1968 $12.00) and "The Force of Women in Japanese History" (*Pubic Affairs Press* 1953 $5.75). The Beards' books were scholarly, well-written, often witty, at times somewhat ponderous. Their "Basic History" is, the *New Yorker* commented, "perhaps, all in all, the best one-volume history that has ever been written about the United States." Among his books still in print are "The Economic Basis of Politics" (1922. *Bks. for Libraries* $7.75) and "The Enduring Federalist" (*Ungar* $7.50 pap. $1.95).

AMERICAN CITY GOVERNMENT: A Survey of Newer Tendencies. 1912. *Arno* 1970 $18.00

SHORT HISTORY OF THE AMERICAN LABOR MOVEMENT. By Mary R. Beard. 1925. *Greenwood* 1968 $10.50

THE SUPREME COURT AND THE CONSTITUTION. 1926. Ed. by A. F. Westin. 1962. *Peter Smith* $4.95

AMERICA THROUGH WOMEN'S EYES. Ed. by Mary R. Beard. 1933. *Greenwood* 1968 $21.50

AN ECONOMIC INTERPRETATION OF THE CONSTITUTION OF THE UNITED STATES. *Macmillan* 1935 $6.95 Free Press 1965 pap. $2.95

(With Mary R. Beard) AMERICA IN MIDPASSAGE. 1939. *Peter Smith* 1966 $12.50

(With Mary R. Beard) THE AMERICAN SPIRIT: A Study of the Idea of Civilization in the United States. 1942. *Macmillan* Collier Bks. pap. $3.95

THE REPUBLIC: Conversations on Fundamentals. *Viking* 1943 $6.00

(With Mary R. Beard) THE BEARDS' NEW BASIC HISTORY OF THE UNITED STATES. 1944. *Doubleday* rev. ed. 1960 $8.95. "New" was added to the title of the rev. ed. by William Beard.

AMERICAN FOREIGN POLICY IN THE MAKING, 1932-1940: A Study in Responsibilities. 1946. *Shoe String Press* 1968 $10.00

PRESIDENT ROOSEVELT AND THE COMING OF THE WAR, 1941: A Study in Appearances and Realities. 1948. *Shoe String Press* 1968 $15.00

Books about the Beards

Charles A. Beard: An Appraisal. Ed. by Howard K. Beale. *Univ. Press of Kentucky* 1953 $4.50
Essays by former students, friends and associates. "The group of appraisals is so excellent, a reviewer hesitates to appraise them severally. . . . Few men have ever presented in a thick volume so complete a picture of a great man"—*(New Republic).*

Charles Beard and the Constitution. By Robert Brown. *Princeton Univ. Press* 1956 $10.00; *Norton* 1965 pap. $2.45

"It is difficult, if not impossible, to refute the specific points made by the author of this painstaking and admirable study. On the other hand, many readers will undoubtedly have some reservations concerning Brown's sweeping indictment"—*(Political Science Quarterly)*.

The Political and Social Thought of Charles A. Beard. By Bernard C. Borning. *Univ. of Washington Press* 1962 $6.75

American Intellectual Histories and Historians. By Robert Allen Skotheim. *Princeton Univ. Press* 1966 $12.00 pap. 1970 $3.95. *(For comment, see listing at beginning of this Section under American History.)*

The Pragmatic Revolt in American History: Carl Becker and Charles Beard. By Cushing Strout. *Cornell Univ. Press* 1966 pap. $1.95

The Progressive Historians: Turner, Beard, Parrington. By Richard Hofstadter. *Knopf* 1968 $8.95; *Random* Vintage Bks. 1970 pap. $2.95. *(For comment, see under entry for Frederick Jackson Turner.)*

Turner and Beard: American Historical Writing Reconsidered. By Lee Benson. *Macmillan* (Free Press) 1965 pap. $1.95

ADAMS, JAMES TRUSLOW. 1878–1949.

James Truslow Adams was not a member of the Henry Adams (*q.v.*) and John Quincy Adams (*q.v.*) family, on which he was the greatest authority. He was descended from Francis Adams, who came to Maryland in 1658 and later settled in Virginia. His first volume, "The Founding of New England," won the Pulitzer Prize in History, though its frank appraisal of the founders became controversial. "The Epic of America" is a compressed account of the American people from the early days of the Spanish explorers, an excellent single-volume history. Adams edited "The Dictionary of American History," "The Atlas of American History" and "Album of American History" (*see Reference Books at the beginning of this Section*). He also wrote "Memorials of Old Bridgehampton" (1916, o.p.) and "History of the Town of Southampton" (1922, o.p.).

THE FOUNDING OF NEW ENGLAND. 1921. *Little* 1963 pap. $2.65; *Peter Smith* $5.00

THE HISTORY OF NEW ENGLAND. 1923. *Scholarly Press* 3 vols. 1971 each $14.50 set $39.50

REVOLUTIONARY NEW ENGLAND, 1691–1776. 1923. *Cooper* 1968 $9.95

NEW ENGLAND IN THE REPUBLIC. 1926. *Scholarly Press* $24.50

PROVINCIAL SOCIETY: 1690–1763. Ed. by Arthur M. Schlesinger and Dixon R. Fox. 1927. *Franklin Watts* pap. $3.45

THE EPIC OF AMERICA. 1931. *Little-Atlantic* rev. ed. 1951 $8.95

THE AMERICAN: The Making of a New Man. 1943. *AMS Press* $21.00

Books about Adams

James Truslow Adams: Historian of the American Dream. By Allan Nevins. *Univ. of Illinois Press* 1968 $6.95

This volume by Adams' friend and fellow historian consists of a 100-page biography and selected correspondence (200 pages). "The biographical section is full of interesting anecdotes, but no major effort is made to evaluate Adams' work or to indicate his significance in American historiography. Perhaps, however, the summaries of those works may make people interested in reading some of Adams' notable books"—*(LJ)*.

THOMAS, NORMAN MATTOON. 1884–1968.

Norman Thomas stands out as the Great Dissenter of our Age, representing as he did, even at 84, half-blind and crippled with arthritis, the reformer whom young people had flocked to hear at 83, the indomitable idealist and fighter for his ideals to the end, charming and humorous always but uncompromising as to his goals. After his death the many organizations and causes he supported (civil liberties, help to the underprivileged—particularly the victims of the ghetto—the ending of the Vietnam war, nuclear arms control) were still sending out the letters signed by him which he had composed in the nursing home where he died. There, too, he had with characteristic energy conferred regularly nearly to the last minute with the editor of his final book, "The Choices." This was dictated to his secretary and carries his last message to an America which had come to love and respect him when it began to understand and catch up with him.

Norman Thomas, born of a family of clergymen, studied at Union Theological Seminary and became himself a Presbyterian clergyman but decided, after a period working as a minister in East Harlem, that the Socialist Party was the only means by which he could try to do something about the poverty and degradation he found there. He became a crusader for Socialism, its strongest and most compelling voice, and ran six times for President on the Socialist ticket, as well as for many other offices—which he never won—and never, indeed, expected to win. As the *N.Y. Times* said in its obituary, "Although he was the voice of the mute and the tribune of the disenfranchised, his brand of Socialism was mild. It shunned class conflict, the dictatorship of the proletariat and the violence of revolution. It was to doctrinal Marxism what Muzak is to Mozart. In Leon Trotsky's celebrated gibe, 'Norman Thomas called himself a Socialist as a result of misunderstanding.' Mr. Thomas, who was anti-Communist and anti-Soviet to a marked degree, wrote extensively on what he regarded as the shortcomings of Marxism. One of his favorite arguments was expressed in question form: 'Can a generation which has had to go far beyond Newtonian physics or atomic chemistry or Darwinian biology be expected to find Marx, who was also the child of his time, infallible?' In his battles Mr. Thomas frequently had the support of many men of intellectual substance—John Dewey, John Haynes Holmes, Rabbi Stephen S. Wise, Reinhold Niebuhr, to mention but a few—but he lacked quantity. Congratulated on the lofty caliber of his campaigns, he replied, 'I appreciate the flowers; only I wish the funeral weren't so complete.' On another occasion he said, 'While I'd rather be right than be President, at any time I'm ready to be both.' "

In his later years Norman Thomas was no longer a "politician" but a fighter for civilized values whenever he saw them jeopardized or betrayed. At his death President Johnson said: "With the passing of Norman Thomas, America loses one of its most eloquent speakers, finest writers and most creative thinkers. Mr. Thomas was once asked what he considered to be his greatest achievements. With characteristic modesty he replied, 'To live to be my age and feel that one has kept the faith or tried to . . . to be able to sleep at night with reasonable satisfaction.' Norman Thomas kept the faith. He was a humane and courageous man who lived to see many of the causes he championed become the law of the land."

IS CONSCIENCE A CRIME? (orig. "The Conscientious Objector in America"). 1927. *Ozer* 1972 $13.50; (and "War's Heretics") *Garland Pub. Co.* $20.00

THE CHOICE BEFORE US: Mankind at the Crossroads. 1934. *AMS Press* 1970 $6.75

SOCIALIST'S FAITH. 1951. *Kennikat* $12.50

THE TEST OF FREEDOM. 1954. *Greenwood* 1974 $10.25

GREAT DISSENTERS. *Norton* 1961 pap. 1970 $1.95

SOCIALISM RE-EXAMINED. *Norton* 1963 $5.75

THE CHOICES. *McKay* (I. Washburn) 1969 $3.50

Books about Thomas

Norman Thomas: Respectable Rebel. By Murray B. Seidler. *Syracuse Univ. Press* 2nd ed. 1967 $7.00. An excellent and comprehensive biography.
Leader at Large: The Long and Fighting Life of Norman Thomas. By Charles Gorham. *Farrar, Straus* 1970 $4.95
Pacifist's Progress: Norman Thomas and the Decline of American Socialism. By Bernard Johnpoll. *Quadrangle* 1970 $8.95
Norman Thomas: Social Realism Through Peace and Democratic Justice. By Bernard Johnpoll. *Garland Pub. Co.* 1974 $15.00
Norman M. Thomas. By James C. Duram. *Twayne* 1974 $7.95
Mister Socialism: Norman Thomas, His Life and Times. By Bright Steward. *Lyle Stuart* 1974 $7.95

MORISON, SAMUEL ELIOT. 1887–

Among our foremost historians, Admiral Morison, now retired from his post at Harvard, writes with authority and an engaging grace of style. The seaman's and the scholar's expert knowledge are perfectly blended in his books, for which he has usually studied the geographical setting at first hand. He prepared for writing "Admiral of the Ocean Sea" (*Little* 1942 $15.00) by four times "following the routes of Columbus' voyages in small sailing vessels comparable in size and rig to those used by Columbus." This magnificent biography was awarded the 1943 Pulitzer Prize. "Christopher Columbus, Mariner" (*Little* 1955 $7.50; *New Am. Lib.* 1957 pap. $.60) is a rewriting of "Admiral of the Ocean Sea" in straight narrative, leaving out lengthy notes and less significant details. Again in 1960 his "John Paul Jones" (*Little* 1959 $10.00 pap. $2.95) won the Pulitzer Biography award. Appointed historian of naval operations by the Navy in 1942, he wrote its 15-volume "History" for World War II, one of the most ambitious government-sponsored historical studies ever undertaken. It received the first Balzan Foundation Award of $51,000 in 1963. His great "Oxford History of the United States, 1783–1917" was written for English college students.

He has written a number of biographies. Besides those already mentioned, important works in this genre are: "Harrison Gray Otis, 1765–1848: The Urbane Federalist," concerning Morison's ancestor (*Houghton* 1968 $12.50) and "Old Bruin: Commodore Matthew C. Perry 1794–1858" (*Little-Atlantic* 1967 $12.50) which Bruce Catton called "a remarkably fine book. . . . Morison presents to us a Perry who was salty, vigorous and highly interesting." John K. Hutchens said of it: "Hearty, brave, forthright, 'Old Bruin' comes back to us, thanks to Professor Morison's diligence and art, in the full-scale portrait he has so long deserved."

Life in early Massachusetts is presented in the admirable "Maritime History of Massachusetts, 1783–1860" (1921. *Houghton* 1961 pap. $2.35), "Builders of the Bay Colony" (*Houghton* 1963 $6.95 pap. $3.95) and "Intellectual Life of Colonial New England" (*New York Univ. Press* 2nd ed. 1956 $8.50; *Cornell Univ. Press* 1960 pap. $2.45). Between 1930 and 1936 *Harvard Univ. Press* published his four volumes on the history of Harvard. Other works are "By Land and By Sea" (*Knopf* 1953 $6.95), "Freedom in Contemporary Society" (1956. *Bks. for Libraries* $7.75) and "An Hour of American History" (*Beacon* 1960 pap. $1.95; *Peter Smith* rev. ed. $3.75). He is also the author of "The Story of Mount Desert Island, Maine" (*Little-Atlantic* 1960 $3.95) and "Spring Tides" (*Houghton* 1965 $4.00).

"One Boy's Boston, 1887–1901" (*Houghton* 1962 $3.75) is a delightful book of reminiscences of his boyhood days in a world rich in material and intellectual gifts.

(Ed.) SOURCES AND DOCUMENTS ILLUSTRATING THE AMERICAN REVOLUTION, 1764–1788 and THE FORMATION OF THE FEDERAL CONSTITUTION. 1923. *Oxford* Galaxy Bks. 2nd ed. 1965 pap. $2.95

THE OXFORD HISTORY OF THE AMERICAN PEOPLE. 1927. *Oxford* 1965 $17.50 text ed. $10.95; *New Am. Lib.* 3 vols. pap. each $1.95

(With Henry Steele Commager). THE GROWTH OF THE AMERICAN REPUBLIC. 1930. *Oxford* 2 vols. 6th ed. 1969 text ed. each $9.95 boxed set $35.00

PORTUGUESE VOYAGERS TO AMERICA IN THE FIFTEENTH CENTURY. 1940. *Octagon* 1965 $9.00

HISTORY OF THE UNITED STATES NAVAL OPERATIONS IN WORLD WAR II: 1939–1945. *Little* 15 vols. 1947–62 each $15.00 (*see publisher's catalog for separate titles*)

(Ed.) OF PLYMOUTH PLANTATION: The Pilgrims in America. By William Bradford. Written c. 1620–1650 first published 1856. *Knopf* 1952 $8.95; *Random* Modern Lib. $2.95; *Putnam* Capricorn Bks. abr. ed. 1962 pap. $1.95; *Peter Smith* abr. $4.00

STRATEGY AND COMPROMISE. *Little* 1958 pap. $1.65 Concise survey of American-British World War II strategy.

THE TWO-OCEAN WAR: A Short History of the United States Navy in the Second World War. *Little* 1963 $15.00. A one-volume condensation of his 15-volume history, concentrating on major battles and campaigns.

VISTAS OF HISTORY. *Knopf* 1964 $4.00

A selection of previously published papers, including "The Experiences and Principles of an Historian"—"a lucid *curriculum vitae* of an intellect"—(*LJ*).

EUROPEAN DISCOVERY OF AMERICA: The Northern Voyages. *Oxford* 1971 $15.00

SAMUEL DE CHAMPLAIN: Father of New France. *Little-Atlantic* 1972 $10.00

EUROPEAN DISCOVERY OF AMERICA: The Southern Voyages. *Oxford* 1974 $17.50

"This sweeping narrative recaptures in sparkling prose the adventures of Columbus, Magellan, Drake, and other explorers of their time"—(*Booklist*).

Books about Morison

American Intellectual Histories and Historians. By Robert Allen Skotheim. *Princeton Univ. Press* 1966 $12.00 pap. 1970 $3.95. (*For comment, see listing at beginning of this Section under American History.*)

SCHLESINGER, ARTHUR M(EIER), SR. 1888–1965.

Called the "leading interpreter of America's past," Professor Schlesinger, born in Xenia, Ohio, and a graduate of Ohio State, taught at Ohio State, Iowa, and for many years at Harvard and went on many "professional pilgrimages to worldwide houses of learning." His volume of essays, "New Viewpoints in American History" (1922, o.p.) was far-reaching in its influence; it marked the turning point in our methods of research. He once said, "In my writing and teaching I have done all I could to disseminate the idea that history should be as inclusive as life itself." Out of print is "The Rise of Modern America, 1865–1951" (1951). His "Learning How to Behave" is a historical study of America's etiquette books (1946. *Cooper Square* 1968 $5.00). Still available are "The Rise of the City, 1878–1898" (1933. *Franklin Watts* 1971 pap. $3.45) and "The American as Reformer" (*Harvard Univ. Press* 2nd ed. 1968 $4.50; *Atheneum* 1968 pap. $1.95.)

He was, of course, the father of a distinguished living American historian. In 1965 Radcliffe College renamed its Women's Archives the Arthur and Elizabeth Schlesinger Library on the History of Women in America because of Mr. Schlesinger's work as the first historian to emphasize the American woman's contribution to history and to honor his wife's work in this field.

PATHS TO THE PRESENT. 1949. *Houghton* 1963 pap. $1.95

(With Dixon R. Fox, Eds.). HISTORY OF AMERICAN LIFE SERIES. *Macmillan* 13 vols. 1950 each $8.95 set $100.00

COLONIAL MERCHANTS AND THE AMERICAN REVOLUTION: 1763–1776. *Ungar* 1957 $12.50; *Atheneum* 1968 pap. $.95

PRELUDE TO INDEPENDENCE: The Newspaper War on Britain, 1764–1776. *Knopf* 1958 $8.95

THE CRITICAL PERIOD IN AMERICAN RELIGION, 1875–1900. *Fortress Press* 1967 pap. $6.00

THE BIRTH OF THE NATION: A Portrait of the American People on the Eve of Independence. With introd. by Arthur M. Schlesinger, Jr. *Knopf* 1968 $7.95

"A masterly summation of a distinguished historian's lifelong study of American national character. It comments wisely and lucidly not only on the traits which helped shape American independence, but also on the enduring characterists of the American people"—(Oscar Handlin).

IN RETROSPECT: The History of a Historian. *Harcourt* 1963 $4.50

"A rewarding autobiographical memoir—an engaging causerie, not a reverie"—(Charles Poore, in the *N.Y. Times*).

LIPPMANN, WALTER. 1889–1974.

"As widely respected by those who differ with his views as by those who agree with them," Walter Lippmann was considered one of the great spokesmen for liberal democracy and the outstanding American political philosopher of this century. Born in New York City, he earned his Harvard B.A. in three years, assisting George Santayana in his fourth year while he studied philosophy in the graduate school. He was associate editor of the *New Republic* in its early days, but left to become Assistant Secretary of War at the outbreak of World War I. Later he helped to prepare data for the Versailles Peace Conference. He served as editor of the New York *World*, and his newspaper column, "Today and Tomorrow," was widely read for many years. His television interviews offered an opportunity for many to listen to his opinion and advice on domestic and world affairs. He received the Pulitzer Prize for International Reporting in 1962, the Presidential Medal of Freedom in 1964, a Special Citation with the Peabody Award to CBS News in 1965 and the Gold Medal for Essays and Criticism from the National Institute of Arts and Letters in 1965. When, at 77, he gave up his regular newspaper column in 1967, he explained, "More and more I have come to wish to get rid of the necessity of knowing, day in and day out, what the blood pressure is at the White House and who said what and who saw whom and who is listened to and who is not listened to." He continued to write longer articles on a more relaxed basis.

THE ESSENTIAL LIPPMANN: A Political Philosophy for Liberal Democracy. Ed. by Clinton Rossiter and James Lare *Random* 1963 $10.00. A selection of Lippmann's writings published over more than half a century issued on the 50th anniversary of "Preface to Politics."

EARLY WRITINGS. *Liveright* 1970 $7.50 pap. 1971 $2.95

PREFACE TO POLITICS. 1913. *Univ. of Michigan Press* 1962 $4.95 pap. $2.25

PUBLIC OPINION. 1922. *Macmillan* (Free Press) 1965 pap. $2.95

THE GOOD SOCIETY. 1937, 1943. *Peter Smith* $5.25; *Greenwood* 1973 $17.25

U.S. FOREIGN POLICY: Shield of the Republic. 1943. *Johnson Reprint* 1971 $16.75

THE PUBLIC PHILOSOPHY. *Little* 1955 $5.95 pap. $2.75; *New Am. Lib.* pap. $.95

THE COMMUNIST WORLD AND OURS. *Little-Atlantic* 1959 $3.95. A report on his Moscow interview with Khrushchev.

DRIFT AND MASTERY: An Attempt to Diagnose the Current Unrest. *Prentice-Hall* 1961 pap. $1.95; *Peter Smith* $4.95

MEN OF DESTINY. *Univ. of Washington Press* 1970 $7.50 pap. $2.95

THE COLD WAR. *Harper* Torchbks. 1972 pap. $2.45

Books about Lippmann

Walter Lippmann: A Study in Personal Journalism. By David E. Weingast. 1949. *Greenwood* $9.00

Crossroads of Liberalism: Croly, Weyl, Lippmann and the Progressive Era, 1900–1925. By Charles Forcey. *Oxford* 1961 Galaxy Bks. 1967 pap. $2.95

Walter Lippmann's Philosophy of International Politics. By Anwar H. Syed. *Univ. of Pennsylvania Press* 1963 $12.00

The Influence of War on Walter Lippmann, 1914–1944. By Francine Curro Cary. *Wisconsin State Historical Society* 1967 $3.25

Twentieth Century Pilgrimage: Walter Lippmann and the Public Philosophy. By Charles Wellborn. *Louisiana State Univ. Press* 1969 $6.50

Lippmann, Liberty and the Press. By John Luskin. *Univ. of Alabama Press* 1972 $7.95

The Intellectual Odyssey of Walter Lippmann. By Hari N. Dam. *Gordon Press* 1973 $34.95

Five Public Philosophies of Walter Lippmann. By Benjamin F. Wright. *Univ. of Texas Press* 1973 $6.75

NEVINS, ALLAN. 1890–1971.

With some 40 books written or edited and two Pulitzer Prizes to his credit, Allan Nevins was a senior associate at the Huntington Library in California, having become emeritus professor of history at Columbia in 1958 after over 25 years on its faculty. Nevins had done editorial work on the *Nation* and several New York newspapers before beginning his teaching career at Cornell in 1927. His biography of Grover Cleveland (*Dodd* 1932 $12.00) won the 1932 Pulitzer award and five years later his "Hamilton Fish" (*Ungar* 2 vols. 1957 set $17.50) was similarly honored. "The Evening Post: A Century of Journalism" (1922), recently reprinted by *Russell & Russell* ($16.00), is a history of the newspaper.

Besides the biographies mentioned, he has written "Abram S. Hewitt: With Some Account of Peter Cooper" (1935. *Octagon* 1967 $8.50) and "John D. Rockefeller" (*Scribner* 1959 $10.00; *Kraus* 2 vols. $60.00). Out of print are his "Ford" (*Scribner* 3 vols. 1954–1963), "Herbert H. Lehmann and His Era" (1963) and "State Universities and Democracy" (*Univ. of Illinois Press* 1962).

THE AMERICAN STATES DURING AND AFTER THE REVOLUTION, 1775–1798. 1924. *Kelley* $17.50

EMERGENCE OF MODERN AMERICA, 1865–1878. 1927. *Scholarly Press* 1971 $19.00

FRÉMONT: Pathmarker of the West. 1928 1939. *Ungar* 2 vols. Vol. 1 Frémont, the Explorer Vol. 2 Frémont in the Civil War set $14.00

AMERICAN PRESS OPINION: Washington to Coolidge. 1928. *Kennikat* 2 vols. set $22.50

(With Henry Steele Commager) POCKET HISTORY OF THE UNITED STATES. 1942. *Simon & Schuster* (Washington Square) 1967 pap. $.95

(With Henry Steele Commager) A SHORT HISTORY OF THE UNITED STATES. 1945. *Knopf* rev. ed. 1966 $10.00 pap. $2.95

THE ORDEAL OF THE UNION. *Scribner* 8 vols. 1947–1971 each $15.00 Vol. 1 The Ordeal of the Union: Fruits of Manifest Destiny, 1847–1852 (1947) Vol. 2 The Ordeal of the Union: A House Dividing, 1852–1857 (1947) Vol. 3 The Emergence of Lincoln: Douglas, Buchanan, and Party Chaos, 1857–1859 (1950) Vol. 4 The Emergence of Lincoln: Prologue to Civil War, 1859–1861 (1950) Vol. 5 The War for the Union: The Improvised War, 1861–1862 (1959) Vol. 6 The War for the Union: War Becomes Revolution, 1862–1863 (1960) Vol. 7 The War for the Union: The Organized War, 1863–1864 (1971) Vol. 8 The War for the Union: The Organized War to Victory, 1864–1865 (1971)

AMERICA THROUGH BRITISH EYES. 1948. *Peter Smith* $6.50

THE UNITED STATES IN A CHAOTIC WORLD. 1950. *U.S. Pubs. Assn.* $3.95

THE STATESMANSHIP OF THE CIVIL WAR. 1953. *Macmillan* Collier Bks. enl. ed. 1962 pap. $.95

THE PLACE OF FRANKLIN D. ROOSEVELT IN HISTORY. *Humanities Press* 1965 pap. $1.50

JAMES TRUSLOW ADAMS: Historian of the American Dream. *Univ. of Illinois Press* 1968 $6.95

BEMIS, SAMUEL FLAGG. 1891–1973.

An outstanding authority on the history of American foreign policy, Professor Bemis was Sterling Professor of Diplomatic History and Inter-American Relations at Yale for nearly 30 years, becoming emeritus professor in 1961. He was a two-time winner of the Pulitzer Prize in history, for "Pinckney's Treaty" in 1926 and for "John Quincy Adams" in 1950. He served as advisory editor on the series "The American Secretaries of State and Their Diplomacy."

Professor Bemis was born in Worcester, Mass., and received his Ph.D. from Harvard. He has been president of the American Historical Association.

JAY'S TREATY: A Study in Commerce and Diplomacy. 1923. *Yale Univ. Press* rev. ed. 1962 pap. $4.95. The first international treaty (with Great Britain, 1794) of Washington's presidency.

PINCKNEY'S TREATY: America's Advantage from Europe's Distress, 1783–1800. 1926. *Greenwood* 1973 repr. 1960 ed. $14.75

(Ed.) THE AMERICAN SECRETARIES OF STATE AND THEIR DIPLOMACY, 1776–1925. 1927. *Cooper* 10 vols. in 5 $50.00

THE HUSSEY-CUMBERLAND MISSION AND AMERICAN INDEPENDENCE. 1931. *Peter Smith* $5.00

THE DIPLOMACY OF THE AMERICAN REVOLUTION. 1935. *Indiana Univ. Press* Midland Bks. 3rd ed. 1957 pap. $1.95; *Peter Smith* 1957 $4.25

(With Grace Gardner Griffin) GUIDE TO THE DIPLOMATIC HISTORY OF THE UNITED STATES, 1775–1921. 1935. *Peter Smith* 1959 $13.50

A SHORT HISTORY OF AMERICAN FOREIGN POLICY AND DIPLOMACY. 1936. *Holt* rev. ed. 1959 $12.50. Short version of "A Diplomatic History of the United States" (1936, o.p.).

THE LATIN AMERICAN POLICY OF THE UNITED STATES: An Historical Interpretation. 1943. *Norton* 1967 pap. $3.45

JOHN QUINCY ADAMS. *Knopf* 2 vols. 1949–56 Vol. 1 John Quincy Adams and the Foundations of American Foreign Policy (1949) Vol. 2 John Quincy Adams and the Union (1965) each $12.50 boxed set $25.00; *Norton* Vol. 1 1973 pap. $4.95

"With 'John Quincy Adams and the Union,' Samuel Flagg Bemis, Professor of Diplomatic History and Inter-American Relations at Yale, completes his superb biography of America's sixth President (the first volume of which, 'John Quincy Adams and the Foundations of American Foreign Policy,' won the Pulitzer Prize in 1950). The second volume opens with Adams' election in 1824. It portrays the stormy years of his administration, sees him go down to defeat before Andrew Jackson, and then describes his extraordinary post-Presidential career in the House of Representatives. The result is a noble picture of one of the noblest of Americans"—(Arthur M. Schlesinger Jr., in the *N.Y. Times*).

AGAR, HERBERT (SEBASTIAN). 1897–

For many years editor of the Louisville *Courier-Journal*, Agar has called himself a "creative conservative." His "harsh dissection of the American Presidency," "The People's Choice" won the Pulitzer History Prize. He was a founder (in 1941) and the first president of Freedom House, an organization for the promotion of peace and international cooperation. "The Saving Remnant: An Account of Jewish Survival" (*Viking* 1960 $5.00) reflected his deep concern with the Nazi aggression. His "Abraham Lincoln" is still available (1952. *Shoe String Press* 1965 $4.00).

THE PEOPLE'S CHOICE. 1933. *Norman S. Berg Pub.* 1968 lib. bdg. $15.00

THE PRICE OF UNION. *Houghton* 1950 $8.50 pap. 1967 $2.85

THE PRICE OF POWER: America since 1945. *Univ. of Chicago Press* 1957 $6.00 pap. $1.95

THE PERILS OF DEMOCRACY. *Dufour* 1966 $4.25; *Putnam* Capricorn Bks. 1968 pap. $1.25

DE VOTO, BERNARD (AUGUSTINE). 1897–1955.

A Harvard graduate and impassioned student and teacher of American history and literature, Bernard De Voto held faculty positions at Northwestern and at Harvard. He was also the second editor of the *Saturday Review of Literature* and conducted "The Editor's Easy Chair" column in *Harper's* Magazine for many years. For "Across the Wide Missouri" he visited the Western trails first blazed by Lewis and Clark. Henry Steele Commager called "The Course of Empire," covering the exploration of America to the year 1805, "the largest of the books, largest in conception and in scope, largest, too, in spirit. It is . . . the best book that has been written about the West since Webb's 'Great Plains' and it is the best written book about the West since Parkman."

THE YEAR OF DECISION: 1846. 1943. *Houghton* 1950 $7.95 Sentry Eds. 1961 pap. $3.95

" 'A monumental narrative,' based on contemporary diaries and other records, of a single but vastly significant year in the history of the American West. His scholarship is sound and thorough, his style vigorous and dramatic"—("Twentieth Century Authors").

ACROSS THE WIDE MISSOURI. *Houghton* 1947 $12.50 Sentry Eds. pap. $3.95

Struthers Burt found that De Voto here expressed "a passion as strong as a Chinook wind—as just and as lucid as the mountain-clearness of the original American idea"—(quoted in "Twentieth Century Authors").

THE COURSE OF EMPIRE. *Houghton* 1952 $8.50

(Ed.) THE JOURNALS OF LEWIS AND CLARK. *Houghton* 1953 $7.50

Books about De Voto

Four Portraits and One Subject: Bernard De Voto. By Catherine Drinker Bowen, Edith Mirrielees, Arthur M. Schlesinger, Jr., and Wallace Stegner. With a Bibliography of his writings prepared by Julius P. Barclay with the collaboration of Elaine Helmer Parnie. *Houghton* 1963 $4.00

Bernard De Voto. By Orlan Sawey. *Twayne* $6.50

The Uneasy Chair: Biography of Bernard De Voto. By Wallace Stegner. *Doubleday* 1974 $12.50

See also Chapter 15, Essays and Criticism, Reader's Adviser, Vol. 1.

DURANT, ARIEL. 1898–   *See under Durant, Will, in Section on Modern and World History, this Chapter.*

CATTON, (CHARLES) BRUCE. 1899–

Bruce Catton, "a journalist turned historian," has made the Civil War his own special bailiwick and has proved himself a master in combining readability with marshaling an amazing number of facts. He was a founding editor of the *American Heritage* magazine from 1954 to 1959 and continued to serve as a senior editor. His "Stillness at Appomattox" won the National Book Award and the Pulitzer Prize in history in 1954. The "Centennial History" has been called "the finest type of popular yet factual historical writing"—(*LJ*). In 1968 he was appointed an honorary consultant in American history by the Library of Congress for a three-year term. He has received honorary degrees from some 20 universities.

MR. LINCOLN'S ARMY. *Doubleday* 1951 $6.95

THE GLORY ROAD: The Bloody Route from Fredericksburg to Gettysburg. *Doubleday* 1952 $6.95

A STILLNESS AT APPOMATTOX. *Doubleday* 1953 $6.95; *Pocket Bks.* pap. $1.50

U. S. GRANT AND THE AMERICAN MILITARY TRADITION. *Little* 1954 $5.00 pap. 1972 $2.95. Grant as man, soldier and president.

THIS HALLOWED GROUND. *Doubleday* 1956 $7.95; *Pocket Bks.* 1972 pap. $1.50. The story of the Union side of the Civil War.

(Ed.) AMERICAN HERITAGE BOOK OF GREAT HISTORIC PLACES. *Simon & Schuster* 1957 $16.50 deluxe ed. $19.00

(Ed.) AMERICAN HERITAGE BOOK OF THE REVOLUTION. 1958. *Simon & Schuster* deluxe ed. $19.00

AMERICA GOES TO WAR: The Civil War and Its Meaning to Americans Today. *Wesleyan Univ. Press* 1958 pap. 1971 $1.75

GRANT MOVES SOUTH. *Little* 1960 $10.95. Vol. 2 in a 3-vol. biography of Grant begun by the late historian, Lloyd Lewis. The first volume was "Captain Sam Grant" (*Little* 1950 $10.95).

GRANT TAKES COMMAND. *Little* 1969 $10.00. Vol. 3, to the end of the war (*see entry just above*).

(Ed.) AMERICAN HERITAGE PICTURE HISTORY OF THE CIVIL WAR. *Doubleday* 1960 $24.95; *Dell* abr. ed. pap. $.95

THE CENTENNIAL HISTORY OF THE CIVIL WAR. *Doubleday* 3 vols. 1961–65 Vol. 1 The Coming Fury, 1860–61 Vol. 2 The Terrible Swift Sword, 1861–62 Vol. 3 Never Call Retreat Vols. 1 and 3 each $10.00 Vol. 2 o.p.; *Pocket Bks.* 1972 Vols. 1 and 2 pap. each $1.50

(With William Catton) TWO ROADS TO SUMTER. *McGraw-Hill* 1963 pap. $2.95

(With others) GRANT, LEE, LINCOLN AND THE RADICALS: Essays on Civil War Leadership. Ed. by Grady McWhitney *Northwestern Univ. Press* 1964 $4.50

THE CIVIL WAR. *McGraw-Hill* 1971 $6.95 pap. $3.95

GETTYSBURG: The Final Fury. *Doubleday* 1974 $8.95

WAITING FOR THE MORNING TRAIN: An American Boyhood. *Doubleday* 1972 $7.95. Autobiographical.

HACKER, LOUIS M(ORTON). 1899–

Professor Hacker, a leading authority on the development of American capitalism, has said, "I write economic history, never losing sight, however, of the close links between politics and economic development." He was born in New York, the son of Austrian immigrants and after considerable hardship was graduated from Columbia and became a free-lance historical writer. He taught at Columbia from 1935 to 1967, when he became professor emeritus. He was Dean of the School of General Studies at Columbia from 1949 to 1958. Mr. Hacker feels "that our civilization is in process of transformation; it is becoming more and more collectivized,with the authority of the central state increasingly powerful. This is the leading question of our time: how to permit collectivization to continue and at the same time hold in check the growth of a state bureaucracy. In America, I feel that it can and will be done: so that the long-term outlook, as I see it, is not dark"—(In "Twentieth Century Authors," 1955).

(With Benjamin B. Kendrick) THE UNITED STATES SINCE 1865. 1932. *Irvington Pubns.* 4th ed. 1949 $14.95

THE TRIUMPH OF AMERICAN CAPITALISM. 1940. *Columbia* 1947 $15.00

THE SHAPING OF THE AMERICAN TRADITION. *Columbia* 1947 $20.00

AMERICAN CAPITALISM: Its Promises and Achievements. 1957. *Peter Smith* $3.25

THE WORLD OF ANDREW CARNEGIE, 1865–1901. *Lippincott* 1968 $8.95

COURSE OF AMERICAN ECONOMIC GROWTH AND DEVELOPMENT. *Wiley* 1970 pap. $6.50

(Ed.) MAJOR DOCUMENTS IN AMERICAN ECONOMIC HISTORY. *Van Nostrand-Reinhold* 2 vols. 1961 Vol. 1 From an Agrarian to an Industrial Economy: 1785–1900 Vol. 2 The Problems of a World Power: The Twentieth Century pap. each $2.95

MILLIS, WALTER. 1899–1968.

For 30 years an editorial writer on the New York *Herald Tribune*, Mr. Millis, whose last years were occupied with the Fund for the Republic, spent most of his adult life examining the genesis and breeding of war in the United States and elsewhere. His "Arms and Men" was reviewed in the *N.Y. Times* as "a book for the years . . . a distinguished job of writing made so by Millis' skill as a narrator, his powers as a penetrative analyst and his ingrained habit of viewing skeptically any idea so long popular that it is accepted as truth." "The Abolition of War," produced under the auspices of the Center for the Study of Democratic Institutions, is a "clear-sighted, penetrating, cogent, passionately worded but rational and hopeful document." Of "An End to Arms" (*Atheneum* 1965, o.p.) Hans J. Morgenthau said, "By presenting his views in so able a manner, he has contributed to bringing about the world that reason requires." In "This Is Pearl! The United States and Japan, 1941" Millis blamed U.S. commanders in Hawaii for the bombing of Pearl Harbor.

Son of a professional soldier and himself an officer in World War I, Mr. Millis became an isolationist until World War II and after it. As the *N.Y. Times* wrote in his obituary, "One of the nation's foremost thinkers in the field of arms control, he was a leading proponent of the view that nuclear weapons make general warfare unthinkable as an instrument of national policy, and many of his late writings were on this theme."

THE ROAD TO WAR: America, 1914–1917. 1935. *Howard Fertig* 1970 $15.50

THIS IS PEARL! The United States and Japan, 1941. 1947. *Greenwood* $17.25

ARMS AND MEN: A Study in American Military History. *Putnam* 1956 pap. 1967 $2.85; *New Am. Lib.* pap. $1.25

ARMS AND THE STATE: Civil-Military Elements in National Policy. 1958. *Kraus* $4.00

(With C. J. Murray, Eds.) FOREIGN POLICY AND THE FREE SOCIETY. *Oceana* 1958 $3.50

(With others) A WORLD WITHOUT WAR. *Washington Square* 1961 pap. $.45

(With James Real) THE ABOLITION OF WAR. *Macmillan* 1963 pap. $1.95

(Ed.) AMERICAN MILITARY THOUGHT. *Bobbs-Merrill* 1966 $7.50 pap. $3.45

COMMAGER, HENRY STEELE. 1902–

Professor Commager, who taught American History at Columbia from 1938 to 1956, is now teaching at Amherst. His writings are popular with both scholars and the general reader, but his specialty is in the field of early American documents. He is said to consider his "Documents of American History" one of his most significant contributions. As a young man he was an American-Scandinavian Foundation fellow in Copenhagen and still maintains an interest in Danish history. Testifying before the Senate Foreign Relations Committee in 1967 (as reported in the *N.Y. Times*), the "dean of American historians" said that "because of a 'moralistic obsession' with Communism," the U.S. "had overextended itself as a world power.... By its Vietnam policies, he said, [it] is risking the loss of world opinion, the possibility of nuclear war and the destruction of the United Nations.... 'We need to cultivate patience, tolerance, the long view and even sympathy with the new nations of the globe.... And if we sometimes think, as doubtless we do,' he said, 'that their methods are violent and misguided and dangerous, we should recall to mind that the Old World thought our methods violent and misguided and dangerous.'"

Among his other works in print are "Theodore Parker, Yankee Crusader" (1936. *Peter Smith* $5.00) and "The Commonwealth of Learning" (*Harper* 1968 $6.95), in which he proposes major reforms in the university structure, asking that it abandom its passive role in favor of showing revolutionary new directions to the society of which it is a part. On the study of history he wrote "The Nature and Study of History" (*Bobbs* 1965 $4.95 pap. $2.50).

(Ed.). DOCUMENTS OF AMERICAN HISTORY. 1934. *Prentice-Hall* 9th ed. 1974 $17.50 2 vols. pap. text ed. each $8.25

(With Allan Nevins). THE HERITAGE OF AMERICA. 1939. *Little* 2nd rev. ed. 1949 $15.00

(With Allan Nevins). POCKET HISTORY OF THE UNTED STATES. 1942. *Simon & Schuster* (Washington Square) 1967 pap. $.95

MAJORITY RULE AND MINORITY RIGHTS. 1943. *Peter Smith* $4.00

(With Allan Nevins). A SHORT HISTORY OF THE UNITED STATES. 1945. *Knopf* rev. ed. 1966 $10.00 pap. $2.95

THE AMERICAN MIND: An Interpretation of American Thought and Character since the 1880's. *Yale Univ. Press* 1950 $17.50 pap. $3.95

(Ed.). THE BLUE AND THE GRAY: The Story of the Civil War as Told by Participants. *Bobbs* 1950 $11.95; *New Am. Lib.* 2 vols. 1973 pap. each $2.25

FREEDOM, LOYALTY, DISSENT. *Oxford* 1954 $5.95

(Ed.). THE PHOTOGRAPHIC HISTORY OF THE CIVIL WAR. *A. S. Barnes* (Yoseloff) 5 vols. 1957 boxed set $60.00

(Ed.). FIFTY BASIC CIVIL WAR DOCUMENTS. *Van Nostrand-Reinhold* Anvil Bks. (orig.) 1965 pap. $2.95

FREEDOM AND ORDER: A Commentary on the American Political Scene. *Braziller* 1966 $6.50; *New Am. Lib.* pap. $2.65

(Ed.). THE STRUGGLE FOR RACIAL EQUALITY: A Documentary Record. 1967. *Peter Smith* $4.75. A selection of writings dealing with the civil rights struggle from the Reconstruction Period to Stokely Carmichael.

(With Richard B. Morris). THE SPIRIT OF 'SEVENTY-SIX: The Story of the American Revolution as Told by Participants. 1958. *Harper* 1967 $20.00

COMMONWEALTH OF LEARNING. *Harper* 1968 $6.95

BRITAIN THROUGH AMERICAN EYES. *McGraw-Hill* 1974 $17.50

JEFFERSON, NATIONALISM, AND THE ENLIGHTENMENT. *Braziller* 1974 $7.50

THE DEFEAT OF AMERICA: Presidential Power and the National Character. *Simon & Schuster* 1975 $7.95 pap. $2.95. (*See comment under United States Government and Politics, this Section.*)

HORGAN, PAUL. 1903–

"Great River" received both the Pulitzer Prize and the Bancroft Prize for history in 1955. It is not only a history of the Rio Grande river but a saga of New Mexico and Texas from ancient to modern times. Mr. Horgan was director of the Center for Advanced Studies in the Liberal Arts, Sciences and Professions at Wesleyan University from 1962 to 1967. In 1969, he became one of the judges of the Book-of-the-Month Club.

GREAT RIVER: The Rio Grande in North American History. *Holt* 1955 2 vols. in 1 rev. ed. 1960 $11.95; *T. Y. Crowell* (Funk & Wagnalls) 2 vols. pap. each $2.95. The history of the Southwest and its four civilizations—the aboriginal Indians, the Spanish, the Mexican and the Anglo-American.

CENTURIES OF SANTA FE. Decorations by the author *Dutton* 1956 pap. $2.25

CONQUISTADORS IN NORTH AMERICAN HISTORY. *Farrar, Straus* 1963 $7.95

KENNAN, GEORGE F(ROST). 1904– *See Modern and World History, this Chapter.*

MILLER, PERRY (GILBERT EDDY). 1905–1963.

"While the late Perry Miller was generally recognized as one of the country's most distinguished intellectual historians, his considerable achievements as an urbane and witty writer were sometimes overshadowed by the originality of his ideas"—(*PW*). Born and educated in Chicago, Perry Miller taught at Harvard for over 30 years until his death. Working with source materials such as diaries and letters, he studied the literature and history of New England in the Colonial era and that of the early Republic. His books, and especially his most popular work, "The New England Mind," should dispel once and for all any impression that the life of American Puritans was dreary. "He respected the Puritans as thinkers, and he regarded them more highly than he did their successors who moderated their teachings"—(Granville Hicks, in *SR*).

A professor of American literature, Miller wrote critical essays and compiled anthologies of early American poetry and prose. "Nature's Nation" (*Harvard Univ. Press* 1967 $7.50) is "a collection of essays and lectures that Miller wrote in the later years of his life. The first six or seven are by-products of his studies of Puritanism, and they show how his mind worked. As he comes down to the nineteenth century his tone grows sharper, and there is a ruthless analysis of the shortcomings of Theodore Parker. He sees the weaknesses of Emerson, too, especially the vestiges of Boston Unitarian snobbishness. . . . Yet in the end he does Emerson justice. He also writes about Thoreau and Melville, and there are two brilliant essays that have not appeared before in book form—'An American Language' and 'Romance and the Novel.' . . . The final essay is amusingly and pointedly entitled 'Sinners in the Hands of a Benevolent God' "—(Hicks).

His other works include "Jonathan Edwards" (1949. *Greenwood* $14.25), "Roger Williams: His Contribution to the American Tradition" (1953. *Atheneum* pap. $1.65; *Peter Smith* $4.50), "Margaret Fuller: American Romantic" (*Cornell Univ. Press* 1970 pap. $2.45) and "The Raven and the Whale" (1956. *Greenwood* 1973 $12.75), a study of Poe and Melville. He also edited "The Complete Writings of Roger Williams" (*Russell & Russell* 7 vols. rev. ed. 1963 set $100.00) and "The Transcendentalists: An Anthology" (*Harvard Univ. Press* 1950 $15.00 pap. $2.95).

ORTHODOXY IN MASSACHUSETTS, 1630–1650. 1933. *Harper* Torchbks. 1970 pap. $2.75; *Peter Smith* $5.50

SOCIETY AND LITERATURE IN AMERICA. 1949. *Folcroft* $4.50

THE NEW ENGLAND MIND. *Harvard Univ. Press* 2 vols. 1953–54 Vol. 1 The Seventeenth Century (1954) o.p. Vol. 2 From Colony to Province (1953) $12.50; *Beacon* 2 vols. 1961 pap. Vol. 1 $3.95 Vol. 2 $4.95

(Ed.) AMERICAN THOUGHT: The Civil War to World War I. *Holt* 1954 pap. $3.95; *Peter Smith* $4.50

(With others) RELIGION AND FREEDOM OF THOUGHT. 1954. *Bks. for Libraries* $6.00

ERRAND INTO THE WILDERNESS. *Harvard Univ. Press* 1956 $7.00; *Harper* Torchbks. pap. $2.50

Essays, mostly on American (Protestant) religion. "For a certain type of specialized reader this book can be endlessly stimulating. Mr. Miller is a man of learning who writes, if not for scholars alone, then for readers who combine a passion for ideas with tireless precision of thought. To such an audience he must rank among the most delightful and rewarding of intellectual historians"— (Robert Peel, in the *Christian Science Monitor*).

(Ed.) AMERICAN PURITANS: Their Prose and Poetry. *Doubleday* Anchor Bks. 1956 pap. $2.50; *Peter Smith* 1959 $4.50

(Ed.) AMERICAN TRANSCENDENTALISTS: Their Prose and Poetry. *Doubleday* Anchor Bks. 1957 pap. $2.50; *Peter Smith* $4.50

THE LIFE OF THE MIND IN AMERICA: From the Revolution to the Civil War. *Harcourt* 1966 pap. 1970 $2.85

"The Enlightenment ideal was that of perfect adaptation of individual to society and society to nature. . . . No more hollow human ideal . . . has ever been conceived; and . . . Perry Miller's discovery that the Enlightenment Sublime was the source of the absurd and disturbing (and oddly touching) American falsity is a great intellectual achievement"—(Morse Peckham, in *SR*). Unfortunately Professor Miller died before he could complete this, planned for several volumes.

(With T. H. Johnson, Eds.) THE PURITANS: A Sourcebook of Their Writings. *Harper* Torchbks. 2 vols. pap. Vol. 1 $2.75 Vol. 2 $2.95; *Peter Smith* 2 vols. each $6.50

(Ed.). THE LEGAL MIND IN AMERICA: From Independence to the Civil War. *Cornell Univ. Press* 1970 pap. $2.45

(With Alan Heimert, Eds.) THE GREAT AWAKENING: Documents Illustrating the Crisis and Its Consequences. *Bobbs* 1967 $7.50 pap. $3.75. About the American religious revival of the 18th-century Colonial Period; it was initiated in New England by Jonathan Edwards.

FAIRBANK, JOHN K(ING). 1907–ﾠ *See Modern and World History, this Chapter.*

WOODWARD, C(OMER) VANN. 1908–

ﾠﾠﾠﾠC. Vann Woodward, the distinguished historian of the South, is Sterling Professor of History at Yale. Born in Arkansas, he graduated from Emory University in 1930 and received his Ph.D. from the University of North Carolina in 1937.

ﾠﾠﾠﾠHis modest volume (the second revised edition is only 205 pages), "The Strange Career of Jim Crow," has become an American classic. First published in 1955, it still sells (in hardback and paper) some 35,000 copies a year. William Styron has called it "one of the most valuable works we have in the entire literature of the American racial dilemma," and the late Ralph McGill wrote of the new edition: "A revised edition of 'The Strange Career of Jim Crow' by C. Vann Woodward to include events of the past decade and to relate them to the past out of which they came is an outstanding service to those wishing to understand the South, the nation, and the traumatic experiences in our slums and in the South. Mr. Vann Woodward is not merely a great American historian, but is without a peer in his knowledge of, and ability to write about, things Southern." "The Burden of Southern History" became a second classic, and it too has recently appeared in revision.

ﾠﾠﾠﾠProfessor Woodward has taught and lectured widely, principally—before his Yale tenure—at Johns Hopkins, from 1946 to 1961. He was Harmsworth Professor at Oxford, 1954–1955, and has won the award of the American Council of Learned Societies, the National Institute of Arts and Letters Award and the Bancroft Prize for his historical writing. With the recent intensification of interest in Afro-American history and the Southern past, he has been much in demand for articles on the subject and has contributed to many periodicals as well as to the *N.Y. Times* Sunday Magazine. He is currently a member of the editorial advisory board for *The American Scholar*.

THE ORIGINS OF THE NEW SOUTH, 1877–1913. *Louisiana State Univ. Press* 1951 rev. ed. 1972 pap. $4.25

"Beyond all question this is the most valuable book that has been written about the South in these years. Because of its freshness of view and its critical scholarship in a period long neglected, it is the most useful volume of 'A History of the South' that has appeared. Although the awkward dates assigned to the volume prevented a clearly defined synthesis, the book clearly establishes the author's primacy among the scholars of the 'New South' (a term which he righteously deplores)"— (W. B. Hesseltine, in the *American Historical Review*).

REUNION AND REACTION: The Compromise of 1877 and the End of Reconstruction. *Little* 1951 rev. ed. 1966 $7.95 pap. $2.45

"Dr. Woodward has tracked down masses of hitherto unknown yet important material, but from it he has articulated a fresh, vital thing, full-bodied, incisive, revealing. At long last we know all the unsavory details of an episode which—even in the incomplete form that we knew in the past—already smelled to high heaven"—*(The Annals)*.

THE STRANGE CAREER OF JIM CROW. *Oxford* 1955 3rd rev. ed. 1974 $8.95 pap. $1.95

This is an "up-to-date edition of one of the most valuable books in the entire canon of race relations in the United States. It was Mr. Woodward who in 1955 reminded a forgetful South that segregation of the Negro was not at all an inviolate tenet of the Southern way of life, that for many years after the Civil War Negroes mixed freely with whites in the South, and that the most rigorous opponents of separation of the races by Jim Crow laws were the leaders of Southern society themselves"—*(New Yorker)*.

THE BURDEN OF SOUTHERN HISTORY. *Louisiana State Univ. Press* 1960 2nd rev. and enl. ed. 1968 $5.95 pap. $2.45; *New Am. Lib.* Mentor Bks. 1969 pap. $.95

"It is in the magnificent flowering of the Southern literary renascence, of course, that Dr. Woodward finds the most perfect expression of the Southern ethic: its haunting sense of guilt, its sense of place, as opposed to the rootlessness of typically American writers like Hemingway and their characters; and most of all, its overwhelming consciousness of the past in the present, as Allen Tate has expressed it. Dr. Woodward overstates his case, somewhat, when he excludes New England authors, generally, from this traditionalism. . . . Stimulating and thoughtful book"—*(SR)*.

(Ed.) THE COMPARATIVE APPROACH TO AMERICAN HISTORY. *Basic Bks.* 1968 $6.50 pap. $2.95

"Until recently, American historians have been accused of parochialism in their approach, of neglecting the comparative method and dwelling on the *in*comparable in our history. In this collection of 24 essays, top-flight historians display their virtuosity in applying the comparative method. They compare the American and French revolutions; the Enlightenment here and in Europe; the differences in slavery in North and South America; the failure of Marxist socialists with the labor movement in the U.S. compared to their success in other countries. From the Colonial period to the Cold War, they find comparisons everywhere. Most of the essays were originally lectures heard over the Voice of America; their foreign-audience slant will give new perspectives to historians and lay readers alike"—*(PW)*.

AMERICAN COUNTERPOINT: Slavery and Race in the North-South Dialogue. *Little* 1971 $7.95 pap. $2.95

(Ed.) THE AMERICAN SOUTH. *Arno* 7 vols. 1973 set $94.00

POTTER, DAVID M(ORRIS). 1910–

Professor Potter, Coe Professor of History at Stanford, was described in the *N.Y. Times* in 1968 by Martin Duberman of Princeton's history department as a man who "may be the greatest living historian of the United States. With the additional evidence of this collection of his essays ['The South and the Sectional Conflict'] I'm glad for the chance to say that in print, not least because Potter is little known outside the historical profession, in part because he has written only a few volumes . . .—and in part because he has always shied away from self-advertisement."

Professor Duberman defends his thesis (and he does not hold it alone): "I believe, first of all, that Potter's eminence has less to do with his special opinions than with the process by which he arrives at them, that his distinction is to be sought in his manner of address to a given problem rather than in the solution he offers for it. In this regard, his most characteristic stance is cautionary—he continually reminds us that history is made by historians. When evaluating a particular interpretation, Potter not only asks the traditional question, 'How well does it fit the known evidence?' but also asks, 'What was there in the background of the historian himself that led him to view the evidence in the way he did?' . . . Recently, historians have been preoccupied with the evils of slavery and the urgency of abolishing it. They have therefore tended to accept the outbreak of war in 1861 as inevitable, as the only possible instrument for destroying slavery. Potter is troubled by historians defending one set of philosophical values as against another, because he believes the historian's proper function is not justification but explanation. He is troubled even when historians try to justify loyalties he himself shares. Though he has deep affection for the South (he was born in Georgia in 1910), he will not sanction any defense of the region that comes at the expense of historical understanding. . . . Potter's fine distinctions, his subtleties of perception, are what the complexities of historical evidence always require but almost never find. To read him is to become aware of a truth that only the greatest historians have been able to show us: that the chief lesson to be derived from a study of the past is that it holds no simple lesson, and that the historian's main responsibility is to prevent anyone from claiming that it does."

Professor Potter graduated from Emory University in 1932 and took his Ph.D. at Yale in 1940. He was Harmsworth Professor at Oxford in 1947–48 and Commonwealth Fund Lecturer at London University in 1963. He has lectured widely and taught at a number of universities in this country, particularly Yale from 1942 to 1961, leaving his Coe professorship at Yale to go to Stanford, also as Coe Professor, in the latter year.

LINCOLN AND HIS PARTY IN THE SECESSION CRISIS. *Yale Univ. Press* 1942 pap. $3.95

"Whether or not the Civil War might have been avoided is a question which Dr. Potter refrains from answering. It is a question constantly posed by his material, and the author's declaration of opinion might have strengthened his book and resolved some of his estimates. But the material is excellently presented, and Dr. Potter's position as the sworn enemy of hindsight lends a freshness and illumination to the treatment"—(*Nation*).

PEOPLE OF PLENTY: Economic Abundance and the American Character. *Univ. of Chicago Press* 1954 $6.75 Phoenix Bks. pap. $1.50

" 'What then is the American, this new man?' For generations this ever fascinating question, asked by Crèvecoeur in 1782, has been repeated the world over. Just how, we ask, does American behavior differ from that of other peoples, and why do we act the way we do? David M. Potter, Coe Professor of American History and Chairman of American Studies at Yale University, has summarized much of the unceasing debate in a brief, important book which lifts the whole problem to a new level of analysis and understanding"—(*Yale Review*).

THE SOUTH AND THE SECTIONAL CONFLICT. *Louisiana State Univ. Press* 1968 $7.50 pap. $2.95. (*See comment above.*)

THE SOUTH AND THE CONCURRENT MAJORITY. Ed. by Don E. Fehrenbacher and Carl N. Delger *Louisiana State Univ. Press* 1972 $4.95

DIVISION AND THE STRESSES OF REUNION: 1845–1876. *Scott, Foresman* 1973 pap. $4.35

HISTORY AND AMERICAN SOCIETY: The Essays of David Potter. Ed. by Don E. Fehrenbacher *Oxford* 1973 $10.95

(With Curtis Grant) EIGHT ISSUES IN AMERICAN HISTORY: Views and Counterviews. *Scott, Foresman* 1966 pap. $4.25

TUCHMAN, BARBARA (WERTHEIM). 1912–   *See Modern and World History, this Chapter.*

BOORSTIN, DANIEL J. 1914–

Dr. Boorstin is the author of more than a dozen scholarly works which have received numerous awards. In 1959 he received Columbia University's Bancroft Prize for "The Americans: The Colonial Experience" the first volume of his trilogy "The Americans." In 1966 he received the Francis Parkman Award for volume 2 "The Americans: The National Experience" and in 1974 he received the Pulitzer Prize for the third volume "The Americans: The Democratic Experience." He has served as Professor of American History at the University of Paris, Cambridge University, and the University of Chicago. In 1969 he left the University of Chicago to assume the position of Director of the National Museum of History and Technology of the Smithsonian Institution. In 1973 he became the Senior Historian of the Smithsonian. In November 1975 he resigned this position to become the Librarian of Congress.

THE MYSTERIOUS SCIENCE OF THE LAW. 1941. 1958. *Peter Smith* $4.25

THE LOST WORLD OF THOMAS JEFFERSON. 1948. *Beacon* 1960 pap. $2.95; *Peter Smith* $4.75

THE GENIUS OF AMERICAN POLITICS. *Univ. of Chicago Press* 1953 $6.50 Phoenix Bks. pap. $1.50

THE AMERICANS. *Random.* 3 vols. 1958–73 Vol. 1 The Colonial Experience (1958) Vol. 2
   The National Experience (1965) Vol. 3 The Democratic Experience (1973) Vols. 1–2
   each $12.50 Vol. 3 $10.00 Vintage Bks. 3 vols. 1958–74 pap. Vol. 1 $3.45 Vol. 2 $2.45
   Vol. 3 $3.95

"An excellent socio-history of the American community. . . . Highly organized, with a wealth of
material never previously drawn from primary sources"—*(LJ)*. Volume 2 received the Francis
Parkman Prize in 1966. In it Dr. Boorstin cites the dominance of our society by wealth and
technology as the origin of illusions and delusions from which America must free itself to meet the
future successfully. Volume 3 is concerned with the democratization of the national character over
the past hundred years and the growth of technology.

AMERICA AND THE IMAGE OF EUROPE: Reflections on American Thought. 1960. *Peter
   Smith* $4.00

IMAGE: A Guide to Pseudo-Events in America. (Orig. "Image, or What Happened to
   the American Dream") *Atheneum* 1962 pap. 1971 $3.95

"An effective phrase-coiner, Dr. Boorstin develops his theme of pseudo-events by compiling an
inventory of commercialized folly"—*(American Historical Review)*.

DECLINE OF RADICALISM: Reflections on America Today. *Random* 1969 $4.95 Vintage
   Bks. 1970 pap. $1.95

SOCIOLOGY OF THE ABSURD. *Simon & Schuster* 1970 $3.95

(Ed.) THE AMERICAN PRIMER. *Univ. of Chicago Press* 2 vols. 1969 set $12.50

(Ed.) TECHNOLOGY AND SOCIETY. *Arno* 53 vols. 1972 set $1,076.00

(Ed.) AMERICAN CIVILIZATION: A Portrait from the Twentieth Century. *McGraw-Hill*
   1972 $35.00

Consists of "interdependent chapters [by 13 authorities] on virtually all phases of the American
experience. These chapters cumulatively describe how the . . . U.S., having achieved materialistic
and technological preeminence and having conquered its own frontiers and outer space, has now
turned increasingly introspective, questioning its destiny"—*(LJ)*.

DEMOCRACY AND ITS DISCONTENTS: Reflections on Everyday America. *Random* 1974
   $5.95

FRANKLIN, JOHN HOPE. 1915–

Professor Franklin, born in Oklahoma, has had a distinguished career as teacher, scholar and
historian of the black experience in America. Son of a lawyer who practiced before the United
States Supreme Court, he was a Phi Beta Kappa graduate of Fisk University and took his Ph.D. at
Harvard in 1941. "He owes his international recognition," says *Current Biography,* "to his books on
American history, including *From Slavery to Freedom* (1947) and *The Militant South* (1956). He is also
known for his work in the classrooms of Fisk University, Howard University, Brooklyn College,
Cambridge University, and other schools, and for his services in professional, civic, and govern-
mental organizations." Of "From Slavery to Freedom," his comprehensive history, the *N.Y. Herald
Tribune* wrote: "Dr. Franklin's book is a mature, balanced, scholarly account of the American
Negro from his African beginnings to his participation in the late war. . . . A rich, absorbing book,
with a clarity of design which all readers will appreciate." The *Saturday Review* said: "Throughout,
the documentation and the bibliography add to the usefulness of the book to students. . . . 'From
Slavery to Freedom' has before it a path of constructive public serviceableness; it will be a long
while until another book in this field supercedes it." Within a short time it was recognized as one of
the most important surveys to have appeared of the history of the black race in this country; it
became a basic textbook in the subject and has been twice revised and brought up to date. Besides
his original work, his national and international teaching assignments at Harvard and Cambridge
(England) and many other universities—he was a Fulbright Professor in Australia in 1960—he has
been chairman of the history department at Brooklyn College (1956–1964) and now occupies the
same post at the University of Chicago. He has been active in many learned and professional
societies, edited many volumes, especially on the Civil War, and served on the editorial boards of
the *Journal of American History* and the *Journal of Negro History.* He is a founding member of the
Black Academy of Arts and Letters and has served on the U.S. Commission for UNESCO. "The
objectivity that assures his integrity as a scholar does not keep him from eloquent and persuasive
argument on occasion, as in an article for the Urban League: 'Not only does his Americanism
compel the Negro to strive to improve his own status by demanding the rights that are his. It also
gives him, as it gives to others committed to the ideals set forth in the American dream, a burning
desire to make the system work' "—*(Current Biography, 1963)*.

THE FREE NEGRO IN NORTH CAROLINA, 1790–1860. 1943. *Norton* 1971 pap. $2.25; *Russell & Russell* 1969 $10.00

"An admirable piece of work"—(*Commonweal*).

FROM SLAVERY TO FREEDOM: A History of American Negroes. *Knopf* 1947 4th ed. 1974 $13.95 pap. $4.50

THE MILITANT SOUTH, 1800–1961. *Harvard Univ. Press* 1956 rev. ed. 1970 $7.50

"John Hope Franklin's study is in many ways a pioneer work. His sources are original, his work is thorough and his book makes a fresh and significant contribution to the understanding of the mind of the South"—(C. Vann Woodward, in the *N.Y. Times*). "John Hope Franklin has assembled an unrivalled body of data on the diverse manifestations of the fighting spirit in the South, and has presented it in a book which enables the reader better to understand a whole range of behavior from the valor of Pickett's charge to the infamy of the Emmett Till murder"—(David M. Potter, in the *Yale Review*).

RECONSTRUCTION AFTER THE CIVIL WAR. *Univ. of Chicago Press* 1961 $6.50 pap. $1.95

An important study in the light of modern scholarship. "A great deal of careful research has gone into the book and the conclusions are set down logically and forcefully. An excellent bibliography adds much to its value"—(*LJ*).

THE EMANCIPATION PROCLAMATION. *Doubleday* 1963 $4.95 Anchor Bks. pap. $1.45

"A work of scholarship that is lucid and attractive to the general reader. With self-restraint and detachment, [Professor Franklin] has more or less successfully abstracted and told the story of the Emancipation Proclamation. There are enough misconceptions about that single great document to justify his attempt to separate its genesis and its content from its indispensable predecessor, the abolitionist movement, from the Civil War itself, and from the bitter aftermath"—(*Commonweal*).

(With Isidore Starr, Eds.) THE NEGRO IN TWENTIETH CENTURY AMERICA: A Reader on the Struggle for Civil Rights. *Random* Vintage Bks. (orig.) 1967 pap. $2.95

(Ed.) COLOR AND RACE. *Houghton* 1969 $6.95; *Beacon* pap. $2.95

"*Daedalus*, the journal of the American Academy of Arts and Sciences, devoted its Spring, 1967, issue to the subject of color and race. Such was the response that now, in an expanded version, the issue appears in book form. Anthropologists, historians, sociologists and psychologists from all over the world have contributed essays"—(*PW*).

ILLUSTRATED HISTORY OF BLACK AMERICANS. *Time-Life* 1970 $7.95

HANDLIN, OSCAR. 1915–

Dr. Handlin, director of the Center for the Study of the History of Liberty at Harvard until 1966, won the Pulitzer Prize in 1952 for "The Uprooted," his study of immigrants in the eastern cities of America. The son of immigrant parents, he made his special field the social history of the immigrant groups who came to America in the 19th-century from central and southern Europe. In "The Americans," as in others of his books, he dispensed with footnotes, bibliography and identification of quotations in favor of "unobstrusive" learning. He edited "Children of the Uprooted" which includes excerpts from various authors on the subject of the "marginality" of immigrants. On the subject of education he wrote "The American University as an Instrument of Republican Culture"(*Humanities Press* 1970 pap. $1.25) and "John Dewey's Challenge to Education: Historical Perspectives on the Cultural Context" (1959. *Greenwood* 1972 $7.25). With his wife, Mary Handlin, he edited "The Popular Sources of Political Authority: Documents on the Massachusetts Constitution of 1780" (*Harvard Univ. Press* 1966 $22.50). Dr. Handlin taught at Harvard for many years where he was Charles Warren Professor of History. He also conducted a book review column for the *Atlantic*.

THE UPROOTED. *Little-Atlantic* 1951 2nd enl. ed. 1973 $8.95 pap. $3.95; *Grosset* Univ. Lib. 1957 pap. $2.50

THE AMERICAN PEOPLE IN THE TWENTIETH CENTURY. *Harvard Univ. Press* 1954 2nd rev. ed. 1966 $7.00; *Beacon* pap. $1.75

ADVENTURES IN FREEDOM. 1954. American History and Culture in the Twentieth Century Ser. *Kennikat* 1971 $11.50

RACE AND NATIONALITY IN AMERICAN LIFE. *Little-Atlantic* 1957 $6.95; *Doubleday* Anchor Bks. 1957 pap. $1.95

AL SMITH AND HIS AMERICA. *Little-Atlantic* 1958 $5.00 pap. $2.75

(Ed.) IMMIGRATION AS A FACTOR IN AMERICAN HISTORY. *Prentice-Hall* Spectrum Bks. 1959 pap. $1.95; *Peter Smith* $4.95

BOSTON'S IMMIGRANTS: A Study of Acculturation. *Harvard Univ. Press* rev. & enl. ed. 1959 $10.00; *Atheneum* 1968 pap. $3.25

NEWCOMERS: Negroes and Puerto Ricans in a Changing Metropolis. *Harvard Univ. Press* 1959 $5.00; *Doubleday* Anchor Bks. pap. $1.95

(With Mary Handlin) THE DIMENSIONS OF LIBERTY. *Harvard Univ. Press* 1961 $5.50; *Atheneum* 1966 pap. $1.75

THE AMERICANS: A New History of the People of the United States. *Little-Atlantic* 1963 $8.95 pap. $2.45. A study of the influence of immigration upon the people of the United States from Leif Ericson to 1962.

FIRE-BELL IN THE NIGHT: The Crisis in Civil Rights. *Little-Atlantic* 1964 $3.95

A CONTINUING TASK. *Random* 1965 $5.00

(Ed.) CHILDREN OF THE UPROOTED. *Braziller* 1966 $8.50; *Grosset* 1968 pap. $3.95
   "In three brief explanatory essays, the editor gives a quick account of types of migration to America and the changing American scene into which the migrants came. He also explains the concept of 'marginality.' . . . Recommended"—(*LJ*).

THE HISTORY OF THE UNITED STATES. *Holt* 2 vols. 1967–68 Vol. 1 o.p. Vol. 2 $12.00

AMERICA: A History. *Holt* 1968 $13.00

A PICTORIAL HISTORY OF IMMIGRATION. *Crown* 1972 $12.50

(Ed.) THIS WAS AMERICA: True Accounts of People and Places, Manners and Customs, as Recorded by European Travelers to the Western Shore in the 18th, 19th and 20th Centuries. *Harvard Univ. Press* 1969 $12.50

(With Mary Handlin) COMMONWEALTH: A Study of the Role of Government in the American Economy, Massachusetts, 1774–1861. *Harvard Univ. Press* rev. ed. 1969 $12.50

(With Mary Handlin) FACING LIFE: Youth and the Family in American History. *Little-Atlantic* 1971 $7.95 pap. $2.95

HOFSTADTER, RICHARD. 1916–

The DeWitt Clinton Professor of History at Columbia is the author of several important volumes on American social history which have cast valuable light upon the intellectual and political heritage of the United States. He received the Pulitzer Prize in history in 1955 for "The Age of Reform." Written in brisk and lucid prose, "it illuminates the whole landscape of American social history and allows its readers to see the intellectuals and the anti-intellectuals as they really exist. . . . His range of experience has been wide, his perception is acute"—(Harold Taylor). He won the 1964 Pulitzer Prize for general nonfiction, the Ralph Waldo Emerson Award of Phi Beta Kappa and the Sidney Hillman Prize Award, all for "Anti-Intellectualism in American Life." He has been a visiting professor at Cambridge University.

His other books include "Academic Freedom in the Age of the College" (*Columbia* 1955 pap. $2.95), with Wilson Smith, "American Higher Education: A Documentary History" (1961. *Univ. of Chicago Press* Phoenix Bks. 2 vols. pap. Vol. 1 $2.95 Vol. 2 $3.45) and with W. P. Metzger, "The Development of Academic Freedom in the United States" (*Columbia* 1955 $15.00).

THE AMERICAN POLITICAL TRADITION. *Knopf* 1948 new ed. 1973 $7.95; *Random* Vintage Bks. pap. $1.95

SOCIAL DARWINISM IN AMERICAN THOUGHT. 1954. *Braziller* rev. ed. 1959 $6.00

THE AGE OF REFORM: From Bryan to F. D. R. *Knopf* 1955 $6.95. This won the 1955 Pulitzer Prize for History.

(With others) THE UNITED STATES: The History of a Republic. *Prentice-Hall* 1957 3rd ed. 1972 $11.50 pap. $6.25

(With others) THE AMERICAN REPUBLIC. *Prentice-Hall* 1959 2 vols. 2nd ed. 1970 Vol. 1 Through Reconstruction Vol. 2 From Reconstruction each $12.50

ANTI-INTELLECTUALISM IN AMERICAN LIFE. *Knopf* 1963 $7.95; *Random* Vintage Bks. pap. $2.95. (*See comment under Supplementary General Reading List, this Section.*)

(Ed.) THE PROGRESSIVE MOVEMENT, 1900–1915. *Prentice-Hall* Spectrum Bks. 1964 pap. $1.95; *Peter Smith* $4.95

(Ed.) TEN MAJOR ISSUES IN AMERICAN POLITICS. *Oxford* 1968 pap. $2.95

(With others) THE STRUCTURE OF AMERICAN HISTORY. *Prentice-Hall* 1964 pap. $5.95 2nd ed. 1973 pap. $6.50

THE PARANOID STYLE IN AMERICAN POLITICS AND OTHER ESSAYS. *Knopf* 1965 $6.95; *Random* Vintage Bks. pap. $1.95

THE PROGRESSIVE HISTORIANS: Turner, Beard, Parrington. *Knopf* 1968 $8.95; *Random* Vintage Bks. 1970 pap. $2.95

Hofstadter "treats Frederick Jackson Turner, Charles A. Beard and Vernon L. Parrington as exemplars of Progressive historiography. These men, Hofstadter asserts, gave Americans the pivotal ideas of the first half of the twentieth century. . . . Turner, Beard and Parrington were influential insofar as they located and rode the crests of current waves of thought and thus met the expressed needs of the politically oriented intellectuals of the time"—(Oscar Handlin, in the *N.Y. Times*).

(With Seymour M. Lipset, Eds.) SOCIOLOGY AND HISTORY: Methods. *Basic Bks.* 1968 $7.95 pap. $3.95

THE IDEA OF A PARTY SYSTEM: The Rise of Legitimate Opposition in the United States, 1780–1840. *Univ. of California Press* 1969 $8.95 pap. $2.45

AMERICA AT 1750: A Social History. *Knopf* 1971 $6.95; *Random* Vintage Bks. 1973 pap. $1.95

McNEILL, WILLIAM H(ARDY). 1917–   *See Modern and World History, this Chapter.*

SCHLESINGER, ARTHUR M(EIER), JR. 1917–

"The Age of Jackson" established its author as one of the most challenging of our younger historians. It was awarded the Pulitzer Prize in 1946. After graduating *summa cum laude* from Harvard in 1938, he returned as a Junior Fellow that year and collected the material for his book on Jackson. He was awarded a Guggenheim fellowship to complete his study of the New Deal and received a grant from the American Academy of Arts and Letters for distinguished writing. In 1947 he was appointed an Associate Professor of History at Harvard where his father (*q.v.*) had been Professor of History. The younger Schlesinger has become the chronicler of the Roosevelt era and was closely associated with the Kennedy administration, having served as Special Assistant to the President from 1961 until Kennedy's death. In 1964 he returned briefly to Harvard. With Morton White he edited "Paths of American Thought" which the *Library Journal* calls "the first full-scale effort to synthesize American intellectual history since Parrington's landmark of the 1920's." He now holds the Albert Schweitzer Chair in the Humanities at the City University of New York and has been a vigorous critic of the Vietnam war. In 1967 Professor Schlesinger received the gold medal for his total literary achievement from the National Institute of Arts and Letters.

THE AGE OF JACKSON. *Little* 1945 $10.00 pap. 1963 $3.95

VITAL CENTER. *Houghton* 1949 Sentry Bks. 1962 pap. $2.95

THE AGE OF ROOSEVELT. *Houghton* 3 vols. 1957–60 Vol. 1 The Crisis of the Old Order (1957) Vol. 2 The Coming of the New Deal (1959) Vol. 3 The Politics of Upheaval (1960) each $10.00 pap. Vol. 1 $2.65 Vols. 2–3 each $3.95

THE POLITICS OF HOPE. *Houghton* 1963 $5.00. A compilation taken from essays, articles, speeches, and reviews over a 13 year span.

(With Morton M. White, Eds.) PATHS OF AMERICAN THOUGHT. *Houghton* 1963 $9.00 Sentry Bks. 1970 pap. $3.75

A THOUSAND DAYS: John F. Kennedy in the White House. *Houghton* 1965 $9.00 ltd. ed. $50.00; *Fawcett* 1971 pap. $1.95

Winner of the 1966 National Book Award for History and Biography and the Pulitzer Prize for Biography.

"A remarkable feat of scholarship and writing, set in the widest historical and intellectual frame—and all the more astounding for having been written in something less than 18 months. . . . The chronicle is fresh, vivid and informative, but what the historian has done is to re-create the historical, political and personal context in which the events take place. . . . He has a sure grasp of the party rivalries, factional quarrels, intellectual and policy differences and quirks of personality in which issues and polices were entangled. . . . This is Authur Schlesinger's best book. A great President has found—perhaps he deliberately chose—a great historian"—(James McGregor Burns, in the *N.Y. Times*).

THE BITTER HERITAGE: Vietnam and American Democracy, 1941–1966. 1966. *Fawcett* rev. ed. 1972 pap. $.95

THE CRISIS OF CONFIDENCE: Ideas, Power and Violence in America. *Houghton* 1969 $5.95

"Whether discussing the role and responsibilities of intellectuals, the anarchist impulse in undergraduate extremism or the prospects for politics in the years ahead, Schlesinger is sensitive to the 'crisis of self-confidence' which this country is undergoing and fully aware of the current rash of despair about our political system. But he gives no quarter to those who would reject the process of reason. . . . To no one's surprise, Professor Schlesinger again shows himself to be as much a man of politics as he is a historian"—(John H. Bunzel, in *SR*).

(With F. L. Israel) THE HISTORY OF AMERICAN PRESIDENTIAL ELECTIONS. *McGraw-Hill* 4 vols. 1971 set $150.00

THE COMING TO POWER: Critical Presidential Elections in American History. *McGraw-Hill* 1972 $12.50

THE IMPERIAL PRESIDENCY. *Houghton* 1973 $10.00; *Popular Lib.* 1974 pap. $2.45

"A survey of nearly 200 years of conflict . . . arising from the Constitution's establishment of an inherently unstable division of powers"—(*Newsweek*).

(Ed.) A HISTORY OF U.S. POLITICAL PARTIES. *Bowker* 4 vols. 1973 Vol. 1 1789–1860, From Factions to Parties Vol. 2 1860–1910, The Gilded Age of Politics Vol. 3 1910–1945, From Square Deal to New Deal Vol. 4 1945–1972, The Politics of Change set $135.00

BARNETT, A(RTHUR) DOAK. 1921– *See Modern and World History, this Chapter.*

KAHN, HERMAN. 1922– *See Chapter 8, Social Sciences, this Vol.*

MODERN AND WORLD HISTORY

H. G. Wells in "The Outline of History" revolutionized the writing of history, or at least the reading of history. He presented for the first time history as a rounded whole. He unified the facts collected by others, and the perspective and foreshortening of the composition are his. He had the vision of "One World." He also insisted on the importance of science at a time when historians as well as other writers remained almost totally ignorant of its significance in our history.

The 1970s have witnessed a rapid fragmentation of the fields of historical scholarship and the introduction of methodological refinements new to the writing of history. Recent findings in psychology, statistics, and the behavioral sciences have provided historians with fresh insights into the basic questions of human motivation. Many hitherto neglected topics such as child rearing, social attitudes toward death and dying, work routines, female fertility and family planning now receive the attention of historians trained in the social sciences. We are riding the crest of an avalanche of revisionist books and articles on American and European social history.

Other historians are applying a humanistic and interdisciplinary approach to the study of cultural values and their diffusion and even to the history of technology. It is unfortunate, however, that many of these books and articles now command the interest of only a fraction of academic historians and perhaps of even fewer members of the general public. We have tried to select from this mass of publications books that combine a lively literary style with a rigorous methodological approach.

Chapters in *"The Reader's Adviser"* complementary to this Section, which now includes Archeology (as a contemporary pursuit, though involving ancient cultures), are, in this volume, Chapter 2, General Biography and Autobiography, which covers memoirs and papers of American presidents and American and foreign statesmen; Chapter 3, Bibles and Related Texts (Bible history, early Jewish history, Bible archeology, the Dead Sea Scrolls); Chapter 4, World Religions; Chapter 7, Science; and Chapter 8, The Social Sciences. Chapter 10, The Lively Arts and Communication, illuminates several facets of contemporary Western experience; Chapter 11, Folklore and Humor, includes material on folklore and folksong throughout the world. The table of contents of Volumes 1 and 2 may be used as detailed subject guides.

Reference Books

See also Section on Reference and Important Series at the beginning of this Chapter.

Barnes, Harry Elmer. An Intellectual and Cultural History of the Western World.1941. *Dover* 3 vols. 3rd rev. ed. 1965 Vol. 1 From Earliest Times through the Middle Ages Vol. 2 From the Renaissance through the Eighteenth Century Vol. 3 From the Nineteenth Century to the Present Day pap. each $3.50 set $10.50; *Peter Smith* 3 vols. 3rd rev. ed. each $6.50 set $20.25

Beatty, John L., and Oliver A. Johnson, Eds. Heritage of Western Civilization: Select Readings. *Prentice-Hall* 2 vols. 3rd ed. 1971 each $8.95 pap. each $5.35

Brock, Clifton. The Literature of Political Science: A Guide for Students, Librarians and Teachers. *Bowker* 1969 $11.50

Brown, Everett Somerville. Manual of Government Publications, United States and Foreign. 1950. *Johnson Reprint* 1965 $6.50 *(see also Chapter 1, Reference Books—General: U.S. Government Publications, this Vol.)*

The Cambridge Medieval History. Planned by J. B. Bury; ed. by H. M. Gwatkin, J. P. Whitney, J. R. Tanner, C. W. Previte-Orton, Z. N. Brooke and others. *Cambridge* 8 vols. Vol. 1 The Christian Roman Empire and the Foundation of the Teutonic Kingdoms (1911) $27.50 Vol. 2 The Rise of the Saracens and the Foundation of the Western Empire (1913) $37.50 Vol. 3 Germany and the Western Empire (1922) $26.50 Vol. 4 The Byzantine Empire 2nd ed. in two pts. ed. by J. M. Hussey with the assistance of D. M. Nicol and G. Cowan Pt. 1 Byzantium and Its Neighbours 2nd ed. (1966) $39.00 Pt 2 Government, Church and Civilization 2nd ed. (1966) $23.50 Vol. 5 Contest of Empire and Papacy (1926) $36.00 Vol. 6 Victory of the Papacy (1929) $36.00 Vol. 7 Decline of the Empire and Papacy (1932) $36.00 Vol. 8 The Close of the Middle Ages (1936) $36.00

  Shorter Cambridge Medieval History. *Cambridge* 2 vols. 1953 boxed set $32.50

Cordier, Andrew W., and Wilder Foote, Eds. Public Papers of the Secretaries-General of the United Nations. *Columbia* 4 vols. 1969–74 Vol. 1 Trygve Lie, 1946–1953 (1969) Vol. 2 Dag Hammarskjöld, 1953–1956 (1972) Vol. 3 Dag Hammarskjöld, 1956–1957 (1973) Vol. 4 Dag Hammarskjöld, 1958–1960 (1974) Vol. 1 $20.00 Vols. 2–4 each $22.50

Davies, Herbert A. An Outline History of the World. *Oxford* 5th rev. ed. 1968 $3.50

Demographic Yearbook 1973. Ed. by the United Nations Statistical Office *Int. Pubns. Service* 1973 $38.00 pap. $30.00

Europa Year Book, 1974. *See Chapter 1, Reference Books—General: Year Books, this Vol.*

Foreign Affairs: An American Quarterly Review. *Council on Foreign Relations, Inc.* (58 East 68 Street, New York, N.Y. 10021) annual subscription $10.00. *(For Foreign Affairs Bibliography, see Section at beginning of this Chapter on Reference and Important Series.)*

Fox, Edward W., Ed. Atlas of European History. *Oxford* 1957 pap. $3.95

Harmon, Robert B. POLITICAL SCIENCE: A Bibliographical Guide to the Literature. *Scarecrow Press* first suppl. 1968 $8.50 2nd suppl. 1972 $17.00 3rd suppl. 1974 $12.50

HARPER ENCYCLOPEDIA OF THE MODERN WORLD: A Concise Reference History from 1760 to the Present. Ed. by Richard B. Morris *Harper* 1972 $17.50

HARVARD HISTORICAL MONOGRAPHS. By the Staff of the Department of History, Harvard University. *Harvard Univ. Press* 60 vols. 1932– *(See publisher's catalog for authors, titles, and prices.)*

HISTORY OF THE MODERN WORLD. *Univ. of Michigan Press* 17 vols. in print 1958– each $7.50–$10.00. *(See publisher's catalog for authors and titles.)* A superb series; well written, authoritative, but balanced; individual titles by important scholars.

Israel, Fred L., Ed. MAJOR PEACE TREATIES OF MODERN HISTORY: 1648–1966. Introd. by Arnold J. Toynbee; commentary by Emanuel Chill *McGraw-Hill* 4 vols. 1967 set $132.00. Treaties from the Westphalia Agreement to the 1966 Treaty of Tashkent between India and Pakistan.

KEESING'S CONTEMPORARY ARCHIVES. 1968– *Scribner* 1968– 5 reports: Africa Independent (1975) $10.00; The Arab-Israeli Conflict (1968) pap. $1.75; Disarmament: Negotiations and Treaties, 1946–1971 (1972) $10.00 pap. $3.95; Germany and Eastern Europe since 1945: From the Potsdam Agreement to Chancellor Brandt's "Ostpolitik" (1973) $9.95; Race Relations in the United States (1969) pap. $2.95

Krikler, Bernard, and Walter Laqueur, Eds. A READER'S GUIDE TO CONTEMPORARY HISTORY. *Quadrangle* 1972 $10.00

It "consists of critical essays by leading British experts on ten areas of the world"—*(LJ)*.

McEvedy, Colin. THE PENGUIN ATLAS OF MODERN HISTORY (to 1815). *Penguin* 1972 pap. $2.50

Mallory, Walter H., Ed. POLITICAL HANDBOOK AND ATLAS OF THE WORLD, 1968. *Simon & Schuster* 41st ed. 1968 $10.00

"The news of the day of any country is at once given its political background and significance"—*(N.Y. Times)*.

Muir, Ramsay. MUIR'S HISTORICAL ATLAS: Medieval and Modern. Ed. by Harold Fullard and R. E. Treharne. 1911. *Harper* (Barnes & Noble) 10th ed. new rev. enl. 1964 $9.00

THE NEW CAMBRIDGE MODERN HISTORY. Planned by Sir George Clark and advisory committee *Cambridge* 12 vols. and atlas 1957– each $23.50 set $250.00. *(See publisher's catalog for titles and authors.)*

NEWS DICTIONARY: An Encyclopedic Summary of Contemporary History. *Facts on File* 1964– Vol. 1 (1964) $7.75 pap. $4.45 Vol. 2 (1965) $7.75 pap. $4.45 Vol. 3 (1966) $7.75 pap. $4.45 Vol. 4 (1967) $7.75 pap. $4.45 Vol. 5 (1968) $7.75 pap. $4.45 Vol. 6 (1969) $9.50 pap. $6.75 Vol. 7 (1970) $9.50 pap. $6.75 Vol. 8 (1971) $9.50 pap $6.75 Vol. 9 (1972) $9.50 pap. $6.75 Vol. 10 (1973) $9.50 pap. $6.75 Vol. 11 (1974) $9.50 pap. $6.75

Pearcy, G. Etzel, and Elvyn A. Stoneman. A HANDBOOK OF NEW NATIONS. *T. Y. Crowell* 1968 $8.95

Roach, John, Ed. A BIBLIOGRAPHY OF MODERN HISTORY. *Cambridge* 1968 $10.95. Intended as a companion to the "New Cambridge Modern History" *(see above)* but useful as a separate volume.

Smith, C. T. AN HISTORICAL GEOGRAPHY OF WESTERN EUROPE BEFORE 1800. *Praeger* 1967 $15.00

"Smith has produced a superior text and has made a superlative contribution to geography in general, and to historical geography in particular"—*(Choice)*.

THE STATESMAN'S YEARBOOK. *See Chapter 1, Reference Books—General: Year Books, this Vol.*

THE STATISTICAL HISTORY OF THE UNITED STATES FROM COLONIAL TIMES TO THE PRESENT. *See Chapter 1, Reference Books—General: Dates and Facts, this Vol.*

Stavrianos, Leften. Epic of Modern Man: A Collection of Readings. *Prentice-Hall* 2nd ed. 1971 pap. $5.95

Man's Past and Present: A Global History. *Prentice-Hall* 1971 $8.95 pap. $6.95

Uden, Grant. A Dictionary of Chivalry. *T. Y. Crowell* 1969 $11.95 A delightful and attractive illustrated work by an expert, suitable for adults and older children.

Wager, W. Warren. Books in World History: A Guide for Teachers and Students. *Indiana Univ. Press* 1973 $4.95

Ware, Caroline F., K. M. Panikkar and J. M. Romein. The Twentieth Century. History of Mankind Ser., Vol. 6, sponsored by UNESCO. *Harper* 1967 $18.50

The Western World in the Twentieth Century: A Source Book. Ed. by Bernard W. Wishey, with Columbia University Contemporary Civilization Staff *Columbia* 1961 $12.50

> This new sourcebook is "an important . . . collection of basic documents of our times from as varied hands as those of H. G. Wells, Leon Trotsky, André Malraux, Wendell Willkie, Neville Chamberlain, John Dewey and scores of others"—(*Christian Century*).

Wiener, Philip P., Ed. Dictionary of the History of Ideas. *Scribner* 4 vols. 1973 each $35.00 set $140.00 Index 1974 $35.00

> "A collection of 311 articles by distinguished scholars on the pivotal and recurrent ideas in the development of Western Thought"—(Publisher's note).

The Yearbook of the United Nations 1974. *See Chapter 1, Reference Books—General: Year Books, this Vol.*

The Year Book of World Affairs. *See Chapter 1, Reference Books—General: Year Books, this Vol.*

Yearbook on International Communist Affairs, 1974. Ed. by Richard F. Staar *Hoover Institution* 1974 $25.00

World History—One- and Two-Volume Surveys

Most serious studies of man's history appear in series volumes which allow a necessary depth and scope to any given period or country. "Only H. G. Wells managed, in the compass of one volume," wrote J. H. Plumb in the *N.Y. Times,* "to convey to millions the whole exciting story of mankind. Inaccurate and old-fashioned as his work is, it remains the best in the field." There are, however several more recent one- and two-volume surveys, McNeill's being one of the most remarkable.

Cantor, Norman F. Western Civilization: Its Genesis and Destiny. *Scott, Foresman* 2 vols. 1969 each $13.25 3 vols. 1970 pap. each $7.95. By the Leff Professor of History at Brandeis University.

Garraty, John A., and Peter Gay, Eds. The Columbia History of the World. *Harper* 1972 $20.00

> "An ambitious undertaking which comes off rather well. Forty scholars, all associated with Columbia at the present time or in the recent past, contributed sections to the book based upon their specialties. The editors have successfully endeavored to fuse the work of the 40 into one"—(*Choice*).

Greenwood, Gordon. The Modern World: A History of Our Time. *Verry* 1969 Vol. 1 From Early European Expansion to the Outbreak of World War II $12.00

> "Useful as a college textbook, or as a reference handbook of facts"—(*LJ*).

Hayes, Carlton J. H., and others. A History of Western Civilization. *Macmillan* 2 vols. 1967 Vol. 1 To 1650 $7.95 Vol. 2 Since 1650 $8.50 1-vol. ed. $10.95

Langer, William L., Ed. An Encyclopedia of World History. *Houghton* 5th ed. 1972 $17.50

(With others) Western Civilization. *Harper* 2 vols. 1968 Vol. 1 Paleolithic Man to the Emergence of European Powers Vol. 2 The Struggle for Empire to Europe in the Modern World each $12.95

Lyon, Bryce, Herbert H. Rowan and Theodore S. Hamerow. A HISTORY OF THE WESTERN WORLD. *Rand McNally* 3 vols. 2nd ed. 1974 pap. each $5.95. Begins with Paleolithic man and emphasizes the period from the Fall of the Roman Empire to the present.

McNeill, William H. THE RISE OF THE WEST: A History of the Human Community. *Univ. of Chicago Press* 1963 $9.95 pap. 1970 $4.25

Hailed by Arnold Toynbee (*q.v.*) as "the most lucid presentation of world history in narrative form that I know," this one volume covers western civilization in 829 hard packed pages and won the 1963 National Book Award for History.

THE SHAPE OF EUROPEAN HISTORY. *Oxford* 1974 $7.50. An overall interpretive scheme for European history—both for scholars and for the general public.

A WORLD HISTORY. *Oxford* 1967 2nd ed. 1971 $15.00 pap. $6.95. A readable one-volume survey of Western history including an introduction to Asian history. *(For further comment see his main entry, this Section.)*

Major, James Russell. AGE OF THE RENAISSANCE AND REFORMATION: A Short History. *Lippincott* 1970 pap. $5.50

(With others) CIVILIZATION IN THE WESTERN WORLD. *Lippincott* 2 vols. 2nd ed. pap. 1971 Vol. 1 Ancient Times to 1715 Vol. 2 1715 to the Present each $7.95 also in 3-vol. ed. Vol. 1 $6.45 Vols. 2–3 each $6.95

Palmer, Robert R., and Joel Colton. A HISTORY OF THE MODERN WORLD. *Knopf* 1950 4th rev. ed. 1971 $16.95. A review of Western civilization from the Renaissance to modern times.

Spengler, Oswald. THE DECLINE OF THE WEST. *Knopf* 2 vols. 1945 set $22.50. A most influential history. *(For further comment see his main entry, this Section.)*

Toynbee, Arnold Joseph. A STUDY OF HISTORY. *Oxford* abr. ed. of Vols. 1–10 in 2 vols. ed. by D. C. Somervell Vols. 1–6 1947 $8.50 Vols. 7–10 1957 $7.50; *Dell* abr. ed. 2 vols. pap. boxed set $2.95

See also his main entry, this Section.

Wallbank, T. Walter, and Alastair M. Taylor. CIVILIZATION: Past and Present. *Scott, Foresman* 2 vols. 6th ed. 1969 each $12.95 3 vols 1970 pap. each $7.75; 1-vol. ed. 1971 $15.25

Wells, H(erbert) G(eorge). THE OUTLINE OF HISTORY. 1920. Rev. and brought up to the end of the Second World War by Raymond Postgate with maps and plans by J. F. Horrabin *Doubleday* new rev. ed. 1971 $9.95

See also his main entry, this Section.

Supplementary Reading List on Modern and World History

This miscellaneous list includes books on general world problems. The titles are in the main new within the last few years, although some older standard titles and Pulitzer Prize winners are included. No attempt has been made to present an exhaustive list, only one that will fill some of the gaps left by the nine selected lists that follow. The subjects and books included in the Modern and World History Section as a whole do represent a slight increase over those covered in our last edition.

Bell, Daniel, Ed. TOWARD THE YEAR 2000: Work in Progress. *Houghton* 1968 $7.95; *Beacon* 1969 pap. $3.95

"With the exception of a paper on violence, this book is a reprint of the summer 1967 issue of *Daedalus*. The papers are tentative and highly speculative, being the first of the Commission on the Year 2000 which was established by the American Academy of Arts and Sciences. The purpose of this work is to bring to the attention of the reader what the Commission has done, its present position, and what it intends to do in the future. It is hoped that this work will serve as a guide to alternative possible futures rather than as a prediction of what is to come. Among the more specific topics dealt with are education, meritocracy, political development, forecasting, violence, youth, privacy, urban development, communications, and democracy. The ideas set forth deserve the consideration of all those interested in shaping the future"—(*LJ*).

Bishop, Morris. THE HORIZON BOOK OF THE MIDDLE AGES. *American Heritage* (dist. by Houghton) 1968 $22.50 de luxe ed. $25.50; (with title "The Middle Ages") abr. and rev. ed. *McGraw-Hill* 1970 $6.95 pap. $2.95

Bowsky, William M., Ed. STUDIES IN MEDIEVAL AND RENAISSANCE HISTORY. *Univ. of Nebraska Press* 10 vols. 1964–1974 Vol. 1 $9.50 Vols. 3–5 each $8.95 Vol. 10 $12.00 Vols. 2, 6–9 o.p.

Cantor, Norman F., Ed. PERSPECTIVES ON THE EUROPEAN PAST: Conversations with Historians. *Macmillan* 1971 $11.95 pap. 2 vols. each $4.95

Clough, Shepard B., and Salvatore Saladino, Eds. A HISTORY OF MODERN ITALY: Documents, Readings and Commentary. *Columbia* 1968 $15.00. Italy in the 19th and 20th centuries.

Evans, Joan, Ed. THE FLOWERING OF THE MIDDLE AGES. *McGraw-Hill* 1966 $34.50

> A "handsome and engaging work" consisting of "essays by nine scholars [that] stress the social, domestic and intellectual achievements of the time rather than the rise and fall of kings and the establishment of empires [with illustrations] so enticing that the reader has to have a will of iron to stay with the text"—(Thomas Lask, in the *N.Y. Times*).

Geiger, Theodore. THE CONFLICTED RELATIONSHIP: The West and the Transformation of Asia, Africa and Latin America. The Atlantic Policy Studies Ser. *McGraw-Hill* 1967 $7.95 pap. $3.95

Gies, Joseph. CRISIS 1918. *Norton* 1974 $7.95

> The author "focuses on the climactic turning point of World War I, namely the little-appreciated events of 1918"—(Publisher's note).

(With Frances Gies) LIFE IN A MEDIEVAL CASTLE. *T. Y. Crowell* 1974 $7.95

Goetzmann, William H. EXPLORATION AND EMPIRE: The Explorer and the Scientist in the Winning of the American West. *Knopf* 1966 $12.50; *Random* Vintage Bks. 1972 pap. $3.95. Winner of the Pulitzer Prize in history, 1967.

Gramont, Sanche de. EPITAPH FOR KINGS. *Putnam* 1968 $6.95; *Dell* 1969 pap. $2.65

> "An engrossing narrative" (*SR*) about the reign of the last three Bourbon kings before the French Revolution.

Halle, Louis J. THE SOCIETY OF MAN. 1965. *Dell* Delta Bks. pap. $1.95

> The conflict between the individual and society set in its historical perspective, with commentary on prospects for the future. A "stimulating and provocative" study—(*LJ*).

Heilbroner, Robert L. THE FUTURE AS HISTORY: The Historic Currents of Our Time and the Direction in Which They are Taking America. *Harper* 1960 $5.95 Torchbks. pap. $1.60. An objective survey of economics and history to help in formulating an assessment of the future.

Horowitz, Irving Louis. THREE WORLDS OF DEVELOPMENT: The Theory and Practice of International Stratification. *Oxford* 1966 2nd ed. 1972 $15.00 pap. $3.95

> "A major work on international development"—(*LJ*). Mr. Horowitz analyzes the U.S. as the first world, the U.S.S.R. and its satellites as the second and the Developing Nations as the third world.

Hudson, G. F. THE HARD AND BITTER PEACE: World Politics since 1945. *Praeger* 1967 pap. $2.95

Jenkins, Romilly. BYZANTIUM: The Imperial Centuries, A.D. 610–1071. *Random* 1967 $15.00 Vintage Bks. 1969 pap. $2.45

> This account of Byzantium at the height of its power, "is authoritative, exceptionally clear, and very readable, and because chronological histories of this period are relatively few, this book is recommended for most libraries"—(*LJ*).

Kahn, Herman, and Anthony J. Wiener. THE YEAR 2000: A Framework for Speculation on the Next Thirty-Three Years. Introd. by Daniel Bell *Macmillan* 1967 $9.95

> "An intelligent, imaginative, and plausible, though not cheerful, book. Starting from where we are, and weighing present trends as best they can, the Messrs. Kahn and Wiener attempt, first, to suggest 'surprise-free' possibilities for the rest of this century"—(*New Yorker*).

Lach, Donald F. ASIA IN THE MAKING OF EUROPE. *Univ. of Chicago Press* 2 vols. 1965 Vol. 1 in 2 pts. The Century of Discovery set $29.50 Vol. 2 Century of Wonder, Bk. 1 The Visual Arts $13.75

Leiden, Carl, and Karl M. Schmitt. THE POLITICS OF VIOLENCE: Revolution in the Modern World. *Prentice-Hall* Spectrum Bks. 1968 pap. $2.95. Four studies of modern revolutions: the Mexican, Turkish, Egyptian and Cuban.

McNeill, William H. THE CONTEMPORARY WORLD: 1914/Present. *Morrow* 1968 $7.00; *Scott, Foresman* 1967 $6.50 pap. 1975 $3.75. An interpretative account of cultural and social developments such as urbanization, war mobilization and peacetime defense planning. Biographical essays on important men of the 20th century are included.

Mair, Lucy. NEW NATIONS. *Univ. of Chicago Press* 1963 $8.50

Mazlish, Bruce, A. D. Kaledin and D. B. Ralston, Eds. REVOLUTION: A Reader. *Macmillan* 1971 pap. $5.95

Palmer, Robert R. THE AGE OF DEMOCRATIC REVOLUTION: A Political History of Europe and America, 1760–1800. *Princeton Univ. Press* 2 vols. 1969–1970 Vol. 1 The Challenge Vol. 2 The Struggle each $15.00 pap. each $3.45

TWELVE WHO RULED: The Year of the Terror in the French Revolution. *Princeton Univ. Press* 1941 $10.00 pap. $2.95

(With Joel Colton) HISTORY OF THE MODERN WORLD. *Knopf* 1950 4th ed. 1971 $12.95

Power, Eileen. MEDIEVAL PEOPLE. *Harper* (Barnes & Noble) 10th rev. and enl. ed. 1963 $6.00 pap. $2.95; *Peter Smith* $4.50. One of the most popular social histories of the Middle Ages.

Rowbotham, Sheila. HIDDEN FROM HISTORY: Rediscovering Women in History from the 17th Century to the Present. *Pantheon* 1975 $7.95

Sanderson, Michael. SEA BATTLES: A Reference Guide. *Wesleyan Univ. Press* 1974 $9.95
"A concise account of the principal sea battles of history from the Graeco-Persian Wars in 499–448 B.C. to the end of the Second World War"—(Publisher's note).

Setton, Kenneth M., Gen. Ed. A HISTORY OF THE CRUSADES. *Univ. of Wisconsin Press* 3 vols. 2nd ed. 1969 Vol. 1 The First Hundred Years ed. by Marshall W. Baldwin Vol. 2 The Later Crusades ed. by Robert Lee Wolff and Harry W. Hazard Vol. 3 The Fourteenth and Fifteenth Centuries ed. by Harry W. Hazard each $25.00

Smith, Preserved. A HISTORY OF MODERN CULTURE. 1930. *Macmillan* Collier Bks. 2 vols. Vol. 1 Origins of Modern Culture, 1543–1687 Vol. 2 Enlightenment, 1687–1776 Vol. 1 o.p. Vol. 2 pap. $1.95; *Peter Smith* 2 vols. set $15.00

Thomas, Hugh. SUEZ. *Harper* 1967 $5.95 pap. 1969 $2.45. An account of the Suez Canal crisis of 1956.

Weill, Herman N., Ed. EUROPEAN DIPLOMATIC HISTORY, 1815–1914: Documents and Interpretations. *Exposition Press* 1973 $15.00

Wright, Quincy. A STUDY OF WAR. *Univ. of Chicago Press* 1942 2nd ed. 1965 $32.50 abr. ed. by Louise Leonard Wright 1964 $12.00 Phoenix Bks. pap. $3.45. Updated by a chapter on war since 1942.

Nine Selected Reading Lists

Contemporary Government and Politics

This listing is concerned largely with ideologies of the modern world—communism, fascism, anarchism and democracy. An interesting series is that of *Harvard Univ. Press* on Comparative Government. *(For other books on communism and its origins, see the listing on Russian History and Soviet Policy; see also the main entries for Marx and Engels in Chapter 8, The Social Sciences, this Vol.)*

Beer, Samuel, Adam B. Ulam, Nicholas Wahl, Harry Eckstein and Herbert J. Spiro.
PATTERNS OF GOVERNMENT: The Major Political Systems of Europe. *Random* 3rd ed.
1972 $10.95

Black, Cyril E. THE DYNAMICS OF MODERNIZATION: A Study in Comparative History.
Harper 1966 Torchbks. 1968 pap. $1.60

> "One of the shortest books . . . on political and social change, both in the developed and in the
> developing countries, and it is the best"—(*N.Y. Times*).

Braham, Randolph L., Ed. DOCUMENTS OF MAJOR EUROPEAN GOVERNMENTS. *Philadelphia
Book Co.* 1972 pap. $2.95

Bromke, Adam, and Philip Uren, Eds. THE COMMUNIST STATES AND THE WEST. *Praeger*
1967 $8.50

> This collection of 12 essays, originally given as lectures at Carleton University in 1965–1966,
> "describes and evaluates changes in the Communist world in terms of East-West relations"—(*LJ*).

Calvert, Peter. REVOLUTION. *Praeger* 1970 $5.00

> This book provides an "outline of the origin and development of revolution as a concept and
> analyzes how the concept is variously applied in present-day political usage"—(Publisher's note).

Cassels, Alan. THE TWO FACES OF FASCISM. *T. Y. Crowell* 1974 $5.75. Traces the devel-
opment of Fascism from Mussolini's Italy to the end of World War II.

Epstein, Leon D. POLITICAL PARTIES IN WESTERN DEMOCRACIES. *Praeger* 1967 pap. $3.95

> A professor of the University of Wisconsin "fully satisfies the need for a comparative study"—
> (*LJ*).

Gellhorn, Walter. OMBUDSMEN AND OTHERS: Citizens' Protectors in Nine Countries.
Harvard Univ. Press 1966 $11.50. The distinguished Columbia professor of law and
political science compares the roles of ombudsmen in Sweden, Norway, Finland,
Denmark, New Zealand, Poland, Yugoslavia, the U.S.S.R. and Japan.

Grimke, Frederick. THE NATURE AND TENDENCY OF FREE INSTITUTIONS. Ed. by John
William Ward. *Harvard Univ. Press* 1968 $15.00. First published in 1848, this
examines America's political institutions as they appeared to the author in the era of
James Polk.

Kohn, Hans. POLITICAL IDEOLOGIES OF THE TWENTIETH CENTURY. *Harper* Torchbks. 1966
pap. $1.95; *Peter Smith* 3rd ed. $4.00

Laidler, Harry W. HISTORY OF SOCIALISM. *Apollo* 1968 pap. $3.95

Laski, Harold J. A GRAMMAR OF POLITICS. *Humanities Press* 5th ed. 1967 pap. $8.00

Lichtheim, George. MARXISM: An Historical and Critical Study. *Praeger* 2nd ed. 1964
$10.00 pap. $4.25

Lipset, Seymour Martin. REVOLUTION AND COUNTER-REVOLUTION: Changes and Persistence in Social Structures. *Doubleday* Anchor Bks. 1970 pap. $1.95. A collection of
11 essays previously published in periodicals.

Macridis, Roy C., and Robert E. Ward. MODERN POLITICAL SYSTEMS: Europe. *Prentice-Hall*
3rd ed. 1972 $12.50

Migdal, Joel S. PEASANTS, POLITICS, AND REVOLUTION: Pressures toward Political and
Social Change in the Third World. *Princeton Univ. Press* 1974 $15.00

Morgenthau, Hans J. POLITICS AMONG NATIONS. *Knopf* 5th ed. 1974 $12.95 text ed.
$10.95

Nolte, Ernst. THREE FACES OF FASCISM: Action Française, Italian Fascism and National
Socialism. Trans. from the German by Leila Vennewitz *Holt* 1966 $7.95; *New Am Lib.*
Mentor Bks. 1969 pap. $1.95

> "An important work"—(*LJ*).

Robertson, Charles L. INTERNATIONAL POLITICS SINCE WORLD WAR II: A Short History.
Wiley 1966 pap. $6.25

Rubinstein, Alvin Z. THE SOVIETS IN INTERNATIONAL ORGANIZATIONS: Changing Policies toward Developing Countries. Fwd. by Philip E. Jacob *Princeton Univ. Press* 1964 $12.50. A study of post-Stalin Soviet policies in regional agencies and economic commissions of the UN; prepared in a special research program at the University of Pennsylvania.

Rush, Myron. HOW COMMUNIST STATES CHANGE THEIR RULERS. *Cornell Univ. Press* 1974 $15.00

> Rush analyzes "13 instances of leadership change in the Soviet bloc of Eastern European nations"—(*Booklist*).

Snyder, Louis L. THE NEW NATIONALISM. *Cornell Univ. Press* 1968 $12.50

Spanier, John. WORLD POLITICS IN AN AGE OF REVOLUTION. *Praeger* 1967 $8.50 pap. $4.95

Triska, Jan F., Ed. CONSTITUTIONS OF THE COMMUNIST PARTY-STATES. *Hoover Institution* 1968 $12.50. Contains the texts of the constitutional documents of the Soviet Union, China, Albania, Bulgaria, Hungary, North Vietnam, East Germany, North Korea, Cuba, Mongolia, Poland, Rumania, Czechoslovakia and Yugoslavia.

Vital, David. THE SURVIVAL OF SMALL STATES: Studies in Small Power—Great Power Conflict. *Oxford* 1972 $7.00

> "Prof. Vital, who teaches at an Israeli university, examines three cases of overt military/political conflict, Czechoslovakia in 1938 . . . the Israeli-Soviet confrontation . . . and Finland vs. Russia"— (*LJ*).

Walter, Eugene V. TERROR AND RESISTANCE: A Study of Political Violence. *Oxford* 1972 pap. $2.95

Wiskemann, Elizabeth. EUROPE OF THE DICTATORS, 1919–1945. *Harper* 1966 Torchbks. pap. $2.25

Wolfe, Bertram D. MARXISM: One Hundred Years in the Life of a Doctrine. *Dial* 1964 $7.50

The Modern World at War

"In reviewing the war systems of the past and describing the present predicament in which we all shudder, . . . it is gruesome to think about these matters. Not to think about them is criminally negligent"—(Orville Prescott, in the *N.Y. Times*). There are an increasing number of books on the two World Wars. Now that we have entered the atomic and space age and contemplate the possibility of World War III—"humanity faces a clear cut choice between demilitarization and destruction"—(Walter Millis and James Real in "The Abolition of War"). A moving title, recently published, which is the antithesis of the events described in this listing is Mark Twain's "The War Prayer" (ill. by John Groth *Harper* 1968 $6.95 pap. 1971 $1.50). *Library Journal* wrote of it: "Unpublished during Twain's life and never separately until now, the devastating *War Prayer* will never seem more timely; its irony and wit, never sharper. John Groth's moving illustrations, the beautiful typography, and the handsome binding are a triumph of design and bookmaking—a rare feat in recent publishing."

Ambrose, Stephen E. THE SUPREME COMMANDER: The War Years of General Dwight D. Eisenhower. Ed. by Sam Vaughan *Doubleday* 1970 $10.00

> "This well written volume includes excellent discussion of such subjects as negotiations with Admiral Darlan, De Gaulle, and the decision not to strike for Berlin"—(*Choice*).

Baldwin, Hanson W. WORLD WAR I: An Outline History. *Harper* 1962 $5.95

> This long-needed history is "compact, concise, authoritative, extremely readable and eminently suitable for adult and young adult collections and will be useful in most academic libraries. . . . It shows extensive research and is well documented"—(*LJ*).

BATTLES LOST AND WON: Great Campaigns of World War II. *Harper* 1966 $10.00; *Avon Bks.* 1967 pap. $1.25

Bekker, Cajus. THE GERMAN NAVY, 1939–1945. *Dial* 1975 $12.50

THE LUFTWAFFE WAR DIARIES. Trans. from the German and ed. by Frank Ziegler 1968. *Ballantine Bks.* 1975 pap. $1.95

Blair, Clay, Jr. SILENT VICTORY: The U.S. Submarine War against Japan. *Lippincott* 1975 $24.95

Blair presents "in very readable form the exciting story of the innovative and silent warriors who very nearly blockaded Japan into surrender in a total war at sea 1941–1945"—(*LJ*).

Blumenson, Martin. THE PATTON PAPERS. *Houghton* 2 vols. 1972–1974 Vol. I 1885–1940 (1972) $17.50 Vol. 2 1940–1945 (1974) $20.00

Buchanan, A. Russell, Ed. THE UNITED STATES AND WORLD WAR II. Ed. by Henry Steele Commager and Richard B. Morris. New American Nation Ser. *Harper* 2 vols. 1964 each $10.00 Torchbks. 1973 pap. $4.95; *Univ. of South Carolina Press* 1972 $9.95

Calder, Nigel, Ed. UNLESS PEACE COMES: A Scientific Forecast of New Weapons. *Viking* 1968 $5.75 Compass Bks. pap. $1.95

Clarke, Robin. THE SCIENCE OF WAR AND PEACE. *McGraw-Hill* 1972 $10.00

THE SILENT WEAPONS: The Realities of Chemical and Biological Warfare. *McKay* 1968 $4.95

Coffman, Edward M. THE WAR TO END ALL WARS: The American Military Experience in World War I. *Oxford* 1968 $12.50

Collier, Basil. A HISTORY OF AIR POWER. *Macmillan* 1974 $10.95

THE LION AND THE EAGLE: British and Anglo American Strategy. *Putnam* 1972 $12.95 Capricorn Giant 1973 pap. $3.50

THE SECOND WORLD WAR: A Military History from Munich to Hiroshima. 1967. *Peter Smith* $7.00

THE WAR IN THE FAR EAST, 1941–1945. *Morrow* 1969 $8.95

Craig, William. ENEMY AT THE GATES: The Battle for Stalingrad. *Reader's Digest Press* (dist. by Dutton) 1973 $10.95; *Ballantine Bks.* 1974 pap. $1.95

"Craig spent five years interviewing survivors of the battle—Germans, Russians, Italians, Rumanians, Austrians, and Hungarians—as well as studying documents, letters, monographs from both sides of the struggle. . . . [He] has brought us a vivid and detailed account of this titanic struggle"—(*Choice*).

Craven, Wesley F., and James L. Cate, Eds. ARMY AIR FORCES IN WORLD WAR II. *Univ. of Chicago Press* 7 vols. 1949–1958 each $15.75

Davidson, Eugene. THE TRIAL OF THE GERMANS. *Macmillan* 1966 $12.50 Collier Bks. 1972 pap. $3.95. Discussion of the war-crimes trials at Nuremberg, with a number of biographical essays on the accused Nazi officials.

Deutsch, Harold C. THE CONSPIRACY AGAINST HITLER IN THE TWILIGHT WAR. *Univ. of Minnesota Press* 1968 $10.00 pap. $3.45

"A magnificent detailed study" (*LJ*) of a 1940 effort—abortive, needless to say.

HITLER AND HIS GENERALS: The Hidden Crisis, January–June 1938. *Univ. of Minnesota Press* 1974 $15.00

Eisenhower, Dwight D. *See his main entry in Chapter 2, General Biography and Autobiography, this Vol.*

Eisenhower, John S. THE BITTER WOODS: A Comprehensive Study of the War in Europe. *Putnam* 1969 $10.00; *Ace Bks.* 1970 pap. $1.95

A study of the German and Allied commands during the European campaign of World War II with emphasis on the Battle of the Bulge. "With an amazing—I almost said overwhelming—grasp of detail, John Eisenhower, a West Pointer and former professional Army officer, tells us what was happening everywhere, at almost every level, within the German as well as the Allied lines"—(Charles Poore, in the *N.Y. Times*).

Feis, Herbert. THE ATOMIC BOMB AND THE END OF WORLD WAR II. *Princeton Univ. Press* rev. ed. 1966 $9.50 pap. $2.95

CHURCHILL, ROOSEVELT, STALIN: The War They Waged and the Peace They Sought. *Princeton Univ. Press* 2nd ed. 1967 $15.00 pap. $3.95

THE ROAD TO PEARL HARBOR. *Princeton Univ. Press* 1950 $12.50 pap. $2.95

Fischer, Fritz. GERMANY'S AIMS IN THE FIRST WORLD WAR. *Norton* 1967 $15.00 pap. $4.50

WAR OF ILLUSIONS: German Policies from 1911 to 1914. Trans. from the German by Marion Jackson *Norton* 1974 $18.95

WORLD POWER OR DECLINE: The Controversy over Germany's Aims in the First World War. Trans. from the German by Lancelot L. Farrar and others *Norton* 1974 $6.95 pap. $1.95

Freidel, Frank. OVER THERE: The Story of America's First Great Overseas Crusade. *Little* 1964 $12.50

Gallagher, Thomas. ASSAULT IN NORWAY: Sabotaging the Nazi Nuclear Bomb. *Harcourt* 1975 $7.50

"An exciting and dramatic episode"—*(LJ)*.

George, Alexander L. THE CHINESE COMMUNIST ARMY IN ACTION: The Korean War. *Columbia* 1969 $10.00

Greenfield, Kent Roberts. AMERICAN STRATEGY IN WORLD WAR II: A Reconsideration. *Johns Hopkins Press* 1963 pap. $2.25

Grunberger, Richard. HITLER'S SS. *Delacorte* 1971 $4.50; *Dell* 1972 pap. $.75

TWELVE-YEAR REICH: A Social History of Nazi Germany, 1933–1945. *Holt* 1971 $10.00

This account of Nazi Germany "showing how Germans lived, worked, relaxed, and regarded themselves and others between 1933 and 1945 [covers such] subjects as education, business, sports, the arts, beauty (no make-up, no dieting), family life in a society where fathers could inform on sons, children on parents"—(Publisher's note).

Hersh, Seymour M. CHEMICAL AND BIOLOGICAL WARFARE: America's Hidden Arsenal. 1968. *Doubleday* Anchor Bks. 1969 pap. $1.95

This is a detailed study and an "admirable" one, "but, of course, no explanation is offered as to why this devilish business must be pursued when a thousand nuclear-tipped missiles stand ready to transform the Soviet Union into one smoking crater"—(Daniel S. Greenberg, in the *N.Y. Times*).

Hitler, Adolf. *See his main entry, this Section.*

James, D. Clayton. THE YEARS OF MACARTHUR: Vol. 1 1880–1941. *Houghton* 1970 $12.50

Jones, James. WORLD WAR II. *Grosset* 1975 $25.00

"There may be more comprehensive illustrated histories of the war, but none is likely to come closer than *World War II* to conveying the feeling of how it was to be there"—*(Time)*.

Kennan, George F. *See his main entry, this Section.*

Kennedy, Ludovic H. PURSUIT: The Chase and Sinking of the Bismarck. *Viking* 1974 $10.00

"The engrossing drama behind the Royal Navy's relentless pursuit of the Bismarck after the German battleship sank the British cruiser Hood in 1941"—*(Booklist)*.

Korbonski, Stefan. FIGHTING WARSAW: The Story of the Polish Underground State, 1939–1945. Trans. by F. B. Czarnomski *T. Y. Crowell* (Funk & Wagnalls) 1968 $6.00 pap. $2.95

Lamont, Lansing. DAY OF TRINITY. *Atheneum* 1965 $6.95

"Human interest reporting of the production and explosion of the first atom bomb"—(ALA).

Landis, Arthur H. THE ABRAHAM LINCOLN BRIGADE: A History of the American Volunteers in the Spanish Civil War. *Citadel Press* 1968 $10.00 pap. $2.95

Lewin, Ronald. MONTGOMERY AS MILITARY COMMANDER. *Stein & Day* 1971 $10.00

ROMMEL AS MILITARY COMMANDER. *Van Nostrand-Reinhold* 1968 $8.95

WAR ON LAND: The British Army in World War II. *Morrow* 1970 $8.95

Liddell Hart, Sir Basil H. HISTORY OF THE SECOND WORLD WAR. *Putnam* 1971 $14.50 Capricorn Giant 2 vols. pap. 1972 Vol. 1 $4.50 Vol. 2 $4.00

"This is a military history on a grand scale . . . Liddell Hart is in command of his material; he is able to sketch an entire campaign in a few paragraphs"—(*LJ*).

THE REAL WAR: 1914–1918. *Little-Atlantic* 1930 pap. 1964 $2.65. A reissue of "*the* most valuable short history of World War I."

Lindbergh, Charles A. THE WARTIME JOURNALS. *Harcourt* 1970 $12.95. (*For comment, see his main entry in Chapter 12, Travel and Adventure, this Vol.*)

McCarthy, Mary. THE SEVENTEENTH DEGREE: How It Went; Vietnam, Hanoi, Medina; Sons of the Morning. *Harcourt* 1974 $7.95. Three of her war-protest pamphlets plus a long autobiographical essay and a critique of David Halberstam's book "The Best and the Brightest."

Macksey, Kenneth J. ANATOMY OF A BATTLE. *Stein & Day* 1974 $8.95

"An authority on modern warfare dissects a single major military encounter—the battle of Normandy, 1944"—(*Booklist*).

Marshall, S. L. A. FIELDS OF BAMBOO: Dongtre, Trung Luong and Hoa Hoi, Three Battles Just Beyond the South China Sea. *Dial* 1971 $6.95

WORLD WAR I. 1964. *McGraw-Hill* 1971 pap. $3.95

May, Ernest R. COMING OF WAR, 1917. Berkeley Readings in American History Ser. Vol. 11. *Rand McNally* 1963 pap. $1.50

WAR, BOOM AND BUST. Life History of the U.S. Ser. Vol. 10. *Time-Life* 1974 $5.95

WORLD WAR AND AMERICAN ISOLATION, 1914–1917. 1959. *Quadrangle-N.Y. Times* 1966 pap. $2.95

Michel, Henri. THE SECOND WORLD WAR. Trans. by Douglas Parmee *Praeger* 1974 $25.00
"Essential for serious libraries"—(*LJ*).

Miller, Marshall Lee. BULGARIA DURING THE SECOND WORLD WAR. *Stanford Univ. Press* 1975 $10.95

Moorehead, Alan. THE MARCH TO TUNIS: The North African War, 1940–1943. *Harper* 1967 $8.50. (*For comment, see his main entry in Chapter 12, Travel and Adventure, this Vol.*)

Morison, Samuel Eliot. THE TWO-OCEAN WAR: A Short History of the United States Navy in the Second World War. *Little-Atlantic* 1963 $15.00; *Ballantine Bks.* pap. $1.95

See also his main entry in Section on American History, this Chapter.

Mosley, Leonard. THE REICH MARSHAL: A Biography of Hermann Goering. *Doubleday* 1974 $12.50

"The book is valuable for it utilizes to good advantage firsthand information and reminiscences from Goering's second wife, his stepson, and many of his close associates"—(*LJ*).

Mydans, Carl, and Shelley Mydans. THE VIOLENT PEACE: A Report on Wars in the Postwar World. *Atheneum* 1968 $12.50. Some 25 eyewitness accounts by correspondents in the Korean war, the Cuban revolution, the Indian border wars, Hungary, Vietnam, etc. bear out the Mydans' contention that the years since the end of World War II have been a "violent peace."

Pavlov, Dmitri V. LENINGRAD 1941: The Blockade. Trans. from the Russian by John Clinton Adams; fwd. by Harrison E. Salisbury *Univ. of Chicago Press* 1965 $7.50

Pogue, Forrest C. GEORGE C. MARSHALL. *Viking* 3 vols. 1963–1973 Vol. 1 Education of a General, 1889–1939 ed. by Gordon Harrison (1963) $10.00 Vol. 2 Ordeal and Hope, 1939–1943 (1966) $12.50 Vol. 3 Organizer of Victory, 1943–1945 (1973) $15.00

Rees, David. KOREA: The Limited War. *Penguin* 1970 pap. $2.45

Ridgway, Matthew B. THE KOREAN WAR. *Doubleday* 1967 $7.95

Rommel, Erwin. THE ROMMEL PAPERS. Ed. by B. H. Liddell Hart *Harcourt* 1953 $14.00. The personal memoirs of one of the most fascinating generals of World War II.

Rose, Steven, Ed. CBW: Chemical and Biological Warfare. *Beacon* 1969 pap. $1.95. Papers presented at a 1968 London conference of international lawyers, scientists and other scholars exploring means for its control.

Ryan, Cornelius. A Bridge Too Far. *Simon & Schuster* 1974 $12.50. The story of the World War II battle for the bridge at Arnhem.

Schmidt, Dana. Armageddon in the Middle East. Ed. by Theodore M. Bernstein. N.Y. Times Survey Ser. *John Day* 1974 $8.95

Shirer, William L. The Rise and Fall of the Third Reich: A History of Nazi Germany. *Simon & Schuster* 1960 $12.50 Touchstone-Clarion Bks. pap. $5.95; *Fawcett* Crest Bks. 1972 pap. $1.95

Smith, Jean Edward. The Defense of Berlin. *Johns Hopkins Press* 1963 $14.00

"This history and analysis of the political and military decisions made from 1941 to May 1962 which led to the present, unresolved situation in Berlin quotes frequently from documents and reports and includes the author's own personal observations and interviews in America and Europe. . . . Not everyone will agree with some conclusions and implications, but this well-written book should be in all college and medium-sized and large public libraries"—(*LJ*).

(Ed.) The Papers of General Lucius D. Clay: Germany 1945–1949. *Indiana Univ. Press* 2 vols. 1974 $35.00

Snyder, Louis L., Ed. Masterpieces of War Reporting: The Great Moments of World War II. *Simon & Schuster* 1962 $10.00. Reports by more than 140 combat correspondents who were there when the battles were fought or the cities were bombed or occupied; well-known names include William L. Shirer, Ernie Pyle, Irwin Shaw, and John Mason Brown.

Stallings, Laurence, Ed. The First World War. 1933. *Simon & Schuster* 1962 $7.50. This reissue of the First World War classic edited by the author of "What Price Glory" now contains more than 500 photographs with captions by Mr. Stallings.

Stein, George H. The Waffen SS: Hitler's Elite Guard at War, 1939–1945. *Cornell Univ. Press* 1966 $12.50

Sulzberger, C. L. The American Heritage Picture History of World War II. Ed. by David G. McCullough; pictorial commentary by Ralph K. Andrist *Simon & Schuster* 1966 $20.00 deluxe ed. $25.00; (with title "World War II") *McGraw-Hill* 1970 $20.00 deluxe ed. $25.00 abr. ed. $6.95 pap. $2.95

The Coldest War: The Russian Game in China. *Harcourt* 1974 $5.95

Taylor, A. J. P. The First World War: An Illustrated History. *Putnam* Capricorn Bks. 1972 pap. $2.95; *Peter Smith* $5.00

See also his main entry, this Section.

Taylor, Telford. The Breaking Wave: The Second World War in the Summer of 1940. *Simon & Schuster* 1967 $10.00

Germany's strategy after the fall of France. "A magnificently revealing and indispensable contribution to our age's story"—(Charles Poore, in the *N.Y. Times*).

Toland, John. Battle: The Story of the Bulge. *Random* 1959 $8.95

The Last 100 Days. *Random* 1966 $10.00; *Bantam* 1970 pap. $1.65

This description of the end of World War II "should join Shirer's 'Rise and Fall of the Third Reich' and Werth's 'Russia at War' . . . on the shelves"—(*Choice*).

The Rising Sun: The Decline and Fall of the Japanese Empire, 1936–45. *Random* 1970 $12.95

Tunney, Christopher. A Biographical Dictionary of World War II. *St. Martin's* 1973 $8.95. Includes over 400 individuals who in some way made noteworthy contributions to the prosecution of the war.

United States Army in World War II Series. *U.S. Army Dept., Office of the Chief of Military History*, Washington, D.C. (*Consult publisher for authors, titles and prices.*) Many vols. by different authors in series and subseries of this official history; the standard of scholarship is high.

Watt, David Cameron. Too Serious a Business: European Armed Forces and the Approach of the Second World War. *Univ. of California Press* 1975 $8.50

"In what were originally six lectures, Watt considers the role of the professional soldier in interwar Europe"—(*LJ*).

Weigley, Russell F. The American Way of War: A History of U.S. Military Strategy and Policy. *Macmillan* 1973 $12.95

History of the United States Army. *Macmillan* 1967 $12.95

Militarism. *Schenkman* 1974 $11.25 pap. $5.95

Towards an American Army: Military Thought from Washington to Marshall. 1962. *Greenwood* 1974 $13.75

America's leaders have always been torn between creating a professional army and an army of civilian soldiers. This study, which traces the controversy from 1776 to 1951, is "carefully documented, and an excellent bibliography is provided as a guide to further study. For college and university libraries, large public libraries, and libraries with large collections on military science"—(*LJ*).

Weingartner, James J. Hitler's Guard: The Story of the *Leibstandarte* S.S. Adolf Hitler, 1933–1945. *Southern Illinois Univ. Press* 1974 $8.95

"A military history of Hitler's special S.S. guard"—(*LJ*).

Werth, Alexander. Russia at War. *Avon* 1964 pap. $1.65

Winterbotham, F. W. The Ultra Secret. *Harper* 1974 $8.95; *Dell* 1975 pap. *(consult publisher's catalog for price)*

"A truly fascinating tale of how England with the help of Polish patriots stole and duplicated Nazi Germany's ultra secret cipher machine"—(*LJ*).

Wright, Gordon. The Ordeal of Total War, 1939–1945. The Rise of Modern Europe Ser. *Harper* 1968 $8.95 pap. $2.75. The impact of World War II on European political and social structure.

Young, Peter. A Short History of World War Two, 1939–1945. *Apollo* 1966 pap. $2.95

"One of the better compact histories of the war"—(Eliot Fremont-Smith, in the *N.Y. Times*).

(Ed.) Atlas of the Second World War. *Putnam* 1974 $17.95

(Ed.) The War Game: Ten Great Battles Recreated from History. Preface by Aram Bakshian, Jr.; war games photographed by Philip O. Stearns *Dutton* 1972 $10.00

"A number of writers have contributed brief accounts of some of the great battles of history—from Thermopylae to El Alamein—illustrated by colour photographs of model battlefields and toy soldiers"—(*TLS, London*).

International Relations and the United Nations

For reference works on international affairs and information on United Nations publications and reference works, see listing on Reference Books, Modern and World History (this Section), and Reference and Important Series at the beginning of this Chapter.

Relevant series are *Oceana*'s Annual Review of U.N. Affairs Series and the Maxwell School Series on the Administration of Foreign Policy through the United Nations. *Praeger* publishes the Library of World Affairs and Studies in International Order. Robert Scholes called Henrietta Buckmaster's novel "The Lion in the Stone" (*Harcourt* 1968, o.p.), about a fictional U.N. crisis, "a modest success" as an "educational effort." "As an introduction to the U.N. it is clearly superior to most textbooks, because it is committed as well as informed, and has sufficient hardness of heart to justify its softness of heart"—(*N.Y. Times*).

Alker, Hayward R., Jr., and Bruce M. Russett. World Politics in the General Assembly. Yale Studies in Political Science Ser. *Yale Univ. Press* 1965 $15.00

"An excellent and well-written study"—(*Choice*).

American Friends Service Committee. IN PLACE OF WAR: An Inquiry into Nonviolent National Defense. *Grossman* 1967 $3.95 pap. $1.95

Aron, Raymond. *See his main entry, this Section.*

Barrat, John, and Michael Louw, Eds. INTERNATIONAL ASPECTS OF OVERPOPULATION. *St. Martin's* 1972 $14.95

Barros, James, Ed. THE UNITED NATIONS: Past, Present, and Future. *Macmillan* (Free Press) 1973 $8.95 pap. $3.45

"Of uniformly high quality, these essays provide an ideal introduction to the subject for graduate students or for specialists on world affairs who wish to brush up on recent thinking and developments in international organization"—*(American Historical Review)*.

Bingham, June. U THANT OF BURMA: The Search for Peace. *Knopf* 1966 $6.95. A biography of the former Secretary-General of the United Nations which tells much about modern Burma as well.

Buckley, William F., Jr. UNITED NATIONS JOURNAL: A Delegate's Odyssey. *Putnam* 1974 $6.95

"This is a day-to-day account of Buckley's experience as a U.S. delegate to the U.N.'s Third Committee of the General Assembly after his appointment in the fall of 1973"—*(LJ)*.

Clark, Grenville, and Louis John. INTRODUCTION TO WORLD PEACE THROUGH WORLD LAW. *World Without War Pubns.* 1973 pap. $1.50

Cordier, Andrew Willington, and Wilder Foote, Eds. THE PUBLIC PAPERS OF THE SECRE-TARIES-GENERAL OF THE UNITED NATIONS. *Columbia* 4 vols. 1969–1974 Vol. 1 $20.00 Vols. 2–4 each $22.50

"The selections are augmented with commentary defining the historical context and giving other background"—*(Booklist)*.

THE QUEST FOR PEACE: The Dag Hammarskjöld Memorial Lectures. *Columbia* 1964 $12.50 pap. $2.95. Contributors include U Thant, Barbara Ward, Madame Pandit, Julius Nyerere, Alva Myrdal, Adlai Stevenson, Paul G. Hoffman and Dean Rusk.

Cruise O'Brien, Conor, and Feliks Topolski. THE UNITED NATIONS: Sacred Drama. *Simon & Schuster* 1968 $7.95

"Two highly individualistic views of the United Nations, one in words and the other in pictures, are presented within these covers . . . Dr. O'Brien argues that the United Nations is a form of sacred drama in which the personages symbolize mighty forces, the audience is mankind, and the theme is the destiny of man"—(Eric Britter, in *SR*).

Dean, Arthur H. TEST BAN AND DISARMAMENT: The Path of Negotiation. Fwd. by John C. Campbell. Policy Book Ser. *Harper* 1966 $3.95. Negotiations involved with the Russians in the signing of the Partial Test-Ban Treaty of 1963. Published for the Council on Foreign Relations.

Dexter, Byron. THE YEARS OF OPPORTUNITY: The League of Nations, 1920–1926. *Viking* 1967 $8.50

Douglas, William O. TOWARDS A GLOBAL FEDERALISM. *New York Univ. Press* 1968 $8.95

Edwards, David V. CREATING A NEW WORLD POLITICS: From Conflict to Cooperation. *McKay* 1973 pap. $2.95

Eichelberger, Clark M. THE UN: The First Twenty-Five Years. *Harper* 4th ed. 1970 $6.95

"A good book for the general undergraduate who wants a quick view of the U.N. and its potential"—*(Choice)*.

Eubank, Keith. THE SUMMIT CONFERENCES, 1919–1960. *Univ. of Oklahoma Press* 1966 $7.95

"In clear, succinct language, he has analyzed each summit conference in terms of the balance of power, personalities, and the prevailing military and political realities"—*(LJ)*.

Frank, Jerome D. SANITY AND SURVIVAL: Psychological Aspects of War and Peace. Pref. by Senator J. William Fulbright *Random* 1967 $5.95

Friedman, Leon. THE LAW OF WAR: A Documentary History. *Random* 2 vols. 1975 set
   $65.00
   "A working collection of 93 carefully selected and critically important primary source documents on the law of war"—(Publisher's note).

Friedmann, Wolfgang, George Kalmanoff and Robert Meagher. INTERNATIONAL FINAN-
   CIAL AID. *Columbia* 1966 $17.50
   "A very comprehensive study of the foreign aid programs of the major nations of the world
   engaged in such activity: United States, Russia, France, United Kingdom, Japan, and West
   Germany. . . . Recommended for serious collections in economics and international affairs"—(*LJ*).

Glick, Edward Bernard. PEACEFUL CONFLICT: The Non-Military Use of the Military.
   Stackpole 1967 $6.50. Dr. Glick looks into the use of soldiery for "civil action" and the
   peaceful resolution of conflict; a thorough study.

Goodrich, Leland M. THE UNITED NATIONS IN A CHANGING WORLD. *Columbia* 1974 $12.95

Gordenker, Leon. THE UN SECRETARY-GENERAL AND THE MAINTENANCE OF PEACE.
   Columbia 1967 $12.50. A discussion of the role he is able to play—in historical
   perspective.

   (Ed.) THE UNITED NATIONS IN INTERNATIONAL POLITICS. *Princeton Univ. Press* 1971
   $8.50

Hammarskjöld, Dag. *See his main entry in Chapter 2, General Biography and Autobiography,
   this Vol.*

Hollins, Elizabeth Jay, Ed. PEACE IS POSSIBLE: A Reader for Laymen. *Grossman* 1966 $6.50
   pap. $3.75
   "The reflective, stimulating pages by the editor of this anthology give unity and movement to
   what might otherwise be just another collection of essays about peace. Most of them are worth
   reading, and some are among the best statements yet made about what Buckminster Fuller has
   termed the human race's unavoidable choice between oblivion and utopia. . . . It would be difficult
   to think of a book about peace which would prove more effectively that many of the best and most
   gifted men of the time have tried to beat on other drums than those of war"—(*SR*). Contributors
   include Paul Tillich, Jerome Frank, George Kenna, Hans Morgenthau, Gunnar Myrdal.

Kay, David A., Ed. THE UNITED NATIONS POLITICAL SYSTEM. *Wiley* 1967 $10.00 pap.
   $6.50
   These essays of "high quality" are written by "distinguished statesmen and professors" (*LJ*) such
   as U Thant, Dag Hammarskjöld, Lester Pearson and Leland Goodrich.

Kenworthy, Leonard S. TELLING THE UN STORY: New Approaches to Teaching about the
   United Nations and Its Related Agencies. *Oceana* 1963 $6.00 pap. $1.75
   Professor Kenworthy, a leading authority, has produced an invaluable guide for teachers. This
   book ranges over the content of the UN and Specialized Agencies and the methodology of the
   teaching profession with remarkable skill. "The appendixes alone are invaluable for their
   reference to UN documentation, nongovernmental organizations, and sources of information
   especially designed for the teacher."

Knapp, Wilfrid F. A HISTORY OF WAR AND PEACE, 1939–1965. *Oxford* 1967 $9.50

Lall, Arthur S. MODERN INTERNATIONAL NEGOTIATION: Principles and Practice. *Columbia*
   1966 $14.00

   THE U.N. AND THE MIDDLE EAST CRISIS, 1967. *Columbia* 1970 $12.50 pap. $2.95
   "Arthur Lall, former Indian Ambassador to the U.N., has made a valiant attempt to inject some
   life—or, at least, liveliness—into the drab records of the U.N. debates by writing a substantial book
   on the Middle East crisis. . . . His book is an eminently fair-minded, judicious, and comprehensive
   account of the crisis, its immediate background, and some of its consequences"—(*SR*).

Lefever, Ernest W. UNCERTAIN MANDATE: Politics of the U.N. Congo Operation. *Johns
   Hopkins Press* 1967 $8.50

Lewin, Leonard C., with notes and introd. REPORT FROM IRON MOUNTAIN: On the
   Possibility and Desirability of Peace. 1967. *Dell* Delta Bks. 1969 pap. $1.95
   "A shocker . . . so substantively original, acute, interesting and horrifying, that it will receive
   serious attention regardless of its origin. Its basic argument is that social stability is, and has always

been, based on a war system; and that, contrary to the 'incorrect assumption that war, as an institution, is subordinate to the social system it is believed to serve . . . war itself is the basic social system.' The prospect the report outlines is truly Orwellian. It includes planned but credible 'threats' from an 'enemy,' a space research program that is deliberately costly and deliberately unproductive, programmed air and water pollution, computer-controlled procreation, the reintroduction of slavery and possibly ritual-killing and genocide"—(Eliot Fremont-Smith, in the *N.Y. Times*).

Macomber, William. THE ANGELS' GAME: A Handbook of Modern Diplomacy. *Stein & Day* 1975 $10.00

"A brief account of past diplomacy and an in-depth discussion of modern diplomacy"—(*LJ*).

Mayer, Arno J. THE POLITICS AND DIPLOMACY OF PEACEMAKING: Containment and Counterrevolution at Versailles, 1918–1919. *Knopf* 1968 $15.00

Mayer, Peter, Ed. THE PACIFIST CONSCIENCE. 1956. *Regnery* Gateway Eds. 1967 pap. $2.95

A "remarkably comprehensive" collection (*PW*) of essays on peace and war by such figures as Lao-Tzu, Gandhi and Martin Luther King, Jr.

Morgenthau, Hans J. POLITICS AMONG NATIONS: The Struggle for Power and Peace. *Knopf* 5th ed. 1974 $12.95 text ed. $10.95. A classic in the field.

Muste, Abraham Johannes. NON-VIOLENCE IN AN AGGRESSIVE WORLD. 1940. *Jerome S. Ozer* 1972 $9.95. A classic by one of this country's most eloquent voices of pacifism and non-violence.

Northedge, F. S., Ed. THE USE OF FORCE IN INTERNATIONAL RELATIONS. *Macmillan* (Free Press) 1974 $12.95

"These nine essays stress that force will remain a pervading factor in international politics as long as sovereign independent nations are ultimately responsible for their own security"—(*LJ*).

Palmer, Norman D., and Howard C. Perkins. INTERNATIONAL RELATIONS: The World Community in Transition. *Houghton* 3rd text ed. 1969 $11.95

Reed, Edward, Ed. BEYOND COEXISTENCE: The Requirements of Peace. Introd. and summary by Robert M. Hutchins *Grossman* 1968 pap. $2.95. Speeches and papers prepared under the aegis of the Center for the Study of Democratic Institutions by 300 distinguished citizens, such as William O. Douglas, Bishop Pike, J. William Fulbright and Martin Luther King, Jr.

Rikhye, Indar J., and others. THE THIN BLUE LINE: International Peacekeeping and Its Future. *Yale Univ. Press* 1974 $12.50

Roosevelt, Eleanor. *See her main entry in Chapter 2, General Biography and Autobiography, this Vol.*

Rosenau, James N., Ed. INTERNATIONAL POLITICS AND FOREIGN POLICY. *Macmillan* (Free Press) 1961 2nd ed. 1969 $10.95

NATIONAL LEADERSHIP AND FOREIGN POLICY. *Princeton Univ Press* 1963 $12.50

Sawczuk, Konstantyn. UKRAINE IN THE UNITED NATIONS ORGANIZATION: A Study in Soviet Foreign Policy, 1944–1950. *Columbia* 1975 $10.00

Schelling, Thomas C. ARMS AND INFLUENCE. *Yale Univ. Press* 1966 pap. $2.95. The influence of military force in world affairs; Mr. Schelling, like Herman Kahn (*q.v.*), "thinks the unthinkable."

Stevenson, Adlai E. *See his main entry, Chapter 2, General Biography and Autobiography, this Vol.*

Stone, Jeremy J. STRATEGIC PERSUASION: Arms Limitation through Dialogue. *Columbia* 1967 $9.00

"A useful and provocative essay about communication between the United States and the Soviet Union affecting arms control and disarmament"—(*SR*).

Twitchett, Kenneth J. THE EVOLVING UNITED NATIONS. *St. Martin's* 1972 $9.95

United Nations. EVERYMAN'S UNITED NATIONS. *United Nations Pubns.* 8th ed. 1968 $6.00 pap. $2.50. A reference book for its first twenty years.

UNITED NATIONS DOCUMENTS INDEX. *United Nations Pubns.* Issued monthly, each issue $1.50

YEARBOOK OF THE UNITED NATIONS. *Int. Pubns. Service* 1971 $35.00. An annual record of the activities of the United Nations and its related agencies. (Back numbers available)

United Nations Association of the U.S.A. WORLD UNDERSTANDING: A Selected Bibliography. Fwd. by Asdrubal Salsamendi; pref. by Frank W. Cyr *Oceana* 1965 $9.00

An "extensive, annotated reading guide on the United Nations and the world of today"—(*LJ*).

UNESCO. INTERNATIONAL GUIDE TO EDUCATIONAL DOCUMENTATION. UNIPUB 2 vols. Vol. 1 1955–1960 (1963) $28.50 Vol. 2 1960–1965 (1972) $35.00. An international guide to the contemporary literature of education.

Wadsworth, James, THE GLASS HOUSE: The United Nations in Action. *Praeger* 1966 $6.00

Yost, Charles W. THE CONDUCT AND MISCONDUCT OF FOREIGN AFFAIRS. *Random* 1972 $7.95

"Mr. Yost carries his faith in organizational and apolitical solutions to a passionate plea for world government"—(*N.Y. Times*).

Young, Oran R. THE INTERMEDIARIES: Third Parties in International Crises. *Princeton Univ. Press* 1967 $14.50. On the efforts of the U.N. and uninvolved nations in crisis situations.

Europe

Auty, Phyllis. TITO: A Biography. 1970. *Ballantine Bks.* 1972 pap. $1.00

"A clear, interesting and very sympathetic account of the Yugoslav Communist leader by a noted British authority on Yugoslavia"—(*Choice*).

Baer, George W. THE COMING OF THE ITALIAN-ETHIOPIAN WAR. *Harvard Univ. Press* 1967 $12.00

Balfour, Michael. THE KAISER AND HIS TIMES. 1964. *Norton* 1972 pap. $3.95

Barker, Elisabeth. AUSTRIA, 1918–1972. *Macmillan* 1973 $12.50

[The author] "maintains a commendable balance while assessing the merits and faults of the chief protagonists"—(*LJ*).

Barry, Joseph A. PASSIONS AND POLITICS: A Biography of Versailles. *Doubleday* 1972 $12.95

This is the story of Versailles "and of the people who lived there, of the passions that assailed them, the politics and forces that motivated and bent them"—(Publisher's note).

Basso, Lelio. ROSA LUXEMBURG: A Reappraisal. *Praeger* 1975 $10.00

"This book comes at a time when interest in Luxemburg is reviving and it will probably become a standard critical work"—(*LJ*)

Batty, Peter. THE HOUSE OF KRUPP. *Stein & Day* 1967 pap. 1969 $2.95

"A hard-hitting exposé of the firm that has played a key role in Europe's military and political history"—(*SR*).

Bendiner, Elmer. A TIME FOR ANGELS: The Tragi-Comic History of the League of Nations. *Knopf* 1975 $12.50

Blum, Jerome, Rondo Cameron and Thomas G. Barnes. THE EUROPEAN WORLD: A History. *Little* 1966 2 vols. 2nd ed. 1970 Vol. 1 The Emergence of the European World Vol. 2 The European World since 1815: Triumph and Transition each $5.95 1-vol. text ed. $6.95

Boxer, Charles Ralph. THE PORTUGUESE SEABORNE EMPIRE, 1415–1825. History of Human Society Ser. *Knopf* 1969 $8.95

Brinton, Crane. *See his main entry, this Section.*

Burden, Hamilton T. THE NUREMBERG PARTY RALLIES: 1923–1939. *Praeger* 1967 $6.00

CAMBRIDGE ECONOMIC HISTORY OF EUROPE. *Cambridge* 6 vols. Vol. 1 The Agrarian Life of the Middle Ages (1941) 2nd ed. by M. M. Postan (1966) $27.50 Vol. 2 Trade and Industry in the Middle Ages (1952) new ed. (in prep.) Vol. 3 Economic Organization and Policies in the Middle Ages ed. by M. M. Postan, E. E. Rich and E. Miller (1963) $23.50 Vol. 4 The Economy of Expanding Europe in the Sixteenth and Seventeenth Centuries ed. by E. E. Rich and C. H. Wilson (1967) $23.50 Vol. 5 (in prep.) Vol. 6 The Industrial Revolutions and After: Incomes, Population and Technological Change in 2 pts. ed. by H. J. Habakkuk and M. M. Postan (1965) set $39.50

Carey, Jane Perry, and Andrew Galbraith Carey. THE WEB OF MODERN GREEK POLITICS. *Columbia* 1968 $10.00

Carlyle, Thomas. *See his main entry, this Section.*

Carr, Raymond. SPAIN: 1808–1939. Oxford History of Modern Europe Ser. *Oxford* 1966 $14.50

Chejne, Anwar G. MUSLIM SPAIN: Its History and Culture. *Univ. of Minnesota Press* 1974 $24.75

Clough, Shepard B. HISTORY OF THE FLEMISH MOVEMENT IN BELGIUM. *Octagon* 1967 $10.50

(With Salvatore Saladino) A HISTORY OF MODERN ITALY: Documents, Readings, and Commentary. *Columbia* 1968 $15.00

(With others) THE EUROPEAN PAST. *Macmillan* 2 vols. 2nd ed. 1970 pap. each $5.50

Cobb, Richard. PARIS AND ITS PROVINCES, 1792–1802. *Oxford* 1974 $17.50

"Social history at its best"—(*TLS*, London).

Compton, James V. THE SWASTIKA AND THE EAGLE: Hitler, the United States and the Origins of World War Two. *Houghton* 1967 $6.95

Crankshaw, Edward. THE FALL OF THE HOUSE OF HABSBURG. 1963. *Popular Lib.* 1971 pap. $1.25

The author, long the Russian correspondent of the London *Observer*, also lived in Vienna for many years. His book, a narrative of 70 critical European years, is built around the long reign of Franz Josef of Austria from his accession in the 1848 Revolution to his death on the verge of Austria's defeat in World War I. It is a combination of the best of political and social history, with portraits of Bismarck, Napoleon III, the Empress Carlotta, and the two lovers who died at Mayerling.

Crawley, Aidan. THE SPOILS OF WAR: The Rise of Western Germany since 1945. *Bobbs* 1973 $7.95

"The author, an unusually well-informed British politician, provides an account that will be helpful primarily to American readers"—(*LJ*).

Cronin, Vincent. THE FLORENTINE RENAISSANCE. *Dutton* 1967 $8.95

Mr. Cronin "covers all aspects of the culture and political life of [the 15th] century in Florence"—(*LJ*).

Davidson, Eugene. THE TRIAL OF THE GERMANS. *Macmillan* 1966 $12.50

"The presentation is scholarly, well-organized, smoothly written. The pen portraits, sketched in acid, are sharp and illuminating"—(Louis L. Snyder, in *SR*).

Davis, Natalie Zemon. SOCIETY AND CULTURE IN EARLY MODERN FRANCE: Eight Essays. *Stanford Univ. Press* 1975 $15.00

The author is "one of the foremost American practitioners of the 'new social history', endeavoring to bring within the purview of historical study the lives of the peasants, laborers, and artisans of pre-Industrial Europe"—(*LJ*).

Delzell, Charles F. MUSSOLINI'S ENEMIES: The Italian Anti-Fascist Resistance. 1961. *Howard Fertig* $16.00. Winner of the George Louis Beer Prize for 1961.

de Rougemont, Denis. THE MEANING OF EUROPE. *Stein & Day* 1965 $3.95

Dornberg, John. THE TWO GERMANYS. *Dial* 1974 $5.95 Mr. Dornberg lived in West Germany working much of the time for *Newsweek*, and made numerous trips to East Germany.

Drew, Katherine F., and Floyd Seward Lear, Eds. PERSPECTIVES IN MEDIEVAL HISTORY. *Univ. of Chicago Press* 1963 $4.85

"Original and thoughtful contributions"—*(LJ)*.

Duveau, Georges. 1848: THE MAKING OF A REVOLUTION. Trans. from the French by Anne Carter *Pantheon* 1966 $8.95; *Random* Vintage Bks. 1968 pap. $1.95

"All that happened in the Paris of 1848 . . . is told in details that are made as vivid as the events at Watts or Saigon"—*(LJ)*.

Eckstein, Harry. DIVISION AND COHESION IN DEMOCRACY: A Study of Norway. *Princeton Univ. Press* 1966 $11.50 pap. $3.45

Erlanger, Philippe. THE AGE OF COURTS AND KINGS: Manners and Morals, 1558–1715. Manners and Morals Ser. *Harper* 1967 $12.50

EUROPEAN BIBLIOGRAPHY. Ed. by Hjalmar Pehrsson and Hanna Wulf *Bowker* 1965 $13.50

"This is a bibliography of about 1,300 books in the areas of history, philosophy, art, economics, etc. Each title is briefly described in English and French, with some additional notes in German, Spanish, Italian and Dutch"—(Publisher's note).

Eyck, Erich. A HISTORY OF THE WEIMAR REPUBLIC. Trans. by Harlan P. Hanson and Robert G. L. Waite *Harvard Univ. Press* 2 vols. 1962–1963 Vol. 1 From the Collapse of the Empire to Hindenburg's Election $11.00 Vol. 2 From the Locarno Conference to Hitler's Seizure of Power $15.00; *Atheneum* 2 vols. 1970 pap. Vol. 1 $3.25 Vol. 2 $3.95

Farnie, D. A. EAST AND WEST OF SUEZ: The Suez Canal in History, 1854–1956. *Oxford* 1969 $41.00

"Not only does it detail the vicissitudes of the canal itself, but it gives enough information on the company, its relation to Egyptian and European politics and economic development of Asia and to the flow of the East-West trade to satisfy the most curious investigator"—*(Choice)*.

Feis, Herbert. BETWEEN WAR AND PEACE: The Potsdam Conference. *Princeton Univ. Press* 1960 $12.50 pap. $3.95. Pulitzer Prize winner, 1961.

Fermi, Laura. MUSSOLINI. *Univ. of Chicago Press* 1961 $10.00 Phoenix Bks. pap. $2.95. A fine study for the general reader.

Ferrero, Guglielmo. THE TWO FRENCH REVOLUTIONS: 1789–1796. Trans. from the French by Samuel J. Hurwitz; ed. by Luc Monnier; fwd. by Crane Brinton *Basic Bks.* 1968 pap. $2.95

"The book fairly bounces with ideas. . . . Not to be missed"—*(New Yorker)*.

Finley, M. I., and Denis Mack Smith. A HISTORY OF SICILY. *Viking* 3 vols. 1968 Vol. 1 Ancient Sicily: To the Arab Conquest, by M. I. Finley Vol. 2 Medieval Sicily: 800–1713 Vol. 3 Modern Sicily: After 1713, by Denis M. Smith Vol. 1 o.p. Vols. 2–3 $20.00.

"M. I. Finley and Denis Mack Smith have produced a history of the island which is cool, complete, and always lively reading; it was something that had to be done, and it could not have been done better"—(Aubrey Menen, in the *N.Y. Times*).

Fischer-Gelati, Stephen. TWENTIETH CENTURY RUMANIA. *Columbia* 1970 $12.00

Flanner, Janet. PARIS JOURNAL. Ed. by William Shawn *Atheneum* 2 vols. 1965–71 Vol. 1 1944–1965 (1965) $10.00 Vol. 2 1965–1971 (1971) $12.50. "Genêt" has been *The New Yorker's* correspondent in France for the last 40 years.

PARIS WAS YESTERDAY, 1925–1939. Ed. by Irving Drutman *Viking* 1972 $8.50; *Popular Lib.* 1973 pap. $1.25

Gallo, Max. MUSSOLINI'S ITALY: Twenty Years of the Fascist Era. Trans. by Charles Markmann *Abelard-Schuman* 1973 $10.95

"A summary in great detail of the last years of Italy's struggle for unity and prestige, years dominated by pomp, bombast, and absurdities"—*(Best Sellers)*.

Gay, Peter. WEIMAR CULTURE: The Outsider as Insider. *Harper* 1968 $5.95 Torchbks. 1970 pap. $1.95

The "themes that Mr. Gay discusses include the strong and 'voluptuous' pull of mysticism and death, the influence of German idealism and the romantic clichés that justified brutalism and unreason, the failure of rebellion to contain any program that would help republican ideals overcome the authoritarian structure of German society . . . a pervasive cynicism and the notion that poetry was higher than politics"—(Eliot Fremont-Smith, in the *N.Y. Times*).

(With Time-Life Bks., Eds.) THE AGE OF ENLIGHTENMENT. Great Ages of Man Ser. *Time-Life Bks.* 1966 lib. bdg. $8.80

"A full and impressive picture of the people, the ideas, the ways of life and thought, the social and cultural conditions of the 18th century"—(*LJ*).

Goebbels, Paul Joseph. THE GOEBBELS DIARIES, 1942–43. Trans. by Louis P. Lochner. 1948. *Greenwood* $18.75

Grunfeld, Frederich V. THE HITLER FILE: A Social History of Germany and the Nazis 1918–45. *Random* 1974 $25.00

"A largely photographic record of Germany from the end of World War I to the finale of the second world conflict in 1945"—(*Booklist*).

Guicciardini, Francesco. THE HISTORY OF ITALY. 1561. Trans. by Austin P. Goddard 1763. *AMS Press* 10 vols. 3rd. ed. each $15.00 set $147.50; trans. and ed. by Sidney Alexander *Macmillan* 1969 $12.50 pap. $3.95

"The [Sidney Alexander] translation of the Italian classic, the first substantial translation in two centuries . . . makes clear the twofold appeal the book has had for its readers since it was first published in 1561, 21 years after the death of the author. It is at once an account of the systematic destruction of the Italian states in the early 16th century [and] also an expression of a philosophical view of politics and political man. . . . Despite its title, 'The History of Italy' only covers the years 1494 to 1534"—(Thomas Lask, in the *N.Y. Times*). "FRANCESCO GUICCIARDINI, the Florentine whose *Storia d'Italia* made him the first modern historian and who was also a great statesman and political thinker, has long been overshadowed by Machiavelli, his contemporary and friend, though while they lived Guicciardini was both more active and more powerful"—(Charles F. Delzell, in *SR*).

Halperin, Samuel William. GERMANY TRIED DEMOCRACY: A Political History of the Reich from 1918 to 1933. 1946. *Norton* 1965 pap. $3.45

Harvey, Donald J. FRANCE SINCE THE REVOLUTION. *Macmillan* (Free Press) 1968 $8.95 pap. $4.95

"A readable, competently written, one-volume history"—(*LJ*).

Hay, Denys, Ed. THE AGE OF THE RENAISSANCE. *McGraw-Hill* 1967 $30.00. Twelve scholars contribute to this attractive book, illustrated mainly in color.

Herold, J. Christopher, and the Editors of *Horizon*. THE HORIZON BOOK OF THE AGE OF NAPOLEON. *Harper* 1963 $18.95

Hibbert, Christopher. GARIBALDI AND HIS ENEMIES: The Clash of Arms and Personalities in the Making of Italy. 1966. *New Am. Lib.* 1970 pap. $3.95

"A very fine history of the *Risorgimento* in 19th-century Italy and the almost fictional wars of revolt led by Giuseppe Garibaldi in his quest for a united Italy"—(*LJ*).

Holborn, Hajo. A HISTORY OF MODERN GERMANY. *Knopf* 2 vols. 1959–69 Vol. 1 The Reformation (1959) $10.00 Vol. 2 1648–1840: On the Crucial Aftermath of the Thirty Years' War (1964) $10.75 Vol. 3 1840–1945 (1969) $13.95 text ed. each $10.95

This Sterling Professor of History at Yale is well equipped to undertake the difficult task of tracing German history to 1945. He taught at Heidelberg and Berlin before coming to the United States in 1933—one of the first anti-Nazi scholars to leave Germany. He deals not only with political events but gives equal attention to social, religious, intellectual and artistic developments.

THE POLITICAL COLLAPSE OF EUROPE. *Knopf* 1951 $3.95

Hoyt, Robert S., Ed. LIFE AND THOUGHT IN THE EARLY MIDDLE AGES. *Univ. of Minnesota Press* 1967 $5.50 pap. $1.95

"A generally excellent group of expanded 'reforming' lectures, the purpose of which is to bring the latest results of medieval research to the attention of the public"—(LJ).

Hughes, H. Stuart. THE OBSTRUCTED PATH: French Social Thought in the Years of Desperation, 1930–1960. *Harper* Torchbks. 1969 pap. $1.95

"Professor Hughes believes that in the course of the twentieth century, French thought, which once offered enlightenment to the whole Western world, became dim, parochial, and unable to create ideas or invent methods that could illuminate contemporary world problems or assist in solving French ones. . . . An attractive, companionable causerie"—(New Yorker).

Jaspers, Karl. THE FUTURE OF GERMANY. Trans. from the German by E. B. Ashton; introd. by Hannah Arendt *Univ. of Chicago Press* 1967 pap. 1974 $6.50

The eminent theologian's "message, as Hannah Arendt sums it up, . . . is that the Federal Republic is 'well on its way to abolishing parliamentary democracy and may be drifting toward some kind of dictatorship' "—(SR).

Johnston, William M. THE AUSTRIAN MIND: An Intellectual and Social History, 1848–1938. *Univ. of California Press* 1972 $17.50

"More than a history of the 'Austrian Mind' it is a multifaceted contribution to general intellectual history. Many of the persons discussed—Freud, Mannheim, Mach, Husserl, Wittgenstein, Buber—are more important to the international community of intellectuals than to Austria"—(Choice).

Jones, Gwyn. A HISTORY OF THE VIKINGS. *Oxford* 1968 $12.50 pap. 1973 $3.95. *(For further material on the Vikings, see Chapter 13, Scandinavian Literature, Reader's Adviser, Vol. 2.)*
Covers the period from 780 to 1070. "A tremendous achievement"—(N.Y. Times).

Kissinger, Henry A. A WORLD RESTORED: Metternich, Castlereagh and the Problems of Peace 1812–22. *Houghton* 1973 pap. $3.95

"His approach to the formulation of policy, the principles on which it should be based, the balances that must be maintained for success"—(TLS, London).

Knodel, John C. THE DECLINE OF FERTILITY IN GERMANY, 1871–1939. *Princeton Univ. Press* 1973 $14.50

Laqueur, Walter. WEIMAR: A Cultural History 1918–1933. *Putnam* 1975 $8.95
"A survey of Weimar culture essentially on political grounds"—(N.Y. Times).

Laslett, Peter, Ed. HOUSEHOLD AND FAMILY IN PAST TIME. *Cambridge* 1972 $37.50. A series of essays based on population studies.

Lefebvre, Georges. THE FRENCH REVOLUTION. *Columbia* 2 vols. 1961–64 Vol. 1 From Its Origins to 1793 trans. by Elizabeth M. Evans (1961) Vol. 2 From 1793 to 1799 trans. by John H. Stewart and James Friguglietti (1964) each $15.00 pap. each $3.45

Lindberg, Leon N. THE POLITICAL DYNAMICS OF EUROPEAN ECONOMIC INTEGRATION. *Stanford Univ. Press* 1963 $10.00

An assistant professor of political science at the University of Wisconsin studies the economic cooperation of the Western European countries to determine the possibilities for eventual political union. He examines the provisions of the Common Market treaty, shows how the Common Market works, giving some examples of decision-making in which major conflicts of interest have been resolved, and considers the implication of political union for these countries, based on the concepts of economic unity.

Lloyd, Alan. THE SPANISH CENTURIES. Mainstream of the Modern World Ser. *Doubleday* 1968 $7.95 pap. 1973 $6.95

"An accomplished British journalist has given us a work that is engagingly readable, historically accurate, and well balanced"—(LJ). Covers the period from 1492 to the present.

Lopez, Robert. THE BIRTH OF EUROPE. *M. Evans* (dist. by Lippincott) 1967 $15.00

"A comprehensive survey of medieval life. . . . Mr. Lopez' scholarship is impeccable and wide-ranging"—(New Yorker).

THREE AGES OF THE ITALIAN RENAISSANCE. *Univ. Press of Virginia* 1970 $7.50; *Little* 1972 pap. $2.95

Macartney, C. A. HUNGARY: A Short History. *Aldine* 1962 $7.50

"Surely the best account to date of Hungarian history in English"—(American Historical Review).

Macaulay, Thomas B. *See his main entry, Section on History of the British Commonwealth, this Chapter.*

Machiavelli, Niccolo. *See his main entry in Chapter 10, Italian Literature*, Reader's Adviser, *Vol. 2.*

McNeill, William H. *See his main entry, this Section.*

McSherry, James E. STALIN, HITLER, AND EUROPE. 1968. *Open Door* 2 vols. 1974 Vol. 1 The Origins of World War Two, 1933–1939 $15.00 Vol. 2 Imbalance of Power, 1939–1941 $17.50. A study of Stalin's policy toward Hitler.

Manchester, William. THE ARMS OF KRUPP, 1587–1968. *Little* 1968 $14.95; *Bantam* 1970 pap. $1.95

A chronicle of the famous German steel dynasty, somewhat overweighted with detail and indignation, but the story is worth the telling. It received much adverse criticism in Germany and was banned in Bavaria. *See also Batty, Peter, above, for less publicized but admirable coverage.*

Marques, Antonio Henrique R. de Oliveira. DAILY LIFE IN PORTUGAL IN THE LATE MIDDLE AGES. Trans. by S. S. Wyatt. *Univ. of Wisconsin Press* 1971 $15.00

HISTORY OF PORTUGAL. *Columbia* 2 vols. 1972 Vol. 1 From Lusitania to Empire Vol. 2 From Empire to Corporate State each $15.00

"Far and away the best general history of Portugal in the English language"—*(Choice).*

Martin, George. THE RED SHIRT AND THE CROSS OF SAVOY: The Story of Italy's Risorgimento, 1748–1871. *Dodd* 1969 $15.00. Includes treatment of Garibaldi, Mazzini, Cavour.

Martinelli, Giuseppe. Ed. THE WORLD OF RENAISSANCE FLORENCE. 1964. Trans. by Walter Darwell *Putnam* 1968 $20.00. Contains color illustrations.

Mattingly, Garrett. THE ARMADA. *Houghton* 1959 $7.50 pap. 1962 $2.65

The late Professor Mattingly of Columbia saw the Armada campaign as "the first great international crisis in modern history." "The Armada" is the classic account of that famous year, 1588, and is a work of art as well as of scholarship. It received a special citation in the Pulitzer Prize Awards for 1960.

RENAISSANCE DIPLOMACY. *Houghton* 1955 1971 pap. $2.45; *Russell & Russell* 1970 $12.00

May, Arthur J. VIENNA IN THE AGE OF FRANZ JOSEPH. *Univ. of Oklahoma Press* 1975 $2.95

Mayer, Hans Eberhard. THE CRUSADES. Trans. from the German by John Gillingham *Oxford* 1972 $10.25 pap. $3.95

"This is essentially a good, short, and up-to-date survey of the Crusades. Mayer is a competent and respected scholar of Crusade history, and the book is the best single-volume account, of the so called 'Official Crusades' between 1095 and 1291"—*(Choice).*

Mayne, Richard. THE COMMUNITY OF EUROPE: Past, Present and Future. *Norton* 1963 pap. $1.95; *Peter Smith* $4.00

A Cambridge historian explains just what the Common Market is, how it functions, the political implications, and its effect upon the U.S.; this "factual, knowledgeable and lucid review" is strongly recommended.

Moraze, Charles. THE TRIUMPH OF THE MIDDLE CLASSES: A Political and Social History of Europe in the Nineteenth Century. 1967. *Doubleday* Anchor Bks. 1968 pap. $2.95; *Peter Smith* $5.00

Mosse, George L., Ed. NAZI CULTURE: Intellectual, Cultural and Social Life in the Third Reich. Trans. by Salvator Attanasio and others *Grosset* 1965 1968 pap. $2.65

Myrdal, Jan. CONFESSIONS OF A DISLOYAL EUROPEAN. *Pantheon* 1968 $5.95; *Random* Vintage Bks. 1969 pap. $1.65

The "Swedish poet, journalist and anthropologist ... presents a coruscating montage of intimate monologues, encounters, dreams, observations and conjectures, a cinematic self-portrait of a precocious rebel. Formidably well-read, traveled and experienced, a political activist from his youth, he finds himself heroic and absurd, guilty, and for all his prolific brillance, impotent. He speaks vividly for the bourgeois Western intellectual who simultaneously condemns and understands the inadequacies and dilemmas of Western society 'from the Urals to California.' On another level Myrdal's 'Confessions' forms an allegory on the unwillingness of the West to act on its knowledge to help poorer societies"—(*N.Y. Times*).

See also Gunnar Myrdal's main entry in Chapter 8, The Social Sciences, this Vol.

Nef, John. THE CONQUEST OF THE MATERIAL WORLD: Essays on the Origins of Industrial Civilization and Their Relations to European History. *Univ. of Chicago Press* 1964 $12.50

Noakes, Jeremy, and Geoffrey Pridham, Comps. DOCUMENTS ON NAZISM, 1919–1945. *Viking* 1975 $12.95

"Basic documents that elucidate the philosophy and rise of Nazism and its responses to the danger of defeat are clearly organized and interpreted"—(*Booklist*).

Olson, Kenneth E. THE HISTORY MAKERS: The Press of Europe from Its Beginnings through 1965. *Louisiana State Univ. Press* 1960 $10.00

"An important book"—(*LJ*).

Palmer, Robert R. THE AGE OF DEMOCRATIC REVOLUTION: A Political History of Europe and America, 1760–1800. *Princeton Univ. Press* 2 vols. 1959 Vol. 1 The Challenge, Vol. 2 The Struggle each $15.00 pap. each $3.45

(With Joel Colton) A HISTORY OF THE MODERN WORLD. *Knopf* 4th ed. 1971 $16.95

Pernoud, Régine. BLANCHE OF CASTILE. Trans. by Henry Noel *Coward* 1974 $8.95

Blanche of Castile, Queen of France "emerges as far more than the stubborn political and domineering mother-in-law of historical tradition"—(*LJ*).

Pflanze, Otto. BISMARCK AND THE DEVELOPMENT OF GERMANY. *Princeton Univ. Press* 2 vols. 1963– Vol. 1 The Period of Unification, 1815–1871 rev. ed (1971) $17.50 pap. $3.95 Vol. 2 The Period of Consolidation, 1871–1890 (in prep.)

The author, now professor of history at the University of Minnesota, presents the first part of a comprehensive new Bismarck interpretation, obviously based on thorough research. "Whether or not one agrees always with Pflanze's verdicts, his book will long be consulted by students of German history. It is strongly recommended for all academic and larger public libraries"—(*LJ*).

Popovic, Nenad D. YUGOSLAVIA: The New Class in Crisis. Introd. by Karl L. Rankin *Syracuse Univ. Press* 1968 $7.00

"This is an outstanding and interesting book written by a Yugoslav and former high official in the Tito regime until his defection to the West in 1961"—(*LJ*).

Prescott, Orville. LORDS OF ITALY: Portraits from the Middle Ages. *Harper* 1972 $10.00

THE PRINCES OF THE RENAISSANCE. 1968. *Int. Pubns. Service* 1970 $11.00

"With genuine enthusiasm, he brings to life the great Princes of the Renaissance who, among other things, were the midwives of magnificence, the progenitors of the glories of Italian art"—(*PW*).

Remond, René. THE RIGHT WING IN FRANCE: From 1815 to de Gaulle. Trans. from the French by James M. Laux *Univ. of Pennsylvania Press* 1966 rev. ed. 1969 $10.00

"A lucid and thought-provoking analysis"—(*LJ*).

Rice, David Talbot. THE DAWN OF EUROPEAN CIVILIZATION: The Dark Ages. *McGraw-Hill* 1965 $28.50

THE RISE OF MODERN EUROPE SERIES. *Harper* 20 vols. projected 1934–   Each of the books published so far in this series is illustrated and has been issued in both hardback and paperback. (*Consult publisher's catalog for individual titles.*)

Rohr, Donald G. THE ORIGINS OF SOCIAL LIBERALISM IN GERMANY. *Univ. of Chicago Press* 1963 $7.50

Roos, Hans. A HISTORY OF MODERN POLAND: From the Foundation of the State in World War I to the Present Day. Trans. from the German by J. R. Frost *Harper* (Barnes & Noble) 1966 $3.75

Rousseas, Stephen, Herman Starobin and Gertrude Lenzer. THE DEATH OF A DEMOCRACY: Greece and the American Conscience. *Grove* 1967 Evergreen Bks. 1968 pap. $1.25

Rudé, George F. The Crowd in the French Revolution. *Oxford* 1959 pap. $2.50

Europe in the Eighteenth Century: Aristocracy and the Bourgeois Challenge, 1715–1789. History of Civilization Ser. *Praeger* 1973 $15.00

Paris and London in the Eighteenth Century: Studies in Popular Protest. *Viking* 1973 $8.95 Compass Bks. pap. $2.75

Revolutionary Europe, 1783–1815. *Harper* 1966 $7.95 Torchbks. pap. $2.95

Runciman, Sir Steven. A History of the Crusades. *Cambridge* 3 vols. 1951–54 Vol. 1 The First Crusade and the Foundation of the Kingdom of Jerusalem Vol. 2 The Kingdom of Jerusalem and the Frankish East Vol. 3 The Kingdom of Acre and the Later Crusades each $16.50

Sampson, Anthony, The Anatomy of Europe. *Harper* 1969 $10.00

"Incredibly informative. It is the first serious profile of the new and yet not so new Europe"—(Peter F. Drucker).

Schwartz, Harry. Eastern Europe in the Soviet Shadow. Ed. by Theodore M. Bernstein. N.Y. Times Survey Ser. *John Day* 1972 $5.95 pap. $1.95

Prague's 200 Days: The Struggle for Democracy in Czechoslovakia. *Praeger* 1969 $7.50. The *N.Y. Times* correspondent gives his account and interpretation of the Czech transformation.

Scobbie, Irene. Sweden. Nations of the Modern World Ser. *Praeger* 1972 $10.00

"Sober, factual, well written, this is a most useful addition to the considerable number of books on Scandinavia"—(*TLS*, London).

Servan-Schreiber, J. J. The American Challenge. Trans. from the French by Ronald Steel; fwd. by Arthur Schlesinger, Jr. *Atheneum* 1968 $6.95; *Avon Bks.* pap. $1.65

"Mr. Servan-Schreiber contends that United States business in Europe succeeds so well because of managerial skill and the complex interplay of big government, big business and big education"—(*LJ*).

Shirer, William Lawrence. The Rise and Fall of the Third Reich: A History of Nazi Germany. *Simon & Schuster* 1960 $12.50 pap. $5.95; *Fawcett* 1972 pap. $1.95

"In spite of the immensity of the task . . . there are no obvious gaps. . . . There are no failures of scholarship, balance, or judgment. . . . There is the appropriate emphasis on those episodes of German history which so many Germans choose to forget. . . . Here is a huge, a grim canvas. Here is history, which may do most good of all in Germany. For nothing comparable has been written there, and if anyone ought to read [this] it is the Germans themselves"—(*Atlantic*). *See also main entry for Adolf Hitler, this Section.*

Soboul, Albert. The French Revolution, 1787–1799. *Random* 1975 $17.95 pap. $5.95

Stern, J. P. Hitler: The Führer and the People. *Univ. of California Press* 1975 pap. $3.65

Symonds, John Addington. The Renaissance in Italy. 1875–1886. *Adler's* 7 vols. 1968–69 set $259.00; *Peter Smith* 3 vols. each $5.50 set $16.50. The major work of the English critic is a classic collection of sketches in cultural history.

Talmon, J. L. Romanticism and Revolt, Europe 1815–1848. History of European Civilization Library Ser. *Harcourt* 1967 pap. $3.95

Taylor, A. J. P. From Sarajevo to Potsdam. History of European Civilization Library Series. *Harcourt* 1967 pap. $3.95

"Perhaps the best short book among the hundreds that deal with the period"—(*LJ*).

See also his main entry, this Section.

Tilly, Charles, and Louise and Richard Tilly. The Rebellious Century, 1830–1930. *Harvard Univ. Press* 1975 $15.00

Vali, Ferenc A. The Quest for a United Germany. *Johns Hopkins Press* 1967 $10.00

"Indispensable"—(*LJ*).

Van De Walle, Etienne. The Female Population of France in the Nineteenth Century: A Reconstruction of 82 Departments. *Princeton Univ. Press* 1974 $21.50

Watt, Richard M. THE KINGS DEPART. The Tragedy of Germany: Versailles and the German Revolution. *Simon & Schuster* 1963 new ed. 1969 $10.00 pap. 1970 $3.45

"An easy narrative filled with pointed details, bright quotes, scene-setting descriptions and quick biographical sketches—all arranged so that personalities focus quickly, issues become instantly clear, and the passive, nonexpert reader is propelled forward by a desire to learn how it all turns out. . . . Watt's book serves to mediate between a complex and important period in modern history and the ill-served reader. And that's what good popular history is all about"— (Christopher Lehmann-Haupt, in the *N.Y. Times*).

Wedgwood, Cicely V. THE THIRTY YEARS WAR. 1938. *Doubleday* Anchor Bks. pap. $1.95; *Fernhill* 1962 $16.50; *Peter Smith* $6.00

Williams, Philip M. FRENCH POLITICIANS AND ELECTIONS, 1951–1968. *Cambridge* 1970 $15.50 pap. $4.95

WARS, PLOTS AND SCANDALS IN POST-WAR FRANCE. *Cambridge* 1970 $11.50

WILLING'S EUROPEAN PRESS GUIDE. *IPC Magazine, Inc.* (205 E. 42 St. New York, N.Y.) 1975 $25.00

Windsor, Philip, and Adam Roberts. CZECHOSLOVAKIA 1968: Reform, Repression and Resistance. *Columbia* 1969 $10.00 pap. $2.50. Essays by the two distinguished scholars.

Woodhouse, C. M., and others. A SHORT HISTORY OF GREECE. *Cambridge* $8.95 pap. $3.45

Zeldin, Theodore. FRANCE, 1848–1945. *Oxford* 1974 Vol. 1 Ambition, Love and Politics $19.50

"Unwilling to accept the frameworks in which the history of France has usually been interpreted, [the author] attacks the traditional myths and generalizations with a wealth of information based on wide reading of contemporary sources and a masterly appreciation of the research in sociology, economics, and politics, as well as history"—(James C. Stone).

Russian History and Soviet Policy

Barghoorn, Frederick C. SOVIET FOREIGN PROPAGANDA. *Princeton Univ. Press* 1964 $10.50

POLITICS IN THE U.S.S.R. *Little* 2nd ed. 1972 pap. $4.95

Ben-Ami. BETWEEN HAMMER AND SICKLE. *The Jewish Publication Society of America* 1968 $6.00. The plight of the Russian Jew.

Berry, Lloyd E., and Robert O. Crummey, Eds. RUDE AND BARBAROUS KINGDOM: Russia in the Accounts of Sixteenth-Century English Voyagers. *Univ. of Wisconsin Press* 1972 $10.00 pap. $4.50

Carmichael, Joel. A SHORT HISTORY OF RUSSIA. *Open Court* 1974 pap. $4.95

Carr, Edward Hallett. A HISTORY OF SOVIET RUSSIA. *Macmillan* 7 vols. 1951–1960 Vols. 1–3 The Bolshevik Revolution 1917–1923 Vol. 4 The Interregnum 1923–1924 Vols. 5–7 Socialism in One Country 1924–1926 Vols. 1–6 each $7.50 Vol. 7 $10.00. This series of volumes promises to become the most comprehensive on the subject in English.

Chermavsky, Michael, Ed. STRUCTURE OF RUSSIAN HISTORY. *Random* 1970 pap. $6.50

Cohen, Stephen F. BUKHARIN AND THE BOLSHEVIK REVOLUTION: A Political Biography, 1888–1938. *Knopf* 1973 $15.00; *Random* Vintage Bks. 1974 pap. $3.95

Conquest, Robert. THE GREAT TERROR: Stalin's Purge of the Thirties. *Macmillan* 1968 rev. ed. 1973 $8.95 Collier Bks. pap. $4.95

The author "knows practically everything about this bloodchilling story. He tells it all, and tells it extraordinarily well. Most wholeheartedly recommended to libraries"—(*LJ*).

POWER AND POLICY IN THE U.S.S.R.: The Struggle for Stalin's Succession, 1945–1960. *Gannon* 1970 $6.50; *Harper* Torchbks. 1960 pap. $2.95

Crankshaw, Edward. KHRUSHCHEV: A Career. *Viking* 1966 $7.50 Compass Bks. pap. $2.75

THE NEW COLD WAR: Moscow v. Peking. 1963. *Bks. for Libraries* $8.00

Dallin, Alexander, and Thomas B. Larson, Eds. SOVIET POLITICS SINCE KHRUSHCHEV. *Prentice-Hall* Spectrum Bks. 1968 pap. $1.95

Deutscher, Issaac. THE UNFINISHED REVOLUTION: Russia 1917–1967. *Oxford* 1967 $3.95 pap. 1969 $1.95

Dukes, Paul. A HISTORY OF RUSSIA: Medieval, Modern, and Contemporary. *McGraw-Hill* 1975 $12.50

Engel, Barbara A., and Clifford N. Rosenthal, Eds. FIVE SISTERS: Women against the Tsar. *Knopf* 1975 $8.95

"The 'sisters' of the title, a quintet of revolutionary precursors of the women's movement, were united through their common struggle against civil oppression during the reign of Alexander II of Russia. . . . Gently bred and scarcely out of their teens, the five were drawn by different routes into the revolutionary ferment of the 1860s and 1870s"—*(LJ)*.

Engels, Friedrich. *See his main entry in Chapter 8, The Social Sciences, this Vol.*

Engle, Eloise, and Lauri A. Poananen. THE WINTER WAR: The Russo-Finnish Conflict 1939–1940. *Scribner* 1973 $7.95

Fainsod, Merle. HOW RUSSIA IS RULED. *Harvard Univ. Press* 1953 rev. ed. 1963 $12.00

Here is a timely, authoritative work with the rare combination of fine scholarship, deep understanding of Russian mentality, well-balanced approach and lucid style. *Current History* calls it "the most authoritative single volume on the Soviet system of government."

Farmborough, Florence. WITH THE ARMIES OF THE CZAR: A Nurse at the Russian Front 1914–1918. *Stein & Day* 1975 $10.00

"An absorbing account of a British nurse in Russia"—(Publisher's note).

Filene, Peter F. AMERICANS AND THE SOVIET EXPERIMENT, 1917–1933. *Harvard Univ. Press* 1967 $11.00

"A well-written, very readable and valuable analysis" *(LJ)* of American attitudes toward the Russian revolution.

Fischer, Louis. THE ROAD TO YALTA: Soviet Foreign Relations, 1941–1945. *Harper* 1972 $8.95

"Fischer, an expert and provocative writer, portrays clearly the leading figures of the time, especially Churchill and Stalin. The practical, hard-headed foreign policy of Stalin is well depicted"—*(Choice)*.

RUSSIA'S ROAD FROM PEACE TO WAR: Soviet Foreign Relations, 1917–1941. *Harper* 1969 $12.50

Golder, F. A. RUSSIAN EXPANSION ON THE PACIFIC, 1641–1850. *Paragon* 1971 $15.00

Gorky, Maxim. UNTIMELY THOUGHTS: Essays on Revolution, Culture, and the Bolsheviks, 1917–1918. Trans. from the Russian with introd. and notes by Herman Ermolaev *Eriksson* 1968 $6.95

"This collection of pieces from the newspaper *Novaya Zhizn* (*New Life*) records, in succession, Gorky's hopefulness just after the Russian Revolution; his horror at the violence, terror, and cruelty that then occurred; his love for his fellow-Russians and his awareness of their difficulties in building a just society; and, last, his dogged, brave, principled opposition to the Bolsheviks, who finally shut down his paper. The collection is something far better than just another anti-Bolshevik witness because of Gorky's simple, concrete, and honest prose"—*(New Yorker)*.

Grey, Ian. THE HORIZON HISTORY OF RUSSIA. *McGraw-Hill* 1970 $22.00 deluxe ed. $25.00

Gruliow, Leo, and The Current Digest of the Soviet Press Staff, Eds. CURRENT SOVIET GOVERNMENT POLICIES No. III: The Documentary Record of the Extraordinary 21st Congress of the Communist Party of the Soviet Union (with a Who's Who of the Central Committee, comp. by Mark Neuweld); No. IV Ed. by Leo Gruliow and Charlotte Saidowski *Columbia* No. 3 1960 No. 4 1962 each $10.00 Vols. 1 (1953) and 2 (1957) o.p.

Gunther, John. INSIDE RUSSIA TODAY. *Harper* rev. ed. 1962 $8.95

Haimson, Leopold H., Ed. THE MENSHEVIKS: From the Revolution of 1917 to the Outbreak of the Second World War. *Univ. of Chicago Press* 1974 $22.50

Hammond, Thomas T., Comp. and ed. SOVIET FOREIGN RELATIONS AND WORLD COMMUNISM: A Selected, Annotated Bibliography of 7,000 Books in 30 Languages. *Princeton Univ. Press* 1965 $32.50

"Because of its judicious selections and careful annotations, this volume will, with periodic updating, doubtless be a standard reference work in the field for years to come"—(*LJ*).

Hendel, Samuel, Ed., with introductory notes. THE SOVIET CRUCIBLE: The Soviet System in Theory and Practice. 1967. *Duxbury Press* 1973 pap. $6.95

Herzen, Alexander. MY PAST AND THOUGHTS: The Memoirs of Alexander Herzen. 1908. Trans. by Constance Garnett; introd. by Isaiah Berlin; rev. by Humphrey Higgens *Gordon Press* 6 vols. $200.00; *Knopf* 4 vols. 1968 boxed set $30.00; *Random* Vintage Bks. pap. $4.95. A wealthy Russian of the 19th century gives a most interesting firsthand account of Russian history in his time.

Hingley, Ronald. A CONCISE HISTORY OF RUSSIA. *Viking* 1972 $10.95

Horecky, Paul L., Ed. RUSSIA AND THE SOVIET UNION: A Bibliographic Guide to Western-Language Publications. *Univ. of Chicago Press* 1965 $12.50

Institute for the Study of the U.S.S.R. PROMINENT PERSONALITIES IN THE U.S.S.R.: A Biographic Directory Containing 6,015 Biographies. Ed. by Edward L. Crowley and others *Scarecrow Press* 1968 $35.00 (annual subscription for quarterly supplements $10.00). A comprehensive and updated reference book which includes quarterly supplements entitled "Portrait of Prominent U.S.S.R. Personalities."

SOVIET DIPLOMATIC CORPS, 1917–1967. *Scarecrow Press* 1970 $7.50

WHO WAS WHO IN THE U.S.S.R.: A Biographic Directory Containing 5,015 Biographies of Prominent Soviet Historical Personalities. Ed. by Heinrich E. Schulz and Paul K. Urban *Scarecrow Press* 1972 $40.00

Jaworskyj, Michael, Comp. and ed. SOVIET POLITICAL THOUGHT: An Anthology. Trans. by the editor *Johns Hopkins Press* 1968 $17.50

Johnson, Priscilla. KHRUSHCHEV AND THE ARTS: The Politics of Soviet Culture, 1962–1964. Documents sel. and ed. by the author and Leopold Labedz *M.I.T. Press* 1965 $12.50

"Miss Johnson presents a balanced and realistic analysis of Khrushchev's handling of the ideological and political issues posed by the relatively independent, unorthodox behavior of [many] Soviet writers. ... Her analysis, together with the valuable documents and notes that comprise the remainder of this useful study, furnish both raw material and orientations helpful to social scientists and to interested citizens generally"—(*Public Opinion Quarterly*).

Kassof, Allen, Ed. PROSPECTS FOR SOVIET SOCIETY. *Praeger* 1968 $10.00 pap. $4.95

Kennan, George F. MARQUIS DE CUSTINE AND HIS RUSSIA IN 1839. *Princeton Univ. Press* 1971 $6.00

See also his main entry, this Section.

Khrushchev, Nikita. *See his main entry in Chapter 2, General Bibliography and Autobiography, this Vol.*

Kluchevsky, Vasilli O. A HISTORY OF RUSSIA. Trans. by C. J. Hogarth. 1911–1931. *Russell & Russell* 5 vols. 1960 set $45.00

Lederer, Ivo J., Ed. RUSSIAN FOREIGN POLICY: Essays in Historical Perspective. *Yale Univ. Press* 1962 $12.50 pap. $2.95

"This well-edited collection of essays looking into the fundamentals of Russian foreign policy pre- and post-revolution stems from the lively conference on 'A Century of Russian Foreign Policy' held at Yale University in Spring 1961. The 'cream' of American Soviet scholars participated and contributed to this book. ... A good addition to any general collection on Soviet affairs"—(*LJ*).

Lenin. *See his main entry, this Section.*

Marx, Karl. *See his main entry in Chapter 8, The Social Sciences, this Vol.*

Massie, Robert K. NICHOLAS AND ALEXANDRA: An Intimate Account of the Last of the Romanovs and the Fall of the Russian Empire. *Atheneum* 1967 $12.95; *Dell* 1971 pap. $1.75. A fine biography.

Masters, Anthony. BAKUNIN: The Father of Anarchism. *Saturday Review Press* 1975 $9.95

Mazour, Anatole G. RUSSIA: Tsarist and Communist. *Van Nostrand* 1962 $12.95

   This revision of an earlier study "Russia Past and Present" (o.p.) is a "massive, richly informative history of Russia"—*(American Historical Review).*

Mills, C. Wright. THE MARXISTS. *Dell* Delta Bks. 1963 pap. $.95. A cogent analysis of Marxist thought and its impact on society.

Mousnier, Roland. PEASANT UPRISINGS IN SEVENTEENTH-CENTURY FRANCE, RUSSIA, AND CHINA. Trans. by Brian Pearce *Harper* Torchbks. 1972 pap. $3.95

Nenarokov, Albert P. RUSSIA IN THE 20TH CENTURY: The View of a Soviet Historian. Trans. by David Windheim. 1968. *Apollo* 1969 pap. $2.50

Nove, Alec. THE SOVIET ECONOMY: An Introduction. *Praeger* 2nd ed. 1969 $8.00 pap. $3.50

Palmer, Alan. ALEXANDER I: Tsar of War and Peace. *Harper* 1974 $15.00

   THE RUSSIA OF WAR AND PEACE. *Macmillan* 1973 $9.95

Parker, W. H. A HISTORICAL GEOGRAPHY OF RUSSIA. *Aldine* 1969 $12.50

   THE SUPERPOWERS: The United States and the Soviet Union Compared. *Halsted Press* 1972 $14.95

Payne, Robert, and Nikita Romanoff. IVAN THE TERRIBLE. *T. Y. Crowell* 1975 price not set

   "A personal, psychological biography of Ivan the Terrible, one of Russia's most controversial czars"—*(LJ).*

Pearson, Michael. THE SEALED TRAIN: Lenin's Eight-Month Journey from Exile to Power. *Putnam* 1974 $8.95

   "A vivid account of the famous and controversial episode of the Russian Revolution—Lenin's passage through Germany to Russia after the overthrow of the Czar in February, 1917"—*(LJ).*

Pipes, Richard E. RUSSIA UNDER THE OLD REGIME. *Scribner* 1975 $17.50 pap. $6.95

   "We put away this book with a feeling of gratitude for the fresh insights it gives us into the broad sweep of Russian history, its unique dilemmas and its pathos"—*(N.Y. Times).*

   (Ed.). REVOLUTIONARY RUSSIA: A Symposium. Russian Research Center Studies Ser. *Harvard Univ. Press* 1968 $9.50. A collection of essays presented at a conference held at Harvard in 1967 commemorating the 50th anniversary of the Russian Revolution.

Reed, John. TEN DAYS THAT SHOOK THE WORLD. 1919. *International Pubs.* 1967 $7.50 pap. $2.45; *Random* Vintage Bks. pap. $1.95

   This "classic example of journalism so perceptive that it approximates history" (Granville Hicks, in *SR*), is therefore still worth reading as an eyewitness account of the Russian Revolution. John Reed (1887–1920), an American journalist with radical leanings, became an exponent of Communism in early youth. He spent much of his life in the Soviet Union and is buried in the Kremlin.

Riasanovsky, Nicholas V. A HISTORY OF RUSSIA. *Oxford* 2nd ed. 1969 $15.00 text ed. $9.95. Written with sober objectivity and notable for its breadth and contemporaneity, it is not for the general reader, but should be considered for large historical and Slavic collections.

Rubin, Ronald I., Ed., with introd. THE UNREDEEMED: Anti-Semitism in the Soviet Union. *Quadrangle* 1968 $10.00

Sakharov, Andrei D. PROGRESS, COEXISTENCE AND INTELLECTUAL FREEDOM. Trans. by the *New York Times*; introd. and notes by Harrison E. Salisbury *Norton* 1968 rev. ed. 1970 $5.95 pap. 1968 $2.50

   "Here is the boldest, most courageous and most starkly expressed statement by a living Russian—or for that matter, by anyone—on the absolute need in a nuclear world for an end to prenuclear politics, partisanship, patriotism, propaganda, and for the real beginnings of freedom, coexistence and even cooperation beteen the two giants, the United States and Soviet Russia. . . . A tremendously important and luminous book"—(*PW*).

See also his main entry in Chapter 7, Science: Scientists, this Vol.

Salisbury, Harrison E. THE 900 DAYS: The Siege of Leningrad. *Harper* 1969 $10.95; *Avon Bks.* pap. $1.45

"Certainly I have read nothing on Leningrad which moved me so totally, so painfully, as Salisbury's magnificent book. This is an account of one of the most horrible, and also one of the most heroic, episodes in human history. Mr. Salisbury has all the qualifications to write it, and he has used them with masterly power. He has lived for a long time in Leningrad, and loves the city and the people. He has read all the published sources, not only the official histories, but also the reminiscences, of which there are a lot"—(C. P. Snow, in the *N.Y. Times*).

RUSSIA. A New York Times Byline Book. *Atheneum* 1965 $3.95 pap. $2.45; *Macmillan* 1965 $2.95 lib. bdg. $2.96

THE SOVIET UNION: The Fifty Years. *Harcourt* 1967 $10.00

"Probably the best all-around book for the general reader"—(Russell Barnes, in *SR*).

Schwarz, Solomon M. THE RUSSIAN REVOLUTION OF 1905: The Workers' Movement and the Formation of Bolshevism and Menshevism. Trans. by Gertrude Vakar *Univ. of Chicago Press* 1967 $12.00

Seton-Watson, Hugh. THE RUSSIAN EMPIRE, 1801–1917. Oxford History of Modern Europe Ser. *Oxford* 1967 $14.95 text ed. $10.95

Simmonds, George W., Ed. SOVIET LEADERS. *T. Y. Crowell* 1967 $10.00

Biographical material on 42 prominent Soviet leaders. "The sketches are accurate and complete, and . . . highly readable"—(*LJ*).

Stalin, Joseph. *See his main entry, this Section.*

Survey Editors. THE STATE OF SOVIET SCIENCE. *M.I.T. Press* 1965 $8.95

A collection of all the articles on Soviet science plus others appearing in the July 1964 issue of the British journal *Survey*. "Lucid, nontechnical accounts of the major developments in astronomy, biology, cybernetics, chemistry as well as in mathematics, medicine, psychology, and space research. Each contributor provides a background of the developments; the result is a panoramic view of scientific thinking in Russia from the early days of Lenin to the present time"—(Publisher's note).

Tatu, Michel. POWER IN THE KREMLIN: From Khrushchev to Kosygin. Trans. by Helen Katel *Viking* 1969 $10.00 Compass Bks. pap. $3.45

"A combination of lucid journalistic style, an instinct for relevant minute details, and a rare understanding of the personal as well as the ideological aspects of Soviet politics contribute to an academically fully acceptable study of remarkable quality"—(*Choice*).

Thomson, Gladys. CATHERINE THE GREAT AND THE EXPANSION OF RUSSIA. 1947. *Macmillan* Collier Bks. 1962 pap. $.95

Trotsky, Leon. *See his main entry, this Section.*

Tucker, Robert C. STALIN AS REVOLUTIONARY, 1879–1929: A Study in History and Personality. *Norton* 1974 $12.95

Ulam, Adam B. THE BOLSHEVIKS: The Intellectual and Political History of the Triumph of Communism in Russia. *Macmillan* 1955 $9.95 Collier Bks. 1968 pap. $2.95

EXPANSION AND COEXISTENCE: Soviet Foreign Policy, 1917–1973. *Praeger* 1968 2nd ed. 1974 $15.95 pap. $6.95

"There have been a few good surveys in English of various periods of Soviet foreign policy, but this massive work is the first to cover the whole 50 years. . . . It will be very useful for reference, being equipped with a moderately good index and not unduly encumbered by footnotes. [It] is admirably accurate"—(Hugh Seton-Watson, in the *N.Y. Times*). "This big, informative work by a Russian expert at Harvard is close to enthralling"—(*New Yorker*).

STALIN: The Man and His Era. *Viking* 1973 $12.95 Compass Bks. 1974 pap. $4.95

Vernadsky, George. *See his main entry, this Section.*

Werth, Alexander. RUSSIA: Hopes and Fears. *Simon & Schuster* 1969 $6.95 Touchstone-Clarion Bks. 1970 pap. $2.95

RUSSIA: The Post-War Years. *Taplinger* 1972 $12.00

Yaney, George L. THE SYSTEMATIZATION OF RUSSIAN GOVERNMENT: Social Evolution in the Domestic Administration of Imperial Russia, 1711–1905. *Univ. of Illinois Press* 1973 $13.50

The Mideast

In this listing will be found political discussion of contemporary Egypt, Israel and other areas in the eastern Mediterranean. For a bibliography of mostly U.S. publications in English on the Arab point of view in the Mideast conflict, write the Fifth of June Society (28 Perfect Building, Tannoukhine St., Beirut, Lebanon). (*See also Supplementary Reading List on Modern and World History; listing on Jewish History, immediately following, and, in* Reader's Adviser, *Vol. 2, Chapter 18, Middle Eastern Literature.*)

Allon, Yigal. THE MAKING OF ISRAEL'S ARMY. *Universe Bks.* 1970 $8.95

"An absorbing account of the development of Israel's army from a band of guerrillas to a modern force"—(Publisher's note).

Berque, Jacques. EGYPT: Imperialism and Revolution. Trans. by Janet Stuart *Praeger* 1972 $38.50

Bose, Tarum C. THE SUPERPOWERS AND THE MIDDLE EAST. *Asia Pub. House* 1972 $6.50

CAMBRIDGE HISTORY OF IRAN. *Cambridge* 8 vols. 1968– Vol. 1 Land of Iran, ed. by W. B. Fisher Vol. 5 The Saljus and Mongol Period, ed. by J. A. Boyle each $22.50 Vols. 2–4, 6–8 (in prep.)

CAMBRIDGE HISTORY OF ISLAM. Ed. by P. M. Holt and others *Cambridge* (1970) Vol. 1 The Central Islamic Lands $27.50 Vol. 2 The Further Islamic Lands: Islamic Society and Civilization $32.50

Carmichael, Joel. THE SHAPING OF THE ARABS: A Study in Ethnic Identity. *Macmillan* 1967 $7.95

Chesnoff, Richard, Edward Klein and Robert Littell. IF ISRAEL LOST THE WAR: A Documentary "Novel." *Coward* 1969 $5.95

A justification for Israel's part in the Six-Day War. "A powerful book"—(Senator Jacob Javits).

Chomsky, Noam. PEACE IN THE MIDDLE EAST? Reflections on Justice and Nationhood. *Pantheon* 1974 $7.95

"Chomsky insists that the concept of socialist binationalism should be accepted by Israel and the Arab states and by the Palestinians to achieve reconciliation"—(*Booklist*).

Cromer, Evelyn B. MODERN EGYPT. *Howard Fertig* 2 vols. 1968 set $32.50

Dayan, Moshe. DIARY OF THE SINAI CAMPAIGN. *Harper* 1966 $7.50; *Schocken* 1967 pap. $1.95. The commander of Israel's forces tells of the 1965 war with the Arabs.

De Novo, John A. AMERICAN INTERESTS AND POLICIES IN THE MIDDLE EAST, 1900–1939. *Univ. of Minnesota Press* 1963 $12.50. A classic study in American foreign policy.

Evron, Yair. THE MIDDLE EAST: Nations, Superpowers, and Wars. *Praeger* 1973 $8.50 pap. $3.50

Field, Michael. $100 MILLION A DAY: The Arabs and Their Money. *St. Martin's* 1975 $10.00

Glubb, John Bagot. PEACE IN THE HOLY LAND: An Historical Analysis of the Palestine Problem. *Int. Pubns. Service* 1971 $12.50; *Verry* 1971 $13.75

A SHORT HISTORY OF THE ARAB PEOPLES. *Stein & Day* 1970 pap. $2.95

SOLDIERS OF FORTUNE: The Story of the Mamlukes. *Stein & Day* $12.50

"This work deals with the Mamlukes who reigned over Egypt and Syria from 1250 to 1517. . . . The Mamlukes were Turks and Circassians from the Russian steppes who were bought from their parents in childhood and brought to Egypt to be trained in the arts of war"—(*Economist*).

SYRIA, LEBANON AND JORDAN. Nations and Peoples Library. *Walker & Co.* 1967 $8.50

Hitti, Philip K. CAPITAL CITIES OF ARAB ISLAM. *Univ. of Minnesota Press* 1973 $7.95

HISTORY OF THE ARABS. *St. Martin's* 10th ed. 1970 $16.95 pap. $8.95

ISLAM: A Way of Life. *Univ. of Minnesota Press* 1970 $6.95; *Regnery* 1971 pap. $1.95

LEBANON IN HISTORY FROM THE EARLIEST TIMES TO THE PRESENT. *St. Martin's* 3rd ed. 1967 $19.95

A SHORT HISTORY OF THE NEAR EAST. *Van Nostrand-Reinhold* 1966 $7.95 pap. $5.50

"Philip Hitti is the most distinguished living Western historian of Arabia and the Near East"—*(LJ)*.

Howard, Harry N. TURKEY, THE STRAITS, AND U.S. POLICY. *Johns Hopkins Press* 1975 $14.50

"An excellent, serious, well-documented analysis of U.S. involvement with and interest in the historic Turkish straits"—*(LJ)*.

Hurewitz, Jacob C. SOVIET-AMERICAN RIVALRY IN THE MIDDLE EAST. *Praeger* 1969 $8.00 pap. $2.95

Issawi, Charles. THE ECONOMIC HISTORY OF IRAN, 1800–1914. Ed. by William R. Polk *Univ. of Chicago Press* 1971 $17.50

(Ed.) THE ECONOMIC HISTORY OF THE MIDDLE EAST, 1800–1914. *Univ. of Chicago Press* 1966 $15.00

"This is a pioneering study in the vast but unexplored field of the economic history of the Middle East by an eminently qualified scholar. Professor Charles Issawi, Ragnar Nurkse Professor of Economics at Columbia University, is familiar with all aspects of the Middle East, as his books and articles, ranging from the philosophy to the politics of the area, testify.... The passages on land tenure, particularly in Iraq and Egypt, and on the transition from subsistence to market economy provide tantalizing and vital information on social and structural changes which accompanied the modernization of the Middle East. Other sections on taxation, financing, banking, population, the introduction of modern systems of transportation, irrigation, and commerce, together with those on industrialization and the occupational habits of ethnic groups, illustrate the broad scope of Professor Issawi's work. [It] consists of a general introduction and sixty-one excerpts, each preceded by a brief introductory passage and accompanied by notes and relevant bibliography. Most of the excerpts are translated from Arabic, Turkish, Russian, Italian, and French, and are made available for the first time to the English reader.... In comparison with Professor Issawi's work, even the better books ... seem outclassed and inadequate"—(Kemal H. Karpat, in *Political Science Quarterly*).

Karpat, Kemal H., Ed. POLITICAL AND SOCIAL THOUGHT IN THE CONTEMPORARY MIDDLE EAST. *Praeger* 1968 $10.00 pap. $3.95

Khouri, Fred J. THE ARAB-ISRAELI DILEMMA. *Syracuse Univ. Press* 1968 pap. $4.25

Kollek, Teddy, and Moshe Pearlman. JERUSALEM: A History of Forty Centuries. *Random* 1968 $15.00. By the mayor of Jerusalem; he acted as a special assistant to Moshe Dayan during the Six-Day War.

Lall, Arthur. THE U.N. AND THE MIDDLE EAST CRISIS. *Columbia* 1970 $12.50 pap. $2.95. By a veteran of the U.N. from India.

Love, Kenneth. SUEZ: The Twice Fought War, a History. *McGraw-Hill* 1970 $10.00

"Should become a classic in modern Middle East history"—*(Choice)*.

McLane, Charles B. SOVIET-MIDDLE EAST RELATIONS. *Columbia* 1973 $15.00

Patai, Raphael. THE ARAB MIND. *Scribner* 1973 $12.50

"In 16 chapters Patai discusses a number of topics, among them, Arab child-rearing practices, Bedouin ethos, sexual behavior, the role of Islam and of the Arabic language ... Arab unity and the Arabs' reactions to, and relations with, the West"—*(Choice)*.

Prittie, Terence. ISRAEL: Miracle in the Desert. *Penguin* rev. ed. 1968 pap. $1.95

Rodinson, Maxine. ISLAM AND CAPITALISM. *Pantheon* 1974 $8.95

ISRAEL AND THE ARABS. Trans. by Michael Perl *Pantheon* 1969 $5.95

Of this "analysis of 70 years of conflict, written with concern for the Arab point of view," Arnold Toynbee has said: "I agree with every word that Professor Rodinson has written here.... I have read it—with admiration and without any dissent whatever, which is a rare experience indeed for any reader of any book on this subject. . . . It is a splendid book; it gives a precise record of the facts; its judgments are discerning; there is in it a deep concern both for justice and for humaneness."

Safran, Nadav. THE UNITED STATES AND ISRAEL. American Foreign Policy Library. *Harvard Univ. Press* 1963 $8.50

Schmidt, Dana Adams. ARMAGEDDON IN THE MIDDLE EAST. Ed. by Theodore M. Berstein *John Day* 1974 $8.95

Shwadran, Benjamin. MIDDLE EAST, OIL AND THE GREAT POWERS. *Halsted Press* 3rd ed. 1974 $20.00

Stephens, Robert. NASSER: A Political Biography. *Simon & Schuster* 1972 $12.50

Thomas, Hugh. SUEZ. *Harper* 1967 $5.95 pap. 1969 $2.45

Wiet, Gaston. BAGHDAD: Metropolis of the Abbased Caliphate. Trans. by S. Feiler *Univ. of Oklahoma Press* 1971 $15.00

Yale, William. THE NEAR EAST: A Modern History. *Univ. of Michigan Press* 1968 $10.00

Jewish History

The following publishers and agencies publish much material on Jewish history: *Philipp Feldheim* (96 E. Broadway, New York, N.Y. 10002), the *Jewish Agency*—American Section (515 Park Ave., New York, N.Y. 10022), the *Jewish Publication Society of America*, the *National Jewish Welfare Board* (145 E. 32 St., New York, N.Y. 10016), *Schocken, Soncino Press* and the *United Synagogue Book Service* (218 E. 70 St., New York, N.Y. 10021). A valuable publication is the *Judaica Book Guide*, published twice a year in fall and spring and available on request (131 E. 23 St., New York, N.Y. 10010). *(For major encyclopedias and histories, see Chapter 4, World Religions—Judaism: Reference Works—History, Criticism and Commentary, this Vol.; for the political life of contemporary Israel, see preceding listing on the Mideast.)*

Ackroyd, Peter R. EXILE AND RESTORATION: A Study of Hebrew Thought in the Sixth Century. *Westminster Press* 1969 $6.50

"A masterly survey of the period running from the eve of the exile to the end of the Sixth Century B.C."—*(TLS*, London).

Agus, Jacob Bernard. THE EVOLUTION OF JEWISH THOUGHT: From Biblical Times to the Opening of the Modern Era. *Arno* 1959 $22.00

This survey is written by a distinguished Hebrew scholar and rabbi. He writes with intellectual verve and a lucidity that makes his book valuable and informative reading.

THE AMERICAN JEWISH YEAR BOOK: An Annual. Ed. by Morris Fine and Milton Himmelfarb; Assoc. Ed. Martha Jelenko *Jewish Publication Society of America* $13.95. *(For comment, see Chapter 1, Reference Books—General: Year Books, this Vol.)*

Arendt, Hannah. EICHMANN IN JERUSALEM: A Report on the Banality of Evil. *Viking* 1963 $6.00 Compass Bks. pap. $1.95. The author covered the trial for the *New Yorker* and the series of articles in that magazine form the bulk of this book.

See also her main entry, this Section.

Avriel, Ehua. OPEN THE GATES!: A Personal Story of 'Illegal' Immigration to Israel. *Atheneum* 1975 $10.00

Avriel "served as an agent of the Mossad (a branch of the Jewish defense underground in Palestine) from 1938 to 1948"—*(LJ)*.

Ben-Ami. BETWEEN HAMMER AND SICKLE. *Jewish Publication Society of America* 1968 $6.00. A report on the present state of Jews in the Soviet Union.

Ben-Gurion, David. ISRAEL: A Personal History. *T. Y. Crowell* (Funk & Wagnalls) 1971 $20.00

(Ed.). JEWS IN THEIR LAND. *Doubleday* 1966 1974 $9.95

Bridger, David, and Samuel J. Wolk. THE NEW JEWISH ENCYCLOPEDIA. *Behrman House* 1962 $15.00. The first new edition since 1925 of this concise encyclopedia with definitions concerning Jewish religion and liturgy, places and people in Jewish history.

Cohen, Hayim J. THE JEWS OF THE MIDDLE EAST, 1860–1972. *Halsted Press* 1973 $12.50
"The history of the Jews in the Middle East is without doubt the most neglected subject in modern Jewish historiography. It is for this reason that any book which deals with this subject in a serious and scholarly manner is to be welcomed"—*(Choice)*.

Cohn, Haim H. JEWISH LAW IN ANCIENT AND MODERN ISRAEL. *KTAV* 1971 $12.50
"A collection of essays from Israeli journals that do not have a wide circulation here"—*(Choice)*.

Cuddihy, John Murray. THE ORDEAL OF CIVILITY: Freud, Marx, Levi-Strauss, and the Jewish Struggle with Modernity. *Basic Bks.* 1974 $11.95
"Analyses Jewish assimilation in post-18th-century Europe and America as a subcultural microcosm of the general global process of modernization"—*(LJ)*.

Davidowicz, Lucy S., Ed. THE GOLDEN TRADITION: Jewish Life and Thought in Eastern Europe. *Holt* 1967 $8.95
"Mrs. Davidowicz, who is the coauthor of *Politics in a Pluralist Democracy* and a frequent contributor to *Commentary, New Leader,* and *Jewish Social Studies*, has captured the pulse of this community in a rich gathering of 'autobiographies, memoirs, reminiscences and letters of some 60 persons whose lives document these East European Jewish responses to modernity.' A brief comment places each author, and the anthology itself is introduced by the editor's penetrating historical review. For the excellence of the selections (many previously unavailable in English) and the high quality of the translations (most are by the editor), this book is highly recommended"—*(LJ)*.

Davis, Moshe, Ed. THE YOM KIPPUR WAR: Israel and the Jewish People. *Arno* 1974 $9.00

Deutscher, Isaac. THE NON-JEWISH JEW AND OTHER ESSAYS. Ed. by Tamara Deutscher. 1968. *Hill & Wang* 1973 pap. $2.65. An expert on Soviet affairs analyzes the question of being a Jew.

Dimont, Max I. THE INDESTRUCTIBLE JEWS: Is There a Manifest Destiny in Jewish History? *Norton* 1971 $8.95; *New Am. Lib.* Signet Bks. 1973 pap. $1.50
Dimont writes "that Jewish history consists of a unique series of events that has preserved the Jews as Jews in exile to fulfill their avowed mission of ushering in the brotherhood of man"—*(LJ)*.

JEWS, GOD AND HISTORY. *Simon & Schuster* 1962 $8.95; *New Am. Lib.* 1972 pap. $1.25

Dinnerstein, Leonard. THE LEO FRANK CASE. *Columbia* 1968 $10.00

Eban, Abba. MY COUNTRY. *Random* 1972 $15.00

VOICE OF ISRAEL. 1957. *Horizon Press* rev. ed. 1969 $7.50. A collection of his speeches.

Eisenberg, Azriel. JEWISH HISTORICAL TREASURES. *Bloch Pub. Co.* 1970 $10.00
"From nearly four millenia of Jewish history the author has chosen . . . objects, artifacts, manuscripts, and instruments with the purpose of illuminating Jewish life through the ages"—*(LJ)*.

Elon, Amos. HERZL. *Holt* 1975 $15.00

THE ISRAELIS: Founders and Sons. *Bantam* 1971 pap. $1.95

Fishman, Priscilla, Ed. THE JEWS OF THE UNITED STATES. *Quadrangle* 1974 $8.95
"One of a number of by-products of the new *Encyclopedia Judaica*"—*(Choice)*.

Friedlander, Albert H., Ed. OUT OF THE WHIRLWIND: A Reader of Holocaust Literature. Ill. by Jacob Landau *Union of American Hebrew Congregations* 1968 $8.65

Gilbert, Martin. ATLAS OF THE ARAB-ISRAELI CONFLICT. *Macmillan* 1975 $6.95
"This concise book of 101 diligently prepared maps covers the creation and continuing existence of the state of Israel"—*(LJ)*.

Goldman, Zeev, and Eva Goldman. A LAND THAT I WILL SHOW THEE: The Jewish People through the Ages. *Putnam* 1968 $25.00

Grant, Michael. THE JEWS IN THE ROMAN WORLD. *Scribner* 1973 $10.00

"Grant traces Jewish history from the Maccabean uprising to the Christianization of the Roman Empire, concentrating on Roman Palestine"—*(Choice)*.

Greenberg, Louis. THE JEWS IN RUSSIA: The Struggle for Emancipation. Fwd. by Alfred Levin. 1944. *AMS Press* 1965 $20.00. A basic work on the subject covering the period from 1772 to 1917.

Heschel, Abraham J. THE INSECURITY OF FREEDOM: Essays on Human Existence. *Farrar, Straus* 1966 $6.95; *Schocken* 1972 pap. $3.45

Hyman, Louis. THE JEWS OF IRELAND FROM EARLIEST TIMES TO THE YEAR 1910. *Irish Academic Press* 1972 $12.50

"The first fully documented history of the Jews of Ireland which traces the origins of the Irish Jewish community from the 11th century until the beginning of the 20th"—*(Choice)*.

Kahler, Erich, and others. THE JEWS AMONG THE NATIONS. *Ungar* 1967 $4.75

"This book is an extraordinary achievement. In 149 pages the author manages to tell the reader more than much larger volumes or even encyclopedias have about the Jews, their history, the problem of their identity, their relationships with various peoples including the Germans and the Arabs, and the attitudes of other nationalities toward them. I have not the least hesitation, having read a representative number of works on the subject, in declaring *The Jews among the Nations* by far the best ever written. It could only have been accomplished by a scholar of Erich Kahler's quality"—(Ashley Montagu, in *SR*).

Kahn, Roger. THE PASSIONATE PEOPLE: What It Means to Be a Jew in America. *Int. Pubns. Service* 1969 $7.50

Kaplan, Chaim A. A SCROLL OF AGONY: The Warsaw Diary of Chaim A. Kaplan. Trans. by Abraham Katsh *Macmillan* 1965 $6.95

Kertzer, Morris N. WHAT IS A JEW? 1953. *Bloch Pub. Co.* 1973 $5.95; *Macmillan* Collier Bks. 1961 pap. $1.25

Laqueur, Walter. HISTORY OF ZIONISM. *Holt* 1972 $10.00

"An extremely important book that could be qualified as unique"—*(Journal of Modern History)*.

Levin, Nora. THE HOLOCAUST: The Destruction of European Jewry, 1933–1945. *T. Y. Crowell* 1968 $12.50; *Schocken* 1973 pap. $6.95

Lumer, Hyman, Ed. LENIN ON THE JEWISH QUESTION. *International Pubs.* 1972 $9.00 pap. $2.95. Contains all his key writings on the Jewish question.

Meir, Golda. A LAND OF OUR OWN: An Oral Autobiography. Ed. by Marie Syrkin *Putnam* 1973 $6.95

Memmi, Albert. THE LIBERATION OF THE JEW. Trans. from the French by Judy Hyun *Grossman* 1966 $4.95; *Viking* Compass Bks. 1973 pap. $2.45. A Tunisian Jew examines the problems of being Jewish in the modern world.

Meyer, Michael A. THE ORIGINS OF THE MODERN JEW: The Jewish Identity and European Culture in Germany, 1749–1824. *Wayne State Univ. Press* 1967 pap. 1972 $3.95

"Professor Meyer, of the California school of the Hebrew Union College-Jewish Institute of Religion, deals with German-Jewish intellectual and religious history during the period starting with Moses Mendelssohn and ending with Leopold Zunz, the period of the Enlightenment and of early German nationalism"—*(LJ)*.

(Ed.) IDEAS OF JEWISH HISTORY. *Behrman* 1974 $12.50

Patai, Raphael. ISRAEL BETWEEN EAST AND WEST. *Greenwood* rev. ed. 1970 $13.00

TENTS OF JACOB: The Diaspora, Yesterday and Today. *Prentice-Hall* 1972 $11.95

"This study of Jewish life outside Israel focuses on the history, customs and culture of the Jews of the Diaspora in its three major divisions—the Oriental, Sephardic, and Ashkenazic"—*(LJ)*.

(With Jennifer Wing) THE MYTH OF THE JEWISH RACE. *Scribner* 1974 $12.50

Porter, Jack N., and Peter Dreier. JEWISH RADICALISM: A Selected Anthology. *Grove* 1973 $7.95 pap. $2.45

"An anthology of articles, poems, and cartoons introducing the themes and ideas of the American-Jewish counter-culture to a wider audience"—(*Choice*).

Rivkin, Ellis. THE SHAPING OF JEWISH HISTORY: A Radical New Interpretation. *Scribner* 1970 $7.95

"Rivkin maintains that in no European society did Jews become emancipated until capitalism . . . acquired a strong foothold"—(Publisher's note).

Rodinson, Maxine. ISRAEL: A Colonial-Settler State? Trans. from the French by David Thorstad *Monad Press* 1973 $4.95 pap. $1.75

"It places the history of Zionism and Israel in the perspective of European expansion and colonialism in the Third World and upholds the view . . . [that Israel is] a 'colonial settler state' imposed by force on an unwilling Palestinian population"—(*Choice*).

Rothenberg, Joshua. THE JEWISH RELIGION IN THE SOVIET UNION. *KTAV* 1972 $10.00

"An extremely informative and interesting book dealing in great detail with the legal, ceremonial, ritualistic, and educational aspects of contemporary Judaism in the Soviet Union"—(*Choice*).

Schwarz, Leo W. GREAT AGES AND IDEAS OF THE JEWISH PEOPLE. *Random* (Modern Lib.) $5.95

Silver, Daniel Jeremy, and Bernard Martin. A HISTORY OF JUDAISM. *Basic Bks.* 2 vols. 1974 Vol. 1 From Abraham to Maimonides Vol. 2 Europe and the New World, by Bernard Martin set $37.00

Singer, Isaac Bashevis. IN MY FATHER'S COURT. *Farrar, Straus* 1966 $5.95 Noonday pap. $1.95

See also his main entry in Chapter 15, Other European Literature—Yiddish Literature, Reader's Adviser, Vol. 2.

Sklare, Marshall, Ed. AMERICA'S JEWS. *Random* 1971 pap. $3.25; *Peter Smith* $5.00

THE JEW IN AMERICAN SOCIETY. Library of Jewish Studies. *Behrman House* 1974 $12.50

THE JEWISH COMMUNITY IN AMERICA. Library of Jewish Studies. *Behrman House* 1974 $12.50

Steiner, Jean-Francois. TREBLINKA. Trans. from the French by Helen Weaver; pref. by Simone de Beauvoir *Simon & Schuster* 1967 $5.95. The best-selling account of the abortive prisoners' revolt in the Treblinka concentration camp.

Syrkin, Marie. GOLDA MEIR: Israel's Leader. *Putnam* 1969 $6.95. A biography of Israel's former Prime Minister.

Weinryb, Bernard D. THE JEWS OF POLAND: A Social and Economic History of the Jewish Community in Poland from 1100 to 1800. *Jewish Publication Society of America* 1972 $10.00

"Weinryb skillfully sets the history of Polish Jewry within the framework of Polish history and records the reactions of the Jews to their social and political environment"—(*Choice*).

Weizmann, Chaim. TRIAL AND ERROR: Autobiography. 1949. *Greenwood* 1972 $17.75; *Schocken* 1966 pap. $3.95. The Life of the first President of Israel.

WHO'S WHO IN WORLD JEWRY. Ed. by I. Carmin Karpman *Pitman* 3rd ed. 1972 $45.00

Wiesel, Elie. THE JEWS OF SILENCE: A Personal Report on Soviet Jewry. Trans. from the French by Neal Kozodoy *Holt* 1966 $4.95; *New Am. Lib.* 1972 pap. $1.95

LEGENDS OF OUR TIME. Trans. by Stephen Donadio *Holt* 1968 $5.95; *Avon Bks.* 1970 pap. $1.25. Myths of 20th-century European Jewry.

Wiesenthal, Simon. THE MURDERERS AMONG US: The Simon Wiesenthal Memoirs. Ed. with introd. by Joseph Wechsberg. 1967. *Bantam* 1973 pap. $1.25. Memoirs of a man who dedicated himself to tracking down Nazi war criminals, 900 of whom he brought to justice.

Wigoder, Geoffrey, Ed. JEWISH ART AND CIVILIZATION. *Walker & Co.* 2 vols. 1972 set $75.00

"These large, expensive, and lavishly illustrated works may be both read and perused for sheer esthetic pleasure"—*(Choice)*.

Wohlgelernter, Maurice. ISRAEL ZANGWILL: A Study. *Columbia* 1964 $10.00. Analysis of the prominent 19th-century British author.

Yaffe, James. THE AMERICAN JEWS. *Random* 1968 $10.95

Asia

Joseph Bram, Professor of Anthropology at New York University, has written: "For a nonspecialist, Southeast Asia is one of the most difficult areas to visualize and to understand." Since our last edition, Vietnam, however, has become a crucial and agonizing preoccupation for Americans, and books on Asia have rapidly multiplied. This interest is reflected in our expanded list and in our two sublistings on Vietnam and China. An excellent and comprehensive bibliography has been published in mimeographed form (60 pages) by the *University of Illinois Graduate School of Library Science* (Publications Office, Urbana, Ill.): Cecil Hobbs, Head of the South Asia Section, Library of Congress, "Understanding the Peoples of Southern Asia: A Bibliographical Essay" (1967 $1.00). *The Asia Society* (112 E. 64 St., New York, N.Y., 10021) published in 1968 a revised edition of its fine bibliography: "Asia: A Guide to Paperbacks" (write publisher for information on this and other materials). *Verry* distributes a number of books written by Indian scholars in English and printed in India. *Asia Publishing House* (dist. by Taplinger), *China Bks.*, *Japan Publications Trading Co.* and *Tuttle* are other sources of Asian books. *(See also Chapter 19, Asian Literature, Reader's Adviser, Vol. 2.)*

Allen, Richard. A SHORT INTRODUCTION TO THE HISTORY AND POLITICS OF SOUTHEAST ASIA. *Oxford* 1970 $7.50

Allworth, Edward A., Ed. CENTRAL ASIA: A Century of Russian Rule. With contributions by the editor, Helen Carrere d'Encausse, Ian Murray Matley, Karl H. Menges, Johanna Spector and Arthur Sprague. *Columbia* 1967 $20.00

ATLAS OF JAPAN: Physical, Economic, and Social. Int. Soc. for Educational Information: *Inter-Culture Assocs.* (Box 277, Thompson, Conn.) 1974 $35.00

"Accurate material drawn from statistical reports of the early 1970's is lucidly presented in the 73 clear and precise maps (48 plates) which illustrate an immense range of information"—*(LJ)*.

Ayub Khan, Mohammad. FRIENDS NOT MASTERS: A Political Autobiography. *Oxford* 1967 $11.00. By the former President of Pakistan.

Basham, A. L. THE WONDER THAT WAS INDIA: A Survey of the History and Culture of the Indian Sub-Continent Before the Coming of the Muslims. *Taplinger* 3rd rev. ed. 1968 $13.50; *Grove* Evergreen Bks. 1959 pap. $6.95

Bhattacharya, Sachchidananda. A DICTIONARY OF INDIAN HISTORY. *Braziller* 1967 $12.50. 2,785 entries in 888 pages. A comprehensive and encyclopedic work, accurate and valuable, by the distinguished Indian professor of history; alphabetical arrangement.

Bloodworth, Dennis. AN EYE FOR THE DRAGON: Southeast Asia Observed, 1954–1970. *Farrar, Straus* 1970 $8.95; *Lancer* pap. $1.75

Bowles, Chester. VIEW FROM NEW DELHI: Selected Speeches and Writings. *Yale Univ. Press* 1969 $10.00 pap. $1.95. By the American Ambassador to the Republic of India.

Butwell, Richard A. SOUTHEAST ASIA: A Political Introduction. *Praeger* 1975 $10.00

Cady, John F. POST WAR SOUTHEAST ASIA: Independence Problems. *Ohio Univ. Press* 1974 $15.00 pap. $8.50

THE CAMBRIDGE HISTORY OF INDIA. Ed. by E. J. Rapson and others *Verry* 6 vols. 1955–1970 each $22.50 Vol. 2 o.p.

Case, C. M. SOUTH ASIAN HISTORY, 1750–1950: A Guide to Periodicals, Dissertations, and Newspapers. *Princeton Univ. Press* 1968 $22.50

Choudhury, G. W. THE LAST DAYS OF UNITED PAKISTAN. *Indiana Univ. Press* 1974 $10.00

PAKISTAN'S RELATIONS WITH INDIA, 1947–1965. *Verry* 1972 $13.25. A Pakistani viewpoint, bitterly hostile to India.

Clyde, Paul H., and Burton F. Beers. THE FAR EAST: A History of the Western Impact and the Eastern Response, 1830–1970. *Prentice-Hall* 5th ed. 1970 $11.95

Coedès, George. THE INDIANIZED STATES OF SOUTHEAST ASIA. Trans. from the French by Susan Brown Cowing; ed. by Walter F. Vella *Univ. Press of Hawaii* (East-West Center) 1968 $12.00

THE MAKING OF SOUTHEAST ASIA. Trans. from the French by H. M. Wright *Univ. of California Press* 1969 $8.00 pap. $2.85. The first translation into English of a brief French work that has become a classic.

Cressey, George B. ASIA'S LANDS AND PEOPLES. *McGraw-Hill* 3rd ed. 1963 $16.00

Dempster, Prue. JAPAN ADVANCES: A Geographical Study. *Harper* (Barnes & Noble) 1967 2nd ed. 1969 $16.50

Dudley, Guilford A. A HISTORY OF EASTERN CIVILIZATION. *Wiley* 1973 $13.95

Edwardes, Michael. BRITISH INDIA, 1772–1947: A Survey of the Nature and Effects of Alien Rules. *Taplinger* 1968 $13.95

THE WEST IN ASIA, 1850–1914. *Putnam* 1967 $5.95 Capricorn Bks. $1.65

Fisher, Charles A. SOUTH-EAST ASIA: A Social, Economic and Political Geography. *Harper* (Barnes & Noble) 2nd ed. 1966 $22.50

Fitzgerald, Charles P. CHINA AND SOUTHEAST ASIA SINCE 1945. *Longman* 1974 $6.50 pap. $3.50

A CONCISE HISTORY OF EAST ASIA. *Praeger* 1966 $8.50

"There are few historians of East Asia today who write as forcefully and gracefully as he does"—(*LJ*).

Fukutake, Tadashi. JAPANESE SOCIETY TODAY. *International Scholarly Bk. Services* 1975 $9.50

"The views of one Japanese scholar and social critic urging his compatriots to face up to problems left in the wake of a century of rapid economic growth"—(*LJ*).

Ghose, Sankar. SOCIALISM AND COMMUNISM IN INDIA. *South Asia Bks.* 1971 $7.50

Gibney, Frank. JAPAN: The Fragile Superpower. *Norton* 1975 $10.00

Grattan, C. Hartley. THE SOUTHWEST PACIFIC. *Univ. of Michigan Press* 2 vols. 1960–1963 Vol. 1 To 1900 $7.50 Vol. 2 Since 1900 $10.00 set $17.50

The scholarly yet readable first volume covers the cultural history of Australia, New Zealand, the Islands—mainly the Fijis, Samoa, New Caledonia, and New Guinea—and Antarctica from the period of exploration to the last half of the century. The activities of the European settlers and politicians are chronicled accurately and due emphasis is given to the problem of the natives.

Greene, Fred. U.S. POLICY AND THE SECURITY OF ASIA. *McGraw-Hill* 1968 $9.95 pap. $3.95

"Highly recommended"—(*LJ*).

Hall, Daniel G. E. A HISTORY OF SOUTH-EAST ASIA. 1955. *St. Martin's* 3rd ed. 1968 $16.95 pap. $8.95. A standard work since publication.

Hall, John Whitney. GOVERNMENT AND LOCAL POWER IN JAPAN, 500 TO 1700: A Study Based on Bizen Province. *Princeton Univ. Press* 1966 $18.50

"One of the most important studies on pre-modern Japanese history ever written by an American scholar"—(*LJ*).

HANDBOOK ON SOUTH AND SOUTHEAST ASIA. *Foreign Policy Assn.* (345 East 46 Street, New York, N.Y. 10017) $1.00. A special feature of INTERCOM, covering the individual countries of the area, activities of the U.S. and the U.N., and books, pamphlets and films on South and Southeast Asia.

Henderson, William, Ed. SOUTHEAST ASIA: Problems of United States Policy. *M.I.T. Press* 1963 $8.95. Essays by thirteen leading specialists on Southeast Asia.

Ho, Robert, and E. C. Chapman, Eds. STUDIES OF CONTEMPORARY THAILAND. *International Scholarly Bk. Services* 1973 pap. $10.50

Htin Aung, M. A HISTORY OF BURMA. *Columbia* 1967 $13.50. The first history in English by a Burmese.

Hughes, John. INDONESIAN UPHEAVAL. *McKay* 1967 $5.95. An account of the fall of Sukarno, by a correspondent of the *Christian Science Monitor*. Mr. Hughes was awarded a 1967 Pulitzer Prize in Journalism for his reporting of the events described in the book.

Iriye, Akira. ACROSS THE PACIFIC: An Inner History of American–East Asian Relations. Introd. by John K. Fairbank *Harcourt* 1967 $9.75 pap. 1969 $2.85
By a Japanese who became a U.S. citizen; an "impressive work"—(*LJ*).

Lamb, Alastair. THE KASHMIR PROBLEM: A Historical Survey. *Praeger* 1967 $5.00
"Short, readable, authoritative"—(*LJ*).

Latourette, Kenneth S. *See his main entry, this Section.*

Lattimore, Owen. NOMADS AND COMMISSARS: Mongolia Revisited. *Oxford* 1962 $7.50. A lively description of a little known country, with historical material.

(With Eleanor Lattimore, Eds., annot. with introd.). SILKS, SPICES AND EMPIRE: Asia Seen Through the Eyes of Its Explorers. Great Explorers Ser. *Dial* (Delacorte) 1968 $8.95; *Dell* 1971 pap. $.95

Lee Chong-Sik. THE POLITICS OF KOREAN NATIONALISM. *Univ. of California Press* 1963 $10.50. An excellent account of the struggle for national independence, 1880–1945; also traces the development of nationalism in Korea during a longer time span.

Lifton, Robert Jay. DEATH IN LIFE: Survivors of Hiroshima. *Random* 1968 Vintage Bks. 1969 pap. $2.95. This psychological study of the survivors of the atomic bomb received a National Book Award in 1969.

Maxwell, Neville. INDIA'S CHINA WAR. *Pantheon* 1971 $10.00
"An account by the former London Times correspondent who covered the Sino-Indian border conflict of 1962. It is based on interviews with authorities and soldiers, unpublished files and government reports and on-the-spot observations"—(Publisher's note).

Michael, Franz H., and George E. Taylor. THE FAR EAST IN THE MODERN WORLD. *Holt* 1956 3rd ed. 1974 $12.95

Moore, Frank J., and Clark D. Neher. THAILAND: Its People, Its Society, Its Culture. *Human Relations Area File Press* 1974 $18.50. Includes chapters on geography, history and government.

Moorhouse, Geoffrey. CALCUTTA. *Harcourt* 1972 $8.95
Moorehouse "has defined and documented the heavy British responsibility for the mess that is modern Calcutta. [He] is horrified by Calcutta but he is also stirred by it"—(*N.Y. Times Bk. Review*).

Morton, W. Scott. JAPAN: Its History and Culture. *T. Y. Crowell* 1970 $7.95

Mueller, Peter G., and Douglas A. Ross. CHINA AND JAPAN—Emerging Global Powers. *Praeger* 1975 $16.50 pap. $5.95

Murdoch, James. A HISTORY OF JAPAN. Introd. by John L. Mish *Ungar* 3 vols. 1964 Vol. 1 (2 pts.) From the Origins to the Arrival of the Portuguese in 1542 A.D. Vol. 2 (2 pts.) During the Century of Early Foreign Intercourse (1542–1651) Vol. 3 (2 pts.) The Tokugawa Epoch (1652–1868) set $75.00
"Murdoch's monumental three-volume work, prepared with collaborators, was for many years the standard English-language history of Japan. In recent years it has been superseded by the three-volume history written by Sir George Sansom [*see below*] but is still useful. This reprint in six volumes, somewhat easier to handle than the original bulky three books, is worth the notice of large libraries"—(*LJ*).

Myrdal, Gunnar. ASIAN DRAMA: An Inquiry into the Poverty of Nations. *Kraus* 3 vols. 1968 set $25.00; *Pantheon* 3 vols. 1968 pap. set $10.00; 1-vol. abr. ed. by Seth King *Pantheon* 1972 $10.00; *Random* Vintage Bks. 1971 pap. $2.45. (*For comment on this monumental work by the Swedish sociologist and statesman, see his main entry in Chapter 8, The Social Sciences, this Vol.*)

Nayar, Kuldip. INDIA: The Critical Years. *International Scholarly Bk. Services* 1971 $6.00

Neumann, William L. AMERICA ENCOUNTERS JAPAN: From Perry to MacArthur. *Johns Hopkins Press* 1963 1969 $12.00 pap. $3.45

"This new one-volume history of Japanese-American relations is a welcome addition to the literature on Japan. . . . Some of [the author's] conclusions and interpretations may be open to question, but this is basically a well-written and valuable discussion of the subject."

New York Times (with O. Edmund Clubb, Advisory Editor). CHINA. Great Contemporary Issues Ser. *Arno* 1972 $35.00

(With Edwin O. Reischauer, Advisory Editor). JAPAN. Great Contemporary Issues Ser. *Arno* new ed. 1974 $35.00

Norbu, Thubten Jigme, and Colin M. Turnbull. TIBET. Drawings by Lobsan Tendzin *Simon & Schuster* 1968 $7.50 pap. 1970 $2.95. By the elder brother of the present Dalai Lama in collaboration with a noted anthropologist.

Pearson, James D. ORIENTAL MANUSCRIPTS IN EUROPE AND NORTH AMERICA. *Int. Pubns. Service* 1971 $27.50

Peffer, Nathaniel. THE FAR EAST: A Modern History. *Univ. of Michigan Press* 1958 rev. & enl. ed. 1968 $8.95

Prawdin, Michael. THE MONGOL EMPIRE: Its Rise and Legacy. Trans. by Eden and Cedar Paul *Barnes & Noble* 2nd ed. 1961 $12.75; *Macmillan* (Free Press) 2nd ed. 1967 pap. $2.95

Pye, Lucian W. SOUTHEAST ASIA'S POLITICAL SYSTEMS. *Prentice-Hall* 1967 2nd ed. 1974 ref. ed. $6.50 pap. $2.95

Reischauer, Edwin O. JAPAN: The Story of a Nation. *Knopf* rev. ed. 1974 $7.95. By our former Ambassador to Japan.

Rudolph, Lloyd I., and Susanne H. Rudolph. THE MODERNITY OF TRADITION: Political Development in India. *Univ. of Chicago Press* 1967 $9.50 pap. $3.25

Sansom, George. A HISTORY OF JAPAN. *Stanford Univ. Press* 3 vols. 1958–1963. Vol. 1 To 1334 (1958) Vol. 2 1334 to 1615 (1961) Vol. 3 1615 to 1867 (1963) Vols. 1–2 each $10.00 Vol. 3 $8.50; pap. Vols. 1–2 each $4.95 Vol. 3 $3.45

Sir George Sansom, the dean of Western scholars on Japan, has produced a monumental work, covering Japan's history from antiquity to the dawn of Japan's modern age. In the final volume he has dealt brilliantly with this fascinating period. "If some of his answers are standard, still others reflect the results of more than a half century's study and thought. The book may well cause moments of bewilderment for the initiate in Japanese history, but patient and methodical study will pay lasting dividends."

Shaplen, Robert. TIME OUT OF HAND: Revolution and Reaction in Southeast Asia. *Harper* 1969 $8.95 rev. ed. 1970 pap. $2.95

"There is probably no Western journalist in Asia so well informed on the war in all its aspects as Shaplen, whose muscular prose has been an ornament to the *New Yorker* for more than a decade. . . . To put the region in context, beginning in Indonesia, he moves briskly through Singapore and Malaysia, the Philippines, Thailand, Cambodia, Laos, and finally, Vietnam. . . . Expert analyses, shrewd and careful"—(Ward Just, in *Book World*).

Smith, Donald Eugene. INDIA AS A SECULAR STATE. *Princeton Univ. Press* 1963 $17.50 pap. $3.45

"The role that religion plays will have considerable impact upon the degree and durability of India's political democracy"—(*Current History*).

Smith, Vincent A. THE OXFORD HISTORY OF INDIA. Ed. by Percival Spear *Oxford* 1958 3rd ed. 1967 $12.00 pap. $7.25

Spear, Percival. A History of India, Vol. 2. *Penguin* Pelican Bks. 1966 pap. $1.45; *Peter Smith* $3.25

"Strongly recommended for advanced students. Its value certainly exceeds its price"—*(Choice)*.

India: A Modern History. *Univ. of Michigan Press* 1961 rev. & enl. ed. 1972 $10.00. Vol. 3 of his "History of India."

"Sir Percival Spear writes from a lifetime of study and work in India and from intimate knowledge of the work of other researchers. From the facts of early civilizations as revealed by recent archaeological discoveries to his own analysis and estimate of Nehru's India, the author presents not only a rich and colorful panorama, but an astute and penetrating analysis of the origins of the religious and *social concepts that have made Indian life so ... exotic to the Westerner.... A superb performance, sound and eminently readable"—*(LJ)*. Volume 3 of Spear's history appeared first, Vol. 2 second; Vol. 1 is not yet published.

Steinberg, David J., and others. In Search of Southeast Asia: A Modern History. *Praeger* 1970 $12.95 pap: $5.95

Stone, Peter B. Japan Surges Ahead: The Story of an Economic Miracle. *Praeger* 1969 $6.95

Tinker, Hugh. South Asia: A Short History. *Praeger* 1966 $7.00 pap. $2.50

Union of Burma. *Oxford* 4th ed. 1967 $10.25

Toland, John. The Rising Sun: The Decline and Fall of the Japanese Empire, 1936–1945. *Random* 1970 $12.95

White, William L. Report on the Asians. *Reynal* 1969 $7.95. A newspaperman tells of his visits to India, Thailand and Vietnam.

Wilber, Donald N., and others. Pakistan: Its People, Its Society, Its Culture. *Human Relations Area File Press* (dist. by Taplinger) 1964 $12.00

Wilcox, Wayne Ayres. Asia and United States Policy. *Prentice-Hall* 1967 $4.95 pap. $2.50

The Emergence of Bangladesh: Problem and Opportunities for a Redefined American Policy in South Asia. *American Enterprise Pubns.* 1973 $3.00

Pakistan: The Consolidation of a Nation. *Columbia* 1963 $11.00. The political evolution presented in a well written study.

Wint, Guy. Asia: A Handbook. *Praeger* 1966 $25.00

Wright, Edward R., Ed. Korean Politics in Transition. *Univ. of Washington Press* 1975 $12.50

Yamamura, Kozo. Economic Policy in Postwar Japan: Growth Versus Economic Democracy. *Univ. of California Press* 1967 $10.00

Yoshida, Shigeru. Japan's Decisive Century: 1867–1967. *Praeger* 1967 $4.95. The former Prime Minister of Japan gives an account of his country's emergence from isolation, growth as an empire, defeat in World War II and postwar emergence as a world power.

China

Barnett, A. Doak. *See his main entry, this Section.*

Baum, Richard. Prelude to Revolution: Mao, the Party, and the Peasant Question. *Columbia* 1975 $10.00

Baum "provides a valuable insight into the working of the party at its higher and lower levels, as well as the mechanisms of mass campaigns, and the problems facing cadres who have to be responsible to the masses below and the party above"—*(LJ)*.

Berton, Peter, and Eugene Wu. Contemporary China: A Research Guide. Bibliographical Ser. *Hoover Institution* 1967 $22.50. Contains 2,226 entries of books, periodicals and theses published mainly after 1949 in Communist China and after 1945 in Taiwan.

Bloodworth, Dennis. THE CHINESE LOOKING GLASS. *Farrar, Straus* 1967 $7.95; *Dell* Delta Bks. pap. $2.45

By the Far East correspondent of the London *Observer*. "Well-informed, charming, crazy-quilt guide to the Chinese character . . . through 30 centuries of turbulent history"—(Eliot Fremont-Smith, in the *N.Y. Times*).

Blum, Robert. THE UNITED STATES AND CHINA IN WORLD AFFAIRS. Ed. by A. Doak Barnett *McGraw-Hill* 1966 $6.50 pap. $2.95. Mr. Blum, who has held several diplomatic posts, believes that the United States should break down the barriers that isolate Communist China.

Buck, Pearl S. CHINA: Past and Present. *John Day* 1972 $8.95

Chai, Winberg. FOREIGN RELATIONS OF THE PEOPLE'S REPUBLIC OF CHINA. *Putnam* 1972 $7.95 Capricorn Giant 1973 pap. $3.75

THE SEARCH FOR A NEW CHINA: A Capsule History, Ideology, and Leadership of the Chinese Communist Party, 1921–1974. *Putnam* 1975 $7.95

"A concise, objective history of the Chinese Communist party drawn from a variety of secondary and primary sources"—(*LJ*).

Ch'ên, Jerome. MAO AND THE CHINESE REVOLUTION: With Thirty-seven Poems by Mao Tse-Tung. Trans. from the Chinese by Michael Bullock and Jerome Ch'ên *Oxford* 1965 $7.50 pap. $2.45

(With Nicholas Tarling, Eds.). STUDIES IN THE SOCIAL HISTORY OF CHINA AND SOUTH-EAST ASIA. *Cambridge* 1970 $19.50

Chen Lung-Chu and Harold D. Lasswell. FORMOSA, CHINA, AND THE UNITED NATIONS: Formosa in the World Community. *St. Martin's* 1967 $8.50

Clubb, O. Edmund. TWENTIETH CENTURY CHINA. *Columbia* 1963 $8.50 pap. $2.75. Written by the last American Consul General in Peiping, this provides a comprehensive history from the Boxer Rebellion to the present.

Eastman, Lloyd E. CHINA UNDER NATIONALIST RULE, 1927–1937. *Harvard Univ. Press* 1975 $16.50

The author "shows why Chiang Kai-shek failed to win the Chinese people or retain full power for long: corruption, over-militarization, currency misjuggling, purges and repressions"—(*N.Y. Times Bk. Review*).

Fairbank, John K. *See his main entry, this Section.*

Fan, K. H., and K. T. Fan, Eds. FROM THE OTHER SIDE OF THE RIVER: A Self Portrait of China Today. *Doubleday* Anchor Bks. 1975 pap. $3.95

"The Chinese introduce their own society in a collection of articles originally published on the mainland"—(*Booklist*).

Fitzgerald, Charles P. THE HORIZON HISTORY OF CHINA. *McGraw-Hill* (American Heritage Press) 1969, o.p. (*See also the companion volume under Horizon, below.*)

THE SOUTHERN EXPANSION OF THE CHINESE PEOPLES. *Praeger* 1972 $8.95

Gittings, John. A CHINESE VIEW OF CHINA. *Pantheon* 1973 $6.95 pap. 1974 $1.95

THE WORLD AND CHINA, 1922–1972. *Harper* 1975 $11.00

"This history of Chinese foreign policy in the twentieth century explores the underlying unity and direction of what may appear to be capricious and doctrinaire decisions dictated by internal requirements"—(*Booklist*).

Granqvist, Hans. THE RED GUARD: A Report on Mao's Revolution. Trans. by Erik J. Friis *Praeger* 1967 $5.95

An analysis "based on visits to China in 1964 and 1966 and other resources. . . . A dispassionate, reasoned, and informed account"—(*LJ*).

Griffith, William E. THE SINO-SOVIET RIFT. *M.I.T. Press* 1963 pap. $3.95

Hébert, Jacques, and Pierre Elliott Trudeau. TWO INNOCENTS IN RED CHINA. Trans. from the French by I. M. Owen *Oxford* 1968 $5.50. A Montreal publisher and Canada's present Prime Minister write of their lighthearted visit to Communist China, at the invitation of the Chinese Government, in the fall of 1960. Contains some valuable insights on that country.

Ho, Ping-Ti. STUDIES ON THE POPULATION OF CHINA, 1368–1953. *Harvard Univ. Press* 1959 $15.00

  (With Tang Tsou, Eds.). CHINA IN CRISIS. *Univ. of Chicago Press* 2 Bks. 1968 Bk. 1 $12.50 Bk. 2 $11.50 pap. 1970 Bk. 1 $3.95 Bk. 2 $3.45

HORIZON. THE HORIZON BOOK OF THE ARTS OF CHINA. Introd. by Hugh Honour *McGraw-Hill* (American Heritage Press) 1969 $20.00 deluxe ed. $23.00. Companion volume to Fitzgerald, *above*.

Hsu, Immanuel C., Ed. READINGS IN MODERN CHINESE HISTORY. *Oxford* 1971 pap. $7.95

Hsu, Kai-Yü. CHOU EN-LAI: China's Gray Eminence. *Doubleday* Anchor Bks. 1969 pap. $1.75. A biography of Mao Tse-Tung's second-in-command.

Jungk, Robert, and others. CHINA AND THE WEST: Mankind Evolving. *Humanities Press* 1970 $6.00

Karol, K. S. CHINA: The Other Communism. Trans. from the French by Tom Baistow; photographs by Marc Riboud *Farrar, Straus* (Hill & Wang) rev. ed. 1968 pap. $3.95. A Polish-born foreign correspondent (for the *New Statesman* and French newspapers), who was once a Soviet citizen, contrasts Communism in China and Russia.

  THE SECOND CHINESE REVOLUTION. Trans. from the French by Mervyn Jones *Farrar, Straus* 1975 $12.95

  "Karol's main argument is that the cultural revolution was not a personal struggle for power, but a genuine policy clash, first over priorities then over timing"—(*N.Y. Times Bk. Review*).

Klein, Donald W., and Anne B. Clark. BIOGRAPHIC DICTIONARY OF CHINESE COMMUNISM, 1921–1965. *Harvard Univ. Press* 2 vols. 1971 set $30.00

  It includes "433 extensive entries, with some 1,750 secondary references, for leaders of the Communist party in China in the period 1921–65"—(*Choice*).

Koningsberger, Hans. LOVE AND HATE IN CHINA. *McGraw-Hill* 1966 1972 pap. $1.95. A fascinating account, part of which first appeared in the *New Yorker*.

Lall, Arthur. HOW COMMUNIST CHINA NEGOTIATES. *Columbia* 1968 $12.00 pap. $2.95. The former Indian Ambassador to the United Nations describes Chinese diplomacy during the 14-month conference on Laos, 1961–1962.

Lifton, Robert Jay. REVOLUTIONARY IMMORTALITY: Mao Tse-Tung and the Chinese Cultural Revolution. *Random* Vintage Bks. 1968 pap. $4.95; *Peter Smith* $4.00

  THOUGHT REFORM AND THE PSYCHOLOGY OF TOTALISM: A Study of 'Brainwashing' in China. *Norton* 1961 $8.50 pap. $3.75

McAleavy, Henry. THE MODERN HISTORY OF CHINA. *Praeger* 1967 $9.00 pap. $4.95

Mao Tse-Tung. QUOTATIONS FROM CHAIRMAN MAO TSE-TUNG. Ed. with introd. and notes by Stuart R. Schram; fwd. by A. Doak Barnett *Praeger* 1967 $5.00; *Bantam* pap. $1.25; *China Bks.* $.60.

  See also his main entry in Chapter 2, General Biography and Autobiography, this Vol.

Meisner, Maurice J. LI TA-CHAO AND THE ORIGINS OF CHINESE MARXISM. *Harvard Univ. Press* 1967 $8.50

Myrdal, Jan. CHINA: The Revolution Continued. Trans. from the Swedish by Paul B. Austin *Pantheon* 1971 $5.95; *Random* Vintage Bks. 1972 pap. $1.95

  CHINESE JOURNEY. *Pantheon* 1965 $9.95; *Beacon* pap. $2.95

  REPORT FROM A CHINESE VILLAGE. Trans. by Maurice Michael *Pantheon* 1965 $8.95; *Random* Vintage Bks. 1972 pap. $2.45

Needham, Joseph, and others. SCIENCE AND CIVILIZATION IN CHINA. *Cambridge* 4 vols. 1954–1970 Vol. 1 Introductory Orientations (1954) $17.50 Vol. 2 History of Scientific Thought $35.00 Vol. 3 Mathematics and the Sciences of the Heavens and the Earth

$47.50 Vol. 4 Physics and Physical Technology, 3 pts.: pt. 1 $27.50 pt. 2 $39.50 pt. 3 (1970) $55.00

Pelissier, Roger. THE AWAKENING OF CHINA, 1793–1949. Trans. from the French and ed. by Martin Kieffer. *Putnam* 1967 $7.95 Capricorn Bks. 1970 pap. $3.25

A survey of China's history from the decline of the Manchu regime to the coming of Communism. "A powerful presentation of a great people. It is, I think, the best that has yet been done"—(Pearl Buck).

Pye, Lucian W. CHINA: An Introduction. *Little* 1972 $10.00 pap. $4.95

THE SPIRIT OF CHINESE POLITICS: A Psychocultural Study of the Crisis in Political Development. *M.I.T. Press* 1968 $10.00 pap. $2.95

WARLORD POLITICS: Conflict and Coalition in the Modernization of Republican China. Library of Chinese Affairs. *Praeger* 1971 $10.00

Rashid Al-Din Tabib. THE SUCCESSORS OF GENGHIS KHAN. Trans. by J. A. Boyle *Columbia* 1972 $12.50

"A translation of an historical work by a Persian physician of Jewish origin (1247–1318) who wrote the first world history for his masters, the Mongol rulers of Persia"—(*Choice*).

Ronning, Chester. A MEMOIR OF CHINA IN REVOLUTION: From the Boxer Rebellion to the People's Republic. *Pantheon* 1974 $10.00

Salisbury, Harrison E. ORBIT OF CHINA. *Harper* 1967 $6.95

"Travelling some 30,000 miles as a journalistic satellite, Mr. Salisbury has made his book 'Orbit of China' a panoramic window looking on events in the Far East. An astute and superbly trained observer, he has written a chilling but rewarding report"—(*LJ*).

To PEKING AND BEYOND: A Report on the New Asia. (Orig. "Report on Red China") *Quadrangle* 1973 $7.95; *Putnam* Capricorn Bks. 1973 pap. $3.25

Schram, Stuart R. MAO TSE-TUNG. *Simon & Schuster* 1967 $7.95; *Penguin* Pelican Bks. 1968 pap. $1.65

"An engrossing account of the momentous Chinese revolution and of the man who brought it off. [This] can be read with profit by specialists and laymen alike"—(*N.Y. Times*). The author concludes that Chairman Mao is no longer answering China's needs.

(Ed.) CHAIRMAN MAO TALKS TO THE PEOPLE: Talks and Letters, 1956–1971. Trans. by John Chinnery and Tieyun *Pantheon* 1975 $10.00 pap. $2.95

"A leading expert on Maoist texts and concepts has selected twenty-six speeches, most of them newly available in recent years"—(*N.Y. Times Bk. Review*).

Schurmann, Franz. IDEOLOGY AND ORGANIZATION IN COMMUNIST CHINA. *Univ. of California Press* 2nd ed. 1968 $12.50 pap. $5.50

(With Orville Schell, Eds.). THE CHINA READER. *Random* 3 vols. 1967 Vol. 1 Imperial China: The Decline of the Last Dynasty and the Origins of Modern China, the 18th and 19th Centuries $8.95 pap. $2.40 Vol. 2 Republican China: Nationalism, War and the Rise of Communism, 1911–1949 $8.95 pap. $1.95 Vol. 3 Communist China: Revolutionary Reconstruction and International Confrontation, 1949 to the Present $10.00 pap. $2.95

Schwartz, Harry. TSARS, MANDARINS AND COMMISSARS: A History of Chinese-Russian Relations. 1964. *Doubleday* Anchor Bks. 1973 pap. $2.50. Emphasizes the conflict between the two countries from the 14th century to the present; by a staff member of the *N.Y. Times*.

Snow, Edgar. THE LONG REVOLUTION. *Random* 1972 $6.95 Vintage Bks. pap. $1.95

RED CHINA TODAY: The Other Side of the River *Random* 1962 rev. ed. 1971 $20.00 Vintage Bks. 1971 pap. $3.45

"Perhaps the definitive, albeit controversial, book on present-day China"—(N.Y.P.L.).

RED STAR OVER CHINA. 1938. *Grove* rev. ed. 1968 $10.00 Black Cat Bks. pap. $2.45. A revised, enlarged edition of his classic work.

Terrill, Ross. 800,000,000: The Real China. *Little-Atlantic* 1972 $7.95 pap. $1.50

Toynbee, Arnold J., Ed. HALF THE WORLD: The History and Culture of China and Japan. *Holt* 1973 $30.00. A lavishly illustrated book with chapters by 13 scholars in this area—E. Glahn, D. C. Twitchett, Owen Lattimore, Wing-tsit Chan, S. Nakayama, James J. Y. Liu, Donald Keene, Jean Chesneaux, etc.

Trager, Frank N., and William Henderson, Eds. COMMUNIST CHINA, 1949–1969: A Twenty Year Assessment. *New York Univ. Press* 1970 $9.50

Tsou Tang. AMERICA'S FAILURE IN CHINA, 1941–1950. *Univ. of Chicago Press* 1963 $15.00 Phoenix Bks. 2 vols. pap. Vol. 1 $2.95 Vol. 2 $2.45

An assessment of the "Open Door" policy in China. "This is *the* book on the subject to date"— (*LJ*).

(With Ping-ti Ho, Eds.). CHINA IN CRISIS. *Univ. of Chicago Press* 2 vols. 1968 Vol. 1 China's Heritage and the Communist Political System $12.50 Vol. 2 China's Policies in Asia and America's Alternatives, fwd. by Charles U. Daly $11.50 Phoenix Bks. 1970 pap. Vol. 1 $3.95 Vol. 2 $3.45

Tuchman, Barbara. STILWELL AND THE AMERICAN EXPERIENCE IN CHINA, 1911–1945. *Macmillan* 1971 $12.50

Twitchett, Dennis, and P. J. M. Geelan. THE TIMES ATLAS OF CHINA. *Quadrangle-N.Y. Times* 1975 $75.00

Young, Arthur N. CHINA AND THE HELPING HAND, 1937–1945. *Harvard Univ. Press* 1963 $13.50

CHINA'S NATION-BUILDING EFFORT, 1927–1937: The Financial and Economic Record. *Hoover Institution* 1971 $19.50

Vietnam

Ashmore, Harry S., and William C. Baggs. MISSION TO HANOI: A Chronicle of Double-Dealing in High Places. Ed. by Elaine H. Burnell *Putnam* 1968 $6.95. This special report of the Center for the Study of Democratic Institutions is an impressive but disheartening account by two distinguished and responsible authors.

Committee on Foreign Relations, U.S. Senate, 90th Congress, 1st Session. BACKGROUND INFORMATION RELATING TO SOUTHEAST ASIA AND VIETNAM. *U.S. Government Printing Office* (Washington, D.C. 20402; *consult publisher for price*)

Fall, Bernard B. HELL IN A VERY SMALL PLACE: The Siege of Dien Bien Phu. Great Battles of History Series. *Lippincott* 1966 $10.00; *Random* Vintage Bks. pap. $2.95

"A thorough account of a brave, sanguinary battle that has turned out to have immense historic importance"—(*New Yorker*).

LAST REFLECTIONS ON A WAR. Pref. by Dorothy Fall, his wife. 1967. *Schocken* 1972 pap. $2.95

THE TWO VIET-NAMS: A Political and Military Analysis. 1963. *Praeger* 2nd rev. ed. 1967 $10.00. The final version of his earlier book.

VIET-NAM WITNESS: 1953–1966. *Praeger* 1966 $7.95. Twenty-six reprints of his articles.

(With Marcus G. Raskin, Eds.). THE VIET-NAM READER. *Random* Vintage Bks. 1965 pap. $2.95

Fitzgerald, Francis. FIRE IN THE LAKE: The Vietnamese and the Americans in Vietnam. *Little-Atlantic* 1972 $12.50 pap. $2.25

Hanh, Thich Nhat. VIETNAM: Lotus in a Sea of Fire. Trans. from the Vietnamese by Alfred Hassler and the author; fwd. by Thomas Merton *Farrar, Straus* (Hill & Wang) 1967 $3.50 pap. $1.65. A Buddhist monk and leading Vietnamese poet proposes a settlement to the war that would maintain Vietnam's identity as a Buddhist nation.

Hersh, Seymour M. My Lai Four: A Report on the Massacre and Its Aftermath. *Random* 1970 $5.95

Ho Chi Minh. Selected Articles and Speeches, 1920–67. Ed. by Jack Woodis; introd. by Bernard B. Fall *International Pubs.* 1970 pap. $1.65

Marxist polemics in prose of "vivid pictorial quality"—(*New Yorker*).

Honey, Patrick J. Communism in North Vietnam. 1963. *Greenwood* 1973 $10.00

"A fascinating picture of the struggle between the pro-Peking and pro-Moscow factions"—(*N.Y. Times*).

Kendrick, Alexander. The Wound Within: America in the Vietnam Years, 1945–1974. *Little* 1974 $12.95

Lacouture, Jean. Ho Chi Minh: A Political Biography. Trans. from the French by Peter Wiles; ed. by Jane Clark Seitz *Random* Vintage Bks. 1968 pap. $1.95

"One of the most detailed portraits yet written of Vietnam's number one Communist"—(*LJ*).

(With Philippe Devillers). End of a War: Indochina, 1954. *Praeger* 1969 $8.95. The final phase of the Indochinese War between French and Asians.

Lamb, Alastair. Mandarin Road to Old Hue: Narratives of Anglo-Vietnamese Diplomacy from the 17th Century to the Eve of the French Conquest. *Shoe String Press* 1970 $14.50

Luce, Don S., and John Sommer. Viet Nam: The Unheard Voices. Fwd. by Edward M. Kennedy *Cornell Univ. Press* 1969 $8.50 pap. $1.95

Two members of the International Volunteer Services in Vietnam, who resigned in protest against American policy, criticize the American role in that country. "Cool, unresentful, objective, impartial, constructive and even, at times, witty"—(*N.Y. Times*).

McCarthy, Mary. Hanoi. *Harcourt* 1968 pap. $1.45. An account of her visit to North Vietnam in March of 1968; she is a "dove" and a sharp observer.

Vietnam. *Harcourt* 1967 pap. $.95

Pike, Douglas. Viet Cong: The Organization and Technique of the National Liberation Front of South Vietnam. *M.I.T. Press* 1966 $12.50 pap. $2.95. By an official of the USIA, stationed for several years in Saigon, who had access to captured NLF documents and intelligence sources.

War, Peace and the Viet Cong. *M.I.T. Press* 1970 $5.95 pap. $2.95

Roy, Jules. The Battle of Dienbienphu. Trans. from the French by Robert Baldick; introd. by David Halberstam *Harper* 1965 $10.00. A bitter analysis, by a French writer, of France's catastrophic defeat in 1954.

Salisbury, Harrison E. Behind the Lines—Hanoi: December 23–January 7. *Harper* 1967 $6.95. The Pulitzer Prize-winning reporter of the *New York Times* writes of his visit to North Vietnam's capital, in an adaptation of his original articles. Awarded the Sidney Hillman Foundation award in 1967 for outstanding achievement in mass communications.

Schell, Jonathan. The Military Half: An Account of Destruction in Quang Ngai and Quang Tin. *Knopf* 1968 $4.95. Similar treatment from the same quarter in two northern provinces of South Vietnam in the summer of 1967.

The Village of Ben Suc. *Knopf* 1967 $4.95. The destruction of a village 30 miles from Saigon by the American military, and the forced evacuation of its 3,500 inhabitants to refugee camps, is described by a correspondent for the *New Yorker*.

Schlesinger, Arthur M., Jr. The Bitter Heritage: Vietnam and American Democracy, 1941–1968. *Fawcett* Premier Bks. rev. ed. 1972 pap. $.95

"In addition to wit, the sharp ring of truth"—(Bernard B. Fall).

Shaplen, Robert. The Road from War: Vietnam 1965–1970. *Harper* 1970 $7.95 pap. $4.45

Sheehan, Susan. TEN VIETNAMESE. *Knopf* 1967 $6.95

"For anyone wishing an insight into the thinking and attitudes of the ordinary Vietnamese, be he farmer or Vietcong, this is an essential book"—(*LJ*).

Vogelsang, Sandy. THE LONG DARK NIGHT OF THE SOUL: The American Intellectual Left and the Vietnam War. *Harper* 1974 $8.95

It "identifies the intellectuals, sources of their alienation from the Kennedy-Johnson presidencies, and the matters they wrote about during this period"—(*Booklist*).

Africa

Africa is rapidly becoming an area of popular interest for Americans. Its history, politics, music, art, and distinctive clothing styles have captured the favorable attention of a large segment of our population, particularly the youth. As more and more Americans travel to Africa, librarians will find it necessary to select both popular and scholarly works on the peoples and cultures of this vast continent. The following titles were selected from several hundred good books that are currently available. *See also Chapter 17, African Literature, Reader's Adviser, Vol. 2, for fiction, poetry and drama by Africans (and white South Africans) as well as other background information and materials.*

General, Historical and Reference Works

Abraham, W. E. THE MIND OF AFRICA. *Univ. of Chicago Press* 1963 $7.50 pap. $3.25

This book is "not aimed at the many who are still struggling with elementary geography and the basic facts of political life in Africa." It is essential reading for those who have already mastered the facts of the modern African social universe.

AFRICA ANNUAL REVIEW. 1972. *Holmes & Meier Pubs.* Africana 1972 pap. $6.50

AFRICA CONTEMPORARY RECORD, 1968– Ed. by Colin Legum *Holmes & Meier Pubs.* Africana 7 vols. 1968–1975 Vols. 1–6 each $55.00 Vol. 7 $50.00. Annual survey and documents.

AFRICA SOUTH OF THE SAHARA, 1970– 5th ed. 1975 *Gale Research Co.* $56.00 *Int. Pubns. Service* $56.00

AFRICAN ENCYCLOPEDIA. Ed. by W. Senteza Kajubi and others *Oxford* 1974 $13.00

Bascom, William R., and Melville J. Herskovits, Eds. CONTINUITY AND CHANGE IN AFRICAN CULTURES. *Univ. of Chicago Press* 1958 $10.00 Phoenix Bks. pap. $2.45

Beetham, T. A. CHRISTIANITY AND THE NEW AFRICA. Library of African Affairs. *Praeger* 1967 $6.00

"Mr. Beetham writes well, with conviction, and, for one so deeply committed, with remarkable objectivity. Whatever may be the solutions it is his opinion that they will and must be made by the Africans themselves"—(*LJ*).

Berque, Jacques. FRENCH NORTH AFRICA: The Maghrib Between Two World Wars. Trans. from the French by Jean Stewart *Praeger* 1967 $12.50. A study of the Maghrib (Arab North Africa) from 1919 to 1939.

Bohannan, Paul, and Philip Curtin. AFRICA AND AFRICANS. *Doubleday* rev. ed. 1971 $7.95 pap. $2.95

Boston University Libraries. CATALOG OF AFRICAN GOVERNMENT DOCUMENTS AND AFRICAN AREA INDEX. *Hall* 2nd ed. 1964 $28.00

Bovill, Edward W., and Robin Hallett. GOLDEN TRADE OF THE MOORS. *Oxford* 2nd ed. 1968 $10.25 pap. 1970 $2.25. A classic history of the trans-Saharan trade in pre-colonial Africa.

Bretton, Henry L. POWER AND POLITICS IN AFRICA. *Aldine* 1973 $15.95 pap. $5.95

Brunschwig, Henri. FRENCH COLONIALISM 1871–1914: Myths and Realities. Trans. by William G. Brown *Praeger* 1966 $9.50

THE CAMBRIDGE HISTORY OF AFRICA: Vol. 4, The Sixteenth and Seventeenth Centuries. Ed. by R. Gray *Cambridge* 1975 $22.50. Vol. 5 From c. 1790 to c. 1870 ed. by J. E. Flint (in prep.)

Carey-Jones, N. S. THE ANATOMY OF UHURU. *Praeger* 1967 $8.50. *"Uhuru"* is "Freedom" in Swahili.

Cartey, Wilfred, and Martin Kilson, Eds. THE AFRICAN READER. *Random* 2 vols. 1970 Vol. 1 Colonial Africa $7.95 pap. $2.40 Vol. 2 Independent Africa $10.00. Vol. 1 spans the last third of the 19th century and the first half of the 20th in selected writings of contemporary African and European writers and historians, government papers and reports by civil servants. Vol. 2 has selections from writers like Aimé Césaire, Nkrumah, Nyerere, Lumumba, Kenyatta, and Wole Soyinca.

Chester, Edward W. CLASH OF TITANS: Africa and U.S. Foreign Policy. *Orbis* 1974 $12.95

Clark, J. Desmond. THE PREHISTORY OF AFRICA. *Praeger* 1970 $10.00

"Within the book's limited compass Clark succeeds in presenting a tremendous amount of information with truly enviable verbal economy and eloquence in a beautifully organized form. The reader will learn a great deal, not only about prehistoric Africa but about the nature of archeological and anthropological research and methodology"—(*Choice*).

(Ed.). ATLAS OF AFRICAN PREHISTORY. *Univ. of Chicago Press* 1967 $35.00

Coleman, James S., and Carl G. Rosberg, Jr., Eds. POLITICAL PARTIES AND NATIONAL INTEGRATION IN TROPICAL AFRICA. *Univ. of California Press* 1964 $14.50

Curtin, Philip D. ATLANTIC SLAVE TRADE: A Census. *Univ. of Wisconsin Press* 1969 $10.00 pap. $3.75

"This is a quantitative analysis of the Atlantic Slave Trade. . . . [The author's task] has been to bring together the pertinent information in the existing literature, to subject accepted data to . . . examination, and to offer a new synthesis of these data"—(Publisher's note).

ECONOMIC CHANGE IN PRE-COLONIAL AFRICA: Senegambia in the Era of the Slave Trade. *Univ. of Wisconsin Press* 2 vols. 1974 each $15.00

(Ed.). AFRICA AND THE WEST: Intellectual Responses to European Culture. *Univ. of Wisconsin Press* 1972 $12.50 pap. 1974 $4.25

(Ed.). AFRICA REMEMBERED: Narratives by West Africans from the Era of the Slave Trade. *Univ. of Wisconsin Press* 1968 $12.50 pap. $3.95

"Professor Curtin, of the University of Wisconsin, states that this book is designed to make more widely available some of the few existing, little known, and difficult to obtain accounts by Africans of the period of the Atlantic slave trade. It is evident that he has accomplished this purpose admirably"—(*LJ*).

Davidson, Basil. AFRICA: History of a Continent. *Macmillan* 1966 rev. ed. 1972 $12.95. Considered to be the best single volume history, a classic by this distinguished expert.

THE AFRICAN GENIUS: An Introduction to Social and Cultural History. *Little-Atlantic* 1970 $8.95 pap. $2.75

THE LOST CITIES OF AFRICA. *Little-Atlantic* 1959 rev. ed. 1970 $10.00 pap. $2.75

(Ed.) THE AFRICAN PAST: Chronicles of Africa from Antiquity to Modern Time. 1964. *Grosset* pap. $2.95. A useful collection of historical documents.

Dickie, John, and Alan Rake. WHO'S WHO IN AFRICA. *Int. Pubns. Service* 1974 $27.50

Dinesen, Isak. OUT OF AFRICA. *Random* 1970 $7.95 Vintage Bks. 1972 pap. $2.45. Beautifully written memories of her life on her Kenya coffee plantation early in the century.

Dumont, René. FALSE START IN AFRICA. Trans. from the French by Phyllis Nauts Ott; introd. by T. Balogh; with a chapter on English-speaking Africa by John Hatch *Praeger* 1966 2nd rev. ed. 1969 $7.50 pap. $3.50

"This is a topical, stimulating book that breaks fresh ground. No other book covers the field of economic and political development so well . . . Every serious library should have a copy"—(*Choice*).

Emerson, Rupert. AFRICA AND UNITED STATES POLICY. *Prentice-Hall* 1967 $4.50 pap. $1.95

(With Martin Kilson, Eds.) THE POLITICAL AWAKENING OF AFRICA. Spectrum Global History Ser. *Prentice-Hall* 1967 pap. $2.50. A collection of passages—from statements, addresses, articles, and books by prominent African politicians.

Fage, J. D. AFRICA DISCOVERS HER PAST. *Oxford* 1970 $3.95 pap. $1.50

"Twelve short essays concerned with the subject of reconstructing Africa's past. Although the essays are of a general nature (most having their origin in a series of broadcasts given in the B.B.C. African Service in 1967), the authors are careful to give actual examples of the subjects under discussion. All contributors are experts in their areas"—(*Choice*).

Fanon, Frantz. BLACK SKIN, WHITE MASKS. Trans. from the French by Charles Lam Markmann *Grove* 1967 $5.00 Black Cat Bks. 1968 pap. $1.95

"About two years ago [1965] Frantz Fanon's 'The Wretched of the Earth' appeared in America, and since then a growing number of both Negroes and whites have found this direct, personal message on the problems of race the most convincing and appealing one around. In that book, written toward the end of his short life (he died of cancer at 36) he tried to show what colonialism does to both victim and oppressor—a subject he was certainly in a position to understand. He had come to France from Martinique, another black man from an overseas 'protectorate' in search of an education and some 'freedom.' He went to medical school, became a psychiatrist and during the Algerian rebellion was sent to Africa, where he soon lost interest in treating French soldiers who were trying to keep one more nation in bondage. Until his death Fanon worked as a doctor for the rebels and, to further their cause, wrote passionate articles, essays and books"—(Robert Coles, in the *N.Y. Times*).

DYING COLONIALISM. Trans. from the French by Haakon Chevalier *Grove* Evergreen Bks. 1967 pap. $2.95

TOWARD THE AFRICAN REVOLUTION. Trans. from the French by Haakon Chevalier. *Grove* Black Cat Bks. 1968 pap. $1.25. A collection of essays originally published between 1952 and 1961.

Farwell, Byron. PRISONERS OF THE MAHDI. 1968. *Tower* 1971 pap. $.95

"Byron Farwell's excursion into 19th-century Anglo-Sudanese history is of the same genre as the Alan Moorehead books on the Nile and Fawn Brodie's account of the travels and adventures of Richard Burton. It is pleasant to report that it is also in the same class"—(Thomas Lask, in the *N.Y. Times*).

Fieldhouse, D. K. THE COLONIAL EMPIRES: A Comparative Survey from the Eighteenth Century. 1966. *Dell* 1971 pap. $2.95

"D. K. Fieldhouse, of Oxford University . . . in this well-written, thoughtful, and authoritative study . . . has carefully analyzed the major and minor colonial empires of Europe from the 18th Century to the present"—(*LJ*). Maps and illustrations are excellent.

First, Ruth. POWER IN AFRICA. *Pantheon* 1970 $10.00; *Penguin* 1972 pap. $2.95

Forde, Daryll, Ed. AFRICAN WORLDS: Studies in the Cosmological Ideas and Social Values of African Peoples. *Oxford* 1954 pap. $3.95

Fortes, Meyer, and Edward E. Evans-Pritchard, Eds. AFRICAN POLITICAL SYSTEMS. *Oxford* 1961 pap. $3.50

France. Institut Géographique National. THE ATLAS OF AFRICA. Ed. by Régine Van Chi-Bonnardel *Macmillan* (Free Press) 1974 $80.00. The first American edition.

Friedland, William H., and Carl G. Rosberg, Jr., Eds. AFRICAN SOCIALISM. *Stanford Univ. Press* 1964 $8.50 pap. $2.95

Gabel, Creighton, and Norman R. Bennett, Eds. RECONSTRUCTING AFRICAN CULTURE HISTORY. *Holmes & Meier Pubs.* Africana 1967 $9.50

"The fields from which contributions were drawn include archaeology, ethnology, linguistics, the study of oral tradition, musicology, art history, physical anthropology, botany, and economics. The authors are all authorities in the various fields"—(*Choice*).

Gailey, Harry A. HISTORY OF AFRICA. *Holt* 2 vols. 1970–1972 pap. Vol. 1 From Earliest Times to 1800 $6.00 Vol. 2 From 1800 to the Present $7.00

Gann, Lewis H., and Peter Duignan, Eds. Burden of Empire: An Appraisal of Western Colonialism in Africa South of the Sahara. *Hoover Institution* 1967 pap. $3.95. Mr. Gann is a senior staff member of the Hoover Institution at Stanford University and Mr. Duignan is director of its African program.

Colonialism in Africa 1870–1960. *Cambridge* 5 vols. 1969–1973 Vol. 1 History and Politics of Colonialism, 1870–1914 Vol. 2 History and Politics of Colonialism, 1914–1960 Vol. 3 Profiles of Change: African Society and Colonial Rule, ed. by V. Turner Vol. 4 o.p. Vol. 5 Bibliography Vols. 1–2 each $22.50 Vol. 3 $19.50 Vol. 5 $27.50

Gibbs, James L., Jr., Ed. Peoples of Africa. *Holt* 1965 $14.00. A collection of essays on African cultures.

Hachten, William A. Muffled Drums: The New Media in Africa. *Iowa State Univ. Press* 1971 $10.50

"A new study of communication media in Africa, the most comprehensive yet published"— (*Choice*).

Hallett, Robin. Africa to 1875: A Modern History. *Univ. of Michigan Press* 1970 $8.95

Africa since 1875: A Modern History. Ed. by Allan Nevins and Howard Ehrmann *Univ. of Michigan Press* 1974 $15.00

Hance, William A. African Economic Development. *Praeger* rev. ed. 1967 pap. $2.50

The Geography of Modern Africa. *Columbia* 1964 $17.50

Population, Migration and Urbanization in Africa. *Columbia* 1970 $15.00

Hanna, William John, and Judith Lynne Hanna, Eds. Urban Dynamics in Black Africa: An Interdisciplinary Approach. *Aldine* 1971 $12.95. A synthesis of the relevant available knowledge, with an extensive bibliography.

Henige, David. The Chronology of Oral Tradition: Quest for a Chimera. *Oxford* 1974 $15.25

"A brilliant work which concentrates solely on the chronological content of oral traditional data"—(*Choice*).

Hodgkin, Thomas. Nationalism in Colonial Africa. *New York Univ. Press* 1957 $7.50 pap. $2.95

Horizon History of Africa. Ed. by Alvin M. Josephy and others *McGraw-Hill* (American Heritage) 1971 $25.00 deluxe ed. $35.00

"It is rare that a book for a popular audience boasts such an outstanding group of scholars and the excellent chapters are informative and readable. 'The Africa Speaks' sections are worthy of special mention: they consist of selections from written and oral sources and give the reader an insight into how history is reconstructed"—(*LJ*).

Ingham, Kenneth, Ed. Foreign Relations of African States. *Shoe String Press* 1974 $32.50

Jahn, Jahnheinz. Muntu: An Outline of the New African Culture. Trans. by Marjorie Grene *Grove* Evergreen Bks. 1961 pap. $3.95

"An illuminating interpretation of African culture, viewed as a great world culture and as the most important factor in the shaping of Africa's destiny"—(NYPL).

July, Robert W. A History of the African People. *Scribner* rev. ed. 1974 $15.00 pap. $6.95

The Origins of Modern African Thought. *Praeger* 1968 $10.00. Its topic is early nationalists in West Africa.

Kamarck, Andrew M. The Economics of African Development. Introd. by Pierre Moussa *Praeger* 1966 rev. ed. 1971 $10.00 pap. $3.95

"An economist for the U.S. Government and the World Bank, [Kamarck] has written a succinct and admirably readable work"—(*LJ*).

Kitchen, Helen, Ed. A Handbook of African Affairs. 1964. *Univ. Place Bk. Shop* pap. $3.50

Legum, Colin, Ed. AFRICA: A Handbook to the Continent. *Praeger* 1962 rev. ed. 1967 $25.00

"Colin Legum, currently Commonwealth correspondent for the *Observer* (London), has been writing about African affairs for more than three decades. The first edition of this invaluable source book appeared only in 1962 but so swift have been the changes in that volatile continent, this revision is badly needed. Some 41 individuals plus the staff of the Economic Commission for Africa, and Legum himself have written the more than 100 articles, half on individual countries, the remainder general surveys of African art, literature, religion, economic situations, and changing cultural patterns affecting education, legal systems, press, trade unions, pan-Africanism, and the African personality"—*(LJ)*.

Lugard, Frederick J. THE DUAL MANDATE IN BRITISH TROPICAL AFRICA. New introd. by Margery Perham *International Scholarly Bk. Services* 1965 $14.00

"Since it was first published in 1922, this book has been regarded as perhaps the most 'authoritative justification of Britain's annexation and government of tropical Africa' "—*(LJ)*. It is, however, a classic assemblage of information found nowhere else.

THE RISE OF OUR EAST AFRICAN EMPIRE: Early Efforts in Nyasaland and Uganda. *International Scholarly Bk. Services* 2 vols. 1968 set $50.00

Lystad, Robert, Ed. THE AFRICAN WORLD: A Survey of Social Research. *Praeger* 1965 $17.50

McCall, Daniel F. AFRICA IN TIME-PERSPECTIVE: A Discussion of Historical Reconstruction from Unwritten Sources. *Oxford* 1969 pap. $1.95

McEwan, Peter J., Ed. AFRICA FROM EARLY TIMES TO 1800. *Oxford* 1968 $10.25

NINETEENTH-CENTURY AFRICA. *Oxford* 1968 $10.25

TWENTIETH CENTURY AFRICA. *Oxford* 1968 $10.25 pap. 1970 $5.50

Mazrui, Ali A. TOWARDS A PAX AFRICANA: A Study of Ideology and Ambition. *Univ. of Chicago Press* 1967 $9.50

"This is the best book on African international politics available today"—*(The Annals)*.

VIOLENCE AND THOUGHT: Essays on Social Tensions in Africa. *Humanities Press* 1969 $8.25 pap. $5.50

Moore, Clement Henry. POLITICS IN NORTH AFRICA: Algeria, Morocco, and Tunisia. *Little* 1970 pap. $4.95

Moorehead, Alan. *See his main entry in Chapter 12, Travel and Adventure, this Vol.*

Morrison, Donald George, and others. BLACK AFRICA: A Comparative Handbook. *Macmillan* (Free Press) 1972 $29.95

Mortimer, Edward. FRANCE AND THE AFRICANS, 1944–1960. *Walker & Co.* 1969 $8.50

Moumouni, Abdou. EDUCATION IN AFRICA. Trans. from the French by Phyllis Nauts Ott *Praeger* 1968 $8.00

"This book of major importance is necessary for any collection concerned with African education"—*(LJ)*.

Mountjoy, Alan B., and Clifford Embleton. AFRICA: A New Geographical Survey. *Praeger* 1967 $12.00 pap. $5.95

"Mr. Mountjoy, a reader in geography at Bedford College, University of London, and Mr. Embleton, a senior lecturer in geography at King's College, University of London, with the assistance of Mr. W. B. Morgan, a lecturer in geography at the University of Birmingham (who contributed to the section on West Africa), have written a vigorous, well-organized geography on Africa, incorporating much recent material"—*(LJ)*.

Mphahlele, Ezekiel. THE AFRICAN IMAGE. *Praeger* 1962 1974 $8.50 pap. $2.95. An examination of writings about Africans by well-known white writers and of the literary stereotypes which developed. By a South African now in self-imposed exile.

Murdock, George Peter. AFRICA: Its Peoples and Their Cultural History. *McGraw-Hill* 1959 $13.50. Unreliable in many details, but still the best anthropological survey in English.

Mwase, George Simeon. STRIKE A BLOW AND DIE: A Narrative of Race Relations in Colonial Africa. Ed. with introd. by Robert I. Rotberg *Harvard Univ. Press* 1967 rev. ed. 1970 $5.50. Biography of John Chilembwe, the first revolutionary of Malawi (then Nyasaland).

Nielsen, Waldemar. AFRICA. *Atheneum* 1966 $3.95 pap. $2.45

Ogunsanwo, Alaba. CHINA'S POLICY IN AFRICA, 1958–1971. *Cambridge* 1974 $19.50

Oliver, Roland, and Anthony Atmore. AFRICA SINCE 1800. *Cambridge* 2nd ed. 1972 $11.95

  (With John D. Fage) A SHORT HISTORY OF AFRICA. *New York Univ. Press* rev. ed. 1963 $9.50; *Penguin* 1962 3rd rev. ed. 1966 pap. $1.95

  (With Caroline Oliver, Eds.) AFRICA IN THE DAYS OF EXPLORATION. *Prentice-Hall* 1965 $4.95 Spectrum Bks. pap. $1.95

Olorunsola, Victor, Ed. POLITICS OF CULTURAL SUB-NATIONALISM IN AFRICA. *Doubleday* Anchor Bks. 1972 pap. $1.95; *Peter Smith* $4.75. Essays on ethnic conflict in Nigeria, Uganda, Sierra Leone, Zaire and Kenya.

OXFORD REGIONAL ECONOMIC ATLAS: Africa. Prepared by P. H. Ady and the Cartographic Dept. of the Clarendon Press *Oxford* 1965 $15.00

Paden, John N., and Edward W. Soja, Eds. THE AFRICAN EXPERIENCE. *Northwestern Univ. Press* 4 vols. 1970 Vol. 1 Essays $15.00 pap. $6.50 Vol. 2 Syllabus $15.00 pap. $4.95 Vol. 3A Bibliography $25.00 Vol. 3B Guide to Resources $5.50

Padmore, George. PAN-AFRICANISM OR COMMUNISM. *Doubleday* 1971 $8.95

  "Padmore is well known as one of the prime movers in the development of Pan-Africanism. He was also an historian of Pan-Africanism and this book displays the unique vitality of the work of a participant as historian"—(*LJ*).

Panofsky, Hans E. A BIBLIOGRAPHY OF AFRICANA. *Greenwood* 1975 $15.00

  "This book delineates the origins and development of African studies in Europe, Africa, and the United States. Factors influencing Africana—for example the role of the church, the state of publishing and the book trade—are examined. Specific emphasis is placed on African studies in the United States"—(Publisher's note).

Paulme, Denise, Ed. WOMEN OF TROPICAL AFRICA. Trans. from the French by H. M. Wright *Univ. of California Press* 1963 $12.50 pap. $3.65

Perham, Margery. COLONIAL SEQUENCE, 1930–1949: A Chronological Commentary Upon British Colonial Policy Especially in Africa. *Harper* (Barnes & Noble) 1968 $11.25. By a distinguished British writer on Africa.

  COLONIAL SEQUENCE, 1949–1969. *Harper* (Barnes & Noble) 1971 $12.75

  (With Jack Simmons, Eds.). AFRICAN DISCOVERY: An Anthology of Exploration. *Northwestern Univ. Press* 1963 $8.50

Robinson, Ronald, John Gallagher and Alice Denny. AFRICA AND THE VICTORIANS: The Official Mind of Imperialism. *Humanities Press* 1967 pap. $9.00

Rodney, Walter. HOW EUROPE UNDERDEVELOPED AFRICA. *Howard Univ. Press* 1974 $10.50

Rotberg, Robert I. POLITICAL HISTORY OF TROPICAL AFRICA. *Harcourt* 1965 $10.95

  (Ed.) REBELLION IN BLACK AFRICA. *Oxford* (orig.) 1971 pap. $2.95

  (With Ali A. Mazrui, Eds.) PROTEST AND POWER IN BLACK AFRICA. *Oxford* 1970 $25.00

  "Various African movements in resistance to alien rule give a new and interesting appraisal of colonial agents and their actions . . . Post independence problems e.g. various coups, the Congo problem, and the difficulties of the Federal Nigerian government are also included"—(*Choice*).

Rubin, Leslie, and Brian Weinstein. INTRODUCTION TO AFRICAN POLITICS: A Continental Approach. *Praeger* 1974 $12.00 pap. $4.95

Samkange, Stanlake. AFRICAN SAGA: A Brief Introduction to African History. *Abingdon* 1972 $5.50 pap. $2.95

Sithole, Ndabaningi. AFRICAN NATIONALISM *Oxford* 1959 2nd ed. 1968 $8.00. Zimbabwe political leaders have called this "our nationalist Bible."

Stamp, Lawrence Dudley, and W. T. Morgan. AFRICA: A Study in Tropical Development. *Wiley* 3rd ed. 1972 $13.25

Stanley, Sir Henry Morton. *See his main entry in Chapter 12, Travel and Adventure, this Vol.*

Stevenson, Robert F. POPULATION AND POLITICAL SYSTEMS IN TROPICAL AFRICA. *Columbia* 1968 $12.00

Taylor, Sidney, Ed. THE NEW AFRICANS: Reuters Guide to the Contemporary History of Emergent Africa and Its Leaders. *Putnam* 1967 $7.50

Van der Post, Laurens. *See his main entry in Chapter 12, Travel and Adventure, this Vol.*

Vansina, Jan. ORAL TRADITION: A Study in Historical Methodology. Trans. by H. M. Wright *Aldine* 1965 $8.95

Venter, Al J. AFRICA AT WAR. *Devin-Adair* 1974 $10.00. Well-illustrated coverage of wars in Nigeria, Chad, southern Africa, Zaire, Sudan, Ethiopia, etc.

Wallerstein, Immanuel. AFRICA: Politics of Independence. 1961. *Random* Vintage Bks. pap. $1.95

    AFRICA, THE POLITICS OF UNITY: An Analysis of a Contemporary Social Movement. *Random* 1967 Vintage Bks. 1969 pap. $1.95. Sequel to the above.

Wellard, James H. THE GREAT SAHARA. 1965. *Tower* 1972 pap. $.95

Wiedner, Donald L. A HISTORY OF AFRICA SOUTH OF THE SAHARA. *Random* 1962 Vintage Bks. pap. $2.95. A useful text.

Independent Countries and Areas

This includes the greater part of the African continent, with the exclusion of the countries and territories noted in the introduction to the list following on southern Africa.

Afrifa, Akwasi A. THE GHANA COUP: 24th February 1966. Introd. by Tibor Szamuely; pref. by K. A. Busia *Humanities Press* 1966 $5.50

    "The detailed story of the planning and successful execution of the actual overthrow of Nkrumah's Government on February 24, 1966. Colonel Afrifa was trained in England's elite officer school at Sandhurst. At first devoted to Nkrumah he gradually became aware of the full meaning of Nkrumah's moves toward dictatorship. By January, 1964, Afrifa had decided that only the Army could bring about the necessary revolt. The plans were well laid, and when Nkrumah left for a visit to a Vietnam Colonel Afrifa and his associates were ready"—(LJ).

Ajayi, J. F., and Michael Crowder, Eds. THE HISTORY OF WEST AFRICA. *Columbia* 2 vols. 1972–74 each $20.00 pap. Vol. 1 $7.50 Vol. 2 $10.00

Amin, Samir. THE MAGHREB IN THE MODERN WORLD: Algeria, Tunisia, Morocco. Trans. by Michael Perl *Gannon* $5.50

    NEO-COLONIALISM IN WEST AFRICA. Trans. from the French by Francis McDonagh *Monthly Review Press* 1974 $11.95

Apter, David E. GHANA IN TRANSITION. *Princeton Univ. Press* 2nd rev. ed. 1972 $13.50 pap. $3.95

    THE POLITICAL KINGDOM IN UGANDA: A Study in Bureaucratic Nationalism. *Princeton Univ. Press* rev. ed. 1967 $16.00

Arkell, Anthony J. A HISTORY OF THE SUDAN. 1961. *Greenwood* 1974 $13.00

Balandier, Georges. AMBIGUOUS AFRICA: Cultures in Collision. Trans. from the French by Helen Weaver *Pantheon* 1965 $7.95

    DAILY LIFE IN THE KINGDOM OF THE KONGO FROM THE 16TH TO THE 18TH CENTURY. Trans. by Helen Weaver *Pantheon* 1968 $8.00

    "A remarkably readable book on the early history of one part of Africa"—(LJ).

Barnett, Donald L., and Karari Njama. MAU MAU FROM WITHIN: Autobiography and Analysis of Kenya's Peasant Revolt. Pref. by B. M. Kaggia and others *Monthly Review Press* pap. 1970 $14.50

"Consisting of a detailed account of the personal experiences of a prominent Mau Mau, Karari Njama, with Barnett—a University of Iowa anthropologist—adding background information and interpretations, this book is a significant contribution to the history of the 1953–56 Mau Mau revolt"—(*LJ*).

Bascom, William. IFA DIVINATION: Communication between Gods and Men in West Africa. *Indiana Univ. Press* 1969 $22.50

"Bascom, professor of anthropology and Director of the Robert L. Lowrie Museum of Anthropology at the University of California, is an outstanding authority on all aspects of West African culture. His exciting book will be difficult reading for the layman but informative for the ethnologist"—(*LJ*).

THE YORUBA OF SOUTHWESTERN NIGERIA. *Holt* 1969 pap. $3.25

Benedict, Burton. MAURITIUS: The Problems of a Plural Society. *Praeger* 1965 $4.00. The best short survey of the island.

Berque, Jacques. EGYPT: Imperialism and Revolution. Trans. by Janet Stuart *Praeger* 1972 $38.50

FRENCH NORTH AFRICA: The Maghrib between Two World Wars. Trans. by Jean Stewart *Praeger* 1967 $12.50

Beshir, Mohamed Omer. REVOLUTION AND NATIONALISM IN THE SUDAN. *Harper* (Barnes & Noble) 1974 $15.00

THE SOUTHERN SUDAN: Background to Conflict. *Humanities Press* 1968 $6.50

Bienen, Henry. KENYA: The Politics of Participation and Control. *Princeton Univ. Press* 1974 $10.00

TANZANIA: Party Transformation and Economic Development. *Princeton Univ. Press* 1967 enl. ed. 1970 $13.50 pap. $3.95

Burns, Sir Alan. HISTORY OF NIGERIA. *Harper* (Barnes & Noble) 1929 8th rev. ed. 1973 $13.50

"Sir Alan was in the Nigerian Civil Service from 1912 to 1934. Then after terms as Governor of British Honduras and of the Gold Coast he was Governor of Nigeria during 1942. This book, which was first published in 1929, has been frequently revised"—(*LJ*).

Cabral, Amilcar. REVOLUTION IN GUINEA: Selected Texts. Ed. and trans. by Richard Handyside *Monthly Review Press* 1972 $4.95 pap. $2.25

Coleman, James S. NIGERIA: Background to Nationalism. 1958. *Univ. of California Press* 1971 $15.50

(With Carl G. Rosberg, Jr., Eds.) POLITICAL PARTIES AND NATIONAL INTEGRATION IN TROPICAL AFRICA. *Univ. of California Press* 1964 $14.50

Collins, Robert O., and Robert L. Tignor. EGYPT AND THE SUDAN. *Prentice-Hall* Spectrum Bks. (orig.) 1967 pap. $1.95

Cowan, L. Gray. THE DILEMMAS OF AFRICAN INDEPENDENCE. *Walker & Co.* rev. ed. 1968 pap. $2.95

"Dr. Cowan is director of the African Studies Program at Columbia University and one of the nation's top scholars in the field. In this informative little book he presents the current problems facing the more than 30 newly, and often suddenly, independent states in Africa"—(*LJ*).

Cox, Richard H. KENYATTA'S COUNTRY. *Praeger* 1966 $5.95

"Richard Cox, foreign correspondent for the *Sunday Times* of London ... writes from a balanced, unprejudiced, and, on the whole, optimistic point of view. His book provides insights into the character and personality of Jomo Kenyatta, an evaluation of the real impact of the Mau Mau, and an estimate of the future possibilities. The book, timely and readable, is for the general reader"—(*LJ*).

Crowder, Michael. WEST AFRICA UNDER COLONIAL RULE. *Northwestern Univ. Press* 1968 $5.00

Davidson, Basil. BLACK STAR: A View of the Life and Times of Kwame Nkrumah. *Praeger* 1974 $7.95

A HISTORY OF EAST AND CENTRAL AFRICA TO THE LATE NINETEENTH CENTURY. *Doubleday* Anchor Bks. 1969 pap. $2.50; *Peter Smith* $4.75

De St. Jorre, John. THE BROTHERS' WAR: Biafra and Nigeria. *Houghton* 1972 $10.00

"This is an account of the Nigerian civil war 1967–70. On January 15, 1966 a group of young officers in Nigeria assassinated some leaders in the army bureaucracy and the civil government . . . They formed the so-called Republic of Biafra. This act of secession . . . led to a civil war. . . . The Republic of Biafra came to an end in January 1970"—*(Best Sellers)*.

Duvignaud, Jean. CHANGE AT SHEBIKA: Report from a North African Village. *Pantheon* 1970 $6.95; *Random* Vintage Bks. 1972 pap. $1.95

Eprile, Cecil. WAR AND PEACE IN THE SUDAN, 1955–1972. *David and Charles* 1974 $15.00. A discussion and assessment of the causes and course of war and peace, based largely on personal contacts.

Fage, John Donnelly. GHANA: A Historical Interpretation. *Univ. of Wisconsin Press* 1959 pap. $2.50

A HISTORY OF WEST AFRICA: An Introductory Survey. *Cambridge* 4th ed. 1969 $10.50 pap. $3.95

Feierman, Steven. THE SHAMBAA KINGDOM: A History. *Univ. of Wisconsin Press* 1974 $12.50. A good example of the use of oral tradition to reconstruct the history of a pre-colonial kingdom near the coast of Tanzania.

Flint, John E. NIGERIA AND GHANA. *Prentice-Hall* Spectrum Bks. (orig.) 1966 pap. $1.95

Furlonge, Geoffrey. THE LANDS OF BARBARY. *Transatlantic* 1968 $7.25. A history of Libya, Morocco, Tunisia, and Algeria.

Gann, Lewis H. CENTRAL AFRICA: The Former British State. *Prentice-Hall* 1971 $5.65 pap. $2.45

"This is easily the most up-to-date treatment of the history of Central Africa"—*(LJ)*.

Gérard-Libois, Jules. KATANGA SECESSION. Trans. by Rebecca Young. *Univ. of Wisconsin Press* 1966 $12.50

Gukiina, Peter M. UGANDA: A Case Study in African Political Development. *Univ. of Notre Dame Press* 1972 $7.95 pap. $3.25

Hargreaves, John D. WEST AFRICA: The Former French States. *Prentice-Hall* 1967 $5.95

"The historical study concentrates on the eight republics of the former Afrique Occidentale Française: Dahomey, Guinea, Ivory Coast, Mali, Mauretania, Niger, Senegal, and Upper Volta; also the former mandate and trust territory of Togo. The survey is especially useful for its coverage of the 15th–19th Centuries; material on the 20th Century includes interesting observations about such figures as Léopold Senghor, Houphouet-Boigny, and Frantz Fanon"—*(LJ)*.

WEST AFRICA PARTITIONED. *Univ. of Wisconsin Press* 1974 Vol. 1 The Loaded Pause, 1885–1889 $15.00

(Ed.) FRANCE AND WEST AFRICA: An Anthology of Historical Documents. *St. Martin's* 1969 $9.95

Henderson, Richard N. THE KING IN EVERY MAN: Evolutionary Trends in Onitsha Ibo Society and Culture. *Yale Univ. Press* 1972 $27.50

The author's objective "is to study the changes occuring in a West African society before its inclusion in a wider British colonial system at the end of the nineteenth century: to reconstruct the evidence of an Ibo community . . . to apply an evolutionary theory of social systems to the interpretation of this history . . . and to describe and analyse the symbols that delineated . . . the society"—*(Choice)*.

Hess, Robert L. Ethiopia: The Modernization of Autocracy. *Cornell Univ. Press* 1970 $8.95 pap. $2.95

Hill, Polly. Studies in Rural Capitalism in West Africa. *Cambridge* 1970 $11.50

"This book is an attempt to provide social anthropologists, economists, and geographers with material relating to the way in which rural people in West Africa order their economic behavior"—(Preface).

A History of East Africa. *Oxford* 2 vols. 1963–65 Vol. 1 ed. by Roland Oliver and Gervase Mathew (1963) $13.00 pap. $5.75 Vol. 2 ed. by Vincent Harlow and E. M. Chilver, assisted by Alison Smith (1965) $17.00

"Its many authors, by combining their diverse talents, have sought to make a dramatic break with the European oriented historiography of East Africa"—(*Choice*). Despite more recent surveys, many chapters are still useful.

Holt, Peter M. Mahdist State in the Sudan, 1881–1898: A Study of Its Origin, Development and Overthrow. *Oxford* 2nd ed. 1970 $9.00

Holt "has profited by the numerous studies by Sudanese scholars, particularly in reference to the origins of the Mahdist idea and the propaganda of the Mahdi. Written with clarity and insight, the book remains of greatest interest to scholars and students of Sudanese history"—(*Choice*).

Hopkins, A. G. An Economic History of West Africa. *Columbia* 1974 $15.00

"The first comprehensive study of this vast area . . . It is therefore a welcome addition by a respected authority to the small but growing literature on African economic history"—(*Choice*).

Johnson, Willard R. The Cameroon Federation: Political Integration in a Fragmentary Society. *Princeton Univ. Press* 1970 $14.50

Julien, C. A. The History of North Africa: From the Arab Conquest to 1830. Trans. from the French by John Petrie *Praeger* 1970 $13.50

Kaunda, Kenneth. A Humanist in Africa: Letters to Colin Morris from Kenneth Kaunda, President of Zambia. *Abingdon* 1968 $3.50

"The informal but carefully expressed views of Kenneth Kaunda about Africa, the African people, and Zambia. His correspondent, Colin Morris, is a missionary, president of the United Church of Zambia. This wise little book is surprisingly profound, considering that the author is a head of state and there are many demands on his time. Besides its obvious importance as a statement of policy, the book has interest to churches because it reaffirms the Christian basis of Kaunda's humanism. It closes with an eloquent declaration of his belief in the eventual possibility of African union"—(*PW*).

Zambia Shall Be Free: An Autobiography. *Humanities Press* 1969 pap. $2.00

Kenyatta, Jomo. The Challenge of Uhuru: The Progress of Kenya, 1968–70. *Int. Pubns. Service* 1971 pap. $3.00

Facing Mt. Kenya: The Tribal Life of the Kikuyu. *Random* Vintage Bks. 1962 pap. $1.95

Suffering Without Bitterness: The Founding of the Kenya Nation. *Int. Pubns. Service* 1968 $8.75

Kilson, Martin. Political Change in a West African State: A Study of the Modernization Process in Sierra Leone. *Harvard Univ. Press* 1966 $8.50; *Atheneum* 1969 pap. $3.25

Lacouture, Jean. Nasser: A Biography. *Knopf* 1973 $10.00

"This account of the career of the President of the U.A.R. from his boyhood to his death in 1970 examines the problems facing Egypt during this period"—(Publisher's note).

Legvold, Robert. Soviet Policy in West Africa. *Harvard Univ. Press* 1970 $13.00

Levine, Donald N. Greater Ethiopia: The Evolution of a Multi-Ethnic Society. *Univ. of Chicago Press* 1974 $12.50

Wax and Gold: Tradition and Innovation in Ethiopian Culture. *Univ. of Chicago Press* 1965 $11.00 pap. 1972 $3.25

Le Vine, Victor T. Cameroon Federal Republic. Ed. by Gwendolen M. Carter *Cornell Univ. Press* 1971 $9.50 pap. $2.45

Levtzion, Nehemia. ANCIENT GHANA AND MALI. *Harper* (Barnes & Noble) 1973 $11.50 pap. $6.50

"Levtzion divides the book into two parts. The first is a chronological account of the history of the western Sudan from the eighth to the sixteenth century; the second part has a . . . discussion of three major themes—government, commerce . . . and the process of Islamization of the region"— (*Choice*).

Lewis, Ian M. THE PEOPLES OF THE HORN OF AFRICA: Somali, Afar and Saho. *Int. Pubns. Service* 1969 $7.50

Liebenow, J. Gus. COLONIAL RULE AND POLITICAL DEVELOPMENT IN TANZANIA: The Case of the Makonde. *Northwestern Univ. Press* 1971 $12.00; *Int. Pubns. Service* 1973 $12.50

LIBERIA: The Evolution of Privilege. *Cornell Univ. Press* 1969 $9.50 pap. $1.95

Ling, Dwight L. TUNISIA: From Protectorate to Republic. *Indiana Univ. Press* 1967 $9.50

Lofchie, Michael F. ZANZIBAR: Background to Revolution. *Princeton Univ. Press* 1965 $12.50 pap. $2.95

"This study describes the historical and social background of the revolution, the general character of politics in Zanzibar, the postwar emergence of Arab nationalism and anticolonial protest, African responses to it, the development of political conflict, the Arab oligarchy's success in establishing popular support among the African majority, the failure of democratic constitutional arrangements to reverse the traditional political relationship, and why force became the only method by which Africans could oust the ruling Arabs and create an African-ruled state"— (*LJ*). Zanzibar joined with Tanganyika to form the new state of Tanzania.

Lumumba, Patrice. LUMUMBA SPEAKS: The Speeches and Writings, 1958–61. Trans. from the French by Helen Lane *Little* 1972 $12.50

Lynch, Hollis R. EDWARD WILMOT BLYDEN: Pan-Negro Patriot, 1832–1912. *Oxford* 1967 pap. 1970 $2.50

MacGaffey, Wyatt. CUSTOM AND GOVERNMENT IN THE LOWER CONGO. *Univ. of California Press* 1970 $6.95

"This book is in the theoretical tradition of American political anthropology and the Manchester School"—(*Choice*).

Marlowe, John. HISTORY OF MODERN EGYPT AND ANGLO-EGYPTIAN RELATIONS 1800–1956. *Shoe String Press* 2nd ed. 1965 $10.00

Mazrui, Ali. A. CULTURAL ENGINEERING AND NATION-BUILDING IN EAST AFRICA. *Northwestern Univ. Press* 1972 $10.00

ON HEROES AND UHURU WORSHIP: Essay on Independent Africa. *Humanities Press* 1967 $7.50 pap. $2.75

Mboya, Tom. THE CHALLENGE OF NATIONHOOD. *Praeger* 1970 $7.50

FREEDOM AND AFTER. *Little* 1963 $6.50. The autobiography of the slain Kenyan leader.

Melady, Thomas Patrick. BURUNDI: The Tragic Years. *Orbis* 1974 $4.95

Merriam, Alan P. AN AFRICAN WORLD: The Basongye Village of Lupupo Ngye. *Indiana Univ. Press* 1974 $12.50

Mofolo, Thomas. CHAKA: An Historical Romance. Trans. by F. H. Dutton *Oxford* 1931 $6.50

CHAKA THE ZULU. *Oxford* 1949 pap. $1.30

Morgan, William B., and J. C. Pugh. WEST AFRICA. *Harper* (Barnes & Noble) 1969 $22.50

Murray-Brown, Jeremy. KENYATTA. *Dutton* 1973 $12.50

Niane, D. T. SUNDIATA: An Epic of Old Mali. Trans. from the French by G. O. Pickett *Humanities Press* 1965 pap. $2.00

Nkrumah, Kwame. GHANA: The Autobiography of Kwame Nkrumah. *International Pubs.* 1971 $7.50 pap. $3.25

Nyerere, Julius K. UJAMAA: Essays on Socialism. *Oxford* 1971 pap. $1.75

Ogot, Bethwell A., and J. A. Kieran, Eds. ZAMANI: A Survey of East African History. *Humanities Press* 1971 $10.00 pap. $4.50

Ostheimer, John M. NIGERIAN POLITICS. *Harper* 1973 pap. $3.95

Ottaway, David, and Marina Ottaway. ALGERIA: The Politics of a Socialist Revolution. *Univ. of California Press* 1970 $10.75

"This book is a study of the Algerian socialist revolution, of those who made it and those who gained by it. The primary focus is on political behavior, on those aspects of the struggle among Algerian leaders which . . . affected the character of the new order"—*(Publisher's note).*

Pachai, Bridglal. MALAWI: The History of the Nation. *Longmans* 1973 $15.00 pap. $5.00

Rosberg, Carl G., Jr., and John Nottingham. THE MYTH OF "MAU MAU": Nationalism in Kenya. *Hoover Institution* 1966 $7.50

Rubin, Neville. CAMEROUN: An African Federation. *Praeger* 1971 $10.00

"Rubin, a lecturer in African law at the University of the Federated Union of Cameroon, provides a readable, concise summary of the political history of Africa's most successful federation"—*(Choice).*

Smith, Robert S. KINGDOM OF THE YORUBA. *Harper* (Barnes & Noble) 1969 pap. $3.50

Smith, William Edgett. WE MUST RUN WHILE THEY WALK: A Portrait of Africa's Julius Nyerere. *Random* 1971 $7.95

"This biography of President Julius Nyerere of Tanzania follows his development from a tribal childhood near the . . . shores of Lake Victoria to his position today as . . . spokesman for African unity, development and nonalignment"—(Publisher's note).

Thompson, Virginia, and Richard Adloff. THE MALAGASY REPUBLIC: Madagascar Today. *Stanford Univ. Press* 1965 $12.50

Turnbull, Colin M. THE FOREST PEOPLE. *Simon & Schuster* 1961 $5.95 Touchstone-Clarion Bks. 1968 pap. $2.95. A readable narrative on the pygmies of the Zaire forest.

THE LONELY AFRICAN. *Simon & Schuster* 1962 $5.50 Touchstone-Clarion Bks. 1968 pap. $2.95. A very readable account of the pressures of modernization and change, with a focus on eastern Zaire.

Ullendorff, Edward. THE ETHIOPIANS: An Introduction to the Country and People. *Oxford* 1960 new ed. 1973 pap. $5.50

Vansina, Jan. THE KINGDOM OF THE MIDDLE CONGO, 1880–1892. *Oxford* 1973 $25.75

KINGDOMS OF THE SAVANNA. *Univ. of Wisconsin Press* 1966 pap. $3.95

Vatikiotis, P. J. MODERN HISTORY OF EGYPT. *Praeger* 1969 $6.95

"Few people can write with authority equal to the contributors of the present volume who succeed in presenting a balanced assessment of the Egyptian experiment since 1952"—*(Choice).*

WEST AFRICA ANNUAL, 1974. *Int. Pubns. Service* 9th ed. 1974 $10.50

Wills, Alfred J. AN INTRODUCTION TO THE HISTORY OF CENTRAL AFRICA. *Oxford* 3rd ed. 1973 $13.00 pap. $6.95

Wolpe, Howard. URBAN POLITICS IN NIGERIA: A Study of Port Harcourt. *Univ. of California Press* 1974 $16.75. A study of the relationship between modernization and communalism from 1913 to 1965.

Young, Crawford. POLITICS IN THE CONGO: Decolonization and Independence. *Princeton Univ. Press* 1965 $12.50

"A remarkably clear and readable account of the tangled politics surrounding and following the most rapid—and least well prepared—transfer of power that has taken place in Africa"—*(Nation).*

Zartman, Ira William. GOVERNMENT AND POLITICS IN NORTHERN AFRICA. *Praeger* 1963 pap. $1.95

Dr. Zartman of the University of South Carolina focuses attention on the eight Arab states: Morrocco, Algeria, Tunisia, Libya, UAR (Egypt), Sudan, Ethiopia, and Somalia, and briefly reviews for each country its history, indigenous political systems, culture, people, and its own struggle for independence. "Against this background he discusses the characteristics of the separate forms of self-government which have been set up, assessing their strength, weaknesses, and chances for success."

(Ed.) MAN, STATE, AND SOCIETY IN THE CONTEMPORARY MAGHRIB. *Praeger* 1973 $15.00 pap. $6.95

Southern Africa: Black vs. White

Southern Africa still contains the seeds of disaster as white minorities cling to power, suppressing black majorities. The latter have resorted to guerilla warfare in Rhodesia, Angola, Mozambique, Namibia and other territories. It is important that Americans begin to understand an area where the flames of racial war, with big-power alignments and involvement, is an ever-present possibility.

Southern Africa is usually considered to include the following, covered in this listing: South Africa; Namibia (the former South West Africa, a Trust Territory under the U.N. to which South Africa clings); Rhodesia, where a white government has declared its independence from Britain, though early in 1969 it was still a member of the British Commonwealth; the former British High Commission Territories of Lesotho, Botswana and Swaziland, now independent but contiguous to or within South Africa; and the Portuguese territories, chiefly Mozambique and Angola, called "overseas provinces" and "integral parts" of Portugal, but in actual fact still Portuguese colonies.

Africa Research Group. RACE TO POWER: The Struggle for Southern Africa. *Doubleday* Anchor Bks. (orig.) 1974 pap. $3.95

Birmingham, David. TRADE AND CONFLICT IN ANGOLA. *Oxford* 1966 $10.25. About Portugal's colony on the southwest coast of Africa, where African guerrillas seek independence.

Bowman, Larry W. POLITICS IN RHODESIA: White Power in an African State. *Harvard Univ. Press* 1973 $9.50

Brookes, Edgar H., Ed. APARTHEID: A Documentary Study of Modern South Africa. *Routledge & Kegan Paul* 1968 $6.25 pap. $3.25

Bull, Theodore, Ed. RHODESIA: Crisis of Color. Introd. by Gwendolen Carter *Quadrangle* 1968 $4.50. The colony that defied Great Britain and declared its independence to keep the white minority in power.

Carter, Gwendolen M., and Thomas Karis with Newell M. Stultz. SOUTH AFRICA'S TRANSKEI: The Politics of Domestic Colonialism. *Northwestern Univ. Press* 1967 $6.50. About a "self-governing Bantustan" or black segregated area.

Chilcote, Ronald H. EMERGING NATIONALISM IN PORTUGUESE AFRICA: Documents. *Hoover Institution* 1972 $25.00

Cole, Ernest, and Thomas Flaherty. HOUSE OF BONDAGE. Introd. by Joseph Lelyveld *Random* 1967 $12.50. Moving photographs of his native land, South Africa, by Mr. Cole, a young African journalist and photographer now in exile.

Davidson, Basil. IN THE EYE OF THE STORM: Angola's People. *Doubleday* 1972 $7.95
"Based on the limited historical sources, available documents, personal observation, and interviews with principals of the struggle for Angolan independence, Davidson's volume is unmatched in its clarification of the central issues of persisting colonial domination in Africa"— (*Choice*).

De Kiewiet, C. W. A HISTORY OF SOUTH AFRICA, SOCIAL AND ECONOMIC. *Oxford* 1941 $12.00 pap. $3.50. An outstanding older history.

Duffy, James E. PORTUGAL IN AFRICA. *Penguin* (orig.) 1963 pap. $.95

ENCYCLOPAEDIA RHODESIA. Ed. by Peter Bridger and others *Rhodesia College Press* 1973 $12.50
This volume "brings together information on Rhodesia, which were it available at all in other sources, would have to be retrieved with considerable effort"—(*College & Research Libs.*).

Feit, Edward. AFRICAN OPPOSITION IN SOUTH AFRICA: The Failure of Passive Resistance. *Hoover Institution* 1967 $7.50. An analysis by a former South African (who now teaches at the University of Massachusetts) of the unsuccessful campaign waged in 1954–55 by the African National Congress against the South African government.

URBAN REVOLT IN SOUTH AFRICA, 1960–1964. *Northwestern Univ. Press* 1971 $11.00

First, Ruth. SOUTH WEST AFRICA. 1963. *Peter Smith* $5.00. A fine, unbiased history of the area now called Namibia, by a South African Communist presently living in London.

(With others) THE SOUTH AFRICAN CONNECTION: Western Investment in Apartheid. *Harper* (Barnes & Noble) 1973 $12.00

Frye, William R. IN WHITEST AFRICA: The Dynamics of Apartheid. *Prentice-Hall* 1968 $6.95

"W. R. Frye, who was chief of the U.N. news bureau of the *Christian Science Monitor* for 13 years, argues that timely intervention by the United States and Western countries in South Africa will perhaps prevent World War IV and 'eliminate a formidable breeding-ground for communism'; he suggests various steps that can be taken to put pressure on the South African government to force a process of peaceful change"—*(LJ)*.

Hance, William A., Ed. SOUTHERN AFRICA AND THE UNITED STATES. *Columbia* 1969 $9.00

"In this little book, four American authorities on Africa—Vernon McKay, Edwin S. Munger. Leo Kuper, and William Hance—examine the political and economic situation in South Africa, Rhodesia, and the former High Commission Territories (Lesotho, Botswana, and Swaziland) and analyze the implications for U.S. and British policy. The four authors disagree on various points, but they do agree that the United States should not relax its pressures and persuasion on South Africa and that it should continue to stand by its long and deeply held principles and ideals supporting human rights and racial equality"—*(PW)*.

Hancock, William K. SMUTS. *Cambridge* 2 vols. 1962–68 Vol. 1 The Sanguine Years, 1870–1919 (1962) Vol. 2 The Fields of Force, 1919–1950 (1968) each $18.50

The life of Jan Christian Smuts, South African soldier, scholar and statesman, by a professor of history at the Australian National University.

Hastings, Adrian. WIRIYAMU: My-Lai in Mozambique. *Orbis* 1974 pap. $3.95

Hepple, Alexander. SOUTH AFRICA: A Political and Economic History. Library of African Affairs *Praeger* 1966 $7.50. By a member of the South African Parliament for 10 years and leader of its Labor Party.

VERWOERD. 1968. *Peter Smith* $3.50

Horwitz, Ralph. THE POLITICAL ECONOMY OF SOUTH AFRICA. *Praeger* 1967 $10.00. By a former member of Parliament, professor at the University of Cape Town, and editor and publisher of business journals.

Houghton, D. Hobart. THE SOUTH AFRICAN ECONOMY. *Oxford* 3rd ed. 1973 $9.75 lib. bdg. $7.70

(With Jenifer Dagut, Eds.) SOURCE MATERIAL ON THE SOUTH AFRICAN ECONOMY: 1860–1970. *Oxford* 2 vols. 1972–73 Vol. 1 $14.00 Vol. 2 $11.75

Isaacman, Allen F. MOZAMBIQUE: The Africanization of a European Institution, the Zambesi Prazos, 1750–1902. *Univ. of Wisconsin Press* 1972 $17.50

The author "has made thorough use of archival sources and has attained a balanced perspective through oral field research in former *prazo* estates. This is a pioneering work in Mozambique history, and it opens up a variety of questions in the field of cross-cultural studies generally"—*(LJ)*.

Kahn, Ely J., Jr. THE SEPARATED PEOPLE: A Look at Contemporary South Africa. *Norton* 1968 $6.95. By the *New Yorker* correspondent.

Keppel-Jones, Arthur. SOUTH AFRICA: A Short History. *Hutchinson Univ. Lib.* (dist. by Hillary House) 1966 $6.00 pap. $2.75

Kuper, Leo. AN AFRICAN BOURGEOISIE: Race, Class, and Politics in South Africa. *Yale Univ. Press* 1965 pap. $2.95

"An outstanding documentation of the impact of repression in South Africa"—*(American Sociological Review)*. Winner of the Herskovits Book Award in 1966.

Legum, Colin, and Margaret Legum. SOUTH AFRICA: Crisis for the West. *Praeger* 1965 $7.50

Luthuli, Albert John. LET MY PEOPLE GO. Introd. by Charles Hooper. 1962. *New Am. Lib.* 1969 pap. $3.95. By the great Zulu chieftain, who was for almost 10 years head of the African National Congress and who was awarded the Nobel Peace Prize in 1960.

Mandela, Nelson. NO EASY WALK TO FREEDOM: Articles, Speeches, and Trial Addresses. Ed. by Ruth First. 1965. *Humanities Press* 1974 pap. $2.25. Nelson Mandela, leader of the South African Pan-Africanist Congress, now banned, spent a number of years imprisoned on Robbens Island after his conviction in the Rivonia treason trial of 1964.

Marquard, Leo. A FEDERATION OF SOUTH AFRICA. *Oxford.* 1972 $6.50

PEOPLES AND POLICIES OF SOUTH AFRICA. *Oxford* 4th ed. 1969 pap. $2.50

A SHORT HISTORY OF SOUTH AFRICA. *Praeger* 1968 $6.50

Morris, Donald R. THE WASHING OF THE SPEARS: The Rise and Fall of the Zulu Nation. *Simon & Schuster* 1965 $12.00 Touchstone-Clarion Bks. 1969 pap. $3.45. A fine re-creation of an abortive African revolt in 1879 in what is now Natal, South Africa.

Omer-Cooper, John D. ZULU AFTERMATH: A Nineteenth Century Revolution in Bantu Africa. *Northwestern Univ. Press* 1966 $7.50

Pachai, Bridglal. THE INTERNATIONAL ASPECTS OF THE SOUTH AFRICAN INDIAN QUESTION, 1860–1970. *Verry* 1971 $22.50

Paton, Alan. APARTHEID AND THE ARCHBISHOP: The Life and Times of Geoffrey Clayton, Archbishop of Cape Town. *Scribner* 1974 $10.00

THE LAND AND PEOPLE OF SOUTH AFRICA. Portraits of the Nations Ser. *Lippincott* rev. ed. 1972 $4.95

THE LONG VIEW. Ed. by Edward Callan *Praeger* 1968 $6.95. Selections from Mr. Paton's writings in *Contact,* a liberal South African journal.

"This collection of essays deals with the problems of South Africa: racism, and the con-catenation of injustices and stupidities that racism creates. Mr. Paton has been on the losing side— or so it appears, at least for the moment—as a leader of a political party (the Liberals) that has been destroyed and as a man locked into his country (his passport has been withdrawn), where, by peculiar South African "banning" laws, he is forbidden to see many of his friends. Nonetheless, Mr. Paton's essays are not gloomy. Neither are they shrill. They are precise, truthtelling, beautifully written reports and comments on a desperate situation by a man who does not despair"—(*New Yorker*).

SOUTH AFRICAN TRAGEDY: The Life and Times of Jan Hofmeyr. *Scribner* 1965 pap. 1970 $2.95. A biography of Prime Minister Smut's wartime deputy, a leading white liberal, who died in 1948.

See also his main entry in Chapter 17, African Literature, Reader's Adviser, *Vol. 2.*

Patterson, Sheila. THE LAST TREK: A Study of the Boer People and the Afrikaner Nation. 1957. *Fernhill* $8.75

Powermaker, Hortense. COPPER TOWN: Changing Africa, the Human Situation on the Rhodesian Copperbelt. 1962. *Greenwood* 1973 $16.00

Ranger, Terence O. AFRICAN VOICE IN SOUTHERN RHODESIA, 1898–1930. *Northwestern Univ. Press* 1970 $9.00; *Int. Pubns. Service* 1970 pap. $5.75

REVOLT IN SOUTHERN RHODESIA, 1896–97. *Northwestern Univ. Press* 1967 $13.50

Reed, Douglas. THE BATTLE FOR RHODESIA. *Devin-Adair* 1967 $3.95

Roberts, Brian. THE ZULU KINGS. *Scribner* 1975 $10.95

"A first-class reassessment of Zulu history"—(*N.Y. Times*).

Rosenthal, Eric. THE ENCYCLOPEDIA OF SOUTHERN AFRICA. *Warne* rev. ed. 1973 $15.00

Sachs, Albert L. JUSTICE IN SOUTH AFRICA. *Univ. of California Press* 1973 $9.00 pap. $3.25. By a young South African lawyer who often defended the victims of apartheid.

Segal, Ronald. THE RACE WAR: The World-Wide Clash of White and Non-White. *Viking* 1967 $6.50

By a fighting liberal, editor of *Africa South*, who was eventually forced to leave South Africa and seek exile in London. "A brilliantly sustained analysis, scrupulously documented"—(Nadine Gordimer).

Simons, H. J., and R. E. Simons. CLASS AND COLOUR IN SOUTH AFRICA, 1850–1950. *Gannon* $8.50

Spiro, Herbert J., Ed. AFRICA: The Primacy of Politics. 1966. *Peter Smith* $4.25

Stevens, Richard P. LESOTHO, BOTSWANA AND SWAZILAND: The Former High Commission Territories in Southern Africa. Library of African Affairs *Praeger* 1967 $9.00. By the director of Lincoln University's African Center.

Stone, John. COLONIST OR UITLANDER: A Study of the British Immigrant in South Africa. *Oxford* new ed. 1973 $16.00

Stultz, Newell M. AFRIKANER POLITICS IN SOUTH AFRICA, 1934–1948. *Univ. of California Press* 1975 $8.00

Taubenfeld, Howard J., and Rita F. Taubenfeld. RACE, PEACE, LAW, AND SOUTHERN AFRICA: Background Paper and Proceedings of the Tenth Hammarskjöld Forum. Ed. by John Carey *Oceana* 1967 $9.00

Thompson, Leonard M., and others. SOUTHERN AFRICAN HISTORY BEFORE 1900: A Select Bibliography of Articles. *Hoover Institution* 1971 $6.50

Were, Gideon S. HISTORY OF SOUTH AFRICA. *Holmes & Meier* (Africana) 1975 $8.95 pap. $4.45

"The author describes the political and economic struggles that lie behind South Africa today and examines the heterogeneous peoples—Bushman, Bantu, Dutch and English—whose roles in the events of the past are manifest in present day isolation and hostility"—(Publisher's note).

Wilson, Monica Hunter, and Leonard Thompson, Eds. OXFORD HISTORY OF SOUTH AFRICA. *Oxford* 2 vols. 1969–1971 each $8.95

Young, Kenneth. RHODESIA AND INDEPENDENCE. *James H. Heineman* 1967 $7.25. A discussion of Rhodesia's unilateral declaration of independence from Britain that is sympathetic to the Ian Smith government.

Archeology

Ashe, Geoffrey, Ed. THE QUEST FOR ARTHUR'S BRITAIN. *Praeger* 1968 $13.50. An account of recent archeological discoveries at Cadbury, Glastonbury and Tintagel in the search for Camelot and the grave of King Arthur.

(With others) THE QUEST FOR AMERICA. *Praeger* 1971 $15.00. Essays on various aspects of the pre-Columbian contacts, by Helge Ingstad, Thor Heyerdahl, J. V. Luce, Bergitta Wallace, Betty J. Meggers, etc.

Bacon, Edward. ARCHAEOLOGY: Discoveries in the 1960's. *Praeger* 1971 $12.50

Bass, George F. ARCHAEOLOGY UNDER WATER. *Praeger* 1966 $8.50; *Penguin* Pelican Bks. 1972 pap. $1.95

Benson, Elizabeth P. THE MAYA WORLD. 1967. *Apollo* 1972 pap. $2.95. By the curator for the pre-Columbian collection at Dumbarton Oaks in Washington, D.C.

Bibby, Geoffrey. THE TESTIMONY OF THE SPADE. *Knopf* 1956 $9.95; *New Am. Lib.* 1974 pap. $2.25. A fascinating account of European archeology north of the Alps.

Binford, Sally R., Ed. NEW PERSPECTIVES IN ARCHEOLOGY. *Aldine* 1970 $9.75

"A series of collected essays concerning new techniques, research strategies, and theoretical approaches which have recently begun to gain prominence. This book emphasizes the role of archaeology as a science, the importance of utilizing a deductive approach for testing archaeological hypotheses, and the necessity for revamping traditional theory and method"—(*Choice*).

Bracegirdle, Brian. THE ARCHAEOLOGY OF THE INDUSTRIAL REVOLUTION. *Fairleigh Dickinson Univ. Press* 1973 $25.00

Bratton, Fred Gladstone. A HISTORY OF EGYPTIAN ARCHAEOLOGY. 1968. *Apollo* 1972 pap. $2.45

"In 12 episodic but connected chapters [the author] has produced not only a history of Egyptology but a rather informal history of Egyptian society. . . . Handsomely illustrated with 40 photographs and nine line drawings [and] five maps"—*(Choice).*

Bray, Warwick. AMERICAN HERITAGE GUIDE TO ARCHAEOLOGY. *American Heritage Press* 1970 $6.95

"The book will prove useful for those whose archeological reading is confined to popular prehistoric archaeology"—*(Choice).*

Ceram, C. W. (pseud. of Kurt W. Marek). *See his main entry, this Section.*

Charles-Picard, Gilbert, Ed. LAROUSSE ENCYCLOPEDIA OF ARCHAEOLOGY. Trans. by Anne Ward *Putnam* 1972 $25.00

"This book defines and explores the science of Archaeology, in addition to describing the results of exploration in the field. Specialists have contributed chapters on their spheres of investigation"—*(SR).*

Clark, Grahame. ASPECTS OF PREHISTORY. *Univ. of California Press* 1970 $5.95

" . . . the expanded texts of three lectures given at the University of California in 1969. Clark devotes much of his space to a lengthy excursus into the early archeological history of a dozen or so different countries around the world"—*(TLS,* London).

Clarke, David L. ANALYTICAL ARCHAEOLOGY. *Harper* (Barnes & Noble) 1969 $23.50

" . . . describes and evaluates the many changes taking place in archaeological methodology"—*(LJ).*

Cottrell, Leonard. IN SEARCH OF THE PHARAOHS. *McKay* 1974 $7.95

LOST CITIES. 1957. *Grosset* Univ. Lib. 1963 pap. $2.25

"Fascinating stories of lost cities, selected from many possible choices on the basis of the element of wonder"—(NYPL).

THE QUEST FOR SUMER. *Putnam* 1965 $5.95

(Ed.) CONCISE ENCYCLOPEDIA OF ARCHAEOLOGY. *Hawthorn* 1971 $16.95

Daniel, Glyn. A HUNDRED AND FIFTY YEARS OF ARCHAEOLOGY. *Duckworth* 1975 $23.00

Deiss, Joseph Jay. HERCULANEUM: Italy's Buried Treasure. Fwd. by Frank E. Brown. 1966. *Apollo* 1969 pap. $4.95. An account of the excavation of a town buried in the eruption of Mt. Vesuvius in 79 A.D.

Deuel, Leo. CONQUISTADORS WITHOUT SWORDS: Archaeologists in the Americas, an Account with Original Narratives. 1967. *Schocken* 1974 pap. $7.50

FLIGHTS INTO YESTERDAY: The Story of Aerial Archaeology. *St. Martin's* 1969 $8.95

TESTAMENTS OF TIME: The Search for Lost Manuscripts and Records. *Knopf* 1965 $10.00

Eydoux, Henri-Paul. IN SEARCH OF LOST WORLDS: The Story of Archaeology. *Collins-World* 1971 $17.50

"This is the work of a genuinely informed enthusiast with admirable and sometimes unfamiliar illustrations. Behind them it covers predictable ground, mainly in the eastern Mediterranean and the Near East"—*(Encounter).*

Giddings, James Louis. ANCIENT MEN OF THE ARCTIC. *Knopf* 1967 $12.50

"This may be the best book written to date by an American archaeologist, in the sense that the reader participates in the suspense, excitement and enthusiasm of the search for evidence of ancient Arctic cultures"—*(PW).*

Hawkes, Jacquetta. *See her main entry, this Section.*

Hawkins, Gerald S. BEYOND STONEHENGE. *Harper* 1972 $10.00

Hawkins' "attempt to reinforce his vision of early man as competent astronomer is not only legitimate but welcome . . . Let us, therefore, honor Professor Hawkins for his persistent essays in communication"—*(N.Y. Times).*

(With John B. White) STONEHENGE DECODED. *Doubleday* 1965 $6.95; *Dell* Delta Bks. 1966 pap. $2.25

Irwin, Constance. FAIR GODS AND STONE FACES. *St. Martin's* 1963 $8.50

"This is a positively fascinating piece of archaeological detective work in which a controversial new theory of the origin of American Indian civilizations is presented." "These are not proofs and have not been so represented; rather, they are implications," the author says regarding her theory of the farsailing early Phoenicians. This book, "intelligently concerned with its thesis, painstakingly researched and lavishly illustrated," is highly recommended.

Johnstone, Paul. THE ARCHAEOLOGY OF SHIPS. *Walck* (dist. by McKay) 1975 $8.75

"This book is very readable . . . Johnstone has traced the development of ships in historical sequence and also covered developments in archaeological technique"—(*TLS*, London).

Leone, Mark P., Ed. CONTEMPORARY ARCHAEOLOGY: A Guide to Theory and Contributions. *Southern Illinois Univ. Press* 1972 $15.00

"Leone has brought together 23 essays, eight of which are original. The first 17 essays deal with the historical background and the theoretical and methodological bases of the new archaeology . . . [the others] present some of the substantive contributions of the new archaeologists"—(*LJ*).

Martin, Paul S., and Fred Plog. THE ARCHAEOLOGY OF ARIZONA: A Study of the Southwest Region. *Doubleday* Natural History Press 1973 $16.95

"Two anthropologists apply innovative theories in archaeological inquiry to prehistoric Arizona"—(*Booklist*).

Marx, Robert F. THE LURE OF SUNKEN TREASURE: Under the Sea with Marine Archaeologists and Treasure Hunters. *McKay* 1973 $9.95

"An intriguing introduction to marine archaeology and treasure hunting"—(*Booklist*).

Meyer, Karl E. THE PLUNDERED PAST. *Atheneum* 1973 $12.95

"The author . . . discusses the illegal international traffic in works of art and antiquities. He considers the case of the acquisition of the Euphronios krater by the Metropolitan Museum of Art, the theft of Mayan archaeological remains [and] the looting of Etruscan and Turkish antiquities"—(Publisher's note).

Noblecourt, Christiane Desroches. TUTANKHAMEN: Life and Death of a Pharaoh. Preface by His Excellency Sarwat Okasha; notes on the color plates by Dr. A. Shoukry *New York Graphic Soc.* 1963 $15.00; *Doubleday* 1965 pap. $2.95

Written by the chief curator of the National Museum of France, this remarkable book is exemplary not only for the fine color plates reproduced with consummate fidelity but also for the quality and quantity of absorbing, essential textual detail. No major work on the subject had appeared before this publication since Howard Carter's own writings after his discovery of the partially rifled tomb in 1922.

Noël-Hume, Ivor. HISTORICAL ARCHAEOLOGY. *Knopf* 1970 $10.00

"This is a handbook for the amateur or student archaeologist interested in excavating and preserving sites . . . [the author] tells how to prospect for a likely spot and how to organize the dig"—(Publisher's note).

Place, Robin. INTRODUCTION TO ARCHAEOLOGY. *Philosophical Lib.* 1969 $6.00

"A smoothly written and entertaining little survey . . . containing a wealth of interesting details"—(*Choice*).

Poole, Lynn, and Gray Poole. MEN WHO DIG UP HISTORY. *Dodd* 1968 $4.00

ONE PASSION, TWO LOVES. *T. Y. Crowell* 1966 $6.95. A biography of Heinrich Schliemann, the remarkable German archeologist who discovered the remains of Troy in 1870, and his wife Sophia.

Robbins, Maurice, and Mary B. Irving. THE AMATEUR ARCHAEOLOGIST'S HANDBOOK. *T. Y. Crowell* 2nd ed. 1973 $7.95

"A practical guide to archaeological techniques and methods for amateurs and professionals; also useful as a college textbook"—(*Booklist*).

Silverberg, Robert. FRONTIERS IN ARCHAEOLOGY. *Chilton* 1966 $4.95

LOST CITIES AND VANISHED CIVILIZATIONS. *Chilton* 1962 $3.95; *Bantam* 1974 pap. $.95

MOUND BUILDERS OF ANCIENT AMERICA: The Archaeology of a Myth. *N.Y. Graphic Soc.* 1968 $12.50

Throckmorton, Peter. SHIPWRECKS AND ARCHAEOLOGY: The Unharvested Sea. *Little* 1970 $7.95

"A vivid glimpse into the world beneath the sea which, through proper archaeological techniques can fill in many missing facets from earlier times"—(*LJ*).

Von Hagen, Victor W. THE GOLDEN MAN. *Saxon House* (dist. by Atheneum) 1974 $13.95

SEARCH FOR THE MAYA: The Story of Stephens and Catherwood. *Saxon House* (dist. by Atheneum) 1974 $10.95

Willey, Gordon R., and Jeremy A. Sabloff. A HISTORY OF AMERICAN ARCHAEOLOGY. *W. H. Freeman* 1974 $9.95 pap. $4.95

"An important contribution to both archaeology and historiography"—(*LJ*).

Wilson, David. THE NEW ARCHEOLOGY. *Random* 1975 $10.00

"In an especially lucid and authoritative popular résumé the science correspondent of the B.B.C. discusses comparatively recent developments of interdisciplinary cooperation in archeology"—(*Booklist*).

FROISSART, JEAN. c. 1337–1410.

This Flemish poet and chronicler, who wrote in French, was educated for the priesthood and ordained. He went to England in his 20's, became a protégé of Queen Philippa, visited Scotland, left England with the Black Prince in 1366 and traveled widely on the Continent. His "Chronicles" are lively imaginative accounts of historic events and great people written mainly from personal observation and conversations with the high-ranking personages who figured in the events he described.

CHRONICLES. Trans. by John Bourchier, Lord Berners (1523–1525) Tudor Translations Ser. 1901–1903. *AMS Press* 6 vols. each $15.00 set $90.00

MÉLIADOR. Ed. by A. Longnon. 1895–1899. *Johnson Reprint* 3 vols. 1965 $84.00 pap. $73.50

Books about Froissart

Froissart and the English Chronicle Play. By Robert M. Smith. 1915. *Blom* $10.00
Froissart, Chronicler and Poet. By F. S. Shears. 1930. *Folcroft* $20.00

SAINT-SIMON, LOUIS DE ROUVRAY, DUC DE. 1675–1755.

Saint-Simon's "Memoirs" are a mine of information about the French Court over a span of 30 years during the reigns of Louis XIV and Louis XV. Based on his own notes begun in 1691 and on contemporary journals and reminiscences, his "Memoirs," "though full of errors [are] an indispensable historical source and remarkable for their psychological observation and brilliant sketches"—(*Columbia Encyclopedia*). "Saint-Simon at Versailles" (sel. and trans. by Lucie Norton, pref. by Nancy Mitford 1959, o.p.) offers an excellent introduction to the diaries. An entertaining discussion of them by Louis Auchincloss appeared in the *N.Y. Times Book Review* of Feb. 21, 1965.

THE AGE OF MAGNIFICENCE: Memoirs. Ed. by Sanché de Gramont *Putnam* abr. ed. 1963 $5.95 pap. $1.85

MEMOIRS OF THE DUC DE SAINT-SIMON. Ed. by W. H. Lewis *Macmillan* 1964 pap. $1.95

THE HISTORICAL MEMOIRS OF THE DUC DE SAINT-SIMON: A Shortened Version. Trans. and ed. by Lucie Norton *Int. Pubns. Service* 3 vols. 1972 Vol. 1 1691–1700 Vol. 2 1710–1715 Vol. 3 1715–1723 Vols. 1–2 each $17.50 Vol. 3 $20.00

LOUIS FOURTEENTH AT VERSAILLES. Trans. by Desmond Flower *Dufour* 1954 $3.95

MONTESQUIEU, CHARLES LOUIS DE SECONDAT, Baron DE LA BREDE ET DE. 1689–1755. *See Chapter 9, French Literature, Reader's Adviser, Vol. 2.*

CARLYLE, THOMAS. 1795–1881.

Carlyle moved to London in 1834 "to be near necessary works of reference for the projected 'French Revolution.' Finally completed in 1837, the book was received with great acclaim. Although it vividly re-creates scenes of the Revolution, it is not a factual account but a poetic rendering of an event in history"—(*Columbia Encyclopedia*). He spent 13 years (1852–1865) on his massive "History of Friedrich II of Prussia, Called Frederick the Great" a survey of a "hero" in accordance with his conviction, expressed in "On Heroes, Hero-Worship and the Heroic in History," that the work of the world is accomplished by natural leaders.

WORKS. Ed. by H. D. Traill. 1896–1901. *Adler's* 30 vols. (in prep.); *AMS Press* 30 vols. 1969 each $17.50 set $525.00; *Scholarly Press* 30 vols. each $19.50 set $495.00; *Richard West* $200.00

SELECTED WORKS, REMINISCENCES AND LETTERS. Ed. by Julian Symons *Harvard Univ. Press* 1970 $12.00 pap. $4.95

THE FRENCH REVOLUTION. 1837. *Dutton* Everyman's 2 vols. 1955 each $3.95

ON HEROES, HERO-WORSHIP AND THE HEROIC IN HISTORY. 1841. *Oxford* World's Class. $5.00; ed. by Carl Niemeyer *Univ. of Nebraska Press* Bison Bks. 1966 pap. $2.95; *Peter Smith* $4.50

HISTORY OF FRIEDRICH II OF PRUSSIA, CALLED FREDERICK THE GREAT. 1858–1865. Ed. by John Clive *Univ. of Chicago Press* 1969 $12.00 pap. $3.45

Books about Carlyle

Thomas Carlyle: A History of the First Forty Years of His Life, 1795–1835. By J. A. Froude. 1882. *Scholarly Press* $29.50; *Richard West* $29.45

Thomas Carlyle: A History of His Life in London, 1834–1881. By James A. Froude. 1884. *Scholarly Press* 2 vols. set $34.50; *Richard West* 2 vols. $34.00

Thomas Carlyle. By G. K. Chesterton and J. E. Hodder Williams. 1902. *Folcroft* 1973 $10.00

A Bibliography of Thomas Carlyle's Writings and Annotations. By Isaac W. Dyer. 1928. *Burt Franklin* $17.50; *Octagon* $19.00; *Somerset Pubs*. $29.50

Thomas Carlyle and the Art of History. By Louise M. Young. 1939. *Octagon* 1971 $10.50

Carlyle and Mill. By Emery Neff. *Octagon* 1964 $14.50

Thomas Carlyle. By David Gascoyne. *British Bk. Centre* $2.95 pap. $1.20

The Carlyles. By John S. Collis. *Dodd* 1973 $6.95

Two Reminiscences of Thomas Carlyle. By John B. Clubbe. *Duke Univ. Press* 1974 $6.95

The Seventh Hero: Thomas Carlyle and the Theory of Radical Activism. By Philip Rosenberg. *Harvard Univ. Press* 1974 $10.00

See also Chapter 15, Essays and Criticism, Reader's Adviser, Vol. 1

BRYCE, JAMES, Viscount.   1838–1922.

His study of the beginning of German history and the relations between Germany and Rome was written while Bryce was Regius Professor of Civil Law at Oxford. He was ambassador to the United States 1907 to 1913, where he was already well known for his classic, "The American Commonwealth" (1888. *AMS Press* 3 vols. set $70.00). Many of his authoritative books on government are now out of print, but still available are his "Reflections on American Institutions" (sel. from "The American Commonwealth" with introd. by H. S. Commager, *Peter Smith* 1962 $4.50), "Social Institutions of the United States" (1891. *Bks. for Libraries* $13.50), and "The Study of American History" (1922. *Greenwood* 1971 $8.75).

THE HOLY ROMAN EMPIRE. 1864. *Norwood* 1911 $25.00; *Schocken* 1961 pap. $3.45

STUDIES IN HISTORY AND JURISPRUDENCE. 1901. *Bks. for Libraries* 2 vols. 1968 set $27.00

STUDIES IN CONTEMPORARY BIOGRAPHY. 1903. *Bks. for Libraries* $15.75

UNIVERSITY AND HISTORICAL ADDRESSES. 1913. *Bks. for Libraries* $11.75

ESSAYS AND ADDRESSES IN WAR TIME. 1918. *Bks. for Libraries* $8.00

INTERNATIONAL RELATIONS. 1922. *Kennikat* $8.50

Books about Bryce

James Bryce. By Herbert A. Fisher. 1927. *Greenwood* 2 vols. $26.00

James Bryce and American Democracy 1870–1922. By Edmund Ions. *Humanities Press* 1970 $14.00

SYMONDS, JOHN ADDINGTON.   1840–1893.

Symonds, an English poet, essayist and literary historian, spent much of his life on the Continent and wrote many travel books and biographies; he is also known for his remarkable translation of Cellini's autobiography (*q.v.*). His major work, "The Renaissance in Italy," is a classic collection of sketches in cultural history.

THE RENAISSANCE IN ITALY. 1875–1886. *Adler's* 7 vols. set $259.00; *Peter Smith* 3 vols. Vol. 1 The Age of the Despots Vol. 2 The Revival of Learning Vol. 3 The Fine Arts each $5.50 set $16.50

A SHORT HISTORY OF THE RENAISSANCE IN ITALY. *Cooper* $6.50

LETTERS AND PAPERS. Ed. by Horatio F. Brown. 1923. *Richard West* $17.50

Books about Symonds

John Addington Symonds: A Biography. By Horatio F. Brown. 1895. *Richard West* 2 vols. set $35.00

Bibliography of the Writings of John Addington Symonds. By Percy L. Babington. 1925. *Burt Franklin* 1967 $18.50; *Richard West* $18.45

John Addington Symonds: A Biographical Study. By Van Wyck Brooks. *Scholarly Press* 1971 $14.50; *Richard West* $25.00

TAYLOR, HENRY OSBORN. 1856–1941.

Henry Osborn Taylor lectured at Harvard but was best known for his masterpiece, "The Medieval Mind," on the subject of his lifetime study. Its sequel, "Thought and Expression in the Sixteenth Century," published in 1920 is out of print as is "Prophets, Poets and Philosopers of the Ancient World" (1919). Still in print are "Freedom of the Mind in History" (1923. *Greenwood* $14.00) and "Historian's Creed" (1939. *Kennikat* 1969 $6.00).

ANCIENT IDEALS: A Study of Intellectual and Spiritual Growth from Early Times to the Establishment of Christianity. 1896. *Norwood* $45.00; *Ungar* 2 vols. 1964 set $15.00

THE CLASSICAL HERITAGE OF THE MIDDLE AGES. 1901. *Ungar* 1958 pap. $2.95

THE MEDIEVAL MIND: A History of the Development of Thought and Emotion in the Middle Ages. 1911. *Harvard Univ. Press* 2 vols. 4th rev. ed. 1959 set $18.50

CROCE, BENEDETTO. 1866–1952.

The philosopher and historian who "emerged from almost twenty years of semi-imprisonment under the Fascist regime to become one of the members of the new Italian government" wrote on the social and moral issues of our time. These books are for the serious reader.

HISTORY: Its Theory and Practice. 1916. Trans. by Douglas Ainslie *Russell & Russell* 1960 $10.00

A HISTORY OF ITALY, 1871–1915. 1929. Trans. by Cecilia M. Ady *Russell & Russell* 1963 $10.00

HISTORY OF EUROPE IN THE NINETEENTH CENTURY. 1933. *Harcourt* 1963 pap. $3.25

HISTORY AS THE STORY OF LIBERTY. 1941. *Humanities Press* 1962 $8.25

PHILOSOPHY, POETRY, HISTORY: An Anthology of Essays. Trans. by Cecil Sprigge *Oxford* 1966 $17.00

HISTORY OF THE KINGDOM OF NAPLES. Trans. by Frances Frenaye; ed. by H. Stuart Hughes *Univ. of Chicago Press* 1970 $11.00 Phoenix Bks. 1972 pap. $2.95

AUTOBIOGRAPHY. Trans. by R. G. Collingwood *Bks. for Libraries* 1927 $7.75

Books about Croce

The Philosophy of Benedetto Croce: The Problem of Art and History. By Herbert W. Carr. 1917. *Russell & Russell* 1969 $8.50

Clio and Mr. Croce. By Allen R. Benham. 1928. *Richard West* 1973 $10.00

See also his main entry in Chapter 10, Italian Literature, Reader's Adviser, *Vol. 2.*

WELLS, H(ERBERT) G(EORGE). 1866–1946.

H. G. Wells revolutionized the writing of history with his great "Outline." He traced life and mankind from Genesis to the future. It sold over two million copies. For it he had the advice and editorial help of Ernest Parker, Sir H. H. Johnston, Sir E. Ray Lankester and Gilbert Murray. "The Shape of Things to Come" (1933, 1945, o.p.), his pseudo-scientific-historical fantasy, Wells called a Short History of the World for "about the next century and a half," 1929 A.D. to the end of the year 2105—an Outline of the Future. Some of his shrewd guesses in earlier works have been impressively right.

THE OUTLINE OF HISTORY. 1920. Rev. and ed. by Raymond Postgate *Doubleday* 1971 $9.95; *Somerset Pubs.* 4 vols. $55.00

Books about Wells

The World of H. G. Wells. By Van Wyck Brooks. 1915. *Gordon Press* 1973 $29.95; *Scholarly Press* 1970 $9.50

The Works of H. G. Wells, 1887–1925: A Bibliography, Dictionary, and Subject Index. By Geoffrey H. Wells. 1926. *Burt Franklin* $15.00

H. G. Wells: A Biography. By Vincent Brome. 1951. *Bks. for Libraries* 1972 $9.75; *Greenwood* $10.75

H. G. Wells. By Norman MacKenzie and Jeanne MacKenzie. *Simon & Schuster* 1973 $10.00 Touchstone-Clarion Bks. 1974 pap. $4.95

H. G. Wells: Critic of Progress. By Jack Williamson. *Mirage Press* 1973 $5.95

See also Chapter 12, Modern British Fiction, Reader's Adviser, *Vol. 1.*

SCHEVILL, FERDINAND. 1868–1954.

A popular and respected teacher at the University of Chicago, from which he retired in 1937, Dr. Schevill wrote a number of books, one of the best known being "A History of Europe: From the Reformation to the Present Day" (1925, o.p.). His "Medici" is a classic of political history of the Medici statesmen who directed Florentine affairs almost without interruption from 1434 to 1537, the last century of the republic. "Medieval and Renaissance Florence" is out of print.

A HISTORY OF THE BALKAN PENINSULA: From the Earliest Times to the Present Day. 1922. *Arno* 1970 $23.00; *Bks. for Libraries* $21.50

FIRST CENTURY OF ITALIAN HUMANISM. 1928. *Gordon Press* $29.95; *Haskell* 1970 pap. $6.95; *Russell & Russell* 1967 $5.00

A HISTORY OF FLORENCE: From the Founding of the City through the Renaissance. 1936. *Ungar* rev. ed. 1961 $12.00

SIENA: The History of a Medieval Commune. *Peter Smith* $5.25

THE MEDICI. 1949. *Harper* Torchbks. pap. $1.95; *Peter Smith* 1960 $4.00

SIX HISTORIANS. *Univ. of Chicago Press* 1957 $7.00

LENIN (born VLADIMIR ILYICH ULYANOV). 1870–1924.

The man who was probably the single most effective influence behind the Russian Revolution of 1917 was described in 1894 by his contemporary, A. N. Potresov: "A great force. But at the same time with a quality of one-sidedness, a kind of single note simplification, a quality of over-simplifying the complexities of life." Believing fervently in the Marxist "rule of the proletariat," Lenin dedicated his life to revolution with a notable lack of personal vanity or ambition and a singular ruthlessness of purpose. "The most highly charged utilitarian who ever came out of the laboratory of history," Trotsky wrote of him in 1924.

Lenin is often found listed as "Nikolai," but this is not a first name used by the founder of the Soviet Union. He was born at Simbirsk, now called after him Ulyanovsk, the son of middle-class parents. His early training was in law. After his brother's execution for involvement in a plot against Czar Alexander III, he dedicated himself entirely to revolutionary causes. He was several times exiled to Siberia and in 1900 went to live in London, where he headed the Bolshevik revolutionary party. He returned to his homeland at the time of the abortive revolution of 1905 but went again abroad in 1907, writing and speaking in Marxist terms to promote the uprising of the Russian working classes. On the outbreak of the 1917 revolution (during World War I he had been living in Switzerland) he returned to Russia and with the victory of the Bolsheviks over the Kerensky government assumed the powerful post of Chairman of the Council of People's Commissars. He played the major role (he was by now also chairman of the Communist Party) in suppressing the Christian churches, establishing the Third International and laying the ground-work for the present form of the Soviet Union. On his death from a stroke in 1924, Stalin became his successor.

SELECTED WORKS. *International Pubs.* 3 vols. 1967 set $25.00. Includes in full such major works as "What Is to Be Done?" "Imperialism" and "State and Revolution." Fully annotated. 1 vol. ed. 1971 pap. $4.95

THE ESSENTIALS OF LENIN. 1947. *Hyperion Press* 2 vols. 1974 $65.00

LENIN ON POLITICS AND REVOLUTION: Selected Writings. Trans. and ed. by James E. Connor *Pegasus* 1968 $7.95 pap. $2.95

WHAT IS TO BE DONE? 1902. *China Bks.* 1973 $1.00; *International Pubs.* 1969 pap. $2.25; trans. by S. V. Utechin *Oxford* 1963 $6.00. His pamphlet on the role of the revolutionary party.

IMPERIALISM: The Highest Stage of Capitalism. 1916. *China Bks.* 1965 pap. $.50; *International Pubs.* 1939 pap. $1.25. His famous treatise on imperialism as the result of finance capital and monopoly.

THE STATE AND REVOLUTION. 1917. *China Bks.* 1965 pap. $.50; *International Pubs.* 1932 pap. $1.00

LENIN ON THE UNITED STATES. Ed. by C. Leiteizen and J. S. Allen *International Pubs.* 1970 pap. $3.65

LETTERS. Trans. and ed. by Elizabeth Hill and Doris Mudie. 1937. *Hyperion Press* $22.00

Books about Lenin

Lenin: Notes for a Biographer. By Leon Trotsky. 1925. Trans. by Tamara Deutscher *Putnam* 1971 $5.95 Capricorn Bks. 1973 pap. $2.95

The Life of Lenin. By Louis Fischer. *Harper* 1964 $12.50 pap. $4.25. Fischer met Lenin in 1922 on his first visit to Russia and is a leading expert on the U.S.S.R.

Impressions of Lenin. By Angelica Balabanoff. Trans. by Isotta Cesari; fwd. by Bertram D. Wolfe *Univ. of Michigan Press* 1964 $5.00 pap. $1.75. Memoirs by one of the early leaders of Soviet Russia. An important primary source, with an excellent foreword.

The Bridge and the Abyss: The Troubled Friendship of Maxim Gorky and V. I. Lenin. By Bertram D. Wolfe. *Praeger* 1967 $15.00

Lenin's Last Struggle. By Moshe Lewin. Trans. from the French by Alan Sheridan Smith *Pantheon* 1968 $4.95; *Random* Vintage Bks. 1970 pap. $1.95

Lenin Today. Ed. by Paul M. Sweezy and Harry Magdoff. *Monthly Review Press* 1970 $5.00

Memories of Lenin. By N. K. Krupskaya. *Beekman Pubs.* 1970 $10.00

Lenin's Childhood. By Isaac Deutscher. *Oxford* 1970 $5.75

Lenin. Ed. by Saul N. Silverman. *Prentice-Hall* 1972 $5.95 Spectrum Bks. pap. $2.45

The Young Lenin. By Leon Trotsky. Trans. by Max Eastman *Doubleday* 1972 $7.95

Moscow under Lenin. By Alfred Rosmer. Trans. from the French by Ian H. Birchall *Monthly Review Press* 1973 $8.95 pap. $3.75

Lenin. By Rolf H. Theen. *Lippincott* 1973 $6.95

Lenin and Trotsky. By John E. Bachman. Ed. by I. E. Cadenhead *Barron's* 1974 pap. $2.95

The Sealed Train: Lenin's Eight-Month Journey from Exile to Power. By Michael Pearson. *Putnam* 1975 $8.95

"A vivid account of the famous and controversial episode of the Russian Revolution—Lenin's passage through Germany to Russia after the overthrow of the Czar in February, 1917. . . . as history, it reveals new data on the controversy surrounding the episode"—*(LJ)*.

GOOCH, GEORGE PEABODY. 1873–1968.

"As one of the two historians to whom the British Government confided the task of editing for publication the British official documents bearing on the First World War . . . Dr. Gooch is, of course, steeped in the international politics of the time"—*(Manchester Guardian)*. He contributed several chapters to the "Cambridge Modern History" and served in Parliament from 1906 to 1910. His autobiography, "Under Six Reigns," extends in time from Queen Victoria to Elizabeth II, and restates the proud creed of the liberal scholar who dares to embrace all men and all history and to seek their common verities. "Dr. Gooch was widely known not only as a historian but also as an authority on methods used to deal with history as a branch of knowledge. He was an opponent of the school that holds that history can be dealt with as a science"—*(N.Y. Times)*. He was editor of the British *Contemporary Review* from 1911 to 1960.

"History of Our Time, 1885–1914" (1911) and "Historical Surveys and Portraits" (1966) are out of print.

ENGLISH DEMOCRATIC IDEAS IN THE SEVENTEENTH CENTURY. 1898. 2nd ed. by H. J. Laski 1927. *Cambridge* $17.00

ANNALS OF POLITICS AND CULTURE, 1492–1899. 1905. *Burt Franklin* 1971 $16.50

HISTORY AND HISTORIANS IN THE 19TH CENTURY. 1913. *Beacon* 1959 pap. $2.75

GERMANY AND THE FRENCH REVOLUTION. 1920. *Russell & Russell* 1966 $10.00

FRANCO-GERMAN RELATIONS, 1871–1914. 1923. *Russell & Russell* 1967 $5.00

STUDIES IN MODERN HISTORY. 1931. *Bks. for Libraries* $11.75

COURTS AND CABINETS. 1944. *Bks. for Libraries* $15.75

FREDERICK THE GREAT: The Ruler, the Writer, the Man. 1947. *Shoe String Press* 1962 $8.50

STUDIES IN GERMAN HISTORY. 1948. *Russell & Russell* 1969 $14.00

MARIA THERESA AND OTHER STUDIES. 1951. *Shoe String Press* 1965 $10.00

CATHERINE THE GREAT AND OTHER STUDIES. 1954. *Shoe String Press* 1973 $8.50

LOUIS XV: The Monarchy in Decline. *Humanities Press* 1966 $7.25

UNDER SIX REIGNS. 1959. *Shoe String Press* 1971 $5.50

STALIN, JOSEPH (VISSARIONOVICH). 1879–1953.

Stalin first became interested in Marxism while he was (briefly) studying for the priesthood. After various periods of arrest and escape or imprisonment, he became a follower of Lenin in the split between the Mensheviks and Bolsheviks in 1903. Originally called Dzhugashvili, he took the name Stalin, "man of steel," about 1913; he was then an editor of the embryo Communist paper *Pravda*. After the October, 1917, revolution, he became people's commissar for nationalities, the leading member of the triumvirate which ruled the U.S.S.R. after Lenin's death. During the period of his dictatorship, which followed, many of his former comrades perished in the "purges."

In 1939 Stalin signed a mutual nonaggression agreement with Nazi Germany, violated in 1941 when the Germans attacked Russia. During the war and after the Allied victory he met with Churchill, Roosevelt and Truman at the Teheran, Yalta and Potsdam Conferences. At his death he received the funeral of a state hero and was buried next to Lenin in Moscow's Red Square. In 1961, after Nikita Khrushchev had denounced Stalin and his policies, his body was moved to the cemetery for heroes near the Kremlin wall. In March 1969, *Pravda* began issuing excerpts from the new novel "They Fought for Their Country" by Mikhail Sholokhov (*q.v.*), which imply that Stalin was unaware of the activities of his secret police in pursuing the purges of the 1930s.

In 1967 his daughter Svetlana Alliluyeva (*q.v.*) caused a sensation when she abandoned the U.S.S.R. and the cruelties she found in the Soviet system, as well as her two nearly grown children, to seek haven in the U.S., where she has since settled. Her "Twenty Letters to a Friend" cast new light on Stalin's private life, her mother's suicide and other matters. In the book she refrains from expressing active hostility to her father and believes that he was to some extent deceived by Beria, chief of his secret police.

Of the many biographical studies of Stalin, one of the most fascinating is that by Leon Trotsky. In the introduction to the 1967 edition, Bertram Wolfe writes: "In all literature there is no more dramatic relationship between author and subject. . . . It is like Robespierre doing a life of Fouché, Kurbsky of Ivan the Terrible, Muenzer of Martin Luther."

WORKS. Ed. by Robert H. McNeal. *Hoover Institution* 3 vols. 1967 set $20.00

SELECTED WORKS. *Cardinal Pubs.* 1971 $9.75

SELECTED WRITINGS. 1942. *Greenwood* $18.75

FOUNDATIONS OF LENINISM. 1939. *International Pubs.* pap. $1.25; *China Bks.* pap. $.50

DIALECTICAL AND HISTORICAL MATERIALISM. 1940. *International Pubs.* pap. $.75

GREAT PATRIOTIC WAR OF THE SOVIET UNION. 1945. *Greenwood* $9.00

ECONOMIC PROBLEMS OF SOCIALISM IN THE U.S.S.R. *China Bks.* pap. $.50

MARXISM AND THE PROBLEM OF LINGUISTICS. *China Bks.* pap. $.35

CORRESPONDENCE WITH CHURCHILL AND ATTLEE. *Putnam* Capricorn Giants 1965 pap. $2.25

CORRESPONDENCE WITH ROOSEVELT AND TRUMAN. *Putnam* Capricorn Giants 1965 pap. $1.95

Books about Stalin

Stalin: An Appraisal of the Man and His Influence. By Leon Trotsky. Trans. and ed. by Charles Malamuth; introd. by Bertram D. Wolfe. 1941. *Stein & Day* 1970 pap. $3.95. The classic biography of his victorious rival.

Stalin: A Political Biography. By Isaac Deutscher. *Oxford* 1949 2nd ed. 1967 $15.00 pap. $3.95 "Highly valuable for its patient and frequently illuminating analysis of the first eight volumes of Stalin's 'Collected Works'. . . . It is by any test stylistically a skillful and well written book"— (Bertram D. Wolfe).

The Rise and Fall of Stalin. By Robert Payne. *Simon & Schuster* 1965 $10.00. A readable and exciting narrative.

The Young Stalin: The Early Years of an Elusive Revolutionary. By Edward Ellis Smith. *Farrar, Straus* 1967 $10.00

Twenty Letters to a Friend: A Memoir. By Svetlana Alliluyeva. Trans. by Priscilla MacMillan *Harper* 1967 $8.50. Recollections by Stalin's daughter of the period up to her father's death.

Stalin and His Generals: Soviet Military Memoirs of World War Two. (Orig. "Stalin's Generals Speak") ed. by Seweryn Bialer *Pegasus* 1967 1969 $10.00

The Great Terror: Stalin's Purge of the Thirties. By Robert Conquest. *Macmillan* rev. ed. 1973 $8.95

Stalin: The Man and His Era. By Adam B. Ulam. *Viking* 1973 $12.95 Compass Bks. 1974 pap. $4.95

Stalin as Revolutionary, 1879–1929: A Study in History and Personality. By Robert C. Tucker. *Norton* 1973 $12.95 pap. 1974 $3.95

Stalin: Man and Legend. By Joseph Hingley. *McGraw-Hill* 1974 $15.00

TROTSKY, LEON (pseud. of Lev Davidovich Bronshtein). 1879–1940.

The son of Jewish parents, Trotsky became a member of a Marxist circle in 1896. Imprisoned many times, he escaped from Siberia by using the name of a jailer called Trotsky on a false passport. During World War I he lived in Switzerland, France and New York City, where he edited the newspaper *Novy Mir* (New World). He went back to Russia in 1917 and joined Lenin in the first, abortive, July revolution of the Bolsheviks. A key organizer of the successful October revolution, he was people's commissar for foreign affairs in the Lenin regime. Antagonism developed between Trotsky and Stalin during the Civil War of 1918–1920; he also had differences with Lenin over control of the workers' union.

Exiled by Stalin after Lenin's death, Trotsky fled across Siberia (carrying with him source material on his experiences in the revolution) to Norway, France and finally Mexico, where he began work on the biography of his bitter enemy Stalin (*q.v.*) in a heavily barred and guarded home in Coyoacan. He realized he was racing against time and was able to complete seven of the twelve chapters before a member of the Soviet secret police managed to work his way into the household by posing as a convert to Trotskyism. Through the latter's agency, Trotsky was killed with a pickaxe at the desk where he was writing "Stalin," and the manuscript was spattered with its author's blood. The construction of the remaining five chapters was accomplished by the translator Charles Malamuth (a son-in-law of Jack London) from notes, worksheets and fragments. His translation of the initial chapters had been completed and checked by Trotsky before his death.

WRITINGS. Ed. by George Breitman, Sarah Lovell, Naomi Allen, Beverly Scott and others *Pathfinder Press, N.Y.* 9 vols. 1970–1974. 1930–1931 (1974) $12.00 pap. $3.95 1932 (1973) $9.95 pap. $3.95 1932–1933 (1973) $8.95 pap. $3.45 1933–1934 (1972) $8.95 pap. $3.45 1934–1935 (1972) $8.95 pap. $3.95 1935–1936 (1970) pap. $2.95 1937–1938 (n.d.) pap. $2.95 1938–1939 (1974) $12.00 pap. $3.95 1939–1940 (1973) $10.00 pap. $3.95

LITERATURE AND REVOLUTION. c.1925. *Univ. of Michigan Press* 1960 $4.95 pap. $2.25

THE RUSSIAN REVOLUTION: The Overthrow of Tsarism and the Triumph of the Soviets. 1932. Trans. by Max Eastman; sel. and ed. by F. W. Dupee (from "The History of the Russian Revolution" trans. by Max Eastman) *Doubleday* 1959 pap. $2.95

THE THIRD INTERNATIONAL AFTER LENIN. 1936. *Pathfinder Press, N.Y.* 1970 $7.95 pap. $3.45

THE STALIN SCHOOL OF FALSIFICATION. 1937. Trans. by John G. Wright; introd. and explanatory notes by Max Schachtman *Pathfinder Press, N.Y.* new rev. ed. 1972 $8.95 pap. $3.45

THE FIRST FIVE YEARS OF THE COMMUNIST INTERNATIONAL. Trans. and ed. by John G. Wright. 1945. *Monad Press* 2 vols. 1973 each $8.95 pap. each $3.75

MARXISM IN OUR TIME. *Pathfinder Press, N.Y.* 1970 pap. $.65

EUROPE AND AMERICA: Two Speeches on Imperialism. Trans. by John G. Wright *Pathfinder Press, N.Y.* 1971 pap. $.95

THE TROTSKY PAPERS 1917–1922. Ed. by Jan M. Meijer *Humanities Press* 2 vols. 1964– 1971 Vol. 1 o.p. Vol. 2 1920–1922 (1971) $47.50. Letters, messages and the like from Trotsky's official Soviet period.

TROTSKY'S DIARY IN EXILE: 1935. Trans. by Elena Ivanovna Zarudnaya *Atheneum* 1964 pap. $3.95

MY LIFE. 1930. *Grosset* Univ. Lib. 1973 pap. $3.85; *Pathfinder Press, N.Y.* new ed. 1970 $12.50 pap. $3.95; *Peter Smith* $6.50

Books about Trotsky

The Prophet Armed: Trotsky, 1879–1921; The Prophet Unarmed: Trotsky, 1921–1929; The Prophet Outcast: Trotsky, 1929–1940. By Isaac Deutscher. *Oxford* 3 vols. 1954–63 each $12.50; *Random* Vintage Bks. pap. each $2.45

Three Who Made a Revolution: A Biographical History. By Bertram D. Wolfe. 1948 rev. ed. 1964 *Dell* Delta Bks. pap. $3.95
"The best book in its field in any language"—(Edmund Wilson).

The Revolutionary Personality: Lenin, Trotsky, and Gandhi. By E. Wolfenstein. *Princeton Univ. Press* 1967 $12.50 pap. 1971 $3.95

Leon Trotsky: The Man and His Works. By Joseph Hansen and others. *Pathfinder Press, N.Y.* 1969 $2.45

The Great Debate Renewed. Ed. by Nicolas Krasso. *Dutton* $8.95

Leon Trotsky and the Politics of Economic Isolation. By R. B. Day. *Cambridge* 1973 $10.95

GUÉRARD, ALBERT LEON.   1880–1959.

Born and educated in France, Professor Guérard came to the United States as a college teacher of French in 1906, and did much to interpret the civilization of his native land. He wrote many excellent volumes which combined erudition and "esprit" with literary elegance, including "Art for Art's Sake" (*Schocken* 1963 $7.00), "Bottle in the Sea" (1954. *Greenwood* 1969 $9.75), "Five Masters of French Romance" (1916. *Richard West* $20.00), and "Literature and Society" (1935. *Cooper* 1971 $12.00). His "France in the Classical Age" has long been a classic. His autobiography "Personal Equation" published in 1948 is now out of print as is his "Testament of a Liberal" of 1956.

FRENCH CIVILIZATION IN THE NINETEENTH CENTURY. 1918. *Cooper* $8.50

FRENCH CIVILIZATION FROM ITS ORIGINS TO THE CLOSE OF THE MIDDLE AGES. 1921. *Cooper* $8.50

BEYOND HATRED: The Democratic Ideal in France and America. 1925. *Negro Univs. Press* $12.50

FRANCE IN THE CLASSICAL AGE: The Life and Death of an Ideal. 1928. *Gannon* 1970 $7.50; *Peter Smith* $4.50

FRANCE: A Short History. *Norton* 1946 $4.95

NAPOLEON III. *Knopf* 1955 $4.50

NAPOLEON I. *Knopf* 1956 $4.95

FRANCE: A Modern History. History of the Modern World Ser. *Univ. of Michigan Press* 1959 rev. & enl. ed. 1969 $10.00

SPENGLER, OSWALD.   1880–1936.

Like Toynbee's great "Study of History," "The Decline of the West" has as its theme the rise and decline of civilizations, but unlike Toynbee, Spengler believed that present Occidental civilization had reached its period of decadence and was about to be conquered by the Mongolian people of Asia. Spengler was a teacher of mathematics who wrote his book in extreme poverty in Munich during the first World War. He revised it in the period of despair following the war and the 1923 edition brought him wealth and fame. At first, because of his dislike of "non-Aryan" peoples, he was popular with the Nazis, but he refused to participate in their anti-Semitic activities. He was allowed to stay in Germany and to keep his property, but the last years of his life were spent under the cloud of official disfavor.

"Man and Technics" (1932) and "Letters: 1913–1936" (1966) are out of print.

THE DECLINE OF THE WEST. 1918. *Knopf* 2 vols. new rev. ed. 1945 set $22.50

THE HOUR OF DECISION. Trans. by Charles Francis Atkinson. 1934. *Knopf* 1963 $6.00

SELECTED ESSAYS. Trans. by Donald O. White *Regnery* 1967 pap. $1.95

APHORISMS. Trans. by Gisela K. O'Brien *Regnery* 1967 pap. $1.25

WOOLLEY, SIR (CHARLES) LEONARD. 1880–1960.

Sir Leonard, knighted in 1935 for his archeological discoveries, was most famous for his excavations at Ur in Iraq (the biblical home of Abraham). He later conducted similar explorations in Syria and Turkey. As an adviser on art and archeology to the Allied armies in Italy during World War II, he contributed to the preservation of ancient monuments in and near Rome. Out of print are "Ur Excavations" (1934), "History Unearthed" (1958), and "Digging Up the Past" (1930).

THE SUMERIANS. 1929. *AMS Press* 1970 $8.50; *Norton* 1965 pap. $3.25

UR OF THE CHALDEES. 1934. *Norton* 1965 pap. $2.25

THE DEVELOPMENT OF SUMERIAN ART. 1935. *Greenwood* $22.00

A FORGOTTEN KINGDOM. 1953. *Norton* 1968 pap. $1.95

HAYES, CARLTON J(OSEPH) H(UNTLEY). 1882–1964.

Professor Hayes, a dramatic and popular lecturer at Columbia (1907–1950), was our Ambassador to Spain, 1942–1945 and wrote unofficially and candidly of his experiences during those wartime years. His writing is distinguished for its impartial, well-rounded viewpoint that combines brilliantly the social, economic, intellectual and cultural with political history. One of his students called his lectures "first-rate theatrical performances, words shot out for emphasis, silences sustained for a moment, gestures and movement deployed like those of a good actor"—("Current Biography"). During the Spanish Civil War he supported the Franco movement, at the same time deploring Fascism, especially for its assumption of racial superiority. He was a strong supporter of international cooperation in such agencies as the United Nations. "Modern Europe to 1870" (1953) and "Contemporary Europe since 1870" (1953) are out of print.

INTRODUCTION TO THE SOURCES RELATING TO THE GERMANIC INVASIONS. 1909. *AMS Press* $10.00

BRITISH SOCIAL POLITICS. 1913. *Bks. for Libraries* $19.00

ESSAYS ON NATIONALISM. 1926. *Russell & Russell* 1966 $13.00

THE HISTORICAL EVOLUTION OF MODERN NATIONALISM. 1931. *Russell & Russell* 1968 $15.00

A GENERATION OF MATERIALISM: 1871–1900. Rise of Modern Europe Ser. *Harper* 1941 $8.95 Torchbks. pap. $3.25

THE UNITED STATES AND SPAIN: An Interpretation. 1951. *Greenwood* $10.50

FRANCE: A Nation of Patriots. *Octagon* 1971 $17.50

(With others) HISTORY OF WESTERN CIVILIZATION SINCE 1500. *Macmillan* 1962 2nd ed. 1967 $9.95

(With others) HISTORY OF WESTERN CIVILIZATION. *Macmillan* 2 vols. 1967 Vol. 1 To 1650 $7.95 Vol. 2 Since 1650 $8.50 1 vol. ed. $10.95

Books about Hayes

Nationalism and Internationalism: Essays Inscribed to Carlton J. H. Hayes. Ed. by Edward M. Earle. 1951. *Octagon* 1974 $17.00

ORTEGA y GASSET, JOSÉ. 1883–1955. *See Chapter 5, Philosophy, this Vol.*

LATOURETTE, KENNETH S(COTT). 1884–1968.

Professor Latourette was an authority on the Far East, an accurate historian and a devoutly religious person, who never "perverted history in the interests of his religious convictions." The author of over 80 books on religious and oriental topics, he served briefly as a missionary in China and helped direct mission activities throughout his lifetime. He was ordained in the Baptist ministry in 1918 and was Professor of Missions and Oriental History at Yale after 1927, becoming Emeritus in 1953. He was decorated by the Chinese Government with the Order of Jade in 1938.

HISTORY OF EARLY RELATIONS BETWEEN THE UNITED STATES AND CHINA, 1784–1844. 1917. *Kraus* $9.50; *Paragon Reprint* 1964 $11.00

A HISTORY OF JAPAN. *Macmillan* 1918 rev. ed. 1957 $6.95

HISTORY OF CHRISTIAN MISSIONS IN CHINA. 1929. *Paragon Reprint* 1966 $16.50; *Russell & Russell* 1967 $22.50

THE CHINESE: Their History and Culture. *Macmillan* 1934 2 vols. in 1 4th rev. ed. 1964 $12.50

A HISTORY OF THE EXPANSION OF CHRISTIANITY. 1937–1945. *Zondervan* 7 vols. pap. each $3.45 set $22.95

GOSPEL, THE CHURCH AND THE WORLD. 1946. *Bks. for Libraries* 10.50

A SHORT HISTORY OF THE FAR EAST. *Macmillan* 1946 4th ed. 1965 $11.95

A HISTORY OF CHRISTIANITY. *Harper* 1953 $11.00

CHRISTIANITY IN A REVOLUTIONARY AGE. 1958–1962. *Greenwood* 5 vols. 1973 $95.00; *Zondervan* 5 vols. pap. each $4.95 set $14.75

CHINA. *Prentice-Hall* 1964 $5.95 Spectrum Bks. pap. $1.95

CHRISTIANITY THROUGH THE AGES. *Harper* Chapel Bks. pap. $3.50; *Peter Smith* $5.75

DURANT, WILL(IAM) (JAMES), 1885–   and ARIEL DURANT, 1898–

Will Durant began his massive "Story of Civilization" in 1927 and by the time the seventh volume was published in 1961 his wife Ariel's assistance had earned her title-page recognition as co-author. Orville Prescott has written of them: "The whole purpose and excuse for being of the Durant series is to introduce intelligent readers who are not professional scholars to the civilizations of the past out of which our own tormented society has grown. To introduce and to popularize is not less worthy an enterprise than to unearth some hitherto unknown facts or to present some new and controversial theory. Many professional historians believe that it is, and some have looked down their noses at the Durants. The truth is that the art of history includes both kinds of writing and needs both. The scholar who delves into obscure archives is essential; without him ignorance would prevail. But the writer who can make history available to the general reader is necessary too"—(in *SR*).

Born in North Adams, Mass., Will Durant was educated in the parochial schools there, earning his undergraduate degree at St. Peter's College in New Jersey. He eventually taught at the libertarian Ferrer Modern School in New York; here he met his wife, then Ada Kaufman, one of his pupils, whom he later preferred to call Ariel. Soon after their marriage in 1913, Dr. Durant earned his Ph.D. in philosophy from Columbia University, where he studied under John Dewey, among others. The Durants have made several world tours to visit the countries they treat in their history and have received countless honorary degrees. In 1968 they received the Pulitzer Prize for "Rousseau and Revolution," the final volume of their magnum opus. Explaining why they stopped at this point in history, they wrote: "We find ourselves exhausted on reaching the French Revolution. We know that this event did not end history, but it ends us." They are currently writing their dual autobiography.

THE STORY OF CIVILIZATION. *Simon & Schuster* 10 vols. 1935–67 each $10.00–$15.00

Pt. 1 Our Oriental Heritage (1935) Pt. 2 The Life of Greece (1939) Pt. 3 Caesar and Christ (1944) Pt. 4 The Age of Faith (1950) Pt. 5 The Renaissance: A History of Civilization in Italy from 1304–1576 A.D. (1953) Pt. 6 The Reformation (1957) Pt. 7 The Age of Reason Begins (1961) Pt. 8 The Age of Louis XIV (1963) Pt. 9 The Age of Voltaire (1965) Pt. 10 Rousseau and Revolution (1967) Pts. 7–10 include Ariel Durant as joint author.

THE LESSONS OF HISTORY. *Simon & Schuster* 1968 $5.00

"A modest, balanced and helpful statement of the beliefs and values that have resulted from the Durants' immersion in historical investigation these many years. Here are their fair-mindedness, their respect for human dignity, their exaltation of reason, their horror of bigotry and their faith in education as the clue to the betterment of the human condition"—(*N.Y. Times*).

INTERPRETATIONS OF LIFE: A Survey of Contemporary Literature. *Simon & Schuster* 1970 $8.95

"The notes of a lifetime's reading . . . in essays about Faulkner, Hemingway, O'Neill, Pound, Sartre, Mann, Kafka, Kazantzakis, Pasternak and over a dozen more"—(*Christian Science Monitor*). "This book obviously will not appeal to literary scholars or critics, but it offers carefully documented, well-written perspective and guidance for the serious general reader"—(*LJ*).

MADARIAGA Y ROJO, SALVADOR DE. 1886–   *See Chapter 11, Spanish Literature, Reader's Adviser, Vol. 2.*

VERNADSKY, GEORGE. 1887–1973.

Professor Emeritus George Vernadsky of Yale was a Russian émigré who settled finally and happily in the United States and became one of the foremost historians on the subject of his native land. His life, he said, fell into three periods, the first of which was his youth in Russia—growing up in Moscow, taking his degree from the University of Moscow, teaching Russian history at the University of Petrograd (from 1914 to 1917) in the stimulating intellectual atmosphere of the former St. Petersburg, and finally studying and teaching in the Urals and Crimea, where, he said, even the Revolution did not unduly disturb the universities. His second period was seven years of teaching in exile, spent in Constantinople, Athens, Prague and Paris. In 1927 he was invited to Yale; he came to the United States and remained in New Haven for the rest of his academic career, gradually producing a monumental body of work on Russian history. "While the transition from one span of my life to another was more or less painful," he said, "the more I think of the course of my life, the more I find that in many respects I should be grateful to Fate for this tortuous path, since it gave me the variety and richness of experience, and since in each of the three spans I was fortunate to meet so many kind and congenial friends."

Professor Vernadsky's major work is, or course, the "History of Russia," of which there are five volumes. Planned as a collaboration between Vernadsky and Michael Karpovich of Harvard, it was originally intended to run to nine volumes, but Dr. Karpovich's death in 1959 ended the possibility of his doing the later sections, and no further volumes appeared. Nevertheless, for the period it covers (to the time of the Renaissance and Reformation in Europe), it is the definitive work. Dr. Vernadsky's shorter "History of Russia" brings Russian history to the nuclear age.

LENIN, RED DICTATOR. 1931. *AMS Press* 1970 $10.50

A HISTORY OF RUSSIA:

Vol. 1, Ancient Russia. *Yale Univ. Press* 1943 $20.00

"So much new material has accumulated that the situation has become ripe for a new synthesis of Russian history on an unprecedented scale. [This promises to provide it.] The first volume, 'Ancient Russia,' has just appeared. . . . It is impossible within the limits of a review to suggest all the ideas, outlooks, insights which 'Ancient Russia' provides. . . . Despite the remoteness of the centuries treated, the reader will find insights of every kind into the Russia of our day. And all who are interested in Russian history will recognize in 'Ancient Russia' a notable achievement of scholarship and interpretation"—(Bertram D. Wolfe, in the *N.Y. Herald Tribune*).

Vol. 2, Kievan Russia. *Yale Univ. Press* 1948 $20.00 pap. $4.45

"As might be expected of such an eminent authority as Professor Vernadsky, this work reflects the same high standards of scholarship, organization, and extent of subject matter as his first volume in the set"—(*The Annals*). "This volume is an outstanding contribution to the understanding of an important period of Russian history. It is bound to have a marked influence on Western opinion about the year in Russian history it treats in such a masterly manner"—(*SR*).

Vol. 3, The Mongols and Russia. *Yale Univ. Press* 1953 $20.00

"A volume distinguished by mature scholarship and based on thorough research and keen synthesis. . . . While scholars may point to minor errors and differ here and there in their interpretations, it is doubtful whether they will be able to oppose successfully the fundamental conclusions reached by the author. . . . It is doubtful whether any or all such criticisms or suggestions can detract from the truly outstanding character of Professor Vernadsky's achievement in this volume"—(R. J. Kerner, in *SR*).

Vol. 4, Russia at the Dawn of the Modern Age. *Yale Univ. Press* 1959 $20.00

"One of the most satisfying pleasures to be found in Russian history is the constant illumination which it sheds upon the Russian present. Too often in this hasty age we are inclined to leap to the conclusion that history in Russia began on November 7, 1917, and that since that day the great land of the Slavs has become a nation made new, a state transformed, a society of men of a new order. But, obviously, this is nonsense—a product in part of Communist propaganda and in part of our own ignorance. The moment one begins to read a careful, scholarly history of Russia, such as the great work which Professor Vernadsky has in progress, the superficiality of so many of our current concepts about Russia becomes apparent. 'Russia at the Dawn of the Modern Age' is Volume IV of the major reexamination of Russian history which Professor Vernadsky has undertaken. It deals for the most part with the foundation for the creation of the modern Russian state which was laid by the predecessors of Ivan the Terrible, Ivan III and Vasili III"—(Harrison Salisbury, in *SR*).

Vol. 5, The Tsardom of Moscow, 1547–1682. *Yale Univ. Press* 2 vols. 1969 set $50.00

"This volume is Professor Vernadsky's final contribution to the ambitious multi-volume 'History of Russia.' . . . The remaining volumes are to be written by other scholars. . . . Vernadsky is the most prolific student of Russian history in the United States, past or present, and he richly deserves our gratitude for the remarkable erudition and energy he has consistently brought to his writings. . . . This work is intended to be a synthesis. The parts are not as well knit together as one might wish however, and the author offers few new interpretations. . . . But students of Russia's Moscow period will certainly need to consult it"—(S. H. Baron, in *American Historical Review*).

(Ed.) MEDIEVAL RUSSIAN LAWS. 1947. *Norton* 1969 pap. $1.95; *Octagon* 1965 $8.50

A HISTORY OF RUSSIA. *Yale Univ. Press* rev. ed. 1961 $20.00 pap. $4.95

"Scholarly, intellectually stimulating, and readable. It is not only a very good guide through the record of Russian development, but it makes one go deeper by the way it raises interesting questions. About the depth, solidity, and honesty of learning, there is of course no possible doubt"—(Frederick C. Barghoorn).

(With Ralph T. Fisher, Jr., Eds.) DICTIONARY OF RUSSIAN HISTORICAL TERMS FROM THE ELEVENTH CENTURY TO 1917. *Yale Univ. Press* 1970 $15.50

(With others, Eds.) A SOURCE BOOK FOR RUSSIAN HISTORY FROM EARLY TIMES TO 1917. *Yale Univ. Press* 3 vols. 1972 Vol. 1 Early Times to Late 17th Century Vol. 2 Peter the Great to Nicholas I Vol. 3 Alexander Second to the February Revolution each $15.00 set $40.00

"The standard collection of primary Russian history materials"—(*Choice*).

HITLER, ADOLF. 1889–1945.

"Mein Kampf" was written early in Hitler's career to describe his ambitions for Germany. "Crude, long-winded, badly written, contradictory, and repetitious," it was "by far the most effective book of the twentieth century," say Norman Cousins, who points out that "for every word . . . 125 lives were to be lost; for every page 4,700 lives; for every chapter, more than 1,200,000 lives." It was the political bible of the German people and guided the policies of the Third Reich from 1933 until the end of World War II. Hitler dictated his "fantastic dream of a frenzied visionary" to his secretary, Rudolf Hess, while in prison as the result of an unsuccessful revolt in Munich (1923), known as the "Beer Hall Putsch." By the outbreak of World War II, 5,000,000 copies had been distributed in Germany alone. Protected by international copyright, the full story was at first restricted by its author to the original German—only a much expurgated version was available in English until 1939. In that year, on the eve of war, two American publishers, one with Hitler's approval and one without, brought out uncensored versions.

In April, 1969, the manuscript of the memoirs of Albert Speer, the wartime Minister of Arms and Munitions who was released in 1965 from his imprisonment as a Nazi war criminal, became available to the *N.Y. Times* on the day *Macmillan* announced its purchase for $250,000 for early publication in English. Speer's acquaintanceship with Hitler lasted from 1930 to Hitler's death in 1945 and in his book he describes the immense and "grandiose" capital Hitler had planned for Berlin—and as a monument to himself—a plan which, of course never materialized. A recent book by the Russian, Lev Bezymenski, "The Death of Adolf Hitler" (1968, o.p.) based on evidence available to the U.S.S.R., has established the fact that Hitler and Eva Braun committed suicide in his Reichschancellery bunker in Berlin by cyanide poisoning.

MEIN KAMPF (My Battle). First Eng. trans. 1933. Trans. by Hurst and Blackett *Angriff Press* $8.00; trans. by Ralph Manheim *Houghton* 1943 $10.00 Sentry Eds. pap. $3.95

MY NEW ORDER. Ed. by Raoul De Roussy de Sales. 1941. *Octagon* 1973 $33.50

HITLER'S SECRET CONVERSATIONS, 1941–1944. *Octagon* $20.00

SPEECHES. Ed. by Norman H. Baynes. 1942. *Howard Fertig* 2 vols. 1969 set $65.00

Books about Hitler

Hitler: A Biography. By Konrad Heiden. Trans. by Winifred Ray. 1936. *AMS Press* $20.00
Hitler: A Study in Tyranny. By Alan Bullock. *Harper* 1953 rev. ed. 1964 $12.50 Torchbks. pap. $4.75 abr. ed. 1971 pap. $1.50
The Last Days of Hitler. By Hugh R. Trevor-Roper. 1956. *Macmillan* Collier Bks. 3rd ed. 1966 pap. $1.25
The Brutal Friendship: Mussolini, Hitler and the Fall of Italian Fascism. By Frederick W. Deakin. *Harper* 1963 $15.00
The Swastika and the Eagle: Hitler, the United States and the Origins of World War II. By James V. Compton. *Houghton* 1967 $6.95
"A thorough and painstaking book. Compton has read extensively in the diplomatic documents and has interviewed and corresponded with many German diplomats. His book is a useful compilation with the virtues of honest and thorough scholarship but it is somewhat lacking in imagination and analytic skill"—(*Book Week*). The most complete book on the period.

Inside the Third Reich: Memoirs. By Albert Speer. *Macmillan* 1970 $12.50; *Avon Bks.* 1974 pap. $1.95

Hitler's S.S. By Richard Grunberger. *Delacorte* 1971 $4.50

Hitler's Battle for Europe. By John Strawson. *Scribner* 1971 $8.95

The Mind of Adolf Hitler: The Secret Wartime Report. By Walter Langer. *Basic Bks.* 1972 $10.00; *New Am. Lib.* 1973 pap. $1.50

The Life and Death of Adolf Hitler. By Robert Payne. *Praeger* 1973 $12.50; *Popular Lib.* 1974 pap. $1.95

The Evolution of Hitler's Germany. By Horst von Maltitz. *McGraw-Hill* 1973 $12.95

Hitler. By Joachim Fest. Trans. by Richard and Clara Winston *Harcourt* 1974 $15.00

Hitler and His Generals: The Hidden Crisis, January–June 1938. By Harold C. Deutsch. *Univ. of Minnesota Press* 1974 $15.00

NEHRU, JAWAHARLAL. 1889–1964.

Nehru, architect of India's freedom and prime minister from independence in 1947 to his death in 1964, wrote widely on Indian nationalist activities. Educated at Harrow and Cambridge, he returned to India in 1912 and joined Gandhi's (*q.v.*) movement in 1919, was second to him in influence and succeeded him as leader of the National Congress party in 1942. He served seven terms (5½ years) in jail from 1921 to 1934. During one stretch of imprisonment, 1930–1933, Nehru whiled away his time by writing letters to his young daughter about man's whole history— enough letters to fill a thousand-page volume, published as "Glimpses of World History." It "retains all of Nehru's philosophical reflections about history, with enough glimpses to illustrate the main course of development in both East and West and their relations today"—(*N.Y. Times*). Early in January 1964, Nehru was fatally stricken by what was called fatigue and high blood pressure at Bhubaneswar, the Orissa state capital, after attending part of the 1964 convention of his ruling Congress Party. After the brief tenure of Prime Minister Shastri, Nehru's daughter, Mrs. Indira Gandhi (no relation to Mahatma Gandhi), succeeded him as Prime Minister.

Much loved and often criticized, Nehru, nurtured by his long periods of contemplation and inaction in prison, was at once revolutionary, philosopher and practical politician. He was perhaps the last great example of the leader who through experience and training—and great literary ability—understood equally, and interpreted through his speeches and writings, the ancient East and modern West. His "Autobiography" (1936) is out of print.

SELECTED WORKS. *Humanities Press* 20 vols. 1973–   Vols. 1–3 each $15.50 Vols. 4–20 (in prep.); ed. by S. Gopal *South Asia Bks.* 7 vols. 1972–1975 Vols. 1–4 each $12.75 Vols. 5–6 each $13.75 Vol. 7 $14.00

SPEECHES, 1946–1964. *Verry* 5 vols. set $26.00

GLIMPSES OF WORLD HISTORY. 1942. *Asia Pub. House* $9.00; (with title "Nehru on World History") abr. by Saul Padover *Indiana Univ. Press* Midland Bks. 1962 pap. $2.45

THE DISCOVERY OF INDIA. 1946. Ed. by Robert I. Crane *Doubleday* Anchor Bks. 1960 pap. $2.95; *Peter Smith* 1960 $5.00

INDEPENDENCE AND AFTER. *Bks. for Libraries* 1950 $15.50

INTERNATIONAL COOPERATION. *Verry* 1966 pap. $2.25

MAHATMA GANDHI. *Asia Pub. House* 1966 1974 $3.95

INDIA'S QUEST: Being Letters on Indian History. *Asia Pub. House* 1967 pap. $2.25

A BUNCH OF OLD LETTERS: From and to Jawaharlal Nehru. *Asia Pub. House* 2nd ed. 1960 $7.25

Books about Nehru

Jawaharlal Nehru's World View: A Theory of International Relations. By Willard Range. *Univ. of Georgia Press* 1961 $5.00. Professor Range analyzes Nehru's published writings, speeches, and interviews. Although some of the author's conclusions are susceptible to argument, his book is helpful in the understanding of a very complex person.

The Trials of Jawaharlal Nehru. By Ram Gopal. *Hillary House* 1962 $6.50

Nehru: A Pictorial Biography. By Michael Edwardes. *Viking* 1963 $6.95. This portrait based in part on material supplied by Nehru's family includes many pictures never before printed.

Jawaharlal Nehru: The Struggle for Independence. By Lord C. H. Butler. *Cambridge* 1967 $.95

Panditji: A Portrait of Jawaharlal Nehru. By Marie Seton. *Taplinger* 1967 $13.95
The author, observing Nehru from the standpoint of an admiring family friend "is very self-consciously a Boswell"—(*N.Y. Times*).

Jawaharlal Nehru—Man of Letters. By V. N. Chhibber. *Verry* 1970 $7.50
Nehru: A Political Biography. By Michael Edwardes. *Praeger* 1972 $8.95
All My Yesterdays. By Prem Bhatia. *International Scholarly Bk. Services* 1973 $5.25
Jawaharlal Nehru. By Chalapathi R. Rau. *South Asia Bks.* 1973 $5.50
The Socialist Thought of Jawaharlal Nehru. By Pradhan Benudhar. *South Asia Bks.* 1974 $17.50
Nehru and Democracy in India. By Miss Neeraj. *Int. Pubns. Service* 1974 $15.00

TOYNBEE, ARNOLD J(OSEPH). 1889–1975.

As Professor Toynbee turned 80, his 12-volume "A Study of History" continued to be acclaimed as "one of the really great works of intellectual history"; it is undoubtedly the best-known history of the century. Charles Poore has written in the *N.Y. Times:* "What gives his many-volumed study of history its status-saturated popularity is the heady sense it conveys of tremendous journeys through half-forgotten ages and newly-discovered realms." Rather than revise the whole ten-volume set (the "Historical Atlas and Gazetteer" is Vol. 11) Toynbee decided to correct errors and refute his critics in "Reconsiderations" (Vol. 12) published in 1961.

"East to West: A Journey Round the World" (*Oxford* 1958 $5.95) is a collection of brilliant world portraits of contemporary affairs and conditions in ancient setting, and "Between Oxus and Jumna" (*Oxford* 1961 $5.75) serves as an unsurpassed travel guide to a little-known, rugged area encompassing Afghanistan, Western Pakistan and Northwest India. Other books about his travels are "Between Niger and Nile" (*Oxford* 1965 $4.75) and "Between Maule and Amazon" (*Oxford* 1967 $5.75).

"Professor Toynbee's approach to history has always been highly controversial, principally because his generalizations have been regarded by some scholars as too sweeping and in-adequately based"—(*N.Y. Times*). He himself has said: "What I am trying to do is explain to Western people that they are only a small minority of the world—the great world is Asia and Africa—outside the West." He continued to express unorthodox opinions: The Americans have been fighting a colonial war in Vietnam; the "native"—of Vietnam, or elsewhere—"is a human being who is treated as not being a human being," and the way to escape being a "native" is to turn Communist. He finds that "there is an absolute stone wall of indifference all over the world these days," which makes those who would be heard resort to violence.

His "Study of History" took him 40 years of steady labor, and at 80 he was still going strong and continuing to work a seven-day week. " 'I suppose that one day I might stop, and if I stopped I might suddenly crumple,' he said. 'It is very important to keep going.' "

THE WESTERN QUESTION IN GREECE AND TURKEY: A Study in the Contrast of Civilization. 1922. *Howard Fertig* 2nd ed. 1970 $13.50

THE WORLD AFTER THE PEACE CONFERENCE. 1925. *Johnson Reprint* 1968 pap. $5.00

ISLAMIC WORLD SINCE THE PEACE SETTLEMENT. 1927. *Johnson Reprint* pap. $30.00

A STUDY OF HISTORY. *Oxford* 12 vols. 1934–1961 Vols. 1–3 Introduction, the Geneses of Civilizations and the Growth of Civilizations 2nd ed. (1935) $24.00 Vols. 4–6 The Disintegration of Civilizations (1939) $24.00 Vol. 7 Universal States, Universal Churches (1954) Vol. 8 Heroic Ages, Contacts between Civilizations in Space (1954) Vol. 9 Contacts between Civilizations in Time, Law and Freedom in History, The Prospects of the Western Civilization (1954) Vol. 10 The Inspirations of Historians (1954) Vols. 7–10 $37.25 Vol. 11 Historical Atlas and Gazetteer (with Edward D. Myers) (1959) $19.25 Vol. 12 Reconsiderations (1961) $10.25 above in green cloth, also boxed sets in maroon cloth: Vols. 1–6 $60.00 Vols. 7–10 $60.00 Vols. 11–12 each $12.50 *Galaxy Bks.* pap. Vols. 7, 8–10, 12 each $4.25

A STUDY OF HISTORY. Abr. ed. by D. C. Somervell *Oxford* 2 vols. 1947–1957 Vol. 1 abr. of Vols. 1–6 (1947) $8.50 Vol. 2 abr. of Vols. 7–10 (1957) $7.50; *Dell* 2 vols. pap. set $2.95; *McGraw-Hill* 1972 $35.00

CIVILIZATION ON TRIAL (1948) and THE WORLD AND THE WEST (1953). *New Am. Lib.* 1958 pap. $3.45

WAR AND CIVILIZATION. Sel. by A. V. Fowler from "A Study of History" *Oxford* 1950 $4.95

THE WORLD AND THE WEST. The Rieth Lectures. *Oxford* 1953 $3.75

HITLER'S EUROPE. 1954. *Johnson Reprint* $32.50 pap. $30.00

THE INDUSTRIAL REVOLUTION. *Beacon* 1956 pap. $2.95; *Peter Smith* 1959 $5.00

AN HISTORIAN'S APPROACH TO RELIGION. *Oxford* 1956 $3.25

AMERICA AND THE WORLD REVOLUTION AND OTHER LECTURES. *Oxford* 1962 $6.50

HANNIBAL'S LEGACY. *Oxford* 2 vols. 1965 $51.00

CHANGE AND HABIT: The Challenge of Our Time. *Oxford* 1966 $6.75

SOME PROBLEMS OF GREEK HISTORY. *Oxford* 1969 $24.00

CITIES ON THE MOVE. *Oxford* 1970 $7.50

CONSTANTINE PORPHYROGENITUS AND HIS WORLD. *Oxford* 1973 $45.00

MANKIND AND MOTHER EARTH: A Narrative History of the World. *Oxford* 1976 $19.50. Toynbee's last book, published posthumously. It emphasizes the interaction of man with his environment and with his fellow man from the beginnings of human life until the 1970s.

ACQUAINTANCES. *Oxford* 1967 $7.95. Biographical sketches of people Toynbee knew.

EXPERIENCES. *Oxford* 1969 $9.50

Autobiographical reminiscences intended as a sequel to "Acquaintances." "He tells of his youth, his career and some personal affairs, always with an eye on more generally valid observations. Then he draws up a balance sheet of human affairs, and finally he shows himself from a new angle: as a poet. . . . Those of us who have been privileged to know him personally will treasure Toynbee's autobiographical chapters especially. For a wider circle of readers—and this brilliant volume deserves many thousands of them—his balance sheet of human affairs in his lifetime may be even more fascinating"—(Felix E. Hirsch, in the *N.Y. Times*).

Books about Toynbee

Toynbee and History: Critical Essays and Reviews. Ed. by M. F. Ashley Montagu. *Sargent* 1956 $7.00

The Intent of Toynbee's History. Ed. by Edward T. Gargan. *Loyola Univ. Press* 1961 $5.00

Arnold J. Toynbee: Historian for an Age in Crisis. By Roland N. Stromberg. *Southern Illinois Univ. Press* 1972 $5.95

An Interpretation of Universal History. By José Ortega y Gasset. Trans. from Spanish by Mildred Adams *Norton* 1973 $8.95. A series of lectures on Toynbee's "A Study of History."

KOHN, HANS. 1891–1971.

"The Idea of Nationalism" established its author as the outstanding authority on the problem it treats. Hans Kohn, who has been called "one of the great teachers of our day," was born in Prague and received his degree as Doctor of Laws from the German University there. Taken prisoner by the Russians in World War I, he was sent to Turkestan and Siberia, where he saw the Russian revolution and civil war. Afterward he settled in Jerusalem and wrote several books on the history and politics of the Middle East. He came to this country in 1931 and, after a period of lecturing at the New School for Social Research in New York, he became Professor of Modern European History at Smith College in 1934. In 1949 he went to City College, New York, where he was made emeritus professor in 1962. "Living in a World Revolution" is a highly personal book in which he discusses the impact on himself and on Western civilization of two world wars, the Russian Revolution and the dissolution of European colonialism. *Library Journal* found the book "full of wisdom and wide perspectives. He writes with a charm rare among present-day historians; he is always frank but also unfailingly tactful."

Out of print are "Pan Slavism" (1953), "American Nationalism" (1957), "The Habsburg Empire, 1804–1918" (1961), "The Age of Nationalism" (1962), "The Modern World, 1858 to the Present" (1963), and "Reflections on Modern History" (1963).

THE HISTORY OF NATIONALISM IN THE EAST. 1929. *Howard Fertig* $13.75; *Scholarly Press* $14.00

NATIONALISM AND IMPERIALISM IN THE HITHER EAST. 1932. *Howard Fertig* $12.50

NATIONALISM IN THE SOVIET UNION. 1933. *AMS Press* $8.50

WESTERN CIVILIZATION IN THE NEAR EAST. Trans. by E. W. Dickes. 1936. *AMS Press* $10.00

REVOLUTIONS AND DICTATORSHIPS. 1939. *Bks. for Libraries* $15.75

NOT BY ARMS ALONE: Essays on Our Time. 1940. *Bks. for Libraries* $8.75

THE IDEA OF NATIONALISM: A Study in Its Origin and Background. *Macmillan* 1944 1967 $7.95 Collier Bks. 1961 pap. $3.95

POLITICAL IDEOLOGIES OF THE TWENTIETH CENTURY. 1949. 3rd rev. ed. 1966. *Peter Smith* $5.00

NATIONALISM: Its Meaning and History. 1955. *Van Nostrand-Reinhold* Anvil Bks. (orig.) rev. ed. 1965 pap. $2.95; *Peter Smith* $5.00

THE MAKING OF THE MODERN FRENCH MIND. *Van Nostrand-Reinhold* Anvil Bks. (orig.) 1955 pap. $2.95; *Peter Smith* $4.00

BASIC HISTORY OF MODERN RUSSIA: Political, Cultural and Social Trends. *Van Nostrand-Reinhold* Anvil Bks. (orig.) 1957 pap. $2.95; *Peter Smith* $4.25

THE MIND OF GERMANY: The Education of a Nation. 1960. *Harper* Torchbks. pap. $2.75

PROPHETS AND PEOPLES: Studies in Nineteenth Century Nationalism. *Macmillan* Collier Bks. 1961 pap. $.95

(Ed.) MIND OF MODERN RUSSIA: Historical and Political Thought of Russia's Great Age. *Harper* 1962 Torchbks. pap. $2.25

LIVING IN A WORLD REVOLUTION: My Encounters with History. *Simon & Schuster* 1964 $4.95 Touchstone-Clarion Bks. 1970 pap. $2.95

(With Wallace Sokolsky) AFRICAN NATIONALISM IN THE TWENTIETH CENTURY. *Van Nostrand-Reinhold* Anvil Bks. 1965 pap. $2.95

ABSOLUTISM AND DEMOCRACY, 1814–1852. *Van Nostrand-Reinhold* Anvil Bks. (orig.) 1965 pap. $2.95

NATIONALISM AND REALISM: 1852–1879. *Van Nostrand-Reinhold* Anvil Bks. (orig.) 1968 pap. $2.95; *Peter Smith* $4.25

(With Daniel Walden). READINGS IN AMERICAN NATIONALISM. *Van Nostrand-Reinhold* Anvil Bks. 1970 pap. $2.95

BRINTON, C(LARENCE) CRANE.   1898–1968.
   "A History of Civilization" is a splendid history of mankind from the pre-historic era to our time by a team of scholars led by Crane Brinton, Harvard's outstanding historian for nearly half a century. The emphasis is on the cultural, intellectual and economic development of the people in the period being discussed, with frequent quotations from the contemporary writings, poetry, orations and documents. In the Introduction on "The Uses of History," the authors maintain that history "can be for any of us who want to study it, a kind of extension in space and time of our own experience, a deepening and widening of our own little private histories."
   Dr. Brinton was born in Winsted, Conn.; he graduated from Harvard and took his Ph.D. in 1923 from Oxford. He spent the rest of his life, until his retirement shortly before his death, teaching at Harvard. "For many years, including the last one, his course on the intellectual history of Europe in the 18th and 19th centuries attracted the largest single class enrollment at the college"—(*N.Y. Times*). Dr. Brinton saw hope in American intellectuals' "growing commitment to social goals" and was planning to teach a course on revolution, on which he was an acknowledged expert, at Dartmouth when death took him.

POLITICAL IDEAS OF THE ENGLISH ROMANTICISTS. 1926. *Univ. of Michigan Press* Ann Arbor Bks. 1966 pap. $1.95; *Russell & Russell* 1962 $7.00

THE JACOBINS: An Essay in the New History. 1930. *Russell & Russell* 1961 $10.00

ENGLISH POLITICAL THOUGHT IN THE 19TH CENTURY. 1933. *Gannon* 1970 $7.50; *Peter Smith* $5.00

DECADE OF REVOLUTION, 1789–1799. 1934. Rise of Modern Europe Ser. *Harper* Torchbks. pap. $2.45

THE ANATOMY OF REVOLUTION. 1938. *Random* Vintage Bks. 1957 pap. $1.95; *Peter Smith* $4.25

THE UNITED STATES AND BRITAIN. 1948. *Greenwood* $13.00

FROM MANY ONE: The Process of Political Integration. 1948. *Greenwood* 1971 $9.25

IDEAS AND MEN: The Story of Western Thought. *Prentice-Hall* 1950 2nd ed. 1963 $11.95

THE TEMPER OF WESTERN EUROPE. 1953. *Greenwood* $8.50

(With others) A HISTORY OF CIVILIZATION. *Prentice-Hall* 2 vols. 1955 4th ed. 1971 Vol. 1 Prehistory to 1715 Vol. 2 1715 to the Present each $12.95 3 vols. pap. Vol. 1 Prehistory to 1300 Vol. 2 1300 to 1815 Vol. 3 1815 to the Present Vols. 1 and 3 each $8.95 Vol. 2 $6.95

(Ed.) THE PORTABLE AGE OF REASON READER. 1956. *Viking* $4.95 pap. $3.35

THE LIVES OF TALLEYRAND. *Norton* 1963 pap. $1.95

THE SHAPING OF MODERN THOUGHT. *Prentice-Hall* Spectrum Bks. (orig.) 1963 pap. $2.45

(With others) CIVILIZATION IN THE WEST. *Prentice-Hall* 1964. 3rd ed. 1973 $12.50 2 vols. pap. each $7.95

THE AMERICANS AND THE FRENCH. American Foreign Policy Lib. *Harvard Univ. Press* 1968 $6.75

"An outspoken discussion of Anglo-French relations since the Second World War"—(*PW*).

KENNAN, GEORGE F(ROST). 1904–

After his graduation from Princeton University in 1925, George Kennan entered the Foreign Service. His diplomatic posts have always found him in critical spots at crucial times. In 1933 he helped reopen the United States embassy in Moscow after our long-delayed recognition of the U.S.S.R.—and witnessed Stalin's purge trials. As Secretary of Legation in Prague in 1938 he watched the German Army occupy the city, and in 1939, when he was assigned to the Berlin embassy, the onset of World War II kept him confined with other Americans for six months. He was Ambassador Averill Harriman's chief aide in Russia from 1944–1946, helped implement the Marshall Plan and was briefly U.S. Ambassador to the Soviet Union in 1952. In 1953 he became a member of the Institute for Advanced Study, Princeton, N.J., and is now a permanent professor there. He has also taught at the University of Chicago and at Oxford. He emerged from official retirement (1961–1963) to be our Ambassador to Yugoslavia.

Within the limitations of his official roles and when free of them, he has been a vocal critic of America's foreign policy. In 1947 his article for *Foreign Affairs*, signed "Mr. X," recommended an American policy of containment towards Russia. (In this, as in other matters, he often failed to convince his superiors of the wisdom of his advice at a given moment.) More recently he called the Johnson Administration's Vietnam policy a "massive miscalculation and error of policy, an error for which it is hard to find any parallels in our history." It is, he continued, "so destructive to civilian life that no conceivable political outcome could justify the attendant suffering and destructiveness." Mr. Kennan is president of the American Academy of Arts and Letters.

AMERICAN DIPLOMACY: 1900–1950. *Univ. of Chicago Press* 1951 $5.95 Phoenix Bks. 1970 pap. $2.95; *New. Am. Lib.* Mentor Bks. 1952 pap. $.95

SOVIET-AMERICAN RELATIONS, 1917–1920. *Princeton Univ. Press* 2 vols. 1956–1958 Vol. 1 Russia Leaves the War (1956) Vol. 2 The Decision to Intervene (1958) each $16.00; *Atheneum* 2 vols. 1967 pap. each $3.95. Vol. 1 won the 1957 Pulitzer Prize for History and the National Book Award.

RUSSIA, THE ATOM AND THE WEST. 1958. *Greenwood* 1974 $8.25

SOVIET FOREIGN POLICY, 1917–1941. *Van Nostrand-Reinhold* Anvil Bks. (orig.) 1960 pap. $2.95

RUSSIA AND THE WEST UNDER LENIN AND STALIN. *Little-Atlantic* 1961 $8.50; *New Am. Lib.* Mentor Bks. pap. $1.50

ON DEALING WITH THE COMMUNIST WORLD. *Harper* 1964 $3.95 Torchbks. pap. $1.45

THE REALITIES OF AMERICAN FOREIGN POLICY. *Norton* 1966 pap. $1.25

FROM PRAGUE AFTER MUNICH: Diplomatic Papers, 1938–1939. *Princeton Univ. Press* 1968 $10.00 pap. $3.95

These are letters, official reports and diary entries written by Kennan as American Secretary of Legation at Prague during the German occupation of Czechoslovakia. "An invaluable eyewitness account and analysis of the dismemberment and destruction of a nation as recorded at the time by a particularly knowledgeble, articulate and sensitive observer"—(*N.Y. Times*). "They reveal an accurate eye and a keen judgment. Above all, Kennan was aware of what he now describes as 'one of humanity's oldest and most recalcitrant dilemmas: the dilemma of a limited collaboration with evil, in the interests of its ultimate mitigation, as opposed to the uncompromising, heroic but suicidal resistance to it, at the expense of the ultimate weakening of the forces capable of acting against it' "—(SR).

MEMOIRS. *Little-Atlantic* 2 vols. Vol. 1 1925–1950 (1967) Vol. 2 1950–1963 (1972) each $12.50

Volume 1 is "a remarkably candid, beautifully written and utterly fascinating intellectual career autobiography of a distinguished diplomat and scholar. . . . There is material here for a dozen books. There are accounts of serpentine negotiations and portraits of the colleagues and statesmen who took part in them and shaped the political world of our time. . . . This is, in short, major history"—(*N.Y. Times*). It won the 1968 National Book Award and Pulitzer Prize. Volume 2 covers "the origins of the Korean War, the cold war mystique of Acheson and Dulles; Moscow in 1952 in the last months of Stalin; how Kennan got thrown out of the Soviet Union for an unguarded remark in a Berlin airport; the McCarthy attack on old friends; the convulsion of the cold warriors over Kennan's Reith Lectures proposing disengagement in central Europe; and his service in Yugoslavia under Kennedy"—(*N.Y. Times Bk. Rev.*).

ARON, RAYMOND. 1905–

Raymond Aron has a far-ranging mind and pen that have explored every facet of human society, including the historical. "Sometimes called 'the Walter Lippmann of France,' [he] is a political scientist, sociologist, economist and philosopher and the author of a dozen books. . . . He comments regularly on the political scene over radio and as a contributor to Le Figaro, the conservative Paris newspaper, and teaches at the École Pratique des Hautes Études in Paris. An expert in international relations, he has used his influence in favor of a French alliance with the United States.

"As a self-styled 'man of the center,' he has been critical of both left and right. His 1957 book 'Opium of the Intellectuals,' which berated Marxism and the French intellectual élite, played a significant role in the debate between Marxists and non-Marxists in France"—(*N.Y. Times*).

"Peace and War" was widely reviewed here and abroad. George Steiner, in a *New Yorker* critique, wrote: "There have always been those who hold, no matter how stoic or disenchanted the tenor of their sensibility, that man's political, public existence can, given sufficient knowledge and practical insight, be both understood and ameliorated. . . . This rationalist tradition springs from Aristotelian logic and the confident sanity of Roman law. In its modern guise, though, it is preeminently French and reflects the long dream of reason from Descartes to Camus. We associate with it the anatomy of civic and national behavior in Montesquieu, the positivist sociology and anthropology of Comte and Durkheim, and, above all, the mixture of ironic scruple and underlying trust in human growth that makes of de Tocqueville the most adult of political thinkers. Today, its representative heir is Raymond Aron."

Describing this "noble, temperate and magisterial book," Martin Wight said (in the *Observer*, London): "The themes are the objects of foreign policy, the stakes of conflict, the nature and assessment of political power, the difficulties of alliances, the conduct and control of war, the Machiavellian question of means in a nuclear world and the Kantian question of attaining universal peace. International relations are carried on by two symbolic individuals: the diplomat and the strategist." Stanley Hoffmann wrote in the *New Republic:* "To dispel error is part of any teacher's job. Aron—whether he deals with world politics or with industrial society—is a great teacher because he brings to his critical task not only a formidable analytical talent but also a piercing common sense—the art of going straight to the heart of an issue, as in his brief discussion of revolutionary wars in which one side loses if it does not win, whereas all that the rebels must do to win is avoid losing—a remark of immediate relevance to Vietnam. At the same time, he manages to see all sides of every problem. [But] there is a coherent vision and a program behind this book after all. Whatever the biological roots of aggressiveness, man lives in communities where conflict is inevitable. . . . Throughout this book (as in all of Aron's major works), ideology is the real villain, both as the enemy of true science and as the enemy of peace. . . . Aron's message is clear. The West, and especially the US if it wants prudence to prevail, should set itself modest goals, particularly in the Third World; for the only truly decisive areas are the arms race and Europe (a lesson we have yet to learn with respect to Southeast Asia). But even if prudence should prevail, the great utopias of 'world peace through world law,' of world federalism, or of universal empire must be dismissed. . . . In the last page . . . Aron reminds us of our two duties: 'to participate in the conflicts that constitute the web of history, and . . . to work for peace.' They often clash. But it is important to remember that we should not shun either, and to be shown that they could be brought together. . . . For all his skepticism and prudence, Aron is the greater optimist. . . . In the last analysis, Aron's great and difficult book teaches us an indispensable lesson: we should not assert more than we know, nor want more than we can possibly achieve."

Not every critic was so favorable, though the space given to Aron by, for example, J. P. Nettl, in a recent *N.Y. Review of Books,* demonstrate that even if Aron "is not a profound or original thinker" he "is the product of a mood, the answer to a need" and therefore a necessary present concern. George Steiner in his long *New Yorker* piece found that "one puts down this book awed by its industry . . . and occasionally moved by its sober reasonableness. But also with a sense of deep tedium . . ." Henry Kissinger, on the other hand, has said (in the *N.Y. Times*): "It is curious that a century dominated by international conflict should be so lacking in theories of international affairs. Now this deficiency has been remedied by Raymond Aron in his profound, civilized, brilliant and difficult work: 'Peace and War.' . . . Henceforth, international theorizing will require reference to Aron." Clearly Professor Aron is worth the serious reader's judging for himself. Professor Aron visited the United States in 1969 as professor-at-large, Cornell University.

THE OPIUM OF THE INTELLECTUALS. 1955. *Norton* 1962 pap. $2.25

(With August Heckscher) DIVERSITY OF WORLDS. 1957. *Greenwood* 1973 $9.25

PEACE AND WAR: A Theory of International Relations. 1962. Trans. by Richard Howard and Annette B. Fox *Doubleday* 1966 $10.00 Anchor Bks. abr. ed. pap. $4.95

ON WAR. Trans. by Terence Kilmartin *Norton* 1968 pap. $1.45

MARXISM AND THE EXISTENTIALISTS. *Harper* 1969 $6.95

ESSAY ON FREEDOM. *Norton* 1970 $7.95; *New Am. Lib.* Merit Bks. pap. $3.95

THE IMPERIAL REPUBLIC: The United Sates and the World 1945–1973. Trans. by Frank Jellinek *Prentice-Hall* 1974 $10.00

See also Chapter 8, The Social Sciences, this Vol.

BOWLE, JOHN. 1905–

Formerly history master at Westminster and Eton, lecturer at Oxford and visiting professor at Columbia and Grinnell College, John Bowle is an eminent historian and the author of numerous books. He is also a frequent contributor to the *Times Literary Supplement* and *Punch.* The *Library Journal* says of his "Man Through the Ages" (1963, o.p.): "This is no ordinary outline world history. . . . It is marked by a gracious and urbane style of writing and by its author's unmistakable flair for compressing a vast amount of material into a logical, closeknit narrative."

"Western Political Thought" and "Politics and Opinion in the Nineteenth Century," both published by *Oxford* in 1948, are out of print as is "England: A Portrait" (1966).

WORLD ORDER OR CATASTROPHE. *Dufour* 1963 pap. $1.50

HENRY VIII: A Study of Power in Action. *Little* 1965 $7.50

"The author has done his work with great precision. His pains are revealed not only in the research and the writing but also in the pictures that adorn his pages. . . . Much of the idiom, of course, will strike the American ear as odd"—(*N.Y. Times*).

UNITY OF EUROPEAN HISTORY: A Political and Cultural Survey. *Oxford* rev. ed. 1970 pap. $3.95

THE ENGLISH EXPERIENCE. *Putnam* 1972 $8.95 Capricorn Giant 1973 pap. $3.25

THE IMPERIAL ACHIEVEMENT: The Rise and Transformation of the British Empire. *Little* 1975 $15.00

"A deeply serious book on a great subject"—(*N.Y. Times*).

MULLER, HERBERT J. 1905–

Author, professor of English and government at the University of Indiana and Distinguished Service Professor from 1959 until his retirement in 1973, he taught earlier at Istanbul and is thoroughly familiar with Asia Minor, past and present. He gained wide acclaim for his brilliant volume of historical interpretation "The Uses of the Past." His ambitious project, the three-volume "History of Freedom," completed in 1966, is out of print. In it he tells the story of freedom in the broadest sense of the word, in its relationship not only to government, but also to mores, technology, commerce, art and religion. Other of his books in print are "Science and Criticism" (1943. *Bks. for Libraries* $12.00), "Spirit of Tragedy" (*Knopf* 1956 $5.95) and "Adlai Stevenson: A Study in Values" (*Harper* 1967 $7.95).

THE USES OF THE PAST: Profiles of Former Societies. *Oxford* 1952 $8.95 Galaxy Bks. 1957 pap. $2.50; *New Am. Lib.* Mentor Bks. 1954 pap. $1.50

THE LOOM OF HISTORY. *Harper* 1958 $10.00; *Oxford* Galaxy Bks. 1966 pap. $2.95

THE ISSUES OF FREEDOM: Paradoxes and Promises. *Harper* 1960 $4.95

RELIGION AND FREEDOM IN THE MODERN WORLD. *Univ. of Chicago Press* 1963 $5.50
Phoenix Bks. pap. $1.50

IN PURSUIT OF RELEVANCE. *Indiana Univ. Press* 1971 $10.95

CHILDREN OF FRANKENSTEIN: A Primer on Modern Technology and Human Values.
Indiana Univ. Press 1971 $12.50 pap. $2.95

THE USES OF THE FUTURE. *Indiana Univ. Press* 1974 $10.00

ARENDT, HANNAH.   1906–1975.

Herself a victim of Nazism who as a Jew fled Germany in 1933, Hannah Arendt's serious and
scholarly bent equipped her superbly to write "The Origins of Totalitarianism," which David
Riesman (*q.v.*) called (in *Commentary*) "not only an achievement in historiography, but also in
political science. . . . It is throughout a densely imaginative work, truly serious, which makes great
demands on the reader, for intellectual readjustments as much as for historical background. I
happen to think such an experience in understanding our times as this book provides is itself a
social force not to be underestimated." Her study of Eichmann at his trial, part of which appeared
originally in the *New Yorker*, was a painfully searching investigation into what made this Nazi
persecutor tick. Of "Men in Dark Times," Marc Slonim wrote (in the *N.Y. Times*): "The three most
important essays, occupying half the book, are on Hermann Broch, Walter Benjamin and Bertolt
Brecht. There are a lively portrait of Isak Dinesen . . . and a very interesting political analysis of
Rosa Luxemburg and her tragic destiny based on J. P. Nettl's excellent 1966 study. Pope John
XXIII's 'Journal of the Soul' offers Miss Arendt a point of departure for a characterization of the
Pontiff that includes colorful reminiscences of contemporaries and anecdotes [she] heard in
Rome. . . . These are intellectual, not psychological or literary, profiles, and although [the work] is
designed as a book about persons and not issues, Miss Arendt is incessantly dealing with problems
of ethics and political behavior, of social change and historical conflicts."

Miss Arendt lived a full and active life. Born in Hanover, Germany, she studied at Marburg and
Freiburg and received her doctorate from Heidelberg. On leaving Germany in the 30's she went to
France, where she helped with the resettlement of Jewish children in Palestine. She emigrated to
the U.S. in 1941 and became an American citizen in 1951. She was Research Director of the
Conference on Jewish Relations, chief editor of Schocken Books, Executive Director of Jewish
Cultural Reconstruction in New York City, a visiting professor at several universities, including
California, Princeton, Columbia, and Chicago, and University Professor at the Graduate Faculty
of The New School for Social Research. She won a number of grants and fellowships and in 1967
received the Sigmund Freud Prize of the German Akademie für Sprache und Dichtung for her
fine scholarly writing. She also wrote the biography "Rahel Varnhagen: The Life of a Jewish
Woman" (1957. *Harcourt* 1974 $7.95 Harvest Bks. 1974 pap. $3.95).

CRISES OF THE REPUBLIC: Lying in Politics, Civil Disobedience, On Violence, Thoughts
on Politics and Revolution. *Harcourt* 1972 $6.95 Harvest Bks. pap. $2.95

THE ORIGINS OF TOTALITARIANISM. 1951. *Harcourt* rev. ed. 1966 $11.00 Harvest Bks.
1973 pap. $4.95 in 3 pts. 1968 Pt. 1 Antisemitism $2.25 Pt. 2 Imperialism $2.65 Pt. 3
Totalitarianism $1.95; *New Am. Lib.* pap. $4.95

THE HUMAN CONDITION: A Study of the Central Dilemmas Facing Modern Man. *Univ.
of Chicago Press* 1958 1969 $5.95 Phoenix Bks. 1970 pap. $3.25

BETWEEN PAST AND FUTURE: Eight Exercises in Political Thought. *Viking* 1961 rev. and
enl. ed. 1968 $5.95 Compass Bks. pap. $2.45

EICHMANN IN JERUSALEM: A Report on the Banality of Evil. *Viking* 1963 $6.00 Compass
Bks. pap. $2.75

ON REVOLUTION. *Viking* 1963 Compass Bks. 1965 pap. $2.95

MEN IN DARK TIMES. *Harcourt* 1968 $6.50 Harvest Bks. 1970 pap. $2.45

ON VIOLENCE. *Harcourt* Harvest Bks. 1970 pap. $2.45

TAYLOR, A(LAN) J(OHN) P(ERCIVALE).   1906–

Fritz Stern wrote of this British historian and his "The Struggle for Mastery in Europe, 1848–
1918" in the *Political Science Quarterly*: "There is something Shavian about A. J. P. Taylor and his
place among academic historians; he is brilliant, erudite, witty, dogmatic, heretical, irritating,
insufferable, and withal inescapable. He sometimes insults and always instructs his fellow-

historians, and never more so than in his present effort to reinterpret the diplomatic history of Europe from 1848 to the end of the First World War. . . . After a brilliant introduction, in which he defines the balance of power and assesses the relative and changing strength of the Great Powers, Mr. Taylor presents a chronological survey, beginning with the diplomacy of revolution (1848) and ending with the diplomacy of war, 1914–1918. . . . [He] writes on two levels. He narrates the history of European diplomacy and compresses it admirably into a single volume. Imposed upon the narrative is his effort to probe the historical meaning of given actions and conditions. . . . He has a peculiar sense of inevitability, growing out of what he regards the logic of a given development, as well as a delicate feeling for live options and alternatives. Mr. Taylor suggests that fear, not aggression, was the dominant impulse of pre-war diplomacy."

"The Origins of the Second World War," again controversial and lively, starts from the premise (in Mr. Taylor's words) that "the war of 1939, far from being premeditated, was a mistake, the result on both sides of diplomatic blunders." The *New Statesman* said of it: "Mr. A. J. P. Taylor is the only English historian now writing who can bend the bow of Gibbon and Macaulay. [This is] a masterpiece: lucid, compassionate, beautifully written in a bare, sparse style, and at the same time deeply disturbing." Writing of the same book in the *New Republic*, Melvin Sheffitz (who points out that Mr. Taylor has "attracted large numbers of readers . . . while also provoking some of his more sober colleagues to attack him as flippant and irresponsible") says: "Many in America and in England and apparently even in Germany have read *The Origins of World War II* mistakenly as a defense of Hitler and of Germany, which is ironic since Taylor in two of his earliest books, the brilliant survey histories, *The Habsburg Monarchy, 1809–1918* (Humanities Press 1941, o.p.) and *The Course of German History*, shows a marked anti-German bias. In effect, Taylor, by de-emphasizing the role of Hitler, was putting Germany itself back on the stage of history. He believes that wars are, in large part, the result of miscalculations and not the result of deliberate, carefully thought out plans. Hitler, according to Taylor, started a war with Poland, but blundered into war with France and England."

"English History, 1914–1945," a volume in the *Oxford History of England Series*, has been widely praised. The *N.Y. Review of Books* greeted it as "an astonishing *tour de force*. It not only deserves, like Macaulay's history, to supersede for a few days the last fashionable novel. . . . It will also be a set book for research students who, as they pounce on misjudgments, will be brought up sharp by the inconvenient contingencies with which Taylor will confound their theories. . . . He is a fearless, not a faceless historian." Allan Nevins, while disagreeing with his account of the origins of World War II, found "English History" the "best" of Mr. Taylor's books to date, "a volume of high merit, rich in insight and offering a marvelously full, but compact, record of perhaps the most eventful period in all English history."

Atheneum summed up Mr. Taylor's career as follows: "Born in Southport, England, in 1906, A. J. P. Taylor attended Oriel College, Oxford. A Fellow of the British Academy, Mr. Taylor was Fords Lecturer in English history at Oxford in 1956, and has been the Leslie Stephen Lecturer at Cambridge. From 1930 to 1938, he lectured in history at Manchester University, and since 1938 has been a Fellow of Magdalen College, Oxford. [He] also gives television lectures, writes for *The Sunday Express* and reviews books for *The Observer*. . . . Mr. Taylor, who lived in Austria from 1928 to 1930, now lives at Magdalen College, Oxford, with his wife."

GERMANY'S FIRST BID FOR COLONIES, 1884–1885: A Move in Bismarck's European Policy. 1938. *Norton* 1970 pap. $1.25; *Shoe String Press* 1967 $4.00

THE COURSE OF GERMAN HISTORY. 1945. *Putnam* Capricorn Bks. 1962 pap. $2.25

FROM NAPOLEON TO LENIN: Historical Essays. 1950. *Harper* Torchbks. pap. $1.60; *Peter Smith* $4.00

THE STRUGGLE FOR MASTERY IN EUROPE, 1848–1918. History of Modern Europe Ser. *Oxford* 1954 $14.50

"What makes this the best study of European diplomacy since W. L. Langer's volumes on the post-1870 period is his ability to keep the major developments of the period clearly before his readers, while at the same time providing them with circumstantial and absorbing accounts of the policies and ambitions of individual powers and statesmen, the changing diplomatic alignments, and the crises and wars which filled the period"—(SR).

BISMARCK: The Man and the Statesman. *Knopf* 1955 $5.95; *Random* Vintage Bks. pap. $1.95

BEAVERBROOK. *Simon & Schuster* $12.95

THE ORIGINS OF THE SECOND WORLD WAR. 1961. *Atheneum* 1962 $6.95; *Fawcett* Premier Bks. rev. ed. 1968 pap. $1.75

THE FIRST WORLD WAR: An Illustrated History. 1963. *Putnam* Capricorn Giants 1972 pap. $2.95; *Peter Smith* $5.25

"One of Britain's foremost historians has chosen to write a taut, cynical, debunking history of World War I and to illustrate it with photographs associated with the accompanying text. The result is a superb job of sparse writing plus an excellent selection of photographs with sometimes sarcastically amusing captions. Mr. Taylor's theme is the futility of the War, its aimless beginning, its futile offensive slaughters, and its stubborn men all believing themselves right. The picture he presents is not pretty, and it will not please romantics or ultranationalists; but it is factual and it is difficult to dispute his interpretations of the facts"—(*LJ*).

ENGLISH HISTORY, 1914–1945. *Oxford* 1965 $12.50 Galaxy Bks. 1970 pap. $4.50

FROM SARAJEVO TO POTSDAM. *Harcourt* 1966 pap. $3.95

"This brief, bright volume is one in a series of summaries of European history. There are few facts in it that, one supposes, most readers do not know by heart, but Mr. Taylor's surprising judgment and originality are irrepressible. Whether he is right is another question—Americans will gasp at his notion that Roosevelt schemed to reduce Great Britain to a second-rate power—yet all his assertions make the reader think. (In this case, in the course of writing about other matters, he makes the reader think about Roosevelt's insistence that America would not fight for the British Empire's sake.) In short, Mr. Taylor offers the pleasure of a historian who simply will not cut and dry his subject"—(*New Yorker*).

FAIRBANK, JOHN K(ING).   1907–

John K. Fairbank, now Francis Lee Higginson Professor of History at Harvard and director of Harvard's East Asian Research Center, has had a distinguished academic career in the field of Asian studies, in which his books are of the first importance. Born in South Dakota, he took his Harvard A.B. *summa cum laude* in 1929 and his Ph.D. at Oxford in 1936. During World War II he worked for the Office of Strategic Services in Washington, was special assistant to the American Ambassador in Chungking (1942–1943), was attached to Washington's Office of War Information (1944–1945) and director of the U.S. Information Service in China (1945–1946). He has been at Harvard—with these intervals—since 1936.

Since the U.S. has begun critically to reexamine its Far Eastern policies, and to reconsider particularly the isolation of China, Professor Fairbank has been an active speaker in conferences on the subject—in early 1969 at a New York City meeting on "The United States and China: The Next Decade"—and has given testimony before the Senate Foreign Relations Committee. He is among those who believe that the isolated China is a danger to world peace, and that mainland China must be drawn again into the community of nations. In pressing for much more teaching about Asia in our schools and colleges (at the American Historical Association meeting, New York, December 1968), Professor Fairbank said: "For the world crisis of the 1970s, to push for world history in general education is not enough. It offers only a prospect of gradual osmosis of ideas, a 'trickle up' theory, that our leadership eventually will be so well educated in things Asian and Chinese, for example, that they will have the wit and wisdom to avoid disaster in our Asian relations—a thin hope, indeed." We need, he believes, much broader knowledge of things Asian as part of the general equipment of every American and the specialized equipment of many more American scholars, civil servants and statesmen.

In addition to the works listed below, he has compiled "Ch'ing Documents: An Introductory Syllabus" (*Harvard Univ. Press* 2 vols. 3rd rev. ed. 1970 pap. set $6.00) and edited "Chinese Thought and Institutions" (*Univ. of Chicago Press* 1957 $8.50 Phoenix Bks. pap. $4.50).

(With Kuang-Ching Liu) MODERN CHINA: A Bibliographical Guide to Chinese Works, 1898–1937. *Harvard Univ. Press* 1950 $8.00

"The books described in this bibliography are in the Chinese language, and deal with affairs in China since the Reform Movement of 1898. The titles are given both in Chinese characters and in romanized form, although all annotations are in English. Students of Chinese affairs, burdened by a difficult language and a voluminous literature, will welcome this convenient and lucid guide. Even those who do not read the language can glean from it much valuable information. It is a challenge to improved scholarship on China in the West"—(*U.S. Quarterly Booklist*). This is a splendid bibliography with abundant notes explaining the merit of each particular item, and doing it very intelligently. It is in fact a catalogue raisonné of a section of the very rich Harvard-Yenching Library, and its existence will greatly increase the practical value of that library"—(*Isis*).

(With Teng Ssu-Yu) CHINA'S RESPONSE TO THE WEST: A Documentary Survey, 1839–1923. 1954. *Atheneum* 1963 pap. $2.95

TRADE AND DIPLOMACY ON THE CHINA COAST: The Opening of the Treaty Ports, 1842–1854. *Harvard Univ. Press* 2 vols. in 1 1954 $18.00; *Stanford Univ. Press* 1969 pap. $4.95

"This is a basic account of the setting up of the treaty system which has dominated the past century in China. It opens up a new field of research in the genesis and growth of that hybrid treaty-port society in which Chinese and western ideas, ways, and interests became so throughly intermixed. The author makes available extensive notes and bibliography, with appendices and a glossary of Chinese names and terms"—(Publisher's note). "The general reader, if he can be induced to look into a work that seems highly specialized, will be rewarded by a beautifully drawn picture of the early negotiator for the Manchu Court, Chi Ying, whose effort was to bring the British barbarian under civilized control by a real sugar plum or two (p. 105) but chiefly by the sugar plums of trade. He will find, also, a neat exposition of the double hypocrisy of the opium trade of the time and may reflect upon the difference in the blinders worn by the Chinese and the British officials. He will find a lively description of the confusion at Shanghai during the Taiping rebellion"—(The Annals).

(With Teng Ssu-Yu) THE CH'ING ADMINISTRATION: Three Studies. Harvard Univ. Press 1960 pap. $5.00

(With Robert R. Bowie) COMMUNIST CHINA 1955–59: Policy Documents with Analysis. Harvard Univ. Press 1962 pap. $12.50

(With Edwin Reischauer) A HISTORY OF EAST ASIAN CIVILIZATION. Houghton 2 vols. 1965 Vol. 1 East Asia: The Great Tradition Vol. 2 East Asia: The Modern Transformation each $13.95

CHINA: The People's Middle Kingdom and the U.S.A. Harvard Univ. Press 1967 $5.00

"In Fairbank's book we find some of the most insightful observations on the impact of China's modern history (especially since her confrontation with the West) and on her present mode of thinking and international posture. . . . Fairbank has given America some highly nutritious food for thought, with her enlightened national interest in mind. One can only hope that there is yet time for his words to be read and acted upon"—(SR). "John K. Fairbank has an admirable mission: to make Everyman an expert on China. To this end, he has assembled a collection of eleven of his speeches and previously published popular articles, most of quite recent vintage. . . . In his ability to capture centuries of Chinese history in a brief essay, he is without peer"—(Journal of American History).

(Ed.) THE CHINESE WORLD ORDER: Traditional China's Foreign Relations. Harvard East Asian Ser. Harvard Univ. Press 1968 $12.00 pap. $5.95

"Nationalist and Communist China," Mr. Fairbank points out, "have inherited a set of institutionalized attitudes and historical precedents not easily conformable to the European tradition of international relations among equally sovereign nation states. Modern China's difficulty of adjustment to the international order of nation states in the nineteenth and twentieth centuries has come partly from the great tradition of the Chinese world order." The N.Y. Times said of it: "Written by (and largely for) professional historians, 'The Chinese World Order' provides the broadest scholarly survey yet available of the workings of the system during the Ch'ing period (1644–1912)."

THE UNITED STATES AND CHINA. Harvard Univ. Press 3rd ed. 1971 $12.00 pap. $4.50

CHINA PERCEIVED: Images and Policies in Chinese-American Relations. Knopf 1974 $7.95

CHINESE-AMERICAN INTERACTIONS: A Historical Summary. Rutgers Univ. Press 1975 $7.50 pap. $2.95

"These essays preserve the casually inserted personal reminiscence, the deliberate understatement, and the ironic aside that mark Fairbank's lectures"—(LJ).

(Ed.) THE MISSIONARY ENTERPRISE IN CHINA AND AMERICA. Univ. of Chicago Press 1975 $7.50

"This collection of essays . . . is based on careful research and it will start the reader's imagination along a number of paths of speculation"—(TLS, London).

HAWKES, JACQUETTA (HOPKINS). 1910–

Stanley Edgar Hyman of the New Yorker has said that Jacquetta Hawkes "writes . . . as a professional archaeologist, an amateur geologist and paleontologist, a furious critic of machine culture along D. H. Lawrence's lines, a poet almost abnormally sensitive to visual beauty, and a passionate woman sometimes unable to distinguish the English rivers and rocks she knows from her own bloodstream and bones." In "Man and the Sun" (1962, o.p.), she ranges widely over civilizations and cultures, describing the origin and evolution of the Sun as a heavenly body. "Today the sun is no longer a divine symbol. Science has dethroned it, and this dethronement, she hopes, will turn out to be temporary, because as she says, 'The present peril and despair of humanity show that we cannot live without religious meaning. . . . If we cannot find God in the world, we lose him in ourselves, we become contemptible in our own eyes. We become mere statistics.' " For "The World of the Past" which she edited, she has contributed a noteworthy 100-page introduction, giving an outline of the history of archeological discovery. "King of the Two Lands" (1966, o.p.) is a novel drawn from the life of Pharaoh Akhenaten who married Nefertiti. In it she re-creates the period of this idealistic young monarch "brilliantly" (*LJ*) and with relevance to our own time. The author is the younger daughter of Sir Frederick Gowland Hopkins, O.M., first cousin of Gerard Manley Hopkins (*q.v.*). She grew up in Cambridge and has always been interested in archeology. At Newnham College, Cambridge, she read archeology and anthropology, held a research scholarship and excavated a number of sites. During World War II she was in the War Cabinet Offices, later transferring to the Ministry of Education when she became British secretary to the British National Commission of UNESCO, but resigned to devote herself to writing. She married J. B. Priestley (*q.v.*) in 1953. "Dawn of the Gods: Minoan and Myceanean Origins of Greece" (1968) is out of print.

(Ed.) THE WORLD OF THE PAST. *Knopf* 2 vols. 1963 set $25.00

This anthology of "enjoyable literature" written by pioneering archeologists will "amuse, excite and inform." Ranging in time from Hesiod and Herodotus to the autumn of 1962, it includes outstanding investigators and two nonprofessionals, William E. Gladstone and D. H. Lawrence. Miss Hawkes has written an enjoyable introductory history.

(With Bernard V. Bothmer) PHARAOHS OF EGYPT. *American Heritage Press* (dist. by Harper) 1965 lib. bdg. $6.89

LAND. *Dufour* 1966 $9.25

NOTHING BUT OR SOMETHING MORE. *Univ. of Washington Press* 1973 $3.95

(Ed.) ATLAS OF ANCIENT ARCHEOLOGY. *McGraw-Hill* 1974 $19.50

"The time span covered is from 1,800,000 B.C. at Olduval Gorge to the 16th century at several new world sites; classical Greece and Rome which have been adequately covered elsewhere, are not included"—(*LJ*).

THE FIRST GREAT CIVILIZATIONS: Life in Mesopotamia, the Indus Valley and Egypt. *Knopf* 1973 $12.50

A "wide-ranging, plausible account of ordinary life in early Mesopotamia, Egypt and the Indus Valley. A difficult task, impressively well done"—(Phoebe Adams, in the *Atlantic*).

DJILAS, MILOVAN. 1911–

The dramatic life of Milovan Djilas, the former Yugoslavian Minister, Vice-President and President of the National Assembly, is likely to become a classic of contemporary history. Leaving his native Montenegro, he joined the Communist party at 18 and soon was imprisoned for his activities in Sremska Mitrovica, which at that time was virtually a Communist university within itself. From it he emerged totally dedicated to the party and embarked on a career of an arch-zealot. His subsequent repudiation of orthodox communism, or even the stringencies of the Yugoslavian variety (of which he himself was the original formulator), makes him one of fanaticism's foremost heretics and one of humanism's most extraordinary converts. In 1954 on the publication of "The New Class," highly critical of the Yugoslav government and its hierarchy, Djilas was expelled from the Central Committee and shortly thereafter resigned from the Communist party. "He began a new life, in which periods of imprisonment marked the pauses and books marked the successive advances in his passionate search for freedom." In 1961 the announcement of the forthcoming publication of "Conversations with Stalin" prompted his fourth arrest, resulting in imprisonment for a term of nine years, later commuted to four.

Once said to be Tito's choice as a successor to himself, Djilas has now become the perpetual and fearless thorn in that leader's side. On his release from his latest imprisonment (1962–1966) he was prevented for five years from publishing in Yugoslavia and from giving press interviews or radio broadcasts. He was allowed, however, in 1968 to come to the U.S. as lecturer at Princeton. Here he received Freedom House's 1968 Freedom Award. Mr. Djilas continued to speak freely while in this country, and the *N.Y. Times* and other media gave much space to his predictions as to the future of communism which he sees as gradually becoming more democratic in nature as governments become more stable. Back in Belgrade, where, according to C. L. Sulzberger of the *N.Y. Times*, he lives (surprisingly) on a generous pension as on "old partisan" and from the foreign royalties on his books (William Jovanovich, president of *Harcourt, Brace*, is his stanch supporter), he supported Yugoslavia's condemnation of the invasion of Czechoslovakia by the U.S.S.R. in the summer of 1968. Mr. Djilas contrives, remarkably, to remain a free spirit and one without bitterness (whom his government, in spite of periodic imprisonment, apparently regards with charity when he appears to "behave"); the impression he gives is one of gentleness, humor and rationality—but of iron integrity.

"Montenegro" (trans. by Kenneth Johnstone *Harcourt* 1963 $5.75) is part history and part fiction. *Library Journal* called his "The Leper and Other Stories" (trans. by Lovett F. Edwards *Harcourt* 1964 $5.95) "an uneven and disturbing collection" which nonetheless shows "a steady artistic and human growth." "Njegos: Poet, Prince, Bishop" (trans. by Michael B. Petrovich *Harcourt* 1966 $10.00) treats a 19th-century Montenegran historical and literary figure (*see Chapter 15, Other Foreign Literature—Yugoslav Literature*, Reader's Adviser, *Vol. 1*). Though an acknowledged atheist, Mr. Djilas spent his latest prison term translating Milton's "Paradise Lost" into Serbian. Of that period he has said (quoted in the *N.Y. Times*): "I have never felt as much at peace with myself and with the outside world as during my last four years and eight months in prison. I was never more reconciled with prison life, with serving my sentence to the end."

THE NEW CLASS: An Analysis of the Communist System. 1954. *Praeger* 1957 $5.95 pap. $1.95

LAND WITHOUT JUSTICE. 1958. *Harcourt* Harvest Bks. 1972 pap. $2.85

CONVERSATIONS WITH STALIN. Trans. by Michael B. Petrovich *Harcourt* Harvest Bks. 1963 pap. $1.95. In three sections, entitled Raptures, Doubts, Disappointments.

THE UNPERFECT SOCIETY: Beyond the New Class. *Harcourt* 1969 $5.75 Harvest Bks. 1970 pap. $2.35

MEMOIR OF A REVOLUTIONARY. *Harcourt* 1973 $12.00

ELLUL, JACQUES. 1912–

Jacques Ellul, a member of the French Resistance movement in World War II and since 1946 professor of the history of law and of social history at the University of Bordeaux, has been variously admired by such men as Paul Tillich, Norman Mailer and Marshall McLuhan for his telling criticism of modern society—particularly *French* society, he reminds us in his "Author's Preface to the English Translation" of "The Political Illusion," but the application of his stringent observation is clearly broad. H. H. Ransom wrote (in *SR*) of "The Technological Society": "The dismal prospect of a society increasingly collectivized, enslaved, and dehumanized by techniques now possible is the main concern of this book. Here is an incisive diagnosis of modern society and its effects on the individual man. . . . True, the problem of balancing liberty and authority is ever more challenging in a technological society. The great value of Mr. Ellul's study is the vivid warning it gives of the consequences of failure to meet this challenge." Marshall McLuhan said of "Propaganda": "Ellul's *The Technological Society* was a rehearsal for this book. . . . The theme of *Propaganda* is quite simply a development of that total technology study—namely, that when our new technology encompasses any culture or society, the result is propaganda. . . . Ellul has made many splendid contributions [here]."

"The Political Illusion," his most comprehensive attack to date on the shibboleths of modern society, sees social man expecting all his problems to be solved by political means—by the gargantuan modern state which is no longer capable of responding to the citizenry, caught up as it is in its own cumbersome, self-perpetuating apparatus. "Ellul's message can be stated simply enough," says Irving Louis Horowitz in *New Politics*: "The essential political illusions are first, that the people *control* the operations of the State; second, that people at least *participate* in the operations of the State; and third, that political solutions are available to all social problems. While rejecting any populist model of politics, Ellul also tends to dismiss the pluralist model of politics as a conflict of interests generated by differing value commitments. Thus, Ellul is left with an elite model of the modern State, and more profoundly left with the problem of what ordinary men can do about this Leviathan. His answer is that to 'dissipate the political illusion' we must 'develop and multiply tensions.' This conflict model is to be stimulated by a juxtaposition of 'private life' versus 'political life.' . . . It is hard to say whether Ellul is counselling resistance to bureaucracy and dehumanization, or acceptance of the inevitable; working to break political illusions by political methods, or by abandoning politics for the private life."

S. K. Oberbeck, book editor of *Newsweek*, wrote (in *Book World*) of the 33 "commonplaces" treated in Ellul's "Critique": "The name Jacques Ellul, like that of Lévi-Strauss or Marcuse, has been steadily climbing on the intellectual hit parade, and for good reason. Ellul is one of those rare, new wide-track cultural critics who transcends linear disciplines and synthesizes a broad range of seemingly eclectic insights into large, important categories. His ideas matter. His past three books dealt brilliantly with man's runaway technological proliferation, with the equally ominous 'politicization' of traditional values and with the pervasive disguises and subtle tyrannies of propaganda. A militant individualist and wily scholar of social and legal history, Ellul writes here in a curiously open style, as with humorous Gallic irony he axes the axioms—what he terms 'commonplaces'—that he feels are synonymous with patent malfunction in society. These are the 'self-evident truths' we often live by, or at least accept unquestioningly; those smug Q.E.D.s that nobody thinks to put to the test of the times, old saws such as 'We must follow the current of history,' 'Public interest comes before private interest,' 'The machine is a neutral object and man is its master' or 'The spiritual side of life cannot develop until the standard of living is raised.' We have all heard them, in one form or another. Ellul, refreshingly, takes them apart."

Not everyone is happy with Ellul's conclusions; some (like Mr. Horowitz) find them "cloudy and confusing"; others (like the *Virginia Quarterly Review*) find that "he is not given to letting facts get in the way of his theorizing, nor does he appear to be willing to examine his theory in light of a broad range of facts." Professor Ellul's greatest virtue is perhaps in the freshness of his dissection of our world; while we may not stand with him entirely, we find that he has hit upon shams and paradoxes we have never squarely faced and has indicated directions through which the thoughtful reader may reorient his own universe.

He has also written a number of books on contemporary religious issues and theology: "Presence of the Kingdom" (*Seabury Press* 1967 pap. $2.25), "False Presence of the Kingdom" (*Seabury Press* $4.95), "Theological Foundation of Law" (*Seabury Press* 1969 pap. $1.95), "To Will and To Do" (*United Church* 1969 $10.00), "Hope in Time of Abandonment" (*Seabury Press* 1973 $8.95), "Judgment of Jonah" (*Eerdmans* 1971 pap. $1.95), "Meaning of the City" (*Eerdmans* 1970 pap. $2.45), "The Politics of God and the Politics of Man" (*Eerdmans* new ed. 1972 pap. $3.45) and "Prayer and Modern Man" (*Seabury Press* 1973 pap. $2.95).

THE TECHNOLOGICAL SOCIETY. 1954. Trans. by John Wilkinson; introd. by Robert K. Merton *Knopf* 1964 $10.95; *Random* Vintage Bks. pap. $2.45

PROPAGANDA: The Formation of Men's Attitudes. 1962. Trans. by Konrad Kellen and Jean Lerner; introd. by Konrad Kellen *Knopf* 1965 $8.95; *Random* Vintage Bks. 1973 pap. $2.45

THE POLITICAL ILLUSION. 1965. Trans. with fwd. by Konrad Kellen and "Author's Preface to the English Translation." 1967. *Random* Vintage Bks. pap. $1.95

THE PRESENCE OF THE KINGDOM. *Seabury Press* 1967 pap. $2.25

A CRITIQUE OF THE NEW COMMONPLACES. 1966. Trans. by Harriet Weaver *Knopf* 1968 $7.95

VIOLENCE: Reflections from a Christian Perspective. *Seabury Press* 1969 $4.95

THE AUTOPSY OF REVOLUTION. *Knopf* 1971 $8.95

TUCHMAN, BARBARA (WERTHEIM). 1912–

Mrs. Tuchman's dramatic retelling of the events of the first 30 days of World War I was a runaway best seller in 1962 and won for its author a Pulitzer Prize. Of her earlier book on the same war, the *N.Y. Times* said: "The value and importance of her book lies in her brilliant use of well known materials, her sureness of insight, and her competent grasp of a complicated chapter of diplomatic history." Oscar Handlin wrote (in the *Atlantic*) that "The Proud Tower," a study of the flaws behind the Edwardian façade, was "consistently interesting. Its author is a skillful and imaginative writer. She has the storyteller's knack for getting the maximum dramatic effect out of the events which crowd her pages."

A daughter of Maurice Wertheim, New York banker, art collector and founder of the Theatre Guild, and granddaughter of Henry Morgenthau, Sr., Mrs. Tuchman lives in her native New York City with her physician husband. Her early volume, "The Bible and the Sword: England and Palestine from the Bronze Age to Balfour" (1956. *Funk & Wagnalls* 1968 $6.95 pap. $2.95), describes the interrelationship between the two countries over the centuries.

THE ZIMMERMANN TELEGRAM. 1958. *Macmillan* 1966 $6.95; *Bantam* 1971 pap. $1.25. A key incident in World War I.

THE GUNS OF AUGUST. *Macmillan* lg.-print ed. 1962 $10.00; *Dell* 1971 pap. $1.75

THE PROUD TOWER. *Macmillan* 1966 $7.95; *Bantam* 1972 pap. $1.45

STILWELL AND THE AMERICAN EXPERIENCE IN CHINA, 1911–1945. *Macmillan* 1971 $12.50; *Bantam* 1972 pap. $2.25

NOTES FROM CHINA. *Macmillan* 1972 pap. $1.25

WARD, BARBARA (LADY JACKSON). 1914–

An outstanding authority on world political, social and economic issues, Barbara Ward (Lady Jackson) has written many books for the general reader. Her "Five Ideas That Change the World" are nationalism, industrialism, colonialism, communism and internationalism. "India and the West" defined the urgency of India's desperate economic requirements and outlined a specific program for their accomplishment. Of it Edward Weeks wrote in the *Atlantic:* "Barbara Ward's new book . . . is in many respects the most important she has ever written. The qualities which she brings to her writing—her gift for historical analysis, her explanation of difficult economic problems, and her reasonable faith in the initiative of the free world—were never more needed."

"The Rich Nations and the Poor Nations" was read by President Johnson, who remarked on how much it "excites and inspires me." Adlai Stevenson found it "exceedingly important." It received a *N.Y. Times Book Review* front-page review in which Eric F. Goldman found it "wondrously lucid, richly informed and trenchantly argued, tough-minded but never failing to assume that intelligence and will can move human society forward. . . . Miss Ward is at her scintillating best in analyzing just how difficult it is for the rich and the poor nations to reach rapport. . . . We could be a good deal more certain [of the future] if Americans would stop feeling overwhelmed by the world long enough to read this wise and inspiriting book."

Miss Ward is a highly trained, widely read observer with much firsthand experience of the Third World, in whose future she is passionately interested—and not only for humanitarian reasons; she realizes that "No man is an island," in John Donne's words, and that if the "poor nations" collapse or catch fire, we, the rich nations, go down with them. Of "Spaceship Earth" *Library Journal* wrote: "The real ideological obstacle to a more stable world, Miss Ward finds, is the mental block that keeps millions from recognizing that the web of interests and activities in which each of us is enmeshed is worldwide and international, but that the narrow base of loyalty remains national. She ends with a plea for *world patriotism.*" "She has" (says *LJ*) "a rare gift of combining genuine economic reasoning with persuasive . . . appeal."

Born in Yorkshire, she was educated in England, Paris, Germany and Somerville College, Oxford, where she took first-class honors in philosophy, politics and economics. She became an editor of the *Economist* in 1939 and remains affiliated with it. "In 1958," say her publishers, "she became a Carnegie Fellow and Visiting Scholar in International Economic Development at Harvard University. In 1968, she went to Columbia University as Albert Schweitzer Professor of International Economic Development. In January 1967 she was appointed by Pope Paul VI to the Pontifical Commission of Justice and Peace. She has received honorary doctorates from Smith College, Columbia, Harvard, Brandeis, Fordham and many other institutions."

"Faith and Freedom" (1954), "Women in the New Asia" (1965), and "Africa in the Making" (1966) are out of print.

THE INTERPLAY OF EAST AND WEST: Points of Conflict and Cooperation. *Norton* 1957 pap. $1.25

FIVE IDEAS THAT CHANGE THE WORLD. *Norton* 1959 pap. $1.75

INDIA AND THE WEST: Pattern for a Common Policy. *Norton* 1961 rev. ed. 1964 pap. $1.45

THE RICH NATIONS AND THE POOR NATIONS. *Norton* 1962 pap. $1.95

NATIONALISM AND IDEOLOGY. *Norton* 1966 $3.75 pap. $1.25

"The author asks for the formation of a world order. Miss Ward suggests that—gradually, if need be, but starting immediately—we should create orders and organizations, federations, and groups below the United Nations and above the nation-state. She sees the necessity for these larger-than-nation-sized units in the fact that the world's economy is international, and in the further fact that the price of war among nations is higher than it has ever been, while the fruits of peace are more varied and abundant. . . . Miss Ward's concluding ideas—on ideological ecumenicity—are particularly appealing"—(*New Yorker*).

SPACESHIP EARTH. *Columbia* 1966 $7.50 pap. $1.95

THE LOPSIDED WORLD. *Norton* 1968 $3.95 pap. $1.25. The needs of the poor nations and the urgency for rich nations to help meet them.

(With Rene Dubos) ONLY ONE EARTH: The Care and Maintenance of a Small Planet. *Norton* 1972 $6.00

(With others, Eds.) WIDENING GAP: Development in the 1970's. *Columbia* 1971 $12.50 pap. $3.95

CERAM, C.' W. (pseud. of Kurt W. Marek). 1915–1972.

Ceram's books about the human side of archeology have found for him a wide audience, and "Gods, Graves and Scholars" remains the classic introduction to the field. (The new edition covers recent discoveries with revisions and added material.) Avowedly nontechnical, his writing is interesting and dramatic. In "Yestermorrow: Notes on Man's Progress" (made up of animated thoughts reported with the continuity one expounds in the free association of ideas), "man's technological advances are contrasted with the threat of his ability to exterminate himself, and juxtaposed to a variety of beliefs in the vision of a better future. Marek has a brilliant and inspiring confidence in the *quality* relationships of technological genius and man's creativeness; he is not too concerned with the *character* of change but rather, as he notes: 'The machine is demonized by those who feel helpless in its presence. Where such demonization occurs today, its authors are neither scientists, nor managers, nor workers, but only outdistanced philosophers and writers sulking in their historical corner' "—*(LJ)*. Mr. Marek's pen name, it will be noted, is a reversal of his true one, C's being substituted for K's.

"The Archaeology of the Cinema" (1965) is out of print.

GODS, GRAVES AND SCHOLARS: The Story of Archaeology. *Knopf* 1951 rev. ed. 1967 $8.95; *Bantam* 2nd rev. ed. 1972 pap. $1.95

THE SECRET OF THE HITTITES: The Discovery of an Ancient Empire. *Knopf* 1956 $8.95; *Schocken* 1973 pap. $3.95

THE MARCH OF ARCHAEOLOGY. *Knopf* 1958 1970 $17.95 pap. $4.95

(Ed.) HANDS ON THE PAST: Pioneer Archaeologists Tell Their Own Story. *Knopf* 1966 $10.00; *Schocken* 1973 pap. $3.95

THE FIRST AMERICAN: A Story of North American Archaeology. *Harcourt* 1971 $9.95; *New Am. Lib.* 1972 pap. $1.95

McNEILL, WILLIAM H(ARDY). 1917–

Toynbee (*q.v.*) has acclaimed "The Rise of the West" as "the most lucid presentation of world history in narrative form that I know." Its Canadian-born author was chairman of the Department of History at the University of Chicago. The volume took nine years of preparation and "was executed with the help of Ford and Carnegie grants, the aid of four student assistants, the advice of twenty-eight specialists here and abroad, and the tolerance of a wife and four children." It won the 1963 National Book Award for history and the Gordon J. Laing Prize of the University of Chicago. His one-volume "World History," which gives equal space to Asia and the West, was greeted as work of major importance by Arnold Toynbee (*see above*), Hans Kohn, Geoffrey Bruun, Stringfellow Barr and John Barkham, among others. He was one of the editors of the Readings in World History Series published by *Oxford*.

HISTORY OF WESTERN CIVILIZATION: A Handbook. *Univ. of Chicago Press* 1948 rev. ed. 1969 $12.00 pap. $5.75

AMERICA, BRITAIN AND RUSSIA: Their Cooperation and Conflict 1941–1946. *Johnson Reprint* 1953 $32.50 pap. $4.95

PAST AND FUTURE. *Univ. of Chicago Press* Phoenix Bks. 1954 pap. $1.75

THE RISE OF THE WEST: A History of the Human Community. *Univ. of Chicago Press* 1963 $9.95 Phoenix Bks. 1970 pap. $4.25

EUROPE'S STEPPE FRONTIER, 1500–1800. *Univ. of Chicago Press* 1964 $7.50

A WORLD HISTORY. *Oxford* 1967 2nd ed. 1971 $15.00 pap. $6.95; *Franklin Watts* lg.-type ed. 1968 $12.50

"He makes the interactions between different civilizations, in all periods of history, the main theme of his book. . . . In fact, he makes a complicated story lucid"—(Arnold Toynbee). It includes an excellent portfolio of colored maps.

THE CONTEMPORARY WORLD, 1914–Present. *Morrow* 1968 $7.00; *Scott, Foresman* 1967 $6.50 rev. ed. 1975 pap. $3.75

ECUMENE: Story of Humanity. *Harper* 1973 $9.88 reader's guide $1.60

THE SHAPE OF EUROPEAN HISTORY. *Oxford* 1974 $7.50

VENICE: The Hinge of Europe 1081–1797. *Univ. of Chicago Press* 1974 $10.75

BARNETT, A(RTHUR) DOAK. 1921–

Born of American parents in Shanghai, Doak Barnett has spent much time in China. After receiving his M.A. from Yale University, he became a correspondent in Hong Kong for the *Chicago Daily News* (1947–1950 and 1952–1953). He was public affairs officer at the American Consulate-General in Hong Kong (1951–1952) and later an associate of the American Universities Field Staff for Asian areas. At first hand "he saw the significance of Communist mass organizations, of their use of group indoctrination. He saw the massive effort to remold the thinking of hundreds of thousands of men and women, saw their sense of drama in carrying out their social campaigns, the shrewd use of their appeal to the ancient sport of public execution and the steady accumulation of the means to exercise total social and political control"—*(N.Y. Times)*.

In "China after Mao" Professor Barnett, "who is a scholar with a knack for writing in a manner comprehensible and interesting to the lay reader, offers a clear-cut discussion of the issues involved in the succession problem and of their implications for the United States"—*(Book Week)*. He was chairman of the foreign area studies department at the U.S. State Department's Foreign Service Institute and is now professor of political science at Columbia University and chairman of the Contemporary China Studies Committee of Columbia's East Asian Institute. A member of, or consultant for, many organizations engaged in China studies, "Professor Barnett is, of course, one of this country's best known and ablest academic China-watchers. [He is in favor of] a flexible American approach, one capable of showing China's leaders that violent, extreme measures will be counterproductive, yet encouraging by positive responses any signs of reasonable and moderate policies in Peking"—(Harry Schwartz, in *SR*).

COMMUNIST CHINA AND ASIA: Challenge to American Policy. 1960. *Verry* $6.95; *Random* Vintage Bks. pap. $1.95

CHINA ON THE EVE OF COMMUNIST TAKEOVER. *Praeger* 1963 pap. $3.50

"Why and how was mainland China lost to the Communists? Here is a highly readable book that throws a great deal of light on the matter. [Professor Barnett] reveals enough of the Communists' doctrinaire ignorance and authoritarianism to indicate why their regime, by now, has become the most rigid, xenophobic dictatorship the Middle Kingdom has ever known"—*(N.Y. Times)*.

COMMUNIST CHINA: The Early Years, 1949–55. *Praeger* 1964 $8.50 pap. $3.50

A collection of previously published articles. "According to the way in which the Chinese Communists see the matter, this book deals with what they call the period of 'reconstruction,' the initial period of 'transition to socialism' and the first two years of the first Five Year Plan. . . . A. Doak Barnett has captured the spirit of these years in a most unusual book, which he rightly says is not a general history or over-all analysis of events. . . . Written in an easy style with caution and modesty, a lack of dogmatism and an obvious zest for digging up facts, these articles stand the test of time very well indeed"—*(N.Y. Times)*.

CHINA AFTER MAO, WITH SELECTED DOCUMENTS. *Princeton Univ. Press* 1967 $8.50 pap. $3.95. Based on the Walter E. Edge Lectures given at Princeton University in 1966.

CADRES, BUREAUCRACY, AND POLITICAL POWER IN COMMUNIST CHINA. *Columbia* 1967 $12.00

"Professor Barnett describes the operations of the Communist system with skill and ingenuity. Although he has used whatever published data exist, his chief sources are exhaustive interviews conducted in 1964–1965 with defectors who had themselves once been part of the system. Such informants are, of course, biased. But Barnett is aware of the danger of uncritical reliance upon their statements and has successfully coped with it. There is no better account of how the Communist government actually operated in 1965"—(Oscar Handlin).

(Ed.) CHINESE COMMUNIST POLITICS IN ACTION: Studies in Chinese Government and Politics. *Univ. of Washington Press* 1969 $12.50 pap. $4.95

(With others, Eds.) THE UNITED STATES AND CHINA: The Next Decade. *Praeger* 1970 $7.95 pap. $2.95

NEW U.S. POLICY TOWARD CHINA. *Brookings* 1971 $5.95 pap. $2.50

UNCERTAIN PASSAGE: China's Transition to the Post-Mao Era. *Brookings* 1974 $9.95 pap. $3.95

Chapter 10

The Lively Arts and Communications

"The multimedia artists (in New York and San Francisco) worked in obscurity . . . producing 'events' which combined film, dance, music, painting, lights. . . . All of the arts seemed suddenly to become possessed with a powerful kinetic urge."
—ELENORE LESTER

"The commands through which we exercise our control over our environment are a kind of information which we impart to it. . . . In control and communication we are always fighting nature's tendency to degrade the organized and to destroy the meaningful."
—NORBERT WIENER

"In this electric age we see ourselves being translated more and more into the form of information, moving toward the technological extension of consciousness."
—MARSHALL MCLUHAN

This chapter reflects the growing interest in dance, opera, and films among many Americans, particularly the younger generations. These once neglected arts deserve more attention and better financial subsidies than they have received in recent years. Government and foundation funds are no longer readily available and inflation has eaten away once substantial endowments. The titles included in this chapter will provide our readers with a good overview of the esthetic and financial status of these lively arts.

Another closely related subject included in this Chapter is Communications which affects our daily lives in many significant ways. Radio, television, and the news media enrich our lives with a seemingly endless flow of entertainment, culture, information, and analysis. We must all learn to understand the goals and the levels of performance of these mass media if we are to become intelligent consumers.

THE LIVELY ARTS

Baumol, William J. THE PERFORMING ARTS: The Economic Dilemma. 1966. *Kraus* $7.50; *M.I.T. Press* 1968 pap. $3.95

Belknap, Sara Yancey, Comp. GUIDE TO THE PERFORMING ARTS. *Scarecrow Press* 1968 $12.50
"Highly recommended for theater, music and dance collections"—(*LJ*).

Filliou, Robert. TEACHING AND LEARNING AS PERFORMING ARTS. *Wittenborn* 1970 pap. $9.50

Gruen, John. THE PARTY'S OVER NOW: Reminiscences of the Fifties—New York's Artists, Writers, Musicians, and Their Friends. *Viking* 1972 $8.95

THE NATIONAL DIRECTORY OF THE PERFORMING ARTS AND CIVIC CENTERS. Ed. by Janet Spencer and Nolanda Turner *Handel & Co.* 2 vols. Vol. 1 (1974) $24.00 Vol. 2 (1975) $40.00

Rachow, Louis, and Katherine Hartley. GUIDE TO THE PERFORMING ARTS. 1968. *Scarecrow Press* 1972 $12.50

Schoolcraft, Ralph N. PERFORMING ARTS BOOKS IN PRINT: An Annotated Bibliography. *Drama Bk. Specialists* 1973 $32.50

Seldes, Gilbert. THE SEVEN LIVELY ARTS. 1924. *A. S. Barnes* 1962 pap. $2.45. A classic in its field.

Sharp, Harold S., and Marjorie Z. Sharp, Eds. INDEX TO CHARACTERS IN THE PERFORMING

ARTS. *Scarecrow Press* 5 vols. 1966–73 Pt. 1 Non-Musical Plays 2 vols. (1966) $36.00 Pt. 2 Operas and Musical Productions (1969) $30.00 Pt. 3 Ballets A to Z and Symbols (1972) $10.00 Pt. 4 Radio and Television (1973) $15.00

Ulanov, Barry. Two WORLDS OF AMERICAN ART. *Macmillan* 1965 $8.95

Weightman, John. CONCEPT OF AVANT-GARDE. *Open Court* (Library Press) 1973 $9.95

Dance

Dance is the oldest of the lively arts. We find pictures of dancing figures on cave walls, on Greek vases, and in ancient Egyptian tombs. Dance serves a number of basic human needs for ritualistic religious worship, esthetic expression, and social enjoyment.

Avant-garde techniques are broadening the base of this art's appeal with the use of "multimedia" such as neon lights, musical tapes, projected film balloons, plastic bubbles and the like—experiments which can be stimulating and successful when they avoid submerging the human form in motion, which must remain central and focal if dance is not to be reduced to spectacle.

The literature on dance continues to increase as interest grows. This list includes works on folk dancing, classical ballet, and modern interpretive dance.

Ambrose, Kay. THE BALLET-LOVER'S COMPANION: Aesthetics without Tears for the Ballet-Lover. Ill. by the author *Knopf* 1949 $3.95. An expanded version of the author's "Pocket-Book."

THE BALLET-LOVER'S POCKET-BOOK: Technique without Tears for the Ballet-Lover. Ill. by the author *Knopf* 1945 $3.95. A brief introduction to ballet as craft, art and entertainment.

Anderson, Jack. DANCE. World of Culture Ser. *McGraw-Hill* (Newsweek Bks.) 1974 $10.00

Anderson "traces the development of dance from the ritual movements of the ancients to the modern and classical choreography of today"—(*LJ*).

Arbeau, Thoinot. ORCHESOGRAPHY. Trans. from the French by Cyril W. Beaumont; pref. by Peter Warlock *Dance Horizons* pap. $3.95; trans. by Mary Evans *Dover* 1966 pap. $3.00; *Peter Smith* $4.50

Arbeau (pseud. of Jehan Tabourot) was an erudite 16th-century cleric. "The *Orchesography*—a manual of the dances, illustrated by drawings and music, of the 16th century—is not only invaluable to dancers, it is indispensable to historians of the period, and to musicologists"—(*LJ*).

Armitage, Merle, Ed. MARTHA GRAHAM. 1937. *Dance Horizons* 1966 pap. $2.95

Sixteen opinions on the great artist of modern dance. "Unqualifiedly recommended"—(*LJ*).

Balanchine, George. BALANCHINE'S NEW COMPLETE STORIES OF THE GREAT BALLETS. Ed. by Francis Mason; ill. by Marta Becket *Doubleday* 1954 rev. ed. 1968 $10.00 1975 pap. $2.95

The Russian-born Balanchine performed with Diaghilev's Ballet Russe (1924–28) as principal dancer and choreographer and came to the U.S. in 1933. He helped in 1934 to found the School of American Ballet and was for three years director of ballet for the Metropolitan Opera. Since 1948 he has been artistic director and choreographer for the New York City Ballet.

Belknap, Sara Yancey, Ed. GUIDE TO DANCE PERIODICALS. 1931–1962. *Univ. of Florida Press* Vol. 1 1931–1935 (1948, 1959) Vol. 5 1951–1952 (1955) Vol. 6 1953–1954 (1956) Vol. 7 1955–1956 (1958) each $7.50. Vols. 2, 3, and 4 o.p.; *Scarecrow Press* Vols. 8–10, o.p. Information since 1965 now incorporated in "Guide to the Performing Arts." (*See Belknap in list following introduction to the Lively Arts.*)

Brinson, Peter, and Clement Crisp. INTERNATIONAL BOOK OF THE BALLET. *Stein & Day* 1970 $8.95

Chujoy, Anatole, and P. W. Manchester, Eds. DANCE ENCYCLOPEDIA. *Simon & Schuster* rev. ed. 1967 $20.00. A broad, general encyclopedia that covers all phases of the dance, with articles by leading specialists of several nations. The present volume is a thorough revision of the 1949 edition; 1,000 pages, 3,000 entries.

Cohen, Selma Jeanne, Ed. Dance as a Theatre Art: Source Readings in Dance History
from 1581 to the Present. *Dodd* 1974 pap. $4.95

Modern Dance: Seven Statements of Belief. *Wesleyan Univ. Press* 1966 pap. $3.95

"A documentary on the modern dance at mid-century as seen by its practitioners"—*(Journal of Aesthetics)*. Contributors include José Limon, Anna Sokolow, Erick Hawkins, Alwin Nikolais, and Paul Taylor, all of whom participated in the "Festival of Dance 1968–69" at the Brooklyn Academy of Music.

De Mille, Agnes. Speak to Me, Dance with Me. *Little-Atlantic* 1973 $8.95; *Popular Lib.* 1974 pap. $1.50

"An exceptionally clever, cosmopolitan tête-à-tête and one of the more intelligent and memorable celebrity memoirs of the decade"—*(LJ)*.

To a Young Dancer: A Handbook. Drawings by Milton Johnson *Little-Atlantic* 1962 $5.95

Miss De Mille's frank and honest advice should benefit youthful dance students considering a professional career as dancers or choreographers. She also has recommendations for students and those teaching dance courses in colleges. The appendixes, listing repertory of major companies, dance films with sources of supply, and colleges included in her study, will add to library usefulness.

Denby, Edwin. Looking at the Dance. 1949. Rev. ed. with introd. by B. H. Haggin
Horizon Press 1968 $7.95; *Curtis Bks.* 1973 pap. $1.50

An eminent critic of the dance discusses "Meaning in Ballet," "Ballet Music and Decoration," modern dancers, recent ballets and other topics. "To read him is an enlightening experience: one comes away with more awareness, more insight, more understanding of what dancing is and means"—(Aaron Copland).

Dolin, Anton. Pas de Deux: The Art of Partnering. 1949. *Dover* 1969 pap. $1.50

Duncan, Irma. The Technique of Isadora Duncan. *Dance Horizons* 1973 pap. $1.95.
The author was a student and "foster child" of the great Isadora.

Duncan, Isadora. The Art of the Dance. *Theatre Arts* $14.95

My Life. 1927. *Liveright* Black and Gold Lib. 1942 $10.00 pap. $3.95; (with title "Isadora") *Universal Pub.* 1968 pap. $.95

Graham, Martha. The Notebooks. *Harcourt* 1973 $25.00

Grant, Gail. Technical Manual and Dictionary of Classical Ballet. 1950. Pref. by
Florence Rogge. With new pref. by Walter J. Ryan *Dover* 1967 pap. $1.50; *Peter Smith* $3.75

The 1950 edition has been expanded to include many new terms and is "considerably enriched by the clear distinctions made among the French, Russian, and Italian (Cecchetti) schools of ballet. The book is useful primarily as a dictionary rather than as a technical manual. It is weak only in its illustrations"—*(Choice)*.

Gruen, John. The Private World of Ballet. *Viking* 1975 $15.00

"In these brief but substantial interviews with more than 70 dancers, choreographers, teachers, and other figures from the dance world, Gruen has been successful in getting his subjects to talk meaningfully about themselves and their work, and to take us to the human side of the silent art. . . . It is impossible to imagine a book done any better than it has been"—*(LJ)*.

Haberman, Martin, and Tobie Garth Meisel, Eds. Dance: An Art in Academe. *Columbia* 1970 $7.95

"An up-to-date cross section of thinking about dance as an important instrumentality in formal education, especially in the education of children"—*(Choice)*.

Haskell, Arnold L. Balletomania: Story of an Obsession. 1934. *AMS Press* $14.50

Horst, Louis. Pre-Classic Dance Forms. *Dance Horizons* 1969 pap. $2.95

(With Carroll Russell) Modern Dance Forms in Relation to the Other Modern
Arts. Fwd. by Martha Graham *Dance Horizons* 1961 pap. $2.95

In this important liberally illustrated book, including musical scores, diagrams, charts, photographs and reproductions of paintings and sculpture, the authors have detailed the relation of all the arts to choreography and the dance. The late Mr. Horst, who began his musical dance career in 1915 as an accompanist for the Denishawn Dancers, was musical director for the great Martha Graham for more than 20 years.

Humphrey, Doris. THE ART OF MAKING DANCES. *Grove* Evergreen Bks. 1962 pap. $2.95. By the famous American dancer and choreographer who served her apprenticeship with the Denishawn Company.

DORIS HUMPHREY: An Artist First. *Wesleyan Univ. Press* 1972 $12.50

"Doris Humphrey is the greatest influence in the wholly native American art, modern dance. This first complete study consists of her unfinished autobiography as completed by Selma Jeanne Cohen"—(*Choice*).

Kahn, Albert E. DAYS WITH ULANOVA. Introd. by Arnold L. Haskell *Simon & Schuster* 1962 $10.00

Ulanova's fame had already preceded her first performance in New York in 1959 with the Bolshoi Ballet from Moscow. This author-photographer became her friend and assembled a pictorial record consisting of some 5,000 photographs depicting every aspect of the dancer's world. The text is a valuable addition to the 300 photographs which he uses. "In its entirety, it is a striking example of how dance can help to make the world one"—(*LJ*).

Kersley, Leo, and Janet Sinclair. A DICTIONARY OF BALLET TERMS. 1953. *Pitman* 3rd ed. 1964 $4.95

"Aimed primarily at the layman and student, this improved edition of one of the most useful of all ballet dictionaries has definitions among the best available, and the explanations do not presuppose much specialist knowledge"—(*LJ*).

Kirstein, Lincoln. DANCE: A Short History of Classic Theatrical Dancing. 1935. *Dance Horizons* 1969 pap. $6.95; *Greenwood* $16.75

MOVEMENT AND METAPHOR: Four Centuries of Ballet. *Praeger* 1971 $17.50

NEW YORK CITY BALLET. *Knopf* 1973 $25.00

NIJINSKY DANCING. *Knopf* 1976 $35.00

The author "offers in this large, visually elegant volume a thoughtful and stirring appreciation and celebration of the legendary Nijinsky for modern ballet lovers"—(*PW*).

THREE PAMPHLETS COLLECTED. *Dance Horizons* 1967 pap. $4.95

The "three incisive and illuminating pamphlets collected here—*Blast at Ballet*, *Ballet Alphabet*, and *What Ballet Is About* (originally issued in small editions and now collectors' items)—are among the most significant writings on ballet in America in the last 40 years"—(*LJ*).

WHAT BALLET IS ABOUT: An American Glossary. 1959. *Johnson Reprint* pap. $5.50

(With Muriel Stuart) THE CLASSIC BALLET. *Knopf* 1952 $10.00

"The basic American reference work on classical technique" by the founder and the general director of the New York City Ballet.

Krokover, Rosalyn. THE NEW BORZOI BOOK OF BALLETS. *Knopf* 1956 $8.95

Notes on 57 current U.S. ballets—covering music, story, choreography, performers and historical position; bibliographic introduction. "For devotees or initiates these chapters will make fine program notes as well as a competent survey of the development of the art"—(*Virginia Kirkus Service*).

Lawson, Joan. THE TEACHING OF CLASSICAL BALLET. *Theatre Arts* 1974 $8.65

Markova, Alicia. GISELLE AND I. Fwd. by Carl Van Vechten *Vanguard* 1961 $5.95. Of wide interest to dancers and historians of the ballet.

Martin, John. AMERICA DANCING: The Background and Personalities of the Modern Dance. 1936. *Dance Horizons* 1968 pap. $4.95. Among the figures included are Isadora Duncan, Martha Graham, Doris Humphrey, Charles Weidman and The Bennington Group.

INTRODUCTION TO THE DANCE. 1939. *Dance Horizons* 1965 pap. $4.95

Mazo, Joseph H. DANCE IS A CONTACT SPORT. *Dutton* 1974 $10.95

"A rewarding tour . . . of the backstage life of a company"—(*Booklist*).

Money, Keith. FONTEYN: The Making of a Legend. *Morrow* 1974 $25.00

Nijinsky, Romola, Ed. THE DIARY OF VASLAV NIJINSKY. *Univ. of California Press* 1968 pap. $2.45

Norris, Dorothy E. K., and Reva P. Shiner. KEYNOTES TO MODERN DANCE. *Burgess* 1965 3rd ed. 1969 pap. $5.75

Noverre, Jean Georges. LETTERS ON DANCING AND BALLETS. Trans. from the French and ed. by Cyril W. Beaumont. First pub. in St. Petersburg, 1803. *Dance Horizons* 1966 pap. $3.95

Jean Georges Noverre, who was active at the turn of the 19th century, was *maitre de ballet* to the Duke of Wurtemberg and had a long career in the European ballet theater. Mr. Beaumont says in the introduction: "Noverre's letters, considered as an exposition of the theories and laws governing ballet and dance representation, and as a contemporary history of dancing, have no equal in the whole of the literature devoted to the art, and no book has exerted so incalculable an influence for good on the manner of production of ballets and dances."

Nureyev, Rudolph. NUREYEV: An Autobiography with Pictures. Introd. by Alexander Bland; photos by Richard Avedon, Michael Peto, Anthony Crickmay and others *Dutton* 1963 $6.95

Nureyev's "dramatic defection from Russia's Kirov company and his position as partner to Margot Fonteyn with Britain's Royal Ballet [made him famous.] While neither his dancing nor his personality are universally admired, his story is a compelling one, and it makes a moving document as here expressed"—(*LJ*). For many, of course, he is perhaps the greatest male dancer of our day.

Roslavleva, Natalia. STANISLAVSKI AND THE BALLET. 1965. *Johnson Reprint* 1973 $8.50

Sachs, Curt. WORLD HISTORY OF THE DANCE. 1937. *Norton* 1957 1963 pap. $2.95. Highly recommended for reference.

Schlundt, Christena L., Ed. PROFESSIONAL APPEARANCES OF RUTH ST. DENIS AND TED SHAWN. *N.Y. Public Lib.* 1962 pap. $3.00

The late Ruth St. Denis and her husband Ted Shawn established the Denishawn Company in 1915. After a 17-year period of touring and of opening schools throughout the country, the company disbanded at the time of the Shawns' separation. Mr. Shawn went on to found the Jacob's Pillow Dance Center at Lee, Mass., and Miss St. Denis to lead the Society of Spiritual Arts in Manhattan. She danced at the Jacob's Pillow summer festivals, however, until 1955. According to Clive Barnes, the Denishawn School, with its revolutionary styles, was the "founding academy of American modern dance"; it trained, among others, Doris Humphrey and Martha Graham. Before Ruth St. Denis, says the *N.Y. Times*, American modern dance "had been an afternoon affair of little prestige."

PROFESSIONAL APPEARANCES OF TED SHAWN AND HIS MEN DANCERS. *N.Y. Public Library* 1967 pap. $3.75. Now o.p. is Mr. Shawn's own "One Thousand and One Night Stands" (1960), an account of his life and career through the U.S., Europe and the Far East.

TAMIRIS: A Chronicle of Her Dance Career, 1929–1955. *N.Y. Public Library* 1972 pap. $8.00

Sorell, Walter. THE DANCER'S IMAGE: Points and Counterpoints. *Columbia* 1971 $15.00. Writings about ballet in four sections: Dance and Dancers, profiles of many famous dancers; Dance and Painters, a survey of artists who have used ballet as subject matter; Dance and Actors, the interactions between ballet and drama; and Dance and Poets, a view of literary reactions to ballet.

(Ed.). THE DANCE HAS MANY FACES. *Columbia* 1951 2nd rev. ed. 1966 $10.00

Twenty-nine articles by various hands. "Valuable as a comprehensive look at the dance of 1967"—(*Choice*).

Stearns, Marshall, and Jean Stearns. JAZZ DANCE: The Story of American Vernacular Dance. *Macmillan* 1968 $9.95. A history of dancing to jazz, from its African origins to the present.

Swift, Mary Grace. THE ART OF THE DANCE IN THE U.S.S.R. *Univ. of Notre Dame Press* 1968 $15.00. This examines the question of whether or not Soviet Ballet has permitted a favored, "free," uncensored development of the art. Includes charts of Russian ballets and an extensive bibliography.

Terry, Walter. THE BALLET COMPANION. *Dodd* 1968 $6.95; *Apollo* 1971 pap. $2.50

Individual chapters are devoted to the various artists responsible for a ballet production. This organization makes for some repetition, but "newcomers of all ages . . . will get a good basic orientation here"—*(LJ)*.

THE BALLET GUIDE. *Dodd* 1975 $15.00

THE DANCE IN AMERICA. *Harper* 1956 rev. ed. 1971 $10.00 Colophon Bks. 1973 pap. $3.25. A brief historical account of dance.

THE LEGACY OF ISADORA DUNCAN AND RUTH ST. DENIS. 1959. *Johnson Reprint* pap. $5.50

MISS RUTH: The More Moving Life of Ruth St. Denis. *Dodd* 1969 $6.95

Vaganova, Agrippina. BASIC PRINCIPLES OF CLASSICAL BALLET. Trans. by Anatole Chujoy and others. 1953. *Dover* rev. ed. 1969 pap. $2.00; *Peter Smith* $4.00

Willis, John, Ed. DANCE WORLD. *Crown* 9 vols. 1966–74 Vols. 1–6 each $10.00 Vols. 7–9 each $15.00. Yearbook of performances in the U.S. of ballet, modern and ethnic companies.

Opera ·

Opera is a drama set to music, often accompanied by dances. This art form traces its origins back to the religious musical dramas and mysteries of the Middle Ages and perhaps even beyond. France, Germany, and Italy each developed a distinctive operatic style, their own great masterpieces, and distinguished composers. These grand operas are now a part of the world's cultural heritage. Today, opera is a declining art in the United States although more people than ever before are attending its performances. This select list includes summaries of the plots, outstanding histories of opera, and criticism.

Ashbrook, William. THE OPERAS OF PUCCINI. *Oxford* 1969 $7.50

"Ashbrook has examined the scores in autograph and supplies information that is not generally known, together with thoughtful insights . . . an indispensable work"—*(Choice)*.

Berges, Ruth. THE BACKGROUNDS AND TRADITIONS OF OPERA. *A. S. Barnes* 1971 $7.95

Borer, Mary Cathcart. COVENT GARDEN. Photographs by A. F. Kersting *Abelard-Schuman* 1967 $6.25

A 700-year history, concentrating on the 17th to 19th centuries, of that area of London containing the famous opera house, Britain's largest produce markets, Drury Lane Theater, Bow Street and St. Paul's Church. *Library Journal* finds particularly rewarding the author's discussions of the literature, drama and music of the Garden's past. The illustrations, old and modern, are attractive.

Brockway, Wallace, and Herbert Weinstock. THE WORLD OF OPERA: The Story of Its Origins and the Lore of Its Performance. *Pantheon* 1962 $12.50

This book, written in a warm readable style for the informed layman, brings together much valuable and up-to-date information. Most of the chapter headings are the same as in their (1941, o.p.) "The Opera: A History of Its Creation and Performance, 1600–1941." There are valuable additions, including a new study on American opera and the brand new "Annals of Performance."

Budden, Julian. THE OPERAS OF VERDI: From Oberto to Rigoletto. *Praeger* 2 vols. 1973 each $20.00

Cross, Milton. NEW COMPLETE STORIES OF THE GREAT OPERAS. *Doubleday* 1947 rev. by Karl Kohrs 1955 $6.95. Includes over 75 operas.

(With Karl Kohrs). MORE STORIES OF THE GREAT OPERAS. *Doubleday* 1971 $7.95

Crosten, William Loran. FRENCH GRAND OPERA: An Art and a Business. 1948. *Da Capo* 1972 $7.95

"The book should be of interest to many readers because of its subject and its non-technical style, and also because it is provocative in calling to mind so many parallel situations between spectacular entertainment in the bourgeois society of the Paris of Louis-Philippe and our American middle-class society of today"—*(Music Library Association Notes)*.

Dent, Edward Joseph. FOUNDATIONS OF ENGLISH OPERA. 1928. *Da Capo* 2nd ed. 1967 $10.50

MOZART'S OPERAS: A Critical Study. *Oxford* 2nd ed. 1947 pap. $4.50

Eaton, Quaintance. OPERA PRODUCTION ONE: A Handbook. 1966. *Da Capo* 1974 $12.50

OPERA PRODUCTION TWO: A Handbook. *Univ. of Minnesota Press* 1974 $12.50

Fellner, Rudolph. OPERA THEMES AND PLOTS. *Simon & Schuster* 1958 Fireside Bks. 1961 pap. $2.25

Gilman, Lawrence. ASPECTS OF MODERN OPERA. 1909. *Haskell* 1969 $12.95. Estimates and inquiries by one of the foremost critics of his time.

WAGNER'S OPERAS. 1937. *Scholarly Press* $14.50.

Gishford, Anthony, Ed. GRAND OPERA: The Story of the World's Leading Opera Houses and Personalities. *Viking* 1972 $14.95

Goldovsky, Boris. BRINGING OPERA TO LIFE: Operatic Acting and Stage Direction. *Prentice-Hall* (Appleton) 1968 $12.95

> "Useful as a handbook, containing a veritable mine of information on the theory and practice of opera staging in all its phases, an indispensable companion to the budding or seasoned opera directors alike"—*(Choice)*.

Grout, Donald Jay. A SHORT HISTORY OF OPERA. *Columbia* 1947 2nd ed. 1965 $13.50

> A comprehensive history of opera from the Greek lyric theater to the present. The 1965 edition has a new chapter on the post-World-War-II period. "The author has fulfilled his purpose admirably. You will find here little or no chitchat about the private lives of composers, singers, conductors and the other people who impinge on the world of opera. The approach is sober, scholarly and based on illuminating musicianship. Here are both the facts and an evaluation of them"—(Howard Taubman, in the *N.Y. Times*). Excellent bibliography.

Hetherington, John. MELBA. *Farrar, Straus* 1968 $7.50

> Dame Nellie Melba (Helen Porter Mitchell Armstrong) was one of the most celebrated divas in the history of opera. "Her career was a long one, covering nearly 40 years at London's Covent Garden. She was also popular in America in opera and in recital. She was a self-assured, colorful, and imperious egoist; but she had style, and in her own way and on her own terms was endearing, if not lovable. The literature about the singer is extensive, but there is room for a thorough and careful study such as this which tries to establish facts and correct myths"—*(LJ)*.

Howard, Patricia. GLUCK AND THE BIRTH OF MODERN OPERA. *St. Martin's* 1963 $8.95

THE OPERAS OF BENJAMIN BRITTEN: An Introduction. *Praeger* 1969 $7.95

Jacobs, Arthur, and Stanley Sadie. OPERA: A Modern Guide. *Drake Pub.* 1972 $9.95; *Int. Pubns. Service* 1972 $15.00

Kerman, Joseph. OPERA AS DRAMA. 1956. *Random* Vintage Bks. 1961 pap. $1.95

> The author demands that opera be treated as an individual art form in its own right. Rejecting the purely musical or purely literary approaches, he defines opera as drama articulated by music. In this light he discusses various works of Monteverdi, Purcell, Metastasio, Mozart, Verdi, Wagner, Stravinsky and Alban Berg.

Kobbé, Gustav. THE NEW KOBBÉ'S COMPLETE OPERA BOOK. 1922. Ed. and rev. by the Earl of Harewood *Putnam* 1954 1963 3rd ed. 1972 $12.95 4th ed. 1976 $20.00. The "Complete Opera Book" provides plots, leading airs and motives in musical notation, notes on the composers, and stage histories of more than 200 operas. This has long been a standard reference book for homes and libraries.

Kolodin, Irving. THE METROPOLITAN OPERA, 1883–1966: A Candid History. *Knopf* 1967 $17.50

> First published in 1936 as "The Metropolitan Opera," this was revised in 1953 as "The Story of the Metropolitan." The 1967 expanded edition retains much of the same material with "many fine pictures" added. Mr. Kolodin's "critical judgment is well known; no one could have done the job with more thoroughness. For the opera buff the book is a hard one to put down; for the music reference librarian it is indispensable"—*(LJ)*.

Lang, Paul Henry. CRITIC AT THE OPERA. *Norton* 1971 $7.95

"An excellent standard resource for students of music history, opera, music drama, and music aesthetics"—(*Choice*).

THE EXPERIENCE OF OPERA. *Norton* 1973 pap. $2.95

Martin, George. THE OPERA COMPANION: A Guide for the Casual Operagoer. Ill. by Everett Raymond Kinstler. 1961. *Apollo* 2 vols. 1970–72 pap. each $2.95; *Peter Smith* $5.00. Information for the layman on opera history, technique, voices, orchestra, ballet, claques, castrati; with synopses of 47 operas and descriptions of 26 modern operas.

Matz, Mary Jane. OPERA STARS IN THE SUN. 1955. *Greenwood* 1973 $15.00

Moore, Frank L. CROWELL'S HANDBOOK OF WORLD OPERA. 1961. *Greenwood* 1974 $27.50. An encyclopedic guide for singers and listeners.

Newman, Ernest. GREAT OPERAS. *Random* Vintage Bks. 2 vols. pap. Vol. 1 $1.95 Vol. 2 $2.40; *Peter Smith* 2 vols. set $8.50. By an eminent opera critic and commentator.

MORE STORIES OF FAMOUS OPERAS. *Knopf* 1943 $10.00

STORIES OF THE GREAT OPERAS AND THEIR COMPOSERS. 1930. *Scholarly Press* 3 vols. in 1 $24.50

WAGNER OPERAS. *Knopf* 1949 $15.00

This is a survey of Wagner's masterpieces from "The Flying Dutchman" to "Parsifal." "The profuse thematic illustrations are very useful, as also Newman's caution to readers not to take literally and exactly the names which officious commentators have given these various themes, or the explanations they have furnished of their 'meanings.' All this, to the Wagnerite, perfect or imperfect, is most informing and suggestive reading"—(*N.Y. Times*). "The great Wagnerian authority and music critic of the London Sunday Times, has produced another definitive and highly readable work that is certain to share in the enthusiastic critical acclaim which greeted his monumental biography of Richard Wagner"—(*San Francisco Chronicle*).

Orrey, Leslie. A CONCISE HISTORY OF OPERA. *Scribner* 1973 $7.95 pap. $4.95

Osborne, Charles. COMPLETE OPERAS OF VERDI. *Knopf* 1970 $10.00

Robinson, Michael F. NAPLES AND NEAPOLITAN OPERA. *Oxford* 1972 $25.75

"This admirably prepared and thoroughly documented volume is recommended for most music libraries"—(*LJ*).

OPERA BEFORE MOZART. *Hillary House* 1966 $5.00; *Apollo* 1967 pap. $1.95. A short historical study of opera from its beginning in 1597 up to the end of the 18th century.

Rosenthal, Harold, and John Warrack. THE CONCISE OXFORD DICTIONARY OF OPERA. *Oxford* 1964 rev. ed. 1972 $8.00

This contains over 3,000 entries with extensive cross-references. "Despite the brevity of the entries, biographical details are often capped with a warm comment on the subject's qualities. For operas of any significance the authors furnish a . . . scene-by-scene synopsis. Characters in operas are also identified, as well as opening lines of popular arias"—(*SR*).

Seltsam, William H., Comp. METROPOLITAN OPERA ANNALS. Introd. by Edward Johnson *Wilson* 1949 $12.00 First Supplement 1947–1957 fwd. by Rudolph Bing 1957 $6.00 Second Supplement 1957–1966 fwd. by Francis Robinson pub. in assoc. with *Metropolitan Opera Guild* 1968 $6.00

A chronicle of artists and performances 1883–1966. "The definitive work on the Met in which the most scrupulous standards of accuracy are maintained; essential for all sizeable music collections"—(*Choice*). The Second Supplement covers the last seasons at the old Metropolitan Opera House and features a complete list of artists' debuts, 1883–1966.

Simon, Henry W. ONE HUNDRED GREAT OPERAS AND THEIR STORIES. (Orig. "Festival of Opera") *Doubleday* rev. ed. 1968 pap. $2.50; *Peter Smith* new and abr. ed. $4.00

(Ed.). TREASURY OF GRAND OPERA. *Simon & Schuster* rev. ed. 1965 $12.50

(Ed.). THE VICTOR BOOK OF THE OPERA. *Simon & Schuster* 13th ed. 1968 $10.00

Sonneck, Oscar George Theodore. EARLY OPERA IN AMERICA. 1915. *Blom* 1964 $15.00; *Gordon Press* $29.95. Covers pre-Revolutionary and post-Revolutionary opera.

Towers, John. DICTIONARY-CATALOGUE OF OPERAS AND OPERETTAS. 1910. *Da Capo* 2 vols. 1967 Vol. 1 Dictionary of Operas and Operettas Vol. 2 Composers and Their Operas set $35.00

Wechsberg, Joseph. THE OPERA. *Macmillan* 1972 $7.95

VERDI. *Putnam* 1974 $15.00

Weisstein, Ulrich Werner, Ed. THE ESSENCE OF OPERA. 1964 *Norton* 1969 pap. $3.95. An anthology of writings on the opera.

Westerman, Gerhart von. OPERA GUIDE. Trans. from the German by Anne Ross; ed. with introd. by Harold Rosenthal *Dutton* 1965 1968 pap. $2.95

"Detailed and helpful synopses of [popular operas] are set in a running text which is in fact a history." Some omissions and unfamiliar emphases stem from the fact that it was written from the German point of view. "But the plan of the book is excellent, and it contains much information not easily available elsewhere"—(*LJ*).

White, Eric Walter. BENJAMIN BRITTEN: His Life and Operas. *Univ. of California Press* 1971 $8.95

"Indispensable for college libraries"—(*Choice*).

Film

Motion pictures, once regarded as a second rate art form, have now achieved intellectual respectability. Film societies are growing steadily in numbers and membership on American college campuses. Many of these societies specialize in the foreign cinema, which has produced some of the major artistic successes of this century; others show only "Old Hollywood" films or even cartoons. Still others feature only recent *avant-garde* pictures. The international film festivals held each year at Cannes and Venice regularly draw as many as 1,500 accredited critics and a large audience of undemanding enthusiasts. Understandably, these festivals vary widely in prestige and popularity. It is argued by film buffs that such esoteric gatherings as the International Experimental Film Festival at Knokke, Belgium, attract a smaller but a more discriminating public.

The commercial film industry is one of the few bright spots in our otherwise gloomy economy. In 1975 the common stocks of the major motion picture firms have generally outperformed the market and their growth potential is enormous (*Film Bulletin,* November 1975). According to *Variety,* the film "Jaws" is inching close to the $100,000,000 mark in returns from film rentals in the United States and Canada. It looks as if the returns from the world market will reach twice that sum. New pictures have been starting in Hollywood and on location at an unprecedented rate, at least for the last decade. The books included in this list cover the origins, the development, and the future of the moving picture industry.

Reference Works

Arnheim, Rudolph. FILM AS ART. 1958. *Univ. of California Press* 1960 pap. $1.95

Bluem, A. William, and Jason E. Squire. THE MOVIE BUSINESS: American Film Industry Practice. *Hastings House* 1972 $12.50 pap. $7.50

Blum, Daniel. *See Willis, John.*

Cohen, Joan. A VISUAL EXPLOSION: The Growth of Film Literature. *Choice* Vol. 10 No. 1, March 1973 pp. 26–40

Cowie, Peter, Ed. INTERNATIONAL FILM GUIDE. International Film Guide Ser. *A. S. Barnes* 10 vols. 1966–1975 pap. each $3.95 (1966, 1973 o.p.)

"Eminently useful, [this] seems well on its way to becoming the authoritative reference source on the growing edge of cinema"—(*SR*).

Dimmitt, Richard Bertrand. ACTOR'S GUIDE TO THE TALKIES: A Comprehensive Listing of 8,000 Feature-Length Films from January 1949, until December 1964. *Scarecrow Press* 2 vols. 1967 set $35.00. Vol. 1 indexes casts of 8,000 films arranged alphabetically by title and includes information for each as to year of production and producing or releasing company. Vol. 2 is a name index of the actors mentioned in Vol. 1.

THE FILM DAILY YEARBOOK OF MOTION PICTURES, 1970. *Arno* 1971 $25.00. An annual, offering vital statistics and facts about the industry as well as brief articles on the "film year."

THE FILM INDEX: Film as Art. Originally published by the *Museum of Modern Art* and *Wilson,* 1941. *Arno* 1966 $22.50. An exhaustive bibliography of film literature and a guide to filmmakers and films from the days of silent cinema through 1936. Superb indexing. The projected accompanying volumes were never completed.

Garbicz, Adam, and Jacek Klinowski. CINEMA, THE MAGIC VEHICLE: A Guide to Its Achievement. *Scarecrow Press* 1975 $8.50

Geduld, Harry M. ILLUSTRATED GLOSSARY OF FILM TERMS. *Holt* 1973 $3.95

Graham, Peter. DICTIONARY OF THE CINEMA. International Film Guide Ser. *A. S. Barnes* 1964 1968 $4.50 pap. $2.25

A "useful . . . international compendium of biographies and definitions"—(*SR*).

Halliwell, Leslie. THE FILMGOER'S COMPANION. *Farrar, Straus* (Hill & Wang) 1966 4th ed. 1974 $25.00

"An indispensable international encyclopedia of films. Over 1,000 pages and over 6,000 entries"—(Publisher's note).

Manchel, Frank. FILM STUDY: A Resource Guide. *Fairleigh Dickinson Univ. Press* 1973 $18.00

"An attempt to list definitively the various sources or materials connected with film study"—(Preface).

Niver, Kemp R. MOTION PICTURES FROM THE LIBRARY OF CONGRESS PAPER PRINT COLLECTION. *Univ. of California Press* 1968 $35.00

A "unique and authoritative study" describing, "often with casts and credits . . . some 3,000 films released in the U.S. between 1894 and 1912"—(*SR*).

Sadoul, Georges. DICTIONARY OF FILM MAKERS. Trans. from the French by Peter Morris *Univ. of California Press* 1972 $14.50 pap. $4.95

"Contains a thousand entries devoted to directors, scriptwriters, cinematographers, art directors, composers, producers, inventors—but not actors and actresses"—(Preface).

DICTIONARY OF FILMS. Trans. by Peter Morris *Univ. of California Press* 1972 $16.50 pap. $5.95

Salem, James M. A GUIDE TO CRITICAL REVIEWS: Pt. 4, The Screenplay from the Jazz Singer to Dr. Strangelove. *Scarecrow Press* 2 vols. 1971 $30.00

Speed, Maurice, Ed. FILM REVIEW: 1973–1974. *Transatlantic* 1974 $12.50. Yearbook. Includes "Necrology," World Film Review, descriptive and pictorial sections and complete Filmographies for all feature productions.

Talbot, Daniel, Ed. FILM: An Anthology. *Univ. of California Press* 2nd ed. 1966 pap. $2.45

University of California, Los Angeles. MOTION PICTURES: A Catalog of Books, Periodicals, Screen Plays and Production Stills. *G. K. Hall* new ed. 1973 $70.00

WHO'S WHO IN HOLLYWOOD, 1900–1975. *Arlington* 2 vols. 1976 set $35.00

Willis, John, Ed. SCREEN WORLD. (Orig. "Daniel Blum's Screen World") *Crown* Vol. 21 (1970) Vol. 23 (1972) Vol. 24 (1973) each $8.95 Vol. 25 (1974) 25th anniv. ed. $9.95 (1959–69, 1971 o.p.). A valuable pictorial and statistical annual founded in 1959 and until 1963 edited by the late Daniel Blum.

History and Criticism

Anderson, Joseph L., and Donald Richie. THE JAPANESE FILM: Art and Industry. *Grove* 1960 Evergreen Bks. pap. $3.95

"A definitive and engrossing work by a scholar and journalist"—(*Journal of the Soc. of Motion Picture and TV Engineers*). Covers the period from 1898 to the present.

Anger, Kenneth. HOLLYWOOD BABYLON. *Straight Arrow* 1975 $14.95

"A delicious 306 page box of poisoned bonbons"—(*N.Y. Times*).

Annan, David. CATASTROPHE! The End in the Cinema. *Crown* 1975 pap. $2.95

"Collects all the overwhelming devastation ever seen on the film into one huge orgy"—(Publisher's note).

Armes, Roy. FILM AND REALITY: An Historical Survey. *Penguin* Pelican Bks. 1974 pap. $1.95

"This study is divided into three parts, each exemplifying a particular view of reality: Pt. 1 Film Realism, indexical, covers the cinema in the earliest, most functional phase . . . Pt. 2 Film Illusion, iconical, covers the fiction film, Hollywood, the stars, the various genres, what most people think of as the movies, and Pt. 3 Film Modernism, symbolic, covers the modern movement from Eisenstein onwards"—(*Encounter*).

THE FRENCH CINEMA SINCE 1946. *A. S. Barnes* 2 vols. 1966. rev. enl. ed. 1970 pap. each $2.95

"A clear and concise analysis and guide"—(NYPL).

PATTERNS OF REALISM: Neo-Realism in Italian Cinema. *A. S. Barnes* 1971 $12.00

Atkins, Thomas R., Ed. SEXUALITY IN THE MOVIES. *Indiana Univ. Press* 1975 $12.50

Balio, Tino. UNITED ARTISTS: The Company Built by the Stars. *Univ. of Wisconsin Press* 1975 $15.00

"This history, which treats those years in which the founders controlled the company, is based on the rich corporate records of United Artists . . . [This] is the first full and scholarly history of a major film company"—(Publisher's note).

Ball, Robert Hamilton. SHAKESPEARE ON SILENT FILM. *Theatre Arts* 1968 $6.25. This gives a rare picture of the early film industry.

Balshofer, Fred J., and Arthur C. Miller with the assistance of Bebe Bergsten. ONE REEL A WEEK. Fwd. by Hugh Kenner *Univ. of California Press* 1968 $7.95

Two cameramen record their 50 years of film experience. "Their intimate accounts of the invidious commercial piracies in the cinema's days of infancy, the attempts to monopolize the making of pictures, and the methods used by independent companies to counteract these endeavors make the book important in the field"—(*LJ*). Photographs.

Barnouw, Erik, and Sukrahmaryan Krishnaswamy. INDIAN FILM. *Columbia* 1963 $12.00. A history of the industry in a social context.

Battcock, Gregory, Ed. THE NEW AMERICAN CINEMA: A Critical Anthology. *Dutton* 1967 pap. $1.95. Twenty-nine articles by filmmakers and directors on underground cinema in the United States.

Bazin, André. WHAT IS CINEMA? Trans. by Hugh Gray *Univ. of California Press* 2 vols. 1967–1971 Vol. 1 (1967) $6.95 Vol. 2 (1971) $7.95 pap. 1968 each $2.45

Significant essays, the first to appear since his death in 1958, of the most important French film critic of his time. "It was Bazin, as the first important editor of the magazine *Cahiers du Cinéma*, who was particularly responsible for the intense dialogue that generated the New Wave, a term now so inclusive as to be empty, but then referring to the films of a group of such friends and disciples as the directors François Truffaut, Alain Resnais and Jean-Luc Godard"—(*N.Y. Times*).

Blum, Daniel. A NEW PICTORIAL HISTORY OF THE TALKIES. 1958. *Putnam* rev. ed. by John Kobal 1968 rev. ed. 1973 $10.00 pap. $5.95

A PICTORIAL HISTORY OF THE SILENT SCREEN. *Grosset* 1955 $7.95; *Putnam* 1972 pap. $4.95

SCREEN WORLD. 1949 1951–1959. *Biblo & Tannen* 10 vols. 1969 set $135.00

Bogle, Donald. TOMS, COONS, MULATTOES, MAMMIES, AND BUCKS: An Interpretive History of Blacks in American Films. *Viking* 1973 $12.50

This "book is a long overdue study of the black contribution to American films. . . . His responses are fresh and well informed. He knows his films and has placed them carefully into a cultural context"—(*Choice*).

Brownlow, Kevin. THE PARADE'S GONE BY . . . *Knopf* 1968 $15.00

This is a serious book about the silent film in America, with interesting dicussions of technique. Arthur Mayer writes in the *N.Y. Times:* "Not since Terry Ramsaye's memorable 'A Million and One Nights' [*see below*] was published back in 1926 have the colorful early days of the movies . . . been re-created and freshly documented with such flair and fervor as here. A must for movie buffs . . . it is also warmly recommended reading" for those who attend less than five new pictures a year. "In a nostalgic melody of praise for the 'golden era' of silent movies from 1916 to 1928," Brownlow combines his own reminiscences with interviews he has held with stars, producers and pioneering directors. The arguable question, according to Mr. Mayer, is Brownlow's thesis that the "art of movies was 'killed' by the advent of sound."

Butler, Ivan. THE WAR FILM. *A. S. Barnes* 1974 $8.95

"A critique of British and U.S. made films, and influential European and Japanese movies, produced from the pre-World War I era to the present"—(*Booklist*).

Clarens, Carlos. AN ILLUSTRATED HISTORY OF THE HORROR FILM. *Putnam* 1967 Capricorn Bks. 1968 pap. $2.95

A "fact-filled compendium" (*SR*) which provides "intelligent and fascinating coverage of one of the movies' great genres"—(*PW*).

Cowie, Peter. FIFTY MAJOR FILM-MAKERS. *A. S. Barnes* 1974 $20.00

HOLLYWOOD, 1920–1970. *A. S. Barnes* 1973 $25.00

(Ed.). CONCISE HISTORY OF THE CINEMA. *A. S. Barnes* 2 vols. 1970 pap. each $3.50

Crowther, Bosley. THE GREAT FILMS: Fifty Golden Years of Motion Pictures. *Putnam* 1967 $10.00 pap. $4.95. A study of 50 significant films by the former *N.Y. Times* film critic.

Durgnat, Raymond. THE CRAZY MIRROR: Hollywood Comedy and the American Image. *Horizon Press* 1970 $12.50

"Discusses both major and minor filmmakers, ranging from Sennett through sophisticated like Lubitsch and Sturges all the way to Jerry Lewis"—(*Choice*).

FILMS AND FEELINGS. *M.I.T. Press* 1967 1971 $6.95 pap. $2.95. The British film critic discusses a popular and cultural art and constructs an aesthetic.

Eames, John Douglas. THE MGM STORY: The Complete History of Fifty Roaring Years. *Crown* 1975 $19.95

"A total of 1,684 films is covered individually in text and picture, all arranged in chronological order"—(Publisher's note).

Evans, Mark. SOUNDTRACK: The Music of the Movies. *Hopkinson & Blake* 1975 $10.00 pap. $6.50

"A young musician attempts to present the highlights of film music history and explain the functions, ethics, and esthetics of film scores"—(*PW*).

Everson, William K. THE BAD GUYS: A Pictorial History of the Movie Villain. *Citadel Press* 1968 pap. $4.95

"A most remarkable rogue's gallery of men you love to hate. . . . The text is written with wit, charm and erudition"—(*LJ*).

CLASSICS OF THE HORROR FILM. *Citadel Press* 1974 $12.00

THE DETECTIVE IN FILM. *Citadel Press* 1972 $9.95 pap. 1974 $4.95

PICTORIAL HISTORY OF THE WESTERN FILM. *Citadel Press* 1971 $10.00 pap. $4.95

Eyles, Allen. THE WESTERN: An Illustrated Index. *A. S. Barnes* 1973 $8.95

(With Pat Billings). HOLLYWOOD TODAY. *A. S. Barnes* 1971 pap. $2.95

Fell, John L. FILM AND THE NARRATIVE TRADITION. *Univ. of Oklahoma Press* 1974 $9.95

Fell "demonstrates how the story film was the logical and interdisciplinary culmination of a technological and aesthetic movement"—(*LJ*).

Fielding, Raymond. THE TECHNIQUE OF SPECIAL EFFECTS CINEMATOGRAPHY. *Hastings House* 3rd rev. & enl. ed. 1972 $18.50

Franklin, Joe. CLASSICS OF THE SILENT SCREEN. *Citadel Press* 1967 pap. $4.95

Friar, Ralph, and Natasha Friar. THE ONLY GOOD INDIAN: The Hollywood Gospel. *Drama Bk. Specialists* 1973 $12.50

Fulton, A. R. MOTION PICTURES: The Development of an Art from Silent Films to the Age of Television. *Univ. of Oklahoma Press* 1960 1970 $6.95

Geduld, Harry M. THE BIRTH OF THE TALKIES: From Edison to Jolson. *Indiana Univ. Press* 1975 $12.50

"The story of the invention of the technology necessary for the talking picture as we know it today"—*(LJ)*.

Gessner, Robert. THE MOVING IMAGE: A Guide to Cinematic Literacy. *Dutton* 1968 $9.95 pap. 1970 $3.95

This book by a film scholar is a comprehensive study of cinematic dramaturgy—of film writing and of the technical process. Mr. Gessner documents his analyses with examples from Hollywood cinema, the "tightly plotted [American and foreign] classics," and from the "scriptless" films of Godard, Resnais and other moderns. "Beautifully planned and executed"—*(PW)*.

Gow, Gordon. HOLLYWOOD IN THE FIFTIES. *A. S. Barnes* 1971 pap. $2.95

SUSPENSE IN THE CINEMA. International Film Guide Ser. *A. S. Barnes* 1968 pap. $2.95; *Paperback Lib.* 1971 pap. $1.25. A British critic documents an interesting study with recent examples from international films.

Greenberg, Harvey R. THE MOVIES ON YOUR MIND: Film Classics on the Couch, from Fellini to Frankenstein. *Saturday Review Press* 1975 $10.95 pap. $4.95

Griffith, Richard, and Arthur Mayer. THE MOVIES: The Definitive Pictorial History of American Motion Pictures. *Simon & Schuster* rev. ed. 1971 $19.95

Hall, Ben M. THE GOLDEN AGE OF THE MOVIE PALACE: The Best Remaining Seats. *Crown* 1975 pap. $4.95

Harmon, Jim, and Donald F. Glut. THE GREAT MOVIE SERIALS: Their Sound and Fury. *Doubleday* 1972 $7.95

Higham, Charles. WARNER BROTHERS. *Scribner* 1975 $9.95

Hochman, Stanley, Ed. AMERICAN FILM DIRECTORS. Library of Film Criticism Ser. *Ungar* 1974 $18.50

"The chronologically arranged excerpts under each director's name are drawn from specialized periodicals, general publications, collections of film [and] private clippings files"—(Foreword).

Houston, Penelope. THE CONTEMPORARY CINEMA, 1945–1963. *Penguin* Pelican 1963 pap. $1.75; *Gannon* $5.00

An excellent introductory study providing "knowledgeable commentary on what has happened in the cinema since World War II"—(NYPL).

Huss, Roy, and Norman Silverstein. THE FILM EXPERIENCE: Elements of Motion Picture Art. *Harper* 1968 $7.95; *Dell* Delta Bks. 1969 pap. $2.25. Examines the art of such directors as Griffith, Lang, Welles and Antonioni.

Huss, Roy, and T. J. Ross, Eds. FOCUS ON THE HORROR FILM. *Prentice-Hall* Spectrum Bks. 1972 pap. $2.45

Jacobs, Lewis, Ed. THE EMERGENCE OF FILM ART: The Evolution and Development of the Motion Picture as an Art, from 1900 to the Present. *Hopkinson and Blake* 1969 $10.00 pap. $5.50

"Jacobs' new anthology is distinguished by the same qualities of clear organization and selective discrimination that have made his previous *Introduction to the Art of the Movies* an invaluable source of information. Covering the whole spectrum of the cinema, he succeeds again in condensing a great amount of substantial material into an easily manageable format"—(George Amberg).

INTRODUCTION TO THE ART OF THE MOVIES. *Farrar, Straus* Noonday 1960 pap. $3.95; *Octagon* 1970 $10.00. An anthology of ideas on the nature of film art.

THE MOVIES AS MEDIUM. *Farrar, Straus* 1970 $8.95 Noonday 1970 pap. $3.65; *Octagon* 1973 $13.50

THE RISE OF THE AMERICAN FILM: A Critical History. Studies in Culture and Communications Ser. *Teachers College* 1968 $12.50 pap. $5.25

Jacobs' work traces movies from the time of their introduction to 1939 and includes an essay entitled "Experimental Cinema in America 1921–1947." "The Rise of the American Film" qualifies at once "not only as an authoritative study of the movie and its growth as a commodity-art and social force but . . . as a vitally interesting and romantic narrative"—(*N.Y. Times*).

Kael, Pauline. DEEPER INTO MOVIES. *Little-Atlantic* 1973 $12.95; *Bantam* 1974 pap. $2.25. Her movie reviews from the *New Yorker* from Sept. 1969 to March 1972.

Kauffman, Stanley. LIVING IMAGES: Film Criticism and Comment. *Harper* 1974 $10.00 pap. $4.95

(With Bruce Henstell, Eds.). AMERICAN FILM CRITICISM FROM THE BEGINNINGS TO CITIZEN KANE. *Liveright* 1973 $12.00 pap. $3.95
"Reviews of significant films at the time they first appeared"—(Publisher's note).

Kerr, Walter. THE SILENT CLOWNS. *Knopf* 1975 $17.95
"A book about the great and near-great comic artists who carried the language of the silent screen to its peak of eloquence"—(*N.Y. Times*).

Knight, Arthur. THE LIVELIEST ART: A Panoramic History of the Movies. *New Am. Lib.* Mentor Bks. 1959 1971 pap. $1.25

Kracauer, Siegfried. FROM CALIGARI TO HITLER: A Psychological History of the German Film. *Princeton Univ. Press* 1947 $11.50 pap. $2.95

THEORY OF FILM: The Redemption of Physical Reality. *Oxford* 1960 Galaxy Bks. 1965 pap. $2.95

Lahue, Kalton C. CONTINUED NEXT WEEK: A History of the Moving Picture Serial. *Univ. of Oklahoma Press* 1964 1969 $6.95
"An informative study"—(*SR*).

RIDERS OF THE RANGE: The Sagebrush Heroes of the Sound Screen. *A. S. Barnes* 1973 $10.00

WORLD OF LAUGHTER: The Motion Picture Comedy Short 1910–1930. *Univ. of Oklahoma Press* 1966 1972 $6.95

(With Terry Brewer, Eds.) KOPS AND CUSTARDS: The Legend of Keystone Films. *Univ. of Oklahoma Press* 1968 $6.95 pap. $2.95
Lahue discusses the creator of Keystone comedies, Mack Sennett, the actors and the company's corporate history. The Keystone shorts (made from 1912 to 1917) "were the pacesetters of early film comedy, and today their name is synonymous with frenzied slapstick in which chases, custard pies, cops, and cuties seem to be involved in a mad ballet"—(*LJ*). An appendix lists all the Keystone films chronologically.

Larkin, Rochelle. HAIL, COLUMBIA. *Arlington House* 1975 $17.95

Lasky, Jesse L., Jr. WHATEVER HAPPENED TO HOLLYWOOD? *T. Y. Crowell* 1975 $8.95

Lawson, John Howard. FILM: The Creative Process. *Farrar, Straus* (Hill & Wang) 1964 2nd ed. 1967 pap. $2.95. By a well-known writer for Hollywood.

Leprohon, Pierre. THE ITALIAN CINEMA. Trans. by R. Greaves and O. Stallybrass *Praeger* 1973 $10.00 pap. $4.95
"Examines the Italian cimena from the earliest Italian inventors of projectors up to the cinema of 1969. . . . [The author's] incredible condensation of critical judgment upon individual films as well as his wealth of background information on filmmakers . . . make this an invaluable reference tool"—(*Choice*).

Leyda, Jay. DIANYING: An Account of Films and the Film Audience in China. *M.I.T. Press* 1972 $12.50

KINO: A History of the Russian and Soviet Film. *Hillary House* 1960 $16.50; *Macmillan* Collier Bks. 1973 pap. $4.95
"A meticulous study of the pre-Soviet and early Soviet silent films with some coverage of the wartime period"—(*Journal of the Society of Motion Picture and TV Engineers*).

LIFE GOES TO THE MOVIES. *Time-Life Bks.* 1975 $19.95. A pictorial review of the extensive coverage *Life* gave to Hollywood during its years of publication.

Low, Rachel. THE HISTORY OF THE BRITISH FILM, 1918–1929. *Bowker* 1974 $18.50
   "A definitive history of the British film industry"—*(Choice)*.

McCaffrey, Donald W. THE GOLDEN AGE OF SOUND COMEDY. *A. S. Barnes* 1973 $15.00

MacCann, Richard Dyer, Ed. FILM: A Montage of Theories. *Dutton* 1966 pap. $2.75.
   Previously published essays by Hitchcock, Sennett, Fellini and Bergman, among
   others.

MacDonald, Dwight. DWIGHT MACDONALD ON MOVIES. *Prentice-Hall* 1969 $9.95
   "A collection of essays on films written during the last 40 years"—*(Choice)*.

Macgowan, Kenneth. BEHIND THE SCREEN: The History and Techniques of the Movies.
   Dell 1965 Delta pap. $3.95. An authority writes on what goes into the making of films.

Madsen, Axel. THE NEW HOLLYWOOD: American Movies in the 70's. *T. Y. Crowell* 1975
   $7.95
   "One of the few books to suggest the relationship of movie art to capitalism"—*(LJ)*.

Michael, Paul. THE ACADEMY AWARDS: A Pictorial History. *Crown* 3rd rev. ed. 1975 $9.95

Murray, Edward. NINE AMERICAN FILM CRITICS: A Study of Theory and Practice. *Ungar*
   1975 $9.50
   "An analysis of nine writers chosen as 'representative' American film critics"—*(LJ)*.

Nilsen, Vladimir. THE CINEMA AS A GRAPHIC ART. *Farrar, Straus* (Hill & Wang) 1959 pap.
   1972 $2.95. An important study on the use of the camera in filmmaking.

O'Leary, Liam. THE SILENT CINEMA. *Dutton* 1965 pap. $1.95. Surveys the international
   scene with brief text and excellent stills.

Pudovkin, V. I. FILM TECHNIQUE AND FILM ACTING. 1928. Trans. from the Russian by
   Ivor Montagu *Crown* 1959 $3.75; *Grove* Black Cat Bks. pap. 1970 $2.25; *Wehman*
   $5.95; *Richard West* repr. of 1949 ed. 1975 $5.75

Ramsaye, Terry. A MILLION AND ONE NIGHTS. 1926. *Simon & Schuster* 1964 $10.00 pap.
   $3.95. A classic early history of Hollywood and all its works.

Reisz, Karel, and Gavin Millar. THE TECHNIQUE OF FILM EDITING. Introd. by Thorold
   Dickinson Library of Communications Technique Ser. *Hastings House* 1953 rev. ed.
   1968 $14.50 pap. $7.20
   This has become a classic of film literature. Extensively expanded to include a study of the 50's
   and 60's, covers developments such as wide-screen photography, *cinéma vérité* and the documentary film of ideas, the "New Wave" and the impact of the individual directors Truffaut, Godard,
   Resnais and Antonioni. "If Part I . . . is standard reading for all serious film students, Part II is a
   revelation for anyone interested in understanding the contemporary cinema"—*(LJ)*.

Renan, Sheldon. AN INTRODUCTION TO THE AMERICAN UNDERGROUND FILM. *Dutton* 1967
   pap. $2.50. Traces its history from the early French and German expressionists to the
   present.

Richie, Donald. JAPANESE CINEMA: Film Style and National Character. *Doubleday* Anchor
   Bks. 1971 pap. $3.95

Robinson, David. THE HISTORY OF WORLD CINEMA. *Stein & Day* 1973 $12.50 pap. 1974
   $4.95
   "An outline of film history—a skeleton chart, with a few landmarks dotted in, on which the
   reader can plot his own experiences of cinema"—(Preface).

Robinson, William R., Ed. MAN AND THE MOVIES. *Louisiana State Univ. Press* 1967 $7.95;
   Penguin Pelican Bks. 1969 pap. $2.95. A sophisticated collection of 20 essays on the
   art of cinema by various hands.

Rosen, Marjorie. POPCORN VENUS: Women, Movies, and the American Dream. *Coward*
   1973 $9.95
   "The first major retrospective on women in films"—(Publisher's note).

Sarris, Andrew. HOLLYWOOD VOICES. *Bobbs* 1972 $7.50

   THE PRIMAL SCREEN: Essays on Film and Related Subjects. *Simon & Schuster* 1973 $9.95

Scheuer, Steven H. THE MOVIE BOOK. *Playboy Press* 1974 $19.95

"A movie buff's delight"—(*Booklist*).

Schickel, Richard. MOVIES: The History of an Art and an Institution. *Basic Bks.* 1964 $6.45

"A stimulating book" by the *Life* film critic. "The coverage is international insofar as foreign films and film-making have had an impact upon America"—(*LJ*).

THE PLATINUM YEARS: On the Set with the Great Movies and Stars of the Last Three Decades. *Random* 1974 $25.00

(Ed.) THE MEN WHO MADE THE MOVIES. *Atheneum* 1975 $12.95

Sennett, Ted. LUNATICS AND LOVERS: A Tribute to the Giddy and Glittering Era of the Screen's "Screwballs" and Romantic Comedies. *Arlington House* 1974 $11.95

WARNER BROTHERS PRESENTS. *Arlington House* 1971 $11.95

Simon, John. MOVIES INTO FILM: Film Criticism 1967–1970. *Dial* 1971 $9.95; *Dell* Delta Bks. 1972 pap. $2.95

PRIVATE SCREENINGS: Views of the Cinema of the Sixties. *Macmillan* 1967 $5.95

This book consists primarily of Mr. Simon's articles written for the *New Leader* between 1963 and 1966. One defines the author's stringent "critical credo," another is devoted to a scathing attack on Godard, Warhol and the underground film-makers for their "sloppy," "mindless" and "arbitrary" creations. Despite its unflinching moral bias, Mr. Simon's work remains a "valuable account of 20th-Century European film-making"—(*LJ*).

Skolsky, Sidney. DON'T GET ME WRONG: I Love Hollywood. *Putnam* 1975 $7.95

"A memoir covering the more than 40 years the author has spent reporting on the movie business"—(*PW*).

Spottiswoode, Raymond. THE FOCAL ENCYCLOPEDIA OF FILM AND TELEVISION: Techniques. *Hastings House* 1974 $37.50

Stephenson, Ralph. THE ANIMATED FILM. *A. S. Barnes* rev. ed. 1973 pap. $2.95

(With Jean R. Debrix) THE CINEMA AS ART. *Penguin* Pelican 1965 pap. $1.65; *Gannon* $4.50. A provocative introductory analysis.

Talbot, Daniel, Comp. FILM: An Anthology. 1959 *Univ. of California Press* 2nd ed. 1966 pap. $2.45. Excellent compilation covering all aspects of motion pictures and their history in the United States, France, Germany and Russia.

Taylor, John Russell. DIRECTORS AND DIRECTIONS: Cinema for the Seventies. *Farrar, Straus* (Hill & Wang) 1975 $10.00 pap. $3.45

"What each of the nine contemporary film directors surveyed in this book has in common is a driving determination 'to explore his own personality' in making films"—(*LJ*).

Tyler, Parker. CLASSICS OF THE FOREIGN FILM. *Citadel* 1962 Corinth Bks. 1967 pap. $4.95. Discussion of 75 films chronologically arranged from 1919 to 1961.

MAGIC AND MYTH OF THE MOVIES. *Simon & Schuster* 1970 $5.95 Touchstone-Clarion Bks. 1970 pap. $1.95

A PICTORIAL HISTORY OF SEX IN FILMS. *Citadel* 1974 $12.00

Wagenknecht, Edward. THE MOVIES IN THE AGE OF INNOCENCE. *Univ. of Oklahoma Press* 1962 $7.95

This recommended critical history of the silent screen is "fortified by well-documented research and recent screenings of many old films." But its special character and its very real charm grow out of this eminent critic's long career as a moviegoer and his personal reactions to early films, directors and stars.

Walker, Alexander. HOLLYWOOD UK: The British Film Industry in the Sixties. *Stein & · Day* 1975 $15.00

"Gives witness to the various shades of creativity tendered by the decade's British filmmakers"—(*Booklist*).

West, Jessamyn. TO SEE THE DREAM. *Harcourt* 1957 $3.95; *Avon Bks.* 1974 pap. $1.25

This tells, with great charm, from the point of view of the writer of a filmed novel, the story of the making of "The Friendly Persuasion," starring Gary Cooper. It is by the well-known author of the book of the same title about a pioneer family of Quakers. Miss West went to Hollywood to write its script and attend its rebirth in movie form.

White, David Manning, and Richard Averson. THE CELLULOID WEAPON: Social Comment in the American Film. *Beacon* 1972 $14.95

Wood, Michael. AMERICA IN THE MOVIES, or Santa Maria It Had Slipped My Mind. *Basic Bks.* 1975 $10.00

"This work has an almost unheard-of combination of virtues for a movie book—lucid, well informed, and obviously written in high spirits"—(*N.Y. Times Bk. Review*).

People in Film–Recent Books

Astor, Mary. LIFE ON FILM. *Dial* (Delacorte) 1971 $7.50

Ayfre, Amedée, and others. THE FILMS OF ROBERT BRESSON. *Praeger* 1970 $4.95 pap. $2.50

"A highly technical, almost adoring collection of articles by various cinema authorities—Bresson's best known film, *Diary of a Country Priest*, is by consensus a masterpiece, and is on most lists of the ten all-time best films"—(*Choice*).

Carter, Randolph. THE WORLD OF FLO ZIEGFIELD. *Praeger* 1974 $14.95

Eyles, Allen. JOHN WAYNE AND THE MOVIES. *A. S. Barnes* 1974 $15.00

Gilliat, Penelope. JEAN RENOIR: Essays, Conversations, Reviews. *McGraw-Hill* 1975 pap. $2.95

Gish, Lillian. DOROTHY AND LILLIAN GISH. *Scribner* 1973 $19.95

Glatzer, Richard, and John Raeburn, Eds. FRANK CAPRA: The Man and His Films. *Univ. of Michigan Press* 1975 pap. $3.95

"A well balanced collection of essays which place Capra's films in their historical setting"—(*LJ*).

Hammond, Paul. MARVELOUS MÉLIÈS. *St. Martin's* 1975 $10.00

"Here is the first book in English devoted to the life and work of this great French filmmaker"—(*LJ*).

Harrison, Rex. REX. *Morrow* 1975 $7.95

"A life well played with zany adventures, reversals of fortune, and echos of tragedy"—(*LJ*).

Lahr, John. NOTES ON A COWARDLY LION: A Biography of Bert Lahr. *Knopf* 1970 $8.95
"A first rate theater biography"—(*Choice*).

Lawrence, Jerome. ACTOR: The Life and Times of Paul Muni. *Putnam* 1974 $10.00
"A highly vivacious biography"—(*Booklist*).

Marx, Arthur. GOLDWYN: A Biography of the Man behind the Myth. *Hawthorn* 1976 $12.50

Marx, Samuel. MAYER AND THALBERG: The Make-Believe Saints. *Random* 1975 $10.00

"The author . . . has penned a study that adds considerably to the lore and legend of Hollywood. . . . Despite their immense power, the pair are portrayed very favorably"—(*LJ*).

Niven, David. BRING ON THE EMPTY HORSES. *Putnam* 1975 $9.95. Engaging memories and anecdotes of bygone Hollywood contemporaries.

THE MOON'S A BALLOON. *Putnam* 1972 $7.95; *Dell* 1973 pap. $1.75

Palmer, Lilli. CHANGE LOBSTERS—AND DANCE: An Autobiography. *Macmillan* 1975 $8.95
"The most enjoyable theater memoir in recent years"—(*LJ*).

Pratley, Gerald. THE CINEMA OF JOHN HUSTON. *A. S. Barnes* 1974 $8.95

Quirk, Lawrence J. THE FILMS OF FREDERICK MARCH. *Citadel Press* 1971 $9.95

THE FILMS OF PAUL NEWMAN. *Citadel Press* 1971 $9.95

Richie, Donald W. GEORGE STEVENS: An American Romantic. *Museum of Modern Art* 1970 pap. $2.50

Robinson, David. BUSTER KEATON. *Indiana Univ. Press* 1969 $6.95 pap. $1.95

Schickel, Richard. HAROLD LLOYD: The Shape of Laughter. *N.Y. Graphic Society* 1974 $35.00

Silver, Charles. MARLENE DIETRICH. *Pyramid Bks.* 1974 pap. $1.75

Swindell, Larry. BODY AND SOUL: The Story of John Garfield. *Morrow* 1975 $8.95

> Garfield was "the prototype for the 'new actor' (the powerful and idiosyncratic Brando, the rebel and loser James Dean, [and] the sexual presences of Newman and McQueen)"—*(LJ)*.

SCREWBALL: The Life of Carole Lombard. *Morrow* 1975 $8.95

> The author "provides many new details in this carefully balanced portrait"—*(LJ)*.

Thomas, Tony. HARRY WARREN AND THE HOLLYWOOD MUSICAL. *Citadel Press* 1975 $17.95

ANTONIONI, MICHELANGELO. 1912–

Michelangelo Antonioni of Italy, a former film critic and screen writer, made his first feature film in 1954. He broke away from the "neo-realism" then in vogue and, in a style rigorously disciplined, distinguished himself as an original artist by his concern with the interior states of isolated man. His subjects are often from the prosperous middle class and his only social criticism oblique. "*L'Avventura*," his sixth film, established his fame. He is the director of the recent "Blow-Up," set in mod London. "Zabriski Point" concerns contemporary American youth and its politics.

L'AVVENTURA. *Grove* 1969 Black Cat Bks. pap. $1.95. A film script.

BLOW-UP. Modern Film Scripts Ser. *Simon & Schuster* 1970 pap. $2.95

ANTONIONI: Four Screenplays. L'Avventura; Il Guido; L'Eclisse; La Notte. *Grossman* 1971 pap. $3.95

RED DESERT. (And "Zabriskie Point") Modern Film Scripts Ser. *Simon & Schuster* 1972 pap. $2.95

Books about Antonioni

Michelangelo Antonioni. By Pierre Leprohon. *Simon & Schuster* 1963 $4.50 pap. $1.95

BERGMAN, INGMAR. 1918–

Ingmar Bergman, Swedish screen writer, playwright, and stage and film director and producer, is a major figure among contemporary "complete filmmakers." "The Seventh Seal" (1956) was the first of many films, sometimes poetic, often bleak and uncompromising in theme, which brought him international recognition. His subject is almost invariably the cosmic relationships of man and God, life and death. Always interesting although not always counted as wholly successful in what he has set out to do, Bergman has been one of those chiefly responsible for the present popularity of film among the American student generation. In 1967 his "Persona" was selected by the National Society of Film Critics as the "best film" of the year with the "best director" and "best actress." In early 1969 his "Shame," a drama of war, received the same awards from that group.

FOUR SCREENPLAYS: Smiles of a Summer Night, The Seventh Seal, Wild Strawberries, The Magician. Trans. from the Swedish by Lars Malmstrom and David Kushner; introd. by the author *Simon & Schuster* 1960 1969 pap. $2.95

THE SEVENTH SEAL. Modern Film Scripts Ser. *Simon & Schuster* 1968 pap. $2.25

WILD STRAWBERRIES. *Simon & Schuster* 1969 pap. $1.95

THREE FILMS. Trans. by Paul B. Austin *Grove* Evergreen Bks. 1969 pap. $2.45. Includes Through a Glass Darkly, Winter Light, The Silence.

PERSONA and SHAME. *Grossman* 1972 $7.95

SCENES FROM A MARRIAGE. Trans. by Alan Blair *Pantheon* 1974 $6.95; *Bantam* 1974 pap. $1.75

BERGMAN ON BERGMAN: Interviews with Ingmar Bergman by Stig Björkman, Torsten Manns, and Jonas Sima. *Simon & Schuster* 1974 $9.95

> "In an extensive interview which spanned a three year period, Bergman reveals clearly and accessibly why it is that he is thought of as one of Europe's greatest filmmakers"—*(Choice)*.

Books about Bergman

The Personal Vision of Ingmar Bergman. By Jörn Donner. Trans. by Holger Lundbergh. 1964. *Bks. for Libraries* $14.50

Ingmar Bergman. By Brigitta Steene. World Authors Ser. *Twayne* 1967 $5.95; *St. Martin's* 1967 pap. $3.95
A somewhat diffuse work which will, however, serve as "a very fine introduction to Bergman for someone who has seen his films, and there is a good selected bibliography"—(*LJ*).
Ingmar Bergman. By Robin Wood. *Praeger* 1969 $5.95
Silence of God: A Creative Response to the Films of Ingmar Bergman. By Arthur Gibson. *Harper* 1969 pap. $2.25
Ingmar Bergman and the Search for Meaning. By Jerry H. Gill. *Eerdmans* 1969 pap. $.95
Cinema Borealis: Ingmar Bergman and the Swedish Ethos. By Vernon Young. *Avon Bks.* 1972 pap. $3.95
Ingmar Bergman Directs: A Visual Analysis by Halcyon. By John Simon. *Harcourt* 1972 $9.95 Harvest Bks. 1974 pap. $3.45
Focus on the Seventh Seal. Ed. by Brigitta Steene. *Prentice-Hall* Spectrum Bks. 1972 pap. $2.45

BOGART, HUMPHREY.   1899–1957.

Bogart first achieved national acclaim as Duke Mantee in the film version of "The Petrified Forest" in 1936. After that success he played a succession of gangster (or some type of tough guy) roles until he was able to shake off that image. Critics respected his outstanding performance in "The Maltese Falcon" and "Casablanca" (both 1942), although he often made light of his talents. "He can drop his accurate English and fall into the clipped jargon of the underworld; he can snarl or cringe, and all apparently without effort"—(*Current Biography*).

Books about Bogart

Bogie. By Joe Hyams. *New Am. Lib.* pap. $1.25
Bogey: The Films of Humphrey Bogart. By Clifford McCarty. *Citadel Press* 1970 pap. $4.95
Humphrey Bogart. By Alan G. Barbour. *Pyramid Bks.* (orig.) 1973 pap. $1.75
Humphrey Bogart. By Nathaniel Benchley. *Little* 1975 $12.50
"Benchley knew Bogart very well and thus we have a good biography of the tough guy"— (*LJ*).

BUÑUEL, LUIS.   1900–

Luis Buñuel made his first films with Salvador Dali, whom he met among other surrealists at Madrid University in the twenties. "*L'Age d'Or*" (1930), the second of these films, is considered a masterpiece and a major key to his later works. After 14 years of relative silence, he won the 1951 Cannes Festival director's prize for "*Los Olvidados*" and again for "*Nazarin*" in 1958. "*Viridiana*" (1960) and "*Belle de Jour*" (1966) established him as a major presence on the European film scene. Buñuel's films are often morbid and violent, sometimes macabre. His art does not purport to be subjective statement; most often he is merely carrying out producer's assignments.

L'AGE D'OR and UN CHIEN ANDALOU. Classic Film Scripts Ser. *Simon & Schuster* 1968 pap. $1.95

BUÑUEL'S SCREENPLAYS. Trans. by Pierguiseppi Bozzetti *Grossman* 1969 $6.95 pap. $3.50

BELLE DE JOUR. Modern Film Scripts Ser. *Simon & Schuster* 1970 $2.95

TRISTANA. Modern Film Scripts Ser. *Simon & Schuster* 1971 pap. $2.95

EXTERMINATING ANGEL; LOS OLVIDADOS; and NAZARIN. Modern Film Scripts Ser. *Simon & Schuster* 1972 pap. $4.95

Books about Buñuel

Luis Buñuel. By Adonis Kyrou. *Simon & Schuster* 1963 $4.50
Luis Buñuel. By Raymond Durgnat. *Univ. of California Press* 1968 pap. $2.45
"Mr. Durgnat eloquently explores the ambiguities and complexities of Buñuel's themes and symbols so that the flavor and character of his art vividly emerges. This is a splendidly conceived and executed critique of a film maker who is both poet and moralist, Freudian and Marxist, humanist and cynic"—(*LJ*). Durgnat says of his subject: "Over thirty-six years, from the hothouse of Parisian Surrealism through the wilderness of cheap Mexican comedies, to his *grande époque* of international celebrity, [Buñuel's] films have explored a body of attitudes and experiences remarkable for its consistency."
The Cinema of Luis Buñuel. By Freddy Buache. International Film Guide Ser. *A. S. Barnes* 1973 pap. $2.95; (with title "Luis Buñuel Cinema") *International Scholarly Bk. Services* 1970 pap. $7.15

CHAPLIN, CHARLES.   1889–

Creator of the legendary "beloved tramp," Charlie Chaplin acted in, directed, produced and wrote his own films. After leaving the Keystone Comedy group (1915), he made movies with D. W.

Griffith, Douglas Fairbanks and Mary Pickford before branching out on his own. Among his most famous productions are "The Gold Rush," "City Lights" and "The Great Dictator." Chaplin is now living in Switzerland.

MY AUTOBIOGRAPHY. *Simon & Schuster* 1964 $6.95; *Pocket Bks.* pap. $1.25

Books about Chaplin

Charlie Chaplin. By Theodore Huff. 1951. *Arno* 1972 $20.00
Charlie Chaplin: His Life and Art. By W. Dodgson Bowman. *Haskell* 1974 $13.95
The Little Fellow: The Life and Works of Charles Chaplin. By Peter Cotes and Thelma Niklaus. *Citadel Press* 1966 pap. $1.95
Charlie Chaplin. By Isabel Quigley. *Dutton* pap. $1.95
Focus on Chaplin. Ed. by Donald W. McCaffrey. *Prentice-Hall* 1971 $5.95 Spectrum Bks. 1971 pap. $2.45
Chaplin: Last of the Clowns. By Parker Tyler. *Horizon Press* 1972 $7.50 pap. $3.95
Chaplin. By Roger Manvell. *Little* 1974 $6.95
Chaplin. By Dennis Gifford. *Doubleday* 1975 $7.50
"A very readable and well-illustrated survey of Chaplin's work"—(*LJ*).

COCTEAU, JEAN. 1889–1963.

A leader of the Paris avant-garde of the twenties and thirties, Cocteau began his film career—one of many outlets for his multiple talents—working in a surrealistic mode. Among his more famous productions are "Blood of a Poet" (1930) and "Beauty and the Beast" (1945), an exciting surrealistic version of Perrault's fairy tale. At the age of 70 he directed his own "testament" in the film "*Testament d'Orphée*." His early discovery of the "poetry" possible in the medium has had a revolutionary influence in the development of, for example, Godard—and of the underground film.

SCREENPLAYS AND OTHER WRITINGS ON THE CINEMA. Trans. by Carol Martin Sperry *Grossman* 1968 $5.95. Includes Blood of a Poet and Testament of Orpheus.

BEAUTY AND THE BEAST: Diary of a Film. *Dover* 1972 pap. $2.75; *Peter Smith* $5.00

COCTEAU: Three Screenplays. *Grossman* 1972 $8.95 pap. $4.95. Includes Beauty and the Beast; Orpheus; The Eternal Return.

COCTEAU ON THE FILM. Trans. by Vera Traill *Dover* 1972 pap. $2.00

JOURNALS. Trans. and introd. by Wallace Fowlie *Peter Smith* $4.50

PROFESSIONAL SECRETS: An Autobiography of Jean Cocteau. Trans. by Richard Howard; ed. by Robert Phelps *Farrar, Straus* 1970 $8.50; *Harper* 1972 pap. $3.25

Books about Cocteau

Jean Cocteau: The History of a Poet's Age. By Wallace Fowlie. *Indiana Univ. Press* 1966 $6.95
Jean Cocteau: The Man and the Mirror. By Elizabeth Sprigge and Jean-Jacques Kihm. *Coward* 1968 $5.95
Jean Cocteau. By René Gilson. Trans. from the French by Ciba Vaughan *Crown* 1969 pap. $2.95
Cocteau: Beauty and the Beast. Ed. by Robert M. Hammond. *New York Univ. Press* 1970 $14.95
Cocteau. By Francis Steegmuller. *Little-Atlantic* 1970 $12.50
Jean Cocteau. By Bettina L. Knapp. World Authors Ser. *Twayne* $6.95
Jean Cocteau and His Films of Orphic Identity. By Arthur B. Evans. *Art Alliance* 1974 $10.00
Sunshine at Midnight: Memories of Picasso and Cocteau. By Genevieve Laporte. Trans. and introd. by Douglas Cooper *Macmillan* 1975 $6.95

See also his main entry in Chapter 9, French Literature, Reader's Adviser, Vol. 2

DISNEY, WALT. 1901–1966.

Walt Disney first gained fame with his cartoon creations, Mickey Mouse and Donald Duck, and with feature length animated films like "Snow White and the Seven Dwarfs," "Fantasia," "Pinocchio," "Bambi," "Alice in Wonderland," and "Lady and the Tramp." In the 1950s he filmed a number of nature films outdoors which were very popular and informative—"Seal Island," "Nature's Half Acre," "The Living Desert" and "The Vanishing Prairie." His production company was also successful with television shows like The Mickey Mouse Club, Davy Crockett, and Disneyland and still produces numerous family type movies.

Books about Disney

The Disney Version: The Life, Times, Art and Commerce of Walt Disney. By Richard Schickel. *Simon & Schuster* 1968 $6.50; *Avon Bks.* 1969 pap. $1.25

In what is less a biography than a cultural study of Walt Disney Productions, Mr. Schickel, film critic for *Life* magazine, studies the impact of Disney's cartoons on American film and society. "A thoroughly satisfying and most informative discussion of all aspects of the Disney legend made particularly rewarding through the author's own astringent and pithy comment on the cultural and aesthetic scene"—(*Harper's*).

The Art of Walt Disney: From Mickey Mouse to the Magic Kingdoms. By Christopher Finch. *Harry N. Abrams* 1973 $45.00

The Disney Films. By Leonard Martin. *Crown* 1973 $9.95

Disneyana: Walt Disney Collectibles. By Cecil Munsey. *Hawthorn* 1974 $19.95

EISENSTEIN, SERGEI. 1898–1948.

"Potemkin" was the great Russian film director's first brilliant "mass epic" (1925), originally commissioned just after the 1918 Russian Revolution to commemorate the 1905 anti-Czarist uprising. In it he developed his "shock-attraction" technique, of which the most famous example is the slaughter on the great flight of steps in Odessa and the slow descent of the baby in baby carriage through the carnage. For a while Eisenstein worked in Hollywood. He found himself often at odds with the Soviet government but in his brief life of 49 years he brought glory to the Soviet people, particularly in "Potemkin," "Ten Days That Shook the World" (1928), "Alexander Nevsky" (1938) and Part 1 of "Ivan the Terrible" (1944).

IVAN THE TERRIBLE. Classic Film Scripts Ser. *Simon & Schuster* 1962 1971 $3.25

POTEMKIN. Trans. by Gillon R. Aitken. Classic Film Scripts Ser. *Simon & Schuster* 1968 pap. $2.25

FILM FORM. *Harcourt* Harvest Bks. 1969 pap. $2.45

FILM SENSE. *Harcourt* Harvest Bks. 1969 pap. $2.45

FILM ESSAYS AND A LECTURE. Trans. by Jay Leyda *Praeger* 1970 $6.95 pap. $2.95

EISENSTEIN: Three Films. Battleship Potemkin; October; Alexander Nevsky. Ed. by Jay Leyda *Harper* 1974 $7.95 pap. $3.95

NOTES OF A FILM DIRECTOR. Trans. by X. Danko *Dover* rev. ed. 1970 pap. $3.00; *Peter Smith* $5.00

Books about Eisenstein

Lessons with Eisenstein. By Vladimir Nizhny. *Farrar, Straus* (Hill & Wang) 1962 $5.75

Sergei Eisenstein. By Leon Moussinac. Trans. by D. Sandy Petrey *Crown* 1970 pap. $2.95

Eisenstein. By Yon Barna. *Indiana Univ. Press* 1974 $10.00

Eisenstein. By Jacques Charriere. *Dutton* 1974 $8.95

FELLINI, FEDERICO. 1920–

Federico Fellini is known for the unique style he early developed, with its ornate visual effects, uninhibited sentiment, mischievous humor and private romantic fantasy. He first attracted attention abroad with "*I Vitelloni*" (1952) and "*La Strada*" (1954), which focuses on the poor, but in a deeply sensitive manner, touched with poetry. The latter brought him international success, as did "*La Dolce Vita*" (1960), with its portrait of the rich and rootless in a decadent Rome, and the autobiographical "8½" (1963). Fellini's penchant for obscurity, his symbolism and sharp satire (of the Church, for example) have made him from time to time controversial, but his imaginative impact is uncontested.

FELLINI: Three Screenplays. Trans. by Judith Green *Grossman* 1970 pap. $3.50. Includes *Il Bidone, I Vitelloni*, The Temptations of Dr. Antonio.

FELLINI'S EARLY SCREENPLAYS: Variety Lights, The White Sheik. Trans. by Judith Green *Grossman* 1971 pap. $2.95

Books about Fellini

Fellini. By Angelo Solmi. Trans. from the Italian by Elizabeth Greenwood *Humanities Press* 1968 $8.25. A historical and thematic study of his films in a biographical framework.

Federico Fellini. By Gilbert Salachas. Trans. from the French by Rosalie Siegel. *Crown* 1969 pap. $2.95. An excellent study in the *Édition Seghers' Cinéma d' Aujourd'hui* (in English) Ser.

On the Set of Fellini Satyricon: A Behind the Scenes Diary. By Eileen L. Hughes. *Morrow* 1970 pap. $2.95

Three European Directors: Buñuel, Fellini, Truffaut. Ed. by James M. Wall. *Eerdmans* 1973 pap. $3.95

Critical Approaches to Federico Fellini's "8½." By Albert E. Benderson. *Arno* 1974 $12.00

The Cinema of Federico Fellini. By Stuart Rosenthal. *A. S. Barnes* 1974 $8.95

FIELDS, W(ILLIAM) C. 1879–1946.

W. C. Fields was a vaudevillian for many years and later joined the Ziegfield Follies. He entered films in 1925, working mainly for Paramount. He wrote many of his later film scripts under a pseudonym and is known for his comic roles in films such as "The Bank Dick," "My Little Chickadee," and "Never Give a Sucker an Even Break."

NEVER TRUST A MAN WHO DOESN'T DRINK. *Random* 1971 $3.00

FIELDS FOR PRESIDENT. Ed. by Michael M. Taylor *Dodd* 1971 $5.95; *Dell* 1972 pap. $1.25

DRAT! Ed. by Richard J. Anobile *New Am. Lib.* Signet 1973 pap. $.95

A FLASK OF FIELDS. Ed. by Richard J. Anobile *Avon Bks.* 1973 pap. $3.95

Books about Fields

The Art of W. C. Fields. By William K. Everson. *Bobbs* Lib. Arts 1967 $7.50
"A leading film historian [writes a] lively and informed analysis of the films and of the on- and off-screen personality of a unique funnyman, one 'with a larcenous heart and wayward feet set firmly on contemporary Yankee soil' "—(*LJ*).
W. C. Fields: His Follies and Fortunes. By Robert L. Taylor. *New Am. Lib.* Signet 1967 pap. $1.25
Films of W. C. Fields. By Donald Deschner. *Citadel Press* $12.00 pap. $4.95
W. C. Fields and Me. By Carlotta Monti and Cy Rice. *Prentice-Hall* 1971 $6.95; *Paperback Lib.* 1973 pap. $1.25
W. C. Fields. By Nicholas Yanni. Ill. History of the Movies Ser. *Pyramid Bks.* (orig.) 1974 pap. $1.75
W. C. Fields by Himself. By Ronald Fields. *Paperback Lib.* 1974 pap. $1.95

FORD, JOHN. 1895–1973.

The American producer and director won awards for "The Informer" (1935), "Grapes of Wrath" (1940), "How Green Was My Valley" (1941) and "The Quiet Man" (1952). His legendary Westerns often starred John Wayne, Ward Bond and Victor McLaglen.

Books about Ford

John Ford. By Peter Bogdanovich. *Univ. of California Press* 1968 pap. $2.45
Based on on-the-scene interviews with the director, this volume represents an "almost ideal approach to John Ford"—(*LJ*).
The Cinema of John Ford. By John Baxter. Int. Film Guide Ser. *A. S. Barnes* 1973 pap. $2.95
The Western Films of John Ford. By J. A. Place. *Citadel Press* 1974 $12.00
"The critiques of Ford's 17 Westerns emphasize the element of legend and romance that sweep through all of his works be it *Stagecoach*—called by many critics the best Western ever made—or *She Wore a Yellow Ribbon*"—(*LJ*).

GARBO, GRETA.

Greta Garbo, the great and lovely Swedish screen actress, stood in her personal life above the hurly-burly of Hollywood, except, perhaps, in her famous love affair with John Gilbert, the "silent" hero. Her shunning of publicity and early retirement matched the high standards of her superlative performances in such films as "Anna Karenina," "Ninotchka" and "Queen Christina," in which she won the hearts of "intellectuals" as well as of movie "fans."

Books about Garbo

The Films of Greta Garbo. By Michael Conway, Dion McGregor and Mark Ricci. Introd. by Parker Tyler *Citadel Press* 1963 1968 pap $4.95
Greta Garbo. By Raymond Durgnat and John Kobal. Studio Vista Pictureback Ser. *Dutton* 1965 pap. $1.95
Garbo: A Pictorial Memoir. By Ture Sjolander. *Harper* 1971 $12.00
Greta Garbo. By Richard Corliss. Ill. History of the Movies Ser. *Pyramid Bks.* 1974 pap. $1.75
Garbo. By Robert Payne. *Praeger* 1976 $12.95

GARLAND, JUDY. 1922–1969.

"Beginning as a juvenile performer in 1933, Judy Garland in the following 15 years while under contract to Metro-Goldwyn-Mayer appeared in some 35 motion pictures, among them "The Wizard of Oz," "Meet Me in St. Louis," and "Easter Parade"—(*Current Biography*). After numerous comebacks, the longest at the Palace Theater in New York City in 1951–1952, Miss Garland died prematurely in 1969.

Books about Garland

Judy: The Films of Judy Garland. By Ed Epstein and Joe Morella. *Citadel Press* 1970 pap. $4.95

Judy: A Remembrance. By David Melton. *Random* 1972 $3.00

Weep No More My Lady. By Mickey Deans and Ann Pinchot. *G. K. Hall* 1972 $9.95; *Hawthorn* 1972 $6.95; *Pyramid Bks.* 1973 pap. $1.50

Little Girl Lost: The Life and Hard Times of Judy Garland. By Al Diorio, Jr. *Arlington House* 1974 $8.95

Judy Garland. By James Tamulis. *Pyramid Bks.* (orig.) 1974 pap. $1.75

Judy Garland: A Biography. By Anne Edwards. *Simon & Schuster* 1975 $9.95

"A reasonably dispassionate version—for the subject—of the old Hollywood success story from a clear-eyed vantage and with a minimum of tears to clog the emotions"—*(Booklist)*.

Judy. By Gerold Frank. *Harper* 1975 $12.50

"A definitive biography that reports the facts rather than repeats the same old tired gossip"—*(LJ)*.

GODARD, JEAN-LUC.   1930–

Jean-Luc Godard is hailed as the most original director of the sixties. A former critic for *Les Cahiers du Cinéma*, Godard has become a liberating force for the young filmmakers, his work being popular chiefly among the small, youthful coterie he seeks to attract. In 1959 he made his directorial debut with "Breathless," which broke new ground and was an immediate international success. Sometimes criticized for an "iconoclastic" and "anarchistic" use of his medium, the New Wave director produces films that are fast-moving, choppy, witty, informal—indeed, a wild collage of contrasting modes. But he has them under absolute control and is, says Stanley Kauffmann a "director to the medium born." Recently he has turned social critic in such films as *"Les Carabiniers"* (1963), *"La Chinoise"* (1967) and *"Weekend"* (1968).

JEAN-LUC GODARD: A Critical Anthology. Ed. by Toby Mussman *Dutton* 1968 pap. $2.45. Contains interviews with Godard, essays on and reviews of his feature films, pieces by the filmmaker himself and the scenarios for *"Vivre Sa Vie"* and "A Woman's a Woman."

ALPHAVILLE. Trans. by Peter Whitehead. Modern Film Scripts Ser. *Simon & Schuster* 1968 pap. $1.95

MASCULINE FEMININE. *Grove* Black Cat Bks. 1969 pap. $2.45

PIERROT LE FOU. Modern Film Scripts Ser. *Simon & Schuster* 1969 pap. $2.25

PETIT SOLDAT. Modern Film Scripts Ser. *Simon & Schuster* 1971 pap. $1.95

WEEKEND and WIND FROM THE EAST. Modern Film Scripts Ser. *Simon & Schuster* 1972 pap. $3.45

GODARD ON GODARD. Trans. and ed. by Tom Milne *Viking* 1972 $10.00 Compass Bks. pap. $3.95

Books about Godard

Godard. By Richard Roud. *Indiana Univ. Press* 1970 $6.95 pap. $2.25

Jean-Luc Godard. By Jean Collet. Trans. by Ciba Vaughan *Crown* 1970 pap. $2.95

Films of Jean-Luc Godard. Ed. by Ian Cameron. *Praeger* 1970 $5.95 pap. $2.95

Focus on Godard. Ed. by Royal S. Brown. *Prentice-Hall* 1972 $5.95 Spectrum Bks. 1972 pap. $2.45

GRIFFITH, D(AVID) W(ARK).   1875–1948.

D. W. Griffith, with "The Birth of a Nation" in 1916, became the father of filmmaking in America. In "The Liveliest Art" Arthur Knight writes: "Between 1908 and 1912 Griffith took the raw elements of movie making as they had evolved up to that time and, singlehanded, wrought from them a medium more intimate than theater, more vivid than literature, more affecting than poetry. He created the art of the film, its language, its syntax." Today "The Birth of a Nation" seems quaint and somewhat reactionary.

INTOLERANCE. Classic Film Scripts Ser. *Simon & Schuster* 1971 pap. $1.95

Books about Griffith

When the Movies Were Young. By Linda A. Griffith (Mrs. D. W. Griffith). 1925. *Blom* 1968 $9.75; *Peter Smith* $5.00

The Movies, Mister Griffith and Me. By Lillian Gish and Ann Pinchot. *Prentice-Hall* 1969 $8.95; *Avon Bks.* 1970 pap. $1.25

Griffith and the Rise of Hollywood. By Paul O'Dell. Int. Film Guide Ser. *A. S. Barnes* 1970 pap. $2.95

D. W. Griffith: The Years at Biograph. By Robert M. Henderson. *Farrar, Straus* 1970 $6.95 Noonday 1971 pap. $2.95

Focus on D. W. Griffith. Ed. by Harry M. Geduld. Film Focus Ser. *Prentice-Hall* 1971 $5.95 Spectrum Bks. 1971 pap. $2.45

D. W. Griffith: His Life and Work. By Robert M. Henderson. *Oxford* 1972 $10.95

The Griffith Actresses. By Anthony Slide. *A. S. Barnes* 1973 $8.95

Adventures with D. W. Griffith. By Karl Brown. *Farrar, Straus* 1974 $8.95

"Brown writes with humor, humanity, and historical sense—but more important, he writes in a prose that attempts to recapture something of what it was to be 17 and in on the birth of movie art"—*(Choice)*.

D. W. Griffith: His Biograph Films in Perspective. By Kemp R. Niver. *Historical Films* 1974 $10.00

The Films of D. W. Griffith. By Edward Wagenknecht. *Crown* 1975 $12.95

HITCHCOCK, ALFRED.   1899–

Alfred Hitchcock has been a maker of thrillers since the thirties, usually playing a small role in his films. Hitchcock's techniques, first encountered by a wide public in "The Lady Vanishes" (1938), have greatly influenced the directors of the fifties and sixties. He first rose to fame in his native England; later he went to work in Hollywood. He is one of those rare artists who has been at once experimental and commercially popular from the start. Some of Hitchcock's more recent successes include "Vertigo" (1958), "Psycho" (1960) and "The Birds" (1963).

Books about Hitchcock

The Films of Alfred Hitchcock. By George S. Perry. *Dutton* 1965 pap. $1.95. Forty-nine are treated.

Hitchcock's Films. By Robin Wood. 1965. *Paperback Lib.* 1970 pap. $1.25

Hitchcock. By François Truffaut. *Simon & Schuster* 1967 $10.00 Touchstone-Clarion Bks. 1969 pap. $3.95

In this dialogue between the French film critic and director and the British master of suspense, "the reader learns much about the making of films and is also exhilarated by the meeting of these minds as they probe the secrets of creating suspense and analyze the methods by which ideas may be expressed in purely visual terms"—*(LJ)*. "One of the most revealing and engrossing books on film art, technique and history ever put together"—*(N.Y. Times)*.

The Strange Case of Alfred Hitchcock. By Raymond Durgnat. *M.I.T. Press* $15.00

Focus on Hitchcock. By Albert J. LaValley. Film Focus Ser. *Prentice-Hall* 1972 $5.95 Spectrum Bks. 1972 pap. $2.45

Hitchcock. By George Perry. *Doubleday* 1975 $7.50

KUBRICK, STANLEY.   1928–

"At age 47, [the American film director, Stanley Kubrick] is the creator of one of cinema's most varied and successful bodies of work: in addition to "2001: A Space Odyssey," it includes "Paths of Glory," "Lolita," "Doctor Strangelove" and "A Clockwork Orange." He enjoys the rare right to final cut of his film without studio advice or interference. . . . About his work Kubrick is the most self-conscious and rational of men. His eccentricities—secretiveness, a great need for privacy—are caused by his intense awareness of time's relentless passage. He wants to use time to 'create a string of masterpieces,' as an acquaintance puts it"—*(Time)*. His latest movie is "Barry Lyndon," a lavish re-creation of the 18th century Thackeray novel.

A CLOCKWORK ORANGE. *Abelard* 1972 $7.95; *Ballantine Bks*. 1972 pap. $3.95

Books about Kubrick

Films of Stanley Kubrick. By Daniel De Vries. *Eerdmans* pap. $1.75

Stanley Kubrick Directs. By Alexander Walker. *Harcourt* 1971 $9.95 Harvest Bks. enl. ed. 1972 pap. $4.45

The Cinema of Stanley Kubrick. By Norman Kagan. *Holt* 1972 $7.95

KUROSAWA, AKIRA.   1910–

Kurosawa is generally recognized as the best of the Japanese filmmakers. He was the first native of his country to gain international recognition for "Rashomon," which received first prize at the Venice Film Festival in 1951, and "The Magnificent Seven" (1959). Since 1960 Kurosawa has headed his own production company in Tokyo.

IKIRU. Modern Film Scripts Ser. *Simon & Schuster* 1968 pap. $1.95

RASHOMON. *Grove* Black Cat Bks. 1969 pap. $1.95

SEVEN SAMURAI. Modern Film Scripts Ser. *Simon & Schuster* 1970 pap. $3.45

Books about Kurosawa

The Films of Akira Kurosawa. By Donald Richie. *Univ. of California Press* 1965 pap. $6.95
"It can be said confidently that this is the best study yet made of a film director's work"—*(LJ)*.
The volume is handsomely and lavishly illustrated with stills from the films of this Japanese
director, the most famous of which are "Rashomon" (1950) and "Yojimbo" (1961). The book
includes an "excellent" filmography—*(LJ)*.
Focus on Rashomon. Ed. by Donald Richie. Film Focus Ser. *Prentice-Hall* Spectrum Bks. 1972
pap. $2.45

LAUREL, STAN, 1890–1965, and OLIVER HARDY, 1892–1957.

Laurel began as a music hall performer in London and later appeared in vaudeville as a comic.
Oliver Hardy began as a silent screen actor at Hollywood. The two met by chance in 1926 and
began their partnership, first with many short films.

Books about Laurel and Hardy

Laurel and Hardy. By Charles Barr. *Univ. of California Press* 1968 pap. $2.95
Films of Laurel and Hardy. By Bill Everson. *Citadel Press* 1969 $12.00 pap. $4.95
Mr. Laurel and Mr. Hardy. By John McCabe. *New Am. Lib.* Signet pap. $1.25
The Comedy World of Stan Laurel. By John McCabe. *Doubleday* 1974 $7.95
Laurel and Hardy. By John McCabe. Ed. by Al Kilgore *Dutton* 1975 $25.00

THE MARX BROTHERS

The Marx Brothers—Groucho, Chico, Harpo and Zeppo (who left the group in 1935)—were
the zany comic team of the thirties and forties who won popular as well as "highbrow" success with
their brilliant combination of pantomime, verbal wit and slapstick. Chico performed at the piano,
the mute Harpo at his harp, while Groucho did the fast talking. The comedies always included
some delectable Hollywood lovelies. Their fans remember particularly "Animal Crackers," "A
Night at the Opera," "A Day at the Races" and "Monkey Business."

MONKEY BUSINESS and DUCK SOUP. Classic Film Scripts Ser. *Simon & Schuster* Touchstone-Clarion Bks. 1972 pap. $3.95

GROUCHO AND ME. By Groucho Marx. *Manor Bks.* 1973 pap. $1.50

THE MARX BROTHERS SCRAPBOOK. Ed. by Groucho Marx and Richard J. Anobile *Darien
House* 1974 $13.95

Books about the Marx Brothers

The Marx Brothers: Their World of Comedy. By Allen Eyles. International Film Guide Ser.
A. S. Barnes pap. 1966 $2.95; *Paperback Lib.* 1971 pap. $1.25
Son of Groucho. By Arthur Marx. *McKay* 1972 $6.95

MONROE, MARILYN. 1926–1962.

Miss Monroe first achieved star billing in 1952 in several films for RKO. Less than a year later
she was the highest paid actress in Hollywood. She later starred in "Gentlemen Prefer Blondes,"
"How to Marry a Millionaire," "Seven Year Itch," and "River of No Return." Married and
divorced several times, she died of an overdose of barbiturates in 1962.

Books about Monroe

The Films of Marilyn Monroe. By Michael Conway and Mark Ricci. *Citadel Press* 1968 $12.00
pap. $4.95
Marilyn: The Tragic Venus. By Edwin P. Hoyt. *Chilton* new ed. 1973 $6.95
Norma Jean: The Life of Marilyn Monroe. By Fred Guiles. *Bantam* 1973 pap. $1.25
Marilyn: An Untold Story. By Norman Rosten. *New Am. Lib.* Signet 1973 pap. $1.25
Marilyn Monroe. By Joan Mellon. *Pyramid Bks.* (orig.) 1973 pap. $1.45
Marilyn Monroe: Her Own Story. By George Carpozi, Jr. *Universal Pub.* 1973 pap. $1.50
Marilyn. By Norman Mailer. *Grosset* 1973 $19.95 pap. 1974 $6.95

TRUFFAUT, FRANÇOIS. 1932–

Truffaut is a former critic for the avant-garde magazine *Les Cahiers du Cinéma*. An admirer of
American B-feature films, he has been much influenced by Hitchcock (*see above*). His own films,
among which "The Four Hundred Blows" is one of the most popular, employ the New Wave
techniques of a personally expressive camera.

THE FOUR HUNDRED BLOWS. *Grove* 1967 Black Cat Bks. 1969 pap. $1.95. A film script.

JULES AND JIM. Trans. from the French by Nicholas Fry. Modern Film Scripts Ser. *Simon & Schuster* 1968 pap. $1.95

THE WILD CHILD. Trans. by Linda Lewin and Christine Lemery *Simon & Schuster* (Washington Square) pap. $.95

FOUR BY TRUFFAUT. *Simon & Schuster* Touchstone-Clarion Bks. 1972 pap. $2.95

THE ADVENTURES OF ANTOINE DOINEL: Four Autobiographical Screenplays. *Simon & Schuster* 1972 $9.95

Books about Truffaut

The Cinema of François Truffaut. By Graham Petrie. Film Guide Ser. *A. S. Barnes* 1970 pap. $2.95

François Truffaut. By C. G. Crisp. *Praeger* 1972 $5.95 pap. $2.95

Three European Directors: Buñuel, Fellini, Truffaut. Ed. by James M. Wall. *Eerdmans* 1973 pap. $3.95

VISCONTI, LUCHINO. 1906–

Visconti has achieved worldwide fame as one of the triumvirate (with Fellini and Antonioni) of great Italian directors. He has been called the father of the Italian neorealistic school. "Just as Visconti combines his aristocratic heritage with a deep social commitment, so does his art blend extreme realism with a sense of the colorful and the spectacular"—(*Contemporary Biography*).

VISCONTI. *Grossman* 2 vols. 1970 pap. set $6.00

VISCONTI—THREE SCREENPLAYS: White Nights, Rocco and His Brothers, The Job. Trans. by Judith Green *Grossman* 1970 pap. $3.50

VISCONTI—TWO SCREENPLAYS: La Terra Treme, Senso. Trans. by Judith Green *Grossman* 1971 pap. $2.50

Books about Visconti

Luchino Visconti. By Geoffrey Nowell-Smith. 1968. *Viking* 1974 $6.95 pap. $3.25. The British film critic examines eight Visconti features. The two best known works of the Italian director are "The Leopard" (1963) and "Rocco and His Brothers" (1960).

VON STERNBERG, JOSEPH. 1894–1969.

Born in Vienna, Sternberg came to the United States at 17 and went to Hollywood where he took on various writing and directorial tasks. His greatest successes were "Morocco" (1931), "Shanghai Express" (1934) and "American Tragedy" (1932). He also returned to Germany to direct "The Blue Angel" starring Marlene Dietrich.

THE BLUE ANGEL. Classic Film Scripts Ser. *Simon & Schuster* 1968 pap. $2.25

SHANGHAI EXPRESS and MOROCCO. Classic Film Scripts Ser. *Simon & Schuster* 1972 pap. $1.95

FUN IN A CHINESE LAUNDRY. *Macmillan* 1965 Collier Bks. 1973 pap. $2.95

Von Sternberg's autobiography is primarily an "inquest" into the nature of his art and work. "No other American director [Sternberg came, however, from Germany] has written so thoughtfully on what a director must do and what he is prevented from doing when he hopes to work as an artist. . . . The title comes from an early film comedy and underscores his disdain for movies in general"—(*LJ*). Von Sternberg discusses actors who have appeared in his films, among them Emil Jannings, Charles Laughton and Marlene Dietrich, the star he discovered.

Books about von Sternberg

Joseph von Sternberg. By Herman G. Weinberg. *Dutton* 1967 pap. $2.25

A "worshipful" biography containing much pertinent detail—(*PW*).

The Films of Joseph von Sternberg. By Andrew Sarris. *Museum of Modern Art* (dist. by N.Y. Graphic Soc.) 1968 $5.95

"A cool and perceptive film-by-film analysis"—(*NYPL*).

VON STROHEIM, ERICH. 1885–1957.

The Austrian-born film figure was known abroad and on the Hollywood scene as an uncompromising artist. An actor during and after World War I, usually playing the sadistic seducer or the villainous German officer, he directed his first film in 1919. "Greed" (1925) was the climax at once of his style of fastidious realism and of his career-long battle with his producers, who objected to the expense of his work and to the all-too-modern morality of his films. When, in the 1940s, producers became unwilling to employ his directing talents, Stroheim returned to acting.

GREED. Classic Film Scripts Ser. *Simon & Schuster* 1970 pap. $4.95

GREED: A Reconstruction of the Complete Erich von Stroheim Film from Stills. Ed. by Herman G. Weinberg. 1971. *Arno* 1972 $50.00; (with title "The Complete Greed of Erich von Stroheim") *Dutton* 1973 pap. $9.95

Books about von Stroheim

Hollywood Scapegoat: The Biography of Erich von Stroheim. By Peter Noble. 1950. *Arno* 1972 $12.00

Stroheim. By Joel Finler. *Univ. of California Press* 1968 pap. $2.45
This is "a pleasant potpourri but not terribly substantial" (*LJ*), which contains, however, an interesting and extensive study of von Stroheim's film "Greed."

Von Stroheim. By Thomas Q. Curtiss. *Farrar, Straus* 1971 $10.00; *Random* Vintage Bks. 1973 pap. $2.45

Stroheim: A Pictorial Record of His Nine Films. By Herman G. Weinberg. *Dover* 1975 pap. $4.95
"A work of lasting value"—(*Choice*).

WELLES, ORSON. 1915–

"By 1941, when he was twenty-six, the protean Orson Welles had become one of the most inventive theatrical directors of his day, had inadvertently launched a nationwide panic with one of his radio plays, and had written, directed, and starred in "Citizen Kane," recently voted the best film in motion-picture history. Since then Welles has demonstrated his virtuosity as actor, director, producer, author, designer, cartoonist, magician, columnist, wit, and bon-vivant"—(*Current Biography*).

TRIAL. Modern Film Scripts Ser. *Simon & Schuster* 1970 pap. $2.95

Books about Welles

Invasion from Mars: A Study in the Psychology of Panic. By Hadley Cantril. *Harper* Torchbks. pap. $2.75

A Ribbon of Dreams: The Cinema of Orson Welles. By Peter Cowie. International Film Guide Ser. *A. S. Barnes* 1965 1973 $12.00
This examines Welles' work in radio, television, theater and the film. His "Citizen Kane" (1941), based on the life of William Randolph Hearst, was an extraordinary film and wide success, which marked the peak of a period of American experimentation with the technical resources of the cinema that had begun in the 30's. The director's innovations in this film, which he has never since equaled, included the use of overlapping dialogue and of functional music.

The Films of Orson Welles. By Charles Higham. *Univ. of California Press* 1970 $10.95 pap. $5.95

Orson Welles. By Maurice Bessy. Trans. by Ciba Vaughan *Crown* 1972 pap. $3.50

Orson Welles. By Joseph McBride. *Viking* 1972 $6.95 pap. $2.95

Mime and Marionettes

This purely silent art consists of acting with dances and gestures rather than words. No one knows precisely when mime originated but it was already a popular form of entertainment at Rome in Augustan times. Modern mime features dramatic performances in which meanings are conveyed solely by means of movement and expression. In recent years such talented artists as Marcel Marceau, Emmet Kelly, and Red Skelton have each in their own way popularized mime in motion pictures and on television. We frequently see mime actors selling products in television commercials and at the other extreme, the American Mime Theatre of New York has endowed mime with a strong social comment.

Alberts, David. PANTOMIME: Elements and Exercises. *Univ. Press of Kansas* 1971 $5.50

Ando, Tsururo. BUNRAKU: The Puppet Theatre. Trans. from the Japanese by Don Kenny *Weatherhill* 1970 $6.50

Arnott, Peter D. PLAYS WITHOUT PEOPLE: Puppetry in Modern and Serious Drama. Introd. by Hubert C. Heffner *Indiana Univ. Press* 1964 $4.95
A history from prehistoric to modern times. Professor Arnott's "contention is that Americans and Englishmen regard marionettes and puppets for the delectation of children only. Continental

Europeans and Orientals have always regarded them as a means of purveying serious drama. They so influenced Gordon Craig that he proposed the abolition of the seen actor and the substitution of giant marionettes with unseen voices accompanying their movements. Tischner's marionettes in Germany and the Yale Puppeteers in New York and Hollywood in the early 1930's opened my eyes to their function as legitimate adult entertainment and fine practitioners of the dramatic art"—(*LJ*).

Aubert, Charles. THE ART OF PANTOMIME. Trans. by Edith Sears, 1927. *Blom* 1969 $10.75

Baird, Bil. THE ART OF THE PUPPET. 1965. *Plays Inc.* 1966 $19.95

"A celebrated puppeteer has produced an elegant panorama of his craft"—(*N.Y. Times*). "In this gorgeous book . . . he outlines the history of puppetry, illustrated with dozens of full-color plates which disclose, better than any words, how ancient and international is the art of the puppet"— (*SR*). "A brilliantly conceived and produced book, stunningly illustrated, . . . a history and survey of puppetry that should become a standard"—(*LJ*).

Batchelder, Marjorie Hope. PUPPET THEATRE HANDBOOK. *Harper* 1947 $8.95

"Miss Batchelder's work on puppet techniques fills a long-felt want, for it treats each point on an elementary and advanced level as no book has before. . . . There are 69 plates and diagrams drawn by Douglas Anderson in a clear and sometimes humorous presentation"—(Paul McPharlin, in *Theatre Arts*).

Beaumont, Cyril W. HISTORY OF HARLEQUIN. 1926. *Blom* 1967 $13.50

Boehn, Max von. DOLLS AND PUPPETS. 1932. Trans. from the German by Josephine Nicoll *Cooper* 1966 $17.50. A history from prehistoric to modern times.

PUPPETS. Trans. from the German by Josephine Nicoll. 1932. *Dover* 1972 pap. $3.50; (with title "Puppets and Automats") *Peter Smith* $5.50

Bohmer, Gunter. WONDERFUL WORLD OF PUPPETS. *Plays, Inc.* 1971 $8.95

Broadbent, R. J. A HISTORY OF PANTOMIME. 1901. *Blom* 1965 $10.75

Bruford, Rose. TEACHING MIME. *Harper* (Barnes & Noble) 1958 $7.00

Crothers, J. Frances. PUPPETEER'S LIBRARY GUIDE, Vol. 1. *Scarecrow Press* 1971 $15.00

Cruikshank, George. PUNCH AND JUDY. 1861. *Finch Press* $9.00

Currell, David. THE COMPLETE BOOK OF PUPPETRY. *Plays, Inc.* 1975 $12.95

Disher, Maurice W. CLOWNS AND PANTOMIMES. 1925. *Blom* 1968 $17.50

Dorcy, Jean. THE MIME: With Essays by Étienne Decroux, Jean-Louis Barrault and Marcel Marceau. Trans. from the French by Robert Speller, Jr. and Pierre de Fontnouvelle *Speller* 1961 $4.95. This is one of the rare books in English about the art of pure pantomime and the role of the artist as mimic.

Enters, Angna. ON MIME. *Wesleyan Univ. Press* 1965 $6.00

"America's foremost exponent of mime" combines a diary of her teaching experience with other material, including extracts from previous books. The result is a "spontaneous highly individual and persuasive reflection of the author's art and artistry. A book for her audience and anyone else who appreciates the mime theater. Her sketches are delightfully piquant"—(*N.Y. Times*).

Fling, Helen. MARIONETTES: How to Make and Work Them. 1930. *Dover* 1973 pap. $2.50; *Peter Smith* $5.00

Fraser, Peter. PUNCH AND JUDY. *Van Nostrand-Reinhold* 1970 $3.95

Hunt, Douglas, and Kari Hunt. PANTOMIME: The Silent Theater. *Atheneum* 1964 $3.95

Hutchings, Margaret. MAKING AND USING FINGER PUPPETS. *Taplinger* 1973 $8.50

Kampmann, Lothar. CREATING WITH PUPPETS. *Van Nostrand-Reinhold* 1972 $5.95

Keene, Donald. BUNRAKU: The Art of the Japanese Puppet Theatre. Introd. by Tanizaki Junichiro; photographs by Kaneko Hiroshi *Kodansha* 1965 $35.00 pap. 1973 $4.95

"The plays have served as bases for many later kabuki and movie epics. This volume successfully joins history, appreciation and mechanics"—(*LJ*). A recording of the traditional music is included.

Kennard, Joseph S. MASKS AND MARIONETTES. 1935. *Kennikat* 1966 $7.50

Kipnis, Claude. THE MIME BOOK. Ed. by Neil Kleinman *Harper* 1974 $12.50

Lawson, Joan. MIME: The Theory and Practice of Expressive Gesture. *Dance Horizons* 1972 pap. $3.95

McPharlin, Marjorie Batchelder. PUPPET THEATRE IN AMERICA: A History, 1524–1948. 1949. With a supplement: Puppetry in America since 1948. *Plays, Inc.* 1969 $12.95

The supplement covers puppetry in a variety of areas such as education, therapy and live performances; and summarizes the careers of important contemporary puppeteers. A bibliography on puppetry and related fields is included.

Mander, Raymond, and Joe Mitchenson. PANTOMIME: A Story in Pictures. *Taplinger* 1973 $14.95

Mayer, David, III. HARLEQUIN IN HIS ELEMENT: The English Pantomime, 1806–1836. *Harvard Univ. Press* 1969 $15.00

Mulholland, John. PRACTICAL PUPPETRY. Drawings by Jack Parker *Arco* 1961 $4.95

Nicoll, Allardyce. MASKS, MIMES, AND MIRACLES. 1931. *Cooper* 1964 $17.50. A history by a brilliant scholar of the theater tracing the popular, nonliterary theater of masks, mimes and miracle plays as far as the *Commedia dell' Arte* in the 17th century.

Niculescu, Margaret, Ed. THE PUPPET THEATRE OF THE MODERN WORLD. Trans. by Ewald Osers and Elizabeth Strick *Plays Inc.* 1967 $14.95

"This handsome, excellently illustrated volume sets forth the case for puppetry as a modern art form. Thirty-six countries are represented in the well-translated words of 19 authors and in 238 photos. . . . This impressive book represents a major contribution to the field"—(*LJ*).

Niklaus, Thelma. HARLEQUIN. *Braziller* 1960 $7.50

Philpott, A. R. DICTIONARY OF PUPPETRY. *Plays, Inc.* 1969 $8.95

Robinson, Stuart, and Patricia Robinson. EXPLORING PUPPETRY. *Taplinger* 1967 $8.50

Sand, Maurice, pseud. THE HISTORY OF THE HARLEQUINADE. 1915. *Blom* 2 vols. 1968 set $18.50. A translation of *"Masques et Bouffons."*

Scott, Adolph Clarence. THE PUPPET THEATRE OF JAPAN. *Tuttle* 1963 1973 pap. $3.50. A historical survey with descriptions of 10 puppet plays.

Shepard, Richmond. MIME: The Techniques of Silence. *Drama Bk. Specialists* 1971 $7.50

Speaight, George. PUNCH AND JUDY: A History. *Plays, Inc.* 1970 $14.95

Walker, Katherine S. EYES ON MIME: Language without Speech. *John Day* 1969 $5.95

Wall, Leonard V., and others. THE PUPPET BOOK. *Plays Inc.* 1950 $7.95

"A splendid puppetry book, one of the best"—(*LJ*). Important information, in 27 "well-integrated" articles, is provided on technique, construction, presentation and use in such fields as psychotherapy.

Wilson, Albert E. PENNY PLAIN TWO PENCE COLOURED: A History of the Juvenile Drama. 1932. *Blom* 1969 $18.75

STORY OF PANTOMIME. 1949. *Rowman* 1974 $8.50

COMMUNICATIONS

We are all "experts" in the field of communication, Professor George N. Gordon wrote recently, although most people can't even define the term properly. Neither an art nor a science, communication is a basic human activity that has become all things to all men. "Many definitions of communication appear in many places and all of them leave something to be desired," Gordon states in his "Communication and Media: Constructing a Cross-Discipline" (*Hastings House* 1975 $4.95). One brave soul who has recently attempted to define and clarify this elusive term is Thomas A. Nilsen. "It is clear enough in conventional usage," he says, "but obscure when we seek to determine the limit of its application." Generally speaking, communication is a response to stimuli directed at us for the purpose of evoking response from us. It includes intercourse by words, letters, thoughts, images, and opinions. It need not be face to face, Nilsen says in the chapter "On Defining Communication" in Kenneth Sereno and C. D. Mortensen "Foundations of Communication Theory" (*Harper* 1970 $3.95).

During the 1960s social scientists confidently predicted the evolution of a "global village" in which the social and cultural differences of nations would be ground down to a bland conformity. This grim prospect has not yet materialized, however, and Wilbur Schramm, Director of the Institute for Communication Research at Stanford University, believes it never will. "People come to the media," he says, "as to other messages seeking what they want, not what the media intends to give them. They still have their defenses up." The mass media make the communication of ideas, opinions, and values possible over great distances but they are merely the "machinery" that brings it about. The basic and equal constituents are the communicator, the message, and the receiver (Wilbur Schramm and Donald F. Roberts "The Process and Effects of Mass Communications" *Univ. of Illinois Press* rev. ed. 1971 $9.75).

So we see that the term, the theory, and some of the key concepts of mass communications have undergone substantial change in recent scientific literature. More than half of all the research ever conducted in human communication, Professor Schramm points out, has become available in the last 18 years. Through this research the media communicators have learned how to record and influence the social and political behavior of individuals and groups. They have also learned how "to illuminate the social pattern of the United States and how to transmit the various facets of our culture from coast to coast." More recently, the mass communicators for the large television networks and metropolitan newspapers have acted as faithful watchdogs over various governmental functions. Consequently, the great and awesome power of mass communications no longer seems so frightening (Edwin Emery and others. "Introduction to Mass Communications" *Dodd* 2nd ed. 1965 $7.45).

General Works

Agee, Warren K., Ed. MASS MEDIA IN A FREE SOCIETY. *Univ. Press of Kansas* 1969 pap. $1.95

Barmash, Isadore. THE WORLD IS FULL OF IT: How We Are Oversold, Overinfluenced and Overwhelmed by the Communications Manipulators. *Dial* (Delacorte) 1974 $7.95

Berelson, Bernard, and Morris Janowitz, Eds. READER IN PUBLIC OPINION AND COMMUNICATION. *Macmillan* (Free Press) 1953 2nd ed. 1966 $12.95

Blum, Eleanor. BASIC BOOKS IN THE MASS MEDIA: An Annotated, Selected Booklist Covering General Communications, Book Publishing, Broadcasting, Film, Magazines, Newspapers, Advertising, Indexes, and Scholarly and Professional Periodicals. *Univ. of Illinois Press* 1972 $8.00

Burch, John S., Jr. INFORMATION SYSTEMS: Theory and Practice. *Wiley* 1973 $12.95

Campbell, James, and Hal Helper. DIMENSION IN COMMUNICATION: Readings. *Wadsworth* 1968 2nd ed. 1970 pap. $5.50

An anthology of 19 articles focusing on the key factor of persuasion in the process of communication. "This paperback contains some of the thinking which is at the cutting edge of new knowledge and still maintains perspective with recent evolutionary landmarks. It is a highly appropriate text in any area dealing with human communication"—(Robert R. Monaghan, Ohio State University).

Chaney, David. PROCESSES OF MASS COMMUNICATION. *Herder & Herder* 1972 $8.95

"A critique of research and theory in mass communication"—(*Choice*). Part 1 concerns audiences and their behavior; Part 2 the reality of production, control and distribution; Part 3 discusses content analysis and its meanings.

Cirino, Robert. DON'T BLAME THE PEOPLE. *Random* 1972 $8.95 Vintage Bks. 1972 pap. $2.45

"Cirino is convinced that the media's failure to inform the public completely is the cause of many social problems and that people would be more moral and humane if they were fully aware of issues"—*(LJ)*.

Dance, Frank E. X. SPEECH COMMUNICATION. *Holt* 1972 $7.95

Daniels, Les. LIVING IN FEAR: A History of Horror in the Mass Media. *Scribner* 1975 $13.00

"A comprehensive and entertaining survey tracing the portrayal of the horrific, weird and supernatural in movies, fiction, TV and radio, pulp magazines, comics, and rock music"—*(PW)*.

Davison, W. Phillips, and Frederick T. Yu. MASS COMMUNICATION RESEARCH: Major Issues and Future Directions. *Praeger* 1974 $15.00

De Fleur, Melvin L. THEORIES OF MASS COMMUNICATION. *McKay* 1966 1970 pap. $2.95

The first half of this text is devoted to the nature and history of the four major media in the United States. The second discusses both classic and contemporary communication theory. Intended for the student, this "short volume of high information density" provides an "orderly introduction to the field"—*(Quarterly Journal of Speech)*.

Duncan, Hugh Dalziel. COMMUNICATION AND SOCIAL ORDER. *Bedminster* 1962 $10.00; *Oxford* 1968 pap. $3.95

Mr. Duncan states as his theme: "Man as a social being exists in and through communication: communication is as basic to man's nature as food and sex; sociation inescapably involves hierarchy; hierarchy involves incongruities which society solves well or ill (as in war, genocide, sadism and masochism); until society masters the dynamics of hierarchy as a set of relationships between superiors, inferiors, and equals, all sociation is in a parlous state; art works offer our best clues for the analyses of these dynamics; and finally students of society must learn how to proceed with such analysis if we are to create a science of human conduct that tells us something about motivation."

SYMBOLS IN SOCIETY. *Oxford* 1968 $7.50 Galaxy Bks. 1972 pap. $2.50. Professor Duncan explores the ways in which "communication by symbols is an essential part of the dynamism of society."

Emery, Edwin, and others. INTRODUCTION TO MASS COMMUNICATIONS. *Dodd* 4th ed. 1973 pap. $7.50

ENCYCLOPAEDIA OF CYBERNETICS. Trans. by G. Gilbertson *A. S. Barnes* 1968 $9.50

"An extremely useful dictionary to have for reference"—*(Choice)*.

Foster, David. THE INTELLIGENT UNIVERSE: A Cybernetic Philosophy. *Putnam* 1975 $7.95

Gerbner, George, and others, Eds. COMMUNICATIONS TECHNOLOGY AND SOCIAL POLICY. *Wiley* 1973 $10.00

Gillmor, Donald M. MASS COMMUNICATION LAW: Cases and Comment. *West Pub. Co.* 2nd ed. 1974

Gordon, George N. COMMUNICATIONS AND MEDIA: Constructing a Cross-Discipline. *Hastings House* 1975 $4.95

Haber, Fred. AN INTRODUCTION TO INFORMATION AND COMMUNICATION THEORY. *Addison-Wesley* 1974 $6.50

Hartmann, Paul, and Charles Husband. RACISM AND THE MASS MEDIA: A Study of the Role of the Mass Media in the Formation of White Beliefs and Attitudes in Britain. *Rowman* 1974 $13.50

"A serious well-documented study"—*(Choice)*.

Hiebert, Ray E., and others. MASS MEDIA: Principles of Modern Communication. *McKay* (orig.) 1974 pap. $7.95

Ingels, Franklin M. INFORMATION AND CODING THEORY. *T. Y. Crowell* (Intext Educ. Pubs.) 1971 $13.25

Jacobs, Norman, Ed. CULTURE FOR THE MILLIONS: Mass Media in Modern Society. Introd. by Paul Lazarfeld *Beacon* 1964 pap. $2.45

Laver, Murray. COMPUTERS, COMMUNICATIONS AND SOCIETY. *Oxford* 1975 $11.25

"An interesting and provocative monograph addressing public policy issues in the merging telecommunications and computer technologies"—(*Choice*).

Lerbinger, Otto. Designs for Persuasive Communication. *Prentice-Hall* 1972 $8.95 pap. $4.95

Lin, Nan. The Study of Human Communication. *Bobbs* 1973 $6.95 pap. $3.25

McLuhan, (Herbert) Marshall. Understanding Media: The Extension of Man. *McGraw-Hill* 1964 $7.95 pap. $1.95; *New Am. Lib.* Signet 1971 pap. $1.25

See also his main entry in Chapter 8, The Social Sciences, this Vol.

Merrill, John C., and Ralph L. Lowenstein. Media, Messages and Men: New Perspectives in Communication. *McKay* 1971 $6.95 pap. $3.95

Merritt, Richard L., Ed. Communication in International Politics. *Univ. of Illinois Press* 1972 $15.00

Miller, George A. Communication, Language and Meaning: Psychological Perspectives. *Basic Bks.* 1973 $7.95

The Psychology of Communications: Seven Essays. 1967. *Penguin* Pelican Bks. 1969 pap. $1.25. Describes several experiments on the relation between psychology and communications.

Moles, Abraham. Information Theory and Esthetic Perception. 1958. Trans. by Joel E. Cohen *Univ. of Illinois Press* 1966 $7.50 pap. $2.45

Mortensen, C. David. Basic Readings in Communication Theory. *Harper* 1973 pap. $4.95

Communication: The Study of Human Interaction. *McGraw-Hill* 1972 $8.50

Ogden, Charles K., and Ivor A. Richards. The Meaning of Meaning: A Study of the Influence of Language upon Thought and of the Science of Symbolism with Supplementary Essays by B. Malinowski and F. G. Crookshank. 1923. *Harcourt* 1959 pap. $2.95

"The most important book on symbolic analysis until the appearance of Mead's and Burke's work in the 30's and 40's—(H. D. Duncan).

Rivers, William L. Mass Media: Reporting, Writing, Editing. 1964. *Harper* 2nd ed. 1974 $12.95

Saracevic, Tefko. Introduction to Information Science. *Bowker* 1970 $28.95

"A compilation of important representative readings in information science. . . . Its purpose is to demonstrate the connection between the theoretical and experimental areas of information science and the practical area of information retrieval, and to effect a more cohesive interaction between the two"—(Publisher's catalog).

Schramm, Wilbur. Men, Messages and Media: A Look at Human Communication. *Harper* 1973 pap. $4.50

(With Donald F. Roberts, Eds.). Process and Effects of Mass Communications. 1954. *Univ. of Illinois Press* rev. ed. 1971 $15.00

"This new edition . . . contains only four articles from the 1954 edition. . . . [It considers] mass communication's media, messages, audience, effects, innovations, and technological future"—(Publisher's note). "This work is another standard reference for all scholars in all fields interested in mass communication process, effects, theory and research"—(*Choice*).

Schreivogel, Paul A. Communications in Crisis. *Nelson* 1971 $4.95

Seiden, Martin H. Who Controls the Mass Media? Popular Myths and Economic Realities. *Basic Bks.* 1974 $8.95

"Seiden . . . contends that through an evolutionary process we have arrived at a desirable (even enviable) position among world communicators, but because of a basic lack of understanding (myths about the media) we stand to lose this position by governmental interference"—(*LJ*)

Seldes, Gilbert. The Public Arts. *Simon & Schuster* 1956 pap. $1.95

A sharply intelligent appraisal of movies, radio and television. The pioneering works of Seldes have "called for, and contributed to, the development of a physics, or perhaps the physical geography, of the popular arts"—(George Gerbner, in Dance's "Human Communication Theory" 1967 o.p.).

THE SEVEN LIVELY ARTS. *A. S. Barnes* 1962 pap. $2.45

Stein, Robert. MEDIA POWER: Who is Shaping Your Picture of the World. (Orig. "Overexposed Society") *Houghton* 1972 $6.95

"An informal and thoughtful critique. ... It makes for interesting, at times informative, reading"—*(Choice)*.

Steinberg, Charles S. COMMUNICATIVE ARTS: An Introduction to Mass Media. *Hastings House* 1970 $10.00 pap. $6.00

"A concise and relevant overview . . . scholarly and extremely readable"—*(Choice)*.

(Ed.). MASS MEDIA AND COMMUNICATION. *Hastings House* 1965 2nd rev. & enl. ed. 1972 $14.50 pap. $8.50

Stephenson, William. THE PLAY THEORY OF MASS COMMUNICATION. *Univ. of Chicago Press* 1967 $7.00

"The theory and the method are so practical and simply profound that the implications of the book are much too inescapable to ignore"—*(Quarterly Journal of Speech)*.

Tebbel, John. THE MEDIA IN AMERICA: A Social and Political History. *T. Y. Crowell* 1974 $10.00

"Focusing on the struggle for freedom, Tebbel aims here to integrate the history of media in America into a social and political framework molded by contemporary events ... [he] adeptly mixes the factual highlights of newspapers, magazines, books, and broadcasting with a defence of . . . the First Amendment"—*(LJ)*.

Voelker, Francis, and Ludmila Voelker. MASS MEDIA: Forces in Our Society. *Harcourt* 2nd ed. 1974 $10.00

"Intended to foster the trend toward intelligent selection and appraisal of the media"— (Preface).

Whitehead, Alfred North. SYMBOLISM: Its Meaning and Effect. 1927. *Putnam* Capricorn Bks. 1959 pap. $1.65

Wiener, Norbert. CYBERNETICS: Or Control and Communication in the Animal and the Machine. 1948. *M.I.T Press* 2nd ed. 1961 $6.50. A classic on the relation of man to the machine in all its ramifications.

THE HUMAN USE OF HUMAN BEINGS: Cybernetics and Society. 1950. *Avon Bks.* 1967 pap. $1.65. An excellent introduction to the field; a classic.

WORLD COMMUNICATIONS: A 200-Country Survey of Press, Radio, Television and Film. *Gower Press* 1975 $9.95

Wright, Charles R. MASS COMMUNICATION: A Sociological Perspective. *Random* 1959 pap. $2.25. An introduction to the field.

Young, John Frederick. INFORMATION THEORY. *Butterworth* 1971 $10.00

Yu, Frederick T. C., Ed. BEHAVIORAL SCIENCES AND THE MASS MEDIA. *Russell Sage Foundation* 1968 $8.00

"Enough dramatic sociological insights are spelled out here to show that the journalist must somehow hook into the knowledge of behavioral scientists to do his job"—*(SR)*.

The News Media

Aronson, James. PACKAGING THE NEWS: A Critical Survey of Press, Radio, TV. *International Pubs.* 1971 pap. $1.45

Batscha, Robert M. FOREIGN AFFAIRS NEWS AND THE BROADCAST JOURNALIST. *Praeger* 1975 $15.00

Blanchard, Robert O. CONGRESS AND THE NEWS MEDIA: Studies in Public Communication. *Hastings House* 1974 $18.50 pap. $10.75

Cirino, Robert. POWER TO PERSUADE: Mass Media and the News. *Bantam* (orig.) 1974 pap. $1.25

Doig, Ivan, and Carol Doig. NEWS: A Consumer's Guide. *Prentice-Hall* 1972 pap. $3.95

Fielding, Raymond. THE AMERICAN NEWSREEL, 1911–1967. *Univ. of Oklahoma Press* 1972 $9.95

"A history of the American newsreel from its inception in Europe and the United States to its demise in the late 1960's, when it was supplanted by TV news"—(Publisher's note).

Hohenberg, John. FOREIGN CORRESPONDENCE: The Great Reporters and Their Times. *Columbia* 1967 $15.00 pap. $2.95

FREE PRESS—FREE PEOPLE: The Best Cause. *Columbia* 1971 $12.50; *Macmillan* (Free Press) 1973 pap. $3.95

THE NEWS MEDIA: A Journalist Looks at His Profession. *Holt* 1968 $6.95

"Detached, professional, and offering many insights, this book ranges over the whole terrain, rather generally, of present-day journalism and pinpoints some of the soft spots—credibility gaps, news management, opinion manipulation. . . . The text of the sermon—and Hohenberg takes a pretty firm stance in the pulpit—is the individual journalist's responsibility 'as a good citizen' "— (*SR*).

Kriegbaum, Hillier. PRESSURES ON THE PRESS. *T. Y. Crowell* 1972 $6.95; *Apollo* 1973 pap. $3.45

Leroy, David J., and Christopher H. Sterling. MASS NEWS: Practices, Controversies and Alternatives. *Prentice-Hall* 1973 $8.95 pap. $5.95

Rucker, Bryce W. TWENTIETH CENTURY REPORTING AT ITS BEST. *Iowa State Univ. Press* 1964 $4.95

Stein, Meyer L. SHAPING THE NEWS: How the Media Function in Today's World. *Simon & Schuster* (Washington Square) (orig.) 1974 pap. $1.25

Journalism

Anderson, Peter J. RESEARCH GUIDE IN JOURNALISM. *General Learning Press* 1974 pap. $3.85

Argyris, Chris. BEHIND THE FRONT PAGE: Organizational Self-Renewal in a Metropolitan Newspaper. *Jossey-Bass* 1974 $12.50

Brown, Lee. THE RELUCTANT REFORMATION: On Criticizing the Press in America. *McKay* 1974 text ed. $6.95 pap. $3.95

Brucker, Herbert. COMMUNICATION IS POWER: Unchanging Values in a Changing Journalism. *Oxford* 1973 $9.50

"A thoughtful, sometimes evocative evaluation of the modern American press"—(*Choice*).

Casey, Ralph D., Ed. THE PRESS IN PERSPECTIVE. *Louisiana State Univ. Press* 1963 $6.00

Collier, Barney. HOPE AND FEAR IN WASHINGTON (The Early Seventies): The Story of the Washington Press Corps. *Dial* 1975 $8.95

Conlin, Joseph R., Ed. THE AMERICAN RADICAL PRESS, 1880–1960. *Greenwood* 2 vols. 1974 set $29.95

These "essays do more than offer a comprehensive view of the radical press of the time; they also make an invaluable contribution to the history of radicalism"—(*LJ*).

Dann, Martin. THE BLACK PRESS, 1820–1890: The Quest for National Identity. *Putnam* 1971 $7.95 Capricorn Giant 1971 pap. $2.95

Davies, Marion. THE TIMES WE HAD: Life with William Randolph Hearst. *Bobbs* 1975 $12.50

Elson, Robert T. TIME INC.: The Intimate History of a Publishing Enterprise, 1923–1941. Ed. by Duncan Norton-Taylor *Atheneum* 1968 $10.00

"The story of the rise of the Luce publishing empire is one of the great sagas of 20th-century American business"—(John Brooks, in the *N.Y. Times*). "Remarkable in its candor. Mr. Elson has set forth a highly detailed but always readable history that steps into personality disputes and reports criticism of the boss above a whisper. . . . A fascinating record" of the founding and business of *Time, Life* and *Fortune*—(Stuart Little, in *SR*). The author occupied high positions in the

Luce Company for over 25 years. A second volume, covering the years of the China Lobby and of Joe McCarthy, follows.

THE WORLD OF TIME INC.: The Intimate History of a Publishing Enterprise, 1941–1960. Ed. by Duncan Norton-Taylor *Atheneum* 1973 $10.00

Emery, Edwin. THE PRESS AND AMERICA. *Prentice-Hall* 2nd ed. 1962 3rd ed. 1972 $12.50

Epstein, Edward J. BETWEEN FACT AND FICTION: The Problems of Journalism. *Random* 1975 pap. $2.95

"Epstein, a political scientist specializing in media analyses, has written these essays to examine the problem of truth in journalism"—*(LJ)*.

Farr, Finis. FAIR ENOUGH: The Life of Westbrook Pegler. *Arlington House* 1975 $8.95

"Easy-to-read informal biography of the termagant Westbrook Pegler, possibly the most damned newspaper columnist in the history of American journalism"—*(Choice)*.

Grant, Jane. ROSS, THE NEW YORKER AND ME. *Reynal* 1968 $5.95

"Miss Grant is constantly, brightly, exuberantly entertaining as she recounts the fun and games of that rowdy and witty era" when she and the *New Yorker* editor were husband and wife—*(SR)*.

Hohenberg, John. PROFESSIONAL JOURNALIST: A Guide to the Principles and Practices of the News Media. *Holt* 3rd ed. 1973 $11.50

THE PULITZER PRIZES. *Columbia* 1974 $14.95

Horton, Russell M. LINCOLN STEFFENS. *Twayne* 1974 $7.50

"An important biography, well suited to the era when newspapers were beginning to sense the need for ethics"—*(Choice)*.

Hudson, Frederic. JOURNALISM IN THE UNITED STATES FROM 1690–1872. 1873. Introd. by Ben Bagdikian *Haskell* 1969 $29.95; *Scholarly Press* $15.00

Hynds, Ernest C. AMERICAN NEWSPAPERS IN THE 1970s. *Hastings House* 1975 $13.95 pap. $7.95

The author "has written a scholarly analysis of newspapers; he examines their historical role to provide background for his analysis of their present operating methods in three areas: business, news and opinion, and production"—*(LJ)*.

Juergens, George. JOSEPH PULITZER AND THE NEW YORK WORLD. *Princeton Univ. Press* 1966 $15.00

Professor Juergens' "impressive book" treats in particular the *World*'s first three years "under Pulitzer's restless and intuitive editorial genius, and indicates how the paper fashioned 'a new style for the dowdy American newspaper' by responding to the hitherto unrecognized popular news needs of a growing urban populace"—*(LJ)*.

Kennedy, Bruce. COMMUNITY JOURNALISM: A Way of Life. *Iowa State Univ. Press* 1974 $7.95

Knightley, Philip. THE FIRST CASUALTY: From the Crimea to Vietnam: The War Correspondent as Hero, Propagandist, and Myth Maker. *Harcourt* 1975 $12.95

"By weaving together the dispatches and exploits of the most notable correspondents and the most outrageous journalistic conjurers, Knightley unfolds a fascinating panorama. . . . [This] is a very readable book that conveys an important well-documented message"—*(SR)*.

Kobre, Sidney J. THE DEVELOPMENT OF AMERICAN JOURNALISM. *W. C. Brown* 1969 $9.95

Kornbluth, Jessie, Ed. NOTES FROM THE NEW UNDERGROUND: An Anthology. *Viking* 1968 $7.50

"Straight-from-the-hip commentary on the much publicized 'underground press,' with a varied selection of its best writing. Represented are such celebrities as Allen Ginsberg, Timothy Leary, and the Beatles"—(Publisher's note). The editor graduated from Harvard in the class of 1968.

Lippmann, Walter. PUBLIC OPINION. 1922. *Macmillan* (Free Press) 1965 pap. $2.95

See also his main entry, Chapter 9, History, Government and Politics: American, this Vol.

Luskin, John. LIPPMANN, LIBERTY, AND THE PRESS. *Univ. of Alabama Press* 1973 $7.95

"Finely and gracefully written, this scholarly appraisal of Lippmann, his work, and the impact of his personality on American society over the past 60 years is a must book"—*(Choice)*.

Lyle, Jack, Ed. THE BLACK AMERICAN AND THE PRESS. *Ward Ritchie* 1968 $4.95 pap. $1.95

Proceedings of a post-Watts symposium. Gunnar Myrdal, Ralph McGill, Dr. John Caughey and Charles Evers were among the participants. The volume "makes urgent reading, whether in Gunnar Myrdal's long-range perspective on the problem, or in the immediate anger and distrusts of blacks dependent upon a white-oriented press"—(SR).

Lyons, Louis M. NEWSPAPER STORY: One Hundred Years of the *Boston Globe*. *Harvard Univ. Press* 1972 $9.95

"This is a work of social history, the intimate account of reporting on Boston and the nation from the era of reconstruction and President Grant to the Viet-Nam War and Nixon"—(*Choice*).

Merrill, John C. THE ELITE PRESS: Great Newspapers of the World. *Pitman* 1969 $7.95 pap. $2.95. A study of 40 newspapers.

THE IMPERATIVE OF FREEDOM: A Philosophy of Journalistic Autonomy. *Hastings House* 1974 $10.00 pap. $5.95

(With others). THE FOREIGN PRESS: A Survey of the World's Journalism. *Louisiana State Univ. Press* rev. ed. 1970 pap. $7.95

Mills, Nicolaus. THE NEW JOURNALISM: A Historical Anthology. *McGraw-Hill* 1973 $9.95 pap. $5.95

Mott, Frank Luther. AMERICAN JOURNALISM: A History, 1690–1960. *Macmillan* 3rd rev. ed. 1962 $11.50. A classic work.

A HISTORY OF AMERICAN MAGAZINES. *Harvard* 5 vols. Vol. 1 1741–1850 (1930) Vol. 2 1850–65 (1938) Vol. 3 1865–85 (1938) Vol. 4 1885–1905 (1957) Vol. 5 1905–1930 (with fwd. by Howard Mumford Jones and autobiographical sketch by Frank Mott, as well as a cumulative index to the 5 vols. (1968) each $17.50

Pollak, Richard, Ed. STOP THE PRESSES, I WANT TO GET OFF: Tales of the News Business from the Pages of *More* Magazine. *Random* 1975 $8.95

"This is a surprisingly solid collection of essays from a magazine often bitingly critical of the journalistic establishment"—(*LJ*).

Potter, Elaine. THE PRESS AS OPPOSITION: The Political Role of South African Newspapers. *Rowman* 1975 $13.75

"Both the undergraduate and graduate students will profit from the reading"—(*Choice*).

Preston, Ivan L. THE GREAT AMERICAN BLOW-UP: Puffery in Advertising and Selling. *Univ. of Wisconsin Press* 1975 $11.95

"This is the story of legalized lying in the marketplace—soft core deception, going under the name of puffery"—(Publisher's note).

Price, Warren C., and Calder M. Pickett. AN ANNOTATED JOURNALISM BIBLIOGRAPHY, 1959–1968. *Univ. of Minnesota Press* 1971 $22.00

"A long awaited, up-to-date journalism bibliography, well-suited to the communications-oriented as well as the how-to-do-it student"—(*Choice*).

Rivers, William L. FREE-LANCER AND STAFF WRITER: Writing Magazine Articles. *Wadsworth Pub.* 1972 $10.00 text ed. $7.50

Smiley, Nixon. KNIGHTS OF THE FOURTH ESTATE: The Story of the *Miami Herald*. *Seemann* 1975 $14.95

"The biography of a newspaper that grew as the city it covers grew"—(*LJ*).

Smith, Anthony, Ed. THE BRITISH PRESS SINCE THE WAR. *Rowman* 1974 $15.00

Swanberg, W. A. CITIZEN HEARST. *Scribner* 1961 $12.95; *Bantam* pap. $1.95

LUCE AND HIS EMPIRE: A Biography. *Scribner* 1972 $12.50; *Dell* 1973 pap. $1.95

PULITZER. *Scribner* 1967 1972 pap. $3.95

"Mr. Swanberg, whose previous biography of Hearst was notoriously denied a Pulitzer Prize, does a sound and thorough job in recounting one of the most exciting chapters in the history of American journalism"—(*N.Y. Times*).

Talese, Gay. THE KINGDOM AND THE POWER. 1966. *Bantam* 1970 pap. $1.50

"Seldom has anyone been so successful in making a newspaper [the *New York Times*] come alive as a human institution"—(*N.Y. Times Bk. Review*).

Tebbel, John. AMERICAN MAGAZINE: A Compact History. *Hawthorn* 1969 $7.95

THE COMPACT HISTORY OF THE AMERICAN NEWSPAPER. *Hawthorn* 1964 1969 $8.95

Van Horne, Harriett. NEVER GO ANYWHERE WITHOUT A PENCIL. *Putnam* 1972 $7.95

"Columnist Van Horne collects some of her newspaper pieces and a few others written from 1968 to 1972 that are commentaries on the passing scene in the late 1960's and early 70's. Her vantage point is New York but her observations range the national scene"—(*Booklist*).

Wilcox, Dennis L., Ed. ENGLISH LANGUAGE NEWSPAPERS ABROAD: A Guide to Daily Newspapers in 56 Non-English Speaking Countries. *Gale Research Co.* 1967 $11.75

"This directory lists 202 newspapers, 167 from Asia and Africa, the remainder from the Middle East, Central America, the Mediterranean, the Pacific, Europe, and South America; most are published only in English though some are bilingual. The arrangement is alphabetical by country. Pertinent criteria include circulation and population figures, editorial and advertising content, format, date of establishment, and addresses of publishers. . . . A convenient guide to the lesser-known newspapers of the world"—(*LJ*).

Wolseley, Roland E. THE BLACK PRESS U.S.A. *Iowa State Univ. Press* 1972 $10.50

"Detailed overview of the black press, a highly neglected subject, by an experienced author and journalism educator"—(*Choice*).

Wood, James P. MAGAZINES IN THE UNITED STATES. *Ronald* 1956 3rd ed. 1971 $9.95

For general histories of publishing, see Chapter 1, Books about Books, Reader's Adviser, *Vol. 1.*

Radio and Television

Arlen, Michael J. LIVING-ROOM WAR. 1969. *Tower* 1971 pap. $.95

A television critique comprised of 40 essays reprinted from the *New Yorker*. "Michael Arlen writes like a waterbug skates and his commentaries, ostensibly on television, are in truth among the best prose poems written on life, love, war, and the state of the nation"—(John Updike).

Aronson, James. DEADLINE FOR THE MEDIA: Today's Challenges to Press, TV and Radio. *Bobbs* 1972 $8.95

Barnouw, Erik. A HISTORY OF BROADCASTING IN THE UNITED STATES. *Oxford Univ. Press* Vol. 1 A Tower in Babel: To 1933 (1966) $8.50 Vol. 2 The Golden Web: 1933–1953 (1968) $9.00 Vol. 3 The Image Empire: From 1950 (1970) each $10.75. The definitive study on this subject.

TUBE OF PLENTY: The Evolution of American Television. *Oxford* 1975 $14.95

"A one-volume condensation of the author's trilogy, 1131 pages boiled down to 518, with some minimal update to accommodate 'Sesame Street' and Richard Nixon at the Watergate"—(*N.Y. Times*).

Barrett, Marvin, Ed. MOMENTS OF TRUTH: The Fifth Alfred I. Dupont—Columbia University Survey of Broadcast Journalism. *T. Y. Crowell* 1975 $6.95

"Analyses and criticism of media treatment of the Watergate scandal and of governmental reaction to commercial and public broadcasts on the crisis"—(*Booklist*).

THE POLITICS OF BROADCASTING: The Alfred I. Dupont—Columbia University Survey of Broadcast Journalism 1971–1972. *T. Y. Crowell* 1973 $5.95

"A valuable book for those concerned with broadcast journalism"—(*Choice*).

Bluem, A. William. DOCUMENTARY IN AMERICAN TELEVISION. *Hastings House* 1964 $8.95. A "classic" in the field.

(Ed.). RELIGIOUS TELEVISION PROGRAMS: A Study in Relevance. *Hastings House* 1968 $4.95

Bogart, Leo. THE AGE OF TELEVISION: A Study of Viewing Habits and the Impact of Television on American Life. *Ungar* 1958 3rd ed. 1972 $14.50

Brown, Ronald. TELECOMMUNICATIONS: The Booming Technology. *Doubleday* 1970 $6.95

Coddington, Robert H. MODERN RADIO BROADCASTING: Management and Operations in Small-to-Medium Markets. *Tab Bks.* 1970 $8.00

"One of the best books about radio station management in small-to-medium markets"—(*Choice*).

Diamant, Lincoln, Ed. THE BROADCAST COMMUNICATIONS DICTIONARY. *Hastings House* 1974 $6.95

"Contains approximately 2,000 clearly defined technical, common, and slang words used frequently in radio, television and film work"—*(Choice)*.

Emery, Alter B. NATIONAL AND INTERNATIONAL SYSTEMS OF BROADCASTING: Their History, Operation, and Control. *Univ. of Michigan Press* 1970 $12.50

"The first book to provide a carefully documented and stimulating study in depth of all the major broadcasting systems in the world"—*(Choice)*.

Fang, Irving E. TELEVISION NEWS: Writing, Filming, Editing, Broadcasting. *Hastings House* 1968 2nd rev. & enl. ed. 1972 $12.50 pap. $7.50. A thorough step-by-step guide to the processes involved in television news coverage.

TELEVISION RADIO NEWS WORKBOOK. *Hastings House* 1974 $6.95

Friendly, Alfred W. DUE TO CIRCUMSTANCES BEYOND OUR CONTROL. *Random* 1967 $8.95 Vintage Bks. 1967 pap. $1.95

"Ed Murrow is the hero of the book," (says Edward Weeks, in the *Atlantic*), "and the early chapters, which are mostly about him, are charged with courage, electricity and affection." *Library Journal* wrote of it: "The place that educational, or non-commercial, or public, television is to fill in American society largely remains to be determined. It has been left considerable latitude by commercial television's inability to solve the dilemma of 'common stock vs. the commonweal,' to borrow one of Fred Friendly's chapter headings. This is the story of how CBS grappled with that problem during Mr. Friendly's tenure, first as producer of *See It Now* and later *CBS Reports*, and then as president of CBS News."

Gelfman, Judith S. WOMEN IN TELEVISION NEWS. *Columbia* 1976 $6.95

The author examines "how women work in a traditionally male field"—*(PW)*.

Head, Sydney W. BROADCASTING IN AMERICA: A Survey of Television and Radio. *Houghton* 2nd ed. 1972 $11.95

Hilliard, Robert L. WRITING FOR TELEVISION AND RADIO. *Hastings House* 1962 2nd ed. 1967 $7.95. Primarily concerned with writing for the nondramatic forms of television and radio.

(Ed.). RADIO BROADCASTING: An Introduction to the Sound Medium. *Hastings House* 1967 2nd rev. & enl. ed. 1974 $8.95 pap. $5.95

(Ed.). UNDERSTANDING TELEVISION: An Introduction to Broadcasting. *Hastings House* $6.95 pap. $3.95

Kahn, Frank J., Ed. DOCUMENTS OF AMERICAN BROADCASTING. *Prentice-Hall* rev. ed. 1973 $12.00

Koenig, Allen E., and Ruane B. Hill, Eds. THE FARTHER VISION: Educational Television Today. *Univ. of Wisconsin Press* 1968 pap. 1969 $4.75

"The use of communications satellites, the effect of federal financing, the educational values of instructional TV, and the rights of teachers in television are among the topics faithfully—if somewhat dully and pedantically—discussed by the 20 authorities, including National Educational Television president John White, in this pioneering volume. . . . An up-to-date, well-documented, thorough study"—*(LJ)*.

LaGuardia, Robert. THE WONDERFUL WORLD OF TV SOAP OPERAS. *Ballantine Bks.* 1974 pap. $1.50

LaGuardia "defends soap operas as representing real life in a fashion instinctively appreciated by an estimated audience of twenty million"—*(Booklist)*.

Lesser, Gerald S. CHILDREN AND TELEVISION: Lessons from Sesame Street. *Random* 1974 $10.00

"Although specifically written to be read by a general audience this readable, scholarly, and well-referenced text promises to serve professional planners, writers, and producers of children's programs for any media. . . . In all, a thought-provoking and scholarly bargain"—*(Choice)*. By the educational director of *Sesame Street*.

Lichty, Lawrence W., and Malachi C. Topping, Eds. AMERICAN BROADCASTING: A Source Book on the History of Radio and Television. *Hastings House* 1974 $26.50 pap. $15.00

Macy, John W. TO IRRIGATE A WASTELAND: The Struggle to Shape a Public Television System in the United States. *Univ. of California Press* 1974 $6.95

"Written by the man who best knows the problems of public broadcasting, the book should become required reading for university radio and television students as well as for anyone who is interested in . . . public broadcasting"—*(Choice)*.

Martin, James T. FUTURE DEVELOPMENTS IN TELECOMMUNICATIONS. *Prentice-Hall* 1972 $14.00

"No one who is intrigued by telecommunications, and no one who wants to look squarely at what that technology can do . . . will be disappointed in this book"—*(Scientific American)*.

Mayer, Martin. ABOUT TELEVISION. *Harper* 1972 $10.00

"A very readable, very popular history of television, centering on the United States and the English speaking world"—*(Best Sellers)*.

Metz, Robert. CBS: Reflections in a Blood-Shot Eye. *Playboy Press* 1975 $13.50

"This is new ground and it is interesting. . . . Mr. Metz does have a sprightly way with a sentence and he is at his best when . . . he deals with the early financial struggles of the company"—*(N.Y. Times)*.

Minow, Newton N., and others. PRESIDENTIAL TELEVISION: A Twentieth Century Fund Report. *Basic Bks.* 1973 $8.95

Owen, Bruce M., and others. TELEVISION ECONOMICS. *Heath* 1974 $15.00

"A comprehensive overview of television policy in the U.S."—*(Choice)*.

Paulu, Burton. RADIO AND TELEVISION BROADCASTING IN EASTERN EUROPE. *Univ. of Minnesota Press* 1974 $22.95

Polsky, Richard M. GETTING TO SESAME STREET: Origins of the Children's Television Workshop. *Praeger* 1974 $11.00

Skornia, Harry J. TELEVISION AND THE NEWS: A Critical Appraisal. *Pacific Books* 1968 pap. 1974 $2.95

Covering a broader range than his title implies, the former president of the National Association of Educational Broadcasters discusses problems of broadcast journalism—from censorship, management and sponsorship to the medium's "rip-and-read" reporting and its stress on conflict and violence.

(With Jack William Kitson, Eds.). PROBLEMS AND CONTROVERSIES IN TELEVISION AND RADIO: Basic Readings. *Pacific Books* 1968 $10.00

More than 50 articles by leaders in broadcasting, advertising, government and education. "A most interesting volume, well edited and provocative as well as nostalgic"—(Eliot Fremont-Smith, in the *N.Y. Times*).

Smith, Anthony. THE SHADOW IN THE CAVE: The Broadcaster, His Audience and the State. *Univ. of Illinois Press* 1974 $8.95

"A well-researched book with a very useful bibliography, it is cogently written and contributes a valuable perspective on the broadcast enterprise"—*(Choice)*.

(Ed.). BRITISH BROADCASTING. *David & Charles* 1974 $15.00

White, David Manning, and Richard Averson, Eds. SIGHT, SOUND, AND SOCIETY: Motion Pictures and Television in America. *Beacon* 1968 $7.50

Wilbur Schramm, Clifford Odets, Arthur Schlesinger Jr., Gilbert Seldes and others discuss aspects of the interrelation between mass communication and American democracy. "Although these essays are reprints, the entire book will appeal to anyone interested in mass communications"—*(LJ)*.

Williams, Raymond. TELEVISION: Technology and Cultural Form. *Schocken* 1975 $7.50 pap. $3.45

The author "is always provocative, sometimes engaging, an English perpetual motion machine for producing radical books about almost everything"—*(N.Y. Times)*.

Wolf, Frank. TELEVISION PROGRAMMING FOR NEWS AND PUBLIC AFFAIRS: A Quantitative Analysis of Networks and Stations. *Praeger* 1972 $15.00

Chapter 11

Folklore and Humor

"Behavior and attitudes become more articulate in folklore than in any other cultural trait, and folklore then tends to crystallize and perpetuate the forms of culture that it has made articulate. . . . It crystallizes the forms that are locally favored or insisted upon, and gives therefore one of the most important available sanctions to the mores of the group. . . . Folklore is literature and like any art it has traditional regional stylistic forms which may be studied like any other art forms."
—RUTH BENEDICT

"Folklore is at once an independent discipline and an intimate associate of sister disciplines in the humanities and social sciences," writes Richard M. Dorson, Distinguished Professor of History and Folklore at Indiana University. "Possessing its own scholarly methods and concepts, folklore requires an apprenticeship and a special aptitude the same as does any other field of study" ("Folklore: Selected Essays" *Indiana Univ. Press* 1972 p. 3).

Folklore emerged as a separate field of learning during the early nineteenth century when antiquarians and philologists began to examine closely the literature, traditions, and folkways of the lower classes. It gradually acquired academic respectability as the rigor of its practitioners' methods increased. In most European countries folklore has been an accepted university discipline, with a faculty and research staff of its own, since the beginning of this century. Folklore gained a foothold in several American universities in the 1940s as a cross disciplinary study offered at the undergraduate level, which grew into a minor concentration and later to a full-fledged undergraduate major. In 1953 Indiana University conferred the first Ph.D. degree in folklore.

During this same period folklore underwent a complete transformation from a "loose and floundering" discipline, dependent on amateur scholars and collectors, to a rigorous, intellectually challenging field of study. Indexing and classification schemes and retrieval systems have recently been developed which enable researchers to organize and to analyze a vast body of transcribed texts and field reports. The raw materials of folklore encompass many forms: narrative songs, cookery, popular drama and dances. The geographical scope of these materials is global. To the layman, and to many social scientists, the formal study of folklore still suggests an element of sentimentality, distortion of meaning, and even fantasy. But these prejudices are rapidly being corrected as so many modern folklorists have exhibited in their works a superb scholarship and a gracious, stimulating literary style.

REFERENCE WORKS ON GENERAL FOLKLORE

Included here are works on general folklore: bibliographies, catalogs, indexes, dictionaries, general anthologies, selected papers, festschrifts, symposia, textbooks, readers and guides. With few exceptions reference works dealing with single types of folklore—Folksong and Dance; Folktale, Legend and Myth; American Regional and Ethnic Folklore; Miscellaneous and Applied Folklore; and Folk and Popular Humor—will be found under their respective heads throughout this Chapter.

Baughman, Ernest W. TYPE AND MOTIF INDEX OF THE FOLKTALES OF ENGLAND AND NORTH AMERICA. *Humanities Press* 1966 pap. $34.50

Bluestein, Gene. THE VOICE OF THE FOLK: Folklore and American Literary Theory. *Univ. of Massachusetts Press* 1972 $9.00

"Wide-ranging series of essays dealing with the effect of 'low culture' folk literature on 'high culture' literary development. . . . An ambitious book, interesting to read, and moderately successful"—(*Choice*).

Botkin, Benjamin A., Ed. A TREASURY OF AMERICAN FOLKLORE: Stories, Ballads and
Traditions of the People. Fwd. by Carl Sandburg. *Crown* 1944 $7.95. More than 500
stories and over 100 songs with music.

Brunvand, Jan Harold. THE STUDY OF AMERICAN FOLKLORE: An Introduction. *Norton*
1968 $8.95

Carvalho Neto, Paulo de. CONCEPT OF FOLKLORE. Trans. by Jacques M. Wilson *Univ. of
Miami Press* 1971 $7.95

Cleveland Public Library, John G. White Dept. THE CATALOG OF FOLKLORE AND FOLK-
SONGS. *Hall* 2 vols. 1964 set $125.00

Coffin, Tristram P., Ed. OUR LIVING TRADITIONS: An Introduction to American Folklore.
Basic Bks. 1968 $7.95
In this generally urbane survey of folklore and folklore scholarship in the U.S., 25 specialists
define and illustrate their specialties so that even nonfolklorists can understand them. It provides
insight into the materials and methods of folklore study as a scholarly pursuit and an appreciation
of the cultural function and values of folklore—(B. A. Botkin).

(With Hennig Cohen, Eds.). FOLKLORE IN AMERICA: Tales, Songs, Superstitions, Proverbs, Riddles, Games, Folk Drama and Folk Festivals, from the *Journal of American
Folklore. Doubleday* 1966 $4.95 Anchor Bks. 1970 pap. $2.50

Daniels, Cora L. ENCYCLOPEDIA OF SUPERSTITIONS, FOLKLORE AND THE OCCULT SCIENCES.
Gordon Press 3 vols. $90.00

Diehl, Katherine. RELIGIONS, MYTHOLOGIES, FOLKLORES: An Annotated Bibliography.
Scarecrow Press 2nd ed. 1962 $12.50

Dorson, Richard M. AMERICA IN LEGEND: Folklore from the Colonial Period to the
Present. *Pantheon* 1973 $15.00 pap. 1974 $5.95
"Profusely documented and critically responsive to the history of collecting folklore, and
written in a style that asserts itself plainly and magnetically, Dorson's book deserves a wide
audience of folk beyond the pale of university walls"—(*LJ*).

AMERICAN FOLKLORE. History of American Civilization Ser. *Univ. of Chicago Press* 1959
$10.00 pap. 1973 $2.95

AMERICAN FOLKLORE AND THE HISTORIAN. *Univ. of Chicago Press* 1971 $8.50

BUYING THE WIND: Regional Folklore in the United States. *Univ. of Chicago Press* 1964
$12.50 Phoenix Bks. 1972 pap. $4.95

FOLKLORE: Selected Essays. *Indiana Univ. Press* 1972 $12.50

FOLKLORE RESEARCH AROUND THE WORLD: A North American Point of View. 1961.
Kennikat $10.00

(Ed.). FOLKLORE AND FOLKLIFE: An Introduction. *Univ. of Chicago Press* 1972 $12.50
This title "maintains a professional, research-oriented tone and still manages to be exciting,
readable, and filled with quaint and interesting facts"—(*LJ*).

Dundes, Alan. THE STUDY OF FOLKLORE. *Prentice-Hall* 1965 $8.95

Emrich, Duncan. FOLKLORE ON THE AMERICAN LAND. *Little* 1972 $15.00
"This book includes such topics as names for places, animals, quilts, cattle brands, etc.,
children's folklore, street cries and gravestone writ, legends and tales, folksongs and ballads, folk
beliefs and superstitions, love songs, sea chanteys and a great deal more"—(*Christian Science
Monitor*).

Goldstein, Kenneth S. A GUIDE FOR FIELD WORKERS IN FOLKLORE. Pref. by Hamish
Henderson. Memoirs of the American Folklore Society, Vol. 52 *Gale Research Co.*
(Folklore Associates) 1964 $6.00
This "first systematic guide to field collecting techniques published in the United States . . .
serves as an introduction to the materials and problems of folklore collection and documentation
for the beginner and the amateur. Even the professional will find it useful and stimulating. . . .
The book makes lively reading and presents a liberal and modern view of folklore investigation"—
(B. A. Botkin, in the *N.Y. Folklore Quarterly*).

Haywood, Charles. A Bibliography of North American Folklore and Folksong. 1951. *Dover* 2 vols. rev. ed. 1961 each $15.00; *Peter Smith* 2 vols. set $30.00

Jackson, Bruce, Ed. Folklore and Society: Essays in Honor of Benjamin A. Botkin. *Norwood Editions* 1966 $15.00

Jobes, Gertrude. Dictionary of Mythology, Folklore and Symbols. *Scarecrow Press* 2 vols. 1961 $40.00

Krappe, Alexander Haggerty. The Science of Folklore. 1930. *Harper* (Barnes & Noble) 1974 $16.75; *Norton* 1964 pap. $4.25

> In spite of some highly personal judgments and heterodox opinions, Alexander Krappe's book is still the most erudite and brilliant eclectic study of folklore treated as literature. He writes: "I conceive of folk-tales and folk-songs as purely literary manifestations of the popular genius, acting under the same impulses as the productive mind of literary men, scholars and artists. The two differ only in much the same things in which different literary schools are apt to be at variance, that is, in questions of taste and methods of technique"—(B. A. Botkin).

Leach, Maria, and Jerome Fried, Eds. The Standard Dictionary of Folklore, Mythology and Legend. *T. Y. Crowell* (Funk & Wagnalls) 1949 text ed. 1972 $17.95

Opie, Iona, and Peter Opie, Eds. The Lore and Language of School Children. *Oxford* 1959 $12.50 pap. 1967 $5.00

Paredes, Américo, and Richard Bauman, Eds. Toward New Perspectives in Folklore. *Univ. of Texas Press* 1971 $8.50

(With Ellen J. Stekert, Eds.). Urban Experience and Folk Tradition. *Univ. of Texas Press* 1972 $6.50

Thompson, Stith, Ed. Motif-Index of Folk Literature. *Indiana Univ. Press* 6 vols. rev. and enl. ed. 1955–59 set $110.00. A classic tool for comparative folktale analysis. Vol. 6 is an alphabetical index.

Wilgus, D. K., and Carol Sommer, Eds. Folklore International: Essays in Traditional Literature, Belief and Custom in Honor of Wayland Debs Hand. *Gale Research Co.* (Folklore Associates) 1967 $15.00

Ziegler, Elsie B. Folklore: An Annotated Bibliography and Index to Single Editions. *Faxon* 1973 $12.00. Indexes mostly juvenile titles.

FOLKSONG AND DANCE

These are general and reference works; collections; critical and historical studies in the field of ballad, folksong and folk dance, with a few relevant titles in popular music. For ethnic and regional titles see Section on American Regional and Ethnic Folklore. Besides the few listed here, there are many singers' songbooks available from *Oak* and other music publishers; Folkways Records (701 7th Ave., New York, N.Y.) issues a catalog of folk and primitive music and documentary recordings. Ray M. Lawless's "Folksingers and Folksongs in America" (*see below*) provides valuable data on recordings, recording companies, singers, archives, periodicals, festivals and the like. *For songs of Afro-Americans see Section on American Regional and Ethnic Folklore: Afro-American Folklore.*

Abrahams, Roger D., Ed. Jump-Rope Rhymes: A Dictionary. *Univ. of Texas Press* 1969 $6.50

Andrews, Edward D. The Gift to Be Simple: Songs, Dances and Rituals of the American Shakers. 1940. *Dover* 1962 pap. $2.00; *Peter Smith* $4.75

Boni, Margaret Bradford, and Norman Lloyd, Eds. The Fireside Book of Folk Songs. 1947. Arr. for the piano by Norman Lloyd; ill. by Alice and Martin Provenson *Simon & Schuster* rev. ed. 1966 $14.95. Ballads, carols, sea chanteys and work songs.

Brand, Oscar. The Ballad Mongers: Rise of the Modern Folk Song. Fwd. by Agnes De Mille *T. Y. Crowell* (Funk & Wagnalls) 1962 1967 pap. $2.95

"A lively, gossipy, informative off-the-cuff personal history of the folksong revival, its sources and popularity. The book gains in immediacy what it loses in objectivity from folksinger, composer and impresario Brand's involvement in all popular phases of the movement"—(B. A. Botkin).

SONGS OF SEVENTY SIX: A Folksinger's History of the Revolution. *M. Evans* 1972 $10.00

Bronson, Bertrand H. THE BALLAD AS SONG. *Univ. of California Press* 1969 $12.50

See also Child, Francis James (below).

Carmer, Carl. AMERICA SINGS: STORIES AND SONGS OF OUR COUNTRY'S GROWING. *Knopf* 1950 $5.75 lib. bdg. $7.99

Child, Francis James. ENGLISH AND SCOTTISH POPULAR BALLADS. 1883–98. Ed. by H. C. Sargent and G. L. Kittredge *Dover* 5 vols. 1965 pap. each $6.00; *Peter Smith* 5 vols. set $37.50

The American scholar Francis James Child (1825–96), a professor of English at Harvard (1876–96), made his great collection with the purpose of including "every obtainable version of every extant English or Scottish ballad, with the fullest possible discussion of related songs or stories in the popular literature of all nations." He had nearly completed it—in ten parts—at his death. A recent book on the subject by Bertrand H. Bronson provides "The Traditional Tunes of the Child Ballads, with Their Texts, According to the Extant Records of Great Britain and America" (*Princeton Univ. Press* 4 vols. 1959–1972 each $40.00). *See also Niles, this list, below.*

Cole, William, Comp. FOLK SONGS OF ENGLAND, IRELAND, SCOTLAND, AND WALES. *Crown* 1975 pap. $4.95

Ewen, David. AMERICAN POPULAR SONGS: From the Revolutionary War to the Present. Fwd. by Sigmund Spaeth *Random* 1966 $10.00. A history.

Fowke, Edith F. LUMBERING SONGS FROM THE NORTHERN WOODS. *Univ. of Texas Press* 1969 $6.50

SALLY GO ROUND THE SUN. *Doubleday* 1970 $6.95

(Ed.). THE PENGUIN BOOK OF CANADIAN FOLK SONGS. *Penguin* 1974 pap. $2.95

"Edited by one of the most respected authorities in the field"—(*Choice*).

(Ed.). TRADITIONAL SINGERS AND SONGS FROM ONTARIO. *Gale Research Co.* 1965 $7.50

(With Joe Glazer). SONGS OF WORK AND PROTEST. (Orig. "Songs of Work and Freedom"). 1960. *Dover* 1973 pap. $3.50; *Peter Smith* $6.75

Fowler, David C. A LITERARY HISTORY OF THE POPULAR BALLAD. *Duke Univ. Press* 1968 $11.75

Friedman, Albert B. THE BALLAD REVIVAL: Studies in the Influence of Popular on Sophisticated Poetry. *Univ. of Chicago Press* 1961 $10.00

(Ed.). THE VIKING BOOK OF FOLK BALLADS OF THE ENGLISH-SPEAKING WORLD. *Viking* 1956 $6.50 Compass Bks. 1962 pap. $2.95

Fuld, James J. THE BOOK OF WORLD-FAMOUS MUSIC: Classical, Folk and Popular. *Crown* 1965 rev. ed. 1971 $15.00. This is a basic reference book containing complete information about almost 1,000 songs and other compositions, including first lines of the music and words. Includes folk material.

Glassie, Henry, and others. FOLKSONGS AND THEIR MAKERS. *Bowling Green Univ. Press* 1971 $5.00 pap. $3.00

Graves, Robert, Ed. ENGLISH AND SCOTTISH BALLADS. 1957. *Harper* (Barnes & Noble) 1969 pap. $2.00

THE ENGLISH BALLAD: A Short Critical Survey. 1927. *Folcroft* $9.75; *Haskell* 1971 $10.95; *Somerset Pub.* $7.50; *Richard West* $7.45

Green, Archie. ONLY A MINER: Studies in Recorded Coal-Mining Songs. *Univ. of Illinois Press* 1972 $12.50

"Green draws on ballad scholarship, labor history, and popular-culture study to explore coal-mining songs and also country music, Negro blues, and problems in current folklore study"—(Publisher's note).

Greenway, John. AMERICAN FOLKSONGS OF PROTEST. 1953. *Octagon* 1970 $13.50

Guthrie, Woody. BORN TO WIN. Ed. by Robert Shelton *Macmillan* 1965 pap. $2.95

"Among the leaders of the folk song revival, Woody Guthrie is unique in the way in which he has contributed autobiographically to his own saga and lengend, beginning with 'Bound for Glory' [*Dutton* 1943 new ed. 1968 $6.95; *New Am. Lib.* Signet 1970 pap. $1.25]. Robert Shelton has sought to bring [Guthrie's] reputation into the light in this revealing and often exciting miscellany, ranging from random fancies, whimsies, impressions, and observations to letters, essays, song lyrics, and free verse poems. . . . What . . . should interest and concern students of American folk song are his notes on the nature and function of song in relation to the American experience and to his own rich and varied participation in America and in the folk song revival"—(B. A. Botkin, in the *N.Y. Folklore Quarterly*). The famous folksinger died after many years of illness in 1968. His son Arlo carries on as a popular folksinger and songwriter.

Hague, Eleanor, Comp. SPANISH-AMERICAN FOLK-SONGS. 1917. *Kraus* $9.00. Ninety-five Spanish folksongs from California, Arizona, Mexico, Cuba, Puerto Rico, Central and South America.

Haywood, Charles. FOLK SONGS OF THE WORLD. Ill. by Carl Smith *John Day* 1966 $12.50

Over 170 songs from 119 countries with tunes, suggested chord accompaniments, translations, comments on individual songs and on the musical tradition of each country. Index, bibliography. For the amateur singer or the serious student, and "essential" (*LJ*) for library folksong collections.

Hugill, Stan, Comp. SHANTIES FROM THE SEVEN SEAS: Shipboard Work-Songs and Songs Used as Work-Songs from the Great Days of Sail. Fwd. by Alan Villiers *Dutton* 1961 $15.95

Jackson, George Pullen, Comp. and ed., with introd. SPIRITUAL FOLK SONGS OF EARLY AMERICA: Two Hundred and Fifty Tunes and Texts. 1937. *Peter Smith* $5.00

Jackson, George Stuyvesant, Ed. EARLY SONGS OF UNCLE SAM. 1933. *Gale Research Co.* 1971 $9.50

Karpeles, Maud, Ed. FOLK SONGS FROM NEWFOUNDLAND. *Shoe String Press* 1970 $20.00

Kraus, Richard G. FOLK DANCING: A Guide for Schools, Colleges and Recreation Groups. *Macmillan* 1962 $8.75

Lawless, Ray M. FOLKSINGERS AND FOLKSONGS IN AMERICA: A Handbook of Biography, Bibliography, and Discography. Ill. from paintings by Thomas Hart Benton and others and from designs in Steuben Glass. 1960. *Hawthorn* 1965 $12.95

An indispensable volume for libraries of all sizes. "Professor Lawless has up-dated this new edition . . . with corrections and a supplement of a bit under 100 pages. Included are more biographies (e.g., Joan Baez, Miriam Makeba, Odetta); descriptions of recent books and magazines in the field; a selective list of about 350 LP records; and other matters too numerous to mention"—(*LJ*).

Laws, G. Malcolm, Jr. AMERICAN BALLADRY FROM BRITISH BROADSIDES: A Guide for Students and Collectors of Traditional Song. Publications of the American Folklore Society, Bibliographical and Special Ser., Vol. 8. *Univ. of Texas Press* (American Folklore Soc.) 1957 $9.95 pap. $4.00

NATIVE AMERICAN BALLADRY: A Descriptive Study and Bibliographical Syllabus. Publications of the American Folklore Society, Bibliographical and Special Ser., Vol. 1. *Univ. of Texas Press* (American Folklore Soc.) rev. ed. 1975 $14.50

Leach, MacEdward, Ed. THE BALLAD BOOK. *A. S. Barnes* 1966 pap. $6.95

(With Tristram P. Coffin, Eds.). THE CRITICS AND THE BALLAD: Readings. *Southern Illinois Univ. Press* 1961 1973 pap. $2.95

Lloyd, A. L. FOLK SONG IN ENGLAND. *International Pubs.* 1968 $10.00 pap. $3.65

Lomax, Alan, Comp. HARD HITTING SONGS FOR HARD-HIT PEOPLE. Notes by Woody Guthrie; music transcribed and ed. by Pete Seeger; fwd. by John Steinbeck. 1967. *Quick Fox* 1975 pap. $6.95

In his "Compiler's Postscript" Alan Lomax relates the topical song-making of the Depression and New Deal years to the earlier American and British traditions of songs of social complaint and protest. The 200 songs in this historical collection run the gamut of hard work, hard times and hard luck—on the farm, on the road, in jails, mines and factories, on strike and the picket line, and on the WPA. As the "logical person to write the commentary," Okie minstrel Woody Guthrie adds the "electric impact" of his personality and his style—(B. A. Botkin).

PENGUIN BOOK OF AMERICAN FOLK SONGS. *Penguin* 1965 pap. $3.95; *Gannon* $6.00

(With Sidney R. Crowell). AMERICAN FOLKSONG AND FOLKLORE: A Regional Bibliography. 1942. *Scholarly Press* 1970 $7.50

Lomax, John A. ADVENTURES OF A BALLAD HUNTER. 1947. *Macmillan* (Hafner) 1971 $12.50

(With Alan Lomax, Eds.). AMERICAN BALLADS AND FOLK SONGS. Fwd. by George Lyman Kittredge *Macmillan* 1934 $10.00

(With Alan Lomax, Eds.). FOLK SONG U.S.A.: The 111 Best American Ballads. Music ed. by Charles Seeger and Ruth Crawford Seeger *Hawthorn* 1948 $12.95; *New Am. Lib.* pap. $4.50

Malone, Bill C. COUNTRY MUSIC U.S.A.: A Fifty-Year History. *Univ. of Texas Press* 1968 1974 $10.00 pap. $4.75

Martin, Gyorgy. HUNGARIAN FOLK DANCES. *Int. Pubns. Service* 1974 $7.50

Mynatt, Constance, and Bernard Kaiman. FOLK DANCING: For Students and Teachers. *William C. Brown* 1969 pap. $3.50

Nettl, Bruno. FOLK AND TRADITIONAL MUSIC OF THE WESTERN CONTINENTS. *Prentice-Hall* 1965 $6.95 2nd ed. 1973 $8.95 pap. $4.95

AN INTRODUCTION TO FOLK MUSIC IN THE UNITED STATES. *Wayne State Univ. Press* 2nd ed. 1962 pap. $3.50

Newell, William Wells, Ed. GAMES AND SONGS OF AMERICAN CHILDREN. 1883. New introd. and index by Carl Withers *Dover* 1963 pap. $2.75; *Peter Smith* $5.50

Niles, John Jacob. THE BALLAD BOOK OF JOHN JACOB NILES. Decorations by William Barss. 1960. *Dover* 1971 pap. $4.95; *Peter Smith* $6.50

Sixty-five Child ballads (*see Child, Francis James, this list, above*) and variants, totaling 110 items, represent a small part of the veteran Kentucky balladeer's collection of over 50 years; includes music. The headnotes contain intriguing anecdotes and bits of mountain life and lore—(B. A. Botkin).

Okun, Milton, Comp. and arr. SOMETHING TO SING ABOUT! The Personal Choices of America's Folk Singers. Introd., commentary and guitar chords by the compiler *Macmillan* 1968 $8.95 Collier Bks. pap. 1970 $3.95

Pound, Louise. AMERICAN SONGS AND BALLADS. *Scribner* 1972 $6.95 pap. $1.95

Quiller-Couch, Sir Arthur. THE OXFORD BOOK OF BALLADS. 1910. *Somerset Pub.* 2 vols. repr. of 1955 ed. $35.50

Rubin, Ruth. A TREASURY OF JEWISH FOLKSONG. Piano settings by Ruth Post; ill. by T. Herzl Rome *Schocken* 1950 $7.50 pap. 1964 $3.50

VOICES OF A PEOPLE: The Story of Yiddish Folk Song. 1963. *McGraw-Hill* 2nd rev. ed. 1973 $9.95

Both a social history of Yiddish folksong and a song-history of East European Jewry, from the *Shtetl* or small town of the Czarist Pale to American and Palestinian immigration, the Soviet Union, Nazi concentration camps and the Warsaw Ghetto. Transliterated texts and literal translations, without tunes—(B. A. Botkin).

Sandburg, Carl. THE AMERICAN SONG BAG. 1927. *Harcourt* 1970 pap. $4.95. Two hundred eighty songs, ballads and ditties.

Scott, John Anthony. THE BALLAD OF AMERICA: The History of the United States in Song and Story. 1967. *Bantam* 1972 pap. $1.25. With the words and music of more than 125 songs.

Seeger, Pete. AMERICAN FAVORITE BALLADS. *Quick Fox* 1961 pap. $2.45

THE INCOMPLEAT FOLKSINGER. Ed. by Jo Metcalf Schwartz *Simon & Schuster* 1972 $12.50

"Capsule biographies, critical commentary, and melodies from a representative repertoire of authentic American folksingers"—(*Choice*).

Silverman, Jerry. FOLK BLUES: One Hundred and Ten American Folk Blues Compiled, Edited and Arranged for Voice, Piano and Guitar. *Macmillan* rev. ed. 1971 $10.00

Simpson, Claude M. THE BRITISH BROADSIDE BALLAD AND ITS MUSIC. *Rutgers Univ. Press* 1966 $20.00

Thede, Marion. THE FIDDLE BOOK: The Comprehensive Book on American Folk Music, Fiddling and Fiddle Styles, Including More Than 150 Traditional Fiddle Tunes, Compiled from Country Fiddlers. *Quick Fox* 1967 $9.95 pap. $4.95

Trask, Willard R. Ed. THE UNWRITTEN SONG: Poetry of the Primitive and Traditional People of the World. *Macmillan* 2 vols. 1966–1967 Vol. 1 The Far North, Africa, Indonesia, Melanesia, Australia Vol. 2 Asia, Polynesia, Micronesian North America, Central America, South America each $8.95. Mr. Trask translated some of the material. No music.

Wilgus, D. K. ANGLO-AMERICAN FOLKSONG SCHOLARSHIP SINCE 1898. *Rutgers Univ. Press* 1959 $12.50

An authoritative, comprehensive, judicious critical history of 20th-century folksong study in Great Britain and North America. An invaluable reference work to the 1950's on all problems and disputes involving origins, authorship, collecting patterns and attitudes, form, style, definitions, function and the like—(B. A. Botkin).

Wimberly, Lowry Charles. FOLKLORE IN THE ENGLISH AND SCOTTISH BALLADS. 1928. *Dover* 1965 pap. $4.00; *Peter Smith* $5.75

Wolf, Edwin, II. AMERICAN SONG SHEETS, SLIP BALLADS AND POETICAL BROADSIDES, 1850–1870: A Catalogue of the Collection of the Library Company of Philadelphia. *Kraus* 1963 $18.00

FOLKTALE, LEGEND AND MYTH

Included here are general studies and collections by country. For American regional, Indian and Afro-American titles, *see Section on American Regional and Ethnic Folklore, with its special subsections covering the two latter areas. For African folktales, see Chapter 17, African Literature,* Reader's Adviser, *Vol. 2.* For classical mythological studies and dictionaries, *see Chapter 3, Reference Books—Literature,* Reader's Adviser, *Vol. 1.* Too numerous to list here are many additional hardcover and paperback reprints—to be found in the catalogs of *Gale Research Co., Dover, Johnson Reprint, Peter Smith,* among others.

An excellent series, to which the reader is referred (*see publisher's catalog for information*), is the *Univ. of Chicago Press's* Folk Tales of the World Series, covering many countries and areas of the world; general editor, Richard M. Dorson.

Aarne, Antti. THE TYPES OF THE FOLKTALE: A Classification and Bibliography. Trans. and ed. by Stith Thompson. 1928. *Burt Franklin* 1971 $17.00. A translation and enlargement of a classic work in German, Aarne's "*Verzeichnis der Märchentypen.*"

Allen, Louis A. TIME BEFORE MORNING: Art and Myth of the Australian Aborigines. *T. Y. Crowell* 1975 $14.95

"The general reader is the beneficiary of his simply told 'tales' which often synthesize the variant versions of different aboriginal groups but do not distort their essential humanity"—(*PW*).

Ausubel, Nathan, Ed., with introd. and commentary. A TREASURY OF JEWISH FOLK-LORE: Stories, Traditions, Legends, Humor, Wisdom and Folk Songs of the Jewish People. *Crown* 1948 $6.95

Beckwith, Martha Warren. HAWAIIAN MYTHOLOGY. *Univ. Press of Hawaii* 1970 $12.00

Boas, Franz. DEVELOPMENT OF FOLK-TALES AND MYTHS. *Finch Press* $15.00

Bonnerjea, Biren. DICTIONARY OF SUPERSTITIONS AND MYTHOLOGY. 1927. *Gale Research Co.* (Singing Tree) 1969 $10.00

Briggs, Katherine M. THE FOLKLORE OF THE COTSWOLDS. *Rowman* 1974 $9.00

(Ed.). A DICTIONARY OF BRITISH FOLK-TALES: Incorporating the F. J. Norton Collection. *Indiana Univ. Press* 2 vols. 1970–71 Pt. A Folk Narratives (1970) Pt. B Folk Legends (1971) each $40.00 set $70.00

"This work will be useful in university literature, folklore, history and social history collections and in all libraries as a basic reference resource"—*(LJ)*.

(With Ruth L. Tongue, Eds.). FOLKTALES OF ENGLAND. Introd. by Katherine M. Briggs; fwd. by Richard M. Dorson. Folktales of the World Ser. *Univ. of Chicago Press* 1965 $7.50 pap. $2.95

Campbell, Joseph. THE MASKS OF GOD. *Viking* 4 vols. 1959–68 Vol. 1 Primitive Mythology (1959) Vol. 2 Oriental Mythology (1962) Vol. 3 Occidental Mythology (1964) Vol. 4 Creative Mythology (1968) boxed set $32.95 Compass Bks. 4 vols. pap. Vol. 1 $3.25 Vols. 2–3 each $3.95 Vol. 4 $4.95

THE MYTHIC IMAGE. *Princeton Univ. Press* 1974 $45.00

MYTHS TO LIVE BY. *Viking* 1972 $6.95; *Bantam* 1973 pap. $1.95

Campbell "explains the necessity of myths to human well-being. . . . He talks of myths of war and myths of peace, myths in schizophrenia, space travel, love and poetry"—*(New Yorker)*.

Chase, Richard, Ed. AMERICAN FOLK TALES AND SONGS. 1956. *Dover* 1971 pap. $2.00; *Peter Smith* $4.00

Christiansen, Reidar Thorwald, Ed., with introd. FOLKTALES OF NORWAY. Trans. by Pat Shaw Iversen; fwd. by Richard M. Dorson. Folktales of the World Ser. *Univ. of Chicago Press* 1964 $9.00 pap. $3.95

Colum, Padraic, Ed. LEGENDS OF HAWAII. *Yale Univ. Press* 1937 $10.00; *Ballantine Bks.* 1973 pap. $1.50

MYTHS OF THE WORLD. *Grosset* 1959 pap. $2.25

A TREASURY OF IRISH FOLKLORE: The Stories, Traditions, Legends, Humor, Wisdom, Ballads and Songs of the Irish People. *Crown* 1954 rev. ed. 1969 $5.95
"An immense fascinating volume"—*(LJ)*.

Courlander, Harold. TALES OF YORUBA GODS AND HEROES. *Crown* 1972 $6.95; *Fawcett Premier Bks.* 1974 pap. $1.50

TREASURY OF AFRICAN FOLKLORE. *Crown* 1974 $14.95

Dégh, Linda. FOLKTALES AND SOCIETY: Story Telling in a Hungarian Peasant Community. Trans. by Emily M. Schossberger *Indiana Univ. Press* rev. ed. 1969 $15.00

(Ed.). FOLKTALES OF HUNGARY. Trans. by Judit Halász; fwd. by Richard M. Dorson. Folktales of the World Ser. *Univ. of Chicago Press* 1965 $10.50 pap. $3.45

Dorson, Richard M. THE BRITISH FOLKLORISTS: A History. *Univ. of Chicago Press* 1969 $15.00

FOLK LEGENDS OF JAPAN: Over 100 Legends Arranged According to Their Geographical Location; Presented in Terms of Their Major Motifs. *Tuttle* 1962 pap. $3.25

(Ed.). AFRICAN FOLKLORE. *Indiana Univ. Press* 1972 $15.00; *Doubleday* Anchor Bks. 1972 pap. $3.50

(Ed.). PEASANT CUSTOMS AND SAVAGE MYTHS: Selections from the British Folklorists. Folk Tales of the World Ser. *Univ. of Chicago Press* 2 vols. 1968 set $25.00

(With Toichi Mabuchi, Eds.). STUDIES IN JAPANESE FOLKLORE. 1963. *Kennikat* 1973 $14.50

Eberhard, Wolfram. CHINESE FAIRY TALES AND FOLK TALES. 1937. *Folcroft* $25.00

STUDIES IN CHINESE FOLKLORE AND RELATED ESSAYS. *Indiana Univ. Press* 1970 pap. $10.00

(Ed.). FOLKTALES OF CHINA. Fwd. by Richard M. Dorson. Folktales of the World Ser. *Univ. of Chicago Press* 1965 $9.00 pap. $3.45; *Simon & Schuster* (Washington Square) pap. $1.25

Feldman, Burton, and Robert D. Richardson, Eds. THE RISE OF MODERN MYTHOLOGY, 1680–1860. *Indiana Univ. Press* 1972 $19.95

"An annotated collection of short excerpts from selected European and American works on the subject of myth published between 1680 and 1860. . . . This collection certainly deserves an audience among folklorists, anthropologists, and others in the humanities and social sciences who enjoy the mythology of myth in Western intellectual history"—*(Am. Anthropologist)*.

Freund, Philip. MYTHS OF CREATION. Ill. by Milton Charles. 1964. *Transatlantic* 1975 pap. $2.95

Gaster, Moses. THE EXEMPLA OF THE RABBIS: A Collection of Exempla, Apologues and Tales Culled from Hebrew Manuscripts and Rare Hebrew Books. 1924. New introd. by William G. Braude *KTAV* 1968 $16.95

Grant, Michael, and John Hazel. GODS AND MORTALS IN CLASSICAL MYTHOLOGY. *Merriam* 1973 $15.00

"Accounts of the characters around whom the myths of Greece and Rome were woven are presented in alphabetical order. The book describes the principal incidents in their mythological careers and records the more significant of the alternative forms which the myths have often assumed"—*(Choice)*.

Graves, Robert. THE GREEK MYTHS. *Braziller* 1959 $7.50; *Penguin* Pelican Bks. 2 vols. 1955 pap. Vol. 1 $1.75 Vol. 2 $1.45

(With Raphael Patai). HEBREW MYTHS: The Book of Genesis. *McGraw-Hill* 1966 pap. $2.95

Greenway, John. THE PRIMITIVE READER: An Anthology of Myths, Tales, Songs, Riddles, and Proverbs of Aboriginal Peoples around the World. *Gale Research Co.* 1965 $5.50

Grimm, Jacob. TEUTONIC MYTHOLOGY. Trans. by James S. Stallybrass *Peter Smith* 4 vols. 4th ed. set $28.00

Hall, Edwin S., Jr. THE ESKIMO STORYTELLER: Folktales from Noatak, Alaska. *Univ. of Tennessee Press* 1975 $18.50

"This book presents 188 folk tales from the Noatak people in northwestern Alaska. The tales were narrated by two elders of the village, translated by other villagers and then recorded without change by Hall"—*(LJ)*.

Hamilton, Edith. MYTHOLOGY. *Little* 1942 $7.95; *Grosset* 1961 pap. $2.50; *New Am. Lib.* 1971 pap. $1.50; *Franklin Watts* 1966 $12.50

Herskovits, Melville J., and Frances S. Herskovits. SURINAME FOLK-LORE. 1936. *AMS Press* 1969 $32.50

Hoogasian-Villa, Susie. 100 ARMENIAN TALES AND THEIR FOLKLORIST RELEVANCE. Fwd. by Thelma G. James *Wayne State Univ. Press* 1966 $11.95

Jacobs, Melville. CONTENT AND STYLE OF AN ORAL LITERATURE: Clackamas Chinook Myth and Tales. *Univ. of Chicago Press* 1959 $9.00

Keightley, Thomas. THE FAIRY MYTHOLOGY: Illustrative of the Romance and Superstition of Various Countries. 1828 rev. and enl. ed. 1850. *AMS Press* 1968 $10.00; *Gale Research Co.* $18.50; *Haskell* 1969 $18.95; *Johnson Reprint* 1969 $21.00

Kellett, Ernst E. THE STORY OF MYTHS. 1927. *Johnson Reprint* 1969 $14.00

Larousse Encyclopedia. THE NEW LAROUSSE ENCYCLOPEDIA OF MYTHOLOGY. Ed. by Felix Guirand *Putnam* rev. ed. 1969 $17.95

Lawson, John C. MODERN GREEK FOLKLORE AND ANCIENT GREEK RELIGION. *University Bks.* 1964 $10.00

Lindfors, Bernth. FOLKLORE IN NIGERIAN LITERATURE. *Holmes & Meier* (Africana Pub. Co.) 1973 $12.50

"A collection of previously published essays brought together because they all seek to define the impact of oral tradition on the emergence of a literary tradition in English in Nigeria. . . . This original and provocative book is indispensable for the serious student and the scholar, for it opens up new directions in critical methodology"—(*Choice*).

MacCulloch, John A., Louis H. Gray and George F. Moore, Eds. THE MYTHOLOGY OF ALL RACES. 1932. *Cooper* 13 vols. $175.00 (*consult publisher's catalog for separate titles*)

Massignon, Geneviève, Ed. FOLKTALES OF FRANCE. Trans. by Jacqueline Hyland; fwd. by Richard M. Dorson. Folktales of the World Ser. *Univ. of Chicago Press* 1968 $9.95

Metayer, Maurice. TALES FROM THE IGLOO. *Books Canada* 1974 $6.95
"Fascinating collection of 22 myths from the oral tradition of the Arctic Coast's Copper Indians"—(Publisher's note).

Murray, Henry A., Ed. MYTH AND MYTHMAKING. *Beacon* 1968 pap. $3.95

Noy, Dov, Ed. FOLKTALES OF ISRAEL. Trans. by Gene Baharav. Folktales of the World Ser. *Univ. of Chicago Press* 1963 $9.95 pap. $2.95

O'Suilleabhain, Sean. HANDBOOK OF IRISH FOLKLORE. 1942. *Gale Research Co.* (Singing Tree) 1970 $19.00

Paredes, Américo. FOLKTALES OF MEXICO. *Univ. of Chicago Press* 1970 $9.75 Phoenix Bks. 1974 pap. $3.95

Patai, Raphael. MYTH AND MODERN MAN. *Prentice-Hall* 1972 $9.95
"Mythic survivals and the mythmaking process in 'modern' society"—(*LJ*).

(With others). STUDIES IN BIBLICAL AND JEWISH FOLKLORE. 1960. *Haskell* 1972 $16.95

Pino-Saavedra, Yolindo, Ed. FOLKTALES OF CHILE. Trans. by Rockwell Gray; fwd. by Richard M. Dorson. Folktales of the World Ser. *Univ. of Chicago Press* 1967 $9.95

Rappoport, Angelo S. FOLKLORE OF THE JEWS. 1937. *Gale Research Co.* $14.00

MYTH AND LEGEND OF ANCIENT ISRAEL. Introd. and notes by Raphael Patai *KTAV* 3 vols. 1966 set $27.50

Rugoff, Milton, Ed. A HARVEST OF WORLD FOLKTALES. Ill. by Joseph Low *Viking* 1949 Compass Bks. 1968 pap. $3.95

Sebeok, Thomas A., Ed. MYTH: A Symposium. *Indiana Univ. Press* 1955 Midland Bks. pap. $2.45; *Peter Smith* $4.75

Seki, Keigo, Ed. FOLKTALES OF JAPAN. Trans. by Robert J. Adams; fwd. by Richard M. Dorson. Folktales of the World Ser. *Univ. of Chicago Press* 1963 $7.50 pap. $2.95

Senungetuk, Joseph E. GIVE OR TAKE A CENTURY: An Eskimo Chronicle. *Indiana Historical Press* 1971 $10.00 pap. $6.00

Skinner, Charles M. MYTHS AND LEGENDS OF OUR OWN LAND. 1896. *Gale Research Co.* (Singing Tree) 2 vols. 1969 $15.00

Sokolov, Yury M. RUSSIAN FOLKLORE. Trans. by Catherine R. Smith. 1966. *Gale Research Co.* 1971 $15.00

Surmelian, Leon. APPLES OF IMMORTALITY: Folktales of Armenia. Ill. by Stewart Irwin *Univ. of California Press* 1968 $8.95

Thompson, Stith. THE FOLKTALE. 1946. *Holt* 1947 1951 $12.00. Includes two appendixes: "Important Works on the Folktale" and "Principal Collections of Folktales," as well as index of Tale Types and index of Motifs.

(Ed.). ONE HUNDRED FAVORITE FOLK TALES. *Indiana Univ. Press* 1968 $15.00 pap. 1974 $5.95. Will appeal especially to young readers.

See also Aarne, Antti, this list.

Werner, Edward T. MYTHS AND LEGENDS OF CHINA. 1922. *Blom* 1971 $13.75

AMERICAN REGIONAL AND ETHNIC FOLKLORE

This is a long and fairly comprehensive listing by regions and groups, arranged as follows: New England; The Middle Atlantic States; The South; The Midwest; The West; American Indian Folklore; Afro-American Folklore. Since every American is perhaps primarily interested in the folklore of his own people or area, considerable space has been allowed for each.

New England

Botkin, B. A., Ed., with introd. and commentary. A Treasury of New England Folklore: Stories, Ballads and Traditions of Yankee Folk. 1947. *Crown* rev. ed. 1965 $7.50

Dorson, Richard M. Jonathan Draws the Long Bow: New England Popular Tales and Legends. 1946. *Russell & Russell* 1970 $11.50

Earle, Alice Morse. Customs and Fashions in Old New England. 1893. *Corner House* 1969 $8.50; *Gale Research Co.* (Singing Tree) 1968 $8.50; *Tuttle* 1971 pap. $3.95

Flanders, Helen Hartness, Comp. and ed. Ancient Ballads Traditionally Sung in New England. With critical analyses by Tristram P. Coffin; music annotations by Bruno Nettl *Univ. of Pennsylvania Press* 4 vols. 1960–65 each $10.00 set $35.00. From the Helen Hartness Flanders Ballad Collection at Middlebury College.

(With George Brown). Vermont Folk-Songs and Ballads. *Gale Research Co.* 1968 $7.50

(With Marguerite Olney, Eds.). Ballads Migrant in New England. 1953. *Bks. for Libraries* $9.50

(With others, Eds.). The New Green Mountain Songster: Traditional Folksongs of Vermont. 1939. *Gale Research Co.* 1966 $7.50

Hazard, Thomas Robinson ("Shepherd Tom"). The Jonny Cake Papers of "Shepherd Tom," Together with Reminiscences of Narragansett School Days. 1915. Rediscovering America Ser. *Johnson Reprint* 1968 $24.50. Includes a biographical sketch and notes by Rowland Gibson Hazard.

Huntington, Gale. Songs the Whalemen Sang. 1964. *Dover* 1968 pap. $3.00

"Approximately 175 songs . . . gleaned from 18th and 19th century diaries, journals, log books and two manuscript song collections . . . assembled by a folk singer from Martha's Vineyard [who] has had to dig [the tunes] out of other sources"—(*LJ*). Photographs from whalemen's journals and photographs of scrimshaw from the Whaling Museum of New Bedford, Mass.

Johnson, Clifton. Old-Time Schools and School Books. 1904. New introd. by Carl Withers; ill. by the author *Dover* 1963 pap. $4.00; *Peter Smith* $6.00

(Comp., with introd.). What They Say in New England and Other New England Folklore. 1896. Ed. with introd. by Carl Withers *Columbia* 1963 $10.00

Kittredge, George Lyman. The Old Farmer and His Almanack: Being Some Observations on Life and Manners in New England a Hundred Years Ago Suggested by Reading the Earlier Numbers of Mr. Robert B. Thomas's Farmer's Almanack, Together with Extracts Curious, Instructive, and Entertaining, as well as a Variety of Miscellaneous Matter, Embellished with Engravings. 1904. *Blom* 1967 $12.75; *Corner House* 1974 $14.00. The author is, of course, the late distinguished Harvard professor of English.

Witchcraft in Old New England. 1929. *Russell & Russell* 1958 $16.00; *Atheneum* 1972 pap. $4.95

Lord, Priscilla Sawyer, and Daniel J. Foley. The Folk Arts and Crafts of New England. Introd. by the authors *Chilton* 1965 1975 $12.50 pap. $8.95

This includes representation of all the arts and crafts for daily use and enjoyment, from spinning, weaving and dyeing to dolls and toys; illustrated with more than 500 pictures from New England's great museums and historical societies—(B. A. Botkin).

Mitchell, Edwin Valentine. Horse and Buggy Age in New England. 1937. *Gale Research Co.* 1974 $9.00

It's an Old State of Maine Custom. *Vanguard* 1949 $3.00

Needham, Walter, and Barrows Mussey. The Book of Country Things. *Stephen Greene Press* 1965 $4.50

The Middle Atlantic States

Bayard, Samuel Preston, Comp. and ed., with introd. Hill Country Tunes: Instrumental Folk Music of Southwestern Pennsylvania. 1944. *Kraus* $9.00

Beck, Henry Charlton. The Roads of Home: Lanes and Legends of New Jersey. Fwd. by Carl Carmer *Rutgers Univ. Press* 1956 $6.00 pap. $2.75

For other titles on New Jersey by Mr. Beck, consult Rutgers Univ. Press catalog.

Carmer, Carl. Dark Trees to the Wind: A Cycle of York State Years. 1949. Decorations by John O'Hara Cosgrave II *McKay* 1965 $4.95 pap. $2.25

Listen for a Lonesome Drum: A York State Chronicle. 1936. Ill. by Cyrus LeRoy Baldridge *McKay* 1966 $4.95 pap. $2.45

Earle, Alice Morse. Colonial Days in Old New York. 1896. *Gale Research Co.* (Singing Tree Press) 1968 $8.50

Korson, George. Black Rock: Mining Folklore of the Pennsylvania Dutch. *Johns Hopkins Press* 1960 $15.00

Coal Dust on the Fiddle: Songs and Stories of the Bituminous Industry. 1943. Introd. by George Korson; fwd. by John Greenway; music transcriptions by Ruth Crawford Seeger *Gale Research Co.* (Folklore Associates) 1965 $8.00. Includes biographies of individual bards and minstrels.

Minstrels of the Mine Patch: Songs and Stories of the Anthracite Industry. 1938. New fwd. by Archie Green; music transcriptions by Melvin Le Mon *Gale Research Co.* (Folklore Associates) 1964 $7.50. Includes biographical sketches of traditional bards and minstrels.

(Ed.). Pennsylvania Songs and Legends. *Johns Hopkins Press* 1960 $15.00

Leach, MacEdward, and Henry Glassie. Guide for Collectors of Oral Traditions and Folk Cultural Materials in Pennsylvania. *Pennsylvania Historical & Museum Comm.* 1973 pap. $.75

Stoudt, John B. The Liberty Bells of Pennsylvania. 1930. *Finch Press* $15.00

Stoudt, John Joseph. Sunbonnets and Shoofly Pies: Pennsylvania Dutch Cultural History. *A. S. Barnes* 1973 $25.00

Thompson, Harold W. New York State Folktales, Legends and Ballads. 1939. *Dover* 2 vols. pap. each $4.00; (with title "Body, Boots and Britches: Folktales, Ballads and Speech from Country New York") *Peter Smith* $5.75

Wyld, Lionel D. Low Bridge!: Folklore and the Erie Canal. *Syracuse Univ. Press* 1962 $5.50

Yoder, Don. Pennsylvania Spirituals. *Gale Research Co.* (Folklore Associates) 1961 $7.50

The South

Anderson, John Q., Ed. With the Bark on: Popular Humor of the Old South. Drawings by Mary Alice Bahler *Vanderbilt Univ. Press* 1967 $7.50. Seventy sketches of backwoods humor in the states of Arkansas, Missouri, Tennessee, Mississippi, Alabama, Georgia and Louisiana from 1835 to 1860.

Botkin, B. A., Ed. A Treasury of Southern Folklore: Stories, Ballads and Traditions of the People of the South. Fwd. by Douglas Southall Freeman *Crown* 1949 $7.50. Includes music.

Brown, Frank C. THE FRANK C. BROWN COLLECTION OF NORTH CAROLINA FOLKLORE. Ed. by Newman Ivey White and others; wood engravings by Clare Leighton *Duke Univ. Press* 7 vols. 1952–64 each $15.00 set $95.00

The folklore of North Carolina was collected by Dr. Frank C. Brown from 1912 to 1943 in collaboration with the North Carolina Folklore Society, of which he was secretary-treasurer 1913–43. Vol. 1 Games and Rhymes, Beliefs and Customs, Riddles, Proverbs, Speech, Tales and Legends Vol. 2 Folk Ballads from North Carolina Vol. 3 Folk Songs from North Carolina Vol. 4 The Music of the Ballads and Songs Vol. 5 The Music of the Folk Songs Vol. 6 Popular Beliefs and Superstitions from North Carolina, Pt. 1 Vol. 7 Popular Beliefs and Superstitions from North Carolina, Pt. 2.

Campbell, Marie. CLOUD-WALKING. *Indiana Univ. Press* 1971 $8.95. Folktales collected by the author in the mountain areas of eastern Kentucky, beginning in 1926.

Chase, Richard, Ed. THE JACK TALES: Told by R. M. Ward and His Kindred in the Beech Mountain Section of Western North Carolina and by Other Descendants of Council Harmon (1803–1896) Elsewhere in the Southern Mountains; with Three Tales from Wise County, Virginia. Appendix comp. by Herbert Halpert; ill. by Berkeley Williams, Jr. *Houghton* 1943 $5.95

These are Southern Appalachian versions of the "Jack" cycle of folktales of the British-American trickster hero, the poor, unpromising, lazy, and often unscrupulous boy who wins out by his cleverness, sharpwittedness and luck, as in "Jack and the Beanstalk" and "Jack the Giant-Killer"—(B. A. Botkin).

Combs, Josiah H. FOLK SONGS OF THE SOUTHERN UNITED STATES. Ed. by D. K. Wilgus from the original French *"Folk-Songs du Midi des États-Unis"* and the English-language manuscript on which it was based. Publications of the American Folklore Society, Bibliographical and Special Ser., Vol. 19 *Univ. of Texas Press* (American Folklore Soc.) 1967 $7.50. Includes music.

Cox, John Harrington, Ed. FOLK-SONGS OF THE SOUTH. 1925. New fwd. by A. K. Davis, Jr.; 29 tunes ed. by Lydia I. Hinkel. Coll. under the auspices of the West Virginia Folklore Society. *Gale Research Co.* (Folklore Associates) 1963 $10.00; *Peter Smith* $6.00. One hundred eighty-five ballads and songs, including some 33 Child ballads. *(See listing on Folksong and Dance under Child, Francis James.)*

Davis, Arthur Kyle, Jr. FOLK-SONGS OF VIRGINIA. 1949. *AMS Press* $16.50

(Ed.). TRADITIONAL BALLADS OF VIRGINIA. 1929. *Univ. Press of Virginia* 1969 $8.50. Coll. under the auspices of the Virginia Folklore Society. Fifty-one Child ballads with variants, totaling 440 items and 148 tunes. *(See list on Folksong and Dance under Child, Francis James.)*

Harris, Joel Chandler. THE COMPLETE TALES OF UNCLE REMUS. Comp. by Richard Chase; ill. by Arthur Burdette Frost and others *Houghton* 1955 $12.50

STORIES OF GEORGIA. 1896. *Cherokee* 1971 $6.50; *Finch Press* $14.00; *Reprint Hse. Intl.* 1972 $15.00

Jackson, George Pullen. WHITE SPIRITUALS IN THE SOUTHERN UPLANDS: The Story of the Fasola Folk, Their Songs, Singing, and "Buckwheat Notes." 1933. New introd. by Don Yoder *Dover* 1965 pap. $4.00; *Gannon* $7.50. Includes music. To his tracing of the spread of "shape-note" music (each note of the scale being individually shaped for quick recognition) from New England to the South and West, Jackson appends his controversial theory of the origin of Negro spirituals in white camp-meeting songs.

Randolph, Vance. OZARK FOLKLORE: A Bibliography. *Indiana Univ. Press* 1972 pap. $25.00

OZARK MAGIC AND FOLKLORE. (Orig. "Ozark Superstitions.") 1947. *Dover* pap. $2.75; *Peter Smith* $5.00

See also his title in Folk and Popular Humor

Roberts, Leonard W. OLD GREASYBEARD: Tales from the Cumberland Gap. *Gale Research Co.* 1969 $6.00

SANG BRANCH SETTLERS: Folksongs and Tales of a Kentucky Mountain Family. *Univ. of Texas Press* 1974 $12.50

Scarborough, Dorothy. A SONG CATCHER IN THE SOUTHERN MOUNTAINS: American Folk Songs of British Ancestry. 1937. *AMS Press* $10.00. Over 200 songs from a collection made in Virginia and North Carolina in 1930. Includes music.

Sharp, Cecil J., and Maud Karpeles, Eds. EIGHTY ENGLISH FOLK SONGS FROM THE SOUTHERN APPALACHIANS. *M.I.T. Press* 1969 pap. $2.45

ENGLISH FOLK SONGS FROM THE SOUTHERN APPALACHIANS: Comprising Two Hundred and Seventy-Three Songs and Ballads, with Nine Hundred and Sixty-Eight Tunes, including Thirty-Nine Tunes contributed by Olive Dame Campbell. *Oxford* 2 vols. 1932 set $38.50

Cecil J. Sharp, English musician and folksong collector, who sought out many folksongs of English origin from this region, was director of the English Folk-Dance Society from its founding in 1911 until his death in 1924.

Thomas, Jeannette. BALLAD MAKIN' IN THE MOUNTAINS OF KENTUCKY. 1939. *Gale Research Co.* $14.00. Music arr. by Walter Kolb. About 120 ballads dealing with current events reflecting or affecting Southern mountain life.

The Midwest

Belden, Henry M., Ed. BALLADS AND SONGS COLLECTED BY THE MISSOURI FOLKLORE SOCIETY. 1940. *Univ. of Missouri Press* 1940 2nd ed. 1955 $10.00. Over 400 songs and ballads, including about 30 Child ballads *(see listing on Folksong and Dance under Child, Francis James)*. Includes music.

Dorson, Richard M. BLOODSTOPPERS AND BEARWALKERS: Folk Traditions of the Upper Peninsula. *Harvard Univ. Press* 1952 $10.00 pap. $3.95

Gard, Robert E., and Elaine Reetz. THE TRAIL OF THE SERPENT: The Fox River Valley Lore and Legend. *Wisconsin House* new ed. 1973 $8.95

Gard, Robert E., and L. G. Sorden. WISCONSIN LORE. *Wisconsin House* 1971 $5.95

Gardner, Emelyn Elizabeth, and Geraldine Jencks Chickering, Comps. and eds. BALLADS AND SONGS OF SOUTHERN MICHIGAN. Introd. by E. E. Gardner; new fwd. by Albert B. Friedman *Gale Research Co.* (Folklore Associates) 1966 $10.00. Two hundred one songs and ballads with music.

Kramer, Frank R. VOICES IN THE VALLEY: Mythmaking and Folk Belief in the Shaping of the Middle West. *Univ. of Wisconsin Press* 1964 $12.50

McIntosh, David S. FOLK SONGS AND SINGING GAMES OF THE ILLINOIS OZARKS. Ed. by Dale R. Whiteside *Southern Illinois Univ. Press* 1974 $8.95

Shephard, Esther. PAUL BUNYAN. *Harcourt* 1941 $5.95

Stevens, James. PAUL BUNYAN. *Knopf* 1948 $5.95

Stout, Earl J. FOLKLORE FROM IOWA. 1936. *Kraus* $12.00

Welsch, Roger L., Comp. A TREASURY OF NEBRASKA PIONEER FOLKLORE. Ill. by Jack Brodie *Univ. of Nebraska Press* 1966 $9.95

"Largely compiled from the thirty *Nebraska Folklore Pamphlets* . . . compiled by workers of the W.P.A. Writers Program of the Works Progress Administration in the State of Nebraska, J. Harris Gable, State Supervisor, and Robert E. Carlsen, Editor," 1937–40.

The West

Boatright, Mody C. FOLK LAUGHTER ON THE AMERICAN FRONTIER. 1949. *Peter Smith* $5.25

FOLKLORE OF THE OIL INDUSTRY. *Southern Methodist Univ. Press* 1963 $5.95

(With William A. Owens). TALES FROM THE DERRICK FLOOR. *Doubleday* 1970 $6.95

(With Wilson M. Hudson and Allen Maxwell, Eds.). FOLK TRAVELERS: Ballads, Tales, and Talk. Texas Folklore Society Publication, No. 25 *Southern Methodist Univ. Press* 1953 $5.95

(With Wilson M. Hudson and Allen Maxwell, Eds.). TEXAS FOLK AND FOLKLORE. Texas Folklore Society Publication, No. 26 *Southern Methodist Univ. Press* 1954 1974 $7.95

For other Texas Folklore Society Publications edited by Dr. Boatright, see Southern Methodist Univ. Press catalog.

Botkin, B. A., Ed. A TREASURY OF WESTERN FOLKLORE. Fwd. by Bernard DeVoto *Crown* 1951 rev. ed. 1975 $9.95

Brunvand, Jan H. GUIDE FOR COLLECTORS OF FOLKLORE IN UTAH. *Univ. of Utah Press* 1971 $6.50 pap. $3.95

Cheney, Thomas E., Ed. MORMON SONGS FROM THE ROCKY MOUNTAINS: A Compilation of Mormon Folksongs. Memoirs of the American Folklore Society, Vol. 53 *Univ. of Texas Press* (American Folklore Soc.) 1968 $7.95

Dobie, J. Frank. CORONADO'S CHILDREN: Tales of Lost Mines and Buried Treasures of the Southwest. Ill. by Ben Carlton Mead *Grosset* 1930 1963 $3.95. Woven out of Dobie's "Legends of Texas." Publications of the American Folklore Society, Vol. 3, 1924 o.p.

FLAVOR OF TEXAS. 1936. *Scholarly Press* 1971 $14.50

LEGENDS OF TEXAS. 1924. *Gale Research Co.* $7.50

THE LONGHORNS. Ill. by Tom Lea *Little* 1941 $10.00; *Grosset* Univ. Lib. 1957 pap. $3.95. The Texas longhorn as maker of history and folklore.

TALES OF OLD-TIME TEXAS. *Little* 1955 $7.50 pap. $2.95

A VAQUERO OF THE BRUSH COUNTRY. 1929. Partly from the reminiscences of John Young. *Little* rev. ed. 1960 $8.95

Discusses the practices of the open range, characteristics of ranch people, the cowboy's belongings; includes tales of longhorns, razorbacks, mustangs and other range yarns, as well as authentic lore of the bloody border and the cattle trail—(B. A. Botkin).

THE VOICE OF THE COYOTE. Ill. by Claus J. Murie *Little* 1949 $6.95; *Univ. of Nebraska Press* Bison Bks. 1961 pap. $2.95. Folklore tales, myths and oddities of the coyote in his own world and the world of man.

(Ed.). GUIDE TO LIFE AND LITERATURE OF THE SOUTHWEST. *Southern Methodist Univ. Press* rev. ed. 1973 $5.95 pap. $2.95

(Ed.). SOUTHWESTERN LORE. Texas Folklore Society Publication, No. 19 *Southern Methodist Univ. Press* 1931 1965 $5.00

(Ed.). TEXAS AND SOUTHWESTERN LORE. Texas Folklore Society Publication, No. 6 *Southern Methodist Univ. Press* 1927 1967 $6.95

For other Texas Folklore Society Publications edited by Mr. Dobie, see Southern Methodist Univ. Press catalog.

Greenway, John, Ed. FOLKLORE OF THE GREAT WEST. *American West* 1969 $10.75

Lingenfelter, Richard E., Richard A. Dwyer, and David Cohen, Eds. SONGS OF THE AMERICAN WEST. Each section has its own introd. by the editors; drawings by Steven M. Johnson. *Univ. of California Press* 1968 $22.50

This collection of nearly 300 songs about the West (an expansion of Dwyer and Lingenfelter's "The Songs of the Gold Rush," 1964) covers almost a century of Western Life from the 1840's to the Depression of the 1930's. Out of the frontier melting pot emerge songs of loneliness and—in contrast—songs of cooperation and union. With their focus on social history, the editors have ignored type distinctions (between folksongs, art songs, broadsides and ballads) and organized their arrangement by occupational or social grouping. As the jacket says, these are "for social and cultural historians, folklorists, musicians, and Western buffs"—(B. A. Botkin).

Moore, Ethel, and Chauncey O. Moore, Eds. BALLADS AND FOLKSONGS OF OKLAHOMA. *Univ. of Oklahoma Press* 1964 pap. 1974 $4.95

BALLADS AND FOLKSONGS OF THE SOUTHWEST. *Univ. of Oklahoma Press* 1964 $15.00

Twenty-five years in the making, this collection, largely urban in its sources and backgrounds, contains 194 titles, 204 texts and 213 tunes.

Paredes, Américo. WITH HIS PISTOL IN HIS HAND: A Border Ballad and Its Hero. Drawings by Jo Alys Downs *Univ. of Texas Press* 1958 $7.50 pap. $2.75

Slotkin, Richard. REGENERATION THROUGH VIOLENCE: The Mythology of the American Frontier, 1600–1860. *Wesleyan Univ. Press* 1973 $25.00 pap. $5.95

"A monumental work . . . pursues this elusive entity through the whole of American mythology"—(*Wassaja*).

Thorp, N. Howard ("Jack"). SONGS OF THE COWBOYS. 1908. With variants, commentary, notes and lexicon by Austin E. and Alta S. Fife *Clarkson N. Potter* 1966 $7.95

The 23 songs of this 1908 collection by "Jack" Thorp, as he was known, are reprinted in facsimile. Included also are the original or reconstructed texts—supplemented with variants and tunes, as well as historical and critical notes—against a backdrop of cowboy culture and the cowboy myth. Bibliography for each song; lexicon and general bibliography. "A feast for cowboy and folksong buffs"—(B. A. Botkin).

American Indian Folklore

Valuable additions to the works below may be found in the representative list of titles in American Indian myth, folktale and folk music published by the Bureau of American Ethnology of the Smithsonian Institution and available from the Government Printing Office, Washington, D.C.

Adamson, Thelma. FOLK-TALES OF THE COAST SALISH. 1934. Memoirs of the American Folklore Society, Vol. 27 *Kraus* $22.00

Alexander, Hartley Burr. NORTH AMERICAN MYTHOLOGY. 1932. Mythology of All Races Ser. *Cooper* 1964 $14.50

WORLD'S RIM: Great Mysteries of the North American Indians. *Univ. of Nebraska Press* Bison Bks. 1967 pap. $1.95

Beck, Horace P. GLUSCAP THE LIAR AND OTHER INDIAN TALES. Ill. by Arthur K. D. Healy *Wheelwright* 1966 $5.95. Forty-one tales of the Penobscot Indians of Maine summarized, with additional material on other Penobscot folklore.

Benedict, Ruth F. THE CONCEPT OF THE GUARDIAN SPIRIT IN NORTH AMERICA. 1923. *Kraus* pap. $6.00

TALES OF THE COCHITI INDIANS. 1931. *Scholarly Press* $14.50

ZUNI MYTHOLOGY. 1935. *AMS Press* 2 vols. 1969 set $47.50; *Finch Press* 2 vols. set $44.00

Boatright, Mody C., Ed. THE SKY IS MY TIPI: Kiowa-Apache Tales and Lore. Texas Folklore Society Publication, No. 22 *Southern Methodist Univ. Press* 1949 1966 $6.95

Burton, Jimalee. INDIAN HERITAGE, INDIAN PRIDE: Stories that Touched My Life. *Univ. of Oklahoma Press* 1974 $12.50

"Burton, part-Cherokee artist, poet, and author, has related 37 memories of her Indian heritage for the expressed purposes of enlightening white men about American Indians and helping to restore to Indian people pride in their heritage"—(*Choice*).

Clark, Ella E. INDIAN LEGENDS FROM THE NORTHERN ROCKIES. Civilization of the American Indian Ser. *Univ. of Oklahoma Press* 1966 1974 $7.95

INDIAN LEGENDS OF THE PACIFIC NORTHWEST. *Univ. of California Press* 1953 pap. $2.45

Clark, LaVerne Harrell. THEY SANG FOR HORSES: The Impact of the Horse on Navajo and Apache Folklore. Ill. by DeGrazia *Univ. of Arizona Press* 1966 pap. $8.50. Myths, songs, rituals, customs and personal narratives concerned with the deification of the horse, the acquisition of horses and their unusual powers.

Coffin, Tristram P., Ed. INDIAN TALES OF NORTH AMERICA: An Anthology for the Adult Reader. *Univ. of Texas Press* 1961 pap. $4.00

de Angulo, Jaime. INDIAN TALES. 1953. *Ballantine Bks.* 1974 pap. $1.65; fwd. by Carl Carmer, ill. by the author *Farrar, Straus* (Hill & Wang) Am. Century 1962 pap. $2.65

Dunn, Dorothy. AMERICAN INDIAN PAINTING OF THE SOUTHWEST AND PLAINS AREA. *Univ. of New Mexico Press* 1968 $30.00

Hausman, Gerald. SITTING ON THE BLUE-EYED BEAR: Navajo Myths and Legends. *Lawrence Hill* 1975 $10.00

"A generous double-grouping of Dineh ceremonial chants, dances and poems along with a number of remarkably playful and roundabout tales drawn from oral tradition"—(PW).

Kroeber, Theodora. THE INLAND WHALE. 1959. Fwd. by Oliver La Farge; ill. by Joseph Crivy *Univ. of California Press* 1959 pap. $2.45; *Peter Smith* $5.00. Nine stories retold from the folklore of California Indian tribes.

Laws, G. Malcolm, Jr. NATIVE AMERICAN BALLADRY. *Univ. of Texas Press* 1975 $14.50

Leland, Charles Godfrey. ALGONQUIN LEGENDS OF NEW ENGLAND. 1884. *Gale Research Co.* (Singing Tree) 1968 $12.50

Marriott, Alice, and Carl K. Rachlin. AMERICAN INDIAN MYTHOLOGY. *T. Y. Crowell* 1968 $10.95; *Apollo* 1972 pap. $2.95; *New Am. Lib.* Mentor Bks. 1972 pap. $1.50

Merriam, Alan P. ETHNOMUSICOLOGY OF THE FLATHEAD INDIANS. *Aldine* 1967 $12.95

"Professor Merriam, one of the nation's outstanding anthropologists, and an authority on American Indian and African affairs, is undoubtedly the leader of current investigations into ethnomusicology. His book, the result of two field trips and a great deal of research, stands as an important work in the literature of primitive music, both for Professor Merriam's insight into Indian beliefs, social thought, customs, and intellectual responsiveness, and for the major contribution he makes towards the developing techniques of ethnomusicology"—(LJ).

Nettl, Bruno. NORTH AMERICAN INDIAN MUSICAL STYLES. 1954. Memoirs of the American Folklore Society, Vol. 45 *Univ. of Texas Press* (American Folklore Soc.) pap. $2.50

Parsons, Elsie Clews. TAOS TALES. 1940. *Kraus* $11.00

 ——— TEWA TALES. 1926. *Kraus* $14.00

 ——— (Ed.). AMERICAN INDIAN LIFE. 1922. Introd. by A. C. Kroeber; ill. by C. Grant LaFarge *Univ. of Nebraska Press* Bison Bks. 1967 pap. $2.95. Twenty-eight essays on North American Indian life in narrative form arranged by regions.

Reichard, Gladys A. NAVAHO RELIGION: A Study of Symbolism. *Princeton Univ. Press* Bollingen Ser. 2 vols. 2nd ed. 1974 $17.50 pap. $6.95

Stevens, James R. SACRED LEGENDS OF THE SANDY LAKE CREE. *McClelland & Stewart* 1971 $6.95

Thompson, Stith, Sel. and annot., with introd. TALES OF THE NORTH AMERICAN INDIANS. 1929. *Indiana Univ. Press* 1966 pap. $3.95; *Peter Smith* $6.00

Ninety-six tales arranged according to type, with "comparative notes, to show the extent of the distribution of each tale and each motif, [presented] in such wise as to be obvious to the general reader"—(Introduction).

Afro-American Folklore

For related listings, see Chapters 8, The Social Sciences: Integration, Racial Problems, Minorities, and 9, History, Government and Politics—American: Afro-American History, this Vol.

Abrahams, Roger D., with introd. DEEP DOWN IN THE JUNGLE: Negro Narrative Folklore from the Streets of Philadelphia. 1964. *Aldine* 1970 $10.95 pap. $3.95

This, preceded by Mr. Abrahams' introduction on "A Method of Folklore Analysis," is "a selected body of obscene folk narrative collected in a single four-block Negro neighborhood in Philadelphia and consisting of playing the dozens, toasts, and jokes. In addition to the treatment of the specific sociological and psychological patterns of urban neighborhood and [mother-centered] family life [and related material], there is much insightful comment on types of the

Negro contest hero developed in this gang subculture"—(B.A. Botkin, in the *N.Y. Folklore Quarterly*). Mr. Abrahams' article on "Playing the Dozens" originally appeared in the September 1962 issue of the *Journal of American Folklore*, to which the interested reader is referred.

Allen, William F., Charles P. Ware, and Lucy McKim Garrison, Eds. SLAVE SONGS OF THE UNITED STATES. 1867. *Bks. for Libraries* $8.75; *Peter Smith* 1960 $4.00

Beckwith, Martha Warren. BLACK ROADWAYS: A Study of Jamaican Folk Life. 1929. *Negro Univs. Press* $14.00

JAMAICA ANANSI STORIES. 1924. *Kraus* $14.00

Blesh, Rudi. SHINING TRUMPETS: A History of Jazz. 1946. *DaCapo* 1975 $20.00

Botkin, B. A., Ed. LAY MY BURDEN DOWN: A Folk History of Slavery. *Univ. of Chicago Press* 1945 $7.50 Phoenix Bks. pap. $2.95. Reminiscences and anecdotes as told by former slaves to workers of the Federal Writers Project in the thirties.

Brewer, J. Mason, Ed. AMERICAN NEGRO FOLKLORE. *Quadrangle Bks.* 1968 1974 pap. $4.95

Brookes, Stella Brewer. JOEL CHANDLER HARRIS—FOLKLORIST. *Univ. of Georgia Press* 1950 $6.00

Carawan, Guy, and Candie Carawan, Eds., with introd. AIN'T YOU GOT A RIGHT TO THE TREE OF LIFE?: The People of Johns Island, South Carolina—Their Faces, Their Words and Their Songs. Photographs by Robert Yellin; music transcribed by Ethel Raim; pref. by Alan Lomax *Simon & Schuster* 1966 $7.95 pap. $3.95

"The life history of an entire [South Carolina Sea Island] community, at work, play, and worship, remembering its cotton plantation slave past . . . and trying to adjust its folk heritage to changing times and patterns. . . . The strongest links with the past are religion [and] the bonds of human 'need and growth' at the grassroots and Tree of Life level. . . . The exciting and dramatic sounds of the spirituals, shouts, folk tales, and children's game songs [are] to be heard on the companion Folkways record, *Been in the Storm So Long*. . . . A landmark among Negro folklore collections"—(B.A. Botkin, in the *N.Y. Folklore Quarterly*).

Chambers, Henry A., Ed. THE TREASURY OF NEGRO SPIRITUALS. Fwd. by Marian Anderson *Emerson Bks.* 1963 $7.50

Charters, Samuel B. POETRY OF THE BLUES. *Avon* 1970 pap. $1.25

Courlander, Harold. THE DRUM AND THE HOE: Life and Lore of the Haitian People. *Univ. of California Press* 1960 1973 $21.50

NEGRO FOLK MUSIC, U.S.A. *Columbia* 1963 $15.00 pap. $3.45

Cuney-Hare, Maud. NEGRO MUSICIANS AND THEIR MUSIC. *Da Capo* 1974 $22.50

Dorson, Richard M. AMERICAN NEGRO FOLKTALES. *Fawcett* 1972 pap. $1.50; *Peter Smith* $3.25

NEGRO FOLKTALES IN MICHIGAN. 1956. *Greenwood* 1974 $12.25

NEGRO TALES FROM PINE BLUFF, ARKANSAS AND CALVIN, MICHIGAN. 1958. *Kraus* $13.00

Dundes, Alan. MOTHER WIT FROM THE LAUGHING BARREL: Readings in the Interpretation of Afro-American Folklore. *Prentice-Hall* 1973 $12.95 pap. $7.95

Edwards, Charles L. BAHAMA SONGS AND STORIES. 1895. *Kraus* $9.00

Fisher, Miles Mark. NEGRO SLAVE SONGS IN THE UNITED STATES. 1953. *Citadel Press* 1969 pap. $2.45; *Russell & Russell* 1968 $13.00

Hughes, Langston, Ed. THE BOOK OF NEGRO HUMOR. *Dodd* 1965 $5.00; *Apollo* 1970 pap. $1.95

(With Arna Bontemps, Eds.). THE BOOK OF NEGRO FOLKLORE. Introd. by Arna Bontemps *Dodd* 1958 $8.00; *Apollo* 1969 pap. $3.45

In compiling the 24 sections of this rewarding anthology the editors discovered that the lore of the Negro turned out to be a deeper vein than was at first suspected. From African prototypes and memories of slavery to "The Jazz Folk" and "Harlem Jive," from "Black Magic and Chance" to "The 'Problem,' " from work songs, sermons and spirituals to songs, poetry and prose "in the folk manner," the book explores the integral relationship between Negro folklore, life, and literature.

Like the slaves, writes Arna Bontemps in his introduction, whose folktales "were actually projections of personal experiences and hopes and defeats in terms of symbols," today's "Negro writers, and the many others who have used the Negro as subject . . . , continue to dip into the richness of Negro folk life"—(B. A. Botkin).

Jackson, Bruce. WAKE UP DEAD MAN: Afro-American Worksongs from Texas Prisons. *Harvard Univ. Press* 1972 $14.95 pap. $4.95

(Ed.). THE NEGRO AND HIS FOLKLORE IN NINETEENTH-CENTURY PERIODICALS. Publications of the American Folklore Society, Bibliographical and Special Series, Vol. 18 *Univ. of Texas Press* (American Folklore Soc.) 1967 $10.00

"Bruce Jackson brings into sharp focus the social and aesthetic values of Negro folklore as seen by white contemporaries from slavery to freedom. Of the 18 periodicals from which the 35 articles, sketches, and reviews have been selected, only one—the *Southern Workman*, established in 1871 at Hampton Institute—represents the (late) emergence of the Negro as collector and student of his own folklore as well as its creator and subject. For the rest, the book deals with the development of changing white attitudes toward the Negro and his folklore, varying from 'paternalistic condescension' and caricature to sympathetic and scientific interest. In tracing this development, . . . Jackson supplies a critical and historical perspective"—(B. A. Botkin, in the *N.Y. Folklore Quarterly*).

Jekyll, Walter, Ed. JAMAICAN SONG AND STORY. 1904. *Dover* 1966 pap. $2.50; *Peter Smith* $5.25

Jones, LeRoi. BLUES PEOPLE: Negro Music in White America. *Morrow* 1963 $8.95 pap. $2.25

Krehbiel, Henry Edward. AFRO-AMERICAN FOLKSONGS: A Study in Racial and National Music. 1914. *Ungar* 1962 $6.50 pap. 1975 $2.95

Odum, Howard W., and Guy B. Johnson. THE NEGRO AND HIS SONGS: A Study of Typical Negro Songs in the South. 1925. *Negro Univs. Press* $13.00

NEGRO WORKADAY SONGS. 1926. *Negro Univs. Press* $12.50

Oliver, Paul. THE MEANING OF THE BLUES. (Orig. "Blues Fell This Morning: The Meaning of the Blues") *Macmillan* 1960 Collier Bks. 1962 pap. $.95

Scarborough, Dorothy. ON THE TRAIL OF NEGRO FOLK SONGS. 1925. *Gale Research Co.* 1963 $8.50

Spalding, Henry D., Ed. ENCYCLOPEDIA OF BLACK FOLKLORE AND HUMOR. *Jonathan David* 1972 $12.95

"The contents consist of anecdotes, stories, songs, poems, proverbs and superstitions, plus a few soul food recipes"—(*LJ*).

White, Newman Ivey. AMERICAN NEGRO FOLK SONGS. 1928. New fwd. by Bruce Jackson *Gale Research Co.* 1965 $10.00

Work, John W. FOLK SONG OF THE AMERICAN NEGRO. 1915. *Negro Univs. Press* $8.50

MISCELLANEOUS AND APPLIED FOLKLORE

The miscellaneous types of folklore sampled in this section have to do with work, play and worship—or everyday life and the supernatural. They include folk arts and crafts, folklife or material culture, beliefs and customs, verbal lore (proverbs, sayings, riddles), games, holidays and festivals. Many of these types involve the application of folklore to other cultural areas and its use in other disciplines in the humanities and social sciences, such as literature, language, history, sociology, psychology and religion. Hence they are also known as applied and interdisciplinary studies.

Bayley, Harold. THE LOST LANGUAGE OF SYMBOLISM: An Inquiry into the Origin of Certain Letters, Words, Names, Fairy-Tales, Folklore, and Mythologies. 1912. *Rowman* 1974 $17.50

Beck, Horace P. FOLKLORE AND THE SEA. *Wesleyan Univ. Press* 1973 $14.95 ltd. ed. $40.00

"A compilation of maritime lore personally collected from individual informants off New England, in the West Indies, and around the British Isles. The book takes as its province . . . traditions pertaining to boats, the ocean, and human life on and by the sea"—(*Choice*).

Botkin, B. A., Ed., with introd. and notes. A CIVIL WAR TREASURY OF TALES, LEGENDS AND FOLKLORE. *Random* 1960 1966 $12.50

Briggs, Katherine M. THE FAIRIES IN ENGLISH TRADITION AND LITERATURE. *Univ. of Chicago Press* 1967 $7.95

PERSONNEL OF FAIRYLAND: A Short Account of the Fairy People of Great Britain for Those Who Tell Stories to Children. 1953. *Gale Research Co.* 1971 $9.00

Coffin, Tristram P. THE BOOK OF CHRISTMAS FOLKLORE. *Seabury Press* 1973 $7.95

ILLUSTRATED BOOK OF CHRISTMAS FOLKLORE. *Seabury Press* rev. ed. 1974 $12.95

UNCERTAIN GLORY: Folklore and the American Revolution. *Gale Research Co.* 1971 $7.00

(With Hennig Cohen, Eds.). FOLKLORE FROM THE WORKING FOLK OF AMERICA. Sel. and ed. from the leading journals and archives of folklore. *Doubleday* 1973 $8.95 Anchor Bks. 1974 pap. $3.50

"This excellent collection provides access to many items from sources that are normally available to only a few scholars"—(*LJ*).

Douglas, Norman. LONDON STREET GAMES. 1931. Folklore and Society Ser. *Johnson Reprint* 2nd rev. and enl. ed. 1969 $8.50 *Gale Research Co.* (Singing Tree Press) 2nd ed. 1968 $6.00

Fishwick, Marshall W. AMERICAN HEROES, MYTH AND REALITY. 1954. *Greenwood* 1972 $11.25

THE HERO, AMERICAN STYLE. *McKay* 1969 $5.95

Gaines, Francis Pendleton. THE SOUTHERN PLANTATION: A Study in the Development and the Accuracy of a Tradition. *Peter Smith* $5.25

Gaster, Theodor H. CUSTOMS AND FOLKWAYS OF JEWISH LIFE. 1955. (Orig. "The Holy and the Profane: The Evolution of Jewish Folkways") *Apollo* 1966 pap. $1.75

FESTIVALS OF THE JEWISH YEAR. *Morrow* 1961 pap. $3.75; *Peter Smith* 1962 $5.50

THESPIS: Ritual, Myth and Drama in the Ancient Near East. *Gordian* 2nd rev. ed. 1975 $15.00

Glassie, Henry. PATTERNS IN THE MATERIAL FOLK CULTURE OF THE EASTERN UNITED STATES. *Univ. of Pennsylvania Press* 1968 rev. ed. 1971 $7.50 pap. $3.45

Hoffman, Daniel G. FORM AND FABLE IN AMERICAN FICTION. 1961. *Norton* 1973 pap. $2.95

Jagendorf, Moritz A. STORIES OF THE ZODIAC. *Vanguard* 1974 $6.95

Kornbluh, Joyce L., Ed. REBEL VOICES: An I.W.W. Anthology. *Univ. of Michigan Press* 1964 $12.50 Ann Arbor Bks. 1968 pap. $4.95

The activities of the Industrial Workers of the World, or Wobblies, early in this century, brought about, says Mrs. Kornbluh, "one of the first social movements in this country to develop an extensive literature and lore all its own." This documentary history, told by the Wobblies themselves, is an outstanding example of applied folklore. Their "songs, poems, stories, anecdotes, skits, language, and visual symbolism" were used to reinforce their goals of industrial unionism within a utopian society. The book is rich in the lore of hoboes, textile workers, harvest stiffs, lumberjacks, and gold, silver, copper and lead miners. There are a chapter on "Joe Hill: Wobbly Bard," and appendix on the "Language of the Migratory Worker" and bibliography—(B. A. Botkin).

Leach, Maria. GOD HAD A DOG: Folklore of the Dog. *Rutgers Univ. Press* 1961 $10.00

Lehner, Ernst, and Johanna Lehner. THE FOLKLORE AND ODYSSEY OF FOOD AND MEDICINAL PLANTS. 1961. *Farrar, Straus* 1973 $8.95 Noonday pap. $3.45

Leland, Charles Godfrey. ENGLISH GYPSIES AND THEIR LANGUAGE. 1874. *Gale Research Co.* 1969 $12.00

GYPSY SORCERY AND FORTUNE TELLING. 1891. *Dover* 1971 pap. $3.00; *Peter Smith* $6.00; *University Bks.* 1963 $10.00

McIlwaine, Shields. THE SOUTHERN POOR-WHITE: From Lubberland to Tobacco Road. 1939. *Cooper* 1971 $8.75

> This treats the evolution over two centuries of a unique social literature around the comic and pathetic type (and stereotype) of the poor-white and his way of life as both a social "cause and a literary vogue"—(B. A. Botkin).

Sloane, Eric. THE CRACKER BARREL. *T. Y. Crowell* (Funk & Wagnalls) 1967 $7.50

THE SECOND BARREL. *T. Y. Crowell* (Funk & Wagnalls) 1969 $7.50

Smith, Elsdon C. A TREASURY OF NAME LORE. *Harper* 1967 $6.95

Wecter, Dixon. THE HERO IN AMERICA: A Chronicle of Hero-Worship. Ill. with headings by Woodi Ishmael. 1941. *Irvington Bks.* 1972 $19.95; *Scribner* 1972 $12.50

Yearsley, Macleod. FOLKLORE OF FAIRY-TALE. 1924. *Gale Research Co.* (Singing Tree) 1968 $9.50

FOLK AND POPULAR HUMOR

The art of humor in its broadest sense encompasses irony, wit, satire, sarcasm, and farce. It also includes situation comedy which is based on the unexpected or incongruous event. The prevalence of folk elements in American humor and of humor in American folklore is sufficient justification, if one were needed, for treating them together in the same chapter. The two have in common what Walter Blair defines and illustrates in "Native American Humor 1800–1900" as "an emphatic native quality: the lore of national and local characterizations revealed in almanacs, jest books, plays . . . newspapers . . . travel books" and local-color fiction from Down East and Southwest. American humorists, borrowing heavily from our democratic frontier traditions, have always acted as catalytic agents for social and political change. This list includes folk and regional humor as well as contemporary comic materials. *(For other regional as well as Negro humor see the Section on American Regional and Ethnic Folklore.)* A number of humorous writers are treated in Chapter 15, Essays and Criticism, *"Reader's Adviser,"* Vol. 1.

Adams, Joey. JOEY ADAMS' ENCYCLOPEDIA OF HUMOR. *Bobbs* 1968 $7.95

> A fully indexed, comprehensive guide for the professional and the amateur humorist, in two parts: one, a manual of joke-telling; two, "The Joey Adams Portable Gag File." Most valuable are the sections on sample routines and repertoires of well-known comedians and on the tricks of the trade—(B. A. Botkin).

JOEY ADAMS' SPEAKER'S BIBLE OF HUMOR. *Doubleday* 1972 $7.95

SON OF ENCYCLOPEDIA OF HUMOR. *Bobbs* 1970 $5.95

Asimov, Isaac. ISAAC ASIMOV'S TREASURY OF HUMOR. *Houghton* 1971 $7.95

Ault, Philip H. HOME BOOK OF WESTERN HUMOR. *Dodd* 1967 $7.50

Ausubel, Nathan, Ed. TREASURY OF JEWISH HUMOR. *Doubleday* 1951 $8.95

Blair, Walter. HORSE SENSE IN AMERICAN HUMOR: From Benjamin Franklin to Ogden Nash. 1942. *Russell & Russell* 1962 $13.50

NATIVE AMERICAN HUMOR (1800–1900). 1937. *T. Y. Crowell* (Chandler Pub.) (dist. by Science Research Assoc.) 1960 pap. $5.95

Blistein, Elmer M. COMEDY IN ACTION. *Duke Univ. Press* 1964 $5.75

> The key word in Blistein's title is "action," referring to comic characters in action in dramatic comedy and to action and reaction in humor generally. In two opening chapters he deals with two kinds of comic character related to the two kinds of laughter: the sympathetic and civil or civilized character, whom we laugh *with* and who in turn identifies with the audience while satirizing, attacking, or poking fun at it; and the comic character as antagonist and victim, whom we laugh *at*, scorn and feel superior to when he is foiled. In three closing chapters he treats "comedy in action" closer to our own time—such sources of humor as cruelty (in slapstick, the practical joke, the sick

joke, the Bloody Mary), love and sex (in burlesque and in the social comedy of films and musicals), politics and social conditions (as in the satire of our stand-up comedians) and dialect (illustrated from yesterday's radio). Blistein regrets the passing of dialect (a staple of American humor) and defends it as a possible source of social empathy through "an understanding of how the other fellow lives [and] thinks [and] what [his] problems are." "More examples of dialect humor," he says, would help "to liberate the comic spirit from at least one of the many, nagging, querulous, artificial restraints"—(B. A. Botkin).

Braude, Jacob Morton. BRAUDE'S TREASURY OF WIT AND HUMOR. *Prentice-Hall* 1964 $6.95

SPEAKER'S AND TOASTMASTER'S HANDBOOK OF ANECDOTES BY AND ABOUT FAMOUS PERSONALITIES. *Prentice-Hall* 1971 $8.95

Couperie, Pierre, and others. A HISTORY OF THE COMIC STRIP. Trans. from the French by Eileen B. Hennessy; created in conjunction with the Exhibition of Comic-Strip Art at the Musée des Arts Décoratifs, Palais du Louvre *Crown* 1968 $6.95 pap. $3.95

Downs, Robert B., Ed. THE BEAR WENT OVER THE MOUNTAIN: Tall Tales of American Animals. 1964. *Gale Research Co.* (Singing Tree) 1971 $9.00

A spirited compilation of over 63 lying, humorous and fantastic tales of American animals, arranged according to region—Yankee, Southern, Ozark, Texan and Western—with the addition of animal-fable and shaggy-dog types. "You'll meet again such favorites as Davy Crockett, Pecos Bill, Brer Rabbit, and others. Among the authors are Mark Twain, Thurber, Benchley, Josh Billings, Vardis Fisher, Saroyan, H. Allen Smith, and a host more. . . . A good anthology, varied and well planned"—(*LJ*). The editor is the distinguished University of Illinois librarian.

Esar, Evan. TWENTY THOUSAND QUIPS AND QUOTES. *Doubleday* 1968 $8.95

In addition to being a useful reference collection of single-sentence wit and wisdom for speakers (in 2,000 categories arranged alphabetically), this latest volume by "humorologist" Esar (as he calls himself) should interest the student of folk and popular humor for its contributions to the history of the quip and witticism. The American folklorist will find here a wealth of material for studying the relation of the "detached saying" to the proverbial saying and of native to sophisticated American humor, from the quips of the horse-sense cracker-box philosopher and newspaper paragrapher to those of our sophisticated wisecrackers and zany comedians. Behavioral scientists would do well to harken to Esar's suggestion that they look into this mirror of "contemporary prejudices" and public attitudes—(B. A. Botkin).

Harris, Joel Chandler. AMERICAN WIT AND HUMOR. 1907. *Folcroft* $10.00

(Ed.). THE WORLD'S WIT AND HUMOR: An Encyclopedia of the Classic Wit and Humor of all Nations. 1905. *Scarecrow Press* 15 vols. in 3 mini-print vols. 1973 $99.50

Hoig, Stan. HUMOR OF THE AMERICAN COWBOY. *Univ. of Nebraska Press* Bison Bks. 1970 pap. $1.95

Hudson, Arthur P., Ed. HUMOR OF THE OLD DEEP SOUTH. 1936. *Kennikat* 2 vols. 1970 set $22.50

Legman, Gershon. NO LAUGHING MATTER: The Rationale of the Dirty Joke, Second Series. *Breaking Point* 1975 $18.00

"A collection of sexual and scatological humor . . . divided under the headings Homosexuality, Prostitution, Sex and Money, Disease and Disgust, Castration, Dysphemism and Insults"—(*Time*).

RATIONALE OF THE DIRTY JOKE: An Analysis of Sexual Humor, First Series. *Grove* 1968 Black Cat Bks. 1968 pap. $2.95

"The jokes of this First Series, which have been called 'the *clean* dirty jokes' will be followed by a Second Series, already completed, of 'the *dirty* dirty jokes' "—(Publisher's note). "Under the mask of humor," writes Mr. Legman, "our society allows infinite aggressions, by everyone and against everyone. . . . Erotic humor is far and away the most popular of all types"—(B. A. Botkin).

Levenson, Sam. IN ONE ERA AND OUT THE OTHER. *G. K. Hall* 1974 $9.95; *Simon & Schuster* 1973 $6.95 (Pocket Bks.) 1974 pap. $1.50

"Comedian and former schoolteacher Levenson presents here scenes and philosophical comments from 'Poor Sammy's Almanac' . . . his poignant stories are beautifully paced, and come through even without listening to him deliver them"—(*LJ*).

Loesser, Arthur. HUMOR IN AMERICAN SONG. 1942. *Gale Research Co.* $14.00

Lynn, Kenneth S., Ed. THE COMIC TRADITION IN AMERICA: An Anthology of American Humor. *Norton* 1968 pap. $2.95

Randolph, Vance. HOT SPRINGS AND HELL AND OTHER FOLK JESTS AND ANECDOTES FROM THE OZARKS. *Gale Research Co.* (Folklore Associates) 1965 1972 $5.95

Other Ozark folklore collections by Mr. Randolph are published by Columbia. See also his titles in Section on American Regional Folklore: The South.

Reik, Theodor. JEWISH WIT. 1964. *Taplinger* $6.00 pap. $2.45

Rosten, Leo. THE JOYS OF YIDDISH: A Relaxed Lexicon of Yiddish, Hebrew and Yinglish Words Often Encountered in English, plus Dozens That Ought to Be with Serendipitous Excursions into Jewish Humor, Habits, Holidays, History, Ceremonies, Folklore, and Cuisine; the Whole Generously Garnished with Stories, Anecdotes, Epigrams, Talmudic Quotations, Folk Sayings and Jokes—from the Days of the Bible to Those of the Beatnik. *McGraw-Hill* 1968 $10.00; *Simon & Schuster* (Pocket Bks.) 1970 pap. $1.95

Tidwell, J. N., Ed. TREASURY OF AMERICAN FOLK HUMOR. *Crown* 1956 $5.00

White, E. B., and Katharine S. White, Eds. A SUBTREASURY OF AMERICAN HUMOR. 1941. *Putnam* Capricorn Bks. abr. ed. 1962 pap. $2.65

"The best assortment of laughable Americana I have ever seen"—(Edward Weeks).

POPULAR CULTURE

Among the newly emerging disciplines at American universities intended to broaden the base of higher education is the rigorous study of cultural materials used by the people rather than the intellectual elite. Popular culture has been defined "as that part of culture abstracted from the total body of intellectual and imaginative work which each generation receives, which is not narrowly elitist or aimed at special audiences, and which is generally (but not necessarily) disseminated via the mass media." (Ray B. Browne). This list includes representative titles by well-known authors in this field.

Ambrosetti, Ronald, and Ray B. Browne. POPULAR CULTURE AND CURRICULA. *Bowling Green Univ.* (Popular Press) rev. ed. 1972 pap. $2.50

"Designed to be used by all persons interested in the various uses of popular culture in the curriculum"—(Publisher's note).

Browne, Ray B. THE POPULAR CULTURE EXPLOSION: Experiencing Mass Media. *W. C. Brown* 1973 $4.95

"A collection of primary sources—articles, cartoons, illustrations, advertisements, stories—from a wide range of mass circulation magazines and periodicals"—(Publisher's note).

(Ed.). POPULAR CULTURE AND THE EXPANDING CONSCIOUSNESS. *Wiley* 1972 $7.50 pap. $4.50

"Examines old attitudes, changing concepts, and expanding awareness in a presentation that helps the selections illuminate each other. By using a thematic disclosure approach to the subject, a fresh view of popular culture reveals itself"—(Publisher's note).

(With Marshall Fishwick). HEROES OF POPULAR CULTURE. *Bowling Green Univ.* (Popular Press) 1972 $6.00 pap. $2.50

"What has happened to the American hero and thus to America since the early 1950's"—(Publisher's note).

Chenoweth, Lawrence. THE AMERICAN DREAM OF SUCCESS: The Search for the Self in the Twentieth Century. *Duxbury Press* 1974 pap. $4.50

"Analyzes over 1800 articles on success from the two most popular magazines of the century, the *Saturday Evening Post* and *Reader's Digest*"—(Publisher's note).

Fishwick, Marshall. PARAMETERS OF POPULAR CULTURE. *Bowling Green Univ.* (Popular Press) 1972 $7.95 pap. $3.00

"The parameters of our culture are electrified, computerized, synchronized, televised. The results are incredible and unpredictable. So the question must be asked: how fares the people's culture—that is popular culture—in the last quarter of the 20th century?"—(Preface).

(With Ray B. Browne). ICONS OF POPULAR CULTURE. *Bowling Green Univ.* (Popular Press) 1970 $5.00 pap. $2.00

Flautz, John. LIFE: The Gentle Satirist. *Bowling Green Univ.* (Popular Press) 1972 $7.95

Goulart, Ron. CHEAP THRILLS: An Informal History of the Pulp Magazines. *Arlington House* 1972 $7.95

"A useful introduction to this literature and its authors"—(*College and Research Libraries*).

MacDonald, Ross. ON CRIME WRITING. *Capra Press* 1971 $2.50

The author "discusses with lucidity and a kind of modest elegance the hard boiled American mystery novel in this small but valuable book"—(*N.Y. Times Bk. Review*).

Nye, Russel B., Ed. NEW DIMENSIONS IN POPULAR CULTURE. *Bowling Green Univ.* (Popular Press) 1970 $10.00

"Examples of what may occur when the traditional techniques of literary study and analyses are applied . . . to popular culture material"—(Publisher's note).

Slout, William J. THEATRE IN A TENT: Development of a Provincial Entertainment. *Bowling Green Univ.* (Popular Press) 1969 $5.00

Stott, William. DOCUMENTARY EXPRESSION AND THIRTIES AMERICA. *Oxford* 1971 $12.50

"Examines America's typical artform the documentary in the period of its greatest flowering in the 1930s"—(Publisher's note).

Chapter 12

Travel and Adventure

"For my part, I travel not to go anywhere, but to go. I travel for travel's sake. The great affair is to move."
—ROBERT LOUIS STEVENSON, "Travels with a Donkey" (1878)

The earliest known work of travel in English literature is "Itinerary Through Wales" (o.p.) by the Welsh ecclesiastical scholar, geographer and historian, Giraldus Cambrensis (Gerald of Wales, 1146?–1220?). He accompanied Archbishop Baldwin, who was preaching on behalf of the Crusades. The account of the journey, written originally in Latin, deals not with religious propaganda but with description of the country. Since that time travelers and explorers have gone to almost all parts of the earth. Tourists are again visiting almost all countries, but it is the mountain climbers, polar explorers, divers and "pioneers in unknown, hostile regions," who are writing of their adventurous search to enrich mankind's heritage.

Despite rising fuel costs many Americans can still spend a three-week—or even briefer—vacation abroad, speeded to their destination by jet. There are still the professional travelers who write winningly of their trips, often for the guidance of the vacationer. And there are the literary travelers, a slightly different breed, who write from the sheer love of the places they have been. Both are represented here.

As to adventure, Space is the new frontier, and the experiences of the highly trained space pilgrims and their elaborate equipment may be investigated in the books covered in Chapter 7, Science: Space and Astronomy. But there are also those like Thor Heyerdahl, or Francis Chichester, or Sir Edmund Hillary, or Robert Falcon Scott and his successors, who deliberately travel with only the basic necessities of life (and often a scientific object in mind) in order to feel themselves pitted against the eternal forces of nature. It has been said that Chichester's lone circumnavigation of the globe rejoiced the hearts of Englishmen because in a world grown technological, bureaucratic and unmanageable, in which human beings often feel themselves pygmies to be manipulated, he had reduced the struggle again to the personal and elemental—man against the sea—and proved that man, with few resources beyond his own wit, strength and skill, could still trimph against tremendous odds—the same odds faced by his ancestors millennia ago.

J. A. Neal's "Reference Guide for Travellers," a guide to guidebooks (*Bowker* 1969 $21.50), provides far greater coverage of travel series than would be possible here. An attractive, clearly organized volume with graceful annotations and evaluations, it covers over 1,200 guidebooks, special guides (museum, shopping and the like) for some 70 countries and all 50 states of the Union. "Arranged by country and city, entries give ordering information, a checklist of subjects covered in the standard guides and a descriptive annotation indicating what the book stresses and how it is arranged. Each geographic section also includes lists of fiction and non-fiction background reading and official travel publications. Appendices give lists of tourist health and medical guides, vocabulary and phrase books, travel periodicals, and a directory of publishers. Also—an author-title index, an index to such special interest travel as camping and skiing, and a gazetteer which keys the world's major points of interest to the guidebooks providing the best information about them"—(Publisher's note). The "Reference Guide" is standard equipment for bookstores, libraries and travel agents. In this edition of *"The Reader's Adviser,"* therefore, we list only a few recent guidebooks per se and have expanded our introductory lists of travel books of the more literary variety—those which convey a flavor of their own, cover a special broad subject or are by distinguished writers known for their books in other fields. Such authors are valuable (for the armchair traveler or potential tourist) as wanderers of sophisticated taste, special historical knowledge or originality of imagination and literary style; they can help the reader choose a destination offering particular rewards to mind and spirit. The listed books on Individual Travels and Exploits have also been chosen—from a great number of worthy candidates—for their qualities of high adventure well described or for literary, imaginative or antiquarian interest.

Following a section on Reference Books and General Works, including mention of some important series, our lists have been subdivided into broad geographical areas: The Americas, North and South; Europe; Africa, Asia, Oceania. The Selected List of Books on Individual Travels or Exploits follows these listings.

REFERENCE BOOKS AND GENERAL WORKS

Adams, Percy G. TRAVELERS AND TRAVEL LIARS: 1600–1800. *Dover* 1962 pap. $2.50. About real travel accounts that contained untruths, armchair trips made to seem real, and the different impressions made when different people described the same places or events.

Allen, Robert T. How TO SURVIVE THE AGE OF TRAVEL. *Doubleday* 1974 $6.95

"Allen's wry narratives of travel experiences center on personal enjoyment of visits to familiar and unfamiliar sites. . . . Allen advises on coping with hotels, airports, and taxi foibles in faraway places"—(*Booklist*).

Andrews, Roy Chapman. THIS BUSINESS OF EXPLORING. 1932. *Finch Press* $12.00

Armstrong, James, Ed. VOYAGES OF DISCOVERY. *Wiley* 1972 pap. $6.50

Bracken, Peg. BUT I WOULDN'T HAVE MISSED IT FOR THE WORLD: The Pleasures and Perils of an Unseasoned Traveler. *Harcourt* 1973 $6.95

"A compilation of random thoughts, peppered with literary quotations about trips [the author] has taken, people she has met, memorable meals she has eaten, her cooking course at Le Cordon Bleu and . . . some recipes. She comments on when to go, what to take, package trips, and jetiquette"—(*LJ*).

Cameron, Ian. ANTARCTICA: The Lost Continent. *Little* 1974 $15.00

ISLAND AT THE TOP OF THE WORLD. (Orig. "Lost Ones") *Avon* 1974 pap. $1.25

THE MOUNTAINS AT THE BOTTOM OF THE WORLD. *Morrow* 1972 $5.95

Casewit, Curtis W., and Dick Pownall. THE MOUNTAINEERING HANDBOOK: An Invitation to Climbing. Introd. by James Ramsey Ullman *Lippincott* 1968 $6.50

Casson, Lionel. ANCIENT MARINERS: Seafarers and Sea Fighters of the Mediterranean in Ancient Times. *Macmillan* 1959 $6.95; *T. Y. Crowell* (Funk & Wagnalls) 1967 pap. $2.75. A lucid and valuable book.

TRAVEL IN THE ANCIENT WORLD. *A. M. Hakkert* 1974 $15.00

Chase, Ilka. WORLDS APART. *Doubleday* 1972 $7.95

"Chatty, informative, and written with Chase's usual good humor the book covers visits to Central and South America, Russia, and Africa to each of which a chapter is devoted"—(*Booklist*).

Cox, Edward Godfrey. A REFERENCE GUIDE TO THE LITERATURE OF TRAVEL: Including Voyages, Geographical Descriptions, Adventures, Shipwrecks and Expeditions. 1935–1949. *Greenwood* 3 vols. Vol. 1 The Old World (1935) Vol. 2 The New World (1938) Vol. 3 Great Britain (1949) set $74.50. These definitive bibliographies list in chronological order from the earliest date to the year 1800 all books on foreign travel *printed in Great Britain*, together with translations from foreign tongues. The final chapters on General Reference Books and Bibliographies include books to 1936.

Doubleday, Nelson, and C. Earl Cooley, Eds. ENCYCLOPEDIA OF WORLD TRAVEL. *Doubleday* 1961 2 vols. 2nd ed. 1973 set $12.95

Dow, George Francis. WHALE SHIPS AND WHALING: A Pictorial History of Whaling during Three Centuries with an Account of the Whale Fishery in Colonial New England. 1925. New introd. by Frank Wood *Argosy-Antiquarian* 1967 $35.00

Elek, Paul, Elizabeth Ele¹ and Moira Johnson, Eds. THE AGE OF THE GRAND TOUR: Containing Sketches of the Manners, Society and Customs of France, Flanders, The United Provinces, Germany, Switzerland and Italy in the Letters, Journals and Writings of the Most Celebrated Voyagers between the Years 1720 and 1820. Introd. by Anthony Burgess; appreciation by Francis Haskell *Crown* 1967 $30.00. The writers include James Boswell, James Fenimore Cooper and Stendhal, among others.

Fuentes, Patricia de, Ed. and trans. with introd. THE CONQUISTADORS: First Person Accounts of the Conquest of Mexico. *Grossman* (dist. by Viking) 1963 $8.95. By the men who actually accompanied Cortes to Mexico and wrote their own personal accounts.

Gordon, Arthur. THE AMERICAN HERITAGE HISTORY OF FLIGHT. *American Heritage Press* (dist. by McGraw-Hill) 1962 $15.00 deluxe ed. $17.50. A basic, comprehensive history of aviation from the earliest times to the beginning of the space age, with excerpts from the reminiscences of the pioneers as well as interviews with those still living.

Halliburton, Richard. COMPLETE BOOK OF MARVELS. *Bobbs* 1937 1960 $7.95. Descriptions and illustrations of many natural and manmade wonders of the Occident and the Orient in a classic work—Golden Gate Bridge, Niagara Falls, Machu Picchu, Matterhorn, Colossus, Mt. Everest, Angkor, etc.

THE ROYAL ROAD TO ROMANCE. 1925. *Greenwood* $22.25

Halliday, William R. AMERICAN CAVES AND CAVING: Techniques, Pleasures, and Safeguards of Modern Cave Exploration. *Harper* 1974 $10.00

DEPTHS OF THE EARTH: Caves and Cavers of the United States. *Harper* 1966 $8.95

Herrmann, Paul. THE GREAT AGE OF DISCOVERY. Trans. from the German by Arnold J. Pomerans. 1958. *Greenwood* 1974 $23.50. An unusual presentation, spanning five centuries, from Columbus to Livingstone in Africa.

Hope, Ronald, Comp. and ed. THE SHOREGOER'S GUIDE TO WORLD PORTS. Fwd. by Sir Donald Anderson. 1964. *Int. Pubns. Service* rev. ed. 1971 $5.25

Horner, David L. TREASURE GALLEONS: Clues to Millions in Sunken Gold and Treasure. *Dodd* 1971 $10.00

Huxley, Anthony, Ed. STANDARD ENCYCLOPEDIA OF THE WORLD'S MOUNTAINS. *Putnam* 1969 $15.00. A typical article gives the salient features of the mountain or range, relates it to the economy of the region, and describes its exploration and famous climbs.

STANDARD ENCYCLOPEDIA OF THE WORLD'S OCEANS AND ISLANDS. *Putnam* 1969 $15.00

Lincoln, Joseph C. SOARING ON THE WIND: A Photographic Essay on the Sport of Soaring. *Northland Press* 1973 $15.00

Lukan, Karl, Ed. THE ALPS AND ALPINISM. Trans. by Hugh Merrick *Coward* 1968 $19.95. Alpine life from Neanderthal times to the present.

McDonald, Kendall. TREASURE BENEATH THE SEA. *A. S. Barnes* 1973 $12.00

Malzberg, Barry N. BEYOND APOLLO. *Random* 1972 $5.95

Morrison, Helen B. THE GOLDEN AGE OF TRAVEL. 1951. *AMS Press* 1972 $22.50

National Geographic Society. THE WORLD BENEATH THE SEA. *National Geographic Society* $4.25

Neatby, Leslie H. THE CONQUEST OF THE LAST FRONTIER. *Ohio Univ. Press* 1966 $12.00

"A most fascinating and well-written account of Arctic exploration beginning with the mid-19th century"—(LJ).

DISCOVERY IN RUSSIAN AND SIBERIAN WATERS. *Ohio Univ. Press* 1973 $8.50

Nesmith, Robert I., and John S. Potter, Jr. TREASURE HUNTER'S GUIDE: How and Where to Find It. 1961. (Orig. "Treasure Hunters") *Arco* rev. ed. 1975 $5.95

Norman, Charles. DISCOVERERS OF AMERICA. *T. Y. Crowell* 1968 $7.95

Parry, John H. THE DISCOVERY OF THE SEA. *Dial* 1974 $20.00

"This book describes the evolution of shipbuilding, navigation, geographical knowledge and trade and politics that made possible the voyages by European seafarers at the end of the fifteenth century and the beginning of the sixteenth [which] established beyond dispute that all the earth's seas were connected"—(Publisher's note).

Penrose, Boies. TRAVEL AND DISCOVERY IN THE RENAISSANCE, 1420–1620. 1955. *Atheneum* 1962 pap. $3.95. Factually sound, clearly written history with good bibliographies.

TUDOR AND EARLY STUART VOYAGING. *Univ. Press of Virginia* 1962 (orig.) pap. $1.50

URBANE TRAVELERS, 1591–1635. *Octagon* 1970 $11.00

Pinney, Roy. QUEST FOR THE UNKNOWN: Explorers of Today. *Lippincott* 1965 $4.50

Rebuffat, Gaston. MEN AND THE MATTERHORN. Trans. from the French by Eleanor Brockett *Oxford* 1973 $17.50. Written with love by a skilled writer and French mountaineer.

ON ICE AND SNOW AND ROCK. Trans. by Patrick Evans *Oxford* 1971 $15.00

"This is a book devoted to the equipment and techniques of mountain climbing . . . but it is also an important book that will be classic in the literature of mountains and mountain climbing"—(LJ).

STARLIGHT AND STORM: The Ascent of Six Great North Faces of the Alps. *Oxford* 1968 $8.00

Rugoff, Milton, Ed., with introds. THE GREAT TRAVELERS: A Collection of Firsthand Narratives of Wayfarers, Wanderers and Explorers in All Parts of the World from 450 B.C. to the Present. *Simon & Schuster* 2 vols. 1960 boxed set $12.50

This handsomely produced and illustrated anthology provides a catholic variety of firsthand accounts, skilfully chosen and organized, that add up to nearly 1,000 pages. The arrangement is as follows. Vol. 1: The Orient: From Persia to Japan; The Levant: From Istanbul to the Arabian Sea; Africa. Vol. 2: A Circuit of Europe; America South; America North; Polar Places. Included is a separate "Map of the Places to Which They Went."

Silverberg, Robert. THE LONGEST VOYAGE: Circumnavigations in the Age of Discovery. *Bobbs* 1972 $10.00

"This book is about the early (1519–1617) circumnavigations of the world. The voyages of Magellan and Drake are described . . . as are the lesser known around-the-world cruises of Thomas Cavendish, Oliver van Noort, Joris van Spilbergen, and William Schouten and Jacob Le Maire . . . also information about pre-Magellan voyages, the European colonization of the Far East, the search for Terra Australia, and the mysterious Patagonian giants"—(LJ).

Thomas, Lowell. BOOK OF THE HIGH MOUNTAINS. *Simon & Schuster* 1964 $10.00 (Fireside) 1969 pap. $3.45

"Unique in the mountain literature of the Western world"—(William O. Douglas).

UNITED NATIONS LIST OF NATIONAL PARKS AND EQUIVALENT RESERVES, WITH ADDENDUM. *Bowker* 1972 $30.00

"Details more than 1,350 national parks and nature reserves in 140 member countries of the United Nations"—(Publisher's note).

Weddell, James. A VOYAGE TOWARD THE SOUTH POLE. *Naval Institute Press* 1971 $9.00

Williams, Neville. CONTRABAND CARGOES: Seven Centuries of Smuggling. *Shoe String Press* 1961 $6.00

THE AMERICAS, NORTH AND SOUTH

Anstee, Margaret J. BOLIVIA: Gate of the Sun. (Orig. "Gate of the Sun: Prospect of Bolivia") *Eriksson* 1971 $7.95

Baird, David M. THE INCREDIBLE GULF. *Verry* 1970 $7.50

Beebe, Charles W. BENEATH TROPIC SEAS: A Record of Diving among the Coral Reefs on Haiti. 1929. *Finch Press* $11.00

Butcher, Devereux. EXPLORING OUR NATIONAL PARKS AND MONUMENTS. *Houghton* 1969 $8.95 pap. $4.95

> OUR NATIONAL PARKS IN COLOR. *Clarkson N. Potter* (dist. by Crown) 1965 3rd rev. ed. 1973 $6.95 pap. $3.95
> "This is very possibly the best available collection of photographs of the national parks"—(*LJ*).

Caccia, Angela. BEYOND LAKE TITICACA. *Int. Pubns. Service* 1969 $10.50

Carmer, Carl, Ed. TAVERN LAMPS ARE BURNING: Literary Journeys through Six Regions and Four Centuries of New York State. *McKay* 1964 $10.00. An anthology of British and American writing describing regions of New York State.

Carter, William E. BOLIVIA: A Profile. *Praeger* 1971 $8.00

Champlain, Samuel de. NARRATIVE OF A VOYAGE TO THE WEST INDIES AND MEXICO IN THE YEARS 1599–1602. Trans. by Alice Wilmere; ed. by Norton Shaw. 1859. *Burt Franklin* $20.00

Chickering, William H. WITHIN THE SOUND OF THESE WAVES: The Story of the Kings of Hawaii Island, Containing a Full Account of the Death of Captain Cook, Together with the Hawaiian Adventures of George Vancouver and Sundry Other Mariners. 1941. *Greenwood* 1971 $16.75

Crampsey, R. A. PUERTO RICO. Islands of the World Ser. *Stackpole* 1973 $8.95

Cumming, William P., and others. THE EXPLORATION OF NORTH AMERICA, 1630–1776. *Putnam* 1974 $30.00

> "Extracts from journals, letters, and manuscripts compiled from the observations of explorers, missionaries, fur trappers, and others from 1630 until the period of the Revolution. Profusely illustrated with colorplates and black-and-white reproductions"—(*Booklist*).

Day, A. Grove, and Carl Stroven, Eds. THE HAWAIIAN READER. *Popular Lib.* pap. $.95. Essays by Mark Twain, James Michener and Jack London, among others, chronologically arranged by the Hawaiian historical events described.

Ellis, William D. LAND OF THE INLAND SEAS: The Historic and Beautiful Great Lakes Country. Great West Ser. *American West Pub. Co.* 1974 $20.00

> "History, natural, human, and industrial, figures prominently in this exploration through word and photograph of the great inland waterway between the United States and Canada"—(*Booklist*).

Espy, Hilda C., and Lex Creamer. ANOTHER WORLD: Central America. *Viking* 1970 $10.00

Freeman, Orville, and Michael Frome. THE NATIONAL FORESTS OF AMERICA. *Putnam* 1968 $12.95

Gaskell, T. F. THE GULF STREAM. *John Day* 1973 $5.95

> "This work traces the history of Gulf Stream research from Benjamin Franklin's time to the present; its influences on navigation, exploration, politics, and climate are made clear in well-written chapters"—(*LJ*).

Guillet, Edwin C. THE GREAT MIGRATION: The Atlantic Crossing by Sailing Ship since 1770. 1937. *Jerome S. Ozer* 1971 $12.95; *Univ. of Toronto Press* 1963 pap. $4.50

Hannau, Hans W. BERMUDA IN FULL COLOR. *Doubleday* rev. ed. 1974 $12.50. This author has done a number of similar guides, including The Caribbean Islands, Puerto Rico, and St. Maarten.

Harner, Michael J. THE JIVARO: People of the Sacred Waterfalls. *Doubleday* 1972 $7.95. About a tribe in Ecuador.

Henfrey, Colin. MANSCAPES: An American Journey. *Gambit* 1973 $7.95

> "An English prose virtuoso's tour of the U.S. in the late 1960's presents often shocking, sometimes predictable, but always germane reactions to what has become of the contemporary American experience"—(*Booklist*).

Herndon, Booton. GREAT LAND: Alaska. *Weybright & Talley* (dist. by McKay) 1971 $6.95

Holton, Isaac F. NEW GRANADA: Twenty Months in the Andes. Ed. by C. Harvey Gardiner *Southern Illinois Univ. Press* 1967 $7.50

Hunte, George. THE WEST INDIAN ISLANDS. *Viking* 1972 $8.95

Logan, Rayford W. HAITI AND THE DOMINICAN REPUBLIC. *Oxford* 1968 $6.75

Lott, Leo. VENEZUELA AND PARAGUAY. *Holt* 1972 pap. $6.00

McBride, Barrie S. AMAZON JOURNEY: Seven Thousand Miles through Peru and Brazil. *Int. Pubns. Service* 1965 $5.25

MacLennan, Hugh. THE COLOUR OF CANADA. *Little* 1968 2nd rev. ed. 1972 $6.95. By the contemporary Canadian novelist.

Marshall, Robert. ALASKA WILDERNESS: Exploring the Central Brooks Range. *Univ. of California Press* 2nd ed. 1970 $8.95 pap. $2.95

Matthews, William H., III. A GUIDE TO THE NATIONAL PARKS: Their Landscape and Geology. Fwd. by Paul M. Tilden *Doubleday* 2 vols. 1968 Vol. 1 The Western Parks $10.95 Vol. 2 The Eastern Parks o.p. Anchor Bks. 2 vols. 1973 pap. each $5.95

Matthiessen, Peter. THE CLOUD FOREST: A Chronicle of the South American Wilderness. *Viking* 1961 $6.50; *Ballantine Bks.* 1973 pap. $1.65

Meyer, Robert, Jr. FESTIVALS U.S.A. AND CANADA. *I. Washburn* (dist. by McKay) rev. ed. 1967 $5.95

Morris, John L., Ed. ALASKA. *Graphic Arts Center* 1972 $25.00

Mowat, Farley. CANADA NORTH. *Little-Atlantic* 1968 $4.95

Muir, John. TRAVELS IN ALASKA. 1915. *AMS Press* 1971 $9.50; *Scholarly Press* $9.50

National Geographic Society. ALASKA. *National Geographic Society* $4.25

Ogburn, Charlton. THE SOUTHERN APPALACHIANS: A Wilderness Quest. *Morrow* 1975 $14.95

"As he makes his way along the trails and roads of the Southern Appalachians from West Virginia to Georgia, Ogburn unfolds the story of the mountains' evolution and of the white man's discovery of them"—(*LJ*).

Olson, Sigurd F. OPEN HORIZONS. *Knopf* 1969 $5.95

"Sigurd Olson's beautifully written book (he has written five others on the Far North) [describes] his youth on a far-northern Wisconsin farm and the love of the lakes, forests and rivers that brought him back, after college, to learn the rugged life of a wilderness guide. Olson is a philosopher as well as a remarkable writer on nature. . . . A spellbinder"—(*PW*).

WILDERNESS DAYS. *Knopf* 1972 $12.50 deluxe ed. $25.00

Parker, Franklin D. TRAVELS IN CENTRAL AMERICA. *Univ. Presses of Florida* 1970 $12.50

Pendle, George. PARAGUAY: A Riverside Nation. *Oxford* 3rd ed. 1967 $4.25

Phelan, Nancy. THE CHILEAN WAY. *British Bk. Centre* 1974 $16.50

Raleigh, Sir Walter. DISCOVERY OF THE LARGE, RICH AND BEAUTIFUL EMPIRE OF GUIANA. 1596. Ed. by V. T. Harlow. 1928. *Da Capo* $25.20; ed. by Richard H. Schomburgk. Hakluyt Society Ser. *Burt Franklin* 1970 $19.50

Robinson, David A. PERU IN FOUR DIMENSIONS. *Blaine Etheridge Bks.* 1968 $10.75

Rodman, Selden. THE MEXICAN TRAVELER. *Hawthorn* 1969 $7.95. By the distinguished American poet and literary critic.

Severin, Timothy. EXPLORERS OF THE MISSISSIPPI. *Knopf* 1968 $7.95

THE GOLDEN ANTILLES. *Knopf* 1970 $8.95

"Severin traces in almost minute detail the life of the myth of El Dorado in the minds of British explorers after 1595. . . . As in the case of each of the travelers he describes he accurately discusses the nature of the expedition, the difficulties it undergoes, and the reasons for its failures"—(*Best Sellers*).

Simon, Kate. MEXICO: Places and Pleasures. *T. Y. Crowell* rev. ed. 1971 $8.95; *New Am. Lib.* pap. $5.95

Smith, Anthony. MATTO GROSSO: The Last Virgin Land. *Dutton* 1971 $17.50

Spiegel, Ted, and Fred Ward. GOLDEN ISLANDS: The Caribbean. *Crown* 1973 $10.00. About the West Indies.

Spring, Norma. ALASKA: The Complete Travel Book. *Macmillan* 1970 $6.95 Collier Bks. 1975 pap. $3.95

Stanton, William. THE GREAT UNITED STATES EXPLORING EXPEDITION OF 1838–1842. *Univ. of California Press* 1975 $14.95

"Professor Stanton ... has written a complex tale of political intrigue, adventure, shipwreck, personality conflicts, professional jealousy—with some ludicrous episodes. ... [The expedition] marked a turning point in American science—when gentlemen naturalists were replaced by professionals and specialists"—*(PW)*.

Stevenson, Robert Louis. TRAVELS IN HAWAII. *Univ. Press of Hawaii* 1973 $8.50

"A collection of Stevenson's writings in, from, and about Hawaii. It includes 10 essays ... , 6 poems and 25 letters by Stevenson and his wife"—*(Choice)*.

Stommel, Henry. THE GULF STREAM: A Physical and Dynamical Description. *Univ. of California Press* 1965 $10.00

Straughan, Robert P. ADVENTURE IN BELIZE. *A. S. Barnes* 1974 $17.50

Teal, John, and Mildred Teal. THE SARGASSO SEA. *Little-Atlantic* 1975 $10.00

"Excerpts from John Teal's diaries of three cruises to the Sargasso (including one dictated during a deep-sea dive) lend immediacy and convey a sense of the painstaking observation which generally builds knowledge out of the once unknown"—*(LJ)*.

Tenison, Marika H. TAGGING ALONG: A Young Woman's Adventure in the Brazilian Jungle with Her Explorer Husband. *Coward* 1972 $6.95

Tilden, Freeman. THE NATIONAL PARKS: What They Mean to You and Me. *Knopf* rev. ed. 1970 $15.00 pap. $4.95

THE STATE PARKS: Their Meaning in American Life. Fwd. by Conrad L. Wirth, Director of the National Park Service *Knopf* 1962 $8.95. Companion volume to "The National Parks."

Toye, William E. BOOK OF CANADA. *Collins-World* $4.95

Toynbee, Arnold J. BETWEEN MAULE AND AMAZON. *Oxford* 1967 $5.75. Both this book and the one following discuss the eminent historian's (*q.v.*) travels through South America.

EAST TO WEST. *Oxford* 1958 $5.95

Ullman, James Ramsey, and Al Dinhofer. THE CARIBBEAN HERE AND NOW: A Complete Guide to 52 Sunny Vacation Spots. *Macmillan* 1970 $8.95

"A pleasant surprise is this combination practical guide and romantic travelog, superbly written and assembled"—*(LJ)*.

United States National Park Service. EXPLORERS AND SETTLERS: Historic Places Commemorating the Early Exploration and Settlement of the United States. 1968. *Finch Press* $15.00

"Part 1 of the present volume covers in a fine narrative style the extension of European civilization into the New World. Part 2 is a splendid survey of historic sites and buildings, copiously illustrated"—*(LJ)*.

Waterton, Charles. WANDERINGS IN SOUTH AMERICA. Introd. by Gilbert Phelps *Transatlantic* 1974 $12.50

Wenkam, Robert. HAWAII: Kauai, Oahu, Maui, Molokai, Lanai and Hawaii. *Rand McNally* 1972 $19.95

KAUAI AND THE PARK COUNTRY OF HAWAII. Ed. by Kenneth Brower; fwd. by David Brower. 1967. *Ballantine Bks.* 1969 pap. $3.95

Wright, Billie. Four Seasons North: A Journal of Life in the Alaskan Wilderness. *Harper* 1973 $7.95

Zochert, Donald, Ed. Walking in America. *Knopf* 1974 $8.95

"Twenty-two essays, covering the period from 1798 to 1971, all about walking—strolling, climbing, rambling, hiking, or even floundering, but always with a general but flexible role"—(*LJ*).

Zwinger, Ann. Run, River, Run: A Naturalist's Journey down One of the Great Rivers of the West. *Harper* 1975 $12.50

"Zwinger explored the Green River from its headwaters to its confluence with the Colorado, and her narrative is punctuated with quotations from earlier explorers, as well as with bits of information from a variety of disciplines (history, archaeology, botany . . .)"—(*LJ*).

EUROPE

Baker, Daisy. Travels in a Donkey Trap. *St. Martin's* 1974 $6.95

"The author describes her travels with a donkey and cart about the countryside of her cottage in Devon, England. She reminisces about the past as she remembers her childhood in the country, her period as between-maid to the bishop's daughters, her first love during the first World War, and her marriage"—(Publisher's note).

Baker, Paul R. The Fortunate Pilgrims: Americans in Italy, 1800–1860. *Harvard Univ. Press* 1964 $5.95

Barzini, Luigi. From Caesar to the Mafia: Sketches of Italian Life. *Open Court* (Library Press) 1971 $8.95. About Italian characters, Italian settings, and Italian problems in a series of character sketches, descriptions and essays.

The Italians. *Atheneum* 1964 $6.95; *Bantam* 1972 pap. $1.25

Berry, Lloyd E., and Robert O. Crummey, Eds. Rude and Barbarous Kingdom: Russia in the Accounts of Sixteenth-Century English Voyagers. *Univ. of Wisconsin Press* 1972 $10.00 pap. $4.50

Bowen, Elizabeth. A Time in Rome. *Knopf* 1960 $5.95. By the distinguished British novelist.

Bradley, David. Lion among Roses: A Memoir of Finland. *Holt* 1965 $5.95

"Penetrates heart and mind"—(*LJ*).

Brockway, Lucile, and George Brockway. Greece: Classical Tour with Extras. *Knopf* 1966 $6.95

"No person who intends to travel to Greece should go without first reading this book"—(*LJ*).

Brossard, Chandler. The Spanish Scene. *Viking* 1968 $4.00. Skillful writing by the avant-garde novelist.

Connery, Donald S. The Irish. *Simon & Schuster* 1968 $7.95 Touchstone-Clarion Bks. 1970 pap. $2.95

The Scandinavians. *Simon & Schuster* 1966 $9.95

Mr. Connery, "a free-lance writer, has done surprisingly well from limited sources and personal observations; he dwells too much on some popular notions of contemporary Scandinavia but dispels most myths about sex, suicides and sin"—(*LJ*).

Deane, Shirley. Corpses in Corsica. *Vanguard* 1969 $5.95

In a Corsican Village. *Vanguard* $5.95

Rocks and Olives. *Transatlantic* $6.95

Denham, H. M. The Adriatic: A Sea-Guide to Its Coasts and Islands. *Transatlantic* 1967 $12.50

"Unique and charming"—(*LJ*).

The Ionian Islands to Rhodes. *Transatlantic* 1972 $15.00

The Tyrrhenian Sea: A Sea-Guide to Its Coasts and Islands. *Transatlantic* 1969 $12.50

Dunn, William J. Enjoy Europe by Train. *Scribner* 1974 $7.95 pap. $3.95

Dunnett, Alastair M., Ed. ALISTAIR MACLEAN INTRODUCES SCOTLAND. *McGraw-Hill* 1972 $8.95

"Several prominent Scotsmen in fiction, journalism, history, and other specialty fields contribute witty and informative essays to a compendium that is geared to the stranger in search of a light-mannered yet informative introduction to Scotland"—*(Booklist)*.

SCOTLAND IN COLOR. *Viking* 1970 $5.95

Durrell, Lawrence. BITTER LEMONS. *Dutton* 1959 pap. $1.65. An evocative account of his life in a Cyprus village.

Gould, John. EUROPE ON SATURDAY NIGHT: The Farmer and His Wife Take a Tour. *Little* 1968 $6.95. The entertaining travels of a Maine couple.

Hall, Ellen, and Emily Hall. THE HALLS OF RAVENSWOOD: Pages from the Journals of Emily and Ellen Hall. Ed. by A. R. Mills *Transatlantic* 1968 $6.95. The yearly travels of a Victorian family.

Hillaby, John D. A WALK THROUGH BRITAIN. *Houghton* 1969 $7.95

The author's journey on foot from Land's End in southwest Cornwall to John O'Groat's in northeast Scotland during the spring and summer of 1966. "Hillaby's interest in and knowledge of, natural life and prehistory gives his book a lively theme and a distinctive flavor in which there is not a trace of the trite or commonplace. He also pleads convincingly for better conservation and recreation practices"—*(LJ)*.

A WALK THROUGH EUROPE. *Houghton* 1972 $6.95

Hillaby "relates matters seen and experienced during a two-month walk from the North Sea to the Mediterranean via the Alps"—*(Booklist)*.

Hürlimann, Martin. ITALY. *Transatlantic* 1972 $18.00

SWITZERLAND: History, Landscape, Architecture. *Int. Pubns. Service* 1974 $32.00

Ingstad, Helge. WESTWARD TO VINLAND. Trans. by Erik J. Friis *St. Martin's* 1969 $6.95; *Harper* Colophon Bks. 1972 pap. $3.45. His account of Norse ruins in Newfoundland.

Innes, Hammond. SEA AND ISLANDS. *Knopf* 1967 $7.95. The British author cruises the islands of the Aegean, Dalmatia and Denmark in a sailboat.

Kane, Robert S. GRAND TOUR A TO Z: The Capitals of Europe. *Doubleday* 1973 $9.95 pap. $6.95

Kimbrough, Emily. FLOATING ISLAND. *Harper* 1968 $6.95. An account of a 12-day barge trip by a group of Americans through the canals of central France.

Kulukundis, Elias. THE FEASTS OF MEMORY: A Journey to a Greek Island. *Holt* 1967 $5.95

"Marvelous recollection" *(LJ)* of the author's trip to Kasos, his ancestral island.

Laxalt, Robert. IN A HUNDRED GRAVES: A Basque Portrait. *Univ. of Nevada Press* 1972 $6.00

SWEET PROMISED LAND. *Harper* 1957 lg.-type ed. $6.95. An old Nevada sheepherder returns to his native village in the Pyrenees for a visit.

Liberman, Alexander. GREECE, GODS, AND ART. Introd. by Robert Graves; texts and commentaries by Iris C. Love *Viking* 1968 $22.50

This "does more to bring the reader close to ancient Greece than would a dozen weary jet flights and bus journeys. A superb technical and imaginative performance"—(Lewis Mumford).

McCarthy, Mary. THE STONES OF FLORENCE. *Harcourt* 1959 $17.50 Harvest Bks. pap. $1.85

VENICE OBSERVED. Ed. by Georges Bernier and Rosamond Bernier *Reynal* (dist. by Morrow) 1956 $15.00; *Harcourt* Harvest Bks. 1963 pap. $2.35. The American novelist's brilliant pen explores past and present aspects of the Queen of the Adriatic.

Mead, William E. THE GRAND TOUR IN THE EIGHTEENTH CENTURY. 1914. *Blom* $13.75

Michener, James A. IBERIA: Spanish Travels and Reflections. *Random* 1968 $12.50; *Fawcett* Crest Bks. 1973 pap. $1.95

"Mr. Michener unfolds a dazzling panorama of Spanish history, character, customs, and art; he discusses sex and bull-fighting, food and wine, picnics, pilgrimages, bird sanctuaries, cathedrals, museums, palaces. Scattered throughout are bright bits about fleabag hotels and delightful rogues"—(*SR*).

Middleton, Dorothy. Victorian Lady Travellers. *Routledge & Kegan Paul* 1965 $5.95

Mullins, Edwin B. The Pilgrimage to Santiago. *Taplinger* 1974 $12.95

"A traditional pilgrimage to Spain, more than a thousand years old, is the base around which a colorful amalgam of history, legend, and travelog are embroidered. Mullins started out from France, traveling alternately by foot and by automobile"—(*Booklist*).

National Geographic Society. This England. Fwd. by Melville Bell Grosvenor *National Geographic Society* 1966 $11.95

"Ten widely known writers, including Alan Villiers, Leonard Cottrell, and H. V. Morton, have contributed affectionate and knowledgeable descriptions, which are illustrated by many superb photographs. Each writer tours a region"—(*LJ*). Makes an excellent guidebook.

Nourissier, François. The French. Trans. from the French by Adrienne Foulke *Knopf* 1968 $6.95

Oakes, George W. Turn Left at the Pub: Walking Tours of the English Countryside. *McKay* 1968 new ed. 1974 $6.95

(With Alexandra Chapman). Turn Right at the Fountain: Walking Tours of London, Oxford, Cambridge, Edinburgh, Copenhagen, Amsterdam, Bruges, Paris, Rome, Florence, Venice, Munich and Geneva. *Holt* 1963 3rd ed. 1971 $5.95

Parkes, Joan. Travel in England in the Seventeenth Century. *Oxford* 1925 $9.75; *Greenwood* $16.00

Pillement, Georges. Unknown Greece. *Int. Pubns. Service* 2 vols. 1973 Vol. 1 Athens and the Peloponnesus Vol. 2 Epirus, Thessaly, Corfu and the Ionian Islands each $10.50. A guide to the less familiar regions of Greece. The author has written similar texts for France, Italy, Portugal, Sardinia and Corsica, Sicily, Spain, Turkey, and Yugoslavia.

Pritchett, Victor S. London Perceived. *Harcourt* 1962 Harvest Bks. 1966 pap. $1.65

(With E. Hofer). Dublin: A Portrait. *Harper* 1967 $15.00. The brilliant English critic and short-story writer provides the text to these books of photographs which evoke each city wonderfully.

Simon, Kate. England's Green and Pleasant Land. *Knopf* 1975 $10.00

Sitwell, Sir Sacheverell. The Netherlands. 1948. *Hastings House* 1974 $8.95

"Recent touring in the Netherlands provided Sitwell with additional information for this updated edition of a travelog that first appeared in 1948"—(*Booklist*).

Skelton, R. A., Thomas E. Marston and George D. Painter. The Vinland Map and the Tartar Relation. Fwd. by Alexander O. Vietor *Yale Univ. Press* 1965 $25.00

Contains a reproduction of the map suggesting that the Norsemen discovered America about 1000 A.D. Here is "printed for the first time Fr. de Bridia's 'Tartar Relation,' a condensed narrative of the extraordinary journey made across Asia by Fr. John de Plano Carpini in 1245–47 A.D. Although the main facts of this journey have long been known from Carpini's and other accounts, de Bridia's narrative adds many new details. George D. Painter has written a most interesting introduction, reviewing what is known about the history of the Mongols in the 13th century"—(*N.Y. Times*).

(Ed.). Country Atlases of the British Isles, 1579–1703: A Bibliography. *British Bk. Centre* 1971 $30.00

Smith, Desmond. Smith's Moscow. *Knopf* 1974 $8.95 pap. $4.95

Stendahl. Travels in the South of France. Trans. from the French by Elisabeth Abbott *Grossman* 1970 $12.50

"This is not a finished book but sketches and notes for a book that Stendahl never polished or published. They record a tour he made in the spring of 1833"—(*New Yorker*).

Stern, Lillian, and Philip Van Doren Stern. BEYOND PARIS: A Touring Guide to the French Provinces. *Norton* 1967 $9.95

An "excellent book for middle-income travelers in France"—*(LJ)*.

Tully, Gerie. FRANCE ESPECIALLY FOR WOMEN. *Abelard* 1974 $8.95

Williams, Lee D. ON THE ROAD THROUGH THE SOVIET UNION. *Lee Williams* (Rochester, N.Y.) 1975 $4.50

A "tale of a Volkswagen bus trip from Calais, France to and through the Soviet Union"—*(Booklist)*.

AFRICA, ASIA, OCEANIA

Adamson, Joy. JOY ADAMSON'S AFRICA. *Harcourt* 1972 $13.95

Allen, Philip M., and Aaron Segal. THE TRAVELER'S AFRICA: A Guide to the Entire Continent. *Dutton* 1973 $12.95; *Hopkinson & Blake* 1973 $12.95

"The first satisfactory guide to Africa as a whole"—*(Choice)*.

Ames, Evelyn. A GLIMPSE OF EDEN. *Houghton* 1967 $5.00; *Franklin Watts* lg.-type ed. $7.95

The experiences of the author and her husband photographing East African wildlife are the substance of this "poetic, moving and memorable book"—*(LJ)*.

IN TIME LIKE GLASS: Reflections on a Journey in Asia. *Houghton* 1974 $6.95

Andrews, Roy Chapman. ACROSS MONGOLIAN PLAINS: A Naturalist's Account of China's "Great Northwest." 1931. *Finch Press* $12.00

ENDS OF THE EARTH. 1929. *Gale Research Co.* 1972 $14.00

Bixler, Norma. BURMESE JOURNEY. *Antioch Press* (dist. by Kent State Univ. Press) 1967 $6.00

"Paul Bixler, the scholarly librarian (now librarian emeritus) of Antioch College, spent the years from 1958 to 1960 setting up the new Social Science Library at the University of Rangoon. His mission there bore results far richer than could have been anticipated, notably, this warm and charming book about the Bixlers in Burma written by his wife, Norma"—*(LJ)*.

Blumenthal, Susan. BRIGHT CONTINENT: A Shoestring Guide to Sub-Saharan Africa. *Doubleday* Anchor Bks. 1974 pap. $5.95

"Basic information for the traveler interested in visiting Africa at reasonable cost with maximum benefit"—*(Booklist)*.

Candlin, Enid S. A TRAVELER'S TALE: Memories of India. *Macmillan* 1974 $12.95

"The parameters of Eastern and Western civilization touch but do not mesh in this picture of the Indian sub-continent when British colonial rule ebbed in the aftermath of World War II"—*(Booklist)*.

Chiang, Yee. THE SILENT TRAVELLER IN JAPAN. *Norton* 1972 $15.00

"Japan and things Japanese as revealed by this distinguished Chinese scholar, artist and poet are experienced in a new dimension, for he sees them in relation to things Western and things Chinese"—(Publisher's note).

Dedmon, Emmett. CHINA JOURNAL. *Rand McNally* 1973 $8.95

"The author, who is Editorial Director of the *Chicago Sun-Times* was one of the first American journalists to tour contemporary China. [He] shares his experiences and insights on this country's unique political and social organization"—(Publisher's note).

Dunmore, John. FRENCH EXPLORERS IN THE PACIFIC. *Oxford* 2 vols. 1965–69 Vol. 1 Eighteenth Century (1965) $13.75 Vol. 2 Nineteenth Century (1969) $18.75

Elisofon, Eliot. TRIBUTE TO AFRICA: The Photographs and the Collection of Eliot Elisofon. Ed. by Warden Robbins *Interbk. Inc.* 1974 pap. $4.00

Fernea, Elizabeth W. GUESTS OF THE SHEIK: An Ethnology of an Iraqi Village. *Doubleday* 1965 Anchor Bks. 1969 pap. $1.75. Life in a tribal settlement on the edge of a village in southern Iraq.

Fernea, Robert A. NUBIANS IN EGYPT: Peaceful People. *Univ. of Texas Press* 1974 $15.00

Gardner, Brian. AFRICAN DREAM. *Putnam* 1970 $7.95. A history of the British experience in Africa, from the late eighteenth century to 1968.

Gide, André. TRAVELS IN THE CONGO. Trans. from the French by Dorothy Bussy *Univ. of California Press* 1957 pap. $1.95

Godden, Jon, and Rumer Godden. SHIVA'S PIGEONS: An Experience of India. Photographs by Stella Snead *Viking* 1972 $17.95

"A fascinating and revealing document which . . . reflects and inter-reflects the ever-changing patterns and colors of an India where their spirits, like Shiva's pigeons, haunt the places they love"—(Publisher's note).

Gunther, John. INSIDE AUSTRALIA. Completed and ed. by William H. Forbis *Harper* 1972 $10.95

Hamilton, Paul, and others. EXPLORING AFRICA AND ASIA. *Doubleday* 1973 $14.95

Harper, Norman. AUSTRALIA, ASIA AND THE PACIFIC. *Verry* 1972 $9.50

Hillaby, John D. JOURNEY TO THE JADE SEA. *Simon & Schuster* 1965 $5.50

"Mr. Hillaby, an English writer and naturalist, engaged a few African companions, borrowed, hired, or bought some sick, tired camels (to carry supplies), and set off on foot for the Jade Sea (Lake Rudolf in Kenya). This is the account of his arduous but successful efforts"—(*LJ*).

Horne, Donald. THE AUSTRALIAN PEOPLE: Biography of a People. *Verry* 1973 $13.75

"Donald Horne is one of the more penetrating writers on contemporary Australian life"—(*LJ*).

Howells, William. THE PACIFIC ISLANDERS. Peoples of the World Ser. *Scribner* 1974 $12.50 pap. $4.95

Huxley, Elspeth. THEIR SHINING ELDORADO: A Journey through Australia. *Morrow* 1967 $7.50

"Having honed her skillful craftsmanship in writing about Africa and other countries, Elspeth Huxley has reached a new peak in this graphic account of Australia"—(*LJ*).

Johnson, Martin Elmer. SAFARI: A Saga of the African Blue. 1928. *Gale Research Co.* 1972 $14.00

Kane, Robert S. AFRICA A TO Z. *Doubleday* 1972 $8.95. This author has written many such guides, including "Asia A to Z" and "South Pacific A to Z."

Lattimore, Owen, and Eleanor Lattimore. SILKS, SPICES AND EMPIRE: Asia Seen through the Eyes of Its Discoverers. Ed. by Evelyn S. Nef *Delacorte* 1968 $8.95; *Dell* Laurel Leaf Lib. 1971 pap. $.95. A fascinating anthology of writings collected by the noted orientalist and his wife.

MacLaine, Shirley. YOU CAN GET THERE FROM HERE. *Norton* 1974 $7.95. An account of a recent journey the author took through China, from Canton to Yenan.

Mowat, Farley. THE SIBERIANS. *Little-Atlantic* 1971 $7.95; *Penguin* 1972 pap. $1.45. A report of two long visits this Canadian author made to Siberia in 1966 and 1969 in which he shows that Siberia has recently become a productive and modern country.

Murphy, Dervla. IN ETHIOPIA WITH A MULE. *Transatlantic* 1970 $7.95

TIBETAN FOOTHOLD. *Transatlantic* 1967 $6.75

THE WAITING LAND: A Spell in Nepal. *Transatlantic* 1969 $6.95

"The 'spell' of the subtitle refers to what the author feels and transmits to her readers, a spell conjured by the friendly hardy people, their customs, and the unspeakable beauty of the country. Miss Murphy, a traveler who breaks all barriers of space, language, religion, food, comfort, and bacteria, writes with love, style, and wit"—(*LJ*).

Norbu, Thubten Jigme, and Colin M. Turnbull. TIBET. *Simon & Schuster* 1968 $7.50 Touchstone-Clarion Bks. 1970 pap. $2.95. The co-authors are the brother of the Dalai Lama and the author of "The Forest People."

Panter-Downes, Mollie. OOTY PRESERVED: A Victorian Hill Station in India. *Farrar, Straus* 1967 $4.95

"The distinguished *New Yorker* correspondent, Miss Panter-Downes, has found an excellent subject in the Old English hill station, Ootacamund, set high up in the Nilgiris. One might have expected such places to disappear after Indian independence. Actually, as I found in Simla, and Miss Panter-Downes has found in Ooty, they are rather surprisingly thriving. Many of the old English residents have lingered on, or even departed for home, only to return, having found post-war, Welfare State conditions intolerable. Then there are the Indians with a taste for such places. They, too, are not too happy in Congress India, and find in hill stations a refuge where they can pretend to themselves that there is still a Viceroy in Delhi, and orders and decorations to be awarded as in the days of the Raj. Of course, as Miss Panter-Downes points out, the effect is ghostly, but sociologically interesting, and with a particular poignancy of its own"—(Malcolm Muggeridge, in the *Observer*, London).

Perham, Margery. AFRICAN APPRENTICESHIP: An Autobiographical Journey in Southern Africa, 1929. *Holmes & Meier Pubs.* (Africana) 1974 $12.50

"Here we see the beginning of her lifetime career and interest in Africa . . . For all levels of libraries with an African interest"—(*Choice*).

(With Jack Simmons, Eds.) AFRICAN DISCOVERY: An Anthology of Exploration. *Northwestern Univ. Press* 1963 $8.50

Planck, Charles E., and Carolyn Planck. PACIFIC PARADISE ON A LOW BUDGET: How Two Toured Hong Kong, Japan, Fiji Islands, Tonga, American Samoa, Western Samoa. *Acropolis* 1973 $3.50

"A refreshing and resourceful couple, aged 63 and 76, describe how they traveled 21,000 miles in 168 days, spending $30 daily for the two"—(*Booklist*).

Rotberg, Robert I. AFRICA AND ITS EXPLORERS: Motives, Methods and Impacts. *Harvard Univ. Press* 1970 $12.95. Essays by nine Africanists on seven British and two German explorers of the 19th century—Barth, Livingstone, Burton, Speke, Baker, Rohlf, Stanley, Cameron, and Thomson.

Salisbury, Charlotte Y. CHINA DIARY. *Walker & Co.* $6.95

RUSSIAN DIARY. *Walker & Co.* 1974 $6.95

(With Alice S. Kandell) MOUNTAINTOP KINGDOM: Sikkim. *Norton* 1971 $20.00

Severin, Timothy. THE AFRICAN ADVENTURE. *Dutton* 1973 $18.00

"The adventures of a variety of explorers, military men, missionaries and sportsmen as they encounter the huge African continent. . . . Severin examines the explorers' varying motives and personalities, basing his account on their numerous publications, covering several centuries and all parts of the continent"—(*LJ*).

Straughan, Robert P. L. JET SAFARI TO AFRICA. *A. S. Barnes* 1973 $17.50

The "scenic wonders in a day-by-day description of his 23,000 mile safari featuring travels on jets and rides on the minibus and landrover across the veldt"—(*Booklist*).

Swaan, Wim. JAPANESE LANTERN. *Taplinger* 1967 1970 $8.95. A cultural guide in the form of essays.

Theroux, Paul. THE GREAT RAILWAY BAZAAR. *Houghton* 1975 $10.00

An account of a four month railroad journey across Asia. "Perhaps not since Mark Twain's "Following the Equator" (1897) have a wanderer's leisurely impressions been hammered into such wry, incisive mots. . . . By word and the seat of his pants Theroux has paid nostalgic homage to the pre-jet era, when men optimistically hoped to bind up the world with bands of steel"—(*Time*).

SELECTED LIST OF BOOKS ON INDIVIDUAL TRAVELS OR EXPLOITS

Adamson, J. H., and H. F. Folland. THE SHEPHERD OF THE OCEAN: Sir Walter Ralegh and His Times. *Gambit* 1969 $8.95. "Ralegh's story has probably never been better told"—(Edward Wagenknecht).

Alsar, Vital, and Enrique H. Lopez. BALSA: The Longest Raft Voyage in History. *Readers Digest Press* (dist. by Dutton) 1973 $7.95

"A member of the four man crew of a balsa wood raft that sailed from Ecuador to Australia, Alsar recounts the course of the voyage with understatement and attention to detail that makes his narrative both informative and engrossing"—(*Booklist*).

Beach, Capt. Edward L. AROUND THE WORLD SUBMERGED: The Voyage of the Triton. *Holt* (Rinehart) 1962 $5.50. An account of the shakedown cruise of the world's largest submarine.

Calderón de la Barca, Frances. LIFE IN MEXICO: The Letters of Fanny Calderón de la Barca. Ed. by Howard T. Fisher and Marion Hall Fisher *Dutton* Everyman's 1968 $3.95

"A definitive edition of this 'quiet persistent classic' has been long overdue. The journals and letters of this Scotswoman comprise one of the liveliest pictures of 19th-century Mexico. She married a Spanish diplomat and spent two busy years (1840–41) in Mexico, mostly in the capital though she traveled to other parts as well"—(*LJ*). The editing is excellent.

Cartier, Jacques. SHORTE AND BRIEFE NARRATIVE OF THE TWO NAVIGATIONS AND DISCOVERIES TO THE NORTHWEST PARTES CALLED NEWE FRANCE. 1580. March of America Ser. *University Microfilms* 1966 $4.55

Champlain, Samuel de. VOYAGES AND EXPLORATIONS, 1604–1616. *AMS Press* 2 vols. $20.00

Drake, Sir Francis. THE WORLD ENCOMPASSED AND ANALAGOUS CONTEMPORARY DOCUMENTS: Concerning Sir Francis Drake's Circumnavigation of the World. 1628. *Cooper* $10.00; ed. by R. Temple *Da Capo* 1926 $18.00; ed. by W. S. Vaux Hakluyt Society Ser. *Burt Franklin* $25.00; *University Microfilms* 1966 $5.75

Eames, Hugh. WINNER LOSE ALL: Dr. Cook and the Theft of the North Pole. *Little* 1973 $8.95

"Certain that Frederick Cook was the first explorer to reach the North Pole, the author presents a convincing, well-written account of Cook's experiences"—(*Booklist*).

Edwards, Hugh. THE WRECK ON THE HALF MOON REEF. *Scribner* 1973 $7.95; *Verry* 1970 $9.00. About Captain James Cook.

Fairfax, John, and Sylvia Cook. OARS ACROSS THE PACIFIC. *Norton* 1973 $6.95

Fairfax "teamed with Sylvia Cook to row across the Pacific from San Francisco to Australia and to write the story of their adventure. Each kept a log and they alternate in describing day-to-day events, meals, weather, mishaps, experiences with marine life, ailments, and visits to several islands"—(*Booklist*).

Fremont, John Charles. REPORT OF THE EXPLORING EXPEDITION TO THE ROCKY MOUNTAINS IN THE YEAR 1842: And to Oregon and North California in the Years 1843–44. 1845. *University Microfilms* 1966 $7.75

Graham, Robin Lee, and Derek L. T. Gill. DOVE. *Harper* 1972 $8.95. The true story of a 16-year old boy who sailed his 24 foot sloop around the world for five years and 33,000 miles to discover adventure and love.

Grant, Rev. George M. OCEAN TO OCEAN: Sandford Fleming's Expedition through Canada in 1872. 1873. *Tuttle* 1967 $3.95

"A stirring account of a small party's journey from Halifax in the east to Victoria in the west in search of a transcontinental railway route. A first-person story of the exhilarations and the hardships of the trip, it compares well with its nearest American counterpart, 'The Journals of Lewis and Clark' "—(*N.Y. Times*).

Haley, Nelson Cole. WHALE HUNT: The Narrative of a Voyage, by Nelson Cole Haley, Harpooner in the Ship Charles W. Morgan, 1849–1853. *I. Washburn* (dist. by McKay) rept. 1967 $5.50

Hiscock, Eric C. ATLANTIC CRUISE IN WANDERER III. *Oxford* 1968 $10.00. The British author and his wife sail their yacht from England to the U.S. by way of the Bahamas, making interesting stops and excursions, meeting interesting people.

SOU'WEST IN WANDERER 4. *Oxford* 1973 $15.00

The "voyage of several years that Hiscock and his wife took on their 49-foot steel ketch from Europe, through the Panama Canal to New Zealand"—(LJ).

VOYAGING UNDER SAIL. *Oxford* 2nd ed. 1970 $14.00

King, William. ADVENTURE IN DEPTH. *Putnam* 1975 $7.95

"King's account of his interrupted solo circumnavigation of the world in his junk-rigged *Galway Blazer II*"—(LJ).

Kingsley, Mary H. TRAVELS IN WEST AFRICA: Congo, Francais, Corisco and Cameroons. 1897. New introd. by John E. Flint *International Scholarly Bk. Services* 1965 $12.50; *Transatlantic* 1974 $8.75

"This is one of the classic writings on African exploration. . . . First published in 1897, it was a sensational success, and a second popular edition appeared in 1900. Both these editions have long been out of print. Mary Kingsley, niece of the novelist Charles, kept house in Cambridge for her father, a physician and amateur anthropologist. Upon his death in 1892 she inherited a small estate and a taste for adventure which led her, quite by chance, to West Africa. Her explorations and account of her first two trips, in 1893 and 1895, were remarkable achievements. And, with far-reaching effects, her intelligent, humanitarian approach to the study of African culture demolished forever the concept of 'savage Africa' and its 'childlike natives.' The book is eminently readable and the introduction by Dr. Flint, of the University of Nigeria, is perceptive and informative"—(LJ).

Ledyard, John. JOURNEY THROUGH RUSSIA AND SIBERIA, 1787–1788: The Journal and Selected Letters. Ed. with introd. by Stephen D. Watrous *Univ. of Wisconsin Press* 1966 $15.00

"John Ledyard was one of the most amazing explorers of all time. A Connecticut Yankee, he first saw the Pacific Northwest with Captain Cook in the 1770's and dreamed of returning there. Enlisting the aid of men like Jefferson, Lafayette, Banks, he conceived the idea of journeying eastward across Europe and Siberia, thence shipping to Alaska and walking across North America to New York. This well-researched, ably edited book describes his journey almost to the Pacific Coast of Siberia, before Catherine the Great ordered him returned to Europe"—(LJ).

Lisi, Albert. MACHAQUILÁ: Through the Mayan Jungle to a Lost City. *Hastings House* 1968 $6.95

"The reader of this remarkable adventure story by a man who set off in search of lost Mayan ruins in an old Rambler with only $300 is in for a vicarious experience seldom found in today's literature"—(LJ).

Morison, Samuel Eliot. SAMUEL DE CHAMPLAIN: Father of New France. *Little-Atlantic* 1972 $10.00

Morwood, William. TRAVELER IN A VANISHED LANDSCAPE: The Life and Times of David Douglas. *Clarkson N. Potter* (dist. by Crown) 1973 $7.95

"A biography of the Scottish naturalist who traveled between 1823 and 1834 as a collector for the Royal Horticultural Society of London through North America. He visited New York State, the Pacific Northwest, California and Hawaii"—(BRD).

Mowat, Farley. THE POLAR PASSION. *Little-Atlantic* 1968 $15.00. Includes extracts from the diaries of the major polar explorers.

(With David Blackwood). WAKE OF THE GREAT SEALERS. Prints and drawings by David Blackwood *Little-Atlantic* 1974 $19.95. The story of the Newfoundland men of the 19th and early 20th centuries who set out in flimsy ships to hunt seals on the treacherous North Atlantic ice fields; lavishly illustrated.

Muenchen, Al. FLYING THE MIDNIGHT SUN: The Exploration of Antarctica by Air. *McKay* 1973 $6.95

"An impressionistic history of the exploration and development of that continent, giving credit to early navigation and polar heroes"—(Booklist).

Nansen, Fridtjof. IN NORTHERN MISTS: Arctic Exploration in Early Times. Trans. from the Norwegian by Arthur G. Chater. 1911. *AMS Press* 2 vols. 1969 set $21.00; *Greenwood* 2 vols. set $38.50

Nott, David. INTO THE LOST WORLD. *Prentice-Hall* 1975 $7.95

A "real-life scientific expedition . . . to a remote Venezuelan jungle plateau"—(LJ).

Pike, Zebuloh Montgomery. ACCOUNT OF EXPEDITIONS TO THE SOURCES OF THE MISSISSIP-
PI, THE SOUTHWEST, ETC. 1810. *Ross* 2 vols. 1965 boxed set $22.50; *University
Microfilms* 1966 $9.95

JOURNALS . . . WITH LETTERS AND RELATED DOCUMENTS. Ed. by Donald Jackson *Univ. of
Oklahoma Press* 2 vols. 1966 set $20.00

Piozzi, Hester Lynch. OBSERVATIONS AND REFLECTIONS: Made in the Course of a Journey
Through France, Italy, and Germany. Ed. by Herbert Barrows *Univ. of Michigan
Press* 1967 $12.50

"A casual observer might well question the wisdom of reprinting a thick volume of travelogue,
written by a woman [before her second marriage Mrs. Thrale] whose principal fame rests upon
her friendship with Dr. Samuel Johnson. But . . . the reader soon discovers that Mrs. Piozzi has a
clear and incisive style, that she possesses good sense in abundance, and that neither prudishness
nor extreme liberalism inhibit her from writing honestly and openly about the persons and
countries which come under her observation"—(*LJ*).

Pizarro, Pedro. RELATION OF THE DISCOVERY AND CONQUEST OF THE KINGDOM OF PERU.
Trans. by Philip A. Means. 1921. *Kraus* 2 vols. in 1 $20.00; *Milford House* 1972 $45.00

Rasmussen, Knud J. ACROSS ARCTIC AMERICA: Narrative of the Fifth Thule Expedition.
1927. *Greenwood* 1968 $28.00

Roberts, David. THE MOUNTAIN OF MY FEAR. *Vanguard* 1968 $6.95. The story of the first
scaling of the west face of Alaska's Mt. Huntington by four Harvard students in 1965.

Roth, Harold. TWO ON A BIG OCEAN: The Story of the First Circumnavigation of the
Pacific Basin in a Small Sailing Ship. *Macmillan* 1972 $8.95

"This book describes the 19 months the Roths spent circumnavigating the Pacific Ocean, from
San Francisco to Tahiti and the South Seas, then to Japan, the sub-Arctic Aleutians and the
mountainous Alaskan and Canadian coasts. In their 35-foot sailboat *Whisper* they traveled 18,538
miles, called at 75 ports, made hundreds of new friends and gained a new understanding of the
sea and the people who live beside it"—(Publisher's note).

Sayre, Woodrow Wilson. FOUR AGAINST EVEREST. *Prentice-Hall* 1964 $5.95; *Tower* 1971
pap. $.95

"Sayre's amazing ascent with three companions almost to the top of Everest was a tremendous
test and magnificent achievement of the human spirit. With the sublime confidence of amateurs,
without governmental permission or the help of Sherpas, and scorning oxygen as offensive to
aesthetic principles and good sportsmanship, they faced unseen hazards but survived. . . . The
chapter 'Why Men Climb' is a masterpiece"—(*LJ*). The controversial author, a professor of
philosophy, was much in the news at the time of this attempt—by some considered foolhardy. But
he has translated his experience into excellent prose with meditations on the philosophy of
mountain-climbing.

Smith, John. TRAVELS AND WORKS OF CAPTAIN JOHN SMITH, PRESIDENT OF VIRGINIA AND
ADMIRAL OF NEW ENGLAND. Ed. by Edward Arber and A. G. Bradley *Burt Franklin* 2
vols. rev. ed. 1965 $42.50

Speke, John Hanning. JOURNAL OF THE DISCOVERY OF THE SOURCE OF THE NILE. 1863.
Dutton Everyman's $3.95; *Greenwood* 1968 $32.00

Teilhard de Chardin, Pierre. LETTERS FROM A TRAVELLER. Ed. by Claude Aragonnes;
introds. by Sir Julian Huxley, Pierre Leroy, S. J., and Claude Aragonnes *Harper* 1962
Torchbks. 1968 pap. $2.45

These are selections from letters written between 1923 and 1955 by Father Teilhard de
Chardin, one of the world's leading paleontologists. His travels took him to China, Java, India,
Ethiopia, South Africa, and the U.S. A person of keen perception and spiritual insight, "he
describes vividly the exotic lands where he searched for prehistoric man."

See also his main entry in Chapter 4, World Religions, this Vol.

Terrell, John Upton. LA SALLE: The Life and Times of an Explorer. *Weybright & Talley*
(dist. by McKay) 1968 $6.95

A "fine historical narrative that should be in all general collections"—(*LJ*).

Waterfield, Gordon. LAYARD OF NINEVEH. *Praeger* 1969 $12.50

"Sir Henry Layard (1817–1894) was one of those larger-than-life Victorians. At 22 years of age he began a ride across the Middle East in search of adventure; ten years later had uncovered the ancient Assyrian cities of Nimrud and Nineveh. Fame swept him into politics where his courage and integrity won him both honor and enemies; he represented Britain at Madrid and Constantinople during periods of revolution and war, and these were but the high points of his active life. Gordon Waterfield, journalist and author, vividly portrays an utterly fascinating man"—(*LJ*).

Weems, John Edward. PEARY: The Explorer and the Man. *Houghton* 1967 $6.95

"This is a well-rounded biography based on Peary's diaries, journals, letters and family papers, which were recently opened for the first time and to which Mr. Weems was given unlimited access. . . . Good biography and very good Arcticana. Recommended for all libraries"—(*LJ*).

Wilson, Edward. DIARY OF THE DISCOVERY EXPEDITION TO THE ANTARCTIC REGIONS, 1901–1904. Ed. by Ann Savours; fwd. by the Duke of Edinburgh *Humanities Press* 1967 $24.75

"Edward Wilson, who died with Scott [*q.v.*] on their return from the South Pole in 1912, first visited the Antarctic some 10 years earlier, keeping a personal and detailed diary, describing the day-to-day work, and the adventures of the scientific expedition. The author, surgeon and scientist of the expedition, was himself a remarkable man, which becomes evident on reading this book. It is illustrated with 47 of Wilson's exquisite watercolors, numerous pencil sketches throughout the text and 5 maps"—(*LJ*).

DIARY OF THE "TERRA NOVA" EXPEDITION TO THE ANTARCTIC: 1910–1912. Ed. by H. R. King *Humanities Press* 1972 $21.50

"The tragic story of Scott's last expedition to the Antarctic . . . as seen through the eyes of Scott's second in command and scientific director"—(*LJ*). "The pictures reproduced in this volume are remarkable by any standard. . . . A hundred reproductions appear in this handsome publication"—(*TLS*, London).

WRITERS ON TRAVEL, EXPLORATION, EXPLOITS

POLO, MARCO. 1254–1323.

Marco Polo was the pioneer explorer of Central Asia and China. His contemporaries refused to believe his story, but time has fully credited the veracity of all he wrote. "The Travels" was written while he was a prison inmate at Genoa during the war between Venice and Genoa. It was dictated to a fellow prisoner entirely in French and almost immediately translated into many languages, the Marsden translation being the first in English. It was followed by the more useful one of Sir Henry Yule, the British Orientalist (1820–1889).

THE TRAVELS OF MARCO POLO. Trans. by William Marsden; ed. by Thomas Wright. 1854. *AMS Press* 1968 $17.50; *Assoc. Booksellers* Airmont Bks. 1968 pap. $.60; introd. by John Masefield *Dutton* Everyman's 1954 $3.95 pap. 1972 $2.25; ed. by Manuel Komroff *Liveright* $6.95; ed. by Ronald Latham *Penguin* 1958 pap. $1.95. The great Venetian's masterful account of his journeyings.

THE BOOK OF SER MARCO POLO, THE VENETIAN: Concerning the Kingdoms and Marvels of the East. Trans. and ed. by Henry Yule *AMS Press* 3 vols. 3rd ed. 1920 set $97.50; *Krishna Press* 2 vols. $100.00

MOST NOBLE AND FAMOUS TRAVELS OF MARCO POLO AND TRAVELS OF NICOLÒ DE CONTI. Trans. by John Frampton; ed. by N. M. Penzer. 1929. *Da Capo* $31.50

THE DESCRIPTION OF THE WORLD. Trans. by Arthur C. Moule and Paul Pelliot. 1938. *AMS Press* 2 vols. $49.50

Books about Marco Polo

Marco Polo and His Books. By E. Denison Ross. 1934. *Folcroft* $5.00
Marco Polo's Asia. By Leonardo Olschki. Trans. by John A. Scott *Univ. of California Press* 1960 $15.00
Marco Polo: Venetian Adventurer. By Henry H. Hart. *Univ. of Oklahoma Press* 1967 $7.95
Contemporaries of Marco Polo. Ed. by Manuel Komroff. *Liveright* $6.95

COLUMBUS, CHRISTOPHER (Cristoforo Colombo). 1446–1506.

A man of imagination, dreams and perseverance, Columbus, the Genoese, persuaded King Ferdinand and Queen Isabella of Spain to sponsor his search for the Orient through a Western route. Columbus made four voyages to the New World, always landing in the West Indies and believing he was very close to the "Island of Cipango" (Japan). Difficulties with his crews and with his native subjects led to his dismissal as Spanish governor of the islands, though King Ferdinand remained an admirer of his nautical prowess.

FERNANDO COLON (Ferdinand Columbus, 1488–1539), his son, wrote "The Life of the Admiral Christopher Columbus" (trans. and ed. by Benjamin Keen *Rutgers Univ. Press* 1959 $10.00). "It is greatly to Ferdinand's credit as an honest biographer that, while trying to show what a hard, sad life his father led, he included so much evidence to suggest that Columbus enjoyed it"—*(New Yorker)*. Ferdinand was a younger and natural son, who accompanied his father on the fourth voyage to America (1502–1504). He was a scholar, writer, bibliographer and founder of the Biblioteca Columbina in Seville. He wrote the biography to refute critics of his father; it was published in Madrid in 1530. The most authoritative modern biography of Columbus is Samuel Eliot Morison's Pulitzer-Prize-winning "Admiral of the Ocean Sea: A Life of Christopher Columbus" *(Little-Atlantic* 1942 $15.00). The author rewrote this in narrative form as "Christopher Columbus, Mariner" *(Little-Atlantic* 1955 $7.50; *New Am. Lib.* Mentor Bks. 1956 pap. $.60). "The Caribbean as Columbus Saw It" (1964, o.p.) is Morison's text based on visits to the area, in collaboration with Mauricio Obregón of Colombia; it includes many photographs.

CHRISTOPHER COLUMBUS: His Life, His Works, His Remains, as Revealed by Original Printed and Manuscript Records. Ed. by John Boyd Thacher. 1903–1904. *AMS Press* 3 vols. 1967 set $125.00; *Kraus* 3 vols. set $125.00

JOURNAL (DURING HIS FIRST VOYAGE, 1492–1493): And Documents Relating to the Voyages of John Cabot and Gasper Corte Real. Ed. by Clements R. Markham. Hakluyt Society Ser. *Burt Franklin* 1972 $22.50

JOURNAL OF FIRST VOYAGE TO AMERICA. 1924. *Bks. for Libraries* 1972 $10.75

FOUR VOYAGES TO THE NEW WORLD. Trans. by R. H. Major; introd. by John E. Flagg *Corinth Bks.* (dist. by Citadel Press) 1961 pap. $1.95; ed. by Jane Cecil. 1930. *Da Capo* $24.00; trans. and ed. by J. M. Cohen *Gannon* $5.00; *Peter Smith* $4.75

LETTER TO RAFAEL SANCHEZ. 1493. *Johnson Reprint* 1970 $4.95

Books about Columbus

The Life and Voyages of Christopher Columbus. By Washington Irving. 1893. *AMS Press* $24.50

Catalogue of the Library of Ferdinand Columbus. Ed. by Archer M. Huntington. 1905. *Kraus* $25.00

Northmen, Columbus and Cabot, 985–1503. Ed. by Julius E. Olson and Edward G. Bourne. 1906. *Harper* (Barnes & Noble) 1959 $6.50

Columbus in the Arctic and Vineland Literature. By J. K. Tornöe. 1965. *Vanous* pap. $4.50

Sails of Hope: The Secret Mission of Christopher Columbus. By Simon Wiesenthal. Trans. from the German by Clara and Richard Winston *Macmillan* 1973 $5.95

Christopher Columbus. By Ernle Bradford. *Viking* 1973 $16.95

Columbus and Related Family Papers, 1451–1902: An Inventory of the Boal Collection. By Richard L. Garner and Donald C. Henderson. *Pennsylvania State Univ. Press* 1974 pap. $3.50

VESPUCCI, AMERIGO. 1451–1512.

The Renaissance Florentine explored the American coast from Florida to Patagonia. He was the first to declare South America a separate continent rather than a part of Asia. As a navigator-mathematician he measured the earth's circumference more exactly than anyone before him and devised an accurate system for ascertaining longitude. His accounts were published in 1507 by Martin Waldseemüller, German geographer, who suggested the new lands be named "America."

LETTERS AND OTHER DOCUMENTS ILLUSTRATIVE OF HIS CAREER. Trans. and ed. by Clements R. Markham. Hakluyt Society Ser. 1894. *Burt Franklin* $20.00

Books about Vespucci

Amerigo Vespucci, Pilot Major. By Frederick J. Pohl. 1944. *Octagon* 1966 $11.00

DÍAZ DEL CASTILLO, BERNAL. 1496–1584.

The Spanish conquistador Díaz went to Mexico in 1519 with Cortes. Believing Lopez de Gomara's history of the conquest of the Aztec Empire to be inaccurate, he wrote his own account of the events. In the "Chronicles" (ed. and trans. by Albert Idell, o.p.) he describes in detailed and idiomatic language the daily life of the average soldier. This living narration was the source for Archibald MacLeish's epic "Conquistador" (*q.v.*, Reader's Adviser, *Vol. 1*), and for Luis Cernudas' poem "Quetzalcoatl."

THE TRUE HISTORY OF THE CONQUEST OF MEXICO: Written in the Year 1568. Trans. by Maurice Keating. 1800. *University Microfilms* 1966 $11.95

THE CONQUEST OF NEW SPAIN. Trans. by John M. Cohen *Penguin* (orig.) 1963 pap. $1.75; *Peter Smith* $4.75

THE DISCOVERY AND CONQUEST OF MEXICO. Ed. by Gerano Garcia; trans. by A. P. Maudslay *Farrar, Straus* 1956 Noonday pap. $4.95

Books about Diaz

How Bernal Diaz's True History Was Reborn. By Ben Grauer. *Between Hours Press* 1960 pap. boxed $5.00

Bernal Diaz: Historian of the Conquest. By Herbert Cerwin. *Univ. of Oklahoma Press* 1963 $7.95. This well-documented biography also contains interesting data on people and places in his life.

CIEZA DE LÉON, PEDRO DE. 1518?–1560.

Cieza, a Spanish soldier, and perhaps one of the most objective of 16th-century Incan historians, spent 17 years traveling, fighting and writing in the New World. His "Chronicle of Peru" is a valuable historical source for the geography and history of the Spanish conquest. The first part (1550) is mainly geographical and anthropological; the sequels, unpublished until the 19th century, describe Inca history and the Peruvian civil wars. Cieza wrote well and with sympathy for the Indians. The edition of "The Incas" is the most complete one in English of the Incan chronicles. Von Hagen's notes and introduction add new valuable information and correct inaccurate accounts of Cieza's life.

THE TRAVELS OF PEDRO DE CIEZA DE LÉON, 1532–1550. Trans. and ed. by Clements R. Markham. 1864. Hakluyt Society Ser. *Burt Franklin* 2 vols. 1964 Vol. 1 From Darien to La Plata Vol. 2 Chronicle of Peru (Pt. 2) set $47.50

THE INCAS OF PEDRO DE CIEZA DE LÉON. Trans. by Harriet de Onis; ed. with introd. by Victor Wolfgang von Hagen *Univ. of Oklahoma Press* 1969 $8.95

THE WAR OF QUITO. Trans. and ed. by Clements R. Markham. 1913. *Kraus*, o.p.

THE CIVIL WARS IN PERU. *Kraus* 2 vols. 1917–1923 Vol. 1 The War of Chupas (1917) Vol. 2 The War of Las Salinas (1923) o.p.

HAKLUYT, RICHARD. 1552–1616.

Hakluyt wrote not of his own travels but of other men's. He was an English divine who took such patriotic pride in the achievements of his countrymen that he devoted his life to preserving the records of all English voyages. They are in three parts—to Russia, to India, and to America. The Hakluyt Society, which republishes records of early voyages and travels, perpetuates his labors as well as his memory.

DIVERS VOYAGES TOUCHING THE DISCOVERIE OF AMERICA and the Ilands Adjacent Unto the Same. Collected and Published by Richard Hakluyt in 1582. Ed. by John W. Jones. 1850. Hakluyt Society Ser. *Burt Franklin* $23.50; *University Microfilms* 1966 $5.75

THE PRINCIPAL NAVIGATIONS, VOYAGES, TRAFFIQUES, AND DISCOVERIES OF THE ENGLISH NATION: Made by Sea or Over Land to the Most Remote and Farthest Distant Quarters of the Earth, at any Time within the Compass of These 1,500 Years. 1589. 3 folio vols. 1598–1600. Text of MacLehose ltd. ed. 1903–05. *AMS Press* 12 vols. 1967 each $16.00 set $190.00; *Kelley* 12 vols. repr. of 1903 ed. set $165.00; ed. with an introd. by David B. Quinn *Cambridge* 2 vols. 1965 set $35.00

HAKLUYT'S VOYAGES TO THE NEW WORLD. Ed. by David F. Hawke. American Historical Landmarks Ser. *Bobbs* 1972 $9.00 pap. $2.95; (with title "The Voyages") introd. by John Masefield 1907. *Dutton* Everyman's 8 vols. 1962 each $3.95 vol. 7 o.p.; (with title "The Portable Hakluyt's Voyages") sel. and ed. with introd. by Irwin R. Blacker *Viking* 1967 $4.95

VOYAGES AND DISCOVERIES. Ed. by Jack Beeching *Gannon* $5.50; *Penguin* 1972 pap. $2.25

VOYAGES AND DOCUMENTS. Ed. by Janet Hampden *Oxford* 1958 $3.00

AUTOBIOGRAPHY: With Selections from His Correspondence. Ed. by M. Bentham-Edwards. 1898. *Kelley*, o.p.

Books about Hakluyt

Richard Hakluyt and the English Voyages. By George B. Parks. 1928. *Ungar* 2nd ed. 1961 $9.50

COOK, CAPTAIN JAMES. 1728–1779.

Captain Cook's voyages round the world resulted in the discovery of the Sandwich Islands, the east coast of Australia, called New South Wales, and other important geographical information. He was killed by savages at Hawaii. An obelisk was erected there in his memory in 1874. Cook's Voyages were written partly by himself and continued by Captain James King after Cook's death.

"It is not too easy at this distance to appreciate fully the impact which Cook's voyages had on the intellectual world of his day. In a period of acute international tension . . . the exploring ships went out, incidentally, with safe conducts from belligerents, and the published reports quickly translated into the principal languages aroused immense enthusiasm. . . . In many ways Cook's second voyage was the high point of his career as an explorer and scientist"—(*LJ*). In the fall of 1960, it was reported that a faded manuscript and log book of Cook's first and second voyages were sold to a London bookseller for $148,400. In early 1969 an expeditionary party of the Academy of Natural Sciences of Philadelphia located some of Captain Cook's cannons in waters 10 fathoms deep off the coast of Australia.

JOURNAL OF A VOYAGE ROUND THE WORLD IN H.M.S. ENDEAVOUR IN THE YEARS 1768–1771. *Da Capo* 1967 $15.75

EXPLORATIONS OF CAPTAIN JAMES COOK IN THE PACIFIC AS TOLD BY SELECTIONS OF HIS OWN JOURNALS, 1768–1779. Ed. by A. Grenfell Price 1957. *Dover* 1972 pap. $4.00; *Peter Smith* $6.00

JOURNAL OF CAPTAIN COOK'S LAST VOYAGE TO THE PACIFIC OCEAN, ON DISCOVERY. 1781. Ed. by John Rickman *Da Capo* 1967 $21.00; *University Microfilms* 1966 $8.95

AUTHENTIC NARRATIVE OF A VOYAGE PERFORMED BY CAPTAIN COOK AND CAPTAIN CLERKE IN HIS MAJESTY'S SHIPS RESOLUTION AND DISCOVERY DURING THE YEARS 1776–1780: In Search of a North-West Passage between the Continents of Asia and America. 1782. Ed. by William Ellis *Da Capo* 1969 2 vols. $48.00

VOYAGES OF DISCOVERY. Ed. by John Barrow; introd. by Guy Pollock. 1906. *Dutton* Everyman's $3.95

Books about Cook

A Bibliography of Captain James Cook. Comp. by the Mitchell Library, Sydney. 1928. *Burt Franklin* $14.50; *Somerset Pub.* $9.50

John Ledyard's Journal of Captain Cook's Last Voyage. Ed. by James Kenneth Munford. Introd. by Sinclair Hitchings with notes by Robert M. Storm and Helen M. Gilkey *Oregon State Univ. Press* 1963 $6.00

"A complete reprint (not facsimile) of the journal published in Hartford, Connecticut, in 1783 under the authorship of the American adventurer who served as corporal of marines with Captain James Cook in his 1776–1780 voyage to the Pacific Ocean"—(Publisher's note).

Captain James Cook: A Definitive Biography. By Alan Villiers. *Scribner* 1967 pap. 1970 $2.45

"Since so little of Cook as a human being, as distinct from the sea captain and explorer, is known, Captain Villiers [himself a veteran seaman] has created a man out of sea and wind, wave and fog, railing storm and gentle airs. . . . His account is marked, as can be expected, by great expertise. . . . The feel of the open sea, of the various weathers and the challenge of the ships can be felt on every page"—(Thomas Lask, in the *N.Y. Times*).

Wreck on the Half-Moon Reef. By Hugh Edwards. *Verry* 1970 $9.00

Captain Cook: Navigator and Scientist. Ed. by G. M. Badger. *Humanities Press* 1970 $7.50

Travels of Captain Cook. By Ronald Syme. *McGraw-Hill* 1971 $12.95

Captain Cook. By Alistair MacLean. *Doubleday* 1972 $9.95

The Life of Captain James Cook. By J. C. Beaglehole. *Stanford Univ. Press* 1974 $18.50. By the editor of "The Journals of Captain James Cook" (1955, o.p.).

Captain Cook's Approach to Oregon. Ed. by T. C. Elliott. *Oregon Historical Society* 1974 pap. $1.00

Captain Cook, R.N. The Resolute Mariner. By Thomas Vaughan and C. M. Murray-Oliver. *Oregon Historical Society* 1974 $12.00 pap. $6.00

MÜNCHHAUSEN, BARON (English corruption spelled Baron Munchausen, pseud. of Rudolf Erich Raspe). 1737–1794.

Baron Munchausen's narrative was written by Rudolf Erich Raspe, a German exile who, while living in England, was befriended by Horace Walpole. The English translation from the German was first published in 1785. The narrative is made up of a collection of fabulous tales, some few founded on the actual adventures of a real Münchhausen—a German who served as an officer in the Russian army, and was noted for his "tall" tales. They gained universal popularity as a monument of methodical lying unparalleled in literature. In 1936 the municipality of Bodenwerder established a museum in the house of the original Karl Friedrich Hieronymus, Baron von Münchhausen. In "The Real Münchhausen" an attempt has been made to separate those tales which were told by the Baron from those falsely attributed to him. One story, "The Sleigh of St. Petersburg," has not previously appeared in any collection.

THE SINGULAR TRAVELS, CAMPAIGNS AND ADVENTURES OF BARON MUNCHAUSEN. By Rudolph Erich Raspe. Ed. by John Carswell. 1948. *Dover* pap. $2.00; *Peter Smith* $3.75

THE REAL MÜNCHHAUSEN: Authentic Tales by the Fabulous Baron of Bodenwerder. Retold by his great-great-great-great-great grandniece, Angelita von Münchhausen; ill. by Harry Carter *Devin-Adair* 1960 $6.00

BARON MUNCHAUSEN AND OTHER TALES FROM GERMANY. *Dutton* $4.50

Books about Münchhausen

The Romantic Rogue: Being the Singular Life and Adventures of Rudolf Erich Raspe. By John Carswell. 1950. *Folcroft* $15.00

BARTRAM, WILLIAM, 1739–1823, and JOHN BARTRAM, 1699–1777. *See Chapter 7, Science, this Vol.*

YOUNG, ARTHUR. 1741–1820. *See Chapter 8, The Social Sciences, this Vol.*

VANCOUVER, GEORGE. 1757–1798.

The English navigator Vancouver began his apprenticeship with Cook (*q.v.*) on his second voyage and went as midshipman on the third. He commanded the "Voyage of Discovery" in search of the fabled Northwest passage and subsequently continued to circumnavigate the globe. He explored the Pacific coast of North America (1792–1794) and surveyed and charted large sections of the coastlines of what are now the States of California, Oregon, Washington, Alaska and Hawaii. Although he died before completing his own account of "A Voyage of Discovery," it was finished by his brother John and one of George Vancouver's officers on the voyage. Now o.p. is "Vancouver in California, 1792–1794" (1954).

A VOYAGE OF DISCOVERY TO THE NORTH PACIFIC OCEAN AND ROUND THE WORLD. 1798. *Da Capo* 3 vols. 1968 $113.75

Books about Vancouver

Vancouver's Discovery of Puget Sound. By Edmond S. Meany. *Binfords* 1957 $6.95
The Life and Voyages of Captain George Vancouver: Surveyor of the Sea. By Bern Anderson. *Univ. of Washington Press* 1960 1966 pap. $2.95
"The present biography is most welcome not only because it is soundly based on the sources and it is well written, but also because the author who is a sailor has covered much of the Northwest Coast in his own ship and has re-created the life of Vancouver from the viewpoint of a practical seaman"—(*LJ*).

MACKENZIE, SIR ALEXANDER. 1763–1820.

Twelve years ahead of the more publicized expedition of Lewis and Clark (*q.v.*), Mackenzie had successfully led a party through some of the roughest terrain in the world to the coast of British Columbia. He is thought to be the first European to accomplish such a passage—one of the great events in the exploration of North America.

VOYAGES FROM MONTREAL, ON THE RIVER ST. LAURENCE, THROUGH THE CONTINENT OF NORTH AMERICA, TO THE FROZEN AND PACIFIC OCEANS IN 1789 AND 1793: With an Account of the Rise and State of the Fur Trade. 1801. *AMS Press* 2 vols. repr. of 1922 ed. $28.50; introd. by Roy Daniells *Tuttle* 1971 $19.25; *University Microfilms* 1966 repr. of 1801 ed. $11.95

EXPLORING THE NORTHWEST TERRITORY: Sir Alexander Mackenzie's Journal of a Voyage by Bark Canoe from Lake Athabasca to the Pacific Ocean in the Summer of 1789. Ed. by T. H. MacDonald *Univ. of Oklahoma Press* 1966 $5.95 pap. $1.95

This and his later version (*see* "First Man West") remain important sources of northern history. The present volume, from the ms. in the British Museum, "while less polished and less readable than the 1801 revision . . . is undoubtedly more accurate. . . . The edition is excellent"—(*LJ*).

FIRST MAN WEST: Alexander Mackenzie's Journal of His Voyage to the Pacific Coast of Canada in 1793. The 1801 edition of his Journal. Ed. by Walter Sheppe 1962, o.p.

"The editor has retraced much of the route and has added supplemental material that makes this a volume that will be enjoyed by the general reader and prove useful to the historian"—(*LJ*).

Books about Mackenzie

Pathfinders of the West. By Agnes C. Laut. 1904. *Bks. for Libraries* $16.75

Alexander Mackenzie and the North West. By Roy Daniells. Great Travellers Ser. *Harper* (Barnes & Noble) 1969 $5.50

Westward Crossings: Balboa, Mackenzie, Lewis and Clark. By Jeanette Mirsky. *Univ. of Chicago Press* Phoenix Bks. 1970 pap. $3.45

CLARK, WILLIAM. 1770–1838. *See* LEWIS, MERIWETHER, 1774–1809, *this Chapter.*

PARK, MUNGO. 1771–1806.

One of the earliest of African explorers, who discovered the Niger River, this Scotsman and his explorations helped to map the interior of Africa. On a second expedition he was lost. His classic account of his adventures was originally published as "Travels in the Interior of Africa." A fascinating study of early African exploration, which touches on Park, is to be found in Alan Moorehead's (*q.v.*) "The White Nile" and "The Blue Nile."

TRAVELS IN THE INTERIOR DISTRICTS OF AFRICA: Performed under the Direction and Patronage of the African Association, in the Years 1795, 1796 and 1797. 1799. *Arno* repr. of 1799 ed. 1971 $15.00; *Scholarly Press* repr. of 1813 ed. 1973 $14.50; (with title "Travels") *Dutton* 1932 1957 $3.95 Everymans pap. 1972 $2.50

JOURNAL OF A MISSION TO THE INTERIOR OF AFRICA. 1815. *Scholarly Press* $19.50

Books about Park

●Mungo Park and the Niger. By Joseph Thomson. *Argosy-Antiquarian* 1970 $15.00

LEWIS, MERIWETHER, 1774–1809, and WILLIAM CLARK, 1770–1838.

The Lewis and Clark expedition was one of the earliest crossings of the United States. Eager to expand the country, President Thomas Jefferson appointed Lewis, formerly his private secretary, to seek a Northwest Passage to the Orient. Lewis and his partner, William Clark, were both seasoned soldiers, expert woodsmen and boatmen. They both kept journals and so did four sergeants and one private in the party of 43 men. They started from St. Louis in 1804 up the Missouri River, across the Rockies and down to the Pacific Coast at the mouth of the Columbia River. The Indian maiden Sacajawea (the Bird Woman), wife of one of the members, gave them valuable help on the hazardous journey, which lasted two years, four months and ten days and cost the U.S. government a total of $38,722.25. Lewis was the better educated of the two captains and his account has "force, color and character." Clark "wrote with a halting pen," and an ingenious phonetic spelling of his own, but "he has a keen eye and little escaped his attention."

The journal of the expedition by Patrick Gass, published in 1807, has recently been republished ("The Journal of Patrick Gass" *Ross & Haines* $10.00). The official edition of the "Journals" (*see below*) did not appear until 1814, when they were edited in two volumes by Nicholas Biddle and Paul Allen. This text, a paraphrase of the journals, was used in various editions until 1904, when R. G. Thwaites edited a full issue (8 vols. 1904–05). De Voto's edition follows the original text, but omits or summarizes the less important passages, making the journals available in all their original freshness.

Early in 1960 it was announced in the *N.Y. Times* that 67 notes written by Clark had been given by Frederick W. Beinecke of New York to the Yale University Library. "The documents, finger-smudged, blotted and blurred with cross-outs, list personal observations previously unknown to historians. . . . The documents, consisting of old letters, envelopes and scraps of paper, were the subject of an unusual legal fight. After the Clark notes were found in an attic in St. Paul, Minn., in 1952, the United States moved to obtain them. The Government contended the documents were part of the official records of Clark while he served the United States. The Federal Court of Appeals in St. Louis dismissed the suit on Jan. 23, 1958. The court test was closely watched by libraries, museums and the American Philosophical Society. Had the Government been upheld, the custody of similar historical documents would have been jeopardized. . . . The Clark documents are being edited for publication by Ernest S. Osgood, a retired professor of Wooster, Ohio."

Shortly after the end of the expedition Lewis was appointed Governor of the Territory of Upper Louisiana. When he at last took up his post he was mysteriously killed—or took his own life—in the lonely wilderness.

HISTORY OF THE EXPEDITION UNDER THE COMMAND OF CAPTAINS LEWIS AND CLARK. Ed. by Nicholas Biddle and Paul Allen. 1814. *University Microfilms* 2 vols. 1966 set $18.95; ed. by Elliott Coues 1893. *AMS Press* 3 vols. repr. of 1922 ed. set $48.00; *Peter Smith* 3 vols. each $8.00 set $22.50

THE ORIGINAL JOURNALS OF THE LEWIS AND CLARK EXPEDITION, 1804–1806. Ed. by Reuben G. Thwaites. 1904–05. *Arno* 8 vols. 1969 set including atlas $135.00

THE JOURNALS OF LEWIS AND CLARK. Ed. by Bernard De Voto *Houghton* 1953 $7.50 Sentry Bks. 1963 pap. $3.95; ed. by John E. Bakeless *New Am. Lib.* (orig.) Mentor Bks. 1964 pap. $1.25

LETTERS OF THE LEWIS AND CLARK EXPEDITION WITH RELATED DOCUMENTS, 1783–1854. Ed. by Donald Jackson *Univ. of Illinois Press* 1962 $10.00

This well-edited collection of source materials is intended to complement the "Journals," drawing together many letters, orders, invoices and similar documents now scattered in both published and unpublished form. There are many detailed and informative annotations which make this volume fascinating and important reading.

Books about Lewis and Clark

Meriwether Lewis, Trail Blazer. By Flora W. Seymour. 1937. *Finch Press* $14.00
The Natural History of the Lewis and Clark Expedition. Ed. with introd. by Raymond Darwin Burroughs. *Michigan State Univ. Press* 1961 $7.50
Lewis and Clark, Partners in Discovery. By John E. Bakeless. *Apollo* 1962 pap. $2.95; *Peter Smith* $5.00
Meriwether Lewis: A Biography. By Richard Dillon. 1965. *Putnam* Capricorn Giant 1968 pap. $2.25
"This is the first full biography of Lewis ever published. For the first time Lewis is separated from 'Lewis and Clark' and the result is excellent"—(*LJ*).
Suicide or Murder: The Strange Death of Governor Meriwether Lewis. By Vardis Fisher. *Swallow* $2.95
In the Footsteps of Lewis and Clark. By the National Geographic Society Editors. *National Geographic Society* $4.25
Lewis & Clark: The Great Adventure. By Donald B. Chidsey. *Crown* 1970 $4.50
Lewis and Clark. By David Holloway. Great Explorers Ser. *Saturday Review Press* 1974 $12.50

SCHOOLCRAFT, HENRY ROWE. 1793–1864.

The American ethnologist Schoolcraft, who made a study of the Indians, especially the Chippewas and Sioux, was Indian agent in the Lake Superior region (1822–1836) and superintendent of Indian affairs for Michigan (1836–1841). Earlier he had explored the mineral deposits of southern Missouri and Arkansas and been with Lewis Cass on an exploring expedition to the beautiful, unspoiled Lake Superior country. In 1820 he discovered the source of the Mississippi River at Lake Itasca.

His wife, MARY H. SCHOOLCRAFT, wrote two books: "Plantation Life: The Narratives of Mrs. Henry Rowe Schoolcraft" (1852–1860. *Negro Univs. Press* $21.50) and "Black Gauntlet: A Tale of Plantation Life in South Carolina" (1860. *AMS Press* $15.00; *Bks. for Libraries* $17.50).

A VIEW OF THE LEAD MINES OF MISSOURI: Including Some Observations on the Mineralogy, Geology, Geography, Antiquities, Soil, Climate, Population and Productions of Missouri and Arkansas, and Other Sections of the Western Country. 1819. *Arno* 1972 $13.00

JOURNAL OF A TOUR INTO THE INTERIOR OF MISSOURI AND ARKANSAS, FROM POTOSI, or Mine à Burton, in Missouri Territory, in a Southwest Direction, toward the Rocky Mountains, Performed in the Years 1818 and 1819. 1821. *AMS Press* $10.00

NARRATIVE JOURNAL OF TRAVELS THROUGH THE NORTHWESTERN REGIONS OF THE UNITED STATES: Extending from Detroit through the Great Chain of American

Lakes to the Sources of the Mississippi River in the Year 1820. 1821. *Arno* 1970 $16.00; *University Microfilms* 1966 $8.95

NOTES ON THE IROQUOIS, or Contributions to American History, Antiquities, and General Ethnology. 1847. *AMS Press* 1974 $31.00

THE INDIAN IN HIS WIGWAM, or Characteristics of the Red Race in America. 1848. *AMS Press* 1974 $29.00

HISTORICAL AND STATISTICAL INFORMATION RESPECTING THE HISTORY, CONDITION AND PROSPECTS OF THE INDIAN TRIBES OF THE UNITED STATES. Ed. by Frances S. Nichols. 1851–1857. *AMS Press* 7 vols. set $1500.00

SUMMARY NARRATIVE OF AN EXPLORATORY EXPEDITION TO THE SOURCES OF THE MISSISSIPPI RIVER, IN 1820. 1855. *Kraus* 1973 $25.00

MYTH OF HIAWATHA AND OTHER ORAL LEGENDS, MYTHOLOGIC AND ALLEGORIC, OF THE NORTH AMERICAN INDIANS. 1856. *Kraus* $14.50

SCHOOLCRAFT'S EXPEDITION TO LAKE ITASCA: The Discovery of the Source of the Mississippi. Ed. by Philip P. Mason *Michigan State Univ. Press* 1958 $7.50

The "Expedition" is the great romantic story of the 1820 journey to discover the source of the Mississippi. Mr. Mason, professor of history and archivist at Wayne State Universtiy has retained and corrected the original texts including the ancillary documents of Dr. Douglas Houghton, the Reverend Mr. William T. Boutwell, the Presbyterian missionary, and Lt. James Allen. The editor has included a great deal of related material, such as newspaper reports of the expedition. There is a good bibliography and notes.

PERSONAL MEMOIRS: Of a Residence of Thirty Years with the Indian Tribes on the American Frontiers, with Brief Notices of Passing Events, Facts and Opinions, A.D. 1812 to A.D. 1842. 1851. *AMS Press* $42.50

Books about Schoolcraft

Schoolcraft: The Literary Voyager. Ed. by Philip P. Mason. *Michigan State Univ. Press* 1962 $5.00

BORROW, GEORGE (HENRY). 1803–1881.

Borrow was employed by the (Protestant) Bible Society to distribute Bibles in Catholic Spain in 1835. He encountered much opposition and was on one occasion imprisoned for three weeks. The famous account of his experience has little to do with the Bible and much to do with the people, land and perils of his journey. "Wild Wales" (1862, o.p.) is a narrative of a trip through Wales in 1854. Borrow is as racy in his descriptions of place as of people—"Lavengro" and its sequel, "The Romany Rye," are like novels in their interest and excitement. They are stories of gypsies, rich in gypsy lore, superstitions and customs. Borrow spent many years in close association with Spanish gypsies, and translated the Gospel of St. Luke into their language. His linguistic abilities were remarkable; he gives much space to word derivations, particularly in "Lavengro." His books abound in pugnacious passages; his attacks on Sir Walter Scott, on prizefighters and on "papists" are indicative of some of his sharp prejudices. But he wrote marvelously, and those who admire him are his devotees for life.

WORKS: The Standard or "Norwich" Edition, Edited with Much Hitherto Unpublished Manuscript. Ed. by Clement Shorter, 1923–1924. *AMS Press* 16 vols. each $20.00 set $300.00

LIFE, WRITINGS AND CORRESPONDENCE: An Account of the Gypsy-Scholar, Traveler, Linguist and Agent for the British and Foreign Bible Society, 1803–1881. Ed. by William Ireland Knapp. 1899. *Gale Research Co.* 2 vols. 1967 set $15.60

THE ZINCALI, or The Gypsies of Spain. 1841. *Dufour* 9th ed. 1966 $4.95

THE BIBLE IN SPAIN. 1843. *Dutton* Everyman's 1907 $3.95

LAVENGRO: The Scholar, the Gypsy, the Priest. 1851. *Dutton* Everyman's $3.95 pap. 1972 $2.25

THE ROMANY RYE. 1857. *Dufour* 1948 $4.50; *Dutton* 1961 $3.95 Everyman's 1972 pap. $2.95

Books about Borrow

George Borrow: The Man and His Work. By R. A. Walling. 1908. *Richard West* 1973 $20.00
Life of George Borrow. Ed. by Herbert Jenkins. 1912. *Kennikat* 1970 $16.00
George Borrow. By Samuel M. Elam. 1929. *Folcroft* 1974 $10.75; *Haskell* 1974 $10.95
George Borrow. By Robert R. Meyers. English Authors Ser. *Twayne* 1966 $6.50
Bibliography of the Writings in Prose and Verse of George Henry Borrow. Ed. by Thomas J. Wise. 1914. *Humanities Press* (Fernhill) 1966 $19.75

KINGLAKE, ALEXANDER (WILLIAM). 1809–1891.

"The Cambridge History of English Literature" regards "Eothen" as "perhaps the best book of travel in the English language." It consists of letters which Kinglake wrote home while making an extensive tour of the East in 1840. It was four years before he could find a publisher. He became the historian of the Crimea in 1863. Eothen is a Greek word meaning "from the early dawn" or "from the East."

EOTHEN. 1844. Introd. by Harold Spender *Dutton* Everyman's 1954 $3.95; *Univ. of Nebraska* Bison Bks. 1970 pap. $2.50; *Peter Smith* $4.50

INVASION OF THE CRIMEA. 1863. *AMS Press* 9 vols. 1972 each $33.35 set $290.00

Books about Kinglake

A. W. Kinglake: A Biographical and Literary Study. By W. Tuckwell. 1902. *Richard West* $20.00
Traveling Gent: The Life of Alexander Kinglake, 1809–1891. By Gerald De Gaury. *Routledge & Kegan Paul* 1972 $10.95

LIVINGSTONE, DAVID. 1813–1873.

One of the most remarkable explorers of the 19th century, the Scotsman Livingstone sought first as a missionary and devout Christian to end the slave trade in Africa and then to locate the source of the Nile. In these attempts he lost his wife, who caught a fever on an expedition in which she joined him. He discovered the Victoria Falls and the lands between Nyasa and Tanganyika, encountering other hardships and tragedies in his double quest, but was much beloved of Africans who knew him, whom he persisted in regarding as human being like himself—an enlightened attitude for the white man of his day. He never abated his efforts in their behalf. His association with Sir Henry Morton Stanley (*q.v.*) is well known. The latter had been sent to find him by an American newspaper when Livingstone was feared lost; the formal approach of Stanley's first remark on finding him in a remote African village, "Dr. Livingstone, I presume?," amused the world and the greeting became a byword. Stanley was with him in northern Tanganyika (now Tanzania), when he died.

The "Missionary Correspondence" is essentially the contemporary record of Livingstone's two journeys to Northwestern Rhodesia in 1851–1853. These letters furnish "priceless source material not only for the student of religious history but for the anthropologist and sociologist. . . . Completely devoted to the cause of Christ, Livingstone was also a realist and a man of unusual intelligence"—(*LJ*). Of "David Livingstone and the Rovuma," (ed. by George A. Shepperson *Aldine* 1965, o.p.) *Library Journal* wrote: "The Rovuma River forms the boundary between Tanzania and Mozambique. To David Livingstone, a century ago, it seemed likely to provide the best entrance into the interior of East Africa and perhaps to Lake Nyasa. During his third unsuccessful attempt late in 1862 to traverse the river, Livingstone kept a small leatherbound field notebook (now in the National Library of Scotland) in which he scribbled notes, maps, and sketches relating to his journey. It appears here in full—together with the despatches Livingstone sent to Earl Russell and with various other related material—scrupulously edited by a noted authority."

MISSIONARY TRAVELS AND RESEARCHES IN SOUTH AFRICA. 1857. *Bks. for Libraries* 1972 $36.00

THE ZAMBESI EXPEDITION, 1858–1863. Ed. by J. P. Wallis *Humanities Press* 2 vols. 1956 set $14.50

NARRATIVE OF AN EXPEDITION TO THE ZAMBEZI AND ITS TRIBUTARIES: And of the Discovery of Lakes Shirwa and Nyasa, 1858–1864. 1866. *Johnson Reprint* $35.00

LIVINGSTONE'S AFRICA. 1872. *Bks. for Libraries* facs. ed. $19.75

LAST JOURNALS OF DAVID LIVINGSTONE IN CENTRAL AFRICA FROM 1865 TO HIS DEATH. Ed. by Horace Waller. 1874. *Greenwood* (Negro Univs. Press) 2 vols. 1968 set $29.50; *Scholarly Press* $29.50

MISSIONARY CORRESPONDENCE, 1841–1856. Ed. with introd. by I. Schapera *Univ. of California Press* 1961 $9.50

FAMILY LETTERS, 1841–1856. Ed. by I. Schapera *Humanities Press* (Fernhill) 2 vols. 1959 set $11.00

SOME LETTERS FROM LIVINGSTONE, 1840–1872. 1940. *Greenwood* (Negro Univs. Press) $14.25

Books about Livingstone

How I Found Livingstone. By Henry M. Stanley. 1872. *Arno* 1970 $30.00

Personal Life of David Livingstone. By William G. Blaikie. 1880. *Greenwood* (Negro Univs. Press) 1969 $18.50

Livingstone the Liberator. By James Macnair. *Collins-World* 1940 $2.50

Livingstone and Africa. By Jack Simmons. *Macmillan* Collier Bks. 1962 pap. $.95

Livingstone's River. By George Martelli. *Simon & Schuster* 1970 $7.50

David Livingstone: His Triumph, Decline and Fall. By Cecil Northcott. *Westminster Press* 1973 $6.95

Livingstone, Man of Africa: Memorial Essays. Ed. by Bridglal Pachai. *Longmans* 1973 $9.00

Livingstone. By Tim Jeal. *Putnam* 1973 $10.00

> "Here was no plastic saint, but a thrusting, opinionated, intolerant and even jealous man who could be relied upon to quarrel with almost any close colleague within a very short time. . . . Livingstone was a man who made great blunders and invariably blamed them on others, who sent other men to their deaths and ascribed the results to their weakness or cowardice"—*(New Statesman)*.

Livingstone and His African Journeys. By Elspeth Huxley. Great Explorers Ser. *Saturday Review Press* (dist. by Dutton) 1974 $12.50

DANA, RICHARD HENRY, JR. 1815–1882

"Two Years before the Mast," the diary of what happened on the brig *Pilgrim* in its voyages round the Horn in 1834–1836—a brig only 86 feet long and registering 180 tons—is a book so pre-eminent in the literature of the sea that England at one time gave a copy of it to every sailor in the Royal Navy.

The author "broke away from Harvard without a degree to become a common sailor," says Allan Nevins (in *SR*). He had "a gift for close observation and character portrayal" and was "an appreciative student of nature," but wrote only one fascinating novel, though he tried others. Of the Journal, Professor Nevins writes: "Robert F. Lucid, who presents the text with admirable care and illuminating annotations, remarks that Dana himself would emphatically agree that his journal does not rank with the diaries of Boswell or Pepys as a document of self-revelation, but adds that it does reveal a great deal about the character of the man." Dana kept the journal from 1841 to 1860. Dana's "Autobiographical Sketch, 1815–1842" (ed. by R. F. Metzdorf with introd. by N. H. Pearson 1953, o.p.) is a brief account of his first 27 years. One of his later activities was "helping to found the Free Soil Party and rescue runaway slaves"—(Nevins).

TWO YEARS BEFORE THE MAST. 1840. *Assoc. Booksellers* Airmont Bks. pap. $.75; *Dutton* Everyman's $3.95 pap. 1972 $2.25

TO CUBA AND BACK. Ed. with introd. by C. Harvey Gardiner *Southern Illinois Univ. Press* 1966 $5.85

> "During Dana's lifetime *To Cuba and Back* was as popular as his *Two Years before the Mast*. It became the standard guidebook for English speaking travelers and was still in print on the eve of World War I. Now a historical curiosity, it is of interest primarily to students of Dana and of Cuban history and to devotees of older travel books. Long out of print, it has needed a new, and preferably scholarly, edition. This publication meets the need only halfway. Its bibliographical and biographical introductions and the supervision of its reprinting have been done by an authority in his field. But Professor Gardiner has tampered with the text (omitting some pages, modernizing certain English spellings, consolidating shorter paragraphs) and in so doing has eliminated the audience for which this work and indeed the entire series seem most suited—the serious student and scholar. In its mutilated and modernized form this perceptive, entertaining, and compelling 19th-century view of Cuba will appeal primarily to the layman"—*(LJ)*.

THE JOURNAL OF RICHARD HENRY DANA, JR. Ed. by Robert F. Lucid *Harvard Univ. Press* 3 vols. 1968 boxed set $40.00

Books about Dana

Richard Henry Dana. By Charles F. Adams. 1890. *Gale Research Co.* 2 vols. 1968 $15.60

Richard Henry Dana, Jr. By Samuel Shapiro. *Michigan State Univ. Press* 1961 $5.00

Richard Henry Dana. By Robert L. Gale. U.S. Authors Ser. *Twayne* 1969 $6.50

BURTON, SIR RICHARD (FRANCIS). 1821–1890.

Sir Richard Burton, the explorer, adventurer, translator, and student of Eastern sexual customs, continues to draw writers "as a honey pot draws bears," says Thomas Lask. Orville Prescott has written (in *SR*): "One of the great explorers of the nineteenth century, Burton disguised himself as a Pathan dervish and doctor in order to penetrate the forbidden cities of Medina and Mecca. He was the first European to reach Harar, the religious capital of Somaliland. He was the discoverer of Lake Tanganyika, and explored in the Congo, the Cameroons, Dahomey, and Brazil. He was a pioneer ethnologist and anthropologist. He was a linguist of dazzling ability, speaking twenty-nine languages and eleven dialects. He wrote forty-three books on his travels, two volumes of poetry, and translated (in addition to *The Arabian Nights*) six volumes of Portuguese literature, two of Latin poetry, and four of Neapolitan, African, and Hindu folklore."

He was also eternally restless and a prey to inner conflicts, and his exploits and personality appealed to the British Foreign Office only to the degree of making him British consul in Trieste for the last 18 years of his life—not the Minister to Morocco, as he longed to be. His wife, Isabel— believed by some to be frigid but to all outward appearances his passionate and loving admirer— was patient and faithful to the end. She burned some of his more erotic literary remainders after his death—for which, in the Victorian age, it is hard to blame her. She had tried to domesticate him, perhaps, but his will was as strong as hers and his difficulties were, in the long run, of his own making. The flamboyance and daring of this learned, paradoxical man of action and accomplishment seem destined to exercise perennial fascination.

Burton's translation of the "Arabian Nights" is the leading and most complete translation in English. "Sir Richard Burton's Kasidah of Haji Abdu el-Yezdi" is a collection of his original poems (1880, o.p.) which were at first supposed to have been translated. He also wrote "Book of the Sword" (1884. *Harper* [Barnes & Noble] 1972 $13.50; *Finch Press* $12.50) and "Vickram and the Vampire: Tales of Hindu Deviltry" (ed. by Isabel Burton 1893. *Dover* 1970 pap. $2.50; *Peter Smith* $5.00).

SINDH AND THE RACES THAT INHABIT THE VALLEY OF THE INDUS. 1851. *Oxford* 1974 $11.00

PERSONAL NARRATIVE OF A PILGRIMAGE TO AL-MADINAH AND MECCAH, 1855–1856. Ed. by Isabel Burton. 1893. *Dover* 2 vols. pap. each $3.50; *Peter Smith* 2 vols. set $10.00; *Richard West* 1913 $20.00

THE LOOK OF THE WEST, 1860: Across the Plains to California. *Peter Smith* $4.25

THE LAKE REGION OF CENTRAL AFRICA: A Picture of Exploration. 1860. *Scholarly Press* 1972 $29.50

THE CITY OF THE SAINTS. 1861. Ed. by Fawn M. Brodie *Knopf* 1963 $10.00; *AMS Press* repr. of 1862 ed. 1972 $25.00. Burton's account of his overland journey in 1860 to the home of the Mormons in Salt Lake City.

WANDERINGS IN WEST AFRICA FROM LIVERPOOL TO FERNANDO PO. 1863. *Johnson Reprint* 2 vols. 1971 set $28.00

THE NILE BASIN. 1864. *Da Capo* 1967 $7.50

EXPLORATIONS OF THE HIGHLANDS OF BRAZIL, 1869: With a Full Account of the Gold and Diamond Mines. *Greenwood* 2 vols. 1968 $32.75

ZANZIBAR: City, Island and Coast. 1872. *Johnson Reprint* 2 vols. set $49.00

TWO TRIPS TO GORILLA LAND AND THE CATARACTS OF THE CONGO. 1876. *Johnson Reprint* 2 vols. in 1 $35.00

(Ed.). WIT AND WISDOM FROM WEST AFRICA: A Book of Proverbial Philosophy, Idioms, Enigmas and Laconisms. 1865. *Biblo & Tannen* 1969 $13.50; *Negro Univs. Press* $15.00

THE EROTIC TRAVELER. Ed. by Edward Leigh *Putnam* 1967 $4.95

"Subtitled 'an astonishing exploration of bizarre sex rites and customs by the great adventurer,' this is sexual anthropology at its most exotic. Here are the customs which provided the material for the *Kama Sutra* and *The Arabian Nights*, as Burton explores the aberrant fetishisms of India, Africa and North and South America. It also gives some background on Burton, the man, as the editor has done a nice job of continuity on Sir Richard's study through the use of a running narrative"—(*Virginia Kirkus Service*).

Books about Burton

The Life of Sir Richard Burton. By Isabel Burton, his wife. 1893. *Milford House* 2 vols. 1973 set $60.00

True Life of Captain Sir Richard F. Burton. By Georgiana M. Stisted. 1896. *Greenwood* (Negro Univs. Press) 1969 $16.00; *Richard West* $13.75

Life of Sir Richard Burton. By Thomas Wright. 1906. *Burt Franklin* 2 vols. 1968 set $28.50

An Annotated Bibliography of Sir Richard Francis Burton. By Norman M. Penzer. 1923. *Burt Franklin* 1970 $14.00

The Arabian Knight: A Study of Sir Richard Burton. By Seton Dearden. 1936. *Richard West* $20.00

Sir Richard Burton's Wife. By Jean Burton. 1942. *Richard West* $20.00

The Devil Drives: A Life of Sir Richard Burton. By Fawn M. Brodie. *Norton* 1967 $6.95
"Richard Burton's career was a bizarre adventure full of failures as well as achievements. It has been told often, but never with such scholarly zeal and judicious detachment as in *The Devil Drives*, by Fawn M. Brodie. This is a fine biography of an extraordinary man. Mrs. Brodie has a taste for and a sympathetic understanding of obsessed men driven by inner devils. . . . She is diligent in research, deft in keeping her narrative moving briskly, and unshockable when confronted by material that can still raise eyebrows even in our outspoken age"—(Orville Prescott, in *SR*).

PARKMAN, FRANCIS. 1823–1893. *See Chapter 9, History Government and Politics— American, this Vol.*

STANLEY, SIR HENRY MORTON. 1841–1904.

Stanley was an American traveler born in Wales, educated in the poorhouse and adopted by a merchant in New Orleans who gave him his name. He fought in the Confederate Army and after the war became a newspaper correspondent. He was commissioned by the *N.Y. Herald* to go in search of Livingstone (*q.v.*) in 1871.

Stanley based one of his most popular books, "Through the Dark Continent" on a series of diaries in which he recorded the progress of his expedition of 1874–1877. They presented the day-to-day account of his journeys undertaken to discover the sources of the Nile and Congo rivers, his circumnavigation of Lakes Victoria and Tanganyika and his dangerous trip down the Congo River to Boma. Recently discovered by Stanley's grandson, "The Exploration Diaries," published for the first time in 1962, is a somewhat revised but continuous version. "Stanley is revealed as not only an ambitious, intrepid leader but also as a fallible human being and a considerate, sympathetic companion"—(*LJ*).

"My Early Travels and Adventures in America and Asia" (2 vols., 1895) is o.p.

How I Found Livingstone. 1872. *Arno* 1970 $30.00; *Greenwood* (Negro Univs. Press) 1970 $23.00

Coomassie and Magdala: The Story of Two British Campaigns in Africa. 1874. *Bks. for Libraries* $19.00

My Kalulu, Prince, King, and Slave: A Story of Central Africa. 1874. *Greenwood* (Negro Univs. Press) $17.25

Through the Dark Continent, or The Sources of the Nile, around the Great Lakes of Equatorial Africa, and down the Livingstone River to the Atlantic Ocean. 1878. *Greenwood* 2 vols. 1968 set $60.75

Congo and the Founding of Its Free State. 1885. *Scholarly Press* 2 vols. set $55.00

The Story of Emin's Rescue as Told in Stanley's Letters. Ed. by J. S. Keltie. 1890. *Greenwood* (Negro Univs. Press) $9.50

My Dark Companions and Their Strange Stories. 1893. *Bks. for Libraries* 1972 $22.50; *Finch Press* $15.00

Africa, Its Partition and Its Future. 1898. *Greenwood* (Negro Univs. Press) $11.00

Exploration Diaries. Ed. by Richard Stanley and Alan Neame *Vanguard* 1962 $8.50

Autobiography. Ed. by Dorothy Stanley. 1909. Introd. by E. Halliday *Greenwood* $26.25

Books about Stanley

Heroes of the Dark Continent. By J. W. Buel. 1889. *Bks. for Libraries* $26.50

Stanley's Story, or Through the Wilds of Africa. By A. G. Feather. 1890. *Metro Bks.* 1969 $27.00
The Man Who Presumed. By Byron Farwell. 1957. *Greenwood* 1974 $15.25
Henry Morton Stanley. By Richard Tames. *Int. Pubns. Service* 1973 pap. $3.00
Stanley: An Adventurer Explored. By Richard Hall. *Houghton* 1975 $12.50

DOUGHTY, CHARLES MONTAGU. 1843–1926.

Doughty is famous as the author of one great book. "Travels in Arabia Deserta" was first published in 1888 in a very small edition. The reviews were all unfavorable, and the book went out of print. Edward Garnett in 1908 rediscovered it and with the sanction of the author abridged it. This, too, went out of print for many years. The first edition is now difficult to obtain and brings a high price. T. E. Lawrence (*q.v.*) calls it "a book not like other books but something particular, a Bible of its kind." Doughty used a stately prose "full of exotic words and archaic turns of expression . . . cunningly contrived to enforce the implicit contrast between the sturdy English Christian and the unstable, fierce and fanatical Moslems of the desert." "The acuteness and wisdom of his observation," says his biographer, "made him the acknowledged master of all later travellers."

TRAVELS IN ARABIA DESERTA. 1888. Ed. and abr. by Edward Garnett. 1908. *Peter Smith* $4.50

MANSOUL, or The Riddle of the World. 1920. *Scholarly Press* 1971 $12.00

Books about Doughty

Charles M. Doughty: A Critical Study. By Barker Fairley. 1927. *Scholarly Press* 1971 $14.50; *Richard West* $20.00
The Life of Charles M. Doughty. By D. G. Hogarth. 1929. *Scholarly Press* 1972 $14.50
Doughty's English. By Walt Taylor. 1939. *Folcroft* $15.00
Three Victorian Travellers: Burton, Blunt and Doughty. By Thomas J. Assad. *Routledge & Kegan Paul* 1964 $5.25

SLOCUM, JOSHUA. 1844–1909?

Captain Slocum, the intrepid mariner who has been called the "Thoreau of the sea," set out in April 1896 to sail around the world alone in a small sloop he had reclaimed from a derelict and named the *Spray.* The voyage took three years, two months and two days. He told the story of this trip in "Sailing Alone around the World." "American Authors and Books 1640–1940" makes the statement that he started on another voyage on Nov. 14, 1909, and was never heard from again. He was legally declared dead as of that date. "Joshua Slocum" by Walter Magnes Teller (*see below*) is an extensively revised and augmented edition of "The Search for Captain Slocum" (1956, o.p.), described at the time of its publication as a definitive biography, "more compact, more revealing and better documented than anything hitherto produced."

THE VOYAGES OF JOSHUA SLOCUM. Ed. with introd. by Walter Magnes Teller *Rutgers Univ Press* 1958 $10.00. Includes all the published works, hitherto unpublished correspondence, a checklist and a selected bibliography.

SAILING ALONE AROUND THE WORLD. 1900. *Dover* 1956 pap. $2.00; *Humanities Press* (Fernhill) $4.75; *Sheridan House* 1954 $7.50

THE VOYAGE OF THE LIBERDADE. 1890. (And "Sailing Alone") *Macmillan* Collier Bks. 1970 pap. $1.25

Books about Slocum

Captain Joshua Slocum: The Adventures of America's Best Known Sailor. By Victor Slocum. *Sheridan House* 1950 $10.00
Joshua Slocum. By Walter Magnes Teller. *Rutgers Univ. Press* 1971 $9.00

PEARY, ROBERT E(DWIN). 1856–1920.

The American discoverer of the North Pole first became interested in Arctic exploration after a trip into the interior of Greenland in 1886. Later trips there funded by the Philadelphia Academy of Natural Sciences proved that Greenland is an island and resulted in his account "Northward over the Great Ice."

"Nearest the Pole" tells of his arctic trip when the "farthest north" record was set about 200 miles from the North Pole. On April 6, 1909 he finally reached the North Pole after a voyage in the specially built ship *Roosevelt* and a long trek over ice via dogsledges. "The North Pole" published in 1910 is his account of that final trip. He retired from the U.S. Navy in 1911 with the rank of rear admiral but again served his country during World War I.

NORTHWARD OVER THE GREAT ICE: A Narrative of Life and Work along the Shores and upon the Interior Ice Cap of Northern Greenland in the Years 1886 and 1891–1897. 1898. *AMS Press* 2 vols. set $87.50

NEAREST THE POLE: A Narrative of the Polar Expedition of the Peary Arctic Club in the S.S. Roosevelt, 1905–1906. 1907. *AMS Press* $40.50

NORTH POLE: Its Discovery in 1909 under the Auspices of the Peary Arctic Club. 1910. *Greenwood* 1968 $26.25; *Somerset Pub.* $14.50

Books about Peary

With Peary near the Pole. By Eivind Astrup. Trans. from the Norwegian by H. J. Bull. 1898. *AMS Press* $22.00

Peary: The Explorer and the Man. By John E. Weems. *Houghton* 1967 $6.95

Black Explorer at the North Pole: An Autobiographical Report by the Negro Who Conquered the Top of the World with Admiral Robert E. Peary. By Matthew A. Henson. *Walker & Co.* 1969 $4.50

Peary at the North Pole: Fact or Fiction? By Dennis Rawlins. *Luce* (dist. by McKay) 1973 $8.95

ROOSEVELT, THEODORE. 1858–1919. (Nobel Peace Prize 1906)

Theodore Roosevelt was as vivid and vigorous when he wrote of adventure as when he lived it. He could re-create for the stay-at-home the dangers of his trips through hitherto unexplored wilderness. Less known were his activities as an ardent field naturalist and conservationist. Two of his well-known titles are out of print at present: "African Game Trails" (1910, 2 vols.) and "Stories of the Great West."

THEODORE ROOSEVELT'S AMERICA: Selections from the Writings of the Oyster Bay Naturalist. Ed. by Farida A. Wiley; introd. essays by John Burroughs and others; fwd. by Ethel Roosevelt Derby. Am. Naturalists Ser. *Devin-Adair* 1955 $7.50

HUNTING TRIPS OF A RANCHMAN. 1885. *Gregg Press* 1970 $12.50

RANCH LIFE IN THE FAR WEST. 1888. Ill. by Frederick Remington *Northland* 1968 $6.00. Six articles reprinted from *Century Magazine*, all published in 1888.

THE WINNING OF THE WEST. 1889–1896. Selections ed. by Harvey Wish *Peter Smith* $5.00; *Somerset Pubs.* repr. of 1900 ed. 6 vols. $72.00

THE ROUGH RIDERS. 1899. Afterword by Lawrence Clark Powell *Corner House Pubs.* 1971 $12.50

RANCH LIFE AND THE HUNTING TRAIL. 1899. *Arno* 1970 $8.00; *University Microfilms* 1966 $8.95

WILDERNESS HUNTER. 1900. *Gregg* 1970 $11.00

THE STRENUOUS LIFE: Essays and Addresses. 1902. *Scholarly Press* $14.50

OUTDOOR PASTIMES OF AN AMERICAN HUNTER. 1905. *Arno* 1970 $16.00

THROUGH THE BRAZILIAN WILDERNESS. 1914. *Greenwood* 1968 $25.75

COWBOYS AND KINGS: Three Great Letters. Introd. by E. E. Morison *Kraus* 1954 1968 $8.00

Books about Roosevelt

Theodore Roosevelt: Outdoorsman. By R. I. Wilson. *Winchester Press* 1970 $12.95

See also Chapter 9, History, Government and Politics—American, this Vol.

SCOTT, ROBERT FALCON. 1868–1912.

After an initial expedition to Antarctica, the British Scott reached the South Pole in 1912 only to find that the Norwegian explorer, Amundsen, had beaten him by a month. Scott and his party perished in a blizzard on the return trip. It was not until the following spring that their bodies and scientific documents were recovered. These two books are valuable as records of scientific research and as human documents. "Scott's Last Expedition" is his own classic diary account of the tragedy together with scientific material gathered on the journey. "Captain Scott kept a precise diary of the bitter days of his last journey South. His hands and feet crippled by frostbite, his eyes and mind befuddled by Antarctic blizzard, he traveled on to final defeat—and, in a way, magnificent triumph. Coming to the South Pole area itself, Scott was overwhelmed to learn that he had been preceded by the Norwegian. He knew full well the shattering implications in terms of personal and national prestige. But, gentleman to the end, he dutifully picked up Amundsen's message to the world (left at the South Pole in case Amundsen did not make it home successfully), and this eventually was conveyed to the King of Norway as proof that the Norwegian had beaten the Briton. Scott's was an act that could have been performed only by a man of honor. It is on the return trip that Scott's diary reaches a poignancy seldom matched in exploration writing"—(SR). Roald E. Amundsen's story is told in his "South Pole: An Account of the Norwegian Antarctic Expedition" (1913. *Finch Press* $18.00).

SIR ERNEST HENRY SHACKLETON (1874–1922), who had accompanied Scott on one of his expeditions, made two other attempts to reach the Pole. He died at sea and was buried at South Georgia in the Antarctic. "South: The Story of Shackleton's Last Expedition, 1914–1917" (1921. *Macmillan*, o.p.) contains his records of the voyage that fixed the magnetic pole. Shackleton also wrote "Heart of the Antarctic, Being the Story of the British Antarctic Expedition, 1907–1909" (1909. *Greenwood* 2 vols. 1968 set $74.50). His story is told in "Shackleton's Voyage" by Donald B. Chidsey (*Universal Pub.* 1974 pap. $1.25). "South with Scott' by Edward Mountevans and "Scott of the Antarctic" by Reginald Pound are out of print at present.

THE VOYAGE OF THE "DISCOVERY." 1905. *Greenwood* 2 vols. 1969 set $48.50

SCOTT'S LAST EXPEDITION. 1913. *Transatlantic* 1951 $9.50

Books about Scott

Diary of the Discovery Expedition to the Antarctic Regions, 1901–1904. By Edward Wilson. Ed. by Ann Savours; fwd. by the Duke of Edinburgh *Humanities Press* 1967 $24.75

Scott and the Discovery of the Antarctic. By Sylvie Nickles. *Grossman* (dist. by Viking) 1972 $3.95

STEFANSSON, VILHJALMUR. 1879–1962.

Stefansson, an American born in Canada of Icelandic parentage and the last of the dogsled explorers, spent many years in the Arctic. His books aim to combat popular misconceptions about the far North. They show that it is a good place for colonization, that human life can be supported there on a diet of seal alone, and that it has possibilities for commercial usefulness. Stefansson's "findings changed many prevailing concepts. By 'humanizing' the icy north, he became known as the man who robbed the Arctic Circle of all its terrors and most of its discomforts"—(*Boston Globe*). Stefansson undertook a medical experiment to prove that a man can remain healthy on an all-meat diet, and in his "Not By Bread Alone" (1946, o.p., enl. as "Fat of the Land," 1956, o.p.) he takes this as his thesis. As far back as 1915 he suggested the feat which the atom-powered *Nautilus* accomplished—submerging under the Arctic ice on the Pacific side and emerging, after two months, on the Atlantic. The whole fascinating story of the search for a Northwest passage is told with scholarly authority in his "Northwest to Fortune." "Clearly and lovingly written, the book brings color and even warmth to regions which for so many of us have seemed wrapped in cold, fog, and ice"—(*Christian Science Monitor*).

Just the week before Stefansson died, he had completed the first draft of his autobiography. *Library Journal* said of it: "His life can be read as a microcosmic reflection of the American experience dating back to the frontier days with the Plains Indians among whom his immigrant family settled. From these small beginnings he grew in importance to know well some of the world's outstanding individuals, many of whom walk through these pages; to help create some of the physical and intellectual changes now received as commonplace, and to participate in some great and small controversies now largely buried. No life which has been lived on many frontiers can fail to be remarkable, but its color is considerably heightened for the reader when it is reported, as his is, in detail with honesty, sincerity, and the half-jest"—(*LJ*). Widely honored, the explorer-historian held honorary degrees from many universities and colleges. He also was awarded Knighthood in the Order of the Falcon by the government of Iceland and was a medalist of the American, National, Philadelphia, Chicago, London, Paris and Berlin Geographical Societies. One of the five islands which he discovered in the Arctic is named for him.

His autobiography "Discovery" (1964), with a postlude by Evelyn Stefansson, is out of print.

MY LIFE WITH THE ESKIMO. 1913. *AMS Press* $46.00; *Macmillan* Collier Bks. 1962 pap. $1.50

THE STEFANSSON-ANDERSON ARCTIC EXPEDITION OF THE AMERICAN MUSEUM OF NATURAL HISTORY: Preliminary Ethnological Report. 1914. *AMS Press* $28.00

HUNTERS OF THE GREAT NORTH. 1922. *AMS Press* $22.00

ADVENTURES IN ERROR. 1936. *Gale Research Co.* 1970 $9.00

UNSOLVED MYSTERIES OF THE ARCTIC. 1938. *Bks. for Libraries* $15.00; *Macmillan* Collier Bks. 1962 pap. $.95

ICELAND: The First American Republic. 1939. *Greenwood* 1971 $14.00

THE FRIENDLY ARCTIC: The Story of Five Years in Polar Regions. 1943. *Greenwood* 1969
$48.75

NORTHWEST TO FORTUNE. 1958. *Greenwood* 1974 $15.00

FREUCHEN, PETER.   1886–1957.

"Vagrant Viking" is a "useful source of twentieth-century polar history," as well as an
entertaining biography of a roving Danish newspaperman, a tough man who truly understood the
unrivaled toughness of life in the North. He made his first trip to the Arctic in 1906. Off and on
for more than two generations he lived, hunted and traveled with the Eskimos, understanding
them better than any other man of our generation. His first wife was an Eskimo, about whom he
wrote "Ivalu, the Eskimo Wife" trans. by Janos Jusztis and Edward P. Ehrich (1935. *AMS Press*
$20.00).

"Fliers enroute from Fort Churchill to distant Arctic air bases can still trace their course by
landmarks he first put on the map." He aided refugees from the Nazis during the late 1930's and
was active in the Underground movement after Denmark was occupied and before his own escape
to Sweden. In 1957 he won the Gold Medal of the International Benjamin Franklin Society for his
"service to mankind in opening new frontiers." Now o.p. are his "Men of the Frozen North"
(1962), "Book of Arctic Exploration" (1962) and "The Arctic Year" (1958). His widow has edited
several posthumous volumes.

THE PETER FREUCHEN READER. Sel. and trans. from the Danish by Dagmar Freuchen;
pref. by David Loth *Simon & Schuster* 1965 $9.95

"Included here are selections from *Vagrant Viking, Book of the Seven Seas, Arctic Adventure,* and
Eskimo, plus a few pieces translated from Danish for this book. They span Peter Freuchen's career
as a polar explorer, fiction writer, journalist, underground fighter, and TV entertainer. The book
deserves to be widely bought and read"—(*LJ*).

ARCTIC ADVENTURE: My Life in the Frozen North. 1935. *AMS Press* $29.00

I SAILED WITH RASMUSSEN: Freuchen's Own Story of the Great Explorer. Trans. by
Arnold Andersen *Simon & Schuster* 1958 $3.95

PETER FREUCHEN'S ADVENTURES IN THE ARCTIC. Ed. by Dagmar Freuchen *Simon &
Schuster* 1960 $4.95

(With David Loth). PETER FREUCHEN'S BOOK OF THE SEVEN SEAS. *Simon & Schuster* 1957
$9.95 deluxe ed. $10.00 1968 pap. $3.95

BOOK OF THE ESKIMOS. 1961. Ed. with pref. by Dagmar Freuchen *Fawcett* Premier Bks.
1973 pap. $1.25. A first-hand portrait of these mysterious people.

VAGRANT VIKING: My Life and Adventures. Trans. from the Danish by Johan Hambro
Simon & Schuster 1953 $5.95

BYRD, RICHARD E(VELYN).   1888–1957.

Rear Admiral Byrd was an American naval officer and aviator, the only person who had flown
over both poles and one of the first men to fly the Atlantic. During the First World War he was Lt.
Commander of the U. S. air forces in Canada. "Skyward" (1928, o.p.) tells of the first airplane
flight made over the North Pole with Floyd Bennett in 1926. "Little America" (1930, o.p.) is a
detailed record of his flight over the South Pole. "Alone" is his remarkable tale of fortitude during
his self-imposed isolation at Advance Base in the Antarctic in 1934. In the spring of 1947 Byrd
returned from his fifth and largest polar expedition, the largest exploring expedition ever
organized—13 ships manned by 4,000 men, entirely naval in personnel.

"America's strategic concept of polar defense is an outgrowth of Admiral Byrd's five exploration
ventures into the Arctic and Antarctic. . . . He was in over-all command of the Naval task force
that, between 1955 and 1959, was to prepare, supply and maintain a series of scientific stations in
Antarctica. . . . He was placed by President Eisenhower in charge of all Antarctic activities of the
United States"—(*N.Y. Times*).

Byrd received a special medal of the National Geographic Society from President Hoover in
1930, the Legion of Merit for "outstanding services" from President Roosevelt in 1945 and the
Defense Department's Medal of Freedom on Feb. 21, 1957. It is thought that he impaired his
health seriously while on the 1933–34 expedition, the basis of "Alone." He was buried with full
military honors in the Arlington National Cemetery.

DISCOVERY: The Story of the Second Byrd Antarctic Expedition. 1935. *Bks. for Libraries*
$25.75; *Gale Research Co.* 1971 $15.00

EXPLORING WITH BYRD: Episodes from an Adventurous Life. 1937. *Gale Research Co.* 1970 $14.00

ALONE. *Putnam* 1938 $6.50

Books about Byrd

Admiral Byrd of Antarctica. By Michael Gladych. *Simon & Schuster* (Messner) 1960 $3.50
Hollow Earth. By Raymond Bernard. *University Books* 1969 $5.95

LAWRENCE, T(HOMAS) E(DWARD) (T. E. Shaw). 1888–1935.

T. E. Lawrence was a soldier, author, archeologist, traveler and translator. He was best known as "Lawrence of Arabia," the man who freed the Arabs from the Turks in World War I. The manuscript of his "Seven Pillars of Wisdom" was lost when two-thirds finished and he rewrote the book from memory in 1919. Because it expressed certain personal and political opinions that Lawrence did not wish to publicize, it was offered for sale in 1926 in England at a prohibitive price. To insure copyright in the United States it was reprinted here by *Doran* (now *Doubleday*) and ten copies offered for sale at $20,000 each, a price "high enough to prevent their ever being sold." In 1935 Lawrence was killed when the motorbike given him by George Bernard Shaw went out of control on an English lane. *Doubleday* then brought out a limited edition and a trade edition, substantially the same as the rare 1926 edition. "Revolt in the Desert" (1927, o.p.) is an abridgment of the "Seven Pillars" which the author made to pay the printing expenses of the original. "The Mint," an account of his service in the Royal Air Force, was published posthumously in an edition of 50 copies, 10 of which were offered for sale at a price of half a million dollars each, to insure no copies being sold. In 1950 a popular edition, in 1955 a limited edition and in 1963 a paperback edition were published. After the war Lawrence enlisted in the Air Corps as Private Ross; in 1927 he became legally T. E. Shaw, under which name he was buried.

Earlier biographers including Lowell Thomas and Robert Graves were enthusiastic and laudatory. Twenty years after Lawrence's death, Richard Aldington wrote "Lawrence of Arabia: A Biographical Enquiry" (1955, o.p.), which "set off a fury of charge and countercharge." But Lawrence's saga has become legend. In tribute to this adventurous, enigmatic genius, who shunned fame, wealth and power, King George V wrote, "His name will live in history." To which Winston Churchill (*q.v.*) added: "That is true; it will live in English letters; it will live in the traditions of the Royal Air Force; it will live in the annals of war and in the legends of Arabia"— (*Time*). Public interest in "the elusive, mysterious and complex young Irishman" who led the Arab revolt, was revived by "Lawrence of Arabia," 1962's most honored film, winner of seven Academy Awards including "Best Picture."

In recent years the picture of Lawrence has changed again with the revelation of his illegitimacy, his readiness to embroider on the truth and other quirks and neuroses; but there were English witnesses to many of his accomplishments and the disagreements among those who knew him have left him undiscredited in any definitive manner; even the Arabs view him with their Arab pride at stake. He remains enigmatic and eccentric and is likely to be the subject of more research and many volumes before the truth about him is fully understood.

THE EVOLUTION OF A REVOLT: Early Postwar Writings. Ed. with introd. by Stanley and Rodelle Weintraub *Pennsylvania State Univ. Press* 1967 $7.50. Newspaper and journal articles from 1918–21.

THE ESSENTIAL T. E. LAWRENCE: Selections from His Writings. Ed. with pref. by David Garnett. 1951. *Viking* Compass Bks 1963 pap. $1.65

THE SEVEN PILLARS OF WISDOM: A Triumph. 1926. *Doubleday* 1935 $6.95; with index and illus. $10.00

THE MINT. (Ltd. ed. 1938) 1950. *Norton* 1963 pap. $1.95

Books about Lawrence

With Lawrence in Arabia. By Lowell Thomas. 1924. With new introd. and afterword by the author *Popular Lib.* 1971 pap. $.75
T. E. Lawrence in Arabia and After. By Basil H. Liddell Hart. 1934. *Greenwood* $20.50. An early biography, but a good one.
Lawrence of Arabia. By R. H. Kiernan. 1935. *Richard West* $20.00
T. E. Lawrence (of Arabia). By Charles Edmonds. 1936. *Richard West* $12.50
T. E. Lawrence by His Friends. Ed. by his brother, A. W. Lawrence. 1937. *Richard West* $25.00
Lawrence: The Rebel. By Edward Robinson. 1946. *Richard West* $15.00
Secret Lives of Lawrence of Arabia. By Philip Knightley and Colin Simpson. *McGraw-Hill* 1970 $8.95

Lawrence of Arabia. By Douglas Orgill. *Ballantine Bks.* (orig.) 1973 pap. $1.00

T. E. Lawrence: A Reader's Guide. By Frank Clements. *Shoe String Press* 1973 $8.50

T. E. Lawrence: A Bibliography. By Jeffrey Meyers. *Garland Pub.* 1974 $10.00

MORTON, H(ENRY CANOVA) V(OLLAM).   1892–

H. V. Morton began writing as an undergraduate in England. By the time he was 19, he became assistant editor of the Birmingham *Gazette and Express.* Later he joined the staff of the *Daily Mail* in London. Returning home from the British Army after World War I, he realized how little he actually knew of his own country. His explorations led him to writing the travel series published by *Dodd* but now out of print: "In Search of England" (1927), "In Search of Scotland" (1929), and "In Search of London" (1951). He has been called "perhaps the greatest living authority on the material being of the British Isles—that is to say, on their landscape, buildings, monuments, customs and history." As a devout churchman, he has also written several books on biblical personages and places. He is an experienced and worldly traveler who has a "unique talent for capturing the essence of lives long past."

H. V. MORTON'S BRITAIN. *Dodd* 1969 $12.95. Selections from his "In Search" books on England, Scotland, Ireland and Wales.

IN THE STEPS OF THE MASTER. 1934. *Folcroft* $10.00

STRANGER IN SPAIN. *Dodd* 1955 $6.00

A TRAVELLER IN ROME. *Dodd* 1957 $6.00

A TRAVELLER IN ITALY. *Dodd* 1964 $10.00

"Well written, well illustrated and really a fine example of the bookmaker's art, this book presents the whole of northern Italy with much skill. The result is a literary feast through the regions of Lombardy and Emilia, the cities of Venice and Florence. Morton is incapable of mere good writing; he is superb. A walk through Verona or a visit to the Pitti Palace or Dante's tomb is turned into a masterpiece of mood mingled with perception. Morton is so effective in evoking the past that it remains no farther away in time than the last ticking of a clock"—*(LJ)*.

A TRAVELLER IN SOUTHERN ITALY. *Dodd* 1969 $10.00

STARK, FREYA (MADELINE).   1893–

Freya Stark was a shy child. Her parents separated when she was young and she was brought up by her mother in northwest Italy. After 1914 she became a wartime censor and then a nurse. She studied Arabic with a Capuchin monk in San Remo and after 1927 began her wanderings into remote parts of the Middle East—alone, usually in poverty and often ill. She was in the British government service, chiefly at Aden, Cairo and Baghdad from 1939 to 1945, and married S. H. Perowne in 1947. In 1952 she traveled about the western coast of Turkey looking at 55 ruined sites.

"Most of all she delighted in southern Arabia, but her passion for Persia comes out in clear, crisp descriptions. . . . For her the light gleams from the ancient temples and the incense found in a Himyaritic tomb two thousand years old still smells sweetly. An enviable life, and her book ("The Freya Stark Story" 1953, o.p.) should be put on the shelf not far from the great Doughty"—*(N.Y. Times).* The *Atlantic* called her "Rome on the Euphrates" (*Harcourt* 1967, o.p.) "an illuminating history of the Roman frontier in Asia Minor and the Middle East. The story sprawls across the events of eight centuries from the Battle of Magnesia in 189 B.C. to the death of Justinian in 565 A.D. The author is not a professional historian, but she has worked through the basic sources with care, and she knows how to tell an interesting story." The *New Statesman* has written: "Miss Freya Stark can astonish us no more. She has long been the first of contemporary English travel writers." Harold Nicolson says, "She has written the best travel books of her generation and her name will survive as an artist in prose."

Also out of print are "A Winter in Arabia" (1940), "Letters from Syria" (1942), "Perseus in the Wind" (1948), and "Dust in the Lion's Paw: Autobiography 1939–1946" (1962) which is her well-documented account of the task that the British Foreign Office set for her in the Near and Middle East and in America.

THE JOURNEY'S ECHO: Selections From Freya Stark. Fwd. by Lawrence Durrell. 1964. *Transatlantic* $6.95

"The reader who comes fresh to Freya Stark through this enchanting work is fortunate. He will go on through her more than 15 books with thanks for this introduction to the Arabic countries and to a world of thought and great beauty"—*(LJ)*.

THE VALLEYS OF THE ASSASSINS. 1934. *Transatlantic* rev. ed. 1972 $12.50

EAST IS WEST. 1945. *Transatlantic* 1953 $6.95

ALEXANDER'S PATH. *Harcourt* Harvest Bks. 1967 pap. $2.25

"From Caria to Cilicia, Miss Stark recreates (although not on foot) the route that Alexander the Great, conqueror of Asia Minor, took in his march through Lycia and Pamphylia. An excellent and absorbing travel book that rewards the reader with its magical mingling of the ancient and the modern"—*(PW)*.

THE ZODIAC ARCH. Woodcuts by Gerald Stone; self-portrait by the author *Harcourt* 1969 $6.95

"Freya Stark is a writer to be savored. She is known not only for her novels but for numerous books of travel and history which communicate her distinctive hallmark, a controlled and sensitive style that is at once immediate in its evocations of scene and keenly interpretive, with flashes of gentle wit. . . . Her new volume . . . is a collection of essays, remembrances and interpretations of journeys she has made and thoughts arising from her travels"—*(PW)*.

GATEWAYS AND CARAVANS: A Portrait of Turkey. Ed. by Alick Bartholomew *Macmillan* 1971 $17.50

MINARET OF DJAM: An Excursion in Afghanistan. *Transatlantic* 1972 $10.00

THE SOUTHERN GATES OF ARABIA: A Journey to the Hadhramaut. *Transatlantic* 1972 $12.50

SITWELL, SIR SACHEVERELL, 6th Bart.   1897–

A writer of "great versatility and urbanity, of vast erudition and the most eclectic tastes," the younger brother of the late Dame Edith and Sir Osbert Sitwell is best known for his prose, expecially his art criticism. This has been described as "a marvel of sustained imaginative, pictorial and interpretative writing." His most recent U.S. publications in the field include "Narrative Pictures: A Survey of English Genre and Its Painters" and "Conversation Pieces: A Survey of English Domestic Portraits and Their Painters" (both *Schocken* 1969 each $12.50). He has also written biographies of musical composers. "Arabesque and Honeycomb" describes his travels to most of the important towns of the Middle East. As he views the monuments of Persia he links them to their counterparts in the West. His aesthetic taste ranges widely here. He has edited "Great Houses of Europe" (*Putnam* 1961, o.p.), calling the 40 private dwellings "the fine flowers of western civilization." He describes them in essays informative about their human history as well as their artistic value. The photographs (many in color) by Edwin Smith show all significant features, including interiors, decorative details, art works and gardens. He is now the only survivor of a colorful family and the successor to his brother Osbert's baronetcy on the latter's death in 1969.

In the absorbing first volume of his "Journey to the Ends of Time" (1959, o.p.), he remembers past experiences and speculates, as an atheist, about life and death. All of the facets of his mind are here—a "rich compound of imagination and experience."

ARABESQUE AND HONEYCOMB: A Travel Chronicle. 1957. *Bks. for Libraries* $16.50

GREAT TEMPLES OF THE EAST: The Wonders of Cambodia, India, Siam and Nepal. *Astor-Honor* 1962 $6.95

BAROQUE AND ROCOCO. *Putnam* 1967 $12.95

"Those familiar with Mr. Sitwell's previous studies of the Baroque know his love for and knowledge of the subject. Here he travels not only in Europe but also in South and Latin America, selecting the triumphs of 16th-Century and 17th-Century architecture, and concentrating on the facades of buildings which he feels are the keystones of style. His descriptions and comparisons of buildings are abetted by stunning illustrations"—*(LJ)*.

GOTHIC EUROPE. *Holt* 1969 $11.95

NETHERLANDS. *Hastings House* 1974 $8.95

(Ed.). GREAT PALACES OF EUROPE. *Putnam* 1964 $22.95

"Thirty palaces in this really elegant book are described and illustrated as the earlier *Great Houses of Europe* was presented. Fourteen countries are chosen, and the jewels are described by authors who are known to be lovers of the past and the authorities on style and decoration—and history . . . . The color plates are magnificent"—*(LJ)*.

ALL SUMMER IN A DAY: An Autobiographical Fantasia. 1926. *Scholarly Press* $14.50

Books about the Sitwells

The Three Sitwells: A Biographical and Critical Study. By J. L. Mégroz. 1927. *Kennikat* 1969 $10.00; *Scholarly Press* 1971 $18.00
A Bibliography of Edith, Osbert and Sacheverell Sitwell. By Richard Fifoot. 1963. *Shoe String Press* 2nd ed. 1971 $15.00

DOUGLAS; WILLIAM O(RVILLE).   1898–

Supreme Court Justice Douglas attended Whitman College in Walla Walla, Wash., and Columbia Law School. He was a Justice of the Supreme Court of the United States from 1939 to 1975. Before his appointment to the Court he served on the law school faculties of Columbia and Yale Universities and was chairman of the Securities and Exchange Commission.

"Of Men and Mountains" tells the story of his boyhood in Yakima, Wash., and his experiences as a mountaineer and fisherman. In "Strange Lands and Friendly People" (*Harper* 1951, o.p.) he reports on his travels through the Near East and India in 1949 and 1950–1951. In 1951 he spent his vacation trekking through the Central Asian country; he wrote of it in "Beyond the High Himalayas" (1952, o.p.). "Russian Journey" (1956, o.p.) tells of his trip to Central Asia and Russia during the summer of 1955. His earnest and enlightened "West of the Indus" (1958, o.p.) is "an exceptional work, one that should be read by anyone who wants an understanding of the Middle East today." "Keenly observant, a competent botanist, knowledgeable on soils, trees and geological formations, he senses a unity with nature, writing with an historical perspective that binds the American people to their land." In such important books as "My Wilderness: The Pacific West" (1960, o.p.) and "My Wilderness: East to Katahdin" he "laments—protests—the depredation of our natural resources, emphasizing the need to preserve an ecological balance 'if we are to survive.' " "Justice Douglas recounts his adventures with modesty, good humor and a sympathetic insight into the customs and the problems of the people he meets along the way"—(*N.Y. Herald Tribune*). In 1965 Justice Douglas was trapped by snow in the mountains near Albuquerque, N. Mex., where he was gathering material for a book on the Southwest mountains. With the rest of his hiking party, he was successfully rescued. The Audubon Society in 1962 awarded him the Audubon Medal for his efforts in the area of conservation.

"Farewell to Texas: A Vanishing Wilderness" (*McGraw-Hill* 1967, o.p.) ends with his eloquent plea for a concerted effort by conservationists in Texas to save the remaining wilderness areas. Justice Douglas suffered a paralytic stroke in 1974, but has recently completed a rehabilitation program.

OF MEN AND MOUNTAINS. *Harper* 1950 $10.00; *Atheneum* 1962 pap. $1.45

MY WILDERNESS: East to Katahdin. 1961. *Pyramid Bks.* 1968 pap. $.75

EXPLORING THE HIMALAYA. *Random* 1958 $2.95 lib. bdg. $3.87. For young people primarily.

MUIR OF THE MOUNTAINS. *Houghton* 1961 $2.95. Intended for high school and junior-high readers.

A WILDERNESS BILL OF RIGHTS. Fwd. from President Lyndon B. Johnson's State of the Union Message *Little* 1965 $7.50 pap. $1.95. His 15th book on travel and/or conservation.

For the political books of Justice Douglas see Chapter 9, History, Government and Politics— American: Civil Liberties and Conscientious Objection, and Modern and World History: International Relations and the United Nations, this Vol.

SAINT EXUPÉRY, ANTOINE DE.   1900–1944.   *See Chapter 9, French Literature, Reader's Adviser, Vol. 2.*

CHICHESTER, SIR FRANCIS.   1901–1972.

When Sir Francis Chichester arrived at Plymouth, England, on May 28, 1967, from his solo voyage round the world in a small yacht, bells were ringing, a thousand newsmen were waiting together with hundreds of thousands of his countrymen, and the Queen in London was preparing to knight him (his knighthood had been announced during his voyage) with Sir Francis Drake's sword in the biggest ceremony since the funeral of Sir Winston Churchill. At the age of 65 he had covered some 29,000 miles (by the "hard" route, heading east around the Cape of Good Hope and Cape Horn) in 226 days on the *Gipsy Moth IV*—a vessel that gave him constant problems—to achieve the fastest circumnavigation ever made in a small boat. Alan Villiers (*q.v.*), writing in the *Saturday Review* gives an idea of his quality: "I first met Sir Francis Chichester—plain Francis then—when he was trying to get backing for an early flight from London to Sydney. [He didn't find it, but he] flew anyway, and got there. It took a long time—six months, I think—and it was a colossal exhibition of guts, endurance, luck, and flying skill. Between long intervals I heard of him from time to time again—trying to fly another minute biplane around the world and smashing into some overhead cables (which he hadn't seen) above a harbor in Japan. He was dragged out of the wreckage, said the news flash, and given ten minutes to live. Ten minutes? That was nearly forty years ago. [More exploits followed. Then] 'Blondie' Hasler, former Marine cockleshell hero, organized the first single-handed yacht race westwards over the North Atlantic in 1960; Francis

Chichester won it. He won the second, too (against himself, failing other entries), and came a creditable second in the third. What next? The man was past sixty. A serious illness was diagnosed as lung cancer. He had a good business publishing maps in London. Anybody else might have sat back. So he dreamt up the idea of a single-handed sail right around the world."

"Gypsy Moth Circles the World" is, of course, his own detailed account of his struggles, triumphs and near-failures on the journey and "one of the great sea stories of all time"—(*PW*). "As J. R. L. Anderson observes in an epilogue," wrote Edmund Fuller in the *Wall Street Journal*, "it was not the technical achievement that had galvanized much of the world, it was the man indomitably pursuing his dream." The *N.Y. Times* asked him "why he had made the dangerous and psychologically difficult journey." Sir Francis replied, "It intensifies life to be living life to the full."

ATLANTIC ADVENTURE. Ed. with introd. by J. R. L. Anderson *De Graff* 1963 $3.95

"Francis Chichester won the first solo Atlantic Ocean Sailing race in 1960. His elapsed time was slightly over 40 days. The year 1962 found Mr. Chichester sailing alone over a similar course in an attempt to break his own record. He did! *Atlantic Adventure* is the detailed account of the preparations involved and the daily hazards faced"—(*LJ*).

ALONG THE CLIPPER WAY. 1967. *Ballantine Bks.* 1973 pap. $1.50

"This title should alert you to the fact that you are embarking in famous company upon a perilous and exciting number of sea voyages. The Great Clipper Way (shown on end-paper maps) covers 28,500 miles, from London around the Cape of Good Hope to Australia, and back to Britain around the notoriously ill-tempered Cape Horn. Every mile is packed with action; there are high winds, tremendous seas, ice floes and gigantic icebergs. Not only is Nature on the rampage, but the denizens of the deep put on a good show too with fights to the death between giant whales and giant squid or octopus, vicious sharks, and swordfish. . . . Enthralling"—(*LJ*). "Highly recommended"—(*New Yorker*).

GIPSY MOTH CIRCLES THE WORLD. *Coward* 1968 $6.95; *Pocket Bks.* 1969 pap. $.95

THE LONELY SEA AND THE SKY: The Autobiography of Francis Chichester. Introd. by J. R. L. Anderson. 1964. *Ballantine Bks.* 1971 pap. $.95

"Many men dream of adventure; some men live it. Into the latter category falls the author of this book, which is both an articulate autobiography and a tale of adventure. In it Chichester relates his adventures as a crewman aboard the ship on which he migrated from England to New Zealand and in New Zealand as a lumberman, farmhand, goldminer, gold prospecter, and partner in a real estate business. Later he piloted his first airplane from England to New Zealand and he made many daring flights including the first solo flight across the Tasman Sea from New Zealand to Australia, and the first solo flight from New Zealand to Japan. After World War II serving with the R.A.F. he became interested in sailing. . . ."—(*LJ*).

THE ROMANTIC CHALLENGE. *Coward* 1972 $7.95; *Ballantine Bks.* 1973 pap. $1.50

"In 1971 the author sailed alone in a ketch between Portuguese Guinea and Nicaragua. His goal was to average 200 miles a day. Though he fell slightly short of that, one quarter of the 4,000 mile voyage was sailed at a speed faster than the goal. Here are chronicled his thoughts and experiences as well as other sailing runs in the Atlantic, in 1970 and 1971 aboard the *Gipsy Moth V*"—(Publisher's note).

Books about Chichester

Francis Chichester: A Biography. By Anita Leslie. *Walker & Co.* 1975 $9.95

GUNTHER, JOHN. 1901–1970.

John Gunther was a war correspondent during World War II and later devoted all his time to writing. "Inside U.S.A." has been translated into 15 or 16 foreign languages. Following a visit to Russia in 1956 (his fourth), he presented important as well as trivial facts in "Inside Russia Today." "The greatest service Mr. Gunther has done is to bring Russia down to a level we can all understand and talk and argue about"—(*N.Y. Times*). In 1958 he received the Geographic Society of Chicago Publication Award for his "Inside" books.

"Inside U.S.A." (1951) and "Inside Africa" (1955) are out of print. He wrote several biographies and a deeply moving account of the death of his young son of a brain tumor: "Death Be Not Proud" (*Harper* 1949 new ed. 1971 $7.95 lib. bdg. $5.82 lg.-type ed. $7.50 pap. $.95; *Modern Library* 1953 $2.95). His "Procession" (*Harper* 1965, o.p.) is a group of sketches of international political figures (not updated) drawn from his "Inside" books and from articles. "Inside Australia," completed and edited by William Forbis, was published posthumously.

INSIDE RUSSIA TODAY. *Harper* 1958 rev. ed. 1962 $8.95

INSIDE EUROPE TODAY. *Harper* 1961 rev. ed. 1962 $8.95

Mr. Gunther established his international reputation with his best seller "Inside Europe." Now in a completely new book, "more seasoned and more searching than the first," he "has made a conscientious effort to interview some of the most important statesmen of our time; he has been conspicuously successful with Adenauer and Macmillan. He has gathered a lot of pertinent observations and characteristic stories about many others, like de Gaulle, Salazar and Tito. He draws also an intriguing pen-portrait of Khrushchev after the collapse of the Paris 'Summit.' . . . In addition to his wealth of biographical information, he introduces his readers to the current problems of each individual country and to the general European issues of our age"—(LJ).

INSIDE SOUTH AMERICA. *Harper* 1967 $8.95

"Guntherization, as it must to all continents, has come again to South America, in another marvelous plum pudding of a book"—(N.Y. Times). *"Inside South America* is John Gunther's report of his trip to ten South American countries in 1965. Using the struggle between democracy and Communism to focus the problems and perspectives facing each nation, he gives general impressions, describes leading personalities whom he met, and sketches historical and descriptive background material. Numerous facts crowd the pages, but despite an extensive bibliography, sources are not always cited"—(LJ).

TWELVE CITIES. *Harper* 1969 $7.95

"Mr. Gunther has a deft hand with atmosphere, the impalpable soul of any great city. He penetrates to the heart of a city's problem and he knows how to identify and analyze the sources of power. The report is quite up-to-date . . . readable, diverting, informative—in a word, Guntherian"—(Clifton Fadiman, in *Book-of-the-Month Club News*).

A FRAGMENT OF AUTOBIOGRAPHY: The Fun of Writing the Inside Books. *Harper* 1962 $4.95

John Gunther is, on a serious level, probably the best known of all American writers on foreign affairs. His books are friendly in approach, authoritative and fair-minded. In his lively and informative "A Fragment of Autobiography," he begins with "Inside Europe" (1936, o.p.) then takes each of his books in turn and "describes how he chose his topics, the preparations he made for his travels, the information he sought, and how he wrote his manuscripts." "In preparing my various books, I visited all the countries of Eastern Europe in 1948, went around the world in 1950, paying particular attention to the development of NATO."

JOHN GUNTHER'S INSIDE AUSTRALIA. Completed and edited by William Forbis *Harper* 1972 $10.95 lib. bdg. $9.89

This book "provides enduring facets of life in Australia and New Zealand"—(*Booklist*).

KEITH, AGNES NEWTON. 1901–

Agnes Newton Keith, born in Oak Park, Ill., writes mainly of her adopted Orient. "Land below the Wind" was her first book. "Three Came Home" tells of the four years that she, her husband and two-year-old son spent in Japanese internment camps after their capture during World War II. "White Man Returns" (*Little* 1951, o.p.) is an account of their return to a devastated North Borneo. In 1951 her husband joined the technical aid program of the United Nations as a forestry expert and they moved to the Philippines. They have continued to move about the world to where his UN duties took her husband. "Children of Allah" was the result of his tenure in Libya as head of an FAO mission to that country. *Time* said of "Bare Feet in the Palace": "Her saving grace is an ability to see men of many colors not as quaint objects, but as individual beings, and a warm faith in Asian friends which is refreshingly free of condescension."

LAND BELOW THE WIND. *Little-Atlantic* 1939 $8.50

THREE CAME HOME. *Little-Atlantic* 1947 $7.50

BARE FEET IN THE PALACE. *Little-Atlantic* 1955 $6.95

CHILDREN OF ALLAH. *Little-Atlantic* 1966 $7.95

"This is the story of a compassionate, intelligent American woman and of how she was drawn to the people of Libya, the citizens of a rugged new Arab state ravaged by war, caught between sea and Sahara and struggling to catch up with the modern world"—(Publisher's note).

BELOVED EXILES. *Little-Atlantic* 1972 $7.95

This story "seen through the eyes of several people living in British North Borneo, centers on the experiences of Sara and Charles Evans from the mid-1930's until 1950, including an account of life in a Japanese prisoner of war camp"—(LJ).

LINDBERGH, CHARLES A(UGUSTUS). 1902–1974.

" 'The Spirit of St. Louis' is a magnificent book. . . . It is a historic document, revealing not only a fascinating individual, but a nation in the throes of whelping an industry which would one day become a source of its power"—(*SR*). "We" was published shortly after the first historic solo, nonstop, transatlantic flight to Paris in 1927. "The Spirit of St. Louis" is the contemplative almost hour-by-hour account of that flight. The first low-priced edition was published to coincide with the release of the motion picture starring James Stewart. During World War II, Lindbergh flew combat missions in the Pacific. Later he worked with Pan American Airways and the National Naval Medical Center. In 1967 the *N.Y. Times* celebrated the 40th anniversary of Lindbergh's transatlantic flight by reprinting the pilot's original account as it appeared in that newspaper on May 23, 1927. Afflicted with incurable cancer, Lindbergh elected to spend his last days at his retreat in the Hawaiian Islands, where he was buried with private ceremonies in an unmarked grave.

WE. *Putnam* 1927 $6.95

THE SPIRIT OF ST. LOUIS. *Scribner* 1953 $9.95

WARTIME JOURNALS. *Harcourt* 1970 $12.95

"In 1937 the author began keeping a diary and he continued it into 1945. The journals therefore cover the pre-World War II period, when the celebrated flier was in Europe surveying military aviation . . . [and] the war years when . . . he served as a civilian aeronautical expert in private industry, and in the Pacific, also managing to work in 50 combat missions; and the weeks just after the Nazi surrender, which found him again in Europe, attached to a Naval Mission studying wartime developments in plane design and missiles"—(*N.Y. Times Bk. Review*).

BOYHOOD ON THE UPPER MISSISSIPPI: A Reminiscent Letter. *Minnesota Historical Society* 1972 $4.50

Books about Lindbergh

The Last Hero: Charles A. Lindbergh. By Walter S. Ross. *Harper* 1968 $7.95
"Since Lindbergh is surely one of the towering individuals of the century, and since his story is packed with an astonishing combination of adventure, triumph, tragedy and conflict, the book is compelling throughout. . . . One of the best things about it is that Mr. Ross, in spite of what must have been repeated temptation, never grovels in hero-worship before his subject. . . . Surely his simplicity and his stubborn drive explain much about Lindbergh, and Ross's book illuminates the surprising ways these traits have kept the hero from ever looking back"—(Loudon Wainwright, in *Life*).
The Flight of the Lone Eagle: Charles Lindbergh Flies Nonstop from New York to Paris. By John T. Foster. *Franklin Watts* 1974 lib. bdg. $3.45
Charles A. Lindbergh and the Battle against American Intervention in World War Two. By Wayne S. Cole. *Harcourt* 1974 $10.00

See also Anne Morrow Lindbergh, this Chapter.

SNOW, EDWARD (ROWE). 1902–

Author, historian and adventurer, Edward Snow is descended from a long line of sea captains, and spent several years of his early life sailing around the world. The *N.Y. Times* has called him "just about the best chronicler of the days of sails alive today." Out of print are: "Mysterious Tales of the New England Coast" (1961) and "Unsolved Mysteries of Sea and Shore" (1963).

MYSTERIES AND ADVENTURES ALONG THE ATLANTIC COAST. 1948. *Bks for Libraries* $14.50

TRUE TALES OF BURIED TREASURE. *Dodd* 1951 $5.95

INCREDIBLE MYSTERIES AND LEGENDS OF THE SEA. *Dodd* 1967 $5.00

FANTASTIC FOLKLORE AND FACT: New England Tales of Land and Sea. *Dodd* 1968 $5.95

GREAT ATLANTIC ADVENTURES. *Dodd* 1970 $5.95

ISLANDS OF BOSTON HARBOR. *Dodd* 1971 $6.95

GHOSTS, GALES AND GOLD. *Dodd* 1972 $5.95

THE LIGHTHOUSES OF NEW ENGLAND. *Dodd* 1973 $7.95

SUPERNATURAL MYSTERIES AND OTHER TALES. *Dodd* 1974 $7.95

CHIANG, YEE. 1903–

"The Silent Traveller" books are unique in their piquant contrast of familiar Western scenes as seen through Chinese eyes. The author-artist is a sharp observer and writes with a quiet humor and unaffected sincerity. He uses Chinese inks and brushes and palette for his delicate but powerful illustrations in line and water color, which are admirably suited to the text.

He is a member of a large family of well-to-do artists and landowners, devoted to the Confucian ideal of moderation. "A Chinese Childhood" (1940, o.p.) tells the delightful story of his first 15 years. Trained as a chemist at Nanking and having served as governor of his native district of Kiu-Kiang, Chiang Yee eventually settled in England. He began writing and illustrating books on Chinese painting, calligraphy, and family life for Western audiences.

THE SILENT TRAVELLER IN PARIS. *Norton* 1956 $7.50

THE SILENT TRAVELLER IN BOSTON. *Norton* 1959 $7.50

THE SILENT TRAVELLER IN SAN FRANCISCO. *Norton* 1964 $12.50

"A refreshing new view of the Bay City and its environs. Nearly all other travelers who have written about San Francisco since 1848 have been Europeans. But Mr. Chiang makes a switch by gracefully using an Oriental tint to coat his unusual narrative. He recalls tales of the Chinese who came to California in the last century to build railroads, dig for gold, operate laundries and work the fields. As he looks at the San Francisco of today he sees things from a Chinese point of view . . . or compares some aspects with those of his native China, or quotes an appropriate saying of some 'celestial' sage, or here and there punctuates his thoughts with an inspired poem that he composes for the occasion. Artist Chiang (he draws and writes with equal sparkle) adds lustre to the book with nearly 100 drawings, some in color"—(*LJ*).

THE SILENT TRAVELLER IN JAPAN. *Norton* 1972 $15.00

"Erudite, graceful, though sometimes discursive, this book combines elements of the travelog with appreciation of qualities inherent in Japanese society, culture and religion especially as these and related aspects of life compare with Chinese historical antecedents"—(*Booklist*).

VILLIERS, ALAN. 1903–

Captain Villiers, an Australian by birth, is a contemporary recorder of life before the mast. "Cruise of the Conrad" (1937, o.p.) is a journal of a voyage around the world in the sailing vessel *Joseph Conrad*, 1934–1936, by way of Good Hope, East Indies, South Seas and Cape Horn. He is an internationally licensed air pilot and during World War II was with the British Navy in antiaircraft work. He was awarded the Portuguese Camões Prize for Literature in 1952 for "The Quest of the Schooner Argus" (1951, o.p.). He is a Commander of the Portuguese Order of St. James of the Sword, and holds the British Distinguished Service Cross.

He was captain of Mayflower II. Given by Englishmen to America, it sailed from Plymouth, England, April 17, 1957, to repeat the journey of the Pilgrim fathers from Plymouth, England to Plymouth, Mass. The company of 33 were fewer than the original 125-odd crew and passengers and they had the comfort and reassurance of radio. "But in many ways they went to sea as the Pilgrims did, eating salt meat, drinking lime juice, living in cramped quarters. They sailed a much longer course (more than 5,000 miles) to get the southerly trades and, while doing so, had to learn the forgotten art of handling a cranky 17th-century ship." Villiers' "Give Me a Ship to Sail" (1959, o.p.) includes the story of this voyage. The *N.Y. Times* said of this title: "Captain Villiers is an unforgettable personality, born to command, at ease among men, great or small. He is also a born writer, fluent and witty. Small wonder then that this book is a tonic thing, fresh, sure and alive."

Villiers edited "Of Ships and Men: A Personal Anthology" (1962, o.p.), a compilation of poetry and prose about the sea from Bible selections to recent news items. "Sons of Sinbad" (1940. rev. ed. 1969, o.p.) tells of his voyage from the Persian Gulf to Zanzibar on an Arabian deep-sea dhow called the *Triumph of Righteousness*.

POSTED MISSING. *Scribner* 1956 rev. ed. 1974 $7.95. A survey of the large number of vessels which have disappeared in recent years despite radio, radar, aircraft, lighthouses and other modern aids.

CAPTAIN JAMES COOK *Scribner* 1967 pap. 1970 $2.45

"One of today's foremost sailing masters, Alan Villiers, has written this outstanding biography of the 18th Century's foremost marine explorer, Captain James Cook." . . . His account with its salt-air authenticity will be a significant addition to most library collections"—(*LJ*). *See also Captain Cook's main entry, this Chapter.*

FALMOUTH FOR ORDERS. *Scribner* rev. ed. 1970 $15.00

WAY OF A SHIP. *Scribner* rev. ed. 1970 $10.00

WAR WITH CAPE HORN. *Scribner* 1971 $10.00

In 1935, Alan Villiers was the master of the *Joseph Conrad*, the last full-rigged ship to round Cape Horn. "Drawing on his own experience, on interviews with old ship masters, and on hitherto unavailable original logs and documents [he] presents an . . . account of the voyages of the great square-riggers fighting to round the Cape . . . [and] recreates the heroic era of the wind-driven sailing ship—the achievements and the disasters"—(Publisher's note).

(With others). MEN, SHIPS AND THE SEA. (Prep. by National Geographic Bk. Serv., Merle Severy, Chief) *National Geographic Society* 1963 1973 $7.95

"Captain Villiers and his associates cover the subject from primitive man through history to the present day. . . . The conclusion brings some good advice on yachting and even the choice of a boat. There are lists of maritime museums and of historic ships still to be seen. . . . A thrilling and worthwhile addition"—(*LJ*).

(With Henri Picard). THE BOUNTY SHIPS OF FRANCE. *Scribner* 1973 $17.50

JOHNSON, IRVING. 1905–

For most of his life Captain Johnson has been a sailor. He was first mate on Sir Thomas Lipton's *Shamrock* on her trip back to England after the races, and sailed in a square rigger around the Horn. With his wife and an amateur crew he cruised around the world in a Dutch pilot schooner *The Yankee*. The story of this trip is told in "Westward Bound in the Schooner *Yankee*" (1936, o.p.). He and his wife, Electa, have made two additional world cruises, described in their books "Sailing to See" (1939, o.p.) and "Yankee Wonder World" (1949, o.p.). "*Yankee* Sails Across Europe" is "the story of the Dutch-built yacht from conception through European cruise." "Yankee's People and Places" (1955) is out of print.

(With Mrs. Irving Johnson). YANKEE SAILS ACROSS EUROPE. *Norton* 1962 $5.95

(With Mrs. Irving Johnson). YANKEE SAILS THE NILE. *Norton* 1966 $7.50

LINDBERGH, ANNE MORROW. 1906–

The first title is a personal account of the Lindberghs' flight to the Orient in the summer of 1931 by the Great Circle Route, the second, the story of their flight across the Atlantic from Africa to Brazil in December, 1933, with maps by Charles A. Lindbergh (*q.v.*). "The Steep Ascent" is a short introspective novel written with great sensitivity and poetic feeling. It describes a perilous flight over the Alps by an American woman and her British airman husband. With Saint-Exupéry (*q.v.*, Chapter 9, French Literature, Reader's Adviser, *Vol*. 2), another poetic flyer, Anne Lindbergh has the power and talent to impart her perceptions to the earthbound.

"Gift from the Sea" is a meditative adventure. In it she explores the human realm of conflicting values—in her own case, the delicate balance between her life as wife and mother and her life as an individual. It "is like a shell itself, in its small and perfect form, the delicate spiraling of its thought, the poetry of its color, and its rhythm from the sea, which tells of light and life and love and the security that lies at the heart of intermittency"—(*N.Y. Times*). In "Dearly Beloved" she continues this line of thought as reflections in a fictional frame. She is also author of "The Unicorn and Other Poems" (*Pantheon* 1956 $5.95).

NORTH TO THE ORIENT. *Harcourt* 1935 Harbrace Modern Classics $2.95 pap. 1966 $.50

LISTEN! THE WIND. *Harcourt* 1938 $6.95

THE STEEP ASCENT. *Harcourt* 1944 $3.00. A novel.

GIFT FROM THE SEA. 1955. *Random* Vintage Bks. pap. $1.65; *Franklin Watts* lg.-type ed. 1966 $7.95

DEARLY BELOVED: A Theme and Variations. *Harcourt* 1962 $6.95; *Popular Lib.* 1967 pap. $.60

EARTH SHINE. *Harcourt* 1969 $6.95 pap. 1970 $2.95

"Two essays showing her reverence for life and her reflections on the beauty of the world. 'The Heron and the Astronaut' tells of the author's visit with Charles to Cape Kennedy to watch the launching of Apollo 8 for its orbit around the moon. She includes her own thoughts about this planet and man's accomplishment in space. The second essay 'Immersion in Life' covers their safari to the animal preserves in East Africa"—(*LJ*).

BRING ME A UNICORN: Diaries and Letters, 1922–1928. *Harcourt* 1972 $6.95; *Hall* 1973 $11.95; *New Am. Lib.* 1974 pap. $1.50

"This first volume covers her formative years as a school girl and a college student, her family life as daughter of the ambassador to Mexico, her meeting in Mexico with Charles Lindbergh, and their courtship"—(Publisher's note).

HOUR OF GOLD, HOUR OF LEAD: Diaries and Letters, 1929–1932. *Harcourt* 1973 $7.95; *Hall* 1974 $12.95; *New Am. Lib.* 1974 pap. $1.75

"This second volume begins with her engagement. She chronicles her hectic schedule of travel and appearances, and tells of a daring flight to the Orient. She describes her experiences learning navigation, sharing her husband's success.... Then came the 'hour of lead', suggesting the numbness caused by grief and bitterness with which she struggled after the kidnapping and death of her first son"—(LJ).

LOCKED ROOMS AND OPEN DOORS: Diaries and Letters, 1933–1935. *Harcourt* 1974 $7.95

"This volume begins with the Hauptmann trial, her first book 'North to the Orient' and her exploration of transatlantic air routes with her husband"—(Publisher's note).

See also Charles A. Lindbergh, this Chapter.

VAN DER POST, LAURENS.   1906–

Colonel Van der Post, a distinguished British subject born in South Africa, has "spent most of his adult life with one foot in Africa and one in England." The beautifully composed "Venture to the Interior" is much more than an account of the plane journey from London to Nyasaland in South Africa, the climbing of Mianje and the exploration of Nyika. It catches the "unique and indefinable spirit of the ancient continent" and explores the interiors of men's minds. His "The Heart of the Hunter" points the way toward a rediscovery of the positive values in our own lives. His extraordinary explorations of African personalities reflect his view that "we all have a dark figure within ourselves, a Negro, a gipsy, an aboriginal with averted back, and, alas! the nearest many of us can get to making terms with him is to strike up these vicarious friendships with him through the black people of Africa."

"A Portrait of All the Russias" (1967), "A Portrait of Japan" (1968), and "The Dark Eye in Africa" (1955), an Afrikaner's discussion of his country's spiritual problems, are out of print.

Novels of Mr. Van der Post, published by *Morrow*, that are out of print are: "In a Province" (1935), about a man in the South Africa of the thirties; "The Seed and the Sower" (1963), about men at war in Africa; and "The Hunter and the Whale: A Tale of Africa" (1967), a rousing sea story of whaling in the 1920's.

"Flamingo Feather" (*McGraw-Hill* 1949 pap. $2.00) is one of his early novels. "Story like the Wind" (*Morrow* 1972 $7.95) is a novel about a boy on a farm in South Africa; its sequel is "A Far-Off Place" (*Morrow* 1974 $7.95).

VENTURE TO THE INTERIOR. 1951. *Greenwood* 1973 $11.25

THE LOST WORLD OF THE KALAHARI. 1958. *Pyramid Bks.* 1972 pap. $.95. An account of an expedition into the remote Kalahari Desert to study the few remaining communities of the Bushmen.

THE HEART OF THE HUNTER. *Morrow* 1961 pap. 1971 $2.50. This study of the heart and soul of the African Bushman started in "The Lost World of the Kalahari."

PATTERNS OF RENEWAL. *Pendle Hill* (orig.) 1962 pap. $.70

A VIEW OF ALL THE RUSSIAS. *Morrow* 1964 $7.95

"This is a fine piece of impressionistic writing, sensitive and perceptive, occasionally accurate, with a strong feeling for nature and many vivid descriptions of landscapes (especially Asian ones), all made to order for the armchair traveler or the nostalgic Russian exile, but hardly the fare for the reader in search of information and insight"—(LJ).

PRISONER AND THE BOMB. (Orig. "Night of the New Moon") *Morrow* 1971 $5.00

Books about Van der Post

Laurens Van der Post. By Frederic I. Carpenter. World Authors Ser. *Twayne* 1969 $6.95

ULLMAN, JAMES RAMSEY.   1907–1971.

James Ramsey Ullman, an American, wrote on a variety of subjects but was most widely known as a specialist in mountains and mountain climbing. His first and best-selling novel, "The White Tower" (*Lippincott* 1945 1959 $5.95; *Popular Lib.* pap. $1.25), a "tense and dramatic story of the ascent of a mountain in the Alps," contains vivid descriptions of climbing. He said of himself in "Twentieth Century Authors": "Over the years I have managed to escape occasionally from the desk and lead something of a double life as traveler and mountaineer, venturing as far afield as Brazil and Hawaii, Russia and South Africa, the Alps and the Andes. And, inevitably, my love of far and high places has strongly influenced my writing. As far back as I can remember, my fondest dream has been to have a try at Mount Everest."

Although he did not achieve this ambition, he did help the simple Himalayan mountain man write *his* autobiography "Tiger of the Snow: the Autobiography of Norgay Sherpa Tenzing" (1955, o.p.) and accompanied the American team sponsored by the National Geographic Society in 1963 as official reporter. "Americans on Everest" (1964, o.p.) is the official account of that expedition which culminated in two successful attempts to reach the summit of Mt. Everest. "Although Ullman, the official scribe, stayed on lower levels, he saw the diaries of the climbers, got constant reports by radio, and utilized verbal accounts. He describes vividly and skillfully the complexities of such an undertaking"—(*LJ*). Justice William O. Douglas has praised "The Age of Mountaineering" as "a beautiful narrative of the conquests of mountains" that is exciting as fiction. "Straight Up: The Life and Death of John Harlin" (1968, o.p.) is the story of a mountaineer on the Eiger.

In addition to "The White Tower," the author's fiction includes the novels "Windom's Way" (*Popular Lib.* pap. $.60), "River of the Sun" (1950, o.p.) and "Banner in the Sky" (*Lippincott* 1954 $5.75), a title for young readers.

THE AGE OF MOUNTAINEERING. *Lippincott* 1954. rev. ed. 1964 $8.95

DOWN THE COLORADO WITH MAJOR POWELL. *Houghton* 1960 $2.95

(With Al Dinhofer). THE CARIBBEAN HERE AND NOW, 1971–1972: Complete Guide to 52 Sunny Vacation Spots. *Macmillan* 1970 $8.95

DIOLÉ, PHILIPPE. 1908–

Diolé writes in a lovely poetic prose. His books of undersea adventure are "highly subjective, philosophical, and at times mystical." Urbane, chatty and restrained, Diolé writes with authority. *Harper's* called "4,000 Years under the Sea" a "careful, scholarly, and yet beautifully evocative account of a new kind of archaeological investigation, the discovery and exploration of sunken ships and cities of antiquity." "Under Sea Adventure" (trans. by Alan Ross 1953–1955) is now o.p. Diolé has also written a novel "Okapi Fever" (1965, o.p.) about three men and two young women on an illegal journey to the Congo River. His work with Jacques Cousteau has produced a number of books giving new information about the creatures of the underwater world.

4,000 YEARS UNDER THE SEA. Trans. by Alan Ross *Simon & Schuster* 1954 $4.50

THE ERRANT ARK: Man's Relationship with Animals. *Putnam* 1974 $8.95

(With Jacques-Yves Cousteau). LIFE AND DEATH IN A CORAL SEA. Trans. by J. F. Bernard *Doubleday* 1971 $8.95

"Although intended apparently for the layman, [this book] is a significant contribution to marine ecology and should be available to students in that area . . . [also covers] diving, coral reefs, coral reef fishes and turtles"—(*Choice*).

(With Jacques-Yves Cousteau). DIVING FOR SUNKEN TREASURE. *Doubleday* 1972 $8.95

(With Jacques-Yves Cousteau). THREE ADVENTURES: Galapagos, Titicaca, the Blue Holes. *Doubleday* 1973 $9.95

"The experience of Jacques Cousteau and his crew of the Calypso as they explore the Galapagos archipelago to record the habits of the marine iguana on film; dive in Peru's Lake Titicaca to find archaeological remains and study the fauna; then investigate the Blue Holes . . . hollowed out rings of coral, in British Honduras and the Bahamas"—(*LJ*).

See also Cousteau, Jacques-Yves, in Chapter 7, Science, this Vol.

HUNT, SIR JOHN. 1910–

"The Conquest of Everest" was this author's first book, although he had written numerous articles for climbing and mountain magazines. Several later ones, now o.p., are "Our Everest Adventure: The Pictorial History From Kathmandu to the Summit" (1954) and "Picture of Everest" (1956). He was born in Simla, India, and educated at Marlborough College and at Sandhurst. The army has been his career and he holds the rank of Colonel (Temporary Brigadier). After the conquest of the world's highest mountain he and Sir Edmund Hillary (*q.v.*) were knighted by Queen Elizabeth II during the Coronation festivities in 1953.

A complement to Sir John's official narrative is Wilfrid Noyce's "South Col, A Personal Story of the Ascent of Everest" (1955, o.p.), which contains an intimate day-by-day account of the adventure. The autobiography of the simple Himalayan mountain man who also achieved fame on this expedition is "Tiger of the Snow" by Norgay Sherpa Tenzing, written in collaboration with James Ramsey Ullman (*q.v.*). James Morris, Special Correspondent to the London *Times* which had exclusive rights to the news of the expedition, has written "Coronation Everest" (1958, o.p.). (*See also Sir Edmund Hillary, this Chapter.*)

THE CONQUEST OF EVEREST: With a Chapter on the Final Assault by Sir Edmund Hillary. Fwd. by H. R. H. the Duke of Edinburgh, now Prince Philip *Dutton* 1954 $8.95

MOOREHEAD, ALAN. 1910–

"Alan Moorehead has put me in a quandary," Gerald Durrell wrote in the *N.Y. Times.* "He has written a book so good that any praise of mine seems inadequate. He writes with such strange brilliance that he evokes the color and scents of the African scene with tremendous power; more than any other book I have read on Africa this one made me feel I was sharing the experiences with the author." The Australian journalist, who went to London in 1937 to become a newspaperman, wrote "No Room in the Ark" after four journeys to Africa. It represents his view of the impact of the white man's civilization on primitive communities and on the wild animals of southern and eastern Africa.

He is "the most remarkable of storytellers," wrote Sir Harold Nicolson. "He knows how to arouse and satisfy expectation; he writes a lucid prose; he has an excellent talent for construction: and his sympathies are ever human and alert." "The White Nile" is a "book about English contact with the 'mightiest river in the world' during the Victorian half century. This was the golden age of African exploration and the heroic age of British imperialism. . . . Speke, Burton, Samuel Baker, Dr. David Livingstone, Stanley, Gen. Charles Gordon, Lord Kitchener—the great names are all here"—(*N.Y. Times*). "The Blue Nile" is the "story of Western exploration and expansion from 1798 through the nineteenth century, into the regions watered by the Nile on its long journey from Lake Tana in Abyssinia to the Mediterranean. These lands have been forgotten since Roman times or had never been known at all." This continually absorbing volume describes the 2,750-mile-long river, the animals and people who live along its banks, and some of the exciting events that took place in Egypt, the Sudan and Ethiopia.

As a foreign correspondent for the London *Daily Express*, Moorehead won an international reputation for his coverage of World War II campaigns in the Middle and Far East, Tunsia, Sicily, Italy and Northwest Europe. In 1950–1951 he served as chief public relations officer in the Ministry of Defense. He and his family now move between Italy and other parts of the world. Out of print are: "Eclipse" (1954), a memoir of the author's war experiences; his historical reconstruction of the famous World War I battle: "Gallipoli" (1956), winner of a number of awards; "Winston Churchill: A Pictorial Biography" (1960), for which he wrote the text on the major events in Churchill's life, and "Fatal Impact: An Account of the Invasion of the South Pacific, 1767–1840" (1966), which "tells of white men's earliest contacts with native life in Tahiti, Australia, and Antarctica ably distilled from primary source materials"—(*LJ*).

THE RUSSIAN REVOLUTION. *Harper* 1958 $10.00 Perenn. Lib. 1965 pap. $1.25

"A popular yet admirably written and absorbing analysis"—(*Foreign Affairs*).

NO ROOM IN THE ARK. *Harper* 1960 $7.95

THE WHITE NILE. *Harper* 1961 1971 deluxe ed. $17.50

THE BLUE NILE. *Harper* 1962 new ed. 1972 deluxe ed. $17.50 pap. 1974 $1.25; *Dell* pap. $.60

COOPER'S CREEK. *Harper* 1964 $7.50

"Here is a graphic account of the first transcontinental crossing of Australia, the 1860–1861 Burke and Wills expedition, the story of which is an Australian classic, little known elsewhere. In the skillful hands of a widely known journalist and war correspondent, the story gains in the retelling. Moorehead knows how to hold his audience: events are presented in the sequence that might be expected in a well-written novel; his characterization, with its goodies and baddies, is excellent; the white man's treatment of the aborigines is food for thought; there are really fine scenic descriptions of the Australian bush; and the near misses at the Cooper's Creek base camp on the return trip are poignantly told"—(*LJ*).

THE MARCH TO TUNIS: The North African War, 1940–1943. (Orig. "African Trilogy"; *see note below*.) Fwd. by Field-Marshal Viscount Montgomery *Harper* 3 vols. in 1 1967 $8.50

"This is one of the finest travel books of the year. The territory it covers goes around the earth—and deep into tough forces that still shake contemporary man"—(*N.Y. Times*). "Alan Moorehead's brilliant reporting job of the North African war first published as three separate works *Mediterranean Front, A Year of Battle,* and the *End in Africa,* is now available again in this compilation. Historians will discuss the fine points of strategy and evaluate the generals on both sides, but the reader will just enjoy this fast paced narrative that gives the excitement and the danger, the political give and take, and great amounts of detail without ever losing sight of the whole picture"—(*LJ*).

DARWIN AND THE BEAGLE. *Harper* 1969 $17.50 pap. $5.95

The five year voyage of the *Beagle* to Brazil, Argentina, Tierra del Fuego, Chile, Peru, the Galapago, Tahiti, New Zealand, Australia and other islands on the way. "The description of scenes, scenery and events during the voyage of the *Beagle* could not be bettered"—(Sir Gavin de Beer, in *Book World*).

LATE EDUCATION. *Harper* 1971 $5.95

HARRER, HEINRICH. 1912–

In 1939 Harrer was a member of the Nanga Parbat Expedition that was interned in India by the British at the outbreak of World War II. He escaped by way of Tibet, and during his seven years there he was unofficial tutor to the Dalai Lama in Lhasa and taught him geography, arithmetic and English. Harrer is an Aus^trian and, during his years at the college and University of Graz he climbed hundreds of walls and ridges in the Alps, some for the first time. "The White Spider" (1960, o.p.) is a history of the nearly impregnable precipice, the Eiger peak in the Bernese Alps. It contains also an analysis of the values and ethics of mountaineering. "Tibet Is My Country" is the autobiography of Thubten Jigme Norbu, brother of the Dalai Lama, as told to Harrer. "This book makes it possible, for virtually the first time, to view Tibetan family, village, and monastic life through the eyes of a Tibetan, uncolored by Western preconceptions, as it was prior to the occupation by Communist China.... When Communist pressures at his monastery became intolerable [Norbu] found a means of joining his family in Lhasa. He then came to the United States for medical treatment and further schooling, and was in New York when news came of the Dalai Lama's flight to India. He immediately returned to India to work with Tibetan refugees. The simplicity and unpretentiousness of the book's style suggests that the translators have carefully avoided embroidering the original"—(*LJ*).

"I Come from the Stone Age" (trans. by Edward Fitzgerald *Dutton* 1965) is out of print.

SEVEN YEARS IN TIBET. Trans. by Richard Graves; introd. by Peter Fleming *Dutton* 1959 $7.95

TIBET IS MY COUNTRY. Trans. by Edward Fitzgerald *Dutton* 1961 $6.95. The oral autobiography of Thubten Jigme Norbu, brother of the Dalai Lama.

HEYERDAHL, THOR. 1914–

"This is an enthralling book," Hamilton Basso wrote in the *New Yorker* of "Kon-Tiki," "and I don't think I can be very far off in calling it the most absorbing sea tale of our time." Mr. Heyerdahl, a Norwegian ethnologist, conceived the theory—not then accepted by other scientists—that Polynesia may have been originally settled by men who crossed the 4,000 miles of ocean from Peru in rafts made of balsa logs. "Kon-Tiki" is the story of how he and five others built the raft, as men of the Stone Age could build it, and traveled in it from Peru to a small island east of Tahiti—a "most fascinating description of intelligent courage."

Mr. Heyerdahl believes that he has at last solved the problem of how natives raised the great statues on Easter Island, and has written a most absorbing account of it in "Aku-Aku." He has adduced further corroboration of his theory from the findings in "The Archeology of Easter Island." In this superb work the editors and staff give full accounts of topography, climatology, flora and fauna, dwellings, artifacts and, incidentally, the solution to several perplexing problems. Though intended for informed scientists and students of archeology and anthropology, this book "cannot fail to appeal to the many who have been fascinated by those mysterious stone statues on the remote island."

In the spring of 1969 Mr. Heyerdahl was engaged in a new experiment, this time planning to cross the Atlantic in a 12-ton papyrus boat—which he and others built themselves in the manner of the ancient Egyptians—from Morocco to Yucatan. In spite of general skepticism as to whether the boat—called the *Ra,* could make the journey without sinking when it became thoroughly watersoaked, Mr. Heyerdahl and six others were going in full confidence, in the effort to demonstrate that Egyptians might have made the journey in this manner four or five thousand years ago and thus have become the precursors of the Incas and Mayas. In July 1969, however, they were forced to abandon their attempt 600 miles short of their goal, near the Virgin Islands, after a series of storms had crippled the *Ra.* They left it drifting in the hope it might reach Barbados on its own. Their second attempt in *Ra II* was successful.

In the intervals between scientific expeditions, lecture tours and other projects, Mr. Heyerdahl has spent much time at his villa on the Italian Riviera.

KON-TIKI: Across the Pacific by Raft. 1948. Trans. by F. H. Lyon *Ballantine Bks.* 1973 pap. $2.95; *Rand McNally* 1950 $8.95; *Simon & Schuster* (Washington Square) 1973 pap. $.95; *Franklin Watts* 1966 lg.-type ed. $7.95

AMERICAN INDIANS IN THE PACIFIC: The Theory behind the Kon-Tiki Expedition. 1952. *Rowman* 1974 $27.50

AKU-AKU: The Secret of Easter Island. *Rand McNally* 1958 $8.95; *Ballantine Bks.* 1974 pap. $2.95; *Simon & Schuster* (Pocket Bks.) 1960 pap. $.95

(With Edwin L. Ferdon, Jr.). THE ARCHAEOLOGY OF EASTER ISLAND: Reports of the Norwegian Archaeological Expedition to Easter Island and the East Pacific, Vol. 1. *Univ. of New Mexico Press* 1961 $15.00

THE RA EXPEDITION. Trans. by Patricia Crampton *Doubleday* 1971 $10.00; *New Am. Lib.* 1972 pap. $1.95. His chronicle of the two voyages across the Atlantic from Morocco to Barbados in a papyrus boat.

FATU-HIVA: Back to Nature on a Pacific Island. *Doubleday* 1975 $10.00

Heyerdahl's "recollection of this colorful period in the infancy of his absorbing career is an attention riveting escape book as well as a revealing, if unnecessarily preachy, easay on what white men have done to a once happy South Sea island, and how the island retaliated against a white couple attempting to settle there . . . it is a valuable contribution to the knowledge of Polynesia"— (*N.Y. Times*).

THE ART OF EASTER ISLAND. *Doubleday* 1976 $35.00

Books about Heyerdahl

Señor Kon-Tiki. By Arnold Jacoby. *Rand McNally* 1967 $7.95

PILKINGTON, ROGER. 1915–

Leisurely and charming, the "Small Boat" books are accounts of explorations of inland waterways aboard the *Commodore*, a 45-foot gasoline-powered vessel that had originally been an admiral's "barge" of the Royal Navy. Wide of beam and shallow of draught, the *Commodore* was as dry and comfortable and spacious as a canal boat. "The author has a lively eye for the amusing, unexpected incident and for the illuminating fragments of history which are either ignored or understressed into dullness by the ordinary guidebook"—(*Manchester Guardian*). The "Small Boat" books cover much of Northern Europe and France; most of the 15 or more titles in the series, published by *St. Martin's*, are out of print at present. Dr. Pilkington, formerly a research scientist at Cambridge, has written a number of books on specialized subjects and on scientific philosophy and religion, some of which have been published by *Macmillan* and *St. Martin's*. His adventure stories for young people are also available from *St. Martin's*.

SMALL BOAT ON THE UPPER RHINE. *St. Martin's* 1971 $9.50

WATERWAYS IN EUROPE: A Guide to Inland Cruising. *Scribner* 1974 $8.95

HERZOG, MAURICE. 1919–

Annapurna, the "story of the nine-man French Expedition which climbed Annapurna (26,493 feet) . . . in 1950 is the most beautiful chapter in mountain literature that I know. . . . Those who have never seen the Himalayas, those who never care to risk an assault will know when they finish this book that they have been a companion of greatness"—(Justice William O. Douglas, in the *N.Y. Times*). This enduring tribute to the spirit of man is the first book by the leader of the nine-man French Expedition. With one companion, he reached the summit of the highest mountain climbed by man at that time. Everest, 29,141 feet and the highest, was conquered in 1953 by the English (*see Sir John Hunt, above*).

ANNAPURNA: First Conquest of an 800-Meter Peak (26,493 feet). Trans. from the French by Nea Martin and Janet Adam Smith; cartographic and photographic documentation by Marcel Ichac; introd. by Eric Shipton *Dutton* 1953 $7.95; *Popular Lib.* 1969 pap. $.75

HILLARY, SIR EDMUND. 1919–

Sir Edmund Hillary wrote the "Chapter on the Final Assault" in "The Conquest of Everest" by Sir John Hunt (*q.v.*). Both were knighted by Queen Elizabeth II during the Coronation festivities of 1953 for their achievement. Before the Everest triumph Sir Edmund had written several books (now o.p.) about his adventures on other famous expeditions. In "No Latitude for Error," (1961, o.p.) he tells of his "personal participation" as a supporting force on the Trans-Antarctic Expedition of 1958, the first crossing of Antarctica by tractor—a fine record of a most hazardous and thrilling achievement. Sir Vivian Fuchs was the leader of the expedition. Starting from opposite sides, they met at the South Pole. The official account was published in Fuchs and Hillary's "The Crossing of Antarctica."

In June 1960, Hillary announced that in the fall he would try an ascent of the 27,790-foot Malaka Peak in Nepal about 20 miles east of Everest. He had two objectives: "first, to determine the effects of high altitude on climbers not equipped with oxygen equipment and, second, to make further efforts to track down the 'Abominable Snowman' "—(*N.Y. Times*). The results are told in "High in the Thin Cold Air" (1962, o.p.), of which Hillary was co-author with Desmond Doig. The results of both efforts were negligible and of one near-tragic, but this expedition established a school at Khumjung which made up for some of the disappointments. A second venture, which resulted in the book "Schoolhouse in the Clouds" (1964, o.p.), is described in *Library Journal's* review: "In response to an appeal for schools similar to the one Hillary had established at Khumjung, the Himalayan Schoolhouse Expedition of 1963 was organized to start schools at Thami and Pangboche, small villages perched more than 13,000 feet high in the Himalayas. The expedition also had plans for long-range medical aid (it arrived in a smallpox epidemic), and to climb some unconquered peaks. Despite many difficulties the two schools were set up. Two climbs are recorded by Jim Wilson and Michael Gill, and Lady Hillary also writes her impressions. . . . A most interesting record, well illustrated."

(With Vivian Fuchs). THE CROSSING OF ANTARCTICA: The Commonwealth Trans-Antarctic Expedition, 1955–1958. 1959. *Greenwood* $23.00

NOTHING VENTURE, NOTHING WIN. *Coward* 1975 $12.95

"The tough, cheery, occasionally irascible New Zealander tells his life story . . . there emerges the portrait of a man ideally suited both in physique and temperament to embrace the hardships, dangers, companionship and loneliness of this highly specialized calling"—*(PW)*. "The conqueror of Everest describes his adventures great and small . . . it's an exciting adventure yarn, particularly when he's describing his early mountaineering exploits"—*(LJ)*.

DURRELL, GERALD. 1925–

"It became plain, a year or so ago, when Gerald Durrell published 'The Overloaded Ark,' that he was a zoological writer with a difference. With 'The Bafut Beagles' the difference blazes in glory. . . . It is beautiful, exciting and funny"—*(SR)*. This brother of Lawrence Durrell has been producing delightful, superbly written books about animals for some time and by now has a large and devoted readership. "Whether you want to know how to capture an ant-eater, an electric eel, a porcupine, a pitful of snakes or a single boa-constrictor, Mr. Durrell is your man." At one time the youngest zoological collector in England, he was born in India and has made several major expeditions to West Africa and British Guiana.

His wife, Jacquie Durrell, is the author of "Beasts in My Bed" (*Atheneum* 1967 $4.95), her story of how she deserted music for mammals and reptiles to become the wife of Gerald the informal zookeeper. His account of his private zoo on the Isle of Jersey, dedicated to the preserving and breeding of dying species, was published as "Menagerie Manor" (1965, o.p.). "Rosy Is My Relative" (*Viking* lg.-type ed. 1968 $7.95) is his novel about an alcoholic elephant's search for a circus—"The effect . . . is of the utmost innocence and good nature"—*(Observer*, London). He has also written books for young people.

"The New Noah" (1955) about his animal collecting adventures in Africa and South America; "The Drunken Forest" (1956), a witty account of a game-collecting expedition in a remote section of Uruguay; and "My Favorite Animal Stories" (1963) are out of print.

THE OVERLOADED ARK. *Viking* 1953 $5.95; *Tower* 1971 pap. $.95; *Franklin Watts* lg.-type ed. $7.95. Two naturalists in the rain forests of the Cameroons collect animals and birds for British zoos.

THREE TICKETS TO ADVENTURE. 1955. *Berkley Pub.* pap. $.75. A young zoologist on safari in the interior of British Guiana.

MY FAMILY AND OTHER ANIMALS. *Viking* 1957 lg.-type ed. $7.95 Compass Bks. 1963 pap. $1.65. Five enchanted boyhood years on the island of Corfu, with the irresistible Durrell family, assorted fauna, tutors and friends.

THE BAFUT BEAGLES. 1954. *Tower* 1971 pap. $.95. An African expedition with a stalwart band from the domain of the enthusiastic Fon of Bafut accompanying Mr. Durrell on his collecting forays.

A ZOO IN MY LUGGAGE. Ill. by Ralph Thompson *Viking* 1960 $5.00. A delightful account of the problems of assembling a private zoo in West Africa and bringing it back to England.

THE WHISPERING LAND. *Viking* 1962 $4.50. An animal collecting adventure in Patagonia and Argentina.

TWO IN THE BUSH. *Viking* 1966 Compass Bks. 1971 pap. $1.95

About a journey to study conservation and the preservation of wildlife. "In this entertaining account of a six-month trip, the reader accompanies Mr. Durrell and his wife, Jacquie, through

New Zealand, Australia and Malaya. The light touch and amusing style that characterize his books on Africa still prevail"—(*LJ*).

BIRDS, BEASTS AND RELATIVES. *Viking* 1969 $5.95 Compass Bks. pap. $2.25. A companion volume to "My Family and Other Animals," more about childhood on Corfu and its animals.

FILLETS OF PLAICE. *Viking* 1971 $5.95

"These incidents from the author's personal life include a boating party at Corfu during which he and his eccentric companions are held captive by Turkish villagers, his experiences as an assistant in a London pet shop, a mad dinner party in Africa, etc."—(*LJ*).

CATCH ME A COLOBUS. *Viking* 1972 $5.95

His adventures managing a zoo on the Isle of Jersey devoted to the preservation of endangered wildlife. "He tells of going on an expedition to secure a Colobus monkey in Sierra Leone, and hunting Teporingo rabbits and thick-billed parrots in Mexico. Some of the difficulties of breeding rare species in captivity are related, including helping a lioness through two deliveries and researching the composition of tapir's milk to feed a newborn tapir"—(*Book Review Digest*).

A BEVY OF BEASTS. *Simon & Schuster* 1973 $7.95

The author recalls his "year as student keeper at Whipsnade Zoo . . . his introduction to the 'bevy of beasts' housed there and to the assortment of men who cared for them. In his epilogue he describes the efforts of his Jersey Wildlife Preservation Trust to save some species from extinction"—(*LJ*).

THOMAS, ELIZABETH MARSHALL. 1931–

"The 'Harmless People' is one of the most fascinating books I have read. It promises to become a classic," Justice William O. Douglas wrote in the *N.Y. Herald Tribune*. Rachel Carson commented that this "fine book lingers in my mind with a dreamlike sense that sometime I myself must have watched the sun set and the moon rise over that austere Kalahari desert and felt the antarctic winds of its winter! The beauty, simplicity and force of her prose delighted me. She has an extraordinary ability, far beyond mere description, to evoke the atmosphere of this strange desert world." Mrs. Thomas was a member of an expedition which, under the auspices of the Peabody Museum of Harvard, went three times to Kalahari, spending there about two years in all. This book deals with the last expedition, when the members came to know the shy and mysterious Bushmen as individuals. "The Warrior Herdsmen" "concerns a [Uganda, East Africa] tribe . . . whose oldest members live just as they did hundreds of years ago, but whose younger members sometimes learn to read and write, and have brushed against the modern world"—(Publisher's note). It has the same personal touch and poetic quality evident in her earlier book. Born in Boston, Mrs. Thomas went to Shady Hill School, Abbott Academy, then Smith College. She transferred to Radcliffe, from which she was graduated. In 1952 she won the *Mademoiselle* College Fiction Contest with a short story "The Hill People," which was later reprinted in Martha Foley's "Best American Short Stories of 1953" (o.p.).

THE HARMLESS PEOPLE. *Knopf* 1959 $6.50; *Random* Vintage Bks. pap. $1.95 lib. bdg. $2.39. An account of the life and customs of the Bushmen of Southwest Africa.

THE WARRIOR HERDSMEN. *Knopf* 1965 $6.95; *Random* Vintage Bks. 1972 pap. $1.95

Author Index

This index includes all authors mentioned in connection with titles of books they have written, whether they appear in introductory essays, general bibliographies at the beginnings of chapters, discussions under the main author headings, or "Books about" sections under main authors. Authors mentioned in passing—to indicate friendships, relationships, etc.—are generally not indexed. Editors are not indexed unless there is no specific author to be named; such books include anthologies, bibliographies, and the like. Translators are not indexed except in those compilations for which the same person acted as both editor and translator. Only last names and initials are listed. If two or more persons with the same surname and initials appear, first names are given in full. Chinese names are also given in full, e.g. Mao Tse-tung. Page numbers for main author headings are given in boldface.

Fuss, P., 319
Futch, O. L., 650

Gabel, C., 751
Gabrieli, F., 159
Gadd, C. J., 603
Gaddis, J. L., 659
Gaddis, T. E., 537
Gaer, J., 134
Gaffney, W. J., 202
Gager, J. G., 182
Gailey, H. A., 751
Gaines, F. P., 854
Galante, P., 74
Galbraith, J. K., 518, **582**
Gale, R. L., 679, 884
Galeano, E., 671
Galen, **444**
Galilei, G., **446**
Galindez Suarez, J. de, 671
Gallagher, J., 754
Gallagher, K. T., 340
Gallagher, T., 713
Gallo, M., 722
Galloway, J., 85
Galston, W. A., 306
Galton, F., **454**
Gambhiranda, Swami, 145
Gambino, R., 524
Gamow, G., 431, 437, **485**
Gandhi, M. K., **62, 238**
Gann, L. H., 752, 757
Gans, H. J., 499
Gantt, W. H., 371
Garbicz, A., 805
Garbo, G., **817**
Garbuny, M., 432
Gard, R. A., 134
Gard, R. E., 848
Gardiner, C. H., 677
Gardiner, M. S., 414
Gardiner, P., 289, 309
Gardiner, S. R., 617
Gardner, B., 870
Gardner, E. E., 848
Gardner, Helen, 17
Gardner, Howard, 362
Gardner, J. L., 682
Gardner, J. W., **588**
Gardner, M., 426
Garfiel, E., 164
Gargan, E. T., 678, 781
Garland, J., **817**
Garner, R. L., 876
Garnett, R. C., 546
Garnsey, P., 604
Garraty, J. A., 12, 632, 639, 675, 706
Garrett, H. E., 362

Garrick, D., **43**
Garrison, L. M., 852
Garrison, W. E., 189
Garrison, W. L., 663
Garvey, R., 129
Gascoyne, D., 768
Gaskell, G. A., 134
Gaskell, T. F., 424, 863
Gaster, M., 843
Gaster, T. H., 115, 119, 854
Gasztold, C. B. de, 129
Gatell, F. O., 586
Gates, G. P., 655
Gates, R., 644
Gaubert, H. B., 212
Gauguin, P., **59**
Gaulle, C. de, **74**
Gaustad, E. S., 189
Gauthier, D. P., 296
Gay, P., 189, 290, 599, 641, 706, 723
Gearhart, S. M., 207
Geba, B., 362
Geddie, J. L., 11
Geddie, W., 11
Geduld, H. M., 805, 808, 819
Geelan, P. J. M., 747
Geelhaar, C., 68
Geertz, C., 159, 499
Gehman, H. S., 112
Geiger, G. R., 321
Geiger, T., 708
Geist, V., 414
Gelfman, J. S., 833
Gellhorn, W., 710
Gelven, M., 339
Gelzer, M., 604, 612
Genovese, E. D., 664
Geoffrey of Monmouth, 620
Georgano, G. N., 440
George, A. L., 713
George, H., **552**
George, H., Jr., 553
George, M., 544
Gérard-Libois, J., 757
Gerbner, G., 826
Germani, G., 531
Gerrish, B. A., 191
Gersh, H., 169
Gerth, H., 148, 547, 591
Gessner, R., 808
Geyelin, P., 81
Geymonat, L., 446
Ghiselin, M. T., 454
Ghose, S., 740
Ghougassian, J. P., 388
Gianakaris, C. J., 611
Gibb, H. A. R., 159
Gibbon, E., **48, 614**
Gibbs, J. L., Jr., 752

Gibbs-Smith, C. H., 440
Gibert, M., 618
Gibney, F., 740
Gibson, A., 814
Gibson, A. M., 647
Gibson, E. J., 363
Gibson, H., 67
Giddens, A., 559
Giddings, J. L., 765
Gide, A., 870
Gies, F., 708
Gies, J., 708
Gifford, D., 815
Gil, F., 671
Gilbert, C., 505
Gilbert, M., 66, 736
Gilbert, M. B., 426
Gilbert, T. F., 426
Gilby, T., 224
Gilkey, L. B., 192, 363
Gill, D. L. T., 872
Gill, J. H., 290, 313, 814
Gill, T. A., 258
Gillan, G., 352
Gillby, T., 224
Gillespie, C. C., 399, 403
Gillespie, E., 129
Gilliat, P., 812
Gillmor, D. M., 826
Gilman, L., 802
Gilson, É., 219, 224, 285, **336**
Gilson, R., 815
Ginger, R., 496
Ginsburg, H., 387, 534
Ginzberg, E., 510, 518, 520, 524, 542
Ginzberg, L., 165
Gipson, L. H., **628**
Girardi, G., 204
Gish, A. G., 207
Gish, L., 812, 818
Gishford, A., 802
Gist, R. R., 504
Gittelson, B., 408
Gittings, J., 744
Gladstone, W. E., 236, 620
Gladwin, T., 534
Gladych, M., 891
Glasenapp, H. von, 151
Glaser, D., 537
Glass, B., 403
Glasscote, R. M., 540
Glasser, W., 363
Glassie, H., 838, 846, 854
Glasson, F. T., 212
Glatzer, N. N., 163, 164, 165, 173, 613
Glatzer, R., 812
Glazer, J., 838

Glazer, M., 515
Glazer, N., 524, 585
Gleason, P., 201
Glemser, B., 429
Glick, E. B., 718
Glick, P., 514
Glick, T. F., 454
Glob, P. V., 499
Glock, C. Y., 363, 515
Glover, T. R., 608
Glubb, J., 159, 220, 733
Gluckman, M., 568
Glueck, E. T., 537
Glueck, S. S., 537
Glut, D. F., 808
Godard, J.-L., **818**
Godbey, A. H., 169
Goddard, D., 151
Goddard, R. H., **464**
Godden, J., 870
Godden, R., 870
Godolphin, F. R. B., 607
Godwin, W., 545
Goebbels, P. J., 723
Goergen, D., 201
Goertzel, M. G., 28
Goertzel, V., 28
Goetzmann, W. H., 648, 708
Goffman, E., 363, **592**
Gofman, J. W., 433
Goguel, M., 182
Golann, S. E., 356
Goldberg, H. S., 443
Goldberg, I., 170
Goldenson, R. M., 356, 363
Golder, F. A., 729
Goldfarb, R., 537
Goldin, J., 162
Golding, L., 212
Goldinger, M., 288
Goldman, E., 736
Goldman, E. F., 81
Goldman, I., 499
Goldman, L., 306
Goldman, P., 30
Goldman, Z., 736
Goldovsky, B., 802
Golds, J., 203
Goldscheider, L., 40
Goldschmidt, E. D., 164
Goldsen, R. K., 591
Goldsmith, M. M., 296
Goldstein, K. S., 836
Goldstein, P., 408
Goldstine, H. H., 440
Goldwater, L. J., 417
Golenpaul, D., 23
Golino, C. L., 447
Gombrich, E. H., 17
Gomme, A. W., 608
Gomperz, T., 274

Title Index

Titles of all books discussed in any section of "The Reader's Adviser" are indexed here, except broad generic titles such as "Complete Works," "Selections," "Poems," "Correspondence," etc. The Viking "Portable . . ." series is not indexed if the author's name is included in the title. In-print volumes of this series will be found under the main heading of the author concerned. In general subtitles are omitted. When two or more identical titles by different authors appear, the last name of each author is given in parentheses following the title. Subject headings are not indexed. We refer the reader to the detailed table of contents for this information.